The Dictionary of Art · volume five

The Dictionary of Art

CONSULTING EDITOR Hugh Brigstocke

EDITOR Jane Turner

5

Brugghen, ter

TO

Casson

GROVE

The Dictionary of Art

edited by JANE TURNER, in thirty-four volumes, 1996

This edition is distributed within the United Kingdom and Europe by Macmillan Publishers Limited, London, and within the United States and Canada by Grove's Dictionaries Inc., New York.

Text keyboarded by Wearset Limited, Sunderland, England
Database management by Pindar plc, York, England
Imagesetting by William Clowes Limited, Suffolk, England
Printed in the United States of America by RR Donnelley & Sons Company, Willard, Ohio

British Library Cataloguing in Publication Data

The dictionary of art
1. Art - Dictionaries 2. Art - History - Dictionaries
I. Turner, Jane
703

ISBN 1-884446-00-0

Library of Congress Cataloging in Publication Data

The dictionary of art / editor, Jane Turner.
p. cm.
Includes bibliographical references and index.
Contents: 1. A to Anckerman
ISBN 1-884446-00-0 (alk. paper)
1. Art—Encyclopedias.
I. Turner, Jane, 1956–
N31.D5 1996 96–13628
703—dc20 CIP

Contents

List of Colour Illustrations vi

General Abbreviations vii

A Note on the Use of the Dictionary xiii

The Dictionary, Volume Five:

Brugghen, ter–Casson 1

Illustration Acknowledgements 926

List of Colour Illustrations

PLATE I. **Carpet**

Savonnerie carpet, wool knotted pile, 6.12×3.58 m, from Paris, 1660–65 (New York, Metropolitan Museum of Art/Photo: Metropolitan Museum of Art, Purchase, Mr and Mrs Charles Wrightsman Gift, no. 1983.268)

PLATE II. **Carpet**

Star Ushak carpet, wool knotted pile, 4.27×2.13 m, from Ushak, Turkey, first half of the 17th century (New York, Metropolitan Museum of Art/Photo: Metropolitan Museum of Art, Gift of Joseph V. McMullan, 1958; no. 58.63)

PLATE III. **Carpet**

Prayer rug, wool knotted pile, 1.65×0.80 m, from Beshir, Turkmenistan, 19th century (Munich, Staatliches Museum für Völkerkunde/Photo: Staatliches Museum für Völkerkunde)

PLATE IV. **Carpet**

Wagner Garden Carpet, wool knotted pile, 5.31×4.32 m, from Iran, 17th century (Glasgow, Burrell Collection/Photo: Glasgow Museums)

General Abbreviations

The abbreviations employed throughout this dictionary, most of which are listed below, do not vary, except for capitalization, regardless of the context in which they are used, including bibliographical citations and for locations of works of art. The principle used to arrive at these abbreviations is that their full form should be easily deducible, and for this reason acronyms have generally been avoided (e.g. Los Angeles Co. Mus. A. instead of LACMA). The same abbreviation is adopted for cognate forms in foreign languages and in most cases for plural and adjectival forms (e.g. A.= Art, Arts, Arte, Arti etc). Not all related forms are listed below. Occasionally, if a name, for instance of an artists' group or exhibiting society, is repeated within the text of one article, it is cited in an abbreviated form after its first mention in full (e.g. The Pre-Raphaelite Brotherhood (PRB) was founded...); the same is true of archaeological periods and eras, which are abbreviated to initial letters in small capitals (e.g. In the Early Minoan (EM) period...). Such abbreviations do not appear in this list. For the reader's convenience, separate full lists of abbreviations for locations, periodical titles and standard reference books and series are included as Appendices A–C in vol. 33.

A.	Art, Arts
A.C.	Arts Council
Acad.	Academy
AD	Anno Domini
Add.	Additional, Addendum
addn	addition
Admin.	Administration
Adv.	Advances, Advanced
Aesth.	Aesthetic(s)
Afr.	African
Afrik.	Afrikaans, Afrikaner
A.G.	Art Gallery
Agrar.	Agrarian
Agric.	Agriculture
Agron.	Agronomy
Agy	Agency
AH	Anno Hegirae
A. Inst.	Art Institute
AK	Alaska (USA)
AL	Alabama (USA)
Alb.	Albanian
Alg.	Algerian
Alta	Alberta (Canada)
Altern.	Alternative
a.m.	ante meridiem [before noon]
Amat.	Amateur
Amer.	American
An.	Annals
Anatol.	Anatolian
Anc.	Ancient
Annu.	Annual
Anon.	Anonymous(ly)
Ant.	Antique
Anthol.	Anthology
Anthropol.	Anthropology
Antiqua.	Antiquarian, Antiquaries
app.	appendix
approx.	approximately
AR	Arkansas (USA)
ARA	Associate of the Royal Academy
Arab.	Arabic
Archaeol.	Archaeology
Archit.	Architecture, Architectural
Archv, Archvs	Archive(s)
Arg.	Argentine
ARHA	Associate of the Royal Hibernian Academy
ARIBA	Associate of the Royal Institute of British Architects
Armen.	Armenian
ARSA	Associate of the Royal Scottish Academy
Asiat.	Asiatic
Assist.	Assistance
Assoc.	Association
Astron.	Astronomy
AT&T	American Telephone & Telegraph Company
attrib.	attribution, attributed to
Aug	August
Aust.	Austrian
Austral.	Australian
Auth.	Author(s)
Auton.	Autonomous
Aux.	Auxiliary
Ave.	Avenue
AZ	Arizona (USA)
Azerbaij.	Azerbaijani
B.	Bartsch [catalogue of Old Master prints]
b	born
BA	Bachelor of Arts
Balt.	Baltic
bapt	baptized
BArch	Bachelor of Architecture
Bart	Baronet
Bask.	Basketry
BBC	British Broadcasting Corporation
BC	Before Christ
BC	British Columbia (Canada)
BE	Buddhist era
Beds	Bedfordshire (GB)
Behav.	Behavioural
Belarus.	Belarusian
Belg.	Belgian
Berks	Berkshire (GB)
Berwicks	Berwickshire (GB; old)
BFA	Bachelor of Fine Arts
Bibl.	Bible, Biblical
Bibliog.	Bibliography, Bibliographical
Biblioph.	Bibliophile
Biog.	Biography, Biographical
Biol.	Biology, Biological
bk, bks	book(s)
Bkbinder	Bookbinder
Bklore	Booklore
Bkshop	Bookshop
BL	British Library
Bld	Build
Bldg	Building

Bldr	Builder
BLitt	Bachelor of Letters/Literature
BM	British Museum
Boh.	Bohemian
Boliv.	Bolivian
Botan.	Botany, Botanical
BP	Before present (1950)
Braz.	Brazilian
BRD	Bundesrepublik Deutschland [Federal Republic of Germany (West Germany)]
Brecons	Breconshire (GB; old)
Brez.	Brezonek [lang. of Brittany]
Brit.	British
Bros	Brothers
BSc	Bachelor of Science
Bucks	Buckinghamshire (GB)
Bulg.	Bulgarian
Bull.	Bulletin
bur	buried
Burm.	Burmese
Byz.	Byzantine
C	Celsius
C.	Century
c.	*circa* [about]
CA	California
Cab.	Cabinet
Caerns	Caernarvonshire (GB; old)
C.A.G.	City Art Gallery
Cal.	Calendar
Callig.	Calligraphy
Cam.	Camera
Cambs	Cambridgeshire (GB)
can	canonized
Can.	Canadian
Cant.	Canton(s), Cantonal
Capt.	Captain
Cards	Cardiganshire (GB; old)
Carib.	Caribbean
Carms	Carmarthenshire (GB; old)
Cartog.	Cartography
Cat.	Catalan
cat.	catalogue
Cath.	Catholic
CBE	Commander of the Order of the British Empire
Celeb.	Celebration
Celt.	Celtic
Cent.	Centre, Central
Centen.	Centennial
Cer.	Ceramic
cf.	confer [compare]
Chap., Chaps	Chapter(s)
Chem.	Chemistry
Ches	Cheshire (GB)
Chil.	Chilean
Chin.	Chinese
Christ.	Christian, Christianity
Chron.	Chronicle
Cie	Compagnie [French]
Cinema.	Cinematography
Circ.	Circle
Civ.	Civil, Civic
Civiliz.	Civilization(s)
Class.	Classic, Classical
Clin.	Clinical
CO	Colorado (USA)
Co.	Company; County
Cod.	Codex, Codices
Col., Cols	Collection(s); Column(s)
Coll.	College
collab.	in collaboration with, collaborated, collaborative
Collct.	Collecting
Colloq.	Colloquies
Colomb.	Colombian
Colon.	Colonies, Colonial
Colr	Collector
Comm.	Commission; Community
Commerc.	Commercial
Communic.	Communications
Comp.	Comparative; compiled by, compiler
Concent.	Concentration
Concr.	Concrete
Confed.	Confederation
Confer.	Conference
Congol.	Congolese
Congr.	Congress
Conserv.	Conservation; Conservatory
Constr.	Construction(al)
cont.	continued
Contemp.	Contemporary
Contrib.	Contributions, Contributor(s)
Convalesc.	Convalescence
Convent.	Convention
Coop.	Cooperation
Coord.	Coordination
Copt.	Coptic
Corp.	Corporation, Corpus
Corr.	Correspondence
Cors.	Corsican
Cost.	Costume
Cret.	Cretan
Crim.	Criminal
Crit.	Critical, Criticism
Croat.	Croatian
CT	Connecticut (USA)
Cttee	Committee
Cub.	Cuban
Cult.	Cultural, Culture
Cumb.	Cumberland (GB; old)
Cur.	Curator, Curatorial, Curatorship
Curr.	Current(s)
CVO	Commander of the [Royal] Victorian Order
Cyclad.	Cycladic
Cyp.	Cypriot
Czech.	Czechoslovak
$	dollars
d	died
d.	denarius, denarii [penny, pence]
Dalmat.	Dalmatian
Dan.	Danish
DBE	Dame Commander of the Order of the British Empire
DC	District of Columbia (USA)
DDR	Deutsche Demokratische Republik [German Democratic Republic (East Germany)]
DE	Delaware (USA)
Dec	December
Dec.	Decorative
ded.	dedication, dedicated to
Democ.	Democracy, Democratic
Demog.	Demography, Demographic
Denbs	Denbighshire (GB; old)
dep.	deposited at
Dept	Department
Dept.	Departmental, Departments
Derbys	Derbyshire (GB)
Des.	Design
destr.	destroyed
Dev.	Development
Devon	Devonshire (GB)
Dial.	Dialogue
diam.	diameter
Diff.	Diffusion
Dig.	Digest
Dip. Eng.	Diploma in Engineering
Dir.	Direction, Directed
Directrt	Directorate
Disc.	Discussion
diss.	dissertation
Distr.	District
Div.	Division
DLitt	Doctor of Letters/Literature
DM	Deutsche Mark
Doc.	Document(s)
Doss.	Dossier
DPhil	Doctor of Philosophy
Dr	Doctor
Drg, Drgs	Drawing(s)
DSc	Doctor of Science/Historical Sciences
Dut.	Dutch
Dwell.	Dwelling
E.	East(ern)

EC	European (Economic) Community
Eccles.	Ecclesiastical
Econ.	Economic, Economies
Ecuad.	Ecuadorean
ed.	editor, edited (by)
edn	edition
eds	editors
Educ.	Education
e.g.	*exempli gratia* [for example]
Egyp.	Egyptian
Elem.	Element(s), Elementary
Emp.	Empirical
Emul.	Emulation
Enc.	Encyclopedia
Encour.	Encouragement
Eng.	English
Engin.	Engineer, Engineering
Engr., Engrs	Engraving(s)
Envmt	Environment
Epig.	Epigraphy
Episc.	Episcopal
Esp.	Especially
Ess.	Essays
est.	established
etc	*etcetera* [and so on]
Ethnog.	Ethnography
Ethnol.	Ethnology
Etrus.	Etruscan
Eur.	European
Evangel.	Evangelical
Exam.	Examination
Excav.	Excavation, Excavated
Exch.	Exchange
Excurs.	Excursion
exh.	exhibition
Exp.	Exposition
Expermntl	Experimental
Explor.	Exploration
Expn	Expansion
Ext.	External
Extn	Extension
f, ff	following page, following pages
F.A.	Fine Art(s)
Fac.	Faculty
facs.	facsimile
Fam.	Family
fasc.	fascicle
fd	feastday (of a saint)
Feb	February
Fed.	Federation, Federal
Fem.	Feminist
Fest.	Festival
fig.	figure (illustration)
Fig.	Figurative
figs	figures
Filip.	Filipina(s), Filipino(s)
Fin.	Finnish
FL	Florida (USA)
fl	*floruit* [he/she flourished]
Flem.	Flemish
Flints	Flintshire (GB; old)
Flk	Folk
Flklore	Folklore
fol., fols	folio(s)
Found.	Foundation
Fr.	French
frag.	fragment
Fri.	Friday
FRIBA	Fellow of the Royal Institute of British Architects
FRS	Fellow of the Royal Society, London
ft	foot, feet
Furn.	Furniture
Futur.	Futurist, Futurism
g	gram(s)
GA	Georgia (USA)
Gael.	Gaelic
Gal., Gals	Gallery, Galleries
Gaz.	Gazette
GB	Great Britain
Gdn, Gdns	Garden(s)
Gdnr(s)	Gardener(s)
Gen.	General
Geneal.	Genealogy, Genealogist
Gent.	Gentleman, Gentlemen
Geog.	Geography
Geol.	Geology
Geom.	Geometry
Georg.	Georgian
Geosci.	Geoscience
Ger.	German, Germanic
G.I.	Government/General Issue (USA)
Glams	Glamorganshire (GB; old)
Glos	Gloucestershire (GB)
Govt	Government
Gr.	Greek
Grad.	Graduate
Graph.	Graphic
Green.	Greenlandic
Gr.-Roman	Greco-Roman
Gt	Great
Gtr	Greater
Guat.	Guatemalan
Gym.	Gymnasium
h.	height
ha	hectare
Hait.	Haitian
Hants	Hampshire (GB)
Hb.	Handbook
Heb.	Hebrew
Hell.	Hellenic
Her.	Heritage
Herald.	Heraldry, Heraldic
Hereford & Worcs	Hereford & Worcester (GB)
Herts	Hertfordshire (GB)
HI	Hawaii (USA)
Hib.	Hibernia
Hisp.	Hispanic
Hist.	History, Historical
HMS	His/Her Majesty's Ship
Hon.	Honorary, Honourable
Horiz.	Horizon
Hort.	Horticulture
Hosp.	Hospital(s)
HRH	His/Her Royal Highness
Human.	Humanities, Humanism
Hung.	Hungarian
Hunts	Huntingdonshire (GB; old)
IA	Iowa
ibid.	*ibidem* [in the same place]
ICA	Institute of Contemporary Arts
Ice.	Icelandic
Iconog.	Iconography
Iconol.	Iconology
ID	Idaho (USA)
i.e.	*id est* [that is]
IL	Illinois (USA)
Illum.	Illumination
illus.	illustrated, illustration
Imp.	Imperial
IN	Indiana (USA)
in., ins	inch(es)
Inc.	Incorporated
inc.	incomplete
incl.	includes, including, inclusive
Incorp.	Incorporation
Ind.	Indian
Indep.	Independent
Indig.	Indigenous
Indol.	Indology
Indon.	Indonesian
Indust.	Industrial
Inf.	Information
Inq.	Inquiry
Inscr.	Inscribed, Inscription
Inst.	Institute(s)
Inst. A.	Institute of Art
Instr.	Instrument, Instrumental
Int.	International
Intell.	Intelligence
Inter.	Interior(s), Internal
Interdiscip.	Interdisciplinary
intro.	introduced by, introduction
inv.	inventory

Inven.	Invention
Invest.	Investigation(s)
Iran.	Iranian
irreg.	irregular(ly)
Islam.	Islamic
Isr.	Israeli
It.	Italian
J.	Journal
Jam.	Jamaican
Jan	January
Jap.	Japanese
Jav.	Javanese
Jew.	Jewish
Jewel.	Jewellery
Jord.	Jordanian
jr	junior
Juris.	Jurisdiction
KBE	Knight Commander of the Order of the British Empire
KCVO	Knight Commander of the Royal Victorian Order
kg	kilogram(s)
kHz	kilohertz
km	kilometre(s)
Knowl.	Knowledge
Kor.	Korean
KS	Kansas (USA)
KY	Kentucky (USA)
Kyrgyz.	Kyrgyzstani
£	libra, librae [pound, pounds sterling]
l.	length
LA	Louisiana (USA)
Lab.	Laboratory
Lancs	Lancashire (GB)
Lang.	Language(s)
Lat.	Latin
Latv.	Latvian
lb, lbs	pound(s) weight
Leb.	Lebanese
Lect.	Lecture
Legis.	Legislative
Leics	Leicestershire (GB)
Lex.	Lexicon
Lg.	Large
Lib., Libs	Library, Libraries
Liber.	Liberian
Libsp	Librarianship
Lincs	Lincolnshire (GB)
Lit.	Literature
Lith.	Lithuanian
Liturg.	Liturgical
LLB	Bachelor of Laws
LLD	Doctor of Laws
Lt	Lieutenant
Lt-Col.	Lieutenant-Colonel
Ltd	Limited
m	metre(s)
m.	married
M.	Monsieur
MA	Master of Arts; Massachusetts (USA)
Mag.	Magazine
Maint.	Maintenance
Malay.	Malaysian
Man.	Manitoba (Canada); Manual
Manuf.	Manufactures
Mar.	Marine, Maritime
Mason.	Masonic
Mat.	Material(s)
Math.	Mathematic
MBE	Member of the Order of the British Empire
MD	Doctor of Medicine; Maryland (USA)
ME	Maine (USA)
Mech.	Mechanical
Med.	Medieval; Medium, Media
Medic.	Medical, Medicine
Medit.	Mediterranean
Mem.	Memorial(s); Memoir(s)
Merions	Merionethshire (GB; old)
Meso-Amer.	Meso-American
Mesop.	Mesopotamian
Met.	Metropolitan
Metal.	Metallurgy
Mex.	Mexican
MFA	Master of Fine Arts
mg	milligram(s)
Mgmt	Management
Mgr	Monsignor
MI	Michigan
Micrones.	Micronesian
Mid. Amer.	Middle American
Middx	Middlesex (GB; old)
Mid. E.	Middle Eastern
Mid. Eng.	Middle English
Mid Glam.	Mid Glamorgan (GB)
Mil.	Military
Mill.	Millenium
Min.	Ministry; Minutes
Misc.	Miscellaneous
Miss.	Mission(s)
Mlle	Mademoiselle
mm	millimetre(s)
Mme	Madame
MN	Minnesota
Mnmt, Mnmts	Monument(s)
Mnmtl	Monumental
MO	Missouri (USA)
Mod.	Modern, Modernist
Moldav.	Moldavian
Moldov.	Moldovan
MOMA	Museum of Modern Art
Mon.	Monday
Mongol.	Mongolian
Mons	Monmouthshire (GB; old)
Montgoms	Montgomeryshire (GB; old)
Mor.	Moral
Morav.	Moravian
Moroc.	Moroccan
Movt	Movement
MP	Member of Parliament
MPhil	Master of Philosophy
MS	Mississippi (USA)
MS., MSS	manuscript(s)
MSc	Master of Science
MT	Montana (USA)
Mt	Mount
Mthly	Monthly
Mun.	Municipal
Mus.	Museum(s)
Mus. A.	Museum of Art
Mus. F.A.	Museum of Fine Art(s)
Music.	Musicology
N.	North(ern); National
n	refractive index of a medium
n.	note
N.A.G.	National Art Gallery
Nat.	Natural, Nature
Naut.	Nautical
NB	New Brunswick (Canada)
NC	North Carolina (USA)
ND	North Dakota (USA)
n.d.	no date
NE	Nebraska; Northeast(ern)
Neth.	Netherlandish
Newslett.	Newsletter
Nfld	Newfoundland (Canada)
N.G.	National Gallery
N.G.A.	National Gallery of Art
NH	New Hampshire (USA)
Niger.	Nigerian
NJ	New Jersey (USA)
NM	New Mexico (USA)
nm	nanometre (109 metre)
nn.	notes
no., nos	number(s)
Nord.	Nordic
Norm.	Normal
Northants	Northamptonshire (GB)
Northumb.	Northumberland (GB)
Norw.	Norwegian
Notts	Nottinghamshire (GB)
Nov	November
n.p.	no place (of publication)
N.P.G.	National Portrait Gallery
nr	near

Nr E.	Near Eastern
NS	New Style; Nova Scotia (Canada)
n. s.	new series
NSW	New South Wales (Australia)
NT	National Trust
Ntbk	Notebook
Numi.	Numismatic(s)
NV	Nevada (USA)
NW	Northwest(ern)
NWT	Northwest Territories (Canada)
NY	New York (USA)
NZ	New Zealand
OBE	Officer of the Order of the British Empire
Obj.	Object(s), Objective
Occas.	Occasional
Occident.	Occidental
Ocean.	Oceania
Oct	October
8vo	octavo
OFM	Order of Friars Minor
OH	Ohio (USA)
OK	Oklahoma (USA)
Olymp.	Olympic
OM	Order of Merit
Ont.	Ontario (Canada)
op.	opus
opp.	opposite; opera [pl. of opus]
OR	Oregon (USA)
Org.	Organization
Orient.	Oriental
Orthdx	Orthodox
OSB	Order of St Benedict
Ott.	Ottoman
Oxon	Oxfordshire (GB)
oz.	ounce(s)
p	pence
p., pp.	page(s)
PA	Pennsylvania (USA)
p.a.	per annum
Pak.	Pakistani
Palaeontol.	Palaeontology, Palaeontological
Palest.	Palestinian
Pap.	Paper(s)
para.	paragraph
Parag.	Paraguayan
Parl.	Parliament
Paroch.	Parochial
Patriarch.	Patriarchate
Patriot.	Patriotic
Patrm.	Patrimony
Pav.	Pavilion
PEI	Prince Edward Island (Canada)
Pembs	Pembrokeshire (GB; old)
Per.	Period
Percep.	Perceptions
Perf.	Performance, Performing, Performed
Period.	Periodical(s)
Pers.	Persian
Persp.	Perspectives
Peru.	Peruvian
PhD	Doctor of Philosophy
Philol.	Philology
Philos.	Philosophy
Phoen.	Phoenician
Phot.	Photograph, Photography, Photographic
Phys.	Physician(s), Physics, Physique, Physical
Physiog.	Physiognomy
Physiol.	Physiology
Pict.	Picture(s), Pictorial
pl.	plate; plural
Plan.	Planning
Planet.	Planetarium
Plast.	Plastic
pls	plates
p.m.	post meridiem [after noon]
Polit.	Political
Poly.	Polytechnic
Polynes.	Polynesian
Pop.	Popular
Port.	Portuguese
Port.	Portfolio
Posth.	Posthumous(ly)
Pott.	Pottery
POW	prisoner of war
PRA	President of the Royal Academy
Pract.	Practical
Prefect.	Prefecture, Prefectural
Preserv.	Preservation
prev.	previous(ly)
priv.	private
PRO	Public Record Office
Prob.	Problem(s)
Proc.	Proceedings
Prod.	Production
Prog.	Progress
Proj.	Project(s)
Promot.	Promotion
Prop.	Property, Properties
Prov.	Province(s), Provincial
Proven.	Provenance
Prt, Prts	Print(s)
Prtg	Printing
pseud.	pseudonym
Psych.	Psychiatry, Psychiatric
Psychol.	Psychology, Psychological
pt	part
Ptg(s)	Painting(s)
Pub.	Public
pubd	published
Publ.	Publicity
pubn(s)	publication(s)
PVA	Polyvinyl acetate
PVC	polyvinyl chloride
Q.	quarterly
4to	quarto
Què.	Quèbec (Canada)
R	reprint
r	*recto*
RA	Royal Academician
Radnors	Radnorshire (GB; old)
RAF	Royal Air Force
Rec.	Record(s)
red.	reduction, reduced for
Ref.	Reference
Refurb.	Refurbishment
reg	*regit* [ruled]
Reg.	Regional
Relig.	Religion, Religious
remod.	remodelled
Ren.	Renaissance
Rep.	Report(s)
repr.	reprint(ed); reproduced, reproduction
Represent.	Representation, Representative
Res.	Research
rest.	restored, restoration
Retro.	Retrospective
rev.	revision, revised (by/for)
Rev.	Reverend; Review
RHA	Royal Hibernian Academician
RI	Rhode Island (USA)
RIBA	Royal Institute of British Architects
RJ	Rio de Janeiro State
Rlwy	Railway
RSA	Royal Scottish Academy
RSFSR	Russian Soviet Federated Socialist Republic
Rt Hon.	Right Honourable
Rur.	Rural
Rus.	Russian
S	San, Santa, Santo, Sant', S o [Saint]
S.	South(ern)
s.	solidus, solidi [shilling(s)]
Sask.	Saskatchewan (Canada)
Sat.	Saturday
SC	South Carolina (USA)
Scand.	Scandinavian
Sch.	School
Sci.	Science(s), Scientific
Scot.	Scottish
Sculp.	Sculpture

SD	South Dakota (USA)
SE	Southeast(ern)
Sect.	Section
Sel.	Selected
Semin.	Seminar(s), Seminary
Semiot.	Semiotic
Semit.	Semitic
Sept	September
Ser.	Series
Serb.	Serbian
Serv.	Service(s)
Sess.	Session, Sessional
Settmt(s)	Settlement(s)
S. Glam.	South Glamorgan (GB)
Siber.	Siberian
Sig.	Signature
Sil.	Silesian
Sin.	Singhala
sing.	singular
SJ	Societas Jesu [Society of Jesus]
Skt	Sanskrit
Slav.	Slavic, Slavonic
Slov.	Slovene, Slovenian
Soc.	Society
Social.	Socialism, Socialist
Sociol.	Sociology
Sov.	Soviet
SP	S o Paulo State
Sp.	Spanish
sq.	square
sr	senior
Sri L.	Sri Lankan
SS	Saints, Santi, Santissima, Santissimo, Santissimi; Steam ship
SSR	Soviet Socialist Republic
St	Saint, Sankt, Sint, Szent
Staffs	Staffordshire (GB)
Ste	Sainte
Stud.	Study, Studies
Subalp.	Subalpine
Sum.	Sumerian
Sun.	Sunday
Sup.	Superior
suppl., suppls	supplement(s), supplementary
Surv.	Survey
SW	Southwest(ern)
Swed.	Swedish
Swi.	Swiss
Symp.	Symposium
Syr.	Syrian
Tap.	Tapestry
Tas.	Tasmanian
Tech.	Technical, Technique
Technol.	Technology
Territ.	Territory
Theat.	Theatre
Theol.	Theology, Theological
Theor.	Theory, Theoretical
Thurs.	Thursday
Tib.	Tibetan
TN	Tennessee (USA)
Top.	Topography
Trad.	Tradition(s), Traditional
trans.	translation, translated by; transactions
Transafr.	Transafrican
Transatlant.	Transatlantic
Transcarpath.	Transcarpathian
transcr.	transcribed by/for
Triq.	Triquarterly
Tropic.	Tropical
Tues.	Tuesday
Turk.	Turkish
Turkmen.	Turkmenistani
TV	Television
TX	Texas (USA)
U.	University
UK	United Kingdom of Great Britain and Northern Ireland
Ukrain.	Ukrainian
Un.	Union
Underwtr	Underwater
UNESCO	United Nations Educational, Scientific and Cultural Organization
Univl	Universal
unpubd	unpublished
Urb.	Urban
Urug.	Uruguayan
US	United States
USA	United States of America
USSR	Union of Soviet Socialist Republics
UT	Utah
v	*verso*
VA	Virginia (USA)
V&A	Victoria and Albert Museum
Var.	Various
Venez.	Venezuelan
Vern.	Vernacular
Vict.	Victorian
Vid.	Video
Viet.	Vietnamese
viz.	*videlicet* [namely]
vol., vols	volume(s)
vs.	versus
VT	Vermont (USA)
Vulg.	Vulgarisation
W.	West(ern)
w.	width
WA	Washington (USA)
Warwicks	Warwickshire (GB)
Wed.	Wednesday
W. Glam.	West Glamorgan (GB)
WI	Wisconsin (USA)
Wilts	Wiltshire (GB)
Wkly	Weekly
W. Midlands	West Midlands (GB)
Worcs	Worcestershire (GB; old)
Wtrcol.	Watercolour
WV	West Virginia (USA)
WY	Wyoming (USA)
Yb., Y.-b.	Yearbook, Year-book
Yem.	Yemeni
Yorks	Yorkshire (GB; old)
Yug.	Yugoslavian
Zamb.	Zambian
Zimb.	Zimbabwean

A Note on the Use of the Dictionary

This note is intended as a short guide to the basic editorial conventions adopted in this dictionary. For a fuller explanation, please refer to the Introduction, vol. 1, pp. xiii–xx.

Abbreviations in general use in the dictionary are listed on pp. vii–xii; those used in bibliographies and for locations of works of art or exhibition venues are listed in the Appendices in vol. 33.

Alphabetization of headings, which are distinguished in bold typeface, is letter by letter up to the first comma (ignoring spaces, hyphens, accents and any parenthesized or bracketed matter); the same principle applies thereafter. Abbreviations of 'Saint' and its foreign equivalents are alphabetized as if spelt out, and headings with the prefix 'Mc' appear under 'Mac'.

Authors' signatures appear at the end of the article or sequence of articles that the authors have contributed; in multipartite articles, any section that is unsigned is by the author of the next signed section. Where the article was compiled by the editors or in the few cases where an author has wished to remain enonymous, this is indicated by a square box (□) instead of a signature.

Bibliographies are arranged chronologically (within section, where divided) by order of year of first publication and, within years, alphabetically by authors' names. Abbreviations have been used for some standard reference books; these are cited in full in Appendix C in vol. 33, as are abbreviations of periodical titles (Appendix B). Abbreviated references to alphabetically arranged dictionaries and encyclopedias appear at the beginning of the bibliography (or section).

Biographical dates when cited in parentheses in running text at the first mention of a personal name indicate that the individual does not have an entry in the dictionary. The presence of parenthesized regnal dates for rulers and popes, however, does not necessarily indicate the lack of a biography of that person. Where no dates are provided for an artist or patron, the reader may assume that there is a biography of that individual in the dictionary (or, more rarely, that the person is so obscure that dates are not readily available).

Cross-references are distinguished by the use of small capital letters, with a large capital to indicate the initial letter of the entry to which the reader is directed; for example, 'He commissioned LEONARDO DA VINCI . . .' means that the entry is alphabetized under 'L'.

B

[continued]

Brugghen [Terbrugghen]**, Hendrick (Jansz.) ter** (*b* ?The Hague, 1588; *d* Utrecht, 1 Nov 1629). Dutch painter and draughtsman. He was, with Gerrit van Honthorst and Dirck van Baburen, one of the leading painters in the group of artists active in Utrecht in the 1620s who came to be known as the UTRECHT CARAVAGGISTI, since they adapted Caravaggio's subject-matter and style to suit the Dutch taste for religious and secular paintings. Ter Brugghen was an important innovator for later Dutch 17th-century genre painting; his recognition as an unorthodox, but significant influence on the work of Johannes Vermeer and others is a relatively recent, 20th-century phenomenon.

1. Life and work. 2. Working methods and technique.

1. LIFE AND WORK.

(i) Background and training in The Hague and Utrecht, before *c.* 1605. (ii) Italy, *c.* 1605–14. (iii) Early Utrecht period, 1615–24. (iv) Mature Utrecht period, 1625 and after.

(i) Background and training in The Hague and Utrecht, before c. *1605.* His grandfather, Egbert ter Brugghen (*d* 1583), was a Catholic priest who came from a prominent Utrecht–Overijssel family and who, in the last years of his life, served as the pastor of the Utrecht village of Ter Aa. Hendrick's father, Jan Egbertz. ter Brugghen (*c.* 1561–?1626), though illegitimate, had a successful career as a civil servant: in 1581 he was appointed secretary to the court of Utrecht by Prince William of Orange and in 1586 he was first bailiff *ordinaris* of the chamber of the Provincial Council of Holland at The Hague. Hendrick's date of birth is derived from the biographical inscription placed on the four frames of his series of the *Four Evangelists* (1621; Deventer, Stadhuis) by Richard ter Brugghen (*c.* 1618–1708/10), the only survivor of his eight children, who presented the canvases to the city of Deventer in 1707.

Hendrick was probably born in The Hague rather than Utrecht, as previously believed, since his father appears regularly in The Hague documents from 1585 to 1602. The young Hendrick probably also received his earliest education in The Hague. However, between 1602—when Hendrick would have been 13 or 14—and 1613, Jan ter Brugghen is again intermittently recorded in Utrecht, where Hendrick studied with Abraham Bloemaert—an indisputable fact supported by such 17th-century sources as Sandrart (1675), who had known the painter while a student in Gerrit van Honthorst's Utrecht workshop *c.* 1625–8. (Bloemaert was also van Honthorst's teacher.) What is unknown, however, is whether ter Brugghen first studied with some as yet unidentified master in The Hague before finishing his training with Bloemaert, or whether, like Rembrandt, he first received a conventional Latin education in preparation for a career as a civil servant. The matter is of some importance since it raises the possibility that ter Brugghen was a relatively late or slow starter, which might account for the problems involved in identifying his early work. Exactly how long Hendrick spent in Bloemaert's workshop also remains unknown, but it is unlikely that his training began before 1602, when his father returned to Utrecht.

(ii) Italy, c. *1605–14.* During the summer of 1614 ter Brugghen, along with another Utrecht artist, Thijman van Galen (*b* 1590), was in Milan preparing for his return journey through St Gotthard's Pass to the northern Netherlands. In a Utrecht legal deposition dated 1 April 1615, concerning a third Utrecht artist they had met on their return journey, Michiel van der Zande (*c.* 1583–before 1643), and his young servant, the future landscape painter Frans van Knibbergen (*c.* 1597–1665 or after), ter Brugghen and van Galen testified that they 'had spent some years in Italy exercising their art'. The ambiguous Dutch term *ettelicke* ('some') used by ter Brugghen in the document usually implies an amount less than ten, thus suggesting that the presently accepted sojourn of ten years should be modified. While ter Brugghen could have spent as little as two or three years in Bloemaert's studio before travelling to Italy *c.* 1604 or 1605, he probably left in the spring or summer of 1605—at the age of 16 or 17. He must have arrived in Rome by 1606, if Cornelis de Bie's statement (1708) that he knew Rubens in that city is correct. If so, then ter Brugghen would have been the only member of the Utrecht Caravaggisti to have arrived in Rome while Caravaggio was still active there. Unfortunately, unlike his compatriots van Honthorst and Dirck van Baburen, there is no trace of ter Brugghen's long stay in Italy—either in the form of a document or a work of art. It may be that his youthful style in Italy was sufficiently different from that which he developed after his return to the northern Netherlands to remain unrecognized.

1. Hendrick ter Brugghen: *Adoration of the Magi*, oil on canvas, 1.34×1.60 m, 1619 (Amsterdam, Rijksmuseum)

(iii) Early Utrecht period, 1615–24. In 1616 ter Brugghen entered the Utrecht Guild of St Luke and on 15 October of the same year he married Jacomijna Verbeeck (*d* 1634), the stepdaughter of his elder brother Jan Jansz. ter Brugghen, a Utrecht innkeeper. Even though Utrecht was a predominantly Catholic centre, the marriage ceremony took place in a Reformed Church, and since the children of this marriage were also baptized in the Reformed Church, it seems likely that the artist was himself Protestant rather than Catholic, as was previously thought. This raises important questions about the subject-matter and function of several of the artist's most important works.

Ter Brugghen's earliest known work, a life-size *Supper at Emmaus* (1616; Toledo, OH, Mus. A.), reveals that he had studied Caravaggio's painting of the same theme (between 1596 and 1602; London, N.G.) as well as another version by an anonymous north Italian artist (Vienna, Ksthist. Mus.). Thus ter Brugghen turned not only to the works of Caravaggio himself but also to his north Italian sources and followers. Indeed, various works by members of the Bassano family and their workshop exerted an ongoing influence on ter Brugghen. The only other known dated painting by ter Brugghen from this early Utrecht phase of his development is the signed and dated *Adoration of the Magi* (1619; Amsterdam, Rijksmus.; see fig. 1), an important picture that betrays the influence of such followers of Caravaggio as Carlo Saraceni.

Several undated works by ter Brugghen can be assigned on stylistic grounds to the period before 1620, including the strikingly coloured, full-length version of the *Calling of St Matthew* (Le Havre, Mus. B.-A.), which ter Brugghen repeated in a more compact, half-length composition with a modified colour scheme (1621; Utrecht, Cent. Mus.). These two paintings and other early works are remarkable for their utilization of early 16th-century Netherlandish physiognomic types and still-life details intermixed with formal elements drawn from Caravaggio's famous painting of the same subject in S Luigi dei Francesi, Rome. In another apparent attempt to modify the Italianate elements of his style and thus make his work more acceptable to conservative Utrecht tastes, ter Brugghen, in the unusual *Christ Crowned with Thorns* (1620; Copenhagen, Stat. Mus. Kst), again tempered his personal form of Caravaggism with native poses and physiognomic features, this time drawn from the prints of Lucas van Leyden.

These traditional Netherlandish insertions largely ended with the return of van Honthorst and van Baburen from Italy during 1620. Together with ter Brugghen, these artists quickly succeeded in transforming the nature of Utrecht art during the following year. Indeed, at the beginning of 1621 ter Brugghen was still producing works such as the *Four Evangelists* (Deventer, Stadhuis), which has the same unusual mixture of Caravaggesque elements and traditional 16th-century Netherlandish still-life details. Later that same year, however, when he came into contact with the latest Italian Caravaggesque ideas brought back by van Baburen (with whom he probably shared a workshop from *c*. 1621 until van Baburen's death early in 1624), ter Brugghen executed two lovely pendant versions of *The Flute-player* (both Kassel, Schloss Wilhelmshöhe), one depicted in a pastoral manner, wearing an *all'antica*, toga-like costume, and the other more theatrically dressed in a flamboyant outfit of the type usually described as 'Burgundian'. These influential works are dependent on the Italian Caravaggesque elements developed by Bartolomeo Manfredi in Rome after ter Brugghen had departed in 1614; they can thus only have been introduced into Utrecht by van Baburen and van Honthorst. Van Baburen, in particular, was an important iconographic and artistic innovator in Utrecht, who provided ter Brugghen and other members of the Utrecht Caravaggisti with both new themes and new approaches to old themes; these were quickly taken up and transformed by ter Brugghen.

Despite their varied sources, the two versions of *The Flute-player* do possess the hallmarks of ter Brugghen's style and personality: a subtle utilization of unusual colour harmonies, lively brushwork and paint surfaces, complex and varied drapery folds and, especially, a certain reticence in the compositional structure, which stands in marked contrast to the more extrovert types and arrangements frequently found in the pictures of van Honthorst and van Baburen. From 1621 ter Brugghen often employed a cool, crisp light source and a sense of form derived as much from the direct observation of the movement of light across surfaces as from such prime Italian followers of Caravaggio as Orazio Gentileschi. A closely similar light quality is found in van Baburen's work, implying that both painters developed this characteristic aspect of their style from their study of Gentileschi in Italy. Interestingly, ter Brugghen only rarely deployed the kind of artificial illumination popularized by van Honthorst.

In an effort to account for the new and up-to-date Italianate elements in the two versions of *The Flute-player* as well as in others, it has been suggested that ter Brugghen made a second journey to Italy (Schuckman). However, the only time when the artist's presence in Utrecht is not documented is between the summer of 1619 and the summer of 1621, hardly long enough for him to accomplish the full agenda of stylistic contacts and influences that some scholars would like to assign to this unconfirmed second sojourn in Italy. Furthermore, since there are more dated works by ter Brugghen from 1621 than almost any other year, it is unlikely that he could have spent any part of that critical year travelling.

After 1621 ter Brugghen produced numerous single-figure genre pictures of the type usually associated with Utrecht: lute-players, musicians, drinkers etc. These are usually rendered with a sensitivity beyond the reach of his Utrecht colleagues (who had originated these themes) and with compositional reticence that is frequently in sharp contrast to the type of activities depicted: the theatrical *Singing Lute-player* (*c*. 1623; Algiers, Mus. N. B.-A.), for example, is depicted in lost profile with his back turned towards the viewer. In the pendant canvases (both 1623) of a *Boy Lighting a Pipe* (Erlau, Lyzeum) and a *Boy Holding a Glass* (Raleigh, NC Mus. A.; see fig. 2), ter Brugghen introduced the northern Caravaggesque device of internal artificial illumination associated in Utrecht with van Honthorst. Characteristically, ter Brugghen imbued these apparently simple genre depictions with ideas developed from popular Dutch beliefs concerning the complementary effects of smoking (hot and dry) and drinking (hot and moist), adding an unusually sensitive investigation of the movement of candlelight across the complex arrangement of fabric and form. Moreover, especially in the better-preserved *Boy Lighting a Pipe*, one of the earliest paintings to focus exclusively on the new activity of tobacco smoking, he introduced idiosyncratic colour relationships quite different from those found in his works from before 1621.

About the same time ter Brugghen took up the traditional northern theme of the *Unequal Lovers* (*c*. 1623; New York, priv. col., see 1986–7 exh. cat., no. 14) in an unusually compact, half-length composition that suggests that he had early 16th-century northern moralizing pictures in mind. Indeed, specific details of the depiction of the old man—including his costume—indicate that ter Brugghen had read the appropriate passages in Erasmus's famous *In Praise of Folly* (1511). Although no longer indulging in the same kind of borrowing of archaic motifs as before, ter Brugghen clearly continued to look to his

2. Hendrick ter Brugghen: *Boy Holding a Glass*, oil on canvas, 673×565 mm, 1623 (Raleigh, NC, North Carolina Museum of Art)

northern artistic antecedents more than his Utrecht contemporaries. At the same time, the picture is also strongly dependent on van Baburen for various stylistic and thematic elements; the two artists obviously had an unusually close working relationship throughout the early 1620s.

In the lovely *Liberation of St Peter* (1624; The Hague, Mauritshuis), with colour and compositional patterns that seem to develop out of the *Boy Lighting a Pipe*, ter Brugghen returned to religious subject-matter and introduced new physical types for both the angel and the saint, types that continued to recur in his works until his death. The new type for the angel, with its declamatory gesture, was probably at least partly indebted to van Baburen, who had used a similar pose for an *Annunciation* (untraced; copy by Jan Janssens, Ghent, Mus. B.-A.).

(iv) Mature Utrecht period, 1625 and after. About 1625 ter Brugghen entered into a new and more mature phase of his artistic development with two of his most important and innovative paintings, the *Crucifixion with the Virgin and St John* (New York, Met.; see fig. 3) and *St Sebastian Tended by Women* (Oberlin, OH, Allen Mem. A. Mus.). Both have monumental compositions and the sort of steep perspective traditionally associated with altarpieces for Catholic churches, although it cannot be proven that either ever served such a religious function. Most striking is the *Crucifixion*, an unusually expressive, but obviously 17th-century recreation of a 15th-century northern Netherlandish work of art. The low horizon line, the simple iconic composition, the star-studded sky and the rendering of the body of Christ, as well as other details, suggest that ter Brugghen—or more likely his patron—wanted an old-fashioned picture that could pass, at least at first glance, for a 15th-century altarpiece. The *St Sebastian*, on the other hand, is a modern Caravaggesque work that clearly reflects elements of Caravaggio's *Entombment* (Rome, Pin. Vaticana) as well as his *Incredulity of Thomas* (Potsdam, Neues Pal.); notable in all these works is the use of powerful descending diagonals and the careful positioning of the three heads. Although the new theme of *St Sebastian Tended by Women* owes something to van Baburen's innovative painting of the same subject (Hamburg, Ksthalle), ter Brugghen's version is one of those rare pictures that completely transcends its formal and iconographic sources, a work whose unusually high level of artistic and expressive perfection was rarely matched in Dutch 17th-century religious painting before the mature works of Rembrandt.

3. Hendrick ter Brugghen: *Crucifixion with the Virgin and St John*, oil on canvas, 1.55×1.02 m, *c.* 1625 (New York, Metropolitan Museum of Art)

One of the most unusual of the extremely varied group of history and genre pictures that ter Brugghen created during the second half of the 1620s is the *Sleeping Mars* (*c.* 1625 or 1626; Utrecht, Cent. Mus.). The picture was enormously popular during the 17th century; around 1650 and even later it was the subject of several didactic poems, although the theme was explained entirely in terms of Dutch political events of that later period. In fact, ter Brugghen's picture was executed a few years after the Twelve Years' Truce between Spain and the revolting northern provinces of the Spanish Netherlands had ended in 1621 and should thus be understood as a plea for peace after the resumption of hostilities. Medallions and tokens with similar images of the sleeping god of war had been struck to commemorate the signing of the truce in Utrecht in 1609, and the artist and his patron would certainly have been aware of the symbolic message of these and other related works.

Ter Brugghen's most beautiful and successful genre paintings, also among his mature works, include the candlelit *Musical Company* (*c.* 1627; London, N.G.; see fig. 4). The composition's unusual formality, in contrast to the everyday activities depicted, along with other details suggest that ter Brugghen was inspired by a musical allegory similar to that found in Caravaggio's *Musicians* (New York, Met.). The choice of the three essential categories of music-making (voice, winds and strings) and the elegantly placed wine and grapes—symbolic of the Bacchic origins of music—support such an interpretation.

In 1627 the great Flemish painter Peter Paul Rubens visited Utrecht and stayed in the inn owned by ter Brugghen's brother (lending some credence to de Bie's report that the two artists had met in Rome). He apparently praised the work of ter Brugghen above that of all the other Utrecht artists. This praise would not be difficult to understand even if Rubens had seen only ter Brugghen's *Musical Company*. Rubens's visit may be at least partly responsible for the renewed use of Italian elements in ter Brugghen's work at this time, as can be seen, for example, in the candlelit *Jacob and Esau* (*c.* 1627; Madrid, Col.

4. Hendrick ter Brugghen: *Musical Company*, oil on canvas, 991×1168 mm, *c.* 1627 (London, National Gallery)

Thyssen-Bornemisza), which, although formally structured like the *Musical Group*, is also strongly indebted to elements borrowed from the Bassano workshop, as is his second version of the same theme (*c.* 1627; Berlin, Bodemus.). The rich and varied surface of the *Musical Company* and other late pictures by ter Brugghen, for instance *Melancholy* (Toronto, A.G. Ont.), make it clear that the master's renewed interest in north Italian painting was not limited to composition alone. The layers of fluid, semi-transparent brushwork, unusually subtle colour harmonies and artificial illumination all combine to produce some of the artist's most engaging works. Furthermore, single-figure compositions such as the candlelit *Old Man Writing* (Northampton, MA, Smith Coll. Mus. A.), with its close investigation of artificial light effects, show that ter Brugghen was still influenced by early 16th-century Netherlandish sources, such as Lucas van Leyden's prints and early Leiden school painting, without resorting to the more obvious stylistic archaisms found in his work before 1621.

In stark contrast to the various late candlelit depictions is another group of late paintings, also from 1627 onwards, such as the *Allegory of Taste* (1627; Malibu, CA, Getty Mus.), which introduce a renewed interest in cool, bright daylight. Although the colour is in some ways indebted to early works such as *The Flute-player* pendants, it also benefits from the master's ongoing investigation of artificially lit surfaces and forms. As ter Brugghen approached the age of 40, he entered a new and more mature phase of his development, which features the cool and pale flesh tones seen in the *Allegory of Taste* and in *The Singer* (1628; Basle, Kstmus.). Interestingly, it is this lesser-known late phase of his activity as a painter that seems to anticipate aspects of Vermeer's style even more than the better-known works of *c.* 1621 usually cited.

During 1628 this new phase manifests itself in the use of bright, but subtle colour harmonies in, for example, the signed and dated *Lute-player and Singing Girl* (1628; Paris, Louvre), as well as in the pendants of ancient philosophers, the *Laughing Democritus* and the *Weeping Heraclitus* (both 1628; Amsterdam, Rijksmus.). The *Democritus* especially, with its beautifully rendered cool yellow highlights on the velveteen drapery, reflects the new and innovative direction of the master's formal and colouristic interests during this late stage in his career.

During the last two years of ter Brugghen's life, with works such as the *Annunciation* (1629; Diest, Stedel.

Mus.), the artist continuously experimented with increasingly rich and varied paint surfaces, complex arrangements of drapery folds, the growing use of richly patterned oriental rugs and fabrics and an unusually subtle study of the movement of light across form—all qualities later present in the works of Vermeer. Several of ter Brugghen's late works, for example the painting of *Jacob, Laban and Leah* (Cologne, Wallraf-Richartz Mus.), also include exceptionally sensitive investigations of still-life elements. Their paint surfaces are also more complex, due to the use of increasingly loose and fluid brushstrokes, which frequently overlay more studied and carefully applied areas as, for example, in *Melancholy* and *The Singer*, suggesting that ter Brugghen's premature death, at the age of only 41, may have cut short the most innovative stage of his artistic development.

2. Working methods and technique. The recurrence of figures, poses, facial types and motifs in works dated four and five years apart would seem to indicate that drawings played an important role in the artist's working procedures. A good example of such a repetition is the figure of the angel that appeared first in the *Liberation of St Peter* of 1624. Ter Brugghen later used a closely related, though full-length figure of the angel for two other paintings, both dated 1629: the *Annunciation* (Diest) and an expressively composed second version of the *Liberation of St Peter* (Schwerin, Staatl. Mus.). Furthermore, a similar, half-length angel also appears in the much repeated *King David with Angels* (1628; Warsaw, N. Mus.), which includes a facial type for King David that resembles that of St Peter from the picture of 1624.

Unfortunately, only three drawings by ter Brugghen have survived, all of which are complete compositions (e.g. *Laughing Democritus*, Rouen, Mus. B.-A.) rather than studies for individual figures or heads. Nevertheless, the pattern of repetition in his paintings does seem to support a method of working similar to that utilized by his teacher, Abraham Bloemaert. Thus, despite the obviously Caravaggesque components of his style, ter Brugghen's working method appears to be rooted in Utrecht Late Mannerist workshop procedures more than that of either the younger van Baburen or van Honthorst, despite the fact that the latter had also been a student of Bloemaert.

BIBLIOGRAPHY

J. von Sandrart: *Teutsche Academie* (1675–9); ed. A. R. Peltzer (1925), pp. 178, 401
C. de Bie: *Den spiegel van der verdrayde werelt* (Antwerp, 1708)
J. J. Dodt van Fl[ensburg]: 'Heyndrick ter Brugghen', *Ber. Hist. Gez. Utrecht*, i (1846), pp. 129–36
M. E. Houch: 'Hendrick Ter Brugghen en zijn *Vier Evengelisten* te Deventer', *Eigen Haard*, 32 (1900), pp. 519–23
H. Voss: 'Vermeer van Delft und die Utrechter Schule', *Mhft. Kstwiss.*, v (1912), pp. 79–83
C. H. Collins Baker: 'Hendrik Terbrugghen and Plein Air', *Burl. Mag.*, l (1927), pp. 196–202
R. Longhi: 'Ter Brugghen e la Parte Nostra', *Vita Artistica*, ii (1927), pp. 105–16
A. von Schneider: 'Entlehnungen Hendrick Ter-Brugghen aus dem Werk Caravaggios', *Oud-Holland*, xliv (1927), pp. 261–9
W. Stechow: 'Zu zwei Bildern des Henrick Terbrugghen', *Oud-Holland*, xlv (1928), pp. 277–81
A. von Schneider: *Caravaggio und die Niederländer* (Marburg, 1933)
G. Isarlo: *Caravage et le caravagisme européen* (Aix-en-Provence, 1941)
Caravaggio en de Nederlanden (exh. cat., Utrecht, Cent. Mus.; Antwerp, Kon. Mus. S. Kst.; 1952); review by H. W. Gerson in *Kunstchronik*, v (1952), pp. 287–93; and by B. Nicolson in *Burl. Mag.*, xciv (1952), pp. 247–52
B. Nicolson: *Hendrick Terbrugghen* (The Hague, 1958)
——: 'Second Thoughts about Terbrugghen', *Burl. Mag.*, cii (1960), pp. 465–73
Hendrick Terbrugghen in America (exh. cat. by L. J. Slatkes, Dayton, OH, A. Inst.; Baltimore, MD, Mus. A.; 1965–6)
B. Nicolson: 'Terbrugghen since 1960', *Album amicorum J. G. van Gelder* (The Hague, 1973), pp. 237–41
——: *The International Caravaggesque Movement* (Oxford, 1979); review by L. J. Slatkes in *Simiolus*, xii (1981–82), pp. 167–83
M. J. Bok and Y. Kobayashi: 'New Data on Hendrick ter Brugghen', *Hoogsteder-Naumann Mercury*, i (1985), pp. 7–34
C. Schuckman: 'Did Hendrick ter Brugghen Revisit Italy? Notes from an Unknown Manuscript by Cornelis de Bie', *Hoogsteder-Naumann Mercury*, iv (1986), pp. 7–22
Holländische Malerei in neuem Licht: Hendrick ter Brugghen und seine Zeitgenossen (exh. cat. by A. Blankert, L. J. Slatkes and others; Utrecht, Cent. Mus.; Brunswick, Herzog Anton Ulrich-Mus.; 1986–7); review by B. Schnackenburg in *Kstchronik*, xl (1987), pp. 169–77

LEONARD J. SLATKES

Brugis, Johannes de. *See* Boudolf, Jan.

Brugnoli. Italian family of architects and engineers. Alvise (Luigi) Brugnoli (*b* 1505–9; *d* Venice, 1560) specialized as a fortifications engineer and acted as executant architect for both Michele Sanmicheli and his nephew Giovanni Girolamo Sanmicheli (1513–58), whose sister Laura he married. From 1534 Alvise worked under Michele on Venetian fortifications, including those at Chiusa da Verona (1551) and Legnago (1554), and at Zara (now Zadar; 1534–50), Sebenico (now Šibenik; 1537–9) and Capodistria (now Koper; *c.* 1550) in Dalmatia. In Cyprus he assisted Giovanni Girolamo in the construction of the governor's loggia at Famagusta (*c.* 1550).

Alvise's son, Bernardino Brugnoli (*b* 1538; *d* Venice, 16 March 1583), worked as a civil rather than military architect and was entrusted with the completion of many projects after the death of Michele Sanmicheli. According to Vasari, he was responsible for saving Sanmicheli's circular design for the church of the Madonna di Campagna (begun 1559) at San Michele Extra, near Verona, from being compromised by the 'miserliness' of the building commissioners. It seems, however, that he was not always so scrupulous in adhering to Sanmicheli's intentions: the window tabernacles (before 1579) of the campanile of S Giorgio in Braida, Verona, have pediments broken by the insertion of a ball on a pedestal, a feature wholly uncharacteristic of Sanmicheli's style. Brugnoli's design for the high altar there has paired Composite columns that support a pediment and the whole follows the curve of the church's apse, like the curved tabernacles in Sanmicheli's Pellegrini Chapel (begun 1527) in S Bernardino, Verona. In 1570 the Bishop of Reggio Emilia chose Bernardino's design for the completion of the cathedral façade, but it was never executed. Bernardino's career reached its zenith in 1580 when Andrea Palladio recommended him for the post of architect to the court of Guglielmo Gonzaga, 3rd Duke of Mantua.

BIBLIOGRAPHY

DBI [with full bibliog.]; Thieme–Becker
G. Vasari: *Vite* (1550, rev. 2/1568); ed. G. Milanesi (1878–85)
E. Langenskiöld: *Michele Sanmicheli: The Architect of Verona* (Uppsala, 1938)

PAUL DAVIES, DAVID HEMSOLL

Brugsal, Alexander van. *See under* MASTERS, ANONYMOUS, AND MONOGRAMMISTS, §III: MASTER S.

Bruguière, Francis (*b* San Francisco, CA, 16 Oct 1880; *d* London, 8 May 1945). American photographer. He studied painting in Europe and trained as a photographer in New York with Frank Eugene. In 1905, after meeting Alfred Stieglitz and the photographers associated with the 291 gallery in New York, he became a member of the Photo-Secession. From then until 1918 he experimented with photography in San Francisco; some of his photographs appeared in *Camera Work* in 1916. In 1919 he opened his own photographic studio in New York. He became well known for his images of alienation—reminiscent of the Cubists—which he achieved by photographing subjects with the help of mirrors. He was an important pioneer of theatre photography, collaborating with Norman Bel Geddes and making an important contribution to the latter's edition of Dante's *Divine Comedy* in 1924. His preoccupation with light led him to create abstract photographs from elements of light, some of which were exhibited at the Sturm-Galerie in Berlin in 1928, on the strength of which he was elected an honorary member of the German Secessionists. The images were also featured in his book *Beyond this Point* (1929). Another product of his experiments with light was his 1930 film *Light Rhythms*. He experimented with multiple exposures, taking a series of photographs of France's cathedrals and Manhattan's skyscrapers. These fascinated his contemporaries from the way in which reality dissolved into abstract patterns. In the 1930s he concentrated on technical experiments, and after 1940 devoted himself to painting.

PHOTOGRAPHIC PUBLICATIONS

with N. Bel Geddes: *Divine Comedy* (New York, 1924)
with L. Sieveking: *Beyond this Point* (London, 1929)

BIBLIOGRAPHY

J. Enyeart: *Bruguière: His Photographs and his Life* (New York, 1977)

ERIKA BILLETER

Brühl, Heinrich, Graf von (*b* Gangloffsömmern, 13 Aug 1700; *d* Dresden, 28 Oct 1763). German statesman and patron. Through his talents as a courtier and diplomat and his knowledge in the field of fine arts, he rose from being a page at the court of Frederick Augustus I of Saxony to the office of chief minister (1746) under Frederick Augustus II, King of Saxony, largely by securing the latter's election as King of Poland. Placed in complete charge of policy, by skilful diplomacy he was able continually to tap new sources of revenue, strengthening the economic and cultural importance of Saxony and acquiring great personal wealth. He built fine houses, including the Brühl Palais and its gardens, Dresden, and acquired an important collection of paintings, drawings and engravings, many by Dutch and Flemish artists. With his crucial collaboration, the royal art collections and court opera (of which he was general director from 1738) in Dresden achieved renown (*see* DRESDEN, §II). He was among those who promoted the Meissen porcelain factory (*see* MEISSEN, §3), becoming chief director in 1739. He can also be credited with the development of the textile industry in Saxony.

His promotion of the alliance between Austria, France and Russia attracted the enmity of Frederick II, King of Prussia, who accused him of intriguing against Prussia and of feathering his own nest, a suspicion that cannot be substantiated. In 1756 Frederick II compelled the Saxon army to capitulate at Pirna, and Brühl and the King of Poland were forced to withdraw to Warsaw, a move by which Brühl's political activities were greatly circumscribed. Hatred of Brühl even led Frederick II to destroy the former's houses and estates. Directly after returning from Poland with his master in 1763, Brühl died, allegedly owing an enormous debt to the state treasury of Saxony. His art collection was bought by Catherine the Great for the Hermitage in St Petersburg.

BIBLIOGRAPHY

ADB; *NDB*
J. G. H. von Justi: *Leben und Charakter des Graf von Brühl*, 3 vols (?Ulm, 1760–64)
F. Neidhart: 'Der Nachlass des kursächsischen Premierministers Reichsgraf Heinrich von Brühl', *Mitt. Ver. Gesch. Dresdens*, viii (1888), pp. 1–26
R. Becker: *Der Dresdner Friede und die Politik Brühls* (Leipzig, 1902)
R. Beyrich: *Kursachsen und die polnische Thronfolge, 1733/36* (Leipzig, 1913)
A. Philipp: *Sulkowski und Brühl und die Entstehung des Premierministeramtes in Sachsen* (1920)
O. E. Schmidt: *Minister Graf Brühl und K. H. von Heinecken, 1733–1763* (Leipzig, 1920)
E. Herrmann: 'Andeutungen über die russische Politik des Reichsgrafen Heinrich von Brühl', *Umění*, ii (1922), pp. 1–60
A. von Boroviczény: *Graf von Brühl* (1929)
R. L. Koehl: 'Heinrich Brühl: A Saxonian Politician of the Eighteenth Century', *J. Cent. Eur. Affairs*, xiii (1954), p. 311

PETRA SCHNIEWIND-MICHEL

Brühl [Augustusburg]**, Schloss.** German Electoral castle, *c.* 8 km west of the Rhine, halfway between Bonn and Cologne. The medieval castle, a massive rectangular building containing a court and surrounded by a moat, was extensively destroyed by Louis XIV's troops in 1689. Elector Joseph Clemens of Cologne decided to rebuild the ruin, and in 1715 his architectural adviser, the Parisian court architect Robert de Cotte, submitted plans for the project. No work had begun, however, when Joseph Clemens died in 1723. His nephew and successor, Clemens August, immediately took over the project, employing an experienced local architect, Johann Conrad Schlaun. In his scheme Schlaun incorporated much of the existing fabric. He duplicated the existing north-west tower with another in the south-west and retained the moat around the whole site, creating a C-shaped building that was open to the east. Construction of the two-storey elevation, set on a one-storey base and capped by a mansard roof, was complete by 1728. Pilasters marked the centres and ends of the wings, and large windows throughout eliminated much of the wall mass, resulting in an exterior that was both monumental and open.

Clemens August, who had visited Versailles in 1725, employed the Bavarian court architect François de Cuvilliés I for the interiors; the latter produced elegant Rococo creations of stucco, including panels with ornamentation that rises above the ceiling coves, and smooth white surfaces. While Cuvilliés worked inside, the gardener Dominique Girard, a pupil of André Le Nôtre, located a terrace and stair along the south wing, filled in the moat and laid out a formal garden with a central axis that stretches from the terrace into the distant landscape. Far from the castle, Cuvilliés built the Falkenlust (1729–34), an intimate pavilion connected to the main complex by a long allée. Closer to the castle stood the Chinese House (1747–53; destr. 1822), a pavilion built to house the porcelain collection, and the Hyazinthenburg (1747–68; destr. 1788). From 1735 Cuvilliés decorated the centrepieces of the east and west façades, removing the towers that had marked the corners of the latter. He added long galleries to the west, establishing a deep court as a counterpoint to the eastern court of the castle.

By *c.* 1740, when Cuvilliés had returned to Munich, the new interiors, modified façades and landscaped setting had transformed Schloss Brühl into a contemporary Residenz. During the 1740s Balthasar Neumann aggrandized this transformation by locating a stately staircase just inside the entrance and reorganizing the rooms on the *piano nobile* that lead to the apartment in the south wing. The stair runs in a single flight to a landing dominated by a tomb-like monument to *Clemens August*, and from there, two return flights rise on bridges supported by caryatid trios at the foot and *faux-marbre* columns over the entrance passage. The ceiling above opens to reveal a circular gallery and a dome-like fresco depicting the *Apotheosis of Clemens August*. Neumann designed the stair, while the upper parts of the stair-hall were from plans by Michel Leveilly and Johann Adolf Biarelle (*fl c.* 1743), stuccoed by Giuseppe Artaria (1697–1769), Carlo Pietro Morsegno (*d* 1754) and Giuseppe Antonio Brilli (*d* 1794), and frescoed by Carlo Carlone (ii). Neumann also remodelled the interior of the adjacent Franciscan church for use by the inhabitants of Schloss Brühl. Decoration of the castle interiors continued into the 1760s, well after the death of Clemens August. The alterations and damage that occurred during the 19th and 20th centuries were later corrected by extensive campaigns to restore the castle and its grounds to their 18th-century appearance.

BIBLIOGRAPHY

E. Renard and F. Wolff Metternich: *Schloss Brühl* (Berlin, 1934)
Kurfürst Clemens August (exh. cat., Brühl, Schloss Augustusburg, 1961)
W. Hansmann: *Das Treppenhaus und das grosse neue Appartement des Brühler Schlosses* (Düsseldorf, 1972)

CHRISTIAN F. OTTO

Brukalski. Polish architects. Stanisław Brukalski (*b* Warsaw, 8 May 1894; *d* 24 Jan 1967) and his wife Barbara Brukalska [née Sokołowska] (*b* Brzeźce, nr Radom, 4 Dec 1899; *d* Warsaw, 3 March 1980) were both members of Praesens, a Polish group of Functionalist architects. He studied architecture (1918–25) in Milan and Warsaw, where she was an architecture student (1921–34) at the Technical University. In 1927 they visited the Netherlands. That year they were engaged by the Warsaw Housing Cooperative to design low-cost blocks of flats in the Żoliborz district of Warsaw, emphasizing such labour-saving devices as central heating, gas supplied to bathrooms and kitchens, built-in cupboards and tiled surfaces. They also designed a 'laboratory kitchen' based on Grete Schütte-Lihotzky's Frankfurt kitchen of *c.* 1928 (*see* MAY, ERNST). The blocks have simple, disciplined forms, the potential monotony of which is relieved by rounded corner balconies or curved staircases projecting in front of the elevation. The entrances to all the blocks are off landscaped courtyards rather than the street. The Warsaw Housing Cooperative development has affinities with German and, especially, Dutch ideas of the time, in particular those of J. J. P. Oud. The Brukalskis' own house (1927–9) at 8 Niegolewskiego Street, Warsaw, is indebted to Neo-plasticist architecture, with elevations and spatial distribution in the spirit of Gerrit Rietveld's Schröder House (1924), Utrecht. From 1929 they were involved with the Polish Society for Housing Reform, which attempted to implement in Poland contemporary developments in urban planning, prefabrication and low-cost housing.

Barbara Brukalska's polemical writings, in which she criticized 'unbridled individualism' in architecture and asserted the need for architects to respond to 'existing (i.e. social) reality', place her among the unmitigated Functionalists. In that capacity she and her husband visited the CIAM conference at Athens in 1933.

Stanisław Brukalski undertook building projects with other partners, for example Józef Szanajca (1902–39), with whom he designed blocks of flats (1930–31) for the Social Insurance Institution in the Żoliborz district. The Polish Pavilion (destr.) that he designed with Bohdan Pniewski for the Exposition Internationale des Arts et Techniques dans la Vie Moderne (Paris, 1937) consisted of a cylindrical tower, clad in rectangular concrete slabs, with a vertical opening to its full height; in contrast to the smoothness of the tower an enclosing wall of roughly hewn stonework was set around its base. After World War II Brukalski was a chief architect at the state-run Miastoprojekt ('city project') where he designed numerous buildings. He taught architectural design at the Warsaw Technical University, where his wife taught design and architectural composition. In 1948 they were both made professors, Barbara Brukalska becoming the first woman professor at that university.

WRITINGS

B. Brukalska: 'Architektura pospolita' [Everyday architecture], *Pion*, iii (1934)
S. Brukalski: 'Uwagi o organizacji pracy projektodawczej dla drobnego budownictwa mieszkaniowego' [Notes on organization of housing design], *Architektura i Budownictwo*, 2 (1934), pp. 54ff
B. Brukalska and S. Brukalski: 'Nasza praca nad mieszkaniem robotniczym' [Our work on working class dwellings], *Dom, Osiedle, Mieszkanie*, viii/10–11 (1936), pp. 16ff

BIBLIOGRAPHY

L. Heyman: *Nowy Żoliborz, 1918–1939* [New Żoliborz, 1918–1939] (Wrocław, 1976)
O. Czerner and H. Listowski: *Awangarda polska* [Polish avant-garde] (Warsaw, 1981)

WANDA KEMP-WELCH

Brukenthal, Samuel, Baron von (*b* Leschkirch, Transylvania, 26 July 1721; *d* Sibiu, 9 March 1803). Transylvanian statesman and collector. He studied law and philosophy at the universities in Halle and Jena (1743–4). He was created a baron by Empress Maria-Theresa (1762) and with her support was appointed Governor of Transylvania (1777–87). His collections were built up mainly in Vienna, where he attended auctions and bought from dealers; he also acquired or received as gifts a few works from the Viennese imperial collections. Unless otherwise stated, works from his collections are held in the Brukenthal Museum in Sibiu. Brukenthal not only bought paintings but also formed archaeological, numismatic and mineralogical collections, a prints collection and an ample library containing many old manuscripts and incunabula and some of the most significant books of the 18th century, among them editions of Immanuel Kant and Johann Gottfried Herder and Diderot's *Encyclopédie*. His most renowned manuscript, however, is the Brukenthal Breviary, with miniatures by early 16th-century Flemish artists. Brukenthal acquired some important Flemish paintings, including van Eyck's *Man with a Blue Cap* (early 1420s) and two portraits by Memling that were subsequently moved to the National Museum of Art, Bucharest, as well as a few works by Jordaens, among them *Summer* (*c*. 1623–5; Bucharest, N. Mus. A.). He also bought still-lifes with game by Jan Fyt and several works by David Teniers II. Among his Dutch paintings were landscapes (Bucharest, N. Mus. A.) by Philips Koninck and Philips Wouwerman, a portrait by Michiel van Mierevelt and some canvases by such Utrecht Caravaggisti as Hendrick Terbrugghen (*David Holding Goliath's Head, Celebrated by Women*; 1623), Jan van Bronchorst and Jan van Bijlert. His Italian paintings included a *Crucifixion* (*c*. 1452–3; Bucharest, N. Mus. A.) by Antonello da Messina and six canvases by Alessandro Magnasco, three of which are now in the National Museum of Art, Bucharest. Brukenthal's interest in Mannerist painting led him to collect mythological compositions by Cornelis Cornelisz. van Haarlem, Hendrick van Balen and Hans von Aachen. He also had French paintings by Jean Raoux and Jean-Baptiste Oudry. The German and Austrian Baroque were particularly well represented in his collection by the allegorical and religious compositions of Johann Michael Rottmayr, battle scenes by Johann Philip Lemke, landscapes by Kilian Fabritius and Johann Christian Brand and some court portraits by Martin Mijtens. A palace built in Sibiu between 1778 and 1786 housed the Brukenthal collections after their removal from Vienna; in 1817 the palace was opened to the public as a museum.

BIBLIOGRAPHY

M. Csaki: *Baron Brukenthalisches Museum: Führer durch die Gemäldegalerie*, rev. 6 (Hermannstadt, 1909)
E. Sigerus: 'Beiträge zur Geschichte des Baron Brukenthalischen Museums', *Mitt. Baron Brukenthal. Mus.*, v (1935), pp. 25–42
T. Ionescu: *Muzeul Brukenthal: Galeria de artă plastică* (Bucharest, 1964)
G. A. Schuller: *Samuel von Brukenthal*, 2 vols (Munich, 1967–8)

REMUS NICULESCU

Brumidi, Constantino (*b* Rome, 26 July 1805; *d* Washington, DC, 19 Feb 1880). American painter of Italian birth. From the age of 13 he studied at the Accademia di San Luca in Rome under the Neo-classical painter, Vincenzo Camuccini. Brumidi's work in Rome included the decoration of the Palazzo Torlonia, the restoration of a loggia and portrait painting at the Vatican, and the murals in the sanctuary of the Madonna dell'Archetto (dedicated in 1851). Jailed for his part in the 1849 republican uprising after the French occupation of Rome, he fled to America in 1852.

After painting altarpieces in Mexico City, Brumidi settled in Washington, DC, where new wings and a dome were being added to the Capitol building. In 1855, in the House of Representatives wing, he demonstrated his skill with *Cincinnatus Being Called from his Plough*, the first true fresco in America. For the next 25 years he decorated committee and reception rooms and the corridors of the Capitol in an Italian Neo-classical style, combining Classical mythology and allegorical figures with American history, technology and wildlife. His masterpiece was the *Apotheosis of George Washington*, painted on the canopy suspended over the eye of the inner dome of the US Capitol (1865; *c*. 19 m diam.; *in situ*; *see* WASHINGTON, DC, §III, 1 and fig. 5). The frescoed frieze at the base of the dome (91 m long) depicts scenes from American history in grisaille. It was begun in 1878 and continued from Brumidi's sketches after his death. These frescoes, hidden for many years under layers of grime and overpaint, were cleaned between 1986 and 1988, revealing Brumidi's radiant colour and mastery of illusionistic mural painting.

BIBLIOGRAPHY

C. Fairman: *Art and Artists of the Capitol of the United States of America* (Washington, DC, 1927)
M. Cheney Murdock: *Constantino Brumidi: Michelangelo of the United States Capitol* (Washington, DC, 1950)

BARBARA ANN BOESE WOLANIN

Brun, Charles-Frédéric [Le Déserteur] (*b* Colmar, Alsace, *c*. 1815; *d* Veysonnaz, Valais, 9 March 1871). Swiss painter. His early life is undocumented; he fled France in 1850 and on reaching Switzerland lived in the canton of Valais, earning food and lodging by painting. Though there are few pieces dated before 1850, the style of his work suggests that he trained in the studio of an ex-voto painter in France. He concentrated almost entirely on religious subjects, often using mountain settings and basing the figures on local people. Painted in bright unmodelled colour, the pictures are in a naive style, neglecting details and employing a shallow pictorial space, as in *St John the Baptist* (1853; Sion, Valais, Dr A. Sierro, priv. col., see Giono, p. 101). In this work, a stretch of water is labelled 'mer morte'; Brun often used such labels for both figures and natural features within the picture. Some of his works were structured as a narrative sequence of separate images, as in *L'Histoire de Geneviève, Comtesse de Brabant, Epouse du Comte Sifrois* (1857; Fully, Valais, priv. col., see Giono, pp. 106–7), which consists of 12 framed and captioned panels. In addition to his religious works he also painted a few portraits, such as *Marie Jeanne Bournissay, Feme a Légier Fragnier, né l'année 1812, mariée l'année 1830* (*sic*: undated; Fully, Valais, Abbé H. Bonvin priv. col., see Giono, p. 53). In this work also religious symbols remain dominant.

BIBLIOGRAPHY

J. Giono: *Le Déserteur* (Lausanne, 1966)

□

Brun, Franz (*fl* ?Strasbourg, *c*. 1559–96). German draughtsman and engraver. He worked in the style of the Nuremberg LITTLE MASTERS. His many known engravings (Bartsch names 111; Passavant, 134) include animal and fencing scenes, military figures (in individual pictures of 1559), Turkish figures, rustic genre scenes, allegories, coats of arms and ornaments. The cycle showing *Christ, the Twelve Apostles and St Paul* (1562–3; B 1–13) is initialled, but Brun also used a monogram, formerly wrongly identified as that of Friedrich Brentel I. He has also been falsely attributed with a copy of Albrecht Dürer's *Passion* engraving, the work of another Franz Brun (*fl* Cologne, 1589–1652).

BIBLIOGRAPHY
Thieme–Becker
A. von Bartsch: *Le Peintre-graveur*, ix (1807), pp. 443–72 [B]
J. D. Passavant: *Le Peintre-graveur*, iv (Leipzig, 1862), pp. 176–8
G. K. Nagler: *Künstler-Lexicon*, ii (1872), p. 167

VERONIKA BRAUNFELS

Brun, Louis-Auguste (*b* Rolle, Vaud, 3 Oct 1758; *d* Paris, 9 Oct 1815). Swiss painter. He came of a prosperous Huguenot family and trained to be a merchant before deciding to become an artist. His first tutor was Nicolas Henri Joseph Fassin, who was staying in Geneva at the time; under his guidance, Brun made copies of Flemish masters. In Geneva he became friendly with Pierre-Louis De La Rive, worked in his Geneva studio and accompanied him on a journey to Mannheim and Dresden. In his own painting Brun soon specialized in charming hunting scenes with Rococo overtones in the style of Philips Wouwerman. In 1779 he set out on an Italian journey that lasted several years. In 1783 he travelled from Turin to Paris, where his hunting scenes soon became very popular with the French court: he painted portraits of *Marie-Antoinette Hunting* and *Louis XVI Hunting*. He became a member of the Académie Royale in Paris in 1788 but in 1792 fled from the French Revolution to his homeland; there he took part in the Vaudois independence movement. He was burgomaster of Versoix from 1801 to 1807, eventually known as 'Brun de Versoix'. In 1815 he returned to Paris after the fall of Napoleon, in order to claim from Louis XVIII the pension that Louis XVI had promised him.

BIBLIOGRAPHY
SKL
D. Agassiz: *Louis Auguste Brun, 1758–1815: Un Peintre suisse à la cour de Louis XVI* (Lausanne, 1931)
F. Zelger: *Stiftung Oskar Reinhart Winterthur*, i (Zurich, 1977), pp. 105–7

MATTHIAS FREHNER

Brunei. Small sultanate (5765 sq. km) on the central part of the north-west coast of the island of Borneo (see fig. 1). Once important for its rubber plantations, this hot, wet, equatorial land of mountains and rain-forests is ruled by the richest man in the world, its sources of wealth being oil and natural gas. Of the population of just over 200,000, 65% are Malay, 23% Chinese. Islam is the official religion.

For map of Peninsular Malaysia, *see* MALAYSIA, fig. 1.

PHILIP STOTT

1. History. 2. Architecture. 3. Metalwork. 4. Ceramics. 5. Coins. 6. Other arts.

1. HISTORY. The kingdom of Brunei, called Po'ni in the early Chinese chronicles, may date to the 7th century AD. It was part of a trading empire along the north-west coast of Borneo where forest products such as camphor, resins and hornbill 'ivory' gathered from the interior were exchanged for imported Chinese porcelain and metalwork. Brunei became increasingly important from the early 15th century, largely as a result of its links with the sultanate of

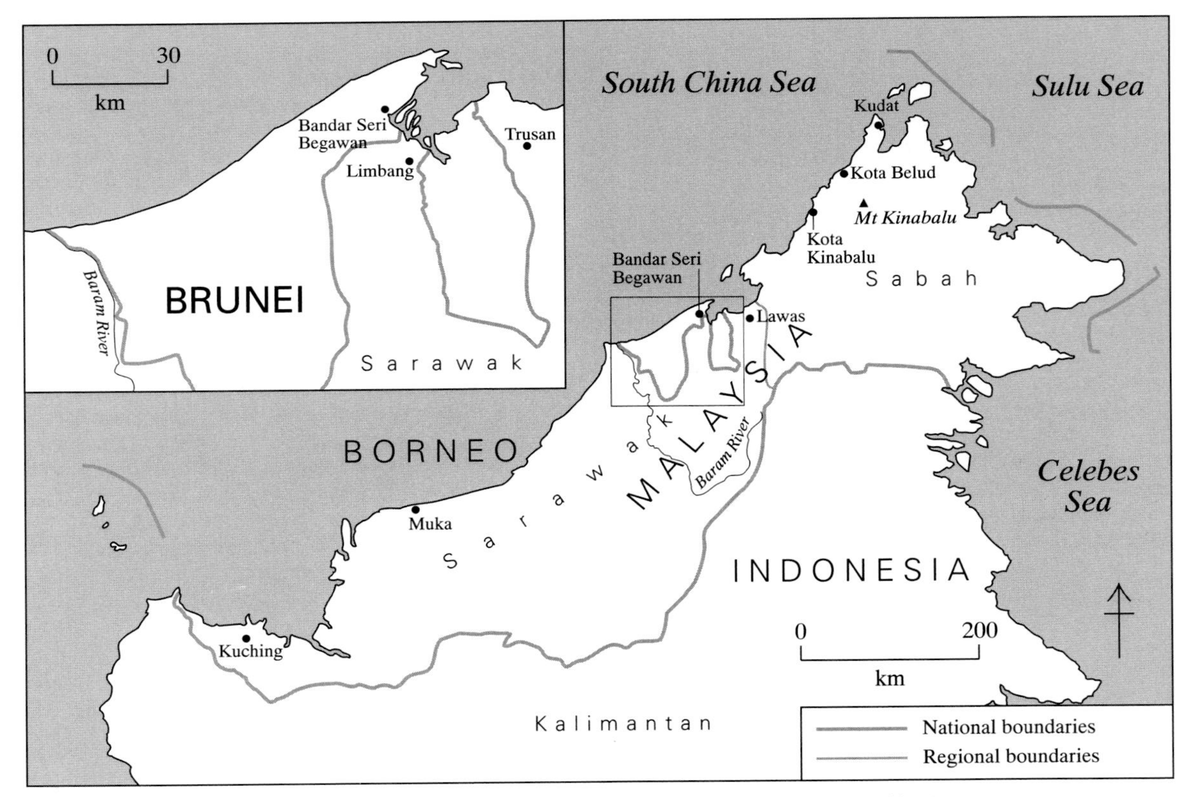

1. Map of Brunei and East Malaysia; those regions with separate entries in this dictionary are distinguished by CROSS-REFERENCE TYPE

Malacca in Peninsular Malaysia. From Malacca, the most important entrepôt in South-east Asia and heartland of Malay culture, Islam was disseminated to other states, including Brunei, which adopted a complex of cultural traits derived from Islam, the Middle East and India: Arabic calligraphy, styles in jewellery and religious architecture, and forms and motifs in metal, wood, cloth and stone. In 1521, Antonio Pigafetta, companion of the Portuguese navigator Ferdinand Magellan, described Brunei as a state of considerable wealth and cultural sophistication, but increasing control of its trade by Europeans led to Brunei's decline from the 16th century onwards. In the 19th century the British rajas of Sarawak, the Brooke family, progressively extended their rule at the expense of the sultanate, and from the 1880s Brunei was also squeezed in the north-east by the expansion of the British North Borneo Chartered Company. Brunei became a British protectorate in 1888; a British Resident was appointed in 1906. The sultanate became fully independent on 1 January 1984, as Negara Brunei Darussalam (Brunei, Abode of Peace). The dominant cultural influence today is Islam, but there are various non-Malay peoples in the rural areas of Brunei, such as the Penan and Iban, who still hold to ancient beliefs in a spirit world.

BIBLIOGRAPHY

D. E. Brown: *Brunei: The Structure and History of a Bornean Malay Sultanate* (Brunei, 1979)

A. V. M. Horton: *The British Residency in Brunei, 1906–1959* (Hull, 1984)

R. Singh: *Brunei, 1839–1983: The Problems of Political Survival* (Singapore, 1984)

J. W. Christie: 'On Po'ni: The Santubong Sites of Sarawak', *Sarawak Mus. J.*, xxxiv/55 (1985), pp. 77–89

2. ARCHITECTURE. The Brunei Malays mainly reside in the capital Bandar Seri Begawan and its environs, especially in Kampong Ayer, the 'water village' of Malay-style family dwellings near the main mosque, raised on wooden stilts above the water in the bay. The traditional house is usually built on a rectangular plan with a front verandah that serves as a reception area, an adjacent living-room and bedrooms at the rear. The kitchen is located at the back of the house, sometimes under the same roof and sometimes separate and connected to the main house by a walkway. Formerly some houses had tiered roofs but by the late 20th century they were all built with a simple pitched roof, either of wooden shingles or, increasingly, of corrugated metal sheeting.

In the past royal buildings were built of planed wood on massive stilts. They had several annexes and pitched and tiered roofs. More recently royal palaces and mosques have been built in mortar, showing a distinct Middle Eastern influence in their characteristic onion-shaped domes and minarets. The main Sultan Ali Saifuddin mosque has an impressive golden dome covered with 3 million pieces of Venetian mosaic and a 51m minaret. Marble is also commonly used for floors and stairways. The Istana Nurul Imam ('palace of the Light of faith'), built to mark Brunei's full independence in 1984, has a marble façade and carved mahogany entrance. Set on a low hill not far from Kampong Ayer near the Brunei River, its large golden dome looms above the Suran (or small mosque) balanced by a smaller dome, and a gracious roof rises to an apex at either end. Within are 1788 rooms and internal courtyards with gardens and fountains.

BIBLIOGRAPHY

Brunei: The Land and its People (Bandar Seri Begawan, n.d.)

A. J. Chalfont (Baron): *By God's Will: A Portrait of the Sultan of Brunei* (London, 1989)

3. METALWORK. The craft of casting brass by the lost-wax process has long been established in Brunei, certainly since the 16th century, and probably earlier. Skills were closely guarded and passed down within specific Brunei Malay families. Guildlike organizations were concentrated in certain parts of the 'water village' on the bay at the capital Bandar Seri Begawan, including Kampong Sumbiling, Sungai Kedayan and Ujong Bukit. The craft may have derived from the Javanese kingdom of Majapahit in the 13th or 14th century, but in addition to local Malay traditions there is also evidence of Chinese, Iranian, Indian and Dongson (North Vietnam) influences. 'Brunei brass' was traditionally made from pure copper or a copper with tin or zinc mix. Its earliest styles are distinguished from other Malay traditions by their decorative ornateness. The court and religious institutions were the main patrons of arts and crafts. Brunei smiths made caskets, salvers, lamps and perfume sprinklers for the wealthy. They also made objects for ordinary domestic and ritual use—betel-nut and tobacco boxes, water and rice containers, kettles and deep-rimmed gongs. However, the most famous articles are the brass cannons. The Brunei Museum in Kota Batu has a collection of over 500 pieces, from large cannons (*bedil*) to miniatures (*mariam*, *boom*). Some were plain, many ornamented. The most distinctive is the *bedil naga* (dragon cannon; see fig. 2), a cannon in the form of a scaly crocodile with protruding feet, a curved tail serving as a rear handle, and a muzzle with teeth. Other cannons had leaf motifs on metal bands around the barrel near the breech, muzzle and lugs.

Among the most remarkable items are the kettles, some of which weigh as much as 30 kg. The designs are usually of Islamic inspiration. The decoration, engraved or embossed, incorporates leaf and flower motifs, including stylized lotus and fig-leaf forms, scrollwork, abstract geometric patterns and Arabic calligraphy. The influence of the Dongson culture is seen in spiral, curvilinear and rhomb motifs. There are also highly ornamental kettles of a non-Islamic kind, decorated with perfect miniatures of lizards, frogs, dragons, serpents, dogs, hornbills and humans fixed on the surface, with decorative handles, knobs in the form of reptiles' heads and spouts in the form of animals' mouths. Kettles were used as water containers on ritual occasions to serve drinking-water and for washing hands and feet. They, like other items of brassware, were passed on as heirlooms or exchanged as dowry articles or in payment of fines.

Silversmithing also dates at least to the 16th century and was practised under royal and religious patronage. Brunei smiths made the magnificent censers in the main mosque, which comprise several hundred small pieces of silver welded together. Originally the silver came from melted-down coinage. Later, strip silver and ingots were used. Java may have been an important early influence on Brunei silversmithing, though skills seem to have come

2. Brass cannon in the form of a crocodile, known as *bedil naga*, 1.99 m, mid-19th century (Kota Batu, Brunei Museum)

ultimately from the Middle East via India and possibly from China.

The main techniques of decoration are chasing and repoussé or embossing. Silver filigree is employed in jewellery manufacture. As with brassware, decorative motifs on the surface of silver objects comprise delicate and stylized floral motifs, especially the leaf-and-tendril design known as *bunga air muleh*. Objects were overwhelmingly for court use and included elaborately ornamented betel-nut boxes, bowls, salvers and pedestal trays. Jewellery included burial headgear, belts, filigree earrings, bracelets, armlets and anklets of beaten silver, buckle-brooches and breast pendants.

BIBLIOGRAPHY

J. S. Lim and P. M. Shariffuddin: 'Brunei Brass: The Traditional Method of Casting', *Brunei Mus. J.*, iii/4 (1976), pp. 142–66

A. A. Choo: *Silver* (Singapore, 1984)

P. H. Ismail bin P. Ibrahim: 'The Craft of the Silversmith in Brunei', *Brunei Mus. J.*, vi/1 (1985), pp. 89–104

B. Singh: *Malay Brassware* (Singapore, 1985)

J. W. Christie and V. T. King: *Metalworking in Borneo: Essays on Iron- and Silverworking in Sarawak* (Hull, 1988)

VICTOR T. KING

4. CERAMICS. Brunei was a major transhipment centre on the international east–west trade route. Quantities of Chinese ceramics found at two primary sites, Sungai Lumut and Kota Batu, attest to its importance. Although a few pieces are as early as the 7th century AD, most date from the late 14th century to the mid-17th. The main types found at Sungai Lumut are early Ming blue and white (*see* CHINA, §VII, 3(vi)) and a few Thai Sawankhalok pieces (*see* THAILAND, §V, 3). At Kota Batu finds include early monochromes, Ming blue and white, celadons, white and brown monochromes, polychromes and Vietnamese blue and white (*see* VIETNAM, §V).

BIBLIOGRAPHY

J. Guy: *Oriental Trade Ceramics in South-east Asia: 9th–16th Century* (Singapore, 1986)

DAWN F. ROONEY

5. COINS. The Boxer Codex, compiled *c.* 1500, contains an enigmatic description of an ancient silver coinage of Brunei, perhaps similar to the sandalwood-flower series of Java (*see* INDONESIA, §VIII, 4). The first surviving coin issues, cast tin-lead alloy pieces, date to the late 16th century. The series was maintained until the early part of the 19th century, when it was replaced by cotton cloth, scrap iron and cannons cast from Chinese copper cash coins. The majority of Brunei's coinage is epigraphic, inscribed with the epithets of Brunei's rulers: *sulṭān al-ādil* ('the just sultan') and *malik al-ẓāhir* ('the acknowledged ruler'), rarely indicating the name of the issuing ruler. None is dated. Brunei coinage is distinctive in that the reverse is often ornamented with a rosette or mill-sail pattern, frequently incorporating the inscription into the design. Others have a recumbent camel or fantastic animal on the obverse.

BIBLIOGRAPHY

R. Hanitsch: 'Tin and Lead Coins from Brunei', *J. Straits Branch Royal Asiat. Soc.*, xlix (1907), pp. 111–14

E. Wodak: 'Old Brunei Coins', *Sarawak Mus. J.*, viii (1958), pp. 278–92
S. Singh and others: *Catalogue of Malaysia, Singapore, and Brunei Coins, 1700–1974* (Singapore, 1974); rev. as *The Standard Catalogue of Coins and Banknotes of Malaysia, Singapore, and Brunei, 1700–1976* (Singapore, 1976)
J. A. Davidson: 'Brunei Coinage', *Brunei Mus. J.*, iv/1 (1977), pp. 43–81
R. S. Wicks: *A Survey of Native South-east Asian Coinage, circa 450–1850: Documentation and Typology* (Ph.D. diss., Ithaca, NY, Cornell U., 1983)

ROBERT S. WICKS

6. OTHER ARTS. Brunei Malays and other, much smaller groups such as the Kedayans are well known for their skills in plaiting rattan carrying-baskets in diagonal weave. Also made are fine-quality *pandan* mats (Malay *pandam*: a member of the plant family Pandanaceae). These are sometimes dyed in pink, green, yellow and blue and woven into patterns with diagonal stripes. Motifs are usually abstract and geometric, composed of triangles, zigzags and keys. *Pandan* fans, purses, bags, sunhats and conical dish covers are also made. Motifs representing flora and fauna appear on baskets woven from bamboo (see fig. 3).

3. Round basket of a type known as *bakul bulat*, bamboo, h. 100 mm, border diam. 190 mm, from Brunei, 20th century (Kota Batu, Brunei Museum)

Some Brunei women are skilled in weaving the sumptuous cloth known as *kain songket*, with its gold- and silver-threaded supplementary weft, using a wooden frame loom and hand-shuttle; this silk or cotton cloth is also found in other parts of the Malay world. The sarong is usually decorated with lozenge or chevron designs in the head-panel across the centre of the cloth, with bamboo-shoot patterns around the upper and lower edges and floral motifs on the body of the *kain*.

Floral designs in the metalware and textiles of Brunei are also found in low-relief wood-carving in decorative panels and friezes, in grilles, doors, door-arches and posts, and in sculptured masonry in public and royal buildings. Motifs include creepers, tendrils, and stylized lotuses and peonies.

BIBLIOGRAPHY

M. Sheppard: *Taman Indera, a Royal Pleasure Ground: Malay Decorative Arts and Pastimes* (London, 1972)

VICTOR T. KING

Brunel, Isambard Kingdom (*b* Portsea, Hants, 9 April 1806; *d* London, 15 Sept 1859). English engineer. In the course of a short, incessantly energetic career, he achieved a reputation as one of the leading engineers of his time. The number and variety of projects for which he took responsibility was astonishing, and the fact that some were failures seemed only to confirm the fertile originality of his overall output. Since his death, particularly in the later 20th century, he has been classed as one of the heroes of England's industrial past.

Brunel's father, Sir Marc Isambard Brunel (1769–1849), was himself an illustrious engineer. Born in France, he fled to America at the time of the French Revolution and from there moved in 1799 to England, where he obtained a naval contract for block-making machinery. He sent his only son to France to be educated, first in Normandy and then at the Lycée Henri-Quatre in Paris. I. K. Brunel remained in Paris and was apprenticed to a clockmaker and instrument maker before being summoned back to England to join his father, who was about to start his most daring project, the making of a tunnel beneath the Thames between Rotherhithe and Wapping in London's docklands. Restarted in 1825, the tunnel had to be abandoned in 1828 half complete (it was not finally finished till 1843), but in the course of the first borings Brunel earned a reputation as a courageous and highly practical engineer.

Brunel's first independent work was the Clifton Suspension Bridge at Bristol (see fig.), for which one of his designs was accepted in 1831. Like his father's tunnel, this was a protracted project and was not in fact completed until 1864, after his death (*see* BARLOW, W.H.). Though bereft of the panels of Egyptian motifs that Brunel intended for the piers, and altered in other minor details, it was essentially his conception of a 214 m span high above the River Avon that was carried out.

In 1833, through his Bristol connections, Brunel was appointed engineer for the railway to link that city with London, soon known as the Great Western Railway. Partly because of his obstinate use of broad-gauge track, but more because of the superb engineering of the line throughout, this railway attracted considerable attention. Through his conscientious regard for every detail, the London to Bristol line and its subsidiary lines to Cornwall, south Wales and the west Midlands were laid out to a coherent pattern of design. Among Brunel's surviving railway works are the original station at Bristol (1839–40), with a castellated masonry exterior and a 22 m-span shed with a cantilever wood and iron roof built to resemble a hammerbeam structure, and the bridge over the Thames at Maidenhead, Berks, two 39 m brick arches that rise only 7 m to their crowns. For the Great Western Railway's second London terminus at Paddington (1850–54; *see* RAILWAY STATION, fig. 2) Brunel sought to apply some of the architectural lessons from the Crystal Palace to a more permanent structure. Aided by some from the team responsible for the exhibition building, notably the contractors Fox Henderson and the architect Matthew Digby Wyatt, he devised a triple-span arched roof, saved from the potential monotony of its immense length by the addition of two transepts. None of the 60 or so timber railway viaducts that he built in Devon and Cornwall has survived, but the railway still crosses the River Tamar on his Royal Albert Bridge (1857–9), Saltash, Devon, which consists of two principal spans of wrought-iron parabolic arches tied by pairs of supension chains, with the railway deck hung from vertical struts (*see* BRIDGE, fig. 1).

The Bristol contacts that led to Brunel's railway career also resulted in his involvement in shipbuilding. At Bristol two ships were built to his design, the timber-hulled paddle steamer *Great Western* (1837) and the iron-hulled screw-propulsion *Great Britain* (1843). But it was at Millwall in London that his most famous ship was built, the colossal 210 m-long *Great Eastern* (1854–9). The construction of this monster, intended for the Indian and Australian trade, was of a scale and novelty that overstretched even Brunel's capacities, and partly accounted for his early death at the age of 53.

In the midst of all these projects Brunel played a part in some of the major public events of his time. As a member of the building committee for the Great Exhibition of 1851, he conceived of housing the event beneath a huge sheet-metal dome, but his design was howled down in favour of the submission by Paxton and Fox Henderson. In 1855 he devised a prefabricated hospital of 1000 beds, erected at Renkioi in Turkey for the casualties of the Crimean War. Though none of its features was particularly original (the roof structure was a variant of his timber viaduct designs), the speed with which he worked brought public acclaim.

The author and social reformer Samuel Smiles (1812–1904) described Brunel as 'the very Napoleon of engineers, thinking more of glory than of profit, and of victory than of dividends'. Brunel was jealous of his fame and his authority, but he inspired great loyalty from his assistants and backers. 'I cannot act under any supervision, or form part of any system which recognizes any other adviser than myself, or any other source of information than mine, on any question connected with the construction or mode of carrying out practically this great project on which I have staked my character', he wrote about the *Great Eastern* during one of the crises in its construction (Rolt, p. 311). Part of his fame has derived from the position he created for himself as a single-handed manager, a role that subsequent generations of engineers have found hard to repeat.

Isambard Kingdom Brunel: Clifton Suspension Bridge, Bristol, completed 1864

BIBLIOGRAPHY

I. Brunel: *The Life of Isambard Kingdom Brunel* (London, 1870)
L. T. C. Rolt: *Isambard Kingdom Brunel* (London, 1957)
R. D. F. Porter Goff: 'Brunel and the Design of the Clifton Suspension Bridge', *Proc. Inst. Civ. Engin.*, i/56 (August 1974), pp. 303–21
R. A. Buchanan: 'Brunel in Bristol', *Essays in Bristol and Gloucestershire History*, ed. P. McGrath and J. Cannon (Bristol, 1976), pp. 217–51
Sir Alfred Pugsley, ed.: *The Works of Isambard Kingdom Brunel* (Bristol, 1976; rev. Cambridge, 1980)
G. S. Emmerson: *John Scott Russell: A Great Victorian Engineer and Naval Architect* (London, 1977)
R. Thorne: 'Paddington Station', *Architects' J.*, xiii (1985), pp. 44–58

ROBERT THORNE

Brunelleschi, Filippo (*b* Florence, 1377; *d* Florence, 16 April 1446). Italian architect and sculptor. He is traditionally regarded as the father of Renaissance architecture who, in the words of Vasari, 'was sent by Heaven to invest architecture with new forms, after it had wandered astray for many centuries'. The 'new forms' were those of Classical antiquity, which Brunelleschi applied to such building types as churches and orphanages for which there were no ancient precedents. In these schemes he was the first to make use of the Classical orders since antiquity (*see* ORDERS, ARCHITECTURAL, §I, 2(iii)(a)); at the same time he employed a proportional system of his own invention, in which all units were related to a simple module, the mathematical characteristics of which informed the entire structure. Brunelleschi worked almost exclusively in Florence, and many features link his architecture with the Romanesque—if not the Gothic—heritage of that city. Nevertheless, he was beyond question responsible for initiating the rediscovery of ancient Roman architecture. He understood its inherent principles and he employed them in an original manner for the building tasks of his own day.

I. Life and work. II. Influence and posthumous reputation.

I. Life and work.

He was the son of the notary Ser Brunellesco di Lippi, an official in the Florentine administration. Brunelleschi's schooling in the liberal arts was of the type that normally preceded training for one of the learned professions, but a gift for drawing led him instead to serve from 1398 as a journeyman in the silk-workers' guild (Por S Maria), which also controlled the craft of goldsmithing. Brunelleschi matriculated as a master goldsmith on 2 July 1404. Surviving work from this period includes silver figures of two *Prophets* (1398–1400) on the altar of S Jacopo, Pistoia Cathedral, and the gilded bronze panel depicting the *Sacrifice of Isaac* (1401; Florence, Bargello) that he submitted in the competition for the east doors of the Baptistery of Florence Cathedral; Brunelleschi's panel places Isaac at the centre of a scene of intense action, in which the main figures are depicted in profile. A wooden Crucifix (1.7×1.7 m, *c.* 1410–15; *see* CRUCIFIX, §3(ii) and fig. 5) by Brunelleschi in the Gondi Chapel of S Maria Novella, Florence, was, according to an early 16th-century account, the outcome of a private competition with Donatello; a wooden Crucifix that has been attributed to the latter hangs in Santa Croce.

According to Brunelleschi's biographer, ANTONIO MANETTI, after Lorenzo Ghiberti had won the competition (1401) for the Baptistery doors, the runners-up, Donatello and Brunelleschi, both left for Rome to study sculpture and architecture respectively. Brunelleschi, who, by family tradition, was a peripheral member of the Florentine political establishment, subsequently took up positions in local political circles, including service on the city council and on advisory committees on the great building works that characterized the emerging oligarchic state at the time and gave new form to the city (*see* FLORENCE, §I, 3). The account of Brunelleschi's visit to Rome is still disputed, but his involvement with Florentine building works and his studies of Classical and of Tuscan Romanesque architecture—exemplified not least in the classicizing details of the Baptistery—must have provided the foundations of his personal *all'antica* language of architectural details, and to his development *c.* 1413 of perspective contruction (*see* PERSPECTIVE, §II) and proportion systems. Brunelleschi's stepson, Buggiano, carved his funeral monument (1447–8; Florence Cathedral; *see* BUGGIANO and fig.).

1. Architecture. 2. Lost works, projects and attributions. 3. Urban planning.

1. ARCHITECTURE.

(i) Dome of Florence Cathedral. (ii) Ospedale degli Innocenti. (iii) Barbadori (Annunziata) Chapel, S Felicità. (iv) S Lorenzo. (v) Pazzi Chapel, Santa Croce. (vi) Palazzo di Parte Guelfa. (vii) Scolari Oratory, S Maria degli Angeli. (viii) Santo Spirito. (ix) Lantern and exedrae of Florence Cathedral.

(i) Dome of Florence Cathedral. Brunelleschi had been consulted on Florence Cathedral as early as 1404, when he was a member of an advisory commission on the construction of one of the buttresses of the northern tribune of the apse, but it was not until 1412 or 1413 that the octagonal opening of the drum was ready for spanning with a dome. In 1417 he was paid for drawings and by the time that a public competition was announced in 1418 for the solution of the problem of the dome, he had already become deeply involved. The wooden model (possibly that in Florence, Mus. Opera Duomo) on which the final scheme was based was submitted to the cathedral works as a collaborative effort of Ghiberti and Brunelleschi. Construction began in 1420 under their joint supervision, but Brunelleschi—subsequently described as the 'inventor and governor'—soon took over and Ghiberti later withdrew or was dismissed. The great dome, which dominates the city of Florence, was completed in 1436 (*see* FLORENCE, fig. 12); its span makes it one of the greatest masonry domes ever built, and his success in its execution constituted the supreme building and engineering achievement of the 15th century.

The basic dimensions, form and curvature of the dome had been determined by 1367; Brunelleschi was constrained by specific guild legislation to accept the existing model, and there is no indication that he was in conflict with its predicated form. The major problem was that of spanning the 42-m opening of the octagonal drum, a space too wide to be bridged by traditional timber centering. Brunelleschi overcame this difficulty by distributing the stresses between eight major ribs, which spring from the angles of the octagon in continuation of the angle piers, and sixteen minor ribs in pairs between them (see fig. 1). The pitch of the inward-curving ribs was kept steep to prevent them from leaning too heavily on the light centering that was employed, while lateral support for the ribs is provided by interstitial binders or horizontal arches with stone, timber and iron tension chains, the whole so contrived as to be self-supporting as it rose, course by course. The statical formula is still a matter for scholarly debate, but a stability was achieved that made it possible to dispense with the massive and expensive falsework, the use of which had appeared unavoidable. The infill between the ribs and binders is of brick laid in a herringbone bond, the dome being constructed with an outer and inner skin on the double-shell principle, the first instance of this usage; stairs between the skins lead up to the lantern.

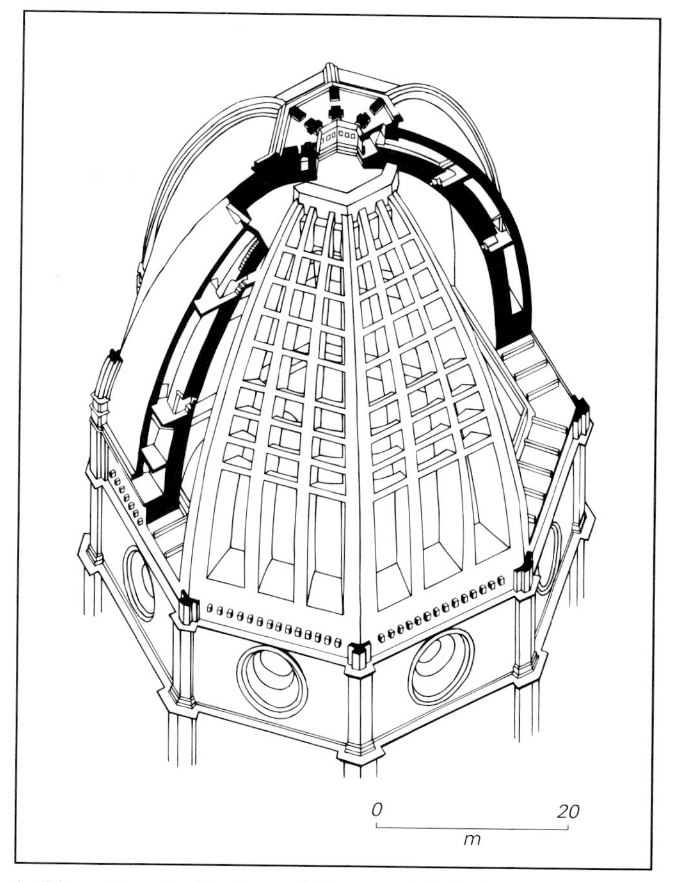

1. Filippo Brunelleschi: dome of Florence Cathedral, 1418–36; diagram showing construction

Brunelleschi designed the scaffolding necessary for the construction work and also invented the hoisting equipment to haul up the building materials. Indeed the entire works, from the dome structure itself to the mechanical accessories used for erecting it, were devised by Brunelleschi himself and are the products of his own ingenuity. In this respect, and in his defence of his radical proposal to the cathedral authorities, he assumed a new status for the architect in relations with both patron and craftsmen, the latter being accorded only a subordinate role. The sources for his technological inspiration, apart from empirical observations and tests, are unclear. Whether or not he visited Rome, when he may have studied Roman construction methods, is still uncertain, but there were in any event no precedents in Rome for the dome of Florence Cathedral: for example, the solid, brick-faced concrete hemispherical dome of the Pantheon (*see* ROME, fig. 26) relies on mass instead of the sophisticated framework of Brunelleschi's dome.

See also DOME, §1.

(ii) Ospedale degli Innocenti. Brunelleschi's first opportunity to apply to a scheme of his own invention the insights he had gained from his studies of Classical and Tuscan Romanesque architecture had come in 1419. In that year his guild asked him to provide a design for an asylum for foundling children that it had undertaken to build. In response, Brunelleschi produced a drawing of a portico façade fronting the Piazza SS Annunziata. The plan of the complex (1419–24) reveals a new order and symmetry; the most revolutionary part of the building, however, is the façade (*see* FLORENCE, fig. 1), which was the first since antiquity to use the vocabulary of Classical Roman architecture and thus constitutes the first structure of the Renaissance. The loggia comprises an arcade of delicate Corinthian columns and wide semicircular arches supporting a deep entablature, with roundels in the spandrels of the arches. The arch faces are not triangular in section, as in a Gothic arch, but are lengths of curved architrave conforming to the profile of the lower part of a Corinthian entablature: in a word, they are classical archivolts. The square portico bays are roofed with a series of simple classical domes (sail vaults) instead of the traditional Gothic form of groined vaults; the domes are borne on the columns at the front and on corbels on the hospital wall at the rear. Corresponding to these bays at the *piano nobile* level of the façade, above the entablature, is a series of rectangular windows framed by moulded architraves and crowned by shallow pediments.

Although Brunelleschi used the stylistic components of ancient architecture at the Ospedale, he applied them to a building type unknown in antiquity and in a manner that differs from ancient usage: for example, the way that such broad arches are supported on such slender columns is as different from the colonnades of the Colosseum in Rome as from any Gothic arcade. The source in this instance was probably the Tuscan proto-Renaissance of the 11th and 12th centuries, as exemplified in S Miniato al Monte, Florence (*see* FLORENCE, §IV, 7), which was then thought to be late Roman or Early Christian. The arcaded elevation of the Ospedale was subsequently imitated on two of the other sides of the Piazza SS Annunziata, namely *c.* 1518 at the Confraternità dei Servi opposite, and in 1599–1604 at the church of SS Annunziata at the north end of the square, although the impulse here was urbanistic rather than architectural.

See also ARCHITECTURAL PROPORTION, §II.

(iii) Barbadori (Annunziata) Chapel, S Felicità. This structure (now known as the Capponi Chapel) is attributed to Brunelleschi by Manetti, who said he designed and executed it for the Barbadori family; late 20th-century research confirms that it was built between 1419 and 1423 by members of that family, and its origins go back to Bartolommeo di Gherardo Barbadori (*d* 1400 of plague). It is the first chapel on the right inside this aisleless church and is thus open in two directions with the help of a corner pier, which is faced with Corinthian pilasters. These support an entablature and flank a minor order of engaged Ionic columns carrying arches. A portico effect is thus created, recalling the loggia setting sometimes shown in depictions of the *Annunciation* (e.g. in S Maria Novella; mid-14th century); a similar scene may have been shown in the original fresco of the *Annunciation* (destr.) on the inner façade wall at S Felicità, which the Barbadori Chapel was intended to frame. The interior of the chapel is roofed by a dome (now truncated) on pendentives with roundels, while the mathematical imperatives of the new system of articulation defined by Brunelleschi are evident in the way that the pilasters in the internal corners are reduced almost to extinction. His design for the chapel served as a model for Michelozzo di Bartolomeo's tabernacle (*c.* 1448) in front of the miraculous image of the *Annunciation* at SS Annunziata, Florence. In 1525–8, after the Barbadori Chapel passed to the Capponi family, redecoration was carried out by Pontormo: his altarpiece of the *Lamentation* (*see* PONTORMO, fig. 2) on the south side may be regarded as a miraculous vision seen by his Virgin Annunciate painted on the inner façade wall, presumably an echo of the original.

2. Filippo Brunelleschi: interior of the Old Sacristy (1419–28), S Lorenzo, Florence

(iv) S Lorenzo. The Old Sacristy at S Lorenzo was also begun by Brunelleschi in this immensely creative period of his life. The project was part of the reconstruction and enlargement of the church, which had been started, according to Manetti, in 1418 with a traditional design. The sacristy was commissioned in 1419 by Giovanni di Averardo de' Medici, probably influenced by his son Cosimo de' Medici; it was built quickly (1421–8), before the new church itself was constructed, and is thus usually considered as an independent structure. The Sacristy exemplifies the mathematical, modular proportioning system adopted by Brunelleschi, as well as his synthesis of Classical forms with innovations of his own devising. It is square in plan and forms a perfect cube in volume, covered by a classical hemispherical dome that is supported on ribs as a twelve-part umbrella dome.

The dome rests on deep pendentives, which lend a semicircular shape to the walls above the ornate entablature (see fig. 2); the latter divides the walls into two equal horizontal zones, the depth of the dome forming a third equal zone above. One of the sides of the cube is also divided into three; the central section opens into an altar space, square in plan and domed over pendentives, and the arch over the opening reflects the semicircular shape of the walls above. As at the Barbadori Chapel, these mathematically proportioned spaces created problems when it came to fitting in the classical articulation of pilasters, as can be seen in the reappearance of the evanescent strips of pilasters at the internal corners.

Brunelleschi's Sacristy became the motive force for reconstructing the whole of S Lorenzo on Renaissance lines instead of traditional Gothic ones. At the instigation of Giovanni di Averardo de' Medici, the patron of the church, Brunelleschi established a scheme (*c.* 1421) for its overall transformation, but work soon lapsed and was not resumed until after 1434. Brunelleschi's involvement probably ceased after completion of the Old Sacristy, and his supervision of the work was thus limited; even his responsibility for the design itself has been challenged in favour of Michelozzo (*see* FLORENCE, §IV, 5). Here it may be said that a simple system of mathematical proportioning informs the plan of S Lorenzo, the forerunner of all the systems—varying in complexity—that numberless Renaissance and Baroque buildings later exploited. The basic unit or module is the square of the crossing (see fig. 3a). This is repeated to form the transepts and choir; four such modules constitute the nave, while an aisle bay is a quarter of a module, as are the chapels grouped around the choir and transepts. In the angle between these chapels are the sacristies (the New Sacristy, 1519–33, was built by Michelangelo as a Mannerist variant of Brunelleschi's model). The nave chapels were originally intended to be square as well, but when construction resumed their dimensions were changed; at this time also the corner chapels were closed between nave aisle and transept, and the chapels at the ends of the transept were doubled. The

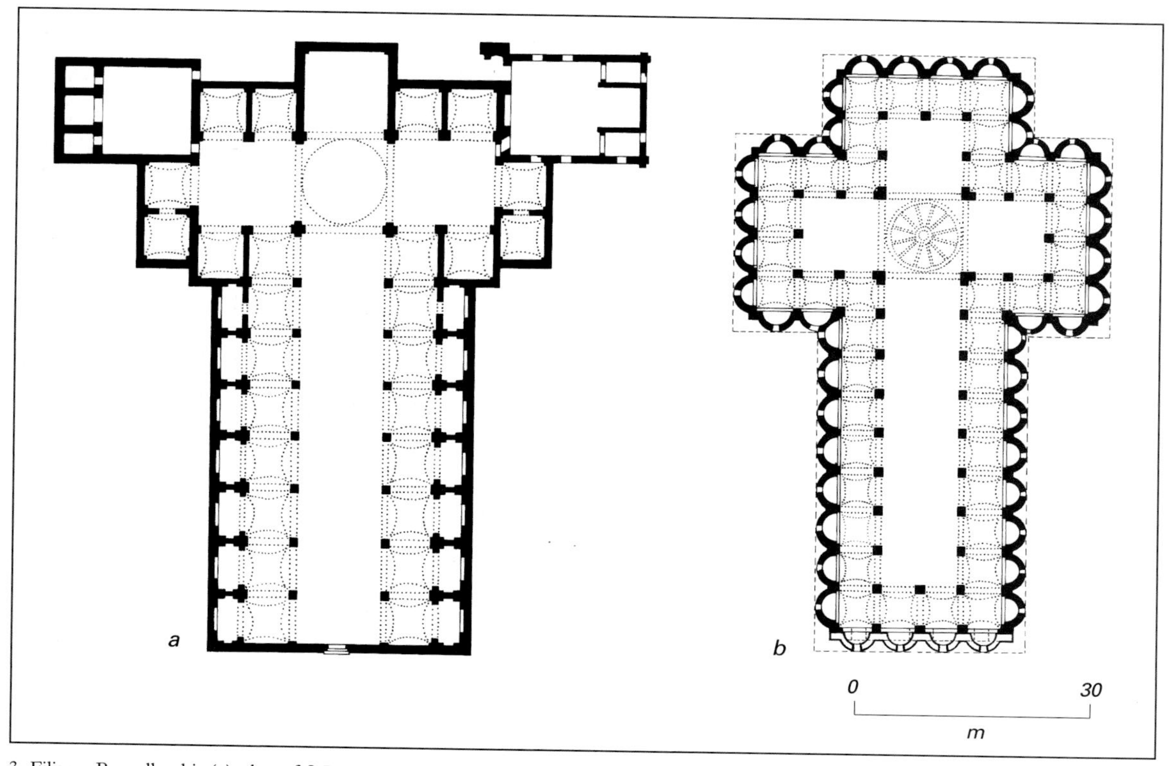

3. Filippo Brunelleschi: (a) plan of S Lorenzo, Florence (after 1434), showing the Old Sacristy (upper left) by Brunelleschi and the New Sacristy (upper right) by Michelangelo: (b) plan of Santo Spirito, Florence (begun 1436), showing proposed design of chapels at west front

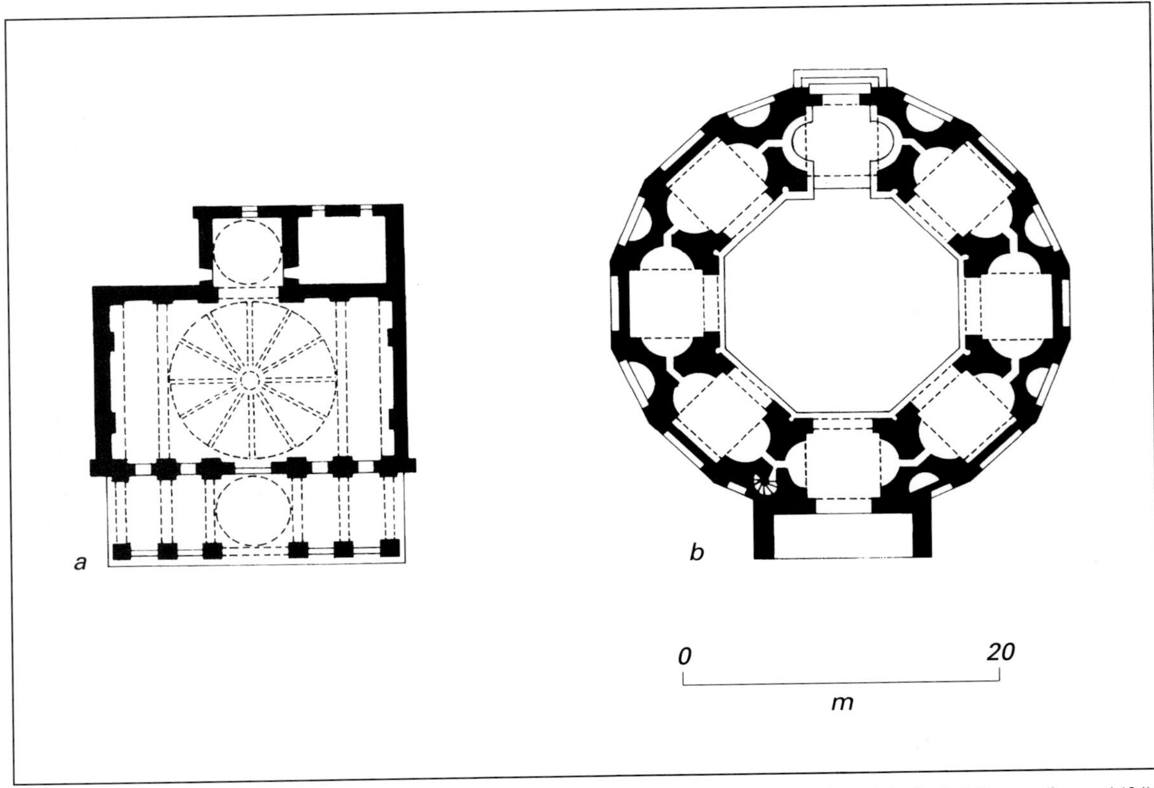

4. Filippo Brunelleschi: (a) plan of the Pazzi Chapel (designed 1420s), Santa Croce, Florence; (b) plan of the Scolari Oratory (begun 1434), S Maria degli Angeli, Florence

overall effect of the proportioning system and the square module used promotes a feeling of serenity and order, even if the precise interrelationship between the parts is only registered subliminally (for illustration of interior *see* FLORENCE, fig. 19).

(v) Pazzi Chapel, Santa Croce. Brunelleschi's design for the chapter house in the cloister of Santa Croce was part of an extensive scheme of rebuilding following a dormitory fire in 1423. Patronage was assumed in 1429 by Andrea di Guglielmo Pazzi (1372–1445), whose family tombs were to be located in a crypt beneath the altar room; the building, generally known as the Pazzi Chapel, was intended to emulate the Old Sacristy at S Lorenzo. A formal commitment to the chapel was made in 1429, but Brunelleschi's design may have been elaborated by 1423–4. It has many features in common with the Sacristy, including the character of the articulation, although the basic shape of the chamber is rectangular rather than square (see fig. 4a). There is, in fact, a square here, formed by the central bay of the building beneath a twelve-part umbrella dome, and it is flanked by narrow 'transeptal' bays marked off by Corinthian pilasters. The dome is supported on pendentives with roundels, like that in the Sacristy, resulting in deep curves in the upper parts of the walls and narrow, coffered barrel vaults over the flanking bays. As at the Sacristy, the east wall is opened up in the centre to reveal a square altar room roofed by a frescoed dome and lit by a large stained-glass window in its far wall. The chapter hall itself is evenly lit by small round windows at the base of the dome, by its lantern-covered oculus and by four tall arched windows in the entrance wall; the latter are echoed in corresponding round-headed panels on the bays of the walls inside.

The front elevation of the Pazzi Chapel (see fig. 5) has a portico extending across its whole width and serving as a continuation of the surrounding cloisters. Its six Corinthian columns support a screen wall that is arched over the central bay and articulated with shallow rectangular panels and pilasters; an attic entablature runs across the top of the wall, above which the porch roof is raised on slender piers. The lateral passage of the portico is barrel-vaulted, with a shallow dome over the central bay; this central domed bay has its counterpart in the altar room on the same axis at the far side of the hall, while the flanking sections of the passage echo the flanking 'transeptal' bays inside.

Owing to the patron's reluctance to make funds available, the Pazzi Chapel was not built until 1442–*c.* 1465, after the death of Pazzi (who was buried in Santa Croce) and mostly after the death of Brunelleschi himself; after *c.* 1450 the work was probably supervised by the workshop of Bernardo Rossellino. Despite theories to the contrary, it is likely that the whole building as executed is substantially that projected by Brunelleschi, including the portico; instead of the executed central dome in the portico, however, he may have planned a sail vault, which would have obviated the raising of the existing porch roof to clear the dome. The completed work, with its subtle adjustment of details and striking contrasts, makes a powerful impression on the visitor. While its spatial organization is clearly expressed in the articulation of the walls and also in the pattern of the marble pavement, an impression of centrality is conveyed by the wider bays at the centre of each side of the room. At the same time, the architectural articulation, with classical pilasters, entablature, semicircular cornices and arches, is emphasized by the colouristic effect of these dark-grey stone elements against the plain white walls (see fig. 6). A similar contrast is provided by the coloured maiolica reliefs in the roundels of the walls (*see* ROBBIA, DELLA, (1), fig. 2); the four polychrome *Evangelists* in the pendentives may have been created by Brunelleschi. This effect was unprecedented, and it helped to promote the influence of the building on subsequent generations. This can be seen not only in such close copies as Giuliano da Sangallo's S Maria delle Carceri (from 1484; *see* SANGALLO, fig. 1), Prato, or in such developments as the oblong room of Bramante's S Maria presso S Satiro (from 1478), Milan, but also in the way it demonstrated the potential of what Michelangelo later called 'the cheerful modern style'.

(vi) Palazzo di Parte Guelfa. This building, Brunelleschi's only extant palazzo, was designed as the assembly hall for the Guelph party, built above a vaulted lower storey to the east of the original palazzo constructed in the years after 1422. Such buildings, like the institutions they served, were modelled on those of the Florentine republic: the Palazzo del Podestà (now the Bargello) and the Palazzo della Signoria (now Palazzo Vecchio). Accommodation was typically centred on a large council hall flanked by administrative offices, all at first-floor level above a vaulted ground floor and accessible by narrow stairs, wholly or partly external for reasons of security. At the height of Guelph power in the 13th century, modest headquarters had sufficed the party; as it declined in influence, however, a building programme was instituted to double the size of its building in a final bid for consolidation of its power.

Brunelleschi's scheme for the assembly hall over the vaulted ground storey, to be joined to the original palazzo by a link block on the Via delle Terme, may have originally been made in the mid-1420s when the new connecting wing was being built. Work was interrupted during the wars with Milan and Lucca (1426–31) and the subsequent factional in-fighting. It was probably when work resumed in 1442 that Brunelleschi intervened with a project for a substantially larger hall in the new east wing, a project that meshed badly with the connecting wing and somewhat overwhelmed the ground-floor structure, but which assured much greater visibility (and hence prestige) for the building from the street. The rectangular hall is articulated on the long (east) wall by four tall, round-headed windows with profiled *all'antica* surrounds, each surmounted by a large circular window; two such units are also featured on the short (south) end. The external angles of the building are clasped by giant unfluted pilasters; these were left incomplete but were probably intended to have Corinthian capitals and an appropriate entablature. There is no central accent in this design, and, characteristically, the number of differentiated parts is reduced to the minimum. None of the internal décor was completed in Brunelleschi's lifetime, but the intention was to support the ceiling (probably coffered) on a classical entablature borne on pilasters between the windows. The existing interior pilasters were executed before *c.* 1456 by Maso di Bartolommeo, an associate of Michelozzo. Work on the upper storey was ended in 1459 when Cosimo de' Medici decided on the permanent degradation of the old institution.

5. Filippo Brunelleschi: Pazzi Chapel (designed 1420s), Santa Croce, Florence

(vii) Scolari Oratory, S Maria degli Angeli. In his design for an oratory in the convent of S Maria degli Angeli, which was funded by the Scolari family and begun in 1434, Brunelleschi introduced yet another important innovation: the first centralized building of the Italian Renaissance. Central planning was traditionally confined to such building types as oratories or martyria, and it was for this reason that Brunelleschi chose a polygonal plan for the building. Centrality had been implicit in his designs for the Sacristy at S Lorenzo and the Pazzi Chapel, although not overtly expressed; the four major projects initiated during the last fifteen years of his life, however, all incorporate centralized symmetry in substance or in essence.

In 1437, three years after construction of the oratory began, the work was suspended and the building left uncompleted. A roof to protect the work was added in 1503, and in 1934 it was 'completed' according to a scheme by the architect Rodolfo Sabatini. Details of Brunelleschi's intentions, particularly with regard to the external elevations, thus derive from documentary sources (see *Filippo Brunelleschi: La sua opera e il suo tempo*, 1980, pp. 477–84). The building is planned as an octagon surrounded by a

6. Filippo Brunelleschi: interior of the Pazzi Chapel (designed 1420s), Santa Croce, Florence

circle of eight chapels (see fig. 4b). Above the central space is a drum and dome supported on a ring of eight angular piers faced by fluted pilasters, probably Corinthian. This central space was intended to contain an altar and to be closed off from the laity by grilles; the monks would have entered from the convent through the eastern chapel, while the laity would have entered through a seven-bay portico on the western side, with access to the interconnected chapels through passageways in the piers. On the sixteen-sided exterior, blank panels alternate with niches set into the outer faces of the pier units.

The sculptural, three-dimensional form of the piers in S Maria degli Angeli gives this design a different character from Brunelleschi's Sacristy and Pazzi Chapel: instead of a space delineated by articulating elements, the spaces in the oratory appear to be moulded from the substance of the building. This is another characteristic of his mature work and is reflected in subsequent designs. A restrained classical vocabulary is used throughout the scheme, with a minimum number of differentiated units and identity of similar parts, but no exact equivalent is traceable to an ancient source, although the ruins of the Temple of Minerva Medica (early 4th century AD), Rome, exhibit a ring of peripheral 'chapels' around a polygonal centre. Many elements seem to be drawn from nearer sources: Florence Cathedral and Baptistery.

(viii) Santo Spirito. Brunelleschi's last great church was begun in 1436 but not finished until 1482, long after his death. It is in many ways similar to S Lorenzo, but without the constraints imposed by working on an existing building. Here he was able to resolve all the inconsistencies inherent in the project for S Lorenzo and, according to Manetti, the Santo Spirito design gave Brunelleschi the most satisfaction. Although retaining the traditional Latin-cross layout required by the clergy, Santo Spirito displays powerful centralizing tendencies and an organic relationship between all of the parts (see fig. 3b; for illustration of the interior *see* RENAISSANCE, fig. 1). The choir and transept arms around the umbrella-domed crossing are of identical dimensions, to which the aisle bays are proportionally related. A ring of identical colonnaded aisle bays (each roofed with a sail vault) and semicircular niched side chapels runs around the entire church—or would have done if Brunelleschi's design had been adhered to: Manetti states that they should have continued across the interior of the entrance front, where there would have been four doors, each opening into a small aisle bay, instead of the existing three. The ring of family chapels, all equal in form and nearly equivalent in prominence of position, made Santo Spirito a classic expression of the 14th-century Florentine ideal of rule by a patriciate of leading families of equivalent power and standing.

The proportions of Santo Spirito were also refined: the height of the nave arcade is the same as the clerestory above, instead of the 5:3 ratio in S Lorenzo, so that the aisle bays of Santo Spirito are half the height of the nave. In addition, the handling of the details reflects a more three-dimensional, sculptural approach, already seen at S Maria degli Angeli and here achieving a monumental, classical grandeur. Instead of flat pilasters flanking the entrances to the side chapels, as at S Lorenzo, for example, in Santo Spirito the equivalent features are half columns that act as responds to the columns in the nave. The semicircular form of the chapels themselves would have been expressed externally by an undulating wall if Brunelleschi's successors had not masked them with planar cladding. The form of the chapels also enabled Brunelleschi to resolve the awkward junction at the corners between the arms flanking the crossing: at Santo Spirito, identical chapels share a three-quarters engaged column at the corner, with the wall between the chapels reduced to a minimum. His perceived aim of achieving homogeneous lighting is satisfied by the careful disposition of windows: round-headed ones in the chapels and clerestory, roundels at the base of the dome, and an oculus at the top of the dome, covered by a lantern, which together ensured a proportional share of lighting throughout.

(ix) Lantern and exedrae of Florence Cathedral. Brunelleschi's chance to contribute his own, mature design approach to the cathedral complex came with the competition (1436) for a lantern to cap the completed dome. Brunelleschi's winning scheme reconciles the essentially Gothic form of the ribbed dome with the Renaissance form of the turret by linking them with a classicized version of flying buttresses (see fig. 7), which clearly express both a structural and an ornamental function. The eight buttresses visually continue the line of the dome ribs with a series of fluted piers, on top of which rest the outer ends of eight decorated volutes—an inversion of the Classical console. Each volute stretches over a pierced, shell-vaulted niche and leans its inner scroll against a Corinthian pilaster folded around the angle of the octagonal turret—a unique

and newly invented way of handling Classical details, never encountered in antiquity. In particular, Brunelleschi's innovative use of the Classical volute or scroll introduced one of the most popular elements of Renaissance architecture. The lantern turret is capped by a delicately moulded entablature, above which rises a stone spire made up of convex panels between pyramidally diminishing angle strips. A gilded ball and cross terminate the composition. The intended effect of this heavy, sculptural structure was to counter the centrifugal forces acting on the 6-m diameter ring at the apex of the dome, which tend to force the stone ribs apart. The lantern was executed (1446–67) under the direction of Michelozzo di Bartolomeo and Bernardo Rossellino.

Brunelleschi's final work at the cathedral, carried out towards the end of his life, was the construction of the exedrae (*tribune morte*) around the base of the drum. These were needed to take up the thrust of the dome on the four free sides of the octagonal substructure, namely the two between the choir and the transepts, and the two between the nave and the transepts. Polygonal exedrae in keeping with those of the choir and transepts had formed part of the original scheme, as embodied in the model of 1367. A revised form for these features was proposed in 1439 by Brunelleschi and accepted by the authorities, with the result that four early Renaissance terminal devices may be seen amid the late medieval complex (see fig. 8). The exedrae are semicircular drums articulated by five shell-vaulted niches, which are separated by pairs of engaged Corinthian columns—the first use of coupled columns in Renaissance architecture. They support a classical entablature beneath a conical tiled roof.

7. Filippo Brunelleschi: lantern (1436–67) of Florence Cathedral

8. Filippo Brunelleschi: semicircular exedra (designed 1439) at the base of the drum, Florence Cathedral

2. LOST WORKS, PROJECTS AND ATTRIBUTIONS. According to Manetti, Brunelleschi was involved with the construction of a house for his kinsman Apollonio Lapi on the Canto de' Ricci, Florence. The existing building there contains octagonal columns and masonry from the first half of the 15th century. Brunelleschi is also reported as having built a chapel for Schiatta Ridolfi in S Jacopo Oltrarno, which Manetti describes as being next to the main chapel, open on two sides (like the Barbadori Chapel) and covered with an umbrella dome. A Baroque reconstruction in 1709 destroyed any remains that may have existed. Other works discussed by Manetti include the office of the Ufficiali del Monte in the Palazzo della Signoria, still existing at the end of the 15th century, and a house in the Borgo San Jacopo, near the Ponte Vecchio, which was built for the Barbadori; remains of what was possibly the latter were destroyed in World War II.

Two perspective panels painted by Brunelleschi were also described by Manetti; they were included in the inventory of the Medici collection at the end of the 15th century but have long since disappeared. One of the panels showed a frontal view of the Baptistery, Florence, seen from the cathedral, which was intended as a graphic illustration of the proportional relationships between similar visual triangles at a scale of about 1:60. Whether the perspective was constructed according to the procedure described in Alberti's *Della pittura* is questionable. Brunelleschi, working inside the central portal of the cathedral, may have painted over the reflection of the building mirrored in the silvered back of the square panel described by Manetti. The proper distance effect was achieved by looking through a hole in the back of the panel and viewing the painting reflected in a mirror held half an arm's length away. It was the correct illustration of the proportional principle, not the perspective illusion, that probably interested Brunelleschi. A second panel, showing the Palazzo della Signoria at an angle, cut out to be seen against real sky, had similar didactic purposes.

According to Vasari, Brunelleschi produced for Cosimo de' Medici a model for the Palazzo Medici, Florence, which was rejected as being too sumptuous (*see* PALAZZO, §2); the palazzo as built was designed in 1444 by Michelozzo. Vasari also attributes three other buildings to Brunelleschi: the Palazzo Pitti and Palazzo Pazzi, Florence, and the Badia in Fiesole. Brunelleschi may have produced an original design for the Palazzo Pitti (*see* PITTI, LUCA DI BONACCORSO), and if uniformity were a criterion of his style, the Palazzo Pitti, as built, would qualify as one of his works. Although he restrained his vocabulary to the least number of differentiated parts, however, his work is never monotonous, nor was large scale in itself the essence of his approach. The elevation of the building (*see* FLORENCE, fig. 23) is characterized by a large expanse of massive, rusticated stone wall, penetrated by three arched openings at ground level, four small rectangular windows on the mezzanine, and, on the two upper floors, by identical arched windows framed by rusticated arches and flanked by almost imperceptible jamb pilasters. There is none of the subtle play of profiled relief against smooth ashlar surfaces, the proportional division of window openings, and the clear separation of wall, window, and pilaster-entablature functions that characterize the Palazzo di Parte Guelfa. Moreover, the Palazzo Pitti was built after 1457/8, and there is no basis for assuming that an old design by Brunelleschi would have been revived 12 years after his death. The Palazzo Pazzi, on which work may have begun in 1462, when the site purchase was completed, or perhaps *c.* 1474, when the Pazzi family became papal bankers, is now usually attributed to Giuliano da Maiano (*see* MAIANO, DA, (1)). However, its plan, elevation and detailing, particularly the dolphin-decorated column capitals of the courtyard, suggest that it may instead have been an early design of Giuliano da Sangallo upon his return from study in Rome. The attribution to Brunelleschi is certainly not sustainable.

The Badia in Fiesole is now attributed to Brunelleschi by few scholars. That the church, an object of Medici patronage built in the decade after 1456, ten years after Brunelleschi's death, should ever have been connected with him is a tribute to the persistence of the Vasari tradition. There are superficial similarities in arch profiles and Corinthian pilaster capitals, but the plan and elevations of the church are in complete contrast with the characteristics of Brunelleschi's style.

3. URBAN PLANNING. Brunelleschi and his patrons never lost sight of the importance of positioning their buildings in such a way as to assure maximum visibility at the longest possible distance. The Ospedale degli Innocenti faced on to the developing piazza in front of the Servite convent of SS Annunziata (*see* FLORENCE, fig. 1). The creation of a suitable piazza in front of S Lorenzo involved demolitions sanctioned by the Signoria in 1433. Brunelleschi's Parte Guelfa project was designed to make the largely hidden building more visible from the nearby main street, Via Por S Maria. The large square next to the oratory at S Maria degli Angeli would have allowed a view of the building from the main street of the Porta di Balla quarter, the Via de' Servi. At Santo Spirito, according to Manetti, Brunelleschi proposed to turn the façade of the church northwards and to create a great piazza extending to the present Via di Santo Spirito, or, possibly, down to the banks of the River Arno, so that travellers coming from Pisa could see the church as they passed on their way into the centre; the resistance of house owners in the quarter sufficed to quash this project, but the building was turned to face the Piazza Santo Spirito. This tendency reflects the spatial effect achieved by the design of such buildings as Santo Spirito, where the composition of repetitive, modular elements, enhanced by a sculptural richness, creates a remarkable visual perspective inside the building.

II. Influence and posthumous reputation.

Brunelleschi's reputation in his own lifetime was unmatched in Italy and has remained high ever since—although 30 years after his death it proved insufficient to ensure the adoption of his scheme for the west-front layout of Santo Spirito. His work exhibits three characteristic features that constituted a new approach to architectural composition: a tendency to reduce to a minimum the number of differentiated parts, as in the repetition of identical windows at the Palazzo di Parte Guelfa; homogeneity of lighting by allocating each part of a building a proportionately scaled window, achieved most notably at Santo Spirito; and a striving for the equivalence of parts, exemplified at the Pazzi Chapel, where a wider domed bay in the portico acts as a counterpart to the domed altar room, and the tall windows are echoed in wall panels. At the same time, many elements of Renaissance architecture now taken for granted are also of his invention: the double-shell dome, the use of curved entablatures as arches over columns, volutes as a linking device, pendentives and coupled orders. The constant recurrence of these features, together with the revived concept of modular design that informs all subsequent architecture in the classical tradition, is testimony to Brunelleschi's influence, which was continued through the elaborations of his successors for the next four centuries.

Brunelleschi's diminishing position in Florentine politics after 1425, when he sat on its highest executive organ, the Priori, and the lack of private commissions in his work after *c.* 1430 indicates that his principal connections were probably with the older generation of Florentines in the more conservative, austere tradition of the 14th century, able to confront problems with a typical ingenuity and persistence. This reflects his architectural vision, which essentially updated the traditional Florentine building repertory with a highly restrained vocabulary—although an entirely novel one—derived from Classical antiquity. His own practical engineering bent ensured that his innovations were not stifled by an excessive devotion to the minutiae of Classical archaeology; instead they served to provide the stylistic guidelines for future generations of Renaissance and Baroque architects. If Alberti became the revolutionary architectural theorist of the early Renaissance, therefore, Brunelleschi remains the uncontested pioneer in the realm of practice, who succeeded, on the basis of his own observations, in reviving a system of architecture extinct for a thousand years and applying it to uses of which the Ancients had never dreamt.

BIBLIOGRAPHY

EARLY SOURCES

A. Manetti: *Vita di Filippo Brunelleschi* (MS. ?1480s; Florence, Bib. N. Cent., MS. II, ii, 325, fols 295*r*–312*v*); Eng. trans., ed. H. Saalman (University Park, PA, 1970)

P. Farulli: *Istoria cronologica del nobile ed antico monastero degli Angioli di Firenze del sacro ordine camaldolese, dal principio della sua fondazione fino al presente giorno* (Lucca, 1710)

G. Richa: *Notizie istoriche delle chiese fiorentine*, 10 vols (Florence, 1754–62)

GENERAL

H. Saalman: 'Early Renaissance Architectural Theory and Practice in Antonio Filarete's "Trattato di architettura"', *A. Bull.*, xli (1959), pp. 89–106

C. Elam: 'Lorenzo de' Medici and the Urban Development of Renaissance Florence', *A. Hist.*, i (1978), pp. 43–66

D. Kent: *The Rise of the Medici: Faction in Florence, 1426–1434* (Oxford, 1978)

A. Brown: 'Pierfrancesco de' Medici (1430–1476): A Radical Alternative to Elder Medicean Supremacy?', *J. Warb. & Court. Inst.*, xli (1979), pp. 81–7

D. F. Zervas: *The Parte Guelfa, Donatello and Brunelleschi* (Locust Valley, NY, 1987)

MONOGRAPHS AND COLLECTIONS OF ESSAYS

H. Folnesicz: *Brunelleschi: Ein Beitrag zur Entwicklungsgeschichte der Frührenaissance-Architektur* (Vienna, 1915)

P. Ginori-Conti: *La basilica di S Lorenzo di Firenze e la famiglia Ginori* (Florence, 1940)

G. C. Argan: *Brunelleschi* (Milan, 1955/*R* 1978)

P. Sanpaolesi: *Brunelleschi* (Milan, 1962)

E. Luporini: *Brunelleschi: Forma e ragione* (Milan, 1964)

G. Morozzi and A. Piccini: *Il restauro dello Spedale di Santa Maria degli Innocenti, 1966–1970* (Florence, 1971)

I. Hyman: *Brunelleschi in Perspective* (Englewood Cliffs, NJ, 1974)

E. Battisti: *Filippo Brunelleschi* (Milan, 1976, rev. 1983)

G. Fanelli: *Brunelleschi* (Florence, 1977)

I. Hyman: *Fifteenth-century Florentine Studies: The Palazzo Medici and a Ledger for the Church of San Lorenzo* (New York and London, 1977)

C. Bozzoni and G. Carbonara: *Filippo Brunelleschi: Saggio di bibliografia*, 2 vols (Rome, 1977–8)

Filippo Brunelleschi: La sua opera e il suo tempo, 2 vols (Florence, 1977–80)

F. Borsi, G. Morolli and F. Quinterno: *Brunelleschiani* (Rome, 1979)

H. Klotz: *Die Frühwerke Brunelleschis und die mittelalterliche Tradition* (Berlin, 1979)

P. Roselli and O. Superchi: *L'edificazione della basilica di San Lorenzo* (Florence, 1980)

H. Saalman: *Filippo Brunelleschi: The Cupola of Santa Maria del Fiore* (London, 1980)

——: *Filippo Brunelleschi: The Buildings* (London, 1993)

SPECIALIST STUDIES

I. del Badia: 'Il vecchio palazzo della Parte Guelfa', *Bull. Assoc. Difesa Firenze Ant.*, iii (1902), pp. 63–74

C. von Fabriczy: 'Brunelleschiana: Urkunden und Forschungen zur Biographie des Meisters', *Jb. Kön.-Preuss. Kstsamml.*, xxviii (1907), pp. 1–84

L. H. Heydenreich: 'Spätwerke Brunelleschis', *J. Preuss. Kstsamml.*, lii (1931), pp. 1–28

G. Marchini: 'Un disegno di Giuliano da Sangallo riproducente l'alzato della rotonda degli Angeli', *Atti del 1. congresso di storia dell'architettura: 1936*, pp. 147–54

D. F. Nyberg: 'Brunelleschi's Use of Proportion in the Pazzi Chapel', *Marsyas*, vii (1957), pp. 1–7

H. Saalman: 'Filippo Brunelleschi: Capital Studies', *A. Bull.*, xl (1958), pp. 113–37

——: 'Further Notes on the Cappella Barbadori in S Felicità', *Burl. Mag.*, c (1958), pp. 270–74

G. Laschi, P. Roselli and P. A. Rossi: 'Indagini sulla Cappella dei Pazzi', *Commentari*, xiii (1962), pp. 24–41

H. Saalman: 'The Authorship of the Pazzi Palace', *A. Bull.*, xlvi (1964), pp. 388–94

M. Cardoso Mendes and G. Dallai: 'Nuove indagini sullo Spedale degli Innocenti a Firenze', *Commentari*, xvii (1966), pp. 83–106

L. Benevolo, S. Chieffi and G. Mezzetti: 'Indagine sul S Spirito di Brunelleschi', *Quad. Ist. Stor. Archit.*, xv (1968), pp. 1–52

P. Waddy: 'Brunelleschi's Design for S Maria degli Angeli in Florence', *Marsyas*, xv (1970–71), pp. 36–45

V. Hoffmann: 'Brunelleschis Architektursystem', *Architectura* [Munich], i (1971), pp. 54–71

A. Bruschi: 'Considerazioni sulla "maniera matura" del Brunelleschi: Con un'appendice sulla rotonda degli Angeli', *Palladio*, n. s., xxii (1972), pp. 89–126

V. Herzner: 'Zur Baugeschichte von San Lorenzo in Florenz', *Z. Kstgesch.*, xxxvii (1974), pp. 89–115

I. Hyman: 'Notes and Speculations on S Lorenzo, Palazzo Medici and an Urban Project by Brunelleschi', *J. Soc. Archit. Historians*, xxxiv (1975), pp. 98–120

G. Miarelli-Mariani: 'I disegni per la rotonda degli Angeli', *Ant. Viva*, xiv (1975), pp. 35–48

——: 'Il Tempio fiorentino degli Scolari: Ipotesi e notizie sopra una irrealizzata imagine brunelleschiana', *Palladio*, n. s., xxiii–xxv (1976), pp. 45–74

R. Mainstone: 'Brunelleschi's Dome', *Archit. Rev.* [London], clxii (1977), pp. 156–66

A. Molho: 'Three Documents Regarding Filippo Brunelleschi', *Burl. Mag.*, cxix (1977), pp. 851–2

H. Saalman: 'San Lorenzo: The 1434 Chapel Project', *Burl. Mag.*, cxx (1978), pp. 361–4

H. Burns: 'San Lorenzo in Florence before the Building of the New Sacristy: An Early Plan', *Mitt. Ksthist. Inst. Florenz*, xxiii (1979), pp. 145–53

C. Elam: 'The Site and the Early Building History of Michelangelo's New Sacristy', *Mitt. Ksthist. Inst. Florenz*, xxiii (1979), pp. 153–86

H.Saalman: 'Designing the Pazzi Chapel: The Problem of Metrical Analysis', *Architectura* [Munich], ix (1979), pp. 1–5

D. Carl: 'Die Kapelle Guidalotti-Mellini im Kreuzgang von S Croce: Ein Beitrag zur Baugeschichte', *Mitt. Ksthist. Inst. Florenz*, xxv (1981), pp. 203–30

C. R. Mack: 'Brunelleschi's Spedale degli Innocenti Rearticulated', *Architectura* [Munich], xi (1981), p. 130

J. Beck: 'Desiderio da Settignano (and Antonio del Pollaiuolo): Problems', *Mitt. Ksthist. Inst. Florenz*, xxviii (1984), pp. 203–24

H. Saalman: 'The New Sacristy of San Lorenzo before Michelangelo', *A. Bull.*, lxvii (1985), pp. 199–228

——: 'Form and Meaning at the Barbadori-Capponi Chapel in Santa Felicità', *Burl. Mag.*, cxxxi (1989), pp. 532–9

M. Kemp: *The Science of Art: Optical Themes in Western Art from Brunelleschi to Seurat* (New Haven and London, 1990)

HAROLD MEEK

Brunet-Debaines, Alfred-Louis (*b* Le Havre, 5 Nov 1845; *d* Hyères, *c*. 1935). French printmaker and painter. He was the son of the architect Charles-Louis-Fortuné Brunet-Debaines (1801–62), and he studied architecture at the Ecole des Beaux-Arts in Paris before he studied painting under Isidore-Alexandre-Augustin Pils. He became interested in etching and engraving and took lessons with Maxime Lalanne, Charles Normand, Jules Jacquemart and Léon Gaucherel (1816–86). After encouragement from Johan Barthold Jongkind, he made his début at the Salon in 1866 with a number of etchings and watercolours. Thereafter he regularly sent works in both media to the Salon, his subjects being flowers, landscapes or architecture. A typical example is the etching of *Nôtre Dame at Bourges* (1869; Paris, Bib. N.). In 1869 he produced plates of the château at Saint Germain-en-Laye for the *Gazette des Beaux-Arts* (e.g. *Chapelle St Louis at the Château St*

Germain, 1869; Paris, Bib. N.) and in 1871 provided engravings for A. de Bullemont's *Catalogue raisonné des peintures, sculptures et objects d'art qui décoraient l'Hôtel de Ville de Paris avant sa destruction* (Paris, 1871). Many of the subjects for his etchings were taken from Paris, Bourgogne, Hyères and Normandy. Among the latter were several views of Rouen (e.g. *Rue de l'Epicerie à Rouen*, 1878; Paris, Bib. N.). From 1884 to 1897 Brunet-Debaines lived in Britain, and in 1878–9 and 1887–8 his views of London, Oxford and Edinburgh appeared in *Portfolio*. After a trip to Tunis, a number of his watercolours painted there were published in the London *Art Journal* in 1903. He also had work published in *L'Illustration* and *Revue de l'art*. In addition to his original work he made many etchings after paintings by Constable, Turner, Canaletto, Corot and others.

BIBLIOGRAPHY

DBF

H. Béraldi: *Les Graveurs du XIXe siècle*, 12 vols (Paris, 1885–92), iv, pp. 22–5

Inventaire du fonds français après 1800 (Paris, Bib. N., 1930–), iii, pp. 478–84

□

Brunetto, Tomás (*b* ?Turin; *d* Rato, 1771). Portuguese potter of Italian birth. He came from Turin, where he probably had some experience of maiolica manufacture. In 1767 he went to Portugal where he became the first director of the REAL FÁBRICA DO RATO in Lisbon. During the early years Brunetto's personality dominated the factory's production. Shapes and patterns were based on Italian prototypes, especially those from the factories in Turin and SAVONA. Production included polychrome table services, tureens in the form of animals, birds (e.g. goose; *see* LISBON, fig. 4), vases, figures and fish tanks supported by dolphins (e.g. of 1767–71; Barnard Castle, Bowes Mus.). Brunetto was succeeded by SEBASTIÃO INÁCIO DE ALMEIDA.

BIBLIOGRAPHY

J. Queirós: *Cerâmica portugesa* (Lisbon, 1907, rev. in 2 vols, 1948/*R* 1987)

A. de Sandão: *Faiança portugesa: Séculos XVIII, XIX* (Oporto, 1976)

LUCIANA ARBACE

Brunfaut. Belgian family of architects. Fernand Brunfaut (*b* Anseremme, 7 July 1886; *d* Brussels, 12 Feb 1972) studied architecture at the Académie Royale des Beaux-Arts, Brussels, as well as sociology and economics at the Université de Bruxelles. From early on he pursued a political career alongside his work as an architect. He was first elected as a local councillor in 1911 and then as a deputy burgomaster (1921–59) was responsible for public works in the communes of Brussels. His architectural works include private and public housing in Brussels, the Maison du Peuple (1922) in Dinant and the workers' clinics in Brussels and Ghent. In 1925 he was elected a socialist Member of Parliament, and in 1949 he drew up the Brunfaut Law, which governed the development of areas of workers' housing in Belgium. From 1930 his buildings were designed in collaboration with his son Maxime Brunfaut (*b* Brussels, 23 May 1902), who had studied with Victor Horta at the Académie Royale des Beaux-Arts in Brussels. For the socialist press they built the head offices of the *Vooruit* newspaper in Ghent (1930) and of *Le Peuple* in Brussels (1931), as well as the head office for the trade union and mutual benefit organization Prévoyance Sociale (1931), Brussels. In all these, and at the Joseph Lemaire Sanatorium (1934–7) at Tombeek, near Wavre, they experimented with an architecture that combined glass, ceramic and concrete to create open perspectives and a bare functional impression. Maxime Brunfaut also worked with Horta on the new central station, Brussels, which he later completed (1946–53), and designed Zaventhem Airport (1958), Brussels.

Gaston Brunfaut (*b* Jemelle, 6 Feb 1894; *d* Brussels, 1 June 1974) studied at the Académie Royale des Beaux-Arts before training with his brother, Fernand Brunfaut. His most characteristic projects were executed between 1930 and 1939. The influence of the theories of the Congrès International d'Architecture Moderne (CIAM) is evident in his designs for workers' housing in Brussels and in numerous competition entries for Functionalist urban planning schemes and communal facilities, such as schools and swimming-pools. Notable realized projects include the seaside children's home (1933–9), Oostduinkerke, several private houses and a hospital, the Instituts Jules Bordet et Paul Héger (1937–9), Brussels, with Stanislas Jasinski (1901–78). As editor (1927–32) of the review *Le Document* he contributed numerous articles on architecture and urban planning as forms of social expression. After World War II he took part in the competition (1947) for the United Nations Organization Building in New York and built several workers' housing blocks.

WRITINGS

G. Brunfaut: 'Confiance en l'architecture moderne', *Le Document*, iv/83 (1931)

——: 'Architecture et pédagogie: L'Ecole moderne', *Babin*, 16 (1934), pp. 589–96

BIBLIOGRAPHY

G. Bekaert and F. Strauven: *La Construction en Belgique* (Brussels, 1971)

P. Puttemans and others: *Modern Architecture in Belgium* (Brussels, 1976)

F. Strauven and others: 'L'architettura in Belgio', *Rass. Archit. & Urb.*, x/34 (1988), pp. 5–88

Brunfaut, Jules (*b* Brussels, 16 Nov 1852; *d* Brussels, 4 Jan 1942). Belgian architect. He studied at the Ecole du Génie Civil in Ghent and then from 1873 to 1879 at the Académie Royale des Beaux-Arts, Brussels. An important early influence was a period spent working with Henri Beyaert, with whom he collaborated closely, acquiring an astonishing virtuosity in the design of façades. The major part of his work, however, can be characterized as derived from Italian and Flemish Renaissance sources, although developed with a rationalist rigour given the limitations of party-wall construction and narrow plots of land with which he had to contend. After the early design for the Ecole Communale (1878–80), Place Anneessens, Brussels, he visited Italy and spent a few years in the early 1880s in Portugal. On his return to Brussels he specialized in designing middle-class homes, large houses for the wealthy, industrial buildings and exhibition halls. However, his outstanding work is the Hôtel Hannon (1902), Rue de la Jonction, Brussels, in which at the instigation of his friend the engineer and photographer Edouard Hannon (1853–1931), he experimented with Art Nouveau. The house was decorated and furnished by Emile Gallé, and forms one of the most beautiful corner buildings of its style in Brussels. Although very different from the rest of his work, it secured Brunfaut a reputation as an exponent of Art Nouveau. In 1885–90 he managed the important Belgian architectural review *L'Emulation*, and in 1887–8 he was president of the Société Centrale d'Architecture de Belgique.

BIBLIOGRAPHY

P. Saintenoy: 'Notice sur Jules Brunfaut, membre de l'Académie', *Annu. Acad. Royale Belgique/Jb. Kon. Acad. België*, cxvi (1950), pp. 137–65

Resurgam: La Reconstruction en Belgique après 1914 (exh. cat., Brussels, Pal. B.-A., 1985), p. 217

ANNETTE NEVE

Bruni, Andrea dei. *See* ANDREA DEI BRUNI.

Bruni, Fyodor [Fidelio] **(Antonovich)** (*b* Milan, 15 Dec 1801; *d* St Petersburg, 11 Sept 1875). Russian painter, etcher, teacher and museum director of Italian birth. He was the son of the Swiss artist Antonio Baroffi Bruni (1767–1825), who moved to Russia with his family in 1807, taking the name Anton Osipovich Bruni. In 1809 he became a pupil at the St Petersburg Academy of Arts, where he studied under Aleksey Yegorov (1776–1851), Andrey Ivanov (1776–1848) and Vasily Shebuyev and graduated in 1818. Between 1819 and 1836 he lived in Italy, principally in Rome, where he perfected his skills by copying works by the Old Masters. He also painted portraits in order to earn a living. In his best-known portrait of this time, *Princess Zinaida Volkonskaya in the Costume of Tancred* (*c.* 1820; St Petersburg, Rus. Mus.), the sitter's fantastical, theatrical knight's costume and her expression of heartfelt languor and radiant sadness are characteristic of Romantic portraiture. In 1824 he completed one of the best-known Russian pictures on a Classical theme, the *Death of Camilla, Sister of Horatius*, also known as the *Triumph of Horatius* (see fig.). The picture was exhibited in Rome to great acclaim, and Bruni was made a member of the Accademia di San Luca. In 1828 he painted *Bacchante Giving Cupid a Drink* (St Petersburg, Rus. Mus.), impressive for its technique but also conveying both the young artist's triumphant love of life and his fascination with the beauty of Italian women.

In 1834 Bruni painted one of the most notable Russian pictures on a biblical subject, *Prayer over the Chalice* (St Petersburg, Rus. Mus.), where he treated his theme in a boldly coloured Romantic style, especially expressive in the image of the saddened Christ. At the end of 1825, on the instructions of the St Petersburg Society for the Encouragement of Artists, Bruni began work on a series of etchings to illustrate *The History of the Russian State* by Nikolay Karamzin. These were conceived as individual compositions recording specific events: the exploits of Prince Svyatoslav, the murder of Boris and Gleb, scenes of the Baptism of Rus' and the death of Andrey Bogolyubsky. The series was issued in 1839 in two albums, *Studies of Events in Russian History*. In September 1834, after exhibiting the *Triumph of Horatius* at the St Petersburg Academy of Arts, Bruni became an Academician. In that year he began to work on his large picture the *Brazen Serpent* (1841; St Petersburg, Rus. Mus.; *see* ST PETERSBURG, fig. 7), one of the most remarkable works of historical Romanticism in Russian art. The biblical

Fyodor Bruni: *Death of Camilla, Sister of Horatius*, oil on canvas, 3.50×5.26 m, 1824 (St Petersburg, Russian Museum)

episode is treated with melodrama and passion, and its real hero is the crowd, a group of individuals discovering the power of fate and punishment. Although Bruni shows the tragic experiences that have befallen the people through their own foolishness and greed, the painting appeals to the viewer's compassion.

In 1836 Bruni returned to St Petersburg where he became Professor of Art History in the Academy of Arts and received many commissions. He painted icons, for example for churches in the Catherine Palace in Tsarskoye Selo (now Pushkin) and in the Winter Palace and Kazan' Cathedral in St Petersburg. At the beginning of the 1840s he was commissioned to paint murals in St Isaac's Cathedral, St Petersburg. He worked on a large scale to provide sketches for the Moscow Cathedral of Christ the Saviour and murals for the main hall of the Old Hermitage and for the private residence of Baron Stieglitz in St Petersburg. Bruni taught at the Academy of Arts between 1836 and 1838 and from 1846 to 1871, instructing a great many of Russia's history painters. From 1855 to 1871 he was Rector of the Academy, from 1866 serving as head of the mosaic studio. He was in charge of the Hermitage Picture Gallery from 1849 to 1864.

BIBLIOGRAPHY

A. Savinov: *F. A. Bruni* (St Petersburg, 1949)
M. Rakova: *Russkaya istoricheskaya zhivopis' XIX veka* [Russian historical art of the 19th century] (Moscow, 1979)
A. Vereshchagina: *Fyodor Antonovich Bruni* (St Petersburg, 1985)

G. A. PRINTSEVA

Bruni, Leonardo [Leonardo Aretino] (*b* Arezzo, 1370; *d* Florence, 9 March 1444). Italian scholar and writer. He was the leading humanist scholar of early 15th-century Florence, widely read in both Latin and Greek and a prolific author and translator. One of the first to attempt an artistically classicizing Latin prose, he brought Aristotle and later Plato, besides others, to the forefront of humanist moral thought in a sustained polemical effort to supersede and augment medieval translations. He was employed as papal secretary (1405–15) to Innocent VII and Gregory XII and as Chancellor of Florence (1427–44). In his writings, notably the treatise *Laudatio florentinae urbis* (*c.* 1400) and the nine-volume *Historia florentini populi* (begun *c.* 1415, pubd 1439), he argued a relationship between the political liberty and cultural flowering of republican Rome and contemporary Florence and promulgated an active engagement of the intellectual with society, after the example of Cicero. The depth and sincerity of this ideology of 'civic humanism' has been much debated by modern scholars. Asked in 1424 for his views on the new bronze doors being designed by Lorenzo Ghiberti for the Baptistery, Florence, Bruni replied that the scenes should be *illustri* (visually ornate) and *significanti* (historically important). His detailed programme for them (Krautheimer), closely modelled on those of the two existing sets of doors, was rejected in favour of a more radical scheme, which possibly owed its iconography to Ambrogio Traversari's patristic exegesis. His tomb (Florence, Santa Croce), erected by the Comune, was designed by Bernardo Rossellino and provided a prototype for many succeeding sepulchral monuments.

WRITINGS

Laudatio florentinae urbis (?Florence, *c.* 1400); ed. V. Zaccaria in *Stud. Med.*, viii (1967), pp. 529–54
Historia florentini populi, 9 vols (Florence, 1439); ed. C. Monzalli as *Storia fiorentina di Leonardo Bruni tradotta in volgare da D. Acciajuoli* (Florence, 1861)

BIBLIOGRAPHY

R. Krautheimer: *Lorenzo Ghiberti*, 2 vols (Princeton, 1956, rev. 1970)
A. M. Schulz: *The Sculpture of B. Rossellino and his Workshop* (Princeton, 1977), pp. 32–51
G. Griffiths, J. Hankins and D. Thompson: *The Humanism of Leonardo Bruni* (Binghamton, NY, 1987)

M. C. DAVIES

Bruni, Lev (Aleksandrovich) (*b* Malaya Vishera, province of Novgorod, 1894; *d* Moscow, 1948). Russian painter and graphic artist. He came from a well-established artistic family and after a brief involvement with avant-garde experimentation he returned to a figurative style. He trained in St Petersburg at Princess Tenisheva's school (1904–9) and at the Academy of Arts (1909–12). He then studied under Henri Laurens at the Académie Julian in Paris (1912–13). Paintings such as *The Rainbow* (1916; St Petersburg, Rus. Mus.) show the influence of Cubism and Futurism. At this time his flat in Petrograd became a meeting-point for various members of the avant-garde, including Vladimir Tatlin. Under Tatlin's influence, Bruni began making purely abstract reliefs and constructions. *Painterly Work with Materials* (1916, destr.; see Lodder, pl. 1.19), which was apparently made from painted wood and metal, explored pictorial relationships of colour and plane, whereas a lost construction of 1917 is more three-dimensional and textural, incorporating very varied materials such as celluloid, aluminium, glass and cloth.

Bruni taught drawing at the A. Stieglitz Central School of Technical Drawing in Petrograd (1920–21), and then in the Graphics Faculty of the Vkhutemas in Moscow (1923–30). During the 1920s he developed a figurative, somewhat lyrical, calligraphic style and joined the Four Arts Society of Artists in 1925. In 1935 he became the Director of the Studio of Monumental Painting at the Moscow Architectural Institute and then at the Academy of Architecture, decorating several pavilions for the 1939 Agricultural Exhibition in Moscow. During the 1930s Bruni also illustrated popular magazines.

BIBLIOGRAPHY

V. Rakitin: *L. A. Bruni* (Moscow, 1970)
C. Lodder: *Russian Constructivism* (New Haven, 1983)

CHRISTINA LODDER

Brüning, Peter (*b* Düsseldorf, 21 Nov 1929; *d* Ratingen, 25 Dec 1970). German painter and sculptor. He studied at the Staatliche Akademie der Bildenden Künste, Stuttgart (1949–52), under Willi Baumeister. In 1953 he joined the Gruppe 53. With Quadriga in Frankfurt and the Zen group in Munich, it was a centre of *Art informel* in Germany. During this period Brüning based his works on biomorphic or representational forms. In 1955, however, he turned to the abstraction of *Art informel*, which was to characterize his work for the next decade. Freely floating patches of colour, to which Brüning gave solidity by adding touches of black, characterized the works he produced *c.* 1957. They also served to relate his previous experiments with structure to his search for simultaneous, spontaneous expressive power. His compositions became increasingly transparent and buoyant until 1964. In these works the pristine white surface of the canvas became an independent element of the composition, and the colour suggested playful energy, for example *Painting 2/63* (1963; Bonn, Städt. Kstmus.).

From the beginning a fundamental aspect of Brüning's work was his interest in landscape, in which he attempted to formulate his notions of space. He continued to explore this area. In 1964 his encounter with Cy Twombly's work and the more concrete, more universal sign-language of cartography inspired him to produce individual abstractions, characterized by gestures. Instead of graduated colours, Brüning painted ciphers: in a two-dimensional way on the pictorial surface, as in the series *Legends* (e.g. *Nos 34–65*, 1964–5; Bonn, Städt. Kstmus.), or in a three-dimensional context, depicting space. In *Strassenwand* (exh. Kassel, *Documenta 4*, 1968), he developed his three-dimensional, energetic expression of space by combining cartographic marks with strips representing streets, luminous bands of colour and aluminium mirrors. On the other hand, he also fulfilled his sociological objective: to find a universally valid language through which to express his views about the effects of industrial civilization on human environment.

BIBLIOGRAPHY

Peter Brüning (exh. cat., Mannheim, Städt. Ksthalle, 1962)
Peter Brüning: Superländer und Signale (exh. cat., Düsseldorf, Kstver., 1970)
Peter Brüning: Bilder, Objekte, Zeichnungen (exh. cat., Bonn, Städt. Kstmus., 1972)
R.-G. Dienst: *Peter Brüning* (Recklinghausen, 1973)

BEATRICE V. BISMARCK

Brünn. *See* BRNO.

Brunner, Johann Michael. *See* PRUNNER, JOHANN MICHAEL.

Brunovský, Albín (*b* Zohor, nr Bratislava, 25 Dec 1935). Slovak printmaker, painter and illustrator. From 1951 to 1955 he studied at the Central School of Industrial Art at Bratislava and at the School of Fine Arts, Bratislava, from 1956 to 1961, completing his training there in 1963–6. In 1967 he was put in charge of the book production department; in 1981 he was appointed professor. His early work as printmaker and illustrator derived its inspiration from the imaginative tradition of Slovak art, which he interpreted in his own version of neo-Surrealism. In 1964 Klee, Kandinsky and Miró began to influence his work, and his illustrations were clearly inspired by Chagall. He gradually developed his own version of Mannerism and adapted his artistic language accordingly, aiming, in his graphic work, at the precise technical mastery of lithography, etching etc. Among his first works with Mannerist traits is *Honour to Arcimboldo* (1965; see Peterajová, no. 18), and the style is fully developed in the cycle *Bella Italia, I–XVIII* (1969–79; Bratislava, Slovak N.G.). While remaining faithful to his imaginative position, he slowly moved towards the rigour of Verismo. In the 1970s, apart from history painting (e.g. *Sisters from Fontainebleau, I–XVIII*, 1972; Dolný Kubín, Oravská Gal.), he produced works in which natural motifs began to appear, inspired by the Slovak countryside, such as a *Walk in Záhorie* (1972; Dolný Kubín, Oravská Gal.). His work began to move away from French and Italian Mannerism and closer to a Flemish style, as in the cycle *Lady in a Hat, I–IX* (1981–2; see Peterajová, nos 115–21). He has illustrated more than 100 books for children and adults, producing paraphrases of texts by way of free improvisation, for example his illustrations for Ovid's *Art of Love* (Bratislava, 1970–72) and Rimbaud's *Le Bateau ivre* (Bratislava, 1981). He developed a combined technique for painting on panel, in which he made full use of the properties of the material, as in the *Third Variant of the Super Large Garden Theatre* (1971; Bratislava, Gal. Capital SR) and *Cruise of Divine Cleopatra's Fans* (1988; Hana Larvová priv. col.). He has also designed bookplates, banknotes and film posters.

BIBLIOGRAPHY

L. Peterajová: *Albín Brunovský* (Bratislava, 1985, rev. 1990) [in Eng.]
L. Petránský: *Moderná slovenská grafika* [Modern Slovak graphic art] (Bratislava, 1985)
B. Stehlíková: 'Albín Brunovský dětem' [Albín Brunovský to children], *Zlatý Máj*, iii (1985)

HANA LARVOVÁ

Brunsberg, Hinrich [Heinrich; Henryk] (*b* ?1360–65; *d* after 1428). German architect. Brunsberg's work represents an important decorative phase of brick Gothic architecture in western Pomerania. There is documentary evidence for his work at St Katharinen, Brandenburg, and a further three buildings are attributed to him on stylistic grounds. His name appears on a brick inscription on the north side of St Katharinen between the Lady chapel portals: *Anno d[o]m[ini] MCCCCI co[n]structa e[st] h[aec] ecc[lesi]a in die assu[m]ptionis Mariae virginis per magistru[m] Hinricu[m] Brunsbergh d[e] Stet[t]in* (Master Hinrich Brunsberg of Szczecin (Ger. Stettin) built St Katharinen in 1401). Brunsberg is also mentioned 28 times in the town records of Szczecin between 1400 and 1428; in each case he is referred to as master in the context of either owing or being owed money. All his architectural activity was concentrated in the area between Brandenburg and Szczecin.

Brunsberg rebuilt the nave of St Katharinen, a five-bay hall construction, after the old nave collapsed in 1395 (for illustration *see* BRANDENBURG). He introduced octagonal piers with delicate shafting, aligned with a series of internal buttresses that divided the side aisles into chapels. These buttresses run the full height of the building (18 m) and are covered on their exteriors by decorated pilaster-strips, the most outstanding characteristics of Brunsberg's style. The brick pilaster-strip decoration is made up of tiers of gabled niches, two of which retain their original sculptures. To the north of the church Brunsberg built a Lady chapel on older foundations, with a north façade decorated in pilaster-strips ending in an elaborate traceried show gable. The chapel was used as the main entrance to the church until *c.* 1434, when a new porch was built on the south side. The east end of St Katharinen was built by a second master and completed in 1434.

The choir of St Mary's, Stargard Szczeciński, Poland (Ger. Stargard; see fig.), is the earliest of the three buildings attributed to Brunsberg and was completed by 1388. It uses the same system of internal buttressing as St Katharinen, but here it is applied to a basilical structure. To

Hinrich Brunsberg: south ambulatory chapels of St Mary, Stargard Szczeciński, completed 1388

strengthen the construction Brunsberg introduced a gallery between the ambulatory buttresses forming vaulted chapels at ground-level. The interior is articulated with decoration: the ambulatory has triradial vaulting, gabled niches are set into the choir piers, and quatrefoil friezes decorate the choir arcade capitals and the triforium string course. The overall impression of the choir exterior is of a tall drum articulated by pilaster-strips; each pilaster has three tiers of lancets, each lancet crowned by a rosette and gable, with small stone heads marking the springing points of the gables.

St Mary's, Chojna, Poland (Ger. Königsberg in Preussen; destr. 1945), is attributed to Brunsberg on grounds of style and the similarity of its cross-section to St Katharinen. The hall construction was begun from the east *c.* 1399 and the choir consecrated in 1407; a second master, introducing minor changes, completed the church in 1457. The six-bay nave is separated from the side aisles by octagonal piers; a polygonal ambulatory opens into chapels formed between the internal buttresses, which are linked by a gallery to strengthen the construction. The treatment is more elaborate than at Stargard Szczeciński, with large openings in the buttresses to permit circulation at gallery level and sculpted consoles supporting the ribs of the chapel vaults. The pilaster-strips that articulate the exterior are similar to those at Stargard Szczeciński; they were added after the outer ambulatory wall was built.

Brunsberg was also responsible for adding an extra south aisle to the basilical structure of St James, Szczecin, Poland, *c.* 1402. The tracery on the exterior follows the layout of St Katharinen but in lower relief. The nave of St James was later converted to a hall structure; the height of Brunsberg's exterior decoration was then reduced and his interior buttressing arrangement altered.

Opinion is divided on the sources of Brunsberg's style. Zaske (1957, 1978) has argued that his background was in the land of the Teutonic Knights; his suggestion that he was employed on decorative work at the Upper Castle, Malbork (Ger. Marienburg), Poland, and St Catherine's, Brodnica, Poland (Ger. Strassburg in Preussen), before moving to Szczecin is controversial. Clasen and Lohman have suggested that he was influenced by stone buildings in southern Germany, such as Holy Cross (1351), Schwäbisch Gmünd, and St Sebaldus (1361–73), Nuremberg, where hall ambulatories are combined with exterior decoration. At Kaisheim Abbey (1352–87), the ambulatory and the ring of chapels are vaulted at a similar height, as in the buildings associated with Brunsberg. The hall choir of St James, Szczecin, completed in 1380, where the ambulatory wall is composed of drawn-in buttresses alternating with tall windows, provides a link between these stone buildings and Brunsberg's work. St James, Szczecin, was particularly significant for Brunsberg: the gallery later introduced into its ambulatory (1380–87) between the internal buttresses became a model for Stargard Szczeciński and Chojna. There is also good local precedent for triradial ambulatory vaulting in the hall choirs of the Marienkirche (*c.* 1367), Frankfurt an der Oder, St James, Szczecin (1380; vaulting destr. 17th century), and St Nikolas (*c.* 1387), Luckau.

The vaulting of the naves of churches by Brunsberg raises many problems, since it is still uncertain which were designed by him and which by his successors. The appearance of stone sculpture and elaborate brick tracery in his churches suggests direct contact with stone-building areas. However, the show gable of the Lady chapel at St Katharinen, Brandenburg, derives from the gables of northern town houses and Lübeck town hall (*c.* 1315).

After Brunsberg's death his workshop completed St Katharinen, Brandenburg, and continued the building of the town hall gable (*c.* 1434) at Tangermünde. By 1430 architects were being drawn independently to Brunsberg's work, adapting his ambitious schemes to a variety of local needs. The most important examples are St Mary (1431–48), Poznań, Poland, SS Peter and Paul (*c.* 1460), Szczecin, and St Stephan (*c.* 1460), Gartz an der Oder. There was a Brunsberg revival in the 19th century, part of a general interest in the Late Gothic period.

BIBLIOGRAPHY

W. Clasen: 'Hinrich Brunsberg und die Parler', *Festschrift Julius Baum* (Stuttgart, 1952)

N. Zaske: 'Heinrich Brunsberg: Ein ordenspreussischer Baumeister der Spätgotik', *Balt. Stud.*, xliv (1957), pp. 49–72

——: 'Henryk Brunsberg: Twórczość i znaczenie' [Hinrich Brunsberg: creation and meaning], *Sztuka Pobrzeżu Bałtkyu* [Art of the Baltic Coast] (1978), pp. 167–201

J. Lohman: *The Case of Hinrich Brunsberg* (diss., U. Manchester, 1982)

JACK LOHMAN

Brunswick [Ger. Braunschweig]. German city in Lower Saxony, formerly the capital of the Duchy of Brunswick.

1. History and urban development. Tradition places the origins of Brunswick in the 9th century when Bruno and Dankward, dukes of Saxony, are said to have founded it (AD 860). Archaeological excavations have uncovered the remains of a series of churches and of a fortified manor house dating back to this period, when merchants first settled at the spot where an important

runswick, view from the east showing (from left to right) St Aegidien, St Magni, St Martin, the cathedral of St Blasius, St Katharina and St Andreas; ing by F. B. Werner, 1729 (Brunswick, Städtisches Museum)

east–west trade route crossed the River Oker. Dankwarderode Castle was subsequently erected on the site of the manor house, and in 1030 the cathedral was founded near by, originally as the collegiate church of St Blasius; the village of Altewiek grew up around it. A century later in 1134 the Benedictines began building the monastery of St Ägidius on a low hill to the south, while on the left bank of the river the merchants' settlement was beginning to spread around the rectangular market of the Altstadt. The regularly planned old town that was built here received its charter from Emperor Lothair III in 1117.

Lothair's grandson Henry the Lion (*see* WELF, (1)) decisively shaped the appearance and development of Brunswick: under his influence, the town assumed the form it still has. In 1142 Henry became Duke of Saxony and enlarged the town to make it his fortified residence. The erection in 1166 of the bronze, formerly gilded, lion (*see* ROMANESQUE, fig. 74) in the castle courtyard (Burgplatz) was a visible expression of his ambitions in north Germany and of his intention to make Brunswick the political and cultural centre of Saxony. The lion is the first large free-standing sculpture north of the Alps. Henry added a further borough to the old town, the Hagen (a drained area of marshland), and surrounded the castle and the existing settlement (except for the Altewiek) with a continuous wall and ditch. Henry also rebuilt Dankwarderode Castle to compete with imperial palaces.

In 1173, on his return from a pilgrimage to Jerusalem, he began building the cathedral of St Blasius, one of the first vaulted buildings in north Germany, to replace the earlier church of St Blasius. He equipped the church (begun 1183, consecrated 1188) with rich furnishings: among his outstanding gifts were the bronze, seven-branched candelabrum (*c.* 1180; h. 4.8 m, w. 4 m; *in situ*), the altar of the Virgin supported on seven bronze columns (before 1180) and the precious Gospels of Henry the Lion (Wolfenbüttel, Herzog August Bib., Cod. Guelf. 105 Noviss. 2°; for illustrations *see* CHRYSOGRAPHY and WOLFENBÜTTEL). Others included the Imerward Cross (*c.* 1160, *in situ*) and the Welf Treasure, which Henry increased (dispersed; mainly in Berlin, Tiergarten Kstgewmus.). The chancel and transept were painted (*c.* 1250); the wall paintings are still largely preserved. Like the important double tomb of Henry and his second wife, Matilda (*c.* 1230), they were produced long after his death. Henry was probably also responsible for the foundation of the Neustadt between the old town and Hagen, primarily occupied by craftsmen and included within the fortifications. As Holy Roman Emperor, his son Otto IV (*reg* 1209–18) added a wall around the Altewiek, so that the four large boroughs, together with a smaller one called Sack, at last formed a unified town. The ducal palace is at the town's centre, an unusual feature as such buildings are generally located at the edge of the town.

Emulating the dukes, the citizens built large parish churches in their individual boroughs (1190–1225). The exteriors, in random rubble built to courses, were modelled on the cathedral, having tall façades with two towers on the west front and a basilica-like interior divided originally into a nave and aisles but later converted to hall construction. In the 13th and 14th centuries each of the five boroughs was given a separate Rathaus (town hall), since each had its own council and burgomaster, until a common council was formed in 1325. The outstanding example is Altstadt Rathaus (begun 1302; rest. after World War II), the two main wings of which meet at an angle to form the corner of the Altstadt market square. The traceried façades, rivalling the churches in their profusion, reduce the 'solid' surfaces to vanishing point. A Dominican monastery had been built on the right bank of the Oker, on the edge of the Hagen district. Other churches were added, so that medieval Brunswick had 25 churches and chapels (see fig.). The medieval fortifications were enlarged and unified, by 1700 taking the form of the bastion (destr. 1797) shown in the illustration.

As a member of the Hanseatic League, Brunswick was a wealthy town, and the opulence of domestic architecture is reflected in its private timber-framed houses, with patterned brick infill (approx. 800 destr. in World War II). Outstanding among them were the Alte Waage (destr.; rebuilt 1993), the surviving 'Zur Hanse' houses and that of the patrician Friedrich Huneborstel (*c.* 1524–52) with its elaborately carved façade timbers. The most important monument from the late Renaissance period is the Gewandhaus, completed in ashlar masonry in 1591, with its magnificent east façade showing Mannerist ornamentation; it was built as a guildhouse under the direct influence of the Flemish architect Hans Vredeman de Vries. In the same period several public buildings and large burghers' houses were given richly ornamented portals, while the churches received costly new interior furnishings. The workshop of the sculptor Jürgen Röttger (1550–1623) played a prominent part in this activity (*c.* 1600).

In the period following the subjection of the town by the Welf dukes in 1671, the most important architectural development was the rebuilding of the castle from 1718 by Hermann Korb (1656–1735). After 1788, the castle again underwent a period of rebuilding. Its last version, a restoration to a scheme (1838) of Karl Theodor Ottmer (1800–43), was bombed in 1944 and later demolished (1960). In the Baroque period also, the Catholic church of St Nicolai was built (1710–12; destr. 1943–5), again by Korb, and important alterations were made to the Neustadt Rathaus (1774–85). The Schlösschen Richmond summer residence was constructed (1768–9) by Duke Carl Wilhelm Ferdinand (Charles II; *reg* 1780–1806) for his English wife, to the designs of Karl Christoph Fleischer (1727–87). Other building projects executed in the second half of the century included the Kammergebäude (1764) and the extension and rebuilding (1773–5 and 1784–6) of the Gothic Neustadtrathaus, both by E. W. Horn, and the former Landschaftliches Haus (1794–9) by C. G. Langwagen.

The razing of the fortifications at the end of the 18th century and their replacement by wide lawns to plans by the architect Peter Joseph Krahe (1758–1840) brought a fundamental change to the appearance of the town. Villas and classical-style gatehouses were put up on the rampart promenades. In 1861 the Staatstheater was built in the same area, followed by the Herzog Anton Ulrich-Museum (1887), the municipal museum, archive and library. The enormous increase in population in the second half of the 19th century caused house building to spread beyond the central area of the city, which had dominated the appearance of Brunswick since the 12th century. In World War II, 40 air raids, especially those of 1944, destroyed over 80% of the city's housing. The great church buildings were saved for the most part, although some roofs were burnt. They have served as the cores for what have been called 'islands of tradition' (mostly groups of restored half-timbered buildings), which give some idea of what the town looked like before its destruction.

BIBLIOGRAPHY

F. Fricke: *Das Bürgerhaus in Braunschweig*, xx of *Das deutsche Bürgerhaus* (Tübingen, 1975)
R. Dorn: *Mittelalterliche Kirchen in Braunschweig* (Hameln, 1978)
Brunswiek 1031—Braunschweig 1981: Die Stadt Heinrichs des Löwen von den Anfängen bis zur Gegenwart (exh. cat., ed. G. Spies; Brunswick, Städt. Mus., 1981)
G. Spies: *Das Gildehaus in Braunschweig: Der Fachwerkbau des Patriziers F. Huneborstel* (Brunswick, 1983)
R. Moderhack: *Braunschweigs Stadtgeschichte*, i of *Braunschweig: Das Bild der Stadt in 900 Jahren, Geschichte und Ansichten* (exh. cat., ed. G. Spies; Brunswick, Städt. Mus., 1985)
M. Puhle and others: *Braunschweigs Stadtbild*, ii of *Braunschweig: Das Bild der Stadt in 900 Jahren, Geschichte und Ansichten* (exh. cat., ed. G. Spies; Brunswick, Städt. Mus., 1985)
H. Rötting: *Stadtarchäologie in Braunschweig: Ein fachübergreifender Arbeitsbericht zu den Grabungen, 1976–1984*, Forschungen der Denkmalpflege in Niedersachsen, iii (Hannover, 1985)
Stadt im Wandel: Kunst und Kultur des Bürgertums in Norddeutschland 1150–1650 (exh. cat., ed. C. Meckseper; Brunswick, Herzog Anton Ulrich-Mus., 1985) i, pp. 56–76
B. Wedemeyer: *Das ehemalige Residenzschloss zu Braunschweig* (Brunswick, 3/1993)

JOHANNES ZAHLTEN

2. CENTRE OF CERAMICS PRODUCTION. The first faience factory in Brunswick was founded in 1707 by Anton Ulrich, Duke of Brunswick-Wolfenbüttel, and directed by Johann Philipp Frantz. Output was extensive and varied, and at first mainly blue-and-white faience, imitative of Delftware, was produced. The large, rather clumsy figures and ewers bearing the ducal monogram are particularly striking. In 1749 the factory was taken over by Johann Erich Behling and Ernst Heinrich Reichard (*d* 1764). The renowned vases and jugs with moulded Rococo decoration painted with bright, high-temperature colours date from this period. In 1776 the factory was bought by Johann Benjamin Heinrich Rabe (*d* 1803) who directed it until his death; the factory closed four years later. The second faience factory was founded in 1747 by Rudolf Anton Chely (*d* 1770) and his sons. Such large items as vases, tureens and figures, which were based on designs by Christoph Rudolf Chely, were a speciality. The factory closed in 1757.

BIBLIOGRAPHY

G. Spies: *Braunschweiger Fayencen* (Brunswick, 1971)
A. Klein: *Deutsche Fayencen* (Brunswick, 1975)

WALTER SPIEGL

Brunswick, House of. *See* WELF, House of.

Brunt, Henry van. *See* VAN BRUNT, HENRY.

Brus, Günter (*b* Ardning, Styria, 27 Sept 1938). Austrian performance artist, draughtsman, painter and film maker. He studied commercial graphic art at the Akademie für Angewandte Kunst in Vienna between 1957 and 1960. Following visits to Spain and the Venice Biennale of 1960, he started to paint gestural abstractions and came into contact with the Austrian painter Alfons Schilling (*b* 1934). In 1961 this development was interrupted when he was called up for military service, after which he found it difficult to return to painting, and by the end of 1962 he had started to concentrate on the act of painting rather than on the finished works themselves. He was persuaded by Otto Muehl to create, with his wife Anni, his first *Aktion* or performance, *Ana*, in November 1964, which he recorded on film in the first of a series of collaborations with the film maker Kurt Kren (*b* 1920). This led to his first self-painting *Aktion*, *Self-painting 1: Painting by Hand, Painting by Head, Painting the Head*, performed the following month. With Muehl, Hermann Nitsch and Rudolf Schwarzkogler he was a founder-member of the AKTIONISMUS group, and with Muehl he helped found the Institut für Direkte Kunst in 1966. To an extent Brus conceived of his *Aktionen* in terms of paintings or tableaux, where the body occupied the centre of a clearly defined space; just as he had scratched and degraded the fabric of the paintings almost to destruction, in his *Aktionen* he portrayed various acts of self-mutilation. This development in Brus's work was encapsulated in the title of his exhibition in 1965 at the Galerie Junge Generation in Vienna, *Malerei, Selbstbemalung, Selbstverstümmelung* (Ger.: painting, self-painting, self-mutilation).

In 1966 Brus collaborated with Muehl on a number of performances. After 1967, however, Brus's *Aktionen* began to push him to further physical and mental extremes as he analysed his own body and its functions, whereas Muehl concentrated on the role of the body in the construction and analysis of psycho-dramas. All symbolism was dispensed with as Brus publicly urinated, defecated and cut himself with a razor-blade. The first of these *Aktionen* to be performed in public was *Citizen Brus Looks at his Own Body*, performed in Aachen and Düsseldorf in 1968, and in June of the same year his *Art and Revolution*, performed at Vienna University, led to his arrest and a six-month prison sentence for degrading the symbols of the State. The culmination of these body-analysis *Aktionen* came in 1970, when Brus stopped making live performances after *Breaking Test* (see fig.) was performed in West Berlin, where Brus had moved the previous year, after his work had been badly received and his life threatened in Austria. This was his most extreme *Aktion* and proved that the continuation of the theme of bodily self-analysis was no longer necessary or possible, since to try and continue realizing this in live actions would have exceeded his own physical limitations. Following this action he returned to painting, drawing and the production of artists' books. In 1971 he held his first exhibition of drawings at the Galerie Michael Werner in Cologne, while his book *Irrwisch* (1971) formed a link between the *Aktion* and the book form by containing the grotesque sexual humour and cathartic intention found in his actions. Many of his books from this period offered narrative depictions of his performances and fantasies. The bleak Expressionism of his *Aktionen* was, however, transformed in his later books into a more romantic form of Expressionism, often using the format of the fairy tale. In such books as *Die Falter des Vorschlafs* (1978) and *Die Garten in der Exosphäre* (1979) Brus revealed the similarity of intention between the sense of enchantment found in tales based on the theme of the 'journey' and the liturgical mythology found particularly in the performances of Nitsch.

Günter Brus: *Breaking Test*, performance, 1970

WRITINGS

Irrwisch (Frankfurt am Main, 1971)
Die Falter des Vorschlafs (Altona and Hohengebraching, 1978)
Die Garten in der Exosphäre (Altona and Hohengebraching, 1979)
Leibvertreib (exh. cat., Düsseldorf, Gal. Heike Curtze, 1989)

BIBLIOGRAPHY

Günter Brus: Zeichnungen und Schriften (exh. cat., text J. Gachnang and A. Meifert; Berne, Ksthalle, 1976)
Günter Brus: Bild-Dichtungen (exh. cat. by A. Meifert, London, Whitechapel A.G.; Hamburg, Kstver.; Lucerne, Kstmus.; Graz, Kulthaus; 1980–81)
Augensternstunden (exh. cat., foreword R. H. Fuchs; Eindhoven, Stedel. Van Abbemus., 1984)
H. Amanhauser and D. Ronte: *Gunter Brus: Der Überblick* (Vienna, 1986)
For further bibliography *see* AKTIONISMUS.

ANDREW WILSON

Brusasorci [Brusasorzi]. Italian family of painters. (1) Domenico Brusasorci was the son of a painter Agostino Riccio, by whom no works are known. Domenico's sons (2) Felice Brusasorci and Giovanni Battista (*b c.* 1544) and his daughter Cecilia (1549–after 1593) were also painters (dal Pozzo; Mantovanelli Stefani).

(1) Domenico Brusasorci [Domenico Riccio] (*b* Verona, *c.* 1515; *d* Verona, 30 March 1567). He probably began his training in his father's shop. Later he studied with Gian Francesco Caroto (Ridolfi, dal Pozzo). Most of Domenico Brusasorci's work was executed in Verona and the surrounding area, and in Vicenza. With Battista del Moro, Domenico belonged to the avant-garde of Veronese painters in the generation before Paolo Veronese.

Brusasorci's frescoes in the choir vault of S Stefano, Verona, painted after 1543, include a *Battle of an Angel and a Demon* that shows his appreciation of the sharply foreshortened figures in the choir vault of Verona Cathedral designed by Giulio Romano and executed by Torbido in 1534. The *Virgin and Child Enthroned with Saints* (Verona, Castelvecchio) and the fresco of *St Ursula and the Virgins* (Verona, Santa Trinità) include Parmigianinesque female figures. In 1552 Brusasorci painted an altarpiece of *St Margaret* for Mantua Cathedral; Battista dell'Angolo del Moro, Paolo Farinati and Paolo Veronese were commissioned to paint for the cathedral at the same time; artists were evidently selected for their modernity, and Brusasorci's *St Margaret*, with her precarious pose and elongated proportions, is an elegant statement of Mannerism.

Among Brusasorci's finest works are the fresco decorations of the Palazzo Fiorio della Seta (later Murari), Verona; the frieze of nymphs in *terra verde* from the façade that faced the River Adige survives (Verona, Castelvecchio). The graceful figures suggest a date in the early 1550s, close to the *St Margaret*. The fresco decoration of 1567 in the Bishop's Palace, Verona, features landscape views and portraits of the bishops of Verona. Brusasorci's abilities as a landscape painter were already demonstrated in 1550 in the small panel paintings of landscapes with distant biblical scenes in the sacristy of S Maria in Organo, Verona.

BIBLIOGRAPHY

DBI; Thieme–Becker
G. Vasari: *Vite* (1550, rev. 2/1568); ed. G. Milanesi (1878–85), vi, pp. 366–8, 488
C. Ridolfi: *Meraviglie* (1648); ed. D. von Hadeln (1914–24), i, p. 298; ii, pp. 108–12
B. dal Pozzo: *Le vite de' pittori, scultori e architetti veronesi* (Verona, 1718), pp. 60–66, 75–6
G. da Re: 'Notizie sui Brusasorzi', *Madonna Verona*, iv (1910), pp. 1–14
R. Montini: 'Per un elenco delle opere di Domenico Brusasorzi', *Boll. Soc. Lett. Verona*, x (1934), pp. 43–8, 83–92
E. Arslan: 'Appunti su Domenico Brusasorzi e la sua cerchia', *Emporium*, cvi (1947), pp. 15–28
L. Crosato: *Gli affreschi nelle ville venete del cinquecento* (Treviso, 1962), pp. 42–3
B. Berenson: *Central and North Italian Schools*, i (London, 1968), pp. 67–9
G. Schweikhart: *Fassadenmalerei in Verona* (Munich, 1973), pp. 236–41
M. Mantovanelli Stefani: 'Una famiglia di artisti, i Brusasorzi: Chiaramenti e aggiunte', *Vita Veron.*, xxxi (1978), pp. 68–88

(2) Felice Brusasorci (*b* Verona, 1539–40; *d* Verona, Feb 1605). Son of (1) Domenico Brusasorci. He was trained by his father in Verona. Felice may have visited Florence early in his career and was documented there in 1597, but most of his extant work is in Verona. His first known altarpiece, the *Virgin and Child Enthroned with Eight Female Saints* (dated 1566; Verona, Santa Trinità), has a polished finish that suggests he was influenced by Florentine Mannerists, whose elongated figures and artificial poses had been adopted earlier by Domenico. The altarpiece of the *Virgin in Glory with Three Archangels* (Verona, S Giorgio Maggiore) was probably executed before 1580; its tonality is lighter and the brushwork freer; the figures are elegantly elongated and fair. This painterly, soft version of Mannerism is evident in the contemporary *Annunciation* and *Four Saints* on the organ shutters of the church of the Madonna di Campagna at San Michele Extra, in the province of Verona, and also in the large *Finding of Moses* (1584; Verona, Castelvecchio). The *Flagellation of Christ* (*c.* 1596; San Michele Extra, Madonna di Campagna) has the same physical types and gestures but is transformed by a delicate luminism (Arslan).

The late works, dating from 1598–1600 onwards, approach a Baroque style and display a more intense religious feeling. In the Giusti Altarpiece of the *Virgin in Glory with Saints* (1598; Verona, S Anastasia) Felice used agitated gestures, although the figures' proportions are more normal, but in the *Christ and the Virgin Appearing to Franciscan Saints* (1600; Bolzano, Chiesa dei Cappuccini) this agitation is replaced by a more effective calm. Felice was locally celebrated for his refinement, delicacy of form and cool tones. He was the teacher of several Veronese Baroque painters, including Sante Creara (*c.* 1572–*c.* 1610–20), Alessandro Turchi, Pasquale Ottino and Marcantonio Bassetti.

BIBLIOGRAPHY

DBI; Thieme–Becker
G. Vasari: *Vite* (1550, rev. 2/1568); ed. G. Milanesi (1878–85), v, p. 379
C. Ridolfi: *Meraviglie* (1648); ed. D. von Hadeln (1914–24), ii, pp. 123–6
B. dal Pozzo: *Le vite de' pittori, scultori e architetti veronesi* (Verona, 1718), pp. 72–5
G. da Re: 'Notizie sui Brusasorzi', *Madonna Verona*, iv (1910), pp. 1–14
E. Arslan: *Il concetto del luminismo e la pittura veneta barocca* (Milan, 1946), pp. 14–15
F. Zava: 'Profilo di Felice Brusasorzi', *A. Ven.*, xxi (1967), pp. 125–43
Cinquant'anni di pittura veronese, 1580–1630 (exh. cat. by L. Magagnato and others, Verona, Gran Guardia, 1974), pp. 51–78

DIANA GISOLFI

Bruselas, Egas de. *See* EGAS, (1).

Bruselas, Hanequin de. *See* HANEQUIN DE BRUSELAS.

Brush. A painting tool made up of a group of fibres bound and inserted into a handle. A brush should hold a quantity of paint and release it gradually as it is applied by the artist to make a consistent mark. The type of fibre, its length and the shape of the brush all affect the type of mark made.

See also CHINA, §XIII, 4; EGYPT, ANCIENT, §X; and JAPAN, §XVI, 4.

1. Materials and manufacture. 2. History. 3. Uses and care.

1. MATERIALS AND MANUFACTURE. Various brush-making materials have been used over the centuries. In ancient Egypt macerated reed fibres were employed. Feathers and human hair have been used in East Asia, as have goat, deer, fox and wolf hair (although Sickman suggested that so-called wolf hair might in fact be that of weasel). The tail fur of the polecat, ermine, mink and sable (all varieties of *Mustela*) are mentioned in many sources as the best material for watercolour brushes (see fig. 1). Miniver, a term used in England up to the 17th century, probably indicated ermine, the winter fur of the stoat. In the West other hair that has been used includes squirrel (tail), ox (ear), badger (back) and bear; the so-called camel hair mentioned in this context is an English misnomer for squirrel. Hair for brushes should be straight, resilient and finely tapered. Kolinsky sable (*Mustela sibirica*) has these characteristics plus good length and a faceted shape that

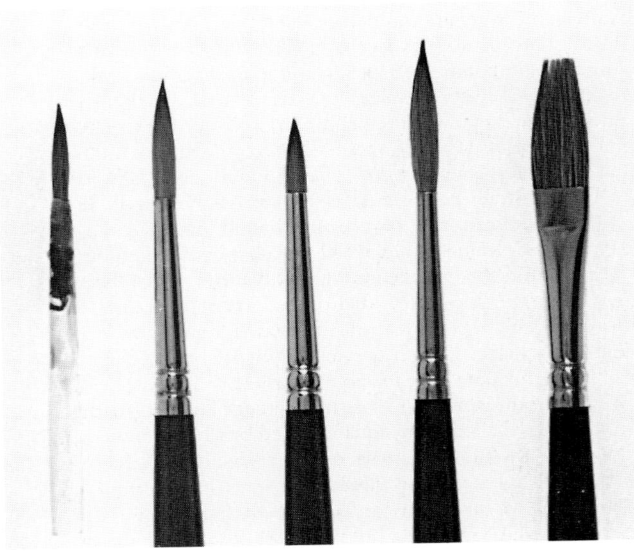

1. Watercolour brushes (from left to right): sable in quill (size 'Duck'); best quality sable with a metal ferrule and wooden handle; short-haired sable for miniature painting; ox/sable mix lettering brush; ox-hair one-stroke brush

allows hairs to hold together well for an easily controlled brush; squirrel is softer, less resilient and has a shape that offers less control; ox-ear hair is coarser and used largely for flat brushes, while badger (now obsolete) was more bristly.

Hog bristle is another natural material that has been used for centuries in both East and West for brushes that need to withstand hard wear. It has a slight natural curve, which is incorporated into the 'turn-in' of a well-shaped bristle brush, and a 'flag' or divided end at the tip, which holds paint well; as long as the bristle is not cut or damaged, this unwinds so that the flag remains as the bristle wears down with use.

Synthetic fibres were introduced to brushmaking in the late 1960s. Initially, inexpensive brushes were made of nylon, but these were unsuitable for high quality painting as they were slippery, did not hold colour well and were poorly tapered. Later, polyester fibre with individually shaped filaments offered an improvement, and for flat brushes the fibre could also be given a splayed tip that facilitated colour holding. By 1980 tapered polyester and sable mixture brushes with good 'point' were produced, combining the toughness of polyester with the resilience and colour-holding properties of sable.

Brush manufacture is a skilled traditional craft. Hair must be sterilized and then 'dressed': taking sable as an example, the end of the tail is broken off and discarded, the hair is cut from the tailbone with scissors, the short, soft hair is combed out from the guard hairs and discarded and the guard hairs are 'dragged' so that the hair is grouped according to length. Blunt or reversed hairs are then removed as the hair in any group must remain with root one end and tip the other; any mixed group is sorted by means of a 'turning stick', a skilful operation that is dependent on the taper of the hair. Small or medium size brushes incorporate a single, uniform length of hair, whereas large sables have several lengths blended together. A quantity of hair is selected, tried for size through the appropriate ferrule, withdrawn, knocked down in a small metal cylinder called a 'cannon' so that the ends are level and then tied and knotted loosely with thread. The hair is then 'domed' for a pointed brush by rotating and shaping it with the fingers, the knot is tightened, the thread cut, and the hair is placed in the ferrule, drawn through and measured for length. The knot and back of the brush are glued into the ferrule, which is then fitted and crimped on to a wooden handle so that it is secure and water is excluded.

Manufacture of hog tools varies a little in that the bristle is obtained in bundles of uniform length and treated so that groups of bristle have a uniform curve. This curve must be incorporated into the 'turn-in' of the brush whether it is to be round or flat; this may be done by manipulation or, for some types of flat brush, by tying two groups together, each of which curves inwards. A round brush has some of the bristle pushed up in the centre to give a rounded shape before being tied and placed in the ferrule. Filbert brushes (a flat brush with a domed shape) are also shaped by manipulation at this stage. Filberts and flat brushes are placed in round ferrules, which are then carefully flattened with pliers, while fan brushes and larger varnish brushes have specially shaped ferrules (see fig. 2).

2. Hog-bristle brushes (from left to right): flat; round; filbert; fan shaped

The older quill mounts, of duck, goose and swan, were boiled to make them pliable while constructing the brush. On drying they contracted to hold the hair tightly and were tied with silk threads, the colours of which denoted different brush sizes. Seamless metal ferrules of nickel-plated brass or cupro-nickel are now very largely used. Brush handles must be smooth and well balanced; Western examples are usually made of hardwood and varnished or enamelled while in East Asia brushes are commonly mounted in bamboo and so no ferrule or handle is needed.

2. History. Since brushmaking is so specialized a craft, it is probable that artists made use of specialist brushmakers from very early on. Although Cennino Cennini, writing in the 1390s in *Il libro dell'arte*, mentions both miniver and bristle brushes, his description of how to make them is perfunctory and hard to follow and does not appear to reflect any first-hand knowledge of the technique. Certainly by the 17th century artists spoke of choosing rather than making brushes for themselves. These would generally have been mounted in quills, with a wooden or bone handle. Bristle brushes could be bound with cord on to a wooden handle or placed in tin holders (*Excellency of Pen and Pencil*, London, 1655, p. 95). Metal ferrules of silver or tin were introduced in the 19th century and encouraged a much greater variety of brush shapes, including the fan shape in sable or bristle.

Historically, any artist's brush, whether of hair or bristle, pointed or 'fitched' (flat, square-ended brushes, known in the USA as 'brights'), was called a 'pencil'. Different shapes and sizes were available for a variety of purposes. Early artists painting in egg tempera would have used a soft hair brush with a fine point to work with fine hatching strokes in this quick-drying medium. Many of the first artists to use oil paint would have employed similar brushes in order to achieve a smooth paint finish and fine details without evidence of brushstrokes. Again, a brush with short length of hair for controlled detail would have been used for miniature painting, while both pointed and fitched pencils were recommended for portrait painting in oil. In the 18th and 19th centuries large brushes made of stiffish badger hair were sold to be used dry for blending oil colours on the canvas (see fig. 3). Known as 'sweeteners' or 'softeners', they were particularly useful in achieving *sfumato* effects and may have been in use earlier than this. Other specialized brushes in sable were known as 'riggers' and had very long hair to paint long, unbroken lines, as, for example, in ships' rigging (*Artist's Repository and Drawing Magazine*, London, 1784–6, p. 63). In the 20th century flat lettering or one-stroke brushes and pointed sables with an extra length of hair became available to commercial artists: the former for flat washes in gouache and the latter allowing long, unbroken application in watercolour.

From the 17th century artists in oil colours could also have made use of brush-washers, to avoid having to clean their brushes completely between use on consecutive days. These ranged from simple slanted metal containers, in which brushes might be laid so that the bristles but not the handles were immersed in oil, to a more sophisticated container that held the brushes between wires so that the bristles were suspended in oil (London, BL, Harley MS.6376, pp. 88–9). This ensured that any residual paint would not harden; however, the brushes had to be prevented from slipping down and bending the bristles.

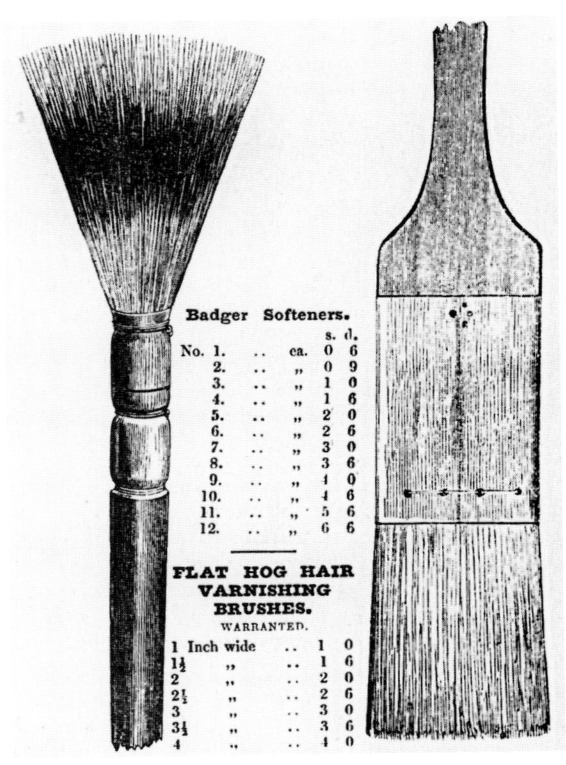

3. Badger-hair softener (left) and hog-bristle varnish brush; from a 19th-century colourman's catalogue

The same containers could also have been used with turpentine. In the 19th century some brush-washers illustrated in colourmen's catalogues were even more elaborate and had a compartment for washing the brushes, with solvent, metal clips for suspending them while drying and a drip tray.

3. Uses and care. The recommended purposes of individual types of brushes are usually explained in colourmen's catalogues. The highest quality sable is reserved for pointed watercolour brushes, made in sizes 000 to 14. These are costly, but, if well cared for and used with traditional watercolour on paper, they will last a long time. A large brush of this kind is versatile in that, being composed of several lengths of hair, it goes from a fat belly to a long, fine point. It is therefore capable of holding a large quantity of colour so that a broad, sweeping wash can be applied, while, if the tip only is used, fine lines are possible. Sable brushes with short hair for absolute control are made for photographic spotting. Flat, soft hair brushes are made up to 25 mm wide for application of broad washes of watercolour; the full width can be used, or a line may be painted with the edge of the brush. Squirrel-hair brushes can be used for broad watercolour washes (some are made in a large mop shape for the purpose) and for watercolour work in which precise detail is not required. Sable brushes that are used with oil or synthetic resin media on canvas or board in order to achieve a smooth finish will wear out rapidly. It is best to use for this purpose sable brushes specifically intended for oil painting, which are made from second-quality sable in round, flat and filbert shapes. Polyester/sable mixture brushes in the same shapes will give even longer wear.

Ox-hair or bristle brushes can be used with aqueous colours when a bold effect with obvious brushstrokes is wanted, but, because of their hard-wearing and good paint-holding properties, bristle brushes are used mainly for painting in oil or alkyd colours. Additionally, the bristles add a varied texture to impastoed paint. A brush with long bristles can produce sweeping strokes of some length, while short, square bristle brushes produce well defined, stubby strokes that are likely to be obvious when looking at the painting. For less definite feathery touches and for blending colours on the painting, a fan brush of sable or bristle can be used.

An artist can achieve certain effects through appropriate choice of brush, but the way the brush is held and moved is another factor, allowing a variety of brushstrokes through variations of technique. Stout (1941) pointed out that representations of early European artists show them with the brush at right-angles to the fingers, a grip that makes full use of elbow and shoulder muscles. The usual modern grip is with the brush parallel to the fingers, as with a writing instrument. This encourages movement with the fingers and wrist. An alternative grip with long-handled bristle brushes is to place the hand further along the handle, holding it as if it were a knife, again giving scope for arm movement.

The care of brushes is applicable to all types. They should be cleaned immediately after use; if paint is allowed to clog the ferrule the brush shape will be spoiled. Brushes for watercolours and acrylics should be washed in cool water. Bristle brushes should be cleaned with white spirit and afterwards washed in soap and water. A soft hair brush should never be allowed to rest on the tip nor be left in water; in the first case the hairs will be permanently deformed and in the second the wooden handle will swell and cause the coating to flake off. Soft hair or bristle brushes should never be trimmed with scissors, but a single stray hair may be broken off with a knife close to the ferrule. Soft hair brushes are subject to moth damage, and any brushes used infrequently should be stored dry, preferably in a metal case, with moth deterrent.

See also AIRBRUSH; for calligraphy *see* CHINA, §IV, 1 and JAPAN, §VII, 1(ii).

BIBLIOGRAPHY

C. Cennini: *Il libro dell'arte*, MS. trans. by D. V. Thompson as *The Craftsman's Handbook* (New Haven, 1933, rev. New York, 2/1960)
L. Sickman: 'Some Chinese Brushes', *Tech. Stud. Field F.A.*, viii (1939), pp. 61–4
G. L. Stout: 'The Grip of the Artist's Brush', *Tech. Stud. Field F.A.*, x (1941), pp. 3–17
R. J. Gettens and G. L. Stout: *Painting Materials: A Short Encyclopaedia* (New York, 1942, rev. 1966), pp. 279–81
R. D. Harley: 'Artists' Brushes—Historical Evidence from the Sixteenth to the Nineteenth Century', *Conservation and Restoration of Pictorial Art*, ed. N. Brommelle and P. Smith (London, 1976), pp. 123–9

R. D. HARLEY

Brush, George de Forest (*b* Shelbyville, TN, 28 Sept 1855; *d* Hanover, NH, 24 April 1941). American painter. He began his formal training at the National Academy of Design in New York and in 1873 entered the atelier of Jean-Léon Gérôme in Paris, studying there and at the Ecole des Beaux-Arts for almost six years. Soon after his return to the USA in 1880 he was elected to the Society of American Artists. Thereafter he spent much time on both sides of the Atlantic, beginning in the American West and including lengthy stays in Paris, Florence, New York and Dublin, NH, where he purchased a farm in 1901.

Brush first attained prominence as a painter of Indian life, which he observed while living in Wyoming and Montana in 1881. His pictures (completed in the studio but frequently based on studies done *in situ*) focus on everyday life and domestic tribal customs, with strict attention paid to documentary detail, a trait adopted from Gérôme and exemplified in *The Moose Chase* (1888; Washington, DC, N. Mus. Amer. A.). In the 1890s Brush painted his first family group, the theme for which he is best known. Invariably his own wife and children posed for these works, for example *Mother and Child* (1894; New York, Met.). Brush imbued this and similar works with a feeling of holiness without the use of Christian iconography.

WRITINGS

'An Artist among the Indians', *C. Illus. Mag.*, xxx (May 1885), pp. 54–7

BIBLIOGRAPHY

N. D. Bowditch: *George de Forest Brush: Recollections of a Joyous Painter* (Peterborough, NH, 1970) [by the artist's daughter]
J. B. Morgan: *George de Forest Brush: Painter of the American Renaissance* (New York, 1985)

ROSS C. ANDERSON

Brushline. At certain times in Western art movements, as, for instance, with Art Nouveau, line has been accorded particular importance. It is also a valued element in Islamic art. However, it is in East Asian art that brushline assumed its most distinctive and universally admired aspect, seen prominently in the brushwork of calligraphy and painting and imitated in woodblock-printing, but also evident in decorated ceramics, lacquerware, architectural tiles and reliefs, and sculpture. Particularly in China, but also in Korea and Japan, viewers of painting traditionally concentrated their appreciation on brushwork, seen in terms of execution or performance and regarded as the most fundamental expression of artistic personality and creative talent, while other elements such as colour and compositional invention were accorded considerably less attention.

From early times, East Asian writers on art have paid great critical and theoretical attention to brushline. The six criteria for the assessment of painting, proposed by the Chinese critic Xie He (*fl c.* AD 500–535) in his essay *Gu huapin lu* ('Classification of painters') and subsequently perpetuated throughout East Asia as the 'Six Canons', placed the 'structural [or "bone"] method of brushwork' (Chin. *gufa yongbi*) second only to 'vitalization through spiritual resonance' (*see* CHINA, §IV, 1). The veneration of brushwork culminated in the writings of the Chinese monk–painter Daoji. In his essay *Huayu lu* ('Remarks on painting'), completed *c.* 1700, he used the term *yihua*—translatable as the 'single', 'unifying' or 'unbroken line'—to liken artistic creativity to nature's spontaneous and indivisible mode of creation. Daoji revealed his preoccupation with the use of brushline as he conveyed the essence of natural substances in paintings such as *Sixteen Luohan* (1667; *see* DAOJI, fig. 1).

The prominent role of brushline in the painting of China, Korea and Japan owes much to the character of the artists' materials, particularly to the flexible brush (see fig. 1a) made of animal or human hair or of birds' feathers (*see* CHINA, §XIII, 4 and JAPAN, §XVI, 4). The brush is placed between the middle and third fingers and steadied by the thumb, with the index finger resting on the handle; it is customarily held in an upright position (1b). The brush allows for the controlled modulation of the thickness of line by lowering the hand, which thereby exposes more of the tapered tuft of hairs; or by raising it, which can reduce the line to the thickness of a single hair; or by tilting the brush diagonally and thereby exposing more of its side (1c). Lines can be made symmetrical by keeping the tip of the brush centred within the stroke, employing the centred-tip (Chin. *zhongfeng*) technique (1d); or assymmetrical by allowing the belly and tip of the brush to trace opposite edges of the line as the brush descends and rises. Beginnings and ends of strokes can be rounded if the brush tip is contained within the stroke by a backward, 'concealing' movement, known as the concealed-tip (Chin. *cangfeng*) technique (1e); angular turns can be avoided by centering the tip in the stroke; or strokes can be pointed and corners made angular if the brush tip is exposed along the edge of the stroke, using the exposed-tip (Chin. *lufeng*) technique (1f and g), or if the brush is held at an angle. The contours of lines can be crisp and regular if the brush is well loaded with ink and the motion is evenly paced; they can be irregular if the ink is drier, if the motion is particularly rapid or if the handle is kept at an angle with the brush hairs perpendicular to the direction of the stroke, which can force the hairs of the brush to separate. (For further discussion of brush technique, *see* CHINA, §IV, 1).

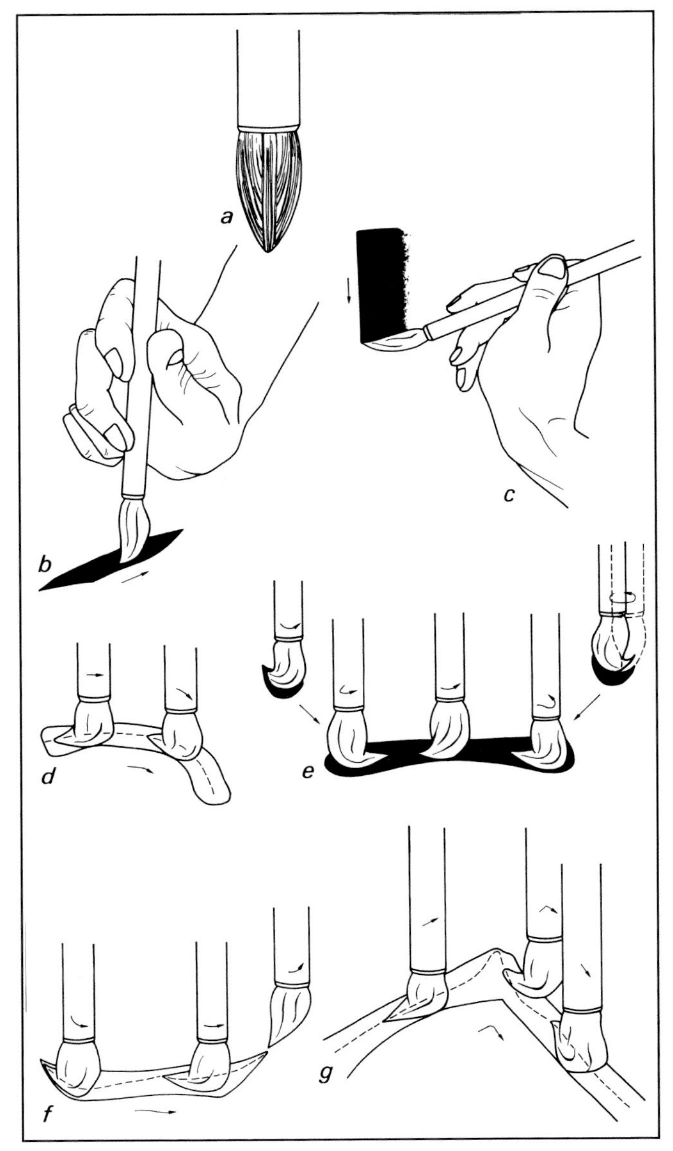

1. East Asian brush, used for painting and calligraphy: (a) sections of the hair; (b) brush held upright; (c) brush held at an angle; (d) centred-tip (Chin. *zhongfeng*) technique, showing direction and positions of brush-tip; (e) concealed-tip (Chin. *cangfeng*) technique; (f) exposed-tip (Chin. *lufeng*) technique; (g) corner stroke, executed using the exposed-tip technique

The traditional painting process was already well established in China by the late Zhou–early Han period (*c.* 4th–2nd centuries BC): the structural outlines were first drawn with linear brushwork in black ink, then secondary additions of colour and ink were applied in broad, smooth planes referred to as washes. Early calligraphy and painting relied solely on brushwork that required strictly maintained pressure. Unmodulated brushwork and rounded lines were characteristic of the seal script (Chin. *zhuanshu*) practised through the Zhou and Qin periods (*c.* 1050–206 BC). In painting, the famous early Chinese scholar-artist Gu Kaizhi was known for his 'firm and tense' brushwork, executed with thin, unmodulated strokes that were likened to strands of silk, while the thicker, unmodulated brushstrokes of many Tang-period (AD 618–907) artists came to be known as 'iron-wire'.

Calligraphy provided the essential first developments in modulated brushwork that initially showed themselves in the clerical script (Chin. *lishu*, Jap. *reisho*) of the Han period (206 BC–AD 220) and then in the regular script (Chin. *kaishu*, Jap. *kaisho*) of the Six Dynasties period (AD 222–589) and the running script (Chin. *xingshu*, Jap. *gyōsho*) and cursive script (Chin. *caoshu*, Jap. *sōsho*) that accompanied regular script (*see* CHINA, §IV, 2(i)–(ii) for further discussion of the evolution of scripts). The epitome of elegant brushwork and the first flowering of calligraphy as a fine art was achieved by Zhong You (AD 151–230), his follower, Wang Xizhi—perhaps the most venerated artist in all East Asian history—and Wang's son, Wang Xianzhi; the full liberation of brushline as a boldly expressive medium was first attained by the Tang calligraphers, Zhang Xu (*fl* AD 713–40) and his followers, Yan Zhenqing and the priest Huaisu. By the early 6th century AD modulated brush techniques had begun to spread to painting, and the Chinese painter Zhang Sengyou (*fl* AD 500–50) had produced works using dots, drag-strokes, hack-strokes and sweeping strokes like those of Chinese calligraphers. In wall painting, since the brushlines created by the master painters were often subsequently covered over by the colourists, the 8th-century Chinese painter Wu Daozi, whose dramatically modulated brushwork was then considered the greatest ever seen, sometimes insisted that his works remain incomplete.

In painting of the Five Dynasties and Song periods (907–1279), modulated brushwork emerged supreme, and newly developed types of brushstrokes became the hallmarks of various styles of painting. Brushwork was adapted to descriptive purposes, rough-edged for natural objects, smooth for drapery, fluctuating to suggest the three-dimensionality of subjects and varied to express the artist's mood and personality. Although given more emphatically calligraphic treatment in later centuries and highlighted by a reduction in the role of ink and colour washes, these techniques remained basic to the Chinese painting vocabulary of later times. They were transmitted to Korea and to Japan in the Kamakura (1185–1333) and Muromachi (1333–1568) periods as Chinese Chan (Jap. Zen) Buddhist priests sought refuge in Japan from unrest within China in the wake of Mongol encroachment and penetration.

Generally, in both painting and calligraphy the Chinese preferred brushwork produced with the brush handle held upright and the tip well centred within the stroke, yielding a smooth-edged, well-rounded effect. In Japan, however, attitudes towards brushwork were far less theoretical. In the classical Japanese *Yamatoe* style, developed in the Heian period (794–1185) as an expression of native aesthetic predilections, line was far less prominent, being unmodulated, subjected to and often hidden beneath semi-opaque washes of colour or simply implied by the crisp juxtaposition of colour planes. Even when working in the Chinese manner of painting or in calligraphy, often with a brush stiffer than the type they generally preferred, Japanese artists tended towards greater and more rapid modulation of brushwork, greater angularity of strokes and a noticeably flatter effect, as exemplified by the 15th-century Japanese priest-painter TŌYŌ SESSHŪ (see fig. 2). At the same time, Japanese brushwork often appears to be simpler and more condensed, as well as remarkably assured in its concentration of emotional effect (*see* JAPAN, §VII, 1(ii)). Moreover, the distinction between the three later forms of writing—regular, running and cursive script—varying from formal to informal in their treatment of structure and line and deeply ingrained aesthetically as alternative modes of expression appropriate to specific occasions, came to be extended to painting and from there to other art forms, from *nō* theatre to the tea ceremony.

Korean artists' use of brushwork showed a similar willingness to break rules in favour of a spontaneous and sometimes individualistic line. Chinese examples undoubtedly influenced the development of calligraphic and painting skills and remained as enduring models, but even in the mural tomb paintings of the Koguryŏ period (37 BC–AD 608) a distinctive flowing line emerges, enhanced by the application of warm colours. Korean brushwork, even at its most delicate, is marked by a confident, vigorous touch. Sometimes, as in the painting by the 17th-century artist Kim Myŏng-guk of the Chan patriarch Bodhidharma (for illustration *see* KIM MYŎNG-GUK), a line of exceptional intensity is achieved. Calligraphy, many of the earliest examples of which are recorded on stelae, is likewise marked by considerable vitality (*see also* KOREA, §V).

2. Tōyō Sesshū: *Winter Landscape*, 451×270 mm, one of a pair of hanging scrolls, ink and colour on paper, 15th century (Tokyo, National Museum)

See also CHINA, §IV; ISLAMIC ART, §III, 2; JAPAN, §VII.

BIBLIOGRAPHY

Kodansha Enc. Japan: 'Calligraphy'
K. Shimonaka, ed.: *Shodō zenshū* [Complete collection of calligraphy], 26 vols, 2 suppls (Tokyo, 2/1954–68); 1st edn ed. Y. Shimonaka (Tokyo, 1930–32) [incl. Chin., Kor. and Jap. works]
W. R. B. Acker: *Some T'ang and pre-T'ang texts on Chinese Painting*, 2 vols (Leiden, 1954–74)
Y. Nakata: *Sho*, Nihon no bijutsu [Arts of Japan], xxvii (Tokyo, 1967); Eng. trans. by A. Woodhull as *The Art of Japanese Calligraphy*, Heibonsha Surv. Jap. A., xxvii (Tokyo, 1973)
Zen Painting and Calligraphy (exh. cat. by J. Fontein and M. L. Hickman, Boston, MA, Mus. F.A., 1970)
Ju-hsi Chou: *In Quest of the Primordial Line: The Genesis and Content of Tao Chi's 'Hua-yu-lu'* (diss., Princeton U., NJ, 1971)
Chinese Calligraphy (exh. cat. by Tseng Yu-ho Ecke, Philadelphia, PA, Mus. A., 1971)
L. Ledderose: 'An Approach to Chinese Calligraphy', *Gugong Jikan*, vii/2 (1972), pp. 1–14
The Courtly Tradition in Japanese Art and Literature: Selections from the Hofer and Hyde Collections (exh. cat. by J. M. Rosenfield and others, Cambridge, MA, Fogg; New York, Japan House Gal.; Chicago, IL, A. Inst.; 1973)
Studies in Connoisseurship: Chinese Paintings from the Arthur M. Sackler Collection in New York and Princeton (exh. cat. by M. Fu and Shen Fu, Princeton U., NJ, A. Mus., 1974)
F. van Briessen: *The Way of the Brush: Painting Techniques of China and Chinese Calligraphy* (New Haven, 1977)
L. Ledderose: *Mi Fu and the Classical Tradition of Chinese Calligraphy* (Princeton, 1979)
J. Silbergeld: *Chinese Painting Style: Media, Methods and Principles of Form* (Seattle, 1980)
Y. Nakata, ed.: *Chūgoku no bijutsu: Shoseki* [Arts of China: calligraphy] (Kyoto, 1982); Eng. trans. as *Chinese Calligraphy* (New York, Tokyo and Kyoto, 1983)
J. Hay: 'The Human Body as a Source of Microcosmic Values in Calligraphy', *Theories of the Arts in China*, ed. S. Bush and C. Murck (Princeton, 1983), pp. 74–102
Masters of Japanese Calligraphy, 8th–19th Century (exh. cat. by Y. Shimizu and J. M. Rosenfield, New York, Japan House Gal. and Asia Soc. Gals; Kansas City, MO, Nelson-Atkins Mus. A.; and elsewhere; 1984–5)

JEROME SILBERGELD

Brusis, Niccolò de. *See* NICCOLÒ PISANO.

Brussel, Jan van. *See* ROOME, JAN VAN.

Brusselmans, Jean (*b* Brussels, 13 June 1884; *d* Dilbeek, 9 Jan 1953). Belgian painter and printmaker. He was apprenticed to an engraver and lithographer and with these skills entered the Académie Royale des Beaux-Arts in Brussels (1897). Soon, however, he transferred to painting and between 1900 and 1906 studied under Guillaume Van Strydonck (1861–1937), Isidore Verheyden and Jean Delville. In 1907 he shared a studio with Rik Wouters and befriended the future Brabant Fauvists, among whom was Auguste Oleffe. He joined the circle known as L'Effort and in 1912 participated in a group exhibition of the Bleus de la G.G.G. (Galerie Georges Giroux in Brussels) with Constant Permeke, Léon Spilliaert, Edgard Tytgat and Wouters. For several years common themes, a bold use of colour and the influence of Cézanne united Brusselmans even more closely with Oleffe, Wouters and Ferdinand Schirren. He had his first one-man show in Antwerp at the Galerie Breckpot in 1921. Three years later he decided to stay in Dilbeek, exhibited at the Expressionist Galerie Le Centaure and became friendly with Louis Thévenet. A founder of the Paruk Clan in 1922 and of *art vivant* in 1930, from 1931 he joined in the enterprise known as Compagnons de l'Art, which he was to commemorate in a painting of the same name (1949; Brussels, Mus. A. Mod.). His influence was particularly strong on certain artists of the Jeune Peinture Belge group (1945). The desire to simplify volumes and planes, which underlies Brusselmans's remarkably structured work, and the vital need to make forms stand out from the canvas by thickening contour lines contrasts with the sensitivity and delicacy of the colours—especially his characteristic grey. Among his best-known paintings are *In the Garden* (1916) and *The Garret I* (1938; both Brussels, Mus. A. Mod.).

BIBLIOGRAPHY

R. L. Delevoy and G. Brys-Schatan: *Jean Brusselmans* (Brussels, 1972) [cat. rais.]

Jean Brusselmans (exh. cat. by W. Van Mulders and others, Brussels, Pal. B.-A., 1979)

Donation Jean Brusselmans (exh. cat. by P. Roberts-Jones, Brussels, Musées Royaux B.-A., 1980)

DANIELLE DERREY-CAPON

Brussels [Flem. Brussel; Fr. Bruxelles]. Capital city and administrative region of Belgium. It is situated in the centre of the country, in the former duchy of Brabant, and grew from a settlement on marshy ground by the River Senne along the trade route between Bruges and Cologne. During the 15th century, under Burgundian rule, it became an important cultural centre. The River Senne was covered over in the the 19th century, at the same time that the principal boulevards were constructed along the line of the medieval fortifications. Although it lies in a principally Flemish-speaking part of the country, Brussels, which has a population of *c.* 1 million, is a bilingual city, with French predominating.

I. History. II. Urban development. III. Art life and organization. IV. Centre of production. V. Buildings.

I. History.

Excavations in the town centre have shown that the site may have been occupied since the Neolithic period (*c.* 2500 BC), and there is evidence for Roman villas and a Merovingian cemetery. Historians, however, are divided as to the early development of the settlement, which became securely established about AD 979 under Charles of France (*reg* 978–91), who was made Duke of Lower Lorraine by Emperor Otto II. As the town grew (*see* §II, 1 below), its inhabitants continued to assert their autonomy and its first charter was granted in 1229 under Henry I, Duke of Brabant (*reg* 1183–1235). Brussels was a centre of the cloth trade and as many markets were established as religious buildings or charitable institutions. The dukes of Burgundy established their court within the city walls in the 15th century and transformed the town into an artistic centre (*see* §III, 1 below). Its renown increased in the 16th century with the manufacture of tapestries and lace (*see* §IV, 1 and 3 below).

Under Habsburg rule—Charles V was both consecrated Emperor and abdicated there—Brussels replaced Mechelen as the seat of government of the Netherlands in the 1530s. From the mid-16th century, however, Spanish rule and the influence of the Inquisition were unpopular, leading to a rebellion by the merchant class, which was put down in 1575. The city prospered under the more enlightened rule (1599–1621) of Archduke Albert of Austria and Archduchess Isabella. In 1695, however, much of the centre was destroyed by a French bombardment. The former Spanish Netherlands were placed under Austrian Habsburg rule in 1713. After the French briefly reoccupied Brussels in 1746, the Austrian Governor General, Charles, Duke of Lorraine (1712–80), encouraged substantial rebuilding in the city, promoting French Neo-classicism. The Austrian Netherlands were annexed by France in 1794.

By the terms of the Congress of Vienna (1814–15), Brussels alternated with The Hague as the capital of the Kingdom of the Netherlands. In 1830, however, the Belgians rebelled against the Dutch and secured their independence, with Brussels as the rapidly developing capital of the new kingdom (*see* §II, 3 below). Throughout the 19th century French architectural influence remained strong. The city was occupied by German forces in both World Wars, although underground resistance was provided each time. Since 1945 the city has taken on a particular international role as the headquarters of the European Community and Euratom (from 1958), and of the North Atlantic Treaty Organization (NATO; from 1967). As part of the Belgian federal reforms, Brussels was recognized as a separate administrative region in 1988.

BIBLIOGRAPHY

A. Henne and A. Wauters: *Histoire de la ville de Bruxelles*, 3 vols (Brussels, 1843–5, rev. 2/1970)

R. Senelle: *The Political, Economic and Social Structure of Belgium* (London, 1970)

M. Martens, ed.: *Histoire de Bruxelles* (Toulouse, 1979)

V. G. Martiny: *Bruxelles*, Cités de Belgique (Brussels, 1980)

II. Urban development.

1. Before 1695. 2. 1695–1829. 3. 1830–1918. 4. After 1918.

1. BEFORE 1695. The layout of the town was established *c.* 979, when Charles of France built a fort on the island of Saint-Géry, where the Steenweg, the trade route between Cologne and Bruges, crossed the Senne. This was rapidly expanded into a stronghold with a harbour and market that became the centre of the region's trade. Lambert II, Comte de Louvain, abandoned the damp valley site and built a second castle (*c.* 1047) on higher ground at Coudenberg. The settlements that had grown up between his two residences, and the oratory of St Michael, which had been built on the side of the hill perhaps as early as the 7th century, were encircled by a crenellated wall (diam. *c.* 4 km) with seven gates and forty defensive towers; the outer ditches were dry around the upper town and water-filled around the lower town.

The entire area within the walls was filled with buildings of stone for the nobility and clergy, and of wood and mud for the commoners. Churches concentrated in the heart of the town included St Nicolas (11th–12th century; belfry destr. 1695; rebuilt 18th century), Notre-Dame de la

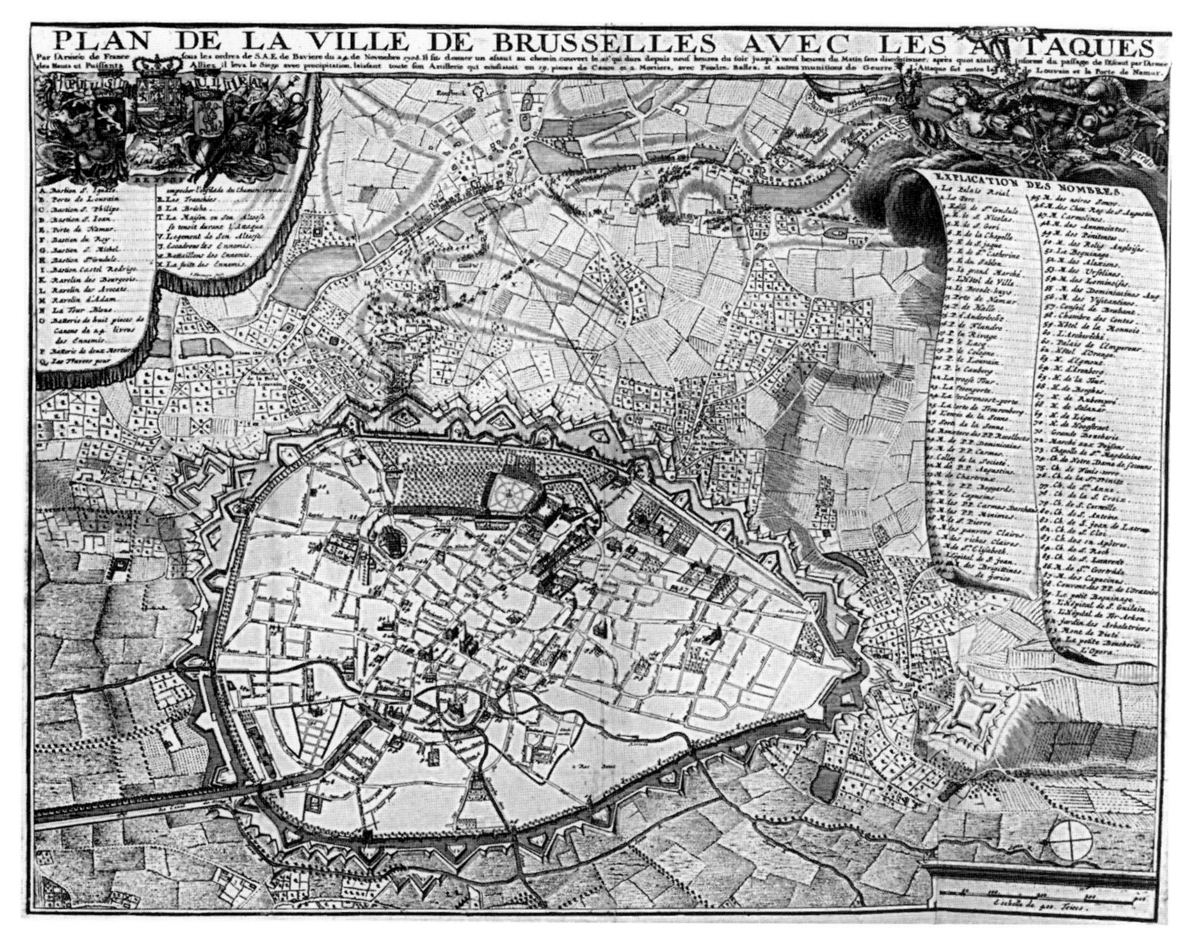

1. Brussels, plan (1708) of the city and the fortifications dating from *c.* 1576 (Brussels, Bibliothèque Royale Albert 1er)

Chapelle (begun *c.* 1190; rebuilt), SS Michel et Gudule (begun *c.* 1225; *see* §V, 1 below) and St Géry (destr. 1798). Settlements that sprang up outside the gates soon rendered the defences ineffective, and another vallum *c.* 1.3 km to the west provided insufficient protection against Louis II, Count of Flanders. After Brussels had ousted Leuven as the capital of the Duchy of Brabant, a second circuit of walls (1357–82; diam. 8 km) was erected, enabling numerous charitable institutions to develop in safety within the outer walls. St Nicolas and other churches were remodelled in Gothic style from the 14th century.

In the 15th century civic buildings, such as the Hôtel de Ville (completed 1455; *see* §V, 2 below) in the Grand-Place, the main market-place, began to compete with the religious buildings in their number and artistic quality. Brussels was a vast building site in which churches were continually rebuilt in Brabantine Gothic, such as the nave (1421–83) of Notre-Dame de la Chapelle, new churches were founded, including Notre-Dame des Victoires (or Notre-Dame du Sablon; choir begun 1436), private residences multiplied, and regulations were enforced to avoid the spread of fire.

The future Emperor Charles V resided in Brussels from 1515, and the city became the capital of the Netherlands in 1531. The Coudenberg Palace (destr. 1731) was rebuilt, and prestigious new buildings were erected, such as the Broodhuys (later Maison du Roi; begun 1515; rebuilt early 17th century; most destr. 1695; rebuilt 1768; rest. 1873–85, by Pierre-Victor Jamaer) and the Nassau Chapel (begun 1530; now part of the Bibliothèque Royale Albert 1er). The Willebroeck Canal, which linked Brussels to the North Sea via Antwerp, was opened in 1561.

In order to counter the advances in artillery and siege techniques, the Hôtel de Ville councillors reinforced the existing defences with earth bastions from *c.* 1576 (see fig. 1). Secure behind its new fortifications, classical, Italianate styles were introduced to the city (*see* BELGIUM, §II, 3 and fig. 5). Church façades, with adjoining bell-towers, were arranged in the classical orders, for example at St Jean-Baptiste au Béguinage (1657–76, by Lucas Faydherbe), while domes were employed at Notre-Dame de Bon Secours (1664–94) and Notre-Dame aux Riches Claires (1665, by Faydherbe). The city's domestic architecture did not escape this trend, as the traditional stepped gables were supplanted by reversed volutes, pilasters and curvilinear pediments. The plan of the city drawn up by Martin de Tailly (*c.* 1592–1652) and engraved by Abraham

Santvoort (*c.* 1624–1669) in 1640 indicates the location of several markets, docks, a commercial warehouse (*mestback*) and numerous culs-de-sac that branched off the winding streets from the Grand-Place to the city gates.

Although 17th-century Brussels was an important commercial centre, it remained vulnerable to warfare. The city's isolation from the surrounding countryside was increased in 1671–2, when the Comte de Monterrey, the Governor General, strengthened the fortifications with a series of bastions, half-moons and ravelins. He also gave his name to a fortress (destr.) on the high ground at Saint-Gilles, south-west of the city. These improvements, however, were unable to withstand the bombardment ordered on 13–15 August 1695 by François de Neufville, Duc de Villeroi (1644–1730), and more than 4000 buildings, especially around the Grand-Place, were destroyed.

2. 1695–1829. The destruction of the city centre by bombardment (see above) had an unexpected consequence. A regulation issued on 24 April 1697, drawn up for aesthetic reasons and enforceable by sanctions, obliged the owners of damaged property to seek a building permit before starting any reconstruction. This ensured that the Grand-Place, in particular, was rebuilt in the Italo-Flemish style that had developed through the 17th century. Its 18th-century appearance has largely survived, although a few 19th-century alterations were made, such as Pierre-Victor Jamaer's rebuilding of the Maison du Roi (1873–5), the demolition of the Maison de l'Etoile in 1850 and its recreation above an arcade in 1897, the complete refurbishment of the Hôtel de Ville's façades and additions to the façades of private houses; these may be identified by comparison with the surviving plans.

French influence, however, was dominant in new buildings erected during the 18th century. The Coudenberg Palace was destroyed by fire in 1731 and Charles of Lorraine, the Governor General, commissioned a new royal residence on the site from 1757. The principal architect was Jean Faulte, working in a severe Neo-classical, although somewhat provincial, style. Almost all the available building land within the city walls had been occupied and there were few opportunities for building with a street frontage, other than on marshland to the south-west and scattered strips that had formerly belonged to large private and ecclesiastical estates, now broken up by political events. The magistrature, indeed, encouraged the shortage by promoting the French urban plan of spacious squares surrounded by buildings to a coordinated design, as had been introduced at Nancy. The Place St Michel (now Place des Martyrs) was laid out after 1775 in the Marolles quarter to designs by Claude Antoine Fisco. Jean-Benoît-Vincent Barré's scheme for the Place Royale, near the royal palace, was executed from 1776 by Barnabé Guimard, who aligned it with the adjoining Parc de Bruxelles, which he laid out from 1773 with Bartholomäus Zinner (*fl* 1720–74). Another architect associated with these schemes was Louis Montoyer, who

2. Brussels, styles of gable along Place Ste Catherine: stepped gables, 17th century; corniced gables, 18th century

built St Jacques sur Coudenberg (1785–6) on the Place Royale and, with Antoine-Marie Payen (1749–93/8), the Schoonberg Castle (1782–4; now the Château Royal), north of the city at Laeken. Available land within the islands created by these grandiose schemes rapidly filled as buildings of all kinds, including modest housing reached via culs-de-sac, known as *bataillons carrés*, were erected behind the main structures. An edict issued in 1784 halted the spread of the cemeteries that had been established around churches in the city.

The dismantling of the city walls and fortifications in order to allow greater freedom of expansion, ordered by Emperor Joseph II (*reg* 1765–90), was to take many years. Work on the replacement of the walls by a peripheral boulevard, suggested by Napoleon in 1803 and ordered by him in 1810, was not started until 1819 under William I, King of the Netherlands, and continued until 1871. While the walls awaited orderly clearance, developments sprang up along the ancient roads leading to the surrounding villages and the citizens inserted breaches in the ramparts, commonly referred to as gates, such as that made at the present Porte de Ninove in 1816. The Porte de Hal is the only surviving gate from the original defences of the 14th century.

The country's successive annexation by the French and the Dutch was reflected in changes to the appearance of the city's buildings. In 1808, for example, the French decreed that all façades in Brussels were to be whitewashed. They also spread the use of pipes to channel water from the roofs to guttering that now ran parallel to the buildings' alignment. Traditional stepped gable designs were supplanted by corniced gables (see fig. 2). In 1819 the Dutch replaced about 2000 oil streetlamps, which had been installed almost a century before, with a public system of gas lighting. They extended the Rue Royale in 1821 to improve access to Laeken and opened up the Rue de la Régence in 1827, creating a prospect south-west from the Place Royale towards Galgenberg, the future site of the Palais de Justice (see below).

3. 1830–1918. The revolution of September 1830 had far-reaching consequences for the urban planning of Brussels, which was influenced by three lines of thought. Initially the government and city council affirmed the city's status as the sole capital of the new kingdom through the construction of prestigious buildings for commerce, administration, justice and education and by the introduction of covered markets and arcades, notably the Galeries St-Hubert (1837–47; *see* CLUYSENAAR, JEAN-PIERRE). The concentration of these buildings at the heart of the city was made possible by expropriations granted by the law of 1858. In the following decade the Banque Nationale (1860–67; *see* BEYAERT, HENRI; *see also* BELGIUM, §II, 4(ii)), the Bourse (1866–83, by Léon-Pierre Suys) and the monumental Palais de Justice (1866–83; *see* POELAERT, JOSEPH) were erected. A concurrent trend emphasized the affirmation of the nation's past through the restoration of most of the important religious and civic buildings within the city's jurisdiction and the promotion of Gothic Revival architecture (*see* JAMAER, PIERRE-VICTOR). Plans were also enacted by the mayor Jules Anspach (1829–79) to improve public health by covering over the Senne (1867) and later the Maelbeek and to open up the centre with the creation of boulevards in imitation of recent developments in Paris (*see* SUYS, (2)).

New industries were established around the outer harbour and along the Willebroeck Canal to the north and the Charleroi Canal (inaugurated 1832) to the south; these developments led to the decline of the small central docks, which were later filled in. Demand for labour resulted in a population explosion that pushed the wealthier citizens towards the suburbs. The city expanded eastwards with the creation of the Quartier Léopold, which covered 75 ha between the Rue de la Loi and the Rue du Trône, and where the Société Civile pour l'Embellissement de Bruxelles (founded 1837) initiated the building of many houses for the middle classes. Between 1849 and 1865 the Avenue Louise was laid out as a triumphal way to the Bois de la Cambre. The first railway services in Europe were inaugurated in May 1835 on the line from Mechelen to a station in the Allée Verte. New areas that combined industry and housing developed around the passenger terminals at the Gare du Nord and Gare du Midi, the freight station to the west, the marshalling yards at Schaerbeek (*see* TENEMENT BUILDING) and the smaller suburban stations.

The anarchic expansion into the surrounding countryside and the later ambitions of King Leopold II to create wide, tree-lined avenues and conserve large areas as public parks lay behind the vast development plans drawn up by a series of outstanding surveyor–inspectors. In 1840, for example, Eugène Charles François Van der Straeten (1802–68) was commissioned to produce a plan for the alignment and levelling of the city and suburbs within 1.5 km of the Hôtel de Ville. Victor Besme (1834–1903)

3. Brussels, Maison Tassel, Rue Paul-Emile Janson, by Victor Horta, 1892–3

devised a plan for the improvement of the whole city in 1866. Suggestions were also made by ALPHONSE BALAT. Some of their recommendations were adopted in such major schemes as the Boulevard Léopold II, which runs north-west from the Willebroeck Canal to the top of the Koekelberg plateau, where the national monument, the basilica of Sacré-Coeur (1905–70), was later built to a design by Albert van Huffel. The Parc du Cinquantenaire was laid out in 1880 for a national exhibition, and beyond this the Avenue de Tervuren (1895–7) linked the Place de Linthout with the Forêt de Soignes. Gédéon Bordiau (1832–1904) designed the area north of the Parc du Cinquantenaire as an effective demonstration of the use of water in landscape. The Rue du Trône was extended as the Avenue de la Couronne to give access to a race-course at Etterbeek, which is now the site of the Free University campus. Connections with the suburbs were improved with the introduction of electric tramways in 1894. Plans were also devised for a north–south road, roughly 5 km east of the inner boulevards, to link the outlying villages; the Boulevard du Souverain, however, was not completed until 1910.

CHARLES BULS was mayor between 1881 and 1899 and actively promoted the restoration of the Grand-Place and attempts to preserve the historical fabric of the city. More innovative trends were evident in the designs of VICTOR HORTA, who was active in the city from 1884, and whose buildings introduced the sinuous lines of Art Nouveau (see fig. 3). The early 20th century, however, was marked by a desperate campaign to demolish the older quarters. This was associated with the wish to create a Mont des Arts, although nothing was achieved until the 1930s, and clear the route for an underground connection between the Gare du Nord and the Gare du Midi. This was agreed by the city and national authorities in 1903 and led to the disappearance of the popular districts of La Putterie, Isabelle, Ter Arken, St Elisabeth and Pachéco.

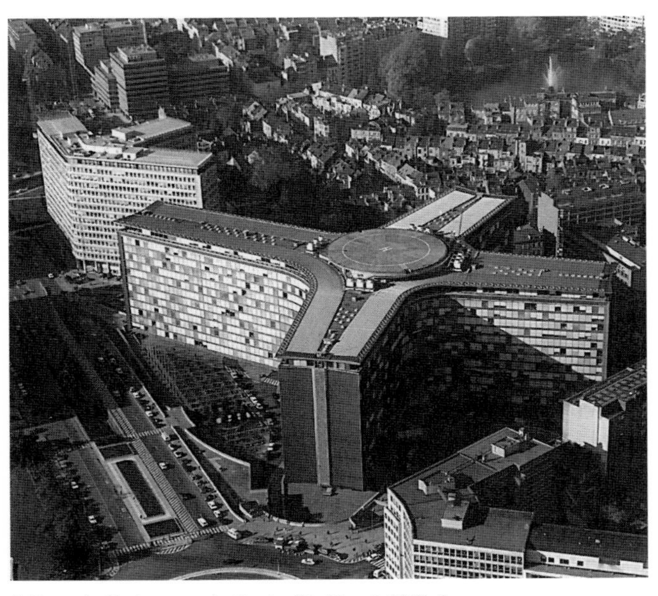

4. Brussels, Barlaymont, by Lucien De Vestel, 1963–9

4. AFTER 1918. Demolition in the central areas (*see* §3 above) recommenced at a greater pace after World War I. Outside the city work continued on covering over the Senne and Maelbeek. The Woluwe Valley was drained and the river transformed into a main sewer. The port of Brussels-Maritime, which was created in 1922 with facilities capable of handling ships of up to 3000 tonnes, was only made possible by the incorporation of the areas of Laeken, Haeren and Neder-Over-Heembeek into the city of Brussels. New factories were established along the widened canal. The major roads built to link the suburbs to the city and the tramway network (which often extended to considerable distances) were lined with building plots that were exploited equally by garden cities and high-rise apartment blocks, which were encouraged by a law of 1924 on joint ownership. The International Exhibition of 1935 was held in the north at Heysel.

During the German occupation from May 1940 to September 1944 there was little development, but this intensified after the liberation. Property developers promoted large residential complexes comprising horizontal blocks with flat roofs, which were scattered freely on the land remaining in joint ownership. The construction of community housing was also encouraged through the so-called laws of Taye and Brunfaut. The proximity of the two types of housing was not always well arranged, however, and a Department of Urban Planning was created in 1945 to maintain some control by obliging the communes to draw up development plans and forcing individuals to seek building permits.

It was some years before the powerful Highways Department, charged with the management of ever increasing road traffic, accepted the need for concerted development. Road tunnels were cut beneath the boulevards of the inner ring to provide access to the 1958 International Exhibition at Heysel. The boulevards of the inner and outer ring-roads were improved to keep traffic moving and to provide access, from well within the urban centre, to motorways to Antwerp, Liège, Namur, Mons and the coast. An administrative centre with a tower 140 m high was built within the north-east angle of the pentagon formed by the inner ring. The headquarters of the European Commission, including the cruciform Barlaymont (1963–9, by Lucien De Vestel; see fig. 4), were laid out at the eastern end of the Rue de la Loi. An outer orbital route was opened in 1976.

Urban planning and development in the region is controlled by the law of 29 March 1962, which introduced the concept of sectoral planning. Brussels was defined in 1971 as an agglomeration of 19 bilingual communes, and the plan approved in 1979 recognizes separate zones, in which the various functions of housing, business, administrative activities, industry, open spaces and shared public services might be integrated. Large shopping centres, which appeared in the 1950s, were laid out close to the access routes and away from the urban centre in areas with sufficient land free for extensive parking. Similar requirements influenced the location of the headquarters of several large companies, such as the Brussels International Trade Markt (1975, by John Portman), the largest commercial centre in Europe. The metro system was opened in 1976 and many outer stations were provided with car-parks to discourage drivers from entering the city centre.

In 1967 the grandiose Manhattan Nord scheme was drawn up to redevelop 53 ha to the west of the Gare du Nord. Some high-rise blocks were built, including the World Trade Center, but the plan was ultimately abandoned. A later project realized during the 1980s was the Espace Bruxelles-Europe, which was constructed over a concrete floor suspended above the railway tracks at the Gare du Luxembourg. In 1989 the urban area of Brussels was granted the status of a separate region within the federation of Belgium. In 1995 an innovative regional development plan was approved that took into account not only ground planning but also economic, social and cultural development

BIBLIOGRAPHY

J. Stengers, ed.: *Bruxelles: Croissance d'une capitale* (Brussels and Antwerp, 1979)

Brussel, breken, bouwen: Architectuur en stedsbverfraaing, 1780–1914 [Brussels, demolition, construction: architecture and urban renewal, 1780–1914] (exh. cat., Brussels, Gemeentekrediet België, 1979)

V. G. Martiny: *Bruxelles: L'Architecture des origines à 1900* (Brussels, 1980)

La Région de Bruxelles: Des villages d'autrefois à la ville d'aujourd'hui (exh. cat., ed. A. Smolar-Meynaert and J. Stengers; Brussels, Crédit Com. Belg., 1989)

V. G. MARTINY

III. Art life and organization.

1. Before 1829. 2. 1830–1918. 3. After 1918.

1. BEFORE 1829. As early as 1306 there was a trade fellowship of painters in Brussels. Gold- and silversmiths were granted privileges by Duke John III of Brabant (*reg* 1312–55), which led to the formation of a guild (*see* §IV, 4 below). Fourteenth-century sculptors belonged to the guild of stonecutters or fellowship of the Quatre Couronnés, which Jan van Mansdale I (*d* 1424/5; *see* KELDERMANS) joined *c*. 1370. Towards the end of the 14th century the Brussels sculptors struck out on a new course, presumably under the influence of CLAUS SLUTER. By 1436 Rogier van der Weyden, originally from Tournai, was living in Brussels, having been officially appointed as painter to the city (*see* WEYDEN, VAN DER, (1)). Among his many pupils and followers were Dieric Bouts in Leuven, Hans Memling in Bruges and VRANCKE VAN DER STOCKT, who succeeded him as painter to the city. In 1447 the tapestry-weavers in Brussels formed a separate guild, and after 1480 Brussels became the most important centre of tapestry-weaving in the southern Netherlands (*see* §IV, 1 below). An important painter working near Brussels from 1475 to 1482 was HUGO VAN DER GOES, who had retreated to a monastery after becoming insane. At this time the painting school of Brussels was characterized by the production of triptychs. From *c*. 1450–*c*. 1550 the production of wood-carved altarpieces in Brabant developed into a true industry (despite Antwerp becoming the main centre of manufacture), reaching its peak with Jan Borman and his family (for illustration *see* BORMAN). The city experienced a period of cultural growth in the 16th century due to economic changes and also the long stay of Desiderius Erasmus in Brabant. Lacemaking flourished (*see* §IV, 3 below), and a generation of painters emerged who were influenced by Italian styles. Bernard van Orley (*see* ORLEY, VAN (i), (2)) studied in Rome, and his pupils included MICHIEL COXCIE and possibly PIETER COECKE VAN AELST I (see fig. 6 below). Pieter Bruegel the elder (*see* BRUEGEL, (1)) probably moved to Brussels on his marriage in 1563.

One of the most prolific sculptors working in Brussels *c*. 1600 was Jérôme Du Quesnoy (*see* DU QUESNOY, (1)). In the 17th century Michiel Sweerts established a drawing academy in the city, but by that time Antwerp had become the artistic capital, with Rubens its central figure. GASPAR DE CRAYER was strongly influenced by Rubens. A school of landscape painting was initiated in Brussels by DENIJS VAN ALSLOOT and LODEWIJK DE VADDER. JACQUES D'ARTHOIS also gave a new impetus to the genre, but it was not until the end of the 17th century that painters such as David Teniers the younger (*see* TENIERS (ii), (2)) broke away from Rubens's influence. In his capacity as court painter Teniers catalogued and painted the collections of the archdukes. It was also in the 17th century that faience workshops were first established in Brussels (*see* §IV, 2 below). Only three tapestry workshops survived the 1695 bombardment of Brussels, an event recorded by Augustin Coppens (*fl c*. 1700) in a series of etchings. It was in the 18th century, however, that the centre of sculptural activity shifted from Antwerp back to Brussels, which, as the residence of the Austrian rulers, assumed a leading position in Europe. The work of JACQUES BERGÉ exemplifies the idealized stylization that became typical towards the end of the century. PIETER PLUMIER made fountains for the town hall with LAURENT DELVAUX, who later became court sculptor. GILLES LAMBERT GODECHARLE, a pupil of Delvaux, was considered to be a prominent representative of Neo-classicism. Charles, Comte de Cobenzl, the Minister Plenipotentiary, was a patron of the arts and played a crucial part in introducing the edict of 1773, which brought an end to restrictive practices within the crafts. Art in Brussels began to show a certain vitality *c*. 1800. In 1816 Jacques-Louis David came to the city as an exile and remained there until his death (*see* DAVID, JACQUES-LOUIS, §I, 4). His most important follower in Brussels was FRANÇOIS-JOSEPH NAVEZ, a Neo-classicist who clashed with the advocates of Romanticism and who led the Académie des Beaux-Arts (founded 1711).

BIBLIOGRAPHY

P. Saintenoy: *Les Arts et les artistes à la cour de Bruxelles*, 3 vols (Brussels, 1931)

J. de Borchgrave D'Altena: *Les Retables brabançons, 1450–1550* (Brussels, 1942)

F. Favresse: *Etudes sur les métiers bruxellois au moyen âge* (Brussels, 1961)

Tapisseries bruxelloises de la pré-renaissance (exh. cat., Brussels, Musées Royaux A. & Hist., 1976)

D. Coekelberghs and A. Vanrie: 'Un Centre de culture: Bruxelles et les arts', *Bruxelles: Croissance d'une capitale*, ed. J. Stengers (Brussels and Antwerp, 1979)

Bruegel: Une Dynastie de peintres (exh. cat., Brussels, Pal. B.-A., 1980)

2. 1830–1918. As a result of Belgium's independence and the rise of Romanticism, sculptors in Brussels developed a liking for subjects with a bearing on national history. GUILLAUME GEEFS led an important workshop, and EUGÈNE SIMONIS made the equestrian statue *Godefroid de Bouillon* (bronze, 1848; Brussels, Pal. Royal), a typically Romantic sculpture. At the Académie des Beaux-Arts,

which played a central role in Belgian painting and sculpture throughout the 19th century, Navez was succeeded by his son-in-law JEAN-FRANÇOIS PORTAELS, who had earlier provided a free studio in Brussels and gave his pupils the freedom to develop in different directions. Belgian painters such as Joseph Stevens (*see* STEVENS, (1)) developed an original form of Realism that—although it was certainly related to Courbet—had its own specific characteristics (*see also* BELGIUM, §III, 4). In 1868 the SOCIÉTÉ LIBRE DES BEAUX-ARTS was founded on the principle that nature should be interpreted freely and individually. The society's members included LOUIS DUBOIS, LOUIS ARTAN, FÉLICIEN ROPS, CHARLES HERMANS, EDOUARD AGNEESENS, CONSTANTIN MEUNIER and ALFRED VERWÉE. Camille Lemonnier (1844–1913) became illustrator of the periodical *Art libre*, which voiced the ideas of the society. They publicly admired the Realism of the French Barbizon school, which had also affected the work of the Tervuren artists, including HIPPOLYTE BOULENGER, painting in the woods near Brussels.

Rodin stayed in Brussels from 1870 to 1877 and made decorations for the Exchange and the Academy buildings. It was early in his career, but he had a strong influence on other sculptors; in the 1870s Julien Dillens (*see* DILLENS, (2)), CHARLES VAN DER STAPPEN, Paul De Vigne (*see* DE VIGNE, (2)) and THOMAS VINÇOTTE won general recognition (*see also* BELGIUM, §IV, 4 and 5). In 1876 Dillens was co-founder of L'ESSOR in Brussels, a society of artists who advocated Realism. Other artists, however, dissociated themselves from the classically orientated art of such groups, and the avant-garde periodical *Art moderne* was founded in 1881. Its editorial secretary was OCTAVE MAUS, a lawyer who became in 1883 the driving force behind Les XX (*see* <VINGT>, LES). This circle was receptive to all trends provided they were independent and original; its members included such diverse figures as FERNAND KHNOPFF, JAMES ENSOR, WILLIAM DEGOUVE DE NUNCQUES, GUILLAUME VOGELS, JEF LAMBEAUX and Théo Van Rysselberghe (*see* VAN RYSSELBERGHE, (2)). The exhibitions held annually by Les XX were used to show both recent work and that of foreign artists such as Cézanne and Seurat. Brussels developed into an international centre for the avant-garde. From 1888 the arts and crafts were also officially represented at the annual exhibitions, including, in 1893, new, experimental work, due largely to the activity of HENRY VAN DE VELDE. For ten years Les XX served as a channel for all the existing movements; when it was disbanded the thread was taken up by the LIBRE ESTHÉTIQUE (1894–1914), again the brainchild of Maus. Impressionists, Pointillists and Symbolists were all given the opportunity to show their ideas. These were the declining years of Realism, and in a few cases the work of Realist painters—some of them orientated towards socialism—became more symbolic, for example that of EUGÈNE LAERMANS, XAVIER MELLERY and LÉON FRÉDERIC. Constantin Meunier became the first Belgian sculptor to receive international recognition for his socially inspired works. Just before the turn of the century the Symbolist movement went through a crisis, when most of the Brussels artists suddenly adopted the sinuous Art Nouveau line. In 1906 the Fauvist movement in Brabant was formed, and from the start it had its own character, as can be seen from the first watercolours by FERDINAND SCHIRREN and RIK WOUTERS. World War I was to cause a slight interruption to the artistic revolution. Libre Esthétique was dissolved in 1914, but it had in any case already been displaced in 1912 by the Galerie Georges Giroux, which supported Fauvists, Cubists, Futurists and Expressionists.

BIBLIOGRAPHY

M.-O. Maus: *Trente années de lutte pour l'art, 1884–1914* (Brussels, 1926)

P. Fierens: *L'Architecture, la sculpture et la peinture au XIXe siècle: L'Art contemporain* (Brussels, rev. 4/1965)

M. Raynal: *Peinture moderne* (Geneva, 1966)

R. L. Delevoy: *Journal du symbolisme* (Geneva, 1977)

Jean Portaels et ses élèves (exh. cat., Brussels, Mus. A. Anc., 1979)

150 ans d'art belge dans les collections des Musées royaux des beaux-arts de Belgique (exh. cat., Brussels, Musées Royaux B.-A., 1981)

H. Liebaers, ed.: *L'Art flamand des origines à nos jours* (Antwerp, 1985)

Académie royale des beaux-arts de Bruxelles: 275 ans d'enseignement (exh. cat., Brussels, Musées Royaux B.-A., 1987)

S. Goyen de Heusch: *L'Impressionnisme et le fauvisme en Belgique* (Antwerp, 1988)

V. Vermeersch and J.-M. Duvosquel, eds: *Musées royaux des beaux-arts de Belgique: Musée d'art moderne de Bruxelles* (Liège, 1988)

3. AFTER 1918. During World War I a dominant style in Brussels besides Fauvism was Flemish Expressionism (*see also* EXPRESSIONISM, §1(ii)), but this did not properly emerge until after 1918. It did not entirely supplant figurative works but was instead supported by a few progressive galleries in Brussels, notably Le Centaure and Sélection, which both published a magazine. Notable Expressionist painters working in the city were JEAN BRUSSELMANS and EDGARD TYTGAT. Others were Ramah (Henri Ramacker; 1887–1947) and Paul Maas (1890–1962), and in sculpture there were OSCAR JESPERS, Henri Puvrez (1893–1971) and Charles Leplae (1903–61). The style of Henri-Victor Wolvens (*b* 1896) was related to that of the Flemish Expressionists, but it lacked their systematic transformation of reality. Another progressive element during the 1920s was the group Zuivere Beelding, formed by the first abstract artists. Their vision was similar to that of the Bauhaus and De Stijl movements, and the most important member was VICTOR SERVRANCKX, who, together with Pierre-Louis Flouquet (1900–67) and VICTOR BOURGEOIS and his brother Pierre, worked for the Brussels magazine *7 Arts* (1922–8).

The opening in 1927 of the Ecole Nationale Supérieure des Arts Visuels at Abbaye de la Cambre in Brussels stimulated the revival of the arts and crafts, but during the 1930s the most important Belgian artistic phenomenon was Surrealism, the influence of which is reflected in the Brussels periodical *Variétés*, published by Paul-Gustave Van Hecke (1887–1967) from Ghent. Van Hecke had previously supported Expressionism; after 1927 he focused his attention on Surrealism and opened the new Epoque Gallery. The most important figure in Belgian Surrealism was RENÉ MAGRITTE. The work of PAUL DELVAUX (see fig. 5) was also linked to the movement, although he was not strictly a Surrealist. In 1927 Magritte had a much criticized exhibition in Le Centaure (he did not gain recognition until after World War II). In 1930 Le Centaure went bankrupt. Magritte moved to Paris but always remained in touch with Brussels, a result being the periodical *Distances*, followed by *Sens propre*.

Luc and Paul Haesaerts founded a new Brussels group, the Compagnons de l'Art, which included Expressionists

5. Paul Delvaux: *Nos Vieux Trams bruxellois*, Bourse metro station, Brussels, oil on panel, 2.35×13.25 m, 1980

and Surrealists as well as representatives of what became known as the Animist style. In July 1945 a generation of artists who had been born *c.* 1910 was promoted through JEUNE PEINTURE BELGE. The group united such different artists as GASTON BERTRAND, Louis Van Lint (1909–86), Anne Bonnet (1908–60), Jean Milo (*b* 1906), Antoine Mortier (*b* 1908) and Marc Mendelson (*b* 1915). The movement lasted until 1948 and defended contemporary art and advocated the liberation of colour. Groupe Surréalisme Révolutionnaire was established in Brussels on 5 April 1947; later this group also branched out into France. The action was laid down in a pamphlet that was signed not only by Magritte but also by the new figures CHRISTIAN DOTREMONT and MARCEL BROODTHAERS. On 8 November 1948 the international COBRA movement, which campaigned against geometrical abstraction, came into being; its most important representative in Brussels was PIERRE ALECHINSKY. One of the places where Cobra took root was the Ateliers du Marais in the centre of Brussels, set up by Alechinsky and Olivier Strebelle (*b* 1927; one of the first artists to become involved in studio pottery). ART ABSTRAIT emerged in 1952, running counter to a regeneration of figurative painting. Among the members of this group were Jo Delahaut (*b* 1911) and Guy Vandenbranden (*b* 1926).

Other movements continued along the lines of the Surrealist experiment. In addition there was the Expressionism in the neo-figurative works of Serge Vandercam (*b* 1924) and the Social Realism of Roger Somville (*b* 1923). In the 1960s public spaces in and around Brussels became the setting for the concrete and steel sculptures of Jacques Moeschal (*b* 1913), and there was also the monumental architecture of Jean-Pierre Ghijsels (*b* 1932) and André Willequet (*b* 1921). After an exhibition at a Brussels gallery in 1964, Broodthaers became an important figure, breaking with conventional ideas on the function of works of art.

BIBLIOGRAPHY

M. Raynal: *Peinture moderne* (Geneva, 1966)
J. Dypreau: *Les Peintures abstraites: L'Art en Belgique* (Brussels, 1968)
E. De Keyser: *La Sculpture contemporaine en Belgique* (Brussels, 1972)
M. Eemans: *L'Art moderne en Belgique* (Brussels, 1974)
W. L. Stokvis: *Cobra* (Amsterdam, 1974)
P. Mertens: *La Jeune Peinture belge, 1945–1948* (Brussels, 1975)
M. Marien: *L'Activité surréaliste en Belgique* (Brussels, 1979)
K. J. Geirlandt, ed.: *L'Art en Belgique depuis 45* (Antwerp, 1983)
H. Liebaers, ed.: *L'Art flamand des origines à nos jours* (Antwerp, 1985)

VÉRONIQUE LAUREYS

IV. Centre of production.

1. Tapestry. 2. Ceramics. 3. Lace. 4. Gold and silver.

1. TAPESTRY.

(i) Before 1600. (ii) 1600 and after.

(i) Before 1600. The tapestry industry in Brussels may well have begun in the 13th century, and the names of several weavers are known from the 14th century. Originally

belonging to the woolworkers' guild, they became increasingly prominent and in 1447 formed an independent guild. The names of many 15th-century tapestry-workers are recorded, which cannot be said of any other city at this time. A membership list shows that between 1417 and 1446 several hundred apprentices, journeymen and master tapestry-workers were registered in the Brussels guild and it includes members of the city board of magistrates. Some of them visited the annual fairs at Bergen op Zoom; others sold expensive tapestries to the governing boards of other Flemish cities or to foreign merchants. Even at this time Brussels tapestries were being delivered to Italian princely courts.

In the 15th century many foreign tapestry-workers came to Brussels, and Brussels natives emigrated to other cities. It is not always possible to reconstruct their movements, since the freemen's records are either missing or incomplete. In Bruges a group of 23 tapestry-weavers gained their citizenship between 1418 and 1496, including 6 natives of Brussels. During the same 78-year period, five weavers from Arras and just one from Tournai gained the freedom of Bruges. The Brussels tapestry-worker Olivier de Barlay was active in Avignon as early as the end of the 14th century. Over the next 100 years, Brussels workers were found throughout the Rhine region, in the Franche-Comté and in Spain. During the 15th century several Brussels weavers were also mentioned in Italy as in the service of the princely courts. Among their number was Reinaut Woutersz. [pseud. Rinaldo Boterame; di Gualtieri; *fl* 1436–81], who was sent to Brussels in 1466 and 1474 by Ludovico II Gonzaga, 2nd Marquess of Mantua, to purchase richly worked tapestries and raw materials. It is certain that the number of émigré Brussels masters was far greater than those documented during the period, and their work abroad was valued perhaps as highly as that from Arras or Tournai.

Such a numerous company of weavers must surely have made and sold much work. The inventory (1420) of Philip the Good, 3rd Duke of Burgundy, refers to two wall hangings (both untraced) with figures, woven in the Duchy of Brabant, presumably in Brussels, at the end of the 13th century. The first piece showed an episode from the *Story of Regnault de Montauban*, the second *Men and Women Playing Games*. It is probable that the tapestries carried the arms of Brabant, a golden lion on a sable field, or some other identifying mark, which would distinguish them from other pieces on the inventory. It is interesting that the origins of the other tapestries, most of which came from Paris or workshops in Arras, are not mentioned.

No Brussels wall hangings have been preserved from the early 15th century. The *Story of Herkinbald* tapestry (Berne, Hist. Mus.) was produced between 1450 and 1460; this was based on the four *Scenes of Justice* panels (*c.* 1439–50; destr. 1695) by Rogier van der Weyden and was originally in the Hôtel de Ville in Brussels. The composition of the *Adoration of the Magi* (Berne, Hist. Mus.) also recalls the work of van der Weyden. The large *Passion* tapestry (Brussels, Musées Royaux A. & Hist.) was probably made in the workshop of Gillis van de Putte (*fl* 1477). While the archaic portrayal of trees, plants and boulders suggests a date of between 1460 and 1480, it also exhibits relationships with the above-mentioned tapestries in the arrangement of the bunches of flowers in the foreground. Documents reveal that the *millefleur* tapestries showing the arms of Philip the Good and Charles the Bold (*c.* 1466; Berne, Hist. Mus.; *see* HERALDRY, colour pl. III, fig. 2) were woven by Jan de Haze (*fl* 1465–72). He was the head of a fairly large Brussels workshop and was also a well-known dealer. His work vividly illustrates the capabilities of the Brussels tapestry industry at this time and shows that certain motifs and stylistic characteristics were not the exclusive property of a particular workshop or city, but were rather common to the tapestry work of the southern Netherlands.

After 1480 Brussels became the principal centre of the tapestry industry in Brabant. It maintained its position until the end of the 18th century, largely due to its favourable situation, an abundance of skilled workers and the activity in the area of painting and other branches of the arts. Production between 1480 and 1490 is stylistically close to that of the sculpted retables of the period. The tapestries are neatly and regularly woven, and progress is evident in the attempts to reproduce certain details and to portray people realistically. Typical examples of this work include the *Allegory of the Blessed Virgin as a Fount of Living Water* and the *Angel's Annunciation to Mary* (both Paris, Louvre). The cartoons for these tapestries are attributed respectively to the Master of the Embroidered Foliage and the Master of the Redemption of the Prado. The arrangement of the figures within the frame of a retable makes a somewhat illogical impression. Once again, flowers fill the foreground of the compositions.

Towards the end of the 15th century there was a reaction against the pictorial trend in tapestry, which was replaced by a monumental style that prevailed until the introduction of Romanism in Brussels. The first group in this new style includes many woven patterns. In a *Mass of St Gregory* (1495; Nuremberg, Ger. Nmus.), which carries the arms of Franz Holzschuher of Nuremberg, a pattern appears on the floor, on the altar and in the clothing of the figures. Around the tapestry there is also a narrow border with representations of precious gemstones. The second group comprises the so-called 'golden' tapestries, in which considerable amounts of gold and silver thread were used (e.g. *Coronation of the Virgin*, *c.* 1502; Madrid, Pal. Real). The third group includes a series of wall hangings that are associated with Jan van Rome (Roome; *fl* 1498–1520), a Brussels painter. Among this group is a piece with the *Story of Herkinbald* (early 16th century; Brussels, Musées Royaux A. & Hist.), which was designed after work by this master. It was ordered in 1513 by the Brotherhood of the Blessed Sacrament and woven in the workshop of Léon de Smet, recorded as a citizen of Brussels in 1490. The border is decorated with flowers, bunches of grapes and the symbols of the Blessed Sacrament. The composition is relatively shallow and is more decorative than earlier works. The figures are unusually stately in their long and luxurious drapes, with deeply sculpted folds. The various scenes in the tapestry are separated by pillars. Another tapestry that belongs to this group portrays the *Finding of the Cross* (Brussels, Musées Royaux A. & Hist.): the threshold of one of the buildings bears the word *Knoest*, the name of the cartoonist who designed the tapestry, Leonard Knoest, who came to

Brussels from Cologne in 1501. All of these tapestries still have a distinctive style and are not so-called 'paintings' in wool and silk, as is the fourth tapestry from the series, the *Legend of Our Lady of Zavel* (Brussels, Musées Royaux A. & Hist.). The composition of this piece is conceived as a triptych and is close to the style of contemporary panel painting. The design is ascribed to Bernard van Orley (*see* ORLEY, VAN (i), (2)) and appears to date from *c.* 1517.

At the beginning of the 16th century, however, there were some instances of serious negligence in tapestry production. The first to react was the City Board of Magistrates, which executed an ordinance in 1528 requiring the addition of the city mark to all tapestries of six square ells (685.8 sq. mm) or more. The mark consisted of two BS (one for Brussels and one for Brabant), surrounding a small red shield. After this, the central government published the imperial ordinance of 1544, which among other things required that all large and expensive tapestries must be signed with the city and the weaver's marks.

Orders for tapestries after cartoons by Italian painters helped to establish a new tapestry style. Between 1513 and 1515 Pope Leo X commissioned Raphael to paint a series of cartoons of the *Acts of the Apostles* (London, V&A). These cartoons, which broke completely with the Flemish tradition, give a good idea of the new trend in painting. Artists now tried to achieve more depth and perspective in their compositions by exploiting large empty spaces and expansive skies. The clothing of the figures was no longer patterned, and the borders featured a series of allegorical figures or scenes related to the life of the patron instead of the earlier decoration of flowers and foliage. It would, however, have been impossible to copy these cartoons exactly; they were conceived as frescoes and went completely against the Flemish style, making them somewhat unsuitable for tapestry work. The tapestry-maker PIETER VAN AELST, who received the commission to weave the tapestries (Rome, Pin. Vaticana) from these cartoons, was an experienced craftsman and managed to circumvent all the difficulties he encountered. He tried to make the entire composition richer, filling the foreground and background with foliage and decorating the cloak of Christ with golden suns. The series was immensely successful and was copied by various workshops throughout Europe until the late 18th century. The best copy (1562–70; Madrid, Pal. Real) was made in the workshop of Jan van Tieghen in Brussels.

Brussels cartoon painters also produced valuable work at this time. Bernard van Orley was the leading figure of Netherlandish Romanism in tapestry production. He broke new ground as a cartoon painter, and his inventive and good-quality designs were very influential. His broadly constructed compositions and sense of monumentality and his familiarity with the work of Raphael enabled him to usher in a new period of tapestry manufacture. He produced cartoons for the two *Passion* series (1520–28; Madrid, Pal. Real; Washington, DC, N.G.A.; Paris, Mus. Jacquemart-André; New York, Met.), the *Hunts of Maximilian* (1528–33; Paris, Louvre) and the *Story of Jacob* (Brussels, Musées Royaux A. & Hist.). The beautiful and decorative borders are sensitively and successfully adapted for tapestry. Van Orley had several students, and such other artists as Lucas van Nevele, to whom the cartoons for the *Months of Lucas* are attributed, followed his example.

Another important cartoon painter was PIETER COECKE VAN AELST I (*see* TAPESTRY, colour pl. II, fig. 1),

6. Tapestry depicting 'Gluttony' from the *Seven Deadly Sins*, designed by Pieter Coecke van Aelst, wool, silk and silver-gilt thread, 3.89×6.78 m, made in Brussels, *c.* 1560–75 (New York, Metropolitan Museum of Art)

7. Tapestry depicting Vertumnus as a haymaker from the *Story of Vertumnus and Pomona*, design attributed to Jan Cornelisz. Vermeyen, gold, silver, silk and wool, 4.3×6.48 m, made in the workshop of Willem de Pannemaker, Brussels, *c.* 1560 (Madrid, Palacio Real de Madrid)

who was active in Antwerp, but lived in Brussels towards the end of his life. Only three series can be definitely traced to his cartoons, the *Story of Joshua* (Vienna, Ksthist. Mus.), the *Life of St Paul* (e.g. Vienna, Ksthist. Mus.) and the suite portraying the *Seven Deadly Sins* (1560–75; examples in Vienna, Ksthist. Mus.; New York, Met.; see fig. 6), although cartoons for the *Tobias* tapestries (Gaasbeek, Kasteel) are also ascribed to him. Coecke's work is more decorative, lively and brilliant than that of van Orley. His crowded scenes are filled with particularly tall, elegant figures with small feet. He also devoted considerable attention to the decoration of the borders, which included grotesques and strapwork.

The importance of Michiel Coxcie as a cartoon painter is indisputable. He studied the Renaissance style in Rome, concentrating particularly on the work of Raphael. For some years Coxcie was the official cartoon painter for the city of Brussels. Among the works credited to him are cartoons for the *Story of the First Human Beings* and the *Life of Noah* (Kraków, N. A. Cols). Although his compositions are very well balanced and he was a skilled master, he had little independence of style. The wonderful borders, filled with all sorts of animals, were very successful and were copied until the early 17th century.

The cartoons for the series the *Conquest of Tunis* (1545–54; Madrid, Patrm. N.) were commissioned from JAN CORNELISZ. VERMEYEN by Emperor Charles V. The tapestries are remarkable for their soft, yellow palette and borders filled with moresques. The cartoons for a series of the *Fables from Ovid* (Madrid, Pal. Real) and another depicting the *Story of Vertumnus and Pomona* (*c*. 1560; Madrid, Pal. Real; see fig. 7) are also attributed to Vermeyen, partly because in both series the borders are decorated with moresques.

The painter PEETER DE KEMPENEER was also an important tapestry designer. At first he lived and worked away from the tapestry industry, but was associated with a few tapestry-workers. He spent some time in Italy and settled in Spain in 1537. He returned in 1564 to Brussels, where he was appointed the official city cartoon painter. The ten cartoons for *SS Peter and Paul* (1556–67; five France, priv. col.; three Ghent, Oudhdknd. Mus. Bijloke), with the arms of the abbey of St Peter, Ghent, and of Abbot François d'Avroult, are attributed to him.

Little is known of the activities of the other cartoon painters of the second half of the 16th century. Nevertheless, there was a noticeable reaction during the last decade against earlier stylistic conceptions: the work became more involved, flatter and more monotonous, with a relatively high horizon. Artists appear to have wanted to return to concepts current *c*. 1500: there was a deliberate retreat from movement and depth in composition and little realism in the depiction of flora. A restricted and monotonous palette, very deep borders and indistinct decoration marked the low level of this work compared to that of the mid-16th century. These Brussels hangings were imitated in other centres, but the colouring was usually less rich and the weave frequently coarser and more cheaply executed.

The Brussels weavers were particularly important in the development of tapestries. Among the most important masters of the first half of the 16th century, in addition to Pieter van Aelst, were Pieter and Willem de Pannemaker (*see* PANNEMAKER, DE), Gabriël van der Tommen (*fl* 1500–25), Frans Geubels (after 1520–before 1585) and Hendrik Tsas (*fl* 1550–1600). The second half of the century was dominated by Jan van Tieghen, Jacob Tseraerts (*c*. 1535–after 1592), Leo van den Hecke (*fl* 1575–1600), Maarten Reynbouts (*fl* 1576–1618) and Jacob Geubels (*d c*. 1605), the son of Frans, as well as the Leyniers family. Those who established tapestry-maker dynasties passed on their technical knowledge and artistic abilities from generation to generation. Their tapestries, however, were not sold from the factory but in the Antwerp Pant. The export of wall hangings abroad was an important part of the industry.

For further illustration *see* TAPESTRY, fig. 6.

(ii) 1600 and after. The designs of Peter Paul Rubens resulted in a revolution in the art of tapestry-weaving, comparable to the one caused by Raphael's *Acts of the Apostles* (*see* §(i) above). His cartoons for the *Story of Decius Mus* (1617–18), which had never been portrayed in tapestry, resulted in numerous orders. The first set of tapestries from these cartoons was made in Brussels for Francisco Cattaneo (*fl* 1600–50) of Genoa. The tapestries were surrounded by a border that was completely independent of the main tapestry. The assignment was a difficult one for weavers to realize: compositions on such a large scale, bursting with energy and blazing with colour. Subsidiary details were reduced to a minimum, and attention was focused on the enormous figures and their muscular bodies. In Rubens's cartoons for the *Story of Achilles* (1630–35; examples Brussels, Musées Royaux A. & Hist.; Boston, MA, Mus. F.A.) the border has lost its independent character and is closely related to the subject. There are herms to the left and right of the central scene, at the bottom, where they appear to stand not on but in front of a plinth, and at the top, where they are connected by a superstructure of putti and garlands, with a richly worked cartouche in the centre.

Rubens's style was spread by his students and followers, including CORNELIS SCHUT I, Theodoor van Thulden, JUSTUS VAN EGMONT and Jan Boeckhorst, but a certain relaxation could already be seen in their work. They adapted more completely to the flatness of the tapestry, designing clear, easy compositions, dominated by concern for detail. Gradually the larger figures disappeared from the designs, resulting in a more harmonious composition. The heavy borders, inspired by architecture and sculpture, disappeared and were replaced by frames filled with flowers and plants. In the designs of Jan van den Hoecke for the *Months*, the *Seasons*, the *Four Elements* and the *Story of Zenobia* (1660; Madrid, Pal. Real; see fig. 8), Rubens's pathos has been completely eliminated. The loving treatment of the abundant details and the sparkling depictions of flowers, fruits and putti prompt the classification of these designs as some of the most successful compositions for tapestry at this time.

A similar evolution can be seen in the tapestry designs of JACOB JORDAENS. He was a highly gifted master with an interest in the decorative character of his art. Throughout his life, however, he was so overwhelmed with

8. Tapestry depicting Zenobia surrounded by various animals from the *Story of Zenobia*, designed by Jan van den Hoecke, wool and silk, 4.08×3.82 m, woven in the workshop of Gerard Peemans, Brussels, *c.* 1660 (Madrid, Palacio Real de Madrid)

commissions that he freely used figures and groups from one series in another. Jordaens is thought to have started painting cartoons as early as 1620. The best and most familiar examples include the *Story of Odysseus* (*c.* 1630–35), the *Story of Alexander the Great* (*c.* 1630–35), *Scenes from Country Life* (*c.* 1635), the *Proverbs* (1644) and the *Riding School* (1645; Vienna, Ksthist. Mus.). His other designs include the series *Famous Women of Antiquity* and the *Story of Charlemagne* (1660s). The compositions are usually well balanced and well adapted to the typical style of tapestry work.

The painter David Teniers the elder was also highly influential in the art of tapestry. Many thousands of tapestries were woven in Brussels, Oudenaarde, Lille, Beauvais and Aubusson, all of which were called *fins Teniers* or *Tenières*, featuring kermesses with rural people returning from the fields or market. It is not clear whether the cartoons for these pieces were painted by David Teniers or whether the scenes were merely inspired by his paintings. It is in any case certain that both he and his son, David Teniers the younger, designed cartoons for allegorical scenes and armorial tapestries.

At the end of the 17th century the increasing influence of the Gobelins factory in Paris is noticeable, particularly in tapestries with mythological and historical scenes and, occasionally, religious scenes. An outstanding example is the beautiful series *Worship of the Gods* (1717; Ghent, Mus. S. Kst.), which came from the Brussels workshops of Urbaan Leyniers (1674–1747), Daniël Leyniers II (1669–1728) and Hendrik Reydams II (1650–1719). The cartoons were painted by the gifted Brussels master Jan van Orley, who took his inspiration not only from the work of Charles Le Brun but from the designs of Antoine Coypel and Charles-Antoine Coypel. The French influence is clear in the elegant, idealized figures, charmingly set in the composition, the rich foreground colouring and the delicate pastels of the background, as well as the virtuosic treatment of the light. The border is filled with foliage in the Louis XIV style and is actually an imitation of the frame of a painted picture. Similarly charming and fashionable figures, lively colours and landscapes constructed like theatrical sets can be seen in a *Story of Psyche* and a series on *Alexander* from the workshop of Jan-Frans van den Hecke (*fl c.* 1660–95), in the *Story of Achilles* signed by Jodocus de Vos and in a suite on the *Life of Christ* (Bruges, St Saviour's Church) from the workshop of Jaspar van der Borght (*fl* 1700–50). All of these works date from the late 17th century or the first half of the 18th and indicate how the Gobelins exercised a growing influence on Brussels tapestry work.

After 1750 decline was rapid, although Jacob van der Borght, son of Jaspar, was still active in Brussels. In 1785 he produced four rather unsuccessful tapestries on the *Legend of the Blessed Sacrament of Miracles* for St Michael's Church, Brussels. He was the last tapestry-maker of Brussels; when he died on 13 March 1794, his workshop was closed down and the contents offered for sale. This meant the end of a once-famous craft in the southern Netherlands. For more than three centuries the Brussels tapestry-weavers had produced work of high artistic quality and had played a leading role in other European countries. Not until the second half of the 19th century was there renewed interest in tapestry work, when workshops like those of Arthur Lambrecht in the Schaerbeek district of Brussels helped to revive an age-old branch of the arts.

BIBLIOGRAPHY

A. Wauters: *Les Tapisseries bruxelloises* (Brussels, 1878)
H. Göbel: *Wandteppiche*, 3 vols (Leipzig, 1923–34; Eng. trans., i, New York, 1924)
J. van Duverger and E. van Duverger: *Artes textiles*, 11 vols (Ghent, 1953–86)
J. Duverger and others: *La Tapisserie flamande aux XVIIe et XVIIIe siècles. Colloque international: Brussels, 1959*
——: *L'Age d'or de la tapisserie flamande. Colloque international: Brussels, 1969*
J. Szablowski and others: *Die flämischen Tapisserien im Wawelschloss in Krakow* (Antwerp, 1972)
E. Duverger: 'Tapisseries et arts textiles', *L'Art flamand des origines à nos jours* (Antwerp, 1985), pp. 189–204, 311–21
E. A. Standen: *European Post-medieval Tapestries and Related Hangings in the Metropolitan Museum of Art*, 2 vols (New York, 1985)
P. Junquera de Vega and C. Herrero Carretero: *Cátalogo de tapices del Patrimonio nacional*, 2 vols (Madrid, 1986)
A. S. Cavallo: *Medieval Tapestries in the Metropolitan Museum of Art* (New York, 1993)

ERIK DUVERGER

2. Ceramics. Several small potteries were in production in Brussels during the mid-17th century. A number of pieces have survived, which are decorated in the style of wares from Delft. During the 18th century, however, more significant manufacturers were established. In 1705 Corneille Mombaers (*d* 1729) obtained a monopoly for the manufacture of faience and with Thierry Witsenburg (*fl* 1705) established a faience factory in Brussels, which manufactured wares for daily use. In 1724 the business was taken over by Mombaers's son, Philippe Mombaers

(1693–1754), who made the concern very successful. In 1754 Philippe Mombaers's son-in-law, Jacques Artoisenet (1719/20–65), also established a factory despite Mombaers's monopoly. The two factories produced similar wares, including such decorative items as tureens in the shape of ducks, fish or vegetables. The factories that most influenced Brussels were Strasbourg and Saint-Amand-les-Eaux, although other centres of production were also inspirational: for example the blue *style rayonnant* was derived from wares from Rouen, while chinoiserie decoration was taken from wares from Sinceny, near Laon. Decoration unique to Brussels consists of dominant green lines, bright-yellow butterflies and snails (*see* BELGIUM, fig. 36). This decorative faience, however, did not resist competition from *faience fine* (lead-glazed pottery) and porcelain. By the end of the 18th century production concentrated solely on everyday wares.

Porcelain was produced in Brussels at the end of the 18th century. The factory of Montplaisir (1786–90) in the Schaerbeek district of Brussels produced wares decorated with sprays of small flowers or landscapes in green. The factory in the Etterbeek district (1787–1803) was established by Chrétien Kühne (*c*. 1744–*c*. 1815). Wares included tablewares decorated with polychrome flowers and chinoiseries.

At the beginning of the 19th century many workshops for decoration were established. Such painters as Louis Cretté (*c*. 1758–1813) ordered pieces of plain white porcelain from Paris, which were then painted with scattered flowers, exotic birds, landscapes and chinoiseries. In 1824 Frédéric Théodore Faber (1782–1844) set up a factory with the sculptor Charles-Christophe Windisch (*d* 1842) in Ixelles, which from 1830 was run by Faber's son Henri Faber (*b* 1808); it was purchased by Jean-Baptiste Cappellemans the elder (1766–1841) in 1849, but closed down in 1870. The factory's most successful wares were those decorated with views of Brussels and genre scenes embellished with gold. In 1833 Windisch set up another factory in Ixelles. He produced white porcelain, which was sometimes gilded, and wares included openwork baskets carried by figures of winged women. Subsequently, a decorative workshop was added. From 1852 to 1901 the factory was managed by the Vermeren-Coché family and until 1959 by their descendants, the Demeuldre-Coché family. Traditional wares were produced but adapted to the various styles in vogue. Decoration included flowers, landscapes, birds and sometimes mythological scenes.

BIBLIOGRAPHY

G. Dansaert: *Les Anciennes Faïences de Bruxelles* (Brussels, 1922/*R* 1979)
M. Lowet de Wotrenge: 'Essai sur la porcelaine dite de Bruxelles', *An. Soc. Royale Archéol. Bruxelles*, xxxvi (1931) [whole issue]
J. Helbig: *La Céramique bruxelloise du bon vieux temps* (Brussels, 1946)
M. Pinckaers: *La Porcelaine de Bruxelles, 1767–1953* (Brussels, 1984)

MIREILLE JOTTRAND

3. LACE. By the second half of the 16th century cutwork, needle lace and bobbin laces were being produced in Brussels, and there were already such competent lace merchants as Jacqueline Masqueliers (*fl c*. 1563–87), who supplied the firm of Plantin in Antwerp between 1563 and 1587. At this time Brussels-made laces were being exported to Paris and elsewhere, and in the 17th century exports grew so phenomenally that many countries tried to prohibit them for economic reasons. Brussels dominated this rapid expansion, early demonstrating its ability to adapt to changing fashions by innovation with the introduction of the flexible part-lace technique, first mentioned in 1646. Bobbin lace now became all-important (*see* LACE, figs 2 and 4), although needle lace continued to be made. In the 17th century Brussels largely followed the practice of the workshops in Venice and then France in design. Leading manufacturers and designers were the Gandussis, father and son, but in the 18th century Brussels had plenty of good designers. Its numerous rich lace merchants now enjoyed considerable standing. The firm of Godefroy-Durondeau supplied the imperial court in Vienna and agents in such cities as Paris, Hamburg and London with all the classic bobbin laces, all made in Brussels, and exquisite, expensive needle lace. The Brussels industry was rescued from the collapse following the French Revolution by Napoleon Bonaparte, who made several visits there, placing large orders. Under the Second Empire (1815–48) prosperity returned, but the dominant firms and the best designers were now based in Paris. In the 1880s leading Brussels firms sought cheaper labour in rural areas, but managed to survive until World War I. In the late 20th century much of the handmade lace sold in Brussels hailed from China, but the city played a leading role in the development of lace as an art form, with its Atelier du XXe Siècle and the International Lace Biennials staged since 1983.

BIBLIOGRAPHY

M. Risselin-Steenebrugen: 'Une Famille de dentelliers bruxellois au XVIIIe siècle', *An. Soc. Royale Archéol. Bruxelles*, xlviii (1948–55), pp. 201–32
——: 'Caroline de Halluin, marchande de dentelles à Bruxelles au XVIIIe siècle', *An. Soc. Royale Archéol. Bruxelles*, xlix (1956–7), pp. 1–15
——: 'Contribution à l'histoire de la dentelle de Bruxelles au XVIIe siècle', *An. Féd. Archéol. & Hist. Belgique* (1968), i, pp. 301–12
——: 'Napoléon et la dentelle de Bruxelles', *An. Féd. Archéol. & Hist. Belgique* (1972), i, pp. 169–86
——: 'Les Débuts de l'industrie dentellière à Bruxelles', *Bull. Mus. Royaux A. & Hist.*, xlviii (1976), pp. 101–20
——: *Les Dentelles belges du XVIe au XVIIIe siècle*, Brussels, Musées Royaux A. & Hist. (Brussels, 1978)

PATRICIA WARDLE

4. GOLD AND SILVER. The gold- and silversmiths of Brussels, of whom the earliest known records date from 1152, were awarded a privilege in the first half of the 14th century by Duke John III of Brabant (*reg* 1312–55), which provided regulations for their guild. On 30 November 1400 his successor, Duchess Joanna (*reg* 1355–1406), reconfirmed the rights awarded by her father; this ordinance also shows that gold and silver objects from Brussels already carried the Lion of Brabant as their hallmark. Before 1462 a second hallmark had already been introduced, derived from the city's coat of arms: the head of the city's patron saint, St Michael, crowned with a small cross. Both marks were used, with some variations in the devices, until the end of the *ancien régime*. A register for the period from 1694 to 1746 also survives, in which the deans of the guild and their corresponding year letters are given. Since no tables or plates of marks have survived, Brussels makers' marks have to be deciphered by using archival data.

The patronage of governors of the Netherlands and their courts, who resided in Brussels from the Renaissance period, enhanced the reputation of the gold- and silversmiths, who already enjoyed the esteem of the Burgundian dukes and the first Habsburg princes, and led to an increase in production. Mary, Queen of Hungary and Regent of the Netherlands (*reg* 1531–55), Albert, Archduke of Austria, and Isabella Clara Eugenia, Archduchess of Austria (*reg* 1598–1633), and the 18th-century Austrian governors as well as the nobility, ecclesiastics and merchants were all notable patrons. In the 18th century silversmiths in Brussels specialized in domestic silver and elaborate services. Production continued throughout the 19th and 20th centuries, particularly in the Art Nouveau and Art Deco period.

See also BELGIUM, §IX, 1.

BIBLIOGRAPHY

Orfèvrerie au poinçon de Bruxelles (exh. cat. by J. Vanwittenbergh, Brussels, Gén. de Banque, 1979)

LEO DE REN

V. Buildings.

1. CATHEDRAL. This former collegiate church, dedicated to SS Michael and Gudule, became a parish church at the Revolution of 1830 and a cathedral in 1962. The present building was begun *c.* 1226, but it was finished only towards the end of the 15th century and has been much altered; it is nevertheless a fine example of Gothic architecture in Brabant. It has a western façade block, a seven-bay aisled nave and shallow side chapels, two-bay transepts with later porches, and a choir of three straight bays and a five-sided hemicycle. The eastern arm is now flanked by two long chapels that replaced the original lateral and radiating chapels in the 16th and 17th centuries. Only the axial chapel survives (rebuilt in the 17th century), although the two restored ambulatory bays on either side have preserved their original layout. The cathedral is built of sandstone and is 110 m long (excluding the axial chapel) and 26.5 m high, measured internally.

In the 7th century the parish of St Michael was founded on a hill dominating the right bank of the River Senne; *c.* 977 the Duke of Lotharingia erected a *castrum* on a nearby island, in the chapel of which he deposited the relics of St Gudule. At the beginning of the 11th century, on the heights of the Coudenberg, a new *castrum* was built, the first enclosure wall embracing the existent pre-urban core. The relics of St Gudule were transferred to St Michael, and a chapter of canons was created in 1047, which perhaps occasioned the rebuilding of the church. This building was probably burnt down in 1072; in any case, a third church was built on the site, the construction of which was finished only *c.* 1200 with the building of a façade block. This had a central tower and two large stair-turrets decorated with blind arcades, which were reconstructed by Brigode after the 1937 excavations as taller than the central part. There was no western entrance. The remains of the façade block are preserved under the second and third bays of the present nave.

About 1226, at the instigation of Henry I, Duke of Brabant, the church was rebuilt in a more up-to-date style, which had already appeared at the cathedrals of Arras and Cambrai (in the diocese of which Brussels lay). In the first campaign, the hemicycle and the two straight bays of the choir were built; the three radiating chapels were separated from one another by an ambulatory bay in the old-fashioned manner followed in the north of Brabant (e.g. Notre-Dame at Saint-Omer). The surviving bays have a rémois passage, which, with the gables over the windows and the quinquepartite ambulatory vaults, must reflect the influence of Cambrai Cathedral. The sanctuary piers are sturdy, paired cylindrical columns, with features derived from Normandy.

9. Brussels Cathedral, west front, begun 14th century

The last bay and the upper parts of the choir were finished in a second campaign from *c.* 1260 to 1294. The triforium has three subdivided openings in the straight bays; its rear wall was originally lit by small oculi, which were blocked when the lateral chapels were built. The tracery of the hemicycle clerestory is a Flamboyant alteration. The quadripartite vaults are supported by two tiers of flying buttresses. The style of the choir is a provincial version of the Gothic of the Champagne region transmitted through Cambrai Cathedral, with additional influences from such buildings as Tournai Cathedral.

Work continued westwards throughout the 14th century on the south side of the building. The west wall of the south transept has two superposed passages and the south façade window is exceptionally large for its date. In the 15th century the northern parts were set out and the nave completed. Despite the apparent unity of style, there are changes to the mouldings and capitals.

The central vessel of the nave built by, among others, Jacob van Tienen, is fully characteristic of Brabantine Gothic, with huge columnar piers 1.47 m in diameter supporting, by contrast, the two fine and delicate upper stages, probably built *c.* 1475. The triforium is reduced to simple mullions, which are an extension of the clerestory mullions, creating a strong play of verticals and contrasting patterns of light and dark. It is unlikely that the triforium, restored in the 19th century, ever had tracery like that of St Pierre in Leuven, as has been suggested. On the exterior the chapels are capped by triangular gables decorated with a large stretched trefoil in a Brabantine fashion begun at Cambrai Cathedral.

The west façade, probably by Gilles van den Bossche (*d* 1460), had been under way since the end of the 14th century, when the Romanesque block was still standing (see fig. 9). The south tower was finished in 1451, and in 1480 only the upper parts of the north tower were unfinished; it was surmounted by a wooden spire in 1534. The vertical lines and balanced architectural masses flanking the central traceried window make this one of the great classic façades; it is exceptional in the Low Countries, where the harmonized façade was not popular, a single western tower being more common.

In the 18th century the building was restored in Baroque style by Dewez; but from 1839 the restorers, including Luis Raeymakers and Louis de Curte, who was responsible for the north transept porch, tried to return it to its original appearance. The monumental stairway in front of the west façade was built in 1860. The church is now in poor condition, however, standing in an urban landscape whose nature has been completely adulterated. It contains fine stained-glass windows, including, in the choir (1522–5) and transepts (1537–8), depictions of rulers of the Empire and their patron saints; the glass on the transept façades was executed from cartoons by Bernard van Orley, as was the *Legend of the Miraculous Host* in the Blessed Sacrament Chapel. The west façade glass depicts the *Last Judgement* (1528), while the chapel of the Virgin contains glass with scenes from the *Life of the Virgin* (1654–63) in the style of Rubens.

BIBLIOGRAPHY

R. Maere: 'L'Eglise Sainte-Gudule à Bruxelles', *Rev. A.* [Brussels], i (1925), pp. 185–99; ii, pp. 13–24, 51–63, 150–69

P. Lefèvre: *La Collégiale des Saints Michel et Gudule à Bruxelles* (Brussels, 1942, 2/1949)

M. Thibaut de Maisères: *Les Eglises gothiques de Bruxelles* (Brussels, 1942)

JACQUES THIEBAUT

2. Hôtel de Ville. Dominating the market-place, the Hôtel de Ville is one of the most important secular Gothic buildings in Brabant. It consists of two wings divided by a tall, central bell-tower (see fig. 10) and was built in at least three campaigns. There is some disagreement over the relation of the bell-tower to the L-shaped left wing, the first of the wings to be built.

In 1301 and 1327 respectively the city magistrature bought two stone houses, 'de Meerte' and 'den Wilden Ever', in which to hold their meetings. The bell-tower may have been built in the second half of the 14th century on the site of 'den Wilden Ever', and acted as the entrance to

10. Brussels, Hôtel de Ville, begun *c.* 1401

the rectangular clothmakers' hall, which was built 1353–1400, further back along what is now Amigostraat. Another view is that the tower was built with the left wing of the Hôtel de Ville, in the first campaign from *c.* 1401 to 1417–21. A bill of 1405, a rare survival, names the architect as Jacob van Thienen (*fl* 1377–1406). At this time the tower reached only to the uppermost balustrade of the building.

About 1435 the city governors decided to add a right wing, for which they acquired more houses, including 'den Scupstoel', 'den Papenkeldere' and 'de Moor', whose cellars survive. Sculptures in the ground-floor gallery refer to their names. The foundation stone was laid on 4 March 1444 by the ten-year-old Duke Charles the Bold, and the building may have been designed by the city architect, Herman de Voghele. This campaign, which lasted only until 1449, was followed immediately by the last phase, which included work on the richly Flamboyant superstructure of the tower. It was finished in 1455 by Jan van Ruysbroeck.

Despite the three campaigns under different architects, the design as a whole transcends the differences of scale and detail. Both wings have an open gallery on the ground-floor, with two upper storeys, topped by a crenellated parapet and a pitched roof. The corners are accented by elegant turrets. The longer left wing has ten bays and includes the original entrance staircase flanked by sculpted lions, which were added in 1770. Between the two upper storeys, with their mullioned windows, there is an imposing row of statues that recalls the galleries of kings on French

High Gothic cathedral façades, such as Notre-Dame, Paris. The figures run on across the tower, implying an architectural and sculptural link between the tower and the left wing. The tower is square at the base, changing above roof level into an openwork, fenestrated octagon, crowned with a weather-vane in the form of a bronze figure of St Michael, patron saint of Brussels, executed by Maarten van Rode in 1454.

The bombardment of 1695 reduced the Hôtel de Ville to a shell, with only the walls surviving, but it was restored relatively quickly to its original form. A new building for the Estates of Brabant was erected on the site of the ruined clothmakers' hall in 1706–17 under the supervision of Cornelis van Nerven (*fl* 1696–1717). As a symbol of the ruling class, however, the town hall was again damaged during the French Revolution (1793–4). It was thoroughly restored during the 19th century under the supervision of Tieleman Franciscus Suys and Victor Jamaer. The entire exterior, including the tower and sculptures, was almost entirely replaced. Inside, rooms such as the so-called Gothic room and the Salle des Mariages were completely redecorated in the Gothic Revival style. In addition to some interesting paintings and sculptures, the town hall contains a collection of 16th- and 18th-century tapestries. Today, as the administrative offices have been transferred to other buildings, the town hall is primarily symbolic.

BIBLIOGRAPHY

M. Calomme-Beginne: *Geïllustreerde catalogus van het stadhuis van Brussel* (Brussels, n.d.)
A. Wauters: *L'Hôtel-de-ville de Bruxelles: L'Epoque de sa construction et la destination de chacune de ses parties* (Ghent, 1841)
G. Des Marez: 'L'Ancien Beffroi de la ville de Bruxelles', *An. Soc. Royale Archéol. Bruxelles*, xxi (1907), pp. 463–75
D. Roggen and L. Verleyen: 'De portaalsculpturen van het Brusselsche stadhuis', *Gent. Bijdr. Kstgesch.*, i (1934), pp. 123–48
P. Bonenfant: 'A propos de 3 chapiteaux de l'Hôtel de ville', *Bull. Soc. Royale Archéol. Bruxelles*, v (1935), pp. 141–53
G. Pergameni: *L'Hôtel de ville de Bruxelles* (Brussels, 1935)
D. Roggen and J. Withof: 'Grondleggers en grootmeesters der Brabantse gotiek', *Gent. Bijdr. Kstgesch.*, x (1944), pp. 83–209
A. Maesschalck and J. Viaene: *Het stadhuis van Brussel*, Mensen en bouwkunst in Boergondisch Brabant (Leuven, 1960)
V. G. Martiny: *Bruxelles: L'Architecture des origines à 1900* (Brussels, 1980) [Fr., Eng. and Dut. text]
——: 'A propos de la restauration de l'escalier des lions de l'Hôtel de ville de Bruxelles: Contribution de Viollet-le-Duc', *An. Soc. Royale Archéol. Bruxelles* (1981), pp. 185–217
M. Goedee: *De standbeelden van het Brusselse stadhuis* (Brussels, 1985)
A. Maesschalck and J. Viaene: 'Jan van Ruysbroeck herdacht, 1486–1986', *Tijdschr. Brussel. Gesch.*, i/2 (1985), pp. 17–110

FRIEDA VAN TYGHEM

Brustolon, Andrea (*b* Belluno, 20 July 1662; *d* Belluno, 25 Oct 1732). Italian sculptor and draughtsman. He worked almost exclusively in wood. His first teacher was his father, Jacopo Brustolon (*d* 1709), also a sculptor, and he then trained with the painter Agostino Ridolfi (1646–1727). In 1677 Andrea was sent to Venice to the workshop of Filippo Parodi, to whose elegance, dynamism and technical virtuosity he was always indebted, although he soon established his own style. Brustolon came from an alpine area that had a long tradition of craftsmanship in wood. His achievement was to transpose techniques that had been associated with everyday craftsmanship on to the highest artistic level.

Brustolon went to Rome, probably in 1679. In 1685 he signed a contract for the execution of the altar of the Souls in S Floriano at Pieve di Zoldo, which suggests that he was already settled in Belluno even while maintaining contacts with Venice. In 1695 he presented a model of a door (unexecuted) for the chapel of the Tesoro at the Santo in Padua, a chapel that had been designed by Parodi, who also supervised its decoration. During the same year Brustolon may have executed a group of angels for the parish church of S Fermo, near Belluno; for the same church he sculpted the group of the *Four Evangelists* and the tabernacle of the high altar. Still in 1695 or 1696 he sculpted the *Custody of St Theodora* in Swiss pine for the Augustinian nuns of Feltre (Feltre, S Giacomo Maggiore), and ecclesiastical commissions in and around Belluno occupied him throughout the late 1690s. In 1696 he was paid for a polished boxwood tabernacle, placed on the high altar of the church of Forno di Canale, and in 1696 or 1697 he modelled another tabernacle (untraced) for S Michele in Valle at La Valle.

In addition to these local commissions, Brustolon made elaborate furniture for Venetian patrician families. Sculpture in wood had already found widespread application in Venice, where Francesco Pianta (*fl c.* 1650–1700) had created the very original decorations of the Scuola di S Rocco and where Giacomo Piazzetta had left such remarkable works as the dossals of the chapel of the Rosario in SS Giovanni e Paolo. Brustolon's works for the Pisani (*c.* 1695) and the Correr (*c.* 1680–85) families and for the Venier family (see fig.), executed in the early years of the

Andrea Brustolon: chair made for the Venier family, ebony and boxwood, h. 1.25 m, 1706–20 (Venice, Ca' Rezzonico); the upholstery, worked in *petit point*, is late 17th century

18th century, won him a high and lasting reputation. For the Pisani he made 12 large chairs in boxwood, incorporating symbols of the *Months* (Rome, Pal. Quirinale). The plant forms that decorate these chairs are of a Baroque magnificence and also possess the lively quality that was to typify elegant Venetian furniture of the 18th century. The forms are turgid and strongly naturalistic. Natural motifs also predominate in the Correr chairs and in the items of furniture, mainly pedestals, for the Venier family, which feature figures—grouped and single—representing the seasons or the elements, warriors and Ethiopian slaves, horses and marine creatures, and Hercules triumphing over the Hydra or Cerberus. The sprightly figures often showed a tendency to elongation that recalls the art of the Hellenistic era. These works (all Venice, Ca' Rezzonica) were made during a time of great creativity and imagination in Brustolon's career.

In 1715 Brustolon's reliquary of *St Innocent* (Hamburg, Mus. Kst & Gew.), carved in boxwood and ebony, was delivered to Polcenigo, Bishop of Feltre. In 1722 the artist was working on the altar of *Our Lady of Sorrows* for the church of Dosoledo di Comelico, for which he continued to be paid until 1729. Probably in 1724 he executed the tabernacle with caryatids and putti for the parish church of Cortina d'Ampezzo. Meanwhile, in 1723, he had signed the contract for the great wooden altarpiece of the *Death of St Francis Xavier* (Belluno, Mus. Civ.) for S Ignazio at Fasola di Belluno. This was commissioned from him by the noble Miari family and completed in 1728. It was the first of the magnificent wooden altarpieces executed during the last period of Brustolon's activity. For the same church he executed an altarpiece of the *Crucifixion* (1729; Belluno, Mus. Civ.). Each such altarpiece reveals his technical proficiency and is composed with his typical assurance. However, certain stylistic peculiarities were laid aside and the compositions appear more structured, moderating the characteristic liveliness of earlier works.

During this period Brustolon continued to carve objects and furniture for private patrons. In 1727 he carved a series of mythological divinities with their accompanying pedestals (priv. col.) for the Piloni, an aristocratic Bellunese family. He continued to produce suites of furniture and had such a productive workshop that for many years dealers attributed to him any piece of furniture of 18th-century origin that happened to include carved figures.

Numerous drawings by Brustolon relating both to known works and to untraced or unrealized projects survive (Belluno, Mus. Civ.). They reveal that he could express himself gracefully and sensitively on paper. His brother, Paolo Brustolon (*d* 1734), worked with him and completed the high altar in S Valentino di Mareson, Andrea's last commission, begun in 1731.

BIBLIOGRAPHY

A. Agosti: *Elogio di A. Brustolon* (Padua, 1833)
G. Biasuz and E. Lacchin: *Andrea Brustolon* (Venice, 1928)
C. Semenzato: 'Andrea Brustolon', *La scultura veneta del seicento e settecento* (Venice, 1966)
G. Biasuz and M. G. Buttignon: *Andrea Brustolon* (Padua, 1969)
A. Forniz: 'Quattro sculture inedite del Brustolon a Rorai Piccolo di Porcia', *A. Ven.*, xxvi (1972), pp. 220–21
G. Biasuz: 'Alla riscoperta di alcune opere del Brustolon nelle chiese scomparse di Belluno', *Archv Stor. Belluno, Feltre & Cadore* (1977)
C. Alberici: *Il mobile veneto* (Milan, 1980)
G. Biasuz: 'Documenti e appunti su alcune opere del Brustolon', *Archv Stor. Belluno, Feltre & Cadore* (1980)

CAMILLO SEMENZATO

Brustolon [Brostoloni; Brustoloni]**, Giambattista** [Giovanni Battista] (*b* Venice, 1712; *d* Venice, 16 Oct 1796). Italian printmaker. His family was from Belluno. He studied with Josef [Giuseppe] Wagner (1706–80) (Moschini). An able reproductive engraver, Brustolon mostly employed a technique that combined etching and engraving, and his work was done for the best Venetian publishers. He is known mainly for his reproductive prints after works by Canaletto. In 1763, for the publisher Ludovico Furlanetto, Brustolon produced a series entitled *Prospectuum aedium, viarumque insigniorum urbis Venetiarum* (see 1983 exh. cat., pp. 83–7, nos 53–8), dedicated to the Doge Marco Foscarini (*reg* 1762–3) and initially composed of 12 views of Venice after Canaletto. It was later completed by the addition of 10 more plates after Michele Giovanni Marieschi and Giambattista Moretti in addition to further plates after Canaletto. Brustolon's most famous series, also published by Furlanetto, was *Feste dogali* (1766–*c*. 1770; see 1983 exh. cat., pp. 87–93, nos 59–66), featuring 12 large engravings of ceremonies and festivals attended by the Doge, derived from drawings by Canaletto. Around 1779 Brustolon started work on a series of 24 architectural capriccios after Canaletto (see 1976 exh. cat., nos 65–8), which was never completed. On 29 September 1780 he asked for the exclusive rights to make a series of 22 prints representing views of Rome, the original drawings of which had been given to him by Canaletto's heirs (London, BM; one Darmstadt, Hess. Landesmus.). The most complete series is in the library of the Correr Museum, Venice, entitled *Varii prospetti di Roma antica e moderna*. Apart from reproductive prints, Brustolon also engraved book illustrations, as for example the plates in Antonio Francesco Gori's *Dactyliotheca Smithiana* (Venice, 1767), a two-volume catalogue of the gem collection of Consul Joseph Smith, published by Giambattista Pasquali.

PRINTS

Prospectuum aedium, viarumque insigniorum urbis Venetiarum (Venice, 1763)
Feste dogali (Venice, 1766–*c*. 1770)
A. F. Gori: *Dactyliotheca Smithiana*, 2 vols (Venice, 1767)

BIBLIOGRAPHY

DBI
G. Moschini: *Dell'incisione in Venezia* (Venice, 1924), pp. 144, 170
L. Alpago Novello: 'Gli incisori bellunesi', *Atti Reale Ist. Ven. Sci., Lett. & A.*, xcix (1939–40), pp. 557–73
R. Gallo: 'L'incisione nel '700 a Venezia e a Bassano', *Ateneo Ven.*, v–vii (1941), pp. 153–214
W. G. Constable: *Canaletto* (Oxford, 1962); rev. by J. G. Links (Oxford, 3/1989), ii, pp. 673–4
Aspetti dell'incisione veneziana del settecento (exh. cat., ed. G. Dillon and R. da Tos; Venice, Scu. Grande S Teodoro, 1976), pp. 23–5
Da Carlevarijs ai Tiepolo: Incisiori veneti e friulani del settecento (exh. cat. by D. Succi, Venice, Correr; Govizia, Mus. Prov. Pal. Attems; 1983), pp. 81–93

DARIO SUCCI

Brutalism. Term applied to the architectural style of exposed rough concrete and large modernist block forms, which flourished in the 1960s and 1970s and which derived from the architecture of Le Corbusier. The term originated from *béton brut* (Fr.: 'raw concrete') and was given overtones of cultural significance not only by Le Corbusier's dictum 'L'architecture, c'est avec des matières brutes établir des rapports émouvants' ('Architecture is the establishing of moving relationships with raw materials'), but also by the *art brut* of Jean Dubuffet and others, which emphasized the material and heavily impastoed surfaces. The epitome of Brutalism in this original sense is seen in the forms and surface treatment of its first major monument, Le Corbusier's Unité d'Habitation de Grandeur Conforme (1948–54; see fig.) in Marseille (for another illustrated example *see* LASDUN, DENYS). The ultimate disgrace of Brutalism in this same sense is to be seen in the innumerable blocks of flats built throughout the world that use the prestige of Le Corbusier's *béton brut* as an excuse for low-cost surface treatments. In Le Corbusier's own buildings exposed concrete is usually very carefully detailed, with particular attention to the surface patterns created by the timber shuttering, and this can be seen in the work of more conscientious followers of the mode such as Lasdun or Atelier 5.

The definition of the compound term New Brutalism is more contentious and was part of the disputes and polemics of British architecture in the 1950s and 1960s. The debate began with Alison and Peter Smithson, who came to prominence in 1949 by winning a competition for the design of a new school at Hunstanton in Norfolk. On completion in 1954 this 'uncompromising' design was clearly seen to be inspired by works of Ludwig Mies van der Rohe, and as such its relatively refined detailing seems far from the usual connotations of the term Brutalism.

Le Corbusier: Unité d'Habitation de Grandeur Conforme, Marseille, 1948–54

However Hunstanton came to be seen as the first step for the more forceful and more obviously Brutalist architecture of Stirling & Gowan and others. During the school's construction period, however, the Smithsons engaged in a variety of architectural polemics, in the course of which Peter Smithson claimed of one of their own unexecuted designs that it would have been the first exponent of New Brutalism in England if it had been built. The project in question was for a small house of simple brick and timber construction, but the term New Brutalism already had overtones beyond meaning unpretentious or unaffected.

Wherever the phrase came from it was clearly intended as a counter to such coinages as 'New Humanism' or 'New Empiricism'. The former was a short-lived term coined by Marxist architects, and the latter was a label invented by the editors of the influential monthly the *Architectural Review* to describe the compromise between traditional and modern domestic architecture that had been developed in Sweden during World War II for large-scale social housing. This style, with its flush wall-surfaces, large windows, projecting balconies, wooden detailing and pitched roofs, was much imitated in post-war England but was also much despised by radical younger architects, for whom the Smithsons became a mouthpiece. The apparent disparity between the elegant steel and glass of the school and the plain blunt brick and timber of the house design underlines the essential aspect of New Brutalism as a polemic: it was not ostensibly concerned with style and was, in the Smithsons' phrase, 'an ethic, not an aesthetic'.

Philip Johnson compared this attitude to that of Adolf Loos, which was perceptive and fair insofar as New Brutalism was not concerned with style but with the making of significant spaces and the honest expression of construction. Its increasing contempt for composition in the traditional sense and its insistence on image were not, however, related to Loos's work. Unlike the rather formal plan of Hunstanton, or the studied axiality of their entry for the Coventry Cathedral competition (1951), later Smithson designs such as the Sugden house (1956) often display a deliberately un-composed quality; the architects were attacked for this, although the designs show a similarity to Le Corbusier's un-composed works of the same period, such as the Maisons Jaoul (1955), which were considered beyond attack. In the Smithsons' view the strength of Le Corbusier was that, over and above the urbanistic and social vision, like Mies van der Rohe he produced works that delivered very powerful visual images. As their work became more preoccupied with visual image, it began to exhibit the qualities of the more generic Brutalism; there is little doubt that their polemics, their teaching and the example of their executed works such as the Economist Building (1964; for illustration *see* SMITHSON) in London, probably the most urbane as well as the most programmatically New Brutalist work, did a great deal to establish the usage of the term Brutalism in good currency. As such it proved a useful way of labelling building as diverse as Louis Kahn's University Art Gallery (1953) at Yale, New Haven, CT, which comes very close to the Smithsons' ideas in some ways, the early housing of Stirling & Gowan (who rejected the term as being bad for client relations) and the 'Brick Brutalist' works of Sigurd Lewerentz or Oswald Mathias Ungers.

It is doubtful if any of the architects mentioned above ever set out deliberately to design Brutalist or New Brutalist buildings. The case of the Italian architect Vittoriano Viganó (*b* 1919) is different; his buildings (1959) for the Istituto Marchiondi Spagliardi, Baggio, were hailed by Italian writers as being specifically New Brutalist and were probably intended so by Viganó, with full acceptance of the Smithsons' stance of ethic not aesthetic.

BIBLIOGRAPHY

Le Corbusier: *L'Unité d'habitation de Marseille* (Paris, 1950); Eng. trans. as *The Marseille Block* (London, 1950)
R. Banham: 'New Brutalism', *Archit. Rev.* [London], cxviii (1955), pp. 355–8
M. Webb: *Architecture in Britain Today* (London, 1964)
A. Smithson and P. Smithson, eds: *Team 10 Primer* (London, 1965)
R. Banham: *The New Brutalism: Ethic or Aesthetic?* (London, 1966)
'Banham's Bumper Book on Brutalism Discussed by Alison and Peter Smithson', *Architects' J.*, cxliv (1966), pp. 1590–91

REYNER BANHAM

Brütt, Adolf (Carl Johannes) (*b* Husum, 10 May 1855; *d* Bad Berka, 9 Nov 1939). German sculptor. He was the son of the miniaturist Barthold Friedrich Brütt (1816–66). After training as a mason (1871–5), he entered service both as a stuccoist and mason, and he trained during the winter semesters of 1875–6, 1876–7 and 1877–8 at the Berlin Akademie under the sculptor Fritz Schaper. In 1878 he worked with Leopold Rau (1847–80); and he exhibited a plaster bust of *Rau* (untraced, see Steckner, p. 14) at the 1880 Akademie exhibition. Brütt's first commission was the bust of *Frederick-Franz II* (1879; untraced; pen sketch, see Steckner, p. 14) and his first public commission the plaster group *Cain and Abel* (1880; untraced). Around 1880 he produced a plaster bust of *Botho Graf Eulenburg* (untraced, see Steckner, p. 16). From 1881 he worked as a mason again, assisting Gustav Eberlein and contributing to the dinner service made for the wedding of Prince William, later Emperor William II (1881; untraced, see sketch for silver jug, Steckner, p. 19).

Brütt spent 1883 in Venice and Florence. His first work to achieve renown was the bronze sculpture *The Fisherman* (or *Saved*; 1887; Flensburg, Mus. Park), which presents a stalwart figure carrying the limp body of a woman saved from drowning. Another important work from this period is the bronze group *Eve with her Children* (1890; Flensburg, Städt. Mus.). In 1892 Brütt was made a member of the Berlin Akademie, where he became a professor in 1896. For the Siegesallee in Berlin he made the marble figures *Otto the Idle* (1899; destr., see Steckner, p. 50) and *Frederick William II* (1900; destr., see Steckner, p. 50), and later (1903) the marble monument to *Emperor Frederick* (destr., see Steckner, p. 50). In 1901 Brütt was one of the founders of the Akademische Schule für Bildende Künste (later the Akademie Fehr) in Berlin. While Brütt continued to provide many official monuments, for example the bronze equestrian monument to *Emperor William I* (1893–6; Kiel) and four marble reliefs on the *Life of William I* (1906; Berlin, Kaiser-Wilhelm-Gedächtniskirche), he also produced dramatic imaginary and symbolic figures, such as the *Woman Wielding a Sword* (1896; Kiel, Rathaus).

Between 1905 and 1910 Brütt had a studio in Weimar, and from 1907 a foundry there. He made sculpture for the Weimar Hoftheater, the University of Jena and the Deutsche Bank in Berlin (1909). His style gradually developed away from the curved forms of the neo-Baroque, and in works such as the symbolic figure group *Night* (1908; untraced, see Steckner, p. 63) his figures became simpler and his arrangements more fluid. With the *Momsen Monument* (1909; now Berlin, Universitätstrasse) he established a much more severe style, adhering strongly to the sense of the stone block and inspired by ancient Egyptian sculpture seen on a journey to Egypt in 1907. Among Brütt's later female figures, however, a softer style was preserved, as in the seated figure *Opus 100* (1909; Berlin, Gerichtstr., Krematorium) and the marble group *Diana with the Wounded Deer* (1913; Berlin, Schöneberg, Rathaus).

BIBLIOGRAPHY

Bénézit; Thieme–Becker
P. Bloch and W. Grzimek: *Das klassische Berlin: Die Berliner Bildhauerschule im 19. Jahrhundert* (Berlin, 1978)
C. Steckner: *Die Sparsamkeit der Alten: Kultureller und technologischer Wandel zwischen 1871 und 1914 in seiner Auswirkung auf die Forschung des Bildhauers Adolf Brütt (1855–1939)* (Frankfurt am Main, 1981)
Von Begas bis Barlach: Bildhauerei im wilhelminischen Berlin (exh. cat., W. Berlin, Kolbe Mus., 1984)
Ethos und Pathos: Die Berliner Bildhauerschule 1786–1914 (exh. cat., ed. P. Bloch, S. Einholz and J. von Simson; Berlin, Staatl. Museen, 1990)

BRIGITTE HÜFLER

Bruyas, Alfred (*b* Montpellier, 15 Aug 1821; *d* Montpellier, 1 Jan 1877). French patron and collector. He was born into a Protestant banking family and received a liberal education. In 1840 he started to take instruction in painting from Charles Mattet (1791–1870), a teacher at the Ecole des Beaux-Arts in Montpellier and curator of the Musée Fabre there. His delicate health (he had tuberculosis) prevented him from taking up a profession, but his private fortune enabled him to devote his time to art and artists. In 1846 he visited Italy and while in Rome frequented the Académie de France at the Villa Medici, where he commissioned his portrait from Alexandre Cabanel (Montpellier, Mus. Fabre). In 1848 he commissioned from Auguste-Barthélémy Glaize a picture showing the *Study of Alfred Bruyas* (Montpellier, Mus. Fabre), and thus for the first time demonstrated publicly his vocation as a patron. Towards the end of 1849 Bruyas left Montpellier for Paris, where he stayed for long periods up to 1854. He was a frequent visitor to museums, the Salon, artists' studios and dealers' galleries. He posed for Thomas Couture and bought works by Jean-Baptiste-Camille Corot, Narcisse Diaz, Jean-François Millet, Théodore Rousseau, Octave Tassaert and Constant Troyon. His most important purchase, however, was the 1849 version of Eugène Delacroix's *Women of Algiers* (Montpellier, Mus. Fabre).

In 1852 Bruyas drew up a first catalogue of his collection, which showed clearly his enthusiasm for contemporary French art. Between then and 1876 he was to publish four additional catalogues. The close friendship that he sought with the artists of his time is well illustrated by a painting by Octave Tassaert dated 1853, *Alfred Bruyas in Tassaert's Studio* (Montpellier, Mus. Fabre), in which Bruyas is standing in front of the easel as if he were the artist. At the Salon of 1853, which was notable for the scandal caused by the works of Gustave Courbet, Bruyas purchased the most controversial painting in the exhibition: *The Bathers* (Montpellier, Mus. Fabre). In addition, he commissioned a portrait of himself from this Realist painter. The high regard he had for Courbet, and his friendship with him, were the major influences on his future as a patron and a collector. The two men shared a profound concern to protect the creativity of the artist from the growing influence both of the art market and of the State. In 1854 Courbet spent several months in Montpellier, and the intensive dialogue that brought the two men together resulted in a continuous succession of portraits and self-portraits. The best known is still *The Meeting* (Montpellier, Mus. Fabre), which was shown at the 1855 Exposition Universelle in Paris, and went down in history with the title of *Bonjour Monsieur Courbet*. Bruyas financed the one-man exhibition that Courbet mounted at the time of the official exhibition as a manifesto of Realism. Bruyas features prominently in Courbet's enormous *Painter's Studio* (Paris, Mus. d'Orsay; *see* COURBET, GUSTAVE, fig. 3), one of the paintings he showed there. In 1868 Bruyas offered his collection to the Musée Fabre in Montpellier, followed up by a legacy in 1877. This important collection of French 19th-century art consists of 142 paintings, including 19 portraits of the donor, as well as 84 drawings and 18 sculptures, of which 17 are bronzes by Antoine-Louis Barye.

BIBLIOGRAPHY

J. Claparède: *Montpellier, Mus. Fabre: Dessins de la collection Alfred Bruyas et autres dessins des XIXe et XXe siècles* (Paris, 1962) [Inventaire des collections publiques françaises No. 6]

Le Roman d'un collectionneur: Alfred Bruyas (1821–1877) (exh. cat. by X. Dejean, Montpellier, Mus. Fabre, 1977)

M. Haedeke: *Alfred Bruyas: Kunstgeschichtliche Studie zum Mäzenatentum im 19. Jahrhundert* (Frankfurt am Main, 1980)

Courbet à Montpellier (exh. cat. by P. Bordes, Montpellier, Mus. Fabre, 1985)

PIERRE CHESSEX

Bruyenne, Justin (*b* Tournai, 1811; *d* Tournai, 1896). Belgian architect. He worked mainly as a church architect, both on new buildings and on restorations, where he was able to exploit his archaeological interests. He is primarily known for his work on the restoration (1851) of Tournai Cathedral, where, following the precepts of Viollet-le-Duc, he inserted into the west front a rose window recognized by later research as an obvious anachronism (*see* TOURNAI, §4(i)). In 1861, following the death of Bruno Renard, he became the leading architect of Tournai. His rise to prominence coincided with the shift in architectural taste away from classicism towards the richer eclecticism characteristic of the second half of the 19th century. His churches at Allain (St Amand, *c*. 1860), Tournai (Redemptorists' Church, 1862), Obigies (St Amand) and Hérinnes (Ste Aldegonde, 1865) were essays in Romanesque Revival. Despite a certain schematic quality and crispness of outline that mark them as modern structures, they are distinguished from earlier Belgian Romanesque Revival monuments by their greater apparent weight, material polychromy and self-consciously antiquarian details. During the 1860s Bruyenne, who was an active member of Belgium's Commission Royale des Monuments et des Sites, was consulted on plans for shoring up or restoring several of the most important medieval and Renaissance monuments in Tournai. In the medieval tower of the church of St Jean he replaced an 18th-century portal with a Gothic Revival one (1863), and he radically modified the windows in the façade of St Nicolas (1868) in order to achieve a more coherent 13th-century appearance. In his restoration work Bruyenne aimed at producing tidy archaeological images, even at the expense of destroying genuine but perhaps visually discordant historical evidence. His later work, mainly in the province of Hainaut, included the Gothic Revival church of St Etienne (1870), Templeuve, additions (1871) to the church at Monceau-sur-Sambre, and churches at Seneffe (1873) and Saint-Sauveur (1882–4). He also designed a hospital (1873) at Sint-Truiden.

BIBLIOGRAPHY

E. de Seyn: *Dictionnaire biographique des sciences, des lettres et des arts en Belgique*, i (Brussels, 1935)

Le Patrimoine monumental de la Belgique, vi (1978) and xiii (1988) (Liège, 1971–) [Prov. de Hainaut: Arrondissement de Tournai, Arrondissement de Ath]

L. Verpoest and G. Bekaert: *België neogotiek* (Antwerp, 1989)

ALFRED WILLIS

Bruyère, Louis (*b* Lyon, 19 March 1758; *d* 31 Dec 1831). French architect, engineer, writer and painter. He worked from an early age in the office of an architect called Maigre, who was a relative of Antoine-Michel Perrache (1726–79), the leading architect and engineer in Lyon of his day. In 1783 Bruyère entered the Ecole des Ponts et Chaussées, Paris, and in 1784 worked on the foundations of the bridge across the Moselle at Frouart. In 1785 he was involved in the design of several bridges in Lyon under the direction of Jean-François Lallié, and the following year became Sous-Ingénieur in Le Mans, where he laid out the Promenade du Greffier and the Promenade des Jacobins (after 1789) and built the grain market.

Bruyère left the Service des Ponts et Chaussées in 1793 to dedicate himself to painting and building. Nothing is known of his painted work, but his buildings include the Maison Boissy on the edge of the Forêt de Montmorency, and in Paris his own house on Rue Chauchat (1798) and further houses on Rue de Ponthieu and at 99 Rue du Faubourg Saint-Honoré. He was appointed Ingénieur Ordinaire and Professeur de Stéréotomie in 1798 at the Ecole des Ponts et Chaussées. From 1801 he was occupied with providing Paris with water. The construction of the Canal de l'Ourcq called for the building of a whole series of fountains, which gained him the post of Ingénieur-en-Chef in 1802. In 1805 commissions in Italy dealing with navigation in the Po Valley led Bruyère to study problems in urban planning; in the same year, he was appointed Secrétaire du Conseil des Ponts et Chaussées. He built his own house at 7 Rue de Port-Mahon (begun 1806), while other work at this time included projects for the Canal de Saint-Maur (1807–8) and crucial reports on the Pont d'Iéna, Paris, and the re-establishment of the Machine de Marly (1810), the means by which water was supplied to the fountains at Versailles.

In 1811 Bruyère was appointed director of public works in Paris and Maître des Requêtes at the Conseil d'Etat, a function he held until 1820. In this capacity he dealt not only with such utilitarian works as markets, granaries, butchers' shops, slaughter-houses and wharves, at a time when particular interest was taken in these types of structures, but also with the great buildings of the Empire, for example La Madeleine, the Bourse, and the Arc de Triomphe. Bruyère's role was that of intermediary and arbitrator between engineers and architects and the various ministers and prefects, but his real part in the conception and execution of these buildings remains undetermined.

Having retired from his posts because of ill health, Bruyère published his various projects as *Etudes relatives à l'art des constructions* (1823–8). It is subdivided into 12 compendia dedicated to such public works as bridges, markets and waterways, and to such private works as houses and a plan for a village. His interest in constructional problems was demonstrated by the inclusion of a section on tiles. His last work included research on mortar, hydraulics, artificial cements and the invention of his so-called *ciment Bruyère*. For want of commissions to build monuments, Bruyère sometimes conceived of counter-projects, such as the transformation of the Arc de Triomphe into a fountain (*c.* 1815). A man of great culture, Bruyère was a pragmatic administrator endowed with great qualities, whose career was not affected by political changes. His systematic and comparativist intellectual approach was close to that of Jean-Nicolas-Louis Durand, without, however, taking on a doctrinaire character. The totality of his work remains to be studied.

WRITINGS

Rapport du 9 floréal an x, sur les moyens de fournir l'eau nécessaire à la ville de Paris, et particulièrement sur la dérivation des rivières de l'Ourcq, de la Beuvronne, de l'Yvette, de la Bièvre, et d'autres (Paris, 1804)
Etudes relatives à l'art des constructions, 2 vols (Paris, 1823–8)

BIBLIOGRAPHY

Michaud
J.-C. Krafft and N. Ransonnette: *Plans, coupes, élévations des plus belles maisons et des hôtels construits à Paris et dans les environs* (Paris, 1801), pl. 59
A. Donnet: *Description des environs de Paris* (Paris, 1824), p. 34, pl. 6
C. Navier: *Notice sur M. Bruyère* (Paris, 1833)
A. Lorion: 'Louis Bruyère et les grands travaux de Paris de 1811 à 1820', *An. Ponts & Chaussées*, vi (1965), pp. 363–72
P. Marachiello and G. Teyssot: *Nascita delle città di stato, ingegneri e architetti sotto il Consolato e l'impero* (Rome, 1983)
J. Eynaud de Fay: 'L'Etape sarthoise de Louis Bruyère', *Rev. Pays Loire*, xii (1987), pp. 110–21
A. Picon: *L'Invention de l'ingénieur moderne: L'Ecole des ponts et chaussées, 1747–1851* (Paris, 1992)

WERNER SZAMBIEN

Bruyn [Bruen; Bruin; Bruns]. German family of painters. (1) Bartholomäus Bruyn (i), either the son-in-law or brother-in-law of JAN JOEST, had three sons. The eldest, Arnt [Arnold] Bruyn (*b* ?1520s; *d* Cologne, 17 Sept 1577), worked in the family shop, collaborating with his father and his more successful younger brother (2) Bartholomäus Bruyn (ii) in 1547 on paintings for Cologne's Karmelitenkloster (see below). He is also attributed with a portrait of *Gerhard Pilgrum*, Mayor of Cologne (1571), and altarpieces in Werden of the *Gathering of the Manna* and the *Angel Bringing Food to Elijah in the Wilderness*, and he is recorded as cleaning altarpieces by Stefan Lochner and Jan Joest. He died of the plague and in debt. The youngest son of Bartholomäus Bruyn (i), Matthias Bruyn, registered to study at the University of Cologne in 1538.

(1) Bartholomäus [Bartel; Bartold] **Bruyn (i)** (*b* Wesel or Cologne, 1493; *d* Cologne 1555). He was the leading portrait painter in Cologne in the 16th century. His birth date is known from Friedrich Hagenauer's portrait medallion of 1539, inscribed BARTHOLOMAUS BRUYN PICTOR COLONIENSIS ANNO AETATIS XLVI. His earliest documented altarpiece, the *Coronation of the Virgin* (1515–16; German priv. col.), was painted for Dr Peter von Clapis, law professor of the University of Cologne, and his wife. On 20 December 1525 he acknowledged receipt of payment for his paintings for the high altar of Essen Cathedral, a commission received in 1522 (of the two pairs of wings one is extant: it has eight panels showing scenes from the *Life of Christ*). On 22 April 1529 he contracted to do a cycle of paintings for the new high altar of St Victor at Xanten, with the *Lives of SS Victor and Helena* and scenes from the *Life of Christ*: he completed the work in 1534. Bruyn received a commission in 1541 to clean Jan Joest's altarpiece at Werden. In 1547 he began a major commission of scenes from the New Testament (all destr., except *Temptation of Christ*; Bonn, Rhein. Landesmus.) for the cloister of Cologne's Karmelitenkloster, which he completed with the assistance of his sons Arnt Bruyn and (2) Bartholomäus Bruyn (ii); he later painted altarpieces (*in situ*) for the churches of St Andrew and St Severin in Cologne.

Bruyn's painting style evolved throughout his career as the styles around him evolved; he seems to have readily assimilated all of the newest trends. His early altarpieces reflect the style of Jan Joest, a relative from whom he received a bequest. Bruyn sometimes utilized Jan Joest's method of placing the light source low within the picture so that the figures are highlighted by the eerie light from below, as in the *Nativity*, a 1516 altar for the von Clapis

1. Bartholomäus Bruyn (i): *Christ Carrying the Cross*, oil on panel, 749×585 mm, *c.* 1512–15 (Munich, Alte Pinakothek)

family (Frankfurt am Main, Städel. Kstinst.). While working on the Essen altarpiece (1522–25), the highpoint of his early work, he continued to rely on Jan Joest's motifs and began to show interest in the work of Joos van Cleve. He adopted that artist's fanciful processions, splendid garments and buildings decorated with classicizing ornament, and he even copied directly some of Joos van Cleve's landscapes. Bruyn's earlier work is filled with active figures, often in exaggerated positions (see fig. 1).

Later, while he worked on the Xanten altar (1529–34), Bruyn emulated the classicizing figures and heroic style of the Italian Renaissance, drawing particularly on Raphael and Michelangelo. For example, on the outside of a portrait diptych of members of the *Rolinxwerth Family* (1529; The Hague, priv. col.) the contrapposto pose of Lucretia is a copy of Raphael's *Galatea* (1511–12; Rome, Villa Farnesina). The figure groups and compositions in the double wings of the Xanten altar, the statuesque saints in the *Lives of SS Victor and Helena*, the *Ecce homo* and the *Resurrection* are early examples of his second-hand Mannerism. Late works feature muscular Italianate figures in affected poses and robust movement. Although some early scholars proposed an Italian trip, it is now generally accepted that these Renaissance forms reached Bruyn by way of the Romanists Jan van Scorel and Martin van Heemskerck, and through Marcantonio Raimondi's prints after Raphael.

Many of the altar panels include group portraits, and Bartholomäus Bruyn (i) is celebrated more for his portraits than for his altars. He founded an important school for portraiture in Cologne, which had not previously had a portrait tradition. Since Bruyn did not sign any of his portraits, and they are not documented as his altarpieces are, scholars have assigned his many attributed portraits by style, based primarily on the Essen and Xanten altarpieces. His portraits, mostly of the patrician citizens of Cologne—mayors, public officials, businessmen and scholars—are lively and expressive, and they show no vain flattery. Bruyn was an honest and direct portrait painter, who represented his fellow citizens with understanding and respect. He began work with preparatory sketches, sometimes catching the likeness in a single sitting. Some of these preparatory sketches are extant (see Rosenberg, 1935; Westhoff-Krummacher, 1965). Often he placed the waist-length figure against a flat green or blue, but occasionally he included drapery or architectural elements, or a landscape, as in the portrait of *Arnold von Brauweiler, Mayor of Cologne* (1535; Cologne, Wallraf-Richartz-Mus.; see fig. 2). Bruyn's portraits focus attention on faces but do not omit any detail of clothing, headdress, or jewellery. Hands are prominent, often gesturing or holding an object that further illuminates the identification, status or character of the sitter. The earlier portraits are in the style of Joos van Cleve; then after 1539 they are influenced by Hans Holbein (ii). In fact, some early inventories attributed his drawings to Holbein. Bruyn's portrait school was very prolific and, through his sons, long-lived.

Throughout his career, Bartholomäus Bruyn was active in civic affairs and was a member of the same upper-middle-class Cologne society that he portrayed with such frankness and dignity. In 1518 and again in 1521 he was elected to Cologne's auxiliary council; in 1549 and 1553

2. Bartholomäus Bruyn (i): *Arnold von Brauweiler, Mayor of Cologne*, oil on panel, 570×405 mm, 1535 (Cologne, Wallraf-Richartz-Museum)

he was elected to the City Council. He is recorded as buying in 1533 the houses 'Carbunckel' and 'Aldegryn', property that had once belonged to the painter Stefan Lochner.

BIBLIOGRAPHY

Thieme–Becker

J. J. Merlo: *Nachrichten von dem Leben und den Werken kölnischer Künstler* (Cologne, 1850) [early archival studies]

E. Firmenich-Richartz: *Bartholomäus Bruyn und seine Schule* (Leipzig, 1891)

J. Rosenberg: 'Bartholomäus Bruyn (1493–1555)', *Old Master Drgs*, x (1935), pp. 52–3

Barthel Bruyn, 1493–1555: Gesamtverzeichnis seiner Bildnisse und Altarwerke: Gedächtnisausstellung aus Anlass seines 400 Todestages (Cologne, 1955)

H.-J. Tümmers: 'Der Manierismus des älteren Bartholomäus Bruyn', *Museion* (1960), pp. 232–6

H. Krummacher: 'Bildniszeichnungen von Bartholomäus Bruyn d. Ä.', *Wallraf-Richartz-Jb.*, xxvi (1964), pp. 59–72 [many attrib.]

P. Pieper: 'Ein Bildnispaar von Barthel Bruyn', *Bonner Jb. Rhein. Landesmus. Bonn & Ver. Altertfreunden Rheinlande*, clxiv (1964), pp. 395–406

H.-J. Tümmers: *Die Altarbilder des älteren Bartholomäus Bruyn* [incl. cat.] (Cologne, 1964)

H. Westhoff-Krummacher: *Barthel Bruyn der Ältere als Bildnismaler*, xxxv of Kunstwissenschaftliche Studien (Munich, 1965)

O. H. Förster: 'Das Salomon-Urteil des Bartholomäus Bruyn', *Wallraf-Richartz-Jb.*, xxviii (1966), pp. 15–30

W. Kemp: 'Vom Segen und Fluch Noahs: Zu einem Bild des Barthel Bruyn im Bonner Landesmuseum', *Rheinisches Landesmus.*, ii (1975), pp. 24–7

H.-J. Tümmers: *Bartholomäus Bruyn der Ältere, 1493–1555: Ein Maler vom Niederrhein* (Cologne, 1982)

——: 'Zwei unbekannte Tafelbilder von Bartholomäus Bruyn dem Älteren', *Wallraf-Richartz-Jb.*, xliii (1982), pp. 115–22
J. M. Collier: 'A Self-portrait by Barthel Bruyn the Elder', *Bull. Mus. A. Archaeol., U. Michigan*, vi (1983–4), pp. 56–63
G. C. Rump: 'Grosse Ankäufe eines kleinen Museums', *Die Weltkunst*, lviii (1988), p. 2818
P. Hacker and C. Kuhl: 'A Portrait of Anne of Cleves', *Burl. Mag.*, cxxxiv (1992), pp. 172–5

(2) Bartholomäus [Barthel] **Bruyn (ii)** (*b* Cologne, *c.* 1530; *d* Cologne, 1607/10). Son of (1) Bartholomäus Bruyn (i). Best known for his portraits of the citizens of Cologne, he trained in the workshop of his father, and inherited the shop and its clientele in 1555. In 1571, following a settlement with his siblings, he attained full possession of the two old houses near the Albankirche, 'Carbunckel' and 'Aldegryn', that comprised the Bruyn shop. Like his father and his older brother Arnt he was active in Cologne affairs, being elected to the City Council in 1567, 1580, and 1607; in 1591 he took on the official position of Bannerherr. About 1590, when his failing eyesight stopped him painting, he closed the workshop.

Bartholomäus worked with his father and with Arnt on paintings (begun 1547) of 57 scenes from the New Testament for the cloisters of Cologne's Karmelitenkloster (only one survives: Bonn, Rhein. Landesmus.). Scheibler (1883) was the first scholar to group the artist's work by style; he named the painter 'Meisters mit den blassen Gesichtern'. Firmenich-Richartz (1891) connected Scheibler's cluster of paintings with the name Bartholomäus Bruyn the younger, and he and other scholars have grouped his works by style around his only signed painting, a diptych for Abbot Peter Ulner of *Christ Carrying the Cross* and *Vanitas* (1560; Bonn, Rhein. Landesmus.). Several entries in 'Das Buch Weinsberg' (ed. Höhlbaum, Lau and Stein) confirm the identification of the name with the style (e.g. portrait of the Carthusian *Laurentius Surius*, ii, p. 87; 1557 altarpiece for Hermann van Weinsberg, iii, p. 7). Through style scholars have continued to attribute to Bartholomäus Bruyn (ii) many portraits and some religious paintings (see Firmenich-Richartz in Thieme–Becker and Tümmers). His portraits, though somewhat more simplified than his father's, are admirable for their pleasing design, precise rendering of details and surface texture, full modelling and enamel-like surfaces. He is noted for his subdued colour harmonies, often limited to black, white, silver grey, browns and delicate flesh tones. Bruyn continued his father's direct, lifelike type of portraiture, long after this originally Netherlandish style was out of fashion.

BIBLIOGRAPHY

Thieme–Becker
L. Scheibler: *Katalog der Königliche Gemälde-Galerie zu Berlin* (Berlin, 1883), p. 317
K. Höhlbaum, F. Lau and J. Stein, eds: 'Das Buch Weinsberg', *Publikationen der Gesellschaft für Rheinische Geschichtskunde* (i, Leipzig, 1886; ii, Leipzig, 1887; iii, Bonn, 1897)
E. Firmenich-Richartz: *Bartholomäus Bruyn und seine Schule* (Leipzig, 1891), pp. 133–47
F. A. Sweet: 'Woman with a Prayer Book by Barthel Bruyn the Younger', *Bull. A. Inst. Chicago*, xxxv (1941), p. 34
H.-J. Tümmers: 'Bartholomäus Bruyn der jüngere', *Wallraf-Richartz-Jb.*, xxxii (1970), pp. 113–34 [life and attrib.]
H. Seifertova: 'Kölner Bildnisse in Böhmen', *Wallraf-Richartz-Jb.*, l (1989), pp. 321–7
M. Didier: 'Le Portrait-obiit de Lambert Lombard représente-t-il réellement le peintre liégeois?', *Wallraf-Richartz-Jb.*, lii (1991), pp. 77–90
German Paintings of the Fifteenth through the Seventeenth Centuries (exh. cat. by J. O. Hand, Washington, DC, N.G.A., 1993), pp. 22–4

JEAN M. CASWELL

Bruyn, de. Flemish family of artists.

BIBLIOGRAPHY

Hollstein: *Dut. & Flem.*; Thieme–Becker; Wurzbach

(1) Abraham de Bruyn (*b* Antwerp, 1540; *d* ?Cologne, 1587). Engraver and publisher. His earliest dated engravings are two series: *Friezes with Hunting Scenes* (1565–6; Hollstein, nos 61–6) and *Ornaments with Figures on a Black Background* (1566, 1569; Hollstein, nos 121–6). From those same years comes an excellent engraving of a *Horseman of the Apocalypse* (1568; Hollstein, no. 42) and a series of *Apostles* (1568; Hollstein, nos 16–27). In 1570 he was working in Breda, where he engraved series of illustrations for Christoph Plantin (e.g. engravings after Pieter van der Borcht IV and Crispijn de Passe I for the *Humanes salutis monumenta* of B. A. Montanus, 1571; Hollstein, nos 384–455, and engravings after van der Borcht for *Officium B. Mariae Virginis*, 1575; Hollstein, nos 32–5). From 1577–*c.* 1580 Abraham was in Cologne, where he published a series of costumes from various countries and continents for the *Omnium poene gentium imagines* (1577) and the *Imperii ac sacerdotii ornatus: Diversarum item gentium peculiaris vestitus* (1578). On his return to Antwerp, he executed a new series of costume studies in *Omnium pene Europae, Asiae, Aphricae atque Americae gentium habitus* (1581; Hollstein, nos 248–306), in which he included several prints unchanged from the 1577 and 1578 publications. A new edition also appeared in 1581, published by J. de Bosscher. These publications provide an important source of information on 16th-century costumes.

After 1580 de Bruyn was back in Antwerp, where he worked for Plantin frequently, producing illustrations for the *François Duc d'Anjou: La Joyeuse et Magnifique Entrée de Monsieur François et sa très renommée ville d'Anvers* (1582; Hollstein, nos 469–89) and a title-page with the figure of Belgium for Guicciardini's *Descrittione di . . . tutti Paesi Bassi* (1581; Hollstein, no. 490). He also engraved ornament designs and mythological scenes and collaborated with Frans Huys on a series of portraits of rulers, which was published by Hans Liefrinck.

BIBLIOGRAPHY

G. K. Nagler: *Neues allgemeines Künstler-Lexikon*, 22 vols (Munich, 1835–52), ii, p. 178
C. Le Blanc: *Manuel de l'amateur d'estampes* (Paris, 1856–88), i, p. 353
G. K. Nagler: *Monogrammisten* (1858–1920), i, pp. 233, 246, 410
J.-C. Brunet: *Manuel de libraire et de l'amateur de livres*, i (Paris, 1860), cols 1287–8
J. J. Merlo: *Leben und Werken kölnischer Künstler* (Düsseldorf, 1893–5), i, p. 67
J. G. T. Graesse: *Trésors de livres rares et précieux*, i (Berlin, 1922), p. 551
M. Funck: *Le Livre belge à gravures* (Paris and Brussels, 1925), p. 287
Vijftien jaar aanwinsten sedert de eerst steenlegging tot de plechtige inwijding van de Bibliotheek [Fifteen years of acquisitions since the ceremonial laying of the foundation-stone of the library] (exh. cat., Brussels, Bib. Royale Albert 1er, 1969), pp. 243–5, no. 247
T. Gerzi: *Netherlandish Drawings in the Budapest Museum: 16th-century Drawings* (Amsterdam, 1971), i, p. 32, no. 3811
Tekeningen en prenten uit Antwerpens Gouden Eeuw (exh. cat.; Nijmegen, Mus. Commanderie St-Jan; Dordrecht, Dordrechts Mus.; Bergen-op-Zoom, Het Markiezenhof; Haarlem, Frans Halsmus.; 1980), nos 58–9

CHRISTINE VAN MULDERS

(2) Nicolaes de Bruyn (*b* Antwerp, 1571; *d* Rotterdam, 1656). Engraver, painter and dealer, son of (1) Abraham de Bruyn. His earliest known works are a series of prints dated 1594 (Hollstein, nos 212–23, 256–73) that continue in his father's tradition; they were published by Assuerus van Londerseel (1572–1635), although de Bruyn later published his own works. He married Assuerus's sister Suzanna van Londerseel, and their brother Jan van Londerseel became his student. De Bruyn was registered in 1601 as a master in Antwerp's Guild of St Luke; by 1617 he is recorded in Rotterdam, where he worked for the rest of his life. An inventory of his possessions in 1632 included a house on the Rijweg in Gouda, a quantity of copper plates and paintings by him and prints by his contemporaries; none of his own paintings has been identified.

De Bruyn's best work dates from the period 1601–10 and consists primarily of engravings after designs by Gillis van Coninxloo and David Vinckboons, both of whom were initially employed by tapestry studios and concentrated on subjects drawn from nature. The compositions are mostly landscaped gardens and formal parks, in which elegant groups of people amuse themselves. When biblical subjects occur, they are subordinated to the landscape settings. In the same style, de Bruyn also engraved a landscape with a deer hunt after Jan Breughel I. He followed the style of van Coninxloo and Vinckboons in his own designs, although these all have biblical subjects and are large (usually 445×650 mm). After 1610, the human figures in de Bruyn's prints became larger and the religious aspects dominated. He no longer drew inspiration from tapestry but from the work of the earlier master Lucas van Leyden, whose compositions he copied closely at a time when others were concentrating on the work of such Mannerists as Bartholomäus Spranger, Hendrick Goltzius and Abraham Bloemart. In common with most engravers of the 16th century and early 17th, he also produced instructional series on such subjects as the Ages of Man, the Seasons, the Four Elements and the Virtues. His series on domestic animals, birds and fish were popular, but these prints are of lesser artistic quality than his others. Throughout his career he was at his best working after the designs of others. Hollstein includes 274 prints in various editions: his publishers included his son-in-law, Frans von Beusecom, Frederick de Wit, Gerard Valck, Pieter Goes, Robert Baudous and, later, Claes Jansz. Visscher I, who published numerous plates in reduced format.

BIBLIOGRAPHY

Hollstein: *Dut. & Flem.*; Thieme–Becker

A. Bredius: *Künstler-Inventäre: Urkunden zur Geschichte der holländischen Kunst des XVI., XVII. und XVIII. Jahrhunderts*, 8 vols (The Hague, 1915–22), v, pp. 1599–603

A. J. J. Delen: *Histoire de la gravure dans les anciens Pays-Bas et dans les provinces belges des origines jusqu'à la fin du XVIIIe siècle* (Paris, 1935)

Nicolaes de Bruyn (1571–1656): Vlaamse elegance in Rotterdam (exh. leaflet by J. Burgers, Rotterdam, Mus. Boymans–van Beuningen, 1986)

JACQUELINE BURGERS

Bruyn van Berendrecht, Michiel de (*b* Utrecht, *c.* 1608; *d* ?London, *c.* 1664). Dutch silversmith. In 1622 he was apprenticed to Adam van Vianen and was admitted to the gold- and silversmiths' guild of Utrecht in 1630. After his marriage to Antonietta van Haerlem in 1636, he set up house in the Mariaplaats, Utrecht. His work was strongly influenced by that of Adam van Vianen and, after the latter's death in 1627, by his son Christiaen van Vianen. A small oval dish with a seated Bacchus on the rim dates from 1637 (Laasne, Cl. D'Allemagne priv. col., see *Zeldzaam zilver uit de gouden eeuw* (exh. cat., Utrecht, Cent. Mus., 1984), no. 103). Bruyn van Berendrecht became known as a producer of Catholic church silver: candelabra, chalices, ewers and salvers, decorated with a mixture of swag ornament and Baroque floral designs. A pair of silver kneeling angels from 1648 is considered one of Bruyn van Berendrecht's most important works, and a pair of Baroque wall sconces of 1653 has wax-catchers in the shape of tulips (Amsterdam, Rijksmus.). In 1660 he formed a partnership with Christiaen van Vianen and accompanied him to England. His son Nicolaes de Bruyn van Berendrecht (apprentice in 1656) was married in London to Aletta, a daughter of Christiaen van Vianen, and was mentioned in a document of 1668 as a 'Jeweller of London' (ter Molen, p. 84).

BIBLIOGRAPHY

J. W. Frederiks: *Dutch Silver*, 4 vols (The Hague, 1952–61)

Nederlands zilver, 1580–1830/Dutch silver, 1580–1830 (exh. cat., ed. A. L. den Blaauwen; Amsterdam, Rijksmus., 1979) [bilingual text], fig. 46

J. R. ter Molen: *Van Vianen: Een Utrechtse familie van zilversmeden met internationale faam* (diss., U. Leiden, 1984)

Kunst uit Oud-Katholieke kerken (exh. cat., ed. P. Dirkse; Utrecht, Catharijneconvent, 1989), nos 94–102

LOUISE E. VAN DEN BERGH-HOOGTERP

Bry, de. Franco-Flemish family of artists, active in Germany.

(1) Theodor de Bry [Dietrich Brey; Dittert Bry] (*b* Liège, 1528; *d* Frankfurt am Main, 29 March 1598). Engraver, printmaker, publisher and goldsmith. He was apparently trained in Liège as a goldsmith and engraver and was active (under the name Dietrich Brey) as a goldsmith in Strasbourg, where in 1560 he married Catherine Esslinger (*d* 1570). He returned to Liège in 1561, where his eldest son, (2) Johann Theodor de Bry, was born, but because of his Lutheran religious convictions de Bry left Liège again to establish citizenship in Strasbourg, where he lived from 1570 to *c.* 1586 and where his second son, Johann Israel de Bry (*b* Liège, before 1570; *d* Frankfurt, 1611), was born. While there he came under the stylistic influence of the Parisian Huguenot Etienne Delaune, who had fled to Strasbourg in 1572. De Bry was married a second time, in 1570, to Catherine, daughter of the Frankfurt goldsmith Hans Rotlinger. In 1588 the de Bry household moved permanently to Frankfurt while Theodor was in England (*c.* 1586–9) making engraved copies after the watercolours of JOHN WHITE of scenes from the New World. These, with his copies after similar works by Jacques Le Moyne de Morgues, are his best-known engravings and were used as illustrations in the ten volumes of American travel literature (*Grands voyages*, Frankfurt am Main, 1590–1618) that he and his sons published. These were a compilation of Girolamo Benzoni's *History of the New World*, Thomas Hariot's *Briefe and True Report of the New Found Land of Virginia* (*see* NATIVE NORTH AMERICAN ART, fig. 51) and a memoir by

Hans Staden of his adventures among the cannibals of Brazil. De Bry's Lutheran bias led him to emphasize the cruelty of the Spanish conquerors toward the natives they encountered in Peru, and his landscape and figure formulae were made to conform to European standards (the influences of Joachim Patinir and Herri met de Bles are particularly striking). These engravings were the medium through which most Europeans came to view the costumes and customs of the American Indians. He also published a series of portraits of famous men—including Gerard Mercator (1512–94) and Copernicus (1473–1543)—engraved after drawings by Jean-Jacques Boissard (*Icones quinquaginta vivorum illustrium doctrine et eruditione praestantium ad vivum effectae*, Frankfurt am Main, 1597–9). The engravings, by a number of different artists, form an important precedent for van Dyck's *Iconographie* of 1632–44.

(2) Johann [Jean] **Theodor de Bry** (*b* Liège, 1561; *d* Frankfurt am Main, 1623). Engraver, etcher, printmaker and publisher, son of (1) Theodor de Bry. He was the most prolific printmaker of the family, practising both engraving and etching. With his father and his brother Johann Israel, he published two popular emblem books: *Emblemata nobilitate et vulgo scitu digna* (Frankfurt am Main, 1593; Paris, 1895) and *Emblemata secularia* (Oppenheim, 1611). With his brother he also published the design of a grotesque and quasi-erotic human alphabet (Hollstein, nos 119–69). His independent work includes reproductive engravings after such masters as Titian, Marten de Vos, Abraham Bloemaert and Sebald Beham.

BIBLIOGRAPHY

Hollstein: *Dut. & Flem.*

H. S. Hüsgen: *Artistisches Magazin, enthaltend das Leben und die Verzeichnisse der Werke hiesiger und anderer Künstler* (Frankfurt am Main, 1790), pp. 93–109

A. M. Hind, M. Corbett and M. Norton: *Engraving in England in the Sixteenth and Seventeenth Centuries: A Descriptive Catalogue with Introduction*, 3 vols (Cambridge, 1952–64), i, pp. 124–37

Lambert Lombard et son temps (exh. cat. by L. Moyano, Liège, Mus. A. Wallon, 1966), pp. xlvii–l, 88–95

The European Vision of America (exh. cat. by H. Honour, Washington, DC, N.G.A.; Cleveland, OH, Mus. A.; Paris, Grand Pal.; 1975–7)

The New Golden Land: European Images of America from the Discoveries to the Present Time (New York, 1975) [based on 1975–7 exh. cat.]

JANE CAMPBELL HUTCHISON

Bryan, Michael (*b* Newcastle upon Tyne, 9 April 1757; *d* London, 21 March 1821). English art historian, connoisseur and dealer. He went to the Continent in 1781 to study art and married Juliana Talbot, sister of Charles Talbot, 15th Earl of Shrewsbury, on 7 June 1784. In London after 1790 he established himself as an authority on painting. In 1798 he negotiated the sale of the Italian and French pictures from the Orléans collection, by then in England, to Francis Egerton, 3rd Duke of Bridgewater, George Granville Leveson-Gower, Earl Gower (later 2nd Marquess of Stafford and 1st Duke of Sutherland) and Frederick Howard, 5th Earl of Carlisle, for the sum of £43,500. The collection was exhibited in London at Bryan's gallery in Pall Mall and at the Lyceum in the Strand. The pictures that the original purchasers did not wish to retain were sold to, among others, John Julius Angerstein, who bought Sebastiano del Piombo's *Raising of Lazarus* (1516–18; London, N.G.). In the course of his commercial activities Bryan built up a collection of his own, which he sold on 17–19 May 1798. Among the pictures in the sale was Gabriel Metsu's *Man and Woman beside a Virginal* (*c.* 1658; London, N.G.). In 1801 he formed a syndicate with Sir Simon Clarke and George Hibbert and purchased 47 pictures from the Robit collection in Paris. The pictures brought to England included works by Murillo, van Dyck, Claude and Rembrandt, a number of which were afterwards offered for sale by Bryan. In 1812 he started work on his authoritative *A Biographical and Critical Dictionary of Painters and Engravers*, which was published in 1816.

WRITINGS

A Biographical and Critical Dictionary of Painters and Engravers, 2 vols (London, 1816); rev. ed. G. C. Williamson; *Bryan's Dictionary of Painters and Engravers*, 5 vols (4/1903/*R* 1920)

BIBLIOGRAPHY

W. Buchanan: *Memoirs of Painting* (London, 1824), i, pp. 18–21, 271–96; ii, p. 35

E. Mackenzie: *A Descriptive and Historical Account of the Town and Country of Newcastle-upon-Tyne*, i (Newcastle upon Tyne, 1827), p. 589

R. Welford: *Men of Mark 'twixt Tyne and Tweed*, i (London, 1895), pp. 422–4

□

Bryans, Lina (*b* Hamburg, 26 Aug 1909). Australian painter of German birth. Untrained, she took up painting in 1936 at the suggestion of William Frater (1890–1974), a pioneer of modernist art in Melbourne who had been much influenced by Post-Impressionism. Over the next decade she developed a close working relationship with Frater. From 1943 to 1948 she lived at Darebin Bridge House, a converted hotel, which became a meeting place for artists and writers and was known as the 'painter's pub': Frater, Ambrose Hallen (1886–1943) and Ian Fairweather had studios there. It was a stimulating and productive period. Her working method was rapid and intuitive. The vitality of her work derives most from the vigorous handling of paint and the strongly felt and immediate response to the subject. Colour was her main interest, and she used it to express mood and emotion. Subjects include cityscapes and a number of fine portraits: one of the best, the *Babe Is Wise* (1940; Melbourne, N.G. Victoria), captures the vibrant personality of the novelist Jean Campbell.

In 1953 Bryans travelled to Europe and America, making contact with Valentine Prax (*b* 1899) and Ossip Zadkine in Paris. Around 1964 she explored the possibilities of abstraction, reducing her landscapes to sensitive floating patterns of colour evocative of the forms and rhythms of the Australian bush, for example in *The Bush 1* (1965; Melbourne, N.G. Victoria). After 1971 she ceased painting.

BIBLIOGRAPHY

B. Burdett: 'Australian Art Today', *The Studio*, cxv (1938), pp. 3–18

——: 'Modern Art in Melbourne', *A. Australia*, n. s. 2, lxxiii (1938), pp. 12–23

Lina Bryans: A Retrospective Exhibition (exh. cat., Melbourne, N.G. Victoria, 1982)

M. Eagle: 'Lina Bryans', *A. & Australia*, xxi (1983), pp. 231–9

JAN MINCHIN

Bryant, Gridley J(ames) F(ox) (*b* Boston, MA, 29 Aug 1816; *d* Boston, 8 June 1899). American architect. He was the son of the engineer and railway pioneer Gridley Bryant. He trained in the office of Alexander Parris and Loammi Baldwin in the 1830s and was practising on his own by the autumn of 1837. In the 1840s he designed railway stations and commercial buildings, for example the Long Wharf Bonded Warehouse (1846; destr.) in Boston. During the next decade he also designed schools and court-houses and was involved in no fewer than 30 asylum projects following the design of his influential Charles Street Jail (1848–51), Boston, in conjunction with the prison reformer, the Rev. Louis Dwight. This adaptation of the Auburn System of prison discipline to a cruciform plan became the first executed American project to be published in the British architectural periodical *The Builder* (vol. VII, 1849, no. 326). When the great fire of 1872 devastated Boston's central business district, destroying 152 buildings designed by Bryant, he received commissions to rebuild 111 of them. He was also responsible for 19 state-capitol and city-hall projects, 95 court-houses, asylums and schools, 16 custom-houses and post offices and eight churches. He worked extensively with ARTHUR DELAVAN GILMAN, who seems to have been responsible for design, while Bryant supervised the construction of such projects as the former Boston City Hall (1862–5), School Street. Primarily remembered as a great commercial architect and a leading figure in the latter stages of the Boston 'granite school', Bryant was also an innovator in an emerging profession. He was one of the first American practitioners to use labour-saving standardized plans, to specialize in particular building types, to develop a large office and to introduce new styles. In the middle decades of the 19th century he presided over a practice that was regional if not quite national in scope.

BIBLIOGRAPHY

MEA

H. T. Bailey: 'An Architect of the Old School', *New England Mag.*, xxv (1901), pp. 326–48

W. H. Kilham: *Boston after Bulfinch* (Cambridge, MA, 1946)

B. Bunting: *Houses of Boston's Back Bay* (Cambridge, MA, 1967)

H. R. Hitchcock and W. Seale: *Temples of Democracy: The State Capitols of the USA* (New York, 1976)

R. B. MacKay: *The Charles Street Jail: Hegemony of a Design* (diss., U. Boston, MA, 1980)

ROBERT B. MACKAY

Bryaxis (*fl* second half of 4th century BC). Greek sculptor. Though his name shows him to have been a native of Caria in Asia Minor, he was trained in Athens. There his name first occurs *c.* 350 BC on a signed marble base (Athens, N. Archaeol. Mus., 1733), which carries a dedication relating to the victories of an Athenian family in the *anthippasia* (a horsemanship contest). On the three subsidiary sides of the base are inferior quality low-relief carvings of horsemen and tripods. Indeed, the base may have supported a bronze tripod. Bryaxis was described as a 'bronzeworker' by Pliny (*Natural History* XXXIV.lxxiii), who recorded two of his works, an *Asklepios* and a portrait of *Seleukos I Nikator* (*reg* 305–281 BC; both untraced). It is not certain if the former was the statue of *Asklepios* by Bryaxis that Pausanias (*Guide to Greece* I.xl.6) saw, together with a statue of *Hygieia* by him in Megara (both untraced).

As a young sculptor Bryaxis is reported to have worked with LEOCHARES, SKOPAS and TIMOTHEOS on the sculptural decoration of the Mausoleum at HALIKARNASSOS (*c.* 360–350 BC), where he undertook the north side of the monument (Pliny: *Natural History* XXXVI.xxx–xxxi; Vitruvius: *On Architecture* VII. Preface xii–xiii). Attempts have been made to assign to him some of the slabs of the *Amazonomachy* frieze, based mainly on the occurrence of the same horse type as on the Athenian base (various slabs in London, BM, have been proposed; e.g. nos 1009 and 1019, or 1018, 1019, 1020 and 1021). The traditional attribution to Bryaxis of the two famous portrait statues from the Mausoleum, known as *Mausolos* and *Artemisia* (both London, BM), is also doubtful.

Bryaxis apparently executed most of his works in Asia Minor. These included a marble statue of *Dionysos* in Knidos (Pliny: *Natural History* XXXVI.xxii), five bronze colossal statues of deities in Rhodes (*Natural History* XXXIV.xlii) and probably also a group of *Zeus and Apollo with Lions* in Patara, Lycia, also ascribed to Pheidias (Clement of Alexandria: *Protreptikos* IV.xlvii; all untraced). One ancient source (Georgios Kedrenos: *Synopsis of Histories* 536 B) states that the colossal cult statue (h. *c.* 12 m) of the standing *Apollo with a Lyre* at Daphne near Antioch was a work of Bryaxis. Since Antioch was founded in 301 BC by Seleukos I Nikator, this work could help to date Bryaxis's later career, although the statue may have been made earlier for another city and transferred to Antioch. Its type is known from a coin of Antiochos IV Epiphanes (*reg* 175–163 BC; ex-R. Jameson priv. col.) and some Roman Imperial coins, as well as through the description of ancient writers (e.g. Libanius: *Oratio* LXI). The *Apollo* was an acrolith with its clothed parts gilded; it depicted the god standing in *peplos* and mantle, holding the lyre with his left hand and a patera in his right. It must have had a great impact on Late Hellenistic and Roman statues of Apollo and the Muses, which probably echo Bryaxis's lost original.

More intricate problems are posed by the colossal seated cult statue (h. *c.* 12 m) of *Sarapis* (a deity combining the Greek Hades and the Egyptian Osiris–Apis) in Alexandria, associated with Bryaxis by Athenodoros of Tarsos (quoted in Clement of Alexandria: *Protreptikos* IV.xliii). The original work was destroyed by Christians in the 4th century AD, but there is an over life-size version in the Graeco-Roman Museum in Alexandria. The original was probably commissioned by Ptolemy I Soter (*reg* 305–283 BC) but if made in the early 3rd century BC, it could hardly have been by the Classical Bryaxis and might have been the work of a younger member of the same family. Some ancient sources (Tacitus: *Histories* IV.lxxxiii–lxxxiv; Plutarch: *Isis and Osiris* XXVIII) suggest that an earlier statue of Hades was made by Bryaxis for the city of Sinope at the Black Sea but transferred to Egypt during the reign of Ptolemy I. Another account (Tacitus: *Histories* IV.lxxxiv) states that the statue was made in the late 4th century BC for Memphis in Egypt and later transferred to Alexandria.

The *Sarapis* consisted of a wooden core, probably covered with a combination of various metals and precious stones, giving its surface a dark blue shade (it may, however, have been chryselephantine; see Hornbostel, 1973). Sarapis was depicted as a god both of fertility and of the underworld, in a manner based on a combination of Greek and non-Greek elements. He wore a tunic and mantle, with a *kalathos* (a standard measure of grain) on his head, and he had thick hair and a full beard. He held a sceptre in his left hand, and his right hand was about to touch one of the three heads of Kerberos standing beside him.

Among copies of other lost works assigned to Bryaxis on the basis of similarities to the head of *Sarapis* is the head of the Otricoli *Zeus* (Rome, Vatican, Mus. Pio-Clementino). Bryaxis is generally regarded as the Late Classical who reinterpreted the figures of the Greek gods and combined Greek form with non-Greek mentality, so that they reflected the emerging Hellenistic civilization.

See also GREECE, ANCIENT, §IV, 2(iv)(b).

BIBLIOGRAPHY

Enc. A. Ant.
G. Lippold: 'Sarapis and Bryaxis', *Festschrift P. Arndt zu seinem sechzigsten Geburtstag*, ed. F. Beckmann (Munich, 1925), pp. 115–27
J. H. Jongkees: 'New Statues by Bryaxis', *J. Hell. Stud.*, lxviii (1948), pp. 29–39
G. Lippold: *Griechische Plastik* (Munich, 1951), pp. 257–60
F. F. Schwarz: *Bryaxis: Eine Studie zur Persönlichkeitsforschung in der bildenden Kunst des 4. Jhs. v. Chr.* (Graz, 1961)
J. Charbonneaux: 'Bryaxis et le Sérapis d'Alexandrie', *Monuments et mémoires: Fondation E. Piot*, LII/ii (1962), pp. 15–26
C. Picard: *Manuel d'archéologie grecque: La Sculpture*, vols i–iv (Paris, 1935–63)
J. J. Pollitt: *The Art of Greece, 1400–31 BC: Sources and Documents* (Englewood Cliffs, 1965, rev. Cambridge, 1990)
W. Hermann: 'Zum Apollo Borghese', *A. Ant.* (1973), pp. 658–63
W. Hornbostel: *Sarapis: Studien zur Ueberlieferungsgeschichte, der Erscheinungsformen und Wandlungen der Gestalt eines Gottes* (Leiden, 1973)
C. M. Robertson: *A History of Greek Art*, 2 vols (Cambridge, 1975)
F. F. Schwarz: 'Nigra maiestas: Bryaxis–Sarapis-Claudian', *Classica e provincialia: Festschrift Erna Diez* (Graz, 1978)
G. B. Waywell: *The Free-standing Sculptures of the Mausoleum at Halicarnassus in the British Museum* (London, 1978)
A. Linfert: 'Der Apollon von Daphne des Bryaxis', *Damas. Mitt.*, i (1983), pp. 165–73
J. J. Pollitt: *Art in the Hellenistic Age* (Cambridge, 1986)
B. S. Ridgway: *Hellenistic Sculpture: The Styles of c. 331–200 BC* (Bristol, 1992), pp. 95–7
L. Todisco: *Scultura greca del IV secolo: Maestri e scuole di statuaria tra classicità ed ellenismo* (Milan, 1993), pp. 88–91

I. LEVENTI

Brydges, James, 1st Duke of Chandos (*b* Dewshall, Hereford & Worcs, 6 Jan 1673; *d* Edgware, Middx, 9 Aug 1744). English patron and collector. He was educated at New College, Oxford, married in 1696 and became MP for Hereford in 1698; in 1705 he was appointed Paymaster-General of the Army abroad. As a result of this appointment he amassed an immense private fortune, part of which he channelled into picture-buying, corresponding with dealers in Amsterdam and buying eclectically on their recommendation.

In 1712 Brydges's wife died; the following year he inherited from her uncle an estate at Cannons, Middx, and soon after he engaged William Talman to design stables for it and George London to lay out new gardens. As was usual with Talman, there were sharp financial altercations, and Brydges replaced him with John James. The north front of the existing house was remodelled by James but he failed to provide a satisfactory design for the south front. By April 1715 Brydges had engaged Sir John Vanbrugh to replace him as principal adviser. The following year James Gibbs was appointed to rebuild the house and chapel. Gibbs appears to have designed the house's south and east elevations and its chapel, but he was dismissed in 1719. During this period Brydges continued to buy pictures: through Henry Davenant, an envoy in Italy, he obtained Guercino's *Samson and Delilah* and Annibale Caracci's *Jupiter and Leda*; via dealers in Rotterdam he bought Alessandro Turchi's *Lot and his Daughters* and two pictures then attributed to Guido Reni—a *Virgin and Child* and the *Angel Awakening Elijah*. These were displayed at Cannons, the interiors of which were enriched with gilding and decorative paintings. The Saloon's ceiling was undertaken by Sir James Thornhill, while Antonio Bellucci was responsible for the ceilings of the State Bedchamber and the Library, in the latter of which he depicted the *Seven Liberal Arts and Sciences*. Bellucci, along with Louis Laguerre, Francesco Sleter (1685–1775) and the carver Grinling Gibbons, all worked on the interior of the neighbouring church of St Lawrence, Little Stanmore, which was almost entirely rebuilt from 1715 with funding from Brydges. Its rich decoration (restored in 1982–5) is a rare example of the full Baroque style in an English parish church, and provided a suitable setting for the composer George Frideric Handel's 'Chandos Anthems', begun in 1716 at Cannons when Handel was serving as director of music there.

In 1719 Brydges was created Duke of Chandos by George I. Although Cannons became a wonder of the age, it was short-lived. On 6 May 1747, three years after Brydges's death, the contents of the house were sold. His collection of pictures, which included works by Sir Peter Lely, the Teniers family and Peter Paul Rubens, was dispersed, along with Joseph Goupy's copies of the Raphael Cartoons and the chapel's decorative paintings and fittings. Two works, by Gerrit Dou and Willem van Mieris, were acquired by Richard, 7th Viscount Fitzwilliam. The house itself was destroyed soon after the sale.

BIBLIOGRAPHY

J. R. Robinson: *The Princely Chandos: A Memoir of James Brydges* (London, 1893)
C. H. Collins Baker and M. I. Baker: *The Life and Circumstances of James Brydges, First Duke of Chandos* (Oxford, 1949)
I. Dunlop: 'Cannons, Middlesex: A Conjectural Reconstruction', *Country Life*, cvi (30 Dec 1949), pp. 1950–54
Treasures for the Nation: Conserving our Heritage (exh. cat., London, BM, 1989), pp. 44–5

CHARLES SAUMAREZ SMITH

Brydon, J(ohn) M(cKean) (*b* Dunfermline, Fife, 1840; *d* London, May 1901). Scottish architect. He began his architectural training in 1856 as an articled student to Douglas Hay of Liverpool. After three years he left to travel in Italy, returning in 1860 to serve with David Bryce (1803–76) in Edinburgh. In 1863 Brydon joined the office of J. J. Stevenson and Campbell Douglas (1828–1910) in Glasgow, a firm that produced many outstanding architects. Through his move in May 1866 to the London office of Richard Norman Shaw and W. E. Nesfield as their chief assistant, Brydon became familiar with the mainstream of the QUEEN ANNE REVIVAL. By 1871, however, he had set up a decorating business in Langham Place with the architects William Wallace and Daniel Cottier (1838–91). In true Arts and Crafts tradition, Brydon specialized in furniture design, and he gave great attention to interior decoration in all his later buildings.

Brydon's design for St Peter's Hospital (1883–4; later Institute of Urology; interior extensively altered) in Henrietta Street, Covent Garden, London, heralded his return to full architectural practice. Carried out in Shaw's redbrick style, St Peter's set a stylistic precedent for Brydon's later hospital buildings in London: the Hospital for Women (1889–94; now the Elizabeth Garrett Anderson Hospital), Euston Road; and the School of Medicine for Women (1896), Judd Street, Bloomsbury. Both of these were undertaken for England's first woman physician, Dr Elizabeth Garrett Anderson (1836–1917).

During the late 1880s and the 1890s Brydon emerged as an outspoken leader of the nationalistic movement to revive English classical architecture in its earlier forms, then regarded as purer. The lectures he delivered at the Architectural Association in London were especially influential in creating a renewed interest in British architecture from Inigo Jones to Charles Robert Cockerell. His buildings reflect this passion for English sources, although he was never loath to introduce elements of Italian Renaissance or support the flowering of the Arts and Crafts as it related to architecture. This blend of classical discipline with the contemporary freedom in the arts marks Brydon's later buildings as fine examples of the Edwardian BAROQUE REVIVAL.

Brydon's addition to the Chelsea Town Hall (1885–7), King's Road, London, and his designs for the nearby Chelsea Free Library, Manresa Road (1889–91; now the Library Building, King's College), and Chelsea Polytechnic (1891–5; now the Medical Centre, King's College) exemplify his work in the Hampton Court style of Christopher Wren. His sympathy for the 18th century, however, reached an apogee in the work he did at Bath. His designs for the extension of the Guildhall (1891–5) are no less than an enhancement of the surviving building of 1776 by Thomas Baldwin (1750–1820), while the Ball Room (1894–5) for the famous Pump Room, the Technical Schools (1895–6) and the Victoria Art Gallery and Library (1899–1900) are in perfect harmony with the fabric of the Georgian city.

In 1898 Brydon received his largest commission, for the New Government Offices (now called Treasury Chambers), Great George Street, London, though he died long before its completion in 1913. This large Portland stone building in Whitehall, which dominates the north side of Parliament Square, has towers inspired by those of St Paul's Cathedral and has a large circular courtyard at its centre. Nowhere is Brydon's overriding concern for the integration of architecture, sculpture and craftsmanship more in evidence, with wrought-iron gates by the Bromsgrove Guild and sculpture by Bertram MacKennell, Paul Raphael Montford and William Silver Frith (1850–1924), who was also responsible for the decorative detailing around windows and doors.

WRITINGS

'The English Renaissance of the Eighteenth Century', *Builder*, lx (1891), pp. 129–31

'William Eden Nesfield, 1835–1883', *Archit. Rev.* [London], i (1896), pp. 235–47, 283–95

'The Work of Professor Cockerell, R. A.', *Builder*, lxxviii (1900), pp. 520–21

BIBLIOGRAPHY

DNB

Obituary, *Builder*, lxxx (1901), pp. 540–41

A. Service: *Edwardian Architecture: A Handbook to Building Design in Britain, 1890–1914* (London, 1977)

A. S. Gray: *Edwardian Architecture: A Biographical Dictionary* (London, 1985)

NEIL R. BINGHAM

Bryen, Camille (*b* Nantes, 17 Sept 1907; *d* Paris, 8 May 1977). French painter, sculptor, draughtsman and poet. He moved in 1926 to Paris, where he became involved with Surrealism, soon afterwards publishing his first collection of poems, *Opoponax* (Paris, 1927). In 1934 he exhibited a series of automatic drawings, which were followed by images produced with the assistance of *objets trouvés*: in *Street Object* (1936; Paris, Pompidou), for instance, he placed a sheet of paper on the road and then drove a car over it so as to leave the imprint of the tyre tracks. Another work of this period consisted of a bus sign bearing the same letters as his initials, so that it could be read as his signature. He also produced assemblages in a Surrealist spirit, such as *Morphology of Desire* (wood, plaster, metal, candle and torch, 1934–7; Paris, Pompidou). After World War II Bryen turned increasingly towards painting, through which he became a leading exponent of ART INFORMEL. His works in this style included drawings in ink and watercolour executed with apparent speed and spontaneity (e.g. *Watercolour No. 307*, 1949; Paris, Pompidou), and oil paintings of fairly modest dimensions, such as *Hépérile* (1951; Paris, Pompidou), for which he used thick paint sometimes straight from the tube. The colour in these dense works is dark and subdued, reflecting the anxieties of the immediate post-war years. This sense was only gradually alleviated in the mid-1950s, when more intense hues and a clearer separation between mark and ground emerged, as in *Informalie* (1954; Le Havre, Mus. B.-A.). Between the linear scaffolding more solid blocks of varied colour asserted themselves in the late 1950s. Although these blocks expanded across the whole surface and the lines became fine and dotted, this formal vocabulary came to characterize all Bryen's subsequent painting. His later paintings, such as *Patron Monet* (1972; Paris, Pompidou), harked back to Impressionism in their overriding concern with the play of light and colour. He also illustrated many texts by contemporary poets.

WRITINGS

Parole . . . parle! (Paris, 1945)

BIBLIOGRAPHY

R. V. Gindertael: *Bryen* (Paris, 1960)

D. Abadie: *Bryen abhomme* (Brussels, 1973)

Bryen (exh. cat., preface J. Leymarie; Paris, Mus. N. A. Mod., 1973)

J. Bouret-Loyer: *Camille Bryen: L'Œuvre peint* (Paris, 1986)

For further bibliography *see* ART INFORMEL.

VANINA COSTA

Bryggman, Erik (William) (*b* Turku, 7 Feb 1891; *d* Turku, 21 Dec 1955). Finnish architect. He studied at the school of the Turku Art Society, then studied architecture at the Technical University in Helsinki (1910–16). While there he travelled to Sweden and Denmark with Hilding Ekelund, and his experience abroad led him to abandon the National Romanticism characteristic of his student architecture projects. In particular he was influenced by Sigurd Lewerentz's unbuilt scheme for a crematorium in

Hälsingborg, Sweden. Several successful competition entries for religious architecture were central to his early work: church, Tammisto, Viborg, Denmark; crematorium, Helsinki (both 1919); church (1929), Sortavala, Russia; and Tehtaanpuisto church (1930) in Helsinki. Common to all these schemes are the clever integration of the landscape and the use of clearly defined, simple architectural elements, in which light is used to create a sacred atmosphere. The Tehtaanpuisto competition sparked a public debate about the suitability of Functionalism for ecclesiastical commissions.

In 1923 Bryggman opened an office in Turku and began creating highly individual designs for blocks of flats and summer houses in the area. The Atrium flats (1927), rising in steps up Yliopistokatu Street, and the hotel Hospitz Betel (1929) are harmoniously set around a small terraced square, reminiscent of Italian vernacular architecture, which had inspired Bryggman during his trips to Italy (the first being in 1920). Towards the end of the 1920s and the beginning of the 1930s he won competitions in which he proposed strikingly pure Functionalist schemes for various building types. The book tower for the library of Åbo Akademi, Turku, completed in 1935, offered a Functionalist solution to the problem presented by a historic site: the six-storey white hexagonal building stands opposite Turku's medieval cathedral, surrounded by mid-19th-century wooden houses.

The funeral chapel (1930) at Parainen was the first of Bryggman's religious buildings to be executed. With a surface of smooth, pale plaster, it is one of the simplest church buildings of the period; under its low, saddleback roof, the chapel is lit by a tall window to one side of the altar. The mature synthesis of Bryggman's church architecture is the idyllic Resurrection Chapel (1938–41) at Turku, the masterpiece of late Finnish functionalism beautifully sited on a hill. One side of the freely styled, barrel-vaulted interior is open along its entire length to the pine forest. The bell-tower forms an independent vertical element beside the church, a traditional feature in Finland.

Throughout his career Bryggman's designs could be compared stylistically to the work of Gunnar Asplund. Bryggman's work of the 1950s continued to show his attention to details as diverse as lighting fixtures, which first became apparent in the funeral chapel at Turku, and exterior surface materials, such as his favourite pebbledash surface on the block of flats (1951) on the banks of the River Aura at Rantakatu 21, Turku. The chemistry laboratory (1951) at Åbo Akademi, Turku, and its Student Union (1950) present a humble beauty that blends in sympathetically with their historic surroundings in the centre of Turku.

BIBLIOGRAPHY

A.-L. Stigell: 'Erik Bryggman', *Finländska gestalter* [Finnish ideas], iv (Ekenäs, 1964)

Erik Bryggman: Näyttelyluettelo (exh. cat. by E. Piironen, Turku, A. Mus., 1967)

Nordisk klassicism, 1910–1930 (exh. cat., ed. S. Paavilainen; Helsinki, Mus. Fin. Archit., 1982), pp. 96–7

Erik Bryggman: Arkkitehti, 1891–1955 (exh. cat., ed. R. Nikula; Helsinki, Mus. Fin. Archit., 1991)

RIITTA NIKULA

Brygos Painter. *See* VASE PAINTERS, §II.

Brymner, William (*b* Greenock, Strathclyde, 14 Dec 1855; *d* Wallasey, Ches, 18 June 1925). Canadian painter and teacher of Scottish birth. He moved with his family to the Eastern Townships, Quebec, in 1857. Brymner's first training was under the architect Richard Cunningham Windeyer (1830–1900) in Montreal and later under Thomas Seaton Scott (1836–95), the Chief Architect for the Department of Public Works in Ottawa. He was one of the first Canadians to travel to Paris for artistic training, arriving there in 1878. He studied at the Académie Julian from 1878 to 1880, under William Bouguereau and Tony Robert-Fleury, and again from 1883 to 1885 and in 1889. The subtle tonal relationships and simple composition of a *Wreath of Flowers* (1884; Ottawa, N.G.), his diploma piece for the Royal Canadian Academy, could be found in works throughout his career. He accepted the position of Master of the School of the Art Association of Montreal in 1886, teaching there until 1921. Brymner became a well-respected teacher, and his students included Clarence Gagnon, Prudence Heward and A. Y. Jackson. In 1892 Brymner was commissioned by Sir William Van Horne to paint a series of pictures of the Canadian Rockies for the Canadian Pacific Railway (e.g. *Mount Cheops, Rogers Pass*, 1898–9; Oshawa, McLaughlin Gal.). The resultant works are ambitious in scale, painted with vigour and a sense of the monumentality of nature. Brymner's friendship with Maurice Cullen modified his early, disciplined approach to painting. He worked in both watercolour and oil and explored such subjects as landscape, figure study and genre scenes. Brymner was President of the Royal Canadian Academy from 1909 to 1917.

BIBLIOGRAPHY

William Brymner, 1855–1925: A Retrospective (exh. cat. by J. Braide, Kingston, Ont., Queen's U., Agnes Etherington A. Cent., 1979)

J. Braide: 'Painter William Brymner and the Ladies', *Can. Colr*, xv/1 (1980), pp. 23–8

LINDA JANSMA

Bryullov. Russian family of artists, of German origin. The family included various artists and craftsmen and settled in Russia in the 18th century. The brothers (1) Aleksandr Bryullov and (2) Karl Bryullov were its most notable members. Aleksandr was one of the originators and leaders of Romanticism and historicism in Russian architecture. Karl briefly became one of the most famous painters in Europe, largely on account of his huge history painting of the *Last Day of Pompeii* (1830–32; St Petersburg, Rus. Mus.); he also produced genre, religious and portrait works. Though much criticized later in the century, he was an outstanding representative of the academic style as combined with a personal response to Romanticism.

(1) Aleksandr (Pavlovich) Bryullov (*b* St Petersburg, 10 Dec 1798; *d* St Petersburg, 21 Jan 1877). Architect. He studied with his father, a craftsman who produced decorative carvings, and then in the St Petersburg Academy of Arts (1810–21) before studying architecture in Italy (1822–6) and France (1826–30). During the 1830s he designed buildings in a variety of styles, which were landmarks in the movement in Russia towards a Romantic picturesqueness. They include the Gothic Revival church in Pargolovo, near St Petersburg, the Gothic Revival house and wooden theatre in the Russian style in Grafskaya Slavyanka, the

Lutheran church of St Peter (1832–8) in the Romanesque Revival style on the Nevsky Prospect, St Petersburg, and the caravanserai for Orenburg in the Mauritanian style. In the building for the Pulkovo Observatory (1834–9), near St Petersburg, Bryullov used the Greek Revival style, combined with an unusual cruciform plan for the main building. He also built the Mikhaylovsky Theatre (1831–3; now the Maly Theatre) and the Guards Headquarters (1837–43), both in St Petersburg. He was a highly talented designer of interior decoration, as can be seen in his restoration of the rooms in the Winter Palace, St Petersburg, after a fire in 1837, where he combined refined Neo-classical decoration with intimate details that could be described as Biedermeier, and in his alterations to interiors of the Marble Palace (1845–9), St Petersburg. His designs for hospital complexes, such as the Aleksandrinsky Hospital (1845–8) and the anatomical building attached to the Medical Surgical Academy (1861), both in St Petersburg, represent one of the earliest attempts in Russia to create styles that were free from the imitation of architecture of the past. Bryullov also painted Romantic watercolour portraits such as that of *Ye. P. Bakunina* (1830–32; Moscow, Tret'yakov Gal.).

BIBLIOGRAPHY

G. A. Ol': *A. P. Bryullov* (Leningrad, 1983)

YE. I. KIRICHENKO

(2) Karl (Pavlovich) Bryullov (*b* St Petersburg, 12 Dec 1799; *d* Marciano, nr Rome, 12 June 1852). Painter. Brother of (1) Aleksandr Bryullov. He showed an outstanding talent for drawing at an early age and at the Academy of Arts, St Petersburg, won the gold medal for his oil painting the *Appearance of Three Angels to Abraham* (1821; St Petersburg, Rus. Mus.). Thanks to the patronage of the newly established Society for the Encouragement of the Arts he spent two years travelling round Europe with his brother and then settled in Rome, where they were rapturously received by various members of the Russian nobility. This patronage proved to be very beneficial, and Bryullov soon developed into one of the most outstanding portraitists of his time. He excelled in both intimate watercolours, such as the portrait of *G. N. and V. A. Olenins* (1827; Moscow, Tret'yakov Gal.), and more ceremonial portraits, such as *Countess Samoilov Leaving the Ball* (*c.* 1839; St Petersburg, Rus. Mus.) and *Giovanna Paccini on Horseback* (or *'The Rider'*, 1832; Moscow, Tret'yakov Gal.). His first genre picture, *Italian Morning* (1823; St Petersburg, Rus. Mus.), which showed a nude at a fountain, revealed a strong debt to the Bolognese school and was generally acclaimed, especially by Emperor Alexander I (*reg* 1801–25), to whom it was presented. On the Emperor's suggestion Bryullov painted its pendant, *Italian Noon* (1827; St Petersburg, Rus. Mus.), which, however, met with open hostility for its triviality and for its deviation from the classical ideal. Although Bryullov defended his right to draw inspiration from nature, the rebuke greatly affected him, and he subsequently restricted his interests in genre to a series of small watercolours.

Karl Bryullov: *Last Day of Pompeii*, oil on canvas, 4.57×6.51 m, 1830–32 (St Petersburg, Russian Museum)

Bryullov knew that a great historical picture was expected of him, and with a commission from Prince Anatole Demidov, with whom he visited Pompeii in 1828, he embarked on his gigantic canvas, the *Last Day of Pompeii* (St Petersburg, Rus. Mus.; see fig.), representing the destruction of the city. He worked in an inspired state and completed the picture in two years (1830–32). In this work, well-balanced groups designed according to the canons of academic art show the most noble expressions of self-sacrifice—children carrying their old father, a man sheltering his family, a mother imploring her son to leave her and save himself—and create a composition of extraordinary power, whose circular movement is emphasized by the use of dramatic lighting. In the centre foreground Bryullov painted a dead woman with a crawling child, a motif borrowed from Pliny's description of one of the most famous pictures of antiquity, by Aristeides, which was intended by Bryullov to symbolize the rebirth of Classical art. Yet, despite its deep debt to Raphael and Guido Reni, Bryullov's picture is too dramatic to comply fully with strict academic rules. The intensity of colour, the movement and the emotions are all pushed to extremes. It was suggested that the painting's Romantic intensity reflected the revolutionary aspirations prevalent in Russia after the Napoleonic Wars, which led to the events of the Decembrist uprising (1825). After it had been shown to huge crowds and received great acclaim in Milan and Paris, Demidov took it to St Petersburg, where he presented it to Emperor Nicholas I (*reg* 1825–55), who gave it a place of honour in the Imperial Hermitage. It was greeted as the highest achievement in Russian art, a contemporary poet claiming that 'the last day of Pompeii became the first day of Russian painting'.

Bryullov returned to St Petersburg through Greece, Turkey and Central Asia, and the last period of his life started with such exalted honours that he began to feel that he would be unable to live up to expectations. He painted a number of altarpieces for various churches, but the main commission was for the 800 sq. m dome of the newly built St Isaac's Cathedral in St Petersburg, showing the Virgin and St John the Baptist and the Apostle John surrounded by the saints whose names were those of the Imperial family. Bryullov was also entrusted with painting the *Twelve Apostles* in the transept and four altarpieces. In between this work and a huge historical picture representing the patriotic subject of the *Siege of Pskov by the Teutonic Knights* (4.82×6.75 m, 1839–43; Moscow, Tret'yakov Gal.), he produced a series of small portraits whose subtlety of colour and psychological depth are in sharp contrast to the icy colours and artificiality of the late religious paintings, for example *Nestor Kukolnik* (1836), *Ivan Krilov* (1841) and a *Self-portrait* (1848; all Moscow, Tret'yakov Gal.). Most of these were left unfinished when in 1849 Bryullov went to Madeira for health reasons, never returning to Russia.

Despite a brief period (1830–32) as one of the most popular artists in Europe, and being the first Russian painter from whom the Uffizi requested a self-portrait, the admiration Bryullov received, especially for the *Last Day of Pompeii*, was shortlived. He subsequently received harsh criticism and seemed to disappoint and irritate his most devoted admirers; this criticism persisted throughout the 19th century.

BIBLIOGRAPHY

P. Konradi: *K. Bryullov* (Kiev and Khar'kov, 1899)
I. Kubasov, ed.: *Arkhiv Bryullovich* (St Petersburg, 1900)
N. G. Mashkovzev: *K. P. Bryullov v pis'makh, dokumentakh i vospominaniyakh sovremennikov* [K. P. Bryullov in letters, documents and the reminiscences of contemporaries] (Moscow, 1961)
E. N. Azarkina: *Karl Pavlovich Bryullov: Zhizn' i tvorchestvo* [Karl Pavlovich Bryullov: life and work] (Moscow, 1963)
M. Rakova: *Bryullov portretist* (Moscow, 1965)
A. Kornilova: *Bryullov v Peterburge* [Bryullov in St Petersburg] (Leningrad, 1974)
G. Leontiyeva: *Karl Bryullov* (Leningrad and Moscow, 1983)
——: *Karl Pavlovich Bryullov* (Leningrad, 1986)
——: *Karl Bryullov: Paintings, Watercolours, Drawings* (Leningrad, 1990)
Proizvedeniya russkikh khudozhnikov iz muzeev i chastnikh kollektsiy Italii [Works of Russian artists from museums and private collections in Italy] (exh. cat., Leningrad; Bologna; Naples; Venice; 1991)

LARISSA HASKELL

Bryusov, Valery (Yakovlevich) (*b* Moscow, 1873; *d* Moscow, 9 Oct 1924). Russian poet and theorist. He is generally seen as the leader of the Russian Symbolist movement in non-visual arts, but he was also closely associated with Symbolist painters and graphic artists through the glossy journals that were mouthpieces for their synthesist philosophy. Thus during 1901–04 he contributed to the literary section of *Mir iskusstva* ('World of Art'), and from 1904 to 1909 he was editor of *Vesy* ('The scales'); in 1906–07 he wrote for *Zolotoye runo* ('Golden fleece') and during 1909–11 for *Apollon*, as well as for several literary journals. Becoming aware as a student of the growing 'decadent' trend in European poetry he set out consciously in 1893 to lead such a movement in Russia, publishing three small poetry collections in 1894–5 with a schoolfriend, A. Miropolsky-Lang. His translations of European poets such as Paul Verlaine initially brought him more respect than his early poems. Drawing heavily on formal and technical innovations abroad, Bryusov developed a theory of artistic synthesis that emphasized technical precision and control of form over mimetic or theosophical concerns. This attention to detail and emphasis on the aesthetic was symptomatic of the 'first generation' of Russian Symbolists, who, under the leadership of Bryusov and Konstantin Bal'mont (1867–1942), influenced such artists as Serge Diaghilev and Mstislav Dobuzhinsky, whose graphic scenes of St Petersburg, Riga and London share the conception in Byusov's urban verse of the modern city as a symbol of creative energy. He fell into dispute with the more metaphysical 'second generation', such as ALEKSANDR BLOK, ANDREY BELY and Vyacheslav Ivanov (1866–1949), who were deeply influenced by the religious philosopher Vladimir Solovyov (1853–1900). This caused Bryusov to distance himself from Symbolist circles after 1910 and move into teaching, publishing further translations. After the Bolshevik revolution of 1917 he adjusted more smoothly to the Soviet regime than former colleagues and had several jobs in the literary bureaucracy of the cultural commisariat NARKOMPROS, as well as publishing textbooks on versification.

BIBLIOGRAPHY

J. E. Bowlt: *The Silver Age: Russian Art of the Early Twentieth Century and the 'World of Art' Group* (Newtonville, MA, 1982)

M. P. Rice: 'Bryusov', *Handbook of Russian Literature*, ed. V. Terras (New Haven and London, 1985), pp. 61–2
J. Graffy: 'Symbolist Literature: Symbolist Writers and the Symbolist Press', *The Twilight of the Tsars: Russian Art at the Turn of the Century*, ed. M. Raeburn (London, 1991), pp. 66–75

CATHERINE COOKE

Brzozowski, Tadeusz (*b* Lwów, 1 Nov 1918; *d* Rome, 13 April 1987). Polish painter. His studies at the Academy of Fine Arts, Kraków (1936–46), were interrupted by World War II, during which he studied in the School of Artistic Trades and acted in the underground theatre of Tadeusz Kantor. From 1954 to 1987 he lived in Zakopane in the Tatra Mountains. His early paintings, for example the *Shark's Funeral* (1948) and *Ninepins* (1957), are at the same time representational and abstract; forms that abandon their narrative context return to it enriched with a wealth of purely painterly meaning.

Brzozowski's technical excellence distinguished him as the leading painter of his generation and allowed him to construct figures in decomposition, often traceable only through individual attributes or titles. These figures reflect isolated aspects of character through the roles they perform or the historic costumes they assume, as in *Cadet* (1958) or *The Recruit* (1970). In *Ceremonies* (1962) and other works from the 1960s the intangibility of the action and feelings suggested by the titles is reflected in the complicated and subtly related abstract forms. Most of Brzozowski's titles are untranslatable, utilizing as they do words torn from their context: idioms, gallicisms and archaisms. Similar to the evanescent narrative element, they recall the theme of decomposition, carrying echoes of a Surrealist richness, and are poetic. Painterly form seems to revive—delicate threads, luminous colours, pulsating areas of colour and impasto networks of dark, barbed lines—and a painterly tension arises, alluding to wounded figures and their interrelations. There is an evident resonance between the deeply revealed structure of the painting, opened out like the interior of a living organism, and the echo of the figure and its 'role'.

BIBLIOGRAPHY

Tadeusz Brzozowski (exh. cat., ed. I. Moderska; Poznań, N. Mus., 1974)
M. Porębski: *Pożegnanie z krytyką* [A farewell to criticism] (Kraków, 1983)
M. Markiewicz: *Tadeusz Brzozowski* (Warsaw, 1986)

EWA MIKINA

bsam yas. *See* SAMYE.

Bteddin. *See* BAYT AL-DIN.

Bubák, Alois (*b* Kosmonosy, Bohemia [now in the Czech Republic], 22 Aug 1824; *d* Prague, 6 March 1870). Bohemian painter. He studied at the Prague Academy of Fine Arts (1844–54), where he was one of the first pupils of Max Haushofer. Bubák's landscapes were often Alpine or idealized, but he also often painted the countryside in his native region north of Prague, especially around Český ráj and České středohoří. These paintings of hilly scenes combined contemporary ideas of the picturesque with the landscape of his own homeland (e.g. the *Craggy Rock*, 1853; Prague, N.G., Convent of St Agnes).

His abiding quality, through many fluctuations of style, was his feeling for the natural structure of a landscape, which led him to work with scientists at the National Museum in Prague, providing them with drawings and watercolours. His work remained conventionally Romantic in its impulses and stylistic repertory, and he eventually began painting large canvases that are tranquil in mood, as in *Summer Afternoon* (1863; Prague, N.G. Convent of St Agnes). These mature oils and watercolours are characterized by a delicate use of colour and diffused light. Together with Adolf Kosárek and Bedřich Havránek, Bubák was one of the leading representatives of landscape painting in Prague during the mid-19th century.

BIBLIOGRAPHY

J. Tomeš: *Alois Bubák* (Prague, 1956)
Alois Bubák a česká krajinomalba 2. poloviny 19. století [Alois Bubák and Czech landscape painting in the second half of the 19th century] (exh. cat., intro. J. Kotalík; ed. N. Blažíčková; Hlinsko, Reg. Mus. & A.G., 1987)

ROMAN PRAHL

Bubastis [Egyp. Per-Bastet; now Tell Basta, nr Zaqāzīq, Egypt]. Site in the eastern Nile Delta 77 km north-east of Cairo. It flourished *c.* 2575 BC–*c.* AD 300. The ancient city of Basta (Gr. Bubastis) was the home of the feline goddess Bastet (Egyp.: 'She of Basta'), often associated in the later periods of Egyptian history with the cat. Both the city and the cult of Bastet date back at least to the beginning of the Old Kingdom (*c.* 2575 BC). Bubastis was a significant political, economic and religious centre, and during the 22nd Dynasty (*c.* 950–*c.* 730 BC) it was home to a family of pharaohs named Osorkon and Shoshenq, who ruled the whole of Egypt. The importance of the city declined with shifting trade routes, changing political structures and above all the appearance of Christianity and later Islam, when the site was abandoned. The great temple to Bastet and her joyous festival are both described by Herodotus (*Histories* II.59–60, 137–8). In the later periods of Egyptian history at least, Bastet was seen as a beneficent deity. The remains of her now largely destroyed temple date to the 22nd Dynasty. Its huge inscribed gateways and columns, with capitals in the form of the head of the goddess Hathor, are all in red granite. They were excavated in the late 19th century.

The city is now best known as a source of the splendid bronze statues of cats (see fig.), which were interred as votive offerings in a series of above-ground, vaulted, mud-brick animal cemeteries (*see* EGYPT, ANCIENT, §VIII, 2(iii)) located on the northern edge of the city. The peculiar religious practice of burying votive objects and mummified animals sacred to a local deity was particularly widespread in Egypt during the centuries preceding the conquest of the country by Alexander the Great (332 BC). Adjacent to the animal cemeteries at Bubastis are the remains of the workshops that produced at least some of the votive objects.

The ancient wealth of the city is reflected by two caches of treasure recovered from the ruins in 1906 and now in museums in Cairo, Berlin and New York. The caches consisted of gold and silver vessels (jugs, cups, bowls, plates and strainers), often elaborately worked, as well as scrap metal and gold jewellery, including a pair of bracelets bearing the name of Ramesses II and adorned with lapis ducks. Given the homogeneity of the contents of the caches and the appearance of the name of Queen Tausert

Bubastis, statue of a cat, bronze, h. 380 mm, *c.* 700–500 BC (London, British Museum)

(*reg c.* 1193–*c.* 1190 BC) on several of them, they may be dated to the end of the 19th Dynasty when they perhaps formed part of the temple treasure.

BIBLIOGRAPHY

E. Naville: *Bubastis (1887–1889)* (London, 1891)

L. Habachi: *Tell Basta* (Cairo, 1957)

W. K. Simpson: 'The Vessels with Engraved Designs and the Repoussé Bowl from the Tell Basta Treasure', *Amer. J. Archaeol.*, lxiii (1959), pp. 29–45

C. C. van Siclen: 'The City of Basta: An Interim Report', *Newslett. Amer. Res. Cent. Egypt*, 128 (1984), pp. 28–39

CHARLES C. VAN SICLEN III

Bubich, Bernardo. *See* BOBIĆ, BERNARDO.

Buccleuch, 5th Duke of. *See* MONTAGU, (3).

Buchanan, William (*b* 1777; *d* 1864). Scottish lawyer and dealer. He was the son of Thomas Buchanan, a wealthy hat manufacturer in Glasgow. While studying law in 1799 the idea of speculating in Old Masters was suggested to him by James Irvine. Buchanan, rather than risk his own money, introduced Irvine to his brother-in-law, Alexander Gordon. In 1802, impressed by the purchases Irvine had made for Gordon, Buchanan invested £2000 of his own in the enterprise. In the same year he invited David Stewart to be his exhibiting and selling agent in London, as he was practising law in Edinburgh. By this time he had become convinced of the interest of English collectors in Old Masters, following the dispersal of the Orléans collection. He was also aware that the Napoleonic invasions were causing great hardship to Italian noblemen who were now willing to part with important pictures from their collections, and that Irvine was able to bring back to England works of the highest quality. Keen both to promote the foundation of a national gallery and to draw attention to the notable paintings that had been acquired for the syndicate in Italy, Buchanan offered three works by Rubens to William Pitt's administration (*see* CHAMPERNOWNE, ARTHUR). The offer was turned down, but the pictures quickly sold, Lady Beaumont in 1803 purchasing *Landscape with a Stone* (*c.* 1636; London, N.G.) for her husband, Sir George Beaumont.

By 1803 Buchanan had invested £12,000 in the business, having negotiated for Arthur Champernowne's half share in Irvine's original speculation. Among the collectors he approached in the following years were John Julius Angerstein and William Petty, 1st Marquess of Lansdowne. Stewart made the initial approach, and Buchanan posed as his man of business. Among the pictures that passed through Buchanan's hands were a number of doubtful attribution and, although he appears from the letters written to his agents to have adopted a somewhat belligerent manner towards collectors, he was not always successful. He suggested to Irvine that they bribe Royal Academicians, whose advice was often sought by collectors, to encourage sales. In 1804 he resorted to sending a number of pictures, including van Dyck's *Head of Charles I in Three Positions* (1636; British Royal Col.), for auction at Christie's, London. In 1805 Stewart resigned.

After various changes of partnership that involved Champernowne and William Holwell Carr, Buchanan asked George Augustus Wallis to make purchases in Spain and Portugal. Wallis succeeded in bringing to England in 1813 Raphael's Alba *Madonna* (*Madonna and Child with St John*; Washington, DC, N.G.A.; for illustration *see* CARPIO, (3)) and Velázquez's *Toilet of Venus* ('Rokeby Venus', 1647–51; London, N.G.; *see* VELÁZQUEZ, DIEGO, fig. 8). Following the downfall of Napoleon I, Buchanan dispensed with his agents on the Continent. In 1817 he succeeded in purchasing the entire collection of Dutch and Flemish paintings from the collection of Charles-Maurice de Talleyrand-Périgord; several of the Dutch paintings were sold to Edward Gray. In 1824 Buchanan published *Memoirs of Painting*, which contains a valuable account of the importation into England of Old Master paintings from the time of the French Revolution. In 1838 his fortunes revived when he was asked to dispose of Gray's collection after the latter's death. One of his later purchases was Giovanni Bellini's *St Francis in Ecstasy* (*c.* 1480; New York, Frick). In 1856 he wrote to the trustees of the National Gallery, London, appealing for recognition of the services he had rendered to the arts in England.

WRITINGS

Memoirs of Painting, 2 vols (London, 1824)

H. Brigstocke, ed.: *William Buchanan and the 19th-century Art Trade: 100 Letters to his Agents in London and Italy* (London, 1982) [incl. lengthy intro.]

BIBLIOGRAPHY

F. Herrmann: *The English as Collectors* (London, 1972)

□

Bucharest. Capital and largest city of Romania, located in the south of the country on the lower reaches of the Dimboviţa River, with a population of *c*. 2 million. It became the Romanian capital in 1861–2, after the country's unification (*see* ROMANIA, §I).

1. HISTORY AND URBAN DEVELOPMENT. Legend ascribes the founding of the city to the shepherd Bucur, but the existence of a small church of the same name puts in doubt the truth of that legend. Archaeological evidence shows habitation of the area from Palaeolithic times, and Neolithic, Bronze- and Iron-Age discoveries abound.

The formation of the present town from the 16th century was based on a fortress built during the reign of Mircea I the Old (*reg* 1386–94), who defeated the Ottoman Bayezid I (*reg* 1389–1402) to maintain the independence of Wallachia. The fortress, located at Curtea Veche, gradually extended to absorb the surrounding villages. For a long time the lifestyle of these 'outskirts' retained a partially rural character. Houses from before the 19th century have generally not been preserved, as a result partly of fires, one of which in 1847 was particularly devastating. Pictures from the period and rare preserved constructions show, however, that they were single-storey dwellings built from earth, straw and bricks, had wooden tile roofs and were surrounded with gardens; only in some central streets in the commercial areas were buildings placed in compact groups without green spaces.

The oldest Bucharest church, the Curţii Vechi, dating from the mid-16th century, is the chapel of the ruined ruler's palace. Also from the 16th century are the monasteries of Mărcuţa and Mihai Vodă (pre-1591); the latter was moved during the Nicolae Ceauşescu dictatorship (1965–89) to make way for a gigantic administrative building. Secular architecture in the 16th century included the Princely Palace, built after 1547 by Patraşcu (*reg* 1544–9) and Mircea V (*reg* 1545–52 and 1552–4).

Dating from the 17th century were the monasteries of Radu Vodă, Plumbuita and Cotroceni, the latter founded by Prince Şerban Cantacuzino (*reg* 1678–88) but later demolished by Ceauşescu. The building was in the so-called 'Brâncoveanu' style, originally named after Constantin Brâncoveanu (*reg* 1688–1714) but subsequently known as the Cantacuzino period. It characterized a number of churches in Bucharest in the early days of the city's new status as capital of Wallachia (1698), including Kretzulescu Church (1722; see fig. 1); it reached its apogee, however, in Văcăreşti monastery (1719–36; demolished under Ceauşescu), founded by Nicolae and Constantin Mavrocordat. The style was characterized by its ornamentation, using motifs and a decorative technique that combined Western Baroque and Eastern features.

1. Bucharest, Kretzulescu Church, 1722

The 19th century was characterized by the adoption of Western Neo-classical formulae, as in Ghika-Tei palace and church (1822) and in the University (1857–69) by Alexandru Orăscu, who had studied in Germany. A Romantic or Gothic Revival style also appeared in such buildings as Şuţu Palace (1830) by Konrad Schwink.

Following the unification of the principalities of Moldavia and Wallachia (1861–2), Bucharest became the capital of the new country; the end of the 19th century and beginning of the 20th were decisive for the urban configuration of the city. Until this time the streets had followed no systematic plan, but the need grew for wide, straight routes. Accordingly two principal arteries were created in the centre of the town, intersecting at University Square. At the same time the town continued to expand, absorbing the villages at its periphery. An architectural eclecticism, exemplified by such buildings as the Savings and Deposit Bank (1896–1909; *see* ROMANIA, fig. 4) by P. Gottereau, competed with a nationalistic Neo-Romanian style, created by ION MINCU and based on popular and old church architecture. The Architecture Institute (see fig. 2) by Grigore Cerchez (1850–1927) exemplified this new style, as did many private houses.

During the 1930s there was an attempt to adopt Modernist architectural forms, with such buildings as the Aro block by Horia Creanga (1893–1943). Some houses were also built in a Cubist style. Following World War II the establishment of the Communist regime transformed all aspects of life in Bucharest, including architecture. The first project of the new regime was the Spark House,

2. Bucharest, Architecture Institute by Grigore Cerchez, early 20th century

copied from Soviet Stalinist models. During the 1960s housing blocks began to appear on the outskirts of the city, and there was an increasing use of metal and glass in construction. Under Ceaușescu the destruction of monuments (e.g. the Simu Museum) reached disastrous proportions, and a large part of the old city centre disappeared to make way for Post-modern developments.

BIBLIOGRAPHY

G. Ionescu: *Istoria arhitecturei în România*, 2 vols (Bucharest, 1965)
F. Georgescu, P. Cernavodeanu and A. Cebuc: *Monumente din București* (Bucharest, 1966)
C. C. Giurescu: *Istoria Bucureștilor* (Bucharest, 1979)
G. Mucenic: *Arhitectura civilă in București in secolul al XIX-lea* (diss., U. Bucharest, 1989)

2. Art life and organization. Until the 17th century the principality of Wallachia followed the medieval tradition of the production of religious art through guilds, which trained the craftsmen. Pārvu Mutu was believed to have opened a private school in Bucharest *c.* 1702, and artistic activity also emanated from various religious institutions. From the late 18th century Bucharest came into contact with the art of the Western tradition, largely through the influence of the Enlightenment in Vienna; Neo-classicism and Romanticism also made their mark on Romanian artists, but it was only in the 1860s, following the unification of the country and Bucharest's establishment as the capital (1861–2), that an active artistic life began in the city. The painters GHEORGHE TATTARESCU and THEODOR AMAN and the sculptor Karl Storck (*see* STORCK (ii), (1)) were instrumental in building the foundations of artistic education and organizing the first collective exhibitions. At the same time the first collectors appeared, such as Mihail Kogalniceanu and Constantin Esarcu, who were more interested in Western than the still young Romanian art. Some painters were also collectors, such as Carol Pop de Szathmari, also a keen traveller and photographer, who established a collection of Western art.

The next important generation of artists was divided between the innovative tendency of NICOLAE GRIGORESCU and the academic style of George Dimitrescu-Mirea (1854–1934), Director of the School of Fine Arts. The former group exhibited at the Salon of Independent Artists and founded the society Ileana (1897) and the group Artistic Youth (Tinerimea Artistică; 1901–47), with whom such notable artists as Constantin Brancusi exhibited. The academicists exhibited at the Official Salon and at the Athenaeum. The first collections of Romanian paintings also appeared during this period, made by such collectors as Alexandru Bogdan Pitești (1871–1922). The first art museum, the Simu Museum, was opened, although it was destroyed in 1960 under the Communist regime and the collection dispersed. Public monuments were commissioned, with the majority of monumental commissions being given to foreigners.

Between the two world wars the official salons and the exhibitions of the Artistic Youth continued. New associations began to appear, including Romanian Art (Arta Română) and The Art (Arta). An avant-garde movement gathered around the Contemporary (Contimporanul), and a folkloristic tendency in painting and decorative arts took shape parallel to the penetration of Art Deco. For the first time artists were organized into the Fine Arts Union (Sindicatul Artelor Frumoase). New monuments were dedicated to the heroes of World War I (e.g. *Triumphal Arch* by the architect Petre Antonescu). Large exhibitions were sent in 1930 to The Hague and Amsterdam, and Romanian artists participated successfully in various international exhibitions.

Following World War II art was subjected to ideological censorship under Communist rule. Republican exhibitions and municipal salons were organized periodically, and artists were organized into the Union of Plastic Artists, which organized exhibitions, managed the letting of studios and administered galleries, grants, prizes and finance. Working in parallel, the Plastic Fund specialized in such commercial aspects as the commissioning of monumental works. It also administered an industrial complex where artists' materials were produced, as well as running typographic works and foundries for the production of, among other things, ceramics, glass and metalwork. The Exhibition Office of the Ministry of Culture organized exhibitions of national interest and international exhibition exchanges.

By the late 20th century there were a large number of museums in Bucharest, including the National History Museum of Romania, the Museum of Art of the Republic, the Museum of Art Collections and various memorial museums to individual artists. The collapse of the Communist regime (1989) initiated a process of transformation in the artistic life of the city, not least in the higher education system, where major structural changes heralded a new era in art education.

BIBLIOGRAPHY

R. Serban and others: *100 de ani de la infiinţarea Institutului de Arte Plastice 'Nicolae Grigorescu'* [100 years from the foundation of the Fine Arts Institute 'Nicolae Grigorescu'] (Bucharest, 1964)

P. Oprea: *Societăţi artistice bucureştene* (Bucharest, 1969)

V. Florea: *Arta românească*, ii (Bucharest, 1982)

ALINA-IOANA ŞERBU

Buchell [Buchel]**, Arnout** [Aernout; Arend] **van** [Buchelius, Arnoldus] (*b* Utrecht, 1565; *d* Utrecht, 1641). Dutch jurist, historian and Classical scholar. He is mainly remembered for his extremely varied collections of excerpts and diary-style notes, many on artists. He studied law in Leiden, Douai and Paris and took his doctorate in 1593. He acquired a basic humanist culture, which he enhanced by travelling to Germany, France and Italy and maintained through detailed correspondence with learned contemporaries, but his main interest lay in the history of Utrecht and especially in ancient monuments and the works of contemporary artists. As a scholar working on his own behalf, he was not dependent on attracting public support or on publishing papers; he lived for his library, which was his 'whole wealth . . . I carry all I possess with me . . . I regard myself as a citizen of the world' (letter to C. van Baerle, June 1627; Utrecht, Bib. Rijksuniv., MS. 983, fol. 158). Buchell's diary and *Res picturiae* contain interesting comments on the arts; they bring together philological studies (excerpts from Plutarch and Pliny), texts by contemporaries with comments on them (Lampsonius and other works in his library), Buchell's own observations (names of artists and their dates, particularly in the field of prints and from his own collection as well) and his own responses (marginal notes on Michelangelo, Dürer and especially on Crispijn de Passe (i) and (ii)). The catalogue of his library and his manuscripts (most of which are unpublished) is in the Bibliotheek der Rijksuniversiteit, Utrecht.

WRITINGS

Diarium van Arend Buchell; ed. G. Brom and L. A. van Langeraid, *Bijdr. & Meded. Hist. Genoot. Utrecht*, n. s. 2, xxi (1907) [with life of Buchell]

[Arnoldus Buchelius] *Res picturiae: Aantekeningen over kunstenaars en kunstwerken, 1583–1639*; ed. G. J. Hoogewerff and J. Q. van Regteren Altena, Quellenstud. Holl. Kstgesch., xv (The Hague, 1928)

'Brieven van Johannes de Wit aan Arend van Buchel en anderen'; ed. A. Hulshof and P. S. Breuning, *Bijdr. & Meded. Hist. Genoot. Utrecht*, lx (1939), pp. 87–208

Notae quotidianae van Aernout van Buchell; ed. J. W. C. van Campen, *Bijdr. & Meded. Hist. Genoot. Utrecht*, n. s. 2, lxx (1940)

'Zes brieven van Joh. de Wit aan Arend van Buchel'; ed. A. Hulshof and P. S. Breuning, *Bijdr. & Meded. Hist. Genoot. Utrecht*, lxi (1940), pp. 60–94

BIBLIOGRAPHY

NBW

H. L. M. Defoer and P. D. Dirkse: 'Het grafmonument van Jan van Scorel' [The tomb of Jan van Scorel], *Oud-Holland*, c (1986), pp. 171–96

J. BECKER

Bucheum. Site of an ancient Egyptian animal necropolis on the west bank of the Nile, immediately to the north of ARMANT, about 15 km south of Luxor. From the 30th Dynasty (380–343 BC) until AD 340, the Bucheum was the burial site of the Buchis (Egyp. *bekh*) bulls, sacred to the war-god Montu. The site was discovered by Robert Mond in 1927.

The burial preparations of the Buchis bulls differ in several ways from those of the Apis bulls at the Saqqara Serapeum (*see* SAQQARA). Judging from the excavated remains of the Buchis bulls and the documentary evidence provided by the Vienna Papyrus (Vienna, Ksthist. Mus.), their viscera were not removed. Whereas the burial chambers at the Serapeum were elaborate and carved from the living rock, those in the Bucheum were built structures, varying greatly both in architectural size and in quantity of burial equipment (only a few of them incorporating a sarcophagus). As at the Serapeum, records were kept of the dates of birth and death of the sacred bulls. Just as the Apis bulls were identified by particular markings, the Buchis bulls were credited with the ability to accomplish hourly changes in the colour of their hides (which are supposed to have grown in the opposite direction to those of normal bulls, according to the Classical writer Macrobius).

BIBLIOGRAPHY

R. Mond and O. H. Myers: *The Bucheum*, 3 vols (London, 1934)

J.-C. Grenier: 'La Stèle funéraire du dernier taureau Bouchis', *Bull. Inst. Fr. Archéol. Orient.*, 83 (1983), pp. 197-208

ELIZABETH L. MEYERS

Buchheister, Carl (*b* Hannover, 17 Oct 1890; *d* Hannover, 2 Feb 1964). German painter. He had no artistic training but began painting in 1919. His friendship with

Kurt Schwitters from 1921 signalled not only a new period of artistic production but also participation in the leading activities of international Constructivism. In 1925 he turned completely to Constructivism, for example *Opus 25A* (oil on canvas, 1925; Hannover, Niedersächs. Landesmus.). His strongly curved forms, comparable to the reliefs of Hans Arp, alternate with squares, in an organic whole conceived in flat, brilliant colours. From the mid-1920s the horizontal–vertical emphasis of his compositions was augmented by the dynamic use of textured surfaces and diagonal grids. The latter featured particularly in the series of *Triangle* pictures on triangular canvases, which anticipated later shaped canvases. Few of his important collages and constructions from these years survive.

The climax of this period was the foundation with Schwitters and others in 1927 of the Hannover group, which Buchheister led from 1928 to 1933. Close contact with the Dessau Bauhaus and the artists of De Stijl brought a new dynamic impulse to European Constructivism. Between 1932 and 1936 Buchheister was a member of Abstraction–Création. However, from 1933 he was considered like many of his German colleagues to be a 'degenerate' artist (*see* ENTARTETE KUNST), and was no longer permitted to paint, although he made detailed realistic drawings. After World War II, working in seclusion, he returned to abstract compositions, in which he developed a looser, more lyrical style, combining collage and the gesture of contemporary *Art informel* painting.

BIBLIOGRAPHY

Carl Buchheister (exh. cat., Ludwigshafen, Hack Mus. & Städt. Kstsamml., 1975)

Carl Buchheister, 1890–1964: Werkverzeichnis der abstrakten Arbeiten, Nuremberg, Ger. Nmus. cat. (Darmstadt, 1984)

Die abstrakte Hannover–Internationale Avantgarde, 1927–1935 (exh. cat., Hannover, Sprengel Mus.; Ludwigshafen, Hack Mus. & Städt. Kstsamml.; 1988)

GOTTLIEB LEINZ

Buchman and Kahn. *See under* KAHN, E.-J.

Buchser, Frank [Franz] (*b* Feldbrunnen, 15 Aug 1828; *d* Feldbrunnen, 22 Nov 1890). Swiss painter. He was self-taught; his career as a painter began in Rome in 1847 while he was serving in the papal Swiss Guard. He lived in Paris between 1849 and 1850 and worked in the studio of his cousin Victor Schnetz. Schnetz's intensely emotive Romantic style influenced Buchser's work for many years, even after he had embraced Realism, as can be seen in *Salvator Rosa among the Robbers* (1857; priv. col., see exh. cat.). He visited England in 1853 and was introduced to landscape painting. Apart from portraits (which accounted for a large proportion of his income throughout his life) Buchser produced several landscapes in England, which already revealed the *plein-air* elements characteristic of such later works as *Landscape near Scarborough* (1874; Winterthur, Samml. Oskar Reinhart) and *Storm at Sea near Scarborough* (1873; Doris Maillard-Buchser priv. col.).

In 1855 Buchser again visited Scarborough in England, where his portraits had already gained him a favourable audience. On his way to England he stopped in Paris, where he saw paintings by Courbet at the Exposition Universelle; his work was to prove a lasting influence. In 1858 he visited Spain, which led to an engagement as a war artist in the Moroccan Rif war of 1860 (e.g. *Spanish Soldier during the Kablia Campaign*, 1860; Berne, Kstmus.). A need for official recognition prompted him to travel to the USA in 1866. However, instead of the projected monumental oil paintings on subjects from the American Civil War intended for the Bundeshaus in Berne, Buchser concentrated mainly on landscapes which he sketched in oil, like diary entries, while travelling (e.g. *Village Street in Woodstock*, 1868; Winterthur, Samml. Oskar Reinhart), and portraits such as *General Lee* (1869; Berne, Kstmus.). Portrayals of black Americans in such paintings as the *Song of Mary Blane* (1871; Solothurn, Kstmus.) were a novelty, but they failed to achieve any notable success in the exhibitions held in various American cities before his departure in 1871.

Buchser again visited England from 1875 to 1877, where he produced a series of pictures depicting fishergirls. He also travelled to Italy (1878–9 and 1882), to Spain and Morocco (1880) and to Dalmatia and Greece (1883, 1884 and 1885). He returned from these journeys with sketches, which he used as a basis for oil paintings executed at home, such as *Spanish Bagpiper* (1882; Lucerne, Kstmus.). Buchser's work occupies a special place in 19th-century Swiss painting: it is both painterly and iconographically rich. In his North-African subjects, such as *Market in Tangier* (1880; Solothurn, Kstmus.), Buchser was one of the few Swiss artists to follow the tradition of European Orientalism. He was also one of the great exponents of *plein-air* painting in Switzerland, as in the portrait of *Miss Wedel in the Sunshine* (1862; Solothurn, Kstmus.). In the last ten years of his life Buchser became a prominent advocate of stronger state support for the arts. It was thanks to his efforts that the Swiss government supported an art exhibition instituted on a regular basis, starting in 1890. His artistic estate went to the Kunstmuseen in Basle (drawings and oil sketches) and Solothurn (oil paintings).

BIBLIOGRAPHY

H. Lüdeke: *Frank Buchsers amerikanische Sendung, 1866–71* (Basle, 1941)

G. Wälchli: *Frank Buchser, 1828–1890: Leben und Werk* (Zurich, 1941)

Frank Buchser, 1828–1890 (exh. cat., Solothurn, Kstmus., 1990) [contains extensive bibliog.]

LUKAS GLOOR

Buck. English family of draughtsmen and engravers. The earliest known publications by Samuel Buck (*b* ?Richmond, N. Yorks, 1696; *d* London, 17 Aug 1779) are engraved prospects of English towns issued in the early 1720s. He was acquainted with the Yorkshire antiquaries Ralph Thoresby (1658–1725) and John Warburton (1682–1759); a volume of over 250 drawings by Buck formerly in Warburton's possession survives (London, BL, Lansdowne MS. 914). By 1724 he had moved to London; that year he issued his first series of engraved views of ancient ruins. The second series, showing ruins in Lincolnshire and Nottinghamshire, was probably based on sketches made *c*. 1724–6 when Buck was drawing antiquities for William Stukeley (e.g. *Gatehouse of Thornton College, Lincs*; Oxford, Bodleian Lib.). From 1728 to 1754 Buck collaborated with his brother Nathaniel Buck (*fl* 1724–after 1753) and others to produce prints of antiquities and town prospects, based on sketches made on their annual tours. Among the earliest and most systematic antiquarian illustrators in Britain, the Bucks were influenced both by the panoramic approach of such Dutch artists active in

England as Jan Wyck and by the compositional detail of French topographers, for example Jean-Baptiste-Claude Chatelain, who worked for the Bucks.

By 1754 Samuel Buck had retired from printmaking and set up as a drawing-master. In the 1760s and 1770s he exhibited flower drawings (untraced) at the Free Society of Artists. In 1774 Robert Sayer (*fl* 1750–80) reissued all the prints by the brothers as *Buck's Antiquities* (for illustration *see* TATTERSHALL); for it Richard Houston produced a mezzotint portrait of them made after a painting by Joseph Highmore. In 1777 Samuel Buck issued proposals for four views in Yorkshire; two years later the antiquary Richard Gough organized a charitable appeal for him.

In their drawings, made in pen outline and shaded with grey wash, the Bucks aimed to give essential information about the appearance of a building (which was always placed centrally in the composition); they did not dwell on its romantic associations in the manner of later 18th-century artists. Their published work was an influential encouragement for the fashion for picturesque tourism, travels that were undertaken in order to view such monuments.

PRINTS

A Collection of Engravings of Castles, Abbeys and Towns in England and Wales, 5 vols (London, 1726–52); repr. as *Buck's Antiquities*, 3 vols (London, 1774)

Bückeburg, Stadtkirche, west façade, 1611–15

BIBLIOGRAPHY

Landscape in Britain, c. 1750–1850 (exh. cat. by L. Parris, London, Tate, 1973), p. 25

Gilded Scenes and Shining Prospects: Panoramic Views of British Towns, 1575–1900 (exh. cat. by R. Hyde, New Haven, Yale Cent. Brit. A., 1985)

R. Hyde: *A Prospect of Britain: The Town Panoramas of Samuel and Nathaniel Buck* (London, 1994)

SUSAN MORRIS

Bückeburg. German town in south-western Lower Saxony. It was until 1918 the residence of the counts (princes from 1807) of Schaumburg-Lippe. The settlement was originally a castle in the water, built by Adolf VI, Graf von Schaumburg (*reg* 1315–53), as a means of controlling the Helweg, an old trade route. Bückeburg was first mentioned in a document of 1304, and by 1365 Graf Adolf VIII (*reg* 1404–27) had granted the settlement around the castle the status of a legal municipality. Bückeburg first achieved significance in 1608, when Ernst, Graf von Schaumburg (from 1619 Prince of the Empire) moved his residence there from neighbouring Stadthagen. In 1609 he granted Bückeburg its town charter and appointed some of the most prominent artists of the time to construct and remodel buildings in the town, including the architect Giovanni Maria Nosseni, the sculptor Adriaen de Vries and the painter Hans Rottenhammer I, as well as such local craftsmen as Ebert Wulff (ii), Jonas Wulff and Hans Wulff from Hildesheim (*see* WULFF; *see also* SCHAUMBURG, ERNST VON). The castle, including older parts of the building such as the 14th-century chapel, was expanded in the Weser Renaissance style and cut off from the town by a splendid Mannerist gate. The market-place, which abutted the castle precincts, was bounded by the town hall, treasury and court buildings. The castle was further remodelled in 1732 following a fire. Its present layout is the result of comprehensive rebuilding in 1893–8, when two buildings were added in a Renaissance Revival style.

The second most striking building constructed at the time of Graf Ernst is the Stadtkirche (1611–15), composed of three aisles of equal height. It represents one of the earliest and most important Protestant church buildings in Germany. The monumental façade, with its Mannerist combination of stylistic elements based on Gothic, Renaissance and early Baroque forms, is one of the most interesting examples of Weser Renaissance work (see fig.). The church contains a bronze font by Adriaen de Vries and a pulpit by Hans Wulff. His brothers Ebert (ii) and Jonas were responsible for important works in the castle, for example the magnificent Door of the Gods (1604) in the Golden Hall.

During the rebuilding of the castle at the end of the 19th century, work was also undertaken on the new palace, intended as the dowager-seat for the mother of the princess and built in a Renaissance Revival style. In 1911–15 the royal mausoleum was built in the grounds of the castle, one of the largest such works in Europe. It was built in a neo-Romantic style and furnished with sumptuous ceiling mosaics in the Byzantine style. The building was designed by Paul Baumgarten from Berlin, a representative of the typically eclectic building style of the Wilhelminian era. In 1905–6 the new Rathaus was built on the site of its predecessor, which had been destroyed. A large theatre auditorium was added to it, also in a Renaissance Revival style.

BIBLIOGRAPHY

J. Habich: *Die künstlerische Gestaltung der Residenz Bückeburg durch den Fürsten Ernst, 1601–1622* (Bückeburg, 1969)

G. Steinwascher and M. Seeliger: *Bückeburg* (Düsseldorf, 1986)

THOMAS SCHWERTFAGER

Buckingham, 1st Duke of. *See* VILLIERS, GEORGE.

Buckingham, 1st Marquess of. *See* GRENVILLE, (2).

Buckingham, Thomas of Woodstock, Earl of. *See* PLANTAGENET, (5).

Buckingham and Chandos, 1st Duke of. *See* GRENVILLE, (3).

Buckland, William (*b* Oxford, 14 Aug 1734; *d* Annapolis, MD, between 16 Nov and 19 Dec 1774). American architect. In 1748 he was apprenticed to his uncle James Buckland, a London joiner; in 1755, after completing his articles, he became an indentured servant to Thomson Mason, who had been studying law in London and had been asked by his brother George Mason (author of the Virginia Bill of Rights) to find a joiner to finish his house in Virginia. Buckland bound himself to serve 'Thomson Mason, his Executors or Assigns in the Plantation of Virginia beyond the Seas, for the Space of Four Years', and thus came to be responsible for all the woodwork, indoors and out, of Gunston Hall (1755–60), Fairfax County, VA. Gunston Hall served as a showpiece for Buckland. The two porches, one an adaptation of the Palladian motif and the other a half-octagon combining a Doric pilaster order with ogee arches, were the first of their kind in colonial America, as was the chinoiserie decoration in the dining room. In designing it, he drew on several books from his own library: *The British Architect* (1745, 1750, 1758) and *A Collection of Designs in Architecture* (1757) by Abraham Swan, *The Gentleman and Cabinet-maker's Director* (1754) by Thomas Chippendale and *The Builder's Companion* (1758) by William Pain.

When Gunston had been completed, Buckland moved to Richmond County, VA, where in 1765 he bought a farm. He moved to Annapolis, MD, in 1771. Buckland's most important work in his Richmond County period was the interior woodwork of Mount Airy (begun 1758, largely destr. 1844), where he was working in 1762. Although documentary evidence is scarce, and it is difficult to be precise about his contribution to the architecture of the period, Buckland is known to have built the county prison and the Lunenburg Parish glebe house. Work in various houses in northern Virginia, including Nanzatico (1767–9), King George County, Menokin (1769–71), Richmond County, and Blandfield (?1769–?72), Essex County, and in Maryland (e.g. Whitehall (begun 1764), Anne Arundel County) has been attributed to him. He was undoubtedly responsible for much of the interior woodwork for the Chase–Lloyd House (1771), Annapolis. The interior has a stately staircase, rising to a half-landing and dividing into two flights with their serpentine underside visible. The dining room has much elaborate carving, mahogany doors with silver handles and panelled window shutters carved with octagonal medallions and rosettes. Buckland was also architect of the Hammond–Harwood House (1773–4), Annapolis, a five-bay house flanked by pavilions with octagonal bays. Although the detail derives from James Gibbs and Swan, the house is an outstanding example of colonial domestic architecture. The interior woodwork is intricately carved, notably in the dining room and ballroom above, with beads, acanthus leaves and scrolls.

At his death, Buckland is recorded as leaving a substantial estate, including 15 books on architecture and closely related subjects.

BIBLIOGRAPHY

Macmillan Enc. Architects

S. F. Limball: 'Gunston Hall', *J. Soc. Archit. Hist.*, xiii (1954), pp. 3–8

R. R. Beirne and J. H. Scarff: *William Buckland, 1734–74: Architect of Virginia and Maryland* (Baltimore, 1958)

W. H. Pierson jr: 'The Hammond–Harwood House: A Colonial Masterpiece', *Antiques*, cxi (1977), pp. 186–93

G. B. Tatum: 'Great Houses from the Golden Age of Annapolis', *Antiques*, cxi (1977), pp. 174–85

MARCUS WHIFFEN

Bückle, Johann Martin (*b* Geisslingen, 7 Feb 1742; *d* Durlach, 1811). German medallist and engraver. In 1768 he began his career in Augsburg, where he exhibited medals of the municipal curators *Langenmantel* and *Amman* and of *Paul von Stetten*. He later went to Karlsruhe, where he became court medallist and die-engraver; he also worked in Durlach. Stylistically, his medals, often initialled J.M.B., closely resemble those of Franz Andreas Schega and Johann Karl Hedlinger. Portrait medals of *Charles V, Duke of Württemberg* and *Charles Frederick, Margrave of Baden* were Bückle's best works. He also executed the commemorative medal of *Count Demetrius Galitzin* (1793) and a silver medal (1773; Domanig, no. 771) depicting a hunting scene, awarded as a prize by the School of Forestry and Hunting Science. His pupil J. H. Boltschhauser became a medal engraver to the Mannheim court.

BIBLIOGRAPHY

H. Bolzenthal: *Skizzen zur Kunstgeschichte der modernen Medaillen-Arbeit (1429–1840)* (Berlin, 1840)

K. Domanig: *Die deutsche Medaille in kunst- und kulturhistorischer Hinsicht* (Vienna, 1907)

HANNELORE HÄGELE

Buckley, Stephen (*b* Leicester, 5 April 1944). English painter and printmaker. From 1962 to 1967 he studied at the University of Newcastle upon Tyne under Richard Hamilton, also benefiting from contact with visiting tutors such as Pop artists Richard Smith (for whom he later worked as an assistant), Joe Tilson and Eduardo Paolozzi. As a student at the University of Reading from 1967 to 1969, Buckley began to present his paintings as substantial physical objects, constructed in frequently eccentric shapes and then decorated. The clues to subject-matter were often indicated in the titles, which could be allusions to places, for example *Rannoch* (1971; AC Eng); to the techniques used, as in *Cut, Burnt and Tied* (1971; London, Brit. Council); or to historic styles, such as Cubism, as in *Head of a Young Girl No. 1* (1974; Liverpool, Walker A.G.). Often Buckley drew upon the everyday environment: in the early work by referring to crazy pavings, tartan patterns and prosaic interiors, and in the later work by alluding to more specific architectural details and by using cardboard tubing and plastic drainpipes as constructional elements. He not only painted with brushes on stretched canvas but also worked with improvised processes such as tearing, folding, stitching, stapling, patching, screwing together, nailing and weaving. Along with traditional artists' materials, he used house paint, shoe polish, liquid linoleum, perspex, carpeting and old clothes. Often admired for the breadth of his reference to other 20th-century art, Buckley, like his friend Howard Hodgkin, used the abstraction of simple marks and bold design to convey specific moods and circumstances.

BIBLIOGRAPHY

Cambridge Works by Stephen Buckley (exh. cat. by R. Morphet and L. Morris, U. Cambridge, Kettle's Yard, 1974)

Stephen Buckley: Many Angles (exh. cat. by M. Livingstone, Oxford, MOMA, 1985) [Retro.]

M. Livingstone, ed.: *Stephen Buckley* (Kyoto, 1989)

MARCO LIVINGSTONE

Bucklin, James C(hamplin) (*b* Pawtucket, RI, 26 July 1801; *d* Providence, RI, 28 Sept 1890). American architect. His early training in architecture was as apprentice to John Holden Greene. When he was 21 he formed a partnership with William Tallman, a builder and timber merchant, and they remained associates until the early 1850s. Russell Warren worked with them between 1827 and the early 1830s, as did Thomas Tefft between 1847 and 1851.

Tallman & Bucklin was a prolific firm. It engaged in speculative residential construction and was awarded some choice local commissions between the late 1820s and 1850s. Most of these were Greek Revival, including the Providence Arcade (1828), a monumental covered shopping mall; Westminster Street Congregational Church (1829; destr.); Rhode Island Hall, Brown University (1840); the Washington Row (1843–5; destr.); and the Providence High School (1844; destr.), all in Providence. The Tudor-style Butler Hospital (1847), Providence, is probably by Tefft, the architectural prodigy who was working for the firm while a student at Brown University.

After 1851 Bucklin practised alone, but the influence of Tefft remained strong. His Renaissance Revival buildings often imitate Tefft's in both detail and format, as in the Third Howard Building (1859; destr.), Providence, and he adapted Tefft's *Rundbogenstil* brickwork for his mills, such as the Monohasset Mill (1868), Providence. The Thomas Davis House (1869; destr.), Providence, a Gothic villa, recalls some of the designs of Tefft who left his papers to Bucklin on his death in 1859.

Bucklin's late work demonstrates his desire to keep up to date in his designs. The Néo-Grec Hoppin Homestead Building (1875; destr.) and the high Victorian Gothic Brownell Building (1878; destr.), both in Providence, were conservative interpretations of current styles.

BIBLIOGRAPHY

D.-B. Nelson: *The Greek Revival Architecture of James C. Bucklin* (diss., Newark, U. DE, 1969)

Buildings on Paper: Rhode Island Architectural Drawings, 1825–1945 (exh. cat., ed. W. H. Jordy and C. P. Monkhouse; Providence, RI, Brown U., Bell Gal., 1982)

W. MCKENZIE WOODWARD

Buckner, Richard (*b* Woolwich, 25 Oct 1812; *d* London, 12 Aug 1883). English painter. He first worked from a studio at his family home in Rumboldswhyke, near Chichester. After a short spell in the army, he went to Rome where he studied under Giovanni Battista Canevari (1789–1876). He set up a studio there and quickly earned a reputation not only for his elegant portraits (e.g. *Lady Charlotte Guest and her Daughter*, priv. col., see Stewart and Cutten, p. 36) but also for his delicate watercolours of Italian peasants. His work attracted the attention of important patrons including Queen Victoria and her husband Albert of Saxe-Coburg-Gotha, Prince Consort; Edward, Prince of Wales; Adelaide, Duchess of Saxe-Meiningen (*fl* 1860s), and William Alexander, 11th Duke of Hamilton.

From 1840 Buckner exhibited works in London, showing at the Royal Academy, the British Institution and the Society of British Artists. In addition he exhibited in Italy and in France. He was able to afford a studio in Rome, and one in Cleveland Row, London, opposite St James's Palace. In Rome he impressed the young Frederic Leighton and advised him on his *Cimabue's Celebrated Madonna is Carried in Procession through the Streets of Florence* (1855; Brit. Royal Col.). Buckner's first £200 commission was a portrait of *Sir Charles Fitzroy, Governor of Australia* (1855; Sydney, Govt House). By the early 1860s his annual income was in excess of £4000 for commissions alone. He usually painted thinly with rapid bravado, and although his lesser works can be poor, his finest paintings have an outstanding quality, which made him the obvious rival of Franz Xaver Winterhalter. As a colourist he was outstanding, using a rich palette of reds and blues. Among works in his collection sold by Christie's, London, on 22 February 1873 were paintings attributed to Anthony van Dyck, Giambattista Tiepolo, Francesco Guardi, Thomas Lawrence and William Etty.

BIBLIOGRAPHY

J. Maas: *Victorian Painters* (London, 1974/*R* 1989)

B. Stewart and M. Cutten: 'Richard Buckner', *Ant. Colr*, lx/4 (1989), pp. 34–41

BRIAN STEWART

Buckridge [Buckeridge], **Bainbrigg** [Baynbrigg] (*b* Northall, Herts, 1668; *d* Hackney, Middx, 1 Jan 1733). English writer and painter. The son of an East India Company merchant, he graduated from St John's College, Oxford, in 1695, intending to be a physician. Instead he took up drawing and painting and travelled to the Netherlands to pursue his interest in art. He was later employed by John Sheffield, 2nd Duke of Buckingham (1648–1721), but the nature of his work is unknown. In 1704 he wrote a poem praising the Duke's pictures at his newly built Buckingham House, London; he addressed another to Antonio Verrio, suggesting a decorative programme for Blenheim Palace, Oxon, to be built for John Churchill, 1st Duke of Marlborough, and begun by John Vanbrugh the following year (see *Poems*, v, pp. 158–76). Buckridge's most important contribution to art is his collection of lives of painters, published in 1706 as part of the first English translation of Roger de Piles's *Abrégé de la vie des peintres* (1699). Previous accounts in English had followed the tradition of Vasari's *Vite* (2/1568) and van Mander's *Schilder-boeck* ([1603]–4) in emphasizing the Italian, Netherlandish and German schools. Although there is some discussion of English artists in Richard Graham's *Short Account of the Most Eminent Painters* (1695), Buckridge's work was the first attempt to construct a history of English painting within this formulaic biographical framework. He borrowed heavily from Graham and others, and his name was not disclosed until the third edition. His notion of an English school embraced foreign artists who had been active in England, for instance Orazio Gentileschi and Hans Holbein (ii), as well as the fashionable court painters Peter Lely and Godfrey Kneller. Examples of his own paintings remain untraced.

WRITINGS

'An Essay towards an English-school, with the Lives, and Characters of above 100 Painters', *The Art of Painting and the Lives of the Painters* (London, 1706, 2/1744, 3/1754/*R* 1969) [Eng. trans. by J. Savage of R. de Piles: *Abrégé de la vie des peintres* (Paris, 1699)]

J. Nichols, ed.: *A Select Collection of Poems*, 8 vols (London, 1780–84)

BIBLIOGRAPHY

[G. Jacob]: *An Historical Account of the Lives and Writings of our Most Considerable English Poets* (London, 1720), pp. 21–2

SHEARER WEST

Bučovice [Ger. Butschowitz]. Moravian town 30 km east of Brno, Czech Republic. It is renowned for the Renaissance palace of Jan Šembera Černohorský z Boskovice (1543–97). The original design, Italian in character, is thought to have been by Jacopo Strada and to date from 1567. It was altered in 1579 at the owner's wish by the master builder Pietro Gabri. The main courtyard was enlarged at the expense of one of the wings, which was transformed into a series of superimposed arcaded galleries, matching the courtyard elevation of two of the remaining three wings. The palace thus lost its original symmetrical layout but gained a three-storey arcaded courtyard of lightness and elegance, Mannerist in style. The palace was also given two lateral courtyards and an extensive Italian garden on its main axis. The whole was bounded by a moat and by a wall with two pairs of gates and with corner bastions that simulate a defensive function, in a typically Mannerist way. When the construction was finished (*c.* 1582) this was one of the most important Renaissance buildings of its time in central Europe and one of the few in the region to be designed on a unified plan with an axially conceived garden.

Five rooms on the ground floor were richly painted by local artists and given stuccoed decoration *c.* 1584. In the Imperial Room (see fig.) busts of four Roman emperors and, most notably, six large three-dimensional polychrome figures representing *Jupiter and the Eagle*, *Leda and the Swan*, *Mars*, *Diana*, the *Rape of Europa* and *Emperor Charles V on Horseback, Trampling a Moor* were incorporated in landscapes painted in the vault lunettes. The precise programme is not entirely understood, but it relates to the glorification of the Habsburgs as heirs of the Roman emperors. These compositions are the only cycle of Mannerist sculpture influenced by Giambologna to have survived from this period in central Europe. Hans Mont, a former assistant of Giambologna, is thought to have been responsible for the extraordinary work; Mont and Bartholomäus Spranger had used the same rare combination of techniques in 1576 at the Neugebäude near Vienna, the summer residence of Emperor Maximilian II (built as an elaborate version of Bučovice by Jacopo Strada in 1568) and in 1577 in the decoration of the Triumphal Arch of Rudolf II, Vienna. Later additions to the palace decoration include a fountain with monsters, attributed to

Bučovice Palace, the Imperial Room, *c.* 1567–84

a sculptor from the circle of Pietro Tacca. It was installed in the main courtyard in 1657.

BIBLIOGRAPHY

J. Krčálová: 'Pietro Ferrabosco und sein Schaffen im Königreich Böhmen, Miscellany Magistri Intelvesi', *Ostbair. Grenzmarken*, xi (Passau, 1969), pp. 183–96

D. Menclová: *Státní zámek Bučovice* [Bučovice palace] (Brno, 1972)

J. Krčálová: *Centrální stavby české renesance* [Centrally planned buildings of the Renaissance in Bohemia] (Prague, 1974), pp. 42–9

——: *Zámek v Bučovicích* [The palace at Bučovice] (Prague, 1979)

——: 'Arts in the Renaissance and Mannerist Periods', *Renaissance Art in Bohemia* (London, New York, Sydney and Toronto, 1979), pp. 49–147

E. Hubala: 'Die Baukunst der mährischen Renaissance', *Renaissance in Böhmen*, ed. F. Seibt (Munich, 1985), pp. 114–67

H. Lietzmann: *Das Neugebäude* (Munich and Berlin, 1987), pp. 76–7, 152, 154–7

J. KRČÁLOVÁ

Bucranium [bucrane; Gk. *boukranion*: 'oxhead']. Motif based on the horned skull of an ox, frequently used to decorate the metopes of a Roman Doric frieze.

□

Buczacz. Town in Podolia, Ukraine, formerly in Polish territory, known as a centre for weaving in the 18th and 19th centuries. In the 18th century the town belonged to the magnate family Potocki, and the art of weaving kilims with floral designs flourished. About 1870 Oskar Potocki founded a large factory to produce wall hangings made of silk interwoven with gold and silver thread. These hangings carried on the Polish tradition of brocade weaving but were made on mechanical looms. They are distinguished by subtle shades of pink, orange and red, with tiny motifs, or are predominantly gold with a beautiful sheen. They were expensive and much prized by connoisseurs. The workshop labels, which give the size of each piece (usually about 1.5×2.5 m), show the Pilawa coat of arms of the Potocki family (a cross with two-and-a-half arms), the name *Buczacz* and sometimes the initials *AP* for Artur Potocki, the manager. These were woven in or stitched on a separate piece of fabric. *Kontush* sashes for the Polish national costume (*see* POLAND, §X, and SŁUCK) were also produced in Buczacz in small quantities. The Potocki factory was in operation until 1939.

BIBLIOGRAPHY

Z. Żygulski jr: *Dzieje polskiego rzemiosła artystycznego* [An outline history of Polish applied art] (Warsaw, 1987), p. 84

ZDZISŁAW ŻYGULSKI JR

Budapest. Capital of Hungary, situated on the River Danube as it flows north–south through the Carpathian Basin. The city, now with a population of more than 2 million, developed at the natural river crossing on the route into western Europe from the east. Modern Budapest is an amalgamation of three cities: Buda on the hills above the right bank, with Óbuda (Old Buda) to the north and Pest occupying the plain on the left bank. The three cities had independent histories of varying importance for almost 2000 years until their unification in 1873 adumbrated the development of modern Budapest.

I. History and urban development. II. Art life and organization. III. Centre of ceramics production. IV. Buda Castle.

I. History and urban development.

1. Before 1541. 2. 1541–1686. 3. 1686–1867. 4. After 1867.

1. BEFORE 1541. Early settlements grew up from mid-Palaeolithic times on the chain of river islands within the boundaries of the modern city. The Eravisci settled there *c.* 55 BC, with their religious cult centre in the south part of what is now Buda. At the Roman conquest of Pannonia in 10 BC, the town of Aquincum was founded on the right bank of the Danube, *c.* 9 km north of Buda. Substantial remains of both the town and the legionary camp were excavated in the 19th century and again in the 1970s, revealing civic buildings, barracks, amphitheatres, floor mosaics (Budapest, Aquincumi Mus.) and an Early Christian basilica outside the walls. The city was rebuilt several times before its abandonment in AD 292 and the construction of Contra Aquincum, a rectangular bridgehead on the left bank.

There are traces of occupation by various peoples during the Migration period before the Magyars conquered the Carpathian Basin *c.* 900. The civic amphitheatre of Aquincum became the site of the castle of Kurszán, the sacred leader of the Magyars. According to medieval tradition, Prince Árpád (*reg* 896–907) was buried in Óbuda near the church of Fehéregyháza (Lat. Alba Ecclesia; the church was incorporated in a 15th-century Pauline monastery and dedicated to the Virgin). After the defeat of the Magyars at Augsburg in 955, the royal residence was moved to the left bank of the river, where there was also a Muslim settlement.

In the following years developments were centred on Óbuda, in the remains of the Roman fortress, known as Budavár. King Peter Orseolo (*reg* 1038–41, 1044–6) founded the royal priory of St Peter, which was completed *c.* 1148 and richly endowed by King Géza II (*reg* 1141–62). Its remains—capitals, corbels and portals decorated with classicizing ornament—show a close stylistic affinity with the royal works at ESZTERGOM, in particular the 12th-century cathedral. From the mid-12th century there was a German trading settlement near the crossing place at Óbuda, and a royal castle next to the priory is recorded in 1212. Its successor, with a rectangular ground-plan and richly moulded gateways, was probably begun *c.* 1226 after the fire that devastated Óbuda in 1223.

Buda and Pest also established their independent identities in the 13th century. The township of Pest, which grew up around the site of Contra Aquincum, already had a Dominican friary in the 1220s, and a German settlement developed to the north, extending across the river south of Óbuda. After the destruction of both cities in the Mongol invasion of 1241–2, a new, fortified city of Nova Mons Pestiensis or Castrum Budiense was founded on the hills south of Óbuda. Intended from the first to be the capital of the kingdom, it was the centre of the royal court, and the mint was transferred there from Esztergom. The inhabitants of Pest were resettled there in 1247–8. Traces of their houses, including the fortified residences of the wealthier citizens, are attested in the records and in surviving details of doors and windows. The early style of Buda was that of the influential second workshop of Óbuda Castle, whose characteristic details appear in several churches, including the mendicant friaries and the German parish church of St Mary (now Matthias Church), which was completed by 1269. Later phases of building in this church show that by *c.* 1260 a new variant of High Gothic, comparable to contemporary Bohemian architecture, had appeared in the city. A simpler church, dedicated to St Mary Magdalene (destr. 1945; tower rest.), was built for the Hungarian congregation in the northern Castle District.

The arrival of Charles Robert of Anjou (*reg* 1308–42) inaugurated the second phase of medieval development in Buda. With the royal residence now in Visegrád, the only major royal building works were in what became Queen Elisabeth Piast's town of Óbuda. Excavations show that the aisled hall church of the Cistercian Order (consecrated 1349) probably had a lierne-vaulted chapter house. The royal building style, rooted in that of the mendicant orders in central Europe, stood comparison with the contemporary court styles of Poland and Bohemia. When, in 1355–6, Elisabeth gave half of Óbuda to the convent chapter, the city began to decline, and by the 18th century it was scarcely more than a village.

From 1346 Buda was no longer ruled by a governor; this increased the power of the city council and affected the city's development, leading to fierce rivalry between the German and Hungarian communities. Construction of Buda Castle (*see* §IV, 1 below) was begun under King Louis the Great (*reg* 1342–82) and further expanded by King Sigismund of Luxembourg (*reg* 1387–1437). The royal workshop was again very influential. From the second half of the 14th century the city was transformed by the building of large town houses and alterations to the churches: St Mary's was converted to a hall church, and the Dominican churches in the city and on Margaret Island were rebuilt. New churches included that of the Brethren of the Cross (partly destr.) and the parish church of Pest, an ambulatory hall church with frescoed scenes of the *Passion*.

Buda was dominated by two styles: that of the 1360s was strongly influenced by the Parler workshop of south Germany (*see* PARLER, (1)), while the second style, associated with Sigismund's works at the royal palace at Buda Castle in the 1420s, was rooted in Prague and Vienna, with some Bavarian characteristics. Sigismund's reign marks the climax of the medieval development of Buda. From then until the end of the Middle Ages the Hungarian aristocracy, the higher clergy and ecclesiastical foundations built palaces alongside the houses of the wealthier citizens, and by 1437 the residential quarters of the city were already so substantial that Sigismund commissioned a report on all the houses in Buda, to prove that the city could accommodate the general Council of the Church, were it to move to Buda from Basle. He also tried unsuccessfully to found a university in Óbuda in 1395.

The next upsurge of building activity occurred only late in the 15th century, in the reign of Matthias Corvinus (*see* HABSBURG, §I, (12)), who wanted to found a university at Buda based on the architectural ideals of Antonio Filarete. In addition to building Matthias's palace at Buda Castle (*see* §IV, 1 below) and his villa at Nyék (destr.), the royal workshop was also employed at Pest, which became a free royal borough in the second half of the 15th century owing to its increasing importance from trading in livestock. The two court styles of this period were a form of Late Gothic originating in Lausitz, Silesia (*see* ARNOLD VON WESTFALEN), which appeared after Matthias was recognized King of Bohemia in 1469; and the ornamental Florentine Renaissance style (primarily that of Benedetto da Maiano and Desiderio da Settignano) brought to Buda by the Florentine builder Chimenti di Leonardo Camicia (1431–before 1505), employed by Matthias on his palace, and exemplified by the high altar and ciborium niches dating from 1507 in the parish church of Pest. In the early 16th century most building work in Buda was concentrated on fortifying the city against the Turks, who reached it soon after their victory at Mohács in 1526 but did not capture it until 1541.

2. 1541–1686. During the Turkish occupation of Buda, the city was the seat of a Turkish *vilayet* (administrative district) and governed by a *beylerbey* (pasha), and the three cities were subject to Turkish administration. Their medieval topography remained, with the addition of two overcrowded settlements, Viziváros and Tabán, outside the walls to the east and south respectively: Óbuda declined sharply. The decay of Buda Castle was precipitated by a succession of gunpowder explosions (1578, 1669 and 1686) and further compounded by an earthquake in 1641. From as early as 1542 unsuccessful attempts were made to recapture Buda, and most of the building work carried out by the Turks was connected with the maintenance and modernization of the fortifications.

Sinan Pasha's personal involvement in the building of the mosque of Pasha Mustafa (destr.) is recorded. Several churches, including St Mary's in Buda, were converted into mosques: traces of this can be seen in the mihrab in the parish church of Pest. The octagonal tomb (rest. 1962) of Gül Baba (*d* 1541), a revered dervish, was built between 1543 and 1548 on Rose Hill, north of Buda. Remains of Toygun Pasha's mosque, built between 1553 and 1556 in Viziváros, have been found in the Capuchin church. Nine Turkish baths, of which four survive, were built on the thermal springs of Buda: the Rudas, Király (King) and Rác (Serbian) baths were built *c.* 1578 under Sokollu Mehmed Pasha. They all preserve their octagonal bath halls. The later Császár (Imperial) Bath, the Bath of Bey Veli, was extended by József Hild in 1841–5 (destr. *c.* 1990). After an unsuccessful siege in 1684, Buda was recaptured by the Habsburgs on 2 September 1686, following an assault that almost completely destroyed both the castle and the city.

3. 1686–1867. After the reconquest, priority was given to building and restoration (see fig. 1). Buda and Pest were granted free borough status in 1703, when their populations were respectively *c.* 11,000 and *c.* 4000. Now ruled from Vienna, they were transformed during the 18th century into Baroque cities, largely at the hands of Austrian and Italian architects. In 1686 Venerio Ceresola began to repair the fortifications of Buda along their existing lines, and from 1692 he also directed building on Buda Town Hall. The residential parts of Buda were rebuilt during the 18th century on the medieval street layout and were repopulated by Germans and Serbian refugees. Viziváros and Tabán, both settled by immigrants, became more urban in character, and the new suburbs of Országút, Ujlak and (from 1770) Krisztinaváros were added to the north and west.

The later 18th-century development of Buda was dictated by efforts to make it the official capital of the Hungarian Province of the Habsburg empire and by moves by Emperor Joseph II (*reg* 1765–90) to secularize the monastic orders. Many government offices were established there, several in disused conventual buildings: the National Assembly was housed in the Clarissan convent, which was converted (1783–5) by Franz Anton Hillebrandt and Johann Josef Thallherr (*d* 1807), second architect of the royal office of works. The most significant architects working in a late Baroque style in Buda were Kristóf Hamon (1693–1748) and Máté Nepauer (*fl* 1749; *d* 1790), who together built the church of St Anne (1740–62).

The rebuilding of the ruined Pest was initially slower than that of Buda. János György Paur (1692–1752), master of the Masons' Guild, played a leading part, building the Town Hall (1721) and churches, including the Franciscan church (1727–43), and from 1725 he added a Baroque nave to the Gothic chancel of the parish church of Pest (now Inner City Church). The medieval walls of Pest were first breached by the city's grandest building enterprise, the hospital for disabled soldiers, begun in 1716 by Prince Eugene of Savoy but never finished. The most impressive religious building of the time was the Pauline Church (now the University Church), built 1722–42 by a follower of Johann Lukas von Hildebrandt, possibly with the assistance of Andreas Mayerhoffer, who became master of the Pest Masons' Guild in 1729 and may have built the church of the Stations of the Cross on the edge of the city in 1744. In 1785 Lipótváros (Ger. Leopoldstadt) was

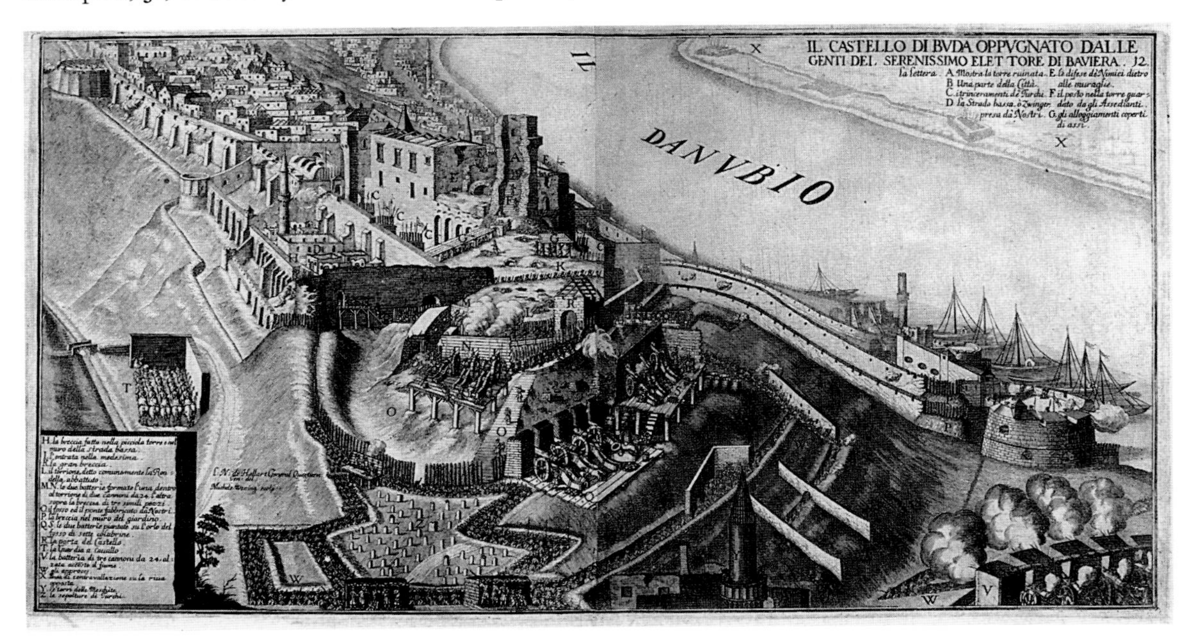

1. Budapest, Buda Castle at the time of its recapture from the Turks in 1686; engraving by M. Wening after L. Hallart, 300×568 mm, 1686

founded north of the city walls, and beyond it, in 1786, Joseph II founded the Imperial-Royal General Hospice–New Building (destr.).

Óbuda, which had 750 inhabitants in 1700, became the centre for the Counts of Zichy, but remained undeveloped, the most important building works being the Trinitarian Monastery (now Kiscell Mus.), built 1744–59 by the Viennese architect Johann Entzenhoffer, with an illusionistic dome painting by Antonio Galli-Bibiena, and the Zichy family mansion (now the Lajos Kassák Mem. Mus.), built 1746–57 by their resident architect, János Henrik Jäger.

In the late 18th century and the first half of the 19th it was Pest that developed most rapidly, to a population of 100,000 in 1847, more than twice that of Buda and ten times larger than Óbuda. The Embellishment Committee of the City of Pest, created in 1808, at once attempted to solve problems of transport and drainage. The greater proportion of Hungarians in Pest made it the centre not only of Enlightenment ideas but also of the rebirth of a Hungarian national culture. Along with the transfer of the university from Buda to Pest in 1790, in recognition of Pest's growing significance, most cultural institutions, such as the Academy of Sciences, literary societies and theatres, were established there. The leading figure behind these initiatives was the reforming liberal Count István Széchenyi (1791–1860).

Around 1800 the Pest townscape was distinctly Neo-classical, Mihály Pollack (*see* POLLACK, (2)) supervising the construction of the Alexander Palace in Buda (1805) and the German theatre in Pest (1808–12), both designed by Johann Aman (1765–1834). In the first half of the 19th century Pollack's buildings were major works of Hungarian Neo-classicism: the Calvinist church (1799–1811), the Ludoviceum (1830–36), the Redoubt (1834) and the Hungarian National Museum (1836–46). Much of the Neo-classical architecture in Pest was the work of local men such as Mátyás Zitterbarth III and JÓZSEF HILD, who built the so-called Lloyd Palace (1827–30; destr. 1945) and the parish church of Lipótváros (designed 1835–47), as well as apartment blocks.

The advent of steamships on the Danube from 1829 and of the railways from the 1840s gave an enormous impetus to the development of Pest. Severely damaged by flooding in 1838 and rebuilt by 1841, the city was permanently linked to Buda by a chain bridge built (1839–49) to the designs of Adam Clark (1811–66). Industrial suburbs grew up around Pest, notably Ujpest, founded in 1840. The National Assembly was transferred to Pest, and the competition for the design of the Parliament House coincided with a reaction against Neo-classicism; it was won in 1846 by FRIGYES FESZL, who produced an eclectic design (unexecuted) of Gothic Revival mixed with other historicist styles. Feszl's greatest historicist design, the Vigadó Concert Hall, was built on the site of the Redoubt in Pest between 1860 and 1864; but in the competition for the design of the Academy of Sciences (1862–5), his type of eclecticism was defeated by the Renaissance Revival design of Friedrich August Stüler.

Although the short-lived independent government of 1848–9 had planned the unification of the three cities, when the Austrians finally regained Pest in 1849 the decree was cancelled. The industrial and urban development of Budapest began only in the 1860s, particularly after the 1867 Compromise with the Austrian government established the Dual Monarchy, when the city became the centre of transport, trade and banking in Hungary.

4. AFTER 1867. Although the three cities were united only in 1873, the Compromise of 1867 provided the

stimulus for development. From 1870 the Metropolitan Council of Public Works co-ordinated urban planning and enforced architectural standards. The international competition for a general city plan in 1871 was won by Lajos Lechner, who proposed three concentric ring roads to link the major routes converging on the city centre. The regulation and embankment of the Danube began in 1871, and Margaret Bridge was built in 1872–6 as part of the second ring road, the Great Ring. Radial Avenue (known after 1885 as Andrássy Road), linking the centre with the City Park, was completed in 1885 and the Great Ring in 1896.

The general aspect of central Budapest was determined by the late historicist-eclectic style of the buildings lining these streets, particularly those designed by Antal Szkalnitzky and Gusztáv Petschacher; the Custom House (1870–77) and the Opera House (1875–83; rest. 1981–4), both by Miklós Ybl; and the headquarters of the Hungarian State Railways Pension Fund (1883), designed by Ödön Lechner and Gyula Pártos (1845–1916). In the 1890s attention was centred on the celebrations in 1896 of the millennium of the Magyar conquest, with the ensemble in Heroes' Square of the Millenary Monument (1894–1900) by György Zala (1858–1937), the Art Hall (1896) and the Museum of Fine Arts (1898–1906), both by Albert Schickedanz. Frigyes Schulek's Gothic Revival restoration (1874–96) of the 13th-century Matthias Church, Buda, and the style of his Fishermen's Bastion in Buda (1895–1903) were also part of the Millenary programme.

Modern Pest (see fig. 2) developed around the mainline railway stations and the business area, rebuilding of which began in 1897. The Western Railway station was built between 1874 and 1877 by August de Serres and Győző Bernardt, while the Eastern Railway station, by Julius Röchlitz (1827–86), was built from 1881. The avenue leading to the Elisabeth Bridge (1897–1903; destr. 1945; rebuilt 1964) cut through the Baroque city centre. The Gothic Revival Parliament Building (*see* HUNGARY, fig. 4) was designed by Imre Steindl in 1883 and completed in 1904, dominating the Danube at the north end of Pest, which, after the demolition of Joseph II's Imperial Hospice, gradually developed into the city's financial district. Most of the infrastructure of Budapest was laid down in this period, and from about 1900 to the 1930s there was little further development. There are many outstanding examples of Art Nouveau buildings from this period, including the Gellért Hotel and Baths, built in 1912 by Ármin Hegedüs (*b* 1869) and Izidor Sterk (*b* 1860).

Two more Danube bridges were proposed in 1929 (and built between 1939 and 1943), and districts of apartment buildings for mass housing rose in their vicinity. The Tabán district of Buda was demolished from 1934. Plans for traffic improvement were thwarted by World War II, in which Budapest was badly bombed. In the winter of 1944–5 it was besieged, the bridges were blown up and Buda Castle was badly damaged. In the late 1940s the Metropolitan Planning Bureau supervised the restoration of the city and the provision of mass housing. In 1950 the suburbs were incorporated to create Greater Budapest, and, with an ever-expanding population, a new development plan was drawn up. Residential areas were built on the edge of the city, and there was further development along the extensions to the underground railway system.

For further discussion and illustration *see* HUNGARY, §II, 4 and fig. 5.

BIBLIOGRAPHY

Budapest régiségei [Ancient monuments of Budapest], 26 vols (Budapest, 1889–)

2. Budapest, general view of Pest, photographed from Buda before World War II

E. Réh: *A régi Buda és Pest épitőmesterei Mária Terézia korában* [Building masters of old Buda and Pest in the time of Maria Theresa] (Budapest, 1932)

A. Schoen: 'Buda és Óbuda XVIII. századi templomai' [18th-century churches in Buda and Obuda], *Történetírás* (1937)

M. Horler, ed.: *Budapest műemlékei* [Monuments in Budapest], 2 vols (Budapest, 1955–62), iv and vi of *Magyarország műemléki topográfiája* [Topography of monuments in Hungary]

B. Boros, A. Sódor and M. Zádor: *Budapest épitészettörténete, városképei és műemlékei* [The architectural history, townscapes and monuments of Budapest] (Budapest, 1959)

G. Preisich: *Budapest városépítésének története* [The history of urban development in Budapest], 3 vols (Budapest, 1960–69)

L. Gerevich, ed.: *Budapest története* [The history of Budapest], 5 vols (Budapest, 1973–80)

J. Gerle, A. Kovács and I. Makovecz: *A Századfordalò magyar épitészete* [Hungarian turn-of-the-century architecture] (Budapest, 1990)

II. Art life and organization.

1. To 1686. In the Middle Ages artistic activity in the three cities was dominated by the royal workshops. In the 12th century and the early 13th the influence of the masons at the royal works at Esztergom was paramount, visible in both the architectural remains and the Early Gothic sculptural fragments from the royal palace at Óbuda (Budapest, Hist. Mus.). The only surviving exception is the style of the stone relief fragments, probably from the rood screen of St Peter's Priory, *c.* 1148, which is strongly influenced by the Emilian sculptor Nicholaus (the most significant piece depicts *Abraham and the Three Angels*, Budapest, N.G.). From about the middle of the 13th century Buda probably became a flourishing centre of goldsmithing, no doubt encouraged by the presence of the royal mint. The court artists specialized in filigree work with added naturalistic details, as seen in the contents of the tomb of *King Stephen V* (*reg* 1270–72) on Margaret Island (Budapest, N. Mus.). These include several crowns, including one later made into a cross (Kraków, Cathedral Mus.).

The Angevin dynasty introduced Italian elements into court works, the white marble shrine of *Princess Margaret Arpád* (*c.* 1330; Budapest, N.G.) showing stylistic affinities to the Neapolitan circle of Tino di Camaino. The numerous red marble tombstones in the churches of Buda, and stylistically related examples from all over medieval Hungary, demonstrate the importance of the Buda workshops, many of which may well have specialized in the production of tombstones.

Masons' and goldsmiths' guilds existed from the beginning of the 15th century, and there is evidence of a considerable presence of traders in textiles and of craftsmen producing luxury goods. There are especially rich finds of pottery, beginning with imported Austrian domestic wares from the 13th century onwards, alongside locally produced material (*see* §III below). Chinese and Syrian ceramics occur sporadically, and from the early 15th century ornamental tableware was imported from Loštice, Dreihausen and Siegburg. A similar picture can be drawn for glassware.

Buda's importance as an artistic centre in the 15th century cannot be demonstrated owing to the almost total destruction of paintings and illuminated manuscripts. Among the few objects that survive are the altarpiece of the *Calvary* (Esztergom, Mus. Christ.) by Tamás Kolozsvári, made in 1427 for Garamszentbenedek Abbey (now Hronský Beňadik, Slovakia). Late Gothic goldsmith work is represented by a scattering of objects (e.g. Budapest, Hist. Mus.; Budapest, Loránd Eötvös U. Lib.). A fairly complete picture of the climax of court artistic production during Matthias Corvinus's reign can be surmised from the survival of reasonably detailed sources, together with architectural and sculptural fragments, manuscripts and luxury goods. Through his circle of Florentine Humanists, Matthias introduced Italian books to his library, the Biblioteca Corviniana, and he also founded a local scriptorium producing works in a Renaissance style. The Renaissance ornament that appeared in architecture (*see* §I, 1 above) was also integrated into tomb sculpture, and later additions to the Biblioteca Corviniana show that it was the north Italian style of Francesco Rosselli and Franciscus de Castello Italico de Mediolano (*fl* 1465) that survived in the letters patent illuminated in the chancellery of Buda, and in Hungarian illumination in general. Although Andreas Hess tried to start a printing press at Buda in Matthias's reign, starting with the *Chronica Hungarorum* (Budapest, 1473), printing began to flourish only in the early 16th century. By then court dominance in art had been lost, and after 1526 it effectively vanished, although there is evidence that Buda artists were still at work. During the Turkish occupation there was a considerable increase around Buda and Pest in the activity of both local craftsmen and those recently arrived from the Balkans. The main branches of Turkish craftsmanship were leatherwork, pottery, wrought iron and goldsmith work.

2. After 1686. After the reconquest architecture was the dominant art form in the cities, and the Masons' Guild was founded as early as 1690. In 1695 the Pest section separated from the Buda Guild. The most significant figure in the early years of the Buda Guild was Johann Hölbling (1660–1736), who was its master from 1700.

As with architects, many sculptors and painters came from outside Hungary, especially Austria, in particular Philipp Ungleich (*d c.* 1736) and Ferenc Antal Hörger (*fl* 1713–37), who made the statue of the *Holy Trinity* (1715–17) for the column in Holy Trinity Square. Jószef Hebenstreit made the high altar (1746) of the Pauline (now the University) church, and the ceiling was frescoed in 1776 by the Viennese, Johann Wenzel Bergl. The two most significant 18th-century painters in Buda, Gábor Kronewetter and Gergely Vogl (1717–82), both studied in Vienna.

The emergence of Pest as the centre for the rebirth of Hungarian national culture was closely followed by its development as an artistic centre. After the transfer of the University in 1790, the Hungarian National Museum was founded in 1807, and the Academy of Sciences in 1825. The most important collection of antiquities in the city was bequeathed to the National Museum in 1832 by Miklós Jankovich (1773–1846), and in 1845 the Museum was further assisted by the formation of the Association for the National Picture Gallery; in 1846 the Gallery acquired the collection of János Lázsló Pyrker, Archbishop of Eger. Pest was also an important centre of printmaking.

From 1804, when Johann Nepomuk Schauff (1757–1827) presented his design for the building of a National Art Academy, the desire to create a 'national art' was strong; however, although Giacomo Marastoni (1804–60) set up a private academy in Pest in 1846, the Akademie der Bildenden Künste remained both the most accessible and the most influential art school. The Artists Association of Pest (active between 1839 and 1869) held regular exhibitions and organized the distribution of prints. Viennese artists such as Peter Krafft, Johann Nepomuk Ender (1793–1854), Friedrich von Amerling and Josef Klieber managed to retain all the large-scale commissions. The first Hungarian to challenge them was the Neo-classical sculptor István Ferenczy, but his ambitious projects, such as the creation of a sculpture academy in 1826 and the erection of a monument to Matthias Corvinus (1839–44), failed to gain acceptance. The first criticism of the prevailing Neo-classicism and the methods pursued by the academies came from the critic Imre Henszlmann (1813–88) in 1841, and this led to the development of Romantic and historicist styles.

The cultural life of the nation could not be fully organized until the Compromise of 1867, but, as Austrian government rule relaxed, in 1858 the Academy of Sciences founded the Archaeological Committee and instituted a series of publications. From 1863 the exhibitions of the Association for Fine Arts were temporarily held in the Academy (later based in the Art Hall), and in 1865 the Esterházy Collection (finally acquired in 1871) was also displayed there.

A national academy for art was achieved in 1870 with the foundation of the Design and Drawing Teachers' Institute, which, together with the Art Teacher Training Institute, became from 1909 the Academy of Fine Arts. In 1872 a Technical University was formed from the reorganization of the József Polytechnic, providing training for architects. The organization and system of training for the building industry and the applied arts were, however, completely overhauled by the Trade and Industry Law of 1872, which ordered the dissolution of the guilds. Art life centred around the Hungarian National Association for Fine Arts. Eclectic historicism, the prevalent style until *c.* 1900, was maintained by artists educated abroad (e.g. in Munich and Vienna), who were highly influential in the art schools: the architects Imre Steindl and Frigyes Schulek, and the painters Bertalan Székely, Gyula Benczúr and Károly Lotz. The same people were given most of the significant commissions in historical and decorative–allegorical works. Twenty-six public statues were erected between 1849 and 1896, with a further fifty-three by 1914. Most of the new sculptures were by leading figures such as Alajos Stróbl (1856–1926), György Zala (1858–1937), Miklós Ligeti (1871–1944) and József Róna (1861–1940).

This was also the great period for the foundation of major museums. An Act of Parliament securing the purchase of the Esterházy Collection in 1871 also instituted the National Picture Gallery, which became the core of the Museum of Fine Arts, founded in 1896. The Arts and Crafts Collection was originally set up in 1872 for educational purposes and to encourage the development of crafts, but by 1896 it had grown into the permanent collection of the Museum of Applied Arts. In 1884 the Hungarian Historical Portrait Gallery became independent and was housed in the Academy of Sciences. Excavation of the Roman remains in Óbuda began in 1880, and the Aquincumi Museum was built on the site of the ancient civilian town in 1894. Later the Metropolitan Museum, planned in 1898, grew up around it; its first exhibition was in 1907. It is now the Budapest Historical Museum. This museum structure has been significantly modified twice during the 20th century, with the foundation of the Metropolitan Gallery in 1932 and the development of the Hungarian National Gallery in 1957 out of the Hungarian collection of the Museum of Fine Arts. Budapest's art life was invigorated around the turn of the 20th century by Art Nouveau, which emerged as a reaction against the prevalent historicism, and also by the proliferation of artists' associations and societies for the organization of exhibitions, such as the National Salon Club (1894), the Artists' Centre (1909) and the Ernst Museum (1912), which paralleled the development of the Art Hall. From the beginning of the 20th century the city accommodated all the trends in Hungarian art, a role that became even more pronounced after World War I, when most of the important provincial cultural and art centres were absorbed by neighbouring countries. As a result Hungarian art life has become concentrated almost exclusively in Budapest. With the changes in the political climate from the late 1980s, there was a greater sense of openness in Budapest art life. The number of private galleries—of both traditional and contemporary art—increased, and many native Hungarian artists who had moved abroad during the Socialist period returned to show their work in Budapest, bringing with them their experience of other Western art centres.

BIBLIOGRAPHY

H. Horváth: *Budapest művészeti emlékei* [Budapest's monuments of art] (Budapest, 1938)

S. Zakariás G.: *Budapest* (1961), iii of *Magyarország művészeti emlékei* [Hungary's monuments of art] (Budapest)

L. Gerevich: *The Art of Buda and Pest in the Middle Ages* (Budapest, 1971)

ERNŐ MAROSÍ

III. Centre of ceramics production.

In the Middle Ages the potters of Buda and Pest produced simple earthenwares: jugs, pots, dishes and plates, as well as fireplace tiles, of which many richly decorated examples remain. The first tin-glazed decorative wall tiles and ornate dishes in Hungary were made in Buda. From 1470 until 1480 faience was produced in a workshop in the Royal Palace of Buda, probably established by Petrus Andrea da Faenza of the bottega Bettini in Faenza. The coloured roof tiles of the Stephansdom in Vienna were made in Buda. In 1785 Domokos Kuny (1754–1822) opened a faience and stoneware factory, and wares were influenced by those of Holics and Tata. The factory closed in 1813. In 1864 Ignác Fisher established a stoneware factory in Pest, which produced high-quality, richly decorated dishes, imitative of wares from the Zsolnay Ceramic Factory, in Pécs; the two factories merged in 1895. The son of Ignác Fisher, Emil Fisher, also owned a stoneware factory. The Drasche Brickworks produced fine porcelain dinner-services and ornamental wares from 1909. The earthenware works in Kispest (est. 1922) produced dinner, tea and coffee services and decorative ornaments; after 1930, under the new title of Granit, the factory also produced porcelain. The Hüttl Porcelain Factory (est. 1854) developed from a small workshop for painting ceramics, and their fine porcelain dinner-services were much sought after. The factory was nationalized in 1948 and continued to operate throughout the 20th century under the name Aquicum. In the 20th century several studio potters including Géza Gorka (1894–1971), Margit Kovács (1902–77) and Hajnalka Zilzer (1893–1957) worked in Budapest.

BIBLIOGRAPHY

L. Gerevich, ed.: *Budapest története* [The history of Budapest], 5 vols (Budapest, 1973–80)

FERENC BATÁRI

IV. Buda Castle.

1. ARCHITECTURE. The postulated existence of a 13th-century precursor to the medieval Royal Palace on the southern part of Castle Hill in Buda is disputed; unresolved problems concern the archaeological interpretation of the oldest walls and the written sources for the location of the *curia regis*. The earliest excavated remains of the palace came from the István Tower, named after Louis I's brother Stephen (1332–54), and therefore probably built in the mid-14th century. Adjoining it, around an inner courtyard, were two wings of the Angevin palace, begun under Louis, which comprised the hall, the treasury and the royal office of records. In the east wing was a double chapel, of which the lower part has been uncovered. King Sigismund of Luxembourg (*reg* 1387–1437) extended the Angevin castle by adding an L-shaped court bounded on the north and east by the so-called Frischer Palace, first mentioned in 1424; according to the written sources this was never completed (*see* §2 below). Flanking this courtyard was an enormous unfinished donjon, the Csonka Tower. The system of defence walls and gate-towers around the castle, still mostly intact, was also built under Sigismund.

3. Budapest Castle, knight wearing chaperon (detail of head no. 46), limestone, h. 410 mm, *c.* 1419–33 (Budapest, Historical Museum)

Construction continued under Matthias Corvinus (*reg* 1458–90), who built a Renaissance palace in the east wing, including his library, the Biblioteca Corviniana, an observatory, living quarters and a throne-room. The earliest recorded date in this building is 1479, the year of the contract to the Florentine builder Chimenti di Leonardo Camicia (1431–before 1505). The remains of terracotta decorations, however, suggest that an architect from Lombardy may have been active in the 1460s; and the architectural decoration indicates the presence of masons from Lausitz in Silesia. Florentine influence is clearest in the portico built around the trapezoid inner court of the Angevin palace. The cistern and hanging garden in the west wing were probably based on similar works in Urbino and were possibly also influenced by the *Trattato de Architettura* of Antonio Filarete. Work on Matthias's palace continued under Vladislav II Jagiellon (*reg* 1490–1516), and the whole was heavily fortified against the Turkish threat by John I (*reg* 1526–40).

Under the Turkish occupation of the 16th and 17th centuries the castle fell into ruin (see fig. 1 above), and the 18th-century palace, which formed the kernel of the later Royal Castle, was built partly on the filled-in medieval ruins. The south wing of the royal palace was built between 1715 and 1735 on the ruins of its predecessor, to a design by Fortunato de Prati (1680–1738); from 1749 the west wing was converted to a Baroque royal residence by Ignác Oraschek, working to designs attributed to the court architects Jean-Nicolas Jadot de Ville-Issey and Nikolaus Pacassi. This had two courtyard blocks joined by a central wing, decorated with rustication and a giant order of pilasters. From 1757 the Hungarian Treasury in the palace was built by Franz Anton Hillebrandt, who had to modify it in 1762 to house the church of the English Young Ladies (Institute of the Blessed Virgin Mary), and again in 1777 for the University, which was transferred from Nagyszombat (now Trnava, Slovakia) until its final establishment in Pest in 1790. The castle was decommissioned in 1875 and at once renovated in a historicist style, beginning with the building of the Castle-Bazaar by Miklós Ybl from 1875 to 1881. Ybl also began the neo-Baroque restoration of the Royal Palace (1883–91), which was continued up to 1905 by Alajos Hauszmann, who doubled the size of the Danube wing. The castle was badly damaged in World War II.

The medieval remains were excavated from 1948 to 1963 and again from 1967, and their partial reconstructions are exhibited in galleries beneath the Széchenyi National Library and the Historical Museum, while the architectural and sculptural fragments, with many smaller finds, are exhibited in the Historical Museum in the south wing.

BIBLIOGRAPHY

J. Balogh: 'A budai királyi várpalota rekonstruálása a történeti források alapján' [The reconstruction of the royal palace in Buda Castle on the basis of historical sources], *Művészettörténeti Értesítő*, i (1952), pp. 29–40

L. Gerevich: *A budai vár feltárása* [The excavation of Buda Castle] (Budapest, 1965)

2. SCULPTURE. The most significant sculptures from the Royal Palace, a group of damaged statues carved from

local limestone, were excavated in the forecourt in 1974. They had been used as infill in the 15th century. Most of the statues were either half-finished or had been broken while being carved, and it is probable that none of them reached the buildings for which they were intended. Similar fragmentary statues were found during earlier excavations at Buda Castle, disputably dated to *c.* 1360/70 or 1400. All the sculptures are now in the Budapest Historical Museum. The group comprises religious figures including saints, the Virgin, Apostles and prophets, secular figures, bishops, royal knights (see fig. 3) and ladies with their retainers and shield-carriers in ceremonial court dress. Stylistically, they are contemporary to King Sigismund's palace (*see* §1 above), and perhaps in particular to work in the main hall of the so-called Frischer Palast. Their unfinished state may be connected to the break in the building work.

The source of the sculptures cannot be directly identified from their inscriptions, but Bertrandon de la Brocquière, the Burgundian envoy to Budapest, mentioned the departure of the masons working at Buda in 1433. The royal arms of Bohemia found on the fragment of a helmet-ornament unearthed with the statues indicates a date after 1419, when Sigismund was crowned King of Bohemia. The statues were probably carved over a relatively short period by a large team of sculptors. Most of the figures show close links with the soft style practised in Lower Austrian sculpture, particularly associated with works by the MASTER OF GROSSLOBMING (*see* MASTERS, ANONYMOUS, AND MONOGRAMMISTS, §I). A smaller group seems to be the work of a master from Brabant, or more specifically from the Lower Rhine region around Cologne and Aachen. The combined styles may have influenced local sculptors, in particular one whose sculpted heads and cubic-type clothes transcend the dominant soft style and who can perhaps be identified with a sculptor of red marble tombs at Buda around 1430 known as the Master of the Stibor grave-slabs. The Castle sculptures' stylistic and iconographic affinities with French court art may demonstrate Sigismund's taste for representational art, presumably acquired during his travels as Holy Roman Emperor through western Europe from 1412 to 1419 in connection with the Council of Konstanz. These statues are the most extensive group of secular sculpture of the period, and their undisputed provenance gives them added significance.

BIBLIOGRAPHY

E. Marosí: 'Vorläufige kunsthistorische Bemerkungen zum Skulpturenfund von 1974 in der Burg von Buda', *Acta Hist. A. Acad. Sci. Hung.*, xx (1976), pp. 333–71

L. Zolnay: 'Der gotische Skulpturenfund von 1974 in der Burg von Buda', *Acta Hist. A. Acad. Sci. Hung.*, xx (1976), pp. 173–331

E. Marosí: 'König Sigismund von Ungarn in Avignon', *Orient und Okzident im Spiegel der Kunst: Festschrift für H. G. Franz zum 70. Geburtstag* (Graz, 1986), pp. 229–49

L. Schultes: 'Der Meister von Grosslobming und die Wiener Plastik des Schönen Stils', *Wien. Jb. Kstgesch.*, xxxix (1986), pp. 1–40, 223–44

M. V. Schwarz: *Höfische Skulptur im 14. Jahrhundert: Entwicklungsphasen und Vermittlungswege im Vorfeld des Weichen Stils* (Worms, 1986), pp. 445ff

Művészet Zsigmond király korában, 1387–1437 [Art in the age of King Sigismund, 1387–1437] (exh. cat., ed. E. Marosi; Budapest, Hist. Mus., 1987), i, pp. 251–68

ERNŐ MAROSÍ

Buddhism. A religious tradition that emerged in India around the 6th to 5th century BC and spread throughout Asia. The term 'Buddhism' is a creation of Western scholarship, in which it is sometimes defined as a philosophy, civilization or culture rather than (or as well as) a religion. The tradition's name is derived from its founder, Siddhartha Gautama, who, on attaining spiritual enlightenment, was known as the Buddha or 'Awakened One'. The art of Buddhism reflects the tradition's ideals and the sophisticated aesthetics of the varied regions and cultures in which it flourished. Its central symbol is the Buddha image, serving as a focus for meditation, devotion or ritual and expressing the peace, harmony and power of enlightenment. Central to Buddhism is the concept of the cycle of rebirth. Three main movements developed within Buddhism: Theravada ('Doctrine of the elders'), Mahayana ('Great vehicle') and Vajrayana ('Thunderbolt vehicle'). Though nearly extinct in India by the 13th century, Buddhism had by that time spread by southern and northern routes to Sri Lanka, Burma, Thailand, Cambodia, Vietnam, Central Asia, China, Tibet, Korea, Japan and Mongolia. Despite the influence of Islam and Christianity and the political upheavals of the 19th and 20th centuries, it remains an important force in much of Asia and a continuing inspiration for the region's art. In the 20th century Buddhism attracted a following in the West, especially in Europe and North America.

I. Introduction. II. Iconography. III. Regional surveys.

I. Introduction.

Buddhism is a complex religion with a variety of doctrines, practices and philosophic paths. Most share an ultimate goal: the attainment of *nirvāṇa* or salvation and escape from the cycle of rebirth. Most also adhere to the Middle Way, the path between severe asceticism and sumptuous living advocated, according to tradition, by the historical Buddha himself. The flexible nature of Buddhism and absence of a single doctrinal authority have enabled the religion to flourish in cultures as varied as those of Sri Lanka, Tibet and Japan. Its adaptation to indigenous cultures has, in turn, contributed to its diversity. Both the continuous thread of the tradition and its regional variations are reflected in Buddhist art.

1. The historical Buddha. 2. *Bodhisattvas* and transcendent Buddhas. 3. Teachings. 4. Literature.

1. THE HISTORICAL BUDDHA. Central to the Theravada tradition and important in most forms of Buddhism is the historical Buddha (*c.* 553 BC, though dates ranging from *c.* 624 BC to *c.* 488 BC have been suggested). According to Buddhist texts, his given name was Siddhartha, his clan name Gautama, and he was a member of the Shakya tribe and thus known in later life as Shakyamuni, the sage of the Shakyas. His father Shuddhodana was the tribal chief, ruling an area straddling the modern India–Nepal border from the city of Kapilavastu.

Little factual material is available documenting the events of the Buddha's life. More important for Buddhism and Buddhist art is the traditional story that has been passed on by followers. According to this frequently illustrated narrative, the birth of an exceptional child was

1. Prince Siddhartha, the future Buddha, going forth from his palace, depicted on a marble relief from Amaravati, 2nd–3rd centuries AD (London, British Museum)

prophesied by the wise men of the court of Kapilavastu on hearing Queen Maya tell of a dream in which a white elephant entered her side. The Queen set out for her mother's home for the delivery, but the child was born along the way in a grove of sal trees at Lumbini (in modern Nepal). The birth scene in Buddhist art is modelled on Indian images of the *yakṣī* or *śālabhañjikā* (Skt: female fertility spirit) represented grasping the branches of a flowering or fruit-laden tree: Queen Maya holds the branches of a sal tree, while the baby emerges from her right side, received by the Hindu god Indra.

Most of the wise men at the court prophesied that Prince Siddhartha would become a great world ruler. One, however, said the sorrows of the world would lead him to become a spiritual teacher. He was thus brought up surrounded by the pleasures of life and shielded from its misery. He was married at the age of 16 to his beautiful cousin Yasodhara, but despite the comforts of his life and the promise of kingship he became disillusioned. He learnt of the vulnerability of the human condition on seeing three signs: an old man, a sick man and a corpse. A further sign, a holy man radiating harmony and inner joy, showed the path he must follow.

Siddhartha renounced the world at the age of 29, soon after the birth of his son, Rahula, to search for the 'supreme state of peace'. This event, a favourite theme of artists, is known as the Great Renunciation or Great Going Forth (*Mahābhiniṣkramaṇa*; see fig. 1). His quest for peace led to apprenticeship under two spiritual masters, performance of sacrificial rituals and extreme self-mortification. Images show him emaciated, with sunken eyes and skeletal frame. When he became dissatisfied with these methods, his comrades deserted him. Finally, intent on gaining enlightenment, he sat locked in meditation beneath a pipal tree at Bodhgaya. Mara, the Buddhist satan, who failed in his attempts to frighten or tempt him, demanded evidence of his worthiness. Siddhartha touched the earth with his hand, a gesture associated in Buddhist art with the enlightenment, and the earth answered in the voice of thunder: 'I am his witness'. At the age of 35, on his 49th day of meditation, he understood the secret of sorrow and how to overcome it; he became enlightened.

After remaining in contemplation for some weeks, the Buddha travelled to Sarnath, near modern Varanasi, where he preached the first sermon to his five former companions. In Buddhist terminology he set the wheel of the doctrine (*dharma*) in motion; in Buddhist art the wheel symbolizes both the first sermon and the doctrine. The Buddha spent the next 45 years as an itinerant monk, preaching mainly in the area now comprising Bihar and eastern Uttar Pradesh. Early in his ministry he founded an order of monks (*bhikṣu saṅgha*) and in the fifth year, after some hesitation, an order of nuns (*bhikṣunī saṅgha*). His teachings are said to have won a large following, including rulers and numerous ordinary citizens, before he died at Kushinara at the age of 80, achieving *nirvāṇa* (see fig. 2). His body was cremated and his relics were divided among various clans, who built tumuli over them. Thus began the tradition of building STUPAS (commemorative mounds) enshrining the relics of Buddhist saints.

According to tradition, the Buddha attained his enlightenment having remained a *bodhisattva* (one on the path towards becoming a Buddha) for several lifetimes, during which he perfected various virtues and meditations. The

2. Buddha achieves *nirvāṇa*, depicted on a stone relief, Gandhara style, 10th century (London, British Museum)

events of the Buddha's previous lives are told in the *avadāna* and *jātaka* stories, many of which are animal fables, some perhaps older than Buddhism. Illustrated copies of the *jātaka* stories remain in use as aids in ethical teaching.

2. *Bodhisattvas* AND TRANSCENDENT BUDDHAS. In the Theravada tradition the historical Buddha is central; in other Buddhist traditions he is accompanied by a host of other Buddhas and *bodhisattvas* and sometimes overshadowed by them. These include Buddhas of past ages who preceded Shakyamuni and are in theory infinite in number. They sometimes appear in wall paintings as a countless Buddha field. Among those frequently depicted individually are the Buddha Dipamkara, seen in Indian, Central Asian and Nepalese art, and the Buddha Prabhutaratna, who occurs mainly in Chinese and Korean art.

More important is the *bodhisattva* Maitreya ('the friendly one'), known by various names throughout the Buddhist world (e.g. Jap. Miroku). In the vast body of literature and mythology that surrounds him, Maitreya is usually described as a disciple of Shakyamuni Buddha now dwelling in the Tushita Heaven, from which he will be reborn to usher in an age of peace and prosperity. Numerous cults and movements have formed around the promise of his coming, especially in China and Korea. Other *bodhisattvas* known and depicted throughout the Buddhist world include Avalokiteshvara, the *bodhisattva* of compassion, and Manjushri, the *bodhisattva* of wisdom.

Though his images are rare in India, the healing Buddha, Bhaishajyaguru, is the focus of veneration in China, Japan and Tibet and is frequently depicted in the art of these countries. It has been argued that Bhaishajyaguru is a manifestation of the historical Buddha, who was given the epithet 'supreme physician', whose good health was noted in texts, and who stressed proper health care and nursed ailing monks. Bhaishajyaguru's name is remembered and repeated to relieve suffering.

Mahayana texts such as the *Saddharmapuṇḍarīka sūtra* ('Lotus of the true law', or Lotus Sutra) assume the existence of Buddhas in other worlds who through their merit have gained the power to aid those who call on them from this world. Among the most powerful and popular is Amitabha (Jap. Amida), who offers rebirth in his Pure Land (Sukhavati), a world indescribably splendid and joyful. Amitabha is said to have been the *bodhisattva* Dharmakara, who saw the suffering of the world and in compassion vowed to create a paradise for those unable to perform difficult austerities in which conditions would be ideal for attaining Buddhahood. Paradise scenes, particularly popular in the art of China, Korea and Japan, often show Amitabha in his Western Pure Land but also depict the paradise of Bhaishajyaguru and the paradise to be ushered in by Maitreya.

By the 6th century AD or earlier the Vajrayana movement, known in Western scholarship also as Tantric or Esoteric Buddhism, had developed in India. By the 8th century it was established in Nepal and Tibet, had reached China (where its elaborate rituals and sexual imagery were less widely accepted) and had gained substantial influence in Japan and Indonesia. The Vajrayana tradition is complex; some texts posit a primordial or central Buddha, the essence of all Buddhahood and the source of a set of Buddhas often conceived of as ruling over the four quarters of the world. The central Buddha is named in texts as Vajradhara or Vairochana or sometimes simply as the Adi ('primordial') Buddha, with Amitabha (west), Akshobhya (east), Amoghasiddhi (north) and Ratnasambhava (south) as the Buddhas of the four quarters. These and other transcendent Buddhas, along with families of deities associated with them, were depicted in art, especially in *maṇḍalas*, the cosmic diagrams invoked in rituals and meditational practices.

Historical figures were also elevated to the position of Buddhas, venerated and depicted in the art of a particular school or region. These include, for instance, Padmasambhava, credited with bringing Buddhism to Tibet, and KŪKAI, founder of the Esoteric Shingon tradition in Japan.

3. TEACHINGS. Buddhism's vast complex of teachings and philosophies is not easily delineated succinctly, but there is a didactic core shared by most manifestations of the tradition. Most important are the Four Noble Truths: the truth of the existence of suffering (*duḥkha*), the truth of the arising of suffering (*samudaya*), the truth of the cessation of suffering (*nirodha*) and the right way of conquering desires (*mārga*). According to the first, life is said to be characterized by *duḥkha*, a term often narrowly translated as suffering but meaning general unsatisfactoriness as well. In saying that life is less than perfect, Buddhism claims it is being realistic and not pessimistic. The second truth explains the cause of this suffering as resulting from desire or craving (*tṛṣṇā*). The third truth establishes that suffering, though painful, is not inevitable, for its cause can be removed. The fourth truth spells out a programme known as the Eightfold Path (*aṣṭāṅgika-mārga*) through which desire can be extinguished and *nirvāṇa* attained. The steps consist of right views, right resolution, right speech, right action, right livelihood, right exertion, right mindfulness and right meditation.

With the Four Noble Truths at its core, the practice of Buddhism by lay followers does not differ greatly between the Theravada, Mahayana and Vajrayana traditions. Where differences exist, they owe more to the indigenous cultures to which Buddhism was adapted. However, the three traditions, although not claiming to be contradictory or mutually exclusive, do differ considerably in their teachings on the possibility and process of salvation. In the Theravada tradition the monastic path is emphasized. The ideal of the monk is to become an *arhat* or fully realized being, who is assured of *nirvāṇa* or total emancipation at the end of his life. The Mahayana tradition saw this view as too conservative and élitist and called itself the Great Vehicle because it claimed to be able to carry a large number, including lay followers, to liberation. It referred to previous traditions as the Hinayana or Lesser Vehicle, as liberation was restricted to the few. Its way to salvation was the *bodhisattva* path, with heavenly *bodhisattvas* available as guides and saviours. Alternatively, transcendent Buddhas, such as Amitabha, offered access to their paradises. The basis for differences in teaching is explained in the Mahayana doctrine of the Buddha's three bodies (*trikāya*), in which the real body is identified as the cosmic body (*dharmakāya*), identical with the universe. The other two, the body of communal enjoyment (*sambhoga-kāya*), through which he delivers sermons to various celestial communities, and the body of transformation (*nirmāṇa-kāya*), the form in which the Buddha appeared on the earth, are manifestations that the Buddha assumes to instruct, expounding his teachings in a way consistent with the ability of the followers to grasp them. The Vajrayana movement emphasizes rituals and meditation techniques aimed at attaining union with cosmic aspects of Buddhahood. Its teachings are esoteric, transmitted from master to disciple. They promise a more direct path to *nirvāṇa*, possibly within a single lifetime.

In none of the three movements is a belief in God relevant. Buddhism is thus often described as atheistic but in a special sense, for it is possible to believe in gods, local or titular deities, who are seen as having attained their special status on account of their *karma* (quality of actions). It also accepts semi-divine beings. *Nat*-worship, for instance, is a significant aspect of Burmese Buddhism, and *yakṣa*s and *yakṣī*s (male and female fertility spirits) regularly appear in India's Buddhist art. Buddhism further rejects belief in a soul, yet this should not be taken to mean that it rejects belief in an afterlife, in morality or a transcendent reality. The portrayal in Tang-period (AD 618–907) Chinese art of the terrors of hell, the elaboration in Buddhist *tangkas* of the workings of *karma* and the universal image of the Buddha wrapped in the realization of *nirvāṇa* are proofs of the presence of these ideas in Buddhism, which otherwise insists that existence is indelibly characterized by impermanence (*anitya*), the absence of any perduring element (*anātman*) and full of suffering (*duḥkha*).

Especially within the Mahayana tradition various schools developed, stressing different aspects of the teachings; they ranged from the Pure Land school, involving devotion to Amitabha, to Chinese and Japanese Chan (Jap. Zen) Buddhism, emphasizing the enlightenment experience. Sectarian movements, such as that founded by the Japanese reformer Nichiren (1222–82), further extended the general pattern of Buddhist teaching.

4. LITERATURE. The canon of Theravada Buddhism, called the *Tripiṭaka* ('Three baskets'), as committed to writing in the 1st century BC in Sri Lanka, consists of the *Sutta piṭaka* (discourse on doctrine), the *Vinaya piṭaka* (the rules of discipline for monks) and the *Abhidhamma piṭaka* (the psychological and logical elaboration of the teachings). These contain further subdivisions. The language of the canon is Pali; commentaries on it, also important, are in Pali, Sinhalese, Burmese and other languages.

The canon of Mahayana Buddhism, larger by comparison, varies in its content and organization with the country where it is found and sometimes according to school or sect. The following texts or classes of text are widely acknowledged: the *Prajñāpāramitā* ('Perfection of wisdom') *sūtra*, the *Saddharmapuṇḍarīka* ('Lotus of the good law') *sūtra*, the *Laṅkāvatāra* ('Entrance of the good doctrine into Lanka') *sūtra*, the *Daśabhūmika* ('Ten stages') *sūtra*, the *Sukhāvatīvyūha* ('Description of the Pure Land'), the *Avataṃsaka* ('Garland') *sūtra*, the *Ratnakūṭa* ('Jewel heaps') *sūtra*, the *Hṛdaya* ('Heart') *sūtra*, the *Vajracchedikā sūtra* or Diamond Sutra and the *Vimalakīrtinirdeśa* ('Exposition of Vimalkirti') *sūtra*. Sanskrit is generally the language of Mahayana Buddhism, but many texts survived only in Chinese, Tibetan or other translations. Commentaries in Sanskrit and other languages are also important.

The revealed texts of the Vajrayana tradition are known as *tantra*s. Among the most important are the *Vairocanābhisaṃbodhi tantra*, the *Tattvasaṃgraha tantra*, the *Hevajra tantra*, the *Guhyasamāji tantra* and the *Kālacakra tantra*. The main languages of texts are Sanskrit, Tibetan and Chinese. Commentaries are particularly important as the texts are obscure, their meaning intended to be explicated by an initiated master. A group of short texts known as *sādhana* give methods for evoking a deity; a number of these are collected in the *Sādhanamālā*. There are also texts on *maṇḍala*s and rituals associated with them, including the *Niṣpannayogāvali*, discussing 26 *maṇḍala*s.

BIBLIOGRAPHY

E. J. Thomas: *The Life of Buddha as Legend and History* (London, 1927, rev. 3/1949)
——: *The History of Buddhist Thought* (London, 1933/*R* 1951)
A. Foucher: *La Vie du Bouddha* (Paris, 1949); abridged Eng. trans. by S. B. Boas (Middletown, CT, 1963)
E. Conze: *Buddhism: Its Essence and Development* (New York, 1951/*R* 1959)
——: *Buddhist Texts through the Ages* (New York, 1954)
T. R. V. Murti: *The Central Philosophy of Buddhism: A Study of the Mādhyamika System* (London, 1955/*R* 1960)
W. T. de Bary, ed.: *Sources of Indian Tradition*, i (New York, 1958)
E. Conze: 'Buddhism: The Mahayana', *The Concise Encyclopedia of Living Faiths*, ed. R. C. Zaehner (Boston, 1959)
I. B. Horner: 'Buddhism: The Theravada', *The Concise Encyclopedia of Living Faiths*, ed. R. C. Zaehner (Boston, 1959)
W. Rahula: *What the Buddha Taught* (New York, 1959, rev. 1974)
D. T. Suzuki: *Outlines of Mahayana Buddhism* (New York, 1963)
D. Goddard, ed.: *A Buddhist Bible* (Boston, 1966)
F. J. Streng: *Emptiness: A Study of Religious Meaning* (Nashville, 1967)
K. K. S. Ch'en: *Buddhism: The Light of Asia* (Woodbury, NY, 1968)
R. H. Robinson and W. L. Johnson: *The Buddhist Religion: A Historical Introduction* (Belmont, 1970, rev. Encino, 3/1982)
M. E. Spiro: *Buddhism and Society* (New York, 1970)
Bhikku Nanamoli: *The Life of Buddha: According to the Pali Canon* (Kandy, 1972/*R* 1978)
T. Ling: *The Buddha: Buddhist Civilization in India and Ceylon* (New York, 1973)
Y. Yoo: *Buddhism: A Subject Index of Periodical Articles in English, 1728–1971* (Metuchen, 1973)
D. J. Kalapahana: *Buddhist Philosophy: A Historical Analysis* (Honolulu, 1976)
H. Nakamura: *Gotama Buddha* (Los Angeles, 1977)
M. Carrithers: *The Buddha* (Oxford, 1983)
H. Bechert and R. Gombrich, eds: *The World of Buddhism* (London, 1984)

ARVIND SHARMA

II. Iconography.

The direct representation of the Buddha in art only became acceptable from the early centuries AD; prior to that, symbols, such as the wheel or the STUPA, were considered more respectful. However, once the principle of figurative representation had been established, a rich iconographic tradition rapidly developed, especially after the emergence of the Mahayana school. In Esoteric and Tantric traditions, such as the Vajrayana, cosmic diagrams (*maṇḍala*s) and images of deities play an important role as aids to meditation (*see* §I above).

1. BUDDHAS. As the founder of Buddhism, the historical Buddha Shakyamuni or Siddhartha Gautama is naturally its most common icon; however, representations of him vary considerably from country to country and over time. In Gandhara sculptures of the 2nd and 3rd centuries AD, for example, he appears in the guise of a Greek nobleman clad in long, draped robes. In the canonical scriptures, Shakyamuni is said to have had 32 major and 84 minor physical characteristics (*lakṣaṇa*), but only some of these appear in Buddhist art, the most prominent being the fleshy protuberance on the crown of his head (*uṣṇīṣa*), originally denoting the turban of a prince, and the curl of hair between his brows (*ūrṇā*), usually sculpted as a round dot. In most images made before the 7th century AD the Buddha is represented as a monk; later he was sometimes shown in royal attire wearing a crown and ornaments. Seated statues of Shakyamuni (*see* INDIAN SUBCONTINENT, fig. 163; *see also* JAPAN, fig. 54) often show him sitting cross-legged in the 'lotus' meditation posture (*padmāsana*), with the left hand resting in his lap while he touches the ground with the right (*bhūmiśparsa mudrā*), a gesture associated with his enlightenment and also with his victory over the evil tempter Mara (*Maravijaya mudrā*; *see* THAILAND, §I, 3 and fig. 15). Other seated figures show him with his hands held in front of his chest, with the index finger of the right hand touching the thumb and the left hand held below, its fingers touching the palm of the right hand in the gesture of teaching or setting the Wheel of Law in motion (*dharmacakra mudrā*). Standing images of Shakyamuni usually show him with a raised right hand (*abhaya mudrā*) and a lowered left hand with the palm turned towards the spectator (*dāna mudrā*), respectively signifying the bestowal of fearlessness and generosity.

In South-east Asia, Shakyamuni is generally the only form of Buddha represented in sculpture, but elsewhere and in other media many other forms occur, particularly in Esoteric and Tantric contexts. Early images of Mahavairochana or Rocana, the absolute (*dharmakāya*) form of Shakyamuni, show him as a monk, with his entire body covered with such images as houses, people, celestial bodies and mountains. Later versions show him seated in meditation posture with his hands in the 'diamond fist' gesture (*vajra mudrā*), which signifies the bestowal of charity. Here the right hand grasps the thumb of the left, signifying the union of all opposites in the absolute. In the Tantric tradition he is often shown crowned and adorned with garlands of jewels. Amitabha (Jap. Amida), the Buddha of the Western Pure Land, is also normally shown in the robes of a monk but with both shoulders covered (*see* JAPAN, fig. 57). Most often his hands assume the teaching gesture, but he is also shown making a peculiar meditation gesture (*dhyāna mudrā*), in which the thumbs of both hands touch the tips of the index fingers (*see* INDIAN SUBCONTINENT, fig. 175). This *mudrā* is very common in Japan. He is also sometimes depicted holding a bowl (*see* JAPAN, §II, 3). Amitabha is sometimes replaced by Amitayus, his blissful form (*sambhogakāya*), who is shown wearing a crown and jewelled ornaments. When depicted in the meditation posture, he holds a vase containing nectar (*amṛta*) in both hands. In Tantric iconography Amitabha is coloured red. Bhaishajyaguru (Jap. Yakushi), the Buddha of healing, is shown wearing a monk's robe; he usually holds a medicine bowl in his left hand, while the right hand proffers medicine. Late examples represent him with a crown and ornaments. In the Tibetan tradition he is shown as blue in colour. Maitreya is the Future Buddha (Jap. Miroku; *see* JAPAN, fig. 56). Early representations from India and China show him sitting on a throne, but by the Tang period (AD 618–907) his form had become established as a Buddha sitting in the European fashion (*pralambhapādasāna*), with both legs touching the ground or a lotus plinth. In East and South-east Asia he is shown as a *bodhisattva* sitting on a throne with one leg placed on the other and his inclined head resting on one hand. The Five Jinas or Dhyani Buddhas of the Five Directions are late additions to Buddhist iconography and occur in the Esoteric context only. They are the white Vairochana of the centre, the blue Akshobya of the east, the yellow Ratnasambhava of the south, the red Amitabha of the west (see above) and the green Amoghasiddhi of the north. They are sometimes depicted seated in sexual union with their consorts in the bliss of non-duality. The Dhyani Buddhas are very important in the Tibetan and Mongolian traditions but are also known in East Asia.

In general the Buddhist attitude to figural imagery is ambivalent, and there can sometimes be no more than a fine line between veneration of the Buddha image and actual worship (*see also* ICONOCLASM).

2. *Bodhisattvas* AND *arhats*. In Mahayana Buddhism a *bodhisattva* is a Buddha-candidate, a higher being who has embarked on the spiritual development but postpones his own *nirvāṇa* in order to help others on the path. In Theravada Buddhism a *bodhisattva* is a being who has reached the state preceding final liberation, which is the attainment of full Buddhahood. As the personification of compassion, Avalokiteshvara (*see* INDIAN SUBCONTINENT, fig. 199) is undoubtedly the most popular *bodhisattva*. A major characteristic is a small image of Amitabha Buddha in his crown or headdress. Originally male, this *bodhisattva* was slowly transformed into a woman in East Asia, a transition that had largely been accomplished by the 11th–12th century. In addition, the Esoteric tradition has produced a number of multi-armed and multi-headed versions of Avalokiteshvara, the most popular of which is the Thousand-armed, Thousand-eyed Avalokiteshvara (*see* VIETNAM, fig. 12). Manjushri is the *bodhisattva* of wisdom (see fig. 3). His usual attribute is the sword, which in East Asia became a sceptre. He is often shown astride a lion, his special mount, and occurs in numerous forms, including a number of Esoteric types; certain Chan Buddhist versions show him as a beggar or a youth clad in a grass robe. Samantabhadra, the *bodhisattva* of goodness, has a white, six-tusked elephant as his special vehicle and may sometimes be shown holding a lotus flower. He rarely occurs alone, often forming a pair with Manjushri. Kshitigarbha, the only *bodhisattva* represented as a monk, is the saviour of those destined for the hells. He is usually shown with a shaved head, although in later Chinese versions he sometimes wears a crown. His attributes are a monk's staff and a translucent pearl. A female *bodhisattva* of great importance in Tibet and Mongolia is Tara (*see* TIBET,

3. The *bodhisattva* Manjushri, shown sitting in a shrine with two worshippers, with his hands in the teaching *mudrā*, Indian palm-leaf manuscript, 10th century (London, British Library, Vikramaśilā MS. Or. 6902)

fig. 14), who is depicted as a young woman seated in a relaxed pose and holding a flower. She is represented in 21 different forms, of which Green Tara (Shyama Tara) is the most popular. She also occurs frequently in Sino-Tibetan art from the Yuan period (1279–1368) onwards.

The monastic disciples of Shakyamuni, the *arhats* (*see* TIBET, fig. 13), constitute a special category within Buddhist iconography. Although they sometimes appear as principal figures, they are often found as attendants to Buddha images in sculptures and paintings. The most important of these disciples are Mahakashyapa, who is depicted as an old monk with a haggard face and long eyebrows, and Ananda, Shakyamuni's nephew, who is shown as a young man with a calm and benevolent face. Other important disciples include Subhuti, the hero of several *sūtras*, Shariputra and Maudgalyayana.

3. PROTECTORS, GODS AND OTHER BEINGS. The Buddhist pantheon also includes a host of protector deities as well as gods, such as Shiva, Brahma and Indra, assimilated from the Hindu pantheon (*see* HINDUISM). In addition to these is the eightfold class of beings consisting of men, gods (*devas*), demigods (*asuras*) and mythical creatures, *nāgas* (serpents), *garuḍas* (eagles with human arms and torsos), demons (*rakṣas*) and heavenly musicians (*gandharvas*, *kinnaris* and *kinnaras*), half-human, half-bird. The beings of the eightfold class are usually shown as part of the assembly in scenes of the Buddha preaching. Prominent among the protector deities are the four guardians of the cardinal points (*lokapālas*) or Four Guardian Kings. These comprise Vaishravana, the Lord of the North, usually shown with a lance in one hand and a pagoda in the other; Dhritarashtra, the Lord of the East, holding a lute; Virupaksha, the Lord of the West, who holds a small dragon and a pearl; and Virudhaka, the Lord of the South, who brandishes a sword. In Esoteric and Tantric Buddhism there is a large number of protectors (*vidyārājās*), of which Mahakala, Yamantaka, Trailokyavijayaraja, Hayagriva, Acala (Jap. Fudō) and Da Yuanshuai are the most popular. They are variously shown with two, four, six or eight arms, in which they brandish various weapons and attributes such as tridents, maces, skull-cups, axes, swords, bows and arrows. They often have three or more faces; each face has three eyes, of which the central one represents wisdom. Some protectors are wrathful, others have benign expressions. Among the latter are Mahamayuri, the Peacock King, and Ushnishavijaya, an eight-armed female deity. Tantric deities are often shown in sexual embrace with their consorts. A lesser category of protecting beings, the guardians of temple gates, are shown as fierce-looking men with muscular bodies.

Countless lesser beings include nature spirits, dragons, denizens of the underworld and various celestial beings. Among these lesser iconographical figures also appear a number of cultural heroes, such as Sudhana, usually shown as a young boy in the company of Avalokiteshvara, the fat, jolly monk Budai (Jap. Hotei), said to be an incarnation of Maitreya, and Bodhidharma, the founder of Chan (Jap. Zen) Buddhism, who is shown as an austere-looking Indian monk with glaring eyes. In Tibet many lamas and local gurus were also included in the pantheon.

BIBLIOGRAPHY

Taisho daizokyo [The Taisho edition of the *Tripiṭaka*], 12 vols (Tokyo, 1923–8) [iconog. suppl.]

A. K. Gordon: *The Iconography of Tibetan Lamaism* (New York, 1939, rev. 1988)

E. D. Saunders: *Mudrā: A Study of Symbolic Gestures in Japanese Buddhist Sculpture* (New York, 1960)

B. Bhattacharyya: *The Indian Buddhist Iconography* (Calcutta, 1968)

J. Okazaki: *Jōdokyōga*, Nihon no bijutsu [Arts of Japan], xxxiii (Tokyo, 1971); Eng. trans. by E. ten Grotenhuis as *Pure Land Buddhist Painting*, Japanese Arts Library, iv, ed. J. Rosenfield (Tokyo and New York, 1977)
B. C. Olschak and others: *Mystik und Kunst Alttibets* (Berne and Stuttgart, 1972)
S. Tenzin and G. Oleshay: 'The Nyingma Icons: A Collection of Line Drawings of 94 Deities and Divinities of Tibet', trans. K. Dowman, *Kailash*, iii/4 (1975), pp. 320–416
T. Bowie and others: *The Sculpture of Thailand* (Canberra, 1976)
S. Gaulier, R. Jera-Bezard and M. Maillard: *Buddhism in Afghanistan and Central Asia*, Iconography of Religions, XIII/xiv (Leiden, 1976)
D. L. Snellgrove, ed.: *The Image of the Buddha* (London and Paris, 1978)
F. M. Asher: *The Art of Eastern India, 300–800* (Minneapolis, 1980)
U. von Schroeder: *Indo-Tibetan Bronzes* (Hong Kong, 1981)
P. Pal and L. Fournier: *A Buddhist Paradise: The Murals of Alchi, Western Himalayas* (Basle and New Delhi, 1982)
Indo kōdai chōkoku ten/Ancient Sculptures of India (Tokyo and Kyoto, 1984)
Nihon bukkyō geijutsu no genryū/Sources of Japanese Buddhist Art, 2 vols (Dohosha, 1984)
Budda Shaka: sono shōgai to zōkei: Nara kokunitsu hakubutsukan, shōwa 59-nen 4-gatsu 29-nichi-6-gatsu 3-nichi/Arts of Buddha Sakyamuni: Special Exhibition (exh. cat., Nara, N. Mus., 1984)
Hong Yiyao, ed.: *Fojiao tuxiang jieshuo huadian* [Pictorial dictionary of Buddhist images with explanation] (Taipei, 1985)
Li Zhenfu: *Dunhuang shouzi* [Hand gestures of Dunhuang] (Changsha, 1985)
Buddhism: Art and Faith (exh. cat., ed. W. Zwalf; London, BM, 1985)
Mun Myŏng-dae: *Sokkuram pulsang chogak ŭi-yŏn'gu* [A study of the Buddhist sculptures in Sokkuram] (Seoul, 1987)
Yu Yunshui, ed.: *Fojiao shouyin tushuo* [Charts of Buddhist *mudrā*s with explanation] (Taipei, 1988)
H. H. Sørensen: *The Iconography of Korean Buddhist Painting*, Iconography of Religions, XII/ix (Leiden, 1989)
E. R. Jansen: *The Book of Buddhas: Ritual Symbolism Used on Buddhist Statuary and Ritual Objects* (Diever, 1990)
Samguk sidae pulgyo chogak [Buddhist sculpture of the Three Kingdoms period], Seoul, N. Mus. (Seoul, 1990)
P. M. Herbert: *The Life of the Buddha* (London, 1992) [Burmese MSS]

HENRIK H. SØRENSEN

III. Regional surveys.

1. Indian subcontinent. 2. Sri Lanka. 3. South-east Asia. 4. Central Asia. 5. Nepal. 6. Tibet. 7. Mongolia. 8. China. 9. Korea. 10. Japan.

1. INDIAN SUBCONTINENT. Less than 1% of the population of modern India is Buddhist. Among those counted in this number are Buddhist communities of Himalayan regions such as Ladakh and Sikkim, refugees to India from Tibet (who number less than 100,000 but include several thousand monks; *see also* §6 below) and converts to Buddhism from the 'scheduled' or 'ex-untouchable' classes. The last group is sometimes known as Neo-Buddhists or Ambedkar Buddhists, after Bhimrao Ambedkar (1891–1956), who led a revival movement advocating Buddhism as an egalitarian Indian religion offering an alternative to caste hierarchies. There is much vitality in the religion and art of these contemporary groups, but little chance of a major resurgence of Buddhism in India.

India's importance for Buddhism (and its art) is thus mainly historical. This was the land where Shakyamuni Buddha lived and taught (*see* §I above), and places associated with events in his life remain important pilgrimage centres. It was the land where the first images of the Buddha were produced (*see* INDIAN SUBCONTINENT, §II, 2(i) and (ii)) and where Buddhist iconography and symbolism evolved, to be elaborated with the spread of the tradition (*see* §II above). From *c.* 200 BC to *c.* AD 200 Buddhism represented an extremely powerful presence on the Indian subcontinent, to judge by the sheer number of artistic remains and relics in comparison with those of other religions.

Over the next few centuries, however, even when other religions, especially Hinduism, began to gain ground, the Indian religious scene remained dominated by the great triad of Indic religions—HINDUISM, Buddhism and JAINISM. From around the 5th century AD the development of Tantra (a system of ritual action thought to lead the practitioner towards salvation) deeply affected all three religions. During the following centuries a rather paradoxical development ensued. On the one hand the Buddhist order of monks and nuns as a separate entity ceased to exist in India; on the other Buddhist ideas and ideals profoundly influenced Hinduism, into which Buddhism was virtually absorbed by the 12th century. Nevertheless, India remains at the heart of Buddhist cultural and doctrinal history: Buddhism's great issues were debated on Indian soil, and its three principal movements—Theravada, Mahayana and Vajrayana—emerged in India to take root in other lands.

(i) Early development, before *c.* 300 BC. (ii) *c.* 300 BC–*c.* AD 300. (iii) After *c.* AD 300.

(i) Early development, before c. *300* BC. The historical Buddha, who spent much of his teaching life in the region that is now Bihar and eastern Uttar Pradesh, is described in texts (committed to writing some centuries later) as exhorting his disciples to go out and preach his gospel in all directions, thereby establishing Buddhism as an explicitly missionary religion. Little documentation exists for early Buddhism, but it appears that as it spread it developed schismatic tendencies.

According to tradition, a First Council was held at Rajagriha (Rajgir) shortly after the Buddha's death, followed by a Second Council at Vaishali 100 years later. Accounts of the Second Council indicate tensions within the tradition, especially between monks living in and around modern Patna (the 'Easterners') and those who lived around modern Ujjain (the 'Westerners'). The *Vinaya piṭaka* suggests that the differences centred on matters of monastic discipline; later Buddhist tradition alludes to doctrinal differences as well. The main monastic point was the acceptance of gold and silver by monks, a practice allowed by the Easterners but censured by the Westerners, who also criticized the Easterners for being deviant in other matters, such as taking food after midday. The main doctrinal issue seems to have been the sinlessness of the *arhat* (Skt: enlightened person); the Easterners considered him capable of lapsing while the Westerners regarded him as fully emancipated. Efforts at mediation failed, with the consequence that the Easterners broke away in protest, possibly as early as the 4th century BC, and came to be known as the Mahasanghika ('Members of the great order'). Although the Mahasanghika originally arose in the east (i.e. Bihar), this region did not become their stronghold. Their relations with Theravada Buddhists are obscure until the 3rd century AD when the Third Buddhist Council met (*see* §(ii) below). The Westerners became known as the followers of Theravada or Sthaviravada ('Way of the elders'). Further splits occurred within these groups, with the result that tradition records some 18 sects by the 3rd century BC.

(ii) c. *300* BC–c. AD *300.*

(a) Emperor Ashoka. Under the patronage of the Mauryan emperor Ashoka (*reg c.* 269–232 BC), Buddhism became a dominant force in the subcontinent. The edicts of Ashoka, carved on pillars and rocks, indicate a tolerance towards all religions but a preference for Buddhism. A Third Council, held during the reign of Ashoka, was dominated, according to Theravada works, by monks of that tradition, who received royal favour. Prominent among the points at issue was the idea that the Buddha was not an ordinary human being, as the Theravada Buddhists maintained, but rather a supramundane being who had manifested himself for the welfare of humanity and whose apparent earthly career was a benign fiction. An altered concept of *bodhisattvas* accompanied this revived conception of the Buddha: they were now also considered supramundane. Similarly, the Buddha's ministry assumed a different aspect: the Buddha was continuously in *samādhi* (trance) and only appeared to deliver sermons, while in fact the words flowed spontaneously from his lips and were compiled in discourses. These discourses were adjusted to the calibre of the disciples.

Royal patronage of the Theravada apparently had the effect of consolidating that group in the north and geographically dispersing the other sects into different parts of India. The Sarvastivada ('Followers of the doctrine that all exists') became popular in the north-west; the Mahasanghika made some gains there and also in the Deccan. The Sarvastivada were doctrinally innovative in their view of the constituents of things existing in all the three dimensions of time (past, present and future), as opposed to the Theravada doctrine that things exist only in the present. They anticipated some Mahayana doctrines, though not to the same extent as the Mahasanghika. The burst of missionary activity under Ashoka is credited with the establishment of Buddhism in Sri Lanka. Tradition records that Ashoka's son, Mahinda, became a Theravada monk and took the tradition in that form to the island.

The legacy of art and architecture from the Mauryan period, though scant, reflects the importance of Buddhism. The elaborate capitals of Mauryan-period pillars display such Buddhist symbols as the wheel (in Buddhism the wheel of the law or *dharma*) and the lion, associated with the historical Buddha, who is described in texts as the 'lion of the Shakyas' (*see also* INDIAN SUBCONTINENT, §IV, 3). Ashoka sponsored the excavation of rock-cut caves (three in the Barabar Hills bear inscriptions) and the raising of STUPAS over relics of the Buddha and revered monks (*see also* INDIAN SUBCONTINENT, §III, 3(ii)). The caves were created to provide shelter for wandering monks and ascetics (Buddhists and others) during the rainy season. By the 2nd century BC pilgrimage centres and monasteries had grown up at stupa sites associated with such events in the Buddha's life as his birth (LUMBINI), enlightenment (Bodhgaya; *see* BODHGAYA AND GAYA), first sermon (SARNATH) and death (KUSHINAGARA). Ashoka had his edicts carved on pillars raised at Buddhist pilgrimage centres and is recorded to have visited such sites.

(b) Foreign adherents. Some foreign rulers of the post-Mauryan period supported Buddhism, possibly with the aim of identifying with their subjects and unifying the divergent cultures of north India. The Greek Menander (*fl c.* 150 BC), known in Buddhist sources as Milinda, is claimed as a convert. The Shakas, a Scythian tribe who arrived on the fringes of the subcontinent *c.* 130 BC and gained control of much of north-west India (*see* SCYTHIAN AND SARMATIAN ART), supported Buddhism, as did the Kushana kings who ruled much of north India from *c.* AD 50–320. It is often claimed (but difficult to prove) that the great king Kanishka (*reg c.* 1st–2nd century AD) was himself a Buddhist. He is said to have called a Fourth Council, probably dominated by the Sarvastivada sect, which was popular in the north-west. The *Mahāvibhāṣā* (*c.* AD 150–200), a commentary that systematized the *abhidharma* (doctrinal elaboration) of the Sarvastivada and is considered a veritable encyclopedia of Buddhist philosophy, may have been redacted at the Fourth Council. Kanishka is said to have presented the Buddha's relics to the Sarvastivada. The stupa erected at his capital near modern Peshawar was renowned as the tallest structure of its type; the Chinese pilgrim Faxian records: 'Of all the stupas and temples which [the travellers] saw in their journeys, there was not one comparable to this in solemn beauty and majestic grandeur'.

(c) Major centres and early figural art. The ruins of the great Buddhist centres that prospered in the north-west in this period (and in many cases earlier and later) have been found at such sites as TAXILA, CHARSADDA and SHA-JI-KI-DHERI, near Peshawar, TAKHT-I-BAHI, SAHRI BAHLOL and JAMALGARHI, near Mardan, and in the Swat Valley at the site of ancient Uddiyana (*see also* INDIAN SUBCONTINENT, §IV, 5(ii) and (iii)). The flourishing state of Buddhism in the region is also evident from the tradition that in the 6th century AD the Huna king Mirpurkhas demolished 1600 Buddhist establishments in north-west India alone.

The support that Buddhism enjoyed in the western Deccan is clear from the sculptural sumptuousness and architectural elaboration of such caves as those at BHAJA, PITALKHORA, BEDSA, KARLE, NASIK and KANHERI (*see also* INDIAN SUBCONTINENT, §IV, 4(iii) and 5(iii)). In most regions new stupas were erected and old stupas renovated, with stone railings and gateways provided to replace wooden ones. The vitality of Buddhism in this period is reflected in the sculpture of such great stupa sites as SANCHI and BHARHUT in central India and AMARAVATI in Andhra Pradesh (see fig. 4; *see also* INDIAN SUBCONTINENT, §IV, 6(vi)).

One of the greatest Buddhist centres was at MATHURA, the Kushana kings' southern capital. (The northern capital was at Taxila in the Gandhara region.) Mathura is surrounded by a cluster of sites, once of royal and religious importance. Faxian noted that within the environs of the city there were some 20 monasteries and 3000 monks. Mathura in the Kushana period is particularly important for art history as a possible place of origin of the Buddha image. The sculpture of early Buddhist monuments such as the stupas at Sanchi and Bharhut seems to represent an aniconic phase in which figural work of great beauty and energy was produced but no images of the Buddha occur. Instead the Buddha was represented by such symbols as the wheel or the stupa. Scholarly debate on where and

4. Slab carved with a stupa with Buddhas and other figures, white marble, h. 1.27 m, from Amaravati, Andhra Pradesh, *c.* late 2nd century AD or early 3rd (London, British Museum)

when the first Buddha images were produced has continued for several decades. Early researchers favoured the north-west region of Gandhara, arguing that the influence of Greco-Roman art was an important factor in the creation of such images and even suggesting that the first Buddha images were made by foreigners, possibly itinerant Roman craftsmen who adapted their repertory to the needs of Buddhism. More recent scholarship sees the *yakṣa* (male nature spirit) as the prototype of the Buddha image, placing the stylistically more 'Indian' images from Mathura as the earliest. While early images from Gandhara show the influence of Mathura, the reverse does not seem to be the case, supporting the argument that the Mathura images evolved first (*see also* INDIAN SUBCONTINENT, §IV, 5(i)). Images of Buddhas and *bodhisattvas* dominate the art of Buddhist monuments from the 2nd century AD onwards, though the Buddha image is often used in conjunction with earlier Buddhist symbols such as the stupa (see fig. 4) and the wheel.

(d) Mahayana Buddhism. Developments in art are related to some extent to the emergence of the Mahayana ('Great vehicle') movement, with its aim of winning salvation for greater numbers, including lay followers. Many Mahayana tenets were anticipated by the Mahasanghika (*see* §(a) above). Mahayana appealed on varied levels: its subtle and complex philosophy offering the doctrine of emptiness (*śūnyatā*) and its popular practice characterized by devotional rituals. The evolution of the Mahayana movement seems to owe something to both internal doctrinal shifts and external social changes. An emphasis on the previous lives of Shakyamuni is already evident in the sculpture of such sites as Bharhut and Sanchi—a trend that culminates in the exaltation of the *bodhisattva* ideal in the Mahayana movement. The changing nature of Indian society as well as Iranian and Central Asian influence may have contributed to the importance of the laity in the Mahayana movement. An emphasis on devotional practices is a general feature of Indian religions of the period. A rising cult of Vishnu with a strong devotional current is evident from the 1st or 2nd century AD. Early images of Jaina saints and Hindu gods and goddesses date to approximately the same period as early Buddha images, suggesting that image-making evolved more or less contemporaneously in these traditions.

The emphasis in Mahayana Buddhism on merit as a factor in the attainment of enlightenment and the belief that merit could be transferred, for instance for the benefit of deceased parents, had important implications for the patronage of art. Inscriptions reveal that sculpture and paintings were financed by donors to gain merit for themselves, for relatives and for all sentient beings. The range of patrons included kings and queens, merchants, artisans, monks and nuns and ordinary lay followers.

(iii) After c. AD *300.*

(a) Beginnings of decline. From the 2nd century AD Hinduism was in the ascendent. Buddhism remained an important force in north India in the Gupta period (319/20–late 5th century), when images of Buddhas and *bodhisattvas* of great splendour were created (*see* INDIAN SUBCONTINENT, §V, 6(i)). Kumaragupta is said to have endowed the great Buddhist monastery at NALANDA in Bihar, which flourished for nearly a thousand years as one of the world's leading institutions of Buddhist scholarship. The Chinese pilgrims Xuanzang and Yijing describe its monasteries, libraries, temples, prayer-halls and observatories as humming with the activity of thousands of monk-scholars. A similar situation seems to have prevailed on the far west coast at the Buddhist university at VALABHI. Inscriptions mention a dozen spacious monasteries inhabited by learned and virtuous monks.

The generous support of Buddhism in the western Deccan in the 5th century is evident from the magnificent sculpture and fine painting from that period at AJANTA, which was within the domains of the Vakataka dynasty. All 27 caves there (some of which date from an earlier phase of *c.* 2nd–1st century BC) are Buddhist dedications. From *c.* 550 AD a new wave of donors embellished older Buddhist sites such as Karli, Nasik and Kanheri with sculptures, mainly of Buddhas and *bodhisattvas*. New caves were excavated in the 5th and 6th centuries at AURANGABAD (where at least one cave dates from an earlier phase of *c.* 1st century BC). At nearby ELLORA there are 34 caves and rock-cut temples, excavated mainly from the 6th to the 9th century: 12 are Buddhist, 17 Hindu and 5 Jaina.

That Buddhist influence remained important as far south as Tamil Nadu (where it was established at the time

5. Scenes from the life of the Buddha, ink and opaque watercolour on palm leaves, 50×535 mm, from manuscript of *Aṣṭasāhasrikā prajñāpāramitā sūtra* ('Perfection of wisdom in 8000 verses'), *c.* AD 1000 (Cambridge, University Library, Add. 1464, fol. 127*v*–128*r*)

of Ashoka) is evident both from surviving images and from Tamil literature. Only three of the five major epics of classical Tamil literature survive. (The two lost texts are attributed to Buddhist authors.) These portray considerable rivalry between Hindus, Buddhists and Jainas. The eponymous heroine of the epic *Maṇimēkalai* is a Hindu who becomes a Buddhist nun, while the *Kuṇṭalakēci*, also named after its heroine, is the story of a Jaina nun who subsequently becomes a follower of Buddhism. Accounts of her life are also found in the commentaries of certain Pali texts. The decline of Buddhism in the south may have set in by the 7th century, though pockets of Buddhism survived until around the 15th century.

(b) Tantra. Ironically, as Buddhism was losing its hold in other parts of India, it underwent a revival in the eastern regions of Bihar and Bengal during the Pala period (8th–12th century). The Buddhism of this period is associated with Tantra, a movement that began to gain momentum after *c.* AD 500 (*see also* §6 below). It affected all parts of India, although some more than others, and all the major religious traditions. To some extent Tantric ritual practices and teachings blurred the distinctions between Hinduism and Buddhism, although Buddhists insist on the uniqueness of their version both doctrinally and iconographically. Like Hindus, Buddhists distinguish between right-handed and left-handed Tantra, on the basis of whether its transgressive sacrality is to be taken metaphorically or literally. Buddhism, like Hinduism in its Tantric manifestation, becomes less respectful of and even directly antithetical to accepted social practices and norms. Despite its radicalism, however, it can be seen as a logical development within Buddhism. Pre-Mahayana Buddhism emphasized the polarity of the mundane and transcendental realms of *saṁsāra* and *nirvāṇa*. Mahayana Buddhism posited a negative identity between them, regarding both as existing only in relation to one another, therefore being empty of independent self-existence and hence identical in their emptiness. Buddhist Tantra or Vajrayana ('Diamond, or thunderbolt, vehicle') converts this negative identity into a positive one and maintains that, if *nirvāṇa* and *saṁsāra* are identical, then not only is one in *nirvāṇa* while one is in *saṁsāra* but an existential realization of this identity, which constitutes *bodhi* or enlightenment, may be triggered by apparently antinomian practices that disabuse the mind of distinctions. Moreover, in Buddhism the law of *karma* (moral cause and effect; quality of actions) is defined mainly in terms of intentionality, so that even deeds that seem sacrilegious, for example sexual intercourse, may lead towards salvation if carried out with that motivation. A third argument is epitomized in the Tantric motto, 'One rises by that by which one falls'; thus negative forces such as attachment and hatred, while destructive in themselves, can promote the spiritual development of the seeker when properly harnessed through Tantric practices. Finally, in keeping with the Mahayana doctrine, since realization is a matter of insight rather than mere morality, the cultivation of gnosis is primary and may be promoted by an iconoclastic attitude towards convention.

Tantra was specially influential in the development of Buddhist art after *c.* 500. Notable features were the role of ritual gestures and devices, the proliferation of deities and the incorporation of their spouses in intimate pictorial representations symbolizing non-duality, the use of *maṇḍala*s (mystic diagrams), visualization as a meditational exercise and the recognition of artistic activity itself as a form of spiritual practice, as in the preparation of *maṇḍala*s and painted hangings. Tantra minimized caste distinctions and emphasized the role of women, thus widening the appeal of Buddhism and of its art. The differences between Hindu and Buddhist Tantra often turn on symbolism, the Hindu Shiva and Shakti being replaced by Upaya ('Skilful means') and his consort Prajna ('Wisdom').

In the Pala period Tantra entered the mainstream of Buddhism and was taught in the great Buddhist universities of eastern India. Inscriptions link the Pala kings with the support of Nalanda as well as the universities of Vikramashila (probably located at ANTICHAK in eastern Bihar) and PAHARPUR. Buddhist manuscripts were copied, illustrated and preserved in such institutions. The earliest known Indian illustrated manuscript, a copy of the *Aṣṭasāhasrikā prajñāpāramitā sūtra* ('Perfection of wisdom in 8000 verses'), was produced in eastern India *c.* AD 1000 (see fig. 5). A great Buddhist university at RATNAGIRI in Orissa flourished from about the 5th century AD to the 12th. Other important Buddhist centres of Orissa were at nearby Lalitagiri and Udayagiri (*see* KHANDAGIRI AND UDAYAGIRI).

(c) Causes of final decline. The reasons for the almost total disappearance of Buddhism in India by the 13th century are complex; a variety of factors no doubt

contributed. The growing popularity of Hinduism, especially Shaivism and Vaishnavism, was important, as was the gradual merging of Hindu and Buddhist ideas and practices. Buddhism's reliance on monastic institutions seems to have proved a weakness when royal and other patronage declined. The destruction of monasteries during the Muslim conquest of north India in the late 12th century, and the flight of monks to Nepal and Tibet, was a final blow from which Buddhism never recovered. Although its great monasteries crumbled into ruins, Buddhism's ideas and ideals profoundly influenced Hinduism, into which it was virtually absorbed.

See also INDIAN SUBCONTINENT, §§I, 7 and II, 2.

BIBLIOGRAPHY

J. Legge, ed. and trans.: *A Record of Buddhistic Kingdoms* (Oxford, 1886/*R* New York, 1965)
T. Watter: *On Yvan Chwang's Travels in India* (London, 1904/*R* New Delhi, 1973)
A. B. Keith: *Buddhist Philosophy in India and Ceylon* (Oxford, 1923)
H. Bhattacharyya, ed.: *The Cultural Heritage of India*, i (Calcutta, 1937)
E. Conze: *A Short History of Buddhism* (Bombay, 1960)
N. Dutt: *Early Monastic Buddhism* (Calcutta, 1960)
E. Conze: *Buddhist Thought in India* (London, 1962)
H. D. Thera: *Buddhism in South India* (Kandy, 1968)
N. Dutt: *Buddhist Sects in India* (Calcutta, 1970)
P. Rawson: *The Art of Tantra* (London, 1973)
A. Wayman: *The Buddhist Tantras* (New York, 1973)
H. Bechert and R. Gombrich, eds: *The World of Buddhism* (London, 1984), pp. 59–98

ARVIND SHARMA

2. Sri Lanka.

(i) Introduction. For more than 2000 years the national identity and culture of Sri Lanka (formerly Ceylon) has been significantly shaped by Theravada Buddhism (*see* §I above), the predominant religion of the Sinhalese majority, followed in the 1990s by approximately 60% of the population. The development of the art, architecture and literature of Sri Lanka was largely inspired by Buddhism and is generally characterized throughout its history by the conservatism and preservation of tradition inherent in Theravada ('Doctrine of the elders'). The Sinhalese chronicles, the *Mahāvaṃsa* ('Great chronicle') and *Culavaṃsa* ('Little chronicle'), relate the history of Buddhism in the island in Pali, the canonical language of Theravada, and reinforce Sri Lanka's image as the supposed 'cradle' of orthodox Buddhism. The chronicles include accounts of three visits the Buddha is said to have made to the island during which he accorded it a particular significance as the future sanctuary of the true (i.e. Theravada) *dhamma* (Pali: 'doctrine'). This role was assumed by Sinhalese Buddhists, and they have attempted to uphold it throughout the centuries (see fig. 6).

Buddhism was originally established in Sri Lanka in the 3rd century BC, when, under the patronage of the Indian emperor Ashoka (*reg c.* 269–232 BC), missions were dispatched to spread the *dhamma* to the border areas of his extensive empire (*see* §1 above). The mission that reached Sri Lanka was headed by the elder Mahinda, traditionally said to have been Ashoka's son, who arrived with a retinue of monks large enough to hold an ordination ceremony. He converted the Sinhalese king, Devanampiya Tissa (*reg c.* 250–210 BC), who ruled from the capital of ANURADHAPURA. The King later founded a stupa to house a

6. Buddhist pilgrimage sites of Sri Lanka, depicted in a wall painting (detail), Talava Temple

relic of the Buddha at nearby MIHINTALE, where his conversion is said to have taken place. He donated a park in Anuradhapura to serve as a monastery, underlining his support for the establishment of Buddhism in the country, for it is the monastic order, the *saṅgha*, which is responsible for preserving and continuing the teaching of the Buddha. The monastery donated by the King was known as the Mahavihara and was the most influential in the early development of Sinhalese Buddhism, the self-proclaimed 'guardian of orthodoxy' where the chronicles were written. Mahinda's sister, the nun Sangha-mitta, later established the first order of nuns, which no longer formally exists in Sri Lanka. She also brought with her a branch from the tree under which the Buddha attained enlightenment; the tree descended from this cutting is still venerated in its shrine at Anuradhapura. Subsequent Sinhalese rulers continued to patronize Buddhism, which rapidly spread and grew in importance. Towards the end of the 1st century BC the Theravada canon, previously transmitted orally, was written down, apparently by a group of monks at the monastery known as Aluvihara near Kandy.

Buddhism in Sri Lanka suffered periods of decline owing to the pressures of foreign invasions from south India and, from the 16th century onwards, from Europe. It also suffered periods of internal decay, which led to the loss in Sri Lanka itself of the indigenous ordination that it had exported to Burma and Thailand (*see* §3 below). In 1753 a mission from Thailand re-established the tradition. The largest of the three main extant bodies of monks in Sri Lanka today, the Siyam Nikaya, are the heirs to that mission. Thousands of Sinhalese Buddhists annually undertake the pilgrimage to the shrine at Kataragama of the god Skanda, one of the four deities assigned Buddhist roles as protectors of Sri Lanka and preservers of the Buddha's doctrine. Thus, while Theravada Buddhism, the backbone of Sri Lanka's culture, is generally conservative, unostentatious and austere, it can also be eclectic.

(ii) Art and architecture. Conventionally both Sri Lanka's history and the development of its art are divided into periods according to the locations of the Sinhalese capitals. The longest-lived of these, during which most of the characteristic features of Sinhalese Buddhism and Buddhist art developed, was the Anuradhapura period (3rd century BC–10th century AD). The early art of this period was closely related to the Indian Andhra tradition of AMARAVATI, especially evident in the large and impressive stupas and early Buddhist images. In Sri Lanka these attained a rigid and austere monumentality that reflected and emphasized the Theravada interpretation of the Buddha's doctrine. During the Polonnaruva period (1070–1250), the artistic traditions of Anuradhapura were revived, and Sri Lanka began to relate to and strongly influence various South-east Asian Theravada communities, in terms of both their art and their religious practice.

The stupa (Sinh. *dāgaba*; 'relic container'; *see also* STUPA, §2), the chief early Buddhist monument, became the hallmark of Buddhism and a focal point for devotional practice, sanctioned by the Theravada canon. The stupa was a symbol of the final *nirvāṇa* and the end of the Buddha's activity in the world. Also a symbol of the eternal *dhamma* realized and taught by the Buddha, it was an object of veneration and pilgrimage, and the ancient stupas around Anuradhapura (*see* SRI LANKA, fig. 3) and elsewhere were particularly venerated and continually renovated. Distinctive circular roofed buildings with concentric rings of pillars were developed to enshrine stupas but retain their free-standing origin and permit circumambulation. The stupa was also the basis for the development of a cult of relics and relic worship. In Sri Lanka this cult inspired a voluminous literature and provided the occasion for the erection of many other types of buildings (*see* SRI LANKA, §III) and for the production of reliquaries often themselves stupa-shaped. In the 4th century AD one of the Buddha's teeth was brought from south India, and it became the principal relic of Sri Lanka. Like other sacred relics, it was moved by successive kings from capital to capital, and it is now enshrined in Kandy. The Temple of the Tooth (Sinh.: Daḷadā Māligāwa) is an imposing late 17th-century structure surrounded by a moat (*see* SRI LANKA, fig. 5). It also houses an important library of palm-leaf manuscripts.

In spite of claims in the chronicles, there do not appear to have been statues of the Buddha in Sri Lanka earlier than the 2nd–3rd century AD. The earliest images were based on the Buddha as a monk, and the traditional attitude of Theravada has generally allowed for little stylistic development in his portrayal in Sri Lanka. Gigantic images of the Buddha, both free-standing and rock-cut, were carved in both the main artistic periods. From the Polonnaruva period the images at the Gal Vihara at Polonnaruva are particularly famous (for illustration *see* POLONNARUVA). Despite its conservatism, Sinhalese Buddhism has accommodated a variety of religious influences, as has its art. The main influence was Hinduism, but both Mahayana Buddhism and folk religious traditions contributed influences. At Buduruvagala, an acknowledged Mahayanist site, a standing Buddha (h. 15 m), flanked by six smaller figures, was carved into a sheer rock face in the 10th century. In the 13th century shrines began to combine worship of Buddha with that of gods identified with Hindu deities, as can be seen at the great rock-cave temples at DAMBULLA.

See also SRI LANKA, §I, 3.

BIBLIOGRAPHY

W. Geiger, trans.: *The Mahāvaṃsa or the Great Chronicle of Ceylon* (Colombo, 1912)
W. Rahula: *History of Buddhism in Ceylon: The Anuradhapura Period* (Colombo, 1956)
J. Boisselier: *Ceylon: Sri Lanka*, Archaeologia Mundi (Geneva, 1979)
Buddhism: Art and Faith (exh. cat., ed. W. Zwalf; London, BM, 1985)
R. F. Gombrich: *Theravada Buddhism: A Social History from Ancient Benares to Modern Colombo* (London, 1988)

SALLY MELLICK

3. SOUTH-EAST ASIA.

(i) Introduction. Buddhism was first introduced into South-east Asia from India in the early centuries AD; it was initially confined to the deltas and coastal areas. It was then carried along the river systems in the region, up the valleys and into the interior. Like Hinduism, Buddhism brought with it not only religious rituals but also artistic concepts and motifs that gave tangible form to the doctrines and thereby enhanced the rituals. (For an account of Buddhism and Buddhist iconography and its relationship to Buddhist art in the countries of South-east Asia *see* BURMA, §I, 3; INDONESIA, §I, 3(iii); LAOS, §I, 3; MALAYSIA, §I, 3; THAILAND, §I, 3; and VIETNAM, §I, 3.) After a while, elements of the material culture of Indian Buddhism became appropriated. The dissemination was gradual and peaceful, and there does not seem to have been an organized or systematic process of evangelization in the region; the ancient texts do not record or even allude to any active proselytizing. In India itself it was chiefly the mercantile class who adopted Buddhism, and this suggests that traders may have been chiefly responsible for its introduction into South-east Asia. The priestly class, who alone possessed the requisite esoteric knowledge, depended on the merchant ships to take them overseas.

Neither Buddhism nor Hinduism superseded existing indigenous religions in South-east Asia; rather, they merged with them in a variety of forms. Moreover, both evolved and changed over the centuries. In South-east Asia the two religions seem to have functioned at different levels, even though doctrinally they complement each other. The art forms relating to each suggest that Buddhism operated more exclusively in the spiritual sphere, while Hinduism concerned itself more with the socio-political context, although in the powerful states that arose in the region, such as the kingdoms that flourished successively in Java, the Khmer empire of Angkor in Cambodia and the Burmese kingdom of Pagan, huge temples were erected for the religious cults of their ruling élites, whether Hindu or Buddhist. Buddhist art in South-east Asia generally displays greater creativity and innovation than Hindu art. This does not necessarily indicate preference for one religion over the other. Indeed, in South-east Asia, as in

India, since both religions are appropriate for certain intentions and in certain circumstances, patrons often treated both with equal honour.

In those South-east Asian countries where Buddhism was adopted by the ruling élite and became the state religion, Buddhist art and architecture acquired an official status. This is especially the case in those countries of mainland South-east Asia where the majority of the population is still Buddhist, unlike insular South-east Asia, which no longer has a significant number of adherents of either Mahayana or Theravada Buddhism.

From the 13th century onwards, Theravada (Skt *sthaviravāda*; 'Doctrine of the elders'), with Pali as its canonical language, became the predominant religion in mainland South-east Asia, establishing itself in Burma, Thailand and Laos both at court and among the people. This doctrine incorporates one of the most important features of early Buddhism, namely the advocacy of the reclusive life of the ascetic (*arhat*), whose ultimate goal is to achieve *nirvāṇa* (extinction). At the same time, variations in doctrine arose as a result of the mythology that had accumulated round the original philosophy and had encrusted it with religious observances. Buddhism, relatively less restricted than the ritually more orthodox and inflexible Hinduism, was more ready to allow popular participation. Moreover, the emergence of original art forms in Indianized South-east Asia through the modification of basic concepts and new interpretations of old themes suggests that South-east Asians themselves were active in spreading Indian cultural ideas at an early stage after their first contact with them. It is therefore futile to search for an Indian prototype for every Buddhist (or Hindu) work of art produced in South-east Asia. The ideology and elements of the technology and even of the aesthetics came initially from India, but inevitably variations soon developed, and it is precisely those variations that give the art of each of the receiving countries its identity. With this spread of Buddhism came the popular cult of the Buddha, first as a semi-divine and then as a fully divine being, making his teachings more accessible to the less educated and less sophisticated and enabling them to be not merely passive receivers of the doctrine but participants. This development led to the production of many different visual personifications and representations of Buddhist beliefs in various media.

Mahayana Buddhism, as it developed in South-east Asia, was characterized by the ease with which it syncretized with Hindu cults, the importance it attached to the idea of redemption of the souls of the dead, which, especially in Java and Bali, blended naturally with indigenous ancestor cults, and its tendency towards mysticism and Tantrism. There is some evidence to suggest that Tantrism, a form of both Hinduism and Buddhism in which magic and sexual symbolism played an important part, was introduced into South-east Asia at an early date—in Burma, for example, well before the reign of King Anawrahta (*reg* 1044–77), when Theravada Buddhism was adopted in Pagan, and in Sumatra perhaps already in the 7th century AD. There is also epigraphic and iconographic evidence of a pronounced Tantric element in the Buddhist cults practised in Java during the Singhasari (1222–92) and Majapahit (1292–*c.* 1500) dynasties and in central Sumatra under the rule of the Minangkabau king Adityavarman in the late 14th century.

(ii) Regional development. The earliest people to adopt Buddhism in Burma were the Pyus in the Irrawaddy basin. They were succeeded by the Mons, based in Lower Burma and round the basin of the Chao Phraya River in Thailand, who were already Buddhists by the 5th century AD. A Buddhist Mon state known as Dvaravati flourished in the Chao Phraya basin from the 6th to the 11th century. From the 5th century the Burmans moved southwards from Tibet, defeated the Pyus in the 8th century and established their capital at Pagan, which was one of the great centres of Buddhist art and architecture in South-east Asia from the 11th century to the late 13th. Although most of the temples of Pagan are today in ruins, Buddhism still survives vigorously in Burma. The Khmer empire of Angkor, which flourished from the 9th to the 15th century and extended at its height from the Mekong delta to the Khorat Plateau and central Thailand, was a Hindu state for most of its history but produced in Jayavarman VII (*reg* 1181–*c.* 1220) one of the greatest Buddhist rulers of South-east Asia. The Thai kingdom of Sukhothai in the 13th and 14th centuries and its successor Ayutthaya (1351–1767) combined several innovative and distinctive features with elements derived from the Mon and Khmer traditions. The development of Buddhist art in northern Thailand stemmed more directly from northern Mon art, which flourished from the late 7th century to the mid-11th in the area round Lamphun and Lampang near Chiang Mai. Finally, Buddhist art in the Ratanakosin period since 1767 has produced a multitude of rich and sumptuously decorated art forms in contrast to the relatively plain, simple and strong lines of Mon, Sukhothai or early Ayutthaya art. Generally speaking, Buddhist art in Vietnam is similar to that of south China, the Vietnamese having been subjected to Chinese rule from the 1st century AD to the 10th.

The island of Java, with its fertile volcanic soil, can support a very dense population, and this made it possible for the rulers to command corvée labour for the building of impressive religious monuments. There were also numerous small Buddhist states in Peninsular Malaysia and the Kra Isthmus and on the island of Sumatra, some of which may have formed part of or been subject to the thalassocratic empire of Srivijaya, which flourished more or less contemporaneously with the Hindu and Buddhist kingdoms of Java from the 7th to the 13th century. In the 7th and 8th centuries, when Mahayana Buddhism was at its height in both Java and Sumatra, Srivijaya was reputed to be a major centre of Buddhist learning. Archaeological excavations, however, have not yet revealed any monuments on a scale to match this reputation, which is derived only from epigraphic and textual sources.

(iii) Architecture and sculpture. The fundamental architectural form of Buddhism, both in India and South-east Asia, is the stupa (*see* STUPA, §3), which is a virtually solid, usually circular reliquary monument that has evolved from the burial tumulus. In South-east Asia it can take many forms, ranging from the high cylindrical dome of some of the stupas built by the Pyus of Srikshetra (5th–9th centuries AD) in Burma (*see* BURMA, §II, 1(i) and fig. 2) to the

7. The *bodhisattva* Lokeshvara, sandstone, h. 1.30 m, Bayon style, from Preah Thkol, late 12th century–early 13th (Paris, Musée Guimet)

elegant bell-shaped stupas (Thai *chedi*) with slender, tapering spires of the Ayutthaya period in Thailand (*see* THAILAND, §II, 1(vi) and fig. 7). The largest and most complex stupa in South-east Asia, if not the world, is Borobudur (for illustration *see* BOROBUDUR), built *c.* 800 in Central Java by a Buddhist ruler of the Shailendra dynasty.

In Buddhist sculpture the Buddha image, both in relief and free-standing, has always been the central subject. The Buddha is portrayed standing, seated, walking and reclining, in all the *mudrā*s (Skt: hand gestures) and all the *āsana*s (sitting postures). Images may be made of stone, bronze, gold, silver, base metals, wood, lacquer, hardstone, crystal or terracotta, although in each country there is a preference for certain iconographic features and for some materials over others. The Khmers have always shown a strong predilection for portraying the Buddha in *dhyāna mudrā* (meditation) after his enlightenment, seated on the coils of the *nāga* (serpent) king Mucilinda, protected from the rain by his seven-headed hood (*see* CAMBODIA, fig. 22). Perhaps the most original of all the varieties of Buddha image in South-east Asian art is the Sukhothai walking Buddha (*see* THAILAND, fig. 16), with its refined features and sinuously elegant figure clad in a diaphanous robe. Another development peculiar to Thai Buddhist iconography is the image of the Buddha riding on various mythical creatures, an idea apparently derived from images of Hindu deities on their mounts (*vāhana*).

In Mahayana Buddhism, images of the *bodhisattva*s (beings destined to attain Buddhahood) became popular. Some scholars have been tempted to see in the fervent Buddhism of Jayavarman VII, the portrait statues of him in meditation (*see* CAMBODIA, fig. 24) and even in the extraordinary face towers of the Bayon (*see* CAMBODIA, fig. 13) an indication that he was the object of a *Buddharāja* cult comparable to the *devarāja* ('the god who is king') cult of his Hindu predecessors (*see* CAMBODIA, §I, 2 and 3), in which he became an embodiment of the *bodhisattva* Avalokiteshvara (Lokeshvara). There is no conclusive evidence to support this conjecture, but it is certain that the cults of Lokeshvara (see fig. 7) and of the feminine *bodhisattva* Prajnaparamita ('Perfection of wisdom') were as popular among the Khmers as in other Mahayana Buddhist countries of South-east Asia, such as Srivijaya. Vietnamese images of the Buddha and of *bodhisattva*s are frequently made of carved wood (see fig. 8) and are generally both iconographically and stylistically similar to those of south China.

BIBLIOGRAPHY

L. P. Briggs: 'The Ancient Khmer Empire', *Trans. Amer. Philos. Soc.*, xli/1 (1951) [whole issue]

8. The *bodhisattva* seated on an elephant, polychrome wood, 13th–15th centuries, Ninh Phuc Temple, Bac Ninh Province, Vietnam

B.-P. Groslier: *Angkor: Hommes et pierres* (Paris, 1956)
A. J. Bernet Kempers: *Ancient Indonesian Art* (Amsterdam and Cambridge, MA, 1959)
L. Frederic: *Sud-Est Asiatique: Ses temples, ses sculptures* (Paris, 1964); Eng. trans. by A. Rosin as *Temples and Sculptures of South East Asia* (London, 1965)
M. Giteau: *Khmer Sculpture and the Angkor Civilization* (London, 1965)
G. H. Luce: *Old Burma, Early Pagan*, 3 vols (Locust Valley, 1969)
J. Fontein: *Ancient Indonesian Art of the Central and Eastern Javanese Periods* (New York, 1971)
T. Bowie, M. C. Subhadradis Diskul and A. B. Griswold, eds: *The Sculpture of Thailand* (New York, 1972)
J. Lowry: *Burmese Art* (London, 1974)
J. Boisselier: *Painting in Thailand* (Fribourg, 1976)
C. Stratton and M. M. Scott: *The Art of Sukhothai: Thailand's Golden Age* (Kuala Lumpur, 1981)
Buddhism: Art and Faith (exh. cat., ed. W. Zwalf; London, BM, 1985)

JOO-EE KHOO

4. Central Asia.

(i) Introduction. During the 1st millennium AD Central Asia was a dominant cultural pivot for the whole Buddhist world. Buddhism was introduced to China, for example, through the mediation of Central Asian monks, and Central Asia probably contributed to the development of Mahayana Buddhism. This past greatness contrasts sharply with the fragile condition of the region's contemporary Buddhist communities, which stem from various reintroductions of Buddhism from Mongolia beginning in the 17th century. The Buddhist tradition preserved by these scattered communities can be traced back further to Tibet (*see* §6 below). Moreover, from their beginnings, these Buddhist communities existed as minority groups facing continual competition from other religions, especially Islam. They also endured governmental intervention and persecution, from the Tsarist regime in Russia to the Communist governments of the former Soviet Union and the People's Republic of China.

This contrast between past and present means that most modern scholarly interest in Central Asian Buddhism is historical in orientation, concerned with the introduction and development of Buddhism during the period in which this religion flourished. Sources for the cultural history of Central Asian Buddhism consist of literary texts in a wide variety of languages, archaeological remains and reports by Chinese pilgrims and later Muslim observers. These sources, however, are often fragmentary and still await systematic study.

The Chinese pilgrim Xuanzang (*c.* AD 600–64) recorded a tradition that Buddhism was brought to Bactria in western Central Asia by two merchant brothers, the first lay disciples of the Buddha. While this legend has no historical confirmation, it does display two typical features in the self-image of Central Asian Buddhism: the prominence of lay people and the association of religion and trade. The first introductions of Buddhism to the region were probably motivated, at least indirectly, by the policies and actions of Ashoka (*reg c.* 269–*c.* 232 BC), the great Mauryan emperor of India (*see* §1 above). Ashoka sponsored missions not only within his own empire but to north-west India and Afghanistan; Buddhist missions to Central Asia later started from these regions. Ashoka also transformed Buddhism from a localized and sectarian, world-rejecting, monastic movement to a religion associated with empire and high civilization, an important factor in the spread of Buddhism throughout Central Asia. After Ashoka, Buddhism offered the vision and prestige of an international civilization that could transcend both cultural differences and geographical distance. The moral universalism of Buddhism was well suited to the cosmopolitanism of the oasis cities along the Silk Route. However, the spread of Buddhism was fostered as much by mercantile as by spiritual concerns.

Buddhist institutions were firmly established by the time of the consolidation of the Kushana empire, centred in Bactria, from north India to the western Tarim Basin *c.* AD 100. Profound changes in Indian Buddhist thought and practice during the Kushana period (*c.* 1st–3rd century AD) can be traced to cultural contacts made possible by the empire's expansion. The cults of the *bodhisattvas* and celestial Buddhas (e.g. Avalokiteshvara and Amitabha) include many features reminiscent of Iranian religions. Cultural contacts within the Kushana empire also encouraged the development of the Gandhara style of Buddhist art, with its Hellenized representation of the Buddha in human form (*see* Indian subcontinent, §V, 5(ii)). Buddhist texts portray the Kushana emperor Kanishka as a second Ashoka, renowned for his promotion of Buddhism. While other evidence suggests that this portrayal is somewhat overstated, there is no doubt that Buddhism benefited both from Kushana patronage and from the prestige of being associated with the empire. Missions from a variety of Buddhist schools, including such Hinayana schools as the Dharmaguptakas and the Sarvastivadins, spread Buddhist texts and institutions beyond the boundaries of the Kushana empire well into eastern Central Asia.

Buddhism was so well established throughout eastern Central Asia by the 3rd century AD that it was not dramatically affected by the collapse of the Kushana empire. Buddhist institutions received material support in the smaller kingdoms to which Buddhism had already been introduced, such as Khotan, Kashgar, Sogdiana and Loulan. New conversions to Buddhism occurred among various peoples, first among the peoples of Tumshuk and the Tokarians, later among the eastern Turks and Uygurs. Missionaries and scholar-monks travelled from kingdom to kingdom along the trade routes, and, although the region remained politically fragmented, considerable cultural cohesiveness was achieved. It is possible to discern literary links between distant sites; much of the known Khotanese and Sogdian literature comes from a library discovered at Dunhuang on the opposite side of the Tarim Basin, and there are Chinese inscriptions at Gilgit in modern Pakistan. Similar patterns of interaction in art are suggested by eastern Central Asian wall painting (*see* Central Asia, §II, 4).

Changes in political alliances, new patterns of commerce and the spread of Islam divided Central Asia as a cultural area, and its unity was irreversibly broken by *c.* AD 1000. The western part became increasingly Islamic, the east more Chinese, although some patterns of Central Asian Buddhism continued in isolated places until at least the 15th century.

(ii) Art and architecture. The centuries after the collapse of the Kushana empire in the 3rd century AD witnessed the greatest achievements of Central Asian Buddhism. Great

monasteries, both free-standing and in cave complexes, were built throughout the region, and some, such as those at Khotan, Gilgit, Turfan, Kucha, Khocho and DUNHUANG, became famous as centres of learning. A glimpse of the educational life of these monasteries is provided by 9th-century wall paintings from Ming-oi, at Shorchuk *c.* 190 km south-west of Turpan (Xinjiang Province, China), depicting student-monks studying books with teachers (see fig. 9). The ruins of monasteries that were not famous for learning, such as Miran, Bezeklik and Fondukistan, give some indication of the general prosperity and splendour of Buddhist institutions in Central Asia during this period. Emblems of civilization itself, sumptuous monasteries were built without any pretence of the ascetic denial that might be expected in the residences of Buddhist monks, with even their most functional parts, such as ceiling beams and doorjambs, richly ornamented. These monasteries were decorated with sculptures and paintings portraying the great beings of the Buddhist pantheon, illustrating scenes from Buddhist history and mythology or depicting donors making gifts to Buddhist monks and monuments (*see* CENTRAL ASIA, figs 68, 69 and 70). Differences in the appearance and dress of the donors in these paintings give vivid evidence of the ethnic pluralism of Buddhist communities in Central Asia.

9. *Buddhist Monks and their Teacher*, wall painting (fragment), 710×455 mm, from Ming-oi, Shorchuk, Xinjiang Province, China, 8th–9th centuries AD (London, British Museum)

Some impression of the varied religious life of Central Asian Buddhism can be gained from the architectural and artistic remains of these monasteries. Some, such as the cave monasteries at Turfan, seem intentionally isolated from worldly affairs, while others, such as those at Khotan, suggest greater secular involvement. As in other areas of the Buddhist world, devotion and merit-making both produced and were focused on stupas (*see* STUPA, §4) and images of the Buddha, and both the latter were prominent features of Central Asian monastic life. Some stupas were large, imposing architectural monuments, painted and decorated with sculptures, but small portable votive stupas were also popular in Central Asia. Stupas and images could be honoured by circumambulation, by ritual offerings of flowers, food and other precious substances and by decorating them with embroidered or painted cloth. Embroidered cloth was also used to decorate the monasteries and to provide a protective wrapping for books. Archaeological evidence indicates that books themselves were used as devotional offerings.

Other works of monastic art may have served as models and supports for particular visualization techniques in Buddhist meditation, such as the recollection of the Buddha and devotional meditations on celestial Buddhas and *bodhisattvas*. The iconography of Central Asian Buddhist art, whether decorative, devotional or meditational, is indicative of the broad, systematic changes in conceptions of the Buddha, the Buddhist path and reality in general that were taking place throughout the Buddhist world. There was an increasing tendency to elevate Buddhahood to greater levels of grandeur and power, until the Buddha was equated with reality itself. This equation was visually represented by superimposing cosmological imagery on to the body of the Buddha (e.g. *see* CENTRAL ASIA, fig. 72). It is possible that the motif of a cosmological Buddha was created in Central Asia.

See also CENTRAL ASIA, §§I, 1(v) and II, 1(v)–(vi).

BIBLIOGRAPHY

D. L. Snellgrove, ed.: *The Image of the Buddha* (Paris and Tokyo, 1978)
L. Sander: 'Central Asia', *Encyclopedia of Buddhism*, ed. J. Dhirasekera (Colombo, 1979), iv, pp. 21–75
Along the Ancient Silk Routes: Central Asian Art from the West Berlin State Museums (exh. cat. by H. Härtel, New York, Met., 1982)
O. von Hinüber: 'Expansion to the North: Afghanistan and Central Asia', *The World of Buddhism*, ed. H. Bechert and R. Gombrich (London, 1984), pp. 99–107
R. E. Emmerick: 'Buddhism in Central Asia', *Encyclopedia of Religion*, ed. M. Eliade (New York, 1987), ii, pp. 400–04

CHARLES HALLISEY

5. NEPAL. While it is conceivable that Buddhism found its way to the Nepal Valley during the lifetime of the Buddha and that the emperor Ashoka (*reg c.* 269–232 BC) visited the region, the first datable contact with India can be placed in the first quarter of the 4th century AD, and the earliest evidence of the presence of Buddhism belongs to the second half of the 5th century. According to Lichchhavi inscriptions the Buddhist ruler Vrishadeva (*fl c.* AD 400) founded a monastery at SVAYAMBHUNATHA (see fig. 10). Although the Lichchhavi kings were generally Hindus, they also contributed to the foundation and

10. Svayambhu Stupa, Svayambhunatha, Nepal, begun 5th century AD

support of Buddhist monasteries. Most Lichchhavi foundations, including that at Svayambhunatha, have disappeared, but a few, such as the Gum Vihara monastery near SANKHU, have survived.

Buddhism in the Nepal Valley developed in a unique way, both because of historical and cultural changes related to the disappearance of Buddhism from India (*see* §1 above) and for social and geographical reasons. After the destruction of the great monastic universities in India, the Newar Buddhist tradition was cut off from its sources, while Newar Buddhists were constantly exposed to the pressure of a caste-dominated society within the narrow boundaries of the valley. Eventually their monastic communities came to constitute a sort of priestly class, the members of which continue to inherit their titles but renounce their vows by means of a special ceremony. In spite of its limitations, Newar Buddhism may be viewed as the survival of Indian Buddhism, just as the sophisticated artistic production of the Nepal Valley represents the continuation of the PALA AND SENA artistic traditions of India.

The traditional style of architecture characterizing most of the 363 monasteries extant in the Nepal Valley can be traced to such early Indian monastic buildings as those found at Sanchi, Ajanta and Ellora. These represent stone prototypes of the brick and wood monasteries of the Nepal Valley, comprising a series of rooms surrounding an open courtyard or assembly hall and a shrine opposite the entry. Few modern Newar monasteries conform in their function to their Indian prototypes, for the rooms surrounding the courtyard have become residential buildings, but all are characterized by three essential elements: a shrine of the Buddha opposite the main entry, which generally faces north, a small stupa in the centre of the courtyard and a Tantric chapel (*āgam*) above the Buddha shrine, where initiated members of the religious community gather to worship the secret tutelary deities of the monastery. Another feature derived from ancient India is the *toraṇa*, originally a decorated arch or arched doorway leading into a shrine; in the Nepal Valley this became a semicircular panel of carved wood or embossed metal placed over the doors of both Buddhist and Hindu shrines. In the centre of the *toraṇa* are represented one or more figures, the chief image portraying either the Buddha or a Tantric deity. The Newar Buddhist pantheon, with its various forms of Buddhas, *bodhisattva*s, goddesses, wrathful protectors and tutelary deities, is largely based on a vast corpus of Indian Tantric literature in which Shaiva, Buddhist and local beliefs and practices merged. Therefore, the iconography of nearly all Tantric deities represented in the Nepal Valley belongs to the Indian tradition, in which Buddhism and Hinduism coexisted and influenced each other for many centuries.

BIBLIOGRAPHY

D. Snellgrove: *Indo-Tibetan Buddhism* (London, 1987)

J. Locke: 'The Unique Features of Newar Buddhism', *The Buddhist Heritage*, ed. T. Skorupski (Tring, 1990)

ERBERTO F. LO BUE

6. TIBET.

(i) Introduction. Tibetan Buddhism is a branch of Buddhism that incorporates, along with earlier doctrines, a form of Mahayanah (Tib. *theg pa chen po*) known as Vajrayana (*rdo rje theg pa*; 'the indestructible path'), called also Mantrayana or Tantrayana. It evolved from a quest for quicker ways to reach enlightenment. Combining ritual and yoga, it is based on revealed texts called *tantra*s (*rgyud*). Visual imagery is intimately linked to the complex meditational practices, such as elements of deity yoga (*lha'i rnal 'byor*), that are transmitted directly from an enlightened teacher, or lama, to his disciple. Through this meditative practice, consisting of ritual, visualization (*see also* TIBET, §I, 5) and *mantra* (a spiritually charged word or phrase), the practitioner develops discriminating wisdom that directly realizes the true nature of phenomena and the emptiness of inherent existence.

The *tantra*s are classed into four groups—*Kriyā tantra* (*bya rgyud*), *Caryā tantra* (*spyod rgyud*), *Yoga tantra* (*rnal 'byor rgyud*) and *Anuttarayoga tantra* (*bla na med rgyud*)—according to their respective deities. Also, because practitioners have different capacities and levels of development, *tantra*s are organized according to different approaches to the realization of Buddhahood (see Tucci, 1980, pp. 71–80, and bsTan 'dzin rgya mtsho). Texts from the *Anuttarayoga tantra* class have been particularly popular since the end of the so-called Second Diffusion of Buddhism (*see* §(iii) below) in Tibet. They include two stages of meditation, one of generation (Skt *utpattikrama*), the second of completion (*sampannakrama*). The latter incorporates the higher initiations (*dbang bskur*; Skt *abhiṣeka*), which include so-called 'sexo-yogic' imagery. When the *yi dam* (*chos kyong;* Skt *dharmapāla*), a tutelary or personal meditation

11. *Kālacakra maṇḍala*, painting on cloth, 830×755 mm, from central Tibet, late 16th century (Paris, Musée Guimet)

deity, is shown embracing his consort, the image is known as *yab yum* ('mother-father'; *see* TIBET, fig. 8); the female deity symbolizes wisdom (Skt *prajñā*), the male deity the means (*upāya*).

In a *tangka* of the *Kālacakra maṇḍala* (see fig. 11) the tutelary deity Kalachakra is depicted embracing his consort, Vishvamata, in the first enclosure in the centre of the *maṇḍala* (*dkyil 'khor*), a circular psychocosmogram in which the essentials of the Tantric teaching are symbolized. The liturgy contains a precise description of the deities and their *maṇḍala*s. In the course of the Tantric initiation ceremony the initiate enters the *maṇḍala* and identifies himself with the essence of Buddhist enlightenment, symbolized by the *yi dam* who presides over the *maṇḍala*. The exact shape of the *maṇḍala* varies according to the central image. Art is best understood as a symbolic expression of Buddhist doctrine and serves the practitioner as an aid in recognizing the ultimate; by manipulating its symbols the mind is able to attain new depths of consciousness.

(ii) First Diffusion, c. *7th–10th century* AD. The introduction of Buddhism, perhaps as early as the 7th century AD, during the reign of the 'first religious king', Songtsen Gampo (srong btsan sgām po; *reg c.* AD 620–49), coincided with the transition in Tibet from a decentralized political system, mostly governed by tribal confederations, to a centralized kingdom. In the 8th century Buddhism became the state religion of Tibet. It is likely that the earliest Buddhist monuments in LHASA (since the 7th century the capital of Tibet), the Ramoche and a chapel on the site of the present Jokhang, date to this period. Despite the testimony of later sources, it is clear that Buddhism fought a long battle against indigenous religions. The contemporaneous situation can in part be understood through the study of the first Tibetan monastery at SAMYE, which demonstrates the influence of two Indian Buddhist traditions: the monastic and the Tantric. The monastery was founded through the combined efforts of the Indian scholar-monk Shantarakshita, the Indian Tantric master Padmasambhava and Trisong Detsen (khri srong lde brtsan; *reg c.* 755–94).

Following the establishment of Samye, the first Tibetan monks were ordained. According to an inscription, noble monks who served as ministers had a higher status than their lay counterparts. Thus, two enduring themes in the political life of Tibet were established: the political role of the clergy and their superior authority. Like later monasteries, Samye was endowed with extensive lands and had a tax-free status. Monasteries became powerful economic and cultural forces that dominated every aspect of life. Until the 1950s monasteries were the primary sources of patronage in the arts (*see also* TIBET, §I, 9).

During the reign of the 'third religious king', Khri gtsug lde brtsan, also known as Ralpachen (*reg* 815–38), there was intensive translation of Buddhist texts. However, anti-Buddhist sentiment gained the upper hand under the next king, the last of the ancient monarchy, Khri gtsug lde btsan, known as Langdarma (*reg c.* 838–42), an apostate who supported the old traditions. He is purported to have destroyed many monasteries and images, and indeed the artistic record before the end of the 10th century is exceedingly meagre. There followed a period of political and economic decline. Small isolated Buddhist communities appear to have survived, particularly in eastern Tibet, but it was not until the 11th century that monastic Buddhism was revived under the patronage of the kings of western Tibet.

(iii) Second Diffusion, 11th century and later. The key figures of this Buddhist revival, known as the Second Diffusion, were the monk Rinchen Sangpo (rin chen bzang po; 958–1055) and his patron, the royal lama Yeshe Ö (ye shes 'od), who abdicated in order to pursue a religious life. They are jointly credited with the patronage of many monasteries and their arts in western Tibet. Archaeological and literary evidence confirms that THOLING was the most important of these monasteries (see Tucci and Ghersi). The best preserved is TABO in the Spiti Valley. At present it consists of nine chapels dating from the 10th to 16th century. The earliest, the assembly hall (*'du khang*), has an inscription recording its foundation in 996 and an extensive renovation in 1042. Bon institutions can be identified from the 11th century, although definite links to the pre-Buddhist religion are difficult to verify. There were also institutions of the Nyingmapa (rnying ma pa), the so-called 'ancients' or 'old translation school', who traced their lineage of transmission to Padmasambhava and his disciples.

From the end of the 10th century there was again intensive interaction between Tibetans and Indian teachers that lasted until the beginning of the 13th century, when Buddhism in India, already in decline, was effectively destroyed by the Muslim conquest. During this period were founded the major Tibetan schools that traced their lineage through Indian Tantric masters and based their doctrines on the texts translated during the Second Diffusion of Buddhism and are thus called 'new translation schools'. It was only in the 13th century that the distinguishing features of these schools, their main monasteries and political roles became evident.

The main disciple of the Indian scholar Atisha (982–1054), the layman Dromton ('brom ston), founded the monastery of Reting (rva sgreng) in 1057 and the Kadampa (bka' gdams pa) school, which later became the foundation for the reformed Gelugpa (dge lugs pa) school. Drokmi ('brog mi; *d* 1074), who studied at Vikramashila Monastery in northern India and with the hermits and Tantric masters Shantipa and Virupa, transmitted the *Hevajra* (*bde mchog*) *tantra*, among other teachings. His student Könchok Gyalpo ('khon dkon mchog rgyal po; 1034–1102), a prince of an ancient line, in 1073 founded SAKYA Monastery, from which the order took its name. Not only did the parent monastery benefit from the lucrative trade with Nepal, but the Sakya monasteries of Tsang developed a distinctive painting style marked by Nepalese influence, as seen in a 15th-century *tangka* depicting four *maṇḍala*s (London, V&A, I.S. 167–1964). Another of Drokmi's pupils was the layman Marpa (*d* 1098), 'the translator'. During his 12 years in India he studied with several Tantric masters, receiving the Six Laws from Naropa (naro chos drug) and from Maitripa the teachings of the *Mahāmudrā* (*phyag rgya chen mo*). Marpa's disciples were the poet–ascetic Milarepa (mi la ras pa; 1040–1123) and Gampopa, who founded the Karmapa branch of the Kagyupa (bka 'brgyud pa) school. Tshurphu, the seat of this school, was founded in 1189. It was among the Karmapa that the principle of reincarnation of the hierarch of the school was first articulated. Such reincarnations are considered a 'form body' (*sprul sku*; Skt *nirmānakāya*) manifestation of the Buddha and hence are called *tulku*. The Dalai Lamas are the incarnate hierarchs of the Gelugpa school, founded by the 'great reformer', Tsong Khapa (1357–1419).

By the early 13th century, Tibetans had translated all of the available Buddhist literature, principally from the Sanskrit but sometimes also from the Chinese. The great scholar and artist Buton (bu ston; 1290–1364) is generally associated with the codification of the canonical literature, primarily the *Kanjur* (*bka' 'gyur*) and *Tanjur* (*bstan 'gyur*), which were deposited in 1334 in the monastery of SHALU, where he was installed as abbot in 1320. The first printed edition made in Beijing in 1410 of this massive collection of texts contained a series of woodblocks of specific deities in the Sino-Tibetan style (see H. Karmay).

As the economic power of the monasteries expanded, the political role of monastic hierarchs increased. The vacuum left after the demise of the monarchy, the feuding of the noble families and the manipulations of the Mongol and Chinese rulers provided numerous opportunities for different religious leaders to evolve their worldly power. It was against this historical background that a remarkable personality, the great fifth Dalai Lama, Ngawang Losang Gyatso (ngag dbang blo bzang rgya mtsho; 1617–82), the first of his line to be considered an incarnation of both his predecessors and the *bodhisattva* Avalokiteshvara, was able to reaffirm the union of political and spiritual power. He built the palace–monastery, the Potala (named after the south Indian mountain where Avalokiteshvara is said to dwell; *see* TIBET, fig. 5), on the site of the palace of the ancient kings, thus reaffirming his connection with the patron deity of Tibet .

Many great monastic complexes were built by the Gelugpa school from the beginning of the 15th century, particularly in central Tibet. They had an enormous impact on cultural life. Narthang in south-central Tibet was the site of an important woodblock-printing workshop. During the first half of the 18th century numerous xylographs were created there, including narrative renditions of the lives of Shakyamuni and Tsong Khapa, to name only two examples, the latter printed on yellow silk and delicately coloured (New Delhi, Tibet House Mus.). Through their inexpensive reproduction and wide distribution these woodblock prints influenced the style and iconography of Tibetan art to the present.

See also TIBET, §§I, 6, II, III and IV.

BIBLIOGRAPHY

Blo bzang rgya mtsho, fifth Dalai Lama: *dKar chag sel dkar me lon*, ed. A. Grünwedel (Heidelberg, 1919)

G. Tucci: *Indo-Tibetica*, 4 vols (Rome, 1932–41/*R*, ed. L. Chandra, New Delhi, 1988–9)

G. Tucci and E. Ghersi: *Secrets of Tibet* (London, 1935)

Blue Annals, pts 1 and 2, trans. G. Roerich (Calcutta, 1949–53/*R* New Delhi, 1979)

D. Snellgrove and H. Richardson: *A Cultural History of Tibet* (New York, 1968, rev. London and Boulder, 1980)

G. Tucci, ed.: *Deb t'er dmar po gsar ma: Tibetan Chronicles by bSod nams grags pa* [The new red annals; Tibetan Chronicles by bSod nams grags pa], i (Rome, 1971)

R. A. Stein: *Tibetan Civilisation* (London, 1972, rev. Paris, 1981)

G. Tucci: *Transhimalaya* (Geneva and London, 1973)

H. Karmay: *Early Sino-Tibetan Art* (Warminster, 1975)

S. G. Karmay: 'A Discussion on the Doctrinal Position of rDzogs-chen from the 10th to the 13th Century', *J. Asiat.*, cclxiii (1975), pp. 147–56

bsTan 'dzin rgya mtsho, fourteenth Dalai Lama: 'Essence of Tantra', *Tsong kha pa: Tantra in Tibet*, trans. J. Hopkins (London, 1977), pp. 13–78

Y. Imaeda: 'Mise au point concernant les éditions chinoises du Kanjur et du Tanjur tibétains', *Essais sur l'art du Tibet*, ed. A. MacDonald and Y. Imaeda (Paris, 1977), pp. 23–51

L. Petech: 'The 'Bri-gun-pa Sect in Western Tibet and Ladakh', *Csoma de Koros Memorial Symposium*, ed. L. Ligetti (Budapest, 1978), pp. 313–25

S. G. Karmay: 'The Ordinance of lHa bLa-ma Ye-shes-'od', *Tibetan Studies in Honour of Hugh Richardson*, ed. M. Aris and Aung San Suu Kyi (Oxford, 1979), pp. 150–63

L. Petech: 'Ya-ts'e, Gu-ge, Pu-ran: A New Study', *Cent. Asiat. J.*, xxiv (1980), pp. 85–111

G. Tucci: *The Religions of Tibet* (London and Berkeley, 1980)

M. Henss: *Tibet: Die Kulturdenkmäler* (Zurich, 1981)

The Silk Route and the Diamond Path: Esoteric Buddhist Art on the Trans-Himalayan Traderoutes (exh. cat. by D. E. Klimburg-Salter, Los Angeles, UCLA; New York, Asia Soc. Gals; Washington, DC, Smithsonian Inst.; 1982–3)

P. Kvaerne: 'Tibet: The Rise and Fall of a Monastic Tradition', *The World of Buddhism*, ed. H. Bechert and R. Gombrich (London, 1984), pp. 253–70

D. E. Klimburg-Salter: 'Reformation and Renaissance: A Study of Indo-Tibetan Monasteries in the 11th Century', *Orientalia Iosephi Tucci Memoriae Dedicata*, ed. G. Gnoli and L. Lanciotti (Rome, 1987), pp. 683–702

Dimore umane, santuari divini: Origini, sviluppo e diffusione dell'architettura tibetana/Demeures des hommes, sanctuaires des dieux: Sources, développement et rayonnement de l'architecture tibétaine (exh. cat., ed. P. M. Vergara and G. Béguin; Rome, La Sapienza; Paris, Mus. Guimet; 1987)

DEBORAH E. KLIMBURG-SALTER

7. MONGOLIA. Buddhism became established in its Tibetan Vajrayana form (*see* §6 above) during the Mongol empire from the 13th century AD. In 1244 the head of the Sakya sect, the Sakya Pandita, Kunga Gyaltsen (1182–1259), was invited to the camp of the Mongol prince Godan as the representative of all Tibet. Together with his nephew Phakpa (1235–80), he surrendered Tibet to the Mongols in order to avoid invasion. Godan was very impressed by Buddhism and appointed the Sakya Pandita his regent in Tibet. On Godan's death in 1221, Kublai (1216–94) assumed command and in 1260 became Emperor of China, founding the Yuan dynasty (1279–1368). He appointed Phakpa as spiritual adviser to the imperial court, thereby strengthening the priest–patron relationship that Godan had started. Although Kublai and his successors did much to spread Buddhism, it was only really practised by the aristocracy of the Yuan court. After the fall of the empire, Buddhism lost its imperial support. Although the Tibetan Sakya sect were the main missionaries in Mongolia, the Kargyu and Nyingma also found favour with certain Mongol chiefs.

The next significant contact with Buddhism was in 1576, when Altan Khan (1507–82) invited the head of the Tibetan Gelugpa sect, Sonam Gyatso, to visit his camp. Altan conferred the title Dalai (Tib.: 'ocean') on the Tibetan lama; it was given retrospectively to his two predecessors and has been held by all subsequent incarnations. Other Mongolian khans also embraced Buddhism, although this was mainly for political prestige. In 1576, Abtai Khan built the first Buddhist monastery at Erdene Zuu. At the Dalai Lama's command, the indigenous SHAMANISM was severely suppressed. Human and animal sacrifices were forbidden, and shamanistic idols (Mong. *onggot*) were replaced by Buddhist deities. However, there were certain parallels between Tantric Buddhism and shamanism that made Mongols more readily accept the new faith: for example the use of exorcist and protective formulae (Skt *mantras*), the use of ritual gestures and implements, the identification with a deity through a special form of meditation and close similarities between the Buddhist oracle priest and the shaman. The fourth Dalai Lama, Yontan Gyatso (1589–1617), was the grandson of Altan Khan. This was politically advantageous for the Mongols, although he spent most of his life in Tibet. To compensate for the loss of the fourth Dalai Lama, the Mongols were given an important reincarnation of their own, who was regarded as an emanation of Maitreya, the Future Buddha: Ondor Gegen Zanabazar (1635–1723) from the family of the Tushet Khan Gombodorj. In 1639 Zanabazar was proclaimed head of the Buddhist faith in Mongolia and formally recognized as the Jebcundamba Hutukhtu (a reincarnate lama) by the fifth Dalai Lama. Zanabazar studied under the Panchen Lama at Tashilhunpo in Tibet and then returned in 1651 to set up the religious centre of Ih huree; this was moved several times before becoming established in 1778 at Urga (now Ulaan Baatar), where it became the accepted capital of Mongolia. Zanabazar was responsible for the overwhelming spread of Buddhism in Mongolia; he was a versatile sculptor and artist and the creator of the Soyombo script (*see* MONGOLIA, §IV, 12 and 13(i)).

The early khans' interest in Buddhism had been more political than spiritual, but from the 17th century the Mongolians adopted the Gelugpa tradition with missionary zeal. There was an overall adherence to the principles of the sect's founder, Tsong Khapa (1357–1419), and many monks were educated in Tibet, particularly at Drepung Monastery. The prominent figures of the time were Ligden Khan (1604–34), Luvsanperenlei of Halh (1642–1714), Ishbaljir (1704–88), Agvaan haidav (1779–1839) and Agvaan balden (1797–1864). Monasteries were built and texts translated, and religious art flourished. The main artistic inspirations came from Tibet, but certain stylistic elements were also borrowed from China. Mongolian art evolved as a synthesis of the two, but iconographically local Mongolian deities were added to the existing Buddhist pantheon (*see* MONGOLIA, §II).

The second Jebcundamba (1724–57) spent most of his life in Beijing, where he was allegedly murdered for supporting Mongol resistance against the Manchus of the Qing dynasty (1644–1911). After his death, most *hutukthus* were found in Tibet and then installed in Beijing, where they received ecclesiastical administrative offices and were given imperial seals. The head lamas for Inner and Outer Mongolia, the Jankya Hutukthu and the Jebcundamba (or Bogd) Hutukthu, were the highest officials, but for political reasons their activities were carefully controlled and manipulated by the Manchus. During the 19th century, the purely religious aspects of Buddhism gradually deteriorated under a Buddhist hierarchy with a more economic and political orientation. The eighth and last Bogd Jebcundamba (1869–1924) emerged as the leader of the anti-Manchu, anti-Chinese national liberation movement and in 1911–20 headed the theocratic monarchy. After the Mongolian People's Revolution in 1921, the Jebcundamba became the constitutional monarch until his death in 1924. Then, under Russian domination, the rapid decline of Buddhism began. During the 1920s and 1930s hundreds of monasteries were destroyed, art works and sacred texts were vandalized, and most monks were shot or expelled. From 1990, a new wave of political freedom resulted in a revival of Buddhism. Monasteries were rebuilt and artists were commissioned to create new religious works of art.

BIBLIOGRAPHY

W. Heissig: *The Religions of Mongolia* (London, 1970)
L. W. Moses: *The Political Role of Buddhism in Mongolia* (Bloomington, 1977)
C. Bawden: *The Modern History of Mongolia* (London, 1989)

ZARA FLEMING

8. CHINA. Buddhism was probably introduced to China in the 1st century AD. Initially it was not accepted as the vehicle of a superior culture, nor was it as a religion considered much different from already established beliefs and practices. The transformation of Buddhism into a truly Chinese religion was a slow process, in the course of which it was adapted to the culture, social norms and political structure of China while contributing considerably to the development of the arts, architecture, mathematics, medicine, historiography, education and the development of Chinese religion and philosophy.

(i) Han (206 BC–AD 220) and Three Kingdoms (AD 220–80) periods. (ii) Northern and Southern Dynasties (310–589). (iii) Sui (581–618) and Tang (618–907) periods. (iv) Five Dynasties period (907–60) to Xixia kingdom (*c.* 990–1227). (v) Song period (960–1279). (vi) Yuan period (1279–1368). (vii) Ming (1368–1644) and Qing (1644–1911) periods. (viii) After 1911.

(i) Han (206 BC–AD *220) and Three Kingdoms (*AD *220–80) periods.* The exact date for the introduction of Buddhism in China is not certain, but there is general agreement that it took place around the 1st century AD. The introduction of Buddhism has traditionally been linked with the dream of Emperor Mingdi (*reg* AD 57–75) about the 'Golden Man of the West' (i.e. Shakyamuni, the historical Buddha) and the subsequent dispatch of officials to India with the purpose of collecting more knowledge about Buddhism. This legend probably indicates the first official recognition of the foreign religion. It also tells of the arrival of two Indian monks in the Han capital, Luoyang, with a white horse carrying Buddhist scriptures. These monks are said to have been installed in a compound outside the capital, where the first Buddhist temple in China, the Baima (White Horse) si, was established. There are, however, relatively strong indications that a Buddhist community under the leadership of Prince Ying existed in the area of northern Jiangsu and Shandong provinces during the second half of the 1st century AD. Around the mid-2nd century AD during the Eastern Han period Buddhism enjoyed some popularity at the court in Luoyang, and historical records refer to the dual worship of Buddha and Huang-Lao (Huang Di ['Yellow emperor'] and Laozi) in the imperial palace.

In the area of modern Shanghai, to the north of the city in the vicinity of Lianyun Harbour, the oldest Buddhist carvings in China, thought to date to the 2nd century AD, consist mainly of deep, incised reliefs in a small rock called Mt Kongwang. Iconographically they are a mixture between Daoist (*see* DAOISM) and Buddhist figures, although the figure of a seated, meditating Buddha and a stylized Great Demise (Skt *mahāparinirvāṇa*) scene showing the disciples surrounding the recumbent Buddha express the clear Buddhist element in the carvings.

The earliest translations of Buddhist texts were made during the 2nd century AD by the Parthian An Shigao (*fl* second half of 2nd century), who stayed in Luoyang during the reign of Emperor Huandi (*reg* 146–68). As many as 90 translations—most of Hinayana scriptures—are attributed to him in a Buddhist canonical catalogue from the early 8th century. A considerable number of these translated works deal with the practice of meditation on breathing (Skt *ānapāna*). One possible reason for the seeming popularity of Buddhist breathing techniques may have been their comparability with similar Daoist practices of the 'inner alchemical' (Chin. *neidan*) type. Following An Shigao, a Scythian monk called Zhi Loujiachan (*fl* 2nd century), who arrived in the Han capital *c.* 167, translated a number of Mahayana texts (Skt *sūtras*) of the *prajñāpāramitā* ('perfection of wisdom') class. These works, which deal with universal emptiness, are more sophisticated on the doctrinal level than the Hinayana texts and in time had a considerable impact on the future of Buddhism in China.

During the Three Kingdoms period (220–80) Buddhism continued to spread in China, and the religion, which previously had been a religion mainly for foreigners, began to attract the Chinese in growing numbers. Before the collapse of the Three Kingdoms, a large number of Mahayana Buddhist scriptures were translated into Chinese, including the *Saddharmapuṇḍarīka* ('Lotus of the wonderful law') *sūtra*, the *Sukhāvatīvyūha* ('Vision of the Western Paradise') and the *Pañcaviṁśatisāhasrika-prajñāpāramitā* ('Perfection of wisdom in 25,000 lines') *sūtra*. By the late 4th century it was common to translate Buddhist terms by using expressions from Chinese literature, mainly from the *Laozi*, otherwise known as the *Daode jing* ('Classic of the way and virtue') and the *Zhuangzi*, another Daoist text, to explain doctrinal meanings. This method was called *geyi* ('matching the meaning'), and it greatly facilitated the assimilation of Buddhist doctrines into Chinese society. However, as this system was tentative rather than explicit, it opened up the possibility of considerable misunderstanding and corruption of traditional Indian Buddhist teachings.

The first Buddhist monastic community (Skt *saṅgha*) with Chinese monks was established as late as the 2nd century. The first Buddhist nuns were not properly ordained until the mid-4th century. Under imperial patronage, Buddhist temples were built throughout the country, and pious emperors, such as Xiaowendi (471–99), Wudi (502–49), Wendi (581–604), Wu Zetian (690–705), Xuanzong (712–56) and Daizong (762–79), had special chapels made within their palace compounds.

During the process of sinicization, Buddhism naturally came into conflict with native traditions. Confucians responded with indignation to such Buddhist norms as celibacy for monks and nuns, which meant a discontinuation of the ancestral line, and the non-productivity of the monastic community, which had to be fed and clothed by the labour of others. Daoists criticized Buddhism for being a barbarian religion, unfit for the Chinese. Relatively early, however, they began to borrow from the better organized Buddhist doctrines and monastic structures. Furthermore, Buddhist art—especially that related to painting and sculpture—played a significant role in the formation of Daoist iconography and themes. Buddhists for their part took up the challenge from the indigenous traditions and stressed such aspects of Buddhism as filial piety (*xiao*) and service to the nation and the ruler in order to appease the Confucians, while they borrowed freely from the Daoist terminology in their translations. On the popular level many local practices, including divination and the use of talismans, were adapted to Buddhism.

(ii) Northern and Southern Dynasties (310–589). Buddhism was already well established by the time China was divided following the collapse of the centralized state at the end of the 4th century. In north China a series of short-lived foreign dynasties supplanted each other until the Northern Wei dynasty (386–534) brought a certain stability to the region. Common to all these foreign dynasties was their support of Buddhism, which, however, was dependent on the emperor. Under the Northern Liang dynasty (396–439), which controlled the Gansu Corridor, a number of Buddhist cave temples, such as Bingling si in the Linxia

region and those at Mt Madi in Minle County and Mt Wenshu in Jinquan County, were made.

A deeper appreciation of the complex and finer points of Mahayana doctrines did not come about until after the teacher and translator–monk Kumarajiva (344–413), a native of Kucha, arrived in Chang'an (now Xian, Shaanxi Province) during the reign of the Northern Liang. He revolutionized Chinese Buddhism through his superior translations, which were largely purged of Daoist terminology but considerably easier to read than the earlier translations. Kumarajiva also introduced the Chinese monastic community to the proper way of understanding wisdom (Skt *prajñā*) and emptiness (*śūnya*). Through a series of eminent successors, Kumarajiva's translations and teaching style spread throughout the realm.

With the exception of a short period of suppression between 446 and 448, partly at Daoist instigation, Buddhism was the state religion of the Northern Wei, and after the suppression stopped, the new head of the community, Tanyao (*fl* second half of 5th century), had the impressive cave-temples at YUNGANG made under imperial patronage. During this period Buddhism enjoyed numerous privileges, and the nobility competed in Buddhist piety by donating lands and slaves to the temples. Under Tanyao *saṅgha* families were established, consisting of pardoned prisoners and slaves, who when owned by the temples were exempt from tax and corvée. These people lived in or around the temples and cultivated their lands, and Buddhist institutions consequently became extremely wealthy and powerful.

In 493–4 Emperor Xiaowendi (*reg* 471–99) moved the capital to Luoyang, where he initiated the carvings at LONGMEN (*see* CHINA, fig. 63). Luoyang became a thriving Buddhist centre with several large monasteries and temples within the city walls and numerous others in the surrounding countryside. Mt Song, south of Luoyang, was a major Buddhist mountain on which more than 10 temples and retreats were located (*see also* CHINA, §II, 4(i)). It is said that the Indian monk Bodhidharma (*d c.* 530), later considered the first patriarch of Chan Buddhism, visited Luoyang at the beginning of the 6th century.

In southern China, Buddhism developed alongside indigenous traditions, CONFUCIANISM and Daoism, resulting in a considerable syncretism of their respective teachings. The south remained largely peaceful throughout the Northern and Southern Dynasties period, with only a few isolated outbreaks of warfare, and the region prospered. In this political climate Buddhism became independent of the state and exercised a great influence at the southern courts. In the state of the Eastern Jin (*fl* 265–420), with its capital at present-day Nanjing, Buddhism enjoyed many privileges, and monks were not forced to bow to the emperor and his officials, as was the norm in the north. Under Emperor Wudi (*reg* 502–49) of Liang (502–57), Buddhism reached its apogee in the south, and countless temples, pagodas and other Buddhist buildings were erected under imperial and noble patronage (*see also* CHINA, §II, 2(iii)). Monks and nuns became more numerous, and it became prestigious for a family to have some of its members enter the monastic community.

(iii) Sui (581–618) and Tang (618–907) periods.

(a) Adoption of Buddhism as state religion. Under the Sui, Buddhism became the state religion, although both Daoism and Confucianism were tolerated. Buddhism spread throughout the country from the capital, Chang'an. Temples grew in size, the monastic community expanded and under imperial patronage several Buddhist sculptural projects were initiated.

It was also under the Sui that the first great school of Chinese Buddhism arose, namely the Tiantai school, with its centre at Guoqing Temple at the foot of Mt Tiantai in Zhejiang Province (*see also* CHINA, §II, 4(i)). The founder was the monk Zheyi (538–97), a master who combined meditation (Chin. *zhiguan*) with the study of the canonical scriptures. The *Saddharmapuṇḍarīka* ('Lotus of the wonderful law') *sūtra*, known as the Lotus Sutra, acquired special importance for this denomination. The Tiantai enjoyed unsurpassed imperial support throughout the Sui period and was the largest of all the Buddhist schools at the time of the founding of the Tang dynasty in 618. Another important school that arose during the Sui was the Sanlun school, chiefly based on the study of wisdom (Skt *prajñā*) and meditation. The main propagator of this school was Jizang (549–623), whose thought greatly influenced the Tiantai school.

With the reunification of the realm under the Tang dynasty, a lengthy period of political stability was inaugurated. During the 7th century the Tang gained control over most of eastern Central Asia, which made travel and trade along the SILK ROUTE considerably easier and more profitable. Although officially linked with Daoism, most of the Tang emperors showed great devotion to Buddhism, which benefited greatly.

Besides patronage from the imperial family and the nobility, for example in the form of land grants, the Buddhist community enjoyed such privileges as tax exemption on lands and produce. Thus many temples rented out their lands or maintained families of tenant farmers in order to strengthen their economy. Others actively engaged in export and import or controlled part of the trade at local markets. Some monasteries ran loan businesses or owned oil presses and water-powered mills.

The size of the monastic community grew dramatically under the Tang, as did the number of slaves owned by temples. It became lucrative for small farmers to become temple tenants, because this meant exemption from taxation and corvée labour. During the later half of the period, when ordination certificates circulated as securities, the community housed many undesirable elements, which eventually caused problems.

Buddhist (and Daoist) temples offered a regular education, providing the only alternative to the official government education, which was accessible to a small, highly privileged number of the Chinese population. In the temple schools novices, both male and female, learnt to read and write and were generally subjected to examinations before being allowed to join the order. Although the curriculum in the temple schools consisted mainly of the traditional Buddhist scriptures, it was common for most novices to study the Chinese classics as well, at least at a rudimentary level.

The Tang period is commonly referred to as the 'golden age of Buddhist translations', for it was during this time that most Indian and Central Asian canonical scriptures were rendered into Chinese. The emperors set up state-sponsored translation teams of eminent monks and scholars, who produced hundreds of high-quality translations. A number of the Tang rulers participated in these translations and in some cases provided the prefaces. In addition, indigenous Chinese Buddhist literature proliferated during the Tang period. Besides the large number of commentaries on the canonical scriptures, scholar-monks produced many original works of their own, including texts on doctrines, histories, encyclopedias, geneaologies, bibliographies and poetry. The Vinaya master Daoxuan (596–667) was an extremely productive writer, and many of his works in several of the categories mentioned survive.

During this period the intellectual milieu developed greatly, and it became common for Confucian scholars and Buddhist monks to engage in friendly debates and exchange views on philosophical and literary matters. This development gained momentum during the An Lushan rebellion (from 756) in the south and spread to the north after peace was restored. A number of prominent Confucian scholars and government officials took part in this exchange, which gave impetus to the classical literature (*guwen*) movement. Among those involved were Bai Juyi (772–846), Li Hua (*d c.* 769), Liu Zongyuan (773–819), Han Yu (768–824) and Pei Xiu (797–870); monks included such eminent masters as Jiaoran (730–99), Zhanran (711–82), Zongmi (780–841) and Xiyun (*d* 850).

(b) Major schools and traditions. With the exception of the Tiantai and Sanlun schools, all the major Chinese Buddhist schools were established during the Tang period. The Vinaya school (Lu zong), centred on the study of the Buddhist disciplinary codices, did not develop a strict sectarian structure. After all, any person wishing to join the monastic community had to undergo some training in the *Vinaya* to be ordained. For this reason all Buddhist monasteries, no matter what their denomination, followed the rules laid down in the *Vinaya*.

Because of its close connection with the ruling house of the previous dynasty, the Tiantai school was denied imperial support during the early Tang period, and patronage was instead extended to the Faxiang school founded by the pilgrim-monk Xuanzang (600–64), who returned to China in 645, bringing with him the Sanskrit scriptures on which he based his teachings. In terms of doctrine the Faxiang school was based on a special branch of Indian *yogācāra* ('practice of Yoga') philosophy, which taught that, whereas phenomena are fundamentally illusory, the mind or consciousness that perceives them is real. A central aspect of this doctrine deals with the classification of the characteristics of the individual phenomena (Skt *dharmalakṣaṇa*), from which the school's name derives.

The prominence of the Faxiang school was shortlived, and under Empress Wu Zetian (*reg* 690–705) two new schools rose to prominence. The first of these was the Huayan school under Fazang (643–712), which based itself on the voluminous *Avataṁsaka sūtra*, and the other was the Chan school, represented by one of the northern lineages under Shenxiu (605–706). The main teachings of the Huayan school focus on the interpenetration of all phenomena and the total integration of the absolute and relative realms, and it is thus one of the most speculative of all the Chinese Buddhist schools. The Chan school, in contrast, is chiefly concerned with the practical realization of the inherent Buddha-nature (Chin. *foxing*) or Buddha-mind (*foxin*) said to be fully present in all beings. As a means to gain awakening to this inherent but not yet 'seen', enlightened nature, meditation is widely recommended, whereas there is a lack of emphasis on the written word. Following a sectarian struggle between various lineages over the right of patriarchal succession, the so-called Southern Chan, consisting of several collateral branches, became the dominant trend. The most important figure in this branch of Chan was the southerner Huineng (638–713), about whose life little is known. Nevertheless, his importance as the figurehead of Chan Buddhism in the mid-Tang period and later was tremendous. Towards the end of the Tang period, Chan Buddhism was divided into five major denominations: the Linji, Guiyang, Caodong, Yunmen and Fayan schools. At that time the anti-textual attitude in Chan gradually weakened and was supplanted by a combined study of the scriptures and meditation.

Pure Land (Jingtu) Buddhism, based on the canonical scriptures pertaining to rebirth in Amitabha Buddha's Western Paradise (Skt Sukhavati), likewise became a major school under the Tang. Traced back to Huiyuan (344–416) and his White Lotus Society on Mt Lu, by the Yangze River in Jiangxi Province, the Pure Land tradition was developed by a number of prominent monks, among whom Shantao (613–81) and Fazhao (*fl* 8th century) were most important. The main practice in this school was the invocation of the name of Amitabha, a method known as *nianfo* ('praying to Buddha'), which is said to secure the believer a rebirth in his paradise and was later adopted by other denominations of Chinese Buddhism.

Perhaps the most widespread form of Buddhism during the Tang period was the largely pan-sectarian Esoteric Buddhist tradition (Mijiao or Zhenyan), whose most prominent representatives were Shubhakarasimha (637–735), Vajrabodhi (669–741) and Amoghavajra (705–74). The last was a highly industrious translator. During the 8th century Esoteric Buddhism exerted a tremendous influence at the Tang court. Several of the largest and most prestigious temples in Chang'an and Luoyang were controlled by adherents of Esoteric Buddhism. At the beginning of the 9th century its transmission was gradually diffused, and Esoteric practices were eventually adapted by the other schools of Chinese Buddhism, in particular by the Tiantai school. By the end of the Tang period Esoteric Buddhism had become extremely popular in Shu (now Sichuan Province), fostering a local variant.

(c) Huichang suppression. Under Emperor Wuzong (*reg* 840–86), whose reign title was Huichang, Buddhism was subjected to the strongest and most far-reaching suppression in Chinese history. In 845 this reached its height in the regions surrounding the two capitals. Many monks and nuns were killed, and several thousand were forced to disrobe and return to lay status. Temples throughout the country were turned over to the government to be used as schools or for storage. Statues and

other metal objects were melted down, and wooden and stone images were destroyed. In this way enormous quantities of religious art were lost. The Huichang suppression signified a radical change in the direction of Chinese Buddhism, as it caused the downfall of the large doctrinal schools, Huayan, Tiantai and Faxiang, and to some extent Esoteric Buddhism, none of which was able to regain its vitality after the suppression ended officially in 858. However, the Chan school and the Pure Land school survived.

(iv) Five Dynasties period (907–60) to Xixia kingdom (c. *990–1227).* In the Five Dynasties period Buddhism flourished once again. The Chan school, which had come relatively intact out of the Huichang suppression, grew rapidly and by the mid-10th century consisted of more than a hundred lineages. Chan became especially strong in southern China and was recognized as the official state creed by a number of states there. In Hangzhou, the capital of the state of Wu–Yue (907–78; in what is now Zhejiang Province), the Fayan school under the masters Fayan Wenyi (885–958) and Yongming Yanshou (904–75) became prominent, and a lively Buddhist interchange was conducted with the kingdom of Koryŏ (*fl* 918–1392) in Korea.

When the Tang dynasty collapsed in 907, there arose in the north, in the area covered by present-day Liaoning Province and part of Hebei Province, the Liao state (907–1125) under the semi-nomadic Khitan (Qidan) people. These people had been exposed to Chinese civilization and culture during the Tang period and had embraced Buddhism as their faith. They established many Buddhist monasteries and sanctuaries, including large brick pagodas, several of which can still be seen in and around Beijing, as well as in various places in Hebei and Liaodong provinces. Life-size polychrome ceramic figures of *luohan* (Skt *arhat*s; 'enlightened men') survive from this period (*see* fig. 12; *see also* CHINA, §VII, 3(iv)(a)). Although few details are known about the history of Buddhism under the Liao, it is clear that Esoteric Buddhism played a leading role. The Khitan produced their own Buddhist canon (Skt *tripiṭaka*) from carved wooden blocks.

More or less contemporaneous with the establishment of the Liao, the Tanguts, a federation of semi-nomadic tribes of Tibeto-Burman descent, established themselves within the bend of the Yellow River in what are now Ningxia, northern Shaanxi and western Shanxi. They had been under Chinese cultural influence for several centuries, and their state of Xixia (*c.* 990–1227) was proclaimed officially in 1038, with Yinchuan as their capital. The Tanguts followed Chinese Buddhism as well as Tibetan Buddhism. Several of the traditional Chinese schools of Buddhism—including the Huayan, Chan, Pure Land and Tiantai—were present in Xixia, as well as Tantric Buddhism introduced from western Tibet. In the later 11th century the Tanguts produced a Buddhist canon in their own language. Both Dunhuang and neighbouring Anxi in north-western Gansu came under Tangut control from the mid-11th century, as is testified by a number of cave temples. KARAKHOTO (now in the Inner Mongolia Autonomous Region) was a thriving frontier town with a large Buddhist community. Archaeological discoveries from the temples in this town include large amounts of Buddhist manuscripts and printed books in both the Xixia script and Chinese. In 1227 the Mongols conquered Xixia, but the Buddhist influence of the state was felt in China during the following century.

(v) Song period (960–1279). This period is viewed by many scholars as the beginning of the decline of Chinese Buddhism. This may hold true with regard to scholastic developments and the close connection to the Indian motherland, but when the level of Buddhist literature, Buddhist art and the size of monasteries are considered, nothing could be more incorrect. In fact the Song period was a time when Buddhism attained the status of a truly Chinese religion.

A few translations from the Sanskrit of mainly Esoteric works were made in the early part of the period, but all the major texts (Skt *sūtra*s) had already been translated by the Tang period (618–907). As the foreign influence waned, the native Buddhist tradition flowered. In the field of literature, Chinese monks and laymen produced a huge amount of Buddhist literature, including commentaries, exegetical works, general histories, sect histories, ritual manuals, encyclopedias, lexicographical studies, dictionaries, biographical works and collections of poems. Temples became increasingly rich, even after the north was lost to the Jin in 1127, and they continued to play a considerable political role at local level throughout the period.

One of the greatest achievements of Buddhism under the Song was the printing of the Buddhist canon. This took place in Sichuan Province in 983, where the *Kaibao tripiṭaka* was carved on wooden blocks and printed. This first printed canon contained 1076 different works, and its fame spread to Korea and Japan, whence embassies came to China to acquire copies.

Although such scholastic Buddhist schools as the Tiantai and Huayan continued to function, the various Chan lineages and the Pure Land school were dominant. At this time Esoteric Buddhism, although no longer existing as an independent school, had permeated Chinese Buddhism, and its teachings and practices were universally followed. Although several of the five schools of Chan—Linji, Guiyang, Caodong, Yunmen and Fayan—had survived well into the Northern Song period (960–1127), by the mid-12th century the Linji lineage formed the dominant trend. A continuous stream of Japanese pilgrim-monks travelled to China to study under Chan masters and on returning to Japan took back examples of Chan Buddhist art and lore.

Where Chan Buddhism was generally more monastic and élitist, the Pure Land tradition catered for the average Chinese with its promise of rebirth in the Western Paradise. During the Song period, Pure Land Buddhism came to be practised in almost all Buddhist temples in the country, and various schemes seeking to integrate Chan with the practice of invoking the name of Amitabha Buddha were developed. This dual practice of Chan and Pure Land became the hallmark of Chinese Buddhism after the Song period.

Buddhist interaction with Confucian scholars continued unbroken in much the same way as it had done under the

12. *Luohan* (Skt *arhat*), polychrome glazed ceramic, h. 1.03 m, from Yizhou, Hebei Province, Liao period (AD 907–1125) (London, British Museum)

Tang, with the exception that the rising Neo-Confucian school was rapidly giving rise to some feelings of animosity towards Buddhism. For Neo-Confucians striving to establish their own philosophy and faith, which borrowed both from Buddhism, especially from the Chan and Huayan schools, and from the Daoist tradition of Laozi and Zhuangzi, Buddhism was seen as a competitor. With the élitist and conservative developments initiated by the philosopher Zhu Xi (1130–1200; *see also* CONFUCIANISM, §2), Neo-Confucianism became generally opposed to Buddhism, although this animosity never resulted in direct persecution. Despite this, many Confucian scholars, including the celebrated poet Su Shi, showed an open interest in Buddhism.

Originally vassals of the Khitan, the Jürchen (Ruzhen)—a Manchurian nomad people with their homeland in what is now Heilongjiang Province—steadily rose to power during the second half of the 11th century. In 1115 they founded the Jin dynasty (1115–1234) and rose against the Liao, whom they defeated with the help of the Song in 1125 before taking the whole of north China (1127). Although not recognized as the state religion, Buddhism enjoyed the patronage of the Jin emperors and the nobility. Buddhist culture generally flourished unabated, with new temples built and old ones renovated.

(vi) Yuan period (1279–1368). With the fall of Hangzhou in 1276 and the subsequent establishment of the Yuan dynasty in 1279, China came under the rule of the Mongols. Although the new rulers favoured Tibetan Buddhism, or Lamaism (*see* §6 above), Chinese Buddhism as a whole prospered. Many temples received special stipends from the emperors and their families, and it again became prestigious for a young man or woman to join the monastic community.

During the early period of Mongol control in northern China following the fall of Jin in 1234, the Quanzhen sect of Daoism became extremely popular. The Daoists started to take over Buddhist temples and in various ways harassed their traditional religious competitors. After the Tibetan lamas of the Sakya sect gained influence at the Yuan court, the Buddhists were able to mount a counter-attack that eventually resulted in the suppression of the Quanzhen Daoists. Under the influence of the Tibetan lamas, the Mongol nobility were brought into contact with Tantric Buddhism with its great love of rituals. Phakpa (1235–80), the nephew of the head of the Sakya sect, enjoyed the confidence of Kublai Khan (*reg* 1260–94) and devised a special script that gained some importance. Sexual *yoga*, which scandalized the average Chinese, is said also to have flourished at the court in Dadu (modern Beijing) during the first half of the 14th century.

Chan Buddhism regained some of its former strength and became influential among the gentry in the southern parts of China. Several Chan monks were noted calligraphers and poets and participated in literary gatherings. One notable example, Zhongfeng Mingben (1263–1323), a Chan master whose fame reached both Korea and Japan, was a close associate of the painter Zhao Mengfu.

With strong support from the Mongols, Buddhist temples were erected all over China (*see* CHINA, §II, 4(i)). Buddhist sculptural projects also were initiated in several places. Famous among these are the sculptures and reliefs at Feilai feng ('Peak that came flying') near Hangzhou, Zhejiang Province, which has some of the oldest Tantric sculptures carved in a Sino-Tibetan style in China. Another important monument is the Juyong guan (Guyong Gate; 1345) of a former temple located near the GREAT WALL OF CHINA at Nankou, north of Beijing, which contains Tantric Buddhist reliefs of Buddhas and the Four Heavenly Kings carved in great slabs of marble.

(vii) Ming (1368–1644) and Qing (1644–1911) periods. During the first 100 years of the Ming period Buddhism continued to enjoy a high status at court and among the general population. Many temples were built, and old ones were renovated. Under the Yongle emperor (*reg* 1403–24) and the Xuande emperor (*reg* 1426–35), the Karma Kagyupa school of Tibetan Buddhism was influential at the imperial court, where elaborate rituals were held, and Tantric Buddhist art flourished in the western and northern parts of the country. More evidence of the prosperity of Buddhism during the early Ming period can be seen in the extraordinarily large number of Buddhist scriptures printed during this period. With the newly invented technique of using movable metal type, books could now be made more cheaply and of a better quality than previously, and new editions of the canon (Skt *tripiṭaka*) as well as popular tracts became readily available.

In the second half of the 15th century Buddhism declined, while both Neo-Confucianism and Daoism prospered. Many Buddhist temples were taken over by the Daoists or appropriated for use by the local government; many others were allowed to fall into ruin.

At the time of the Wanli emperor (*reg* 1573–1620) Buddhism experienced a brief revival under several famous Chan monks. Among these were Hanshan Deqing (1546–1623), Zhuhong (1535–1615) and Zhenke (1543–1604), who rebuilt and established temples, mainly in southern China (see fig. 13). At that time the Jesuits were attempting

13. Chinese Buddhist altar in the library of the Huiju Temple, Mt Baohua, Jiangsu Province, late Ming period (1368–1644)

to gain a foothold in China, and Zhuhong and his followers became involved in a religious war of words with them.

Following the demise of the great Ming masters, Buddhism entered a new period of decline that continued into the Qing period (1644–1911). The Manchu emperors of the Qing dynasty were officially followers of Mongolian Lamaism (*see* §7 above) and worshipped the *bodhisattva* Manjushri as their tutelary divinity. For this reason Mt Wutai, the mountain consecrated to this *bodhisattva*, held a special meaning for the Manchu imperial line. The Qing emperors supported Buddhism in general and Lamaism in particular and contributed to the upkeep of lamaseries in Manchuria, Inner Mongolia and Tibet. Among the Qing emperors the most serious Buddhist was the Yongzheng emperor (*reg* 1723–35). He participated in the compilation of Buddhist works and wrote a number of prefaces for them. He appears to have been especially fond of Chan Buddhism. His official residence in Beijing was converted into a Lamaist temple in 1744. A replica of the Potala Palace in Lhasa was constructed near the imperial summer resort at Jehol (now Chengde) under the Qianlong emperor (*reg* 1736–96).

(viii) After 1911. Buddhism experienced a brief revival towards the end of the Qing period that lasted well into the Republican period (1911–49). This revival took two forms: there was, on the one hand, a reaffirmation of traditional practices and beliefs among the members of the monastic community and, on the other, a trend towards modernization and reformation of the community, based partly on the Japanese model. The traditionalist movement was led by such eminent Chan masters as Xuyun (1849–1959), Laiguo (1880–1953) and the Vinaya master Hongyi (1880–1942), a noted calligrapher and painter. The modernizers were led by the controversial monk Taixu (1890–1947), who, despite a general failure to reform and renovate Buddhism, was able to attract a number of prominent lay persons to his cause. As a result of the Buddhist renaissance many lay Buddhist societies came into being in the large cities.

With the collapse of the Republican army in 1949 and the establishment of the People's Republic of China, Buddhism and other religions were persecuted. This culminated in the so-called Cultural Revolution (1966–76), when many monks were killed. After 1980 the Communist government eased restrictions on Buddhist temples and became generally supportive of old Buddhist sites, including temples and sites with sculptures, protecting and preserving them.

See also CHINA, §§I, 5; II, 4(i); III, 1; V, 3(i) and (ii).

BIBLIOGRAPHY

Chou Yi-liang: 'Tantrism in China', *Harvard J. Asiat. Stud.*, viii (1945), pp. 241–332

J. Gernet: *Les Aspects économiques du bouddhisme dans la société chinoise du Ve au Xe siècle* (Saigon, 1956)

E. Zürcher: *The Buddhist Conquest of China: The Spread and Adaptation of Buddhism in Early Medieval China*, 2 vols, Sinica Leidensia, 11 (Leiden, 1959/*R* 1972)

J. Thiel: 'Der Streit der Buddhisten und Taoisten zur Mongolenzeit', *Mnmt Serica*, xx (1961), pp. 1–81

Jan Yün-hua: 'Buddhist Historiography in Sung China', *Z. Dt. Mrgländ. Ges.*, mxiv (1964), pp. 360–81

K. Ch'en: *Buddhism in China: A Historical Survey* (Princeton, 1964–73)

Jan Yün-hua: 'Buddhist Relations between India and Sung China', *History of Religions*, vi (1966), pt 1, pp. 24–42; pt 2, pp. 135–68

Jan Yün-hua, ed.: *A Chronicle of Buddhism in China 581–960 A.D.: Translations from Monk Chih-p'an's 'Fo-tsu T'ung-chi'* (Santiniketan, 1966)

H. Welch: *The Practice of Chinese Buddhism 1900–1950*, Harvard East Asian Studies, xxvi (Cambridge, MA, 1967)

——: *The Buddhist Revival in China*, Harvard East Asian Studies, xxxiii (Cambridge, MA, 1968)

——: *Buddhism under Mao*, Harvard East Asian Studies, lxix (Cambridge, MA, 1972)

K. Ch'en: *The Chinese Transformation of Buddhism* (Princeton, 1973)

D. L. Overmyer: *Folk Buddhist Religion: Dissenting Sects in Late Traditional China*, Harvard East Asian Studies, lxxxiii (Cambridge, MA, and London, 1976)

Chün-fang Yü: *The Renewal of Buddhism in China: Chu-hung and the Late Ming Synthesis* (New York, 1981)

H. Franke: 'Tibetans in Yüan China', *China under Mongol Rule*, ed. J. D. Langlois (Princeton, 1981), pp. 296–328

Guo Peng: *Song Yuan fojiao* [Buddhism under the Song and Yuan] (Fuzhou, 1981)

——: *Ming Qing fojiao* [Buddhism under the Ming and Qing] (Fuzhou, 1982)

Z. Tsukamoto: *A History of Early Chinese Buddhism*, 2 vols (Tokyo and New York, 1985)

E. Zürcher: 'Chinese Ch'an and Confucianism', *Zen in China, Japan, East Asian Art* (Zurich, 1985), pp. 29–46

Jan Yün-hua: 'Patterns of Chinese Assimilation of Buddhist Thought: A Comparative Study of No-thought (*wu-nien*) in Indian and Chinese Texts', *J. Orient. Stud.*, xxiv (1986), pp. 21–36

P. N. Gregory, ed.: *Traditions of Meditation in Chinese Buddhism*, Studies in East Asian Buddhism, iv (Honolulu, 1986)

J. R. McRae: *The Northern School and the Formation of Early Ch'an Buddhism*, Studies in East Asian Buddhism, iii (Honolulu, 1986)

D. W. Chappell, ed.: *Buddhist and Taoist Practice in Medieval Chinese Society* (1987), ii of *Buddhist and Taoist Studies*, Asian Studies at Hawaii, 34 (Honolulu)

S. Weinstein: *Buddhism under the T'ang* (Cambridge, 1987)

H. H. Sørensen: *A Survey of the Religious Sculptures of Anyue* (Copenhagen, 1989)

R. Whitfield: 'Buddhist Monuments in China and Some Recent Finds', *The Buddhist Heritage*, ed. T. Skorupski, Buddhica Britannica, i (Tring, 1989), pp. 129–42

E. Zürcher: 'The Impact of Buddhism on Chinese Culture in an Historical Perspective', *The Buddhist Heritage*, ed. T. Skorupski, Buddhica Britannica, i (Tring, 1989), pp. 117–28

K. K. Tanaka: *The Dawn of Chinese Pure Land Buddhist Doctrine* (Albany, 1990)

HENRIK H. SØRENSEN

9. KOREA.

(i) Before AD *668.* The traditional dates for the introduction of Buddhism by monks from China to the courts of the Korean kingdoms of Koguryŏ (37 BC–AD 668) and Paekche (18 BC–AD 660) are given as AD 372 and 384 respectively in the *Samguk sagi* ('History of the Three Kingdoms'), compiled in 1145. Silla (57 BC–AD 668), the third of Korea's Three Kingdoms, is said not to have formally sanctioned the practice of Buddhism until AD 528, although this date falls well after the surreptitious introduction of the religion from Koguryŏ. In all three kingdoms Buddhism officially began as a religion espoused by the royal court. The meagre surviving textual and material evidence of the 4th and 5th centuries indicates that in Koguryŏ and Paekche it remained essentially, until the early 6th century, a cult limited to the court. Thereafter, however, possibly following the example of China, Korean kings seem to have become convinced of the utility of Buddhism in encouraging the development of a centralized state. Throughout the peninsula the increasingly close association of state and Buddhism was publicized through

the building of temples and the endowing of images at royal expense. In 527, for example, Taet'ong Temple was built at the then Paekche capital of Ungjin (modern Kongju) in what is now South Ch'ungch'ŏng Province, and in 553 construction was begun at the Silla capital of Kyŏngju of Hwangyong Temple (*see* KOREA, §II, 3(i)(a)). Its nine-storey pagoda and sixteen-foot image of the Buddha were to become two of the kingdom's three protective national treasures.

During the late 6th century and early 7th, a number of Korean monks travelled to study in China, whence they returned, bearing religious texts, icons and relics, to spread the teachings gained abroad. Prominent among these was the late 6th-century monk Hyŏn'gwang from Paekche, who studied under Huisi (515–77), the second patriarch of the Tiantai (Kor. Ch'ŏnt'ae) sect of Buddhism (*see* §8 above). Hyŏn'gwang was followed in the early 7th century by two monks from Silla: Anham, who returned with copies of the *Laṅkāvatāra sūtra* and the *Śrīmālā siṃhanāda sūtra*, and Chajang, who is credited with founding the Vinaya (Kor. Kyeyul) sect in Korea and is said to have brought Buddhist images and scriptures from China. None of the art or texts brought to Korea from Sui (581–618) or early Tang (618–907) China have survived, yet the imprint of Chinese artistic models of this period remained pronounced throughout 7th-century Buddhist culture in the Korean peninsula. Illustration is provided by the exquisite mid-7th-century sculpted image of *Avalokiteshvara* (Kor. Kwanseŭm), one of a stone triad, with *Shakyamuni* and *Maitreya* (Kor. Mirŭk), at Unsan in Sŏsan District, South Ch'ungchŏng Province. Although sectarian distinctions may have had little importance in Korea at that time, the teachings of several sects were introduced into the peninsula: Vinaya texts concerning clerical and lay discipline, the fundamental tenets of the Nirvana (Kor. Yŏlban) and Madhyamika (Kor. Samnon) sects, basic Pure Land beliefs (Kor. Chŏngt'o) and even some early Tiantai meditational techniques.

Especially pronounced in the Buddhism of the Korean Three Kingdoms were practices aimed at protecting the state, such as those connected with the nationalistic Hwarang cult dedicated to Maitreya, the Future Buddha, which developed among the young men of Silla. The popularity throughout Korea of Maitreya is apparent from the number and quality of sculptures surviving from the Three Kingdoms period that depict this *bodhisattva*, generally in a pensive pose. Such are the large bronze images in the National Museum of Korea (see fig. 14; *see also* KOREA, fig. 21). Closely allied to the concept of defending the state were such government-sponsored rituals as the 'Assembly of the One Hundred Seats of the Benevolent Kings' (Kor. Inwang paekkojwa-hoe) and the 'Assembly of Eight Commandments' (Kor. P'algwan-hoe). Korea's critical role in the transmission of both the doctrine and the culture of Buddhism to Japan was similarly underpinned by political as well as religious motives. The religion was formally introduced to the Japanese court as part of a Paekche diplomatic initiative in the mid-6th century (*see* §10 below), and the greater number of Japan's best-known monks and Buddhist artisans of the 6th and 7th centuries were from Koguryŏ and Paekche, some being sent to Japan at government behest.

14. Korean figure of Maitreya, the Future Buddha, gilt-bronze, h. 910 mm, early 7th century AD, Three Kingdoms period, (Seoul, National Museum of Korea)

(ii) AD *668 and after.* For the first time in its history the Korean peninsula was ruled as a unified state when Silla, backed by massive Chinese military assistance, finally asserted its hegemony in 668. With the ardent support of the court, Korean Buddhism in the Unified Silla period (668–918) entered a phase of unparalleled scholarly achievement, institutional development and expansion through all social classes. The 7th and 8th centuries witnessed many profound doctrinal advances in China; together with stylistic and iconographic innovations in Buddhist art, these were transmitted to Korea by the numerous Korean monks studying in Chinese monasteries.

During this period of growth several of the historically most influential sectarian traditions of Korean Buddhism became institutionalized, some based closely on Chinese models, others more substantially informed by the theological innovations of eminent Korean monks. Five sects in which textual authority was uppermost attained particular importance during the Unified Silla period: the Vinaya, Nirvana, Dharma Nature (Kor. Pŏpsŏng), Avatamsaka (Kor. Hwaŏm or Wŏnyung) and Yogacara (Kor. Pŏpsang) sects. In addition, the meditative tradition of Sŏn (Chin. Chan; Jap. Zen) was securely established in Korea by the end of the 8th century. The Avatamsaka (Hwaŏm) sect, with its emphasis on order and cohesion around a central Buddha, was pre-eminent among the aristocracy. Among the common folk Buddhism, particularly in the form of Pure Land Buddhism, for the first time gained a widespread following. This transformation of Buddhism from a belief of the élite to a popular religion was accomplished at least in part through the proselytizing of such individuals as the monk Wŏnhyo (617–86), a scholar and active propagator of Pure Land teachings in the countryside.

The importance of the Avatamsaka and Pure Land sects is reflected in the comparatively large numbers of representations of the Vairochana (Kor. Pirojana) Buddha, associated with the first sect, and Amitabha (Kor. Amit'a) Buddha, favoured by the Pure Land sect, among extant Unified Silla sculptures (*see* KOREA, figs 22 and 24). Also numerically prominent but without specific sectarian implications are images of Bhaishajyaguru (Kor. Yaksa), the medicine Buddha. Throughout the Unified Silla period, Buddhist rituals to strengthen and protect the state were regularly performed at court and in the major temples of the land. Important works of art were commissioned with the same purpose, for example Sach'ŏnwang (Four Heavenly Kings) Temple, built in the late 7th century to bolster resistance against Chinese encroachment, and the 8th-century shrine of Sŏkkuram (*see* KOREA, §III, 1(ii) and fig. 24), created in part to protect the Korean coastline from Japanese marauders.

The close relationship between Buddhism and the national government characteristic of the Unified Silla period was perpetuated and intensified under the succeeding KORYŎ dynasty (918–1392), when the major sects counted among the most powerful political forces in the land. Buddhist ceremonies were deemed essential to the commonweal and defence of the state. The vast enterprise of carving woodblocks for a complete edition of the Buddhist canon (*Tripitaka*) was twice undertaken at court expense, partly motivated in both instances by the hope of securing divine aid against foreign invaders. The second set of these woodblocks, completed in 1251 as protection against the Mongols, is preserved at Haein Temple in South Kyŏngsang Province. Government esteem for Buddhism was reflected in the rapid proliferation of large temple estates exempt from tax and in the creation of a hierarchy of posts for clerics within the official bureaucracy. Appointment to these posts depended on success in a special civil service examination restricted to the clergy.

In spite of its great social and economic prosperity, Koryŏ Buddhism proved less spiritually and intellectually vibrant than the Buddhism of the Unified Silla period. Tensions between the increasing appeal of Sŏn meditative traditions and the text-centred practices of the five established sects were never satisfactorily resolved, despite the ecumenical efforts of the monk Ŭich'ŏn (1055–1101), founder of the Ch'ŏnt'ae sect in Korea, who attempted to use his encompassing perspective to harmonize the differences within Koryŏ Buddhism. Following Ŭich'ŏn's death, theological innovation became primarily associated with Sŏn Buddhism. The Chogye sect of Sŏn, formed around the distinctive teachings of the monk Chinul (1158–1210), took root and has endured. Despite the persistence of Sŏn, no example of Koryŏ art that can be exclusively associated with the sect has been preserved. Rather, surviving examples of Koryŏ Buddhist sculpture (e.g. *see* KOREA, fig. 27) and painting display an iconography more appropriate to the text-centred sects and reveal the imprint of Chinese stylistic influence of the Song (960–1279) and Yuan (1279–1368) periods.

As part of the systematic efforts of the early kings of the Chosŏn dynasty (1392–1910) to create an orthodox Neo-Confucian state, Buddhism was placed under such severe restrictions concerning its rights, the size of its clergy, the number of its temples and the extent of its land-holdings that its role as a major political and cultural force in Korea was effectively terminated. In 1424 regulations were enacted that officially placed all existing temples within only two legally recognized divisions of Korean Buddhism, the Kyo ('textual') and the Sŏn ('meditative') schools. In the late 20th century, no longer subject to the crippling restrictions it suffered in the Chosŏn period, Buddhism is slowly regaining a footing in Korean society.

See also KOREA, §I, 4.

BIBLIOGRAPHY

Kakhun: *Lives of Eminent Korean Monks: The Haedong kosŭng chŏn* (1215); Eng. trans. by P. H. Lee, Harvard–Yenching Institute Studies, xxv (Cambridge, MA, 1969)
Iryon: *Samguk Yusa: Legends and History of the Three Kingdoms of Ancient Korea* (late 13th century); Eng. trans. by Ha Taehung and G. K. Mintz (Seoul, 1972)
Yi Nŭng-hwa: *Chosŏn pulgyo t'ongsa* [A comprehensive history of Korean Buddhism] (Seoul, 1918)
Han Ki-du: *Hanguk pulgyo sasang* [Korean Buddhist thought] (Iri, 1973)
I. Nakagiri: *Kaitō no bukkyō* [Korean Buddhism] (Tokyo, 1973)
Chun Shin-yang [Chŏn Sin-yong], ed.: *Buddhist Culture in Korea*, Korean Culture Series, iii (Seoul, 1974)
Sungsan Pak Kilchin paksa hwagap kinyŏm: Hanguk pulgyo sasangsa [Essays in honour of the 60th birthday of Professor Pak Kilchin: a history of Korean Buddhist thought] (Iri, 1975)
An Kye-hyŏn: *Hanguk pulgyosa yŏn'gu* [Researches in Korean Buddhist history] (Seoul, 1982)
R. E. Buswell: *The Korean Approach to Zen: The Collected Works of Chinul* (Honolulu, 1983)
J. H. Grayson: *Early Buddhism and Christianity in Korea*, Studies in the History of Religion, xlvii (Leiden, 1985)

JONATHAN W. BEST

10. JAPAN. The impact of Buddhism on Japanese cultural and artistic life cannot be overestimated. Six-sevenths of the population of modern Japan nominally profess the faith and are usually buried with its rites. The Buddhism that was introduced into Japan in the mid-6th century AD (*see also* JAPAN, §II, 3) reflected a thousand years of evolution in India and continental East Asia. After a period of uncertainty as to whether or not the court would adopt the new religion, the pro-Buddhist forces, led by the Soga clan, crushed the anti-Buddhist Mononobe family, and the assimilation of Buddhism was officially encouraged. The religion found a true champion in Prince SHŌTOKU, regent of Japan, who founded a number of

monasteries, including HŌRYŪJI, near Nara (*see* §(i) below).

(i) Early development. (ii) Tantric. (iii) Pure Land. (iv) Zen. (v) Development after 1600.

(i) Early development. During the Nara period (AD 710–94), six sects (Nanto Rokushū; Six Sects of the Southern Capital) flourished within Japanese Buddhism: the Hossō, Jōjitsu, Kusha, Sanron, Kegon and Ritsu. All six preached the doctrines of Mahayana ('Great vehicle') Buddhism, which had appeared in India around the beginning of the Common Era and spread northwards through Central Asia to China, Korea and Japan (*see* §§4, 8 and 9 above). Mahayana is distinguished from the more conservative tradition, sometimes derogatorily termed Hinayana ('Lesser vehicle'), which survives today primarily as the Theravada ('School of the elders') in South-east Asia.

Although the conservative tradition was introduced into Japan, the Japanese, like the Chinese, were more attracted to Mahayana Buddhism, which offered a broader spectrum of teachings at both doctrinal and devotional levels and emphasized the role of the laity. Whereas Hinayana acknowledged only one Buddha in this world cycle, the historical Buddha Shakyamuni (Jap. Shaka), Mahayana posited the existence of countless Buddhas, perfectly enlightened beings, emancipated from the ignorance, craving and aggression that bind ordinary people to the painful cycle of birth, death and rebirth. These Buddhas are usually depicted in painting and sculpture (*see* JAPAN, §§V, 3 and VI, 3(i)) dressed in monks' garb, although they show such distinguishing bodily marks as the cranial protuberance of wisdom (Skt *uṣṇīṣa*) and the tuft between the eyebrows (*ūrṇā*). Mahayana Buddhism also developed the imagery of a group of deities called *bodhisattvas* (Jap. *bosatsu*), embodiments of the ideal of compassion, who postpone their own complete emancipation from the world until they can save all beings. *Bodhisattvas* are usually bejewelled and dressed in regal garments to show their willing involvement with the mundane world.

Hōryūji (originally Wakakusadera) was completed in the first decade of the 7th century AD. Its originally modest precincts were rebuilt after a fire in 670 and expanded, especially during the late 7th century and early 8th, when the monastery was associated with the Hossō sect. The architectural setting and the works of art found in Hōryūji reflect the teachings of Mahayana Buddhism as well as the stylistic influences of 6th–7th-century China. Like other early monasteries, Hōryūji was built according to Chinese geomantic principles, orientated to the four cardinal directions, with the main entrance facing south. An early monastic compound such as Hōryūji consisted of a minimum of seven buildings (Jap. *shichidō garan*; 'communal dwelling of seven structures'). The *tō* or pagoda (*see* PAGODA, §3), a multi-storey tower with a holy relic in its foundation, was the East Asian form of the Indian STUPA, the hemispherical mound erected over the remains or relics of an exalted person and the most ancient type of Buddhist monument. The other five of the seven basic monastic structures were the *korō*, a bell or drum tower, the *kyōzō* (*sūtra* repository), the *kōdō* (lecture hall), the *sōbō* (dormitories) and the *jikidō*, a dining hall where vegetarian meals were served. As the faith evolved, new kinds of structures were added to this ceremonial core.

One of the deities depicted in the wall paintings in the Kondō (Golden Hall) at Hōryūji was the *bodhisattva* Kannon with eleven heads (Jūichimen Kannon). Especially associated with Amida (Skt Amitabha; the Buddha of the Western Pure Land), Kannon (Skt Avalokiteshvara; the *bodhisattva* of compassion) has the ability to assume many guises as an agent of salvation. This manifestation with eleven heads suggests the beginning of the Tantric movement within Buddhism that developed and spread rapidly throughout East Asia in the 8th century. The deities of Tantrism are often characterized by multiple heads and limbs, to show their supernatural power. Tantric images are also found at Tōdaiji, the other great monastery of early Buddhism (*see* NARA, §III, 4), built to be the head temple of a system of officially sponsored monasteries in each provincial capital. Tōdaiji was a monument to the fusion of political and religious ideals of state Buddhism in the Nara period.

(ii) Tantric. In 784, partly to counter the growing power of the Nara monastic establishment and particularly the monks of Tōdaiji, the capital of the country was moved to Nagaoka before being moved again to Heian (now Kyoto) in 794. At the same time, Tantric Buddhism (*mikkyō*; 'secret or esoteric teachings') was introduced to Japan. The secret teachings are revealed only to those of sufficiently developed spiritual training and awareness. The Tantric Mantrayana Shingon sect was brought to Japan from China by the monk KŪKAI (Kōbō Daishi). The eclectic Tendai sect, with its esotericizing tendencies, was introduced by the monk Saichō (Dengyō Daishi; 762–822).

Kūkai, who had studied in China from 804 to 806 under the Tantric patriarch Huiguo (746–805), was awarded the abbacies of Takaosanji (now Jingoji) in Kyoto Prefecture and of Tōji (officially Kyōōgokokuji), Kyoto; but the monastery that is most associated with his memory is a large architectural complex on the remote Mt Kōya (Wakayama Prefect.), popularly called Kōyasan, although its main temple is the KONGŌBUJI. Construction of this monastery began in 817. Kūkai, enshrined at Kōyasan after his death in 835, is believed to be suspended in a state of profound meditation awaiting the coming of the Future Buddha, Miroku (Skt Maitreya).

Kōyasan, like other Mahayana monasteries, was built for practices directed towards attaining a state of enlightenment, which, in the Tantric context, was understood to be identification of the practitioner (the microcosm) with the cosmic Buddha principle (the macrocosm). It was believed that enlightenment could be realized in the present without waiting for many more lives to pass or for rebirth in a distant, paradise-like pure land. Through the practice of the Three Secrets or Mysteries (Jap. *sanmitsu*) of body, speech and mind, individuals hoped to identify their own body, speech and mind with those of universal Buddhahood. Body is represented by *mudrās* (Skt: symbolic hand gestures), speech by *mantras* (spiritually charged syllables or phrases) and mind by internal visualization, usually of *maṇḍalas* (diagrammatic representations of the realm of enlightenment). The Tantric pantheon was expanded, often with deities associated with Hinduism whose own religion had also been influenced by Tantric concepts.

The monastery buildings on Kōyasan were placed less regularly than at other locations, because of the mountainous terrain, but were still usually orientated to the cardinal directions. Buildings appeared for the worship of new, often fierce and multi-limbed Tantric deities divinities such as the Go Daimyōō (Skt *vidyārājā*s; five great wisdom kings) and for new rites, such as the initiation ceremony that took place in a hall called the *kanjōdō*. Other buildings were modified, for example the pagoda, called, in Tantric monasteries, the *tahōtō* ('multi-jewelled pagoda'). Reflecting the renewed Indian influence in Tantrism, this pagoda shows beneath its main roof a large, usually white, dome like element, suggesting the old hemispherical Indian stupa.

The importance of *mantra*s is reflected in the name Shingon, which means 'true word'. Another of the Three Secrets or Mysteries, the *maṇḍala* (Jap. *mandara*), is found in several forms on Kōyasan. A *maṇḍala* may be defined as a sacred centre, in Shingon belief the locus for the identification of practitioner and Buddha. It can assume a three-dimensional form, as in an architectural plan or in the arrangement of statues on an altar, or a two-dimensional form, as in usually geometric compositions that show deities or their symbols disposed in relation to other deities in a timeless, cosmic setting. The two most important *maṇḍala*s in Shingon and esotericized Tendai Buddhism are the *Taizō* ('womb' or 'matrix') *maṇḍala* and the *Kongōkai* ('Diamond world') *maṇḍala*, together called the *Ryōgai mandara* ('Mandala of the two worlds'). Each focuses on the primordial Buddha Dainichi (Skt Mahavairochana; 'Great Illuminator'), the supreme Buddha of the East Asian Tantric hierarchy, who, unlike most Buddhas, is shown crowned and bejewelled. The *Taizōkai maṇḍala* represents truth in its nurturing, protective aspect and also expresses Dainichi's great compassion as it is revealed in the conditioned world. It shows Dainichi seated in the centre of an arrangement of 12 halls or mansions in which more than 400 figures appear. The *Kongōkai maṇḍala*, with over 1400 deities or their symbols, represents Dainichi's wisdom as it is revealed in the unconditioned Buddha realm. Dainichi is presented in his actualized or active aspect, dominating from the top central square (called an 'assembly') the configuration of nine small, almost square assemblies (three to a register). The topographical layout of Kōyasan itself, with over 100 monastic buildings centring on Kongōbuji, is meant to symbolize the *Ryōgai mandara*. Other two-dimensional *maṇḍala*s, called *besson* ('individual deities') *maṇḍala*s, can focus on deities other than Dainichi. Paintings and sculptures of single deities, some of a wrathful nature, were also created. Feminine deities were particularly honoured in Tantric Buddhism. Many Tantric deities were *hibutsu* ('secret images') and were not displayed to the uninitiated.

Although sectarian differences characterize the history of Japanese Buddhism, a non-exclusive eclecticism is also apparent. During the Nara period, Tantric and Pure Land elements existed within the general Mahayana Buddhist movement. As soon as the formal esotericized schools were introduced in the early Heian period (794–1185), they began to influence and to be influenced by already existing traditions. In particular, interaction with the indigenous tradition now known as SHINTO (*see also* JAPAN, §II, 2) became more pronounced and took, for the first time, visible shape in works of art—sculpture and later painting— that honoured Shinto deities and the relationships between Shinto and Buddhist deities. Potential tensions between the two religions were resolved doctrinally by the theory of *honji-suijaku* (*see* JAPAN, §II, 2), which explained that the Shinto deities were in fact manifestations of Buddhist deities. Shinto shrines were often linked to Buddhist temples, which were assumed to offer them protection, as in the association between the

15. *Maṇḍala* from the Kasuga shrine, Nara, hanging scroll, ink, colours and gold on silk, 998×350 mm, 14th century (London, British Museum)

Kasuga Grand Shrine in Nara and the Buddhist temple Kōfukuji (see fig. 15; *see also* JAPAN, §VI, 3(ii)(b)). When Kūkai built his monastic retreat in the mountains away from the capital, he helped foster the mountain asceticism that developed into a hybrid Shinto–Buddhist religious system called Shugendō (*see* JAPAN, §II, 7). Saichō's establishment of his monastic headquarters at ENRYAKUJI on top of Mt Hiei to the north-east of Kyoto ensured that local Shinto deities would be incorporated into the Tendai school. When 9th-century Tantric Buddhist sculptors began to leave unpainted the surfaces of solid wooden images, they were perhaps in part reflecting the Shinto belief that, because the sacred resides in natural elements such as trees, the material should be left in as natural a form as possible.

(iii) Pure Land. Pure Land Buddhism developed in India in the first few centuries AD and became prominent in China from the 6th century. Its teachings and practice had a longer history in East Asia than those of Tantric Buddhism. One of the earliest Japanese depictions of the Western Pure Land of the Buddha Amida—the goal after death for Pure Land devotees—appears as a wall painting in the Kondō at Hōryūji (*c.* 700). It was not until the 13th century, however, that Pure Land (Jōdo) sects began to emerge as distinct entities. In the early Heian period, veneration of Amida and his Pure Land was only one of many practices, particularly encouraged by eclectic Tendai Buddhists in their hermitages on Mt Hiei.

(a) Beliefs and practices. The Tendai-sect monk Genshin (942–1017) contributed greatly to the popularization of Pure Land teachings with his monumental essay, the *Ōjō yōshū* ('Essentials of salvation'; 985), which inspired numerous works of art and contains vivid and horrifying descriptions of the six realms into which beings must continually be incarnated until they are freed from bondage to the wheel of birth and death. The six realms are those of hell, hungry ghosts, angry demons, beasts, human beings and heavenly (but not enlightened) beings. Genshin contrasts the filth, decay and suffering of the six realms with the glorious perfection of Amida's Western Pure Land, where the faithful are born after death in one of nine levels, depending on their degree of merit. The most holy will quickly experience enlightenment through the guidance of Amida's teachings; repentant evil-doers too are promised enlightenment, although this will take much longer to accomplish. Genshin described, and artists often represented, the descent of Amida and his celestial company (*raigō*; 'coming to welcome'; see fig. 16) to the bedsides of dying believers to guide them back to the Western Pure Land. The monk also devoted many passages to a discussion of the *nenbutsu*, the mantric phrase 'Namu Amida Butsu' ('Homage to Amida Buddha'), whose devout recitation would help assure birth in the Pure Land.

In the 11th century, Japanese Buddhists believed that the 'end of the Buddhist Law' (*mappō*) was imminent. The third and last stage—the degenerate age—was calculated to begin in 1052. This century thus saw a flurry of *sūtra*-copying, temple building and temple embellishment to gain merit, as well as the burying of holy texts for preservation until the coming of the Future Buddha. It is significant that one of the loveliest places expressing Pure Land beliefs, the BYŌDŌIN at Uji near Kyoto, was consecrated in 1053.

16. *Descent of Amida and Bodhisattvas*, ink, colour and gold on silk, 1.70×0.85 m, 15th century (Cleveland, OH, Cleveland Museum of Art)

(b) Art and architecture. The Byōdōin was converted from a family villa into a temple by Fujiwara no Yorimichi (990–1074) to promote the auspicious rebirth of his father, the statesman Fujiwara no Michinaga (966–1028). The Amida hall (Amidadō), popularly called the Hōōdō or Phoenix Hall, was meant to evoke the glorious palatial setting of the Western Pure Land. Like most of the Amida halls built in the 11th and 12th centuries, its scale was small. Pure Land scriptures speak of the magnificent lake of the Pure Land in which devotees are born seated on lotus flowers, a symbol of spiritual purity. Lotus flowers,

representing enlightenment, rise high above their roots in the mud, representing the everyday world. The lotus continues to be an important motif in Buddist art. Ponds filled with lotus flowers were usually situated in front of Amida halls. At the Byōdōin a pond roughly shaped like the Sanskrit character for A, signifying Amida, encircles the Phoenix Hall. Devotees may have worshipped the Amida enshrined in the hall, facing west from a point of land across the pond or enacted symbolic journeys to the Western Pure Land by poling their boats westward across the pond to the Amida hall. From this time onwards, landscape design became an important element in Japanese temple construction, as it had been for centuries in domestic gardens in China and Japan.

The object of devotion in the Phoenix Hall is a graceful gilt-wood statue, 2.8 m high, of Amida seated in meditation beneath a canopy (*see* JAPAN, §V, 3(iii) and fig. 61). This image, created by the sculptor JŌCHŌ, was dedicated in 1053. Attached to the upper part of the walls of the hall are 52 exquisite little figures of adoring and music-making *bodhisattvas*, the celestial company described in Pure Land scriptures. *Raigō* scenes of the nine degrees of birth are painted on the interior walls and doors of the Phoenix Hall, completing the vision of the Western Pure Land.

Other surviving buildings that express Pure Land beliefs include the 11th-century Amida hall of Hōkaiji, built by the Hino family not far from the Byōdōin, the 12th-century Konjikidō (Golden Hall) of Chūsonji at Hiraizumi, Iwate Prefecture (*see* HIRAIZUMI, §2(i)), and the 12th-century Amida hall at Fukiji, Ōita Prefecture. The fact that Amida halls are found in remote provinces to the north and south of the capital attests to the diffusion of Buddhist culture (and especially Pure Land beliefs) throughout Japan in the late Heian period.

Amida was the focus of devotion in many painted and sculpted visions of the Pure Land, such as the Taima *maṇḍala*, whose Japanese name *mandara* reflects the lingering influence of Tantric nomenclature. The original Taima *maṇḍala*, named after the temple south of Nara where it is kept, is a large tapestry woven in China and brought to Japan in the mid-8th century. After the early 13th century, when it became the primary icon of the nascent Pure Land sect, this composition was copied repeatedly in painted and woodblock-printed versions. In other kinds of painting, Amida was often shown in a *raigō* pose, as, for example, in the famous *Descent of Amida and the Celestial Multitude* (three hanging scrolls; late 12th century; Mt Kōya, Yūshi Hachimankō Jūhakkain). Sometimes Amida was shown descending alone or with only two attendants. Some of the portable paintings were taken to the bedsides of dying believers to help turn their thoughts towards the Pure Land. Cords that the devotees could hold might be attached to the hands of Amida.

Other paintings depicting Pure Land beliefs include handscrolls and hanging scrolls of the six realms of existence. Notable among these are the late 12th-century *Jigoku zōshi* ('Scrolls of hell'; Tokyo, N. Mus. and Nara, N. Mus.) and the *Gaki zōshi* ('Scrolls of hungry ghosts'; Tokyo, N. Mus. and Kyoto, N. Mus; *see* JAPAN, fig. 8), which complement with horrific pictures corresponding literary passages in Genshin's *Ōjō yōshū* and in other texts.

Pure Land beliefs emerged out of a Tendai matrix and influenced Tantric Buddhism in return. In the mid-12th century, Mt Kōya became almost as strong a community for the practice of Pure Land beliefs as Mt Hiei. A Shingon monk named Kakuban (1095–1143) preached a reform movement called Shingi ('new doctrine') Shingon, in which Amida replaced Dainichi at the apex of the Tantric hierarchy, and many Pure Land devotees settled on Mt Kōya. In 1288 Kakuban's followers were hounded from Mt Kōya, but, even there, Pure Land beliefs continued to enter eclectic teachings. Nevertheless, the Amida halls of the late Heian period were usually subsidiary buildings in larger monastic compounds. Until the 14th century, for example, the Byōdōin was affiliated with the Jimon branch of the Tendai sect, and a statue of Dainichi (untraced), not Amida, was the chief icon of the entire temple.

The Pure Land sects—the Jōdo sect founded by Hōnen (1133–1212), the Jōdo Shin (True Pure Land) sect founded by Shinran (1173–1263) and the Ji (Time) sect established by Ippen (1239–89)—reflected the politics of the Kamakura period (1185–1333). Power had shifted from the aristocratic to the warrior class, and Buddhism, which hitherto had been orientated towards the aristocratic class, began to permeate the lives of common people. The Nichiren sect, founded by the nationalist priest Nichiren (1222–82) and based on the Lotus *sūtra* (Jap. *Hokkekyō* or *Myōhō renge kyō*), was another populist sect. The popularization of the faith is shown by the proliferation of narrative painting, often depicting the legends of the origins of particular holy sites, the lives of holy people or the miracles performed by deities. Shinto paintings of sacred places (loosely called *maṇḍalas*) were sometimes modelled on Pure Land visions, although many of the paintings showing relationships between Buddhist and Shinto deities displayed Tantric influences as well.

(iv) Zen.

(a) Introduction. The Chan ('meditation'; Jap. Zen) sects of Buddhism, introduced from China in the early Kamakura period (*see also* §8 above), soon found an eager response, especially among the warriors living in the new capital of Kamakura, but also among the Kyoto aristocracy and the educated classes in general. The primary practice in Zen is formal, seated meditation inspired by the example of the historical Buddha Shakyamuni. The Chinese Linji (Jap. Rinzai) sect was introduced by the monk Eisai (1141–1215) and the Caodong (Jap. Sōtō) sect by the monk Dōgen (1200–53). The Rinzai sect, especially syncretic in character, had absorbed many of the secular artistic and literary influences current in Hangzhou, the Chinese capital during the Southern Song period (1127–1279). Linji monasteries from that vicinity sent missionary monks to Japan, who built temples, advised leaders and introduced ink painting (Jap. *suibokuga*; *see* JAPAN, §VI, 4(iii)). The Zen tradition, particularly in its Rinzai form, was to influence subsequent Japanese culture significantly, encouraging expression in the secular arts of calligraphy, Chinese-style poetry, the *nō* theatre, landscape gardening and the tea ceremony (*see* JAPAN, §§VII, XIII and XIV).

(b) Art and architecture. Zen monasteries, most of them established in Kamakura and Kyoto, became centres of culture and education, especially between the 13th and 16th centuries. In the early 14th century a Rinzai monastery called Daitokuji (*see* KYOTO, §IV, 5) was built in the northern part of Kyoto, which became the capital of the country again after 1336. Daitokuji is a representative example of the culture associated with Zen Buddhism. The ceremonial buildings of Zen monasteries were typically axially arranged. Leading into the complex was the imposing Triple Gate (Sanmon); in its second-storey hall images of *arhats* (Jap. *rakan*; monk-disciples of the historical Buddha), flanking a figure of the White-robed (Byakue) Kannon, were often found. Further along this central axis was the Butsuden (Buddha hall) where public ceremonies were held, the *hattō* (Dharma hall) where monks assembled for lectures or interviews and the *hōjō*, the abbot's quarters. Zen monasteries were built in the *Karayō* (Chinese) style, as distinct from the established Japanese style (Wayō) of temple-building. In general, *Karayō* was smaller in scale, more complex in detail and more delicate in effect, with complex roof supports, intricate transom windows and masonry floors instead of the traditional wooden floors.

A characteristic feature of medieval Japanese Zen monasteries was the *tatchū* or subsidiary temple, a small, semi-autonomous group of enclosed buildings housing a little community of monks and separated from the ceremonial core of the monastery. In the quiet, meditative privacy of the *tatchū*, monks and their lay patrons and disciples practised calligraphy and ink painting, held poetry meetings and perfected such arts as the tea ceremony and landscape gardening. Especially after 1600, the *tatchū* were built in the mature *Shoin* style of architecture (*see* JAPAN, §III, 4(ii)(a)). Within Daitokuji there remain some 20 *tatchū*. The *tatchū* Daisen'in is renowned for its dry-landscape gardens (*kare sansui*), which re-create in miniature a vast natural scene of mountains and river landscape leading to a broad, calm sea; raked white gravel is used to suggest water. This kind of garden, which is not a stroll garden, may be used for contemplation.

Zen Buddhists revered many Mahayana deities, but certain forms of these deities have come to be especially associated with the tradition. One example is the White-robed Kannon, an image of the *bodhisattva* of compassion seated informally on a rocky crag beside a turbulent ocean. One of the earliest existing Chinese examples of this theme, painted in pale washes of black ink on silk by the 13th-century monk–painter Muqi, is found in Daitokuji. Chinese landscape paintings by Muqi and others helped legitimize the concept that landscape painting could express deep spiritual values.

The Zen tradition also contributed its own holy figures to Buddhism, including the semi-legendary 6th-century Indian monk Bodhidharma (Jap. Daruma), who was supposed to have introduced Zen teachings from India to China, and the pot-bellied, 10th-century Chinese Chan monk Budai (Jap. Hotei), who was believed to be an incarnation of the Future Buddha. Imaginary portraits were created, sometimes in sculpture but more often in painting, of Bodhidharma and the Chinese patriarchs. One example is the famous painting by TŌYŌ SESSHŪ (hanging scroll; 1496; Aichi Prefect., Sainenji) of a man, destined to become the second patriarch of the sect in China, offering his severed arm to Bodhidharma to show his intense desire for religious instruction. Another type of painted or sculpted portrait (Jap. *chinsō*) shows a historical monk and often served as an object of veneration.

(v) Development after 1600. With the establishment of the Tokugawa military government in Edo (now Tokyo) at the beginning of the Edo period (1600–1868), subtle changes occurred in the intellectual and religious life of the country. The rationally orientated teachings of Neo-Confucianism became virtually a state ideology, and a much more secular feeling began to permeate the most creative of the arts. Buddhism was still munificently patronized—the number of *tatchū* at Daitokuji sponsored by private patrons, for example, swelled to about 60—but the religion was not at the forefront of innovative intellectual and artistic activity. However, a kind of abbreviated and frequently humorous form of ink painting called in the 20th century *Zenga* ('Zen painting'; *see* JAPAN, §VI, 4(vii)) was produced as a form of religious expression, often by Zen monks who were amateur painters. Takuan Sōhō, Hakuin Ekaku, who helped revitalize the Rinzai sect, and Sengai Gibon were notable *Zenga* painters. The spirit underlying *Zenga* influenced other artists, both amateur and professional, and a new Zen sect introduced from China in the 17th century called Ōbaku (Chin. Huangbo), an offshoot of the Linji school, provided fresh religious and artistic stimulation.

Although much traditional Buddhist sculpture continued to be produced during the Edo period, most of it was derivative and lacking in dynamism or creative expressiveness. A few sculptors, monks who were also amateur artists, created works that were rough and powerful, translations into sculpture of the same tendencies seen in *Zenga*. Among those renowned for their simple, arresting images were the wandering monk Enkū and Myōman Mokujiki, a devotee of both Shingon and Pure Land teachings.

After the Meiji Restoration of 1868 and the resumption of Japan's interaction with the outside world following some two centuries of near isolation, the Japanese struggled to define themselves, partly in relation to the West. The traditional religions of Buddhism and Shinto endured, although efforts at industrialization and modernization seem to have absorbed the energies that in earlier centuries were directed towards spiritual goals. Nevertheless, new Buddhist groups emerged in the 20th century, chiefly offshoots of the Nichiren sect; the largest and most powerful is Soka Gakkai, claiming to have over six million adherents in Japan. The permeation of traditional Buddhist values in Japanese culture today might best be seen in secular activities like the tea ceremony which originally had roots in a religious context.

BIBLIOGRAPHY

H. H. Coates and R. Ishizuka: *Hōnen, the Buddhist Saint: His Life and Teaching* (Kyoto, 1925)
M. Anesaki: *History of Japanese Religion* (London, 1930)
L. Warner: *The Enduring Art of Japan* (Cambridge, MA, 1952)
S. Hisamatsu: *Zen to bijutsu* (Kyoto, 1958/*R* 1976); Eng. trans. by G. Tokiwa as *Zen and the Fine Arts* (Tokyo, 1971)
R. Tsunoda and others: *Sources of the Japanese Tradition* (New York, 1958)
D. T. Suzuki: *Zen and Japanese Culture* (New York, 1959)

E. D. Saunders: *Mudrā: A Study of Symbolic Gestures in Japanese Buddhist Sculpture* (Princeton, 1960)
T. Sawa: *Mikkyō no bijutsu* [*Mikkyō* arts], Nihon no bijutsu [Arts of Japan], viii (Tokyo, 1964); Eng. trans. by R. L. Gage as *Art in Japanese Esoteric Buddhism*, Heibonsha Surv. Jap. A., viii (New York and Tokyo, 1982)
D. Seckel: *The Art of Buddhism*; Eng. trans. by A. Keep, Arts of the World, xiv (New York, 1964)
J. M. Kitagawa: *Religion in Japanese History* (New York, 1966)
W. T. de Bary, ed.: *The Buddhist Tradition in India, China and Japan* (New York, 1969)
Y. Awakawa: *Zen Painting*; Eng. trans. by J. Bester (Tokyo and Palo Alto, 1970)
The Zen Master Hakuin: Selected Writings; Eng. trans. by P. B. Yampolsky, Records of Civilization, Sources and Studies, lxxxvi (New York, 1971)
Y. S. Hakeda: *Kūkai: Major Works Translated, with an Account of his Life and a Study of his Thought* (New York, 1972)
A. A. Andrews: *The Teachings Essential for Rebirth: A Study of Genshin's 'Ōjō Yōshū'* (Tokyo, 1973)
J. Covell and S. Yamada: *Zen at Daitoku-ji* (Tokyo, 1974)
D. Matsunaga and A. Matsunaga: *Foundation of Japanese Buddhism*, 2 vols (Los Angeles and Tokyo, 1974–6)
Y. Yokoi: *Zen Master Mōgen* (New York, 1976)
M. Kiyota: *Shingon Buddhism* (Los Angeles, 1977)
M. Collcutt: *Five Mountains: The Rinzai Zen Monastic Tradition in Medieval Japan* (Cambridge, MA, 1981)
J. M. Kitagawa: *On Understanding Japanese Religion* (Princeton, NJ, 1987)
T. Yamasaki: *Shingon: Japanese Esoteric Buddhism* (Boston and London, 1988)
H. Dumoulin: *Zen Buddhism: A History*, ii (London, 1990)
B. Faure: *The Rhetoric of Immediacy* (Princeton, NJ, 1991)
R. E. Fisher: *Buddhist Art and Architecture* (London, 1993)
M. Yiengpruksawan: 'The Phoenix Hall at Uji and the Symmetries of Replication', *A. Bull.*, 77 (1995), pp. 647–72

ELIZABETH TEN GROTENHUIS

Budeşti, Nicolae Ghika. *See* GHIKA-BUDEŞTI, NICOLAE.

Budhanilkantha [Buḍhā Nilkaṇṭha]. Village 8 km north of Kathmandu, Nepal. It is the site of a stone image of the Hindu god Vishnu lying on the coiled mass of the serpent Ananta (l. 7 m), the largest sculpture in the Kathmandu Valley and one of its outstanding masterpieces (see fig.).

The Jalashayana Narayana of Budhanilkantha village is second in importance only to CHANGU NARAYAN in the worship of Vishnu in Nepal. It was carved from a single block of a variety of basalt found a few kilometres outside the Kathmandu Valley. Several artists must have contributed to the sculpture, although it appears to have been conceived by a single mind. Notwithstanding its huge size, the figure is well proportioned and seems to float in the spring-fed pool surrounding the cushion-like coils of Ananta, who shelters the god under the canopy of his eleven hoods. The statue was consecrated in AD 641–2 by Vishnugupta, a *de facto* ruler who wielded power during the reign of the Lichchhavi king Bhimarjunadeva.

BIBLIOGRAPHY

P. Pal: *Vaiṣṇava Iconology in Nepal: A Study of Art and Religion* (Calcutta, 1970)
——: *The Arts of Nepal*, i: *Sculpture* (Leiden, 1974)
M. S. Slusser: *Nepal Mandala: A Cultural Study of the Kathmandu Valley*, 2 vols (Princeton, 1982)

ERBERTO F. LO BUE

Budich, Bernardo. *See* BOBIĆ, BERNARDO.

Budzyniewicz [Budziniewicz], **Wojciech** [Adalbert] (*fl* first half of the 17th century; *d* after 1672). Polish goldsmith. He moved from Kraków to Poznań, where he was probably apprenticed to Wojciech Schwartz, whose stepdaughter he married. He was a master in the goldsmiths' guild from 1632 to 1672. His work is almost exclusively ecclesiastical, including monstrances, ciboria, altar crosses, chalices and reliquaries. These works show the evolution from the Mannerist forms, in which abstract motifs and shell-like decoration predominate, to the fully developed Baroque style. He adopted early the type of monstrance with radial aureola (examples in parish church of Ptaszkowo, 1665; Franciscan Church, Poznań, 1671), rejecting the architectonic, retable-like form popular among goldsmiths in Poznań in the mid-17th century. He is also known to have produced jewellery, especially chains and bells used in the Polish national costume and on church vessels as decoration (e.g. altar cross in Pakośó).

BIBLIOGRAPHY

J. Eckhardt: 'Złotnictwo poznańskie w dobie Odrodzenia' [Goldsmithing in Poznań in the Renaissance], *Stud. Muz.*, ii (1957), pp. 121–2
A. Wasilkowska: 'O złotnikach wyszkolonych w Krakowie, a działających w Poznaniu w XVII wieku' [Goldsmiths trained in Kraków and working

Budhanilkantha, Nepal, figure of Vishnu reclining on the serpent Ananta (Jalashayana Narayana), basalt, l. 7 m, AD 641–2

in Poznań in the 17th century], *Biul. Hist. Sztuki*, xxxvi (1974), pp. 352–3

TADEUSZ CHRZANOWSKI

Bueckelaer, Joachim. *See* BEUCKELAER, JOACHIM.

Bueno, Diego López. *See* LÓPEZ BUENO, DIEGO.

Bueno, Mauricio (*b* Quito, 8 Sept 1939). Ecuadorean painter, graphic designer, sculptor, installation artist, architect and teacher. He studied architecture at the Universidad Nacional de Bogotá, Colombia. He worked for the Graham Foundation and the National Endowment for the Arts, Washington, DC, and received a grant to attend the Center for Advanced Visual Studies at Massachusetts Institute of Technology, Cambridge, MA, where he worked with Gyorgy Kepes. Later he became a professor at the arts faculty of the Universidad Central, Quito. Bueno worked first in graphic design before going on to experiment with the incorporation of technology into art, using laser beams, mechanical pumps, plastic, glass and such elements as water, fire and air, for example in *49 Tubes*, exhibited at the Bienal de Arte Coltejer in Medellín in 1972. He also combined visual art with music in such works as *Flame Orchards*, with music by Paul Earls, which won joint first prize with Kepes in the same exhibition. Exploration into ecological and environmental art led him to experiment with the idea of an aerial view of the urban landscape incorporating military camouflage sheets.

BIBLIOGRAPHY

H. Rodríguez Castelo: 'Mauricio Bueno', *Rev. Diners*, 6 (1981), pp. 36–44

CECILIA SUÁREZ

Buenos Aires. Capital and largest city of Argentina, located on the south-western bank of the River Plate estuary. It has a metropolitan population of 11 million, almost entirely of European (especially Italian) descent; indeed the cultural development of the city was largely influenced by the wave of Italian immigrants who arrived in the 1870s. Buenos Aires was first founded by Spanish colonizers in 1536, but it was not until 1580 that a lasting settlement was organized. During the first two centuries of colonial occupation, the city of CÓRDOBA (ii) was of greater importance, but in 1776 Buenos Aires became the centre of the new Viceroyalty of the River Plate, and since then it has grown continually in size and importance. The few remaining buildings from the colonial period display a range of influences, including Spanish Baroque, Portuguese Manueline style and the Rococo style of Lima (*see also* ARGENTINA, §II, 1). One of the most notable early structures was the cathedral (1593), subsequently rebuilt (1689–1791) by Antonio Masella and others (Andrea Bianchi and Giovanni Battista Primoli executed the façade) as a three-aisled church with a dome at the crossing. The Cabildo, first built in 1608 but rebuilt from 1719 by Primoli, is also notable. The Jesuit church of S Ignacio, La Compañia, was built from 1710 by Juan Kraus of Bohemia, while La Merced and S Francisco (completed 1754) were both worked on by Bianchi.

Planning initiatives in the late 19th century led to Buenos Aires taking on the Beaux-Arts classicism of Paris. Giovanni Antonio Buschiazzo (1846–1917), notably, opened up the Avenida de Mayo in 1880. The opera house, the Teatro Colón (see fig.), was rebuilt in 1908; it plays a central role in the cultural life of Buenos Aires. Designed

Buenos Aires, Teatro Colón, by Vittorio Meano and Jules Dormal, 1908

by Vittorio Meano and completed after his death by Jules Dormal (1846–1924), it is neo-classical in style, using Ionic and Corinthian orders. It combines the effective planning and solidity of German architecture with French decorative charm and variety; with a capacity of 3570, the theatre is well known for its perfect acoustics. ALEJANDRO BUSTILLO, reflecting a 20th-century revivalist tendency, also created many notable neo-classical buildings in Buenos Aires, including La Continental hotel (1927), the Chade Volta building (1930) and the Banco de la Nación (1944), but the city has felt other progressive influences, such as Art Nouveau, and, more importantly, Modernism itself. Le Corbusier visited the city in 1929 and drew up a plan envisaging skyscrapers set in green areas. While this was not implemented *per se*, a project in 1936 created plazas along the Avenida de Mayo (which runs from the Palacio del Congreso to the Casa Rosada; for an illustration of the latter, *see* ARGENTINA, fig. 3), dramatically widening the street; in 1990, however, renovation work began to return the avenue to its neo-classical splendour.

Several structures built in the late 20th century greatly enhanced the architectural environment of Buenos Aires. In 1987 Eduardo Leston designed a gymnasium and swimming pool complex as part of the Parque Deportivo Jorge Newbery: the building is ideally suited to the surrounding greenery, with the strong horizontal lines contrasting with the verticality of the trees. Aldo Rossi and Gianni Braghieri designed the office building Techint (1984) in the city centre and combined the city's European traditions with Modernism to form a uniquely Argentine style. The first floor is raised by over 4 m on each of the lateral sections to allow viewing of the church and convent of S Catalina and to allow space for public gatherings.

Buenos Aires has many notable museums (*see also* ARGENTINA, §VI), of which the Museo Nacional de Bellas Artes is the largest and most important, with some galleries devoted to Argentine painting of the 19th and 20th centuries. The Museo Nacional de Arte Decorativo, housed in an elegant neo-classical mansion designed by Tené Sergent and Achille Duchesne, has an impressive collection of antique furnishings, musical instruments, silver and weapons from the 16th to 19th centuries, as well as a collection of Oriental art. Specialist museums of colonial gold- and silverware include the Museo de Arte Issac Fernandez Blanco. Buenos Aires has a strong tradition as a centre of activity for artists, and various avant-garde groups have been based there in the 20th century. Notable among the artists working in the city at the end of the century were the painter and sculptor Juan Carlos Distéfano and the sculptors Jorge Michel and Hernán Dompé (*see also* ARGENTINA, §III, 2).

BIBLIOGRAPHY

J. A. Pillado: *Buenos Aires colonial* (Buenos Aires, 1910)
J. Glusberg, ed.: *Arquitectos de Buenos Aires* (Buenos Aires, 1979)
A. R. Williams: 'Eighty Years of Elegance and Excellence', *Américas* (Sept–Oct 1987), pp. 14–19
'The Friends of Museums of Argentina Make the Arts and Collections of their Country Known', *Museum*, xxxix/2 (1987), pp. 120–21
J. Goldman: 'Argentine Renaissance', *Archit. Rec.*, clxxxi (Jan 1993), pp. 44–6

ANN McKEIGHAN LEE

Bufalo, del. Italian family of patrons. Marchese Ottavio del Bufalo (*d* Rome, 1612) lived in a palace (now the Palazzo Ferraioli) on the south side of Piazza Colonna, Rome, but at the end of the 16th century he began to shift the centre of his family's patronage further east to the neighbourhood known as Capo le Case. In 1600 he bought the villa formerly owned by Angelo Colocci (1474–1549) behind the Trevi Fountain, which had a casino (destr. 1885) frescoed externally by Polidoro da Caravaggio (1525; fragments now Rome, Pal. Braschi). This became the site of the second Palazzo del Bufalo, sometimes attributed to Giacomo del Duca. The nearby church of the Italian Minims, S Andrea delle Fratte, was begun in 1604 to the design of Gaspare Guerra (1560–1622); when the friars ran into financial difficulties in 1610 they turned to Ottavio del Bufalo, who assumed the expenses of the church and façade until his death. Ottavio's marriage to Veturia Santacroce proved childless; both his estate and his commitments to the Minims therefore passed to his nephew, Marchese Paolo del Bufalo (*d* 1665), who later engaged Borromini to build the crossing, dome and campanile of S Andrea (*see* BORROMINI, FRANCESCO, §I, 10). Work was begun in 1653 but remained unfinished after the deaths of both the patron and the architect in the 1660s. Sketches by Filippo Juvarra (e.g. New York, Met.) show Borromini's ideas for finishing the cupola. The dome was closed with a provisional roof in 1686–91, but only the campanile received the final stucco decorations; its finial features, among other symbols, a buffalo's head as a heraldic device called *arma parlante*.

UNPUBLISHED SOURCES

Rome, Bib. Casanatense, MS. 966 [G. Marocchi: *Istoria della nobilissima, ed antichissima famiglia del Bufalo di Roma*, 1824]

BIBLIOGRAPHY

T. Amayden: *La storia delle famiglie romane* [*c.* 1650]; ed. C. A. Bertini (Rome, 1910), i, pp. 187–97
R. Kultzen: 'Die Malereien Polidoros da Caravaggio im Giardino del Bufalo in Rom', *Mitt. Ksthist. Inst. Florenz*, iv (1959–60), pp. 99–120
A. Blunt: *Guide to Baroque Rome* (London, 1982), pp. 8–10
H. A. Millon: *Filippo Juvarra: Drawings from the Roman Period, 1704–1724* (Rome, 1984), pl. 47
A. Barghini: *Juvarra a Roma: Disegni dell'atelier di Carlo Fontana* (Turin, 1994), fol. 19*r*

JOSEPH CONNORS

Buffalmacco [Bonamico; Buonamico di Martino] (*fl c.* 1315–36). Italian painter. He is recorded as 'Bonamichus magistri Martini' among the painters in the Florentine Matricola dei Medici e Speziali of 1320, but he was first recorded there *c.* 1315 (Hueck). He was in Pisa in 1336 (Bacci, 1917). According to a document of 1341, some time previously he had painted a fresco in Arezzo Cathedral (Pasqui). The record of 'Buonamico Cristofani detto Buffalmacco' in the Compagnia dei Pittori of Florence in 1351 is a forgery (Bacci, 1911).

Bonamico, who was nicknamed 'Buffalmacco' (Sacchetti) was not only a painter noted for his practical jokes in tales by Boccaccio (*Decameron* VIII.3, 6 and 9; IX.5) and Sacchetti (*Il trecentonovelle* CXXXVI, CLXI, CLXIX, CXCI, CXCII) but was also an artist whose greatness was affirmed by Lorenzo Ghiberti. No authenticated work by him survives, however. Some early attributions derive from Vasari's *vita* of Buffalmacco, but this is very unreliable. The frescoes dated 1315 in the Cappella Spini in the

Badia at Settimo, near Florence, which were attributed to him by Ghiberti, are too poorly preserved to assess the artist's style, even though they once gave rise to a theory that identified Buffalmacco as the St Cecilia Master (Sirén). A fragmentary fresco of the *Virgin and Child with Saints* in a tomb niche on the south wall of Arezzo Cathedral (partly hidden by a 16th-century altar) has been plausibly attributed to him on the basis of the Arezzo document of 1341 (Donati).

More recently Buffalmacco has been identified as the Master of the Triumph of Death (Bellosi), the painter of an extensive fresco cycle in the Camposanto of Pisa, often attributed to the Pisan Francesco Traini (*see* MASTERS, ANONYMOUS, AND MONOGRAMMISTS, §I: MASTER OF THE TRIUMPH OF DEATH). The argument is based on the following points: the absence from the Pisan frescoes of the Sienese characteristics that are so distinct a feature of Traini's work; the stylistic affinity with the fresco of the *Virgin and Child with Saints* attributed to Buffalmacco in Arezzo Cathedral; the evidence of Ghiberti who mentions 'numerous scenes' painted by Buffalmacco in the Camposanto at Pisa (these can be identified as being among the frescoes visible in the Camposanto in the 15th century, of which there is the evidence of a short poem by Michelangelo di Cristofano da Volterra, and not among those mentioned by later authors as being destroyed); Ghiberti's description of Buffalmacco's activity in S Paolo a Ripa d'Arno, Pisa, in which there are two frescoed figures of saints evidently by the Master of the Triumph of Death; Ghiberti's report that Buffalmacco was also active in Bologna and the strong links discerned between Bolognese painting and the work of the Master of the Triumph of Death; and the notable correspondence between the documented date of 1336 when Buffalmacco was in Pisa (living in the chapel of S Maria Maggiore where the masters employed by the Cathedral Works were lodged) and the most probable date of the *Triumph of Death* cycle (mid-1330s), based on deductions made from the costumes. The identification of Buffalmacco as the Master of the Triumph of Death seems to have been generally accepted, despite one attempt to defend Millard Meiss's attribution to Traini (Maginnis).

BIBLIOGRAPHY

G. Vasari: *Vite* (1550, rev. 2/1568); ed. G. Milanesi (1878–85), i, pp. 154–63

A. and U. Pasqui: *La cattedrale aretina e i suoi monumenti* (Arezzo, 1880), p. 171

I. B. Supino: *Il Camposanto di Pisa* (Florence, 1896) [incl. descriptions of the Camposanto decorations by Michelangelo di Cristofano da Volterra and others]

A. Venturi: *Storia* (1901–40/*R* 1967), v, pp. 288–90

P. Bacci: 'Gli affreschi di Buffalmacco scoperti nella chiesa di Badia a Firenze', *Boll. A.*, v (1911), pp. 1–27

L. Ghiberti: *I commentarii*, ed. J. von Schlosser, i (Berlin, 1912), pp. 38–9

P. Bacci: 'Bonamico Buffalmacco pittore e la critica tedesca: Un documento pisano del 1336', *Marzocco*, xxii (June 1917)

O. Sirén: 'A Great Contemporary of Giotto', *Burl. Mag.*, xxxv (1919), pp. 229–36; xxxvi (1920), pp. 4–11

——: 'The Buffalmacco Hypothesis: Some Additional Remarks', *Burl. Mag.*, xxxvii (1920), pp. 176–84

P. P. Donati: 'Proposta per Buffalmacco', *Commentari*, xviii (1967), pp. 290–96

I. Hueck: 'Le matricole dei pittori fiorentini prima e dopo il 1320', *Boll. A.*, lvii (1972), pp. 114–21

L. Bellosi: *Buffalmacco e il Trionfo della Morte* (Turin, 1974); review by H. B. J. Maginnis in *A. Bull.*, lviii (1976), pp. 126–8

M. Boskovits: *Pittura fiorentina alla vigilia del rinascimento* (Florence, 1975), p. 197

A. Smart: *The Dawn of Italian Painting* (Oxford, 1978), pp. 118–20

A. Caleca: *Pisa: Museo delle Sinopie del Camposanto Monumentale* (Pisa, 1979), pp. 55–7

W. Prinz: 'Bemerkungen zur "storia" im Triumph des Todes im Camposanto von Pisa', *Scritti in onore di Roberto Salvini* (Florence, 1984), pp. 202–10

LUCIANO BELLOSI

Buffalo. American city and seat of Erie County in the state of New York. It is situated at the eastern end of Lake Erie, where the lake flows into the Niagara River, and has a population of *c.* 328,000. Designed as a village for the Holland Land Co. in 1803 by Joseph Ellicott (1760–1826), the settlement grew rapidly after the opening of the Erie Canal in 1825, developing into a major port, rail centre, livestock and grain market and becoming known as the gateway to the Midwest. The migration to the suburbs in the 1950s was detrimental to architectural development. The city's notable buildings include St Paul's Episcopal cathedral by Richard Upjohn (spire 1870; church rebuilt after the fire of 1888 by R. W. Gibson (1854–1927)); the State Hospital (1872–7) by H. H. Richardson; and the Guaranty (1894–6; now Prudential) Building by Dankmar Adler and Louis Sullivan, which is considered to be one of their finest buildings (*see* SULLIVAN, LOUIS, fig. 1). In 1904 Frank Lloyd Wright designed the offices of the Larkin Soap Co. (1903–6; destr. 1950) and the Darwin Martin House (1903–6), an example of his 'prairie houses'. Pilot Field, stadium for the Bisons, was designed by Hellmuth, Obata & Kassabaum in 1988. Buffalo has two significant art museums. The Albright–Knox Art Gallery (1900–05) was designed by Edward B. Green (1855–1950), and an extension by Skidmore, Owings & Merrill was added in 1962. The museum is best known for its collection of American and European contemporary art and also contains 18th-century English and 19th-century French and American paintings. The Burchfield Art Center (previously Rockwell Hall), founded in 1966 at State University College of New York at Buffalo, is noted mainly for its collection of 77 paintings by CHARLES BURCHFIELD.

BIBLIOGRAPHY

M. Goldman: *High Hopes: The Rise and Decline of Buffalo, New York* (Albany, 1983)

S. Doubilet: 'In the Empire State', *Prog. Archit.*, xi (1984), pp. 88–94

S. Webster: 'Pattern and Decoration in the Public Eye', *A. America*, lxxv (Feb 1987), pp. 118–25

E. Lica: 'Burchfield and Friends', *ARTnews*, lxxxix (1990), p. 62

ANN McKEIGHAN LEE

Buffalo Meat (*b* Southern Plains, *c.* 1847; *d* nr Kingfisher, OK, 2 Oct 1917). Native American Southern Cheyenne artist. In his younger years he lived the ordinary life of the buffalo-hunting Plains Indians. He married *c.* 1867. On 3 April 1875 he was arrested at the Cheyenne Agency, Indian Territory, OK, with the charge of participating in the murder of a Euro-American immigrant family. He was sentenced to imprisonment without a trial or hearing, along with 71 other Native American Indians. They arrived at Fort Marion, FL, on 21 May 1875. Encouraged by the fort's commander, 26 of the younger prisoners started to produce an enormous amount of pencil, ink and crayon drawings depicting their former lives. It became known as 'ledger book art' and soon a white market developed for it (*see also* NATIVE NORTH AMERICAN ART, §IV, 1(iv)). Buffalo Meat made his first known drawings during this imprisonment, although he probably produced some art before his arrest. He departed for the reservation on 11 April 1878, where he became a policeman, labourer for the agent, then a worker and deacon in the Baptist church. There is no record of his artistic occupation after his homecoming. In 1917 he died of tuberculosis. Among the 44 drawings assigned to him, the attribution of 16 drawings (before 1878; Washington, DC, Smithsonian Inst., Archvs Amer. A.), 'BAEC', is uncertain, although these are definitely the work of a Kiowa artist. A set of 8 pages of drawings (before 12 March 1878; Fort Worth, TX, Amon Carter Mus.) depicts scenes of Native American life. The other set, of six drawings, includes his best-known work, *Buffalo Meat in his Sunday Clothes* (crayon and coloured inks, 160×110 mm, before 12 March 1878; Oklahoma City, OK Hist. Soc.), which shows an attempt to represent spatial depth.

BIBLIOGRAPHY

K. D. Petersen: *Plains Indian Art from Fort Marion* (Norman, 1971)
M. F. Harris: *Between Two Cultures* (St Paul, 1989)

IMRE NAGY

Buffet, Bernard (*b* Paris, 10 July 1928). French painter, illustrator and printmaker. After studying at the Ecole des Jésuites, he entered the Lycée Carnot in Paris in 1939. His antipathy to academic study led to his expulsion in 1943, in which year he attended an evening class in drawing. In December 1943 he gained a place at the Ecole Nationale Supérieure des Beaux-Arts in Paris, working in the studio of Eugène Narbonne (*b* 1885). On leaving the Ecole des Beaux-Arts in 1945 he travelled to Brittany with his mother, but after her sudden death he returned to Paris, where he devoted himself to painting. He then moved to Massy-Palaiseau, just south of Paris, to work with his friend Robert Mantienne, a French painter, and painted the *Deposition from the Cross* (*c.* 1945; Paris, Pompidou). This early work, with its restrained grey-toned colours and gaunt, anxious human figures, already bears many of the hallmarks of his later painting; both in spirit and colouring it shows the influence of Francis Gruber. In 1946 he met the writer Pierre Descargues, who became one of his earliest and most ardent supporters, writing the catalogue preface for his first one-man show in 1947.

In 1948, after failing to win the Prix de la Jeune Peinture, Buffet shared the Prix de la Critique with a much older French painter, Bernard Lorjou (*b* 1908). The award ensured him early public recognition. He began illustrating books, for example producing 25 drypoints for an edition of the Comte de Lautréamont's *Les Chants de Maldoror* (Paris, 1952). He exhibited annually in Paris from 1949, first at the Galerie Drouant-David, then at the Galerie David et Garnier and, from 1968, at the Galerie Maurice Garnier. From 1951 he gave each of these exhibitions a specific theme; in 1955, for example, he exhibited the *Horror of War*, a series of watercolours and oil paintings executed during the previous year. Typical of these was the *Hanged Men* (1954; priv. col.; see Le Pichon, pl. 267), which presents a series of brutal massacres and hangings against the panoramic background of a town. Characteristically, the emaciated figures were painted with angular, dark outlines, and the victims were given expressions of hopeless despair. Apart from the apocalyptic, glowing red horizon, the colours are muted greens, browns and greys. Such a catalogue of the atrocities of war was inevitably reminiscent of Goya's *Disasters of War* etchings.

Buffet's tremendous early success was doubtless partly due to the accessibility of his works; they have little of the innovative quality usually associated with modern art, relying rather on more conservative artistic traditions. His stylized and spiky draughtsmanship, together with a tendency to sentimentality, sometimes bordered on kitsch, but it was precisely these elements that satisfied a popular conception of 'modernity'. Furthermore, the anxiety found in his work resonated with the then popular philosophy of Existentialism. Indeed, the angst-ridden figures in many paintings by Buffet represent superficial paradigms, if not caricatures, of the 'Existential man' described in that philosophy.

In 1961 Buffet painted a series of scenes from the life of Christ, such as the *Deposition from the Cross* (1961; Rome, Pin. Vaticana), using a thick impasto and occasional areas of rich red and blue colouring. These were initially intended to hang in the chapel of Château l'Arc, his own residence near Aix-en-Provence, but were then requested for the Vatican. His naturally expressive style here found an ideal theme, resulting in a powerful reworking of familiar subjects. In 1965 he held an exhibition (Paris, Gal. David & Garnier) of works based on the subject of flayed human figures, as in *Flayed Man Seen from the Front* (1964; Nagaizumi-cho, Shizuoka Prefect., Mus. Bernard Buffet). These again recalled the horrors of World War II, especially the destruction of Hiroshima and Nagasaki by nuclear bombs. However, the staring, skeletal figures, painted in reds and oranges, seem too contrived to produce any genuine emotional impact on the viewer, a flaw that also applies to some of his other works.

In 1973 the Musée Bernard Buffet was opened in Shizuoka Prefecture, Nagaizumi-cho, in the Suragadaira Nature Park in Japan, devoted entirely to his work and demonstrating his popularity in that country. Among other series of the 1970s, he produced a series of drypoints and oil paintings illustrating Dante's *Inferno* (1976), such as *The Harpies* (1976; priv. col.; see Le Pichon, pl. 819). Throughout his career Buffet's style remained largely unchanged, though in his later works the expressive power seems much diminished. Many, such as *Sumo Rikishi* (1980–1; Nagaizumi-cho, Shizuoka Prefect., Mus. Bernard Buffet), which was part of a Japanese series, are little more than decorative. Landscape, also a subject of earlier paintings, became increasingly dominant, as in *Villereau* (1976; priv. col.; see Le Pichon, pl. 798), so further extending the decorative trend of his work.

BIBLIOGRAPHY

P. Descargues: *Bernard Buffet* (Paris, 1952)
J. Giono: *Bernard Buffet* (Paris, 1956)
M. Druon: *Bernard Buffet* (Paris, 1964)
P. Cabanne: *Bernard Buffet* (Paris, 1966)
F. Mourlot: *Bernard Buffet: Lithographies de 1952 à 1966* (Paris, 1967)
Y. Le Pichon: *Bernard Buffet*, 2 vols (Paris, 1986)

□

Buffington, LeRoy Sunderland (*b* Cincinnati, OH, 22 Sept 1847; *d* Minneapolis, MN, 6 Feb 1931). American architect. From 1864 to 1871 he was employed by several Cincinnati architectural firms, most notably that of Anderson & Hannaford. Moving to St Paul, MN, in 1871 Buffington first served as the local superintendent of construction for the new United States Customs House. In 1872 he formed a partnership with A. H. Radcliffe (1827–86) and two years later established an independent practice in nearby Minneapolis. Within a few years he was known as the best architect in the state and certainly one of the busiest; he produced dozens of residential, commercial, civic and church designs.

Buffington's Queen Anne style designs included the Boston Block (1880–84; destr.), the Pillsbury 'A' Mill (1880–83), the West Hotel (1881–4; destr.), the Tribune Building (1883–4; destr.), the Mechanic Arts Building (1885–6; now Eddy Hall) at the University of Minnesota, all in Minneapolis, and the North Dakota State Capitol (begun 1880; destr.) in Bismarck. Subsequent designs in the Romanesque style of H. H. Richardson, such as those for Pillsbury Hall (1886–9) at the University of Minnesota, the Charles Pillsbury residence (1887), the Samuel Gale residence (1888), all in Minneapolis, and the Tainter Memorial (1889) in Menomonie, WI, propelled the Buffington office to national fame because of their publication in *American Architect and Building News* and *Inland Architect*. These designs and many other unrealized ones also in the style of Richardson were all done by office employees, most notably Francis W. Fitzpatrick (1864–1931), Harvey Ellis and Edgar Eugene Joralemon (1858–1934).

Buffington claimed that he had invented skyscraper construction, that is a skeletal metal framing system for tall buildings, between the winters of 1880–81 and 1883–4. On 22 May 1888 the United States Patent Office granted him patent no. 383170 for his 'cloudscraper', as he called it, although it used an iron construction that was essentially standard. In 1892 he founded the Buffington Iron Building Company to license use of his system. When his practice declined after 1893 Buffington began to gain notoriety because of his repeated legal attempts, unsuccessful except in the instance of the Foshay Tower (1926–9), Minneapolis, by Magney & Tussler, to collect royalties from other architects who were designing tall buildings.

UNPUBLISHED SOURCES

Minneapolis, U. MN, *Memories* [1931, ed. M. B. Christison as MA thesis, 1941]
Minneapolis, U. MN Libs, NW Archit. Archvs [drawings and memorabilia]

BIBLIOGRAPHY

'Buffington, Leroy Sunderland', *The National Cyclopedia of American Biography*, xxii (New York, 1932), p. 364
E. M. Upjohn: 'Buffington and the Skyscraper', *A. Bull.*, xx (1935), pp. 48–70
M. B. Christison: 'How Buffington Staked his Claim', *A. Bull.*, xxvi (1944), pp. 267–76
D. Tselos: 'The Enigma of Buffington's Skyscraper', *A. Bull.*, xxvi (1944), pp. 3–12
E. Manning: *The Architectural Designs of Harvey Ellis* (diss., U. MN, 1953), pp. 19–44

EILEEN MICHELS

Bugatti. Italian family of artists. (1) Carlo Bugatti is best known for his highly original furniture designs. About 1904 he moved from Milan to Paris, probably to advance the careers of his sons (2) Rembrandt Bugatti and Ettore Bugatti (*b* Milan, 15 Sept 1881; *d* Paris, 21 Aug 1947). Although Rembrandt originally trained in his father's workshop, he subsequently became a sculptor whose most common subjects were animals. Ettore revealed a talent for mechanics at an early age and went on to become internationally known as a designer of exclusive cars and racing cars. Ettore's son Jean Bugatti (*b* 6 Jan 1909; *d* 11 Aug 1939) worked with his father as a designer until his death in a car crash.

BIBLIOGRAPHY

P. Garner, M. Harvey and H. Conway: *The Amazing Bugattis* (London, 1979)
P. Dejean: *Carlo, Rembrandt, Ettore, Jean Bugatti* (Milan, 1982)
Die Bugattis (exh. cat., ed. A. von Saldern; Hamburg, Mus. Kst & Gew., 1983)
I Bugatti (exh. cat. by R. Bossaglia, M. F. Giubilei and U. Hucke, Ferrara, Gal. Civ. A. Mod., 1988)

(1) Carlo Bugatti (*b* Milan, 16 Feb 1856; *d* Molsheim, Alsace, April 1940). Designer, active also in France. His biography, based largely on poorly documented family tradition, remains sketchy. His father Giovanni Luigi Bugatti was a decorative stone-carver. Carlo Bugatti registered at the Accademia di Brera in Milan in 1875, and is said later to have been at the Ecole des Beaux-Arts in Paris. He painted and showed an interest in architecture, producing designs for buildings and elements of interior architecture at several points in his career, although no structures designed by him are recorded as having been executed. In 1880 he returned to Milan, where he lived for approximately 25 years. At this time his sister formed a union with the painter Giovanni Segantini, with whom he had studied at the Brera; for them he designed a small group of furniture (see Garner, Harvey and Conway, p. 18), which, although said to have been made in 1880, probably dates to about 1885 or slightly later. The first clear visual evidence of Bugatti's activities as a furniture designer and manufacturer is contained in some illustrations related to the display of his work at the Italian Exhibition at Earl's Court, London, in 1888 (see Garner, Harvey and Conway, p. 22, and 1983 exh. cat., p. 32).

Bugatti's furniture is self-consciously original in design, though sources for its style can be found in the Islamic and Japanese decorative traditions and in Romanesque architecture. He often covered his pieces with vellum or parchment, with inlays of brass and pewter in the wooden supporting members. In his earlier work the vellum is sometimes painted in brown monochrome with Japanese-inspired motifs, but after about 1900 he favoured painted, polychrome geometric designs. Elaborate fringes and tassels often decorate his pieces. Circles, round arches and, later, curving planes are usually encountered in his furniture designs. Once his formal vocabulary was established, Bugatti produced a varied series of works using a limited number of motifs. A stylistic progression is observable in his designs towards unified, plastic forms, which culminated in the organic shapes of the tables and chairs (e.g. mahogany and parchment chair, 1902; Paris, Mus. d'Orsay) of the Snail Room, shown at the Esposizione Internazionale d'Arte Decorativa of 1902 in Turin. The precise chronology of this development is not clear, and it seems that early designs continued to be manufactured over a long period of time.

About 1904 Bugatti and his family moved to Paris. He sold his Milanese furniture-making shop to the De Vecchi firm, and this and other Italian firms made furniture after his designs or in his style for some years after his departure. In France he turned his attention primarily to designing silver, often incorporating fantastic human and animal forms, which was exhibited and sold by the Parisian firm of Adrien Hébrard. Some furniture designed by Bugatti was produced in France but probably not in large quantity. He also made plaster models for interior architectural schemes, but they seem not to have been realized. (Many of his plaster models for silver and architecture are in the Musée d'Orsay, Paris.) After 1910 he seems to have lived essentially in retirement in Pierrefonds, Oise, painting occasionally, for example family portraits (see Rossi-Sacchetti and Garner, Harvey and Conway, p. 31), but virtually ceasing his design activities. In 1937 he moved to Molsheim, Alsace, to be near his son Ettore.

BIBLIOGRAPHY

V. Rossi-Sacchetti: 'L'Art de Carlo Bugatti', *A. Déc.*, xxv (1911), pp. 301–8

P. Dejean: *Bugatti* (Paris, 1981; Eng. trans., New York, 1982)

HENRY HAWLEY

(2) Rembrandt Bugatti (*b* Milan, 16 Oct 1884 or 1885; *d* Paris, 8 Jan 1916). Sculptor and draughtsman, son of (1) Carlo Bugatti. He produced his first works in metal and wood at the age of 15 in his father's studio. He subsequently studied under Paolo Troubetskoy, from whom he learnt the technique of modelling forms directly using 'thumbstrokes', as can be seen in *The Dromedary* (*c.* 1904; Paris, Lesieutre priv. col., see exh. cat.), which like the majority of his works was cast in bronze using the lost-wax technique.

When the Bugatti family moved to Paris *c.* 1904, Rembrandt met the businessman Adrien Hébrard, who was responsible for casting many of his sculptures. In 1907 Rembrandt moved to Antwerp; at the city zoo he was provided with a studio where he could make his animal sculptures. These were included in many exhibitions, and some were acquired by the administrators of the zoo as the nucleus of their newly established animal museum. In addition to his sculptures, Bugatti also produced drawings and caricatures of considerable quality, as shown by his *Self-portrait* (*c.* 1910; Paris, Lesieutre priv. col., see exh. cat.), which, with its disquieting symbolism, could be compared with some contemporary works by Schiele. A combination of financial problems and depression led him to commit suicide in Paris in 1916.

BIBLIOGRAPHY

J. Chalom Des Cordes and V. Chalom Des Cordes: *Rembrandt Bugatti: Catalogue raisonné, la vie, l'oeuvre* (Paris, 1987)

SAVERIO SIMI DE BURGIS

Bugatto, Zanetto (*b* Milan, ?1433; *d* Pavia or Milan, 1476). Italian painter. He is one of the best-documented court portrait painters of the 15th century and worked for the Dukes of Milan for 15 years, producing numerous family likenesses on panel and in fresco. Yet, despite many attempts, no work of art has been convincingly linked with his name. Bugatto's name appears in the account-books of Milan Cathedral in 1458 for minor work produced for a procession. His first commission for the court, a portrait of *Ippolita Sforza* (untraced), Francesco and Bianca Maria Sforza's eldest daughter, was undertaken in 1460. That year his patrons sent him to Brussels to study under Rogier van der Weyden. Bugatto remained in northern Europe for three years, but his relations with Rogier were not always ideal; the Milanese ambassador reported that Bugatto had left his master's studio and that the Dauphin, later Louis XI of France, had intervened to reconcile the two artists. Nonetheless, Rogier's influence must have been profound, and Bianca Maria wrote him a warm letter of thanks on Bugatto's return to Milan in 1463.

On the basis of this sojourn, Sterling has associated two pictures with Bugatto: a *Portrait of a Young Man* (Châteauroux, Mus. B.-A.) and the *Virgin with Symbols of the Passion* (Paris, priv. col., see Sterling, fig. 174), both of which combine Rogier-like characteristics with north Italian mannerisms. A small panel of *St Jerome* (Bergamo, Gal. Accad. Carrara) has also been connected, less convincingly, with this stay in northern Europe; it reproduces in colour the grisaille exterior of the Sforza Triptych (mid-1440s; Brussels, Mus. A. Anc.), a work commissioned by Alessandro Sforza and once considered to be by Rogier, but now usually attributed to Hans Memling.

Bugatto's name appears frequently in Sforza correspondence after his return to Milan. The documents provide an excellent account of the services a court portrait painter was expected to undertake. He was sent to France in 1468 to portray Bona of Savoy, Galeazzo Maria Sforza's intended bride. Bugatto also profited from the trip by taking with him a double portrait of *Francesco and Galeazzo Maria Sforza* (untraced), which he sold to Louis XI. While in Milan, he designed coins and medals as well as easel portraits. In July 1471 Galeazzo Maria called him to Gonzaga, near Mantua, where he met Andrea Mantegna. The two artists returned together to Mantua, and Bugatto probably had a chance to study Mantegna's masterly portraits in the frescoes in the Camera degli Sposi in the Palazzo Ducale.

It is unclear whether Bugatto produced anything else apart from portraits. He often worked in association with other artists on larger commissions, but he may have specialized in the production of donor figures. In 1472 he collaborated with Bonifacio Bembo and Leonardo Ponzoni (*fl* 1472–7) on S Maria delle Grazie (destr.) outside Vigevano, where figures of the ducal family were frescoed along with religious scenes. In 1474 Bugatto joined with Bembo and Vincenzo Foppa to compete for a contract to paint a new chapel in the Castello Sforza in Pavia. Shortly before his death, he began working with these two painters on a large fresco cycle depicting scenes from the *Life of Christ* in the church of S Giacomo fuori Pavia.

When Bugatto died, Galeazzo Maria Sforza tried to obtain the services of Antonello da Messina as his new court portrait painter. There is no indication that Antonello moved to Milan or served Galeazzo Maria for the short period before the Duke was assassinated in December 1476. But his interest suggests that Bugatto's works may have had the same appeal as the Flemish-style portraits Antonello produced. With this in mind, scholars have attributed two other paintings with Flemish qualities to Bugatto: the *Virgin and Child* (Gazzada, Mus. Villa Cagnola) and the badly damaged portrait of *Galeazzo*

Zanetto Bugatto (attrib.): *Galeazzo Maria Sforza*, 430×390 mm (Milan, Museo Civico di Milano)

Buggiano: funerary monument to *Filippo Brunelleschi*, marble, 1447–8, Florence Cathedral

Maria Sforza (see fig.). Each of these works is problematic, however, and, unless new documentation or a signed work emerges, Bugatto will remain an enigmatic figure.

BIBLIOGRAPHY

DBI

F. Malaguzzi Valeri: *I pittori lombardi del quattrocento* (Milan, 1902), pp. 125–36

P. Durrieu: 'Achat par le roi de France, Louis XI, d'un tableau du peintre milanais Zanetto Bugatto', *Chron. A. & Curiosité* (1904), pp. 231–2

F. Malaguzzi Valeri: 'Zanetto Bugatto', *Ant. Viva*, 11 (1911), pp. 193–5

——: 'Ancora di Zanetto Bugatto e de suoi soci', *Ant. Viva*, 12 (1912), p. 48

F. Bologna: 'Un *San Girolamo* lombardo del quattrocento', *Paragone*, xlix (1954), p. 49

F. Zeri: 'Un'aggiunta al problema della Madonna Cagnola', *Paragone*, xciii (1957), pp. 11–16

P. Wechser: 'Zanetto Bugatto e Rogier van der Weyden', *A. Q.* [Detroit], xxv (1962), pp. 209–13

C. Siracusano: 'Zanetto Bugatto?', *Antonello da Messina* (Rome, 1981), pp. 198–200

C. Sterling: 'A la recherche des oeuvres de Zanetto Bugatto: Une Nouvelle Piste', *Scritti di storia dell'arte in onore di Federico Zeri* (Florence, 1984), i, pp. 163–78

E. SAMUELS WELCH

Buggiano [Andrea di Lazzaro Cavalcanti] (*b* Borgo a Buggiano, Pistoia, 1412; *d* Florence, 21 Feb 1461/2). Italian decorator and sculptor. He was the son of Lazzaro Cavalcanti but was adopted at the age of seven by Filippo Brunelleschi and lived with him near S Michele Berteldi, where from an early age Brunelleschi put him to work at the cathedral in nearby Florence. As an apprentice he carved the marble cornices for the windows of the tribunes (1429). Two years later he worked on the sacristy chapel of Cosimo de' Medici (the Old Sacristy) in S Lorenzo, Florence, where he executed the marble altar, which is decorated with three panels, separated with marble semi-colonettes, one of which includes figures of the Virgin and Child. In the same chapel he executed the tomb of Cosimo's father, *Giovanni di Averardo*, which takes the form of an antique sarcophagus decorated with garlands and groups of putti carrying scrolls. In 1433 Buggiano fled to Naples with his payment for this work, which had been withheld by Brunelleschi, and met up with some Florentine sculptors from the circle of Donatello. Through the intervention of Pope Eugene IV and Giovanna II, Queen of Naples, Brunelleschi resolved the matter within a year. By 1438 Buggiano was back in Florence working on a marble lavabo in the Sagrestia delle Messe in the cathedral, a commission that had been given to Brunelleschi in 1432. This work, conceived as a Classical aedicula surrounding two putti in low relief sitting on a cushion and surmounted with a triangular pediment, was completed in 1440. In 1442 Buggiano began work on a similar marble lavabo for the Sagrestia dei Canonici of the cathedral. This version is more lively, both in its subject-matter and decoration, while the handling shows the influence of Donatello. In the same period, Buggiano carved other works in marble for the cathedral, including a tabernacle of *Corpus Christi* (1443), eventually placed in the lateral tribune on the north side; the fluted columns and cornice of the altar of the SS Sacramento (1446), based on a design by Michelozzo di Bartolommeo and located in the same tribune; and the funerary monument to *Filippo Brunelleschi* (see fig.), consisting of a tondo containing his bust (1447–8). The features of the bust repeat those of the plaster death mask

(Florence, Mus. Opera Duomo), which may have been made by Buggiano.

In 1443 Buggiano had begun to carve a circular marble pulpit for the church of S Maria Novella, Florence, based on a model by Brunelleschi and financed by the monk Andrea Rucellai. The pulpit, with its richly carved mouldings, betrays an element of ingenuity and repetition in the four panels depicting scenes of the Life of the Virgin; the work was completed in 1452, after much delay, and was assembled and evaluated by Antonio Rossellino and Desiderio da Settignano. Buggiano was also paid modest sums for unspecified work in S Lorenzo between 1445 and 1447. On Brunelleschi's death Buggiano inherited his entire estate, but offers of work diminished. His final documented work is an evaluation carried out for Luca della Robbia on the execution of the tomb of *Bishop Benozzo Federighi* (now in Florence, Santa Trìnita), following a dispute between della Robbia and his patron; Buggiano gave his full supoort to Luca's claims (1459).

Gaye suggested that Buggiano had also been an architect, but to date there is no documentary proof for this. In particular, the Oratory of the Madonna Piè di Piazza, Pescia (Pistoia), founded in 1447, and the Cardini Chapel in the church of S Francesco at Pescia, which is similar in appearance to the painted architecture of Masaccio's *Trinity* fresco in the church of S Maria Novella, Florence, are attributed to him. Both buildings are judged to be immature and provincial creations, but are distinguished by virtue of being the first in the Renaissance style outside Florence. In addition, Schlegel (1957) attributed to Buggiano a contribution to Brunelleschi's Barbadori Chapel in the church of S Felicità, because of certain inadequacies in the handling of the proportions and decorations, as well as work in the Carnesecchi Chapel in S Maria Maggiore and on the marble tabernacle in the church of S Ambrogio (*c.* 1433), all in Florence. Schlegel (1962) also attributed to him four stucco reliefs of the *Virgin and Child*, while Schöttmuller attributed to him two terracotta statues (all Berlin, Skulpgal.).

BIBLIOGRAPHY

DBI

G. Gaye: *Carteggio inedito d'artisti dei secoli XIV, XV, XVI*, i (Florence, 1839), p. 144

K. von Stegmann and H. F. von Geymüller: *Die Architektur der Renaissance in Toscana* (Munich, 1885–1907), i, pp. 3, 53, 61, 62; ii, p. 1

C. von Fabriczy: *Filippo Brunelleschi: Sein Leben und seine Werke* (Stuttgart, 1892)

G. Poggi: 'Il duomo di Firenze', *It. Forsch. Kstgesch.*, ii (1909), pp. 10, 12, 14, 18, 220

G. Calamari: *Andrea di Lazzaro Cavalcanti e la sua opera in Pescia* (Pescia, 1923)

F. Schöttmuller: *Die italienischen und spanischen Bildwerke der Renaissance und des Barock, i: Die Bildwerke in Stein, Holz, Ton u. Wachs*, Staatliche Museen zu Berlin, Bildwerke des Kaiser Friedrich-Museums (Berlin and Leipzig, 1933)

U. Schlegel: 'La Cappella Barbadori e l'architettura fiorentina del primo Rinascimento', *Riv. A.*, xxxii (1957), pp. 77–106

——: 'Vier Madonnen Reliefs des Andrea di Lazzaro gennant Buggiano', *Berlin. Mus: Ber. Staatl. Mus. Preuss. Kultbes.*, xii (1962), pp. 4–9

F. Borsi, G. Morolli and F. Quinterio: *Brunelleschiani* (Rome, 1979), pp. 25–33, 247–59

Atti del convegno su Andrea Cavalcanti detto 'Il Buggiano': Buggiano Castello, 1979

FRANCESCO QUINTERIO

Bugiardini, Giuliano (di Piero di Simone) (*b* Florence, 29 Jan 1475; *d* Florence, 17 Feb 1554). Italian painter and draughtsman. He trained in Florence in the workshop of Domenico Ghirlandaio. The influence of Ghirlandaio is apparent in his earliest known works, datable between *c.* 1495 and 1500, which include part of the altarpiece of the *Nativity* (Florence, Santa Croce) painted for the Castellani family. Apart from Ghirlandaio, his two most important early influences were Fra Bartolommeo and Mariotto Albertinelli. In 1503 Bugiardini joined the Compagnia di S Luca and began an association with Albertinelli that continued until 1509 when Albertinelli moved to the workshop of Fra Bartolommeo. Bugiardini's paintings of the *Virgin and Child* (e.g. *c.* 1510; Kansas City, MO, Nelson–Atkins Mus. A.) show the influence of the balanced classical compositions executed by Raphael in Florence between 1504 and 1508 (e.g. the *Madonna of the Meadow*, 1505, Vienna, Ksthist. Mus.; *La Belle Jardinière*, 1507, Paris, Louvre). From Ghirlandaio's workshop and his study of antique sculpture in the Medici garden, Bugiardini would have known Michelangelo early in his career. Vasari mentioned Bugiardini as among the artists who went to Rome in 1508 to assist Michelangelo with the painting of the ceiling of the Sistine Chapel (Vatican) and who were almost immediately sent back to Florence. The influence of Franciabigio is clear in such works as the *Birth of John the Baptist* (1512; Stockholm U., Kstsaml.; autograph copy, Modena, Gal. & Mus. Estense) in which nature is not idealized, as compared to contemporary works in Rome. The signed and dated *Madonna della palma* (*Virgin and Child with the Infant John the Baptist*, 1520; Florence, Uffizi) suggests his familiarity with such contemporary Roman paintings by Raphael and his workshop as the *Madonna of Divine Love* (Naples, Capodimonte) or the *Madonna of the Rose* (*c.* 1518; Madrid, Prado). The development of Bugiardini's mature style continued in the 1520s with such ambitious compositions as the *Virgin and Child with the Infant John the Baptist* (*c.* 1522; Leipzig, Mus. Bild. Kst).

Bugiardini was probably in Bologna *c.* 1523–5, where he began to return to the ideals of equilibrium and formal perfection that inspired him in his youth. The *Mystic Marriage of St Catherine* (*c.* 1525; Bologna, Pin. N.) is similar to many of Fra Bartolommeo's *Sacre conversazioni* (e.g. Paris, Louvre; Florence, Accad.) and also to Andrea del Sarto's *Mystic Marriage of St Catherine* (1512–13; Dresden, Gemäldegal. Alte Meister). The influence of Raphael and Fra Bartolommeo was revived in the *Martyrdom of St Catherine* (1530–40; Florence, S Maria Novella), which Bugiardini worked on intermittently for a decade, according to Vasari from drawings supplied by Michelangelo. The use of lucid and dense colours seems also to stem from Michelangelo and possibly from Agnolo Bronzino. In his most impressive surviving late work, the *Virgin and St Mary Magdalene with St John the Baptist* (*c.* 1540; New York, Met.), Bugiardini employed the style of Fra Bartolommeo with a new fluency and breadth of form derived from Michelangelo.

Many drawings once attributed to Bugiardini are now given to others. Several, however, can be linked to specific paintings, such as the delicate drawing of a woman's head (Paris, Louvre, 10965), probably a study for the *Virgin and Child* (*c.* 1523–5; Allentown PA, A. Mus.), also known as the Allentown *Madonna*.

BIBLIOGRAPHY

DBI; Thieme–Becker

G. Vasari: *Vite* (1550, rev. 2/1568); ed. G. Milanesi (1878–85), ii, pp. 214, 643; v, p. 25; vi, pp. 201–9, 211, 612–13; vii, pp. 175, 258

A. Venturi: 'Un disegno di Michelangelo e una tavola del Bugiardini', *L'Arte*, ii (1899), pp. 259–61

L. Dami: *Vita di Giuliano Bugiardini* (Florence, 1915)

O. Sirén: 'Alcuni quadri sconosciuti di Giuliano Bugiardini', *Dédalo*, iii (1926), pp. 773–83

E. Zahle: 'Bugiardini Caritas', *Kstmus. Årsskr.*, xix (1932), pp. 48–52

D. Redig de Campos: 'Das Porträt Michelangelos mit dem Turban von Giuliano Bugiardini', *Festschrift für Hubert von Einem zum 16. Februar 1965* (Berlin, 1965)

F. Zeri and E. E. Gardner: *The Metropolitan Museum of Art: Italian Painting: Florentine School* (London, 1971)

S. J. Freedberg: *Painting in Italy, 1500–1600*, Pelican Hist. A. (Harmondsworth, 2/1983), pp. 101, 238

L. Pagnotta: *Giuliano Bugiardini* (Milan, 1987)

□

Buglioni. Italian family of sculptors. Active in Florence and elsewhere in Italy from the late 15th century to the 16th, they were particularly noted for works in glazed terracotta. (1) Benedetto Buglioni worked with his brother Francesco Buglioni (1462–1520) and with another relative, (2) Santi Buglioni.

BIBLIOGRAPHY

A. Marquand: *Benedetto and Santi Buglioni* (Princeton, 1921/*R* New York, 1972)

G. Gentilini: *I Della Robbia: La scultura invetriata nel rinascimento* (Florence, 1992), pp. 390–449

(1) Benedetto Buglioni (*b* Florence, 1459/60; *d* Florence, 7 March 1521). The son of the sculptor Giovanni di Bernardo (1429/30–*c.* 1510) and possibly a pupil of Andrea Verrocchio, he probably worked with Andrea della Robbia, whose glazing techniques he learnt. In the early 1480s he opened his own shop, producing works in the style of della Robbia, often with compositions after Verrocchio, Antonia Rossellino or Benedetto da Maiano. His first documented work dates from 1484: a relief of the *Descent into Limbo* (untraced) for SS Annunziata in Florence. From 1487 to 1490 he and his brother Francesco went to Perugia, where he executed for the cathedral the stone altar of the Holy Ring, of which only the busts of *Isaiah* and *David* are extant, and many works in glazed terracotta for the monastery of S Pietro dei Cassinesi, including a pulpit and a basin with *Christ and the Samaritans* (both *in situ*). Among works from the 1490s are: the glazed altarpiece of the *Resurrection* (1490; Pistoia, Mus. Civ.) for Pistoia Cathedral; a frieze (*c.* 1493; London, V&A) for the main chapel of S Chiara in Florence; an altarpiece of the *Crucifixion* (1490–95; Radicofani, S Pietro); and the lunette with *St Mary of Egypt* (Florence, Mus. Opera Duomo). Also in this period he and his brother executed many projects for the sanctuary of S Cristina in Bolsena, rebuilt by order of Cardinal Giovanni de' Medici, notably the stone façade (1493–5), the effigy on the saint's tomb and an impressive tabernacle, the 'altar of St Christina'. The important decoration (1500) of the oratory of S Maria delle Grazie near Stia (Arezzo) was among many commissions from the Florentine prelate Leonardo Buonafede (*c.* 1450–1544). Buglioni was one of those appointed to decide the location of Michelangelo's *David* (Florence, Accad.) in 1504, probably the year he produced the glazed decoration (destr.) of the Del Bianco Chapel in the Badia Fiorentina. From *c.* 1500 his workshop produced terracottas with naturalistic colourings, such as the *Virgin with SS Jerome and Nicholas of Bari* (1502; Amsterdam, Rijksmus.) and the *Virgin with SS John the Baptist and Anthony Abbot* (S Casciano, nr Florence, S Giovanni in Sugana). Probably *c.* 1510 he executed the *Coronation of the Virgin* over the portal of Ognissanti and the *St Lucy Adored by Angels* over the portal of S Lucia dei Magnoli (both Florence). His last documented work is the *Virgin with Child and Four Saints*, commissioned by Buonafede for S Michele at Badia Tedalda, Arezzo (*in situ*), for which he was paid in 1517. From 1510–20 he produced many polychrome altarpieces, for example the *Nativity* (Montaione, S Vivaldo) and the *Assumption* (Barga, S Elisabetta), the latest being the *Virgin and Saints* for S Miniato al Montanino near Figline (dated 1520; Florence, Mus. Osp. Innocenti).

BIBLIOGRAPHY

DBI; Thieme–Becker

F. T. Fagliasi Zeni Buchicchio: 'Santa Cristina a Bolsena e gli autori della sua facciata', *Stor. Archit.*, III/1–2 (1978), pp. 79–100

M. Moscini: *Il miracolo di Bolsena* (Bolsena, 1987), pp. 62, 157–61

F. Domestici: 'Il mecenatismo di Leonardo Buonafede per l'arredo del Santuario delle Grazie in Casentino', *Ant. Viva*, xxvii/3–4 (1988), pp. 35–40

G. Gentilini: *Sculture robbiane a Figline* (Florence, 1990), pp. 13, 37–8

(2) Santi (di Michele Viviano) Buglioni (*b* Florence, 20 Dec 1494; *d* Florence, 27 Nov 1576). Relative of (1) Benedetto Buglioni. He collaborated with Benedetto and inherited his workshop and name. He soon developed a more modern style than Benedetto, reflecting his interest in Mannerism. His hand can be seen in such workshop productions from 1510–20 as the altarpiece of S Giovanni in S Casciano Sugana and the lunette of the *Virgin with Child and Saints* (Arezzo, Badia Tedalda). His more independent works include the *Virgin and Child with Four Saints* (Antona, Massa, S Gimignano), the *Adoration of the Shepherds* (Chicago, IL, A. Inst.) and a lavabo (1520; Prato, S Niccolò da Tolentino). Payments to him are first recorded for a tabernacle with *Christ Blessing*, an altarpiece with the *Virgin of the Girdle*, and another with *SS Sebastian, Giuliano, Antonio Abate* and the *Annunciation* (all 1521–2) for Badia Tedalda, Arezzo (all *in situ*), works previously attributed to Benedetto. The polychrome altarpiece with *SS Peter and Paul Adoring the Eucharist* (mid-1520s; Greve in Chianti, S Maria a la Panca) shows his taste for elaborate Mannerist inventions. The compositional scheme of the painted terracotta *Lamentation* with a glazed frame (mid-1520s; Greve in Chianti, S Francesco) is repeated in the Franciscan churches of La Verna (*c.* 1532), S Salvatore al Monte in Florence, and the Osservanza in Siena. Among numerous monumental glazed altarpieces of the 1520s and 1530s are: the *Ecce agnus dei* (before 1529; Bibbiena, S Maria del Sasso); two arched anconas of the *Noli me tangere* (both Florence, Bargello); and variants of the *Virgin with Saints* (Florence, Pal. Bardi di Vernio; Arezzo, Oratory of the Madonna del Ponte (1531); Vallombrosa Monastery). Lunettes include the *Annunciation* (before 1527; Florence, Compagnia della SS Annunziata) and the *Virgin with Child and SS Peter and Paul* (Florence, S Piero a Ponti).

Buglioni's best-known work is the glazed and painted terracotta frieze (1526–8) on the portico of the Ospedale del Ceppo in Pistoia. Commissioned by Leonardo Buonafede, it depicts the *Seven Works of Mercy* in scenes of great narrative effectiveness. After the plague of 1527, he was the only artist in Florence who knew the secret of della Robbia glazes. Also from this period is the important, animated ancona depicting the *Stigmata of St Francis* (Città di Castello, S Francesco). Buglioni worked with Michelangelo's pupil Niccolò Tribolo on the decorations for the wedding of Cosimo I, Duke of Florence, and Eleonora of Toledo in 1539 and on the pavement (1548–54) of the library at S Lorenzo, Florence. He also designed numerous pavements (1555–60) in the Palazzo Vecchio and in the Boboli Gardens, Florence. Works probably of the mid-16th century include the altarpiece of *Meeting of Mary and Joseph* (Florence, S Maria at Dicomano), the Virgin and Saints (after 1530; Carnertino, church of the Capuchins), the *Pietà* and the *Madonna della Cintola* (Villafranca, Lumigiana, S Francesco) and the *Annunciation* (Bevagna, SS Annunziata). He modelled portraits of Michelangelo for the latter's funeral ceremonies in Florence in 1564 and, in 1565, with Lorenzo Marignolli (*fl c.* 1542–65), he executed stucco decorations for the Palazzo Vecchio in Florence for the wedding of Francesco de' Medici, later Grand Duke of Tuscany, and Joanna of Austria.

BIBLIOGRAPHY

DBI
G. Vasari: *Vite* (1550, rev. 2/1568); ed. G. Milanesi (1878–85), ii, p. 184; iii, p. 376; vi, p. 88; ix, p. 40
E. Allegri and A. Cecchi: *Guida storica: Palazzo Vecchio e i Medici* (Florence, 1980)
F. Gurrieri and A. Amendola: *Il fregio robbiano dell'Ospedale del Ceppo a Pistoia* (Pistoia, 1982)
M. I. Catalano: *Il pavimento della Biblioteca Mediceo Laurenziana* (Florence, 1992)

GIANCARLO GENTILINI

Buhagiar, Emanuele (*b* 1876; *d* 1962). Maltese cabinet-maker and designer. He was trained exclusively in Malta, where one of his teachers was the painter Lazzaro Pisani. He was a gifted wood-carver, but his speciality was wood inlay, for which he developed his own distinctive technique. He designed and executed many items of church furniture, developing and elaborating a richly ornate Baroque style that reflects the Maltese love of exuberant decoration. He also produced designs for liturgical objects in precious metals and for church brocades.

Buhagiar, Gian Nicola (*b* Haz Zebbug, 1698; *d* 1725). Maltese painter. He was the son of a stone-carver and spent most of his life in Valletta. In many respects the artistic heir of Alesso Erardi, whose pupil he may well have been, he was, after Francesco Zahra, the most significant representative of the Maltese Baroque school. His work is uneven in quality, and his paintings often contain weak and arid details, which reflect the provincial insularity of his art. His most ambitious undertaking was the vast composition of the *Lamentation* in the apse in the north transept of Zejtun Parish Church, which was painted directly in oil on the primed stonework. It was completed in 1739 in competition with the young Zahra, who worked on the south transept in the same church. The two painters shared many qualities, and it is sometimes difficult to differentiate between their work.

MARIO BUHAGIAR

Bühler. *See* BILLER.

Bühler, Wolfgang. *See under* MASTERS, ANONYMOUS, AND MONOGRAMMISTS, §III: MASTER WB.

Buhot, Félix(-Hilaire) (*b* Valognes, Normandy, 9 July 1847; *d* Paris, 26 April 1898). French printmaker, painter, draughtsman and writer. He moved to Paris in 1866 and enrolled at the Ecole des Beaux-Arts, where he studied under Isidore-Alexandre-Augustin Pils. In 1867 he enrolled in a drawing course run by Horace Lecoq de Boisbaudran, and the following year he studied with the marine painter Jules Noël (1815–81). He learnt the techniques of etching from Louis Monziès (*b* 1849) and Adolphe Lalauze (1838–1905) around 1873, producing his first etching later that year. He concentrated on landscapes and urban scenes such as *Cabs, a Winter Morning at the Quai de l'Hôtel-Dieu* (1876; Washington, DC, N.G.A.). Many of these etchings combine a central image with a margin of supplementary illustrations, which the artist described as either anecdotal or 'symphonic', the latter being evocative additions rather than narrative extensions to the main image. They were published in *L'Art*, then directed by Léon Gaucherel, and also in Roger Lesclide's *Paris à l'eau-forte.* Buhot also illustrated books such as Jules Barbey d'Aurevilly's novels *Une Vieille Maîtresse* (Paris, 1879) and *L'Ensorcelée* (Paris, 1897), Alphonse Daudet's *Lettres de mon moulin* (Paris, 1882) and Octave Uzanne's *Les Zigzags d'un curieux* (Paris, 1888).

Buhot first exhibited at the Salon in 1875 and in the late 1870s and early 1880s he concentrated on painting, producing works such as *La Butte des Moulins during the Demolition for the Avenue de l'Opéra* (1878; Paris, Carnavalet). He had a great love for England, which he first visited in 1876, returning in 1879 and on other occasions. His second visit inspired *Landing in England* (1879; Caen, Mus. B.-A.), an atmospheric etching which the artist considered characteristic of his work: it shows its links with Romanticism through its depiction of the power and grandeur of nature (in this case a storm at a landing pier on the coast). By the early 1880s Buhot's graphic output had begun to decrease, though his reputation was growing. Helped by his acquaintance with the print dealer Frederick Keppel (1845–1912) in New York, he found a large market in the USA. Throughout much of his life Buhot wrote essays; he also contributed to the *Journal des Arts* between 1884 and 1892. In 1890 he succumbed to a profound depression and by 1892 had given up etching altogether, producing only a handful of lithographs.

BIBLIOGRAPHY

G. Bourcard: *Félix Buhot: Catalogue descriptif de son oeuvre gravé* (Paris, 1899/*R* New York, 1979)
A. Fontaine: *Félix Buhot: Peintre graveur* (Paris, 1932/*R* Paris, 1982)
Félix Buhot: Peintre graveur (exh. cat. by J. M. Fisher and C. Baxter, Baltimore, MD, Mus. A., 1983)

□

Bührle, Emil Georg (*b* Pforzheim, 31 Aug 1890; *d* Zurich, 28 Nov 1956). Swiss industrialist and collector of German birth. He studied literature, art history and philosophy at the Albert-Ludwigs-Universität in Freiburg im Breisgau, where Wilhelm Vöge awakened his interest in medieval sculpture. Bührle first saw masterpieces of

French Impressionism in the Nationalgalerie in Berlin, an experience that made him wish to own similar paintings. The outbreak of World War I interrupted his studies, and he served as an officer until the end of the war. His wartime experiences and the uncertainties of the post-war years persuaded him to go into commerce instead of resuming his studies. In 1924 he took over a small engine-tool factory in Oerlikon and settled in nearby Zurich. Within a few years he had succeeded in building up a large industrial concern, now Bührle Holding. With his new wealth he began to create an important art collection, centred on French painting of the second half of the 19th century and the early 20th, and including major works by Cézanne, Manet, Degas, Monet and van Gogh. He also collected Dutch and Venetian art, and medieval painting and sculpture. In 1944 Bührle was made a trustee of the Kunsthaus Zürich, and in 1953 he became vice-president of its board, endowing an extension to the museum and arranging to buy for it Monet's *Waterlilies* (*c*. 1910). He also sponsored the Swiss Award for Painting from 1941 to 1949. After his death the Bührle Collection was exhibited at the Kunsthaus Zürich (1958). A large part of the collection, administered by a foundation established in 1960, is now open to public view.

WRITINGS

Neujbl. Zürch. Kstlergesellschaft (1957) [incl. three autobiographical essays]

BIBLIOGRAPHY

Sammlung Emil Georg Bührle (exh. cat., Zurich, Ksthaus, 1958)

L. Reidemeister and others: *Stiftung Sammlung E. G. Bührle* (Munich, 1973)

The Passionate Eye: Impressionist and Other Master Paintings from the E. G. Bührle Collection (exh. cat. by H. Anda-Bührle, M. Hahnloser-Ingold and C. Bührle, Washington, DC, N.G.A.; Montreal, Mus. F.A.; Yokohama, Kamakura A. Mus.; London, RA; 1990–91)

RENÉ WEHRLI

Buijs [Buys], **Jan (Willem Eduard)** (*b* Surakarta, Java, 26 Aug 1889; *d* The Hague, 19 Oct 1961). Dutch architect. After graduating in architecture at the Technische Hoogeschool, Delft (1919), he joined the Public Works Department of Haarlem, where he remained until 1924. There he met the architect Joan B. Lürsen (*b* 1894), with whom he worked until 1955, sometimes in partnership, sometimes on a consultancy basis. His major work was the building for the Socialist cooperative, De Volharding (1927–8), The Hague. A multi-purpose corner building containing shops, dental clinic and administrative offices, it represented a splendid synthesis of avant-garde ideas: Cubo-Futurist fascination with movement and transparency; Expressionist celebration of glass as a building material; De Stijl compositional principles; and Constructivist incorporation of graphic means of communication into architecture for the proletariat.

Buijs's development can be seen as a summary of the most important trends in 20th-century European architecture. His first commissions, numerous houses in the environs of The Hague, were related to the work of the Amsterdam school. He was then influenced by Frank Lloyd Wright and De Stijl. When Neue Sachlichkeit became dominant in the late 1920s, he worked in that style but thereafter responded to the renewed traditionalism that entered the mainstream in the 1930s. A member of the Sociaal Democratische Arbeiders Partij (SDAP) until 1931, his most compelling buildings were realized for Socialist organizations (e.g. office building and printing plant, 1929–31, for De Arbeiderspers, Amsterdam; destr., see Rehorst, 1983, pp. 72–3, 78–9), although he also made two powerful designs for Rudolf Steiner's Anthroposophical Society in The Hague, a project for a clubhouse (1924; see Rehorst, 1983, p. 42) and the executed Rudolph Steiner Clinic (1926–8), Nieuwe Parklaan.

BIBLIOGRAPHY

Uitgevoerde werken van bouwkundige ingenieurs (Amsterdam, 1956)

C. Rehorst: *Jan Buijs, architect van de Volharding* (The Hague, 1983) [summary in English, extensive bibliog.]

——: 'Jan Buijs and De Volharding, The Hague, Holland', *J. Soc. Archit. Hist.*, xliv/2 (1985), pp. 147–60

HELEN SEARING

Building machinery. *See* CONSTRUCTION MACHINERY.

Building regulations. Laws controlling the layout of buildings and the materials used in their construction to ensure the strength and durability of the fabric as well as the health and safety of the occupants. While building regulations are stipulated by governments, building standards are voluntarily agreed technical norms that define and help coordinate the highly dispersed design and construction professions and industries. Although legally distinguishable, building standards and building regulations are intimately intertwined in practice, and each is better understood when presented in light of one another.

1. Purpose and extent. 2. The governance of building technology. 3. Evolution of building regulation. 4. Approaches and trends.

1. PURPOSE AND EXTENT. Building standards are a modern, formally documented means of communicating the detailed knowledge of precedent that each generation of building design and construction professionals has imparted, both orally and manually, to the next since prehistoric times. They are agreements that describe the design, performance and other characteristics of materials, products, systems and services. Designers use standards as one means of communication with constructers during the course of a building project. Prospective buyers or tenants of buildings may use standard terms and definitions in communicating their needs to building owners or operators. Most technical standards are descriptive rather than prescriptive. It is when specific levels of performance begin to be stipulated that some hitherto voluntary standards, whether originating in building lore or cultural norms, or in modern research and technology, become part of a society's regulatory process.

Building regulations are those practices that are found to be so useful and that satisfy such widely felt needs for safety and security that they become the subject of enforceable government legislation. Governments not only determine what minimum levels of performance are necessary to ensure a building inventory that will meet public needs but also define those needs in respect of buildings. Regulations must accommodate two sets of imperatives: technical feasibility and social expectations. These must be linked, but they are tempered by different criteria. Technical feasibilities are interpreted by specialists and professionals, usually within the building industry and organized into trade and professional associations, who

Date	Object	Method	Initiators
1880	Curtail typhoid and noisome nuisance.	Protected water supply; sewage treatment.	Sanitary engineers, public health physicians.
1890	Improvements in housing and health.	Indoor plumbing.	Housing reformers, plumbers.
1900	Prevent conflagrations.	Sprinkler protection of individual structures; fire service to built-up districts; fire endurance concept.	Fire insurance underwriters.
1920	Confine fire to building of origin.	Fire endurance concept.	Fire researchers, services and underwriters.
1965	Confine fire to room and floor of origin.	Fire zones in buildings.	Fire researchers, services and underwriters.
1974	Reduction of death, injury and property loss via the Housing and Community Development Act of 1974.	Federal pre-emptive regulation of mobile homes.	Low-income households (initially); housing and mobile home producers (later).
1975	Energy conservation.	Energy use targets for entire buildings and/or components.	Resource conservation groups.
1978	Historic preservation.	Alternative regulatory devices.	Architectural and local history amateurs and professionals.
1980	Accessibility.	Performance requirements of prescriptive geometries.	Architects, paralyzed veterans, disabled citizens and gerontologists.
1990	Indoor environmental quality.	Air management; real-time monitoring.	Office worker unions; health organizations.

1. Chronological chart showing the widening scope of building regulations in the USA

continually create technical or design options and characterize, classify and otherwise manage them through the systems of voluntary codes and standards. Social expectations, which include aesthetics and appropriateness, come from outside the building industry but are also realized within the context of regulations. These expectations have increased with the growth in environmental awareness, and they manifest themselves through building committees and social critics.

Reaching public consensus on the characteristics of a desirable environment is necessarily an incremental process and is typically open-ended. The consensus is never perfect, either on the attributes of the environment that merit regulation in the public interest or on required performance levels. A high degree of consensus may nevertheless be quickly attained where a widely shared cultural value, such as public safety, is directly or discernibly threatened by an errant technology or practice. Regulations may require longer gestation on more contentious issues, such as aesthetics or the public convenience of buildings, for example in terms of access by disabled people. This longer gestation reflects not only the likely breadth of opinion but also the intractability of the issues. The regulatory purview is also widening as experts identify the effects of environments on users and occupants. This was particularly apparent in the second half of the 20th century, as can be seen in the USA, for example (see fig. 1). The scope of regulation seems destined to grow further as technology presents designers with wider choices, as science reliably identifies more effects and as societies become increasingly differentiated in tastes.

2. The governance of building technology. The phrase 'social control of building technology' is a sensitive one for many in the building industry. Design professionals, for example, may fear their autonomy compromised or the scope of their creative freedom restricted as the regulatory system pervades the form and

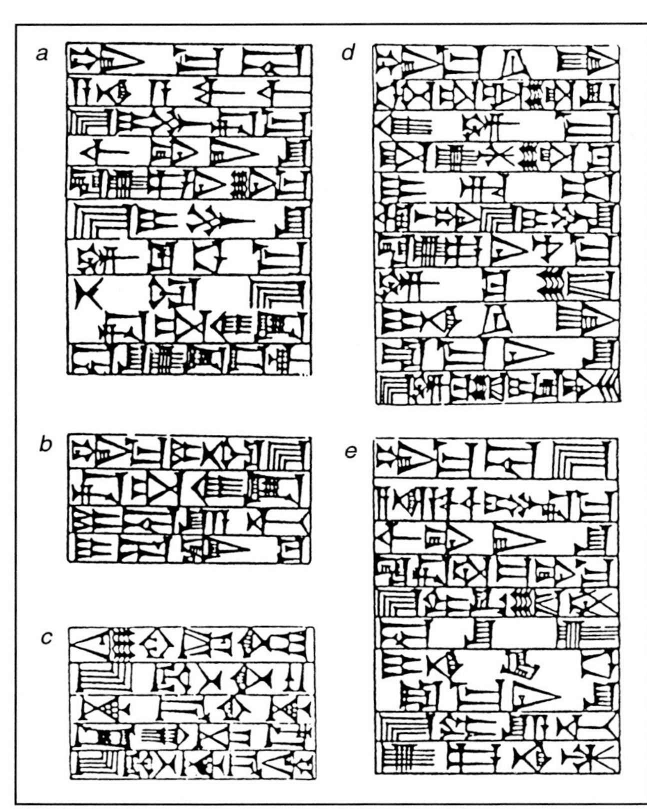

2. Code of Hammurabi, King of Babylon (*reg* 1792–1750 BC), inscribed on the Law-Code Stele (Paris, Musée du Louvre) showing sections dealing with buildings: (a) 'If a builder has built a house for a man and his work is not strong, and if the house he has built falls in and kills the householder, that builder shall be slain'; (b) 'If the child of the householder be killed, the child of that builder shall be slain'; (c) 'If the slave of the householder be killed, he shall give slave for slave to the householder'; (d) 'If goods have been destroyed, he shall replace all that has been destroyed; and because the house that he built was not made strong, and it has fallen in, he shall restore the fallen house out of his own material'; (e) 'If a builder has built a house for a man, and his work is not done properly and a wall shifts, then that builder shall make that wall good with his own silver'

content of the built environment, bringing the coercive authority of the state to bear on them. Social control of building has always existed, however; only its form and degree have changed. Throughout history, social needs and technological possibilities have forced changes in the scope, depth and formality of building regulation.

In the earliest times building rituals responded simultaneously to both earthly needs and sacred pursuits. The rites, skills and customs of building were conveyed by example and emulation from one generation to the next as a natural part of everyday life. Preferred practices survived, while unsatisfactory ones were explicitly proscribed or allowed to fall into disuse. With labour specialization and urbanization, however, the formalization of building standards and, later, regulations became inevitable. The growth of technical knowledge opened a gap between specialists and less knowledgeable building users and the government officials responsible for assessing taxes on completed structures. Building also became more of a commercial transaction, dominated by specialists whose competence was vouched for by fellow practitioners, specifically by the guild members who controlled entry to and training in the building arts. The potential for mischief and malfeasance was manifest in this interaction between builder and user, and it was in this context that the first explicit and formal social control over building was asserted more than 3600 years ago.

The Code of Hammurabi, King of Babylon (*reg* 1792–1750 BC), inscribed on the Law-Code Stele (Paris, Louvre; see fig. 2; *see also* MESOPOTAMIA, fig. 14), is widely but incorrectly referred to as the first written building code. It did not stipulate a required level of building performance consistent with the public interest, but it socialized building decisions and the risks associated with building construction by extending the law of retaliation to cover relations between builder and client. A builder whose structure failed was subject to retribution: if the householder was killed through the builder's negligence, the builder too lost his life; if the householder's child was killed, the builder's child was slain; and so on through the householder's retinue of slaves and chattels. Hammurabi thus established a public presence in order to protect the interests of individuals who were not able to discern either the competence of specialist builders or the adequacy of the structure. As building technology became more arcane, the need for consumer protection grew more acute, since incipient or even potential construction failures were detectable by the trained eye only. Modern legislation on regulatory reform reflects the need to assure consumers that the largest single expenditure of their lives—their homes—will be adequate not only for their physical safety and health but for their economic and psychological well-being too.

3. EVOLUTION OF BUILDING REGULATION. The establishment of cities increased the need to formalize not only the relationship between builder and occupant but also the builder's obligations to previously unaffected third parties: immediate neighbours at first, but eventually the entire community. Buildings clearly have external effects reaching beyond a single private transaction on a specific site, and the community as a whole must be protected from injury caused by failure or malpractice by contracting private parties. This was evident in large cities, where combustible multi-storey, mixed-occupancy buildings resulted in many catastrophic conflagrations that often permanently altered city life and building technology. To mitigate these losses, ancient cities promulgated laws stipulating the use of non-combustible materials, supplementing the earlier requirements for structural integrity. After the devastating fire of AD 64 in Rome, for example, Emperor Nero issued regulations banning party walls (*parietes communes*) and limiting the height of multi-storey apartment buildings to four of five storeys (*see* INSULA); porticos were required to have accessible flat roofs for fire-fighting and each householder to have his own fire-fighting equipment. The use of timber in buildings was also restricted by regulation, and fire-resistant masonry was encouraged (*see also* ROME, ANCIENT, §II, 1(i)(c) and (ii)(c)).

The particular Roman contribution was the extension of the regulatory purview into sanitation, water supply and sewage disposal. In ancient Rome tenements were required to be separated from one another by 3 m: the *insulae* were islands in a sea of space and were considered sacrosanct, consecrated to the 'god of enclosure'. Party walls were permitted in the *Lex Julia de modo aedificiorum* (*c.* 46–44 BC), although subsequently banned after the great fire in Rome. The Pandects (*c.* AD 533) of Justinian I formalized the relations between adjacent structures, establishing 'servitudes' (easements) in order to assure light, air and access to more Roman citizens. The prescience and persistence of these Roman regulators controlled fire and kept contagion and plague out of their populous cities for centuries.

In the towns of medieval Europe building was carried out within a statutory framework that the communes, seeking autonomy, placed between themselves and the feudal lords who ruled life outside the city walls. Such laws were needed because in urban settlements populations were concentrated at higher densities in more or less contiguous structures. These city building rules gave initial impetus and sustained character to some of the world's most remarkable cities, including Beijing as well as such European cities as Paris, Bologna, Prague, Edinburgh and Vienna. The variety of legal and quasi-legal approaches adopted by such cities is striking, as is their persistent reliance on them throughout their histories.

Social controls over building technology, contained in the teaching of elders, were not formalized until building became a specialist occupation. In China, for example, this line was crossed during the Song Dynasty (AD 960–1279) with the publication of *Yingzao fashi* ('Building standards'; 1103), which codified building technology, calculations, foundations, carpentry, joinery and the manufacture of a number of building materials, such as masonry, tiles, paints, mortars and plasters (*see* CHINA, §II, 2(v)). Drawings of buildings, types of construction and decoration were also included. *Yingzao fashi* was intended to impose controls and standards, not to instruct craftsmen; for example, the book includes calculations for estimating manpower and materials usage.

In London, within living memory of the fire of 1136, the city's first Lord Mayor, Fitz-Alwyne, promulgated an Assize (1189) that recommended methods for constructing conflagration-containing party walls for 'appeasing contentions which sometimes arise among neighbours'. In Siena—a city with renowned urban beauty—the spacing between buildings and even fenestration, the form and pattern of wall openings, had been regulated by 1295. The manufacture of materials used in construction had also come under regulation by several Italian municipalities in the 12th and 13th centuries and by Dutch towns by the 14th. Initially only the location of brickyards was regulated: they were proscribed from the city territory itself according to the communal statutes of Florence. Later, the brickyards supplying Florence, wherever they might be located, were required to display—and make available for annual inspection—model brick moulds (*modani*) that were bound in iron and bore a city seal. These rules were enforced by guild agents, the *ricercatori* ('searchers') who attended firings and spot-checked construction sites while work was in progress. In England a statute of 1477 required that clay for bricks be dug before 1 November, 'stirred and turned' before 1 February and 'wrought' after 1 March, presumably to utilize the winter rains and frost to break down the clay.

By 1592, in the reign of Queen Elizabeth I, London had grown so rapidly that an act was passed forbidding the location of new construction within three miles (*c.* 5 km) of the city's perimeter. The act's preamble referred to the 'evils of crowding', but another stimulus was the apprehension of the building guilds, who sought, through legislation, to keep away from the lucrative market of central London the building tradesmen who were migrating to the thriving city from the hinterlands. Another indication of the strength of the building guilds was the granting by the Queen of a monopoly to the Tile and Brickmakers' Company of London, an action subsequently vitiated by the establishment (1725) of brick manufacturing standards available to all, not just to guild members. Construction itself was not subject to coercive rules until Charles II signed the act for rebuilding the City of London after the Great Fire of 1666, which prohibited timber-framed and half-timbered houses and inflammable roof coverings. Moreover, the act authorized the appointment of inspectors to ensure that buildings within the four regulatory districts of the city conformed to each district's specific requirements for height, spacing, materials selection and minimum wall thicknesses.

Most of the components of the modern regulatory system were thus in place by the time of the European colonization of the New World. Controls had already existed there in Pre-Columbian civilizations: during the brief period of Inca supremacy in South America in the late 14th century and early 15th, for example, all construction relating to imperial administration had been controlled through a central bureaucracy, and standardized architectural form and construction techniques were imposed on the entire Andean region (*see* SOUTH AMERICA, PRE-COLUMBIAN, §III, 2(iv)(c)). In turn the Leyes de Indias (1573), the colonization ordinances imposed by Spain on all its territories in the Americas, included standards for the manufacture and use of materials, installation under the supervision of licensed professionals, the subdivision of larger territories into districts with specific building requirements and enforcement by delegated officers of the local government. In North America, the Dutch established a code for buildings at New Amsterdam (now New York) in 1625.

Regulatory systems were subsequently enlarged to cover new building types, methods and materials, while the scope of regulations was widened to accommodate evolving consensus about what societies wanted from their buildings. In 19th-century England a succession of legislative measures aimed at improving the social conditions of the population included stricter controls over the quality and reliability of buildings, particularly through the Public Health Acts of 1848 and 1875, which ensured that even the smallest new house was subject to detailed planning and building regulations. The development of high-rise building technology led to a variety of controls: in the late 19th century in Paris height restrictions were relaxed and new regulations coordinated by Louis Bonnier and

3. Building regulations as a determinant of form: set-back rule of New York's Zoning Law (1916) expressed in the McGraw-Hill Building, New York, by Raymond Hood, Frederick Godley and J. André Fouilhoux, 1931–2

adopted in 1902 (in force until the 1950s) authorized buildings to greater heights, with more vertical profiles. In New York the rapid development of skyscrapers led to controls in the Zoning Law (1916) over the three-dimensional form of such buildings, requiring that they be stepped back above a certain height to ensure that adequate light and air reached the streets below (see fig. 3). In many European cities the construction of high-rise buildings was later restricted to specific areas to conserve historic centres. The control of earthquake damage was also the subject of building regulation, particularly in Japan and also in such cities as San Francisco; there the wave of high-rise construction in the 1970s and 1980s led to the formulation of some of the USA's most stringent planning and earthquake-proof construction guidelines, as well as architectural design review processes, which strictly controlled new construction. Building regulation thus became an accepted element of the powers by which governments assumed increased responsibility for the health, safety and welfare of their citizens and of their built environments.

4. Approaches and trends. Building standards may be either performance-related or prescriptive in nature. A well-written performance specification or regulation states the problem and the criteria for evaluating the solution, leaving the designer or manufacturer free to provide any response that meets them; the traditional prescriptive standard, on the other hand, provides for both the problem and the solution. The performance approach has been adopted in a piecemeal fashion by many sectors of the building enterprise: owners, designers, contractors, regulators and the suppliers of building products. It permits designers or contractors a much wider choice of technologies to satisfy users' or regulators' requirements, thus encouraging the building products industry to continue to innovate.

Those who adopt the performance approach depend on four kinds of information, which force all participants to maintain the integrity of their historic role in the process while requiring higher-quality communications between them. Owners or users and their designers first need to set out clearly the scope of a performance-orientated provision in a technical document: what fundamental requirements—often stated qualitatively—need to be satisfied by the intended material, component, system or service? A precise—usually quantitative—statement of criteria is then provided to indicate the threshold level of performance that must be crossed to assure that requirements have been met. An evaluation method is next identified, whereby all concerned can determine when the criteria have been met. This may include analytic methods, physical testing or expert judgement. Finally, a commentary is required to assist in clarifying the intent, methodology or implementation of either the requirement, criterion or method of evaluation. What matters is that the methods be documented, accessible and replicable for all to see.

A 'model code' is a standard or performance-based code developed and promulgated with the recommendation that it be adopted for regulatory application by a local government. Model codes, dealing with fire, electrical, boiler and pressure vessel, and accessibility, are written by those with an abiding interest in such building codes. In the USA, for example, they may be written by the Building Officials and Code Administrators International (National Building Code); the Southern Building Code Congress International (Standard Building Code); the International Conference of Building Officials (Uniform Building Code); the National Fire Protection Association (Life Safety Code and National Electrical Code); the American Society of Mechanical Engineers (Boiler and Pressure Vessel Code); the American Society of Testing and Materials (ASTM) and the American National Standards Institute (ANSI) for accessibility.

At the end of the 20th century two principal concerns were discernible in the field of building regulations: building diagnostics, and regulations in newly industrialized countries. Building diagnostics is defined as a 'process in which a skilled expert draws on available knowledge, techniques and instruments in order to predict a building's likely performance over a period of time'. Building diagnosticians are primarily concerned with 'sick buildings', those that have a less than favourable combined impact on their environment—notably indoor environmental quality—and ways to get them 'healthy'. This entails monitoring a building throughout its life, from conception to demolition. Building diagnostics examines four principal areas in the life of a building: structure, envelope, interior spaces and services. All four must be at or above the standards in order to foster and maintain the well-being of occupants. Criteria for the four areas—whether performance or prescriptive—must also be consistent throughout the building's life. Newly industrialized countries need a series of standards and regulations that will bring them into conformity with those of the industrialized community at large, thus enabling them to participate in the global economy.

See also URBAN PLANNING, §§II, IV, V and VI.

BIBLIOGRAPHY

W. R. Davidge: 'The Development of London and the London Building Acts', *RIBA J.*, 3rd ser., xxi/11 (1914), pp. 333–69
C. S. Rhyne: *Survey of the Law of Building Codes* (Washington, DC, 1960)
H. J. Cowan: *The Masterbuilders: A History of Structural and Environmental Design from Ancient Egypt to the Nineteenth Century* (New York, 1977)
R. A. Goldthwaite: *The Building of Renaissance Florence* (Baltimore, 1980)
E. Gallon: 'Chinese Building Standards in the 12th Century', *Sci. American*, ccxliv (1981), pp. 162–73
Working with the Performance Approach in Building, International Council for Building Research, Studies and Documentation (Rotterdam, 1982)
Building Diagnostic: A Conceptual Framework, Building Research Board (Washington, DC, 1985)
R. T.-Y. Lai: *The Law in Urban Design and Planning* (New York, 1987)
G. Davis and F. T. Ventre: *Performance of Buildings and Serviceability of Facilities, STP 1029* (Philadelphia, 1990)
F. T. Ventre: *Regulation: A Realization of Social Ethics* (New York, 1990)

FRANCIS T. VENTRE

Building services. *See under* SKYSCRAPER, §1.

Building speculation. *See* PROPERTY DEVELOPMENT.

Bukhara [Bukhārā]. City in Uzbekistan.

1. History, urban development and art life. 2. Buildings.

1. HISTORY, URBAN DEVELOPMENT AND ART LIFE. The development of irrigation on the lower reaches of the Zarafshan River in the 1st millennium BC allowed the population of the region to expand, and the earliest settlement levels at the site of Bukhara are datable to the 5th–2nd century BC, when the citadel on a hill was separated by a ditch from a sprawling settlement on the east. The city came under the control of an indigenous Sogdian dynasty, the Bukhar-khudat, who in the 7th century AD restored and enlarged the citadel and constructed new walls around the residential quarters. At the beginning of the 8th century the two quarters were joined: the city proper was roughly square and covered some 30–55 ha. The two streets that crossed in the centre divided the town into quadrants, and the original four gates were increased to seven. Within were workshops, bazaars, shops, houses, palaces and houses of worship for a variety of sects, including Zoroastrians, Nestorian Christians, Buddhists, Manichaeans, ancestor and idol worshippers and those following the cult of Prince Siyavush. The Rud-i Zar Canal ran through the town. The citadel (3.5 ha) lay 120 m to the north-west of the city proper and contained the palace of the governors, a temple, armouries, a mint, a chancellery, a treasury and a prison. A street linked the eastern gate, which led to the city proper, with the western gate, which opened on to the market square known as the Registan. The suburbs contained the estates of the landowners with their fortified castles, at one time numbering 700. In front of these castles were gardens and service quarters.

The city paid tribute to the first Arab armies to cross the Oxus River in 673–4, but permanent Arab control of Bukhara was established only in the early 8th century. The main Buddhist or Zoroastrian temple in the citadel was rebuilt as a mosque (712–13) and the townspeople were paid to attend Muslim worship. There were regular uprisings of the indigenous Turks and Sogdians against Muslim rule, and the first ring of walls connecting the citadel, city and inner suburb was built in the 8th century, while the second ring (849–50) encompassed a far wider territory, including the outer suburb (*see* CENTRAL ASIA, fig. 17).

As capital of the quasi-independent SAMANID dynasty (*reg* 875–1005 in Transoxiana) Bukhara developed into a major cultural centre for Arabic learning and New Persian literature. In the 10th century many religious and civic buildings were erected, including two mosques (902, 951) and the Farjak Madrasa (937), one of the earliest institutions of higher learning in Central Asia. Court life moved from the citadel to the Registan, on which the amir's palace and ten chancelleries were erected with a bath and a madrasa near by, and suburban parks and gardens were made. The Samanid dynastic mausoleum (*see* §2(i) below), one of the earliest known secular mausolea in the Islamic lands, was erected to the west of the centre. Between the citadel and the city proper stood the congregational mosque and its minaret and weavers' workshops. Close by the palaces and religious buildings were squalid slums; contemporaries called Bukhara 'the cesspool of the country'.

Although the Qarakhanid Turks (*reg* 992–1211) transferred the capital to Samarkand in 999, they sponsored many constructions in Bukhara during the 11th and 12th centuries. The walls of the inner suburb were repaired and those of the outer suburb and citadel revetted with baked brick in 1164–5. Several new religious structures were erected, such as the Magoki Attari Mosque (early 12th century; *see* §2(ii) below), which replaced the older Mokh Mosque, and the Kalan Mosque and adjacent minaret (1127; *see* §2(iii) below). An outdoor praying place for festivals (Pers. *namāzgāh*; Arab. *muṣallā*) was built in a former garden in the southern suburb. The Qarakhanids also improved the facilities linking Bukhara with other cities, such as the caravanserai Ribat-i Malik on the road to Samarkand. Bukhara was temporarily under the rule of Qara Khitay (Western Liao) in 1141 and was seized in 1207 by the Khwarazmshah Muhammad, who repaired the citadel and erected new buildings there. The city was plundered and destroyed by the Mongols in 1220, but by the end of the century building activity had resumed, to judge from the construction of two large madrasas, the Masʿudiyya (destr. 1273) and the Khaniyya (destr.).

Under the Chaghatayid (*reg* 1227–1370) and TIMURID (*reg* 1370–1506) dynasties, Bukhara became the religious centre of the country, largely due to the activity of the Nakshbandi order of Sufis. The mausolea of Buyan Quli (*reg* 1348–59), one of the last Chaghatayid khans, and of Sayf al-Din Bakharzi (*d* 1261; *see* §2(iv) below), a theologian and poet, were erected in a cemetery on the eastern outskirts of the city. The Chashma-yi Ayyub shrine, a rectangular building with a tent dome over the well that supposedly appeared when the prophet Job struck the ground with his staff, was built by Timur in 1379–80. His grandson Ulughbeg built madrasas in Bukhara (1417–20) and in nearby Ghujdivan (1432–3). The Kalan Mosque was also rebuilt under the Timurids.

Under the SHAYBANID dynasty (*reg* 1500–98), Bukhara again became a capital of western Central Asia, and many new buildings and ensembles, ranging from mosques and madrasas to caravanserais, cisterns and broad subterranean irrigation canals, were erected within and without the city (*see also* CENTRAL ASIA, §I, 2(i)(f)). The city walls were partly restored and partly rebuilt, and domed retail markets (Pers. *chahārsū, ṭāq*) were erected at major crossroads (*see* ISLAMIC ART, fig. 73). The largest, the Taq-i Zargaran (Goldsmiths' Market), had more than 30 shops and an adjacent caravanserai and hammam (bath). Several large madrasas were constructed in ensembles, for example the Mir-i ʿArab Madrasa (1530–36) opposite the Kalan Mosque and the ʿAbdallah Khan Madrasa (1588–90) opposite the Madar-i Khan (or Qush) Madrasa built by his mother in 1566–7. The madrasa of Qul Baba Kukaltash (1569) was built by an amir of ʿAbdallah Khan. The Char Bakr ensemble (1559–69), 6 km west of the city centre, honours four early religious scholars from Bukhara named Abu Bakr; it comprises a mosque and hospice (Arab. *khānaqāh*) linked by cells and a central iwan to form a court open on the east. The Faizabad *khānaqāh* (1598–9) was erected to the east of the city walls; its interior is decorated with carved stucco.

There was somewhat less construction in the 17th and 18th centuries. Nadr Divan Begi Arlat constructed a madrasa, *khānaqāh* (1619–23) and reservoir (Pers. *ḥawẓ*) facing the Kukaltash Madrasa to create the Lab-i Hawz ensemble, and ʿAbd al-ʿAziz (*reg* 1647–80) constructed the largest madrasa (1651–2) in the city opposite that of Ulughbeg on the Registan (*see also* CENTRAL ASIA, §I, 2(ii)(b)). The Magoki Kurpa, a second congregational mosque, was erected, while in the south-west part of the city the Khiyaban Madrasa and Jubari Kalan were completed. Feudal strife and economic crises in the 18th century led to a decline in the quantity and quality of construction, although mosques, madrasas, shrines (*mazār*) and cisterns were still erected. Under the last amirs of Bukhara the city became a leading centre of Islamic theology. The amirs' summer palace outside the city walls is a museum of pottery, porcelain, carpets and other local crafts (Bukhara, Reg. Mus.). After the Russian annexation of Central Asia in the 1880s, Russian engineers introduced western-style buildings and country houses. Two-storey residential structures were erected, particularly in the city centre. The city centre has been designated a state reserve in which the building of new structures is not permitted and the old monuments are being restored.

The Bukhara oasis was a centre of textile production from the 6th century AD. A group of compound-woven silks (7th–9th century) has been assigned to the region on the basis of an inscription penned in Sogdian identifying one as *zandanījī*, that is derived from the town of Zandane near Bukhara (*see* ISLAMIC ART, §VI, 2(i)(b)). Silk-weaving remained a major art into the 20th century, and the city is known for its ikat silks and fine embroideries (*sūzanī*; *see* ISLAMIC ART, §VI, 2(iii)(d) and CENTRAL ASIA, fig. 48). Many examples are displayed in the museum of local lore, history and economy in the citadel. Bukhara was also the

1. *Mihr Entertaining King Kayman*, manuscript illustration from ʿAssar's *Mihr and Mushtari*, opaque pigment on paper, page size 265×170 mm, Bukhara, 1523 (Washington, DC, Freer Gallery of Art)

main centre for the sale of carpets knotted by Turkoman nomads, and the name Bukhara (Bokara) has come to identify a distinctive red-ground carpet with geometric designs (*see* ISLAMIC ART, §VI, 4(iv)(e)). In the 16th century Bukhara became a centre for the production of illustrated manuscripts (see fig. 1) when artists fled Herat after the fall of the Timurids. Many of the manuscripts produced under Shaybanid patronage closely follow models established under the Timurids (*see* ISLAMIC ART, §III, 4(vi)(c) and CENTRAL ASIA, §I, 4(vi)), and Bukharan painters participated in the transfer of Persian styles of painting to Mughal India. Many traditional crafts are still practised in the city.

BIBLIOGRAPHY

Enc. Iran.; *Enc. Islam/2*

Narshakhī: *Tārīkh-i Bukhārā* (AD 943–4); Eng. trans. by R. N. Frye as *The History of Bukhara* (Cambridge, MA, 1954)

V. A. Shishkin: *Arkhitekturnye pamyatniki Bukhary* [Architectural monuments of Bukhara] (Tashkent, 1936)

V. A. Nil'sen: *Monumental'naya arkhitektura Bukharskogo oazisa* [Monumental architecture of the Bukhara Oasis] (Tashkent, 1956)

O. A. Sukhareva: *K istorii gorodov Bukharskogo khanstva* [On the history of the towns of the Bukhara khanate] (Tashkent, 1958)

D. G. Shepherd and W. Henning: 'Zandaniji Identified?', *Aus der Welt der islamischen Kunst: Festschrift für Ernst Kühnel* (Berlin, 1959), pp. 15–40
L. I. Rempel': 'Iz istorii gradostroitel'stva na Vostoke: Materialy po planirovke staroy Bukhary' [From the history of town planning in the Orient: material on the planning of old Bukhara], *Iskusstvo zodchikh Uzbekistana* [The art of the architects of Uzbekistan] (Tashkent, 1962)
R. N. Frye: *Bukhara: The Medieval Achievement* (Norman, 1965)
G. A. Pugachenkova: *Samarkand, Bukhara (po drevnim pamyatnikam)* [Samarkand, Bukhara (through its ancient buildings)] (Moscow, 1968); Ger. trans. as *Samarkand, Buchara* (Berlin, 1975)
Istoriya Bukhary s drevneyshikh vremyon do nashikh dney [History of Bukhara from ancient times to the present] (Tashkent, 1976)
R. D. McChesney: 'Economic and Social Aspects of the Public Architecture of Bukhara in the 1560s and 1570s', *Islam. A.*, ii (1987), pp. 217–42

2. Buildings.

(i) Mausoleum of the Samanids. Lying to the west of medieval Bukhara opposite the citadel, the mausoleum is one of the oldest examples of commemorative architecture in the Islamic world. According to tradition and later sources, it was built by Isma'il I (*reg* 892–907) for his father Nasr I who had been governor of Samarkand, but some scholars have read the name of Nasr II (*reg* 914–43) on a wooden lintel above the eastern entrance. The mausoleum, constructed and decorated in fired brick, is a small cube (10.8×10.7×10.8 m) covered with a dome (diam. 9.25 m) with smaller domes at the corners. The four façades are identical. The 1.8 m thick walls are pierced along their axes by four arches, while the corners are marked by powerful three-quarter columns. Running along the top of the walls is a gallery with ten arched openings per side. Squinches support an octagonal zone of transition on which the dome rests. Despite the simple forms, the decoration of the building is notable: the whole of the interior and exterior has designs of creamy-coloured bricks (230×230×30 mm) laid in patterns. The walls and columns are covered with a chequer-board pattern, while architectural details are emphasized with carved flowers, pearls and other shapes and combined with carved plaster. The use of the same ornamental devices on interior and exterior lends an integrity to the building. The simplicity of mass, unified composition of façades and balance among parts make the mausoleum a major monument in the history of Central Asian and Islamic architecture (*see* Islamic art, fig. 27).

BIBLIOGRAPHY

M. S. Bulatov: *Mavzoley Samanidov: Zhemchuzhina arkhitektury sredney Azii* [Mausoleum of the Samanids: a pearl of Central Asian architecture] (Tashkent, 1976)
S. S. Blair: *The Monumental Inscriptions of Early Islamic Iran and Transoxiana* (Leiden, 1992), pp. 25–9

(ii) Magoki Attari Mosque [Pers. *masjid-i maghak-i 'aṭṭārī*: 'recessed mosque of the perfumers']. Small mosque on the southern outskirts of the medieval city centre, known as the Magoki Attari on account of the surrounding land's having risen some 3–4 m over the centuries. Documents from the 10th century and excavations in the mosque itself suggest that the building was originally the Mokh Mosque erected in the 10th century on the site of the Mokh Bazaar and temple of idol worshippers, but was rebuilt in the 12th and 16th centuries. The present structure incorporates a 16th-century rectangular hall with 6 piers supporting 12 domes; the plan roughly repeats the 10th-century original. Excavations have revealed fragments of carved plaster (9th–10th century, perhaps from the Mokh Mosque) and mud-brick (perhaps from the pre-Islamic temple) below. The most notable element of the mosque is its southern portal (12th century; see fig. 2). Two slightly projecting piers once carried an arch enclosing a smaller arched niche and a door. Each pier is formed of two addorsed quarter-columns, an original device with roots in pre-Islamic buildings in which walls were commonly decorated with closely set half columns. Virtually all of the portal was faced with glazed and unglazed tiles arranged in various patterns, including strapwork (itself decorated with carved vegetal ornament). A foundation inscription (partly destr.) in blue glazed tile decorates the archivolts of the inner arch, and the hood within has three tiers of *muqarnas* made of patterned brick; both are early examples.

2. Bukhara, Magoki Attari Mosque, portal, 12th century

BIBLIOGRAPHY

V. A. Shishkin: 'Mechet' Magaki-Attari v Bukhare' [The Magok-i 'Attari Mosque at Bukhara], *Materialy po arkheologii Uzbekistana* (1948), i of *Trudy Instituta Istorii Arkhitektury Akademii Nauk Uzbekskoi SSR* (Tashkent, 1948–), pp. 3–21

(iii) Kalan complex. Ensemble comprising a congregational mosque, minaret and madrasa, which took on its final shape in the 16th century. The original mosque and minaret were erected in 1121–2 in the south-west part of medieval Bukhara at the instigation of the Qarakhanid ruler Arslan Khan Muhammad II (*reg* 1102–29). After the minaret collapsed, destroying two-thirds of the mosque, the mosque was rebuilt and a new minaret erected (see fig. 3). Set on an octagonal socle above a foundation 10 m deep, the minaret has a tapering cylindrical shaft (h. 45.6 m; diam. at base 9 m) with an internal spiral stair of 105 steps. The shaft is decorated with bands of bricks set in relief to

3. Bukhara, Kalan Minaret, 1127–9

form geometric patterns. An inscription band in the middle gives the name of the patron, Arslan Khan, and the date of construction, 1127. A second inscription band in blue glazed tile, set at the top of the shaft, gives the date of completion, 1129. The lantern at the top is set between tiers of *muqarnas* and has 16 open arches decorated with half columns. Known as the Kalan (Pers. 'large', 'high'; Rus. *kalyan*) Minaret, the tower dominates the skyline and lends its name to the surrounding complex, known as the Pa-i Kalan ('foot of the Kalan').

The mosque, one of the largest in western Central Asia (130×80 m), has a spacious courtyard with four iwans connected by a columnar hall with 288 domes. It has a clear and simple form and restrained decoration of brick and glazed tile. It was rebuilt *c.* 1430, to judge from the tile revetment on the interior. The entrance portal, with bevelled corners, a *muqarnas* semi-dome and fine tile mosaic, is dated by inscription to 1514. The elaborate mihrab of tile mosaic, signed by Bayazid Purani, also dates to the 16th century. Further decoration was added in the 1530s, for some of the revetment beneath the plaster on the façade is contemporary with the third building in the complex, the Mir-i Arab Madrasa erected opposite in 1530–36. Built in honour of the shaykh Mir-i ʿArab, who is buried in the corner room, the madrasa is remarkable for its symmetrical plan (73×55 m), balance and formal harmony. The building has a court (37×33 m) with bevelled corners and four iwans connected by two storeys of cells. The main façade consists of a monumental portal with a lancet-shaped arch flanked by towers at the corners; it is covered with fine tile decoration. Large interior spaces are covered by an intricate system of vaulting in which four arches springing from the corners intersect in nets below a *muqarnas* frieze and support a lantern drum. Interior surfaces are faced with white plaster highlighted with polished brick and tile insets around the edges.

BIBLIOGRAPHY

L. Golombek and D. Wilber: *The Timurid Architecture of Iran and Turan*, 2 vols (Princeton, 1988)

(iv) Mausolea of Buyan Quli and Sayf al-Din Bakharzi. Two mausolea that mark the graves of the Chaghatayid khan Buyan Quli (*reg* 1348–59) and the shaykh, poet and theologian Sayf al-Din Bakharzi (*d* 1261). The two buildings, set at right angles to each other in the eastern suburb of Fathabad, create an effective contrast in plan and decoration: the monumental mausoleum of Buyan Quli is remarkable for its unusual plan, spatial organization and rich decoration of carved and glazed terracotta, while the mausoleum of Sayf al-Din Bakharzi has elegant proportions and polychrome lattice decoration recalling earlier tombs in the Shah-i Zinda (*see* SAMARKAND, §3(i)). Written records suggest that in the 13th century and early 14th another mausoleum linked with the shaykh's tomb stood on the site along with other religious buildings. Like early medieval castles in western Central Asia, the cubic mass of the tomb of Buyan Quli stands on a broad stylobate (1.5 m) that projects 2.4 m from the walls. The portal is emphasized only by a slightly raised frame around the arch. The entrance leads into the central hall (6.2 m sq) with a dome on squinches. Opposite the entrance is a tomb room (3.00×1.95 m) that once accommodated a small tiled cenotaph. Doors on the sides of the tomb room lead to narrow corridors (750 mm) running along the building and leading to the roof. The purpose of these corridors is unclear. Glazed terracotta varying from greenish-blue to violet-brown covers the walls and dome of both interior and exterior, and the revetment suggests a date in the mid-14th century.

Excavations in the 1960s showed that the mausoleum to the south-east marking the grave of Sayf al-Din Bakharzi was built later, not earlier than that of Buyan Quli, probably during the late 14th century or early 15th. The building comprises a portal, memorial mosque (Pers. *ziyārat-khāna*) and tomb (*gūr-khāna*) set along a central axis. The monumental portal (*pīshṭāq*), rebuilt in the 16th century, is crowned by an open arcade with seven lancet arches and flanked by towers at the corners. The two rooms are covered by ovoid domes set on small drums pierced with windows. In both rooms the openings at the corners of the octagon and the 16-sided drum are decorated with stucco *muqarnas*. The walls of the mosque are revetted with stucco, while the tomb housed a carved wooden cenotaph (Bukhara, Reg. Mus.) inscribed with the name of Sayf al-Din Bakharzi's grandson (*d* 1336) and tiled and marble tombstones.

BIBLIOGRAPHY

L. Golombek and D. Wilber: *The Timurid Architecture of Iran and Turan*, 2 vols (Princeton, 1988)

N. B. Nemtseva: 'Arkhitekturnyy kompleks na okraine Bukhary: Kul'tura srednego Vostoka' [An architectural complex on the outskirts of Bukhara: the culture of the Middle East], *Gradostroitel'stvo i arkhitektura* [Town planning and architecture] (Tashkent, 1989), pp. 104–14

N. B. NEMTSEVA

Bukharin, Nikolay (Ivanovich) (*b* Moscow, 9 Oct 1888; *d* Moscow, 15 March 1938). Russian politician and theorist. He was editor of the Communist Party newspaper *Pravda* from the 1917 Revolution and took over as the main theoretician of the Comintern (Communist International) after Lenin's death in 1924. He was interested in art as both a political means and as an amateur artist (an exhibition of his paintings was held in the Tret'yakov Gallery, Moscow, in 1935–6). Before the 1920s he subscribed to Aleksandr Bogdanov's ideas concerning proletarian art, which he viewed as a cultural form arising during the transition from Capitalism to Communism. However, he disagreed with the Proletkul't's desire for independence from the Party, and in *Proletarian Revolution and Culture* (1923) he abandoned his earlier, more radical ideas and posited the creation of the proletariat as new agents of culture—living machines with a Communist ideology, by whom artists and writers belonging to the old bourgeois social order would be ousted. Bukharin is recognized as the author of the Central Committee decree on the Party policy on literature in 1925, which recognized the educative role of 'fellow travellers' (e.g. non-Party writers) in the evolution of a proletarian culture; the Russian avant-garde thus remained a powerful but divided force until 1929, when Bukharinism was finally defeated. Bukharin opposed Formalism and promoted a social approach to art in several essays, though in the 1930s he came into conflict with Stalin, who destroyed pluralist culture and its agents. In his speech on poetics, poetry and the aims of poetic work in the USSR in 1934, Bukharin rejected the 'creative work' of proletarian writers and artists, calling for higher artistic quality, freedom of competition and an end to propaganda art. He propounded the notion of 'socialist humanism', which was used after World War II in reformist policies.

WRITINGS

Proletarskaya revolyutsiya i kul'tura [Proletarian revolution and culture] (Petrograd, 1923)

Voprosy kul'tury pri diktature proletariate [Problems of culture under a proletarian dictatorship] (Moscow, 1925)

Leninizm i problema kul'turnoy revolyutsii [Leninism and the problem of cultural revolution] (Moscow, 1928)

Culture in Two Worlds (New York, 1934)

Les Problèmes fondamentaux de la culture contemporaine (Paris, 1936)

BIBLIOGRAPHY

S. Cohen: *Bukharin and the Bolshevik Revolution: A Political Biography, 1888–1938* (Oxford, 1980)

A. Kovalev: 'N. I. Bukharin: Estetika, kritika, strategiya kul'turnoy revolyutsii', *Iskusstvo*, xii (1988), pp. 21–5

SERGEY KUZNETSOV

Bukhvostov, Yakov [Yanka; Yakushka] **(Grigor'yevich)** (*b* Nikol'skoye-Sverchkovo village, nr Moscow; *fl* 1690–1704). Russian architect. He was active in Moscow, and his distinctive brick buildings, displaying a picturesque, tiered treatment of volumes with an abundance of white-stone decorative details, are highly characteristic works of the contemporary Moscow school of architecture. The decorative handling of the orders, complex, frequently broken profiles, bold, inset, carved ornamentation with foliage and fruit motifs, and the overall liveliness of the composition are all features characteristic of Naryshkin Baroque (named after the Naryshkins, the family on whose estates in and around Moscow many of its most striking examples were built), a style that makes extensive use of western European Baroque forms but that adheres to the general tectonic rules of earlier Russian architecture. Among the best-known buildings ascribed to Bukhvostov are the church of the Trinity (1698–1704) in Troitse-Lykovo, the walls, wall-towers and gate chapel of the New Jerusalem Monastery (1690–97; destr. World War II; now restored) and the church of the Saviour (1694–7) in the village of Ubory, near Moscow. A number of buildings associated with his name have also survived in and around Ryazan', including the church of the Holy Spirit (1688–9) and the gate chapel (1688–99) at the Solotcha Monastery and the cathedral of the Dormition (1693–9).

BIBLIOGRAPHY

M. A. Il'in: *Zodchiy Ya. Bukhvostov* [The architect Y. Bukhvostov] (Moscow, 1959)

P. A. Tel'tevskiy: *Zodchiy Bukhvostov* [The architect Bukhvostov] (Moscow, 1960)

A. I. KOMECH

Bukovac, Vlaho (*b* Cavtat, 4 Aug 1855; *d* Prague, 23 April 1922). Croatian painter. After travels in the Americas, he studied in Paris at the Ecole des Beaux-Arts under Alexandre Cabanel from 1877 and exhibited in the Paris Salon from 1878, achieving his greatest success with *La Grande Iza* (1882; Novi Sad, Pavla Beljanskog Mem. Col.). He completed his studies in 1880 and stayed in Paris for the next 13 years; his paintings of this period showed academicist realism on the one hand and elements of Impressionism on the other. Two periods of portraiture in England (1886 and 1888), where he worked *en plein air*, were important factors in the gradual lightening of his palette. On his return to Zagreb in 1893 Bukovac became the leader of a group of young artists who soon won an international reputation as the Zagreb 'colourful school', with a brighter palette and freer technique than their predecessors; he was a founder of the Society of Croatian Artists and the instigator of the building of the Art Pavilion in Zagreb (1898). Bukovac applied his technical skill to painting such large-format compositions as *Gundulić's Dream* (1894; Zagreb, Gal. Mod. A.; *see* CROATIA, fig. 4). He exhibited at the Venice Biennale and at the first exhibition of the Vienna Secession. In 1903 he became a professor at the Prague Academy of Fine Arts. Here, after a brief encounter with Art Nouveau, he adopted a technique of short vertical brushstrokes, arriving in his last years at a type of Pointillism.

BIBLIOGRAPHY

V. Kružić Uchytil: *Vlaho Bukovac* (Zagreb, 1968)

ZDENKO RUS

Bulatov, Erik (Vladimirovich) (*b* Sverdlovsk, 5 Sept 1933). Russian painter and draughtsman. He trained at the Surikov Art Institute in Moscow (1952–8), after which, in his own words, he 're-trained', drawing on the advice of Robert Fal'k and Vladimir Favorsky, and he developed a sturdy independence in relation to the official doctrine of Socialist Realism. He illustrated many children's books, his teacher in this field being Il'ya Kabakov. Bulatov's independent style crystallized in the late 1960s, after experiments in different styles with varying degrees of affinity to Pop art. Combining a conventional naturalistic, intentionally anonymous image with a vivid posterlike symbol or inscription, the artist achieved strong parodic effects. Thus, in *Red Horizon* (1971–2; Paris, priv. col., see 1989 exh. cat., pp. 50–51) a red Soviet medal ribbon cuts across a distant seascape, while the inscription *Slava KPSS* ('Glory to the CPSU') in the painting of that name (1975; priv. col., see 1989 exh. cat., p. 63) blots out a blue sky. In emphasizing the contrast between propaganda and reality, Bulatov's work approaches the satirical images of SOTS ART; his paintings are not limited to satire, however; they are structuralist meditations on the boundaries of art and reality, conceptual works that demythologize, using poster stereotypes merely as raw material. His 'philosophical Sots art' in the second half of the 1980s earned him wide renown as the 'artist of *perestroyka*' (political and economic transformation), whose work symbolized the advent of a new stage in Russian art.

BIBLIOGRAPHY

Eric Bulatow (exh. cat., Zurich, Ksthalle, 1988)
Erik Bulatov, Moscow (exh. cat. by C. Jolles, V. Misiano, V. Nekrassov and texts by the artist, London, ICA; Boston, MA Inst. Technol., List Visual A. Cent.; Newport Beach, CA, Harbor A. Mus.; U. Chicago, IL, Ren. Soc.; 1989)

M. N. SOKOLOV

Büler, Wolfgang. *See under* MASTERS, ANONYMOUS, AND MONOGRAMMISTS, §III: MASTER WB.

Bulfinch, Charles (*b* Boston, MA, 8 August 1763; *d* Boston, 15 April 1844). American architect. He was a leading architect of the Federal period in America, but had no formal architectural training.

1. BEFORE 1795. Born to an aristocratic Boston family, Bulfinch graduated from Harvard College in 1781. In 1785 he embarked on a two-year tour of Italy, France and England, during which he developed a special enthusiasm for the Neo-classical style of Robert Adam. On his return he married a wealthy cousin and, by his own account, spent the following eight years 'pursuing no business but giving gratuitous advice in architecture'. Bulfinch designed approximately 15 buildings during this early period, including three churches, a theatre, a state house for Connecticut, seven detached houses and a group of row houses. The style derives clearly from Adam, but it is noticeably shallow and linear, owing perhaps to the American use of wood and brick rather than stone, and to Bulfinch's probable reliance on sketches and engravings of the English models. It is also likely that, at this stage of his career, Bulfinch did not supervise his buildings but merely provided elevations and floor plans to builders who constructed them.

Notable among his early works are two churches for Pittsfield and Taunton, MA (both begun in 1790), in which Bulfinch placed a belfry at the join of the principal roof of the building and the lower gable of the entrance porch so as to interlock the three principal masses, an innovation that became a popular standard for New England churches for many decades.

In 1793 Bulfinch designed the Tontine Crescent, a sweeping arc of connected town houses (destr.), which derived its general configuration from John Wood II's Royal Crescent at Bath and its detailing from Robert Adam's Adelphi Terrace in London. The failure of this venture, which was Bulfinch's first attempt at large-scale improvement to the Boston townscape, eradicated his fortune, forced him to declare bankruptcy and concluded his amateur status in architecture.

2. 1795–1816. Bulfinch's commission (1795) for the Massachusetts State House in Boston was second only to the United States Capitol as the largest and most complex building in America in the 1790s (*see* BOSTON, fig. 1). The elevation of his seven-bay projecting centre is reworked from the design for the centre of the main range to the river of Somerset House (1776–86), London, by Sir William Chambers. It has a tall arched arcade at ground-level, a first-floor colonnade with the outer bay to either side emphasized by coupled columns and a five-bay pedimented attic storey with the dome surmounted by a cupola. The building has a slight awkwardness of proportion, characteristic of Bulfinch's large-scale commissions. Documents indicate that he was paid about £600 over a three-year period as supervising architect of the building, a sum that provided only marginal subsistence to the Bulfinch family. In 1799 Bulfinch was made Chairman of the Board of Selectmen and Superintendent of Police of the Town of Boston, a position similar to that of mayor, which he held for nearly 20 years.

With this assurance and a modicum of economic stability (the position paid £600 per year, later raised to £1000), Bulfinch designed approximately five churches, 21 houses and 23 civic and commercial buildings between 1799 and 1817, many in Boston. India Wharf (1803), Faneuil Hall (1906) and Boylston Hall and Market (1809), with inadequate decorative elements on a scale more appropriate to domestic buildings, show again his awkward handling of large buildings. He was most confident with domestic architecture, his refined sense of proportion and restrained use of Neo-classical detail culminating in the three houses designed for Harrison Gray Otis between 1795 and 1805. His third house for Otis (1805), on Beacon Street, has a superbly proportioned symmetrical façade, with cast-iron balconies in a handsome fretwork design; behind the façade lies an unexpectedly varied plan. His New South Church, Boston (1814, destr.), was an elegant Neo-classical restatement of one of James Gibbs's alternative designs for St Martin-in-the-Fields, London. His finest work, the church of Christ in rural Lancaster, MA (1816; see fig.), is a red brick building with white wooden Neo-classical detail, but its distinction lies in the daringly over-scaled massing of the portico with its three tall arches divided by pilasters, attic block and tall cupola which nearly hide the main hall with a powerful design of abstract shapes.

Despite his active involvement in architecture and the financial support given by the town of Boston, Bulfinch's financial situation remained tenuous, and in 1811 he was again forced to declare bankruptcy and spent a brief period in jail.

3. 1817–29. Bulfinch finally achieved full professional status as an architect in 1817, when President James Monroe summoned him to Washington and appointed him Architect of the United States Capitol at an annual salary of £2500. Bulfinch was initially daunted by the prospect of carrying out the work begun by Benjamin Henry Latrobe, whose training and abilities were so clearly superior to his own, but he persevered and brought the building to completion in 1829, contributing the old Library of Congress (destr. 1851), the dome (replaced) and the west front. The Capitol building was Bulfinch's crowning achievement in its scale, but it is not his finest work. Under pressure from members of the President's Cabinet he raised the central dome considerably higher than he wanted, and the west front, which is on a falling site and a full storey taller than the east front, is marred by fussy detail.

Charles Bulfinch: church of Christ, Lancaster, Massachusetts, 1816

Bulfinch returned to Boston in 1829; he lived there in retirement until his death. His last commission, the State House for Augusta, ME, of 1829, follows the general configuration of the Massachusetts State House of 1795, but the details are thickened in response to the developing Greek Revival.

BIBLIOGRAPHY

C. A. Cummings: 'Architecture in Boston', *The Memorial History of Boston*, ed. J. Winsor, iv (Boston, 1881), pp. 465–88
A. R. Willard: 'Charles Bulfinch, the Architect', *New England Mag.*, iii (1890), pp. 272–99
S. E. Bulfinch: *The Life and Letters of Charles Bulfinch* (Boston, 1896)
A. S. Roe: 'The Massachusetts State House', *New England Mag.*, xix (1899), pp. 659–77
C. A. Place: *Charles Bulfinch: Architect and Citizen* (Boston, 1925)
W. Kilham: *Boston after Bulfinch* (Cambridge, 1946)
A. L. Cummings: 'Charles Bulfinch and Boston's Vanishing West End', *Old-Time New England*, lii (1961), pp. 31–47
——: 'The Beginnings of India Wharf', *Proceedings of the Bostonian Society: Boston, 1962*, pp. 17–24 [annual meeting]
H. and J. Kirker: *Bulfinch's Boston: 1787–1817* (New York, 1964)
H. Kirker: *The Architecture of Charles Bulfinch* (Cambridge, 1969)
B. Pickens: 'Wyatt's Pantheon, the State House in Boston and a New View of Bulfinch', *J. Soc. Archit. Hist.*, xxix (1970), pp. 124–31
W. Pierson: *American Buildings and their Architects: The Colonial and Neo-classical Styles* (New York, 1970), pp. 240–85
R. Nylander: 'First Harrison Gray Otis House', *Antiques*, cvii (1975), pp. 1130
F. C. Detwiller: 'Thomas Dawes's Church in Brattle Square', *Old-Time New England*, lxix (1979), pp. 1–17
J. F. Quinan: 'Asher Benjamin and Charles Bulfinch: An Examination of Baroque Forms in Federal Style Architecture', *New England Meeting House and Church: 1630–1850* (Boston, 1980), pp. 18–29
J. Frew: 'Bulfinch on Gothic', *J. Soc. Archit. Hist.*, xlv (1986), pp. 161–3
R. Nylander: 'The First Harrison Gray Otis House, Boston, Massachusetts', *Antiques*, cxxix (1986), pp. 618–21

JACK QUINAN

Bulgaria. Country in the Balkan peninsula, in south-eastern Europe. It is bordered by Romania, Turkey, Greece, Macedonia and Serbia. The territory of Bulgaria covers *c.* 111,720 sq. km and extends from the shores of the Black Sea in the east to the River Struma in the west. Its northern frontier is formed by the River Danube and the southern frontier by the southern slopes of the Rodopi Mountains (see fig. 1). Other geographic regions include a plain stretching east–west to the south of the Danube, succeeded further south by the Stara Planina ('the Old Mountain'); the latter is separated from the Rodopi Mountains to the south by another fertile plain. This is watered by the River Maritsa and its tributary the River Tundzha, which empty into the Aegean. Bulgaria lies at the core of what was a much larger area inhabited by the Thracian people (*see* THRACIAN AND DACIAN ART). This article includes brief information on early periods but covers predominantly the art produced in the country after the establishment of the First Bulgarian Kingdom in AD 681.

I. Introduction. II. Architecture. III. Painting and graphic arts. IV. Sculpture. V. Interior decoration. VI. Furniture. VII. Ceramics. VIII. Glass. IX. Metalwork. X. Textiles. XI. Patronage. XII. Museums, collections and art libraries. XIII. Art education and historiography.

I. Introduction.

The gradual hellenization of ancient Thrace began in the 7th century BC with the establishment of Greek colonies on the Black Sea coast (*see* BLACK SEA COLONIES). The

1. Map of Bulgaria; those sites with separate entries in this dictionary are distinguished by CROSS-REFERENCE TYPE

spread of an urban-based culture continued under the Romans, who in AD 15 and AD 46 created the two provinces of Moesia and Thracia respectively. Starting in the early 3rd century AD, the Karps, Goths, Sarmatians and other peoples invaded the country.

In the 5th and 6th centuries the Huns, Slavs and Bulgars infiltrated Bulgaria in increasing numbers (*see* MIGRATION PERIOD). Their settlement of the region resulted in the establishment of the First Bulgarian Kingdom with a capital at Pliska under Asparuch (*reg* 681–702), who gained official recognition of his state from the Byzantine emperor Constantine IV (*reg* 668–85). The union of the Slavs and Bulgars was reinforced with the adoption of Christianity and the creation of a Slavonic script (the Glagolitic alphabet) in 864/5. The Bulgarian kingdom was in close contact with the Byzantine empire, which was at some times a dangerous adversary and at others a peaceful neighbour wielding considerable cultural influence over the Bulgars.

In 893 Preslav replaced Pliska as the capital of the Bulgarian kingdom. From the second half of the 10th century, however, Byzantium began to gain the political upper hand in the Balkan peninsula and in 971 the Byzantine emperor John I Tzimiskis (*reg* 969–76) captured Preslav. Although the Bulgarian Tsar Samuel (*reg* 976–1014) succeeded in establishing a separate kingdom on the island base in Little Prespa Lake (*see* PRESPA), by 1018 the whole of Bulgaria had been incorporated into the Byzantine empire. Bulgaria challenged Byzantine supremacy several times until, in 1188, the area of Bulgaria north of the Stara Planina regained its independence with a capital at Tărnovo (now Veliko Turnovo). In 1193 much of central Thrace was annexed and the Second Bulgarian Kingdom emerged. Despite the extension of its western frontier as far as Dyrrhachion on the Adriatic in 1230, the country's lack of economic unity and internal stability resulted in several revolts. The increasing encroachment of the Ottomans from 1370 led in 1393 to Bulgaria's invasion and annexation by Bayezid I (*reg* 1389–1403).

In 1878, during the Russo-Turkish wars, Bulgaria was liberated from Turkish supremacy by Russia, but it gained full independence only in 1908 when Ferdinand of Coburg proclaimed himself king (*reg* 1908–18). The country aligned itself with the German side in World War I and again in World War II, until its occupation by the Soviet Union in 1944. In 1946 the monarchy was abolished and a People's Republic was proclaimed. In 1989 mass unrest brought the Communist Party's monopoly of power to an end and free elections took place in 1990.

BIBLIOGRAPHY

A. Protich: *Fine Art in Bulgaria* (London, 1907)

N. Trufeshev: *Monumentalnite izkustva i arkhitekturata v Balgariya* [Monumental arts and architecture in Bulgaria] (Sofia, 1968)
A. Bozhkov: *Die bulgarische Malerei* (Berlin, 1969)
R. Browning: *Byzantium and Bulgaria* (Berkeley, 1975)
Encyclopedia Bulgaria, 12 vols (Sofia, 1976–88)
I. Dujcev and others: *Histoire de la Bulgarie* (Roanne, 1977)
Entsiklopediya na izobrazitelnite izkustva v Bălgariya [Encyclopedia of the fine arts in Bulgaria], 2 vols (Sofia, 1980–87)
M. Stancheva, ed.: *The Bulgarian Contribution to the World Culture Heritage* (Sofia, 1989)

KARA HATTERSLEY-SMITH

II. Architecture.

1. Before AD 681. 2. AD 681–1393. 3. 1394–1878. 4. After 1878.

1. BEFORE AD 681. Among the most impressive examples of Thracian architecture are the excavated remains from the cities of Seuthopolis and Kabyle, and the burial mounds containing tombs of hewn stone or brick construction (4th century BC), as at KAZANLUK and Mezek (*see* THRACIAN AND DACIAN ART). Of the Greek city states established along the Black Sea coast (*see* BLACK SEA COLONIES, §2), public and domestic buildings have been recovered at NESEBĂR, Pomorie (anc. Anchialos), Sozopol (anc. Apollonia), Varna (anc. Odessos) and Balchik (anc. Dionysianopolis). Under the Romans many cities along the coast and in the interior (e.g. Philippopolis, now Plovdiv; Kabyle; and Beroe-Augusta Trajana, now Stara Zagora) were refortified and their buildings renewed, while at the same time new cities were founded: Nikopolis ad Istrum (near Veliko Turnovo), Marcianopolis (now Devnja) and Serdika (now Sofia). Military camps along the Danube frontier also developed into civic settlements, as at Ricaria (now Archar, near Vidin), Oeskus (now Gigen, near Pleven) and Abritus (now Razgrad). These cities were organized along the familiar grid-plan system of streets surrounded by strongly fortified walls, and they contained the usual component of public buildings such as baths, theatres and stadia. The excavated town house (first half of the 4th century AD) at Stara Zagora and the large villa (2nd century AD–*c*. 376) near the cliffs of Madara are just two examples of richly decorated peristyle residences with mosaic floors and marble revetted walls.

With the establishment of Christianity as the official religion of the Empire (381), church building became widespread in Bulgaria. Although most churches are only known through excavation or survive as ruins, they nevertheless indicate that various church types were erected: single-aisle churches and three-aisled basilicas, as well as cruciform and centrally planned churches. Most single-aisle churches date to the 4th century and were often replaced by larger three-aisled basilicas in the 5th century. The three-aisled plan was adapted in numerous ways as architectural influences from other parts of the empire were merged with local elements. For example, the introduction of the tripartite narthex and the semicircular

2. 'Red Church', Perushtitsa, Bulgaria, *c*. AD 500

apse with three-sided external walls, as in the Old Metropolis (late 5th century or early 6th) at Nesebăr, is usually thought to follow the construction of St John Stoudios in Constantinople (*see* ISTANBUL, §III, 6). The substantial remains of the three-aisled basilica (late 5th century–early 6th) at Belovo also reveal a tripartite narthex, but instead of a single three-sided apse, all three aisles terminate in ovoid apses. The central apse had a three-stepped synthronon, while the smaller side apses presumably served as *prothesis* and *diakonikon*. Another feature of the Belovo basilica was the series of square brick piers, four on each side, that separated the nave from the aisles. They supported groin vaults over the aisles and probably a barrel vault over the nave.

The Elenska basilica (early 6th century; now roofless) north-east of Pirdop combines features found in the Old Metropolis and the Belovo basilica with new structural features. To the west the nave and two aisles are preceded by a tripartite narthex, while to the east the central three-sided apse is flanked by two chambers (a *diakonikon* and a *prothesis*) with semicircular apses, thus forming a triple sanctuary similar to that in the Episcopal Basilica (*c.* 525–50) at Caričin Grad. Another particularly noteworthy feature of the Elenska basilica is the system of three pairs of piers that separate the nave and aisles and also divide the nave into two square halves. Although the piers clearly formed the supports of a dome over the nave's eastern half, it is not certain whether the western half was domed or barrel-vaulted.

Churches with cruciform plans survive in a variety of forms. At Delidoushka, near Preslav, the three-aisled basilica has two rectangular side-chambers projecting from the east ends of the side aisles, while in the single-aisle churches near Ivanyani (first half of the 6th century) and at Tsurkvishte (5th or 6th century) the chambers project from the nave. The line of the nave continued beyond the chambers to form a short choir before the apse. This plan is also found in the fifth phase of St Sophia (6th century; present church) in Sofia, where it has been incorporated into a domed transept basilica with galleries.

One of the most unusual churches in Bulgaria is the ruined 'Red Church' (*c.* 500; see fig. 2) at PERUSHTITSA, which was a domed quatrefoil. The adoption of this form probably reflects the influence of contemporary trends in Constantinople and the transition from the basilical to the centralized plan. Further developments in Bulgaria's architecture during the late 6th century and the 7th remain obscure.

2. AD 681–1393. During the period of the First Bulgarian Kingdom (681–1018) several large fortified cities were either founded or rebuilt, such as those of PLISKA, PRESLAV, Madara and OHRID. They were surrounded by defensive walls interspersed with towers and contained secular and ecclesiastical buildings that survive either as excavated remains, ruins or preserved structures. Some of the most remarkable monuments are the palaces at Pliska and Preslav, both of which served as capitals of the First Bulgarian Kingdom (681–893 and 893–971 respectively). A characteristic feature is the construction technique using well-hewn blocks of stone, the origin of which remains a mystery, particularly since the Bulgars were essentially a nomadic people until the 9th century and were not therefore builders by tradition. Byzantine influence is, however, suggested by certain decorative elements, such as the mosaic floors at Preslav, and by the provision of a water supply and drainage system at both sites.

Research on the ecclesiastical architecture of the period has revealed three main church types: single-aisle churches and three-aisled basilicas, and centrally planned churches (*see* EARLY CHRISTIAN AND BYZANTINE ART, §II, 2(iii)(b)). The first type is represented by small barrel-vaulted halls with walls of unhewn stone and mortar. A number of such churches have been excavated at or near Pliska, and their plans are reminiscent of certain 10th- or early 11th-century churches at KASTORIA. Three-aisled basilicas are more common. One variant of this type has shortened aisles with a high pitched roof over the central aisle, one or two apses to the east and a narthex at the opposite end. Ornamental brickwork usually decorates the external walls, as in St Stephen (10th century) at Nesebăr and St Vrachi and St Stephen (both 10th century) at Kostur. A second variant is the large three-aisled basilica with one or two narthexes to the west and usually three apses to the east. The earliest example is the 'Great Basilica' at Pliska, which probably served as the royal church in the 9th century. Its archaic features and general design, however, may indicate a 5th- or 6th-century foundation. The Bulgarian Tsar Samuel (*reg* 976–1014) adopted a similar basilical plan for the cathedral of Hagios Achilleos (*c.* 990–1000; destr.) on his island base in Little Prespa Lake (*see* PRESPA). Another example of a large three-aisled basilica is that of St Sophia at Ohrid. Opinion is divided as to its date of construction. A possible sequence of phases begins with a building dated to the second half of the 9th century but constructed on the site of an Early Christian church, followed by the first of several alterations in the mid-11th century.

From the early 10th century the centrally planned church began to replace the basilica as the most popular church type. The Round Church (*c.* 900; diam. 11 m) at Preslav is the earliest example; its unusual domed and circular design, with eight semicircular conches protruding outward on either side of the main apse, may have been inspired by Constantinopolitan models. On a smaller scale are several domed triconch chapels (e.g. St Panteleimon, *c.* 893, Ohrid) and square-planned churches with lateral conches (e.g. Vinitsa, *c.* 950). Most centrally planned churches are cross-in-square structures with and without free-standing supports for the dome. In the latter category are St Nikola (10th century) at Sapareva Banya, with its shallow lateral arms, and the church (?10th century) at Delidoushka, near Preslav, the arms of which protrude to form a pronounced cross shape. In the former category the free-standing supports are either piers or columns. In churches 3 and 4 in Selishte at Preslav only the western side of the dome rests on free-standing supports. Most other churches, however, have two pairs of supports, as in St John the Baptist (probably 10th century) at Nesebăr and St John the Theologian (11th century) at ZEMEN. In both these churches the dome rests on a tall cylindrical drum and the east end terminates in three semicircular apses preceded by clearly marked forechoirs. The sides of the buildings are articulated with blind-arched niches corresponding to the interior arrangement, but whereas the walls of St John the Baptist are made of rough stone and brick with ornamental brickwork, St John the Theologian is constructed of ashlar blocks.

Similar plans appear in the excavated churches around Preslav, as for example Avradak Church 1 (10th century) and the Patleina Monastery church (*c*. 907). In both these structures, however, the apses are polygonal on the outside. The Patleina church also reveals a variation in its internal design in which the inward corners of the four dome supports are curved. Another noteworthy feature is its decoration of glazed tiles, which originally spread over the floors and walls. This may have been considered an acceptable substitute for the unobtainable marble veneer and mosaic decoration.

During the period of Byzantine rule (1018–1193) the development of Bulgarian architecture was to some degree retarded. With the re-emergence of Bulgaria as a dominant force in the Balkans and the establishment of the Second Bulgarian Kingdom (1193–1393), there was a corresponding upsurge of architectural activity. The political instability of the region is reflected in the refortification of old cities (e.g. Vidin, Sredets, Tărnovo (now Veliko Turnovo)) and the establishment of new settlements on naturally protected sites (e.g. Cherven, Lovech). The defensive character of these settlements was further enhanced by the construction of stone walls from 1 to 3 m thick and up to 12 m high, with solid towers and bastions. Most buildings excavated within these fortifications have been dated to the 12th century onwards, including the remains of the royal and patriarchal palaces at Veliko Turnovo.

The most significant example of ecclesiastical architecture that can be firmly dated to the period of Byzantine rule is the charnel-house (1083) in BACHKOVO MONASTERY (*see* §III, 2(i) below). This single-aisle, two-storey building, with walls of alternating bands of brick and stone and façades articulated with niches, combines local building tradition with Georgian influences that reflect the origin of the monastery's founders. The extension of existing monasteries and the erection of new ones (e.g. the Great Lavra at Veliko Turnovo and DRAGALEVTSI MONASTERY CHURCH) was encouraged particularly in the 13th and 14th centuries. Although these monasteries all consisted of a fortified enclosure with a church in the middle, some were more like fortresses and had defensive towers, such as the Khrelyu Tower (1335) in the RILA MONASTERY.

Numerous churches of various types are preserved or have been recovered in the monasteries and cities of the Second Bulgarian Kingdom. Among the few examples of three-aisled basilicas from this period are the late 12th-century St Nikola at Melnik and the mid-13th-century church of the Forty Martyrs Monastery at Veliko Turnovo. Single-aisle churches without domes are just as rare, although in the case of St Paraskeva (first half of the 13th century or 14th) at Nesebăr this type of plan is combined with the elaborately decorated façades of alternating bands of brick and stone and with glazed ceramic shapes that were typical of contemporary Bulgarian architecture.

Centrally planned churches are the most common type and appear in many variants. One variant is the cruciform church with a dome supported on pendentives that rest directly on the walls of the structure, as in SS Nicholas and Panteleimon (1259) at BOYANA. Another variant is the barrel-vaulted single-aisle church with a central dome on a high drum and a bell-tower over the narthex, as in St Dimiter (1186) at Veliko Turnovo, churches 1 and 2 (probably 13th century) at Cherven, and the Petrichka Virgin (late 12th century or early 13th) at Asenovgrad. The development of this variant can be seen in the church of the Archangels Michael and Gabriel (14th century), in which a second dome rises above the narthex. A less frequent form is the domed triconch, as in St Nikola in Oryahovo Monastery at Peshtera and St John the Theologian in Poganovo Monastery.

The most complex of the centrally planned types is the domed cross-in-square, outstanding examples of which are SS Peter and Paul (13th century; reconstructed 1980) at Veliko Turnovo and St John Aleitourgetos and the Pantokrator (both 14th century) at Nesebăr. The last two provide the best indication of Late Byzantine architectural developments (*see* EARLY CHRISTIAN AND BYZANTINE ART, §II, 2(iv)(c)) in Bulgaria. Their highly decorative façades, with arcades and niched pilasters, stone, brick and glazed ceramic ornament and corbel-table friezes, represent the apogee of this trend in Bulgarian architecture.

BIBLIOGRAPHY

B. Berbenliev: *The Architectural Heritage of the Lands of Bulgaria* (Sofia, n.d.)

K. Miyatev: *The Architecture of Medieval Bulgaria* (Sofia, 1965)

R. F. Hoddinott: *Bulgaria in Antiquity: An Archaeological Introduction* (London and Tonbridge, 1975)

M. Stancheva, ed.: *The Bulgarian Contribution to the World Cultural Heritage* (Sofia, 1989)

3. 1394–1878. The Ottoman occupation of Bulgaria resulted in the destruction of many individual buildings as well as numerous towns and villages. The construction and restoration of churches was officially prohibited until the end of the 16th century, thus retarding the development of local Bulgarian architecture. In some of the more remote monasteries, however, new churches were built in the second half of the 15th century. A more general wave of construction began in the late 16th century with the breakdown of the Ottoman military system and the subsequent growth in importance and prosperity of the cities and smaller towns. This upsurge is often referred to as the Period of Revival and is attested by all categories of building, including domestic architecture, Ottoman public architecture and Bulgarian churches and monasteries.

Ottoman and indigenous Bulgarian traditions of domestic architecture developed side by side, resulting in a style similar to that found in towns and villages throughout the Balkans where there was a mixed Muslim and Christian population. Until the 16th century, most houses were single-storey structures with one or two rooms and a verandah, such as the Pavlikyanski House at Koprivshtitsa. Gradually their layout became more complex and they acquired one or two more storeys. Houses of the 16th and 17th centuries that survive at Bansko and Arbanassi are mostly two-storey structures with storage space below and living quarters and an open verandah above. These look

3. Nikola Fichev: Hadji Nikoli Inn, Veliko Turnovo, Bulgaria, 1858

out on to a large yard surrounded by stone walls and agricultural buildings. On the outside the houses have high closed façades, giving them a fortress-like appearance. As economic prosperity spread to other towns and regions of Bulgaria in the 18th and 19th centuries, so the houses became larger, often with the addition of a third storey; there was also a trend towards greater symmetry in layout, as in the Kableshkov House (1845) at Koprivshtitsa. Timber overhangs and eaves are characteristic features of these houses, many of which also survive at Plovdiv, Veliko Turnovo and in the towns of the Rodopi and Kotel regions. One of the defining features of an Ottoman house was its division into a women's and a men's section, and perhaps the inclusion of a bath.

Much more distinctive are the surviving monuments of Ottoman public architecture, including mosques, schools, tombs, caravanserais, covered markets, water fountains, clock-towers, bridges and baths. Some churches were initially converted to mosques, but numerous large mosques were also built anew, such as that of Yamboul (1420s; dome diam. *c.* 25 m) and the Djumaya Mosque (probably 1423) and Imaret Mosque (1444–5) at Plovdiv. The only preserved example of a covered market is the 15th-century one at Yamboul. The Ottomans continued to build throughout their occupation, learning to adapt local construction techniques to suit their needs, as in the mid-19th-century Bayraklı Mosque at Samokov, with its timber dome supported on four wooden columns. They often employed Bulgarian builders, for example Nikola Fichev (*b* 1836), who constructed the Hadji Nikoli Inn (1858) and the *konak* (town hall; 1872) at Veliko Turnovo. The former is situated on steep terrain and is centred on a courtyard, two sides of which are lined by wings three storeys high. The ground floor is of solid stone construction but the two upper storeys are fronted by arcades supported on columns, which imparts a certain elegance to the whole structure (see fig. 3). In the *konak* at Veliko Turnovo, Fichev had to adapt the building's cruciform plan to the steep terrain. He was also responsible for the covered bridge (1865–7) over the River Ossum at Lovech.

Bulgarian monasteries and churches constitute the other important category of architecture from this period. Some of the earliest churches are SS Peter and Paul (1469–78) in the Orlitsa Hermitage, which lies 22 km west of its parent Rila Monastery, the church of the Virgin (1493) in Dragalevstsi Monastery, and St George (*c.* 1493) in Kremikovtsi Monastery. According to an inscription, this last church was paid for by Radivoi, a wealthy boyar from Sofia. The most common church type initially was a vaulted single-aisle structure, which may be partially dug into the ground. Numerous examples of this type were built both inside and outside monastic precincts, such as St Petka Samardjiiska (1578–81; now a museum) in Sofia, which was funded by the saddlers' guild, St Nikola (end of the 16th century) at Maritsa, and the church of the Nativity (late 16th century) at Arbanassi.

From the late 16th century onwards, however, these small single-aisle churches were largely replaced by three-aisled basilicas such as the church of the Virgin (1597) in the Rozhen Monastery. This type became particularly widespread outside the monasteries and in some cases continued to be partially dug into the ground. The nave and aisles are sometimes separated by arcades on masonry piers, as in SS Theodore Tyron and Theodore Stratilat (1614) at Dobursko, and sometimes by colonnades, either of stone, as in St Nikola (1756) at Melnik and the Holy Archangels (1819) at Tryavna, or of plastered wooden columns, as in the metropolitan church of the Dormition (1793–1805) at Samokov. A single pitched roof usually covered the entire church, although in the 19th century it became common to add one or more domes. In St Dimiter (1831) at Peshtera, for example, a dome rises above the centre of the nave, while in St George (1848) at Asenovgrad the nave is surmounted by a central dome and two smaller domes at the north and south ends. The eastern apse in both these churches is semicircular, as it is in most other three-aisled basilicas. By contrast, the three-aisled churches of the Holy Trinity (1865–7) at Svishtov and SS Konstantin and Elena (1873) at Veliko Turnovo, built by Nikola Fichev, each have a yoke-shaped eastern apse and two semicircular apses on the north and south sides. Both churches have a dome above the central bay of the nave, and the Holy Trinity church also has smaller domes above the apses.

Domed churches constructed in the monasteries are often more varied in ground-plan. The church of the Virgin (1607) in Bachkovo Monastery is a cross-in-square with apses to the east, north and south. Four columns support a central dome. The Troyan Monastery church (1837) and the churches of the Transfiguration and of the Virgin (both mid-19th century) at Preobrazhenie Monastery are closer to domed triconches in plan. More daring in design is the large church of the Virgin (1834) built by Pavel in the Rila Monastery. It is a three-aisled basilica, the longitudinal east–west axis of which is interrupted by two chambers that protrude from the centre of its north and south sides and by north and south apses at its east end. It is surmounted by a large central dome and four smaller domes. An open portico flanks its west side as well as the western end of its north and south sides.

BIBLIOGRAPHY

B. Berbenliev: *The Architectural Heritage of the Lands of Bulgaria* (Sofia, n.d.)

A. Protich: *Denationalizirane i văzrazhdane na bălgarskoto izkustvo prez turskoto robstro ot, 1393–1879* [Denationalization and revival of Bulgarian art, 1393–1879] (Sofia, 1929)

S. Cmouykob: *The Architecture of the Town of Koprivshtitsa* (Sofia, 1977)

A. Roshkovska: *Die Bajraklı Moschee* (Sofia, 1977)

Entsiklopediya na izobrazitelnite izkustva v Bălgariya [Encyclopedia of the fine arts in Bulgaria], i (Sofia, 1980)

M. Kiel: *Art and Society of Bulgaria in the Turkish Period* (Assen and Maastricht, 1985)

4. AFTER 1878. In the decades before World War I, Bulgarian architecture was influenced by such western European trends as the Renaissance Revival, Neo-classicism, neo-Baroque and Art Nouveau as well as by the Russian Empire style, introduced by foreign architects and Bulgarian architects who had studied abroad. Houses built in these styles survive at Rousse, Bourgas and Sofia, and often have elaborate overhangs, as in Yablanski House and Surmdyiev House in Sofia. Public buildings display the same variety of influences, usually combined with rich sculptural ornament. The Army Club (1895–1900) in Sofia designed by the Czech architect Kolar combines elements of Renaissance Revival architecture, as in the two storeys of arcaded loggias on the main façade, with sculptural decoration in the Empire style. Also in Sofia are the Alexander Nevski Church (1904–12, consecrated 1924; see fig. 4) and the National Theatre (1906). The former is a three-aisled transept basilica with a dome (diam. 46 m) over the crossing. 'Byzantine' and Russian Empire influences are evident in the design, which is largely the work of the Russian Aleksandr Pomerantsev. In the National Theatre, FERDINAND FELLNER and Hermann Helmer (1849–1919) combined Renaissance, Baroque and Art Nouveau styles to create a symmetrically planned building with an imposing porticoed entrance.

At the beginning of the 20th century, various Bulgarian architects, including Momchilov, Milanov, Nikola Lazarov and Torlov, reintroduced the architecture of the Period of Revival (*see* §3 above). Two examples are the Mineral Baths (1908–10) and the Holy Synod building (1910), both in Sofia. The latter is particularly representative, with its wings of three storeys arranged around an inner courtyard. Although this trend continued in the period between World War I and the end of World War II, it conflicted with the growing interest in neo-classicism and the modernist trends of Functionalism and Constructivism. Several of Sofia's most important buildings are in the neo-classical style, including the Court of Justice (1928–36; by P. Koichev), the Bulgarian National Bank (1934–9), the Cyril and Methodius Library (1942–54; both by IVAN VASSILYOV and D. Tzolov) and the Bulgaria Hotel and Concert Hall (1934–7; by Stancho Belkovski).

In the decades after World War II the need to provide housing resulted in the development of new principles in urban planning. The radial squares and axial urban plans of the early 20th century were abandoned and replaced by

4. Aleksandr Pomerantsev: Alexander Nevski Church, Sofia, Bulgaria, 1904–12, consecrated 1924

estates containing domestic and public buildings (e.g. schools, hospitals, shopping centres) set in areas of greenery. Impressive buildings were erected in the centres of major cities, for example the Trimoncium Hotel in Plovdiv, with elements derived from STALINIST ARCHITECTURE, and the Library–Museum (1939–52) at Veliko Turnovo, with arcades and overhangs that recall Renaissance architecture. By 1956 Sofia's centre was also dominated by such buildings as the Central Department Store, the Party Building and the Sheraton Hotel, all in an impressive, monumental style.

Among the numerous housing projects between 1954 and 1990, the two most successful examples are the Zaimov at Sofia and Chayka at Varna. The country's largest cities also acquired theatres and art galleries, such as those (1981) at Smolyan, which were adapted to the natural amphitheatre shape of the land and included elements of traditional Rodopi architecture. In Sofia the National Palace of Culture (1981; by Aleksandr Barov) is a synthesis of finely decorated interiors and a monumental style of architecture that served a variety of functions (e.g. congress centre, concert hall, theatre). The Gallery for International Art (1986; by Nikola Nikolov), also in Sofia, is an impressive example of the neo-classical style.

With the growth of tourism, several resorts were built along the Black Sea coast. Druzba, Zlatny Pyasutsy and Sluntchev Bryag are characterized by their high-rise buildings, while at Alben and Rousalka the structure of the buildings is clearly expressed in their design. Villas and small-scale construction with elements of Bulgarian Revival architecture predominate at Duni and Eleni (1985–7).

BIBLIOGRAPHY

M. P. Tsapenko: *Arkhitektura Bălgarii* [The architecture of Bulgaria] (Moscow, 1958)
Entsiklopediya na izobrazitelnite izkustva v Bălgariya [Encyclopedia of the Fine Arts in Bulgaria], i (Sofia, 1980)
K. Stefanov and M. Kirov: *Savremenno balgarsko monumentalno izkustvo, 1956–1986* [Contemporary Bulgarian monumental art, 1956–1986] (Sofia, 1986)

MARIANA KATZAROVA

III. Painting and graphic arts.

1. Before AD 681. 2. AD 681–1393. 3. 1394–1878. 4. After 1878.

1. BEFORE AD 681. The best-preserved examples of painted decoration from this period survive in underground burial chambers of the 4th–3rd century BC and the 4th century AD. Among the earliest monuments are the Thracian tombs of KAZANLUK and Sveshtari, which were painted with scenes from the life of the deceased and depictions of the funeral ceremony and meal. The quality of the decoration, which at Sveshtari is combined with elaborate architectural and sculptural ornament, suggests that both tombs were meant for members of the Thracian nobility.

Another well-preserved example of funerary art is the vaulted tomb (4th century AD) at Silistra (anc. Durostorum), which is completely covered in paintings. They consist of 11 panels of full-length figures around the walls, geometric ornament on the vault, floral motifs, birds and hunting scenes. Fragments of wall painting (second half of the 4th century; Sofia, N. Archaeol. Mus.) have also been recovered from the cemetery tombs around Hissar (anc. Diocletianopolis). Paintings (4th–5th century) of an obviously Christian character, including chi–rho motifs, and the busts of four archangels decorate the brick-built subterranean tombs in the ancient cemetery at Sofia. At Perushtitsa traces of a complex painted scheme of the 6th century are still *in situ* in the Red Church.

BIBLIOGRAPHY

B. Berbenliev: *The Architectural Heritage of the Lands of Bulgaria* (Sofia, n.d.)

2. AD 681–1393.

(i) Monumental. (ii) Icon. (iii) Manuscript.

(i) Monumental. Although fragments of 10th-century painting are preserved in the church of St George in Sofia, the earliest important group is in the charnel-house (1083) of BACHKOVO MONASTERY, which was founded by the Georgian brothers Grigori and Apazi Pakuriani and became a centre of Georgian culture. The iconographic programme is both original and coherent. The most important compositions, namely the *Deësis* in the apse, *Ezekiel's Vision of the Dry Bones*, the *Vision of Ezekiel beside the Kebar River*, the *Last Judgement* and the *Melismos* (the breaking of bread in Eucharist), reflect the funerary function of the building and reveal a theological thinking of unusual breadth. The heavy linear style of painting is also evident in the groups of *All Saints* (*see* EARLY CHRISTIAN AND BYZANTINE ART, fig. 43) and has been dated to the second half of the 12th century; a few portraits are attributed to the 14th.

The effect of the classicizing revival in Byzantine art during the 13th century (*see* EARLY CHRISTIAN AND BYZANTINE ART, §III, 5(i)) is evident in the painted church of SS Nicholas and Panteleimon (1259) at BOYANA, for example the *Life of St Nicholas* (see Grabar, fig. 26). Figures are delicately modelled, revealing a sculptural approach to volume and a certain statuesque quality, as is evident in the portrait of the founder *Sebastokrator Kaloyan* (see fig. 5). Some iconographic details are of Western origin. A striking characteristic of several 13th-century chapels on the Trapesitsa Hill at VELIKO TURNOVO (formerly Tărnovo) is the number of paintings of standing military saints. Other vestiges of 13th-century painting survive in St Dimiter and the church of the Forty Martyrs (the latter includes a *Menologian*) at Veliko Turnovo, and in the church of Gospodov Dol, near Cherven.

Some of the most significant paintings of the 14th century are in the rock-cut chapel known as Crkvata ('the church') near IVANOVO. The sophisticated and progressive nature of this art, although surprising given its setting within an anchorite community, is explained by the portrait of Tsar Ivan Alexander (*reg* 1331–71), who founded the church. The influence of contemporary Byzantine trends is attested by the number of semi-naked bodies, the presence of nude caryatids in scenes from the Passion, the foreshortening, the unusual postures of the slender and elongated figures, the importance of landscape and architectural ornament and the rich and subtly shaded colours. A few interesting painted fragments (14th century) also survive in the nearby rock-cut church of Moskov Dol, as well as in the church of the Forty Martyrs at Veliko Turnovo.

5. Wall painting of *Sebastokrator Kaloyan*, SS Nicholas and Panteleimon, Boyana, Bulgaria, 1259

The portrait of the Bulgarian tsar Michael Shishman (*reg* 1323–30) determines the date and origins of the church of the Virgin at Dolna Kamenica (Serbia); the style and iconography of the paintings lack unity but not originality. A singularly lively and dramatic *Lamentation* is painted next to a plain *Melismos* and *Mounted Military Saints*, the prominent position of which is unusual in Balkan art and recalls the art of the regions of the eastern Byzantine frontier, particularly that of Cappadocia, Coptic Egypt and Georgia. The paintings in the chapel of Khrelyu Tower (1335) in RILA MONASTERY display a particularly academic iconography, including scenes from the Psalms and a representation of *Christ the Wisdom of God*.

In St George at Sofia the animated and dramatic figures of the *Prophets* (end of the 14th century) around the dome drum and certain other compositions brilliantly reproduce most of the features that characterize Late Palaiologan art (*see* EARLY CHRISTIAN AND BYZANTINE ART, §III, 5). The same is true of the donor portrait (14th century) in St John the Baptist at Nesebăr and the painted fragments (14th century) in the Petrichka Virgin Church at Asenovgrad and in St Nikola at Melnik. The paintings in St Peter (?14th century) at Berende reflect both the influence of Palaiologan art and local iconographic tradition. Some decorative backgrounds, while reminiscent of motifs common in contemporary Italian art, are in fact borrowed from Iranian art.

Despite their poor state of preservation, the paintings (*c*. 1360) in St John the Theologian at ZEMEN include a highly developed Passion cycle in which the images are larger than those in the rest of the church. The cycle also contains elements that reflect Western influence, as in the *Raising of the Cross*. The painting style is somewhat clumsy and archaic, with a linear quality and most figures in fully frontal poses. Similar in style are the 14th-century paintings in St Theodore Tiron at Boboshevo, St Marina and St Nicholas, also known as 'Gligora' at KARLUKOVO, and the church at Ritlite, near Lyutibrod.

Apart from Bachkovo, almost all the paintings mentioned above are accompanied by inscriptions in Church Slavonic, reflecting the fact that the liturgy was also celebrated in that language.

BIBLIOGRAPHY

A. Grabar: *La Peinture religieuse en Bulgarie* (Sofia, 1925, rev. Paris, 1928)
L. Prashkov: *Khrelyovata kula* [Khrelyu's tower] (Sofia, 1973)
E. Bakalova: *Bachkovskata kostnica* [The charnel-house at Bachkovo] (Sofia, 1977)
L. Mavrodinova: *Zemenskata tsurkva* [The church at Zemen] (Sofia, 1980)

(ii) Icon. Of the few icons that have survived from before 1393, the earliest is the ceramic icon of *St Theodore* (570×470 mm, *c*. 900; Sofia, N. Gal. Dec. & Applied A.), with a Slavonic inscription, from the Patleina Monastery, near Preslav. The saint is represented to shoulder level and his face corresponds more to the type common in the Byzantine East than to a Hellenistic model. Small carved icons in alabaster (e.g. *St George*, 12th century; Plovdiv, Archaeol. Mus.), silver (e.g. *SS Constantine and Helena*, 12th–13th century; Sofia, N. Archaeol. Mus.) and steatite (*St John the Evangelist*, 12th–13th century) have also been preserved. These icons were intended for private worship, especially during journeys, as protection against danger.

A 12th- or 13th-century icon (900×830 mm; Sofia, N. Gal. Dec. & Applied A.) from the iconostasis of St Nicholas at Melnik depicts a deacon in bust form, holding a precious reliquary or receptacle decorated with gems. He wears a curious red bonnet. The body is flattened, with a complete absence of modelling, while the face conveys an inner peace, accentuated by the profound expression of the eyes. The same flattening of the body is evident in the 13th-century icon of *St Nicholas* (1.02×0.81 m; Nesebăr, Mun. Archaeol. Mus.), which represents a bust of the saint clothed in an omophorion. He holds a closed copy of the Gospels and his right hand is raised in benediction. Unlike earlier icons, the face is no longer encircled by a hard contour.

The classicizing style of the Palaiologan period appears in the double-sided icon with a bust of *Christ Pantokrator* on one side and the *Virgin Eleousa* ('merciful') on the other (1.19×0.97 m, 13th–14th century; Sofia, N. Gal. Dec. & Applied A.). Christ is flanked by two medallions with angels, as well as by six standing prophets on the frame. His wide shoulders, finely modelled face and reflective expression are characteristic features of contemporary Byzantine painting. The *Virgin Eleousa* is based on the earliest and most renowned icon of this type, the *Virgin of Vladimir* (*c*. 1131). The child tenderly presses his cheek against that of the Virgin. Six standing prophets are preserved on one side of the frame, while the two angels in the upper corners are later additions.

An icon of the *Hodegetria* ('Virgin who points the way'; 1.30×1.07 m, 1342; Sofia, N. Archaeol. Mus.) is particularly interesting for its silver revetment embossed with two archangels in medallions and with scenes from the life of the Virgin, and decorated with enamel cloisonné. This cover is also inscribed with quotations from sacred texts. The faces of the Virgin and Christ were repainted at a later date. An embossed bronze icon (14th century; Plovdiv, A.G.) from Mihailovo represents a full-length *Virgin Eleousa* holding the Child in both hands. A 14th-century icon (770×550 mm) of special importance is that of the Bulgarian hermit *St John of Rila*, which was found in Rila Monastery and is now in the monastery museum. The saint appears in bust form, holding a cross in his right hand and a scroll in his left. The work is of a high standard, with fine modelling and painted in warm, exceptionally harmonious colours. It recalls early 14th-century wall paintings in the churches of Thessaloniki and Macedonia (*see* EARLY CHRISTIAN AND BYZANTINE ART, §III, 5(ii)(b)).

The most beautiful icon in the Bulgarian collections, and one of particular significance for Byzantine painting, is the double-sided icon from Poganovo Monastery (*see* EARLY CHRISTIAN AND BYZANTINE ART, §VI, 4(ii)). The icon depicts the *Virgin Katafigi* ('refuge') and *St John the Evangelist* on one side, and the *Vision of Ezekiel beside the Kebar River* on the reverse (see fig. 6), and it was given to the monastery in 1395 by its founder, Empress Eleni, wife of Emperor Manuel II (*reg* 1391–1425). The standing Virgin with her head inclined to one side has an expression of incomparable sadness, while the face of St John, who leans slightly towards her, is full of sorrow. The modelling of the figures is admirable and the body of St John resembles a Classical statue. In the *Vision of Ezekiel beside the Kebar River*, a Hellenistic-style landscape is surmounted by Christ seated within a circle made up of seven spherical bands in shades of blue and grey and surrounded by the symbols of the Evangelists.

6. Icon of the *Vision of Ezekiel beside the Kebar River*, tempera on panel, 930×610 mm, before 1395 (Sofia, National Art Gallery at Alexander Nevski Cathedral)

BIBLIOGRAPHY

K. Weitzmann and others: *Frühe Ikonen: Sinai–Griechenland–Bulgarien–Jugoslawien* (Vienna and Munich, 1965)
Icônes bulgares (exh. cat., Paris, Petit Pal., 1976)
A. Bozhkov: *Bălgarskata ikona* [Bulgarian icons] (Sofia, 1984)
T. Totev: *Preslavskata keramichna ikona* [Preslav's ceramic tiles] (Sofia, 1988)

(iii) Manuscript. Following Bulgaria's conversion to Christianity (864/5), the production of manuscripts, which were often illustrated, became a matter of urgency. Greek texts and illustrations came from Byzantine sources until the brothers Cyril and Methodios from Thessaloniki gave the Slav peoples, including the Bulgarians, their first alphabet for the writing of Church Slavonic, known as Glagolitic (*see* §I above). Although manuscripts of the late 9th century and 10th were written in this alphabet, by the early 11th century it was almost completely supplanted by the Cyrillic alphabet. Workshops were first set up at Preslav and Ohrid, and subsequently at Tărnovo (now Veliko Turnovo), where the decoration and illustration of manuscripts were practised with great mastery.

Manuscripts of the 9th and 10th centuries contain geometric-type ornament rather than miniatures and are similar to the manuscripts from Syria (*see* EARLY CHRISTIAN AND BYZANTINE ART, §V, 3) and southern Italy. One of the most interesting examples is the Assemani Gospels (10th century; Rome, Vatican, Bib. Apostolica, MS. Vat. Slav. 3), which has initials decorated with human figures and episodes from the Gospels, as well as geometric ornament often in the form of plaited tresses (e.g. fols 112*v*, 157*v*, 158*r*). The Mariinsko Gospels (10th–11th century; Moscow, Rus. Lib., Grig, 6M1689) has a miniature representing the *Evangelist Luke* (see Dzhurova, fig. 18) and decoration based on plant and geometric-type motifs, as well as some zoomorphic representations.

From the 11th century onwards the Cyrillic alphabet was widely used, and from the 12th century zoomorphic decoration was popular. The first stage in this development can be seen in the 11th-century Sava Gospel book (Moscow, Cent. Archv Anc. Doc., f. 166*r*), where the zoomorphic and vegetal elements complement each other (e.g. fols 149*v*, 150*r*). In the 12th century initials were richly decorated with plant and animal motifs; this development continued in later centuries.

The flowering of Bulgarian illustrated manuscripts in the 13th and 14th centuries has its roots in the establishment of the Second Bulgarian Kingdom, with its capital at Tărnovo. The city's royal workshops and several great monasteries (e.g. Rila, Kilifarevo, Bachkovo, Ivanovo)

7. Miniature of *Tsar Ivan Alexander with his Family*, from the London (or Curzon) Gospels, 1356 (London, British Library, Add. MS. 39627, fol. 3*r*)

were centres of manuscript production. Two particularly noteworthy examples are a 13th-century Gospel book (Rila Monastery, N. Mus., MS. 1, 13) and the Argirov Triddon (Sofia, Cyril Methodius N. Lib., MS. 497), both of which contain illustrations in a painting style close to that of 11th- and 12th-century Constantinople. Another stylistic development is characterized by the manner in which grotesque vegetal, zoomorphic and anthropomorphic elements intertwine around the initials, as in the Dobreisho Gospels (Sofia, Nat. Lib., MS. 18, fols 19*v*, 73*v*).

In the 14th century manuscripts were richly illustrated and filled with miniatures. Most manuscripts were made in or near Tărnovo, including two works commissioned by Tsar Ivan Alexander (*reg* 1331–71). The first is the Chronicle of Constantine Manassès (1344–5; Rome, Vatican, Bib. Apostolica, MS. Vat. Slav. 2, fol. 2*r*), which comprises three illustrated cycles of unequal length. The Chronicle itself begins with the *Creation of Eve* (fol. 2*r*) and includes the greatest number of miniatures; the second cycle covers the history of Bulgaria (fols 145*v*, 145*r*, 148*v*, 163*v*, 172*v*, 174*r*, 175*r*, 178*v*, 178*r*, 183*v*, 183*r*); and the third contains three portraits of Ivan Alexander (fols 1*r*, 2*v*, 205*r*) and two scenes relating to the death of his son Asen (fols 2*r*, 2*v*). The execution of the miniatures is somewhat careless and attests the work of several artists.

The second work is the London Gospels, also known as the Curzon Gospels (London, BL, Add. MS. 39627), which was probably produced at Kilifarevo Monastery (near Veliko Turnovo) in 1356. Its prototype is a well-known Greek Gospel book of the late 11th century (Paris, Bib. N., MS. gr. 74; *see* EARLY CHRISTIAN AND BYZANTINE ART, §V, 2(ii)(b)). The style is particularly refined, with gold backgrounds, and is heavily influenced by the classicizing appearance of its model. The portrait of *Tsar Ivan Alexander with his Family* occupies a double page (fols 2*v*, 3*r*; see fig. 7) and demonstrates his pretentions and self-awareness.

The miniatures in the Tomich Psalter (*c.* 1360; Moscow, Hist. Mus., MS. 2752) reveal great theological subtlety as well as the will to fight against the heresies that were rampant in the country. These miniatures correspond to the Palaiologan style of painting, which is marked by a sense of volume, architecture and landscape and is sometimes combined with a more monumental style of composition, as in *Miriam and Other Women Celebrating the Crossing of the Red Sea.* The complex decoration is evident in various ornamental borders and headpieces and particularly in the title-pages, which are based on a group of Byzantine illuminated manuscripts (*c.* 1275–*c.* 1325) that are themselves derived from works of the 10th to the 12th century. With the Turkish invasion of 1393, the development of manuscript illustration at Tărnovo was interrupted.

BIBLIOGRAPHY

A. Grabar: *Recherches sur les influences orientales dans l'art balkanique* (Paris, 1928)

I. Dujchev: *Letopista na Konstantin Manasi* [The Chronicle of Constantine Manassès] (Sofia, 1963)

M. V. Shchepkina: *Bolgarskaya miniatyura XIV veka* [The Bulgarian miniatures of the 14th century] (Moscow, 1963)

A. Dzhurova: *Khiljada godini bălgarska rakopisna kniga: Ornament i miniatjura* [1000-year-old Bulgarian manuscripts: ornaments and miniatures] (Sofia, 1981)

TANIA VELMANS

3. 1394–1878. As a result of the Ottoman invasion in 1393, many Bulgarian painters fled the country. In the second half of the 15th century, however, the painting of icons and of churches and monasteries was revived (*see* POST-BYZANTINE ART, §III, 1 and 2(ii)). Traditional Byzantine styles, often combined with Western motifs and painting techniques, predominated. The wall paintings in the church of the Virgin (1476) in the DRAGALEVTSI MONASTERY CHURCH and in St Dimiter (1488) in Boboshevo Monastery recall the early 14th-century Macedonian school (*see* EARLY CHRISTIAN AND BYZANTINE ART, §III, 5(ii)(b)), while those in SS Peter and Paul (1491) in the Orlitsa Hermitage near the Rila Monastery are closer to the Palaiologan tradition. An outstanding synthesis of the Byzantine and Italian traditions is achieved in St John the Theologian (1500) in the Poganovo Monastery (now in Serbia).

In the late 16th century and in the 17th there was a major revival in wall painting, some examples of which include those in the monastery church (1596) of Kurilo, St Stephen (1599) at Nesebăr, the rock-cut chapels (14th century; partially repainted 1602) at Karlukovo, the church of the Virgin (1607) in Bachkovo Monastery, and St Petka (1649) at Tărnovo (now Veliko Turnovo).

Icon painting went through similar stages of development, but by the 17th century the Byzantine tradition was to some extent replaced by styles derived from folk art. A number of icons are still housed in such monasteries as Bachkovo and Poganovo, and in the churches of certain towns, for example Nesebăr (St Stephen and church of the Weeping Virgin), Veliko Turnovo and Sozopol (*Resurrection*, early 17th century, church of the Virgin). Most icons, however, are part of museum collections, notably *St George Killing the Dragon* (1684; Sofia, N.A.G.).

In the 18th century, painting played a significant part in the revival of Bulgarian heritage. Portrait painting and the painting of historical and revolutionary scenes, with Gothic, Renaissance, Baroque and Rococo elements, became popular. Religious wall and icon painting also flourished, particularly under the BANSKO SCHOOL founded by Toma Vishanov (*b c.* 1750), called Molera, and the SAMOKOV SCHOOL founded by Khristo Dimitrov (*d* 1819). Artists from these schools painted the monasteries of Rila, Bachkovo, Troyan and Preobrazhenski, and they were the first to introduce secular elements into sacred scenes. Groups from both schools also specialized in the decoration of houses with genre and landscape compositions.

The development of graphic art, connected with that of book printing, led in the 18th century to the production of engravings with pictures of religious scenes produced initially in the monasteries. At the Rila Monastery, for example, the pictures were mainly of the monastery's patron, St Ivan Rilsky, and of the monastery itself. Samokov benefited from its proximity to the monastery to become one of the main centres for the production of illustrated printed books, and it was here that in 1828 Bulgaria's first printing press was established. Woodcuts and engravings were used to produce colourful pictures based on folk art.

One of the most outstanding secular painters and lithographers of the 19th century was Nikolay Pavlovich (1835–94), whose style reflects Western Neo-classical and Romantic influences (e.g. *Self-portrait*, 1865; Sofia, N.A.G.). Another important artist was Khristo Tsokev (1847–83), whose technique in portrait painting was influenced by Rembrandt and whose technique in landscapes was influenced by the Impressionists (e.g. *The Monk*, 1867; Sofia, N.A.G.).

BIBLIOGRAPHY

N. Mavrodinov: *Izkustvoto na Bălgarskoto Natsionalno Văzrazhdane* [Art of the Bulgarian National Revival] (Sofia, 1957)

A. Vasiliev: *Bălgarski văzrozhdenski maystori* [Bulgarian artists of the Revival] (Sofia, 1965)

V. Sachariev: *Graphische Schule von Samokov* (Dresden, 1968)

4. AFTER 1878. One of the most significant developments of the late 19th century was the decline of icon painting, which had by tradition been associated with certain families. Art education became the concern of the state, and from 1880 onwards art teachers, mainly from abroad, were appointed in schools. There was a general trend away from religious art to secular painting. In 1885 the first such painting exhibition was held in the National Assembly building in Sofia by Ivan Dimitrov, who had trained in Paris and whose style approached European academicism with elements of classicism and realism (e.g. *Portrait of the Prime Minister Stephan Stambolov*, 1886; Sofia, N.A.G.).

In the period from 1896, when the Art Academy was founded, to 1944, numerous trends in painting developed simultaneously. At the beginning of the 20th century battle pictures and military scenes by the academicist Dimiter Giudjenov (1891–1979; e.g. *Tsar Boris I Receives St Clement in Preslav*, 1934; Sofia, N.A.G.) and the more classical Nikola Kojuharov (1892–1971; e.g. *A Dragon Loves me, Mother*, 1922; Sofia, N.A.G.) were particularly popular. From the late 19th century to the early 1930s, there was a trend in portrait painting that attempted to achieve a balance between spiritual harmony and the model's physical characteristics. Some of the best-known painters who practised this were Stefan Ivanov (1875–1951), NIKOLA MIHAILOV, Tseno Todorov (1877–1953), Boris Mitov (1891–1963), Nikola Ganushev (1889–1958) and Nikola Marinov (1879–1948). Their artistic aims were further developed by Ilya Petrov (1903–75), Nenko Balkanski (1907–77) and DECHKO UZUNOV. In his landscapes, Jaroslav Veshin (1860–1915), one of the founders of the National Academy of Arts, eschewed contemporary academicism to paint in a more spontaneously impressionistic manner (e.g. *Returning from the Market*, 1898; Sofia, N.A.G.). Other landscape painters included Khristo Standchev (1870–1950), Elena Karamihailova (1875–

8. Zlatyu Boyadjiev: *Autumn*, oil on canvas, 1.01×0.72 m, 1941 (Sofia, National Art Gallery)

1961), Nikola Petrov (1881–1916), Konstantin Sturkelov (1889–1961), Boris Denev (1883–1969), Nikola Tanev (1890–1962) and Danail Dechev (1891–1962).

During the 1920s such artists as VLADIMIR DIMITROV-MAISTORA, SYRAK SKITNIK, IVAN MILEV and VASSIL ZAKHARIEV developed the concepts of a national school in which their subject-matter was based on traditional folk-tales and legends and executed in a stylized manner. This was combined with the techniques learnt from Impressionism and the treatment of form in a synthesized and monumental manner, as in *Autumn* (1941; Sofia, N.A.G.; see fig. 8) by ZLATYU BOYADJIEV. The development of these tendencies resulted in a distinctive national style that found expression not only in painting but also in graphic art. Until 1919, this was largely limited to lithographs portraying historic scenes, after which the techniques of etching and aquatint were introduced to the Academy. It was not until the 1930s, however, that complex and multi-figured compositions were developed, as in the work of Zakhariev. Three-dimensional effect was mastered by Vesselin Staikov (1906–70), who created the impression of sculptural form and space through a careful balance of black and white (e.g. the two series *Bansko* (1936) and *Melnik* (1937–8), both Sofia, N.A.G.).

After 1944 Socialist Realism predominated in art and was the main obstacle to the free development of artistic expression among several generations of Bulgarian artists. In the 1960s, painting and graphic art entered a new phase in which artists were able to develop new styles reflecting contemporary trends and technical skill.

BIBLIOGRAPHY

A. Protich: *Fifty Years of Bulgarian Art*, 2 vols (Sofia, 1933–4)
N. Mavrodinov: *The New Bulgarian Painting* (Sofia, 1947)
E. Tomov: *Bulgarian Graphics* (Sofia, 1955)
I. Mihalcheva: *The Portrait in Bulgarian Painting*, 2 vols (Sofia, 1968–71)
P. Chuklev: *Contemporary Bulgarian Graphics* (Sofia, 1971)

JULIANA NEDEVA-WEGENER

IV. Sculpture.

1. BEFORE 1393. Some of the best-known examples of Thracian sculptural work are the gold and silver vessels with figured reliefs that have been found in treasure hoards (*see* THRACIAN AND DACIAN ART). Stone sculpture has also survived as an important decorative element in some Thracian funerary tombs, such as the Strelcha and Sveshtari tombs (4th–3rd century BC; *see* BLACK SEA COLONIES, §2). In the latter tomb the decoration is particularly impressive and consists of 14 carved caryatid-type figures (h. 1.2 m) around the walls, their arms raised to support the frieze above. Other elements of architectural sculpture include columns, painted capitals, metopes and triglyphs. Many Hellenistic and Roman works survive as relief sculpture on stelae, as statues in bronze and marble, and as architectural sculpture (Sofia, N. Archaeol. Mus.) from the excavated remains of ancient cities such as Nesebăr (anc. Mesembria), Plovdiv (anc. Philippopolis) and Nikopolis ad Istrum (nr Veliko Turnovo).

Excavations of several Early Christian churches (5th–6th century) have revealed numerous architectural fragments such as capitals and altar-screen plaques with carved decoration, mostly in relief. The capitals (Vratsa, Hist. Mus.) from the Early Christian basilica at Lyutibrod are decorated with reliefs of crosses, sheep and simple acanthus and vine motifs. Deeply cut acanthus-leaf capitals (Sofia, N. Archaeol. Mus.) have, however, been found in the Early Christian basilicas at Maryan and Bluskovtsi. Altar-screen plaques also reveal a variety of designs, such as that of a single peacock facing a cup from the Early Christian basilica at Ossenovo (Varna, Hist. & A. Mus.) and the geometric and vine designs from Basilica 2 at Hissar (Sofia, N. Archaeol. Mus.).

Funerary reliefs dating from the 8th century AD onwards have been found near Pliska and Preslav; known as the 'stone grannies', they depict the deceased. The rock-cut relief 23 m above ground at Madara (early 8th century) shows a horseman thrusting a spear into a lion beneath him, with a dog following behind. Only one of the three Greek inscriptions accompanying the relief is contemporary with it; the others are later. The flattened style of the carving characterizes Bulgarian sculpture of the 8th to the 11th century. Despite the stiff and formal appearance of the composition, the sculptor has conveyed a powerful image of heroism through the depiction of a hunting triumph. A similar style is evident in the sculptural ornament of the 10th- and 11th-century palaces and churches at Pliska and Preslav. Griffins, winged lions, palm trees and bunches of grapes are some of the motifs that decorate the stone cornices, friezes and corbels of these buildings. While these patterns recall Sasanian decoration, others, such as the egg-and-dart and palmette friezes on the cornices of the Round Church (10th century) at Preslav, suggest copies from antique models. Other examples of flattened sculptural reliefs are represented by the birds, animals, garlands and crosses on the door friezes and altar-screen plaques in Hagios Achilleos (*c.* 990–*c.* 1000) in Little Prespa Lake, St Sophia (10th century) at Ohrid, the church of the Virgin (late 10th century) at Boyana and St Vrachi (11th century) at Kostur.

Although there is little evidence for stone sculpture after the 11th century, examples of wood-carving survive from the 14th. One of the most important works is the full-length wood-carving in high relief of St Clement in the eponymous church at Ohrid. It shows the saint in his bishop's vestments, holding a closed book in his left hand and raising his right in benediction. On the wooden doors of the Slepche Monastery church, near Bitola, interlace designs divide the nine panels on which are depicted individual saints, the Virgin and various mythological animals (e.g. dragons and a unicorn) in low relief.

BIBLIOGRAPHY

G. Katzarov: *Bulgaria in Antiquity* (Sofia, 1926)
K. Miyatev: *Bulgarian Art in the 9th–10th Centuries: The Madara Rider* (Sofia, 1930)
D. Angelov and others: *Medieval Bulgarian Culture* (Sofia, 1964)

2. 1393–1878. In the 15th and 16th centuries the tradition of carved wooden church decoration spread throughout Bulgaria. Stone altar screens were largely replaced by richly carved wooden iconostases (*see* SCREEN (i), §2) and Royal Doors such as those in St Petka (15th or 16th century) at Veliko Turnovo. The flat and shallow ornament on the doors consists of complex interlace bands surrounding panels of the Virgin, Christ, saints and various mythological animals. This decorative system continued into the 17th century, as attested by the Royal

Doors from the church at Bozhenitsa (Sofia, N. Mus. Eccles. Hist. & Archaeol.) and those in St Theodore at Dobursko. In the 18th century the wood-carving became more three-dimensional, as in the iconostasis in the south aisle of the Rozhen Monastery church. Here, animals (e.g. two-headed eagles, lions, dragons, birds) and Old Testament scenes blend in with the rhythmic ornamental scheme of acanthus leaf, rosettes and palmettes. A similar combination of floral motifs and figural compositions decorate the iconostasis and Royal Doors (late 18th century) in the church of the Virgin at Sozopol.

By the early 19th century, schools of wood-carving were established at Debăr, Tryavna, Bansko and Samokov. Artists incorporated Renaissance, Baroque and Rococo elements into their designs, as in the bishop's chair in the church of the Annunciation at Gare and the iconostasis (1800–07) in Biger Monastery, both by Peter Garka of the Debar School. He also worked with Atanas Teladur of the SAMOKOV SCHOOL on the iconostasis in the church of the Virgin in Rila Monastery. Lavishly carved iconostases are found in the church of the Transfiguration (*c.* 1820) in Preobrazhenski Monastery, the church of the Virgin (1837) at Pazardjik, the Troyan Monastery church (1838–9) and St Marina (1853) at Plovdiv. In the church of the Archangel Michael (1846) at Stoudena, some of the carved floral motifs on the wooden iconostasis appear in stone relief around the door frames on the south and west façades.

Wood-carving was also used to decorate Revival houses of the 19th century. Ceilings with moulded decoration and recesses were particularly popular, as in the Lizotov House (1854) at Koprivshtitsa, the Sarafska House (mid-19th century) at Samokov and the Sarafkina House (mid-19th century) at Veliko Turnovo. From the mid-19th century onwards such architects as Nikola Fichev (*b* 1836) used stone sculptural reliefs of nymphs, griffins, lions and two-headed eagles to decorate public buildings, including fountains and bridges (e.g. bridge over the River Yantro at Byala; 1865).

BIBLIOGRAPHY

N. Mavrodinov: *Izkustvoto na Bălgarskoto Natsionalno Văzrazhdane* [Art of the Bulgarian National Revival] (Sofia, 1957)

A. Vasiliev: *Bălgarski văzrozhdenski maystori* [Bulgarian artists of the Revival] (Sofia, 1965)

A. Slavov: *Darvorezbite na Rozhenskir manastir* [The wood-carvings of the Rozhen monastery] (n.p., 1968)

V. Ivanova and M. Koeva: *The Sculptural Richness of Renaissance Ecclesiastical Wood-carving* (Sofia, 1979)

3. AFTER 1878. Following the liberation of Bulgaria from Ottoman rule in 1878, over 400 sculptures and public monuments in stone, concrete and metal were erected as memorials to the event. Most are in the form of obelisks decorated with sculptural reliefs in a mixture of styles current between the late 19th century and early 20th (e.g. neo-Baroque, Renaissance, Neo-classical). Some representative examples include the *Monument of Freedom* (1894) at Sevlievo and the *Monument of Freedom* (1925; by Aleksandr Andreev) at Shipka Peak. The latter consists of statues of a lion, a Bulgarian and a Russian (the last two in marble). Also in memory of Bulgaria's liberation are two particularly impressive monuments by the Florentine sculptor Arnoldo Giocchi. One of these is the *Tsar Liberator* (h. 12 m; 1907) in the National Assembly Square in Sofia, which consists of a bronze equestrian statue (h. 4.5 m) of Tsar Alexander II (*reg* 1858–81) and reliefs symbolizing the Bulgarian people led by a female figure in Classical garb personifying Victory. His other work, the *Monument of Freedom* (1909) in Rousse, consists of a female figure (h. 3 m) personifying Freedom, two lions with a broken chain in their mouths and sculptural reliefs depicting the Bulgarians fighting the Ottomans.

Between the late 19th century and the early 20th, urban spaces and parks were decorated with sculptures and fountains by such artists as Mina Ivanov, BORIS SCHATZ and ANDREY NIKOLOV. The sculpting of smaller works has developed since the 1910s under the impetus of artists such as IVAN LAZAROV, who produced majolica figures and reliefs, Atanas Dudolov, known for his wooden statuettes, and Yanko Pavlov, whose satirical and humorous works are in ceramic or stone.

Although small-scale sculpture in different materials has become a popular art form since the 1960s, only a few artists work exclusively as sculptors, for example Khristo Pesev (in terracotta and stone), Valentin Starchev (in bronze), Krum Damyanov (in bronze and wood), Georgi Tchapkonov (in bronze and silver) and Stavri Kalinov (in bronze).

In the late 1970s and early 1980s a number of monumental sculptures were created celebrating 1300 years since the foundation of the Bulgarian state. Krum Damyanov erected the monumental sculptures of *1300 Years of the Bulgarian State* (1981; in concrete, granite, bronze, mosaic stones and stained glass) at Shoumen, which consist of four equestrian figures (each h. 6 m) surrounding an upright sword, and *Assenovtzi* (1985) at Veliko Turnovo. In 1981 Valentin Starchev completed the sculpture of *Bulgaria: Past, Present and Future* (in granite and bronze) in front of the National Palace of Culture in Sofia and the *Monument of the Unknown Soldier* at Bourgas. Also in this year Andrey Nikolov completed the *Monument of the Unknown Soldier* (begun in 1933) in Sofia, which is dominated by a marble figure of a reclining lion, facing east.

BIBLIOGRAPHY

N. Ganev: *The Monuments of the Capital* (n.p., 1939)

V. Ivanova: *Contemporary Bulgarian Sculpture* (Sofia, 1971)

K. Stefanov and M. Kirov: *Savremenno bălgarsko monumentalno izkustvo, 1956–1986* [Contemporary Bulgarian monumental art, 1956–1986] [Eng. summary] (Sofia, 1986)

MARIANA KATZAROVA

V. Interior decoration.

At the end of the 18th century and the beginning of the 19th, Bulgarian houses of the Period of Revival, whether symmetrical (four rooms arranged in a square), asymmetrical, one- or two-storey, had a main 'at home' room (*kùschi*) with inside balconies (*chardak*), bedrooms or guest rooms (*sòba*) and larders (*kiler*). The main room contained the fireplace, the chest for storing flour, and most of the household cutlery. There were niches, cupboards and narrow, open, wooden shelves on the white-washed walls, the floor was made of hard clay or of planks, and the ceiling was of sawn beams or split planks. This room served as a sitting-room, kitchen and everyday parlour. It led to the *sòba*, which was usually directly behind the wall on which the fireplace was situated so that it was heated by the fireplace or by a special stove (*sòba*), which gave the room its name. The entrance to the other rooms was either from the *chardak* or from the 'at home' room. The *sòba* and other rooms had whitewashed walls, plain, waxed wooden floors and relatively low ceilings. Often one wall was entirely occupied by built-in cupboards (*dolap*) with carved doors. Narrow open shelves were used to display and store plates, pans, pots and other kitchenware. The wooden ceilings in the *sòba* of wealthy households were beautifully carved with such ornamentation as huge central suns (symbols of life and freedom), or geometric straight lines, or rosettes and tracery (e.g. the Daskalov house (1804) and the Raikov house (1846); both in Sofia). The interiors were sparsely furnished with three-legged stools, low beds (*odăr*)—which were used both for sitting and sleeping and were covered with rugs made of sheep's wool—built-in cupboards and chests (*rakla*). Food was served on a low table (*sofra*) in the centre of the *sòba*. Furniture such as beds, tables and chairs tended to be functional rather than decorative. However, the decorated chest (*rakla*), of ancient origin, given to a bride by her father, was carved or decorated with coloured ornamentation; *rakla* of the Period of Revival, the richest from the Sredna Gora Mountains and north-west Bulgaria, were found in known Revival houses (e.g. the Daskalov, the Raikov, the Plovdiv (Kuyumdzhioglu; 1847), the Genshov (1860) and others; all in Sofia). For the most part decorative impulses found expression in curtains and tablecloths, in embroidered pillows, in the design of tufted and fleecy rugs, in carefully wrought fire-irons and in the circles and stars on earthenware jugs, spoons and low tables. Other ornamental items were the icons and the icon-lamps suspended in one corner in most rooms, and the occasional engraved icon-stand. Decoration of stylized twigs, leaves, buds and fruits was used on cupboards, shelves, ceilings, earthenware and copper jugs; icon-stands were sometimes engraved with sunflowers, grapes, vine-leaves, blossoms and birds, and the decorative elements were built mainly on the rhythmic repetition of motifs or identical forms.

The Plovdiv region flourished during the Period of Revival. Trade developed, and such wealthy merchants as Arghir Kuyumdzhioglou commissioned fine houses from the master-builder Hadji Georgi (e.g. 1847; now the Ethnographic Museum). The Plovdiv bourgeois house of the Period of Revival had no interior balcony or hearth. Ceilings and cupboards were virtually identical to those described above, but the walls were painted with decorative motifs borrowed from other cultural traditions, for example strange landscapes of distant towns and ports or brightly coloured flowers and bouquets. There were low beds, but the movable furniture was based on Turkish and European models.

Traditional folk art was influenced by contact with foreign cultures through merchants and craftsmen travelling abroad to such places as Mt Athos, Istanbul and other towns in the Ottoman Empire. Contact with Romania, Italy and Greece influenced architecture and wood-carving; furniture reflected contact with western Europe (see fig. 9). With the development of capitalism and increasing division of labour, a class of professional decorative artists with specialized training emerged.

9. Parlour in the house of a Plovdiv merchant, 19th century (Plovdiv, Ethnographic Museum)

Until the 1940s towns in Bulgaria were small, their population consisting mainly of craftsmen, officials and shopkeepers. The standard one-family house might have one or two storeys with a parlour, a bedroom, a kitchen that also served as a sitting-room, and an outside bathroom and lavatory. Rooms had a fireplace, two or more high windows, and walls painted with distemper in pastel colours, often with designs imitating wallpaper; ceilings were whitewashed. The panelled doors and the window-frames were painted or impregnated with linseed oil to preserve the light brown colour of the wood. Household furnishings included rugs and carpets of wool, cotton or hemp; copper and glass utensils; wooden and silver cutlery; tablecloths of heavy damask cloth or draped plush with tassels, tulle curtains and cotton bedspreads; and mirrors with elaborate frames. There was a profusion of handmade lace and crochet work, embroidered cushions, knitted coverlets, small carpets and tablecloths. After about 1900 furniture and mass-produced articles generally followed Western styles; homemade work used native motifs or those inspired by Viennese *Sezessionstil* and the English Arts and Crafts Movement. The kitchen/dining-room contained a kitchen cupboard, a table and chairs, a bed and a stove. Bedrooms were furnished simply with high beds and wardrobes. The parlour was the best room and reflected family status. It had a table in the centre, with a lamp hanging above it, and many small decorative objects.

VI. Furniture.

During the late 18th and early 19th centuries schools of furniture-making emerged at Tryavna, Debăr, Samokov, Kalofer and Razlog. Their development was stimulated by such technological improvements as the establishment of water-powered saw mills. Powerful guilds defended the interests of craftsmen, journeymen and apprentices. The

Tryavna wood-carvers produced a variety of small tables, chairs, spoons, forks and decorated doors, ceilings and icon-stands. The Vitanov family of craftsmen (18th–19th century), notably Koyu Vitanov (1821–91), was among the most famous of the Tryavna school. Furniture at this time was mostly made of pine or beech. Three-legged stools and low beds were used for seating. After World War II the low wooden tables were replaced by ones of normal height and high beds became more common. Built-in food cupboards and open shelves for kitchenware became standard. The *rakla*, a free-standing chest in the form of a parallelepiped (*see* §V above) was still used to store new clothes, textiles and valuables. The fronts of many chests were either painted or carved. Furniture hardware—hinges, knobs, handles and locks—was hammered out of mild iron, or cast brass. Wealthy families in towns along the Danube acquired furniture from abroad; Viennese pieces were much sought after.

From the 1920s to the 1940s furniture in Bulgaria was very diverse: 'Revival' *raklas* with domed lids, 'Viennese' chairs in Secessionist style, 'English' iron beds with brass decoration, painted decoration reminiscent of the Biedermeier style, tables, chests, wardrobes, shelves etc. Parlour furniture was upholstered and covered with heavy damask. From 1945 furniture was made from French models in the Art Nouveau style and from German models in the *Jugendstil* style. After the 1950s state enterprises for furniture were established that produced utilitarian pieces using wood, imported synthetic materials, decorative textiles, glass, metal etc. The Institute for Furniture and Furnishing at the Ministry of Forests and Forestry was founded in 1965. Such architects as Aleksandăr Dorosiev (*b* 1915), Emil Dimchev I, Lilyana Boseva (*b* 1913) and such other craftsmen and interior designers as Dimităr Mekhandzhiyski (*b* 1916) and Ivan Radev (*b* 1921) produced furniture designs. Traditional furniture with carved decoration was produced by such artists as Petăr Kănchev (1874–1958), Asen Vasilev (1909–83) and Slavyan Vasilev (*b* 1947).

In the late 20th century mass-produced commercial furniture was produced in large quantities, although one-off designer pieces were also made. There was an interest in reviving classical styles and the traditional styles that make use of carving, intarsia, decorative turning and damask upholstery. There were furniture factories in Troyan, Bansko, Cherven Bryag, Velingrad, Plovdiv and Stara Zagora. Chairs were produced in the 'Khemus' Factory in Troyan, and the 'Pirin' Factory in Bansko, kitchen furniture in the 'N. Vaptsarov' Factory in Cherven Bryag, section furniture in the 'Napredăk' Factory in Plovdiv and the 'Mebel' Factory in Stara Zagora. New furniture designs for commercial production were provided by the Institute for Furniture and Furnishing, which also produced prototypes for the State 'Mebel' Corporation, and by the design departments in the factories themselves. Designs were approved by the Council for Design of Furniture at the Ministry of Forests and Forestry.

BIBLIOGRAPHY

T. Zlatev: *Bălgarskata kăshta prez epokhata na Văzrazhdaneto* [Bulgarian houses during the Period of Revival] (Sofia, 1955)
K. Peev: *Plovdivskata kăshta prez epokhata na Văzrazhdaneto* [The Plovdiv house during the Period of Revival] (Sofia, 1960)
I. Kitov and S. Kostov: *Novi vidove mebeli* [New types of furniture] (Sofia, 1964)
A. Vasilev: *Bălgarski văzrozhdenski maystori* [Bulgarian artists of the Revival] (Sofia, 1965)
G. Kozhukharov: *Bălgarskata kăshta prez pet stoletiya* [Bulgarian houses during five centuries] (Sofia, 1967)
G. Kyuchukov: *Konstruirane na mebeli* [Furniture construction] (Sofia, 1975)
G. Arbaliev: *Stroitelni i khudozhestveni traditsii na bălgarskata arkhitektura* [Building and artistic traditions in Bulgarian architecture] (Sofia, 1977)

VII. Ceramics.

About the middle of the 19th century, under the influence of social and cultural changes, Bulgarian crafts, including ceramics, reached a high artistic level. The art of pottery-making was widespread: the centres of production, which chiefly made kitchenware, were in the area of Trăn and included Busintsi (Pernik district), Razlog, Bansko, Troyan and Gabrovo. Local varieties of well-known and frequently produced types of kitchen utensil were created. Multicoloured lead glazes and traditional decorative techniques including *sgraffito* were applied to the wares. The motifs included simple floral, zoomorphic and anthropomorphic designs. The limited use of decoration, the high quality of the products and their functionalism were characteristic of the work of the Bulgarian craftsmen from all centres of ceramic production.

During this period different types of machine-made and handmade articles for everyday life were produced. However, the production of handmade wares was quite different from that of machine-made wares. Traditional methods of production were supplanted by the introduction of foreign methods and imitations of foreign ceramic wares. Potters were either retrained in the new ceramic factories or remained in their workshops and continued to use traditional methods of production. The artistic quality of the pottery began to diminish, which was also caused by the very basic level of the available machinery in the workshops. In these poor conditions the attempts by potters to introduce faience using traditional methods failed.

After the liberation of Bulgaria from Ottoman rule in 1878, the traditions of Bulgarian ceramics were assimilated with western European knowledge, and production expanded. In addition to traditional pottery-making, the production of mass-produced, architectural ceramics began. In 1888 a pottery department at the State Educational Workshop for Crafts in the village of Knyazhevo (now part of Sofia) was opened. In 1904 a department for ceramics was established at the State Painting School (now the Nikolaj Pavlovich Higher Institute of Fine Arts, Sofia). From 1921 ceramic exhibitions were organized, while Bulgarian potters started to participate in European exhibitions. Stefan Dimitrov (1871–1937) was a very active potter at the beginning of the 20th century. In the 1920s and 1930s the most important part of the potters' work was the use of ceramics for interior decoration. Especially notable at that time were the works of Stoyan Raynov (1894–1978) and Georgi Bakărdzhiev (1899–1972).

After World War II ceramics developed both as an art and as an industry. Artists experimented with new ways of applying ceramics, especially in architecture. Sculptors and potters turned their attention to figured terracotta murals that were particularly used in public buildings. The most prominent artists included Bakărdzhiev and Jova Raevska and, later, Antonina Konzova (*b* 1939) and Mikhayl Nedkov (*b* 1947).

In the early 1970s artistic experiments centred on the ceramic panel. These were used either in decorative wall panels in a rectangular or irregularly shaped composition, as seen in the still-lifes of Zdravka Olekova (*b* 1936) in the Vitosha-New Othany Hotel; or, alternatively, as a sculptural relief panel where the ideological content was important, as seen in *Strike* by Mito Ganovski (*b* 1925) in the House of Culture, Pernik, or in *The Letters* by Nikolina Dzhelebova (*b* 1944) in the House of Teachers, Sofia. Walls were also entirely covered in ceramic tiles: they were designed in modules and resemble mosaics. The best examples include those in the Cherno More Hotel, Varna, by Milka Stoyanova (*b* 1920) and that of Olya Kolcheva (*b* 1939) in the Vitosha-New Othany Hotel, Sofia, which was constructed in modules of soft-paste porcelain. Ceramic screens were used to divide space and were a permanent element in the structure of the building. The best examples include the screens in the Sandanski Hotel (1982), Sandanski, by Nikolina Dzhelebova and those in the National Swimming Complex, Sofia, by Blagovest Petkov (*b* 1940). Others were conceived as independent works not installed in buildings, and they were closely linked with painting and sculpture. The most prominent ceramic artists, all of whom produced panels, include Georgi Kolarov (*b* 1908), Venko Kolev (*b* 1909), Yova Raevska (*b* 1918), Zdravko Manolov (*b* 1920), Evelina Pireva (*b* 1946), Ekaterina Zolotova (*b* 1923), Evgeniya Racheva-Manolova (*b* 1930; see fig. 10), Olya Kolcheva and, from the next generation, Irena Dimova (*b* 1951), Krasimir Dzhidrov (*b* 1947) and Bozhidar Bonchev (*b* 1956).

10. Ceramic panel showing a female potter by Evgeniya Racheva-Manolova, 1983 (Sofia, National Gallery of Decorative and Applied Arts)

Potters also collaborated with glassmakers, for example at the Dyanko Stefanov Glass and Porcelain Factory, Razgrad, and in the Kosta Yordanov Porcelain Factory, Vidin. The design of modern Bulgarian ceramics is determined by prominent artists and decorators who both work in traditional ways and are also influenced by wares from other countries.

BIBLIOGRAPHY

N. Mavrodinov: *Izkustvoto na bălgarskoto Văzrazhdane* [The art of the Bulgarian Revival] (Sofia, 1955)

G. Bakărdzhiev: *Bălgarska keramika* (Sofia, 1956)

N. Trufeshev: *Monumentalnite izkustva i arkhitekturata v Bălgariya* [Monumental arts and architecture in Bulgaria] (Sofia, 1968)

V. Angelov: *Izkustvoto i okolnata sreda* [Art and environment] (Sofia, 1975)

V. Angelov, D. G. Dimitrov and S. Lozanova: *Săvremenni dekorativno prilozhni izkustva v Bălgariya* [Modern decorative and applied arts in Bulgaria] (Sofia, 1989)

VIII. Glass.

Storage, pharmaceutical, window and decorative glass have been produced for many years in Bulgaria. The first industrial glass factories were founded in Samokov in 1881 and near Gebedzhe (now Beloslav) in 1893. The Dyanko Stefanov Factory in Razgrad was established in 1961 and produced glassware including sheet and ornamental glass; in 1966 the General Ivan Vinarov Factory in Pleven was established and produced storage glass; in 1978 the Deveti Septemvri Factory in Elena was established for hollow-ware. At the same time old factories were re-established, including the Stind Factory in Sofia, which produced kitchenware and sheet glass, and the Kitka Factory in Novi Pazar, which produced hollow-ware and cut lead-crystal. At the Stoyko Peev Factory in Beloslav, production included medical and coloured ornamental glass; the designer Stoyan Gaydarov (*b* 1956) worked at the factory and experimented with the production of new models and designs.

Art glass and stained glass were also produced in Bulgaria. Examples of stained glass can be found mainly in buildings from the 1930s and 1940s, for example St Kliment Okhridski University and the Palace of Justice, both in Sofia. Artists working later in stained glass, who produced works with brighter, richer colours and more dynamic forms, included Nikolay Bukov (*b* 1931), Nikolay Drachev (*b* 1951) and Vilyam Getov (*b* 1934). Ekaterina Getsova (*b* 1944) used glass in three-dimensional sculpture, while Dimo Zaymov (*b* 1930) incorporated thick cast glass into concrete constructions.

BIBLIOGRAPHY

V. Angelov, D. G. Dimitrov and S. Lozanova: *Săvremenno dekorativno monumentalno izkustvo v Bălgariya* [Modern decorative and monumental art in Bulgaria] (Sofia, 1989)

TATYANA YANKOVA

IX. Metalwork.

After the Ottoman conquest of the Bulgarian lands in 1396 metalwork suffered a temporary decline, but demand from the Bulgarian population and the Ottomans ensured that the metalwork trade soon recovered. The majority of the objects made in precious metals were ecclesiastical. Although the church canons imposed some limitations on the design of objects—in the case of Gospel book covers, for example, the front had to represent the scene of the Crucifixion, while the back had to represent the Descent into Hell—the works produced by Bulgarian goldsmiths were of high quality. Two such items made in the 16th century were produced by Matey Zlatar from Sofia: the gold and silver cover of the Krupnik Gospels (1577; see fig. 11) and the cover of the Gospel book in the church of St Petka in Sofia (1581; *in situ*).

There are many more extant ecclesiastical works dating from the 17th and 18th centuries: covers for church books, ciboria, icon facings, crosses and communion cups. They were produced in the major goldsmithing centres of Vratsa, Chiprovtsi, Vidin, Sofia, Plovdiv and Tarnovo. Characteristic features of metalwork made in the 17th and 18th centuries are detailed inscriptions, a combination of different materials and the use of several colours, which can be seen on an alms dish (1644) from the Bachkovo Monastery (*in situ*), made by the craftsman Petăr from Chiprovtsi in silver and gold with filigree, enamel and gemstone decoration, and on a silver ciborium (1637; Bachkovo monastery) in the form of a church made by Zafir Zlati. Domestic silver was also produced (e.g. silver bowl, 37×136mm, from Chiprovtsi, 16th century; Sofia, N. Hist. Mus.).

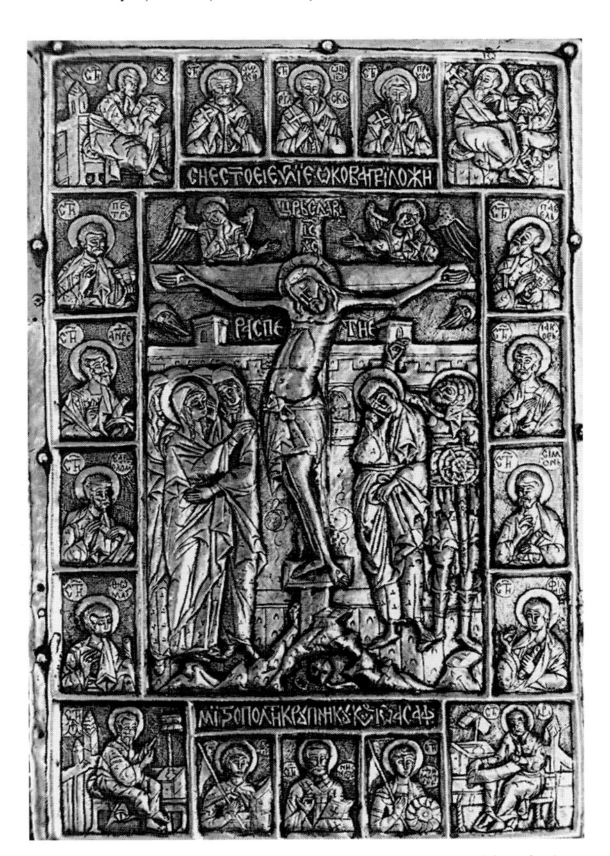

11. Cover of the Krupnik Gospels by Matey Zlatar, gold and silver, 410×285×120 mm, 1577 (Rila Monestry, National Museum)

Few copper utensils have survived as they were often melted down. Until the end of the 17th century the decoration of these objects (floral and geometrical motifs) was similar to the ornament in ancient Bulgarian manuscripts. During the 18th century Islamic and Turkish ornament was introduced. Plain forms were also made. The great variety in the decoration of copper utensils was due to the combination of Bulgarian and Islamic ornament. An important work dating from the 18th century is the copper baptismal font (1752) in the Rila Monastery (*in situ*), inscribed with the names of its makers Guran and Nikola and those of their assistants. Craftsmen were given official state protection in 1773 by the sultan Mustafa III's decree regulating crafts organizations within the Ottoman Empire, and the guilds subsequently became more powerful. At the end of the 18th century and during the 19th, western European cultural trends influenced Bulgarian craftsmen specializing in metalwork. The import of English sheet copper in the 19th century, however, led to the introduction of cheap semi-manufactured products that considerably reduced the value of wrought copper.

Besides ecclesiastical objects and copper utensils, jewellery was made, although gold was rarely used as silver jewellery was more popular among the wealthy. In the 18th and 19th centuries brass was also used and was combined with such other metals as copper, silver and bronze. Brass bracelets, earrings, necklaces, adornments for the head, brooches and buckles were gold- or silver-plated. The use of coloured stones, coloured paste and beads enriched and contributed to the variety of articles produced. Different techniques, for example casting, filigree and granulating, were used. During the 19th century brass was also used for the covers of church books. Floral ornament was predominant, with late Baroque elements.

During the 19th century the production of pewter articles reached its peak. The lack of tin-ore deposits in Bulgaria made craftsmen dependent on imports. There were only three centres of pewter production: Teteven, Etropole and Karlovo. Pewter articles were often modelled on imported Islamic objects. Pewter utensils for drinking *rakiya* (a fruit drink) and special vessels (*băklitsa*) and flasks (*pavurche*) for both domestic and ritual use were the most common. In their shape and decoration there are elements of both Christian and Islamic art. The geometrical and floral decoration—carnations, tulips and cypresses—were derived from Islamic art, while representations of St George and St Demetrius, as well as the double-headed eagles, were distinctly Bulgarian features.

The production of wrought-iron articles increased in the 19th century due to the boom in building. Hinges for locks, handles, door-knockers, candlesticks, chandeliers and gratings for windows were made. Geometric and naturalistic motifs were used in the decoration. Inscriptions with the name of the craftsman or of the owner were often forged, but the year of production was not usually included, since wrought-iron articles were not regarded as valuable.

After the liberation of Bulgaria from Ottoman rule in 1878, the production of articles in wrought iron, copper and gold continued, but on a smaller scale. Cheaper western European metal articles were imported, causing a decline in the production of metalwork and jewellery. In the 1960s, however, the metalwork crafts were revived, and two tendencies clearly emerged: the continuing use of traditional forms and techniques and a pursuit of new means of expression. Notable modern artists include Dimo Zaimov (*b* 1930) and Angelo Krasini (*b* 1954). A great variety of objects in both precious and base metals were made, from jewellery to wrought-iron gratings and decorative metalwork in abstract forms for the interiors of public buildings. Such metals as aluminium were used, as well as bronze and copper.

BIBLIOGRAPHY

G. Bakărdzhiev: *Kovana med* [Wrought copper] (Sofia, 1957)

A. Bozhinov, Kh. Vakarelski and D. Drumev: *Kovano zhelyazo: Khudozhestveni tvorbi na bălgarskite kovachi predi Osvobozhdenieto* [Wrought iron: artistic works of Bulgarian blacksmiths before the Liberation] (Sofia, 1957)

S. Georgieva and D. Buchinski: *Staroto zlatarstvo văv Vratsa* [The old goldsmiths' trade in Vratsa] (Sofia, 1959)

M. Ivanov: *Zlatarskite proizvedeniya ot XVI–XIX v. v muzeya na Bachkovskiya manastir* [Goldsmiths' products from the 16th to the 19th century in the museum of the Bachkovo monastery] (Sofia, 1967)

N. Trufeshev: *Monumentalnite izkustva i arkhitekturata v Bălgariya* [Monumental arts and architecture in Bulgaria] (Sofia, 1968)

D. Drumev: *Zlatarsko izkustvo* [Goldsmiths' art] (Sofia, 1976)

V. Pandurski: *Pametnitsi na izkustvoto v Tsărkovniya istoriko-arkheologicheski muzey—Sofia* [Monuments of art in the Church Historical and Archaeological Museum in Sofia] (Sofia, 1977)

P. Petrova-Golyska, ed.: *Narodnite hudozhestveni zanyati v Bălgariya: Bibliografski ukazatel* [National cultural handicrafts in Bulgaria: a bibliographical index] (Lovech, 1984)

M. Stefanov and M. Kirov: *Savremenno bălgarsko monumentalno izkustvo, 1956–1986* [Contemporary Bulgarian monumental art, 1956–1986] (Sofia, 1986) [Eng. summary]

X. Textiles.

From the 6th century to the 10th Bulgarian textiles show a strong, Slav preference for abstract geometric designs. Woven textiles, especially linen, were exported during the second Bulgarian Kingdom, and it is probable that luxury textiles were also produced, but none survives. In the 16th century, under Ottoman rule, Kotel and Sliven were centres of textile production, from which woollen bedding and coverlets were exported to all parts of the empire. The importance of textiles in the country's economy did not diminish until the mid-18th century. By then Russia was an important outside influence. In the 19th century the transition to industrial production started in the areas with traditions in weaving; the first textile mill opened in Sliven in 1834. Originally linen and hemp were used for clothing and household textiles, but in the 19th century the production of cotton and silk increased. Wool had an important role in everyday life and was used for carpets, rugs, pillows, bedspreads, tablecloths, bags and towels. Most were woven on the horizontal loom, although tablet-woven belts were also produced.

The decoration of textiles featured patterns and motifs that were specific to each region of Bulgaria. Embroidery was worked with crewel wool, with cotton, silk and metal threads. In the domestic embroidery of the 18th and 19th centuries geometric patterns predominated, reflecting the Slav influence. Stylized flowers (e.g. carnations, roses and tulips) had recognizable roots in Turkish embroidery. Figures of animals and people also appear. Embroidery was used to decorate women's clothes and household furnishings. The vestments of the Greek Orthodox Church were decorated with figurative embroidery in an archaic Byzantine style (e.g. Sofia, N. Mus. Eccles. Hist. & Archeol.). Subjects included the *Entombment*, the *Lamentation* and the *Evangelists*. The embroidery was almost entirely worked in metal thread (sometimes twisted with coloured silk to give a faint coloured sheen) on a silk ground. The technique of surface couching was used, and in the best pieces the couching stitches form decorative patterns. Faces were worked in split stitch and silk thread to give a detailed, realistic effect.

The Bulgarian form of bobbin lace is worked in polychrome as well as white threads. The motifs are very varied: the sun, rhomboids and rosettes are archaic stylized images, while there are also more expressive and lively floral patterns. During the 19th century the technique of *bibila* lace was introduced to Bulgaria from Turkey. These delicate, needle-made edgings were worked in silk or cotton thread and were brightly coloured. They were used to decorate clothes and small textiles in some parts of the country, but the technique was not widely adopted by Bulgarian women. At the end of the 19th century and the beginning of the 20th more solid, tape-based laces appeared, influenced by Russia and western Europe; the figurative designs often show religious or pastoral scenes.

Flat-woven carpets, or kilims, of a high standard were produced in Bulgaria during the period of Turkish rule and exported to other countries. Towards the end of the 19th century they began to deviate from the traditional folk designs, and new styles influenced by Persian and Anatolian carpets were introduced. The main centres of the industry were Kotel and Chiprovtsi. The basic material was wool, but from the 1920s cotton was also used.

In the mid-20th century there was a revival of interest in traditional handmade textiles. The Guild of Masters of Folk Crafts, founded in 1967, encouraged the use of folk art in contemporary settings. While products were made in the 1950s and 1960s that still used traditional motifs, as in the *White Horseman* (1968; Sofia, N. Gal. Dec. & Applied A.; see fig. 12) by Mara Yosifova (*b* 1905), at the same time some textile artists, following the international development of fibre art, experimented with synthetic fibres, different textures and new forms, to the extent that by the 1980s their work was often completely separate from the wall. However, the wall hanging remained, in the later 20th century, the principal medium for Bulgarian textile artists (most in Sofia, N. Gal. Dec. & Applied A.). Notable modern artists included Mariu Vărbanov (1932–89; e.g. *Dawn*, wool, plain weave, 3.2×2.6 m, 1972; Sofia, N. Gal. Dec. & Applied A.), Tzvetana Petrova (*b* 1943; e.g. *Before the Spring Comes*, linen and silk, mixed technique, 2.05×2.0 m, 1983; Sofia, N. Gal. Dec. & Applied A.), Vladimir Ovtcharov (*b* 1938; e.g. *Chair*, 800×500×500 mm, 1983; Montana, Art Gallery) and Zdravko Mavrodiev (*b* 1936; e.g. *Antithese II*, wool and silk, mixed technique, 1982; Sofia, N. Gal. Dec. & Applied A.).

12. Flat-woven wall hanging, *White Horseman* by Mara Yosifova, 1.83×1.53 m, 1968 (Sofia, National Gallery of Decorative and Applied Arts)

BIBLIOGRAPHY

S. I. Kostov and E. Peteva: *Bălgarski narodni shevitsi* [Bulgarian folk embroidery] (Sofia, 1928)

I. Koev: *Bălgarska vezbena ornamentika* [Bulgarian motifs in embroidery] (Sofia, 1951)

D. Velev: *Bălgarski kilimi do kraya na XIX v.* [Bulgarian carpets until the end of the 19th century] (Sofia, 1960)

Kh. Vakarelski: *Bălgarsko narodno izkustvo* [Bulgarian folk art] (Sofia, 1969)

D. Stankov: *Chergi i kilimi* [Rugs and carpets] (Sofia, 1975)

P. Puntev: *Bălgarski narodni vezbeni ornamenti* [Bulgarian folk designs in embroidery] (Sofia, 1977)

P. Johnstone: 'Central and South-eastern Europe', *Needlework: An Illustrated History*, ed. H. Bridgeman and E. Drury (New York and London, 1978), pp. 267–301

G. Krăsteva-Nozharova: *Domashno traditsionno tăkachestvo i ornamentirano tăkane v Bălgariya* [Traditional domestic textiles and decorative weaving in Bulgaria] (Sofia, 1982)

Plastichnite izkustva i zhilishtnata sreda [Decorative arts and interiors] (Sofia, 1983)

K. Popov: *Bălgarski narodni ornamenti: Vezba, pletiva, tăkani* [Bulgarian folk designs: embroidery, crochet, fabrics] (Sofia, 1986)

DOTCHKA KISIJOVA

XI. Patronage.

The arts flourished under the personal patronage of Simeon I (*reg* 893–927). Ohrid and Preslav became centres of illustrated manuscript production, and following on from Simeon's example, successive kings founded palaces, churches, libraries and public buildings (*see* §II, 3 above). During the Second Bulgarian Kingdom (1193–1393) kings, clerics and boyars sponsored numerous works of art and architecture, particularly in the new capital of Tărnovo (now Veliko Turnovo). One of the city's 13th-century buildings is the church of the Forty Martyrs, which John Asen II (*reg* 1218–41) erected in memory of his victory in 1230 over the feudal lord Theodore Komnin. The earliest donor portraits are the wall paintings of *Sebastokrator Kaloyan* (see fig. 5 above) and his wife Dessislava in SS Nicholas and Panteleimon, which they founded in 1259 at BOYANA. Several portraits of Tsar Ivan Alexander (*reg* 1331–71) appear in two illustrated manuscripts made for him in or near Tărnovo (*see* §III, 2(iii) above): the Chronicle of Manassès (1344–5; Rome, Vatican, Bib. Apostolica, MS. Vat. Slav. 2) and the London Gospels (1356; London, BL, Add. MS. 39627; see fig. 7).

Under the Ottoman empire, the churches and monasteries were the principal patrons of ecclesiastical buildings, as well as for painting and graphic art (*see* §III, 3 above). In the 18th century Samokov and the Rila Monastery developed into centres of graphic art production. A group of clerics led by Neophit of Rila (1793–1881) held courses on the graphic design of books and organized the monastery's archive of over 41,000 items, including documents granting it privileges, works of art and endowments from Bulgarian, Serbian and Greek clerics as well as from the Bulgarian kings.

After Bulgaria's liberation from Ottoman rule (1878), the National Assembly commissioned numerous commemorative monuments and buildings to the war (*see* §IV, 3 above), including the Alexander Nevski Church (1904–12; see fig. 4 above) in Sofia. Between 1944 and 1989, the ruling Communist Party built memorials and monuments to its more popular leaders who were patrons of youth organizations and factories. Until the early 1960s Socialist Realism remained the prevalent style, after which other styles were adopted, such as Expressionism, Hyper-realism, Surrealism and fully abstract art. In 1981, the government celebrated Bulgaria's 1300th anniversary by commissioning the monumental sculptures of *1300 Years of the Bulgarian State* (reinforced concrete, granite, bronze, mosaic stones and stained glass; by Krum Damyanov (*b* 1937)) in Shoumen and *Bulgaria: Past, Present and Future* (granite and bronze; by Valentin Starchev (*b* 1935)) in Sofia.

BIBLIOGRAPHY

Encyclopedia Bulgaria, 12 vols (Sofia, 1976–88)

Entsiklopediya na izobrazitelnite iskustva v Bălgariya [Encyclopedia of the fine arts in Bulgaria], 2 vols (Sofia, 1980–87)

JULIANA NEDEVA-WEGENER

XII. Museums, collections and art libraries.

After 1393 Bulgaria's churches and monasteries became the storehouses of important documents, religious works of art, manuscripts and early printed books that were mostly donated by feudal lords, members of the clergy and lay men and women. During the Period of Revival (late 16th century–19th), awareness of the value of these collections grew, as did general interest in the archaeology, ethnography and art history of Bulgaria. The first exhibitions of Bulgarian culture were held in the newly founded museums of Svishtov and Veliko Turnovo (formerly Tărnovo) in 1856 and 1872 respectively.

Following the overthrow of Ottoman rule in 1878, numerous museums and art libraries were founded. One of the first was the Cyril and Methodius National Library,

Sofia (1878), which contains rich collections of art books, Bulgarian illustrated manuscripts and early printed books, as well as portraits and photographs mainly from the Period of Revival. Its Oriental department has many beautiful examples of calligraphy and illustrated Persian, Arabic and Ottoman manuscripts. The library also holds a significant collection of prints and lithographs, including the oldest print with Roman script of *St Ivan the Wonder Worker* (1791).

The excavation of the old Bulgarian capitals of Pliska, Preslav and Tărnovo between 1895 and 1914 by Russian and Czech archaeologists (including the Škorpil brothers, Hermingild (1851–1907) and Karel Václav (1859–1944)) led to the construction of museums at these sites. By 1944 there were 34 museums in the country, only 13 of which were permanently staffed or recognized by the state. One of the most important private collections to come to light between 1878 and 1944 was a collection of western European prints from the 17th to the 19th century acquired by Khristo Zographski (1841–1919), the son of Zakhary Zograph. It was catalogued in 1927 in Plovdiv; much of the collection is in the National Art Gallery, Sofia.

After World War II a network of museums and art galleries was created throughout the country. In 1948 the National Art Gallery was opened in the Old Royal Palace in Sofia and is largely devoted to Bulgarian painting. In 1952 the first laws were passed that dealt with the establishment and organization of museums and art galleries and with the use of churches, cultural institutes and universities as venues for permanent and temporary art exhibitions. Since 1965, the crypt of Alexander Nevski Church in Sofia has served as an annexe of the National Art Gallery for the display of old Bulgarian icons. A gallery of foreign art was opened in 1981 by the International Foundation of SS Cyril and Methodius. Specialist art libraries exist within the Art Academy and the Institute of Architecture in Sofia. Bulgaria's largest photographic collection is housed in the Central State Photo Archive, although smaller documentary photographic collections are held by the National History Museum in Sofia and the Museum of Sofia's History. Some of their most important photographs are of central Sofia before its destruction in 1944. By the end of 1990 Bulgaria had 220 museums, 35 civic art galleries, 15 exhibition centres for contemporary Bulgarian painters and sculptors, and over 450 exhibitions at other venues.

A large number of private individuals began to collect art in the early 1970s. One of the most renowned collectors was the painter Svetlin Russev (*b* 1933), who acquired works by 20th-century Bulgarian painters, graphic artists and sculptors, old Bulgarian icons, prints and wood-carvings, French paintings (including works by André Derain and Honoré Daumier) and Indian, Mexican and African art objects. In 1987 he donated part of his collection to the museum in Pleven, where it appears on permanent display. Another collector of repute is Bogomil Rainov (*b* 1919), whose collection includes old Bulgarian icons and wood-carvings, modern Bulgarian paintings, French and Belgian graphic art of the 19th and 20th centuries and Chinese works of art. Works from his graphic art collection by Daumier and Frans Masereel were donated to the museum at Sliven in 1978. The former world and Olympic wrestling champion Boyan Radev (*b* 1942) acquired a sizeable collection of works by Bulgarian artists, including Ivan Milev, Bencho Obreshkov, Kiril Tsonev, SYRAK SKITNIK, ZLATYU BOYADJIEV, Ivan Nenov, Dechko Uzunov and Georgi Baev.

Although most artists sell their work directly from their studios or through agents, sales of art are often organized at the Sheraton Hotel, Sofia, or through the Union of Bulgarian Artists (*see* NATIONAL ART SOCIETY OF BULGARIA). After 1990, when Bulgaria embraced democratic reforms, new legislation was introduced so as better to regulate the sale and export of art objects and antiquities.

BIBLIOGRAPHY

A. Protich: 'Denatsionalirsirane i văzrazhdane na bălgarskoto iskustvo (1393–1879)' [Denationalizing and the revival of Bulgarian art (1393–1879)], *Bulgaria: 1000 godini, 927–1927* [Bulgaria: 1000 years, 927–1927] (Sofia, 1930)

Musei i pametnitsi v Bălgariya [Museums and monuments in Bulgaria] (Sofia, 1959)

Bălgarsko Photo (1966–90)

T. Silyanovska-Novikova: *Osnovi na museyznanieto* [The basics of museum science] (Sofia, 1970)

K. Kalaydzhieva: *Narodnata biblioteka Cyril i Methodius* [The Cyril and Methodius National Library] (Sofia, 1973)

Museyte i organisatsia na museyte v Bălgariya [Museums and museum organization in Bulgaria] (Sofia, 1977)

Svetlin Russev (exh. cat., Pleven, A.G., 1987)

J. Nedeva: 'Isloyba na chastni kolektsii v Sofiiskata gradska hudozhestvenna galeriya' [Private collections exhibited at the Sofia City Art Gallery], *Kartinna Gal.*, 5 (1990), pp. 14–21

MARIANA KATZAROVA, JULIANA NEDEVA-WEGENER

XIII. Art education and historiography.

Among the first writers of Bulgarian art history were Lyuben Karavelov and Marin Drinov in the 1860s. There was a significant development in the subject after 1878, when Czech art historians, including the Škorpil brothers, began to research the art and architecture of Bulgaria. Between 1895 and 1930 several art periodicals were established, including *Izkustvo*, *Hudozhnik* and *Hudzhestvena kultura*, to which artists and art historians such as Simeon Radev (1879–1967), Krustyu Miyatev (1892–1966), Andrey Protich (1875–1959), Kiril Krustev (1904–92), Nikolay Rainov and Syrak Skitnik contributed. One of the most eminent foreign scholars to write about Bulgarian art was André Grabar.

In 1896 the School of Drawing (renamed the Art Academy by 1924) was founded in Sofia. It attracted international recognition in 1900 by winning the gold medal for art education at the Exposition Universelle in Paris. In 1924 the two departments of the Art Academy were established: the fine arts department with classes in painting, graphic art, sculpture, art history and theory, and the department of applied arts with classes in wall painting, architectural sculpture, stage design, ceramics, carving, fashion, and poster, textile and industrial design.

With the imposition of Communist rule in 1944, art historical research developed along Marxist lines. Not until the 1960s was there a move away from this kind of interpretation, by such writers as Asen Vassiliev, Irina Mihalcheva, Atanass Bozhkov and Dimiter Avramov. During the 1970s and 1980s numerous monographs on Bulgarian art were published inside and outside Bulgaria;

the most notable works in the latter category are those by Tania Velmans and Dora Valie.

Interest in Bulgarian art is also reflected in the number of specialist secondary schools in Sofia, Plovdiv and Varna that offer courses in painting, graphic art, sculpture and the decorative arts. In 1973 Veliko Turnovo University introduced a course on painting.

BIBLIOGRAPHY

A. Protich: *Fine Art in Bulgaria* (London, 1907)
A. Grabar: *La Peinture religieuse en Bulgarie* (Sofia, 1925, rev. Paris, 1928)
A. Bozhkov: *The Bulgarian Art Academy* (Sofia, 1962)
K. Miyatev: *The Architecture of Medieval Bulgaria* (Sofia, 1965)
I. Mihalcheva: *The Portrait in Bulgarian Painting*, 2 vols (Sofia, 1968–71)
D. Avramov: *Aesthetics of Modern Art* (Sofia, 1969)
A. Bozhkov: *Die bulgarische Malerei* (Berlin, 1969)
Reference Book for Prospective Students, 1992–1993, Ministry of Culture (Sofia, 1992)

MARIANA KATZAROVA

Bulgarini, Bartolommeo [Bartolomeo] [Ovile Master] (*fl* Siena, 1337; *d* Siena, 4 Sept 1378). Italian painter. Many of his paintings were attributed by Berenson to an anonymous master he called 'Ugolino–Lorenzetti', because of the artist's obvious indebtedness to the work of Ugolino di Nerio and Pietro Lorenzetti. A group of paintings that partially overlapped with these was attributed by Dewald to an artist he called the Ovile Master, after a painting formerly in S Pietro a Ovile, Siena. In 1931 Meiss recognized that these works formed the oeuvre of a single artist, and in 1936 he identified this figure as Bartolommeo Bulgarini. Subsequent discoveries have confirmed Meiss's hypothesis and established a dated work around which the rest of Bulgarini's paintings can be studied. A 16th-century inventory of Siena Cathedral names Bulgarini as the artist of a *Nativity* that stood on the altar of St Victor (one of four altars dedicated to the city's patron saints). This must have been a prestigious commission, since the other altarpieces in the cycle are all major works by important artists: the *Annunciation* by Simone Martini and Lippo Memmi (Florence, Uffizi), the *Birth of the Virgin* by Pietro Lorenzetti (Siena, Mus. Opera Duomo) and the *Purification of the Virgin* by Ambrogio Lorenzetti (Florence, Uffizi). Bulgarini's work has been identified with the *Adoration of the Shepherds* (*c.* 1350; Cambridge, MA, Fogg; see fig.), which has been cut down and restored several times. Stylistically it marks a turning point in his development: the unusual composition balances a feeling for depth and monumental form derived from the Lorenzetti with a rigorous two-dimensional organization of the surface. Bulgarini himself executed the central portion and predella, while the lateral panels were painted by an anonymous follower of Simone Martini, known as the Master of the Palazzo Venezia Madonna (*fl* 1335–55).

Bulgarini's earlier works—such as the polyptych of *c.* 1340 that Vasari saw in Santa Croce (Florence, Fortezza Basso) or that of *c.* 1345, now divided between Lucca (Villa Guinigi), Rome (Mus. Capitolino) and Washington, DC (N.G.A.)—reflect the influence of late Duccesque painting in the figure types and the graceful but restrained rhythms of the draperies. The hard, linear definition of forms and the pronounced highlights are, however, close to the more mannered works of Ugolino di Nerio, as are the facial types. These recur throughout Bulgarini's work. The debt to Pietro Lorenzetti is revealed in the dynamic

Bartolommeo Bulgarini: *Adoration of the Shepherds*, tempera on panel, 1.72×1.23 m, *c.* 1350 (Cambridge, MA, Fogg Art Museum)

depiction of the Christ Child, the breadth of the forms, the experiments with the interrelation of figure and frame and the use of plain, unornamented surfaces. The sombre but emotionally unexpressive figures parallel those of Niccolò di Segna (*fl* 1331–5), with whom Bulgarini may have worked.

After the *Adoration of the Shepherds*, Bulgarini, like many other Sienese artists of the 1350s, began to use the *sgraffito* technique developed by Simone Martini to provide more extensive surface decoration in his paintings. He also employed a more fluent, undulating line, characteristic of Simone and his followers. These stylistic changes may have been stimulated by his contact with the Master of the Palazzo Venezia Madonna, but Bulgarini fused Simone's style of surface decoration with the illusionism of the Lorenzetti to create subtle tensions between three- and two-dimensional effects. This development in his painting casts doubt on prevailing notions of a conservative regression in Sienese art after the outbreak of the Black Death in 1348. In fact, Bulgarini's most influential contribution to 14th-century painting, his use of a cusped frame as both a decorative and an illusionistic device, was probably made after this date. The *Virgin and Child*, made *c.* 1355 for the hospital church of S Maria della Scala, Siena (Siena, Pin. N., 76), was the first to use the cusp openings as windows into the picture space. The idea was refined in the Ovile *Madonna* (Siena, Semin.) and culminated in the *Virgin and Child* (Siena, Pin. N., 80) of *c.* 1359–60, which was part of another altarpiece for S Maria della

Scala. Here angels and cusps are interwoven in an exquisite design that rises pyramidally to the apex of the arch. The *Assumption of the Virgin* (Siena, Pin. N., 61), datable *c.* 1360–61 and also from S Maria della Scala, is Bulgarini's last surviving work and serves as a fitting final expression of his desire to synthesize seemingly opposing artistic values. The entire surface is covered with gold leaf that threatens to dissolve the three-dimensional forms as it envelops them. The radiant splendour of Bulgarini's works for this church may reflect the wishes of the institution itself, which had then acquired great wealth and prestige. In total, Bulgarini executed at least five altarpieces for S Maria della Scala, and in 1370 he and his wife Bartolommea became lay members of its charitable society. Like other Sienese artists, he held minor public offices as well as carrying out artistic commissions for the city. With the exception of a possible sojourn in Rome, Bulgarini apparently spent his entire career in Tuscany, largely in Siena, although he is also known to have worked in Florence, San Gimignano, Pienza, Grosseto and possibly Lucca and Pisa.

BIBLIOGRAPHY

G. Vasari: *Vite* (1550, rev. 2/1586); ed. G. Milanesi (1878–85)
B. Berenson: 'Ugolino–Lorenzetti', *A. America*, v (1916–17), pp. 259–75; vi (1917–18), pp. 25–52
E. T. Dewald: 'The Master of the Ovile Madonna', *A. Stud.*, i (1923), pp. 45–54
M. Meiss: 'Ugolino–Lorenzetti', *A. Bull.*, xiii (1931), pp. 376–97
——: 'Bartolomeo Bulgarini altrimenti detto "Ugolino Lorenzetti"?', *Riv. A.*, xviii (1936), pp. 113–36
E. Skaug: 'Punch-marks—What are they Worth? Problems of Tuscan Workshop Interrelationships in the Mid-fourteenth Century: The Ovile Master and Giovanni da Milano', *La pittura nel XIV e XV secolo. Il contributo dell'analisi tecnica alla storia dell'arte. Atti del XXIV congresso internazionale di storia dell'arte: Bologna, 1982*, iii, pp. 253–82
E. Beatson, N. Muller and J. Steinhoff: 'The St Victor Altarpiece in Siena Cathedral: A Reconstruction', *A. Bull.*, lxviii (1986), pp. 610–31
J. Steinhoff-Morrison: *Bartolomeo Bulgarini and Sienese Painting of the Mid-fourteenth Century* (diss., Princeton U., 1989)

J. STEINHOFF-MORRISON

Bull, Georg (Andreas) (*b* Bergen, 26 March 1829; *d* Aker [now Oslo], 1 Feb 1917). Norwegian architect. He trained as a draughtsman in Bergen (1843–5) and was educated as a mechanical engineer in Hannover (1846–50) and as an architect in Berlin (1855–6). He was an assistant to Christian Heinrich Grosch in Christiania (now Oslo) from 1856 to 1857, after which he established his own practice, later taking such official posts as Architect to the State Railway (1863–72) and City Architect of Christiania (1865–1903). In the numerous town houses he designed for the Homansby district of Christiania (1858–66) he used a variety of styles, including Gothic, classical and Islamic: the large villa at 13 Josefines Gate (1860) has a round corner tower, hipped roof and such elaborately Gothic decorations as ogee-arched door canopies, producing an effect vaguely reminiscent of a French Renaissance château; the nearby house at 17 Oscars Gate (1863) uses 'Norman' motifs. The Venetian Renaissance effect of Bull's design for Christiania's Western Railway station (1872) is not dissipated by the grand towers flanking its main façade; his Eastern Railway station (1878–82; now incorporated in Oslo Central Station) is an essay in the Renaissance Revival in the contemporary Berlin manner. Bull's wooden buildings outside Christiania were influenced by the prevailing 'Swiss style'. His most important contribution to the growth of Christiania was his development plan (begun 1861) for the Grünerløkka area; a regular street grid left undeveloped green spaces between others built up over the next four decades with three- and four-storey blocks.

BIBLIOGRAPHY

NKL
U. Hamran: 'G. A. Bull: Homansbyens arkitekt', *Foreningen til Norske Fortidsminners Bevarings Årbok* (1959)
T. Thiis-Evensen: *Steder i Oslo* [Places in Oslo] (Oslo, 1976)

Bull, Henrik (*b* Christiania [now Oslo], 28 March 1864; *d* Oslo, 2 June 1953). Norwegian architect and designer. He was trained as a draughtsman and technician in Christiania (1883–4) and completed his education as an architect in Berlin (1884–7). He started his own practice in Christiania in 1888, serving also as a teacher at the Royal School of Design there from 1908 and as director from 1912 to 1934. Early on he demonstrated an extraordinary ability as a draughtsman and a thorough knowledge of architectural history; he was equally interested in the traditional buildings of his own country and international contemporary trends. Bull's first buildings in Christiania, such as the Paulus Church (1889–92) and Mogens Thorsen's home for the elderly (1896–8; destr.), are historicist, although freely so. The high spire of the Gothic-Revival church, which is of red brick with details in glazed tiles, provides a landmark for Georg Bull's earlier Grünerløkka development. In the National Theatre (1891–9), Christiania, however, the search for a more personal style can be recognized. The aim of his mature works was to create a distinctively Norwegian *Jugendstil* comparable to the architecture of Lars Sonck and Eliel Saarinen in Finland: the exterior, of yellow brick with both roughly dressed and fine-cut granite elements, stylistically resembles the regular, orthogonal, Neo-classical buildings Bull would have seen in Berlin. Inside, however, walls and details curve in a Baroque manner, which occasionally achieves the fluidity of *Jugendstil*. In the Historisk Museum (1898–1902; *see* NORWAY, fig. 4), Christiania, this style is fully developed; the building is an important example of Scandinavian *Jugendstil* architecture, where fluid curves combine with the intricate ornaments inspired by the 'Dragon style' (*see* MUNTHE, HOLM), splendidly interpreted by Bull. The interiors provide a successful setting for the fine collection of medieval stave church portals. Bull's work culminated in the great project for the Government Building (1899–1906), Christiania, of which only one wing was executed. Here a huge mass of granite is subtly articulated with the controlled use of roughly dressed granite, a technique (also used on part of the National Theatre façade) that became characteristic of Scandinavian National Romanticism: *Jugendstil* forms and 'national' ornament. Bull won a Gold Medal at the Exposition Universelle in Paris in 1900, where he exhibited a dining-room in Norwegian *Jugendstil* (Oslo, Norsk Flkmus.).

After the Norwegian Centennial Exhibition, held in Christiania in 1914, Bull turned to a more classical mode of expression exemplified in the Villa Wilhelmsen (1916) and the Hannevig Building (1917, later heightened; both in Oslo). He remained active, but could not adapt to the ascetic, inter-war Functionalism: during this period his work was even attacked by younger colleagues for being old-fashioned. Bull was later recognized, in Norway and abroad, as a major architect of the turn of the century. He also designed furniture, cutlery, emblems and coins. The latter, in common use in Norway for more than 50 years, testify in particular to his exceptional talent.

BIBLIOGRAPHY

NKL
C. Norberg-Schulz: 'Henrik Bull', *Bygkst*, xlviii (1966), pp. 70–81
T. Thiis-Evensen: *Henrik Bull: Arkitekt og formgiver* [Henrik Bull: architect and designer] (Oslo, 1975)
S. Tschudi-Madsen: *Henrik Bull*, intro. C. Jencks (Oslo, 1983)

CHRISTIAN NORBERG-SCHULZ

Bullant, Jean [Jehan] (*b* ?Amiens, *c*. 1515; *d* Ecouen, 1578). French architect and mason. His family were prominent master masons in Picardy, and he combined the skills of the master mason with a mastery of Classical architecture. According to the preface of his *Reigle généralle d'architecture* (1564), he made measured drawings of ancient monuments while in Rome (*c*. 1540–45). From *c*. 1550 to 1567 Bullant was in the service of the Constable ANNE MONTMORENCY and resided at Montmorency's château of Ecouen (Val-d'Oise) from 1556 to 1578, where he produced his major works. He began with the exterior façade of the north wing, basing the composition directly on Roman models as well as on Vitruvian doctrine. His monumental entry pavilion on the east wing, with its triumphal arch motif composed of superimposed orders (1555–60; destr. 1787, but known through an engraving by Jacques Androuet I Du Cerceau; for illustration *see* ECOUEN), recalls Philibert de L'Orme's portico at Anet (Eure-et-Loire). Bullant used the Giant order for the first time in France in the entry portal to the south wing of the court (*c*. 1560); although modelled on that of the Corinthian portico of the Pantheon in Rome, its context here was not strictly classical. Michelangelo's two white marble slaves, once destined for the tomb of Julius II, adorned the niches.

Bullant's liking for scenographic effects revives the spirit of antiquity in the galleries of the viaduct over the valley of the château of Fère-en-Tardenois (Aisne) that join the château to its attendant buildings. Dating from 1552 to 1562, this work prefigures Vasari's bridge and gallery over the Arno in Florence (1560s), connecting the Uffizi and Pitti palaces. The articulation of the château's façade with its interlocking system of pediments above the windows, which in turn intrude on the entablature, was further developed in the Petit Château (*c*. 1560) at Chantilly, Oise.

During a lull in his building work for Montmorency, Bullant turned to a study of architectural treatises and technical matters and to writing three tracts that are largely a compilation of his research. In the *Reigle généralle d'architecture* Bullant addressed practising architects, providing them with a rational means of constructing the orders and with magnificently detailed drawings, advising architects to seek 'in ruins the true forms of ancient buildings'.

As Supervisor of the King's Buildings, Bullant appears in the royal accounts from 1557 to 1559 but does not reappear until after de L'Orme's death in 1570, when he was appointed architect to Catherine de' Medici (1519–89). In this capacity in Paris he probably designed the south-west pavilion of the Tuileries (1571; destr.) and supervised work begun by Francesco Primaticcio on the Valois Chapel in Saint-Denis (1572–8; destr.). He designed the immense Hôtel de la Reine (1572–8; later the Hôtel de Soissons; destr.), whose surviving Doric column (h. 25 m) stood in the middle of the court, near the Halle au Blé, its summit perhaps serving as an observatory for the Queen or as a memorial. Bullant was also in charge of additions to the château of Saint-Maur-des-Fossés, near Paris (1575–9; destr.). The gallery on the bridge spanning the Cher at the château of Chenonceau, Indre-et-Loire (1576), was part of his scheme to add to the château's sense of scale by creating dramatic axial approaches. Various works have been attributed to Bullant, including alterations for Montmorency to the Hôtel Neuf, Paris (1558–61; today Hôtel d'Albret, altered 18th century), the façade of the abbey church of St Martin de Montmorency (1563), the monument dedicated to the heart of the Constable (1571–6) executed with Barthélemy Prieur and alterations to the châteaux of Gandelu, Aisne (1563–73; destr. except terrace), and Offémont, Haut-Rhin (1567–9; destr.; see James).

Bullant's style has a licence within the rules that is characteristic of Mannerism; the coexistence of this licence with an element of fantasy perpetuates the medieval heritage of the master masons. His unparalleled dexterity as a stone cutter, joined to his flair for the dramatic in architecture, is compatible with the mentality of his patron Montmorency. Bullant, perhaps, following his principal mentor de L'Orme in the quest for antiquity, was reaching for a new classical architecture, one that would be distinctly modern and uniquely French.

WRITINGS

Recueil d'horlogiographie, contenant la description, fabrication et usage des horloges solaires (Paris, 1561)
Petit traicté de géométrie et d'horlogiographie pratique (Paris, 1562)
Reigle générale d'architecture des cinq manières de colonnes,... à l'exemple de l'antique suivant les reigles & doctrine de Vitruve (Paris, 1564, rev. 1619)

BIBLIOGRAPHY

Bauchal
A. de Montaiglon: 'Jehan Bullant architecte: Analyse du compte des dépenses faites pour le château des Tuileries en 1571', *Archvs A. Fr.*, ix (1857–8), pp. 1–13
——: 'Jean Bullant, architecte du connétable de Montmorency: Actes extraits des registres de la mairie d'Ecouen (1556–78)', *Archvs A. Fr.*, xi (1858–60), pp. 305–39
R. Blomfield: *A History of French Architecture, 1494–1661*, i (London, 1911/*R* New York, 1974), pp. 93–107
F. Gebelin: *Les Châteaux de la Renaissance en France* (Paris, 1927), pp. 32–4, 76–8, 83–8, 90–96, 105–37
A. Blunt: *Art and Architecture in France, 1500–1700*, Pelican Hist. A. (Harmondsworth, 1953/*R* 1982), pp. 135–40
F.-C. James: 'Jean Bullant: Recherches sur l'architecture française du XVIe siècle', *Ecole Nationale de Chartres: Positions des thèses* (Paris, 1968), pp. 101–9
V. Hoffmann: 'Artisti francesi a Roma: Philibert Delorme e Jean Bullant', *Colloq. Sodalizo*, n. s. 2, iv (1973–4), pp. 55–68

NAOMI MILLER

Bullet. French family of architects.

UNPUBLISHED SOURCES

Stockholm, Nmus. [drawings by Pierre Bullet and Jean-Baptiste Bullet]

BIBLIOGRAPHY

R. Strandberg: *Pierre Bullet et J.-B. de Chamblain à la lumière des dessins de la collection Tessin-Hårleman du Musée National de Stockholm* (Stockholm, 1971)

(1) Pierre Bullet (*b* 1639; *d* Paris, before 23 Nov 1716). He was the son of a Parisian master builder, Martin Bullet (*fl* 1608; *d* after 1639), and rapidly made his reputation as an architectural draughtsman, producing a plan of Paris for the city council (1665; Paris, Archvs N.). In 1672 he was admitted to the Académie Royale d'Architecture, where he became a disciple of the director François Blondel. He was appointed as a draughtsman to the Académie in 1673, with a full fellowship in 1685. In 1672 Bullet completed the triumphal arch of the Porte St-Denis, designed by Blondel, on the new, tree-lined boulevard with which Louis XIV replaced the former rampart, and two years later he built the Porte St-Martin to his own design.

Bullet's experience with Blondel also led to a commission from the city council for a new map of Paris (1676, reprinted in 1700 and 1707), showing the improvements decided upon by the king. He also collaborated actively on municipal works in Paris, such as the first St-Michel fountain in 1684 and the Quai Pelletier and Quai de Gesvres, a daring overhanging construction above the River Seine. His contribution to religious architecture was also significant. In 1675 he designed the main altar in the church of the Sorbonne and the altars in the transept chapels of St-Germain-des-Prés, and in 1676 he submitted a project for Les Invalides in collaboration with Jules Hardouin Mansart. He worked for various religious orders, including, in 1681, the Ursulines of Bourges and the Visitandines of Chaillot; he also worked on the reformed Jacobins' noviciate in the Faubourg St Germain in 1682–3 and, from 1712 to 1720, on the priory of St-Martin-des-Champs.

Bullet's reputation, however, is based mainly on the building of châteaux and town houses, especially the design of their façades. One of his first commissions was for the palace (1681) in Bourges for Archbishop Phélypeaux de La Vrillière, only one wing of which was completed. He also produced plans for the archepiscopal palace in Cambrai, but his major work was the Château d'Issy (destr. 1870) at Portes de Paris (Hauts-de-Seine). In 1686 Bullet built an isolated house of almost square plan for Denis Talon, the Assistant Public Prosecutor at Châtelet. Among his surviving Parisian town houses are those of Le Peletier de Souzy (29 Rue de Sévigné, 1686–7); Amelot de Chaillou (78 Rue des Archives, 1702); and Vouvray (57 Rue Cuvier, 1708).

Bullet also played a major role, with Jules Hardouin Mansart, in the development of the Place Vendôme. In 1699 he suggested a plan for the transformation of the square (around which he had bought several plots of land), and many buyers entrusted him with the task of building their town houses behind the uniform façades. Bullet was forced to modify the traditional arrangement of apartments that he had used in the Le Peletier and Amelot de Chaillou residences in order to give the rooms an attractive outlook over the square and, at the same time, to provide these residences with all the conveniences of an independent hôtel arranged around one or two courtyards. Thus, at the Hôtel d'Evreux (no. 19) the coachman's passage, situated in one of the cut-off corners of the building, leads to a rectangular court with a semicircular end, beyond which stands the *corps de logis* between court and garden. Bullet's plans show the changing axes of the apartments skilfully articulated within circular or oval halls.

Bullet was interested in all technical problems affecting the work of architects and engineers. His *Architecture pratique* was used by builders for over a century as a convenient handbook containing descriptions and appraisals of architectural works and incorporating elementary primers on geometry and public law. Although Blondel remained a lasting influence, Bullet's remaining works and numerous drawings, collected by Carl Hårleman, reveal his borrowings from Vitruvius and his debts to Vignola and, particularly, Palladio. The buildings of his contemporaries Bernini, Louis Le Vau, François Mansart and Jules Hardouin Mansart also influenced him but left scope for the personal expression that created his characteristic style, a blend of restraint and austerity. His use of columns was restricted to a few projecting parts of his façades, while the rhythm was obtained by using arcades on the ground floor, rows of pilasters, and even more by the noble simplicity of the channelled stonework. Decoration was applied to the large triangular pediments surmounting the usual three-part frontal sections of the building and to the circular medallions applied to the façades (as at the Hôtel Amelot). His majestic internal staircases, for example at the Hôtel Amelot and Hôtel Le Peletier (where, as a surprising novelty the banister is in cast iron), rank with those of François Mansart, Jules Hardouin Mansart and Robert de Cotte.

WRITINGS

Traité de l'usage du pantomètre (Paris, 1675)
Traité du nivellement (Paris, 1688)
L'Architecture pratique qui comprend le détail du toise et du devis des ouvrages (Paris, 1691, *R*/1838)
Observations sur la nature et sur les effets de la mauvais odeur de lieux d'aisances et cloaques (Paris, 1692)

BIBLIOGRAPHY

Från Ludwig XIV Paris: Pierre Bullet originalritingingar [From Louis XIV's Paris: Pierre Bullet's original drawings] (exh. cat. by E. Bier, Stockholm, Nmus., 1945)
E. Langenskiöld: *Pierre Bullet, the Royal Architect* (Stockholm, 1959)
R. Strandberg: 'Les Projets d'autel conçus par Pierre Bullet pour St-Germain-des-Prés', *Gaz. B.-A.*, lxxi (1968), p. 33
J.-P. Babelon: 'Une Oeuvre mal connue de Pierre Bullet: L'Hôtel Amelot de Chaillou', *Bull. Mnmtl*, cxxxvi/4 (1978), pp. 325–39

(2) Jean-Baptiste Bullet (de Chamblain) (*b* Paris, 1665; *d* Paris, 1726). Son of (1) Pierre Bullet. He was trained by his father and followed the teachings of the Académie Royale d'Architecture, where he was appointed a fellow in 1699. An excellent draughtsman, he first worked with his father on a project for St-Germain-des-Prés (*c.* 1704) and later produced designs for St-Sulpice (*c.* 1725) and St-Roche (1722–6). At the Place Vendôme he was involved in the construction of the Villemaré, Poisson and Bourvalais houses (nos 9 and 11–13). An examination of the drawings of Pierre and Jean-Baptiste Bullet reveals how Jean-Baptiste gradually broke away from the Louis XIV style of his father to develop a style characteristic of the French Regency period or of early Rococo, both in his façades, which were decorated with sculpted mascarons or consoles and balconies, and in the interior decorations, which were executed in a livelier style. His two best-known works are the Château de Champs (1703–6; Champs-sur-Marne; *see* CHAREAU, fig. 3) for the financier Paul Poisson of Bourvalais, on a plan inspired by the château at Vaux-le-Vicomte, with a large oval saloon on the garden side of the building, and the Hôtel Dodun (21 Rue de Richelieu), built a little after 1715. The former displays a rigorous approach in the rhythm of the wings, the uniform Gothic roofs and the sobriety of ornamentation typified by the apartments' large pilasters, similar to those at Versailles and Trianon, and yet the affluence and grace of the 18th century are apparent. At the Hôtel Dodun a freer inventive spirit was expressed in the extraordinary staircase and in the panelling of the apartments (now installed in the Irish embassy in Paris and at Waddesdon Manor, Bucks).

BIBLIOGRAPHY

L. Hautecoeur: *Architecture classique*, ii, pt 1 (1948), pp. 689–93; ii, pt 2 (1948), pp. 516–17; iii (1950), p. 148

R. Strandberg: 'Jean-Baptiste Bullet de Chamblain, Architecte du Roi', *Bull. Soc. Hist. A. Fr.* (1962), p. 193

M. Gallet: *Paris Domestic Architecture of the 18th Century* (London, 1972), p. 147

JEAN-PIERRE BABELON

Bullinger, Johann Balthasar, I (*b* Langnau, 30 Nov 1713; *d* Zurich, 31 March 1793). Swiss painter, draughtsman and printmaker. He spent an unproductive period of training with the engraver Melchior Füssli (1677–1736) and from 1729 served a three-year apprenticeship with the painter Johann Simmler (1693–1748). Bullinger travelled in northern Italy and from 1733 to 1735 was a pupil of Giambattista Tiepolo in Venice. He returned to Zurich in 1735, then from 1736 to 1737 travelled on foot through Solothurn, Neuenburg and Berne, painting landscapes and portraits. In 1738 he went to Düsseldorf, then began three years of study in Amsterdam. In 1742 he settled in Zurich, where he painted interiors and began etching. In 1756 he published a collection of landscapes after Johann Franz Ermels (1641–93), the landscape painter Felix Meyer (1653–1713) and his own drawings, and in 1770 a similar collection of *100 Schweizer Prospekten.* Bullinger's work became known in Paris through the engraver and collector Jean-Georges Wille. Bullinger's landscapes, unlike those of his Swiss contemporaries, were based on German Baroque models; they were studio pieces of fantastical composition, which did not aim to reflect observed reality. The compositions are clearly divided into foreground, middle ground and background and are assembled from props—rocks, trees, clouds, figure and animal groups—like stage sets. In 1773 he became a professor at the newly founded art academy in Zurich, a post he held until his death.

His grandson Johann Balthasar Bullinger II (1777–1844), a clergyman and dilettante artist, was more important as a collector. Johann Balthasar II's landscape drawings and etchings are of little significance. Some of his drawings were engraved by Heinrich Meyer (1802–77) and Johann Hürlimann (1793–1850). He assembled an important collection of 5200 landscape engravings by Heinrich Meyer, Johann Jakob Biedermann and S. Kobell and two volumes of drawings by his grandfather.

BIBLIOGRAPHY

SKL; Thieme–Becker

J. Gantner and A. Reinle: *Die Kunst der Renaissance, des Barock, des Klassizismus* (1956), iii of *Kunstgeschichte der Schweiz von den Anfängen bis zum Beginn des 20. Jahrhunderts* (Frauenfeld and Leipzig, 1936–62), pp. 326–8

CHRISTINA FREHNER-BÜHLER

Bullion, Claude de (*b c.* 1570; *d* Paris, 22 Dec 1640). French administrator and patron. He came from a distinguished family of lawyers and himself achieved high office, becoming Maître des Requêtes, Conseiller in the Parlement and in 1632 Surintendant des Finances. He appears to have been an able minister; he was awarded the Cordon Bleu of the Order of St Esprit in recognition of his creation of the *louis*, a gold coin worth 10 livres. The largest part of his expenditure on the arts was devoted to his residences: the hôtel particulier in the Rue Plâtrière, Paris (now Rue J. J. Rousseau), which he acquired in 1613, and the château of Wideville, Yvelines, built in 1580, which he purchased from René de Longueil in 1630. He entrusted the town house to Salomon de Brosse, who enlarged and transformed it. There were two galleries for paintings; for the lower one Bullion commissioned from Jacques Blanchard in 1634 a set of allegorical paintings of *The Months*, painted in the artist's characteristically sensuous manner. By 1765 Antoine-Nicolas Dezallier d'Argenville noted that the paintings had been badly damaged by damp; they no longer survive. In 1634 Bullion also commissioned Simon Vouet to decorate the vaulted upper gallery with a series of 24 paintings of the *Adventures of Ulysses* (destr.). The stucco frames were executed by Jacques Sarazin. In 1639 Bullion commissioned Philibert Le Roy (*fl* 1623–44) to carry out some improvements for the interior of the château of Wideville and expended considerable sums on embellishing the grounds with new pools, fountains and statues, commissioned from Sarazin and Philippe de Buyster, and with a grotto or nymphaeum (1635), decorated by Vouet and Sarazin. Shortly before his death Bullion commissioned Vouet to decorate other parts of the estate, a gallery and an aviary.

BIBLIOGRAPHY

G. Brice: *Description nouvelle de ce qu'il y a de plus remarquable dans la ville de Paris* (Paris, 1684, rev. 7/1752), pp. 470–71

H. Sauval: *Histoire et recherches des antiquités de la ville de Paris*, ed. C.-B. Rousseau, ii (Paris, 1724/*R* 1733, 1750), p. 192

A. -N. Dezallier d'Argenville: *Voyage pittoresque de Paris ou indication de tout ce qu'il y a de plus beau dans cette grande ville en peinture, sculpture et architecture* (Paris, 1749, rev. 4/1765), pp. 173–5

G. Tallemant des Réaux: *Historiettes*, ii (Paris, 1834, rev. 1854–8), pp. 145–50, 151–60

E. Bonnaffé: *Dictionnaire des amateurs français du XVIIème siècle* (Paris, 1884)

M. Digard: *Jacques Sarazzin* (Paris, 1934)

C. Grodecki: 'La Construction du château de Wideville et sa place dans l'architecture française au dernier quart du XVIIe siècle', *Bull. Mnmtl*, cxxxvi (1978), pp. 135–78

Vouet (exh. cat. by J. Thuillier, B. Brejon de Lavergnée and D. Lavalle, Paris, Grand Pal., 1990–91)

PIERRE CHALEIX

Bullock, George (*b* 1778 or 1782–3; *d* London, 1 May 1818). English cabinetmaker and sculptor. He seems to have acquired an early training in sculpture from his mother, who made a display of life-size waxwork figures, exhibited in and around Birmingham from 1794. By 1798 he had gained a reputation as a portrait sculptor and soon set up independently as a 'Miniature-painter and Portrait-modeller in Rice-paste'. His brother, William Bullock, opened a 'Cabinet of Curiosites' in Birmingham in 1800, moving to Liverpool in 1801. Bullock joined him there and by 1804 had gone into partnership with a looking-glass maker, William Stoakes of Church Street, Liverpool. They advertised themselves as 'Cabinet Makers, General Furnishers and Marble Workers' and in 1805 supplied Gothic furniture designed by Bullock to Cholmondeley Castle, Ches (*in situ*). The following year Bullock set up on his own in Bold Street, Liverpool, selling furniture and bronze ornaments. By 1806 he had acquired the Mona Marble quarries in Anglesey and sold 'fashionable and elegant Sculptured and Plain Chimney Pieces' at a separate showroom in Church Street.

In 1804 Bullock exhibited six busts at the Royal Academy, London, including those of *Henry Blundell* (marble), *William Roscoe* (plaster) and *Sir James Edward Smith* (plaster; all Liverpool, Walker A.G.). In 1810 he showed nine busts at the Liverpool Academy, of which he was founding president (1810–12). Around 1809 or 1810 Bullock was briefly in partnership with the architect Joseph Michael Gandy, as 'architects, modellers, sculptors, marble masons, cabinet-makers and upholsterers', probably working together at Storrs Hall, on Lake Windermere, Cumbria, and Bolton Hall, N. Yorks, both for Colonel John Bolton (1756–1837). Gandy may have been involved in Bullock's antiquarian refurbishment of Speke Hall, Liverpool, for Richard Watt (*d* 1812) in 1811.

Between 1812 and 1814 Bullock transferred his business to London, again following his brother, who had left Liverpool in 1810 to create a renowned museum (including his large collection of arms and armour) at the Egyptian Hall, Piccadilly. In 1813 George Bullock set up his own Grecian Rooms in the Egyptian Hall, but moved the following year to a large house in Tenterden Street, with manufacturing premises in Oxford Street adjoining his back garden. These included polishing rooms for marble and a Calico Room for printing upholstery fabrics in addition to furniture workshops. Bullock's major furnishing commissions during the remainder of his life were at Blair Castle, Tayside, for John Murray, 4th Duke of Atholl (begun 1814); Longwood, St Helena, for the use of Napoleon Bonaparte (1815); Tew Park, Oxon, for Matthew Robinson Boulton; Abbotsford (nr Melrose, Borders) for Sir Walter Scott; and Battle Abbey, E. Sussex, for Sir Godfrey Webster (all from 1816). The designer Richard Bridgens, who had known Bullock in Liverpool, was involved in the antiquarian schemes at both Abbotsford and Battle Abbey.

The majority of Bullock's furniture is in a massive Regency Neo-classical style, although he also designed in the Gothic, Elizabethan and Jacobean manners. He pioneered the use of native British materials, using such woods as larch for cabinets at Blair Castle, and Mona and Scottish marbles. His Neo-classical furniture is often finely decorated with stylized marquetry of various woods and metals, and splendid brass or ormolu mounts. After Bullock's sudden death in 1818 the workshops continued to operate until the following May, when the stock-in-trade, including 290 drawings and designs for furniture by Bullock, was sold by Christie's (3–5 May, 13–15 May). One purchaser was a 'Wilkinson', who may be linked to the book of tracings by Thomas Wilkinson 'from the designs of the late Mr George Bullock, 1820' (Birmingham, Mus. & A.G.), which constitutes the major source of information on Bullock's work.

UNPUBLISHED SOURCES

Birmingham, Mus. & A.G. [bk of tracings by T. Wilkinson after Bullock's designs]

BIBLIOGRAPHY

G. Beard and C. Gilbert, eds: *Dictionary of English Furniture Makers* (London, 1986)

George Bullock: Cabinet Maker (exh. cat., London, Blairman & Sons; Liverpool, Sudley A.G.; 1988)

ROSAMOND ALLWOOD

Bullock, Wynn [Percy Wingfield] (*b* Chicago, IL, 18 April 1902; *d* Monterey, CA, 16 Nov 1975). American photographer. He was brought up in South Pasadena, CA, and he moved to New York in the early 1920s to attend Columbia University and to study singing and music. He was a professional tenor before moving in 1928 to Paris, where he lived for two years and became increasingly interested in the visual arts and photography. He bought his first camera to document his intermittent tours around the Continent. Returning to the USA in 1931, Bullock briefly considered a career in real estate or law before enrolling in the Los Angeles Art Center School in 1938. There he studied photography with Edward Kaminski (1895–1964), who encouraged the creative use of the medium, in particular surrealistic experimentation.

Bullock's early work reflected the experimental approach of his teacher. He developed a solarization technique, patenting it in 1948, which photographically produced a line drawing of the outlines of objects rather than a conventional continuous tone image. He also worked in the carbro colour print process, a complex technique used to produce brilliant, highly focused colour prints (*see* PHOTOGRAPHY, §I). His first one-man show was held in 1941 at the Los Angeles County Museum, where he exhibited his Art Center School photographs. In 1940–41 he also studied with the semanticist Alfred Korzybski (1879–1950), who stressed the principle that words as labels interfere with perception. Bullock became increasingly concerned with the philosophical aspects of photography and the meaningfulness of his photographs as symbols.

In 1946 Bullock settled in the coastal town of Monterey, CA, and opened a commercial photography studio. After meeting the photographer Edward Weston in 1948, Bullock radically changed his artistic direction and decided to explore natural imagery. The Californian coastline provided him with an abundance of richly textured environments for solitary nature studies and as backgrounds for his provocative nudes. Edward Steichen, as Director of the Department of Photography at the Museum of Modern Art in New York, was an early enthusiast of Bullock's work and featured his *Child in the Forest* (1951; Tucson, U. AZ, Cent. Creative Phot.) in the Museum's landmark exhibition, the *Family of Man*, in 1955.

Bullock claimed that he was always an intuitive photographer, who only much later developed the concepts to substantiate his work. He believed that the principles of 'space-time' and 'opposites' were important visual tools with which we could better perceive the world. These beliefs are illustrated in his juxtaposition of nude flesh against foliage and timber and in his time exposures, which juxtapose static and mobile elements such as trees and creeping mist, and which were achieved by using filters, small lens aperture sizes and lengthy exposures. His finest prints impart a mystical connotation within the framework of a straight photograph.

WRITINGS

The Photograph as Symbol (Capitola, 1976)

BIBLIOGRAPHY

B. Bullock: *Wynn Bullock* (San Francisco, 1971)
Wynn Bullock: 20 Color Photographs/Light Abstractions (exh. cat., Santa Clara U., CA, De Saisset Mus., 1972)
L. DeCock, ed.: *Wynn Bullock: Photography, A Way of Life* (Dobbs Ferry, 1973)
D. Fuess: *Wynn Bullock* (Millerton, 1976)
H. Jones, ed.: 'Wynn Bullock: American Lyric Tenor', *Cent. Creative Phot.*, 2 (Sept 1976) [whole issue]
C. Lamb and C. Ludlow, eds: *Wynn Bullock Archive*, Cent. Creative Phot., Guide Ser., 6 (Tucson, 1982)
B. Bullock-Wilson and E. Bullock, eds: *Wynn Bullock: Photographing the Nude* (Salt Lake City, 1984)

RICHARD LORENZ

Bull's eye. *See* OEIL-DE-BOEUF.

Buls, Charles [Karel] **(François Gommaire)** (*b* Brussels, 13 Oct 1837; *d* Uccle, 13 July 1914). Belgian urban planner and writer. The son of a jeweller, he spent a somewhat isolated youth: poor health enhanced a shyness, which set him apart from other children. Although he completed secondary schooling, in terms of his vocation he was largely self-taught. After nearly two years of artistic training in Paris and Italy, he gave up plans to follow in his father's trade, choosing instead to take up the cause of educational reform. With some of his liberal friends he founded in 1864 the Ligue de l'Enseignement, a pressure group with close ties to Masonic circles. He particularly devoted himself to drawing primary instruction away from ecclesiastical influence and to setting up a new teaching method based on comprehension and experience rather than on learning by rote. In 1875 he became the first director of a successful model school created according to these new didactical objectives.

All the while Buls was deeply concerned with the development of the decorative arts. Disappointment with the appeal of the artistic production of his time made him turn to history for roots and principles that might provide a more invigorating approach. Influenced by the mid-19th-century German art historians, Karl Schnaase and Wilhelm Lübke, and by the aesthetic theories of Gottfried Semper, he soon adopted their rationalist thesis whereby each of the decorative arts was to be determined by its use, the properties of its materials and the method of construction. Philosophical considerations by Kant and Schopenhauer convinced him that eternal ideas were the foundation of aesthetical contemplation, ideas that Buls related to the inherent nature and tradition of the population and the place from which the artistic expression emanated. He thus arrived at the concept of a national art that he was to defend for the rest of his life.

Buls's election to the Brussels city council in 1877 initiated a rapid political ascent. By 1879 he had been placed in charge of education and became mayor in 1881. Even when elected to parliament (1882–4 and 1886–94), he continued to administer the Belgian capital, until he voluntarily resigned in 1899. During his period as mayor Buls drastically changed the policy of great urban transformations, such as the covering of the River Senne and slum clearance, initiated by his predecessor Anspach. He continued to modernize the city but resorted to more effective small-scale operations, which appealed to middle-class proprietors. Particularly innovative were his overall attempts to preserve the historical texture of the city. These efforts fundamentally served the same policy of upgrading the city centre but introduced a cultural alternative to the stereotypical solutions of the technocratical planning of the time. His conservation scheme for the Grand-Place, the historic central square of Brussels, which was restored to its ancient splendour during his mayoralty, secured him an international reputation.

In response to a proposal of King Leopold II, who intended to replace the vivid commercial district of Montagne de la Cour, Brussels, with a more insular and academic complex of museums and archives, Buls published his famous pamphlet *Esthétique des villes* (1893). In this text, which was later translated into German, English and Italian, Buls not only argued against the project but systematically drew up the theoretical foundation for an artistic conception of urban planning policy. He applied his rationalist approach towards art in general to planning and asserted that the integration of development with existing local conditions far better served the functional requirements of a city than the stultifying uniformity of the usual aprioristic schemes. Against their artificial rigidity, he proposed the organic development that had characterized cities in the past. These ideas were closely connected with the new aesthetic principles of such German and Austrian urban planners as Camillo Sitte and Cornelius Gurlitt. Buls reviewed and translated their principal contributions and acted as an important intermediary for the circulation of their rationalist approach to the aesthetics of urban planning in French-speaking Europe. As a recognized authority his advice was notably followed in conservation projects for the Piazza Navona in Rome, and the surroundings of the cathedral of Ste Gudule (La Collégiale des SS Michel-et-Gudule) in Brussels.

After Buls retired from politics, the more functional and constructive rationality that had characterized his earlier arguments gave way to a greater emphasis on preservation and on determining rules to achieve picturesque settings. References to national tradition and character predominate in his later writings, affiliations that inspired him to make serious criticisms of Otto Wagner's famous theoretical study for the development of a big city, *Die Grossstadt: Eine Studie über diese* (1911).

WRITINGS

L'Architecture moderne', *Rev. Belgique* (1874), pp. 324–7
'Histoire de l'architecture', *Patria Belgica*, iii (1875), pp. 577–612
'Esthétique des arts industriels', *Rev. Belgique* (1876), pp. 305–15; (1877), pp. 197–210; (1878), pp. 66–92
Esthétique des villes (Brussels, 1893)
La Restauration des monuments anciens (Brussels, 1903)
'L'Esthétique de Rome', *Rev. U. Bruxelles* (1903), pp. 401–10

De la disposition et du développement des rues et des espaces libres dans les villes (Brussels, 1906)
L'Evolution du pignon à Bruxelles (Brussels, 1908)
L'Isolement des vieilles églises (Brussels, 1910)

BIBLIOGRAPHY

M. Martens: *Charles Buls, ses papiers conservés aux archives de la ville* (Brussels, 1958)
M. Smets: *L'Avènement de la cité-jardin en Belgique* (Brussels, 1958)
——: *Pierres et rues: Bruxelles croissance urbaine, 1780–1980* (Brussels, 1982)
M. Bots, ed.: *Het dagboek van C. Buls* (Brussels, 1987)
M. Bots and others: *Karel Buls, wereldreiziger met een hart voor Brussel* (Brussels, 1987)

MARCEL SMETS

Bunbury, Henry William (*b* Mildenhall, Suffolk, 1750; *d* Keswick, Cumberland [now Cumbria], 10 May 1811). English draughtsman. He was the younger son of the Rev. Sir William Bunbury and was educated at Westminster School and Cambridge. After a Grand Tour in the late 1760s he began a military career with a colonelcy in the Suffolk Militia, purchased for him by his brother. In 1787 he was appointed equerry to Frederick, Duke of York, and became a familiar and popular figure at court. Bunbury's artistic career began at Westminster with a drawing of a *Boy Riding on a Pig* (London, BM). He worked in pencil and crayon, treating subjects from his experiences that were largely shared by his patrons, including Cambridge (the *Hopes of the Family*, 1773; see George, pl. 73); the Grand Tour (a *Tour to Foreign Parts*, 1778; G pl. 136); military life (*Visit to the Camp*; 1779; G pl. 52); and particularly horsemanship: he published *An Academy for Grown Horsemen* (1787) and *Annals of Horsemanship* (1791) under the pseudonym Geoffrey Gambado. His caricatures are gentle social satires, and only one example, *A Chop House* (1781; London, BM; G pl. 120), includes identifiable portraits, those of Samuel Johnson and James Boswell. In 1792 Bunbury was commissioned by Thomas Macklin to illustrate a *Shakespeare Gallery* in competition to that of John Boydell. The final plate appeared in 1796, by which time the market had been depressed by the war with France, and the series remained incomplete; the female figures owe a debt to Francis Wheatley. Bunbury's friends included Joshua Reynolds, who was his second son's godfather, Oliver Goldsmith and David Garrick. His position as a gentleman and courtier undoubtedly increased his prestige in the eyes of his contemporaries; Horace Walpole compared him favourably to William Hogarth.

BIBLIOGRAPHY

M. D. George: *Catalogue of Political and Personal Satires Preserved in the Department of Prints and Drawings in the British Museum*, 7 vols (London, 1935–54/*R* 1978)
——: *Hogarth to Cruikshank: Social Change in Graphic Satire* (London, 1967) [G]
J. Riely: 'Horace Walpole and "the Second Hogarth"', *18th C. Stud.*, ix (Autumn 1975), pp. 28–44
J. Bailey, ed.: *A Folio of Shakespeare Engravings Taken from the Drawings of Henry William Bunbury* (London, 1978)
Henry William Bunbury (exh. cat. by H. Belsey, Sudbury, Gainsborough's House, 1983)
English Caricature: 1620 to the Present (exh. cat., ed. R. Godfrey; London, V&A, 1984)

DAVID RODGERS

Bunchō (i). *See* TANI BUNCHŌ.

Bunchō (ii). *See* IPPITSUSAI BUNCHŌ.

Bundi. City in Rajasthan, India. It flourished in the 17th–18th centuries AD as capital of the state of the same name. It contains a wide variety of palaces, mansions (*hāvelīs*), temples, stepwells and gardens. The city is dominated by the Taragarh hill-fort, founded by the Rajput king Rao Deva in 1241; the palace on the hillside below contains many attractive structures, including the Ratan Mahal, built by Rao Ratan Singh (*reg* 1607–31), the beautifully painted Chatar Mahal by Rao Chatarsal (*reg* 1631–58) and the Chitra Shali by Rao Umed Singh (*reg* 1739–70) (*see* INDIAN SUBCONTINENT, §III, 7(ii)(b) and fig. 115). Bundi was also a centre of manuscript painting from the 17th century (*see* INDIAN SUBCONTINENT, §V, 4(iii)(c)).

BIBLIOGRAPHY

H. C. Ray: *Dynastic History of Northern India*, 2 vols (Calcutta, 1931)
K. C. Jain: *Ancient Cities and Towns of Rajasthan* (Delhi, 1972)
G. H. R. Tillotson: *The Rajput Palaces: The Development of an Architectural Style, 1450–1750* (London, 1987)

ASOK KUMAR DAS

Bundura, Cristoforo. *See* BONADURA, CRISTOFORO.

Bundzhikat [Bunjikath]. Site near the town of Shakhristan (Shahristan) in northern Tajikistan. Capital of the medieval state of Ustrushana, which occupied the region between the Syr River and the Hisar Range from Samarkand to Khodzhent, Bundzhikat was described in 10th to 12th-century sources as a large and densely populated town in a beautiful location with plenty of water and gardens. The city proper was surrounded by a special wall with two gates, while the nearby citadel had its own fortifications and the suburb its own wall with four gates. All three parts of the city, as well as the country palaces, houses, gardens and vineyards, were surrounded by an enceinte. Among the largest buildings were the central mosque in the city, the prison in the citadel and the king's palace in the suburb. The town got its water from the small Sarin River and six canals leading from it, along which there were over ten mills.

Archaeological investigation under the guidance of Professor N. Negmatov from the 1950s to the 1980s at the site of Kala-i Kakhkakh uncovered remains of this large Central Asian town, which flourished from the 7th to the 12th century, and many examples of metalwork, jewellery, textiles, ceramics, wall painting and wood-carving (*see* CENTRAL ASIA, §I, 3(iii)(a)). Within powerful fortifications, residential and artisanal quarters were found as well as multi-roomed buildings such as palaces, barracks and castles. In addition to pre-Islamic public and religious structures, there were mosques and mausolea. Buildings were decorated with superb polychrome wall paintings, both ornamental and figural, as well as wooden sculptures, furnishings and architectural fittings such as columns, balusters, friezes and cornices. Terracotta ornament and cut bricks were also used.

Among the masterpieces found at the site (all Dushanbe, Tajikistan Acad. Sci., Donish Inst. Hist., Archaeol. & Ethnog.) is a 6 m-long wall painting (7th century); depicting a Sogdian version of Romulus and Remus suckled by a she-wolf, a fragmentary scene of a goddess riding a lion (see fig.), as well as narrative scenes from the Ustrushana

Bundzhikat, fragment of a wall painting depicting a goddess riding a lion, 8th century AD (Dushanbe, Tajikistan Academy of Sciences, Donish Institute of History, Archaeology and Ethnography)

pantheon, battling demons, winged warriors, a king in a chariot, musician warriors and harpists (*see* CENTRAL ASIA, §I, 4(iv)(a)). A superb carved wooden panel (1.43×2.93 m) from the tympanum of the palace entrance bears an image of the battle between Good and Evil from the Iranian epic tradition. Other finds include glass carafes decorated with partridges, a glazed ceramic aquamanile in the form of a beast, sphero-conical ceramic vessels, a bronze platter and several ewers (one signed by master Ahmad), gold signet rings and other pieces of jewellery.

BIBLIOGRAPHY

N. N. Negmatov and S. G. Khmel'nitskiy: *Srednevekovyy Shakhristan* [Medieval Shakhristan] (Dushanbe, 1966)

V. L. Voronina and N. N. Negmatov: 'Otkrytiye Ustrushany' [The discovery of Ustrushana], *Nauka i chelovechestvo: 1975* [Science and humanity: 1975] (Moscow, 1974), pp. 51–72

N. N. Negmatov and V. M. Sokolovskiy: ' "Kapitoliyskaya volchitsa" v Tadzhikistane i legendy Yevrazii' ["The Capitoline Wolf" in Tajikistan and Eurasian legends], *Pamyatniki kul'tury: Novyye otkyritiye* [Cultural monuments: new discoveries] (Moscow, 1975), pp. 438–58

N. N. Negmatov: 'Reznoye panno dvortsa afshinov Ustrushany' [A carved panel from the Afshin Palace in Ustrushana], *Pamyatniki kul'tury: Novyye otkyritiye* [Cultural monuments: new discoveries] (Moscow, 1977), pp. 353–62

E. V. Kil'chevskaya and N. N. Negmatov: 'Shedevry torevtiki Ustrushany' [Masterpieces of Ustrushana metalwork], *Pamyatniki kul'tury: Novyye otkyritiye* [Cultural monuments: new discoveries] (Leningrad, 1979), pp. 458–70

Drevnosti tadzhikistana [Antiquities of Tajikistan] (exh. cat., ed. Ye. V. Zeymal'; Leningrad, Hermitage, 1985), nos 681–714, 806, 808–15, 820–22

N. N. NEGMATOV

Bunel, Jacob (*b* Blois, *bapt* 6 Oct 1558; *d* Paris, before 8 Oct 1614). French painter and draughtsman. He was the son of the painter François Bunel the elder (*d c.* 1580) and the brother of François Bunel the younger (1552–before 1599). According to his pupil Claude Vignon, he travelled to Spain early in his career, where he worked for Philip II at the Escorial and studied the works of Titian. Jacob then went to Rome, where he is said to have worked with Federico Zuccaro and Niccolò Pomarancio. By 1595 he had returned to France and from 1601 he was active in Paris at the Tuileries Palace, where he painted perspective decorations and views of towns captured by French troops (destr.), and at the Louvre, where he was Toussaint Dubreuil's principal collaborator on the decoration of the ceiling of the Petite Galerie (destr. 1661). After Dubreuil's death in 1602, Bunel's role in the decoration of the gallery was considerable, and from 1607, in collaboration with his wife, Marguerite Bahuche (*d c.* 1630), he executed a set of 28 life-size portraits of the kings and queens of France from the time of St Louis. This formed the principal decoration of the walls of the Petite Galerie. A preparatory drawing of *Henry IV* (Paris, Louvre) is all that remains of Bunel's contribution to this important scheme, which also included smaller portraits of the principal personages of each reign. Nothing survives of his other major decorative works for the Louvre, nor of the altarpieces for Paris churches mentioned by André Félibien and in other early sources, such as the *Pentecost* for the church of the Grands Augustins. A small number of drawings by him survive, including the *Head of a Man* and a *Sleeping Warrior* (both Paris, Louvre), as well as engravings after his portraits of *Henry IV* (by Thomas de Leu, 1605) and of the sculptor *Pietro Francavilla* (by Pieter de Jode I, 1613), and one after a mythological subject (by Hendrik Oldeland, *fl* 1636–43). Too little remains to give any real idea of the style of a painter who was clearly highly esteemed in his own day.

BIBLIOGRAPHY

Thieme–Becker

A. Félibien: *Entretien sur les vies et sur les oeuvres des plus excellens peintres anciens et modernes* (Trévoux, 1725/*R* London, 1967)

L. Dimier: *Histoire de la peinture de portrait en France au XVIe siècle*, 3 vols (Paris and Brussels, 1924–6), i, pp. 168, 188, 142, 189, 194; ii (1925), pp. 286–8

L.-H. Collard and E.-J. Ciprut: *Nouveaux Documents sur le Louvre* (Paris, 1963)

S. Béguin: 'Toussaint Dubreuil, premier peintre de Henri IV', *A. France*, iv (1964), pp. 86–107

M.-A. Fleury: *Documents du minutier central concernant les peintres, les sculpteurs et les graveurs au XVIIe siècle 1600–1650* (Paris, 1969)

F. Bardon: *Le Portrait mythologique à la cour de France sous Henri IV et Louis XIII* (Paris, 1974), p. 86

S. Béguin: 'Nouvelles Attributions à Toussaint Dubreuil', *Etudes d'art français offertes à Charles Sterling* (Paris, 1975), pp. 165–74

Dessins français du XVIIe siècle (exh. cat., ed. R. Bacou; Paris, Louvre, 1984–5), p. 10

Torquato Tasso tra letteratura, musica, teatro et arti figurative (exh. cat., ed. A. Buzzoni; Ferrara, Castello Estense, 1985), pp. 238–45

J. Pérot: '*Henri IV à la bataille d'Arques*, peinture de J. Bunel?', *Bull. Soc. Amis Château Pau*, 99–100 (1985), pp. 6–7

C. de Mérindol: 'La *Pietà* de Nouans et le triptyque de l'Hôtel Jacques-Coeur à Bourges', *Rev. A.* [Paris], lxvii (1985), pp. 49–58
D. Cordellier: 'Toussaint Dubreuil, "singulier en son art"', *Bull. Soc. Hist. A. Fr.* (1987), pp. 7–33
C. Scaillérez: 'Le grand Cabinet de la Reine au Louvre: Le Part de Gabriel Honnet et de Guillaume Dumée', *Rev. Louvre*, no. 3 (1989), pp. 156–63
S. Béguin: 'Tradition et modernité dans les arts graphiques', *Henri IV et la reconstruction du royaume* (exh. cat., Pau, Mus. N. Chateau, 1989, and Paris, Archvs N.: Hôtel de Rohan, 1989–90), pp. 327–43
D. Cordellier: 'Un Modèle de Dubreuil pour les portraits de la Petite Galerie du Louvre', *Rev. Louvre*, no. 6 (1990), pp. 484–8

PHILIPPE ROUILLARD

Bungalow. Detached or free-standing dwelling, usually of one storey and frequently having a verandah; in southern Asia and Africa it denotes a detached dwelling of modern design, not necessarily of one storey. The bungalow functions as a permanent suburban and country home, as a vacation home and as a building type associated with the elderly and retired. Originally a form of dwelling native to Bengal, the bungalow was adapted by the British during their imperial rule over India and transplanted to Britain in the late 19th century. It subsequently became part of the suburban vernacular of the British Isles, North America, Australasia and other areas of the world influenced by British colonialism. To a lesser extent it has also been adopted in Europe and elsewhere.

Bangla was a Hindi or Mahratti term meaning 'of or belonging to Bengal' used in the 17th century to describe the type of dwelling-hut built by Bengal peasants. Its distinguishing features were the raised plinth and roof structure made from two bent bamboo poles, which, when thatched, resulted in two sloping sides forming the segment of a circle and resembling an overturned boat. The first known reference in English to such dwellings dates from 1659, but this form clearly has a longer history. Europeans in India made use of this structure, but with the permanent settlement of the British after their military victory at Plassey (1757) another version of the peasants' hut was appropriated and adapted for use by British army officers and colonial administrators.

According to the English artist William Hodges, the bungalows in 18th-century India were 'generally raised on a base of brick, one, two or three feet from the ground, and consist of only one storey; the plan of them usually is a large room in the centre for an eating and sitting room, and rooms at each corner for sleeping; the whole is covered with one general thatch which comes low to each side; the spaces between the angle rooms are *viranders* or open porticoes to sit in during the evenings' (*Travels in India*, 1793). The thatched version, extensive in size, was supplemented in the 19th century by a more classical design, built in brick and stucco with a flat roof and pillared verandah and with a more extended plan. Located in large compounds of two, ten or twenty acres, the bungalow became the archetypal dwelling of the colonial regime, used widely in civil stations and military cantonments.

This classical version of the bungalow formed the basic residential unit in the planning of New Delhi from 1911. In India and British colonies elsewhere the bungalow became a symbol of imperial power but also, in its separation from the indigenous settlement, a vehicle for economic and cultural change, paving the way for new social and spatial forms in the Indian city. Today in India the term bungalow refers not just to a one-storey house but also to any detached, Western-style dwelling.

Britain's colonial connections at a time of urban expansion in Britain brought about the introduction of the bungalow, both in name and single-storey form, to the West. The first few were built between 1869 and the mid-1870s on the north Kent coast of England, two hours by train from London, at the exclusive resorts of Westgate and Birchington. These large and spacious dwellings were an early instance of the purpose-built second or vacation home, part of a new-style type of leisure resort created from the surplus wealth generated by industrial capitalism. The connections enjoyed by the architects John Taylor (1833–1912) and J. P. Seddon with artistic circles in London brought the ailing Dante Gabriel Rossetti to Birchington to become, perhaps, the first person to die (1882) in a bungalow in England.

With the development of prefabricated wood and iron versions from the 1870s, the bungalow quickly became popular. For better-off members of an increasingly complex urban society, the seaside bungalow offered novel simplicity and a carefree outdoor life. From the 1890s Bungalow Town was developed at Shoreham-by-Sea, W. Sussex; H. G. Wells described it as 'a fruit of the reaction of artistic-minded and carelessly-living people against the costly and uncomfortable social stiffness of the more formal seaside resorts . . . a fashion with a certain Bohemian-spirited class' (*In the Days of the Comet*, 1906).

The introduction of the innovative architectural form of the bungalow into the countryside (see fig.) owed much to the Arts and Crafts architect Robert Alexander Briggs (1858–1916), whose *Bungalows and Country Residences* (1891)—which was in its fifth edition by 1901—popularized the idea on both sides of the Atlantic. Varied in form, generally having one floor though often with bedrooms in the roofspace, designs by 'Bungalow' Briggs as well as by numerous others were meant for middle-class weekend homes in the country as well as the wealthier suburbs.

The bungalow achieved its greatest popularity in North America. In three decades after 1905, improved and developed by innumerable anonymous builders as well as by known architects, notably GREENE & GREENE, it became the most characteristic form of domestic architecture in California, among many other places. In suburban Los Angeles the attraction lay in its potential for formal variety, low cost and artistic design; it also combined the virtues of indoor and outdoor life. In such a developed free-market economy as that of the USA, where a detached family home is part of the American dream, the one-and-a-half-storey bungalow spread rapidly through the suburbs as far as Canada, becoming one of the first truly nationwide housing forms, the predecessor of another popular building type, the ranch-house.

The popularity of the bungalow in Britain became widespread between *c.* 1920 and 1939 and again after World War II. Its smaller size and lower cost as well as the convenience of single-storey living were deemed attractive by people at many social levels, especially with the decline of domestic service. With its penetration of the countryside preserves of the landed classes, the cheaply

Country bungalow designed by Arthur W. Yeomans, Hawkchurch, Devon, 1904; from *Building News*, 22 April 1904

built bungalow became a subject of contention, and 'bungaloid' a term of abuse. New town and country planning laws controlled its development and, while preserving the countryside for the bourgeoisie, also helped to contain an urban proletariat in the towns. At the end of the 20th century, as the population continued to move from the terraced housing of declining post-industrial cities to the expanding car-based suburbs or country towns, the one- or two-car bungalow became established in the British Isles. The presence of the bungalow elsewhere in the world can be ascribed to similar political, economic, social and cultural developments.

BIBLIOGRAPHY

A. D. King: *Colonial Urban Development* (London, 1976)
J. Pott: *Old Bungalows in Bangalore* (London, 1977)
G. Herbert: *Pioneers of Prefabrication* (Princeton, 1978)
A. D. King: 'A Time for Space and a Space for Time: The Social Production of the Vacation House', *Buildings and Society*, ed. A. D. King (London, 1980), pp. 193-227
R. Winter: *The California Bungalow* (Los Angeles, 1980)
A. D. King: *The Bungalow: The Production of a Global Culture* (London, 1984)
C. Lancaster: *The American Bungalow* (New York, 1985)
A. L. Reeve: *From Hacienda to Bungalow: Northern New Mexico Houses, 1850–1912* (New Mexico, 1988)
G. Stickley: *Craftsman Bungalows* (New York, 1988)
J. Jakle and R. W. Bastian: *Common Houses in America's Small Towns: The Atlantic Seaboard to the Mississippi Valley* (Athens, GA, 1989)
A. D. King: *Urbanism, Colonialism and the World Economy* (London, 1990)
R. D. Parker: 'The Californian Bungalow and the Tyrolean Chalet: The Ill-fated Life of an American Vernacular', *J. Amer. Cult.*, xv/4 (1992), pp. 1–16

See also CHALET.

ANTHONY D. KING

Bunker, Dennis Miller (*b* New York, 6 Nov 1861; *d* Boston, MA, 28 Dec 1890). American painter. He was a founder-member of the 'Boston school' of painters and was the first artist to bring the Impressionist style to New England. From *c*. 1878 to 1881 he studied with William Merritt Chase, and from 1881 he studied in Paris with Jean-Léon Gérôme, returning to America in the autumn of 1885 to teach at the Cowles Art School in Boston. Although he held this post for only five years, he influenced many Bostonians (among them Isabella Stewart Gardner, founder of the Gardner Museum in Boston) to be more open to European ideas in art. After spending the summer of 1888 at Calcott, Salop, England, painting *plein-air* landscapes with John Singer Sargent, who was working closely with Claude Monet at the time, his colours became brighter and his brushwork grew looser. However, he always maintained the careful drawing he had learnt from Gérôme. Bunker's best-known works date from the last year or two of his life, such as *Jessica* (Boston, MA, Mus. F.A.) and the *Roadside Cottage: Medfield* (both 1890; Duxbury, MA, A. Complex Mus.). Bunker, whom Sargent once called the most gifted young American, died at 29 of influenza, just a few years after his first solo exhibition.

BIBLIOGRAPHY

R. H. I. Gammell: *Dennis Miller Bunker* (New York, 1953)
Dennis Miller Bunker (1861–1890) Rediscovered (exh. cat., ed. C. Ferguson; New Britain, CT, Mus. Amer. A., 1978)

MARK W. SULLIVAN

Bunny, Rupert (Charles Wulsten) [Charles Rupert Wulsten] (*b* St Kilda, nr Melbourne, 29 Sept 1864;

d Melbourne, 26 May 1947). Australian painter. After studying in Melbourne under G. F. Folingsby (*d* 1891), he moved to Europe in 1884 and studied in London under P. H. Calderon and in Paris under Jean-Paul Laurens, who introduced him to the Société des Artistes Français in 1887. His early works consisted mainly of mythological subjects and graceful images of pleasant Symbolist landscapes (e.g. *Pastoral*, *c.* 1893; Canberra, N.G.); he defected to the New Salon in 1901 and produced some less decorative works, including images of biblical subjects (e.g. the *Prodigal Son*, *c.* 1903; Melbourne, Wesley Church). A long series of paintings of women followed (e.g. the *Distant Song*, *c.* 1909; Canberra, N.G.), but his style again changed abruptly when in 1913 he exhibited at the Salon d'Automne a series of images of dancers, *The Rite* (untraced; repr. in *A. & Déc.*, xxxiv (1913), p. 170), that shows the influence of Primitivism. Although not attracted to the avant-garde, Bunny showed an adventurous spirit in his unusual sense of colour, sense of rhythm and witty use of his subjects' poses. He continued to live in Paris and London until 1933, when he returned to Melbourne, following the death of his French wife.

BIBLIOGRAPHY

D. Thomas: *Rupert Bunny, 1864–1947* (Melbourne, 1970)
M. Eagle: *The Art of Rupert Bunny* (Canberra, 1991)

MARY EAGLE

Bunsei [Kor. Mun-ch'ŏng] (*fl c.* 1450–60). Zen monk and ink painter, active in Japan. He may have come to Japan from Korea, where his work is also known: a couple of paintings in the National Museum of Korea in Seoul bear his seal. Moreover, some of his extant landscapes in Japan were done in Korean style. His seal, which appears on only a handful of paintings, is similar to that used by JOSETSU, with whom until the mid-20th century he was sometimes confused. Bunsei is thought to have worked at Daitokuji in Kyoto.

Bunsei's extant works suggest the influence of TENSHO SHŪBUN. They show a range of subjects, including several landscapes (Osaka, Masaki A. Mus.; Boston, MA, Mus. F.A.), a portrait of *Abbot Yosō of Daitokuji* (1452) and the popular ecumenical subject *Three Laughers of the Tiger Ravine* (Powers priv. col.). Bunsei's masterpiece is a painting of the famous *Buddhist Layman Yuima* (1457; Nara, Yamato Bunkakan). Whether in landscapes or figure compositions, Bunsei's delicate touch and sure sense of composition distinguish him as one of the greatest and most mysterious Muromachi period (1333–1568) ink painters (*see* JAPAN, §VI, 4(iii)).

BIBLIOGRAPHY

S. Shimizu and C. Wheelwright, eds: *Japanese Ink Painting* (Princeton, 1976)

KEN BROWN

Bunshaft, Gordon (*b* Buffalo, NY, 9 May 1909; *d* New York, 6 Aug 1990). American architect. He graduated in architecture at the Massachusetts Institute of Technology, Cambridge (BArch, 1933; MArch, 1935). In 1935–7 he was in Europe and North Africa on the Rotch Traveling Scholarship. On his return to New York in 1937 he joined the firm of SKIDMORE, OWINGS & MERRILL (SOM). In 1938, with Robert A. Green (*b* 1910), he submitted a design in the well-known Wheaton College Art Center (Illinois) competition, which aimed at bringing Modernism to the American campus. The scheme, which won an Honorable Mention, derived from Impington Village College (1936–9) by Walter Gropius and E. Maxwell Fry in Cambs, England, and the Bunshaft and Green design confirmed their acceptance of the International Style idiom. Bunshaft was thus among the first American architects to embrace European Modernism, but unlike others, such as Edward Durrell Stone, Philip Johnson and Eero Saarinen, he never rejected its machine-age imperatives. More pragmatic and vernacular in his approach, he never entered the arena of architectural theory, history or criticism.

Bunshaft served during World War II, returning to SOM in 1946 and becoming a partner in 1949. He remained a major designer in the firm until his retirement in the 1980s. His greatest success came with the construction of Lever House (1950–52), New York, one of the first completely Modernist high-rises in any American city (*see* INTERNATIONAL STYLE, fig. 2). It became the precedent for literally hundreds of similarly designed and constructed high-rises that characterize most American cities and many around the world. Its prefabricated aluminium and plate-glass curtain walls hang shorn of any hint of the craftsmanship necessary with walls of brick, stone or terracotta. Its specially designed movable scaffolding enables its sheath to be regularly and mechanically washed with Lever Brothers' products. Such a design quickly won support from the country's aggressive, expanding corporate establishment. The building's stilts are also significant since they open up much space at ground-level. Pedestrians are thereby enabled to abandon the gridiron flow pattern of New York's streets and freely cut across the space. This concept was, and continues to be, widely imitated, although some have suggested that such planning can contribute to a loss of sense of direction as well as clarity in the urban landscape if insensitively handled. The 24-storey building was later threatened by a scheme to build a yet higher structure on its site; many Post-modernists were in favour of demolishing the building that symbolized the 'less is a bore', glass-box type of Modernist architecture. However, the new scheme was rejected.

The success of Lever House brought Bunshaft and the firm many corporate commissions, to such an extent that offices were opened in Chicago and San Francisco in order to handle the volume of work, and with over 2000 staff the firm reached a size hitherto unprecedented. With the design of the Connecticut General Life Insurance complex (1957), Bloomfield, Bunshaft produced another design option for corporate architecture: sited on *c.* 250 acres, landscaped in the picturesque mode, the scheme was widely influential on firms wanting suburban or rural locations.

Among the urban buildings credited to Bunshaft are the Pepsi-Cola (now Olivetti) Building (1960), Chase Manhattan Bank (1962), Marine Midland Bank (1967) and the W. R. Grace Building (1973), 1114 Avenue of the Americas, all in New York. The last of these pioneered the concave sloped façade as a solution to the setback requirements of the city's zoning laws. Bunshaft also had international commissions: Banque Lambert (1965), Brussels; the Haj Terminal (1982) at King ʿAbd al-ʿAziz International Airport, near Mecca, Saudi Arabia (for illustration *see* AIRPORT); and the National Commercial Bank (1982), Jiddah, Saudi Arabia. His monumental commissions included the Lyndon Baines Johnson and Sid W. Richardson Library (1971), University of Texas at Austin, and the Hirshhorn Museum and Sculpture Garden (1974), Washington, DC.

BIBLIOGRAPHY

'Wheaton College Art Center', *Archit. Forum*, lxix/2 (1938), p. 155
'Batiment de bureaux, Bloomfield, Connecticut, Etats-Unis', *Archit. Aujourd'hui*, xxxv/48 (1965), pp. 8–10
'Banque Lambert, Brussels', *Archit. Rev.* [London], cxxxix/829 (1966), pp. 193–200
'In Praise of a Monument to Lyndon B. Johnson', *Archit. Rec.*, cl/1 (1971), pp. 113–20
D. Jacobs: 'The Establishment's Architect-plus', *NY Times Mag.* (23 July 1972), pp. 12–23
S. Stephens: 'Big Deals and Bitter Endings', *Artforum*, xiii/6 (1975), pp. 56–62
——: 'Museum as Monument', *Prog. Archit.*, lvi/3 (1975), pp. 42–7
C. Stoloff: 'Art Gallery and Sculpture Garden, Washington, DC', *Architect & Bldr*, xxv (March 1975), pp. 18–20
S. Abercrombie: 'Twenty-five Year Award Goes to Lever House', *AIA J.*, lxix/3 (1980), pp. 76–9

JAMES D. KORNWOLF

Bunt. *See* REVOLT GROUP.

Buon [Bon] **(i).** Italian family of sculptors and architects. They were active in Venice from the late 14th century to the late 15th. Giovanni Buon (*b c.* 1360; *d* 1442) ran a large workshop in Venice, where his son (1) Bartolomeo Buon was probably trained. Father and son took on a number of joint commissions until Giovanni's death, but the latter's contribution seems to have been a minor one. Attributions to Giovanni and Bartolomeo are many and so diverse that no consensus has been reached on their oeuvre. A complete lack of secure attributions to Giovanni has meant that there is no reliable basis for a reconstruction and appraisal of his career. In Bartolomeo's case the documents are more numerous, with several relating directly to specific works, although these works often show irreconcilable differences of style and quality. This uncertainty has led to widely differing accounts of his career (e.g. Wolters, 1976; Markham Schulz, 1978).

(1) Bartolomeo Buon (*b c.* 1400–10; *d c.* 1464–7). He is first mentioned as a sculptor in 1425. In 1427 he produced figures for the well-head of the Cà d'Oro, a sumptuous Gothic palace (1424–31) built in Venice for Marino Contarini. In this early work the drapery of the allegories of the *Virtues* shows clear allusions to the portal of the Corner Chapel in S Maria Gloriosa dei Frari, a work by the Master of the Mascoli Altar (*see* VENICE, §IV, 4). In another early work, the *Annunciation* (Frankfurt am Main, Liebieghaus), there are references to one of the saints on the Mascoli Altar in S Marco, Venice (*see* VENICE, §IV, 1(ii)). Agreement has not been reached on the attribution of the group of the *Judgement of Solomon*, situated on the north-west corner of the Doge's Palace (*see* VENICE, §IV, 6(i)). Probably created in the 1430s, it is considered by some scholars to be Bartolomeo's finest sculptural work and by others to be the creation of Nanni di Bartolo.

In the late 1430s Bartolomeo seems to have turned increasingly to architecture. In 1438 father and son took on the contract for the Porta della Carta, a monumental entrance to the Doge's Palace; Bartolomeo, who signed the portal after his father's death, was probably responsible for the design, which was entirely in the traditional style of mature Venetian Gothic. In 1441 the sculptural group *Justice* was set in place on the right of the portal (see fig.); it is one of the few works almost unanimously attributed to Bartolomeo (like the portrait bust of *Doge Francesco Foscari*; Venice, Mus. Opera Pal.) and is an excellent example of his expressive, psychologically astute style. When the *Justice* was put in position, most of the figures were still missing, including the *Virtues* in the niches, although these were soon supplied, possibly by four collaborators. There are notable stylistic similarities in this group of the *Judgement of Solomon* to the figures (e.g. *St*

Bartolomeo Buon: Porta della Carta, Doge's Palace, Venice, *c.* 1438, with the sculptural group *Justice* (attrib.; installed 1441) to the right

Francis) attributed to Bartolomeo on the main portal of S Maria Gloriosa dei Frari (?1440s). During the 1440s Bartolomeo worked as an architect and sculptor at S Maria della Carità, where his tracery windows on the façade (destr.) were imitated by the anonymous architect of S Gregorio, Venice, as early as 1450. He was commissioned to carve the relief (now in the sacristy of S Maria della Salute; *see* VENICE, §IV, 5) on the portal of the same church, for which he was paid in 1442–4, although it was executed by an assistant. The same is true of his commission to carve the Virgin for the loggia at Udine in 1448, and probably of the relief of the *Madonna of Mercy* on the portal of the Scuola Grande di S Maria della Misericordia (London, V&A; *see* VENICE, fig. 29), which is likely to have come from his workshop. Bartolomeo's portal for SS Giovanni e Paolo (1458; *see* VENICE, §IV, 3) and above all, his main architectural work, the Cà del Duca palace, are evidence that he was the founder of Renaissance architecture in Venice. Only fragments of the Cà del Duca were built, as work was suspended in 1461, but the rusticated plinth in Istrian stone, surmounted by panels of facet-cut masonry, imply a design that has completed the transition from Gothic to early Renaissance. Bartolomeo Buon was undoubtedly the most important sculptor–architect active in Venice before the emergence of the sculptor Antonio Rizzo and the architect Mauro Codussi.

BIBLIOGRAPHY

Macmillan Enc. Architects; Thieme–Becker

P. Paoletti: *L'architettura e la scultura del rinascimento a Venezia* (Venice, 1893)

L. Planiscig: *Venezianische Bildhauer der Renaissance* (Vienna, 1921)

G. Fiocco: 'I Lamberti a Venezia, III: Imitatori e seguaci', *Dedalo*, viii (1927–8), pp. 432–58

L. Planiscig: 'Die Bildhauer Venedigs in der ersten Hälfte des Quattrocento', *Jb. Ksthist. Samml. Wien*, n. s. 4 (1930), pp. 47–120

G. Fogolari: 'Ancora di Bartolomeo Bon scultore veneziano', *L'Arte*, xxxv (1932), pp. 27–45

R. Gallo: 'L'architettura di transizione dal gotico al rinascimento e Bartolomeo Bon', *Atti Ist. Ven. Sci., Lett. & A.*, cxx (1961–2), pp. 187–204

E. Arslan: *Venezia gotica* (Milan, 1970); Eng. trans. by A. Engel as *Gothic Architecture in Venice* (London and New York, 1971)

W. Wolters: *La scultura veneziana gotica (1300–1460)* (Milan, 1976) [contains a list of attributions made to Giovanni and Bartolomeo Buon up to 1976]

A. Markham Schulz: 'The Sculpture of Giovanni and Bartolomeo Bon and their Workshop', *Trans. Amer. Philos. Soc.*, lxviii/3 (1978), pp. 1–81

D. Howard: *The Architectural History of Venice* (New York and London, 1980)

WOLFGANG WOLTERS

Buon [Bon] **(ii).** Italian family of architects and sculptors. The lives and careers of Bartolomeo Buon (*b* Bergamo, *c.* 1450; *d* Venice, ?1509) and Pietro Buon (*d* Venice, 15 March 1529) are closely linked, with many details remaining conjectural; it is almost certain, however, that Pietro was Bartolomeo's son. Much of the work traditionally ascribed to Bartolomeo, notably at the Scuola Grande di S Rocco, Venice, has been reattributed by modern scholars to Pietro. The Buons were strongly influenced by Mauro Codussi, to whom they may have been related, and Pietro may have been the latter's pupil. The Buons' style is also linked to the decorative tradition of Pietro Lombardo, which is characterized by refined low-relief decoration and the use of rare marbles set within stone panelling. Their nickname of 'i Bergamaschi' reflects their Lombard origins and serves to distinguish them from the earlier, Venetian Buon family (*see* BUON (i)). Also referred to sometimes as one of 'i Bergamaschi' is Guglielmo de' Grigi (*see* GRIGI, DE', (1)), who was also from Bergamo and worked with Pietro Buon in Venice.

The first record of Bartolomeo Buon in Venice is from 1485, as an employee of the Provveditori al Sal, a government agency responsible for funding state building works. His first important scheme was the church of S Rocco (begun 1489; consecrated 1508). However, only the apses and high altar have survived; the rest of the church was rebuilt in the 18th century. The apses are simple forms in the manner of Codussi, and records of the lost façade show that it too was a straightforward work in Codussi's style, although of awkward proportions. The remains of the portal survive (on the north wall), decorated with pilasters similar to Lombardo's style. The high altar is later and considerably richer, inset with rare marbles. It dates from *c.* 1520 and must therefore be the work of Pietro. The careers of the two artists in the 1490s are difficult to disentangle. In 1492 Bartolomeo, still employed by the Provveditori al Sal, was sent abroad for two years on government business, but he resumed the post on his return. This was followed by a second foreign mission in 1496, at which time Pietro seems to have replaced him as *proto* (chief surveyor or architect), perhaps initially on a temporary basis.

In 1505 a 'maistro Bon' was appointed to the most senior post of *proto* of the Procuracy of S Marco, responsible for all state buildings on and near the Piazza S Marco. This seems to have been Pietro, to whom several works around the piazza from 1510 to 1517 are thus attributable. They include supervision of the completion of the Torre dell'Orologio (begun 1496–1500), generally believed to have been designed by Mauro Codussi. Pietro was also responsible for reconstructing (1511–14) the uppermost stage of the campanile of S Marco, which had been badly damaged by lightning in 1489; there he broadly followed an initial design by Giorgio Spavento, who had died in 1509. His last work on the piazza was the supervision of the rebuilding of the Procuratie Vecchie, the long structure on the north side of the piazza built to house the apartments of the Procurators of S Marco. A few bays of the older Procuratie had been demolished earlier to make room for the Torre, but in 1513 reconstruction began on the remainder. It is likely that Pietro followed original designs by Codussi, although as *proto* he had considerable authority to modify or refine detailing, subject to government approval. The lower two storeys were complete by 1518, while the second floor was added by Guglielmo de' Grigi, again under Pietro's supervision; this was completed by 1525. The repetitive rhythm of the arcades echoes the earlier Byzantine structure, while the detailing appears to retain Codussi's refined sense of proportion. Because none of these works represents an original design by Pietro, however, his own style cannot be clearly identified in them. It is only at the Scuola Grande di S Rocco (for illustration *see* SCARPAGNINO, ANTONIO) that his own character emerges with clarity. The foundation stone for the Scuola was laid in 1515, but construction took 50 years under a succession of *proti*, whose relationship with the

Scuola was often strained and occasionally broken. Pietro was appointed (unpaid) *proto* in 1517 and remained in office for nine years; he was responsible for the ground-plan and notably for the characteristic ground-floor hall, as well as the lower order of the façade. This fine, rich work incorporates motifs in the style of Codussi, such as the paired windows (by then a little archaic) together with more florid elements derived from Pietro Lombardo, notably the complex entrance portal with its rich marbles. Work had been completed up to the first floor by 1524, when Pietro had a dispute with the Scuola and was summarily dismissed, to be replaced first by Sante Lombardo and then by Antonio Scarpagnino, who completed the first floor. Little is known of Pietro's last years.

Several other works in Venice have been attributed to either Pietro or Bartolomeo, all from the first two decades of the 16th century. One is the Palazzo Cappello Trevisan, a particularly richly decorated Lombard-style palace, also sometimes attributed to de' Grigi. Bartolomeo had served under Admiral Melchior Trevisan for two years, and the house was built for the latter's family. It may thus be the work of both the Buons and de' Grigi. The campanile of the Madonna dell'Orto has often been ascribed to the Buons, but with no documentary evidence. The style of the Buons is difficult to classify. Pietro in particular seems to have been somewhat eclectic and in some ways characteristic of the later part of the first wave of Renaissance architects in Venice: more robust and less purely decorative than Pietro Lombardo, his work is more richly decorated and decorative than the purer forms of Codussi. He is thus best seen as a transitional figure, and although his work has a fairly strong architectural framework, its rather excessive richness prompted the next generation of architects in Venice to develop a more disciplined classicism.

BIBLIOGRAPHY

G. Soravia: *Le chiese di Venezia descritte e illustrate* (Venice, 1824)
E. A. Cicogna: *Delle iscrizioni veneziane*, 6 vols (Venice, 1824–53)
P. Paoletti: *L'architettura e la scultura del rinascimento in Venezia* (Venice, 1897)
A. Venturi: *Storia* (1901–40)
A. Mazzucato: *La Scuola Grande e la chiesa di S Rocco in Venezia* (Venice, 1953)
J. McAndrew: *Venetian Architecture of the Early Renaissance* (Cambridge, MA, and London, 1980)
S. Mariani: *Vita e opere dei proti Bon, Bartolomeo e Pietro* (diss., Venice, Ist. U. Archit., 1983)
M. Tafuri: *Venice and the Renaissance* (Cambridge, MA, and London, 1989)

RICHARD J. GOY

Buonaccorsi, Pietro. *See* PERINO DEL VAGA.

Buonaccorsi [Bonaccorsi]**, Raimondo** (*b* Macerata, 1669; *d* Macerata, 1743). Italian patron. A member of a noble Marchigian family, he embarked in the early 18th century on an ambitious programme of art patronage. In 1701 he commissioned the Roman architect Giovanni Battista Contini to rebuild the family palace in Macerata (now the Accademia, Via Don Minzoni); once the building was completed, he devoted particular attention to the decoration of the new long gallery, the theme of which was the story of Aeneas. In 1707 the Bolognese fresco painters Carlo Antonio Rambaldi (1680–1717) and Antonio Dardani (1677–1735) painted the *Apotheosis of Aeneas* on the gallery ceiling. The story was then developed in a series of 12 canvases commissioned between 1708 and 1717 from artists in the principal Italian art centres. They included the Bolognese artists Marcantonio Franceschini and Giovanni Gioseffo dal Sole, the Venetian Gregorio Lazzarini, Antonio Balestra of Verona and the Neapolitan Francesco Solimena, whose *Dido and Aeneas* (Macerata, Pal. Buonaccorsi) arrived in 1714. (Many of the *Aeneid* paintings remain *in situ* but some were dispersed before the commune of Macerata purchased the palace in 1967.) The reason for Buonaccorsi's selection of the Virgilian theme is unknown, but his choice of artists suggests a wish to bring together and compare works by those belonging to the most prominent Italian regional schools of the day, whether individually famous or not. The gallery apart, his taste extended also to the more informal kind of art exemplified by the work of the Bolognese painter Giuseppe Maria Crespi, who was represented in Buonaccorsi's collection by four commissioned pictures, among them *Leto Turning the Shepherds into Frogs* (Bologna, Pin. N.). Two pastoral scenes commissioned from another Bolognese, Giuseppe Gambarini, were the *Birth of Adonis* and its companion, the *Nurture of Jupiter* (Bologna, Maccafferi priv. col.). Buonaccorsi's initiative does not seem to have stimulated comparable ventures in art patronage in 18th-century Macerata and, isolated as it was, it attracted relatively little outside attention, though the Bolognese writer Marcello Oretti, who visited the region *c*. 1777, did take note of the paintings (Bologna, Bib. Com. Archiginnasio, MS. B. 291: 'Pitture delle città della Umbria e della Marca'). Nevertheless, Buonaccorsi, like his contemporary Stefano Conti in Lucca, is an interesting representative of Italian provincial taste in the early 18th century.

BIBLIOGRAPHY

S. Ubaldi: *I Buonaccorsi a Macerata, cenni storici* (Macerata, 1950)
F. Haskell: *Patrons and Painters: A Study in the Relations between Italian Art and Society in the Age of the Baroque* (London, 1963, rev. New Haven, 1980), pp. 223–5, 404
D. Miller: 'The Gallery of Aeneid in the Palazzo Bonaccorsi at Macerata', *A. Ant. & Mod.*, vi (1963), pp. 153–8; vii (1964), p. 113
Urbino—Restauri nelle Marche: Testimonianze, acquisti e recuperi (exh. cat., ed. P. Torriti; Urbino, Pal. Ducale, 1973), pp. 532–52

JANET SOUTHORN

Buonaccorso, Niccolò di. *See* NICCOLÒ DI BUONACCORSO.

Buonamici, Agostino. *See* TASSI, AGOSTINO.

Buonamico di Martino. *See* BUFFALMACCO.

Buonaparte. *See* BONAPARTE.

Buonarotti, Michelangelo. *See* MICHELANGELO.

Buonarroti, Michelangelo, the younger (*b* Florence, *bapt* 4 Nov 1568; *d* Florence, 11 Jan 1646). Italian scholar and patron. A great-nephew of the great MICHELANGELO, he studied from 1586 to 1591 in Pisa, where for a while he shared lodgings with Maffeo Barberini, the future Pope Urban VIII. On his return to Florence, he frequented literary circles and the Medici court. He was elected to the Accademia della Crusca in 1589 and became a member of the Accademia Fiorentina in 1591. He worked on both the first (1612) and the second (1623) editions of the *Vocabolario della Crusca*.

Buonarroti was friendly with many artists, including Cristofano Allori, Luigi Arrigucci, Lodovico Cigoli, Sigismondo Coccapani, Cosimo Gamberucci (*fl* 1600–19) and, after 1637, Pietro da Cortona. He was frequently asked to give opinions in artistic matters and was an *operaio* (member of the cathedral building committee) for the projected façade of S Maria del Fiore, Florence. Later, in his proposals for the Palazzo Barberini in Rome, he combined literary and artistic interests in proposing an architecture that would have the quality of *sprezzatura*, a carefully contrived naturalness and variety previously foreign to the formality of palace design. He was instrumental in the Medici commissioning of Pietro da Cortona to paint the Sala della Stufa (from 1637) in the Palazzo Pitti, Florence, a project for which he provided a programme combining texts from Ovid and allegorical allusions to the Medici. Buonarroti remodelled and redecorated (1612–38) his own house, the Casa Buonarroti in Via Ghibellina, Florence, and made it a veritable compendium of contemporary Florentine painting. Four rooms were decorated with a series of paintings celebrating Michelangelo, the Buonarroti family and aspects of Florentine life, spiritual, ecclesiastical, intellectual and military. The decoration of the house includes works by JACOPO DA EMPOLI, GIOVANNI DA SAN GIOVANNI, DOMENICO PASSIGNANO, MATTEO ROSSELLI and JACOPO VIGNALI. It is now a museum.

BIBLIOGRAPHY

M. G. Masera: *Michelangelo Buonarroti il Giovane* (Turin, 1941)
U. Procacci: *La Casa Buonarroti a Firenze* (Milan, 1965)
P. Waddy: 'Michelangelo Buonarroti the Younger, *sprezzatura*, and Palazzo Barberini', *Architectura*, v (1975), pp. 101–22
M. Campbell: *Pietro da Cortona at the Pitti Palace*, Princeton Monographs A. & Archaeol., xli (Princeton, 1977)

PATRICIA WADDY

Buonconsiglio, Giovanni [il Marescalco] (*b* Vicenza, ?1465–70; *d* Venice, ?1535–8). Italian painter. Probably apprenticed in Vicenza to Bartolommeo Montagna by 1484, he was influenced by many painters during his formative years. He is documented as having settled in Venice on 22 January 1495, where he may have revived a friendship with Cima da Conegliano, whom he may have known in Vicenza. The few works predating 1497 that have been identified as Buonconsiglio's are dominated by Lombard influences, the spatial and monumental qualities of Antonello da Messina and Mantegna being particularly evident, as well as the influence of Bramante. Among these early works are the signed *Pietà* (*c.* 1495; Vicenza, Mus. Civ. A. & Stor.; see fig.) and a related drawing depicting *Christ at the Column* (Paris, Louvre). Generally considered to be his masterpiece, the *Pietà* reaches a level of perfection he was never to surpass nor often even to approach (Borenius, p. 161). The awkward figure of Christ lies rigidly at an angle to the picture plane, receding into it at the left, with head and shoulders resting against the Virgin, who is seated on a low, natural stone bench. Balancing these figures are those of St John the Evangelist and Mary Magdalene, respectively standing and kneeling to the right of the picture's centre. Greys, blues and olives predominate, with the bright red of St John's mantle and the gold and green of Mary Magdalene's elaborate garments in sharp contrast. The landscape background of

Giovanni Buonconsiglio: *Pietà*, tempera on panel, 1.77×1.60 m, *c.* 1495 (Vicenza, Museo Civico d'Arte e Storia)

this early masterpiece shows that Buonconsiglio must have known Mantegna or Domenico Morone well; Bramante's influence is especially clear in the figure of St John. Also from this early period are the *Beheading of St Paul* (Vicenza, S Lorenzo) and a corresponding drawing of *A Soldier* (ex-Koenig Col., Haarlem), fresco fragments in Montagnana Cathedral, the *St Catherine of Alexandria* (Vicenza, Mus. Civ. A. & Stor.) and a monochrome frieze (Venice, Col. Cini). A fragment from an altarpiece, signed and dated 1497, depicting *SS Benedict, Tecla and Cosmas* (Venice, Accad.), shows the dominating influence of Giovanni Bellini.

Buonconsiglio's development in the first decade of the 16th century can be summarized by comparing two altarpieces with similar compositions: the large *Virgin and Child Enthroned with SS Paul, Peter, Dominic and Sebastian* (Vicenza, Mus. Civ. A. & Stor.) is signed and dated 1502; the *Virgin and Child Enthroned with Saints* (Montagnana Cathedral) dates from 1507. Both depict the Virgin and Child enthroned on a raised pedestal flanked by equal groups of saints, and, as was typically Venetian, the figures are placed in a church aedicule. The earlier painting owes a great deal to Giovanni Bellini: the figures of the Virgin and Child and SS Dominic and Sebastian, and the setting (a chapel covered in golden mosaics), are direct quotations from his S Giobbe altarpiece (Venice, Accad.). In the later painting, which shows Buonconsiglio having reached his maturity, the pedestal supporting the Virgin and Child has been lowered, resulting in a more nearly horizontal composition. Most impressive, however, is the difference in the structure and modelling of the figures in the two *sacre conversazioni*. In the earlier all surfaces are hard-edged and clearly differentiated, almost incised, while in the latter the figures, now more anatomically correct, are modelled with an almost *sfumato* technique. Buonconsiglio's *Virgin and Child with SS John the Baptist and Catherine* (*c*. 1508; Padua, Cassa di Risparmio) is notable for a landscape background that assimilates the influence of Dürer. Among Buonconsiglio's portraits is an impressive *Self-portrait* (*c*. 1500; Rome, Mus. Capitolino).

Another important group of paintings spans the years between 1510 and 1515; *St Sebastian with SS Lawrence and Roch* (*c*. 1510; Venice, S Giacomo dell'Orio), the *Virgin and Child with SS Sebastian and Roch* (1511; Montagnana Cathedral) and *Christ the Redeemer with SS Jerome and George* (*c*. 1513; Venice, Spirito Santo). Although the last two paintings show a certain fatigue, passages of real beauty may be seen in the altarpiece of *St Catherine with the Archangel Raphael and Tobias and St Nicholas of Tolentino* (1513; Montagnana Cathedral), which takes Cima da Conegliano as a model. Buonconsiglio frescoed the apse and left transept wall in Montagnana Cathedral between *c*. 1511 and 1513 with, respectively, an *Assumption* (possibly derived from the apse painting by Melozzo da Forlì in Rome, SS Apostoli) and a *Circumcision*. Both survive *in situ*, although the *Circumcision* is in extremely poor condition. Buonconsiglio's latest significant works are the altarpiece of the *Virgin and Child Enthroned with SS John the Baptist and Stephen* (Warsaw, N. Mus.) and that for the church of St Peter in Montecchio Maggiore (1519), his last signed and dated work.

BIBLIOGRAPHY

Thieme–Becker
T. Borenius: *The Painters of Vicenza, 1480–1550* (London, 1909), pp. 155–204
R. Longhi: *Viatico per cinque secoli di pittura veneziana* (Florence, 1946), pp. 15, 60
G. Spettoli: 'Buonconsiglio: Due frammenti d'affresco', *Paragone*, i/2 (1950), pp. 58–60
F. Barbieri: *Museo civico di Vicenza: Dipinti e scultura dal XIV al XV secolo* (Venice, 1962), pp. 93–100
L. Puppi: 'Giovanni Buonconsiglio detto il Marescalco', *Riv. Ist. N. Archeol. & Stor. A.*, xiii–xiv (1964–5), pp. 297–374
R. Pallucchini: 'Una nuova opera del Marescalco', *A. Ven.*, xxvi (1973), pp. 31–8
V. Sgarbi: *Giovanni Buonconsiglio* (diss., U. Bologna, 1974)
F. Zeri: 'Il capitolo "bramantesco" di Giovanni Buonconsiglio', *Diari di lavoro 2* (Turin, 1976), pp. 58–70
V. Sgarbi: 'Le due culture di Giovanni Buonconsiglio', *Boll. A.*, lxv/7 (1980), pp. 31–64 [with full bibliog.]

ALEXANDRA HERZ

Buonconsiglio [Buon Consiglio; Trent; Trento] **Castle.** Vast monumental complex built between the north and east gates of the ancient city walls (*c*. 1200–20) of Trent, the capital of Trentino in Italy. It has three main nuclei: the Castelvecchio, the Magno Palazzo and the Giunta Albertiana. The oldest part, Castelvecchio, was built (1239–55) around the strong donjon, the Torre d'Augusto, by the Imperial Podestà of Trent, Sodegerio da Tito (*d* 1255), who took up office in 1238. Its function was predominantly military. In 1277 it passed to the Church and became the residence of the prince-bishop of Trent. In subsequent centuries a series of modifications and extensions have brought the castle to its present form (see fig.). Of fundamental importance were the works completed in 1475 by Giovanni Hinderbach (*d* 1486) with the aid of Venetian craftsmen, who built the Renaissance Gothic internal court with tiered open galleries and the small loggia on the third floor. At that time the walls of the upper loggia were frescoed with portraits of the bishops of Trent from the city's origin to the year 1000; the series was completed in the adjoining room with portraits of the bishops since the millennium. The frescoed festoons (1476) on the outside of the galleries were the work of Bartolomeo Sacchetto of Verona. The appearance of the castle in the 15th century is known from a watercolour (1494; London, BM) by Albrecht Dürer.

Between 1528 and 1536 Bernhard von Cles (1485–1539; prince-bishop, 1514; cardinal, 1530) had the Castel Nuovo built beside the medieval structure; it was called the 'Magno Palazzo' by Pietro Andrea Mattioli. Cles was linked by close ties of loyalty to the Austrian monarchy, which considered the episcopal principality of Trent as the southern outpost of the empire. He chose to have his new residence built according to the dictates of Renaissance architecture, enriched by extensive decorations based on humanist themes, following the example of other Italian courts.

Documents provide the names of a few architects, including Lodovico Zaffran (*fl c*. 1527) and Alessio Longhi (*fl* 1522–50), as well as those of craftsmen who took part in the building of the palace under the careful guidance of Cles. It became a great Renaissance princely residence. The painters Gerolamo Romanino (*see* ROMANINO, GEROLAMO and fig.), Dosso Dossi, Battista Dossi, Marcello Fogolino, Matteo Fogolino (*fl* 1523–48) and Bartholomäus Dill Riemenschneider (*fl c*. 1525–50) worked on the decorations (damaged) from 1531, creating some of their masterpieces there. Sculptors included Vincenzo Grandi, Alessio Longhi and Zaccaria Zacchi.

Prince-Bishop Francesco Alberti Poja (*reg* 1677–89) added the Giunta Albertiana, linking the two preceding structures. Externally it resembles the Magno Palazzo, while the interior is decorated in splendid Baroque style. In the two first-floor salons, frescoed by Giuseppe Alberti (1640–1716), exuberant stucco decoration surrounds historical and allegorical paintings celebrating the victory over the Turks in 1683, while the second floor has richly carved and gilded wooden ceilings.

The Torre Aquila (*c*. 1200–20) is an ancient watch-tower overlooking the east gate of the city. Prince-Bishop Georg von Liechtenstein (*reg* 1390–1416) turned it into an elegant private residence, accessible from the castle via the path running along the city walls. Around 1400 George had the salon on the middle floor of the tower frescoed with the famous Late Gothic *Twelve Months* cycle (*see* DRESS, fig. 21). There are other frescoes on secular themes in the Torre del Falco, with scenes of hunting and outdoor life (*c*. 1530–32) that are attributable to Bartholomäus Dill Riemenschneider.

With the Napoleonic Wars (1803–15) the principality was suppressed, and Buonconsiglio Castle entered a period of decline. It was occupied in turn by the Austrians, the French and the Bavarians, then converted into a barracks for the Austrians. The Trent Irredentists Cesare Battisti, Damiano Chiesa and Fabio Filzi died there. The castle later became the seat of the Museo Nazionale and the

Buonconsiglio Castle, view from the south-west, showing the tower (completed 1475) by Giovanni Hinderbach incorporated into the Castel Nuovo ('Magno Palazzo'; 1528–36), and the top of the Torre d'Augusto (begun 1239) beyond, to the left

Museo Trentino del Risorgimento e della Lotta per la Libertà. In 1973 it came under the control of the autonomous province of Trent, and in 1975 it became the Museo Provinciale d'Arte. At the same time important restoration work began, together with the reorganization of the collections. The museum has been very active in conservation, cataloguing and restoration, as well as in producing exhibitions and publications.

BIBLIOGRAPHY

P. A. Mattioli: *Il Magno Palazzo del Cardinale di Trento* (Venice, 1539)

H. Semper: *Il Castello del Buon Consiglio a Trento: Documenti concernenti la fabbrica nel periodo closiano, 1527–1536* (Trent, 1914)

C. Ausserer and G. Gerola: *I documenti clesiani del Buonconsiglio*, ii of *Miscellanea veneto tridentina della regia deputazione di storia patria* (Venice, 1924)

G. Gerola: *Il Castello del Buonconsiglio e il Museo nazionale di Trento* (Rome, 1934)

N. Rasmo: *Il Castello del Buonconsiglio a Trento* (Rome, 1975, rev. Trent, 2/1982)

Bernardo Cles e l'arte del Rinascimento nel Trentino (exh. cat., ed. E. Chini and F. de Gramatica; Trent, Castello Buonconsiglio, 1985–6)

E. Castelnuovo: *I mesi di Trento* (Trent, 1986)

E. Chini: *Il Romanino a Trento: Gli affreschi nella loggia del Buonconsiglio* (Milan, 1988)

MARIA ANGELA MATTEVI

Buondelmonte, Christopher (*b* Florence, *c.* 1375; *d* Rhodes, *c.* 1435). Italian cartographer and priest. After his ordination he travelled in the Aegean between 1415 and 1422 and then settled in Rhodes, where his tombstone stands. His early education probably acquainted him with Ptolemy's *Geography* (2nd century AD). His own two geographical works are the earliest deliberate, disciplined attempts to set down in words and on maps detailed first-hand knowledge of terrain. For the *Description of Crete* (written by 1417) Buondelmonte circumnavigated and then traversed the island. The original map survives only in copies. The *Book of Islands*, dedicated in 1420 to Cardinal Orsini, describes 74 islands in the Greek archipelago. Accompanying maps show the mountains in black, the plains in white and the sea in green. The schematic coastlines are more accurate and on a larger scale than portulan charts, although in the earliest manuscripts places marked are few and symbols recognizably Classical in character. Later copyists were uninhibited, embellishing their originals and sometimes drawing inspiration from the text. The work's popularity caused it to be elaborated and enlarged throughout the 15th century. As many as 64 manuscripts are known, some of great beauty, representing three traditions. Both text and maps were plagiarized by writers over the next two centuries, the maps in particular by Henricus Martellus, Bartolomeo Sonetti and Benedetto Bordone. Buondelmonte also drew a map of Constantinople (now Istanbul) for Vitold, Duke of Lithuania, one of very few depictions of towns. This is not known to survive, but it probably influenced Pietro Massaio, who illustrated Ptolemy's *Geography* (1468 and 1472).

WRITINGS

E. Legrand, ed.: *Descriptions des Iles de l'Archipel* (Paris, 1897)

M.-A. van Spitael, ed.: *Descriptio insule Crete et liber insularum* (Herakleion, 1981)

BIBLIOGRAPHY

DBI

A. Luttrell: *The Later History of the Maussoleion and its Utilization in the Hospitaller Castle at Bodrum*, Jutland Archaeological Society Publications, ii (Copenhagen, 1986), pp. 189–94, 210–11

H. L. Turner: 'Christopher Buondelmonti and the Isolario', *Terr. Incog.*, xix (1988), pp. 11–28

HILARY LOUISE TURNER

Buoneri, Francesco. *See* CARAVAGGIO, CECCO DEL.

Buonfigli, Benedetto. *See* BONFIGLI, BENEDETTO.

Buoni, Giacomo Antonio. *See* BONI, GIACOMO ANTONIO.

Buono [Bonii, Bono]. Italian family of sculptors. The earliest recorded work by Carlo Antonio Buono (*fl* Milan, 1634–73) is a stucco high relief of the *Beheading of St John the Baptist* (1634; destr., known through a photograph) for S Giovanni in Laterano (destr.), Milan. He is documented as working in Milan Cathedral and in the workshops of the Camposanto and in 1645 was appointed sculptor to the cathedral workshop. He contributed to the sculptural enrichment of the cathedral's façade (from 1645), for which his works include a low relief of *Ruth and Boaz* for the tympanum of the second window on the left (terracotta model, Milan, Mus. Duomo). At the end of the 1650s he began to work in stucco as well as marble for the cathedral, and between 1646 and 1649 he produced one of the figures of the *Four Crowned Saints* and terracotta models of the prophets *Isaiah* and *Jeremiah* (realized in marble in 1652). For the chapel of the Madonna dell' Albero in the cathedral he produced life-size angels with musical instruments and cherubs (1654–7) for the vault, and in 1662 a prophet for the pilaster on the left and *King Josiah*, the latter now moved to the external wall of the north transept, which also holds his figures of the prophet *Amos* (1668) and *St Margaret* (1673). His style unites Lombard realism with the more expressionistic tendencies of medieval north European art, a union characteristic of the Milanese Baroque. His son Giuseppe Buono (*fl* Milan, 1670–1709/21) began his career by collaborating with his father in the workshop of Milan Cathedral, from 1670. After his father's death, despite the contraction of the workshop, he, along with two other sculptors, Carlo Simonetta (*d* 1693) and Giuseppe Rusnati (*d* 1713), managed to retain his post and to win further commissions. In 1681 he sculpted one of the marble figures of *Four Crowned Saints*. From 1682 he worked alternately in Germany and in Italy; at Linz he directed the execution of the sculpture for the high altar of the monastery church of St Florian, and in 1683 the execution, in plaster, of statues of the *Four Seasons* and, in marble, of heraldic shields for the new summer residence of the same monastery.

UNPUBLISHED SOURCES

Milan, Archv Stor. Fabbrica Duomo, cartt./40, 141ff

BIBLIOGRAPHY

An. Fabbrica Duomo, v (Milan, 1883), pp. 308, 316, 320; (1885), pp. 1, 5, 37, 40, 48, 51, 59, 68, 74, 76, 82

A. Czerny: *Kunst und Kunstgewerbe im Stifte St Florian* (Linz, 1886) pp. 165ff

U. Nebbia: *La scultura del Duomo di Milano* (Milan, 1908), pp. 217, 262ff

G. G. Dehio: *Handbuch der Oberösterreich* (Vienna, 1958), pp. 266ff

G. Nicodemi: 'La scultura lombarda dal 1630 al 1706', *Stor. Milano*, xi (Milan, 1958), pp. 541, 546ff

R. Bossaglia: *La scultura: Il duomo di Milano* (Milan, 1973)

GABRIELLA FERRI PICCALUGA

Buono di Jacopo, Mariano del. *See* MARIANO DEL BUONO DI JACOPO.

Buontalenti, Bernardo [Bernardo delle Girandole] (*b* Florence, *c.* 1531; *d* Florence, 6 June 1608). Italian architect, engineer, designer, painter and inventor. He was one of the great Renaissance polymaths and was not only admired but also liked by his contemporaries. A friend of princes, he spent most of his life at the Tuscan court, but his influence stretched throughout Europe.

1. TRAINING AND EARLY WORK, BEFORE 1570. After his parents were drowned he was brought up at the court of Cosimo I de' Medici. As an apprentice he trained first with Francesco Salviati, then with Agnolo Bronzino, Giorgio Vasari and finally Don Giulio Clovio. His education must have been broadly based as he was appointed tutor at the age of 15 to the future Francesco I de' Medici, to whom he taught not only drawing, colouring and perspective but also architecture and engineering. This was the beginning of a lifelong friendship, in which they shared a passionate interest in the natural sciences.

Buontalenti's earliest known work was a wooden crucifix (destr.) for the church of S Maria degli Angeli, Florence. On 1 February 1550 a document refers to his work as a pyrotechnist, from which he earned his nickname. In 1556 he was sent as a specialist adviser in engineering to Fernando Alvárez de Toledo, Duke of Alba, for whom he designed fortifications at Civetta del Trono. He also built the much-feared Florentine cannon nicknamed 'Scacciadiavoli' (destr.). In 1562–3, with Francesco de' Medici, he visited Madrid, where both men admired the oriental porcelain collection of Philip II of Spain. Buontalenti is credited with the creation of two soft-porcelain pieces (*c.*1565) in Florence. He is also recorded as working in Madrid as a miniaturist, executing a number of portraits and paintings of the Virgin for the King.

Buontalenti's first recorded secular architectural work (1567) was the house for Bianca Capello, mistress and later wife of Francesco de' Medici. This was followed in 1569 by the commission for the villa and gardens at PRATOLINO, just outside Florence (now mostly destr.), to which a visit was almost obligatory for visitors to Tuscany. As a result Pratolino had a major influence on European garden design and was studied through contemporary descriptions and engravings. The villa had evolved from ideas current at the time and discussed at the Medici court, and it epitomized Mannerist art. The villa's design was novel, anticipating Buontalenti's numerous experiments with the form over the following 20 years. The internal courtyard was omitted, the north and south façades were treated differently, and the central portion was raised considerably higher than the flanking wings. The vertical axis was emphasized by the two formal terraces leading down to the long avenue surrounded by the wild garden. The letters of Benedetto Uguccioni (Florence, Archv Stat.), who supervised the building works, give an insight into Buontalenti's working methods. Work began on the villa before he had decided on the form of the main entrance, and this seems to have been a typical practice in later works. Two drawings for the doorway survive in the Uffizi, Florence. The garden was a combination of formal walks, punctuated with pools, grottoes and fountains, and wild groves dotted with architectural caprices. Here Buontalenti's skill as an engineer was particularly useful in transporting over five miles the huge amount of water needed to service the fountains. The six main grottoes were on two levels beneath the terraces by the house. The most admired was the Grotto of Galatea, with Galatea appearing on a golden shell pulled by dolphins, preceded by a Triton rising from the rocks blowing a trumpet.

2. ARCHITECTURAL WORK, AFTER 1570. Buontalenti's ability as an engineer continued to shape his career. During the 1570s he is recorded as working on the fortifications at various cities including Pisa, Siena, Prato (*c.* 1574) and Livorno (1576), where he was responsible for the design of the harbour that helped make Livorno the second most important port in the Mediterranean by the end of the 16th century. He also constructed the canal (1573) between Livorno and Pisa.

Buontalenti's next major architectural commission was the Casino de' Medici (1574; now the Palazzo delle Corte d'Appello), again for Francesco de' Medici. It was built as a garden house opening on to an orchard, on the outskirts of Florence. The window arrangement is typical of Buontalenti's work, especially the elaborate detailing, where consoles flank carved shells and drapery swags beneath the ground-floor windows. However, the overall effect is of simplicity and harmony. His capricious spirit is evident in another work begun in 1574, the chancel of Santa Trìnità (which has since been transferred to S Stefano). Here the steps of the chancel fan outwards like heavy folds of drapery from a pleat, contrasting with a very precise balustrade above.

On the death of Vasari in 1574, Buontalenti became chief architect to the Tuscan court. In this capacity he oversaw the conversion of the top floors of the Uffizi into the grand ducal art gallery. Around 1580 he designed the Tribuna in the Uffizi for the display of Francesco de' Medici's greatest art treasures. The room is octagonal with a diffused light issuing from windows in the drum, which in turn is reflected by the mother-of-pearl inlaid into the vault. He also completed the great grotto (see fig. 1) in the Boboli Gardens, Florence, adding the elaborate upper storey, which incorporated natural rock formations and foliage framing the Medici coat of arms. The interior of the grotto housed Michelangelo's four *Slaves* (Florence, Accademia), which had recently been acquired by the Medici. They were set in the corners of the interior space amid roughly carved rocks, natural rock formations such as stalactites and frescoes of fantastic Alpine landscapes by Bernardino Poccetti.

Buontalenti's major architectural works of the 1580s and 1590s include villas at Le Marignolle (1587), Castello (1592) and Artimino (1597), where in keeping with his working method at Pratolino he did not design the doors, chimney and fireplace until the first floor was complete. Like other Florentine villas of the time, these buildings were less grandiose and massive and had a neater, more controlled appearance than similar buildings in Rome, with smooth light surfaces ornamented with sparing dark patterns. Buontalenti's villas, however, have a stronger sense of volume than the typical Florentine villa. They are articulated more strongly using towers and loggias, and the windows are more definite elements in the patterning of wall surfaces. Buontalenti introduced more detail and a more inventive manner, as in the fantastic array of chimneys at the Villa Artimino, Signa. There is visual movement—often no more than the arrangement of windows, but this gives an air of vitality and lightness balancing the almost fortress-like architectural elements—yet there is a strong overall sense of balance and order. Towards the end of his life, Buontalenti had two architectural failures: the façade of the cathedral and the Cappella dei Principi at the church of S Lorenzo, Florence. His proposed designs (Florence, Uffizi) were too inventive, and as a result of the consequent incoherence they remained unexecuted.

1. Bernardo Buontalenti: façade of the great grotto, Boboli Gardens, Florence (upper part by Buontalenti, from 1583; lower part by Giorgio Vasari, 1556–60)

3. OTHER ACTIVITIES. In addition to his architectural achievements, Buontalenti excelled as a theatrical designer. His career in this area began with a period as assistant to Vasari; he is first mentioned in connection with the celebrations for the visit (1569) of Grand Duke Charles of Austria, when he was responsible for costumes transforming peasants into frogs. His skill as a designer was

2. Bernardo Buontalenti: *Inferno*, design for the intermezzo of the *Music of Hell*, 1589 (Paris, Musée du Louvre)

also required at state ceremonies such as baptisms and funerals, which in their lavishness attempted to bolster Medici claims as the rulers of Tuscany and as European powers. For the obsequies of Grand Duke Cosimo de' Medici, Buontalenti designed a stepped baldacchino laden with 3000 candles, for which the immediate precedent was the funeral of Emperor Charles V in 1558. However, such designs can be traced back to the funeral pyres of the Roman Empire, mentioned in Tommaso Porcecchi's treatise *Funerali antiche di diversi popoli et natione* (1574). Other elaborate settings were executed with just as much pomp and display, for example for such celebrations as the baptism of Filippo de' Medici in 1577. On that occasion the medieval interior of the Baptistery in Florence was ripped out and replaced by an elaborate double ramping staircase (destr.) leading to the tribune, where a new font and a platform of *pietra dura* for the child were placed. For the same celebrations he designed a number of firework-breathing monsters.

In 1586 Buontalenti built the Teatro Mediceo (capacity 3000) on the top floor of the Uffizi. The inaugural performance was during the wedding festivities for Virginia de' Medici and Cesare d'Este, Duke of Modena. Contemporary accounts mention that he used bold colours for costumes and that he experimented with lighting, producing a more united and convincing effect than had previously been achieved. The audience was enthusiastic about the perspective view of Rome, which Buontalenti painted on a range of stage flats and backcloths, and which were viewed through a proscenium arch. In 1589, for the month-long celebration of the marriage of the Grand Duke Ferdinand I de' Medici to Christina of Lorraine, Buontalenti designed a series of intermezzi on fantastic, mythological and cosmological themes, in which music, dance and scenic effects were combined (see fig. 2). For his Great Naval Battle, another part of the same celebration, the entertainment began with an elaborate tournament in the courtyard of the Palazzo Pitti; when the guests returned from dinner they found the courtyard flooded and 18 galleons ready for a mock battle. The records for *Il rapimento di Cefalo* in 1600 describe it as having the most marvellous machines that had ever been seen and compared it to the spectacles of ancient Rome: Buontalenti apparently produced mountains that rose from the earth, flying Cupids, gods on clouds and elaborate sea scenes with leaping fish and whales.

Few of Buontalenti's paintings survive, although there is a *Self-portrait* (Florence, Pitti) and a miniature of the *Holy Family* (Florence, Uffizi). He was also known for his skill with gemstones, and a lapis lazuli vase (*see* ITALY, fig. 95) designed by him is in the Palazzo Pitti, Florence.

See also LIVORNO.

BIBLIOGRAPHY

G. Vasari: *Vite* (1550, rev. 2/1568); ed. G. Milanesi (1878–85)
F. de' Vieri: *Delle maravigliose opere di Pratolino* (Florence, 1586)
R. Borghini: *Il riposo* (Florence, 1589), ii, pp. 26ff
F. Baldinucci: *Notizie* (1681–1728); ed. F. Ranalli (1845–7), ii, pp. 490–532
B. Sgrilli: *Descrizione della Regia Villa, fontane e fabbriche di Pratolino* (Florence, 1742)
V. Giovannozzi: 'La vita di Bernardo Buontalenti, scritta da Gherado Silvani', *Riv. A.*, xiv (1932), pp. 505–24
A. Colasanti: 'Una miniatura di Bernardo Buontalenti', *Miscellanea di storia dell'arte in onore di I. B. Supino* (1933)

V. Giovannozzi: 'Ricerche su Bernardo Buontalenti', *Riv. A.*, xv (1933), pp. 297–327
M. de Montaigne: *Journal de voyage à l'Italie par la Suisse et l'Allemagne en 1580–81*, ed. C. Dedeyan (Paris, 1946), pp. 185–6
L. Giori Montanelli: 'Giudizio sul Buontalenti architetto', *Quad. Ist. Stor. Archit.*, xxxl–xlviii (1961), pp. 207ff
W. Smith: 'Pratolino', *J. Soc. Archit. Hist.*, xx (1961), pp. 155–68
A. Nagler: *Theatre Festivals of the Medici* (London, 1964)
D. Heikamp: 'La Tribuna degli Uffizi: Come era nel cinquecento', *Ant. Viva*, iii (1964)
E. Borsook: 'Art and Politics at the Medici Court I: The Funeral of Cosimo I de' Medici', *Mitt. Ksthist. Inst. Florenz*, xii (1965), pp. 31–54
D. Heikamp: 'La grotta grande del Giardino di Boboli', *Ant. Viva*, iv (1965), pp. 27–43
E. Borsook: 'Art and Politics at the Medici Court II: The Baptism of Filippo de' Medici in 1577', *Mitt. Ksthist. Inst. Florenz*, xiii (1967), pp. 95–114
Mostra di disegno di Bernardo Buontalenti (exh. cat. by I. M. Botto, Florence, Uffizi, 1968)
N. Bemporad: 'Gli Uffizi e la scala buontalentiana', *L'Architettura*, xiv (1968), pp. 610–19
D. Heikamp: 'Pratolino suoi giorni splendidi', *Ant. Viva*, viii (1969), pp. 14–34
——: 'Il teatro mediceo degli Uffizi', *Boll. Cent. Int. Stud. Archit. Andrea Palladio*, xvi (1974), pp. 323–32
A. Fara: 'Le ville di Bernardo Buontalenti nel tardo rinascimento toscana', *Stor. A.* (1977)
——: 'L'architettura delle ville buontalentiane attraverso i documenti', *Citta, ville, fortezze della Toscana nel XVI secolo* (Florence, 1978)
——: *Buontalenti architettura e teatro* (Florence, 1979)

ALICE DUGDALE

Buonvisi Painter. *See under* FREDIANI, VINCENZO.

Bupalos and Athenis (*fl c.* 540–*c.* 537 BC). Greek sculptors of the Archaic period from Chios. Pliny's date for their activity in the 60th Olympiad (540–537 BC) is corroborated by the epigraphically established date (mid-6th century BC) of their father Archermos of Chios, the probable sculptor of the *Nike* of Delos (Athens, N. Archaeol. Mus., 21). Knowledge of their work is derived entirely from literary sources. Most famous was their image of the Ephesian poet Hipponax, who was apparently incensed by its unflattering realism and responded with verses so bitter that the artists were driven to suicide (Pliny: *Natural History* XXXVI.xi–xiii). This anecdote was known to late commentators but was already questioned by Pliny, who knew of later works by the two at Iasos, Chios and Delos. Since brutally realistic portraits seem alien to 6th-century sculpture, the reference may be to some informal caricature. Pliny also mentioned sculptures by Bupalos and Athenis *in fastigio* (probably pedimental rather than acroteria) on Augustus' Temple of Palatine Apollo (ded. 28 BC), as on all Augustus' temples. Some may have been copies or archaistic works, but a fragmentary head of *Athena* in genuine East Greek Archaic style has been found on the Palatine (Rome, Antiqua. Palatino). Pausanias twice mentioned a sculptor Bupalos alone, whose works included a *Tyche* at Smyrna (IV.xxx.6; apparently the first to be shown with *polos* (headdress) and cornucopia) and groups of *Charites* at Smyrna and Pergamon (IX.xxxv.6). The subjects and locations of these works may imply the existence of a second sculptor Bupalos, active in the Hellenistic period, with whom Heidenreich associated works of an East Greek archaizing Hellenistic style.

BIBLIOGRAPHY

Pausanias: *Guide to Greece*
R. Heidenreich: 'Bupalos und Pergamon', *Archäol. Anz.* (1935), pp. 668–701
A. Rumpf: 'Zu Bupalos und Athenis', *Archäol. Anz.* (1936), pp. 52–63
M. D. Fullerton: 'Archaistic Statuary of the Hellenistic Period', *Mitt.: Dt. Archäol. Inst.: Athen. Abt.*, cii (1987), pp. 259–78
P. Zanker: *The Power of Images in the Age of Augustus* (Ann Arbor, 1988), pp. 242–3

MARK D. FULLERTON

Buqras [Bouqras]. Site of an ancient Near Eastern Neolithic village, occupied mainly between 6400 and 5900 BC, located on a terrace overlooking the River Euphrates near Dayr al-Zawr in north-eastern Syria. At this site (2.7 ha in area) the transition from Aceramic to Ceramic Neolithic was exhibited in an area midway between the Levant and northern Iraq cultural zones. There were soundings in 1965 by H. de Contenson and J. W. van Liere, and the site was jointly excavated in 1976–8 by the Universities of Amsterdam and Groningen. Finds are in the National Museum in Damascus and in the Dayr al-Zawr Museum.

The inhabitants of Buqras, of whom there were probably between 600 and 1000, were fully agricultural, with domesticated animals and plants. Even though the village was located beyond the limits of rain-fed agriculture, their economic resources enabled them to ornament house and person and to experiment with ceramic technology. Excavations revealed that the later building phases comprised orderly, rectangular, mud-brick detached dwellings set in parallel rows along streets or in blocks around courtyards. Most were divided into nine small oblong or square rooms, up to *c.* 3 m across, entered sometimes from the roof. White plaster was used to form storage bins or hearths or to line the interior floors and walls. The latter areas were often decorated with designs in red ochre: a frieze of ostriches on one wall was reminiscent of the onager frieze at UMM DABAGHIYA in Iraq (*c.* 5500 BC). On another wall there was a human head in relief with eyes of inlaid obsidian. These works may represent pure decoration but could also refer to hunting magic. At first, vessels were made in gypsum plaster (White Ware; *see* SYRIA-PALESTINE, §V, 1), but gradually a ceramic industry developed. Bowls and basins in simple shapes, sometimes carinated, were made of light-coloured fine clay; the surfaces were treated variously by burnishing, slipping, appliqué, incisions filled with white plaster, or by painting with simple geometric designs (triangles, chevrons, zigzags etc).

Quantities of beads and pendants in bone, shell, stone, amber and clay were found, including 'butterfly beads' (stone tubes with lateral wings), a type known also from Abu Hureyra. Other objects in baked clay or stone were plentiful, including human and animal figurines of alabaster or limestone that may indicate religious practices. The finest craftsmanship, however, produced stone vessels in the form of bowls and platters, often footed. These were usually made of local limestone, but foreign rocks of granite, alabaster or greenstone were fashioned, sometimes in the shape of animals (see fig.), and polished to bring out the beauty of the veining. Even the more utilitarian items, such as greenstone axes and mortars, were well polished.

Impressions left in clay or plaster indicate that other crafts using perishable materials were practised, such as

Buqras, alabaster hedgehog, h. 66 mm, *c.* 6400–5900 BC

basketry and matting. Installations found in the long rooms of some houses suggest that textile weaving (perhaps using wool and hemp) was done. Bone articles (awls, needles, spatulas) and flint tools and weapons (javelins, arrowheads, borers, engravers, knives of flint and obsidian) were fashioned. The site gives a valuable glimpse of a well-adapted and organized late Euphrates Pre-pottery Neolithic and early pottery Neolithic village.

BIBLIOGRAPHY

P. A. Akkermans, H. Fokkens and H. T. Waterbolk: 'Stratigraphy, Architecture and Lay-out of Bouqras', *Préhistoire du Levant* (Lyon, 1981), pp. 485–501

P. A. Akkermans and others: 'Bouqras Revisited: Preliminary Report on the Project in Eastern Syria', *Proc. Prehist. Soc.*, xl (1983), pp. 335–72

M. Lemière: *Les Premières Céramiques du Moyen-Euphrate* (diss., Lyon, Université-Lumière/Lyon II, 1986)

J. J. Roodenberg: *Le Mobilier en pierre de Bouqras* (Istanbul, 1986)

LORRAINE COPELAND

Burana [formerly Balasaghun; Balasagun; Kuz-Balyk; Kuz-Ordu]. Medieval site 12 km south of Tokmak and 6 km from AK-BESHIM in the eastern part of the Chu Valley in northern Kyrgyzstan. Identified with Balasaghun, the capital of the Qarakhanid dynasty (*reg* 940–1211), Burana takes its name from the surviving minaret (10th–11th century) called *Manār-i burāna* by the 16th-century historian Mirza Muhammad-Haydar Dughlat. Archaeological investigation of the site, which was destroyed by earthquakes in the 14th and 15th centuries, has been conducted since 1927. The central group of ruins, identified by Masson as the city proper, covers an area 600×560–80 m and includes a palace complex, the minaret and various buildings dating from the 10th to the 14th century. This was the administrative and religious centre of medieval Balasaghun. The minaret (h. 24 m; rest. 1974) has a square base, octagonal socle and tapering cylindrical shaft articulated by bands of decoration. A door 5 m above ground level (indicating the height of the roof of the now-destroyed mosque) leads to an internal spiral stair. Near by were the tombs of the Qarakhanids (destr.), of which three have been excavated. One was an octagonal prism with a dome or conical cap; the two others were cylinders with monumental portals and either a dome or conical cap. They were decorated with bricks laid in patterns, terracotta and carved plaster. A *khānaqāh* complex, containing a single-room mosque, was repeatedly remodelled from the early 11th century to the 14th.

Excavations outside the city proper uncovered a series of houses, workshops, water conduits and a bath. Two rings of walls girdled the town and its gardens, an area of 28 sq. km. The buildings were constructed of baked- or mud-brick and boasted rich decoration in the form of wall paintings and carved plaster combined with patterned flooring and panelling. Houses had public rooms, apartments for men and women and service rooms, grouped around internal courtyards. Small flat gravestones (Rus. *kairak*) inscribed in Arabic and Nestorian Christian funerary monuments inscribed in Syriac date from the 12th to the 14th century. There is an open-air museum at the site, and many of the finds are in the Kyrgyzstan Historical Museum in Bishkek.

BIBLIOGRAPHY

Enc. Iran.: 'Balāsāgūn'; *Enc. Islam/2*: 'Balāsāghūn'

Mirza Muhammad-Haydar Dughlat (1500–51): *Tārīkh-i rashīdī* ['The Rashidian history']; Eng. trans. by N. Elias and E. D. Ross as *A History of the Moghuls of Central Asia* (London, 1895/*R* 1972), pp. 364–5

V. D. Goryacheva: *Srednevekovyye gorodskiye tsentry i arkhitekturnyye ansambli kirgizii (Burana, Uzgen, Safid-Bulan)* [Medieval urban centres and architectural ensembles of Kyrgyzstan (Burana, Uzgen, Safid-Bulan)] (Frunze, 1983), pp. 21–66

M. Ye. Masson and V. D. Goryacheva: *Burana: Istoriya izucheniya gorodischa i yego arkhitekturnykh pamyatnikov* [Burana: a history of the investigation of the site and its architectural monuments] (Frunze, 1985)

V. D. GORYACHEVA

Buratti, Carlo (*b* Novazzano, nr Como, *c.* 1651; *d* Rome, ?1734). Italian architect. Following his arrival in Rome at an unknown date, he became a pupil of Carlo Fontana. His first known work was the renovation in 1695 of the theatre (destr.) in the Palazzo Capranica. In 1698 he was elected a member of the Accademia di S Luca, where he served both as an instructor of architecture and as a judge for student competitions held between 1704 and 1708. In 1702 he went to Benevento to assist in the rebuilding of the city, which had been damaged by an earthquake; in 1705 he redesigned the piazza in front of S Sofia and placed a monumental portal on an axis with the entrance of the church (destr. 1809). He restored the medieval cathedrals of Salerno (1703–4) and Aversa (1703–15); he also remodelled the interior of Albano Cathedral (*c.* 1720) following the model of SS Apostoli in Rome, incorporating the existing columns of the nave into large square piers articulated with pilasters. The new façade of the cathedral was articulated with a giant order derived from Gianlorenzo Bernini's sanctuary at Galloro and Fontana's S Maria dell'Umilità, Rome. Among Buratti's few independent works are the new seminary in Aversa (1713), whose flat expanses of wall and simple pilaster articulation reflect his classical training, and the church of the Bambino Gesù in Rome (begun 1731); although this was completed by Ferdinando Fuga, the design is essentially Buratti's. The church is arranged as a small Greek cross with a dome over the crossing. Except for the broken pediment, the façade is close to that of Albano Cathedral.

BIBLIOGRAPHY

A. Schiavo: 'L'architetto Carlo Buratti', *Studi offerti a Giovanni Incisa della Rocchetta* (Rome, 1973), pp. 503–10

J. Garms: *Il Bambin Gesù*, Chiese di Roma Illustrate, 135 (Rome, 1975)

CATHIE C. KELLY

Burch, Edward (*bapt* London, 30 Oct 1730; *d* London, Feb 1814). English gem-engraver, medallist, wax modeller and miniature painter. Of humble origins, he was self-taught as an engraver but studied drawing and modelling at the St Martin's Lane Academy and in the gallery of casts belonging to Charles Lennox, 3rd Duke of Richmond, known as the Duke of Richmond's Academy. He exhibited with the Society of Artists, of which he was a director, from 1760 until 1769, and gained three premiums from the Society of Arts between 1763 and 1766. In 1769 he enrolled at the Royal Academy as a student, became an ARA the following year and in 1771 was the first of the elected Academicians, presenting as his diploma work a cornelian intaglio of *Neptune* (London, RA). He enjoyed great success and attracted wide patronage for more than two decades, engraving principally antique subjects (e.g. *Sabina*, yellow sard intaglio; Baltimore, MD, Walters A.G.), allegorical scenes (e.g. *Sacrifice to Minerva*, chalcedony intaglio; St Petersburg, Hermitage) and portraits of worthies (e.g. *Shakespeare*, version attrib., cornelian intaglio; Cambridge, Fitzwilliam; *Newton*, chalcedony intaglio; sale cat. London, Christie's, 4 Oct 1989, lot 435). He prided himself particularly on his figure studies (e.g. *Hercules*, citrine intaglio ; London, BM), inspired by the anatomy lectures of Dr William Hunter, for whom he modelled a wax anatomical figure (248 mm, before 1769; U. Glasgow, Hunterian Mus.) and created two medals (1775; London, BM, and Oxford, Ashmolean; and 1786; untraced). Among his other works are 19 horses modelled (*c*. 1789) for Wedgwood's jasper ware and prize medals for Göttingen University (1785, 1786; bronze copies, London, BM and Oxford, Ashmolean). He exhibited at the Royal Academy until 1808, but his career had already begun to decline by 1788. Almost destitute, he was appointed Librarian to the Royal Academy in 1794; the publication the following year of a catalogue of his gems, many of them for sale, did not restore his fortunes, while failing eyesight prevented him from continuing as an engraver. He took up miniature painting late in life (examples, London, V&A; see Foskett, pls 31, 97 and 98).

Both of Burch's sons, Edward (*fl* 1789–1804) and Henry Jacob (*b* 1763), followed in his footsteps: Edward exhibited at the Royal Academy from 1789 to 1804, while Henry turned to painting miniatures, including a portrait of his father (exh. RA 1814; untraced).

WRITINGS

A Catalogue of One Hundred Proofs from Gems, Engraved in England, by E. Burch, RA (London, 1795)

BIBLIOGRAPHY

DNB; Foskett; Thieme–Becker

L. Brown: *Bristol Historical Medals*, i (1980)

G. Seidmann: 'Nathaniel Marchant, Gem-Engraver', *Walpole Soc.*, liii (1987), pp. 1–105

——: 'A Cornelian Intaglio Antinous by Edward Burch', *Antiqua. J.*, lxxiii (1993)

GERTRUD SEIDMANN

Burch [Burgh], **Hendrick van der** (*b* Naaldwijk, nr Delft, *bapt* 27 June 1627; *d* after 1666). Dutch painter. One of his sisters seems to have been Jannetje van der Burch, the wife of Pieter de Hooch, whose genre scenes of guard-rooms, domestic interiors and courtyards closely resemble those of van der Burch. Van der Burch was living in Delft by 1642 and joined the Guild of St Luke in 1649. He cosigned documents with de Hooch in 1652, 1654 and 1655. Probably in imitation of de Hooch, van der Burch developed an interest in the expressive use of highly ordered, geometric space and sophisticated lighting effects, often employing a view to an adjoining space through a doorway or window. However, his command of perspective was never so certain and his lighting effects rarely so subtle as de Hooch's. Van der Burch moved to Leiden in 1655 and acquired a house opposite the university; one of his rare signed paintings depicts a *Graduation Procession at the University of Leiden* (Amsterdam, Rijksmus.). He had moved to Amsterdam by May 1659 but in the 1660s is recorded in both Leiden and Delft. Besides his genre scenes, he painted at least one group portrait and a river scene; a *Susanna* by van der Burch appeared in an inventory of 1703.

BIBLIOGRAPHY

W. R. Valentiner: *Pieter de Hooch: Des Meisters Gemälde in 180 Abbildungen mit einem Anhang über die Genremaler um Pieter de Hooch und die Kunst Hendrik van der Burch*, Klass. Kst Gesamtausgeben, xxxv (Stuttgart, 1929), pp. xxxvii–lii

P. C. Sutton: 'Hendrick van der Burch', *Burl. Mag.*, cxxii/926 (1980), pp. 315–26

PETER C. SUTTON

Burchard, Ludwig (*b* Mainz, 31 May 1886; *d* London, 7 Sept 1960). British art historian of German birth. He studied at the universities of Munich, Heidelberg and Halle am Saale. In 1912 he received his doctorate under Adolph Goldschmidt with a dissertation on the art of etching in Holland before Rembrandt. In 1922 he began to compile a new critical catalogue of the works of Rubens, and thereafter he devoted his career to the work of this artist. In 1935 the rising power of the National Socialists forced him to move to London and in 1948 he became a British citizen. During World War II and later, his ill-health prevented Burchard from publishing the material he had assembled during nearly 50 years for his catalogue raisonné. Since 1963, the vast amount of documentary material he left behind, mainly related to Rubens and 17th-century Flemish art, has formed an essential part of the library and the files of the Rubenianum, a centre for the study of 16th- and 17th-century Flemish art, adjacent to Rubens's house in Antwerp. It also provided the basic groundwork for the multi-volume *Corpus Rubenianum Ludwig Burchard* (Brussels and London, 1971–).

WRITINGS

Die holländischen Radierer vor Rembrandt (Berlin, 1917)

with R. A. d'Hulst: *Rubens Drawings*, 2 vols (Brussels, 1963)

BIBLIOGRAPHY

F. Baudouin: 'Dr Ludwig Burchard (1886–1960) en zijn betekenis voor de studie van Rubens en van de Vlaamse kunst van de 17de eeuw', *Acad. Anlct.: Kl. S. Kst.*, xlviii/1 (1987), pp. 67–100 [with full list of his publications]

FRANS BAUDOUIN

Burchard, Pablo (*b* Santiago, 1875; *d* Santiago, 1964). Chilean painter. He studied at the Escuela de Bellas Artes in Santiago under Pedro Lira and Miguel Campos (1844–99) and under the influence of Juan Francisco González developed an Impressionistic approach to painting that was rational in its emphasis on technique and precise drawing, but also romantic in the poetry animating his landscapes and in its delicate range of enveloping colour. His approach was one of humility, befitting his personality, and it took shape, mainly from the example of Cézanne, in clear patches of colour: light, evocative and with their own unique poetic spirit. Nevertheless his tendency to synthesize different elements placed him in the avant-garde as a young man, and he had a profound influence on the Grupo Montparnasse a short time later (*see* MORI, CAMILO). Rightly considered one of the founders of modern Chilean art, he influenced later generations both through his teaching at the Escuela de Bellas Artes (of which he was director from 1932 to 1935) and through the expressive and abstract qualities of his painting. He won various awards including the Premio Nacional de Arte in 1944. His son, Pablo Burchard Aguayo (*b* 1919), also established his reputation as a painter, especially with several large murals in Santiago (e.g. for the Banco Central) and on the basis of his later abstract work.

BIBLIOGRAPHY

Art of Latin America since Independence (exh. cat. by S. L. Catlin and T. Grieder, New Haven, CT, Yale U. A.G.; Austin, U. TX, A. Mus.; San Francisco, CA, Mus. A.; and elsewhere; 1966), pp. 91, 143, 157, 163–4, 222

CARLOS LASTARRIA HERMOSILLA

Charles Burchfield: *The Insect Chorus*, watercolour, 487×387 mm, 1917 (Utica, NY, Munson-Williams-Proctor Institute)

Burchfield, Charles (Ephraim) (*b* Ashtabula Harbor, OH, 9 April 1893; *d* West Seneca, NY, 10 Jan 1967). American painter. At five he moved with his family to Salem, OH, where he spent his youth. From 1912 to 1916 he studied at the Cleveland School of Art, OH. He was awarded a scholarship to the National Academy of Design, New York, where he went in October 1916 but left after one day of classes. He returned to Salem in November, where he supported himself by working at a local metal-fabricating plant, and painted during his lunch-hours and at weekends.

Between 1915 and 1918 Burchfield painted small watercolours marked by their fantasy and arbitrary colour. In these he often painted either visual equivalents of sounds in nature, as in *The Insect Chorus* (1917; Utica, NY, Munson–Williams–Proctor Inst.; see fig.), or re-created childhood emotions, such as fear of the dark in *Church Bells Ringing, Rainy Winter Night* (1917; Cleveland, OH, Mus. A.). For these works he invented symbols in a sketchbook entitled *Conventions for Abstract Thoughts* (New York, Kennedy Gals) in which he identified his motifs with such labels as 'Fear', 'Dangerous Brooding' and 'Fascination of Evil'. Other watercolours from this period reflect his deep love of nature, as in *Dandelion Seed Balls and Trees* (1917; New York, Met.). All Burchfield's early watercolours have a strong decorative quality derived in part from oriental art, which he had admired at the Cleveland Museum of Art during his student days. However his use of expressive colour and distortion of form was achieved independently of the example of European modernism, with which he was not familiar until much later.

In July 1918 Burchfield was drafted into the US Army and was released in January 1919. In 1921 he became a designer for the wallpaper firm of M. H. Birge & Sons in Buffalo, NY, and in 1922 married Bertha L. Kenreich. In 1925 he moved to a small house in Gardenville, a suburb of Buffalo, where he spent the rest of his life. In 1929 he left Birge to paint full-time. The period 1919 to 1929 was an interlude of experiment and change in Burchfield's work. In 1924 Guy Pène du Bois referred to Burchfield as depicting 'the American scene' in his paintings of provincial America (*see* AMERICAN SCENE PAINTING). From 1929 to 1943 he developed a predominantly realist style, in which he largely abandoned fantasy and concentrated on urban subjects. The paintings were larger in scale and more realistically handled than his earlier works on paper. He occasionally painted in oil, for example *Old House by Creek* (1932–8; New York, Whitney), but his preferred medium was always watercolour. He developed a distinctive watercolour technique using heavy, overlapping brushstrokes that gave the medium a notable weight and density rather than its customary transparency and sparkle. His subject-matter was the architecture and industry of Buffalo: its grim Victorian houses, the façades of which he painted to evoke faces of corresponding mood, for example *Rainy Night* (1929–30; San Diego, CA, Mus. A.); its industrial scenes, such as *Black Iron* (1935; New York, Mrs John D. Rockefeller III priv. col.); and its piles of rusty debris, which can be seen in *Scrap Iron* (1929; Lockport, NY, Charles Rand Penney priv. col.). Between 1936 and 1937 *Fortune* magazine commissioned him to paint railway yards in Pennsylvania and coal-mines in Texas and West Virginia. By 1943 Burchfield felt he had exhausted this style and made a conscious effort to revive the imaginative quality of his early work on a larger scale.

Burchfield's late, expressionist period lasted from 1943 to 1967. He enlarged some early watercolours by pasting strips of paper around them in a style consistent with their fantasy, for example *Sun and Rocks* (1918, enlarged 1950; Buffalo, NY, Albright-Knox A.G.). Other watercolours followed that were not reconstructions but the result of a direct approach to nature. In these, he adapted the broad, solid technique of his middle period to expressionist rather than realist ends. By freely distorting form and colour he interpreted the moods he felt in all the changing aspects of the landscape in different seasons, light and weather. The large watercolours of this last period (often over 1.25 m wide) were the clearest expression of his faith in the ultimate spiritual meaning of nature. Outstanding examples are *An April Mood* (1946–55; New York, Whitney), *Arctic Owl and Winter Moon* (1960; Montgomery, AL, Blount Col.), *Orion in Winter* (1962; Lugano, Col. Thyssen-Bornemisza), *Dandelion Seed Heads and the Moon* (1961–5; Wayne, NJ, Irwin Goldstein priv. col., see Trovato, p. 311). In these Burchfield affirmed unmistakably the pantheism that had informed so much of his work. He was one of the last of many American pantheists and belonged to a tradition that began in the 19th century with writers such as Ralph Waldo Emerson and painters of the Hudson River school, and that later embraced the Luminists and even natural historians, including John Burroughs (1837–1921) and John Muir (1838–1914).

BIBLIOGRAPHY

J. I. H. Baur: *Charles Burchfield* (New York, 1956)
J. S. Trovato: *Charles Burchfield: Catalogue of Paintings in Public and Private Collections* (Utica, 1970)
M. Baigell: *Charles Burchfield* (New York, 1976)
J. I. H. Baur: *The Inlander: Life and Work of Charles Burchfield, 1893–1967* (East Brunswick, NJ, 1982)

JOHN I. H. BAUR

Burckhardt, Jacob (Christoph) (*b* Basle, 25 May 1818; *d* Basle, 8 Aug 1897). Swiss historian and art historian. He was born into one of the leading families of Basle and was the son of the chief pastor. Raised on the neohumanist Humboldtian ideals adopted for the city's schools by the ruling bourgeoisie in the aftermath of the French Revolution, he saw his world transformed by the rise of modern industrial society and the spread of social democracy and aggressive nationalism. His work reflects an intense experience of his own time by a citizen of one of the last city-republics in Europe.

Burckhardt first studied theology but lost his faith and switched to history and philosophy at the University of Berlin (1839–43). He took courses in art history, then a new discipline, from Franz Kugler, to whom he remained attached all his life. He also spent a term in Bonn, then a centre of German Romanticism. Later celebrated as the historian and admirer of the Italian Renaissance, he began his career as a German nationalist, a medievalist and an enthusiastic champion of the Gothic.

Although he became well known as a historian of culture, Burckhardt was also a pioneer art historian. His first course as a teacher at the University of Basle, in 1844, was on the history of architecture. At the newly founded Eidgenössische Technische Hochschule (ETH) in Zurich, where he was appointed to the first chair of art history in Switzerland in 1855, he taught a cycle of three courses on ancient art, Christian art and the architecture of the Renaissance. Even after he was recalled to Basle to fill the chair of history in 1858, he continued to offer courses in art history almost every year until he became the first occupant of a new chair in art history in 1886. Because of his neohumanist conviction that the study of history must contribute to *Bildung* rather than *Wissenschaft*, Burckhardt always tried to reach a general educated audience, often lecturing to non-specialists. He contributed hundreds of articles on art history to the ninth edition of the Brockhaus Encyclopaedia and throughout his life gave public lectures at Basle on subjects of history, art and literature.

Burckhardt despised the fact-grubbing approach to art history. Like Kugler, he adopted a broadly Hegelian periodization of world history but rejected the idea of historical progress, focusing rather on the characteristics that distinguish the art of one period from that of another and on the way particular styles and forms express key features of the cultures they belong to. The goal of his books and classes was *Genuss*, by which he meant not so much pleasure as the experience, through art, of order and harmony. To that experience, in an age he considered to be increasingly characterized by violence and cultural vulgarity, Burckhardt attributed the highest human and moral value.

Much of Burckhardt's writing, like his teaching, was devoted to the history of art. *Die Kunstwerke der belgischen Städte* already demonstrated a characteristic propensity to concentrate on formal relations and on the internal organization of individual works. Four years later, his revision of Kugler's *Handbuch der Geschichte der Malerei* (1837; 2/Berlin, 1847) initiated a retreat from the Romantic view of art as the expression of the popular spirit, according to which the Germans were the true successors of the Greeks; Greek art and the 'German' art of the Middle Ages (i.e. Gothic) were uniquely 'organic', 'original' and truly 'classical' in their perfect harmony of form and function; and Roman and Italian Renaissance art were derivative and secondary. Burckhardt emphasized instead an aspect of Renaissance art and culture that anticipated the later *Cultur der Renaissance in Italien*: the emergence of an original secular view of the world, resulting in a new sense of the concrete and the real, a new individual artistic consciousness and the progressive autonomization of art.

Burckhardt identified Michelangelo as the prototypical 'modern' artist, in whom this process had gone so far that it threatened the balance of energy and order, individuality and shared values and assumptions on which the particular beauty of Renaissance art rested. Tintoretto, Correggio and Rembrandt had similarly been unable or unwilling to set limits to 'das Empörende' ('the force rising up from below'), the very energy that had made the Renaissance possible in the first place; and in all four the process of autonomization had transformed art into a medium for exploring not a subject-matter but the artist's subjectivity or the problems of his art. Burckhardt's lifelong admiration for Rubens, culminating in the posthumously published *Erinnerungen aus Rubens*, was due to the success with which he believed Rubens had given shape, form and harmony to a world of daemonic energies. It seems likely that he admired the work of his contemporary Arnold Böcklin (also from Basle) for similar reasons. The re-evaluation of Renaissance art was completed in *Der Cicerone*, in which Burckhardt presented Italian art as a continuous tradition from Late Antiquity, and the art of 'die eigentliche Renaissance' not as a copying of Antiquity but as the product of a fruitful tension between the spontaneous creative energies of a new world and norms inherited from Classical antiquity. He identified a 'golden age' (*c.* 1500–1540), which he designated as 'classical'; by this he meant an art based on the creative use of borrowed forms, the product of individual imagination regulated by normative cultural traditions rather than—as at an earlier stage in his career—an 'organic' or 'original' expression of popular spirit. In the aftermath of the Revolution of 1848 Burckhardt was not as enthusiastic about the popular spirit.

The *Geschichte der neueren Baukunst*, the material of which was originally intended for inclusion in *Die Cultur der Renaissance in Italien*, confirmed Burckhardt's view of the Renaissance and his interest in form as the locus of meaning in art. By 1839–40 he had distinguished 'two avenues for the history of art. Either it becomes a handmaiden of cultural history or it starts out from the beautiful itself and uses cultural history only to enhance understanding of the work of art'. He followed both approaches—that of cultural history and that of art history—without ever fusing them. As an art historian he emphasized 'the history of styles, i.e. of the modes of expression of the beautiful in art'. This meant treating each art form from the point of view of its own traditions, problems and internal development, showing how specific artistic or architectural tasks found different solutions in the hands of different artists or schools. He described this approach to art history as the history of art 'nach Aufgaben' ('according to tasks'). History, as it was understood in his time (i.e. the political evolution of peoples and nations), did not 'explain' art in Burckhardt's view: art and politics were equally part of culture. Thus Burckhardt's practice, as a historian, of substituting a cross-sectional synchronic mode of historical analysis for the traditional narrative or diachronic mode, may be indebted to his practice of art history. Likewise, the cultural history he preferred to traditional political history corresponded to his intention to write art history as a 'history without names' rather than a history of artistic personalities.

Though less productive than those of his student and successor at Basle, Heinrich Wölfflin, Burckhardt's formal categories of 'organic style' and 'spatial style'—the former dominated by a single building type closely connected with communal religious practice, the latter borrowing freely and recombining formal elements detached from their 'organic' models to create new and original designs—ultimately led him to question art-historical orthodoxies about the 'degeneracy' of the later stages of an artistic tradition and to begin the rehabilitation of Late Antiquity and the Baroque that became a dominant theme of his later work. His classicism was not timorous or academic: he admired energy and inventiveness even where he believed they jeopardized the equilibrium that to him was the supreme achievement of Classical art. He even came to see some virtue in the fragmentation and the general breakdown of traditions in his own time that he otherwise denounced unremittingly. If it had produced a demi-culture based on mass education, the press, fashion and the market and had made artistic cohesion almost unattainable, it had also vastly expanded the viewer's receptiveness to a wide range of artistic styles and had created the conditions in which art history itself could develop.

WRITINGS

Die Kunstwerke der belgischen Städte (Düsseldorf, 1842)
Die Zeit Konstantins des Grossen (Basle, 1853; Eng. trans., London, 1949)
Der Cicerone: Eine Anleitung zum Genuss der Kunstwerke Italiens (Basle, 1855; Eng. trans., London, 1873)
Die Kultur der Renaissance in Italien (Basle, 1860; Eng. trans., London, 1878)
Geschichte der neueren Baukunst (Stuttgart, 1867); as *Geschichte der Renaissance in Italien* (Stuttgart, 1878)
Erinnerungen aus Rubens (Basle, 1898; Eng. trans., London, 1950)
Griechische Kulturgeschichte (Berlin and Stuttgart, 1898–1902; Eng. trans., abridged, London, 1963)
Weltgeschichtliche Betrachtungen (Berlin and Stuttgart, 1905; Eng. trans., London, 1943)
E. Durr and others, eds: *Gesamtausgabe*, 14 vols (Stuttgart, Leipzig and Berlin, 1929–34)
M. Burckhardt, ed.: *Briefe*, 10 vols (Basle, 1949–86)
H. Ritter, ed.: *Die Kunst der Betrachtung: Aufsätze und Vorträge zur bildenden Kunst* (Cologne, 1984)

BIBLIOGRAPHY

W. Waetzoldt: *Von Passavant bis Justi* (1924, 2/1965), ii of *Deutsche Kunsthistoriker* (Berlin, 1921–4, 2/1965), pp. 172–209
C. Neumann: *Jacob Burckhardt* (Munich, 1927)
H. Wölfflin: 'Jacob Burckhardt und die Kunst'; 'Jacob Burckhardt und die systematische Kunstgeschichte'; 'Jacob Burckhardt zum 100. Geburtstag, 25 Mai 1918', *Gedanken zur Kunstgeschichte* (Basle, 1940)
W. Kaegi: *Jacob Burckhardt: Eine Biographie*, 7 vols (Basle, 1947–82)
K. Berger: 'Jacob Burckhardt as Art Historian', *Jacob Burckhardt and the Renaissance: 100 Years After* (Lawrence, 1960), pp. 38–44
K. Löwith: *Jacob Burckhardt* (Stuttgart, 1966)
J. Wenzel: *Jacob Burckhardt in der Krise seiner Zeit* (Berlin, 1967)
F. Gilbert: 'Jacob Burckhardt's Student Years: The Road to Cultural History', *J. Hist. Ideas*, xlvii (1986), pp. 251–73
I. Siebert: *Jacob Burckhardt: Studien zur Kunst- und Kulturgeschichtschreibung* (Basle, 1991)
F. Haskell: *History and its Images: Art and the Interpretation of the Past* (New Haven and London, 1993), pp. 331–46

LIONEL GOSSMAN

Burckhardt, Jean-Louis [John Lewis; Johann Ludwig] (*b* Lausanne, 24 Nov 1784; *d* Cairo, 15 Oct 1817). Swiss explorer. He was born into a distinguished Basle family and attended the university at Leipzig (1800) and subsequently at Göttingen (1804). He arrived in England in 1806 where, through the influence of Sir JOSEPH BANKS, he was adopted by the African Society to search for the source of the River Niger. In 1809 he departed for the Middle East where, at Aleppo, he perfected his Arabic and undertook a protracted induction into Muslim theology, practice and culture. In 1812 he set out for Cairo, *en route* discovering the ancient city of PETRA. His subsequent exploration of the Upper Nile led to his discovery of the Great and Small Temples of Ramesses II at ABU SIMBEL. Accepted as a Muslim after rigorous cross-examination, he visited Mecca and Medina in 1814, the first European to have done so. Further travels ensued, but after his return to Cairo in 1817 he died after a short illness. He was a man of great modesty and splendid personal qualities, including toughness and dedication, whose achievement was remarkable. His *Travels* were to open up to European interest lands then still as 'dark' as the Africa he had hoped to explore but never reached.

WRITINGS
Travels in Nubia (London, 1819, 2/1822) [1st edn incl. biog. preface]
Travels in Syria and the Holy Land (London, 1822)
Travels in Arabia (London, 1829)

BIBLIOGRAPHY
K. Sim: *Jean-Louis Burckhardt: A Biography* (London, 1981)

IAIN BROWNING

Bureau. Type of furniture used for writing, typically a writing-table incorporating drawers or a type of case furniture with a hinged writing surface. The first furniture types to bear the name bureau evolved in France in the middle of the 17th century. Their antecedents, however, existed in the early medieval period, and the word 'bureau' is a corruption of the medieval French for a kind of coarse linen used as a surface for writing. In Sweden a simple desk has been preserved (*c.* 1200; Gotland, Vallstena Church), which has a sloping writing surface supported on the turned uprights typical of Romanesque furniture. Most medieval desks, however, were not free-standing and took the form of a writing-box with a hinged, sloping writing surface. Cabinets with a drop-leaf writing surface appeared in Italy during the Renaissance, and in Spain the *vargueño*—a cabinet, often carved and gilded, with a drop-leaf concealing an elaborate arrangement of drawers—began to appear at around the same time (e.g. walnut and gilt *vargueño*, first half 16th century; London V&A).

An early type of bureau developed in France in the mid-17th century, sometimes known as a bureau Mazarin, took the form of a writing-table, initially pushed against the wall like a pier table. Below the writing surface were two banks of drawers flanking a central kneehole. The drawers were carried on an arrangement of eight tapering legs joined by stretchers. Many examples survive, typically decorated with boulle inlay or floral marquetry. A variation of this type was the *bureau brisé*, which had a hinged horizontal top that concealed a writing surface and an arrangement of small drawers. During the early 18th century the bureau Mazarin gradually evolved into the more elegant form known as the *bureau plat* (e.g. *bureau plat*, attributed to André-Charles Boulle, 1710–15; Paris, Louvre). The banks of drawers were replaced by single drawers flanking a shallow drawer in the kneehole, while the complex arrangement of eight legs was replaced by four sinuous cabriole supports. The *bureau plat* was one of the most successful French furniture types of the 18th century. Although its elegant curving contours were straightened with the advent of Neo-classicism, its overall configuration remained almost unchanged into the 1820s.

In England the bureau had, typically, a hinged sloping flap that enclosed a fitted interior and opened out into a writing surface. Some early models were raised on legs, but by 1700 most bureaux were carried on an arrangement of drawers reaching almost to the floor. A particularly successful variation on this type was the bureau-cabinet, where the bureau supported a tall cabinet with one or two doors often faced with mirrored panels. Although such pieces were usually given the restrained boxlike form of 18th-century English case furniture, the grander examples were enlivened by architectural outlines with scroll pediments or arched crestings, while the doors could be flanked by pilasters. Until the 1730s most examples were veneered with walnut, although some of the most decorative examples were japanned in bright colours (e.g. bureau-cabinet japanned in blue and gold, *c.* 1745–9; London, V&A). After *c.* 1730 mahogany succeeded walnut as the timber most commonly used.

The English type of bureau and bureau-cabinet was adopted widely throughout northern Europe, although its form was often altered beyond recognition. Initially Dutch bureaux and bureau-cabinets were almost indistinguishable from their English counterparts, but during the second quarter of the century they acquired complex *bombe* profiles and broad, canted corners. The cabinets that surmounted them were usually given domed outlines. From 1750 to 1775 the form of the Dutch bureau-cabinet became more restrained, and a cylinder replaced the simple sloping flap. Mahogany again replaced walnut as the favoured timber.

In German-speaking countries bureaux assumed complex serpentine forms contained within broad canted corners. The cabinets or banks of drawers that surmounted them were usually slightly narrower than the bureau and were often divided into three parts with a slightly higher central section. These *Schreibschränke* were normally veneered with walnut inlaid with strapwork or panels of

1. Bureau by Johann Philip Raab, *Schreibschrank* design, walnut with maple marquetry, 2.63×1.59×0.73 m, 1764 (Karlsruhe, Badisches Landesmuseum)

burr-wood or marquetry. In Mainz the development of the *Schreibschrank* reached a peak in the 1760s when its elaborate form was framed by detached scrolling volutes (e.g. *Schreibschrank*, 1764; Karlsruhe, Bad. Landesmus; see fig. 1). Although such bureaux were to lose their popularity towards the end of the century, the form persisted in Neo-classical guise in northern Germany. In Denmark, the bureau-cabinet with a roll-top and tripartite superstructures known as a *chatol* was still one of the more important household pieces around 1800.

The bureau-cabinet was also widely popular in Italy, where it was adapted to regional characteristics. In Genoa the gently swelling forms were decorated with finely figured veneers laid in contrasting directions; in Venice lacquering and japanning were a common form of decoration, although walnut was widely favoured. Some of the most extraordinary bureaux were made in Piedmont. In the Rococo era Pietro Piffetti created a series of fantastic pieces of elaborate *bombe* and serpentine form inlaid with rare woods and ivory (e.g. bureau-cabinet, 1738; Rome, Pal. Quirinale). In the Neo-classical period Giuseppe Maria Bonzanigo produced a fabulous bureau-cabinet (*c.* 1780; Stupinigi, Mus. A. & Ammobil.) decorated with delicately carved white-painted grotesques set against a turquoise background.

The bureau-cabinets and bureaux closest to English prototypes were made in the USA. Although inspired by English pattern books, they were given regional inflections. Those in Newport, for example, had blocked fronts with convex and concave panels headed by shell lunettes (*see* UNITED STATES OF AMERICA, fig. 32). Such cabinetmakers as John Cogswell (*fl* 1769–1818) from Boston gave their bureaux a pronounced *bombe* profile.

2. Bureau of King Louis XV by Jean-François Oeben and Jean-Henri Riesener, oak with marquetry of holly, box and other woods on pear-wood panels, 1.43×1.83×0.97 m, 1769 (Paris, Musée du Louvre)

Towards the middle of the 18th century in France such *ébénistes* as Bernard van Risamburgh (ii) produced small writing-tables known as *secrétaires en pente* for the luxury end of the market. The *secrétaire en pente* was rather smaller than the *bureau plat*, and its writing surface and fitted interior were concealed beneath a sloping fall-front. It was carried on cabriole legs rather than banks of drawers (e.g. *secrétaire en pente*, 18th century; Paris, Mus. Jacquemart-André). The luxurious *bureau à cylindre*, pioneered by Jean-François Oeben, reached its apogee with the bureau of King Louis XV commissioned from Oeben in 1760 and finished and delivered to Louis XV by Jean-Henri Riesener in 1769 (Paris, Louvre; see fig. 2). Other famous *bureaux à cylindre* were made by David Roentgen (e.g. 1785; Paris, Louvre). The *secrétaire à abattant*, also known as the *secrétaire en armoire*, was a shoulder-height piece of case furniture that stood against the wall, with a vertical fall-front enclosing a fitted interior above a cupboard. Although Rococo secrétaires of this type exist, its boxlike form suited the rectangular shapes of Neo-classicism (*see* WOOD, colour pl. I, fig. 1), and it achieved pre-eminence in the later part of the 18th century, often being made *en suite* with a commode. Its rectangular form was ideal for trellis parquetry and floral and pictorial marquetry. Riesener made several examples distinguished by the extraordinary quality of their gilt-bronze mounts, including a lacquered commode and secrétaire (1784; New York, Met.) for Marie-Antoinette's appartements at Saint Cloud. During the late 1780s and 1790s finely figured veneers framed with simple gilt-bronze or brass mounts were increasingly favoured as an alternative to complex marquetry (e.g. *secrétaire à abattant* by Riesener, *c.* 1783; London, Wallace).

By the 1790s the *secrétaire à abattant* had replaced the bureau throughout most of Europe. In the Netherlands such secrétaires were often of satin-wood decorated with marquetry or set with panels of lacquer or *verre églomisé*. In German-speaking and Scandinavian countries the *secrétaire à abattant* was particularly suited to the simple geometric forms of the Biedermeier style.

In England the bureau-cabinet had become outmoded by the 1780s, although bureaux continued to be produced until the turn of the century. It was replaced by the secrétaire-bookcase, which substituted a fitted secrétaire drawer for the sloping fall-front of the bureau. The doors of the cabinet were usually glazed and divided by thin astragals arranged in elegant patterns. Although mahogany remained the primary timber, rosewood and satinwood were also used. Such designers as Thomas Sheraton, however, drew inspiration from such French types as the *bonheur-du-jour*, the most successful of which was the D-shaped Carlton House writing-table, with a bank of drawers surrounding a writing surface (the original was supposed to have been supplied to the Prince Regent, later George IV, at Carlton House, London). The importance of the library grew during the Regency period, and there was a concomitant development of a variety of small writing-tables carried on legs or end standards. The Davenport—a small desk with a sloping writing-surface above a single bank of drawers—was particularly popular from 1800 to 1875. For much of the 19th century, however, the writing-tables and pedestal desks developed during the 18th century replaced bureaux and secrétaires, although the Sheraton revival at the end of the century caused a return to favour of the Carlton House desk.

During the same period such French luxury manufacturers as François Linke (1855–1945) continued to produce a wide range of bureaux and secrétaires that drew their inspiration freely from 18th-century types. Other *ébénistes*, notably Henri Dasson (1825–96), produced high-quality replicas of 18th-century originals. During the Art Nouveau period such designers as Henry Van de Velde and Louis Majorelle successfully reinterpreted the bureau form through the sinuous abstractions of the Art Nouveau style.

BIBLIOGRAPHY

W. H. Odom: *A History of Italian Furniture from the Fourteenth to the Early Nineteenth Centuries*, 2 vols (New York, 1918–19, 2/1966–7)
F. de Salverte: *Les Ebénistes du XVIIIe siècle* (Paris, 1923, rev. 3/1934)
P. Macquoid and R. Edwards: *The Dictionary of English Furniture*, 3 vols (London, 1924–7, rev. 1954/*R* 1983)
G. H. Burr: *Hispanic Furniture from the Fifteenth through the Eighteenth Century* (New York, 1941, rev. 2/1964)
D. Ledoux-Lebard: *Les Ebénistes parisiens, 1795–1830* (Paris, 1951)
H. Kreisel: *Die Kunst des deutschen Möbels*, 3 vols (Munich, 1968–73)
S. Jervis: *Printed Furniture Designs before 1650* (Leeds, 1974)
P. Thornton: *Seventeenth Century Interior Decoration in England, France and Holland* (New Haven and London, 1978)
A. Gonzàles-Palacios: *Il tempio del gusto*, 2 vols (Milan, 1984)
P. Thornton: *Authentic Decor: The Domestic Interior, 1620–1920* (London, 1984)
N. de Reyniès: *Le Mobilier domestique*, i (Paris, 1987)

J. W. TAYLOR

Buren, Alexander von. *See* PASQUALINI, (1).

Buren, Daniel (*b* Boulogne-Billancourt, Seine-et-Oise, 25 March 1938). French painter and conceptual artist. He graduated from the Ecole Nationale Supérieure des Métiers d'Art, Paris, in 1960. After 1966 he developed an aesthetic form that rejected all formal exploration and gave importance solely to the positioning of the work of art. In particular he devised the formula of alternating white and coloured vertical stripes. This became his exclusive mark, at first as a member of the BMPT group with Olivier Mosset (*b* 1944), Parmentier and Niele Toroni (*b* 1937). He painted his stripes on a whole range of different supports in various inappropriate settings. After abandoning the idea of painting as object he proposed a critical analysis of painting that would henceforth be like wallpaper pasted up in the streets of Paris, rather like the huge canvas stretched across the middle of the Guggenheim Museum in New York (1971). In his many installations in galleries and museums as well as in the open or in the city, he responded to the surrounding space or the context of an exhibition with great acuity. His work often has a decorative quality, as can be seen in his controversial creation in the courtyard of the Palais Royal in Paris, *The Two Plateaux* (1985–6).

For illustration of his work *see* ENVIRONMENTAL ART.

WRITINGS

Limites critiques (Paris, 1970)
Rebondissements (Brussels, 1977)

BIBLIOGRAPHY

Daniel Buren (exh. cat., ed. D. Buren and P. Robert; Venice, Biennale, 1986)
A. Baldassari: *Daniel Buren: Entrevue* (Paris, 1987)
C. Francklin: *Daniel Buren* (Paris, 1987)

ALFRED PACQUEMENT

Burgee, John. *See under* JOHNSON, PHILIP.

Burger, Nikolaus. *See* JUNG, MORIZ.

Bürger, W(illem). *See* THORÉ, THÉOPHILE.

Burges, William (*b* London, 2 Dec 1827; *d* London, 20 April 1881). English architect and designer. His flamboyant and original High Victorian architectural style was influenced by French 13th-century Gothic, but he drew also on sources of many other periods. He is best known for his work at Cardiff Castle and Castell Coch for his patron, the Marquess of Bute. His designs for the decorative arts, particularly furniture and metalwork, are equally inventive and elaborate. He was friendly with the leaders of the Pre-Raphaelite movement, employing a number of Pre-Raphaelite artists and craftsmen in his decorative work.

1. Training and early work. 2. Commissions for the Marquess of Bute. 3. Other architectural work, 1869–81. 4. Interior design, furniture and metalwork.

1. TRAINING AND EARLY WORK. He was the eldest son of Alfred Burges, a marine engineer and partner of James Walker (1781–1862). Walker & Burges were government engineers for many military and civil projects. Alfred Burges was immensely successful and the family wealth later enabled William to be selective in his commissions.

William Burges attended King's College School, London, from 1839; here he was a contemporary of Dante Gabriel Rossetti and studied under John Sell Cotman. In 1843 he began to study engineering, but after a year took up articles with Edward Blore, who was Surveyor of Westminster Abbey. He worked with Blore on restoration work at the Abbey; together they uncovered the 13th-century retable. In 1849 Burges moved to the office of Matthew Digby Wyatt, who was Special Commissioner and Secretary to the Great Exhibition of 1851, held in Hyde Park, London. Burges assisted Wyatt in assessing the competition entries for the design of the exhibition building and later in the production of *The Industrial Arts of the Nineteenth Century* (2 vols, 1851–3), a record of the Great Exhibition to which he contributed 14 articles.

In the early 1850s Burges was better known as an archaeologist than an architect. In 1851 he became assistant to Henry Clutton, working on drawings for Clutton's *Remarks with Illustrations on the Domestic Architecture of France* (1853), and various ecclesiastical and domestic commissions, including the restoration of the Chapter House at Salisbury Cathedral (1854–6). In 1855 Clutton and Burges became partners and together won the competition for Lille Cathedral, although the design was never executed. In 1856 the partnership was dissolved.

Burges was deeply influenced by A. W. N. Pugin, whose theory, buildings and decorative work he knew principally through Pugin's writing. Like Pugin, he travelled extensively to further his architectural studies, visiting and sketching medieval buildings and artefacts. From 1845 he travelled in southern and eastern England and from 1849 he travelled regularly in France, Belgium, Germany and Italy. He embarked on a major tour in 1853, studying the cathedral towns around Paris and the decorative work of medieval secular buildings in Italy and Sicily. In 1859 he visited Constantinople, returning home via Greece. Throughout the 1860s and early 1870s he continued to travel widely in Europe. He was greatly influenced by Islamic and oriental art and architecture, also becoming familiar with them through his reading and through imported goods. The rejection of the design for Lille caused a scandal that brought Burges to the attention of the public. In 1856, having started in practice on his own, he won the competition for the Crimea Memorial Church, Constantinople. Although he laid its foundation stone, Burges ran into trouble with the committee and his design was never executed. His design for Brisbane Cathedral of 1859 also remained unexecuted, but in that year Burges received his first major commission from Robert John, 2nd Lord Carrington at Gayhurst, Bucks. Burges worked on the commission until 1860, decorating interior rooms (now largely altered) and making additions, most notably a servants' privy, a circular building surmounted by a carving of *Cerberus*.

1. William Burges: Summer Smoking Room, Clock Tower, Cardiff Castle, 1871–4

In 1860 Burges undertook restorations at Waltham Abbey, Essex, remodelling the east wall and inserting a large wheel window; his alterations are heavy and insensitive, but the reredos (1861–75), executed by Thomas Nicholls, is spectacular. The work prompted Burges to enter the competition for Cork Cathedral, which he won in 1863. St Finbar's Cathedral was begun in 1865 and further funds were gradually raised, enabling almost all of Burges's original ideas to be fulfilled and completed by 1876. The compact, bulky building, derived from French Gothic cathedrals, has three great towers, a curved apse and enormous wheel windows in the west end and transepts. While Burges was waiting for work on Cork Cathedral to start, he took on the redecoration of Worcester College Chapel, Oxford (1864), in an elaborate High Renaissance style of about 1500, with Pre-Raphaelite style windows by Henry Holiday, sculpture by Thomas Nicholls and a mosaic floor inspired by ancient Rome.

2. Commissions for the Marquess of Bute. In 1864 Burges met John Patrick Crichton Stuart, 3rd Marquess of Bute (*see* Stuart, (2)), a scholarly and sympathetic patron with the financial resources to realize Burges's ambitious and indulgent designs. From 1865 until his death Burges was continually at work at Cardiff Castle for the Marquess and put it before all other commissions. After his death, work continued to his designs.

At Cardiff, Burges found the ruins of the medieval castle, a landscape scheme by Lancelot Brown and a residential wing by Henry Holland and Sir Robert Smirke. Burges reported to the Bute Trustees in 1866 and work began when the Marquess came of age in 1868. The foundation stone of the Clock Tower in the south-western corner of the site was laid in 1868 and with its elaborate interiors it took seven years to complete. The Bute Tower was started in 1873, the Herbert Tower in 1876 and the Guest Tower, Library and Banqueting Hall in 1877. The work of Holland and Smirke was demolished or completely reclad. Cardiff Castle has a dramatic exterior, bristling with towers, pinnacles, crenellations and with steeply pitched roofs in a domestic French style. The interior was sumptuously fitted out with elaborate iconographic schemes by a team of artists and a workshop of specially trained craftsmen. The Summer Smoking Room (1871–4; see fig. 1), at the top of the Clock Tower, has elaborate fittings, all connected with the symbolism of summer. These include carving on the fireplace and capitals, executed by Nicholls, pictorial tiles by W. B. Simpson, and a chandelier by James Redfern representing the rays of the sun.

In 1871–2 Burges undertook a further commission for the Marquess, reporting on the ruins of the 13th-century Castell Coch, just outside Cardiff. Work began on the reconstruction of the castle in 1875, and the exterior was complete by the end of 1879, although the interiors (largely completed to his designs) were scarcely begun when Burges died. Castell Coch (*see* Castle, fig. 11) was designed as an occasional summer residence but was seldom used and never equipped with stables or offices. It is a re-creation rather than a restoration of a medieval castle, a folly with an inventive, colourful interior.

2. William Burges: garden façade of Knightshayes, Tiverton, Devon, 1869–74

3. OTHER ARCHITECTURAL WORK, 1869–81. In 1869 the foundation stone was laid at Knightshayes, Tiverton, Devon, Burges's largest country house, for John Heathcoate Amory, MP. The garden front, with its three-storey bay windows in either wing, is almost symmetrical, and despite its pointed windows, quatrefoils and gabled dormers, it is surprisingly unobtrusive (see fig. 2). The interior was never finished to Burges's designs, John Dibblee Crace taking over in 1874 with more modest designs.

Burges's other important domestic buildings were James McConnochie's house (1872–3, interior 1880) in Cardiff, and his own Tower house (1875–81) in Melbury Road, west London. Knightshayes and the McConnochie house illustrate Burges's restrained exterior domestic manner. The Tower House has bold expanses of brickwork with stone dressings and a prominent staircase tower with a conical roof. The interior is as fantastic as Cardiff Castle, though on a smaller scale. Each room is designed around a different theme with elaborate painted ceilings, stencilled and painted walls, and huge sculptured chimney-pieces. It ignores the developments of R. Norman Shaw and the Queen Anne Revival and is the result of Burges's vivid imagination combined with his extensive architectural and archaeological knowledge.

In the 1870s Burges also designed two churches, Christ the Consoler (1870–76), Skelton, W. Yorks, and St Mary's (1870–78), Studley Royal, W. Yorks, both similar in scale and plan. Skelton was commissioned by Lady Mary Vyner as a memorial to her son Frederick Grantham Vyner, who was murdered in Greece by bandits in 1870, and no expense was spared. Studley Royal, built by George Frederick Robinson, 1st Marquess of Ripon (1827–1909), also as a memorial to Vyner, is widely regarded as Burges's ecclesiastical masterpiece, benefiting from a parkland setting on a hill at the end of a great avenue. The interior has elaborate sculpture and painted and polychromatic decoration of the highest quality.

Burges was too medieval and too rigorously artistic to attract commissions for major public buildings, never achieving the success of Alfred Waterhouse, Cuthbert Brodrick or T. E. Collcutt in this field. His ambitious entry for the competition to design the Law Courts in London in 1866 (*see* COMPETITION, fig. 1), beaten by G. E. Street, proposed a picturesque skyline with towers and turrets and rows of Gothic windows and arcades. He designed the Speech Room (1871–7) for Harrow School, north London, with geometric clarity. The auditorium is on a D-plan, like a Greek amphitheatre, but his decorative schemes were not executed. His designs for Trinity College (1873–82), Hartford, CT, were diluted during execution in Burges's absence.

Burges's exteriors frequently surprise by their simplicity. Despite such *tours de force* as the east end of Studley Royal, they rely for effect on mass and boldly handled forms, such as square towers at Cardiff Castle (rebuilt from 1867), round towers at Castell Coch (rebuilt from 1875; *see* CASTLE, fig. 11), the D-plan of Harrow School's Speech Room and the round tower pinned on to an L-plan at the Tower House. His interiors, on the other hand, are dazzling.

4. INTERIOR DESIGN, FURNITURE AND METALWORK. Burges tightly controlled details of interior design, and numerous detailed drawings in his hand survive

for woodwork, stonework, sculpture and wall decoration. His control was all-pervading and minute. From the Law Courts competition of 1866 until his death, he did, however, rely on AXEL HERRMAN HAIG to interpret his designs in immensely impressive perspectives, which were regularly exhibited.

Burges also designed his furniture and metalwork in detail before his craftsmen set to work. His furniture is heavy and massively sculptural, with elaborate carving. It is richly painted and highly architectural. Cabinets have pitched roofs, dormers, chimneys and gables. Shelves are supported by Gothic columns, beds have Gothic arcades and many pieces are capped with crenellations. There are figurative panels with painted medieval scenes and there is a lavish use of geometric and stylized stencilled work. His furniture is witty, inventive and erudite. Among his earliest pieces of painted furniture was the first Yatman Cabinet (1858; London, V&A), which was decorated by Edward John Poynter. Other examples of his furniture are the Vita Nuova washstand and Golden Bed (both London, V & A) from the Guest Bedroom, Tower House. At the International Exhibition of 1862 in London, Burges laid out the Medieval Court for the Ecclesiological Society. The work of many Gothic Revival artists and craftsmen was exhibited, including painted furniture by Burges himself and by William Morris, whose furniture was particularly influenced by Burges. His metalwork shows a similar witty invention, evident in his church plate as well as his elephant inkstand (untraced). Good examples are his two decanters of 1865 (Bedford, Cecil Higgins A.G. and Cambridge, Fitzwilliam). He rejected mechanized manufacture and designed almost exclusively for wealthy private clients.

Burges's art and architecture were resoundingly élitist. He indulged himself and his clients, and although admired by his contemporaries, he was in many ways outside the Victorian mainstream. 'Burges, with his roots in the past, designed nothing from which the future could benefit,' wrote Charles Handley-Read, 'his work embodies no architectural advances of any kind.'

WRITINGS

Art Applied to Industry (Oxford and London, 1865)
'Art and Religion', *The Church and the World: Essays on Questions of the Day*, ed. O. Shipley (London, 1868), pp. 574–98
Architectural Drawings (London, 1870)

BIBLIOGRAPHY

C. Handley-Read: 'William Burges', *Victorian Architecture*, ed. P. Ferriday (London, 1963)
J. M. Crook: *William Burges and the High Victorian Dream* (London, 1981)
The Strange Genius of William Burges, 'Art-Architect', 1827–1881 (exh. cat., ed. J. M. Crook; Cardiff, N. Mus., 1981)
J. Cooper: *Victorian and Edwardian Furniture and Interiors* (London, 1987)

DAVID PROUT

Burgess, Gregory (*b* Newcastle, NSW, 8 Aug 1945). Australian architect. He graduated from the University of Melbourne (1970) and worked for Daryl Jackson Evan Walker Architects before starting his own practice in 1972. Burgess's architecture, inspired by esoteric literature, particularly Asian writings, and by the ideas of Rudolf Steiner, was concerned with human responses to form and space, the expansion of human consciousness and encouraging a sense of spiritual wholeness. He was also influenced by the Melbourne tradition of improvisatory 'bush' architecture and perhaps by the geometrical plans of such architects as Roy Grounds in the 1950s. Burgess's buildings generally have strong, complex geometries, often combined with more intuitive organic forms, conveying a sense of spiritual struggle in a contradictory modern world. He designed many houses, often largely in timber, for example the Hackford House (1981), Traralgon, Victoria, with a central stair tower that symbolically links earth and sky. His many public commissions included several school buildings; the church of St Michael and St John (1987), Horsham; Brambuk Living Cultural Centre (1989), Halls Gap, designed for an Aboriginal community, all in Victoria; the exuberant Boxhill Community Arts Centre (1990), Melbourne, with patterned brickwork and coloured glazed tiles produced in collaboration with an artist and the local community; and studios (1991) for the School of Art and Design, Bundoora Campus, Royal Melbourne Institute of Technology.

BIBLIOGRAPHY

M. Tawa: 'Greg Burgess: The Way of Transformation', *Transition* [Austral.], iv/1 (1984), pp. 14–19
——: 'Primordial Reality', *Tension*, 10 (1986), pp. 29–31
J. Taylor: *Australian Architecture since 1960* (Sydney, 1986, rev. 2/1990)

RORY SPENCE

Burgess, James (*b* Kirkmahoe, Dumfriesshire [now Dumfries & Galloway], 14 Aug 1832; *d* Edinburgh, 3 Oct 1916). Scottish art historian, active in India. He was educated in Dumfries, Glasgow and Edinburgh, and he went to India in 1855 as professor of mathematics at Doveton College, Calcutta. In 1861 he became head of the Sir Jamsetjee Jejeebhoy Parsee Benevolent Institution, Bombay, and here, in his spare time, he began his architectural and archaeological studies. In the years 1868 to 1873 he was secretary of the Bombay Geographical Society, and in 1872 he founded the journal *Indian Antiquary*, which he edited until 1884. He was appointed Archaeological Surveyor and Reporter to Government for Western India in 1874, and Southern India was added to his brief in 1881. As a result, over a period of 30 years he wrote a variety of important reports. He was promoted to Director-General of the Archaeological Survey of India in 1886 and took up residence in Calcutta. In this position he restructured archaeological enquiry in India and initiated the *Epigraphia Indica*, a journal dedicated to a systematic presentation of inscriptions. Although he retired from government service in 1889 and left India for Edinburgh, he continued to work on a variety of projects.

In his approach to the study of Indian architecture, Burgess was essentially a disciple of James Fergusson, and he followed Fergusson's classification of monuments as 'Hindu', 'Buddhist' and 'Jaina'. His most notable achievements are his detailed and accurate descriptions of monuments and his pioneering work in relating one monument to another. He was also skilled as a draughtsman and photographer.

WRITINGS

The Temples of Satruñjaya (Bombay, 1869)
The Rock Temples of Elephanta (Bombay, 1871)
Regular reports for the *Archaeological Survey of India* (1874–1905)
with J. Fergusson: *The Cave Temples of India* (London, 1880)

with P. Phene Spiers: rev. edn of J. Fergusson: *History of Indian and Eastern Architecture* (London, 1910)

BIBLIOGRAPHY

C. E. Buckland: *Dictionary of Indian Biography* (London, 1906), p. 61
J. F. Fleet: Obituary, *Ind. Antiqua.*, xlvi (1917), pp. 1–4
R. Sewell: Obituary, *J. Royal Asiat. Soc. GB & Ireland*, i (1917), pp. 195–9
P. Chandra: *On the Study of Indian Art* (Cambridge, MA, 1983)

S. J. VERNOIT

Burgh, Thomas (*b* Dromkeen, Co. Limerick, 1670; *d* Oldtown, Naas, Co. Kildare, 18 Dec 1730). Irish architect. He emerged from a background of military engineering to become one of the most prominent architects in Ireland in the first two decades of the 18th century. In 1700 he succeeded William Robinson as 'Engineer, Overseer, Surveyor & Director Generall of all. . .Fortifications, buildings' etc in Ireland, a life appointment with responsibility (not always clearly defined) for erecting and maintaining most government, and some military, buildings.

Burgh's most important works are public rather than domestic buildings, though it is difficult to tell to what extent this view depends on the uneven survival of records. His earliest building of consequence was the Royal (now Collins) Barracks, Dublin, begun shortly after 1700. Arranged around four open squares, Burgh's ranges (partly destr.) display his characteristic astylar classicism, derived from William Robinson and from English 17th-century architects such as Roger Pratt. The elements of this style, adaptable to barracks, country houses, custom houses or hospitals, include façades of two or three storeys with central and end projections (sometimes pedimented), quoins and continuous string courses, rusticated ground-floor arcades and sometimes a top storey of dormers. This reticent, flexible, economic and undeniably prosaic formula was popularized by Burgh and dominated pre-Palladian architecture in Ireland, where there are few parallels to the work of English Baroque architects.

Burgh's next important commission was for a new Custom House in Dublin (1704–8; destr. 1815), built beside Essex Bridge. By the 1770s its condition was described as unstable and it was replaced by James Gandon's more elaborate building on a new site further downstream in the 1780s. Burgh began work at Dublin Castle *c.* 1705. His principal contribution was the building from *c.* 1712 onwards of the east and west ranges of the Upper Yard (the east range survives only in the form of a modern reproduction) and the Treasury block, which is the northern range of the Lower Castle Yard. The chronology of his work at the Castle is obscure in detail.

The most impressive of Burgh's buildings is his library for Trinity College, Dublin (1712–33) related in form to Wren's Trinity College Library, Cambridge (1676–84). The Dublin building is externally severe and astylar, while inside, the Long Room is articulated with a rich Corinthian order. This bright, galleried and flat-ceilinged room was completed some years after Burgh's death; together with a few Palladian interiors by Edward Lovett Pearce, it set new standards for classical monumentality in interiors in Ireland. Burgh's last important building, designed in 1718, was Dr Steevens' Hospital in Dublin. Its exterior is similar to his work elsewhere, while the plan derives from that of Robinson's Royal Hospital, Kilmainham, Co. Dublin (1680–87).

Though he was Surveyor-General, Burgh did not receive the commission for the Parliament House in Dublin, awarded in 1728–9 to Edward Lovett Pearce. On artistic grounds, Pearce no doubt deserved the commission. Burgh had been a worthy but not pioneering successor to Robinson; he consolidated the classical tradition initiated by Robinson in the Royal Hospital, but he did not significantly develop it.

WRITINGS

A Method to Determine the Areas of Right-lined Figures Universally (Dublin, 1724)

BIBLIOGRAPHY

C. Brooking: *A Map of the City and Suburbs of Dublin* (London, 1728)
R. Loeber: *A Biographical Dictionary of Architects in Ireland, 1600–1720* (London, 1981)
A. Crookshank: 'The Long Room', *Treasures of the Library, Trinity College Dublin*, ed. P. Fox (Dublin, 1986), pp. 16–28

EDWARD McPARLAND

Burghausen, Hans von. *See* HANS VON BURGHAUSEN.

Burghley, 1st Baron. *See* CECIL, (1).

Burgin, Victor (*b* Sheffield, 24 July 1941). English conceptual artist, writer and photographer. He studied painting at the Royal College of Art from 1962 to 1965 and philosophy and fine art at Yale University from 1965 to 1967. From the late 1960s he adhered to CONCEPTUAL ART using combinations of photographic images and printed texts to examine the relationship between apparent and implicit meaning. In his *Lei Feng* series (1973; London, Tate), for example, he drew on semiotic, psychoanalytic and feminist theory to decode structures of representation. A teacher and theoretician, he published numerous writings on art theory and criticism, with particular concern for Post-modernist aesthetics.

WRITINGS

Work and Commentary (1969–1973) (London, 1973)
Victor Burgin (exh. cat., Eindhoven, Stedel. Van Abbemus., 1977)
Between (Oxford, 1986) [writings and visual work 1975–86]
The End of Art Theory (London, 1986)

HILARY GRESTY

Burgkmair. German family of artists. The Augsburg painter (1) Thoman Burgkmair was the father of one of the city's most important artists, (2) Hans Burgkmair I. Hans married Anna Allerlay, a furrier's daughter, in 1497; their son Hans Burgkmair II (*c.* 1500–62) took over the family workshop in 1531, but his only known works are a few designs for woodcut book illustrations (Hollstein, nos 1–4) and some miniature paintings, mostly after his father's works (e.g. a series of tournament participants, Munich, Staatl. Graph. Samml.).

BIBLIOGRAPHY

Hollstein: *Ger.*; Thieme–Becker
H. Pallmann: *Hans Burgkmair des Jüngeren Turnierbuch von 1529* (Leipzig, 1910)

(1) Thoman Burgkmair [Master of the Augsburg Legend of St Benedict] (*b* Augsburg, 1444–6; *d* Augsburg, 1525). Painter. Around 1460 he was apprenticed to Johannes Bämler, scribe, miniature painter and later an important book printer in Augsburg. Marriage *c.* 1469 with the daughter of a sculptor allowed Burgkmair to become a member of the Augsburg painters', glaziers' and sculptors' guild, in which he played a leading role. When the guild acquired its own house in 1472, he began to write the first Augsburg *Malerbuch* (Augsburg, Stadarchv), a record of events in the life of the guild.

The only authenticated painting by Burgkmair is a portrait of the Italian Franciscan monk and travelling preacher *Johannes Capistranus* (*c.* 1500; Prague, N.G., Šternberk Pal.), whose impressive sermons in Augsburg he had heard as a child aged eight in 1452, according to the inscription on the back of the picture. Though painted after Italian models, the profile view clearly portrays the fanatical preacher and indicates Burgkmair's ability. The marriage portrait of *Jakob Fugger and Sibylla Arzet* (1498; priv. col., see Buchner and Feuchtmayr, pp. 80–81) is another historically interesting work and is superior as a painting; it is debatable, however, whether it is by Thoman or by his son (2) Hans Burgkmair.

The remainder of the painted oeuvre consists of about a dozen panels: fragments of altarpieces and devotional paintings, compiled by Buchner, who ascribed them to Thoman Burgkmair. The most significant of these are four panels of the *Legend of St Benedict* (Augsburg, St Stephan, destr. World War II), after which the master was previously named, which show him to have retained a carefully crafted but dry, Late Gothic narrative style. In 1488 the Augsburg Cathedral chapter commissioned him to paint a historical series of portraits of bishops (of which the earlier ones survive only in late copies; all Augsburg Cathedral), and he also worked for Duke Christopher of Bavaria (1449–93); but no drawings or designs for woodcut book illustrations can be convincingly ascribed to him. His expressive powers declined considerably after 1500. There is a striking portrait of him as an old man, drawn by Hans Burgkmair with an inscription *maler, krank* ('painter, ill'; 1520; ex-Kupferstichkab., Dresden; missing after 1945; see Buchner and Feuchtmayr, p. 91).

BIBLIOGRAPHY

Thieme–Becker: 'Burgkmair, Thoman'; 'Meister der Augsburger Benedikt-Legende'
E. Buchner and K. Feuchtmayr, eds: *Beiträge zur Geschichte der deutschen Kunst*, ii (Augsburg, 1928), pp. 65–92
P. Wescher: 'Die Illustrationen der Augsburger Schedelchronik und ihr Meister', *Gutenberg Jb.* (1933), pp. 62–8
E. Buchner: 'Meister mit Notnamen und Monogrammisten', *Z. Kst*, iv (1950), p. 310
H. Müller: 'Die Malerfamilie Burgkmair', *Lebensbild. Bayer. Schwaben*, iv (1955), pp. 44–9
A. Stange: *Deutsche Malerei der Gotik*, viii (Munich and Berlin, 1957), pp. 48–51
Hans Holbein der Ältere und die Kunst der Spätgotik (exh. cat., Augsburg, Städt. Kstsammlungen, 1965), nos 122–3, 169
T. Falk: *Hans Burgkmair: Studien zu Leben und Werk des Augsburger Marlers* (Munich, 1968), pp. 10–12, 16–18

(2) Hans Burgkmair I [the elder] (*b* Augsburg, 1473; *d* Augsburg, May–Aug 1531). Painter, woodcut designer and draughtsman, son of (1) Thoman Burgkmair. He belongs in the first rank of German early 16th-century artists alongside Dürer, Lucas Cranach (i), Albrecht Altdorfer and Matthias Grünewald. While his drawings have received little attention, the approximately 800 woodcuts after his designs bear witness to his imagination, productivity and success. Through his decisive adoption of the forms of the Venetian Renaissance (he and Dürer were the first German artists to establish this connection), his links with the circle of artists and humanists around Emperor Maximilian I and his leading position in Augsburg, he played a decisive role in the blossoming of German art *c.* 1500. His only significant follower in Augsburg was Christoph Amberger.

1. EARLY WORKS, BEFORE 1508. Burgkmair's father, probably his first teacher, sent him in 1488–9 to Martin Schongauer, then the most famous painter and graphic artist in the Upper Rhine; this is confirmed in the inscription on Hans's posthumous portrait of *Martin Schongauer* (Munich, Alte Pin.). He concentrated on painting there—he appears never to have engraved—but soon after his return to Augsburg he was busy as a draughtsman, designing woodcuts for the printer Erhart Ratdolt. Ratdolt had worked in Venice from 1476 to 1486, but despite his receptiveness to Renaissance models, he achieved fame for superb large-format liturgical printed works in the Late Gothic tradition, which he produced for many dioceses. It was probably Burgkmair's task to design full-page woodcuts of canonized and patron saints. The clarity of these (unsigned) compositions and the increasingly individual appearance of his saints indicate his growing artistic maturity in the decade 1493–1504.

Burgkmair's first surviving painted works are portraits: *Geiler von Kaysersberg*, a preacher at Strasbourg Cathedral (perhaps painted while he was still on the Upper Rhine), and his friend the Bishop of Augsburg, *Friedrich von Zollern* (both 1490; Augsburg, Schaezlerpal.). Although rather awkward youthful works, they suggest his ambitiousness and indicate his early contacts with high-ranking church patrons. On his marriage in 1497 Burgkmair depicted himself in fine clothing in an unusual double *Self-portrait* drawing (Vienna, Albertina), signing his marriage contract and on his wedding day. The following year he acquired his master's certificate and was henceforth an established citizen of Augsburg.

Around the turn of the century Burgkmair received his first known large commission from the Church, for three of the six large paintings (all Augsburg, Schaezlerpal.) of the seven pilgrims' churches in Rome; these were in the shape of a Gothic arch, commissioned by the Dominican nuns of the former St Katharina Convent (now in Schaezlerpal.) in Augsburg for their refectory. Two pictures are by Hans Holbein the elder and one is by an unknown painter. In each, an image of one of the basilicas is linked with the legend of the associated saint. Burgkmair's first picture, *St Peter's Basilica*, which made special reference to the Holy Year 1500 in Rome, shows the first pure Renaissance forms to appear in a German painting, in the *porta santa* on the church façade. In a solemn *sacra conversazione* St Peter sits enthroned before his church, removed from all temporal concerns, surrounded by saints and auxiliary saints. The *Basilica S Giovanni in Laterano* (1502) presents a number of episodes from the story of St John the Evangelist, and the last picture represents the *Basilica S Croce* (1504) as a Romanesque church similar to that in Cologne, with the *Crucifixion* above, and at the side the legend of *St Ursula and the Maidens*, in front of Cologne's city walls. There is no evidence of Burgkmair in Augsburg during 1503, probably because he travelled to Cologne and on to the Netherlands; a group of early outline sketches survives, after works by Rogier der Weyden, Stefan Lochner and others from the Lower Rhine and the Netherlands. Burgkmair's reputation as a painter spread quickly; in 1505 the Elector of Saxony, Frederick the Wise, commissioned a triptych for the new castle chapel in Wittenberg, for which Lucas Cranach (i) and Dürer were also working. Among Burgkmair's portraits from this period, those of the merchant *Hans Schellenberger* (1505) and his wife *Barbara Schellenberger* (1507) are noteworthy (both Cologne, Wallraf-Richartz-Mus.).

Burgkmair travelled to Italy in 1507, a journey that had a decisive effect on his style and turned him away from the influences of the Upper and Lower Rhine. He stayed in Venice and may have spent time in Florence, Milan and Pavia. Woodcuts made soon after, such as *St Luke Painting the Virgin* (1507; B. 24) and the companion pieces *St George* (B. 23) and the equestrian *Emperor Maximilian* (B. 32; both 1508), reveal a freer concept of space and include elements of Renaissance architecture and ornamentation that had not hitherto been seen in Germany. In his paintings the bright Late Gothic colouring typical of southern Germany was increasingly replaced by Venetian *sfumato*. The *Virgin in a Landscape* (1509; Nuremberg, Ger. Nmus.) is his best painting of these years; iconographically it is still indebted to such life-size Late Gothic pictures of Mary as Schongauer's *Virgin of the Rose Bower* (1473; Colmar, Dominican Church). The colouring, landscape motifs and Mary's marble Renaissance throne are very Italianate, whereas the figures, particularly the naturalistically helpless baby Jesus, remain far removed from the ideal types of Giovanni Bellini or Raphael.

2. MATURE WORKS, 1508–20. Between 1508 and 1512 Burgkmair designed a series of technically innovative woodcuts using colour, with the help of an expert woodcutter from Antwerp, Jost de Negker. They experimented with printing in gold and silver, then made woodcuts using two or three tint blocks, which are among the earliest examples of chiaroscuro in woodblock printing. The graphic commissions placed by Maximilian were almost all executed in Augsburg under the supervision of the humanist scholar Conrad Peutinger, even when the designs were produced by artists from elsewhere. The first series on the genealogy of the House of Habsburg comprises 92 imagined ancestors of the Emperor going back to Classical and biblical times; Burgkmair designed it in 1509–10 (B. 79). Next came *Theuerdanck*, the first of Maximilian's essays in autobiography, romantically elaborating the adventures of his youth; printed with specially designed lettering, it is one of the most beautiful books of the 16th century. Burgkmair designed only 15 of the 118 illustrations for it (*c.* 1509–12; Hollstein, nos 416–30), but his designs had considerable influence on the style and mood of the whole series. Then followed illustrations for the *Weisskunig*, the wars and political fortunes of Maximilian. Some of the qualities of the approximately 118 (out of a total 251) woodcuts designed here by Burgkmair (executed *c.* 1514–18; B. 80) appear in the scene of the *Emperor Visiting the Armourers* (see fig. 1). And finally there was *Maximilian's Triumphal Procession* (*c.* 1516–18; B. 81), a

1. Hans Burgkmair I: *Emperor Visiting the Armourers*, woodcut for the *Weisskunig* of Emperor Maximilian I, 220×195 mm, *c.* 1514–18 (London, British Museum)

woodcut series of 139 prints conceived as a frieze, so arranged that they would extend 54 m. Here Burgkmair, who designed about half the scenes, was working in competition with such artists as Albrecht Altdorfer. Burgkmair proved to be the most inventive and the one best able to interpret the Emperor's wishes; his work is exuberantly imaginative and shows understanding of the difficult task of intermingling historical, allegorical and real people and situations. Except for the *Theuerdanck*, these series were not completed and published in the Emperor's lifetime; yet they brought Burgkmair great fame, causing him to be regarded with Dürer as the most important graphic artist working for Maximilian.

After these major achievements in woodcut, which ended with the Emperor's death in January 1519, Burgkmair returned to painting and drawing. His best church paintings are the *St John* altarpiece (1518; see fig. 2) and the *Crucifixion* altarpiece (1519; both Munich, Alte Pin.), the latter donated by the Peutinger family. Unlike earlier altarpieces (and some later ones) produced in south Germany in the Late Gothic tradition, which emphasize detail, these large panels have simple rectangular outlines, solemn, statuesque figures and warm colours influenced by Venetian painting. In each the central subject and the wings are linked by a background landscape that extends across the three panels. The exotic plants in *St John on Patmos*, the central panel of the *St John* altarpiece, may be based on studies Burgkmair made in the gardens of the Fugger family.

2. Hans Burgkmair I: *St John* altarpiece, oil on panel, 4.47×2.17 m, 1518 (Munich, Alte Pinakothek)

When Dürer and Burgkmair met (not for the first time) in 1518 they made portrait drawings of each other. Only Dürer's, on which Burgkmair wrote an inscription, survives (Oxford, Ashmolean). Most of Burgkmair's 90 known drawings (few of them for print designs) use chalk or charcoal; their broader lines give something of the effect of a painting, as in the *Adoration of the Shepherds* (Turin, Bib. Reale) and portrait studies (e.g. Berlin, Kupferstichkab.; Cambridge, Fitzwilliam; Chatsworth, Derbys; Dresden, Kupferstichkab.; London, BM). He was more concerned with light effects and decorative elegance than with linear precision as Dürer understood it.

3. LATE WORKS, AFTER 1520. The quantity and quality of Burgkmair's paintings declined in his final decade. Working with such wood-carvers as Sebastian Loscher (*fl* 1510–*c.* 1548), he produced conventional altarpieces for Nuremberg (Rochuskapelle), Rauris near Salzburg (untraced) and elsewhere (*Passion*, side panels, Stuttgart, Staatsgal.). The *Holy Family with St John the Baptist as a Boy* (Berlin, Gemäldegal.) clearly shows familiarity with motifs used by Raphael.

Burgkmair's attitude towards the Reformation is unknown, but the upheaval seems not to have caused him hardship. His continued work in religious woodcuts (*see* WOODCUT, §II, 3) included illustrations of the *Apocalypse* (Hollstein, nos 7–39) for the reissue of Luther's translation of the New Testament (Augsburg, 1523), which are notable for their close correlation with the German text, unlike Cranach's and Dürer's famous woodcuts on that theme. Towards the end of his life Burgkmair contributed to the series of history paintings for the Munich Residenz of Duke William IV of Bavaria. His *Battle at Cannae* (1529; *in situ*) contains many authentic details, while *Esther before Ahasuerus* (1528; *in situ*) is one of the best pictures in the entire battle and biblical series. In the latter his narrative skill and striving for authenticity are combined with a display of oriental splendour and intense colour in the Venetian manner.

BIBLIOGRAPHY

Hollstein: *Ger.*; Thieme–Becker

H. Rupé: *Beiträge zum Werke Hans Burgkmairs des Älteren* (Leipzig, 1912)

E. Buchner and K. Feuchtmayr, eds: *Beiträge zur Geschichte der deutschen Kunst*, i (Augsburg, 1924), pp. 194–223

Das Malerwerk Hans Burgkmairs von Augsburg (exh. cat., ed. K. Feuchtmayr; Munich, Alte Pin.; Augsburg, Schaezlerpal.; 1931)

A. Burkhard: *Hans Burgkmair d. Ä.*, Meister der Graphik, xv (Berlin, 1932)

——: *Hans Burgkmair d. Ä.* (Leipzig, [1934])

F. Winkler: 'Hans Burgkmairs früheste Holzschnitte', *Z. Kstwiss.*, i (1947), pp. 39–50

H. Müller: 'Die Malerfamilie Burgkmair', *Lebensbild. Bayer. Schwaben*, iv (1955), pp. 44–66

P. Halm: 'Hans Burgkmair als Zeichner', *Münchn. Jb. Bild. Kst*, xiii (1962), pp. 75–162

S. Appelbaum, ed.: *The Triumph of Maximilian I* (New York, 1964)

T. Falk: *Hans Burgkmair: Studien zu Leben und Werk des Augsburger Malers* (Munich, 1968)

G. von der Osten and H. Vey: *Painting and Sculpture in Germany and the Netherlands, 1500–1600*, Pelican Hist. A. (Harmondsworth, 1969)

Hans Burgkmair, 1473–1973: Das graphische Werk (exh. cat., Augsburg, Städt. Kstsammlungen; Stuttgart, Staatsgal.; 1973)

Hans Burgkmair, 1473–1531 (exh. cat., ed. W. Schade; E. Berlin, Staatl. Museen, 1974)

T. Falk: *Sixteenth Century German Artists*, 11 [VII/ii] of *The Illustrated Bartsch*, ed. W. L. Strauss (New York, 1980) [B.]

The German Renaissance Print (exh. cat. by G. Bartram, London, BM, 1995)

TILMAN FALK

Burgos. Spanish city and provincial capital in Old Castile.

1. History and urban development. 2. Buildings.

1. HISTORY AND URBAN DEVELOPMENT. Situated on either side of the River Arlanzón, under a hill (h. 800 m) that makes a strong natural defensive position, Burgos commands a route from the north coast of Spain through the Pancorbo Pass on to the plateau of Old Castile, and lies on the pilgrimage road from Navarre to Santiago de Compostela in Galicia. It is said to have been founded by a Castilian count, Diego Rodríguez Porcelos, in 884. In its early days it seems to have consisted of six hamlets, each with its *alcalde* (mayor), grouped together in the Arlanzón valley under the protection of the castle on the hill, which served as the palace of the counts of Castile in the 10th century. Burgos may well have been organized against Arab attacks on the orders of King Alfonso III of Asturias (*reg* 866–910). It became the chief town of Castile; and a village near by, Vivar del Cid, was the traditional birthplace of the Castilian hero Rodrigo (or Ruy) Díaz de Vivar (1026–99), called El Cid. From 1074 Burgos was the seat of a diocese that had the standing of an archbishopric, depending directly on the Holy See. Already by the time of the Arab geographer al-Idrisi (*d* 1165/6) it was described as a big city divided into two parts. In 1187 Alfonso VIII of Castile (*reg* 1158–1214) and Queen Eleanor founded the Cistercian convent of Las Huelgas there as the royal mausoleum (*see* §2(ii) below). Burgos was represented in the Cortes, and by *c.* 1300 it was one of the most prosperous cities of Castile. This was reflected in its cathedral, begun in 1221 to replace its Romanesque predecessor (*see* §2(i) below).

The city's prosperity was above all linked to the wool trade. Its commercial position was enhanced towards the end of the 15th century by the privileges granted to it by the Catholic monarchs, Ferdinand and Isabella, which purported to give it the control of the monopoly of the trade in fine wool. These privileges were resisted by the port of Bilbao, however, and a long rivalry between the two cities ensued, regulated from time to time by compacts (such as that in 1499). Burgos enjoyed exemption from certain royal tributes and from contributions voted in the Cortes. The monarch personally appointed the governor of the castle, such was the importance of its fortress.

Burgos was not only an industrial centre; it also encouraged business, and its merchants imported goods from abroad, forwarding them to the fair at Medina del Campo. From the 13th century onwards it had a *consorcio* or *compañía comercial*, which traded with Brittany, Normandy, England and above all with Flanders, through Bruges. The site of one of the six mints in Castile, the city had thirteen banks of exchange, and its fourteen craft guilds included one for masters of works and masons who were Jews and Moors.

Around 1440 Bishop Alonso de Cartagena (*reg* 1415–56) brought Juan de Colonia to Burgos (*see* COLONIA, DE, (1)). He worked at the cathedral and in 1454 began the church of the Carthusian monastery of Miraflores, which lies 3 km east of Burgos. The church, with a single-cell, five-bay nave and polygonal, star-vaulted apse, was completed by his son Simón and consecrated in 1496. It contains the alabaster tombs of *King John II of Castile* (*reg* 1406–54), his wife *Isabella of Portugal* and their son *Alfonso* (*d* 1468). Both the tombs (begun 1489) and the magnificent high altar retable were the work of Gil de Siloé, the father of Diego de Siloé (*see* SILOÉ, DE). The most important churches in Burgos are S Esteban (1280–1350), which has a sculptured west portal surmounted by a rose window and imposing tower; S Gil (1399 and later additions), with its octagonal, star-vaulted chapel of the Natividad by Felipe Vigarny and Diego de Siloé; and S Nicolás, rebuilt from 1408, which has a fine retable (*c.* 1503–5) by Francisco de Colonia and contains tombs of the Polanco family.

The noble family of Velasco had a town palace in Burgos, the Casa del Cordón (*see* VELASCO, PEDRO FERNÁNDEZ DE), as did the Condes de Miranda. The former, begun in 1482, was a royal residence from the time of Ferdinand and Isabella until the mid-18th century. The rectangular façade has corner towers and decorative cresting; its portal incorporates *Mudéjar* motifs and is framed by the knotted girdle that gives the palace its name. The patio has two storeys (with a third on the north side), decorated with coats of arms, monograms and inscriptions. The palace has been much altered, but restorations were begun in the 1980s. The Casa de Miranda (1545), which has a richly decorated two-storey patio as well as a fine Plateresque staircase, now houses the provincial museum. Other notable buildings of this period are the Hospital del Rey, founded by Alfonso VIII for pilgrims to Santiago and reconstructed in the 16th century, which has a rich Plateresque portal, the Puerta de los Romeros (1526) and the mid-16th-century Hospital de la Concepción, with one Plateresque façade and one in the classicizing style of Juan de Herrera.

Stretches of the fortifications begun under Alfonso X in 1276 to the south-west of the castle survive, as well as some of the city gates, including the Moorish Arco de S Martín and the fine castellated gateway known as the Puerta (or Arco) de S María (see fig. 1). The last was erected in 1534–6 to mark the failure of the Revolt of the 'Comuneros' (1520–21) and the reconciliation of Burgos with Charles V; the statues in the niches above the arch include representations of the Emperor and prominent figures in Burgos's history, such as El Cid. Another arch, the Arco de Fernán González, was erected in the Doric style in 1592 by Philip II to commemorate the 10th-century leader of Burgos, Conde Fernán González of Castile. Burgos enjoyed the title of 'Cabeza' (head) of Castile, and was sufficiently influential to dissuade the government of Charles V from limiting its wool exports in order to encourage the native cloth industry, but it was not strong enough to affect the decision of Philip II to make Madrid his capital. The rivalry of Bilbao, and with the rise of Seville, the collapse of the fair of Medina del Campo combined with the growing importance of Madrid to bring about the rapid decline of Burgos, and by the end of the 17th century its trade in wool was in confusion. During the Peninsular War the French stood siege successfully in the castle, the interior of which had been

1. Burgos, Puerta de S María, 1534–6

severely burnt in 1736. When Arthur Wellesley, later 1st Duke of Wellington, raised the siege (1812–13), the French mined and destroyed the castle and its fortifications before they retreated.

Some of the most notable buildings of Burgos's later history are the Baroque Jesuit church of S Lorenzo, built on an octagonal plan; the Neo-classical Casas Consistoriales, begun in 1791 to designs by Ventura Rodríguez; and the Palacio del Paseo de la Isla, of the last quarter of the 19th century, by Arturo Mélida y Alinari. The city had a modern revival after the Revolt of 1936, when it became temporarily the Nationalist capital.

BIBLIOGRAPHY

J. Klein: *The Mesta: A Study in Spanish Economic History, 1273–1836* (Cambridge, MA, 1920)
T. López Mata: *La ciudad y el castillo de Burgos* (Burgos, 1949)
——: *Geografía urbana burgalesa en los siglos XV y XVI* (Burgos, 1952)
J. M. Lacarra: 'Orientation des études d'histoire urbaine en Espagne entre 1940 et 1957', *Moyen Age*, lxiv (1958), pp. 317–39
M. Basas Fernández: *El consulado de Burgos en el siglo XVI* (Madrid, 1963)
J. M. Lacarra: 'Les Villes frontières dans l'Espagne des XIe et XIIe siècles', *Moyen Age*, lxix (1963), pp. 205–22
J. G. Sainz de Baranda: *La ciudad de Burgos y su concejo en la Edad Media* (Burgos, 1967)
M. del Carmen Carlé: *Del concejo medieval castellano-leonés* (Buenos Aires, 1968)
E. A. Gutkind: *Urban Development in Southern Europe, Spain and Portugal*, International History of City Development, iii (New York, 1969)
L. G. de Valdeavellano: *Orígenes de la burguesía en la España medieval* (Madrid, 1969)
J. Pérez: *La Révolution des 'Comunidades' de Castille (1520–1521)* (Bordeaux, 1970)
R. S. Smith: *The Spanish Guild Merchant: A History of the Consulado, 1250–1700* (New York, 1972)
M. del Carmen Carlé: 'La ciudad y su contorno en León y Castilla (siglos X–XIII)', *Anu. Estud. Med.*, viii (1972–3), pp. 69–103
J. A. Bonacha Hernando: *El concejo de Burgos en la baja Edad Media, 1345–1426* (Valladolid, 1978)
Urbanismo e historia urbana en España, 3 vols (Madrid, 1979–83)
E. Sánchez, ed.: *La ciudad hispánica durante los siglos XIII al XVI*, 3 vols (Madrid, 1985–7)

J. R. L. HIGHFIELD

2. Buildings.

(i) Cathedral. (ii) Las Huelgas Abbey.

(i) Cathedral.

(a) Architecture. (b) Sculpture. (c) Stained glass.

(a) Architecture. The foundation stone of the present building, dedicated to the Virgin, was laid by Bishop Maurice of Burgos (*reg* 1217–38) on 20 July 1221. Work proceeded rapidly owing to an indulgence granted by Pope Honorius III on 25 July 1223 to all who contributed towards its cost. The first campaign ended in 1230: the constitution given by Bishop Maurice to his chapter in November indicates that the canons had just moved into the choir. The transept chapels were then half-built: in 1230 Chanter Pedro Pérez de Villahoz bequeathed 200 maravedís for the completion of the chapel of S Nicolas off the north transept; the south jamb of its entrance arch has the socle moulding of the choir, but the north jamb does not, and the south transept chapel mirrors this arrangement. Karge (1989) believed that the blind arcade at the bottom of the south transept portal had also just been constructed. The second campaign followed, work proceeding from east to west, in the 1240s and 1250s: Bishop Juan of Burgos (*reg* 1240–46) bequeathed 400 maravedís for the work, and two donations of Alfonso X on 11 November 1257 indicate that both transept portals were by then in place. It was at this time that the Romanesque cathedral (1075–96), which lay on the site of the present nave, must have been destroyed. Little remained to be done when the Cathedral was consecrated on 20 July 1260. Built of limestone from Hontoria (Burgos), it is 115 m long and 27 m high.

The original plan consisted of an aisled nave ending in a two-towered façade, projecting transept with a single, square eastern chapel off the inner bay of each arm, and a deep chevet. The ambulatory belongs to the first campaign, but, as Branner pointed out, the radiating chapels are later. However, Karge has demonstrated that there were originally five small radiating chapels as at Bourges Cathedral. He has also established the chronology of the galleries of the transept (*c.* 1260), the west façade's third storey (*c.* 1265), the two-storey cloister (*c.* 1265–70) and the oldest of the later radiating chapels (*c.* 1270–80). The elevation is the same throughout, consisting of an arcade, a triforium resembling a tribune gallery and a clerestory with plate tracery (see fig. 2). In the French High Gothic Context the cathedrals's plan and elevation are old-fashioned. Since Burgos was on the pilgrimage route to Galicia, however, they make the cathedral a latter-day pilgrimage church, with its three façades, gallery and extra chapels. When the building was conceived, Castile and Leon were separate kingdoms, and Castile, having just won a resounding victory over Islam at Las Navas de Tolosa (1212), was in assertive mood. Burgos was surely

2. Burgos Cathedral, begun 1221, interior of crossing and south transept

intended by Bishop Maurice as Castile's answer to Santiago de Compostela.

The cathedral is first indebted to Bourges Cathedral. There are the original chapels of the chevet; the elevations of the two buildings have the same components. The piers with cylindrical cores rising through the elevations, and the eight evenly-spaced, attached colonettes of two sizes, the largest on the main axis, are similar. The flattened, mural, character of the elevation, however, is closer to those of the chevet at St Etienne, Caen, or the nave of St Leu d'Esserent, Oise; the choir's flying buttresses are like those of the nave of Notre-Dame-de-Paris; and the longitudinal ridge ribs in the main vessels seem inspired by the decorative vaults of Anjou. Karge suggested that the architect came from Tours, where the chevet of the Abbey of St Martin had just been rebuilt in the Bourges style. The embellishment of the cathedral from *c.* 1260 employed a more modern French style befitting the kingdom's leading city, which was associated with the kings of France. The façades had galleries filled with statues like the transept façades of Reims Cathedral, the Capetian coronation church; and the cloister's upper-storey arcade has the same pattern as the windows of the Sainte-Chapelle (1241–6), Paris, a monument of Parisian Rayonnant style. Stylistically, however, the cathedral is hardly a French import. Indeed, its Castilian character seems to have grown over the years: the decoration of the triforium in the choir is tame in comparison with that of the nave. By the time the cloister was conceived a distinctively Castilian Gothic style had appeared, half-Rayonnant, concerned with the display of sculpture.

Burgos was the most influential of the 13th-century Castilian cathedrals. Such details as oculi pierced through the webbing of hemicycle vaults—derived from Bourges—and the longitudinal ridge ribs are found in minor churches throughout Old Castile and further afield. The Castilian decorative style occurs in the cathedrals of Cuenca (nave and west façade) and Toledo (choir). Details reveal the presence of a Burgalese Master in the cathedral of León (begun *c.* 1255) and the recently-discovered chevet of the cathedral of Santiago de Compostela (1258–*c.* 1276). The cloister was copied at the cathedral of Oviedo (begun *c.* 1296–1301).

In the 15th and 16th centuries the building was transformed. First spires were added to the western towers between 1442 and 1458 by Juan de Colonia at the expense of Bishop Alonso de Cartagena. They were modelled on the spires of Germany, Juan's homeland, such as the single spire of Freiburg-im-Breisgau Minster. Then sepulchral chapels were built around the cathedral by various eminent Burgalese. Bishop Alonso's chapel of the Visitación (1440–42) off the south transept, attributed to Juan de Colonia, was followed by the chapel of S Ana (1477–88), off the north transept, ordered by Bishop Luis Acuña (*reg* 1457–95) and also probably by Juan de Colonia. The chapel of the Presentación, built on a site off the south aisle ceded in 1520 by Canon Gonzalo de Lerma, is attributed to Felipe Vigarny. These chapels are all surpassed, however, by the chapel of the Condestable, begun in 1482 off the axial bay of the ambulatory. It was founded by the Constable of Castile, Pedro Fernández de Velasco, and his wife Dona Mencia de Mendoza and designed by Simón de Colonia. Each chapel centres on the tombs of its founders and is stamped with their escutcheons. The chapels have notable Late Gothic vaults: those of the chapels of the Condestable and the Presentación have tracery rather than webbing in the middle. The Condestable Chapel was widely imitated, as in the apse of the Convento de S Clara, Briviesca, begun in 1523 by the Constable's daughter. At the same time, the 13th-century fabric was embellished. Felipe Vigarny was hired on 17 July 1498 to carve the *trascoro* and in 1507 he was at work on the choir-stalls. These were moved from the presbytery to the nave with the *coro* in 1535. Francisco de Colonia in 1516 erected the Puerta de la Pellejería on the east side of the north transept, giving access at the cathedral's floor level, and Diego de Siloé built the Escalera Dorada in the early 1520s. This staircase, modelled on the stairway of Bramante's terraced Cortile Belvedere in the Vatican, bridges the gap between the cathedral pavement and the north transept portal, the Puerta de la Coronería, which is set at a higher level.

Lastly the crossing was given a *cimborio.* The one built at the expense of Bishop Luis Acuña fell on 4 March 1539 but it was immediately rebuilt by Felipe Vigarny and Juan de Vallejo (*fl* *c.* 1518–69) after they had repaired and remodelled the crossing piers and adjacent bays. Finished in 1568, it was probably designed by Juan de Langres (*fl c.* 1522–40). Rising above enormous drum piers, the *cimborio* is a pinnacled, two-storey octagonal lantern decorated with Gothic and Renaissance motifs, gargoyles and herms, and enlivened by inscriptions, escutcheons and Old Testament figures. It is dazzlingly rich, accentuated by the vault, a copy of that of the Condestable Chapel but entirely covered by tracery.

Later building activity was aimed at making the cathedral more serviceable. The *coro* was enclosed by walls (the side ones date to 1656–9), and the parish church was moved elsewhere on 26 April 1731, because it was too dingy. Its site was swallowed up by the magnificent Churrigueresque chapel of S Tecla (finished in 1734). Finally, the west façade was restored at the expense of its Gothic sculpture and the lavish sacristy constructed (1761–7).

See also ENRIQUE, MASTER; COLONIA, DE.

BIBLIOGRAPHY

M. Martínez y Sanz: *Historia del templo catedral de Burgos* (Burgos, 1866/*R* 1983)

E. Lambert: *L'Art gothique en Espagne aux XIIe et XIIIe siècles* (Paris, 1931)

R. Branner: *La Cathédrale de Bourges et sa place dans l'architecture gothique* (Paris, 1962)

H. Karge: *Die Kathedrale von Burgos und die spanische Architektur des 13. Jahrhunderts: Französische Hochgotik in Kastilien und Leon* (Berlin, 1989)

——: 'La Cathédrale de Burgos: Organisation et technique de la construction', *Les Bâtisseurs des cathédrales gothiques* (exh. cat., ed. R. Recht; Strasbourg, Musées Ville, 1989), pp. 139–63

C. P. G. Welander: 'The Architecture of the Cloister of Burgos Cathedral', *Medieval Architecture and its Intellectual Context: Studies in Honour of Peter Kidson*, ed. E. Fernie and P. Crossley (Hambledon, 1990), pp. 159–68

3. Burgos Cathedral, statues on the cloister wall, probably of Ferdinando III and Queen Beatrice of Swabia, almost life-size, *c.* 1270

(*b*) *Sculpture.* The cathedral bears all the sculpted embellishments of a French High Gothic cathedral. The south transept portal, the Puerta del Sarmental, was carved *c.* 1235–40. Its iconography, the *Last Judgement*, is derived from the central portal of the west façade of Chartres Cathedral, and its style shows that its two main sculptors came from Amiens Cathedral. The north transept portal, the Puerta de la Coronería, dates from *c.* 1245. Its iconography, also the *Last Judgement* (for illustration *see* GOTHIC, fig. 47), comes from Chartres Cathedral as well, but as interpreted in the more recent central portal of the south transept there. The sculptor of the tympanum, although he was indebted to the Amiens masters, possessed his own style, characterized by introspective expressions and voluminous draperies. The sculpture of the three west façade portals was lost during the 18th-century restorations. The statues of angels, kings and youths adorning the roofs, façades and western towers were carved *c.* 1260–65 in a style related to that of the so-called 'Philip Augustus' figure on the north transept of Reims Cathedral.

Inside, the sculpted decoration is more unusual. The hood-moulding of the triforium is decorated with heads executed by 1260, and the cloister, entered through a portal in the south transept, has numerous statues, both on the jambs of the portal and lining its walls. Two of the latter are thought by many to represent Ferdinand III and Queen Beatrice of Swabia (*c.* 1270; see fig. 3). *David* and *Isaiah* on the south jamb of the portal are in a new style, that of the JOSEPH MASTER at Reims (*see* MASTERS, ANONYMOUS, AND MONOGRAMMISTS, §I), but the others are in either the style of the tower statues or that of the north transept tympanum. In Spain the amount of surviving 13th-century sculpture at Burgos is surpassed only by that at León Cathedral. It is closer to the French prototypes, however, and was just as influential: the style of the north transept Puerta de la Coronería appears in León with Nuestra Señora La Blanca.

There was much sculptural activity in the cathedral during the 15th and 16th centuries. The completion of the tomb of *Bishop Alonso de Cartagena* in the chapel of the Visitación is documented in 1447–9, but scholars are agreed that the style of the present effigy is of *c.* 1475. With its decorative drapery style and robust realism, it was the first masterpiece to be carved in Burgos in the Late Gothic style imported from the Netherlands. The niche tomb of *Pedro Fernández de Villegas* (*d* 1536) was carved by one of Simon de Colonia's assistants on the chapel of the Condestable. At the same time, the greatest Late Gothic sculptor in Burgos, Gil de Siloé, was active in the Cathedral. His love of jewelled costumes is manifest in the documented *Tree of Jesse* retable (1486–8) in the chapel of S Ana, on which he collaborated with Diego de la Cruz, and the retable of *St Anne* of *c.* 1500–05 in the chapel of the Condestable (*see* RETABLE, fig. 1).

In the alabaster reliefs for the *trascoro* (begun 1498), Felipe Vigarny from Langres (Champagne) introduced Italian Renaissance sculpture to Burgos. He was followed by Diego de Siloé with his alabaster tomb of Bishop Luis Acuña in the chapel of S Ana (1519) and in the decoration of the Escalera Dorada (1519–23), both of which show the influence of Michelangelo. They collaborated on the retable (1523–6) of the chapel of the Condestable, Vigarny providing the design (a Renaissance version of a Gothic retable) and Siloé contributing figures such as the Virgin and Child of the *Presentation* scene.

BIBLIOGRAPHY
F. B. Deknatel: 'The Thirteenth-century Gothic Sculpture of the Cathedrals of Burgos and León', *A. Bull.*, xvii (1935), pp. 243–388
H. E. Wethey: *Gil de Siloe and his School: A Study of Late Gothic Sculpture* (Cambridge, MA, 1936)
——: 'The Early Works of Bartolomé Ordóñez and Diego de Siloé', *A. Bull.*, xv (1943), pp. 226–38, 325–45
B. G. Proske: *Castilian Sculpture: Gothic to Renaissance* (New York, 1951)
A. Durán Sanpere and J. Ainaud de Lasarte: *Escultura gotica*, A. Hisp., viii (Madrid, 1956)

CHRISTOPHER WELANDER

(c) Stained glass. Burgos Cathedral was designed to incorporate the type of glazing scheme characteristic of the 13th-century Ile-de-France. 15th-century documents referring to the glaziers' workshops in the city indicate that not only the cathedral glass but also windows for other cathedral cities were the work of glaziers from south Netherlands. The French master glazier Juan de Arqr, who also worked at León (*see* LEÓN, §II, 1(iii)), is known to have been at Burgos in the early 15th century. There are remains of a 15th-century programme, but unfortunately the cathedral lost most of its medieval glass in 1813 during the Peninsular War, when retreating French soldiers blew up a powder magazine inside the building. The marble pavements were described as being strewn with fragments of glass, which were collected and, where possible, reinserted in new areas.

The main surviving 15th-century remains are in the chapel of the Condestable. There are two rows of windows, eight in the upper and six in the lower tier, with three lancets each. Seven contain standing figures under canopies painted in a German style. Two lancets over the crossing also retain some fragments. The two rose windows are almost entirely restored, but the one in the south transept has some medieval pieces in outer semicircular openings.

BIBLIOGRAPHY
J. A. Gade: *Cathedrals of Spain* (London, 1911)
C. H. Sherrill: *Stained Glass Tours in Spain and Flanders* (London, 1924)
L. Lee, G. Seddon and F. Stephens: *Stained Glass* (London, 1976)

CAROLA HICKS

(ii) Las Huelgas Abbey. The Cistercian abbey of Las Huelgas was founded in 1187 by Alfonso VIII of Castile (*reg* 1158–1214) and Queen Eleanor. Its site, next to the royal palace, was an unusual choice for a Cistercian foundation; and only aristocratic young women from the kingdom were admitted as nuns. The monastery was wealthy, and for many centuries the abbess played an important part in the economic and political life of Castile.

The construction of Las Huelgas continued throughout the 13th century, but a precise chronology is difficult to establish. The church must have been begun *c.* 1220, and it was probably built by the Master Ricardo, who had been a protegé of Alfonso VIII. It was completed in 1279, when several altars and the burial places of the kings and their families in the nave were consecrated.

The church is built of limestone and has a cruciform plan with a narrow, projecting transept and an aisled nave that served as the nuns' choir. The east end has a deep *capilla mayor* of three rectangular bays and a seven-sided apse with two rows of windows. On either side of the *capilla mayor* and opening on to the transept are two rectangular chapels. They contain the most original vault designs in the church: the first bay has a quadripartite vault, but the second bay has six ribs radiating over an irregular hexagon formed by the insertion of small, rib-vaulted triangles in each of the far corners. There are sexpartite vaults in the *capilla mayor* and an octopartite vault over the crossing. The main entrance to the church is in the north transept façade, with a portico and the entrance to the chapel of S Juan. A rib-vaulted loggia runs along the north side of the church. Parallels for features at Las Huelgas have been found at the Hospice of Roncesvalles (Navarra), Cuenca Cathedral, the earliest stages of Burgos Cathedral and at S María de Huerta (Soria), all of which show Angevin influence (Azcárate).

The poorly preserved cloister of S Fernando on the south side of the nave is covered by pointed barrel vaults of brick. They show traces of *Mudéjar* stucco decoration and bear the date 1275. The chapter house is an elegant, rib-vaulted building of nine bays; its four piers have cylindrical cores surrounded by eight detached shafts, but the capitals have been left uncarved. The second, smaller cloister, 'Las Claustrillas', is Romanesque in appearance and provides access to the chapel of the Assumption, which was built for the burial of Alfonso VIII's son Fernando (*d* 1211). Its centralized plan is typical of Christian funerary monuments, but its architecture shows Almohad influence.

Although Las Huelgas was used as a royal burial place until the 16th century, most of the burials are of the founders and their descendants. The sarcophagi are mainly plain stone caskets decorated with simple pictorial compositions, except for the twin tombs of *Alfonso VIII* and *Queen Eleanor* (both *d* 1214), situated in the centre of the nuns' choir, which bear rich heraldic decoration, and those of *Doña Berenguela* (*d* 1279) and *Don Fernando de la Cerda* (*d* 1275). The tomb of *Dona Berenguela* is the most interesting: instead of an effigy, the lid has a sculptured cycle of the *Infancy of Christ*, from the *Annunciation* to the *Flight into Egypt*, set under arcades; the sarcophagus itself bears the *Adoration of the Magi* and the *Massacre of the Innocents*. Although the style is characteristic of its period, it is difficult to identify it with that of contemporary sculpture in Burgos Cathedral, as has been suggested. The sculpted *Calvary* in the arch that frames the sarcophagus of *Don Fernando de la Cerda* is executed in the style of *c.* 1200 and thus seems markedly archaic.

The clothes of the deceased and the textiles that once covered the coffins have been preserved. They provide valuable evidence for 13th-century Spanish textiles and are of *Mudéjar*, Christian and Islamic origin, some with delicate borders. Also preserved is the banner captured at the Battle of Las Navas de Tolosa (1212), a fine example of Almohad textile manufacture.

BIBLIOGRAPHY
G. E. Street: *Some Account of Gothic Architecture in Spain* (London, 1865, 2/1869; rev. G. G. King, 2 vols, 1914)
J. Agapito y Revilla: *El real monasterio de las Huelgas de Burgos* (Valladolid, 1903)
A. Rodriguez Lopez: *El real monasterio de las Huelgas en Burgos y el Hospital del Rey* (Burgos, 1907)

E. Lambert: *L'Art gothique en Espagne aux XIIe et XIIIe siècles* (Paris, 1931)
G. Avila y Diez de Ubierna: *El real monasterio de las Huelgas: Su origen y fundación y descripción de su parte artística* (Burgos, 1941)
M. Gomez Moreno: *El Panteón real de las Huelgas de Burgos* (Madrid, 1946)
J. Gonzalez: 'Un arquitecto de las Huelgas de Burgos', *Rev. Archvs, Bib. & Mus.* (1947), pp. 47–50
S. Sebastian: 'Nuevas fechas sobre la erección del famoso cenobio de las Huelgas', *Bol. Inst. Fernán González* (1948), pp. 199–200
L. Torres Balbás: *Arquitectura gótica*, A. Hisp., vii (Madrid, 1952)
J. Azcárate: *El protogótico hispánico* (Madrid, 1974)
J. M. Lizoain Garrido: *Documentación del monasterio de las Huelgas de Burgos*, 2 vols (Burgos, 1985)

I. G. BANGO TORVISO

Burgos Mantilla, Francisco de (*b* Burgos, 1612; *d* Madrid, 1 April 1672). Spanish painter. He was in Madrid from 1618, where he trained under Pedro de las Cuevas, and he later became a disciple of Velázquez. Though renowned for his portraits, his only known work is the small *Still-life with Dried Fruit*, signed and dated 1631 (New Haven, CT, Yale U. A.G.). The picture's restrained tonal range and painterly technique clearly betray Burgos Mantilla's admiration for Velázquez. Depicting an apparently casual arrangement of packets of dried fruit and nuts, its intuitive composition is closer to still-lifes by Italian followers of Caravaggio than to the studied artifice found in those by such Spanish painters as Juan van der Hamen y León. Burgos Mantilla may have been encouraged in this direction by Velázquez, who returned from Italy in the year that the former's picture was painted. However, a similar naturalness is found in still-lifes by such contemporaries of Burgos Mantilla as Juan Bautista de Espinosa, the artist's friend, and Antonio de Pereda, a fellow pupil of Pedro de las Cuevas.

BIBLIOGRAPHY

M. Agulló and A. E. Pérez Sánchez: 'Francisco de Burgos Mantilla', *Bol. Semin. Estud. A. & Arqueol.*, xlvii (1981), pp. 359–82
Spanish Still-life in the Golden Age, 1600–1650 (exh. cat. by W. B. Jordan, Fort Worth, TX, Kimbell A. Mus., 1985) [excellent plate]
P. Cherry: *Still-life and Genre Painting in Spain during the First Half of the Seventeenth Century* (diss., U. London, Courtauld Inst., 1991)
Spanish Still-life from Velázquez to Goya (exh. cat. by W. B. Jordan and P. Cherry, London, N.G., 1995)

PETER CHERRY

Burgundy, House of. French dynasty of rulers and patrons. They were a cadet branch of the French royal house of VALOIS. After the death of the last Capetian duke, Philippe de Rouvres, in 1361, the Duchy of Burgundy, a region to the south-east of Paris, was given by King Charles V to his brother (1) Philip the Bold in 1363. Philip acquired the counties of Flanders, Artois, Rethel, Burgundy (Franche-Comté) and Nevers at the death of his father-in-law, Louis de Mâle, in 1384; the dukes then became vassals of the Holy Roman Emperor as well as of the king of France. Both Philip the Bold and his son (2) John the Fearless were heavily involved in the politics of France. The alliance formed with England by John's son (3) Philip the Good increased Burgundian power at a time of French weakness during the Hundred Years War. Philip extended his lands to include Namur, Zeeland, Holland, Hainault and Luxembourg, while his son (5) Charles the Bold attempted to link the northern and southern possessions of the house by the conquest of the Duchy of Lorraine. Charles was defeated by the Swiss Confederation in 1477, and at his death the Duchy of Burgundy reverted to France, while the Netherlands passed to the Habsburgs through the marriage of his daughter (6) Mary, Duchess of Burgundy, to Maximilian, later Holy Roman Emperor.

The artistic and political emphasis of the Burgundians gradually turned from their capital at Dijon to the Netherlands, where they ruled the towns of Ypres, Bruges and Ghent and on which their wealth was founded. Charles the Bold eventually established the seat of government at Mechelen (Fr. Malines). Much of the dukes' patronage can be linked directly to their political aspirations, which for Charles the Bold included the achievement of royal status. The dukes attracted Netherlandish artists to Dijon, and the peripatetic court acted as a focus for a variety of nobles, ambassadors, officials and merchants who supported the artists of the so-called northern Renaissance. Of Philip the Good's illegitimate sons, (4) Antoine was an important patron of manuscripts, while (7) Philip of Burgundy, Bishop of Utrecht, was a humanist and a patron of Jan Gossart.

BIBLIOGRAPHY

R. Vaughan: *Valois Burgundy* (London, 1975)
W. Prevenier and W. Blockmans: *Les Pays-Bas bourguignons* (Antwerp, 1984; Eng. trans., Cambridge, 1986)

GILES CLIFFORD

(1) Philip the Bold [Philip II; Philippe le Hardi], 1st Valois Duke of Burgundy (*b* Pontoise, 17 Jan 1342; *d* Halle, 27 April 1404). He was the fourth and last son of King John II of France (*reg* 1350–64) and Bonne of Luxembourg. In 1356 Philip, then Duc de Touraine, earned his epithet 'the Bold' while at his father's side at the Battle of Poitiers. After the death of the last Capetian duke of Burgundy, Philippe de Rouvres, in 1361, King John laid claim to the duchy, investing his youngest son with this wealthy fief in 1364 and creating him first peer of France (for a representation of Philip haranguing his troops, see fig.).

1. Introduction. 2. Architechture and related work. 3. Tapestries, manuscripts and paintings.

1. INTRODUCTION. Philip the Bold was to become a most powerful prince, his ambitions served by his sagacity and diplomatic skills. He also commanded vast financial resources. Two factors were essential in this respect: his marriage on 19 June 1369 to Margaret of Flanders (1350–1405), who by January 1384 inherited from her father, Louis de Mâle, Count of Flanders, the counties of Flanders, Artois, Rethel, Burgundy and Nevers; and Philip's skill at appropriating portions of the royal revenues during the reign of his nephew, Charles VI, especially after 1392 when the young King fell victim to bouts of insanity.

With extensive means at his disposal, Philip was also a discriminating patron, and his commissions were unequalled during the period 1380–1404. If, with the works he ordered, the Duke sought to create a fitting setting for his dynastic ambitions, his involvement in their selection and visits to work-sites also point to genuine interest. He availed himself of the most accomplished artists to be found in France and his own dominions. His main architect was the Parisian Drouet de Dammartin; his official sculptors were JEAN DE MARVILLE and CLAUS SLUTER from

Haarlem; his bronze-founder was Colard Joseph of Dinant, his wood-carver Jean de Liège; his court painters were, successively, Jean d'Arbois, Jean de Beaumetz from Artois and Jean Malouel from Guelders; his glassmaker was Jean de Thioys of Cambrai and his goldsmiths Hennequin de Haacht from Liège and Josset de Halle; his tapestry weavers were Pierre de Beaumetz and Jehan Cosset of Arras. At the death of his father-in-law, Philip reappointed to his own service Netherlandish artists who had worked for Louis de Mâle, among whom were the painters Jean de Hasselt and Melchior Broederlam, the sculptor Jacques de Baerze and the goldsmiths Jean de Brabant and Herman Ruissel. The Duke also employed artists on a temporary basis, such as the sculptor Claus de Haine and the painter Herman of Cologne.

2. Architecture and related work. The palace, a sprawling building complex in the capital of Dijon, had deteriorated during the last decades of Capetian rule. Beginning in the 1360s, Philip the Bold ordered restorations and rebuilding works, the only surviving example of which is the three-storey tower, the Tour de Bar, which formed the heart of the new ducal apartments. Though massive and sparsely ornamented, the structure is less forbidding than earlier examples such as the castle at Vincennes. Philip's main artists had their workshop at the palace, allowing for greater ducal supervision. From 1391 to 1399 important structural work was completed on the palace chapel (Sainte-Chapelle; begun 1172).

Foremost among the Duke's artistic projects was the construction and embellishment of the Carthusian monastery at Champmol on the outskirts of Dijon, founded in 1385 as a mausoleum for Philip and his descendants (*see* Dijon, §IV, 1). Its nucleus was a single-nave church begun in 1388 to house the funerary monuments. The Carthusians were to pray for the souls of those buried in the church and to protect their tombs. Philip spared neither expense nor effort for his foundation, determining each step and personally engaging most of the artists. With the exception of his own tomb, the complex was completed before his death.

Although the Charterhouse was his main concern, Philip frequently diverted the efforts of artists at his service to projects in his residences, mainly at Montbard (ruined), Rouvres, Talant and Argilly (all destr.), the last an important complex favoured by the Duke for hunting. Jean de Beaumetz and his workshop embellished the chapel there and probably painted an altarpiece for it, as did the Artois painter Huchon de Boulogne. The sculptor Jean de Liège made a *Virgin* (destr.) for the main altar, and by 1388 Jean de Marville furnished statues of the *Virgin* and *St Christopher* for the portal of the castle and may also have carved life-size statues of *Apostles* for the chapel (all untraced).

In the decade 1381–91 an entirely new castle (altered) was built for the Duchess Margaret of Flanders at Germolles, near Chalon-sur-Saône. Drouet de Dammartin was responsible for the plans and supervised its construction by masons from Champmol; sculptors and painters who had worked at the monastery were also employed at Germolles. The traditional fortified castle plan was only partially followed for the new residence: with its adjoining

Philip the Bold Haranguing his Troops, miniature by the Master of the Policratique of Charles V, 1384 (Brussels, Bibliothèque Royale Albert 1er, MS. 11042, fol. 12*r*)

sheep-rearing and farming complex, the structure, marked by large windows and a wealth of surface decoration, was one of the first to be conceived as a manor. It appeared to reflect the lyric and bucolic mood that pervaded late 14th-century aristocratic circles: wall decorations included ducal ciphers, amatory emblems and, principally, numerous images of ewes painted by Arnoul Picornet. Among recovered fragments of over 15,000 floor tiles manufactured for Germolles, the most frequently recurring iconographic motif is that of sheep resting under a shady elm. Several tapestries reinforced the theme. The most striking embodiment of Margaret's interest in sheep-rearing was a carved group (untraced) with no known counterpart in medieval sculpture: it consisted of two life-size figures representing Philip and Margaret standing among a flock of sheep under a golden elm tree. The group, made by Claus Sluter and his workshop, was installed in 1393 in a prominent position near the entrance to the ducal apartments.

In 1384 Philip and Margaret inherited Louis de Mâle's residences in Flanders and Artois and those he had owned in Paris, the Hôtel de Flandre and the Hôtel d'Artois. The latter became Philip's main residence, and it was accordingly enlarged and refurbished, including new sculpture for the altar of its chapel; the tower, known as the Tour Jean sans Peur, probably planned by Duke Philip, is one of the last vestiges of late medieval civil architecture in Paris. In Artois, the castle of Hesdin (destr.) was the favourite ducal residence. There, Melchior Broederlam was commissioned to repaint an unusual series of automatons as well as to paint screens and, probably, an altarpiece for the chapel.

3. TAPESTRIES, MANUSCRIPTS AND PAINTINGS. Philip the Bold and his wife owned over 100 tapestries. They commissioned more high warps than anyone else in the 14th and early 15th centuries. Many depicted religious and literary themes and historical events, while others bore heraldic motifs and stylized plants and animal life (*verdure*). They were often composed of several panels, and some, such as the *Credo* tapestry (90 sq. m) delivered by Pierre de Beaumetz and Jacques Dourdin in 1388, were of enormous proportions. Also impressive was the large ducal collection of embroidered antependia and vestments for the chapels.

By 1404 Philip and Margaret owned a combined library of over 200 volumes, one of the richest private collections of illuminated manuscripts. While many of the books were inherited or received as gifts, from 1376 Philip started to commission illuminated manuscripts and proved himself to be an avid bibliophile. His principal Book of Hours, the Grandes Heures (vol. 1: Cambridge, Fitzwilliam, MSS 3–1954; vol. 2: Brussels, Bib. Royale Albert 1er, MSS 13092, 110035–7), ordered through the Parisian copyist Jean l'Avenant, contains, despite losses, a cycle of 117 miniatures produced by the two most important Parisian illuminators at this time, the Master of the Boqueteaux and the Master of the Coronation Book of Charles V. In addition to enlarging his library and ordering liturgical volumes for his chapels and oratories, Philip also made substantial purchases of books for the Carthusians at Champmol. He was the protector of authors, several of whom presented him with illuminated copies of their work, such as Honoré Bouvet, Gaston Phoebus, Philippe de Mézières and especially Christine de Pizan, who gave the prince three manuscripts (e.g. Brussels, Bib. Royale Albert 1er, MS. 9508) with miniatures by the Master of the Epître d'Othéa and the Master of the Roman de la Rose of Valencia. In the last four years of his life Philip acquired, through Dino and Jacques Rapondi, merchants of Lucca settled in Paris and Bruges, lavish volumes with miniatures produced by the most stylistically innovative painters active in Paris, Perrin Remy and the Master of the Livre des Femmes Nobles et Renommées. Beginning in 1402, the Duke commissioned Pol and Jean de Limbourg, nephews of his painter Jean Malouel, to illustrate a large *Bible moralisée* (usually identified with the Paris, Bib. N., MS. fr. 166; *see* LIMBOURG, DE, fig. 1); so exclusive was the contract that the artists had to reside in the house of the ducal physician. By early 1404, Jacques Coene and Haincelin de Hagenau (the possible identities of the Boucicaut and Bedford Masters) were also contributing miniatures to Philip's Bible.

Philip was also of considerable importance for the development of panel painting in France; the few surviving pictures of the period that are held to be French have generally been connected with artists active at his court. Philip also fostered the development of portraiture, judging from the statues of himself and his wife commissioned from Claus Sluter for the portal of Champmol (*see* DIJON, fig.4), the *miniatures* in his Grandes Heures, the profile portrait (Versailles, Château) showing the aged Duke (the lost original probably by Malouel) and commissions such as the sculptures for Germolles and the tapestries of the *Battle of Roosebecke* and of the *Twelve Peers* (all untraced), in which Philip himself, Charles VI and Louis de Mâle were realistically depicted at Philip's command. Philip's politics required lavish ceremonies involving the services of painters, goldsmiths and tapestry weavers. The most notable examples were the weddings held in Cambrai in 1388 and Charles VI's visit to Dijon in 1390. The following year, when Philip planned to invade England from Sluis, his ship was fitted with precious tapestries, altarpieces, embroidered pennons and numerous multicoloured flags decorated by Beaumetz and Broederlam. The latter decorated the mainsail with daisies (*marguerites*) and the ducal motto 'Il me tarde' on a ground of shimmering gold.

Orchestrating much of the policy-making of France, Philip the Bold in his last years lived primarily in Paris, while Margaret chose to reside in Arras until her death on 21 March 1405. Philip died as the result of double-pneumonia on a trip to Brabant to secure that duchy for his second son, Antoine. His body, garbed in the white cowl of a Carthusian and accompanied by 60 torch-bearing mourners uniformly dressed in black, was brought to rest at Champmol (for an illustration of his tomb *see* WEEPER). Philip was succeeded by his eldest son, (2) John the Fearless.

BIBLIOGRAPHY

C. Dehaisnes: *Documents et extraits divers concernant l'histoire de l'art dans la Flandre, l'Artois et le Hainaut avant le XVe siècle*, 2 vols (Lille, 1886)
C. Monget: *La Chartreuse de Dijon d'après les documents des archives de Dijon*, 3 vols (Montreuil-sur-Mer, 1898–1905)
B. Prost and H. Prost: *Inventaires mobiliers et extraits des comptes des ducs de Bourgogne de la Maison de Valois, 1363–1477*, 2 vols (Paris, 1902–8)
H. David: *Philippe le Hardi, duc de Bourgogne, protecteur des arts* (Dijon, 1937)
R. Vaughan: *Philip the Bold* (Cambridge, MA, 1962)
P. de Winter: *The Patronage of Philippe le Hardi, Duke of Burgundy (1364–1404)* (diss., New York U., 1976)
——: 'The "Grandes Heures" of Philip the Bold, Duke of Burgundy: The Copyist Jean L'Avenant and his Patrons at the French Court', *Speculum*, lvii (1982), pp. 786–842
——: 'Castles and Town Residences of Philip the Bold, Duke of Burgundy, 1364–1404', *Artibus & Hist.*, viii (1983), pp. 95–118
——: *La Bibliothèque de Philippe le Hardi, duc de Bourgogne (1364–1404): Etude sur les manuscrits à peintures d'une collection princière à l'époque du 'style gothique international'* (Paris, 1985)
——: 'Art from the Duchy of Burgundy', *Bull. Cleveland Mus. A.*, lxxiv (1987), pp. 406–51

PATRICK M. DE WINTER

(2) John the Fearless [Jean sans Peur], 2nd Valois Duke of Burgundy (*b* Rouvres, 28 May 1371; *d* Montereau-faut-Yonne, 10 Sept 1419). Son of (1) Philip the Bold. Much of John's energy and funds as Duke of Burgundy (from 1404) were directed towards maintaining his status in France. He struggled for the control of the country with Louis, Duke of Orléans, brother of the ailing king Charles VI, and arranged for his murder in 1407. The subsequent opposition of the 'Armagnac' faction eventually led to John's assassination in 1419 by the Dauphin (later Charles VII), who saw him as a threat to royal authority. John's patronage was largely a means of supporting his political ambitions, but although for a brief period he controlled the finances of France, his personal finances were not especially strong or stable, and he was less extravagant than either Philip the Bold or his uncle Jean, Duc de Berry. There seems to be no characteristic touch in his choice of artists, many of whom had been employed by his father, nor in the types of work commissioned, which follow largely in the mould of other appanagiste dukes; many of his artists came, however, from his possessions in the southern Netherlands.

John the Fearless funded few architectural works. The Tour de Jean sans Peur added to the Hôtel d'Artois, the Burgundian residence in Paris, is decorated with John's emblem, the plane (he claimed that it would render ineffective the knotty club that was the symbol of Orléans), but it may have been planned by Philip the Bold (*see* (1) above). John continued the family patronage of the Charterhouse of Champmol outside Dijon, constructing a roof to protect Claus Sluter's Well of Moses in the cloister. Sluter was employed until his death in 1406, when his nephew Claus de Werve became the ducal sculptor, continuing work on the tomb of *Philip the Bold* (Dijon, Mus. B.-A.; for illustration *see* WEEPER). John granted de Werve a bonus for his efforts on the tomb after seeing it in 1409, but work slowed thereafter, and commissions executed by the sculptor for other patrons in the period 1413–15 suggest a lack of continuing ducal support.

Philip's painter Jean Malouel was also retained in John's service. He coloured the tomb effigies of *Philip the Bold* and *Margaret of Flanders* and in 1412 painted a portrait of *John the Fearless* (untraced) as a gift to King John I of Portugal. The *Martyrdom of St Denis* (Paris, Louvre) is almost certainly identifiable as one of the works John commissioned from Malouel to decorate the Charterhouse, but it was apparently executed by HENRI BELLECHOSE, who became court painter and 'varlet de chambre' after Malouel's death in 1415. It is probably the only painting commissioned by John to survive. Bellechose, like the Duke's other painters, carried out much decorative work, including painting banners for the ducal castle of Talant near Dijon in 1416. The peripatetic Burgundian court made much use of tapestries from Arras, Paris and later Tournai, and the collection included one commemorating the Duke's victory at Othée in 1407. An early copy of a contemporary portrait of *John the Fearless* (Paris, Louvre) shows him displaying a ring, the symbol of his ducal power.

The best preserved evidence of John's patronage is his library (most MSS in Brussels, Bib. Royale Albert Ier). He increased the existing ducal collection to *c.* 250 books, moving it from Paris to Dijon. Unlike Jean, Duc de Berry, whose finest manuscripts were illuminated by painters in his service, John the Fearless commissioned books through agents, especially Dino and Jacques Raponde, merchants and bankers in Bruges. His manuscripts were illuminated by both Netherlandish and Parisian artists. A Book of Hours (Paris, Bib N., MS. nouv. acq. lat. 3055) is from the region of Ypres or Ghent, while the Breviary of Jean sans Peur (*c.* 1413–19; London, BL, Harley MS. 2897 and Add. MS. 35311; for illustration *see* BREVIARY) was evidently made by an associate of the Limbourg brothers. The Boucicaut Master was involved in the illumination of the *Livre des merveilles* (Paris, Bib. N., MS. fr. 2810), which bears the arms, device and a portrait of the Duke (fol. 226*r*) and an inscription recording that the manuscript was presented to Jean de Berry in January 1413; it was one of many gifts exchanged between the Duke and his uncle. John's wife, Margaret of Bavaria, whom he married in 1385, influenced some purchases. A French *Bible historiale* (Brussels, Bib. Royale Albert Ier, MSS 9024–5) was acquired at her request in 1415, and in May 1412 he gave her 300 francs to purchase a Breviary.

BIBLIOGRAPHY

L. de Laborde: *Les Ducs de Bourgogne* (Paris, 1849–52)
P. Durrieu: 'Manuscrits de luxe exécutés pour les princes et grands seigneurs français', *Manuscrit*, ii (1895)
A. Humbert: *La Sculpture sous les ducs de Bourgogne* (Paris, 1913)
R. Vaughan: *John the Fearless* (London, 1966)

GILES CLIFFORD

(3) Philip the Good [Philippe le Bon, Philip III], 3rd Valois Duke of Burgundy (*b* Dijon, 31 July 1396; *d* Bruges, 15 June 1467). Son of (2) John the Fearless.

1. Introduction. 2. Architecture and sculpture. 3. Panels and manuscripts. 4. Tapestries and other arts.

1. INTRODUCTION. From his accession on 20 September 1419 the first half of Philip the Good's reign was occupied by relations with France, culminating in the Treaty of Arras to end the Hundred Years War, and by the expansion of his territory until he acquired Luxembourg in 1443; during the second half he established some internal institutions and cultivated relations with other states. To persuade his subjects of his policies and authority required the constant use of propaganda, through paid agents and factions, letters, charters, his Order of the Golden Fleece (founded 1430) and the arts. Philip patronized all the arts, using his enormous revenues and the taxes levied on prosperous towns. His exceptionally fine court chapel (*see* §2 below), with the composer Gilles de Binchois (*c.* 1400–60) among the chaplains, was the font of the *Ars nova*, spreading Netherlandish musicians to all the courts of Europe. Philip also presided over a literary revival devoted to making Old French and Latin texts readily available. For example, among his official writers, Jean Wauquelin turned verse epics into prose and translated Latin and Netherlandish chronicles. Public festivities constituted an important aspect of the Duke's patronage. He was responsible for the week-long celebration of his third wedding in 1430, the regular assemblies of the Order of the Golden Fleece and the three-day Feast of the Pheasant staged at Lille in 1454 to launch his great crusade. For these occasions carpenters were employed, writers composed poems and devised dumb shows, and scores of artists made decorations and machinery.

Inspired by his grandfather, (1) Philip the Bold, from whom he had inherited the ducal residences, library and tapestry collection, the themes of Philip the Good's patronage reflected his wider policies: his magnificence, his authority derived from illustrious ancestors and predecessors, the acquisition of the provinces of Lotharingia and crusading. He was a highly active patron. He followed the production of his works, designing entertainment machines for Hesdin, visiting Jan van Eyck at work in his shop, inspecting new texts before their final transcription and buying the *Gideon* tapestry cartoons (*see* §3 below) to prevent their reuse. He watched his workmen for hours, even on the last day of his life. This care, combined with the magnitude of his commissions, made him an exemplar of magnificence throughout Europe. More important, his patronage built up the art industries of the Netherlands, especially in books and tapestries, creating an international success that long outlived the state he intended to create.

2. ARCHITECTURE AND SCULPTURE. Philip's building activity has been underestimated because so little survives. His only new ecclesiastical structure was the chapel of Nôtre-Dame de la Treille in St Peter (destr. 1793), Lille, which was the site of the first assembly of the Order of the Golden Fleece and of the tomb he had made for Louis II de Mâle, Count of Flanders and Duke of Brabant (see below). The work on the ducal residences, however, contributed to the flourishing of Netherlandish domestic architecture. In Lille, Philip enlarged the Hôtel de la Salle and built the new Hôtel du Rihour (ruined); he expanded the Prinsenhof in Bruges, where he bought and rebuilt the Hôtel Vert for his private use. In Brussels, Gilles Joes (*d* 10 Feb 1460) designed a much enlarged palace (destr. 1695) on the Coudenberg, to which Willem de Voghel (*fl* 1452–69) added a great hall in the 1450s, without central columns and so large (17×45 m) that huge beams and extraordinary joinery were needed to support the upper storey. In Dijon Philip rebuilt the Palais des Ducs (now part of the Mus. B.-A.), adding a high tower and the Salle des Gardes, and rebuilt the Sainte-Chapelle (destr. 1802) as the sanctuary for the Order of the Golden Fleece; two of the knights' armorial shields from the stalls survive (Dijon, Mus. B.-A.). In his country castle of Hesdin (destr. 1553), where according to the chronicler Du Clercq some construction was always under way, Philip enlarged the gallery of mechanical entertainments and built a dining house on wheels for the park.

Philip's sculptural projects included the tomb of his parents, *John the Fearless and Margaret of Bavaria* (Dijon, Mus. B.-A.), in the Charterhouse at Champmol and that of his sister, *Anne of Burgundy* (destr.; effigy, Paris, Louvre), at the convent of the Celestins, Paris, both probably commissioned in 1435. The former, closely modelled on Claus Sluter's tomb for *Philip the Bold* (Dijon, Mus. B.-A.; for illustration *see* WEEPER), follows the French royal type with a row of mourners, here a procession of members of the ducal household, around the base. Juan de la Huerta was hired in 1443 to carve the figures, but he accomplished so little that he was dismissed and in 1462 was replaced by Antoine Le Moiturier, who finished the work in 1469. Visual records indicate that Guillaume Vluten's tomb for *Anne of Burgundy* was in the form of a wall tomb, with Philip the Good and probably Anne's husband, John, Duke of Bedford, in a row of mourners on the base.

The finest of the tombs was the bronze tomb of *Louis de Mâle* (destr. 1793), cast by Jacques de Gérines (*fl* 1428; *d* 1463/4) of Brussels in 1455 from figures probably designed by Rogier van der Weyden. Commissioned in 1453, three months after Philip had crushed the revolt of Ghent, the figures on the base of the tomb included Philip among two generations of the descendants of the counts of Flanders, a visual assertion of his rights as Count of Flanders. In 1459 Philip bought the wooden figures from Gérines for the tomb of *Joanna*, Duchess of Brabant (Brussels, church of the Minorites, destr. 1695), and had them repaired by the sculptor Jean Delemer (*fl* 1428–59) and painted by van der Weyden.

3. PANELS AND MANUSCRIPTS. Among Philip's several court painters were, in Dijon, first HENRI BELLECHOSE and then Jean de Maisoncelles, who painted the Duke's portrait (1436) for Champmol (untraced; possible copy, 16th century; Cincinnati, OH, A. Mus.) and a *Dance of Death* (1436–7; destr. 1803) in the cloister of the Sainte-Chapelle. For heraldic decorations Philip employed Hue de Boulogne (*c.* 1379–1451) in Hesdin, Jacques Daret's brother Daniel (*fl* 1431–9) briefly in Tournai and Pierre Coustain in Bruges. The painter–engineer Colard le Voleur (*c.* 1400–69) maintained the entertainments at Hesdin and made table fountains for the feast in Lille.

The Duke's favourite painter, however, was Jan van Eyck, who travelled extensively on Philip's behalf (*see* EYCK, VAN, (2)). Van Eyck's work, probably wall painting, in the residences in Lille and Brussels involved designing secular subjects on a large scale, and Philip encouraged such inventions as the ingenious world map described by Bartolomeo Fazio. Little remains of the ducal assignments. Among these is a drawing reproducing the betrothal portrait of *Isabella of Portugal* (Germany, priv. col.) and fragments of two paintings that Philip may have given to Champmol: a *Virgin and Child in a Niche* (Paris, Mus. A. Déc.) for his private chapel and a triptych (*Annunciation* panel, Washington, DC, N.G.A.).

Philip's second contribution to Netherlandish painting was to make Rogier van der Weyden his unofficial portrait painter in the late 1440s, effectively when he was given a rash of commissions: Philip in bust-length, with hat and without hat, in two much-copied portraits (untraced; best copies, Dijon, Mus. B.-A. and Bruges, Groeningemus.; and Antwerp, Kon. Mus. S. Kst, respectively); standing among his court, in the frontispiece of Wauquelin's *Chronicles of Hainault* (Brussels, Bib. Royale Albert 1er, MS. 9242, fol. 1; see fig.); and kneeling, in the altarpiece (untraced; drawing, Lisbon, Mus. N. A. Ant.) for Batalha Abbey, Portugal. The Batalha altarpiece included Duchess Isabella (1397–1472) and Philip's son, Charles the Bold, who is also in the *Chronicles* frontispiece. Shortly afterwards Rogier made an independent portrait of *Duchess Isabella* (untraced; copy, Malibu, CA, Getty Mus.) and in the early 1450s painted Philip and Charles together in a diptych or triptych (untraced; copies, Arras, Bib. Ville). Philip's courtiers followed suit, with commissions on single panels and in diptychs and triptychs. These elegant images, idealized by straightened postures, lengthened noses and raised brows, perfectly expressed the princely Burgundian ideal and determined the form of Netherlandish portraits for the rest of the century.

Philip had the largest library in northern Europe, which grew from the 250 books he had inherited to around 1000

Philip the Good, Duke of Burgundy, and his Court, probably by Rogier van der Weyden; frontispiece miniature from the *Chronicles of Hainault*, 211×152 mm, 1448 (Brussels, Bibliothèque Royale Albert 1er, MS. 9242, fol. 1)

at the time of his death. The library, most of it housed in his residence and chapel in Bruges, included liturgical books, devotional texts, didactic and practical works and a great many histories and historical romances, most of which were epics of revolt (*see* BELGIUM, §III, 1 and 2). Significantly, Philip began his major expansion of the library in 1446, at the time of his negotiations with the German Emperor, commissioning works on the deeds of such as Girart de Roussillon and the first Duke of Burgundy under Charles the Bold, and a translation of De Dynter's *Chronicle of Brabant*; clearly Philip wanted sumptuous copies of documentation for his claim to the Carolingian middle realm. Likewise, most of his books on crusading and the related story of Jason were commissioned while he was agitating for the crusade.

About half of these books were illustrated. The texts were transcribed in the new large Burgundian *hybrida* script, for ease in reading aloud, with wide margins and generous spaces for miniatures. The large volumes were then filled with rich borders and bold pictures by such artists as DREUX JEAN, the official illuminator charged with the library's initial expansion, the Master of Mansel, SIMON MARMION, JEAN LE TAVERNIER, WILLEM VRELANT, LIEVEN VAN LATHEM and LOYSET LIÉDET. The artists met the need to produce as many as *c.* 100 new miniatures, since the texts had never been so fully illustrated. The resulting volumes are handsome, effective embodiments of the Duke's favourite themes.

4. TAPESTRIES AND OTHER ARTS. Many of the same romances were illustrated in Philip's collection of tapestries, which grew from 63 sets in 1430 to nearly 1000. Woven with gold and silver thread and silk as well as fine wool, these hangings made Philip the chief customer of the tapestry industry. At first he continued his predecessors' support of the Arras industry, which used designs by Jacques Daret and BAUDUIN DE BAILLEUL. After the death of the principal dealer, Jean Walois, Philip turned to PASQUIER GRENIER in Tournai, beginning in 1449–52 with the famous cycle of the *History of Gideon* (destr. 1794), eight huge pieces woven on Bailleul's designs at a cost of 8960 gold crowns. Grenier provided several more suites in the following years, including a six-piece chamber of *Alexander the Great* for 5000 crowns (two pieces, Rome, Pal. Doria-Pamphili) and the *Legend of the Swan Knight* (two pieces, Krakow, N.A. Cols and Vienna, Österreich. Mus. Angewandte Kst). Philip also supported the growing industry of Brussels, buying among other things a set of *verdure* from Jean de Haze (fragment, Berne, Hist. Mus.; *see* HERALDRY, colour pl. III, fig. 2).

The subject-matter of his tapestries ranged from such *verdure* and heraldry to genre scenes of hunting, woodsmen, orange pickers, children going to school and outdoor court festivities. They were largely housed in a depository in Arras, with a staff of keepers to send the panels wherever the Duke required. They were often displayed with political intent. The panel of John the Fearless's victorious battle at Liège hung in the banquet hall, probably as a warning against the failure of negotiations during the council of Arras. The *Gideon* tapestry was exhibited regularly during the assemblies of the Order of the Golden Fleece at Lille, and the *Labours of Hercules* in the banqueting hall encouraged pledges for the crusade. During the coronation of Louis XI the suites of *Gideon* and *Alexander* perhaps reminded viewers of Philip's character as a virtuous knight and ruler as they were displayed on the façade of his residence in Paris.

Philip's collection of metalwork and jewels was legendary, most of it bought from Jean Peutin (*fl* 1424–36) and other goldsmiths in Bruges. At the end of his life Leo of Rozmital reported that three days were required to examine all the pieces. A very few items survive (e.g. Solothurn, Mus. Altes Zeughaus; Fribourg Cathedral; Vienna, Ksthist. Mus.).

BIBLIOGRAPHY

G. Doutrepont: *La Littérature française à la cour de Bourgogne* (Paris, 1909/*R* Geneva, 1970)
P. Saintenoy: *Les Arts et les artistes à la cour de Bruxelles, 2: Le Palais des ducs de Bourgogne à Bruxelles du règne d'Antoine de Bourgogne à celui de Charles-Quint* (Mém. Acad. Royale Belgique, Cl. B.-A.), 2nd ser., v (Brussels, 1934)
A. Zuylen van Nyevelt: *Episodes de la vie des ducs de Bourgogne à Bruges* (Bruges, 1937)
Bruxelles au XVe siècle (exh. cat. by P. Bonenfaut and others, Brussels, Mus. Com. Brussels, 1953)
Le Siècle d'or de la miniature flamande: Le Mécénat de Philippe le Bon (exh. cat., ed. L. M. J. Delaissé; Brussels, Pal. B.-A., 1959)
La Sainte Chapelle de Dijon (exh. cat., ed. P. Quarré; Dijon, Mus. B.-A., 1962)
S. Schneebalg-Perelman: 'Les Sources de l'histoire de la tapisserie bruxelloise et la tapisserie en tant que source', *An. Soc. Royale Archéol. Bruxelles*, lxi (1966), pp. 279–337
La Librairie de Philippe le Bon (exh. cat., ed. G. Dogaer and M. Debae; Brussels, Bib. Royale Albert 1er, 1967)
J. Gardelles: 'L'Art à Lille—les monuments', *Histoire de Lille, I: Des origines à l'avènement de Charles Quint* (Lille, 1970)
R. Vaughan: *Philip the Good* (London, 1970)
Y. Lacaze: 'Le Rôle des traditions dans la genèse d'un sentiment national au XVe siècle: La Bourgogne de Philippe le Bon', *Bib. Ecole Chartres*, cxxix (1971), pp. 303–85
J. C. Smith: *The Artistic Patronage of Philip the Good, Duke of Burgundy (1419–1467)* (diss., New York, Columbia U.; microfilm, Ann Arbor, 1979)
A. H. van Buren: 'The Model Roll of the Golden Fleece', *A. Bull.*, lxi (1979), pp. 359–76
W. Prevenier and W. Blockmans: *Les Pays-Bas bourguignons* (Antwerp, 1985; Eng. trans., Cambridge, 1986)
A. H. van Buren: 'La Roulotte de Philippe le Bon', *Liber amicorum: Etudes historiques offertes à Pierre Bougard* (Arras, 1987), pp. 115–22
L. Campbell: 'The Tomb of Joanna, Duchess of Brabant', *Ren. Stud.*, ii (1988), pp. 163–72
J. C. Smith: 'Portable Propaganda—Tapestries as Princely Metaphors at the Courts of Philip the Good and Charles the Bold', *A. J.* [New York], xlviii (1989), pp. 123–9

ANNE HAGOPIAN VAN BUREN

(4) Burgundy, Antoine of [Le Grand Bâtard] (*b* 1421; *d* Bruges, 1504). Illegitimate son of (3) Philip the Good. He was soon granted authority over a number of his father's territories. In 1456 he became a Knight of the Order of the Golden Fleece. In 1464–5 he conducted the crusade to Ceuta, Morocco. He was captured at the Battle of Nancy (5 Jan 1477) and handed over to Louis XI of France, in whose service he remained until his death. Antoine was a great bibliophile. Practically all of the numerous manuscripts he collected in his castle at La Roche-en-Ardenne (ruined), Belgium, bear his *ex libris* vignette with the motto *Nul ne s'y frote*. What happened to his collection of books after his death remains obscure, but a number of manuscripts (in various libraries, including Brussels, Bib. Royale Albert 1er; London, BL; Paris, Bib. Arsenal; Louvre) apparently stayed in the family: they are marked with the phrase *A. de Bourgogne. Nul ne l'aproche*, which refers to Antoine's grandson, Adolphe of Burgundy. One of the most important manuscripts commissioned by Antoine is a splendid version of Jean Froissart's *Chronicles* (1468/9; Berlin, Staatsbib. Preuss. Kultbes., Dep. Breslau MS. 1), which was probably made in the Bruges workshop of Loyset Liédet. Two portraits of Antoine survive (Chantilly, Mus. Condé, and Dresden, Gemäldegal. Alte Meister).

BIBLIOGRAPHY

DBF
A. Boinet: 'Un Bibliophile du XVe siècle: Le Grand Bâtard de Bourgogne', *Bib. Ecole Chartes*, lxvii (1906), pp. 255–69
A. M. Menschaert: *Verluchte handschriften gemaakt in opdracht van Antoon, de grote bastaard van Boergondië* [Illuminated manuscripts commissioned by Anthony, the great bastard of Burgundy] (diss., Ghent U., 1971)

L. BOONEN

(5) Charles the Bold [Charles le Hardi; Charles le Téméraire], 4th Duke of Burgundy (*b* Dijon, 10 Nov 1433; *d* Nancy, 5 Jan 1477). Son of (3) Philip the Good. He was the last Valois Duke of Burgundy (*reg* 1467–77). He sought the expansion of Burgundian power, and his reign was dominated by the quest for personal glory; his pretensions to kingly status are illustrated by the forward-facing style of helm used on his stalls in Notre-Dame, Bruges. The epithet 'Le Téméraire' ('the rash') was applied to him after his death, which effectively brought to an end the Burgundian independence he had fostered; he was killed at the siege of Nancy during an attempt to recapture upper Alsace and Lorraine. His Netherlandish lands then passed to his daughter, (5) Mary, but the Burgundian territories in France reverted to the French crown as he had no male heir. The emphasis of Charles's patronage was on material display, but expenditure on warfare in the second half of his reign much reduced his sponsorship of the arts.

Charles was an accomplished musician and had a knowledge of Italian, Latin and possibly Flemish. His literary tastes show a preference for works on military subjects by such Classical authors as Livy and Valerius Maximus, and his speeches referred frequently to Hannibal, Alexander the Great and Julius Caesar. He hung tapestries of *Alexander* in Bruges for his wedding (1468) to Margaret of York; in Brussels when he received homage from the citizens of Ghent (1469); and in the hall in Trier where he was to receive the German Emperor (1473). For his wedding in Bruges he commissioned tapestries depicting the coronation of the Merovingian king Clovis, and 166 painters and sculptors, including Hugo van der Goes and Jacques Daret, were employed on the decoration of banners, props, mechanical devices and sets for tableaux vivants, under the supervision of Jean Hennecart and Pierre Coustain.

Charles's painters were occupied principally on such decorative tasks. The Duke acquired tapestries and plate and kept large numbers of artefacts in his baggage train on campaigns; many were captured by the Swiss in 1476–7 (some now Berne, Hist. Mus.). One fine surviving example of metalwork commissioned by the Duke is the gold and enamel reliquary by GERARD LOYET, which bears statuettes of Charles with St George (completed 1466–7; Liège Cathedral; see fig.). It was given to St Lambert's, Liège, after the Duke's destruction of the city in 1471. Loyet, described in the accounts as 'orfebre et graveur de sceaux' and the Duke's 'varlet de chambre' from 1470, was also involved in the embellishment of clothing and hats with jewels, as well as making life-size silver statues and portrait busts of him (untraced).

Charles the Bold with St George, reliquary by Gerard Loyet, silver, gold and enamel, completed 1466–7 (Liège Cathedral)

Italian influence at the Burgundian court increased during Charles's reign, with the presence of ambassadors, papal emissaries and merchants from Italy reflecting the alliances he formed with Naples (1471), Venice (1472) and Milan (1475) and his commercial agreement with the papacy (1468–73). In 1474 King Louis XI gave Charles a book about Charlemagne, written in Italian, 'knowing that he was deeply devoted to the customs, ways of life and methods of government of the Italians'. Italian influence seems to have had only a superficial impact on Charles, however, affecting his taste in such matters as costume and hats; his literary acquisitions were nearly all translations, and he cannot be considered responsible for the spread of humanist learning in northern Europe. The medallist Giovanni Candida was employed from 1472 as a secretary and diplomat, not for his artistic skills, and the two medals of the Duke attributed to him were apparently not the result of a commission.

Charles the Bold commissioned and acquired only a few manuscripts, but their artistic quality is very high. He instigated the completion of several manuscripts left unfinished at the death of Philip the Good, a number of them from LOYSET LIÉDET. Payments were made in 1468 to Willem Vrelant of Bruges and Liédet for the illumination of the second and third volumes respectively of the *Chronicles of Hainault* (Brussels, Bib. Royale Albert 1er, MSS 9243–4), and in 1472 Liédet was paid for the completion of the *Histoire de Charles Martel* (Brussels, Bib. Royale Albert 1er, MSS 8–9), which bears his signature (MS. 9, fol. 7*r*). Philippe de Mazerolles was appointed the ducal 'enlumineur et varlet de chambre' in 1467, the year in which he completed a Book of Hours (possibly Vienna, Österreich. Nbib., Cod. 1856; *see also* PHILIPPE DE MAZEROLLES) on black parchment for presentation to the Duke by the citizens of Bruges on his entry into the city. In 1475 he was paid for illuminating 21 copies of military ordinances for Charles to give to officials; six of these survive (e.g. London, BL, Add. MS. 36619). Ordinances for the Master of the Horse (Vienna, Österreich. Nbib., Cod. S. n. 2616) were produced by the scribe Nicolas Spierinck of Antwerp and contain illumination showing the influence of Hugo van der Goes. Other ducal illuminators include Simon Marmion, who in 1470 received final payments for a Breviary begun for Philip the Good; Lieven van Lathem, who was paid for a prayerbook in 1469, probably the Little Hours of Charles the Bold (Larrivière, Charnace priv. col.); and Jean Hennecart, who was in Charles's service before his accession and in 1470 was paid for illuminating two copies of the *Instruction d'un jeune prince*; the surviving copy, with three miniatures (Paris, Bib. Arsenal, MS. 5104), bears the initials of Charles the Bold and Margaret of York (fol. 66*r*). Margaret seems to have exercised more in the way of personal taste than her husband and was responsible for the Breviary decorated by the MASTER OF MARY OF BURGUNDY (Cambridge, St John's Coll., MS. H. 13; London, BL, Cotton MS. Tiberius A. 11, fol. 1*r*; *see* MASTERS, ANONYMOUS, AND MONOGRAMMISTS, §I) and for the initial commission for the Hours of Mary of Burgundy (Vienna, Österreich. Nbib., Cod. 1857; for illustration *see* LIEVEN VAN LATHEM), which contains work by Vrelant, van Lathem and Marmion. The Duchess was also an important patron of William Caxton, but, although printing was well developed in the Burgundian territories, Charles the Bold seems not to have collected printed books. Charles is sometimes represented in manuscripts, but one of the few surviving portraits (Berlin, Gemäldegal.) depicts him at the age of 27, before his succession; it is probably a copy after Rogier van der Weyden.

BIBLIOGRAPHY

Marguerite d'York et son temps (exh. cat. by M. R. Thielemans, Brussels, Banque-Lambert, 1967)

R. Vaughan: *Charles the Bold: The Last Valois Duke of Burgundy* (London, 1973) [full bibliog.]

R. Walsh: 'The Coming of Humanism to the Low Countries: Italian Influences at the Court of Charles the Bold', *Human. Lovan.*, xxxv (1976), pp. 146–97

Charles le Téméraire (exh. cat. by P. Cockshaw and others, Brussels, Bib. Royale Albert 1er, 1977)

Cinqcentième anniversaire de la bataille de Nancy. Colloque: Nancy, 1979 [articles by C. A. J. Armstrong and J. Bartier]

G. Dogaer: *Flemish Miniature Painting of the 15th and 16th Centuries* (Amsterdam, 1987)

(6) Mary, Duchess of Burgundy (*b* Brussels, 13 Feb 1457; *d* Bruges, 27 March 1482). Daughter of (5) Charles the Bold. She was his only child and inherited the Burgundian lands in the Netherlands in 1477. Her mother was Isabella of Portugal. She married Maximilian, later Holy Roman Emperor, in 1477. Brought up mainly in Ghent and Bruges, she received a Classical education and from 1468 was influenced by her bibliophile stepmother, Margaret of York. Before her accession Mary saw to the construction of her mother's tomb (completed 1476; now in Antwerp Cathedral) in St Michael's Abbey, Antwerp. It was surrounded by bronze figures (Amsterdam, Rijksmus.) in a funeral procession, in imitation of the tomb of Mary's ancestor, *Louis de Mâle* (destr.). She also commissioned an Alphabet Book (copies, Paris, Louvre, and Brussels, Bib. Royale Albert 1er) and arranged the completion of the Hours of Mary of Burgundy (Vienna, Österreich. Nbib., Cod. 1857), which was originally commissioned by Margaret of York, probably as a gift to Mary (*see* MASTERS, ANONYMOUS, AND MONOGRAMMISTS, §I: MASTER OF MARY OF BURGUNDY and fig. 1). After her accession on 5 January 1477 Mary's patronage followed the normal course of her ducal predecessors, with such artists as Hugo van der Goes engaged for the decoration of banners and the paraphernalia of state occasions. Pierre Coustain continued in her service, and GIOVANNI CANDIDA was re-employed in August 1477; he produced several medals of Mary and Maximilian. Mary's patronage was adversely affected, however, by the war with France (1477–9) and economic depression, which resulted in the loss of Candida's services in 1480 and the need to give the Medici bank in Bruges some 32 pictures in repayment for a loan.

BIBLIOGRAPHY

L. Hommel: *Marie de Bourgogne ou le grand héritage* (Brussels, 1951)

G.-H. Dumont: *Marie de Bourgogne* (Brussels, 1982) [with bibliog.]

GILES CLIFFORD

(7) Philip, Bishop of Utrecht (*b* Brussels, 1466; *d* Duurstede, nr Wijk, 7 April 1524). Illegitimate son of (3) Philip the Good and Margaretha van Post. He fostered the development of an indigenous Renaissance culture in the north Netherlands and was particularly influential for the development of the style of JAN GOSSART. Philip was raised at the court of Mary of Burgundy and in 1484 matriculated at the University of Louvain. According to his biographer, the humanist Gerard Geldenhauer (1482–1542), in his youth he also acquired the rudiments of the arts of painting and goldsmithing. He was knighted in 1486 and granted the lordships of Sommeldijk, Blaton and Cruybecque. In 1501 he was awarded the collar of the Order of the Golden Fleece and, as admiral of Flanders (1498), travelled to Spain with Archduke Philip the Fair (later Philip I of Spain). In the further capacity of head of the Archduke's household, in 1504 Philip arranged for the painter Hieronymus Bosch to receive a commission for a panel of the *Last Judgement* (untraced). Apparently, he also personally owned two of Bosch's works; one, the *Stone Operation*, may be the version in Madrid (Prado; *see* BOSCH, HIERONYMUS, fig. 7). As imperial legate, Philip left Mechelen (Fr. Malines) for Italy on 26 November 1508, travelling through Verona and Florence to Rome. He was accompanied by a retinue that included Geldenhauer as his secretary and the painter Jan Gossart, whom he commissioned to record the sculptures and ruins of ancient Rome in a series of drawings (dispersed). Impressed by the broad learning of the legate, Pope Julius II gave him ancient statues of *Julius Caesar* and of *Hadrian* (both untraced). Following his return to the Netherlands by June 1509, Philip introduced both Gossart and the Venetian painter and printmaker Jacopo de' Barbari to the court of the regent, Margaret of Austria, at Mechelen.

Independently wealthy through inheritances from siblings, Philip, in emulation of Italian princes, encouraged the gathering of scholars at his castle of Suytborg (now Souberg, Walcheren Island). These included Erasmus (who dedicated his *Querimonia pacis* (Basle, 1517–20) to Philip) and Geldenhauer, the latter under the pen-name Noviomagus fostering the study of epigraphy, numismatics and Vitruvius's architectural treatises. Among artists in that circle were de' Barbari, the sculptor Conrat Meit and especially Gossart, who, under Philip's intellectual directive, created large paintings of mythological subjects, prominently featuring nude figures *all'antica*. Gossart's panel of *Neptune and Amphitrite* (1516; Berlin, Gemäldegal; *see* GOSSART, JAN, fig. 3) probably formed part of this scheme. Philip of Burgundy's name and motto A.PLVS. SERA appears prominently on the picture, and its subject may refer to his admiralty. According to Geldenhauer, Philip composed inscriptions for paintings and on at least one occasion provided verses for allegories in connection with a state pageantry held in Brussels. A 16th-century drawing (Arras, Bib. Ville) that records a bust-length panel of Philip before his accession to the Utrecht bishopric in 1517 is probably after a lost work of Gossart. The sitter's features are corroborated in a die-cast medal commemorating his episcopal investiture. Once bishop, Philip resided within his see at the castle of Wijk-bij-Duurstede, some 30 km south of Utrecht. Here, while diligently seeing to his administration, he and his retainers pursued humanist interests. Philip also commissioned large mythological paintings for the castle, probably from Gossart. According to the cursory and incomplete inventory drawn up on his death, Philip had amassed a considerable library as well as antiquities, tapestries and paintings of religious and mythological subjects, much of which was passed on to his nephew Adolf (*d* 1540), son of (4) Antoine of Burgundy; Adolf succeded his uncle as admiral in Zeeland.

BIBLIOGRAPHY

G. Noviomagus [G. Geldenhauer]: *Vita clarrisimi principis Philippi a Burgundia* (Strasbourg, 1529)

G. Marlier: *Erasme et la peinture flamande de son temps* (Damme, 1954)

J. Sterk: *Philips van Bourgondië (1465–1524): Bisschop van Utrecht als protagonist van de Renaissance, zijn leven en maecenaat* (Zutphen, 1980)

PATRICK M. DE WINTER

Buri, Max (Alfred) (*b* Burgdorf, 24 July 1868; *d* Interlaken, 21 May 1915). Swiss painter. While still at school he was given drawing lessons by Paul Volmar (1832–1906) in Berne. From 1883 he was a pupil of Fritz Schider (1846–1907) in Basle, where he became acquainted with the works of Hans Holbein the younger and Arnold Böcklin. In 1886 he went to the Akademie der Bildenden Künste in Munich, transferring in 1887 to Simon Hollósy's painting school. After seeing the works of the French Impressionists exhibited in Munich, he moved to the Académie Julian in Paris in 1889. He made several journeys to Algeria, Holland, Belgium and England, and in 1893 he returned to Munich to study under Albert von Keller. In 1898 he settled in Switzerland, living first at Lucerne, then from 1903 in Brienz, near Interlaken. About 1900, influenced by the paintings of Ferdinand Hodler, Buri moved on from his early genre pictures, which were in mawkish shades of pink in the style of Keller and Hóllosy, to achieve an individual style that brought him great popularity. He established his reputation with *Village Politicians* (1904; Basle, Kstmus.). He painted mainly the landscape and people of the Bernese Oberland, often depicting single figures and groups in front of bare indoor walls in realistic everyday scenes. The expressiveness of the compositions is achieved by clear contours and powerful clearly differentiated surfaces in local colours. Buri's works are essentially populist rather than intellectual and avoid Hodler's strict parallelism and Symbolist content.

BIBLIOGRAPHY

H. Graber: *Max Buri: Sein Leben und Werk* (Basle, 1916)

M. Huggler: *Max Buri: Der Maler von Brienz* (Berne, 1981)

FRANZ MÜLLER

Burin [graver]. Tool for incising lines into a metal plate to create an engraving (*see* ENGRAVING, fig. 1a–d). It consists of a sharpened steel point with a diamond-shaped cross section, mounted in a wooden handle. A burin gouges out a thin section of metal, leaving an incised groove with a shape depending on the size and width of the point and the force of application.

RUPERT FEATHERSTONE

Burke, Edmund (*b* Dublin, 12 Jan 1729; *d* Beaconsfield, Bucks, 9 July 1797). British statesman, philosopher and writer. Following studies at Trinity College, Dublin, he enrolled in 1750 at the Middle Temple, London, but soon abandoned the study of law and devoted the rest of his life to politics and writing. In 1765 he became MP for Wendover, and his eloquence and ability enabled him to rise rapidly in the Whig party; his political writings were widely admired. In 1756 he published, anonymously, *A Philosophical Enquiry into the Origin of our Ideas of the Sublime and the Beautiful.* The major influence on writers on taste during the 18th century was Longinus's Greek treatise *On the Sublime* (1st century AD). Longinus defined the Sublime as differing from beauty, and invoking more intense emotions by vastness, a quality that inspires awe. The term came into general use in the 18th century and was used particularly in relation to landscape painting, the works of Salvator Rosa being considered the foremost examples among the Old Masters. The Sublime was discussed by, among others, Jonathan Richardson sr, the Abbé Jean-Baptiste Dubos and John Baillie. Burke was the first to examine and substantiate the link between terror and the Sublime; he also drew a distinction between beauty and the Sublime (for a fuller discussion *see* THE SUBLIME). He believed that both were perceived emotionally, thus rejecting the long-standing theories that beauty was the result of proportion, utility or perfection. In the second edition (1759) of his work he added an *Essay on Taste* to explain his views further. The subject of taste was of deep interest to 18th-century intellectuals; the philosopher David Hume agreed with Burke that taste is the result of the imagination reacting to sensibility and refined by knowledge and judgement (*Dissertation on Taste*, 1756). However, Burke differed from Hume in believing that taste operates identically in all mankind—'The pleasure of all the senses ... is the same in all, high and low, learned and unlearned'—and is therefore determinable, whereas Hume was sceptical of a scientifically established standard of taste.

Burke's *Enquiry* had an overwhelming influence on both the theory and the practice of art. Joshua Reynolds, James Barry and Henry Fuseli propagated Burke's theories through their Royal Academy lectures; Uvedale Price incorporated Burke's ideas in his theory of the PICTURESQUE; and, on the Continent, they were enthusiastically accepted by Gotthold Ephraim Lessing. In 1763 Burke met Barry, who had already read the *Enquiry*, in Dublin; he encouraged Barry's ambition to be a history painter and financed his stay in Rome from 1765 to 1770. Barry painted Burke's portrait (*c.* 1771; Dublin, Trinity Coll.); and although the two men became estranged in 1774, Burke appeared two years later in Barry's allegorical history painting *Portraits of Barry and Burke in the Characters of Ulysses and a Companion Fleeing from the Cave of Polyphemus* (Cork, Crawford Mun. A.G.). Burke also used his influence to further the career of the landscape painter George Barret.

WRITINGS

A Philosophical Enquiry into the Origin of our Ideas of the Sublime and the Beautiful, ed. J. T. Boulton (London, 1958)

BIBLIOGRAPHY

S. H. Monk: *The Sublime: A Study of Critical Theories in Eighteenth-century England* (New York, 1935; rev. 1960)

DAVID RODGERS

Burke, John (*b* Clonmel, Co. Tipperary, 11 May 1946). Irish sculptor. He attended the Crawford Municipal School of Art from 1964 to 1967, winning the Cork Arts Society Award in 1967 and the McCauley Fellowship in 1970. This took him to London, where he worked for a year as assistant to Bryan Kneale (*b* 1930). His study of early 20th-century Constructivism and of the work of David Smith led him to produce welded steel sculptures in which colour provided a final incidental and decorative element that disguised scrap-metal forms that would otherwise have been too readily recognizable. His interest in musical rhythm was manifested in the fluidity and counterpoint of form in sculptures such as *Etsumi* (1973; Belfast, Ulster Mus.), which create a sense of space enveloping the form irrespective of the organic volume.

Burke's work had an enormous impact on public sculpture in Cork, where he was largely based and where most of his large outdoor commissions are on public view. His huge untitled black sculpture (painted steel, h. 5 m, 1984) at Wilton Roundabout, Cork, creates a provocative pattern in space, with paradoxical twists of direction and counter-shapes. Among his major sculptures outside Cork are those at the Bank of Ireland headquarters in Dublin and at Dunmanway and Fermoy (both Co. Cork).

BIBLIOGRAPHY

Irish Art, 1943–1973 (exh. cat. by C. Barrett, Cork, Crawford Mun. A.G., 1980)

Cork Art Now '85 (exh. cat. by V. Ryan, Cork, Crawford Mun. A.G.; Amsterdam, Heineken Gal.; 1985)

HILARY PYLE

Burke, Selma Hortense (*b* Mooresville, NC, 1 Jan 1907; *d* New Hope, PA, 29 Aug 1995). American sculptor, teacher and writer. She initially trained as a nurse at the Women's Medical College, NC, before studying philosophy at Columbia University, New York (1936–41). During the 1930s she became one of a few prominent black American sculptors (*see* AFRICAN AMERICAN ART, §2) participating in the Works Progress Administration's Federal Art Projects. She also became an instructor in sculpture at the Harlem Community Art Centre and a frequent contributor to periodicals and newspapers, and she worked with Aristide Maillol in Paris and Hans Reiss (*b* 1885) in New York. In 1940 she was awarded a Rosenwald Fellowship and in 1943–6 was director of the Student's School of Sculpture, New York. Her sculpture is characterized by an idealistic intent in sensitively moulded stone carvings on humanistic themes, for example *Lafayette* and *Salome*, exhibited at the McMillen Galleries, New York, in November 1941. In later works the artist evoked the timeless spirit of such universal subjects as *Mother and Child* (1968; Los Angeles, CA, Co. Mus. A.), in which the smooth surfaces of intertwined figures play against rhythmic drapery. There were major exhibitions in 1945 held at the Carlen Galleries, Philadelphia, and the McMillen Galleries and Modernage Gallery, New York. Works are held in the New York Public Library, New York Public School, Bethune College, New York, Teachers College, Winston-Salem, NC, and the Recorder of Deeds Building, Washington, DC.

BIBLIOGRAPHY

Two Centuries of Black American Art (exh. cat. by D. D. Driscoll, Los Angeles, CA, Co. Mus. A., 1976)

G. B. Opitz, ed.: *Dictionary of American Painters, Sculptors and Engravers* (New York, 1986)

P. Chiarmonte: *Women Artists in the United States* (Boston, 1990)

□

Burke, Thomas (*b* Dublin, 1749; *d* London, 31 Dec 1815). Irish engraver, active in England. He first trained, according to Carey, in the Dublin Society's Schools under Robert West, moving *c.* 1770 to London, where he studied mezzotint-engraving under John Dixon. Most of Burke's mezzotints were engraved after Angelica Kauffman for William Wynne Ryland, although other examples included a mezzotint in 1773 of the racehorse *Eclipse* after George Stubbs for the publisher Robert Sayer. Burke presumably learnt stipple-engraving from Ryland, and in 1775 he gave up mezzotint for this newer technique, engraving many fine plates for Ryland after Kauffman, who according to an obituary of Burke in *New Monthly Magazine* had 'always preferred him to engrave her designs'. Francesco Bartolozzi is said to have praised proofs of these prints in terms of the 'mellowness, delicacy, power and richness of their effect' (Carey). Burke's *Lady Rushout* (O'Donoghue, ii) after Kauffman, published by William Dickinson in 1784, is one of his finest prints. *The Nightmare*, engraved in 1783 after Johann Heinrich Füseli, was so successful that it was reputed to have made £500 for its publisher, John Raphael Smith. Other well-known plates, after such painters as William Redmore Bigg and Henry Singleton, include Bigg's *Saturday Morning*, engraved in 1797. He engraved one plate, *Cymbeline*, after William Hamilton for John Boydell's 'Shakespeare Gallery'. Burke, who nearly always preferred to work for publishers rather than issue prints himself, was principally an engraver of subject pictures, although he did engrave some 30 portraits. He produced little after the mid-1790s owing to ill-health.

BIBLIOGRAPHY

O'Donoghue; Thieme–Becker

W. P. Carey: 'Bartolozzi', *Eur. Mag.*, lxviii (1815), pp. 309–14

Obituary, *New Mthly Mag.*, iv/22 (Dec 1815), p. 361

C. Le Blanc: *Manuel de l'amateur d'estampes* (Paris, 1854–89), i, pp. 550–51

J. C. Smith: *English Mezzotinto Portraits* (London, 1878–83), i, pp. 133–6

J. Frankau: *Eighteenth-century Colour Prints* (London, 1900), pp. 77–9

DAVID ALEXANDER

Burkina Faso [République Démocratique Populaire de Burkina Faso; formerly Upper Volta, Haute-Volta]. Country of *c.* 274,200 sq. km in West Africa, bordered by Mali to the west and north, Niger to the east and Côte d'Ivoire, Ghana, Togo and Benin to the south. The capital is Ouagadougou. Conquered by the French in 1896, it remained under their control until 1960, when it became independent. Until 1984 it was called Haute-Volta or Upper Volta. Its population (*c.* 8,509,000; UN estimate, 1988) is made up of *c.* 30 distinct ethnic groups. Although the official language is French, large numbers of people use Moore, the language of the Mossi people (the most numerous group in the country); Jula, the language of traders from the north-west; or Fulfulde, the language of the Fulani herders, as common languages. The peoples of Burkina Faso can be divided into two major language groups: the peoples in the centre and east, including the Bwa, Gurunsi and Mossi, speak Voltaic languages, while the peoples in the west, principally the Bobo and Marka, speak Mande languages. Although most traders are Muslim, and many city-dwellers, especially those working in government and education, are Christian, more than 80% of the country's population continue to practise the traditional religions of their ancestors. This entry covers the art produced in the country since colonial times. For art of the area in earlier periods, *see* AFRICA, §VII, 3.

The high percentage of the population still practising indigenous religions, combined with the former French colonial policy of underdevelopment, has resulted in the survival of many traditional forms. Many of the sculptural forms that were so abundant at the end of the 19th century have continued to be produced and used into the late 20th century. The Mossi political élite, for example, continue to make wood figures, while the other Mossi make masks like those that their ancestors produced (*see* MOSSI, figs 1 and 2). Figures and masks are produced in large numbers by many other peoples and appear in numerous celebrations during the dry season (October to May). These masks and figures represent the spirits of nature that give life and power to the natural environment. There is also a flourishing production of earthen pottery by women and of narrow-loom textiles, baskets and iron tools by men. Some Burkinabe peoples, especially the Gurunsi, have appeared with their masks at public celebrations and political rallies, as frequently happens elsewhere in West Africa. Many other peoples, however, especially the Mossi, Bwa and Bobo, have refused to allow their sacred objects to be seen in secular or popular contexts.

Until the 1900s the Mossi brass-casters (*nyogsin*) of Ouagadougou cast only stirrups, bits and buckles for the Mossi cavalry and funerary portraits of Mossi emperors. With the arrival of the French they began to produce large numbers of cast-brass scenes of everyday life, depicting such themes as drummers, dancers and women pounding millet or administering enemas to their children. In the early 1970s the Centre National des Arts in Ouagadougou, created and staffed by American Peace Corps Volunteers, organized local artisans to sell their art to tourists (see fig.). The new art forms that developed included scenes of everyday life reproduced on cloth using the batik technique.

During the late colonial period a large and important collection of the art and material culture of the peoples of Burkina Faso was gathered together by the French scholar Guy LeMoal and housed at the Institut Français de l'Afrique Noire (IFAN) in Ouagadougou. In 1961 the direction of the museum passed to one of LeMoal's former assistants, Toumani Triande, and the collection was removed from the old IFAN building and housed temporarily in the principal hotel in Ouagadougou. As administrative responsibility for the museum was shuttled from one ministry to another, the collection suffered loss and damage. Interest in caring for this important collection was revived by Bouriema Diamatani. In the 1990s plans existed to house the works in a new, climate-controlled building that would allow them to become the focus of new programmes for study, collecting and education. Diamatani also created new branch museums in old colonial buildings and other disused structures in Burkina Faso's second city, Bobo Dioulasso (Musée), and in the capital of Lobi country, Gaoua (Mus. Civilis. S.-Ouest). These small museums house art made locally and make it available to visitors and school-children.

See also BWA AND GURUNSI, BOBO, FULANI, LOBI and MOSSI.

Apprentice Mossi brass-casters, *nyogsin*, forming wax moulds for casting at the Centre National des Arts, Ouagadougou, Burkina Faso, 1972

BIBLIOGRAPHY

J. Anquetil: *Haute-Volta: Artisanat créateur* (Paris, 1977)
——: *Sénégal, Mali, Niger, Haute-Volta, Côte d'Ivoire: Artisanat créateur* (Paris, 1977)
J. Etienne-Nugue: *Artisanat traditionnel: Haute-Volta* (Dakar, 1982)

CHRISTOPHER D. ROY

Bürklein, Friedrich (*b* Burk, 30 March 1813; *d* Werneck, 4 Dec 1872). German architect and teacher. He studied at the Munich Akademie from 1828 as a pupil of Friedrich von Gärtner and subsequently became the latter's assistant. In 1840–41 he travelled with him to Greece, where he was briefly involved in building the royal palace (1836–41) in Athens. Bürklein adopted Gärtner's stylistic principles and from 1840 he built a large number of private houses in Munich, influenced by the *Rundbogenstil.* He also designed the Rathaus (1840–43) in Fürth, derived loosely from the Palazzo Vecchio in Florence. In 1846 he was sent abroad by the Bavarian government to study the design of railway stations and on his return he designed the new main railway station (1847–9; destr. 1945) in Munich. While the exterior derived from Italian Romanesque churches, the concourse had a daring and highly advanced timber roof structure (altered 1883). The building's success earned Bürklein the favour of Maximilian II, King of Bavaria (*reg* 1848–64), who appointed him professor (from 1850) at the Technische Hochschule, Munich. After an unsuccessful attempt to stimulate the creation of a new architectural style through an international competition (1850), Maximilian commissioned Bürklein (1852) to plan a model street for Munich, designed uniformly in a new style. Over the next few years, in an idiom of predominantly Gothic forms, Bürklein created most of the buildings on the Maximilianstrasse, including the Regierungs-Gebäude (1856–64), and, facing down its length, the Maximilianeum (1857–74; for illustration *see* ECLECTICISM), built as a school for royal pages and now the Bavarian provincial parliament. Following one of Maximilian's predilections, the most important buildings were faced with terracotta slabs, although neither this technique nor the 'Maximilian style' was much imitated.

WRITINGS

Architektonische Entwürfe zu Pracht- und Zivilgebäuden (Munich, 1846)

BIBLIOGRAPHY

Thieme–Becker; Wasmuth
H. Gollwitzer: *100 Jahre Maximilianeum, 1852–1952* (Munich, 1953)
A. Hahn: *Der Maximilianstil in München* (Munich, 1982)

DIETRICH NEUMANN

Burle Marx, Roberto (*b* São Paulo, 4 Aug 1909). Brazilian landscape architect, painter and designer. He studied painting at a private school in Berlin from 1928 to 1929 and during this time he frequently went to the Botanical Gardens at Dahlem to study the collections of plants that were arranged in geographical groupings, providing useful lessons in botany and ecology. He thus learnt to appreciate fully many examples of the flora of Brazil that were rarely used in Brazilian gardens, an experience that had a lasting effect on him. In 1930 he entered the Escola Nacional de Belas Artes in Rio de Janeiro to study painting and he also took a course in ecology at the Botanical Gardens in Rio. In 1934 he was invited to become Director of Parks and Gardens at Recife, a position he held until 1937 when he established his own practice as a landscape architect in Rio de Janeiro. To this period belong the gardens of the Casa do Forte, where aquatic plants predominate, and the gardens he designed for the Praça Euclides da Cunha, where his studies of the *caatinga*, the low, open, sandy forests of Brazil, led him to make extensive use of species from arid climates.

Roberto Burle Marx: garden of the Ministry of Foreign Affairs building, Brasília, 1965

In 1938 Burle Marx came into contact with the Modernist architects who led the revival of Brazilian architecture from the 1930s when, working in association with Lúcio Costa and his team, he was commissioned to design the gardens for the Le Corbusier Ministry of Education and Health building (now the Palácio da Cultura) in Rio de Janeiro. He was associated with another Modernist architectural group, M. M. Roberto, when he designed the roof garden for the Brazilian Press Association (ABI) building and the gardens for Praça Salgado Filho at Santos Dumont Airport (both 1938; Rio de Janeiro). The gardens for the airport and for the Roberto Marinho house (1938) in Rio were works that greatly impressed Oscar Niemeyer and from 1941 Burle Marx worked on the design of the park at Niemeyer's Pampulha complex at Belo Horizonte, Minas Gerais, producing a work of great beauty and international renown.

In 1943 Burle Marx created a park at Araxá, Minas Gerais. Divided into 25 sections, each demonstrating different ecological systems, this work was inspired by the botanist Henrique L. de Mello Barreto, who taught Burle Marx to appreciate that plants do not live in isolation but in associations, and to be aware of the natural habitats of plants before attempting to use them in gardens. With Mello Barreto he visited many parts of Brazil to study the flora of the different geological regions—ferriferous clay, sandstone, quartzite, calcareous rocks—and of such areas as *cerrado*, or open pastureland with stunted vegetation. Another garden based on this principle was the park, designed in 1948, attached to the Odette Monteiro house at Correas, Rio de Janeiro; situated near the Serra dos Orgãos, the gardens were planned in accordance with their mountain environment and were integrated with the native vegetation of the region.

In 1949 Burle Marx acquired the S António da Bica site in Campo Grande, Rio de Janeiro, where he gradually built up one of the greatest collections of living plants in the world. During years of patient work, he gathered together classified groups of plants collected on journeys systematically undertaken throughout Brazil in the company of botanists from whom he acquired a profound knowledge of tropical plants. This extensive study formed the basis of several landscaping projects of considerable complexity and size, such as the 70 ha Parque del Este (1956) in Caracas and a series of works in Brasília, in collaboration with Oscar Niemeyer. These included the Parque Zoobotánico (1961), in which Burle Marx demonstrated the relationship between animals, plants and rocks of the same region in a sequence of ecological settings; the garden of the Ministry of Foreign Affairs building (1965; see fig.), in which a large lake with waterlilies surrounds the Palácio dos Arcos, providing reflections and creating a lush microclimate within the arid environment of the new capital; the Army and Justice Ministries (1970) and the Rogério Pithon Serejo Farias Recreation Park (1974).

Burle Marx was a prolific designer. Other notable works include gardens for the Civic Centre of Santo André (1967; design Rino Levi), São Paulo, in which Portuguese tiles are used to unify squares, terraces and parks in a restrained plan of curved and straight lines; features include three large concrete bas-reliefs at the theatre entrance and a tapestry 26 m long. From 1954 he collaborated with the architect Affonso Eduardo Reidy on the design for a 1.2 million sq. m area of the Flamengo waterfront in Rio de Janeiro, in which the gardens for the Museu de Arte Moderna and the Monument to the Dead of World War II are outstanding.

The magnificent promenades (1970) of the Copacabana beach embankment in Rio, where abstract, flowing mosaic designs in white, black and brown Portuguese tiles establish a dialogue between the paving, the sea and the groups of trees growing along the foreshore are typical of Burle Marx's painterly approach. In these large-scale works it is clear that he is preoccupied with questions of form, colour, geometry and rhythm; he continued to paint with intensity and, just as he treated plants and gardens with a painter's vision, so his studies of flora enriched his work as a painter. However, he made a clear distinction between the two activities, recognizing the effect on a garden of a complex range of environmental factors and the variability of colour under different conditions of light and weather. Burle Marx was outspoken in defence of the flora and fauna threatened with destruction and pollution, using his position to advise the government on more effective legislation to protect the environment. His work, including sculpture and tapestry design as well as painting and landscape design, was exhibited in galleries and museums around the world on numerous occasions, and he received many awards and honours during his career.

WRITINGS

Arte & paisagem: Conferências escolhidas [Art & landscape: selected lectures] (São Paulo, 1987)

BIBLIOGRAPHY

C. Vincent: 'The Modern Garden in Brazil', *Archit. Rev.* [London], ci/605 (1947), pp. 165–72

H. R. Hitchcock: *Latin American Architecture since 1945* (New York, 1955)

H. E. Mindlin: *Modern Architecture in Brazil* (Rio de Janeiro, 1956)

'Rapporto Brasile', *Zodiac*, 6 (1960), pp. 118–27

P. M. Bardi: *The Tropical Gardens of Burle Marx* (Amsterdam, 1964)

D. Bayón and P. Gasparini: *Panorámica de la arquitectura latino-americana* (Barcelona, 1977; Eng. trans., New York, 1979)

F. L. Motta, ed.: *Roberto Burle Marx e a nova visão da paisagem* (São Paulo, 1984)

E. Eliovson: *The Gardens of Roberto Burle Marx* (London, 1991)

PAULO J. V. BRUNA

Burlington, 3rd Earl of. *See* BOYLE, (2).

Burlyuk [Burliuk]. Ukrainian family of artists. All six children in the family showed artistic or literary talent, but (1) David Burlyuk, the eldest, and (2) Vladimir Burlyuk are especially noted for their contributions to avant-garde movements in Russia in the early 20th century, in particular to Russian Futurism.

(1) David (Davidovich) Burlyuk (*b* Kharkiv, Ukraine, 21 July 1882; *d* Southampton, Long Island, NJ, 15 Jan 1967). Painter and writer. He studied art in Kazan' and Odessa from 1899 to 1901, when he left for Munich to study with Anton Ažbé. In 1904 he attended the Ecole des Beaux-Arts, Paris, under Fernand Cormon. Returning to Russia, he settled in Moscow but again studied at the Odessa School of Art from 1910 to 1911 and then entered the Moscow School of Painting, Sculpture and Architecture, from which he was expelled in 1914.

From 1908 David had been active in organizing exhibitions promoting the new art that was emerging in Russia. In that year he published his first polemical article, 'Golos impressionista: V zashchitu zhivopisi' ('The voice of an Impressionist: in defence of painting'). In this article he rejected the realistic style of the Wanderers, the outmoded rules of the Academy of Art in St Petersburg and the retrospection of the World of Art (Mir Iskusstva) group, in favour of the styles of the Western Post-Impressionists (whom he here called Impressionists), especially Cézanne and van Gogh. He helped organize and contributed to the controversial Jack of Diamonds exhibitions in Moscow from 1910 to 1917. There he exhibited such works as *Bridge (Landscape from Four Points of View)* (1911; St Petersburg, Rus. Mus.), which is clearly indebted to French Cubism, both in the title and in the displaced planes with which the landscape is constructed. *A Landscape* (1912; Lugano, Col. Thyssen-Bornemisza), with rough-textured, spike-like tree shapes in dark green, blues, tan and yellow, is closer to contemporary German Expressionist painting; but this painting also reveals the interest of both David and Vladimir Burlyuk in the simplified outlines of prehistoric art and their practice of rolling their canvases in mud to give them a texture very different from the slick surfaces of academic painting and one intended to reinforce the emotional content of the paintings. In the *Headless Barber* (*c.* 1912; priv. col., see exh. cat., fig. 9), he used Cubist planes and displacements to surreal effect, separating the head of the barber from his body and showing it sitting on a nearby table.

David also contributed poetry, prose and illustrations to anthologies of the new Russian writing, later called Russian Futurism. His most influential essay, however, 'Die "Wilden" Russlands', was one he sent to the almanac *Der Blaue Reiter* in 1912, on the invitation of Vasily Kandinsky. There he praised the 'barbaric' art of Egypt, Assyria and the Scythians, and he reproduced works of Russian folk art. David's article and the works by young Russian artists reproduced in the almanac brought the iconoclastic ideas of the Russian Futurists to the attention of a wider circle of non-Russian-speaking artists and critics. The degree of their iconoclasm may be indicated by the title of one of the anthologies that David helped produce: *Poshchechina obshchestvennomu vkusu* ('A slap in the face of public taste'; 1912). David's contribution to Russian literary Futurism as organizer and polemicist, which led to the appellation 'the father of Russian Futurism', was greater than his work as an artist or writer. As early as 1908, the emerging artists Mikhail Larionov and Natal'ya Goncharova broke with David over what they perceived as his excessive commitment to the styles of Western Europe.

After the October Revolution of 1917, David moved first to Siberia and then to Japan, where he again organized exhibitions, gave lectures and wrote poetry. In 1922 he moved to the USA and settled in New York, where he continued to write and paint. In 1930 he established the journal *Color and Rhyme*, in which many of his later works were reproduced. The last issue appeared in 1966.

See also CUBO-FUTURISM and PERFORMANCE ART.

WRITINGS

'Golos impressionista: V zashchitu zhivopisi' [The voice of an Impressionist: in defence of painting], *Zveno* [Link] (exh. cat., Kiev, 1908); Eng. trans., extract, in Bowlt, pp. 10–11

'Die "Wilden" Russlands', *Der Blaue Reiter* (Munich, 1912; rev. 2, ed. K. Lankenheit, 1965; Eng. trans. H. Falkenstein, London, 1974)

Poshchechina obshchestvennomu vkusu [A slap in the face of public taste] (Moscow, 1912); Eng. trans. in V. Markov: *Russian Futurism: A History* (London, 1969), pp. 45–6

BIBLIOGRAPHY

Russian Avant-garde (exh. cat., New York, Leonard Hutton Gal., 1971)

J. Bowlt: *Russian Art of the Avant-garde: Theory and Criticism, 1902–1934* (New York, 1976)

K. Passuth: 'David Burliuk, Paintings, 1907–1966', *Cah. Mus. Nat. A. Mod.* 2 (1979), p. 282

' "A *Slap* in the *Face* of Public Taste": A Jubilee for David Burliuk and the Cause of Russian Futurism', *Can.-Amer. Slav. Stud.*, xx/1–2 (1986) [issue devoted to David Burlyuk]

(2) Vladimir (Davidovich) Burlyuk (*b* Chernyanka, Ukraine, 27 March 1887; *d* Salonika, Greece, 1917). Painter, brother of (1) David Burlyuk. He first studied at the Odessa School of Art and then, in 1903, with Anton Ažbé in Munich. After his return to Russia, he became an active contributor to many of the newly formed exhibition groups there, among them Jack of Diamonds and Union of Youth. He also contributed to exhibitions in Munich and Berlin and was well aware of the latest developments in European painting, although he preferred to appear as an untaught 'savage'. Mikhail Larionov's primitivizing portrait of *Vladimir*, probably from the summer of 1910 (Lyon, Mus. B.-A.), shows him in a peasant shirt, carrying the heavy lifting weights that he brought along to poetry readings and art exhibitions.

Vladimir's portrait of the poet *Benedikt Livshits* (1911; New York, Ella Jaffe Freidus priv. col.; see Livshits, p. 49) is organized in Cubist planes, though without fragmentation. However, a slightly later work, *Landscape with Trees* (1912; Moscow, Tret'yakov Gal., ex-G. Costakis priv. col.), with its stylized trees and background patterned like stained glass, betrays the continuing influence of the *Jugendstil*, then prevalent in Munich. Vladimir also contributed illustrations, firstly primitivizing, then Cubist, to the many Russian Futurist publications that appeared during these years. These included *Sadok sudey* ('A trap for judges'; St Petersburg, 1910), which contains relatively traditional portraits of most of the contributors, while *Sadok sudey 2* (St Petersburg, 1913) contains a portrait by Vladimir that shows how a Cubist head can be transformed into an abstract design (see Compton, pls 74–5). From 1915 he was on active duty with the Russian army; he was killed in action in 1917.

BIBLIOGRAPHY

B. Livshits: *Polutoraglazyy strelets* [The one-and-a-half-eyed archer] (Leningrad, 1933; Eng. trans. J. E. Bowlt, Newtonville, 1977), p. 49

S. Compton: *The World Backwards: Russian Futurist Books, 1912–16* (London, 1978), pls 42, 74–5, 106

A. Rudenstine, ed.: *Russian Avant-garde Art: The George Costakis Collection* (New York, 1981), p. 81

MARIAN BURLEIGH-MOTLEY

Burma [Myan ma; Myanmar]. Country in South-east Asia occupying the westernmost part of the Indo-Chinese Peninsula, with a seacoast on the Bay of Bengal. (For the regional context of Burmese art forms *see* SOUTH-EAST ASIA, §I.)

I. Introduction. II. Architecture. III. City planning. IV. Sculpture. V. Painting. VI. Textiles. VII. Dress and body decoration. VIII. Theatre. IX. Other arts. X. Folk and village art. XI. Art education.

I. Introduction.

1. Geography, peoples and languages. 2. History. 3. Religion, iconography and subject-matter.

1. GEOGRAPHY, PEOPLES AND LANGUAGES. The wide variety of styles and forms, techniques, materials and subject-matter found in the art of Burma through the centuries has to a great extent been determined by the geography of the country, its links with its neighbours, particularly India, the ethnic and linguistic diversity of its inhabitants and their early adoption of Buddhism. The geographical heart of Burma is a dry central zone, drained by the Irrawaddy River. This is surrounded on three sides by high mountains, which border, from west to east, Bangladesh, India, China, Laos and Thailand (see fig. 1). Originally, much of the mountain country was clothed with tropical semi-evergreen rain-forest and hill evergreen forest, while the central plain, being sheltered from the monsoon rains, was much drier, with savanna forest and thorn scrub. The intermediate zones provided monsoon forest with teak, a supreme wood for building and carving. The dry central plain became the historic core of the country, where an early use of irrigation allowed the development of such great civilizations as PAGAN, based on the cultivation of rice.

The population of almost 40 million is ethnically and linguistically one of the most diverse in South-east Asia. The indigenous inhabitants, who entered Burma from the north and east, are closely related to each other and speak languages of the Tibeto-Burman, Mon-Khmer and Tai groups. The most important non-indigenous groups are the Indians and the Chinese. Burmese is the official language. The majority of the population (85%) are Theravada Buddhists, and there are small minorities of animists, Muslims, Hindus and Christians. The dominant Buddhist Burmans (65%) control the central plain and the capital city, Rangoon.

In the mountains, by contrast, there is a mosaic of peoples with different languages, dress and cultures, including the Karens (11%), the Shan-Tai (8.5%), and the Kachins (3.5%), as well as many others, such as the Chins, the Lahus and the Nagas. Because these groups have retained a substantial degree of cultural autonomy and still remain largely independent of the government, the arts of Burma are extremely varied both in their origins and style (*see* §X below).

BIBLIOGRAPHY

H. Chhibber: *The Physiography of Burma* (Calcutta and London, 1933/*R* New York, 1975)

C. Fisher: *South-east Asia: A Social, Economic and Political Geography* (London, 1964/*R* 1971)

F. Le Bar, G. Hickey and J. Musgrave: *Ethnic Groups of Mainland Southeast Asia* (New Haven, 1964)

E. Dobby: *Southeast Asia* (London, 1975)

G. Lubeigt: *La Birmanie*, Que sais-je?, no. 1620 (Paris, 1975)

PHILIP STOTT

2. HISTORY. The history of Burmese art may be divided into three main periods: the centuries from the prehistoric

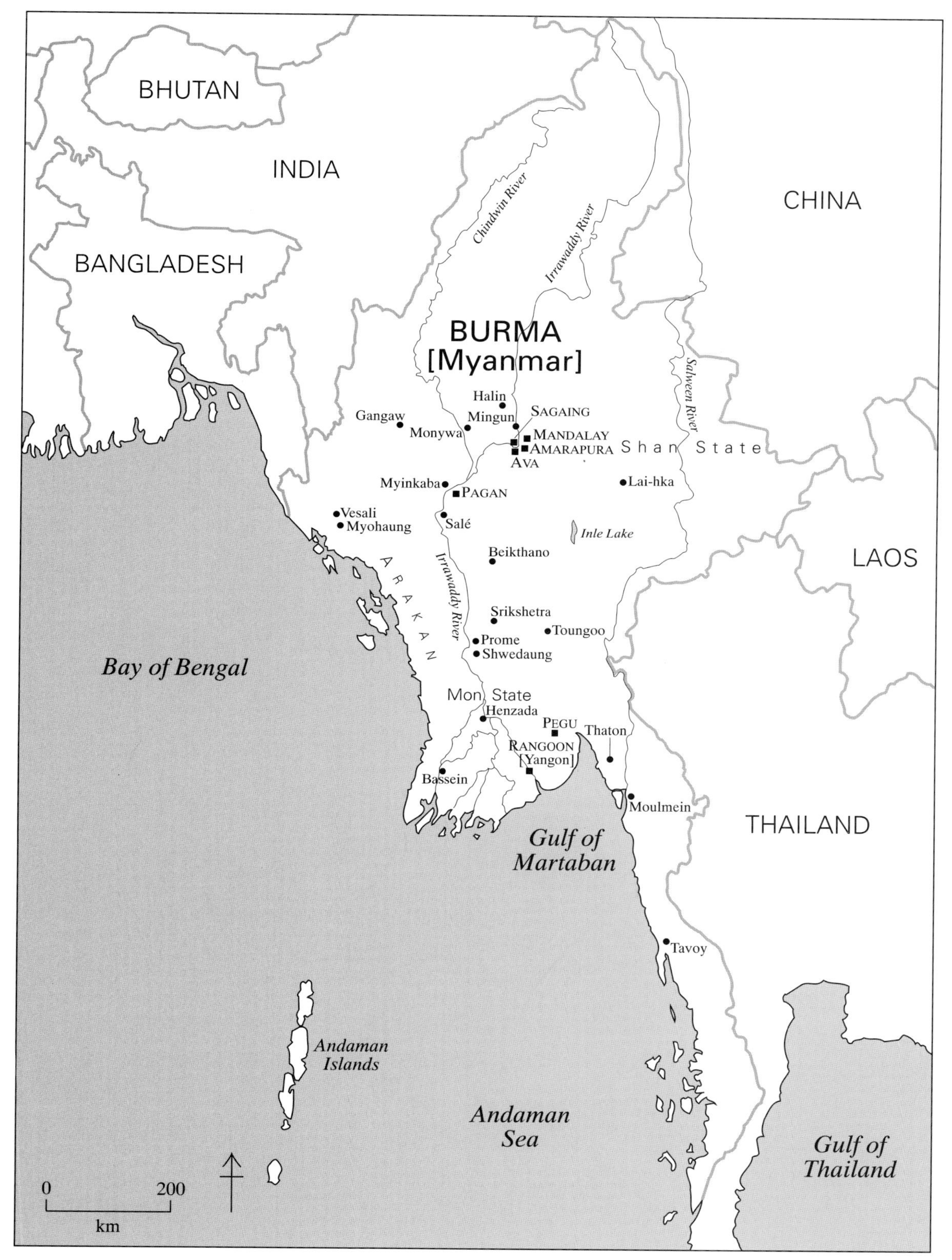

1. Map of Burma; those areas with separate entries in this dictionary are distinguished by CROSS-REFERENCE TYPE

period to the emergence of a distinctively Burmese civilization with the establishment of the Pagan kingdom in central Burma in the mid-9th century AD, the 400 years during which Pagan was a major centre of Buddhist religion and culture, and the period from the abandonment of Pagan some years after the Mongol conquest of 1287 up to the present day.

(i) Before 9th century AD. The archaeological evidence suggests the existence of Palaeolithic and early Neolithic cultures dating back to *c.* 11,000 BC; firmer information is available for the period after the beginning of the Christian era when several city-states flourished, of which Beikthano (*see* §II, 1(i) below) is the best known. The first Indianized peoples in Burma were the Mons and their northern neighbours the Pyus. The Mons, a people of Indonesian stock related to the Khmers, settled in Lower Burma and established their capital at Thaton. The main centre of the Pyus, a Tibeto-Burman people, was at Srikshetra (modern Hmawza), near Prome, north of the delta of the Irrawaddy River. From the 5th century AD the Burmans, also of Tibeto-Burman stock, moved southwards from eastern Tibet into the Irrawaddy Valley, overthrew the Pyus in the mid-8th century and established their capital at Pagan.

(ii) 9th–14th centuries. The greatest flowering of Burmese art and architecture took place during the period from the accession of King Anawrahta (*reg* 1044–77), the first historical ruler of Pagan, to the Mongol conquest of 1287. Anawrahta's conquest of Thaton *c.* 1057 led to the establishment of orthodox Theravada Buddhism as the state religion of Pagan and marked the beginning of a long era of almost ceaseless royal temple-building. Mon influence was chiefly confined to religion and literature and had little effect on the temple architecture of Pagan.

Most of the major religious monuments of Pagan were built in the century following the death of Anawrahta. Among these were the Ananda (*see* PAGAN, §2(iii)) founded by Anawrahta's son, Kyanzittha (*reg* 1084–1112), which is one of the few temples in Pagan to have remained continuously in use since its consecration, and the Sulamani, the Gadaw-palin and the Dhamma-yazika, all three of which were founded by King Narapatisithu (*reg* 1170–73). During the 12th century Pagan also became celebrated as a centre of Buddhist learning, a development encouraged by the decay of Buddhism in India and by the arrival in Burma of many scholars from the great Buddhist university and missionary centre of Nalanda in Bihar.

The enormous sums spent on the establishment and maintenance of religious foundations in Pagan during the 13th century seriously undermined the economy of the kingdom and weakened its power. The last important Buddhist monument to be built in Pagan was the Mingalazedi (see fig. 6 below), which was consecrated by King Narathihapati in 1274. Thirteen years later the Mongols invaded Pagan and Narathihapati fled. The political unity of Burma was thus destroyed, not to be regained until the 17th century, although the religious and cultural life of Pagan seems to have continued more or less unchanged at least until the mid-14th century.

(iii) 14th–20th centuries. The collapse of the Pagan monarchy led to a period of decentralization of power in central Burma, allowing for greater autonomy for the more distant political centres. Sometimes referred to as the period of Shan domination, this era was characterized by petty states competing for supremacy. By the second half of the 14th century, one of these states was able to establish a new dynasty centred on AVA.

Ava, although founded as early as 1365, did not hold sway over the major part of Burma until the period between 1597 and 1626. It was described by European visitors as well as by the Burmese as 'Golden Ava, the dwelling of kings'. Though the fortifications of Ava are irregular in form, the inner citadel, with the palace at its centre, is laid out, like all Burmese capitals until Rangoon, on cosmological principles. Ava's control of the Irrawaddy Valley trade provided the city with much of its power.

The fall of the Ava empire came as the result of the establishment of another and more powerful rival in the south at Toungoo. By linking the economic power of the lower Irrawaddy Valley with the additional resources that came from involvement in foreign trade, the rulers at Toungoo soon gained control of the whole country. By the mid-17th century the Toungoo dynasty was able to move the capital back to the central dry zone, the seat of earlier empires and the cultural heart of the society. The court returned to Ava, which remained the capital until 1752, when it was sacked by more powerful rivals, once more from the south. The consolidation of central and southern Burma under powerful kings and the increasing importance of trade for the wealth of the court and the strength of its armies resulted in a geographical shift of interest on the part of the State.

Soon after the fall of the Toungoo dynasty, a new line was founded by a dynamic lower official of the old order named Alaungpaya. The dynasty he established, the Konbaung, also made its capitals in the central dry zone, moving from place to place but always reconstructing the splendour of the State in the centre of the territory that had formed the heart of the Pagan kingdom nearly a thousand years earlier.

Like its predecessors, the Konbaung dynasty presided over a society and economy where strong sumptuary laws restricted the possession of wealth and power to the ruling dynasty and to the individuals appointed by it to administer the provinces. Village headmen (the only hereditary figures of authority other than the king) and court officials were permitted greater displays in their dress and their houses.

The most powerful institution of either classical or early modern Burma was the Buddhist monkhood (Skt and Pali *saṅgha*). As the legitimacy of the king and his state was demonstrated by his support and reverence for the Buddhist faith and its institutions, the court turned over vast amounts of land, taxes and labour for the construction of stupas, temples, monasteries and libraries. While simple literacy in Buddhist texts was reasonably widespread among the male population, it was usually only the court and the monkhood that could appreciate and maintain the high culture of these periods.

The fall of the Konbaung dynasty to the British Indian empire came as the result of defeat in three wars in 1824–6, 1852 and 1885. When Burma was finally annexed as a province of British India, the monarchy was destroyed and replaced by a functional bureaucracy largely staffed by British and Indian officials. In 1937 Burma was made a separate colony under the Secretary of State for India and Burma, but Indian influences remained strong until the Japanese invasion of the country in 1942. After three years of Japanese occupation, the British returned but found that it was impossible to re-establish the old colonial order in the face of widespread nationalism and organized political resistance. After three years of negotiations, Burma regained its independence on 4 January 1948.

Almost immediately the country was thrust into four years of civil war between a secular, Western-orientated government, a variety of ethnic separatist groups and an initially popular Communist Party. With the help of the army, the civilian government led by U Nu was able to control but not defeat the various opposition groups. When the civilian politicians began to squabble among themselves, the army intervened and established new governments, from 1958 to 1960 and again in 1962. After the second coup, the military under General Ne Win attempted to establish a one-party state and follow socialist economic policies predicated on avoiding both foreign investment and involvement in world trade cycles. After 25 years the inappropriateness of this strategy became apparent and in the middle of 1988 the socialist experiment ended in several weeks of demonstrations and bloody reprisals followed by another military coup.

The fall of the Konbaung dynasty in the 19th century had profound effects on the economy and structure of Burmese society. No longer dependent on the State for its major support, the Buddhist *saṅgha* and its institutions became much more variegated and responsive to individual donors for support. Education was no longer the prerogative of the monkhood but became largely a state enterprise with a functional and secular orientation. New art forms and technology were imported from the West; for example, the popular short story and novel became widespread. While the military/socialist government of the post-1962 period placed many restrictions on the arts and literature, the styles and forms developed during the first half of the 20th century have persisted.

BIBLIOGRAPHY

J. F. Cady: *A History of Modern Burma* (Ithaca, 1958)

D. E. Smith: *Religion and Politics in Burma* (Princeton, 1965)

F. S. V. Donnison: *Burma* (New York, 1970)

V. B. Lieberman: *Burmese Administrative Cycles: Anarchy and Conquest c. 1580–1760* (Princeton, 1984)

M. Aung Thwin: *Pagan: The Origins of Modern Burma* (Honolulu, 1985)

R. H. Taylor: *The State in Burma* (London, 1987)

R. H. TAYLOR

3. RELIGION, ICONOGRAPHY AND SUBJECT-MATTER. Human and animal figures dating to the Stone Age found at Taungthaman near Amarapura in the 1970s may have been used in religious ceremonies and are possibly Burma's oldest religious artefacts. From at least the early centuries AD two religions originating in neighbouring India are evident: Brahmanism and Buddhism. Since the 11th century the latter, in its Theravada (Doctrine of the Elders) form, has been practised by a majority of the Burmese (*see* BUDDHISM, §§I and III, 3). Co-existing peacefully with Buddhism is an indigenous tradition involving a belief in and propitiation of the *nat* (spirits). Over the centuries the *nat* pantheon has come to include not only indigenous spirits but also Indian Hindu and Buddhist deities (Skt *devas*).

Excavations at Beikthano ('city of Vishnu'), a Pyu capital that flourished from the 1st to the 5th centuries AD, show that both Brahmanism and Buddhism were practised. Though little in the way of religious art has been uncovered, symbols associated with Shiva and the remains of stupas and monasteries have been found (*see* §II, 1(i) below). Halin, another Pyu city further north, has yielded more objects, among them a damaged stele showing courtiers seated with hands joined in an attitude of prayer or respect possibly before a Buddha image (see fig. 11 below).

At the southern capital of Srikshetra, near modern Prome, iconographic material relating to both Theravada and Mahayana Buddhism as well as to Brahmanism has been found. Excavations have revealed Mahayana bronze Buddhist figures of *bodhisattvas* (Skt: 'beings of enlightenment') dressed as royal personages with diadems and elaborate jewellery. The Pyus, while adopting the teachings of Buddhism, also worshipped local spirits.

The Burmans, who had succeeded the Pyus as the dominant people in Upper Burma by the mid-8th century and by the mid-11th century had established Pagan as their capital, adopted both Buddhism and the Pyu spirit cult. Theravada Buddhism became the principal tradition in Pagan as a result of King Anawrahta's conquest of the Mon Kingdom of Thaton (Sudhammavati) *c.* 1057. Anawrahta is said to have brought back Mon craftsmen and scholars to Pagan. He introduced a purer form of the Theravada doctrine and also collected images of *nat* from their cult centres near his capital, allocating them places within the grounds of the Shwe-zigon Temple. These are known as the 37 Lords of the Inner Circle, i.e. spirits within the enclosure of the Shwe-zigon. The most prominent among the figures is a wooden icon almost 2.5 m high of Sakka (the Hindu god Indra), who is chief of the spirits. Some of the *nat* have poetic names, such as Lady Golden Face (Shwe-myet-hnar), a Pyu queen, and her sister, Lady Three Times Beautiful (Thon-pan-hla), who was believed to be beautiful at dawn, midday and at night. Beyond the boundary of the Shwe-zigon pagoda were lesser *nat*, each important to the locality from which its cult emerged. These became known as Lords of the Outer Circle. Among them is the malignant Lady of the Tame Waters (Ye-yin-kadaw), noted for her spitefulness.

The centre of village and urban religious life is the *zedi* (Burm.: 'stupa'), which is usually built of bricks and painted white and sometimes gilded all over by the devout in order to gain merit. Built to a prescribed pattern, stupas vary in size from the minute to such huge monuments as the Shwe-dagon in Rangoon, which is almost 100 m high (for illustration *see* RANGOON). The base, usually square and believed to represent Mount Meru, is surmounted by an inverted bowl, which is divided into two parts signifying the worlds of form and formlessness. This is the area where sacred relics are normally enshrined. Above this are rings, piled one above the other, gradually decreasing in size and crowned by bands of lotus petals, which terminate in a bud. Fixed to the tip is a metal *hti* (Burm.: 'tiered umbrella'), usually decorated with precious stones and hung with tiny bells. The stupa to some represents the

Buddha and to others nirvana. Attached to many temples are wooden or brick monasteries with the traditional multi-tiered roof.

Thousands of images, in a variety of materials, postures (Skt *āsana*), gestures (*mudrā*) and sizes can be seen all over Burma. The craftsmen who make them follow a systematic scheme of proportions handed down from ancient times. The three most common forms of Buddha image in Burma are the seated Buddha in *bhūmisparśa mudrā* (gesture of calling the earth to witness), the standing Buddha with the right hand raised in *abhaya mudrā* (dispelling fear) and the reclining Buddha, with his cheek resting on his right palm as he enters nirvana. Influences from eastern India and China and from Khmer and Thai sources are also apparent in another type of image known as the *jambupati*, which portrays the Buddha crowned and attired in royal robes. The *jātaka*s (stories of previous lives of the historical Buddha) and the life of Gautama Buddha are frequently represented in murals, stone sculpture and terracotta plaques.

Nat images are normally carved out of *yamanei* (*Gmelina arborea*) and gilded. They are depicted either seated or standing on an animal, a demon or a lotus and, if kept at home, are placed well below any Buddha image. *Nat* shrines are also often found within the grounds of a temple, as it is claimed that the spirits come to worship and be near the Enlightened One. Since their social backgrounds vary, the figures are shown appropriately dressed, each holding an attribute associated with it. Female *nat* whose deaths have been caused in an unpleasant way usually have a hand on the left breast, a traditional sign of grief. Rituals vary from district to district, but offerings, usually of food, flowers and finery, are accompanied by music and dancing. Professional mediums travel around the country, officiating at the annual celebrations of each cult centre.

The architecture of the large cities reflects not only the predominance of Buddhism but also the existence of important minority communities of Hindus, Muslims and Christians. In Rangoon, for example, the spire of the Sule Stupa soars into the sky together with the steeple of a Baptist church, the elegant minarets of a Sunni mosque and a vividly exuberant Hindu temple.

BIBLIOGRAPHY

R. Temple: *The Thirty-seven Nats of Burma* (London, 1906)
Taw Sein Ko: *Burmese Sketches* (Rangoon, 1913)
G. E. Harvey: *History of Burma* (London, 1925/*R* 1967)
G. H. Luce: *Man Shu* [Book of the southern barbarians] (Ithaca, 1961)
U. Mya: *Shay-haung-oak-khwet-yoke-pwar-sin-du-daw-myar* [Votive tablets of Burma], pts I and II (Rangoon, 1961)
Htin Aung: *Folk Elements in Burmese Buddhism* (Oxford, 1962)
U Aung Thaw: *Excavations at Beikthano* (Rangoon, 1968)
G. H. Luce: *Old Burma, Early Pagan*, 3 vols (Locust Valley, NY, 1969) [*Artibus Asiae* suppl. 25]
U Aung Thaw: *Historical Sites in Burma* (Rangoon, 1972/*R* 1978)

NOEL F. SINGER

II. Architecture.

Burma's cultural links with India are nowhere more clearly revealed than in architecture, which in Burma already by the late 5th century AD was characterized by a blending of Indian and indigenous elements.

GENERAL BIBLIOGRAPHY

H. Yule: *A Narrative of the Mission Sent by the Governor-General of India to the Court of Ava in 1855* (London, 1858)
J. Fergusson: *History of Indian and Eastern Architecture* (London, 1876), rev. by J. Burgess, 2 vols (London, 1910)
E. Forchhammer: *Report on the Antiquities of Arakan* (Rangoon, 1892)
L. de Beylié: *L'Architecture hindoue en Extrême-Orient* (Paris, 1907)
——: *Prome et Samara: Voyage archéologique en Birmanie et en Mésopotamie* (Paris, 1907)
V. C. Scott O'Connor: *Mandalay and Other Cities of the Past in Burma* (London, 1907/*R* Bangkok, 1987)
C. Duroiselle: 'Pictorial Representations of the Jatakas in Burma', *Archaeol. Surv. India, Annu. Rep.* (1912–13), pp. 87–119
Amended List of Ancient Monuments in Burma (Rangoon, 1921/*R* 1960)
H. Marchal: 'Notes d'architecture birmane', *Bull. Ecole Fr. Extrême-Orient*, xl (1940), pp. 422–37
——: *L'Architecture comparée dans l'Inde et l'Extrême-Orient* (Paris, 1944)
G. Coedès: *Les États hindouisés d'Indochine et d'Indonésie* (Hanoi, 1944/*R* Paris, 1964); Eng. trans. by S. Cowing as *The Indianized States of Southeast Asia* (Honolulu and Kuala Lumpur, 1968, rev. Honolulu, 1971)
H. Parmentier: *L'Art architectural hindou dans l'Inde et en Extrême-Orient* (Paris, 1948)
A. B. Griswold, C. Kim and P. H. Pott: *Burma, Korea, Tibet* (London, 1964)
U Aung Thaw: *Historical Sites in Burma* (Rangoon, 1972/*R* 1978)
San Tha Aung: *The Buddhist Art of Ancient Arakan* (Rangoon, 1979)
B. L. Smith: 'The Pagan Period (1044–1287): A Bibliographic Note', *Contrib. Asian Stud.*, xvi (1981), pp. 112–30
Pagan Newslett. (Paris and Pondicherry, 1982–) [1989 issue contains preliminary UNDP–UNESCO map of 2230 Pagan mnmts]
J. Boisselier: *Il sud-est asiatico* (Turin, 1986)
N. Oshegowa and S. Oshegow: *Kunst in Burma: 2000 Jahre Architektur, Malerei und Plastik im Zeichen des Buddhismus und Animismus* (Leipzig, 1988; Ger. trans. from Rus. ed. of 1985 [*Iskusstvo Birmy*])
P. Strachan, ed.: *Essays on the History and Buddhism of Burma by Professor Than Tun* (Arran, 1988)
P. Pichard: *Inventory of Monuments at Pagan* (Paris and Gartmore, 1992–)

1. Religious and formal. 2. Domestic.

1. RELIGIOUS AND FORMAL. Virtually all the surviving monuments of Burma are religious—temples, stupas and monasteries. Nothing remains of any royal palaces or other secular and domestic buildings before the modern period, as these were all constructed of wood and other perishable materials. The form of the stupa, a solid edifice enshrining a sacred relic or image of the Buddha (*see* STUPA, §3), in Burma, as in most South-east Asian countries, is highly distinctive. Another feature of Burmese religious monuments is the arch, which before modern times was ribbed and voussoired, whereas elsewhere in South-east Asia it was corbelled.

(i) 1st–11th centuries. (ii) 11th–14th centuries. (iii) 14th–20th centuries.

(i) 1st–11th centuries. Little of the architecture of Burma before the Pagan period has survived. Several sites have been identified, but excavations have provided more information on sculpture, artefacts and coins than on architecture: only the floor and the base of the walls have been recovered in most buildings, yielding little evidence of their original appearance.

Beikthano ('city of Vishnu'), the earliest known Pyu city, appears to have been occupied from the 1st to the 5th century AD. Only a few of the hundred or so debris mounds have been excavated, revealing bases of buildings made of large baked bricks, among them two halls with evidence of wooden pillars, a large rectangular monastery with multiple cells and the foundations of several circular stupas, a few of them on square bases. These stupas were in several cases associated with numerous burial urns containing the ashes of cremated human bodies.

At Halin, a Pyu city in northern Burma that seems to have flourished from the 2nd to the 6th century AD, preliminary explorations were performed in 1904–5 and 1929–30, and excavations conducted from 1962 to 1967. These yielded burial urns, stone sculptures, metal implements and a few lines of Pyu inscriptions but little architectural evidence other than the bases of some square or rectangular brick buildings. Stupas do not seem to have been erected in Halin.

There is more evidence for Pyu architecture in Srikshetra, the capital city of a Pyu kingdom from the 5th to the 9th century AD. The large oval city wall was provided with several fortified gateways. The former palace is indicated by a rectangular enclosure approximately at the centre of the walled area. Several stupas are still standing outside the city wall, the best preserved being the Bawbaw-gyi, which has a high, cylindrical profile and rests on five low, circular terraces (see fig. 2). Exceptionally, the dome has an interior space up to about two-thirds of its height that can be entered by an opening at its base. Also outside the city wall are the Paya-gyi and Paya-ma stupas, which have a slightly ogival profile and are set on low, circular terraces. The upper parts of these three stupas, with their small finials, are not original. Stupas of different shapes are known: two, represented on stone slabs, have a hemispherical dome and a square crowning element and are similar to the votive stupas of Nalanda and Ratnagiri in India; others with a bell-shaped dome, found sometimes in the form of a small plastered stupa encased within a larger, ruined one, foreshadow the characteristic stupa type of Pagan.

2. Bawbaw-gyi Stupa, Srikshetra, Pyu, 5th–9th centuries AD

Inside the city is a small temple, the East Ze-gu, with a central, square shrine and a porch to the east. Two other temples stand outside—the Le-myet-hna, which has a solid core surrounded by a narrow corridor and four porches, and the Bebe, which has a central shrine. Built of brick and already vaulted using the same technique that was to be used later in Pagan, they are considered to be the forerunners of the Pagan temples. However, as they bear traces of repeated alterations, their date is difficult to ascertain, and it is possible that, just as temples were still built in Pagan under later Burmese dynasties, these temples were erected or completely restored long after the fall of the Srikshetra kingdom as provincial foundations of Pagan. Other temples in Srikshetra are now reduced to the base of their walls. In Pagan itself a few Pyu structures, identified by the Pyu letters marked on their bricks, were transformed or incorporated into new buildings during the Pagan period. The Mon kingdom of Ramannadesa in south Burma was in contact with the Buddhist cultures of south India and Sri Lanka as well as with the other Mon states that now form part of modern Thailand, especially Dvaravati. Apart from the rectangular city wall, no important architectural remains of this period have been found at its capital, Thaton (Sudhammavati), where all the monuments have been later modernized or reconstructed. Similarly, in the first city of Pegu, which is said to date from the 9th century AD, only the surrounding moat and traces of the wall have survived.

In ARAKAN, the cities of Dhannavati (Dinnyawadi) and Vesali were active centres from the 1st century AD to the 9th. Excavations at Vesali in 1980–84 revealed the bases of several religious brick buildings. Most of them are rectangular and were probably monasteries or ordination halls. There too the city was enclosed by two concentric walls supplemented by defensive moats connected with the nearby rivers.

BIBLIOGRAPHY

C. Duroiselle: 'Excavations at Hmawza', *Archaeol. Surv. India, Annu. Rep.* (1926–7), pp. 171–83

——: 'Excavations at Halin', *Archaeol. Surv. India, Annu. Rep.* (1929–30), pp. 151–4

——: 'Excavations at Hmawza', *Archaeol. Surv. India, Annu. Rep.* (1929–30), pp. 127–35

P. C. Gutman: *Ancient Arakan, with Special Reference to its Cultural History between the 5th and 11th Centuries* (diss., Canberra, Austral. N. U., 1977)

U Kan Hla [S. Ozhegov]: 'Ancient Cities in Burma', *J. Soc. Archit. Hist.*, xxxviii/2 (1979), pp. 95–102

J. Stargardt: *Early Pyu Cities in a Man-made Landscape*, i of *The Ancient Pyu of Burma* (Cambridge, 1990)

(ii) 11th–14th centuries. Between the 11th and the 14th centuries a distinctively Burmese style of architecture developed, together with the establishment of Theravada Buddhism as the national religion of the Pagan kingdom. The religious monuments of PAGAN display a skilful balance between uniformity and diversity. They achieve uniformity by their common vocabulary of architectural and decorative patterns, the general use of brick and

similar construction methods. Their diversity arises from differences of scale, type, form and decoration.

The monuments range in scale from buildings no larger than a one-room hut to such impressive stupas as the Shwe-zigon or such famous temples as the That-byin-nyu, which has four storeys, two tiers of receding terraces and a square tower, with a total height of 61 m, equivalent to a modern 20-storey building. Most studies so far published have focused on these very large and highly venerated monuments, although they are not necessarily architecturally the most significant; as important places of worship and pilgrimage, attracting large public donations, they have been regularly maintained and periodically renovated, if not altered. Scattered all over Pagan is a huge number of smaller monuments, generally nameless and only identified by their inventory number, some in fair condition and others more or less dilapidated, and these provide a more reliable architectural and historical record of the Pagan period.

To chart the evolution of Pagan architecture accurately is a difficult task, chiefly because only a few monuments can be securely dated from contemporary stone inscriptions. In some cases, these inscriptions are extremely detailed, providing the very days when the construction began and ended. For instance, the Shwe-gu-gyi, a medium-sized temple, was built in seven and a half months in 1231, and the Dhamma-yazika, a very large stupa, in little more than one year (1197–8). The inscriptions sometimes also provide precise data about building costs and processes, but the vast majority of the monuments lack inscriptions and can only be tentatively dated on stylistic grounds and by reference to dated buildings. Even this method has limitations, because some stylistic features continued without change throughout the Pagan period, and some of the earlier features were later revived as deliberate archaisms, while some monuments were repaired or renovated even before the fall of Pagan. Moreover, this evolution does not progress from the simplest to the most elaborate type: because they were founded by the first kings and queens, the design of the earliest temples such as the Ananda is of exceptional elaboration. The royal example was later followed by other classes of Pagan society. Smaller simpler structures were built all over Pagan for non-royal patrons, while more sophisticated structures continued to be built as royal foundations.

(a) Materials and techniques. (b) Building types.

(a) Materials and techniques. With the exception of the Shwe-zigon Stupa, which is entirely built of sandstone, and of two temples where a stone facing has been applied on the brick wall, Pagan monuments are made of brick plastered with stucco. The bricks are usually well baked and regularly shaped and rather large in size, ranging from 280×140×35 mm to 430×210×80mm, the most usual size being around 360×180×50 mm. Different sizes may occur in a single temple, and there are instances of small or secondary buildings, particularly monasteries, entirely built with broken or half bricks, probably left over after the completion of a large monument near by. Although many bricks were made in Pagan, as is shown by the large depressions dug in the clay on the riverbank, others were made in distant places, the names of which were stamped on them, and were brought by boat to Pagan. It is, however, difficult to assess the respective proportions of production.

The brick facing was carefully done, with the joints as thin as possible, whereas the inner part of the walls was built with thicker joints and a higher proportion of broken bricks and debris, though it cannot be described as mere filling. The binding mortar was simple clay, sometimes with a large admixture of sand. It is traditionally said that vegetal resin, glue and various other products were mixed with the clay to improve its strength. No modern analysis so far has provided evidence of this, but the possibility cannot be ruled out since these organic materials would have disappeared with time. Thanks, however, to their great thickness, the walls have proved strong enough to bear the weight of the structure and the lateral strain of the vaults, as well as to resist several earthquakes. Problems arise if this clay becomes wet, as a result of cracks developing in the roof and plaster, in which case it becomes slippery and tends to expand. The Pagan architects were evidently concerned with the durability of their buildings, but, curiously, the high-quality mortar used for plastering the monuments was never employed as a binding agent for the masonry itself, although this would have greatly increased its resistance.

Stone was scarcely used except in specific contexts—for example for thresholds, anchorings for door pivots and paving the inside of temples. In the most strongly built monuments, such as royal foundations, long keystones were inserted at intervals as binders to attach the brick facing to the inner wall. In such important monuments, stone was also sometimes used for corner anchors or as a whole course at the head of a wall to support its brick cornice. In some earlier temples, such as the Ananda and the Naga-yon, stone voussoirs were alternated with bricks to strengthen the arches. Stone plinths and sockets were also used under timber posts in wooden buildings and pavilions, and stone slabs, perforated in various decorative patterns, were placed upright in the windows of some temples and monasteries to control light and ventilation.

The most specific characteristic of Pagan temples and monasteries is the general use of voussoired vaults and arches, which distinguishes them from contemporary monuments elsewhere in south and South-east Asia. Various hypotheses, none of them conclusive, have been advanced for their origin, from China to Mesopotamia or Rome. Though the vault was rarely used in India before the arrival of Islam at the end of the 12th century, it was known, as is shown by the small temple of BHITARGAON, which has been assigned to the 6th century. Numerous ancient Buddhist monasteries of India have been excavated, but usually nothing but their plan is discernible, since only the bases of the walls remain, and there is little evidence of the form of their upper parts or the techniques used in constructing them. Brick vaults are, however, recorded in Nalanda, and excavations carried out in 1956 and 1966 at Ratnagiri, a Buddhist site in Orissa, have revealed two monasteries where the springs of vaults can clearly be seen above corridors and cells. Technically, these brick vaults are similar to the Pagan ones, and the stylistic and archaeological evidence suggests that they date from the 7th century, possibly earlier. There is therefore a strong probability that this technique of brick vaulting was transmitted from the Buddhist communities of Orissa to Pagan via the contemporary Pyu kingdom of Srikshetra, which, only 260 km from Pagan, was also Buddhist, and where several small vaulted temples are known (*see* §(i) above).

It was, however, in Pagan that the technique was successfully developed and improved. The vaults of Ratnagiri seem to have been simple barrel vaults with spans not exceeding 2.5 m, and it is remarkable that some of the earliest monuments of Pagan, for instance the Ananda and the Naga-yon temples, have large halls and shrines where the vaulting technique has already been perfectly mastered and over quite wide spans. The most common types are the cloister vault, on a square or rectangular plan, and all the varieties of barrel vault, whether full, half or three-quarter. Cupolas were also built above circular shrines. Composite vaults on different levels and intersecting vaults at the corners of corridors were also used, providing diversity, hierarchy and subtlety in the interior spaces. The vaulting technique is quite different from that used in Roman and European architecture. The bricks are placed vertically, each brick shaped into a trapezium with its sides radially disposed, forming parallel, juxtaposed arches, which could be erected with no, or only very limited, timber centering. In several structures, relieving vaults and diaphragm arches were systematically used, and such difficult features as sloping vaults over staircases or voussoired flat arches were successfully attempted. In addition, the corbelled 'false' vault or arch was sometimes used, particularly in monasteries.

(b) Building types. The major traditional distinction among Pagan monuments is that between temple and stupa. Temples (Burm. *gu*) have an interior vaulted space, sheltering one or more Buddha images, while stupas (*zedi*) are solid monuments. There are borderline cases, however, such as stupas with niches sheltering Buddha images, or temples built on a circular plan and crowned by the bell-shaped dome of a stupa but provided with an internal shrine accessible through a single porch. A third widely represented type of monument is the monastery, which can be either an isolated building or a large complex. Other structures, such as ordination halls and libraries are far less numerous.

Both temples and stupas were generally planned as single monuments: even where two or more monuments are built close to each other, there is usually no clear alignment or connection between them. Occasionally, however, a spatial relationship was sought: one of the finest examples of this is the Sein-nyet Ama Temple and the Sein-nyet Nyi-ma Stupa, which are aligned on a single west–east axis in a rectangular enclosure. There are, however, a few instances of multiple monuments aligned on a common platform, such as the four small temples of the Pe-natha group or the five stupas of Min-o-chantha, and sometimes interconnected by corridors, such as the Paya-thon-zu Temple with its three shrines.

Only the largest or most important monuments were surrounded by a boundary wall. This was usually square and had an elaborate gateway on each side, the chief purpose of which, according to contemporary inscriptions, was to provide protection against fire. This is one of the rare indications that dwelling quarters were located in the vicinity. The main building, whether temple or stupa, was in the middle of this large enclosure, sometimes on a raised platform, and smaller satellite structures were generally built round it.

Temples. There are two main types of temple, one with a central shrine and the other with a solid core and circumambulatory corridor. The two types are sometimes combined in a single building. The simplest type, of which there are several hundreds scattered all over the site, is a small single-storey temple with a square central shrine and a small vestibule and porch on one side, usually the east, although north and west entrances are not uncommon. The statue of the Buddha, seated against the back wall, faces the entrance. A cloister vault covers the shrine, and a slightly pointed barrel vault the vestibule and porch. A variant is seen in circular temples, the exterior shape of which is quite similar to a stupa but with the addition of the porch: in such temples the central shrine may be either square or circular. An enlarged version of the type with a central shrine features an entrance hall instead of a vestibule. This hall is covered by a barrel vault, frequently hipped on the outside, and is separated from the shrine by a doorway, adorned with pilasters and a pediment on the inside (see fig. 3). Other temples of this type are built on a cruciform plan and have a central shrine accessible from all four sides, through a vestibule and a porch, sometimes with four Buddha images seated back to back at the centre. More often, one of these four vestibules is

3. Temple 2070, entrance hall and Buddha image, Pagan, 13th century

4. Kubyauk-gyi, Wetkyi-in, Pagan, *c.* 1200; view of the temple from the east

developed into an entrance hall, and a single, seated image is placed against a screen wall built inside the shrine, facing the main entrance. Pagan also contains numerous image houses, rectangular brick buildings in which the image faces the entrance and which are therefore not very different in appearance from a simple temple but even less elaborate in design and without its characteristic upper parts.

In the solid-core type, the main interior space is the circumambulatory vaulted corridor running right round the core, with Buddha images on each side of the core, set either against its faces or inside niches. The more usual design is on a square plan, with four images, each facing one entrance, representing either the four previous Buddhas of the present era or different scenes of the historical Gautama Buddha's life. In several cases, the future Buddha, Maitreya, has been added, resulting in a pentagonal plan with five images and porches. Variants of these types emphasize the space round each image by means of a vault higher than the vault on the corridor, resulting in a temple with four or five shrines, which may even be independent in the few cases where the corridor has been suppressed. In a more frequent variation, greater importance is given to one side, generally the eastern one, by placing an entrance hall on it and providing the others only with vestibules and porches. In at least two instances, Temple 1790 and Temple 1359, a circular plan has been adopted, with four porches and a corridor around the square solid core.

A subtle combination of the two main types is seen in such temples as the Kubyauk-gyi (see fig. 4) at Wetkyi-in or the Thabeik-hmauk, where the large entrance hall is at the same time the shrine, since it shelters the main Buddha image, facing the entrance and seated against one side of the solid core. The corridor runs only round the three other sides of the core, connected to a vestibule and a porch on each side and to the hall-shrine by lateral passages on both sides of the image. In its classical form, this design was adopted for some of the greatest temples of Pagan, such as the Hti-lo-min-lo, Sula-mani and the Gadaw-palin, but with the shrine sometimes set into the core. In such large temples, the entrance halls are usually more complex, with a central nave and side aisles.

The Ananda, one of the largest and earliest Pagan temples, is of this type, with the important difference that the same pattern repeats itself on each of the four sides, resulting in a cruciform plan (*see* PAGAN, fig. 2). Its four, high-vaulted shrines shelter standing Buddha images and are interconnected by two concentric corridors, with numerous niches on each side displaying a rich collection of stone sculptures. The light effects inside this great temple are carefully and skilfully controlled, from the wide, brightly lit entrance halls to the dim shrines, where a small aperture in the roof projects a concentrated ray on the Buddha's head, while windows pierced in the thick walls provide rich internal perspectives and a well-modulated light in the corridors. A similar plan on a larger scale was later adopted for the Dhamma-yan-gyi, although its exterior design differs.

The two main types are also combined in temples with a square central shrine surrounded by a circumambulatory corridor. These temples, most of them among the earliest in Pagan, have an entrance hall and porch on one side and windows on the three other sides to illuminate the corridor. The main Buddha image is in the central shrine, seated facing the entrance, and several smaller images depicting either major scenes in the life of the historical Buddha or the 28 previous Buddhas are placed in niches along the walls of the corridor (as in the Naga-yon). A unique example is the Nat-hlaung-kyaung, the only Pagan temple of which the iconography is fully Hindu and not Buddhist, where two concentric corridors surround the central shrine. The vault of the outer corridor collapsed long ago, together with the exterior wall, but its traces are still clearly visible on the upper parts of the monument.

Pagan architects carried out further experiments in design with multi-storey temples. The earliest, such as the Pahto-thamya and the Kubyauk-gyi at Wetkyi-in are basically single-storey monuments with a small shrine, on the model of the simplest independent temples, built on the roof of the entrance hall, in front of the main tower above the central shrine. These small shrines tended to be integrated with the tower, as for instance in the Mye-bon-tha, and ultimately developed into a whole upper storey, although always smaller than the ground-floor. Access to this upper storey and also to the upper terraces is provided by steep, narrow staircases built into the thickness of the walls. The ground-floor always consists of a solid core and a circumambulatory corridor, but the upper storey sometimes has a central shrine under the tower, as for instance in the South Gu-ni, offering rich possibilities for images. In the Thein-mazi, the four statues on the ground-floor represent Gautama Buddha seated on the east and south sides, standing on the north and reclining on the west, while the image in the central shrine of the upper storey is in the usual seated posture, facing the main eastern entrance. More often, two-storey temples have a solid core and circumambulatory corridors on both floors, as in the That-tei-gu and the North Gu-ni, and this became the standard design of the larger temples, such as the Sulamani, Hti-lo-min-lo and Gadaw-palin.

Three- or four-storey temples are quite exceptional. The Thissa-wadi is a classical two-storey temple, with a solid core, a circumambulatory corridor and an entrance hall on the east on each level, but a third storey with a central shrine and porches on the east, south and north sides has been added under the central tower. The That-byin-nyu, the tallest of the Pagan temples, has four storeys: on the ground-floor, the main eastern porch opens into a wide entrance hall, from which an axial staircase ascends, while side passages connect the hall with a circumambulatory corridor and porches on the other three sides; the next storey features two concentric corridors running round the core, from which further stairs climb up to the main storey, where the wide central shrine shelters the principal image, with an entrance hall to the east, a circumambulatory corridor and porches to the south, west and north; finally, more stairs give access to the fourth storey, a single vaulted corridor, and to the upper terraces.

The very few underground temples were usually hollowed out under a cliff. Although only partially underground, the most famous example is the Kyaukku-ohn-min, which has a raised central shrine with a vault supported by two high pillars that separate it from a similarly vaulted aisle. The main image is seated and faces a single porch on the north side, and there are numerous smaller images in the niches of the outer wall. Immediately behind the shrine, a circumambulatory corridor and several tunnels have been dug under the cliff. The main northern façade, the porch and the shrine are built near the bottom of a canyon, and the upper floor is level with the alluvial plateau. Another temple, the Thein-hwet-ohn-min, is entirely underground, with seven porches opening at the base of the cliff and leading to seven shrines connected by a corridor parallel to its face. The Buddha images, all seated, were sculpted out of the rock when the temple was first hollowed out.

There is no clear relationship between the plan (whether with a central shrine or a solid core) and the external design of the temple. The main body is usually more or less cubical (but occasionally circular or polygonal), the walls being generally adorned with pilasters, a base and a cornice and, more rarely, pierced by windows. On one or more sides there may be a central projection, which is more or less developed, depending on whether or not there is an entrance hall between the shrine and the porch. Always lower than the main body, these foreparts are usually covered by a flat, terraced roof, or by a sloping roof in some of the earliest temples (Naga-yon, Ananda).

Similar sloping roofs, made of bricks laid so that they form a curved profile, were constructed over the main body of early temples (11th and early 12th centuries), but these were later replaced by receding terraces (usually three), providing a stepped pyramidal profile embellished at all corners on each level by small stupas or turrets. A niche or an arch above a narrow stairway sometimes marks the axis of each face of these terraces. The uppermost terrace is crowned either by a stupa-like dome or by a square tower with a curvilinear profile, which is undoubtedly derived from the shikhara of the Orissan temples of India. Throughout the Pagan period, both these designs were adopted; in some cases, though not invariably, there is a connection between the plan of a temple and the shape of its superstructure. Temples built on a single axis, with a wide entrance hall on one side only and smaller foreparts, if any, on the other sides, are generally crowned by a shikhara, while temples with two axes or built symmetrically on a more or less cruciform plan tend to culminate in a stupa dome. Furthermore, large temples are generally provided with a shikhara, rather than a dome (the Ananda, though built on a cruciform plan, has an imposing shikhara). There is more variety among smaller temples: for instance, in a cluster of five small temples built during the 13th century on the east side of Pagan village, two, 1843 and 1845, are crowned by a shikhara and the three others, 1844, 1846 and 1847, by a bell-shaped dome, although they are similar in size and plan, with a central shrine and a single vestibule and porch (see fig. 5). It may be noted, however, that the two temples

5. Temples 1843, 1845 and 1844, Pagan, 13th century

surmounted by a shikhara are also the only two which face east, as 1844 faces north and 1846 and 1847 face west. Standing alone 200 m west of this group is Temple 1890, with a square shikhara, which is partly destroyed and so severely cracked that the original dome has been revealed. This was evidently encased in a shikhara at the time it was built or only a few years later, which clearly shows that the dome and the shikhara were interchangeable.

Multi-storey temples appear to have only two storeys, even in the few cases where there are in fact more than two. The ground-floor is topped by the usual three receding terraces, on which rises the body of the upper storey, itself designed like a single-storey temple and usually crowned by a shikhara—one notable exception being Temple 357 in the Wuthana-daw group, which is crowned by a small, bell-shaped dome.

The exterior decoration of almost all the temples of Pagan consists of stucco applied to the brick surfaces and sculpted. The stucco is enhanced by mouldings along the major lines of the building and decorative elements at selected places. The mouldings were first roughly profiled by courses of protruding bricks and then finished with stucco, which may either be undecorated or adorned with lotus petals, pearls, rosettes, diamonds, tassels or foliations. Typically, the base is adorned with large lotus petals and surmounted by a dado of small upright triangles along the undecorated wall. The wall is topped by a frieze of *kīrttimukha*s (Skt: stylized demon masks), from which hang garlands forming swags that alternate with floral pendants, a motif probably inspired by the temples of Orissa. Above this frieze is a projecting cornice, supported by lotus petals and with its own foliated decoration and monster heads protruding at each corner and terminating in a crenellated acroterion. The plain surfaces of the walls are vertically divided by pilasters, each with its own decorated base and capital and symmetrically disposed diagonal beaded lines. Variations of this general pattern include friezes with praying figures inside the garland, or even animals and flowers, or again with pointed oval leaves on a delicately carved foliated background. Sometimes figures of animals or mythological beings are sculpted on the corners of pilasters or in recesses.

The pediments on the foreparts, and sometimes above niches and windows also, have elaborate stucco decoration. The arch of each porch is divided into four, six, eight or ten smaller sinuous curves by down-pointing cusps, a specifically Burmese evolution of the Indian gable model comparable to contemporary Khmer or Javanese pediment designs. Above this sinuous arch rise high vertical flame motifs, the central one usually containing a figure in relief of the praying *Sakka* (the Hindu god Indra), while lions or *makara*s (Skt: aquatic monsters) are symmetrically disposed on either side. In such early temples as the Mye-bon-tha or the Kubyauk-gyi, these pediments are framed by a reduced elevation of a temple, with receding terraces and finials. On the temple itself the small stupa or tower adorning each corner of the terraces is ornamented with plaster mouldings. A final concentration of finely sculpted stucco occurs at the top of the temple, either on the lancets of the square tower, which have rich floral motifs often surmounted by a central figure, or round the bell-shaped dome, treated in the same way as a stupa.

On several monuments, glazed terracotta plaques are embedded in the mortar, usually set in horizontal rows along the base and terraces. Sometimes these, with their vivid touches of colour, provide the main decorative elements, for instance on the pediments of the Sula-mani. Yellow and green were the most usual colours and the terracotta plaques were either plain or decorated, as in the Ananda. In some instances glazed sandstone pieces were also used, as on the Shwe-zigon Stupa or on Temple 1756, but this was a rare and difficult technological achievement.

Interior decoration was mostly confined to painting, although the focal point is always the principal Buddha image, seated facing the entrance in the canonical earth-touching position (*bhūmisparśa mudrā*). Above and around the image, the Bodhi (enlightenment) tree is realistically painted on the wall behind and framed by a curved pediment, and on both sides of it are grouped the Buddha's disciples and attendants. The other walls contain architectural elements similar to those sculpted in stucco outside, such as corner pilasters, capitals, friezes and pediments above arches, but they are painted almost in *trompe l'oeil* and are enlivened with fantastic birds and animal or human figures. The areas between the divisions usually contain rows of small panels illustrating scenes from the 550 *jātaka*s (stories of the Buddha's previous lives) or representations of the 28 previous Buddhas or depictions of the most important episodes of the Gautama Buddha's life and of the history of Buddhism.

Vaults are also painted all over, their quadrants outlined by decorative diagonal bands culminating in a large rosetted lotus and filled with various patterns composed of touching or intersecting circles, lozenges and quatrefoils or rows of small figures. In some temples these recurring patterns cover walls and vaults alike. Special motifs were used in the apexes of the vaults over vestibules and porches, the most frequent one being the sacred footprints of the Buddha. In addition, representations of famous Buddhist buildings, maps and sections of the universe and traditional horoscopes of the Buddha's life are not uncommon on the walls, while a number of these illustrations have painted captions to help the layman to interpret them.

While the evolution of the temple is complex, some general developments can be ascertained. Temples built before the first quarter of the 12th century, with the notable exception of the Ananda (which dates from about 1105 and was built on a cruciform plan), are characterized by an entrance hall and porch on one side only, the three other sides being provided with windows but no foreparts. They usually belong to the type combining a central shrine with a circumambulatory corridor. Where a caption is painted on the walls of these early temples, it is in the Mon language. (The earliest appearance of written Burmese is the famous Mya-zedi inscription, which dates from 1113 and has parallel texts in Pyu, Mon, Pali and Burmese.) Smaller and simpler temples with central shrines and one porch apparently first occur in the second quarter of the 12th century with the Loka-hteik-pan, together with larger temples having a single entrance hall and a forepart with porch on the three other sides (Shwe-gu-gyi, 1131). From that time up to the 13th century the range of types, forms and dimensions gradually widened.

Stupas. The form of the Pagan stupa was clearly derived from the earliest examples in India and Sri Lanka, but, as it evolved, the base and terraces became proportionally more important and the general outline became more continuous and pyramidal, although the dome remained the major architectural element. As early as the second half of the 11th century, the classical model of the great stupa had become fixed in Pagan by two outstanding monuments, the Shwe-hsan-daw and the Shwe-zigon. The former has five high, square receding terraces and the latter three. These terraces, linked by a medial stairway in each face, support one or two octagonal terraces, on which rests the bell-shaped dome, circular in plan and culminating in a conical, ringed spire. Built near the end of the Pagan dynasty, the Mingala-zedi (see fig. 6) is very similar in design and size to the Shwe-zigon. A notable variation is provided by the Dhamma-yazika, completed in 1198, which has three terraces built on a pentagonal plan.

This model, however, though generally presented as typical, is restricted to a few monuments of exceptional size. All over Pagan there are hundreds of smaller stupas in a great variety of distinctive forms and profiles. Some stupas closely derived from Orissan and Singhalese models have circular terraces, without a stairway and supporting a hemispherical dome crowned by a masonry block, usually square in plan, and a conical spire. Such are the Sapada and Stupa 495 near Minnanthu. This crowning block, clearly inspired by the *harmikā* of India and Sri Lanka, may be elaborately indented and decorated and 'burmanized' by being placed on a series of square or octagonal receding terraces, usually without stairways, as in the Setana-gyi and the Hpyat-sa Stupa. Another variation in the profile of the dome is seen in the bulbous stupas, entirely circular in plan, some of which are among the oldest in Pagan and are probably of Pyu origin. Even stupas with the typical bell-shaped dome are sometimes built on a totally circular plan from base to summit.

In some stupas the base is treated like a temple wall, crowned by a frieze and a cornice and supporting two or three terraces and the bell-shaped dome. In such cases, the plan of the base is usually square with two projections on each side, with the single exception of the Zedi-she, which is built on an octagonal plan.

The form of stupa most frequently found is rather slender and of modest size, without stairways and set on two square terraces, slightly receding and with two projections on each side, below a third, shallower transitional terrace. This terrace is most commonly an irregular dodecagon with a single projection on each side—a sensible way of linking the circular plan of the upper parts with the square terraces below. Octagons and 16- or 20-sided polygons are also sometimes used. As a further variation, a vertex instead of a side of this upper terrace is occasionally set on the axis of each face. This uppermost terrace supports the bell-shaped dome, which is crowned by the conical, ringed spire. Today, all maintained Burmese religious monuments are surmounted by a metal *hti* (Burm.: 'tiered umbrella'), and this also appears to have been the case during the Pagan period. Stupas without *hti* have been recorded in Pagan, but they may have been unfinished, since the erection of *hti* is also recorded in contemporary stone inscriptions, and what appear to be representations of monuments with *hti* occur in Pagan paintings.

6. Mingala-zedi Stupa from the north-east, Pagan, completed 1274

Numerous instances of small stupas subsequently encased in larger ones occur in Pagan, many of which remain concealed as long as the outer structure is in good condition. When the later stupa becomes ruined, the inner one is revealed, usually in perfect condition. In some cases, two small stupas have been engulfed in a single large one. The form of the monument sometimes changes in the process, for instance in Stupa 1754, where a hemispherical dome has been encased in a bell-shaped stupa. In the general absence of epigraphic evidence, it is impossible to know how much time elapsed between the two phases, although in a few cases (Stupa 1982 for instance) the process was adopted as a corrective measure to enlarge the dome before its completion.

Like temples, stupas were covered with stucco decoration. The decorative vocabulary is similar, its most conspicuous feature being the frieze with *kīrttimukha*s or demon masks and festoons, which on stupas is located under the band round the waist of the dome. The wall of each terrace has prominent mouldings, either plain or richly decorated and set symmetrically round a central recess, which in important foundations such as the Shwe-zigon, the Dhamma-yazika and the Mingala-zedi, contains a series of glazed, decorated plaques depicting scenes from the 550 *jātaka*s. Similar but unglazed plaques are set in the walls of the corridor round the twin East and West Hpet-leik stupas. The Somin-gyi Stupa, a short distance to the north of the Somin-gyi ok-kyaung, is exceptional in having horizontal bands of glazed terracotta, decorated with floral volutes that emphasize each of the three high terraces with continuous lines of colour, while two other stupas, the Nga-kywe-na-daung and the Shin-pahto, have domes entirely covered with glazed bricks.

The corners of the main terraces are adorned with special elements, usually miniature replicas of the main stupa, but in several cases water-pots (*kalaśa*) or turrets are used instead. Occasionally, inaccessible niches are found midway up the side of the dome, at the cardinal points, each housing an image framed by the elevation of a temple. The best examples of this are on the Sein-nyet-nyi-ma, the West Hpet-leik and the Hpyat-sa stupas.

Monasteries and other structures. The buildings that housed the monastic communities that served and maintained the temples are of two main types. The simplest and most common type is the single-cell monastery, a more or less cubical brick building with a single vaulted room under a flat, terraced roof (see fig. 7). Built against its main façade (usually on the east) was a timber pavilion, with a tiled or shingle roof sheltering the front doorways. These pavilions have now disappeared, but their form can be securely ascertained from their stone border plinths, the stone sockets that supported their wooden posts and the decoration at the points at which their roofs were joined to the face of the brick building. In some larger buildings of this type, a barrel-vaulted corridor surrounds the central cell, and there are projecting foreparts on the three sides not occupied by the timber pavilion. Most of these monasteries either had two brick-vaulted storeys, each on a roughly similar plan, or an entresol with wooden beams and joists inside the structure. Narrow staircases were usually inserted inside the walls to give access to the upper storey and to the roof, linked by blind, narrow corridors with corbelled vaults at the level of the upper main vault.

The second type, the multiple-cell monastery, is, in plan, the local version of ancient Indian Buddhist monasteries (Nalanda, Ratnagiri, Mainamati). A single entrance leads through a hall into a central courtyard on to which open small, square cells. Facing the entrance on the opposite side of the courtyard, one cell has been developed into a shrine, sometimes surrounded by a circumambulatory corridor. Such monasteries, the best known being the Somin-gyi, were often two-storey. In a more compact version, the central courtyard becomes a vaulted hall giving access to the multiple cells either directly or through a corridor (for instance monasteries 1111 and 1112 at Tamani).

In its underground version, the multiple-cell monastery is similarly hollowed out round a central courtyard dug into the soil and open to the sky. All that can be seen at ground-level is a small gateway and a low parapet around the courtyard. Stairs descend directly from the gateway to the courtyard, from which interconnected tunnels give access to small, subterranean cells.

7. Monastery 449, Minnanthu, Pagan, 13th century

Many of the monasteries in Pagan were either isolated or satellites of large temples, sometimes built inside their enclosure walls as at the Dhamma-yan-gyi and the Ku-byauk-ngè at Myinkaba. From the 13th century large monastic complexes began to appear. They may owe their conception to the great monasteries of ANURADHAPURA in Sri Lanka since they also have two concentric, rectangular boundary walls, the inner one enclosing a cluster of different buildings. One such is the Le-myet-hna, which consists of a temple, a multiple-cell building that may have been the monastic school, a large central-cell monastery and an ordination hall; another is the Hsu-taung-pyit, where there is the same grouping but with a stupa instead of a temple, and the space between the two boundary walls contains numerous small single-cell buildings. Such complexes were still being built or enlarged during the 14th century, long after the fall of the Pagan dynasty.

Monasteries are much less profusely decorated than temples or stupas. Apart from the usual wall friezes, stucco decoration is generally restricted to the main front of the building, above the junction with the roof of the timber pavilion (where it is sometimes extremely ornate). Mural paintings are uncommon, and when they occur they are simple.

The great monastic complexes had ordination halls usually consisting of a large roof supported on wooden posts. All that remains is a rectangular platform, accessible from the sides by stone steps and bordered by a stone plinth, with rows of circular stone sockets which supported the timber posts. Around this platform, a set of boundary stones (Pali. *sīmā*) delimits the sacred area. Another type of ordination hall is represented by the Upali Thein, a rectangular brick building famous for its mural paintings. The paintings date from the 18th century, and the building itself, if not first constructed, was at least completely renovated at that time.

Libraries were also built in the Pagan period. In 1783 the Pitaka-taik, a manuscript library, was renovated, and its upper parts were greatly modified in the process. Another library built in stone during the Pagan period was totally destroyed in the early 20th century. Other structures at Pagan include the brick city wall, which encloses only a small area of the archaeological site. Of the several gates that pierced it, only the eastern one, a large structure previously vaulted, survives. Other identifiable non-religious structures are several kilns, half-underground vaulted ovens for glazing pottery or other materials used for decoration.

BIBLIOGRAPHY

E. Forchhammer: *Pagan I. The Kyaukku Temple* (Rangoon, 1891/*R* 1910)
C. Duroiselle: 'The Nat-hlaung-kyaung, Pagan', *Archaeol. Surv. India, Annu. Rep.* (1906–7), pp. 136–9
Taw Sein Ko: 'The Plaques Found at the Hpetleik Pagoda, Pagan', *Archaeol. Surv. India, Annu. Rep.* (1906–7), pp. 127–37
E. Huber: 'Les Bas-reliefs du temple d'Ananda à Pagan', *Bull. Ecole Fr. Extrême-Orient*, xi (1911), pp. 1–5
C. Duroiselle: 'The Stone Sculptures in the Ananda Temple at Pagan', *Archaeol. Surv. India, Annu. Rep.* (1913–14), pp. 63–97

G. H. Luce: 'The Greater Temples of Pagan', *J. Burma Res. Soc.* viii/3 (1918), pp. 189–98/*R* 50th anniv. pubn, l/2 (1960), pp. 169–78
——: 'The Smaller Temples of Pagan', *J. Burma Res. Soc.*, x/2 (1920), pp. 41–8/*R* 50th anniv. pubn, l/2 (1960), pp. 179–91
W. B. Sinclair: 'Monasteries of Pagan', *J. Burma Res. Soc.*, x/1 (1920), pp. 1–10/*R* 50th anniv. pubn, l/2 (1960), pp. 505–15
T. Thomann: *Pagan, ein Jahrtausend buddhistischer Tempelkunst* (Stuttgart, 1923)
U Mya: 'A Note on the Nanpaya Temple and the Images of Brahma Carved on the Pillars inside it, Myinpayan, Pagan', *Archaeol. Surv. India, Annu. Rep.* (1934–5), pp. 101–6
C. Duroiselle: *The Ananda Temple at Pagan*, Mem. Archaeol. Surv. India, lvi (Delhi, 1937)
U Lu Pe Win: *Pictorial Guide to Pagan* (Rangoon, 1955/*R* 1975)
G. H. Luce: 'The 550 Jatakas in Old Burma', *Artibus Asiae*, xix/3–4 (1956), pp. 291–307
S. Wickremasingh: 'Ceylon's Relations with South-east Asia, with Special Reference to Burma', *Ceylon J. Hist. & Soc. Stud.*, iii (1960), pp. 38–58
G. H. Luce and Ba Shin: 'Pagan Myinkaba Kubyauk-gyi Temple of Rajakumar (1113 AD) and the Old Mon Writings on its Walls', *Bull. Burma Hist. Comm.*, ii (1961), pp. 277–416
Ba Shin and G. H. Luce: *The Lokahteikpan, an Early Burmese Pagan Temple* (Rangoon, 1962)
G. H. Luce: *Old Burma, Early Pagan*, 3 vols (Locust Valley, NY, 1969) [*Artibus Asiae* suppl. 25; contains comprehensive bibliog.]
Ba Shin, K. J. Whitbread and G. H. Luce: 'Pagan Wetkyi-in Kubyauk-gyi, an Early Burmese Temple with Ink Glosses', *Artibus Asiae*, xxxiii (1971), pp. 194–200
She-haung a shauk a-u-myasa ying [List of ancient monuments maintained by the Dept. of Archaeology], Dept. of Archaeology (Rangoon, 1972)
U Kan Hla [S. Ozhegov]: 'Pagan: Development and Town Planning', *J. Soc. Archit. Historians*, xxxvi/1 (1977), pp. 15–29
——: 'Traditional Town Planning in Burma', *J. Soc. Archit. Historians*, xxvii/2 (1978), pp. 92–104
H. G. Franz: 'Ambulatory Temples in Buddhism and Hinduism', *S. Asian Archaeol.* [Scandinavian Institute of Asian Studies, occas. pap. no. 4] (1979), pp. 449–58
——: *Von Gandhara bis Pagan* (Graz, 1979)
U Bokay: *Pagan Thutethana Lan-hnyun* [Research guide to Pagan] (Rangoon, 1981)
U Aung-Kyaing: *Pagan-khit bi-thuka let-ya-mya* [Architectural ornamentation of the Pagan period] (Rangoon, 1985)
M. Aung Thwin: *Pagan: The Origins of Modern Burma* (Honolulu, 1985)
E. Guillon: *L'Armée de Mara au pied de l'Ananda (Pagan–Birmanie)* (Paris, 1985)
P. Pichard: 'Les Monuments sur plan pentagone à Pagan', *Bull. Ecole Fr. Extrême-Orient*, lxxiv (1985), pp. 305–408
Traditional Burmese Architecture, Dept. of Higher Education (Rangoon, 1986)
Cultural Heritage of Asia, iv: *Study on Pagan*, Organizing Committee, Pagan Symposium, Tokyo (Tokyo, 1989)
P. Strachan: *Pagan: Art and Architecture of Old Burma* (Arran, 1989)
P. Pichard: *The Pentagonal Monuments of Pagan* (Bangkok, 1991)
——: *Inventory of Monuments at Pagan* (Paris and Gartmore, 1992–)
——: 'La Composition architecturale des temples de Pagan', *Acad. Inscr. & B.-Lett.: C. R. Séances* (April–June, 1992), pp. 357–74
——: 'Sous les voûtes de Pagan', *A. Asiatiques*, xlviii (1993), pp. 86–109

(iii) 14th–20th centuries. The style of Burmese architecture after the fall of Pagan in 1287 evolved from types, forms and decorative elements and patterns developed during the intensively creative Pagan period. It is difficult to gain a precise view of this evolution: buildings of perishable materials such as wood have disappeared, others in brick have been renovated, or destroyed, or severely damaged by a series of earthquakes in the 19th and 20th centuries. As a general trend, however, it can be shown that Indian influence gradually declined, as specifically Burmese motifs gained favour. For instance, the square tower with a curvilinear profile, so characteristic of the Pagan temples where it represents the local version of the Orissan shikhara, becomes quite rare after the 15th century, and is replaced either by a stupa-like finial, or by a *pyatthat* (Burm.: a multi-tiered pavilion on a square plan), which occurs during the Pagan period only on a few monuments and more usually on monasteries than on temples.

The divisions of Burmese art history after the Pagan period (1044–1287) continue to be identified by the name of the capital of the then dominant kingdom or of the ruling dynasty: the Pinya period (14th century), the first Ava period (15th century), the Toungoo and second Ava periods (16th century) and the Nyaungyan and Konbaung periods (17th to 19th centuries). Such divisions, however, have little relevance from the point of view of stylistic development. In the city of Pakhan-gyi for instance, which is enclosed by an impressive brick rampart, there are several small brick temples built during the 14th century that are quite similar to those at Pagan, at least as far as can be inferred given their present poor condition.

The types of buildings are basically the same as those that were developed at Pagan: the temple, the stupa and the monastery. To these must be added the royal palace with its large halls and ancillary buildings, a complex certainly present in Pagan but for which more evidence is available from later periods.

(a) Temples. (b) Stupas. (c) Monasteries. (d) Palaces.

(a) Temples. Large temples of the kind built during the Pagan period are exceptional in later times, and it is the simplest form, a square central shrine with a porch on one side, generally the east, which becomes the norm, though temples with doors on three or four sides are not uncommon. The general design is thus a cube crowned by a pyramidal or conical superstructure. Except in Arakan, the type with a solid core and circumambulatory corridor (*see* §(ii)(b) above) appears to be a conscious archaism, the most famous example being the Kyauk-taw-gyi in Amarapura, built in 1847 on the model of the Ananda temple of Pagan.

Until the early 20th century, all these temples were made of brick, plastered with carved stucco and regularly whitewashed. The motifs in the stucco derive from Pagan models, though the decoration tends to be simpler on the walls, with plain mouldings at base and cornice, and more elaborate on the superstructure, with a greater number of niches, antefixes and corner decorative elements, which show the influence of wooden architecture. Porches conserve their general design, with two pilasters under a pediment with flame ornaments, the main element of which is an axial bulb in the form of the stylized breast of a peacock flanked by flamboyant horns. Inside, the voussoired cloister vault still occurs widely, though the corbelled brick vault tends to replace it in smaller temples, and walls as well as vaults are generally plastered and painted.

In Amarapura, where a large number of temples are still standing, the great variety of shapes and designs testifies to the inventiveness and creativity of the Burmese architects. This is seen, for instance, in the Naga-yon, the superstructure of which is in the shape of a gigantic dragon sheltering the building as, according to the legend, the *nāga* king Mucalinda did for the Buddha, and in the Phaya-nga-zu, a cruciform complex of five temples crowned by a central stupa and four tiered pyramids.

(b) Stupas. Unlike the temples, stupas of large size were regularly built in Burma, and many ancient ones were substantially and repeatedly enlarged from the 14th century onwards. The present shape of most of the great Burmese stupas, such as the Shwe-dagon in Rangoon, the Shwe-maw-daw in Pegu and the Shwe-hsan-daw in Prome, is relatively late, even if the original monument, now hidden and encased at its core, is of ancient origin. These large stupas are designed on the classical Pagan model, but their relative proportions have evolved with time. The Htupa-yon (*c.* 1460) in Sagaing keeps the bell-shaped dome of the Pagan period, but its circular terraces with rows of niches are a new element (see fig. 8). In the 17th century, close relations with Sri Lanka gave impetus to the building of stupas derived from the great stupas of ANURADHAPURA, with a large, hemispherical dome resting on low terraces, such as the Kaung-hmu-daw (1636) in Sagaing. Some stupas in Upper Burma, for instance the Eindaw-ya in Mandalay, are closer to the Pagan model, with the lower terraces constructed on a square plan and accessible by stairways on each side. On this pattern, the Pato-daw-gyi Stupa in Amarapura, built 1819–20, maintains the Pagan tradition of depicting the *jātaka* stories, in this case sculptured on marble plates around its three terraces. The general trend, however, is to merge the separate elements of the Pagan stupa into a continuous, conical profile. This can be achieved by multiplying the number of small stepped tiers under the dome, as in the Thakya-man-aung, the Lin-ban-pyauk or the Teza-rama in Myohaung (Arakan), and giving an inclined outline to the lower and octagonal terraces, as in the Shwe-dagon (for illustration, *see* RANGOON) and Shwe-maw-daw (Pegu). In the later types and especially in the numerous small stupas built in the 18th and 19th centuries, the bell-shaped dome itself is gradually reduced and integrated into the conical profile, crowned by a slender spire. In 1790 King Bodawpaya began the construction of a stupa at Mingun, intended to be the highest Buddhist monument in the world and to reach a height of 150 m. Only its base had been completed when the project was abandoned at the King's death in 1819, but the form of the projected building, with a gigantic dome built on a square plan on the model of a Pagan shikhara, can be conjectured from the masonry model standing in front of it.

9. Tham-bude-hpaya Stupa, Amarapura, 1782

8. Htupa-yon Stupa, Sagaing, *c.* 1460

The distinction between temple and stupa, already quite unclear in some Pagan monuments, was further blurred in later examples, one of the most impressive being the Hsin-byu-me stupa built in Mingun in 1816, where a circular shrine, crowned by the dome of a stupa, stands on top of seven circular terraces with undulating parapets. On a much smaller scale, the Tham-bude-hpaya in Amarapura, built in 1782, is a conical stupa with four adjacent shrines, crowned by a spire and with rows of small niches, each containing a Buddha image, at regular intervals on the façade (see fig. 9).

(c) Monasteries. The typical Pagan monastery, a cubical brick building with a timber pavilion built against its main

façade, disappears after the 14th century, but it provided the model for the linear composition that is the basic design of the Burmese monastery up to the beginning of the 20th century. The design of these large wooden monasteries is peculiar to Burmese architecture and they were built in great numbers all over central Burma. They take the form of a single, long building, sometimes complemented by ancillary structures in the same compound for monks and pilgrims. The main building is raised on wooden posts, the unpaved ground-level being, as in the traditional Burmese house, a continuation of the surrounding courtyard rather than an interior space. Around the building are several ornamented staircases, usually six or eight in number, which are the only parts of the complex built in plastered brick and which act as buttresses for the structure. They give access to the main platform, which is made of wooden boards and runs around the building proper. The building is composed of several parts aligned on a common axis, generally from east to west. The first part is the *pyatthat hsaung*, crowned by a tall spire, where images of the Buddha and sacred books are kept. The *pyatthat hsaung* is linked to the main part, the *marabin hsaung*, by a transitional and lower space, the *sanú*, where the abbot resides. The *marabin hsaung* houses the two main halls under a single structure, divided by a transverse partition which clearly marks the limit between the laymen's area and the monks'. The first hall, which contains another Buddha image, is used for preaching and rituals involving both monks and laymen, the second for ceremonies restricted to the monastic community. Behind it, the storage hall (*bàw-gá hsaung*) may be independent or linked to the main halls by another covered space (*sanú* or *khaung-gàn*). These divisions are clearly marked by the hierarchically distinct volumes of the building: the tiered spire of the *pyatthat hsaung* at one end, the high roofs of the central halls, and at the other end the transverse roof of the *bàw-gá hsaung*, while its unity is enhanced by the continuous horizontal lines of the surrounding platform and of the edges of the roofs.

Such buildings are sometimes very large, up to 75 m long by 45 m wide. The technique of their construction is simple and effective. Vertical posts are placed in several long, parallel rows. Horizontal beams inserted through these cylindrical posts provide bracing and support the floors, the walls, the ceilings and the roofs. Depending on their location, these one-piece wooden posts may be only 3 m high at the periphery, where they merely support the platform, or as much as 20 m under the central roof. Walls, floors and roofs are made of wooden boards, the division of roofs into several tiers allowing each span to be covered by a single board, without any cross-joint.

Outside, the monastery is lavishly decorated with wood carving, enhancing the main lines of the building. Finely carved boards frame the balustrade round the platform, the corners and nodal points of which are adorned with wood sculptures, often in high relief, illustrating the *jātaka* stories with scenes from contemporary daily life, thus giving an extremely vivid insight into Burmese society in the 18th century and 19th, with its different classes, houses, dress and implements (loom, ox-cart, boat etc). Between the platform and the roof the walls are usually divided into regular square panels and their decoration is restricted to sculptured frames round each door and window, with intricate floral or animal motifs and guardian deities. The whole outline of the roof is also profusely adorned with flame-like motifs round the gables, on the eaves and the ridge, all of them offering opportunities for the sculptor to express his fantasy by carving small human figures, birds, lizards, monkeys or mythical beings in all sorts of postures.

For bibliography *see* §(d) below.

(d) Palaces. The royal palaces of Burma were built on a model formerly found throughout South-east Asia, composed of groups of timber-frame buildings on masonry platforms within a well-guarded enclosure. Royal palaces were prime targets in time of war, so most of them have disappeared and are known only from their representation in contemporary mural paintings and from descriptions in chronicles and travellers' accounts. However, their platforms, when still extant, as in Pegu or Myohaung, give a reliable indication of their plan and size. The last representative of this tradition was the palace at Mandalay, which was founded in 1857 and incorporated many elements transported from the palace of AMARAPURA. It was totally destroyed by shelling and bombing during World War II, but it is fortunately well documented in old photographs and architectural surveys. The palace was at the centre of three concentric enclosures, the outermost one of which, a huge brick rampart, is still standing. The area of the second enclosure was 36 ha and was surrounded by a teak stockade with a brick wall running parallel to it. Inside there were palm-groves and ornamental gardens with canals and ponds to the north and south, while at its centre stood the palace itself, enclosed by a rectangular wall measuring about 400 m from east to west and 210 m from north to south. The various buildings of the palace stood on a single masonry platform, 2 m high, accessible by several stairways. The main entrance was in the centre of the east face, this east–west line being the major axis of the whole composition and the most important buildings.

The great audience hall formed the eastern front of the palace. It was a symmetrical composition with a central hall and two lateral wings on north and south. Immediately following it on the main axis was the Hall of the Lion Throne, above which was the tallest spire of the palace in the form of a seven-tiered *pyatthat* about 55 m high. Here the most solemn ceremonies of the kingdom were performed. Throne halls were built to the same design as the main halls of contemporary monasteries, consisting of a rectangular building divided by a central partition running from north to south, against which the throne was set. The king climbed up to the throne from the room behind, using a flight of steps and a richly decorated door in the dividing wall, and sat facing the audience, who were prostrated before him in the other, eastern room. There were eight of these thrones, each one named after the decoration of its pedestal, for example the Goose Throne, the Peacock Throne etc, and each housed in a separate hall. The five most important were aligned on the main axis, from the Lion Throne Hall at the eastern end to the Lily Throne Hall, which was reserved for the first queen's audiences, at the western end. The most lavishly decorated, with lacquered or gilded wooden carvings, mirrors and

10. Shwe-nan-daw Monastery, Mandalay, 1880 (formerly part of Mandalay Palace)

glass ornaments, were the Lion Throne Hall and the Bee Throne Hall, also known as the Glass Palace. All these buildings were rectangular, single-storey timber halls, with teak floors and multiple roofs supported by tall wooden posts. They followed the general design of contemporary timber monasteries so closely that the apartment of King Mindon, which had formed part of the palace, was dismantled in 1880 after his death by his son and successor King Thibaw (*reg* 1878–85), and re-erected in the city as the Shwe-nan-daw Monastery (see fig. 10).

The throne halls were connected by passages used as guard-rooms and antechambers. In addition, several buildings stood in spacious gardens to the south and north sides of the central axis, including the apartments of minor queens, the treasury, the armoury, the theatre and recreation rooms, and the elegant watch-tower, a cylindrical wooden structure encircled by a spiral staircase.

BIBLIOGRAPHY

J. G. Scott [Shway Yoe]: *The Burman: His Life and Notions* (London, 1882/*R* New York, 1963/*R* Arran, 1989)

Taw Sein Ko: 'The Mandalay Palace', *Archaeol. Surv. India, Annu. Rep.* (1902–3), pp. 95–103

C. Duroiselle: 'Taitkaw and Sangyaung Monasteries, Mandalay', *Archaeol. Surv. India, Annu. Rep.* (1912–13), pp. 87–119

Taw Sein Ko: 'The Sangyaung Monasteries of Amarapura', *Archaeol. Surv. India, Annu. Rep.* (1914–15), pp. 56–65

C. Duroiselle: *Guide to the Mandalay Palace* (Rangoon, 1925/*R* 1963) [reprint illustrated]

U Myo Myint Sein and others: 'Kòn-baùng hkit hnaùng phòn-gyì kyaùng-myà' [Monasteries of the later Konbaung period], *Tekkathou pyinnya padetha sa Sheì Myan-ma ein-myà zaung*, v (1970), pp. 269–92

U Win Pe: *Shwe Dagon* (Rangoon, 1972)

U Kan Hla [S. Ozhegov]: 'Traditional Town Planning in Burma', *J. Soc. Archit. Historians*, xxxvii/2 (1978), pp. 92–104

G. Garachon: *Lexique de l'architecture birmane traditionnelle en matériaux légers* (diss., U. Paris III, 1983)

U Maung Shwe: *The Linear Composition of a Konbaung Monastery* (Rangoon, 1985) [typescript]

F. K. Lehman: 'Monasteries, Palaces and Ambiguities: Burmese Sacred and Secular Space', *Contrib. Ind. Sociol.*, xxi/1 (1987), pp. 169–86

2. DOMESTIC. Traditional Burmese houses are built with local materials, on a light timber frame, with walls made of wood for the affluent and of bamboo matting for most of the villagers. The material used for roofs depends on the climatic area: panels of grass or rice straw in the central plain and parts of the deltas, of split bamboo or palmyra leaves in the dry zone and of water-palm leaves along the seashore, especially in ARAKAN.

Houses are built on wooden posts with a height of between 0.6 m and 2.5 m. Only the upper floor constitutes the house proper, the ground-floor, which is unpaved, being used as a daytime resting-place and a storage area for farm implements. The kitchen with its fireplace is usually at ground-level and forms a small unit, sometimes connected with the main building.

The plan of the house is rectangular, under a roof with a gable at each end. Formerly, only the king, the nobility and religious and other high dignitaries were permitted to build a staircase perpendicular to the façade. The staircase is thus more usually set longitudinally, parallel to the main façade and running from one corner of the house towards its centre, giving access to a covered verandah, which runs all the length of the upper floor of the building, with two or three rooms opening off it. This staircase is covered by a corner of the roof and is visually enhanced by a kind of arched wooden curtain wall, which shows clearly the relative orientation of the whole house. The two ends of the house are called the head and the foot gable, according to the direction of the staircase. Space hierarchy, from the unclean and public to the sacred and private, is marked by the relative elevation of the floors: for instance, there is generally a step from the verandah to the rooms.

The general orientation depends largely on the configuration of the street, the ridge of the roof being parallel to the street, and even in ancient villages, where the street pattern is not regular, all houses tend to be parallel to each other. Theoretically, the size, location and orientation of a new house should be calculated by an astrologer, chiefly from the date and time of the owner's birth, and the first post is ritually erected at the south-east corner of the future house, or at least on its southern side. Later, the small altar for offering coconuts and flowers to the spirit of the house will be attached to this south-east post, while the Buddha's altar will be located on the east side. At nightfall the family lay out their mats on the floor of the upper level, taking care to sleep with their heads towards the east or, failing that, the north. There is little furniture other than the mats and a few storage boxes and jars. (For a discussion of the similar orientation of traditional Thai houses *see* THAILAND, §II, 2.)

In central Burma villages are compact and enclosed by a thick and thorny hedge, carefully maintained. There are generally four village gates, which are closed each night by the people of the house nearest to them. Each family has its own compound, also enclosed by a hedge or a fence and large enough to accommodate the main house, the kitchen, the cattle pen, the oil mill and the straw stack, a few trees and sometimes a barn or a granary. Outside the village, often near one corner of its boundary, stands the monastery, which is traditionally the village school and is also a wooden building on posts. Other public amenities are few, apart from the *zayat* (Burm.: an open-sided shelter for travellers) and occasionally a covered bridge. This pattern may of course be altered by local conditions, for instance in Arakan and in the deltas, where linear villages are located alongside the canals and rivers. Outside central Burma, where the Burman house dominates, each ethnic minority has developed its traditional type of house and village, with specific forms and configurations.

Traditionally, most cities in Burma were little more than large villages, and their houses were built on the same model. The commercial area was centred on the local market, and increasingly the open ground-floor under the surrounding houses was walled and used for shops or workshops. Later, higher urban densities led to the building of terraces of houses in a continuous row on each side of the street. Masonry houses have appeared only in modern times. In Rangoon and some other administrative centres, fine mansions from the colonial period can be seen, built either entirely of wood or with a masonry ground-floor under a timber upper storey, elaborately adorned with verandahs, balconies and bow windows and covered by huge roofs of teak shingles.

BIBLIOGRAPHY

J. G. Scott [Shway Yoe]: *The Burman: His Life and Notions* (London, 1882/*R* New York, 1963/*R* Arran, 1989)

V. C. Scott O'Connor: *Mandalay and Other Cities of the Past in Burma* (London, 1907/*R* Bangkok, 1987)

L. Sherman: 'Wohnhaustypen in Birma und Assam', *Archv Anthropol.*, n. s. xiv (1915), pp. 203–4

U Myo Myint Sein and others: 'Rhe mran ma im mya' [Ancient Burmese houses], *Tekkathou pyinnya padetha sa Sheì Myan-ma ein-myà zaung*, v (1970), pp. 496–520

G. Lubeigt: 'Les Villages de Birmanie centrale', *Etud. Rur.*, liii–lvi (1975), pp. 259–99

G. Garachon: *Lexique de l'architecture birmane traditionelle en matériaux légers* (diss., U. Paris III, 1983)

B. Brac de la Perrière: *Etude d'une communauté urbaine de Basse Birmanie* (diss., Paris, Ecole Hautes Etud. Sci. Soc., 1984)

PIERRE PICHARD

III. City planning.

The city plans of Burma appear to have been influenced by early Indian ideas. The Vedic and Hindu concept of the universe is of a square. The capital city and the royal palace, which in turn represent the universe, should therefore also be square. However, in the *Arthaśāstra*, an early Indian text on statecraft attributed to Kautilya, the minister of Chandragupta Maurya (*reg c.* 321–*c.* 297 BC) allowed for a practical approach; the fortress constituting the nucleus of the city could be round, oval or square, depending on the nature of the site. There should be three royal streets running from east to west and three from north to south and a total of 12 gates, three on each side. The *Arthaśāstra* also suggests that the chief temples should be located at the centre of the city with the royal complex or 'inner city' set to the north; excavations of ancient Indian cities show that in many cases the palace complex, often fortified, was placed at or near the centre.

The Pyu cities are the best-known early examples in Burma. The capitals of distinct but related kingdoms, they were all similarly planned, covering a wide area enclosed by a brick wall and moat, with a second defensive wall round the restricted central area where the royal palace is thought to have been. Although located along the Irrawaddy Valley, many of these cities were built away from the river, in sharp contrast to later Burmese cities (Pagan, Ava, Amarapura, Mandalay), which were built on the river bank.

Beikthano ('city of Vishnu'), the earliest known Pyu city, appears to have been occupied from the 1st to the 5th century AD. The outer city wall was of brick and roughly rhomboid, with an area of about 2.8 sq. km enclosing a rectangular palace area (450×320 m) somewhat to the north of the centre. The northern Pyu city of Halin, north of Mandalay, which flourished probably from the 2nd to the 6th century AD, has a rectangular enclosure wall (*c.* 3.2×1.5 km) with 12 gates. The fortified wall of Srikshetra, the capital city of a Pyu kingdom from about the 5th to the 9th century AD, was roughly oval, enclosing an area with a mean diameter of 4 km, and was pierced by several gateways. Some sections of the wall are over 4.5 m high. Approximately at its centre is the palace site in a rectangular enclosure (*c.* 520×345 m).

The Glass Palace Chronicle of the Kings of Burma, written in the early 19th century, attempts to make Srikshetra fit the pattern of the ideal Buddhist royal city—modelled on Sudarsana, the heavenly city of Indra on the summit of Mount Meru at the centre of the universe. Indra's palace is at the centre of the city, and around it are the palaces of 32 other gods. In Buddhist iconography the capital thus becomes a representation of the Heaven of the Thirty-Three Gods (Pali: *Tāvatiṃsa*). The chronicle states that Srikshetra had all the things needed for a city: '32 main gates, 32 small gates, moats, ditches, barbicans, machicolations, four-cornered towers with graduated roofs over the gates, turrets along the walls' and so forth. However, in his work at the site G. H. Luce identified only 19 gates. In later Burmese capitals, the gates of the city represented, and were often named after, the chief vassals or provincial governors of the realm, with the king at the centre corresponding to Indra.

PAGAN, capital of the first Burmese kingdom (11th–14th centuries), was enclosed in a square brick wall and moat. Of the entrances, only the main eastern Sarabha Gate survives. A substantial part of the west of the city has been washed away by the Irrawaddy River. As was almost always the case in traditional South-east Asian royal cities, the walled city was a citadel, containing only the royal palace, court buildings and some religious monuments; merchants, artisans and cultivators lived outside—a separation that had been advised in the *Arthaśāstra*.

Cities of the post-Pagan period follow Pagan in many respects but also exhibit important differences. The royal city of AVA, founded by Thadominbya, a Shan prince, *c.* 1365 and serving again as capital for almost 150 years in the 17th to the 19th centuries, was irregular in shape and hugged the Irrawaddy River to the west. The palace was built in the north-west, next to the river. The area reserved for the royal court was small; a large wall with 18 gates gave protection to the populace.

The moat and traces of the wall are discernible in the first city of PEGU, said to have been founded by two Mon brothers from Thaton in the 9th century. The 16th-century city of Pegu, built in 1566 by King Bayinnaung 1 km to the west, had a rectangular city wall and moat and a grid plan of streets. European traders of the time praised its broad avenues and walls pierced by five gates on each side.

The royal city of Alaungpaya (*reg* 1752–60) at Shwebo (Moksobo) was bounded by a brick-and-mud wall and had 12 gates, four of which were to the north and two to the east. The palace was north of the centre. Outside was a town protected by a mud rampart with 43 gates, many of them named after towns in Burma.

The royal city at AMARAPURA (capital 1782–1823, 1837–60) was square and laid out on a grid plan, as was its successor at Mandalay. Moated MANDALAY (capital 1860–85) had 12 fortified gates, three on each side. Each gate had a post beside it bearing a sign of the zodiac indicating that the city was an image of the Tavatimsa Heaven, with the constellations encircling the central Mount Meru represented by the royal palace. In the eastern, most sacred part of the palace stood the Lion Throne (*see* §II, 1(iii)(d) above) under a seven-tiered *pyatthat* that corresponded to the peak of Mount Meru and was decorated with figures of the 33 gods of Indra's celestial city. The straight streets intersected at right angles and led from gate to gate. The large, moated royal sites in Amarapura and Mandalay were reserved strictly for activities related to the monarchy. The populace lived outside, without protecting walls.

BIBLIOGRAPHY

H. Yule: *A Narrative of the Mission to the Court of Ava in 1855* (London, 1858/*R* Kuala Lumpur, 1968)
R. Hakluyt: *The Principal Navigations Voyages Traffiques & Discoveries of the English Nation*, v (Glasgow, 1904), p. 420
V. C. Scott O'Connor: *Mandalay and Other Cities of the Past in Burma* (London, 1907/*R* Bangkok, 1987)
J. S. Furnivall: 'The Record of the Province of Hanthawaddy in the Year 64', *J. Burma Res. Soc.*, vi/3 (1911), pp. 213–16
J. A. Stewart: 'Excavation and Exploration in Pegu', *J. Burma Res. Soc.*, vii/1 (1917)
Pe Maung Tin and G. H. Luce: *The Glass Palace Chronicle of the Kings of Burma* (Rangoon, 1922)
J. J. Meyer: *Das Altindische Buch vom Welt- und Staatsleben: Das Arthaçāstra des Kautilya* (Graz, 1926/*R* 1977), pp. 64–9
R. R. Langham-Carter: 'Alompra's Shwebo', *J. Burma Res. Soc.*, xxiii/1 (1933), pp. 1–12
The Mandalay Palace, Directorate of Archaeological Survey (Rangoon, 1963)
U Aung Thaw: *Excavations at Beikthano* (Rangoon, 1968)
U Kan Hla [S. Ozhegov]: 'Pagan: Development and Town Planning', *J. Soc. Archit. Historians*, xxxvi/1 (1977), pp. 15–29
H. G. Quaritch Wales: *The Universe around Them: Cosmology and Cosmic Renewal in Indianized South-east Asia* (London, 1977)
U Kan Hla [S. Ozhegov]: 'Traditional Town Planning in Burma', *J. Soc. Archit. Historians*, xxxvii/2 (1978), pp. 92–104
——: 'Ancient Cities in Burma', *J. Soc. Archit. Historians*, xxxviii/2 (1979), pp. 95–102
San Tha Aung: *The Buddhist Art of Ancient Arakan* (Rangoon, 1979)
U Win: 'Lu nay kyi htwa toe tet nay thi Pegu ii myo myay toe che yay ko pahtapiwin shu daung hma laylar thone that chet' [Geographical analysis of the expansion of Pegu, a growing city], *Tekkatho Thutethana Sarsaung* [University research journal], i (1979)
Ye Myint: 'Hanthawaddy nanmyodaw panetpon' [Ground-plan of the Hanthawaddy royal city], *Nyanlin* [Light of knowledge] (December 1984)
G. H. Luce: *Phases of Pre-Pagan Burma, Languages and History*, ii (Oxford, 1985)
J. Stargardt: *Early Pyu Cities in a Man-made Landscape*, i of *The Ancient Pyu of Burma* (Cambridge, 1990)

VIRGINIA DI CROCCO, PIERRE PICHARD

IV. Sculpture.

Burmese sculpture has diverse styles and iconographic origins. Since the establishment of the Pagan kingdom in the 9th century AD, it has been predominantly Theravada Buddhist and so largely confined to Buddha images or scenes from Buddhist mythology in bronze, stone, stuccoed brick, wood, dry lacquer and terracotta.

BIBLIOGRAPHY

R. Braun and I. Braun: *Opium-Gewichte: Opium Weights: Poids d'Asie* (Landau, 1983) [trilingual text]
O. Karow: *Burmese Buddhist Sculpture: The Johan Möger Collection* (Bangkok, 1991)
H. Hassan: *Ancient Buddhist Art Forms: Burma* (Bangkok, 1993)

1. 3rd–9th centuries AD. 2. 9th–13th centuries. 3. 13th–20th centuries.

1. 3RD–9TH CENTURIES AD. In this early period sculpture was produced in the Mon kingdom of Thaton in the south, the Pyu kingdoms of central Burma and the Arakanese kingdoms on the eastern coast of the Bay of Bengal. Although predominantly Buddhist, these kingdoms were also influenced by Brahmanism, particularly by Vaishnavite cults.

The study of Mon sculpture *in situ* and in local museums has been disrupted by the virtual impossibility of travelling in Lower Burma during the period after the establishment of the military regime in 1962. A number of Buddha images are well documented though photographs seldom exist, but certain late 19th-century publications provide the only evidence that in Thaton and such nearby sites as Kogun and P'agat there are also Brahmanic stone stelae. These include three representations (*c.* 9th century) of Vishnu asleep on the serpent of eternity, Ananta, with three lotuses in full bloom issuing from his navel, carrying seated figures of Brahma, Vishnu and Shiva respectively.

The sculpture of the Pyu realms is more accessible, but the poor condition of many of the large bas-reliefs in stone and the impossibility of translating the inscriptions that occur on some of them make them difficult to identify. One example of this is a relief at Halin, the lower half of which is occupied by rows of small figures with heads raised and hands joined, venerating a figure seated above them of whom only the legs and a hand remain (see fig. 11). Some clearly Buddhist stelae dating from the 5th to the 7th century are still preserved in Srikshetra temples (Bebe, Le-myet-hna) as well as in the local museum of Hmawza. In these the Buddha, more often than not, is seated with legs crossed and the right leg lying sole upwards over the left leg in the *vīrāsana* (Skt: 'hero') position or with legs hanging down in the so-called European position (*pralambapādāsana*). His gesture is either the *bhūmisparśa mudrā* (calling the earth to witness), sometimes with the left hand, or the *dhyāna mudrā* (meditation) or the *vitarka mudrā* (teaching). He is surrounded by praying figures or stupas. Sometimes, in a symbolic representation of the

11. Stone stele with inscription in Pyu, h. 1.17 m, Halin, 8th or 9th century AD

First Sermon in Sarnath, the Buddha is depicted above a Wheel of the Law and two deer. Two large sandstone stelae at Srikshetra have as their principal motif a gigantic stupa, the base of which is decorated with five niches occupied by five small Buddhas in meditation. The Hindu deity most frequently depicted is Vishnu standing with his attributes (conch, mace) or on his mount, Garuda, or asleep on Ananta giving birth to the Brahmanic triad.

Pyu Buddha images have rounded faces, and evenly disposed curls of hair covering a cranial protuberance (*uṣṇīṣa*) that is barely visible. The robe is smooth and clings to the body and the right shoulder is sometimes bare. Images in the round are of small dimensions and in gold, silver or bronze. Images in bronze include a statuette of the *bodhisattva* Avalokiteshvara ('The Lord who looks down with compassion') and five other small images of musicians and dancers, all finely executed. Several beautiful reliquaries in chased silver are decorated with images of the Buddha.

At Dhannavati in Arakan the sanctuary of the Mahamuni still possesses a series of stelae decorated with *dvārapāla*s (door guardians), *nāgarāja*s (serpent kings) or *kinnara* (heavenly beings, part human and part animal or bird). There are also five small rectangular bas-reliefs in stone dating from the 5th century, three of which show a strong Gupta influence in the depiction of the Buddha. In the Archaeological Museum, Myohaung (Myauk U), carved pillars, statues of Vishnu and the sun god Surya in stone and an assortment of small adorned Buddhas in bronze originating from Vesali have been preserved.

2. 9TH–13TH CENTURIES. The sculpture of the Pagan period (9th–13th centuries) is relatively homogeneous in style, and this seems to reflect the great cohesion of the Burmans who, soon after they arrived in the area, were converted to Theravada Buddhism.

(i) Temple decoration. The sculptors of Pagan swiftly adopted the iconographic traditions of Theravada Buddhism and continued them, while at the same time giving them a distinctive character. This can be seen in the stucco decoration of buildings, where animals typical of the iconographic repertory of the Indianized world, such as the *siṁha* ('lion'), *haṁsa* ('goose'), *kīrttimukha* (demon mask) and *makara* (mythological aquatic beast) appear in the foliated stucco scrolls. It can also be seen in the series of small square, often glazed terracotta plaques depicting scenes from the *jātaka*s (previous lives of the Buddha) that run along the tiered terraces of certain stupas (e.g. Shwe-zigon, Mingala-zedi) or the exterior of certain temples (e.g. Ananda). The most beautiful of these, which date from the late 11th century and portray people and animals with picturesque naivety, are still *in situ* in the two stupas East Hpet-leik and West Hpet-leik to the south of the village of Thiripyitsaya. Belonging to the same period are numerous stone stelae placed on the foreparts (e.g. Naga-yon) and in the corridors of the temples (e.g. Ananda) that recount seven of the eight principal episodes in the life of the Buddha: his *Birth*, the *First Sermon in the Deer Park at Sarnath*, the *Descent from the Heaven of the Thirty-three Gods* (Pali *Tāvatiṃsa*), the *Great Miracle of Shravasti*, the *Meditation in the Forest of Parileyyaka*, the *Submission of the Nalagiri Elephant* and the *Death of the Buddha and his Entry into Mahāparinirvāṇa* ('complete nirvana'). The 28 previous Buddhas are also depicted on the Naga-yon. They are seated on a throne or under the bodhi tree, either in meditation (*samādhi*) or calling the earth to witness (*bhūmisparśa mudrā*).

(ii) Statuary. The characteristic elements of the Pagan style are most clearly evident in statuary. Images of the Buddha, particularly those in bronze, have distinctive facial features and dress (see fig. 12). The typical face with its pointed chin and its relatively flat cranium resembles an inverted isosceles triangle, a little distorted by the slight rounding of the cheeks. The mouth is small and smiling; the fine nose is quite long and often aquiline; the eyes are fully open underneath a long brow ridge and are symmetrically elongated towards the temples into 'butterfly wings'. The mole or mark between the eyebrows (*ūrṇā*) is about the size of a pellet and set in low relief on the forehead above the bridge of the nose. The hair is arranged in small curls, sometimes quite pointed, which cover a central, well-defined *uṣṇīṣa* in the centre of the cranium. The protuberance is always surmounted by a small triangular ornament, which sometimes has the appearance of a flattened flame. The monastic robe, comprising two pieces of smooth cloth, clings to the contours of the body. In the seated images the right shoulder is naked and the end of the overgarment forms a pleated flap over the left shoulder.

12. Seated Buddha in *bhūmisparśa mudrā*, bronze, h. 350 mm, 11th or 12th century (Rangoon, National Museum)

By contrast, in the standing images the shoulders are covered, the robe falls symmetrically the whole length of the body, forming regular folds on each side of the legs, and the end of the flap is held in the right hand.

The positions (*āsana*) and the gestures (*mudrā*) follow the canonical rules and are therefore similar to those of all images of the Buddha. However, in the seated images, the *Māravijaya* position (Victory over Mara) is the more common, with legs crossed and right hand calling the earth to witness (*bhūmisparśa mudrā*). In the stelae the Buddha is also occasionally depicted walking. The action of walking is suggested not by the position of the feet, which remain flat on the ground, but by the robe, which flares out naturalistically on one side.

Some Pagan images are colossal, the largest being an 11th-century reclining Buddha (Shinbinthalyaung; approx. 18 m), which is housed in a rectangular, brick building in the enclosure wall of the Shwe-hsan-daw Stupa. However, the enormous statues for worship that sit majestically enthroned in the heart of each temple are generally even more impressive. The four Buddhas almost 10 m tall standing with their backs against the central core of the Ananda are in this category—although only the sandalwood images on the north and south sides date from the Pagan period—and the impact of their great height and the gilding of the four images in the semi-darkness unfailingly command respect. The images facing north and south are in the *dharmachakra mudrā* (setting the Wheel of the Law in motion), the later east image holds the myrobalan fruit in the right hand and the west image is in the *abhaya mudrā* (dispelling fear). The use of these *mudrā* in standing images of the Buddha is unique to Burma.

Some crowned and adorned stone Buddhas dating from this epoch have been preserved in the Archaeological Museum, Pagan. They are seated and carry on their heads a high diadem composed of juxtaposed triangular motifs, sometimes with a tall and highly decorated finial ornament at the level of the *uṣṇīṣa*. They wear long hanging earrings and an elaborate pectoral ornament. Adorned images in bronze are rarely found, but some fine standing Buddhas of this type in wood are held in private collections.

The Votive tablets were made in great quantities and they have a varied iconography; most are in terracotta, but some are in stone and these show the remarkable skill of the Pagan sculptors in engraving on a small surface, as they range in size from as little as 100 mm to 200 mm. The most appealing show the central image of a Buddha seated on a lotus, calling the earth to witness and surrounded by miniature scenes of the seven principal episodes of his life. This taste for delicate engraving is also evident in the craftsmanship of some metal objects, principally in beautiful bronze lotuses. These have movable petals each with a miniature sculpture carved on it. When open they reveal, among other things, a tiny Buddha image or a stupa at the heart of the flower.

According to the Shwe-zigon inscription (1086), King Kyanzittha was deemed to be an incarnation of Vishnu, while still being a devout Theravada Buddhist. This Brahmanic cult, which was well tolerated by the highest authorities in the realm, had repercussions in the art of Pagan. In the Nan-hpaya Temple, for example, beautiful Brahmanic images, sculpted in shallow relief, decorate the four pillars of the cella. In the Nat-hlaung-kyaung, the only Vaishnavite temple in Pagan, seven of the original reliefs, representing the avatars or incarnations of Vishnu, are still *in situ* in the niches that decorate the exterior walls at regular intervals. By contrast, all that remains of the principal group of sculptures showing Vishnu asleep on the serpent Ananta giving birth to the Brahmanic triad, which once occupied the interior cella, is the figure of Shiva seated on a lotus. Still recognizable is a figure of Vishnu mounted on Garuda set in a niche above a pilaster, but the effigies of deities in bas-relief surrounding the central core have deteriorated to such an extent that they are no longer identifiable. Some statuettes and stelae preserved in the Archaeological Museum, Pagan, also represent Brahmanic deities. The earliest known statues of *nat* spirits date from this period.

3. 13TH–20TH CENTURIES. For three centuries after the fall of Pagan the political situation in Burma was unstable, as various kingdoms tried to establish supremacy over each other, and art does not appear to have flourished.

In the 15th century the Mon kingdom of PEGU experienced relative prosperity and a religious revival, particularly during the reign of Dammazedi (Ramadhipati, *reg* 1472–92). The little museum built on the platform of the Shwe-maw-daw Stupa at Pegu houses a beautiful collection of Buddhist statuettes, some of which date back to this period. The most celebrated sculptures of this period, however, are colossal images such as the great reclining Buddha (Shwethalyaung) at Pegu. This image

(h. 16 m, l. 54 m) was sculpted at the end of the 10th century AD and appears to have been entirely restored in the 15th century. Equally impressive are the four Buddhas, each of them 30 m high, seated in the *Māravijaya* position, with their backs against the sides of the enormous, central core of the Kyaik-pun Temple (1476). From the Shwe-gu-gyi Temple, built by Dammazedi in imitation of the temple at Bodhgaya in India, comes a series of beautiful bas-reliefs in glazed terracotta, between 450 mm and 480 mm high, some representing Mara's daughters and others his warriors with animal heads. They are preserved in various Western museums (e.g. Berlin, Mus. Ind. Kst; London, V&A).

In ARAKAN, the geographical position of the kingdom of Myohaung (Myauk U), founded in 1430, enabled it to enjoy, until its annexation by the Burmese at the end of 1784, a measure of independence that allowed it to develop a particular style of architecture and sculpture. The bas-reliefs that decorate the corridors of the Shitthaung Temple (1535), with their series of animals, numerous little genre scenes of daily life and deities, are a valuable source of information on the fauna, the local population and the religious life of the time. Similarly, an idea of 16th-century Arakanese fashions can be gained from the sculptures of the Htuk-kaw-thein (1571), where richly dressed male and female dignitaries are shown kneeling on each side of niches placed at regular intervals along the sombre, vaulted corridors. The representations of the Buddha are numerous and of all sizes. Those inside the temples are in stone and mostly seated, with legs crossed and making the gesture of calling the earth to witness (*bhūmisparśa mudrā*); an impression of bulk is conveyed by their thickset bodies and their almost rectangular, square-jawed heads bearing a large *uṣṇīṣa*, flattened at the top. The bronze images preserved in the museums and monasteries of Sittwe and Myohaung provide more variety, both in their attire and in their gestures. Sometimes the Buddha is portrayed bare-chested and wearing only a lower garment, but he is also frequently adorned and may be compared in this respect to certain images of Pala-period art. The famous bronze image of Mahamuni, taken during the Burmese war in 1784 and venerated thereafter in Mandalay, was for centuries the supreme god in Arakan. Large bas-reliefs showing door guardians (*dvārapālas*), formerly in the royal palace, can be seen in the Archaeological Museum, Myohaung.

The remarkable collection of stone Buddhist sculpture in the famous grotto-sanctuaries of Pindaya, near Kalaw and Taung-gyi, in the Shan States, was probably first formed in the early 16th century. Buddha images of Shan type have a distinctive physiognomy and are characterized by the enlarged lotus bud that rises from the *uṣṇīṣa* as well as by the drape of the monastic robe. In seated images, the latter, which is often trimmed with braid, is always draped so that it falls forwards over the bare right shoulder.

Burmese sculpture underwent a revival during the Konbaung period (1752–1885). The Mon kings of the Alaungpaya dynasty filled their successive capitals (SAGAING, AVA, AMARAPURA, MANDALAY) with numerous works of art. Wood-carving was highly esteemed and used frequently in the decoration of buildings. Palaces and monasteries, such as the Shwe-nan-daw and Shwe-In-Bin in Mandalay and the Bagaya-kyaung in Ava, built of teak and constructed on piles, are veritable examples of lace-work in wood, though much of the decoration of the exterior has been lost as a result of exposure to the elements. The doors are decorated with carved deities (see fig. 13); the walls are ornamented with various decorative motifs; in the balustrades the spaces between the balusters are filled with lavish arabesques; and the festooned and fretted edges of the tiered roofs are outlined against the sky. The same high level of craftsmanship is found in the chased and engraved silver and gold objects from the royal treasure in Mandalay, which are preserved in the National Museum, Rangoon.

Though images of the Buddha were still sometimes made in bronze, more frequently they were of lacquered and gilded wood or marble. Sculptures of the Buddha seated in the *Māravijaya* position, with legs crossed in the *vajrāsana* position and the right hand calling the earth to witness, were made in enormous numbers. Standing Buddhas are less numerous and show more diversity; for example, they sometimes hold between their fingers the tapering oval fruit of the myrobalan (a gesture already found in Arakanese and Shan seated images), or even, as

13. Carved wooden doorway, Shwe-In-Bin Monastery, Mandalay, 19th century

in the colossal statue on Mandalay Hill, with the right arm outstretched and the index finger pointing. The number of adorned images increased: their headdresses became more and more elaborate, with large, intricately worked wings spread out on either side of the diadem. Finally, the so-called Chinese-style Buddha images display a different iconography. The face has mongoloid features and is adorned below the hairline by a narrow ornamented band; the curls of the hair are extremely small and cover a rounded *uṣṇīsa*, clearly visible but devoid of embellishment; the monastic robe, bordered by a decorated band, is draped loosely and falls in large, irregular undulations around the body. This iconography is still current, as the modern Buddha images in gilded metal in the temples of Rangoon demonstrate.

BIBLIOGRAPHY

R. C. Temple: 'Notes on Antiquities in Ramannadesa (The Talaing Country of Burma)', *Ind. Antiqua.*, xxii (1893), pp. 327–66
C. Duroiselle: 'The Stone Sculptures in the Ananda Temple at Pagan', *Archaeol. Surv. India, Annu. Rep.* (1913–14), pp. 63–97
G. H. Luce: *Old Burma, Early Pagan*, 3 vols (Locust Valley, NY, 1969) [*Artibus Asiae* suppl. 25]
U Aung Thaw: *Historical Sites in Burma* (Rangoon, 1972/*R* 1978)
J. Lowry: *Burmese Art* (London, 1974)
San Tha Aung: *The Buddhist Art of Ancient Arakan* (Rangoon, 1979)
S. Fraser-Lu: 'Buddha Images from Burma', *A. Asia*, xl (1981), no. 1 'Sculptured in Stone', pp. 72–82; no. 2 'Bronze and Related Metals', pp. 62–72; no. 3 'Wood and Lacquer', pp. 129–36
M. Gatellier: 'L'Image du Buddha dans la statuaire birmane', *A. Asiatiques*, xl (1985), pp. 32–40
E. Guillon: *L'Armée de Mara au pied de l'Ananda (Pagan-Birmanie)* (Paris, 1985)

MARIE GATELLIER

V. Painting.

The Burmese have long excelled at painting, and the paintings that decorate the walls of many of the temples of Pagan and elsewhere in Burma constitute perhaps their most distinctive contribution to the Buddhist art of South-east Asia. The technical skill of Burmese artists is demonstrated not only in the elaborate decoration and complex iconography of these wall paintings but also in the highly stylized painted manuscripts of Buddhist texts and, since the late 19th century, in paintings of secular subjects, many of them in oils or watercolour and depicting Burmese scenes in a realistic, Western style.

1. Wall painting. 2. Manuscript. 3. Modern.

1. WALL PAINTING. Pagan is the most ancient Burmese site where a large corpus of wall paintings is still extant. Several painted caves in Burma may be earlier than the 11th century but they have not been securely dated, and no systematic survey of them has yet been carried out. The paintings are extremely sensitive to humidity, and the dry climate and sandy soil of the Pagan area account for their exceptional degree of preservation, even more than of the monuments. It is highly probable that there were paintings in Pyu or Mon temples in other regions of Burma that have now totally vanished. There are 347 temples in Pagan and some 40 more in Salé and Hsalè, the earliest of them dating from the 11th century, that still preserve substantial parts of the wall paintings which previously covered most of their walls and vaults.

☐

(i) Techniques. The inscriptions provide reliable evidence that the temples and their wall paintings were completed in a short time, and this in turn presupposes a high degree of organization. The painting surface was composed of a layer of mud applied to the brick wall (from the 12th century onwards the brick surface was first chipped), on which a thin layer (1–3 mm) of lime mixed with finely sieved sand was carefully smoothed. The mud layer was replaced after the 13th century by several layers of stucco, which formed a render that was more resistant to insects and weathering. Few traces of vertical or horizontal joins are found in the render. The unfinished paintings show that the preparatory work included tracing the main lines of the composition by snapping a colour-soaked string. At places, a square grid was used for the enlargement of the models, which were probably drawn on paper or on cloth, similar to the 12th-century cloth painting found in 1984 in Temple 315. Some sort of stencil was probably used for repeated motifs. Painting was executed on the dry lime render, beginning with light colours (white lime, yellow ochre and pale yellow orpiment) and progressing to burnt or red ochres, vermilion and minium, green (produced by mixing yellow ochre and black), blue (probably obtained from indigo) and carbon or animal black. A thick layer of white pigment (lime) was used for eyes, flowers etc, and the finishing touches were provided by neat outlines in black, red lacquer or red ochre. The binder for the pigments was probably a vegetal gum or glue diluted in water. In the 13th century the paint layer seems to have become thinner, and new pigments were added, such as red and purple lacquers, chrysocolla and copper-based green. In the 18th and 19th centuries a priming white coat of clay or chalk was applied to the lime render before painting, and new and more vivid pigments came into use, such as Prussian blue and artificial ultramarine.

(ii) Subject-matter and decorative motifs. Throughout the Pagan period, three major themes provided the subject-matter of wall painting: illustrations of the great events of the Buddha's life, historical or mythological personages and depictions of the *jātaka*s (previous lives of the Buddha). These were combined with a variety of decorative elements.

The eight great events of the Buddha's life, each corresponding to one of the chief places of Buddhist pilgrimage in north India, are traditionally: the Birth, the Enlightenment, the First Sermon, the Twin Miracles, the Descent from the Heaven of the Thirty-three Gods, the Parileyyaka Meditation, the Submission of the Nalagiri Elephant, and the Death of the Buddha and his Entry into *mahāparinirvāṇa* (complete nirvana). These eight scenes were popularized in Indian Buddhist art as early as the Gandhara period and continuously thereafter, and are better known to us in sculpture than in painting because of the greater durability of the former medium. In the 8th century the Pala school of Bengal and Orissa illustrated these scenes in a single composition dominated by a central and larger representation, usually of the Enlightenment, in stone sculpture or on small terracotta tablets that were often carried away by pilgrims as mementos. Tablets based on this model were also made in Srikshetra and in Pagan and gave inspiration to sculptors and painters.

14. Painted *jātaka* panels (detail) on west wall of shrine, Loka-hteik-pan Temple, Pagan, 12th century

For example, in the Loka-hteik-pan Temple in Pagan, built in the first half of the 12th century, the wall paintings on the back wall of the shrine illustrate the eight scenes according to the Pala model, with the exception of the central scene, which, since the Enlightenment is portrayed by the sculptured image in the foreground at the centre of the shrine, is occupied by a window.

In the large temples built at the beginning of the Pagan period, such as the Ananda or the Naga-yon, these scenes were mostly represented by numerous stone sculptures placed in niches, with the addition of other episodes of the life of the Buddha. Slightly later, for instance in the Kubyauk-gyi Temple at Myinkaba (1113), wall paintings began to portray these themes. Scenes were added, one of the most popular in all the Pagan temples being the assault by Mara's army, with its numerous soldiers, wild beasts and monsters. Scenes from the history of Buddhism were also added, such as the great Buddhist councils and depictions of legendary Indian kings.

Both in sculpture and in painting, such scenes are composed round a large, central figure about whom are grouped secondary personages, portrayed on a smaller scale. The major figures, who still show the influence of Pala sculpture, are painted with animation, though in hieratic postures, with expressive faces and bodies and finely executed details of patterned clothing and of jewellery or coiffure. The background is filled with various motifs such as trees, buildings or decorative flowers, scrolls and festoons, no attempt being made to set them in a realistic landscape. The representation is often diachronic, juxtaposing several successive episodes in a single composition.

Historical or mythological personages are portrayed in separate framed panels, generally rectangular but sometimes circular, or in continuous rows. The most widely represented are the 28 successive Buddhas of the past (the historical Gautama Buddha being the 28th), each seated under a specific tree, but portraits of Buddha's famous disciples, of *bodhisattvas*, of legendary kings or Hindu gods (as in the Pahto-tha-mya and Abe-yadana temples) are also to be seen. In many cases, the personage is painted in front of a detailed elevation of a contemporary Pagan stupa or temple.

The *jātakas* have always been a great source of inspiration for Burmese painters and wood-carvers. Like the great events, the earliest representations of the *jātakas* in Pagan were carved on stone or clay plaques (as in the Shwe-zigon and the two Hpet-leik stupas), but they came to constitute one of the main motifs of the wall paintings. Each *jātaka* is illustrated in a square panel, using its chief characters or a selected episode (a few personages or animals, a tree, a boat, a house etc) to evoke the whole and sometimes complex story, in a precise but usually not centred composition. Such square panels, the sides of which can vary from 80 to 400 mm, are juxtaposed in regular rows and columns covering all the walls of the temples (see fig. 14). In many cases, the subject of the paintings is identified by a small painted caption in Mon or Old Burmese. The study of these has greatly contributed to the knowledge of these ancient languages as well as to the identification of the literary sources from India or Sri Lanka known in Burma at that time.

Paintings based on these themes are integrated into a complete decorative composition that emphasizes the interior design. A few of the architecturally important motifs may be sculptured in relief on the plaster, for example as on the pilasters and pediment framing the main door from the hall to the shrine or the corridor, and such elements, for instance in the Kubyauk-gyi at Myinkaba, are treated polychromatically, with vivid colours underlining the mouldings. More commonly, the main lines of the interior architecture are emphasized with *trompe l'oeil* elements, reproducing the architectural decoration of the exterior: arches are decorated on the plain stucco with a painted pediment, pilasters are painted at the corners of the shrine, and a decorative frieze runs all round the building at the junction of the wall and the vault. Above the square shrine, the cluster vault is divided into four triangles by diagonal corner bands culminating in a central lotus flower. These elements are generally enlivened by an intricate foliate background and a variety of small creatures, such as parrots, peacocks, deer or rabbits, dragons and monsters, half-animal and half-human, or even half-vegetal, while familiar birds and ritual objects are painted under the frieze.

Under the vaults, regular decorative patterns were used to form a network of touching or intersecting circles, squares, diamonds and octagons, sometimes with a small Buddha figure at the centre of each motif. Another popular pattern, which in several of the smaller temples unifies the whole surface from the base of the walls to the top of the vault, is known as the 'Thousand Buddhas': it is composed of innumerable rows of seated Buddha figures, sometimes no more than 20 mm high, the final effect being somewhat similar to a wallpaper. These regular patterns may be interrupted by various larger symbolic motifs, such as the sacred footprints, the horoscope of the Buddha's life or the map of the Buddhist universe, with its central Mt Meru surrounded by seven concentric mountain ranges and its four islands on the surrounding ocean. The main sculpture of the seated Buddha is often framed by a large tree of enlightenment painted on the wall behind.

After the Pagan period, these major themes are still present, but the general composition tends to be less rigidly divided. The regular square *jātaka* panels are replaced by a composition consisting of long horizontal registers, and pre-eminence is given to episodes from the ten last *jātaka*s. These are told in more detail, and illustrations of the various episodes may occupy a whole wall. At the same time, they portray more details from everyday life in Burma, with numerous palace scenes, but also subsidiary scenes featuring fishermen in the river, women at their looms, and again a profusion of familiar trees and animals, which Burmese painters always liked to represent. Decorative patterns continued to be painted under the vaults and became increasingly elaborate. Owing to the introduction of new pigments, the colour scheme is generally richer, as in the Tilawka-guru Monastery in Sagaing (1672) or in the Ananda Ok-kyaung Monastery in Pagan (1785), but some examples, for instance the 18th-century paintings in the Sula-mani Temple of Pagan, have very light and transparent colouring, not unlike a kind of mural watercolour. Also in the 18th century, perspective began to be used for painting buildings and landscape, possibly under Chinese influence, and during the 19th century European perspective was increasingly adopted, for instance in the paintings of landscapes and Buddhist monuments in the Kyauk-taw-gyi Temple of Amarapura (1847).

BIBLIOGRAPHY

C. Duroiselle: 'The Nat-hlaung-kyaung, Pagan', *Archaeol. Surv. India, Annu. Rep.* (1906–7), pp. 136–9
——: 'Pictorial Representations of the Jatakas in Burma', *Archaeol. Surv. India, Annu. Rep.* (1912–13), pp. 87–119
G. H. Luce: 'The Smaller Temples of Pagan', *J. Burma Res. Soc.*, x/2 (1920), pp. 41–8/*R* 50th anniv. pubn. 1/2 (1960), pp. 179–91
T. Thomann: *Pagan, ein Jahrtausend buddhistischer Tempelkunst* (Stuttgart, 1923)
U Lu Pe Win: *Pictorial Guide to Pagan* (Rangoon, 1955/*R* 1975)
G. H. Luce: 'The 550 Jatakas in Old Burma', *Artibus Asiae*, xix/3–4 (1956), pp. 291–307
P. Coremans: *Report of Unesco Mission to the Union of Burma* (Paris, 1961)
G. H. Luce and Ba Shin: 'Pagan Myinkaba Kubyauk-gyi Temple of Rajakumar (1113 AD) and the Old Mon Writings on its Walls', *Bull. Burma Hist. Comm.*, ii (1961), pp. 277–416
Ba Shin and G. H. Luce: *The Lokahteikpan, an Early Burmese Pagan Temple* (Rangoon, 1962)
A. B. Griswold, C. Kim and C. H. Pott: *Burma: Korea: Tibet* (London, 1964)
P. de Hénau and U Ba Tint: *Contributions à l'étude des peintures murales de Pagan en Birmanie* (Brussels, 1969)
G. H. Luce: *Old Burma: Early Pagan*, 3 vols (Locust Valley, NY, 1969) [*Artibus Asiae* suppl. 25]
Ba Shin, K. J. Whitbread and G. H. Luce: 'Pagan Wetkyi-in Kubyauk-gyi, an Early Burmese Temple with Ink Glosses', *Artibus Asiae*, xxxiii (1971), pp. 194–200
U Aung Thaw: *Historical Sites in Burma* (Rangoon, 1972/*R* 1978)
H. G. Quaritch Wales: *Early Burma–Old Siam: A Comparative Commentary* (London, 1973)
U Tin Lwin: 'Old Burmese Painting', *Oriens Extrem.*, ii/2 (1974), pp. 237–59 [Eng. trans. of *Shei yo Myan-ma baji* (Rangoon, *c.* 1966)]
J. T. Bailey: 'Some Burmese Paintings of the Seventeenth Century and Later—Part I: A Seventeenth-century Painting Style near Sagaing', *Artibus Asiae*, xxxviii (1976), pp. 267–86
K. Wenk: *Murals in Burma*, i of *Painting from Pagan of the Late Period, 18th Century* (Zurich, 1977)
J. T. Bailey: 'Some Burmese Paintings of the Seventeenth Century and Later—Part II: The Return to Pagan', *Artibus Asiae*, xl (1978), pp. 41–61
T. Ono and T. Inoue: *Mural Paintings of the Buddhist Temples in Burma* (Tokyo, 1978) [Jap. and Eng. text]
J. T. Bailey: 'Some Burmese Paintings of the Seventeenth Century and Later—Part III: Nineteenth-century Murals at the Taungthaman Kyauktawgyi', *Artibus Asiae*, xli (1979), pp. 41–63
U Bokay: *Pagan Thutethana Lan-hnyun* [Research guide to Pagan] (Rangoon, 1981)
Pagan Newslett. (Paris and Pondicherry, 1982–)
P. Schwartzbaum and others: *Conservation of Mural Paintings and Stuccoes, Pagan, Burma* (Rome, 1982–91)
J. Boisselier: *Il sud-est asiatico* (Turin, 1986)
G. Giantomassi and D. Zari: *Report on the Restoration Interventions on a 12th Century Cloth-painting from Pagan, Burma* (Rome, 1987)
Y. Ishizawa, Y. Kono and others, ed.: *Study on Pagan*, Cultural Heritage in Asia, iv (Tokyo, 1989), pp. 165–71
P. Strachan: *Pagan: Art and Architecture of Old Burma* (Arran, 1989)
P. Pichard: *Inventory of Monuments at Pagan* (Paris and Gartmore, 1992–)

RUDOLPHO LUJAN, PIERRE PICHARD

2. MANUSCRIPT. Although there are references to manuscripts of different kinds in the ancient inscriptions of Burma, little is known of Burmese manuscript art before the beginning of the Konbaung dynasty in 1752. The ravages of war, fire, climate and insects have repeatedly destroyed Burma's manuscripts through the centuries. Most of the surviving manuscripts are not illustrated but

are plain palm-leaf texts dating from the 18th and 19th centuries.

(i) Palm-leaf manuscripts. Decoration of palm-leaf manuscripts is largely confined to the gilding of the edges of the leaves and to the wooden cover boards, which sometimes have decoration in black or red lacquer or gilding. More elaborately ornamented manuscripts are the *Kammāwasā*, or Buddhist ordination texts, used in the performance of monastic ceremonies. The leaves of the *Kammāwasā* manuscripts may be made of palm-leaf, metal or ivory, and all have gilded and lacquered decoration both on the surface of the leaves and on the cover boards, with the Pali text written in raised lacquer Burmese square script or tamarind seed characters.

(ii) Folding books. The main medium for Burmese manuscript painting is the *parabaik* (Burm.: 'paper folding book'). These, if opened out, may extend to as much as 30 m. However, they were not intended to be viewed in a single display but to be kept folded concertina fashion and viewed one page at a time. There are two kinds of *parabaik*: the black, on which the text is written with a white steatite crayon, and the white or cream, used for special documents and, above all, for painted illustrations. Black *parabaik* were mostly used as working notebooks and are sometimes illustrated with astrological and cabbalistic diagrams and, more rarely, maps. The white *parabaik* were usually given a thin coating of white priming to prepare the paper surface for painting, and the unpainted marginal areas were often coloured bright yellow. The text or captions were written under the scenes against this yellow background in black ink. The painting procedure followed was for the outline to be drawn first, usually in red or black, and then filled in with colour—the whole having a flat, linear appearance. The use of bright colours and of plentiful gilding is characteristic of Burmese manuscript painting. Scenes have multiple perspectives and are often not painted in chronological sequence but grouped according to the location of a scene. Thus, two events separated in time will appear together because they share the same setting. Sometimes the division of scenes is made naturalistically by lines of trees or buildings or by rows of figures who play some part in the narrative. The devices of a coordinated perspective and horizon and also of shading only began to appear under Western influence in the 19th century. In early Burmese manuscript paintings there is great attention to detail and faces have an individuality of expression that by the late 19th century had largely been lost. Scenes in later manuscripts also lose their crowded vitality and become more spaced and sequential.

The subjects most frequently depicted in Burmese manuscript painting are scenes from the *Rāmāyaṇa* (see fig. 15), the Life of the Buddha (see fig. 16), the *jātakas* (stories of the Buddha's previous lives), Buddhist cosmology and court entertainments, such as festivals, boatraces, games, cockfighting, elephant-training, royal processions and ceremonies. Some manuscripts record objects in use at the palace, costumes, hairstyles, buildings, royal barges etc and thus provide information about the kingdom's sumptuary laws. A feature of Burmese representations of the life of the Buddha and of the *jātakas* is that the artist depicted them in contemporary terms, so that scenes portray the costumes and hairstyles, architecture and life of the time in which they were painted. Thus the Buddha in one of his previous incarnations may be depicted aboard

15. *Abduction of Sita* (detail); miniature from a Burmese *Rāmāyaṇa* manuscript, mid-19th century (London, British Library, Or. MS. 14178, fol. 10)

16. *Descent from the Heaven of the Thirty-three Gods*; miniature from a Burmese *Life of the Buddha* manuscript, early 19th century (London, India Office Library, Or. MS. 5757, fols 17–18)

a paddle-steamer, Western figures may appear, and palace structures may be roofed in corrugated iron. It is extremely rare for an illustrated manuscript to be signed or dated, and although the names of several court artists are known, few manuscripts can be attributed to a particular individual, so that this incorporation of contemporary elements is an important stylistic aid to the dating of Burmese manuscripts. The composition, use of perspective and range of colours also assist in dating, as does comparison with dated temple murals.

Most surviving Burmese painted *parabaik* date from the mid- to late 19th century, with comparatively few examples attributable to the late 18th or early 19th century. Most manuscripts were produced at the Burmese court under royal or official patronage. Artists worked in teams on manuscript series of the Life of the Buddha, the *jātaka*s and scenes of court festivities, with several artists contributing to a single manuscript according to their individual talents. It is known that King Mindon (*reg* 1853–78) employed 15 to 18 artists, of whom the most celebrated was U Kya Nyunt (*d* 1881). U Kya Nyunt's son, Hsaya Sa (Tsa), succeeded him briefly as court artist, and a former pupil, Hsaya Chone, later became pre-eminent. The last reigning monarch of the Konbaung dynasty, King Thibaw (*reg* 1878–85), had two Italian painters in his employ at court. Burmese manuscript painting did not cease entirely with the British annexation of Upper Burma in 1886 and the consequent loss of royal patronage. It lingered on into the 20th century and increasingly adapted its style to the more limited market provided by Western and secular patrons.

BIBLIOGRAPHY

U Tin Lwin: 'Old Burmese Painting', *Oriens Extrem.*, ii/2 (1974), pp. 237–59 [Eng. trans. of *Shei yo Myan-ma baji* (Rangoon, *c.* 1966)]

P. M. Herbert: *The Life of the Buddha* (London, 1993)

PATRICIA M. HERBERT

3. MODERN. After the annexation of Upper Burma by Britain in 1885, most of the court artists began to tour the country, painting idealized portraits of royalty that were exhibited at religious and secular functions. Decorated fans and other items for the Raj tourists were also sold through foreign dealers specializing in Burmese crafts. In the 1890s U Khanti, the 'hermit' of Mandalay Hill, regrouped some of the artists, and under his direction hundreds of Buddhist scenes were painted for buildings attached to important temples in Upper Burma. Among the artists Saya Aye was noted for his portraits, which were painted using both Western and traditional techniques.

The visit to Burma about 1900 of R. Talbot Kelly and J. R. Middleton (painters of watercolours and oils respectively) is considered by many to have been a turning-point in the Westernization of painting styles in Rangoon, with the reputations of local artists gaining considerably from their association with the two men. The leading Burmese watercolour artists of the day were M. T. Hla, Ba Ohn and Mg Gyi, who exhibited at some of Rangoon's leading hotels. In 1920 the first government-sponsored Arts and Crafts Exhibition was held at the Jubilee Hall in Rangoon. Twelve artists, whose works totalled 120 paintings in both watercolours and oil, are known to have exhibited. It was also in the 1920s that U Ba Nyan and U Ba Zaw were sent to study art in England. Realistic paintings of native scenes in oil and watercolour became popular (see fig. 17). Sales, however, were made mostly to resident Europeans and tourists, with the moat at Mandalay and the Shwe-dagon in Rangoon being the bestselling subjects.

The years after World War II were dominated by the artists Yadanabon Mg Su, a watercolourist, and U Ngwe Gaing, an oil painter, who, among others, specialized in paintings of ethnic groups and country scenes. In the late 1950s and early 1960s the annual art exhibition at the Burma Translation Society attracted the best painters in the land, with Western-influenced paintings now being sought after and bought by the Burmese.

In 1963 the Council for Art and Sculpture was founded, with headquarters at Mandalay and Rangoon. Watercolours predominated at exhibitions, but by the mid-1970s the numbers had fallen and there was an alarming drop in quality, while oil paintings became extremely popular. Established watercolourists expressed concern, and in 1977 the Council succeeded in arranging the first exhibition of watercolours in Rangoon. At Monywa, in Upper Burma, members of the Chindwin Yekyi Society are noted for their outstanding work in this medium. Although traditional values have been revived, there are many Burmese artists who have experimented with the variety of styles prevalent in the West, and some have adopted them permanently.

BIBLIOGRAPHY

R. T. Kelly: *Burma* (London, 1905)
J. Laughlin: *Perspective of Burma* (New York, 1958)
U Hla Tin Htun: *Art and Sculpture Bulletin for 1979* (Rangoon, 1979)
P. Herbert: *The Buddha is Born* (New York, 1985)

NOEL F. SINGER

VI. Textiles.

Evidence for the history of Burmese textiles is scant. Chinese sources describe clothing in the Pyu period (5th–8th centuries AD); stone inscriptions of the Pagan period (1044–1287) refer to cotton and silk; fragments of painted cloth banners and cloth manuscript wrappers of the period have been found. European descriptions date from as early as the 16th century but are more numerous from the 18th and 19th centuries.

Until the 20th century most cloth was produced in the home for local use. Both in the plains and among the hill peoples, women and unmarried girls spun yarn and wove cloth for clothing, blankets and bags. Weaving was done on back-strap looms, tensioned by the weaver's own body, and light frame looms. Cotton, hemp, wool and silk were traditionally used. Cotton is grown in the central Mandalay–Sagaing area and by some hill people on slash-and-burn plots. Hemp is grown in remote hill areas. Wool was traditionally used by such groups as the Kachins in the north for the weft yarns of their cloths, but it has been replaced to some extent by acrylic. Silk was mainly imported from India or China in yarn form and dyed locally, but some silk was produced in the Pegu Yoma hill range east of the lower Irrawaddy. In the 20th century natural dyes gave way to synthetic dyes, but indigo and lac are still used by a few hill groups.

Mon, Shan, Arakanese and Burman rulers at different periods established communities of specialist weavers and embroiderers and imported luxury cloths from India and China. Weaving centres that probably had such origins include those at Amarapura, first capital (1782–1823) of the Konbaung dynasty, south of Mandalay; Henzada, north-east of Rangoon; and Tavoy in the Mon area to the south—all still known for silk production—and Shwedaung, south of Prome, which was formerly a major silk centre.

17. Lar Ban: *Burmese Village Scene*, watercolour, 229×178 mm, *c.* 1935 (London, private collection)

Domestic production continues among some hill communities, but many 'traditional' handloom cloths are produced commercially for regional markets in such centres as Amarapura and the Inle Lake region in the Shan States. The former silk-weaving centre of Shwedaung produces plaid cotton cloths on a large scale. There is still a demand for handloom textiles in the hills. In the plains men still use mainly Burmese handloom silks and cottons in geometrical designs, stripes and checks, although women favour floral patterns and imported textiles.

1. Special woven cloths.

(i) Supplementary weft cloths. Arakan is known for men's cloths with strong geometrical patterns composed of combinations of stripes, squares and circles. They are created by the application of a loose, continuous supplementary weft on a plain, striped or check ground. Black is used on a lighter ground, white or light colours on a dark ground. Main centres of production are Kyaukpyu, Thandwei, Sittwe and Sandoway. 'Arakan' cloths are also produced in Amarapura and in Mudon, south of Moulmein (Tenasserim). Gangaw produces silk and cotton textiles with a light supplementary weft on a dark ground, men's designs having small repetitive patterns in a diamond frame. Arakan women's cloths have small traditional and European floral motifs and Burmese *acheik* (wave) designs (*see* §(ii) below); Gangaw cloths have flowers, peacocks and swastikas.

Karen, Shan, Kachin and Chin and other hill communities, like related groups in northern Thailand and Laos, use the supplementary weft technique, sometimes with ikat, embroidery or appliqué, on cloths that have a plain ground or are patterned with alternating colour stripes. Among the Karens the woman's blouse may be decorated with diamond patterns. Supplementary weft is also used on men's headcloths and modern sarongs. The Shan women's shirts and headdresses have patterns of large and small diamonds filled with ornate swastikas and stylized flower patterns. Kachin women's sarongs and shoulder-bags are decorated with geometric, zigzag, diamond and

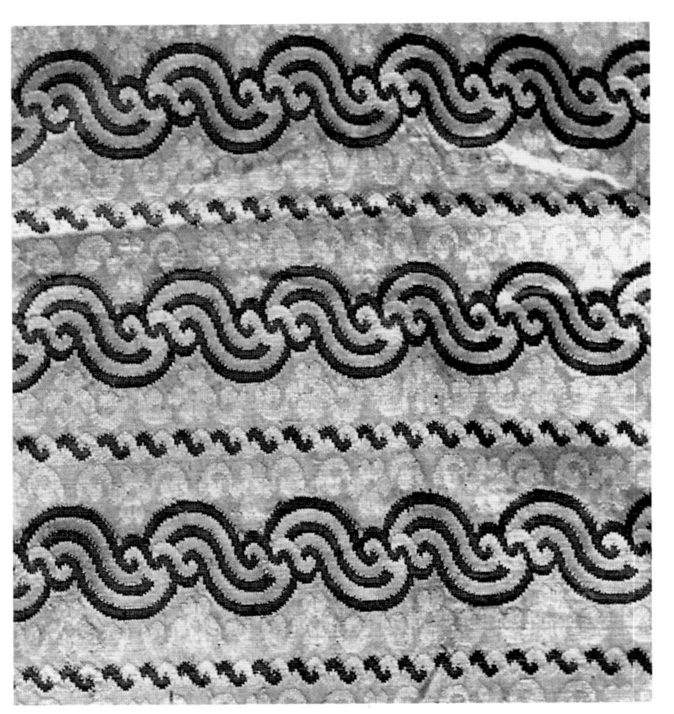

18. Detail of a child's lower garment (*hta-mein*) of *lùn-taya* weave, from Mandalay Palace, *c.* 1890 (Brighton, Art Gallery and Museum)

Chinese-inspired key patterns. The Haka Chin weave silk and cotton blankets with chains of diamonds and zigzags on coloured warp stripes.

(ii) Tapestry weave. Burma's most famous specialist silk cloth is a horizontal wave-patterned silk cloth in interlocking tapestry weave (see fig. 18). It is commonly referred to as *lùn-taya* ('100 shuttles') or *acheik* ('wave design'). This cloth is woven in Amarapura. The *acheik* pattern consists of bands of parallel S-shaped wavy and zigzag lines. Complicated wave designs may have up to five or seven stripes. Frequent colours are reds, purples, pinks, greens and yellows; two or three shades of a small colour range are often used together, sometimes with silver thread.

The origin of the cloth is unclear. Wave-like patterns can be traced back to the Bronze Age Dongson culture in what is now northern Vietnam. The technique may have been introduced by weavers brought to Burma from neighbouring Manipur in India in the second half of the 18th century, following the conquest of that region, but it is more likely to have been introduced from China via Yunnan. The weaving of *acheik* cloths was subject to sumptuary rules established by the court at Mandalay. Since the fall of the Konbaung dynasty in 1885 *acheik* cloths have come to be used for wear on special occasions by all who can afford them. The same weaving technique is also used occasionally for silk hangings.

(iii) Ikat. In ikat cloths a pattern is produced by tie-dyeing either the warp or the weft threads (occasionally both) before weaving. Old weft ikats are woven from imported silk in weft-faced twill weave in subdued yellows, reds and greens with hook, rhomb and diagonal cross patterns. They were probably inspired by royal Cambodian weft ikat cloths that imitated the Indian *patola* (*see* INDIAN SUBCONTINENT, §VII, 3(iii)(a)) and were used by Shan princes. The industry was revived and modernized in the 1930s and now uses lightweight Chinese imported silk in twill and plain weaves, together with chemical dyes and fly shuttles. Weft ikats are called *zìn-me* (Burmese for Chiang Mai, over the border in Thailand). They have close-patterned, repetitive designs, sometimes with border patterns and vertical panels; or sometimes modern designs.

There are several centres of ikat production. The Intha of Inle Lake in the Shan States, who originally came from Tavoy (Mon State), are notable ikat weavers. Twill-weave weft ikats of Indian cotton yarn chemically dyed and warp ikat designs on a striped weft are produced in San Khan, near Mandalay. At Kyi Thei near Shwedaung (northern Pegu) cotton warp ikats are made with simple floral patterns on plain backgrounds and streaking zigzag designs like those of San Khan. For the Sgaw and Pwo Karens in the south, who create ikat cloths incorporating a python motif for women's sarongs, the production of ikat is subject to secret ritual.

2. APPLIQUÉ AND EMBROIDERY. Embroidered and appliqué hangings (*kalaga*) of silk, velvet or coloured felt with added sequin and tinsel decoration were produced in the Rangoon region in the second half of the 19th century (see fig. 19 below). The technique probably derives from both Indian and European sources. *Kalaga* cloths became popular among Burmese, who commissioned them for festive occasions and offered them as merit-making gifts to monasteries. They were displayed in temples and monasteries, in private houses and gardens and on carts. *Kalaga* depict scenes from the *jātaka* stories (previous lives of the Buddha) and the *Rāmāyaṇa* (Sanskrit epic of Rama) as well as secular themes and have such decorative motifs as the peacock. The designs resemble paintings in the treatment of narrative, figures and landscape.

In the 19th century sequin-embroidered decoration was also used on court costume. Among the hill peoples today the Shans use some embroidery on women's skirts. The Kachins use needle decoration in imitation of brocade weaving and decorate the edges of garments with embroidery and pompoms, silver bosses and coins and adorn their bags with silver ornaments and tassels. Tibeto-Burman groups near the Chinese border apply pieces of Chinese plain or brocade silk trim. The Lahu people trim the edges of coats and sarongs, the Akha and the Palaung decorate cloth with colourful appliqué. The Karens embroider with cotton yarns and apply rick-rack (decorative braid) in chevrons, zigzags, rosettes and stars, as well as the shiny white seeds of the grass *Coix lachryma-jobi* ('Job's tears') as necklace beads.

3. IMPORTED TEXTILES. Chinese accounts indicate that silk was imported into Burma from China in the Tang period (618–907 AD) or earlier. It is likely that some cotton was also imported from India in the same period. Sixteenth-century European accounts show that the Mon

kingdom (13th–16th centuries) centred on Pegu in southern Burma was on the main Arab trade route in South-east Asia and that it imported printed and woven cotton and silk cloths from Bengal, the Coromandel Coast and Gujarat. In the same period plaid cloths, gold and silver thread and some embroidery techniques and styles were similarly introduced into Burma. From the 19th century until the mid-20th some British mill-produced cloth was imported. Subsequently the main source of imported cloth has been China. Among the hill peoples of the Shan Hills Chinese silk brocade and European red flannel have been used in small quantities as appliqué decoration.

BIBLIOGRAPHY

J. Lowry: *Burmese Art* (London, 1974)
M. A. Stanislaw: *Kalagas: The Wall Hangings of South-east Asia* (Menlo Park, 1987)
S. Fraser-Lu: *Handwoven Textiles of South-east Asia* (Singapore, 1988)
R. Maxwell: *Textiles of South-east Asia: Tradition, Trade and Transformation* (Melbourne, 1990)
S. Conway: *Thai Textiles* (London, 1992)

VII. Dress and body decoration.

Burmese traditional dress is similar to that of other South-east Asian countries. Paintings, sculptures and travellers' accounts give some idea of court dress in earlier periods. Its main elements—a wrapped or tubular, sewn lower garment and stole, a breast- or shoulder-cloth and a sewn jacket—relate respectively to the Indian and Chinese traditions. Modern dress is an adaptation of 19th-century forms. The wearing of jewellery plays an important part in Burmese life and different ethnic groups wear different forms and designs. A notable type of body ornamentation in Burma is tattooing.

1. DRESS. Everyday garments at the Mandalay court of the Konbaung dynasty in the 19th century (see fig. 19) were the same as those of the people, though of costlier material. Women wore a long rectangular waistcloth (*htamein*) folded to overlap slightly in front, consisting of three horizontal panels of cloth sewn together—a waist-band, a colourful central panel of cotton or silk woven in *lùn-taya* or *acheik* weave (*see* §VI, 1(ii) above) and a train of light-coloured silk or cotton. Above the waist a semi-transparent, tight-fitting jacket (*eìn-gyi*) of muslin or lace was worn over a long breast-cloth (*tabet*) of silk or cotton. Men wore a double-length waistcloth (*pahsò*), sometimes of *acheik* design, with a large portion of the cloth draped in folds at the front for formal wear or passed through the legs for more active wear. An *eìn-gyi* of muslin or quilted cotton and a turban (*gaung-baung*) completed the costume.

In the 20th century both men and women began to wear a tubular sarong (*long-gyi*), worn folded into a front pleat tucked into the waist or fastened with a knot. Women also began to wear a fitted blouse with or without sleeves, which may be fastened Chinese-style diagonally across the front with jewellery studs or cloth buttons; men wear a collarless Chinese-style jacket (both are called *eìn-gyi*). In the cities some men adopted Western dress. On special occasions women wear a silk (sometimes *acheik*) *lon-gyi* and fitted blouse with the *tabet* as a stole, and men wear the *pahsò* and collarless jacket and a *gaung-baung*.

The Konbaung kings wore ceremonial dress for state occasions, similar to that of the kings of Thailand but

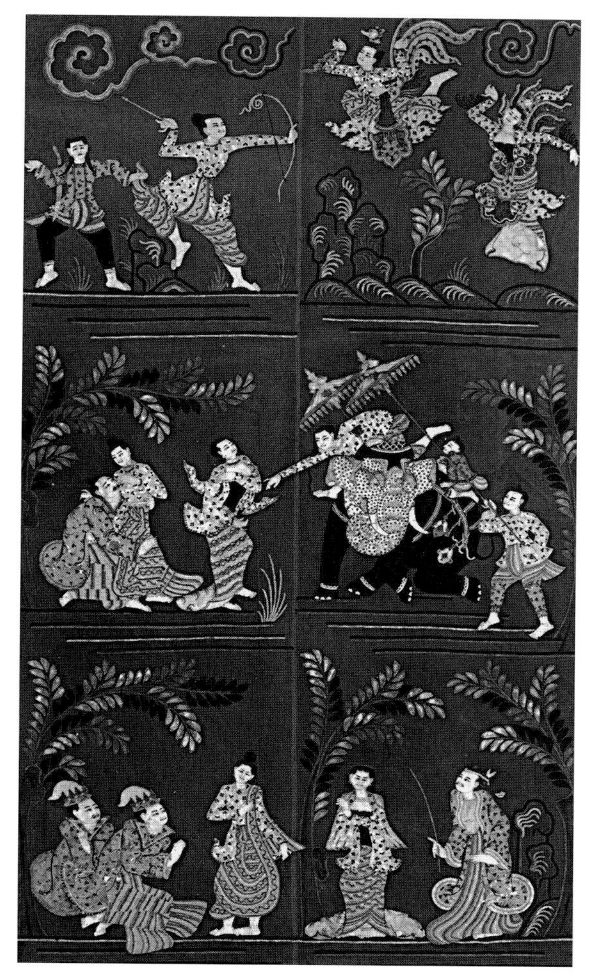

19. Figures in the everyday court dress of the Konbaung dynasty (1752–1885) as depicted on a detail from a textile hanging (*kalaga*) of green wool with wool and cotton appliqué, silver sequins and other ornamentation, 3.66×2.67 m, *c.* 1880 (London, Victoria and Albert Museum)

different in finish. These robes of state consisted of gold and silk thread appliqué and jewel-studded embroidery on flat and layered costumes shaped and stiffened by stretching fabric over bamboo frames, with frontal pieces ending in fishtails, the cloud collar motif and winged epaulettes. Similar decoration ornamented the elaborate headdresses of kings, queens and ministers. These costumes were made of Indian and Chinese silk and gold brocades, *maśru*s (silk and cotton mixtures), muslins, or European, Turkish, Chinese or Russian velvets, embroidered with gold thread and sequins. The style was possibly derived from sculptural depictions of draped cloths on royal images of the god-king of the Khmer Vishnu and subsequent South-east Asian traditions, with additional features from representations of *bodhisattva*s and costumes of the Mongolian, Central Asian and Chinese traditions.

The traditional clothing of the hill peoples is related to that of the peoples of Nagaland, northern Thailand and

Laos. Women of each group have a distinctive dress, consisting of various open or tubular-sewn wrap-around lower garments (*lon-gyi*) of different lengths and jackets of varying length, cut and decoration. Additional features are cane belts, sashes and cloth leggings. Men wear either *lon-gyi*s, often similar to those worn by plainsmen, a type of baggy 'hill' trousers or Western trousers. Distinctive headdresses are worn by Karen men, Shan men and women, Pa O, Lahu and Palaung women.

BIBLIOGRAPHY

R. A. Innes: *Costumes of Upper Burma and the Shan States* (Halifax, 1957)

F. Franklin and D. Swallow: 'Identifying with the Gods: Burmese Court Costume', *Hali Annu.* (1994), pp. 48–61

N. F. Singer: 'Maha Bandula the Younger: Burmese Court Costumes in the West', *A. Asia*, xxiv (1994), no. 6, pp. 101–9

D. A. SWALLOW

2. JEWELLERY. In Burma ear ornaments are especially significant. Burman girls formerly had their ears pierced on coming of age. The holes in the lobes were widened with earplugs until there was sufficient room to insert prized cylinders, known as *na doung*. Amber earplugs were also valued, and sometimes bundles of German-made glass tubes were inserted in the lobes. At the court of King Thebaw (*reg* 1878–85) in Mandalay there were strict rules concerning the use of gold ear-tubes set with jewels. High-born women also wore finger-rings set with diamonds, emeralds or rubies, while royal dancers wore gilded head-dresses and leg ornaments. Elaborate jewellery is worn by most of the peoples of the border zone between Burma, Thailand and Laos known as the Golden Triangle. Jewellery is often worn to display the family's wealth, and the finest pieces may be seen during New Year festivities. Lisu women, for example, wear black vests covered with silver buttons, over which are worn cloth collars with many dangles. They also wear layers of neckrings and necklaces, as well as earrings linked by silver chains and wide bracelets with bevelled edges. Akha women are equally splendidly attired and are known for their tall headdresses festooned with chased and repoussé silverwork. They also wear multicoloured strings of beads round their headdresses or as necklaces. Lahu women are distinguished by their red and white beaded necklaces. Various Karen groups also incorporate Chinese beads into female jewellery, which may include silver tiaras, hairpins and bracelets, boar's tusk combs, bracelets made of white buttons and brass and copper bracelets. Padaung women traditionally encase their necks in metal rings that press down on their shoulders and give the impression that their necks have been elongated. In the 1980s Padaung women began to cross the border into Thailand to have their neckrings removed under medical supervision.

Jewellery plays an important part in courtship rituals: bracelets, for example, are exchanged by Lisu courting couples. It is also believed that a person possessed by a weretiger can make the essence of the beast move into a valuable object, such as a piece of jewellery. The jewellery may then be disposed of on a piece of waste ground, but anybody who picks it up risks becoming possessed in turn by the weretiger. Among the Haka Chins, who live on Burma's north-western borders, jewellery is included in the payments made before marriage. Prestige is accorded families who own old and beautiful beads; these are known as *pumtek* and have a high exchange value. Unmarried Haka Chin women wear necklaces decorated with *pumtek*, as well as wooden hairpins decorated with red, black and grey geometric designs or made in the form of models of weapons.

BIBLIOGRAPHY

G. T. Gascoigne: *Among Pagodas and Fair Ladies: An Account of a Tour through Burma* (London, 1898)

E. Lewis and P. Lewis: *Peoples of the Golden Triangle* (London, 1984)

J. Mack, ed.: *Ethnic Jewellery* (London, 1988) [intro.], pp. 42–65; pp. 57, 66–115

MICHAEL HITCHCOCK

3. TATTOO DESIGNS. The art of decorating the body with tattoos is said to have been introduced, as a form of protection, by the monk U Ottama Sri of Srikshetra (modern Hmawza), capital of the Pyus, some time before the 8th century AD. The designs, originally simple, evolved into representations of animals, birds, mythological creatures and vegetal patterns. By the 18th century tattooing had become an accepted part of initiation into manhood for all classes. Women encouraged it, for they believed that if a young man were brave enough to go through the ordeal he would make a better provider and be prepared to face the hardships life might thrust upon him.

The tattooing ceremony, which was held after the end of the rains in November, was accompanied by elaborate preparations. A decorated structure, to which only males were admitted, was built with two entrances. The doorway chosen by a young man conveyed to the tattooist whether the patterns required were purely ornamental or of a protective nature. Female friends sang and shouted encouragement and showed their appreciation if the initiate emerged unaided, slapping his biceps to show his bravery in the traditional challenge threat.

By the 1880s a choice of over 60 designs had been created for the thigh area alone. Ovals composed of either words or rays enclosed a variety of characters, including alchemists, dancing demons, yawning cats, hump-backed pigs and peacocks. Personal selection resulted in an individual overall design for every male (fig. 20). Since the written Burmese character lends itself to the formation of figures, spells were made up in the shape of Buddha images and celestial beings. These were always tattooed above the waist, usually on monks and members of religious sects. Magic squares, protective deities, tigers and dragons were also tattooed on appropriate parts of the body using a stylus (fig. 20b) to ward off attacks by wild beasts or reptiles. Occasionally the ink was mixed with elaborate concoctions composed of rare and expensive herbs that were beyond the means of most people. Love charm designs were popular. Males had themselves tattooed with a variety of potent designs on the lower part of the body. Beautiful young women, afraid of falling victim to enchantment, countered by having the tips of their tongues and fingers marked with protective spells.

Young men called up for military service were tattooed with their regimental symbol, which might be a cannon, a horse or a demon. Certain grades of civil servant were also tattooed on the neck with the palace mark for easy identification. Criminals had the names of their crimes permanently tattooed on their forehead, chest and palms. Felons were ringed on each cheek, making them outcasts

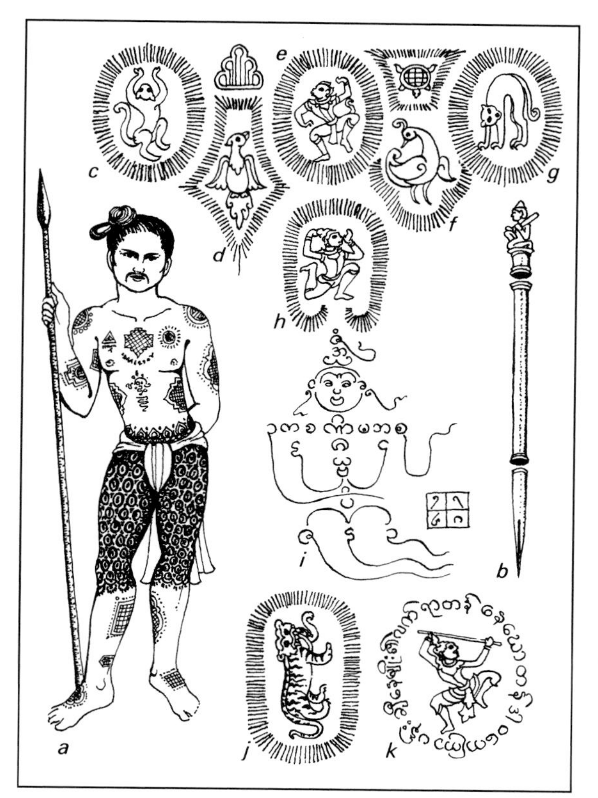

20. Burmese tattoos: (a) tattooed figure; (b) tattoo instrument; (c) yawning cat; (d) bird; (e) monkey; (f) bird; (g) arched cat; (h) demon; (i) cabbalistic design of a goddess; (j) tiger; (k) demon; copied by the author from various 19th-century manuscripts (Burma, private collections)

for life, forced to do work other people shunned. Burglars had magical cats and other symbols, cunningly hidden among innocuous tendrils and birds.

Tattooing in the old style and the symbolism of the once popular patterns are now obsolete. In larger towns and at fairgrounds the introduction of battery-operated instruments from the West has produced a rash of tattoo parlours offering 'modern' designs that have little affinity with the traditional arts of the country.

BIBLIOGRAPHY

A. Flytche: *Burma Past and Present* (London, 1878/*R* New York, 1963/*R* London, 1989)

J. G. Scott [Shway Yoe]: *The Burman: His Life and Notions* (London, 1882/*R* New York, 1963/*R* Arran, 1989)

Father Sangermano: *The Burmese Empire* (London, 1893)

E. Hart: *Picturesque Burma* (London, 1897)

H. T. White: *Burma* (Cambridge, 1923)

Aung Thein: *Myanmar Htogwin* [Burmese tattoo] (Rangoon, 1986)

N. F. Singer: 'Tattoo Weights from Burma', *A. Asia*, lxxxviii/2 (1988), pp. 70–79

VIII. Theatre.

The principal form of theatre in Burma is dance drama in which the actors wear masks. Other categories of dance are folk dances, and trance dances traditionally associated with *nat* (spirit) worship. Each of these three styles has its own distinctive set of costumes, which follow traditional designs. Another typical Burmese genre is the marionette show, which enjoyed great popularity and illustrious patronage in the past but is now nearly extinct.

1. MASKS AND COSTUMES. The earliest reference to dancing is in a Chinese report of a tribute mission from Burma to the Tang emperor in AD 802. The dancers, sumptuously dressed and adorned with jewels, performed to music provided by an orchestra of 19 different instruments. Wall-paintings, terracotta plaques and stone inscriptions indicate that subsequently music and dancing continued to feature prominently in the life of the country.

Masks of animals, birds and demons were first used in religious pageants (*nibat-khin*), which flourished from the 15th century to the early part of the 20th century. The costumed players travelled in bullock carts from village to village, where they acted scenes from the life of the historical Buddha and *jātaka* stories of his previous lives.

It was not until the Burmese conquest in 1767 of Ayutthaya, the Thai capital, and the subsequent introduction by captured court dancers of dance drama based on the *Rāmāyaṇa* that the age of the mask really began. The novelty and presentation of this dance drama so impressed the Burmese court that for the first ten years or so the design of the costumes and masks remained Thai. Inevitably, Burmese influences crept in until the two styles became quite distinct. This is noticeable in the shape of the headdress worn by most of the characters in the epic. The Thai crown tapers to a thin point, whereas the Burmese crown is thicker and shorter, a difference that is echoed in the temple architecture of the two countries.

Most Burmese masks are made of woven bamboo, cloth or paper, which is moulded with a mixture of sawdust, ash and lacquer. Once dry, the mask is painted, gilded and ornamented with tiny pieces of multicoloured glass. On the completion of masks that portray important characters, the dancers perform a 'consecration' ceremony that is believed to endow these inanimate objects with a life of their own. Masks that represent good and evil forces are kept apart from each other. The two groups of masks are arranged on racks decorated with offerings of fruit and flowers. During a performance, the actors who take part also keep to the appropriate side of the stage.

Three 19th-century manuscripts containing designs of masks from the *Rāmāyaṇa* (see fig. 21) have survived. Two are in a private collection in Burma and the third is in Dublin (Chester Beatty Lib., 1201).

A study of dancing figures in wall-paintings suggests that costume became more elaborate as time went by, culminating in robes of extravagant design by the second half of the 19th century. The quality of the cloth depended on the status of the performer, and court dancers wore apparel made of rich foreign materials. Sequins for decorating ceremonial and theatrical dress at court were imported from India or punched out of thin sheets of gold, silver, tin or brass by goldsmiths in the palace workshops, the less valuable metals being worn by dancers. In the 18th century members of itinerant troupes used ornaments of gilded brass and the gold and green wing-cases of beetles to decorate their costumes.

Burmese plays are peopled by a rich assortment of characters from supernatural beings, heroes and princesses

21. Masks used in Burmese dance drama (*Rāmāyaṇa*): (a) Ravana; (b) Rama; (c) Hanuman; (d) Sita; copied by the author from tracings and drawings by Saya Saing and U Shwe Taung (Rangoon, private collection) of the original 19th-century manuscripts (untraced)

in distress to animals, each wearing a costume that can be instantly recognized by the audience. Most of the stories are set in the legendary Indian kingdoms, but the players always appear in their own native dress.

The traditional costume of a male dancer for an energetic dance consists of a tight-fitting jacket and calf-length trousers, over which is worn a *pahsò* (waistcloth) tucked up between the legs. For singing duets and dancing with a female dancer, the long piece of material in front, part of the *pahsò*, is left hanging from the waist. Depending on his role, he wears either a *gaung-baung* (turban) or a pointed headdress. By the beginning of the 19th century, principal male characters had begun wearing large collars with scalloped edges and, at the waist, richly embroidered panels (*bon*) that hung down in curling, flame-like patterns. This was an amalgam of ideas borrowed from the Thai court, Burmese paintings and carved figures of celestial beings, often found within temple precincts.

The costume of the female dancer has remained basically the same for 250 years or more, only the richness of the material and jewellery distinguishing the heroine from her maid. It consists of a tight long-sleeved jacket, open in front. The trailing skirt, secured under the armpits or around the hips, is often enhanced with a richly decorated breast-cloth. Strings of pearls and beads are worn in profusion. The dancer rarely wears a headdress, unless she is playing a named role. Her long hair is dressed in an elaborately knotted coiffure, encircled with a tiara of tiny flowers and jewelled hair ornaments. Since the 18th century, the *pawa* (shawl) has been an important accessory employed to enhance the dancer's supple movements.

BIBLIOGRAPHY

G. E. Harvey: *History of Burma* (London, 1925)
Maung Htin Aung: *Burmese Drama* (Oxford, 1956)
Dances and Music from Burma, Ministry of Union Culture (Rangoon, 1957)
G. H. Luce: *Old Burma: Early Pagan*, 3 vols (Locust Valley, NY, 1969) [*Artibus Asiae* suppl. 25]

NOEL F. SINGER

2. PUPPETS. Unlike the rod- and shadow-puppets more common elsewhere in South-east Asia, the Burmese puppet tradition uses marionettes (*yok theì*). A single marionette may be manipulated by as many as 40 strings, enabling a skilled puppeteer to endow a figure with extraordinary grace.

There were marionettes in Burma at least as early as the 15th century. A poem of that date alludes to the way the puppeteer pulls the strings to lower and raise the puppet. In the early 19th century, King Bodawgyi's Minister for Performances promulgated regulations for the conduct of marionette performances that are still observed. Later in the century the court in Mandalay supported two marionette troupes, one by appointment to the king, the other to the queen. A puppet troupe was said to have enjoyed greater liberty to criticize the king's policies than other performers (Withey). However, with the loss of royal patronage and the eclipse of the aristocracy following Upper Burma's annexation by the British, the art form slowly declined. The last famous troupe, headed by Shweibou Tin Maung, disbanded shortly after his death in 1980. Temple festival committees that until the 1980s included puppet plays as part of their annual celebrations hire other types of troupe or show films instead. A few traditional performances still take place, as well as brief shows for tourists, but many old puppets (as well as cheaply made new ones) are being sold off within Burma and abroad. As puppeteers train ever fewer students, it is unlikely the tradition will last.

The jointed puppets are made of wood and cloth (see fig. 22). The principal human characters, such as the prince and princess, and the horse and the *nat* (spirit) were traditionally made of the light wood called *yamaneí* (*Gmelina arborea*). In lesser puppets only the head, or the head, hands and feet, were wooden; their torsos, upper arms and thighs were of cloth stuffed with cotton. The carved heads and limbs were coated in layers of chalk mixed with the resin of the tamar or neem tree (*Azadirachta indica*): the sticky fluid bound the chalk to the surface. Once dry, the features were painted in red and finished in black.

Typically puppets range in height from 150 mm to 650 mm and within a set vary according to an iconographic principle which makes their size inversely proportional to status and refinement. The leading prince and princess are the smallest in stature. They have pale complexions, refined features and luxurious costumes. Ogres and servants are larger and coarser. Ogres are painted in bright colours,

22. Puppet figure, painted wood and embroidered silk decorated with sequins, glass beads and pieces of mirror, h. 635 mm, Mandalay, late 19th century (London, Victoria and Albert Museum)

servants dress in old-fashioned commoners' clothes. The princely hero is clean-shaven, but other male characters often have bushy moustaches and eyebrows; the diminutive, bejewelled princess contrasts with her large, round-eyed maidservants in their plain costumes.

The subject-matter of marionette plays is drawn from the life of the Buddha, his previous lives (*jātaka* stories), tales of mythical heroes, Burmese royal chronicles and, after the Burmese conquest of the Thai kingdom of Ayutthaya in 1767, from the Thai version of the Hindu epic the *Rāmāyaṇa*. In the past a puppet troupe would have from four to ten stories in a season's repertory. A full troupe consists of about twenty-five people: four puppeteers, about twelve people to speak the puppets' parts, seven musicians and one or two lighting technicians. Formerly, female parts were sung and spoken by men.

Traditionally, marionette performances were held on a large stage, 12 m wide tapering to 6.5 m at the rear. In later years a less elaborate stage came to be used. A backdrop was hung behind the puppets and another curtain above the performance area, to hide the puppeteers from view. A full-scale performance might last for two or three successive nights. The musicians started to play at seven in the evening, the puppets began to dance at nine, and the performance ended at sunrise the next morning.

BIBLIOGRAPHY

J. A. Stewart: 'The Burmese Stage', *J. Royal Soc. A.*, lxxxii (1939), pp. 761–76

U Ba Cho Deedok: 'Burmese Marionettes', *Burmese Culture: General and Particular*, ed. U Khin Zaw (Rangoon, 1951)

K. Sein and J. Withey: *The Great Po Sein* (Bloomington, 1965)

Hla Thamein: *Myan-má youk-theì thabin* [Burmese marionette theatre] (Rangoon, 1968); trans. with additions by A. Bruns and Hla Thamein as *Birmanisches Marionettentheater* (Berlin, 1990)

'Youk thei' [Marionettes], *Myan-má swe-soun kyàn* [Burmese encyclopedia], xi (Rangoon, 1970)

WARD KEELER

IX. Other arts.

The Burmese excel in ceramics, lacquerwork, ivory carving and a variety of other art forms and in the production of a range of functional but beautiful objects (betel sets, loom pulleys, weights), many of which have become collectors' items. In this section a selection of outstanding and unusual art forms and objects is discussed.

1. Bells. 2. Betel sets. 3. Boats. 4. Ceramics. 5. Coins. 6. Ephemeral art. 7. Gilded glass inlay. 8. Ivory. 9. Karen drums. 10. Lacquer. 11. Loom pulleys. 12. Musical instruments. 13. Silver. 14. Weapons. 15. Weights. 16. Wood-carving.

1. BELLS. Several types of idiophone are used in Burma for both sacred and profane purposes. Small, hollow bronze bells with interior clappers are attached to the metal umbrellas (*hti*) that crown the spires of stupas and to the eaves of temples and monasteries. Larger royal examples may warrant a separate pavilion. The sound of these bells, whether initiated by wind or man, is believed to call forth the spirits (*nat*) of heaven and earth to witness the devotions of the Buddhist faithful. Large bells are located near alms chests and are struck by donors when they give money. The more elaborate examples of this type usually have four semicircular suspension lugs in the form of serpent deities (*nāga*) or protective lions (*chinthei*). Pali or Burmese inscriptions on a bell's exterior may record the date of casting, the donor's name, the desire to achieve nirvana and curses on those who would destroy the bell. Enormous bells have been used in Buddhist ritual since the Pagan period, as shown by the massive bell-pillars standing outside the 12th-century That-byin-nyu Temple (*see* PAGAN, §2(iv)). Bronze bell production has been located at Amarapura, near Mandalay, since the 18th century. In 1790 King Bodawpaya commissioned the great bell at Mingun near Mandalay, the largest bell ever successfully cast. It is 3.7 m in height and 5 m in width and weighs 87 tons. There are similar but smaller bells in the compounds of major Buddhist monuments, such as the Shwe-dagon in Rangoon.

Suspended, triangular percussion plaques, which are struck with a wooden or staghorn mallet, may also be used in Buddhist ritual. The contour of these plaques is associated by devotees with the seated Buddha or the crescent moon.

Although bells are not found within the Burmese home, they are used for domesticated animals: hung round the necks of elephants, horses and cattle and, among the Shans in the east of the country, mounted in a rattan case on the shoulders of pack animals to monitor the movement of trade caravans.

BIBLIOGRAPHY

J. G. Scott [Shway Yoe]: *The Burman: His Life and Notions* (London, 1882/*R* New York, 1963/*R* Arran, 1989)

M. Ferrars and B. Ferrars: *Burma* (London, 1901)

C. Sachs: *Die Musikinstrumente Birmas und Assams im K. Ethnographischen Museum zu München* (Munich, 1917)

RICHARD M. COOLER

2. BETEL SETS. Betel chewing, an ancient and widespread habit, is an integral part of Burmese culture and social customs. A typical betel set consists of a large box with individual containers for the ingredients, cutters for paring the areca-nuts and a serving tray. The material, style and decoration of a betel set vary according to the wealth and status of the user. Lacquer is the primary material used, although silver is popular for small containers. Ceremonial betel sets are made of silver or gold and inset with precious stones.

A characteristic lacquer betel box is made of woven bamboo, cylindrically shaped with a cover approximately the same size as the body and fitted with trays and small containers. The size of the box varies, depending on whether it is for personal or collective use.

Designs are traditionally black and red and characterized by complexity, repetition, panelling and horizontal rings. Themes derive from Buddhist mythology and folklore; Burmese animals of the week and zoomorphic signs of the zodiac are also popular.

Repoussé, the process of producing a design in relief by hammering on the reverse side, is the most widely used technique for silverwork betel containers, although the lost-wax process and niello are also popular. Silver shapes are simple geometric forms. Designs reflect the decorative styles and iconography of Burma. Mythical animals, Buddhist symbols and themes from nature are typical.

BIBLIOGRAPHY

S. Fraser-Lu: 'Burmese Silverware', *A. Asia*, x (March–April 1980), pp. 77–83

——: *Burmese Lacquerware* (Bangkok, 1985)

H. Brownrigg: *Betel Cutters from the Samuel Eilenberg Collection* (London, 1992)

DAWN F. ROONEY

3. BOATS. Rivers have always been the main channels of communication in Burma. Boats range from simple log canoes (*launggo*) to the elaborate state barges used by royalty. Boats used far inland are generally long and narrow and propelled by single paddles. Although most are unadorned, some racing boats may be brightly painted; other types have eyes painted on the bows. Some of the large plank-built craft used further south have stem- and stern-posts simply carved; on others the posts have carved figureheads of peacocks, human and other figures, gilded and inlaid with mirrors. The steersman's platform of some boats is carved with plant motifs.

Traditional royal boats were more elaborate. *Hlawhadaw* or *hlawga* (dispatch boats) were gilded, and *hpaungnaw* (express boats) often had a figure of Garuda, the mount of Vishnu, on the bows. The state boats carrying ministers and royalty were usually carved and gilded, particularly at the prow and stern, which often swept up to form animal heads and tails. The king's barge was double-keeled with huge figureheads of mythical creatures and twin sterns sweeping up to form carved and pierced panels. A pavilion with a seven-tiered roof straddled the double keel, and the whole structure was covered with gold leaf.

BIBLIOGRAPHY

J. G. Scott [Shway Yoe]: *The Burman: His Life and Notions* (London, 1882/*R* New York, 1963/*R* Arran, 1989)

R. Raven-Hart: *Canoe to Mandalay* (London, 1939)

SIAN E. JAY

4. CERAMICS. Abundant sources of clay and numerous pottery centres in most parts of modern Burma suggest a long and continuous history of ceramics manufacture. The earliest known Burmese ceramics are earthenware pots and funerary urns of the Pyu people in central Burma (1st–7th centuries AD) and unglazed vessels for domestic use from Mon sites in Lower Burma (1st–5th centuries AD). Chinese sources mention glazed ware in the 9th century, but the technique of applying a glaze is likely to have been introduced earlier, probably by the Mons, since many modern Burmese potting terms derive from the Mon language. In modern Burma ceramics kilns produce mainly vessels for everyday use; jars for domestic storage of liquids and foods are the most common. The three main groups of ceramics for which Burma is especially known are discussed below.

(i) Plaques. Both unglazed and glazed plaques are a common architectural feature on religious monuments throughout the period from the 11th to the 18th century. The technique may have originated in Thaton, capital of a Mon kingdom, and spread to later Burmese capitals at Pagan (where the Ananda Temple had some 1500 plaques;

23. Glazed earthenware tile, *Warriors from the Army of Mara*, 455×305 mm, from Shwegugyi Stupa region, Pegu, late 15th century or early 16th (Boston, MA, Museum of Fine Arts)

see PAGAN, §2(iii)) and Pegu. The earthenware plaques are characteristically thick and weighty, modelled in relief or moulded and lead-glazed. Pictorial plaques portray *jātakas*, episodes from the Buddha's former lives. Pairs of mythical figures, such as door guardians (Skt *dvārapāla*) or warriors with bird or animal heads (see fig. 23), are also typical. These plaques are square or rectangular with a green glaze that varies from pale to bluish, depending on the quantity of tin and copper used, with smaller areas of white, reddish-orange and brown. Geometric plaques are square, round or octagonal and characteristically decorated with a circle of impressed lotus leaves or a moulded lozenge. Typical glaze colours are bright or bluish-green with yellow and white accents.

(ii) Martaban jars. Large glazed storage jars, known as *martaban*, were made from the 14th century near the town in southern Burma after which they were named. The jars, used on ships, achieved such acclaim that they acquired magical attributes. A typical jar is bulbous with lug handles, a grainy, reddish body and a shiny, dark-brown glaze. A distinctive horizontal ridge resulting from joining two separately potted parts together encircles the centre of the body. Characteristic decoration consists of vertical bands with raised buttons modelled from a light-coloured clay extending between the neck and the mid-section.

(iii) Green-and-white ware. This provisional classification is based on a comparative analysis of shards from Pagan and burial wares found in north-central Thailand in 1984. The class has been tentatively dated to the 14th to the 16th century. It is wheel-thrown, low-fired, lead-glazed earthenware made from a reddish, porous clay. Two types, monochromes (white, celadon, red, brown, blue) and painted ware, dominate. Plates and bowls are the most common forms. Decoration on the monochrome ware is minimal, consisting merely of a small stamped floral or geometric design in the centre. Painted motifs—in green on a white background—are derived from nature. The decoration is divided into sections with a design in the centre and on the walls, rim and exterior.

BIBLIOGRAPHY

S. Adhyatman: *Burmese Ceramics*; A. Ridho: *White Kendis* (Jakarta, 1985) [publication of Himpunan Keramik Indonesia (Ceramic Society of Indonesia); two monographs bound as one book]

J. C. Shaw: *Introducing Thai Ceramics, also Burmese and Khmer* (Chiang Mai, 1987)

DAWN F. ROONEY

5. COINS. A 5th-century silver coinage showing the conch and *śrīvatsa* (a shield-like symbol associated with good fortune and divinity) originating in Pegu in southern Burma was the model for nearly all coinage in mainland South-east Asia during the remainder of the first millennium AD. The Pyu, further north, struck a derivative series in several main varieties up to the end of the 8th century. This silver series with *bhadrapīṭha* (throne) and *śrīvatsa* has been found at a number of sites in central and upper Burma, including Srikshetra (modern Hmawza), Halin, Beikthano and elsewhere. It is possible that the as yet unattributed series with the rising sun and *śrīvatsa*, widely distributed from Burma to southern Vietnam, was struck by the Pyus or by the Mons in the south. From the 11th to the 13th century Pagan issued no coins, preferring instead to use silver and copper bars as media of exchange. Coinage was not used again in Burma proper until the end of the 18th century.

The Chandra rulers of Arakan to the west began issuing silver coins with the bull and *triśūla* (trident) by the middle of the 5th century AD under their fourth ruler, Devachandra, who had earlier struck a coin with conch and *śrīvatsa*. The bull and *triśūla* type continued to be made by rulers of the main Chandra dynasty until their demise in the late 6th century and was subsequently revived on a number of occasions by their successors in Arakan and south-eastern Bengal (Bangladesh) until the early 11th century.

Between the 15th and the 18th centuries, until their conquest by the Burmese king Bodawpaya in 1784, Arakanese rulers of Myohaung (Myauk-U) struck a silver coinage heavily influenced by the Islamic issues of Bengal. Some of the earliest coins have trilingual inscriptions in Arakanese, Arabic and Bengali. Others are inscribed only in Arakanese with the same inscription on both sides. The coins were typically issued at the accession of each ruler and distributed as largesse following the coronation ceremony.

Cast tin-lead coins associated with Martaban, Tavoy and Mergui (Tenasserim) were reported by European observers in the late 16th century and continued to be made until the early 19th century. Issues ascribed to Tenasserim are frequently quite broad (diam. 60–70 mm), with the design of a fantastic animal (*tò*), dragon (*tò-nayà*), sacred goose (*hìn-tha*) or cockerel on the obverse and a Pali inscription or geometric design on the reverse. Pegu coins, similar in design, are considerably smaller (diam. 24–7 mm).

Bodawpaya had ordered the mint at Calcutta to strike silver and copper coins for him in 1797, but the first Burmese mint on European lines was established by King Mindon at Mandalay in 1866; it struck the famous peacock coins designed by Ralph Heaton & Son of Birmingham, England.

BIBLIOGRAPHY

A. P. Phayre: *The Coins of Arakan, of Pegu and of Burma* (London, 1882)

M. Robinson and L. A. Shaw: *The Coins and Banknotes of Burma* (Manchester, 1980)

R. S. Wicks: 'The Ancient Coinage of Mainland Southeast Asia', *J. SE Asian Stud.*, xvi/2 (1985), pp. 195–225

M. Robinson: *The Lead and Tin Coins of Pegu and Tenasserim* (Sale, 1986)

ROBERT S. WICKS

6. EPHEMERAL ART. Burma's best known ephemeral art is *sat bagyi*, the construction out of bamboo and paper of brilliantly decorated temporary structures in the form of buildings or figures. Although the art was practised well before the 18th century using local material, it was not until the introduction of foreign coloured paper and gold and silver foil, in the late 19th century, that craftsmen were able to produce the ambitious and dazzling creations that have made *sat bagyi* famous.

Sat bagyi workers make floats of fantastic shapes and decorate marquees for numerous secular and religious ceremonies. The designs vary according to the area of the country and the occasion being celebrated. Traditionally, the most elaborate *sat bagyi* was seen at the death of a venerated monk. The monk's body, coated with wax and covered in gold leaf, was placed in a hollowed-out log, then laid in a lavishly decorated sarcophagus, which was taken to the 'monastery of the dead', a huge structure with a seven-tiered roof. The body lay in state for months, while festivals and theatrical performances were held to entertain a constant stream of pilgrims. Around the central building were arranged large effigies of animals and mythical beasts—frequently including white elephants (with the trunks and ears hinged to move with the slightest breeze) carrying elaborate howdahs.

On the last day, the sarcophagus was hoisted to the platform on top of another tall bamboo building filled with combustible material. The funeral pyre of the monk was set alight by firing rockets (*dohn*) made from hollowed-out tree-trunks at it. The rockets were mounted on wheels and decorated with a demon or animal figure made of paper. Occasionally guide-ropes were attached to direct the rockets, but it was normal practice simply to aim and fire. Eventually, the huge, colourful pyre was ignited and in a matter of minutes the flames would destroy the creations of many months. The immense effigies were also burnt. It was said that when a famous monk died the people of his village became destitute, so great was the religious fervour to provide a magnificent farewell for a venerated man.

BIBLIOGRAPHY

C. A. Gordon: *Our Trip to Burmah* (London, 1875)

J. G. Scott [Shway Yoe]: *The Burman: His Life and Notions* (London, 1882/*R* New York, 1963/*R* Arran, 1989)

J. Nisbet: *Burma under British Rule and Before* (London, 1901)

Aung Thein: *Sat Panchee* [Bamboo and paper art] (Rangoon, 1982)

NOEL F. SINGER

7. Gilded glass inlay. Widely used throughout Burma to decorate religious objects and places of worship, gilded glass inlay (*hman-zi shwei-chá*) was formerly used in a secular context only by Burmese royalty, because of the lavish application of gold. In preparation for glass inlay, the surface is made smooth with a coating of raw lacquer and powdered sawdust mixed with a glue of boiled rice. The prepared area is embellished with sprigs of flowers, small, lively figures, undulating threads and minute strings of beads deftly modelled from *thayò*, a putty-like mixture of bone ash and lacquer, to create the impression of wood-carving in low relief. These moulded designs are then highlighted with fragments of coloured mirror glass cut into various geometric shapes and carefully cemented in place with lacquer. Once the glass is in place, the object is gilded with gold leaf to create an overall sumptuous effect.

This technique is thought to have originated around the 12th century in China; it became popular in Burma during the late 18th century. The earliest example recovered in Burma is the cover of a palm-leaf book with a date equivalent to 1790. In early examples the glass used is thick, chunky and cloudy in colour, held in place by ridges of gilded *thayò*. The glass pieces on later examples are smaller, finer and more even in shape, owing to the advent of improved cutting tools from Europe in the mid-19th century and the introduction of mirror glass.

Objects decorated in this technique include manuscript chests (*sadaik*), Buddha images, votive food containers (*hsùn-ok*), cosmetic and betel boxes, monks' ceremonial fans, musical instruments, couches, shrines, screens, doorways, pillars, ceilings and architraves of buildings. Motifs include vegetal designs, such as flowers (*pan-shwei*), orchid tendrils (*tha-zin-gwei*) and lotus petals (*kya-hmauk* and *kya-lan*), as well as such geometric motifs as diamond-shaped (*hman-gu-gwet*), triangular (*phet-htok*), wave (*ach-eik*) and beaded (*ywè-dán*) designs. Pictorial designs feature episodes from the life of the Buddha, *jātaka* stories of the Buddha's previous lives, Burmese folk-tales and popular local motifs, such as the lion (*chin-theí*), the dragon (*tò-nayà*), heavenly beings and peacocks.

Mandalay is the modern centre for gilded glass inlay. Some work is also produced at Lai-hka in the Shan States and at Kyauk-ka in the Monywa district.

BIBLIOGRAPHY

H. L. Tilly: *Glass Mosaic of Burma* (Rangoon, 1900)

Burma: A Handbook on Burma with Special Reference to Burmese Customs, History, Economic Resources, Education, Famous Pagodas and Cities, Directorate of Information (Rangoon, 1959)

Maung Myat Daung: 'The Art of Glass Inlaying and Gilding', *Forward*, iii/3 (1964), pp. 14–15

S. Fraser-Lu: 'Sadaik: Burmese Manuscript Chests', *A. Asia* (May–June, 1984), pp. 69–74

——: *Burmese Lacquerware* (Bangkok, 1985)

Thuteti Myint Tun: 'Hman-zi-shwei-chá' [Burmese gilded glass inlay], *Thu-ta Shwe-zon* [Encyclopedia of knowledge] (Rangoon, 1986)

——: *Burmese Crafts Past and Present* (Kuala Lumpur, 1994)

8. Ivory. The softness and regularity of local elephant ivory made it the preferred material of Burmese craftsmen, who specialized in carving complex scenes from Buddhist folklore in open tracery and deep undercut high relief reminiscent of wood-carving. Some examples, rivalling Chinese work in intricacy, were commissioned from whole tusks and presented to monasteries as an act of merit. The handles of ceremonial swords and daggers were carved in fine detail in open work and low relief. Burmese ivory-workers also delighted in sculpting small figurines in the round, particularly elephants, Buddha images and figures of Burmese saints, some of which, although a little stiff, exhibit a delightfully whimsical quality. Platelets of ivory in low relief were used to decorate boxes and picture-frames. In pre-colonial times Moulmein in southern Burma was famous for ivory carving; late 20th-century centres include Mandalay and Rangoon, where craft workers specialize in making items for the tourist trade.

BIBLIOGRAPHY

H. S. Pratt: *Monograph on Ivory Carving in Burma* (Rangoon, 1901)

U Tun Yin: 'Ivory Carving', *Burma: A Handbook* (Rangoon, 1959)

S. Fraser-Lu: *Burmese Crafts Past and Present (Kuala Lumpur, 1994)*

SYLVIA FRASER-LU

9. Karen drums. The use and manufacture of bronze drums, the oldest continuous art tradition in South-east Asia, began some time before the 6th century BC in northern Vietnam and later spread to other areas of South-east Asia and China. By AD 1056, the ritual use of these bronze drums had been adopted by various peoples living in Burma who are collectively known as the Karen. During this long period of adoption and transfer, the drum type was progressively altered from that found in northern Vietnam (Dong Son or Heger Type I; *see* Vietnam, §VI, 6), to produce a separate Karen type (Heger Type III). Distinguishing features of this Karen type include a less

bulbous shape and a tympanum with a markedly protruding lip. The drums are known as frog drums (*hpà-si*), after the images of frogs that invariably appear at four equidistant points on the circumference of the tympanum. On one side of the body-shell insects and animals are represented descending the trunk of a stylized tree. The numerous changes of motif in the two-dimensional ornamentation of the drums have been used to establish a relative chronology for the development of the Karen drum type (Cooler, 1994).

Although the drums were cast primarily for use by groups of non-Buddhist hill people, they were used by the kings of Burma and Thailand as musical instruments at court and as appropriate gifts to Buddhist institutions; the first known record of them is an inscription of the Mon king Manuha at Thaton, dated 1056. The ritual use of Karen drums in lowland royal courts and monasteries continued during the centuries that followed and is an important instance of inversion of the direction in which cultural influences usually flow from the lowlands to the hills.

Bronze drums were used among the Karen as a device to assure prosperity by summoning rain, by taking the spirit of the dead into the after-life and by assembling groups for funerals, marriages and house-entering ceremonies. They were a form of currency that could be traded for slaves, goods or services and were often used in marriage exchanges. They were also a symbol of status, and no Karen could be considered wealthy without one. The drums were held in such high esteem that drum fragments were placed in tombs to accompany the spirit of the deceased into the after-life. Consequently, few ancient drums remain in perfect condition.

The town of Nwe Daung, 15 km south of Loikaw, capital of Kayah (formerly Karenni) State, is the only recorded casting site in Burma. Drums were made there for the Karens by Shan craftsmen in the 19th century until the town burned in 1889. They were cast by the lost-wax technique using a five-metal, bronze alloy. Several later attempts by the Karens to revive the casting of drums failed. From the late 19th century non-Karen hill people, attracted to the area by the prospect of work with British teak loggers, bought large numbers of Karen drums and transported them to Thailand and Laos. These works are frequently wrongly identified by collectors.

BIBLIOGRAPHY

F. Heger: *Alte Metalltrommeln aus Südost-Asien* (Leipzig, 1902)

H. I. Marshall: *The Karen People of Burma: A Study in Anthropology and Ethnology* (Columbus, 1922)

——: 'Karen Bronze Drums', *J. Burma Res. Soc.*, xix (1929), pp. 1–14

R. M. Cooler: 'The Use of Karen Bronze Drums in the Royal Courts and Buddhist Temples of Burma and Thailand: A Continuing Mon Tradition?', *Papers from a Conference on Thai Studies in Honor of William J. Gedney* (Michigan Papers on South and Southeast Asia, 25) (Ann Arbor, 1986), pp. 107–20

——: *The Karen Bronze Drums of Burma: Types, Iconography, Manufacture and Use* (Leiden, 1994)

RICHARD M. COOLER

10. LACQUER. This characteristic Burmese art was probably introduced from China either directly or indirectly via neighbouring states, but the process and date of transmission are subject to conjecture. According to travellers' accounts, it has been a leading craft for at least 300 years. Lacquerware was a popular gift to foreign envoys from Burmese royalty, banquets were served on lacquer dishes and royal letters and jewellery were kept in lacquer containers. Lacquerware was also important in Buddhist religious ceremonies and for presenting food to monasteries on festival days. In Burma, porcelain and glass were rare, so there was widespread use of sturdy lacquer containers for food, refreshments, clothing, cosmetics and flowers.

Lacquer (*thit-sì*) comes from the sap of *Melanorrhoea usitata*, a tree native to South-east Asia that grows wild at altitudes of up to 1000 m in the drier forest areas of the Shan States. Lacquered articles are made from a base of coiled and woven bamboo, wood or sheet metal to which layers of lacquer and fine ash are first applied until a smooth finish is obtained, followed by thin coats of lacquer mixed with colouring (usually red or green). Burma is famous for a unique style of lacquer decoration called *yùn*, in which the surface decoration is engraved with a fine

24. Lacquer tiffin basket, *yùn* ware from Pagan, red with an incised design in black, yellow and green, h. 340 mm, diam. 230 mm, *c.* 1910–20 (London, Victoria and Albert Museum)

stylus and the incisions are filled with colouring matter (see fig. 24). The technique may have been introduced from Thailand (*see* THAILAND, §VII). Other techniques include painting, gold-leaf decoration (*shwei-zawa*), moulded lacquer (*thayò*), glass-inlay work (*hman-zi shwei-chá*; *see* §7 above) and dry lacquer (*man-hpayà*). The latter is a modelling technique where a Buddha image is formed from *thayò* (a mixture of lacquer, sawdust and bone ash) applied over a clay cone.

Secular lacquerware objects include circular containers for betel-chewing paraphernalia, pickled tea, tiffin, cheroots and cosmetics; plates; low round tables; oil containers; water pots; covered bowls for condiments; storage boxes and musical instruments. Religious objects made of lacquer include dry-lacquer Buddha images, votive food containers (such as the tapering and multi-tiered *hsùn-ok*), monks' bowls (*thabeik*) and betel-leaf containers on stands, flower vases, reclining couches, screens, shrines, thrones, pedestals and intricately decorated manuscript boxes (*sa-daik*), which contain elaborately decorated *Kammāwas-ā* manuscripts used for monastic ceremonies (*see* §V, 2(i) above).

Decorative motifs on Burmese lacquer are drawn from the rich reservoir of Buddhist mythology and Burmese folklore. They include episodes from the *Rāmāyaṇa*, the life of the Buddha and *jātaka* stories of the Buddha's previous lives, and from the Mandalay court. Animals feature in the eight-planet design (*gyo-shit-lòn*), with a creature for each day of the week, and for the months of the Burmese zodiac. Decoration abounds with lions (*chin-thei*), elephants, peacocks, the Brahmani duck (*hìn-tha*), celestial beings half-human and half-bird or -animal (*kein-naya*, Skt *kinnara*), fabulous dragon-like creatures (*tò-nayà* and *pyin-sá-yùpâ*), spirits, gods, ogres (*balù*) and magicians (*zaw-gyi*). The Burmese love of ornamentation is evident in the wide variety of floral motifs that form the background and border patterns on most types of lacquerware. Repetition and complexity, panelling and horizontal bands are characteristic features of the Burmese lacquerware design.

Pagan, which specializes in *yùn* and gold-leaf, is the largest and oldest centre of lacquerware production in Burma. Second in importance is Kyauk-ka near Monywa in Upper Burma, which is noted for sturdy utilitarian black and red wares. Mandalay specializes in moulded lacquer and gilded glass inlay work. Some lacquer is also produced at Lai-hka, Inle and Kengtung in the Shan States.

BIBLIOGRAPHY

H. Burney: 'Some Account of the Lacquered or Japanned Ware of Ava', *J. Asiat. Soc. Bengal*, i/5 (1882), pp. 169–87
A. P. Morris: 'The Lacquerware Industry of Burma', *J. Burma Res. Soc.*, x (1919), pp. 1–13
Kyaw Dun: 'Lacquerware Called Yun', *J. Burma Res. Soc.*, xi (1920), pp. 75–7
Khin Maung Gyi: 'Burmese Lacquerware', *Forward*, i/18 (1963), pp. 16–21
Maung Theikpa: 'The Beauty of Lacquerware', *Forward*, iii/17 (1963), pp. 16–18
Hla Gyi: 'Lacquerware, Symbol of the Culture of Old Pagan', *Forward*, iv/12 (1966), pp. 17–19
G. Prunner: *Meisterwerke Burmanischer Lackkunst* (Hamburg, 1966)
U Maung Ko [Thabyei-Nyo]: *Myan-ma yo-ya yun let-hmu pyin-nya* [The art of traditional Burmese lacquer] (Rangoon, 1971)
S. Mann: 'Burmese Lacquerware', *Forward*, x/21 (1972), pp. 22–3
Hla Gyi: *Myan-ma-pàn-yùn* [Burmese lacquer] (Rangoon, 1981)
S. Fraser-Lu: *Burmese Lacquerware* (Bangkok, 1985)
——: 'Pagan Lacquer Museum', *A. Asia* (July–August 1985), pp. 104–11

11. LOOM PULLEYS. The Burmese traditional floor loom (*ya-kan*) makes use of a pair of wooden or bronze pulleys with grooved rims in which the cords that suspend the heddles from the top of the frame are manipulated so as to raise and lower the odd and even warp threads. Burmese loom pulleys are of interest because they are traditionally surmounted by a figure of a bird such as the Brahmani duck (*hìn-tha*) or parrot, or a mythical creature such as the half-human and half-bird or -animal *kein-naya* (Skt: *kinnara*). Some of these are of exquisite proportions and show a mastery of carving or casting to rank as art objects in their own right. Others less finely crafted possess a strong, lively, robust quality and are excellent examples of time-hallowed folk–craft tradition where the local blacksmith and cultivator-cum-woodcarver delighted in producing well-crafted utilitarian objects in imaginative vegetal and zoomorphic forms for the use of family and fellow villagers.

BIBLIOGRAPHY

J. Lowry: *Burmese Art* (London, 1974)
S. Fraser-Lu: *Burmese Crafts Past and Present* (Kuala Lumpur, 1994)

SYLVIA FRASER-LU

12. MUSICAL INSTRUMENTS. The oldest extant musical instruments in Burma are the large bronze Karen drums (*see* §9 above) that derive from Dong Son originals (*see* SOUTH-EAST ASIA, §I, 2). Both Karen drums and bells (*see* §1 above) are chiefly important for their ritual and ceremonial use, rather than as performance instruments.

The instruments of the traditional Burmese orchestra are derived from both Pyu and Mon sources but also display certain Indian influences. Many of the instruments are common to most countries of South-east Asia, but others are uniquely Burmese. Metallophones, xylophones and other wooden percussion instruments, drums, wind and string instruments are all represented. Some instruments are lavishly decorated.

The leading instrument of the orchestra, the *pat-waìng*, comprises 21 tuned drums mounted on a circular frame about 1 m high. The player sits in the centre. The wooden frame has carved and pierced panels and may be lacquered, gilded and inlaid with glass. Plumed birds and mythical creatures called *tò-nayà* are popular motifs. The *pat-waìng* or *hsaìng-waìng* (the latter name also denotes the whole orchestra) is rarely found outside Burma. Another drum, the large, barrel-shaped *pat-má*, is suspended from an elaborate frame often decorated with another mythical creature called *pyin-sa-yu-pa*.

The *kyì-waìng* is a gong-chime of 21 knobbed gongs set in a circular frame, which may be of turned wood or wood elaborately carved and gilded. The player sits in the centre. Gong-chimes called *maùng-zaìng* are mounted in five rows, usually on plain wooden frames. Large knobbed gongs (*maùng*) are hung in lacquered and gilded frames. Mon gongs are mounted in a boat-shaped frame, also heavily carved and gilded, and the stand may be in the form of an animal. Xylophones (*pat-talà*) are similarly mounted and decorated.

Stringed instruments include a three-stringed zither (*mí-gyaùng*) unique to Burma, the wooden body of which is carved in the form of a crocodile and may be lacquered. The Burmese harp (*saùng-gauk*) is a 14-stringed, boat-shaped instrument with an arched neck. The *saùng-gauk* in the Victoria and Albert Museum, London, is of lacquered wood decorated with scenes from the *Rāmāyaṇa* in gold leaf and set with red, green and white mirror-glass inlay (see fig. 25).

BIBLIOGRAPHY

J. G. Scott [Shway Yoe]: *The Burman: His Life and Notions* (London, 1882/*R* New York, 1963/*R* Arran, 1989), pp. 316–27
C. Sachs: *Die Musikinstrumente Birmas und Assams im K. Ethnographischen Museum zu München* (Munich, 1917)
D. C. Twitchett and A. H. Christie: 'A Medieval Burmese Orchestra', *Asia Major*, n. s., vii (1959), pp. 176–95
J. Lowry: *Burmese Art* (London, 1974), p. 38
S. Fraser-Lu: *Burmese Lacquerware* (Bangkok, 1985), pp. 82–4
E. Taylor: *Musical Instruments of South-east Asia* (Oxford, 1989)

SIAN E. JAY

13. SILVER. Burma has a long history of crafting silver dating back to the Pyu period (5th–9th centuries AD). The excavation of a Pyu relic chamber near Prome in 1926 led to the discovery of silver guardian figures, miniature pagodas, lotus flowers and delicately wrought caskets with Buddha images in high relief. A number of silver alloy coins from the same period, featuring such symbols as the *śrīvatsa* (a sign associated with good fortune and divinity), *vajra* (thunderbolt), *śaṅkha* (conch) and the rising sun, have been recovered in Burma as well as in Thailand and Cambodia (*see* §5 above). Influences from Gupta India are clearly visible in the Buddhist figures and in the Brahmanical symbols on these early coins, indicating strong Indian influences in early Burmese silverwork.

Silver was important in royal ceremonies. Betel sets (*see* §2 above), vases, bowls, spittoons and ceremonial weapons (*see* §14 below) in the palace were of gold or silver, as were items of the king's regalia and the insignia of the nobility, such as the *salwe* chest ornament. Silver receptacles were widely used, for example by the well-to-do at important events, such as the *shin-byú* ceremony when a son entered a monastery or at the *nà-htwìn* or ear-piercing ceremony to celebrate a young girl's attainment of womanhood. Silver bowls were used to carry water for washing Buddha images in the temples.

Burmese silversmiths traditionally excel in repoussé, chasing and openwork. Simple objects covered with lively figures and detailed scrolling in high relief are reminiscent of the silverwork of southern India. The Burmese are masters at casting small Buddha images and lively figurines in silver, and at one time they also practised the art of niello. The silver used traditionally came from a variety of sources: ore from the Bawdwin mines in the Shan States, recycled antique silver and European, Indian and Chinese coins acquired through foreign trade.

Decoration on Burmese silver usually depicts scenes from the Buddhist *jātaka* stories, the *Rāmāyaṇa*, Burmese folk-tales and astrology. Episodes in pictorial scenes may be continuous or separated by spandrels of foliage and bounded by bands of stylized lotus petals. The base of the object may be engraved with lively figures encircled by an inscription in Burmese, expressing a salutation or the name of the person who commissioned the object and the date of its completion. There may also be a stamp indicating that the silver used is 95% pure.

25. Burmese harp (*saùng-gauk*), lacquered wood decorated with scenes from the *Rāmāyaṇa* in gold leaf inlaid with red, green and white mirror glass, 610×725 mm, from Prome, Lower Burma, 19th century (London, Victoria and Albert Museum)

With the coming of the British, in the 19th century, the Victorian love of ornamentation influenced the appearance of Burmese silverware, and new items, such as tea and coffee sets, tankards and teaspoons, were added to the Burmese silversmith's repertory.

The Shan people of eastern Burma, who are closely related to the Thais, have a distinct silver tradition, modelling in lower relief than the Burman silversmiths, and specialize in making silver bowls, cylindrical betel boxes and lime boxes. They are master swordsmiths and show great skill in decorating scabbards with fine sheets of silver embellished with simple motifs in filigree and enamel. Shan silversmiths also make hemispherical studs, buckles and distinctive jewellery for neighbouring hill people.

For further details relating to jewellery and weapons *see* §§VII, 2 above and IX, 14 below.

BIBLIOGRAPHY

H. L. Tilly: *The Silverwork of Burma* (Rangoon, 1902)
——: *Modern Burmese Silverwork* (Rangoon, 1904)
Myint Tun: 'Silversmith's Craft', *Forward*, xvii/1 (1978), pp. 16–18
S. Fraser-Lu: 'Burmese Silverware', *A. Asia*, x (March–April 1980), pp. 77–83
——: *Silverware of South-east Asia* (Singapore and Oxford, 1989)
——: *Burmese Crafts Past and Present* (Kuala Lumpur, 1994)

SYLVIA FRASER-LU

14. WEAPONS. According to British sources, 19th-century Burmese soldiers were equipped with spears, swords, crossbows and fire-arms called *jinjal*. Of these the most significant artistically are the various two-handed and one-handed swords known as *dà* (*dha*). This group includes not only weapons but also general-purpose knives

for chopping, trimming and clearing foliage. Similar weapons are found in neighbouring countries. The blade of the *dà* is usually single-edged and slightly curved with a blunt or tapering point. The characteristic long handle does not have a guard but may be richly ornamented. Sheaths are usually of wood bound with metal and are sometimes embellished with silver or silver gilt. The scabbard may have a heavy cord wound round it, which can be fastened with a knot leaving a loop that may be worn over the shoulder. The blades, grips and sheaths of *dà* used for warfare and ceremonial purposes are decorated with various techniques. Blades are sometimes deeply engraved and the sunken areas darkened to show foliage and figurative patterns in sharp relief. The raised areas are gilded to provide contrasting designs in black, silver and gold. Similar methods are used to decorate hilts. Ivory handles may have intricate designs made with much undercutting similar to that found in wood-carving. Some of the best Burmese ivorywork rivals that of the Chinese. Hilts are also made from horn or shark skin, and ferrules may be inlaid with brass. *Dà* also have embossed and engraved silver grips, and their sheaths may be set with semi-precious stones. British sources describe the quality of Burmese steel as poor, and there are reports of swords being bent in combat. Small curved swords like *dà* served as daggers.

The traditional arms of the Karens resemble those of the Burmese. The Karens, however, use poisoned crossbow arrows tipped with the juice of the Pegu upas tree (*Antiaris ovalifolia* or *Atoxicaria*). Karen weapons also serve a ritual purpose and are used to consolidate agreements. It is the Karen custom to scrape steel from a gun, sword or spear into a bowl filled with spirits. The contracting parties then hold the weapons in the liquid and drink it off.

26. Bronze weight (1 *viss*) in the form of a Brahmani duck (*hìn-tha* bird), h. 127 mm, diam. 114 mm, early 18th century (USA, collection of Mr and Mrs George Lu)

BIBLIOGRAPHY

W. Egerton: *An Illustrated Handbook of Indian Arms and those of Nepal, Burma, Thailand and Malaya* (London, 1880/*R* Bangkok, 1981)

G. C. Stone: *A Glossary of the Construction, Decoration and Use of Arms and Armor in All Countries and in All Times together with Some Closely Related Subjects* (New York, 1961)

J. Lowry: *Burmese Art* (London, 1974)

MICHAEL HITCHCOCK

15. WEIGHTS. In successive Burmese kingdoms boldly modelled zoomorphic bronze weights—often incorrectly called 'opium' weights—were used with a beam balance to weigh food and other basic commodities. Historical texts indicate that such weights were used during the Ava period in the 14th and 15th centuries. The earliest examples recovered in Burma date from the 16th or 17th century. Weights were subject to close scrutiny by royal officials, who had a master set made at the beginning of each reign, in the form of an animal of the king's choosing.

Weights traditionally consist of sets of 10, based on the Indian system. The largest (about 1.6 kg) is the *peik-tha* or *viss* (Tamil: *vīsai*, 'division') made up of 100 *tical* or *kyat*. This is followed by 50, 20, 10, 5, 2 and 1 *tical* weights, ending with $\frac{1}{2}$, $\frac{1}{4}$, and $\frac{1}{8}$ *tical*. Later sets may have 10, 5 and $2\frac{1}{2}$ *peik-tha* weights. Weights above 20 *tical* usually have handles for easier lifting.

Weights consist of a figure of an animal or bird set on a sturdy base. The Brahmani duck (*hìn-tha*; see fig. 26), Burmese crane (*karaweik*) and a mythical bull-like creature resembling a lion (*tò-aung*) are the most common; the elephant, chicken, horse, tortoise, spider and fish are rare. The weights were cast from lead piece-moulds by the lost-wax process using carefully pre-weighed ingredients. Surface features may be emphasized by incised decoration.

Various features indicate the date of the weights. In 16th- and 17th-century examples the animal sits directly on a large pumpkin-shaped base, which may be embossed at the front with a small circular effigy of the animal. There may also be square seals, letters and numbers on the sides of the base. The weight often has a reddish hue owing to the relatively high copper content of the alloy.

Weights from the 18th century usually have a smaller, round base. There may be a small pointed niche on the front, faintly imprinted with a minuscule image of the animal. The *hìn-tha* bird has a sprig of foliage suspended from its bill-like beak, the neck feathers lie flat and tail feathers are upturned. Larger weights have a simple hook-shaped handle. The *karaweik* has a streamlined body, pointed beak and upturned neck feathers. The *tò-aung*, which stands with hooves on a small octagonal base, is plump and sturdy with bared teeth, small horns, pointed ears and a long tail; sometimes sprigs of foliage issue from the mouth and curvilinear mouldings on the body. These weights often have a silvery hue owing to the high tin content of the alloy.

Examples from the 19th century are set on sloping hexagonal and octagonal bases. Upturned feathers, manes and tails are more flamboyant than on older weights; handles are more elaborate. There may be incised marks on the base, such as a simple flower with a varying number of petals.

BIBLIOGRAPHY

S. Fraser-Lu: 'Burmese "Opium" Weights', *A. Asia* (Jan–Feb 1982), pp. 73–81

R. Braun and I. Braun: *Opium Weights* (Landau, 1983) [Eng., Ger. and Fr. text]

SYLVIA FRASER-LU

16. WOOD-CARVING. The Burmese have long excelled at wood-carving. The subject-matter of early carvings was the 37 *nat* (spirits) that included a Buddha of later origin. Some of the finest and oldest extant examples of carving are in the 11th-century Shwe-zigon Temple at Pagan. A few standing images of the Buddha in wood survive from the Pagan period (*see* §IV, 2 above) and there are gilded and lacquered wooden Buddha images from the Konbaung period (18th–19th centuries; *see* §IV, 3 above). A great door, possibly dating to the 11th century, has also been discovered, the leaves of which are decorated with floral designs and dancing human figures.

Because of the danger from earthquakes and the plentiful supply of timber, most habitations were built of wood. The structures and the decorated parts of the exterior of buildings were made from teak, but a softer wood called *yamaneí* (*Gmelina arborea*) was also used for carving. Figures of the Buddha and of spirits and creatures from mythology that guarded royal cities were made from the wood of auspicious trees, such as *thabyei* (*Eugenia grandis*, rose-apple), *sandagu* (*Santalum album*, sandalwood), *sagà* (*Michelia champaca*), *thin-gàn-thà* (*Hopea odorata*), *karawei* (*Cinnamomum camphora*, camphorwood) and *pyin-nyaung* (*Ficus indica*, bo or banyan tree). These magically charged icons were placed in carved wooden shrines along the city walls to give maximum protection to the inhabitants.

Such specialist crafts as wood-carving were handed down from father to son, and service at court was compulsory during certain times of the year for outstanding craftsmen. Apprentices prepared the wood; the design was drawn in charcoal, then cut out with a chisel and completed by journeymen under the supervision of the master carver. In the older surviving carvings, the ornamental scrollwork is not deeply cut; however, by the end of the 19th century a free-standing, open-cut style had become fashionable. The traditional tools of the wood-carver—chisel, gouge and mallet—originally came from China, but by the second half of the 19th century many Western tools were also being used.

Strict observance was demanded of the sumptuary laws (*yazagaìng*) governing the use of designs on the dwellings, palanquins, barges and other paraphernalia of the royal family and civil servants. Only the sovereign and the most senior monk had the right to a seven-tiered roof supported by huge, gilded wooden pillars. A certain floral design, the *chù pàn*, was exclusively reserved for the carvings on royal thrones. The majority of the population used wood oil to coat interior and exterior decorative carvings; the upper classes were permitted the use of plain black or red lacquer and, for the élite, part-gilding of fixtures and fittings was allowed. Within the inner palace gold was used lavishly, and walls, ceilings and furniture were decorated with small fragments of multicoloured glass and semi-precious stones set in gesso.

In the 18th and 19th centuries wooden monasteries and palaces were decorated with carving on the doors, walls, pillars, balustrades and bargeboards (*see* §§II, 1(iii)(c) and (d) and IV, 3, above). At Mandalay in the late 19th century court ceremonial revolved around nine intricately carved and gilded thrones, made of different types of wood and decorated with a host of carvings depicting mythological beasts and benevolent deities. The principal, the *Theehathana* (Pali: 'Lion Throne'; destr.), had rows of lions (*chin-theí*) placed before it (see fig. 27) and was housed in a huge, tapering wooden structure embellished with glass mosaic and gilding, known as the 'Centre of the Universe'. An identical throne, which stood in the *Hlutdaw* ('privy council'), is in the National Museum in Rangoon. The wood-carver's art probably reached its zenith during the 1850s in Amarapura. Some examples of this work are recorded in photographs of monasteries in Amarapura taken by an Englishman, Linnaeus Tripe, in 1855 (London, BL, photo 61, Acta Renans, xxxiv, 3450–3568).

27. Wood-carving of a *chin-theí* ('lion'), gilded, h. 500 mm, from the Theehathana ('Lion Throne'), Royal Palace, Mandalay, 19th century (UK, private collection)

With the coming of the British Raj in Upper Burma, in 1885, the central control and discipline of the wood-carvers dissipated. Building of lavish monasteries ceased, and there was a rush to the rich towns of the south. An 1897 guidebook to Burma (see Bird) states that wood-carving was carried out chiefly at Henzada, Mandalay and Moulmein; prisoners in the jails of these towns turned out excellent examples of furniture and *objets d'art*. In Rangoon, activity seems to have centred on Godwin (now Lanmadaw) Road and the vast platform of the Shwedagon pagoda, where newly acquired wealth was flaunted by the commissioning of ostentatious pavilions, which were covered in a frenzy of carvings depicting scenes from the Buddhist *jātaka* stories and the *Rāmāyaṇa*. Examples of work from this period by Saya Khin and U Po Nyun—both famed for their carving—survive.

Foreign entrepreneurs, such as Felice Beato, commissioned extravagant 'Burmese Victoriana' for the European market. Such items included tables, chairs, easels and screens, all decked in a riot of incongruous creatures from mythology. Designs that would not have been tolerated within a Burmese household were passed off as the best products of the country. During the years before World War II there was a steep decline in the quality of workmanship, but since the 1970s, with encouragement from the Burmese Ministry of Fine Arts, there has been a gradual return to traditional art forms.

Several treatises on design, such as the *Yazaw-wada Kyan* (see Ferrars), together with illustrated paper folding books (*parabaik*) compiled in the 19th century from earlier material, exist in private collections and at the University Library, Rangoon. In 1987 a selection of the more popular scrollwork used by wood-carvers since the 11th century was collated and published by Ko Ko Naing.

BIBLIOGRAPHY

G. W. Bird: *Wanderings in Burma* (London, 1897)
M. Ferrars and B. Ferrars: *Burma* (London, 1900), pp. 111–21
J. Nisbet: *Burma under British Rule and Before* (London, 1901)
H. L. Tilly: *Wood Carving of Burma* (Rangoon, 1903)
Daw Yi Yi: 'The Thrones of the Burmese Kings', *J. Burma Res. Soc.*, xliii (1960), pp. 97–123
J. Lowry: *Burmese Art* (London, 1974)
Linnaeus Tripe, Photographer of British India, 1854–1870 (exh. cat. by J. Dewan and M.-M. Sutnik; Toronto, A.G. Ont., 1986–7)
Ko Ko Naing: *Myanma Pàn Bú* [Burmese wood-carving] (Rangoon, 1987)
N. F. Singer: 'Survivors from a Burmese Palace', *A. Asia*, xviii/1 (1988)

NOEL F. SINGER

X. Folk and village art.

The hill peoples of Burma belong to a cultural tradition that remained relatively little influenced by Indianization. They have developed social systems, religious concepts and political systems characteristic of other indigenous South-east Asian cultures, and they represent certain of these concepts in a particular iconography. Burmese groups that belong to this tradition are the Kachin, Karen, Lisu, Lahu, Shan and Akha peoples, as well as the numerous Naga groups that live on the Indian border. As little is known of the art of these peoples in Burma, accounts of Naga material culture and arts in Assam in north-east India (*see* INDIAN SUBCONTINENT, §XI) and descriptions of the hill peoples who live in northern Thailand as well as Burma (*see* THAILAND, §VIII, 2) are valuable sources of information. National frontiers are in any case artificial, for these Tibeto-Burman and Tai-speaking peoples inhabit Yunnan (south China) and Assam as well as Burma and Thailand.

In all these societies political organization focuses on the village, and the economy is based on shifting cultivation, with rice as the main staple crop. Religious beliefs are concerned with fertility and cosmic balance and lack the Buddhist notion of renunciation. Traditionally, many groups practised headhunting as a way of increasing the community's 'fertility', a custom once found in other indigenous South-east Asian societies, notably in eastern Indonesia and the Philippines. The artistic forms that have emerged are all village-based. Buildings are of wood, occasionally with ornaments added in relief carving. The iconography concentrates on ancestor and animal representations. Among the Nagas in particular the *mithan*, a large buffalo, is depicted, as well as the tiger. The buffalo is as important for the Nagas as it is in parts of Indonesia. It is their major sacrificial animal and is associated with concepts of fertility and the well-being of the lineage. The Naga men's house (*morung*) is built with great care and may be decorated with carvings or painting. Stone temples are completely lacking.

Aesthetic endeavour concentrates on personal adornment, costume and jewellery. The textiles are decorated in a technique common to much of South-east Asia: supplementary weft predominates, but ikat and embroidery are also found (*see* §VI, above). Certain of the more complex geometric or spiral designs have apparently been part of South-east Asian artistic forms since the area's Bronze Age. In hill regions fabrics are woven on looms in which the weaver keeps the threads taut by means of a back strap, similar to a type that occurs in Indonesia. Decorative metalwork is confined chiefly to jewellery. Silver and brass ornaments are combined with imported beads and shells to create multiple strings of necklaces, bracelets and other body ornaments. The smithing technique used for working the metals is also related to that of maritime South-east Asia.

The wearing of certain costumes is linked with ethnic identity but is also associated with inherited or acquired status. The Nagas, in particular, have developed elaborate systems of dress appropriate for specific individuals. In the past, headhunting and feasts of merit, also familiar from Indonesia, were determining factors in this respect. The manner of wearing certain costumes, in particular headdresses, may relate to the buffalo cult. One example is the headdress of Lisu women, from the southern Shan States. This is comparable in style to the ceremonial headdress of Minangkabau women from Sumatra.

BIBLIOGRAPHY

F. M. LeBar, G. Hickey and J. Musgrave: *Ethnic Groups of Mainland Southeast Asia* (New Haven, 1964)
J. H. Hutton: 'The Mixed Culture of the Naga Tribes', *J. Royal Anthropol. Inst. GB & Ireland*, xcv (1965), pp. 16–43
R. Heine-Geldern: 'Some Tribal Art Styles of Southeast Asia: An Experiment in Art History', *The Many Faces of Primitive Art*, ed. D. Fraser (Englewood Cliffs, 1966), pp. 165–221
W. G. Solheim: 'A Look at "L'Art prébouddhique de la Chine et de l'Asie du Sud-est et son influence en Océanie" Forty Years After', *Asian Persp.*, xxii (1979) [published 1982], pp. 165–205
P. Lewis and E. Lewis: *Peoples of the Golden Triangle: Six Tribes in Thailand* (London, 1984)
J. P. Barbier: *Art of Nagaland: The Barbier-Müller Collection, Geneva* (Los Angeles, 1985)
S. Fraser-Lu: *Handwoven Textiles of South-east Asia* (Oxford, 1988)
M. Gittinger and H. L. Lefferts: *Textiles and the Thai Experience in South-east Asia* (Washington, 1992)

RUTH BARNES

XI. Art education.

Traditionally, specialist crafts were passed down within families. The only way for a young person with an interest in the arts to acquire knowledge outside the family was to apprentice himself to a master (*hsaya*). This applied to all the arts, of which there were officially ten, known as the ten flowers (*bahse myò*). These were: building with brick (*bayan*), wood-carving (*babû*), wood-turning (*babut*), painting (*bagyi*), gold- and silverwork (*badein*), smithing (*babair*), lacquerwork (*bayùn*), work in cement or stucco (*badáw*), brassworking (*badîn*) and stone sculpture (*bata-máw*). Apprentice craftsmen sometimes lived with the *hsaya*, acting as his servants in return for food and clothing. The bond thus established between pupil and teacher was rarely broken.

Manuals on various arts survive. These were sometimes kept in monastic collections, from which students might acquire further knowledge. In the past, Burmese art was almost exclusively religious, and scholarly monks kept a critical eye on work to ensure religious requirements were met.

About 1900 some artists came into contact with British amateur painters in Rangoon, who introduced Western techniques (*see* §V, 3 above). In 1953 a State School for Fine Arts was opened in Mandalay and another in Rangoon. The curriculum originally consisted of painting (watercolours and oil), sculpture (wood and clay) and music and dance, with emphasis on traditional styles. By the early 1980s new subjects, such as illustration and poster and cartoon drawing, had been added. Art classes were introduced into most schools and teachers' training colleges. Small state and private schools were also opened in the provinces, offering training in local traditional arts: lacquerware in Pagan, glazed pottery in Pegu and Shwegu and weaving at Inle and Amarapura. On completion of their studies, students usually work with established members of their chosen profession.

BIBLIOGRAPHY

J. G. Scott [Shway Yoe]: *The Burman: His Life and Notions* (London, 1882/*R* New York, 1963/*R* Arran, 1989)
J. Laughlin: *Perspective of Burma*, *Atlantic Mthly*, suppl. (New York, 1958)
U Hla Tin Htun: 'Myan-má Yesay Pan Chee Hloke Shar Hmu' [The evolution of Burmese watercolour painting], *Panchee Pan Bu Sarsaung* (1979), pp. 107–10
U Tun Shein: *Mandalay Yinkyaihmu Ahnu Pyinnya* [Crafts of Mandalay] (Rangoon, 1979)
U Khin Zaw: *Burmese Culture* (Rangoon, 1981)

NOEL F. SINGER

Burman, Thomas (*b* 1617–18; *d* London, 17 March 1674). English sculptor. He was apprenticed to Edward Marshall in 1632–3 under the auspices of the Masons' Company of London, which he later served twice as Warden (1668–9, 1673–4). His first known work was the funeral effigy of *Robert Devereux, 3rd Earl of Essex* (1646; destr. that year). In 1651–2, when he was said to be 'poore', he submitted designs for Sir Ralph Verney's family church monument, but the commission went to his former master. A bust supplied by John Stone to Sir William Paston was completed *c*. 1652 by Burman, and he may well have worked on tombs such as that of *Sir Edward and Lady Hungerford* (*c*. 1648; Farleigh House, Somerset) that can be stylistically associated with both the Stone workshop and Burman's own later memorials. That to *John Dutton* (1661; Sherborne, Glos, St Mary Magdalen) is a mediocre imitation of the famous *John Donne* by Nicholas Stone (i), while *Bartholomew Beale and his Wife* (1672; Walton, Bucks, St Michael) derives ultimately from an ancient Roman type with busts in hemispherical niches. Burman also made the statue of *Mary, Countess of Shrewsbury* (1671) and probably that of *Lady Margaret Beaufort* (1674), both at St John's College, Cambridge.

BIBLIOGRAPHY

Gunnis
L. Stone: 'The Verney Tomb at Middle Claydon', *Rec. Bucks*, xvi (1955–6), pp. 67–82 (68–70, 74–8)
M. Whinney: *Sculpture in Britain 1530–1830*, Pelican Hist. A. (Harmondsworth, 1964, rev. 2/1987), pp. 41–2

ADAM WHITE

Burn, William (*b* Edinburgh, 20 Dec 1789; *d* London, 15 Feb 1870). Scottish architect. He was the leading country-house specialist in Scotland between 1820 and 1844 and a dominant influence on Scottish architecture. He trained first with his father Robert Burn (1752–1815) before joining in 1808 the London office of Sir Robert Smirke, where he learnt meticulous accuracy of draughtsmanship on the drawings for Lowther Castle (1806–11), Cumbria, and the practical problems of running a large contract at Covent Garden Theatre (1808–9; destr.), London. He returned to Scotland in 1811 or 1812 when he undertook the building of Smirke's design for the country house Kinmount (1812), Dumfries & Galloway.

These three buildings were the formative influences on Burn's early career. The elevations of Merchant Maiden Hospital (1816; destr.) and John Watson's School (1825; now the National Gallery of Modern Art), both in Edinburgh, and the Custom House (1817) at Greenock, Strathclyde, all derive from Covent Garden. Similarly, Smirke's plan of Eastnor Castle (1812–20), Hereford & Worcs, and Kinmount, with a central saloon and lantern tower, provided the basic arrangement of his first major country houses, Saltoun (1818), East Lothian, in a neo-Tudor style, and Camperdown (1821; revised 1824), near Dundee, Tayside, which has Ionic details. The Camperdown plan, in which all the principal apartments were logically planned *en suite* from the family bedroom to the dining-room, was continually refined and set new standards of privacy which soon brought an average of five major domestic commissions a year. Burn also drew inspiration from William Wilkins's Greek Revival Grange Park (*c*. 1808–9) for Camperdown and, in Strathclyde, for his neo-Tudor work for Blairquhan (1820), Straiton, Carstairs (1822), and Garscube (1826; destr.); Edward Blore's Cotswold neo-Tudor Corehouse (1824–7), Strathclyde, was the model for his influential cottage houses in Tayside at Snaigow (destr.) and Pitcairns, Dunning (both 1827).

At Dupplin, Tayside, and St Fort, Forgan, Fife (1828 and 1829; destr.), both in a neo-Jacobean style, the central saloon is superseded by a hall-corridor with the principal apartments ranged along the garden front. Entrance elevations were invariably asymmetrical, neatly composed with refined detail and balanced by a lower service wing, often at right angles to create a sheltered forecourt.

With encouragement from Sir Walter Scott, Burn began experimenting with Scottish motifs. At Brodie (1824), Grampian, and Lauriston (1827), Edinburgh, old tower houses were made the dominant elements of otherwise new houses, establishing a compositional formula that David Bryce, his assistant, and from 1841 partner, later exploited in his new houses. By 1829 Burn himself had begun to build neo-Jacobean houses with Scottish turrets and crow-steps at Milton Lockhart (1829–36; destr.), Carluke, Strathclyde, achieving pure 17th-century Scottish detailing by 1838 in his addition to Castle Menzies, Tayside. The same year Burn was commissioned to complete Anthony Salvin's Harlaxton Manor, Lincs. This work, together with his study of original Jacobean houses, produced a series of outstandingly fine houses designed in a neo-Jacobean style. These commissions, coming from Scotland, England and Ireland, resulted in the transfer of his practice to London in 1844 and a decision to accept country-house work only.

After the vast scheme for Fonthill (1849) was abandoned, the quality of Burn's work declined, with the exception of Montagu House (1853–9; destr.), Whitehall, London, for his great patron Walter Francis Montagu-Douglas-Scott, 5th Duke of Buccleuch. Most of his later work involved the improvement of existing houses, with rich interiors in a range of styles. Burn was forthright in manner, and his extreme scrupulousness in his dealings with clients and his refusal to allow his work to be exhibited or published were major factors in his success. His presentation drawings are invariably small in scale, usually in pencil but sometimes in pen and wash, occasionally watercolour.

Johann Bernhard Fischer von Erlach and Lodovico Burnacini: Trinity Column, Graben, Vienna, completed 1692

BIBLIOGRAPHY

A. J. Youngson: *The Making of Classical Edinburgh* (Edinburgh, 1966)
J. M. Macaulay: *The Gothic Revival: 1745–1845* (Glasgow, 1975), pp. 318–37
J. Fawcett, ed.: *Seven Victorian Architects* (London, 1976), pp. 8–31
V. Fiddes and A. J. Rowan, eds: *Mr David Bryce* (Edinburgh, 1976)
M. Girouard: *The Victorian Country House* (London, 1979)
J. Franklin: *The Gentleman's Country House and its Plan: 1835–1914* (London, 1981)
N. Allen, ed.: *Scottish Pioneers of the Greek Revival* (Edinburgh, 1984), pp. 3–35

DAVID WALKER

Burnacini, Lodovico [Ludovico] **(Ottavio)** (*b* Mantua, 1636; *d* Vienna, 1707). Italian architect and stage designer, active in Austria. He went to Vienna in 1651 as the apprentice of his father, Giovanni Burnacini (*d* 1655), the Venetian theatre architect who introduced to Vienna the system of stage design developed by Giovanni Battista Aleotti and who produced stage sets in the Florentine–Venetian style of Giulio and Alfonso Parigi and Giacomo Torelli. Lodovico Burnacini was his father's assistant until the latter's death and succeeded him in the office of theatre architect and imperial court engineer to Emperor Leopold I. Although he participated in the construction of various imperial castles in the vicinity of Vienna, Burnacini was mainly engaged in theatre design, developing his father's style of stage settings and becoming the founder of the Viennese style, which had considerable influence on German theatre. Designs for 115 compositions and plays have survived, and many of Burnacini's designs were reproduced as engravings in luxury editions of the libretti. Holograph drawings are preserved (Vienna, Österreich. Nbib.). They include religious themes, physiognomic sketches, figurines and grotesques as well as narrative illustrations.

In 1665 Burnacini designed and built the first free-standing, combined opera and playhouse in the German-speaking region, the Comödihauss auf der Cortina (destr. 1683), a timber-framed building on a stone base on the site of the present Hofbibliothek. It was a square, four-storey galleried building; inside, three tiers without boxes provided 2000 seats, and there was also a raised upper circle reserved for the imperial family. The theatre was equipped with every imaginable technical refinement and extended the usual Italian sequence of proscenium, stage, pit and backdrop. The stage itself, measuring *c*. 65 m in total length, had a depth of *c*. 30 m, comprising proscenium, apron, pit and lowerable middle backdrop, ramped rear stage and closing backdrop with several workshops and green rooms behind. Machinery and five pairs of wings made it possible to have 50 different set changes during a single production, and there was room for up to 2000 performers on the stage. The theatre was built for the performance of Pietro Antonio Cesti's opera *Il pomo d'oro*, which was the climax of a succession of festivities to mark the marriage of Leopold I with the Infanta Margherita of Spain, celebrated from 1666 to 1668. The stage settings were after Burnacini's designs and required complicated technical apparatus for which none of the existing Viennese theatres was sufficiently equipped. The Italian libretto by Francesco Sbarra was published in

Vienna (1668) and has 25 engravings after Burnacini's designs, giving an impression of the theatre building and its sets. The illusionistically painted ceiling can also be seen, the first of its kind in Vienna. Burnacini liked investigating allegory and symbolism, and in *Il pomo d'oro* he reached the apogee of Baroque stage design.

From 1687 Burnacini was Senior Court Engineer, in which capacity he supervised the construction of the Trinity Column in Vienna (see fig.), a memorial to victims of the plague. Johann Bernhard Fischer von Erlach was responsible for changes (1686) to the original design (1682) by Mathias Rauchmillar, and Burnacini executed Fischer von Erlach's plans with considerable artistic intervention, seen in various preserved plans and designs (Vienna, Österreich. Nbib.). Burnacini's reputation, however, was primarily established through his theatre productions, and he was awarded numerous imperial honours.

UNPUBLISHED SOURCES

Vienna, Österreich. Nbib. [drawings for set designs and plans for the Trinity Column, Cod. min. 29, fols 63a/3, 63a/2, 58a/2, 65b/1]

PRINTS

F. Sbarra: *Il pomo d'oro* (Vienna, 1668)

BIBLIOGRAPHY

F. Biach-Schiffmann: *Giovanni und Ludovico Burnacini: Theater und Feste am Wiener Hof* (Vienna and Berlin, 1931)
G. Schikola: 'Ludovico Burnacinis Entwürfe für die Wiener Pestsäule', *Wien. Jb. Kunstgesch.*, xxv (1972), pp. 247–58
S. Solf: *Festdekoration und Groteske: Der Wiener Bühnenbildner Lodovico Ottavio Burnacini: Inszenierung barocker Kunstvorstellung*, Stud. Dt. Kstgesch., 355 (Baden-Baden, 1975)

CAROLA WENZEL

Burnand, Eugène (*b* Moudon, Vaud, 30 Aug 1850; *d* Paris, 4 Feb 1921). Swiss painter and illustrator. Having studied with Barthélemy Menn at the Ecole des Beaux-Arts in Geneva, he went to Paris in 1872 and joined Jean-Léon Gérôme's studio. After a visit to Rome in 1876–7, he returned to live in Paris in 1878. Burnand was primarily a landscape painter. Works such as the *Village Pump* (1879; Neuchâtel, Mus. A. & Hist.), *Bull in the Alps* (1884; Lausanne, Pal. Rumine) and *Day's End* (1896; Lucerne, Kstmus.) reveal his debt to the Realism of Millet and Courbet and express a genuine attentiveness and great sensitivity to nature. This Realism is also present in his religious works, for example the *Apostles Peter and John Running to the Sepulchre* (1898; Paris, Mus. d'Orsay). After learning engraving with Paul Girardet (1821–93) in Versailles, Burnand also produced many illustrations for such newspapers as *L'Illustration* and *Tour du monde*. In addition he illustrated editions of numerous literary works: Alphonse Daudet's *Contes choisis* (Paris, 1883), Frédéric Mistral's *Mireille* (Paris, 1884), Cérésole's *Légendes des Alpes vaudoises* (Lausanne, 1885), George Sand's *François le champi* (Paris, 1888), Olivier's *L'Orphelin* (Lausanne, n.d.) and the *Paraboles de l'Evangile* (Paris-Nancy, 1908). He won a third-class medal for engraving in the Paris Salon of 1882, a gold medal in the Exposition Universelle of 1889 in Paris and another in 1900. Burnand lived in Montpellier between 1895 and 1903 and then between 1903 and 1907 at Hauterive in Neuenburgsee. In 1914 he organized an important exhibition of works which he had painted in Assisi.

BIBLIOGRAPHY

M. V. Grellet: *Eugène Burnand: Sa vie, son oeuvre* (Lausanne, 1921)
R. Burnand: *Eugène Burnand: L'Homme, l'artiste et son oeuvre* (Paris, 1926)
——: *Jeunesse de peintres: Eugène Burnand et ses amis* (Lausanne, 1949)

A. DAGUERRE DE HUREAUX

Burne-Jones, Sir **Edward (Coley)** (*b* Birmingham, 28 Aug 1833; *d* London, 17 June 1898). English painter and decorative artist. He was the leading figure in the second phase of the Pre-Raphaelite movement. His paintings of subjects from medieval legend and Classical mythology and his designs for stained glass, tapestry and many other media played an important part in the Aesthetic Movement and the history of international Symbolism.

1. Life and work. 2. Working methods and technique.

1. LIFE AND WORK.

(i) Training, to 1855. He was the only surviving child of Edward Richard Jones, who ran a small carving and gilding business in the centre of Birmingham, and Elizabeth Coley, the daughter of a prosperous jeweller. Christened Edward Coley Burne Jones, he was called simply Edward Jones until *c.* 1860 when he adopted the surname Burne-Jones. From an early age he drew prolifically but with little guidance and no intention of becoming an artist. In 1844 he entered the local grammar school, King Edward's, destined for a career in engineering. It was probably in this connection that in 1848 he attended evening classes at the Birmingham School of Design. By the time he left school in 1852, having come under the influence of John Henry Newman, he had decided to enter the Church.

In January 1853 he went up to Exeter College, Oxford, where he met his lifelong friend and working associate, William Morris. As Anglo-Catholics, steeped in Romantic literature and fascinated by everything medieval, they were thrilled by the outward appearance of the still unreformed university. However, they were dismayed to discover that the religious fervour of the Tractarian heyday had abated and were soon looking for leadership elsewhere. Inspired by the work ethic of Thomas Carlyle, they joined with other friends in planning the *Oxford and Cambridge Magazine*; this ran for twelve issues in 1856, Burne-Jones contributing two stories and several reviews. Meanwhile they experienced the more important influence of John Ruskin, whose emphasis on the prophetic role of the artist showed them that art, no less than the Church, could be the vehicle of their idealism. Burne-Jones cultivated his talent for drawing by going into the Oxfordshire countryside to make careful studies from nature in the prescribed Ruskinian manner. In 1854 he received his first commission, to illustrate *The Fairy Family*, a collection of fairy tales by Archibald Maclaren. Ruskin's writings also introduced Burne-Jones and Morris to the paintings of the early Italian painters and the Pre-Raphaelite Brotherhood. At the Royal Academy exhibition of 1854 they saw William Holman Hunt's work for the first time, but it was Dante Gabriel Rossetti's watercolour *Dante Drawing an Angel* (Oxford, Ashmolean) that impressed them most when they saw it in Thomas Combe's collection in Oxford in 1855. Returning from a tour of the French cathedrals in the long vacation that year, they finally decided to devote themselves to art.

(ii) Early successes, 1856–70. In January 1856 Burne-Jones secured an introduction to Rossetti, and in May he left Oxford without taking his degree and settled in London to begin his artistic career. Rossetti gave him informal lessons, and for several years he attended evening life classes at the school run by James Matthews Leigh (1808–60); otherwise he was virtually self-taught. From November 1856 to September 1858 he and Morris shared rooms at 17 Red Lion Square, formerly occupied by Rossetti and Walter Deverell. They were in constant touch with Rossetti at this period, forming together a bohemian clique passionately devoted to the Middle Ages. Burne-Jones's main contribution was a series of small, highly finished pen-and-ink drawings inspired by Malory and Froissart and closely related to both Rossetti's contemporary watercolours and the poems in Morris's *Defence of Guenevere* (1858). In 1857–8 he collaborated with Rossetti and others in decorating the debating chamber of the new Oxford Union with murals illustrating the *Morte d'Arthur*.

From the start Burne-Jones enjoyed success, his work being seen at the exhibitions of the Hogarth Club and attracting the attention of patrons, notably the Leeds stockbroker T. E. Plint. His sense of design was already pronounced, and during these early years he was associated with many progressive architects of the Gothic Revival, including William Butterfield, William Burges and G. F. Bodley. Stained glass was his particular forte; in 1857 he designed the first of a number of windows for James Powell & Sons, and he also worked for the rival firm of Lavers & Barraud. From 1859 to 1861 he taught at the Working Men's College.

In the summer of 1858 he spent several months recovering from nervous exhaustion at Little Holland House, where G. F. Watts urged him to adopt a broader basis of style. The same course was encouraged by Ruskin, whom he met in November 1856. Influenced by both men, he made his first visit to Italy in the autumn of 1859 with Watts's pupil Val Prinsep. The tour included Genoa, Pisa, Florence, Siena, Padua and Venice, and wherever he went he made copies of 14th- and 15th-century paintings (Cambridge, Fitzwilliam).

In June 1860 he married Georgiana Macdonald (1840–1920); their first child, Philip (1861–1926), was later a minor painter of portraits and subject pictures. Shortly after his marriage Burne-Jones painted murals at Red House, Morris's new home in Kent, and in April 1861 he helped to found the firm of Morris, Marshall, Faulkner & Co., 'Fine Art Workmen', soon becoming their chief designer of figure subjects for stained glass (*see* STAINED GLASS, fig. 11 and colour pl. VI, fig. 2) and tiles.

From May to July 1862 the Burne-Joneses were in north Italy with Ruskin, who commissioned the artist to copy paintings in Venice, Padua and Milan. This marks the climax of Ruskin's attempt to influence Burne-Jones's development and of a Venetian tendency that his work exhibits in the early 1860s, like that of many artists in his circle. The copies of Bernardino Luini's paintings that he made in Milan had a bearing on the evolution of his later facial type.

About 1860 Burne-Jones turned to watercolour as his primary medium, and in 1864 he was elected an Associate of the Old Water-Colour Society (OWCS). This brought his work before a wide public for the first time. It was never popular with the more conservative members and was often savagely attacked in the press. Nonetheless he began to be seen as the leader of a new school. The mystical feeling of such paintings as *The Merciful Knight* (1863; Birmingham, Mus. & A.G.) gained him eager followers, including the young Walter Crane. They also attracted new patrons, notably William Graham, a wealthy businessman and MP for Glasgow, and F. R. Leyland, the Liverpool shipowner. At the end of 1864 the Burne-Joneses moved to 41 Kensington Square, and in 1867 they settled at The Grange, North End Lane, Fulham, where they remained until Burne-Jones's death.

During the late 1860s Burne-Jones adopted a more professional approach, partly in order to meet his new commitments and the ever-growing demands of the firm, partly in response to press criticism and Watts's advice that he must improve his drawing, and partly to compete with academically trained artists such as Frederic Leighton and Edward Poynter, who married one of Georgiana's sisters in 1866. Though his work lost some of its early intensity, by studying the nude and the Antique he became a much better draughtsman, while his handling of watercolour and, increasingly, oil grew more proficient. In 1865 he began a series of designs for an illustrated edition of Morris's cycle of narrative poems *The Earthly Paradise*; the scheme fell through, but it was to provide him with compositions for pictures until the end of his life. His work of this period also has close links with the poetry of A. C. Swinburne, who dedicated his *Poems and Ballads* to him in 1866, and it reflects the prevailing classic and aesthetic trends in painting, inviting comparison with Albert Moore and James McNeill Whistler. Major examples are *The Lament* (1866; London, William Morris Gal.) and *The Wine of Circe* (priv. col., see Bell, p. 98), a picture exhibited at the OWCS in 1869 that did much to advance his reputation.

Despite outward success, Burne-Jones faced a personal and professional crisis in the years around 1870. His private life was clouded by his affair with the Greek beauty Mary Zambaco, although this episode found many echoes in his work. He also suffered from an acute sense of artistic isolation. In 1870 he resigned from the OWCS when objections were raised to the male nude figure in *Phyllis and Demophoön* (1870; Birmingham, Mus. & A.G.), and the following year he quarrelled with Ruskin over their different views on Michelangelo. His friendship with Rossetti declined after Rossetti's breakdown in June 1872, and with Morris too there was less sympathy than before. In 1875 the firm of Morris, Marshall, Faulkner & Co. in its original form was dissolved.

For reassurance Burne-Jones turned to the Italian Renaissance painters who had assumed increasing importance for him in the 1860s, and he decided to return to Italy in September 1871. He revisited Genoa, Florence and Pisa and saw for the first time San Gimignano, Orvieto and Rome, besides Assisi, Perugia, Cortona and Arezzo. As on previous visits, he made many copies of paintings, as well as paying careful attention to architecture and landscape. On his return he wrote that his favourite painters were now Giotto, Andrea di Cione Orcagna, Paolo Uccello, Piero della Francesca, Andrea Mantegna,

Luca Signorelli, Sandro Botticelli, Michelangelo and Andrea del Sarto. He made a fourth and final visit in the spring of 1873, seeing Siena, Florence and Ravenna.

His enthusiasm for Italy is abundantly clear in the work of this period. The outstanding example is the Troy triptych (Birmingham, Mus. & A.G.), conceived in 1870 but never completed, though several of its component designs were later worked up as independent pictures. Two of these are perhaps the most Italianate works he ever conceived: the unfinished *Venus Discordia* (begun 1873; Cardiff, N. Mus.), with its echoes of Antonio del Pollaiuolo and Luca Signorelli, and *The Wheel of Fortune* (1875–83; Paris, Mus. d'Orsay), which celebrates his passion for Michelangelo.

(iii) Maturity and late work, 1870–98. For seven years after resigning from the OWCS Burne-Jones hardly exhibited, but at the opening exhibition at the Grosvenor Gallery, London, in 1877, he showed eight large works, including *The Beguiling of Merlin* (1873–7; Port Sunlight, Lady Lever A.G.) and *The Mirror of Venus* (1873–7; Lisbon, Mus. Gulbenkian), both of which belonged to Leyland, and *The Days of Creation* (1871–76; Cambridge, MA, Fogg), which had been purchased by Graham. This dramatic revelation of his mature powers established him overnight as the star of the Grosvenor, a key figure in the Aesthetic Movement and one of the leading artists of the day.

Further exhibitions at the Grosvenor confirmed his reputation. In 1878 he showed *Laus Veneris* (1873–8; Newcastle upon Tyne, Laing A.G.) and *Le Chant d'amour* (1868–77; New York, Met., see fig. 1), two richly coloured Giorgionesque compositions that reflect the taste of their owner, Graham. These were followed in 1879–80 by a group of works in a rather cold, classical style: the *Pygmalion* series (completed 1879; Birmingham, Mus. & A.G.), *The Annunciation* (1876–9; Port Sunlight, Lady Lever A.G.) and *The Golden Stairs* (1876–80; London, Tate). In 1882 he exhibited *The Mill* (London, V&A), a sombre, romantic picture that was bought by Constantine Ionides, the leader of the Anglo-Greek community in London, followed in 1883 by *The Wheel of Fortune* (Paris, Mus. d'Orsay) and *The Hours* (Sheffield, Mappin A.G.) and in 1884 by *King Cophetua and the Beggar Maid* (London, Tate; see fig. 2). This was at once recognized as a new peak in his career, and it has remained probably his single most famous work.

In 1880 Burne-Jones was able to buy a country retreat at Rottingdean on the Sussex coast. In 1883 Ruskin, as Slade Professor at Oxford, devoted a lecture to him in his 'Art of England' series, and in 1885 Burne-Jones accepted the presidency of the Birmingham Society of Artists and

1. Edward Burne-Jones: *Le Chant d'amour*, oil on canvas, 1.12×1.53 m, 1868–77 (New York, Metropolitan Museum of Art)

2. Edward Burne-Jones: *King Cophetua and the Beggar Maid*, oil on canvas, 2.93×1.36 m, 1884 (London, Tate Gallery)

was elected ARA. However, the Royal Academy was never his spiritual home, and having exhibited only one picture there—*The Depths of the Sea* (priv. col., see 1975–6 exh. cat., p. 57) in 1886—he resigned in 1893. In 1886 he was re-elected to the OWCS.

In 1887 a dispute arose over the policy of the Grosvenor Gallery. Burne-Jones sided with the directors, Charles Hallé and J. Comyns Carr, and they pledged support for the New Gallery, which opened in Regent Street the following year. At the first exhibition he showed *Danaë and the Brazen Tower* (1887–8; Glasgow, A.G. & Mus.) and two of the *Perseus* series (completed 1888; Stuttgart, Staatsgal.), which had been commissioned by the politician and philosopher A. J. Balfour in 1875.

In the 1890s Burne-Jones also enjoyed an international reputation. His work was first seen in Paris, when he showed *The Beguiling of Merlin* at the Exposition Universelle of 1878. It made little impact, but *King Cophetua* was a great success when it appeared at the Exposition Universelle of 1889, earning the artist the cross of the Légion d'honneur. He continued to exhibit in Paris until 1896 and was much admired in Symbolist circles. His work was also acclaimed in Belgium, Germany, Spain, America and Russia.

Although it did not come easily to him, in later life he made several attempts at portraiture, the most ambitious being a full-length likeness of *Lady Windsor* (1891–5; priv. col., see 1975–6 exh. cat., p. 78). Like Balfour, the sitter was a leading member of The Souls, a group with which Burne-Jones was closely associated. It was also at this time that his talents as a decorative artist reached their fullest development. He still provided Morris with a seemingly endless flow of stained-glass cartoons, their work in this field culminating in the four enormous windows made for St Philip's Cathedral, Birmingham (1885–97). During the 1880s Morris turned his attention to tapestry; again Burne-Jones supplied the designs, their greatest achievement being the Holy Grail series completed in 1894 for Stanmore Hall, Uxbridge, near London (*see* TAPESTRY, colour pl. III, fig. 2). But the Morris firm accounted for only part of his decorative output. In 1879–80, collaborating with Broadwood, he designed and painted the 'Orpheus' piano (priv. col., see 1975–6 exh. cat., p. 71) for Graham's daughter Frances, a close friend of later years. In 1881 he was commissioned to design mosaics for G. E. Street's American Episcopal church of St Paul in Rome, adopting a Byzantine idiom that permeated much of his work in the ensuing period. Nor did his invention stop here, embracing needlework, gesso panels, jewellery, tombstones, ceremonial seals, stage design, book covers, even shoes and garden seats. Many of his later designs were shown at the exhibitions of the Arts and Crafts Exhibition Society, founded in 1888.

In 1890 Morris launched his last great venture, the Kelmscott Press. Once more Burne-Jones was closely involved, illustrating 12 books. By far the most important was the celebrated edition of Chaucer's works (May 1896), for which he made 87 designs (*see* MORRIS, WILLIAM, fig. 4).

Burne-Jones's career reached its climax in 1890 with the popular exhibition of the four large *Briar Rose* paintings (1870–90; Buscot Park, Oxon, NT) at the Bond Street premises of his dealers, Agnew's. In 1892–3 a retrospective exhibition of his work was held at the New Gallery, and in 1894 he accepted a baronetcy from his old friend W. E. Gladstone.

His late work shows him retreating into himself, evolving a mannered and highly personal style and returning to his early interest in Malory. The chief expression of this private world is *The Sleep of King Arthur in Avalon* (begun 1881; Ponce, Mus. A.), the colossal unfinished canvas on which he was working at his death. By the end of his life there were already signs that his popularity was waning:

Love Leading the Pilgrim (1877–97; London, Tate), exhibited at the New Gallery in 1897, returned to his studio unsold. Morris's death in October 1896 further increased his isolation, and he died of a heart attack two years later.

2. WORKING METHODS AND TECHNIQUE. Burne-Jones's working methods often seem wilfully perverse, the result, no doubt, of his lack of formal training. His early drawings for Maclaren's *Fairy Family*, meticulously worked in pen and ink and grey wash, have the appearance of steel engravings, and indeed were inspired by conventional book illustrations of the day. The pen drawings of the late 1850s were again influenced by engravings, those of Albrecht Dürer. When Burne-Jones turned to watercolour he handled it like oil, with a plentiful use of body colour; while with oil he eschewed painterly effects, preferring to work up the forms and colours by means of scumbles and glazes over a monochrome underpainting.

From the first he tended to blur the boundaries between his painting and decorative work; pictures were developed from designs for glass, tapestry and even mosaic, and occasionally were painted on top of a glass cartoon. While this could make his decorative designs dangerously pictorial, it accounts for some of the salient features of his style as a painter: his fondness for restricted spatial recession, for surface texture and pattern, and for tall upright compositions like the lights of a stained-glass window. It also had a bearing on the scale of his pictures, which grew steadily larger throughout his career. Increasingly he came to feel that his easel pictures were no more than substitutes for the frescoes he would have been painting if he had lived in a society with the priorities of Renaissance Florence.

His paintings were similarly influenced by his book illustrations, which encouraged him to think in terms of series of linked designs; for example, the *Pygmalion* series consists of four canvases based on his illustrations to Morris's *Earthly Paradise*.

Despite his poor health, Burne-Jones was a tireless worker. His fertile imagination generated far more ideas than he could bring to fruition, and his studio was littered with works at every stage of development. Since he liked to work slowly, putting one picture aside when another claimed his attention, they often took years to complete; his last exhibited picture, *The Prioress's Tale* (Wilmington, DE, A. Mus.), was begun in 1869 and had been designed a decade earlier. In the course of this long gestation, he often started other versions to try out some alternative approach, while at every stage studies were made, particularly of nudes, heads, drapery and armour. These drawings have the character of independent works of art and Burne-Jones clearly saw them as such, exhibiting many in his lifetime. His passion for drawing also had an unofficial aspect, making him a prolific and delightfully whimsical caricaturist.

His sense of line was powerful; the serpentine rhythms he developed under the influence of Botticelli are especially characteristic and were to prove an important source for Art Nouveau. He was also a fine colourist. His early watercolours are rich and glowing, revealing his connection with High Victorian decorative schemes and the influence of Venetian painting. In the mid-1860s he adopted a rather chalky palette, in keeping with the classicism of the time, but in his mature works he returned to a stronger range of tones, making great play with shot colours that enabled him to maintain a chromatic harmony across a large canvas. However, his cartoons for stained glass and tapestries, whether in sepia wash or charcoal, seldom indicate the colours to be used; this was Morris's responsibility.

The pressures that Burne-Jones faced by the mid-1860s led him to employ assistants. The first was Charles Fairfax Murray, who began working for him in November 1866 and was soon followed by others, the most important being Thomas Matthews Rooke (1842–1942), who stayed with his master to the end, and John Melhuish Strudwick (1849–1937), who joined the studio for a period in the 1870s. Like Murray, both became artists of note, Rooke as a painter of Old Testament subjects and a fine topographical draughtsman, Strudwick as a somewhat anaemic exponent of the Burne-Jones style. Though he carried out the most important pictures himself, Burne-Jones was prepared for others to be executed partly or even wholly from his designs. Failure to understand this working principle has sometimes led to confusion, and indeed the demarcation between the hands of the master himself and his coadjutors is not always easy to determine.

The sale of his studio contents was held at Christie's, London, 16 and 18 July 1898; a second studio sale took place at Christie's, 5 June 1919.

For further illustration *see* TAPESTRY, fig. 12.

UNPUBLISHED SOURCES

An autograph notebook containing Burne-Jones's own record of his works and two autograph pass-books containing his accounts with Morris & Co. (1861–98) are in the Fitzwilliam Museum, Cambridge. Burne-Jones's numerous letters are widely scattered; collections are in the British Library, London, the Fitzwilliam Museum, Cambridge, and the Bodleian Library, Oxford.

BIBLIOGRAPHY

A. Maclaren: *The Fairy Family* (London, 1857, rev. 2/1985) [rev. contains an add. 85 illus. and an intro. by J. Christian]

M. Bell: *Sir Edward Burne-Jones: A Record and Review* (London, 1892, rev. 2/1898) [standard early monograph]

A. Vallance: 'The Decorative Art of Sir Edward Burne-Jones, Bt.', *A. Annu.* (1900) [special Easter no. of the *Art Journal*]

G. B[urne]-J[ones]: *Memorials of Edward Burne-Jones*, 2 vols (London, 1904) [widow's biog.]; repr., intro. by J. Christian (1993)

F. De Lisle: *Burne-Jones* (London, 1904) [informative early monograph]

The Flower Book (London, 1905) [facs. repr. of the 38 wtrcol. thus entitled in the British Museum]

T. Martin Wood: *Drawings of Sir Edward Burne-Jones* (London, 1907)

R. Ironside: 'Burne-Jones and Gustave Moreau', *Horizon*, i (1940), pp. 406–24

D. Cecil: *Visionary and Dreamer: Samuel Palmer and Edward Burne-Jones* (Princeton, 1969)

Burne-Jones (exh. cat., by W. S. Taylor, Sheffield, Mappin A.G., 1971)

J. Christian: 'Early German sources for Pre-Raphaelite designs', *A. Q.*, xxxvi (1973), pp. 56–83

M. Harrison and B. Waters: *Burne-Jones* (London, 1973)

K.Löcher: *Der Perseus-Zyklus von Edward Burne-Jones* (Stuttgart, 1973)

A. C. Sewter: *The Stained Glass of William Morris and his Circle*, 2 vols (New Haven, 1974–5) [cat., incl. all Burne-Jones's windows]

P. Fitzgerald: *Edward Burne-Jones: A Biography* (London, 1975)

Apollo, cii/165 (1975) [articles by nine scholars to coincide with ACGB exhibition]

Burne-Jones (exh. cat. by J. Christian, ACGB, 1975–6)

J. Christian, ed.: *The Little Holland House Album* (North Berwick, 1981) [formerly unpubd. early drgs]

M. Lago, ed.: *Burne-Jones Talking* (London, 1981) [the artist's studio conversation, 1895–8]

J. Christian: '*La Roue de la fortune* de Burne-Jones', *Rev. Louvre*, iii (1984), pp. 204–11 [reproduces all versions]
——: '"A serious talk": Ruskin's place in Burne-Jones's artistic development', *Pre-Raphaelite Papers*, ed. L. Parris (London, 1984), pp. 184–205
The Pre-Raphaelites (exh. cat., ed. L. Parris; London, Tate, 1984) [incl. 16 major works by Burne-Jones]
C. Poulson: 'Costume Designs by Burne-Jones for Irving's Production of *King Arthur*', *Burl. Mag.*, cxxviii (1986), pp. 18–24
K. Powell: 'Burne-Jones and the Legend of the Briar Rose', *J. Pre-Raphaelite Stud.*, vi (1986), pp. 15–28
Burne-Jones (exh. cat. by M. T. Benedetti and G. Piantoni, Rome, G.N.A. Mod., 1986)
Burne-Jones and his Followers (exh. cat. by J. Christian, circulated in Japan by the *Tokyo Shimbun*, 1987)
The Last Romantics: The Romantic Tradition in British Art: Burne-Jones to Stanley Spencer (exh. cat. by J. Christian, London, Barbican A. G., 1989)
P. Fitzgerald: 'Within a Magic Circle', *TLS* (22 October 1993), p. 18

For further bibliography see W. E. Fredeman: *Pre-Raphaelitism: A Bibliocritical Study* (Cambridge, MA, 1965), pp. 155–62.

For general works on the Pre-Raphaelites, *see* PRE-RAPHAELITISM.

JOHN CHRISTIAN

Burnell, Robert (*b* Acton Burnell, Salop, *c.* 1230; *d* Berwick-upon-Tweed, 1292). Bishop of Bath and Wells, Chancellor of England and patron. He was the younger son of a minor Shropshire landowner. After entering the Church and training as a lawyer, he became attached to the household of the future King Edward I (*reg* 1272–1307), with whom he built up a close relationship in the 1260s. After Edward's accession he rapidly became the chief figure in the political life of the kingdom: appointed Chancellor in 1274 and elected Bishop of Bath and Wells in 1275. He used his wealth to create a great estate centred on his birthplace, which he rebuilt as Acton Burnell 'Castle' (1284–6), and added a great chapel and aisled hall (40×21 m) to the Bishop's Palace at Wells (*c.* 1280–92). Both works, though partly ruined, are remarkable survivals of courtier houses of the late 13th century; battlemented more for display than fortification and with elegant windows that are early examples of ecclesiastical tracery applied to secular buildings. The style indicates that Burnell employed masons familiar with the latest Rayonnant works in London (e.g. Old St Paul's Cathedral) and with Edward I's castles in North Wales. The style also relates to contemporary cathedral works at Wells and Exeter, and his craftsmen were probably responsible for introducing a more refined version of early Decorated style to south-west England. His career is an outstanding early example of a churchman who, like his contemporaries bishops Merton of Rochester and Kirkby of Ely, rose through royal favour to become a major patron of architecture and a forerunner of the great courtier–prelates of the 14th century, such as William of Wykeham.

BIBLIOGRAPHY

DNB
C. A. R. Radford: *Acton Burnell Castle* (London, 1966)
R. K. Morris: 'The Remodelling of the Hereford Aisles', *J. Brit. Archaeol. Assoc.*, xxxviii (1974), pp. 21–39 (32–6)
J. West: 'Acton Burnell Castle, Shropshire', *Collectanea historica: Essays in Memory of Stuart Rigold* (Maidstone, 1981), pp. 85–92

R. K. MORRIS

Burnet, Sir **J(ohn) J(ames)** (*b* Glasgow, 31 March 1857; *d* Colinton, Edinburgh, 2 July 1938). Scottish architect. The son of the Glasgow architect John Burnet (1814–1900), he was a Beaux-Arts-trained classicist who became a modernist. Encouraged by R. Phené Spiers (1838–1916) to study at the Atelier Jean-Louis Pascal, Paris, during his time there (1875–7) he formed life-long friendships with Pascal and Henri-Paul Nénot. The first building wholly to his design was the Glasgow Fine Art Institute (1878–80, destr.), followed by the Clyde Navigation Trust (1883), Robertson Street, Glasgow, the Edinburgh International Exhibition building and the Glasgow Athenaeum, St George's Place (both 1886). All four were pure Beaux-Arts designs in which sculpture played an important role, the first two being Greco-Renaissance, the third a variant of the design by Léopold Hardy (1829-94) for the Exposition Universelle of 1878 in Paris, and the fourth a highly simplified Roman.

In 1886 another Pascal pupil, John Archibald Campbell (1859–1909), became Burnet's partner, and the practice began to develop in other directions. First, J. L. Pearson selected their design, derived from his own for St John's, Red Lion Square, London, for Barony Church (1886–9, 1898–1900), Glasgow, and secondly Burnet, whose first essay in Arts and Crafts design had been the studio house at Kilneiss (1884), Moniaive, Dumfries & Galloway, began to look across the Atlantic for inspiration in his designs for Corrienessan (1886), Loch Ard, Central, which had an American verandah plan. An important series of low, broad-eaved churches with squat Romanesque towers and Late Gothic detail followed, beginning with Shiskine (1887), Arran, for the Church of Scotland and culminating in the Gardner Memorial Church (1896–1900; now Southesk), Brechin, Tayside, and the McLaren Memorial Church and Manse (1897–1907), Stenhousemuir, Central. In 1888 Campbell combined low proportions with Scottish Renaissance detail at the Ewing Gilmour Institute, Alexandria, Strathclyde, evolving an individual manner that Burnet took up enthusiastically at Alloa Baths (1895), Clackmannan, Central, and Campbeltown Library, Strathclyde.

In 1891 Burnet designed Charing Cross Mansions, Glasgow, in a 16th-century French manner. Thereafter his Beaux-Arts training was more evident in his theoretical approach and in nuances of detailing than in style. His influential Athenaeum Theatre (1891), Glasgow, had a narrow street façade. The bold, arched recess with cantilevered canted window, derived from R. Norman Shaw, became a recurring theme in Glasgow, while the mullioned treatment of the theatre's stair and lift-shaft tower became a Burnet hallmark. At the Glasgow Savings Bank (1895), Ingram Street, his Baroque detailing, with sculpture by George Frampton, was strengthened by a visit to Italy in 1895; it became characteristic of his larger urban buildings for the following decade.

In 1897 the Burnet and Campbell partnership was dissolved. In 1895 Burnet had met Charles McKim and seen the work of Louis Sullivan during a visit to the USA. His subsequent commercial designs show the influence of this visit, notably in Atlantic Chambers (1899), Hope Street, and the more complex Waterloo Chambers (1899), Waterloo Street (both in Glasgow), and 30 Princes Street (1905–7), Edinburgh, which has a full steel frame.

In 1903 Burnet was selected to execute the Edward VII Galleries (1907) at the British Museum, London, in the Beaux-Arts Greek Revival style. An office was opened in London, the Glasgow practice becoming in 1909 a separate partnership with the Paris-trained Norman Aitken Dick (1883–1948). Of his subsequent commercial designs, the façade of General Buildings (1909), 99 Aldwych, London, uses broken pediments and decorative sculpture, while McGeoch's Warehouse (1905–6, destr.), Glasgow, had grid fenestration derived from Louis Sullivan. The Kodak Building (1910–11), 65 Kingsway, London, was developed into its final form by THOMAS TAIT, who had become Burnet's assistant in 1903. Between the greatly simplified pilasters of the street façade the spaces are filled with windows and metal panels. Adelaide House (1924–5), London Bridge Approach, London, returned to a grid with Greco-Egyptian detailing. In Glasgow, influenced by American architects such as Albert Kahn, Dwight Perkins (*b* 1867) and Richard Schmidt (1865–1958), Burnet evolved a powerful brick style that he used at the Alhambra Theatre (1910–11, destr.) and the Wallace Scott Tailoring Institute (1913–22), Cathcart, Strathclyde, the first garden factory in Britain. This style was widely used by the partnership Burnet, Tait & Lorne in the early 1930s. Burnet's later career is inseparable from that of Tait. It was much taken up with official appointments as assessor and juror, notably at the League of Nations, Geneva (1927). He was knighted in 1914 and awarded the Royal Gold Medal in 1923.

BIBLIOGRAPHY

DNB
'Men Who Build: No. 65, John James Burnet, A.R.S.A.', *Bldr's J.*, xiv (1901), pp. 138–47
H. S. Goodhart-Rendel: 'The Work of Sir John Burnet, Royal Gold Medallist', *Architects' J.*, lvii (1923), pp. 1066–1109
P. Waterhouse: 'The Royal Gold Medal Address', *RIBA J.*, xxx (1923), pp. 509–16
E. J. Burrows & Co.: *Modern Architectural Art: Sir John J. Burnet & Partners*, 2 pts (Cheltenham and London, 1924)
The Architectural Work of Sir John Burnet & Partners (Geneva, 1927)
T. Fyfe: Obituary, *RIBA J.*, xlv (1938), pp. 941–3
T. S. Tait and A. N. Paterson: Obituary, *RIBA J.*, xlv (1938), pp. 893–6
R. B. Rankin: 'Sir John J. Burnet, R.A., R.S.A., LL.D., and his Works', *Royal Incorp. Architects Scotland, Q.*, xciv (1953), pp. 27–39
J. M. Crook: *The British Museum* (London, 1972), pp. 211–16
L. K. Eaton: *American Architecture Comes of Age* (Cambridge, MA, and London, 1972), pp. 38–49
A. Service: *Edwardian Architecture and its Origins* (London, 1975), pp. 192–215
A. S. Gray: *Edwardian Architecture* (London, 1985), pp. 128–32

DAVID WALKER

Burnet, John (*b* Edinburgh, 20 March 1784; *d* London, 29 April 1868). Scottish engraver, painter and writer. He trained as an engraver in Edinburgh with Robert Scott (1771–1841) and also studied at the Trustees Academy under John Graham (1754–1817) in the same city, where he was a contemporary of David Wilkie. In 1806 he moved to London where he greatly enhanced Wilkie's reputation by producing engravings after several of the latter's early works. In the same period he also engraved original works, including illustrations to the poems of Robert Burns. He engraved a number of works after Rembrandt for *Engravings from the Pictures of the National Gallery*, which was published in London between 1830 and 1840 by an association of engravers, and contributed to Cadell's illustrated edition of Walter Scott's *Waverley* novels. As a painter he produced landscape, genre and history works, his most ambitious painting being *Greenwich Pensioners Commemorating the Anniversary of the Battle of Trafalgar* (London, Apsley House). Painted in the early 1830s, this was a rather unhappy pendant to Wilkie's *Chelsea Pensioners Reading the Despatch of the Battle of Waterloo* (exh. RA 1822; London, Apsley House).

Burnet was also a prolific writer, especially of books on the techniques of painting. A collection of four of these was published as *A Practical Treatise on Painting* (1843). *Practical Essays on Various Branches of the Fine Arts* (1848) contained, among others, essays on the practicalities of history painting, portrait painting and fancy painting and closed with an essay in which he attacked both the limited interest taken in art in Britain and also the negligence with which the national collections were treated. His other publications include monographs on Rembrandt (1849) and Turner (1852), both of which are marked by the technical approach found in his other works. *The Progress of a Painter in the Nineteenth Century* (1854) is a semi-fictionalized account of the career of his younger brother James Burnet (1788–1816), who greatly influenced his style. James Burnet trained briefly at the Trustees Academy and then joined his brother in London in 1810. He had a brief career as a landscape painter, producing works influenced by such 17th-century Dutch artists as Paulus Potter (i) and Aelbert Cuyp (e.g. *Old Chelsea Bridge*, Aberdeen, A.G.).

WRITINGS

A Practical Treatise on Painting, Consisting of an Essay on the Education of the Eye with Reference to Painting, and Practical Hints on Composition, Chiaroscuro and Colour (London, 1843)
Practical Essays on Various Branches of the Fine Arts (London, 1848)
Rembrandt and his Works (London, 1849, 2/1859)
'Autobiography of John Burnet', *A. J.* [London], xii (1850), pp. 275–6
Turner and his Works (London, 1852, 2/1859)
The Progress of a Painter in the Nineteenth Century, 2 vols (London, 1854)
'Recollections of my Contemporaries: The Early Days of Wilkie', *A. J.* [London], n. s. 1, vi (1860), pp. 236–7

BIBLIOGRAPHY

DNB
D. Irwin and F. Irwin: *Scottish Painters at Home and Abroad* (London, 1975), pp. 195–6, 237–8

DUNCAN MACMILLAN

Burney, Edward Francesco [Francis] (*b* Worcester, 7 Sept 1760; *d* London, 16 Dec 1848). English painter and illustrator. He studied at the Royal Academy Schools, London, from 1777. The work of James Barry and Henry Fuseli was an influence on his style, which often strained unsuccessfully towards heroic effects, but a more mundane technical proficiency was gained from copying portraits by Sir Joshua Reynolds. There are several accomplished versions of Reynolds's 1781 portrait of *Dr Charles Burney*, Edward's uncle (e.g. Oxford, Ashmolean), and the best of his few original portraits depicts his cousin, the novelist *Fanny Burney* (1782; London, N.P.G.). Burney's first exhibited works were three drawings of scenes from Fanny Burney's novel *Evelina* (exh. RA 1780; untraced), and his literary connections may have encouraged his work as an illustrator. Nevertheless, he had dreams of working on a larger scale and made sketches for a *St Paul at Ephesus* (*c.* 1800; New Haven, CT, Yale U., A.G.) in the manner of the Raphael Cartoons (London, V&A). Burney's early drawings, such as the watercolour (1782; London, BM) of Loutherbourg's Eidophusikon (a miniature theatre with light effects and translucent screens giving an impression of motion), are quaint, nervous and spiky but, perhaps

Edward Francesco Burney: *Elegant Establishment*, watercolour, 502×727 mm (London, Victoria and Albert Museum)

assisted by extensive copying at the annual Royal Academy exhibitions, his technique became seductively curvilinear and extremely sophisticated. His sketchbooks of 1780–84 are in the Huntington Library, San Marino, CA.

Burney began to work for the serial publishers Harrison & Bell in the mid-1780s. Several commissions were shared with Thomas Stothard, whose reticent style seems to have been preferred by contemporaries to the baroque contortions of Burney's illustrations for an edition of Thomson's plays (1788) and the miniaturized epic quality of his drawings for Fénelon's *Telemachus* (1792). Burney's bravest attempt at history painting on a small scale is perhaps his series of 13 illustrations to *Paradise Lost* (1799; Princeton U., NJ, A. Mus.). The designs are bold, powerful and vigorous, reminiscent of Fuseli's illustrations to Milton and Shakespeare. However, Burney's most attractive work is in a lighter vein, and his illustrations to Harrison's *Novelist's Magazine* (1785–7) and John Bell's second edition of Shakespeare (1784–8), for instance, show a delicate touch as well as a whimsical sense of narrative and an eye for amusing detail. His undulating female forms have been interpreted as showing an application of Hogarth's 'Line of Beauty' (Crown). Burney's bolder drawings are usually in red chalk, but the designs for book illustrations are often finished in watercolour with grey wash decorative borders.

From 1780 to 1803 Burney exhibited regularly at the Royal Academy, sending some of his more imposing illustrations and a few family portraits. Thereafter his work became increasingly eccentric as he developed his literary talents. In the 1820s he wrote a sequel to William Cowper's *John Gilpin*, with illustrations that include scenes on the Grand Junction Canal (San Marino, CA, Huntington Lib.), and an illustrated scientific adventure story, *Q.Q. es'Qre.* In a more serious vein, Burney also completed a series of large watercolours (*c.* 1820) that perhaps reflect the revival of interest in Hogarth that occurred in the second decade of the 19th century. Burney's drawings the *Elegant Establishment* (see fig.), *The Waltz* and the *Glee Club* (all London, V&A) and *Amateurs of Tye Wig Music* (New Haven, CT, Yale Cent.) satirize contemporary hypocrisies through allusion, sexual innuendo and double meaning. They are over-crowded, littered with notes and messages, and their ultimate meaning remains opaque. However, with their strong sense of hidden symmetry, their strange iconography and their limited palette with flashes of acidic blues and yellows, they are Burney's most original contribution to English art.

BIBLIOGRAPHY

H. Hammelmann and T. S. R. Boase: *Book Illustration in Eighteenth Century England* (London, 1975)

P. D. Crown: *Edward F. Burney: An Historical Study in English Romantic Art* (diss., Los Angeles, UCLA, 1977)

GEOFFREY ASHTON

Burnham, Daniel H(udson) (*b* Henderson, NY, 4 Sept 1846; *d* Heidelberg, Germany, 1 June 1912). American architect, urban planner and writer. The most active and successful architect, urban planner and organizer in the years around 1900, Burnham, with his partner JOHN

WELLBORN ROOT, created a series of original and distinctive early skyscrapers in Chicago in the 1880s. Burnham's urban plans, particularly those for Washington, DC (1901–2), and Chicago (1906–9), made a crucial contribution to the creation of monumental city centres with a great emphasis on parks.

1. Architectural work, to 1892. 2. Urban plans for the World's Columbian Exposition, 1890–93. 3. Architectural work, 1893 and after. 4. Urban plans, 1901 and after. 5. Critical reception and posthumous reputation.

1. ARCHITECTURAL WORK, TO 1892. In 1854 Burnham's established New England family settled in Chicago. His father, ambitious for his son, sent him for tutoring and to a preparatory school in Waltham, MA (1863). He failed the entrance examinations for both Harvard University, Cambridge, MA, and Yale University, New Haven, CT, before returning in 1867 to Chicago where his father placed him temporarily in the office of the engineer and architect William Le Baron Jenney. After two years of fruitless adventures in the West (1869–70), he worked for other architects in Chicago, and in 1872 he was presented by his father to Peter Bonnett Wight of Carter, Drake & Wight (*fl* 1872–4). There he met Root, who was chief draughtsman, and in 1873 they set up their own firm of Burnham & Root, with Burnham in charge of business and planning and Root of design. Initially they received only house commissions, the first being that in 1874 (destr.) for the businessman and organizer of the Union Stock Yards, John B. Sherman, whose daughter Burnham married in 1876. The firm's domestic commissions for a fashionable clientele were executed in an accurate Ruskinian Gothic Revival style, which Root had learnt from Wight.

From 1880 Burnham & Root emerged as the principal designers of the new ten-storey skyscraper office buildings (*see* SKYSCRAPER, §2(i)), especially with the Montauk Block (1881–2; destr.), Chicago. Here and in some two dozen subsequent structures in the city, the firm perfected 'raft' foundations to support tall buildings on the muddy Chicago soil, iron (and eventually steel) skeletal frames to lighten and expedite their construction, and a frank, unfussy treatment of façades in red brick, terracotta and sandstone to express this new technological creation. The Rookery Building (1885–8; for illustration *see* ROOT, JOHN WELLBORN) was their next prominent work, at the south-east corner of La Salle and Adams Streets, followed by the Rand–McNally Building (1888–90; destr.) with a complete steel frame lightly clad only in terracotta, the Monadnock Building (1889–92) at the south-west corner of Dearborn and Jackson Streets, with a brick exterior ornamented only by the elegant batter of its walls and cavetto cornice, and finally the steel and terracotta Masonic Temple (1890–92; destr.), at 22 storeys then the tallest building in the world.

2. URBAN PLANS FOR THE WORLD'S COLUMBIAN EXPOSITION, 1890–93. In 1890 Burnham & Root were appointed consulting architects to the World's Columbian Exposition, a world fair in commemoration of the discovery of America in 1492. The fair was snatched away from

1. Daniel H. Burnham: Court of Honor, World's Columbian Exposition, Chicago, 1891–3 (destr.); from a photograph by C. D. Arnold

2. Daniel H. Burnham: Union Station, Washington, DC, 1907

New York by Chicago and held a year late, in 1893, because of construction time. Preliminary plans were worked out in late 1890 by Burnham & Root and the landscape partnership of Frederick Law Olmsted and Henry Sargent Codman (1867–93). In December 1890 it was decided that detailed designs for the pavilions were to be executed by a board of five of the most prestigious architectural firms in the country: Richard Morris Hunt (*see* HUNT, (2)), George Browne Post and McKim, Mead & White, all from New York; Peabody & Stearns of Boston; and Van Brunt & Howe of Kansas City. In the face of local dismay that no Chicago architects were included an equal number of Chicago practices were added: Adler & Sullivan, Solon S. Beman, Henry Ives Cobb, Jenney & Mundie and Burling & Whitehouse (*fl* 1880s). The board of architects met in Chicago in January 1891 to divide the work. The first five firms and Beman were given the task of designing the pavilions around the monumental Court of Honor, sketched out by Root and Olmsted, and they agreed to adhere to common façade and cornice lines and to adopt a consistent Greco-Roman style, executed in a kind of plaster known as staff. The Chicago firms were mostly assigned structures behind the Court of Honor, and they produced freer designs, especially Louis Sullivan's Transportation and Cobb's Fisheries Buildings. Root died unexpectedly of pneumonia just after the first meeting of the board of architects, but Burnham carried the project through with legendary assiduousness as Director of Construction, employing CHARLES B. ATWOOD of New York to design structures not envisioned in the initial plans, most notably the celebrated Fine Arts Building. Although Burnham did not design the complex, he was responsible for its execution, deciding such important secondary questions as the painting of the buildings in a uniform ivory white and their illumination at night.

The opening of the Exposition on 1 May 1893 was a triumph for Burnham. The monumental harmony, the classical nostalgia and the white cleanliness of the Court of Honor (see fig. 1) made a tremendous impression on Americans as a vision of what a great orderly city might be.

3. ARCHITECTURAL WORK, 1893 AND AFTER. In the light of all the activity after Root's death, Burnham's day-to-day practice of architecture as the senior partner of one of the largest firms in the country is easily forgotten. He had virtually closed his practice during the erection of the World's Columbian Exposition buildings. When he reopened it in 1893, he organized it around his Exposition staff, with Atwood in charge of design (until 1895) and with a 27% interest in the partnership, and Ernest Graham controlling the draughting room and Edward Shankland (1854–1924) responsible for engineering, who both held a 10% interest.

Atwood withdrew in December 1895 and Shankland in January 1900, after which Graham and Burnham split the firm 40:60. In 1900 Peirce Anderson (1870–1924) returned from the Ecole des Beaux-Arts, Paris, to take charge of design and in 1908 he became a partner. In 1910 Burnham's sons Hubert Burnham (1887–1974) and Daniel Hudson Burnham jr (1886–1961) also entered the firm. After Burnham's death in 1912 the firm was reorganized as Graham, Burnham & Co.; in 1917, when Burnham's sons left the practice, it took the name GRAHAM, ANDERSON, PROBST & WHITE.

It is easy to imagine that Burnham had little impact on the artistic production of the firm, but his contemporaries were vehement in denying this. 'When a man has no time to make large drawings,' wrote Peter Bonnett Wight in *Construction News* on Burnham's death, 'he has to make small ones, and he has to reduce the size of his sheets as the demands upon his time increase. That is what Burnham did. He could lay out the plan for a large office building on sheets six inches square; and he would not only make one plan but would use sheets enough to lay it out according to every arrangement he could conceive of until he found the best one to recommend to his client.'

The production of the firm after 1893 was almost exclusively office buildings and department stores, particularly the large and expensive sort: the Reliance Building (lower storeys, 1889–91; upper storeys, 1894–5), 32 North State Street, Chicago (*see* SKYSCRAPER, fig. 1); the Ellicott Square Building (1894), Buffalo, NY; the Frick Building (1901), Pittsburgh, PA; the Flatiron Building (1903), intersection of Broadway and Fifth Avenue, New York; the Railway Exchange (1903) and People's Gas buildings (1910), both Chicago; the department stores Selfridge's (1906), London, and Wanamaker's (1909), Philadelphia. Although widely scattered, these buildings displayed a remarkably consistent vocabulary of a few classical motifs applied over a clearly expressed steel skeleton, small variations in the costliness of materials and extensiveness of ornament responding to the budget and pretences of particular cases. The designs of Burnham & Co. were considered practical and fashionable, the 'latest thing' from Chicago. The firm's few monumental commissions included the Union Station (1907; see fig. 2) in Washington, DC, of which Peirce Anderson was in charge. It is a remarkably spacious and successful composition of characteristic volumes without, however, any individuality or 'punch' in its details.

4. URBAN PLANS, 1901 AND AFTER. The World's Columbian Exposition ultimately inspired a movement that supported monumental municipal planning in New York, Philadelphia and elsewhere. Burnham and his new friend McKim were honoured and consulted, and Burnham was awarded honorary degrees from Yale, Harvard and Northwestern universities. In 1901–2 Senator James McMillan, chairman of the congressional committee administering the national capital, the District of Columbia, commissioned a new plan for the city, based on the 18th-century Baroque scheme of Pierre-Charles L'Enfant (*see* WASHINGTON, DC, §I). Burnham, McKim and Frederick Law Olmsted jr (1870–1957) were appointed to a three-man planning commission and, in collaboration with government authorities, they worked out a scheme of low Greco-Roman masses set in broad parks along L'Enfant's monumental axes, which was followed in the rebuilding of Washington during the next half century. In 1902–3 Burnham headed a commission to advise on the rebuilding of the centre of Cleveland, a project promoted by the mayor Tom Johnson who supported municipal reform. In 1905 Burnham produced an elaborate plan for San Francisco; the plan was not, however, adopted when the city was rebuilt after the earthquake of 1906, though small fragments of it appeared, as in a portion of Telegraph Hill. In 1904–5 the United States government dispatched him to the newly pacified Philippines to redesign Manila and to lay out a summer capital at Baguio. Finally, and most importantly, between 1906 and 1909 Burnham, together with Edward H. Bennett (1874–1954), oversaw a plan for the rebuilding and expansion of Chicago, which they published as *Plan of Chicago* (1909), a magnificent volume with architectural designs by the Frenchman Fernand Janin (1880–1912) and renderings by the American Jules Guérin (1866–1946). The Chicago plan was Burnham's last as well as his greatest work. It provided for streets laid out on a grid with radial and concentric boulevards, monumental civic buildings and efficient transport systems, a greater number of parks and a lakefront park system stretching 20 miles along Lake Michigan. The drawings were displayed around the world, with Burnham himself presenting them at the Town Planning Conference held in London in 1910.

Burnham consolidated his increasing reputation as a planner with a number of professional posts, some of which were created for him. In 1884 he was a founder and officer of the Western Association of Architects. After it amalgamated with the American Institute of Architects (1889), he served as the AIA's President in 1894 and 1895, pushing for application of the Tarsney Act of 1893 which provided for the competitive award of public commissions. In 1894 Burnham and McKim were the prime movers in the founding of the American School of Architecture in Rome (later the American Academy). In 1910 he was appointed Chairman of the National Council of Fine Arts to oversee all public building and art in Washington, DC.

5. CRITICAL RECEPTION AND POSTHUMOUS REPUTATION. Burnham's critical reputation, both as an architect and as a planner, has fluctuated over time. His contemporaries depicted him as a brilliant planner who conceived initial layouts of buildings in consultation with the clients, and as an omnipresent and incisive critic who controlled his battalion of draughtsmen with great effectiveness. He is often remembered for the words his associate Willis Jefferson Polk attributed to him: 'Make no little plans, they have no magic to stir men's blood.... Make big plans . . . remembering that a noble, logical diagram once recorded will never die but long after we are gone will be a living thing asserting itself with ever growing intensity.' His older professional contemporary Wight summarized his accomplishment more succinctly: 'For the practice of the profession of architecture, he did this: he made [his profession] known and respected by millions who had never heard of an architect in all their lives.'

Burnham was tremendously admired at the time of his death, although as a planner rather than as an artist. His initial schemes for Washington and Chicago determined urban development in both cities until the 1950s: the Mall and Federal Triangle projects in Washington and the Lakefront parks and Chicago River quays and bridges in Chicago. In the 1920s advocates of the European International Style praised Burnham's reticent skyscrapers, especially the Reliance Building, while decrying the formality of his urban plans. Today the harmony and expressiveness of his great schemes—the Court of Honor, the Washington Mall, Grant Park in Chicago—have come to seem preferable to the starkness and individuality of post-war Modernism. Yet as early as 1924 concern was expressed by Louis Sullivan in his *Autobiography of an Idea* and later by Thomas Hines in his *Burnham of Chicago* (1974) that Burnham sought a least common denominator and that, for all the efficiency of his execution, his building designs and city plans remain uncommitted either socially or aesthetically.

See also CHICAGO SCHOOL.

UNPUBLISHED SOURCES

Chicago, IL, A. Inst. [Daniel H. Burnham Papers]

WRITINGS

The Improvement of the Park System of the District of Columbia (Washington, DC, 1902)

with J. M. Carrere and A. Brunner: 'The Grouping of Public Buildings at Cleveland', *Inland Architect & News Rec.*, xlii (Sept 1903), pp. 13–15

Report on a Plan for San Francisco, ed. E. F. O'Day (San Francisco, 1905)

with E. H. Bennett: *Plan of Chicago* (Chicago, 1909, *R* New York, 1970)

'A City of the Future under a Democratic Government', *Trans. of the Town Planning Conference, Royal Institute of British Architects: London, 1910*, pp. 368–78

BIBLIOGRAPHY

H. Monroe: *John Wellborn Root: A Study of his Life and Work* (Boston, 1896)

C. Moore: *Daniel H. Burnham: Architect, Planner of Cities*, 2 vols (Boston, 1921)

L. H. Sullivan: *The Autobiography of an Idea* (New York, 1924)

T. Tallmadge: *Architecture in Old Chicago* (Chicago, 1941)

C. Condit: *The Rise of the Skyscraper* (Chicago, 1952)

D. Hoffmann: *The Architecture of John Wellborn Root* (Baltimore, 1973)

T. Hines: *Burnham of Chicago* (Chicago, 1974)

J. E. Draper: 'Paris by the Lake: Sources of Burnham's Plan of Chicago', *Chicago Architecture, 1872–1922: Birth of a Metropolis*, ed. J. Zakowsky (Munich, 1987)

DAVID VAN ZANTEN

Burnisher. Tool with a hard, smooth, tip, mounted in a wooden handle, used for smoothing or polishing. In water gilding, a burnisher of polished agate is used to smooth the underlying gesso and bole after the gold is applied, giving a highly reflective surface. Burnishers used to burnish ancient pots are depicted in Egyptian wall paintings from the 14th century BC. In 13th-century Italy, burnishers of haematite or dog's tooth were recommended. A steel-bladed burnisher (*see* ENGRAVING, fig. 1f) is used in intaglio printing for the correction of errors or scratches on the metal plate or for the reduction of dark areas (*see also* PRINTS, §III, 2).

RUPERT FEATHERSTONE

Burnsides, Tom (*b* Pine Springs, AZ, *c.* 1910; *d* New Mexico, 1957). Native American Navajo silversmith. He learnt the art as a young man from his half-brother John and an older Navajo, Left Handed Red, then branched out on his own. He became a successful silversmith, and with his wife Mabel was one of the most active craftsmen in the area, not far from the Hubbell Trading Post, AZ. During the fieldwork of ethnographer John Adair (*b* 1913) they became well acquainted, and Burnsides was a primary source for most of Adair's study; Adair's subsequent publication (1944) gave Burnsides a status that caused collectors to prize his work. Tom and Mabel were frequently called upon to tour and demonstrate their silversmithing and weaving skills, and they made several world trips under the auspices of the US Government Office of Information and of the State Department. Both were killed in a car accident.

BIBLIOGRAPHY

J. Adair: *The Navajo and Pueblo Silversmiths* (Norman, 1944)

——: 'Navajo Tom Burnsides Sandcasts a Silver Pendant', *Craft Horiz.*, xviii/4 (1957), pp. 38–9

FREDERICK J. DOCKSTADER

Burov, Andrey (Konstantinovich) (*b* Moscow, 15 Oct 1900; *d* Moscow, 7 May 1957). Russian architect. He was born into a family of architects and in 1918 he entered the Moscow School of Painting, Sculpture and Architecture. In 1920 he entered the VKHUTEMAS into which the school had been absorbed and there he worked in the studio of Aleksandr Vesnin. Several pavilions of the Moscow Agriculture and Craft Fair were built to Burov's designs, as were a garden square near the Kremlin and ship's cabins for the Leningrad–London line. He became known for his schemes using modern technology, in particular the railway station that he designed as a student in 1925. In the same year he became an assistant lecturer at the Vkhutemas and joined the ranks of the Constructivists, among whom, however, he remained a solitary figure. He became widely known with the temporary agricultural buildings that he produced in 1926–7 for Sergey Eisenstein's film *The Old and the New*, later retitled *The General Line*, where the forms of a battery of American grain silos are associated with those of Le Corbusier's villas. When Le Corbusier visited Moscow in 1928, Burov took him round the city and introduced him into avant-garde circles.

From 1930 to 1931 Burov was responsible for the construction of the large tractor factory in Chelyabinsk, on which the American company of Albert Kahn Associates, very much involved in the programmes of the first Five-Year Plan, had been consulted. He went to Detroit for several months to familiarize himself with industrial construction techniques, and from there he wrote interesting letters to his family. In 1935 he went to Greece, Italy and France. These journeys gave him a first-hand knowledge both of historical architecture and of such major contemporary figures as Le Corbusier and Auguste Perret, and set him apart from other Russian architects of his generation. He designed the scenery for a number of theatre productions and retained a fairly theatrical concept of architecture.

In Moscow between 1937 and 1939 Burov carried out the renovation of the interiors of the Historical Museum on Red Square, and in 1941 he built the façade of the House of Architects in Shchusev Street using the vivid colours of traditional Russian architecture and incorporating decoration designed by Vladimir Favorsky. In 1939 and 1941, with Boris Blokhin, Burov became involved in the design of heavy prefabrication and built several blocks of flats in Moscow using reinforced concrete panels, though keeping to the aesthetic precepts then in force. In the building on Leningradsky Prospect (1940), he dressed the exterior of the supporting panels with quite superfluous moulded arabesques, which later appeared to be an explicit criticism of the decorative excesses of Stalinist architecture. During World War II Burov continued his research into architecture and technology, designing houses composed of plaster panels that could be dismantled, as well as grandiose monuments to the Red Army. In 1944 and 1945 he worked on a plan for the reconstruction of Yalta based on the separation of pedestrians and vehicles and on the creation of a skyline punctuated by curious skyscrapers of various styles. After 1945 he resumed the design of mass-produced residential buildings, made all the more necessary by the pressure of reconstruction. He devoted himself mainly, however, to teaching and to research into new building materials, in particular on the use of plastic raw materials. He filed a considerable number of patents on this subject.

WRITINGS

Ob arkhitekture (Moscow, 1960)

BIBLIOGRAPHY

R. Burova and O. I. Rzhekhina: *Andrey Konstantinovich Burov* (Moscow, 1980)

R. Blashkevich, R. Burova and O. Rzhekhina: *A. K. Burov* (Moscow, 1984)

JEAN-LOUIS COHEN

Burr. Term applied in printmaking to the sharp ridge of metal raised especially by a drypoint needle as it scratches the plate; it can also be produced by the action of a burin in engraving but is usually removed. Burr prints as a rich, slightly smudged line or area, as the curled metal holds a quantity of ink; eventually the metal fragments flake off in printing, so the effect, which was exploited by artists such as Rembrandt, is limited to a small number of early impressions (for illustration *see* DRYPOINT). The effect can be easily detected with a magnifying glass and contrasts with sharp and precise engraved lines.

□

Burra, Edward (*b* London, 29 March 1905; *d* Hastings, 22 Oct 1976). English painter, illustrator and stage designer. As a student at the Chelsea Polytechnic (1921–3) and the Royal College of Art (1923–5) he became a talented figure draughtsman. In the second half of the decade he spent much time in France painting intricately detailed urban scenes, which depicted the low life of Toulon and Marseille. Works such as the watercolour *Toulon* (1927; priv. col., see Causey, cat. no. 33) were executed in a meticulously finished and vividly coloured decorative style. Burra usually used watercolour and tempera and occasionally collage oil paints.

Burra took ideas from Cubism, Dada (notably George Grosz) and, especially, Surrealism, but his work is also linked with the English satirical tradition of William Hogarth, Thomas Rowlandson and Isaac Cruikshank: Burra loved burlesque and poked fun at people's pretensions and excesses of style and behaviour, as in *John Deth (Homage to Conrad Aiken)* (1931; U. Manchester, Whitworth A.G.; see fig.). His first one-man show at the Leicester Galleries, London, in 1929 gained him a personal following, and his place in the English modern movement was acknowledged by his inclusion in the avant-garde Unit One exhibition in London in 1934. Burra was also a member of the Surrealist group in England and exhibited at the International Surrealist Exhibition in London in 1936, but otherwise he remained independent. He was interested in artists such as Stanley Spencer and William Roberts, who also favoured modern life scenes, but there are no close parallels between Burra and his English contemporaries.

Edward Burra: *John Deth (Homage to Conrad Aiken)*, pencil and gouache, 365×785 mm, 1931 (Manchester, University of Manchester, Whitworth Art Gallery)

In the 1930s Burra focused his interest on Spain, where he spent much time between 1933 and 1936; the USA, which he visited in 1933–4 and 1937; and Mexico, where he and the American poet Conrad Aiken stayed with the novelist Malcolm Lowry in 1937. In Granada in 1933 Burra witnessed the outbreak of violence in the wave of anti-clericalism that preceded the Spanish Civil War. Brutality and destruction, deprivation and poverty became frequent subjects in his art, for instance in the watercolour *Old Iron* (*c.* 1938; ex-Alex Reid & Lefevre Ltd, London, 1988). Burra was politically non-partisan, and his work is polemical only in the sense that it attacked all forms of cruelty and repression. While some of his paintings relate specifically to Spain, almost all were affected by the general unrest of the late 1930s, and he would often introduce other cultural traditions, such as Mexican art, into his depictions of contemporary European events.

During World War II Burra was unable to travel, and his work focused for the first time since the mid-1920s on English subjects. Landscape painting, which he began to explore in such watercolours as *Blasted Oak* (1942; AC Eng), was to dominate his work during the rest of his career. He travelled less as he grew older, though bar scenes in Boston, where he stayed with Aiken in the 1950s, are among his best works: an example is *Izzy Ort's* (1955; Edinburgh, N.G. Mod. A.). Unlike earlier 20th-century landscape painters such as Paul Nash (whom he met in 1927), who painted only southern England, Burra looked back to Romanticism and the search for grandeur and solitude, discovering many of his subjects in the sparsely populated peripheries of the British Isles. In the late 1930s he had begun to paint very large watercolours (up to 1.55 × 1.10 m) and continued in his late landscapes a technique of joining together several sheets of paper that he had worked on separately. His sparse drawing and broad washes of colour, for example in *River Rother, Early Morning* (1962–3; priv. col., see Causey, cat. no. 291), give a commanding presence to his late landscapes, in complete contrast to his early small, crowded figure designs.

Burra's occasional excursions into book illustration were very successful, but his main professional activity apart from painting was stage design. Through many friends in theatre and ballet he received a steady stream of commissions for set and costume designs for Covent Garden, Sadlers Wells and elsewhere between 1932 and 1958.

BIBLIOGRAPHY

J. Rothenstein: *Edward Burra*, Penguin Mod. Masters (Harmondsworth, 1945)

Edward Burra (exh. cat., London, Tate, 1973)

A. Causey: *Edward Burra: Complete Catalogue* (Oxford, 1985)

W. Chappell, ed.: *Well Dearie! The Letters of Edward Burra* (London, 1985)

Edward Burra (exh. cat., ACGB, 1985)

ANDREW CAUSEY

Burrell, Sir **William** (*b* Glasgow, 9 July 1861; *d* Berwick-upon-Tweed, 29 March 1958). Scottish businessman, collector and philanthropist. He was born into a ship-owning family of Northumbrian origin who later settled in Glasgow. The family firm, although originally small-scale and dealing in canal cargoes, had expanded into a prosperous international shipping business by the time he joined it in 1876. With the outbreak of World War I the fleet was sold to meet the demand for ships, and from 1916 he devoted the remainder of his life to collecting works of art.

Burrell had begun collecting as a boy, and in his maturity he was probably influenced by a number of other Glasgow businessmen who were also collectors, for example Arthur Kay, Alexander Young and W. A. Coats. Like them, Burrell called on the services of a number of trusted dealers, for example Daniel Cottier and Alex Reid, both of whom had galleries in Glasgow. By 1901 Burrell's collection was already important enough for him to loan more than 200 items to the International Exhibition held at Kelvingrove Park that year. From 1911 to 1957 he kept a detailed record of his purchases in a series of school exercise-books. As well as documenting what he bought, when and from whom, the books indicate how much he paid. On average, he spent £20,000 per annum, but there were peaks in his expenditure: in 1936 he spent £80,000 and in 1948 £60,000. His shrewdness in business carried over into his purchase of works of art, and he often bought when the art market was depressed and would frequently haggle over prices. On the whole he bought well, and all the works of art described below are in the Burrell Collection. In the field of painting, Burrell collected more than 20 works by Degas, including *The Rehearsal* (*c.* 1877) and *Jockeys in the Rain* (*c.* 1886), a rare early Cézanne—the *Château de Medan* (1880)—and works by Courbet, Gericault, Delacroix, Honoré Daumier, Henri Fantin-Latour, Francisque Millet, Eugène Boudin, Manet, Alfred Sisley and The Hague school. He also purchased an early Rembrandt *Self-portrait* (1632) and paintings by Lucas Cranach the elder (e.g. *The Stag-hunt*, 1529), Memling and Giovanni Bellini (e.g. *Virgin and Child*, *c.* 1488–90). He amassed one of the finest collections of late Gothic and early Renaissance works of art from northern Europe, comprising stained glass, tapestries, wood and stone sculpture, ivories, furniture and metalwork. He also collected East Asian art: Chinese ceramics, jades, bronzes and sculpture from the Neolithic period to the Qing dynasty, Japanese prints, Islamic ceramics and metalwork, carpets from Persia, the Indian subcontinent and Central Asia, and other textiles. His collection of Chinese ceramics was particularly comprehensive, and he succeeded in acquiring many 17th-century Persian carpets, including the so-called Wagner Garden Carpet (*see* CARPET, colour pl. IV).

Although Burrell was a very private man, he was extremely active in public life and was a Glasgow city councillor and a trustee of the National Gallery of Scotland, Edinburgh, and the Tate Gallery, London. His services to the public were recognized in 1927 with the conferment of a knighthood. In 1944 he gave some 6000 items of his collection to the City of Glasgow. Between 1944 and 1957 he continued to buy, primarily art of the Ancient Near East—an area in which he had not previously collected—and the final gift totalled more than 8000 items. The Burrell Collection is now housed in a purpose-built gallery (1972–83) in Pollok Park, which was opened to the public in 1983 (*see* SCOTLAND, §II and fig. 7).

BIBLIOGRAPHY

G. Seligman: *Merchants of Art* (New York, 1961), pp. 201–3

W. Wells: 'Sir William Burrell's Purchase Books', *Scot. Rev.*, ix (1963), pp. 19–22

T. J. Honeyman: *Art and Audacity* (Glasgow, 1971)
W. Wells: 'Sir William Burrell and his Collection', *Mus. J.*, lxxii (1972), pp. 101–3
——: *Treasures from the Burrell Collection* (exh. cat., ACGB, 1975)
K. Clark: 'Sir William Burrell: A Personal Reminiscence', *Scot. Rev.*, ii (1977), no. 6, pp. 15–16
P. Savage: 'Through the Eyes of a Friend: William Burrell, Collector (1861–1958)', *Country Life*, clxi (27 Jan 1977), pp. 15–16
——: *Lorimer and the Edinburgh Craft Designers* (Edinburgh, 1980)
R. Marks: *Burrell: A Portrait of a Collector* (Glasgow, 1983, rev. 1988)
——: *The Burrell Collection* (London and Glasgow, 1983)
Ten Years of the Burrell Collection: A Celebration of Art in Nature (exh. cat., Glasgow, Burrell Col., 1993)

NICHOLAS PEARCE

Burri, Alberto (*b* Città di Castello, 12 March 1915). Italian painter and sculptor. Trained as a physician, he began painting during his internment as a prisoner of war in Hereford, TX. He abandoned medicine and settled in Rome upon repatriation in 1946. Burri's first solo exhibition in 1947 at La Margherita in Rome featured expressionistic landscapes (e.g. 1947; Città di Castello, priv. col., see cat. rais., p. 15) and still-lifes. In his earliest abstractions (1948–9) the inspiration of Joan Miró, Paul Klee, Hans Arp and Enrico Prampolini is discernible, although the addition of tar, pumice, sand, enamel and collage elements to the oil in such works as *Composition* (1948; priv. col., see cat. rais., p. 19) was more significant. A protagonist of *Art informel*, Burri's career evolved through series that overlapped chronologically, in which he used unorthodox materials and processes. In this he was a precursor of Arte Povera. In 1950 he produced his first *Sacks*, paintings that displayed broad expanses of worn and stained sacking (see fig.). Colour was restricted to red and black, which enhanced the effect of desolation. Burri's use of 'poor' materials offered an alternative to the hermetic painted surfaces of the contemporary geometric 'post-Cubist' Concrete art movement. In contrast to idealist aesthetics of the Fascist era, Burri's works signified a re-engagement with life without recourse to realism. Burri remained aloof from the contemporary debates in Italy about the political significance of abstract and realist art and refused to offer a metaphorical reading of his art. With Mario Ballocco (*b* 1913), Ettore Colla and Giuseppe Capogrossi he founded the Gruppo Origine in 1951, which declared a commitment to an anti-decorative and non-referential art of pure abstract fundamentals.

From the late 1940s Burri expanded the frontiers of painting by cutting, layering, and burning diverse materials. With few exceptions his works were named after their constituent materials or formative processes: for example the dark, sticky *Tars* of the late 1940s (e.g. 1949; priv. col., see cat. rais., p. 21), and the burnt surfaces of the *Combustions* of the later 1950s and early 1960s. At this time Burri departed from overtly sensuous and expressionistic effects in the more restrained and physically resilient *Woods* and *Irons*. From the mid-1960s the effects of fire were explored in the draped, scorched membranes of the *Plastics*. However, the 1970s were marked by more austere works, such as the cracked, desiccated *Clays* (e.g. *Black Clay G.4.*, 1975; Città di Castello, Col. Burri). In the same period the *Cellotex* series consisted of works made from industrial fibreboard that divided the pictorial field into flat zones differentiated by texture and colour. While the dimensions

Alberto Burri: *Sack and Red*, acrylic and sacking, 0.86×1.00 m, 1954 (London, Tate Gallery)

of early works ranged greatly, a more consistent monumentality prevailed from the 1970s. In the 1980s Burri's work included the highly colourful *Sextant* series (e.g. *Sextant 7*, 1982; priv. col., see cat. rais., p. 317). However, this sensuality was followed by a return to the *Blacks* series, re-exploring concerns of the 1950s. Burri also produced such sculptures as the *Large Iron* (5.18×1.98×0.61 m, 1980; Città di Castello, Col. Burri).

BIBLIOGRAPHY

G. C. Argan: 'Alberto Burri', *Catalogo della XXX Biennale* (exh. cat., Venice, Biennale, 1960), pp. 65–8
C. Brandi: *Alberto Burri* (Rome, 1963)
M. Calvesi: *Alberto Burri* (Milan, 1971)
Alberto Burri (exh. cat., ed. C. Pirovano; Milan, Brera, 1985)
G. P. Zamboni and others: *Alberto Burri: Contributi al catalogo sistematico* (Città di Castello, 1990) [cat. rais.]

MARCIA E. VETROCQ

Burri, René (*b* Zurich, 9 April 1933). Swiss photographer and film maker. He studied photography under Hans Finsler at the Kunstgewerbeschule in Zurich (1949–53), where he also studied film making. After 1955 he worked as a freelance photojournalist for large-circulation illustrated magazines such as *Life*, *Paris Match* and *Stern*. In 1956 he became a correspondent for Magnum Photos in Paris and New York. His reputation as a photojournalist was based on his ability to grasp situations requiring a rapid response, while retaining in his photographs a clear structure and composition in such a way that chance itself appears to be constructed. This is apparent in the work undertaken on foreign assignments in the 1950s and 1960s, to places such as Egypt during the Suez crisis (1956), Greece and Turkey (1957), Korea and Japan (1961) and Vietnam (1963). As a film maker he is best known for *What's It All About?* (1967).

PHOTOGRAPHIC PUBLICATIONS

Die Deutschen/Les Allemands (Zurich and Paris, 1962)

BIBLIOGRAPHY

Die Deutschen: René Burri (exh. cat., Cologne, Gal. Kicken & Pauseback, 1981)

ERIKA BILLETER

Burrini, Gian Antonio (*b* Bologna, 25 April 1656; *d* Bologna, 5 Jan 1727). Italian painter. He was among the most original and gifted Bolognese painters of his time, and his Baroque style, colourfully dramatic, impetuous and passionate, opposed the cool refinement of the classical art of Carlo Cignani and Marcantonio Franceschini. Until 1672 he trained in the studio of Domenico Maria Canuti, a brilliant exponent of grand-scale fresco decoration, and then with Lorenzo Pasinelli, the creator of subtly beautiful easel paintings of biblical and mythological scenes for a sophisticated patrician clientele.

Burrini followed the conventional course of studies for a Bolognese painter of this period, studying the celebrated fresco cycles by the Carracci in the Palazzo Fava and the Palazzo Magnani and famous pictures in the various churches and palazzi of the city. He received generous help from his patron, Giulio Cesare Venenti (1642–97), himself an amateur engraver, who supported these studies for several years and also offered his protégé lodging in his residence. Burrini visited Venice (Zanotti), and his study of the pictures of Titian and Veronese inspired in his own work a sumptuousness of colouring and rich painterly handling that were unusual in the Bolognese tradition. With his teacher, Pasinelli, he was in the vanguard of a neo-Venetian current in Bolognese painting in the late 17th century.

Gian Antonio Burrini: *Fall of the Giants* (1681–4), ceiling fresco in the Villa Albergati, Zola Predosa, near Bologna

Burrini began as a fresco decorator, producing some of the most vigorous and imaginative frescoes of the period. He usually collaborated with a *quadratura* specialist, and his earliest work of this type, a frieze of small wall paintings in the Casa Marchesini, Bologna, was carried out with the assistance of the *quadraturista* Marcantonio Chiarini (1652–1730). Among his earliest known works are his most brilliant surviving frescoes: the ceiling decorations (1681–4) for six rooms in the Villa Albergati at Zola Predosa, near Bologna, again with *quadratura* settings by Chiarini. These frescoes show mythological scenes, including the *Fall of the Giants* (see fig.), and are distinguished by their bold and brilliant Baroque illusionism and rich colouring. In the same period Burrini established his reputation as a painter of altarpieces. In 1682–3 the Duca di Mirandola commissioned the *Martyrdom of St Victoria* (Compiègne, Château) for the cathedral in Mirandola, an energetic and colourful work indebted to Veronese. There followed the *Virgin with SS Petronius and Dionysius the Areopagite* (1684) for the church of S Giacomo Maggiore, Bologna (now in Monghidoro, parish church), his first public work in Bologna and closer to the art of the Carracci. It was commissioned by the Ratta family, who also ordered an *Adoration of the Magi* (Cambridge, MA, Fogg), which, when taken to Rome by Monsignor Ratta, was admired by Carlo Maratti. In 1685 Burrini decorated the palace of the Duca di Novellara (untraced). On his return from Novellara he shared a studio with Giuseppe Maria Crespi for two years (1686–8) and was possibly influential in encouraging the development of Crespi's forceful and painterly style. In 1688 Burrini decorated the Franchi Chapel in the Bolognese church of S Giovanni dei Celestini (destr.) and in the same year, on the invitation of Prince Filiberto di Carignano, went to Turin accompanied by the *quadraturista* Tommaso Aldrovandini (1653–1736), though nothing now remains of their work there.

Burrini's easel paintings of the late 1680s and early 1690s are extraordinarily free and spontaneous in execution and markedly Venetian in style. They show a variety of subjects from biblical history, such as *Susanna and the Elders* (*c.* 1686–90; Paris, priv. col.), and scenes from mythology and epic poetry, such as *Erminia and the Shepherds* (*c.* 1686–90; Bologna, Pin. N.) and *Diana and Endymion* (*c.* 1690; York, C.A.G.). The *Erminia* and a *Bacchus and Ariadne* (early 1690s; priv. col., see 1986 exh. cat., no. 127) have landscape settings loosely brushed with liquid impastos that reveal Burrini's unusual capacity in this regard. In the *Landscape with St Jerome*, where a small figure of St Jerome is seen in a vast landscape panorama, he developed the landscape more extensively. Zanotti noted that this picture was inspired by Titian's *St Jerome* (Paris, Louvre). Burrini also executed zestful oil sketches of heads in genre-like groupings, such as the *Genre Scene* (Bologna, Pin. N.).

In 1690, with Chiarini, Burrini executed huge wall paintings and a ceiling painting in the *salone* of the Palazzo Pini Alamandini, Bologna, with scenes from the *Myth of Phaeton* and representations of the *Continents* and the *Elements*. These are less daring and less Baroque than his earlier frescoes, and closer to the Bolognese classical tradition. The period 1680–95 was the most felicitous and productive of Burrini's career. In 1696, at the age of 40, he married and was thereafter weighed down with the responsibility of a large family. Zanotti, who knew him well, said that this caused him to paint with less thought. He was further demoralized by his estrangement from his daughter Barbara (*b* 1700), whom he had taught to be a painter. Letters survive that pathetically reflect this dissension in the artist's family (Bologna, Bib. Com. Archiginnasio, Autografi XI no. 3424). Zanotti's assertions about Burrini's decline are unverifiable as little survives of the artist's later work. His *Martyrdom of St Catherine* (Bologna, S Caterina di Saragozza; see 1979 exh. cat., no. 6), however, is a vigorous work, described as 'una delle ultime opere' in Malvasia/Zanotti *Le pitture di Bologna* (1732). Burrini was among the artists who founded the Accademia Clementina in Bologna in 1709. He took an active part in its affairs and was its seventh director (1723–4).

BIBLIOGRAPHY

DBI; Thieme–Becker

G. P. Zanotti: *Storia dell'Accademia Clementina di Bologna*, 2 vols (Bologna, 1739), i, pp. 319–31

L. Crespi: *Vite de' pittori bolognesi non descritte nella Felsina pittrice* (Rome, 1769), pp. 48, 58, 204

L. Lanzi: *Storia pittorica della Italia* (Florence, 1834), pp. 137, 144

A. Arfelli: 'Gian Antonio Burrini', *Com. Bologna*, xxxi/11 (1934), pp. 67–75

Mostra del settecento bolognese (exh. cat. by R. Longhi and G. Zucchini, Bologna, Pal. Com., 1935), pp. 5–6

O. Kurz: *Bolognese Drawings at Windsor Castle* (London, 1955), pp. 81–2

E. Riccomini: 'Gian Antonio Burrini', *A. Ant. & Mod.*, 6 (1959), pp. 219–27

Maestri della pittura del seicento emiliano (exh. cat., ed. F. Arcangeli and others; Bologna. Pal. Archiginnasio, 1959), pp. 191–6

H. Brigstocke: 'Antonio Burrini, *Diana and Endymion* at York', *Burl. Mag.*, xcii (1970), p. 760

L'arte del settecento emiliano: La pittura; l'Accademia Clementina (exh. cat., ed. A. Emiliani; Bologna, Pal. Podestà, 1979), p. 7, no. 6

Bolognese Drawings in North American Collections, 1500–1800 (exh. cat. by C. Johnston and M. Cazort, Ottawa, N.G., 1982), pp. 120–22

C. Thiem: *Disegni di artisti bolognesi dal seicento all'ottocento* (Bologna, 1983), pp. 114–19

The Age of Correggio and the Carracci: Emilian Painting of the 16th and 17th Centuries (exh. cat., Washington, N.G.A.; New York, Met.; Bologna, Pin. N.; 1986), pp. 385–91

DWIGHT C. MILLER

Bursa [anc. Prusa; Fr. Brousse]. City in north-west Turkey. Located on the northern foothills of Mysian Olympus (Mt Ulu Dağ), the ancient city of Prusa was a spa town of note and the capital of Bithynia. The city prospered under Roman and Byzantine rule and changed hands frequently between Christians and Muslims in the 11th and 12th centuries. In 1326 it was taken by the Ottoman sultan Orhan (*reg c.* 1324–60) and served as the capital of the Ottoman empire until 1402. The several important buildings preserved from the early Ottoman period exemplify the Ottoman pattern of urbanization whereby sultans successively built architectural complexes (*see* KÜLLIYE) in unurbanized parts of the city, which then became the nuclei of new quarters. The city was also an international centre for the silk and textile trade.

Orhan began his complex of mosque, kitchen, bath and caravanserai in 1339–40, near the Byzantine citadel in the area that later became the commercial centre of the city.

Bursa, Green mosque, 1412–24; interior

The mosque (rest.) is an early example of the Bursa- or *zāwiya*-type (*see* ISLAMIC ART, §II, 6(ii)(b)): it has a five-bay porch on the north leading to a domed vestibule and a central domed hall. Flanked by small iwans with adjoining rectangular rooms for itinerant dervishes, the hall opens to the main iwan (9.30×8.65 m) on the south, used for prayer. Orhan's successor Murad I Hudavendigar (*reg* 1360–89) built his complex (1366–85) on a hill in the western suburb of Çekirge. The two-storey building combines a typical Bursa-type mosque on the ground floor with a madrasa above (*see* ISLAMIC ART, fig. 55). Bayezid i Yıldırım (*reg* 1389–1402) chose a hill to the east of the city for his complex (1390–95), which comprises a Bursa-type mosque, madrasa, tomb for the founder and bath, along with a kitchen, hospital and palace (destr.). In the commercial centre he commissioned the congregational mosque (Ulu Cami; 1396–1400), a large (68×56 m) rectangular building with 12 piers supporting 20 domed bays. Opposite is the covered market (Turk. *bedesten*), and near by are such other commercial establishments as the Sipahiler Çarsı, the covered market of the cavalry soldiers, built under Mehmed I (*reg* 1403–21), and the Koza Han (silk cocoon caravanserai; 1451).

Another urban nucleus on the east side of town is centred around the Green complex (Turk. *yeşil*; 1412–24) of Mehmed I. It comprises a mosque, tomb, madrasa, kitchen and bath and takes its name from its superb decoration in *cuerda seca* tile. The mosque (rest.) is similar in plan to that of Bayezid but has second-storey lodges on the north for the sultan and his family. The magnificent tiles in the mihrab are signed by the Masters of Tabriz (see fig; *see also* ISLAMIC ART, §V, 4(iii)). The octagonal tomb (rest.) also has rich decoration, including a tiled mihrab and cenotaph and elaborately carved doors. The madrasa, which houses a collection of Turkish and Islamic art, consists of a courtyard enclosed by cells on three sides and a domed hall on the fourth. The last of the large royal complexes (1424–6) was that built by Murad II (*reg* 1421–51 with interruption) west of the citadel. It includes the standard Bursa-type mosque, a madrasa, a kitchen and a tomb with an open oculus, the largest of 12 in the royal cemetery.

BIBLIOGRAPHY

Enc. Islam/2

A. Gabriel: *Une Capitale turque: Brousse*, 2 vols (Paris, 1958)

A. Kuran: *The Mosque in Early Ottoman Architecture* (Chicago, 1968), pp. 98–103, 110–23, 151–3, 161–4

G. Godwin: *A History of Ottoman Architecture* (Baltimore, 1971), pp. 34–91

ÇIGDEM KAFESÇIOGLU

Burton, Alfred (Henry) (*b* England, 1834; *d* Dunedin, 1914). New Zealand photographer. At the age of 34 he travelled to join his younger brother, Walter Burton, who had established a photographic business in Dunedin, New Zealand. Under the name of Burton Bros. they practised photography together until their partnership was dissolved by mutual consent in 1876. Alfred continued to trade under the firm's name until 1898, at which point he sold his remaining interests to two former associates, Muir and Moodie. A great deal of anecdotal information about his life can be found in the self-promoting articles that he supplied to various Dunedin newspapers and publications. He is remembered above all for his trip up the Wanganui River in April and May in 1885. This North Island river gave access to the hinterland known as the King Country, a place where Maori tribes had retreated after the New Zealand Wars of the 1860s. Photographing as he went, Burton documented the villages and people of the area in 250 plates. These images are among the most important social documents on Maori life to have survived from this period. Burton marketed his views in albums, which he called *Maori at Home*. Although very few of these remain in their original form, the bulk of his negatives survives in the National Museum, Wellington.

WILLIAM MAIN

Burton, Decimus (*b* London, 30 Sept 1800; *d* London, 14 Dec 1881). English architect. An extremely prolific classical architect and urban planner who continued the Picturesque tradition established by John Nash, he was trained by his father James Burton (1761–1837), the builder of Nash's Regent's Park terraces, and by George Maddox (1760–1843). Achieving early success through the joint patronage of his father and of Nash, he was responsible, under Nash, for the design of Clarence and Cornwall Terraces, Regent's Park, London, at the age of 20. His other contributions to Regent's Park were several elegant villas, including the Holme (1819) for his father, the Colosseum (1823–7; destr.) and buildings and gardens for the Zoological Society (1826–41) and the Royal Botanical Society (1840–59). The Colosseum, a Greek Doric version of the Pantheon in Rome with a dome slightly larger than that of St Paul's Cathedral, was an ambitious construction for which Burton was much admired. The function of the building was to exhibit the popular panoramas and dioramas, the Picturesque precursors of modern *son et lumière* performances. His numerous contributions to London in an adaptable but scholarly Greek Revival manner, which are in some ways analogous to the achievement of Karl Friedrich Schinkel in Berlin, include the Ionic screen at Hyde Park Corner (1824–5) and the archway on Constitution Hill (1827–8), the Athenaeum Club (1827–8), with its full-size copy of the Parthenon's Panathenaic frieze, and the former Charing Cross Hospital (1831–4). The screen and arch at Hyde Park Corner were commissioned by the Office of Woods and Forests as part of an ambition to extend to the gates of the park the monumentality of Buckingham Palace as newly enlarged by Nash. Burton's arch is a version of the Arch of Titus in Rome, while his chaste Ionic screen may have been inspired by Henry Holland's at Carlton House, which was being demolished at about this time. In 1888 the arch was unfortunately moved to a position on the axis of Constitution Hill, thus destroying its relation to the screen.

The most attractive work by Burton outside London is the Calverley Estate at Tunbridge Wells, Kent, begun in 1828 as an attempt to exploit the themes initiated by Nash at Park Villages East and West in Regent's Park. Burton's schemes provided 24 villas, chiefly in Greek and Italianate styles, following a curved private road and overlooking a miniature landscaped park which appears from each house to belong to it alone.

Burton's churches are unattractive, for he was never sympathetic to the Gothic style in which he was obliged to design them, and he was best in his numerous small country houses and villas. A commission to remodel Grimston, N. Yorks, in 1840 gave him an opportunity to create an ambitious country house in a dignified Italianate style, with sumptuous interiors and a fine conservatory. He was noted for his skill as an architect of large glazed structures, for example his conservatory in Regent's Park (1845; destr. 1932), the Palm House at Kew Gardens, Surrey (1845–8; rest. 1984–91), and, with Sir Joseph Paxton, the Great Conservatory at Chatsworth, Derbys (1836–40; destr. 1920). The bold clean lines of the Palm House at Kew were established by Burton in direct opposition to the first design by the iron-founder Richard Turner, which was in the Gothic style with numerous crockets and perforated parapets. Burton's Palm House (l. 110 m, h. 19 m in the centre) is one of the most arresting iron-and-glass constructions of 19th-century Britain, its billowing curved forms resembling those of the contemporary crinoline dresses with their steel frames. The building was a milestone on the path that led from the iron-and-glass conservatories of the Regency period to the great glazed sheds of the mid-Victorian railway stations.

BIBLIOGRAPHY

Colvin
J. Elmes: *Metropolitan Improvements* (London, 1831)
J. Britton: *Descriptive Sketches of Tunbridge Wells and the Calverley Estate* (London, 1832)
Obituary, *Builder*, xli (1881), p. 779
R. P. Jones: 'The Life and Work of Decimus Burton', *Archit. Rev.* [London], xvii (1905), pp. 109–18, 155–64
C. Hussey: *English Country Houses: Late Georgian* (London, 1958)
Survey of London, xxix–xxx (London, 1960)
G. F. Chadwick: *The Works of Sir Joseph Paxton* (London, 1961)
H. M. Colvin, ed.: *History of the King's Works*, vi (London, 1973)

DAVID WATKIN

Burton, Sir **Frederic William** (*b* Corofin, Co. Clare, 8 April 1816; *d* London, 16 March 1900). Irish painter and museum director. He was taught painting by the Brocas brothers in Dublin and, like them, he specialized in watercolours. He soon established himself as a portrait painter, and he had many notable sitters in Dublin. He made a charming portrait of *Helen Faucit as Antigone* (Dublin, N.G.) in 1849 and also designed the gold and emerald fibula (Dublin, N. Mus.) presented to her by a group of Dublin gentlemen. Burton became friendly with George Petrie, who encouraged his interest in Irish life and antiquities, which gave rise to such pictures as the *Aran Fisherman's Drowned Child* (1841; Dublin, N.G.). This work combines careful observation of the costume and habits of the people of the west of Ireland with dramatic composition and gestures derived less from life than from the Old Masters. Like many of his other subject-pictures in watercolour, it is very densely and richly painted. Burton was elected Royal Hibernian Academician in 1839 at the age of 23. In 1851 he settled in Munich, from where he made sketching trips and visits to the German art galleries. He subsequently settled in London, where he continued to devote himself to the study of art history and to portrait painting. His portrait of *George Eliot* (London, N.P.G.) was exhibited at the Royal Academy in 1867.

From 1874 to 1894 Burton was Director of the National Gallery in London and gave up painting completely. His appointment was an unexpected one, but his scholarship, discrimination and wide experience of European painting equipped him well for the job. He made sound purchases over a remarkably wide range; he bought Italian Renaissance works, including Leonardo's *Virgin of the Rocks*, Piero della Francesca's *Nativity* and Raphael's Ansidei *Madonna* (*Madonna and Child with SS John the Baptist and Nicholas of Bari*), but he also bought 18th-century Italian works, the gallery's first painting by Vermeer, *Young Woman Standing at a Virginal*, and Velázquez's *Philip IV in Brown and Silver* (all London, N.G.).

BIBLIOGRAPHY

DNB
H. Potterton: 'A Director with Discrimination', *Country Life*, clv (9 May 1974), pp. 1140–41
M. Bourke: 'The *Aran Fisherman's Drowned Child*', *Irish A. Rev. Yb.* (1988), pp. 190–96
A. Crookshank and The Knight of Glin: *The Watercolours of Ireland* (London, 1994)

JEANNE SHEEHY

Burton, Mildred (*b* Paraná, Entre Ríos, 28 Dec 1942). Argentine painter, draughtsman, watercolourist and collagist. She studied at the Escuela Provincial de Artes Visuales in Paraná and at the Escuela Superior de Bellas Artes (Ernesto de la Cárcova) in Buenos Aires. Taking the cue for her well-crafted works from Surrealism but concentrating her attention on fortuitous encounters in everyday life, she fluctuated between a meticulously detailed photographic realism and an artificial imagery of old porcelain dolls and turn-of-the-century postcards, posters and advertising handbills. Generally working in series, she combined the sinister and the humorous, sometimes in a single work, as in *Sublime Portrait of my Mother* (1978; see Glusberg, p. 455), a frontal view of a masked woman with a vacant and enigmatic smile. An early triptych, the *Family of the Condemned* (1974), is in the national collection in Buenos Aires (Mus. N. B.A.).

BIBLIOGRAPHY

J. Glusberg: *Del Pop-art a la Nueva Imagen* (Buenos Aires, 1985), pp. 455–8

JORGE GLUSBERG

Burton, William Shakespeare (*b* London, 1 June 1826; *d* London, 26 Jan 1916). English painter. He was the son of the dramatist William Evans Burton (1802–60). After studying at the Government School of Design at Somerset House, he entered the Royal Academy Schools in 1846. He exhibited intermittently from that year until 1897 at the Royal Academy and was a member of the Hogarth Club, a predominantly Pre-Raphaelite institution. He was befriended by the critic Tom Taylor and through him was offered work designing capital letters for *Punch* early in his career, which helped alleviate serious financial hardship. In 1852 he exhibited *Delilah Begging the Forgiveness of Samson in Captivity* at the Royal Academy, where it won a gold medal. Four years later Burton's most popular work, the *Wounded Cavalier* (London, Guildhall A.G.), was shown there. It was well received by critics, who commented on its apparent debt to Pre-Raphaelitism. Burton had only slight personal contact with Pre-Raphaelite circles, but the style of the *Wounded Cavalier* and the choice of a Civil War subject similar to John Everett Millais's earlier *Proscribed Royalist, 1651* (1853; priv. col., see 1984 exh. cat., no. 46) suggest close familiarity with their work.

Despite his success, Burton found it increasingly difficult to establish himself as an artist. From 1868 until 1876 he lived and worked in Italy. On returning to England he suffered ill-health and was for a time unable to paint. Towards the end of the 1880s he started painting again, and in the following decade there was a revival of interest in his work. In his later years he painted religious subjects.

BIBLIOGRAPHY

E. Rimbault Dibdin: 'William Shakespeare Burton', *Mag. A.*, xxiii (1899), pp. 289–98
W. Gaunt: 'The Lesser-known Pre-Raphaelite Painters', *Apollo Annual* (1948), pp. 5–9
A. Staley: *Pre-Raphaelite Landscape* (Oxford, 1973), p. 89
The Pre-Raphaelites (exh. cat., ed. L. Parris; London, Tate, 1984), p. 29
For further bibliography *see* PRE-RAPHAELITISM.

JENNY ELKAN

Burty, Philippe (*b* Paris, 11 Feb 1830; *d* Parays, Tarn-et-Garonne, 3 June 1890). French critic, collector and etcher. He studied drawing and painting before becoming art critic of the *Gazette des Beaux-Arts* in 1859. His extensive articles examined such issues as the etching revival (*see* ETCHING, §V), modernization of the industrial arts, the cult of JAPONISME and Impressionism. With his notices in the newspaper *Le Rappel* (1869–71) and the avant-garde journal *La Renaissance littéraire et artistique* (1871–2), the periodical of the emerging Symbolist poets, Burty passionately espoused the taste for Japanese art and culture and coined the term Japonisme in 1872. His apartment, which contained a vast collection of Japanese works of art, attracted many collectors also fascinated by Japan, including Edmond de Goncourt, Félix Bracquemond and Edgar Degas. Burty's meetings and his collection and staunch advocacy of Japonisme influenced many, including his Impressionist friends, in whose compositions the subtle assimilation of Japanese print design is evident. The marriage of Burty's daughter Madeleine to the entrepreneur Charles Haviland, a director of Haviland & Co., porcelain manufacturers of Limoges, assured the use of Japoniste decoration by ceramicists. Burty also prompted Haviland to collect Japanese artefacts.

Burty avidly championed the Impressionist cause through personal contacts and with articles in such publications as *La République française* and the English *Academy* (1874). His reviews defended the Impressionists' techniques and motivations against prevailing critical reserve or sarcasm. Burty saw their spontaneous appreciation of nature, their light-filled canvases and their sketch-like compositions as some of the most promising qualities for the future of painting. Burty is thus recognized as one of the few popular journalists to have openly advocated innovation and independent creativity. Burty's support of these characteristics was abetted by his own proclivity as a draughtsman; his small landscape sketches (France, priv. col.), in pencil or charcoal, reveal an awareness of light and subtle atmospheric conditions developed from observation.

Burty was a major advocate of the etching revival, and himself etched (e.g. *Japanese Objects from the Collection of Philippe Burty*, *c.* 1873; Boston, MA, Mus. F.A.). He was a founder-member of the Société des Aquafortistes (1862). As Burty knew many etchers, he had a fine collection, including prints by Bracquemond, Charles Meryon and Whistler. During the late 1870s he auctioned a large portion of his contemporary print collection in London and used the money raised to enlarge his collection of Japanese objects. Burty was a latent Romantic and a staunch advocate of the works of Delacroix, whose letters he edited, but by the beginning of the 1880s his collection consumed more of his time than his writing. Everything Burty was motivated by or accomplished, especially late in life, was nourished by Japan, and when he died he was seen as the leading popularizer of Japonisme in France.

WRITINGS

Les Emaux cloisonnés anciens et modernes (Paris, 1868)
'Japonisme', *Ren. Litt. & A.*, i (1872), pp. 25–6, 59–60, 83–4, 106–7, 122–3; ii (1873), pp. 3–5
'Japonisme', *L'Art*, ii (1875), pp. 1–7, 330–42; v (1876), pp. 49–58, 278–82; vi (1876), pp. 150–55
ed.: *Lettres d'Eugène Delacroix* (Paris, 1878, rev., 2 vols, 1880)
Regular contributions to *Gaz. B.-A.* (1859), *Le Rappel* (1869–71), *Rev. Litt. & A.* (1871–2), *République Fr.* (1874), *Academy* (1874) and *L'Art* (1870s)

BIBLIOGRAPHY

M. Tourneux: 'Philippe Burty', *Gaz. B.-A.*, n. s. 3, xxxvii (1907), pp. 388–402
G. P. Weisberg: *The Early Years of Philippe Burty: Art Critic, Amateur and Japoniste, 1855–1875* (diss., Baltimore, MD, Johns Hopkins U., 1967)
——: 'Philippe Burty: A Notable Critic of the Nineteenth Century', *Apollo*, xci (1970), pp. 296–300
——: 'Philippe Burty and Early *Japonisme*', *Japonisme in Art: An International Symposium: Tokyo, 1980*, pp. 109–25
——: *The Independent Critic: Philippe Burty and the Visual Arts of Mid-nineteenth-century France* (Berne and New York, 1993)

GABRIEL P. WEISBERG

Burundi, Republic of [République de Burundi]. Small, densely populated and mountainous country in eastern Africa, formerly part of Ruanda-Urundi. Burundi is bordered by Rwanda to the north, Tanzania to the east and Zaïre to the west; Lake Tanganyika defines its south-eastern border. The capital is Bujumbura (formerly Usumbura); its national languages are Kirundi and French, while Swahili is also spoken. A poor infrastructure and a long history of civil turbulence have made Burundi one of Africa's poorest nations. The population (5,302,000; UN estimate, 1989) is made up of Hutu (85%), Tutsi (14%) and Twa (1%). The peoples of Burundi have lived together according to a model of social organization established by the Tutsi monarchy at the end of the 18th century, which lasted until its abolition in 1966. The resulting strong cultural unity and geographical protection enabled Burundi to resist not only the raids of Arab slave traders but also German occupation (following the Treaty of Kiganda in 1903) and the control of Belgium, beginning in 1923, which attached Burundi to the administration of the Congo (1925–62). This entry covers the art produced in Burundi since colonial times. For art of the region in earlier periods *see* AFRICA, §VII, 7.

Much art and architecture in modern Burundi continues traditions from the precolonial period. Although advanced government systems might be expected to have resulted in new building styles that reflected the country's political and administrative sophistication, instead the traditional family compound of round houses encircled by walls (Kirundi *rugo*) continues to be the most prevalent expression of indigenous architecture. While monotheism and the lack of forests for wood help to explain the absence of precolonial sculptural and masking traditions, the Tutsi monarchy and its aristocratic protectionism led to highly developed musical traditions and a sophisticated art of drum-making. Other traditional arts are concerned mainly with production of utilitarian objects and items for personal adornment, such as collars, bracelets and delicate objects associated with elegance. Such arts are well represented in the numerous regional craft centres, including those at Gishubi, famous for its pottery, Bugarama, which produces much basketry, and Ngozi, specializing in matting. Modern decorative arts have been developed under the auspices of Christian missionary institutions, which encouraged religious statuary and painting.

The School of Art at Giheta and the Professional Centre at Gitega teach painting, sculpture and ceramics, influenced by the training developed in the former Belgian Congo. Late 20th-century painters include Mopela Gahungu and Pierre Gahungu. The best-known modern Burundi sculptors are Antoine Manirampa, Léonidas Bayenyeye and Julien Banza, although 35 sculptors were known to the Burundi Ministry of Culture in 1982. Among the other art forms produced are, at Nyakabiga, tableaux made from banana leaves glued to wood panels. Overall, however, no school of original expression has emerged in Burundi. The poverty of the people must be one factor, while others include a historical lack of patronage, scarcity of exhibition space, the relative dearth of art education and the sometimes violent political troubles. Tourists have become the main market for contemporary Burundi art, and this may also be seen as limiting. The fullest collection of national art is held in the Living Museum, Bujumbura, which opened in 1977 and continues to be traditional in scope.

BIBLIOGRAPHY

G. Celis: 'The Decorative Arts in Rwanda and Burundi', *Afr. A.*, iv/1 (1970), pp. 40–42

J. Anquetil: *Burundi: L'Artisanat créateur* (Paris, 1982)

J.-L. Acquier and C. Seignobis: *Le Burundi*, Collection architectures traditionnelles, 3 (Marseille, 1986)

A. Nijembazi: 'La Poterie au Burundi', *Cult. & Soc.*, x (1988), pp. 48–60

P.-C. Sendegeya: *Anthologie des sculpteurs et peintres burundais contemporains* (Paris, 1989)

PIERRE HAFFNER

Bury, château of. Château near Blois (Loir-et-Cher), France. Although ruined in the 17th century, this Renaissance château, built by Florimond ROBERTET, Secretary of Finance to Charles VIII, Louis XII and Francis I, still dominates the village of Bury. It was long considered to be one of the lesser architectural creations of 16th-century France, but this evaluation depended on an erroneously late dating of its construction and a misunderstanding of its original appearance. It has now been established that the building was begun in 1511 (possibly to the designs of Fra Giovanni Giocondo) and that it was nearly complete by January 1515; it can thus no longer be considered to be an imitation of the Francis I wing of the château of Blois. If Bury was built as it appears in the engravings of Jacques Androuet Du Cerceau (i) (*see* GARDEN, fig. 41), it was in certain respects the precursor of the great châteaux of the Loire valley built between 1515 and 1525, such as Chenonceau, Azay-le-Rideau and Chambord.

The buildings at Bury were grouped around a square court, with round towers under high roofs at the corners. This arrangement was, however, distinguished from its medieval predecessors by a new emphasis on regularity (the staircases, for instance, did not jut out from the façades), by an axial arrangement connecting the gardens and the *cour d'honneur*, and by an emphasis on the *corps de logis* achieved by reducing the entrance wing to a single-storey arcaded cloister. The three elevations of the *cour d'honneur* were marked by the first appearance of the gridlike articulation of superimposed pilasters and horizontal string courses typical of early Renaissance architecture in France. The rhythm of the bays was also a novelty, with the decoratively carved window bays that culminated in elaborate dormer windows in the steep roofs being separated by double-width sections of wall.

This attempt to achieve a monumental effect, taken in conjunction with the precocious, semi-classicizing design of the entrance portico, underlines the unusual depth of Italian influence at Bury, echoes of which may be found in the more advanced classicizing châteaux of the 1530s, such as Villandry (Indre-et-Loire) and Ecouen (Val-d'Oise).

BIBLIOGRAPHY

J. A. Du Cerceau: *Les Plus Excellents Bastiments de France* (Paris, 1576–9/*R* London, 1972)

P. Lesueur: 'Le Château de Bury et l'architecte Fra Giocondo', *Gaz. B.-A.*, n. s. 4, xii (1925), pp. 337–57

M. Garczynska: 'Le Château de Bury-en-Blésois', *Inf. Hist. A.*, 2 (1965), pp. 84–5

J.-M. Pérouse de Montclos: *Architectures en région centre*, Le Guide du patrimoine (Paris, 1987), pp. 235–8

MARTINE TISSIER DE MALLERAIS

Bury, Friedrich (*b* Hanau, 13 March 1763; *d* Aachen, 18 May 1823). German painter and dealer. He was taught to draw by his father, Jean Jacques Bury (1731–85), a goldsmith and engraver born in Strasbourg, who also taught at the Hanau Zeichnenakademie. After taking painting lessons from Anton Wilhelm Tischbein (1730–1804), in 1780 Bury attended the Kunstakademie in Düsseldorf, where he practised copying from the work of the Old Masters, especially Peter Paul Rubens, in the gallery belonging to the Elector Palatine Charles Theodore. In 1782 Bury went to Italy with his friend Heinrich Lips (1758–1817), a copperplate-engraver, staying until 1799. His contented and enthusiastic character endeared him to the German artists in Rome, and he became especially close to Wilhelm Tischbein, nephew of his former painting teacher, who introduced him to Goethe in 1786. Goethe often subsequently referred to Bury as a 'child' and bought many of the drawings and watercolours based on the work of Raphael, Michelangelo and other Old Masters that Bury produced in Rome (Weimar, Goethe-Nmus.). In turn Goethe recommended Bury to Anna Amalia of Saxe-Weimar, who was in Italy from 1788 to 1790 and who became Bury's patron. Bury accompanied her to Naples in 1789–90, making drawings of antiquities and famous paintings for her (Weimar, Schlossmus.). While travelling with her on her return journey to Weimar, Bury again met Goethe in northern Italy, and the two visited several towns together. Goethe then commissioned Bury to make copies of works by Andrea Mantegna and Giulio Romano in Mantua.

On his return to Rome, Bury worked principally as an art dealer. Frederick of Hanover, third son of George III, became his patron. In 1800 Bury spent almost a year in Weimar, hoping vainly that Goethe would give him further help. Goethe, however, claimed to find only moderate merit in Bury's work, even though he praised the purity of his watercolour style and his treatment of light and shade. Bury worked as a portrait painter in Weimar, making portrait drawings of *Goethe* and of *Christiane Vulpius* (both Weimar, Goethe-Nmus.). At the end of 1800, he moved to Berlin, where he earned his living by giving drawing lessons at the Prussian court. Queen Louisa, Duchess of Mecklenburg-Strelitz, bought Bury's copy (Potsdam, Schloss Sanssouci) of Raphael's *Sistine Madonna* (Dresden, Gemäldegal. Alte Meister). From 1800 Bury regularly exhibited at the exhibitions held by the Akademie der Künste, becoming a member in 1811. He remained in the service of both Princess Wilhelmina, when she became Queen of the Netherlands, and her sister Augusta, Electress of Hesse-Kassel, and he alternated between living in Kassel, Brussels, The Hague and his home town of Hanau. His portraits continued to be in high demand. He also painted rather austere, academic paintings on mythological and historical themes: *Cupid Triumphant* and the *Oath Sworn by the Swiss* (both The Hague, Mauritshuis). Bury's letters to Goethe (Weimar, Goethe- & Schiller-Archv) are an excellent source of information about him, both as an artist and as a man.

BIBLIOGRAPHY

NDB; Thieme–Becker

H. Börsch-Supan, ed.: *Die Kataloge der Berliner Akademie-Ausstellungen, 1786–1850* (Berlin, 1971)

'Es ist nur ein Rom in der Welt': Zeichnungen und Bildnisse deutscher Künstler in Rom um 1800 (exh. cat., Kassel, Staatl. Kstsammlungen, 1977)

INGRID SATTEL BERNARDINI

Bury, Pol (*b* Haine-Saint-Pierre, nr La Louvière, 26 April 1922). Belgian painter and sculptor. After attending the Académie des Beaux-Arts in Mons he met the poet Achille Chavée at La Louvière in 1939 and joined the Surrealist group Rupture. His first paintings were influenced by Magritte and Yves Tanguy. In 1947 he joined the Jeune Peinture Belge group in Brussels and met Christian Dotremont and Pierre Alechinsky; he was also close to the Cobra group until 1951. When he discovered the art of Alexander Calder he joined the group Art Abstrait (1952). Attracted by movement, he created the *Mobile Planes* (1953) and the *Multiplanes* (1957), which were moved by electric motors. He was also developing an aesthetic of slowness, which led in 1959 to 1961 to the *Luminous Punctuations* and the *Erectile Punctuations*. After moving to France he published *La Boule et le trou* (1961).

In 1963 Bury created his first actual sculptures, 'furniture' in waxed wood incorporating balls, cubes and cylinders. In 1964 he visited New York and began his first *Cinematizations*. After this he ceaselessly developed secret and complicated mechanisms, attempting to fix the imperceptible moment between movement and immobility as the balls moved over sloping or curved planes. From 1967 onwards stainless or Corten steel led him to monumentality as well as to formal and technical perfection, the reflections responding to movements that were now magnetically controlled and apparently even freer than previously. In 1972, with the support of the Renault company, he created a group of 50 mobile columns, each 3 m high. In 1976 he began work on hydraulic sculptures that were moved by the weight of water. These were followed by many works integrated with architecture, such as the two fountains installed in 1985 in the courtyard of the Palais-Royal in Paris.

WRITINGS

La Boule et le trou (Brussels, 1961)

L'Art à bicyclette et la révolution à cheval (Paris, 1972)

BIBLIOGRAPHY

D. Ashton: *Pol Bury* (Paris, 1970)

E. Ionesco and A. Balthazar: *Pol Bury* (Brussels, 1976)

PIERRE BAUDSON

Buryatia. *See under* RUSSIA, §XII, 4.

Bury St Edmunds [St Edmundsbury]. Town in Suffolk, England.

1. HISTORY AND URBAN DEVELOPMENT. A medieval town with a Georgian face, Bury grew beside one of England's richest abbeys, founded *c.* AD 663. After Edmund, King of East Anglia, was martyred by the Danes in 869, his tomb became the focus for pilgrims and patrons, King Cnut installing Benedictines in the Abbey in 1020. Until the Reformation, the Abbey both owned and controlled the town. The population grew restless and in 1327 attacked and burnt the Abbey, which responded by allowing guilds to run the town, the monks running the guilds. As medieval East Anglia grew rich on the wool trade Bury entered a period of growth: the 1523 Subsidy

Returns show that its wealth equalled that of Canterbury and was ahead of Lincoln and York. Much of the surviving urban fabric dates from this prosperous period, though now concealed behind Georgian façades. During the 19th century Bury had no industry and was overshadowed by Ipswich and Cambridge; it remained solid, moneyed and agrarian. Since 1945 it has expanded, enjoying economic growth.

The Anglo-Saxon abbey, which included several centralized churches, was rebuilt by Abbot Baldwin (1065–97). The Romanesque abbey church was 188 m long, nearly 20 m longer than Norwich Cathedral. It had an apse and ambulatory plan with radiating chapels and a four-bay choir, all raised on a crypt, comparable to such buildings as St Augustine's, Canterbury. The transept was long, with a single, eastern aisle as at Lincoln Cathedral, but also eastern apsidal chapels. Like the choir, the ten-bay nave had a tall gallery, such as is found at Ely Cathedral. The extended west front, completed *c.* 1140, was nearly 85 m wide, with five arches, a central tower (rebuilt after 1430) and polygonal terminals. It was a multi-storey structure similar to the west block of Lincoln, but much bigger. The picturesque remains now contain houses. Very few additions were made to the Romanesque church before the fire of 1463, after which high stone vaults were inserted. The church was demolished after the Dissolution (1536–40). The monastic complex was large, but only fragments survive.

Other monastic remains include two gate-houses and two churches, St James and St Mary's, which the monastery provided for the town. The Romanesque gate-tower (*c.* 1130) stands directly to the west of the abbey church and has a great gabled portal and three upper floors, richly arcaded and decorated, including the motif of blind arches and windows within Giant orders. It was once battlemented. The second gate was built by the penitential townspeople after the riots of 1327. Formerly vaulted, it is solid and fortified but exquisitely worked. Triangular gables and nodding ogee canopies climb the sides and are arranged across the upper façade. The Romanesque gate-tower acts as the bell-tower to St James. A cathedral since 1914, this church has a 16th-century nave and an eastern extension by S. E. Dykes Bower (begun 1960). The whitewashed nave has tall, slender arcades, many aisle windows and a closely packed clerestory. The roof (1865–9) is by the elder George Gilbert Scott. Massive and expensive, St Mary's is the classic East Anglian church, only the tower predating the 15th-century reconstruction. The nave has tall arcades and disproportionately high aisles (see fig. 1). The clerestory level, which is almost entirely of glass, lights the famous roof with its high arch-braces resting on canopied saints and huge, jutting wooden angels. The south aisle chapel has a ceiling with tiny mirrors, and the chancel roof has painted scenes.

The Normans replanned Bury on a grid-pattern with two rectangular markets. Civic buildings include the two so-called Jews houses of stone (*c.* 1190), the 15th-century Guildhall with a door of *c.* 1230, the cruciform Town Hall (1774) by Robert Adam in grey brick and stone and the Theatre Royal (1819) by William Wilkins with an intact Georgian interior. Bury has two notable post-medieval churches, the Baroque Presbyterian Chapel (1711), of

1. Bury St Edmunds, St Mary, interior facing north-east, 15th century

polished red brick, and St Edmund's Catholic Church (1837), an example of Greek Revival, with interesting fittings.

Bury is rich in domestic architecture, especially late medieval and Georgian. Hall houses survive tucked away in, for example, Lower Baxter Street, and other timber ranges are being uncovered, for example 17 Mustow Street. Most are hidden from view, but the best example is 56 Abbeygate Street, where a blank Regency exterior conceals a huge timber-framed merchant house (*c.* 1525) with carved corner posts and elaborate moulded ceilings. Cupola House (1693) in The Traverse is the first of a magnificent array of classical houses, some paired and grouped with great invention. Some of the best occur in Guildhall Street, St Mary's Square and Honey Hill, including Manor House (*c.* 1720) by James Burrough (1691–1764). Two outstanding mansions are near Bury St Edmunds: Hengrave Hall (1525–38) and the eccentric Ickworth, begun in 1796 by Francis Sandys (*fl* 1788–1814) and Mario Asprucci (1760–1804).

BIBLIOGRAPHY

S. Tymms: *An Architectural and Historical Account of the Church of St Mary, Bury St Edmunds* (Bury St Edmunds, 1854)

M. R. James: 'On the Abbey of St Edmund at Bury', *Cambs Antiqua. Soc. 8vo Pubns*, xxviii (1895) [whole issue]

M. D. Lobel: *The Borough of Bury St Edmunds* (Oxford, 1935)

M. Beresford and J. St Joseph: *Medieval England: An Aerial Survey* (Cambridge, 1958, 2/1979)

N. Pevsner: *Suffolk*, Bldgs England (Harmondsworth, 1961, 2/1974)

L. Butler and C. Given-Wilson: *Medieval Monasteries of Great Britain* (London, 1979)

FRANCIS WOODMAN

2. CENTRE OF MANUSCRIPT PRODUCTION. During the late 11th century and the 12th, Bury St Edmunds Abbey was one of the most important centres of manuscript production in England. In the earlier part of this period the various activities involved in the making of books were carried out by the monks themselves, but increasingly during the 12th century lay scribes and artists were employed in the scriptorium of the abbey. By the end of the 12th century, although the production of illuminated manuscripts had by then fallen off, a large library had been built up, and this continued to grow throughout the medieval period, mainly as a result of acquiring books from outside the abbey. Over 100 books from the 12th-century library still survive. There is some evidence for book production in the town of Bury St Edmunds in the 15th century, but this does not seem necessarily to have been centred on the abbey. Over 300 books survive from the medieval library disseminated at the Dissolution of the Monasteries, a major part of which was given to Pembroke College, Cambridge, in 1599 by William Smart of Ipswich.

The evidence for manuscript production at the abbey in the Anglo-Saxon period is limited, since its foundation in 1020 was late compared with that of the other great English Benedictine houses. In the four decades before the Norman Conquest (1066) books for Bury were probably acquired from established centres such as Christ Church, Canterbury. A Gospel book (London, BL, Harley MS. 76) and a Psalter (Rome, Vatican, Bib. Apostolica, MS. Reg. lat. 12) of the second quarter of the 11th century seem to have been produced at Christ Church for Bury. By the end of the 11th century Bury was producing its own books: for example a Herbal (*c.* 1100; Oxford, Bodleian Lib., MS. Bodley 130), which is illustrated by tinted drawings. Other books of this early period have only minor decorated initials. In the second decade of the 12th century more books were produced with more decoration, and active production continued until the end of the century when it seems to have declined rapidly. The books of the period *c.* 1110–40 have decorated and historiated initials and in some cases framed illustrations in tinted drawing: for example a Missal (Laon, Bib. Mun., MS. 238) and 12 leaves added to a New Testament book (Cambridge, Pembroke Coll., MS. 120). The latter were probably executed *c.* 1130 and comprise full-page framed illustrations of the *Life of Christ.* In the period *c.* 1125–35, under the influence of the style of illumination at St Albans Abbey, a *Life and Miracles of St Edmund* (New York, Pierpont Morgan Lib., MS. M. 736) was produced with 32 painted full-page miniatures (see fig. 2). This St Albans style (*see* ST ALBANS, §2) is also evident in the tinted drawings in the New Testament manuscript and became established at Bury, continuing to be evident in the illumination produced there well into the second half of the century.

A new phase in book illumination at Bury began with the production of the BURY ST EDMUNDS BIBLE (*c.* 1135; Cambridge, Corpus Christi Coll., MS. 2; *see* ROMANESQUE, fig. 64). This introduced a Byzantinizing figure style, which was used in other books from Bury of the period *c.* 1140–60, such as in the historiated initials in St Gregory's *Homilies on the Gospels* (Cambridge, Pembroke Coll., MS. 16). During the second half of the 12th century relatively few books were produced at Bury and very few of these were decorated with anything but ornamental initials. During the 13th and 14th centuries there seem to have been hardly any books produced there.

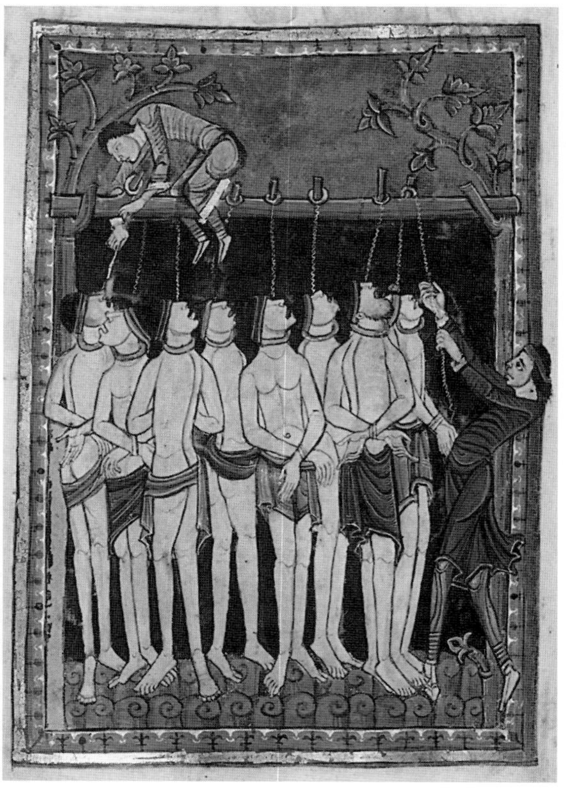

2. *Execution of Eight Thieves*; miniature from the *Life and Miracles of St Edmund*, 273×184 mm, *c.* 1125–35 (New York, Pierpont Morgan Library, MS. M. 736, p. 36)

In the early 15th century a Psalter (Bury St Edmunds, Co. Upper Sch., on dep. Suffolk Rec. Office) for liturgical use at the Abbey was probably made there. In 1433–4 a presentation copy of the *Life of SS Edmund and Fremund* by the Bury monk John Lydgate, with 120 framed miniatures, was presented to King Henry VI when he visited the abbey. This and another product of the same workshop, a Book of Hours (Cambridge, Fitzwilliam, MS. 3-1979), seem to be a later continuation of the style of the earlier Psalter.

BIBLIOGRAPHY

R. M. Thomson: 'The Library of Bury St Edmunds Abbey in the Eleventh and Twelfth Centuries', *Speculum*, xlvii (1972), pp. 617–45
C. M. Kauffmann: *Romanesque Manuscripts, 1066–1190* (1975), iii of *A Survey of Manuscripts Illuminated in the British Isles*, ed. J. J. G. Alexander (London, 1975–), nos 11, 34–5, 56–8
E. Temple: *Anglo-Saxon Manuscripts, 900–1066* (1976), ii of *A Survey of Manuscripts Illuminated in the British Isles*, ed. J. J. G. Alexander (London, 1975–), nos 75, 84

K. R. Bateman: 'Pembroke 120 and Morgan 736: A Reexamination of the St Albans–Bury St Edmunds Manuscript Dilemma', *Gesta*, xvii (1978), pp. 19–26
E. P. McLachlan: 'The Scriptorium of Bury St Edmunds in the 3rd and 4th Decades of the Twelfth Century', *Med. Stud.*, xl (1978), pp. 328–48
B. Abou-El-Haj: 'Bury St Edmunds Abbey between 1070 and 1124: A History of Property, Privilege and Monastic Art Production', *A. Hist.*, vi (1983), pp. 1–29
E. P. McLachlan: *The Scriptorium of Bury St Edmunds in the Twelfth Century* (New York, 1986)
N. J. Rogers: 'Fitzwilliam Museum MS. 3–1979: A Bury St Edmunds Book of Hours and the Origins of the Bury Style', *England in the Fifteenth Century. Proceedings of the 1986 Harlaxton Symposium: Harlaxton, 1986*, pp. 229–43

NIGEL J. MORGAN

Bury St Edmunds Bible. Manuscript (514×353 mm; Cambridge, Corpus Christi Coll., MS. 2) identified with a Bible recorded in the *Gesta sacristarum* of Bury St Edmunds Abbey. It is described as having been commissioned by the Sacrist, Hervey, in the time of his brother, Prior Talbot (*c.* 1125–38), and illuminated by MASTER HUGO. From this information a date of *c.* 1135 has been suggested for its production. Full-page painted miniatures (*see* ROMANESQUE, §IV, 2(vi) and fig. 64) survive at the beginning of six of the biblical books, and there are also historiated initials. These are painted in strong colours dominated by reds, blues, greens and purple. Although this palette is in some ways similar to that of the St Albans style evident in the *Life and Miracles of St Edmund* (New York, Pierpont Morgan Lib., MS. M. 736; *see* BURY ST EDMUNDS, fig. 2), a manuscript produced at Bury a few years earlier and probably painted by the artist of the St Albans Psalter (*see* ST ALBANS, §2), the colours are much brighter and more thickly applied. Master Hugo's figure style also depends to some extent on this same St Albans style, but with a characteristic new way of treating folds in patterned areas to reflect the positions of the limbs. This so-called dampfold style is ultimately of Byzantine origin, but was probably known to Master Hugo through French, German or Italian intermediaries. Its sources and development over many parts of Europe during the second quarter of the 12th century are controversial issues. In the 1130s and 1140s it appears at Canterbury and St Albans, and both these centres of book illumination are interrelated with Bury St Edmunds during this period.

BIBLIOGRAPHY

C. M. Kauffmann: 'The Bury Bible', *J. Warb. & Court. Inst.*, xxix (1966), pp. 60–81
R. M. Thomson: 'The Dates of the Pierpont Morgan *Vita sancti Edmundi* and the Bury Bible', *Viator*, ii (1971), pp. 211–25
——: 'The Date of the Bury Bible Reexamined', *Viator*, vi (1975), pp. 51–8

NIGEL J. MORGAN

Busati, Andrea (*fl* Venice, 1503–28). Italian painter. None of the published documents provides any information about Busati's activity as a painter. He was a member of two of the Venetian *scuole grandi* and made his will in 1528. Three signed works are known; on one, a *Lamentation* (London, N.G.), the painter appears to call himself a pupil of Giovanni Bellini. A fourth painting, the *Virgin and Child with SS Peter and John the Baptist* (ex-Cavendish Beutinck priv. col.), apparently signed and dated 1522, has disappeared and it is not now possible to check the authenticity of the inscription. However, the stylistic evidence of the three extant works indicates that Busati was much more closely associated with Cima da Conegliano than with Giovanni Bellini. The *Lamentation* includes a landscape motif borrowed from the Bellini workshop, but its composition and figure types are based on Cima's *Lamentation* altarpiece (Modena, Gal. & Mus. Estense). Compared with Cima's figures, Busati's tend to be schematized, with pudgy faces and wooden draperies, and despite the somewhat pedantic accumulation of animals and buildings, his landscapes appear arid, without air or natural light. Similar stylistic features are present in a handful of unsigned works that may be reasonably attributed to Busati. Perhaps the best of them is a *Pietà* in the village church of San Pietro d'Orzio, near Bergamo. He probably also had a hand in a number of works attributed to Cima's workshop.

BIBLIOGRAPHY

DBI; Thieme–Becker
B. Cecchetti: 'Saggio di cognomi ed autografi di artisti in Venezia', *Archv Veneto*, xxxiii (1887), p. 402; xxxiv (1887), p. 205 [docs]
G. Ludwig: 'Archivalische Beiträge zur Geschichte der venezianischen Malerei', *Jb. Kön.-Preuss. Kstsamml.*, xxvi (1905), pp. 98–100
M. Davies: *The Earlier Italian Schools*, London, N.G. cat. (London, 1951, 2/1961/*R* 1986), pp. 129–32
S. Moschini Marconi: *Gallerie dell'Accademia di Venezia: Opere d'arte dei secoli XIV e XV* (Rome, 1955), pp. 95–6
B. Berenson: *Venetian School*, i (1957), p. 51
L. Coletti: *Cima da Conegliano* (Venice, 1959), pp. 67, 98
R. Pallucchini: 'Appunti alla mostra di Cima da Conegliano', *A. Veneta*, xvi (1962), p. 227
P. Zampetti: *A Dictionary of Venetian Painters*, ii (Leigh-on-Sea, 1970), p. 37
L. Menegazzi: *Cima da Conegliano* (Treviso, 1981)
P. Humfrey: *Cima da Conegliano* (Cambridge, 1983)

PETER HUMFREY

Busca, Antonio (*b* Milan, 28 July 1625; *d* Milan, 23 Dec 1684). Italian painter and draughtsman. A prolific artist, he painted altarpieces and frescoes of religious scenes in Milan and Lombardy. He was trained by Panfilo Nuvolone and Ercole Procaccini (ii) and his *Apparition of the Virgin to St Felix* (Orta San Giulio, S Nicolao) may date from the 1640s. In 1650–51, accompanied by Giovanni Ghisolfi, with whom he frequently collaborated, Busca studied in Rome. This visit was decisive for his art and encouraged him to develop an academic style that united elements of Milanese Mannerism with Roman and Bolognese classicism, as in his crowded *Raising of the Cross* (mid-1650s; Milan, S Marco). In 1661, with Ercole Procaccini, he worked in Turin at the court of the House of Savoy, but no trace of their activity remains. In 1664 Busca frescoed the chapel of S Siro in the Certosa di Pavia, with scenes from the *Life of St Siro*, and in 1669 the chapel of the Arese in S Vittore al Corpo, Milan, with figures of *Prophets*. Also in 1669 Busca was appointed director of painting at the reopened Accademia Ambrosiana, Milan, and his colleague Dionigi Bussola became director of sculpture. In 1670 Busca executed the fresco of the *Crucifixion* in chapel X and frescoes in the oratory of the Blessed Giuliana and Caterina, all for the Sacromonte at Varese (*in situ*). Some time before 1674 he painted two canvases for the Sala dei Senatori in the Palazzo Ducale, Milan: one of these, the *Tribute Money* (Milan, Brera, on dep. Milan, S Marco), a strikingly classical work both in the figure style and in the grandiose architectural setting, survives. His career ended with the frescoes of *St Francis in Glory* in chapel XX of the Sacromonte at Orta. Among his pupils were Filippo Abbiati (1640–1713), Andrea Lanzani and Giovanni Ambrogio Besozzi (1648–1706), but he was not popular with the succeeding generation and his teaching methods were resented as too dictatorial. There are collections of his drawings in the Ambrosiana, Milan, and in the Musei Civici, Milan.

BIBLIOGRAPHY

DBI [with sources and bibliog.]
C. Torre: *Il ritratto di Milano* (Milan, 1674, rev. 1714), pp. 34, 160, 197, 238–9, 253
G. Rossi: 'Notizie su Antonio Busca', *A. Lombarda*, iv/2 (1959), pp. 314–22 [with bibliog. and illus.]
G. Melzi d'Eril: 'Sacro Monte d'Orta', *Isola San Giulio e Sacro Monte d'Orta* (Turin, 1977), pp. 79, 203, 206, 212

SIMONETTA COPPA

Busch, Wilhelm (*b* Wiedensahl, 15 April 1832; *d* Mechtshausen, 9 Jan 1908). German draughtsman, painter and writer. A grocer's son and the first of seven children, he enrolled at the Polytechnische Schule in Hannover to train (1847–51) as an engineer but, while there, decided to become an artist. In 1851 he transferred to the Akademie in Düsseldorf where he remained for a year, attending elementary classes in life drawing with Carl Ferdinand Sohn and studying proportion and anatomy with Heinrich Anton Mücke (1806–91). In May 1852 he moved to the less severely doctrinaire Academy in Antwerp, but the obsessive concern for precision of his tutor, the genre painter Joseph-Laurent Dyckmans (1811–88), did not appeal to him. As he conceded in 1886 in his autobiography, *Was mich betrifft*, he was assailed by doubts about his talent as a painter, not because of the demands of an academic training but because of the apparently unsurpassable example of Frans Hals and other Old Masters whose works he had studied in the Koninklijk Museum in Antwerp. During this period Busch produced several studies of heads in oils on cardboard that were freer in execution than his work in Düsseldorf, for example *Portrait of a Young Man* (*c.* 1852; Hannover, Wilhelm-Busch-Mus.), as well as drawings of views of Antwerp. In May 1853, after an attack of typhoid, he returned home to Wiedensahl, where he lived for the next 18 months, collecting legends and fairy tales of the Weser region and making drawings of gravestones and antiques in the area for a scholar in Berlin. He also painted oil studies of peasants in Bückeburg and portraits of members of his family, for example *Domestic Studies: Otto Busch Reading* (*c.* 1854; Hannover, Wilhelm-Busch-Mus.).

From 1854 to 1858 Busch attended the Munich Akademie, but he found the tuition unsatisfactory and did not take his final examinations. Every summer until 1858 he went back to Wiedensahl where he made sketchbook studies of local motifs (Hannover, Wilhelm-Busch-Mus.). He also made a number of oil studies, revealing a fascination for the detail of woodland plants, stones and tree stumps. Motifs from the farmhouses in upper Bavaria also interested him as seen in *Grindstone* (mid-1850s; Brunswick, Städt. Mus.). His Munich colleagues regarded him as an outsider, although they much appreciated his aphorisms.

In Munich Busch also secured his first real employment: he became a draughtsman and cartoonist for Caspar Braun, editor of the magazines *Fliegende Blätter* and *Münchner Bilderbogen*. He retained these posts until 1870 although after the early 1860s he generally lived away from Munich. Busch's first work for Braun took the form of cartoons without captions for *Fliegende Blätter*. These were followed by caricatures with brief prose commentaries, including, in 1865, the first *Max und Moritz* cartoon strip, which has remained his most popular work. As printed on the page, the cartoons represented a crude simplification of the subtly drawn originals, which nevertheless began in the style of 'stick-men'. Caspar Braun's wood-engravers were not skilful enough to cut into the hard wooden block against the grain. Accordingly, the impact of these early, fairly long strip cartoons, with chapter divisions, lay in their novel achievement of unity between exuberant pictorial and poetic fantasy. Busch presented his turbulent events not in the moralistic, finger-wagging spirit of children's education at that period but with obvious delight in a child's unbridled imagination, in undomesticated cruelty and in ironic parody of adult behaviour. Even at this time his work suggests a fundamental pessimism, probably owing a good deal to the philosophy of Arthur Schopenhauer to which he was introduced by his brother Otto. Busch also made very successful use of the street ballad technique, unillustrated, but with a prologue and conclusion that prepared the reader for the often cruel, if comic, fate that awaited the protagonists. These were generally established social types: farmers, clergymen, scholars, artists. They may have derived, in part, from the English 18th-century satirical caricatures popularized in Hannover by Johann Heinrich Ramberg. Busch's types were not especially representative of his age; their settings have a strong element of the folk-tale and Busch rarely took up political issues from contemporary life.

In 1868 Busch moved to Frankfurt to join his brother Otto who was a private tutor there. During the next three years or so Busch was especially prolific, producing in rapid succession the strip cartoons *Hans Huckebein, der Unglücksrabe*, *Schnurrdiburr oder die Bienen* and the cartoon banned by the Catholic Church, *Der Heilige Antonius von Padua*. Busch also worked for the publisher Otto Bassermann, producing *Die Fromme Helene*, *Die Jobsiade* and *Pater Filuzius*. Under pressure from Johanna Kessler, the wife of Otto's employer, Busch made one last foray into the career he had originally planned, that of painter. In formats that were unusually large for his financial circumstances—sometimes on canvas—he copied or created still-lifes in the style of the Leibl circle, for example *Still-life with Candle* (1869–72; Hannover, Wilhelm-Busch-Mus.), and he painted two self-portraits, one in the style of Frans Hals.

Two years after his mother's death in 1870, Busch settled in Wiedensahl. He travelled to Munich every winter and, in 1873, joined the artists' association Allotria, where the painter Franz Lenbach became his friend. He was now better able to assess the real nature of his talents. In a philosophically coloured correspondence with the Dutch writer Maria Anderson, he explained the circumstances of his life. He then painted a touching sequence of small-scale portraits of a country girl, Lina Weissenborn, and during the next few years produced various versions of rural subjects, combining a background applied in thinly scratched strokes with firmly executed figures and objects. Towards the end of this period, *c.* 1876 Busch used his brush to create swirling, revolving forms. In the years 1874–8 his drawing and painting styles were very close. The strip cartoons *Dideldum* (1874), *Abenteuer eines Junggesellen* (1875), *Herr und Frau Knopp* (1876), *Julchen* (1877) and, above all, the short sequence *Der Haarbeutel* (1878; see fig.) marked the peak of Busch's achievement as a cartoonist. He was now able to transfer his drawings photomechanically directly on to the wooden block, and Bassermann's wood-engravers were so skilful that the work in print was very close in quality to the originals. During Busch's last visits to Munich, in the winter months of 1877–80, many friends, in particular Lenbach, urged him to continue with his painting. In Munich Lenbach took him to Richard Wagner's operas *Lohengrin* and *Tannhäuser.* Although the world of theatre was fundamentally alien to him, Busch produced an eloquent response in *Halloween* (late 1870s; Hannover, Wilhelm-Busch-Mus.), an oil sketch in tones of bottle green and brownish red. In 1881 Busch left Munich for good. In both paintings and drawings he now produced long series of variations on basic themes: the landscape near his birthplace with animals—especially cows—and people. Gradually landscape swallowed up other details and by around 1889 the human figure was present only as a blob of colour, as with the red jacket in *View through Trees: Landscape Sketch* (1890s; Hannover, Wilhelm-Busch-Mus.). Busch also turned to rustic genre scenes, influenced by the work of David Teniers (ii) and Adriaen Brouwer. The local figures in *Farmers Drinking* (*c.* 1890; Hannover, Wilhelm-Busch-Mus.) are painted in dark, unbroken reds and blues. Such works were very different from the gently humorous genre scenes more typical of Munich at this time. By 1884 Busch had already delivered his last strip cartoon, *Maler Klecksel,* an ironic gloss on the career he was unable to follow. His last dated painting is from 1892 and shortly after this he also stopped drawing. In the 1890s he began to write thought-provoking fairy tales: *Eduards Traum* (1891), *Der Schmetterling* (1895) and the volumes of poems *Zu guterletzt* and *Schein und Sein* (1899). None of these was illustrated.

Wilhelm Busch: illustration for the story 'Vierhändig', from *Der Haarbeutel* (Heidelberg, 1878), p. 46

WRITINGS

F. Bohne, ed.: *Wilhelm Busch: Sämtliche Briefe,* 2 vols (Hannover, 1968–9)

BIBLIOGRAPHY

F. Bohne: *Leben-Werk-Schicksal* (Zurich, 1958)

G. Veding: *Wilhelm Busch: Das 19. Jahrhundert in Miniature* (Frankfurt am Main, 1977)

H. G. Gmelin: *Wilhelm Busch als Maler* (Berlin, 1980/ *R* 1981)

Die Bildergeschichten zwischen Flugblatt und Kartoon (exh. cat., Hannover, Orangerie, 1982)

Wilhelm Busch als Maler in seiner Zeit (exh. cat., Hannover, Niedersächs. Landesmus., 1982)

Wilhelm Busch als Zeichner nach der Natur (exh. cat., Hannover, Wilhelm-Busch-Mus., 1982)

HANS GEORG GMELIN

Buschetto [Boschetto; Busketus] (*fl* Pisa, *c.* 1064–1110). Italian architect. According to the inscription on his tomb (now set in the northernmost arch of the cathedral façade), he was responsible for the construction of Pisa Cathedral. The verses celebrate his art and technical ability, comparing them with those of the mythical Ulysses and Daedalus, and praise the expertise with which he organized the dangerous transport of the enormous columns by sea and by land, avoiding hostile ambushes and using machines of his own invention that could even be operated by two young girls.

Two documents, dated 1104 and 1110, mention Buschetto as one of the *Operai* (administrators) of Pisa Cathedral. He is considered responsible for its original plan, however, and he must have been active by 1064, when construction work began. The cathedral shows at least two building phases. The eastern sections of the building are built mainly of dark marble, but the walls to the west of the breaks are largely of white stone. Since Buschetto's epigraph refers to a 'temple of white marble', at least some of these walls must have been executed under his direction. He was therefore probably responsible for the modification of the west end and the widening of the new façade, which was executed by Rainaldo and his school.

Stylistic analysis of Pisa Cathedral indicates that Buschetto had studied Early Christian, Byzantine and Islamic buildings at first hand. His presence in Rome was recorded in an epigraph (untraced) commemorating his work on the erection of the Vatican obelisk, and in its overall design the cathedral resembles the great Roman basilicas, such as Old St Peter's and S Paolo fuori le Mura. At the same time, it represents a singular mixture of structural solutions and decorative elements inspired by the architecture of Asia Minor (e.g. the three-aisled transepts and the confluence of the four wings of the building into a central space, as at Qal'at Sim'ăn in Syria) and by Islamic buildings, especially those of Spain and the Maghreb (e.g. the stilted arches of the aisles, the use of the pointed arch and the alternation of black and white voussoirs, as in the Madinat al-Zahra, Córdoba, and the Great Mosque at Kairouan). The sculptural decoration was limited in the first construction phase to such elements as cornices and capitals, the latter skilfully realized in accordance with Classical models.

For further discussion *see* PISA, §III, 1(i) and figs.

BIBLIOGRAPHY

S. Monini: *Buscheto pisano* (Pisa, 1896)
I. B. Supino: *Arte pisana* (Florence, 1903)
M. Salmi: *L'architettura romanica in Toscana* (Milan, 1927)
L. Chiappelli: *Storia di Pistoia nell'alto medioevo* (Pistoia, 1932)
P. C. Claussen: 'Früher Künstlerstolz: Mittelalterliche Signaturen als Quelle der Kunstsoziologie', *Colloquium. Bauwerk und Bildwerk im Hochmittelalter: Marburg, 1979*, pp. 7–34
E. Carli, ed.: *Il Duomo di Pisa. Il Battistero. Il Campanile* (Florence, 1989)

ROSSELLA CARUSO

Bush, Jack (Hamilton) (*b* Toronto, 20 March 1909; *d* Toronto, 24 Jan 1977). Canadian painter. He studied initially in Montreal and then at the Ontario College of Art, Toronto. His earliest paintings from the 1930s and 1940s were influenced by the landscapes of the Group of Seven. While working full-time for a commercial art firm until 1968, Bush established his reputation through figurative paintings which he exhibited with the major art societies in Canada. In the late 1940s he began painting expressionistic works with emotional and religious themes, partly resulting from an exposure to European art and his dissatisfaction with the artistic establishment. After a period of wide experimentation, Bush developed a personal abstract style in which his strength as a colourist and his preference for eccentric shapes are evident.

During the 1950s Bush allied himself with PAINTERS ELEVEN, a group of abstract painters. In 1957 he began to free himself from the influence of Abstract Expressionism after meeting the American art critic Clement Greenberg, who encouraged Bush to duplicate in oils the effects of his innovative watercolours of 1956, for example *Painting with Red* (1957; Oshawa, McLaughlin Gal.). Over the next decade Bush explored colour relationships through a number of series, notably *Thrust* (e.g. *Top Spin*, 1961; Boston, MA, Mus. F.A.), *Funnel*, *Sash* and *Column*, (e.g. *School Tie*, 1965; Edmonton, Alta, A.G.) and *Fringe* (e.g. *Irish Rock No. 1*, 1969; Wellesley Coll., MA, Mus.). This development culminated in the 1970s in paintings based on musical themes (e.g. *Polyphonic Fugue*, 1975; Edmonton, Alta, A.G.), in which independent strokes of colour dance against a mottled background applied to raw canvas with sponges and rollers.

One of the foremost abstract painters in Canada, Bush received international acclaim for his large canvases of the 1960s and 1970s. He represented Canada at the São Paolo Bienal (1967), was awarded a Guggenheim Fellowship in 1968 and in 1976 was made an Officer of the Order of Canada.

BIBLIOGRAPHY

Jack Bush: A Retrospective (exh. cat. by T. Fenton, Toronto, A.G. Ont., 1976)
Jack Bush: Paintings and Drawings, 1955–76 (exh. cat., ACGB, 1980)
K. Wilkin, ed.: *Jack Bush* (Toronto, 1984)
Jack Bush: Early Work (exh. cat. by C. Boyanoski, Toronto, A.G. Ont., 1985)
Jack Bush on Paper (exh. cat., ed. K. Wilkin; Toronto, Koffler Gal., 1985)

CHRISTINE BOYANOSKI

Bush Barrow. Early Bronze Age round burial mound on Normanton Down, near Stonehenge, Wilts (Wilsford G.5 in L. V. Grinsell's numbering). The Bush Barrow grave finds represent the finest flowering of Early Bronze Age craftsmanship in Britain. When excavated by William Cunnington in 1808, it contained 'the skeleton of a tall and stout man' and a variety of grave goods, including a bronze flanged axe, three bronze daggers, a stone macehead with bronze fitting, cylindrical bone mounts with toothed edges, a gold belt-hook cover, two lozenge-shaped plates of gold foil and a number of 'brass rivets intermixed with wood' (London, BM; on loan from Devizes Mus.). The grave and its objects are taken as typical of the Wessex Culture, identified from a group of burial finds centred on central-southern England and dating to the mid-2nd millennium BC. The site's position within sight of Stonehenge lends weight to the suggestion that it was a major centre for social, artistic and religious activity during this period.

The most spectacular objects are the belt-hook cover and the lozenge-shaped plates. The former consists of a quadrilateral piece of gold sheet with convex sides and concave ends, the edges folded over to grip an organic backing. Four bands, each of three grooves, decorate the surface. The hook itself, a separate piece of hollow metal, protrudes tonguelike from the front and is decorated with grooves on the sides and end. Of the two lozenges, the larger (185×157 mm) is decorated by four bands of four grooves, the outer space being filled with a zigzag line and the centre by a two-line lattice. There are perforations top and bottom, and the edges are folded over and decorated with a groove. The smaller lozenge (317×195 mm) is decorated with three concentric grooves. Recent restoration and study of these objects have led to the conclusion that they were all slightly domed in profile.

The macehead is made of a rare fossiliferous limestone believed to have come from the Teignmouth area of Devon. It is highly polished and was originally fastened to a wooden handle by a metal ring and pin. The toothed bone mounts, probably from the handle of the mace, resemble a grave find from Mycenae dated to *c.* 1600 BC, and small gold versions of such objects are known from Brittany. One of the daggers was broken and corroded, with a hilt into which numerous minute gold pins had been hammered. This hilt has been compared with a group of such finds from Brittany. The pins are so small that it has been suggested that the craftsman would have had to use a crystal lens to work with them.

See also PREHISTORIC EUROPE, §V, 4 and 8.

BIBLIOGRAPHY

L. V. Grinsell: *The Stonehenge Barrow Groups* (Salisbury, n.d.), pp. 31–5

R. C. Hoare: *Ancient Wiltshire: I, South* (1812), pp. 202–4

S. Gerloff: *The Early Bronze Age Daggers in Great Britain, and a Reconsideration of the Wessex Culture*, Prähistorische Bronzefunde, vi/2 (Munich, 1975)

J. J. Taylor: *Bronze Age Goldwork of the British Isles* (Cambridge, 1980), pp. 45–50, pl. 25

I. A. Kinnes and others: 'Bush Barrow Gold', *Antiquity*, lxii (1988), pp. 24–39

C. A. Shell and P. Robinson: 'The Recent Reconstruction of the Bush Barrow Lozenge Plates', *Antiquity*, lxii (1988), pp. 248–58

A. F. HARDING

Bushell, Stephen Wooton (*b* Ash, Kent, 28 July 1844; *d* London, 18 Dec 1908). English art historian. Trained in medicine, he became interested in the history of Chinese ceramics during his many years as physician to the British embassy in Beijing. In 1891 he drafted a translation (pubd 1910) of Zhu Yan's *Tao shuo* ('Description of Chinese pottery and porcelain', 1774), the first comprehensive account of Chinese ceramics written for connoisseurs by a Chinese critic. Bushell's greatest achievement was his catalogue of the William T. Walters Collection in Baltimore, sumptuously published in ten folio volumes in 1897; its text, published as a single volume in 1899, is the earliest systematic study in English of Chinese ceramics in which the subject is treated chronologically and in which particular aspects such as reign marks, forms, technical matters and decorative motifs are considered separately. Bushell also translated a handwritten copy of Xiang Yuanbian's *Lidai mingci tupu* ('Illustrated description of the celebrated porcelain of different dynasties', *c.* 1575), with illustrations that were purported to be 16th-century ones but were later revealed as fakes by Percival David (P. David: 'Hsiang and his Album', *Trans. Orient. Cer. Soc.*, xi (1933–4), pp. 22–47). They had been copied from woodcut book illustrations of Chinese art collections such as the *Bogu tulu* ('Illustrated record of antiquities'; compiled by Wang Fu, *c.* 1120) that were known from later reprints. As the first English authority to have any knowledge of the Chinese language, Bushell was one of the most important pioneers in the study of Chinese ceramics.

WRITINGS

Oriental Ceramic Art: Illustrated by Examples from the Collection of W. T. Walters, 10 vols (New York, 1897); text only as *Oriental Ceramic Art: Collection of W. T. Walters* (New York, 1899/*R* London, 1981)

Chinese Art, London, V&A handbook, 2 vols (London, 1904–6/*R*)

ed.: *Chinese Porcelain: Sixteenth-century Coloured Illustrations with Chinese Manuscript Text* (Oxford, 1908); trans. of Xiang Yuanbian: *Lidai mingci tupu* [Illustrated description of the celebrated porcelain of different dynasties] (*c.* 1575)

ed.: *Description of Chinese Pottery and Porcelain: Being a Translation of the 'Tao shuo'* (Oxford, 1910); trans. of Zhu Yan: *Tao shuo* (1744)

MARGARET MEDLEY

Bush hammer. *See* BOUCHARDE.

Bushmen. *See* SAN.

Bushnell, John (*d* London, 15 May 1701). English sculptor. The son of a plumber, he was apprenticed to the sculptor Thomas Burman (*d* 1674). Before he had served his time he was forced to marry a servant seduced by Burman, but he stole £15 and escaped to Europe when sent to set up a Burman monument outside London. He worked his way as a journeyman-mason in France, the Netherlands and Italy and settled in Venice; there he was employed in 1663–4 to assist on the huge monument to *Alvise Mocenigo* designed by Giuseppe Sardi in S Lazzaro dei Mendicanti, some of the figures of which are signed by Josse de Corte. Bushnell's prolonged stay permitted him to absorb a feeling for the Baroque (he was one of the first Englishmen to do so), and undoubtedly he would have seen the work of Bernini in Rome.

Bushnell was eventually persuaded to return to England (where he was promptly sued by Burman for theft). By 1670 he was working on statues of *Charles II* and *Queen Catherine* for Temple Bar, London (*in situ*), for which he was paid £440, and in the following year on the stone or marble figures of *Charles I*, *Charles II* and *Sir Thomas Gresham* for the new Royal Exchange (building destr. 1838; statues now London, Old Bailey). On learning that Caius Gabriel Cibber had applied to carve statues for the building, Bushnell haughtily refused to do any more, as he considered himself to be superior to any other sculptor then working in London. The superb terracotta bust of *Charles II* (Cambridge, Fitzwilliam) and two of his monuments of the 1670s, the standing figure of *John, Viscount Mordaunt* (marble, *c.* 1675; London, Fulham, All Saints; *see* ENGLAND, fig. 29), and the dramatic group erected by William Ashburnham in 1675 to himself and his wife (Ashburnham, E. Sussex, St Peter), demonstrate his ability when at the height of his powers. His monument to *Lady May* (*d* 1681) was buried beneath the chancel of St Nicholas, Mid-Lavant, W. Sussex, in 1871–2 during the church's restoration. The effigy of *Lady May*, her face carved as if pitted by smallpox as it had been in life, was disinterred undamaged in 1981.

In later life Bushnell became increasingly eccentric. He began to speculate unsuccessfully, built himself a large house on the site of what is now Apsley House, Hyde Park Corner, London, and constructed a huge model of the Trojan Horse, said to have had its eyes as windows and to have accommodated 12 men in its head. He died bankrupt and mad in Paddington, London. Even allowing for Bushnell's unbalanced state of mind, it is difficult to appreciate that so accomplished a sculptor could be responsible for the grotesque and ill-proportioned figures kneeling frontally on the monument to *Henry O'Brien, 7th Earl of Thomond*, erected in 1700 in St Andrew's, Great Billing, Northants.

Among Bushnell's extant works are the monuments to Samuel Pepys's wife (*d* 1669; London, Hart Street, St Olave); *Sir Palmes Fairborne*, governor of Tangiers (*d* 1680; London, Westminster Abbey), now shorn of its reliefs of Moorish towns and the busts of *Thomas Bruce, 1st Earl of Elgin*, and his grandson *Edward Bruce*, formerly in the Bruce Mausoleum, Maulden, Beds (now Deene Park, Northants). He made the plaster and wax effigy of *General Monck, 1st Duke of Albemarle* for his funeral (1670), the head of which survives in Westminster Abbey. Attributed to him are the effigy of *Lionel Lockyer* (*d* 1672; London, Southwark Cathedral) and the monument to *Lady Jane Clifford* (*d* 1679; London, Westminster Abbey).

BIBLIOGRAPHY

Gunnis

K. A. Esdaile: 'John Bushnell, Sculptor', *Walpole Soc.*, xv (1927), pp. 21–45

——: 'Additional Notes to John Bushnell, Sculptor', *Walpole Soc.*, xxi (1933), pp. 105–8
M. D. Whinney: *Sculpture in Britain, 1530–1830,* Pelican Hist. A. (Harmondsworth, 1964, rev. J. Physick, 1988)

JOHN PHYSICK

Busi, Giovanni de'. *See* CARIANI, GIOVANNI.

Büsinck, Ludolph (*b* Hanoversch Münden, 1599 or 1602; *d* Hanoversch Münden, 1669). German engraver, draughtsman and painter. His presence in the northern Netherlands *c.* 1620 is suggested by the woodcut *Holy Family under a Tree* (Hollstein, no. 4), which renders a design taken from Abraham Bloemaert in a chiaroscuro produced with one line and two tone blocks—a technique developed by Hendrick Goltzius. Between 1623 and 1629–30 Büsinck lived in Paris, producing woodcuts for the publisher Melchior Tavernier (1564–1641) after drawings by Georges Lallemand (see fig.). The *Holy Family with the Infant St John* (1623; H 3) shows a more Italian technique, restricting contours to the black line and placing less emphasis on the use of the tone blocks. Subsequent work, such as the *Moses* (H 1) and the *Apostles* series (H 5–19) after Lallemand, synthesizes the clear black outlines of the Italian tradition with a lively decorative sway characteristic of the Dutch 17th-century style; while the systematic layers of parallel lines and crosshatching used in the *Flute-player* (H 23) derive from the style of the Gerrit van Honthorst circle.

Büsinck settled in Münden *c.* 1630, marrying there. He continued to produce chiaroscuro woodcuts largely based on Lallemand, such as the *Lute-player* (1630). The adaptation of the chiaroscuro technique to his draughtsmanship is shown in a drawing of the *Holy Family* (priv. col.; see exh. cat., ii, p. 141). The figures are rendered in rough but animated painterly brushstrokes; undulating drapery folds suggesting the body weight beneath give the composition a Baroque monumentality. Büsinck's one extant painting, the *Crucifixion* (1636; Göttingen, Pauluskirche), again draws on Lallemand in the broad modelling of the figures. It also relates to the Hamburg and Lower Saxon school represented by Matthias Scheits and Otto Wagenfeldt. A large painting of the *Capture of Münden by General Tilly in 1626*, which Büsinck promised the Münden merchants' guild when he joined it in 1639, is untraced. He is documented as a customs officer from 1647. His later work, such as the *Peasant Figures* (H 30–35) and *Standing Cavalier* (1630; Berlin, Kupferstichkab.), is simpler and more sober, concentrating on outline and abandoning the tone-block technique. Büsinck's son was the painter Wilhelm Büsinck (1632–73).

BIBLIOGRAPHY

Hollstein: *Ger.* [H]
W. Stechow: 'Ludolph Büsinck, Maler von Münden, und sein Hochaltar für die Göttinger Johanniskirche', *Neues Gött. Jb.*, iv (1933–4), pp. 5–12
——: 'Ludolph Büsinck', *Prt Colr Q.*, xxv (1938), pp. 392–419
——: 'Catalogue of the Woodcuts by Ludolph Büsinck', *Prt Colr Q.*, xxvi (1939), pp. 348–59
Zeichnung in Deutschland, 2 vols (exh. cat., ed. H. Geissler; Stuttgart, Staatsgal., 1979–80)

Busiri, Giovanni Battista (*b* Rome, 1698; *d* 1757). Italian painter and draughtsman. His tentative beginnings *c.* 1720 as an amateur painter of perspectival and architectural

Ludolph Büsinck: *The Procuress*, chiaroscuro woodcut, 220×341 mm (London, British Museum), after a drawing by Georges Lallemand

vedute representing Rome and its environs are documented by, among other works, four paintings in tempera showing the *Colosseum*, the *Piazza del Pantheon*, the *Pyramid of Cestius* and the *Ponte Rotto* (all Newark, Cambs, Hildyard priv. col., see Busiri Vici, pp. 26–7). Busiri preferred working in that medium rather than oil, and many of his finest tempera paintings, including those in the Hildyard collection, were acquired by English and Scottish collectors in Rome during the 18th century. Among his mature works is the notable *View of the Environs of Rome* (*c.* 1730–35; Glasgow, A.G. & Mus.); this was formerly attributed to Jan Frans van Bloemen, whose style it closely resembles. In 1735 Busiri was documented as residing in the parish of S Lorenzo in Lucina, Rome, and in 1739 and 1740 some of his best-known pictures were acquired by the English collector William Windham (*b* 1717), in Rome, almost certainly through commissions to the artist. Windham purchased six oil paintings, all dating from just before 1740, including the *View of a Waterfall*, showing the influence of Gaspard Dughet. He also bought 26 tempera paintings, 11 dating from 1739 (e.g. *Cascade at Tivoli*) and 10 dating from 1740 (e.g. *Bridge of S Rocco at Tivoli*). These pictures are all still in Windham's residence (Felbrigg Hall, Norfolk, NT).

Many notable paintings by Busiri that were formerly in Lord Dartmouth's collection are now in the Busiri Vici collection in Rome. These include the exceptional *External View of the Casino at the Villa Borghese* (*c.* 1753; see Busiri Vici, pl. viii). A number of his paintings were engraved by other artists, including three views of Rome: *Ponte Rotto* (see Busiri Vici, p. 58), the *Colosseum* and the *Temple of Minerva Medica* (see Busiri Vici, both pl. xiii), which were reproduced by the engravers Thomas Smith (*d* 1769) and Francis Vivares (1709–80) and published in London (1746).

Busiri was also an excellent draughtsman, and two important collections of his drawings, primarily rapid pen sketches, are in the Fitzwilliam Museum, Cambridge, and the British Museum, London. The drawings represent imaginary and topographical views of Rome, its monuments and surrounding countryside, and are distinguished by their freshness and vivacity.

BIBLIOGRAPHY

DBI; Bolaffi

Eighteenth Century Italy and the Grand Tour (exh. cat., ed. F. W. Hawcroft; Norwich, Castle Mus., 1958), p. 14

F. W. Hawcroft: 'Giovanni Battista Busiri', *Gaz. B.-A.*, liii (1959), pp. 295–304

A. Busiri Vici: *Giovanni Battista Busiri: Vedutista romano del '700* (Rome, 1966)

Mostra di disegni italiani: Paesaggio del seicento e del settecento (exh. cat. by M. Chiarini, Florence, Uffizi, 1973), nos 87–8, pp. 66–7

□

Busler [Bustler]**, Petrus.** *See* BORSSELER, PIETER.

Buṣrā. *See* BOSRA.

Bussaert [Bussart; Bussert]**, Martin** [Morten] (*d* Copenhagen, 1553). Danish sculptor and architect. His sculptural work shows a precocious awareness of early Renaissance art, suggesting that he trained in the workshop of Claus Berg in Odense. He first served Christian II, King of Denmark (*reg* 1512–23), as architect and sculptor and had settled in Copenhagen by 1523. His tombstone sculptures equal or surpass his architectural successes. The first in his series of gravestone reliefs was of *Elisabeth of Habsburg* (*c.* 1523; Copenhagen, Nmus.), Christian II's queen, a pendant to an earlier representation of *King John* (1503; Copenhagen, Nmus.), sculpted by Adam van Düren . The limestone high relief had a conventional Gothic framework but hinted at Bussaert's mature work in the more naturalistic folds of Elisabeth's gown. After Christian II fled to the Netherlands in 1523, Bussaert elected to remain in Copenhagen in the employ of the newly crowned Frederick I (*reg* 1523–34). Frederick rewarded Bussaert well, naming him master builder in *c.* 1525 and endowing him and his wife with a living at Slangerup Cloister in 1529. Bussaert's major period of productivity began when the Lutheran King Christian III (*reg* 1534–59) assumed Denmark's throne. Among Bussaert's architectural achievements were the Tøjhus (the Royal Arsenal); the Krempe Fortress (1549; with Jakob Binck) in Schleswig-Holstein, Germany; and the spire of Århus Cathedral (1550). He is credited with creating the Herreborg style of stepped or curved-gable manor house as seen at Hesselagergård in Fyn. As a sculptor, Bussaert fulfilled his early promise in the tombstone relief of *Mourits Olufsen Kragnos* (4.1×2.1 m, *c.* 1550; Ringsted Church). In this he was not content to portray static images of the deceased, his mother and widow, instead linking them both compositionally and emotionally. It is this human touch that distinguished his work from that in the same genre by such contemporaries and followers as Hans Malen of Roskilde and the Dutchman Gert van Grøningen, who worked in Århus. He also abandoned the pointed Gothic framework for a rectilinear boundary. Bussaert's willingness to go beyond the Gothic, combined with his skill in translating the new Renaissance vocabulary into Danish forms, placed him in the vanguard of 16th-century Danish art.

BIBLIOGRAPHY

C. A. Jensen: 'Sculpture, 1500–1700', *Danish Art through the Ages*, ed. P. Nörlund (Copenhagen, n. d.)

F. Beckett: *Renaissancen og kunstens historie i Danmark* [The Renaissance and the history of art in Denmark] (Copenhagen, 1897)

W. Lorenzen: *Studier i dansk herregaards arkitektur 16. og 17. aarhundrede* [Studies in Danish manor architecture in the 16th and 17th centuries] (Copenhagen, 1921)

E. Lassen: 'Absalonstenen mester' [The master of the Absalon stone], *Billedkunst og skulptur: Riget maend lader sig male, 1500–1700* [Painting and sculpture: officials who commissioned portraits, 1500–1700], Dan. Ksthist., ii (Copenhagen, 1973), pp. 18–20

ROBIN A. BRANSTATOR

Bussi, Santino de (*b* Bissone, Ticino, 28 Aug 1664; *d* Vienna, 1737). Italian stuccoist. He was taught to draw by his father, the painter Giovanni Francesco Bussi, but then concentrated on developing a career as a stuccoist. He began his career in Milan, where he worked on the decoration of numerous palaces, but was then summoned to Vienna by Eugene, Prince of Savoy. From 1695 to 1704 he worked under the architect Domenico Martinelli at the palace of Count Dominik Andreas Kaunitz (now the Liechtenstein Palace) in Bankgasse, Vienna, which had been acquired by Prince Andrew of Liechtenstein in 1694. Here Bussi decorated twenty-two rooms, two cabinets, the great hall, the staircase and the two vestibules. The elegance and lightness that he imparted to the staircase with his vivid leaf and vine scroll decoration were impaired, however, during the modernization of the building by Alois II, Prince of Liechtenstein, and his English architect Peter Hubert Desvignes *c.* 1840. At around the same time he also worked at the Franciscan church (destr.) in Feldsberg, Bohemia, and the Prinz-Eugen-Palais (now the Finance Ministry) in Himmelspfortgasse, Vienna, where he executed stucco overdoors showing the *Labours of Hercules*.

In the first decade of the 18th century Bussi was active at the priory church of St Dorothea (1702–5), in the Schattenkloster and in the former Questenberg-Kaunitz-Palais (1705) in Johannesgasse, all in Vienna. From September 1704 to August 1705 he stuccoed the vault of the ground-floor chapel at the Liechtenstein Garden Palace in the Fürstengasse, and in 1706 he decorated the two staircases, the Marmorsaal, the Galeriesaal and the other six rooms on the main floor. In March 1713 he signed a contract with Johann Lukas von Hildebrandt to execute stuccowork in the renovated *sala terrena* and on the façade of Schloss Mirabell in Salzburg. However, by this time he was much in demand and therefore expensive to employ, with the result that Hildebrandt sent back the sketches Bussi had submitted for work in Schloss Mirabell. That year he was summoned to Ansbach, where he executed stuccowork in the stairwell of the palace, and in 1715 he worked with Johann-Jacob Castelli on the main staircase at St Florian Abbey. From 1717 he is documented as working at Melk Abbey, where he later (1724–5) provided the stucco decoration for the stairwell and the monastery's sumptuous collection of paintings. Other notable projects of the 1720s include work in the Upper Belvedere in Vienna, where he decorated the garden façade and a stucco field in the *sala terrena* (1722–3), at Schloss Schlosshof (1722–5) in Lower Austria, at the priory building at Dürnstein (1723–4), also in Lower Austria, and at the church at Abtsdorf (1727) in Bavaria.

In 1728 Bussi received 515 florins and 5 kronen for work in the Harrach Garden Palace in the Ungargasse, Vienna, designed by Hildebrandt. The portal before the *cour d'honneur* was completed in November 1729, and on 10 December 1729 Bussi received 5 florins for 'a head with leaf work on the large stone portal in the courtyard'. In 1730 the stucco of the vestibule was finished, and the following year the interior decoration of the palace was completed. Other late works include reliefs and other works (from 1729) at the church of Klosterneuburg Abbey and the marbling of the altarpiece at the church of St Peter, Vienna, which he also decorated with statues and reliefs and for which he executed stuccoes in the chancel (1730).

BIBLIOGRAPHY

L. Sailer: *Die Stukkateure*, i of *Die Künstler Wiens* (Vienna and Munich, 1943)
B. Grimschitz: *Wiener Barockpalaste* (Vienna, 1947)
A. Machatschek: 'Die Rekonstruktion der Decke und die Restaurierung der Feststiege im Stadtpalais Liechtenstein', *Österr. Z. Kst & Dkmlpf.*, xxxi (1977), pp. 51–7
G. Wacha: 'Die Stukkateure in den Kalendernotizen des Propstes Hieronymus Übelbacher von Dürnstein, 1716–39', *Unsere Heimat*, 1/4 (1979), pp. 196–203
G. Beard: *Stucco and Decorative Plasterwork in Europe* (London, 1983), pp. 63–4
K. Drexler: *Stucco-dekorationen in dem reg. Chorherrenstifte Klosterneuberg bei Wien* (Vienna, 1986)
G. Beard: *Stuck: Die Entwicklung plastischer Dekoration* (Zurich, 1988)
W. G. Rizzi: 'Ergänzungen zur Baugeschichte des Stadt-palais Liechtenstein in Wien, Bankgasse', *Österr. Z. Kst & Dkmlpf.* (1988), p. 135

BIRGIT ROTH

Bussière, Gaston (*b* Cuisery, Saône-et-Loire, 24 April 1862; *d* Saulieu, Côte d'Or, 29 Oct 1928). French painter, illustrator and printmaker. He was taught by his father, Victor Bussière, a decorative painter in Mâcon. He went to the Ecole des Beaux-Arts in Lyon and then to Paris, where he studied in the atelier of Alexandre Cabanel. During further studies under Puvis de Chavannes, he came into contact with Gustave Moreau. Symbolist paintings followed, drawing on French legend, as in the *Song of Roland* (exh. Salon 1892), and Nordic myth (*Valkyries*, exh. Salon 1894); he exhibited at the Symbolist Salon de la Rose+Croix, 1893–5. In 1905 he rented a studio at Grez-sur-Loing on the edge of the Forest of Fontainebleau. Paintings such as the *Rhine Maidens* (1906; Mâcon, Mus. Mun. Ursulines) drew on observations of the forest, populating its streams with adolescent water nymphs. Such studies of the female nude—a lifelong speciality of Bussière's—uphold a rigorous draughtsmanship that is yet not devoid of sensuality.

Bussière was also a prolific illustrator, having learnt the art of engraving on the advice of Luc Olivier Merson. He worked for 15 years with the publisher Ferroud, for whom he illustrated Flaubert (*Hérodias*, 1913; *Salammbô*, 1921), Théophile Gautier, Balzac and Anatole France (Abeille, 1927). The Musée Municipal des Ursulines, Mâcon, has a large collection of his work.

BIBLIOGRAPHY

E. Bussière: *La Vie et l'oeuvre de Gaston Bussière, peintre, illustrateur, graveur* (Paris, 1932)

COLETTE E. BIDON

Bussola, Dionigi (*b* Milan, 1615; *d* Milan, 15 Sept 1687). Italian sculptor. He and his son, Cesare Bussola (*b* Milan, 1653; *d* after 1735), were involved in the major sculptural projects of 17th-century Lombardy, and their elaborate and theatrical sculptural decorations brilliantly expressed the spirit and objectives of the Counter-Reformation. Dionigi was trained in Rome, where he was influenced by Ercole Ferrata and by the academic training promulgated by the Accademia di S Luca. He returned from Rome in 1645, and between 1645 and 1651 worked at Milan Cathedral, where he completed Gaspare Vismara's statues of *St Martin* and *St Andrew* (1651). Later (1655–9) he executed part of the sculptural decoration of the vault of the chapel of the Madonna dell'Albero. In 1658 he became leader of the team of sculptors working in the cathedral and in the same year executed three low reliefs for the façade, showing scenes from the *Life of Elijah*, which formed a prelude to his intense activity for the sacrimonti of Piedmont and Lombardy (*see* SACROMONTE). These reliefs show the beginnings of a dynamic, passionate style, indebted to Gianlorenzo Bernini, yet still restrained by the vestiges of Mannerist formulae, while in the works for the sacrimonti he drew on his knowledge of Roman art, above all of the illusionist decorative frescoes of Pietro da Cortona and Giovanni Lanfranco, to attain a new theatrical power. The series of works for the sacrimonti opened with the large and elaborate *Assumption of the Virgin* (1661; Varallo, Basilica dell'Assunta), which unites painting and sculpture, incorporating 140 realistically coloured statues. There followed the terracotta group of the *Crucifixion* (1660–70) in Chapel X of the sacromonte at Varese, which is perfectly united with the frescoed decoration by Antonio Busca, and the group of terracotta statues (*c.* 1670) distributed between at least ten chapels of the sacromonte at Orta, which depict, with intense theatrical rhetoric, scenes from the *Life of St Francis of Assisi.* In the same period Bussola continued to work for Milan Cathedral, creating statues of various subjects in 1661, 1662 and 1663; he collaborated with his son Cesare, and the attribution of some of the more refined works, such as *St Dorothy* (1667) and *Habakuk*, remains uncertain.

In 1669 Bussola was appointed Director of Sculpture at the newly reopened Accademia Ambrosiana in Milan. In 1670 he executed several terracotta statues—*Grammar, Theology, Philosophy, Jurisprudence, Mathematics, Astrology* and *Medicine*—for the Accademia (Milan, Bib. Ambrosiana, Salone Pio XI), and in the same year the bronze and copper statue of *St Carlo Borromeo* (Milan, Piazza Borromeo). Other works include *Two Angels* for S Maria della Vittoria, Milan; statues of the *Virgin* and *Four Angels* for the façade of the Santuario della Madonna dei Miracoli, Saronno (in collaboration with Carlo Antonio Buono); and the *Madonna of the Rosary* (1673) for the Santuario di S Pietro Martire, Seveso. In 1674 Bussola was appointed to direct the sculptors working at the Certosa di Pavia, where he worked with Cesare. Dionigi's independent works there include the altar frontal, the *Massacre of the Innocents* (1667 or 1677), in the chapel of S Giuseppe, and the marble balustrade surrounding the high altar. In the decade before his death he collaborated yet more closely with Cesare, and his independent career virtually finished in the early 1670s.

Dionigi was a successful and prolific artist, yet there is no evidence that he controlled a large workshop. He was, however, assisted by his son and occasionally by other artists from the Milan Cathedral workshop. Cesare's career was dominated by his father, who enrolled him at an early age in the drawing class at the Accademia Ambrosiana, Milan, and in 1677 introduced him to the cathedral works. It seems that Cesare was the more conservative artist, and where the two artists worked together, as at the Certosa di Pavia, the weaker works, such as the statues of *St Ambrose* and *St John* (1674), are attributed to him. After the death of Dionigi, Cesare continued to work at Milan Cathedral, where his last documented work, the *St Agatha* (1735), reveals his continuing adherence to an outdated Mannerist style.

BIBLIOGRAPHY

DBI; Thieme–Becker

Annali della Fabbrica del duomo di Milano, v (1883), vi (1885)

U. Nebbia: *La scultura nel duomo di Milano* (Milan, 1908)

G. Nicodemi: 'L'accademia di pittura . . . all'Ambrosiana', *Studi in onore di C. Castiglioni* (Milan, 1957), pp. 651–96

——: 'La scultura milanese nel XVIII secolo', *Stor. Milano*, xii (1959), pp. 775–91

R. Bossaglia: *La Certosa di Pavia* (Milan, 1968)

——: 'La scultura', *Il duomo di Milano* (Milan, 1973), pp. 65–176

GABRIELLA FERRI PICCALUGA

Bussy, Nicolás de (*b* Strasbourg, 1650–51; *d* Valencia, Dec 1706). French–German sculptor active in Spain. He arrived in Valencia in 1672, and although he is thought of as a Spanish sculptor, the influences on his work of Bernini and southern German Baroque sculpture indicate his non-Spanish origins. He may have visited Italy, although this is undocumented. His activity was mainly confined to eastern Spain, in Valencia, Alicante, Elche and Murcia. It is probable that he also lived in Madrid, as in a document of 1689 he styled himself as 'Escultor de Cámara de Su Magestad'.

Bussy worked in stone and polychromed wood and specialized in naturalistic, free-standing figures. His *Cristo de la Sangre* (1693; Murcia, Iglesia del Carmen), now much restored, was made in polychromed wood as a processional image for the Cofradía de la Preciósa Sangre in Murcia. Iconographically the work is innovative in the medium of sculpture: the figure of Christ on the cross is shown as alive and appears to be walking. An angel catches the blood from his side in a chalice, a symbolic reference to the Mass. Bussy's processional works were a seminal influence in Murcia, particularly on Nicolás Salzillo (1672–1727).

BIBLIOGRAPHY

J. Sánchez Moreno: *D. Nicolás de Bussy, escultor* (Murcia, 1944)

J. C. López Jiménez: 'El escultor Don Nicolás de Bussy', *Archv A. Valenc.*, xxiv (1963), pp. 64–77

J. J. Martín González: *Escultura barroca en España, 1600–1770* (Madrid, 1983), pp. 342–6

MARJORIE TRUSTED

Bust. Type of sculpture, commonly but not always a portrait, that includes the chest or part of the chest, as well as the head. In this sense the word has been used for only about three centuries in English, and for many years writers on art in England preferred to use the Italian term *busto*, which reflects the fact that this type of sculpture was regarded as of Italian origin.

Generally, a sculptured bust does not include the arms, although it does often include a suggestion of their existence. Usually a substantial portion of the upper chest is also included, thus outweighing the head, which it supports. There are, however, sculptures that include only a small, rounded portion of the chest as a base for the neck, and there are truncated statues that include arms as well as a chest. Such variants are commonly referred to as busts since there are no other established terms with which to describe them.

I. Ancient origins: Egyptian, Greek and Roman. II. Early Christian, Byzantine and medieval. III. Renaissance and Baroque. IV. Rococo and Neo-classical. V. Modern.

I. Ancient origins: Egyptian, Greek and Roman.

In many civilizations masks have played an important part in magical rites or sacred ceremonies. Such masks enable the wearer to represent a god or spirit: consequently divine power is embodied in the face. The spirit could be an ancestor, and thus the veneration of that ancestor could be identified with a mask. The materials for masks include metal and stone, but there were obvious advantages to lighter materials, some of which could be cast from moulds, and such moulds could be taken from the faces of the dead. Some scholars believe that some of the Egyptian plaster casts discovered at Amarna and dating from *c.* 1340 BC were made in this way. The practice of basing sculptural portraits closely on such casts was certainly known in Greece in the 4th century BC and was later believed to be an innovation of that date.

Whether the Romans and other Italic peoples were familiar with the ancient traditions of making naturalistic masks or borrowed some new techniques of mould-making from Greece is uncertain; they certainly kept wax likenesses of the heads of their ancestors, some of which were remarkably naturalistic, in domestic shrines. These heads could be more conveniently and decently displayed and could be more easily carried in funeral processions if they included necks and a portion of chest. None of these wax portraits has survived, but a famous full-length marble statue of a Roman patrician, known as the *Barberini Togatus* (1st century AD; Rome, Pal. Conserv., Braccio Nuovo), carrying two such effigies provides an idea of their appearance. Numerous marble portraits similar to those featured here do survive, and no doubt it became fashionable to translate existing wax heads into the newly imported Greek white marble. In any case, the earliest Roman portrait busts tended to be commemorative in character and complemented the cinerary urn and the inscription in the suburban *columbaria* of late Republican Rome. These busts existed in great number and were not confined to the most wealthy or powerful sections of society but also commemorated tradesmen and even artisans, as in the busts representing a *Blacksmith* and a *Carpenter* (*c.* 25–20 BC; London, BM). This relief sculpture replicates not only the wax portraits but also, it seems, the circumstances in which such busts were displayed or stored. Since stone busts were no longer easily portable, there was perhaps no longer felt to be any need to make them fully in the round; many, however, were made in the round (*see also* ROME, ANCIENT, §IV, 1(iv)(b)).

The story of the European portrait bust usually starts with Roman sepulchral carvings of the late Republic such as these. There are, however, ancient Egyptian sculptures as close as these, or closer, to some of the bust portraits made in later centuries, or indeed to those made in Imperial Rome. The most celebrated of these must certainly be the painted limestone bust of *Queen Nefertiti* made *c.* 1350 BC and discovered with the plaster casts already mentioned (for illustration *see* NEFERTITI). This, however, may not have been regarded as a finished work of art, but rather as a sculptor's model. At a much earlier date, during the reign of Cheops (*reg c.* 2551–*c.* 2528 BC) in the 4th Dynasty of the Old Kingdom and for a short while thereafter, 'reserve heads' (as they are known to archaeologists)—simplified, hairless, painted or unpainted, approximately life-size and naturalistic—apparently recording individuals but without any very idiosyncratic features, were enclosed in burial chambers (*see* EGYPT, ANCIENT, fig. 47). Also of relevance are the canopic jars in which the embalmed viscera of the deceased were kept (*see* EGYPT, ANCIENT, fig. 81). These vessels, sometimes made of alabaster, were occasionally supplied with lids in the form of portrait busts of the deceased, which, although idealized, are nevertheless recognizable forerunners of the Etruscan clay burial urns, the lids of which took the form of highly realistic heads.

It has been noted that 'the bodiless head as an independent work of art is an Italian and not a Greek idea' and that 'Greek portrait statues were, certainly in the Classical period, always full-length figures' (Robertson). The former statement must be qualified with some reference to the conventions of ancient Egyptian art such as the canopic jar (familiar to and apparently imitated by some Greek pottery) and to the prevalence of masks in many non-Italian civilizations. The author also seems to forget one of the arts that the Greeks did most to develop—that of metal coinage.

In ancient Greece cities marked their coins with either the image of a patron deity or a sacred badge and commonly identified the former by the head alone, generally in profile (*see* GREECE, ANCIENT, §X, 2). Here, certainly, the bodiless head was used as an independent work of art. These were not portrait heads, but outside Greece where the sovereign power was embodied by an individual ruler, that ruler's head took the place of the god. The heads of the kings of Lycia and of some satraps of the Persian empire that appear on coins in the 5th century BC were the work of Greek artists; the Greek city states, however, resisted the innovation. So too did the Macedonian conqueror Alexander the Great. At first Alexander's 'successors' (*diadochi*) depicted his head on their coins (*see* GREECE, ANCIENT, fig. 161), but before long they also represented themselves, while still alive, in this manner.

Some of these Hellenistic coin portraits are obviously idealized and represent the ruler as a god; thus the boy-king Antiochos VI of the Seleucid dynasty in Syria was represented *c.* 140 BC with the rays of the sun god Helios and a look of sublime detachment. Mithridates III, King of Pontus (*c.* 220–185 BC), however, was not idealized, or at least not beautified, for the rugged features and frown of stern command may be conventional. Even if the portrait bust was unknown in Hellenistic sculpture during Rome's rise to Mediterranean dominance in the 1st century BC, the idea of partial or abbreviated portraiture may not have seemed an extraordinary step to take.

The HERM, another convention of Greek sculpture, should also be mentioned in this connection. This was an image of the god Hermes and took the form of a post or pillar crowned by a bearded head and a phallus in relief attached to the front of the pillar. In origin this was no doubt a primitive fertility symbol, but it remained popular in a period when most images of the gods were naturalistic. During the 5th century BC there were many images of this sort in Athens. Here too the Greeks showed their ability to consider the head as separate from the body. By the time the marble portrait bust became popular in the burial places of Roman freedmen, the herm form was employed to reproduce the heads of the classics of Greek sculpture: for example the head of Polykleitos' famous bronze statue of the *Doryphoros* (*c.* 440–*c.* 435 BC; copy in Minneapolis, MN, Inst. A.; *see* POLYKLEITOS, fig. 1) was adapted to a herm bust (Naples, Mus. Archeol. N.) by the Greek sculptor Apollonios in 30 BC. By the same date full-length portrait statues of public figures, which the Greeks had erected since the late 6th century BC, were reproduced as heads in this way—the veneration for Classical art and for great men being here combined.

From the 1st century AD the bust was one of the most common forms of sculpture in the Roman Empire. Public and private libraries, academies and gardens, for example, were adorned with herms of famous orators and poets. At the same time, the shelves of tombs and family shrines were filled with busts or contained relief carvings of busts that gave the impression of being shelved. These two categories were quite distinct, but neither was regarded as 'high' art. The former were, for the most part at least, reproductions of 'old masters', the latter were doubtless often not regarded as art at all. There would probably have been some resistance to innovation in both categories. There were, however, busts that belonged to neither category—most notably portraits of the emperor, members of his family or a powerful patron commissioned as an expression of piety, loyalty or attachment, sometimes for entirely public and sometimes for domestic circumstances. These represented a new type of art. The subjects were often alive, and there was every reason for their presentation to be fashionable as well as artistic.

It was this type of bust that began to display more of the chest and shoulders, the truncation concealed or softened with folds of drapery and the whole balanced on a socle, sometimes joined to the bust with a scrolled tablet, and designed to be supported by a columnar pedestal or perhaps a console. By the end of the 1st century AD a sculptural form had been invented in which the life-size and more or less naturalistic partial portrait was made into an elegant and ornamental unit for the first time. This invention is perhaps the single most original one in the history of Roman sculpture. Such portrait busts were by no means always life-size, however; small bronzes were made, and, for the court at least, miniature busts were fashioned out of chalcedony and other hardstones.

A typical example of such Roman portraiture is the bust of an *Antonine Lady* (*c.* AD 150; Malibu, CA, Getty Mus.; see fig. 1), her hair dressed in the style made fashionable by Empress Faustina. The solemn but intimate mood is common to many such portraits of her, and the exquisite handling of the Carrara marble, with passages of eloquent low relief in the eyes and of ingenious undercutting in the drapery, is exceptional. The subtlety of expression and responsive turn of the head suggest that, even if the bust were commemorative, it was displayed in some domestic environment in the company of the living rather than the dead. The highly refined execution and polish suggest that it was also displayed as a work of art—not stored on a shelf, treated as an architectural accessory or item of high-class interior decoration. Some bust sculpture was more ambitious, most notably the portrait of *Emperor Commodus* (*reg* AD 180–92; Rome, Mus. Conserv.), which is more of a truncated statue with both arms included. In one hand the Emperor holds the apples of the Hesperides, in the other the club of Hercules; the lion's pelt, another attribute of Hercules, is tied around his neck and mantles his intricately curled hair. The Emperor is therefore identified with a Greek deified hero and as immortal (the apples granted eternal life). He is venerated as a god, just as emperors were on Roman coinage, imitating in this respect the 'successors' of Alexander. The sublime, or at least

1. Bust of an *Antonine Lady*, Carrara marble, h. 675 mm, *c.* AD 150 (Malibu, CA, J. Paul Getty Museum)

hyperbolic, character of the bust is in some ways disturbing: the tiny supporting figures of the Victories make the body seem colossal, the fragility of the supporting elements makes the torso seem miraculously to float, the porcellaneous surface finish, contrasted with the very dark shadows of the deep virtuoso drilling, make the body appear to shine as flesh cannot.

II. Early Christian, Byzantine and medieval.

The portrait bust, like the portrait statue, disappeared in the western Roman Empire after the introduction of new burial practices and attitudes towards personal commemoration and with the diminished civic life that came with the establishment of Christianity and the emergencies of foreign invasions. In Byzantium, however, conventions of bust portraiture survived. Although some coins showed the emperor's head in profile truncated at the neck or together with the chest (as had been common in previous centuries), in others the emperor was depicted in a frontal pose with both hands included, as in the gold multiple solidus struck at Nicomedia *c.* AD 355, in which the

2. Bust of *Piero I de' Medici, Lord of Florence* by Mino da Fiesole, marble, 1453 (Florence, Museo Nazionale del Bargello)

emperor Constantius II (*reg* 337–61) holds a statuette of Victory and a lance. The same frontality, staring eyes, prominent diadem and absence of real substance in the torso (which also feature in cameo portraits of the same emperor) are found on the coins of his successors for over the next 500 years. This was also the manner in which saints and indeed Christ were often represented on repoussé silver bowls, on coins (e.g. Christ Pantokrator on coins of Justinian II (*reg* 685–9, 705–11)) and in the roundels or medallions on ivories, mosaics and enamels. Byzantine works of this kind (the enamels perhaps especially; *see* EARLY CHRISTIAN AND BYZANTINE ART, fig. 73) determined the way in which saints were represented in the upper registers of altarpieces, including painted altarpieces, which became so popular in the Christian West during the 14th century. Such works of art, however, are either in low relief or two-dimensional; no such continuous popularity was enjoyed by sculpture in the round.

The rebirth of the three-dimensional bust relates to the increasing value attached to relics in Europe during the late Middle Ages. Reliquaries frequently took the form of hollow, truncated bodies, often with the top of the head forming a hinged lid (*see* RELIQUARY, fig. 3). Sometimes such reliquary busts contained the whole or parts of the skull of the represented saint, which may explain the origin of the form; many of them, however, contained other sorts of relic, which could sometimes be glimpsed through a setting of rock crystal in the chest. These reliquaries were often made of wood but also of beaten copper with painted, gilded and jewelled surfaces. They were never of stone, which was difficult to hollow and which even so would have been too heavy to transpose to the altar or other place of display, or to carry in procession.

III. Renaissance and Baroque.

During the 15th century the sculptured portrait bust was revived, at first and chiefly in Florence. Such a revival may have owed something to the knowledge that such sculpture was popular in ancient Rome, but it was more influenced in form by the reliquary busts of saints. This is less surprising when bearing in mind the numerous busts made of saints, Christ and the Virgin. One of the earliest Florentine portrait busts and the earliest of all dated marble busts of the Renaissance is the portrait of *Piero I de' Medici, Lord of Florence* (1453; Florence, Bargello; see fig. 2) by Mino da Fiesole. It is known that it was placed over a door in a room within the family palace, and other 15th-century busts seem to have been displayed in a similar way. The manner of their truncation would have given them extra security in such a location.

It has been claimed that 15th-century Florentine portrait busts differed radically from ancient Roman ones, which had either depicted people of rank displayed in or on public buildings or had been sepulchral effigies. 'In all its uses [the bust in the ancient Roman world] was basically an idol, a cult image—for ruler or hero worship in the case of public portraits, for ancestor worship in the case of private portraits' (Lavin). This is most certainly an exaggeration, as it is impossible to believe that the finest Antonine portrait busts, such as that of a woman discussed above, were expected to stimulate either form of worship. Moreover, since the Roman ancestor portraits were kept in the house as well as in the tomb, the domestic setting of Florentine portrait busts does not appear to be very different. Furthermore, there is one very important similarity between the marble portrait bust in the late Roman Republic and in 15th-century Florence: in both cases the portraiture owed something to the practice of making wax death-masks. Vasari explicitly documented the revival of this practice in 15th-century Florence, and there are terracotta busts that clearly reflect the use of such masks.

At the end of the 15th century Italian sculptors began to imitate the type of truncation found in Roman bust portraiture where the shoulders are often cut off as well as the chest, which is terminated with a variety of curves. This style was imitated in bronze busts of such ancient Romans as *Marcus Aurelius* (*c.* 1500; Munich, Bayer. Nmus.) and *Antoninus Pius* (*c.* 1500; Paris, Louvre) made by Antico for the Mantuan court; in the case of *Antoninus Pius* the truncation follows the line of a cloak. Before this date this style of bust is recorded in the reconstructions of the ancient world in paintings by Mantegna.

The only 15th-century marble bust that has both sharply cut shoulders and an antique-style socle is the bust of *Beatrice d'Este* (*c.* 1490; Paris, Louvre) made in Mantua by Gian Cristoforo Romano; and yet it resembles no known antique example, not least because the socle is so large in relation to the bust it supports. The manner in which rounded truncation was combined with a small socle—often with a scrolled tablet between these two elements—so common in Roman Imperial bust portraiture of the 2nd century AD, seems never to have been imitated, and

3. Bust of *Rudolf II* by Adriaen de Vries, bronze, 1603 (Vienna, Kunsthistorisches Museum)

perhaps never even depicted, in 15th-century Italy. It does occur in the early 16th century, at first in small bronze sculptures of ancient Roman subjects and then in marble. When executed in marble, such busts departed radically from the 15th-century concept of the bust as a solid form carved on both sides (even if generally only visible on one). In order to be supported by such a slender means the bust generally had to be hollowed out from behind; it was also convenient for bronze busts to be open behind the chest.

By the mid-16th century the conventions of Roman Imperial bust portraiture had been fully assimilated by the leading Italian sculptors. The portrait busts (both 1540s; Florence, Bargello) of *Cosimo I, Grand Duke of Tuscany* by Benvenuto Cellini and Baccio Bandinelli have often been contrasted: Cellini's more vital bronze creation is now invariably preferred, although Cosimo seems to have preferred Bandinelli's marble version. The two works have, however, much in common: a turned and waisted socle (in Bandinelli's case with a scrolled tablet as well), an antique-style breastplate, a turned head and a commanding frown fixed on some distant prospect. These are portraits of rulers, imposing public images of a kind unknown in the 15th century but familiar in antiquity. Cellini's bust was installed over the entrance of the fortress at the port of Portoferraio on Elba—not a location the artist intended, but he certainly did make the portrait as an image that people looked up to.

Bronze busts, on account of their expense, were most commonly commissioned by princes (*see* METAL, colour pl. II, fig. 4), and those made of the emperor *Charles V* (1551–5; Madrid, Prado) and *Prince Philip* by Leone Leoni (1549–51; Madrid, Prado), later imitated by Jacques Jonghelinck in his bust of the *Duke of Alba* (1571; New York, Frick) and by Adriaen de Vries in his bust of *Rudolf II* (1603; Vienna, Ksthist. Mus.; see fig. 3), possess a similar grandeur to the bust of *Commodus* discussed above. They are not nude like Commodus, but the truncation of the bust, which corresponds with the end of the breastplate, is in most cases supported by figures and an eagle of an entirely different scale, reminiscent of the supporters of the *Commodus* bust.

The next major development of the bust depicting a ruler occurred in Italy in the mid-17th century, when Gianlorenzo Bernini created his marble portrait of *Francesco I d'Este* (1650–51; Modena, Gal. & Mus. Estense; see fig. 4). The grandeur in this case is not created by the emphatic verticality of the composition but by an entirely novel horizontal movement of drapery, a cloak pulled tight across the breast plate, blown wildly over the arm, thus dramatizing the turning of the head. Cloaks had been used before to soften the truncation of the bust, or rather to disguise it, but never to provide a spectacular and irregular frame of this kind. Bernini repeated this formula in his bust of *Louis XIV* of France (Versailles, Château). It was then adopted by sculptors all over Europe but with particular skill by French court sculptors, especially Antoine Coyzevox. None of them, however, went further than, and few went as far as, Bernini himself; the formula was one of those that established at its foundation its own most extreme potential. Some of Bernini's other earlier male busts were more convivial, even conversational—most notably that of *Scipione Borghese* (Rome, Gal. Borghese; for illustration *see* BORGHESE, (2))—but these also tended to be broader than those made at an earlier date. Such busts were displayed on pedestals, and generally on pedestals that tapered and thus compensated for the spreading form of the bust. The height at which they were displayed was crucial to their effect—again these were busts to view from below.

Neither in the 16th century nor in the 17th was the bust portrait a particularly popular form—not least because a bust in marble or bronze was far more expensive than a painted portrait. In the second half of the 15th century the leading Florentine merchant families had had busts made in terracotta, presumably for a relatively low price and for their palace interiors, but this fashion seems not to have continued. The most common place for portrait busts to be displayed in the 16th and 17th centuries was in church. As abbreviated effigies they had obvious advantages for small or medium-sized tombs and were often preferred by great and wealthy patrons who were

4. Bust of *Francesco I d'Este* by Gianlorenzo Bernini, marble, life-size, 1650–51 (Modena, Galleria e Museo Estense)

careful not to emulate the full-length effigies of their lords. This type of tomb first received widespread success in Venice and the Veneto, and it is no coincidence that it was a Venetian artist, ALESSANDRO VITTORIA, who seems to have been the first modern European sculptor whose reputation depended chiefly on his work as a bust portraitist.

Although busts of similar composition were made for both domestic and sepulchral settings, and indeed busts were sometimes transferred from the home to the church, in many cases the nature of tomb architecture determined the shape of the bust. The magnificent bust of *Piero Bembo* (1547) by Danese Cattaneo in the nave of the Santo in Padua had to be impressive enough not to be dominated by the tall and elegant columnar aedicula designed by the architect Michele Sanmicheli. It was enhanced by the shadows of the niche with a shell heading within which it was lodged and was carefully calculated in relation to the inscribed pedestal on which it rests. Many aspects of the bust's composition were determined by the architecture—the slope of the shoulders, the verticality (much emphasized by the long beard), the truncation (which uses the line of the Cardinal's *mozzetta* just as busts of rulers sometimes used the breastplate). In smaller tombs the bust was often displayed within an upright oval or a round frame. The latter could be small and encouraged both the use of very little chest and an almost semicircular or U-shaped truncation. When a bust is removed from such a setting and given a more orthodox socle, it looks mean—as is the case with the superb Roman bust of a *Cardinal* (*c.* 1700; Oxford, Ashmolean), perhaps by Pierre Legros (ii).

Fifteenth-century bust portraits in Florence were, it seems, generally displayed over doors, and this remained a common location for busts both inside and outside a palace over the next two centuries. Another popular elevated position during the 18th century, which in fact originated earlier, was the cornice of the monumental library bookcase. This was considered a particularly appropriate setting for busts of the great poets and thinkers of antiquity, often copied from antique sculpture, and of great modern writers.

IV. Rococo and Neo-classical.

The 18th century was, however, above all the period when the bust was brought down to a lower level and the informal bust was displayed on a low pedestal or side table (or sometimes on a bracket or a chimney-piece), often below the eye-level of a standing man. Such busts were designed to play an active part in a domestic interior—to seem responsive to the relaxed sedentary conversation of the salon. Accordingly, in French, British and Dutch sculpture especially, the sitters were often represented not only with interrogative brows, seemingly sparkling eyes, hovering smiles and parted lips, but often *en négligé*, wearing nightcaps and shirts and coats unbuttoned, as in the great *Self-portrait* (*c.* 1761; London, N.P.G.) by Louis-François Roubiliac. Bust portraits of women and children became more common, and in the work of the leading portrait sculptors of the late 18th century—Joseph Nollekens in London and Jean-Antoine Houdon in Paris—there were almost as many female as there were male sitters. The quiet, intimate mood of ancient Roman busts, such as the portrait of a lady of the Antonine period discussed above, were often emulated in the busts of the late 18th century.

Sympathy with ancient sculpture also led some sitters to be represented with bare chests, as in Joseph Wilton's bust of the *Fourth Earl of Chesterfield* (1757; London, V&A). This prompted the widespread adoption, by the end of the century, of Classical drapery, often of a generalized kind, for both sexes. In a few exceptional cases, such as the *Artist's Father* (1759; Stockholm, Nmus.; see fig. 5) by Johan Tobias Sergel, the herm form was revived; this tended to be used more frequently, however, for copies of antique busts than for modern portraits. Among those devoted to the imitation of antique sculpture there were some who abjured ancient Roman art and preferred the herm as an earlier and purer form: 'the Grecian method of cutting the chest square, and placing the whole mass immediately on a term or other solid support, seems much preferable to the more prevailing one of finishing or rounding off that chest, and balancing its centre only on a slender and tottering pivot', declared Thomas Hope in his polemical introduction to *Household Furniture and Interior Decoration* (London, 1807). Herm busts became more popular in the first decades of the 19th century, but they were more commonly used for portraits of the dead than the living, were far more popular for men than for women, and are more frequently found in busts made for tombs or gardens than for the home.

5. Bust of the *Artist's Father* by Johan Tobias Sergel, marble, life-size, 1759 (Stockholm, Nationalmuseum)

V. Modern.

The bust portrait continued as a highly popular art form throughout the 19th century. In the early 19th century new types of patronage emerged: busts of eminent men were commissioned for such professional institutions as the Royal College of Physicians in London and such seats of local government as the town hall in Manchester. Public monuments, many of them erected by subscription, which greatly proliferated in Britain after *c.* 1830, Italy after *c.* 1850 and France after *c.* 1880, included many bust portraits of politicians, philanthropists and generals, sometimes endowed with allegorical accessories and often erected in public gardens. Such monuments often had a political meaning, and the private ownership of a bust became an important means of demonstrating political allegiance; by the late 18th century, for example, supporters of the charismatic opposition politician Charles James Fox owned copies or casts of his bust by Nollekens, just as those sympathetic to secular and liberal ideas in France would own a bust of Voltaire. Throughout the 19th century patriotic, political and ideological allegiance was stimulated by the circulation of busts of such heroes as Napoleon, Nelson, Pitt the younger, Shakespeare and Goethe.

This use of the bust as a sort of political badge, together with the inevitable association of the bust with official and often pompous male portraiture, encouraged the development of the antithetical caricature bust by French sculptors after the July Revolution (1830) in Paris. From 1832 HONORÉ DAUMIER began to produce his clay *bustes chargés*, which represented the politicians in favour under Louis-Philippe. These, however, were only enjoyed by a close circle of friends—they were not fired and were only reproduced posthumously as casts in plaster or bronze (examples in Paris, Mus. d'Orsay). The grotesque nature of these sculptures partly derives from their exploitation of the ugliness implicit in the severed chest without any artifice of curving line, composed cloak or elegant socle. Better-natured and also more inventive are the caricature busts of such celebrities as *Victor Hugo* (1832; Paris, Carnavalet; see fig. 6) by Jean-Pierre Dantan; these were more widely known than those by Daumier and not without some echo in the contemporary portraits of geniuses made by the Romantic sculptor David d'Angers, whose *Paganini* (1830; Angers, Mus. B.-A.), for example, with wild hair, huge brow and straining neck comes daringly close to comedy in its striving for sublimity and in its sketchy plasticity.

Romanticism, as well as licensing some extraordinary and novel experiments in bust portraiture, also encouraged the revival of archaic conventions and in particular the 15th-century style of the Florentine bust portrait. Just as the accurate revival of antique Roman bust forms was first

6. Bust of *Victor Hugo* by Jean-Pierre Dantan, plaster, h. 172 mm, 1832 (Paris, Musée Carnavalet)

employed during the Renaissance in busts with Roman subject-matter, so the accurate revival of the 15th-century style was at first confined to poetic busts of historical or literary figures from that period, one of the earliest examples being the imaginary portrait of *Bernardino Cenci* (1870; Lyon, Mus. B.-A.) by Charles-Jean-Marie Degeorges. By the end of the 19th century this convention was occasionally adopted for portraits of modern people, albeit usually children or women, poetically depicted. Such sculptures were exceptional, but they were symptomatic of a reaction against the Antique as the ultimate source of inspiration for this class of sculpture. Generalized drapery, to say nothing of toga, cuirass and bare chest, was rejected by most leading sculptors (an exception being Adolf von Hildebrand) in favour of contemporary dress.

During the second half of the 19th century there was a revived interest in 17th-century Baroque sculpture on the part of both Italian and French sculptors who revelled in virtuoso modelling in clay and cutting in marble, not only rendering flamboyant drapery but also highly realistic fashionable haberdashery. This revival was accompanied by a greater interest in the rhetorical potential of the bust: the figures were represented in action or their action was implied, and they were given fleeting and evanescent expressions. The marble bust portrait of *Mme Turner* (1871; London, V&A) by Jean-Baptiste Carpeaux is an example of the trend, all the more interesting on account of the soulful undercurrent to the sitter's vivacity.

Auguste Rodin's portrait bust of *Mme Morla Vicuña* (1884; Paris, Mus. Rodin; see fig. 7), wife of the Chilean Ambassador to France, owes much to the example of Carpeaux's high-society portraiture, but here the dress and bouquet are merely suggested in the 'unfinished' block of marble out of which head and shoulders emerge. The effect is reminiscent of the sketchy oil portraits by Giovanni Boldini in which background and accessories were deliberately left unfinished; in Rodin's portrait, however, the whole device is more artificial since the sculpture and the whole conceit of its incompleteness were not invented in marble but in clay. Rodin was also interested in the work of art as an eloquent fragment (a device that had long been exploited by the Romantic poets). The application of this to bust portraiture provided a solution to the problem of how to truncate the figure. The bust was now conceived of as something either unfinished or as broken or torn from a larger work. Rodin's bronze mask of the *Man with a Broken Nose* (original terracotta, 1863–4; Antwerp, Kon. Mus. S. Kst.; numerous bronzes) and his *Honoré de Balzac* (1897; e.g. Oxford, Ashmolean) are two examples of portraits by him that resemble fragments. Since the late 19th century portrait sculpture in general has been presented in this way. The public, conditioned by the uncompromising presentation of antique sculptural fragments in modern museums, have come to accept this solution to the perennial one posed by the partial or abbreviated sculptural portrait.

7. Bust of *Mme Morla Vicuña* by Auguste Rodin, marble, life-size, 1884 (Paris, Musée Auguste Rodin)

BIBLIOGRAPHY

P. Bienkowski: 'Note sur l'histoire du buste dans l'antiquité', *Rev. Archéol.*, xxvii (1895), pp. 293ff

W. von Bode: 'Die Ausbildung des Sockles bei den Büsten der italienischen Renaissance', *Amtl. Ber. Preusz. Kstsamml.*, xl (1918–19), pp. 100–120

A. N. Zadkos and J. Jitta: *Ancestral Portraiture in Rome* (Amsterdam, 1932)

J. Burckhardt: 'Skulptur der Renaissance', *Gesamtausgabe*, ii (Stuttgart, 1937), cols 639ff

E. T. Newell: *Royal Greek Portrait Coins* (London, 1937)

M. Wegner: *Die Herrscherbildnisse in antoninischer Zeit*, Römische Herrscherbild (Berlin, 1939)

A. Boëthius: 'On the Ancestral Masks of the Romans', *Acta Archaeol.*, xiii (1942), pp. 226–35

G. Daltrop: *Die stadtrömischen männlichen Privatbildnisse trajanischer und hadrianischer Zeit* (Münster, 1958)

J. Pope-Hennessy: *Italian Renaissance Sculpture* (London, 1958)

S. Ferri: 'Busti fittili di Magna Grecia e l'origine dell'erma', *Rendi. Adunanze Solenni: Accad. N. Lincei*, xviii (1963), pp. 29–62

J. Pope-Hennessy: *Italian High Renaissance and Baroque Sculpture* (London, 1963)

E. Kovàcs: *Kopfreliquiare des Mittelalters* (Budapest, 1964)

T. Lorenz: *Galerien von griechischen Philosophen- und Dichterbildnissen* (Mainz, 1965)

G. Daltrop, U. Hausmann and M. Wegner: *Die Flavier*, Römische Herrscherbild (Berlin, 1966)

J. Pope-Hennessy: *The Portrait in the Renaissance* (London and New York, 1966)

I. Lavin: 'On the Sources and Meaning of the Renaissance Portrait Bust', *A.Q.* [Detroit], xxxiii (1970), pp. 207–26

R. Wittkower: *Art and Architecture in Italy, 1600–1750*, Pelican Hist. A. (Harmondsworth, 1973)

M. Robertson: *A History of Greek Art*, 2 vols (Cambridge, 1975)

D. E. E. Kleiner: *Roman Group Portraiture: The Funerary Reliefs of the Late Republic and Early Empire* (New York, 1977)

I. Carradice: *Ancient Greek Portrait Coins* (London, 1978)

J. M. C. Toynbee: *Roman Historical Portraits* (London, 1978)

J. Holderbaum: 'Portrait Sculpture', *The Romantics to Rodin* (exh. cat., ed. P. Fusco and H. W. Janson; Los Angeles, CA, Co. Mus. A., 1980), pp. 36–51

H. W. Janson: *Nineteenth Century Sculpture* (London, 1985)

A. Hannah: 'The Emperor's Star: The Conservatori Portrait of Commodus', *Amer. J. Archaeol.*, xc (1986), pp. 337–42

NICHOLAS PENNY

Bustamante (Herrera), Bartolomé (de) (*b* Alcalá de Henares, Madrid, 23 Aug 1501; *d* Trigueros, Huelva, 21 June 1570). Spanish architect. He began his career as an ecclesiastic in the parish of Caravaña, Madrid. After studying in Alcalá de Henares he served Cardinal Juan Pardo de Tavera as secretary (1534–6) and chaplain (1536–45) and travelled to Italy as his diplomatic envoy (1536). Tavera appointed him Inspector of Works for the archbishopric of Toledo, where he advised on the layout of the Hospital de S Juan Bautista (1541–50; *see* COVARRUBIAS, ALONSO DE, fig. 1), which was founded by Tavera and built to Covarrubias's designs. As the administrator (and rector) of the project (from 1549), Bustamante's main responsibility lay with the organization of construction; his criticism of the different schemes confirms his actual absence from the planning process. In 1551 Bustamante left Toledo to join the Jesuit Order, becoming secretary (1552–4) to Francisco Borja (1510–72), Provincial of Andalusia (1555–61), general of the Jesuit Order (1565–72), Inspector of the Jesuit provinces of Andalusia and Toledo (1566–8) and founder of various houses and schools. In 1565 he returned to Rome, where he took part in the II General Congregation (the chief governing body of the Jesuit Order) and was a member of the buildings committee. His participation in architectural matters during this period was again restricted more to organization and administration than to planning. At most he designed small college buildings, their emphasis on function rather than style in accordance with the ideals of simplicity and austerity expressed by the Jesuit Order during the first decades of its existence.

The documentary evidence of Bustamante's works, which include the Jesuit colleges of Burgos and Medina del Campo, Valladolid (1553), Plasencia (1554), Murcia (1555), Granada and Marchena, Seville (1556), Seville (1557), Villarejo de Fuentes, Cuenca (1562), Trigueros (1563), Córdoba (1564), Ocaña and Alcalá de Henares (1567), and Caravaca, Murcia and Segura de la Sierra, Jaén (1569), shows that he was principally active in planning extremely simple houses and small chapels for these communities, while outlining ideas for local architects to develop, following his recommendations on function and layout. Most of Bustamante's buildings have disappeared, having been erected during the early years of the Jesuit Order and then gradually replaced by more imposing structures with greater artistic pretensions. Any attempt by Bustamante to bring new ideas to Spanish Renaissance architecture would have been thwarted not only by economic strictures but by the Spanish Jesuits' absolute commitment to austerity. His correspondingly sober style was part of a general movement in early 16th-century Spanish architecture that may have contributed to the development of the reductive classicism of some of the work produced during the reign of Philip II (*reg* 1556–98).

BIBLIOGRAPHY

M. Pereda de la Reguera: *Bartolomé de Bustamante Herrera* (Santander, 1950)

F. Chueca Goitia: *Arquitectura del siglo XVI*, A. Hisp., xi (Madrid, 1953)

A. Rodríguez G. de Ceballos: 'El Padre Bustamante, iniciador de la arquitectura jesuítica en España (1501–1570)', *Archv Hist. Soc. Iesu*, xxxii (1963), pp. 3–102

——: *Bartolomé de Bustamante (1501–1570) y los orígenes de la arquitectura jesuítica en España* (Rome, 1967)

C. Wilkinson: *The Hospital of Cardinal Tavera in Toledo: A Documentary and Stylistic Study on Spanish Architecture in the Mid-sixteenth Century* (New York and London, 1976)

F. Marías: *La arquitectura del Renacimiento en Toledo (1541–1631)*, 4 vols (Toledo, 1983–6)

——: 'L'ospedale del Cardinale Tavera a Toledo: Da *hospitium pauperum a domus infirmorum*', *Ric. Stor. A.*, 32 (1987), pp. 27–44

FERNANDO MARÍAS

Bustelli, Franz Anton (*b* Locarno, ?1723; *d* Munich, April 1763). German porcelain modeller of Swiss birth. Although little is known about his early life, he is recorded as joining the Neudeck factory near Munich in November 1754 as Modellmeister; the factory was later moved to the Nymphenburg Palace, from which it then took its name. From that time until his death he produced one of the most remarkable series of porcelain figures ever modelled. Beginning with small Ovidian gods (e.g. *Flora*, 1755–8; Frankfurt am Main, Mus. Ksthandwk), nude putti with various classical attributes on fairly simple bases, he then made a series of figures of street vendors including an egg seller (e.g. *c.* 1755; Hamburg, Mus. Kst & Gew.) and a mushroom seller. These early figures do not reflect the full Rococo movement of Bustelli's later work. They do, however, display one essential characteristic of his entire oeuvre: a tendency to conceive his figures with faceted planiform surfaces, more reminiscent of wood-carving than clay-modelling, which may suggest that he was trained as a wood-carver. His figures seem to carry on in porcelain the rich traditions of the south German Rococo, and his first major compositions, including a Crucifix, a Virgin and a St John, are all in the direct tradition of south German ecclesiastical sculpture; at one time they were even ascribed to the sculptor Ignaz Gunther.

Bustelli's greatest period, however, began with his Chinese and Turkish figures, whose rich and vigorously scrolled bases surrounding and supporting them were to assume an important part of the whole creation. This phenomenon is also a vital feature of Bustelli's groups the *Sleeper Disturbed* and *Lovers among Ruins* (e.g. 1756; Hamburg, Mus. Kst & Gew.), in which the figures play an almost subsidiary role to their Rococo surroundings. His reputation as one of the greatest porcelain modellers was secured by his characters from the *commedia dell'arte*; the series (1759–60), consisting of 16 figures, is the most extensive and is considered the most daring and beautiful of its kind. The figures are arranged in eight pairs, each of a male and a female character. The two people in each couple appear to react physically as they gaze at one another across the space framed by each integral composition. Bustelli departed from the canon of the *commedia dell'arte* in porcelain by the inclusion of the characters Ottavio, Corine, Anselmo, Julia, Leda (e.g. 1759–60; Hamburg, Mus. Kst & Gew.), Lalage, Lucinda and Donna Martina. Corine and Anselmo are paired together, while the others are matched with the more usual members of the cast of the Comedy. Unusually, too, these figures bear the Wittelsbach shield, impressed into the scrolls on which they stand.

Bustelli was little concerned with the factory's wares; his only extant creations are a very Rococo clockcase and holy-water stoup. He produced few portraits from life, and his only extant work is the outstanding bust of *Graf*

Sigmund von Haimhausen (*d* 1793) who was the director of the factory and very influential in its workings. After his death Bustelli was succeeded by Dominikus Auliczek (1734–1804). Bustelli's work, however, one of the definitive expressions of the Bavarian Rococo, found no real successor.

For illustration of work *see* GERMANY, fig. 55.

BIBLIOGRAPHY
F. Hohhmann: *Geschichte der Porzellan Manufaktur Nymphenburg* (Leipzig, 1921)
W. B. Honey: *German Porcelain* (London, 1947)
R. Ruckert: *Bustelli* (Munich, 1963)
HUGO MORLEY-FLETCHER

Busti, Agostino. *See* BAMBAIA.

Bustillo, Alejandro (*b* Buenos Aires, 18 March 1889; *d* ?Buenos Aires, ?1982). Argentine architect. He won a national award for painting (1912) while still a student of architecture at the Universidad de Buenos Aires, where he graduated in 1913. He visited Europe in 1920. A classicist, he favoured the Greek Revival (he went to Greece as a guest of honour in 1970), but he worked in many styles in his vast oeuvre of more than 200 buildings. Bustillo's declared aim of producing original designs within the traditional styles brought him a wide range of commissions. In Buenos Aires, as well as many apartment buildings constructed both before and after World War II, he designed offices, hotels and banks, including the Banco de la Nación (1944), which boasts a central glass-covered banking hall with a span of 50 m. Elsewhere he designed the Casino and Hotel Provincial (1936), Mar del Plata; Bariloche Cathedral (begun 1932) and the Llao Llao Hotel (1939), also in Bariloche, South Andes; and numerous rural estancias in the colonial manner. He was also responsible for two buildings in Paris and a hotel in Brussels.

WRITINGS
Alejandro Bustillo (Buenos Aires, 1944)

BIBLIOGRAPHY
F. Bullrich: *Arquitectura latino-americana, 1930–1970* (Barcelona, 1969)
LUDOVICO C. KOPPMANN

Bustos, Hermenegildo (*b* Purísima del Rincón, Guanajuato, 13 April 1832; *d* Purísima del Rincón, 28 June 1907). Mexican painter. He was mainly self-taught as an artist and painted small-format portraits, still-lifes, ex-votos and retables. His portraits were realistic and closely observed; he generally portrayed villagers, but his *Self-portrait* (1891; Mexico City, Inst. N. B.A.) makes skilful use of light and shade to construct and highlight shapes. His still-lifes are distinguished by their presentation of Mexican fruit and objects, laid out as if for a botanical illustration (e.g. *Still-life with Fruit and Frog*, 1874; Guanajuato, Mus. Granaditas). The small ex-votos show wit, spontaneity and fantasy, and constitute valuable historical records of the faith and customs of the period. Bustos was one of the most popular artists of his time, and his work is notable for its precision of line, sensitivity, skill and sobriety of colour.

BIBLIOGRAPHY
R. Tibol: *Hermenegildo Bustos: Pintor del pueblo* (Guanajuato, 1981)
Art in Latin America: The Modern Era, 1820–1980 (exh. cat. by D. Ades and others, London, Hayward Gal., 1989), pp. 91–2
R. Tibol and others: *Hermenegildo Bustos, 1832–1907* (Mexico City, 1992)
ELISA GARCÍA BARRAGÁN

Busuttil, Salvatore (1798–1854). Maltese painter. He was the son of the painter Michele Busuttil. He studied at the Accademia Nazionale di San Luca in Rome, where he eventually established himself as an artist. The altarpiece of *St Gregory Interceding with the Virgin for the Plague-stricken* (Kercem, parish church) is his most important work in Malta. It reveals his affinities with Purismo, the anti-Baroque school of whom Tommaso Minardi was a leader, and is remarkable for its painstaking execution and the serene calmness of its harmonious composition.

BIBLIOGRAPHY
M. Buhagiar, ed.: *St Catherine of Alexandria: Her Churches, Paintings and Statues in the Maltese Islands* (Valletta, 1979)
MARIO BUHAGIAR

Bute, Earls and Marquesses of. *See* STUART.

Buthe, Michael (*b* Sonthofen, Allgäu, 1 Aug 1944). German painter, sculptor and environmental artist. He studied in Kassel between 1964 and 1967, first at the Werkkunstschule and then at the Hochschule für Bildende Künste with Arnold Bode. In 1969 he moved to Cologne. His first journey to Morocco in 1970 was decisive for the course of his artistic development, and thereafter Marrakesh was his second home. At *Documenta 5* in Kassel (1972) Buthe was one of the artists whose work was grouped under the heading of 'Individuelle Mythologien', exhibiting the environment *Homage to the Sun* (see von Weise, p. 21).

Buthe's works cannot be characterized by one style, but rather they emerge from an attitude that makes no differentiation between art and life. The artist builds spaces (for himself), using a large variety of materials, which may be transitory, 'poor', or precious (e.g. gold), as well as trivia: everyday objects as well as keepsakes become cult objects, fetishes, linked to folk myths and fairy tales. Murals or installations were built up on a collage principle, and earlier works could be reworked with a new status. Sumptuous colours and imagery such as stars, suns, palm-trees and stylized flowers reveal the influence of Africa, for example *Mask* (1973; Cologne, Mus. Ludwig). As well as the figurative paintings, which place Buthe close to the 'archaeological' painters Nikolaus Lang, Anne Poirier and Patrick Poirier, he produced environmental formations in space, in which he himself lived, for example the installation of his Cologne studio as the *Echnaton Museum* (1976; see von Weise, pp. 33–4, 55). He used artistic media such as photography, engraving, collage, painting, object-art and installations, as well as language poetry, to take his life far from everyday norms. All his works have a fragmentary character, and, as in the *Arabian Nights*, they have no beginning, no end, no main or subsidiary subject-matter; everything occurs in the great flow of autobiographical history.

WRITINGS
Die wundersame Reise des Saladin Ben Ismael (Cologne, 1977)

BIBLIOGRAPHY

When Attitudes Become Form (exh. cat., Berne, Ksthalle; Krefeld, Mus. Hans Lange; London, ICA; 1969)

Michael Buthe: Le Dieu de Babylone (exh. cat., Cologne, Kstver., 1973)

Michael Buthe: Die endlose Reise der Bilder (exh. cat., Essen, Mus. Flkwang, 1980)

S. von Wiese: *Michael Buthe: Skulptura in Deo Fabulosa* (Munich, 1983)

Michael Buthe (exh. cat., Ghent, Mus. Hedendaagse Kst; Munich, Villa Stuck; 1984)

EVA MEYER-HERMANN

Butinone, Bernardino (*b c.* 1450; *d* Treviglio, before 6 Nov 1510). Italian painter. He was the son of the painter Jacopo Butinone of Treviglio. His training was probably based on the study of such painters as Andrea Mantegna, Cosimo Tura, Francesco del Cossa, from whom he learnt an expressive and refined style, and Vincenzo Foppa. The earliest works, probably from the early 1480s, include a panel of the *Crucifixion* (Rome, G.N.A. Mod.), in which the incisive drawing and dramatic atmosphere suggest Mantegna's influence. Also from this period is the *Virgin and Child with Angels* (Milan, Gallarati-Scotti priv. col.), inspired by Tura and Cossa. Butinone is documented in Milan from 1484, probably the year he painted the triptych of the *Virgin and Child with SS Leonard and Bernardino of Siena* (Milan, Brera; see fig.), which reflects the realistic style of Foppa.

In 1485 Butinone and Bernardo Zenale signed a contract for the *St Martin* altarpiece (Treviglio, S Martino), for which Butinone probably painted the figures of SS Stephen, Peter and Paul. In this period the two painters, possibly with Giovanni Donato da Montorfano, executed the frescoes of *Dominican Saints and Blesseds* in S Maria delle Grazie in Milan. Butinone, Zenale and other artists executed decorations (destr.) for the Sala della Balla in the Castello Sforzesco, Milan, in 1490, for the wedding of Ludovico Sforza. Between 1490 and 1493 Butinone and Zenale frescoed stories from the *Life of St Ambrose* in the Griffi chapel of S Pietro in Gessate, Milan. Also probably from the 1490s is Butinone's *Virgin and Child with Angels and SS John the Baptist and Justine* (Isola Bella, Mus. Borromeo), influenced by Donato Bramante. Small panels, including the *Circumcision* (Bergamo, Accad. Carrara B.A.),

Bernardino Butinone: *Virgin and Child with SS Leonard and Bernardino of Siena*, oil on panel, 1.10×1.19 m, *c.* 1484 (Milan, Accademia di Belle Arti di Brera)

the *Adoration of the Shepherds* (London, N.G.), the *Flight into Egypt* (Chicago, IL, A. Inst.) and the *Incredulity of Thomas* (Pavia, Pin. Malaspina), probably made up a portable altar similar to the later one with scenes from the *Life of Christ* (Milan, Castello Sforzesco). Early in the 16th century he frescoed *Angel Musicians and Doctors of the Church* on the ceiling of the baptistry of S Martino in Treviglio, and also (perhaps with collaborators) the stories from the *Life of St Mary Magdalene* in the church of the Camuzzago monastery at Ornago (Monza). Towards the end of his life he entered the Franciscan convent of the Annunziata in Treviglio and devoted his last years to the illumination of codices. His elegant and expressive style influenced Bramantino.

BIBLIOGRAPHY

DBI

Arte lombarda dai Visconti agli Sforza (exh. cat., Milan, Pal. Reale, 1958), pp. 147–50, 153–4 [entries by F. Mazzini]

F. Mazzini: *Affreschi lombardi del quattrocento* (Milan, 1965), pp. 473–6, 627–8

B. Berenson: *Central and North Italian Schools* (1968), i, pp. 69–72

Zenale e Leonardo: Tradizione e rinnovamento della pittura lombarda (exh. cat., Milan, Mus. Poldi Pezzoli, 1982), pp. 50–52, 150–51 [entries by M. Natale]

M. Gregori, ed.: *Pittura tra Adda e Serio: Lodi, Treviglio, Caravaggio, Crema* (Milan, 1987), pp. 163–6, 169–70

F. Zeri, ed.: *Pinacoteca di Brera: Scuole lombarda e piemontese, 1300–1500* (Milan, 1988), pp. 142–6

ANNA MARIA FERRARI

Butkara [from Pers. *butkada*, 'house of images']. Group of three sites east of Saidu Sharif, Swat, Pakistan. The sacred precinct of the great Buddhist stupa at Butkara I (3rd century BC–10th century AD) and the graveyard known as Butkara II (*c*. 4th century BC) were excavated by the Istituto Italiano per il Medio ed Extremo Oriente; Butkara III, a smaller Buddhist site (*c*. 1st–4th century AD), was excavated by the Department of Archaeology, Peshawar University. Finds are in the Swat Museum, Saidu Sharif, the Istituto Italiano per il Medio ed Estremo Oriente, Rome, and the Department of Archaeology Museum at Peshawar University.

Butkara II, a necropolis of 48 tombs, pre-dates the arrival of Buddhism in the area. The burials were of two types: inhumation, with funeral vases, some jewellery and, occasionally, weapons or working utensils; and cremation, the burnt bones being placed in a large closed jar encircled by funerary vases. The red or grey wheelmade pottery was glazed and polished, with some incised decoration. Only one painted fragment and two terracotta figurines (one animal, one human) were found. The graves were identified by Giuseppe Tucci as belonging to the Assakenoi, against whom Alexander the Great fought after crossing the Panjkora River.

Butkara I has been identified as Tuoluo, the largest and richest monastery of ancient Udyana, visited by the Chinese pilgrim Songyun in AD 520 (Chavannes, p. 410). The foundation of the original core stupa with a relic cell in the centre is dated by a coin of Chandragupta Maurya to the 3rd century BC. The stupa resembles in plan other wheel-shaped stupas such as Dharmarajika at Taxila but utilizes earlier building techniques. In the 2nd century BC a circular base was added, with a niche at each cardinal point; that on the south side was either a podium or, more probably, steps. The entire structure was encased around the beginning of the 1st century AD within a greatly enlarged stupa comprising a circular base with steps at the cardinal points and two superimposed cylindrical drums, the upper berm being subsequently decorated with pilasters. The dome of this stupa has not survived. Some of the numerous coats of plaster on the upper drum bore traces of having been painted red or pink, while one layer had a decorative garland in red. The black or grey schist used throughout the earlier phases of construction had been replaced by soapstone for facings and green schist for decorative elements.

A fourth enlargement in the time of the Kushana king Huvishka (*c*. 2nd century) again completely enclosed this stupa. The new base had 16 niches, each with a small reliquary recess, fronted by large reused schist reliefs from the earlier monument depicting scenes from the life of the Buddha. As the schist panels decayed, the wall surface was coated instead with successive layers of plaster, the second layer having the painted motif of a red-and-black undulating garland with lotus flowers in the volutes. Stucco statues were placed against the wall. The stupa was encircled by an ambulatory (Skt *pradakṣiṇāpatha*), which was enclosed in turn by a ring of votive stupas, shrines and columns, variously dating from the earliest period. Two of the original four gates to the ambulatory were later blocked by additional structures. The square enclosure of the

1. Butkara I, arched false gable, framing the figure of Nanda who offers a necklace to Sundart, holding a mirror, green schist, 533×340×70 mm, *c*. 1st century AD (Saidu Sharif, Swat Museum)

2. Butkara I, head of a *bodhisattva* wearing a turban decorated with an open lotus flower and an animal protome, green schist, 450×430×130 mm, *c.* 2nd century AD (Saidu Sharif, Swat Museum)

surrounding sacred precinct contained more than 200 monuments, primarily votive stupas. Reliefs found *in situ* on stupas 14 and 17 are datable from archaeological evidence to *c.* 1st century AD and provide a benchmark for analysis of Gandharan sculptures from the site. The sculptures fit broadly into three stylistic groups, the development of which can be traced through a number of schist slabs that were worked on one side, then later cut and reused on the other side. An arched false gable with the figures of Nanda and Sundart holding a mirror, a gift associated with marriage (see fig. 1), may be dated *c.* 1st century AD, for the relief was found close to Stupa 14 and probably originally belonged to that monument. It is clear that the schist sculptures were highly valued: those found *in situ* on later monuments had all been reused, even when in a broken or fragmentary condition. A *bodhisattva* head of *c.* 2nd century (see fig. 2) appears to be an example of this, for it is associated by its findspot with one of the *c.* 4th-century stupas 89 and 90. Following the destruction of all the monuments in the sacred precinct, probably by an earthquake, the main stupa was rebuilt in a simplified form for a fifth time in the late 7th century or the 8th. Occupation of the site continued until the arrival of the Muslims under Mahmud of Ghazna (*reg* 998–1030).

The site of Butkara III is bisected by a seasonal stream, the Nari Khwar. Partial excavation on the western part of the site revealed a row of six rooms cut out of the clay deposit in the hillside. The excavated area (54×48 m) on the eastern side comprised an open courtyard containing ten stupas of various sizes, all with square bases, and a row of two monastic buildings (*vihāras*) and six shrines on the east and north sides, again all cut out of the clay hillside and fronted by a masonry wall. A sculpture workshop contained a number of unfinished reliefs and architectural elements. Each shrine comprised a vaulted porch and a domed inner chamber. One porch contained a row of three small stupas coated with red-and-blue painted plaster; the others had a plinth against the walls for clay sculptures. All the square inner chambers contained a circular stupa (max. h. 3.2 m including dome; diam. *c.* 2.7 m), again with a plastered façade painted in blue and red, and also decorated with phyllite and green schist reliefs. Every stupa was crowned with a square railing (*harmikā*) with carved decoration on the sides and three umbrellas. In Shrine D, it was possible to ascertain the original position of the sculptures by recording the different levels of the finds and matching corresponding tenon holes in the reliefs and stupa surface. Each panel appears to have been conceived as an independent unit, and there was no continuity of subject-matter between adjoining reliefs.

Excavation uncovered four structural phases at the site but only two coins: one of Soter Megas providing a *c.* mid-1st-century date for phase II; another of the Kushana ruler Vasudeva, suggesting a 2nd-century date for phase III. Although numismatic evidence is lacking, a gradual extension of the site appears to have continued long after the 2nd century. Buddhist occupants were replaced subsequently by non-Buddhists, who levelled some of the stupas and used the structures for domestic purposes.

See also INDIAN SUBCONTINENT, §IV, 5(ii)(c).

BIBLIOGRAPHY

E. Chavannes: 'Voyage de Song Yun dans l'Udyāna et le Gandhāra 518–522 AD', *Bull. Ecole Fr. Extrême-Orient*, iii (1903), pp. 379–441
D. Faccenna: 'Mingora: Site of Butkara I', *Reports on the Campaigns 1956–1958 in Swāt (Pakistan)*, Ist. It. Med. & Estrem. Oriente. Rep. & Mem., i (Rome, 1962), pp. 3–169
D. Faccenna and M. Taddei: *Sculptures from the Sacred Area of Butkara I (Swāt, W. Pakistan)*, 2 vols, Ist. It. Med. & Estrem. Oriente. Rep. & Mem., ii/2–3 (Rome, 1962–4)
C. Silvi Antonini: 'Preliminary Notes on the Excavations of the Necropolises Found in Western Pakistan', *E. & W.*, xiv (1963), pp. 13–26
G. Tucci: 'The Tombs of the Asvakayana–Assakenoi', *E. & W.*, xiv (1963), pp. 27–8
G. Alciati: *Butkara II*, Ist. It. Med. & Estrem. Oriente. Rep. & Mem., viii/1 (Rome, 1967); rev. by G. Genna, *Genus*, xxv/1–4 (1969), pp. 343–57
R. Göbl: *A Catalogue of Coins from Butkara I (Swāt, Pakistan)*, Ist. It. Med. & Estrem. Oriente. Rep. & Mem., iv (Rome, 1976)
D. Faccenna: *Butkara I (Swāt, Pakistan) 1956–1962*, 5 vols, Ist. It. Med. & Estrem. Oriente. Rep. & Mem., iii/1–5.2 (Rome, 1980–81)
C. Fabrègues: 'The Indo-Parthian Beginnings of Gandhara Sculpture', *Bull. Asia Inst.*, i (1987), pp. 33–43
Abdur Rahman: 'Butkara III: A Preliminary Report', *South Asian Studies 1987*, ii, ed. M. Taddei (Rome, 1990), pp. 693–706

E. ERRINGTON

Butler. Irish family of architects. William Deane Butler (*fl* 1828; *d* Dublin, 28 Nov 1857) was apprenticed to a Mr Beazley (possibly Samuel Beazley (1786–1857), architect of London theatres). By 1839 he was a member of the committee of the Civil Engineers Society of Ireland (later the Institute of Civil Engineers of Ireland) and the only Irish Fellow of the Royal Institute of British Architects. His work typifies the eclecticism of the period. St Kieran's College (1836–9), Kilkenny, is in Tudor style, whereas his proposals for a hotel at Kingsbridge, Dublin (unexecuted; drawing, Dublin, Irish Archit. Archv, 75/2/ 1), reveal the classical influence of Charles Barry. Butler was indeed responsible for the first building in this Italianate style in Dublin, the Amiens Street Train Station (1844; now

Connolly Station), a two-storey composition in silver Wicklow granite raised on a deep podium. A colonnade links the entrance bays to terminal pavilions that rise above the roof-line to form belvederes. The grand entrance, treated as a triumphal arch, also has a one-bay tower and crowning belvedere. Butler executed the enormous Sligo Lunatic Asylum (1856; disused) again in an early 16th-century style, with decorated gables and ornate chimney-stacks as salient features on the roof-line.

William Deane Butler's son, James (John) Sterling Butler (*fl* 1854–78), had an extensive practice and exhibited frequently at the Royal Hibernian Academy. He was responsible for many Catholic churches, completing work begun by his father, such as St Cronin (1843–50, 1860), Roscrea, Co. Tipperary, which is in a Gothic Revival style. His orphanage (1858–60; destr.) at Glasnevin, Dublin, for the Society of St Vincent de Paul, showed some influence of his father's Amiens Street Train Station, particularly its central tower. He was responsible for the New County Hall (1866), Carrick-on-Shannon, Co. Leitrim, and was Dublin City Architect between 1866 and 1878, in which year he resigned.

BIBLIOGRAPHY

Builder (9 Feb 1856), p. 74 ['Inquiry into. . . .Irish Lunatic Asylums': mention of W. Deane Butler]

M. Craig: *Dublin, 1660–1860* (Dublin, 1952/*R* 1980), p. 299

J. Graby, ed.: *150 Years of Architecture in Ireland: RIAI 1839–1989* (Dublin, 1989)

HUGH MAGUIRE

Butler, Lady [née Thompson, Elizabeth Southerden] (*b* Lausanne, 3 Nov 1846; *d* Gormanston, Ireland, 2 Oct 1933). English painter. She was the elder daughter of Thomas James and Christiana (née Weller) Thompson, members of London's literary and artistic circles and close friends of Charles Dickens. Both she and her sister (the poet and essayist Alice Meynell) were educated by their father. She spent much of her childhood in Italy, but the family returned to England in 1860 so that she could have professional tuition. She became a student in the elementary class at the Female School of Art, South Kensington, London, and, after a further interval of travel and residence on the Continent, obtained a place in the antique and life classes at the school in 1866. Her main rival for academic honours there was Kate Greenaway. In 1869 the family lived in Florence, where she studied drawing at the Accademia di Belle Arti with Giuseppe Bellucci (1827–82). Her first recorded painting was a religious work, *The Magnificat* (1869–71; Ventnor, St Wilfred), executed after her conversion to Roman Catholicism. The work was refused by the hanging committee of the Royal Academy, London, in 1871, and this may have deterred her from attempting any other religious painting.

A visit to Paris in the aftermath of the Franco-Prussian War (1870–71) inspired her to work on a military subject. She noted that, although there was a thriving school of military painting in France, the field was comparatively neglected in England, providing a great opportunity for an ambitious painter to 'distinguish herself from the ruck'. Her first large oil painting on a military theme, *Missing* (1872; untraced, see 1987 exh. cat., p. 26), was exhibited at the Royal Academy in 1873. It shows two French soldiers travelling through a bleak landscape during the Franco-Prussian War. *Calling the Roll after an Engagement, Crimea*, generally known as the *Roll Call* (1874; Brit. Royal Col.; *see* BATTLE PICTURES AND MILITARY SCENES, fig. 2), is a retrospective and romanticized representation of soldiers during the Crimean War (1854–6). It depicts a row of soldiers dazed but heroically disciplined after a battle. The work was phenomenally successful with the public and Queen Victoria purchased it, although it had been commissioned by Charles Galloway, a Manchester industrialist. The artist's reputation was undoubtedly boosted by the approval of the royal family, and her work inspired a generation of battle painters, including Ernest Crofts (1847–1911), William Wollen (1857–1936) and Richard Caton Woodville (ii). Her next picture, the *28th Regiment at Quatre-Bras* (1875; Melbourne, N.G. Victoria), was praised by Ruskin, who claimed that it was 'Pre-Raphaelite'. The popularity of this and other paintings during the 1870s may be gauged by the high prices paid for reproduction rights. The Fine Art Society bought the engraving copyright to the *Roll Call*, *Quatre-Bras* and *Balaclava* (1876; Manchester, C.A.G) and promoted her career by exhibiting and publicizing these works.

Elizabeth Thompson married the military hero Major (later Lt-Gen. Sir) William Francis Butler in 1877. His unconventionally radical views on colonial policy and army administration, as well as his many books on military history, influenced her art. She produced a number of little-known pictures that passionately attacked English policy in Ireland, her husband's home. *Evicted* (1890; Dublin, U. Coll.) received very little critical attention at the Royal Academy of 1890 and was dismissed as being melodramatic. Her reputation rested on more conventional battle pictures, which depicted events from the Crimean War, the Peninsula and Waterloo campaigns and, in the 1880s, from contemporary colonial wars. *Scotland for Ever!* (1881; Leeds C.A.G.) was begun in 1879 in response to an exhibition at the Grosvenor Gallery, which Lady Butler denigrated as 'the home of the "Aesthetes"'. This surprisingly small work (1.0×1.9 m) depicts the charge of the Scots Greys at the Battle of Waterloo, with over 20 horses galloping towards the spectator in an excellent representation of equine action.

Despite her popularity and royal patronage, in 1879 Butler was narrowly defeated in the election for associateship of the Royal Academy. The rules were subsequently changed to exclude women. Her style remained unchanged until she ceased to exhibit in the early 1920s. Her art fell out of favour with the emergence of English Impressionism but enjoyed a revival during World War I, when her patriotic scenes of heroic soldiery on horseback were a welcome antidote to depictions of trench warfare. A major solo show of her work, held at the Leicester Gallery in 1915 to celebrate the centenary of Waterloo, had *Scotland for Ever!* as its centrepiece. Her art always manifested a devotion to the heroic aspects of war, concentrating on the elevated personal qualities that she believed it called forth, rather than the bloody realities. Her patrons were mostly industrialists from the north of England. There are examples of her work at the city galleries of Manchester, Leeds and Hull.

WRITINGS

Letters from the Holy Land (London, 1903)
From Sketchbook and Diary (London, 1909)
An Autobiography (London, 1922)

BIBLIOGRAPHY

DNB
E. Clayton: *English Female Artists*, ii (London, 1876), pp. 139–43
J. Oldcastle: 'Our Living Artists: Elizabeth Butler (née Thompson)', *Mag. A.*, ii (1879), pp. 257–62
W. Meynell: 'The Life and Work of Lady Butler', *A. Annu.* (1898) [Christmas issue]
J. Ruskin: *Academy Notes, Ruskin's Works*, ed. E. T. Cook and A. Wedderburn (London, 1903–12), xiv, pp. 306, 308
J. Hichberger: *A Victorian Amazon: The Life and Work of Lady Butler* (diss., U. Leicester, 1980)
R. Hamilton: *Representing the Victorian Army in 1874: The 'Roll Call', Elizabeth Thompson, and Military Discourses* (diss., U. Leeds, 1984)
Lady Butler: Battle Artist, 1846–1933 (exh. cat. by P. Usherwood and J. Spencer-Smith, London, N. Army Mus., 1987)

JOAN HICHBERGER

Butler, Charles (*b* 1822; *d* 29 June 1910). English collector. Director of the Royal Insurance Company and, at his death, a millionaire, he amassed a large and wide-ranging collection of paintings, sculptures and other objects. In November 1890 financial difficulties obliged him to sell some of his paintings; the rest of his collection, including illuminated manuscripts, Limoges enamels, antique and Renaissance Italian bronzes, maiolica, Chinese porcelain and ivory carvings, was sold after his death by Christie, Manson & Woods, London. The painting collection was particularly strong in Italian works: Botticelli, Bronzino, the Carracci, Giotto, Filippino Lippi, Mantegna, Orcagna, Raphael, Andrea del Sarto, Tiepolo, Titian, Tintoretto, Uccello and Palma Vecchio were all represented. Paintings from other countries included works by William Dobson, Richard Wilson, Peter Lely, Nicolas Poussin, Zurbarán, Dürer, Rubens, Aelbert Cuyp and van Dyck. Particularly well-known items in his collection were Nicolas Poussin's *Pan and Syrinx* (*c.* 1637; Dresden, Gemäldegal. Alte Meister), Rubens's the *Departure of Lot and his Family from Sodom* (*c.* 1613–15; Sarasota, FL, Ringling Mus. A.) and the *Madonna di Casa Colonna* (Berlin, Gemäldegal.), attributed to Raphael.

BIBLIOGRAPHY

Catalogue of Art, Porcelain and Faience: The Property of the Late Charles Butler Esq. Removed from 3 Connaught Place, Hyde Park (sale cat., London, Christie's, 22–24 May 1911)
Catalogue of Highly Important Pictures by Old Masters: The Property of the Late Charles Butler Esq. Removed from 3 Connaught Place, Hyde Park (sale cat., London, Christie's, 25–26 May 1911)
Catalogue of Italian Pictures at 16 South Street, Park Lane, London and Buckhurst in Sussex: Collected by Robert and Evelyn Benson (London, 1914)

□

Butler, Cotterell. *See under* BUTLER, REG.

Butler, Horacio (*b* Buenos Aires, 28 Aug 1897; *d* Buenos Aires, 17 March 1983). Argentine painter, tapestry designer and stage designer. From 1922 to 1933 he lived in Europe, where he studied first in Germany at the artistic colony in Worpswede and then in Paris under André Lhote and Othon Friesz. He was untouched by the violence of German Expressionism, but he assimilated various influences in France, structuring forms in the manner of Cézanne, and combining these with the audacious colouring of Fauvism and the strict sense of order in Cubism, as in *The Siesta* (1926; Buenos Aires, Mus. N. B.A.).

On his return to Argentina, Butler applied these European influences to lyrical landscapes of the islands in the Parana Delta of the Tigre region near Buenos Aires, selecting unusual scenes into which he incorporated childhood reminiscences in the figures. Using arabesques to link nature and people in his essentially flat pictures, he projected himself on to the scenery of which he was so fond in pictures such as the *House of the Trees* (1960) and *Nocturne* (1972; both Buenos Aires, Mus. Mun. A. Plást. Sívori). He also designed tapestries, notably one of monumental size (12×8 m), an *Allegory of St Francis*, for the wall behind the altar in the church of S Francisco in Buenos Aires, and stage sets for the Teatro Colón in Buenos Aires, the Teatro Solís in Montevideo and La Scala in Milan.

WRITINGS

La pintura y mi tiempo (Buenos Aires, 1966)

BIBLIOGRAPHY

C. Córdoba Iturburu: *80 años de pintura argentina* (Buenos Aires, 1978), p. 38

NELLY PERAZZO

Butler, Howard Crosby (*b* Croton Falls, New York, 7 March 1872; *d* Paris, 13 Aug 1922). American archaeologist and teacher. After receiving his MA in 1893 from Princeton University with a fellowship in archaeology, he studied architecture at Columbia University. From 1895 until his death he held various appointments at Princeton in architecture, archaeology and art: his teaching of architecture as one of the fine arts led to the creation of the Princeton School of Architecture, of which he became the founding director in 1922. He was one of the most influential American archaeologists of his time, owing to his discoveries in Syria and at Sardis. His work in Syria was inspired by Melchior de Vogüé's explorations there in the 1860s. Butler organized and led an American expedition in 1899 with the intention of verifying, photographing and adding to the list of de Vogüé's sites. His work in Syria continued until 1909 and resulted in several important publications on the Early Christian architecture. In 1910 he began excavating at Sardis, uncovering the Artemis Temple and a number of important Lydian objects, until 1914, when the outbreak of World War I halted work. He was occupied with his commitments at Princeton and the American Institute of Archaeology until 1922, when he returned to Sardis for a season of excavating. He died unexpectedly on his journey home, leaving his greatest dream, the excavation of Palmyra, unrealized.

WRITINGS

Architecture and Other Arts (New York, 1903)
Ancient Architecture in Syria, 2 vols (Leiden, 1919–20)
Sardis I: The Excavations, Part I: 1910–1914 (Leiden, 1922)
Sardis II: Architecture, Part I: The Temple of Artemis (Leiden, 1925)
E. Baldwin Smith, ed.: *Early Churches in Syria: Fourth to Seventh Centuries* (Princeton, 1929)

BIBLIOGRAPHY

Howard Crosby Butler, 1872–1922, Princeton University (Princeton, 1923)
H. S. Leach: *A Bibliography of Howard Crosby Butler, 1872–1922* (Princeton, 1924)

LAWRENCE E. BUTLER

Butler, James. *See under* HEATON, BUTLER & BAYNE.

Butler, James, 1st Duke of Ormonde (*b* London, 19 Oct 1610; *d* Kingston Hall, Dorset, 21 July 1688). Irish administrator and collector. Though coming of a powerful old Anglo-Irish family, he was born and educated in England. In 1632 he succeeded his grandfather as the 12th Earl of Ormonde and Ossory. He was a consistent supporter of Charles I during the 1641 rebellion in Ireland and was Lord Lieutenant from 1643 to 1644. Under the Commonwealth he followed the future Charles II into exile in France; with the Restoration, he returned with great pomp to Ireland as Lord Lieutenant in 1662. This marked a new beginning for the arts in Ireland. While in France, Ormonde would have seen the leading architecture and painting of the day; subsequently he was in contact with such prominent artistic figures in England as Peter Lely, Grinling Gibbons and Hugh May and had an English artist, James Gandy (1619–89), in his entourage. Ormonde commissioned furnishings (of which few survive) for his family seat at Kilkenny Castle, Kilkenny, and for his house (destr. 18th century) at Dunmore, Kilkenny; the surviving inventories (Dubin, N. Lib.) indicate the luxury of the interiors, which were decorated with Spanish leather, tapestries, court portraits, silver furniture, plate, upholstery and hangings. There were also decorative wall and ceiling paintings. Ormonde was also instrumental in the building of the Royal Hospital in Kilmainham, Dublin, and of other military buildings, such as the Charles Fort in Kinsale, Cork; he gave a new impetus to the architectural development of Dublin. He was a man of upright character, refinement and taste, distinguished also by his love of fine dress. Jealous rivals forced his resignation as Lord Lieutenant in 1669, although he occupied the post again from 1677 to 1685.

BIBLIOGRAPHY

DNB

A. Crookshank and the Knight of Glin: *The Painters of Ireland, c. 1660–1920* (London, 1978), pp. 16, 20

J. Fenlon: 'Kilkenny Castle', *Decantations: Tribute to Maurice Craig* (Dublin, 1992), pp. 29–37

JOHN TURPIN

Butler, Reg(inald Cotterell) (*b* Buntingford, Herts, 28 April 1913; *d* Berkhamsted, Herts, 23 Oct 1981). English sculptor, draughtsman, architect and writer. After training as an architect from 1933 to 1936, he taught at the Architectural Association in London and practised as an architect as Cotterell Butler until 1939; among the buildings designed by him were two houses at Bushey (1935) and Great Munden, Herts (1939), as well as the clock-tower of Slough Town Hall (1936), designed while working for C. H. James & Bywaters & Roland Pierce (for illustrations, see exh. cat., p. 9). From 1941 to the end of World War II he worked as a blacksmith in Iping, West Sussex, as a conscientious objector; from 1946 until 1950 he worked as a technical editor for the Architectural Press, acted as consultant to various firms, including Ove Arup and Partners, and attended life-classes at Chelsea School of Art.

Butler began to sculpt in 1944, without having had any formal training, and held his first one-man show at the Hanover Gallery, London, in 1949. Works such as the skeletal, insect-like *Woman* (forged and welded iron, 1949; London, Tate) were influenced both by his training as a blacksmith and by constructions by sculptors such as Alexander Calder and Julio González. While working at the University of Leeds as the first Gregory Fellow in Sculpture from 1950 to 1953 he had time to mature as a sculptor, turning to modelling in clay, plaster or wax instead of welding, and casting in a thin-shell bronze technique of his own. In early works such as *Girl and Boy* (forged and welded iron, 1950–51; AC Eng) he criticized the dominant aesthetic of Henry Moore and Barbara Hepworth, rejecting their cult of natural materials and organic form as too remote from modern urban existence.

Butler took part in many international exhibitions from 1952, including the Venice Biennale (1952 and 1954), and by the mid-1950s he was considered one of the most promising British sculptors of a generation that included Lynn Chadwick and Kenneth Armitage. In 1953 he won first prize in an international competition for a monument to the *Unknown Political Prisoner*, which culminated in a working model (h. 2.24 m, 1955–6; London, Tate). It was never realized at its full envisaged height of 18 m. Its thin skeletal forms encasing a highly stylized figure create an abstract box-like structure reminiscent of the early Surrealist work of Alberto Giacometti. In the late 1950s, under the influence of Germaine Richier, Butler returned to a more directly figurative style, concentrating on bronze female figures sometimes encased in a framework of metal bars that contrasted with the softness and vulnerability of the figures; in works such as *Girl* (h. 1.49 m, 1956–7; Leeds, C.A.G.) he typically presented the nude figure with arms outstretched in the act of undressing.

During the 1960s Butler's production decreased dramatically to around three or four sculptures a year and his style underwent a radical change. Taking young women as his main subject, he often subjected them to extreme contortions, distorting their anatomy to stress their sensuousness. They were cast in polyester resin or bronze and often painted or supplemented by elements such as real hair in order to achieve a physical immediacy, as in *Girl on Back (Study for the Battersea Figure)* (painted bronze and hair on velvet-covered foam base, 1975–81; priv. col., see exh. cat., p. 71). These late sculptures, which were preceded by detailed preparatory drawings, frequently took years to complete. Butler explained his working methods at length in his Townsend Memorial Lecture of 1980; he also published *Creative Development* (1962), in which he criticized the formalist bias of most modern art and art training, emphasized the importance of historical context and declared that modernism would be followed by a 'post-modernist' or open phase.

WRITINGS

Creative Development: Five Lectures to Art Students (London, 1962)

BIBLIOGRAPHY

P. Heron: *The Changing Forms of Art* (London, 1955), pp. 43–4, 226–32

B. Robertson, J. Russell and Lord Snowdon: *Private View* (London, 1965), pp. 82–5

W. Schwartz: *The Hand and Eye of the Sculptor* (London, 1969), pp. 2–27

Reg Butler (exh. cat., ed. R. Calvocoressi; London, Tate, 1983) [incl. Butler's William Townsend Memorial Lect., 1980, 'The Venus of Lespugue and Other Naked Ladies']

KENNETH G. HAY

Butmir. Prehistoric settlement and cultural typesite of the 6th–5th millennia BC, on the fringes of the VINČA culture, in the upper Neretva Valley, near Sarajevo in Bosnia. The Late Neolithic site has yielded interesting handmade decorated pottery and plain fired clay figurines with unusually realistically modelled heads. It was partially excavated in 1893–6 by Viclav Radimský and his colleagues, and material recovered is in the National Museum, Sarajevo. Pottery from Butmir and other more recently excavated sites such as Obre, near Zenica, comprises a range of globular and pear-shaped vessels with spiral motifs incised and painted in red and white after firing. There are also small fired clay anthropomorphic figurines in the general Balkan tradition, but some are distinctive for having realistically modelled heads. Foreheads, eyes, lips and chins are delineated as well as noses and ears. Most archaeologists, however, would regard these primarily as cult or ritual objects rather than artistic representations; some suggest that they represent figures in a pantheon of deities.

For further discussion of Neolithic European pottery *see* PREHISTORIC EUROPE, §IV, 4.

BIBLIOGRAPHY

V. Radimský and M. Hoernes: *Die neolithische Station von Butmir*, i (Vienna, 1895)
F. Fiala and M. Hoernes: *Die neolithische Station von Butmir*, ii (Vienna, 1898)
R. Tringham: *Hunters, Fishers and Farmers of Eastern Europe: 6000–3000 BC* (London, 1971)
M. Gimbutas: *The Goddesses and Gods of Old Europe* (London, 1982)

ALASDAIR WHITTLE

Buto. *See* FARAIN, TELL EL-.

Butrint [It. Butrinto; anc. Gr. Bouthroton; Lat. Buthrotum]. Site in southern Albania, set on a hill beside a coastal lagoon connected to the sea by a natural channel. The city flourished in Greek, Roman and Byzantine times. Excavation and display of its extensive and deserted remains, begun by the Italians in 1928, have been continued by Albanian archaeologists; finds are displayed in the site museum (renovated 1988) and in the National Historical Museum, Tiranë. It was probably a colony of Kerkyra (Corfu), from which its site is visible. Earliest occupation on the hilltop is shown by Corinthian pottery of the 7th–6th century BC and a wall of polygonal masonry, rebuilt in the 5th century BC. By the following century the expanding city required new walls, which survive up to 9 m high and include the Lion Gate, named after the Archaic relief reused as its lintel (6th century BC). Butrint became a centre for the surrounding Epirot people, the Prasaiboi, as is shown by similar fortifications at nearby sites and by the slave-manumission inscriptions on the theatre walls. The theatre (4th century BC) could seat 1500 people; several marble statues were found there. The theatre's stage building and the adjoining temple of Asklepios were rebuilt in the 2nd century AD. Adjacent to them are the remains of a Hellenistic peristyle house and the Roman public baths, and other smaller bathhouses, a gymnasium and a nymphaeum have been uncovered. The aqueduct that supplied the city is shown on its 1st-century AD coins.

Surviving Early Christian buildings (6th century AD) include a baptistery, circular internally with two concentric rings of columns and a figured mosaic pavement, and an apsidal basilica with walls standing nearly to full height. A castle was built on the acropolis during the Middle Ages, and new city walls were built in the 11th–13th centuries; after 1205 it was an important stronghold of the Despots of Epiros and subsequently a Venetian dependency (1384–1796). Ali Pasha added defensive works after capturing it from the French in 1807.

BIBLIOGRAPHY

L. M. Ugolini: *L'acropoli di Butrinto* (1942), iii of *Albania Antica* (Rome, 1927–42)
P. Cabanes: 'Recherches archéologiques en Albanie 1945–1985', *Rev. Archéol.* (1986), pp. 107–42
A. Baçe and D. Çondi: *Buthrote* (Tiranë, 1987)

T. F. C. BLAGG

Butrón, Juan Alonso de (*b* 1603; *fl* 1620s). Spanish writer, theorist and administrator. He was a lawyer on the Council of Castile and the author of the treatise *Discursos apologéticos en que se defiende la ingenuidad del arte de la pintura, que es liberal y noble de todos los derechos* (Madrid, 1626). Based on philosophical and juridical arguments influenced by the ideology of the Counter-Reformation, this critical discussion demonstrated that painting was a liberal science by comparison with the traditional liberal arts. This was an important and polemical subject in Spain during the 17th century and was connected with the *pleitos de alcabala* (sales tax disputes) that concerned the imposition of taxes and other obligations on the practice and commerce of painting. Butrón's *Epístola dirigida al rey suplicando protección para la Academia de los pintores* (Madrid, 1626) gives valuable information on the little-known Academia de los Pintores in Madrid at the beginning of the 17th century. He was also the author of one of the petitions (*Memoriales*) in defence of painting that Vicente Carducho (*see* CARDUCHO, (2)) appended to his *Diálogos de la pintura* (Madrid, 1633).

BIBLIOGRAPHY

F. J. Sánchez Cantón: *Fuentes literarias para la historia del arte español*, ii (Madrid, 1933)
P. Ballesteros: *Los pintores ante el fisco* (Madrid, 1942)
E. Lafuente Ferrari: 'Borrascas de la pintura y triunfo de su excelencia', *Archv Esp. A.*, lxi (1944), pp. 402–6
J. A. Gaya Nuño: *Historia de la crítica de arte en España* (Madrid, 1975)
J. Gállego: *El pintor de artesano a artista* (Granada, 1976)
F. Calvo Serraller: *Teoría de la pintura del siglo de oro* (Madrid, 1981)

FRANCISCO CALVO SERRALLER

Butschowitz. *See* BUČOVICE.

Butterfield, William (*b* London, 7 Sept 1814; *d* London, 23 Feb 1900). English architect and designer. He committed his feelings and creative energies to the High Anglicanism of the Oxford Movement from the early 1840s and to its expression through the revival of Gothic architecture and design, then vociferously advocated by the Ecclesiological Society, of which he became an active member. Butterfield's extensive output was almost exclusively confined to the building and restoration of churches and associated buildings, such as vicarages and schools.

1. Early career. 2. All Saints (1849–59), Margaret Street. 3. Other mature work. 4. Late work.

1. Early career. He was the eldest son of a London chemist, and his parents were Nonconformists. From 1831 to 1833 Butterfield was articled to a Pimlico builder, Thomas Arber, from whom he must have derived the detailed understanding of practical building that was to be basic to his architectural practice. Between 1833 and 1836 he was the pupil of E. L. Blackburne, a London architect with strong antiquarian interests, and in 1838–9 he became assistant to a Worcester architect, probably Harvey Eginton, whose practice included church building and restoration. During this period Butterfield must have begun to acquire the profound knowledge of medieval architecture that was to underlie all his work. In 1840 Butterfield returned to London. Having first contacted the Cambridge Camden (from 1845, Ecclesiological) Society in 1842, he was elected a member two years later. He immediately assumed a leading role in its activities, providing all the designs for the first series of the Society's *Instrumenta ecclesiastica* (1844–7) and editing the second series (1850–52, 2/1856). These specimen designs for ecclesiological furnishings, though firmly based on medieval precedents, often reveal something of the angularity and boldness that were to become typical of Butterfield's work. Their influence on Victorian ecclesiastical fittings was pervasive, particularly in the design of plate, where Butterfield's examples were decisive in effecting a change in character.

1. William Butterfield: All Saints, Margaret Street, London, 1849–59, exterior from the street

Also in 1844 Butterfield designed his first Anglican church group, St Saviour's church and parsonage, Coalpit Heath, Glos (*see* GOTHIC REVIVAL, fig. 3) and received his first major commission, for St Augustine's Missionary College, Canterbury, from A. J. B. Hope, the Society's president. St Saviour's is a workmanlike and well-understood exercise in the Decorated Gothic advocated by A. W. N. Pugin and the Ecclesiologists. More strikingly, its parsonage combines vernacular materials and a range of historical precedents in a functionally expressive design that stresses the formal and often awkward discreteness of its parts. All these characteristics were developed in buildings over the next few years: Wilmcote School and Parsonage (1845), Warwicks, Aston Cantlow School (1847–8), Warwicks, with its markedly vernacular master's house, Ogbourne St Andrew Parsonage (1848), Wilts, and the school and house at Alfington (1849), Devon, where the compact massing and angular division of parts look forward to developments of the 1850s. St Augustine's College, Canterbury, was also prophetic: the style is Decorated, but the unbroken roof lines, the sheer wall surfaces and the use of flush tracery anticipate the vocabulary of High Victorian Gothic.

Butterfield's success at St Augustine's and his High Church credentials brought commissions for conventual buildings, which posed similar problems of complex planning, notably St Dunstan's Abbey (1850), Plymouth, and Cumbrae College (1844–51), Bute, Strathclyde, where forceful detailing and a strong asymmetrical plan brilliantly play off against a spectacular landscape setting. Butterfield also provided designs for Adelaide Cathedral (1847; built 1869–78 to revised plans) in Australia, and completed Fredericton Cathedral (1848–53), New Brunswick, Canada. Finally, in the 1840s he produced the first of over 160 church restorations and refittings: the most important include those at Dorchester Abbey (1846–53), Oxon, Merton College Chapel (1849–51), Oxford, and Ottery St Mary (1849–50), Devon, this last commission secured through the Coleridge family, who remained among Butterfield's very few close friends. As Thompson (1971) has shown, and contrary to many 20th-century assertions, these restorations were conservative by the standards of the time and carried out with a scrupulous concern for the medieval fabric. (Among later major restorations were SS Mary and Melor (1852–3), Amesbury, Wilts, a long series of works at Winchester College (1857–82), including reconstruction of the chapel tower (1858), St Cross Hospital (largely 1858–65), Winchester, SS Peter and Paul (1865–7), Heytesbury, Wilts, All Saints (1869–70), Hastings, E. Sussex, and St Mary's (1883–6), Warwick.)

2. All Saints (1849–59), Margaret Street. In the late 1840s the Ecclesiologists, backed by Hope's money, decided to commission a model town church. It was to be High Anglican in ritual arrangement and to embody the latest stylistic thinking, particularly the idea of structural polychromy, using differently coloured materials for both construction and decoration, as advocated by John Ruskin. Accordingly, in 1849 Butterfield designed All Saints, Margaret Street, London; this became, unquestionably, one of the most influential churches of the 19th century and is a building of startling originality (see fig. 1).

Its brick construction was an explicit statement of urbanism and contemporaneity; its external massing—church, clergy house and school tightly packed around a small courtyard dominated by a massively sheer steeple —was entirely novel; although the avowed style was Decorated, the spire was based on German examples, the chancel vaulting on Assisi, while other details were essentially ahistorical; internally, Butterfield's surprisingly grand arcade, tall nave and taller chancel created a spatial complex as exciting as it was unmedieval. His use of structural polychromy was, however, the most dramatic feature at All Saints. The exterior red brick was patterned with bands and zig-zags of black, variously related or unrelated to windows, doors and buttresses. Internally, the variety of patterns and materials is astonishing: big geometrical roundels of matt-coloured tiles in the spandrels of the nave arcade, hard polished granite for the piers, decorations in red and black brick above the chancel arch, gleaming marbles inlaid in bright abstract patterns for the pulpit. Some contemporaries, including the irritable Hope, found the overall effect bewildering, and some modern critics have interpreted All Saints as aggressive and even brutalist. Although, as Thompson (1971) has rightly argued, deliberate ugliness was no part of Butterfield's intention, the scheme does exploit abruptness and discontinuity, with sharp contrasts between material textures, collisions between pattern forms, and inconsistent connections between decorative organization and plastic features. By such methods he made conflict and ambiguity and their resolution central architectural issues; in so doing, he also created an architectural language uniquely appropriate to the broader cultural dynamics of Victorian Britain.

3. OTHER MATURE WORK. While All Saints was paradigmatic for all High Victorian Gothic, nobody developed its vocabulary as consistently as Butterfield himself. Many of the country churches he built subsequently have important decorative schemes, often executed in tiles and mastic, and frequently based on a sophisticated use of echoic patterns and geometric forms. These included St Mary's (1854–5), Langley, Kent, St James's (1855–7), Baldersby, N. Yorks, St James's (1855–7), Waresley, Beds, and St Anne's (1864–6), Dropmore, Bucks. St Laurence's (1857–61), Alvechurch, Hereford & Worcs, Holy Saviour (1863–6), Hitchin, Herts, and St Augustine's (1864–6), Penarth, Cardiff, all have fine polychromatic brick patterning throughout the nave. The most elaborate of these decorative schemes was that of All Saints (1865–74), Babbacombe, Devon, where a web of raised stone ribs covering the nave and chancel walls was repeated in analogous forms and patterns throughout the building, unifying decoration and structure in an unmistakable yet ambiguous system of architectural echoes. Simultaneously, Butterfield was exploring the three-dimensional geometry of architectural massing: while he kept the component parts of his buildings separately articulated, he counterpointed this by increasing compression, so that forms and volumes were often telescoped or compacted together. Hence the forcefulness and sense of tension that characterize his great urban churches (all built in brick): St Matthias (1849–53), Stoke Newington, London; St Alban's (1859–62; interior destr.), Holborn, London, its massive saddleback tower, buttressed by elongated transepts and stair turret, stretching the full width of the church; St Cross (1862–6), Clayton, Manchester; and St Augustine's (1870–77), Kensington, London, where the tightly packed plasticity of its west front rises sheer from the street. Similar characteristics are evident in the substantial parsonages Butterfield designed for Sheen (1852), Staffs, and for Alvechurch (1855), Hereford & Worcs, and in the taut composition of his only complete country house, Milton Ernest Hall (1853–6), Beds, built for his brother-in-law Benjamin Starey. On a small scale the process of simultaneous articulation and compression produced the delightful interlocking masses of country churches such as St Paul's (1853–4), Hensall, N. Yorks, St Mary's (1854–6), Milton, Oxon, and Elerch (1865–8), Dyfed; on a large scale it enabled Butterfield to achieve formal concentration even in such a large building as the Hampshire County Hospital (1863–8), Winchester.

Butterfield's pursuit of pattern had resulted in the bright geometry of his decorative schemes: so also his fascination with three-dimensional form led to sculptural abstraction, most evident in the design of his fonts, which were often stripped of historicist detail, so that the sharp play of mass and plane emerged with great clarity. Representative examples are at All Saints (1854–5), Braishfield, Hants, St John the Baptist's (1858–61), Latton, Wilts, St Sebastian's (1864–5), Wokingham, Berks, St Barnabas's (1867–8), Horton cum Studley, Oxon, St George's (1874–5), Morebath, Devon, and St Catherine's (1876–7), Netherhampton, Wilts. If Butterfield's fonts were his most abstract designs, his most functional plans were for the estate housing designed during the 1850s, much of it commissioned by William Dawnay, 7th Viscount Downe, in Yorkshire and the Midlands. Yet here he was as original as elsewhere, reinterpreting his own responses to form, material and style through the traditions of vernacular building. Cottages (1855–9) at Baldersby, N. Yorks, combined hipped gables, big chimneys and fine brickwork, with tellingly simplified Gothic detail; in his cottage terrace (*c.* 1858) at Ashwell, Leics, historicism is present only in the brick moulding on the doorcases and in a single band of differently coloured brickwork; in the terraces of 1859 at Braunstone and Kirby Muxloe, both Leics, overt Gothic references have disappeared entirely. Parallel developments occurred in a number of smaller parsonages: Great Woolstone (1851), Bucks, Pollington (1854), Humberside, and Bamford (1862), Derbys. These modest houses, deceptively simple in massing, consciously vernacular in reference, greatly impressed the young Philip Webb; through him they came to be a seminal influence on the whole development of later Victorian domestic architecture.

4. LATE WORK. Butterfield's late career was dominated by major commissions for Rugby School (1860–85), Warwicks, and Keble College (1867–83), Oxford. Of a dozen buildings he designed for Rugby, three may be mentioned as outstanding: New Schools (1867–70; *see* POLYCHROMY, colour pl. I, fig. 2), with its arrestingly complex street elevations; the Chapel (1870–72), the impressive tower of which was built up in a sequence of

vigorously compressed masses; and New Big School (1884–5), a moving contrast to the other two in its compact, rather dumpy profile. Keble College, like Rugby, was also built in brick, a conscious assertion of modernity and a challenge to the university's conservatism. Although planned, traditionally enough, around a quadrangle, the college's enclosure is firmly broken at two points; its buildings, their red-brown brickwork banded and diapered in black and white, are asymmetrical in elevation and disposition, and its principal axes are off-centre. The Chapel (1873–6) dominates, its lower walls without windows below the eaves-level of the other buildings, its clerestory climbing high above their slate roofs, its decoration and plasticity progressively enriched as it rises (see fig 2). The single-vaulted space of the Chapel interior (see fig. 3), with a lavish but carefully orchestrated decorative scheme, is among the most impressive Butterfield ever designed.

Keble College was the summation of his career, just as the London Law Courts were that of G. E. Street, and it is as much a masterpiece. Ironically, however, by the 1870s Butterfield was already isolated from contemporary architectural developments. Even so, he produced both major buildings and new stylistic departures in his late years. St Andrew's (1875–9), Rugby, Warwicks, St Mark's (1876–8 and 1889–91), Dundela, Belfast, and his second Australian cathedral, St Paul's (1877–91), Melbourne, are particularly notable; they are big-boned churches, generously proportioned, and they retain all Butterfield's clarity of structural expression. Their polychromy is, however, disposed more broadly, and the interiors have a balance, a repose even, that gives them a quite different expressive character from that of his earlier churches. At the same time, curling, foliate forms, graceful yet remote, appeared in his designs for metalwork, as in the great chancel screen (1886–7) of St Bee's, Cumbria, and mosaics, as in the delicate Coleridge Memorial (1878–9) at Ottery St Mary, Devon, and at St Mary-sub-Castro (1888–9), Dover, and All Saints (1889–92), Harrow Weald, London. Despite this evidence of continuing creative vigour, Butterfield was an old man and an increasingly lonely one, particularly after the death of his elder sister Anne in 1891. He retired from active practice in 1892. He was buried in Tottenham Cemetery, London, under a tombstone that he had designed himself.

UNPUBLISHED SOURCES

Most of Butterfield's surviving letters, drawings and account books are owned by members of the Starey family. A set of notebooks that he gave to W. D. Caroë is owned by Caroë's descendants.

London, RIBA [drawings]

WRITINGS

Details of St John's Shottesbrooke by William Butterfield Esq. (Oxford, 1844)

Church Seats and Kneeling Boards (London, 1885)

BIBLIOGRAPHY

C. L. Eastlake: *A History of the Gothic Revival* (London, 1872, *R* Leicester, 1970)

H. Ricardo: 'William Butterfield', *Archit. Rev.* [London], vii (1900), pp. 259–63; viii (1900), pp. 15–23 [obituary]

H. S. Goodhart-Rendel: 'English Gothic Architecture of the Nineteenth Century', *RIBA J.*, xxxi (1924), pp. 321–44

W. R. Lethaby: *Philip Webb and his Work* (Oxford, 1935, *R* London, 1979)

2. William Butterfield: exterior of the Keble College Chapel, Oxford, 1873–6

H. Redfern: 'Some Recollections of William Butterfield', *Architect & Bldg News*, clxxviii (1944), pp. 21–2, 44–5, 57–60
J. Summerson: 'William Butterfield, or the Glory of Ugliness', *Archit. Rev.* [London], xcviii (1945), pp. 166–75; repr. in *Heavenly Mansions* (London, 1949)
H.-R. Hitchcock: *Early Victorian Architecture in Britain*, 2 vols (London, 1954)
J. P. H. House: 'The Architecture of William Butterfield, 1814–1900', *Trans. Anc. Mnmt Soc.*, xi (1963), pp. 109–30
P. Thompson: 'All Saints Church, Margaret Street, Reconsidered', *Archit. Hist.*, viii (1965), pp. 73–9
Copy or Creation? Victorian Treasures from English Churches (exh. cat., London, Goldsmiths' Co. and Victorian Soc., 1967) [includes a catalogue of plate]
P. Thompson: *William Butterfield* (London, 1971)
Victorian Church Art (exh. cat., London, V&A, 1971)
S. Muthesius: *The High Victorian Movement in Architecture, 1850–1870* (London, 1972)
C. Brooks: *Signs for the Times: Symbolic Realism in the Mid-Victorian World* (London, 1984)

CHRIS BROOKS

3. William Butterfield: interior of Keble College Chapel, Oxford, 1873–6

Butteri, Giovanni Maria (*b* Florence, *c.* 1540; *d* Florence, 4 Oct 1606 or 1608). Italian painter. After he trained under Agnolo Bronzino (as did his brother, Cresci Butteri; *fl* 1551–89), in 1564 he entered the newly founded Accademia del Disegno in Florence, in which he was very active. He worked mainly in Florence and for the Medici on commissions for paintings, decorations for buildings and court occasions (many untraced); these included *Michelangelo the Poet with Apollo and the Muses* for the funeral of the artist (1564) and *Poets and Writers* for the wedding (1565) of Grand Duke Cosimo I de' Medici's son Francesco (later Francesco I de' Medici, Grand Duke of Tuscany) and Joanna of Austria (1547–78). For the *studiolo* (Florence, Pal. Vecchio) of Francesco I de' Medici he painted (1570–71) *Aeneas Arriving in Italy* and the *Glassblowers' Workshop.* He worked on a number of commissions under the supervision of another Bronzino protégé, Alessandro Allori (*see* ALLORI, (1)), including decorations for the Villa Medici at Poggio a Caiano (1579–82), for the first corridor of the Galleria degli Uffizi (1581) in Florence and for the wedding of Grand Duke Ferdinand I de' Medici and Christine of Lorraine (1589), as well as cartoons (1590s) for the Arazzeria Medicea or tapestry works. Numerous portraits by Butteri are documented: *Bianca Cappello* (Arezzo, Mus. Casa Vasari); the *Virgin and Child with Saints* (1575), which contains portraits of Eleonora de' Medici, Cosimo I de' Medici and their sons; and *Simone Corsi*, Luocotenente of the Accademia del Disegno (1596; both Florence, Depositi Gal.). Other works include the decoration (1578–81), with Allori, of the Palazzo Salviati in Florence (now the Banca Toscana), the *Christ and the Centurion* (Florence, Santa Maria del Carmine), the *Coronation of the Virgin* (Florence, Santo Spirito), six frescoes (begun 1582) in the large cloister of S Maria Novella, Florence, and paintings at the Badia of Passignano (1581; *in situ*), the *Miracle of St Giovanni Gualberto* and the *Trial of St Peter Igneus.* Butteri was a Tuscan Mannerist comparable to such other Bronzino followers as Allori. His paintings are characterized by bright diffused light, metallic colours and figures that show stylized forms and features deriving from Bronzino.

BIBLIOGRAPHY

Colnaghi; *DBI*; Thieme–Becker
G. Vasari: *Vite* (1550, rev. 2/1568); ed. G. Milanesi (1878–85), vi, p. 6; vii, pp. 305, 608; viii, p. 617
F. Baldinucci: *Notizie* (1681–1728); ed. F. Ranalli (1845–7), iii, pp. 500–01
A. Schiavo: 'La Badia di San Michele Arcangelo a Passignano in Val di Pesa', *Benedictina*, viii (1954), p. 266
M. Collareta and K. Langedijk: 'Giovanni Maria Butteri', *Palazzo Vecchio: Committenza e collezionismo medicei, 1537–1610* (exh. cat., ed. C. Beltramo Ceppi and N. Conforto; Florence, Pal. Vecchio, 1980), pp. 289–90
A. Petrioli Tofani: 'Contributi allo studio degli apparati e delle feste medicee', *Firenze e la Toscana dei Medici nell'Europa del '500: Firenze, 1980*, ii, pp. 645–61
Il primato del disegno (exh. cat., ed. L. Berti; Florence, Pal. Strozzi, 1980), p. 92 [entry by M. Mosco]
R. Scorza: 'A New Drawing for the Florentine "apparato" of 1565: Borghini, Butteri and the Tuscan Poets', *Burl. Mag.*, cxxvii (1985), pp. 887–90
From Studio to Studiolo: Florentine Draftsmanship under the First Medici Grand Dukes (essay K.-E. Barzman, exh. cat. ed. L. J. Feinberg; Oberlin Coll., OH, Allen Mem. A. Mus., 1991)

MILES L. CHAPPELL

Buttress. Mass of masonry or brickwork projecting perpendicularly from a wall to give additional support to that wall along its length or at the corners.

1. WALL. A buttress built either as a part of the wall (engaged) or against it.

Angle. Two buttresses meeting at an angle of 90°, usually on a corner or an acute angle of a building (see fig. (a)). This kind of buttressing was common throughout the

Types of buttress: (a) angle: Creil, St Evremont, 12th century; (b) clasping: Allonne parish church, late 11th century; (c) diagonal: Le Mans Cathedral, 1217–54; (d) setback: Caen, St Etienne, west façade, 1090–1100; (e) flying: Saint-Denis Abbey, nave, 1231–81

Middle Ages, usually in towers; good examples include the west towers of Chartres Cathedral (*c.* 1140s; *see* CHARTRES, §I, 1) and that of Holy Cross (rebuilt 1519, rest. 1872), Great Ponton, Lincs.

Clasping. A buttress that encases a corner or an acute angle on a building (see fig. (b)). It is common in ashlar construction beginning in the Roman and Late Antique periods and can be found in numerous examples, including S Vitale (consecrated AD 547), Ravenna, St Lawrence (?10th century AD), Bradford-on-Avon, Wilts, St Pantaleon (consecrated AD 980), Cologne, and St Philibert (11th century), Tournus.

Diagonal. A buttress placed against the right angle or corner formed by two walls (see fig. (c)). Diagonal buttressing was more common in the Late Gothic period, such as on the west tower of St James (altered late 15th century), Chipping Campden, Glos.

Internal. An interior buttress that serves to rigidify the wall and is usually disguised as an architectural element; or a buttress built within the wall that does not visibly project on either interior or exterior. The first is common on large ashlar walls in buildings as diverse as the cathedral of Ste Croix (destr. 989), Orléans, S Vicente (consecrated 1040), Cardona, Speyer Cathedral (consecrated 1061) and Jumièges Abbey (1040–67).

Setback. A buttress set back from the corner or the angle (see fig. (d)). Setback buttressing was common throughout the Middle Ages, with examples ranging from such early Asturian churches as S Miguel de Lillo, Oviedo (9th century AD; *see* ASTURIAN ARCHITECTURE), to such Late Gothic parish churches as SS Peter and Paul (*c.* 14th century), Lavenham, Suffolk.

2. FLYING. A buttress consisting of two parts (see fig. (e)): the flyer arch, either segmental or quadrant, transmits thrusts from the vault and the high, exposed timber roof of a Gothic building across the aisle to the outer, upright support or buttress (Fr.: culée; *see* MASONRY, §III, 3(vi) and figs 6 and 7). The flying buttress adumbrated in such buildings as the Basilica of Maxentius in Rome (early 4th century AD) was developed in the Ile-de-France from the second half of the 12th century. By 1200 the flying buttress had become the most identifiable exterior component of churches in France; by 1250 it was known all over Europe.

The origins and structural function of the flying buttress have preoccupied scholars since Viollet-le-Duc. After him, the first serious attempt to investigate its origins and development was that of Lefèvre-Pontalis in 1919, who followed Viollet-le-Duc's structural explanation. With only a few modifications (largely in the realm of dating the earlier examples), his account remained the standard one until the 1970s, when scholars began to add previously unrecognized early examples to the list. The most important of Prache's additions (1973) are the flying buttresses of the chevet of St Remi, Reims (1162–81; *see* REIMS, §IV, 3(i)), as well as the possibility that flyers were intended for its new westernmost nave bay, which predates the chevet. The problem with these suggestions is that it cannot be demonstrated that flyers were intended when construction of the chevet was begun or that they were built on the west bay before the vault itself, which was built only when the nave was vaulted after the completion of the east end. Claims have also been advanced for early flying buttresses at St Martin, Etampes (Henriet, 1978), and Sens Cathedral (*c.* 1140–68; Henriet, 1982; *see* SENS, §1(i)), but for these and various other suggestions such as those of Wilson (1990), confirming archaeological evidence is either wholly lacking or, at best, equivocal for every example earlier than *c.* 1170.

Priority and identification of the first flying buttresses are, however, considerably less important than recognizing the examples that unquestionably had the greatest impact on the history of Gothic architecture: those that appeared at gallery level on the nave (*c.* 1170–75) of Notre-Dame, Paris (*see* PARIS, §V, 1(i); Clark and Mark, 1984). They had an almost immediate impact, not only on buildings then under construction (including the unfinished chevet at Paris, the cathedrals of Laon (begun *c.* 1155–60; *see* LAON, §1(i)) and Canterbury (1175–84), St Remi at Reims and Notre-Dame (*c.* 1170–1220) at Mantes) or in the planning stages, but even on those recently completed (e.g. the chevet of St Germain-des-Prés (*c.* 1145–55), Paris, and, most likely, the chevet of Sens Cathedral). The rebuilding of the early buttressing of Notre-Dame at Paris *c.* 1220–25 spurred another wave of changes in the buttressing systems at Mantes, the cathedrals of Chartres and Bourges, and elsewhere. This had an enormous influence on 13th-century architecture in France and, ultimately, throughout Europe.

BIBLIOGRAPHY

E.-E. Viollet-le-Duc: *Dictionnaire raisonné de l'architecture française du XIe au XVIe siècle* (Paris, 1854–68): i, pp. 60–83; iv, pp. 284–306

E. Lefèvre-Pontalis: 'L'Origine des arcs-boutants', *Congr. Archéol. France*, lxxxii (1919), pp. 367–96

P. Abraham: *Viollet-le-Duc et le rationalisme médiéval* (Paris, 1934)

A. Prache: 'Les Arcs-boutants du chevet de Saint-Remi de Reims', *Bull. Soc. N. Antiqua. France* (1973), pp. 41–3

——: 'Les Arcs-boutants au XIIe siècle', *Gesta*, xv (1976), pp. 31–42

J. Henriet: 'Recherches sur les premiers arcs-boutants: Un Jalon: Saint-Martin d'Etampes', *Bull. Mnmtl.*, cxxxvi (1978), pp. 309–23

——: 'La Cathédrale Saint-Etienne de Sens: Le Parti du premier maître et les campagnes du XIIe siècle', *Bull. Mnmtl.*, cxl (1982), pp. 81–168

R. Mark: *Experiments in Gothic Structure* (Cambridge, MA, 1982)

——: *High Gothic Structure: A Technological Reinterpretation* (Princeton, 1984)

W. Clark and R. Mark: 'The First Flying Buttress: A New Reconstruction of the Nave of Notre-Dame de Paris', *A. Bull.*, lxvi (1984), pp. 47–65

——: 'Gothic Structural Experimentation', *Sci. American*, ccli/5 (1984), pp. 144–6

C. Bruzelius: 'The Construction of Notre-Dame in Paris', *A. Bull.*, lxix (1987), pp. 540–69

W. Clark and R. Mark: 'Le Chevet et la nef de Notre-Dame de Paris: Une Comparaison entre les premières élévations', *J. Hist. Archit.*, ii (1989), pp. 69–88

R. Mark: *Light, Wind and Structure* (Cambridge, MA, 1990)

C. Wilson: *The Gothic Cathedral* (London, 1990)

C. Hardy: 'Les Roses dans l'élévation de Notre-Dame de Paris', *Bull. Mnmtl*, cxlix (1991), pp. 153–99

WILLIAM W. CLARK

Buvelot, Abram-Louis (*b* Morges, Vaud, 3 March 1814; *d* Melbourne, Victoria, 30 May 1888). Swiss painter, lithographer and photographer, active in Brazil and Australia. He attended a drawing school in Lausanne, where his teacher may have been Marc-Louis Arlaud (1772–1845), and is thought to have spent some time with the landscape painter Camille Flers in Paris *c.* 1836 *en route* to Bahia (Salvador), Brazil. In 1840 he moved to Rio de Janeiro, where he established himself as a painter of local views. He exhibited with the Imperial Academy of Fine Arts, Rio. His Brazilian landscapes, of which the *View of Gamboa* (1852; Rio de Janeiro, Mus. N. B.A.) is an example, received critical acclaim for their vivacious lighting. As a photographer he fulfilled commissions in daguerreotype for Emperor Peter II, and with the figure painter Auguste Moreau he produced a set of 18 lithographs, *Picturesque Rio de Janeiro*, published in 1843–4. In Switzerland from 1852 to 1864 he worked as a portrait photographer and from 1855 to 1864 as a teacher of art in La Chaux de Fonds, Neuchâtel, associating and exhibiting his landscapes with the Swiss followers of Corot. In 1865 Buvelot settled in Melbourne, Victoria, and worked for a year as a portrait photographer. From 1866 to *c.* 1884, painting both in oils and watercolours, he depicted sunny and peaceful landscapes, creating images of the countryside that were familiar and domesticated, as in *St Kilda Park* (*c.* 1878; Adelaide, A.G. S. Australia). His manner was identified as French because of its relative freedom of touch. He was accorded the highest respect by Australian patrons and critics and by younger artists, in particular those of the Heidelberg school.

BIBLIOGRAPHY

Louis Buvelot: Landscape and Portrait Photographer (exh. cat. by J. Gray, Melbourne, Gal. E. Hill, 1970)

J. Gray: *Louis Buvelot: His Life and Work* (MA thesis, U. Melbourne, 1977)

——: 'Abram-Louis Buvelot and the Art of the French Painters of Barbizon', *A. & Australia*, xvi/12 (1978), pp. 152–8

F. Ansermoz-Dubois and V. Ansermoz-Dubois: *Louis Buvelot* (Lausanne, 1984)

JOCELYN FRAILLON GRAY

Buwayhid. *See* BUYID.

Bux [Buksh], **Allah** (*b* Wazirabad, 1895; *d* Lahore, 1978). Pakistani painter and etcher. Apprenticed at age five to Master Abdulla, a Mughal miniature artist of Lahore, by age fourteen Bux had become an accomplished signboard painter. He worked as a carriage painter for Mughalpura Railway and as a scene painter for Agha Hasher Kashmiri's theatrical company. In 1914 he went to Bombay, where he was employed as a photographer, retouch artist and portrait and landscape painter at the Bombay Art Studio. After returning to Lahore in 1919, he became a fine art painter who supported himself as a commercial artist.

Bux was known as the 'Krishna painter', after one of his favourite themes, and until 1947 was readily patronized by the Hindu community of Lahore. Panoramic fantasies filled with earthly and floating figures and brightly coloured realistic or abstract landscapes recall Maxfield Parrish, Gustave Moreau and the Symbolists. Bux had access to Western originals in the collection of Bhupindra Singh, ruler of Patiala, for whom he worked part-time for several years.

After Pakistan was created in 1947, Bux recognized the need to adapt his themes to the requirements of a Muslim nation. He painted Punjabi village life: celebrations, dances, marriage festivals and work in the fields. His academic paintings (*see* ACADEMY) anticipate the realist pictures of the Lahore Landscape Movement that evolved in the 1970s (*see* PAKISTAN, §III). In that city in 1976 he inaugurated the Allah Bux Academy, which has perpetuated the European academic tradition in Pakistan, and where a collection of his paintings is on display. Immensely popular with the public, Bux was a dedicated teacher and frequent prize-winner. In his later years blindness hindered his work. While some critics labelled him a provincial painter, the current generation recognizes the depth of his influence. He was a recipient of the Presidential Medal for Pride of Performance. Other institutions holding examples of his work include the Lahore Museum and the National Gallery of Art in Islamabad.

BIBLIOGRAPHY

Exhibition of Paintings Ustad Allah Bux (exh. cat. by A. S. Khurshid, Rawalpindi, Soc. Contemp. A. Gals, 1962)

M. Barbar: 'First Ever Allah Bux Show in Islamabad', *Mag* (17–23 April 1986), p. 9

Paintings from Pakistan (Idara Saqafat-e Pakistan and UNESCO: Islamabad, 1988)

A. ul-Hasan: *Painting in Pakistan* (Lahore, 1991)

M. Nesom-Sirhandi: *Contemporary Painting in Pakistan* (Lahore, 1992)

MARCELLA NESOM-SIRHANDI

Buxböm, Hans. *See* PUCHSPAUM, HANS.

Buyck, Pierre François (*b* Bruges, 23 March 1805; *d* Bruges, 31 Dec 1877). Belgian architect. He came from a family of architects who had been working in public service for several generations. After studying at the Academie voor Schone Kunsten in Bruges he accepted an administrative job with the Department of Public Works under the Dutch government; then in 1831 he left to become Inspector of Public Works in Bruges under the supervision of the architect J.-B. Rudd (1792–1870). He also taught at the Academie for a while. In 1842 Buyck went back into government service as provincial architect for the district of Bruges; he built numerous churches, presbyteries, town halls, schools and hospitals in the north of West Flanders. In addition he did restoration work on St Salvator Cathedral in Bruges, the churches of Our Lady in Lissewege and in Damme, the lighthouse in Nieuwpoort, the 'het Brugse Vrije' (now a museum) and other buildings. His buildings are characteristic of the group of architects who worked in public service and initiated the revivalist styles in Belgium during the second quarter of the 19th century. He designed churches in a Neo-classical style (Zedelgem, 1846), in the *Rundbogenstil* (Bovekerke, 1848) as well as in a Gothic Revival style (Gits, 1847; Eernegem, 1852; Gistel, 1853; Moerkerke, 1867; Bredene, St Rijkers, 1871; Heist, 1871). His first buildings were designed with an element of fantasy, including stuccoed details, but gradually their appearance conformed to the new archaeological norms. His role in the rise of the archaeological Gothic Revival style, of which Bruges became the centre, is especially interesting. As early as 1844 he collaborated with R. D. Chantrell (1793–1872), the English architect, on the Romanesque Revival spire of St Salvator Cathedral in Bruges. In 1850 his plans for the Magdalenakerk, Staelyserplaats, in Bruges, were fiercely criticized by THOMAS HARPER KING, who substantially influenced their eventual execution. His son, René Buyck (1850–1923), succeeded him as provincial architect from 1878 to 1883.

BIBLIOGRAPHY
Thieme–Becker
J. van Cleven: 'Buyck, Pierre François', *Nationaal Biografisch Woordenboek*, x (Brussels, 1983), pp. 82–4

JEAN VAN CLEVEN

Buyid [Buwayhid]. Islamic dynasty that ruled in Iran and Iraq from AD 932 to 1062. Civil wars, the erosion of caliphal power by a Turkish military caste, corrupt administration and racial tensions during the 9th century terminally damaged the ABBASID state, and gradually the extremities of the empire in North Africa, Spain, Central Asia and Afghanistan established a *de facto* independence. In Iran, burgeoning national sentiment found expression in the Shuʿubiyya (the controversy over the respective merits of the Arab and Persian literary traditions), in heterodox religious movements and in a revival of pre-Islamic Persian culture, notably among the breakaway Tahirid (*reg* AD 821–73), Saffarid (*reg* AD 867–*c*. 1495) and SAMANID dynasties. These tendencies crystallized after 932 with the gradual rise to power of Abu Shuja' Buya and his clan of condottieri from the mountainous area south of the Caspian Sea. He and his three formidable sons masterminded the liberation of western Iran and Iraq from caliphal control. The youngest son, Muʿizz al-Dawla (*reg* AD 936–67), became commander-in-chief of the caliphal armies in 945 and quickly reduced the caliph to the status of a puppet, though his titular authority was maintained. Muʿizz al-Dawla controlled both the army and the state finances, appointed the vizier and chief of police and took the new title *sulṭān* (Arab.: 'power') to indicate his executive role. Subsequent Buyid rulers adopted regnal titles featuring the word *dawla* ('state') and had their names proclaimed in the Friday bidding-prayer (*khuṭba*) and on the coinage, thereby usurping traditional caliphal privileges. Determined to legitimize their rule, they fabricated a genealogy linking themselves to the Sasanians, propagated the Sasanian notion of the divine right of kings, carved their inscriptions at the ancient Persian capital of Persepolis and had their pottery decorated with fire altars and pseudo-Pahlavi inscriptions. As fervent Twelver Shiʿites, they introduced Shiʿite festivals to Baghdad, built special colleges to propagate Shiʿite theology and honoured the burial places of the Shiʿite martyrs. This confessional orientation hastened their downfall at the hands of the GHAZNAVID dynasty and the SALJUQS OF IRAN, orthodox Sunnis of Turkish stock who successively controlled eastern Iran.

To finance their military machine, the Buyids exploited the already extant system whereby, in lieu of pay, army commanders were allotted whatever tax revenues they could mulct from a given territory. This despoiled the land, often made the tax farmer more powerful than the provincial governor and compromised the financial stability of the whole regime. Altogether the Buyid regime underlined the primacy of the army in medieval Iranian politics, opened the way for the growing spiritual authority of the caliphate—and thus the revival of orthodoxy—by accelerating its decline as a temporal institution, inaugurated the recurrent Iranian link between political dominion and Shiʿism and spearheaded the strongest revival of Persian national consciousness since the Arab conquest in the 7th century AD. Thus Iranian culture was definitively emancipated from Arab domination and Iran sundered from the Arab world.

So little of Buyid art has survived that it is difficult to define its nature. In architecture (*see* ISLAMIC ART, §II, 5(i)(a)), the Jurjir Portal and the hypostyle Friday mosques at Isfahan (*see* ISFAHAN, §3(i)) and NA'IN show that, alongside stucco designs that are clearly in thrall to Abbasid Iraqi modes, there had developed a taste for small-scale bricks used in decorative lays on façades, niches and even multifoil columns. In addition the Jurjir Portal displays a remarkably sophisticated spatial sense in its syncopated counterpoint of salients and recesses. The dome chamber of the congregational mosque at NATANZ (999) shows that the *maqṣūra* dome so typical of Saljuq architecture was already known in Buyid times, and the domed square chamber at Qurva (?1013) may offer further evidence on that score. The congregational mosque at Nayriz (?973) is an early example of the iwan mosque and is presumably derived from local Sasanian palace architecture. Buyid inscriptions survive at the congregational mosques of Sava and Ardistan and at Shiraz, Persepolis, Naqsh-i Rustam and Tang-i Buraq. A gigantic 12-sided mausoleum excavated near Rayy fleshes out the admiring reference by the geographer al-Maqdisi (985) to the high domes of the Buyid royal mausolea there. Nothing remains of the 360-room royal palace at Shiraz that he described, and indeed the real character of Buyid architecture remains elusive.

Buyid metalwork (*see* ISLAMIC ART, §IV, 2(ii)), with the occasional exception such as the gold jug with the name of a Buyid amir (Washington, DC, Freer) or the silver wine-set with the name of the amir Valgin (*c*. 1000; Tehran, Archaeol. Mus.), is bedevilled by still unsolved problems of authenticity, dating and provenance. Much of the bronze and silver wares commonly dubbed post-Sasanian and displaying degenerate Sasanian iconography—fabulous beasts, royal audiences and princely hunters—is probably Buyid, but the necessary iconographic and stylistic analysis has yet to be achieved. Medieval texts mention gold presentation medals of prodigious size minted by the Buyids, but the surviving pieces are much smaller. Their iconography includes images of princes seated cross-legged and entertained by musicians, portrait busts of rulers wearing crowns of pseudo-Sasanian type, mounted horsemen, and the ancient royal motif of the lion bringing down a bull. Some bear Pahlavi inscriptions and use the ancient Persian title *shāhanshāh* ('king of kings'). All this indicates a radical departure from the norms of Muslim numismatics. Some architectural elements in carved woodwork (Cairo, Mus. Islam. A. and elsewhere) bear inscriptions of apparently Buyid date (*see* ISLAMIC ART, §VII, 1(ii)).

In ceramics nothing was produced to equal the contemporary Samanid wares of Samarkand and Nishapur, and there was no significant technical breakthrough. The 10th- and 11th-century wares of Sari make up in vigour and colour what they lack in finesse; their painted designs of birds and animals are mere daubs, examples of folk art. Garrus wares employ a debased princely cycle and even legendary themes. The other major Buyid ceramic type, often associated with RAYY, is more elaborate, comprising incised designs clearly derived from metalwork: radiating and interlocking or concentric designs dominate, often with a central zoomorphic motif. It illustrates how aristocratic themes, even if in debased form and humble materials, could infiltrate popular taste. No high-level luxury ceramics can be linked with certainty to the Buyids, though at least in Iraq they probably used lustreware of the Samarra' type.

The most controversial art form associated with the Buyids is textiles (*see* ISLAMIC ART, §VI, 2(i)(b)). Scores of elaborate palls, hangings and garments are purportedly of Buyid origin, although spirited disagreements about their authenticity have continued among scientists and art historians since they first reached the market, in part at least through clandestine excavations at Rayy in the 1920s. A few pieces are widely accepted as genuine, and their iconography not only reveals, as would be expected, strong Sasanian associations but also builds on these to create dynamic new versions of the themes of post-Sasanian metalwork. All in all textiles are revealed as a principal art of the period—closely challenged by Koranic calligraphy. A fragmentary Koran (AD 993; from Isfahan; London, Nour priv. col.), written on paper but using an exceptional horizontal format, provides valuable evidence that the New Abbasid style of calligraphy was practised in Buyid domains (*see* ISLAMIC ART, §III, 2(iii)(a)). The paper manuscript of the Koran (1000–01; Baghdad; Dublin, Chester Beatty Lib., MS. 1431) copied by the renowned master IBN AL-BAWWAB is a bench-mark for the art of cursive calligraphy. The diminutive size of the manuscript cannot dim the well-nigh endlessly varied splendour of its ornamental palmettes, its frontispieces and finispieces conceived like the leaves of doors and structured with a prosperous, recondite rhythm around a theme of exploding interlaced semicircles. The only illustrated manuscript of the period is a copy of al-Sufi's astronomical treatise (1009–10; Baghdad; Oxford, Bodleian Lib., Marsh 144) with drawings of constellation images in a style mixing Central Asian and Abbasid elements (*see* ISLAMIC ART, §III, 4(iii)).

BIBLIOGRAPHY

Enc. Islam/2: 'Buwayhids'

E. Kühnel: 'Die Kunst Persiens unter den Buyiden', *Z. Dt. Mrgländ. Ges.*, cvi (1956), pp. 78–92

E. Kühnel and D. G. Shepherd: 'Buyid Silks', *Proceedings of the IVth International Congress of Iranian Art and Archeology: New York, Philadelphia, Baltimore & Washington DC, 1960*

G. C. Miles: 'A Portrait of the Buyid Prince Rukn al-Dawlah', *Amer. Numi. Soc. Mus. Notes*, xi (1964), pp. 283–93

O. Grabar: 'The Earliest Islamic Commemorative Structures', *A. Orient.*, vi (1966), pp. 7–46

Bull. Liaison Cent. Int. Etud. Textiles Anc., xxxvii (1973) and xxxviii (1973) [two issues devoted to the 'Buyid' silks in the Abegg-Stiftung, Riggisberg]

O. Grabar: 'The Visual Arts', *From the Arab Invasion to the Saljuqs*, ed. R. N. Frye (1975), iv of *The Cambridge History of Iran* (Cambridge, 1968–91), pp. 329–63

R. Hillenbrand: 'Abbasid Mosques in Iran', *Riv. Stud. Orient.*, lix (1985), pp. 175–212

G. D. Lowry: 'On the Gold Jug Ascribed to Abu Mansur al-Amir Bakhtiyar ibn Mu'izz al-Dawla in the Freer Gallery of Art', *A. Orient.*, xix (1989), pp. 103–15

S. S. Blair: *The Monumental Inscriptions of Early Islamic Iran and Transoxiana* (Leiden, 1992)

F. Déroche: *The Abbasid Tradition: Qur'ans of the 8th to the 10th Centuries AD* (1992), i of *The Nasser D. Khalili Collection of Islamic Art*, ed. J. Raby (London and Oxford, 1992–)

S. S. Blair, J. M. Bloom and A. E. Wardwell: 'Reevaluating the Date of the "Buyid" Silks', *A. Orient.*, xxii (1993), pp. 1–42

ROBERT HILLENBRAND

Buys, Cornelis, the elder. *See* MASTERS, ANONYMOUS, AND MONOGRAMMISTS, §I: MASTER OF ALKMAAR.

Buys, Jacobus (*bapt* Amsterdam, 19 Nov 1724; *d* Amsterdam, 7 April 1801). Dutch draughtsman, painter and printmaker. He was the son of a wig-maker. Up to the age of 19 he worked for a solicitor. Both his employer's son and the poet and collector Sybrand Feitama encouraged him to take lessons with Cornelis Pronk and at the Amsterdam Drawing Academy. He studied, among other things, Jacob de Wit's work and, after further training with Cornelis Troost, established himself as an independent artist in 1745, enrolling in Amsterdam's Guild of St Luke in 1750. Initially he made pastel portraits and painted theatre scenery, from 1755 to 1760 living in Mijdrecht. During the 1770s he began to work on book illustration, the field in which he became famous. He illustrated Martinus Stuart's *Romeinse geschiedenissen* ('Roman histories'; 17 vols, Amsterdam, 1793–1810), J. Kok's *Vaderlandsch woordenboek* ('Dictionary of the national language'; 35 vols, Amsterdam, 1785–96) and the work of numerous other Dutch writers. His drawings were engraved by Jan Punt, Reinier Vinkeles and many others. CORNELIS PLOOS VAN AMSTEL, an acquaintance whose family he portrayed (1756; Cape Town, S. Afr. Cult. Hist. Mus.), assembled an enormous collection of his drawings, including copies after Dutch 17th-century masters. Buys was expert at copying drawings and paintings in the style of Ploos's *prenttekeningen* (print-drawings).

In 1768 Buys became a co-director of the city's drawing school, the Amsterdamse Stadstekenacademie, where he gave three lectures on art theory, which were published. His few surviving paintings mostly represent scenes from contemporary plays, done in the style favoured by Dutch 17th-century painters of interiors. His most famous pupils were his son Cornelis Buys (1745–1826) and Egbert van Marum. His paintings, drawings and prints were sold at auction in Amsterdam on 16 February 1802.

WRITINGS

Teekenen naar het naakt en antieke beelden . . . [Drawing from the nude and antique sculpture] (Amsterdam, 1767 and 1769) [pubd lectures]

BIBLIOGRAPHY

Dutch Masterpieces from the Eighteenth Century: Paintings and Drawings, 1700–1800 (exh. cat., ed. E. R. Mandle, with essay by J. W. Niemeijer; Minneapolis, Inst. A.; Toledo, OH, Mus. A.; Philadelphia, Mus. A.; 1971–2), pp. 30–32

L. Buijnsters-Smets: 'Jacobus Buys als boekillustrator', *Docbld Werkgroep 18de Eeuw*, xvi/2 (1984), pp. 91–107

P. KNOLLE

Buys, Jan. *See* BUIJS, JAN.

Buyster, Philippe de (*b* Antwerp, 1595; *d* Paris, 16 March 1688). Flemish sculptor, active in France. He trained in Antwerp as a carver of wooden altarpieces and around 1620 arrived in Paris, where he first found work decorating carriages; at this time he made his first religious sculptures (untraced). In 1622 he was received into the Communauté des Peintres et Sculpteurs, becoming a member of the Académie Royale de Peinture et de Sculpture in 1651. The

Flemish realism of de Buyster's work was modified by exposure to the classicism of Jacques Sarazin, who returned to France from Rome in 1628 and with whom he collaborated extensively. The influence of Sarazin was also probably responsible for the element of Mannerist expression in his work.

Around 1635 de Buyster executed a group of stone, allegorical female statues, characterized by bucolic vigour, for the park of the Château de Wideville (nr Versailles), of which seven survive *in situ*. Between 1639 and 1642 de Buyster carved four classicizing caryatids and a relief of *Fame* based on designs by Sarazin for the right-hand portion of the façade of the Pavillon de l'Horloge of the Louvre, Paris (*see* PARIS, §V, 6), and between 1643 and 1650 he was again one of Sarazin's collaborators on the sculptural decoration of the Château de Maisons, Yvelines, built by François Mansart, where he executed four allegorical groups of naked children full of vigour and cheerful verve on the staircase (stucco; *in situ*). Between 1646 and 1664 he contributed numerous works to the decoration of the church and convent of the Val-de-Grâce, Paris. These include 16 free-standing stone angels 2.13 m tall and 16 candelabras around the dome, as well as the marble Solomonic columns of the baldacchino.

De Buyster also produced several tombs with praying effigies of the deceased. Among them are those of *Madeleine de Crèvecoeur* (marble, 1634; Paris, Louvre) and *Cardinal de La Rochefoucauld* (marble, 1656; Ivry-sur-Seine, Val-de-Marne, hospice), with sumptuous draperies, as well as the recumbent figure of *Bishop Claude de Rueil* (marble, 1650; Angers Cathedral) leaning on one elbow. His last important work, *c*. 1675, was the allegorical statue representing *Satirical Poetry* for the Parterre d'Eau at the Château de Versailles (*in situ*), a marble sculpture 2.13 m tall, which humorously pastiches the Antique.

BIBLIOGRAPHY

G. Brice: *Nouvelle description de la ville de Paris* (Paris, 1752), ii, p. 489; iii, pp. 129, 135, 478
Guillet de Saint-Georges: *Mémoires inédits sur la vie et les ouvrages des membres de l'Académie royale de peinture et de sculpture*, 2 vols (Paris, 1854)
R. Crozet: *La Vie artistique en France au XVIIe siècle* (Paris, 1954)
P. Chaleix: *Philippe de Buyster, sculpteur, 1595–1688* (Paris, 1967)
C. Mignot: 'L'Eglise du Val-de-Grâce: Architecture et décor', *Bull. Soc. Hist. A. Fr.* (1975), pp. 104–8

PIERRE CHALEIX

Buytewech, Willem (Pietersz.) (*b* Rotterdam, 1591–2; *d* Rotterdam, 23 Sept 1624). Dutch painter, draughtsman and etcher. Although he was born and died in Rotterdam, stylistically he belongs to the generation of young artists working in Haarlem at the beginning of the 17th century. He was nicknamed 'Geestige Willem' (Dut.: 'inventive, or witty, Willem') by his contemporaries, and during his short career he made an important and highly personal contribution to the new approach to realism in Dutch art. He was one of the first to paint interiors with merry companies (*see* CONVERSATION PIECE) and is primarily known for his lively and spontaneous drawings and etchings on a wide range of subjects.

1. Life and work. 2. Working methods and technique. 3. Critical reception and posthumous reputation.

1. LIFE AND WORK. The name Buytewech may derive from (Buiten)achterweg ('outer back road'), where Willem's father, the cobbler Pieter Jacobsz., was living on 3 February 1591 when he married Jutgen Willemsdr. Buytewech's earliest work, a signed engraving of the *Flute-player* (1606), carries an inscription that connects it with an inn just outside Rotterdam. In style it shows the influence of the previous generation of Dutch printmakers (Crispijn van de Passe I and Hendrick Goltzius, possibly through the work of Jacob Matham). Buytewech is next mentioned in 1612 when, with Esaias van de Velde (i) and Hercules Segers, he entered the Haarlem Guild of St Luke. Two years later the engraver Jan II van de Velde (i) also became a member. Buytewech remained in close contact with him for the rest of his life, even after returning to Rotterdam in 1617.

On 16 September 1624, in his early thirties, Buytewech—'sick in body'—drew up his will. He died a week later and was buried in Rotterdam's Grote Kerk. After his death his wife, Aaltje Jacobsdr. van Amerongen, whom he had married in Haarlem in 1613, gave birth to Willem Willemsz. Buytewech (*b* Rotterdam, *bapt* 4 Jan 1625; *bur* Rotterdam, between 20 and 26 April 1670), who also became an artist. Six landscape paintings, mostly on panel (London, N.G.), and at least one drawing (*Goats in a Landscape*, 1652; Vienna, Albertina) by him are known. His speciality was Christmas nocturnes with animals (*Karsnagten en beesjes*), according to the painters index (1669–78) made by the Amsterdam city doctor Jan Sysmus (A. Bredius: 'Het schildersregister van Jan Sysmus, stads doctor van Amsterdam', *Oud-Holland*, viii (1890), pp. 1–8; xiii (1895), p. 113), such as the *Annunciation to the Shepherds* (1664; untraced, see Naumann, fig. 5), which is in the style of Benjamin Gerritsz. Cuyp. His landscapes show the influence of Jan Asselijn and Jan Wijnants (e.g. *Dune Landscape*, London, N.G.), under whose names many may still be known.

(i) Drawings. Buytewech's highly praised versatility emerges not only from his use of different techniques but also from his great range of subjects, especially in his drawings: religious and historical scenes, figures, interiors, scenes of everyday life, allegories, groups, architectural features, landscapes, designs for book illustrations etc. Only a few works are dated, making it difficult to establish a chronological and stylistic development, especially as they were produced over such a short period. Thus his oeuvre is usually treated thematically. The *c*. 125 drawings attributed to him include religious scenes with striking contrasts of light and dark (e.g. the *Holy Family*; Amsterdam, Rijksmus.). His sketches of fashionably dressed dandies and young women, some of which often seem almost grotesque (e.g. the *Standing Man*; Hamburg, Ksthalle; Haverkamp-Begemann, 1959, no. 53), are executed with great freedom, giving the impression of drawings from life. The same can be said of the *Sleeping Woman* (Paris, Fond Custodia, Inst. Néer.), a subject rarely depicted at that time. The carefully executed *Interior with a Family by the Fire* (1617; Hamburg, Ksthalle; see fig. 1) also seems to represent an actual scene but was based on

1. Willem Buytewech: *Interior with a Family by the Fire*, pen and brown ink, grey and brown wash, 188×290 mm, 1617 (Hamburg, Hamburger Kunsthalle)

a much sketchier drawing (Berlin, Kupferstichkab.). The many corrections (done by means of overlaid pieces of paper) and altered details demonstrate the contrived nature of the final version. By contrast, Buytewech's drawing of the scene when a sperm whale was stranded on the beach between Scheveningen and Katwijk in January 1617 must have been done on the spot (Berlin, Kupferstichkab.). The same sketchy manner of drawing recurs in the *Anatomy Demonstration at Leiden* (Rotterdam, Boymans–van Beuningen). Two drawings representing a *Fool with Herrings and Sausages round his Neck* (both Paris, Fond Custodia, Inst. Néer.) show familiarity with the work of Frans Hals, as the figure in these drawings was taken from Hals's painting *Shrovetide Revellers* (*c.* 1615; New York, Met.).

Besides the many sketches showing groups of women and children there are a number of precise, detailed drawings intended for prints. Most of these date from Buytewech's period in Rotterdam when he had, apparently, given up making etchings. Among them is a series of designs for regional costumes, first engraved in Haarlem by Gillis van Scheyndel. A carefully worked-out scene of an *Interior with Dancing Couples and Musicians* (Paris, Fond Custodia, Inst. Néer.) served as a preparatory drawing for Cornelis Koning (*fl* 1608–33), another engraver and publisher working in Haarlem. Buytewech also provided designs for the title-pages of two books, Johan Baptist Houwaert's *Den handel der amoureusheyt* ('Amorous trade'; Rotterdam, 1621) and *Alle de spelen* ('The complete plays') by G. A. Bredero (Rotterdam, 1622). Both were engraved by Jan van de Velde. Apart from engraving a number of biblical or religious subjects after designs by Buytewech, van de Velde was also responsible for two series representing the *Four Elements.* Two of the designs for these series survive; one of them, the *Vinkebaan* (shooting and trapping range for small birds; Rotterdam, Boymans–van Beuningen), symbolizes *Air.* The figures are set in a landscape similar to that found near Haarlem. The drawing belongs to a small group in which the subject forms a remarkable unity with the landscape.

A different impression is created by a pair of drawings depicting a wooded landscape by a lake (both London, BM), which are regarded as Buytewech's earliest known landscapes. In these, the influence of Adam Elsheimer (undoubtedly transmitted through the engravings of Hendrick Goudt) is unmistakable. But the drawing of the trees, with their cauliflower-like crowns and twisted branches, is a distinctive and highly personal feature of Buytewech's landscapes, in which the presence of human beings is entirely subordinated to the scenery (further examples, U. London, Courtauld Inst. Gals, Cambridge, Fitzwilliam, and Washington, DC, N.G.A.). Figures are omitted altogether in some drawings of buildings or landscape, for example *Landscape with a Row of Trees* (Berlin, Altes Mus.). In total contrast are the sketchy drawings of easily recognizable motifs in a more spacious setting (e.g. *View of Scheveningen*; Rotterdam, Boymans–van Beuningen).

(ii) Etchings. Buytewech's most original contribution to Dutch landscape imagery is his series of ten etchings (including the title-page) of *Various Little Landscapes* (*c.* 1616; Hollstein, nos 35–44). Made immediately after those of Esaias and Jan van de Velde (1612 and 1615), it exemplifies his new and highly personal interpretation of the landscape. Three of the nine sheets show a ruin; in the remaining six, trees are the main motif, their twisted trunks rhythmically rendered and their branches fanning out at the top (see fig. 2).

In all, 32 prints by Buytewech are known. They were presumably made in Haarlem between 1612 and 1617 and are almost all pure etchings. Three prints with religious subjects are included among the early works; two of these, *Cain and Abel* (Hollstein, no. 1) and *St Francis* (Hollstein, no. 9), are copies after, respectively, Peter Paul Rubens and John Matham. Two of the three etchings of *Bathsheba* (*c.* 1615–16; Hollstein, nos 2–4) also demonstrate Buytewech's familiarity with Rubens's work. As with the drawings of biblical subjects, these prints show strong contrasts of lighting, particularly evident in the dramatic image of *Bathsheba Reading David's Letter* (*c.* 1616; Hollstein, no. 4). A comparable dynamic treatment can be found in *Lucelle and Ascagnes* (Hollstein, no. 17), which was intended as an illustration for Bredero's translation (1616) of François-Louis Le Jars's play *Lucelle* (Paris, 1576). In both prints the underlying theme is that of *vanitas.* The etchings of stranded sperm whales (1614, 1617; Hollstein, nos 14, 13) have also been given a moralizing interpretation, since the incidents were regarded by contemporaries as bad omens or punishment for sin; but Buytewech's purpose would seem to have been mainly documentary. In the print of 1614 are the same elegantly dressed figures as in the series of *Seven Noblemen* (Hollstein, nos 21–7), which represents young noblemen of seven nationalities. These are Buytewech's most personal etchings. The lively manner in which the modish figures are depicted was unmatched in his time.

(iii) Paintings. Figures are also the subjects of all of Buytewech's paintings. His oeuvre is presently thought to comprise ten paintings, previously attributed to Frans or Dirck Hals. They are neither signed nor dated, but the costumes and stylistic parallels with his graphic work suggest that they were painted in the last years of his life, between 1616 and 1624. Although he borrowed subjects from Frans Hals (as in his *Merry Company in the Open Air*, *c.* 1616–17; Berlin, priv. col., on loan to Berlin, Gemäldegal.), he developed a genre of his own in four depictions of merry companies in interiors. In three of these paintings, fashionably dressed young men and women are set in a room, the main motif of which is a map on the back wall (Rotterdam, Boymans–van Beuningen; The Hague, Mus. Bredius; Budapest, Mus. F.A.). The activities portrayed, such as smoking, drinking and card playing, symbolized worldly pleasure, giving these pictures a moralizing message. Erotic allusions such as rosebuds, a fountain and a cobweb occur in the *Formal Courtship* (*c.* 1616–17; Amsterdam, Rijksmus.). A striking feature is the balanced, almost classical composition in which the exaggeratedly stylish figures are represented. In contrast to the apparent freedom with which he drew figures and their settings, his paintings are obviously contrived. The stiff appearance of the figures, which often seem large for the space, suggests that he used lay figures.

2. Willem Buytewech: *The Charcoal-burner*, etching, 89×125 mm, 1616 (London, British Museum)

2. Working methods and technique. The majority of Willem Buytewech's drawings are executed in pen and ink. The religious scenes have strong lines and broadly washed areas in graduated tones. Pen sketches, apparently drawn from life, are often reworked with a fine brush. The designs for his prints are carefully executed compositions in pen and brush, often in combination with black chalk, a medium he sometimes used on its own, for example in the *Surgeon* and the *Bleeding* (both 1616; Haarlem, Teylers Mus.). He used red chalk only occasionally. The group of landscape drawings without figures shows highly original handling: small loops and circles drawn with a pen to represent foliage, as found in Hercules Segers's etchings.

Buytewech's own etchings, which were initially executed with a mixed technique, display an exceptionally supple line. With Esaias van de Velde he was one of the first to use the etching needle alone, in a manner not suggestive of the burin. His use of pointillé next to heavy shadows and the combination of swelling lines and short, sharp hooks, lend great variety.

Buytewech's paintings on canvas show a remarkably thin use of paint, and the colours are clearly separated from each other. In comparison with Dirck Hals, his painting technique is crisper, and his figures look rather linear. His paintings lack the lively highlights so characteristic of Hals's work.

3. Critical reception and posthumous reputation. From an early date Buytewech's drawings and etchings and the prints made after his work were regarded as collectors' items. They are mentioned in Rembrandt's estate inventory of 1656 ('A ditto [book] full of prints by Frans Floris, Buijtewech, Goltseus, and Abraham Bloemer') and Jan van de Capelle's inventory of 1680 ('A ditto [portfolio] with 86 drawings by Willem Buijtewech' and 'a ditto [portfolio] with 161 sketches by Buijtewech and Gout'). The auction (14 May 1736) of the collection of

Samuel van Huls (1655–1734), burgomaster of The Hague, included no less than 120 drawings by 'Geestige Willem'. The Delft collector Valerius Röver found the *Interior with a Family by the Fire* 'so far removed (*'buiten de weg'*) from the usual manner of drawing that I cannot think of anything like it'.

Little is said about Buytewech in early art-historical literature. Apart from Orlers's account of Jan Lievens, who made drawings in 1618 after 'prints of Geestighe Willem', the next reference is by Houbraken (1719), who described him as a painter of 'companies of young ladies, gentlemen and peasants'. After this the artist and his work seem to have been forgotten. His paintings were attributed to other artists, while his drawings and prints were dispersed in various collections. The 'rediscovery' of Buytewech at the beginning of the 20th century led to various publications (e.g. Goldschmidt, Martin and the catalogue raisonné of the etchings by van Gelder). Haverkamp-Begemann's catalogue of the complete works (1959) is now regarded as the standard reference work on 'Geestige Willem'.

BIBLIOGRAPHY

Hollstein: *Dut. & Flem.*, iv, pp. 53–77
J. Orlers: *Beschrijvinge der stadt Leyden...* (Leiden, 1641), p. 376
A. Houbraken: *De groote schouburgh* (1718–21), ii, p. 90
A. Goldschmidt: 'Willem Buytewech', *Jb. Kön.-Preuss. Kstsamml.*, xxiii (1902), pp. 100–17
W. Martin: 'Hoe schilderde Willem Buytewech', *Oud-Holland*, xxxiv (1916), pp. 197–203
L. Burchard: *Die holländischen Radierer vor Rembrandt* (Berlin, 1917), pp. 52–9
G. Poensgen: 'Beiträge zur Kunst des Willem Buytewech', *Jb. Kön.-Preuss. Kstsamml.*, xlvii (1926), pp. 87–102
G. Knuttel Wzn: 'Willem Buytewech', *Meded. Dienst Kst & Wetsch. Gemeente 's-Gravenhage*, iv (1928), pp. 116–24
——: 'Willem Buytewech: Van manierisme tot naturalisme', *Meded. Dienst Kst & Wetsch. Gemeente 's-Gravenhage*, v–vi (1928), pp. 181–98
J. G. van Gelder: 'De etsen van Willem Buytewech', *Oud-Holland*, xlviii (1931), pp. 49–72
E. Haverkamp-Begemann: *Willem Buytewech* (Amsterdam, 1959)
J. S. Kunstreich: *Der geistreiche Willem: Studien zur Willem Buytewech, 1591–1624* (Cologne, 1959)
E. Haverkamp-Begemann: 'The Etchings of Willem Buytewech', *Prints*, ed. C. Zigrosser (New York, 1962), pp. 55–81
Willem Buytewech, 1591–1624 (exh. cat. by J. Giltay and others; intro. E. Haverkamp-Begemann; Rotterdam, Boymans–van Beuningen; Paris, Inst. Néer., 1974–5) [excellent plates of almost all the graphic work by and after Buytewech]
O. Naumann: 'Willem Buytewech the Younger', *Essays in Northern Art Presented to Egbert Haverkamp-Begemann*, ed. A. M. Logan (Doornspijk, 1983), pp. 194–8
J. A. Welu: 'The Maps of Willem Buytewech', *Hoogsteder-Naumann Mercury*, v (1987), pp. 21–8
Dawn of the Golden Age (exh. cat., ed. G. Luijten and others; Amsterdam, Rijksmus., 1993–4)

MARIA VAN BERGE-GERBAUD

Buyuklijski, Dimitar [Mitchy] (*b* Sofia, 7 Sept 1943). Bulgarian painter. From 1958 to 1962 he studied at the High School for Arts and in 1969 graduated from the National Academy of Arts (Natsionalna Hudozhestvena Academia) in Sofia, specializing in painting. His work is characterized by a careful, classical sense of composition and a clear ordering of space. The underlying geometric order, reminiscent of the work of Cézanne, is offset by warm, vibrant colours and gentle, rhythmic lines that describe figures and volumes. Brushstrokes are smoothly and carefully applied. All his subjects appear initially similar, although subtle differences become evident after several moments' viewing. The solid, lithe bodies of his figures are filled with an inner tension. Buyuklijski's paintings are collected in the National Art Gallery, Sofia, and in many collections internationally.

BIBLIOGRAPHY

Natsionalna Hudozhestvena Galeriya [National Art Gallery], cat. (Sofia, 1980)

JULIANA NEDEVA-WEGENER

Buza, Abdurrahim (*b* Üsküb [now Skopje], 22 Dec 1905; *d* Tiranë, 7 Nov 1986). Albanian painter and draughtsman. He began his studies in painting at the Accademia Albertina di Belle Arti in Turin in 1928, and he continued his artistic training at the Accademia di Belle Arti in Florence (1929–33). After his return to Albania he worked as a teacher of drawing in the State Gymnasium of Tiranë. His works of the 1930s are in a loose, impressionist style, with broad brushstrokes and bright colours, and are imbued with the tense spirit of the War of National Liberation. His drawings of this period depict the unemployed, the poor, refugees and orphans, and there is even an aura of desperation in such works as *Self-portrait* (oil on canvas, 300×400 mm, 1934; Tiranë, A.G.) and in some of his numerous landscapes. After the war, however, Buza discovered a new optimism. He taught at the Jordan Misja Arts Lyceum in Tiranë (1946–66) and produced many of his best works at this time, tackling such themes as the right of the Albanian people to self-determination and producing works that celebrated the dramatic reconstruction of Albania in the aftermath of World War II, such as *Volunteer Workers* (oil on canvas, 660×480 mm, 1948; Tiranë, A.G.). He continued to treat historical subjects in such later works as the *Convention of the Albanian League of Prizren* (oil on canvas, 590×400 mm, 1978; Tiranë, A.G.). He was fascinated by life in the countryside and the people, scenery and customs of the Kosovo region. Many of his later canvases have a single monochrome background upon which Buza experimented with traditional Albanian patterns and shapes, while his drawings (e.g. portrait of *Sulejman Vokshi*; pen and black ink, 1978; Tiranë, A.G.) are characterized by their studious, precise line and dynamic, expressive and psychologically eloquent outline.

For illustration *see* ALBANIA, fig. 3.

UNPUBLISHED SOURCES

Tiranë, A.G. (MSS)

BIBLIOGRAPHY

H. Bani: 'Lufta kunder rrethimit armik në një tablo' [The battle against the encirclement of enemies in painting], *Drita* (10 Sept 1978), p. 7
Abdurrahim Buza piktor i popullit [Abdurrahim Buza people's painter] (exh. cat., Tiranë, A.G., 1980)
'Me frymë të thellë realiste e kombëtare' [With deep realistic and national spirit], *Drita* (31 Aug 1980), p. 11

GJERGJ FRASHËRI

Buzas, Stefan. *See under* CUBITT, JAMES.

Buzzi. Italian family of marble masons and sculptors. From the 16th century until 1772 the family workshop in Viggiù provided marble masons and sculptors who worked at the Fabbrica del Duomo in Milan. (1) Elia Vincenzo Buzzi was active in the workshop of his brother Giuseppe Maria Buzzi, a marble mason, whose son (2) Giuseppe Buzzi he strongly influenced.

(1) Elia Vincenzo Buzzi (*b* Viggiù, nr Varese, 1704; *d* Viggiù, 1780). Sculptor. He began his apprenticeship under Carlo Beretta (1716–64), and later worked with Carlo Francesco Mellone (*d* 1736), both of whom were *protostatuari*, or directors of sculpture, for the Fabbrica del Duomo in Milan. In 1728 Buzzi began working as a sculptor in the Camposanto sculpture yard, after producing a successful test-piece *bozzetto* in terracotta of *Diana Awakened by Endymion* (Milan, Mus. Duomo). The high professional quality of Buzzi's work, and his marked sensitivity to the poetry of the Roman Baroque—introduced to Milan by Mellone—won him a series of commissions. At first Buzzi carried on his activity in the workshop of his brother Giuseppe Maria, who was also active in the cathedral as a marble mason. Elia Vincenzo did not open his own workshop until 1741, on the death of the sculptor F. Zarabatta. He was also active in other workshops, including those at the Milanese churches of S Maria alla Porta (1740), S Vittore (1755) and S Giuseppe (1763). In 1753 he rose to the rank of *protostatuario*, the most prestigious position in the Fabbrica del Duomo. For the rest of his career Buzzi continued to produce important statuary both for the outside and for the interior of Milan Cathedral. By the end of his career the Neo-classical aesthetic had already taken precedence over the Rococo sensibility that had been so masterfully interpreted and transmitted by Buzzi. As *protostatuario* he played an important role in training young sculptors in his bottega and in the Fabbrica del Duomo.

BIBLIOGRAPHY

G. Ferri Piccaluga: 'Elia Vincenzo Buzzi', *Commentari*, xviii (1967), pp. 207–24

(2) Giuseppe Buzzi (*fl* 1791–1835). Sculptor, nephew of (1) Elia Vincenzo Buzzi. His mature production was marked by his 'provincial' training in the family workshops and in particular by his uncle's Rococo style, as well as by his own later activity in Milan Cathedral. In 1791 he designed and executed the marble main altar in the church of S Maria di Campagna at Piacenza. From 1792 he was active at the Fabbrica del Duomo in Milan. The statues that he produced there were particularly numerous after a decree issued by the Emperor Napoleon in 1805 forced the administration to complete the cathedral's façade and its sculptural decoration in a very short time. The stylistic heterogeneity that characterizes Buzzi's whole production reflects his uncertainty at a time when Milanese sculpture was dominated by the conflicting styles of the Rococo and Neo-classicism. At times Buzzi followed a Neo-classical aesthetic, as in the statues of *St John the Evangelist* and *St James the Less* (both 1812), designed by Camillo Pacetti for the cathedral. However, he was still tied to the reigning traditions of Rococo grace and Lombard verism, as can be seen in the statues of *St Severinus* or *St Secundus* (1824) and *St Sylvia* (1825), also for the cathedral. His numerous works there are also interesting as examples of the iconographic choices made by the Council of the Fabbrica in those years.

BIBLIOGRAPHY

DBI
An. Fabbrica Duomo, vi (Milan, 1885), pp. 113–97, 223–6, app. no. ii, p. 231
U. Nebbia: *La scultura nel Duomo di Milano* (Milan, 1908)
R. Bossaglia: 'La scultura', *Il Duomo di Milano* (Milan, 1973), pp. 65–176

GABRIELLA FERRI PICCALUGA

Buzzi, Carlo (*b* ?1608; *d* Milan, 23 Sept 1658). Italian architect. He should not be confused with the painter of the same name, who was the son of Lelio Buzzi. He was an exponent of the Milanese Baroque style of Galeazzo Alessi and Francesco Maria Ricchini, although he strongly supported the continuation of Gothic forms at Milan Cathedral, of which he was architect between 1638 and 1658. The late date for the earliest work on the building (1385) meant that Gothic design had continued into the Renaissance, and controversy raged between 'Classicists' and 'Goths' over the correct way to finish it. Buzzi made several designs for the façade in a conservative Gothic style, based on the existing side elevations but incorporating the Renaissance window details already constructed. One of these projects was accepted, but a strongly argued preference expressed by Gianlorenzo Bernini (1656) for an alternative scheme by Francesco Castelli in a Gothicized classical style brought work to a standstill. The façade was ultimately completed (1806–13) to one of Buzzi's designs (slightly modified) on the orders of Napoleon.

Buzzi worked extensively in and around Milan. His extant works include the octagonal nucleus (1641), later significantly altered, of the sanctuary of S Maria del Bosco, Imbersago; a new campanile (1643) for S Stefano Maggiore, Milan; the reconstruction (1645) of the Scuole Palatine, Piazza dei Mercanti, with an ornate façade consisting of a rusticated upper storey resting on an arcade of paired columns in imitation of the nearby Palazzo dei Giureconsulti (1558–68) by Vincenzo Seregni; and the nave, campanile and façade of S Ambrogio (1648; unfinished), Merate, in severe Roman style.

BIBLIOGRAPHY

L. Grassi: *Province del Barocco e del Rococo* (Milan, 1966)
R. Wittkower: *Gothic versus Classic* (London, 1974)
A. M. Buratti, ed.: *Milano nel settecento* (Milan, 1976)

□

Buzzi, Lelio (*b* Viggiù, nr Varese, 1553; *d* ?1608). Italian architect. He worked first as an assistant to Pellegrino Tibaldi but came under the influence of Francesco Maria Ricchini. From 1569 he worked in several capacities at the cathedral in Milan, where he also started work on the Biblioteca Ambrosiana. He was a member of the Collegio degli Ingegneri e Architetti di Milano from 1590 to 1608. Buzzi was appointed Master of Works of the cathedral in 1591 and served as acting architect between 1593 and 1603. A design (*c.* 1603; Milan, Mus. Duomo) for the main façade has been attributed to him (Wittkower). It is highly ornate, articulated by clusters of engaged columns, but poorly organized: a projecting wall, perforated with niches, appears to support the portico, a device misused from Ricchino's proposal of 1603. Other buildings outside Milan on which Buzzi worked as a Master of Works included the Collegio Borromeo (begun 1585), Pavia; the façade (1596) of the Sanctuary, Soronno, in collaboration with Giacomo Borroni, to the design of Tibaldi; the

Palazzo Nuovo, Bergamo (*c.* 1600) by Vincenzo Scamozzi; and Brescia Cathedral (*c.* 1603) by Giovanni Battista Lantana (1581–1627). Buzzi started work for Cardinal Federico Borromeo, Archbishop of Milan, in 1602; the following year he started work in the Biblioteca Ambrosiana. Only the vestibule and reading-room were executed; the latter (26 m×13.6 m) was barrel-vaulted in the Roman manner, which was considered very modern. It was completed by Fabio Mangone (1587–1629) after 1608 and was subsequently radically altered.

BIBLIOGRAPHY

DBI
V. Ingegnoli: 'Origini dell'Ambrosiana: Lelio Buzzi e Fabio Mangone', *A. Lombarda*, x (1965), pp. 103–6
L. Grassi: *Province del Barocco e del Rococo* (Milan, 1966)
R. Wittkower: *Gothic versus Classic* (London, 1974)
A. M. Buratti, ed.: *Milano nel settecento* (Milan, 1976)

ZILAH QUEZADO DECKKER

Bwa and Gurunsi. Group of Voltaic-speaking peoples living in Burkina Faso and Mali. There has been much confusion in literature about the identity of these peoples and the relations between them. They are discussed together in this entry because of the similarity of their art forms. Ideally, however, their traditions should be discussed separately and the pseudo-ethnonym 'Gurunsi' abandoned.

1. Introduction. 2. Masks and masquerades. 3. Figure sculpture and divination instruments.

1. INTRODUCTION. The Gurunsi, who live between the Red Volta and Black Volta rivers in the centre of the country, are the most prolific and influential sculptors in Burkina Faso. They have also heavily influenced the mask traditions of their neighbours to the west, the southern Bwa, who carve the largest wooden masks in Black Africa.

The name 'Gurunsi' is a pejorative name applied by the neighbouring Mossi to a number of peoples who call themselves Nunuma, Nuna, Winiama, Lela, Sisala and Kasena and who together number *c.* 200,000. Their lands are sparsely inhabited, with large areas of dry, uncultivated bush separating small villages. Their major crops are millet, sorghum and maize. Their political systems are very democratic, with all decisions made by a council of male elders, in contrast to the stratified, centralized kingship system of the Mossi. Most Gurunsi retain no traditions of immigration into the area and claim to be the first inhabitants of the land. The Nunama, Nuna, Lela and Winiama carve masks, figures, furniture, musical instruments and jewellery. Both figures and masks are covered with geometric patterns in red, white, and black pigments.

In addition to the difficulty surrounding the name 'Gurunsi' further confusion has arisen from the practice of early French ethnographers of referring to the Bwa as 'Bobo' or 'Bobo-Oulé', with the implication that they are related to the Bobo-Fing or Bobo. The term 'Bobo-Oulé' is a Jula name for the Bwa.

There are *c.* 300,000 Bwa in total, with 125,000 in Mali and 175,000 in Burkina Faso. They speak Bwamu, a Voltaic language with numerous local dialects. The neighbours of the Bwa are the Bobo to the west, the Bamana to the north, the Marka Dafing to the east, and the Gurunsi and Lobi to the south. The territory of the Bwa extends from the banks of the Bani River in Mali in the north almost to Diébougou and the Ghana-Burkina Faso border in the south. Bwa country is made up of two major zones of occupation: the northern stretching from the Bani River to the city of Nouna; and the southern from Dédougou and Solenzo to Houndé in the south.

The Bwa are farmers and consider farming to be the most noble of occupations. Most work in the fields is done by men, although women help out occasionally during planting and some harvests, and by carrying harvested crops to the village. The Bwa grow cotton, grains, root crops, ground peas and peanuts. The annual gathering by the women of wild crops contributes substantially to their diet. Like the Gurunsi the Bwa live in independent villages devoid of central political authority. All decisions are made by a council of the male elders of the local lineages, and all external authority is strongly resisted. The independence and authority of the lineages are submerged to the good of the community.

2. MASKS AND MASQUERADES. While there is some stylistic variation in Gurunsi masks, overall there is a degree of homogeneity. Masks represent spirits in the forms of animals from the bush, humans, or in monstrous agglomerations of human, animal and supernatural forms. Many masks have a short, rectangular plank that supports human figures or is itself supported by a large human figure. Downward-curving hooks protrude from the front and back of the plank, and the eyes are surrounded by red, white and black concentric circles, sometimes known as the 'Upper Volta target motif'. Geometric patterns carved in low relief include triangles, rectangles, crescents, circles, concentric circles and parallel lines, painted red, white and black. Red pigment is made from ground haematite, black is a vegetable extract made by boiling the seed pods of the acacia, and white is made from lizard excrement found concentrated in burrows and mixed with a binder of gum Arabic.

Gurunsi masks can be distinguished from those of their Bwa neighbours by a system of lines that radiate from the eyes of the masks, like the petals of a flower; these do not appear in the Bwa style. Bwa masks are also larger than Gurunsi masks and tend to be less complex in composition, with fewer geometric patterns. Otherwise the styles are quite similar, because the Bwa have acquired wooden masks from the Nunuma and Nuna.

The Bwa are receptive to change and quick to adopt institutions they admire from their neighbours. In the late 19th century they decided that the magic of their Nuna neighbours, especially their control of spirits through carved wooden masks, was more powerful than the magic of their own masks of leaves and vines dedicated to the cult of Do. By purchase, theft and outright copying from their eastern neighbours, the southern Bwa, especially in the villages of Boni, Dossi, Bagassi and Pa, between 1870 and 1900 acquired the right to carve wooden masks. They also incorporated the spirits that these masks represented into their own cults or carved other masks to represent new spirits they encountered in the bush surrounding their villages.

The spirits that control the lives and well-being of the Gurunsi and Bwa take many forms. They may appear as animal or human or may take no recognizable natural shape. Animal characters include Lalo, the bush buffalo, Kan, the antelope, Basi, the fish, Doho, the serpent, and many others. The serpent mask in the village of Pa is over six metres tall. Plank masks half a metre wide and two metres tall called Nwantantay (see fig. 1) or Wama represent flying spirits associated with the pools of fresh water that remain after the first rains of spring. Plank masks are carved according to two basic patterns. Most consist of a large, flat, oval facial area with a protuberant round mouth (see fig. 2) through which the masker can see. Below the mouth are three black leaf shapes (triangles), and above are two great target eyes. The face is connected to the plank above by a diamond or lozenge, from which protrudes a downward-curving and very prominent hook. The plank is a large, vertical rectangle marked with geometric patterns in black and white, and occasionally red. This is, in turn, surmounted by a large crescent opening upward. The second major plank type has a diamond-shaped mouth, and the large plank is bisected horizontally by openwork triangles half-way up the plank, effectively forming two smaller planks.

All plank masks are covered with geometric patterns, especially chequerboards and large crosses. Both the Bwa and the Nuna call the patterns scars, and these have the same meanings as have the scars applied to the human body at an early age. The patterns and their meanings are part of esoteric initiatory language that is first taught at the earliest stages of initiation, and in which both men and women gain further knowledge with increasing age. For example, the black-and-white squares of the chequerboard represent the separation of knowledge from innocence, the black squares representing the old, soiled hides on which the wise elders sit, and the white squares the clean white hides on which the new initiates sit during mask performances and sacrifices. Aspects of the mask form itself also have meanings. For example, the hook that protrudes from the joint between the plank and face of the mask represents the beak of the hornbill, a bird associated with magic, divination and witchcraft.

Masks play key roles in initiation in both Bwa and Gurunsi villages. Initiates are told the secrets of the mask cult, are taught how to make the fibre costumes that cover the maskers' bodies and are given instruction in the secret initiatory languages, including an analysis of the moral messages communicated by the patterns that cover each mask. Initiation sometimes includes a form of combat between the boys and a mask and often ends with celebratory performances attended by the entire community in which each boy wears a mask. Before initiation children are considered to be under the control of the spirits of the bush, but as initiated adults they submit to the rules for proper behaviour in the village.

Among the southern Bwa wooden masks are a tradition from between 1870 and 1900. In many families this has replaced the ancient cult of Do, the son of the creator God, a spirit of the wild bush and of the vital energy of nature who is represented by masks of leaves and vines. Traditionally, at least, leaf masks appeared in all Bwa villages in the spring, when they participated in rites of renewal called Loponu. These celebrations are held just before the first steady rains, when the fields are cleared

1. Nwantantay plank mask at a village purification ceremony in the Bwa town of Boni; from a photograph by Christopher D. Roy, 1984

and planted. Groups of young men go into the bush to cut wild grasses, vines and leaves. The body of the masker is wrapped in a spiral covering of vines, then small bundles of green leaves are bound to this structure. The head is covered by a sagittal crest. In northern areas this may include a disc-shaped crest of thick grasses, while in southern areas it may include dozens of white feathers (*see* AFRICA, fig. 124). The maskers are assembled before dawn and they enter the village from the east with the rising sun. They dance and participate in sacrifices throughout the day and leave the village towards the setting sun. The mask costumes are then secretly cut up and burnt.

There is much friction and conflict, even fighting, between the clans that continue the old leaf-mask traditions and the cult of Do and the clans that have adopted the wooden masks. In many villages, notably Dossi and Bagassi, clans using each type live side by side. Those who have continued to honour Do with leaf masks look on the adoption of wooden masks as heretical and as

2. Winiama plank masks at a New Year purification ceremony in Ouri, a village in central Burkina Faso; from a photograph by Christopher D. Roy, 1985

an attempt to wrest religious authority from its traditional source, the local earth-priest. Clans that have adopted wooden masks and magic from their Winiama and Nuna or Nunuma neighbours are aggressive and proselytizing. In their songs accompanying the performances of wooden masks they insult the clans that persist in using leaf masks, referring to them as dirty and ignorant savages.

3. Figure sculpture and divination instruments. While wooden masks are both numerous and highly visible in Bwa and Gurunsi villages, figure sculpture is numerous but much less visible. Figures are kept hidden in homes, on family altars or on the shrines of diviners. Like masks, wooden figures represent spirits that men encounter in the wild bush, far from cultivated fields. The most powerful and dangerous spirits appear to men who possess special skill as manipulators or users of supernatural forces. These men are greatly feared in their communities because they can use their powers both to help their clients and to harm their enemies. Each diviner may possess one or several spirits that he or his male ancestors encountered in the bush, and that are embodied in magical objects. These objects may be simple balls of sacrificial materials, concoctions of clay, animal and plant parts, such manmade objects as bottles or iron or stone blades, canes of various shapes bearing carved figures, or they may be figures of wood or brass. All such objects are kept hidden in the diviner's home. In many cases large areas of the figures are covered with thick accumulations of sacrificial and magical material that feeds the spirit embodied in the figure. The sacrificial materials and bits of animal parts used in the magical bundles give them a sickening stench. A diviner's equipment may also include long wooden staves, bearing midway up the staff naturalistic human figures that represent spirits. During the divination process, the client and the diviner may together grasp the handle of a smaller hook-shaped staff or wand that bears a carved figure at the angle of the handle and hook. Such staffs are tapped against the ground as the diviner chants, in a secret language, the spirit's response to the client's questions.

Among the Bwa diviners also use carved wooden figures as well as figures modelled in clay, although fully carved anthropomorphic figures are much less common among the Bwa than among the Gurunsi. They place the figures on shrines that embody protective bush spirits. The supernatural power of these spirits can be manipulated by the diviner for his clients' benefit. Brass or copper bracelets with a pair of small spirit figures standing together and projecting upwards from the bracelet are essential tools of the Bwa diviner. These are placed next to the larger carved or modelled figures during consultations with the spirits.

Among the Bwa, both free-standing figures and figures carved on canes are used in fertility rites. For example, a large wooden figure from the village of Boni bears low-relief geometric patterns on the head, shoulders and arms; these are also painted red, white and black. The figure is of a female and is used in annual sacrifices of purification of the village and consecration of masks. The figure is a symbol of fertility, bestowing good harvests and healthy children. Infertile women offer sacrifices to ask for children. Accompanied by the large wooden masks, the figure is carried from compound to compound once a year, blessing each in turn.

BIBLIOGRAPHY

J. Cremer: *Les Bobo: La Vie sociale* (Paris, 1924)

——: *Les Bobo: La Mentalité mystique* (Paris, 1927)

J. Capron: 'Quelques notes sur la société du Do chez les populations bwa du Cercle de San', *J. Soc. Africanistes*, xxvii/1 (1957), pp. 81–129

G. Manessy: *Tâches quotidiennes et travaux saisonniers en pays bwa*, Publications de la Section de Langues et Littératures, Faculté des Lettres et Sciences Humaines, Université de Dakar, 5 (Dakar, 1960)

J. Capron: 'Univers religieux et cohésion interne dans les communautés villageoises *bwa* traditionnelles', *Africa*, xxxii/2 (1962), pp. 132–71

M. Fortes and others: *Colloque sur les cultures voltaïques*, Recherches voltaïques, 8 (Paris and Ouagadougou, 1967)

H. Haselberger: 'Bemerkungen zum Kunsthandwerk in der Republik Haute Volta: Gourounsi und Altvölker des äussersten Südwestens', *Z. Ethnol.*, xciv/2 (1969), pp. 171–246

J. Capron: *Communautés villageoises bwa: Mali, Haute-Volta* (Paris, 1973)

G. Pallier: *Géographie générale de la Haute-Volta* (Limoges, 1978, rev. 1981)

A.-M. Duperray: *Les Gourounsi de Haute-Volta* (Stuttgart, 1984)

Oumarou Nao: *Masques et société chez les Nouna de Zawara* (MA thesis, U. Ouagadougou, 1984)

Art and Life in Africa: Selections from the Stanley Collection (exh. cat. by C. D. Roy, Iowa City, U. IA Mus. A., 1985)

C. D. Roy: *The Art of the Upper Volta Rivers* (Meudon, 1987)

CHRISTOPHER D. ROY

Byam Shaw. *See* SHAW, BYAM.

Byblos [anc. Gebal, Gabla; now Gebeil, Jbeil]. Ancient city built on a low cliff (h. 24 m) on the Mediterranean coast *c.* 40 km north of Beirut, Lebanon. Founded in the 6th millennium BC as a fishing village, it later developed into a cosmopolitan centre where trade and various industries flourished. During the 3rd and 2nd millennia BC it was the foremost harbour town in the eastern Mediterranean. The Phoenician alphabet was developed there (*see* ANCIENT NEAR EAST, §I, 3.). The word 'Bible' is derived from the Greeks' name for the city whence they obtained the parchment (Gr. *biblos*) from which they made books (*biblia*). The site was excavated from 1921 onwards by Pierre Montet (until 1924) and Maurice Dunand. Most of the finds were deposited in the Musée National in Beirut.

1. ARCHITECTURE. The flimsy houses of the Neolithic and Chalcolithic periods (6th–4th millennia BC) consisted of one big room, rounded or oval for the earlier period, rectangular or apsidal for the later. In the Early Bronze Age (*c.* 3000–*c.* 2000 BC) a system of construction was devised that shows great elasticity and resistance to earthquakes. Byblos is situated in an area famous for its tall conifers (cedars of Lebanon), and stone was also readily available; thick, low stone walls served as stylobates for a timber framework reinforced by wooden posts placed on stone bases, and an axial row of wooden columns supported the roof. The most characteristic house consisted of a set of rooms on either side of a long hall, a ground-plan that continued in use throughout Lebanon until modern times. There is evidence that during the 2nd millennium BC buildings were at least two storeys high, the ground-floor being used for storage, while the upper floor was reserved for residential purposes. It is probable that houses in later periods also consisted of several storeys.

The major temple of the city, the Baalat-Gebal, was built in the mid-3rd millennium BC on three terraces that sloped from north to south. The eastern entrance consisted of a double gateway with piers on either side, leading to the central cella. The southern entrance was connected to an open porch by a long ramp. The cornice of the temple and the frieze of sacred uraei (cobras) were borrowed directly from Egypt, but contrary to Egyptian arrangement (where the frieze of sacred uraei was always set above the cornice), the Byblite architect chose to carve the frieze within the curve of the cornice. Similar architectonic elements were still to be found in the Roman period.

Towards the end of the 3rd millennium BC Byblos was destroyed but quickly rebuilt with sacred architecture mainly of the MEGARON type, with the altar facing east. These megara were either square or of the long-room type, and both were present in Temple XIV of the Obelisk complex, dating to the Middle Bronze Age (*c.* 2000–*c.* 1500 BC). They were preceded by columns set *in antis* or by a low porch wall, and they may have been the antecedents of Greek temples: Temple XIV is very similar to the Hellenistic triple-shrined temple at OLD PAPHOS in Cyprus, although they are separated by 2000 years. At the beginning of the 2nd millennium BC, hypaethral sanctuaries with standing stone columns or obelisks were introduced alongside the megaron-style temple.

Unfortunately, Late Bronze Age and Phoenician architecture is absent from Byblos, but information can be gleaned from texts. It was probably at the beginning of the Late Bronze Age (*c.* 1500 BC) that metal started to play an important role in the decoration of sacred architecture. In a letter to Pharaoh Akhenaten (*reg c.* 1353–*c.* 1336 BC), Rib-Addi, a prince of Byblos, stated '. . .there is much silver and gold (in the city);. . .in its temple, there is much wealth'. About 450 BC Yehaw-Milk had the following inscribed on a stele: '. . .I made for my lady Baalat-Gebal a bronze altar, which is in the court,. . .a golden door, facing my door, (and) surmounted by a lintel with a golden disc in the middle. . .and this portico and columns topped by capitals. . .'. This description seems to fit the temple depicted on a Roman coin (see fig.) of Emperor Macrinus (*reg* AD 217–18). This representation is of special interest because it shows the fusion of Byblite temple styles that had appeared throughout the city's long history: the two main entrances perpendicular to each other, the portico or the passage *in antis* (features of the Byblite megara), the open-air sanctuary with a baetyl in the middle, and Egyptian architectonic elements. Four Egyptianizing stone colossi were discovered flanking the passage *in antis* that led to the cella of the Roman Baalat-Gebal temple, but it is believed that the colossi are much earlier; according to Benjamin of Tudela (*c.* AD 1200), they were covered with gold leaf.

Roman Byblos had a second important temple superimposed on the Middle Bronze Age Obelisk complex. It had a tripartite arrangement, the antecedents of which had appeared in the megara of the late 3rd millennium BC. The nympheum has elegant niches for statues. It was connected by a stairway with the theatre, which was modelled according to Greek principles of design and was originally built above the main gate of the 3rd millennium BC. (The theatre was moved so that the gate (24×4 m) could be excavated. The gate was paved with flagstones, equipped with a portcullis and may have been vaulted.) A narrow road paved with flagstones led to a huge basilica built over the Early Bronze Age fortifications. In the north-west

Byblos, bronze coin of Emperor Macrinus struck from an engraved die of a temple, diam. 30 mm, early 3rd century AD (London, British Museum)

sector of the city, Roman baths were built above the Bronze Age royal necropolis. Roman Byblos was surrounded by a colonnade.

In AD 551 an earthquake ruined the coastal cities of Phoenicia. Later the crusaders used the temples and colonnades as quarries, and granite columns were laid horizontally as binders in their constructions. The church of St John was built in the Romanesque style *c.* 1215, and there is a crusader castle that lies south-west of the Roman nympheum.

2. METALWORK AND SCULPTURE. The first stone and clay idols of the 6th millennium BC are crude. By the 4th millennium BC, however, copper, silver, gold, bone and ivory products display skill and evidence of foreign contacts; for example, a bone statuette of a woman has affinities with the Beersheba bone and ivory industries of southern Palestine. A bone idol in the shape of a violin is a splendid abstraction of the fertility goddess.

During the Early Bronze Age, stags' heads were incised on copper ceremonial daggers that were found in the cella of the Baalat-Gebal temple. Byblos was open to different cultures because its seafarers traded to all parts of the ancient world. Its craftsmen responded to foreign stimuli and incorporated new motifs into their local traditions, resulting in masterpieces in gold marked by delicate use of filigree and granulation. This is especially evident on the shafts of gold fenestrated axes (2nd millennium BC). They excelled also in relief work on metal; other techniques, such as cloisonné, were of Egyptian origin, but polychromy in metal (niello) seems to have been a local invention. It can best be seen on a bronze scimitar of the Middle Bronze Age, the mid-rib of which, represented by a sacred uraeus, was inlaid with gold wire, and hieroglyphic inscriptions were applied in gold and silver. Gold leaf was used to cover mass-produced bronze votive figurines and other works of art.

Ivories from the shaft grave of King Ahiram (*reg c.* 1000 BC) date to the 13th century BC. One represents a crested griffin attacking a bull (Paris, Louvre), the other is a disc incised with confronted leaping griffins. King Ahiram's sarcophagus may have dated to the 13th century BC, although Porada has argued that it was not reused but was carved in the 9th century BC. The reliefs on it show a local tradition of mourning the dead with women tearing their hair, beating their bare breasts and wailing, while the dead king sits on a throne protected by winged sphinxes. In front of him is a table laden with food probably associated with the Egyptian funerary feast; a procession of men approach the King and lift their hands in worship. Egyptian influence is also seen in the lotus frieze above the scene. Four crudely carved lions support the sarcophagus, and on the lid the King and his son appear in their local costumes, the space between them filled with two elongated lions. The inscription naming Ahiram is the earliest datable example in the Phoenician alphabet. From the port of Byblos the alphabet spread to Greece and beyond, and it is the source of modern Western alphabets.

BIBLIOGRAPHY

R. Dussaud: 'Le Sanctuaire phénicien de Byblos d'après Benjamin de Tudèle', *Syria*, vii (1927), pp. 247–56
——: 'Note additionnelle aux rapports de MM. Dunand et Pillet', *Syria*, viii (1928), pp. 113–25
P. Montet: *Byblos et l'Egypte*, 2 vols (Paris, 1928–9)
M. Dunand: *Fouilles de Byblos*, 5 vols (Paris, 1937–73)
H. Frankfort: *The Art and Architecture of the Ancient Orient*, Pelican Hist. A. (Harmondsworth, 1954, rev. 4/1970)
D. Harden: *The Phoenicians* (London, 1963, 2/1971)
W. F. Albright: 'Further Light on the History of Middle Bronze Byblos', *Bull. Amer. Sch. Orient. Res.*, clxxix (1965), pp. 38–43
W. Culican: *The First Merchant Venturers: The Ancient Levant in History and Commerce* (London, 1966)
O. Tufnell and W. A. Ward: 'Relations between Byblos, Egypt and Mesopotamia at the End of the Third Millennium BC: A Study of the Montet Jar', *Syria*, xliii (1966), pp. 165–241
K. A. Kitchen: 'Byblos, Egypt and Mari in the Early Second Millennium BC', *Orientalia*, n. s., xxxvi (1967)
M. Durand: *Byblos: Son Histoire, ses ruines, ses légendes* (Paris, 1968)
N. Jidejian: *Byblos through the Ages* (Beirut, 1968)
P. Cintas: *Manuel d'archéologie punique*, i (Paris, 1970)
E. Porada: 'Notes on the Sarcophagus of Ahiram', *J. Anc. Nr E. Soc.*, v (1973), pp. 355–72
A. Parrot, M. H. Chéhab and S. Moscati: *Les Phéniciens: L'Expansion phénicienne. Carthage*, A. Mankind (Paris, 1975)
A. I. Baumgarten: *The Phoenician History of Philo of Byblos* (Leiden, 1981)
U. Finkbeiner: 'Untersuchungen zur Stratigraphie des Obelisken Tempels in Byblos', *Baghdad. Mitt.*, xii (1981)
M. Saghieh: *Byblos in the Third Millennium BC* (Warminster, 1983)

MUNTAHA SAGHIE

Byelorussia [Byelarus']. *See* BELARUS'.

Bykovsky. Russian family of architects.

(1) Mikhail (Dorimedontovich) [Dormidontovich] **Bykovsky** (*b* Moscow, 10 Nov 1801; *d* Moscow, 21 Nov 1885). He studied under Domenico Gillardi from 1816 and in the 1820s worked as his assistant on the Golitsyn family estates of Grebnevo and Kus'minki and the Volkonsky family estate, Sukhanovo (all Moscow region). His first independent commissions were also mansion house and park ensembles, most notably for the Panin family, first (late 1820s, early 1830s) at Dugino (Smolensk prov.)

and then (1831–46) at Marfino (Moscow prov.). Conceived in the spirit of Romanticism, these accorded with the local geography and the personality of the landowner. At Marfino, his masterpiece, Bykovsky redesigned and rebuilt the existing house, its wings, the winter and summer churches, and the bridge over the lake. The latter, with its complex interplay of Russian and Italian medieval forms, was a key element in the picturesque effect of the ensemble. He also built from new a landing-stage, with an ornate pair of monumental griffins, and a cattle-yard. The appearance of most of the buildings was transformed in the course of this synthesis of the existing, Neo-classical plans with Gothic Revival detailing, and the result rivalled Edward Blore's Alupka Palace (1833–7), Crimea, and Adam Menelas's Aleksandriya Park ensemble (1832–6), Peterhof, as the most important achievement of the Russian Gothic Revival. Bykovsky's eclectic approach allowed him to incorporate elements derived from early Victorian mansion houses in England, with borrowings from Tuscan architecture of the 14th and 15th centuries (the latter alluding to the legendary origins of the Panin (Panini) family) in his design for the main façade.

Bykovsky's work as an architect demonstrated the theory he expounded at the Moscow Imperial Architectural Institute, where he was a lecturer from 1828 and became director in 1836. His published speech of 1834 expressed his reservations concerning the suitability of Classical architecture as a universal model and called for the creation of a new school of Russian architecture, which he sought to establish through the combination of historical sources and new house types. He proposed the rehabilitation of other styles, in particular the Gothic, but as free, eclectic interpretation rather than straight imitation of the past.

In the late 1830s, however, as Moscow's chief architect (since 1830) and following his travels through western Europe (1838–9), Bykovsky moved away from his championship of Gothic Revival. This was first evident in the Golitsyn Arcade (1835–42; destr.), Moscow, with its shops and theatre. Roofed in glass, this, in Bykovsky's words, was 'a grandiose bazaar building with a theatre resembling the Palais Royal'. Its remarkably light and airy interior, created in late Neo-classical style, was the first example of a new era of rationalism in Russian architecture. His other Moscow buildings built on similar principles included the Stock Exchange (1836–9; reconstructed 1873–5 by A. S. Kaminsky (1829–97)), Il'inka Lane, and the Gorikhvostov Refuge House (1839) in the Khamovniki quarter. He also utilized the forms of the Italian Renaissance, notably in the Loris-Melikov house in Milyutin Lane, Moscow, and the Vonlyarlyarsky house on Blagoveshchensky Bridge, St Petersburg (both 1850s). Eclecticism dominated his ecclesiastical architecture in Moscow, and his fusion of Renaissance, Romanesque and Byzantine forms can be found in the walls and bell-tower of the Strastnoy monastery (1848–55); the buildings of the Ivanovsky monastery (1861–78); and the bell-tower of the Nikitsky monastery (1868; destr.). His bell-towers were built on a grand scale, returning them to their traditional domination of surrounding buildings and community. His churches in Moscow included the church of Nikita the Martyr 'in Old Tolmachakh' (1858) in Kuznetskaya Street and the church of the Trinity on the Mire (1868) in Pokrovka Street. Of particular significance was his reconstruction of Moscow's Petrovsky Park complex, with its theatre, circus, coffee and tea houses, amusement pavilions and 'Vauxhall' concert hall (destr.). The latter was an enormous Neo-classical structure with a dance-hall and auditorium that could seat over 1000 spectators.

In 1844 Bykovsky reorganized the art class at the Moscow Arts Society, which subsequently (1865) became the Moscow Institute of Painting, Sculpture and Architecture. He was also the founder and first chairman of the Moscow Architectural Society (1867–9).

WRITINGS

Rech' o neosnovatel'nosti mneniya, chto arkhitektura grecheskaya ili grekorimskaya mozhet byt' vseobshchuyu i chto krasota arkhitektury osnovyvaetsya na pyati izvestnykh chinopolozheniyakh [Speech on the groundlessness of the opinion that Greek or Greco-Roman architecture must be universal and that the beauty of architecture is based on five famous orders] (Moscow, 1834)

BIBLIOGRAPHY

N. Khomutetsky: 'Vydayushchiysya russkiy zodchiy M. D. Bykovskiy (1801–1885)', *Arkhitekturnaya praktika i istoriya arkhitektury: Sbornik nauchnykh trudov Leningradskogo inzhenerno-stroitel'nogo instituta* [Architectural practice and the history of architecture: collected scientific papers of the Leningrad Engineering and Construction Institute], xxi (1958), pp. 135–44

Y. Kirichenko: *Mikhail Bykovsky* (Moscow, 1990)

JEREMY HOWARD, SERGEY KUZNETSOV

(2) Konstantin (Mikhaylovich) Bykovsky (*b* Moscow, 3 April 1841; *d* Moscow, 3 Oct 1906). Son of (1) Mikhail Bykovsky. He studied at the Moscow School of Painting, Sculpture and Architecture (1859) and at the St Petersburg Academy of Arts (1859–66) under Nikolay Benois; he then worked (1866–8) as Benois's assistant before becoming his father's assistant (1868–70). In 1880 he was granted the title of academician and in 1893 was made professor of architecture. For two extended periods (1870–81, 1895–1906) he taught architecture and the history of art at the Moscow School of Painting, Sculpture and Architecture and at various times also taught in the School of Fine Arts and the Stroganov School of Technical Drawing. He helped organize the section concerned with the history of Russian architecture in the Polytechnical Exhibition (1872) in Moscow and as chairman (1893–1900) of the Moscow Society of Art Lovers helped organize the first congress of artists (1894) in Moscow, held to mark the donation (1893) to the city of Moscow of the gallery of Russian art collected by the Tret'yakov brothers (now the Tret'yakov State Gallery). Between 1882 and 1906 Bykovsky was vice-president of the Committee for the Preservation of Ancient Monuments of the Moscow Archaeological Society, taking part in all its major restoration and specialist work. He also served as chairman of the Moscow Architectural Society (1894–7, 1904–5).

In his work Bykovsky emphasized his belief that artistic forms are the result of a reinterpretation of the design and utilitarian principle of a structure in accordance with the laws of beauty. He saw the main achievements of 19th-century architecture as being the development of new design and constructional systems, democracy, humanity and the satisfaction of broad social requirements, contrasting them with imitativeness or empty eclecticism, what he called an 'architectural masquerade'. Feeling that the reasons for the disastrous position of architecture lay in the absence of a unifying idea and in the mould of contemporary life, he nevertheless rejected the aspirations of radicals, who were inspired by 'a preconceived idea of originality'. His policy was to meet the spiritual and material needs of contemporary existence through the strength derived from modern progress in scientific knowledge and the assimilation of past constructional experience.

As architect to Moscow University, Bykovsky worked mainly on designing large public buildings and complexes. The Moscow University clinics at Maiden's Field, or Devich'ye Pole (1885–99), in their time the best in Europe, are an impressive ensemble in terms of their size and imposing appearance on a site 1.5 km long. Their construction marked the beginning of the development of a large region on the outskirts of Moscow. More than 15 buildings were freely arranged on the site. Concern for creating the best conditions for medical health and teaching was combined with a concern to create a significant group of buildings: most expressive and ceremonial is the side of the complex facing the street, which presents a mature, solemn, symmetrical composition. The university library (1901), the botanical and zoological blocks and the Zoological Museum (1902), the lecture block (1904) and the teachers' building were located in direct proximity to the old university buildings, intensifying the classical order of the latter, which date from the beginning of the 19th century; the Physiology Institute and the laboratory block were built in the middle of the site. One example of the ceremonial public buildings in Moscow designed in the solemn forms of the Italian Renaissance is the State Bank building (1890–94) on Neglinnaya, with a large main courtyard in front of the main façade. The Ol'ginskaya Hospital (1886; now the Khludovskaya Children's Hospital) on Pervaya Meshchanskaya Street (now Prospect Mira) and the university students' residence (1897) on Bol'shaya Gruzinskaya Street were also built to his designs. Stylistically Bykovsky was a Renaissance Revivalist, drawing mainly on 16th-century Italian models, principally the work of the Sangallos, Sansovino and Vincenzo Scamozzi.

WRITINGS

'O znachenii izucheniya drevnikh pamyatnikov dlya sovremennogo zodchestva' [Concerning the importance for modern architecture of studying ancient monuments], *Trudy pervogo s'yezda russkikh zodchikh v Moskve: Moscow, 1896* [Transactions of the first congress of Russian architects in Moscow: Moscow, 1896]

'Zadachi arkhitektury XIX veka' [The problems of 19th-century architecture], *Trudy II c'yezda russkikh zodchikh v Moskve: Moscow, 1899* [Transactions of the II congress of Russian architects in Moscow: Moscow, 1899]

BIBLIOGRAPHY

A. Novitsky: 'Pamyati K. M. Bykovskogo' [In memory of K. M. Bykovsky], *Zapiski Moskov. Arkhit. Obshchestva*, i/3 (1905–6)

N. V. Nekrasov: 'Nekotoryye dannyye o deyatel'nosti K. M. Bykovskogo' [Details of the work of K. M. Bykovsky], *Drevnosti*, i (1907)

YE. I. KIRICHENKO

Bylert, Jan van. *See* BIJLERT, JAN VAN.

Bylivert. *See* BIJLIVERT.

Byōdōin [Asahiyama]. Japanese Buddhist temple in the city of Uji, *c.* 18 km south of Kyoto. It occupies 1.65 ha of woodland along the western bank of the River Uji. Its 'mountain name' (*sangō*) and identifier prefix is Asahiyama.

1. INTRODUCTION. Byōdōin is an independent temple affiliated with the Jōdo (Pure land) school of the Tendai sect of Esoteric BUDDHISM and has been in operation since the late Heian period (AD 794–1185). Its principal building, the *Amidadō* or hall for the worship of Amida (Skt Amitābha), is called the Hōōdō (Phoenix Hall; see fig.) and is widely recognized as exemplifying the type of religious art commissioned by the Heian period aristocracy, who were profoundly affected by the popularization of the Jōdo belief and praxis in conjunction with extended emphasis on the Lotus sutra (Jap. *Hokkekyō* or *Myōhō renge kyō*) as a salvational vehicle.

Uji has long been noted for its picturesque setting on the river. From at least the late Nara period (710–94) it also served as an important trade stop between Yamato and Yamashiro provinces (now Kyoto Prefect.). By the 9th century Uji had been developed as a 'resort' for the villas (*sansō*) of the nobility, most notably the Fujiwara family (*see* FUJIWARA (ii)). After the regency of Fujiwara no Michinaga (966–1028), Uji became the nearly exclusive holding of the Sekkanke ('House of the regents and chancellors to the throne'), the most powerful of the several Fujiwara lineages.

Michinaga's son Yorimichi (990–1074) inherited his family's villa at Uji *c.* 1027. In 1052 he converted it into a temple, which he named Byōdōin and used as his private grounds for meditation and prayer. Historical sources indicate that a *hondō* ('main hall') and the resplendent Hōōdō had been completed by early 1053. A *Hokkedō* (hall for meditations on the *Hokkekyō*) was built in 1056. In 1061 Yorimichi's daughter Kanshi (1036–1121), wife of Emperor Reizei (*reg* 1045–68), sponsored a *tahōtō* (two-storey pagoda with pent roofs on the first floor and a drum covering the second) that enshrined figures of the *Five Wisdom Buddhas* (*Gochi Nyorai*) by Kakujo. In 1066 Yorimichi commissioned a *Godaidō* (hall for the worship of the Go Daimyōō or Five Great Kings of the True Word; Skt Vidyārāja), and by 1073 a *kyōzō* (*sūtra* repository) had been constructed, and Minamoto no Morofusa (?1005–77) had dedicated a *Fudōdō* (hall for the worship of Fudō; Skt Acalanātha) for Yorimichi.

Although Byōdōin was maintained by the Sekkanke well into the 12th century, it was severely damaged during the Taira–Minamoto wars (1177–81). During the Kamakura period (1185–1333) Byōdōin declined into a minor regional temple. In 1335, with the exception of Hōōdō and a 13th-century *Kannondō* or hall for the worship of Kannon (Skt Avalokiteshvara), Byōdōin was destroyed by fire. The current temple consists of the original Hōōdō and *Kannondō* and a group of late 20th-century restorations of earlier halls.

2. HŌŌDŌ ('PHOENIX HALL'). This building is an unusual construction as a Buddhist hall. It consists of a central chapel (*chūdō*), to which are attached L-shaped, turreted wings (*yokurō*) on its north and south sides, and a straight, covered corridor, the *birō* ('tail corridor'), which extends directly west from its western side. The building is on an island in a large artificial pond surrounded by gardens. It opens on the eastern side, over the pond, and the corner segments of its two wings also face east. Because the layout of the structure suggests a bird with

Byōdōin, Hōōdō (Phoenix Hall), completed by 1053; view from the north

wings and tail outspread—perhaps a mythical phoenix—many believe that the name derives from the hall's shape. However, most scholars now hold that the name Hōōdō probably originated during restorations in the Edo period (1600–1868), when two new gilt-bronze finials, each in the form of a phoenix, were affixed to the hall's roof.

(i) Architecture and decoration. The hall's central chapel of 3×2 bays is built in the hip-and-gable roof construction style (*irimoya zukuri*), with tile roofing and a surrounding *mokoshi* (lean-to pent roof construction). Each of the two wings is five bays long and three bays deep and is in the gabled-roof construction style (*kirizuma zukuri*), with tile roofing. The two-storey turret over each wing corner is in the pyramidal-roof construction style (*hōgyō zukuri*), also with tile roofing. The *birō* measures seven bays in length and one bay in depth and is built in the gabled-roof mode, with tile roofing. Important architectural features at the Hōōdō include three-stepped bracket complexes, circular base rafters and squared flying rafters in the chapel; chamfering in the pillars, bracket complexes and rafters of the *mokoshi*; and a foundation paved with squared stone slabs. Originally the hall's exterior was painted brightly in cinnabar, yellow ochre and white, with the doors of the main façade lacquered in vermilion; some of this polychrome has been restored.

The interior of the central chapel preserves the hall's original opulence to a significant degree. The *honzon* (principal object of worship), a gilt-wood sculpture (h. 2.8 m) of *Amida* by the master sculptor Jōchō, is situated on a central dais inlaid with floral motifs in mother-of-pearl. A gilt-wood ritual canopy with elaborate, peony-like, floral designs called *hōsōge* ('Buddha-visage flowers') in intricate *sukashibori* (openwork carving) is suspended above the canopy. The lower walls and the doors surrounding the *honzon* are decorated with a series of paintings illustrating the teachings of the *Kanmuryōjukyō* ('Visualization Sutra'). The upper walls are mounted with wood-relief figures called the *Unchū Kuyō Bosatsu* ('Worshipful *bodhisattvas* on clouds'), which were probably sculpted to complement the chapel's paradise scenes. The pillars, bracketing and ceiling of the chapel were originally decorated in contrasting shades of vermilion and ultramarine, highlighted with gold.

(ii) Interpretation and context. Aside from its technical and stylistic sophistication, the Hōōdō is significant because it was clearly conceived to provide an inspired symbolic articulation of Amida enthroned in his Western Paradise (Jap. Gokuraku; Skt Sukhāvatī). Many scholars suggest that Jōchō was responsible for this design. Jōchō and apprentices from his Kyoto studio worked in close cooperation with Yorimichi and priestly advisers. The organization of the hall is based on a learned reading of Buddhist

scripture, specifically on the descriptions of paradise in the *Muryōjukyō* (Skt [Larger] *Sukhāvatīvyūha*) and the *Kanmuryōjukyō*. It is also a three-dimensional extrapolation from the paradisal theme as presented in Jōdo *maṇḍalas* (called *hensōzu*, 'pictorial transfigurations'), which depict various notions of Amida's world realm. The principal example of this genre is the Nara period *Taima Maṇḍala* at the temple of Taimadera in Nara prefecture. The unusual layout and construction of the Hōōdō, although clearly related to the architecture of the Heian period Daigokuden ('Great audience hall') at the Heian Daidairi ('Palace compound'; *see* KYOTO, §I), are reminiscent of portrayals of Amida's palace in the *Taima Maṇḍala* and other Buddhist paintings.

As a symbolic presentation of Amida in heaven, and again in faithful observance of the core teaching of the *Kanmuryōjukyō*, the Hōōdō marks the creation of an environment well suited to meditation on Amida and his paradise as described in Jōdo scripture. Thus the building is perhaps the key late Heian period example of the extended role assigned to the visual arts in Jōdo belief and practice, particularly in the form of contemplation called *kansō nenbutsu* (Buddha ideation through chanting and visualization). It also serves to underscore the high level of aestheticism inherent in much of Jōdo scripture, with its emphasis on the sublime beauty of Amida and paradise (*see also* JAPAN, §II, 3). Furthermore the extravagance of the hall reflects the belief, developed most conclusively among the courtiers and prelates of the Heian period aristocracy, that temples and their art works function as 'good works' or 'virtue' (*kudoku*) in a salvational scheme predicated on the accumulation of merit as a means to paradise.

It must be emphasized that Byōdōin differs fundamentally from the vast contemporary shrine–temple complexes, such as ENRYAKUJI and KONGŌBUJI, whose monastic communities set the intellectual and spiritual direction of mainstream Heian period Buddhist culture. Rather, it belongs to a class of privately commissioned temples, whose sponsors and patrons built them in accordance with a highly aestheticized understanding of scripture and used them as halls for their individualized religious exercise. Not surprisingly, many such temples, Byōdōin included, were also the residences of their sponsors or had been converted from earlier villas or detached halls. Thus the Hōōdō is also recognized as an important example of the influence on Buddhist architecture of contemporary aristocratic residences, known as *shinden zukuri* (sleeping-hall construction; *see* JAPAN, §III, 3(iii)).

BIBLIOGRAPHY

T. Fukuyama: 'Byōdōin to Chūsonji', *Nihon no bijutsu* [Arts of Japan], ix (Tokyo, 1964); Eng. trans. by R. K. Jones as *Heian Temples: Byodo-in and Chuson-ji*, Heibonsha Surv. Jap. A., ix (New York and Tokyo, 1976)

K. Suzuki: 'Todai no jiin kenchiku' [Early Buddhist architecture], *Nihon no bijutsu* [Arts of Japan], lxvi (1971); Eng. trans. by M. N. Parent and N. S. Steinhardt as *Early Buddhist Architecture*, Japanese Arts Library, ix (New York and Tokyo, 1980)

S. Murayama: *Jōdokyō geijutsu to Mida shinkō* [Amida worship and the arts of Pure Land Buddhism] (Tokyo, 1977)

K. Mizuno, ed.: 'Daibusshi Jōchō' [The Buddhist master sculptor Jōchō], *Nihon no bijutsu* [Arts of Japan], clxiv (1980)

H. Ōta, K. Suzuki, T. Fukuyama and T. Akiyama, eds: *Byōdōin taikan*, 3 vols (Tokyo, 1987–92)

H. Shimizu: *Heian jidai bukkyō kenchikushī no kenkyū* [Research on Buddhist architects of the Heian period] (Tokyo, 1992)

MIMI HALL YIENGPRUKSAWAN

Byrd [Bird]**, William** (*b* Gloucester, *bapt* 1 June 1624; *d* ?1690). English sculptor and architect. Byrd served an eight-year apprenticeship to Walter Nicholls, a mason of Gloucester. About the year 1647 he moved to Oxford, where he discovered a process for painting and staining marble (1658) and made the ornamental centrepiece for the fountain in the Great ('Tom') Quadrangle at Christ Church (1670; removed 1695; destr.). He claimed to have worked on 'several noble buildings' in different counties but most of those with which he can be specifically associated are in Oxford. By 1656 he had been appointed mason at Wadham College, and from 1666 to 1669 he supplied the ornamental carving for Wren's Sheldonian Theatre, including the 14 'Emperors' heads' which adorn the screen on the street front (now recut). He stated that he built the chapel of St Edmund Hall (1680–85/6), and he also designed and partly built the Garden Quadrangle at New College (1682–5) according to a plan that was probably influenced by Wren's design for the palace of Charles II at Winchester, of which Byrd undertook to erect most of the south wing in 1683.

Byrd also made church monuments; they are generally competent, but unmistakably provincial. *Bishop Brideoake* is represented by a Baroque reclining effigy (*c.* 1678; Windsor, Berks, St George's Chapel), while the Fettiplace memorial (*c.* 1686; Swinbrook, Oxon, St Mary) was clearly designed to match an earlier monument in the church to members of the same family, with three reclining effigies, one above the other.

BIBLIOGRAPHY

Colvin; Gunnis

J. C. Cole: 'William Byrd, Stonecutter and Mason', *Oxoniensia*, xiv (1949), pp. 63–74

ADAM WHITE

Byres, James (*b* Tonley, Aberdeenshire [now Grampian], 1734; *d* Tonley, Sept 1817). Scottish antiquarian, dealer and architect, active in Italy. As the son of a Catholic Jacobite laird obliged to flee in the aftermath of the rebellion of 1745 he was educated in France. After returning briefly to Britain, he decided to travel to Rome to study painting, where he became a pupil of Anton Raphael Mengs. Richard Hayward, in his list of artists visiting Rome (London, BM), and Robert Strange both gave 1758 as the date of his arrival, but there is evidence to suggest he was in Rome by 1756 (Ford, p. 447). Deciding that his talents lay elsewhere, he turned to architecture, in 1762 causing interest in Britain by winning a prize in the Concorso Clementino at the Accademia di S Luca, Rome, with a design for a palace in the rather heavy late Baroque style characteristic of Ferdinando Fuga and Luigi Vanvitelli. Byres never established a practice, though he designed a series of buildings for British visitors to Rome, none of which was executed. He was elected to the Accademia di S Luca in 1768. By 1763/4 Byres had decided to become an antiquarian and cicerone, and for the next quarter of a century he was regarded as the principal antiquarian to British visitors to Rome, featuring prominently in the diaries of many Grand Tourists. In

1764 he spent several weeks guiding the historian Edward Gibbon and in 1770, for example, he was closely involved in assisting Charles Burney in his researches on ancient musical instruments. Byres's exhaustive courses could last up to six weeks, and he was regarded as expensive.

Parallel to these activities Byres was active as a dealer. One of his greatest coups was the purchase in 1785 of the first series of the *Seven Sacraments* by Nicolas Poussin from the Bonapaduli collection, which he then sold to Charles Manners, 4th Duke of Rutland. But it is as a dealer in antiquities that he is best remembered. Byres did not compete with his rival Thomas Jenkins as a dealer in large and expensive marble statues, but specialized in coins, gems, bronzes and Etruscan vases, which brought him into contact with such scholarly collectors as Charles Townley, Cracherode and Richard Payne Knight, to all of whom he sold regularly. He is also known to have supplied coins to Charles Watson-Wentworth, 2nd Marquess of Rockingham, and gems to Catherine II, Empress of Russia.

Byres's scholarly interests were serious and wide-ranging. In 1766 he undertook an extensive journey in southern Italy and Sicily in the company of a member of the Wilbraham family, probably Roger Wilbraham, of which he kept a diary (Edinburgh, N. Lib.). He developed a pioneering interest in the Etruscan sites at Tarquinia, and while one reason for this was the acquisition of items for sale, he also took care to record the tombs he saw. In 1767 he tried unsuccessfully to publish his work on the Etruscan antiquities of Corneto, with plates engraved by his friend and business partner Christopher Norton, but he failed to find enough support; it finally appeared posthumously in 1842 under the title *Hypogaei.* His most memorable purchase, *c.* 1780, was the celebrated cameo-glass vase from the Palazzo Barberini, Rome, the Portland Vase (London, BM; *see* GLASS, fig. 5), which he sold to Sir William Hamilton, who in turn sold it to Margaret Bentinck, Duchess of Portland, in 1784. Like Jenkins, Byres took a strong interest in young British artists, to whom he regularly offered hospitality and whose works he promoted. In 1790 Byres left Rome permanently and thereafter lived in quiet retirement in Scotland on the family estate at Tonley.

UNPUBLISHED SOURCES

Edinburgh, N. Lib., MS. 4448 [diary, 1766]

WRITINGS

Hypogaei or Sepulchral Caverns of Tarquinia (London, 1842) [pubd posthumously]

BIBLIOGRAPHY

Colvin

B. Skinner: *Scots in Italy in the 18th Century* (Edinburgh, 1966), pp. 16–17

B. Ford: 'James Byres: Principal Antiquarian for the English Visitors to Rome', *Apollo*, xcix (1974), pp. 446–61

GERARD VAUGHAN

Byrne, (Francis) Barry (*b* Chicago, IL, 19 Dec 1892; *d* Chicago, 17 Dec 1967). American architect. He was apprenticed to Frank Lloyd Wright from 1902 to 1909, then spent a year in Seattle, WA. During a brief period in 1913 in California, he met the sculptor Alfonso Ianelli (1888–1965), who later provided ornament for several of Byrne's buildings. Byrne took over Walter Burley Griffin's American practice from 1913 to 1922, after the latter's departure to Australia. Later he founded his own building company (1922–9) and a small practice in Wilmette, IL (1930–32). From 1932 until his return to Chicago in 1945 he had an office in New York, where in addition to practising architecture he published articles and reviews on architectural aesthetics and church design.

Byrne's secular work shows his individual synthesis of the PRAIRIE SCHOOL, Expressionism and Modernism in libraries, schools and private dwellings, notably the Kenna Apartments, 2214 East 69th Street (1916), Chicago, where the brick is used in a planar way, and Immaculata High School, Irving Park Road and Marine Drive (1922), Chicago, with its special attention to the edges where the masonry planes join. Byrne's churches are particularly expressive of his architectural ideas. By integrating the nave and sanctuary spaces he devised new spatial environments to express the liturgical reform movement in the Roman Catholic Church, anticipating by 40 years the changes that followed the Vatican II Councils of the 1960s. The church of St Thomas the Apostle at 55th and Kimbark (1922), Chicago, is the beginning of this development, which continued in the church of Christ the King (Tulsa, OK, 1926) and in a concrete church also called Christ the King (Cork, Ireland, 1929).

In his later churches in the USA Byrne showed a continuing sensitivity to light and colour as well as to space, giving architectural expression to the ideas of peace and fulfilment that he felt were appropriate to the spiritual expression embodied in the Mass.

WRITINGS

'Plan for a Church', *Liturg. A.*, x (May 1942)
'On Training for Architecture', *Liturg. A.*, xiii (May 1945)
'This Modernism', *Liturg. A.*, xix (Feb 1951)
'From These Roots', *Amer. Benedictine Rev.*, ii (Summer 1951)

BIBLIOGRAPHY

S. A. Kitt Chappell: *Barry Byrne: Architecture and Writings* (diss., Evanston, Northwestern U., 1968; microfilm, Ann Arbor, 1969)

S. A. Kitt Chappell and A. Van Zanten: *Barry Byrne and John Lloyd Wright: Architecture and Design* (Chicago, 1982) [incl. a select bibliog. of articles and reviews by Byrne]

SALLY A. KITT CHAPPELL

Byrne, Patrick (*b* 1783; *d* Dublin, 10 Jan 1864). Irish architect. He was deeply influenced by his training in the Schools of the Dublin Society under Henry Aaron Baker. He made some elegant watercolour perspectives (e.g. *Trinity College and the Portus of the House of Lords*, 1819; Dublin, N.G.) of James Gandon's Dublin work in 1818 and 1819. Byrne is best known for the churches he designed for the Catholic archdiocese of Dublin from 1830, in which the stylistic and religious pressures of the time are well illustrated. His earliest works are classical, on a T plan, with clear spacious interiors. St Paul's (begun 1835), Dublin, has an Ionic portico surmounted by a bell tower with a cupola. Inside, the east end is given focus by use of a Doric screen. St Audoen's (begun 1841), Dublin, is even grander, with a sumptuous interior articulated by Corinthian pilasters. Byrne turned to the Gothic Revival style, however, for the church of St John the Baptist (1842), Blackrock, Co. Dublin, influenced by A. W. N. Pugin's articles in the *Dublin Review* (1841). On the whole he preferred later Perpendicular forms and deviated from Pugin's principles in his use of plaster for pretty Gothic vaults and moulded decoration. From then on all his churches were Gothic Revival, except for Our Lady of Refuge (1850), Rathmines, Dublin, and the Three Patrons (1860), Rathgar, Dublin, where the parish priest insisted on classical buildings. Byrne was a man of genial disposition, popular with his colleagues. Professionally successful, he was a member of the Royal Institute of Architects of Ireland and one of its three vice-presidents from 1852 until his death. He became a Royal Hibernian Academician in 1860.

BIBLIOGRAPHY

Obituary, *Irish Bldr*, v (1864), p. 9
C. P. Curran: 'Patrick Byrne: Architect', *Stud.: Irish Q. Rev. Lett., Philos. & Sci.*, xxxiii (1944), pp. 193–203
P. Raftery: 'The Last of the Traditionalists: Patrick Byrne (1783–1864)', *Bull. Irish Georg. Soc.*, vii/2–4 (1964), pp. 48–67

JEANNE SHEEHY

Byron, Robert (*b* London, 26 Feb 1905; *d* off Stornaway, 24 Feb 1941). British writer and traveller. His travels in Greece in 1925–7 resulted in two books, *The Station* and *The Byzantine Achievement*, in which he presented readers brought up on the culture of Classical antiquity with a novel view of the importance of the civilization of Byzantium and the seminal influence of its art on the later development of European painting. In *The Birth of Western Painting* he developed this line of thought with a reassessment of El Greco as the 'last and greatest flower of Byzantine genius'. His best-known book is *The Road to Oxiana*, a record of travels through Persia and Afghanistan in 1933–4 in search of the origins of Islamic architecture and culture. He contributed a conspectus of Timurid architecture and photographs taken on his journeys to the *Survey of Persian Art.* Although his views were often coloured by personal enthusiasm and prejudices (for example his hatred of the historical writings of Gibbon) a surprising number of his insights into Byzantine and Islamic culture have been confirmed by later scholarship, and he played a major role in bringing these cultures to the attention of educated readers. He was also a founder-member of the Georgian Group and a tireless campaigner for the preservation of English 18th-century architecture, publishing in this connection his notable protest against the destruction of Georgian London, *How we Celebrate the Coronation.*

WRITINGS

The Station, Athos: Treasures and Men (London, 1928)
The Byzantine Achievement (London, 1929, 2/1987)
with D. T. Rice: *The Birth of Western Painting* (London, 1930)
An Essay on India (London, 1931)
'New Delhi', *Archit. Rev.* [London], lxix (1931), pp. 1–30
First Russia, then Tibet (London, 1933)
How we Celebrate the Coronation (London, 1937)
The Road to Oxiana (London, 1937, 2/1981)
'Timurid Architecture: General Trends', *A Survey of Persian Art*, ed. A. U. Pope, ii (London, 1939), pp. 1119–43

BIBLIOGRAPHY

C. Sykes: *Four Studies in Loyalty* (London, 1946), pp. 80–179
C. Hussey: *The Life of Sir Edwin Lutyens* (London, 1950)
A. Powell: *The Memoirs of Anthony Powell* (London, 1976–82), i, pp. 109–15
P. Fussell: *Abroad: British Literary Travelling between the Wars* (New York, 1980), pp. 79–112

□

Byss [Bys], **Johann Rudolf** (*b* Chur, 11 May 1660; *d* Würzburg, 11 Dec 1738). Swiss painter, active in Prague and Franconia. He was a pupil of his father, Johann Joseph Byss, in Solothurn. In the 1680s he made a study trip to Germany, England and the Netherlands. From 1689 he was employed by Count Hermann Jakob Černín (*d* 1710) in Prague as court painter and administrator of the Count's picture gallery, and that year he also married Maximiliana Wagner, the daughter of one of the Emperor's clerks. Byss introduced to Prague many of the stylistic tendencies of Netherlandish and Italian classicism: for example in his altar painting of 1691, *John of God* (Prague, church of the Brothers of Mercy). A Netherlandish orientation is again seen in the easel painting *Vestal Claudia Quinta* (1692; Prague, N.G., convent of St George). In 1692 Byss became a citizen of Prague, and in 1694 he was admitted to the painters' guild, where he subsequently became a master. His versatility and speed soon brought him a number of commissions. In easel paintings he treated historical themes, and he painted landscapes inspired by the work of the Dutch followers of Nicolaes Berchem. He also painted notable still-lifes, at first following the example of the game-pieces by Jan Baptist Weenix and Willem Gouw Ferguson, for example *Shot Partridge* (1693; sold Amsterdam, Christie's, 1985). The *Bust of a Child Wreathed with Flowers* (1695; Munich, Alte Pin.) reveals a more original approach to still-life, as well as a liking for elaborate detail and paler colours. A companion piece for this work was painted in 1703 by Johann Adalbert Angermeyer (1674–*c.* 1740), a pupil of Byss and the first Prague still-life specialist.

After 1700 Byss generally painted pictures in a small format, taking his model from Netherlandish painting of the early 17th century, as in *Bouquet in a Vase* (1702; Kassel, Schloss Wilhelmshöhe) or such figural compositions as the *Four Elements* (1708–11; Pommersfelden, Schloss Weissenstein), where he closely followed the work of Jan Breughel II and Hendrick van Balen. By 1700 Byss had also begun to decorate Prague palace interiors. In the palace of Petr Straka von Nedabylice he proved his versatility in his choice of themes: alongside commemorative allegories inspired especially by the work of Gérard de Lairesse, he favoured decorative devices such as illusory architectural vistas, *trompe l'oeil* still-lifes and, on a wall of the main hall, a view into a picture gallery with scenes of landscapes, genre paintings and portraits. In 1707 Byss travelled to Italy, where he was received by Pope Clement XI. In 1708 he decorated the Antikenkabinett in the Sternberg Palais, Prague. His work in Prague established his reputation for excellence in both decorative and easel painting and Lothar Franz von Schönborn, Archbishop and Elector of Mainz (1655–1729), subsequently appointed him court painter at Bamberg. From 1713 to 1717 Byss was active in the Schönborn Castle in Pommersfelden together with Johann Michael Rottmayr, being also engaged there as administrator of the art gallery, for which he published the first printed museum catalogue in Germany (1719). After 1721 he painted wall decorations in the Tettnang Castle, near Ravensburg. In 1721 he also made a journey to his native Switzerland. In 1722 he carried out the decoration of the main hall of Hatzfeld Palace (destr.) in Breslau (now Wrocław, Poland). Between 1723 and 1730 Byss worked in Vienna again, on the decoration of the building of the imperial office (destr.).

In 1729, after the death of Lothar Franz, Byss entered into the service of his successor, Friedrich Karl von Schönborn, who charged him with the decoration of the most important halls of the monastery in Gottweig. In 1731–3 Byss took part in the decoration of the Schönborn Chapel in the cathedral of St Kilian in Würzburg. For the new Schönborn Residenz in Würzburg he devised a programme for the wall paintings, produced detailed sketches and patterns and designed stucco decorations, wall coverings and furniture. His pupils Johann Baptist Thalhofer (*d* 1777) and Anton Joseph Högler (*c.* 1705–*c.* 1786) assisted in the execution of these.

Byss often drew on the examples of Italian and Netherlandish painting, and he was able to meet his patrons' demands for large-scale decorative painting as well as virtuoso displays of painting on a small scale. In his ability to combine elements from different art traditions, the intimacy of his small-scale work and his preference for pale colours, Byss prepared the way for the style and sentiment of the Rococo.

BIBLIOGRAPHY

L. Broder: 'Der Solothurner Maler Johann Rudolf Byss', *Z. Schweiz. Archäol. & Kstgesch.*, i (1939), pp. 1–14
——: 'Johann Rudolf Byss als Stillebenmaler', *Z. Schweiz. Archäol. & Kstgesch.*, i (1939), pp. 193–203
O. J. Blážíček: 'Johann Rudolf Bys v Praze', *Umění*, x (1962), pp. 537–608
Schweizer Stilleben im Barock (exh. cat., Zurich, Haus Rechberg, 1973), pp. 59–65
G. Adriani: *Deutsche Malerei im 17. Jahrhundert* (Cologne, 1977), pp. 178–9
H. Seifertová: 'Barockstilleben in Böhmen und Mähren', *Mitt. Österreich. Gal.*, xxi (1977), pp. 46–9
G. Krämer: *Deutsche Barockgalerie* (Augsburg, 1984), pp. 45–6
B. M. Mayer: *Johann Rudolf Bys (1622–1738)* (diss., Berlin, 1990)

HANA SEIFERTOVÁ

Byström, Johan Niklas (*b* Filipstad, Värmland, 18 Dec 1783; *d* Rome, 13 March 1848). Swedish sculptor. He studied under Johan Tobias Sergel at the Konstakademi in Stockholm from 1803 to 1809, and in 1810 moved to Rome where he lived thereafter when not working or teaching in Sweden. In Italy he owned a marble quarry at Carrara and thus executed most of his sculptures in this high-quality stone. In Rome he studied antique sculpture and made copies of works there, such as *Head of Bacchus* (Stockholm, Nmus.). In his own work he invariably used subjects derived from Classical mythology, executing them in a Neo-classical style influenced by Antonio Canova, as in *Juno with the Baby Hercules* (1818; Stockholm, Nmus.), of which various versions exist. In this large work Juno is shown asleep with the young Hercules playing by her side. The outstretched goddess is elegantly carved and the drapery is especially fine, though the overall composition is rather heavy and lifeless, a fault of much of Byström's work.

Apart from mythological sculptures, Byström also produced a number of portrait busts, largely of royalty, such as the marble *Karl XIV* (1818; Stockholm, Nmus.). He also designed various public monuments with portrait statues, such as that to the great botanist *Carolus Linnaeus* for the Orangery of the botanical garden in Uppsala, which was unveiled in 1829. He also designed the colossal bronze bust of the poet and musician *Carl Michael Bellman* for the Djurgarden park in Stockholm, which was erected in 1829. In 1831 he created a plaster altarpiece showing *Jesus with Faith, Love and Hope* for Linköping church, a copy of which was also made for Skeppholm church in Stockholm. After having been appointed assistant professor at the Stockholm Konstakademi in 1816 he became a full professor in 1832.

BIBLIOGRAPHY

SBL
T. Nyman: *Johan Niklas Byström* (Uppsala, 1939)

□

Byzantine art. *See* EARLY CHRISTIAN AND BYZANTINE ART.

Byzantine blossom [Ger. *Byzantinische Blüthenblatt*]. Term used to describe a wide range of 'floral' motifs prominent in Western art from the 11th century to the end of the 12th. The German term was first used to describe generically similar motifs that appear in 10th-century Byzantine art, for example in the Hippiatrika Codex (Berlin, Preuss. Staatsbib. Kultbes., cod. Phillipps 1538, fol. 39*v*). The early 12th-century reference by Theophilus to 'folia graeca' may refer to Byzantine 'leaf-flowers' although the term is not documented in other sources. The variation of the constituent leaves is common to both Eastern and Western ornaments. Unlike the rosette, the leaves typically rise from the junction of the flower and stem. Their origins may lie in the Classical palmette, although Sasanian ornaments provide the immediate models for the Byzantine flowers. Whereas in Byzantine art the flowers are conservative in form and detail, Western blossoms are characteristically individualized. In the decorated headpieces of Byzantine manuscripts (see above), the flowers occupy the centres and interstitial spaces of series of delicately painted roundels. In both Middle Byzantine metalwork and Western art the flowers are used as the decorative terminals of running scrollwork.

The trefoil is a rarity in Byzantine art but occurs in Western art with increasing frequency from the 8th century AD, being a common Romanesque floral ornament from *c.* 1050 to *c.* 1150, and takes its origins from the trefoil vine scroll. Evidence of a new departure towards a more ornate flower, based ultimately on Byzantine ornament and composed of tiers of leafage, often wound around the encircling scrollwork, is found in the Bury Bible (*c.* 1135; Cambridge, Corpus Christi Coll. Lib., MS. 2). The stimulus for these highly individualized flowers lies in the sub-Byzantine flowers of late 11th-century German ornament. By *c.* 1170–80 a shift of emphasis from the flower to the intricate patterning of the scroll marks the final, 'mannerist' phase of the Byzantine blossom in Western art.

BIBLIOGRAPHY

K. Weitzmann: *Die byzantinische Buchmalerei des 9. und 10. Jahrhunderts* (Berlin, 1935)
C. M. Kauffmann: *Romanesque Manuscripts, 1066–1190* (1975), iii of *A Survey of Manuscripts Illuminated in the British Isles*, ed. J. J. A. Alexander (London, 1975–)

JEFFREY WEST

Byzantine Revival. Term applied to a revivalist style that affected all the arts (including visual and literary), but primarily architecture and the decorative arts. The style was prevalent in Western and Eastern Europe and North

America during the second half of the 19th century and into the early 20th. Its international nature was appropriate to the multi-cultural identity and geographical range of the Byzantine empire (early 4th century AD–1453). The initial impetus for the Revival came from 18th- and 19th-century accounts of travels to Italy, Greece and Turkey, containing descriptions of Early Christian and Byzantine buildings, and from early specialist books on Byzantine and Early Christian architecture. It received an additional stimulus from the fashion for the *Rundbogenstil*, which originated in Germany during the 1820s.

The growth of serious academic and architectural interest in the Byzantine style began in the 1830s. Thomas Hope's *An Historical Essay on Architecture* (1835) devoted 20 chapters to Early Christian and Byzantine architecture (*see* HOPE, (1)). ALEXANDER LINDSAY allocated a large section of *Sketches in the History of Christian Art* (1847) to Early Christian art. Both books received critical attention, notably from JOHN RUSKIN, stimulating further publication in this field. Ruskin's own three-volume *The Seven Lamps of Architecture* (1849) and *The Stones of Venice* (1851) were also both highly influential: the latter prompted an international public outcry over the restoration of the basilica of S Marco, Venice. The widespread public acceptance of the style dates from the 1850s. Matthew Digby Wyatt designed the Byzantine and Early Christian Court (1854; destr. 1936) in the Crystal Palace, London, as part of a series of historical displays created after the palace's re-erection at Sydenham. The University Church (1854–6), Dublin, conceived by JOHN HENRY NEWMAN and designed and decorated by John Hungerford Pollen was strongly based on the Early Christian basilicas of Ravenna. In mosaic decoration the Byzantine Revival was promoted by the Venetian firm of Salviati (founded 1859), who led an international revival of mosaic mural decoration, combining Byzantine pictorial imagery with industrialized methods of production (*see also* MOSAIC, §II, 3).

By 1880 a more specific use of Byzantine as opposed to Early Christian idioms emerged. At Cardiff Castle, Wales, John Patrick Crichton-Stuart, 3rd Marquess of Bute, a leading patron of the Byzantine Revival, commissioned a private chapel, designed by William Burges. It contains a Byzantine-inspired baldacchino, and on its dome is depicted Christ Pantocrator in a Victorianized version of 12th-century Sicilian and Greek Byzantine decoration. The Greek Orthodox cathedral of St Sophia (1877–9), London, designed by John Oldrid Scott, has a centralized cruciform plan, surmounted by a dome supported on pendentives, and a full programme of mosaic decoration, based on 12th-century Greek Byzantine models. In Bavaria, King Ludwig II commissioned a richly decorated Byzantinesque throne-room (1885–6), also with strong Sicilian overtones, as part of his palace of Neuschwanstein, designed by Eduard Riedel (1813–85) and Georg von Dollmann.

The peak of the Byzantine Revival was between 1890 and 1914. W. R. Lethaby and Harold Swainson's monograph *The Church of Sancta Sophia, Constantinople* (1894) identified the mystical quality and symbolic spiritual significance of Byzantine architecture, pinpointing its *fin-de-siècle* appeal. The book provided a vital source for the design of the Roman Catholic Westminster Cathedral (begun 1895; for discussion and illustration *see* BENTLEY, JOHN FRANCIS), London. The major study by Charles Texier and RICHARD POPPLEWELL PULLAN, *Byzantine Architecture* (1864), was the inspiration for Rice University (begun 1912), Houston, TX, by Ralph Adams Cram.

BIBLIOGRAPHY

M. Praz: *The Romantic Agony* (London, 1933, rev. 2/1970), pp. 303–474
P. Julian: *Dreamers of Decadence* (London, 1971), pp. 149–61
D. Talbot Rice: *The Appreciation of Byzantine Art* (London, 1972)
Romantik und Restauration: Architektur in Bayern zur Zeit Ludwigs I., 1825–1848 (exh. cat., ed. W. Nerdinger; Munich, Stadtmus., 1987)
M. P. Dristel: *Representing Belief: Religion, Art and Society in Nineteenth Century France* (Philadelphia, 1992)

DOROTHY BOSOMWORTH

C

Ça Anglada, Pere [Sanglada, Pedro] (*fl* 1386–1407). Catalan sculptor and wood-carver. He has been associated with Girona (Sp. Gerona), but his style, particularly that of the figures peopling the choir-stalls he carved for Barcelona Cathedral (1394–9; pulpit completed 1403), reflects his travels in France and the Netherlands. Ça Anglada was primarily concerned with the direction of the cathedral workshops and with projects for the city of Barcelona. In the early years of the 15th century he carried out various works for the Casa de la Ciutat (the Town Hall), including the carvings in the Saló de Cent and probably also the *St Raphael* on the Gothic façade of the building. An *Annunciation* in the choir of Barcelona Cathedral is partly the work of the sculptor Jordi di Deu (*fl c.* 1361–1418); but the decisive role is that of Ça Anglada, who gave an innovative refashioning, on International Gothic lines, to the subjects of this Italianizing master. In 1406 Ça Anglada was working on the alabaster tomb of *St Olaguer* in Barcelona Cathedral. The following year he received a commission for the *Virgin* centring the retable at Monreale Cathedral, Sicily, an indication of his widespread fame. Attributions stylistically linking the tombs of *Arnau* and *Bertran de Montrodo* in Girona Cathedral with the throne in Barcelona Cathedral as Ça Anglada's work have now been discredited, as has his authorship of two sculptures of *St Peter* (Barcelona, Gudiol priv. col.; Barcelona, Mus. Marés) and of a *Virgin* for the high altar retable of Santes Creus Abbey (Tarragona, Mus. Dioc.).

BIBLIOGRAPHY

M. R. Terés: 'Pere Ça Anglada maestro del coro de la catedral de Barcelona: Aspectos documentales y formales', *D'Art* [Barcelona], 5 (1979), pp. 51–9

——: *Pere Ça Anglada i la introducció de l'estil internacional a l'escultura catalana* (Barcelona, 1987)

ROSA ALCOY

Caballero, José (*b* Huelva, 1916; *d* Madrid, 1991). Spanish painter. He studied painting at the Academia de Bellas Artes de San Fernando and in Daniel Vázquez Díaz's studio, Madrid (1933). His friendship with poets and artists including Pablo Neruda and Joaquín Torres García drew him towards Surrealism. He designed theatre sets and illustrated books of poetry, for example Lorca's *Llanto por Ignacio Sánchez Mejias* (Madrid, 1935). After the Spanish Civil War he gave up painting. Following his return to Spain in 1945, his work became abstract, and from 1970 he used calligraphic elements with strong symbolic and expressive force, as in *Machine for Capturing Planets* (1972; Madrid, Mus. N. Cent. A. Reina Sofía).

He had numerous exhibitions in Europe, Latin America and the USA, and his work can be found in international museums. He was awarded the Premio Nacional de Artes Plásticas in 1984.

BIBLIOGRAPHY

R. Faraldo: *José Caballero* (Madrid, 1958)

José Caballero (exh. cat., Lisbon, Fund. Gulbenkian, 1973)

R. Chavarri: *José Caballero* (Madrid, 1974)

José Caballero (exh. cat., Madrid, Cent. Cult. Villà Madrid, 1992)

JUAN PÉREZ DE AYALA

Caballero, Luis (*b* Bogotá, 1943). Colombian painter. His earliest paintings, executed in oil on paper in the late 1960s, represent large and energetic nudes—influenced by the work of Francis Bacon—among gestural splashes of intense colour. He subsequently toned down his use of colour and began to work from life, showing the human body in varied postures indicative of emotion and energy. He used sexuality and his own erotic pleasure as a means of heightening the impact of his nude figures, which he described as painted 'with semen, not turpentine'. His exclusive subjects in later paintings were athletic young men in recumbent positions, their expressions suggestive of a state of sexual trance or death. Violence, blood and suffering dominate images of figures piled together in dramatic orgies and states of sadness and desire, projecting an intensity of emotion rooted in Romanticism.

WRITINGS

Me tocó ser así (Bogotá, 1986)

BIBLIOGRAPHY

Cien años de arte colombiano (exh. cat. by E. Serrano, Bogotá, Mus. A. Mod., 1985)

EDUARDO SERRANO

Caballettus [de Cabaleto]**, Giovanni Battista.** *See* CAVALLETTO, GIOVANNI BATTISTA.

Cabaña, La. *See* LA CABAÑA.

Cabanel, Alexandre (*b* Montpellier, 28 Sept 1823; *d* Paris, 23 Jan 1889). French painter and teacher. His skill in drawing was apparently evident by the age of 11. His father could not afford his training, but in 1839 his département gave him a grant to go to Paris. This enabled him to register at the Ecole des Beaux-Arts the following October as a pupil of François-Edouard Picot. At his first Salon in 1843 he presented *Agony in the Garden* (Valenciennes, Mus. B.-A.) and won second place in the Prix de

Rome competition (after Léon Bénouville, also a pupil of Picot) in 1845 with *Christ at the Praetorium* (Paris, Ecole N. Sup. B.-A.). Both Cabanel and Bénouville were able to go to Rome, as there was a vacancy from the previous year. Cabanel's *Death of Moses* (untraced), an academic composition, painted to comply with the regulations of the Ecole de Rome, was exhibited at the Salon of 1852. The pictures he painted for Alfred Bruyas, his chief patron at this time (and, like Cabanel, a native of Montpellier), showed more clearly the direction his art had taken during his stay in Italy. *Albaydé, Angel of the Evening, Chiarruccia* and *Velleda* (all in Montpellier, Mus. Fabre) were the first of many mysterious or tragic heroines painted by Cabanel and show his taste for the elegiac types and suave finish of the Florentine Mannerists.

On Cabanel's return to Paris, the architect Jean-Baptiste Cicéron Lesueur (1794–1883) commissioned him to decorate 12 pendentives in the Salon des Caryatides in the Hôtel de Ville (destr. 1871). Several major decorative commissions followed, which included work on the Hôtel Pereire, the Hôtel Say and the Louvre. Much has been destroyed, but the ceiling in the Cabinet des Dessins in the Louvre, *The Triumph of Flora*, which combines the hard contours and careful finish of Ingres's school with a composition and colour that recalls the ceilings of the French Rococo, is probably typical of Cabanel's talent for achieving sumptuous effects.

In 1855 Cabanel exhibited *Christian Martyr* (Carcassonne, Mus. B.-A.), *Glorification of St Louis* (Lunéville, Mus. Lunéville) and *Autumn Evening* (untraced), establishing his academic and official credentials. In 1855 he received the Légion d'honneur and in 1863 he was elected to the Institut and nominated professor (along with Jean-Léon Gérôme and Isidore-Alexandre-Augustin Pils) at the reorganized Ecole des Beaux-Arts in Paris. He won the Grande Médaille d'Honneur at the Salons of 1865, 1867 and 1878. His dark-eyed heroines, thinly painted, usually in muted colours, and immaculately drawn, were popular with collectors on both sides of the Atlantic; likewise his mythological paintings, which were a by-product of his decorative works. *Nymph Abducted by a Faun* (1860, exh. Salon, 1861; Lille, Mus. B.-A.; see fig.) is a solid, decorative group in the manner of Charles Coypel or François Lemoyne. He exhibited the *Birth of Venus* (1862; Paris, Mus. d'Orsay) in 1863 to widespread acclaim. It is composed like an overdoor by Boucher, although it has been suggested that it was influenced by Ingres's *Odalisque and her Slave* (1839; Cambridge, MA, Fogg). Both paintings were acquired by Napoleon III. In 1867 he painted a huge *Paradise Lost* (Munich, Maximilianum) for Ludwig II, the King of Bavaria, and in 1868 *Ruth* (untraced) for the Empress Eugénie. The full-length portrait of the Emperor that Cabanel painted for the Tuileries in 1865 was liked by critics less than Hippolyte Flandrin's dreamy portrait exhibited in 1863 (*c.* 1860–61; Versailles, Château), but it was much more popular at court. Cabanel's portraits were already in demand, and he rivalled Edouard Dubufe and Franz Xavier Winterhalter as portrait painter to the Napoleonic aristocracy.

Cabanel was also a successful teacher. His pupils (like those of his master, Picot) often won the Prix de Rome; among the best known are Jules Bastien-Lepage, Edouard

Alexandre Cabanel: *Nymph Abducted by a Faun*, oil on canvas, 2.45×1.47 m, 1860 (Lille, Musée des Beaux-Arts)

Debat-Ponsan, Edouard Théophile Blanchard (1844–79), Henri Gervex and Lodewijk Royer. He was elected regularly to the Salon jury, and his pupils could be counted by the hundred at the Salons. Through them, Cabanel did more than any other artist of his generation to form the character of 'belle époque' French painting. Cabanel's pictures were always drawn and painted with a high degree of academic virtuosity, combined with an undercurrent of strong feeling, as in the *Death of Francesca da Rimini and Paolo Malatesta* (1870; Paris, Mus. d'Orsay). This made him popular in his lifetime, but it was the wrong combination for the tastes of later generations. After his death his reputation collapsed.

BIBLIOGRAPHY

A. Meynell: 'Our Living Artists: Alexandre Cabanel', *Mag. A.*, ix (1886), pp. 271–6

G. Lafenestre: 'Alexandre Cabanel', *Gaz. B.-A.*, n.s. 3, i (1889), pp. 265–80

J. Nougaret: *Alexandre Cabanel: Sa vie, son oeuvre* (diss., U. Montpellier, 1962)

Alexandre Cabanel (exh. cat., Montpellier, Mus. Fabre, 1975)

JON WHITELEY

Cabat, (Nicolas-)Louis (*b* Paris, 12 Dec 1812; *d* Paris, 13 March 1893). French painter. From 1825 to 1828 he was apprenticed as a decorator of porcelain at the Gouverneur Factory in Paris. He then studied under Camille Flers, who taught him to paint landscape *en plein air* and compelled him to sharpen his powers of observation of nature at the expense of the rules of classical landscape. In 1830 he visited Normandy and on his return to Paris he associated with two avant-garde painters, Philippe-Auguste Jeanron, founder of the Société Libre de Peinture et de Sculpture, and Jules Dupré. The latter was a committed member of the Barbizon school who sought to portray the truthfulness of nature in his landscapes rather than an arranged composition (*see* BARBIZON SCHOOL). In order to deepen their study of nature, Cabat and Dupré painted together in the Forest of Fontainebleau. In 1832 they also visited the region of Berry. The following year, Cabat exhibited for the first time at the Salon in Paris, where until 1891 he showed landscapes inspired by his travels to Normandy, Picardy, Berry, the Ile de France and Italy (e.g. *Farm in Normandy*; Nantes, Mus. B.-A.). His paintings feature trees and ponds and often show the influence of the Dutch school of the 17th century. Around 1840 the honest emotion and sincerity of his early works began to be superseded by a conventional manner that gained him some official honours and cost him the friendship of other members of the Barbizon school. He was a member of the Institut de France in 1867 and was Director of the Académie de France in Rome from 1877 to 1885. His paintings embody a confrontation between two tendencies prominent at that time: realism and classicism.

BIBLIOGRAPHY
Bellier de La Chavignerie–Auvray
M.-M. Aubrun: 'La Tradition du paysage historique et le paysage naturaliste dans la première moitié du XIXe siècle français', *Inf. Hist. A.*, xiii (1968), pp. 63–73
The Realist Tradition: French Painting and Drawing, 1830–1900 (exh. cat. by G. Weisberg, Cleveland, OH, Mus. A.; New York, Brooklyn Mus.; St Louis, MO, A. Mus.; Glasgow, A.G. & Mus.; 1980–82), pp. 277–8
Louis Cabat, 1812–1893 (exh. cat., Troyes, Mus. B.-A. & Archéol., 1987)
ANNIE SCOTTEZ-DE WAMBRECHIES

Cabel [Kabel]**, Adriaan** [Adriaen; Ary] **van der** [Corydon; Geestigheit] (*b* Rijswijk, nr The Hague, 1630–31; *d* Lyon, *bur* 16 June 1705). Dutch painter, etcher and draughtsman. He studied with Jan van Goyen, whose influence is reflected in early paintings such as *Dune Landscape with Peasants beside a Cottage* (ex-Semenoff priv. col., St Petersburg). He travelled to Rome around 1655, stopping at Paris and Lyon on the way. He met Willem Schellinks in 1664, by which time he had joined the Schildersbent, the confraternity of Dutch artists in Rome. Once in Italy he was influenced by Claude Lorrain, Pier Francesco Mola (ii) and Salvator Rosa. Besides many pastoral landscape drawings with sheep and herdsmen, he drew views of Sicilian sites, indicating a possible stay there. From 7 December 1688 until his death he was registered in Lyon, a view of which he depicted in a drawing now in the Institut Néerlandais, Paris. His 60 or 70 etchings, representing either classical landscapes or harbour scenes, were made after his own designs and show a confident hand. His painted work also comprises seascapes, several still-lifes, figure pieces and portraits (e.g. *Jean Estival*; Lyon, Mus. B.-A.).

BIBLIOGRAPHY
Hollstein: *Dut. & Flem.*
A. Houbraken: *De groote schouburgh* (1718–21), ii, pp. 235, 268–9; iii, pp. 217–18, 341
R. de Cazenove: *Le Peintre Van der Kabel* (Paris, 1888)
L. J. Bol: *Holländische Maler des 17. Jahrhunderts, Landschaften und Stilleben* (Brunswick, 1969), p. 183
——: *Die holländische Marinemalerei des 17. Jahrhunderts* (Brunswick, 1973), pp. 161–2
Printmaking in the Age of Rembrandt (exh. cat., ed. C. S. Ackley; Boston, MA, Mus. F.A., 1980–81), no. 206
CHRISTIAAN SCHUCKMAN

Cabello, Francisco Gutiérrez. *See* GUTIÉRREZ CABELLO, FRANCISCO.

Cabezalero, Juan Martín (*b* Almadén, Ciudad Real, 1633; *d* Madrid, 1673). Spanish painter. He entered the studio of Juan Carreño de Miranda in Madrid as pupil and assistant and remained on close terms with his master, for in 1666 he was still living in Carreño's house. Palomino praises his modest and studious temperament and laments that he died young. Few works by Cabezalero survive; although little is known of his development, his paintings are of high quality. His signed *St Jerome* (1666; Dallas, TX, S. Methodist U., Meadows Mus. & Gal.) is a good example of his adherence to Carreño and their common admiration for Anthony van Dyck. The large canvases of scenes from the Passion (1667–8; Madrid, Chapel of the Venerable Third Order of St Francis) are another tacit tribute to van Dyck, whose figures and sense of composition Cabezalero was able to absorb and mark with his own personality. They show his characteristic system of modelling by means of broad planes of light, with strong outlines. He was an excellent colourist, preferring light, intense colours with individual tones of blue, orange-yellows and vibrant, pearly whites. The *Assumption of the Virgin* (*c.* 1670; Madrid, Prado), formerly attributed to Mateo Cerezo, has been recognized as an important work by Cabezalero.

BIBLIOGRAPHY
A. A. Palomino de Castro y Velasco: *Museo pictórico* (1715–24/*R* 1947), p. 974
L. Alonso: 'Cabezalero', *Bol. Soc. Esp. Excurs.*, xxiii (1915), pp. 32–50
A. E. Pérez Sánchez: 'Precisiones sobre Juan Martin Cabezalero', *Velázques y el arte de su tiempo* (Madrid, 1991)
ALFONSO E. PÉREZ SÁNCHEZ

Cabianca, Francesco (*b* Venice, 1665; *d* Venice, 15 April 1737). Italian sculptor. His first known work is the marble *St Benedict* (1695) for S Michele in Isola, Venice. Illness forced him to move around 1698 to Dalmatia, where he stayed at Ragusa (now Dubrovnik) and at Cattaro. There he completed the high altar with *SS John, Dominic, Bruno and Chiara* for S Chiara, an altar for S Giuseppe and the marble altar of the chapel of S Trifone for S Trifone. He returned to Venice in 1708 but retained contacts with Dalmatia. In 1711 he executed his best-known work, the reliquary, with panels representing the *Crucifixion*, the *Deposition* and the *Pietà*, for the sacristy of S Maria Gloriosa dei Frari in Venice. He also worked in Gorizia. In Venice he carved a figure of *Bellona* in stone for the entrance to the Arsenal and statues of the *Trinity*, *SS Peter and Paul* and other figures for the courtyard of the Frari. On the façade of the church of the Gesuiti are *St John the*

Evangelist and *St James* in niches and *St Andrew* on the crowning balustrade. His low relief of the martyrdoms of *SS Simon and Jude* is placed in the tympanum of the church of SS Simeone e Giuda, and on the great staircase of the Seminario Patriarcale are low reliefs of *Jacob's Dream* and the *Vision of the Orphan*. He carved a marble figure of *Saturn* for the Summer Gardens in St Petersburg. In his most significant works, the altar of S Trifone at Cattaro and the three low reliefs on the reliquary in the sacristy of S Maria Gloriosa dei Frari in Venice, Cabianca demonstrates a dynamism that points to contact with Filippo Parodi (1630–1702) and a classical sense akin to that of Pietro Baratta, whose works his own most resemble. Cabianca's works are not of a consistent formal quality, and it is known that the sculptor died in great poverty, which suggests a certain disorder in his life.

BIBLIOGRAPHY

T. Temanza: *Zibaldone*, ed. N. Ivanoff (Venice, 1963)

C. Semenzato: 'Francesco Cabianca', *La scultura veneta del seicento e del settecento* (Venice, 1966)

K. Prijatelj: 'Contributi per la scultura barocca a Ragusa, II', *A. Ven.*, xxiv (1970), pp. 238–43

A. Niero: 'Episodi della scultura barocca del seicento veneziano: Lo scalone del Seminario Patriarcale', *Ateneo Ven.* (1977)

CAMILLO SEMENZATO

Cabinet (i). Small and often highly decorated room meant for private use and often housing a collection of small works of art or other objects of interest. The word was first used in the late 15th century in France and from the beginning of the 16th century spread to the rest of Europe. During the 17th century it came to be used to denote not only a particular sort of room but also the collection of objects contained therein. The definitions given in 17th- and 18th-century French and German dictionaries indicate that the term has also been used with a wide range of other meanings, all of which, however, convey the fundamental idea of seclusion and privacy.

1. Location and purpose. 2. Contents and arrangement. 3. Decoration. 4. Important types.

1. LOCATION AND PURPOSE. The first cabinets were small rooms, usually adjoining a bedchamber, in the most private part of a castle, palace or apartment, meant for the private use of the master of the house. It is difficult to construct a universal and precise typology for the position of cabinets within a building. Sometimes, following the tradition of the STUDIOLO, they were placed on the north side. Cabinets with a view of the garden were greatly favoured. They were usually placed at the corners of a building, especially in towers or pavilions. Pierre Le Muet's plan for the château of Pont-sur-Seine (1638–44; destr. 1814), Aube, clearly shows that the spaces on the first floor inside the four corner towers were occupied by the chapel, two cabinets and a garderobe, all communicating with bedchambers. A similar arrangement is found in the Upper Belvedere (1721–3) built outside Vienna for Eugene, Prince of Savoy, where three of the four corner pavilions contained the cabinet of mirrors (the Goldenes Zimmer or Spiegelzimmer), the marble cabinet (Marmoriertes Kabinett) and the painted cabinet (Gemahlenes Kabinett), while the fourth pavilion was occupied by the upper part of the chapel. The Marmoriertes Kabinett and the Spiegelzimmer had a view of the garden; under each of them, on the ground floor, there was an 'open cabinet' that gave directly on to the garden. On the south side of the first floor of the Belvedere there was also another cabinet (the Bilderzimmer), which was the only one directly adjoining a bedchamber and contained a collection of pictures.

It was also common to find a cabinet at each end of a gallery, for example at the ends of the Galerie des Glaces at Versailles (*see* §4(ii) below) and the gallery (begun 1654 by Antonio del Grande) of the Palazzo Colonna in Rome. César-Pierre Richelet (1631–98) referred to such an arrangement in the primary definition of the word cabinet in his *Dictionnaire françois* of 1680: 'Petit endroit qu'on met souvent au bout d'une galerie, et que Vitruve apelle *exedra*'. Long before Richelet, however, Louis Savot had clearly maintained, in *L'Architecture françoise des bastimens particuliers* (Paris, 1624), that every gallery must always have a cabinet at one of its ends.

Although it almost always had the quality of a private place, the cabinet did not always have the same function. It might be the place where the master of the house attended to his most personal affairs, or, as is suggested by Richelet's reference to the Vitruvian exedra, it could be used as a room for conversation and audience. The word was also used to designate the room where people retired to meditate and study in solitude, or where they kept collections of objects, uses in which the derivation from the Italian model of the *studiolo* is evident (*see* §2 below). Indeed Diderot's *Encyclopédie* (1751–72) emphasized the necessity for a great aristocrat to have several cabinets in his residence, each with a specific function. First, there had to be a *grand cabinet* in which he could discuss private matters with those who called upon him because of his social position; and in this same room he might have kept his pictures and curiosities. There also had to be an *arrière-cabinet* for his books and writing-table; this was his place of work, but also the room where he received guests of higher rank towards whom he wanted to show special respect. In another cabinet documents, contracts and money could be kept safe, and lastly there was a *cabinet de toilette* containing dressing and sanitary facilities. In his *Architecture françoise* (1752–6), however, Jacques-François Blondel divides the cabinets into two categories: firstly there were those that served basically the same function as the *grand cabinet* and *arrière-cabinet* above; and secondly there were those used as oratories and boudoirs and containing dressing and sanitary facilities.

By the end of the 17th century certain structures or decorative elements in gardens had also become known as cabinets. Thomas Corneille's *Dictionnaire des arts et des sciences* (1694), for example, lists three types: the *cabinet de jardin*, a small isolated pavilion open on all sides to serve as a cool retreat; the *cabinet de treillage*, a small pergola made of interwoven iron bars overgrown with honeysuckle; and the *cabinet de verdure*, another type of pergola made of the intertwined branches of a tree. Indeed, as a repository for collections the cabinet had a close relationship with the garden in the 16th and 17th centuries: both were places for the display of artifice and of nature, places that lent themselves to the comparison of, and competition between, art and nature. John Evelyn, when visiting Italian villas and palazzi in the late 1640s, found it quite normal to pass directly from the cabinet to the garden; he conceived the latter as a natural extension of the former, and in both places he expected to see notable curiosities.

2. CONTENTS AND ARRANGEMENT. In the 17th century it became common to refer to a whole suite of several rooms containing a collection as a cabinet. For example, the traveller Maximilien Misson (*c.* 1650–1722), when describing his visit to Lodovico Moscardo in Verona in December 1687, did not hesitate to call Moscardo's museum a cabinet even though it consisted of 'a gallery and six rooms, all full of the most marvellous objects in the field of Art and in that of Nature'. Collections of all types, from the encyclopedic to the specialized, might be held in such cabinets. In his awed comment on the great variety of the collections in Amsterdam, Charles Patin wrote: 'one seems to pass not from one Cabinet to another, but from one world to another'. Cabinets of pictures were very common (in French these were called *cabinets de tableaux*) and often also contained sculptures. These were usually small or medium-sized works, while large ones were displayed in the gallery. The pictures were usually hung in a symmetrical arrangement, one immediately beside the other, so that every wall was completely covered with pictures (*see* CABINET PICTURE). In the cabinet in the north-west corner of the first floor of the Mauritshuis, the residence of John Maurits, Count of Nassau-Siegen, at The Hague, the upper part of the walls contained almost a hundred pictures, regularly arranged in four rows; they were all of the same small size with the same type of frame, and together they gave the impression of a sort of chequer-board. Each one depicted an illustrious person, following the tradition established by the Italian humanist PAOLO GIOVIO.

An idea of the furnishing of another very fashionable type of cabinet, containing coins and medals, is given by the cabinet in the castle of Gotha. This became important and famous only in 1712, when Duke Frederick II bought the collection of Prince Anton Günther von Schwarzburg in Arnstadt for 100,000 thalers. After the imperial collection in Vienna, it was the finest in the German regions. Frederick had the last room at the south end of his palace fitted up as his Münzkabinett, a view of which was engraved by I. D. Schilbach (*fl* 1727–30) at the beginning of the *Gotha numaria* by Christian Sigismund Liebe (Amsterdam, 1730). The ceiling of the cabinet was decorated with paintings, while the walls were divided by pilasters. The Duke's old collection of medals was contained in a single, enormous cupboard at the end of the room, standing between two windows and surmounted by a gilded statuette of himself. The great purchase of 1712 made it necessary to construct 14 additional cupboards, similar to the old one but smaller. These were placed along the two main walls of the room, seven on each side; they were surmounted by busts of emperors and copies of

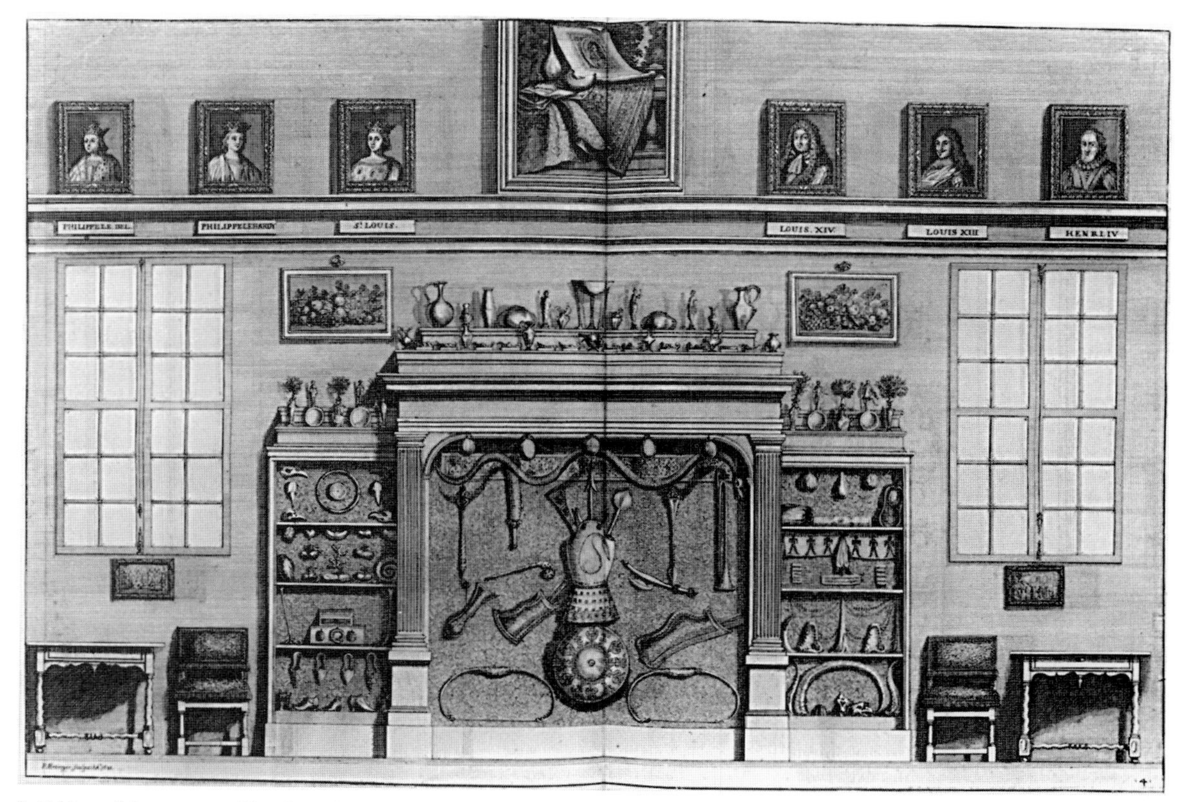

1. Cabinet of the convent of Ste Geneviève, Paris, *c.* 1675; engraving by Frans Ertinger, from Claude Du Molinet: *Le Cabinet de la Bibliothèque de Sainte Geneviève divisé en deux parties* (Paris, 1692)

antique and Renaissance statues or sculptural groups. The lower part of each one, ornamented with inlay work, contained books, while coins and medals were kept in the upper part. The arrangement was highly rational, because it enabled access to both the objects of study and the relevant literature at the same time.

The cabinets most often visited, those that most satisfied the thirst for novelty of travellers on the Grand Tour, were undoubtedly the cabinets of curiosities, containing rare and bizarre objects, both natural and artificial. In 1727 Antoine-Joseph Dezallier d'Argenville laid down a set of criteria for the organization of such cabinets. He provided a long list of objects that might legitimately attract the interest of the curious collector: paintings, prints, drawings, books, medals, engraved stones, antiques, porcelain, armour, ancient and foreign footwear, objects representing the three realms of nature and scientific instruments. An example of this approach was the cabinet 'of rare and curious pieces' at the convent of Ste Geneviève (see fig. 1), Paris, created around 1675 by Father Claude Du Molinet. At the height of the Enlightenment cabinets of curiosities were quite widespread throughout Europe, and they were only partially modified by the increasingly scientific interest in natural history. Even the owners of cabinets of natural history often gave preference to unusual or surprising items and tried to obtain items for their prestige value rather than for purposes of research. Instead of arranging the different materials on the basis of systematic criteria, they sought first of all to create a variety of forms and colours to delight the eye. However, the same period saw the beginnings of criticism by real scientists of these curiosities of natural history and the collections that held them, just as in the field of art the true connoisseurs were criticizing the amateurs. In such writings as Denis Diderot's entry 'Cabinet d'histoire naturelle' for the *Encyclopédie* or the preface by Philipp L. Müller to Georg Wolfgang Knorr's *Deliciae naturae selectae*, there was already an explicit condemnation of those who collected only beautiful and rare things rather than specimens that were really useful for the serious study of nature. The cabinet of natural history, with its complete sets of materials including more common objects, was beginning to take shape as a specialized instrument for scientific research.

See also KUNSTKAMMER and MUSEUM, §I.

3. DECORATION. Whatever specific use was made of it, the cabinet reflected the personal tastes of the owner more than any other room. From the mid-17th century, the decoration tended to become increasingly complex and sumptuous, making the cabinet an instrument of self-affirmation, in which the master of the house celebrated himself and his family. There were two reasons for the increasing care given to the decoration of this room. On the one hand the original character of the cabinet as an intimate and private place meant that it could be used for experiments in completely new forms of ornament, and these were often quite extravagant and bizarre. On the other hand the cabinet increasingly assumed a public dimension: first of all the *grand cabinet* became progressively larger until it was one of the main reception rooms of the apartment. Even the more intimate cabinets were opened to guests, however, and in fact it was mainly these rooms and their decorations that were designed to arouse astonishment and wonder. They were conceived as precious, hidden treasure chests, to which only the most privileged visitors could be admitted. Inside this precious coffer the visitor was likely to find another: a small item of furniture with numerous little drawers and cupboards, often richly ornamented with intaglios, ivory inlays, panels of pietra dura and tortoise-shell (for further discussion *see* CABINET (ii)).

At the beginning of the 17th century the structure of the 16th-century French cabinet in castles served as a model for those in aristocratic town houses, especially in Paris. The walls of the room were usually completely covered in wood, painted in bright colours with grotesques, arabesques, emblems, plant motifs and landscapes. The painted decoration was continued on the ceiling beams. The wooden walls (e.g. in the *Cabinet des dames* at the château of Pibrac (1540–45), near Toulouse, by Nicolas Bachelier) were often divided into horizontal zones. The lower zone was a base or wainscoting that extended from the floor almost halfway up the walls. At times the painted decoration on the lower part of this base (grotesques and emblems) might differ from that of the upper part (landscapes or compositions of fruit and flowers). Above this was a thick moulded cornice, usually decorated with plant motifs, which divided the lower part of the walls from the upper part. The latter was reserved for paintings on board or canvas. Apart from the wooden wall coverings, wide use was made of cloth hangings and of embossed and gilded leather. In the mid-17th century the decoration of cabinets changed, becoming more unified and more opulent. The whole wall, often divided by pilasters that accentuated the verticals, was filled with ornamental motifs in a dense network of arabesques and grotesques. Painting began to take second place to wood-carving and sculpture but was used on the ceiling, where coffering, which replaced the earlier beam-work, provided spaces suitable for paintings. Later the whole ceiling was filled with paintings or frescoes, mostly on mythological subjects. Often these paintings had a symbolic meaning connected with the patron's social position, intellectual ambitions or achievements.

Unlike other typical rooms in the great house, such as the gallery, the cabinet was often in danger of seeming too closed, dark and suffocating. One way round this was to site the room where it had a good view from its windows. Another technique was to simulate openings by means of mirrors and by painting real or imaginary landscapes on the walls (e.g. cabinets in Hôtel Lauzun and Hôtel Lambert, Paris). In country houses there were also cabinets completely decorated with a dense network of flowers, leaves, fruits and birds, designed to make the room into a sort of prolongation of the garden, or a substitute for it, and to emphasize the close relationship between the two (*see* §1 above). In other cases, rather than seeking solutions or artifices to brighten up the cabinet, an architect might choose the opposite approach: by exploiting the smallness of the space it was possible to accentuate the impression of seclusion and transform the room into a mysterious and magic recess, completely isolated from the world.

During the Baroque and Rococo period the decoration of the cabinet reached unprecedented levels of ostentation and originality. Walls were decorated with a profusion of gilt and stucco, precious materials and objects (*see* §4 and fig. 2 below). The cabinet increasingly acquired the role of a status symbol and indeed was often the main attraction of a house. The 18th-century vogue for exotic decorations was epitomized by the 'Chinese cabinet'. Here, not only were the walls covered in expensive lacquerwork, silk tapestries or wallpaper with Chinese motifs: the furniture, *objets d'art* and ceramics were also often of East Asian origin or inspiration. By the early 19th century, however, the cabinet was beginning to pass from favour. The Chinese cabinet gradually gave way to Greek (often erroneously called Etruscan) or Pompeian designs. The Neo-classical period and the period of the Empire style, despite some setbacks and subsequent revivals, perhaps represented the last era in which the cabinet still at least partly retained its original functions. It subsequently lost nearly all those decorations that were meant to make an impression on visitors as it was transformed into the study and became a real work place, with furnishings that were simpler but functional for the owner's scholarly or professional work.

BIBLIOGRAPHY

C. Patin: *Relations historiques et curieuses de voyages en Allemagne, Angleterre, Hollande, Bohême, Suisse* (Lyon, 1676)
M. Misson: *Nouveau voyage d'Italie, fait en l'année 1688*, 2 vols (The Hague, 1691)
C. du Molinet: *Le Cabinet de la Bibliothèque de Sainte Geneviève divisé en deux parties* (Paris, 1692)
A. J. Dezallier d'Argenville: 'Lettre sur le choix et l'arrangement d'un cabinet curieux', *Mercure France* (June 1727), pp. 1295–330
C. F. Neickel: *Museographia oder Anleitung zum rechten Begriff und nützlicher Anlegung der Museorum, oder Raritäten-Kammern* (Leipzig, 1727)
A. J. Dezallier d'Argenville: *L'Histoire naturelle éclaircie dans deux de ses parties principales, la lithologie et la conchyliologie* (Paris, 1742)
J.-F. Blondel: *Architecture françoise, ou recueil des plans, élévations, coupes et profils des églises, maisons royales, palais . . . de la France*, i (Paris, 1752–6)
G. W. Knorr: *Deliciae naturae selectae: Oder auserlesenes Natüraliencabinet, welches aus den drey Reichen der Natur zeiget was von cüriosen Liebhabern aufbehalten und gesammlet zu werden verdienet . . . beschrieben von Philipp Ludwig Müller* (Nuremberg, 1766–7)
B. Pick: 'Das Gothaer Münzkabinett, 1712–1912', *Coburg-gothaischen Landen: Heimatblätter*, viii (1912), pp. 1–13
P. Smit, A. P. M. Sanders and J. P. F. van der Veer, eds: 'Hendrik Engel's Alphabetical List of Dutch Zoological Cabinets and Menageries', *Bijdr. Dierknd*, xxvii (1939), pp. 247–346; as book (Amsterdam, 2/1986)
S. Speth-Holterhoff: *Les Peintres flamands de cabinets d'amateurs au XVIIe siècle* (Brussels, 1957)
Y. Laissus: 'Les Cabinets d'histoire naturelle', *Enseignement et diffusion des sciences en France au XVIIIe siècle*, ed. R. Taton (Paris, 1964), pp. 659–712
F. Zehnacker and N. Petit, eds: *Le Cabinet de l'Amour de l'Hôtel Lambert*, Musée du Louvre, Dossier du Département des Peintures, no. 3 (Paris, 1972)
M. Roland Michel: 'Le Cabinet de Bonnier de la Mosson et la participation de Lajoue à son décor', *Bull. Soc. Hist. A. Fr.* (1975), pp. 211–21
T. H. Lunsingh Scheurleer: 'The Mauritshuis as "domus cosmografica" I', *Johan Maurits van Nassau-Siegen 1604–1679: A Humanist Prince in Europe and Brazil*, ed. E. van den Boogaart with H. R. Hoetink and P. J. P. Whitehead (The Hague, 1979), pp. 143–89
H. Beck and others, eds: *Antikensammlungen im 18. Jahrhundert* (Berlin, 1981)
H. Beck and P. C. Bol, eds: *Forschungen zur Villa Albani: Antike Kunst und die Epoche der Aufklärung* (Berlin, 1982)
P. Thornton: *Authentic Decor: The Domestic Interior 1620–1920* (London, 1984)
O. Impey and A. MacGregor, eds: *The Origins of Museums: The Cabinet of Curiosities in Sixteenth and Seventeenth-century Europe* (Oxford, 1985)
K. Pomian: *Collectionneurs, amateurs et curieux: Paris, Venise, XVIe–XVIIIe siècle* (Paris, 1987)
A. Schnapper: *Le Géant, la licorne et la tulipe: Collections et collectionneurs dans la France du XVIIe siècle* (Paris, 1988–)
J.-P. Balelon and others, eds: *Le Cabinet de curiosités de la Bibliothèque Sainte-Geneviève: Des origines à nos jours* (Paris, 1989)
A. Mérot: 'Le Cabinet: Décor et espace d'illusion', *XVIIe Siècle*, xli (1989), pp. 37–51

GIUSEPPE OLMI

4. IMPORTANT TYPES. The most spectacular cabinets were undoubtedly those decorated with porcelain or mirrors, or with a combination of these two (and possibly other) materials.

(i) Porcelain. The massed display of porcelain in special rooms became fashionable in Europe during the 17th and 18th centuries. At first East Asian porcelain was used, but once porcelain had begun to be made in Europe (Meissen, 1710), some rooms were furnished with European porcelain. It is generally considered that this form of decoration was Dutch in origin. Between 1663 and 1765 porcelain rooms were created in royal palaces in Germany and throughout most of Europe, with the exception of France. Porcelain rooms were frequently embellished with such other luxurious materials as lacquer and mirrors. Many German rooms were called mirror cabinets (Spiegelkabinette) and were as much a showcase for the plate-glass mirrors as for the porcelain (*see* §(ii) below). Such decorative ideas were disseminated by the engraved designs of such artists as Daniel Marot I, Paul Decker I, Christof Pitzler and Salomon Kleiner.

The earliest documented porcelain rooms were associated with female Dutch royalty. The first was designed in 1663 by the Dutch-trained architect Johann Gregor Memhardt (*d* 1678) at Schloss Oranienburg (destr.), near Berlin, for Louise-Henrietta of Brandenburg-Prussia, the daughter of Frederick Henry, Prince of Orange Nassau, and Amalia, Countess of Solms-Braunfels, who also had an extensive collection of porcelain; it is not known, however, how she displayed these items. This room established the tradition in the Prussian Royal family for porcelain rooms for four generations. Oranienburg was rebuilt by Frederick I of Prussia between 1688 and 1695. It included a new porcelain room (destr. 18th century) after designs by Christof Pitzler. Some porcelain from this room was later used in a spectacular Porzellankabinett (1703–6; destr. 1943; rest. from 1945) designed by Johann Friedrich Eosander for the Electress Sophia Charlotte at Schloss Charlottenburg in Berlin. Queen Mary Stuart is associated with the use of massed porcelain in palaces in the Netherlands and England, almost certainly with the assistance of Marot. However, her collection of porcelain was dispersed after her death as part of her disposable property.

The fashion for exoticism spread quickly in the early 18th century, particularly in Germany and Austria. Collecting porcelain and assembling porcelain rooms continued to be a favoured pursuit of noblewomen, but men also quickly become involved with their creation. Porcelain rooms became so fashionable that princes vied to outdo one another. One of the finest extant porcelain rooms was created in 1719 by Ferdinand Plitzner at Schloss Weissenstein in Pommersfelden, South Germany, for Lothar Franz von Schönborn, Elector-Archbishop of Mainz and Prince-

Bishop of Bamberg. The Prince-Bishop's prized collection of East Asian porcelain, which included Japanese and Chinese Imari and blue-and-white Kang xi porcelain, was clustered in groups on brackets (see fig. 2). The Prince-Bishop was well aware of and possibly inspired by the Porzellankabinett (*c.* 1713; rest.) in the Lower Belvedere in Vienna, which was created by Prince Eugene of Savoy. The most ambitious porcelain interior, however, was planned by Frederick-Augustus I, Elector of Saxony (Augustus II, King of Poland). In 1719, inspired by an earlier visit to Schloss Charlottenburg and by the founding in 1710 of his own porcelain factory at Meissen, Frederick-Augustus decided to renovate the Holländisches Palais in Dresden as the showplace for his collection of East Asian and Meissen porcelain. By 1728 the palace was unable to contain the burgeoning collection, and it was gradually reconstructed and renamed the Japanisches Palais (1729–37). The interior was designed by Matthäus Daniel Pöppelman and Zacharius Longuelune; it was to have contained over 57,000 pieces of porcelain. The project was abandoned a few years after Frederick-Augustus's death in 1733.

By the 1730s most of the great princely families of Germany and Austria had created porcelain rooms in their palaces, and they were emulated in many of the smaller principalities; few examples, however, survive. There were porcelain rooms in such palaces as the Residenz in Munich (1693; 1731–3); the Dubsky Zimmer in the Schloss Dubsky, in Brno, Moravia (1720–25; now Vienna, Österreich. Mus. Angewandte Kst); the Falkenlust, Brühl Castle (*c.* 1730); the Residenz in Ansbach (*c.* 1730); Schloss Saarbrücken (*c.* 1747) and Schloss Monbijou in Berlin (1753–4). Porcelain rooms were also created in Russia, for example in the Montplaisir, Peterhof, St Petersburg (1713–16). There is also a single curious and early example of a ceiling lined with Chinese porcelain in the palace of the counts of Azurara in Lisbon (1680s; Lisbon, Mus. A. Dec. Fund. Espirito Sante). The apotheosis of the porcelain room was the Salottino di Porcellana in the Palazzo Reale in Pórtici, near Naples (1757–9; Naples, Capodimonte; *see* ITALY, fig. 7). This room, created (1724–60) for Maria Amalia of Naples by Guiseppe Gricci and Stefano Gricci, comprises 3000 interlocking pieces of porcelain made at the factory of Capodimonte. A larger version of this room, the Gabinete de la Porcelana (1763–5; *in situ*) was also made by Guiseppe Gricci with porcelain from the Fábrica del Buen Retiro for the Aranjuez Palace, near Madrid; another is situated in the Palacio Real, Madrid.

BIBLIOGRAPHY

J. L. Sponsel: *Kabinettstücke der Meissner Porzellan-Manufaktur* (Leipzig, 1900)
R. Schmidt: *Das Porzellan als Kunstwerk und Kulturspiegel* (Munich, 1925)
F. H. Hoffman: *Das Porzellan* (Berlin, 1932)
L. Reidmeister: 'Die Porzellankabinette der brandenburgisch-preussischen Schlösser', *Jb. Preuss. Kstsamml.*, i (1933), pp. 262–72
P. Thornton: *Seventeenth-century Interior Decoration in England, France & Holland* (New Haven and London, 1978)
L. Rosenfeld Shulsky: 'Queen Mary's Collection of Porcelain and Delft in its Display at Kensington Palace', *Amer. Cer. Circ. Bull.*, vii (1989), pp. 51–74
J. Ayers and others: *Porcelain for Palaces: The Fashion for Japan in Europe* (London, 1990)
H. Brautigan and others: *Porzellan aus China und Japan: Die Porzellangalerie der Landgrafen von Hessen-Kassel* (Berlin, 1990)
G. Heres: *Dresdener Kunst-Sammlungen im 18. Jahrhundert* (Leipzig, 1991)

2. Porcelain and mirror cabinet, Schloss Weissenstein, Pommersfelden, designed by Ferdinand Plitzner, 1719; engraving by Salomon Kleiner, Augsburg, 1728

M. Chilton: 'Rooms of Porcelain', *International Ceramics Fair and Seminar* (London, 1992), pp. 24–33

MEREDITH CHILTON

(ii) Mirror. Small showpiece rooms with mirrored surfaces were popular in European royal and aristocratic palaces in the 17th and 18th centuries, as mirror-glass was regarded as a luxury material. Mirrored surfaces of various sizes that were incorporated into panelling or the plasterwork or that were placed on the walls extended the confines of the room and created light-enhancing effects. The 17th-century French *cabinets des glaces* were rooms in which the panelling was fitted with small, framed mirrors or mirror tiles placed together, for example in the Dauphin's mirror cabinet (1670s; destr.) at Versailles. In a similar way mirrored surfaces in gilt plasterwork and stucco panels were integrated with painted grotesque ornament in the oval *cabinet des glaces* (1651) of the Château de Maisons, near Paris, by François Mansart. It was not until large sheets of cast plate-glass were developed in the royal factory (*c.* 1680) that it was possible for rooms to be transformed into spacious fields of mirrors. The most spectacular example is the Galerie des Glaces (begun 1678) at Versailles by Jules Hardouin Mansart and Charles Le Brun; as the symbol of the power of the absolute monarchy, it was copied throughout Europe. Mirror cabinets were also found in the Netherlands in the 17th century. The combination of the fashion for mirrors with that for chinoiserie resulted in the creation of exotic, intricately fitted cabinets, possibly inspired by 17th-century Turkish and Persian 'mirror mosaics' (e.g. Chihil Sutun at Isfahan). Exotic lacquered cabinets with mirrored ceilings were created for the princes of Orange Nassau; in these, East Asian porcelain was displayed in front of mirrored chimney-breasts, for example in the Lacquer Cabinet (1645–52) of the Huis ten Bosch, The Hague; the 'Indiaense Cabinet' (*c.* 1685) at Honselaarsdijk, by Daniel Marot I; and the Library (*c.* 1692) at Het Loo, also by Marot.

In the late Baroque period in Germany the mirror cabinet reached its most elaborate form, serving as a spectacular conclusion to the suite of state apartments. Early examples in Prussia followed the Dutch example in linking the fashion for chinoiserie with that for mirrors (e.g. the porcelain room at Schloss Oranienburg, built in 1695 (destr.); or that designed by Johann Friedrich Eosander at Schloss Charlottenburg, Berlin, in 1703–6 (destr. 1943; rest. from 1945)). Large mirrored surfaces were set into gilt panels to provide reflective backdrops for the display of large quantities of porcelain, which became a distinctive feature of German mirror cabinets. The Gläsernes Schlafgemach (*c.* 1706) by Johann Friedrich Eosander in the Schloss Charlottenburg, in which mirrored pilaster strips alternated with bands of green damask, however, drew its inspiration from France.

In the early 18th century the variety with which mirrors could be used in interior decoration increased. The use of large sheets of mirror panels was popular in France in salons (e.g. the Salon des Glaces (1706) by Robert de Cotte, Grand Trianon, Versailles), and in bedrooms, boudoirs or bathrooms. Architectural theorists such as Paul Decker I published designs (e.g. *Fürstlicher Baumeister oder Architectura Civilis*, Augsburg, 1711) that combine the Dutch 'Indiaense Cabinet' with chinoiserie and French grotesques in the style of Jean Bérain I. Mirror cabinets in Vienna and South Germany became increasingly extravagant during this period: with a few exceptions that were purely mirror cabinets, for example the Spiegelkabinett (*c.* 1719; destr.) of the Schönbrunn Palace, Vienna, and the Goldenes Zimmer (*c.* 1721) of the Upper Belvedere, Vienna, by Johann Lükas von Hildebrandt, these rooms were combined mirror and porcelain cabinets. In the Vergultes Zimmer (1709–13; destr.) in Schloss Gaibach mirrored pilaster strips alternated with gilt panels of grotesques and sheets of glass using red-and-black *verre églomisé.* The Spiegelkabinett (1719) by Ferdinand Plitzner at Schloss Weissenstein, Pommersfelden, incorporates gilt wood-carvings with grotesque ornament on a background of walnut and mirror panels (see fig. 2 above). Combinations of mirror with other luxury materials became more varied and exaggerated throughout the 18th century. The German princes were particularly fond of using distorting mirrors, for example in the Spiegelkabinett (*c.* 1711) of the residence 'Favorite', near Rastatt, by Johann Michael Ludwig Rohrer. They also preferred mirrors with Bérain-style grotesques and figures from the *commedia dell'arte* (e.g. bedroom, Schloss Ludwigsburg, 1716) or created elaborate lighting effects using gilt stucco and wood and mirrors (e.g. Spiegelkabinett, Würzburg, Residenz, 1740–45; destr. 1945; rest. from 1987 to the original design by Johann Wolfgang von der Auwera).

The Rococo style emanating from France influenced many richly decorated mirror rooms throughout Europe, for example the Mirror Salon in the Palazzo Isnardi, Castello. This style was popular in Germany and Austria, and led to the elegant mirror cabinets designed by François de Cuvilliés I (examples at the Falkenlust, Brühl Castle, *c.* 1730; and Munich, Residenz, 1731–3) and the mirror cabinets in the Residenzschloss at Ansbach (*c.* 1740) and in the Residenzschloss at Fulda (1757). The mirror cabinets in the Altes Schloss Eremitage (*c.* 1750) and the Neues Schloss (*c.* 1755) at Bayreuth are fitted out with fragments of mirror, Rococo and chinoiserie decoration. Nikolaus Pacassi designed the Rococo Spiegelsaal (1761) in the Schönbrunn Palace, Vienna. Rooms with mirrored walls, for example the Mirror Room (*c.* 1780) in the palace of Tsarkoye Selo (now Pushkin), Russia by Charles Cameron, or with glass walls backed with painted panels (e.g. Glass Drawing Room, Northumberland House, by Robert Adam, *c.* 1773–5; London, V&A) remained an important aspect of interior decoration in aristocratic houses throughout the Neo-classical period and into the 19th century (e.g. the Spiegelkabinett in the Linderhof, Oberammergau, 1870s).

BIBLIOGRAPHY

H. Kreisel: *Deutsche Spiegelkabinette* (Darmstadt, 1953)

S. Roche and P. Devinoy: *Miroirs, galeries et cabinets des glaces* (Paris, 1956); rev. in Ger. by S. Roche, G. Courage and P. Devinoy as *Spiegel, Spiegelgalerien, Spiegelkabinette, Hand- und Wandspiegel* (Tübingen, 1985)

H.-D. Lohneis: *Die deutschen Spiegelkabinette: Studien zu den Räumen des späten 17. und des frühen 18. Jahrhunderts* (Munich, 1985)

W. Loibl: 'Ideen im Spiegel: Die Spiegelkabinette in den fränkischen Schönborn-Schlössern', *Die Grafen von Schönborn, Kirchenfürsten, Sammler, Mäzene* (exh. cat., Nüremberg, Ger. Nmus., 1989), pp. 80–90

FRIEDERIKE WAPPENSCHMIDT

Cabinet (ii). Small piece of furniture, shaped like a sloping desk, that contains drawers and pigeon-holes for the storage of small precious objects. The name is derived from the French *cabinet*, which came into use *c.* 1500, and can also mean a small private room (*see* CABINET (i), §1). Three basic furniture archetypes, the bed, the table and the chair, answer physical needs—sleep, food and rest during the day. By contrast, the chest, a space enclosed by a lid, and the cupboard, a space enclosed by doors, are for the protection of possessions. The chest, because it is impractical for the retrieval of individual objects, which have to be stored under others, has been largely superseded, replaced by a multiplicity of forms incorporating drawers. This family of forms has yet to be fully disentangled, but the principal catalyst for their development was the cabinet.

The form seems to have originated in Spain, where a Moorish tradition of piecing together small refined wooden objects survived (*see* SPAIN, §VI, 1 and 2), in contrast to the more structural carpentry tradition of northern Europe. About 1500 a new form appeared, the *cofre de Valencia*, outwardly resembling a chest, but with on one side a door concealing a nest of small drawers. The next development seems to have been the *escritorio*, a box filled with drawers whose fall-front, when let down and resting on a table, or on lopers incorporated in a stand, served as a writing surface. Such a practical portable combination of document case and writing-desk circulated rapidly through the Habsburg Empire, and the form now known as a *Schreibtisch* was produced in quantity in the great mercantile cities of Augsburg and Nuremberg. In 1603 Philip III of Spain was driven to forbid the import of Nuremberg cabinets, and around 1600 *cabinets d'Alemagne* often crop up in French inventories. The form was also copied in Japan. By this date the fall-front had usually given way to doors, and the cabinet was associated with the princely cult of the precious microcosm, which was so important an aspect of Mannerism. Thus in 1568 Bernardo Buontalenti designed an octagonal cabinet (untraced) for the centre of the Tribuna of the Uffizi, Florence (Italian terms were *studiolo*, *stipo*, or in Naples, reflecting the trade with Spain, *scritorio*), and in the early 17th century PHILIPP HAINHOFER, an Augsburg merchant, orchestrated the production of a series of monumental cabinets packed with works of art and nature.

From the 1570s ebony was the preferred material for cabinets, whether they were made in Augsburg (*see* GERMANY, fig. 45), Naples or Florence. In Paris ebony cabinets began to be made in the 1630s (*see* GOBELINS, fig. 2): hence the French word for cabinetmaker is *ébéniste* (It. *ebanista*). At this date cabinets were much larger, and their stands were a more integral part of their composition. In many cases the doors were dispensed with, and the cabinet, once a miniature and secretive form, became increasingly monumental and splendid, decorated with paintings, gilt and silver mounts, tortoiseshell, marquetry, lacquer and pietre dure, a process that culminated in the magnificent cabinet (priv. col.), 3.8 m high, delivered from the Grand Ducal workshops in Florence to Henry Somerset, 3rd Duke of Beaufort (1707–45), in 1732. Cabinets of this form continued to be made: one was presented by the City of Paris to Marie-Antoinette in 1787 (Versailles, Château), and Henri Fourdinois (1830–1907) showed an elaborate Fontainebleau-style cabinet (London, V&A; see fig.) at the Exposition Universelle of 1867 in Paris. New cabinet types also emerged, however: at Gripsholm Castle in Sweden, for instance, there is an amber cabinet dated 1712, which looks back to the 16th century, shown in a possibly contemporary glazed cabinet. Secrétaires, however various in outward form, often preserved an interior arrangement, including secret drawers, ultimately inherited from the 16th-century cabinet. Thus, although few modern cabinetmakers know what a cabinet is, the form has entered their craft sub-conscious as the most complex and various of furniture forms, and the only furniture type to possess an internal anatomy.

Fontainebleau-style cabinet by Henri Fourdinois, walnut, 2.74×1.27 m, 1855 (London, Victoria and Albert Museum)

BIBLIOGRAPHY

S. Jervis: 'A Tortoise-shell Cabinet and its Precursors', *V&A Mus. Bull.*, iv (1968), pp. 132–43

G. Himmelheber: *Kabinettschränke* (Munich, 1977)
P. Thornton: *Seventeenth-century Interior Decoration in England, France and Holland* (New Haven and London, 1978), pp. 244–7
D. Alfter: *Die Geschichte des Augsburger Kabinettschranks* (Augsburg, 1986)

SIMON JERVIS

Cabinet card. *See under* PHOTOGRAPHY, §I.

Cabinet picture. Small painting of the type hung in a KUNSTKAMMER—an art collection formed by a connoisseur in northern Europe at the end of the 16th and especially in the 17th century. It can, in addition, refer to painted depictions of these collections.

1. Pictures for collections. 2. Pictures of collections.

1. PICTURES FOR COLLECTIONS. Encyclopedic collections (*Kunstkammern*) were popular at the beginning of the 17th century in the southern Netherlands and particularly in Antwerp (*see* BELGIUM, §XIII), although similar types of *Kunstkammern* also existed in the northern Netherlands, as can be seen from the inventory of Rembrandt's collection. At the same time, the place accorded to pictures in such private collections in Antwerp increased in importance; paintings clearly formed the bulk of the inventory of the collection of Arnold Lunden, the Antwerp banker and brother-in-law of Peter Paul Rubens, which was drawn up in 176 sections between 1639 and 1649. Besides pictures by all the chief Flemish masters of his time, it included masterpieces of the Antwerp school and works by Italian artists of the 16th and 17th centuries. Antwerp burghers were fully aware of the aristocratic pretensions of such connoisseurship. Besides originals, they collected copies of famous or characteristic works by well-known artists. There was a predominance of painters in the Antwerp Guild of St Luke and the dominance of pupils over masters is probably explained by this demand for copies. During the 17th century there was a great increase in the export of small cabinet paintings from Antwerp to all parts of Europe, probably because their small format made transport easy, but also because Antwerp was recognized as an international art centre.

The restricted size of bourgeois houses necessitated small pictures; Rubens, in a letter of 1611 to Johann Faber, remarked on the popularity of '*cose piccole*'. Sometimes the paintings were hung symmetrically around one or two larger works; as pictures of collections show (e.g. Willem van Herp I's '*Art Gallery of Rubens*'; Florence, Pitti; see fig. 1), the custom was to fill the wall with them, edge to edge. These pictures of galleries, together with contemporary inventories, provide a valuable (if not always completely accurate) record of collectors' taste and the methods of display they preferred. The Antwerp collectors were interested in all types of subjects: biblical, allegorical and historical themes, portraits, landscapes, sea-pieces and still-lifes. During the first quarter of the 17th century each of these groups was methodically subdivided: still-lifes, for instance, into flowers, shells, fish or spoils of the chase; landscapes into woodland, winter or village scenes. Representations of the seasons, hitherto created by the artist as series, now tended to be single works: in the 17th century, for example, a winter landscape by Gysbrecht

1. Willem van Herp I: '*Art Gallery of Rubens*', 730×1850 mm, after 1640 (Florence, Palazzo Pitti)

Lytens (1586–1643/56) was hung opposite a summer landscape by Josse de Momper II. Painters of cabinet pictures began to specialize; thus there were painters of figures or architecture (e.g. Frans Francken II, Hendrick van Balen and Sebastiaen Vrancx), landscapes (e.g. Josse de Momper II and Abraham Govaerts), and flowers, animals and still-lifes (e.g. Osias Beert I, Alexander Adriaenssen and Clara Peeters). This specialization was accompanied by a readiness to collaborate with specialists in other fields (e.g. Jan Breughel the elder and Frans Francken II worked together). The subdivision of genres made it possible for a small cabinet painting, by reason of its subject, to replace or represent one aspect of the encyclopedic principle of collection; for example, a still-life of flowers would represent *natura*, or one of coins *antiquitas*. Cabinet paintings were seldom assembled according to artists but rather by genre and subject, with the general aim of comprehensiveness.

Such collections also became popular in Prague during the reign (1576–1612) of Emperor Rudolf II (*see* CZECH REPUBLIC, §XII). These collections were, however, dominated by portraits, contemporary or posthumous, of the owner, his family or the ruling families, and can be seen as an expression of the collector's increasing self-confidence (Pesek, 1987). The Antwerp burghers, with their cosmopolitan outlook and extensive economic connections, were concerned with display; by contrast, those of Prague were more interested in the close ties of a familiar cultural tradition. Although comparable galleries of small pictures thus developed outside Antwerp at the beginning of the 17th century, it was only in Antwerp itself that pictures of collections (see below) developed into a popular genre.

BIBLIOGRAPHY

J. von Schlosser: *Die Kunst- und Wunderkammern der Spätrenaissance* (Leipzig, 1908, rev. Brunswick, 1978)
J. Denucé; *Kunstausfuhr Antwerpens im 17. Jahrhundert: Die Firma Forchoudt* (Antwerp, 1931)
——: 'De Antwerpsche konstkamers', *Inventarissen van kunstverzamelingen te Antwerpen in de 16e en 17e eeuwen* (Amsterdam, 1932)
E. Duverger: 'Nieuwe gegevens betreffende de Kunsthandel van Matthijs Musson en Maria Fourmenois te Antwerpen tussen 1633 en 1681' [New information concerning the art firm of Matthijs Musson and Maria Fourmenois in Antwerp between 1633 and 1681], *Gent. Bijdr. Kstgesch. & Oudhdknd.*, xxi (1968) [complete issue]
W. Schade: 'Maler am Hofe Moritz von Sachsen', *Z. Dt. Ver. Kstwiss.*, xxii (1968), pp. 29–44
R. W. Scheller: 'Rembrandt and the Encyclopaedic Collection', *Oud-Holland*, lxxxiv (1969), pp. 81–147
J. Stockbauer: 'Die Kunstbestrebungen am bairischen Hof', *Quellenschr. Kstgesch.*, viii (1970)
G. Dogaer: 'De inventaris van Diego Duarte', *Jb.: Kon. Mus. S. Kst.* (1971), pp. 195–222
E. Duverger: 'De verzameling schilderijen van de Antwerpse zijde- en tapijthandelaar Peter van Hecke de Jonge, schoonbroer van P. P. Rubens, naar een inventaris van 1646' [The collection of paintings owned by the Antwerp dealer in silks and carpets, Peter van Hecke, brother-in-law of P. P. Rubens, according to an inventory of 1646], *Jb.: Kon. Mus. S. Kst.* (1971), pp. 143–73
W. Liebenwein: 'Studiolo', *Frankfurt. Forsch.*, vi (Berlin, 1977)
H. Vlieghe: 'Une Grande Collection anversoise du dix-septième siècle: Le Cabinet d'Arnold Lunden, beau-frère de Rubens', *Der Mensch um 1500: Werke aus Kirchen und Kunstkammern* (exh. cat., Berlin, Skulpgal., 1977), pp. 172–204
K. Ertz: *Jan Brueghel I: Die Gemälde* (Cologne, 1979)
Stilleben in Europa (exh. cat., Münster, Westfäl. Landesmus.; Baden-Baden, Staatl. Ksthalle; 1980)
U. Härting: *Studien zur Kabinettbildmalerei des Frans Francken II* (Hildesheim and New York, 1983)
The Collector's Cabinet: Flemish Paintings from New England Private Collections (exh. cat., Worcester, MA, A. Mus., 1983–4)
J. Pánek: 'Zwei Arten böhmischen Adelsmäzenatentums in der Zeit Rudolfs II', *Prag um 1600: Beiträge zur Kunst und Kultur am Hofe Rudolfs II: Prague, 1987*, pp. 218–31
J. Pesek: 'Porträts in den Bürgerhäusern des Rudolfinischen Prags', *Prag um 1600: Beiträge zur Kunst und Kultur am Hofe Rudolfs II: Prague, 1987*, pp. 244–8
U. Härting: *Frans Francken II: Die Gemälde* (Freren, 1989)
The Age of the Marvelous (exh. cat., ed. J. Kenseth; Hanover, NH, Dartmouth Coll., Hood Mus. A., 1991)
H. Bredekamp: *Antikensehnsucht und Maschinenglauben: Die Geschichte der Kunstkammer und die Zukunft der Kunstgeschichte* (Berlin, 1993)

2. PICTURES OF COLLECTIONS. At about the same time as cabinet pictures became widespread, there arose in the southern Netherlands, especially in bourgeois Antwerp, a new type of painting, which depicted the private galleries, or *Kunstkammern*, themselves. The predecessors of such works include the perspective studies of Hans Vredeman de Vries, Abel Grimmer's indoor scenes with biblical figures and the 'dancing parties' of Hieronymus Francken, Frans Francken II and Marten Pepijn. The gallery paintings depict a room in peep-show style, its walls hung decoratively with cabinet pictures. There is generally a side table with shells lying on it; on another table are scientific instruments and sculptures; scholars and connoisseurs can be seen engaged in debate. A distinction has to be drawn between allegorical pictures of imaginary galleries, depictions of art dealers' establishments and pictures of actual collections. Among Flemish artists who specialized in such interiors were Cornelis de Baellieur, Hans Jordaens III, Jan van Kessel, Gonzales Coques and, subsequently, Balthasar van den Bosche.

The different types of gallery paintings have led to differing views as to their content and purpose, as the various modes of portrayal were not clearly distinguished. The earliest such paintings were produced in Antwerp in the first decade of the 17th century by Frans Francken (ii), who specialized in small figures. Special forms like the *Preziosenwand*, or, properly, 'encyclopedic still-life', also developed at this time. These depict a table or similar piece of furniture, partly cut off by the lower picture-edge, on which *Kunstkammer* items are displayed in a still-life: shells, dried flowers in glass cylinders, coins, small sculptures, porcelain and books. On the wall behind the table are paintings, drawings and miniatures: the effect is to present a cross-section of a *Kunstkammer*, indicating its encyclopedic scope. Often the artist depicts an adjoining room with scholars debating, or an artist's studio. In paintings of this type, as in the more complete depictions of *Kunstkammern*, scientific investigation and scholarship are seen as forming the basis of a universal collection.

A parallel development of the gallery picture showed scholars and *ânes iconoclastes* ('iconoclastic donkeys'). This type of gallery interior was popularized by Frans Francken II (see fig. 2) and represents an allegory on knowledge and ignorance: on the one hand, debating scholars and connoisseurs; on the other, men with asses' heads destroying works of art and scientific instruments.

The earliest dated picture of a collection is a *Kunstkammer with Debating Scholars* (1612; ex-Sotheby's, London, 19 April 1967). It is not a picture of an actual gallery, but an allegory of the meritorious studies of the learned men,

2. Frans Francken II: *Art Gallery with Scholars and 'Anes Iconoclastes'*, oil on copper, 525×740 mm, *c.* 1615–18 (Rome, Palazzo Barberini)

with their globe and *objets d'art*, with particular reference to biblical history painting. The study of objects in the collection, and especially the contemplation of the painted histories, has as its final purpose the recognition of the greatness of God. The main part in this is played by paintings of biblical stories, which can depict virtuous and pious conduct in a convincing and intelligible manner; painting gives material shape to all ideas. Taking up Francken's lead, Jan Breughel the elder and Peter Paul Rubens executed the kaleidoscopic cycle of the *Five Senses*, now in the Prado, Madrid. The first picture is an *Allegory of Sight* (1617), showing an encyclopedic *Kunstkammer* with a personification of Sight.

Besides such pictures of imaginary galleries, with very complex allegorical content, there are also 'portraits' of collections that can be identified along with their owners (e.g. the *Kunstkammer of Nicolaas Rockox* by Frans Francken II; Munich, Alte Pin.; *see* FRANCKEN, (5), fig. 1). The earliest work of this kind seems to be the *Cabinet of Cornelis van der Geest of Antwerp* (1628; Antwerp, Rubenshuis) by Willem van Haecht II, in which not only the pictures but also those visiting the gallery can be identified. They include the Archdukes, Albert and Isabella, Rubens, Anthony van Dyck and other contemporary artists. In this first work of its kind the *Kunstkammer* with its rich collection serves to enhance the prestige of van der Geest, a patron of the arts, who is further honoured by the visit of the viceregal couple. This self-advertising element is found in all successive pictures of this format.

In addition to this first portrait of van der Geest's collection, van Haecht painted an almost equally important scene of *Alexander the Great Visiting the Studio of Apelles* (The Hague, Mauritshuis; *see* DISPLAY OF ART, fig. 4), which combines an episode from ancient history with traditional allegory. Alexander is seen as a patron of the arts; he is presented as a learned, intellectual connoisseur. But at the same time the artist at his easel appears as a scholar and intellectual, for his cabinet, full of antique sculptures, scientific instruments and books, is evidence of learning and the thirst for knowledge.

About the middle of the 17th century there developed from these types of cabinet picture portraits of artists in which it is difficult to distinguish a portrait of an artist in his studio from a self-portrait set in a *Kunstkammer* (e.g. '*Art Gallery of Rubens*'; see fig. 1 above). From this time onward the artist's self-presentation is strongly marked by the striving after culture; he is no longer a mere producer of works of art, but also an owner and connoisseur. In an etching of 1771, the *Painter's Study* (Stuttgart, Staatsgal.), Daniel Nikolaus Chodowiecki shows a painter in front of a wall covered with pictures; in the room are his wife and children sitting at a table and looking attentively at pictures. This *cabinet d'un peintre* is probably no more than a piece of stage scenery designed to indicate the artist's intellectual and social status.

A new period of prestigious 'portraits' of collections began with the 12 works of this kind that David Teniers II painted in Brussels after 1651, as court painter and keeper of the collection of Archduke Leopold William (versions Brussels, Mus. A. Anc.; Vienna, Ksthist. Mus.; for illustration *see* HABSBURG, §I(18); Petworth House, W. Sussex, NT; *see* TENIERS, (2), fig. 3). The pictures of the collection surround the Archduke and enhance his prestige. Again, while Cardinal Silvio Valenti Gonzaga appears inconspicuous in the 1749 picture of his collection (Hartford, CT, Wadsworth Atheneum) by Giovanni Paolo Panini, nevertheless the great painters' names redound to his credit.

Panini's huge imaginary picture galleries hung with painted views of the architectural monuments of Rome subordinate the gallery structure to the glorification of the painted architecture, with an almost surreal decrease in the picture's legibility. A series of four paintings was commissioned by the French Ambassador to the Vatican, Etienne François, Duc de Choiseul, to enhance his own reputation as a connoisseur. Panini thus created a compendium of painted Roman architecture in his *Ancient Rome* (Stuttgart, Württemberg. Landesmus.) and *Modern Rome* (Boston, Mus. F.A.), together with the companion works depicting the interior and exterior of St Peter's with the visit of the Duc. The allegorical aspect is subordinated to the decorative, but the patron's self-advertisement is well to the fore.

Paintings of art dealers' galleries, real or imaginary, probably originated *c.* 1615–20. A delightful masterpiece of this genre is Antoine Watteau's *L'Enseigne de Gersaint* (1720; Berlin, Schloss Charlottenburg; *see* DRESS, fig. 43). Among the paintings exhibited by the Paris dealer are works by Watteau's artistic forebears, the 16th-century Venetian and 17th-century Flemish painters.

In depictions of the French *salons* (e.g. Gabriel-Jacques de Saint-Aubin, *Paris Salon of 1767*; Paris, priv. col., see 1982–3 exh. cat., pl. 304) there are paintings that can still be identified, such is the artist's realism; but he gives the scene a further dimension by introducing Apollo, as patron of the arts, in a glory above the picture zone. With this allegorical touch Saint-Aubin recalls the early forms of *Kunstkammer* depiction.

This type of painting was not continued to any significant extent after the mid-18th century, as the fame of private collections diminished owing to political enlightenment and the expansion of public collections in museums. However, there has of late been a revival of the custom of depicting individual patrons amid their collections, either in painting or photographically (e.g. Baron Hans Heinrich von Thyssen-Bornemisza, Lugano, and Peter Ludwig, Aachen).

BIBLIOGRAPHY

E. Dacier: *Gabriel de Saint-Aubin* (Paris, 1929–31)
L. van Puyvelde: 'Willem van Haecht en zijn *Galerij van Cornelis van der Geest*', *Rev. Belge Archéol. & Hist. A.*, xxiv (1955)
J. Held: 'Artis pictoriae amator: An Antwerp Art Patron and his Collection', *Gaz. B.-A.*, n. s. 5, i (1957), pp. 53–84; also in *Studies by Julius Held* (Princeton, 1982), pp. 35–64
S. Speth-Holterhoff: *Les Peintres flamands de cabinets d'amateurs* (Brussels, 1957)
M. Winner: *Die Quellen der Pictura-Allegorien in gemalten Bildergalerien des 17. Jahrhunderts zu Antwerpen* (diss., U. Cologne, 1957)
F. Arisi: *Gian Paolo Panini* (Piacenza, 1961)
M. Winner: 'Gemalte Kunsttheorie', *Jb. Berlin. Mus.*, iv (1962), pp. 151–83
R. W. Scheller: 'Rembrandt and the Encyclopaedic Collection', *Oud-Holland*, lxxxiv (1969), pp. 81–147
K. Ertz: *Jan Breughel I: Die Gemälde* (Cologne, 1979)
J. Briels: 'Amator pictoriae artis—De Antwerpse kunstverzamelaar Peeter Stevens (1590–1668) en zijn Constkamer', *Jb.: Kon. Mus. S. Kst.* (1980), pp. 137–226
Bruegel: Une Dynastie de peintres (exh. cat., intro. M. Klinge; Brussels, Pal. B.-A., 1980)
La Peinture dans la peinture (exh. cat., ed. P. Georgel and A. M. Lecoq; Dijon, Mus. B.-A., 1982–3)
M. Smith Podles: 'Virtue and Vice: Paintings and Sculpture in Two Pictures from the Walters Collection', *J. Walters A.G.*, xli (1983), pp. 29–44
J. Müller Hofstede: 'Non saturatur oculus visu—zur *Allegorie des Gesichts* von Peter Paul Rubens und Jan Breughel der Ältere', *Wort und Bild in der niederländischen Kunst und Literatur des 16. und 17. Jahrhunderts*, eds H. W. J. Vekeman and J. Müller Hofstede (Erstadt, 1984), pp. 243–89
H.-J. Raupp: *Untersuchungen zu Künstlerbildnis und Künstlerdarstellung in den Niederlanden im 17. Jahrhundert* (Hildesheim and New York, 1984)
Watteau, 1684–1721 (exh. cat., Washington, DC, N.G.A.; Paris, Grand Pal.; W. Berlin, Schloss Charlottenburg; 1984–5)
E. Larsen: *Seventeenth-century Flemish Painting* (Freren, 1985)
Z. Z. Filipczak: *Picturing Art in Antwerp, 1550–1700* (Princeton, 1987)
S. Slive: 'Dutch Pictures in the Collection of Cardinal Silvio Valenti Gonzaga', *Simiolus*, xvii (1987), pp. 169–87
U. Härting: *Frans Francken II: Die Gemälde* (Freren, 1989)
——: ' "Doctrina et pietas"—über frühe Galeriebilder', *Jb: Kon. Mus. S. Kst.* (in preparation)

URSULA HÄRTING

Cable moulding. *See* ROPEWORK.

Cabré, Manuel (*b* Barcelona, Spain, 25 Jan 1890; *d* Caracas, 5 Feb 1984). Venezuelan painter. From 1896 he lived in Venezuela and studied at the Academia de Bellas Artes, Caracas (1904–9), under Emilio Mauri (1855–1908) and Antonio Herrera Toro. In 1912 he was a founder-member with Antonio Edmundo Monsanto and others of the Círculo de Bellas Artes in Caracas, a group that made landscape painting the leading genre in Venezuelan art in the first half of the 20th century. Between 1916 and 1919 the influence of Samys Mützner, Nicolas Ferdinandov and Emilio Boggio had a marked effect on his palette and composition. He travelled to France in 1920 to consolidate his artistic training, attending the Académie Colarossi and the Académie de la Grande Chaumière and executing several works. In 1931 he returned to Venezuela and held an exhibition of his French paintings. From then on he dedicated himself fully to studying the Venezuelan landscape, in particular the mountain El Avila. In 1951 he was awarded the national painting prize, which confirmed his position as a leading representative of Venezuelan landscape painting and as the originator of a school of painting. An example of his work from this period is *La Silla Seen from La Urbina* (1955; Caracas, Mus. A. Contemp. Sofía Imber).

WRITINGS

Cabré por Cabré (Caracas, 1980)

BIBLIOGRAPHY

A. Amengual: *Cabré, el niño* (Caracas, 1980)
J. Calzadilla: *Cabré* (Caracas, 1980)

YASMINY PÉREZ SILVA

Cabrera, Enríquez de. *See under* CASTILLA.

Cabrera, Francisco (*b* Guatemala City, 16 Sept 1781; *d* Guatemala City, 21 Nov 1845). Guatemalan painter, printmaker and medallist. He entered the mint in 1795 as an apprentice engraver but on the recommendation of its director, Pedro Garci Aguirre, also became Master Corrector at the Escuela de Dibujo de la Sociedad Económica de Amigos del Paìs, Guatemala City, in 1796, holding the post until 1804. He continued working at the mint until 1809 and demonstrated outstanding skill both as a medallist and engraver of coins and as an engraver and etcher. He returned to the mint in 1823 as second engraver, remaining in the post until his death.

Despite the quality of his work as a printmaker and medallist, Cabrera gained artistic recognition only as a miniature painter, working mostly in watercolour on ivory in a meticulous technique. He produced some miniatures on religious themes and others of birds, but the majority, measuring no more than 50 mm in height or width, were portraits of members of the Guatemalan aristocracy and bourgeoisie. It is not known exactly how many he produced, but from the middle of the 1830s he began to number them, starting from 500; the highest known number of the approximately 200 authenticated miniatures is 745. Although he suffered some illness, he was most productive during the last five years of his life. An evolution can be discerned from his earliest works, dating from *c.* 1810, in which he painted in compact and smooth vertical strokes on grey backgrounds tinged with green, through to the extraordinarily fine quality of anatomical drawing in his final works, with pale blue backgrounds. He had several students, including Justo Letona, José Letona, Delfina Luna and Leocadia Santa Cruz, but none rivalled him in quality. As a miniature painter he remained an essentially solitary figure, following no local precedents and leaving no substantial legacy.

BIBLIOGRAPHY

H. Garavito: *Francisco Cabrera: Miniaturista guatemalteco* (Guatemala City, 1945)

Francisco Cabrera (1781–1845) (exh. cat. by J. Luján Muñoz, Guatemala City, Bib. N., 1984)

JORGE LUJÁN-MUÑOZ

Cabrera, Geles (*b* Mexico City, 2 Aug 1929). Mexican sculptor. She studied at the Academia de Bellas Artes de San Carlos, Mexico City, from 1944 to 1946, and in 1947 at the Academia de San Alejandro in Havana, Cuba, where she received a number of awards. She held her first one-woman exhibition in 1950. Her sensitive sculpture addressed human emotions and situations, including motherhood, love and solitude. Taking inspiration for her sculptures from prehistoric art, she worked first in terracotta and then in bronze and with direct carving in stone, using clean contours to stress the curves and sensuality of the human form. Later she used newspapers as a sculptural material. From 1975, in association with other Mexican sculptors such as Angela Gurría, Mathias Goeritz, Juan Luis Díaz (*b* 1939) and Sebastián, she began also to conceive sculptures for urban settings.

BIBLIOGRAPHY

Geles Cabrera (Mexico City, 1977)

L. Kassner: *Diccionario de escultura mexicana* (Mexico City, 1983), p. 55

LOUISE NOELLE

Cabrera, Germán (*b* Las Piedras, nr Montevideo, 2 May 1903; *d* Montevideo, 30 May 1990). Uruguayan sculptor. He studied under the Argentinian sculptor Luis Falcini (1899–1973) from 1918 to 1926 at the Círculo de Bellas Artes in Montevideo, and in Paris from 1926 to 1928 under Charles Despiau at the Académie Colarossi and under Emile-Antoine Bourdelle at the Académie de la Grande Chaumière. He lived again in Uruguay (1928–36), and in Paris (1936–8), before moving to Caracas (1938–44). After travelling extensively in Europe, Mexico and the USA he settled in Madrid in 1975 to the end of the decade.

Cabrera's sculptures, such as *Untitled* (1963; Montevideo, Estación Goes), depend on a dramatic tension between spatial, geometrical and mechanical elements and biomorphic and organic forms suggestive of the human body. He used a great variety of materials, including scrap iron, concrete, marble and combinations of wood and metal, sometimes left in their natural state and sometimes modified, painted or assembled. In Montevideo many of his works are displayed in architectural settings. He took part in a number of exhibitions, including the São Paulo Biennale in 1961 and the Venice Biennale in 1962.

BIBLIOGRAPHY

R. Huyghe: *El arte y el hombre*, iii (1967/*R* Madrid, 1975), p. 549

F. García Esteban: *Artes plásticas del Uruguay del siglo XX* (Montevideo, 1970)

A. Kalenberg: *Reencuentro y recuperación de lo monstruoso* (Montevideo, 1976)

Germán Cabrera (exh. cat., ed. A. Haber; Montevideo, Salón Mun. Exp., 1992)

ANGEL KALENBERG

Cabrera, Miguel (*b* Antequera [now Oaxaca], 27 Feb 1695; *d* Mexico City, 16 May 1768). Mexican painter. He studied under Juan Correa and made indiscriminate use in his paintings of old engravings from different European schools. He is known to have painted a number of pictures during the 1740s, but it was after 1750 that he received his most important commissions, including the series dedicated to the life of St Ignatius Loyola for the Colegio de San Ignacio y San Francisco Javier in Querétaro, for the Templo de La Profesa in Mexico City and for the Jesuit college at Tepotzotlán near Mexico City. In the 1760s Cabrera painted a *Virgin of the Apocalypse* (Mexico City, Pin. Virreinal), basing the image on an engraving after a work by Rubens that was very popular in Mexico during the colonial period. He also designed funerary pyres commemorating the deaths of Maria Amalia of Saxony (1761), the Archbishop Rubio y Salinas (1765) and Isabel Farnese (1767). In addition he explored genres known as 'castes' and 'half-castes', representations of family groups comprising individuals with ethnic differences (e.g. Madrid, Mus. América).

Cabrera was among the painters who in 1754 participated in the formation of a society or academy of art in Mexico City. In his book *Maravilla americana y conjunto de raras maravillas* (1756) he described one of his paintings, a representation of the *Virgin of Guadalupe*, and the opinions of contemporary artists on that subject. His prolific production and reliance on stereotypical models had considerable influence on his contemporaries.

WRITINGS

Maravilla americana y conjunto de raras maravillas (1756, rev. Madrid/1785)

BIBLIOGRAPHY
J. Castro Mantecón: *Miguel Cabrera, pintor oaxaqueño del siglo XVIII* (Mexico City, 1958)
A. Carrillo y Gariel: *El pintor Miguel Cabrera* (Mexico City, 1966)

MARIA CONCEPCIÓN GARCÍA SÁIZ

Cabrera, Roberto (*b* Guatemala City, 11 Dec 1937). Guatemalan painter and printmaker. He studied at the Escuela Nacional de Artes Plásticas in Guatemala City from 1953 to 1958 and displayed great originality from an early age, mixing styles as diverse as Expressionism and Surrealism and ranging from a traditional figuration to avant-garde modes in a variety of media, including drawing, printmaking, painting and collage. His interest in archaic styles led him to use Pre-Columbian sources as well as their modern popular and indigenous counterparts. He also addressed himself, both personally and artistically, to political and social problems on both a national and an international level. Together with Marco Augusto Quiroa and Elmar René Rojas he founded the Vértebra group, which held a number of exhibitions from 1965 to 1968. In the early 1980s he settled in Costa Rica, where he devoted himself primarily to teaching and aesthetic theory.

BIBLIOGRAPHY
L. Méndez Dávila: *Arte vanguardia Guatemala* (Guatemala City, 1969), pp.v-vi
Roberto Cabrera: Su producción artística (exh. cat., Guatemala City, Escuela N.A. Plást., 1976)

JORGE LUJÁN-MUÑOZ

Cabriole [Fr.: 'caper'; Lat. *capreolus*: 'goat']. Form of furniture leg that resembles the foreleg of a capering animal and curves and narrows downwards, ending in a club, hoof or paw. It is characteristic of the designs of Thomas Chippendale (i), among others (*see* UNITED STATES OF AMERICA, fig. 31).

□

Cacault, François (*b* Nantes, 10 Feb 1743; *d* Clisson, 10 Oct 1805). French diplomat, patron and collector. His military service at the Ecole Militaire, Paris (1767–9), and under the Maréchal de Lussan, Commander-in-Chief of Brittany (1775–85), was punctuated by a Grand Tour of Europe and England. His diplomatic career included the posts of Secretary at the French Embassy, Naples (1785–91), Special Envoy to Rome (1793–6) and Ambassador to the Papal States (1800–03). In 1804 he became Senator for the Loire-Inférieure. His brother Pierre Cacault (1744–1810), a painter and pupil of Joseph-Marie Vien, lived for a period in Rome that coincided with François's diplomatic appointments. It is thought that François Cacault began collecting art works as early as the 1770s. His ambition to create a collection surveying the history of European art for the benefit of art education became public in 1800 when buildings were erected at Clisson, near Nantes, as the nucleus of a museum and school of art under one roof, a *musée-école*. Before his death, the collection included works on loan from the state. Pierre Cacault inherited the museum and school and commenced protracted negotiations to sell them to the nation. At his death in 1810, the collection was acquired by the City of Nantes, forming the nucleus of the Musée des Beaux-Arts. Apart from engravings numbered in excess of 10,000, and more than 60 sculptures, the Cacault collection consists of a group of paintings that includes an interesting selection of early Italian works, among them a *Virgin and Child with Saints* by Bernardo Daddi and a panel with *SS Anthony and Sebastian* by Perugino, as well as a group of three important paintings by Georges de La Tour: the *Hurdy-Gurdy Player*, the *Dream of St Joseph* and the *Denial of St Peter*. Among Cacault's pictures by 18th-century French artists is *Harlequin Emperor of the Moon*, attributed to Antoine Watteau, and a *View of Mount Vesuvius* by Pierre-Jacques Volaire. He also bought a number of paintings in Naples, ranging from an oil sketch for an altarpiece of the *Mystic Marriage of St Catherine* by Francesco Solimena to a still-life of fish by Giuseppe Recco.

BIBLIOGRAPHY
H. de Saint-Georges: *Notice historique sur le musée de peinture de Nantes* (Nantes, 1858), pp. 33–111
A. Bourdeaut: 'François et Pierre Cacault: Les Origines du Concordat et le Musée des beaux-arts de Nantes', *Mém. Soc. Hist. & Archéol. Bretagne* (1936), pp. 75–182
C. Souviron: *Musée des beaux-arts de Nantes, 60 peintures* (Nantes, 1981)
C. Cosneau: 'La Collection Cacault ou du Musée-école au Musée des beaux-arts', *Rev. Pays Loire* (1985), pp. 6–31
——: 'Musée: Nantes', *Beaux-A.* [20th C.], xxxvii (1986), pp. 48–53

PETER ROLFE MONKS

Cacaxtla. Pre-Columbian site in Tlaxcala, central Mexico. It flourished *c.* 250 BC–*c.* AD 900 and is notable for its wall paintings (*in situ*).

1. INTRODUCTION. The ruins of Cacaxtla lie in the hilly uplands between Tlaxcala and Puebla, *c.* 100 km east of Mexico City, on ancient routes of communication between the Central Highlands and both the Gulf Coast region and the Southern Highlands of Mixteca. Only a small part of the site has been excavated, and its history is not yet fully understood. Archaeological evidence indicates human occupation since the Late Pre-Classic period (*c.* 300 BC–*c.* AD 250), with two phases of more intense occupation during the Classic period (*c.* AD 250–*c.* 900). Pottery, traces of Teotihuacán TALUD–TABLERO architecture and residential structures suggest that Cacaxtla may have served during part of the Classic period (*c.* AD 400–*c.* 600) as a stage on the trade routes controlled by TEOTIHUACÁN. Very different cultural affiliations are indicated by the surface ruins, which appear to be heavily fortified and date from the Late Classic period (*c.* AD 600–*c.* 900) and into the Early Post-Classic period (*c.* AD 900–*c.* 1200), a time of instability and strife in the Central Highlands. The wall paintings for which the site is famous have been attributed to the early part of this second phase (*c.* AD 750–*c.* 900). They are located in two structures (designated Building A and Building B) at the north end of a large open plaza. Other buildings enclose this space, the most elaborate being to the south where a complex of small rooms, called the Palace, surrounds a second and smaller court. An unexcavated pyramidal mound lies to the north. The architecture, associated pottery and wall paintings have a distinctive local character but also reflect strong external influences, including other Central Highland, Southern Highland and Maya styles.

2. WALL PAINTINGS. Pending further excavation, the wall paintings provide the richest source of information

for the interpretation of the site. They fall into two distinctive sets: battle scenes on the substructure of Building B (see fig.), and near life-size representations of elaborately clothed individuals on either side of the doorway and adjoining doorjambs of the portico of Building A. The superposition of floors suggests that the battle scenes are slightly earlier than those of the portico.

The battle scenes of Building B cover *c.* 25 m of a *talud–tablero* wall that is bisected by a stairway. In its central area the polychrome paintings, in vivid reds, yellows, blues, black and white, are well-preserved and stand 1.80 m high, but towards the two extremities their condition deteriorates sharply, and little more than the lower metre survives. The 48 participants depicted can be divided into two groups, both of which stand out from the vivid turquoise blue background: the victors, armed with spears, knives and round shields, stand in a variety of aggressive poses. They are simply dressed, some with jaguar-skin jerkins or accessories, and wear headbands with short feathers. The vanquished are almost all prone, dead or horribly wounded; they are naked and unarmed but wear elaborate headdresses in the form of birds' heads with long trailing feathers, and rich ornaments such as jade pectorals, nose plugs and other accessories. Only two sumptuously clothed 'bird' warriors remain standing, in attitudes of apparent resignation close to the centre of the wall painting on either side of the stairway.

The portico paintings of Building A are different in character, although there is a thematic continuity with the battle scene in that the individuals portrayed in the main panels are dressed in jaguar and avian costumes, recalling those of the two groups of warriors. There is, however, nothing violent about their poses, which have a statuesque quality. The paintings combine the depiction of symbols of water and fertility with the representation of concepts related to fundamental Mesoamerican religious myths (*see* MESOAMERICA, PRE-COLUMBIAN, §I, 4). Among the pictographic signs, symbols and numerals used is the 'serpent eye' glyph, which also appears at Teotihuacán and is probably calendrical in meaning. The bar and dot numbering system (using a horizontal bar to indicate the value of five) is used in a similar way in the carved stone reliefs of XOCHICALCO and is also characteristic of ZAPOTEC writing. Venus symbols, including the eyed, five-pointed half-star symbol, abound. These panels have therefore generally been interpreted as a symbolic reconciliation of the opponents depicted in the battle scenes, and perhaps the apotheosis of their leaders.

The Cacaxtla wall paintings have been admired for the fidelity and individuality of their depiction of the human figure, which verges on portraiture, as well as for their compositional dynamism. Both aspects represent a break with the artistic conventions of the Central and Southern Highlands, and are exceptional even by Maya standards. They are eclectic, revealing a harmonious blend of influences from many parts of Mesoamerica: Teotihuacán, Xochicalco, the Gulf Coast region, the Maya region and other areas. Scholars generally agree that the formal style of the wall paintings is closest to the MAYA tradition, for example as at BONAMPAK, and that the vanquished 'bird' warriors display ethnic and iconographic traits that are essentially Maya. They also agree that the depictions of victorious 'jaguar' warriors, with their costumes and weapons, show a strong Highland influence. This has directed attention to ethnohistorical evidence that the decline of Teotihuacán in the 8th century AD was followed by the occupation of the Cholula–Tlaxcala area by peoples called the Olmeca–Xicalanca. Little is known about them, but tradition places their origin in the south-east Gulf Coast region. They have been identified with the Putún Maya,

Cacaxtla, wall painting from Building B showing a battle scene (detail, line drawing), *c.* 1.8×22 m, *c.* AD 750–*c.* 900

who were seafarers and traders inhabiting the estuary of the Usumacinta River. They are thought to have had extensive contacts, especially through trade, with the Central Highlands and to have played a decisive role in the transmission of Highland traits to many cities of the Usumacinta watershed before the collapse of Classic-Period Maya culture.

The blend of Highland and Maya influences is so evident in the Cacaxtla murals that the latter are held to confirm the primacy of the Olmeca–Xicalanca at the site. It has also been suggested that the paintings depict either real or mythical episodes from their past. If this is the case, they depict ancestral rather than contemporary history at Cacaxtla, for there is no ethnohistorical evidence that the Classic Maya were involved in contention for the site, and the glyphic material interspersed among the figures can almost all be traced back to a Central or Southern Highland source. Most glyphs derive from Teotihuacán, although there is also a stylistic link with glyphs at Xochicalco; other glyphs, and some of the numerals, display a MIXTEC influence. However, several of the signs, notably the year sign and Tláloc (god of rain) emblems associated with the two leaders of the victorious 'jaguar' warriors, take a form clearly identified with the Lowland Maya area, notably the Usumacinta watershed after the intrusion of the Putún. Some 8th-century monuments, such as those at YAXCHILÁN, display the blend of pictorial and symbolic elements characteristic of Cacaxtla, suggesting the possibility of a common historical source for the scenes depicted.

For discussion of Mesoamerican wall painting *see also* MESOAMERICA, PRE-COLUMBIAN, §VI.

BIBLIOGRAPHY

R. Abascal and others: 'El mural del Palacio, Estructura II-1 del sitio T-280 Cacaxtla', *Comunic. Proy. Puebla–Tlaxcala*, suppl. ii (1976), pp. 23–53
D. López and D. Molina: 'Los murales de Cacaxtla', *Bol. INAH*, n.s., xv (1976), pp. 3–8
M. Foncerrada de Molina: 'The Cacaxtla Murals: An Example of Cultural Contact', *Ibero-Amer. Archv*, n.s., iv/2 (1978), pp. 141–60
D. McVicker: 'The "Mayanized" Mexicans', *Amer. Ant.*, l (1985), pp. 82–101
O. Baddeley: *The Cacaxtla Murals: The Problems they Raise for Mesoamerican Art History* (diss., Colchester, U. Essex, 1986)
A. García Cook: *Cacaxtla–Tizatlán: Guía oficial* (Mexico City, 1986)
S. Lombardo de Ruíz and others: *Cacaxtla: El lugar donde muere la lluvia en la tierra* (Tlaxcala, 1986)
G. E. Stuart and E. Ferorelli: 'Mural Masterpieces of Ancient Cacaxtla', *N. Geog.*, clxxii (1992), pp. 120–36

J. C. LANGLEY

Caccavello, Annibale (*b* Naples, *c.* 1515; *d* after 22 March 1570). Italian sculptor. The son of a supplier of marble, he was one of the most important Neapolitan artists of the 16th century. His earliest work was probably executed in the workshop of Giovanni Marigliano, where he made the acquaintance of Giovan Domenico d'Auria (*see* AURIA, (1)) with whom he later formed a partnership and frequently collaborated. The marble statues of the *Risen Christ*, *St Nicholas of Bari*, *St Francis* and the two *Angels* on the tomb of *Sigismondo Sanseverino di Saponara* (Naples, SS Severino e Sossio) probably belong to this early period, as do many of the bas-reliefs depicting *Episodes in the Conquest of the Kingdom of Naples* on the base of the tomb of the Viceroy of Naples, *Don Pedro de Toledo* (Naples, S Giacomo degli Spagnoli). The relief depicting the *Conversion of St Paul* (1539; Naples, S Maria delle Grazie a Caponapoli) is documented as by Giovan Domenico d'Auria but sometimes attributed to Caccavello. From 1547 to 1567 Caccavello kept a full diary of his career. The Tuscan Mannerism of Giovanni Angelo Montorsoli emerges in a number of works, for example certain parts of the monument to *Don Pedro de Toledo*, the decoration of the tomb of *Nicola Antonio Caracciolo, Marchese di Vico* (*c.* 1547; Naples, S Giovanni a Carbonara, Cappella Caracciolo di Vico), the relief depicting the *Virgin and Child in Glory with Souls in Purgatory* (1550; Capua, Mus. Prov. Campano), executed in collaboration with Giovan Domenico d'Auria, the tombs of *Odetto di Foix, Comte de Lautrec* and *Pietro Navarro* (1551; Naples, S Maria la Nova) and the tomb of *Alfonso Basurto* (1554; Naples, S Giacomo degli Spagnoli). In collaborating with d'Auria, Caccavello experimented with Mannerist decoration and forms of portrait iconography then unfamiliar but later used in 17th-century Neapolitan sculpture. In the tombs of *Hans Walter von Hiernheim* (1557; Naples, S Giacomo degli Spagnoli) and *Scipione Somma* (1557; Naples, S Giovanni a Carbonara) the emphasis on portraiture is subordinated to the decorative scheme. Caccavello's last works were mostly finished by his brother Desiato Caccavello and by another relative, Salvatore Caccavello.

WRITINGS

A. Filangieri di Candida, ed.: *Il diario di Annibale Caccavello, scultore napoletano del XVI secolo* (Naples, 1896)

BIBLIOGRAPHY

DBI; Thieme–Becker
O. Morisani: 'Giovanni Miriliano da Nola', *Archv Stor. Prov. Napolet.*, lxvi (1941), pp. 282–327 (319–25)
Sculture lignee nella Campania (exh. cat. by F. Bologna and R. Causa, Naples, Pal. Reale, 1950), pp. 74, 113, 159
O. Morisani: 'La scultura del cinquecento a Napoli', *Storia di Napoli*, V/ii, ed. E. Pontieri (Cava dei Tirreni, 1972), pp. 719–80 (763–70)
R. Pane: *Il rinascimento nell'Italia meridionale*, ii (Milan, 1977), pp. 127, 170, 189, 193, 194
F. Abbate: [review of G. Weise: *Studi sulla scultura napoletana del primo cinquecento* (Naples, 1977)], *Prospettiva*, 13 (1978), pp. 67–74
——: 'Un possibile episodio valdesiano a Napoli: La tomba di *Galeazzo Caracciolo* in San Giovanni a Carbonara', *Boll. A.*, 6th series, lxiv/2 (1979), pp. 97–102

For further bibliography *see* AURIA, D'.

RICCARDO LATTUADA

Caccia, Guglielmo. *See* MONCALVO, IL.

Caccianiga, Francesco (*b* Milan, 6 Aug 1700; *d* Rome, 1781). Italian painter. A diligent craftsman of little originality, he created art that derived from the traditions of classical Bologna and Baroque Rome. In 1717 he moved to Bologna, where he studied with Ferdinando Galli-Bibbiena and probably with Carlo Cignani and Marcantonio Franceschini. In 1719 he was commissioned by Conte Calderari to paint the *Martyrdom of St Catherine* (untraced) for the church of S Maria Beltrade (destr.), Milan, and the same patron commissioned three biblical scenes for his Milanese palazzo. After this Caccianiga settled in Rome, where in 1727 he won first prize for drawing in a competition organized by the Accademia di S Luca with a *Belshazzar's Feast* (Rome, Gal. Accad. N. S. Luca). His painting of *St Celso Triumphing over the Pagan Priests* (1736–8) for the main chapel of SS Celso e Giuliano,

Rome, demonstrates the influence of the proto-Neo-classical culture then fashionable in Rome. In 1740 Caccianiga was elected into both the Virtuosi del Pantheon and the Accademia di S Luca, in which he held various posts. A bitter disagreement with Cardinal Furietti made it difficult for him to further his career in Rome, so for a period he worked in the Papal States (Ancona, Morrovalle and Camerano), in Milan and in Portugal. He also painted four overdoors (untraced) for Charles-Emanuel III of Savoy, King of Sardinia, that were important in the development of Neo-classicism. After 1760 he was again working in Rome, on decorations at Casa Gavotti and at Palazzo Vidoni. It was presumably at this time that he executed his paintings for the University Chapel of Salamanca in Spain. In 1773–4 he painted his best-known work, the *Aurora* in Palazzo Borghese, and five years later the *Fall of Phaethon* for a ceiling at the Villa Borghese, his last work.

BIBLIOGRAPHY

Bolaffi; *DBI*; Thieme–Becker

I. Faldi: 'Gli inizi del Neoclassicismo in pittura nella prima metà del '700', *Nuove idee e nuova arte nel '700 italiano: Atti dei convegni lincei: Roma, 1977*, p. 507

J. Urrea Fernández: *La pintura italiana del siglo XVIII en España* (Valladolid, 1977), pp. 251–3

S. Rudolph: *La pittura del settecento a Roma* (Milan, 1983), p. 754

A. M. Rybko: 'Francesco Caccianiga', *La pittura in Italia: Il settecento*, ed. G. Briganti, 2 vols (Milan, 1989, rev. 1990), pp. 642–3

G. Sestiere: *Repertorio delle pitture romane della fine del seicento e del settecento*, i (Turin, 1994), p. 38

ANA MARIA RYBKO

Caccini, Giovanni Battista (*b* Rome, 24 Oct 1556; *bur* Florence, 17 March 1613). Italian sculptor and architect. He was the pupil and assistant of Giovanni Antonio Dosio and probably moved with his master from Rome to Florence in November 1575, spending the rest of his life in Florence. From Dosio he learnt the techniques of marble-carving, stucco and antique restoration and the principles of architecture, benefiting from Dosio's intense interest in Greek and Roman antiquity. He spent much of his early career engaged in the restoration of sculptures, although he also produced significant original work at this time. He had become fully established by the late 1590s, and his predominance as a sculptor in Florence was assured by the move of his rival, Pietro Francavilla, to France in 1601. Of a secondary nature, Caccini's rather obscurely documented work as an architect began in the 1590s and continued until his death.

1. SCULPTURE. Caccini became a member of the Accademia del Disegno in Florence on 12 October 1578, while still employed by Dosio, and between 1578 and 1580 he carried out his first important commission, for the reclining tomb effigy of *St John Gualberto* (Passignano, Abbey of S Michele). The effigy reveals that the influence of Dosio and Bartolomeo Ammanati persisted for some years after Caccini moved to Florence. This work, together with the statues of *Temperance* (*c.* 1578–84; New York, Met.; see fig. 1) for the Bishop of Marsia and of *St Bartholomew* and *St Zenobius* (*c.* 1580–85) for the Carnesecchi Chapel, S Maria Maggiore, Florence, was praised by Raffaele Borghini as presaging an illustrious career, yet no further commissions of importance are known for the 1570s.

1. Giovanni Battista Caccini: *Temperance*, marble, h. 1.83m, *c.* 1578–84 (New York, Metropolitan Museum of Art)

Caccini's works of the early 1580s show the influence of Giambologna. The faithful reproduction not only of Giambologna's stylistic idiom but also of his models before they took their final form in bronze, as in the case of *Temperance*, suggests that Caccini had very close links with Giambologna's studio in the Borgo Pinti. Caccini's main activity during this period was the restoration of antique statuary, which is recorded by Borghini and documented in the Medici archives between 1583 and 1590. Two of his restorations for the Medici survive: an *Apollo Sauroktonos* and *Hercules and a Centaur* (both Florence, Uffizi). An undocumented restoration of a *Bacchus and Faun* group (Florence, Uffizi) has also been attributed to him; it reveals a gentle, poetic sensibility that otherwise emerges only in Caccini's religious busts.

Baldinucci recorded Caccini's industry as a portrait sculptor, but only five busts can be securely identified: the *Baccio Valori* (1584; Florence, Bargello) is the earliest and best known of these. His earliest religious works are also in the form of busts, such as the *Christ* (1587) in Via de' Cerretani, Florence.

On 8 May 1586 Caccini was elected a consul of the Accademia del Disegno. His contribution of papier mâché statues, including that of *St John Gualberto* (1588–9; Florence Cathedral) for the wedding festivities of Ferdinando I de' Medici, brought him court patronage, but he still remained in the shadow of Giambologna. In 1590 he obtained a commission for a marble statue of *St James the Greater* (1591) for Orvieto Cathedral (*in situ*). The statue demonstrates his virtuosity in the carving of marble, yet Caccini could not challenge the predominance of Pietro Francavilla in this material in Florence, and he did not manage to obtain a supervisory role in a major commission until the end of the 1590s. However, by 1593 he had more work than he could easily manage alone. The works of the 1590s demonstrate a superlative technique and elegance of design but little originality. They are marked by a deeply mannered, intellectual approach that all but excluded reality. Caccini reduced Giambologna's drapery idiom to the simplified, almost relief-like planes of Dosio's style.

In 1592, on the occasion of the baptismal ceremonies of Ferdinand I, the Grand Duke of Tuscany's eldest son, Caccini made a terracotta *modello* of the kneeling figure of Charles V for a marble group of the *Coronation of Charles V by Clement VII*. It had been begun by Baccio Bandinelli for the Salone dei Cinquecento in the Palazzo Vecchio, Florence, but left incomplete. For the same occasion and site Caccini also provided a terracotta statue of *Francesco I de' Medici*. He executed both statues in marble between 1593 and 1594. His garden sculptures *Summer* and *Autumn* (*c*. 1592–3), commissioned by Alessandro Acciaioli, were later purchased by Ferdinando I to ornament Ponte Santa Trìnita (*in situ*) in 1608 for the wedding festivities of Cosimo de' Medici (later Cosimo II). Four of the undocumented garden figures in the Boboli Gardens in Florence have been attributed to Caccini: *Aesculapius and Hippolytus*, *Prudence* (*Autumn*), a female figure of *Summer* and a male figure of *Autumn*. It is possible that a further two, *Young Jupiter* and *Flora*, may be by his workshop. In 1594 he contracted to execute a relief of the *Trinity* for the façade of Santa Trìnita, Florence, designed by Bernardo Buontalenti. He may also have been responsible for the undocumented statue of *St Alexis* on the façade, which was presumably executed concurrently with the relief. In 1593 he gained a commission for statues of *St John the Baptist*, *St Paul*, *St Peter* and *St Bruno* for Dosio's renovation of S Martino, Naples (all *in situ*), but did not begin work on them until 1609. These statues, left unfinished at his death, were completed by Cosimo Fanzago in 1631. A statue of *Purity* (*Contemplative Life*) in the same church has also been attributed to Caccini.

In 1597 Caccini was commissioned to provide reliefs for the bronze doors of Pisa Cathedral, designed by Raffaello Pagni (*fl* 1588–97). The project involved all the foremost sculptors in Tuscany, including Pietro Francavilla, Hans Reichle and Pietro Tacca. Caccini was asked to provide 20 reliefs, more than any other sculptor, but his other commitments allowed him to model only 4. A fifth relief, the *Assumption of the Virgin*, was modelled by a pupil after his design. For the frames Caccini designed and made wax models of figurines, emblem and motto reliefs, foliage, cartouches and architectural niches, for which he received payment between May 1599 and May 1600. Of a series of nine marble busts of saints in S Maria degli Angeli, Florence, begun by Francavilla in 1599, those of the *Blessed Michael* (1602), *St Boniface* and *St James the Greater* are signed by Caccini. Two more of this series, the *Christ* and the *Virgin*, have also been attributed to him.

Caccini's position in the vanguard of his profession was assured as Francavilla became increasingly active in France from 1601. The splendid high altar erected for Giovanni Battista Michelozzi in Santo Spirito, Florence, on which he worked from 1599 to 1613, is the fullest expression of Caccini's art and shows him to be as technically assured as Francavilla. Its design may have been influenced by Buontalenti's original design (untraced), and it is possible that he was also assisted by Dosio. Above the columns of the edifice enclosing the altar are four marble statues of *St Peter*, *St John the Baptist*, *St John the Evangelist* and *St Augustine*, all studio works. The niches of the ciborium contain four bronze statuettes of the Evangelists. The corners of the enclosing parapet support marble statues of the *Virgin*, *St John the Evangelist* and six angels bearing candelabra. According to early sources, of the four angels completed and installed before Caccini's death, the pair nearest the altar were executed by Gherardo Silvani, Caccini's principal assistant, after his master's models while the front pair are by Caccini. The rear two angels, the *Virgin* and the *Evangelist* were left unfinished at Caccini's death, and, though based on his designs, their style of execution indicates a later hand; they were installed in 1745. The *Baptist* above the altar is probably by Silvani.

Caccini's two angels bearing candelabra (designed by 1601; see fig. 2) appear to alight on their pedestals in a graceful gliding motion. Their design is based upon that of Giambologna's angels (1599–1603) for Pisa Cathedral, although Caccini has a fundamentally new approach. Inspired by Giambologna's *Hope* (1579–80; Genoa, Grimaldi Chapel), Caccini invested the draperies with an expressive, fluttering motion, dramatically enhanced by the flickering play of light over abstracted patterns of deeply cut, sharp-edged curves that fall into triangular facets. Slim, tendril-like hands emerge from this brittle shell, while the angels' mobile features are exquisitely carved to imitate the waxy softness and subtle planes of youthful flesh, framed by streaming lines of thick hair. Their expressions are of divine rapture, tempered by melancholy. These qualities of movement, dramatically expressive pictorial detail and poetic intensity anticipate aspects of the Baroque, and illustrate the innovative artistic undercurrents at the turn of the 17th century, emerging concurrently in Rome in the works of Camillo Mariani, Nicolas Cordier and Francesco Mochi and merging in the work of Bernini.

The imposing wall-tomb of *Antonio Peri* in SS Annunziata, Florence, completed in 1601, was also carried out

2. Giovanni Battista Caccini: *Angel Bearing a Candelabrum*, one of a pair from the high altar, marble, designed by 1601 (Florence, Santo Spirito)

by Caccini's studio. Despite conflicting traditions regarding the attribution of the statue of *St Peter* on this monument, and of the *St Paul* on the identical wall-tomb of *Caterina Pandolfini* opposite (1609), the quality of the former suggests that Caccini participated in its execution, while the latter was probably executed by Silvani after Caccini's model. The combination of technical brilliance and spiritual expression achieved by Caccini in his angels for Santo Spirito is apparent in his last completed works, the statues of *St Agnes* and *St Lucy* (*c.* 1603–9; Florence, Santa Trìnita, Strozzi Chapel), which are undoubtedly by him.

2. Architecture. Much of Caccini's architectural activity remains obscure. The first records of his work in this field concern his (rejected) designs for the projected renovations of the choir and sacristy of Pisa Cathedral in 1596. His earliest extant works are the elegant portico of SS Annunziata, Florence (1599–1604), which follows Michelozzo di Bartolomeo's design, and the sculptural and architectural additions that formed part of the renovation of the adjacent oratory of S Sebastiano (1605–15), commissioned by Roberto Pucci and completed by Silvani. Other architectural works include the renovation of the Strozzi Chapel in Santa Trìnita, Florence, and of the Inghirami Chapel (1607–15) in Volterra Cathedral, also completed by Silvani; the redesigning of the choir and vault of S Domenico, Fiesole (1603–6), and the supervising of the completion of Buontalenti's Palazzo Nonfinito, Florence (*c.* 1600–10), for which he had executed a richly detailed coat of arms *c.* 1592. He was also responsible for the ceiling stuccos of the reliquary chapel of S Giovanni Gualberto in Santa Trìnita (1593–4). The six herms of poets and humanists on the façade of the Palazzo Valori (now Palazzo Altoviti), Florence, completed before 1603, have also been attributed to him, while Morrogh assigned three architectural drawings (Florence, Uffizi) to Caccini.

Caccini's architecture relies heavily on Dosio's synthesis of classical and contemporary influences and reflects the fashion set by Francesco I, Grand Duke of Tuscany, for the lavish use of pietra dura in panels and intricate mosaic designs. His most ambitious scheme, the high altar complex for Santo Spirito, is important not only for the richness of its detail but also because its design is influenced by Buontalenti and Dosio's unrealized plans for the high altar of the Cappella de' Principi in S Lorenzo, and it therefore provides a visual document of their ideas.

3. Influence. None of Caccini's pupils was of sufficient calibre to exploit or develop their master's innovative ideas, but the progressive style of Domenico Pieratti was formed in his school. Caccini also influenced Pietro Bernini and Hans Reichle, as is evident in the latter's works in Augsburg. In the field of marble sculpture Caccini established a secondary stylistic line in Florence, which appears in the works of Antonio Novelli, Bartolomeo Cennini and many other sculptors.

UNPUBLISHED SOURCES

London, Courtauld Inst., Conway Lib. [phot. by P. Ward-Jackson]

BIBLIOGRAPHY

DBI; Thieme–Becker

R. Borghini: *Il riposo* (Florence, 1584), p. 647

F. Baldinucci: *Notizie* (1681–1728); ed. F. Ranalli (1845–7)

A. Venturi: *Storia* (1901–40), X/iii, pp. 792–816

A. Grünwald: 'Über einige unechte Werke Michelangelos', *Münchn. Jb. Bild. Kst.*, v (1910), pp. 10–22, 68–70

E. Mandowski: 'Two Menelaus and Patroclus Replicas in Florence', *A. Bull.*, xxviii (1946), pp. 115–18

A. Morini: *Giovanni Caccini, scultore e architetto fiorentino* (diss., U. Florence, 1946)

J. Holderbaum: 'Surviving Colossal Sculpture for the Florentine Wedding Festivities of 1589', *J. Soc. Archit. Hist.*, xxvii (1968), pp. 210–11

J. K. Schmidt: 'Le statue per la facciata di S Maria del Fiore in occasione delle nozze di Ferdinando I', *Ant. Viva*, vii/5 (1968), pp. 43–53

——: *Studien zum statuarischen Werk des Giovanni Battista Caccini* (Cologne, 1971)

C. J. Valone: *Giovanni Antonio Dosio and his Patrons* (diss., Evanston, IL, Northwestern U., 1972), pp. 191, 204–7, 252, n. 99

C. Caneva: *Il giardino di Boboli*, Lo Studiolo (Florence, 1982), p. 42, nos 38–9

A. D. Morogh: *The Early History of the Cappella de' Principi, Florence* (diss., U. London, 1983), pp. 120, 123–4, 136, 422, n. 3

M. I. Catalano: 'Scultori toscani a Napoli alla fine del cinquecento: Considerazioni e problemi', *Stor. A.*, 54 (1985), pp. 127–31

Il seicento fiorentino: Arte a Firenze da Ferdinando I a Cosimo III (exh. cat., Florence, Pal. Strozzi, 1986)

ANTHEA BROOK

Cáceres. Spanish city and capital of the province of the same name in the region of Extremadura. It has a population of *c.* 74,000 and occupies a long ridge running east–west. It has been fortified since Roman times (when it was the Colonia Norbensis Caesarina) and is now chiefly notable for the good state of preservation of its medieval core. Remaining from the Roman period is the Puente de Alcántara. From the 15th century Cáceres was a *ciudad caballeresco* ('knightly town'), where many eminent families chose to maintain residences; a large number of these remain. Alfonso VII of León (*reg* 1126–57) conquered Cáceres from the Moors in 1141, but in 1143 the city was retaken. It changed hands again in 1180, 1184 and 1196, before being definitively reconquered by Alfonso IX of León (*reg* 1188–1230) in 1229. The city walls incorporate Roman, Moorish and medieval Christian masonry and are well preserved; the towers are square, apart from two octagonal Moorish ones, and there are four medieval gateways.

The church of S María la Mayor (completed 1550s) stands in the middle of the old town. It was built to replace a medieval building and is externally severely plain, being built from the local granite (the hardness of which tends to restrict architectural ornament). It has a high nave and wide aisles of almost equal height covered in fine vaults. The great wooden retable, on three sides of the main apse, is by the Fleming Rocque Balduc with Guillén Ferrán. The church of S Mateo, in the highest part of the town, is also 16th century and is built of severe ashlar masonry on the site of a former mosque; it contains a large number of 16th-century funerary monuments, including the tomb of the *Marqués de Valdepuentes*. Also of interest is the church of Santiago, outside the city walls to the east, which dates from the 12th century but was largely rebuilt *c.* 1550 at the expense of Francisco de Carvajal, a churchman and member of an eminent local family. The architect was Rodrigo Gil de Hontañón (*see* GIL DE HONTAÑÓN, (3), §1). It contains an important retable by Alonso Berruguete (*see* BERRUGUETE, (2)), with three small and six large panels in high relief; begun in 1557, it was completed in 1562 by Berruguete's workshop after his death. Part of the chancel, transepts and tower remain of the Romanesque building.

Cáceres never had a cathedral (it is in the see of Coria), but from the 13th century the bishops of Coria maintained an episcopal palace there, close to S María la Mayor. The present Palacio Episcopal dates to between *c.* 1400 and *c.* 1600. It is free-standing, of rubble masonry, with a Plateresque portal dating to *c.* 1579 (see fig.) and an arcaded patio from *c.* 1600. At least as early as *c.* 1400 Cáceres attracted noble families, whose palaces or houses (they were often on quite a modest scale) tended to be irregularly shaped buildings constructed around two-storey patios; their severe façades were usually of rubble masonry and ornamentation was usually concentrated around the portal, although sometimes around windows. A large number of these buildings remain: perhaps the finest is the early 16th-century Casa de los Golfines, in finely cut granite, mixing Late Gothic ornament around the portal with Renaissance balustrading on top. The Casa de Solís, Casa de Carvajal and several others have entrance arches distinguished by their plain but massive voussoir blocks, a feature seen in many noble residences in other parts of the Extremadura region. Several palaces have fine arcaded Renaissance patios, most notably the former Casa de Roco, built by Francisco de Godoy, a follower of the conquistador Francisco Pizarro (*c.* 1475–1541). The Casa de Ovando is notable for its 16th-century Plateresque portal.

Cáceres, Palacio Episcopal, façade with Plateresque portal, *c.* 1579

BIBLIOGRAPHY

F. N. Mehling, ed.: *Spain: A Phaidon Cultural Guide* (Oxford, 1985/*R* 1986), pp. 135–8

STEPHEN BRINDLE

Cachet, C. A. Lion. *See* LION CACHET, C. A.

Cacheux, François-Joseph-Emile (*b* Mulhouse, 1844; *d* 1923). French philanthropist, industrialist and writer. After studying as an engineer at the Ecole Centrale des Arts et Métiers, Paris, he directed a chemical works in Mulhouse, one of the pioneering centres of social reform in France. He soon returned to Paris, however, where he married the daughter of a public works contractor and as a result became proprietor of 500 flats in the city. Shocked at the housing conditions he found in his properties, he began a lifelong involvement in housing reform, as a designer, builder, pamphleteer, writer and public campaigner. His aim was to enable every working family to become proprietor of a house and garden, an aim based on the avowed intentions of improving workers' living conditions while simultaneously reinforcing the existing social order. Such housing was to be a bastion against Communism and stood at the opposite social pole to Fourierism, a cooperative theory of social organizations.

The model for Cacheux's conservative ideal of housing reform was the workers' housing built in Mulhouse from 1852, financed by the city's industrialists. Its designer, EMILE MÜLLER, was Cacheux's teacher in Paris, and in 1879 the two men collaborated on the production of a pattern book for builders of cheap housing. He published another book with plans in 1882. In 1889 Cacheux was among the founder-members of the Société Française des Habitations à Bon Marché. This organization gave the housing reform movement in France official status and espoused Cacheux's ideals, promoting the first legislation (1894) to encourage the production of such housing. His role in this movement emphasizes the relative lack of interest of the architectural profession in the question of social housing before the 20th century; in the late 19th century it was engineers and industrialists who defined the politically acceptable form of cheap housing.

WRITINGS

with E. Müller: *Les Habitations ouvrières en tous pays: Situation en 1878, avenir* (Paris, 1879, rev. 1889)

Le Philanthrope pratique: Première partie. Habitations ouvrières: Etudes avec plans, sur les habitations isolées, maisons à étages, hôtels pour ouvriers (Paris, 1882)

L'Economiste pratique (Paris, 1885)

Etat des habitations ouvrières à la fin du XIXe siècle (Paris, 1891)

BIBLIOGRAPHY

DBF

J. JAMES READ

Cacialli, Giuseppe (*b* Florence, 1770; *d* Florence, 6 Oct 1828). Italian architect and teacher. He studied architecture at the Accademia di Belle Arti in Florence together with Pasquale Poccianti and Luigi de Cambray Digny; all three were pupils of the leading figure in Tuscan Neo-classicism, Gaspero Maria Paoletti. At barely 15 years of age Cacialli won the second prize for architecture with a measured drawing of the chapel of S Andrea Corsini in the Florentine church of S Maria del Carmine. Having completed his studies, in 1795 he was appointed first an assistant and then Accademico Professore di Prima Classe at the Accademia. During the period of French rule in Tuscany, Cacialli rose to a position of prominence in Tuscan architectural affairs; in March 1808 Elisa Bonaparte, Grand Duchess of Tuscany, appointed him Architetto delli Regie Fabbriche, and in 1813, together with the painter Pietro Benvenuti, the sculptor Giovanni Antonio Santarelli and his fellow architect Giuseppe Manetti (1762–1817), he was appointed to the commission to design a monument (unexecuted) to *Napoleon* at Moncenisio. After the restoration in 1814 of the House of Lorraine in Tuscany, he was appointed architect to the Scrittoio delle Reali Fabbriche, a position he held until he retired in January 1827.

Cacialli's architectural work was mainly connected with the administration of important restoration and rebuilding projects commissioned first by Elisa Bonaparte and then by Grand Duke Ferdinand III (*reg* 1814–24), notably at the Villa di Poggio Imperiale and the Palazzo Pitti, which are documented by two volumes of engravings published by Cacialli in 1823. In 1807 he began working at the Villa di Poggio Imperiale, on the southern outskirts of Florence, which was designed by Giulio Parigi in 1622 and remodelled between 1766 and *c.* 1782 by Paoletti. Cacialli completed the vast entrance front begun *c.* 1804 by Poccianti, and he constructed the Loggetta del Peristilio (1807–14) on the first floor, and the elegant and original Neo-classical chapel (1812), the Sala Verde, the offices of the Vice-Director (1818) and the Sala d'Achille (1821–2). At the Palazzo Pitti, among other works he rearranged the pavilion of La Meridiana (1808–10), designed the Sala dell'Iliade (1815) and the Grand Duchess's bathroom (1819), rearranged the Palatine apartments (1823) and redecorated the Sala d'Ercole (1828). He also renovated parts of the Boboli Gardens, especially the botanical garden, including the new Portone d'Annalena and adjacent Palazzina (1821). Between 1808 and 1826 Cacialli also directed important restoration projects at several Medici villas, including Castello, where he remodelled the Grand Duchess's apartments and completed works in the garden; Petraia; Pratolino, where he constructed water conduits and restored Giambologna's *Colossus of the Appenines*; and, in particular, the Villa di Poggio a Caiano, where he replanned the park and designed an iron bridge over the River Ombrone.

In addition to his royal commissions, Cacialli directed numerous other works in Florence, including the rebuilding of the Teatro degli Intrepidi or Teatro Nuovo (1809–10) and work on the Uffizi Galleries (1811–12); in his capacity as architect to Florence Cathedral (1820–23) he planned the restoration of the Baptistery roof (1821) and created an elegant entrance to the cloister and adjoining structures of the monumental complex of S Pancrazio. Cacialli's publications document the enormous range of his projects and teaching activity; they also reveal the extent to which his brand of Tuscan Neo-classicism was indebted to architects of the French Enlightenment, such as Etienne-Louis Boullée, Claude-Nicolas Ledoux and Jean-Nicolas-Louis Durand.

UNPUBLISHED SOURCES

Florence, Uffizi, nn. 6290–95 [architectural designs]

WRITINGS

Raccolta dei progetti architettonici, ideati dall'Arch. Giuseppe Cacialli (Florence, 1827)

PRINTS

Collezione dei disegni di nuove fabbriche e ornati fatti nella Regia Villa del Poggio Imperiale (Florence, 1823)

Parte seconda dell'opera architettonica di Giuseppe Cacciali la quale contiene i disegni dei nuovi ornamenti aggiunta e da aggiungersi all'I. e. R. Palazzo Pitti (Florence, 1823)

BIBLIOGRAPHY

DBI

C. L. V. Meeks: *Italian Architecture, 1750–1914* (New Haven and London, 1966), pp. 142–4

Disegni di fabbriche brunelleschiane, Florence, Uffizi cat. (Florence, 1977), pp. 146–53

C. Cresti and L. Zangheri: *Architetti e ingegneri nella Toscana dell'ottocento* (Florence, 1978), pp. 40–41, 267–8

MARIO BENCIVENNI

Cadart, Alfred [Alphonse] (*b* St Omer, Pas-de-Calais, 5 April 1828; *d* Paris, 1875). French dealer and print publisher. He was the son of an innkeeper and joined the army in 1848. After spending several years in Lyon, he returned to St Omer and in 1859 married the sister of the printmaker and painter François Chifflart. In that year he gave up his modest position with a railway company and set up in Paris in the Rue de Richelieu as a print dealer and print publisher. His first publication appeared in May 1859 and was an album of Chifflart's works illustrated with photographs, lithographs and etchings. He also launched two illustrated periodicals, *Paris mystérieux* (1861) and *Paris qui s'en va* (1859; only one issue published). In 1861 he went into partnership with the photographer Félix Chevalier, and in August of that year they held an exhibition of photographs of the principal pictures of the Salon, as well as an exhibition of paintings that included landscapes by Corot and Claudius Jacquand from Lyon, the latter an artist in whom they took an interest. In that year they also published their first original etchings, a set of prints (*Esquisses à l'eau-forte*) by Alphonse Legros. In 1862 they began to publish monthly issues of the Société des Aquafortistes (*Eaux-fortes modernes: Oeuvres inédites et originales*, 5 vols (Paris, 1862–7)), which included work by Legros, Manet, Félix Bracquemond, Johan Barthold Jongkind and François Bonvin. That year Cadart also hoped to encourage the production of original lithographs by distributing three stones each to Legros, Manet, Bracquemond, Théodule Ribot and Henri Fantin-Latour for them to work on. Manet's *The Balloon* (1862) was one of the results of the experiment, but the projected set was never published. However, Cadart published most of Manet's original etchings.

In April 1863 Cadart's association with Chevalier ended and in October he formed a partnership with Jules Luquet (*b* 1824), owner of the Hôtel de la Grande-Bretagne in Paris and a collector of pictures. This association marked a new direction for the firm; it became the first to take an interest in Eugène Boudin's *plein-air* studies and when it exhibited Manet's *Battle between the 'Kearsage' and the 'Alabama'* (1864; Philadelphia, PA, Mus. F. A.), a press notice described the firm as being 'a permanent Salon for the new school'. At the Decamps sale (Paris, 23–4 Jan 1865) they bought a set of four decorative panels by Corot (Lockinge House, Oxon) and exhibited them, together with several other of Corot's landscapes. In 1866 the firm commissioned a smaller version (probably ex-Simu Mus., Bucharest) of *Camille* (Bremen, Ksthalle), Monet's successful painting in the Salon of that year, which they sent to an exhibition in the USA. A second, unsuccessful, trip to the USA resulted in financial collapse and eventual dissolution in 1867, also ending the Société des Aquafortistes. Cadart then took an employee called Luce as his partner, and in 1868 they launched *L'Illustration nouvelle*, a monthly periodical dedicated to etching. From 1874 (one year before Cadart's death) to 1881 the firm published an annual album of between 30 and 40 etched plates, for which the critic Philippe Burty wrote the prefaces. After Cadart's death, his widow Célonie-Sophie and his son Léon (1856–85) continued the business, but it eventually declined, ending in bankruptcy in January 1882.

BIBLIOGRAPHY

J. Bailly-Herzberg: *L'Eau-forte de peintre au dix-neuvième siècle: La Société des aquafortistes, 1862–1867* (Paris, 1972)

LINDA WHITELEY

Cadaval, Duques de [de Melo]. Portuguese family of statesmen, patrons and collectors. The Cadaval family was related by descent to the Condes de Tentugal and the Marquêses de Ferreira and owned the Paço das Cinco Quinas, also known as the Palacio Condes de Cadaval, in Évora, a gift from John I (*reg* 1385–1433) to Martim Afonso de Melo (*d* 1432) in 1390. The family pantheon (1485–91) was built by Rodrigo de Melo (*d* 1487) in the church of the convent of S João Evangelista dos Loios, located on an adjoining site.

The title of Duque de Cadaval was created on 18 July 1648 by John IV as a reward for the family's services during the period of the restoration of the Portuguese Crown after the Spanish Domination (1580–1640). Nuno Alvares Pereira de Melo (*b* Évora, 4 Nov 1638; *d* Pedrouços, Lisbon, 27 Jan 1727) was the first to receive it, although the hereditary title had been offered to Francisco de Melo, his father. During the war against Spain the 1st Duque took part in the frontier wars (1658), in which he was wounded. He was then appointed Conselheiro de Estado (Counsellor of State) and Ministro de Despacho (Minister of Public Affairs) of the Junta Nocturna. During the reign of Alfonso VI (*reg* 1656–83), he sided with Dom Pedro de Braganza (later Pedro II), the King's brother, and when through court intrigue Alfonso was ousted from power and Pedro was sworn in as Regent by the Cortes of 1668, Dom Nuno was present as Condestável do Reino (Constable of the Kingdom). The respect that he earned and his dedication to matters of state ensured his appointment to many posts of major importance, and, after members of the royal family, he became the most significant person in Portugal.

His scholarly interest in history was well known, as he formed a collection of rare and unusual papers and manuscripts concerning Portugal (Muge, Arquiv. Casa Cadaval), which was added to by his son, Jaime de Melo (*d* 1749), 3rd Duque de Cadaval. At the time of the French invasions in 1807 Napoleon I's general Andoche took a small number of these documents to Paris, where they now form the Fonds Portuguais of the Bibliothèque Nationale, Paris. The 1st Duque also built the Palácio de Muge, Santarém, and a country house (destr.) at Pedrouços; the latter was sometimes used as a residence by Peter II. His death was sadly felt by John V, who commissioned an eulogy of him from Dom Jaime. This work, which gives an account of the Duque's last years, is a sumptuous volume illustrated with a portrait of Dom Nuno by the painter Pierre-Antoine Quillard and also contains engravings by Quillard and others of scenes of his impressive funeral rites.

Dom Nuno was succeeded first by his son Luis de Melo (1679–1700), 2nd Duque de Cadaval, and then, on Luis's death, by his son Jaime de Melo, 3rd Duque de Cadaval, who kept alive the memory and the example of his father. His position as Estribeiro Mor (Chief Equerry) of Portugal during the reign of John V required him to be present at important events, of which he left memoirs in manuscript form, recorded (1741) by Barbosa de Machado. He also commissioned works of art, especially portraits, and encouraged the most outstanding artists working for the King. The two portraits of his father (Lisbon, Arquiv. N.; Lisbon, Tarouca col.) are copies or original works of art by Domenico Dupra, for many years the official court portrait painter, who is known to have been commissioned by Dom Jaime to paint a portrait for his father's funeral. The equestrian portrait of *Jaime de Melo* (Évora, Pal. Condes de Cadaval) is attributed to Quillard, from whom

Dom Jaime also purchased paintings and drawings (Muge, Arquiv. Casa Cadaval).

UNPUBLISHED SOURCES

Muge, Arquiv. Casa Cadaval [MS. by D. Jaime de Melo: *Históricas da fundação do real convento de N. Senhora e Sto António da Vila de Mafra* (1730)]

WRITINGS

J. de Melo: *Ultimas acções do Duque D. Nuno Alvares Pereira* (Lisbon, 1730)

BIBLIOGRAPHY

A. Ayres de Carvalho: *D. João V e a arte do seu tempo* (Lisbon, n.d.) [disc. of the authorship of the portraits of the Duques]
D. Barbosa de Machado: *Biblioteca lusitana*, 4 vols (Lisbon, 1741–59)
A. Caetano de Sousa: *História genealógica da casa real portuguesa*, x (Lisbon, 1743) [incl. biog. of the Duques de Cadaval]
V. Rao and F. Gomes da Silva: *Os manuscritos do arquivo da Casa du Cadaval respeitantes ao Brasil*, 2 vols (Coimbra, 1956–8)
T. Espanca: 'História da Casa de Cadaval', *A Cidade de Évora*, 43 (1960–61) [suppl.]
J. V. Serrao: *História de Portugal*, v (Lisbon, 1980)
——: 'Cadaval', *Dicionário da história de Portugal*, ed. L. Figueiriuhas (Oporto, *c.* 1980)
J.-A. França: *O retrato na arte portuguesa* (Lisbon, 1981)

LUISA ARRUDA

Cadbury, George (*b* Birmingham, 19 Sept 1839; *d* Birmingham, 24 Oct 1922). English industrialist, philanthropist, patron and newspaper proprietor. He was the third son of John Cadbury (1801–89), a Birmingham tea and coffee dealer, cocoa manufacturer and Quaker. With his brother, Richard Cadbury (1835–99), George Cadbury took over their father's ailing firm in 1861. Prosperity returned in the mid-1860s, and by 1879 a new factory was needed for cocoa manufacture. They moved to the healthier environment of Bournville, four miles south of Birmingham. Between 1893 and 1900 George Cadbury purchased 300 acres of land adjacent to the new factory and began to build a model village, employing the 22-year-old W. Alexander Harvey as architect from 1897. By 1900 300 houses had been constructed. The Bournville Village Trust was then established to use any profits for the benefit of the experiment in urban planning. Bournville is informally planned, with large public spaces and good-sized gardens. Schools, meeting halls, a Quaker Meeting House and parish church were built between 1905 and 1925. Although preceded as a model town by Port Sunlight, Cheshire, Bournville is important because it was set up on a sound economic and commercial basis. At Port Sunlight the architecture is extravagant and expensive, at Bournville it is simple and economical, and rents pay for the cost of construction and maintenance. Also unlike at Port Sunlight, residents of Bournville were not limited to those working for the Cadburys. Cadbury became the chief proprietor of the *Daily News* in 1901.

BIBLIOGRAPHY

DNB
A. G. Gardiner: *Life of George Cadbury* (London, 1923)
The Bournville Village Trust, 1900–1955 (Birmingham, 1956)
G. E. Cherry: *Cities and Plans: The Shaping of Urban Britain in the 19th and 20th Centuries* (London, 1988)

DAVID PROUT

Caddinet. Small, flat, rectangular stand, of gold, silver or silver gilt, with a box standing proud at its end to hold personal cutlery, napkins and condiments. It probably originated in the 16th-century French court as a *cadenas* (Fr.: 'padlock', 'clasp') and was used by royal families and high nobility. English caddinets are recorded from *c.* 1660 although the trencher-of-state recorded in the 16th century may be a precursor. There are two extant English examples that are engraved with the royal arms of William and Mary (e.g. of silver gilt by Anthony Nelme, 1689; London, Tower). The caddinet appears to have become obsolete by the early 18th century.

□

Cadena, Luis (*b* Machachi, Pichincha, 12 Jan 1830; *d* Quito, 1889). Ecuadorean painter. He studied under Antonio Salas (1780–1860) and lived in Santiago de Chile from 1852 to 1856, painting lavish, sentimental portraits under the tutelage of the French painter Raymond Monvoisin (1809–70). In 1857 he went to Rome with a government grant to attend the Accademia Nazionale di S Luca; he worked with the painter Alejandro Marini and made a series of academic studies of nudes and typical Italian characters. His interest in establishing greater academic training in Ecuador, which was still the centre of a prolonged colonial Baroque style in the arts, led him in 1861 to become Director of the Academia de Dibujo y Pintura in Quito. Between 1872 and 1875 he directed the Escuela de Bellas Artes, also in Quito. Cadena dedicated much of his prolific career to executing portraits of leading figures of the period, such as *Nicolás Martínez* (late 19th century; Quito, Mus. Aurelio Espinosa Pólit). His academic style and accuracy of draughtsmanship and composition are evident in the numerous works executed for the Roman Catholic Church. Outstanding are the series on the *Life of St Augustine* (1864; Quito, Convento S Augustín) and the *Mysteries of the Virgin of the Rosary* (1888; Quito, Convent of S Domingo).

BIBLIOGRAPHY

J. M. Vargas: *Los pintores quiteños del siglo XIX* (Quito, 1971), pp. 24–7
J. G. Navarro: *La pintura en el Ecuador del XVI al XIX* (Quito, 1991), pp. 190–92

ALEXANDRA KENNEDY TROYA

Cades, Giuseppe (*b* Rome, 4 March 1750; *d* Rome, 8 Dec 1799). Italian painter and draughtsman. He was an important history painter and decorator, whose paintings and drawings vary in manner from the Baroque to Neo-classical, and who anticipated Romantic historicism. His subjects are taken from Greek and Roman literature, 16th- and 17th-century religious history and Italian literature of the early and High Renaissance; his many drawings include preparatory studies, caricatures, genre scenes and portraits. He trained under Domenico Corvi at the Accademia di S Luca, where he won prizes with drawings such as the mannered and brilliant *Tobias Healing his Blind Father* (1766; Rome, Accad. N. S Luca). However, Cades had to leave Corvi's studio *c.* 1766, as Corvi apparently resented his pupil's excessive independence (Lanzi).

In the early 1770s Cades started to receive important commissions. His first large canvases were the *Martyrdom of St Benignus* (1774; San Benigno Canavese, Fruttuaria Abbey), which continues the classical tradition of late 17th-century Italian painting, and the *Ecstasy of St Joseph of Copertino* (1777; Rome, SS Apostoli), influenced by Venetian painting. Between 1774 and 1781, however, Cades's style as a draughtsman was deeply influenced by the circle of northern artists who gathered in Rome around

Johann Heinrich Füseli and Johan Tobias Sergel. He broke with the Late Baroque formulae, deriving from Carlo Maratti, to create a Romantic style, influenced both by the Antique and by Mannerist and Renaissance painting, in rich and powerful drawings such as *Ulysses, Achilles and Patroclus* (Paris, Louvre), *Achilles and Briseis* (1776; Montpellier, Mus. Fabre) and *Mars and Venus* (Florence, Mus. Horne, on dep. Florence, Uffizi). (Sergel kept a sketchbook of Cades's drawings after the Antique and after Roman painting; Stockholm, Nmus..) Four canvases from these years take subjects from ancient history: *Ulysses, Achilles and Patroclus, Cornelia, Mother of the Gracchi* (both Paris, Louvre), *Lucretia, Tarquin and Collatinus* (France, priv. col., see Caracciolo, 1984, fig. 3) and *Pontifex Maximus among the Vestals* (untraced). These were acquired before 1789 by the Toulouse collector Nicolas Joseph Marcassus, Baron de Puymaurin. They suggest an interest in the achievements of contemporary Neo-classical painters, both from France and northern Europe.

Between 1776 and 1779 Cades began working with the architect Giacomo Quarenghi, painting a *Deposition* for the altar of the chapel at Wardour Castle (now Cranbourne Chase School), Wilts, on a commission from Henry, 8th Baron Arundell of Wardour. In 1779 they completed the new music room, commissioned by Don Abbondio Rezzonico, for the Palazzo Senatorio in Rome. In the same year Cades also made a portrait drawing of *Giovanni Battista Piranesi*, which Piranesi's son, Francesco (1758–1810), later engraved.

In the 1780s Cades consolidated his position in the official art world of Rome. His *St Peter Appearing to SS Lucy and Agatha* (Ascoli Piceno, Pin. Civ.) dates from 1781, and in 1782 he painted a ceiling in the Palazzo Ruspoli, Rome, with *Venus Weeping over the Body of Adonis* (*in situ*). He also responded to the new interest of contemporary French painters in costume pieces, as in his etching, the *Death of Leonardo da Vinci in the Arms of Francis I* (1783; plate, Rome, Calcografia N.; preparatory drawings, Oxford, Ashmolean, and Lisbon, Mus. N. A. Ant.), which was inspired by Vasari's *Vite* and shows figures sumptuously clad in Renaissance dress. In 1784 Cades was commissioned, through Quarenghi, who was working in Russia, to paint four canvases with the theme of *Ceres* for Empress Catherine II, to decorate the music pavilion in the park at Tsarskoye Selo. Also in 1784 he worked on the Neo-classical decoration of the Sala delle Muse in the Palazzo Chigi, Rome (destr.); in 1785 there followed the vast and richly ornamented Neo-classical *Birth of the Virgin* (Genoa, S Maria delle Vigne). Cades was elected an academician at the Accademia di S Luca in 1786; a *Self-portrait* (Rome, Accad. N. S Luca), dated 1786, but probably painted at an earlier date, was given to the Accademia by the artist's wife after his death.

Cades made a study tour of northern Italy *c.* 1785, visiting Florence, Bologna, Cento, Ferrara and Venice. A volume of drawings which belonged to Bertel Thorvaldsen (Copenhagen, Thorvaldsens Mus.) contains sketches that reveal Cades's great admiration for late 16th- and 17th-century Venetian and Bolognese painters, particularly Veronese and Guercino. He was extremely busy in the late 1780s on decorative schemes. The most important of these were the decoration of the Neo-classical apartments in the Palazzo Altieri, Rome (1787 and 1791); the ceiling of a small room on the second floor of the Villa Borghese, Rome, with a scene (1787) from Boccaccio's *Decameron*, the *Recognition of Count Gautier of Angers*; and the decoration of the Sala dell'Ariosto in the Palazzo Chigi at Ariccia, commissioned by Prince Sigismondo Chigi, with scenes (1788–90) from Ariosto's *Orlando furioso* (see fig.). These paintings epitomize his mature style: the colours are light and fresh, the compositions classically balanced, yet enriched by a dramatic, neo-Mannerist quality that is most evident in the preparatory drawings (Budapest, Mus. F.A.; copies of the drawings, Archv Chigi, Rome, Vatican, Bib. Apostolica).

Religious paintings largely occupied Cades from the late 1780s onwards, often with subjects from 16th- and 17th-century religious history. He executed five large paintings

Giuseppe Cades: *Triumph of Bradamante*, a scene from Ariosto's *Orlando furioso*, wall painting, tempera, 1788–90 (Ariccia, Palazzo Chigi, Sala dell'Ariosto)

(1790) for the convent of S Francesco at Fabriano: *St Lucy and St Apollonia*, *St Anthony of Padua* and *St Joseph of Copertino* (all Fabriano, S Agostino) and the *Virgin Appearing to Five Saints* and the *Blessed F. Venimbeni* (Fabriano, S Caterina). Other subjects include a *Virgin with the Blessed G. De Bono and N. da Longobardi* (1791; Rome, S Andrea delle Fratte); *SS Francis and Bonaventure* (1796; Bagnoregio, S Francesco); and the *Blessed Angelina of Marsciano* (1798; Foligno, S Francesco), for which there is a drawing dated 1795 (Lisbon, Mus. N. A. Ant.). In his late works Cades's interest in Romantic historicism, and in the elegant cavaliers of Anthony van Dyck and the women of Rubens, is increasingly marked, as in the drawing *St Elizabeth of Portugal Reconciling her Son and her Husband* (Lisbon, Mus. N. A. Ant.), made for an altarpiece for S Antonio dei Portoghesi in Rome (*in situ*), which was finished after Cades's death by Luigi Agricola (*b* 1750). Important collections of drawings by Cades are in the Lisbon Museu Nacional de Arte Antiga (a volume formerly owned by Domingos António de Sequeira); Berlin, Kupferstichkabinett (originally in the collection of Vincenzo Pacetti); and in the Hermitage, St Petersburg.

BIBLIOGRAPHY

DBI

L. Lanzi: *Storia pittorica della Italia*, 6 vols (Bassano, 1809); ed. M. Capucci, i (Florence, 1968), pp. 422–4

Il settecento a Roma (exh. cat., ed. S. de Luca; Rome, Pal. Espos., 1959), pp. 71–3

A. M. Clark: 'An Introduction to the Drawings of Giuseppe Cades', *Master Drgs*, ii (1964), pp. 18–26

Painting in Italy in the 18th Century: Rococo to Romanticism (exh. cat., Chicago, IL, A. Inst., 1970), p. 184

M. T. Caracciolo: 'Per Giuseppe Cades', *A. Illus.*, iv (1973), pp. 2–14

——: 'Giuseppe Cades, pittore e disegnatore', *Colloqui del Sodalizio fra Studiosi dell'Arte: Roma, 1975*, ii, pp. 125–33

——: 'L'ispirazione letteraria di Giuseppe Cades', *Antol. B. A.*, i/3 (1977), pp. 248–65

——: 'Storia antica e mitologia nell'arte di Giuseppe Cades', *Quaderni sul Neoclassico*, iv (Rome, 1978), pp. 73–84

——: 'Un album di Giuseppe Cades: Appunti di viaggio e disegni', *Meddel. Thorvaldsens Mus.* (1978), pp. 7–47

A Scholar Collects: Selection from the Anthony Morris Clark Bequest (exh. cat., ed. U. W. Hiesinger and A. Percy; Philadelphia, PA, Mus. A., 1980–81), pp. 78–86

A. Czere: 'Esquisses nouvellement découvertes de Giuseppe Cades aux peintures murales à Ariccia', *Bull. Mus. N. Hong. B.-A.*, lvi–lvii (1981), pp. 153–75

M. T. Caracciolo: 'Giuseppe Cades, 1750–99: L'Expérience française d'un peintre romain', *Rev. Louvre*, v–vi (1984), pp. 353–8, pl. 221

——: 'Francesi e svedesi a Roma: Episodi di storia ed arte settecentesca', *Antol. B. A.*, n. s., xxxiii–xxxiv (1988), pp. 42–51

——: 'Giuseppe Cades tra Bergamo e la Russia', *Osservatorio delle Arti*, 1 (1988), pp. 68–73

G. L. Mellini: 'Addenda per Giuseppe Cades', *Labyrinthos*, vi/12 (1988), pp. 3–19

M. T. Caracciolo: 'Due opere di Giuseppe Cades nelle collezioni comunali', *Boll. Mus. Com. Roma*, n. s., iv (1990), pp. 69–74

——: *Giuseppe Cades (1750–1799) et la Rome de son temps* (Paris, 1992)

MARIA TERESA CARACCIOLO

Cadillac. French town in the Gironde département, on the River Garonne. A notable tapestry workshop was briefly in existence at the château of Cadillac in the 17th century. The Director, Claude de la Pierre (1605–60), previously head of a workshop in the Faubourg S Marcel, Paris, had been engaged by the Duc d'Epernon (1554–1642) in March 1632. The following year eight other Parisian weavers joined him. With the three workers already there they completed the twenty-seven pieces depicting the *Life of Henry III*, of which only the *Battle of Jarnac* (1632–7; Paris, Louvre) still exists. The cartoon maker for these works is unknown. The archaic composition juxtaposes with a certain lack of skill several successive episodes in the action. The weaving is fine and regular, with subdued colours in blue and yellow. The ruin of the House of Epernon led to the closure of the Cadillac workshop in 1637.

BIBLIOGRAPHY

C. Braquehaye: 'La Manufacture de tapisserie de Cadillac-sur-Garone', *Gaz. B.-A.*, xxxvi (1887), pp. 328–39

——: 'Claude de la Pierre', *Réun. Soc. B.-A. Dépt.*, xvi (1892), pp. 462–83

H. Gobel: *Wandteppiche: Die romanischen Länder*, ii (Leipzig, 1923–4), pp. 351–4

R.-A. Weigert: *French Tapestry* (London, 1962)

ISABELLE DENIS

Cádiz [anc. Gadir, Gaddir, Gadeira, Gades]. Spanish port and city, the capital of the province of the same name. It is situated on a peninsula in the south-west of the country, and its naturally protected harbour has helped make it the principal port of the region, with a population of *c.* 158,000. Cádiz is one of the oldest cities in Western Europe, having been founded in 1104 BC by the Phoenicians. The Phoenician city (Gadir) probably comprised tall houses built in close proximity, with terraces and balconies. The city was occupied in the late 6th century BC by the Carthaginians, who made it an important commercial centre, but it rose to splendour in the 1st century BC, when Lucius Cornelius Balbus (*fl c.* 40 BC) built the new city (Gades). Hidden under the houses of the modern city is the fully preserved Roman theatre; near it was the amphitheatre, of which only fragments remain.

From the 3rd century AD to the 13th, Cádiz suffered a serious reversal of fortunes, its former splendour eclipsed by Visigothic and subsequent Moorish occupation. It is not clear what the Muslim city comprised, but many of its buildings probably continued to be used after the reconquest of the city by Alfonso X (*reg* 1252–84), who built the Christian city on the highest part of the peninsula. A defensive wall was built on the east, north and west sides, each one with a gate. Inside the city, the cathedral was built in the south-western corner and the castle (destr.) in the south-east. The streets were short and narrow, and the squares small and few in number. During the 14th and 15th centuries Cádiz was repeatedly enlarged and modified, and this gradual expansion gave rise to two new suburbs, Santa María, to the east, and Santiago, to the west. By the 16th century it was once more beginning to flourish, its population including a high percentage of foreign migrants, mostly traders.

In 1596 Cádiz was destroyed by the 2nd Earl of Essex, leading to its almost total rebuilding on a grid plan that has been partly maintained; the first major work was to rebuild the cathedral (the Catedral Vieja, dedicated to La Santa Cruz), which was completed in 1602. Among the major artists active in the city during the 17th century was Bartolomé Murillo, whose *Marriage of S Catalina* (1681) is in the church of S Catalina; it was while executing this work that the artist fell from the scaffolding, sustaining the injuries that led to his death. In the 18th century the power of the wealthy traders in the city secured the supremacy of Cádiz over Seville in their rivalry for the

Cádiz, aerial view of the Catedral Nueva, by Vicente Acero and others, 1722–1860

monopoly of commerce with the Americas: the Casa de Contratación de Indias, governing trade with the Indies, was transferred from Seville to Cádiz in 1717. During the period of prosperity that followed, a new cathedral (the Catedral Nueva) was begun in the Baroque style in 1722 by Vicente Acero (*d* 1738) (completed 1860; see fig.). The fortifications of the city were completed, and the dominant features of its civil architecture began to take shape: such important buildings as the Casa de la Aduana (by Juan Caballero, 1763; now the Diputación) and the Neo-classical Ayuntamiento (1779–1825) and the Cárcel Real (1789; both by Torcuato José Benjumeda (1757–1836)) were erected, and new districts, such as San Carlos and La Vina, were created. Francisco de Goya was active in the city around this time, painting three frescoes in the elliptical chapel of La Santa Cueva, and in 1794 the Academia de Nobles Artes was also established.

From 1796, however, Cádiz lost its dominance as the primary Spanish port, and although it played a prominent role in the Spanish War of Independence or Peninsular War (1808–13), when the first liberal Spanish parliament assembled there, in the 19th century it suffered a decline in fortunes, hastened by the loss of the Spanish colonies. It remained a centre of political agitation in the 19th century, playing a leading role in the liberal uprisings of 1820 and 1868, but in the 20th century Cádiz came to rely economically on the transportation of sherry (from nearby Jerez) and agricultural products and on ship-building and food processing. It still provides some important museums, however, most notably the Museo Provincial, which contains works by such painters as Zurbarán, Murillo and Ribera.

BIBLIOGRAPHY

T. Falcón: *Torcuato Benjumeda y la arquitectura neoclásica en Cádiz* (Cádiz, 1974)

J. Sánchez Herrero: *Cádiz: La ciudad medieval y cristiana* (Córdoba, 1981)

R. Corzo Sánchez: 'Sobre la topografía de Cádiz en la edad media', *Rev. Dept. Hist. Med.*, i (1982), pp. 147–54

——: 'Cádiz y la arqueología fenicia', *An. Real Acad. B.A. Cádiz*, i (1983), pp. 5–29

J. Rodríguez-Pinero Bravo-Ferrer, ed.: *Cádiz y su provincia*, 4 vols (Seville, 1984–5)

MARÍA ÁNGELES RAYA RAYA

Cadmus, Paul (*b* New York, 17 Dec 1904). American painter. He studied in New York at the National Academy of Design (1919–26) and at the Art Students League (1928). With the painter Jared French (*b* 1905) he travelled in Italy from 1931 to 1933. His deep admiration for Italian Renaissance painting, for skilled draughtsmanship and classical composition led him to learn the technique of egg tempera, which he often combined with oil. His social concerns informed his often critical view of contemporary life as in *Sailors and Floosies* (1938; New York, Whitney). Sexually ambiguous themes, which were often satirical and affectionate, pervade works such as *Bar Italia* (1952–5; Washington, DC, N. Mus. Amer. A.).

BIBLIOGRAPHY

Paul Cadmus, Yesterday and Today (exh. cat. by P. Eliasoph, Oxford, OH, Miami U., A. Mus., 1981) [retrospective exhibition]

L. Kirstein: *Paul Cadmus* (New York, 1984)

EMMANUEL COOPER

Cadouin Abbey. Former Cistercian abbey dedicated to Notre-Dame de la Nativité, in Périgord, France. The abbey is particularly famous for its cloister. Cadouin, on the River Dordogne, fell under the control of the Cistercians directly after its foundation in 1115. The acquisition of a famous relic (the 'Saint Suaire' or Holy Shroud) led to the establishment of a flourishing pilgrimage to the site. The church dates from the 12th century, but the monastic complex, heavily damaged in the Hundred Years War, was rebuilt in the 15th and 16th centuries. The cloister, a relatively small structure (six bays by five; 19×16 m), was begun under Abbot Pierre V de Gaing (1455–75). During the troubled period of the wars the relic of the Holy Shroud was alienated and went to Toulouse, but Pierre de Gaing re-established possession of it and regained many of the lost domaines of the monastery. He initiated major campaigns of construction on the cloister, building the north, south and east walks. It was completed in the early 16th century (see fig.).

It was this remarkable cloister that led to the revival of interest in the monastery, which had become derelict after the French Revolution: in the 1830s its state of abandonment, fantastic tracery and sculptural forms attracted the attention of the liberal Catholic Charles-Forbes-René, Comte de Montalembert, who helped engineer the purchase of the monument for the département, while in the 1840s Baron de Guilhermy studied the iconography of the sculpture. The cloister walks are entirely vaulted, and the supports have an appropriately massive structure with substantial buttresses against their outer edges. The star-shaped patterns of the vaults result from the use of tiercerons and liernes, and the main points of intersection are marked by pendent keystones, many of which have disappeared. The points of support are expressed not by bundles of applied shafts but by sculptural motifs that sometimes embody a canopy and base designed to shelter small statues and sometimes depict crenellated tower motifs. Unglazed Flamboyant tracery fills the openings into the cloister garth: the flickering shapes appear to have no means of support, and prismatic mouldings and bases are carved with the precise but rich detail of 15th-century Flamboyant.

There is a lavish programme of architectural and figurative sculpture: several highly decorated portals, five groups of statues, more than thirty decorated corbels and a complex series of reliefs in the north wall. These reliefs were placed in relation to the abbot's throne below a great *Calvary* (destr.). To the left of the throne is a representation of the monastic community processing from a tower, led by their abbot, Pierre de Gaing, and the Magdalene depicted at the foot of the cross; to the right of the throne were placed three further reliefs: *Soldiers Casting Lots*, the *Road to Calvary* and the *Holy Women*. Surviving fragments provide evidence of an extensive programme of mural painting. The whole construction was made possible not only through the revival of the pilgrimage and the reorganization of the monastic domaines but also through the patronage of Louis XI, who gave 4000 pounds to the monastery in 1482. The popularity of the place as a pilgrimage centre has continued.

Cadouin Abbey, cloister, east walk, mid-15th century to the early 16th

BIBLIOGRAPHY

G. Delluc and J. Secret: *Cadouin: Une Aventure cistercienne en Périgord* (Périgueux, n.d.)

Baron de Guilhermy: 'Iconographie des fabliaux: Aristote et Virgile', *An. Archéol.*, vi (1847), pp. 147–57

F. de Verneilh: 'Causerie archéologique', *Bull. Soc. Archéol. & Hist. Périgord*, xv (1888), pp. 385–97

J. Sigala: *Cadouin-en-Périgueux* (Bordeaux, 1950)

R. Issartel: *Abbaye de Cadouin en Périgord* (Périgueux, 1968)

J. Gardelles: L'Abbaye de Cadouin', *Congr. Archéol. France*, cxxxvii (1979), pp. 146–78

STEPHEN MURRAY

Caen [Gallic Catumagos; Lat. Cadomus; Med. Fr. Cathim, Cathom, Chaem]. Capital city of the Calvados département in Normandy, France. Little is known of its early history, but excavations have revealed Gallo-Roman and Merovingian remains on the sites of St Etienne, St Martin and St Gilles. The existence of a large village at the confluence of the rivers Orne and Odon was recorded in a charter of Duke Richard II of Normandy (*reg* 996–1027) in 1025. It was the capital of the Duchy under William the Conqueror (*reg* 1035–87). Around 1060 he built his castle there and founded the abbey of St Etienne, and his wife founded the abbey of La Trinité (*see* §§1 and 2 below); this decided the city's future and attracted settlement. From the Norman conquest of England (1066) to the death of Henry I of England (1135) Caen was virtually a building site, with the construction of the fortifications and the Vieux Palais (*c.* 1100), the keep (under Henry I, *reg* 1100–35), the two abbeys and a number of churches, such as St Nicolas, St Georges, St Gilles and Sainte Paix. The city was taken by the French in 1203–4, and after 1204 Philip II Augustus of France (*reg* 1180–1223) built a curtain wall flanked by four towers around the keep.

The town was besieged and conquered in 1346 by Edward III of England (*reg* 1327–77), and additional fortifications were built in 1354, though it reverted to French hands soon afterwards. Caen was retaken in 1417 by Henry V (*reg* 1413–22), who settled there, but it was restored to the King of France in 1450 at the Battle of Formigny. In spite of being pillaged during the Wars of Religion (1562–3), the town and its port flourished from the 16th century to the 18th. The restoration of the churches of St Jean, St Sauveur and St Pierre (13th–16th centuries) was completed during the Renaissance. Some handsome mansions were also built at this time, including the Hôtel d'Escoville (1538), built for Nicolas Le Valois, and also a large number of high-quality half-timbered houses. With the Maurist reforms, the two abbeys were endowed with new conventual buildings during the 17th and 18th centuries following plans drawn up by Guillaume de la Tremblaye (1644–1715). New sanctuaries were built, such as Notre-Dame-de-la-Gloriette.

Although the damage caused during the Revolution was partly repaired by the 19th-century restorations, the Allied bombardments of 1944 had more dramatic consequences: St Gilles was destroyed, together with entire neighbourhoods, particularly around the castle. All the monuments were damaged to some extent, but they were later restored, thanks to a policy designed to enhance the town's artistic heritage. Caen is now a centre for such industries as iron and steel, textiles and electronic equipment.

BIBLIOGRAPHY

C. de Bourgeville, Sieur de Bras: *Les Richesses et antiquitez de la ville de Caen* (Caen, 1588)

F. G. S. Trebutien: *Caen, son histoire, ses monuments* (Caen, 1847)

Congr. Archéol. France, lxxv (1908); cxxxii (1974)

M. de Bouard: *Le Château de Caen* (Caen, 1980)

G. Désert, ed.: *Histoire de Caen* (Toulouse, 1985)

1. St Etienne. 2. La Trinité.

1. ST ETIENNE. The Benedictine abbey of St Etienne was founded *c.* 1060 by William the Conqueror in expiation for his marriage to his cousin Matilda of Flanders. The first abbot was Lanfranc (*d* 1089), who became Archbishop of Canterbury in 1070. The church seems to have been begun *c.* 1066; its large scale was probably the result of the financial gains made from William's conquest of England. Three consecrations mark the stages of construction, carried out from east to west: 1073, 1077 (the choir, transepts and two bays of the nave) and 1081 (the remaining six nave bays); the façade towers and the western nave bay were built in the last decade of the 11th century. The Romanesque east end was replaced in the later 12th century. The crossing tower collapsed in 1566, and from 1601 to 1626 Dom Jehan de Baillehache carried out important restorations on the crossing, transept and choir and added the quatrefoil balustrade to the nave. The monastic community was dispersed in 1790, and the church used as a temple of the Supreme Being (1793–4). It became a parish church in the 19th century and was restored by the architects Guy (in 1825–30) and Victor-Marie-Charles Ruprich-Robert (after 1863).

(i) Architecture. St Etienne is built of Caen stone. It is 110 m long and has an aisled nave of nine bays (one façade bay between the towers and four double bays with subtly alternating piers), a crossing tower and projecting transepts with tribune galleries across the end of each arm. The plan of the Romanesque choir is known approximately from Carlson's excavations: in the 11th century it had two aisled bays terminating in three apses in echelon (the outer apses perhaps square externally) and a two-storey chapel opening on to each transept arm.

The three-storey nave elevation has a tall arcade of round arches in two orders with angle rolls; tribune galleries almost the same height as the arcades; and a clerestory with a passage fronted by an arcade of small arches, four to each double bay (see fig. 1). These arches were originally of the same height and evenly spaced, but they were altered in the 12th century to accommodate the vault springers. In the proportions and the equal height of the lower two storeys, the elevation of St Etienne differs substantially from that of La Trinité (*see* §2 below) and even of Jumièges Abbey. It was to influence the arrangement at Cérisy-la-Forêt (Normandy) and, in England, the Romanesque cathedral at Lincoln, Winchester Cathedral, Blyth Priory (Notts) and Ely Cathedral.

The wall structure is very advanced for the years 1060–80, perfecting the thick-wall technique (Bony; *see* THICK-WALL STRUCTURE) already partially introduced in the transepts at Bernay Abbey and Jumièges (Notre-Dame and St Pierre; *see* JUMIÈGES ABBEY). The whole structure of the wall at St Etienne contributes to this system: the pier alternation (the strong piers are distinguished by a dosseret behind the attached shafts facing the main vessel), the internal reinforcement of the gallery piers, and at clerestory level the hollowed-out walls preserve a very dense masonry section above the strong piers, where the passage is very narrow. In every second bay a half-shaft

1. Caen, St Etienne, interior looking east, begun *c.* 1066

runs the full height of the elevation acting as an interior buttress, which allows the wall to be further opened up. Quadrant vaults over the tribune reinforce this structure and buttress the upper nave wall. The transept, which has a tribune gallery across the end of each arm (as later at St Nicolas in Caen, Cérisy-la-Forêt and Winchester Cathedral) and a clerestory wall passage, linked the nave with the Romanesque choir at all levels; the wall passage probably ran all around the eastern arm. As usual in 11th-century Norman great churches, the nave and transepts were wooden-roofed, and only the aisles had groin vaults (replaced by rib vaults *c.* 1120).

Slightly later, but planned from the start (as can be seen from the layout of the first courses of masonry), is the façade block, articulated by broad buttresses (see fig. 2).

2. Caen, St Etienne, west façade, late 11th century

Its two towers are in the same plane as the central gable. The respective widths of the towers and the central façade bay, and the proportions of the three storeys pierced by round-headed openings, exactly reflect the internal widths and elevation of the nave and aisles. It is one of the earliest examples of the integrated façade, with no suggestion of the transverse westwork with porch and tribune still being built *c.* 1070–80 at La Trinité and St Nicolas in Caen. On the interior of the façade a narrow passage provides communication between the north and south nave galleries.

New experiments in rib vaulting were made at Caen, after those carried out *c.* 1093–1100 at Durham Cathedral and Lessay Abbey (Normandy). Around 1120 the nave of St Etienne was spanned by sexpartite rib vaults, one of the first known uses of this form, although there may have been an earlier experiment in the choir of Durham. Quadripartite vaults cover the transept.

The Romanesque church of St Etienne is of great significance for the history of medieval architecture: its influence can be seen first of all in the general spread of the apse-echelon plan in both Normandy and England (e.g. St Albans Cathedral); two-storey chapels linked to the tribune galleries appear in the transepts of such churches as Cérisy-la-Forêt, St Vigor in Bayeux and St Ouen in Rouen. The clerestory wall passage and thick-wall technique were adopted in most Norman and English churches (e.g. Cérisy, Lessay, St Albans, Peterborough, Ely and Gloucester). The sexpartite vaults were, with the experiments of Durham and St Lucien at Beauvais, an important step towards the development of Gothic, as was the harmonized façade, which anticipated numerous Gothic west fronts.

The eastern arm was rebuilt by an architect named Guillelmus with an extended choir of four bays, ambulatory and seven contiguous, radiating chapels. The proportions of the Romanesque nave elevation with tribune gallery and clerestory passage were retained. The galleries open on to the choir with paired pointed openings under round containing arches (pointed in the hemicycle), and most are lit by oculi. At clerestory level the wall passage runs behind a pointed triple-arcaded screen carried on tall, slender shafts. The rectangular bays of the nave are spanned by quadripartite rib vaults, and there is no alternation; the straight bays are buttressed by double-span flyers, and four stair-turrets mark the turn of the apse. The design of St Etienne combines elements from indigenous, Norman building traditions (e.g. Fécamp Abbey, St Laurent, Eu) with those derived from the Gothic churches of the Ile de France (e.g. Notre-Dame, Paris). There are also stylistic similarities with buildings that reflect in varying degrees the choir of Saint-Denis Abbey: Pontigny Abbey and Ste Madeleine, Vézelay, in Burgundy (arcades screening the lower masonry of the buttresses between the interconnecting radiating chapels, elbow corbels etc) and the choir of the Cistercian abbey of Mortemer in Normandy (begun 1174; ruined). Connections with Canterbury Cathedral are apparent in some of the details, particularly of articulation. No documents relating to the construction of the choir survive, but the design sources have suggested a date in the mid-1180s (Grant).

The choir of St Etienne established a new approach to Gothic architecture in Normandy, and its influence there was far-reaching; it is evident at Lisieux Cathedral (choir, last campaign), at Coutances Cathedral and in the choir of Bayeux Cathedral. The spires that crown the Romanesque western towers are contemporary with the new choir and were imitated in several churches in the Bessin, such as Tour, Audrieu, Bernières-sur-Mer and Secqueville.

(ii) Sculpture. The sculptural decoration of St Etienne was carried out by different workshops, corresponding to the building campaigns. The sculptures of the transept and nave (*c.* 1066–81) have been much restored, but their characteristics can nevertheless be discerned. They are related to work at La Trinité and Sainte Paix, Caen (*c.* 1060–80), but the proportions of the capitals are slightly taller. They are also distinguished by the frequent use of double rows of leaves and the sparseness of decoration, for example simple masks, sometimes with bodies, like those at Bernay Abbey. In the capitals of the façade block (*c.* 1090–1100) the volutes hug the block, and the masks are more schematic, indicating a tendency towards simplicity of form that is already discernible in the sculptures of St Nicolas, Caen, and Cérisy-la-Forêt. The decoration of the clerestory wall passages (*c.* 1120–25) is quite different and comprises several different groups: capitals covered with basketweave or interlace with animal terminations, suggesting both Italian and Anglo-Scandinavian influence; flared capitals with slightly projecting scallops; and volute capitals bearing figures and symmetrically arranged monsters, also found on contemporary tympana at the Norman churches of Colleville-sur-Mer and Authie.

BIBLIOGRAPHY

V. Ruprich-Robert: *L'Eglise Sainte-Trinité et l'église Saint-Etienne à Caen* (Caen, 1864)

G. Bouet: *Analyse architecturale de l'abbaye de Saint-Etienne de Caen* (Caen, 1868) [previously published in *Bull. Mnmtl.*, xxi (1865), pp. 417–79, 637–80; xxxiii (1867), pp. 254–303, 546–92, 761–801]

J. Bony: 'La Technique normande du mur épais à l'époque romane', *Bull. Mnmtl.*, xcviii (1939), pp. 153–88

E. G. Carlson: *The Abbey-church of Saint-Etienne at Caen in the Eleventh and Early Twelfth Centuries* (diss., New Haven, CT, Yale U., 1968)

——: 'Excavations at Saint-Etienne, Caen', *Gesta*, x (1971), pp. 23–30

L. M. Grant: 'The Choir of St Etienne at Caen', *Medieval Architecture in its Intellectual Context: Essays for Peter Kidson* (London, 1990), pp. 113–25

3. Caen, La Trinité, capital of south-west crossing pier, *c.* 1060–80

2. LA TRINITÉ. The abbey was founded *c.* 1060 by Matilda, wife of William the Conqueror, as a convent for women. There was a consecration in 1066, and Matilda was buried in the choir in 1083. Work continued until *c.* 1130, when the nave received its unusual false sexpartite vaults. The church has a crypt at the east end, an aisled nave of nine bays with a twin-tower façade block, projecting transepts with an eastern apsidal chapel on each arm (that opening on to the south transept was replaced *c.* 1260 by a Gothic rectangular chapel) and a two-bay, groin-vaulted choir separated from the flanking aisles by a solid wall. Originally there were three eastern apses in echelon, but the main apse was replaced by a two-storey hemicycle in the early 12th century. The nave has a three-storey elevation, with a narrow, false triforium and a clerestory passage.

La Trinité, like St Etienne, Caen, was decorated by several different workshops of sculptors. The capitals of the nave arcade and crossing arches survive from the campaign of *c.* 1060–80, although they have been much restored. They are distantly based on the Corinthian form, with angle volutes, one or two rows of smooth leaves, foliate surface decoration in low relief or masks connected by stems. The last are related to capitals in the crypt of Bayeux Cathedral and to Romanesque fragments at Rouen Cathedral. The sculptures of this campaign are distinguished by their variety and originality; they were influential both in Normandy (e.g. at the churches of Guibray and Cérisy-la-Forêt) and in England (e.g. Blyth Priory, Notts, St Mary's, Stogursey, Somerset, and York Minster). The rams and rams' heads on the crossing capitals (see fig. 3) derive from Byzantine and Italian examples (e.g. Pieve S Martino a Vado at Strado, nr Arezzo). This workshop was also active at Sainte Paix, Caen, and introduced into Normandy sunk-star motifs and fret ornament, part of the Norman taste for geometric decoration that became widespread at the end of the 11th century. In the crypt capitals (*c.* 1090) the forms used in the nave became simpler and more schematic, with small volutes pressed against the capital, rings of smooth leaves and large, flat crosses; like the exterior capitals of the apse, they are related to sculpture at Lessay Abbey.

The early 12th-century hemicycle capitals are in a different style. They bear symmetrically arranged zoomorphic motifs (e.g. dogs with fish heads, ducks and cranes), rinceaux inhabited by lions or whales, an elephant and castle, and a figure driving lions, the last probably inspired by bestiaries, which were very popular in Caen at the beginning of the 12th century. The decoration is in low relief but with subtle modelling, demonstrating a taste for ornamental beaded stems. The style of these works is related to illuminated manuscripts of the St Ouen at Rouen group (e.g. Bayeux, Bib. Chapitre, MSS 57–8; Durham, Cathedral Lib., MS. A.II.4) and to contemporary sculptures in the crypt of Canterbury Cathedral, England (particularly in St Gabriel's chapel).

The sculpture of the clerestory passages of the nave and transept (*c.* 1130) depended on a very different style. Although restored and rearranged, the scallop capitals are decorated with beading, heads and volutes that illustrate general trends in Norman sculpture *c.* 1130. Their influence can be seen in a number of country churches in Normandy, particularly at Bernières-sur-Mer, Creully and Saint-Gabriel, and in England, especially at Canterbury Cathedral.

BIBLIOGRAPHY

V. Ruprich-Robert: *L'Architecture normande*, i, ii (Paris, 1883)
L. Musset: *Normandie romane*, i, Nuit Temps (La Pierre-qui-vire, 1967)
M. Baylé: *La Trinité de Caen* (Paris and Geneva, 1979)

MAYLIS BAYLÉ

Caere. *See* CERVETERI.

Caernarfon [Caernarvon] **Castle.** Royal fortress and palace in Gwynedd, Wales. It was begun in 1283 on the site of a Norman predecessor, built *c.* 1090 by Hugh, Earl of Chester, and is the most splendid and important of the royal castles built in connection with Edward I's Welsh wars. The castle made an impact on the development of both secular and religious architecture in early 14th-century England and successfully emulated one of the great works of antiquity.

1. HISTORY. The royal building accounts have been analysed by Taylor (1952) to establish a chronology, which is divided into two phases. The full length of the south curtain wall from the Eagle Tower to the North-East Tower was constructed between 1283 and 1292. This completed the enclosure of the town walls, which were built simultaneously. Associated work on the north curtain wall was suspended after the excavation of a substantial ditch and the laying of the lower masonry courses. Welsh forces led by Prince Madoc overran these unfinished defences in 1294, set fire to the timber structures of the castle and seriously damaged the town walls. Work began again in 1296, and, in a prolonged campaign that lasted until 1323, most of the north curtain wall, the upper parts of the Eagle Tower and adjacent south curtain were completed. At the same time, the town walls were repaired.

The overall design of the castle has been ascribed to JAMES OF ST GEORGE, although WALTER OF HEREFORD is known to have been in charge of the work from 1295 until 1309, when he was succeeded by his assistant Henry of Ellerton. It is possible, however, that Walter of Hereford may also have been executant architect for the first building campaign and that it was his responsibility to detail and carry out the plans of Master James, his superior in the King's Works in Wales. The wave mouldings that occur on doorways and other arches in the earliest work are unlike the profiles found in those castles with which James of St George's name is directly connected by documents, but fragments from Vale Royal Abbey, Cheshire, show that these early Caernarfon mouldings were part of Walter of Hereford's vocabulary. The absence of certain vital documents relating to this early work means, however, that the question of authorship must remain unresolved.

The castle survived three sieges by the Parliamentary forces in the Civil War and today is exceptionally well preserved. The only major loss was the removal of Earl Hugh's motte from the upper ward in 1870, after which the castle was extensively and sympathetically repaired by Sir Llewelyn Turner for the government.

2. ARCHITECTURE. The plan loosely resembles that of Conwy in so far as it is arranged as a pair of adjacent

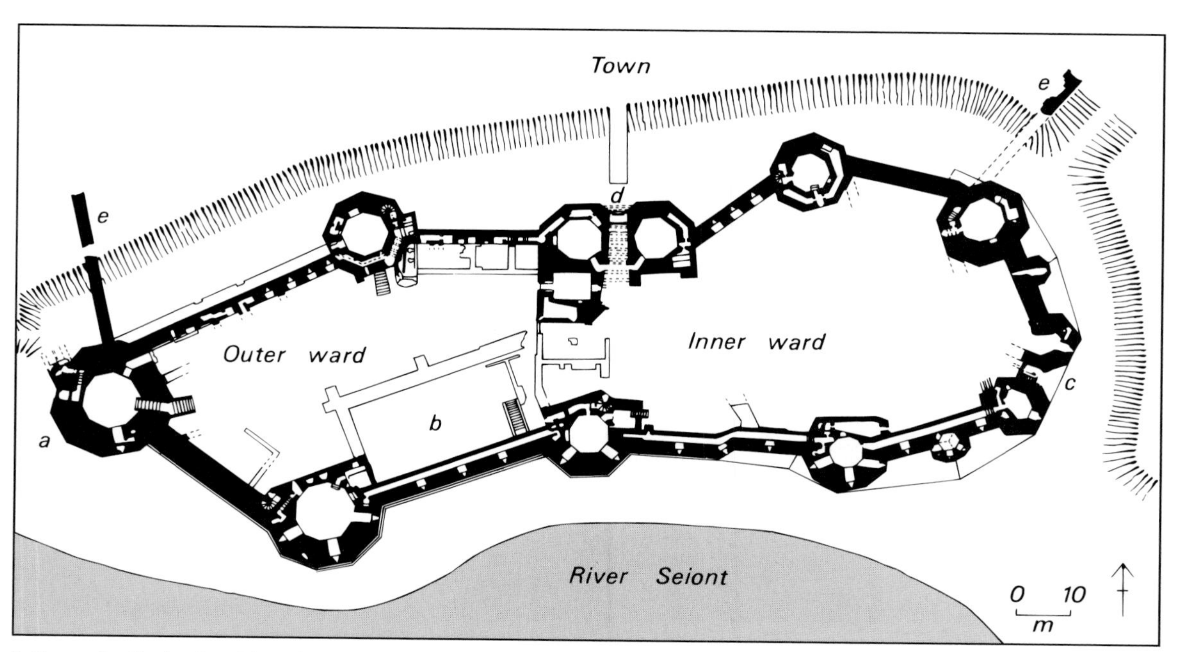

1. Caernarfon Castle, plan: (a) Eagle Tower; (b) hall; (c) Queen's Gate; (d) King's Gate; (e) town wall

2. Caernarfon Castle, view from the south, begun 1283

wards, but the shape of the site and the decision to retain the Norman motte at the eastern end necessitated an irregular layout (see fig. 1). The castle is built of limestone. The walls are defended by seven large towers and two twin-towered gatehouses. The King's Gate in the centre of the north curtain wall was the principal entrance from the town while the Queen's Gate, originally approached by a long stone ramp, gave access to the inner ward from the field. The use of polygonal towers, though not unique to Caernarfon, differentiates it from most of Edward's other castles, although most elements of the design exhibit a generic relationship with them. The massive, ten-sided Eagle Tower that dominates the outer ward is a relative of the donjon at Flint, Clwyd, and one can recognize in the planning of the Queen's Gate and its adjacent walls something of the layout of Rhuddlan, Clwyd. The later work of the north curtain wall on the other hand shows significant technical advances in its defensive features. Many of these were measures devised to cope with its proximity to the buildings of the town. Widely splayed arrow loops with three internal firing positions commanded an unusually wide and shallow field, and in the King's Gate a long entrance passage, defended by a succession of doors, portcullises, arrow slits and machicolations, controlled entry to the castle, a role that in more spacious conditions would have been performed by an open barbican like those of Conwy, Harlech or Beaumaris, Gwynedd. There is evidence that it was intended, like the similar but more compact gatehouse at Denbigh, to terminate in a central octagonal chamber with a passage to the outer ward, but this feature was never completed.

The design was intended to convey that, for Edward I, Caernarfon was also a royal palace, the seat of English government in medieval Wales and the residence of his justiciar. It expresses the King's characteristic interest in the exploitation of historical precedent. Although polygonal towers had been used by James of St George to distinguish Count Philip I's palace at St Georges-d'Espéranche in Savoy from his other fortresses, the combination of these shapes at Caernarfon, with walls striped in horizontal bands of light and dark masonry in the south curtain wall, has been interpreted as a deliberate and successful attempt to reproduce the 5th-century land walls of Constantinople (now Istanbul; see fig. 2). Welsh legends ascribed the foundation of Roman Caernarfon to Constantine's son, the Emperor Magnus Maximus, and described how he saw, in a dream, a coloured fort at the mouth of a river set in a land of high mountains. The remarkable accuracy with which Edward was able to imitate the walls of Constantinople in 13th-century Caernarfon shows the degree to which European engineers had assimilated knowledge of Eastern fortification gained during the Crusades. Comparably impressive Byzantine features appear in other late 13th-century castles, for example Caerphilly Castle, Gwent, but never so self-consciously. The large, nichelike entrances of the King's Gate and the Queen's Gate satisfy various military necessities but also possess strong imperial overtones, recalling the great niches in the westwork of Charlemagne's palatine chapel at Aachen (792–805) and the entrance to the Exarch's palace at Ravenna (after 712). The special status of Caernarfon is also reflected in its extensive use of carved and moulded masonry.

3. INFLUENCE. Caernarfon is crucial to the development of the Decorated style, which in its churches and monuments shows an interest in unusual polygonal plans. The early 14th-century hexagonal porches of St Mary Redcliffe, Bristol, and St Lawrence, Ludlow, Salop, are probably derived from the sequence of passageways and hexagonal chambers in the Eagle Tower and from the plan of the King's Gate; it is also conceivable that the

polygonal plans of Eleanor crosses in the 1290s at Waltham, Essex, and Hardingstone and Geddington, Northants, are related in some way to the spatial concepts of Caernarfon. The two most frequently-used new mouldings in Decorated architecture, the wave and sunk chamfer, are used extensively at Caernarfon, and they can be found in the greatest concentrations in the 14th-century churches of western England, the hinterland of Edward's massive late 13th-century castle-building campaign. The decorative parapet figures of Caernarfon's battlements, one of which at least was being fixed to the Eagle Tower in 1316–17, are found in various Decorated buildings in Yorkshire, though it is not possible to be certain whether these are earlier or later than those of the castle.

Caernarfon's influence on military architecture has yet to be positively identified. The polygonal towers of the barbican at Caerphilly and Newport Castle, Gwent, the barbicans and gatehouses at Arundel, W. Sussex, and Alnwick, Northumb., and the Chapel tower at Kidwelly, Dyfed, all resemble Caernarfon in their planning or masonry decoration; it is difficult, however, to determine what is derivation and what represents simply shared knowledge of Eastern work. Caernarfon, as the great new royal palace of the late 13th century, must have been influential in establishing the multi-angular tower as a symbol of opulence in castle design, and the English 14th-century vogue for fortified dwellings with polygonal towers (of which Stokesay Castle (1291), Salop, is perhaps the earliest instance) was almost certainly inspired by Caernarfon's example.

BIBLIOGRAPHY

A. J. Taylor: 'The Date of Caernarvon Castle', *Antiquity*, xxvi (1952), pp. 25–34

Inventory of the Ancient Monuments in Caernarvonshire, Royal Commission on Ancient and Historical Monuments in Wales and Monmouthshire, ii (London, 1960), pp. 115–56

A. J. Taylor: 'The King's Works in Wales', *The History of the King's Works*, ed. H. H. Colvin (London, 1963), pp. 369–95; as book (London, 1974)

J. M. MADDISON

Caesar, (Gaius) Julius (*b* Rome, 13 July ?102 BC; *d* Rome, 15 March 44 BC). Roman dictator, general and patron. After defeating Pompey and his followers in the Civil War he was named dictator (*reg* 49–44 BC), but was assassinated by conspirators. Caesar renovated the centre of Rome with important works in the Forum Romanum, for example the Basilica Julia, begun in 54 BC and opened, still incomplete, eight years later. His most important building project, however, was the construction of the Forum Julium (*see* ROME, §V, 2), conceived as an extension of the Forum Romanum and as a model of urban renewal for the old parts of the town centre. It established the pattern for the later Imperial Fora. The rectangular, porticoed court of the forum had shops on the north-east and south-west sides. In the centre of the short north-west side a temple was erected to Venus Genetrix, the patroness of the *gens* Julia, whose cult statue was by the sculptor ARKESILAOS. The middle of the court was dominated by an equestrian statue of Caesar (now lost). A plan for the development of the city, possibly drawn up by an Athenian architect, called for a diversion of the Tiber from the Pons Mulvius (now Ponte Milvio) to the foot of the Vatican hills, and for the building of the Campus Martius. The Campus Vaticanus was to be used for the military functions of the Campus Martius. The death of Caesar forestalled the realization of many of these works, but his ideas, and many unfinished buildings, were taken over by AUGUSTUS and AGRIPPA.

BIBLIOGRAPHY

G. Fuchs: 'Zur Baugeschichte der Basilica Aemilia in republikanischer Zeit', *Mitt. Dt. Archäol. Inst.: Röm. Abt.*, lxiii (1956), pp. 14–25

G. Fiorani: 'Problemi architettonici del Foro di Cesare', *Quad. Ist. Top.*, v (1968), pp. 91–103

G. A. Mansuelli: *Roma e il mondo romano*, i (Turin, 1981), pp. 87–9, 113–37

LUCA LEONCINI

Caesar Aelius Hadrianus Antoninus Pius. *See* ANTONINUS PIUS.

Caesarea. *See* CHERCHEL.

Caetano de Sousa, Manuel (*b* Mafra, 26 Jan 1742; *d* Lisbon, 24 May 1802). Portuguese architect and draughtsman. He was the son of the master builder Caetano Tomás de Sousa (*fl* 1718–64). He held appointments as architect to the military orders (1766–85) and to the Casa do Infantado (1786–91), the Casa do Risco (office of works in Lisbon; 1792), the royal palaces of Mafra and Queluz, near Lisbon (1785–92) and the Ajuda Palace in Lisbon (from 1796 until his death).

Much of his work is distinctly Baroque, sometimes characterized by a kind of Rococo style that is linear and symmetrical. In this category are his many drawings for altarpieces, engravings, fountains, funerary monuments and ephemeral constructions for festivals and other celebrations at Queluz and Lisbon. He also designed the last Baroque tower in Lisbon, that of the royal chapel at the Ajuda Palace, in 1792. The rest of his work, however, is more problematical. He tried to synthesize Neo-classical ideas, incompletely understood, with Baroque, producing eclectic hybrids. Although he eliminated towers in his church designs and simplified elevations, he retained Baroque decorations, and his façades, with their emphatic upper sections, tended to lack articulation.

Between 1785 and 1787 Caetano de Sousa designed the south wing of Queluz Palace, the most eclectic part of the building. In 1785 he also planned a *palacete* or small palace for Queen Maria I at Queluz, but this was never built. In 1787 he designed the Manteigueiro Palace in Lisbon, a house with a rectangular plan and a high, flat façade in which the openings are profusely decorated with Baroque mouldings. He also designed the chapel in the Bemposta Palace in Lisbon (completed 1793). The façade of this single-nave or 'box' church has large windows and a *perron*, a double approach stairway that is symmetrical in a Baroque fashion, deriving from Mateus Vicente de Oliveira's work at Queluz; but it is made top-heavy by the triangular pediment, the balustrade and torchlike stone ornaments. Nossa Senhora de Encarnação (begun 1792) in Lisbon is also a 'box' church, with a single nave, customary in Portugal, and a flat façade that is disproportionately high and decorated with Baroque ornament. The heavy triangular pediment was added later but is in keeping with the general style of the building.

Caetano de Sousa was heavily criticized by advocates of Neo-classicism. The critic Cyrillo Volkmar Machado

(1748–1823) considered him to be representative of 'German bad taste', a term which for him covered all manifestations of Baroque deriving from the early 18th-century palace-convent of Mafra. In 1796 work started on the Ajuda Palace in Lisbon, under the direction of Caetano de Sousa. His unrealized plans were for a vast square with six domed towers, a central lantern and a grand stairway, inspired by Luigi Vanvitelli's palace at Caserta, near Naples. However, he was accused of various forms of dishonesty and criticized for his excessive use of ornament, and he found himself obliged to accept the collaboration of two Neo-classical architects, JOSÉ DA COSTA E SILVA and FRANCESCO SAVERIO FABRI, whose plans were ultimately preferred to his own. Legend has it that he died in the middle of an interview with the Inspector General of Public Works, Rodrigo de Sousa Coutinho, while defending his architectural plans and his professional probity. With him died Portuguese Baroque architecture. The palatial wing and tower opposite the Queluz Palace were built to his designs by his elder son, Francisco António de Sousa.

BIBLIOGRAPHY

J.-A. França: *A arte em Portugal no século XIX*, 2 vols (Lisbon, 1966)
——: 'La Fin du goût baroque au Portugal', *Actas do Congresso André Soares* (Braga, 1973–4), ii, pp. 370–76
A. de Carvalho: *Os três arquitectos da Ajuda: Entre o rocócó e o neo-clássico* (Lisbon, 1979)
P. Varela Gomes: *O essencial sobre a arquitectura barroca em Portugal* (Lisbon, 1987)
L. Ferrão: 'Manuel Caetano de Sousa', *Dicionário da arte barroca em Portugal*, ed. J. Fernandes Perreira (Lisbon, 1989), pp. 462–4

PAULO VARELA GOMES

Cafaggiolo Ceramic Factory. Italian ceramic factory. In 1498 a maiolica factory was established in the Medici villa of Cafaggiolo, in the Mugello near Florence, by the brothers Piero Schiavon and Stefano SCHIAVON from Montelupo, a famous Tuscan centre of ceramics production. The factory was in production throughout the 16th century, and the products made for the grand dukes of Tuscany and other noble Florentine families reveal a remarkable pictorial zeal, which developed from decorative schemes influenced by the style of wares from Faenza, including *alla porcellana* (blue-and-white decoration inspired by Chinese porcelain) and grotesques and the rather showy and heraldic *istoriato* (narrative) scenes. Many of these works are stamped or marked underneath with the words *in Chafagiollo* or *Chafaguotto* or sometimes stamped with the famous SP monogram, by tradition ascribed to the Fattorini family (e.g. jug with a portrait of Leo X, *c*. 1515; Faenza, Mus. Int. Cer.). The strong incentive of an important, rich clientele lasted for several decades. When it declined, however, the factory's production became increasingly mediocre during the 16th century and was finally supplanted by MONTELUPO, which was able to expand its production considerably in the 16th and 17th centuries. During the second half of the 16th century, after a period of intense activity to which the long lists of potters' names testify, only Jacopo di Stefano, Francesco di Stefano and Michele di Stefano were still active; Michele was working until at least 1599. From this point, however, the potters who had trained at Cafaggiolo seem to have transferred to other centres of production in the surrounding area.

BIBLIOGRAPHY

G. Guasti: *Di Cafaggiolo e d'altre fabbriche in Toscana* (Florence, 1902)
G. Cora: *Storia della maiolica di Firenze e del contado* (Florence, 1973)
G. Cora and A. Fanfani: *La maiolica di Cafaggiolo* (Florence, 1982)

CARMEN RAVANELLI GUIDOTTI

Café Gresham group. *See* GRESHAM GROUP.

Caffa [Cafà; Cofà; Gafar]**, Melchiorre** (*b* Vittoriosa, nr Mdina, 1638; *d* Rome, before 10 Sept 1667). Maltese sculptor and draughtsman active in Italy. He was the son of Marco Caffa, and his elder brother Lorenzo (1630–1710) was an architect. Melchiorre Caffa was the most significant figure in Italian Baroque sculpture in the generation after Gianlorenzo Bernini, his small but artistically important output marking the beginnings of the late Baroque period. He had completed very few of his works before his early death in a foundry accident.

Some time before 1660 Caffa joined the workshop, in Rome, of the sculptor Ercole Ferrata, with whom he remained connected even after becoming an independent master. Ferrata passed on to Caffa the moderated Baroque style of his own teacher, Alessandro Algardi, but more important was the impression made by the works of Bernini. Caffa's first known independent commission, awarded in December 1660 by Prince Camillo Pamphili, was for a monumental marble relief of the *Martyrdom of St Eustace* for the Pamphili family church in Rome, S Agnese in Agone. Caffa's original conception can be seen only in the terracotta sketch model (Rome, Pal. Venezia); the marble relief, apart from the main figure, was completed with major alterations after his death by Ferrata's workshop and by Giovanni Francesco Rossi (*fl* 1640–77). The work adheres closely to Bernini's illusionistic conception of the relief, but the freedom of composition and modelling seems to proclaim a new, late Baroque manner.

In 1661 Caffa produced a wooden statue of the *Madonna of the Rosary* (Rabat, Malta, S Domenico) for his native island. The following year he was admitted as a member of the Accademia di S Luca, Rome, though he declined to become its *principe*. In 1663 he began the over life-size marble group of the *Charity of St Thomas of Villanova* for the altar (constructed by Giovanni Maria Baratta) of the Pamphili family chapel in S Agostino, Rome. Here, too, Caffa completed only the figure of the saint before his death; the remainder of his scheme was carried out, in changed and reduced form, by Ferrata. A terracotta sketch model (Valletta, N. Mus.) and a dedication print by the painter Pietro del Po (1610–92), based on a drawing by Caffa, give an idea of Caffa's intention to transform the traditional type of niche statue into a *tableau vivant* and thus create a pictorial altar sculpture emancipated from architecture. Floating cherubim and obliquely introduced daylight give the scene a miraculous quality, drawing on altars with hidden light sources by Bernini (Rome, S Maria della Vittoria, Cornaro Chapel) and by Pietro da Cortona (model of the high altar, Rome, S Giovanni dei Fiorentini).

In 1666 Caffa's ambitious and costly project for the high altar of Valletta Cathedral was approved. Again, the scheme, embracing marble architecture and bronze sculpture, was interrupted by his death, by which time only the models, from which the main group—an over-life-size *Baptism of Christ*—was to be cast, had been completed. The project was realized *c.* 1700 by Caffa's pupil Giuseppe Mazzuoli and by Lorenzo Caffa, but in a substantially changed form. It is not clear whether a small signed bronze by Caffa of the *Baptism of Christ* (ex-Sestieri, Rome) reproduces the original form of the main group. A wooden statue of *St Paul* (Valletta, S Paolo Naufrago), intended for use in processions and based on Caffa's sketch model (terracotta; Valletta, Raphael Bonnici Calì priv. col.), is undated; a marble statue of *St Paul* (Rabat, Malta, St Paul's Grotto) was begun in 1666 and completed after Caffa's death by Ferrata's workshop. At about this time, following a design by the architect Giovanni Antonio de Rossi, Caffa produced the model (untraced) for the high altar of S Maria in Campitelli, Rome, which clearly reflects the influence of Bernini's *Cathedra Petri* (Rome, St Peter's).

In the first half of 1667, on a commission from Cardinal Flavio Chigi, Caffa created one of the finest papal portraits of the century: the bust of *Alexander VII* (bronze versions, Siena Cathedral, sacristy, and New York, Met.; terracotta model, Ariccia, Pal. Chigi). A new, intimate conception of portraiture is revealed in this work, involving a penetrating psychological treatment rendered by loose and richly complex modelling and diverging from the portraits of the High Baroque as represented by Bernini and Algardi. The same is true of the marble memorial statue of *Alexander III* (Siena Cathedral), in which the traditional pattern of the enthroned pope, presented from the front, is fundamentally reinterpreted. Equally innovative is the relief showing the *Ecstasy of St Catherine of Siena* for the high altar of S Caterina da Siena a Monte Magnanapoli, Rome (completed 1667; see fig.), in which Caffa isolated the white marble relief against a background of various coloured marbles to achieve a strongly painterly effect: as the almost free-standing figure of the saint, elevated ecstatically on clouds, seems to float out of the framed, brightly coloured background, the traditional boundaries between the genres of painting and sculpture are suspended. The life-size marble group of *St Rosa of Lima* (Lima, S Domingo; terracotta sketch model, Rome, Pal. Venezia), which shows the death of the first New World saint, introduced a new realm of feeling to Baroque sculpture.

Melchiorre Caffa: *Ecstasy of St Catherine of Siena*, marble relief, 1667 (Rome, S Caterina da Siena a Monte Magnanapoli)

Caffa was especially gifted as a modeller of preparatory sketches (*bozzetti*): further examples include those for the façade statues of *St Andrew* and *the Blessed Andrea Avellino* (terracottas, St Petersburg, Hermitage) at S Andrea della Valle, Rome, the full-size versions of which were executed by Ferrata's workshop; *St John the Baptist* (terracotta, Rome, Pal. Venezia); two *Martyrs* (terracotta, Valletta, N. Mus.); and *Justice*, *Charity* and *Clemency* (terracottas, St Petersburg, Hermitage). A small number of drawings by Caffa are known (e.g. those in Paris, Louvre and Bib. N.; London, BM; and Vienna, Albertina). The only known portrait of Caffa (Stockholm, Nmus.) bears the inscription *pictor, sculptor et architectus*, but no painting by him has been identified, and the attribution of his architectural designs remains doubtful, the only certain ones being the projects for the choirs of S Nicola di Bari and S Giovanni Battista in Valletta. The architecture of the high altar of S Caterina da Siena a Monte Manganapoli in Rome has also been attributed to him.

BIBLIOGRAPHY

DBI

F. Baldinucci: *Notizie* (1681–1728); ed. F. Ranalli (1845–7), v, p. 391

P. A. Orlandi: *Abecedario pittorico* (Bologna, 1704), p. 285

N. Pio: *Vite* (1724); ed. C. Enggass and R. Enggass (1977), pp. 111–12

L. Pascoli: *Vite* (1730–36), i, pp. 256–8

M. Missirini: *Memorie per servire alla storia della Romana Accademia di S Luca fino alla morte di A. Canova* (Rome, 1823), p. 123

S. Tizocci: *Dizionario degli architetti, scultori, pittori*, i (Milan, 1830), pp. 244–5

R. Wittkower: 'Eine Bronzegruppe des Melchiorre Caffa', *Z. Bild. Kst*, lxii (1928–9), pp. 227–31

V. Golzio: 'Artisti, pittori e scultori nella chiesa di S Agnese a Piazza Navona, Roma', *Archv Italia*, i (1933–4), pp. 300–10

——: 'Lo "studio" di Ercole Ferrata', *Archv Italia*, ii (1935), pp. 64–5

A. Riccoboni: *Roma nell'arte: La scultura nell'evo moderno* (Rome, 1942), pp. 225–6

J. Fleming: 'A Note on Melchiorre Caffa', *Burl. Mag.* (1947), pp. 85–9

A. Santangelo: *Museo di Palazzo Venezia: Catalogo delle sculture* (Rome, 1954), pp. 83–4, 88, 91

A. Nava Cellini: 'Contributi a Melchiorre Caffa', *Paragone*, vii/83 (1956), pp. 17–31

Il seicento europeo (exh. cat., Rome, Pal. Espos., 1956), pp. 259–60

E. Sammut: 'Melchior Gafà, Maltese Sculptor of the Baroque: Further Biographical Notes', *Scientia*, xxiii (1957), pp. 117–39

R. Wittkower: 'Melchiorre Caffa's Bust of *Alexander VII*', *Bull. Met.*, 17 (1959), pp. 197–204

E. Sammut: 'A Bozzetto by Melchiorre Caffa for the Church of St John, Valletta', *Anu. Ordre Souverain Mil. Malte* (1960), pp. 27–30

L. I. Latt: 'Melchior Kaffà i ego proizvedenia v Ermitazhe' [Melchiorre Caffa and his exhibits in the Hermitage], *Trudy Gosudarstvennogo Ermitazha*, viii (1964), pp. 61–83

G. Spagnesi: *Giovanni Antonio de Rossi: Architetto romano* (Rome, 1964), pp. 119–20, 132, 237–8

A. Clark: 'The Portraits of Artists Drawn for Nicola Pio', *Master Drgs*, v (1967), p. 12

R. Preimesberger: 'Ein Bozzetto Melchiorre Caffas", *Wien. Jb. Kstgesch.*, xxii (1969), pp. 178–83

G. Eimer: *La fabbrica di S Agnese in Navona*, ii (Stockholm, 1971), pp. 496, 499, 532

J. Garms: *Quellen aus dem Archiv Doria-Pamphilj zur Kunsttätigkeit in Rom unter Innozenz X* (Rome and Vienna, 1972), docs 54, 86, 253, 749, 918
J. Montagu: 'Le *Baptême du Christ* d'Alessandro Algardi', *Rev. A.* [Paris], 15 (1972), pp. 64–78
R. Preimesberger and M. Weil: 'The Pamphili Chapel in Sant'Agostino', *Röm. Jb. Kstgesch.*, xv (1975), pp. 183–98
U. Schlegel: *Die italienische Bildwerke des 17. und 18. Jahrhunderts* (1978), i of *Die Bildwerke der Skulpturengalerie Berlin* (Berlin, 1978–88), pp. 46–57
M. Butzek: 'Papstmonumente im Dom von Siena', *Mitt. Ksthist. Inst. Florenz*, xxiv (1980), pp. 40–41
D. Jemma: 'Inediti e documenti di Melchiorre Caffà', *Paragone*, xxvii/379 (1981), pp. 53–8
J. Montagu: 'The Graphic Work of Melchior Cafà', *Paragone*, xxx/413 (1984), pp. 50–61

RUDOLF PREIMESBERGER

Caffarelli, Scipione. *See* BORGHESE, (2).

Cafferata, Francisco (*b* Buenos Aires, 28 Feb 1861; *d* Buenos Aires, 28 Nov 1890). Argentine sculptor. He studied in Buenos Aires under Julio Laguens before travelling in 1877 to Florence, where he studied sculpture under the Italian sculptors Urbano Lucchesi (1844–1906) and Augusto Passaglia (1838–1918). His *Slave* (bronze), now in the Jardines del Parque 3 de Febrero in Buenos Aires, was awarded a gold medal at the Exposición Continental, Buenos Aires, in 1882. In 1885 he returned to Argentina with his monument to *Admiral Guillermo Brown* (bronze; Adrogué, Plaza Almirante Brown), unveiled in 1886; as the first monument by a native artist to be erected in Argentina it received an enthusiastic reception.

Cafferata also produced busts of his father, of the revolutionary Spanish ideologist Mariano Moreno and of the poet José de Espronceda, and he was one of the few 19th-century artists in Argentina to recognize the role of the negro in his society, for example in a monument to the popular hero *Falucho*, which was unfinished when he committed suicide; the conception was taken over by Lucio Correa Morales in his bronze sculpture *Falucho* (Buenos Aires, Plazoleta Falucho). Cafferata's sculpture is characterized by powerful modelling and by a dramatic expressiveness that places him beyond the bounds of academic sculpture.

BIBLIOGRAPHY

J. M. Taverna Irigoyen: *Escultura argentina de este siglo* (Santa Fé, 1977), p. 10
E. B. Rodríguez: *Visiones de la escultura argentina* (Buenos Aires, 1983), pp. 13–14

NELLY PERAZZO

Caffi, Ippolito (*b* Belluno, 16 Oct 1809; *d* at sea, Lissa, 20 July 1866). Italian painter. After training initially in Belluno (1821–5), then in Padua with his cousin Pietro Paoletti (1801–47), Caffi attended the Accademia di Belle Arti in Venice (1827–31), studying under Teodoro Matteini (1754–1831), Francesco Bagnara (1784–1866) and Tranquillo Orsi (1771–1845). In 1832 he moved to Rome, acquiring immediate fame as a *vedutista.* He displayed a virtuoso command of spatial construction; in 1835 he published a textbook on perspective, *Lezioni di prospettiva pratica*, with Antonio Bianchini. Caffi modernized the *veduta* vocabulary inherited from Canaletto, selecting new points of view, and he showed an interest in nocturnal scenes with artificial or lunar illumination, in recording the effects of light and atmosphere at particular times, and in chronicling unusual events such as eclipses and balloon flights. His most famous work, the *Last Hour of Carnevale in Rome (The Candles)* (1837; Venice, Ca' Pesaro), displays the originality of his style. Rome appears as an illusionistically vast stage on which human figures are simply sparks of light and patches of vivid colour. Exhibited in Venice, it met with enormous success; Caffi executed 42 replicas, a practice he adopted for other popular subjects. Veiled light and heavy atmosphere are the main elements of *Venice in the Snow* (1850; Trieste, Mus. Civ. Revoltella).

Caffi travelled extensively in Italy, the Orient (1843–4) and around Europe (1850s), recording his experiences in numerous sketches. Extremely prolific, he received many commissions for paintings and frescoes throughout Italy. A fervent patriot, he painted many episodes of the Risorgimento (e.g. the *Arrival of Victor Emanuel II in Naples*, 1860–61; Venice, Ca' Pesaro; large version, Turin, Mus. N. Ris. It.) and died attempting to record the battle of Lissa.

BIBLIOGRAPHY

M. Pittaluga: *Il pittore Ippolito Caffi* (Vicenza, 1971)
G. Perocco: *Ippolito Caffi (1809–1866)* (Venice, 1979)
Ippolito Caffi, 1809–1866 (exh. cat., ed. E. di Majo and S. Susinno; Copenhagen, Thorvaldsens Mus., 1986)

EFREM GISELLA CALINGAERT

Caffi, Margherita (*b* ?Vicenza, *fl* 1662–1700). Italian painter. Around 30 flower paintings by her, dated between 1662 and 1700, have been identified (two of which are in Florence, Uffizi, and were damaged by the bomb in May 1993). Her father, Vincenzo Volò, and her husband, Francesco [?Lodovico] Caffi of Cremona, were both still-life painters. She was patronized by the Medici in Florence and by the Habsburgs in Madrid and Innsbruck, especially the latter, where she is said to have lived for an extensive period.

Caffi's paintings are remarkable for their freedom of composition and the loose, fluid technique that resembles 18th-century decorative painting rather than the work of her contemporaries. But the dark backgrounds that give strength to her preferred colour scheme for flowers of blue, red and white mark these works as Baroque rather than Rococo. Her flowers are not always accurately depicted, or even identifiable; she was less interested in the scientific (or symbolic) content of still-lifes than in their potential for a decorative composition, as, for example, in the *Still-life with Flowers in a Landscape* (1662; sold London, Sotheby's, 15 July 1970, lot 90; see sale cat. for illus.). The exuberant virtuosity of her technique makes her work an interesting link between the styles of earlier north Italian 17th-century painters such as Giovanni Benedetto Castiglione, Bernardo Strozzi and Domenico Fetti, who also used free, fluid brushwork and impasto (*pittura di tocco*), and Venetian 18th-century painters such as Francesco Guardi and Giovanni Battista Tiepolo, who perfected this style.

BIBLIOGRAPHY

G. B. Zaist: *Notizie istoriche de' pittori, scultori ed architetti cremonesi* (Cremona, 1774), ii, p. 124
G. Grasselli: *Abecedario biografico de' pittori . . . cremonesi* (Milan, 1827), p. 71
La natura morta italiana (exh. cat. by S. Bottari and others, Naples, Pal. Reale, 1964), pp. 112–13, nos 261–5

The Twilight of the Medici (exh. cat., Detroit, MI, Inst. A.; Florence, Pitti; 1974), pp. 198–9

Women Artists, 1550–1950 (exh. cat. by A. Sutherland Harris and L. Nochlin, Los Angeles, CA, Co. Mus. A., 1977), pp. 151–2

ANN SUTHERLAND HARRIS

Caffiéri [Caffieri; Caffier]. French family of artists of Italian descent. (1) Philippe Caffiéri (i), the son of Daniele Caffiéri (1603–39), chief engineer to Pope Urban VIII, left Rome for Paris in 1660. His virtuosity of craftsmanship and mastery of detail were characteristics that were shared by other members of the family, as was employment as a sculptor in the naval yards. Philippe was associated with Le Havre while his eldest son, François-Charles Caffiéri (1667–1729), François-Charles's own son, Charles-Philippe Caffiéri (*b* 1695), and grandson, Charles-Marie Caffiéri (*b* 1736), all worked as sculptors in the naval yards of Le Havre and Brest. (2) Jacques Caffiéri, another of Philippe's sons, was one of the most celebrated bronzeworkers in the reign of Louis XV. Jacques's eldest son, (3) Philippe Caffiéri (ii), was also a bronze-caster and chaser and had a large private clientele in France that included the Marquise de Pompadour, the Prince de Condé and Mme du Barry. Jacques's younger son, (4) Jean-Jacques Caffiéri, became one of the most eminent sculptors of the second half of the 18th century, producing monumental works as well as small-scale allegorical groups and some of the liveliest and most elegant portrait busts of the time.

BIBLIOGRAPHY

J. Guiffrey: *Les Caffiéri: Sculpteurs et fondeurs-ciseleurs* (Paris, 1877)

(1) Philippe [Filippo] **Caffiéri (i)** (*b* Rome, 1634; *d* Paris, 7 Sept 1716). Sculptor, wood-carver and bronze-founder. In 1660 he was summoned to Paris by Cardinal Mazarin. There he was based at the Gobelins manufactory, where he was associated with Domenico Cucci (1635–1705) and worked for the Bâtiments du Roi under Charles Le Brun. In 1665 he was described in his naturalization papers as 'Sculpteur Ordinaire des Meubles de la Couronne'. He was principally a wood-carver, contributing decorative carving to the Tuileries (1666) and the Louvre (1668)—sometimes working in collaboration with Mathieu Lespagnandelle (1617–89)—and also to the Château de St-Germain-en-Laye, Yvelines, where in 1669 he provided carvings for the chapel; none of this work survives. At Versailles he executed many carvings, most notably for the sumptuous Appartement des Bains of Louis XIV and for the queen's oratory (both destr.), as well as providing carved doors and furniture for the king's apartments. He seems also to have specialized in frame-making and between 1682 and 1683 was paid for 50 frames for paintings in the Cabinet du Roi. The carved and gilded frames on Guido Reni's series of the *Labours of Hercules* (Paris, Louvre) have been attributed to him. In 1680 he provided bronze architectural ornaments after models by Le Brun in the Galerie des Glaces (*in situ*), Versailles, and bronze Ionic capitals for pilasters on the Escalier des Ambassadeurs (destr. 1750). In 1687 he was appointed Maître-sculpteur to the royal fleet at Le Havre. His work is typical of the ponderous and magnificent style evolved by Le Brun and his associates for Louis XIV.

GUILHEM SCHERF

(2) Jacques Caffiéri (*b* Paris, 25 Aug 1678; *d* Paris, 23 Nov 1755). Bronze-caster, sculptor and designer, son of (1) Philippe Caffiéri (i). He was the nephew of Charles Le Brun and had two sons by his marriage to Marie-Anne Rousseau, (3) Philippe Caffiéri (ii) and (4) Jean-Jacques Caffiéri. Jacques became one of the most prominent bronzeworkers in the reign of Louis XV. A member of the Académie de Saint-Luc, Paris, he became a master bronze-caster and chaser in Paris before 1715 and, on an unknown earlier date, received the title of Sculpteur et Ciseleur Ordinaire des Bâtiments du Roi. It is probable that one of his teachers was Domenico Cucci, who was Ebéniste et Fondeur du Roi and with whom the Caffiéri family was closely linked. Jacques also received training in sculpture, as evidenced by his busts of *Baron de Besenval* (1735) and *Baron de Brunstadt* (1737). It was in the decorative arts, however, that he achieved his reputation.

In 1740 his wife bought the warrant of Marchande Doreuse Privilégiée du Roi suivant la Cour, which allowed them to continue the processes of bronze-casting and gilding, which would normally have been performed by separate businesses, within the same workshop. In 1747 his son Philippe Caffiéri (ii) joined him as an associate. Jacques had clients in the city of Paris and at court, including the royal family. He also became Maître Sculpteur et Dessinateur des Vaisseaux du Roi. Of his bronzework only small, decorative pieces are extant. He is known to have made gilt-bronze mantelpieces (destr.) for four chimney-pieces commissioned for the château of Versailles in 1747, but only those from the Dauphin's Bedchamber survive. Similarly, the numerous bronze ornaments for coaches, including those commissioned by the court, are lost. Of his work for cabinetmakers, only the bronzes for the commode (1739; London, Wallace; for illustration *see* COMMODE) by Antoine-Robert Gaudreaus for Louis XV are extant, although those for the desk (Baron Edmond de Rothschild priv. col.) for the Duc de Choiseul have also been attributed to him.

Jacques Caffiéri specialized in the Louis XV style. Animals and fantastic beasts, figures of gods and heroes inspired by Ovid's *Metamorphoses* and genre subjects, all combined with elaborate curves that are emphasized by leafy, flowered branches, typical of the asymmetrical Louis XV style, feature prominently in his earlier works. Examples with this type of decoration include the *Diana* and *Apollo* clocks (Pushkin, Pal.–Mus.; Duke of Buccleuch, priv. col.); the *Diana and Endymion* cartel-clock (Amsterdam, Rijksmus.); Queen Marie Leczinska's candelabra (Paris, Louvre); wall-lights (Malibu, CA, Getty Mus.) made for the Infanta Elizabeth, Louis XV's daughter (1727–59); fire-dogs decorated with hunters (Rome, Pal. Quirinale); and the chandeliers (Paris, Bib. Mazarine) of the Marquise de Pompadour, which include putti playing among bouquets of roses, as well as representations of castles similar to those that feature on the Marquise's coat of arms. Caffiéri's later works are in the symmetrical version of the Louis XV style, for example the chandelier (1751; London, Wallace) from the collection of the dukes of Parma and the Passament astronomical clock (1753; Versailles, Château) for Louis XV.

(3) Philippe Caffiéri (ii) (*b* Paris, 19 Feb 1714; *d* Paris, 8 Oct 1774). Bronze-caster, collector and designer, son of (2) Jacques Caffiéri. He succeeded his mother as Marchand Doreur Privilégié du Roi in 1743. Trained by his father, and an associate in his business from 1747, he continued the workshop and succeeded his father as Sculpteur et Ciseleur Ordinaire des Bâtiments du Roi. In 1754 he was admitted to the Académie de Saint-Luc, Paris, and on 16 January 1756 became a master bronze-caster and chaser. Under his direction the Caffiéri workshop continued to prosper by working for a prestigious clientele, and Philippe became wealthy. He was able to form a collection that included drawings and paintings by Rembrandt, David Teniers (ii), Jean-Baptiste Oudry, Chardin, François de Troy (ii), Louis Lagrenée, Boucher and Jean-Honoré Fragonard and sculptures by Jacques-François-Joseph de Saly, Etienne-Maurice Falconet and Michel-Ange Challe.

Caffiéri rejected the Louis XV style in which his father had worked, favouring instead the richly decorative technique of black patination with gilding, which he used particularly for Neo-classical works. Both his own works and those carried out under the supervision of various architects show his freely interpreted versions of canons of the 'Greek style', which lack the often dogmatic stylistic vocabulary apparent in the work of some of his contemporaries. After 1756 Caffiéri modelled bronzes based on the designs of Louis-Joseph Le Lorrain for the desk (Chantilly, Mus. Condé) of Ange-Laurent de La Live de Jully, which is one of the finest examples of French Neo-classical furniture. Caffiéri later produced the mantelpiece, designed by Ange-Jacques Gabriel, for the chimney-piece of the Salle des Maréchaux in the Ecole Militaire, Paris, which, with its lions' heads, draperies and frieze with a repeating scroll motif, incorporates most of the decorative themes of the Neo-classical style. The lamp brackets (1759; Rome, Pal. Quirinale) with trophies of the Arts and the Sciences also illustrate Caffiéri's modernism.

Following the example of his father, Caffiéri produced many different types of bronzework. He made the bronzes for a medal-cabinet by Jean-François Oeben for François Boucher and decorated pendulum clocks (New York, Frick; Versailles, Château) made by Berthoud and Lieutaud with bronze bas-reliefs, including one of the *Chariots of Apollo.* He also modelled vase and pedestal decorations for the Duc d'Aumont (Paris, Louvre), Paul Randon de Boisset, La Live de Jully and Stanislav II Poniatowski, King of Poland. Caffiéri also designed a toilet-table for the Princess of the Asturias in 1765, altar bronzes for the cathedral of Notre-Dame and the church of St Nicolas du Chardonnet, Paris, and for Bayeux Cathedral, as well as numerous works at Versailles. Some of his most notable bronzes are those commissioned for the Palais-Bourbon, Paris, for which only the designs (Chantilly, Mus. Condé) are extant, and the candelabra mounted around Martin Desjardins's statues (London, Buckingham Pal., Royal Col.) illustrating the *Four Seasons*, for the Comte d'Orsay. From 1766 to 1768 Caffiéri took part in the redecoration of the Łazienki Palace, Warsaw, for Stanislav II, together with Jean-Louis Prieur and Victor Louis, providing ornaments for four chimney-pieces, six tripod candelabra with cornucopias and a set of wall-lights with illusionistic drapery (all Warsaw, Royal Castle).

BIBLIOGRAPHY

J. Guiffrey: *Les Caffiéri: Sculpteurs et fondeurs-ciseleurs* (Paris, 1877)
S. Eriksen: *Early Neo-classicism* (London, 1974)

JEAN-DOMINIQUE AUGARDE

(4) Jean-Jacques Caffiéri (*b* Paris, 30 April 1725; *d* Paris, 21 June 1792). Sculptor, son of (2) Jacques Caffiéri. He trained with his father and later with Jean-Baptiste Lemoyne (ii), whose lively portrait style he absorbed. In 1748 he won the Prix de Rome with the bas-relief *Cain Killing Abel*, and in 1749 he left for Rome; he remained in Italy until 1753, possibly travelling to Naples in that year, where he was disappointed in his desire to participate in the sculptural decoration of Luigi Vanvitelli's royal palace at Caserta. While in Italy he modelled a number of portrait busts, most notably those of the *Abbé Leblanc* (1751; untraced) and *Benedict XIV* (1751; untraced), but his principal Roman work was the large stucco high-relief group of the *Trinity* crowning the pediment of the high altar of S Luigi dei Francesi, which was commissioned in 1752 by the French ambassador, the Abbé de Canilliac. Executed with the advice of Charles-Joseph Natoire, the director of the Académie de France in Rome, it shows the influence of the Roman Baroque.

Caffiéri returned to his native Paris in 1754 and was approved (*agréé*) at the Académie Royale in 1757 and received (*reçu*) as a full member in 1759 with a skilfully posed *River God* (plaster, exh. Salon 1757; marble, 1759; Paris, Louvre). He was a keen petitioner for work and was given State commissions for statues of *St Sylvia*, *St Satyrus* and *St Alipius* (all marble, 1774–88; destr.) for the church of the Dôme des Invalides, Paris; for statues of *Pierre Corneille* (marble, exh. Salon 1779; Paris, Louvre; terracotta version, Rouen, Mus. B.-A.) and *Molière* (marble, exh. Salon 1787; Paris, Louvre) for the series of *Illustrious Frenchmen* commissioned by Charles-Claude de Flahaut de la Billarderie, Comte d'Angiviller, director of the Bâtiments du Roi; for monumental allegorical statues of *Air* and *Water* (stone, *in situ*; terracotta models, exh. Salon 1771; untraced) for the façade of the Hôtel de la Monnaie, Paris; and for a pair of life-size lead *Angels* for Rouen Cathedral (*c.* 1787; *in situ*).

Caffiéri also had numerous discerning private clients. Mme du Barry commissioned the life-size and light-hearted allegorical group *Friendship Surprised by Love* (plaster, exh. Salon 1773; terracotta, Lugano, coll. Thyssen-Bornemisza), influenced by one of his masterworks, *Hope Nourishing Love* (marble, 1769; Malibu, CA, Getty Mus.). The Abbé de Voisenon, distraught at the death of the actress Mme Favart, commissioned the small *Monument to Mme Favart* (marble; Paris, Louvre), the terracotta that caused a scandal at the 1773 Salon. For the Abbé Terray, briefly director of the Bâtiments and a noted collector of sculpture, Caffiéri carved the marble group of *Geometry and Architecture* represented as children (marble, *c.* 1776; Waddesdon Manor, Bucks, NT) and executed a pair of small bronzes, *Cupid Vanquishing Pan* (1777; London, Wallace; see fig.; terracotta model, exh. Salon 1771) and a reduction of Mme du Barry's group (1777; Toledo, OH, Mus. A.). These last two subjects seem to

Jean-Jacques Caffiéri: *Cupid Vanquishing Pan*, bronze, h. 425 mm, 1777 (London, Wallace Collection)

have been particularly popular and are typical of the skill with which Caffiéri satisfied the contemporary fashionable taste for the sentimental.

However, Jean-Jacques Caffiéri's skills found their finest expression in his vivacious and naturalistic portraits. He showed himself a worthy successor to Lemoyne, whom he surpassed in the virtuosity of his handling of marble if not in his sympathetic presentation of character. He made many lively and perceptive busts of his contemporaries, of which the best, such as that of *Canon Pingré* (terracotta, 1788; Paris, Louvre), rival those of his younger contemporary Jean-Antoine Houdon. He was also the greatest 18th-century specialist in the genre of the posthumous portrait, examples of which can be seen at the Comédie Française, Paris, including busts of such actors and writers as *Buirette de Belloy* (marble, 1771), *Alexis Piron* (marble, 1775), *Jean de la Fontaine* (terracotta, exh. Salon 1779), *Jean de Rotrou* (marble, 1783) and *Jean-Baptiste Rousseau* (marble, 1787), many of which were donated by Caffiéri in return for free admission to the theatre during his lifetime. The sculptor's habit of making casts from his own work and presenting them to institutions has meant that a record has been preserved of a number of lost marbles, including his famous bust of the composer *Jean-Philippe Rameau* (plaster; Paris, Bib. Ste-Geneviève), which was highly praised by Diderot when it was shown at the Salon of 1771.

BIBLIOGRAPHY

J. Guiffrey: *Les Caffiéri: Sculpteurs et fondeurs-ciseleurs* (Paris, 1877)

Diderot et l'art de Boucher à David (exh. cat., Paris, Admin. Monnaies & Médailles, 1984–5), pp. 441–5

P. Verlet: *Les Bronzes dorés français du XVIIIe siècle* (Paris, 1987)

GUILHEM SCHERF

Cage, John (*b* Los Angeles, 5 Sept 1912; *d* New York, 12 Aug 1992). American composer, philosopher, writer and printmaker. He was educated in California and then made a study tour of Europe (1930–31), concentrating on art, architecture and music. On his return to the USA he studied music with Richard Buhlig, Adolph Weiss, Henry Cowell and Arnold Schoenberg; in 1934 he abandoned abstract painting for music. An interest in extending the existing range of percussion instruments led him, in 1940, to devise the 'prepared piano' (in which the sound is transformed by the insertion of various objects between the strings) and to pioneer electronic sound sources.

Cage's studies of Zen Buddhism and Indian philosophy during the 1940s resulted in a decision to remove intention, memory and personal taste from music, based on the Oriental concern with process rather than result. According equal status to both structured sound and noise, he treated silence (the absence of intentional sounds) as an element in its own right. In the early 1950s he began his close collaboration with the pianist David Tudor and, with the composers Morton Feldman, Earle Brown and Christian Wolff, they worked on his Project of Music for Magnetic Tapes (1951–3). In the winter of 1950–51 Wolff gave Cage a copy of his father's publication of the *Yi jing* (*I Ching*), the Chinese Book of Changes, which he used in his work thereafter as a source of 'chance operations' to obtain numerical values (for which Cage had earlier devised mathematical charts) that could be applied to any facet of musical or artistic composition. In the following year Cage produced his *4'33"* (shortly after Robert Rauschenberg's 'white canvases'), in which the performer(s) make no sounds but only delineate the work's three movements.

Also in 1952 Cage organized an untitled event at BLACK MOUNTAIN COLLEGE which foreshadowed the 'happenings' of the following decade and initiated an approach to performance in collaboration with the dancer and choreographer MERCE CUNNINGHAM, in which music and movement were conceived separately and performed simultaneously. Many later works make use of concurrent layers of independent musical or non-musical activities. Cage also pioneered aspects of live electronic music and offered the performer greater creative freedom.

Cage was influential not only as a composer but also as a thinker, profoundly influencing artists working in other media. He was a friend of visual artists such as Mark Tobey, Morris Graves, Max Ernst, Richard Lippold, Willem de Kooning, Robert Motherwell, Rauschenberg, Jasper Johns, Joan Miró and, in particular, Marcel Duchamp, and wrote about and collaborated with most of them. In his own scores after 1950 Cage frequently incorporated visual elements, such as superimpositions of transparent sheets covered with straight and curved lines, circles and dots; coloured wavy lines to represent melodic outlines; and graphlike notations. In some scores he determined the positioning of pitches on a more or less conventional staff by the superimposition of star charts, or he based it on observations of imperfections in the paper. During the 1950s Cage also worked for a time as art director for a textile company.

From 1949 Cage began to introduce new elements into the presentation of lectures, beginning with *Lecture on Nothing*, by juxtaposing passages of text and sometimes also of music with silences and physical gestures. This was extended in the mid-1960s by the exploratory use of non-syntactical texts and texts printed in a variety of different typefaces. From 1963 Cage developed a new poetic form that he called the 'mesostic', in which new words were formed vertically by highlighting one character within each line of the horizontal text. An example of this is the score of a composition for unaccompanied, amplified voice, *62 Mesostics re Merce Cunningham* (1971), which uses more than 700 different Letraset typefaces and sizes. A new visual element—the fragmentary drawings from nature scattered throughout Thoreau's *Journal*—is included in the published text of Cage's *Empty Words* and in the compositions *Score (40 Drawings by Thoreau) and 23 Parts* (1974) and *Renga* (1976; based on 361 paintings), for any instruments or voices.

Cage's increasing involvement in the graphic presentation of his work also led him to create purely visual works that have no musical connections. These are largely in the form of limited editions, mostly carried out in the etching studio of Crown Point Press in Oakland, CA, where he created 28 series of prints in the course of fairly regular visits between 1978 and his death in 1992. The earliest such work was *Not Wanting to Say Anything about Marcel* (1969), produced in collaboration with Calvin Sumsion. It consists of eight parts (referred to as plexigrams), each comprising a base in which eight parallel Perspex sheets are fitted; fragments of printed text and images are silkscreened on to the sheets. Cage's etchings became increasingly complex as he used the *Yi jing* as a means of making formal decisions and of selecting a variety of printmaking techniques. In *Changes and Disappearances* (1979–82) up to 45 different, irregularly shaped etching plates were used in each of the 35 etchings, and the final print contains 298 colours. Until 1982 most of his prints included reproductions of drawings by Thoreau in whole or in part; thereafter his images were inspired by the four elements of earth, air, fire and water, as well as the shapes of stones and rocks. In 1982, as part of his 70th birthday celebrations, the exhibition *John Cage: Scores and Prints* was mounted at the Whitney Museum of American Art, New York.

WRITINGS

Silence: Lectures and Writings (Middletown, CT, 1961/*R* London, 1968)
A Year from Monday: New Lectures and Writings by John Cage (Middletown, CT, 1967/*R* London, 1968)
To Describe the Process of Composition Used in 'Not Wanting to Say Anything about Marcel' (Cincinnati, 1969)
with C. Sumsion: 'Plexigram IV: Not Wanting to Say Anything about Marcel', *Source: Music of the Avant-garde*, iv/7–8 (1970), pp. 1–20
M: Writings, '67–'72 (Middletown, CT, 1973/*R* London, 1973)
Empty Words: Writings, '73–'78 (Middletown, CT, 1979/*R* London, 1980)
X: Writings, '79–'82 (Middletown, CT, 1983/*R* London, 1987)
J.-J. Nattiez, ed.: *Pierre Boulez/John Cage: Correspondance et documents* (Winterthur, 1990) [bilingual text]; Fr. trans. (Paris, 1991); Eng. trans. as *The Boulez-Cage Correspondence* (Cambridge, 1993) [exchange of letters between 1949 and 1954]
R. Kostelanetz, ed.: *John Cage, Writer: Previously Uncollected Pieces* (New York, 1993)

BIBLIOGRAPHY

Grove 6; Grove Amer. Music; Grove Instr.
C. Tomkins: 'Figure in an Imaginary Landscape', *New Yorker* (28 Nov 1964), pp. 64–128; rev. as 'John Cage' in *The Bride and the Bachelors* (New York, 1965); Eng. edn as *Ahead of the Game: Four Versions of the Avant-garde* (London, 1965), pp. 69–138
R. Kostelanetz, ed.: *John Cage* (New York, 1970/*R* London, 1971); rev. as *John Cage: An Anthology* (New York, 1991) [incl. 'Cage's Visual Art', p. 219, a list of graphic works to 1989]
D. Charles: 'Cage et Duchamp', *L'Arc*, 59 (Oct-Dec 1974), pp. 72–9 [repr. in *Gloses sur John Cage* (Paris, 1978), pp. 183–96]
Pour les oiseaux: Entretiens avec Daniel Charles (Paris, 1976; Eng. trans. London and Boston, MA, 1981) [based on interviews pubd in *Rev. Esthét.*, xxi/2–4 (1968)]
H.-K. Metzger and R. Riehn, eds: *John Cage I* (Munich, 1978), pp. 65–91, 132–46 [well illus.; rev. 1990]
Tri-Quarterly, 54 (Spring 1982) [issue ded. Cage], pp. 62–232; also as *A John Cage Reader*, ed. P. Gena and J. Brent (New York, London and Frankfurt, 1982) [illus., incl. 8 colour pls from *Changes and Disappearances*]
John Cage: Etchings, 1978–1982 (exh. cat., Oakland, CA, Crown Point Gal., 1982) [with introductory essay and chronology; incl. items by L. Toland and K. Brown orig. pubd in *Tri-Quarterly*, 54 (Spring 1982)]
R. Kostelanetz, ed.: *Conversing with Cage* (New York, 1988/*R* London, 1989), pp. 173–90 [selections from interviews, esp. since 1965]
H.-K. Metzger and R. Riehn, eds: *John Cage II* (Munich, 1990) [well illus.; incl. M. Erdmann: 'Chronologisches Verzeichnis', pp. 305–41, an annotated list (to 1988) of compositions, graphic works and writings]
R. Kostelanetz: 'John Cage: The Development of his Visual Art', *Musicworks*, 52 (Spring 1992), pp. 40–42 [graphic works to 1969, in special Cage issue]
D. Revill: *The Roaring Silence: John Cage, a Life* (London, 1992), pp. 261–5, 273–7, *passim* [first biography, incl. list of compositions (to early 1992) and 'Chronology of Visual Works', pp. 367–8]
J. Pritchett: *The Music of John Cage* (Cambridge, 1993), pp. 180–89

HUGH DAVIES

Cagli, Corrado (*b* Ancona, 22 Feb 1910; *d* Rome, 28 March 1976). Italian painter and stage designer. He studied at the Accademia di Belle Arti in Rome. Cagli exhibited for the first time as a painter in 1932 at the Galleria di Roma and the Galleria Il Milione in Milan, with Giuseppe Capogrossi and Emanuele Cavalli (1904–81). After a further group exhibition at the Galerie Bonjean in Paris in 1933, Cagli and his colleagues were among members of the second phase of the informal group the SCUOLA ROMANA. During this period Cagli became particularly close to Mirko, who married his sister in 1938. In an article of 1933 Cagli opposed the classical ideals of Novecento Italiano, putting forward his own preoccupation with the mythical and primordial. Nevertheless he expressed this within the current orthodoxy of a monumental figurative style. In the *Battle of San Martino and Solferino* (encaustic, 5.5×6.6 m, 1936; Florence, Uffizi), executed for the Milan Triennale, the re-expression of a mural technique and of an ancient epic form is fragmented into episodes that follow free associations and psychological analogies.

As a result of anti-semitic persecution Cagli moved to Paris at the end of 1938 and to New York in the following year; he remained there until 1948, although he served in the army during the Normandy landings. Exile proved to be the means to a widening of Cagli's artistic experience: in particular the post-Cubist works of Picasso and Braque, and the Surrealism of Max Ernst and André Masson contributed, once he had returned to Rome in 1948, towards new developments in his painting. From this time his eclectic, experimental work included both figurative and geometric abstract styles that focused on the nature of materials and signs such as *Y & X4* (1948; priv. col., see 1989 Verona exh. cat., p. 83). Towards the end of his career, he concentrated on stage designs for ballets.

WRITINGS

'Anticipi sulla scuola di Roma', *Quadrante*, 6 (Sept 1933), p. 36

BIBLIOGRAPHY

La Fondazione Cagli per Firenze (exh. cat. by C. L. Ragghianti, Florence, Pal. Strozzi, 1979)
I percorsi di Cagli (exh. cat., ed. E. Crispolti; Naples, Castel Ovo, 1982)
Il Cagli romano (exh. cat., Siena, Pal. Pub. and Magazzini del Sale, 1985)
Cagli, immaginare la libertà (exh. cat., ed. I. Reale; Udine, Gal. A. Ant. & Mod., 1989)
Corrado Cagli: Mostra antologica (exh. cat. by G. Cortenova, E. Crispolti and E. Mascelloni, Verona, Pal. Forti, 1989)

SILVIA LUCCHESI

Cagnacci, Guido (*b* Sant'Arcangelo di Romagna, 19 Jan 1601; *d* Vienna, 1663). Italian painter. He studied in Bologna in 1618–21 with an unidentified teacher, went to Rome in 1621 and finished an apprenticeship with Guercino in 1622. His earliest documented work, the *Procession of the Holy Sacrament* (1627; Saludecio, parish church), was to have been part of a larger decorative cycle that was never completed. At about the same time he painted an altarpiece depicting *St Sixtus II* (Saludecio, parish church). In 1628, at which time he was living in Rimini with his family, he attempted to elope with a widowed noblewoman, Teodora Stivivi, intending to force her family to consent to their marriage. The attempt was a failure but had long-lasting repercussions that affected the course of his career. He was obliged to leave Rimini for a while but returned in 1631 and painted some important works, characterized by a dramatic chiaroscuro that suggests direct contact with the followers of Caravaggio in Rome. Particularly noteworthy are his altarpieces of the *Virgin and Child with Three Carmelite Saints* (*c.* 1631; Rimini, S Giovanni Battista), the *Calling of St Matthew* (Rimini, Pin. Com. & Mus. Civ.) and *Christ with SS Joseph and Eloi* (1635; Sant'Arcangelo di Romagna, Collegiata).

In the following years Cagnacci executed several paintings in Urbania, Pesaro, the city from which his family originated. These are clearly inspired by Bolognese art, specifically that of Guido Reni, whose influence is evident

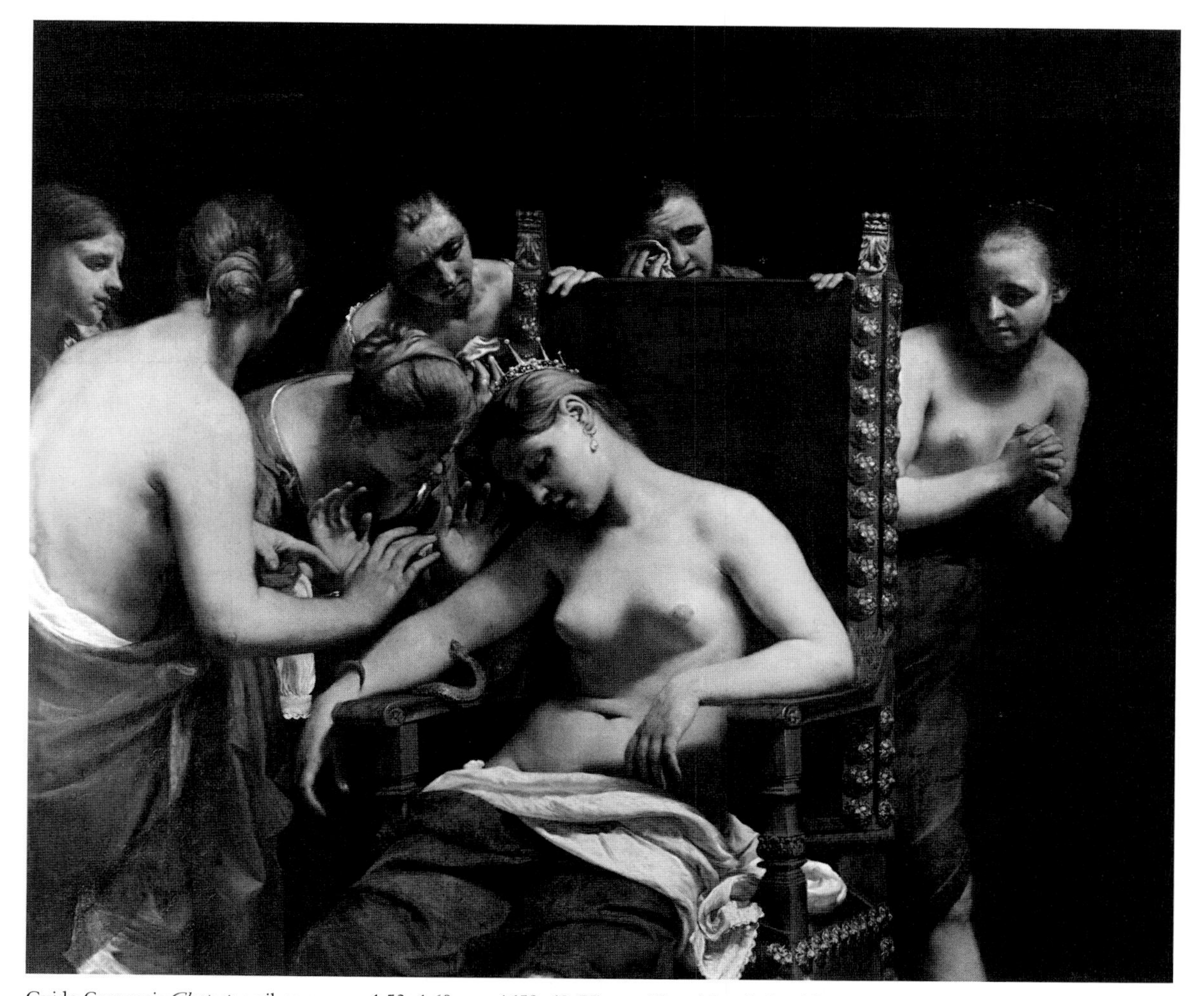

Guido Cagnacci: *Cleopatra*, oil on canvas, 1.53×1.69 m, *c.* 1659–62 (Vienna, Kunsthistorisches Museum)

especially in the altarpiece of *St Mary Magdalene in Ecstasy* (1637; Urbania, S Maria Maddalena). This period of Cagnacci's life remains a mystery; he may have lived in Tuscany, Emilia or the Veneto. Evidently he paid increased attention to the late work of Reni and to the classicizing manner of Guercino and deepened his knowledge of the art of Correggio, Veronese and Giovanni Lanfranco, for he abandoned the Caravaggesque chiaroscuro of his early works in favour of a more naturalistic manner, with figures limpidly realized in warm, deep and luminous colours.

In 1642 Cagnacci was in Forlì, where he executed a *St Joseph* for the high altar of the oratory of S Giuseppe, and a *St Anthony Preaching* for the cathedral (both *in situ*). In the cathedral he was commissioned to decorate the dome of the chapel of the Madonna del Fuoco with an *Assumption of the Virgin* in the cupola and two large canvases of the patron saints of the city, *St Valerian* and *St Mercury* (both 1643–4; Forlì, Pin. Civ.), on the drum. Only the latter two were completed. They represent Cagnacci's achievement of stylistic maturity in their lively rhythmic composition and brilliant colouring. His stay in Forlì seems to have been abruptly interrupted, since he did not complete the commission. The reason for his continual moves and for his eventual flight from the Papal States probably had something to do with his involvement with the widow Stivivi.

After 1645 Cagnacci received no more official commissions for religious works and relied principally on private patrons, for whom he produced paintings of modest dimensions, usually featuring secular subjects, for example *Vanitas*, another of his female nudes (*c*. 1645; Cesena, Cassa di Risparmio; Amiens, Mus. Picardie). He had also begun a long succession of half-length figures of nude or partially clad women, for example *Lucretia* (*c*. 1640; Forlì, priv. col., see Pasini, 1986, no. 38d), *Portia* (Milan, priv. col.), *Faith* (untraced) and *Human Life* (version, England, priv. col., see Pasini, 1986, pl. xxxviii). They are well-considered studies of the female nude, open and direct and dignified by their sensual beauty.

In 1646 Cagnacci was in Cesena and in 1647 at Faenza, where he seems to have made a vain attempt to enter the service of Pope Innocent X through the recommendation of Cardinal Bernardino Spada. Finally, *c*. 1650, he went to Venice, where he lived at first under an assumed name: Guido Baldo Canlassi. In Venice, Cagnacci maintained a workshop and took on pupils for a decade. His Venetian paintings are characterized by intense colours, rich texture and attention to detail. His forms developed an astonishing clarity and naturalness. Among his finest works are two versions of the *Assumption of the Magdalene* (1650s; Florence, Pitti; Munich, Alte Pin.), a *Woman Striking Two Dogs* (Novara, priv. col., see Pasini, 1986, pls xliii–xliv) and *Jacob between Leah and Rachel* (1650s; London, Hampton Court, Royal Col.). He also continued to paint half-length figures of women (e.g. another *Lucretia*, *c*. 1650, Bologna, Pin. N.; *Europa*, 1650s, Bologna, priv. col., see Pasini, 1986, pl. xli). Cagnacci found himself in competition with many other painters, notably Pietro Liberi, but his art was highly appreciated, as is demonstrated by contemporary eulogies (Mazzoni, and Martinioni in Sansovino) and by the summons (*c*. 1660) to Vienna to be court painter to Emperor Leopold I.

In his last years in Venice, or at the start of his period in Vienna, Cagnacci produced works celebrated for their sensuality, such as two versions of *Cleopatra* (*c*. 1659–62; Milan, Brera; Vienna, Ksthist. Mus.; see fig.) and the *Conversion of Mary Magdalene* (Pasadena, CA, Norton Simon Mus.), an extraordinary blend of refined and sensuous nudes, sumptuous still-life details and complex symbols and allusions. Other works from his Viennese period are the portrait of *Emperor Leopold I in his Coronation Armour*, *St Jerome* (both Vienna, Ksthist. Mus.) and *Artemisia* (Dresden, Gemäldegal. Alte Meister).

BIBLIOGRAPHY

F. Scannelli: *Il microcosmo della pittura* (Cesena, 1657), pp. 368–9
S. Mazzoni: *Il tempo perduto, scherzi sconcertanti* (Venice, 1661)
F. Sansovino: *Venetia città nobilissima et singolare*, suppl. G. Martinioni (Venice, 1663), p. 22
G. B. Costa: 'Lettere varie e documenti autentici intorno le opere, e vero nome, cognome, e patria di Guido Cagnacci pittore', *Raccolta d'opuscoli scientifici e filologici*, ed. A. Calogiera, xlvii (Venice, 1752), pp. 119–61
G. Bottari and S. Ticozzi: *Raccolta di lettere sulla pittura, scultura, ed architettura*, vii (Milan, 1822), pp. 482–5
C. Ricci: 'Il Cagnacci e Lucrezia Romana', *Annu. Reale Accad. S Luca* (1913–14), pp. 1–25
C. Gnudi: 'Note sullo stile di Guido Cagnacci', *Riv. Com. Bologna* (Feb–March, 1937), pp. 34–9
Mostra della pittura del '600 riminese (exh. cat., ed. F. Arcangeli, C. Gnudi and C. Ravaioli; Rimini, Pal. Arengo, 1952/*R* Rimini, 1982)
Mostra della pittura del seicento emiliano (exh. cat., ed. F. Arcangeli and others; Bologna, Pal. Archiginnasio, 1959), pp. 274–88
R. Buscaroli: *Il pittore Guido Cagnacci* (Forlì, 1962)
M. Zuffa: 'Novità per Guido Cagnacci', *A. Ant. & Mod.*, 24 (1963), pp. 357–81
P. G. Pasini: 'Note ed aggiunte a Guido Cagnacci', *Boll. A.*, ii (1967), pp. 78–89
——: *Guido Cagnacci pittore* (Rimini, 1986)
——: 'Le donne del Cagnacci', *Romagna A. & Stor.*, xxi (1987), pp. 65–84
A. Brejon De Lavergnée and N. Volle: *Musées de France: Répertoire des peintures italiennes du XVII siècle* (Paris, 1988)
P. G. Pasini: *Le donne del Cagnacci* (Rimini, 1993)
Guido Cagnacci (exh. cat. by D. Benati and M. Bona Catelloti, Rimini, Mus. Com., 1993)

PIER GIORGIO PASINI

Cagnola, Luigi (*b* Milan, 9 June 1762; *d* Inverigo, Como, 14 Aug 1833). Italian architect and diplomat. From 1776 he attended the Collegio Pio Clementino, Rome, and while there he developed an interest in architecture, studying ancient buildings and monuments. Following his return to Milan (*c*. 1780) his geometrical designs for Neo-classical buildings attracted attention. This interest in architecture was combined with his study of law at the University of Padua (1781–2) and the later holding of various public offices, in keeping with his noble birth, including that of commissioner to the Austrian armed forces (until 1796). He presented a design for a toll-gate for the Porta Orientale, Milan, in competition with Giuseppe Piermarini. He also contributed a series of measured drawings to the first volume of Angelo Fumagalli's *Delle antichità longobardico–milanesi* (1792), which probably depict the remains of the Imperial Baths of Hercules. From an early date in his career it was clear that when working on historic buildings his guiding principle was to conform to the style of the original architecture, whatever its period. He followed this criterion in his designs for the façade of Milan Cathedral (1790) and for completing the Shrine at Rho (1795).

When the French entered Milan in 1796 Cagnola took refuge in Venice, where he studied Palladio and Sansovino and designed his first executed building, the Villa Zurla at Vaiano. In 1801 he returned to Milan and was appointed to the city council. In this capacity he was responsible for designing the temporary monuments erected for such celebrations as the coronation of Napoleon. To celebrate the victory of Marengo (1800) he organized the construction of the so-called Atrium of Porta Marengo (1801–14), producing a design that incorporated the entire Corso di Porta Ticinese. His plan allowed for three pairs of symmetrical buildings (two market arcades, two toll-houses and two other edifices to replace the medieval gate). Only the Atrium on the bridge and the two toll-houses were built, however. During this period the Rationalist principles of Cagnola's training became integrated with his study of Palladio, although his interpretation of the latter resulted in works that were more austere in design and use of materials, such as his project for a triangular casino (*c.* 1787; plans at Milan, Castello Sforzesco).

The first Arco della Pace (1806) near Porta Orientale was temporary, built by Cagnola to celebrate the marriage of the Viceroy Eugène de Beauharnais to Amalia of Bavaria. It was so admired, however, that it was rebuilt in marble (1807; *see* MILAN, fig. 6) and placed at the entrance to the Foro Bonaparte on the Strada del Sempione. The arch resembles the contemporary Arc de Triomphe du Carrousel (1806), Paris, by Charles Percier and Pierre-François-Léonard Fontaine, but it is particularly distinguished for its statues, low reliefs and decorative details carried out by Milan's leading artists, including Camillo Pacetti (1758–1826), Pompeo Marchesi and Benedetto Cacciatori (1794–1871).

In 1807 Cagnola was appointed a member of the Commissione d'Ornato of Milan, the body created to regulate building activities in the city. He drew up the Commission's *Piano dei Rettifili*, which would have radically altered the city with a multi-centric network of roads, based in part on those of ancient Rome. Although the plan was not put into effect, Cagnola was able to influence Milanese urban planning. Among his proposals were a project for a botanic garden, intended to occupy a vast area outside the Porta Nuova, and a plan for a Temple of Fame (1809–14) involving a spacious arcaded complex connected to the city walls, which would have replaced the cemetery of the Ospedale Maggiore. Cagnola also designed a vast portico composed of 144 columns to be built at the Moncenisio Pass (1813), in the western Alps, as a monument commemorating Napoleon's gratitude towards the French and Italian people after the battle of Wurtchen (1813). After the fall of Napoleon, however, Cagnola had few opportunities to express himself in the grand, celebratory manner of the previous 15 years. Although he remained an eminent architect, he was no longer able to intervene as frequently in civic building.

At the church of Concorezzo (begun 1818), Cagnola modified his Palladian design by reducing the amount of decoration, and at the church of Ghisalba (1822–33), near Bergamo, he adopted a massive Pantheon theme. His designs for the enlargement of the Hofburg and the Burgtor in Vienna (both 1818–24), the latter executed by Pietro Nobile with substantial modifications, are massive and impersonal. In 1825 Emperor Francis I visited Milan; this provided Cagnola with a second opportunity to realize his proposals for the layout of the Porta Orientale, where he planned to rebuild the Arco del Sempione, which had been left unfinished after the fall of Napoleon, and to build a triumphal atrium in stone. However, only a gilt bronze model (Milan, Bib. Ambrosiana), to the scale 1:28, was executed under his own direction.

Luigi Cagnola: villa at Inverigo, near Como, 1813–33

Several of Cagnola's most successful works were produced in the last 20 years of his life, including the campanile at Urgnano and his own villa at Inverigo, near Como, in which he employed unusual architectural forms and materials. The ground-plan of the Urgnano campanile (1824–9) is circular, with a series of superimposed orders rising from a podium and crowned with a small tempietto-like structure, with caryatids supporting a small hemispherical dome. The villa at Inverigo (1813–33; see fig.) stands on a hill and is loosely based on Palladio's Villa Rotonda. The colonnaded portico of white stucco, approached by a staircase, the rear façade with atlantids sculpted by Pompeo Marchesi, the arcades imitating Roman aqueducts, the 'Egyptian' hall and portal and the triumphal arch entrances all create a succession of remarkable contrasting views and spaces. Cagnola's influence on the next generation of architects, including Nicola Dordoni (*fl c.* 1840) and Pietro Bianchi (ii), was considerable.

UNPUBLISHED SOURCES

Milan, Castello Sforzesco [large col. of Cagnola's drgs]

BIBLIOGRAPHY

DBI

R. Gironi: 'Necrologia del marchese Luigi Cagnola', *Bib. It. G. Lett. Sci. & A.*, lxxi (1833), pp. 127–43

P. Mezzanotte: *Le architetture di Luigi Cagnola*, Quaderni di architettura del sindicato fascista architetti di Milano, i (Milan, 1930)

——: 'L'architettura dal 1796 alla caduta del regno italico', *Stor. Milano*, xiii (1959), pp. 478–522

L'età neoclassica in Lombardia (exh. cat., ed. A. Ottino Della Chiesa; Como, Villa Olmo, 1959), pp. 30, 63

P. Mezzanotte: 'L'edilizia milanese dalla caduta del regno italico alla prima guerra mondiale', *Stor. Milano*, xv (1962), pp. 322–35

C. L. V. Meeks: *Italian Architecture, 1750–1914* (New Haven and London, 1966), p. 112

G. Mezzanotte: *Architettura neoclassica in Lombardia* (Naples, 1966), pp. 317–70

The Age of Neoclassicism (exh. cat., London, RA and V&A, 1972), pp. 964–6
Mostra dei maestri di Brera (exh. cat., Milan, Pal. Permanente, 1975), pp. 74–6

GIANNI MEZZANOTTE

Cāhamāna. *See* CHAHAMANA.

Cahill, Holger [Bjarnason, Sveinn Kristján] (*b* Snæfellsnessýsla, Iceland, 13 Jan 1887; *d* Stockbridge, MA, 8 July 1960). American arts administrator and writer of Icelandic birth. His parents emigrated to Canada, later moving to North Dakota. He moved to New York *c.* 1918, having changed his name, and became a journalist. At Columbia University he was exposed to JOHN DEWEY's theories of art and education, and at the New School for Social Research he learnt to appreciate handicraft as art. In 1922 he went to the Newark Museum where he was responsible for educational programmes and the modern art collection. He organized influential exhibitions of American primitive painting and folk sculpture, before moving to the Museum of Modern Art as director of exhibitions in 1932.

From 1935 to 1941 he was head of the Works Progress Administration's Federal Art Project (WPA/FAP; *see* UNITED STATES OF AMERICA, §XII), the US government's most extensive art programme. By employing artists who were registered on relief rolls during the Depression, the FAP brought art to millions of Americans, commissioning murals, paintings, prints, posters, photographs and sculpture. From 1935 Cahill organized the Index of American Design, which recorded in 22,000 watercolour illustrations objects of American folk art from public and private collections. When the FAP ended in 1943, he returned to writing, mainly fiction.

WRITINGS

American Folk Art: The Art of the Common Man in America, 1750–1900 (exh. cat., New York, MOMA, 1932)
ed., with A. H. Barr jr: *Art in America: A Complete Survey* (New York, 1933, rev. 1935)

BIBLIOGRAPHY

DAB
F. V. O'Connor, ed.: *The New Deal Art Projects: An Anthology of Memoirs* (Washington, DC, 1972)
R. D. McKinzie: *The New Deal for Artists* (Princeton, 1973)

ALAN M. FERN

Cahn, Miriam (*b* Basle, 21 July 1949). Swiss draughtswoman and painter. She studied at the Gewerbeschule in Basle from 1968 to 1975 and made her first public appearance in 1979 with a 'night action', *Being a Woman Is my Public Role* (see 1983 exh. cat.), which consisted of personal, intimate signs drawn on the anonymous concrete walls of the motorway leading to Basle. Her concern with the image of women in the male social and artistic tradition, and with a search for specifically female signs, led to two series, *Classical Love* (exh. Basle, 1983, see 1986 exh. cat.) and *Wild Love* (exh. 1984, see 1985 exh. cat., pp. 22–3). In these she presented the male world in the form of drawings of rockets, war and merchant ships, skyscrapers, computers and pornographic images, while symbolizing the female world by tables, menstruation houses and faces with wide open mouths. Her works are always shown in groups so as to stress the open-ended and incomplete quality of the process, which leads to further questions. Cahn sought to express her psychological and physical disposition in her drawings by working on the floor with her eyes closed. In a later series of installations, *Relations* (exh. Wiesbaden, 1989/90, see 1990 exh. cat. pp. 98–9), she juxtaposed traditional oil paintings representing such structures as nuclear power plants and chemical factories with landscapes, plants and animals in the form of drawings made with black chalk dust. As in her earlier works she made use of confrontation and contradiction, while also demonstrating the close relationship between growth and destruction.

BIBLIOGRAPHY

Miriam Cahn: Arbeiten 1979–1983 (exh. cat., Basle, Ksthalle, 1983)
Cross-currents in Swiss Art (exh. cat. by R. Calvocoressi, London, Serpentine Gal., 1985), pp. 5–6, 8–9, 20–23
Miriam Cahn: Strategische Orte (exh. cat., Bonn, Städt. Kstmus., 1986)
Miriam Cahn: Lesen in Staub (exh. cat., W. Berlin, Haus Waldsee; and Hannover, Kstver., 1988)
Künstlerinnen des 20. Jahrhunderts (exh. cat., Wiesbaden, Mus. Wiesbaden, 1990), pp. 98–102, 338

ASTRID SCHMETTERLING

Cahokia. Site in the USA in East St Louis, IL, of a huge Pre-Columbian city. Founded *c.* AD 700, it was the largest prehistoric city ever built north of Mexico and was probably influenced by political and civic ideas from PRE-COLUMBIAN MESOAMERICA. At its height, between *c.* AD 1050 and *c.* 1250, Cahokia encompassed *c.* 13 sq. km and had a population of *c.* 10–15,000. Although located in the north-west part of the middle Mississippi Southern Cult area, it was the political, economic and religious centre for more than 50 towns (*see* NATIVE NORTH AMERICAN ART, §I, 4(v)). The exact nature of its power or rule, however, is uncertain. A potential rival in the south-east of the cult area was Moundville, AL, nearly as large. Cahokia began to decline after *c.* 1250, although some of its satellite towns, at such sites as Angel, Aztatlan, Dickson and Kinkaid, continued to flourish as local centres. A drastic population decline *c.* 1450 led to the abandonment or severe diminishment of many sites before European contact.

Cahokia lay in the American Bottomlands—the middle Mississippi Valley and confluence of the Mississippi, Missouri and Illinois rivers—a fertile alluvial valley region of light, fertile soils suitable for hoe-using agriculture. Archaeological evidence in the form of artefacts and skeletal remains (Springfield, IL, State Mus.) suggests that Mesoamerican influence began to penetrate this south-east woodlands region from *c.* AD 700. Later Mesoamerican influence brought about the construction of civic mounds. By *c.* 1200 Cahokia comprised a Central Plaza (see fig. (a)) formed by 17 major mound structures of rammed earth, and over 80 other mounds. Dominating the north side of the Central Plaza is Monks Mound (b), begun perhaps two centuries earlier and constructed in 14 stages to a height of more than 30 m. In its final configuration it comprised a complex rectangle with sloping sides (241×316 m at the base and more than 600,000 m^3 of earth). A ramp set slightly off-centre on the south side led up to a wide platform across the south quarter. Higher stages were formed running north–south along the east and west sides, with two further platforms above these. Around the Central Plaza stood a four-sided timber palisade (c) enclosing *c.* 120 ha. The ends of the long east

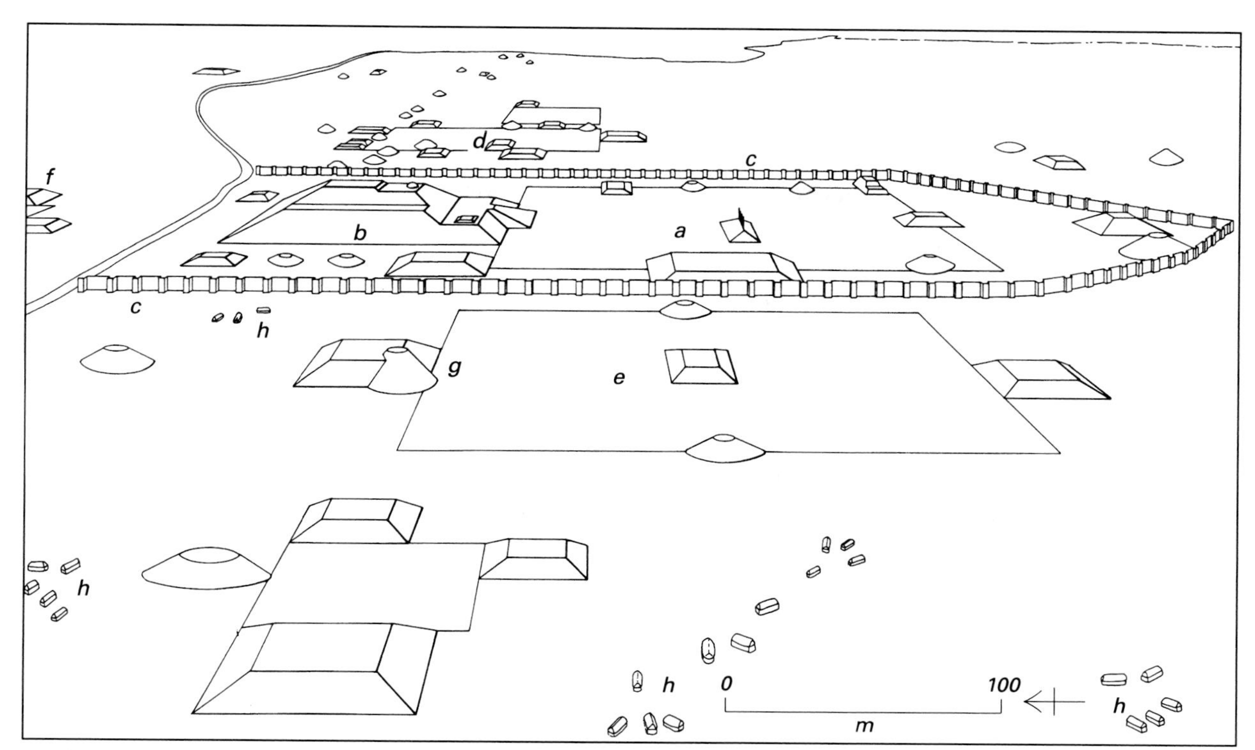

Cahokia, reconstruction drawing of the site *c.* 1200, looking east: (a) Central Plaza; (b) Monks Mound; (c) palisade; (d) Ramey Plaza; (e) Merrell Plaza; (f) North Plaza; (g) square mound and truncated cone; (h) longhouses

and west sections of the stockade ended at the edge of Cahokia Creek, forming the north side of the ceremonial area. The two southern sections of the palisade formed an offset point. Opinion differs as to whether the palisade was defensive or merely a ceremonial screen.

Groups of mounds formed further plazas immediately outside the palisade to east (Ramey Plaza (d)) and west (Merrell Plaza (e)), and across Cahokia Creek (North Plaza (f)). The mounds, also slope-sided, were flat-topped and square, rectangular or circular. In one case in the west plaza a truncated cone (g) was set against the south-west corner of a square mound. When exacavated, many mounds, including Monks Mound, bore traces of wooden structures presumed to be temples on their summits. Traces of ordinary longhouses (h) built of upright logs were found scattered on the outskirts of the plazas.

Some mounds contained burials of élite citizens, while the cemeteries of non-élites formed several clusters around the Central Plaza and to the south-west of it. One élite burial contained two men surrounded by bundles of disarticulated bones. Another comprised an élite person wrapped in a robe of some 12,000 shell beads; around him were caches of polished stones, mica and arrowheads, and six male retainers. A pit near by contained the mass burial of 53 women, and in another pit were four decapitated men with amputated hands. The Wilson Mound, more than 1 km north-west of the Central Plaza, covered a mortuary chamber (4.25×5.50 m) containing hundreds of disarticulated bones grouped into bundles of several individuals each, and a single dog skeleton. Scattered among the bundles were large whelk shells and disc-shaped marine shell beads.

BIBLIOGRAPHY

W. K. Moorehead: *The Cahokia Mounds*, Bulletin of the University of Illinois, xxvi/4 (Urbana, 1928)

M. L. Fowler: *Cahokia: Ancient Capital of the Midwest* (Menlo Park, CA, 1974)

J. Pfeiffer: 'America's First City', *Horizon*, xvi/2 (1974), pp. 58–63

C. Hudson: *The Southeastern Indians* (Knoxville, 1976)

D. Snow: *The Archaeology of North America: American Indians and their Origins* (London and New York, 1976, rev. 1980)

W. N. Morgan: *Prehistoric Architecture in the Eastern United States* (Cambridge, MA, 1980)

M. Coe, D. Snow and E. Benson: *Atlas of Ancient America* (Oxford, 1986), pp. 55–60

C. Scarre, ed.: *Past Worlds: The Times Atlas of Archaeology* (London, 1988), pp. 230–31

DAVID M. JONES

Cahors. City in Lot département, south-western France. The history of the ancient site of Divona Cadurcorum is controversial. The southern half of a peninsula embraced by a broad curve in the River Lot was urbanized in the time of Augustus, but only traces of a theatre and baths survive. The name suggests that it was a cult centre related perhaps to a shrine on Mt Saint-Cyr, the site of a crossroads with commercial routes radiating to Bordeaux, Toulouse, Limoges and Clermont. The medieval city's importance stemmed from its commerce and an episcopal seat. During the episcopacy of St Didier (630–55) much building was carried out, and the city was defined by ramparts. The cathedral, dedicated to St Stephen and the first of ten churches within the city, lay on the main street that crossed the Pont Vieux to the south, whereas the site of the death of Rusticus, the brother and predecessor of Didier, lay across the Pont Neuf to the east. The surviving 14th-century Pont Valentré (*see* §2 below) crosses the Lot to the west from the district of St Gery (the resting-place of Didier), while the suburb of La Citadelle adjoins the city to the north across a walled moat dominated by the Tour St Jean.

BIBLIOGRAPHY

C. Higounet, J. B. Marquet and P. Wolff, eds: *Atlas historique des villes de France* (Paris, 1983)

1. CATHEDRAL. The present cathedral was begun after the reform of the chapter sometime between 1083 and 1112, and an altar was consecrated during the visit of Pope Calixtus II in 1119. The altar stood within a giant hemicycle with three radiating chapels, to which was added a nave composed of two domed bays, each 20×20 m, the largest in France (*see* ROMANESQUE, fig. 15). The upper choir was rebuilt between 1282 and 1293, and the west wall was replaced with a massive façade after 1300. A deep porch on the north side, once facing the ancient forum, overlaps the buttress dividing the two nave bays. Walled up in 1732, the portal was discovered in 1841 and finally restored by 1912. Figured sculpture was applied to the tympanum and archivolt only, the flanking walls being decorated instead with rows of rosettes in blind arcading. The *Ascension* is represented on the tympanum above the Virgin and the Apostles framed within trefoil arcades. The theophany is flanked by compositions in two tiers depicting the trial and vision of the patron, St Stephen, thus combining episodes from Acts of the Apostles 1 and 7. The original style, characterized by well-proportioned, firmly drawn and supplely animated figures, contributes to the anecdotal character of the martyrdom and the frieze decorating the hood-mould. The sculptures are executed in limestone. The master's debt to St Pierre, Moissac, and Souillac Abbey for the drapery style and ornament and to Angoulême Cathedral (and, indirectly, to St Sernin, Toulouse) for the poses and proportions of the figures suggests that the programme should be dated around 1140. The artist's influence has been detected in the Cantal in the churches at La Graulière, Ydes, Collonges and Mauriac. The porch type is derived from Moissac, as are the earlier capitals that decorate the radiating chapels.

BIBLIOGRAPHY

F.-A. Calvet: 'Etudes sur le Lot: La Cathédrale de Cahors', *Annuaire statistique et administratif du département du Lot* (Cahors, 1841)
R. Rey: *La Cathédrale de Cahors et les origines de l'architecture à coupoles d'Aquitaine* (Cahors, 1925)
A. Shaver-Crandell: 'The North Portal of the Cathedral of Cahors' (diss., New York, Columbia U., 1974)
E. Bratke: *Das Nordportal der Kathedrale Saint-Etienne in Cahors* (Freiburg-im-Breisgau, 1977)
M. Durliat: 'La Cathédrale Saint-Etienne de Cahors: Architecture et sculpture', *Bull. Mnmtl.*, cxxxvii (1979), pp. 285–340

THOMAS W. LYMAN

2. PONT VALENTRÉ. Few medieval cities in France could have prided themselves, like Cahors, in possessing three stone bridges, each spanning over 300 m and fortified by strong towered gates. Although the last of the works and not the most important, the Pont Valentré, built outside the walls by the city between 1306 and 1355, is the only one to survive. It is remarkably homogeneous, with six main spans, each 16.5 m wide; at each end a tower acts as an abutment and is connected to the river bank by an arch of narrower span. Despite the thickness of the abutment piers (5.5–6.25 m) and the depressed profile of the ribs, a sense of verticality is created by the continuation of the cut-waters up to the level of the parapet and by the tall towers. Like other French medieval bridges, the vertical lines were reinforced by the lack of emphasis on the parapet. The hood-mould accentuating the outline of the arches is a rare feature in medieval French bridge architecture, however, and it had an exclusively decorative function.

There is one curious detail, which appears to be unique in France and may be related to the construction process: all the cut-waters, with the exception of the first from the right bank, are pierced by passages at the springing level of the arches. They were connected by wooden gangways and may have been intended to facilitate the transport of materials and perhaps to secure a crossing while awaiting the completion of the vaulting.

The bridge was securely fortified by an outwork barring access on each side and above all by its three gate-towers, which give it the character of a small, independent fortress. The two end towers are alike. They have four floors above a vaulted passage with a portcullis: the first floor is accessible by exterior stairs, the others are served by an interior wooden staircase. The first and second floors have arrow loops in all four walls; the third floor is defended by three bartizans, and the fourth is crenellated. The defensive potential is less developed in the middle tower, which is crenellated only at the top, while its lower floors have windows.

The Pont Valentré is an outstanding example of a series of works with defensive towers that multiplied in France between 1250 and 1350 (e.g. Montauban, Villeneuve-sur-Lot, Cahors-pont-vieux, Cahors-pont-neuf and Orthez); it is remarkable for its perfect state of preservation and is one of the finest examples of a fortified bridge in Europe.

BIBLIOGRAPHY

F. de Dartein: *Etudes sur les ponts en pierre remarquables par leur décoration antérieurs au XIXe siècle*, i (Paris, 1912), pp. 7–14
R. Rey: 'Le Pont Valentré à Cahors', *Congr. Archéol. France*, c (1937), pp. 270–76

JEAN MESQUI

Cahrs, Paul. *See* CASSIRER, PAUL.

Cahuachi [Kawachi]. Major site of the Pre-Columbian NAZCA culture in the Nazca Valley on the south coast of Peru. It was the capital of a brilliant civilization that flourished *c.* AD 1–*c.* 400. The site covers 150 ha and comprises some 40 artificial and semi-artificial mounds of various sizes, the largest of which measure some 20 m high and 140 m per side at the base. There are also walled and open plaza areas and Nazca and post-Nazca burial grounds.

William Strong's fieldwork of 1952–3 determined that Cahuachi was first settled in the early 1st century AD, when the inhabitants lived in wattle and daub houses. Approximately a century later temple mounds began to be built. Cahuachi did not, however, grow into a great city: Helaine Silverman's excavations of 1984–5 indicate that even at its height Cahuachi had only a small permanent population, perhaps consisting of the Nazca élite and their retainers, although frequent pilgrimage activity meant that the site could fill up with thousands of transient inhabitants.

Cahuachi's architecture was largely civic and ceremonial rather than domestic. Many of the truncated mounds were the temples of the various Nazca social groups who worshipped at the site. Some mounds also functioned as burial terraces. Although most tombs have been looted, a series of intact burials was located by Silverman on one small mound on the western side of the site. These contained offerings of Nazca pottery, pyro-engraved gourds and other material; two mummy bundles were found wrapped in rich textiles.

Construction at Cahuachi ceased around AD 400, and the site was abandoned. However, in the latest Nazca times—around AD 750—Cahuachi received renewed attention when an abandoned temple room on the western side of the site was ritually entombed in clean sand by the HUACA DEL LORO people (alternatively identified as Nazca 8 people). Sixteen whole pots and other items were left as offerings in the sand in which the room was buried. The shapes and iconography of the pots indicate that the people who interred the room had strong connections with the adjacent highland area of Ayacucho. It remains to be determined why, hundreds of years after the abandonment of Cahuachi, these people felt obliged to bury ceremonially a non-functioning structure.

BIBLIOGRAPHY

W. D. Strong: 'Paracas, Nazca and Tiahuanacoid Cultural Relationships on the South Coast of Peru', *Mem. Soc. Amer. Archaeol.*, xiii (Salt Lake City, 1957)

H. Silverman: *Cahuachi in the Ancient Nasca World* (Iowa City, 1993)

HELAINE SILVERMAN

Caiger-Smith, Alan (*b* Buenos Aires, 8 Feb 1930). English potter. He became interested in pottery while at King's College, Cambridge (1949–52), and took pottery evening classes at the Central School of Arts and Crafts, London (1954–5). In 1955 he founded Aldermaston Pottery, Berks, a cooperative workshop (closed down in 1993) of about seven potters making functional domesticware and tiles, as well as individual commissions and one-off pots. By trial and error he revived and perfected two virtually lost techniques: the use of tin glaze and painted pigments on red earthenware clay, and the firing of lustres on to tin glazes (e.g. earthenware bowl, 1968; London, V&A). He has also written extensively on both techniques.

WRITINGS

Tin-glaze Pottery in Europe and the Islamic World: The Tradition of 1,000 Years in Maiolica, Faience and Delftware (London, 1973)

with R. Lightbown, trans.: G. Piccolpasso: *I tre libri dell'arte del vasaio* (1548) as *The Three Books of the Potter's Art* (London, 1980)

Lustre Pottery (London, 1985)

BIBLIOGRAPHY

Tin Glaze and Smoked Lustre; Pottery by Alan Caiger-Smith and Aldermaston Potters (exh. cat., ed. K. Niblett; Stoke-on-Trent, City Mus. & A.G., 1985)

KATHY NIBLETT

Cai Jing [Ts'ai Ching; *zi* Yuanchang] (*b* Xianyou County, Fujian Province, 1046; *d* Tanzhou [now in Changsha Municipality], Hunan Province, 1126). Chinese calligrapher and scholar–official. He passed the national civil-service examination to become a *jinshi* in 1070 and began his official career in provincial posts. He was transferred to the capital, Bianliang (now Kaifeng) in 1082, where he became involved in political factionalism as a supporter of Wang Anshi's (1021–86) radical reforms. Cai is traditionally vilified as the evil minister responsible for the fall of the Northern Song (960–1127). He was exiled after the Jin invasion in 1125 and soon died; the male members of his family were executed. His considerable accomplishments as a calligrapher and litterateur have received scant attention from traditional critics, who believed that good calligraphy could be written only by men of fine character.

The few surviving examples of Cai's calligraphy suggest that he excelled in running script (*xingshu*) and large character writing. According to his son's account, Cai initially imitated the style of a distant relative, CAI XIANG. After meeting SU SHI, he changed to the plumper modes of Xu Hao (AD 703–82) and Shen Chuanshi (*fl* early 9th century AD). In about 1093 he studied Ouyang Xun (557–641) and finally he took up the elegant styles of Wang Xizhi and Wang Xianzhi (*see* WANG (i), (1) and (2)). Cai served as prime minister four times under the emperor Huizong, for nearly 16 years in all. He encouraged Huizong's artistic interests and enjoyed the rare privilege of inscribing the emperor's writings and paintings. One of Cai's surviving works is his monumental title for the emperor's *Imperial Stele of the Daguan Era* (*Daguan sheng zuo bei*; 1108). It is unusual in being executed in the informal Song regular script (Song *kai*), while the emperor's text is in the more formal slender gold style (*shoujinti*). Huizong and Cai Jing both inscribed poems, using the same rhymes, on the anonymous court painting *Literary Gathering* (hanging scrolls, ink and colour on silk; Taipei, N. Pal. Mus.), an early example of the integration of poetry, calligraphy and painting.

BIBLIOGRAPHY

Franke: 'Ts'ai Ching'

K. Shimonaka, ed.: *Shodō zenshū* [Complete collection of calligraphy], xv (Tokyo, 2/1954), pp. 37–44, 176, 185 and pl. 117

R. Trauzettel: *Ts'ai Ching (1046–1126) als Typus des illegitimen Ministers* (Bamberg, 1964)

Tuotuo and others: *Song shi* [History of the Song] (Beijing, 1977), *juan*, cdlxxii, pp. 13721–8

JULIA K. MURRAY

Caillebotte, Gustave (*b* Paris, 18 Aug 1848; *d* Gennevilliers, nr Paris, 21 Feb 1894). French painter and collector.

1. LIFE AND WORK. Caillebotte's parents, of Norman descent, were wealthy members of the Parisian upper middle class, and his paintings often evoke his family background. After studying classics at the Lycée Louis Le Grand, he obtained a law degree in 1870, and during the Franco-Prussian War he was drafted into the Seine Garde Mobile (1870–71). He joined Léon Bonnat's studio in 1872 and passed the entrance examination for the Ecole des Beaux-Arts on 18 March 1873. The records of the Ecole make no mention of his work there, and his attendance seems to have been short-lived. He was very soon attracted by the innovative experiments, against academic teaching, of the young rebels who were to become known as the Impressionists. In 1874 Edgar Degas, whom Caillebotte had met at the house of their

mutual friend Giuseppe de Nittis, asked him to take part in the First Impressionist Exhibition at the Nadar Gallery in the Boulevard des Capucines in Paris. However, it was only at the time of their second exhibition in April 1876 that, at Auguste Renoir's invitation, Caillebotte joined the Impressionist group. From then on he was one of the most regular participants in their exhibitions (1877, 1879, 1880, 1882). He organized the show of 1877 and made great efforts to restore the cohesion of the group by persuading Claude Monet to exhibit in 1879. Having inherited a large fortune from his parents, Caillebotte had no need to sell his pictures and could afford to provide crucial financial assistance for his artist friends. He purchased their work, much disparaged at the time, and amassed the famous collection of Impressionist masterpieces that he left to the State (*see* §2 below).

Caillebotte's first important painting, *Planing the Floor* (1875; Paris, Mus. d'Orsay), shows that he was involved in the search for a new Realism that was to a great extent the catalyst of the Impressionist revolution. The subject seems to have been suggested by work being carried out in his Paris home, 77 Rue de Miromesnil. In the choice of subject rather than the manner of its execution, this image of working-class life marked Caillebotte's rejection of academic conventions. The sombre palette and traditional technique with which he described the carefully foreshortened torsos of the kneeling floor-scrapers (recorded in preliminary crayon and charcoal drawings; see Varnedoe, 1987, p. 56) recall his training in Bonnat's atelier. The composition, however, is more unusual, emphasizing the receding right angles of the floor-planking in a way that he was to repeat in many later works. Apparently turned down by the jury of the Salon in 1875, the painting formed part of Caillebotte's submission to the Impressionist exhibition of 1876.

Until 1881 most of Caillebotte's paintings depicted the contemporary urban life of Paris (e.g. *Housepainters*, 1877; priv. col., see Berhaut, 1978, cat. no. 48) or the everyday domestic existence of his family and friends (e.g. *Luncheon*, 1876; priv. col., see Berhaut, 1978, cat. no. 32). His *plein-air* studies executed during summer visits to his family property at Yerres (Seine-et-Oise) from 1871 to 1878 more often than not have a similarly modern touch, as in the depiction of skips in *Canoes on the Yerres* (1878; Rennes, Mus. B.-A). These themes were widely represented in Caillebotte's contributions to the Impressionist exhibitions, where he was dealt with by the critics as harshly as his friends; however, this wide press coverage indicates the interest his painting aroused. He was considered one of the painters most responsive to the ideas of French Realist writers. There is a particularly close correspondence between the theories on the representation of contemporary life expressed by Edmond Duranty in *La Nouvelle Peinture* (1876) and such pictures by Caillebotte as *Young Man at his Window* (1876; priv. col., see Berhaut, 1978, cat. no. 26). Emile Zola hailed him as 'a painter of the highest courage' (*Le Sémaphore de Marseille*, 19 April 1877) and Joris-Karl Huysmans, his most enthusiastic commentator, linked his name with that of Degas in contrasting their art with the 'factitious and anecdotal art' of the Realist painters in the official Salons ('Salon des Indépendans (1882)' in *L'Art moderne*, 1883). Caillebotte's two great Parisian street scenes at the Impressionist exhibition of 1877, *Pont de l'Europe* (1876; Geneva, Petit Pal.; see fig.) and *Paris Street: Rainy Weather* (1877; Chicago, IL, A. Inst.), illustrate his characteristically individual use of plunging recession and firmly Realist choice of contemporary urban subject-matter.

In 1878 Caillebotte moved to 31 Boulevard Haussmann behind the Opéra. In this district, recently transformed by the urban planning of the Second Empire, Caillebotte's vision was renewed. His earlier Realist painting gave way to more sensitive interpretations of the Parisian scene. His chosen subjects dealt with the play of light and shade and are reminiscent of contemporary cityscapes by Monet and Renoir. Caillebotte was less interested in the movement of crowds under the shade of great trees than in the architectural rhythm expressed in the rigorous alignment of tall apartment blocks, seen for example in *Boulevard des Italiens* (*c.* 1880; priv. col., see Berhaut, 1978, cat. no. 135). On long balconies that emphasize the rising perspective, figures in top hats—sometimes seen from the rear, with their back to the light or framed in windows—convey the note of Parisian modernism always important to Caillebotte (e.g. *Balcony*, 1880; priv. col., see Berhaut, 1978, cat. no. 136). This series of views of Paris was completed in 1880 and includes two works that appear to have been painted from a point overhanging Caillebotte's apartment on the Boulevard Haussmann: *Traffic Island, Boulevard Haussmann* (1880; priv. col., see Berhaut, 1978, cat. no. 141) and *Boulevard Seen from Above* (1880; priv. col., see Berhaut, 1978, cat. no. 143). These were the boldest spatial interpretations of the Impressionist era. Pierre Bonnard and Edouard Vuillard were perhaps inspired by these works during their Nabi period, and they even foreshadow the photographic experiments of the early 20th century.

Disillusioned by disagreements that resulted in the breakup of the Impressionist group, Caillebotte took little part in Parisian artistic life after 1882. He settled in Petit-Gennevilliers near Argenteuil, which had been an important site for Impressionist painting some years earlier. The Parisian landscape no longer featured in his work, except for some snow scenes executed in 1886 and 1888; he was almost alone among the Impressionists in his interest in depicting the effects of snow in an urban setting, most notably in his *Rooftops of Paris* series painted around 1878 (e.g. *Rooftops (Snow)*, 1878; Paris, Mus. d'Orsay).

An important group of paintings of the Normandy coast, dating from the summers of 1880 to 1884, marked the transition from Caillebotte's Paris period to that of Gennevilliers. The seaside villas of Trouville, Villers and Villerville, situated below the level of the overhanging road, provided him with bird's-eye views reminiscent of his Parisian compositions (e.g. *Cottage, Trouville*, 1882; Chicago, IL, A. Inst.). He used unexpected angles to show to advantage the typical Normandy architecture of that period. He also produced many paintings of the Seine, the Normandy countryside and gardens, and seascapes (e.g. *Seascape: Regatta at Villers*, 1880; priv. col., see Berhaut, 1978, cat. no. 152), which capture changing effects of light and atmosphere with broken Impressionist brushwork and a high-key palette particularly indebted to Monet.

Gustave Caillebotte: *Pont de l'Europe*, oil on canvas, 1.24×1.80 m, 1876 (Geneva, Musée du Petit Palais)

However, his representation of fleeting atmospheric changes never led him to sacrifice the permanence of forms and the rhythm of structures. He was also always conscious of the unexpected, sometimes peculiar angles that his chosen subject might offer. His series of regatta pictures testifies to his increasing enthusiasm for yachting (e.g. *Regattas at Argenteuil*, 1893; priv. col., see Berhaut, 1978, cat. no. 447).

Like Monet at Giverny, Caillebotte lavished much care on his garden at Petit-Gennevilliers. In his final years in Paris he had painted still-lifes of cut flowers and fruit (e.g. *Fruit on Display*, 1881; Boston, MA, Mus. F.A.). At Petit-Gennevilliers he often preferred to paint in his garden directly from the subject (e.g. *Dahlias, the Garden at Petit-Gennevilliers*, 1893; priv. col., see Berhaut, 1978, cat. no. 443). Roses and gladioli, dahlias and chrysanthemums, painted in a freer technique, retain on canvas the brilliance of daylight. The exotic plants in his greenhouse provided the theme for a series of decorative panels begun in 1893 and intended for the dining-room at Petit-Gennevilliers (priv. col., see Berhaut, 1978, cat. nos 464–74). In a very original decorative effect, the orchids appear to be entwined in the metal structure of the greenhouse where they hang. Caillebotte died from apoplexy at the age of 45 before he was able to finish the last two panels. Most of his paintings remained in the collections of his family and friends, and for many years his bequest provoked more comment than his artistic achievement, which has only been reassessed since the 1970s.

2. THE CAILLEBOTTE COLLECTION AND BEQUEST. Caillebotte began to buy his friends' paintings very soon after they were created. During the period of the Impressionist exhibitions he acquired such masterpieces as Renoir's *Moulin de la Galette* (1876), Monet's *Gare St-Lazare* (1877), Edouard Manet's *Balcony* (1869) and Degas's *Dancer on the Stage* (*c.* 1878; all Paris, Mus. d'Orsay). From an early stage Caillebotte was determined that at his death his collection should be accepted in its entirety by the Musée du Luxembourg in Paris, and later the Louvre, even if a period of 20 years or more should elapse before this was possible. He made his first will on 3 November 1876 and confirmed his intentions on 20 November 1883. As Caillebotte had anticipated, his bequest raised great problems. Laborious negotiations between his executors, his brother Martial and Renoir, and the State representatives, Henry Roujon and Léonce Bénédite, finally ended in compromise in 1896. Of the 67 Impressionist works in the collection, the State accepted 38: two by Paul Cézanne, seven by Degas, eight by Monet, seven by Camille Pissarro, two by Manet, six by Alfred Sisley and six by Renoir. Although the bequest was only partially accepted, it provoked numerous and violent protests from political and artistic circles when it was first shown at the Musée du Luxembourg in January 1897. It subsequently moved to the Musée d'Orsay, Paris, where it forms the core of the Impressionist collection.

BIBLIOGRAPHY

A. Tabarant: 'Le Peintre Caillebotte et sa collection', *Bull. Vie A.*, xv (1921), pp. 405–13

Gustave Caillebotte, 1848–1894 (exh. cat. by D. Sutton, London, Wildenstein's, 1966)
M. Berhaut: *Caillebotte, l'Impressionniste* (Paris and Lausanne, 1968)
K. Varnedoe: 'Caillebotte's *Pont de l'Europe*: A New Slant', *A. Int.*, xviii/4 (1974), pp. 28–9
——: 'Gustave Caillebotte in Context', *A. Mag.*, i/9 (1976), pp. 94–9
Gustave Caillebotte: A Retrospective Exhibition (exh. cat. by K. Varnedoe and T. P. Lee, Houston, Mus. F.A., 1976)
M. Berhaut: 'Gustave Caillebotte et le réalisme impressionniste', *L'Oeil*, 68 (1977), pp. 42–9
——: *Gustave Caillebotte: Sa Vie et son oeuvre* (Paris, 1978, rev. 1994 as *Catalogue raisonné de Gustave Caillebotte*)
——: 'Le Legs Caillebotte, vérités et contre-vérités', *Bull. Soc. Hist. A. Fr.* (1983), pp. 209–39
P. Vaisse: 'Le legs Caillebotte d'après les documents', *Bull. Soc. Hist. A. Fr.* (1983), pp. 201–8
K. Varnedoe: *Gustave Caillebotte* (New Haven, 1987)

For further bibliography *see* IMPRESSIONISM.

MARIE BERHAUT

Cailleteau. *See* LASSURANCE.

Cailleux, (Achille-Alexandre) Alphonse de (*b* Rouen, 31 Dec 1788; *d* Paris, 24 May 1876). French museum curator. He was initially trained as an architect but changed direction and joined the army. He was made a lieutenant in the Garde Royale and became aide-de-camp to General J.-A.-B. Law, Marquis de Lauriston. When the latter was appointed Ministère de la Maison du Roi in 1820, he made Cailleux Secrétaire Général des Musées, which led to a long-held appointment as Directeur Adjoint des Musées and finally to the post of Directeur Général des Musées (1841–8). His fame largely rests with his transformation of the château of Versailles into a museum devoted to 'all the glories of France'. Work began on this project in 1833 and the museum, though not finished, opened in 1837, with displays largely representative of the academic art of the day. In 1845 Cailleux succeeded the Comte de Vaublanc as 'membre libre' of the Académie des Beaux-Arts. After the Revolution of 1848, he lost his posts and faded into obscurity. He collaborated with his friend Baron Isidore-Justin-Séverin Taylor and with Charles Nodier (1783–1844) on *Voyages pittoresques et romantiques dans l'ancienne France* (Paris, 1820–78), a 19-volume publication, copiously illustrated with lithographs, surveying the art and history of various areas of France and intended especially to provide a record of rapidly disappearing medieval art. Cailleux worked mainly on the sections on Normandy and Brittany.

BIBLIOGRAPHY

DBF
A. Soubies: *Les Membres de l'Académie des beaux-arts* (Paris, 1906), ii, pp. 266–8

Caillot, Claude-Augustin. *See* CAYOT, CLAUDE-AUGUSTIN.

Cain, Auguste-Nicolas (*b* Paris, 10 Nov 1821; *d* Paris, 6 Aug 1894). French sculptor and designer. After working in his father's butchery, he entered the studio of Alexandre Guionnet (*fl* 1831–53), an animal sculptor who worked in wood, and then became a pupil of François Rude; he augmented his training by drawing animals in the Jardin des Plantes, Paris. During the 1840s he worked for the goldsmiths François-Auguste Fannière (1818–1900) and his brother François-Joseph-Louis (1822–97) and also made models for the jewellers Frédéric-Jules Rudolphi and the house of Christofle. He exhibited small-scale animal sculptures at the Salon from 1846 onwards, making his début with the wax group *Warblers Defending their Nest against a Dormouse* (untraced). He went into partnership with the sculptor Pierre-Jules Mène (whose daughter he married in 1852), casting many of his own works in bronze at their foundry; he also made casts of his father-in-law's works, continuing to do so after Mène's death. Among the utilitarian objects he made, usually featuring animal motifs, were matchboxes and cigarette cases, ashtrays decorated with frogs or rats, as well as goblets and candlesticks.

Cain began to receive official commissions in the 1850s, making animal sculptures to decorate the Egyptian department in the Louvre, the grounds of the château of Fontainebleau, the palaces of the Tuileries (where he also provided four sculptural groups for the gardens, e.g. *Family of Tigers*, bronze, 1876), the Louvre and the Elysée, as well as the Jeu de Paume at Versailles. He was also involved in the decoration of the Opéra, the Hôtel de Ville and the Palais du Trocadéro (destr.), all in Paris, as well as the grounds of the château of Chantilly and the Hôtel de Ville in Poitiers. Outside France, Cain is represented in public sites in New York, Buenos Aires and in Geneva, where he erected the colossal red marble monument to *Charles II, Duke of Brunswick* (*d* 1873), in the form of a copy of the 14th-century tombs to the della Scala family in Verona.

BIBLIOGRAPHY

Lami

LAURE DE MARGERIE

Caipler, Jan. *See* CEYPLER, JAN.

Caire, Nicholas (John) (*b* Guernsey, Channel Islands, 28 Feb 1837; *d* Melbourne, 13 Feb 1918). Australian photographer of Guernsey birth. After his arrival in South Australia *c.* 1858, he pursued his interest in photography while working as a hairdresser, becoming a professional photographer in Adelaide in 1867. Economic recession led him to move in 1870 to the neighbouring colony of Victoria, where he worked as hairdresser and photographer in the goldfields settlement of Talbot. By 1871 he was able to open a studio in the larger town of Bendigo, achieving commercial success with *carte-de-visite* portraits and local views. He had an interest in art, having tried his hand at painting, and became a precursor of Pictorial photography, converting the formally posed group portrait into the conversation piece and producing landscape scenes with human interest genre subjects and picturesque effects to meet a growing nationalistic demand.

To take advantage of his increasing success Caire moved to Melbourne in 1876 to exploit its rapid urban growth as subject-matter, and to use it as a base for forays into the countryside, seeking novel or spectacular subjects. Expansion of the railway system and his adoption of the dry plate process gave him greater mobility, and he was able to photograph increasingly remote localities, culminating in an expedition to Mt Buffalo, in 1888, organized by the Alpine Club, which subsequently used his photographs to advertise the area. He was an admirer of pioneering life and the 'bush' poets; and an advocate of the benefits of healthy outdoor living, which he publicized by frequent lantern lectures using his own photographs. His work was recognized by his authorization in 1880 as one of three official photographers to the Melbourne International Exhibition and by subsequent accreditation as photographer by special appointment to the government of Victoria.

BIBLIOGRAPHY

J. Cato: *The Story of the Camera in Australia* (Melbourne, 1955)

A. Pitkethly and D. Pitkethly: *N. J. Caire: Landscape Photographer* (Melbourne, 1988)

ROBERT SMITH

Cairo [al-Qahira; Fr. Le Caire, Ger. Kairo; colloquial Arab. Miṣr, Maṣr]. Capital city of Egypt. Founded in AD 641 as al-Fustat, it was successively the seat of the TULUNID, FATIMID, AYYUBID and MAMLUK dynasties. Following the Ottoman conquest in 1517, it remained one of the pre-eminent centres of Arab culture and is now the largest metropolis in the Arab world.

I. History and urban development. II. Art life and organization. III. Buildings.

I. History and urban development.

Cairo is strategically sited at the meeting of Lower and Upper Egypt, at the head of the Nile Delta and at the crossing of ancient routes that linked Arabia and Syria–Palestine with North Africa and Mediterranean coastal centres with inner Africa. The main urban area of Fustat, the old city, extended about 6 km along the eastern bank of the Nile between its course and the scarp of the desert plateau (al-Muqattam) overlooking the valley (see fig. 1). The later satellite towns of al-ʿAskar, al-Qata'iʿ and al-Qahira extended several kilometres further north. Western and northern parts of the city were located on low and flat alluvial grounds created as the course of the Nile moved to the west over the centuries, while the eastern and southern quarters were rocky and gradually rose eastwards towards the slopes of the Muqattam (h. 200 m), the lower extensions of which were the hills of the citadel and the Istabl ʿAntar.

Sources for the history and arts of Cairo are probably more abundant than for any other medieval metropolis. Over 600 architectural monuments have been registered and classified, certainly the richest source of information on architecture and building techniques in any town in the Islamic world. The Egyptian Mission extensively excavated Fustat between 1913 and 1920, and the American Fustat Expedition conducted a more scientific excavation between 1964 and 1980. Smaller-scale rescue operations and those ancillary to the restoration of monuments have also provided information. Written sources, mainly in Arabic, include topographies, geographies, biographies of important people, encyclopedias, secretarial handbooks for bureaucrats, medical works, travel accounts and guidebooks, in addition to general histories and chronicles. A significant quantity has been published and even translated into European languages, but much of this material is still unpublished and not easily available for study. Many important works on urban topography are lost, but 15th-century authors such as Ibn Duqmāq (*d* 1406) or al-Maqrīzī (1364–1442) quoted them extensively. The writings of Christian and Jewish authors, usually based on independent sources, often provide a correlative to these works. In addition, the foundation deeds for Islamic religious buildings (Arab. *waqf*), the unique cache of medieval documents found in the storeroom (Heb. *geniza*) of the synagogue in Fustat, and epigraphic sources, including inscriptions on buildings, tombstones, artefacts and coins, provide important dates and biographical details for the history of the city.

See also ISLAMIC ART, §II, 10(i).

BIBLIOGRAPHY

Enc. Islam/2: 'al-Ḳāhira' [Cairo]

Ibn Duqmāq (*d* 1406): *Kitāb al-intiṣār li-wāsiṭat ʿiqd al-amṣār* [A ten-volume history of the ten largest cities], vol. iv trans. by K. Vollers as *Description de l'Egypte par Ibn Doukmak* (Cairo, 1983)

Aḥmad ibn ʿAlī al-Maqrīzī (1364–1442): *al-Mawāʿiẓ wa'l-iʿtibār bi-dhikr al-khiṭaṭ wa'l-āthār* [Exhortations and consideration for the mention of districts and monuments], 2 vols (Cairo, 1853)

ʿAlī Mubārak: *al-Khiṭaṭ al-jadīda al-tawfīqiyya li-Miṣr al-Qāhira* [Continuation of al-Maqrīzī's 'Khitat'], 20 vols (Cairo, 1888–9)

S. Lane-Poole: *The Story of Cairo* (London, 1902/*R* 1906)

K. A. C. Creswell: *Early Muslim Architecture*, 2 vols (Oxford, 1932–40; 2nd edn of vol. i, Oxford, 1969/*R* New York, 1979)

L. Hautecoeur and G. Wiet: *Les Mosquées du Caire*, 2 vols (Paris, 1932)

M. Clerget: *Le Caire: Etude de géographie urbaine et d'histoire économique*, 2 vols (Cairo, 1934)

Index to Mohammedan Monuments Appearing on the Special 1:5000 Scale Maps of Cairo, Survey of Egypt (Cairo, 1951)

K. A. C. Creswell: *The Muslim Architecture of Egypt*, 2 vols (Oxford, 1952–9/*R* New York, 1978)

L. Massignon: 'La Cité des morts au Caire (Qarâfa-Darb al-Aḥmar)', *Bull. Inst. Fr. Archéol. Orient.* [Cairo], lvii (1958), pp. 25–79

G. Wiet: *Cairo: City of Art and Commerce* (Norman, 1964)

S. D. Goitein: *A Mediterranean Society*, 5 vols (Berkeley, 1967–88)

Colloque international sur l'histoire du Caire: Le Caire, 1969

J. Abu-Lughod: *Cairo: 1001 Years of the City Victorious* (Princeton, 1971)

R. B. Parker and R. Sabin: *Islamic Monuments in Cairo: A Practical Guide*, 3rd edn rev. and enlarged by C. Williams (Cairo, 1985)

D. Behrens-Abouseif: *Islamic Architecture in Cairo: An Introduction* (Leiden, 1989)

1. To *c.* 1250. 2. *c.* 1250–*c.* 1517. 3. *c.* 1517–*c.* 1800. 4. After *c.* 1800.

1. TO *c.* 1250. Several statues mentioned in Arabic sources leave little doubt that some Pharaonic monuments existed in the vicinity of Cairo, possibly as part of the suburbs of Memphis that lay on the east bank of the Nile. The fortress and town of Babylon (see fig. 1a) was apparently built *c.* AD 100 by Trajan to defend a bridge of boats across the Nile and the mouth of the Amnis Trajani (later known as the Khalij Misri; 1b), a canal leading to the Red Sea. During the later Roman and Byzantine periods it was a centre of Byzantine administration and Coptic religion and was evidently rebuilt several times. At the time of the Arab investment, Babylon stood on the Nile bank opposite an island later known as al-Rawda (colloquial Roda: 'the Garden'). The fortress, usually known to the Arabs as Qasr al-Shamʿ, preserves several old basilican churches, such as Sitt Barbara, al-Muʿallaqa and St Sergius (where the Holy Family are reputed to have stayed on the Flight into Egypt) as well as the Coptic Museum, one of the richest collections of Coptic art in the world.

The urban history of Cairo began with the foundation of al-Fustat (probably derived from the Greco-Roman

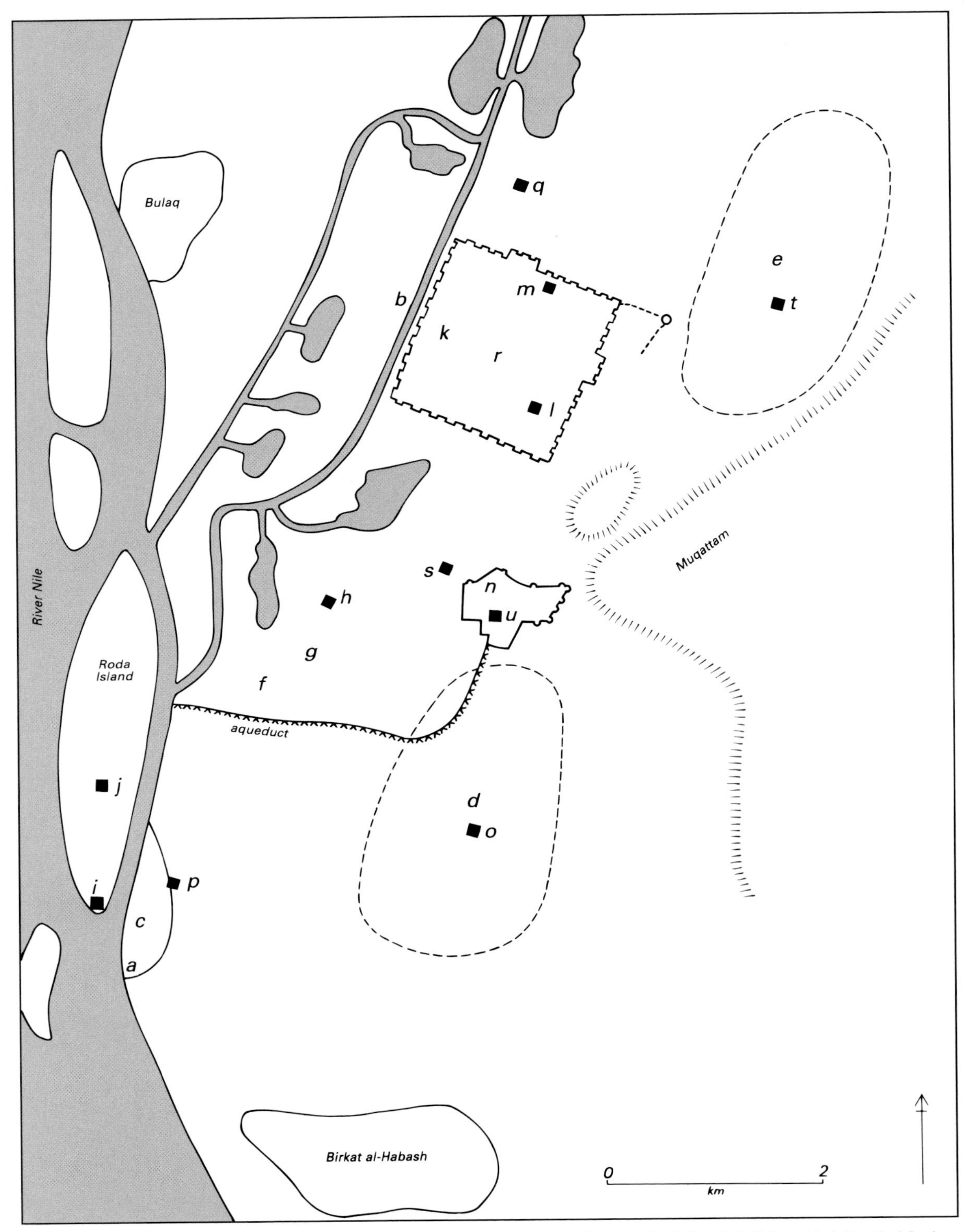

1. Map of Cairo: (a) Babylon (Qasr al-Sham); (b) Amnis Trajani (Khalij Misri); (c) al-Fustat; (d) al-Qarafa al-Kubra; (e) al-Qarafa al-Sughra; (f) al-ʿAskar; (g) al-Qataʾi; (h) mosque of Ibn Tulun; (i) Nilometer; (j) fortress; (k) al-Qahira; (l) al-Azhar Mosque; (m) mosque of al-Hakim; (n) citadel; (o) tomb of al-Shafiʿi; (p) mosque of ʿAmr; (q) mosque of Baybars; (r) complex of Qalaʾun; (s) complex of Sultan Hasan; (t) complex of Qaʾitbay; (u) mosque of Muhammad ʿAli

fossatum: 'ditch'; 1c) as an Arab military camp and provincial capital after the Islamic conquest of Egypt in AD 641 by ʿAmr ibn al-ʿAs. The Muslim soldiers and their families had semi-permanent dwellings there, and the tribal army units were given portions of land (Arab. *khiṭaṭ*), which retained their tribal names for several centuries as they later became city quarters. The settlement was like all other Arab military towns except that an older and alien settlement (which long kept its predominantly Christian character) lay at its centre. The Arab quarters soon lost their temporary form as footpaths became streets and permanent houses were built, some with a certain architectural distinction. Each quarter had a mosque and buildings for both military and communal uses. The army commanders and aristocracy settled in the central quarter near Babylon, where an official residence was erected and the tribal mosque was enlarged to become the congregational mosque for the entire city (1p; *see* §III, 1 below). The quarter also included the main bazaars and commercial structures, baths, the army office and the mint. Palaces were erected along the Nile; one of them, called 'the Gilded House' or 'the City', was erected in 686–7 by ʿAbd al-ʿAziz ibn Marwan, the brother of the Umayyad caliph and all-powerful governor of the western empire. Ordinary houses followed either the Mediterranean pattern, with a central courtyard and an upper storey, or the Coptic style, with thick mud-brick walls and vaulted rooms, but multistorey houses were possibly modelled on South Arabian prototypes. Unlike the early Arab settlements in Iraq, burials at Fustat lay outside the urban area. The cemeteries that extended to the east and south of Fustat, al-Qarafa al-Kubra (1d) and al-Qarafa al-Sughra (1e), continued to be used throughout the medieval era.

Fustat was burned by order of the last Umayyad caliph, Marwan II (*reg* 744–50), as he fled before the victorious Abbasid army in 750, but the city remained the foremost economic, cultural and artistic centre in Egypt. The Abbasid government founded a new administrative and garrison suburb, al-ʿAskar ('the Army'; 1f). Its exact location is unknown, but it probably extended to the north of the mouth of the canal. A new congregational mosque was built, as well as a governor's residence, administrative buildings and army barracks. Yet al-ʿAskar never superseded Fustat. Some Abbasid governors resided in Fustat, taking part of the administration with them. They also enlarged and adorned the congregational mosque in Fustat, indicating their continuing interest in the older city. At this time the Nile receded westward, leaving a large new stretch of land; the relatively distant quarter of al-ʿAskar may have become superfluous, and whatever remained of it merged with Fustat.

In 870 Ahmad ibn Tulun, the semi-independent TULUNID governor of Egypt and Syria for the Abbasids, built yet another suburb. As at the Abbasid capitals at BAGHDAD and SAMARRA' in Iraq, a large army of mixed descent had to be separated from the civil population, and the ruler required a palatial complex equal to his rank. Since there was no room at Fustat, al-Qata'iʿ ('the Allotments'; 1g) was built away from the Nile on the high, healthier grounds of Jabal Yashkur. Ahmad ibn Tulun built a large mosque still known by his name (*see* §III, 2 below; 1h), a government house (*dār al-imāra*) adjacent to it, a civil hospital and an aqueduct that brought water from the Birkat al-Habash on the southern fringes of Fustat. At the foot of the hill he also built a splendid palace, which was later enlarged by his son. Barracks were erected for different army detachments, as were administrative buildings and houses for officers and notables, but everything except the mosque was destroyed when the dynasty was overthrown in 905. Ahmad ibn Tulun also repaired the Nilometer (1i) on Roda Island in 861 and built a fortress (destr.; 1j) there. Tulunid rule brought security, economic prosperity and artistic development to Egypt and its capital. The few surviving pieces of pottery, glass, woodwork, textiles, architecture and decoration datable to this period show a marked change in taste from the Late Antique styles of the Mediterranean lands to the abstract style of decoration associated with Samarra'.

The development of the city and its arts is somewhat obscure in the period between the fall of the Tulunids and the advent of the FATIMID dynasty in 969, but the Fatimids soon brought about momentous changes in both (*see* ISLAMIC ART, §II, 5(ii)(c)). They had ruled North Africa for several generations; their conquest of Egypt brought about the interplay of North African and imperial Abbasid models for architecture and art, allowing for fuller and more mature expressions. Upon conquering Egypt, the Fatimid general Jawhar immediately founded a suburban garrison measuring 1200×1150 m about 2 km north of Fustat. It quickly became known as al-Qahira ('the Victorious', whence Cairo; 1k), and this satellite town housing the caliph, his attendants, bodyguards and administration was destined to surpass the older quarters. It was smaller than al-Qita'iʿ, but from the start it was strongly fortified with a moat and eight gates in a high mud-brick wall, broad enough for two horses to ride abreast. The eastern Fatimid palace was built for the caliph al-Muʿizz (*reg* 953–75) in the middle of the enclosure, but it was repeatedly modified and enlarged. Separated from the city by another

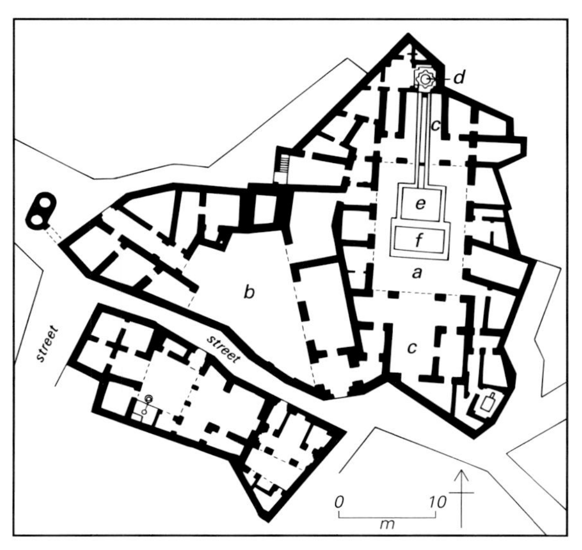

2. Cairo, Fustat, ground-plan of house, 9th–10th centuries: (a) central or main court; (b) secondary court; (c) iwans; (d) fountain; (e) pool; (f) sunken garden

3. Cairo, Bab al-Nasr, 1087–92

wall, it had 12 pavilions and allegedly covered 10 ha. On the other side of the main north–south road, known as Bayn al-Qasrayn ('Between the Two Palaces', now Shariʿ Muʿizz li-Din Allah), al-ʿAziz (*reg* 975–96) built the Small Western Palace in front of a vast garden. The only architectural monuments of this period to remain are al-Azhar Mosque (970; 1l), and the mosque of al-Hakim (990–1013; 1m), built just outside the city walls (*see* §III, 3 and 4 below). Houses and public buildings soon crowded the new walled city, but for another century only officials and soldiers carrying special authorization were allowed to live there. Even merchants and artisans were not allowed to spend nights there, and the bulk of the population remained at Fustat, which continued to be the centre of economic and artistic activity. Houses built in an Iraqi style with central courtyards and iwans have been excavated in Fustat (see fig. 2), as well as a bathhouse decorated with a figural fresco similar in style to the paintings decorating the Cappella Palatina in Palermo (*see* PALERMO, §II, 2(ii) and ISLAMIC ART, §II, 9(iii)). The thousands of artefacts excavated include locally produced underglaze-painted sgraffito and overglaze-painted lustre pottery, glass and metal objects, carvings in wood, bone and stone, and jewellery. Textiles, however, were produced in provincial towns (*see* ISLAMIC ART, §VI, 2(i)).

Famine and pestilence ravaged Egypt between 1066 and 1072, depopulating Fustat and ending many of its flourishing craft industries as artisans either left the town or died. About two-thirds of it was completely deserted; only the quarters close to the Nile survived for another century. Taking advantage of the liberal policies of Badr al-Jamali, vizier to al-Mustansir (*reg* 1036–94), the survivors settled in Cairo and created a new class of artisans and artists. Vigorous growth brought Cairo all the administrative, military, economic and cultural qualities of a city. The territory expanded beyond the new and larger city wall (1087–92) built by Badr al-Jamali, which, with its three gates (Bab al-Nasr (see fig. 3), Bab al-Futuh and Bab Zuwayla), is regarded as one of the finest examples of pre-Crusader military construction (*see also* MILITARY ARCHITECTURE AND FORTIFICATION, §IV, 2). The city was embellished with new buildings with richly decorated façades, a novelty in Egyptian architecture. Among the best known are the Aqmar Mosque (1125; *see* ISLAMIC ART, fig. 37) and the mosque of Salih Talaʾiʿ (1160). Many remarkable funerary buildings were erected outside the city, including the martyrium (*mashhad*) of Badr al-Jamali (1085; also known as the mosque of al-Jiyushi; *see* ISLAMIC ART, fig. 38) on the Muqattam scarp and the mausoleum of Sayyida Ruqayya (1133) in the Qarafa al-Kubra cemetery.

The surviving quarters of Fustat were set ablaze in 1168 to prevent their falling to the Crusaders. In 1171 Egypt passed to the AYYUBID dynasty, and the quarters close to the Nile were rebuilt for industrial and commercial use. Salah al-Din (*reg* 1171–93) envisioned a single defence system of powerful walls connecting the harbours and industry of Fustat with the centre of power in Cairo. This brilliant project never got beyond the initial stages of construction, but an impregnable citadel (1n) included in the system was built on the western projection of the Muqattam (*see* §III, 5 below). Strategic considerations also dictated the construction of an 80-arch viaduct beyond al-Giza, Cairo's suburb on the west bank of the Nile, to raise the essential route to the west above the Nile floods. The Crusader threat led al-ʿAdil (*reg* 1200–18) to strengthen the citadel's defences and build another fortress on Roda Island, which later became the house of the Bahri Mamluks. The Ayyubids introduced the institution of the MADRASA to Egypt to propagate their Sunni beliefs, but only that built on the site of the eastern Fatimid palace by al-Salih Najm al-Din Ayyub (*reg* 1240–49) remains, albeit in a much ruined state. They also enlarged the tomb of the imam al-Shafiʿi (*d* 820; 1o), the prominent jurisconsult, although many of its details were later redone (*see* §III, 6 below).

BIBLIOGRAPHY

P. Ravaisse: *Essai sur l'histoire et sur la topographie du Caire d'après Maḳrîzî* (Cairo, 1886–9)

G. Salmon: *Etude sur la topographie du Caire: Le Kal'at Al-Kabsch et la Birkat Al-Fîl* (Cairo, 1902)

P. Casanova: *Essai de reconstitution topographique de la ville d'al-Fousṭâṭ au Miṣr* (Cairo, 1913–19)

A. J. Butler: *Babylon of Egypt* (Oxford, 1914)

K. A. C. Creswell: *The Muslim Architecture of Egypt*, 2 vols (Oxford, 1952–9/*R* New York, 1978)

S. D. Goitein: 'Cairo: An Islamic City in the Light of Geniza Documents', *Middle Eastern Cities*, ed. I. M. Lapidus (Berkeley, 1969), pp. 80–96

O. V. Volkoff: *Le Caire, 969–1969: Histoire de la ville des 'Mille et une nuits'* (Cairo, 1971)

W. B. Kubiak and G. T. Scanlon: 'Fustat: Redating Bahgat's Houses and the Aqueduct', *A. & Archaeol. Res. Pap.*, iv (1973), pp. 138–48

G. T. Scanlon: 'The Pits of Fusṭâṭ: Problems of Chronology', *J. Egyp. Archaeol.*, lx (1974), pp. 60–78

W. B. Kubiak: 'The Burning of Miṣr al-Fusṭāṭ in 1168: A Reconsideration of Historical Evidence', *Afr. Bull.*, xxv (1976), pp. 51–64

A. A. Ostrasz: 'The Archaeological Material for the Study of the Domestic Architecture at Fustat', *Afr. Bull.*, xxvi (1977), pp. 57–86

W. B. Kubiak: 'The Circulation Tracks of al-Fustat: One Aspect of the Physiognomy of a Mediaeval Arab City', *Afr. Bull.*, xxviii (1979), pp. 7–28

G. T. Scanlon: 'Municipal Planning and Archaeology: The Case of Fustat (Old Cairo)', *The Arab City*, ed. I. Serageldin and S. el-Sadek (Riyadh, 1982), pp. 230–34

W. B. Kubiak: *Al-Fustat: Its Foundation and Early Urban Development* (Cairo, 1987)
N. D. MacKenzie: *Ayyubid Cairo: A Topographical Study* (Cairo, 1992)

WLADYSŁAW B. KUBIAK

2. *c.* 1250–*c.* 1517. Under the rule of the MAMLUK sequence of sultans, the development of Cairo depended largely on Salah al-Din's foundation of the citadel on a hill between al-Qahira and Fustat. The role of the citadel as army headquarters, barracks and residence of the rulers led to the urbanization of the quarters located between the citadel and Bab Zuwayla, the southern gate of al-Qahira. This southern neighbourhood flourished and expanded throughout subsequent centuries. Markets for horses, weapons and military equipment were clustered at the foot of the citadel. The Saliba, which connected the citadel with the banks of the Khalij, similarly attracted the building zeal of the ruling aristocracy.

Al-Qahira became the main focus for commercial, residential and religious building, as Fustat never regained the glamour it had had in earlier periods. Al-Qahira's main avenue and processional road (Arab. *qaṣaba*) was extended beyond the southern walls of the Fatimid city and bordered on both sides by residences and charitable foundations erected by the Mamluk sultans (*see* ISLAMIC ART, §II, 6(iii)(a)). These institutions might include a mosque for prayer, madrasa for teaching or KHĀNAQĀH for Sufis, and they had dwellings for the communities attached to them as well as the tomb of the founder. That of Qala'un (*reg* 1280–90; *see* §III, 8 below) on the western side of the *qaṣaba* had a world-famous hospital, while the complex of Hasan (*reg* 1347–61 with interruption; *see* §III, 9 below) at the foot of the citadel was the largest such foundation in Cairo. As Friday prayer was no longer restricted to a few major mosques, many neighbourhood mosques were erected throughout the city so that the inhabitants could attend Friday prayer within their quarter. Virtually all religious buildings, including colleges and monasteries, had an attached fountain (*sabīl*) to provide drinking water to passers-by, as well as a primary school (*maktab*) for boys.

Around these buildings were concentrated the most prestigious markets of the capital, either as shops and stalls along the street or within commercial structures (known as *wakāla*, *qayṣariyya* and *khān*; *see* CARAVANSERAI). These commercial buildings existed in large numbers in the city centre and near the gates, both inside and outside the walls. As elsewhere in the Islamic world, the markets in Cairo were arranged according to specializations; unlike in other Islamic cities, the markets were always connected to dwellings. The commercial structures were multi-storey courtyard buildings: the lower floors were used for selling, storing or manufacturing goods, while the upper storeys comprised an apartment complex (*rab*ʿ) accessible from a separate entrance. The characteristic housing for the middle-class of Cairo in pre-modern times, the *rab*ʿ could also be located above a line of shops. Stalls for the sale of cooked food occupied an important place among the trades of the city centre, as they provided people in the markets and those who had no kitchen with ready meals. Markets also surrounded the residences of the Bahri Mamluk amirs (1250–1382) built within the confines of the Fatimid city; these residences sometimes overlooked a square (*raḥaba*).

The construction of a new congregational mosque by Baybars I (*reg* 1260–77) between 1266 and 1269 to the north-east of al-Qahira on the site of a hippodrome near the Khalij did not have significant consequences for the city's subsequent development (*see* §III, 7 below). The location of the mosque does not seem to have been chosen according to any urban criteria, and it remained isolated in a green suburb for centuries. To the east of the mosque and west of the cemetery of Bab al-Nasr lay the quarter of al-Husayniyya, which developed with the influx of refugees fleeing the Mongol invasions. Cairo expanded greatly during the reign of al-Nasir Muhammad (*reg* 1294–1340 with interruptions), a noted patron of architecture. His long and prosperous reign allowed him to shape the capital according to his ambitions. He destroyed and rebuilt many of his predecessors' buildings, especially the palaces of the citadel, which were designed to be the stage for a sophisticated court ceremonial. Al-Nasir encouraged his amirs to develop the land to the west of the Khalij, which was mainly occupied by orchards, by giving them long-term leases, but the western bank was not truly urbanized until the Ottoman period.

An economic depression at the end of the 14th century led to the shrinking of the areas that had been expanded by al-Nasir's activities, and the only road that persisted was the one connecting al-Qahira to the port of Bulaq on the Nile. The Khalij remained the western boundary of the city until the end of the Mamluk period. This canal fed a number of ponds (*birka*) in the western, northern and southern outskirts, which the Nile flooded in summer, leaving their beds green with vegetation when the waters receded. The coolness and greenery made these areas resorts for the Cairenes, who would go boating or sit in tents erected along the shores to celebrate their feasts. Many princely residences, with various types of loggias to take advantage of the scenery, were built near these ponds, particularly the Birkat al-Fil in the south. Cairo's domestic architecture, unlike that of many other Islamic cities, was extroverted: windows screened with panels of turned wood (*mashrabiyya*; *see* ISLAMIC ART, §VII) characterized the façades of apartment complexes, houses and palaces.

The cemeteries of Cairo always included dwellings for the staff of the religious foundations and the aristocracy. In the 14th century several amirs erected mausolea with adjacent religious foundations in the desert on the eastern side of the city. This cemetery had been transformed by al-Nasir Muhammad from a hippodrome that Baybars had established. In the 15th century several sultans, such as Faraj ibn Barquq (*reg* 1399–1412 with interruption) and Qa'itbay (*reg* 1468–96), had their funerary complexes erected there (*see* §III, 10 below).

The long reign of Qa'itbay in the second half of the 15th century had a great impact on the development of Cairo, not only because of his own buildings and restorations throughout the city but also because of the urbanization projects of his amirs. Yashbak min Mahdi, for example, expanded the processional route to the northern outskirts, where he built a dome to commemorate Qa'itbay's pilgrimage to Mecca. It stood to the north of the quarter of al-Husayniyya within a plaisance complex and overlooked a hippodrome, known as the Birds' Feeding Ground (*maṭʿam al-ṭayr*), which had played an important role in Mamluk ceremonial and sports since the beginning of the 15th century. Azbak, another Mamluk amir, founded the Azbakiyya quarter along the shores of a large pond that he dug to embellish the landscape on the western bank of the Khalij. The area was not fully urbanized until the 19th century. Many other amirs of the 15th century established smaller residences outside the Fatimid city.

BIBLIOGRAPHY

J. Revault and B. Maury: *Palais et maisons du Caire du XIVe au XVIIIe siècle*, 3 vols (Paris, 1975–9)
L. ʿAli Ibrahim: 'Middle-class Living Units in Mamluk Cairo', *A. & Archaeol. Res. Pap.*, xiv (1978), pp. 24–30
D. Behrens-Abouseif: 'A Circassian Mamluk Suburb North of Cairo', *A. & Archaeol. Res. Pap.*, xiv (1978), pp. 14–23
A. Raymond and G. Wiet: *Les Marchés du Caire: Traduction annotée du texte de Maqrīzī* (Cairo, 1979)
D. Behrens-Abouseif: 'The North-eastern Extension of Cairo under the Mamluks', *An. Islam.*, xvii (1981), pp. 157–89
N. Hanna: *An Urban History of Bulaq in the Mamluk and Ottoman Periods* (Cairo, 1983)
A. Raymond: 'Cairo's Area and Population in the Early Fifteenth Century', *Muqarnas*, ii (1984), pp. 21–31
J. A. Williams: 'Urbanization and Monument Construction in Mamluk Cairo', *Muqarnas*, ii (1984), pp. 33–45
D. Behrens-Abouseif: *Azbakiyya and its Environs, from Azbak to Ismaʿil, 1476–1879* (Cairo, 1985)
——: 'Locations of Non-Muslim Quarters in Medieval Cairo', *An. Islam.*, xxii (1986), pp. 117–32

3. *c.* 1517–*c.* 1800. Cairo lost its status as capital of the Mamluk sultanate and became a provincial centre after the Ottomans conquered Egypt in 1517. This change did not have any radical impact on the character of the city, and it excluded great architectural innovation. The most visible differences were the introduction of the metropolitan Ottoman style of architecture (*see* ISLAMIC ART, §II, 7(i)(c)), particularly domed mosques and pencil-shaped minarets, and the spread of coffee-houses after the introduction of coffee-drinking in the early 16th century.

As the port of Cairo and gateway to the capital at Istanbul, the Bulaq district expanded under Ottoman rule, whereas the port at Fustat declined. At Bulaq, Egyptian agricultural products were dispatched to the sultan, and the Ottoman governors who embarked and disembarked there erected several warehouses (Arab. *wakāla*) and mosques. The impressive mosque (1571) built by Sinan Pasha on the banks of the Nile is a successful amalgamation of Ottoman and Mamluk architectural styles. In erecting charitable foundations, the Ottoman pashas and other officials avoided the old city, which was already built up. Süleyman Pasha, for example, built a mosque at the citadel (1528) and a madrasa in the southern quarter of Qusun (1543). Safiya, the wife of the Ottoman sultan Murad III (*reg* 1574–95), erected a mosque at Dawudiyya near by. The fountain of Khusraw Pasha (1535) remained the only building erected by an Ottoman pasha in the heart of the old city of Cairo for more than three centuries. With a few exceptions, however, Ottoman architecture in Cairo was faithful to the Mamluk architectural traditions until the 18th century, when styles of decoration began to follow more closely those of the Ottoman court in Istanbul.

Under the Ottoman governors, Mamluk buildings, which were sturdy constructions, were used and restored rather than replaced. The old city continued to be the main business centre, crowded with commercial establishments that flourished under Ottoman rule, particularly because of the new trade in coffee from south Arabia. Khan al-Khalili (1382) in the heart of al-Qahira continued to be the centre for luxury goods. Industrial establishments, such as mills, oil presses and gypsum factories, were located on the western bank of the Khalij and in Fustat, where small mosques were founded by members of the religious establishment.

With the increasing concentration of commercial activities in the old city since the 15th century, the aristocracy tended to dwell outside the main centre. The notables of the Ottoman period dwelt in the southern quarters neighbouring the citadel and along the shores of the Khalij, often using buildings erected by their Mamluk predecessors. After the shores of the Birkat al-Fil were built up, the Azbakiyya neighbourhood started to become fashionable in the 18th century. The orchards on the western bank of the Khalij were gradually urbanized. The northern cemeteries no longer attracted sponsors of religious foundations; rather the shrines of the southern cemeteries interested Ottoman patrons who built or restored religious foundations there, such as the mosque of Sidi ʿUqba and the tomb of Dhu'l-Nun (1655). The Rumayla Square and hippodrome at the foot of the citadel was the only true public square throughout the Mamluk and Ottoman periods. It was the site of parades and such religious celebrations as the departure of the pilgrimage caravan.

Non-Muslim minorities had lived outside the confines of al-Qahira since the Mamluk period, although churches had existed since the Fatimid period in the quarters located on either side of the *qaṣaba*. Because Islamic law tolerated pre-existing churches but did not easily allow the foundation of new ones, the quarter of al-Maqs, which was located north of Azbakiyya and was the most important Christian agglomeration of Ottoman Cairo, remained without churches until the 19th century. In contrast, Old Cairo retained several churches and monasteries that had been located there since pre-Islamic times, but it had only a small Christian and Jewish community, for most non-Muslims had left the district to follow the centre of economic activities. Harat Zuwayla, established in Fatimid times between the *qaṣaba* and the Khalij, continued to contain the main Jewish community of Cairo as well as a Christian quarter. Another Christian quarter was located north of Bab Zuwayla in al-Qahira. In contrast to their predecessors, the Ottomans allowed European merchants to settle in the city, and the European quarter was located on the western bank of the Khalij near the Muski bridge. Local, Syrian and Armenian Christians also dwelt there.

The amirs of the Ottoman period were more interested in upgrading existing marginal quarters than in initiating prestigious pioneer projects as their Mamluk predecessors had done (*see* ISLAMIC ART, fig. 85). ʿAbdin Bey urbanized the quarter of Suwayqat Safiyya, which became the quarter of ʿAbdin on the western bank of the Khalij, and Ridwan Bey (*d* 1656) developed the street south of Bab Zuwayla, which became Qasabat Ridwan. Ibrahim Agha (*d* 1654) upgraded Tabbana south of Bab Zuwayla, and Dawud Agha founded the quarter of Dawudiyya east of the Birkat

4. Cairo, fountain and elementary school (*sabīl-kuttāb*) of ʿAbd al-Rahman Katkhuda, 1744

al-Fil. Such projects usually included the restoration of existing mosques or shrines and the construction of a public fountain with a primary school for boys on the upper floor; these were usually independent structures not attached to a religious building. The most prominent restorer was ʿAbd al-Rahman Katkhuda (*d* 1776), an officer in the janissary corps, who rebuilt and restored most of the important shrines of Cairo and a number of mosques scattered all over the city. He also built several fountains and elementary schools, the most famous of which (1744; see fig. 4), stands at a bifurcation of the *qaṣaba* in the centre of al-Qahira.

BIBLIOGRAPHY

A. Raymond: 'Essai de géographie des quartiers de résidence aristocratique au Caire au XVIIIème siècle', *J. Econ. & Soc. Hist. Orient*, vi (1963), pp. 58–103

——: 'Les Constructions de l'émir ʿAbd al-Raḥmān Katḫudā au Caire', *An. Islam.*, xi (1972), pp. 235–52

N. Hanna: *An Urban History of Bulaq in the Mamluk and Ottoman Periods* (Cairo, 1983)

A. Raymond and others: *Palais et maisons du Caire: Epoque ottomane (XVIe–XVIIIe siècles)* (Paris, 1983)

D. Behrens-Abouseif: *Azbakiyya and its Environs, from Azbak to Ismaʿil, 1476–1879* (Cairo, 1985)

A. Raymond: *Les Grandes Villes arabes à l'époque ottomane* (Paris, 1985)

M. Al-Asad: 'The Mosque of al-Rifaʿi in Cairo', *Muqarnas*, x (1993), pp. 108–24

4. After *c.* 1800. The history of modern Cairo began with Napoleon's expedition to Egypt (1798–1801), when drastic changes were made to the city by the French occupiers for strategic reasons. Napoleon's headquarters were located on the western shore of the Azbakiyya pond, whence access to the port of Bulaq was direct and easy. To facilitate the movement of his army throughout the city, he planned new roads to connect Azbakiyya with Bulaq to the west and the old city, via the Muski bridge, to the east. Existing streets were widened and straightened, and the city walls were cleared and used as forts so that the French army could control the rebellious population. In the course of these measures, several mosques and monuments were destroyed and the medieval barricades of the quarters (Arab. *ḥāra*), which were closed at night to protect the inhabitants against intruders, were demolished. The Husayniyya and Azbakiyya quarters were partly demolished by cannon shells directed against rebels. The French divided Cairo into eight districts administered by a central organization (*dīwān*) to replace the 53 self-governing quarters. During the three-year French rule, regulations were issued concerning hygiene, sanitation and the elimination of cemeteries from urban areas.

The brief French occupation introduced Egyptians to European lifestyles and technology, and Muhammad ʿAli (*reg* 1805–48), the new ruler, confirmed the trend established by the occupation and continued an intensive modernization programme. He established new regulations to clean the streets, level the rubbish mounds that surrounded the city and fill in the ponds, which were considered swampy and unsanitary. The disappearance of the ponds marked the end of a characteristic aspect of medieval life in Cairo. European domestic architecture was introduced, and the pasha's own palaces were built and decorated in the new fashion. The windows with grilles of turned wood (*mashrabiyya*) characteristic of medieval houses were prohibited on the grounds that they constituted a fire hazard. The street that the French had pierced to the Muski district was adapted to wheeled traffic and became the new commercial centre, with European-style hotels, restaurants and shops selling imported goods. The Mamluk palaces in the citadel were ruthlessly destroyed for the mosque of Muhammad ʿAli (*see* §III, 11 below), residences, offices and barracks. These were all built in mixed Turkish and European styles without the least concession to the local tradition, which the pasha aimed at annihilating as he had the Mamluks.

Under ʿAbbas I (*reg* 1848–54), the first Egyptian railway was built to connect Cairo with Alexandria, and the terminus was erected to the north-west of the old city at Bab al-Hadid. ʿAbbas also founded the quarter of ʿAbbasiyya in the north-east outskirts on the site of Raydaniyya. Planned as a garrison city, it soon became a residential quarter and opened the way to Cairo's northern extension. Khedive Ismaʿil (*reg* 1863–79) sought to make Egypt a part of Europe and Cairo as glamorous as a European metropolis. His education and European travels opened the way for European architects and engineers, who were invited to shape the modern Egyptian capital. Azbakiyya became a European-style square and the centre of new radiating thoroughfares. European consulates, great hotels such as Shepheard's, bars, restaurants, banks and fashionable shops were established around it. A park planned to imitate Parc Monceau in Paris included the first modern theatres in Egypt as well as the Opera House (1869), built in Italian style to celebrate the opening of the Suez Canal. From Azbakiyya, Muhammad ʿAli Street, designed in imitation of the Rue de Rivoli, connected the European city with the citadel. On the west bank of the Nile another paved road connected the modern city with the Pyramids in Giza. The Ismaʿiliyya Canal was dug to facilitate the northern and western extensions of the city. The Ismaʿiliyya quarter was established to the west of Azbakiyya as the new business centre, and the ʿAbdin quarter was established as the administrative centre around the khedival palace. Several modern squares were planned, some in the old city to enhance the view of its monuments. Through concessions given to French companies, Cairo acquired modern municipal water and gas mains. Many of the European architects employed by Ismaʿil discovered the aesthetic values of the medieval city and contributed to the preservation of its architectural heritage, which they saw threatened by modernism. Their Orientalist style can still be seen, for example, in the Museum of Islamic Art, founded as the Arab Museum in 1883.

Britain established a protectorate over Egypt in 1882, but the character of Egyptian cities owes little to British influence, apart from the quarter of Garden City, built along the Nile to the west of ʿAbdin and around the British Embassy for the European community. It was planned for villas with gardens and still has several Art Deco buildings designed by European architects in the 1930s. The quarter of Heliopolis was founded at the beginning of the 20th century by the Belgian Baron Edouard d'Empain in the north-east outskirts of the city and became one of the most successful western urban planning projects in Cairo. Its mixture of architectural styles, including Orientalism, makes it one of the most charming districts of Cairo. The demographic explosion since the beginning of the 20th century has opened a new chapter in the history of the city. This historic centre, which occupies only a small portion of greater Cairo, has been designated by UNESCO a City of Human Heritage. Although it has not lost its economic vitality, overpopulation and a boom of small industries overload its insufficient infrastructure and threaten its historic monuments.

See also EGYPT.

BIBLIOGRAPHY

R. Owen: 'The Cairo Building Industry and the Building Boom of 1897 to 1907', *Colloque international sur l'histoire du Caire: Le Caire, 1969*, pp. 337–50

R. Ilbert: *Héliopolis: Le Caire, 1905–1922: Genèse d'une ville* (Paris, 1981)

The Expanding Metropolis Coping with the Urban Growth of Cairo: Proceedings of Seminar Nine: Cairo, 1984

M. Volait: *L'Architecture moderne en Egypte et la Revue al-ʿImara, 1939–1959* (Cairo, 1987)

M. Scharabi: *Kairo: Stadt und Architektur im Zeitalter des europäischen Kolonialismus* (Tübingen, 1989)

D. Behrens-Abouseif: 'The ʿAbd al-Raḥmān Katkhudā Style in 18th-century Cairo', *An. Islam.*, xxvi (1992), pp. 117–26

——: *Egypt's Adjustment to Ottoman Rule: Institutions, Waqf and Architecture in Cairo, 16th and 17th Centuries* (Leiden, 1994)

DORIS BEHRENS-ABOUSEIF

II. Art life and organization.

For most of its history Cairo was a pre-eminent centre of artistic production not only for Egypt, where it was the major city, but also for the entire Islamic world. From the advent of the TULUNID dynasty in 868 to the Ottoman conquest in 1517, court patrons in Cairo sponsored the manufacture, use and trade of exquisite luxury goods. The most brilliant periods were the century between 969 and 1067 under the patronage of the FATIMID dynasty and the period from 1260 to 1382 under the MAMLUK sultans of the Bahri line, particularly the third reign of al-Nasir Muhammad (*reg* 1309–40). From *c.* 1820 to *c.* 1920 artistic life in the city was dominated by Europeans and European arts, but since 1920 Egyptians have revived local artistic traditions and developed indigenous traditions of easel painting and sculpture in the round.

Under the Muslim dynasties of Egypt, the techniques of the loom, the kiln and the crucible of Pharaonic, Hellenistic and Coptic times were continued, but new themes and techniques were added. Contemporary authors give few specifics of this production or of the workshops that were responsible for it, but archaeological excavations and inscriptions on objects allow general typologies and chronologies to be established. The manufacture of textiles, comprising the production of fibres, the dyeing and weaving processes and the decoration of the finished cloth, was the major industry of the medieval Islamic world, and Egypt and its capital were major centres of this industry (*see* ISLAMIC ART, §VI). Special factories (*see* TIRAZ), often located in the nearby towns of the Delta, produced much of the cloth woven for the ruler and his court as robes of honour and state gifts. Founded in Fatimid times, these factories continued to operate throughout the Mamluk period. Ceramics were always produced in Cairo for domestic consumption, but high-quality wares decorated with lustre painting are particularly associated with the 11th and 12th centuries, as are the many wasters of sgraffito ware excavated at Fustat (*see* ISLAMIC ART, §V, 3(i)). Although some early bronzes have been ascribed to the Fatimid period, the most notable metalwares produced at Cairo were vessels of copper alloy inlaid with silver and gold made during the early Mamluk period (*see* ISLAMIC ART, §IV, 3(iii)(a)).

In addition to these three traditional media, other industries and art forms were associated with the city in the Islamic period. Carved and inlaid furnishings and fixtures of wood decorated public and private buildings. Some early pieces are decorated with ivory marquetry set in geometric designs or with the Bevelled style of carving introduced under the Tulunids, but under the Fatimids a more naturalistic style of carving emerged, only to be replaced in the 12th century by large-scale strapwork designs executed in joinery and inlay (*see* ISLAMIC ART, §VII, 1(i)(b) and 2(ii)). Rock crystal was superbly carved into ewers and other luxury objects in the 10th and 11th centuries (*see* ISLAMIC ART, §VIII, 13(i); for illustration *see* FATIMID). Cairo was an enduring centre of Muslim scholarship, and the arts of the book flourished there. Finely calligraphed, decorated and bound copies of the Koran were made at Cairo, particularly under the patronage of the Mamluk sultans (*see* ISLAMIC ART, §III, 2(iii)(c); 3(i) and 7), although the illustrated book was never as important as it was in eastern Islamic lands. A distinct group of pile carpets, distinguished by S-spun wool (and, rarely, silk), the use of an asymmetrical knot and a centralized design revolving around one or more octagonal medallions, was produced in the late 15th century and in the 16th; they are known as Mamluk Carpets and are usually ascribed to Cairo (*see* ISLAMIC ART, §VI, 4(iii)(b)).

Patterns and techniques were often transferred from one medium or one context to another. The same star-centred geometric design can be found on a bronze door or a wooden minbar; the same pattern of inlaid marble can be found in a fountain of a private reception room or over a mihrab in a mosque; and the same inlaid geometric pattern can be found on a stand for a manuscript of the Koran or on a chancel screen in a church. Changes in style and form resulted from new regional alliances and the movement of artisans rather than from dynastic affiliations. The Tulunids, for example, brought Samarran styles with them from Iraq, while the Fatimids brought the styles of the Mediterranean and Byzantine lands with which they were linked by trade and diplomacy. Skilled artisans were usually attracted to Cairo by the luxury and stability of the court, but when the Ottomans conquered Cairo in 1517, many master craftsmen were transferred to Istanbul.

Members of a craft often had communal, occupational and spatial bonds, as well as an informal hierarchy of apprentice, journeyman and master, but from the 9th century to the 15th there were no guilds in the European sense of voluntary associations of craftsmen who policed their own work. Rather it was the state, first by a representative of the police and from the 13th century by the superintendent of the market (Arab. *muḥtasib*), that exerted rigorous external controls over production. An overseer appointed by each craft and trade assisted this official in his political, economic, fiscal and moral duties. Craft guilds were introduced only under the Ottomans: from the 16th century to the 19th there were 250 specialized craft guilds (e.g. of knot-tiers and tassel-makers) for an active population of 100,000 craftsmen and tradesmen in a city of 250,000 people.

Under Muhammad ʿAli (*reg* 1805–48) and his successors, the Egyptian government, which had formerly been medieval, Mamluk and introverted, looked outward and westward. European writers, archaeologists, explorers, travellers and painters came to Egypt and discovered its Pharaonic and Islamic past. Of those who depicted urban Cairo with a brush, DAVID ROBERTS and John Frederick Lewis (*see* LEWIS (i), (1)) are outstanding; they accurately portrayed the traditional urban scene that was in danger of disappearing. Photographers such as FRANCIS FRITH were also active in the city. From the mid-19th century, artists from various European countries visited Cairo and responded enthusiastically to the human and architectural scenes, as well as to the dazzling interplay of light and texture. The most distinguished was JEAN-LÉON GÉRÔME, who specialized in realistic genre scenes of the devout at worship and natives in intricate costumes.

Europeans were also involved as preservers of the past. The Egyptian Museum was the brainchild of the colourful French archaeologist Auguste Mariette (1821–81), who was perturbed by the wholesale disappearance of Egyptian antiquities. The present sandstone structure near the Qasr al-Nil barracks was designed by the French architect Marcel Dourgnon (1858–1911) in the Neo-classical style. Opened in 1902, the museum now contains the most important collection of Egyptian antiquities, with more than 120,000 items. Similarly, a collection of Islamic artefacts was formed because of a growing concern about the destruction of Islamic monuments and the export of items to Europe. To preserve the Islamic architectural heritage, the Committee for the Conservation of the Monuments of Arab Art (usually known as the Comité) was created in 1881. Materials collected from mosques and secular buildings formed the genesis of their collection, which was housed initially in makeshift quarters in the mosque of al-Hakim. In 1903 the Museum of Arab Art moved to a new structure in Neo-Mamluk style, which also housed the collection of manuscripts begun by Khedive Ismaʿil (*reg* 1863–79) on the upper floor. The museum, renamed the Museum of Islamic Art in 1952, contains almost 80,000 items in addition to the manuscripts, which were moved to the new National Library (Dar al-Kutub) in 1984. The third of the great museums in Cairo, the Coptic Museum, was founded in 1910 by Morcos Simaika on a site donated by the Coptic patriarch within the ancient walls of Babylon and adjacent to six of the oldest Coptic churches in the city.

The Modern Art Museum (est. 1929) found a permanent home in 1966. It houses works by MAHMUD MUKHTAR, the first major figure in modern Egyptian art, and by his contemporaries and successors MAHMUD SAID, Muhammad Naghi, Raghib Ayyad, Fuad Kamil, Ramsis Yunan, ʿABD AL-HADI AL-GAZZAR and Hamid Nada. The works range in style from neo-Pharaonic to folk-realist. The Khalil Museum, designed by Ramses Wissa-Wassef (*d* 1974), houses a collection of paintings by Degas, Gauguin, Monet, Camille Pissarro and Henri Rousseau and sculptures collected by Muhammad Mahmoud Khalil during his sojourn in France. Wissa-Wassef, a friend and colleague of the noted Egyptian architect HASSAN FATHY, also designed the mud-brick vaulted Museum of Wissa-Wassef Tapestries and planned the village of Harrania near Giza as a living-producing complex built in the beautiful vernacular style of Egypt. The tapestries, worked in wool dyed with vibrantly coloured vegetal dyes, depict village themes.

See also EGYPT.

BIBLIOGRAPHY

Islamic Art in Egypt (969–1517) (exh. cat., Cairo, Mus. Islam. A., 1969)
Orientalism: The Near East in French Painting, 1800–1880 (exh. cat. by D. A. Rosenthal, U. Rochester, NY, Mem. A.G., 1982)
R. Anderson and I. Fawzy, eds: *Egypt Revealed: Scenes from Napoleon's 'Description de l'Egypte'* (Cairo, 1987)
L. Karnouk: *Modern Egyptian Art: The Emergence of a National Style* (Cairo, 1988)
J. Sweetman: *The Oriental Obsession: Islamic Inspiration in British and American Art and Architecture, 1500–1920* (Cambridge, 1988)
D. M. Reid: 'Cultural Imperialism and Nationalism: The Struggle to Define and Control the Heritage of Arab Art in Egypt', *Int. J. Mid. E. Stud.*, xxiv (1992), pp. 57–76

CAROLINE WILLIAMS

III. Buildings.

1. Mosque of ʿAmr. 2. Mosque of Ibn Tulun. 3. Al-Azhar Mosque. 4. Mosque of al-Hakim. 5. Citadel. 6. Tomb of al-Shafiʿi. 7. Mosque of Baybars. 8. Complex of Qalaʾun. 9. Complex of Sultan Hasan. 10. Complex of Qaʾitbay. 11. Mosque of Muhammad ʿAli.

1. MOSQUE OF ʿAMR. The mosque founded in Fustat in AD 641 by ʿAmr ibn al-ʿAs enjoys a certain prestige as the first mosque in Egypt and one of the oldest in the

world, but the building has suffered from long neglect and repeated reconstruction and preserves very little older than the 19th century (see fig. 1p above). Originally it was a small rectangular building (*c*. 15×25 m). A courtyard was added in 673 when the mosque was replaced with a larger one. Four small structures like sentry boxes (Arab. *ṣawmaʿa*; *see* MINARET) were built at the corners of the roof to shelter the muezzins. Further additions were made in 696–7 or 698–9 and in 710–12 to accommodate the burgeoning population of Fustat. In 827 the last major campaign doubled the area of the mosque to the south-west, making it a roughly square building with a rectangular courtyard. These successive enlargements were made possible by the typical plan of the hypostyle mosque in the early Islamic period, but the building was unusual in having the same number of arcades (seven) on the qibla side as on the side opposite. This layout was perhaps inspired by the mosque of MEDINA as restored in the early 8th century. The earliest remains in the mosque of ʿAmr, a wooden architrave carved with vine scrolls and a very stylized acanthus (identical to those in the nearby monastery of Dayr Abu'l-Sufayn), are from the south-west half of the mosque and cannot be earlier than 827. An early 14th-century mihrab, the only other medieval remnant, was destroyed in the 1970s when an attempt was made to transport it.

2. MOSQUE OF IBN TULUN. The mosque of Ahmad ibn Tulun (AD 876–9; *see* TULUNID) comprises a vast courtyard (92×92 m) surrounded by wooden-roofed arcades, five aisles deep on the qibla side and two on each of the other sides, the whole enclosed in a walled precinct (Arab. *ziyāda*; 122×140 m) on three sides (see fig. 1h above). Features such as the precinct, the use of brick, the stucco decoration of the arcades and the helicoidal form of the original minaret that stood in the precinct opposite the mihrab derive from contemporary Abbasid architecture in Iraq, but the basic form of the mosque does not resemble either of the mosques at Samarra', the Abbasid capital. Wooden lintels are carved in the Bevelled style popular in many media at Samarra', and narrow wooden friezes of Koranic inscriptions in kufic script decorated the interior. Most of the stucco window grilles date from the restoration of the mosque in 1296 by the Mamluk ruler Lajin (*reg* 1297–9), when the domed pavilion in the centre of the court and the present minaret were built. Nevertheless the basic form of the mosque has remained relatively unaltered. The precinct still isolates the prayer-hall from the noise of the surrounding city, and the resulting peace encourages contemplation of the beauty of the architecture. The harmonious proportions and the multiplication of the single arched unit into endless vistas allowed by the vast size of the hypostyle plan result in a building that many deem the aesthetic highpoint of architecture not only in Cairo but in the entire Islamic world (*see* ISLAMIC ART, fig. 24).

3. AL-AZHAR MOSQUE. The mosque known as al-Azhar ('the Radiant') was begun in AD 970 as the principal mosque of al-Qahira (see fig. 1l above). Completed in 972, it was made a teaching institution in 988–9, and its present renown is due to the prestige of its almost unbroken tradition as an educational centre. The original mosque was a rectangle (*c*. 85×70 m) with arcades on three sides of a court. There was no arcade opposite the qibla, but there may have been a monumental portal like that at the earlier mosque built by the Fatimids at MAHDIA in Tunisia or the later Cairene mosque of al-Hakim (*see* §4 below). At the centre of the qibla side a raised transept on paired columns leads to a dome over the mihrab bay, an arrangement recalling Mahdia, and domes cover the back corners of the hypostyle prayer-hall, otherwise covered with a flat wooden roof. The mosque walls preserve a considerable amount of the original stucco decoration, which has the peculiarity of being exclusively epigraphic or vegetal, omitting the interlaced geometric motifs found at the mosques of Ibn Tulun and al-Hakim (*see* ISLAMIC ART, §II, 5(ii)(c)). Nothing of the original exterior remains, as the mosque was repeatedly restored and enlarged with additional prayer-halls, minarets, madrasas, shops and places for ablution.

4. MOSQUE OF AL-HAKIM. The Fatimid caliph al-ʿAziz (*reg* 975–96) began construction in 989 or 990 of a huge mosque (120×113 m) just outside the north wall of al-Qahira (see fig. 1m above); his son al-Hakim (*reg* 996–1021) completed the building in 1013. It was erected to accommodate not only the ever-burgeoning population of Cairo but also Fatimid pageantry, for the imams visited successive mosques on religious festival days, accompanied by much cermonial pomp. The mosque (*see* ISLAMIC ART, fig. 36) shares with al-Azhar the basic plan, one of transept with clerestory and three domes along the qibla wall, but differs in materials (brick piers and rubble-faced walls) and in its entrance façade, which has two minarets flanking a monumental portal, all finely decorated with carved stone arabesques and inscriptions. The bastions erected in 1010–11 to encase the minarets are the most enigmatic feature of the mosque. Bloom suggested that the shape of the minarets (square bases leading to polygonal or circular shafts) deliberately alluded to that of those on the Haram in Mecca, but after Fatimid–Meccan relations deteriorated, al-Hakim prohibited his subjects from visiting Mecca and ordered the minarets to be concealed. The interior of the mosque was quite plain except for long bands of Koranic inscriptions carved in stucco just below the ceiling (*see* ISLAMIC ART, fig. 83). In later centuries the mosque was repeatedly allowed to deteriorate and was then restored; it was turned into a fortress during the French occupation, and from 1880 to 1896 it housed the Arab Museum. In 1980 the mosque was again restored in inappropriate gilt and gleaming marble.

BIBLIOGRAPHY

J. M. Bloom: 'The Mosque of al-Ḥākim in Cairo', *Muqarnas*, i (1983), pp. 14–36

5. CITADEL. In 1176 the Ayyubid sultan Salah al-Din (*reg* 1171–93) began to erect a citadel on a spur of the Muqattam Hills overlooking Cairo (see fig. 1n above), probably as a precaution against internal revolt. The citadel supplanted the Fatimid palaces as the residence for the rulers of Egypt, and it attracted urban development to the area, slowing the northward expansion of the city. Most

of the curtain wall was finished at the time of Salah al-Din's death; his brother al-ʿAdil (*reg* 1200–18) added strongly fortified towers like those of the fortresses he built or restored in Aleppo, Damascus and Bosra. The masonry of the citadel is inferior to that of the Fatimid gates of Cairo, but its bent entrances are more sophisticated for defence. A well (Bi'r Yusuf) having a staircase sufficiently wide to accommodate oxen was dug 87 m through bedrock to the water table, an astonishing feat of engineering. The Mamluk sultan Baybars I (*reg* 1260–77) divided the citadel into two enclosures, the southernmost of which, as developed by him and by later Mamluk rulers, was less heavily fortified because the need for protection against the local inhabitants had diminished. It contained the palaces and state buildings, of which the most impressive was the dome chamber of the Dar al-ʿAdl, built by the Mamluk sultan al-Nasir Muhammad (*reg* 1294–1340 with interruptions) in 1333–4. Known through an early 19th-century engraving as the 'Divan of Joseph', much of it was destroyed in an explosion in 1824, and the rest was cleared to make way for the mosque of Muhammad ʿAli (*see* §11 below).

BIBLIOGRAPHY

The Citadel of Cairo, 1176–1341: Reconstructing Architecture from Texts (diss., Cambridge, MA, MIT, 1991)

6. TOMB OF AL-SHAFIʿI. The tomb of the imam al-Shafiʿi (*d* 820), founder of one of the orthodox schools of Islamic law, in the Qarafa al-Kubra cemetery (see fig. 1o above), was a natural focus for the Ayyubid campaign against the heterodox Fatimid ideology. In 1176–7 Salah al-Din (*reg* 1171–93) ordered a madrasa (destr.) to be built near the grave of al-Shafiʿi, and in 1211 Salah al-Din's nephew al-Kamil built the present mausoleum in his mother's honour. It consists of a 20 m square base, with 2.75 m thick walls (stone below, brick above); they greatly exceed the support necessary for the double wooden dome, which at 29 m high is one of the most imposing in Egypt. The exterior (see fig. 5), divided into two storeys below the dome, preserves some of its original carved stucco decoration. The use of stucco motifs from Spain and North Africa suggests the presence of refugee artisans. The lead-sheathed dome (rebuilt 1772) is crowned by a metal boat-shaped finial. The spacious interior preserves many examples of Ayyubid woodwork, among which are al-Shafiʿi's cenotaph (1178–9) and the cenotaph of al-Kamil's mother, which retains only a small fragment of a powerful openwork inscription in kufic. The mausoleum still has its system of wooden beams and brackets from which lamps were hung. The earliest example of its type in Cairo, it is carved with geometric decoration and kufic inscriptions on a vegetal ground. The soffit over the original entrance (now a window) has octagonal coffers in a style that was to remain popular for the next two centuries

5. Cairo, tomb of al-Shafiʿi, 1211

7. MOSQUE OF BAYBARS. The mosque that the Mamluk sultan Baybars I (*reg* 1260–77; *see* MAMLUK, §II, 2(1)) built between 1266 and 1269 in the Husayniyya district (see fig. 1q above) has many similarities to the mosque of al-Hakim, but it differs in having a single minaret over the portal opposite the qibla, in the axial bays leading from the courtyard to each portal and in an enormous dome chamber in front of the mihrab. The idea of incorporating such a huge dome within the mosque may have been inspired by Iranian mosque plans, but it may also have been intended to symbolize the new ascendancy of the Hanafi school of law, which Baybars favoured over the Shafiʿi school traditional in Egypt. Baybars expressly specified that the dome was to be as large as that over al-Shafiʿi's tomb—the mosque stood amid the homes of recent, probably Hanafi, refugees from the Mongol invasions—and he appointed a Hanafi preacher to the mosque, the location of which in Husayniyya was also due undoubtedly to its proximity to the residence (*zāwiya*) of Baybars's spiritual adviser, Shaykh Khidr. Spoils from the citadel of Jaffa, which he captured from the Crusaders while the mosque was being erected, were incorporated in the dome chamber to symbolize Islam's victory over Christianity. The portal crowned by a single minaret may have been a visual reference to the minarets of the Haram in Mecca, a likelihood increased by the portal inscription referring to Baybars as 'servant of the two noble sanctuaries' (i.e. Mecca and Medina). Most of the interior decoration of the mosque has vanished, but what remains shows new Syrian features such as striped masonry on the portals and broad interlacing bands on the inner spandrels of the main portal.

BIBLIOGRAPHY

J. M. Bloom: 'The Mosque of Baybars al-Bunduqdārī in Cairo', *An. Islam.*, xviii (1982), pp. 45–78

8. COMPLEX OF QALA'UN. The complex of the Mamluk sultan Qala'un (*reg* 1280–90) was built in 1284–5

on the site of the former Fatimid palace (see fig. 1r above). It comprises a hospital, madrasa, mausoleum and minaret. The cruciform hospital was built in fulfilment of a vow Qala'un had made when he received treatment at the hospital of Nur al-Din in Damascus. From the ruined state of Qala'un's hospital, it is difficult to determine the extent to which parts of the palace were incorporated. The madrasa has an unusual four-iwan plan with two vestigial iwans on the sides; it anticipates those popular for madrasas in later centuries. A triple-arched façade of Syrian inspiration fronted the qibla iwan, which was divided by granite columns into three aisles, an arrangement later copied in the nearby madrasa built by the Mamluk sultan Barquq in 1384–6. The mihrab hood was decorated with glass mosaic, another feature more common to Syria. The unique plan of the mausoleum comprises a dome supported on four piers and four columns within a square ambulatory (*see* ISLAMIC ART, fig. 56). Meinecke has plausibly suggested that the building and its marble revetment were inspired by the Dome of the Rock in Jerusalem in an attempt to underscore Qala'un's claim to be the spiritual heir to the glory of the Umayyads. The marble and mother-of-pearl mosaic decoration of the mihrab, with arched colonnades capped by scallop shells, set the fashion for Mamluk decoration in Cairo even as late as the mausoleum of al-Ashraf Barsbay (1423–4). The papyrus cornices of the upper storeys of the minaret (the uppermost by Qala'un's son al-Nasir Muhammad) are a most unusual example of Pharaonic motifs in Egyptian Islamic art.

6. Cairo, mosque of Muhammad ʿAli, 1828–*c.* 1857

BIBLIOGRAPHY

M. Meinecke: 'Das Mausoleum des Qalā'ūn in Kairo: Untersuchungen zur Genese der mamlukischen Architekturdekoration', *Mitt. Dt. Archäol. Inst.: Abt. Kairo*, xxvii/1 (1971), pp. 47–80

9. COMPLEX OF SULTAN HASAN. The complex erected between 1356 and 1362 by the Mamluk sultan Hasan (*reg* 1347–61 with interruption) is the largest and most impressive of all Mamluk buildings in Cairo, but it is not clear why such an impressive building should have been erected by a man who accomplished little else of note in his lifetime. Admittedly, some of his unpopularity resulted from his squeezing the state treasury and his amirs for building funds. Located on the square below the citadel (see fig. 1s above), the building comprises a four-iwan congregational mosque (*see* ISLAMIC ART, fig. 57) with four madrasas of varying size crammed into its corners, a huge domed mausoleum flanked by twin minarets behind the qibla iwan and, at a lower level, a market and water-tower. The once bulbous dome has been rebuilt. The massive stone exterior, punctuated by the dome and minarets, is articulated with thin vertical niches and crowned by a bold *muqarnas* cornice. The 28 m-high portal, designed with twin minarets above and based roughly on Anatolian models, was cleverly angled to be visible from the citadel. Its unfinished decoration gives valuable evidence of contemporary working practices. The bronze doors were the finest in medieval Cairo; in 1416 the Mamluk sultan Mu'ayyad paid a paltry sum to have them transferred to his own mosque. The enormous domed vestibule is elaborately decorated; a panel of inlaid marble can only have been the work of a craftsman trained in Damascus, giving support to historical accounts that Hasan invited architects from all over the Islamic world to work on the building.

BIBLIOGRAPHY

M. Meinecke: 'Mamluk Architecture: Regional Architectural Traditions: Evolution and Interrelations', *Damas. Mitt.*, ii (1985), pp. 163–75

10. COMPLEX OF QA'ITBAY. The complex built by the Mamluk sultan Qa'itbay (*reg* 1468–96) between 1472 and 1474 in the northern cemetery comprised his mausoleum (*see* MUQARNAS, fig. 2), a madrasa, fountain and elementary school (Arab. *sabīl-kuttāb*), an apartment complex (*rabʿ*) and a water trough within an enclosure wall with two portals (see fig. 1t above). The complex is notable for its wealth of detail and the delicate balance between the parts, rather than for its size. The view from the north-east, most frequently drawn and photographed (*see* ISLAMIC ART, fig. 58), is most successful, for the elaborate decoration of the minaret beside the portal balances the mausoleum's dome. The dome is the cynosure of carved stone domes in Cairo: its decoration interweaves foliate arabesques with eight-pointed stars on an ever-decreasing surface. The way in which the eave of the *sabīl-kuttāb* is extended to shade the entrance portal is an effective and innovative feature, and the carving of the brackets supporting the sills of the fountain and the bulbous fleuron at the base of the dome shows equal attention to detail. The lantern-covered courtyard of the madrasa, the vestigial side iwans and the lateral extension of the qibla iwan show that later Cairene religious architecture borrowed many features from domestic architecture, such as the reception

room (*qāʿa*) of the palace of Beshtak (1334–9). The interior decoration of the complex is even more elaborate—or, arguably, excessive. Coffered ceilings are painted and gilded, windows filled with coloured glass in stucco grilles and window hoods decorated with carved stucco. Only the marble dado has not survived.

11. MOSQUE OF MUHAMMAD ʿALI. The mosque erected by Muhammad ʿAli (*reg* 1805–48) is the most prominent monument in Cairo (see fig. 6). Its commanding location on the citadel (see fig. 1u above) enables its soaring minarets to be seen throughout the city, and the combination of dome and semi-domes is successful as silhouette. As early as 1820, Muhammad ʿAli broached the idea of building a new mosque on the site with PASCAL-XAVIER COSTE, who would hardly have deemed a mosque in the Ottoman metropolitan style (*see* ISLAMIC ART, §II, 7(i)) appropriate. Work started in late 1828 under Yusuf Bushnaq, a Greek from Istanbul, and continued for at least nine years after Muhammad ʿAli's death. Although such centrally planned mosques in Istanbul as that of Sultan Ahmed (*see* ISTANBUL, §III, 11) have been cited as models, the copyist was blind to any of the subtleties of the originals. The interior of the mosque of Muhammad ʿAli may recreate the wonderful sense of space that characterizes mosques in Istanbul, but the way in which the four semi-domes are attached to the blank walls of the exterior without any transitional zone is extremely crude. The alabaster revetment of the mosque, which rises to 11 m, is another major aesthetic flaw; as even some contemporaries suspected, its poor weathering qualities have resulted in discolouration and pitting. The building served as Muhammad ʿAli's mausoleum, as he had intended.

BIBLIOGRAPHY

G. Wiet: *Mohammed Ali et les beaux-arts* (Cairo, 1949), pp. 265–88

M. Al-Asad: 'The Mosque of Muhammad ʿAli in Cairo', *Muqarnas*, ix (1992), pp. 39–55

BERNARD O'KANE

Cairo, Francesco [del] (*b* Milan, 26 Sept 1607; *d* Milan, 27 July 1665). Italian painter. He led a successful career as court painter at Turin and painted many large altarpieces for religious orders; the range of his stylistic development during nearly 40 years is enormous, yet his early cabinet pictures, of macabre and morbid subjects, remain his most fascinating achievement. They mark the end of the brilliant originality and passionate feeling that had distinguished early 17th-century Milanese painting.

1. LIFE AND WORK.

(i) Before 1639: early years in Lombardy and as court painter at Turin. Cairo's teacher is usually supposed to have been Morazzone, a stylistically credible idea. Cairo's earliest known altarpiece, *St Teresa's Vision of SS Peter and Paul* (late 1620s; Pavia, Certosa di Pavia, New Sacristy; see fig. 1), was previously attributed to Morazzone and is indebted to him in its colouring, based upon sharply lit oranges, browns and greens. The picture also shows the influence of the late work of Giovanni Battista Crespi. Cairo's *Death of the Blessed Andrea Avellino* (*c*. 1630; Milan, S Antonio Abate) is a more integrated composition, its sources less apparent. These works represent mystical

1. Francesco Cairo: *St Teresa's Vision of SS Peter and Paul*, oil on canvas, 331×213 mm, late 1620s (Pavia, Certosa di Pavia, New Sacristy)

visions with the intense emotion that is characteristic of Baroque devotional iconography. Their dramatic lighting, richly worked surfaces and shallow pictorial space are typical of Milanese painting of the 1620s, yet a new clarity of space and gesture suggests a fresh response to early 17th-century Bolognese art. They were painted for religious orders, and the Carmelites in particular remained important patrons of the artist.

In 1633 Cairo was called to Turin as court painter to Victor-Amadeus I, Duke of Savoy. A group of pictures now in the Galleria Sabauda, Turin, is mentioned in the 1635 inventory of the Savoy collection and probably postdates his summons there; included are *Christ in the Garden of Gethsemane* (other versions in Milan, Brera; Milan, Castello Sforzesco), *Herodias with the Head of St John the Baptist* (*see* ITALY, fig. 39; other versions in Boston, MA, Mus. F.A.; New York, Met.; Vicenza, Mus. Civ. A. & Stor.), a *Martyrdom of St Agnes* and a *Death of Lucretia*. These pictures typify one aspect of Cairo's art: they are rather small, rarely more than a metre high, with one or, at most, two figures placed close to the picture plane; they are carefully and smoothly painted with a sophisticated palette based on muted browns, oranges and greens, sharpened by whites and yellows. In most cases they depict an equivocal moment of extreme emotion, and the painted series of tragic heroines reveals a morbid fascination with violence and death. The executioner plunges his knife into the pallid breast of an ecstatic St Agnes; in a disturbingly erotic work a richly jewelled Herodias, veiled in dark shadows, half swoons in rapture or in anguish over the lurid severed head of the dead Baptist. Stylistically similar works, such as the anguished, spectral *St Francis in Ecstasy* (Milan, Castello Sforzesco) or the eerie *Dream of St Joseph* (Berlin, Bodemus.), are probably close in date. In both devotional and lay literature of the period there are specific parallels and sources for this expression of the senses pushed beyond the limits of reason.

Such a sumptuous mixture of the dramatic, the macabre and the ecstatic was popular with private collectors. By the late 1630s Cairo's pictures were collected in Venice, and his reputation was spreading to England. His success at the ducal court in Turin was marked by his enrolment in the Order of SS Maurice and Lazarus in 1634 and by the grant by the Duke of Savoy of a regular stipend in 1635. In 1637 he went to Rome at the expense of the ducal family. He remained there a year, but no pictures have been identified from this period.

(ii) 1639–47: further activity in Lombardy and Turin. By early 1639 Cairo was back in Turin. Around 1640 he married a well-born Piedmontese, Ludovica Piossasca di Sculaghi. From 1641 to 1643 several documents attest to his presence in Lombardy. In 1644 Christina of France, the widow of Victor-Amadeus I, ordered his return to regular paid service in Turin. The works dating from his return north from Rome mark a decisive stylistic change. The concentrated experience of painting in Rome undoubtedly caused Cairo to renew his art; he was influenced by the grand, decorative style and warm Venetian colour of Pietro da Cortona and by the glowing surfaces and tender sentiment of Genoese painters, particularly Giovanni Benedetto Castiglione and the Fleming Anthony van Dyck, who had worked in Genoa (Gregori, in 1983 exh. cat.). Cairo's *Mystic Marriage of St Catherine* (early 1640s; Toulouse, Mus. Augustins) is inspired by Correggio's *Madonna of St Jerome* (1527–8; Parma, G.N.); another altarpiece, the *Virgin and Child with SS Catherine of Alexandria and Catherine of Siena* (completed by 1645; Pavia, Certosa), which is indebted to van Dyck for the figures, is grander and more Roman. The composition is clear and symmetrical, and the background is enriched with noble Classical architecture. Thus by the early 1640s Cairo's art had become less idiosyncratic and began to follow the dominant tendencies of Seicento painting. His colours became lighter in tone, no longer playing on sharp contrasts of light and dark, and his figures fuller, inhabiting a more ample pictorial space. His technique also changed, the pigments becoming thinner and his brushwork looser and more painterly.

The pictures painted for Christina of France in the mid-1640s, *Moses Brought to Pharaoh's Daughter* (completed by 1645; Turin, Gal. Sabauda), *Christ Appearing to SS Christine and Valentine* (begun 1645; Turin, Gal. Sabauda) and the *Virgin Appearing to Petrina Tesio* (1647; Savigliano, Santuario Apparizione), developed the new tendencies of Cairo's art. The grandeur of *SS Augustine, Francis, Bernard and Dominic* (Milan, S Vittore al Corpo) suggests that this picture may date from the end of the 1640s; the figures are framed by monumental niches and unite the striking realism of Cairo's early works with the greater dignity and richer, more brilliant surfaces of the period around the middle of the century.

2. Francesco Cairo: *Death of Lucretia*, 1.23×1.20 m, 1640s (Madrid, Museo del Prado)

This change in style, which occurred in the work of other Milanese painters during the 1640s, was accompanied in Cairo's art by a change in expression. The formal and emotional excesses of his earlier pictures lessened. His paintings for private patrons during the 1640s illustrate this new direction. The languidly voluptuous *Death of Lucretia* (Madrid, Prado; see fig. 2) recalls similar subjects of tragic heroines by Guido Reni; the *Death of Cleopatra* (Milan, Bib. Ambrosiana) and *Pandora* (Pavia, Pin. Malaspina) reflect a study of 16th-century Venetian art.

(iii) 1648–65: later years in Milan. By 1648 Cairo had left Turin and had returned permanently to Milan. However, he continued until 1651 to hold property granted him in 1646 by Christine of France (which carried with it the title of count); and in 1652 her son Charles-Emmanuel II, Duke of Savoy, commissioned Cairo to advise about pictures on the Milanese art market. In 1654 he received payment for an altarpiece painted for the Venetian Carmelite church, the *Ecstasy of St Teresa* (Venice, S Maria di Nazareth). The sharp yellows, browns, reds and blues of this turbulent, visionary work are an interpretation of the neo-Venetian colouring of van Dyck. In other pictures the influence of 16th-century Venetian painting deepened and became more direct; he knew Venetian paintings in Milan and Turin and may also have visited Venice. Already by the late 17th century and the early 18th, critics described Cairo's later work as inspired by Titian and Veronese. His portraits particularly were considered Venetian; one of the two so far identified, the *Portrait of a Man* (Milan, Bib.

Ambrosiana; catalogued as Sebastiano Mazzoni), is markedly Venetian in character, with its streaked sky, studied reflections and rich colouring.

Otherwise Cairo continued to draw on the same Emilian and Genoese sources as in the 1640s. Van Dyck remained a constant inspiration, as is shown in Cairo's *St Francis Xavier Preaching to the Indians* (early 1650s; Modena, S Bartolomeo) and the *Assumption of the Virgin* (1662; San Giulio d'Orta, S Giulio all'Isola). Central Italian influences are also apparent. The *Martyrdom of St Stephen* exists in two versions (one dated 1660; Casale, S Stefano; the other Milan, S Stefano), both close variants of Pietro da Cortona's rendering of the same subject (St Petersburg, Hermitage). The mark of Cairo's late style is the increasing thinning out of form and pigment so that his painting loses its earlier solidity. His best late works are sensitive and diaphanous, with a high-keyed range of thinly applied blues, reds and yellows; others show a marked decline and can be vacuously derivative.

2. CRITICAL RECEPTION AND POSTHUMOUS REPUTATION. Cairo worked for a wide market and enjoyed handsome financial and social rewards. The sympathy he inspired in members of the House of Savoy played a major role in his career. In 1662, long after he had stopped working for them regularly, he asked Charles-Emmanuel II for a dowry to enable his daughter to enter a convent. The day after his death his widow notified the House of Savoy. The inventory of his collection drawn up two days after his death records an enormous stock, and it is possible that he also dealt in paintings. The contents are divided into two sections (see Colombo, in 1983 exh. cat.): the first, with 294 entries, records Cairo's own pictures and those by other artists, including Rubens, van Dyck, Guido Reni, Paris Bordone, Giulio Cesare Procaccini and Salvator Rosa; the second part lists 129 *abbozzi* (sketches) by Cairo, some on panel.

Some collectors, such as the churchman Cesare Biandrate (*d* after 14 March 1660), seem to have specialized in Cairo's work; others commissioned copies of his paintings not long after his death (Basso). Such references offer brief glimpses of his position in the rich, complex and fluid Seicento art market.

BIBLIOGRAPHY

C. Torre: *Il ritratto di Milano* (Milan, 1674, 2/1714/*R* 1973)
P. A. Orlandi: *Abecedario pittorico* (Bologna, 1701)
S. Matalon: 'Francesco del Cairo', *Riv. A.*, xii (1930), pp. 497–532
A. Baudi de Vesme: 'L'arte in Piemonte dal 1580 al 1650', *Atti Soc. Piemont. Archeol. & B.A.*, xiv/1 (1932), pp. 148–67; rev. as *Schede Vesme: L'arte in Piemonte dal XVI al XVIII secolo*, i (Turin, 1963–8), pp. 233–9
G. Testori: 'Su Francesco del Cairo', *Paragone*, iii/27 (1952), pp. 24–43
Mostra del manierismo piemontese e lombardo del seicento (exh. cat., ed. G. Testori; Turin, Mus. Civ. A. Art., 1955)
M. G. Brunori: 'Considerazioni sul primo tempo di Francesco Del Cairo', *Boll. A.*, xlix/3 (1964), pp. 236–45
——: 'Per Francesco Del Cairo (dal 1639 al 1665)', *Commentari*, xvi (1964), pp. 232–45
G. Grandi: 'L'ultimo Cairo a Torino', *Boll. Soc. Piemont. Archeol. & B.A.*, xviii (1964), pp. 110–19
S. Savini Branca: *Il collezionismo veneziano nel '600* (Padua, 1965)
Il seicento lombardo: Catalogo dei dipinti e delle sculture (exh. cat., ed. M. Valsecchi; Milan, Pal. Reale [1973])
Lombard Paintings, c. 1595–c. 1630: The Age of Federico Borromeo (exh. cat., ed. P. Cannon-Brookes; Birmingham, A.G., 1974)
Francesco Cairo, 1607–65 (exh. cat., ed. G. Testori; Varese, Mus. Civ. Villa Mirabello, 1983)
L. Basso: 'Aggiunte al catalogo di Francesco Cairo', *A. Lombarda*, lxxiii–lxxv (1985), pp. 81–7
P. Skakeshaft: ' "To Much Bewiched with those Intysing Things" ': The Letters of James, Third Marques of Hamilton and Basil, Viscount Fielding', *Burl. Mag.*, cxxvii (1986), pp. 114–32
F. Porzio and others: *Pinacoteca di Brera: Scuola lombarda, ligure e piemontese, 1535–1796* (Milan, 1989), pp. 176–90

NANCY WARD NEILSON

Caisra. *See* CERVETERI.

Cai Xiang [Ts'ai Hsiang; *zi* Junmo] (*b* Xianyou County, Fujian Province, 1012; *d* Xianyou County, 1067). Chinese calligrapher, scholar–official and poet. From an undistinguished provincial family, he rose to prominence as an official after passing the national civil-service examination to become a *jinshi* in 1030. He attained his highest posts at the courts of the emperors Renzong (*reg* 1023–63) and Yingzong (*reg* 1064–7) during the ascendency of the reform faction led by Fan Zhongyan (989–1052) and OUYANG XIU. Cai is traditionally designated one of the Four Great Calligraphers of the Northern Song (960–1127), along with Su Shi, Huang Tingjian and Mi Fu (*see* CHINA, §IV, 2(iv)(a)). The oldest of the four, Cai played an important role in setting the direction for the development of Song (960–1279) calligraphy and was praised by Su Shi as the greatest calligrapher of the period.

As a calligrapher, Cai achieved distinction in several established scripts: regular script (*kaishu*), running script (*xingshu*), cursive script (*caoshu*) and clerical script (*lishu*). He is best known, however, for his pioneering contribution to Song regular script (Song *kai*), also called running regular script (*xing kaishu*). Song regular script combined naturalness and informality of execution with clarity of structure, permitted variations in stroke formation, including abbreviations and ligatures, and, like running script, displayed an exposed brushtip (*see* CHINA, §IV, 1(ii)). It was dominant from the late Northern Song until the end of the Southern Song (1127–1279), and Cai's influence is clearly visible in the writing style of the Southern Song emperor GAOZONG and the calligrapher Zhang Jizhi (1186–1266). Cai probably studied initially with Zhou Yue (*fl c.* 1023–48), who is thought to have practised the imperially sanctioned style of Wang Xizhi (*see* WANG (i), (1)). Later, Cai encountered the more muscular and disciplined calligraphy of YAN ZHENQING, some examples of which were owned by his friend Ouyang Xiu. Eventually he was also able to examine good copies of Wang Xizhi's calligraphy, including the *Lanting xu* ('Orchid pavilion preface'; destr.; *see* CHINA, §IV, 2(ii)(d)). Cai's mature style achieved a synthesis of the elegant fluency of Wang Xizhi and the precise character structures and disciplined stroke shapes of Yan Zhenqing. Cai's achievement in synthesizing the Yan and Wang styles is probably best represented by his informal letters of the 1060s, written in Song regular script and running script (Taipei, N. Pal. Mus.). Cai's most famous surviving work is perhaps his *Xie ci yushu shibiao* ('Poem-memorial of gratitude for a gift of imperial calligraphy'; 1052; Tokyo, Mus. Callig.). Written in small, angular regular script, the calligraphy is unusually formal because it was intended as a submission to Renzong, who had honoured Cai by personally writing out his style-name (*zi*). The *Xie ci yushu shibiao* exhibits the firm control and precision associated with Yan Zhenqing, but the languidly elongated diagonal stroke (*na*) comes from the Wang tradition.

BIBLIOGRAPHY

Franke: 'Ts'ai Hsiang'
K. Shimonaka, ed.: *Shodō zenshū* [Complete collection of calligraphy], xv (Tokyo, 2/1954), pp. 8–9, 161–3, 181, pls 8–21
'Song Cai Xiang moji' [Calligraphy of Cai Xiang of the Song], *Gugong fashu* [Calligraphy in the National Palace Museum], viii (exh. cat., Taipei, 1965)
H. Franke, ed.: *Sung Biographies*, iv (Wiesbaden, 1976), pp. 1026–9
Tuotuo and others: *Song shi* [History of the Song] (Beijing, 1977), *juan* cccxx, pp. 10397–401
Cai Xiang moji jingpin [Masterpieces of Cai Xiang's calligraphy] (Shanghai, 1981)
Shan Guoqiang: 'Cai Xiang de jijian cunshi moji' [Some extant pieces of calligraphy by Cai Xiang], *Shufa congkan* [Journal of calligraphy], i (Beijing, 1981), pp. 20–22
Shui Laiyou: *Cai Xiang shufa shiliao ji* [Collected historical materials for Cai Xiang's calligraphy] (Shanghai, 1983)
A. McNair: 'The Sung Calligrapher Ts'ai Hsiang', *Bulletin of Sung–Yuan Studies*, xviii (Ithaca, NY, 1986), pp. 61–75

JULIA K. MURRAY

Caja-espiga [Sp.: 'peg-and-socket joint']. Construction method that enables an exact joint to be made between two pieces of wood, stone or other material by means of a tenon or peg (*espiga*) on one piece fitted into a corresponding mortice or socket (*caja*) in the other. In Pre-Columbian Mesoamerica the *caja-espiga* joint was used particularly in sculpture, both free-standing and architectural. Its origins probably lie in OLMEC sculpture, as represented in Monument 34 from SAN LORENZO TENOCHTITLÁN, the figure of a kneeling man carved in andesite (h. 790 mm, *c.* 1200–750 BC; Mexico City, Mus. N. Antropol.). A cavity in the left shoulder shows where a tenon in the arm, either fixed or articulated, would have been inserted.

At TEOTIHUACÁN (*fl c.* 250 BC–AD 800) in the Basin of Mexico this type of joint was used for assembling blocks of carved stone, strengthening the vertical elements and resisting lateral movement. It was commonly used for fixing the stone ring markers to the walls of ballcourts (*see* BALLCOURT, §1) or to free-standing carved upright shafts, also probably ballcourt markers, as in the case of the misnamed Stele of La Ventilla (a compound at Teotihuacán), where *caja-espiga* joints were used to fix the ring and its three-part shaft together (Mexico City, Mus. N. Antropol.). *Caja-espiga* joints were used in other sculptures at the Palace of Quetzalpapálotl. From the Early Post-Classic period (*c.* AD 900–*c.* 1200) the Toltecs in TULA changed the practice of using internal wooden supports in buildings, inherited from Teotihuacán, frequently substituting *caja-espiga* joints in the assembly of the parts of pillars or columns. The best-known examples are the four Atlantean figures, square pillars and serpent columns of the Temple of Tlahuizcalpantecuhtli (*in situ*; see fig.).

In the high cultures of the central Andes the *caja-espiga* was used to fix carved stone masks or heads to the walls of temples and pyramidal platforms. Some of the best-known examples are the grotesque masks fixed on the terrace facings on Initial period (*c.* 1800–*c.* 900 BC) CHAVÍN DE HUÁNTAR and the hollow-eyed heads attached to the walls of the sunken court at Middle Horizon TIAHUANACO.

BIBLIOGRAPHY

I. Marquina: *Arquitectura prehispánica* (Mexico City, 1950, 2/1964/*R* 1981)
J. R. Acosta: *El Palacio de Quetzalpapálotl* (Mexico City, 1964)
B. de la Fuente: *Escultura monumental olmeca* (Mexico City, 1973)
D. Heyden and P. Gendrop: *Pre-Columbian Architecture in Mesoamerica* (New York, 1975)
M. E. Miller: *The Art of Mesoamerica from Olmec to Aztec* (London, 1986)
M. E. Moseley: *The Incas and their Ancestors: The Archaeology of Peru* (London, 1992)

PAUL GENDROP

Cajahuaringa, José Milner (*b* Huarochirí, nr Lima, 29 Feb 1932). Peruvian painter. He graduated from the Escuela Nacional Superior de Bellas Artes in Lima in 1959, winning a gold medal, and taught there from 1972. In his paintings he played with the complementary colours, trapezoidal images and geometrical forms that typify the architecture of ancient Tahuantinsuyu and with the warm tonalities used in native weaving. He maintained a steady balance in his work between abstraction and figuration, although the representational aspect became more dominant in later years.

BIBLIOGRAPHY

J. M. Ugarte Eléspuru: *Pintura y escultura en el Perú contemporáneo* (Lima, 1970)
L. E. Tord: 'Historia de las artes plásticas en el Perú', *Historia del Perú*, ix (Lima, 1980)

LUIS ENRIQUE TORD

Cajal, Santiago Ramón y. *See* RAMÓN Y CAJAL, SANTIAGO.

Cajamarca. Peruvian city and capital of the department of Cajamarca in northern Peru. It is also notable for being the site of a Pre-Columbian culture and the centre of distribution of a ceramic style. It is situated at an altitude of *c.* 2750 m in a fertile Andean valley and has a population of *c.* 70,000. Settlements dating back to the Early Horizon or Chavín period (*c.* 900–*c.* 200 BC), such as Huaca Loma and Layzón, have been discovered on the outskirts of the town. In the hills above the town, 14 km to the south-west, the Cumbe Mayo aqueduct, which is 7.8 km long and probably contemporary with Chavín culture, feeds the fertile Cajamarca valley. Also in the vicinity is the site of Otuzco, with its Middle Horizon cemetery, comprising mainly niches carved into the stone and an associated fortress. The modern city is a popular holiday destination for Peruvians.

1. PRE-COLUMBIAN CULTURE. This is represented primarily by a localized pottery style dated *c.* AD 400–*c.* 1000. The ceramic style was first defined in 1949 by Henri and Paule Reichlen, who described four phases (Cajamarca I–IV). Commonly associated with the city, however, is the Cajamarca Cursive style of painted pottery, which had a wide distribution, first in the mountains and later on the coast. The success of Cajamarca pottery was rooted in its raw material, a high-grade kaolinite clay. In the last few centuries BC, South American potters learnt how to fire this to sufficiently high temperatures to produce a thin, hard, very white paste. Between *c.* 200 BC and *c.* AD 600 other highland cultures, especially to the

Caja-espiga construction used in the assembly of Atlantean figures, square pillars and round columns at the Temple of Tlahuizcalpantecuhtli, Tula, Early Post-Classic period, *c.* AD 900–1200

south, also experimented with kaolin clays, but the Cajamarca artisans were the most skilled. Cajamarca potters produced simple shapes. Open bowls measuring *c.* 120–240 mm in diameter were the commonest early form, and angled bowls with low straight sides, usually provided with low ring bases, were also popular. More hemispherical forms appeared somewhat later, and tripod legs were added after *c.* AD 800. Ceramic spoons in many different sizes and shapes were also produced in large numbers.

Unlike many of the better-known ceramic styles of the Central Andean area (*see* SOUTH AMERICA, PRE-COLUMBIAN, §III, 5), the Cajamarca sequence includes a narrow range of naturalistic representation, and modelling is exceptionally rare. Instead, vessel decoration is based on geometric design. The style is an exuberant one, pleasing in its symmetry and attention to detail. The 'Cursive' style was so named by A. L. Kroeber because it is typified by small hooks, loops and spirals quickly and lightly drawn with a soft brush to produce a close resemblance to cursive writing. Generally both the interiors and exteriors of bowls were painted. Bowls with rounded sides had panels defined by horizontal lines running around the entire circumference of the vessel on both the inner and outer surfaces. Angled plates presented three design fields: the exterior wall, interior wall and the bottom of the plate. These fields were usually further subdivided and the resultant spaces filled with short curved lines and other cursive elements. The most frequent colouring was brown or black on the natural white background, but a red or reddish brown was also often used.

Anthropomorphic and zoomorphic figures frequently occur in the Cajamarca Cursive style; they are usually small and often repeated symmetrically on the vessel. Human faces are rendered schematically with only a circle and a few curved lines representing the nose and eyes. Complete figures have block-like bodies, with fine lines representing the disproportionately small hands and feet. Such figures are usually repeated in a line around the vessel wall, often with hands linked, as if for dancing. Animal figures are shown with their bodies in profile and their heads either in profile or in frontal view. Some of those represented are felines, with claws and teeth emphasized, while others resemble the local viscacha (a type of rodent).

From *c.* AD 400 onward, Cajamarca pottery was a prestigious trade commodity in the sierra, appearing as far south as Huari. In its later, more decadent form, the style influenced north coast pottery after the waning of the MOCHE style; between *c.* AD 800 and *c.* 1000 pieces modelled according to north coast tradition were painted with fine cursive elements typical of the Cajamarca style.

BIBLIOGRAPHY

H. Reichlen and P. Reichlen: 'Recherches archéologiques dans les Andes de Cajamarca: Premier rapport de la Mission Ethnologique Française au Pérou septentrional', *J. Soc. Américanistes*, xxxviii (1949), pp. 137–74

K. Terada and Y. Onuki: *Excavations at Huacaloma in the Cajamarca Valley, Peru, 1979* (Tokyo, 1982)

THERESA LANGE TOPIC

2. LATER HISTORY AND URBAN DEVELOPMENT. The town was built around the hill known as Ingaconga in Quechua (later San Francisco de Monte Alverna; now Santa Apolonia), which is crowned by a shrine that is probably Early Horizon. After its capture *c.* 1460 by the Inca, the town served as a base for the conquest of the Chimú kingdom. Under the Inca the shrine was fortified and the town below enlarged. Inca remains include the polygonal-style so-called Incas' Palace on Jirón Amalia Puga. Some sources suggest that Cajamarca had a triangular main square (although trapezoidal is more likely), with a ceremonial dais (*usnu* or *ushnu*) surrounded by assembly halls (*kallankas*) with an associated Temple of the Sun and *Akllawasi* (Quechua: House of the Chosen Women). After Pizarro's arrival (1532) and the ambush and execution of the Inca Atahuallpa (1533), a grid plan of streets was laid out around a central Plaza de Armas, largely obliterating evidence of the Inca settlement.

The modern city retains many of its colonial buildings. In the centre are mansions, churches and the cathedral, which developed from an earlier adobe chapel, apparently constructed in three days. A royal decree (1665) ordered the construction of a more substantial, stone building (1682–1762; *see* PERU, §III, 1), with a barrel vault over the nave. The plan is simple, but there is rich decoration, including figures and vines, grapes and clusters of fruit, spiralling up the columns. The church became a cathedral in 1908. S Francisco (or S Antonio de Padua) was built from 1699 on the site of the Temple of the Sun; Matías Pérez Palomino began the project, which was completed by José Manuel and Francisco de Tapia. It has an unusually tall Baroque Plateresque façade. The central portal is richly carved. A belfry was added in 1941, and the towers were completed in the 1960s. The adjacent Capilla de la Virgén de los Dolores contains some fine stonework and catacombs.

The church of El Belén (or Belém; 1684–1744) has a tall, narrow retable façade flanked by an expanse of undecorated stone. Inside, the large, stone cupola is punctuated by windows and a ring of sculpted and painted winged angels that appear to support the roof. The upper portion of the cupola is decorated by multicoloured, intricate, chainlike garlands on a pale blue background. Alongside the church is an attractive courtyard and two hospitals, one for men (1763) and the other for women (1774), built by Juan de Belém. The Colegio de Belém (1672), on the opposite side of the street from the church, has a small belfry and a richly ornamented façade. Other colonial churches include La Recoleta (1668–78), La Inmaculada (1747–1806) and S José (1681–3). Cajamarca has at least 104 decorated stone portals, notable examples of which include those of the Casona de los Condes de Uceda (now a bank), the Palacio de Espinache and the Casa de los Castañeda. Colonial architecture in Cajamarca incorporates both interesting features from the coastal area and fine stone ornamentation typical of the Central and Southern Andes. The city has few outstanding examples of early republican architecture; styles are essentially local and functional or, in a few cases, refer to North American examples.

BIBLIOGRAPHY

P. F. Cortázar: *Cajamarca* (1971), vi of *Documental del Perú* (Lima, 1966–)

J. Dammert Bellido: 'Trabajo indígena bajo el Virreynato', *La Prensa* [Lima] (29 Oct 1976), p. 19

R. Ravines: *Cajamarca prehispánica* (Lima, 1985)

W. IAIN MACKAY

Cajés [Caxés, Caxesi, Caxete]. Italian family of artists, active in Spain.

(1) Patricio [Patrizio] **Cajés** (*b* Arezzo, *c.* 1540; *d* Madrid, 14 May 1612). Painter and designer. He is first known to have painted in Rome, where in 1567 he and Romulo Cincinato (*c.* 1502–93) were engaged by Luis de Requesens, Ambassador to Philip III, to work for three years at the Spanish royal court. The two artists painted mythological frescoes (*c.* 1568; destr.) in Philip's hunting lodges at the Palacio del Pardo and at the Palacio de Valsaín, Segovia, and also executed scenes of imaginary architecture (*c.* 1568; destr.) in some rooms of the Alcázar (destr.) in Madrid. Cajés also drew up the plan *c.* 1570 for the altarpiece (1599) of S Felipe el Real, Madrid. After the court moved to Valladolid in 1601, he, Bartolomé Carducho and Fabrizio Castello (i) were commissioned to decorate (*c.* 1605) a large ballroom in the palace of the Conde de Miranda (destr.), Valladolid, a building acquired by Philip III around that time. Cajés's last fresco, executed in the Galería de la Reina of the Palacio del Pardo, depicts several scenes from the *Life of Joseph* (1608–12; destr.). While at work on the fresco, he became seriously ill and was incapacitated; he was taken to Madrid but failed to recover. As most of his works have been lost, little is known about his style of painting. He was also interested in architecture, translated Jacopo Vignola's treatise *Regola delli cinque ordini d'architettura* and designed a number of projects that were never realized (e.g. plan for the joining of El Pardo with the Casa de Campo, Madrid; Madrid, Bib. Pal. Real).

WRITINGS

trans.: J. Vignola: *Regola delli cinque ordini d'architettura* (Rome, 1562) as *La regla de las cinco órdenes de arquitectura* (Madrid, 1593)

BIBLIOGRAPHY

Ceán Bermúdez
Llaguno y Amirola: *Noticias* (1829), iii, pp. 111–13
J. Martí y Monsó: *Estudios histórico-artísticos* (Valladolid, 1901), pp. 278, 607
J. J. Martín González: 'Arte y artistas del siglo XVII en la corte', *Archv Esp. A.*, xxxi (1958), pp. 125–42

TRINIDAD DE ANTONIO SÁENZ

(2) Eugenio Cajés (*b* Madrid, 1575; *d* Madrid, 15 Dec 1634). Painter and draughtsman, son of (1) Patricio Cajés. He undoubtedly served his apprenticeship with his father, with whom he also collaborated on his earliest commissions. Eugenio Cajés's *Meeting of Joachim and Anne* (Madrid, Real Acad. S Fernando, Mus.) was probably painted for an altarpiece that his father contracted for in 1604. It reveals, in both the sense of monumentality and the rather mannered lines of the drapery, the influence of the fresco paintings carried out by Pellegrino Tibaldi at the Escorial.

Eugenio Cajés began working for Philip III in the Palacio del Pardo in 1608 and was appointed Painter to the King in 1612. His first important work is the fresco decoration of the chapel of the Virgen del Sagrario, Toledo Cathedral, carried out in collaboration with Vicente Carducho in 1615–16. The subjects painted by Cajés include saints (*St Sebastian* and *St Athanasius* on the altar, for example); the *Immaculate Conception* and the *Birth of the Virgin*; and, on the ceilings, *Allegories*. In these he subjugated his personal style to the need for uniformity, but the canvases he did for the lateral chapels of the Sagrario are more individual. *St Leocadia* reveals his interest in the effects of light. The angels in the foreground epitomize the softness of modelling for which he was noted by his contemporaries and which is derived from his study of Correggio; while the angels above, dramatically foreshortened and defined by hard contours, suggest an interest in the art of Caravaggio (perhaps through Juan Bautista Maino's paintings for S Pedro Martir, Toledo, begun in 1612). This tendency towards greater naturalism characterizes the paintings of Cajés's maturity.

There are *c.* 100 known drawings by Cajés, an unusually rich collection in comparison with the numbers of drawings left by other contemporaneous painters in Spain. His drawings, like the paintings, reflect the influence of the Escorial school, especially Federico Zuccaro. The figures tend to be elongated, and dramatic chiaroscuro effects are achieved through the use of pen and sepia wash over black chalk on white paper, while in *Virgin of the Sagrario* (*c.* 1615; Madrid, Bib. N.) he used red ochre on buff paper.

Cajés continued to work for the court, painting mythological subjects, including the *Story of Agamemnon* (1631) for the Alcázar (destr.), Madrid, and working in fresco and gilded stucco for the Palacio del Pardo. He contributed two paintings to the series of victories commissioned from various artists for the Hall of Realms of the Buen Retiro Palace: *Recapture of San Juan, Puerto Rico* (1633–4; Madrid, Prado) and *Recapture of St Martin* (untraced).

BIBLIOGRAPHY

D. Angulo Iñiguez and A. E. Pérez Sánchez: *Historia de la pintura española: Escuela madrileña del primer tercio del siglo XVII* (Madrid, 1969)
——: *A Corpus of Spanish Drawings: Madrid, 1600–50* (London, 1977)

SUZANNE STRATTON

Calakmul. Site of the Pre-Columbian MAYA culture in Campeche, Mexico. It was the largest and most populous Maya city ever built and is notable for the number of stelae and monoliths erected by its ancient inhabitants. It was occupied from the Middle Pre-Classic period (*c.* 1000–*c.* 300 BC) onwards and flourished in the Late Classic period (*c.* AD 600–*c.* 900) as one of several powerful Maya states. Some of its carved stelae, columns and figures are in the Museo Arqueológico, Etnográfico e Histórico del Estado, Campeche.

Calakmul was rediscovered in 1931 by C. L. Lundell and studied by various scholars, including Sylvanus Morley and Karl Ruppert in the 1930s and 1940s. Since the late 1970s, William Folan and numerous Mexican scholars have mapped some 6500 structures at the site and determined that the ancient city covered *c.* 30 sq. km. Regional analysis shows that Calakmul was the centre of an independent political sphere, possibly with a certain deference paid to the Maya city of TIKAL, to the south in the Guatemalan Petén. At the contemporary Maya site of COPÁN city name-glyphs have been identified on Stele A designating Calakmul, Tikal, Copán and PALENQUE as four Maya regional capitals of the 8th century AD. As such, Calakmul was surrounded by smaller, dependent sites, which together exemplify a politico-economically ranked settlement pattern. The sites of Oxpemul (to the north), Muñeca (north-east), Altamíra, Balakbal, Naachtún, MIRADOR, Uxul and Sasilha comprised second-rank centres, each with its own cluster of smaller, dependent towns. The rulers of Calakmul probably held sway over a territory of between 5000 and 8000 sq. km.

The architectural core of Calakmul comprises numerous plazas and courtyards formed by raised platforms and multi-roomed, pyramid-towered buildings forming several clusters, including a ballcourt. One section includes a 6-m high wall. Abel Morales Lopez's analysis of the central area indicates that the civic centre may have been laid out as an enormous sundial. Form and façade decoration is in RÍO BEC style but is less ornate than in examples found at Río Bec itself or at Becán or Xpuhil. Structure III (20.5×16.0 m), for example, dated by associated inscriptions to the 7th century AD, comprises at least 12 intercommunicating rooms beneath a central tower and two smaller flanking towers supporting false temples, each with an elaborate roof-comb. Two royal tombs have been found at Calakmul, one containing a jadeite portrait mask (Campeche, Mus. Arqueol. Etnog. & Hist. Estado) with thick-lipped, drooping mouth, corpulent cheeks and inlaid eyes, wearing a hood or helmet-like headpiece with an elaborate, protruding top. Most of Calakmul's 108 stelae and monoliths were erected in the site nucleus. Only 30 stelae are either plain or so heavily eroded that their carvings are obscured. A total of 25 comparatively smaller stelae have been found at 18 of the surrounding sites. Inscriptions on the stelae not only give dates generally within the 7th and 8th centuries AD but also include the dates of AD 514 and 810. Additional inscriptions describe nobles and other important personages and their marriages and alliances and include one of the first mentions of Motul, a Late Classic Maya centre in the far north of Yucatán, indicating the range of Calakmul's contacts. Figures on the stelae represent Maya lords, standing with their feet at 180°, their faces in profile, within rectangular frames and groups of inscriptions. Many stand over smaller, captive figures, resembling stelae at PIEDRAS NEGRAS and YAXCHILÁN. Their costumes are elaborate and include complex, multi-faceted headdresses and jewellery. Many figures hold staffs or insignia of office.

BIBLIOGRAPHY

I. Marquina: *Arquitectura prehispánica* (Mexico City, 1950, 2/1964/*R* 1981), pp. 571–6

G. Kubler: *The Art and Architecture of Ancient America*, Pelican Hist. A. (Harmondsworth, 1962, rev. 3/1984), p. 228

M. P. Weaver: *The Aztecs, Maya and their Predecessors: Archaeology of Mesoamerica* (New York, 1972, rev. 2/1981), pp. 180, 282, 329, 352, 355

J. S. Henderson: *The World of the Ancient Maya* (Ithaca, 1981), pp. 165–6

W. J. Folan: 'Calakmul, Campeche: Su centro urbano, estado y región en relación al concepto del resto de la Gran Mesoamérica', *Información*, ix (1985), pp. 161–85

J. Marcus: *The Inscription of Calakmul: Royal Marriage at a Maya City in Campeche, Mexico*, University of Michigan, Museum of Anthropology Technical Report, xxi (Ann Arbor, 1987)

W. J. Folan: 'Calakmul, Campeche: El nacimiento de la tradición clásica en la Gran Mesoamérica', *Información*, xiii (1988), pp. 122–90

M. Coyoc Ramírez: 'Los enterramientos humanos asociados a la Estructura III de Calakmul, Campeche', *Primer Congreso Internacional de Mayistas, Homenaje a Alberto Ruz Lhuiller: San Cristobal de las Casas, Chiapas, Mexico, 1989*

J. May Hau and others: *El mapa de las ruinas de Calakmul, Campeche, Mexico* (Campeche, 1990)

W. J. Folan: 'Calakmul, Campeche: A Centralized Urban Administrative Center in the Northern Petén', *World Archaeol.*, xxiv (1992), pp. 158–68

DAVID M. JONES

Calamatta, Luigi (*b* Civitavecchia, 21 June 1802; *d* Milan, 8 March 1869). Italian printmaker. He studied in Rome under Antonio Ricciani (1775–1836) and Domenico Marchetti (1780–1838). In 1823 he went to Paris, where he became friendly with Ingres, whom he had met when the painter was working in Florence in 1820. After participating in the 1830 Revolution against Charles X, Calamatta was recommended by Ingres to the new king, Louis-Philippe, to direct publication of the catalogue of history paintings at Versailles, *Catalogue des planches gravées composant les fonds de la Calcographie* (Paris, 1881). In 1834 he became famous for his engraving of the *Death Mask of Napoleon I*. From 1838 to 1860 he was a professor at the Académie Royale des Beaux-Arts in Brussels, and subsequently at the Accademia di Brera in Milan. In Brussels he perfected the technique of steel-facing copper-plates so as to obtain the maximum number of un-retouched prints from a single plate. Many of the plates for his engravings from Old Masters, such as Leonardo da Vinci's *Mona Lisa* (1855), are preserved in the Calcografia Nazionale, Rome, and the Museo Nazionale in Civitavecchia.

BIBLIOGRAPHY

V. Corbucci: *Luigi Calamatta, incisore* (Civitavecchia, 1886)

S. Bastanelli: *Collezione comunale delle incisioni di Luigi Calamatta* (Civitavecchia, 1951)

L. Servolini: 'Luigi Calamatta', *Dizionario illustrato degli incisori italiani moderni e contemporanei* (Milan, 1955), pp. 142–3

STEFANIA MASSARI

Calame, Alexandre (*b* Vevey, Vaud, 28 May 1810; *d* Menton, 17 March 1864). Swiss painter, draughtsman and printmaker. He studied under François Diday in Geneva and then travelled to Paris (1837), to the Netherlands and Düsseldorf (1838), to Italy (1844) and to London (1850). Despite his frail health he spent each summer painting in the mountains of the Bernese Oberland and central Switzerland, where he produced the drawings and studies from nature that were later used in his studio compositions. A fervent Calvinist, he saw his subjects—the grandiose forces of nature, stormy summits and torrents as well as calm lakes—as expressions of Divine power. He enjoyed success during his lifetime, partly due to a firm adherence to a conventional landscape painting tradition. Among his best-known pictures are *Storm at Handeck* (1839; Geneva, Mus. A. & Hist.), *Sunlight on the Upper Alps of the Valais, Opposite the Range of Mont-Rose* (1843–4; Neuchâtel, Mus. A. & Hist.), *Ruins of the Temples of Paestum* (1847; Leipzig, Mus. Bild. Kst.) and *Lake of the Four Cantons* (1855; Riggisberg, Abegg-Stift.). Calame also left a large number of prints, notably lithographs, and a quantity of drawings (Geneva, Cab. Est. Mus. A. & Hist. and elsewhere).

BIBLIOGRAPHY

E. Rambert: *Alexandre Calame: Sa vie et son oeuvre d'après les sources originales* (Paris, 1894)

A. Schreiber-Favre: *Alexandre Calame: Peintre, paysagiste, graveur et lithographe* (Geneva, 1934)

A. Calabi and A. Schreiber-Favre: 'Les Eaux-fortes et les lithographies d'Alexandre Calame', *Graph. Kst.*, ii (1937), pp. 64–77, 110–17

A. Schreiber-Favre: *La Lithographie artistique en Suisse au 19e siècle: Alexandre Calame, le paysage* (Neuchâtel, 1966)

V. Anker: *Alexandre Calame: Vie et oeuvre*, Geneva, Mus. Rath. cat. (Fribourg, 1987) [cat. rais. of the ptgs]

Dessins d'Alexandre Calame (1810–64) (exh. cat., Geneva, Mus. A. & Hist., 1987)

VALENTINA ANKER

Calamelli, Virgiliotto [Virgilio] (*fl* Faenza, 1531; *d* Faenza, *c.* 1570). Italian potter. He was the son of Giovanni da Calamello, and there are plenty of documents relating to him, especially after 1540, when as a practising potter he went to sell his wares in Bologna. He was so successful that citizenship was conferred on him. In FAENZA his workshop was situated in the S Vitale quarter, where there were many other potteries during the 16th century. An inventory of 1556 (Grigioni, pp. 143–51) describes his economic position and the progress of his workshop. Apparently his was among the most well-established workshops in Faenza, able to produce huge table-services, including water jugs, salt-cellars, dishes and vases (e.g. vase with lion handles, *c.* 1550–60; Brunswick, Herzog Anton Ulrich-Mus.). In 1563, for health reasons, he handed his shop over to Leonardo Bettisi, known as Don Pino (*fl* 1563–89), also from Faenza. Calamelli is recognized as an important exponent of the *Compendiario* (sketchy) style, which was typical of the so-called *bianchi di Faenza* wares. His most important works were stamped with the monogram VR FA.

BIBLIOGRAPHY
C. Grigioni: 'I Calamelli maiolicari di Faenza: Documenti', *Faenza*, xxii (1934), pp. 50–54, 88–90, 143–53
G. Gennari: 'Virgiliotto Calamelli e la sua bottega', *Faenza*, xlii (1956), pp. 57–60

CARMEN RAVANELLI GUIDOTTI

Calandra, Davide (*b* Turin, 21 Oct 1856; *d* Turin, 8 Sept 1915). Italian sculptor. He studied at the Accademia Albertina di Belle Arti in Turin, where he was a pupil of Alfonso Balzico and Odoardo Tabacchi. In 1880 he participated for the first time in a public exhibition, held in the Parco del Valentino, Turin, with a plaster study representing *Penelope's Vigil.* This was immediately well received by both the public and critics, and he continued to be highly regarded, although the ease of his success, due partly to his personal qualities, prevented him from reaching a full expressive development. His early works were largely limited to realistic plaster or terracotta studies with unconventional themes (e.g. *Royal Tiger*, exh. Munich, 1883; ex-Chiesa priv. col., Turin, see Micheli, p. 145). In the period that followed Calandra worked on rural subjects, for example the bronze *Plough* (1888; Rome, G.N.A. Mod.); some were historical and all were executed in a sketchy realist style. Calandra then adopted a more ambitious symbolism for large celebratory sculptures. He beat Leonardo Bistolfi in a competition for the execution of the monument to *Prince Amedeo d'Aosta* in Turin in 1892: the work was realized in 1902 in the Parco del Valentino. The monument to *Giuseppe Zanardelli* (1906–9) in Brescia was executed in a more monumental manner and with greater attention to its setting. It was built of marble and bronze with a classical scenic background. In 1907 Calandra worked with Edoardo Rubino on the monument to *Gen. Bartolomeo Nitre* in Avenida Alvear, Buenos Aires, and the following year he was commissioned to produce a gigantic bronze relief depicting the *Apotheosis of the House of Savoy* for the parliamentary chamber at Montecitorio in Rome. This was completed in 1912 and exhibited at the International Exhibition in Amsterdam. Calandra produced designs for coins and continued to produce portraits and funerary monuments, as well as works expressing his personal taste, for example the equestrian bronze *Conqueror* (1904; Turin, Gal. Civ. A. Mod.), which may be considered his masterpiece. In 1902, with Bistolfi, he was among the founders of the Turin review *L'arte decorativa moderna*, which conducted a vigorous battle for the affirmation of contemporary art.

BIBLIOGRAPHY
DBI
C. Ricci: *Davide Calandra* (Milan, 1916)
L. Caramel and C. Pirovano: *Galleria d'arte moderna di Milano*, v (Milan, 1975), p. 36
G. Panazza: 'La scultura', *Brescia postromantica e liberty: 1880–1915* (Brescia, 1985), pp. 172, 264
G. Dainotti: 'Davide Calandra', *Il liberty nell'altra Torino* (Turin, 1987), p. 28
M. de Micheli: *La scultura dell'ottocento* (Turin, 1992), pp. 145–9

VALERIO TERRAROLI

Calandrelli, Alexander (Emil Lodovico) (*b* Berlin, 9 May 1834; *d* Berlin, 26 May 1903). German sculptor. He was the son of an Italian lapidary who taught at the Gewerbe-Institut in Berlin. He began to study sculpture at the Königliche Akademie der Künste in Berlin in 1847 but had to leave three years later because of financial problems, and after 1852 Friedrich Drake became his mentor and teacher. Between 1855 and 1863 Calandrelli worked in the studio of August Fischer, where he produced small-scale sculpture, and during the same period he began to exhibit his work in Berlin. In 1864 he set up his own workshop, initially producing mostly decorative work, and in 1871 he achieved recognition with his first major public commission. This was for one of the four reliefs for the *Triumphal Column* in Berlin, which depicted scenes from the war of Prussia and Austria with Denmark (1864). Other important commissions followed. In 1874 he received a professorship, in 1887 he was elected to the Senat of the Akademie in Berlin and from then on he also enjoyed royal patronage. Calandrelli contributed to many decorative schemes of public buildings, producing, for example, the terracotta reliefs (1879) for the town hall in Berlin. Among his many statues were a marble figure of the painter *Peter Cornelius* (1880; Berlin, Altes Mus.) and the equestrian monuments of *King Frederick William IV* (1886) and of *Emperor William I* (1893). With his bronze statuette of *Elector Frederick I of Hohenzollern* (1891) he entered the competition for a monument of the Elector for Friesach. This was originally won by Johannes Boese, but the decision was overruled by the emperor in favour of Calandrelli.

BIBLIOGRAPHY
Thieme–Becker
P. Bloch and W. Grzimek: *Das klassische Berlin: Die Berliner Bildhauerschule im neunzehnten Jahrhundert* (Berlin, Frankfurt am Main and Vienna, 1978), cols 173–6
Ethos und Pathos: Die Berliner Bildhauerschule, 1786–1914, 2 vols (exh. cat., ed. P. Bloch, S. Einholz and J. von Simson; Berlin, Staatl. Museen Preuss. Kultbes., 1990), esp., pp. 65–7

HANNELORE HÄGELE

Calandrucci, Giacinto (*b* Palermo, 1646; *d* Palermo, 1707). Italian painter and draughtsman. He was trained in Rome, where he was first a pupil of the painter and engraver Pietro del Pò (1610–92), who also came from Palermo. At an unknown date he moved to the studio of Carlo Maratti and, with Giuseppe Passeri, became a favourite pupil. He was clearly linked to Maratti's workshop for a long period and perfectly assimilated his teacher's idiom, though without attaining his elegance and precision. In the 1680s Calandrucci executed various decorative frescoes in Roman palazzi: the *Four Seasons* in the Palazzo Lante; mythological frescoes in the gallery of the Palazzo Muti–Papazzurri; the decoration (untraced) of the gallery of the Palazzo Strozzi–Besso; and a ceiling fresco, the *Sacrifice of Ceres*, in the Villa Falconieri at Frascati. He also painted idyllic pastoral scenes, among them two pictures at Burghley House, Stamford, England. His secular decorations are more successful than the sometimes clumsy and banal altarpieces and ceiling frescoes that he executed in Roman churches. These include the high altar, the *Virgin and Child with Saints*, a *Baptism* and ceiling frescoes, all in the Cimini Chapel of S Antonio del Portoghesi (from 1682), a *Virgin and Child with St Anne and Saints* in frescoes and canvases in S Bonaventura (before 1686), a *Holy Family with St Anne* and *St Anthony of Padua*, both in S Paolo della Regola (*c.* 1700), and frescoes in S Maria dell'Orto (*c.* 1700–05). In 1705 he returned to Palermo, where he began the decoration of the oratory of S Lorenzo. Of over 1500 surviving drawings by Calandrucci, the great majority are in the Kunstmuseum, Düsseldorf, and in the Cabinet des Dessins of the Louvre. Many of his sketches record paintings that the artist planned and probably executed, though these have not yet been traced.

BIBLIOGRAPHY

N. Pio: *Vite* (1724); ed. C. Enggass and R. Enggass (1977), pp. 225–6
L. Pascoli: *Vite* (1730–36), ii, pp. 308–17
F. Schulze: 'Appunti su Giacinto Calandrucci', *An. Scu. Norm. Sup. Pisa*, n. s. 2, iii (1973), pp. 213–19
E. K. Waterhouse: *Roman Baroque Painting* (Oxford, 1976) [incl. a list of works]
D. Graf: *Die Handzeichnungen von Giacinto Calandrucci*, 2 vols, Düsseldorf, Kstmus. cat. (Düsseldorf, 1986)

DIETER GRAF

Calatrava, Santiago (*b* Benimamet, nr Valencia, 28 July 1951). Spanish architect and engineer. He studied architecture and urban planning at the Escuela Technica Superior de Arquitectura in Valencia (1969–74) and then civil engineering at the Eidgenössische Technische Hochschule (ETH), Zurich (1975–9). Between 1979 and 1981 he worked at the ETH and obtained a doctorate on the technology of space frames. After establishing an independent architectural and engineering practice in Zurich in 1981, he rapidly gained an international reputation for his integration of technology and aesthetics, producing dynamic structural forms that challenged traditional practice in both architecture and engineering. His approach to bridge design, for example, is based on the view that bridges can be used 'to add energy to the landscape', as seen in the elegant, slender steel arch of his Lusitania Bridge (1988–91), Mérida, Spain, and the graceful continuous span of the tied steel arch projected for the East London River Crossing (1990; unexecuted). The single tilted steel arch of the small pedestrian La Devesa Bridge (1989–91), Ripoll, near Barcelona, the single inclined pylons with cable stays supporting the decks of the Alamillo Bridge (1987–92), Seville, and the pedestrian Trinity Bridge (begun 1993), Salford, Lancs, are dramatic, cantilevered designs that express the same view. Calatrava's most important building designs include the Stadelhofen Railway Station (1983–90), Zurich, a long, curving, three-level structure that includes a basement underpass and upper-level walkway with connecting bridges. The nature of these spaces is emphasized by the structure: the basement is dominated by heavy, inclined concrete supports, and the upper walkway by the skeletal steel ribs of its cantilevered glazed roof. Lyon Airport Railway Station (1989–94) was designed with 500 m-long platform vaults of latticed concrete ribs; the station hall rising above them at the centre has complex, angled roofs in the form of outstretched wings. Similar curved and skeletal forms feature in other projects, such as the Science Museum (1991), Valencia; the Kuwait Pavilion at Expo 92, Seville, with a roof formed of scimitar-shaped concrete ribs that could be hydraulically manoeuvred to different angles; and a project (1991) for the completion of the cathedral of St John the Divine, New York, which includes an extraordinary, organic, skeletal structure for the transepts and a high-level garden under a glazed roof. Calatrava's work was exhibited widely in Europe and the USA in the 1980s and after, and he received several international awards, including the Gold Medal of the Institution of Structural Engineers, London (1992).

BIBLIOGRAPHY

W. Blaser, ed.: *Santiago Calatrava: Engineering-Architecture* (Basle, 1987)
F. Candela: 'Calatrava's Graceful Shapes', *World Archit.*, 13 (1991), pp. 46–57
D. Sharp, ed.: *Santiago Calatrava* (London, 1992, rev. 1994)
K. Frampton and others: *Calatrava Bridges* (Zurich and London, 1993)

VALERIE A. CLACK

Calcagni, Antonio (di Bernardino) (*b* Recanati, 18 Dec 1536; *d* Loreto, 9 Sept 1593). Italian sculptor and bronze-caster. Of noble birth, he showed a precocious drawing talent and at a young age was apprenticed to the sculptors Girolamo Lombardo and Aurelio Lombardo in Recanati. He became a favoured student of Girolamo, learning to work bronze, silver, gold and terracotta. In 1574 he settled in Loreto, where he remained until his death. The foundry he owned with his brothers was renowned for the quality of its bronze-casting. Most of his early works were executed under his teachers' commissions, including a bronze baptismal font (destr.) for Penna Cathedral, Naples, and a fountain decoration (destr.) for the Doge's Palace, Venice. The bronze statue of *Gregory XIII* for Ascoli Piceno (destr. 1798; drawing, Ascoli Piceno, Mus. Dioc.), which Calcagni completed after Aurelio's death, established his reputation. His first independent work, a stucco *Virgin and Child*, was executed in 1574 for the Cavaliere Agostino Filago. This led to similar commissions from the religious community, such as figures of *Christ* for the Fraternità of Castelnuovo, and a figure of *Christ* and a silver *Crucifix* adorned with crystal for the Fraternità of Camerino. He also created a stone and bronze sepulchre for *Monsignor Francesco Alberici* (1574; bust only extant, Recanati, Mus. Dioc.), the bronze memorial to *Cavaliere Agostino Filago*, and a silver *Crucifix* and twelve *Apostles* (destr.) for Monsignor Casali, Governatore of Loreto. In this period Calcagni created perhaps his greatest work, the bust of the humanist *Annibal Caro* (London, V&A; see fig.), commissioned by his family in 1566. Dated either 1574 or between 1566 and 1572, it was executed from a portrait of Caro by Jacopino del Conte and is a marvel of vitality and strength of character, of an immediacy belying its posthumous execution. Masterfully cast in bronze and fitted to a body of crimson breccia stained with white, it rests on a plinth of rich orange-red and white marble, with a *cartellino* of black marble. According to Pope-Hennessy, it is 'one of the masterpieces of bronze portraiture of the later 16th century'.

Calcagni's name is indissolubly linked with the basilica and the Santa Casa in Loreto (*see* LORETO, §II, 1), and most of his surviving work is there. The restriction of his activity to this relatively provincial area kept his reputation local. Works in the basilica include the oval relief of the *Crucifixion* with angels and doves, cast in 1578 for the Altar of the Pietà, and five bronze panels commissioned by Gregorio Massilla of San Ginesio for the chapel of the Pietà. These consist of a relief of the *Deposition* and relief portraits of Massilla, his wife and daughter and Antonio Rogato, cast in 1582.

Calcagni created two major works in bronze for the basilica. The first, the magnificent statue of *Sixtus V* for the piazza, was commissioned by the city in honour of the election of the Marchese Cardinal Peretti-Montalto as

Antonio Calcagni: *Annibal Caro*, bronze, marble and breccia, h. 768mm, commissioned 1566 (London, Victoria and Albert Museum)

pope in 1585. Calcagni was awarded the commission over Girolamo Lombardo, whom he had succeeded as head of the Recanati school. The statue was rapidly executed, and installed by 1589. A seated figure, with arm raised in the act of benediction, the statue appears both beneficent and powerful. The pedestal is adorned with four small statues of Charity, Peace, Faith and Justice and two low reliefs of the *Entry into Jerusalem* and *Christ Driving the Money-changers from the Temple.* For its 'total perfection' he was awarded an additional 1300 scudi by the city. The second major work, the south door of the basilica, was commissioned 28 February 1590 by Cardinal Antonio Maria Gallo, Protector of Santa Casa, with the main door assigned to Antonio Lombardo, son of Girolamo, and the north door to Tiburzio Vergelli. Calcagni had executed the designs and terracotta models (Ancona, Mus. Dioc.) for the panels before his death. The door was completed by his students and inaugurated in 1600. Each of the two parts has five panels of scenes from the Old and New Testaments, ovals holding statues of the Prophets, and figures of the Virtues, putti, acantha flowers and fruit.

BIBLIOGRAPHY

DBI; Thieme–Becker

F. Baldinucci: *Notizie* (1681–1728); ed. F. Ranalli (1845–7), iii, pp. 101–24

A. Venturi: *Storia* (1901–40), x, pp. 721–34

G. Gennari: 'Un bassorilievo in terracotta di Antonio Calcagni da Recanati', *L'Arte*, xli (1938), pp. 298–300

J. Pope-Hennessy: 'Sculpture for the Victoria and Albert Museum', *Apollo*, lxxx (1964), pp. 458–65

——: 'Antonio Calcagni's Bust of Annibale Caro', *Arte in Europa: Scritti di storia dell'arte in onore di Edoardo Arslan*, 2 vols (Pavia, 1965–6), i, pp. 577–80; ii, pls 374–5; repr. in *V&A Mus. Bull.*, 3 (1967), pp. 13–17

F. Grimaldi and K. Sordi: *Scultori a Loreto: Fratelli Lombardi, Antonio Calcagni e Tiburzio Vergelli: Documenti* (Ancona, 1987), pp. 113–236, 297–308

——: *Pittori a Loreto. Committenze tra '500 e '600* (Ancona, 1988)

B. K. GRINDSTAFF

Calcar, Jan Joest von. *See* JOEST, JAN.

Calcar, Jan Steven [Johannes Stephanus] **van** (*b* Calcar [now Kalkar], ?1499; *d* Naples, ?1546). North Netherlandish painter and draughtsman, active in Italy. He was a pupil of Titian's in Venice, *c.* 1536 or 1537, though not necessarily the pupil referred to as 'Stefano' by Marcantonio Michiel in 1532. The only identifiable work by van Calcar mentioned in such early sources as Vasari, Lomazzo and van Mander is the series of designs for the highly influential woodcut illustrations in the anatomical treatise *De humani corporis fabrica* (Basle, 1543; *see* BOOK ILLUSTRATION, fig. 2) by ANDREAS VESALIUS, who held the chair of surgery in Padua from 1537; van Calcar's precise share in the project, however, is not clear. The strongly Titianesque character of the illustrations coincides with another old tradition, which dates back at least to Annibal Caro in the 1540s, crediting Titian himself with the designs for the treatise.

The association between van Calcar and Vesalius is firmly documented in two earlier instances: one for the production, which van Calcar financed, of six woodcuts published in *Tabulae anatomicae sex* (Venice, 1538 onwards), with skeletons drawn by him and illustrations of the vascular system by Vesalius. The other is Vesalius's

Venesection Epistle of 1539, in which he praised 'Johannes Stephanus' and requested his assistance for the illustrations to his anatomical treatise.

Van Calcar subsequently settled in Naples, where in 1545 he befriended Vasari, who considered him one of the few northern painters able to produce wholly Italian-looking works. Van Calcar must also have excelled in portraiture, since Hendrick Goltzius mistook his works for originals by Titian. These few facts, together with the otherwise undocumented portrait of *Vesalius* on the second frontispiece of the anatomical treatise, have led to the attribution of a number of painted portraits to van Calcar. Logical among these are such Titianesque portraits as that of *Vesalius* (St Petersburg, Hermitage) and that of *Melchior von Braunweiler* (1540; Paris, Louvre), which was listed as by van Calcar in the collection of Louis XIV; other likely candidates include three more male portraits (two in Paris, Louvre; and one in Berlin, Gemäldegal.; see Suida) and the *Portrait of Three Men and a Girl* (London, N.G.). Stylistically they are close enough to have been painted by the same hand as the *Portrait of a Man* (Vienna, Ksthist. Mus.), so far his only known signed work; according to its inscription, it was painted in Naples. Other attributed portraits (see Wurzbach, Thieme–Becker and Suida, among others) are doubtful, while genuine portraits by van Calcar may still be hiding under attributions to Titian and his followers. A fresco with the *Lamentation of St Roch* in the oratory of S Rocco, Padua, has also been ascribed to van Calcar (see Rinaldi), though the basis for the attribution is the first frontispiece of Vesalius's treatise, which was actually drawn by Domenico Campagnola.

BIBLIOGRAPHY

Thieme–Becker; Wurzbach
M. A. Michiel: *Notizia d'opere di disegno nella prima metà del secolo XVI* (MS., 1521–43); ed. J. Morelli (Bassano, 1800); rev. and augmented by F. Ftizzoni (Bologna, 1884), p. 147
G. Vasari: *Vite* (1550, rev. 2/1568); ed. G. Milanesi (1878–85), v, p. 435; vii, pp. 461, 582
G. P. Lomazzo: *Trattato dell'arte della pittura* (Milan, 1584)
K. van Mander: *Schilder-boeck* ([1603]–1604), fols 217–18
F. M. G. de Feiffer: 'Jan Steven van Calcar (Johannes Stephanus), 1499–1546', *Ned. Tijdschr. Geneesknd.*, iii/31 (1933), cols 3562–79
W. Suida: 'Fremde Meister um Tizian', *Belvedere*, xii (1934–7), pp. 12–13
H. Cushing: *A Bio-bibliography of Andreas Vesalius* (New York, 1943), pp. xxviii–xxxvii, *passim*
E. Tietze-Conrat: 'Neglected Contemporary Sources Relating to Michelangelo and Titian', *A. Bull.*, xxv (1943), pp. 157–8
J. B. Saunders and C. D. O'Malley: *The Illustrations from the Works of Andreas Vesalius* (Cleveland and New York, 1950/*R* 1973)
S. M. Rinaldi: 'Un affresco del Calcar a Padova', *A. Ven.*, xx (1966), pp. 241–3
R. Pallucchini: *Il Tiziano* (Florence, 1969), pp. 213–14
Verzeichnis Gemäldegal. Ksthist. Mus., Wien (1973), p. 36, pl. 28
F. Heinemann: 'La bottega de Tiziano', *Tiziano e Venezia. Convegno internazionale di studi Venezia: Venezia, 1976*, p. 435
M. Muraro: 'Tiziano e le anatomie del Vesalio', *Tiziano e Venezia. Convegno internazionale di studi Venezia: Venezia, 1976*, pp. 307–16
Tiziano e la silografia veneziana del cinquecento (exh. cat. by M. Muraro and D. Rosand, Venice, Doge's Pal.; Washington, DC, N.G.A.; 1976), pp. 123–33
M. Lucco: 'Dopo Mantegna', *Paragone*, cccxiii (1977), pp. 124–5
A. Brejon de Lavergnée: 'L'Inventaire Le Brun de 1683: La Collection des tableaux de Louis XIV', *Notes et documents des musées de France*, xvii (Paris, 1987), p. 126, fig. 48

BERT W. MEIJER

Calcar, St Nikolai. *See* KALKAR, ST NIKOLAI.

Calcutta. Indian port city, capital of the state of West Bengal, sited on the Hooghly River, 128 km north of the Bay of Bengal.

1. History. 2. Urban development. 3. Art life and organization.

1. HISTORY. Calcutta was founded in 1690 by Job Charnock, an English merchant of the East India Company, on insalubrious mud flats near the Temple of Kalighat at Sutanuti on the Hooghly River. The site was unhealthy, with a high mortality rate, and prone to devastating cyclones. The earliest settlement was established in defiance of the authority of the Nawab of Bengal and without the benefit of an imperial *farmān* from the Mughal emperor in Delhi. Despite these circumstances, Charnock's resolve to establish an English presence in Bengal was successful. In less than 20 years this precarious foothold had grown to be a thriving commercial enclave, one that was to become the capital of British India and the second city of the British Empire.

Although the early 18th century was a period of quiet consolidation and expansion, the slow decline of the Mughal empire left a dangerous political vacuum. By the 1740s, although the Nawabs of Bengal paid nominal allegiance to Delhi, they exercised increasing independence, as Mughal rule diminished to a nominal suzerainty. In 1756 the Nawab Surajal-Daula attacked Calcutta with an army of 50,000, and on 20 June the city fell. A total of 146 European prisoners was taken, of which only 23 are alleged to have survived the following night in the notorious Black Hole, a dungeon of Fort William. A force under the command of Admiral Watson and Robert Clive recaptured the city, and Clive went on to defeat the Nawab at Plassey on 2 January 1757. A nominee, Mir Jafar, was installed in place of the Nawab, and suddenly the East India Company found itself master of Bengal, with its merchants having free reign throughout the province. Following the Regulating Act of Parliament in 1773 the Governor of Calcutta, assisted by a Council, became Governor-General of all India, a notable enhancement of the city's function. Calcutta replaced Murshidabad as the political and commercial centre of Bengal.

From the earliest days immigrants had been encouraged: initially Armenians and Portuguese, but later Dutch, Danes, Chinese and Jews all responded in large numbers, mixed with Bengalis, Punjabis, Gujaratis and others who swelled the ranks of the Indian population, eager to capitalize on the opportunity for trade and commerce. An ethnic mix developed that conferred a distinct cosmopolitan character that is still evident, which had a profound impact on the literary, religious, social and intellectual life of India.

By 1820 British paramountcy was firmly established. This was nobly reflected in the urban form and development of Calcutta as the capital city of British India (*see* §2 below). In the later 19th century, with the opening of more direct routes from Europe and the growth of Bombay on the west coast, Calcutta lost some of its commercial pre-eminence. This was compounded in 1905 by the partition of Bengal, which aroused violent resistance, and finally in 1910 by the momentous decision to create a new imperial capital at Delhi. In spite of these setbacks, Calcutta continued to play a leading role in political life, symbolized by the completion of the Victoria Memorial in 1921 and then, ironically, by its emergence as a centre for reformist sympathies and incipient nationalism. In the 20th century the overcrowded city has become a byword for urban deprivation.

BIBLIOGRAPHY

E. Fay: *Original Letters from India, 1779–1815* (London, 1819)
G. N. Curzon: *British Government in India* (London, 1925)
G. Moorhouse; *Calcutta* (London, 1971)
P. Pal, ed.: *Changing Visions, Lasting Images—Calcutta through 300 Years* (Bombay, 1990)

2. URBAN DEVELOPMENT.

(i) 1690–1845. The initial foothold of makeshift huts and boats established by Charnock soon gave way to a more conventional settlement. Charnock's own tomb (*c.* 1695), in the churchyard of St John's, Council House Street and Hastings Street, built of granite from Pallavaram, near Madras, is the oldest European structure surviving in the city.

European settlements were regarded at this time as useful bulwarks of Mughal authority in an area where it was difficult to exercise central control from a distance, and in 1697 the English merchants were permitted to fortify the town. This was the origin of Old Fort William, a robust redbrick enclosure in the shape of an irregular tetragon. The fort offered security, which in turn generated local commercial confidence. In 1700 Calcutta became a presidency, an area under the control of a president of the East India Company. Six years later the President's or Governor's House was completed, with a fine pilastered range raised on a high podium dominating the river frontage. By 1710 the town had a hospital, barracks and an Anglican church, St Anne's. The old pond, Lal Dighee, was deepened and cleaned to provide a central reservoir of drinking water, an urban feature that has survived as Tank Square at the centre of the city. Although many of the houses of the period were simple, with thatched roofs based on local vernacular huts or bungalows, some had rectangular windows and balustraded roofs set in garden areas, the only concession to the climate being the use of cane rather than glass in the windows.

In 1742 marauding Maratha horsemen swept through Orissa and Bengal and briefly threatened the city. These raids prompted the construction of a three-mile ditch around outlying areas, a feature later perpetuated in the Circular Road. A huge new Fort William, designed by Captain John Brohier (*fl* 1740–65), was built from 1757 (*see* MILITARY ARCHITECTURE AND FORTIFICATION, fig. 19b) and dictated a major change in the pattern of urban development. Buildings were no longer concentrated inside the walls; instead the city expanded beneath the protective ramparts of the most impressive European fortifications in Asia. The new fort altered the entire plan of Calcutta, for in order to command an open field of fire a vast space was cleared to create, by 1780, the Maidan and Esplanade (see fig. 1), which not only rendered the fort unassailable but also provided an enormous vista around which a series of splendid houses and public buildings arose. The merchant classes expressed their new wealth in houses that reflected their emerging status. Old bamboo and thatch bungalows were replaced by elegant classical colonial villas, with colonnaded verandahs, pedimented centrepieces and pilastered walls, all faced in chunam, a form of local stucco. In Chowringhee, east of the Maidan, Alipur to the south and Garden Reach to the

1. Calcutta, Esplanade, from a photograph of *c.* 1880

south-west, entire districts arose that reflected the mercantile spirit of the age. They offered a stunning prospect and were considered by Viscount George Valentia in 1803 as 'the finest view I ever beheld in any city'.

These elegant merchant houses marked an important stage in the evolution of European forms of architecture to an Indian context. Most followed a conventional pattern, a well-proportioned block of two or three storeys set in its own garden compound, with the inner rooms protected from the heat by colonnaded verandahs or porticos. The siting of these houses in their own gardens was as much a reflection of good planning, to promote a cool flow of air and reduce the risk of diseases, as of the desire for exaggerated individual impact. As a result, settlement was widely dispersed with considerable distances between houses, transport being by palanquin or carriage. Entrance porches became *porte-cochères*, often of enormous proportions to accommodate the elephants of visiting dignitaries.

In time central residential areas such as Chowringhee and the Esplanade acquired a continuous street frontage of boundary walls, screens and gates complementing the grandeur of the houses. As European styles were refined and adapted to local conditions, intercolumniation was adjusted to provide greater shade, proportions were altered, and louvred screens or cane tatties of moist plaited grass were hung between the columns to cool the air. Surviving examples include the Loretto Convent in Middleton Row, once the home of Henry Vansittart, Governor of Bengal (1760–64), the nearby Royal Calcutta Turf Club (1820), the Bishop's Palace (1825), Warren Hastings's house at Alipur (1777), the Tollygunge Club (*c.* 1780) and Belvedere (*c.* 1770; now the National Library).

In spite of the surface grandeur, the mortality rate remained devastating. Until 1800 the European residents met annually on 15 November to celebrate having survived another season. For many, life in Calcutta lasted just two monsoons. Park Street Cemetery (opened 1767) contains the graves of many famous Calcutta citizens of the period and is a fascinating repository of Neo-classical funerary sculpture.

By 1773 the city was the effective capital of British India, and the East India Company began to erect public buildings that expressed its self-confidence. These were designed by military engineers or amateur enthusiasts using available architectural pattern books. They made allusions to Classical antiquity in a conscious attempt to identify the expanding Company presence with the civilizing values of the ancient world.

In 1780 Thomas Lyon's Writers' Buildings (refronted 1880) were erected to house the junior clerks of the East India Company. They were followed by St John's Church (1787), built by Lt James Agg (*c.* 1758–1828) and based, as were many Anglican churches in India, on James Gibbs's St Martin-in-the-Fields (1720–26), London. By far the most opulent was Government House (1803). Designed by Captain Charles Wyatt (1758–1819) for Marquess Wellesley, Governor-General from 1798 to 1805, it was modelled on Robert Adam's Kedleston Hall (1759–70), Derbyshire, but adapted to the climate and context. It created new standards of architectural splendour, with its grand approach through triumphal gateways surmounted by sphinxes and lions, and set the precedent for many other government houses and residencies throughout India for using architecture as a conscious instrument of policy to create an aura of power and wealth.

As the city grew, a whole series of classical perspectives was created with vistas terminated by prominent public buildings and monuments. European ideas on planning and townscape were imposed on an unprecedented scale. The Town Hall (1811), designed by Colonel John Garstin (1756–1820), complemented Government House. St Andrew's Kirk (1818), by Burn, Currie and Co., closed the vista from Council House Street, but by the 1820s a more austere form of Neo-classicism prevailed. The new Silver Mint (1831) by Major William Nairn Forbes (1796–1855) adopted a severe Greek Revival style with a central portico copied in half size from the Parthenon in Athens. The boys' school of La Martinière (1835) was embellished with a handsome Ionic order, while Metcalfe Hall (1840–44), by C. K. Robison (*fl* 1835–50), was designed in a similar vein with the capitals on the principal west front based on the Tower of the Winds in Athens. The huge Ochterlony Column (1828), designed by J. P. Parker (*fl* 1820–40) and raised as a focal point at the north end of the Maidan, combined a curious mixture of Egyptian and Greek styles.

(ii) After 1845. The classical tradition persisted in Calcutta throughout the 19th century. The General Post Office (1868), Indian Museum (1875) and university buildings (1866–72; destr. 1961) were the work of Walter L. B. Granville (1819–74), an accomplished and versatile architect who acted as consulting architect to the government of India from 1863 to 1868. The East India Railway Offices (*c.* 1880), by Roskell Bayne (*fl* 1870-95), were modelled in part on the Farnese Palace in Rome. As late as 1916 public buildings, such as the Royal Exchange by T. S. Gregson (*fl* 1870-95), were being built in the classical style and faced in chunam. However, there were exceptions to this tradition. At the south end of the Maidan, St Paul's Cathedral was completed in 1847 in English Perpendicular Gothic adapted to the climate. It was the first major church in India to break away from the influence of Gibbs. Designed by William Nairn Forbes, the original tower and spire were modelled on Norwich Cathedral, but following an earthquake they were recast in 1934 to resemble Bell Harry Tower at Canterbury. A significant departure from the classical tradition was the High Court (1872) by Granville (*see* LAW COURT, fig. 2), a great Gothic range modelled on Sir George Gilbert Scott's designs for the Town Hall at Hamburg, which in turn had reflected the great medieval prototype of the Cloth Hall at Ypres. However, when plans were laid by Lord Curzon, Viceroy from 1899 to 1905, for a great memorial to Queen Victoria, he argued strongly for a building in the classical tradition and turned to William Emerson, President of the RIBA, to prepare a scheme. The Victoria Memorial (see fig. 2), built as a museum and art gallery, is the architectural climax of the city and an imposing symbol of imperial power. Consciously influenced by English civic Baroque Revival architecture, and in particular by A. Brumwell Thomas's Belfast City Hall (1897–1906), its huge marble dome, crowned by a revolving figure of Victory, dominates

2. Calcutta, Victoria Memorial by William Emerson (opened 1921), seen through Edward VII Memorial Arch (by Bertram Mackennal)

the entire city. Construction was delayed by World War I, and it was not opened until 1921.

The most significant later addition to the city was the great Howrah Bridge, built by Hubert Shirley-Smith (1901-81) in 1943 to replace an earlier pontoon bridge. This improved lateral communications between the east and west banks and access to Howrah Station (1900–08), a huge, cavernous Arts and Crafts complex by Halsey Ricardo. The bridge rapidly became a potent symbol of the city. As late as 1947 the New Mint, designed by Henry Medd, used a stripped classical style.

BIBLIOGRAPHY

T. Daniell: *Views of Calcutta* (Calcutta, 1786–8)

R. Heber: *Narrative of a Journey from Calcutta to the Upper Provinces of India: From Calcutta to Bombay, 1824–25* (London, 1828)

J. Long: *Calcutta and its Neighbourhood* (Calcutta, 1874)

W. K. Firminger: *Thacker's Guide to Calcutta* (Calcutta, 1906)

C. R. Wilson: *Old Fort William in Bengal* (London, 1906)

H. E. A. Cotton: *Calcutta Old and New* (Calcutta, 1907)

H. E. Busteed: *Echoes of Old Calcutta* (London, 1908)

H. A. Newell: *Guide to Calcutta* (Calcutta, 1920)

S. Nilsson: *European Architecture in India, 1750–1850* (London, 1968)

M. Bence-Jones: *Palaces of the Raj* (London, 1973)

P. H. Davies: *Splendours of the Raj: British Architecture in India, 1660–1947* (London, 1985)

——: *The Penguin Guide to the Monuments of India, Volume II: Islamic, Rajput, European* (London, 1989)

Calcutta, City of Palaces: A Survey of the City in the Days of the East India Company, 1690–1858 (exh. cat. by J. P. Lusty, London, BL, 1990)

PHILIP DAVIES

3. ART LIFE AND ORGANIZATION.

(i) 1690–1900. In its early development Calcutta retained a colonial stamp. Art as defined in European terms came into existence with the arrival of visiting British artists. The city received its first visual treatment in the engravings of Thomas and William DANIELL, who made Calcutta their base in 1786–7 before setting out across India. The panoramic vision of the Daniell engravings was complemented by other views of Calcutta, produced by such resident artists as James Baillie Fraser (1783–1856) and Sir Charles D'Oyly (1781–1845) in the 1830s and 1840s. At the same time that these views projected the colonial archetype of Calcutta, European portrait painters in the city (the most prominent being JOHAN ZOFFANY, who worked there between 1783 and 1789) created some of the most representative images of British imperial power. These artists also established Western-style oil painting as the medium to be preferred over indigenous pictorial conventions.

As an exclusive European domain of high art, the first amateur art society, the Brush Club, inaugurated a chain of 'fine art' exhibitions. Held in the Town Hall in 1831–2 and later in the new premises of the Indian Museum and the Government School of Art, these exhibitions featured the works of British painters and copies of Old Masters and, over time, admitted a few art school-trained Indians. Some wealthy Bengalis also found a niche as collectors and lenders. Throughout the mid- and late 19th century, large collections of Western Neo-classical painting and sculpture amassed in rich Bengali homes buttressed this colonial art world, carefully segregating it from the arena of 'bazaar' art.

Defined through exclusion, the city's 'bazaar' artists had their two main centres in Kalighat (the vicinity of the Kali temple; see fig. 3 for an example of their output) and Bat-tala (the hub of early Bengali printing and publishing). In the late 18th century and early 19th, several displaced court painters from Murshidabad and Patna arrived in Calcutta to meet British demands for studies of Indian topography, ethnology, architecture and natural history, orientating their skills to satisfy their patrons' tastes for naturalism and precision. Examples of such work (termed 'Company painting') declined in the latter half of the century (*see* INDIAN SUBCONTINENT, §VI, 4(ix)(b)–(d)). During the same period an indigenous clientele kept alive the trade in religious, mythological and the new genre of satirical pictures, produced by the migrant village painters (*paṭuās*) of Kalighat and the metal- and wood-engravers of Bat-tala. Around Bat-tala oil paintings also were produced, crudely adapting both the medium and realist techniques to Hindu mythological themes. Such trends gained full momentum towards the end of the century, resulting in a flood of popular 'realistic' lithographs.

Outside this domain of 'bazaar' picture production, the School of Art in Calcutta—begun in 1854 as a private British endeavour and converted to a full government institution in 1864—provided training for a new category of middle-class artists. The possibilities for Bengalis were limited, however, since the curriculum was chiefly technical and craft-orientated, and patrons supported few Indians except as portrait painters or copyists. Unlike Bombay,

3. Calcutta, Kalighat district, the goddess Kali by a 'bazaar' artist, opaque colour on paper, 19th century (London, Victoria and Albert Museum)

Calcutta did not develop a prominent group of professional academic oil painters (*see* BOMBAY, §2). Until the end of the 19th century most graduates of the School of Art became drawing-masters, draughtsmen, lithographers and engravers, with some of them turning their new skills towards satisfying the flourishing popular market for religious pictures, prints and illustrations.

(ii) 1900–50. Calcutta gained a place in India's modern art history at the turn of the century, when a nationalist movement in painting was inaugurated by Abanindranath Tagore (*see* TAGORE, (3)) in reaction against both the 'imitativeness' of academically inspired art and the 'vulgarities' of 'bazaar' pictures. Inspired by the new Orientalist valorization of Indian art, particularly the writings of Ernest Binfield Havell (*see* HAVELL, (3)) and ANANDA KENTISH COOMARASWAMY, this movement sought to reconstruct an Indian style of painting, in keeping with what was thought of as the classical themes and spiritual essence of Indian aesthetics. Coinciding with the Swadeshi boycott of British goods in Bengal (1905–8), Abanindranath Tagore's New School of Indian Painting won acclaimed status as 'national art'. His student following grew after he became vice-principal of the School of Art in 1905. The movement found unofficial support in the home of the Tagore family and at the Indian Society of Oriental Art, founded in 1907 by Orientalist and nationalist art enthusiasts.

After 1920 Calcutta ceased to be the main venue of this movement, known by then as the Bengal School. The movement found a new direction and locus in the university established by Rabindranath Tagore (*see* TAGORE, (1)) at Santiniketan. Abanindranath's prized student NANDALAL BOSE, who was in charge of teaching at the Santiniketan Kala Bhavan in 1920, replaced his master as the chief representative of 'Indian' painting. While Santiniketan became an important site of artistic innovation, Calcutta remained split during the 1920s and 1930s between Western academic practice and the lingering Bengal School stereotype of Indian painting.

A powerful reaction against both these stagnating trends manifested itself in the figure of JAMINI ROY. Having trained at the School of Art, he returned to the rural roots of Bengali folk painting (*paṭacitrās*) to evolve a distinctive style. Ranging from the boldly primitive to the colourfully decorative, Roy's style soon became standardized. His paintings captured the middle-class art market of Bengal and became the symbol of 'progressive' art. With World War II, the climax of the campaign for independence and the disastrous famine of the early 1940s, art activities in Calcutta again claimed national attention. The Calcutta Group, formed in 1943 out of the leftist cultural movement and Anti-Fascist Association of Writers and Artists, included painters and sculptors such as Gopal Ghosh (1913–80), Nirode Majumdar (1916–82), Pradosh Dasgupta (*b* 1913) and Paritosh Sen (*b* 1918). The group was unified not by style but by a modernist and internationalist thrust and a desire to engage with the stark social realities of the city. Images of famine, of the trauma of partition and of the refugee influx became the hallmarks of Calcutta's visual arts, their major proponents being Communist printmakers such as Chittaprasad Bhattacharya (1913–78) and SOMNATH HORE.

The nationalist art movement had heralded the growth of voluntary art societies and organizations that attempted to carve out a space for artists, critics and the public outside the orbit of official or individual patronage. Havell's programme of Indianizing the teaching at the Government School of Art led, in 1905, to the temporary formation of the breakaway Jubilee Art Academy to preserve the tenets of Western academic training. Another private Bengali enterprise, the Indian Art School, begun in the 1890s with the same aim, survives today as the city's second art-training centre. The dominant Orientalist/nationalist art lobby had continuous (though short-lived) rivals in parallel groupings of Academic artists such as the Indian Academy of Art (est. 1920) and the Society of Fine Arts (est. 1921). Calcutta's thriving tradition of reproducing artists' work in journals reached a peak with the publication of the prestigious art journal *Rupam* beginning in 1920. Exhibitions found a long-lasting forum in the Academy of Fine Arts, founded in 1933 by a body of wealthy Bengali patrons. Throughout the 1940s and 1950s galleries at 15 Park Street (Artistry House) and 1 Chowringhee Terrace served as important exhibition premises, hosting, for instance, the displays of the Calcutta Group.

After 1947 the Academy of Fine Arts acquired its own quarters, galleries and a permanent collection of modern art and so became the focus of the city's art life.

(iii) After 1950. Although the Calcutta Group had dissolved by 1953, its most important artists continued to dominate the art scene for a long time afterwards. Among the many artists' groups that were formed in the subsequent period the most important was the Society of Contemporary Artists, which had its first group show in 1960 and soon drew in some of contemporary Calcutta's senior and best-known artists. These included such painters as Ganesh Haloi (*b* 1936), Ganesh Pyne (*b* 1937), Shyamal Dutta Roy (*b* 1934) and Bikash Bhattacharya (*b* 1940), such printmakers as Amitabha Banerjee (*b* 1929) and Sanat Kar (*b* 1935) and such sculptors as Sarbari Roychowdhury (*b* 1933). The Academy of Fine Arts was partially eclipsed in importance by the Birla Academy of Art and Culture, begun in 1968 by a family of collectors. The latter had greater resources and a stronger organization, and its exhibitions (including its annual all-India shows) and permanent collection of traditional and modern Indian art gave it prominence.

Unlike its Delhi counterpart, the state wing of the Lalit Kala Akademi, set up in Calcutta in the 1980s, functioned mainly as a studio for sculptors and graphic artists. The state government developed another exhibition centre and permanent gallery of work by 20th-century Calcutta artists, the Gaganendra Shilpa Pradarshanshala, named after the painter and designer Gaganendranath Tagore (*see* TAGORE, (2)). By far the most striking development in the 1990s was an unprecedented boom in privately owned, commercially run galleries, which provided the main means of promoting artists, drawing a clientele and controlling prices.

See also INDIAN SUBCONTINENT, §XII.

BIBLIOGRAPHY

B. Dey and J. Irwin: *Jamini Roy* (Calcutta, 1941)

M. Archer and W. G. Archer: *Indian Painting for the British, 1775–1880* (Oxford, 1955)

J. Appasamy: *Abanindranath Tagore and the Art of his Times* (Delhi, 1968)

W. G. Archer: *Kalighat Paintings* (London, 1971)

M. Archer: *India and British Portraiture, 1770–1825* (Delhi and Karachi, 1979)

A. Paul, ed.: *Woodcut Prints of Nineteenth Century Calcutta* (Calcutta, 1983)

R. Chattopadhyay: *From the Karkhana to the Studio: Changing Social Roles of Artists and Patrons in Bengal* (Delhi, 1990)

T. Guha-Thakurta: 'Art in Old Calcutta: The Melting Pot of Western Styles', *Calcutta: The Living City, Vol. I: The Past*, ed. S. Chauduri (Calcutta, 1990), pp. 146–55

R. P. Gupta: 'Art in Old Calcutta: Indian Styles', *Calcutta: The Living City, Vol. I: The Past*, ed. S. Chauduri (Calcutta, 1990), pp. 137–45

T. Mitra: 'Art and Artists in Twentieth Century Calcutta', *Calcutta: The Living City, Vol. II: The Present and the Future*, ed. S. Chauduri (Calcutta, 1990), pp. 260–69

T. Guha-Thakurta: *The Making of a New 'Indian' Art: Artists, Aesthetics and Nationalism in Bengal, c. 1850–1920* (Cambridge, 1992)

B. Khanna: *Kalighat, Indian Popular Painting, 1800–1930* (London, 1993)

TAPATI GUHA-THAKURTA

Caldara, Polidoro. *See* POLIDORO DA CARAVAGGIO.

Caldarium. *See under* BATH (ii), §1.

Caldas da Rainha. Portuguese centre of ceramic production. Documents record kilns operating in the town in 1488, and the first potters were Álvaro Annes, Vicente Annes and Francisco Lopes. However, the modern ceramics tradition with which the town is associated dates to the time of a certain D. Maria 'dos Cacos', who is recorded as having attempted to sell his wares in fairs all over Portugal between 1820 and 1853. Pieces attributed to him are rare. He was succeeded by Manuel Cipriano Gomes (*fl* 1853–7) from Mafra. In addition to producing faience that resembled wares made in the Oporto factories (*see* OPORTO, §2), Gomes also produced a body of wares that were strongly influenced by the work of BERNARD PALISSY.

In 1884 the Fábrica de Faianças das Caldas da Rainha was established in Lisbon, under the artistic direction of the painter Rafael Bordalo Pinheiro (*see* BORDALO PINHEIRO, (1)), who transferred the concern to Caldas da Rainha. Production began in June 1885 after colour and glazing experiments had been carried out in the factory of Francisco Gomes d'Alvelar (*fl* 1875–97) in Caldas da Rainha. Bordalo Pinheiro's mastery in the art of translating caricature into moulded clay coupled with his innate ability to apply naturalistic relief decoration to his pieces is clearly discernible in the early period. In the Palissy tradition the majority of such pieces as jars, pots and plates feature vegetation, crustacea, fish and reptiles. Bordalo Pinheiro's large sculpture *St George and the Dragon* (Lisbon, Mus. Bordalo Pinheiro) dates from this period, and in 1887 he began his series of statues for the *Stations of the Cross* (Caldas da Rainha, Mus. Malhoa). Although financial difficulties led to a temporary closure of the factory in 1891, the last decade of the 19th century was one of resounding success. It was during this period that he produced the large Beethoven Vase (1895; Rio de Janeiro, Mus. N.) and figures of such popular Portuguese characters as Zé Povinho in various postures. Bordalo Pinheiro's son Manuel Gustavo Bordalo Pinheiro assisted his father during this period and after his father's death continued the tradition of relief decoration. Economic decline led to the sale of the factory at auction to Manuel Godinho Leal in 1908, after which nothing was produced.

BIBLIOGRAPHY

J. de Vasconcellos: *A Fábrica de faiança das Caldas da Rainha* (Oporto, 1891)

Exposição de cerâmica e olaria das Caldas da Rainha (exh. cat., ed. J. Ferrão; Lisbon, Mus. N. A. Ant., 1963)

A. de Sandão: *Faiança portuguesa, séculos XVIII, XIX* (Oporto, 1976)

Catálogo da exposição Caldas, 1977 (exh. cat., ed. R. S. Calado; Caldas da Rainha, Mus. Malhoa, 1977)

Catálogo da exposição cerâmica das Caldas (exh. cat., Lisbon, Mus. N. A. Ant., 1978)

J. A. França: *Rafael Bordalo Pinheiro: O Português tal e qual* (Lisbon, 1981)

BERNADETTE NELSON

Caldecott, Randolph (*b* Chester, 22 March 1846; *d* St Augustine, FL, 12 Feb 1886). English illustrator, painter and sculptor. Caldecott worked as a bank clerk in Whitchurch and Manchester and attended evening classes at the Manchester School of Art. He moved to London in 1872 and studied briefly at the Slade School of Fine Art. Through the painter Thomas Armstrong, he was introduced to London editors and publishers. He collaborated with Armstrong and W. E. Nesfield on decorative paintings for aesthetic interiors, notably at Bank Hall (1872–3), Derbys. Caldecott was taught to model by Jules Dalou, later modelling the gilt capitals of birds for the Arab Hall (1877–9) at Leighton House, London. Outstanding among Caldecott's work were his illustrations to Washington Irving's books, such as *Old Christmas* (1875), and the jolly Christmas stories and illustrated letters from abroad commissioned by the *Graphic*. However, his reputation rests on the frequently reprinted series of 16 picture books for children published between 1878 and 1885.

Caldecott was one of the first illustrators to eschew the heavy black-and-white effects of the 1860s. Taking advantage of the skilful colour woodblock printing carried out by the firm of Edmund Evans, he was able to preserve in his printed books the verve and economy of his line drawings and the delicacy of his watercolours; in contrast, his oils are laboured. Caldecott set his nursery rhymes and stories amid the vernacular architecture and gentle landscapes of his childhood, but his nostalgic vision of red-coated huntsmen and dairymaids in Regency costume was tempered by a lively sense of humour. His drawing of animals was particularly spirited; examples were owned by Beatrix Potter, whose work was indebted to his. Van Gogh and Gauguin were also admirers of his work. Caldecott is commemorated in a charming memorial by Alfred Gilbert at St Paul's Cathedral, London.

BIBLIOGRAPHY

R. K. Engen: *Randolph Caldecott: 'Lord of the Nursery'* (London, 1976) [incl. full bibliog.]
M. Hutchins, ed.: *Pictorially Yours: Illustrated Letters of Randolph Caldecott* (London, 1976)
Randolph Caldecott (exh. cat., ed. J. Treuherz; Manchester, C.A.G., 1977)
N. Finlay: *Randolph Caldecott: A Checklist of the Caroline Miller Parker Collection in the Houghton Library* (Cambridge, MA, 1986)

JULIAN TREUHERZ

Calder. American family of artists. (1) Alexander Milne Calder, of Scottish birth, moved to Philadelphia in his early 20s and produced several important sculptural works for the city. His son (2) Alexander Stirling Calder was also a sculptor. The family's greatest success came in the third generation, however, with (3) Alexander Calder, best known for his kinetic sculptures or mobiles.

(1) Alexander Milne Calder (*b* Aberdeen, 23 Aug 1846; *d* Philadelphia, PA, 14 June 1923). Sculptor. The son of a stone-cutter, he studied carving at the Royal Institute of Arts in Edinburgh and also in Paris and in London, where he later worked on the carving of the Albert Memorial. In 1868 he went to Philadelphia and studied at the Pennsylvania Academy of the Fine Arts with Thomas Eakins. In 1873 he began a 20-year project to design and execute sculptural decorations for Philadelphia's new City Hall. This is his most significant work, and the elaborate reliefs, statues and panels of statesmen and early settlers form perhaps the most ambitious decorative programme ever executed for a building by a single sculptor in the USA. The bronze statue of *William Penn* (over 11 m high), placed on top of City Hall in 1894, is a well-known landmark in Philadelphia and was until the 1980s the highest point in the city. Calder exhibited several figures and a carved stone panel (untraced) at the Centennial Exhibition in Philadelphia in 1876. Other notable works include a bronze portrait of *General George Gordon Meade* (Fairmount Park, Philadelphia) and the Hayden Memorial Geological Fund medal for the Academy of Natural Sciences (bronze, 1888).

BIBLIOGRAPHY

W. Craven: *Sculpture in America* (New York, 1968, rev. Newark, New York and London, 1984), pp. 483–6
Sculpture of a City: Philadelphia's Treasures in Bronze and Stone (New York, 1974), pp. 94–109
Philadelphia: Three Centuries of American Art (exh. cat., ed. G. Marcus and D. Sewell; Philadelphia, PA, Mus. A., 1976), pp. 432–3

(2) Alexander Stirling Calder (*b* Philadelphia, PA, 11 Jan 1870; *d* New York, 6 Jan 1945). Sculptor, son of (1) Alexander Milne Calder. He studied at the Pennsylvania Academy of the Fine Arts under Thomas Eakins and Thomas Anshutz and later in Paris at the Académie Julian and the Ecole des Beaux-Arts. Returning to Philadelphia in 1892 he won the gold medal of the Philadelphia Art Club and became an assistant instructor in modelling at the Pennsylvania Academy. His first commission, in 1893, was for a portrait statue in marble of the eminent surgeon *Dr Samuel Gross* to go in front of the Army Medical Museum, Washington, DC (now Washington, DC, Armed Forces Inst. Pathology, N. Mus. Health & Medic., on loan to Philadelphia, PA, Thomas Jefferson U., Medic. Col.). In 1903 he began teaching at the Pennsylvania School of Industrial Art in Philadelphia. His first national recognition came after he won a silver medal for a statue of the explorer *Philippe François Renault* at the World's Fair of 1904 in St Louis, MO. Moving to New York in 1910 he taught at the National Academy of Design and later the Art Students League. Calder was in charge of the sculptural decoration for the Panama Pacific International Exposition of 1915 in San Francisco after the death of Karl Bitter (1867–1915). Although he was largely trained in the French academic tradition, he transcended its limits in some of his better pieces, such as the marble figure of *George Washington* (1918) for the Washington Arch in New York and the Swann Memorial Fountain (bronze, 1924) in Logan Circle, Philadelphia. Among his other notable works are the sculptures for Viscaya in Miami, FL, and the bronze statue of the Norse explorer *Leif Ericsson*, presented to Iceland by the USA in 1932 and placed on Skolavoeroduholt, the highest hill above Reykjavík.

BIBLIOGRAPHY

J. Bowes: 'The Sculpture of Stirling Calder', *Amer. Mag. A.*, xvi (1925), pp. 231, 234–5
W. Craven: *Sculpture in America* (New York, 1968, rev. Newark, New York and London, 1984), pp. 570–73
Sculpture of a City: Philadelphia's Treasures in Bronze and Stone (New York, 1974), pp. 230–39
Philadelphia: Three Centuries of American Art (exh. cat., ed. G. Marcus and D. Sewell; Philadelphia, PA, Mus. A., 1976), pp. 525–6

ABIGAIL SCHADE GARY

(3) Alexander Calder (*b* Philadelphia, PA, 22 July 1898; *d* New York, 11 Nov 1976). Sculptor, painter, illustrator, printmaker and designer, son of (2) Alexander Stirling Calder. He graduated from Stevens Institute of Technology, Hoboken, NJ, with a degree in mechanical engineering in 1919. In 1923 he enrolled at the Art Students League in New York, where he was inspired by his teacher, John Sloan, to produce oil paintings. He became a freelance artist for the *National Police Gazette* in 1924, sketching sporting events and circus performances. His first illustrated book, *Animal Sketching* (New York, 1926), was based on studies made at the Bronx and Central Park Zoos in New York. The illustrations are brush and ink studies of animals in motion, with an accompanying text by the artist.

In 1926 Calder began his sojourns in Paris, where he attended sketching classes at the Académie de la Grande Chaumière. He was particularly influenced by the inventive collages of Joan Miró and by the whimsical art of Paul Klee, to which he was introduced by Miró. In Paris Calder made wood and wire animals with movable parts and designed the first pieces of his miniature *Circus* (1926–32; New York, Whitney). Performances of this hand-operated circus helped to introduce Calder to the Parisian avant-garde and to potential patrons. From 1927 to 1930 he constructed figures, animals and portrait heads in wire and carved similar subjects in wood.

After visiting Piet Mondrian's studio in 1930, Calder began to experiment with abstract constructions. He was invited to join Abstraction-Création in 1931 and was one of the few Americans to be actively involved with the group. In Paris in 1931 he exhibited his first non-objective construction, and in the following year he showed hand-cranked and motorized mobiles, marking the beginning of his development as a leading exponent of KINETIC ART. His major contribution to modern sculpture was the MOBILE, a kinetic construction of disparate elements that describe individual movements. *A Universe* (1934; New York, MOMA) is an open sphere made of steel wire containing two smaller spheres in constant motion. With this motorized sculpture and related examples he demonstrated his indebtedness to astronomical instruments of the past, including the armillary sphere and the mechanical orrery. In addition, he used his knowledge of laboratory instruments from his college training in kinetics.

Calder remained fully committed to abstraction during the 1930s and was encouraged by European modernists. After an initial involvement with geometric elements and machine imagery, he introduced biomorphic forms into his kinetic sculptures. Both the painted constructions and the brightly coloured mobiles synthesized Constructivist methods and materials with abstract forms derived from Surrealist imagery. While his American contemporaries were only beginning to discover Constructivism, Calder was already exhibiting such work, both in the USA and in Europe. In 1938 he bought a farm in Roxbury, CT, and thereafter divided his time between visits abroad and longer periods of residence in the USA. He refined his wind-driven mobiles in subsequent years to produce elegant, space-encompassing abstractions of gracefully bending wires. *Lobster Trap and Fish Tail* (1939; New York, MOMA) is an example of the delicate balance that he achieved in deploying various forms from painted sheet metal and wire. His production of the 1930s included 'plastic interludes', which were circles and spirals performing on an empty stage during the intermissions of Martha Graham's ballets. He also designed a mobile set for Erik

Alexander Calder: *Big Red*, painted sheet aluminium, steel rods and wire, 1.88×2.90 m, 1959 (New York, Whitney Museum of American Art)

Satie's symphonic drama, *Socrate* (1936), held at the Wadsworth Atheneum, Hartford, CT. In his later years he created costumes and set designs for various ballets and theatrical productions. Stabiles, large-scale constructions in cut and painted metal sheets, the first of which he created in the 1930s, appeared in substantial numbers from the 1950s. In his mature years his production included paintings, drawings, prints, book illustrations, jewellery and tapestries, all of which were composed of bold, abstract elements in primary colours. During the 1950s Calder continued to produce such mobiles as *Big Red* (1959; New York, Whitney; see fig.) and *125* (1957; John F. Kennedy International Airport, New York; for illustration *see* MOBILE), as well as producing new forms, including the *Towers*, wire constructions attached to the wall, with moving elements, and *Gongs*, metal pieces intended to produce various sounds. In spring 1954 Calder established a new studio and remodelled a house in Saché, France, where his family settled.

During the 1960s and 1970s colossal stabiles were commissioned for public sites around the world. Calder's arching forms, dynamic surfaces and biomorphic imagery were the appropriate complement for the geometric regularity and severity of modern architectural complexes. *Teodelapio*, a stabile originally made for an exhibition in Spoleto, Italy, in 1962, served as a monumental gateway to the city. He designed *Man* for the World's Fair, Montreal, in 1967. Stabiles of 15 m and more were installed in many American and European cities. The frequent allusions to animal forms in these stabiles can be traced back to his formative years and his interest in Miró and Klee's fantastic imagery. One of the finest stabiles is *Flamingo* (1973), located at Federal Center Plaza in Chicago, IL. Positioned outside federal office buildings designed by Mies van der Rohe, it provides a visual transition between human scale and the colossal proportions of two monolithic skyscrapers that are adjacent. The red stabile complements the black steel and glass of the towers, and the curving forms counterpoise the severe geometry of the architect's design. Like a giant bird poised on spindly legs with beak lowered to the ground, it attracts the attention of pedestrians and encourages movement beneath the space it occupies. Shortly before his death Calder completed a colossal stabile, *La Défense*, at the Rond Point de La Défense Métro station in Paris. His allusions to fantastic animal forms in brightly painted sheets of metal attracted the attention of sculptors interested in whimsical creatures in polychrome. As the first American artist to achieve international success for his Constructivist/ Surrealist sculpture, he exerted a strong influence on younger artists committed to abstraction.

See also ART LEGISLATION.

WRITINGS

An Autobiography with Pictures (New York, 1966)

BIBLIOGRAPHY

H. H. Arnason: *Calder* (New York, 1966)
H. H. Arnason and U. Mulas: *Calder* (New York, 1971)
J. Lipman: *Calder's Universe* (New York, 1976)
J. Marter: 'Alexander Calder: Cosmic Imagery and the Use of Scientific Instruments', *Arts* [New York], liii (1978), pp. 108–13
J. Marter, R. Tarbell and J. Wechsler: *Vanguard American Sculpture, 1913–1939* (New Brunswick, 1979)
G. Carandente: *Calder* (Milan, 1983)
J. Marter: *Alexander Calder* (Cambridge, New York and Melbourne, 1991)

JOAN MARTER

Calderari [Calderatti]**,** Conte **Ottone Maria** (*b* Vicenza, ?18 Sept 1730; *d* Vicenza, 26 Oct 1803). Italian architect and writer. He was a pupil of Domenico Cerato, developing an extremely conservative trend of Neo-classicism based on Palladio but assimilating contemporary ideas of prismatic form and functional planning; he was heavily influenced by the contemporary publication of Ottavio Bertotti Scamozzi's *Le fabbriche e i disegni di Andrea Palladio raccolti e illustrati* (1776–83). Bertotti Scamozzi regarded him as having 'appropriated' rather then 'imitated' Palladio; Antoine Quatremère de Quincy called him a 'rejuvenated Palladio'. He was a prolific architect, building numerous palazzi, villas and churches in the Veneto, and was elected a member of the Institut de France.

Calderari's unexecuted design (1756) for the façade of the church of Padri Scalzi, Vicenza, exemplifies his manner. The composition followed closely that by Palladio for S Giorgio Maggiore (begun 1566), Venice, but the flat planes and the decoration of the frieze were resolutely Neo-classical. The chapels of the Casa Monza (1760), Breganze, and the Villa Porto (1774), Pilastroni di Vivaro, have severe temple façades, with four engaged columns supporting a pediment, but somewhat subordinate wings. The church of S Orso (1777), near Vicenza, is centrally planned with an apsidal sanctuary; it was derived from Palladio's unexecuted design for S Nicola da Tolentino (1579), Venice, but with extended chapels. The principal elevation is a reduced version of S Giorgio Maggiore; the decoration and niches appear to be incised in the façade.

Calderari designed a number of magnificent palazzi in Vicenza, each a variation on those by Palladio but more pragmatically planned. The Palazzo Cordellina (1776; partially executed; now Scuola Media) is regarded as his masterpiece. The ground floor and *piano nobile* of the principal façade feature engaged columns, as at the Palazzo Barbarano-Da Porto (1570–75) by Palladio. Two magnificent courtyards are separated by a central block containing a cruciform atrium; the cross axis opens on one side to a garden and on the other to an enormous staircase leading to a *salone* lit by thermal windows. Calderari's other palaces in Vicenza were based on Palladio's Palazzo da Porto-Festa (*c.* 1547): they include the Palazzo Quinto (n.d.; unexecuted), the Palazzo Loschi (1782), with three projecting central bays, and the Palazzo Salvi (1784; partially executed), also with three projecting central bays and an unusual oval staircase in a tower rising above the adjacent roofs. Calderari's villas were usually modelled on Palladio's Villa Foscari (*c.* 1558): they include the Casino Todaro (1785; now Dolcetta), Campedello, the Villa Anti (1772; partially executed) and the Casino Fontanella (designed 1766, executed 1799; now Girotto). The Villa Porto (1776–8; partially executed), Pilastroni di Vivaro, however, was derived from Palladio's Villa Cornaro (1551–3) but with more dominant wings. Calderari designed several more modest dwellings, such as the Palazzo Bonin (1785), with an Ionic colonnade supporting the upper storeys, the Casa Capra (1803; now Lampertico), the Casa Disconzi (*c* 1802), and the Casa Zanchi (1773), Padua. Calderari acted as consultant on the restoration of several buildings by Palladio, in particular the Basilica (1778) and the Teatro Olimpico, on which he also wrote a treatise; in 1762 he proposed painting the ceiling of the auditorium as a velarium (executed 1827–8; destr. 1914).

WRITINGS

Disegni e scritti di architettura, 2 vols (Vicenza, 1808–15/*R* Bologna, 1978)

'Discorso sopra la copertura del Teatro Olimpico', *Scritture inedite in materia di architettura*, ed. Antonio Magini (Padua, 1847)

BIBLIOGRAPHY

DBI

F. Barbieri: 'Il neoclassico vicentino: Ottone Calderari', *A. Ven.*, vii (1953), pp. 63–78

R. Cevese: 'L'architettura neoclassica vicentina e Ottone Calderari', *Boll. Cent. Stud. Stor. Archit.*, v (1963), pp. 144–51

F. Cataldi: 'Il Santuario di Santorso a Vicenza', *Archit.: Cron. & Stor.*, x (1965), pp. 624–31

F. Barbieri: 'Ottone Calderari', *Illuministi e neoclassici a Vicenza* (Vicenza, 1971), pp. 93–144

□

Calderini, Guglielmo (*b* Perugia, 3 March 1837; *d* Rome, 12 Feb 1916). Italian architect and writer. He studied engineering at the University of Turin under Carlo Promis and received a diploma in architectural engineering at Rome, before working in Perugia for nine years. There he was named honorary engineer (1869) for his contributions to the study and restoration of Umbria's historic buildings. Throughout his career, Calderini frequently entered competitions for civic works, demonstrating sensitivity to the integration of historic and contemporary elements in both design and building techniques, as shown in his college (1879) at Nocera Umbra, and the completion of Savona's 16th-century cathedral (1880–86). His Palazzo delle Belle Arti (begun 1880; destr. during World War II) in Turin, Palazzo di Giustizia (1882–1910) in Rome and Palazzo Comunale (begun 1910) in Messina, along with his numerous, handsomely executed competition designs, chronicle the exuberant, revivalist spirit of the new Kingdom of Italy. By the turn of the century, Calderini was regarded as the leading exponent of a style that fused the ancient, Renaissance and Baroque architecture of Rome with the social and aesthetic needs of a unified Italian people.

In 1882 Calderini began his lengthy association with the Palazzo di Giustizia, Rome, which started with a highly publicized, two-stage competition, continued with the complicated construction supervision (1888–97), and concluded with the legal resolution of difficulties encountered with the still-incomplete building in 1908. The project was hampered from the beginning by an unstable building site and by rapidly rising construction costs. The building was opened in 1910, lacking the bronze quadriga by Ettore Ximenes, which was finally completed in 1917; it was evacuated in 1970 due to imminent collapse. Extensive reinforcement and renovation were completed in 1992. The conspicuous site and important function of the huge palazzo commanded attention as perhaps the most prominent architectural symbol of the 'third Rome' and new Italy. Placed directly on the north end of the monumental Ponte Umberto I, near the Castel Sant'Angelo, the sumptuously decorated white marble structure seems to sit above a base formed by the Tiber's stone embankment. On approach, a central archway reveals the vast interior entrance court with twin, curved flights of stairs. This foil to the heavy façade hints at the plan; the massive two-storey block encloses a symmetrical series of ten smaller courts, giving light and grace to the interior offices.

While working on the Palazzo di Giustizia, Calderini also had important projects in Perugia, and between 1888 and 1904 these included the Palazzo Bianchi, the public baths, market portico and the church of S Costanzo (1890). He also built the Palazzo Cesaroni (1908; later a hotel). In Rome he became in 1893 the fourth architect to supervise the rebuilding of the basilica of S Paolo fuori le Mura, which had burnt down in 1823. There he completed the façade and the fourth side of the great quadriporticus (1893–1910). As director of the Uffizio Regionale per la Conservazione dei Monumenti di Roma, Aquila e Chieti he also restored the Romanesque cloisters there and at S Giovanni in Laterano. Calderini was professor of architecture at the Accademia di Perugia (1870–80) and University of Pisa (1881) and was later instructor (1891–1912) at the engineering college in Rome. For his writings, he won three times the prize instituted by Luigi Poletti at the Accademia di S Luca.

WRITINGS

Michelangelo Buonarroti e l'architettura moderna (Perugia, 1875)

Sull'insegnamento dell'architettura nelle regie università italiane (Perugia, 1881)

Il Palazzo di Giustizia di Roma (Rome, 1890)

Sulla riforma delle scuole di belle arti (Rome, 1907)

Scritti di architettura (Rome, 1991)

BIBLIOGRAPHY

DBI

C. L. V. Meeks: *Italian Architecture, 1750–1914* (New Haven and London, 1966)

G. Accasto: *L'architettura di Roma capitale, 1870–1970* (Rome, 1973)

P. Marconi: *Calderini* (Rome, 1975)

GRETCHEN G. FOX

Calderini, Marco (*b* Turin, 20 July 1850; *d* Turin, 26 Feb 1941). Italian painter, critic and writer. From 1867 to 1873 he studied at the Accademia Albertina di Belle Arti in Turin, and when Antonio Fontanesi arrived in 1869 to teach landscape painting, Calderini became one of his first and most able pupils. He took a studio with a fellow student, Francesco Mosso (1849–77), and in 1870 made his début at the Società Promotrice with *Solitary Statues* (Rome, G.N.A. Mod.), a painting depicting the statues and gardens of the Palazzo Reale in Turin after rainfall. Fontanesi's expressive and fluid style with its emphasis on the sensuous qualities of a particular landscape (e.g. *Stillness*, 1860; Turin, Gal. Civ. A. Mod.) inspired Calderini to approach landscape painting in a similarly evocative manner (e.g. *Spring, Hills near Turin*, 1878; see Lombroso, p. 251). However, he created an equilibrium between Fontanesi's lyricism and his own more objective portrayal of nature. He shared the older artist's fervent belief in direct experience and would not paint a landscape unless he had spent at least six months in the area. Together with Fontanesi, he introduced an expressive naturalism into Piedmontese landscape painting in contrast to the finely 'finished' landscapes of Massimo D'Azeglio. Effects of light and colour at different times of day and at different seasons are the subjects of a number of works, including *Summer in the Lower Alps* (1885), the *Po in May* (1898) and *Sunset in November* (1900; all Turin, Gal. Civ. A. Mod.). In 1881, together with Domenico Morelli, he became a member of the Commissione Permanente di

Belle Arti. He exhibited frequently in Italy, especially at the Società Promotrice in Turin until 1939, and had many patrons, although few in Turin. His honest approach to painting is reflected in his critical writings that appeared in *La stampa*, *La gazzetta letteraria di Torino* and *Gazette des beaux-arts*, among others. His biographical publications on friends, such as that on Fontanesi (1901), are perceptive and unsentimental.

WRITINGS

Regular contributions to *Gaz. B.-A.*, *Gaz. Lett. Torino*, *Rass. N.* and *La Stampa* (1873–88)

Le memorie postume di Francesco Mosso (Turin, 1885)

Antonio Fontanesi: Pittore paesista, 1818–1882 (Turin, 1901, 2/1925)

BIBLIOGRAPHY

P. Lombroso: 'Marco Calderini', *Emporium*, viii/40 (1898), pp. 241–56

A. Griseri: *Il paesaggio nella pittura piemontese dell'ottocento* (Milan, 1967)

L. Mallé, ed.: *I dipinti della Galleria d'Arte Moderna*, Turin, Mus. Civ. cat. (Turin, 1968), p. 104

□

Calderón, Coqui [Constancia] (*b* Panama City, 17 Jan 1937). Panamanian painter and printmaker. She studied from 1955 to 1959 at Rosemont College in Philadelphia, PA, and in Paris at the Académie de la Grande Chaumière (1959–61) and from 1960 to 1961 at the Académie Julian and the Sorbonne. Her early paintings were figurative, with sombre colours and textured surfaces. She held her first solo exhibition in Panama in 1960, followed by others in Munich and Paris, and established her reputation with an international art prize in San Salvador in 1967. In the 1960s she lived in New York, where she came under the influence of Pop art in paintings such as *555–1212* (1967; Panama City, Mus. A. Contemp.), which depict positive/negative images in strident, fluorescent colours. In the 1970s she produced paintings, drawings, screenprints and embossed prints based on patterns created through the repetition of an image, often a part of the body. There was humour in acrylic paintings such as *Tribute to the Letter 'A' No. 2* (1976; Washington, DC, A. Mus. Americas), in which the lines of the letters were softened and curved until they looked like shapely human torsos.

The smooth surfaces of Calderón's abstract paintings were often airbrushed with acrylic paint; shapes could be sharp and stencilled in appearance or soft and diffused. This technique is apparent even in her sometimes politically inspired later works and in her sensuous and colourful landscapes and still-lifes of the 1980s. Calderón was an important promoter of the arts in Panama. In 1983 she was awarded the Order of Vasco Nuñez de Balboa for her work with the Instituto Panameño de Arte.

BIBLIOGRAPHY

Coqui Calderón: Protesta '84 (exh. cat. by G. Guardia, Panama City, Gal. Etcétera, 1984)

Calderón, 1985–1986 (exh. cat., ed. M. E. Kupfer; Panama City, Mus. A. Contemp., 1986)

MONICA E. KUPFER

Calderón, Juan Carlos (*b* La Paz, 2 June 1932). Bolivian architect. He studied architecture at Oklahoma State University, Stillwater, and lectured in the architecture faculties of the University of Utah, Salt Lake City, and Florida State University, Tallahassee, in the 1960s. Unlike his slightly younger contemporary Gustavo Medeiros, Calderón was educated in the USA during the period of American influence immediately after the revolution of 1952, but he returned to do his main work in La Paz in the 1970s and 1980s. He designed a number of important buildings that tend towards an organic style sensitive to context. Among his best-known private commissions are the multi-storey HANSA headquarters (1975), the Plaza Hotel (1976) and the Illimani and S Teresa apartment blocks (1979–80), all in La Paz. Major government buildings followed, for example the Edificio Nacional de Correos (1983) and the Ministerio de Transportes y Communicaciones (1975–90) in La Paz. There are suggestions of Post-modernism in Calderón's later work in the 1980s.

WRITINGS

Juan Carlos Calderón, arquitecto (Mexico City, 1986)

TERESA GISBERT

Calderon, Philip Hermogenes (*b* Poitiers, 3 May 1833; *d* London, 30 April 1898). English painter of Spanish and French descent. His father, at one time a Roman Catholic priest, was Professor of Spanish Literature at King's College, London. Calderon studied at James M. Leigh's school in London in 1850, then in Paris at the studio of François-Edouard Picot. He lived near by in Montmartre, sharing a room with fellow art student Henry Stacy Marks. He exhibited his first Royal Academy painting, *By the Waters of Babylon* (London, Tate), in 1853 and thereafter became a regular exhibitor until 1897. He first made his name with *Broken Vows* (London, Tate), exhibited in 1857. The painting shows a woman overhearing through a garden fence her lover betraying her and was painted in the detailed, clean-cut style associated with the Pre-Raphaelites. It was successful with critics and public alike and was engraved in 1859.

Calderon was elected RA in 1867. By this date he had become an established artist and one of the founder-members of the ST JOHN'S WOOD CLIQUE. The artists belonging to this group specialized in historical or biblical scenes depicted in a romantic or dramatic light, as in Calderon's *Ruth and Naomi* (1886; Liverpool, Walker A.G.). In 1887 Calderon was appointed Keeper at the Royal Academy. When he exhibited the *Renunciation of St Elizabeth of Hungary* (London, Tate) in 1891, the depiction of the Saint kneeling naked in front of the altar provoked criticism from Roman Catholic circles. In general, however, his good draughtsmanship, attractive colouring and interesting choice of subjects made him popular in his day.

BIBLIOGRAPHY

H. S. Marks: *Pen and Pencil Sketches*, 2 vols (London, 1894)

G. A. Storey: 'Philip Hermogenes Calderon, RA', *Mag. A.*, xxii (1898), pp. 446–52

S. Casteras: *Down the Garden Path* (diss., New Haven, Yale U., 1977)

For further bibliography *see* PRE-RAPHAELITISM and ST JOHN'S WOOD CLIQUE.

JENNY ELKAN

Calderón, Rodrigo (*b* Antwerp, *c.* 1576; *d* Madrid, 21 Oct 1621). Spanish politician, patron and collector. At an early age he entered the service of Francisco Gómez de Sandoval y Rojas, Marqués de Denia and the future Duque de Lerma, and became his close confidant. He led the negotiations in Paris and Flanders to arrange two marriages, of Prince Philip, the future Philip IV, with Elizabeth of Bourbon (1602–44), and of the Spanish Infanta, Ana

(1601–66), with Louis XIII of France; he returned to Spain in 1612, receiving successively the title of Conde de la Oliva and Marqués de Siete Iglesias. The Duque de Lerma's fall from favour in 1618 entailed that of Calderón, and having been found guilty of the charges made against him, he was executed in Madrid. His possessions were sold at public auction, some being reserved for the royal house. Calderón's patronage is notable for his foundation of the convent of Nuestra Señora de Porta Coeli (1606–7) in Valladolid, containing his tomb and that of his wife and her parents, built by Diego de Praves; and the convent of Nuestra Señora de la Merced and the chapel of S Teresa de Jesús in the Carmelite convent, both in Madrid. He endowed these buildings with many of the gifts received for favours from the Duque de Lerma: at Porta Coeli these include the custodia; the principal retable, associated with Juan de Muñiátegui (*d* 1612) and Gregorio Fernández; the four family funerary busts (attributed to Taddeo Carlone); and the doors and mantelpieces of Genoa marble (all *c.* 1607–14; *in situ*). In 1611 Calderón received, perhaps from the Duque de Taurisano, Spanish Ambassador to the Holy See, 12 paintings by ORAZIO BORGIANNI for the retable of the church of the convent of the Porta Coeli (*in situ*), Valladolid. Calderón's palaces in Madrid and Valladolid contained Flemish tapestries and paintings, including 40 canvases depicting the *Legend of the Infantes de Lara* commissioned from Otto van Veen in Flanders. These, together with others depicting the *Wonders of the World*, also by van Veen, were subsequently acquired by Philip IV. The *Adoration of the Magi* (1609; Madrid, Prado), an early painting by Rubens, of whose works he possessed others, was a gift to Calderón from the municipality of Antwerp and was confiscated and placed in the Alcázar, Madrid, on the orders of Philip IV in 1621.

BIBLIOGRAPHY

G. Gascón de Torquemada: *Nacimiento, vida, prisión y muerte de Don Rodrigo Calderón, Marqués de Siete Iglesias, Conde de la Oliva* (Madrid, 1789)

F. de Quevedo: *Grandes anales de quince días, obras completas*, i (Madrid, 1958)

J. J. Martín González: 'Bienes artísticos de don Rodrigo Calderón', *Bol. Semin. Estud. A. & Arqueol.*, liv (1988), pp. 267–92

NATIVIDAD SÁNCHEZ ESTEBAN

Calderon Site. *See* HATILLO, EL.

Calendar. As applied to medieval manuscripts, a list of the principal feast days of the Church and the commemorative feasts of the saints throughout the liturgical year. It was an essential part of books used to celebrate Mass (the MISSAL, Pontifical and Benedictional) and the Divine Office (the PSALTER and BREVIARY), as well as of books of prayers used for private devotion (e.g. BOOK OF HOURS). Major Church feasts (e.g. Christmas and Easter), the commemorative days of the Apostles and other major saints or the names of saints particularly important in the diocese for which the book was made might be highlighted by being written in red, gold or blue. The text usually begins with an embellished KL (for Kalends, the Latin name for the first day of the month); the days of the week are indicated by lower-case letters a–g, accompanied by abbreviations of Ides and Nones. Golden numbers (i–xix) might also appear in the left column for calculating the date of the Paschal moon. Normally the text for such a calendar, with a line allocated to each day, occupied the *recto* and *verso* of 12 folios.

1. EARLY DEVELOPMENT. It became customary to decorate calendars in illustrated manuscripts with the Signs of the Zodiac, signifying the passage of celestial time, and the Labours of the Months, indicating Man's toil on the earth and the passage of terrestrial time. Such representations evolved from the personifications of the Months, sometimes in conjunction with the Signs of the Zodiac, as a manifestation of the cyclical passing of the seasons; this theme had been used in Classical art from as early as the 2nd or 1st century BC, for example in a Hellenistic frieze (partly destr.) in Panagia Gorgoepikoos, Athens, and in Roman floor mosaics, such as one from Carthage (London, BM). Single-figure personifications of the Months, shown in a labelled architectural frame, are found in the Calendar of AD 354, which is known from 15th- and 17th-century drawings after a Carolingian copy (Vienna, Österreich. Nbib., Cod. 3416, and Rome, Vatican, Bib. Apostolica, MS. Barb. lat. 2154; *see* ICONOGRAPHY AND ICONOLOGY, fig. 2). A circular diagram containing personifications of the Months and the Signs of the Zodiac, which had prototypes in Roman mosaic decoration, also appears in a Carolingian manuscript of Ptolemy (*c.* AD 813–20; Rome, Vatican, Bib. Apostolica, MS. Vat. gr. 1291). The earliest extant representations of figures performing the Labours of the Months occur in calendars in two Carolingian manuscripts containing astronomical treatises and the *De rerum natura* of Bede (*c.* 818; Munich, Bayer. Staatsbib., Clm. 210; and before 830; Vienna, Österreich. Nbib., Cod. 387, respectively), in which all 12 Labours are depicted on a single folio. A mid-9th-century poem by Wandalbert, Abbot of Prüm, on the occupations and astrological and meteorological characteristics of each month may have added impetus to this developing tradition. Thus derived from antique sources and elaborated in a variety of secular and astrological treatises, by the 12th century the paired representations of the Signs of the Zodiac and Labours of the Months became commonplace in church decoration (*see* ASTROLOGICAL AND ASTRONOMICAL MANUSCRIPTS). They are found in carved capitals (e.g. Brescia, Mus. Civ. Crist.), in floor mosaics (e.g. Aosta Cathedral) and in the sculpted reliefs and archivolts of numerous Romanesque and Gothic churches, usually in connection with the iconographical programmes of portal sculpture. These representations were intended to serve as reminders of the passage of celestial and terrestrial time until the Second Coming and the Last Judgement.

2. MANUSCRIPT ILLUSTRATIONS. In many illustrated calendars throughout the Middle Ages single figures representing the Signs of the Zodiac and the Labours of the Months were paired, without any further elaboration of setting or season. In the calendar of the Queen Ingeborg Psalter (*c.* 1195; Chantilly, Mus. Condé, MS. 1695), paired medallions containing these representations on a gold ground appear on the opening side of the folio for each month. Shown in various formats, such simplified representations were the most common until the 15th century. The specific labour associated with each month varied

according to the region and the period, but by the end of the Middle Ages a more or less standard sequence of representations had evolved:

January	Feasting	Aquarius
February	Warming by a fire	Pisces
March	Pruning	Aries
April	Planting or picking flowers	Taurus
May	Hawking	Cancer
June	Harvesting hay	Gemini
July	Reaping corn	Leo
August	Threshing wheat	Virgo
September	Harvesting grapes	Libra
October	Ploughing and sowing	Scorpio
November	Gathering acorns for pigs	Sagittarius
December	Killing a pig or baking bread	Capricorn

When not restricted to single-figure personifications, the depictions of the Labours of the Months soon reflected the various agricultural practices and provide glimpses of secular life at the time. Remarkable early examples of the Labours depicted in some detail and set in a rudimentary landscape can be found in an early 11th-century calendar inserted in a hymnal, possibly from Canterbury (London, BL, Cotton MS. Jul. A. VI; see fig. 1), in which the vibrant pen drawings reflect the style of the Utrecht Psalter (Utrecht, Bib. Rijksuniv., MS. 32). This is the earliest known English 'occupational' calendar, and in turn it may have served as a source for some of the painted illustrations in a slightly later calendar prefacing an astronomical treatise (London, BL, Cotton MS. Tib. B. V). Although inferior in execution, the miniatures in this manuscript show greater attention to the details of the agricultural setting and the narrative effect.

Sometimes iconographical elements were introduced that were focused more on religious than on secular concerns. In the calendar of the Belleville Breviary (1323–6; Paris, Bib. N., MSS lat. 10483–4), the Labours of the Months and Signs of the Zodiac are accompanied by allegorical representations of the establishment of the Articles of Christian Faith: on folio 6*v*, for example, St Paul is depicted above the text preaching to the nations of the earth while the Virgin waves a banner from a city gate; below, in the *bas-de-page*, a prophet removes a brick from a disintegrating synagogue and hands a veiled prophecy to an Apostle who unveils it.

With the growing interest in the representation of landscape from the end of the 14th century, accompanied by the assimilation of the aesthetic of panel painting into manuscript illumination, calendar scenes occasionally expanded into detailed depictions of the activities and settings of daily life. This is particularly true of the full-page miniatures illustrating the calendar of the TRÈS RICHES HEURES (Chantilly, Mus. Condé, MS. 65) begun in 1411–13 by the Limbourg brothers for Jean, Duc de Berry (for illustration *see* LIMBOURG, DE, fig. 2, and VALOIS, (3)). Each miniature faces the relevant page of calendar text. Capped by astronomical data, representations of both Signs of the Zodiac that are dominant in any given month (e.g. Aquarius and Pisces in February) and an image of Apollo driving the chariot of the sun across the heavens, the miniatures contain meticulous depictions of the activities of nobles at play and peasants at work. The landscape detail, the precise observation of tools, the atmospheric quality of the seasons (such as the snow-laden sky for February) and the accurate representation of recognizable landmarks (such as the buildings of Paris and the Duc de Berry's châteaux; *see* MILITARY ARCHITECTURE AND FORTIFICATION, fig. 1) make these the first truly effective landscape paintings in north European art.

Although the traditional abbreviated paintings of Signs and Labours continued to be used, the example of the calendar scenes of the Très Riches Heures was copied by French and south Netherlandish illuminators of the late 15th century and the early 16th, as in the calendar of the Grimani Breviary (1510–20; Venice, Bib. N. Marciana, MS. lat. I. 99). In the Spinola Hours (Malibu, CA, Getty Mus., MS. 83), illuminated in Bruges or Ghent by 1515, the standard programme of the calendar was expanded to provide additional scenes and depictions of the contemporary landscape and agricultural customs based on close observation. These are found in the margins of the relevant pages: for example, in *May* (see fig. 2) nobles enjoy festivities in a boat, while others embark on a falconry

1. Calendar illustration, *June*; from a metrical calendar, 195×125 mm, ?Canterbury, early 11th century (London, British Library, Cotton MS. Jul. A. VI, fol. 5*v*)

2. Calendar illustration, *May*; from the Spinola Hours, 232×166 mm, south Netherlands, before 1515 (Malibu, CA, J. Paul Getty Museum, MS. 83, fol. 3*v*)

party over a bridge with a farm and castle in the background. In the lower left-hand corner is the sign of *Gemini*, while two roundels above showing *SS Philip and James* and the *Discovery of the True Cross* indicate major feasts, which are written in red in the text.

BIBLIOGRAPHY

A. Riegl: 'Die mittelalterliche Kalanderillustration', *Mitt. Österreich. Inst. Geschforsch.*, x (1889), pp. 1–74

J. Le Sénécal: 'Les Occupations des mois dans l'iconographie du moyen-âge', *Bull. Soc. Antiqua. Normandie*, xxxv (1921–3), pp. 1–218

M. J. Husung: 'Über die Entwicklung der Monatsbilder in Kalanders', *Buch und Bucheinband: Aufsätze und graphische Blätter zum 60. Geburtstage von Hans Loubier* (Leipzig, 1923), pp. 13–32

J. F. Willard: 'Occupations of the Months in Medieval Calendars', *Bodleian Q. Rec.*, vii (1932), pp. 33–9

J. C. Webster: *The Labours of the Months in Antique and Medieval Art to the End of the Twelfth Century* (Princeton, 1938)

O. Pächt: 'Early Italian Nature Studies and the Early Calendar Landscape', *J. Warb. & Court. Inst.*, xiii (1950), pp. 13–47

ROBERT G. CALKINS

Calendario [Chalandarjo; Kalandario]**, Filippo** (*b* before 1315; *d* Venice, 16 April 1355). Italian architect and sculptor. Reliable Venetian chronicles from the 15th century onwards not only praise him as the architect of the Doge's Palace in Venice and as a sculptor but also record that the Venetian government ('Signoria dogal') valued his advice when building palaces, towers and other public works. He was the most important sculptor and architect of the 14th century in Venice, although no building other than the Doge's Palace can now be attributed to him.

It is probable that Calendario, like many Venetian masons, traded in stone, for he owned *marani*, large boats suitable for its transport. When he lost three *marani* in 1343, he was given State support. Calendario became known above all for his part in the 'conspiracy' of Doge Marin Falier (*reg* 1354–5), as a result of which he was condemned to death and hanged between two columns of the Doge's Palace.

The decision to build a new Sala del Maggior Consiglio, which involved rebuilding the south wing of the Doge's Palace, was taken on 28 December 1340, and building started in 1341. In 1344 *incisores lapidum* were mentioned, perhaps a reference to the masons engaged in carving the capitals. One of the west façade capitals is dated 1344, which almost certainly dates this part of the building. The roof seems to have been put on in 1348, although as late as 1362 the work still had not been completed.

Among the many 14th-century sculptures on both façades of the Doge's Palace there are considerable discrepancies of quality, though fewer differences of style. In some 19th-century and later literature the sculptural decoration has often been dated later than the documented dates, but this interpretation is based on a misreading of its style. The corner groups of the *Drunkenness of Noah* (see fig.) and of *Adam and Eve*, the allegorical figure of *Venice* and some of the capitals (e.g. those depicting the *Life of Man*, the *Zodiac* and the *Creation of Adam*) can be attributed to Filippo Calendario as the master in charge of the work; contrary to the usual Venetian practice, however, he seems to have ensured that his assistants, of whom there were probably many, followed his style. Calendario's ability to capture the most subtle emotional expressions by the attitudes and gestures of the figures, as well as to record accurate observations of nature in stone, distinguish him from his better-known Venetian contemporary Andriolo de Santi. With his relief of *Venice* in a tondo on the west façade of the Doge's Palace, near the junction of the building campaigns, Calendario created the earliest monumental depiction of Venice under the guise of Justice, an allegorical representation of the Republic that was to become widespread in later years; the complex and encyclopaedic programme of sculptural decoration of the Palazzo, however, was unlikely to have been devised by the sculptor. Whether Calendario introduced the figured capital to Venice is uncertain. Among the spoils included in the façades of S Marco, however, there is only one example, on the upper loggia of the west façade, but it seems possible that figured capitals may have been employed in the previous Doge's Palace built under Doge Sebastiano Ziani (*reg* 1172–8).

The roots of Calendario's style as a sculptor and the inspiration and models for many of his characteristic physiognomies are probably to be sought primarily in Venice, and the influence of contemporary Venetian painting (Paolo Veneziano) is also likely. The striking gestures of the *Noah* group have their origin in a similar depiction of the theme in the narthex mosaics of S Marco. There was no sculptural tradition in Venice for many of the themes depicted, and some of the capital designs may be based on manuscript illuminations, occasionally on

Filippo Calendario (attrib.): *Drunkenness of Noah*, Istrian stone, façade of the Doge's Palace, Venice, begun *c.* 1341

French examples circulating in Venice (e.g. Venice, Bib. N. Marciana, MS. francese XVII(230), fols 10*v*, 11*r*). Attempts to trace the roots of Calendario's style to Tuscany (Florence or Pisa) have so far proved unsuccessful. The splendid, variegated foliage of the capitals, for example, seems to derive from Venetian rather than Tuscan or Lombard models (e.g. from the circle of the Pisani or Giovanni di Balduccio, in whose work figured capitals are frequent). Tuscan elements are often found in Venetian sculpture before 1340, as in the tomb of St Simon (1318; Venice, S Simeone Grande), which was probably an important influence on Calendario's work.

BIBLIOGRAPHY

Thieme–Becker
J. Ruskin: *The Stones of Venice*, ii (New York, 1851), pp. 293–366
P. Paoletti: *L'architettura e la scultura del rinascimento a Venezia* (Venice, 1893), p. 10
V. Lazzarini: *Filippo Calendario l'architetto della tradizione del Palazzo Ducale*, Nuovo Archivio Veneto, iv (Venice, 1894), pp. 429–46
——: *Marino Falier: la congiura*, Nuovo Archivio Veneto, vii (Venice, 1897), pp. 5–107, 277–374
G. Fogolari: 'La prima deca di Tito Livio illustrata nel trecento a Venezia', *L'Arte*, x (1907), pp. 330–45 (345)
E. Bassi: 'Appunti per la storia del Palazzo Ducale di Venezia', *Crit. A.*, ix (1962), pp. 25–38
——: 'L'architettura gotica a Venezia', *Boll. Cent. Int. Stud. Archit. Andrea Palladio*, vii (1965), pp. 185–206
E. Arslan: *Venezia gotica* (Milan, 1970), pp. 137–76
W. Wolters: *La scultura veneziana gotica (1300–1460)* (Milan, 1976), pp. 40–48, 172–9

WOLFGANG WOLTERS

Caletti, Giuseppe [il Cremonese] (*b* ?Cremona, *c.* 1595; *d* Ferrara, 1660). Italian painter, draughtsman and etcher. His artistic formation was complex. He knew contemporary Emilian art, from Giacomo Cavedoni to Lionello Spada and Guercino, and was intensely interested in 16th-century painters from Venice and the Po Valley, ranging from Giorgione to Titian, from Altobello Meloni to Romanino and of course Dosso Dossi. Caletti was mainly interested, as was Pietro della Vecchia, in a revival of 16th-century Venetian art, and, like della Vecchia, although at times he produced forgeries of 16th-century pictures, he more often interpreted such sources with irony and powerful emotion, as in the *St Sebastian* (Cento, Taddei priv. col.), which is modelled on Titian's figure of St Sebastian in the Averoldi polyptych of the *Resurrection* (1522; Brescia, SS Nazaro and Celso).

In a rare public commission, a depiction of *St Mark* (*c.* 1630; Ferrara, Pin. N.), Caletti grew closer to Guercino. He was attracted by the bold Venetian colour of Guercino's early manner, the influence of which is apparent in this work and in *Jael and Sisera* (Ferrara, Pin. N.). Caletti's sketchy and vivid style as a draughtsman and etcher, revealed in his drawings, for example *St Roch* (Windsor Castle, Berks, Royal Lib.) and in such etchings as *The Lovers* (B. 9) and *Samson and Delilah* (B. 4), remains suggestive of Guercino, as are many of his cabinet pictures. The latter form the greatest part of Caletti's work and include many macabre renderings of *David with the Head of Goliath* (e.g. Florence, priv. col., see Fioravanti Baraldi, p. 123). His last works must be the small panels with scenes from the *Life of St John the Baptist* (Ferrara, S Giovanni Battista). These paintings (most in Ferrara, Mus. Civ.) are distinguished by a sketchy, almost awkwardly careless style.

BIBLIOGRAPHY

G. Baruffaldi: *Vite de' pittori e scultori ferraresi, 1697–1722*; ed. G. Boschini, ii (Ferrara, 1846), pp. 209–16
A. von Bartsch: *Le Peintre-graveur* (1803–21) [B.]
N. Ivanoff: 'Giuseppe Caletti detto il Cremonese, 1600(?)–1660', *Emporium* (Aug 1951), pp. 73–8
G. Raimondi: 'Appunto su Giuseppe Caletti, il "Cremonese"', *A. Ant. & Mod.*, iv/13–16 (1961), pp. 279–84
E. Riccomini: *Il seicento ferrarese* (Cinisello Balsamo, 1969), pp. 41–7
C. Savonuzzi: 'Il Caletti, di nuovo', *Mus. Ferrar.: Boll. Annu.*, ii (1972), pp. 31–6
A. M. Fioravanti Baraldi: 'La pittura a Ferrara nel secolo XVII', *La chiesa di S Giovanni Battista e la cultura ferrarese del seicento* (exh. cat., ed. A. F. Toselli; Ferrara, Pal. Schifanoia, 1981), pp. 112–35
M. Tanzi: 'Un inedito cremonese di Giuseppe Caletti', *Mus. Ferrar.: Boll. Annu.*, xiii (1983–4), pp. 133–8

UGO RUGGERI

Calì, Giuseppe (*b* Valletta, 14 Aug 1846; *d* Valletta, 1 March 1930). Maltese painter. He was the nephew of Antonio Calì (1788–1866) and the cousin of Beniamino Calì (*b* 1832), both of whom achieved fame as sculptors in Naples in the 19th century. Because of unrest in Italy during the Risorgimento (1796–1870), his parents moved to Malta shortly before his birth. In 1863 he studied in

Naples at the Accademia di Belle Arti e Liceo Artistico under Giuseppe Mancinelli (1813–75) and then in the studio of Domenico Morelli, whose dynamic and sensuous work made a lasting impression on him. Another important formative influence was the work of Delacroix, which inspired Calì's early *Death of Dragut* (1867; Valletta, Fort St Elmo, War Mus.). This painting, remarkable for its superb colours and vigour, made Calì Malta's most popular artist. He was extremely versatile and prodigiously prolific, painting in a Romantic style. His output ranges from easel paintings and altarpieces to large-scale decorations for church vaults. His vast oeuvre is uneven in quality and some of his works are spoiled by a sickly morbidity, although he was an excellent draughtsman. His best works are boldly and freely rendered with an exciting exuberant spontaneity. He is best known for the huge ceiling painting of the *Apotheosis of St Francis* (1907; Valletta, St Francis), which was painted specifically to demonstrate his virtuosity in the face of competition by foreign artists of lesser merit, including Attilio Palombi (*c.* 1860–1913). He is best remembered as an artist who worked for the Church but he was also a talented portrait painter. Among his finest portraits are *Sir Adrian Dingli* (1896; Valletta, Chamber of Commerce) and *Sir Giuseppe Carbone* (1915; Valletta, Casino Maltese). He also executed a large number of exquisitely poetic genre paintings whose Victorian charm is often tinged with a pleasing sensuality (e.g. *Girl by the Stream*; Valletta, Mus. F.A.). His son Ramiro Raffaele Calì (1882–1945) was also a painter.

BIBLIOGRAPHY

G. Calì: Centenary Exhibition, 1846–1946 (exh. cat., ed. R. Bonnici Calì; Valletta, Salle Pal., 1946)

M. Buhagiar, ed.: *St Catherine of Alexandria: Her Churches, Paintings and Statues in the Maltese Islands* (Valletta, 1979), p. 212

M. Buhagiar: *The Iconography of the Maltese Islands, 1400–1900: Painting* (Valletta, 1988), pp. 178–85

E. Fiorentino and L. A. Grasso: *Giuseppe Calì, 1846–1930* (Valletta, 1991)

MARIO BUHAGIAR

Caliari. Italian family of painters. The most accomplished member of the family, Paolo Caliari, is better known as PAOLO VERONESE, from his birthplace. After his death in 1588, his workshop (*see* VERONESE, PAOLO, §II, 3) was run by his brother (1) Benedetto Caliari and his sons (2) Carlo Caliari and Gabriele Caliari (*b* Venice, 1568; *d* 1631), using the signature *Haeredes Pauli.* Only one signed work by Gabriele is known: an altarpiece of the *Virgin and St Anne* (Liettoli, parish church); its physical types are related to Veronese's but are rather awkward and heavy.

(1) Benedetto Caliari (*b* Verona, 1538; *d* Venice, 1598). In 1556, at age 18, he was recorded as the assistant of his elder brother, Paolo Veronese, decorating the ceiling (*in situ*; *see* VERONESE, PAOLO, §I, 2(i)) of the church of S Sebastiano, Venice, and it is thought that he was Veronese's principal collaborator at the Villa Barbaro at Maser (*c.* 1561; *see* VERONESE, PAOLO, §I, 3(i)), producing much of the illusionistic architecture there and some of the landscapes (*in situ*). Frescoes (*c.* 1564–77) in the Vescovado, Treviso (*in situ*), offer the first known instance of his independent work; the Sala there is an echo of the Sala Crociera at Maser, with landscape views seen through a painted arcade. Benedetto Caliari is attributed with the decoration of the Villa Corner-Piacentini, Sant'Andrea (*in situ*), with some of the frescoes (after 1575) of the Villa Giusti at Magnadola (*in situ*) and with easel paintings (late 1560s) of *St Peter Visiting St Agatha in Prison* (Murano, S Pietro) and the *Flight into Egypt* (Caen, Mus. B.-A.). He assisted Veronese with two commissions at the Doge's Palace, Venice (1574–82; *see* VERONESE, PAOLO, §I, 4(i)), and in 1575 he was in Padua, helping Veronese with the *Martyrdom of St Justine* (Padua, S Giustina), a work that clearly shows his hand. The *Birth of the Virgin* (1577; Venice, Accad., on dep. Venice, Gal. Farsetti), commissioned for the Scuola dei Mercanti, is one of the few paintings documented as designed and executed by Benedetto Caliari, the forms are heavy, strongly modelled versions of Veronese's types, and the hand is somewhat mechanical.

(2) Carlo [Carletto] **Caliari** (*b* Venice, 1567–70; *d* Venice, 1592–6). Nephew of (1) Benedetto Caliari and son of Paolo Veronese. As the most talented member of his father's workshop, he undoubtedly executed many works that are attributed to his father. Works that have been clearly isolated as Carlo's own are more precise and delicate, both technically and in the physical types; they lack Veronese's bravura, whether in the line and wash of a chiaroscuro drawing or in the richly layered pigments that make an embroidered drape. His early signed works show the influence of both his father and the Bassano family by whom he was trained. They include *Angelica and Medoro* (*c.* 1584; Padua, Barbieri priv. col.), which has a preciousness in the landscape and in details of foliage and coiffures that sets it apart from Veronese's work. The signed *Nativity* (*c.* 1588; Brescia, S Afra) combines narrative detail typical of the Bassano with morphological similarities to Veronese. There are similar characteristics in frescoes at the Villa Loredan, Sant'Urbano, Padua, that are assigned to Carlo by Crosato. Other signed paintings—the *Virgin in Glory with SS Margaret, Mary Magdalene and Frediano* (*c.* 1588–90; Florence, Uffizi), *St Agnes* (Madrid, Prado) and the *Vanity* (London, priv. col.)—share facial type, a smooth finish and the somewhat mannered gestures also found in the attributed *St Catherine* (Florence, Pitti). More closely resembling works by Veronese, and perhaps later, are the signed *St Augustine Giving the Rules of his Order to the Irregular Canons Lateran* (Venice, Accad.) and the *Virgin in Glory with Saints* (*c.* 1602; Venice, Fond. Cini; attributed to Carlo by Boschini). The signed *Resurrection of Lazarus* (Venice, Accad.) is rather refined, delicate and static, qualities also found in its preparatory drawing (Vienna, Albertina).

BIBLIOGRAPHY

Thieme–Becker

C. Ridolfi: *Meraviglie* (1648); ed. D. von Hadeln, i (1914–24), pp. 353–61

M. Boschini: *La carta del navegar pittoresca* (Venice, 1660), pp. 280, 435–9

——: *Le ricche miniere* (Venice, 1674), pp. 27, 50

B. dal Pozzo: *Le vite dei pittori, scultori e architetti veronesi* (Verona, 1718), pp. 114, 122

L. Coletti: 'I paesi di Paolo Veronese', *Dedalo*, vi (1925), pp. 404–10

L. Crosato: *Gli affreschi nelle ville venete del cinquecento* (Treviso, 1962), figs 109–20, 129–31

L. Crosato Larcher: 'Per Gabriele Caliari', *A. Ven.*, xviii (1964), pp. 174–5

——: 'Per Carletto Caliari', *A. Ven.*, xxi (1967), pp. 108–24

——: 'Note su Benedetto Caliari', *A. Ven.*, xxiii (1969), pp. 115–30

R. Brenzoni: *Dizionario di artisti veneti* (Florence, 1972), p. 67

T. Formiciova: 'Opere di allievi del Veronese nella collezione dell'Ermitage: Nuove attribuzioni', *A. Ven.*, xxxiii (1979), pp. 131–6
A. Cuozzo: 'Una inedita *Natività della Vergine* di Benedetto Caliari', *A. Ven.*, xxxiv (1985), pp. 145–6

DIANA GISOLFI

Caliari, Paolo (i). *See* VERONESE, PAOLO.

Caliari, Paolo [Paolino] **(ii)** (*b* Verona, 1763; *d* Verona, 23 April 1835). Italian painter and draughtsman. He is usually known in Verona as Paolino Caliari, in order to distinguish him from his great ancestor, Paolo Veronese, whose family name was Caliari. His father, Domenico Caliari, a book dealer and engraver of some means, gladly allowed him to study art, as was the family tradition. Caliari trained under Prospero Schiavi (1730–1803), a pupil of Giambettino Cignaroli. On 30 August 1788 he graduated from the Accademia di Pittura e Scultura in Verona. He developed great skill in copying Renaissance masters, imitating their techniques as well as their compositions. His copies attracted the interest of Marchese Maurizio Gherardini, also from Verona, who helped him win a commission from Victor Amadeus, Prince of Carignano, to make copies of great paintings throughout Italy, as well as to provide works of his own invention. This project ended, however, with the French Revolution and with Gherardini's death in 1796.

For three consecutive years Caliari won the Lorgna prize at the Accademia di Verona, with works in encaustic of *Hebe* (1792), an *Ecce homo* (1793) and the *Hesperides* (1794). In 1808 he was designated master at the Accademia Cignaroli in Verona, where he taught for the rest of his life. Understanding how artificial the art of his own time had become, he advocated a return to the great masters of the 15th and 16th centuries. He championed simple compositions and discouraged his colleagues and students from following that style, which, especially at the end of the 18th century, sacrificed all reason and propriety to a system requiring pyramidal compositions and highly contrasting, bright colours.

In 1815 Caliari's series of 40 pen drawings (Verona, Bib. Civ.) illustrating the collection of his cousin Giovanni Albarelli were published as a volume of engravings: *Gabinetto di quadri o raccolta di pezzi originali esistenti in Verona presso il sig. Gio. Albarelli disegnati da P.C. con illustrazioni* (Verona, 1815). Among the artists represented in Albarelli's collection were Giovanni Bellini, Mantegna, Cima da Conegliano, Pellegrino da San Daniele, Correggio, Titian, Palma Giovane, Guido Reni, Guercino and van Dyck. Caliari also had a busy career as a decorator, painting coats of arms, furniture, ceramics and carriages. In this he was assisted by his son and pupil, Giovanni Caliari. In addition, Paolo executed frescoes on ceilings, walls and doors, painting landscapes, mythological subjects, arabesques, *trompe l'oeil* bas-reliefs, garlands of fruit and flowers, and groups of fawns and putti. Portrait painting formed another aspect of his activities.

BIBLIOGRAPHY

Bénézit; Bolaffi; *DBI* [with bibliog.]; Thieme–Becker
L. Simeoni: *Verona* (Verona, 1909), pp. xxxiii, 158, 178, 238, 278, 323
P. Caliari: 'Paolo Caliari pittore (1763–1835)', *Madonna Verona*, vi/24 (1912), pp. 37–42

ALEXANDRA HERZ

Calicut [now Kozhikode]. City on the Malabar Coast of Kerala, India. According to the 14th-century Moroccan traveller Ibn Battuta, Calicut, a major port by 1342, was India's principal entrepôt for the spice trade. Attracting traders from both east and west of India, Arab merchants in the town had gained a monopoly on foreign commerce by the 15th century, by which time Calicut had a sizeable Muslim population. This monopoly was briefly challenged by Vasco da Gama, who between 1498 and 1510 attempted to establish Portuguese authority over the port. By 1515 the Portuguese had departed after much destruction. The Muslims maintained commercial control for several centuries, until the advent of the British and the devastations of Tipu Sultan (*reg* 1782–99). Calicut and its environs were ruled from *c*. AD 826 to 1766 by the Zamorins, a local Hindu dynasty that seems, for the most part, to have maintained cordial relations with the Muslim community.

Hindu monuments in Calicut are few. The Shiva Temple at Tiruvanur, on the outskirts, has an apsidal plan and laterite foundations. Two phases of construction occurred between *c*. AD 800 and 1200. The Tali Temple (early 15th century), near the Zamorins' palace in Calicut proper, combines traditional Kerala and NAYAKA stylistic features. The exterior of the sanctum has murals and high-relief stuccowork, giving the walls an almost brocaded effect.

More numerous are the mosques and tombs built by wealthy Muslim merchants during the 14th and 15th centuries. These structures are generally well preserved and retain most of their original features. In general the plans of the mosques include a colonnaded porch, an antechamber and a prayer-hall. Upper storeys housed schools (*see* MADRASA), administrative offices or storage space. Exteriors evoke Kerala with their tiered roofs, surrounding corridors and use of wood. Traditional Islamic features include arched doorways and prayer niches (*see* MIHRAB) and spacious interior pillared halls. Some of the more notable works are the Mithqalpalli (Makhuda Mithqal Masjid; 14th century), a sizeable structure with a three-tiered wooden roof (*see* INDIAN SUBCONTINENT, fig. 96); the Jamiʿ Masjid (restored and renovated in 1480–81 (AH 885) according to an *in situ* inscription), the largest mosque in Calicut; and the Muchchandipalli (13th–14th century), a small, well-preserved mosque with a carved wooden ceiling (in the Kerala tradition but without human figures) in its front hall.

The Kohenur Masjid at the University of Kozhikode, completed in the late 1970s, attempts to harmonize Islamic and Kerala features with modern construction techniques. The V. K. Krishna Menon Museum and Art Gallery has a collection of modern Indian paintings, carved ivory artefacts and wood-carvings. The Pazhassiraja Museum houses copies of palace and temple murals and collections of bronze sculptures and ancient coins.

See also INDIAN SUBCONTINENT, §III, 6(ii)(f).

BIBLIOGRAPHY

K. V. Krishna Ayyar: *The Zamorins of Calicut* (Calicut, 1938)
H. Sarkar: *An Architectural Survey of Temples of Kerala* (New Delhi, 1978)
T. P. Kuttiammu: 'The Mosques of Kerala', *Marq*, xxxii (1978–9), pp. 85–9
S. F. Dale: *Islamic Society on the South Asian Frontier* (Oxford, 1980)
R. Bernier: *The Temple Arts of Kerala* (New Delhi, 1982)
R. Ptak: 'China and Calicut in the Early Ming Period: Envoys and Tribute Embassies', *J. Royal Asiat. Soc. GB & Ireland* (1989), pp. 81–111

M. Shokoohy: 'Architecture of the Sultanate of Ma'bar in Madura, and Other Muslim Monuments in South India', *J. Royal Asiat. Soc. GB & Ireland*, 3rd ser., i, pt 1 (April 1991), pp. 31–92

WALTER SMITH

California bungalow. *See under* LOS ANGELES, §1; *see also* BUNGALOW.

Călineşti, Gheorghe Iliescu. *See* ILIESCU-CĂLINEȘTI, GHEORGHE.

Calixtlahuaca. Site in the Toluca Valley, Mexico. It was the capital and principal ceremonial centre of the Matlazinca people. The name derives from *calli* (Náhuatl: house) and *ixtlahuaca* (field or plain), thus 'Place of houses on the plain'. Calixtlahuaca is one of the few Matlazinca sites known with substantial remains, and its architectural ruins, scattered on the hillside between the modern villages of Calixtlahuaca and Tecaxic, combine elements from central and northern Mesoamerica. Most of the site lies beneath the villages or the fields between the villages. Surface survey and excavations were carried out between 1930 and 1938 by José García Payón.

Calixtlahuaca was occupied between *c.* 1700 BC and AD 1510, when it was destroyed by AZTEC forces. After the Spanish Conquest, Matlazinca survivors returned and established the two villages. Occupation has been divided by archaeologists into five periods: from *c.* 1700 BC–*c.* 200 BC, Pre-Classic remains represented by figurines and traces of terrace walls; from *c.* 200 BC–8th century AD, Classic period influences from TEOTIHUACÁN, especially 4th to 8th centuries, and construction of the first Temple to Quetzalcóatl; from *c.* 900–1200, Early Post-Classic TOLTEC influence, polychrome pottery with geometric designs, and construction of the second Temple to Quetzalcóatl; from 1200–1474, principal Matlazinca ceremonial centre, and construction of the third Temple to Quetzalcóatl; and from 1474–1510, captured and made subject to the México Aztecs, and the construction of the fourth Temple of Quetzalcóatl and other Aztec structures. From Toltec times the Temple of Quetzalcóatl was dedicated to his guise as Éhecatl, the wind god. Complexes of rooms on platforms were built in the valley, and the town may have paid tribute to TULA. The Toltecs used the Toluca Valley as a trade route into southern Mexico, and contact with the Basin of Mexico remained strong in the succeeding period. In the Aztec period conflict between Matlazinca factions aided invasion by the México, who captured several towns, establishing garrisons and colonies of México in them. After three rebellions (AD 1475, 1482, 1510) Calixtlahuaca was razed, the Matlazinca were forced to flee west into refuge among the TARASCAN people, and a permanent colony of Aztecs was established.

Most monuments now visible are Aztec. Defence was a main concern, with terracing, cisterns and water-collection channels, and food stores on the hillside and dwellings in the valley. Ceremonial plazas were therefore small and scattered among the terraces. Seventeen principal structures have been excavated and three principal groups restored. The Temple of Quetzalcóatl–Éhecatl is a series of four superimposed, tiered, circular temple platforms, each with a staircase up the eastern side. The first, *c.* AD 300, was 10 m in diameter and 5.5 m high in five tiers, with a 2.5 m-wide staircase. The second comprised four tiers 16.5 m in diameter and 7.5 m high, with a 3.4 m-wide staircase. The third, of the 13th or 14th century AD, also had four tiers, 17.3 m in diameter and 9.75 m high, with a 6.5 m-wide staircase. Ornamental serpent heads were carved on the vertical faces of each step and originally painted in bright colours. The temple was destroyed by earthquake in 1475. The final, Aztec, temple (four tiers 22 m in diameter; full height estimated at *c.* 12 m) incorporated a projection to support the staircase, with low platforms on either side. The 8.4 m-wide staircase forms two flights, with two stone pedestals for braziers at the base and a rectangular stone altar at the centre of the landing between flights. A rare Aztec statue of Éhecatl–Quetzalcóatl was found within the foundations of the platform and can now be seen in the Museo Arqueológico del Estado de México in Tenango, near Toluca. It represents a human wearing a duck-billed mask symbol of Éhecatl, a loincloth and sandals.

The Temple of Tláloc forms the west side of another small plaza. Built in red and black *tezontle* (volcanic stone), it comprised three tiers, with a foundation tier on the downhill side. The second tier formed the base of the platform (27×20 m) and supported a pyramid (19×18 m); the entire structure stood 12 m high. A 7 m-wide staircase formed two flights up the east side, flanked by ramps and square pedestals for braziers at the foot. The Altar of Skulls stands opposite and is also of red and black *tezontle.* It is cruciform in plan with a rounded eastern arm, *c.* 9 m wide east–west; 469 protruding pegs and carved skulls decorate its sides. Different interpretations claim that it provided a warning of sacrifice to the rebellious Matlazinca or that it was used in ceremonies dedicated to the death of the sun in the 52-year Mesoamerican calendrical cycle (*see* MESOAMERICA, PRE-COLUMBIAN, §I, 4(i)). At the base of the hill the Aztecs built what is thought to be a *calmecac*, a 'college' for training selected youths for government, military and religious offices. It comprises a large rectangular enclosure (40×28 m) with surrounding platforms and staircases leading to room complexes, built of adobe and stone, probably in the third archaeological period, but burnt in AD 1510 by order of Motecuhzuma II. Other structures scattered on the hillside are unrestored, but from a plaza at the summit came a statue of Coatlícue, Aztec Earth goddess and mother of the Moon, now in the Museo Nacional de Antropología in Mexico City.

For discussion of the arts of Pre-Columbian Mexico *see also* MESOAMERICA, PRE-COLUMBIAN.

BIBLIOGRAPHY

J. García Payón: *La zona arqueológica de Tecaxic–Calixtlahuaca* (Mexico City, 1936)

——: 'La cerámica del Valle de Toluca', *Rev. Mex. Estud. Antropol.*, v (1941), pp. 209–38

I. Marquina: *Arquitectura prehispánica* (Mexico City, 1950, 2/1964/*R* 1981), pp. 223–35

Calixtlahuaca: Official Guide (Mexico City, 1969)

M. P. Weaver: *The Aztecs, Maya and their Predecessors: Archaeology of Mesoamerica* (New York, 1972, rev. 2/1981)

C. B. Hunter: *A Guide to Ancient Mexican Ruins* (Norman, 1977), pp. 121–9

J. Kelly: *The Complete Visitor's Guide to Mesoamerican Ruins* (Norman, 1982), pp. 48–51

DAVID M. JONES, JAIME LITVAK KING

Calixtus III, Pope. *See* BORGIA, (1).

Callahan, Harry (*b* Detroit, 22 Oct 1912). American photographer. He took up photography in 1938, at the relatively late age of 26. Ansel Adams visited the Detroit Photo Guild in 1941 and Callahan was inspired by his emphasis on craftsmanship and his majestic images. Callahan's earliest works focused on the calligraphic details of landscape, such as the patterns of grass against snow or telephone wires against the sky, or explored the effects of multiple exposures. Later subjects included studies of his wife Eleanor, a series of portraits made on Chicago's State Street in 1950, a series of houses at Providence, RI, and Cape Cod beachscapes begun in the 1960s. Whether working in black and white or, later, in colour, as in *Harry Callahan: Color* (New York, 1980), Callahan was committed in all his work to what he called 'the moment that people can't always see'.

In 1946 Callahan joined the staff at the Institute of Design in Chicago. Colleagues such as the architect Mies van der Rohe, the artist Hugo Weber (1918–71) and fellow photographer Arthur Siegel (*b* 1913) brought him into contact with an innovative attitude towards art that emphasized the formal elements of composition and structure. He was acclaimed not only as a teacher at Chicago and later at the Rhode Island School of Design but also for the refinement and rigour of his vision.

BIBLIOGRAPHY

P. Sherman: *Harry Callahan* (New York, 1967)
J. Szarkowski, ed.: *Harry Callahan* (Millerton, NY, 1976)
P. C. Bunnell: *Harry Callahan* (New York, 1978)
Harry Callahan: Photographs (exh. cat., ed. K. F. Davis; Lawrence, KS, Spencer Mus. A.; Albuquerque, U. NM, A. Mus.; Durham, NC, Duke U., Mus. A.; 1981)

MERRY A. FORESTA

Callcott. English painter and writer. (1) Augustus Wall Callcott was a painter of landscapes and marine scenes, and engravings after his drawings were used to illustrate works written by his wife, the traveller and writer (2) Maria Callcott.

(1) Sir **Augustus Wall Callcott** (*b* London, 20 Feb 1779, *d* London, 2 Nov 1844). Though originally intended for a musical career, he entered the Royal Academy Schools, London, in 1797 and studied with the portrait painter John Hoppner. His first Academy exhibits were portraits, but by the beginning of the 19th century he had turned to landscape. In 1801 Callcott was a member of the Sketching Society (also known as The Brothers), and some of his earliest landscapes were watercolours. He produced three for Edward, Viscount Lascelles (*d* 1820), in 1804, but he preferred to paint ideal and picturesque landscapes in oils than to work on topographical watercolours. From 1805 he developed a rustic picturesque style dependent on Dutch artistic traditions and on Gainsborough that immediately proved popular with the major patrons of the day, including Sir John Leicester, Richard Payne Knight and Sir Richard Colt Hoare.

Callcott's rivalry with J. M. W. Turner was noticed as early as 1805, but he was no mere pasticheur. His reputation was founded on a style recognizably his own, and he formed a genuine friendship with Turner based on mutual respect. The interest in effects of light and atmosphere that brought them together was developed by each independently, and the characteristic pale colours and vaporous effects that provoked Sir George Beaumont's attacks on the two artists as 'white painters' were first apparent in Callcott's two coast scenes exhibited at the Royal Academy in 1806: *Sea-coast, with Figures Bargaining for Fish* (priv. col., see 1981 exh. cat., p. 56) and *Calm, with Figures: Shrimping* (priv. col., see 1981 exh. cat., p. 58).

Callcott's career advanced rapidly in its early years. He was elected ARA in 1806 and RA in 1810, but by the end of the decade Beaumont's criticism had proved damaging. In 1813 and 1814 Callcott declined to exhibit at the Academy, while protesting vigorously at the monopoly Beaumont's opinions were gaining among connoisseurs now that his taste had become enshrined in the rival British Institution. But it was an exhibition of Dutch pictures at the Institution in 1815 that helped to lay the foundations of patronage and taste for the next and most important phase of Callcott's work. Thus far he had painted mainly the pastoral or picturesque, with an excursion into historic landscape around 1811–12. In 1815, however, a large marine painting, *Passage and Luggage Boats* (untraced), proved resoundingly successful when it was exhibited at the Academy, and the next decade was devoted mainly to similar works. His masterpiece in this genre was *Entrance to the Pool of London* (Bowood House, Wilts), shown in 1816, the composition and cool golden tonality of which were derived from the river scenes of Aelbert Cuyp and were in turn used by Turner in *Dort Packet-boat from Rotterdam Becalmed* (exh. RA 1818; New Haven, CT, Yale Cent. Brit. A.). Other marine paintings by Callcott, mostly views of Rotterdam and Antwerp, have affinities with Turner's paintings of continental seaports of the same decade. Contemporaries regarded their careful execution and sober colouring as a more acceptable alternative to Turner's increasingly bold style.

Callcott married the writer and traveller Maria Graham in 1827. Until her death in 1842 the Callcotts' house in Kensington was one of London's more important cultural salons. Callcott had close links with many continental artists. His interests, which included German and Italian primitives as well as the German Nazarenes, proved a formative influence on younger friends, including William Dyce and Charles Lock Eastlake. Callcott's connoisseurship and social gifts were much sought after on committees during the 1830s. He was knighted in 1837 and appointed Surveyor of the Queen's Pictures in 1843. Callcott's artistic production failed to keep pace with his reputation during his last years. He worked on smaller marine paintings and landscapes in the style of Claude, depicting Italy and the Alps, and experimented with the narrative genre popularized by his friends David Wilkie and William Mulready. Although these often appeared to be pot-boilers, he did execute two huge historical compositions, *Raphael and the Fornarina* (exh. RA 1837; untraced; for engraving by Lumb Stocks see 1981 exh. cat., p. 90) and *Milton Dictating to his Daughters* (exh. RA 1840; untraced). His later work, though popular with contemporaries, has not stood the test of time and has obscured the more substantial achievements of his earlier years.

BIBLIOGRAPHY

T. C. Dibdin: *Sir Augustus Wall Callcott's Italian and English Landscapes Lithographed by T. C. Dibdin* (London, 1847)

J. C. Dafforne: *Pictures by Sir Augustus Wall Callcott RA, with a Biographical Memoir* (London, 1876)

Augustus Wall Callcott (exh. cat., by D. B. Brown, London, Tate, 1981) [biography and reassessment of Callcott's work and relationship with Turner with note on archival sources]

DAVID BLAYNEY BROWN

(2) Maria, Lady **Callcott** [Maria Graham; née Dundas] (*b* Papcastle, nr Cockermouth, Cumb., 19 July 1785; *d* London, 21 Nov 1842). Wife of (1) Augustus Wall Callcott. A daughter of Rear-Admiral George Dundas, as a child she spent long periods with her uncle Sir David Dundas in Richmond, Surrey, where the guests included Thomas Lawrence and the poet Thomas Campbell. In 1808 she sailed for India, where her father was then stationed, and there married Captain Thomas Graham the following year. She returned to England in 1811 and published *Journal of a Residence in India* (Edinburgh, 1812), the first of several travel-based books. She visited Italy in 1819, and in 1820 published *Memoirs of the Life of Nicholas Poussin*, a biography with a catalogue of the artist's works and the first study of Poussin in English. She visited Brazil and Chile from 1821 to 1823, by now a widow, since her husband had died on the way to South America. In 1827 she married the painter Augustus Wall Callcott and honeymooned with him in Italy and Germany in 1828. In 1831, a victim of tuberculosis, she burst a blood vessel, which left her incapacitated but not inactive. In 1835 she published the short *Descriptions of the Annunziata dell' Arena: Or Giotto's Chapel, in Padua*, illustrated by engravings after her husband's drawings, and a history book for children, *Little Arthur's History of England*, which became very popular. In *Essays towards the History of Painting* (1836) she described the origins of painting in Egyptian, Indian, Chinese and Chaldean civilizations and went on to discuss its subsequent development in the Etruscan and Greek cultures, examining the painting techniques and materials used. The brief *Continuation of Essays towards the History of Painting* (1838) extended the earlier work up to the 13th century, but illness prevented Lady Callcott from completing the project.

WRITINGS

M. Graham: *Memoirs of the Life of Nicolas Poussin* (London and Edinburgh, 1820)

Descriptions of the Annunziata dell'Arena: Or Giotto's Chapel, in Padua (London, 1835)

Essays towards the History of Painting (London, 1836)

Continuation of Essays towards the History of Painting (London, 1838)

BIBLIOGRAPHY

DNB

R. B. Gotch: *Maria, Lady Callcott: The Creator of 'Little Arthur'* (London, 1937)

□

Calle, Benjamín de la (*b* Yarumal, 1869; *d* Medellín, 1934). Colombian photographer. After studying photography with Emiliano Mejía he established a photographic studio in Yarumal in 1898, working there until his move in 1903 to Medellín. He added the prefixes to his surname, Calle, to declare his identification with other people 'of the street': nonconformists, bohemians and those marginalized by society. He openly aligned himself with the underprivileged social classes in his photographs, stating his opposition to the arbitrary and vengeful aspects of his society by recording some of the most moving events of his day including the last executions by firing squad to take place in Colombia. This series included photographs of prisoners awaiting their deaths while facing their coffins and as bullet-ridden corpses.

De la Calle was also an exceptional portraitist, usually of anonymous and unsophisticated people to whom he gave great dignity, such as proudly barefooted peasants who boldly displayed the instruments and tools of their work. He sometimes presented his figures with elements such as revolvers and cartridge belts to indicate his political and social rebellion. Through such perceptive images he recorded the urban, industrial and commercial development of Medellín.

BIBLIOGRAPHY

Historia de la fotografía en Colombia (exh. cat. by E. Serrano, Bogotá, Mus. A. Mod., 1983)

EDUARDO SERRANO

Calle, Sophie (*b* Paris, 1953). French photographer. After completing her schooling she travelled for seven years. When she returned to Paris in 1979 she began a series of projects to acquaint herself again both with the city and people of Paris and with herself. These sought to construct identities by offering documentary 'proof' in the form of photographs. Her work was seen to have roots in the tradition of conceptual art because the emphasis was on the artistic idea rather than the finished object. One of her well-known pieces, *Suite Vénitienne* (1980), involved following someone that she had met at a party in Paris to Venice without his knowledge. The photographic documentation of the project raised questions as to whether the man's identity could be revealed by his day-to-day movements through the city, as well as imitating ironically the behaviour of unrequited love. The French writer Jean Baudrillard wrote an essay (1988) that described this project in terms of a reciprocal loss of will on the part of both pursued and pursuer. Another project, *Detective* (1980), consisted of Calle being followed for a day by a private detective, who had been hired (at Calle's request) by her mother. Calle proceeded to lead the unwitting detective around parts of Paris that were particularly important for her, thereby reversing the expected position of the observed subject. Such projects, with their suggestions of intimacy, also questioned the role of the spectator, with viewers often feeling a sense of unease as they became the unwitting collaborators in these violations of privacy. Moreover, the deliberately constructed and thus in one sense artificial nature of the documentary 'evidence' used in Calle's work questioned the nature of all truths.

PHOTOGRAPHIC PUBLICATIONS

Suite vénitienne (Seattle, 1988) [incl. essay by J. Baudrillard]

BIBLIOGRAPHY

Sophie Calle: A Survey (exh. cat., essay by D. Irmas; Santa Monica, CA, Fred Hoffman Gal., 1989)

□

Calleja, Andrés de la (*b* La Rioja, 1705; *d* Madrid, 2 Jan 1785). Spanish painter. He trained in Madrid with Jerónimo de Ezquerra and Miguel Jacinto Meléndez and was soon patronized by the Prince of Asturias, the future Ferdinand VI. Calleja painted two canvases derived from sketches by Meléndez for S Felipe el Real in Madrid (untraced) and portraits of several members of the royal family, similar in style to the work of Jean Ranc. In 1744 Philip V appointed Calleja Honorary Director of the preparatory board of the Academia de Bellas Artes de S Fernando in Madrid, which was established in 1752, and in 1778 Ferdinand VI, for whom Calleja had already made a portable altar (untraced), appointed him Director General. He was also made Pintor de Cámara, and his knowledge of painting techniques led to his being charged with the restoration of the pictures in the royal residences, in particular those that survived the fire in the Alcázar of Madrid in 1734. He also made inventories and appraisals of the royal collections and tapestry cartoons for the Real Fábrica de Tapices, such as *The Farm* (*c.* 1766; Madrid, Prado, on dep. U. de Valladolid).

Calleja's portraits and his religious and allegorical works show the influence of late 17th-century thought and of Louis-Michel van Loo and Anton Raphael Mengs. Prominent among his official portraits are *José de Carvajal Bestowing a Medal on Mariano Sánchez* (1745; Madrid, Real Acad. S Fernando) and *Charles III on Horseback* (Mariefred, Gripsholms Slott), while his allegorical works include *Time Revealing Truth* (Madrid, Real Acad. S Fernando).

BIBLIOGRAPHY

F. J. Sánchez Cantón: *Los pintores de cámara de los reyes de España* (Madrid, 1916)

J. Held: *Die Genrebilder der Madrider Teppichmanufaktur und die Anfänge Goyas* (Berlin, 1971)

C. Bedat: *L'Académie des beaux-arts de Madrid, 1744–1808* (Toulouse, 1974)

JUAN J. LUNA

Callet, Antoine-François (*b* Paris, 1741; *d* Paris, 1823). French painter. He studied under Antoine Boizot, attending drawing classes at the Académie Royale. In 1764, with his painting *Epponina and Sabinus Condemned by Vespasian* (Paris, Ecole N. Sup. B.-A.), he won the Prix de Rome, which allowed him to complete his artistic education at the Académie de France in Rome. Callet remained in Italy until 1772, when he executed a ceiling painting for the ballroom of the Palazzo Spinola in Genoa, which shows the influence of Veronese and the Bolognese school. His first major work on returning to Paris was the decoration of the cupola of the Salon de Compagnie in the Petits Appartements of the Palais Bourbon (1774; destr. 1864; painting of the decoration by the artist, Paris, Musées Nationaux). Its mythological scenes, with classicizing figure types, virtuoso foreshortenings and *trompe l'oeil* effects, again draw on Italian models. Another ceiling painting, the *Triumph of Flora* (1775), is known from an oil sketch (Cholet, Mus. A.) and a small replica (Paris, Louvre).

In 1781 Callet's *Allegory of Spring*, intended for the Galerie d'Apollon of the Louvre, gained him membership of the Académie: the Baroque *sotto in sù* composition of this monumental ceiling painting is preserved in a preparatory sketch (priv. col.). A portrait of *Louis XVI* (versions, Paris, Carnavalet; Clermont-Ferrand, Mus. Bargoin) was one of Callet's best-known and most frequently reproduced works; he remained, however, a much sought after artist after the Revolution, adapting a Neo-classical style in such works as the axially structured oil sketch of the *Rape of Europa* (1790; Meaux, Mus. Bossuet) and meeting the demands of the Napoleonic era in such paintings as the *Installation of the First Consul in Lyon* (1804; untraced; preparatory sketch, Lyon, Mus. Hist.). Callet's work has been compared with that of Jean-Honoré Fragonard but has a more official and imposing character.

BIBLIOGRAPHY

Bénézit; Thieme–Becker

P. Rosenberg, N. Reynaud and I. Compin: *Ecole française, XVIIe et XVIIIe siècles*, i of *Catalogue illustré des peintures: Musée du Louvre* (Paris, 1974)

M. C. Chaudonneret: 'A propos des tableaux du Palais Saint Pierre détruits en 1816', *Bull. Mus. & Mnmts Lyon.*, vi/1 (1977), pp. 9–18

J. Wilhelm: 'La Coupole peinte par Antoine Callet pour le Salon de Compagnie des Petits Appartements du Palais Bourbon', *Bull. Soc. Hist. A. Fr.* (1979), pp. 167–77

B. Gallini: 'Acquisitions des Musées de Cholet et de Meaux: Les Esquisses d'Antoine-François Callet (1741–1823)', *Rev. Louvre*, xxxiii/2 (1983), pp. 134–7

CATHRIN KLINGSÖHR LE ROY

Calleva Atrebatum [now Silchester, Hampshire]. Roman site, 13 km south-west of Reading. The town was capital of the tribal *civitas* of the Atrebates, succeeding an earlier native settlement. It flourished from *c.* AD 68 to the late 5th century and was abandoned during the Saxon period in favour of Reading. By the time of the excavations of 1890–1909, the results of which were of fundamental importance for the understanding of Roman urban development in Britain, the defensive walls and the embankment of the amphitheatre were all that remained above ground. The excavations uncovered the forum, its west side enclosed by a basilica, public baths, five Romano-Celtic temples and a probable Early Christian church. About 20 substantial town houses, built around courtyards, were also found, as well as many smaller houses and shops. The city was laid out on a rectangular grid of streets, with evidence of an early realignment. The forum plan has proved to be typical of the arrangement found in other British *civitas* capitals in having a basilica on one side, shops and offices behind the colonnades on the other three, the entrance opposite the basilica but, in contrast with other provinces, no Capitolium temple.

Further excavations carried out by M. G. Fulford discovered an earlier forum basilica of timber; the stone building is now dated to the late 1st century AD or early 2nd. The amphitheatre has seating supported on an earth bank, revetted at first in timber and later heightened and walled in stone; it was a much simpler structure than the amphitheatres of the Mediterranean provinces. The defensive walls were built in the 3rd century, enclosing an irregular polygon 67 ha in area; there were earlier earthwork defences on slightly different alignments. Inscriptions record benefactions by local guilds and dignitaries, and sculpture from the site includes a large bronze eagle, perhaps from an Imperial statuary group (Reading, Mus. & A.G.).

BIBLIOGRAPHY

G. C. Boon: *Silchester: The Roman Town of Calleva* (Newton Abbot, 1974)

M. G. Fulford: 'Excavations on the Sites of the Amphitheatre and Forum Basilica at Silchester, Hampshire: An Interim Report', *Antiqua. J.*, lxv (1985), pp. 39–81

T. F. C. BLAGG

Çallı, Ibrahim (*b* Çal, Denizli province, 1882; *d* Istanbul, 1960). Turkish painter. He lived in Çal during his youth but went to Istanbul, where Ahmet Ali helped to get him enrolled at the Fine Arts Academy. In 1910 he won first prize in a competition for a European scholarship and went to Paris, where he studied under Fernand Cormon. He returned to Turkey in 1914 and was assigned a teaching post at the Fine Arts Academy. At this time he became recognized as the foremost figure in the Çallı group, named after him. Inspired by Impressionism and other European movements, he lightened his palette and worked straight on to canvas without preliminary studies. The artists of the Çallı group also painted *en plein air* and introduced new themes to Turkish painting, including 'multi-figured' and narrative compositions. In 1914 they started to exhibit work at the Galatasaray Lycée in Istanbul. During World War I Çallı became a war artist and was taken to the Gelibolu–Bolayır front. His works of that period include *Night Ambush* (*c*. 1916; Istanbul, Mil. Mus.). After the War he achieved success as a portrait painter, and his portraits of *Kemal Atatürk* and *Ismet Inönü* were reproduced and hung in government offices. His subject-matter also included still-lifes, for example *Magnolias* (1933), scenes from daily life, such as *Sewing* (1927; both Istanbul, Mimar Sinan U., Mus. Ptg & Sculp.), nudes and landscapes. He was highly influential in training younger artists during his 33 years of teaching.

BIBLIOGRAPHY

Z. Güvemli: *The Sabancı Collection of Paintings* (Istanbul, 1984) [Turk. and Eng. text]

S. Tansuğ: *Çağdaş Türk sanatı* [Contemporary Turkish art] (Istanbul, 1986)

G. Renda and others: *A History of Turkish Painting* (Geneva, Seattle and London, 1988)

Callicrates. *See* KALLIKRATES.

Calligraphy. The art of fine writing with brush and ink or pen and ink, frequently used as a means of decoration and artistic expression as well as written communication. For detailed surveys of different traditions of calligraphic art *see under* CHINA, JAPAN, KOREA, INDIAN SUBCONTINENT and ISLAMIC ART; for the art of fine penmanship in the West *see* SCRIPT.

□

Callimachus. *See* KALLIMACHOS.

Callipers. Pair of hinged jaws, of wood or metal, used to take measurements from a figure, model or drawing. Proportional callipers, which possess a movable pivot with jaws at both ends, can be employed to reduce or increase measurements when making a copy from an original.

RUPERT FEATHERSTONE

Callisto da Lodi. *See* PIAZZA, (1).

Callot, Jacques (*b* Nancy, March–Aug 1592; *d* Nancy, 25 March 1635). French etcher, engraver and draughtsman. He was one of the most accomplished printmakers in the Western tradition and one of the major exponents of the Mannerist style in the early 17th century. His often fantastic compositions combine grotesque and elegant elements in a compelling and personal manner. He greatly advanced both the technical and the aesthetic possibilities of etching through his invention of a chip-resistant ground for copperplates and his consummate skill in making repeated bitings of a single plate.

1. LIFE AND WORK. Callot was the son of a herald to Charles III, Duke of Lorraine. In 1607 he entered into a four-year apprenticeship with Domange Crocq (*fl* 1608–34; *d* 1637), a medallist in Nancy, but may have left for Rome before 1611. His earliest known print is an engraving of *Charles III* dated 1607 (see Lieure, no. 1). According to Félibien and others, he became an apprentice in Rome to the engraver Philippe Thomassin. With Antonio Tempesta and Rafaello Schiaminossi he made a set of 29 etchings commemorating the funeral of the Queen of Spain (L 52–69), published in 1612 in Florence; he was certainly living in Florence by October 1614, when he was recorded as receiving funds from the Medici court and working in the Uffizi. For the next seven years he created many drawings, single prints and prints in suites. He recorded, in a highly animated style, court-sponsored pageants and theatrical productions, among them the *Guerra d'amore* (1616; L 169–72) and *Il Ventaglio* (1619; Florence, Uffizi), both of which were public, outdoor festivals, and the intermezzi (1617; L 185–7) staged in the

1. Jacques Callot: *Zanni*, etching and engraving, from *Three Italian Comedians*, *c*. 1618–20 (Washington, DC, National Gallery of Art)

Uffizi theatre for an élite audience. The Florentine architect, engineer and court impresario Giulio Parigi (1571–1635) designed these productions and, according to Baldinucci, Callot was his pupil and learnt perspective from him. By this time he had become expert at evoking a deep sense of space, partly through the use of dark animated figures that were placed in the foregrounds to act as repoussoir elements for the scenes beyond them. He was also combining acute observation of reality with a taste for grotesque or bizarre aspects of life and his own fanciful imagination; the sophisticated Florentine theatre was an important stimulus for him (see fig. 1). Callot's major work in Florence was the *Fair at Impruneta* (L 361), dated 1620 and dedicated to Cosimo II, Grand Duke of Tuscany; this large plate (436×678 mm) contains an astonishing 1300 human and animal figures. The representation of this huge crowd, engaged in myriad activities, is subtly but rigorously ordered through the use of perspective and light and dark tones.

Following Cosimo's premature death in 1621, Callot, like many other artists, lost court funding; he reluctantly returned to Nancy. His earliest works in Nancy were of Florence-inspired subjects: one was the *Gobbi* series (L 279, 407–26), depicting dwarf entertainers, and another was *Balli di Sfessania* (L 379–402), 24 images of performers, inspired by the *commedia dell'arte*. Drawings for the former and perhaps the latter were made in Florence, primarily in the studio rather than from life. Callot also etched a second *Fair at Impruneta* (L 478), virtually identical to the first. In 1623 he began to receive support from Henry II, Duke of Lorraine; from then on he frequently worked on commissions, mostly from the court and religious orders. There are few theatrical or festival prints from this period; a notable exception is the *Combat at the Barrier* (L 575–88), prints commemorating a festival ordered by the Duke in 1627 in honour of Marie, Duchesse de Chevreuse. Callot and Claude Deruet organized and designed this fête. In 1626 Callot worked on six plates for the *Siege of Breda* (L 593), commissioned to celebrate the victory in 1625 of the Spanish army, led by the Marqués de Spinola, over the Dutch. Callot's virtuoso work combined cartography and scenography into a visually cohesive whole. The imagery was mostly based on a published account of the battle by Hermannus Hugo, field chaplain to Spinola. Callot later made two siege maps for King Louis XIII of France, celebrating victories over the Huguenots: the *Siege of La Rochelle* (L 655, 660–61) and the *Siege of St-Martin-de-Ré* (L 654, 656–9). By January 1629 Callot was in Paris. In 1633 Callot's friend Israël Henriet published in Paris his famous suite of 18 prints, the *Miseries and Misfortunes of War* (*Les Misères et les malheurs de la guerre*; L 1339–56), in which soldiers are shown fighting, raping and pillaging; some are punished or gravely wounded, and a few are rewarded for victory.

Between 1631 and 1634 Callot executed more than 600 religious works, many of which were commissioned and others produced for sale to the public, Lorraine being a stronghold of Roman Catholicism. The second version of

2. Jacques Callot: *Temptation of St Antony*, etching (second version), 1635 (Washington, DC, National Gallery of Art)

the *Temptation of St Antony* (L 1416; see fig. 2; the first version is dated *c.* 1616–17), is dated 1635, the year Callot died of a painful stomach ailment, and may have been personally motivated; it represents a fearsome Hell scene set within a rocky proscenium arch and is dominated at upper centre by a chained, Satan-like monster. St Antony is a tiny figure in the middle distance, tempted by a female nude and tormented by devils. This work, in its linear perfection, strong light and dark effects and its vivid imaginative imagery, is a summation of Callot's technical and stylistic expertise. His oeuvre consists of more than 1400 prints and 2000 drawings, which include the *Agony in the Garden* (Chatsworth, Derbys). Many of his copper-plates are preserved in the Musée Historique Lorrain, Nancy.

2. WORKING METHODS AND TECHNIQUE. Many of Callot's extant drawings were made as detailed studies for his prints (e.g. three studies (*c.* 1617) for the *Fair at Impruneta*; Florence, Uffizi, and Vienna, Albertina; and two studies (*c.* 1625) for the *Palace Gardens at Nancy*; St Petersburg, Hermitage, and Nancy, Mus. Hist. Lorrain), indicating his methodical preparation for etching. In Florence, he favoured both pen and ink and chalk for drawing. Later in Lorraine he increasingly used brilliant washes over light chalk underdrawing, but the final preparatory drawings were then often translated into linear networks in pen and ink. His hard ground for etching was made of mastic and linseed oil: it both reduced foul-biting (acid accidentally penetrating the ground to the copper) and provided an excellent surface for metal drawing tools. For working on the plate Callot preferred the *échoppe* to etching needles; he exploited this oval-shaped tool for creating lines that swell and diminish, effectively suggesting volumetric form and vigorous physical movement. Occasionally he used the burin, an engraving tool, to strengthen lines further after biting the plate and before printing. In skilfully rebiting the plate while covering some areas with stopping-out varnish, he achieved a wide range of tone and line in his images, far surpassing 16th-century etchers. It remained for Rembrandt to move away from linear to painterly evocation of form in etching. However, Callot's methods remained influential, owing in part to Abraham Bosse's treatise of 1645, which was substantially based on them: it was frequently reprinted and translated into several languages.

BIBLIOGRAPHY

F. Baldinucci: *Notizie* (1681–1728); ed. F. Ranalli (1845–7)
A. de Félibien: *Entretien sur les vies et les ouvrages des plus excellens peintres, anciens et modernes* (Paris, 1685), iv
J. Lieure: *Jacques Callot*, 8 vols (Paris, 1924–7/*R* New York, 1969) [L]
D. Ternois: *L'Art de Jacques Callot* (Paris, 1962)
——: *Jacques Callot: Catalogue complet de son oeuvre dessiné* (Paris, 1962)
G. Sadoul: *Jacques Callot: Miroir de son temps* (Paris, 1969)
P. Marot: 'Jacques Callot, sa vie, son travail, ses éditions: Nouvelles recherches', *Gaz. B.-A.*, lxxxv (1975), pp. 3–38, 153–74; lxxxvi (1975), pp. 185–98
Jacques Callot: Prints and Related Drawings (exh. cat. by H. D. Russell, J. Blanchard and J. Krill, Washington, DC, N.G.A., 1975)
D. Posner: 'Jacques Callot and the Dances Called *Sfessania*', *A. Bull.*, lix (1977), pp. 203–16
O. J. Rothrock and E. Van Gullick: 'Seeing and Meaning: Observations on the Theatre of Callot's *Primo Intermedio*', *NM Stud. F.A.*, iv (1979), pp. 16–35
Claude Lorrain e i pittori lorenesi nel XVII secolo (exh. cat., Rome, Acad. France, 1982), pp. 135–79
S. Zurawski: 'New Sources for Jacques Callot's *Map of the Siege of Breda*', *A. Bull.*, lxx (1988), pp. 621–39
Jacques Callot 1592–1635 (exh. cat. by P. Choné, D. Ternois and others, Nancy, Mus. Hist. Lorrain, 1992)

H. DIANE RUSSELL

Callow, William (*b* Greenwich, nr London, 28 July 1812; *d* Great Missenden, Bucks, 20 Feb 1908). English painter and engraver. The son of a carpenter and builder, Callow was apprenticed at the age of 11 to Theodore Fielding, with whom he remained for two years. Copley Fielding also took an interest in his progress. In 1825 Callow was articled to Theodore Fielding for eight years' instruction in watercolour drawing and aquatint engraving. However, in 1829 he left for Paris, at the invitation of Thales Fielding, to work for the publisher J. F. d'Ostervald. He lived and worked with Newton Fielding until 1830, when the events of the July Revolution forced them back to Britain. Callow was again in Paris by February 1831 and returned to London only in 1841. He settled there until 1854 when he bought a cottage at Great Missenden, Bucks.

Callow's work was profoundly influenced by that of Richard Parkes Bonington and Thomas Shotter Boys. Callow accompanied Boys regularly on sketching expeditions, stepping into the place left vacant by the death of Bonington in 1828. In 1833 Callow shared Boys's studio in the Rue du Bouloi, Paris. Callow's work was noticed at the 1834 Salon, and in the same year he was appointed drawing-master to the family of King Louis-Philippe. His watercolours of the 1830s and 1840s, particularly his seascapes and Venetian views (e.g. *The Grand Canal, Venice*, 1842; engraved in the London *Art Union Prize Annual*, 1845), satisfied a popular early Victorian taste for travel imagery. Callow adopted Bonington's clarity of construction and choice of motif, reinforcing them with a degree of elaboration and finish to suit the Victorian market. His brother John Callow (1822–78) was a skilled watercolourist and drawing-master.

BIBLIOGRAPHY

H. M. Cundall: *William Callow, RWS, FRGS* (London, 1908)
J. Reynolds: *William Callow, RWS* (London, 1980)

MARCIA POINTON

Calonne, Charles-Alexandre de (*b* Douai, 20 Jan 1734; *d* Paris, 20 Oct 1802). French administrator and collector. He was the son of a magistrate of Douai and rose rapidly to prominence, holding various legal and administrative posts in the French government. In 1783 he became Contrôleur-Général des Finances. His official residence in Paris, the Hôtel du Contrôleur-Général, was richly decorated with furniture by André-Charles Boulle. Calonne collected Chinese clocks, rare turquoise-blue Chinese porcelain and decorative terracotta groups by Clodion, such as *Poetry and Music* (Washington, DC, N.G.A.). He possessed numerous paintings; as well as Dutch cabinet paintings, he owned paintings by Claude and by contemporary French painters (e.g. Boucher's *Toilet of Venus*, 1751; New York, Met.). He also owned works by Murillo, including the *Flower Girl* (*c.* 1670; London, Dulwich Pict. Gal.), and paintings by contemporary English painters who were his friends, including Reynolds's *Mrs Siddons as the Tragic Muse* (1784; San Marino, CA, Huntington A.G.; signed copy 1789; London, Dulwich Pict. Gal.). Elisabeth-Louise Vigée-Le Brun, who was reputed to be a close friend, painted an elegant portrait of him (1784; Windsor Castle, Berks, Royal Col.). Calonne's efforts to reform the financial system of France by increasing the taxes on the nobility and clergy resulted in 1787 in his dismissal. He left for England, where he had a close friend in Edmund Burke; following his departure, his house in Paris and his possessions, including many paintings, were sold in 1788 (Paris, Jean-Baptiste-Pierre Le Brun, 21–30 April). Mme de Harvelay, whom he subsequently married in England, purchased some 200 paintings at the sale. Calonne was highly critical of the French Revolution, and acted as counsellor to members of the nobility who had taken refuge in England. Further sales of his property were held in London: the furnishings were sold in 1793 (London, Christie's, 13 May); and silver, jewellery and musical instruments in 1794 (London, Christie's, 2 May). There was a sale of paintings, drawings, miniatures and prints in 1795 (London, Skinner and Sykes, 23–8 March). Calonne returned to France shortly before his death. A posthumous sale in 1803 (London, Christie's, 9 July) included paintings, mathematical instruments, minerals and shells.

BIBLIOGRAPHY

Museum Calonnianum: Specification of the Various Articles which Compose the Magnificent Museum of Natural History by M. de Calonne in France, and Lately his Property: . . . All of which Now Exhibiting at Saville House . . . Previous to the Sale thereof (London, 1797) [compiled by G. Humphreys]
P. Joly: *Calonne* (Paris, 1949)
R. Lacour-Gayet: *Calonne: Financier, réformateur, contre-révolutionnaire, 1734–1802* (Paris, 1963)
B. Scott: 'Charles Alexandre de Calonne: Economist and Collector', *Apollo*, xcvii (1973), pp. 86–91

□

Calotype. *See under* PHOTOGRAPHY, §I.

Calpe. *See* GIBRALTAR.

Calraet [Kalraet], **Abraham (Pietersz.) van** (*bapt* Dordrecht, 12 Oct 1642; *bur* Dordrecht, 12 June 1722). Dutch painter. He was the eldest son of Pieter Jansz. van Calraet (*c.* 1620–81), a sculptor from Utrecht. According to Houbraken, Abraham was taught by the Dordrecht sculptors Aemilius and Samuel Huppe, although nothing is known of his activity as a sculptor. Houbraken also stated that Abraham learnt to paint figures and fruit and that his brother Barent van Calraet (1649–1737), who specialized at first in horse paintings but later imitated the Rhine landscapes of Herman Saftleven, was a pupil of Aelbert Cuyp (*see* CUYP, (3)). The known signed works by Barent confirm this. A painting of two horses in a stable, initialled APK (Rotterdam, Mus. Boymans–van Beuningen), indicates that Abraham, too, must have been well acquainted with Cuyp and provides the basis for identifying Abraham's painting style. A large number of landscapes with horses, paintings of livestock in stables and still-lifes, all initialled A.C. and formerly attributed to Aelbert Cuyp, are now generally considered to be the work of van Calraet, although many of these are in fact copies after him.

In van Calraet's studio were several paintings by Cuyp and after him, as well as copies after Philips Wouwerman, Jan Both and other landscape artists. Van Calraet himself often painted cattle and horses (e.g. *Horse with a Saddle beside it*, London, N.G.) or *Horses before an Inn* (St Petersburg, Hermitage). Closely related to Cuyp's work, van Calraet's handling is nonetheless smoother, broader and more monochromatic. To some extent, the oeuvres of the two artists remain confused. Some works by van Calraet, such as the *River Landscape* (London, N.G., 53, as Cuyp), are close in concept to Cuyp's work and must have been meant as imitations. His paintings of stable interiors (e.g. 1851; London, N.G.) are strongly indebted to Wouwerman. A *Battle Scene* (Amsterdam, Rijksmus.) is of a more independent impulse, although still based ultimately on Cuyp. Van Calraet showed greater willingness than Cuyp to tackle figural subjects, as in his *Christ Entering Jerusalem* (Glasgow, C.A.G.). Most original and striking among van Calraet's paintings are his delicate, deeply shadowed still-lifes, usually showing fruit on a table, with brilliantly coloured butterflies (e.g. Otterlo, Rijksmus. Kröller-Müller). Although these are widely believed to have been derived from Cuyp's work, in fact no securely attributable still-life by Cuyp has been located.

Van Calraet married Anna, daughter of the Dordrecht painter Cornelis Bisschop, on 30 June 1680.

BIBLIOGRAPHY

Thieme-Becker
A. Houbraken: *De groote schouburgh* (1718–21), iii, pp. 181, 292
G. H. Veth: 'Aanteekeningen omtrent eenige, Dordrechtsche schilders: Barent van Kalraet', *Oud-Holland*, vii (1889), pp. 304–5
A. Bredius: 'Der Stillebenmaler Abraham (van) Calraet', *Kunstchronik*, xxv (1914), pp. 93–4
——: *Künstler-Inventare*, i (The Hague, 1915), pp. 307–20
——: 'The Still-life Painter Abraham Calraet', *Burl. Mag.*, xxx (1917), pp. 172–9
F. Schmidt-Degener: 'Kalraet in Boymans', *Oude Kst*, iv (1918–19), pp. 285–91
J. L. van Dalen: 'De familie van Calraet', *Oud-Holland*, xlii (1925), pp. 172–5
J. G. van Gelder: 'A. Calraet, niet Cuyp', *Ksthist. Meded. Rijksbureau Ksthist. Doc.*, i (1946), pp. 7–8
L. J. Bol: *Goede onbekenden*, ii (The Hague, 1979, 2/Utrecht, 1982), pp. 14–20
De zichtbaare wereld (exh. cat., Dordrecht, Dordrechts Mus., 1992), pp. 106–13

ALAN CHONG

Cals, Adolphe-Félix (*b* Paris, 17 Oct 1810; *d* Honfleur, 3 Oct 1880). French painter and printmaker. A workman's son, he was apprenticed to the engraver Jean-Louis Anselin (1754–1823) at the age of 12. On his master's death he went to the workshop of Ponce and Bosc, where he learnt to use the burin. He also lithographed works by François Boucher and Devéria. In 1828 he joined the studio of Léon Cogniet. Cals was never attracted by the brand of history painting practised by Cogniet, who failed to recognize his talent and compared him with Jean-Baptiste-Camille Corot. This conventional apprenticeship, therefore, had no influence on his art. At the beginning of the 1830s he drew and painted landscapes, and he made his début in the Salon in 1835 with a genre painting, *Poor Woman* (untraced), and several portraits. He exhibited regularly in the Salon until 1870.

Cals painted his landscapes in front of the motif, in the outskirts of Paris, at Argenteuil, Versailles and Saint-Cyr, initially with a rather firm and heavy touch. He depicted models he came across in everyday life, favouring tired faces and expressions of melancholy and restrained sorrow. His relative poverty in the 1840s brought him close to the poor, and his earliest, little-known works reveal an

Adolphe-Félix Cals: *Peasant Woman and her Child*, oil on canvas, 464×378 mm, 1846 (Barnard Castle, Bowes Museum)

interest in peasant life, sometimes anticipating Jean-François Millet. In 1846 he exhibited 11 canvases in the Salon, probably including *Peasant Woman and her Child* (Barnard Castle, Bowes Mus.; see fig.). Cals treated the deprivation of the figures (echoed by the bareness of the setting) with a sentimentality that he never entirely shook off and which distinguishes him from Gustave Courbet.

In the 1850s Cals specialized in peaceful scenes of family life, painted in a manner similar to contemporary works by Octave Tassaert and Edouard Frère. *Young Girl Knitting* (1850; Reims, Mus. St-Denis) shows the influence of Dutch art in the simplicity of the pose and use of chiaroscuro. Cals was also interested in still-lifes of rustic objects and domestic themes, as in *Woman Plucking a Duck* (1854; Barnard Castle, Bowes Mus.). These intimist scenes, in which he depicted the activities of his daughter Marie or children playing, also indicate the influence of Jean-Siméon Chardin. The technique used in panels such as *Portrait of a Young Woman* (Honfleur, Mus. Boudin) was looser and more sketchlike than in his earlier work. Chiaroscuro tended to mask the sad expressions of his subjects, while his lighter touch blended the colours in a misty harmony. Although he was accepted by the Salon, his pictures were little valued, badly hung and ignored by the critics.

In 1848 Cals met the dealer Père Martin, who sold the works of Corot, Millet and Cals in his Paris shop in the Rue Mogador, later in the Rue Laffitte. In 1858 Père Martin introduced Cals to Count Armand Doria, who became his most important patron and invited him often to his château at Orrouy, until 1868. The second half of Cals's career coincided with a more settled life, which he divided between Paris and Orrouy. These new circumstances explain the commissions he received for portraits and the importance of the works he painted for Doria (sold, 4 May 1899). He continued to work on intimist genre scenes: *The Caress* and *Reading* (1867; priv. col.), *The Nurse and the Child* (1869; priv. col.) and *Woman Mending Nets* (after 1873; Dijon, Mus. B.-A.,). His paintings of the 1860s had a greater freedom and the colour was organized in less brilliant harmonies than the more patiently executed earlier panels. Representation of light became his major concern, particularly in the landscapes produced in the Nièvre (1861), at Saint-Valéry-en-Caux (1864) and at Elbeuf-en-Bray (1869), in which his brushwork became more vaporous and transparent; for example, *Bend in the Marne* (Lyon, Mus. B.-A.).

In 1871 Cals met Adolphe Hervier, Eugène Boudin and Johan Barthold Jongkind at Honfleur, where he settled. He became increasingly interested in landscape and developed a greater spontaneity of expression with which to describe different times of day, using a lighter range of colours. He took part in the Salon des Refusés in 1863 and exhibited with the Impressionists in 1874, 1876, 1877 and 1879. *Woman in an Orchard* (1875; Paris, Mus. d'Orsay) revealed his interest in the new artistic developments in France in the 1870s. Although he was a friend of Claude Monet he remained closer in spirit to the precursors of the Impressionist movement such as Auguste Ravier and the painters of the Barbizon school, Charles-François Daubigny and the group who met at the Saint Siméon farm, where he often stayed.

BIBLIOGRAPHY

A. Alexandre: *A.-F. Cals ou le bonheur de peindre* (Paris, 1900)
L'oeuvre de A.-F. Cals (exh. cat., Paris, Gal. Petit, 1901)
V. Jannesson: *Le Peintre A.-F. Cals* (Paris, 1913)
Exposition de peintures de A.-F. Cals (rétrospective) et de sculptures de Paul Paulin (exh. cat., Paris, Gal. Louis-le-Grand, 1914)
Exposition rétrospective de A.-F. Cals (exh. cat., Paris, Gal. Druet, 1930)
Exposition rétrospective de A.-F. Cals (exh. cat., Paris, Gal. Dubourg, 1943)
A. Doria: 'Un Peintre injustement oublié: Adolphe-Félix Cals', *A. Basse-Normandie*, 22 (1961)
A.-F. Cals (exh. cat., London, Hazlitt, Gooden & Fox, 1969)
Cals, 1810–1880 (exh. cat. by F. Delestre, Paris, Gal. Delestre, 1975)

VALÉRIE M. C. BAJOU

Cāḷukyas of Kalyāṇa or Kalyāṇi. *See* CHALUKYA, §2.

Calvaert [Caluwaert], **Denys** [Denijs, Denis] [Dionisio Fiamingo] (*b* Antwerp, *c.* 1540; *d* Bologna, 16 April 1619). Flemish painter and draughtsman, active in Italy. In 1556–7 he was inscribed in the registers of the painters' corporation in Antwerp as a pupil of the landscape painter Kerstiaen van Queboorn (1515–78). Calvaert went to Bologna *c.* 1560, where he was to remain for the rest of his life. There he came under the protection of the influential Bolognini family and entered the workshop of Prospero Fontana the elder. After about two years he left Fontana to work with Lorenzo Sabatini, with whom he collaborated on several pictures, including the *Holy Family with the Archangel St Michael* (Bologna, S Giacomo Maggiore) and an *Assumption* (Bologna, Pin. N.). Calvaert's oeuvre is composed almost exclusively of religious works, ranging in size from vast altarpieces to small devotional pictures on copper. This sets him apart from other Netherlandish painters, notably those of the school of

Prague, for whom Classical mythology was a constant source of inspiration. His first signed and dated work was *Vigilance* (1568; Bologna, Pin. N.); thereafter he developed a more original style, as in the *Noli me tangere* (Bologna, Pin. N.). However, these early works reveal Calvaert's inexperience in painting figures and the influence of Marten de Vos, whose work Calvaert must have seen in Antwerp before leaving for Italy.

In 1572 Pope Gregory XIII called Sabatini to Rome; Calvaert accompanied him and received a payment for a *Battle of Lepanto.* From 1572 to 1575 Calvaert remained in Rome, where he made numerous drawings, mainly studies after such Old Masters as Michelangelo, Sebastiano del Piombo and Raphael, whose *St Cecilia* he later copied. Calvaert's drawings are characterized by their thickset figures, reminiscent of the work of Michiel Coxcie, and detailed execution, as in the red chalk study for the *Ascension* (Amsterdam, Rijksmus.). Another sheet with two studies of apostles on the *recto* and *verso* (Florence, Uffizi), annotated *Dionisio fiamingo*, shows a technique that resembles that of his red-and-black chalk drawing dated 1570 or 1578, *Moses and the Daughters of Jethro* (Paris, Louvre), which was engraved by Agostino Carracci in 1581. Calvaert also made drawings after the Antique: a pen-and-ink *Study of a Nude Man* (Amsterdam, Rijskmus.) is modelled on the Farnese *Hercules* (Naples, Mus. N.). Calvaert's composition drawings are hard to distinguish from those of his Italian contemporaries, whereas his studies of single figures come very close to those of the northern artist Peter Candid. Calvaert's painted copies of Old Masters have also sometimes created confusion, and art dealers have sold Calvaert's copies as originals.

Denys Calvaert: *Virgin Appearing to SS Francis and Dominic*, oil on canvas, 1.60×1.25 m, 1598 (Dresden, Gemäldegalerie Alte Meister)

In 1575 Calvaert returned to Bologna, where he founded a painting school seven years before the Accademia degli Incamminati of the Carracci brothers. His method of instruction seems to have been based on extensive knowledge of 16th-century Italian art and culture, much of it gained through the study of prints. Among Calvaert's pupils were Guido Reni and Domenichino, both of whom transferred to the rival Accademia degli Incamminati in 1582. Calvaert's *Mystic Marriage of St Catherine* (1590; Rome, Pin. Capitolina) is typical of his second Bolognese period. His initial response to the style of Parmigianino, which characterized his early works and those of many other Flemish painters on their arrival in Italy, was modified by a knowledge of the work of Federico Barocci. In the *Virgin Appearing to SS Francis and Dominic* (1598; Dresden, Gemäldegal. Alte Meister; see fig.) Calvaert combined the chiaroscuro and exaggerated poses of Correggio with a panoramic landscape of a distinctly northern character in the background. Barocci's influence is evident in the softly rounded feminine faces, the skin tones and the use of a range of soft colours of pearly hue.

Together with Barocci, Calvaert contributed to the revival of the Correggesque manner of painting in Bologna during the last quarter of the 16th century. Throughout his career he remained faithful to the Mannerist style of painting, even when it was already out of fashion. His work contributed to the particular form of classicism that developed in Bologna and the Emilia in the early 17th century.

BIBLIOGRAPHY

BNB; Thieme–Becker

C. C. Malvasia: *Felsina pittrice* (1678); ed. M. Brascaglia (1971)

S. Bergmans: *Catalogue critique des oeuvres du peintre Denis Calvaert* (Brussels, 1932)

F. Lugt: *Inventaire général des dessins des écoles du nord: Musée du Louvre* (Paris, 1968), pp. 125–9, nos 606–24

A. Emiliani, ed.: *Scritti originali del Conte Carlo Cesare Malvasia spettanti alla sua Felsina pittrice* (Bologna, 1983), pp. 124, 202, 211–12, 218–29, 262, 272, 324, 381, 385, 387

T. Montella: 'Dionisio Calvart', *Pittura bolognese del '500*, ed. V. Fortunati Pietrantonio (Bologna, 1986), ii, pp. 683–708

N. Dacos: 'Denys Calvaert', *The Age of Correggio and Carracci: Emilian Painting of the Sixteenth and Seventeenth Centuries* (exh. cat., Washington, DC, N.G.A., 1986), pp. 77–81

HANS J. VAN MIEGROET

Calvary [Lat. *Calvaria*: 'skull'; Aramaic Golgotha]. Site in Jerusalem where the crucifixion of Christ took place and name given to representations of that event. It is identified as the Place of the Skull in the New Testament Gospels and was at that time located outside the city walls, not far from a gate and near a road, a garden and at least one tomb. These landmarks of Christ's death, burial and resurrection have been revered by Christians since at least the 4th century, when Emperor Constantine the Great excavated the area and erected on top of it the basilican church of the Holy Sepulchre (*c.* 325–36; *see* JERUSALEM, §II, 2). The rock of Calvary, originally 4 m high, was cut and reshaped to serve in the basilica as a pedestal for a great jewelled cross placed on top of it. Calvary's elevation does not appear in the earliest depictions of Christ's crucifixion, but it gradually develops in art, for example in the Rabbula Gospels of 586 (Florence, Bib. Medicea-Laurenziana, MS. Plut. I.56) and the Utrecht Psalter of *c.* 830 (Utrecht, Bib. Rijksuniv., MS. 32), reaching at times absurd proportions, as in the painting by Lucas van Valckenborch, *Landscape with Jerusalem, Christ Carrying the Cross and Preparations on the Hill of Calvary* (1567; sold London, Christie's, 6 July 1984).

Various explanations have been offered as to why the site came to be identified with the skull. Some authors have suggested that this was owing to the shape of the rounded, rocky hillock. St Jerome theorized that the skulls of executed criminals lay about the place unburied, a theory exemplified in Antonello da Messina's *Crucifixion* (London, N.G.). An early Christian legend cited by Origen (*fl c.* 185–254) and Basil, Bishop of Caesarea (*fl c.* 330–79), claimed that the site was so named because it was the burial place of Adam, although a more ancient Jewish tradition located Adam's burial place at Mt Moriah, where Abraham was later ordered to sacrifice Isaac and where Solomon built his magnificent temple. In the 2nd century, mystic speculation springing from the Judeo–Christian milieu of Jerusalem assimilated Jewish notions of the history of salvation and divine covenant by transferring Adam's tomb from the altar of the temple on Mt Moriah to the place of Christ's cross on Calvary. This mirrored the theology of St Paul, who saw in Christ the 'New Adam' and saw his death on Calvary as the expiatory sacrifice for the Original Sin of the first Adam and his descendants. In Christian art, Adam's skull and bones were commonly depicted inside the mound beneath the foot of Christ's cross, as found in Giotto's *Crucifixion* (Padua, Arena Chapel) and Cimabue's *Crucifixion* (Assisi, S Francesco), or placed outside the mound as in Andrea del Castagno's *Crucifixion with Four Saints* (S Apollonia, Florence).

Advocates of St Paul's theological concept further elaborated on it in legend and art by associating the wood of the cross on Calvary with a miraculous tree found in the Garden of Eden. Along these lines, the *Golden Legend* of Jacopo da Voragine recounted the tale found in the apocryphal gospel of Nicodemus, wherein an ailing and aged Adam sent his son Seth to the gate of the Garden of Eden to ask for a few drops of oil from the tree of mercy to restore his health. In the common version of the story, the Archangel Michael gave a branch of the tree to Seth, telling him that on the day the tree bore fruit, his father would be made whole. But Seth returned to his father to find him already dead. He planted the branch over Adam's grave and it flourished until the reign of King Solomon, when it was cut down for use in the construction of his temple. Discarded by workers who had cut it too short, it was thrown over a small pond to serve as a bridge. The Queen of Sheba on her visit to Solomon refused to set foot on the bridge, claiming she foresaw that the Saviour would one day hang upon it, bringing to an end the kingdom of the Jews. On hearing this, Solomon had the tree buried deep in the earth, where it gave rise to the healing pond called Probatica. By the time of Christ's death, the tree had floated to the surface of the pond and was formed into the cross used by his executioners. Afterwards it was discarded in a cistern near Calvary, where it lay buried for hundreds of years. Voragine cautioned his readers that such tales were not to be found in any authentic chronicle or history. Nevertheless, these stories of the grave and tree at Calvary were often depicted in art, as in the Hours of Catherine of Cleves (New York, Pierpont Morgan Lib., MSS M. 917, fol. 97, pl. 82; M. 945; see fig.), a masterpiece of Netherlandish miniature painting made for the Duchess of Guelders around 1440. Such legends are linked to the account of the Emperor Constantine's desire to uncover the True Cross, sending for this purpose his mother, Helena, who led an expedition to Jerusalem. When her excavations unearthed three crosses at Calvary, the True Cross was determined when it revivified a corpse. This is the subject of the fresco cycle by Agnolo Gaddi (*c.* 1388–93; Florence, Santa Croce; *see* GADDI (i), (4), fig. 1), and of that by Piero della Francesca (1453–4; Arezzo, S Francesco).

Calvary, miniature from the Hours of Catherine of Cleves, *c.* 1440 (New York, Pierpont Morgan Library, MSS M. 917, M. 945)

Architecturally, the Calvary site has undergone numerous transformations. The Constantinian church was burned by the Persians in 614, restored in 628 and brought down to its very foundations by Hakem, Caliph of Egypt, in 1009. The Crusaders devoted half a century (1099–1149) to the reconstruction of the church, and it is this Romanesque edifice, with its various alterations, repairs, consolidations and devotional chapels, that today covers the spot where Christ's death is venerated.

BIBLIOGRAPHY

W. Staude: 'Le Crâne-calice au pied de la Croix', *Rev. des A.*, iv/3 (1954), pp. 137–42

A. Parrot: *Golgotha et Saint-Sépulcre* (Neuchâtel, 1955; Eng. trans., 1957)
R. Krautheimer: *Early Christian and Byzantine Architecture* (Baltimore, MD, 1965)
C. Coüasnon: *The Church of the Holy Sepulchre in Jerusalem* (London, 1974)
S. De Sandoli: *Il Calvario e il S Sepolcro* (Jerusalem, 1974; Eng. trans., 1977)
R. Milburn: *Early Christian Art and Architecture* (Berkeley, 1988)

MICHAEL MORRIS

Calvert, Edward (*b* Appledore, Devon, 20 Sept 1799; *d* London, 14 July 1883). English wood-engraver and painter. The son of a soldier, he entered the Navy but left the service after the death in action of his closest friend. He studied drawing in Plymouth with Thomas (or James) Ball and with Turner's champion Ambrose Bowden Johns (1776–1858). In 1824 he moved to London and entered the Royal Academy Schools. Through John Giles, Samuel Palmer's cousin, Calvert met William Blake and the Shoreham circle of the Ancients. He visited Shoreham and, supported by private means, escaped from his Academy studies to pursue his interest in wood-engraving. Rich in Arcadian imagery and chiaroscuro, Calvert's 11 miniature prints, produced between 1827 and 1831, are masterpieces of the medium and are among the most intense expressions of the Ancients' artistic sensibility. Like Palmer, he was inspired by Blake's illustrations to Thornton's edition of Virgil, but the figural content of Calvert's prints, of which the finest is the *Chamber Idyll* (1831), is more akin to his friend and fellow student George Richmond's interpretation of Blake than to Palmer's. Unlike the other Shoreham artists, Calvert did not base his pastoral visions on religious poetry such as that of Milton or Bunyan, but found inspiration in Theocritus and other pagan idylls. Early states of his prints frequently incorporated Christian sentences (e.g. the *Cyder Feast*) apparently less out of conviction than a desire to refute charges of paganism, since he removed them from later states.

After 1831 and Blake's death, Calvert's pastoral vision faded but his interest in ancient Greece developed into a more classical sentiment. He abandoned printmaking and for the rest of his life painted mainly for pleasure, working in oil, watercolour and gouache. He took his subjects chiefly from pagan mythology, aspiring to a 'beautiful ideal' drawn from ancient Greek art, and he visited Greece where he sketched prolifically. In later years Calvert became a recluse with a suitably picturesque appearance.

BIBLIOGRAPHY

S. Calvert: *Memoir of Edward Calvert* (London, 1893)
L. Binyon: *The Followers of William Blake* (London, 1925)
A. J. Finberg: 'Edward Calvert's Engravings', *Pr. Colr Q*, xvii (1930), pp. 139–53
R. Lister: *Edward Calvert* (London, 1962)
Samuel Palmer and 'the Ancients' (exh. cat. by R. Lister, Cambridge, Fitzwilliam, 1984), pp. 78–86

DAVID BLAYNEY BROWN

Calvi, Girolamo-Luigi (*b* Milan, 1791; *d* Milan, 28 March 1872). Italian painter and art historian. He was trained as a painter in the Neo-classical school of Giuseppe Bossi, and by Vincenzo Camuccini and Pietro Benvenuti. He was the author of *Notizie sulla vita...e degli Sforza*, the first great history of Milanese art of the 14th to the 16th century, which largely established the canon of early Milanese artists. Calvi's book was founded on his perceptive connoisseurship of painting and sculpture, and a good understanding of secondary literature. He made a thorough, intelligent use of primary sources including lapidary inscriptions, documents from the archives of Milan and Pavia, and also the then unpublished manuscript (compiled *c*. 1775) of Antonio Francesco Albuzzi. This work consisted of a collection of notes on the lives of Milanese artists, its author being the first secretary of the Accademia Braidense, where Giuseppe Bossi taught. Both Bossi and Calvi possessed copies of Albuzzi's manuscript.

WRITINGS

Notizie sulla vita e sulle opere dei principali architetti, scultori e pittori che fiorirono in Milano durante il governo dei Visconti e degli Sforza, 3 vols (Milan, 1859–69)

BIBLIOGRAPHY

Thieme–Becker
M. Caffi: 'Necrologia: Girolamo-Luigi Calvi', *Archv Stor. It.*, 3rd ser., xv (1872), pp. 363–4
C. R. Morscheck: *Relief Sculpture for the Façade of the Certosa di Pavia, 1473–1499* (New York and London, 1978), pp. 157–61

CHARLES R. MORSCHECK JR

Calvi, Jacopo Alessandro [il Sordino] (*b* Bologna, 23 Feb 1740; *d* Bologna, 5 May 1815). Italian painter, biographer, draughtsman and engraver. He was a pupil of Giuseppe Varotti (1715–80). While a student at the Accademia Clementina, Bologna, he received two awards, including the Premio Marsili for the *Sacrifice of Noah* (1758; Bologna, Accad. B.A. & Liceo A.). He pursued literary interests throughout his life and became a member of the avant-garde Accademia Letteraria degli 'Ingomiti' in Bologna in 1763. His early paintings, notably the *St Francis de Sales* (1764; Bologna, Ospizio dei Preti), continue the strict classical strain within the Bolognese figurative tradition; they show the influences of Ercole Graziani, Marc Antonio Franceschini and Donato Creti. Calvi primarily painted sacred subjects, receiving numerous, mainly local, commissions. From about 1770 onwards many pictures, including his superb *Self-portrait* (1770; Bologna, Pin. N.), became increasingly austere and Raphaelesque in both style and design, anticipating 19th-century Bolognese Neo-classicism. In 1766 he frescoed an *Assumption of the Virgin* (Bologna, S Luca), for which Giovan Pietro Zanotti, Calvi's lifelong associate, composed a laudatory sonnet. Paintings from the late 1770s and 1780s, for example the *Blessed Corsini, Ramuzzi and Malvezzi* (1779; Bologna, S Maria dei Servi), often betray the somewhat academic classicism of, among others, Gaetano Gandolfi.

Calvi also made engravings and was considered an excellent draughtsman. His best-known engravings were after frescoes by Ludovico Carracci in S Michele in Bosco, Bologna. The same frescoes were the subject of a study first published in 1776 by Zanotti, of which Calvi edited a second edition, eventually published in 1847. His literary pursuits are in fact of a certain art-historical interest. He published biographical studies of three Bolognese artists: Guercino, Mauro Antonio Tesi and Francesco Francia. There is also an unpublished manuscript by him on Ubaldo and Gaetano Gandolfi.

UNPUBLISHED SOURCES

U. Vienna, Inst. Kstgesch. [Calvi MS. Inv. Nr. 11334: *Succinte notizie dei due celebri professori di pittura Ubaldo e Gaetano Gandolfi . . . Bologna, 30 giugno 1802*]

WRITINGS

Raccolta di disegni originali di Mauro Tesi estratti da diverse collezioni (Bologna, 1787/*R* Farnborough, Hants, 1970)

Notizie della vita e delle opere del Cavaliere Gioan Francesco Barbieri detto il Guercino da Cento (Bologna, 1808); also in C. C. Malvasia: *Felsina pittrice*, ed. G. Zanotti (Bologna, 1841), ii, pp. 275–343

Memorie della vita e delle opere di Francesco Raibolini detto il Francia (Bologna, 1812)

ed.: G. P. Zanotti: *Le pitture di Lodovico Carracci. . . . nel chiostro della chiesa di S Michele in Bosco*, 2nd edn (Bologna, 1847)

See also UNPUBLISHED SOURCES above.

BIBLIOGRAPHY

G. B. Grilli Rossi: *Vita di J. A. Calvi detto il Sordino* (Bologna, 1825)

A. Emiliani and F. Varignana: *Le collezioni d'arte della Cassa di Risparmio in Bologna dal cinquecento al neoclassicismo: I disegni*, i (Bologna, 1973), nos 329–50, pp. 360–68

□

Calvière, Charles-François, Marquis de (*b* Avignon, 22 April 1698; *d* Vézénobres, Gard, 16 Nov 1777). French nobleman, patron and collector. In the course of his military career he rose from page under Louis XIV to Lieutenant Général of the armies of Louis XV (1748); he was on familiar terms with the court and even the King. In 1753 he retired to his estates in southern France, having had erected a magnificent château near Uzès, built to the design of Guillaume Rollin (1685–1761), an architect from Nîmes. There he housed the collections he had assembled in Paris of pictures, drawings, coins and medals: in forming it, his association since 1747 with the Académie Royale de Peinture et de Sculpture had proved useful.

After his retirement, Calvière continued to acquire drawings in Paris, for example at the time of the Mariette sale in 1775, through the agency of François-Claude Joullain; but he devoted himself particularly to his collections of coins and medals, and to archaeology in general. This is demonstrated by the correspondence he conducted with two well-known *antiquaires*, F. E. Séguier (1714–84; letters, Nîmes, Bib. Mun.) and Esprit Calvet (1728–1810; letters, Avignon, Médiathèque). After Calvière's death his heirs made over his archaeological collections to Calvet, which thus eventually found their way to the Musée Calvet, Avignon; they included an important Egyptian *Head of a Vizier* in green basalt and a fragment of the mosaic from La Daurade, Toulouse. Calvière's books were sold in Avignon, while his paintings and drawings were dispersed, for the most part, by Joullain, in a sale in Paris (5–20 May 1779). It totalled 674 items, including more than 600 drawings from the three main schools. Some 120 sheets, acquired by the Comte d'Orsay and Etienne Bourgevin Vialart, Comte de Saint-Morys (1772–1817) are now in the Cabinet des Dessins in the Louvre and may be identified by inscriptions in Calvière's hand.

BIBLIOGRAPHY

Les Collections du Comte d'Orsay: Dessins du Musée du Louvre (exh. cat., ed. J.-F. Mejanès; Paris, Louvre, 1983)

F. Arquié-Bruley, J. Labbé and L. Bicart-Sée: *La Collection Saint-Morys au Cabinet des Dessins du Musée du Louvre* (Paris, 1987)

M.-F. Perez: 'Les Collections numismatiques du Marquis de Calvière (1698–1777)', *Anticomanie? La Collection d'antiquités en France aux XVIIIe et XIXe siècles: Montpellier, 1988*

MARIE-FÉLICIE PÉREZ

Calvinism. Religious movement within Western Christendom, originating in the teaching of Jean Calvin (1509–64). In various contexts it is referred to as Presbyterianism, Puritanism or the Reformed Church; its French adherents were known as HUGUENOTS.

1. Origins: Jean Calvin. 2. Spread. 3. Iconography.

1. ORIGINS: JEAN CALVIN. There was no single or charismatic leader in the origins of Reformed Protestantism, which was a distinct movement within the pre-Reformation Church represented by Huldrych Zwingli (1484–1531), Heinrich Bullinger (1504–75), Martin Bucer (1491–1551) and Guillaume Farel (1489–1565). In its second generation, however, the French scholar and churchman Jean Calvin emerged as the most influential theologian and spokesman for Reformed Protestantism. He was the only one of the reformers to be trained as both a lawyer and a humanist. Before 4 May 1534 he had made his break with Roman Catholicism, being influenced by Christian humanism, Martin Luther's texts and his personal experience of the Bible as the Word of God. Under threat of persecution, he left France between 1534 and 1535 for haven in Basle. During this self-imposed exile, he wrote the *Christianae religionis institutio* (Basle, 1536), an explanation of French Protestantism, which became the representative statement of Reformed Christianity. He first settled in Geneva in 1536, but liturgical disputes there led him to spend 1538–41 as a pastor in Strasbourg, where he prepared several influential scriptural exegeses and revised the *Institutio.* His return to Geneva barely preceded the approval of his new constitution, *Ordonnances ecclésiastiques*, which established a type of theocracy and formed the basic charter of Calvinist or Presbyterian polity. Between 1555 and 1564 Calvin firmly controlled the leadership of the Reformed Church in Geneva. In 1559 he established the Academy of Geneva (now university) as a seminary for preachers and published the final edition of the *Institutio.* He was succeeded in his role at Geneva by Theodore Beza (1519–1605). The dominating influence of the reformers on the city is commemorated in the Reformation Monument (see fig.).

The four central concepts of Calvin's theology were the absolute sovereign will of God, Christocentricism, Scripture as the supreme rule of faith and life, and the Church. God's majesty and providence, the foundation of his systematic theology, governed everything, including the destiny of humanity. Following the Augustinian model, Calvin's doctrine of election and predestination emphasized human depravity and the mystery of God's merciful grace. Arguing for a vigorous morality, he held a pessimistic view of humanity but an optimistic view of history as a doctrine of progress. He interpreted the Scriptures as the inerrant laws God created for human salvation and the Church as essential for that salvation through the Word and the sacraments.

Calvin promoted a more thorough reform of both church worship and organization than Martin Luther had done. The pulpit with an open Bible became the focal point of Calvinist worship, which centred on preaching, prayer and hymns. He recognized two sacraments: baptism and the Lord's Supper, which he interpreted as the spiritual

Jean Calvin, with fellow reformers Favel, Beza and Knox as the central figures of the Reformation Monument, Geneva, by Henri Bouchard and Paul Landowski, stone, 8.50×4.57×120.0 m, 1909–17

presence of Christ performing a work of grace for the recipients. Premised on his removal of the restriction on usury and the economic values of the rising middle class, his social ethics have been seen as the religious foundation of modern capitalism. Calvin's covenant theology was a striking fusion of aristocracy and democracy. His tenet of representative Church government followed the New Testament model, in which the secular State should not dictate to the Church but rather existed to maintain and protect the Church. Geneva became Calvin's vision of a city totally dedicated to the glorification of God. This model of Reformed Protestantism flourished only in the European colonies. Where the constituted authorities opposed total revision of the governmental system, Calvinism supported its manifestation of the glory of God through personal morality, diligence and industry.

2. SPREAD.

(i) Germany and Switzerland. Luther's support for the repression of the Peasant Revolt (1524–6) resulted in the acceptance of Calvinism in the Rhineland as well as such major cities as Strasbourg and Konstanz. Under Frederick III, Elector of Saxony, the University of Heidelberg became a theological haven for Calvinism. The *Heidelberg Confession* (1562) became the creed of the German Reformed Church and supported the Reformed tradition in Poland, Bohemia, Hungary and Moravia. The *Consensus Tigurinus* (1549), formulated by Bullinger and Calvin, supported the general acceptance of Calvinism throughout Switzerland. Bullinger later wrote the *Second Helvetic Confession* (1566), which was published in the name of all the Swiss Cantons except Basle and Neuchâtel. Into the 20th century, the Swiss Reformed Church claimed the majority of the population as members. Following World War I, Switzerland again became the theological centre of Calvinism with the establishment of the neo-orthodox theology of Karl Barth (1886–1968), who reasserted human finitude and guilt, the need for salvific grace and the transcendent majesty of God in his widely influential *Die kirchliche Dogmatik* (Munich, 1932).

(ii) The Netherlands. From 1555 Philip II, King of Spain, a devout Roman Catholic, attempted to eradicate Dutch Protestantism, especially the newly introduced Calvinism, by introducing the Inquisition. However, Dutch Calvinism gathered enough strength to call a synod in 1560 and published the *Belgic Confession* in 1561, establishing the Dutch Reformed Church. The Synod of Emden (1571) perfected the Church's organization and operation. In 1566 William I, Prince of Orange, led an armed revolt against Spanish rule, and a period of violent iconoclasm began in the Netherlands. The Union of Utrecht (1579) decreed Calvinism as the official religion of the Netherlands and affirmed iconoclasm. The Declaration of Independence of the Netherlands' five northern provinces was issued in 1581, and their total independence from Spanish rule was achieved in 1609. Religious toleration was granted to Lutherans and Anabaptists but denied to Roman Catholics. The Netherlands became a religious haven for persecuted Protestants, including Anabaptists, Huguenots, Scottish Covenanters and English Puritans and Separatists. At independence the Netherlands was a major European trading power with an extensive merchant marine, which spread the Dutch Reformed Church throughout the Far East and West Indies, into Dutch American colonies, especially New Amsterdam [New York], and to the Dutch settlements in South Africa.

(iii) Britain and Ireland. Calvinism was influential from the mid-16th century in both England and Scotland. The Scottish preacher John Knox (*c.* 1513–72), who had visited Geneva, returned to Scotland in 1559 and rapidly established a Calvinist dominance in the Lowland towns. His *First Book of Discipline* (Edinburgh, 1560) defined the organization and administration of Scottish Presbyterianism and supported the acceptance of the Confession of Faith by the Scots Parliament (1560). James VI, King of Scotland from 1568 (and of England from 1603), promised economic advantage to Scots Presbyterians who settled in Ulster in the early 17th century to aid his control over Ireland, but after settlement the Stuart government imposed severe economic and political pressure on them, so that many fled to the American colonies. Presbyterian doctrines in England ('Puritanism') were delineated in the 1572 'Admonition to Parliament'. They underlay the 'Millenary Petition' (1603), a formal list of liturgical and theological abuses within the Church of England. The only response of King James was to order preparation of the Authorized Version of the Bible (the King James Bible, 1611). Committed to Calvin's organic society, in which all citizens must do the will of God and which required rule by the 'holy and regenerate', large numbers of English Puritans migrated to New England in the 1620s and 1630s. The *Westminster Confession* (1646) was influenced by Presbyterian acceptance of Calvin's sovereignty of God, authority of scripture and double predestination, and Puritanism dominated the Commonwealth of 1649–60; subsequently, however, it became marginalized in England.

(iv) France. The Huguenots of France were the most severely persecuted of all Calvinist groups. Initially receiving little opposition, the Huguenots called the Synod of Paris (1559), which issued the *Gallican Confession.* However, the Wars of Religion that followed their slaughter in the Massacre of St Bartholomew's Day (1572) continued until 1593. In 1598 Henry IV issued the Edict of Toleration. In 1685, after a period of relative religious stability, Louis XIV, dedicated to 'one nation, one faith', revoked the Edict of Toleration: French Huguenots fled to Holland, Switzerland, England, Prussia and the American colonies. The Reformed Church was granted toleration and legal status in France in 1802.

(v) America. Migrations from the European Reformed Churches into the American colonies influenced the development of socio-political and religious attitudes. The federal theology of the New England Puritans supported rule by the 'holy and regenerate' and included the tenets of freedom of conscience based on clear and explicit scriptural teaching, rule by fundamental law (the Bible) and government by consent of the governed. The establishment of Presbyterian, Congregationalist, Baptist and Colonial Anglican churches affirmed the fundamental pluralism and religious toleration of the new nation, which espoused freedom of human rights and of religion and separation of Church and State. The Great Awakening (1740) affirmed the Reformed Confessions and established 'denominationalism' as the American Protestant model. 18th- and 19th-century modifications stressed human initiative and independence. The 20th-century move towards ecumenism and fundamentalism initiated a revival among the Reformed Churches.

3. ICONOGRAPHY. Though fundamentally iconoclastic, Calvin formulated a median position on the visual image. In 'It is unlawful to attribute a visible form to God, and generally whoever sets up idols revolts against the true God', he clarified his position against the worship of false idols (*Institutio* I.11). He prohibited depictions of God and of any event, scriptural or theological, that was not historical. He argued that, since painting and carving, like all things, came from God, they cannot be denied. However, the 'practice of art should be kept pure and lawful'—this referred, in effect, to instructive or admonitive depictions of history. Calvin advised a certain restricted value in the arts while authorizing the removal of images from worship, especially devotional art dedicated to Christ and the Virgin. He permitted the use of the empty cross in churches but not the crucifix. Rearranging the church interior, he gave primacy to the pulpit and secondary rank to the altar (for an illustration of the interior of a Calvinist church *see* CHURCH, fig. 10). The central image of Calvinism was the open Bible on the pulpit.

No longer patronized by the Church, artists in Calvinist society turned to the rising middle class for economic support by creating themes appropriate to domestic environments: landscapes, portraiture and genre scenes flourished in 16th- and 17th-century Holland and Germany. Nonetheless, religious art did not disappear totally from Calvinist cultures. Rather, it was transformed into history painting, which featured narrative scriptural events as opposed to such mystical or transcendent moments as the Resurrection. The retrieval of scriptural typology by Reformed exegesis led to a visual emphasis on Old Testament morality themes, including the *Fall of Man* (e.g. etching by Rembrandt, 1638; Washington DC, N.G.A.), the *Sacrifice of Isaac* and *Solomon's Idolatry.* Iconographic innovations included depictions of Christ's sermons and parables, especially *Suffer Little Children* (Matt. 19:14), for example *Christ Blessing the Children* by Nicolaes Maes (1650s; London, N.G.). Given the prevalent antipathy within Protestantism to sculpture and painting, the print became the primary mode for Reformed iconography, especially for Bible illustrations. Series of moralizing prints, especially of scriptural themes, supported Calvinism's moral fervour. More often than not, the violent iconoclasm generally associated with Calvinism, such as the destruction of ecclesiastical buildings and religious images in France, Holland, England and Scotland, arose as a protest against Catholicism as well as a spiritual fear of images. Public support for Calvinist iconoclasm developed from the vernacular texts of popular authors.

BIBLIOGRAPHY

J. Calvin: *Christianae religionis institutio* (Basle, 1536; rev. Geneva, 1559); Eng. trans. in *Library of Christian Classics*, xxi–xxii (Philadelphia, 1960)
G. G. Coulton: *Art and the Reformation* (Oxford, 1928)
J. Dillenberger and C. Welch: *Protestant Christianity* (New York, 1954)
W. Hudson: *Religion in America* (New York, 1965)
E. Panofsky: 'Comments on Art and Reformation', *Symbols in Transformation: Themes at the Time of the Reformation* (Princeton, 1969)
S. E. Ahlstrom: *A Religious History of the American People* (New Haven and London, 1972)
J. Gutmann, ed.: *The Image and the Word: Confrontations in Judaism, Christianity, and Islam* (Missoula, 1972)
C. Harbison: 'Reformation Iconography: Problems and Attitudes', *Prt Rev.*, v (1976), pp. 78–86
A. C. Moore: *Iconography of Religions* (Philadelphia, 1977)
C. Trumpel: 'Religious History Painting', *Gods, Saints and Heroes: Dutch Painting in the Age of Iconoclasm* (Washington, DC, 1980)
G. Heyer: *Signs of Our Times: Theological Essays on Art in the Twentieth Century* (Grand Rapids, 1981)
D. Freedberg: 'The Hidden God: Image and Interdiction in the Netherlands in the Sixteenth Century', *A. Hist.*, v (1982), pp. 133–53
W. H. Halewood: *Six Subjects of Reformation Art: A Preface to Rembrandt* (Toronto, 1982)

DIANE APOSTOLOS-CAPPADONA

Calvit, Mario (*b* Panama City, 29 Jan 1933). Panamanian sculptor and painter. He studied at the Escuela Nacional de Artes Plásticas in Panama City (1950–53) and established his reputation with abstract or semi-abstract sculptural constructions of soldered unfinished iron. Although the metal surface is sometimes painted, most pieces have a rusty finish, for example *Marine Flight* (1972; Panama City, Mus. A. Contemp.). The lyrical realism of his paintings, such as *Mythical Trainers of a Lipizzaner Horse* (1982; Panama City, artist's col., see E. Wolfschoon: *Las manifestaciones artísticas en Panamá*, Panama City, 1983, p. 401), is comparable to that of the Mexicans Francisco Corzas and Pedro Coronel, often with poetic or literary associations.

BIBLIOGRAPHY

R. Oviero: 'Calvit del otro lado del lienzo', *A. Visual*, i/2 (1985), pp. 17–20
Encuentro de escultura (exh. cat., ed. M. E. Kupfer; Panama City, Mus. A. Contemp., 1987), pp. 22–3

MONICA E. KUPFER

Calvo, Marco Fabio (*b* *c.* 1450; *d* Rome, 1527). Italian philologist and antiquarian. He was probably born near Ravenna. 'Calvus' was a classical cognomen; the family name 'de Fabii' can be traced to Forlì. By 1511 Calvo had entered the employ of Federico II Gonzaga, Marquess of Mantua, as a private tutor of geometry and Greek; he was already preparing an omnibus translation of Hippocrates into Latin (pubd 1525). At the request of Pope Julius II, Calvo settled in Rome in 1512. His reputation as a philologist brought him into contact with Raphael, who asked him to stay as a guest in his palazzo and to translate Vitruvius. Raphael might have used Calvo's work in progress when he wrote to Baldassare Castiglione in 1514 that he had 'probed Vitruvius, but still yearned for more'. Presumably Calvo completed the translation by November 1516, when he turned his attention to an edition and commentary of Galen's *Epidemiorum*, which occupied him until December 1518. Calvo's autograph of Vitruvius is lost. There are two manuscripts in the Bayerische Staatsbibliothek, Munich (Cod. Ital. 37a and 37b). Raphael added sparse marginalia to books 3 and 4, and illustrations for woodcuts. Despite his stoic and retiring character, Calvo remained almost like a mentor and father ('quasi praeceptorem et patrem'; Calcagnini Ferrariensis) to Raphael.

Calvo's last years were devoted to reviving the commission Raphael had begun for Leo X graphically to reconstruct ancient Rome in a series of *piante*—a project that had been cut short at the artist's premature death in April 1520. In February 1527 Calvo was still receiving a stipend from the Camera Apostolica. Two months later his illustrated atlas was published in Rome by Ludovico Arrighi, subsidized by the papal treasurer, Cardinal Francesco Armellini. The *Antiquae urbis Romae cum regionibus simulachrum* comprises 24 woodcuts in folio with a brief text and captions, beginning with composite maps of Rome during four historical periods: the Roma Quadrata of Romulus, the Republican city under Servius Tullius, Augustan Rome and the city at the time of Pliny the elder. Calvo drew upon ancient land-surveying treatises, most notably the recently discovered Codex Arcerianus, as a source for these idealized cityscapes. Next follows a map of the Capitoline and a prologue to the central section, consisting of individual site-plans of the 14 regions from Imperial Rome. Many of the reconstructions of specific monuments are based on the reverses of ancient coins. The last two folios depict an ancient bathhouse (*balneum*) and a diagram of the circus. The *Simulachrum* was reprinted only five years later by the Brescian printer, Valerius Dorichus, with an introduction by the author's nephew, Fabio Timotheo. From this we learn that Calvo had begun on a more comprehensive guide to the antiquities of Rome on the scale of Andrea Fulvio's *Antiquitates urbis* (1527), although the draft of this work perished that year in the sack of the city. One of the plates of the *Simulachrum* was reused by Sebastian Münster for his edition of Solinus' *Polyhistoria* in 1538.

BIBLIOGRAPHY

C. Calcagnini Ferrariensis: *Protonotarii Apostolici opera aliquot* [About the work of the Protonotarii Apostolici] (Basle, 1544), p. 101
P. Valeriano: *Contarenus, sive de litteratorum infelicitate libri II* [Contarenus, or the unhappiness of men of letters, in two books] (Leipzig, 1707), pp. 360–70
G. Mercati: 'Appunti su Marco Fabio Calvo', *Notizie varie di antica letteratura medica e di bibliografia* (Rome, 1917), pp. 67–71
——: 'Altre notizie di M. Fabio Calvo', *Bessarione*, xiii (1919), pp. 158–61
A. P. Frutaz: *Le piante di Roma*, i, ii (Rome, 1962)
F. Castagnoli: 'Raphael and Ancient Rome', *Complete Works of Raphael*, ed. M. Salmi (New York, 1969), pp. 569–84
R. Weiss: *The Renaissance Discovery of Classical Antiquity* (Oxford, 1969), pp. 86–9
V. Fontana and P. Morachiello: *Vitruvio e Raffaello: Il 'De Architectura' di Vitruvio nella traduzione inedita di Fabio Calvo Ravennate* (Rome, 1975) [bibliog. of Calvo's pubd works and sources for his life]
P. N. Pagliara: 'La Roma antica di Fabio Calvo: Note sulla cultura antiquaria e architettonica', *Psicon: Riv. Int. Archit.*, viii-ix/3 (1976), pp. 31ff
P. J. Jacks: 'The *Simulachrum* of Fabio Calvo: A View of Roman Architecture *all'antica* in 1527', *A. Bull.*, lxxii (1990), pp. 453–81
——: *The Antiquarian and the Myth of Antiquity: The Origins of Rome in Renaissance Thought* (Cambridge, 1993), pp. 184–204

PHILIP J. JACKS

Calydon. *See* KALYDON.

Calyx [kalyx] **krater.** Ancient form of vessel, used as a mixing bowl (*see* GREECE, ANCIENT, figs 70, 71(ii)c, 113, 123 and 124).

Calzada, Humberto (*b* Havana, 25 May 1944). Cuban painter, active in the USA. He moved to the USA in 1960, settling in Miami. Self-taught as an artist, he had his first one-man show at the Bacardi Art Gallery in Miami in 1975. He is known principally for acrylic paintings showing architectural images or themes of the infinite in a hard-edge style, as in his series of the 1980s *A World Within* (e.g. *No. 14*, 1984; see 1988–9 exh. cat., p. 27), which employs a 'painting-within-a-painting' technique. In his works he drew upon Renaissance perspective; the spaces of Giorgio De Chirico and Luis Barragán; the stained-glass images of Amelia Peláez; and colonial Caribbean architecture. The buildings that Calzada depicted are non-functional; they comprise detached façades and windows, labyrinthine walls and stairs, and portions of columns arranged in courtyards, with projections of shadow and perspective. Calzada exhibited throughout the Americas, and his work is held in a number of North American museums and in the Museo de Arte de Ponce, Puerto Rico.

For illustration *see* LATIN AMERICAN ARTISTS OF THE USA, fig. 3.

BIBLIOGRAPHY

R. Pau-Llosa: 'Calzada's Architecture of Memory', *Carib. Rev.*, xiii/2 (1984), pp. 38–9
——: 'Image du bâti', *Conn. A.*, 384 (1984), pp. 52–7
Outside Cuba (exh. cat. by I. Fuentes Pérez and others, New York, Mus. Contemp. Hisp. A.; Oxford, OH, Miami U., A. Mus.; Ponce, Mus. A.; and elsewhere; 1987–9), pp. 212–17
¡Mira! Canadian Club Hispanic Art Tour (exh. cat. by R. Pau-Llosa, S. Torruella Leval and I. Lockpez, Dallas, TX, S. Methodist U., Meadows Mus. & Gal.; and elsewhere; 1988–9)

RICARDO PAU-LLOSA

Calzetti, Matteo. *See* WITHOOS, MATTHIAS.

Camacho, Jorge (*b* Havana, 5 Jan 1934). Cuban painter. A self-taught artist, he forsook law studies in 1952 to dedicate himself to painting and held his first individual exhibition in the Galería Cubana in Havana in 1955. In 1959 he settled in Paris where he became an important figure in the circle of Latin American émigré artists. In 1961 he met André Breton and joined what was left of the Surrealist group.

Camacho derived his stylized organic forms from the quasi-abstract Surrealism of Yves Tanguy, and his totemistic images from Wifredo Lam. Gradually he integrated into his complex and enigmatic art other interests such as alchemy, jazz and flamenco, as well as the bird life of French Guiana and Venezuela (which he studied at first hand in 1974 and 1975), as in, for example, *Bird, Night* (1980; Mario Amignet priv. col., see 1987 exh. cat.). His subtle tropes and allusions had a particularly strong appeal to poets like Joyce Mansour and Reinaldo Arenas, with whom he collaborated on numerous projects.

BIBLIOGRAPHY

A. Breton: *Le Surréalisme et la peinture* (Paris, 1928, rev. 1965; Eng. trans., London and New York, 1972)
Outside Cuba/Fuera de Cuba (exh. cat., New Brunswick, NJ, Rutgers U., Zimmerli A. Mus., 1987), p. 125

RICARDO PAU-LLOSA

Camagüey [formerly Santa María del Puerto Príncipe]. Cuban city situated between the Tinima and Hatibonico rivers. The original settlement of Santa María del Puerto Príncipe, one of the first seven towns founded by the Spaniards in CUBA, was established in 1514 at Punta del Guincho on the central north coast of the island. The vulnerability of this location led to the settlement being transferred in 1516 to Caonao, where it was subsequently destroyed by a native uprising. It was finally relocated at the inland site, later renamed Camagüey, in 1528. The population was sparse in the 16th century, and the town comprised a line of buildings stretching between its first two churches, the monastery of San Francisco de Paula (rebuilt 1720) and La Merced. In the 17th century the number of inhabitants grew to 3000, but the town was destroyed by Henry Morgan, the English pirate, in 1668. During the 18th century the population expanded to almost 30,000 as a result of new prosperity from cattle-rearing, smuggling and the growing sugar industry. Significant monuments of this period include the church of Santo Cristo del Buen Viaje (1723), the monastery and hospital of S Juan de Dios (1728), the sanctuary of La Caridad (1734) and the hermitage and hospital of S Lázaro (1737). The district of La Caridad was the first area to apply the grid system of urban planning, in contrast to the winding streets and irregular squares of the old town centre. When the Spanish Royal Tribunal was transferred from Santo Domingo (*see* DOMINICAN REPUBLIC) to Puerto Príncipe in 1800, the population increased yet again; by the end of the 19th century it had reached 60,000. In 1817 Ferdinand VII made the town a city; following Cuban independence in 1898 it was renamed Camagüey in 1903 and became the capital of a province of the same name.

The emergence of a rich landholding middle class created new residential districts, such as La Vigía, La Zambrana and Garrido; from the 1940s these were joined by Vista Hermosa, Puerto Príncipe and Montecarlo. Following the Revolution of 1959 the growth of the capital HAVANA was restricted and provincial development encouraged, leading to further growth in the population; by 1990 there were 300,000 inhabitants. Peripheral expansion in the city has allowed the protection of the historical centre, which is undergoing restoration.

BIBLIOGRAPHY

J. Juárez Cano: *Apuntes de Camagüey* (Camagüey, 1929)
A. Pérez: *El Camagüey legendario* (Camagüey, 1944)
'Camagüey, otra carga al machete', *Cuba Int.*, vi/56 (1974) [special issue]
L. Gómez Consuegra and others: *Centro histórico de Camagüey* (Camagüey, 1989)

ROBERTO SEGRE

Camaieu [Fr. *en camaieu*: 'like a cameo']. Painting with a single colour (monochrome) in two or three tones only (*see* BELGIUM, fig. 37); the technique is often employed to give the spectator, the illusion that the image is carved (*see also* GRISAILLE).

□

Camaino, Tino di. *See* TINO DI CAMAINO.

Camaldolese, Simone. *See* SIMONE CAMALDOLESE, Don.

Camaldolese Order. Religious order of hermit-monks.

1. INTRODUCTION. The Order was founded by St Romuald (*c.* 950–1027; *can* 1595), a Benedictine monk from Ravenna, who wanted to return to the purity of St Benedict's original ideas (*see* BENEDICTINE ORDER, §I) and combine an austere form of monastic community with the mystical simplicity of the hermit's life. In 1022–3 he established a community at Camaldoli, near Poppi, where solitary eremitical cells (the Sacro Eremo) were grouped above a cenobitical monastery (Fontebono), an arrangement that later inspired the Carthusians. It would appear that he did not intend to originate an order based specifically at Camaldoli, for he later founded other communities. His ideas directly influenced St Peter Damian (1007–72) and St John Gualberto (*d* 1073), who founded the Vallombrosans. The Constitutions and Rule of the Camaldolensians were written by Rudolph, 4th Prior of Camaldoli (*reg* 1074–89). The Rule was followed at numerous monasteries, both male and female, in central and northern Italy. Although the sites chosen gradually tended to be nearer to or even within towns, the internal discipline rarely diverged from Romuald's ideal combination of penitent isolation with communal austerity.

The Order's contemplative mysticism found early expression in creative scholarship, for example the systematization of canon law by Gratian (*d c.* 1179) and the *Decretals* of the Camaldolese Pope Gregory IX (*reg* 1227–41). The production of books was considered eminently appropriate to the contemplative life, and there was a celebrated scriptorium at Camaldoli. In the 14th century a school of manuscript illumination was established in S Maria degli Angeli (founded 1295), Florence. At first this important Camaldolese foundation was involved in the anti-humanist religious revival of the Florentine Observance, but by 1431, when he was elected General of the Order, AMBROGIO TRAVERSARI had reconciled revived religious feeling with respect for humanist scholarship and art. In the following century reform movements encouraged the consolidation of eremitical orders, and the

Camaldolese iconography: *St Benedict Presents the Rule to St Romuald*, altarpiece predella by an artist of the Pisan school, tempera on panel, 14th century (Florence, Galleria degli Uffizi)

community at Fonte Avellana, refounded by St Peter Damian, united with the Camaldolese in 1549. Houses in Rome and Turin were established in the 17th century, and the Order has continued into the late 20th century.

2. ICONOGRAPHY. The most distinctive image of Camaldolese tradition was St Romuald's vision of white-robed monks ascending a ladder to Heaven, which prompted him to select the spot for his community. Early representations were restricted to altarpiece predellas showing Romuald asleep, alone or with a companion, and the vision beside him (e.g. 14th century; Florence, Accad.; Florence, Uffizi), in which the symbols of the Eucharist and an altar prefigure the foundation of the monastery. During the Counter-Reformation revival of medieval imagery, the *Dream of St Romuald*, suitably elaborated, was considered appropriate for large narratives and altarpieces, for example by ANTIVEDUTO GRAMATICA (*c.* 1620; Frascati, S Romualdo di Camaldoli) and Andrea Sacchi (1631; Rome, Pin. Vaticana; *see* SACCHI, ANDREA, fig. 2). The latter was imitated, more dynamically, on the ceiling (*c.* 1700) of S Maria degli Angeli, Florence (for illustration *see* GHERARDINI, ALESSANDRO). Later in the 18th century Antonio Zanchi's *St Romuald* (Venice, Correr) returned to a simpler iconography, showing the Saint asleep and alone, but for the inspiring angel and his vision.

Romuald is usually shown in white robes, as is St Benedict in Camaldolese iconography, for example on a Pisan school predella of *St Benedict Presents the Rule to St Romuald* (14th century; Florence, Uffizi; see fig.). Although scenes from the *Life of St Benedict*, such as Uccello's lost frescoes in S Maria degli Angeli, frequently decorated Camaldolese monasteries, Romuald's life was rarely depicted: a panel by a follower of Fra Angelico shows *Emperor Otto III Confessing to St Romuald* (15th century; Antwerp, Kon. Mus. S. Kst.). After the Counter-Reformation, however, such subjects became more important, for example Guercino's *Angel Liberating St Romuald from a Demon* (Ravenna, Accad. B.A.), and cycles of the Saint's life, death, burial and translation appeared throughout the 17th and 18th centuries.

In early representations Romuald chiefly appears on Camaldolese altarpieces as a supporting saint, often with St Benedict. On the *Coronation of the Virgin* triptych (1414; Florence, Uffizi), painted by LORENZO MONACO for S Maria degli Angeli, Romuald bears his customary attribute of a T-shaped staff. The two saints also appear in the fresco, originally in the same monastery, of the *Crucifixion with the Virgin and SS John the Evangelist, Benedict, Romuald and Mary Magdalene* (*c.* 1442; Florence, S Maria Nuova; *see* CASTAGNO, ANDREA DEL,§1 (i)). In Francesco Salviati's *Virgin and Child Enthroned with Saints* (1540; Bologna, S Cristina) St Romuald kneels in adoration, carrying his secondary attribute, a model of the Sacro Eremo. Both staff and model feature on the frontispiece of an edition (Florence, 1513) of St Peter Damian's mid-11th-century *Life of the Blessed Romuald*, together with the Eucharistic symbol of a chalice flanked by doves, the badge or crest of Camaldoli.

3. PATRONAGE. The only distinctive provision in the Order's churches, as was usual for enclosed orders, was a separate monks' choir. This was the sole feature specified in the design of its most unusual church, Brunelleschi's oratory at S Maria degli Angeli (from 1434); although the form of the main oratory may have been influenced by Ambrogio Traversari, it was chiefly an expression of secular humanism.

Manuscripts produced by the informal school at S Maria degli Angeli are eclectic in style, combining elements from the followers of Giotto and the Sienese school. Its distinguished practitioners included SILVESTRO DEI GHERARDUCCI, SIMONE CAMALDOLESE and Lorenzo Monaco, who was allowed to leave the monastery in 1399 to set up his studio outside, while remaining in minor orders. Traversari's appreciation of humanist art may be partly attributable to his brother Girolamo Traversari (*d* 1433), another painter in S Maria degli Angeli. The only later Camaldolese artist of distinction was Bartolomeo della Gatta.

During the 16th century S Maria degli Angeli benefited from Medici patronage, represented by Vasari's *Deposition* triptych (1540; now Camaldoli, SS Donato ed Ilariano). Between 1570 and 1600 the church was rebuilt by Bartolomeo Ammanati. The Order's 17th-century expansion into Lazio produced more original results, such as the paintings by Gramatica (*see* §2 above) and Carlo Saraceni's *Rest on the Flight into Egypt* (1606; both Frascati, S Romualdo di Camaldoli). Less distinguished were the later 17th-century fresco cycles at Val di Castro and Fabriano (1674), and in the second remodelling (from 1676) of S Maria degli Angeli. At Camaldoli itself, the work of Anton Domenico Gabbiani (1695) was followed by the redecoration of both churches, culminating in the *Apotheosis of St Romuald* (*c.* 1775) on the vault of SS Donato ed Ilariano by Sante Pacini (1735–*c.* 1800).

BIBLIOGRAPHY

Peter Damian: *Life of the Blessed Romuald* (mid-11th century); ed. G. Tabacco (Rome, 1957)
A. Forturio: *Historiarum Camaldulensium libri tres*, 2 vols (Florence, 1575–9)
P. Fanelli: *Istoria cronologica del nobile ed antico monastero degli Angioli di Firenze del sacro ordine Camaldolese dal principio della sua fondazione fino al presente giorno* (Lucca, 1710)
G. B. Mittarelli and A. Costadoni: *Annales Camaldulenses*, 9 vols (Venice, 1755–73; facs. Farnborough, 1970)
W. Paatz and E. Paatz: *Kirchen* (1940–57)
G. Tabacco and P. Cannata: 'Romualdo', *Bibliotheca Sanctorum*, xi (Rome, 1968), pp. 366–83
C. Stinger: 'Ambrogio Traversari and the "Tempio degli Scolari" at S Maria degli Angeli in Florence', *Essays Presented to Myron P. Gilmore*, ed. S. Bertelli and G. Remakus (Florence, 1978), i, pp. 271–86
M. E. Magheri Cataluccio and A. U. Fossa: *Biblioteca e cultura a Camaldoli* (Rome, 1979)
P.-R. Gaussin: *L'Europe des ordres et des congrégations* (Saint-Etienne, 1984)
H. Leyser: *Hermits and the New Monasticism* (London, 1984)

NIGEL GAUK-ROGER

Camarena, Jorge González (*b* Guadalajara, Mexico, 24 March 1908; *d* Mexico City, 24 May 1980). Mexican painter and sculptor. He studied painting at the Academia de San Carlos, Mexico City (1922–30), and later devoted himself to illustrating advertisements and especially to painting murals. In 1932–3 he worked on the restoration of a 16th-century fresco in the monastery at Huejotzingo, which allowed him to study earlier techniques in detail. After various mural experiments in the 1940s he was commissioned in 1950 to decorate the main building of the Instituto Mexicano del Seguro Social in the Paseo de la Reforma, Mexico City; here, his mural painting and the sculptural groups on either side of the door were perfectly integrated with the architecture of the building. Camarena developed his own technique based on 'harmonizing geometry' (*geométrica armónica*), in which the whole composition and construction of figures derives from the laws of elementary geometry, a term applied by a critic, but based on the artist's own words. This, together with the singular colouring inspired by the work of Rufino Tamayo, gave a freshness and originality to his murals. His use of dramatic foreshortening and stylized realism are sometimes reminiscent of the work of David Alfaro Siqueiros, while the mural of *The Fight against Tyranny: Tribute to Belisario Domínguez* (1958) in the Senate in Mexico City has more anguish and strength.

BIBLIOGRAPHY

A. Luna Arroyo: *Jorge González Camarena en la plástica mexicana* (Mexico City, 1981)
E. Acevedo and others: *Guía de murales del centro historico de la ciudad de México* (Mexico City, 1984), p. 49

ESPERANZA GARRIDO

Camargo, Iberê (*b* Restinga Seca, 18 Nov 1914). Brazilian painter and engraver. He settled in Rio de Janeiro in 1943, travelling to Europe in 1947 to complete his painting studies in Paris and Rome with André Lhote and Giorgio De Chirico and his engraving studies with Carlo Petrucci (*b* 1881). Camargo resisted changing fashions, continuing to produce figurative works such as *Riacho Landscape* (1946; Pôrto Alegre, Mus. A. Rio Grande do Sul) and *Lapa* (1947; Rio de Janeiro, Mus. N. B.A.) long after abstraction took hold in Brazil in the late 1940s. Conversely he practised abstraction, for example in *Structure* (1961; Rio de Janeiro, Mus. N. B.A.), when figurative art was in the ascendancy in the 1960s. In 1966 he painted an abstract panel (7.0×7.0 m) for the headquarters of the World Health Organization in Geneva. His interpretation of Neo-Expressionism in the 1980s was likewise a highly personal one. Throughout these changes his painting retained an atmosphere of violence conveyed through colour and convulsive shapes. In 1982 he resettled in Pôrto Alegre in southern Brazil while still making frequent visits to Rio de Janeiro.

BIBLIOGRAPHY

J. Teixeira Leite: *A gravura brasileira contemporânea* [Contemporary Brazilian engraving] (Rio de Janeiro, 1965)
E. Berg and others: *Iberê Camargo* (Rio de Janeiro, 1985)
J. Maurício: 'Abstração', *Seis décadas de arte moderna na Coleção Roberto Marinho* (Rio de Janeiro, 1985), pp. 332–9

Camargo, Sérgio de (*b* Rio de Janeiro, 8 April 1930; *d* Rio de Janeiro, 10 Jan 1991). Brazilian sculptor. He studied with Emilio Petorutti (1892–1971) and Lucio Fontana in the Academia Altamira in Buenos Aires and in 1948 left for Paris. There he saw the work of Constantin Brancusi, Arp and Georges Vantongerloo, who became important influences on his work. From 1953 to 1961 he lived in Brazil where at the São Paulo Biennale in 1965 he won the prize for best national sculptor, before settling again in Paris. His active participation in the Parisian milieu, extended through exhibitions in Europe and the USA, led to his recognition, with Jesús Rafael Soto, Julio le Parc and Carlos Cruz-Diez, as a leading figure within the Latin American Constructivist movement. His brand of Kinetic art, however, was never concerned purely with optical effects. At first his rigorously non-figurative route led him to carry out a reductive exercise of variations on the same problem and subject. But in the long series of reliefs begun in 1963 with wooden modules, usually cylindrical and painted white, and in the wood and marble sculptures that he produced after his return to Brazil in 1974 (*Relevo 351*, 1974; Rio de Janeiro, Col. Gilberto Chateaubriand), he demonstrated the inexhaustible diversity of solutions arising out of an exclusive, restricted nucleus of research. In 1968 he finished a vast concrete panel (untitled) for the interior of the Palácio dos Arcos in Brasília.

BIBLIOGRAPHY

P. Chevalier: 'Sérgio de Camargo', *Aujourd'hui*, 46 (1964)

Sérgio de Camargo (exh. cat. by J. Clay, Caracas, Estud. Actual, 1972)

R. Pontual: *Entre dois séculos—Arte brasileira do século XX na Coleção Gilberto Chateaubriand* [Between two centuries—Brazilian art of the 20th century in the Gilberto Chateaubriand collection] (Rio de Janeiro, 1987)

ROBERTO PONTUAL

Camarín. Decorated room or chapel behind the altar of a Spanish church, in which an image, often of the Virgin, or its accoutrements are kept. It is sometimes at a higher level than the nave.

Camaro, Alexander (*b* Breslau, Silesia [now Wrocław, Poland], 27 Sept 1901; *d* Berlin, 1992). German painter and printmaker. He studied under Otto Mueller in Breslau from 1920. Camaro also studied music and spent some time as a cabaret performer. He later trained as a dancer, concentrating on contemporary rather than classical dance. After 1930 he was a painter in Berlin, and he travelled widely in France, Greece, Holland and Norway. However, he did not show his work until 1946, exhibiting a series of 19 paintings entitled *Wooden Theatre* in West Berlin at the Galerie Gerd Rosen (e.g. *Box No. 7*, 1946; artist's col.). After 1951 he taught at the Akademie der Künste in West Berlin. He had one-man shows at the Kleine Galerie Schüler in Hamburg (1947), the Haus am Waldsee in West Berlin (1951) and at the Kunstverein in Hannover (1952). His gentle style and early preference for tempera owes much to the example of Mueller, which is evident in such works as *Girl on a Balcony* (Halle, Staatl. Gal. Moritzburg). Camaro's subjects, such as *In the Morning: Reclining Girl* (1948; artist's col., see 1983 exh. cat., pl. 16), often derive their lyrical power from the tension that they evoke between dream and reality. However, in the mid-1960s Camaro's preference for planar compositions resulted in the exclusion of external references and emphasis on gesture and colour. This coincided with extensive travels in Spain, Corfu, Malta and Sardinia, which influenced his archaic and ritualistic imagery in such works as *Tam Tam* (1967; artist's col., see 1983 exh. cat., pl. 60) and *Animal Ikon* (1980; artist's col., see 1983 exh. cat., pl. 86). These signs also paved the way for a reintroduction of the figure in subsequent works.

BIBLIOGRAPHY

Alexander Camaro (exh. cat. by W. Grohmann, W. Berlin, Haus Waldsee, 1951)

Alexander Camaro (exh. cat., Wolfsburg, Kstver., 1961)

Camaro Ölbilder, Aquarelle, Zeichnungen (exh. cat. by A. Camaro and L. Schauer, W. Berlin, Neuer Berlin. Kstver., 1983)

□

Camarón. Spanish family of artists. Nicolás Camarón was a sculptor and architect originally from Aragon. His son (1) José Camarón y Boronat and his grandson (2) José Camarón Meliá were both painters and draughtsmen.

(1) José Camarón y Boronat (*b* Segorbe, 1731; *d* Valencia, 1803). Painter and draughtsman. He first trained in his father's workshop, and in 1749 he went to Valencia. In 1752 he moved to Madrid, where he probably studied in the workshop of Francisco Bonay, a Valencian landscape artist and miniaturist, and may have attended the Real Academia de S Fernando, although his name does not appear in the matriculation books for those years. During this period he devoted himself almost exclusively to painting landscapes and miniatures and to copying works by such masters as Titian, Rubens, van Dyck and Murillo.

In 1753 Camarón y Boronat returned to Valencia, where he was appointed teacher of painting at the recently opened Academia de S Bárbara. In 1762 he was elected Académico de Mérito of the Real Academia de S Fernando, and in 1768 he received the same honour from the Academia de S Carlos in Valencia. He became Director of Painting at the Academia, Valencia, when Cristóbal Valero died in 1790, and from 1796 to 1801 he held the post of Director General. Camarón y Boronat completed many religious paintings as well as works of a festive nature. His ability as a draughtsman is evident in the many preparatory works that he executed both for painted compositions and for engravings.

BIBLIOGRAPHY

R. Rodríguez Cuelbras: *José Camarón y Boronat, 1731–1803: Ein valencianischer Maler zur Zeit Goyas* (Munich, 1968)

A. Espinós Díaz: 'Dos lienzos de José Camarón y Boronat en el Museo del Prado', *Bol. Mus. Prado*, iii/9 (1982)

JUAN J. LUNA

(2) José Camarón Meliá (*b* Segorbe, 1760; *d* Madrid, 1819). Painter and draughtsman, son of (1) José Camarón y Boronat. His training began in his father's studio and continued at the Academia de S Carlos, Valencia. In 1778 his name appears in the minutes of the Real Academia de S Fernando, Madrid, where in 1779 he competed for a scholarship to Rome. From 1779 until 1785 he lived in Italy, and works painted during this period include *David and Goliath* (1781; copy of a painting by Guido Cagnacci) and *Moses Giving the Law* (1785; both Madrid, Real Acad. S Fernando, Mus.).

In 1786 Camarón Meliá was named Académico de Mérito by the academies in both Valencia and Madrid. He also began working that year with the Real Fábrica de Tapices de S Bárbara, producing the cartoon *Two Women with a Child* (Madrid, Prado, on dep. London, Sp. Embassy), which was made under the direction of Mariano Maella for the dining-room of the Infantas at the Palacio del Pardo, Madrid, and which shows the influence of his father's style. The two cartoons *View of the Paseo del Prado with a Street Seller* and *View of the Canal with Boat Building* (both 1787; Madrid, Prado, on dep. Madrid, Min. Econ. & Hacienda) were also painted under the direction of Maella for the Palacio del Pardo. In 1788 he collaborated on a series of 32 paintings for the cloister of the convent of S Francisco el Grande, Madrid. The series, which had been begun in 1781, was based on Franciscan iconography and was executed by a group of leading artists that included Camarón Meliá's father, Zacarías González Velázquez, Manuel de la Cruz (1750–92) and Antonio Carnicero. Camarón Meliá painted *St Francis Comforted by Angels* and *St Francis Begging on Behalf of the Poor* (both 1788; *in situ*).

His *Holy Family*, painted for a side altar of the church of Caballero de Gracia, Madrid (*in situ*), can also be dated to 1788.

Shortly after 1793 Camarón Meliá broke off relations with the Real Fábrica, but his increasing reputation in Madrid must have led to the commission at the oratory of Santa Cueva, Cádiz, for which he painted the *Gathering of Manna* (1795; *in situ*), part of a series on which the artist collaborated with Goya and Zacarías González Velázquez. In 1799 he was appointed director of painting at the Galería de Pintura de la Fábrica de Porcelana del Buen Retiro, but he relinquished his position in 1805 on being asked by Manuel Godoy to take part in a project to produce engravings after masterpieces in the Spanish royal collections. In 1805 he was appointed Pintor de Cámara, after which his most important work was for the 'Queen's room' in the Palacio Real, Madrid, where he painted *Queen Isabella the Catholic Giving her Jewels to Columbus* (1817; *in situ*), part of a series of five in grisaille on which Zacarías González Velázquez, Vicente López y Portana and Goya also worked.

BIBLIOGRAPHY

J. Held: *Die Genrebilder der Madrider Teppichmanufaktur und die Anfänge Goyas* (Berlin, 1971)

A. Espinós Díaz: 'José Camarón Meliá (1760–1819): Pintor de cámara de Carlos III', *El arte en las cortes europeas del siglo XVIII* (Madrid, 1987), pp. 256–62

——: 'José Camarón Meliá (1760–1819): Artista valenciano establecido en la corte', *III Jornadas de arte: Cinco siglos de arte en Madrid (XV–XX)* (Madrid, 1991), pp. 219–32

ADELA ESPINÓS DÍAZ

Camars. *See* CHIUSI.

Camassei, Andrea (*b* Bevagna, Umbria, *bapt* 1 Dec 1602; *d* Rome, 18 Aug 1649). Italian painter and printmaker. He was first recorded in Rome in 1626 and was apparently trained there by Domenichino (Bellori; Passeri; Pascoli). His earliest surviving commission is the decoration of the chapel of St Philip Neri in S Margarita, Bevagna, with canvases showing scenes from the life of the saint (1627; *in situ*). In 1628 he worked with Andrea Sacchi, under Pietro da Cortona, on the decoration of the Villa Sacchetti at Castelfusano. He received his first commission from the Barberini family, for chiaroscuro room decorations in the Palazzo Barberini (*see* ROME, §VI, 24), in 1631, by which time he had already been commissioned to paint a large overdoor fresco in St Peter's; the composition of the lost *Baptism of SS Processus and Martinianus* (1630–35; destr. before 1700) is recorded in a modello (USA, priv. col., see Sutherland Harris, 1970, pl. 10). After completing two frescoed ceilings in the Palazzo Barberini—*Apollo and the Muses on Mt Parnassus* (1631; destr.) and *God the Father Dividing the Angel Hierarchies* (1632)—Camassei

Andrea Camassei: *Death of the Niobids*, oil on canvas, 3.01×4.10m, 1640 (Rome, Palazzo Barberini)

seemed on the verge of a major career when he was commissioned to paint the ceiling of the Gran Salone. However, according to Passeri, Camassei (whom he knew) declined the commission because he realized that it was beyond his talents. Instead it was awarded to Pietro da Cortona. A drawing at Chatsworth shows Camassei's preliminary scheme for part of the ceiling (see Sutherland Harris, 1988).

The Barberini, especially Don Taddeo Barberini, continued to patronize Camassei during the papacy of Urban VIII. They commissioned him to participate, along with such established artists as Guido Reni, Andrea Sacchi, Giovanni Lanfranco and Pietro da Cortona, in the decoration of S Maria della Concezione, Rome (1631–8), to which Camassei contributed an altarpiece of the *Lamentation* (*c*. 1631; *in situ*). They also ordered religious and mythological paintings for their own collection (see fig.) and designs for book illustrations, such as the frontispiece for Girolamo Teti's description of the Palazzo Barberini, *Aedes Barberinae ad Quirinalem* (Rome, 1642). On the death of Urban VIII in 1644, his disgraced nephews fled into exile in France, and Camassei lacked steady patronage. In 1646–7 he was employed by Sacchi to paint two large frescoes for the Lateran Baptistery: the *Triumph of Constantine* and the *Battle of the Milvian Bridge* (both *in situ*). For the composition of the latter, perhaps again because he found large compositions difficult, he turned for guidance to Raphael's fresco of the same subject (completed by Raphael's studio after his death, 1523–4; Rome, Vatican, Sala di Costantino). In 1648–9 he painted friezes illustrating the story of *Bacchus and Ariadne* in the Palazzo Pamphili, Rome.

Camassei's training with Domenichino, his aversion to large decorative commissions and the conventional rhetoric of his narratives link him with those painters in Rome, for example Giovanni Francesco Romanelli and Giacinto Gimignani, whose reserved manner offered a foil to the more flamboyant, decorative approach of Pietro da Cortona and his circle. Camassei's style, with its emphasis on pastel colours, reflects his admiration for the work produced *c*. 1630 by Nicolas Poussin, Sacchi and Lanfranco, although his narratives lack the psychological acuity of either Poussin or Sacchi. The gently curved poses of his figures recall those of the Flemish sculptor François Du Quesnoy.

Camassei's drawings are mainly in red chalk, although there are some in black chalk and a few pen-and-wash studies. Characteristic red chalk studies include those (New York, Met.) for the *Martyrdom of St Sebastian* (1633; Rome, S Sebastiano alla Polviera) and the *St Peter Meditating* (Florence, Uffizi). Although his reputation faded after his death, he was given a brief biography at the end of Bellori's life of Domenichino as well as biographies by Passeri and Pascoli.

BIBLIOGRAPHY

G. P. Bellori: *Vite* (1672); ed. E. Borea (1976)
G. B. Passeri: *Vite* (1679); ed. J. Hess (1934)
L. Pascoli: *Vite de' pittori, scultori ed architetti moderni*, 2 vols (Rome, 1730–36)
A. Presenzini: *Vita ed opera di Andrea Camassei* (Assisi, 1880)
O. Pollak: *Die Kunsttätigkeit unter Urban VIII*, 2 vols (Vienna, 1928–31)
E. K. Waterhouse: *Baroque Painting in Rome* (London, 1937)
C. Pietrangeli: *Guida da Bevagna* (Spoleto, 1959)
A. F. Blunt and H. L. Cooke: *Roman Drawings in the Collection of Her Majesty the Queen at Windsor Castle* (London, 1960)
G. di Domenico Cortese: 'La vicenda artistica di Andrea Camassei', *Commentari*, xix (1969), pp. 281–98
A. Sutherland Harris: 'A Contribution to Andrea Camassei Studies', *A. Bull.*, lii (1970), pp. 49–70
L. Barroero: 'Andrea Camassei, Giovambattista Speranza e Marco Caprinozzi a San Lorenzo in Fonte in Roma', *Boll. A.*, n. s. vi (1979), no. 1, pp. 65–76
A. Sutherland Harris: 'Camassei et Cortona au Palazzo Barberini', *Rev. A.* [Paris], (1988), no.82
J. Beldon Scott: *Images of Nepotism: The Painted Ceilings of the Palazzo Barberini* (Princeton, 1991), pp. 95–101

ANN SUTHERLAND HARRIS

Cambay. *See* KHAMBHAT.

Cambi, Ulisse (*b* Florence, 22 Sept 1807; *d* Florence, 7 April 1895). Italian sculptor. The son of the sculptor Pietro Cambi, he studied at the Accademia di Belle Arti e Liceo Artistico in Florence and in 1833, after winning a four-year stipendium, continued his training in Rome. While there he completed several works in gesso, including a *Daphnis and Chloe* (1834; Florence, Pitti; marble version, 1841) executed in an academic classical style. He returned to Florence about 1837 and for a time struggled to gain recognition, but by 1841, after having been nominated to, and given a professorship in, the Accademia, he began to obtain numerous important commissions. He gained esteem for his funerary monuments, among them one to the painter *Luigi Sabatelli* (1844; Florence, Santa Croce) that is noted for its unsparingly realistic depiction of the dying man's wasted body. Commissions for other memorials followed: *Benvenuto Cellini* (1845; Florence, Uffizi) and the dramatist *Carlo Goldoni* (1873) in Piazza Goldoni, Florence. By tempering Neo-classical severity with a lively naturalism, he produced images that attained great popularity. *Love as a Beggar*, displayed at the Exposition Universelle in Paris in 1855, generated the demand for over 30 copies. His depictions of children, such as those appearing in the group *Eve and her Sons* (1857), proved especially appealing to a 19th-century audience. Throughout his prolific career he fluctuated between Neo-classical and realistic impulses, usually eschewing a grand manner in favour of engaging but sometimes overly prettified works.

BIBLIOGRAPHY

A. De Gubernatis: *Dizionario degli artisti italiani viventi: Pittori, scultori, e architetti* (Florence, 1892)

□

Cambiaso, Luca (*b* Moneglia, Genoa, 18 Oct 1527; *d* Madrid, 6 Sept 1585). Italian painter and draughtsman. He was the leading artist in Genoa in the 16th century and the founder of the Genoese school. His many grandiose decorative schemes in churches and palazzi established a tradition of historical fresco painting in Genoa. He was also famous for his poetic night scenes. Among his many drawings, some are unusual for their figures being reduced to geometric (often cubic) forms.

1. TRAINING AND EARLY WORK, TO 1550. Luca's father, Giovanni Cambiaso (1495–1579), although aware of the new style introduced to Genoa by Perino del Vaga at the Palazzo Doria (begun 1528), remained a limited and

provincial painter. Yet he was important to the artistic development of his son, which was also determined by constant practice in drawing and by a study of the Genoese works of Perino del Vaga, Pordenone and Domenico Beccafumi, and of Giulio Romano's *Stoning of St Stephen* (1530; Genoa, S Stefano). Luca probably visited Rome between 1547 and 1550, when he might have met Pellegrino Tibaldi and Daniele da Volterra; certainly Michelangelo's work had a significant impact on his formation. He also learnt to model, which his father considered essential to an understanding of the technique of painting. At this stage of his career Luca was closely associated with his father and depended on him for commissions.

Soprani (1674), whose biography is based on an account by the Venetian painter Valerio Corte (1530–80), a close friend of Cambiaso's, described his early style as 'too bold and proud' and 'rich in invention'. Confident in his power as a draughtsman, Cambiaso indulged in bold foreshortenings and exaggerated gestures. The forms in his *Resurrection* (1547; Imperia, SS Giacomo e Filippo) are heavy and muscular, the poses mannered and dramatic. Such features are yet more marked in his early frescoes, notably in the *Battle between Hercules and the Amazons* and *Apollo Shooting the Greeks with Arrows before Troy* (dated 1545–7 by Rotondi and 1550 by Calì; Genoa, Prefettura), which were painted for the Palazzo Doria, and in the *Last Judgement* (1550; Chiavari, S Maria delle Grazie). An early altarpiece, the *Adoration of the Magi* (Turin, Gal. Sabauda), is distinguished by the elaborate poses and an unusually low viewpoint. Cambiaso clarified his style in many ebullient and energetic drawings in which a serpentine outline encloses rounded volumes with colossal figures and extravagant foreshortenings. His fresco technique was unusually spontaneous, allowing him to proceed from small drawings to full-size sketches executed on the walls without the aid of cartoons.

2. Artistic maturity, 1551–69. After 1551 Cambiaso became established as an independent artist. In these years he was influenced by the architect Galeazzo Alessi, who encouraged him to moderate the excesses of his early style and to develop a 'softer, and more harmonious' manner (Soprani, ed. Ratti). This new phase opened with a fresco for the church of S Maria degli Angeli, Genoa, of the *Beheading of St John the Baptist* (1552; destr.), for which Cambiaso modified his usual practice and prepared a cartoon.

In the following years Cambiaso collaborated with Giovanni Battista Castello on a series of commissions for decorative fresco cycles (*see* Castello (i), (1)). Castello, a learned painter with a deep knowledge of Emilian art and of Raphael, was also a decorator and architect and introduced Cambiaso to a wider artistic culture. In the 1550s they worked together in the loggia of the *piano nobile* of a villa built by Alessi for Luca Giustiniani (now the Villa Giustiniani Cambiaso, Genoa), where Cambiaso's *Diana* and Castello's *Apollo* face each other from opposite lunettes. Around 1560 Cambiaso painted a series of frescoes in the Palazzo Imperiale in Campetto, Genoa. Here the fame of the artists' collaboration led Vincenzo Imperiale to commission Cambiaso and Castello to work side by side on a ceiling fresco consisting of two scenes from the *Life of Cleopatra* (both destr. World War II). In this Cambiaso gave new importance to setting complex groups of figures in an elaborate and spacious architectural setting. Stylistically close to this work are the *Resurrection* (1559) and the *Transfiguration* (1561; both Genoa, S Bartolommeo), symmetrical and taut designs in which light and colour radiate from the central figure of Christ. In the mid-1560s Cambiaso continued to work with Castello on the decoration of some of the most prestigious Genoese palazzi: before 1565 he painted the *Rape of the Sabines* (see fig.1) on the ceiling of the *salone* in the Villa Cattaneo (now Villa Imperiale di Terralba); and shortly afterwards in the Palazzo Meridiana, where the stucco ornaments were designed by Castello in 1565, he painted another ceiling fresco, the *Return of Ulysses.* Both these narrative scenes have elaborate displays of figures set within grandiose classical architecture from a centralized perspective viewpoint; in the *Return of Ulysses* the symmetry is more marked, and the figures are less crowded.

Although by now his style had matured, Cambiaso remained open to new ideas. Above all he was influenced

1. Luca Cambiaso: *Rape of the Sabines* (before 1565), ceiling fresco, Villa Imperiale di Terralba, Genoa

by Valerio Corte, who was not only a portrait painter but a distinguished collector who owned works by Titian, Paolo Veronese and Andrea del Sarto. The composition of *St Benedict Enthroned between SS John the Baptist and Luke* (1562; Genoa Cathedral) is indebted to Venetian painting, with a richer, more refined use of colour and more painterly surfaces. The *Virgin and Child with St John the Baptist, Angels and God the Father* (*c.* 1563; Genoa-Sampierdarena, S Maria della Cella) in which the sacred subject is treated in a naturalistic manner, almost as an idyll, is similarly indebted to Venetian painting, and to Correggio. Venetian influence is apparent, too, in the sensuous mythological paintings that Cambiaso was producing at this time, such as the openly erotic *Venus and Adonis* (*c.* 1562; Rome, Gal. Borghese), and even more so in another painting of this subject (Genoa, priv. col; SM&S, fig. 113), which was clearly influenced by Veronese.

In the mid-1560s Cambiaso began to use simplified cubic shapes in his drawings, possibly influenced by an encounter with similar drawings in the work of German artists (for example, Albrecht Dürer) or in illustrated theoretical treatises, such as Erhard Schön's *Underweissung Proportion* (Nuremberg, 1538). The most famous of such drawings is *Fighting Figures* (Florence, Uffizi), in which the figures have the simplified forms of mannequins.

This formal simplification is also evident in the paintings. Cambiaso began to use more restrained gesture and expression and to organize his composition through clear and simple geometric shapes, as in the fresco of the *Construction of the Warehouse at Trebizond* (Genoa, Pal. Parodi). Similar concerns are apparent in his work for the Lercari Chapel in Genoa Cathedral, for which he produced frescoes (*Marriage of the Virgin*; *Purification of the Virgin*), probably painted after Castello's departure for Spain in 1567, as well as canvases (*Virgin and Child with SS John the Baptist and Lawrence* for the high altar, now in the baptistery; *Adoration of the Magi*; *Adoration of the Shepherds*). He is also documented as having executed a marble statue of *Prudence* for the chapel. The paintings, highly concentrated and meditative in feeling, convey a new spiritual vision that Cambiaso developed further in the 1570s.

3. Late years in Genoa and Spain, 1570–85. In these years Cambiaso had less interest in decorative fresco painting. His *Celebration of the Synod* (*c.* 1574; Genoa, Pal. Arcivescovile), painted for his friend Cipriano Pallavicino, Bishop of Genoa, is his only fresco of the 1570s and shows a monotonous series of figures in a rigidly symmetrical framework. A mythological work of this period, *Venus Weeping over the Body of Adonis* (*c.* 1570–75; Rome, Pal. Barberini), is no longer a joyous celebration of the senses, but a meditation on death. He was now more interested in religious painting and, increasingly, in a

2. Luca Cambiaso: *Gloria*, fresco, 26×14 m, 1584 (Madrid, Escorial)

correct expression of theological ideas. His style became yet more simplified, each scene being reduced to its essential features to produce austere and meditative compositions in a limited chromatic range. He may have been aware of the movement for Catholic reform, which spread in Genoa before the Council of Trent, and was perhaps familiar with Ignatius Loyola's *Spiritual Exercises* (1521–35). His *Pietà* (*c.* 1572; Genoa, S Maria in Carignano) is a starkly simple narrative, showing the patron in meditation within the picture, as if to emphasize the role of painting as a spiritual aid.

In these years Cambiaso painted many devotional subjects for private collectors, many of them night scenes. These include the celebrated *Madonna with a Candle* (Genoa, Pal. Bianco), in which the light, as though itself the imagination, reveals the sacred characters as rustic, simple and close to the spectator. The same sense of immediacy characterizes the delicate *Holy Family with Angels and Donor* (Genoa, Mus. Accad. Ligustica B.A.). Cambiaso's increasing concern with nocturnal settings also led him to concentrate on subject-matter drawn from the Passion: in *Christ before Caiaphas* (Genoa, Mus. Accad. Ligustica B.A.) he used thick brushstrokes to emphasize the fall of light on folds and profiles; *Christ at the Column* (Genoa, Pal. Bianco) and the *Agony in the Garden* (Portoria, Annunziata) are closely related in this respect; he also produced a series of drawings (1570–75; Florence, Uffizi). In his later paintings, such as the *Deposition* (1575–80; Genoa, Mus. Accad. Ligustica B.A.), the *Pietà* (1575–80; Genoa, Pal. Rosso) and *Christ Bleeding from his Wounds* (after 1580; Genoa Cathedral), he demonstrated an even greater concern with theological rectitude.

In September 1583 Cambiaso accepted an invitation to work for Philip II of Spain, the result of a test piece he had sent from Genoa in 1581—the *Martyrdom of St Lawrence* (Madrid, Escorial)—which had evidently convinced the King's advisers that Cambiaso's artistic taste coincided with their ruler's. He was commissioned to decorate the church of S Lorenzo in the Hieronymite monastery of the Escorial in accordance with an erudite theological programme. The *Gloria* (1584; see fig. 2) that he painted on the sacristy vault and modified to comply with suggestions from the court, is an icily rigid representation of the Trinity and the Church Triumphant, disconcerting to modern taste and, indeed, an interesting case of the total subjection of art to the dictates of ideology. He worked unceasingly in S Lorenzo, assisted by many others, including his son Orazio, Lazzaro Tavarone (a pupil from Genoa) and some of the artists who had already been working in Spain with Cambiaso's former collaborator, Castello, notably the latter's son, Fabrizio, and Nicolas Granello. By May 1584 he had completed four large canvases of *St Anne*, *The Sermon of St John the Baptist*, *St Ursula and the Ten Thousand Virgins* and the *Archangel Michael* (*in situ*). In the spring of 1585 most of the frescoes for the Capilla Mayor and the sacristy were finished. Their hasty execution and the involvement of many collaborators provides sufficient explanation for the many weak passages that make them disappointing examples of Cambiaso's skill.

BIBLIOGRAPHY

DBI; Thieme–Becker
R. Soprani: *Vite* (1674), pp. 35–51; ed. C. G. Ratti (1768–9/*R* 1965), i, pp. 76–97
F. Alizeri: *Notizie dei professori del disegno in Liguria*, iii (Genoa, 1876), pp. 459–66
B. Suida Manning: 'The Nocturnes of Luca Cambiaso', *A. Q.* [Detroit], xv (1952), pp. 197–200
P. Rotondi: 'Appunti sull'attività giovanile di Luca Cambiaso', *Quad. Sopr. Gal. Liguria*, iv (1956)
B. Suida Manning and W. Suida: *Luca Cambiaso: La vita e le opere* (Milan, 1958) [with complete cat. of works, documentary sources, illustrations and bibliog.] [SM&S]
P. Torriti: *Luca Cambiaso: Disegni* (Genoa, 1966)
L. Profumo Müller: 'Le opere geometrizzate di Luca Cambiaso', *A. Lombarda*, xv/2 (1970), pp. 33–40
P. Torriti: 'Luca Cambiaso', *La pittura a Genova e in Liguria* (Genoa, 1970, rev. 1987), i, pp. 209–40
E. Gavazza: *La grande decorazione a Genova* (Genoa, 1974), pp. 18–36
L. Profumo Müller: 'L'architettura "ficta" negli affreschi di Luca Cambiaso', *A. Lombarda*, xix/4 (1974), pp. 51–76
L. Magnani: 'Luca Cambiaso tra due "riforme"', *A. Lombarda*, xxiv/50 (1978), pp. 87–94
M. Calì: *Da Michelangelo all'Escorial: Momenti del dibattito religioso nell'arte del cinquecento* (Turin, 1980), pp. 169–81
G. Fusconi, ed.: *Disegni genovesi dal XVI al XVIII secolo* (Rome, 1980), pp. 15–22, 111–12
G. Frabetti: 'Luca Cambiaso', *Il Museo dell'Accademia Ligustica di belle arti: La Pinacoteca* (Genoa, 1983), pp. 26–8
L. Magnani: 'Committenza e arte sacra a Genova dopo il Concilio di Trento', *Stud. Stor. A.*, v (1983–5), pp. 133–84 (145–53)
G. Biavati: 'Affreschi inediti di Luca Cambiaso', *Bol. Mus. Civ. Genov.*, vi/16–18 (1984), pp. 25–51
G. Biavati Frabetti: 'Luca Cambiaso e il Bergamasco: Una "nobile gara"', *Bol. Mus. Civ. Genov.*, vii/19–21 (1985), pp. 5–27
Omaggio a Luca Cambiaso (exh. cat. by E. Gavazza and G. Rotondi Terminiello, Moneglia, oratory of Santa Croce, 1985) [with full bibliog.]
R. Mulcahy: *'A la mayor gloria de Dios y el Rey': La decoración de la Real Basilica del Monasterio di El Escorial* (Madrid, 1992)
M. di Giampaolo, ed.: *Los frescos italianos de El Escorial* (Madrid, 1993), pp. 28–33, 42–51
L. Magnani: *Luca Cambiaso: Da Genova all'Escorial* (Genoa, 1995)

LAURO MAGNANI

Cambio, Arnolfo di. *See* ARNOLFO DI CAMBIO.

Cambodia [Kampuchea]. Country in South-east Asia, bordering Thailand, Laos and Vietnam, with a seacoast on the Gulf of Thailand (see fig. 1). Cambodia was the heartland of the Khmer empire of Angkor, which flourished between the 9th and the 15th centuries AD.

I. Introduction. II. Architecture. III. Sculpture. IV. Painting. V. Textiles. VI. Theatre. VII. Ceramics. VIII. Other arts.

DETAILED TABLE OF CONTENTS

I. Introduction 459
1. Geography and peoples 459
2. History 459
3. Religion, iconography and subject-matter 461
(i) Animism 461
(ii) Hinduism 461
(iii) Buddhism 462
II. Architecture 463
1. Religious and formal 463
(i) Pre-Angkor period (before *c.* AD 889) 463
(a) 6th century 463
(b) Early 7th century: Sambor Prei Kuk style 464
(c) Later 7th century to the 8th: Prei Khmeng and Kompong Preah styles 464
(d) Early to mid-9th century: Kulen style 464

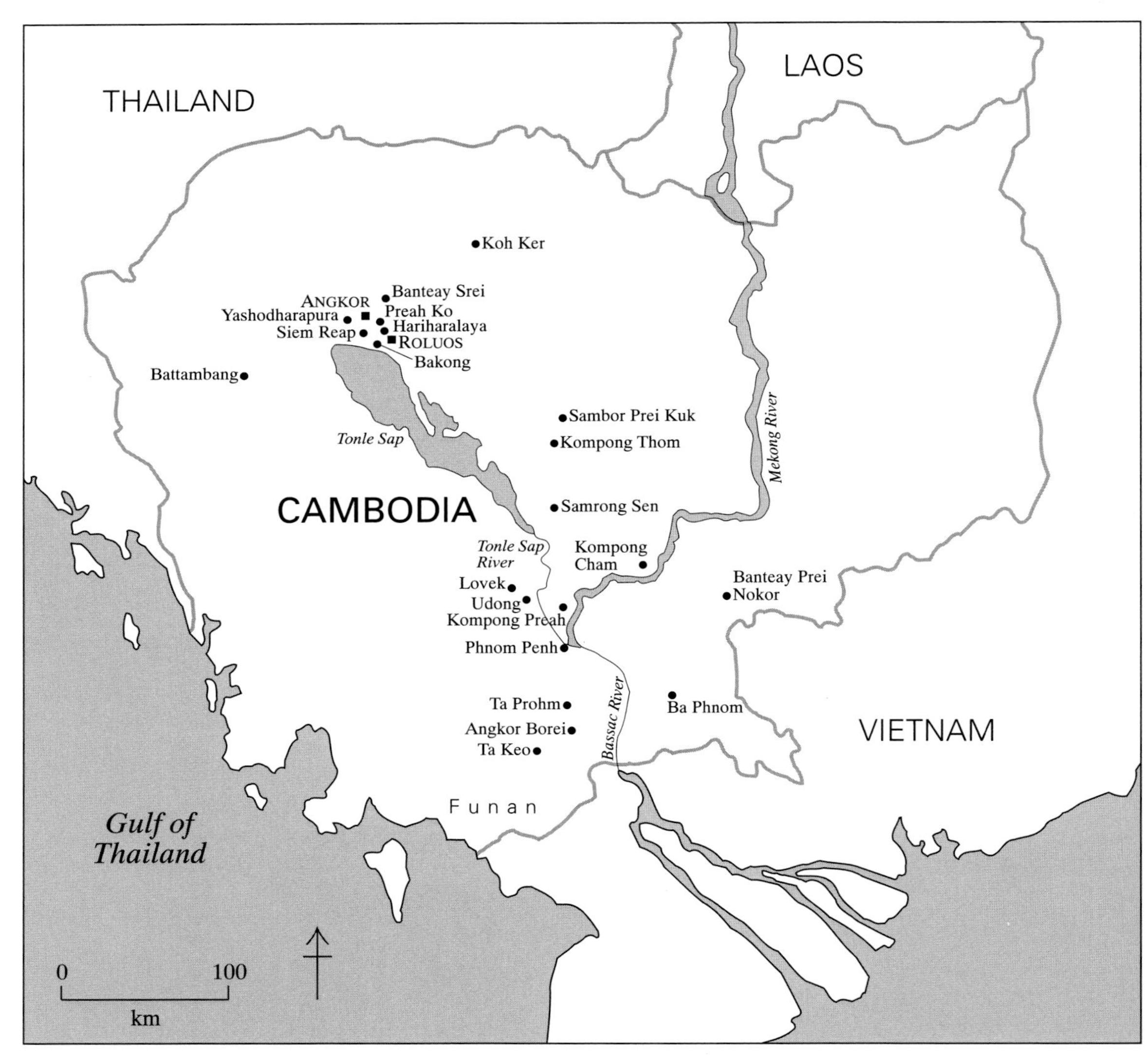

1. Map of Cambodia; those sites with separate entries in this dictionary are distinguished by CROSS-REFERENCE TYPE

(e) Later 9th century: Preah Ko style 464
(ii) Early Angkor period (*c.* 889–*c.* 1080) 467
(a) Late 9th century to the mid-10th: first style of Angkor 467
(b) Later 10th century: Banteay Srei style 470
(c) Late 10th century to the 11th: Baphuon style 471
(iii) Middle Angkor period (*c.* 1080–*c.* 1181): Angkor Vat style 473
(a) Introduction 473
(b) Function and cosmology 473
(c) Building techniques and design 474
(d) Architectural decoration 475
(iv) Late Angkor period (*c.* 1181–*c.* 1431) 476
(a) Introduction 476
(b) *c.* 1181–*c.* 1191 477
(c) *c.* 1191–*c.* 1200 477
(d) *c.* 1200–*c.* 1220 479
(e) *c.* 1220–*c.* 1431 480
(v) Post-Angkor period (after *c.* 1431) 481
(a) *c.* 1431–*c.* 1863 481
(b) After *c.* 1863 481
2. Domestic 483
III. Sculpture 483
1. Pre-Angkor period (before *c.* 889) 484
2. Early Angkor period (*c.* 889–*c.* 1080) 486
(i) Late 9th century to the mid-10th: first style of Angkor 486
(ii) Later 10th century: Banteay Srei style 487
(iii) Late 10th century to the 11th: Baphuon style 489
3. Middle Angkor period (*c.* 1080–*c.* 1181): Angkor Vat style 490
(i) Narrative reliefs of Angkor Vat 490
(a) Introduction 490
(b) Description 491
(ii) Other relief sculpture 492
(iii) Sculpture in the round 493

(a) Stone 493
(b) Bronze 494
4. Bayon style (*c.* 1181–*c.*1220) 495
(i) Reliefs 495
(ii) Sculpture in the round 496
(a) Stone 496
(b) Bronze 497
5. After *c.* 1220 498
(i) Late 13th century–the 16th 498
(ii) 17th–19th centuries 499
(iii) 19th–20th centuries 500
IV. Painting 501
V. Textiles 502
1. Khmer 502
2. Minority peoples 503
VI. Theatre 503
1. Costumes and masks 504
2. Puppets 504
VII. Ceramics 506
VIII. Other arts 507
1. Coins 507
2. Crematory pavilions 507
3. Metalwork 507
(i) Betel sets 508
(ii) Other objects 508
4. Musical instruments 508
5. Wood-carving 509

I. Introduction.

1. Geography and peoples. 2. History. 3. Religion, iconography and subject-matter.

1. Geography and peoples. The geography of Cambodia is dominated by the Mekong River and its tributaries. Three-quarters of the country consists of a rich alluvial plain, the largest in South-east Asia. The lowlands are hemmed in by high mountains, once densely forested, which border Thailand, Laos and Vietnam. In the centre of the plain lies the Tonle Sap (Great Lake), which in the dry season is 208 km long and has an average depth of only 2.2 m, but during the wet season of the south-west monsoon (May to early October) can quadruple in size. When this occurs, the flow of the Tonle Sap River, which joins the Mekong at Phnom Penh, is reversed and much of the Mekong floodwater is diverted into the lake. The ensuing flood provides water for rice production and an abundant harvest of fish. Situated to the north of the lake are the remains of the successive capital cities of the empire of Angkor, for which floodwater-retreat agriculture was the economic base. Sandstone hills to the north of the Tonle Sap provided the building material for the many religious monuments of Angkor, along with brick and laterite. After the decline of Angkor, the centre of the kingdom shifted to Phnom Penh, the present capital, which governs the confluence of the Tonle Sap, Bassac and Mekong rivers.

The management of water and its symbolic significance have always played a crucial part in Khmer economic, social and religious life. Not only did each family use or share a pond, where the ritual of daily bathing would take place, but elaborate systems of *baray* (reservoirs), ponds and canals, some of them on a gigantic scale, were created by the Khmer rulers for their capitals. There is still much controversy among scholars regarding the actual use of these hydraulic systems. One view is that Angkor was a classic example of a hydraulic society, the prosperity of which depended on the creation and maintenance of large-scale irrigation works adapted to the monsoon climate. This interpretation has also been appropriated by Marxist scholars, who see Angkor as an example of the so-called 'Asiatic mode of production', whereby the need to control water led to the employment of large, sometimes disproportionate, manpower resources on hydraulic works and the consequent development of a despotic society.

Both views have been countered by the theory that the hydraulic systems of Angkor were not constructed for irrigation purposes at all, but as symbolic representations of the cosmic oceans surrounding the universe, and as purely urban systems, for transport, fishing, bathing and design. Some water engineers have argued that despite the impressive size of the works, they would not have provided enough water to produce more than a fraction of the rice needed to support such a rich and powerful state. Moreover, there is little evidence, either on the ground or in aerial photographs, to suggest that there was a system of distribution of water to the fields, and in any case the flooding of the Tonle Sap in the wet season provides a natural system of floodwater-retreat agriculture. Zhou Daguan, a Chinese emissary to Angkor in 1296–7, observed that farmers noted when the rice was ripe and the height to which the water then rose in flood, and timed their sowing accordingly, but he never mentioned the use of the water for irrigation.

The population of approximately seven million is dominated by the Khmers (90%). Other important ethnic groups are the Vietnamese, Chinese and Chams, while various hill peoples inhabit the mountain fringes of the state. The main language is Khmer, a non-tonal language with two registers, closely related to Mon. The word 'Cambodia' derives from the Sanskrit Kambuja, the name of a north Indian tribe associated with a myth of the origin of Cambodia.

BIBLIOGRAPHY

J. Delvert: *Le Paysan cambodgien* (Paris, 1961)
C. Fisher: *South-east Asia: A Social, Economic and Political Geography* (London, 1964/*R* 1971)
F. Le Bar, G. Hickey and J. Musgrave: *Ethnic Groups of Mainland Southeast Asia* (New Haven, 1964)
L. Sedov: 'La Société angkorienne et le problème du mode de production asiatique', *Sur le 'mode de production asiatique'* (Paris, 1969), pp. 327–44
D. P. Chandler: *The Land and People of Cambodia* (Philadelphia, 1972)
J. M. Jacob: 'The Ecology of Angkor', *Nature and Man in South East Asia*, ed. P. Stott (London, 1978), pp. 109–27
B. P. Groslier: 'La Cité hydraulique angkorienne: Exploitation ou surexploitation du sol', *Bull. Ecole Fr. Extrême-Orient*, lxvi (1979), pp. 161–202
W. J. van Liere: 'Traditional Water Management in the Lower Mekong Basin', *World Archaeol.*, xi/3 (1980), pp. 265–80
P. Stott: 'Angkor: Shifting the Hydraulic Paradigm', *The Gift of Water*, ed. J. Rigg (London, 1992)

PHILIP STOTT

2. History. The first inhabitants of the lower Mekong Valley were probably Indonesian (*c.* 3rd millennium BC); their culture was megalithic, and they built circular forts. At the Neolithic site of Samrong Sen, south-east of the Tonle Sap, bronze bracelets (Siem Reap, Conserv. Mnmts Angkor) and elsewhere anklets, urns and a drum of Dong

SON type (all Phnom Penh, N. Mus.) have been found. The first kingdom in this area of which there is any record was known to the Chinese as Funan, and Chinese histories, Sanskrit inscriptions and Indianized statuary provide most of what is known about it. Its centre was in the Mekong delta in southern Vietnam, and at its greatest it probably extended as far as the middle Mekong and Chao Phraya valleys and peninsular Malaysia. Chinese sources say that it had a 'port of a thousand rivers'; this may have been OC EO, on the west coast of the delta region, north of Rach Gia. The Chinese records relate how in the 1st century AD a certain Huntian came by ship; he shot a magic arrow at the vessel of the queen of the country, who submitted and became his wife, thus establishing the ruling dynasty. According to a Sanskrit version of this story the adventurer was an Indian Brahman, Kaundinya, who threw his spear to mark where he should build his capital, then married Soma, daughter of the *nāgarāja* ('serpent king') of that place, who helped him to conquer the kingdom and changed its name to Kambuja. Almost all later rulers in Cambodia traced their genealogies back to the dynasty founded by Kaundinya and Soma.

There seems to have been a second wave of Indian immigration beginning in the late 4th century. One of the few kings of Funan about whom anything is known was Jayavarman (*reg c.* 478–*c.* 514), a Shaivite who waged war against neighbouring Champa and sent embassies to China. Jayavarman moved the capital to Vyadhapura, probably Ba Phnom in south-east Cambodia, but this was destroyed by a new enemy from the north, the Khmer kingdom of Zhenla, and the capital moved again to Angkor Borei, west of the Mekong. By *c.* 630 the kingdom of Funan had been absorbed by Zhenla, and the population had become predominantly Khmer.

The greatest king of Zhenla, Jayavarman I (*reg c.* 657–*c.* 681), reigned at Angkor Borei, where several inscriptions in Sanskrit and Khmer survive. Administration and religion were organized on the Hindu model, and the Indian epics, the *Mahābhārata* and *Rāmāyaṇa*, became widely known. After 707 Zhenla was evidently divided into two kingdoms, Zhenla of the Land in the north and Zhenla of the Water in the south. In the late 8th century the Javanese Shailendra dynasty established suzerainty over Zhenla of the Water; however, a Khmer prince came from 'Java', threw off the suzerainty of the Shailendras and was consecrated *cakravartin* (Skt: universal monarch) as Jayavarman II (*reg* 802–50), an event that is generally considered to mark the foundation of the Khmer empire of Angkor. His principal capital, however, was Hariharalaya (*see* ROLUOS), about 15 km south-east of Angkor, where he established the cult of the *devarāja*, the 'god who is king', the deity charged with the protection of the kingdom through the worship of Shiva in the form of a *liṅga* in a multi-terraced temple-pyramid representing the sacred mountain Mt Meru. Yashovarman I (*reg* 889–*c.* 900) founded Yashodharapura (*see* ANGKOR), which continued as capital for 500 years, apart from a short period when Jayavarman IV (*reg* 921[928]–44) moved it to Koh Ker, near Kompong Thom. The history of the Angkor empire was marked by frequent wars with Annam (Vietnam), Champa, the Mon kingdoms and latterly the Thais, as well as by civil disorders, often arising from a disputed succession. In 1010 Suryavarman I (*reg* 1002–50) was consecrated as supreme ruler after a dynastic struggle. During his reign Khmer rule extended as far as Lopburi and Sukhothai in central Thailand and the Lao states on the Mekong. Suryavarman II (*reg* 1113–*c.* 1150) was a great warrior-king who extended the Khmer empire and founded numerous temples, including Angkor Vat.

During the reign of the usurper Tribhuvanadityavarman (*reg* 1165–77), the Chams invaded Cambodia, pillaging Angkor in 1177. This event marked the beginning of the decline of the empire. There was a revival, however, under Jayavarman VII (*reg* 1181–*c.* 1220), who expelled the Chams from Angkor, restored the capital and defeated Champa, making it a Khmer province from 1203 to 1220. His architectural works at Angkor were extensive, and included the Bayon temple in the middle of the royal city of Angkor Thom. In 1296–7, in the reign of Indravarman III (*reg* 1295–1308), the Chinese envoy Zhou Daguan visited Angkor and wrote an account that provides a full and vivid description of Khmer life and culture at this time.

Although the Cambodian royal chronicles begin *c.* 1350, the documentary evidence for the following two centuries of Cambodian history is scanty. The Thais repeatedly invaded Angkor, finally capturing it in 1431–2. The Khmers abandoned the city soon after and moved their capital first to Phnom Penh at the confluence of the Mekong and Tonle Sap rivers, later to Lovek, then Udong on the Tonle Sap River and finally back to Phnom Penh. The Khmers reverted to a simpler, mainly agrarian life, and Theravada Buddhism became the established religion. In the 16th century Portuguese and Spanish missionaries and traders arrived, and in the 17th century the Dutch and English set up trading posts at Lovek. The Vietnamese invaded in 1658–9, and by 1700 the delta region of the Mekong River had passed from Khmer to Vietnamese rule. During the late 18th century and the earlier 19th Cambodia was constantly at war, either with the Thais or the Vietnamese, and fell under the tutelage now of one and now of the other, until in 1845 it was put under joint Vietnamese and Thai protection.

In the 1860s the French became interested in extending control over Cambodia and the other states of mainland south-east Asia. In 1858 the ruins of Angkor, which had been swallowed up by the jungle, were rediscovered by the French naturalist Henri Mouhot, and thereafter the French not only took a lead in the study of Khmer art and civilization, but also became interested in acquiring possession of the site of Angkor itself. In 1863 the French Protectorate was imposed, and in 1887 the French Indo-Chinese Union was established by decree, embracing Cambodia, Laos and the Vietnamese provinces. During the reigns of Norodom (*reg* 1860–1904) and his brother Sisovath (*reg* 1904–28), the French gradually gained complete domination over the Cambodian administration and reduced the power of the monarchy. In 1941 they installed the 18-year-old Sihanouk on the throne. The French granted Cambodia independence in 1953, and Sihanouk became prime minister. In 1970, partly as a result of increasing involvement in the Vietnam War, he was deposed and the Khmer Republic was formed; civil war followed in 1973 (locations cited for works of art in this survey may not now be correct due to theft and the destruction of war). The ensuing Communist regime of Pol Pot (1975–9) brought about a rapid and almost total devastation of the culture and economy of Cambodia. This reign of terror ended when the Vietnamese captured Phnom Penh in 1979 and proclaimed a People's Republic. The Vietnamese withdrew their forces in 1989, and economic and cultural life began to revive under a transitional government supervised by the United Nations.

BIBLIOGRAPHY

F. Garnier: 'Chronique royale du Cambodge', *J. A.* [Paris], vi/18 (1871), pp. 336–85; vi/20 (1872), pp. 112–44

C. Lemire: *Etablissement du protectorat français au Cambodge* (Paris, 1879)

A. Barth and A. Bergaigne: *Inscriptions sanscrites du Cambodge et du Champa*, 3 vols (Paris, 1885–93)

R. R. Chatterji: *Indian Influences in Cambodia* (Calcutta, 1928)

G. Coedès: *Inscriptions du Cambodge*, 8 vols (Paris, 1937–66)

L. P. Briggs: 'The Ancient Khmer Empire', *Trans. Amer. Philos. Soc.*, xli/1 (1951) [whole issue]

P. Pelliot: *Mémoires sur les coutumes du Cambodge de Tcheo Ta-Kuan: Version nouvelle* (Paris, 1951)

L. Malleret: *L'Archéologie du delta du Mékong*, 4 vols (Paris, 1959–74)

J. Boisselier: *Manuel d'archéologie d'Extrême Orient: Le Cambodge* (Paris, 1966)

B. P. Groslier: *Angkor: Art and Civilization* (London, 1966)

I. W. Mabbett: 'Devaraja', *J. SE Asian Hist.*, x/2 (1969), pp. 202–23

M. E. Osborne: *The French Presence in Cochinchina and Cambodia: Rule and Response (1859–1905)* (Ithaca and London, 1969)

V. M. Reddi: *A History of the Cambodian Independence Movement, 1863–1955* (Tirupati, 1970)

Nidhi Aeusrivongse: 'The *Devaraja* Cult and Khmer Kingship at Angkor', *Explorations in Early Southeast Asian History: The Origins of Southeast Asian Statecraft*, eds K. R. Hall and J. K. Whitmore (Ann Arbor, 1976), pp. 107–48

M. T. Vickery: *Cambodia after Angkor: The Chronicular Evidence from the Fourteenth to the Sixteenth Centuries* (Ann Arbor, 1977)

H. Kulke: *The Devaraja Cult*, Eng. trans. by I. W. Mabbett (Ithaca, 1978)

C. Jacques: '"Funan", "Zhenla": The Reality Concealed by these Chinese Views of Indochina', *Early South East Asia*, eds R. B. Smith and W. Watson (London, 1979), pp. 371–9

W. Shawcross: *Sideshow: Kissinger, Nixon and the Destruction of Cambodia* (London, 1979)

D. P. Chandler: *A History of Cambodia* (Boulder, CO, 1983, rev. 1992)

C. Etcheson: *The Rise and Demise of Democratic Kampuchea* (Boulder, CO, 1984)

W. Shawcross: *The Quality of Mercy: Cambodia, Holocaust and Modern Conscience* (London, 1984)

M. Macdonald: *Angkor and the Khmers* (Singapore, 1987)

C. Higham: *The Archaeology of Mainland Southeast Asia from 10,000 BC to the Fall of Angkor* (Cambridge, 1989)

3. RELIGION, ICONOGRAPHY AND SUBJECT-MATTER. In prehistoric times the people of Cambodia were animists, and elements of animism persisted into later times. In the historical era, the main forms of religious expression derived from India. At first, Hinduism was dominant and favoured by the rulers. Buddhism was also present from early times, but it was not until the 13th century that it prevailed for a period, and it only finally triumphed in the 15th century after the fall of Angkor.

(i) Animism. In Neolithic times, the people had animistic beliefs related to rice-growing and water spirits, including *nāga*s and *nāgī*s (serpents), which were thought to inhabit rivers, lakes and irrigated fields. In the myth of the origin of Funan (*see* §2 above), the Brahman adventurer Kaundinya married the local ruling queen, who was a *nāgī* and guardian of the treasures. The union between the ruler and the *nāga* of the state temple became part of the royal cult, and *nāga*s have always played a prominent part in Cambodian architecture and iconography.

(ii) Hinduism. During the Funan period (1st century AD–*c.* 500) Hindu cult figures included Vishnu, the Preserver, in various *avatāra*s or incarnations, such as Balarama, the patron of warriors and elder brother of Krishna; Krishna himself, who in a fine stele from Angkor Borei (Phnom Penh, N. Mus.) is shown lifting Mt Govardhana; and Kalkin, the future saviour, represented as a horse or a knight mounted on a horse. The most remarkable Hindu images of this period are of Harihara, a combination of Shiva (Hara) and Vishnu (Hari), reflecting a syncretic tendency to represent the essential unity of the supreme deity. In sculpture, he is shown with the right side in the image of Shiva and the left side in the image of Vishnu, both sharing the cylindrical mitre, but the former distinguished by a high plaited chignon (see fig. 16 below). In Sanskrit literature, the cult of Harihara is linked with the *Harivaṃśa*, a long appendix to the *Mahābhārata* epic, which is believed to have originated among the Bhagavatas, a Vaishnavite sect in southern India.

During the Zhenla period (*c.* 500–802) the worship of Shiva, the Destroyer and Renewer, predominated in the form of the *liṅga* (Skt: the symbolic representation of Shiva as a stylized phallus, which became the palladium of the Khmer rulers). The cult of Surya, the sun-god, also had some followers; and the goddess Lakshmi, or Sri, the beautiful consort of Vishnu, was favoured as the patroness of fortune and of the fertility of the rice harvest.

In the Angkor period (802–*c.* 1431) most of the rulers were Shaivite, and the royal worship was expressed in the cult of the *devarāja*, established by Jayavarman II (*reg* 802–50) at Phnom Kulen; its symbol was the Shiva *liṅga*, placed in the temple at the summit of the royal temple-mountain. Sometimes Shiva was represented as an ascetic in meditation, with a beard and high crown of plaited hair; or in royal form, with a tiara and crown and a third eye set vertically in his forehead, enabling him to beam destruction on his enemies. The gods were surrounded by heavenly beings, richly represented in Khmer art, including *apsarasas* (celestial dancers or courtesans), *asura*s (demons) and *garuḍa*s (mythical birds with human arms and torso, and head, wings and claws of an eagle). The *nāga*s are generally found forming the balustrades that flank the causeways approaching temple complexes, and in sculptures of Vishnu asleep upon the cosmic serpent Ananta.

The temple-mountains represented Mt Meru, centre of the universe and abode of the gods (*see also* §II, 1(ii) below). They were constructed on a *maṇḍala* (cosmic diagram) plan, and as such were centres of magical power. This was thought to enable the king to sustain the good order and welfare of the state and to fend off enemies, thus producing unity and self-confidence among his subjects. Some scholars believe that when a king died his temple became his funerary monument; this practice, perhaps a survival of ancestor worship from pre-Hindu times, would also explain why each succeeding king constructed his own royal temple. At Banteay Srei, built in 967, the central shrine is dedicated to Shiva under the title of Tribhuvanamaheshvara ('Great Lord of the Three Worlds'), and the flanking shrines to Brahma and Vishnu, the other two members of the Hindu Trimurti (Trinity). The decoration of the temple includes depictions of incidents from the Hindu epics, the *Mahābhārata*, the *Harivaṃsa* and the *Rāmāyaṇa* (*see* §III, 2(ii) below). Angkor Vat was the work of Suryavarman II (*reg* 1113–*c.* 1150), a Vaishnavite who was attracted to the *bhakti* devotional cult, which emphasizes love and surrender to the deity and was at that time popular in India. The series of reliefs on the walls of the outer gallery depict such scenes from Hindu mythology as the *Churning of the Ocean of Milk*, scenes of heaven and hell, the *Battle of Kurukshetra* from the *Mahābhārata* and episodes from the *Rāmāyaṇa* (*see* §III, 3(i) below), as well as portraits of himself.

By the time Angkor was finally abandoned after 1431, the cult of the *devarāja* had ceased to be significant, and Hinduism had been displaced by Theravada Buddhism. However, Hinduism still played a part in court ceremonies, in the *Reamker* (the Khmer *Rāmāyaṇa*) and in the royal dances based upon it. Hinduism as practised in Cambodia was a life-affirming system, full of vigour and movement, conscious of the beauty of creation and seeing in king and kingdom a reflection of heaven and the gods. This idealism inspired great art and literature.

(iii) Buddhism. Hinayana Buddhists of the Sanskrit Sarvastivada school came to Funan in the 3rd century AD, and sandstone Buddha images of the Gupta type dating from the early 6th century have survived. Mahayana Buddhism is evident from the 8th century: an inscription of 791 mentions the erection of an image of the *bodhisattva* Lokeshvara (the 'Lord of the World').

During most of the Angkor period, Buddhism played a subsidiary role. Kavindrarimathana, one of the ministers of Rajendravarman II (*reg* 944–68), was a Mahayana Buddhist, who at Bat Chum erected images of the Buddha, the *bodhisattva* of divine compassion, Avalokiteshvara-Padmapani (usually known as Lokeshvara), and the feminine *bhodisattva* Prajnaparamita ('Perfection of Wisdom'). There was a further advance of Buddhism during and after the reign of Jayavarman V (*reg* 968–1001), with an image of the *Buddha Meditating, Seated on the Serpent Muchalinda*, second half of the 12th century (see fig. 2), but Buddhism did not prevail until the reign of Jayavarman VII (*reg* 1181–*c.* 1220). When Cambodia was defeated by the Chams, he rallied support by appealing to the Buddhism of the ordinary people. He followed the cult of Lokeshvara, who may be depicted in the colossal heads on the towers of his monuments (*see* §II, 1(iv) below). He also built several monasteries, notably Ta Prohm. The most characteristic representation of the Buddha by Jayavarman VII's time is of him seated in meditation on the seven-headed *nāga* Muchilinda, who shades him with his hood (see also fig. 22 below). Jayavarman favoured the teaching of Prajnaparamita, of whom there are images in the form of a beautiful kneeling woman at Preah Khan. At Prei Montei, Roluos, an altar was found with bronze images of the Buddha flanked by Lokeshvara and Prajnaparamita.

After the fall of Angkor in 1431, Theravada Buddhism became the state religion, largely through the influence of the neighbouring Thais, who had established close links with Sri Lanka, the centre of orthodox Theravada doctrine. Popular devotion no longer centred on the *devarāja* but on monastic communities, which provided education and where all young men were expected to spend some time as monks. The Pali scriptures, incised or written on palm leaves, were studied, and Buddhist works were composed

2. *Buddha Meditating, Seated on the Serpent Muchalinda*, sandstone, h. 2.30 m, Angkor Vat style, from Phnom Srók, second half of the 12th century AD (Paris, Musée Guimet)

in Khmer, such as the *Story of Vorvong and Saurivong*, which the Khmers include among the *jātaka*s (tales of the previous lives of the Buddha). However, Hinduism remains in the *Reamker*, in which Rama is represented as an incarnation of both Vishnu and the Buddha.

Under Pol Pot, from 1975 to 1979, Buddhism was ruthlessly suppressed, the monks were sent to work in the fields, monasteries and temples were desecrated and Buddha images were destroyed. This violent disruption of religious life, however, was only temporary, and since 1979 the Khmer people have continued in their traditional loyalty to Buddhist faith and practice.

BIBLIOGRAPHY

A. Leclère: *Le Bouddhisme au Cambodge* (Paris, 1899)
P. Stern: *Le Bayon d'Angkor Thom et l'évolution de l'art khmer* (Paris, 1927)
G. Porée and E. Maspéro: *Traditions and Customs of the Khmer* (New Haven, 1953)
E. Porée-Maspero: 'Notes sur les particularités du culte chez les Cambodgiens', *Bull. Ecole Fr. Extrême-Orient*, xliv/2 (1954), pp. 63–71
D. J. Steinberg: *Cambodia: Its People, its Society, its Culture* (New Haven, 1957)
R. de Berval, ed.: *Présence du Bouddhisme*, France–Asie, 153–7 (Saigon, 1959)
E. Porée-Maspero: *Etude sur les rites agraires des Cambodgiens* (Paris, 1962)
C. Pym: *The Ancient Civilization of Angkor* (New York, 1967)
A. Bareau: 'Le Monastère bouddhique de Tep Pranam à Oudong', *Bull. Ecole Fr. Extrême-Orient*, lxvi (1969), pp. 34–9
——: 'Quelques ermitages et centres de méditation bouddhiques du Cambodge', *Bull. Ecole Fr. Extrême-Orient*, lxvi (1969), pp. 107–21
H. Kulke: 'Der Devaraja-Kult', *Saeculum*, xxv/1 (1974), pp. 24–55 (Eng. trans., Ithaca, 1978)
M. Giteau: *L'Iconographie du Cambodge post-angkorien* (Paris, 1975)
S. Pou: *Etude sur le Ramakirti* (Paris, 1977)
J. M. Jacob: *Reamker (Rāmakerti): The Cambodian Version of the Rāmāyaṇa* (London, 1986)

G. E. MARRISON

II. Architecture.

Virtually all the surviving monuments of the successive Khmer kingdoms that flourished in the area covered by modern Cambodia and beyond are religious, and almost nothing remains of any royal palaces or other secular buildings before the modern period, as these were constructed of perishable materials.

1. Religious and formal. 2. Domestic.

1. Religious and formal. The most fundamental characteristic of Khmer religious architecture is its cosmological and symbolic character. The constituent elements of the Khmer temple—halls, 'libraries', shrines, terraces, galleries and enclosures—and its decorative features—lintels, pediments, colonnettes and pilasters—therefore have a symbolic function as well as a structural and aesthetic one. It is such functions that determine their form, rather than considerations of congregational worship, for which they were not intended. The strictly symmetrical arrangement of concentric or axial courtyards, enclosures and ancillary buildings round the central sanctuary (*prasat*), which is almost invariably raised on a platform and is sometimes built on the summit of a tiered pyramid representing the sacred mountain, Mt Meru, and the tendency to reduce architectural decoration on buildings the further they are from the central sanctuary, are instances of this rigorous adherence to Hindu and Buddhist cosomological precepts.

BIBLIOGRAPHY

L. Delaporte: *Voyage au Cambodge: L'Architecture khmère* (Paris, 1880)
E. Lunet de Lajonquière: *Inventaire descriptif des monuments du Cambodge*, Pubns Ecole Fr. Extrême-Orient, iv, viii and ix (Paris, 1902–11)
E. Aymonier: *Le Groupe d'Angkor et l'histoire* (1903), iii of *Le Cambodge*, 3 vols (Paris, 1901–3)
J. Commaille: *Guide aux ruines d'Angkor* (Paris, 1912)
G. Coedès: *Pour mieux comprendre Angkor* (Hanoi, 1943, rev. Paris, 2/1947); rev. with Eng. trans. by E. F. Gardiner as *Angkor: An Introduction* (London and New York, 1963)
M. Glaize: *Les Monuments du groupe d'Angkor* (Saigon, 1944, rev. Paris, 3/1964)
H. Stierlin: *Angkor* (Fribourg, 1970)
D. Mazzeo and C. S. Antonini: *Grandi monumenti: Civiltà khmer* (Tokyo, 1972); Eng. trans. as *Monuments of Civilization: Ancient Cambodia* (New York, 1978)
M. Giteau: *Angkor: Un Peuple, un art* (Paris, 1976)
B. Dagens: *Angkor: La Forêt de pierre* (Paris, 1989)
A. Le Bonheur: *Cambodge, Angkor: Temples en péril* (Paris, 1989)
M. Freeman and R. Warner: *Angkor: The Hidden Glories* (Boston, London and Melbourne, 1990)
C. Jacques with R. Dumont: *Angkor* (Paris, 1990)

(i) Pre-Angkor period (before *c.* AD 889). (ii) Early Angkor period (*c.* 889–*c.* 1080). (iii) Middle Angkor period (*c.* 1080–*c.* 1181): Angkor Vat style. (iv) Late Angkor period (*c.* 1181–*c.* 1431). (v) Post-Angkor period (after *c.* 1431).

(i) Pre-Angkor period (before c. *AD 889).* Most religious monuments of the period before the accession of Yashovarman I (*reg* 889–*c.* 900) and the foundation of the first Khmer capital at Angkor were built of brick, although sandstone and laterite were also employed for foundations and walls and sometimes for entire sanctuaries, and sandstone was used for such architectural features as lintels and colonnettes framing doorways. The earliest inscriptions, which are undated, indicate the importance to the rulers of various Hindu deities, particularly Shiva. This emphasis on the worship of Shiva, especially under his vocable of Girisha, 'he who reigns on the mountain', and in the form of the *liṅga* (Skt: the symbolic representation of Shiva as a stylized phallus, which became the palladium of the Khmer rulers), may have owed its popularity to the existence of earlier indigenous fertility and mountain-worship cults that were assimilated into Shaivite cults. The earliest surviving temples are Hindu and followed the basic Indian Gupta and post-Gupta plan: a small square or rectangular cella for the sacred image, usually facing east, surmounted by a multi-storey tower with a corbelled vault. A few sanctuaries have vestibules in front of the cella. Larger complexes are rare and typically consist of a central tower of the same type surrounded by a number of smaller towers, with the main orientation again to the east, and standing within a walled enclosure. Through the French system of analysing various architectural and sculptural elements, particularly in the work of Stern and de Coral Rémusat, a stylistic sequence has been established that makes it possible to date with some exactitude monuments that cannot be dated from epigraphic or other evidence. Each style is named after a monument that typifies it.

(a) 6th century. (b) Early 7th century: Sambor Prei Kuk style. (c) Later 7th century to the 8th: Prei Khmeng and Kompong Preah styles. (d) Early to mid-9th century: Kulen style. (e) Later 9th century: Preah Ko style.

(a) 6th century. The simplest and perhaps the oldest of the surviving temples, such as Prasat Preah Theat Toc in

the citadel of Banteay Prei Nokor, Hanchey and Kok Preah Theat (all in Kompong Cham, *c.* 70 km north of Banam), and Asram Maharosei on Phnom Da near Angkor Borei, may date to the late 6th century or early 7th. They are small in scale (usually under 4 m square), with very plain walls except for some decorated pilasters. The multi-storeyed towers, reminiscent of the early south Indian *dravida* style, are ornamented primarily with small *kūdu* (niche, generally containing a head) motifs or triangular antefixes based on that motif. Benisti (1968) has suggested that some lintels from the region of Thala Borivat, on the Mekong River near its confluence with the Se San, which have certain similarities with the lintels of these simple buildings, are primitive versions of those found at Sambor Prei Kuk (*see* §(b) below) and may even date to the late 6th century. The appearance of dated inscriptions in both Sanskrit and Khmer in the early 7th century has made possible a more accurate dating for 7th- to 9th-century architecture, as well as providing a firmer historical context for individual monuments.

(b) Early 7th century: Sambor Prei Kuk style. The most important architectural site from this period is the complex of Sambor Prei Kuk, 35 km from Kompong Thom, apparently once the religious centre of Ishanapura, the capital of Ishanavarman I (*reg c.* 615–after 635). The city of Ishanapura was enclosed by a moat and a double earth rampart measuring 1.6×1.6 km. The ruins of the religious complex consist of three main groups of brick buildings, known as the south, central and north groups (the central sanctuaries of each designated respectively as S1, C1 and N1), each within its own enclosure, with some additional buildings or clusters of buildings outside. Most of the temples at Sambor Prei Kuk seem to have been built in the first half of the 7th century, although there were some important additions and renovations at later periods. De Coral Rémusat placed C1 in the 9th-century Kulen style, and Benisti (1977) has reassigned S1 to a transitional phase between the Sambor Prei Kuk and Prei Khmeng styles. These structures are prototypes for later Khmer temple architecture. The individual buildings are single-celled, square, rectangular or occasionally octagonal in plan and surmounted by multi-storey pyramidal towers. Each storey of the tower repeats on a diminishing scale the basic design of the main temple façade. The scale is impressive: according to Parmentier's scale drawings (1927), when intact N1 was nearly 10 m square; N8, one of the four smaller sanctuaries surrounding N1 to form a quincunx, was 7×9 m in plan and nearly 12 m high; and S1 was 12.75×17.0 m in plan and over 21 m high.

The exterior walls at Sambor Prei Kuk were originally stuccoed. Most of the plaster has disappeared, but it is still possible to see from the remaining brick surfaces that the walls stood on an elaborately moulded base and were divided into vertical panels by pilasters and ornamented with false doorways, niches and relief panels. As in the larger wall reliefs, the decoration of the pediments apparently included miniature representations of buildings. The doorway decoration is in stone and consists of finely carved lintels supported by circular colonnettes. A typical lintel from the site shows an arched band with an overall floral pattern interrupted by three circular medallions, each enclosing an image of a deity or auspicious creature. The band, along with small figures of lions, spouts from the mouths of *makara* (mythical sea monster combining the features of a crocodile and a dolphin and having an elephant's trunk); these are covered with floral decoration and their tails turn into exuberant floral swirls. Swags of jewels and flowers hang from the arch.

(c) Later 7th century to the 8th: Prei Khmeng and Kompong Preah styles. The two major extant monuments from the later 7th century and the 8th, Prei Khmeng and Kompong Preah, are less ambitious than Sambor Prei Kuk and differ from it primarily in the details of the lintels and colonnettes. Figures occur in the Prei Khmeng lintels, but the design of those at Kompong Preah consists entirely, and rather monotonously, of leaves and foliate bands. The decoration of the colonnettes is spread over a larger area than at Sambor Prei Kuk.

(d) Early to mid-9th century: Kulen style. In the first half of the 9th century Jayavarman II (*reg* 802–50) founded a series of capitals in the fertile Angkor plain. The Kulen style is so called after Phnom Kulen, a hill overlooking the plain where Jayavarman II founded his ceremonial capital, Mahendraparvata, 'the Mountain of the Great Indra', and where he initiated the Shaivite cult of the *devarāja* ('god who is king') and declared the Khmer realm free of Javanese tutelage. The basic form of such sanctuaries on Phnom Kulen as Prasat Thma Dap changed little from that of the 7th and 8th centuries, although the decoration, especially of tympana and lintels, became considerably more varied, with some motifs introduced from Java and Champa. Some tympana contain larger figures of deities; lintels again have *makara* at their ends, though often facing outwards, and various small images appear in the centre of their flat foliate band, including tiny *kalā* heads (grimacing lionlike masks with no lower jaw) in a pale reflection of the giant *kalā* heads crowning the doorways of contemporary central Javanese temples. Square and octagonal colonnettes also appear.

Traces survive of two interesting monuments in the Angkor area that indicate that the building of temple-mountains symbolizing Mt Meru had already begun in the time of Jayavarman II. Prasat Ak Yom, the earliest of these temple-mountains, later partly buried in the dike of the West Baray at Angkor and restored by Georges Trouvé in 1932, and Rong Chen on Phnom Kulen both consisted of tower-sanctuaries on a three-tiered pyramid base.

(e) Later 9th century: Preah Ko style. The two most important extant 9th-century monuments built before Yashovarman I moved the capital to Angkor itself are Preah Ko and Bakong, which were founded by his father Indravarman I (*reg* 877–89) at Hariharalaya (*see* ROLUOS). As soon as Indravarman I became king, he established a pattern of royal behaviour (as noted by Stern) that was followed by almost all subsequent Khmer rulers. He began in the year of his consecration with a major irrigation project, the construction of a great *baray* (reservoir) called Indratataka, now known as the Loley Baray, which provided water for an enlarged irrigation system as well as for the temples, the royal palace and the city. Then, just to the

south of the Indratataka, he dedicated a temple, Preah Ko, to his ancestors. Finally, he constructed to the south of Preah Ko a personal temple, the Bakong, in which to continue the cult of the *devarāja*.

Preah Ko, which was completed in 879, consists of a group of six brick tower-sanctuaries facing east, set in two rows on a low platform (see fig. 3). The three towers in the front row contained statues of Shiva and in the second row those of Gauri, consort of Shiva. The central tower of the front row was dedicated to Jayavarman II under his posthumous name of Parameshvara; the central tower of the second row was dedicated to the wife of Jayavarman II under the vocable of Dharanindradevi, and the other towers to the parents and maternal grandparents of Indravarman I.

Preah Ko is larger and more impressive than any earlier surviving Khmer temple complex, although the basic form of each tower-sanctuary is the same. There are four concentric enclosures surrounding the sanctuaries at the centre. The outer one is a moat measuring about 450×800 m, within which are two ponds. The next three are surrounded by walls with gateways on the east and west axes. Between the innermost wall (about 60 m square) and the next (about 95 m square) there were a number of subsidiary buildings.

The sanctuaries are reached by three short stairways, flanked by seated lions, on the east side of the platform, and faced at ground level by three large sculptures of the bull Nandi, Shiva's mount. This is probably the first occurrence of Nandi in a Khmer monument and may account for the name of the temple, Preah Ko ('sacred ox'). Each sanctuary is raised on its own small square base, with steps on all four sides leading up to an entrance on the east side and false doorways on the other three. Bands of moulding run along the base between the doorframes. Some of the stucco finish on the walls remains, including the intricately decorated pilasters at the corners of the towers and the areas over the arched niches that flank the doorways. These niches, carved from stone slabs, contain figures of *dvārapāla*s ('door guardians'). The upper storeys of the towers were also decorated with pilasters, mouldings and niches containing figures in relief, few traces of which remain.

The doorways are the main focal point for each façade, with an elaborate lintel supported by ornate octagonal colonnettes. A sculptured frieze separates the lintel from the relief on the tympanum within an inverted U-shaped arch. The badly damaged frames of the arches still reveal traces of the lobed outline edged with *makara-* or *nāga* (serpent)-heads facing outwards. The reliefs on the tympanum are also very badly damaged, but traces of scenes of deities and worshippers remain. The decoration of the lintels is characteristic of the Preah Ko style, which typically consists of a horizontal foliate scroll, its ends often accented by *nāga-* or *makara-*heads turning outwards. Large leaf motifs or foliate swags hang below the flat

3. Preah Ko, Roluos, completed AD 879

section of the scroll, sometimes alternating with jewelled pendants. The centre of the foliate band is often accented by a small figure of a deity.

The Bakong (see fig. 4), built to contain Indravarman I's royal *liṅga* Indreshvara and dedicated in 881, is extremely important as the first reasonably complete temple-mountain of which Ak Yom and Rong Chen are earlier examples. It is also much larger and more elaborate in plan than any earlier Khmer temple complex, including Preah Ko. The outermost enclosure is bounded by a moat 30 m wide with embankments, and measures about 650×860 m. It is traversed by four medial causeways, although the main orientation of the whole complex and the main axial approach are to the east. Within this enclosure are traces of 22 small brick tower-sanctuaries. The next enclosure has a laterite wall with *gopuras* (entrance pavilions), and a large moat traversed on the east and west by a causeway with *nāga* balustrades, occurring here for the first time. Inside this is another laterite wall with four gateways enclosing the central complex in an area of about 120×160 m. These concentric enclosures surround a five-tiered pyramid, faced with sandstone, roughly 65 m square at the base and 14 m high, to which a sandstone sanctuary-tower was added in the 12th century, replacing an earlier one. An axial stairway preceded by a covered gateway leads up each side, flanked at each level by a pair of seated lions. Set diagonally at each corner of each level are half-size figures of elephants. Twelve small stone shrines are set around the fourth tier. Eight brick tower-sanctuaries stand at the base of the pyramid, two on each side. These may also have held *liṅgas*; the dedicatory inscription of the temple describes eight forms of Shiva enshrined in the complex, manifested through the eight elements.

Although the stepped pyramid plan of the Bakong does not echo the configuration of Mt Meru so specifically as do later Khmer temples, with their five shrines in quincunx on the summit, it is generally accepted as a temple-mountain (*see* §(ii)(a) below). Its enclosing walls and moats correspond to the concentric rings of mountains and oceans that surround Mt Meru. By building his state temple as a representation of the cosmos, Indravarman I was declaring that his capital and kingdom were the centre of the world and that he was a *cakravartin* (Skt: 'universal monarch').

The last temple of the Roluos group, Loley, although it was not completed until 893 in the reign of Yashovarman I, still belongs to the Preah Ko style. It consists of four brick towers (two others were planned, but never completed) on a low platform and stands on an artificial island in the middle of the Loley Baray. As at Preah Ko, the two front towers were dedicated to Shiva in honour of the King's father and maternal grandfather, and the two rear

4. The Bakong, Roluos, aerial view from the east, consecrated AD 881

towers to Gauri, in honour of his mother and maternal grandmother.

BIBLIOGRAPHY

H. Parmentier: 'L'Art d'Indravarman', *Bull. Ecole Fr. Extrême-Orient*, xix (1919), pp. 1–98

——: *L'Art khmer primitif*, 2 vols, Pubns Ecole Fr. Extrême-Orient, xxi and xxii (Paris, 1927)

——: 'L'Art présumé du Fou-nan', *Bull. Ecole Fr. Extrême-Orient*, xxxii (1932), pp. 183–9

P. Stern: 'Hariharalaya et Indrapura', *Bull. Ecole Fr. Extrême-Orient*, xxxviii (1938), pp. 175–97

G. de Coral Rémusat: *L'Art khmer: Les Grandes Etapes de son évolution* (Paris, 1940, rev. 2/1951)

P. Dupont: 'La Dislocation du Tchen-la et la formation du Cambodge (VII–IXe siècles)', *Bull. Ecole Fr. Extrême-Orient*, xliii (1943), pp. 17–55

P. Stern: 'Diversité et rythme des fondations royales khmères', *Bull. Ecole Fr. Extrême-Orient*, xliv/2 (1954), pp. 649–85

M. Benisti: 'Recherches sur le premier art khmer, I: Les Linteaux dits de Thala Borivat', *A. Asiatiques*, xviii (1968), pp. 85–101

——: *Rapports entre le premier art khmer et l'art indien*, Pubns Ecole Fr. Extrême-Orient (Paris, 1970)

——: 'Recherches sur le premier art khmer, III: Aux confins des styles de Prei Kmeng et de Kompong Preah', *A. Asiatiques*, xxiii (1971), pp. 93–134

——: 'Recherches sur le premier art khmer, VII: Le Problème de Sambor S. 1', *A. Asiatiques*, xxxiii (1977), pp. 25–56

*(ii) Early Angkor period (*c*. 889–*c*. 1080).* The religious architecture of this period, from the reign of Yashovarman I (*reg* 889–*c*. 900) to that of Harshavarman III (*reg c*. 1066–1080), continued, and developed elements already present in the architecture of the pre-Angkor period. Brick, laterite and sandstone remained the building materials. The basic unit was still a single-celled sanctuary with a tiered pyramidal superstructure, based on the early Hindu sanctuaries of India. The cell doorway was almost always on the east side of the building, with false doorways, or occasionally true doors, on the other three sides. The principal sanctuary or group of sanctuaries was placed on a raised platform and surrounded by a variety of subsidiary buildings, *gopura*s, enclosure walls and moats. Corbelled arches were used to span interior spaces, thus limiting their width and encouraging the construction of long, narrow galleries and clusters of smaller structures.

The monuments can be divided into two types according to their function and symbolism. The first of these types is the temple-mountain, the monument dedicated by the ruler as the symbolic centre of his kingdom. Sometimes built on the summit of a natural hill, it was in the form of a terraced pyramid that provided a base for the central sanctuary in which the *liṅga* or other image symbolizing the king's power was placed; it also represented the sacred mountain, Mt Meru, centre of the Hindu and Buddhist cosmos and axis of the world. The great majority of extant temples, however, whether dedicated by rulers or by members of the aristocracy, were built directly on flat ground and followed the model of most Indian and Khmer temples, where one or more sanctuaries were placed on a single low platform. In both these types the plan was usually elaborated by other elements, including subsidiary shrines, 'libraries' (so called because it is thought they may have been built for the storage of sacred texts), galleries, *gopura*s, *baray*, causeways and enclosure walls.

Stylistically, the architecture and sculpture of this period has been divided by Gilberte de Coral Rémusat and Philippe Stern as follows: Bakheng style (late 9th century to early 10th); Koh Ker style (second quarter of the 10th century); Banteay Srei style (second half of the 10th century); style of the Khleangs (late 10th century to early 11th); and Baphuon style (11th century). Such transitional styles as the Pre Rup style (mid-10th century), characterized by other monuments, occur between most of these main periods. It is generally preferable, however, to divide the period more broadly into the first style of Angkor, the Banteay Srei style and the Baphuon style (*see also* §III, 2 below).

(a) Late 9th century to the mid-10th: first style of Angkor. (b) Later 10th century: Banteay Srei style. (c) Late 10th century to the 11th: Baphuon style.

(a) Late 9th century to the mid-10th: first style of Angkor. Yashovarman I reigned at first at his father's capital Hariharalaya, where he followed the example of his predecessors by constructing a temple to his ancestors (Loley; *see* §(i)(e) above). The agricultural possibilities of the Roluos area had, however, evidently already been fully exploited, so Yashovarman founded a new capital, Yashodharapura ('City of Yashovarman'), in the immediate Angkor area about 15 km north-west of Roluos. This area was to remain the centre of the Khmer kingdom until the 15th century, except for a brief hiatus between 921 and 944. Again following his predecessors' example, Yashovarman constructed a gigantic reservoir at Yashodharapura, the Yashodharatataka ('Lake of Yashovarman', the modern East Baray). This reservoir, about 1.8×7.0 km, fed by the Siem Reap River flowing from Phnom Kulen, has a surface area roughly four times that of the Loley reservoir at Roluos. Yashovarman also built minor temples on low platforms on three small hills in the Angkor area; the temple on Phnom Dei is dedicated to Harihara, those on Phnom Krom and Phnom Bok to Vishnu, Shiva and Brahma, the Hindu Trimurti (Trinity).

His major monument, however, is the central temple-mountain Yashodharagiri ('Mountain of Yashovarman'), known as Phnom Bakheng, which he built in 893 for the practice of the *devarāja* cult on the highest of the low hills of the area, Phnom Bakheng, and which formed the centre of the new city (*see* ANGKOR, §2(i)). Phnom Bakheng is a monument of great complexity, consisting of a five-tiered pyramid faced with sandstone and surmounted by five sandstone sanctuaries in quincunx. On each of the five terrace levels are 12 small sandstone sanctuaries, making a total of 60. There are 44 larger brick towers round the base of the pyramid and *gopura*s at the cardinal points of the enclosure. This complex plan and in particular the great number of small shrines, of which those on the west terraces are extremely difficult to enter because their doorways face into the wall of the terrace above, seems to have been dictated by considerations of the symbolism of the monument rather than any function as a place of worship. Filliozat is the first to have analysed the plan of Phnom Bakheng in terms of Hindu cosmology and as a representation of the cosmic mountain, Mt Meru. Mt Meru was usually described as having a central peak surrounded by four lesser peaks at the cardinal points and an additional four at the intermediate points, and this accounts for the quincuncial arrangement of the five tower-sanctuaries, a common feature of Indian and South-east Asian architecture generally and of the Khmer temple-mountain in particular. Mt Meru was also sometimes described as having seven levels, which are represented at Phnom Bakheng by the enclosure at the ground level, the five terraces and the square platform on top of the five terraces. The brick temples and the moat that surround the base of the pyramid and the moat and embankment of the city itself, enclosing an area of *c.* 16 sq. km, may also represent the concentric rings of mountains and oceans surrounding Mt Meru.

Filliozat thought that the 108 small shrines surrounding the central one had a chronological symbolism, 108 being equal to four times the lunar cycle of 27 days, and that the 60 towers on the five terraces could symbolize the complete cycle of time, because in Indian astronomy it was believed that the planet Jupiter took 60 years to complete its orbit through the heavens. He further pointed out that only 33 shrines can be seen at one time from the centre of each side of the monument and linked this aspect of the plan to the 33 gods thought to inhabit the 33 levels of Indra's heaven on Mt Meru. As Heine-Geldern first noted, by building a temple complex at the centre of his capital that was a representation of Mt Meru, Yashovarman was, like many South-east Asian rulers, simultaneously establishing his capital and his kingdom as a model of the cosmos and as the symbolic centre of his world.

Under Yashovarman's son and successor, Harshavarman I (*reg c.* 900–21), construction seems to have been considerably more modest. He probably began the construction of Baksei Chamkrong, a small temple in laterite, brick and sandstone, composed of a four-storey pyramid only 27 m sq. at the base and 12 m high, on a platform with axial stairways up each side and crowned by a single brick sanctuary about 11 m high. The stucco ornament that formerly decorated the laterite base and the sanctuary was probably typical of the period, with small figures and much swirling foliage. To the same period belongs Prasat Kravan, a group of five brick sanctuaries set in a row on a north–south axis, all facing east, on a low base. This temple was dedicated to Vishnu in 921 by a group of court dignitaries. Unusually also at this early period, the inside walls of the towers are decorated with large reliefs carved in brick and covered by a thin layer of plaster (*see* §III, 2(i) below).

Baksei Chamkrong was far exceeded and even Phnom Bakheng was rivalled in scale and ambition by Prasat Thom, the temple complex built by the usurper Jayavarman IV (*reg* 921 [928]–44) when he set up his capital in 921 at Chok Gargyar, also called Lingapura, modern Koh Ker. On this site, now a rather infertile plain about 100 km north-east of Angkor, Jayavarman IV first built an artificial lake or reservoir (560×1200 m), the Rahal, presumably to supply water for agricultural development. The orientation both of this reservoir, some 15 degrees west of north, and of the walled enclosure, which was probably the capital, with the Prasat Thom complex within it to the north of the Rahal, was dictated by the terrain rather than by strict cosmological symbolism, indicating the importance attached by Khmer rulers to ensuring the food supply. The plan of Prasat Thom represents an interesting variation on the type for the temple-mountain established by the builders of the Bakong and Bakheng. At Prasat Thom the subsidiary buildings and shrines, which in the Bakong and Phnom Bakheng are grouped round the central sanctuary and within the immediate enclosure round the stepped pyramid, are strung along either side of the approach axis leading to a seven-tiered pyramid dressed in sandstone. Moreover, at Prasat Thom, as at Baksei Chamkrong, this pyramid was the base for only a single sanctuary.

At the beginning of the approach are two groups of buildings, sometimes described as palaces, one on either side, then a space of some 170 m leading to a large *gopura*. The extension of this *gopura* on each side is perhaps the first instance of the surrounding gallery that was to become so characteristic of later Khmer temples. Beyond the *gopura* are two laterite enclosures, one behind the other, each about 170×150 m. The first enclosure, entered through a very large and impressive red brick *gopura*, contains a moat traversed by causeways on the east and west. On either side of these causeways, and stretching along their entire length, is a balustrade composed of a *nāga*, with a huge image of a *garuḍa* (mythical bird with human arms and torso, and the head, wings and claws of an eagle), traditional enemy of the *nāga*s, behind it as if in pursuit. Within the moat two more walled enclosures (one laterite and one sandstone) contain a series of buildings on an elongated rectilinear plan, forming an almost uninterrupted ring round the middle enclosure. This also foreshadows the development of the surrounding gallery. The innermost courtyard contains 21 small brick sanctuaries, of which nine are arranged in two rows of five and four on the central terrace, with 12 smaller sanctuaries in four groups of three just off the corners of the terrace. A rectangular antechamber (*maṇḍapa*) precedes the sanctuary in the centre of the front row. The rear enclosure contains only the seven-tiered pyramid, set back within the western half of the compound, with only one stairway approach, on the east side. On the summit of the pyramid, which is 62×64 m at the base and 36 m high, and so much larger than any previous Khmer pyramid, once stood a sanctuary containing a colossal *liṅga*, perhaps as high as 4.5 m, under the vocable of Tribhuvaneshvara. The carved base of the sanctuary survives and is 17 m sq., which suggests that the height of the sanctuary may have been as much as 24 m.

The design of sanctuaries in the Bakheng and Koh Ker periods followed a model that had already evolved by the end of the pre-Angkor period. The base of the structure was accentuated by a series of horizontal mouldings; the wall area above was then divided into vertical panels by pilasters, with niches flanking the doors or false doors in the centre of each side of the sanctuary. These niches contained standing images in high relief of guardian figures, both male and female. Above them in the niche or on the wall above the niche small flying figures of celestial beings were frequently carved. The pilasters and wall areas were filled with overall relief decoration of foliage swirls, jewel bands and similar patterns. The sandstone tympana, lintels and colonnettes flanking the doorways also provided surfaces for relief sculpture. Lintels were covered with foliage swags hanging from a horizontal foliated scroll that dipped at the middle under a small motif such as a *kalā* head or the figure of a deity. In the Koh Ker period the central motif on the lintel was sometimes a small scene, rather than a single figure, and the colonnettes tended to become even more filled with leaf and jewel patterns. The frames of the pediments above the doorways were of two different forms: one a flattened horseshoe or U-shape, the other higher, with an undulating outline. The lower corners of the pediments generally ended in a *makara* head. The figures of deities in the tympana tended to be engulfed in the foliage framing them. A triangular pediment, its shape derived from wooden gables and its tympanum also filled with foliage patterns, appeared in the Koh Ker period. The superstructures of the sandstone sanctuaries of Phnom Bakheng have been lost, and those of the stucco-covered brick sanctuaries of most of the monuments of the first 70 years of the early Angkor period are so damaged that little of their form or decoration can be determined beyond the tiered structure and the presence of small niches and miniature temple replicas.

The capital was moved back to the Angkor area by Rajendravarman II (*reg* 944–68) who, however, also continued to make dedications in the Koh Ker area, as did some of his officials. At Angkor, Rajendravarman II is thought to have completed the small pyramid temple of Baksei Chamkrong, probably begun by Harshavarman I, but his most ambitious projects were the East Mebon (ded. 953), set on an artificial island in the East Baray, and Pre Rup (961; see fig. 5), located just south of the East Baray. These two complexes are very similar in form and it is not entirely clear whether both were intended as a combination of ancestor-temple and temple-mountain or whether the slightly earlier and smaller East Mebon was an ancestor-temple, while Pre Rup was, like the Bakong and the Bakheng, a temple-mountain. The construction of the East Mebon may have been in deliberate imitation of Yashovarman's ancestor-temple of Loley in the centre of the Indratataka *baray* at Roluos and, if so, this reinforces the idea that it was also an ancestor-temple.

The island on which the East Mebon was built is only 120 m sq., limiting the scale of the complex. The temple consists of a three-tiered pyramid in laterite surmounted by five square brick sanctuary towers in quincunx on a 30 m sq. upper terrace. Large free-standing sculptures of elephants are set diagonally at the corners of each terrace. A *liṅga* under the vocable of Rajendreshvara was placed in the central sanctuary and images dedicated to Rajendravarman's ancestors in the four corner sanctuaries. Similarly, at Pre Rup a group of five brick sanctuaries in quincunx was built for the royal *liṅga* Rajendrabhadreshvara, for images of Shiva, Vishnu and Uma representing ancestors or predecessors of Rajendravarman, and for another image of Shiva in the south-east tower. At Pre Rup there are eight additional small sanctuaries on the first level of the three-tiered pyramid, which is 12 m high and 50×50 m at its base. The pyramid stands on two concentric terraces, each enclosed by a laterite wall with axial gateways and containing various subsidiary buildings and an additional five shrines (six were originally intended) on the east side of the first courtyard. The four axial stairways are guarded by lions at each level. None of the pediments or the reliefs on the tympana has survived,

5. Pre Rup, Angkor, aerial view from the north-east, consecrated AD 961

although some of the guardian figures in the niches flanking the doorways can still be made out.

It may have been during the reign of Rajendravarman II that the first major buildings in permanent materials were constructed at Preah Vihear (Thai: Khao Phra Wihan), although there is some uncertainty about the origins of this remarkable complex, most of which dates from the period between the reigns of Suryavarman I (*reg* 1002–50) and Suryavarman II (*reg* 1113–*c.* 1150). Preah Vihear consists, not of concentric enclosures, but of a series of courts and *gopuras* strung out on a longitudinal axis over a distance of approximately 850 m on the top of a sloping promontory 600 m above sea-level in the Dangkrek mountains on the Thai-Cambodian frontier. Also dating from the reign of Rajendravarman II are two small Mahayana Buddhist temples at Angkor, south of the East Baray, Prasat Lak Nan and Prasat Bat Chum, as well as the oldest parts of Prasat Khna, Kompong Thom Province.

(b) Later 10th century: Banteay Srei style. Perhaps the most interesting monument constructed in Rajendravarman II's reign is Banteay Srei (Citadel of the Women; see fig. 6), which was evidently largely finished by 967 but not dedicated until 968, at the beginning of the reign of Jayavarman V (*reg* 968–1001). This miniature Shaivite temple, located on the Siem Reap River about 20 km north-east of Angkor, was founded by the Brahman Yajnavaraha and his younger brother, Vishnukumara. Yajnavaraha, a grandson of Harshavarman I, was tutor to both Rajendravarman II and his son, Jayavarman V, and was the founder of a number of temples. Banteay Srei, meticulously restored by the French archaeological service and almost unscathed during the Communist regime, is the best preserved of all the monuments of Angkor up to that date. Like Prasat Thom and Preah Vihear, Banteay Srei is built on a longitudinal axis. A processional causeway leads through three quadrangular enclosures to the three sanctuaries at the centre. These stand on a low platform in a line running north–south, with two 'libraries' in front. (For a detailed description of the temple *see* ANGKOR, §2(ii).)

6. Banteay Srei, Angkor, consecrated AD 968

Banteay Srei is built almost entirely of fine pink sandstone, carefully colour-matched. The small, almost miniature scale of the complex, judged by Stierlin to be less than one-half normal size, may account for the meticulous execution of the sculptural decoration and for its quantity: virtually every surface of the main buildings is covered in finely detailed relief carving. All three of the multi-tiered towers of the sanctuaries have four storeys separated by strong horizontal cornices, the whole crowned by a circular coping-stone that may once have had a metal finial. Each level of the tower repeats the basic composition of the main walls of the temple, with a horseshoe-shaped pediment placed directly above the fronton of the doorway below and flanked by pilasters and figures in niches in the body of the tower. Standing free at each corner is a miniature model of a temple, and between these, in front of the wall of the tower, are antefixes with a foliate arch surrounding a standing or seated figure.

The pediments of the sanctuaries are in the more simple horseshoe shape found in earlier Khmer architecture, but the double and triple pediments above the second enclosure gateway and the 'library' doorways have the more undulating, polylobed frame that is characteristic of later Khmer temple pediments. This accumulation of pediments behind and above each other was to become a major characteristic of Khmer temple architecture in the 12th century. The ends of the pediments are more varied than those of the earlier 10th century, which ended either in *makaras* or in *nāgas*. Some of the Banteay Srei pediments do end simply with *makaras* spouting jewels, but others have *makaras* on each face of the corner, spouting either a multi-headed *nāga* or a standing lion, which thus provides the pivot for the corner. The design of the pediment of the gateway in the outer laterite wall is the same as at Koh Ker. Instead of the more conventional towered structure with a series of horseshoe or polylobed pediments, this gateway has a triangular pediment, here set on columns, in imitation of the gable ends of the timber-framed, tile-roofed long halls of Khmer architecture. Its edges echo the diagonal timber beams that meet at the ridge of a timber-framed roof, with a diamond-shaped ridge-point motif capped with a flame or leaf-shaped motif. The outer ends of the beams swirl up in a reverse-curve volute like the coil of a serpent's tail. The supporting columns are almost entirely plain, as are the laterite walls of the enclosure, setting off the delicate foliage and jewel motifs of the pediment and its frame even more effectively.

Among the most remarkable features of the decoration of Banteay Srei are the apparently deliberate archaism of some elements and the narrative content of the major bas-reliefs. These archaizing elements, which have often been attributed to the influence of the founder, Yajnavaraha, include round colonnettes and relief figures of guardians in the niches flanking the sanctuary doorways in a style related to those of the pre-Angkor period. The large-scale narrative relief scenes, found on the tympana of the pediments of the 'libraries' and some of the ancillary buildings are almost unprecedented in earlier Khmer architecture (*see* §III, 2(ii) below). This archaizing tendency suggests that the Khmers had already by this period acquired a sense of the historical development of styles in their own art, although it is unclear whether the motives for this revival were purely aesthetic or political and doctrinal. It has been noted, however, by some art historians, that there are archaic features in the planning and location of the East Mebon and in some of the decorative elements of the East Mebon and Pre Rup that echo the styles of Preah Ko and Phnom Bakheng. The appearance of archaic elements at Banteay Srei may thus be part of a general trend in the later 10th century.

(c) Late 10th century to the 11th: Baphuon style. Only two small monuments in the style of Banteay Srei survive at Angkor: Prasat Sralau and the monument behind the North Khleang. Most of the monuments of the late 10th century are closer in style to the Bakheng and Koh Ker. The round colonnettes have disappeared; the designs on the tympana, such as those at the Khleangs (*see* ANGKOR, §1), are basically foliage patterns, certainly not narrative figural relief scenes; and the foliate scroll of the lintels on the Khleangs dips into a distinctive broad U-form at the centre, containing small figures of divinities or scenes, a style that continued into the Baphuon period but that had also begun to occur in a few lintels at Banteay Srei.

The two major constructions of the late 10th century and early 11th were Ta Keo and the Phimeanakas, both possibly founded by Jayavarman V, but with later additions early in the 11th century. Both are temple-mountains, and inscriptions of the period refer to the erection of two such monuments, the Hemasringagiri (Mountain of the Golden Horn), which is thought to be the Phimeanakas, and the Hemagiri (Mountain of Gold), which may be identified with Ta Keo. Ta Keo is built almost entirely of sandstone and is colossal in scale (see fig. 7). The 22 m-high pyramid base has five levels, of which the three upper ones form a three-tiered pyramid set back on two concentric terraces.

7. Ta Keo, Angkor, aerial view from the east, *c.* 1000

The first terrace, measuring 96×112 m, is enclosed by a wall and the second by a continuous gallery that was probably originally covered by a corbelled brick roof. False windows with balusters decorate the exterior of the gallery. There are four entrance gateways on each of these levels. Two long buildings stand on either side of the eastern gateway at each of these levels, and there are two 'libraries' on the second level flanking the eastern gate. Five sanctuaries, each with a cruciform plan made by the four true doors with antechambers that lead into the cell from each side, stand in quincunx on the 40 m sq. top terrace. The ornamentation of Ta Keo was left unfinished, and only those elements that were carved before being set in place, such as the colonnettes, have any decorative detail. The Phimeanakas is enclosed by a 250×600 m wall and stands on a rectangular, three-tiered, laterite base (35×28 m). It has an extremely steep profile, the uppermost terrace being at a height of 12 m, yet measuring 30×23 m. There are staircases at the centre of each side, flanked by lions at each level and with elephants set at the corners of the terraces. The single central shrine has disappeared, but there is still a continuous covered gallery, built entirely in sandstone, around the top terrace. These, the earliest surviving galleries with stone vaults, are very narrow as a result, just over 1 m wide.

Suryavarman I (*reg* 1002–50) does not appear to have firmly established his control at Angkor until *c.* 1011, and much of the construction carried out in his reign seems to have consisted of the repair, completion or embellishment of earlier monuments, such as the Phimeanakas, as well as the repair and enlargement of the irrigation system of Angkor. Late in his reign, outside Angkor, he added to such monuments as Preah Vihear, Prasat Neak Buos and Vat Phu, the last in what is now southern Laos and an important sacred site since the earliest pre-Angkor period. These monuments and Prasat Phnom Chisor, one of Suryavarman I's few new constructions, were all chosen as sacred sites because of their dramatic natural settings and their association with sacred mountains. Prasat Phnom Chisor is located at a height of 120 m on a mountain in Bati Province, to the north-west of the pre-Angkor capital of Angkor Borei. An enclosure approximately 45×50 m is approached by a long stairway and causeway running up the east slope of the mountain from the plain below, where a large artificial water basin is located. Vat Phu is also situated on the slope of a mountain, Phu Bassac, about 8 km south of Champassac, called in a 7th-century inscription Lingaparvata (Mountain of the Linga) because of the vaguely phallic rock formation crowning its summit. A large number of later additions were made to the original 7th-century brick temple to create an ensemble on a longitudinal plan that stretches about 800 m, from a 200×600 m basin through a series of causeways, stairs and courtyards up the slope, to end in the sanctuary courtyard at the foot of the mountain. Other foundations of Suryavarman I include Vat Ek, Vat Baset and Chau Srei Vibol.

Suryavarman I also built the West Baray, an enormous reservoir approximately 2.2×8.0 km in area, with a capacity of about 40 million cubic m. The eastern edge of this reservoir overlapped the western edge of Yashovarman I's capital and buried several earlier monuments, notably Ak Yom. Udayadityavarman II (*reg* 1050–*c.* 1066) built the West Mebon on an artificial circular island between 150 and 200 m in diameter, in the middle of this lake, following the pattern established by Yashovarman I and Rajendravarman II at Loley and the East Mebon. Its construction is rather unusual. In the centre of the island is an enclosure about 70×70 m, with a sandstone wall between 2 and 3 m high provided with porticos and towers decorated with bas-reliefs of animals and various scenes. Inside is a pond with a causeway leading to its centre, where there is a cruciform platform on which a sanctuary may once have stood. Little is known about this complex, but it was undoubtedly dedicated to Vishnu. An enormous but fragmentary bronze of Vishnu lying asleep on the cosmic serpent Ananta (Phnom Penh, N. Mus.), discovered in 1936 at the complex, must have been the image that the late 13th-century Chinese envoy, Zhou Daguan, saw and described as a bronze Buddha from which water flowed continuously.

Udayadityavarman II also built the Baphuon, which of all the monuments of Angkor is second only to Angkor Vat in ground area. Unfortunately, it is also one of the most ruined. Its outer wall (425×125 m) is pierced by a large *gopura* on the east, leading to a raised causeway about 200 m long that traverses a large pond. The base of the five-stepped pyramid is approximately 120×100 m and is surrounded by a vaulted sandstone gallery, with large entrance pavilions at the cardinal points and towers at the corners, as are the middle and top terraces. The eastern and western gateways are flanked by cruciform 'libraries', which are connected to each other and the gateways by walkways raised on short pillars. A single sanctuary formerly stood at the centre of the top terrace. The upper levels rise very steeply from the terrace, with four axial stairs and two additional stairs at each corner leading up to the top corner towers. The steepness of the base, combined with the weight of the galleries running along the edges of the upper terrace, may be responsible for the particularly ruinous condition of the Baphuon. Undoubtedly, water from the monsoon rain seeping into the fill and the growth of tropical vegetation on the structure after Angkor was abandoned also weakened the retaining walls of the terraces. The wooden beams encased in stone, employed to lighten the spans in the galleries, eventually decayed and contributed to their collapse, and much of the material of the galleries was carried away at some time for use elsewhere. The Baphuon was, however, still standing at the end of the 13th century when Zhou Daguan saw it and was much impressed by its great size and its 'tower of copper'.

Much of the pyramid base is decorated with a continuous series of mouldings, so that there is no space for reliefs. The *gopura*s, however, have a large number of small figural relief panels arranged in vertical rows (*see* §III, 2(iii) below), and a few scenes and figures also occur on the lintels. The pediments at the Baphuon are decorated primarily with foliage motifs, although a few figures do occur. The undulating upper edges of the Baphuon pediments have the appearance of a serpent's body, appropriate for the *nāga* heads that continued to be placed at the pediment ends.

BIBLIOGRAPHY

L. Finot, V. Goloubew and H. Parmentier: *Le Temple d'Içvarapura (Bantay Srei, Cambodge)*, Pubns Ecole Fr. Extrême-Orient, i (Paris, 1926)

H. Parmentier: *L'Art khmer primitif*, 2 vols, Pubns Ecole Fr. Extrême-Orient, xxi and xxii (Paris, 1927)
R. Heine-Geldern: 'Conceptions of State and Kingship in Southeast Asia', *Far E. Q.*, ii (1942), pp. 15–30
J. Filliozat: 'Le Symbolisme du monument du Phnom Bakheng', *Bull. Ecole Fr. Extrême-Orient*, xliv (1954), p. 527
P. Stern: 'Diversité et rythmes des fondations royales khmères', *Bull. Ecole Fr. Extrême-Orient*, xliv/2 (1954), pp. 649–85
H. Stierlin: *Angkor* (Fribourg, 1970)
J. Dumarçay: *Ta Kev: Etude architecturale du temple*, Pubns Ecole Fr. Extrême-Orient, vi (Paris, 1971)
——: *Phnom Bakheng: Etude architecturale du temple*, Pubns Ecole Fr. Extrême-Orient, vii (Paris, 1972)
M. Giteau: *Angkor: Un Peuple, un art* (Paris, 1976)

JUDITH PATT

*(iii) Middle Angkor period (*c. *1080–*c. *1181): Angkor Vat style.* The Angkor Vat style is the last but one of the 12 styles in the sequence of Khmer art, established by Stern and de Coral Rémusat and refined by Boisselier, in which each style is named after a building that typifies it.

(a) Introduction. (b) Function and cosmology. (c) Building techniques and design. (d) Architectural decoration.

(a) Introduction. The Angkor Vat style covers the reigns of Dharanīndravarman I (*reg* 1107–13), Sūryavarman II (*reg* 1113–*c.* 1150), Yashovarman II (*reg c.* 1150–65) and Tribhuvanādityavarman (*reg* 1165–77). Nine temple complexes are generally considered as belonging in whole or in part to the style: Phimai (*see also* THAILAND, §II, 1(iii)(b)), Preah Pithu, Thommanon, Angkor Vat (see figs 8 and 9; *see also* ANGKOR, §2(iii)), Beng Mealea, Banteay Samré, Preah Palilay, Chau Say Tevoda and Vat Athvea. They are all in the immediate vicinity of Angkor, except Beng Mealea, which is about 40 km to the east of Angkor in a forest just south of the eastern end of Phnom Kulen; Vat Athvea, which is between Siem Reap and the Tonle Sap (Great Lake); and Phimai, which is far to the north-west on the Khorat Plateau in north-east Thailand. Angkor Vat is a royal foundation and is the only one of the nine monuments to have been built as a temple-mountain raised on a platform (see fig. 8); all the others are 'flat' temples built on level ground.

Phimai is the earliest of the nine and is the main example of the transitional style between the Baphuon and Angkor Vat styles; the inscriptions indicate that it dates from the reign of Jayavarman VI (*reg* 1080–1107). Preah Pithu seems also to have been begun at that period. Thommanon is thought to be somewhat earlier than Angkor Vat (built by Sūryavarman II), while Banteay Samré and Vat Athvea were contemporary with it and Preah Palilay and Chau Say Tevoda were built soon after. According to Boisselier, Beng Mealea was started before Angkor Vat but not completed until after it. In spite of its ruinous condition, it plays an important role in the chronology since, as well as being a prototype for the Angkor Vat style in its general layout, it already shows in various details of building technique and decoration characteristics of the Bayon style that followed it in the reign of Jayavarman VII (*reg* 1181–*c.* 1220).

(b) Function and cosmology. Of the nine temples classified as being in the Angkor Vat style, only Phimai, Preah Pithu and Preah Palilay are certainly Buddhist; all the rest are Hindu, the last important Hindu temples to be built at Angkor before the rise to supremacy of Mahayana Buddhism in the reign of Jayavarman VII. However, it is not always clear to which god they were dedicated, for as a rule there are no cult images in the cella, and the inscriptions are ambiguous. In the religious beliefs of the Khmer people there had been a tendency from very early times to regard the two great Hindu deities Shiva and Vishnu as a unity (hence their predilection for Harihara, a combination of the two in a single image), and this syncretism also influenced the decoration of the temples. There was a similar syncretic tendency between Shaivism and Mahayana Buddhism, and pictorial representations of legends relating to Hindu or Buddhist deities may likewise appear together on the same buildings. Vaishnavite subjects seem to have been especially popular at the time of the Angkor Vat style, and two predominantly Vaishnavite epics, the *Mahābhārata* and the *Rāmāyaṇa*, were the main sources for the scenes depicted. This can perhaps be explained by

8. Angkor Vat, Angkor, view from the west, early 12th century

the fact that Sūryavarman II, in whose reign the most important monuments in this style were erected, was himself a Vaishnavite.

The plan of Angkor Vat shows more impressively than any other Khmer religious monument how Hindu cosmological concepts were reproduced in microcosm in the temple-mountain, with the moat representing the mythical oceans, the surrounding wall the belt of mountains, and the uppermost level, with its five towers in quincunx, the five peaks of Mt Meru (*see also* §(ii)(a) and §I, 3 above). The *nāga* balustrades flanking the causeways that lead across the moat towards the main entrance, a feature first found in the Bakong at the end of the 9th century, also have an important cosmological significance. In Indian mythology the *nāga* was compared to the rainbow that formed the bridge from the human world to the heaven of the gods, over which Indra presided. Walking towards the temple that is the abode of the god, borne along by the *nāga*s, one leaves behind the earthly world and enters the celestial sphere. The theory that the *nāga* balustrades represent the myth of the churning of the Ocean of Milk to produce the elixir of immortality (*amṛta*) is no longer held.

(c) Building techniques and design. All the temple complexes were built of laterite and sandstone, as was customary from the 10th century. The sandstone was quarried on the Kulen plateau to the north-east of Angkor. The walls and towers of the buildings were built predominantly of sandstone, but laterite continued to be used for the substructure and the massive inner areas of the terraces and foundations, which were then clad with sandstone. Even for parts of the buildings where great strength was needed, such as the foundations, the inner core was made of laterite and the outer part of sandstone, and almost invariably the vaulting and roofs of buildings in the Angkor Vat style were made of sandstone. In the *gopuras* at Chau Say Tevoda and Thommanon brick was used, but this is exceptional. For the construction of ceilings beneath the corbelled sandstone vaulting, rafters of a very hard wood resembling oak were used. Some of these rafters have been partially preserved, for example at Preah Palilay, but in most buildings the ceilings have completely disappeared to reveal the corbelled vaulting.

A distinguishing feature of the building technique of this period is the use of blocks rather than pegs for joining joists and columns, as in Angkor Vat itself and in parts of Beng Mealea. Pegs were used in all buildings in the subsequent Bayon style and in the later parts of Beng Mealea. Presumably this was due to the haste with which the later buildings at Angkor were erected. By contrast, buildings in the Angkor Vat style, especially Angkor Vat itself and Beng Mealea, were evidently constructed with great care.

The three structures that traditionally constituted the principal elements of the Khmer temple—the terrace as a base or foundation, the tower and the gallery—were developed architecturally into a great variety of forms. The temple enclosure was built symmetrically round the central shrine. All the angles are right angles. The orientation to the east was still obligatory, except in cases where for religious reasons, in connection with funerary cults, a westward orientation was required, as at Angkor Vat and Vat Athvea, or where, as at Phimai, which faces south-east, the temple was built looking towards the city of Angkor. The principal shrine consists of a square, windowless cella and a tower with corbelled vaulting above it. The base of the shrine is constructed in a series of steps to emphasize the tower-like character of the whole building. The cella often has four doors, each preceded by a vestibule with several horizontal and vertical stages; sometimes all four doors are real entrances (Angkor Vat), sometimes three are false but still have porches (Thommanon, Banteay Samré). The development of the porches to become antechambers or entrance passages with several stepped levels is characteristic.

Angkor Vat as a temple-mountain and Beng Mealea as a 'flat' temple built on one level epitomize the two typical ground-plans of Khmer temples, which could already be observed in embryonic form in the preceding Baphuon period. However, the fully evolved ground-plan for this type of complex did not emerge until the beginning of the Angkor Vat style and continued to be used until the first period of the Bayon style. Its most distinctive feature is the three rectangular galleries that run round the three concentric inner courts of the temple precinct, with the main shrine, raised on its stepped base, standing in the innermost court. The corner pavilions of the innermost gallery developed into secondary shrines with tower superstructures and were sometimes linked to the main sanctuary by galleries positioned axially to form a cross, as at Angkor Vat. At Phimai, Beng Mealea and Banteay Samré an elongated *gopura* was built in front of the principal, eastern entrance to the cella; in some cases this forms the only link to the innermost gallery.

These surrounding galleries, which occur for the first time at the Phimeanakas (*see* §(ii)(c) above), were extended in later temples into an elaborate and ingenious system of interlinked passageways. Corner pavilions were built at the points of intersection, and on the axial entrances there were numerous doorways and porticos, often made up of several parts and having side wings. The most important innovation of the Angkor Vat style is the cruciform forecourt supported by covered galleries with pillars. This is found most notably at Beng Mealea, Phimai, Preah Palilay and Angkor Vat (see fig. 9). The exteriors of the barrel-vaulted roofs were decorated with snake motifs running down in parallel lines, each ending in a small hood with a tiny *garuḍa* figure in it. The walls might have blind or real windows on one or both sides, with balusters that, in the estimation of many scholars, are the finest in Khmer art. Some of the galleries had wide vaults supported on the inner side by a wall and on the other by a single or double row of pillars. The wall, being thus illuminated by natural light, would be decorated with bas-reliefs. This type of gallery, which first appears at Beng Mealea and was perfected at Banteay Samré and Angkor Vat, can also be found in buildings in the subsequent Bayon style.

Ceremonial causeways and terraces raised on square or octagonal pillars are also characteristic of the Angkor Vat style. They are found most frequently at Beng Mealea; at Chau Say Tevoda they are square, and at Angkor Vat both square and octagonal pillars occur. The terraces are in the shape of a Latin cross (with a longer upright) and interrupt

9. Angkor Vat, Angkor, aerial view of cruciform galleries from the north-east, early 12th century

the causeway in front of the main entrance of the sanctuary. They are further elaborated with projecting and recessed parts. The causeways and terraces are flanked by *nāga* balustrades and completely paved with stone slabs. Such paving, which had been occasionally used since the 11th century, was now used consistently. A wide moat formed the outermost enclosure of the temple complex, outside a wall punctuated by axial entrances that in turn enclosed the rectangular temple precinct; the doorway of the main entrance was of special grandeur. The main sanctuary was not placed at the dead centre of the rectangle, but slightly nearer the back on the side opposite the main entrance. Each of the three concentric galleries within the enclosure was likewise set back a little. This remarkable architectural subtlety has the effect of preventing the viewer who approaches the monument slowly from gaining the impression that the walls and the tower are leaning towards him. It shows, moreover, that the temple complexes were designed to be viewed from a specific, ideal vantage point.

(d) Architectural decoration. As Boisselier has pointed out, a precise indication of the date of a Khmer building can often be gained from a careful analysis of the decorative elements of its parts. Traditionally, each architectural feature bears certain decorative motifs, for example the lintels above doors generally have vine decoration and the pilasters on either side of them foliage, and changes in these, although they are often only detectable in minute details, make it possible not only to distinguish between styles but to establish the chronological sequence of buildings within a style. Throughout the history of Khmer art the decoration of doorways has received special attention, in particular the lintels, colonnettes, pilasters and, in the case of false doors, sunken panels at the sides. In the Angkor Vat style they are given very diverse treatment, being sometimes overladen with detail but usually very carefully executed.

The lintels of Angkor Vat and Thommanon frequently show scenes, while at Beng Mealea they show only a single vine. This vine, with four U-curves, is essentially the same as those found on lintels in the Baphuon style of the 11th century but is more complex, as it is enriched with a multitude of tiny human figures that sometimes also appear on pediments, pilasters and socles at the bases of columns. At Beng Mealea and Banteay Samré *haṁsa*s (sacred geese) with crests are to be seen at the centre of the vine or within its loops, a motif also characteristic of the subsequent Bayon style. These motifs are found on most door lintels of the Angkor Vat style, and they continue into the early Bayon style. A new feature of the Angkor Vat style is the lintel without the vine motif; it is embellished instead with vertical, parallel scrolls of foliage. This motif disappears after Angkor Vat but recurs in a similar form in the second phase of the Bayon style.

The colonnettes of the Angkor Vat style are the most profusely decorated in the whole of Khmer art. They have up to ten rings, each one clearly articulated. The deeply recessed smooth sections are decorated with tiny zigzag leaf motifs. There are only a few deviations from this type, for example at Preah Palilay, where relatively large smooth sections similar to those of the 10th-century Banteay Srei style are found, and at Angkor Vat, where some of the colonnettes have sixteen sides instead of eight, so that they appear almost round.

Throughout the period of the Angkor Vat and Bayon styles, the carved tympana in the pediments over the doors or on the gables of the stepped roofs always depict a scene that may be either a unified composition or divided into registers. The pediment arches, which are always trilobate, can be dated more precisely. The smooth arches ending directly in a many-headed *nāga* hood, characteristic of the Baphuon style, disappear at the beginning of the Angkor Vat style and become convex, with leaf ornamentation in relief. At their ends the five-headed *nāga*s emerge again from the mouths of *makara*, with neck ruffs, stylized fins and a forked tongue. On some temples, for example Thommanon and Chau Say Tevoda, the snakes have pearl necklaces with pendants round their necks, and their mouths are narrowed into snouts, in a manner typical of the Bayon style. In Khmer iconography, the snake, living in the underworld and gaining access to the human world through water, has a primordial place, and its wide hood with several heads is therefore one of the most common decorative motifs in Khmer architecture. Also characteristic of the Angkor Vat style are the small figures incorporated into the lancet-leaf ornamentation on the outer edges of the pediment arches.

A reliable aid to dating is provided by the ridge at the base of the pediment, which in the Angkor Vat style is bent down at right angles at the corners, while the ornamental bands run straight on, whereas in the Bayon style it is bent down at an oblique angle and the ornamental bands grow steadily narrower. Other decorative elements that can be adduced for dating include the vertical ridge with flower ornamentation (*hampe à fleuron*) forming a chevron with the leaves projecting at the sides, which appears on doorway pilasters and is repeated at regular intervals. In the Angkor Vat style it is shorter than in the Baphuon style and has a small figure in its upper part. In the Bayon style it is formed in exactly the same way, but the leaf arches at Angkor Vat curl upwards, whereas they curl downwards at the Bayon. Scenic depictions on the bases of pilasters are frequent in the Angkor Vat style and become the rule in the Bayon style.

Wall decoration is in very shallow relief, no longer reminiscent of wood-carving, as in earlier buildings, but rather of elaborate embroidery. Rosettes, diamonds or chevrons are repeated at regular intervals. The centre of the design is often a grimacing *kala* head, which first appeared in the 9th century and is frequently employed as a symbol of protection and good fortune, its fearsome appearance being intended to drive away evil spirits. The pair of additional fangs jutting vertically from the corners of the mouth provides a sure means of dating, as these first occur in the Angkor Vat period and become universal in the Bayon style. Another typical decorative motif found on door and window jambs and many pilasters consists of vine scrolls encircling figural scenes from the Hindu epics and mythology, in which the figures can be identified individually.

BIBLIOGRAPHY

J. de Mecquenem: 'Les Bâtiments annexés de Ben Mala', *Bull. Ecole Fr. Extrême-Orient*, xiii/2 (1913), pp. 1–22

H. Marchal: 'Le Temple de Prah Palilay', *Bull. Ecole Fr. Extrême-Orient*, xxii (1922), pp. 101–34

G. Coedès, L. Finot and V. Goloubew: *Le Temple d'Angkor Vat*, 7 vols, Pubns Ecole Fr. Extrême-Orient (Paris, 1929–32), ii

F. D. K. Bosch: 'Notes archéologiques, IV: Le Temple d'Angkor Vat', *Bull. Ecole Fr. Extrême-Orient*, xxxii (1932), pp. 7–21

G. Coedès: 'Angkor Vat, temple ou tombe?', *Bull. Ecole Fr. Extrême-Orient*, xxxiii (1933), pp. 303–9

G. de Coral Rémusat: *L'Art khmer: Les Grandes Etapes de son évolution* (Paris, 1940, 2/1951)

J. Boisselier: 'Běň Mālā et la chronologie des monuments du style d'Aṅkor Vat', *Bull. Ecole Fr. Extrême-Orient*, xlvi (1952), pp. 187-226

G. Nafilyan: *Angkor Vat: Description graphique du temple*, Pubns Ecole Fr. Extrême-Orient, Mémoire Archéologique, iv (Paris, 1969)

WIBKE LOBO

*(iv) Late Angkor period (*c. *1181–*c. *1431).* Three phases can be discerned in the development of architectural style during the extraordinary burst of frenzied building activity that marked the reign of Jayavarman VII (*reg* 1181–*c.* 1220). From his death until the abandonment of Angkor soon after the Thai invasion of 1431–2, only a few stone buildings were erected and those few of only minor importance.

(a) Introduction. (b) *c.* 1181–*c.* 1191. (c) *c.* 1191–*c.* 1200. (d) *c.* 1200–*c.* 1220. (e) *c.* 1220–*c.* 1431.

(a) Introduction. It is probable that when Angkor was sacked by the Chams in 1177, the future King Jayavarman VII was in the neighbourhood of the temple of Preah Khan of Kompong Svay in Kompong Thom Province, about 100 km east of Beng Mealea, awaiting a propitious moment to intervene and establish his authority by force of arms over Angkor and the Khmer empire. This he seems to have achieved by 1181, the year of his consecration as supreme ruler, at the age of about 50. He immediately embarked upon an ambitious building programme, establishing new foundations and renovating and adapting old ones throughout the empire, and this programme continued until the end of his long reign, culminating in the Bayon, the great temple-mountain at the centre of his capital, Angkor Thom, that gave its name to the style of the whole reign. At the same time, Jayavarman VII reorganized the Khmer state and the monarchy on a new religious basis by instituting Mahayana Buddhism as the state religion, and this led to important changes in both the design and the decoration of religious monuments, giving them a grandeur and an ebullience they had never before attained. It is probable also that from the outset of his reign Jayavarman VII, like his predecessors, undertook a number of public works, such as the digging of reservoirs and the construction or restoration of roads and canals.

At the beginning of the reign, architecture continued in the style of Angkor Vat, but before long decoration began to assume more importance than design, which lost its sense of grandeur and proportion and became concerned chiefly with facile effects of sheer size. At the same time, the human scale, so well understood in the art of Angkor Vat, tended to be replaced by an exaggerated symbolism. Khmer architecture had always been strongly symbolical, but nothing on the colossal scale of the buildings of the ambitious and profoundly religious Jayavarman VII had ever been attempted before. His monuments were the expression of a centralized authority and an omnipresent state in which the religion of the mass of the people seems to have played little part.

(b) c. *1181*–c. *1191.* This period may be defined as a period of homage to the ancestors. It began with the consecration of Jayavarman VII as supreme ruler of the Khmer empire *c.* 1181 and ended with the establishment of Buddhism as the state religion *c.* 1191. The architecture of this period followed the style of Angkor Vat and was largely confined to foundations in honour of the King's parents and his guru (spiritual teacher). According to an inscription, at the very beginning of his reign he built the temple of Banteay Kdei at Angkor in honour of his guru. This temple is not a temple-mountain, but a 'flat' temple built entirely at ground-level (see fig. 10). It is orientated to the east and opens on to the reservoir of Sras Sang. It was extended after 1191 by the construction of an outer enclosure, and after 1220 by the addition of a gallery and halls or chapels containing images.

In 1186 Jayavarman VII founded the temple-monastery of Ta Prohm, dedicated to his mother (see fig. 11). It is situated to the north-west of Banteay Kdei and is also a 'flat' temple and, like Banteay Kdei, it was extended by the addition of an enclosure surrounding the monastery domain and of a gallery and chapels during the second and third periods of Jayavarman VII's reign. In 1191 Jayavarman VII founded the temple of Preah Khan (*see* ANGKOR, §2(iv)), which he dedicated to his father, Dharanindravarman II. In plan Preah Khan is similar to Ta Prohm, but unlike Ta Prohm it was all built at the same time within an enclosure surrounded by a wall decorated with monumental figures of *garuḍa*s in the guise of telamones. At Preah Khan for the first time the causeways leading to the fourth enclosure were flanked by 108 giants holding *nāga*s. This is an allusion to the 108 revolutions of the cosmos. At about the same time work was begun on the important temple of Preah Khan of Kompong Svay. This is the earliest Khmer temple to have a sanctuary with a superstructure decorated with a colossal face on each of its four sides representing the omnipresence both of the compassionate *bodhisattva* Lokeshvara and of the king, and it is indeed the first occurrence of these 'face-towers' in Khmer architecture. Probably also dating from this period is the first form of the exquisite, small sanctuary known as Neak Pean (Coiled Serpents) after the *nāga*s coiled round its base (see fig. 12). Situated in the middle of the *baray* that adjoins Preah Khan to the east, it stands in the middle of an axial pool flanked by four smaller pools, the whole symbolizing the cosmic Lake Anavatapta, from which the four great rivers of the universe spring. Facing the sanctuary in the first pool is a figure of the horse Balaha, an avatar of Lokeshvara. The other temples built during this first period, such as Ta Som, Banteay Prei and Ta Nei, are less important.

(c) c. *1191*–c. *1200.* This period is characterized by the profound cultural changes that accompanied the establishment of Buddhism as the state religion in 1191. It is not known whether Jayavarman VII was converted to Buddhism by masters from Nalanda in Bengal who had been

10. Banteay Kdei, Angkor, east entrance pavilion, late 12th century to the early 13th

11. Ta Prohm, Angkor, west entrance pavilion and causeway, mid-12th century to the early 13th

12. Neak Pean, Angkor, view from the south, late 12th century

13. The Bayon, Angkor Thom, general view from the east, late 12th century

forced to leave about 1190 by the advent of Islam, but it was they who taught the Mahayana Buddhist doctrine, with Sanskrit as its sacred language and with special emphasis on honouring Lokeshvara and Prajnaparamita. Jayavarman VII rallied his subjects round these new religious ideas, which were given expression in the architecture of this second and highly innovative period of his reign. Major royal building schemes were inaugurated throughout the empire, and the use of architectural symbolism on a gigantic scale was further developed. The chief manifestations of this symbolism in the architecture of this period are the face-towers representing the omnipresence of Buddhism and of the ruler, and the causeways bordered by 108 giants holding the cosmic *nāga*.

The rebuilding of the city of Angkor Thom (*see* ANGKOR, §2(v)) was probably begun early in Jayavarman VII's reign, but it was only in the second period that it acquired its final form as a fortified city. The enclosure, which is about 3 km square, is surrounded by a rampart 7.8 m high with a road running round the inside. Access to the city is by means of gates surmounted by three face-towers on the axis of each of the four sides. A fifth gate, now called the Gate of Victories, leads on the east side to the Royal Palace. On the axis of each gate, raised 200 m above the moat, is a causeway flanked on either side by 54 colossal statues—on the left 54 *devatā*s (deities) and on the right 54 *asura*s (demons)—holding under their arms the body of a *nāga*.

At the same time, Jayavarman VII began the construction of the Bayon (see fig. 13), his temple-mountain dedicated to the Buddha. The Bayon is his most astonishing creation and the most complete expression of monumental symbolism, as well as being perhaps the finest of all surviving Khmer temples, with its 54 towers and 192 faces looking out to the four quarters. It has three quadrangular enclosures, of which the innermost one has a cruciform plan. The central sanctuary is built on a circular plan and rises 43 m above the causeway leading up to it. It originally housed at its centre a statue of the Buddha in meditation seated on the *nāga*, perhaps a portrait-statue of Jayavarman VII himself (Phnom Penh, N. Mus.). It only reached its final form in the third period of Jayavarman VII's reign (*see* §(d) below).

The major monument of this period is unquestionably the great temple of Banteay Chhmar in the far north-west of Cambodia, built by the king in memory of his son, killed in battle. It is a huge temple, laid out, like Ta Prohm and Preah Khan, on a single level, with four enclosures, the outermost one measuring about 2.0×2.5 km. It contains face-towers and is approached by causeways flanked by 108 giants. The second enclosure is similar to the third enclosure of Angkor Vat and is decorated with a continuous bas-relief. Unusually, the entire temple complex was built at the same time and therefore has an exceptional degree of stylistic unity.

During this period many additions were made to earlier temples, for example the outer enclosures of Preah Khan of Kompong Svay, Banteay Kdei, Ta Prohm, Ta Nei, Ta Som and Vat Nokor, and the chapels of the 102 hospitals built by Jayavarman VII and of the 120 travellers' rest-houses (*dharmaśālā*) at the staging posts on the great roads traversing the empire.

(d) c. 1200–c. 1220. The third period of the art of Jayavarman VII's reign begins a little after 1200 and ends with his death *c.* 1220. It is marked by the completion of the Bayon and the laying out of the Royal Square. The numerous additions and modifications made to earlier temples in this period, often carried out hastily and clumsily, had a coarsening effect on the architecture.

The base of the Bayon was initially in the form of a Greek cross surrounded by an inner enclosure on the same plan. Soon after, this base was raised and enlarged, the outside corners were blocked by galleries set at right angles to form a rectangle, 70×80 m, constituting a second enclosure attached to the *gopura*s of the first enclosure, which are thus shared between the two enclosures. The whole was then surrounded by a third gallery forming another enclosure, 140×160 m, which was entirely covered with sculptures in bas-relief.

Meanwhile, 16 small passage halls with vestibules at either end were built between the two galleries, probably before the execution of the bas-reliefs of the third enclosure, as is demonstrated by the constricted style of the relief-carving to the right of the doors leading into the halls. In the middle a colossal sanctuary was built on a circular plan with 12 radiating chapels round it, each of which contained the image of a high dignitary of the kingdom, who thus became associated with the royal cult that the Bayon embodied. Each sanctuary and chapel is surmounted by a tower, 54 in all, with the faces of Lokeshvara on them in the image of the king facing the four quarters and omnipresent in his kingdom and the world. In the most important provincial temples this royal presence was embodied in the portrait-statues of the king that were placed there.

In the last years of his reign Jayavarman VII also laid out the Royal Square to the north of Bayon. This consists mainly of the terraces in front of the Royal Palace and the Terrace of the Leper King, extending about 300 m to the north. The terraces of the Royal Palace, often called the Terraces of the Elephants, located on either side of a central stairway, are decorated with standing *garuḍa*s and lions, which indicate that the terraces formed the base of a royal tribune. The Terrace of the Leper King, situated immediately to the north and forming an extension to the Terraces of the Elephants, is of more modest dimensions. It consists of a redented block 25 m square and is supported by two parallel walls 6 m high with a space of 600 mm between them. The two walls are entirely covered with sculpture. The wall behind has reliefs of deities carrying in their headdresses numerous *nāga*s, and at regular intervals there are *nāga* images with seven or nine heads. Probably the sole purpose of this hidden wall was to symbolize the subterranean worlds, unless it was part of an earlier terrace that was later enlarged, following the Khmers' frequent practice of modifying the design of their buildings during construction. The precise function of the terrace has never been established, but there are strong grounds for believing it was used for royal cremations.

This last period of Jayavarman VII's reign was also marked by the addition to many temples of chapels, passage-halls and galleries surrounding or connecting enclosures. These additions seem to have been hastily and inexpertly executed and have the effect of giving the plan of the temples a cluttered and labyrinthine appearance.

(e) c. *1220*–c. *1431.* In spite of some signs of revival at the end of Jayavarman VII's reign, the architecture of that period was essentially the expression of the will of one man, and after his death no major monuments were built at Angkor. It seems that from the mid-13th century the Khmers lacked both the means and the religious fervour necessary to carry out ambitious building schemes. A further change in the state religion from Mahayana to Theravada Buddhism led to important changes in religious architecture. Buildings were no longer designed to enhance the power of the king or of his god nor to perpetuate the royal personality cult, which had hitherto been expressed by the use of durable materials. On the contrary, the need of the new religion was for places where monks and laypeople could meet for prayer in the presence of an image of the Buddha. The durability of such buildings was unimportant and so it did not matter what material was used to construct them.

There was already a tendency before the end of Jayavarman VII's reign to add to temple buildings a proliferation of timber-frame structures with tiled roofs. Since these met the requirements of the new style of religious worship admirably, they were soon generally adopted; thereafter, all buildings were made of light materials. The ravages of the climate, of insects and of man have ensured that no trace of them remains except their stone bases, which are difficult to date, for example the Buddhist terraces of Angkor Thom, Tep Pranam and Preah Pithu or Temple 486. An idea of their architecture can, however, be gained from the representations of buildings in the bas-reliefs of the Bayon and Banteay Chhmar.

Only two small buildings dating from this period have survived. The first of these is Temple 487, usually called the Mangalartha, built in the reign of Jayavarman VIII (*reg c.* 1243–95), who, unlike his predecessors, was a Hindu. The Mangalartha is possibly a reconstruction on the site of an older temple dating from the reign of Yashovarman I. It is in the north-east quarter of Angkor Thom, between the Avenue of Death and the Avenue of Victory. According to an inscription dated 1295, it is dedicated to his mother and to a Brahman named Jaya Mangalartha ('Prince of Professors'), a dignitary of high rank, signally honoured by several Khmer rulers, whom he had served during a long life of 104 years. The Mangalartha, which is built entirely of sandstone, is orientated to the east on a cruciform plan with four foreparts preceded on the east by a vestibule. It has a number of features characteristic of the third period of the Bayon style. The iconography is both Buddhist and Brahmanic, demonstrating the habitual tendency of the Khmers towards religious syncretism.

Like the Mangalartha, the second small monument, which is identified only by the number 486, is within the city of Angkor Thom and is also a reconstruction of an earlier monument, perhaps dating from the 10th century. Again like the Mangalartha, its iconography is both Buddhist and Brahmanic. Behind the sanctuary is a badly ruined building in which some colonnettes and lintels of pink sandstone in the style of Banteay Srei (late 10th century) have been incorporated. There are two other late sanctuaries, one on either side of the central sanctuary. In front of the temple is a terrace that appears to have had a Buddhist function, as it is surrounded by *sema* (sacred boundary stones). It probably formed the base of a wooden structure that has disappeared.

BIBLIOGRAPHY

H. Dufour and others: *Le Bayon d'Angkor Thom*, 2 vols (Paris, 1910–14)

L. Finot and V. Goloubew: 'Le Symbolisme de Neak Pean', *Bull. Ecole Fr. Extrême-Orient*, xxiii (1923), pp. 401–5

P. Stern: 'Le Bayon d'Angkor et l'évolution de l'art khmer', *An. Mus. Guimet*, xlvii (Paris, 1927)

P. Mus: *Symbolisme à Angkor Thom: Le 'Grand Miracle' du Bayon* (Paris, 1936)
——: *Les Monuments khmers du style du Bayon et Jayavarman VII*, Pubns Ecole Fr. Extrême-Orient (Paris, 1965)
J. Dumarçay: *Le Bayon*, 2 vols, Pubns Ecole Fr. Extrême-Orient, iii (Paris, 1967–73)

(v) Post-Angkor period (after c. *1431).*

(a) *c.* 1431–*c.* 1863. (b) After *c.* 1863.

(a) c. *1431–*c. *1863.* The post-Angkor period, between the capture of Angkor in 1431 and the establishment of the French protectorate in 1863, was a time of great confusion and there are almost no surviving traces of its architecture apart from a few stupas and a number of monasteries, of which even the oldest barely date back further than the second half of the 19th century. Royal residences were built as the king and his court moved from one place to another, and their existence was recorded by both 16th- and 17th-century European travellers and in the royal chronicles. These indicate that there were royal palaces, or residences at Srei Santhor, at Udong and then in 1528 in the reign of King Ang Chan I (*reg c.* 1510–*c.* 1560) at Lovek, and again at Udong, where King Chei Chettha II (*reg* 1618–22) took refuge in 1620. It was he who gave the site the name of Udong. King Ang Eng (*reg* 1779–96) had his royal palace built there in 1794, and he made the city the capital of the kingdom, which it remained until the French protectorate was ratified in 1864. The only surviving evidence of these royal residences is provided by a few land surveys, such as the one made at Lovek, which mentions the enclosure, and a few basins which have more or less completely silted up. The references to them in travellers' accounts are too brief to provide any precise information, and it is therefore not possible to speak about their architecture, even by extrapolation.

The problem posed by the Buddhist monasteries is different. Although no traces survive from this period, their appearance can easily be deduced from the evidence of the monasteries dating from the late 19th century which are reconstructions of older monasteries that had been destroyed. These monasteries were generally established, wherever possible, in the immediate vicinity of an ancient temple, and often in fact actually integrated into an existing temple, as in the case of Angkor Vat, Bakong, Lolei or Ta Prohm in Bati. The main building (Skt *vihāra*) at Vat Prasat Andet, for example, was built adjoining the 7th-century AD shrine, and at Vat Prasat Phum Prasat, which dates from 706, a monastery was constructed at the beginning of the 20th century. Buddhist monasteries usually comprise a group of buildings set together inside an enclosure which is either of masonry or built in the form of a stockade. The group includes the living quarters for the monks, the *kuti*, and one or more *sala* or pavilions, almost invariably open-sided, which are used for assemblies of monks and worshippers. Some *sala* may also be used by the monks for teaching children to read and write. The group also includes the *vihāra*, the principal building of the monastery complex, where images of the Buddha are housed and religious ceremonies are celebrated. The *vihāra* is usually richly decorated and consists essentially of a large rectangular hall on an east–west orientation and open at its eastern end. It is usually built in the south-eastern quadrant of the monastery. It has a central nave, usually with a ceiling, flanked by low sides or *robieng*, recalling the central gallery of the cruciform cloister of the second enclosure of the temple of Angkor Vat. On the outside, a peristyle or portico runs round the whole building, which is set on top of a masonry base. The roof is built with two slopes in layers exactly like the roof of a classical Khmer temple. It has gables with pediments and tympana, which are usually decorated with relief sculptures in the traditional style of classical Khmer architecture. The interior walls and ceilings are often painted in a manner suggesting a strong Thai influence.

Khmer monasteries usually have a number of stupas, the base of which may either be laid out in the form of a redented square or a circle. In Cambodia, as in Thailand, their dominant line is vertical, with a bell-shaped *aṇḍa* (main body) and numerous stylized parasols. The base is imposingly high and forms an important part of the whole. The stupa is by definition a memorial monument, either because it houses funerary remains or relics or because it is associated with the memory of a place. It is therefore often the oldest building in the monastery. Stupas are usually built out of brick covered with plaster. One of the oldest stupas in Cambodia is the Phnom Stupa in Phnom Penh, which is thought to date from the 16th century. It was restored in 1816 by King Ang Chan II (*reg* 1806–34) and again in 1890–94. It is said to house the remains of Lady Penh, the founder of the city. There is also a stupa at Srei Santhor which dates from the same period. The late stupa built close to the eastern part of the third enclosure of Angkor Vat dates from 1702. The royal stupas of Udong, which date from the mid-19th century, have bases in the form of a redented square, a clearly marked *harmika* (box-like element, sometimes colonnaded, between the base and the spire of the stupa) and a prominent *chattravali* (triple parasol) above, which reveal the influence of Thai art of the Ayutthaya and Ratanakosin periods.

Since nothing except these few stupas has survived, it is only possible to advance hypotheses concerning the architecture of this period. It may be assumed that the influence of Ayutthaya was strong and that it combined with local architectural traditions directly derived from classical Khmer art, particularly with regard to the wooden architecture that was used in association with stone architecture in the temples of the Angkor period.

(b) After c. *1863.* After the French protectorate was established in 1863 Cambodia entered a period of peace and renewal. The country was opened up to the influence of Western culture and the European economy. In 1865 the royal palace was established in Phnom Penh, thus marking its birth as the country's first great city since the fall of Angkor. Both the sovereign and the French administration supported the establishment of Phnom Penh as the capital. The city was laid out in the French style, with wide avenues running along the axes formed by public buildings or by monuments and creating handsome vistas. The development of Phnom Phenh prompted a renaissance of fine architecture in Cambodia.

Until the 1880s, architecture remained essentially traditional and wood continued to be the principal building material; even the royal palace was built in light materials. It was not until the 1890s that the first Western-style buildings in masonry and concrete appeared. From this point onwards the two types of architecture developed in parallel. Although traditional architecture in wood was progressively revitalized, the use of wood for walls was gradually replaced by masonry joined with mortar and by structures in reinforced concrete. The traditional tiled roofs, however, remained unchanged and were either left in their natural colour or painted and varnished.

The royal palace, which was originally built of wood in the 1870s, was rebuilt in more durable materials by King Sisovath (*reg* 1904–27). Work started in 1907 and the palace was inaugurated on 16 May 1919. Its architecture was purely traditional, with layered roofs, ridge-poles ending in double curves, pediments with curves and counter-curves and multicoloured, varnished, tiling. The whole could have been an illustration for the descriptions of the monuments of Angkor at the end of the 14th century by the Chinese chronicler Zhou Daguan. It was restored for the return of Prince Norodom Sihanouk to Cambodia in 1991. Vat Peah Keo (also known as the Silver Pagoda because its floor is made of sheets of silver) was built by order of King Norodom (*reg* 1860–1904) in 1902 in the immediate vicinity of the royal palace. It is an elegant and well-proportioned building. The monastery of Vat Botum Vodei was built a little further away but also in line with the royal palace. It dates from between 1868 and 1874 and is a reconstruction of an earlier pagoda on the same site. The pagoda of Vat Onalum, the home of the Mohanikay sect, which is the largest in Cambodia, is more recent, but it too is built to a purely traditional architectural design, as indeed are most modern religious edifices in Cambodia. Other buildings belonging to this current traditional architecture include the National Museum designed and executed by George Groslier. Work started on this site in 1917 and it was officially inaugurated in 1920. The National Museum not only houses a fine collection of Khmer art but is itself a notably successful work of art with a design admirably suited to its function. Another striking modern building in traditional style is the Buddhist Institute, opened in 1930.

14. Vann Molyvann: Chakdomukh Hall, Phnom Penh, 1962

A style of colonial architecture imported directly from Europe and particularly from France also developed in Cambodia during this period. Some colonial buildings were ill-adapted to the constraints of the climatic conditions of Cambodia, but they had the merit of disseminating modern construction techniques and providing examples of new forms which revitalized traditional art. A good example of this is the pavilion donated to Cambodia by France *c.* 1876. It is a light construction, executed in metal, standing within the enclosure of the royal palace. The city's main post office is thought to date from the last few years of the 19th century, and its architecture is typical of a certain colonial style of that period.

Several striking buildings were erected during the 1930s, including the Hôtel Royal, which was heavily influenced by contemporary French construction in Vietnam. With its overhanging roof, this building remains a milestone in the history of Phnom Penh's architecture and urban development. Almost contemporary with the Hôtel Royal is the central market, which was built between 1934 and 1935. Though its construction was thought to be too ambitious at the time, it is now barely adequate to meet present needs. In the fashion of its day, the market is somewhat Germanic in appearance, and its completely open reinforced concrete structure is well suited to the local climate. It has a cruciform layout with four identical sections and can easily accommodate the milling crowds typical of an Asian market-place. The same design was also used very successfully for a market in Kompong Cham. Two other important buildings of imported architectural design belonging to this period in Phnom Penh are the railway station, which is in the style of the French railway stations of the 1930s, and the cathedral, which had no well-defined architecture or style and was destroyed during the Pol Pot regime.

These two architectural currents were combined under the influence of the French-trained Vann Molyvann (*b* 1926), who came to dominate architecture in Cambodia in the second half of the 20th century. He studied at the Ecole Nationale Supérieure des Beaux-Arts in Paris and took the prize for the best foreign diploma of his year before returning to Cambodia, where Prince Norodom Sihanouk gave him the position and the means to generate a renaissance in modern Khmer architecture. His work attempts both to forge links with the ancient traditions of Angkor and to translate those traditional forms into a modern architectural language, while at the same time taking account of the constraints of the Cambodian climate. His first work was the Independence Monument, a handsome academic exercise, the most outstanding feature of which is the way it reproduces a Khmer sanctuary tower (*prasat*) on exactly the right scale for the crossroads it adorns. It reveals a sense of the monumental worthy of his predecessors and was the promising beginning of a whole series of exceptional construction projects. In 1962 Molyvann designed the Chakdomukh Hall (see fig. 14), for which he made use of a series of triangular pediments, derived from the traditional Khmer temple roof. Its good natural ventilation means that it can be used at all times of the year without air-conditioning. In 1963–4 he executed the National Sports Complex, with its 60,000 capacity stadium, eight tennis courts, gymnasium, sports centre and 4,000 capacity Olympic swimming pool. This was perhaps his most Khmer achievement; its vistas and ornamental ponds, its embankments, terraces and staircases combine to make it strikingly reminiscent of the great temple complexes of Angkor. It was officially opened by Prince Norodom Sihanouk on 12 Dec 1964. In 1965–6 Molyvann built the Kompong Sam State Brewery, in which for the first time in Cambodia he introduced suspended structures, and in 1966 the Chamcar Mon State Palace for official receptions by the head of state. This building is regarded by many as one of the finest expressions of the new Khmer architecture. In 1967–8 Molyvann was responsible for the Municipal Theatre, with its 1600 seats and a stage facing in two directions so that it can be used for either indoor or outdoor performances. The building has excellent natural ventilation. In the great entrance hall on the first floor, one wall has an opening at eye-level which stretches the whole length of the façade and gives a panoramic view of the mouth of the four branches of the Mekong River.

Two other Cambodian architects deserve mention. Lu Ban Hap (*b* 1931) designed and executed the Cambodiana Hotel complex on the banks of the Mekong. Work began on this site between 1967 and 1968, but it was only completed in 1992. The architecture of this hotel is an attempt to combine traditional roof shapes with a modern outline. Oug Sadam (*b* 1943), who graduated from the Ecole Nationale Supérieure des Beaux-Arts in Paris, has executed several designs for branches of the Inadanajati Bank, as well as private houses in a more overtly modern style.

GUY NAFILYAN

2. DOMESTIC. The simplest Khmer house is rectangular in plan with an area of about 60 sq. m and is built on wooden stilts to avoid flooding. The interior is not partitioned unless there is a newly born child, when the mother and child are temporarily separated from the rest of the family by a partition in a corner. The floor has several levels; the kitchen is on the upper part, and smoke from the hearth escapes through the thatched roof. Openings that serve as windows are made in the bamboo matting walls (see fig. 15). The dwellings of the wealthy are more complex in plan, though still rectangular (up to 100 sq. m) and raised on stilts. In front, on one of the short sides, is an open terrace, also on stilts, which leads into the main room. All the other rooms open on to this and some also lead into each other. Individual rooms serve no specified purpose; the inhabitants of the house occupy them as they see fit. Wealthier families, however, have their kitchen in a separate building outside. Partitions and external walls are made of vertical planks nailed on to joists that also hold the doors and windows in place. On the finest houses, if they are of sufficient height, the outsides of the windows have a fretwork pediment. The stringers of the access stairways are decorated with either the bodies of *nāga*s or volutes. The gables are also decorated, occasionally with a fine design of foliated scrolls

15. Village houses of wood and thatch, near Siem Reap, Cambodia

but more often with decorative beamwork usually associated with larger buildings. Inside, the beamwork is partly hidden by a wooden ceiling that is sometimes painted with large geometric or floral designs with lotus-flowers. Outside the windows, which open inward, is a small wooden balustrade resting on a base, visible both outside and inside, which represents the extremities of an animal, ending in either the claws of a tiger or the talons of a bird of prey. In mountain areas the houses are usually small (60 sq. m or less), but they sometimes have an upper storey. The area between the ceiling and the roof forms a loft where the men in the family sleep.

BIBLIOGRAPHY

M. Giteau: 'Un Court Traité d'architecture cambodgienne moderne', *A. Asiat.*, xxiv (1971), pp. 103–48

J. Dumarçay: *Charpentes et tuiles khmères* (Paris, 1973)

——: *The House in South-east Asia*, ed. and trans. M. Smithies (Singapore, 1987)

J. DUMARÇAY

III. Sculpture.

The fine quality and originality of Khmer Hindu and Buddhist sculpture, in both stone and bronze, both free-standing and in relief, from the late Funan period in the mid-6th century AD through the Angkor period and beyond, is generally recognized, but its stylistic evolution and consequently its dating have been the subject of much argument, and its chronology difficult to establish. However, following the pioneer work of Philippe Stern, Pierre Dupont and Gilberte de Coral Rémusat in the 1920s, refined in the 1950s by Jean Boisselier, it has been possible to classify most Khmer sculptures according to the same stylistic periods established for architecture. (The decoration of architectural elements, e.g. lintels, is discussed in §II, 1 above.)

BIBLIOGRAPHY

J. Commaille: 'Notes sur la décoration cambodgienne', *Bull. Ecole Fr. Extrême-Orient*, xiii/3 (1913), pp. 1–34

G. Groslier: 'Les Collections khmères du Musée Albert Sarraut à Phnom Penh', *A. Asiatiques.*, xvi (1927) [whole issue]; as book (Paris, 1931)

G. de Coral Rémusat: *L'Art khmer: Les Grandes Etapes de son évolution* (Paris, 1940, 2/1951)

J. Boisselier: 'Garuda dans l'art khmer', *Bull. Ecole Fr. Extrême-Orient*, xliv (1951), pp. 55–87

H. Marchal: *Le Décor et la sculpture khmère* (Paris, 1951)

J. Boisselier: *La Statuaire khmère et son évolution*, 2 vols, Pubns Ecole Fr. Extrême-Orient, xxxvii (Saigon, 1955)

——: *Tendances de l'art khmer* (Paris, 1956); Eng. trans., rev. and ed. by N. Eilenberg and M. Elliott (Ithaca, NY, 1989)

M. Giteau: *Guide du Musée National, I: Sculpture* (Phnom Penh, 1960)

——: *Khmer Sculpture and the Angkor Civilization* (Fribourg, Paris and New York, 1965)
J. Boisselier: 'Notes sur l'art du bronze dans l'ancien Cambodge', *Artibus Asiae*, xxix (1968), pp. 275–334
S. E. Lee: *Ancient Cambodian Sculpture* (New York, 1969)
Das Zeitlose Bildnis: Plastische Kunst der Khmer und Thai/Sculptures of the Khmer and Thai (exh. cat. by Piriya Krairiksh, Cologne, Rautenstrauch-Joest-Mus., 1984) [bilingual text]
W. Felten and M. Lerner: *Thai and Cambodian Sculpture: From the 6th to the 14th Centuries* (London, 1989)
The Age of Angkor: Treasures from the National Museum of Cambodia (exh. cat. by M. Brand and Chuch Phoeurn, Canberra, N.G., 1992)

1. Pre-Angkor period (before *c.* 889). 2. Early Angkor period (*c.* 889–*c.* 1080). 3. Middle Angkor period (*c.* 1080–*c.* 1181): Angkor Vat style. 4. Bayon style (*c.* 1181–*c.* 1220). 5. After *c.* 1220.

1. PRE-ANGKOR PERIOD (BEFORE *c.* 889). The earliest surviving Cambodian sculptures, typically in sandstone, are thought to date from the 5th or 6th century AD; they are already mature works, technically sophisticated and often large in scale, suggesting that there may have been an earlier sculptural tradition in less permanent materials in the area. Two large wooden Buddha images (ex-N. Mus. S. Vietnam, Saigon) from southern Vietnam, thought by Groslier to date perhaps to the 4th or 5th century owing to their 'Gupta inspiration', provide evidence of this theory.

Although Buddhism appears to have played only a minor role in Cambodia until the reign of Jayavarman VII, the sculptures of the pre-Angkor period are both Hindu and Buddhist. The early Buddhist sculptures have not yet been systematically studied, and their dating is still rather uncertain, often based on similarities to Indian and Sri Lankan styles and images that are themselves not very precisely dated. Benisti attributed a more precise date of 750–820 to one of the major stone sculptures, the Avalokiteshvara of Rach Gia (Paris, Baronne Didelot priv. col.), through the similarity of the treatment of its necklace to architectural motifs, but this is an exceptional case. Our understanding of the dating and stylistic sequence of the Hindu images is much more precise, thanks to the studies of French scholars and especially to Boisselier's *La Statuaire khmère et son évolution* (1955). Boisselier's meticulous analysis of such details as garments, jewellery and hairstyles enabled him to establish a sequence of styles, which covers the period before the move of the capital by Yashovarman I (*reg* 889–*c.* 900) to Angkor: Phnom Da style (6th century); Sambor Prei Kuk style (first half of the 7th century); Prei Khmeng style (later 7th century); Prasat Andet style (late 7th century to early 8th); Kompong Preah style (8th century); Kulen style (mid-9th century); and Preah Ko style (last quarter of the 9th century). Sculptures relating to these styles have also been found in Thailand (Phra Kon Chai, Si Thep), Laos and Vietnam.

Despite the stylistic differences that mark these periods in the pre-Angkor Hindu sculptural tradition, the sculptures share a number of common characteristics. Even in this early period the Khmer sculptors were evidently determined to create sculpture in the round, despite the problems that this caused in carving stone images, especially multi-armed Hindu deities, and in contrast to their Indian models, where, until much later, stone sculpture was typically in high relief, with a stone stele used to give structural support to the figure. The sculpture from Vat Romlok of *Krishna Holding up Mt Govardhana* (Phnom Penh, N. Mus.) is a pre-Angkor example of this type of high-relief image, but it is an exception. The sculptors of the pre-Angkor period generally had to resort to horseshoe-shaped arches, arm props or other supports for multi-armed figures, but the sculptures still function satisfactorily as works in the round.

There is also a subtle realism in the sculpture of this period. This is clearly visible in the Krishna image, with its careful attention to anatomical proportion and the rendering of such features as the collar-bone, elbows, knees and ankles, and even including such details as tear-ducts. Nevertheless, this 'realism' is very simple and often stylized, and its total effect is of refined elegance and grace. The handling of the surface of the stone to represent skin is especially sophisticated and delicate. The broad, smooth areas of the torso and other planes of the body are subtly modelled and polished to produce an effect of tautness. The drapery is incised or carved in very low relief and clings to the body, clearly revealing the limbs below. The tension of the finished surface is barely disturbed by the details of garments or jewellery, again in strong contrast to the treatment of these details in contemporary Indian sculpture.

The image of Harihara from Asram Maharosei (sandstone, h. 1.68 m; Paris, Mus. Guimet), the half-Vishnu, half-Shiva deity popular at this period, dating from the mid-6th century and in the Phnom Da style, is a fine example of these general characteristics. The shoulders are broad, the hips narrow, the rather short legs slim, the smooth, somewhat abstract modelling of the torso emphasized by the fine polish. The pose is uncharacteristic, however; it is frontal, with virtually none of the sense of weight shift (the Indian *tribhaṅga* or triple flexion) that can be seen in such early pre-Angkor sculptures as the Rama and Balarama from Phnom Da, the Vishnu from Tuol Dai Buon and the Harihara and female torso from Sambor Prei Kuk (all Phnom Penh, N. Mus.). The quite realistic treatment of the fleshiness of the abdomen of the Asram Maharosei Harihara is slightly accentuated by the edge of the rectangular cloth garment or *sampot* worn low on the hips and tied in front. The crisp detailing of the garment, with its delicate folds on the right (Vishnu) and a feline head on the left (Shiva), creates an almost transparent effect. The face is oval, with a finely modelled aquiline nose and wide mouth. The eyes are elongated with lightly incised lids and pupils; the brows are subtly modelled. The total impression of serenity and elegance is emphasized by the fine polish of the stone and the delicate carving of a limited number of details.

The most important surviving images of the Sambor period are female, and these appear somewhat harder and more stylized in their treatment of the anatomy. The Lakshmi from Koh Krieng (Phnom Penh, N. Mus.) still conveys a sense of real fleshiness in contrast to the fine linear detail of the jewelled belt, hair and garment folds. Later male images still have broad shoulders and long, slim legs, as, for example, the elegant figure of Harihara in the Prasat Andet style (see fig. 16). The torso, hips and buttocks of this figure are slightly harder and heavier, but the modelling and sense of anatomy are still superb. The face is slightly more square-jawed than that of the earlier

16. Harihara, sandstone, h. 1.94 m, from Prasat Andet, late 7th century to the early 8th (Phnom Penh, National Museum)

Harihara and the eyes have rather heavy upper and lower lids that give the image a fixed stare, but the stylistic differences are confined chiefly to such details as the handling of the garment and the appearance of a moustache on the upper lip, the latter a characteristic of virtually all later Khmer male images. Other male sculptures of this period convey far less sense of weight shift and anatomical realism. The subdued realism found in 7th-century female images also decreases in the 8th century.

By the 9th century, Khmer sculptors had abandoned the horseshoe arch and other awkward supports and created free-standing images in the round; this development did, however, necessitate some thickening of the legs and ankles, which is echoed in the heavier torsos. The images are thus more powerful but less graceful and elegant. Two images in the Kulen style, the Vishnu of Prasat Damrei Krap (Phnom Penh, N. Mus.) and the torso of Vishnu (Paris, Mus. Guimet), are typical. The modelling of the muscles of the torso is more stylized, the total effect harder and less naturalistic. The folds of the *sampot* at the hips and the fastening are in higher relief. The modelling of the face is broader and the moustache is also in higher relief. The Preah Ko-style triad of Vishnu and two consorts, probably Sri and Bhu, formerly thought to represent Shiva, Uma and Ganga, from the Bakong, Roluos (Angkor, Depôt Conserv. Mnmts), is an excellent example of the increasingly hieratic and abstract quality that typifies later Khmer sculpture. The three figures are frontal, stiff and thick-bodied, with only a few deeply incised lines under the breasts remaining of the earlier sensitive modelling of the torso. There is no attempt at anatomical realism in the elephantine legs of Vishnu. The garments also appear heavier, with folds more prominent and in higher relief.

Pre-Angkor Buddha and *bodhisattva* images display the same preferences as the Hindu images for thin drapery over sensitively modelled bodies. The poses of some standing images, such as the Avalokiteshvara of Rach Gia and the Buddhas from Vat Romlok and Tuol Preah Theat (Phnom Penh, N. Mus.), display a weight shift or bend that gives the images a more relaxed, natural air than that of their Indian prototypes. Although these images can be related to Indian styles, especially the Sarnath Gupta and post-Gupta, they have a freshness and sense of life that demonstrates the ability of the Khmer sculptors to synthesize imported models into something new and impressive. The little extant relief sculpture from the period includes some fragments of a bas-relief frieze portraying mythological scenes, on the wall of the fifth tier of the Bakong.

A few small pre-Angkor Buddhist images in bronze exist, and a number of fragments of colossal bronzes, of which some date to the pre-Angkor period (Boisselier, 1967). The discovery of a hoard of bronze Mahayana Buddhist images from Phra Kon Chai in Thailand, including a number of larger images in styles related to 7th- and 8th-century pre-Angkor styles, revealed that earlier Khmer sculptors achieved an equal mastery in bronze. Giteau has suggested that many Khmer stone images, both Hindu and Buddhist, were originally gilded, while Lee has proposed a close connection between the style of the images of bronze, which was the primary sculptural medium, and of stone, of which there are more surviving examples. Such special characteristics of pre-Angkor Hindu and Buddhist stone sculpture as the remarkable plastic quality of the modelling, the crisply incised details and the taut surface of the highly polished stone, may in fact owe much to the qualities found in the bronze images originally imported from abroad that served as both iconographic and aesthetic models for the Khmers.

BIBLIOGRAPHY

H. Parmentier: 'L'Art présumé du Fou-nan', *Bull. Ecole Fr. Extrême-Orient*, xxxii (1932), pp. 183–9

P. Dupont: 'La Dislocation du Tchen-la et la formation du Cambodge angkorien (VII–IXe siècles)', *Bull. Ecole Fr. Extrême-Orient*, xliii (1943), pp. 17–55
——: 'Tchen-la et Panduranga', *Bull. Soc. Etud. Indochin.*, xxiv (1949), pp. 21–37
——: 'Les Linteaux khmers du VIIIe siècle', *Artibus Asiae*, xv (1952), pp. 561–70
——: 'La Statuaire préangkorienne', *Artibus Asiae*, suppl. xv (1955)
B. P. Groslier: *Hinterindien* (Baden-Baden, 1960); Fr. trans. as *Indochine: Carrefour des arts* (Paris, 1961)
M. Giteau: *Khmer Sculpture and the Angkor Civilization* (New York, 1965)
J. Boisselier: 'Notes sur l'art du bronze dans l'ancien Cambodge', *Artibus Asiae*, xxix/4 (1967), pp. 275–334
M. Benisti: 'Recherches sur le premier art khmer, II. La Bande à chatons, critère chronologiques?', *A. Asiatiques*, xx (1969), pp. 99–120
S. E. Lee: *Ancient Cambodian Sculpture* (New York, 1969)
E. C. Bunker: 'Pre-Angkor Period Bronzes from Pra Kon Chai', *Archvs Asian A.*, v/25 (1971–2), pp. 67–76

2. Early Angkor period (*c*. 889–*c*. 1080). The sculpture of the early Angkor period, from the shift of the capital to Angkor from Roluos by Yashovarman I (*reg* 889–*c*. 900) to the beginning of the reign of Jayavarman VI (*reg* 1080–1107), includes some of the finest of all extant Khmer sculpture. It has been subjected to the same meticulous stylistic analysis by French scholars as that of other periods, particularly by de Coral Rémusat and Boisselier, who have established a series of stylistic periods, linked to each other with transitional periods. The main styles in the early Angkor period are the Bakheng style (late 9th century to early 10th); the Koh Ker style (second quarter of the 10th century); the Banteay Srei style (second half of the 10th century); the style of the Khleangs (late 10th century to early 11th); and the Baphuon style (11th century). Differentiation between these various styles often depends on minute changes in the handling of garments, hairstyles and jewellery. Although this helps to date more precisely otherwise undated works, the styles of Bakheng and Koh Ker and such transitional styles as the Pre Rup style (mid-10th century) are usually so similar, while the sculptural remains of the Khleang period are so sparse and so close stylistically to works in the later Baphuon style, that Sherman Lee's broader division into first style of Angkor and Baphuon style, with Banteay Srei as a pivotal transitional link between the two, seems generally preferable.

(i) Late 9th century to the mid-10th: first style of Angkor. (ii) Later 10th century: Banteay Srei style. (iii) Late 10th century to the 11th: Baphuon style.

(i) Late 9th century to the mid-10th: first style of Angkor. The sculpture of the first 70 or 80 years of the early Angkor period, that is, from the sculptures of the Loley (889) and Bakheng temples (893) up to those of Banteay Srei (968), was a natural continuation and evolution of 9th-century styles and particularly of the Preah Ko style. It is generally seen as the most hieratic and formal of all Khmer styles of sculpture. Lee has commented that in the first style of Angkor the 'polished subtlety of the fleshy areas' of pre-Angkor sculptures was 'modified to achieve almost abstract and architectonic ends rather than to indicate bone and joint, hence the imposing and awesome inhumanity of these early Angkor images of major Hindu deities' (Lee, p. 22). Outstanding examples of this first style of Angkor include a free-standing stone image of Brahma in the Bakheng style, reputedly from Prasat Prei Prasat (New York, Met.); a headless male torso from Phnom Bakheng; a headless female deity from Prasat Neang Khmau, a shrine dated to 928; the monumental (over 2.5 m high) battling monkeys, Valin and Sugriva, from Koh Ker (all Phnom Penh, N. Mus.); a seated Brahma from Phnom Baset (sandstone, 1.1 m; Paris, Mus. Guimet); and a damaged four-armed Vishnu in the style of Pre Rup (San Francisco, CA, Asian A. Mus.). There are also a few smaller bronzes, one of the most interesting being a figure of Durga, the fierce aspect of Devi, standing on a pedestal ornamented with the head of the buffalo Mahisha that she has slain, while the goddess herself holds the attributes of Vishnu.

Characteristics that these works share are frontality and stiffness and the imposing sense of power noted by Lee. The shoulders are broad and straight and the torsos, hips and legs heavy, with no trace of sensuous fleshiness. Faces are broad and, in the later works, increasingly square-jawed. The eyebrow ridge, which has a slight natural curve in the earlier sculptures, becomes almost straight and totally abstract in the later works. Details of eyes, lips, beard and moustache are lightly but crisply incised, giving a linear accent to the smooth mass of the face. The headdress of a deity is typically a diadem framing a cylindrical or conical chignon (*mukuṭa*), with finely incised details of jewel or hair patterns, again giving a fine linear decoration to the simple three-dimensional form. These figures are generally without jewels carved in the stone, except the Brahma from Phnom Baset and the monkeys from Koh Ker, which have earrings and armlets; it is possible that the other sculptures were once adorned with actual jewellery. The male images wear the *sampot* and the females a long skirt, both of which have even, fine and quite deeply incised vertical pleats. In both male and female figures, the edge of the garment above the belt stands out slightly from the hips, producing a distinct, almost horizontal line that echoes that of the shoulders and sets off the smoothly polished torso. In the female figures the effect of a broad apron is created by a fold of cloth of even depth over the belt across the whole front of the hips, increasing the horizontal accent of the edge of the skirt. In the male figures the tail of the *sampot* is brought through the legs and looped over the belt so that it falls in folds to form the shape of two anchors, one above the other, far less realistic in appearance than the fish-tail fold of Kulen- and Preah Ko-style figures.

The pose of the battling monkeys from Koh Ker is strikingly different, although their general proportions and the details of their headdresses and garments are characteristic of the first style of Angkor. The figures are arrested in action, legs bent, arms extended, and they not only interact with the space around them but frame it between their bodies. The dynamic pose, combined with the huge scale, is extremely impressive. Such action poses and scenes of struggle are virtually unknown in earlier Khmer sculpture, although the relief fragment from the Bakong showing a battle scene indicates that such subjects had been treated earlier. Large, free-standing sculptures of lions and elephants were used in the early Angkor period as well as later to decorate a number of temples, including the East Mebon, but there are none extant depicting such dynamic action from any sites other than Koh Ker, where,

17. *Lakshmi and Two Worshippers*, brick relief, h. 1.66 m, Bakheng/Koh Ker style, west wall of north sanctuary, Prasat Kravan, Angkor, *c.* AD 925

in addition to the Valin and Sugriva sculpture, a large-scale fragment of wrestling or struggling figures, a *garuḍa* (mythical bird with human arms and torso, and head, wings and claws of an eagle) behind a *nāga* (serpent) that formed part of a balustrade, and fragments of a large dancing Shiva have all been discovered (all Phnom Penh, N. Mus.).

Relief sculptures in the first style of Angkor also generally continue and develop the style of 9th-century relief decoration. The decoration of lintels, niches and doorways is still chiefly foliate (*see* §II, 1(ii)(a) above), and in the Koh Ker period profuse foliate motifs begin to appear around the figures of deities and attendants in the tympana above the lintels. The guardian figures in the niches flanking doorways, such as the *devatā*s (deities) on the central sanctuary of the Bakheng, share the general physical type and treatment of garments and hair found in free-standing sculptures. At Prasat Kravan (dedicated 921), a Vaishnavite temple at Angkor, there are monumental carved brick reliefs of Vishnu and Lakshmi in the interiors of the sanctuaries (see fig. 17). These reliefs were originally covered by a thin layer of stucco and may also have been painted. They show the same body, garment and jewel types found in the free-standing sculpture of the period. A certain stiffness and awkwardness results from the two-dimensional depiction of three-dimensional poses.

(ii) Later 10th century: Banteay Srei style. The temple of Banteay Srei helped to initiate and gave its name to a new style at Angkor. In the later 10th century and during the 11th this style, which was partly based on a conscious revival of the pre-Angkor sculptural styles of the 7th and 8th centuries, was fully developed in the sculptures of the Baphuon style. Banteay Srei is built almost entirely in fine pink sandstone, evidently carefully selected by the masons, and its carved decoration is of the finest design and workmanship. After restoration by the Ecole Française d'Extrême-Orient, its reliefs and other carvings are in a far better state of preservation than most 10th-century monuments at Angkor, which are largely constructed in brick and laterite and decorated with stucco, so that much of their fine detail has been badly damaged or entirely lost. At Banteay Srei, the small scale, fine craftsmanship and extreme elaboration of the relief decoration together create an impression of jewel-like beauty (*see also* §II, 1(ii)(b) above). While many of the tympanum reliefs within the pediments continue to feature large figures of a major deity accompanied by smaller figures, all engulfed in swirling foliage, six of the tympana contain complex and lively narrative reliefs of scenes from tales of Shiva and of two incarnations of Vishnu, Krishna and Rama. Although narrative scenes occasionally appear on lintels before this time, and there is some evidence for narrative friezes (the Bakong fragment) and a wall painting tradition (extremely damaged fragments at Prasat Neang Khmau; *see* §IV below), the quite sophisticated composition of these narrative reliefs at Banteay Srei is almost without precedent. There are no surviving Khmer reliefs of equal sophistication until those of Angkor Vat.

Perhaps the most successful of these reliefs at Banteay Srei is that on the east wall of the south 'library' (so called because it is thought that it may have been built for the storage of sacred texts), showing Ravana shaking Mt Kailasa while Shiva, seated on top of the mountain with Parvati at his side, quells the shaking with the pressure of his big toe alone. It is particularly interesting for its depiction of Mt Kailasa as a multi-tiered stepped pyramid like the pyramidal base of a Khmer temple-mountain representing Mt Meru. The stepped pyramid mountain form fits well into the curvilinear triangular shape of the pediment; the three leaf-shaped trees framing Shiva and Parvati not only gracefully fill the empty space at the top of the tympanum, but their curving branches and delicate leaf patterns also contrast very effectively with the rectilinear shape of the mountain and the horizontal lines of the mouldings of each level of the pyramid. Various *ṛṣi*s (sages) and animal- and bird-headed figures in lively, interactive poses, showing alarm at Ravana's threat, populate the intermediate levels of the pyramid. At the bottom, a powerful, seven-headed, twenty-armed Ravana struggles to lift the mountain, while animals flee on either side. Ravana's pose as he kneels on one knee with torso and shoulders tilted and arms outstretched, the fleeing animals and the quieter gestures of the *ṛṣi*s and of Shiva and Parvati are well observed and, considering the stylizing tendency of Khmer art and Hindu art in general, convincingly natural. The carving of the relief is shallow, and the total effect strongly linear, again suggesting that there was already a well-developed drawing or painting tradition at Angkor.

The other reliefs dealing with Shiva and Krishna themes also use a multi-level setting, with many small figures in carefully studied and convincingly realistic poses. The depiction of Kama, the god of love, shooting Shiva with an arrow on the west end of the south 'library' is almost identical to the Ravana relief; it has the same stepped pyramid-mountain setting and the same disposition of numerous small figures on the lower levels, with a larger figure of Shiva above. However, the absence of a large figure of the struggling Ravana at the base makes this relief more static. The *Krishna Slaying Kamsa*, depicted on the west end of the north 'library', is set in a multi-storey wooden palace, with its towered superstructure conforming to the space contained within the triangular tympanum (see fig. 18). The tympanum relief at the east end of the north 'library' is also a multi-level composition, depicting at the top Indra riding Airavata, his three-headed elephant, framed by a number of small figures paying him homage; successive bands of waves, rain and birds below; and at the bottom a delightful forest scene with numerous human and animal figures flanked by two incarnations of Vishnu, Krishna and Balarama. However, the static horizontal bands dividing the two figural areas make this a less cohesive and successful composition than the three discussed above. The other two narrative reliefs, one still *in situ* on an ancillary building, the other in the Musée Guimet in Paris, are quite different in conception. They depict scenes from the *Rāmāyaṇa*, with larger-scale figures on a single plane, set against simpler backgrounds. The poses and sense of movement are admirably caught, although the space is shallow, and despite the relatively deep relief the linear quality of the outline tends to predominate.

The treatment of the garments, the hair and the facial features of the figures in these and other tympanum and lintel reliefs at Banteay Srei generally follows the style of earlier 10th-century sculpture, although some of the faces in the reliefs are slightly softer and rounder. Both male and female figures wear garments with an apron-like flap folded forward over the belt and narrow, vertical pleats covering this and the *sampot* and skirt. The free-standing sculptures of Shiva and his consort found in the central sanctuary (Phnom Penh, N. Mus.), the guardian figures

18. *Krishna Slaying Kamsa*, sandstone relief carving on west pediment of north 'library', Banteay Srei style, Banteay Srei, third quarter of the 10th century AD

and a standing Vishnu from the north sanctuary all wear jewelled diadems. A head of a male deity found near the main sanctuary (Phnom Penh, N. Mus.) has no diadem, however, and the hair is arranged in fine braids, following the profile of the skull and pulled up into a cylindrical topknot. This hairstyle is close to that of the male guardians in high relief in the niches flanking the sanctuary doorways, and it is also found in a number of the small relief figures in the lintels and pediments. This head also differs in other ways: the chin is more pointed, and the contours of the face are slightly softer and more naturalistic than in the square-jawed Shiva image.

Both the head and the guardian figures in the niches of the sanctuary contrast stylistically with most of the free-standing and relief sculpture from Banteay Srei and more closely resemble the pre-Angkor styles of the late 6th century to the 8th, with their slimmer, more naturalistically modelled torsos, narrower heads with more gentle, rounded chins and generally sweeter and more youthful air. The handling of garments, hairstyles and jewellery shows that this resemblance is not accidental. The garments, for example, lack the narrow vertical pleats and the apron effect of the 10th century and instead cling to the body and have the same fold and pocket details as in earlier styles. The reasons for this apparently deliberate archaism have not yet been explored. Some art historians have assumed that the patron's tastes or background may have been influential, although there is no documentary evidence for this. Since most of the extant works from the pre-Angkor period come from outside the Angkor region, which did not become a major settlement area until the 9th century, the question of how the sculptors acquired familiarity with this style is particularly intriguing. It is possible that they used easily transportable metal images from the earlier periods as their models or that sculptors from centres outside the Angkor area, where stone sculptures in the earlier styles were still to be seen, were brought into work at Banteay Srei. The distribution of the different hairstyles among the small relief figures in both 10th-century and earlier sculptures may be random, but the consistency of style among the guardian figures, including those in the archaizing group, suggests a conscious choice of style for specific groups. The head of a male deity in the archaic style seems to be an exception, however, as it is the only surviving example of a free-standing sculpture in this style.

(iii) Late 10th century to the 11th: Baphuon style. The carved decoration of two small temples at Angkor, Prasat Sralau and the structure behind the North Khleang, carry on the Banteay Srei style. The tympana of other surviving late 10th- and early 11th-century monuments at Angkor, such as the Khleangs, the Phimeanakas and Ta Keo, have the non-narrative foliage motifs found in early 10th-century decoration. Little sculpture in the round exists from this period. Some pieces, such as the Shiva from Phum Bavel (Battambang, Mus. Povéal) and a female torso from Banteay Kdei (Angkor, Depôt Conserv. Mnmts), both dated by Giteau to the first half of the 11th century, also have some of the characteristic features of the earlier 10th-century style, with the broad-shouldered, more heavily mature body and the thick, vertically pleated garment. Other works dated by Lee to the first half of the 11th century, such as a Shiva (Cleveland, OH, Mus. A.) and another Shiva and two female torsos in private collections, follow the Banteay Srei archaizing prototype, with slimmer, more youthful figures, rounder chins, absence of diadems, and the garment rendered so as to appear thin and clinging, with no heavy ridge of cloth at the waist, the hem dipping below the navel at the front and rising at the back. All these characteristics occur fully developed in the later part of the 11th century and typify the Baphuon style, which is marked by great subtlety and refinement.

19. *Shiva and Uma*, sandstone, h. 1.12 m and 1.04 m, Baphuon style, late 11th century (San Francisco, CA, Asian Art Museum of San Francisco)

Among the loveliest of the sculptures in this style are a *Shiva and Uma* (San Francisco, CA, Asian A. Mus.; see fig. 19). Although they have both lost their forearms, the Shiva much of his legs and Uma her ankles and feet, their surfaces are exceptionally well preserved and still retain the contrast of the crisp linear detail of jewels, hair and the finely incised vertical pleats of the garments with the taut, polished surface of the fleshy areas. Both have broad shoulders, but their general slimness and their rounded faces with slightly dimpled or cleft chins gives them an air of youthfulness. The long eyes, the lips and Shiva's beard are defined by finely incised lines. The two figures have identical hairstyles; the curve of the low, rounded chignon of plaited hair enhances the sweet and gentle expression of the faces.

Eleventh-century relief sculpture survives in a number of lintels and tympana. Among the most important of these are the lintel at Vat Ek, near Battambang, depicting the *Churning of the Ocean of Milk*, and the tympanum above, portraying *Sita in Ravana's Palace Garden*. Both are lively scenes, but they have a somewhat provincial air; the heads of the figures are too large for the bodies, and the bends in the rather tubular limbs of Sita and her companions are anatomically incorrect. Unlike the Banteay Srei tympana, the small square and rectangular relief panels on the corner towers and gateways of the Baphuon that illustrate scenes from the lives of Rama and Krishna also seem to be more concerned with the vivid portrayal of movement than with anatomical accuracy. Arms and legs are often extremely out of proportion, trees and rocks highly schematized and the whole scene depicted on one plane, even though this necessitates some overlapping of the figures or of figures with the minimal background elements. The general form and style of these reliefs, especially the absence of the more detailed and elaborate settings found in the Banteay Srei reliefs, are more reminiscent of the contemporary terracotta relief plaques illustrating *jātaka*s (tales of the previous lives of the Buddha) at Pagan (*see* BURMA, §IV, 2(i)) than either the earlier Bakong or Banteay Srei reliefs. Groslier has suggested that the awkwardness of the Baphuon reliefs may be either due to the sculptors' lack of experience in dealing with narrative reliefs or the result of an intentional naivety.

Buddhist sculptures continued to be produced during this period. Surviving examples include both Buddha images and images of the *bodhisattva* Avalokiteshvara (Lokeshvara), such as the very fine Lokeshvara in the Baphuon style (Paris, Mus. Guimet) and the Buddha sheltered by the *nāga* Muchilinda from Peam Cheang (Phnom Penh, N. Mus.), also in the Baphuon style. The latter, like many mid-10th century and later Buddhist images, shows the influence of Hindu sculpture in its details; the hair is not in small snail-shell curls, but in fine braids pulled up to a conical *uṣṇīṣa* (cranial protuberance), similar to the *mukuṭa* of Hindu images.

A number of 11th-century images and fragments in bronze have also survived, the most remarkable being the colossal fragment of Vishnu resting on the cosmic snake Ananta from the West Mebon (Phnom Penh, N. Mus.), which consists of the shoulders, head and two right arms that together form a section 1.14 m high and more than 2 m long. Despite its damaged condition, this fragment still has the elegance characteristic of the Baphuon style, although the face seems heavier and broader than those of such images as the Shiva and consort. The eyes and eyebrows were evidently once inlaid, another indication of the elaboration and elegance of the sculpture of this period. Another large gilt bronze fragment, a head of Shiva (Siem Reap, Conserv. Mnmts Angkor), 320 mm in height, from Por Loboeuk, Kralanh, 50 km north-east of Angkor, is further proof of the technical mastery that Khmer bronzeworkers had achieved by this period. It, too, was once decorated with inlay and enamel. The smaller bronzes from the Baphuon period are also remarkable for their quality and the variety of their subject-matter, including a delightful monkey and a charming figure of a kneeling girl (Phnom Penh, N. Mus.).

BIBLIOGRAPHY

L. Finot, V. Goloubew and H. Parmentier: *Le Temple d'Içvarapura (Bantay Srei, Cambodge)*, Pubns Ecole Fr. Extrême-Orient, i (Paris, 1926)

P. Dupont: 'L'Art du Kulen et les débuts de la statuaire angkorienne', *Bull. Ecole Fr. Extrême-Orient*, xxxvi (1936), pp. 415–26

G. de Coral Rémusat: *L'Art khmer: Les Grandes Etapes de son évolution* (Paris, 1940, 2/1951)

J. Boisselier: *La Statuaire khmère et son évolution*, 2 vols, Pubns Ecole Fr. Extrême-Orient, xxxvii (Saigon, 1955)

——: *Tendances de l'art khmer* (Paris, 1956); Eng. trans., rev. and ed. by N. Eilenberg and M. Elliott (Ithaca, NY, 1989)

G. P. Groslier: *The Art of Indochina* (New York, 1962)

M. Giteau: *Khmer Sculpture and the Angkor Civilization* (Fribourg, Paris and New York, 1965)

S. E. Lee: *Ancient Cambodian Sculpture* (New York, 1969)

JUDITH PATT

3. MIDDLE ANGKOR PERIOD (*c.* 1080–*c.* 1181): ANGKOR VAT STYLE. Perhaps the finest sculpture of the middle Angkor period is to be found in the bas-reliefs, especially those of Angkor Vat. By contrast, sculpture in the round seems to have played only a minor role.

(i) Narrative reliefs of Angkor Vat. (ii) Other relief sculpture. (iii) Sculpture in the round.

(i) Narrative reliefs of Angkor Vat. The reliefs of Angkor Vat (*see* ANGKOR, §2(iii)), most of which were carved during the reign of Suryavarman II (*reg* 1113–*c.* 1150), are rightly regarded as marking the finest achievement of Khmer relief sculpture. In their profusion and delicacy of execution they are unsurpassed.

(a) Introduction. (b) Description.

(a) Introduction. The lower gallery of the temple precinct, barely 5 m wide, is bordered on the outside by a double row of columns. On the inside, however, is a stone wall on which the reliefs are carved running round the entire temple complex. They are about 2 m high and more than 500 m long and cover an area of well over 1000 sq. m. The relief is so shallow that they have been described as 'frescoes in stone', and originally they may indeed have been partly painted. The figures of gods, for example, were distinguished by being painted red, the colour of veneration, while eminent personages were in other bright colours, and especially important details were covered in gold leaf. This use of very shallow relief was clearly intended to ensure that the restless, whirling figures of the frieze would not disturb the clear lines of the architecture. They are only visible to someone looking directly at them, and anyone gazing down the long vista of the gallery is not distracted. The long corridors are interrupted at the intersections of the axes of the main sanctuary by staircases that meet to form pavilions. In this way eight wall sections of about 55, 66 and as much as 98 m in length are created. The reliefs are conceived as a continuous series of scenes flowing into each other without interruption and without a centimetre of the surface being left uncarved. Their narrative zest, communicative urge and a royal desire for display give them an explosive force. The mythical scenes are all of Vaishnavite subjects and at the same time illustrate the heroic deeds of Suryavarman II, who had identified himself with the god Vishnu, the ideal model of kingship. Six of the friezes depict stories from the *Mahābhārata*, the *Rāmāyaṇa* and other Hindu epics; one shows

Suryavarman II participating in a parade of kings and another depicts the dead on their journey to the beyond.

Each frieze has its own composition, determined by the exigencies of the central episode of its theme. The gigantic scale gives an opportunity to recount the legends in exhaustive detail, so that it is possible to find texts from the epics or the Puranas that correspond to most of the scenes depicted. At first the density of the images is confusing, but the composition is carefully planned, generally making use of undulating and diagonal lines to relieve the monotony of the very long, narrow friezes. The just characters (gods, kings, dignitaries) always have regular features and well-proportioned bodies, while the wicked (demons, sinners) are given such ugly and frightening attributes as unkempt hair, round, protuberant eyes, fangs or misshapen bodies. Gods wear conical crowns and demons crests of hair. The movements of the human figures are elegant and vigorous, and the details of such features as crowns and jewels, battle-chariots and the patterns on clothing and parasols are executed with great delicacy.

Six of the friezes, to judge by their style and technical mastery, are contemporaneous with the building of the temple in the 12th century. Two, however, were evidently not completed until the mid-16th century, when the Khmer kings returned to Angkor after a lapse of two centuries (*see also* §5 below). Although in many parts they are based on 12th-century originals, they fall far short of the others in artistic quality. The relief is carelessly executed, the lines are hard and the modelling crude and inexpressive. The bodies often seem clumsy and ill-proportioned, the faces angular, the movements erratic and unnatural. Faces and bodies give an impression of caricature. As Boisselier (1962) has demonstrated, they show the influence of Thai art, especially of wall paintings of 15th- and 16th-century Ayutthaya. Certain Chinese elements, such as cloud shapes, were also adopted through the intermediary of Thai art. In some places, even in the earlier reliefs, it seems as if the sculptors have not completed the detail, as whole groups of figures are shown in outline only.

The allocation of subjects to particular sections of the gallery has a symbolic significance, so that the iconographic and architectural aspects are interdependent. Correct orientation is of great importance, as it was determined by the role of Angkor Vat as a funerary temple, which meant that the ritual pacing-out of the gallery had to be performed in an anti-clockwise direction, contrary to the course of the sun.

(b) Description. The dramatic climax of the *Rāmāyaṇa* is shown on a frieze 54 m long in the north wing of the west gallery. Rama and his brother Lakshmana fight, with the help of the army of monkeys and bears, against the demon ruler of Lanka, Ravana and his army, to free the abducted Sita. The surging battle scene moves from one end of the frieze to the other in an uninterrupted stream. All the soldiers have human bodies but animals' or demons' heads. The seemingly inextricable tangle of bodies is carefully structured. At intervals of two or three metres a larger figure of a leader stands on a chariot drawn by fabulous beasts and forms a fixed point that allows the eye to regain its bearings. Some can be identified by characteristic iconographic features. The rearing animals drawing the chariots and the warriors standing on them and lunging forward form diagonal lines that cut across the undulating mass of interlocked fighters. In this way, the effect of a violent but not chaotic battle is produced.

In the south wing of the west gallery, the *Battle of the Gods and Demons* from the *Mahābhārata* is depicted on another frieze 54 m long. From either end of the frieze the armies move towards each other. Archers stand on chariots drawn by horses. Among them the foot-soldiers whirl about with raised swords and lances. Here too the chariots advancing in two offset rows one above the other (i.e. one behind the other) and the galloping horses form diagonals within the horizontal composition of the relief. The agitated scene, suggesting breakneck speed, is given optical stability by a continuous chain of soldiers at the bottom edge of the frieze, who first march in closed formation towards the middle, then engage each other. The clashing of the two armies at the centre of the frieze is indicated only by the disintegration of this chain and the reversal of the direction of the chariots, and not by emphasizing any special scene. None of the leaders, as descendants of a royal house, has individual features that might reveal their identities. However, a few scenes can be identified, such as the mourning for the dead Bhisma on his bed of arrows.

In the west wing of the south gallery is a parade of kings, 98 m long, which shows not mythological but historical events. 18 Khmer kings with their retinues and troops are portrayed. Unusually, numerous inscriptions in Old Khmer give information on the people, as well as the posthumous names of the kings in Sanskrit. The parade starts at the west corner of the gallery and moves without interruption from west to east to the end of the wing. Characteristic of this frieze is the careful rendering of vegetation. Treetops fill most of the upper part of the picture, and trees stand as scene dividers between each king. The first 15 scenes are divided into two registers. The lower one shows men and women straining forward in loose groups, the upper one seated dignitaries armed with spears, all looking towards the king, who sits on a throne under many parasols and fans. According to the inscription, he is assembling his troops. With one hand he points forwards to where the twofold division of the frieze breaks off and a group of soldiers climbs steeply downwards. These join an almost unbroken chain of armed men who form the lower edge of the relief and stretch to the end of the frieze, interrupted at regular intervals by dignitaries on horseback. The armed men wear the typical clothes and headgear of Khmer warriors, though a group of Thais is also shown, described as Siamese in an inscription and conspicuous by their foreign dress. The middle of the picture is taken up by depictions of the kings on their elephants. Most of them stand on howdahs in the pose of victors, with bow and arrow or sword and shield.

In the east wing of the south gallery a frieze 66 m long shows the dead marching to the court of Yama, the god of death, and their subsequent sojourns in heaven and hell. Here again the action moves in a stream from left to right. At the beginning the frieze is divided into three

20. The god of war Skanda (Kārttikeya) in the *Battle of the Gods and Demons* (detail), sandstone relief carving, Angkor Vat style, west wing of north gallery, Angkor Vat, first half of the 12th century

registers. Short inscriptions in Old Khmer explain that the two upper registers show the dead on the path to heaven, while the lower one shows them on the path to hell. On the upper paths well-proportioned, bejewelled men and women set out on their journey to the beyond in ordered lines on foot or borne on litters and always screened by parasols. Those on the path to hell are emaciated, pitiful figures driven violently by servants of hell through a forest full of ferocious wild beasts. After about 17 m Yama appears seated on his water-buffalo, taking up the full height of the two upper registers. While in the upper register he is followed by the continuation of the path to heaven, in the middle and lower registers Yama's retinue is to be seen. Further on, the frieze continues in two registers. In the upper one are ranged the palaces of heaven, borne by *garuḍa*s, in which the blessed are seated. The lower register shows the 32 hells and their torments, which pilgrims were intended to interpret also as punishments that the ruler might mete out to them in this world.

The south wing of the east gallery has a frieze 54 m long showing the gods and demons churning the Ocean of Milk to create the nectar of immortality (*amṛta*). In the centre is Vishnu, here portrayed on three different levels of being: at the bottom as the divine tortoise, Kurma, forming the base of the cosmic churning pole, Mt Mandara; in the middle as the four-armed god Vasudeva; and hovering at the top as the absolute god Narayana. Round Mt Mandara lies the body of the world-snake, Vasuki, which stretches to each side across the whole relief. At the head the demons pull to the left, at the tail the gods pull to the right. The frieze is arranged in three registers. At the bottom the sea is represented by fishes and reptiles; the wide middle register is filled by the gods and demons pulling on the snake's body; at the top hovering nymphs indicate heaven. A local variant not found in Indian texts or depictions is the appearance of the monkey-general, Hanuman, hero of the *Rāmāyaṇa*, at the end of the line of gods. As an image of the Vaishnavite myth of creation, this scene is of primordial importance in Cambodia; the layout of the city of Angkor Thom illustrates it in monumental form. The frieze faces east towards the sunrise, the source of life.

In the north wing of the east gallery Vishnu's fight with the demon armies of Naraka is depicted in a 16th-century frieze 54 m long, arranged in two registers. From the right and left ends of the gallery two armies of foot-soldiers, chariots and elephants, each exactly matching the other, move towards the middle to fight together against the god Vishnu, who stands on the shoulders of his mount, Garuda, at the centre of the relief, confronting his assailants alone. He has just felled four demon warriors on elephants, whom Vishnu in his incarnation as Krishna vanquishes before the gates of his city. In another 16th-century frieze (66 m long) in the east wing of the north gallery, Krishna, Balarama and Pradyumna, standing on the shoulders and wings of a giant *garuḍa*, fight against Bana.

The frieze in the west wing of the north gallery is 98 m long and also depicts the *Battle of the Gods and Demons.* Many of the gods are recognizable by their characteristic iconographic features, such as Kubera, god of riches, on a *yakṣa* (protective genie); Agni, god of fire, on a rhinoceros; Vishnu on Garuda; Skanda, child of Shiva and god of war, on a peacock (see fig. 20); Indra, god of storms, on the three-headed elephant Airavata; Yama, god of death, on a chariot drawn by a buffalo; Shiva on a chariot drawn by the bull Nandi; Brahma on a *haṁsa* (sacred goose); Surya, the sun-god, before the disc of the sun; and Varuna, god of rain and waters, on a serpent. Only the chief demon, Kalanemi, can be identified. There are no divisions between the individual duels, and the entire space is filled with a confused mêlée of foot-soldiers, horsemen and charioteers. The duel between Vishnu and Kalanemi in the centre, which is described in the legend as the decisive episode in the battle between gods and demons that followed the churning of the Ocean of Milk, may be seen as the focal point of the frieze.

Only the two pavilions at the west corner of the south and north galleries are decorated with reliefs. These cover the entire walls from a low socle up to the cornice. Subsidiary figures are arranged schematically in registers, but the main scenes break through these limits. Between the figural scenes trees and foliage are inserted. Most of the scenes are of episodes in the stories of Rama and Krishna. The sequence of reliefs does not seem to be based on any system relating to their subject-matter.

(ii) Other relief sculpture. The relief figures of *apsarasas* and other deities in the Angkor Vat style are of two types, one earlier and one later. The earlier type is found at Beng Mealea and Thommanon, where some of them are portrayed wearing the traditional pleated, waist-high garment with a long fold hanging down at the front and a diadem with only one decorative disc. In the later type, which is also represented in these two temples and almost everywhere in Angkor Vat (see fig. 21), the garment is only slightly pleated but is decorated with flower patterns and worn with a wide, gathered sash with fluttering ends in front of the right hip and a narrow sash on the left. The

21. *Apsaras* (celestial dancer), sandstone relief carving, from Angkor Vat, 12th century (Paris, Musée Guimet)

top edge of the garment may be straight or folded over the belt, which has pendants and a large buckle at the front. At Thommanon and Chau Say Tevoda the traditional dress is reserved for the figures in the sanctuary, a distinction that is also observed, although less strictly, at Angkor Vat. At Beng Mealea, however, and in sculptures in the subsequent Bayon style, it is not found at all. Images wearing this later type of garment also have ornate diadems with many decorative discs and usually three tall points and have bizarre, elaborately knotted hairstyles, which are also no longer found at Beng Mealea or later. The deities show a wide diversity of gestures. The arms and legs are full of movement, but the torsos have a tendency towards the stiff frontality characteristic of contemporary sculpture in the round. Flexion of the hips is entirely absent. Occasionally the figures stand under an arch, which is often replaced by a vine arrangement, e.g. on the third level at Angkor Vat.

*Dvārapāla*s ('door guardians') in relief in the Angkor Vat style occur at Beng Mealea, Banteay Samré, Thommanon and the second enclosure of Banteay Srei. In Angkor Vat itself there are none. *Dvārapāla*s in the round become common only in the Bayon period. The *sampot* of relief *dvārapāla*s is the same as that worn by male gods. They hold their weapon, a club, with both hands waist-high in front of their bodies. Their hairstyles and faces differ widely, according to whether they are fearsome or benign. The latter always have a diadem with a conical crown, but the former have their hair in bosses or tufts. Fearsome *dvārapāla*s, jewelled but without diadems or conical ear-pendants, are typical of the Angkor Vat style but do not occur either before or later.

Representations of the *garuḍa* in the Angkor Vat style are also mainly in relief. They can be dated primarily by their jewellery (Boisselier, 1966). In this period it occurs for the first time in association with the *nāga* (serpent) hoods terminating the balustrades, either in miniature in the foliage above the *nāga*'s heads or standing in front, often taking up the whole middle section (Angkor Vat, Preah Pithu). The bas-reliefs of Angkor Vat often show a *garuḍa* as a mount (*vāhana*) carrying a god on his outstretched wings (*see* §(i)(b) above).

(iii) Sculpture in the round.

(a) Stone. Few sculptures in the round have survived from the Angkor Vat period, and few of those are still *in situ.* The two triads from Banteay Srei are an exception and were probably produced at the time of a restoration of the temple by Divākara in the 12th century, which is recorded in the inscriptions. Apart from images of Hindu gods and Buddha figures, there are *dvārapāla*s, guardian lions and *nāga*s that form an integral part of the architecture; in some cases these too are still *in situ.*

The style of sculpture in the round differs considerably from that of reliefs, and its stylistic evolution was slower. The images of deities, after the freedom of the Baphuon style, demonstrate a return to the hieratic, strictly frontal representation that was typical of the Bakheng style. The bodies are stocky, the legs thick. The slightly arched and sharply defined eyebrows give the broad faces a severe expression. The slightly bulging eyes have a second line round them, and the pupil is always indicated. The large mouth has fleshy lips. The cleft chin, typical of the Baphuon style, has disappeared. Towards the end of the period the faces grow softer. The earlier male figures wear the *sampot* just reaching the knees; in the later figures it is shorter and decorated with pearls along the hem. The gathered material is held by a belt with pendant ornaments. The 'pocket' at the side disappears completely in the course of the period. The cloth sometimes hangs in a semicircle over the belt at the front, and its ends hang down to the edge to form a double anchor. The square belt buckle is often embellished with floral motifs at front or back. The long skirt of the female deities follows the traditional form, without sashes at the sides and pleated. Only during the transition to the Bayon style is the material sometimes also flowered on the free-standing figures. In the front, a semicircular fold or a fold ending in a fishtail is typical. The decorative folds below the breast disappear entirely. Jewellery occurs more frequently and is more lavish in both Hindu and Buddhist figures than in any other style except the Koh Ker. The band of the diadem is either plain or decorated with lotus leaves, pearls, lozenges and half-lozenges; sometimes there is a second pearl band and a serrated upper edge. For the first time, the necklace has leaf-shaped pendants; these are still to be found in the Bayon style. The heavy, conical ear-pendants, falling from a flower calyx, are almost always supported at the neck.

Among the most frequent of the Buddhist figures is the Buddha seated on the *nāga* with three coils, known since the 10th century (see fig. 22). For the first time in this period the Buddha takes on the appearance and attributes of a Brahmanic deity. His torso is uncovered, and he wears a diadem surmounted by a conical crown (a feature that ceases to appear in the Bayon style) and neck and ear jewellery. The facial features, at first severe, grow softer in the course of the 12th century and foreshadow the charming expression typical of Buddhist figures of the Bayon style. *Nāga*s with broad hoods and usually seven heads form the balustrades bordering the causeways leading to the sanctuaries. During this period several types of *nāga* occur, sometimes more than one type appearing in a single monument. Apart from the classical *nāga* heads there are others with the appearance of a dragon with horns, snout and a beard. The seven heads sometimes share a single nimbus strongly marked with lines and flat, geometric patterns (Beng Mealea) or deeply cut, leaf-shaped decoration (Angkor Vat). Sometimes each *nāga* head has a separate nimbus, so that the hood takes on a serrated edge (Preah Pithu). At the front a lotus blossom embellishes the *nāga*'s neck. Sometimes there is a *makara* (mythological sea monster combining the features of a crocodile and a dolphin and having an elephant's trunk) in low relief round the neck, symbolizing the ocean (Preah Palilay, Preah Pithu, Banteay Samré). Another type has a *kala* head instead of a *makara* on the nape (Angkor Vat, Preah Pithu); this feature also occurs in the Bayon style. Free-standing lion guards on the terraces and at the entrances to the sanctuaries became common in the 12th century. Unlike earlier representations, they stand in a fierce posture, poised to spring on all fours (Angkor Vat, Banteay Samré). The mane is highly stylized and surrounds the head like a wig; at the breast it has the appearance of a flat, decorative ribbon. They have all lost their tails, but in general these do not seem, as in earlier lion figures, to have rested on their backs, with the exception of those at Chau Say Tevoda, which show precisely this feature. In the early 12th century fangs, as in the *kala* images, frequently appear in the lions' mouths, which are open, with the jaws at right angles. The bull Nandi, the mount of Shiva, at Chau Say Tevoda is the last known three-dimensional sculpture of this period. He seems to have lost all his strength, his body and hump are out of proportion and his head is shaped like a horse's. One foreleg is lifted, with the hoof touching the ground. His broad neck-band has leaf-shaped pendants resembling the necklaces typical of the Angkor Vat style.

22. *Crowned Buddha on Snake*, sandstone, h. 870 mm, Angkor Vat style, first half of the 12th century (Phnom Penh, National Museum)

(b) Bronze. Detailed study of the bronze images of this period has yet to be made, and the features characteristic of the stone sculpture can only be applied to the bronzes with reservations. Roughly speaking, those bronze figures that show clear characteristics neither of the Baphuon nor of the Bayon styles, but approximate broadly to the reliefs and free-standing sculptures of Angkor Vat, are included in the latter style. More detailed analysis is needed of how the bronzes of this period from the metropolitan area differ from those of Lopburi and other western provinces (*see* THAILAND, §IV, 3). In general, the figures with severe, angular features are ascribed to Angkor and those with a gentle, smiling expression to Lopburi. Some features of dress and jewellery found on stone sculpture of the Angkor Vat style occur also in bronze figures up to the 13th century and merge with those of the Bayon style. A fairly large number of bronzes of Brahmanic gods, especially Vishnu, have survived from this period. The statuette (Phnom Penh, N. Mus.) of the god Vishnu–Vasudeva–Narayana, 380 mm high (incorrectly described as Hari-hara), found in Angkor Thom, may be regarded as typical.

Small figures of Vishnu standing on the shoulders of his mount, Garuda, are also common.

Bronze implements such as censers, bells, holy-water vessels, hooks, jewellery and mirrors are difficult to date accurately, as they often lack characteristic details, and most of the known pieces can only be assigned broadly to the 12th century. As with the bronze images, certain decorative elements of these objects are also found on 13th-century bronze implements, notably the lotus, the *garuḍa* and the *nāga*.

BIBLIOGRAPHY

L. Finot: 'Les Bas-reliefs du Baphuon', *Bull. Comm. Archéol. Indochine*, i (1910), pp. 155–61

G. Coedès: 'Les Bas-reliefs d'Angkor Vat', *Bull. Comm. Archéol. Indochine*, ii (1911), pp. 170–220

——: 'Note sur l'iconographie de Ben Mala', *Bull. Ecole Fr. Extrême-Orient*, iii (1913), pp. 23–8

J. Boisselier: 'Précisions sur la statuaire du style d'Ankor Vat', *Bull. Ecole Fr. Extrême-Orient*, xlvi (1952), pp. 227–52

——: 'Note sur les bas-reliefs tardifs d'Ankor Vat', *J. Asiat.*, ccl (1962), pp. 235–48

——: *Le Cambodge* (1966), I/i of *Manuel d'archéologie d'Extrême-Orient* (Paris, 1966–)

L. Sunnary: 'Etude iconographique du temple khmer de Thommanon (Dhammananda)', *A. Asiatiques.*, xxv (1972), pp. 155–87

WIBKE LOBO

4. BAYON STYLE (*c.* 1181–*c.* 1220). The sculptors of the Bayon style, contemporaneous with the reign of Jayavarman VII (*reg* 1181–*c.* 1220), favoured naturalism and the expression of spirituality, in contrast to their predecessors in the Angkor Vat style, who had adopted a return to a more hieratic style marked by rather formal poses and set facial expressions. This stylistic change corresponded to a religious transformation. In 1177 the Chams had captured Angkor and in 1181 King Jayavarman VII, who was a fervent Mahayana Buddhist, having regained his kingdom, rebuilt his capital according to Mahayana Buddhist precepts. All the major foundations of Jayavarman VII's reign are Mahayana Buddhist rather than dedicated to a Hindu deity, as had usually been the case hitherto.

The *bodhisattva* most venerated by the Khmers was Avalokiteshvara (or Lokeshvara), who, out of compassion, helps those who suffer by protecting them from danger and leading them towards final deliverance. He is distinguished by the small image he carries in his hair of the Buddha Amitabha ('Infinite Light'), the transcendental Buddha of the northern region of the universe. He is represented in the round with four or eight arms. In his 'radiant' manifestation his torso and clothes are covered with tiny figures, usually seated in meditation. On a bas-relief at Banteay Chhmar, the images of Avalokiteshvara have several heads and arms. Among other *bodhisattvas* popular in this period were Vajrapani ('Thunder in Hand') holding the *vajra*, a symbol of thunder, and Manjushri. An important place was accorded to Prajnaparamita ('Perfection of Wisdom'), a female *bodhisattva* associated with Avalokiteshvara and, like him, wearing an image of Amitabha in her hair. Numerous small stelae represent the Buddha protected by the *nāga*, between Avalokiteshvara and Prajnaparamita. Although at this time Hinduism was not as important as Buddhism, there are many images of this period that have lost their distinctive signs and attributes and that may represent Brahmanic deities; furthermore, bas-reliefs, particularly on pediments and lintels, show scenes from Hindu mythology.

(i) Reliefs. (ii) Sculpture in the round.

(i) Reliefs. The pediments of monuments of Jayavarman VII's reign are generally carved with narrative scenes. In addition, some lintels contain a figure or even a small scene in the centre. In buildings in the Angkor Vat style, a mythical event is often shown on the base of pilasters, but the sculptors of the Bayon style confined themselves here to the representation of meditating ascetics or dancing deities. On the other hand, narrative scenes sometimes occur in ornamental borders of foliage, friezes or decoration at ground-level, as for example on a pilaster at Ta Prohm, Jayavarman VII's first temple-monastery (1186), where a foliage border frames episodes from the Life of the Buddha. As at Angkor Vat, the most important reliefs are on walls; indeed, in the Bayon they cover the internal walls, not only of the two enclosing galleries, but also the *gopuras* (entrance pavilions) and the corner pavilions. Extensive reliefs also cover the walls of the grand gallery at Banteay Chhmar, the great temple founded by Jayavarman VII early in his reign 160 km north-west of Angkor. On the external walls of other temples the reliefs only occupy a relatively modest space (for example the reliefs of *gopura* IV at Ta Prohm, and the false doors sculpted with large images of the *bodhisattva* Avalokiteshvara at Neak Pean). On the other hand, important reliefs cover the walls of some terraces (the Royal Terrace, Elephant Terrace and Terrace of the Leper King on the Royal Square at Angkor Thom; the supporting wall of the causeway to Preah Khan of Angkor; the steps of the pond of the Royal Palace at Angkor Thom), and there are three-headed elephants on the corners of the gates of Angkor Thom.

The sculptures on the walls of the Bayon and Banteay Chhmar are true bas-reliefs with only a shallow projection, as at Angkor Vat. On some of the terrace walls, however, they are in much higher relief, as, for example, the female images on the Terrace of the Leper King, or the large *garuḍas* (mythical birds) alternating with standing lions on the Royal Terrace and the giant three-headed elephant antefixes, mounts of the god Indra, at the corners of the gates to Angkor Thom. At the corner of an inner wall of the Royal Terrace is a relief of an elephant seizing with his trunk an unfortunate terror-stricken warrior, who is depicted in the round.

The division of the composition into registers, apparent on some reliefs at Angkor Vat, had become general by the Bayon period. This arrangement is particularly successful on the south side of the eastern external gallery of the Bayon, where it creates an impression of a long parade of different parts of a marching army. In other compositions there are important personages, who therefore take up the whole height of the wall and so break the monotony of this horizontal arrangement, as at Banteay Chhmar, where eight large images of Avalokiteshvara harmonize the composition, dominating the small figures of humans and deities that surround them.

The iconography of reliefs in the Bayon style is very varied, as their subject-matter is sometimes Buddhist, sometimes Hindu and occasionally historical. Episodes in

23. War elephants and foot-soldiers, sandstone relief carving, Bayon style, west wing of south gallery, Bayon, late 12th century to the early 13th

the life of the Buddha rarely appear except on pediments (e.g. Preah Palilay) or in the decorations, and exceptionally on the reliefs of Ta Prohm, where the Buddha's victory over Mara is portrayed. Of Mahayana Buddhist subjects the most remarkable are the representations of Avalokiteshvara at Banteay Chhmar and Neak Pean. Most of the subjects are difficult to identify and, indeed, little is known about Khmer Mahayana Buddhism in this period. However, it seems that certain historical events were considered as re-enactments of Buddhist legends. For example, Jayavarman VII's reconquest of Angkor from the Chams, which echoed the victory of the gods over their enemies, the *asuras* (demons), is portrayed in a large and superbly executed bas-relief covering almost the whole eastern wall of the southern external gallery of the Bayon and is also represented on the wall of one of the galleries at Banteay Chhmar. Above the Bayon relief, the king, whose simply sketched outline recalls the large statues thought to be portraits of Jayavarman VII (*see* §(ii)(a) below), commands the battle raging beneath him: the short-haired Khmers in their boats attack the Chams, who wear helmets shaped like upside-down flowers, evoking the *asuras*' hairstyles. Wounded or dead warriors fall into the water, prey for the crocodiles. Right at the bottom of the relief is a kind of frieze portraying the daily life of the Khmer villagers liberated from the Cham invasion by this victory. Intimate details that only appear tentatively on the Angkor Vat bas-reliefs, for example in the depiction of Krishna's childhood, are numerous in the Bayon reliefs. In one, below the relief of the naval combat, carpenters at work, people selling goods at the market and villagers at home are shown. In another a rich landowner receives his guests, while the servants busy themselves in the kitchens. Leisure activities are also portrayed, such as cock-fighting, games of chess, music and dancing. Animals are also frequently portrayed. In the battle scenes, horses and elephants are prominent (see fig. 23). On the Elephant Terrace in Angkor Thom, elephants are shown bearing warriors, and deer, tigers and panthers are depicted in the hunting scenes. At the corners of the gates to Angkor Thom, the three-headed elephants pull up clumps of lotus with their trunks. Finally, on the steps of the pond of the Royal Palace, fish and fantastic sea monsters mingle in a watery world. Other beasts portrayed in the reliefs include *garuḍas*, *nāgas* and highly stylized lions.

The reliefs of this period are not all of the same quality. Most are of high quality, although those dating from the end of the period were often produced in haste by artists of mediocre talent. They provide much information about Khmer daily life in both palace and village during the last great period of the Angkor kingdom and give valuable details of technologies, armaments, means of transport and even such religious ceremonies as rites of homage and buffalo sacrifices. They display lively and realistic poses, elegant lines and a keen sense of the picturesque and humorous. The reliefs depicting religious subjects are generally imbued with Buddhist spirituality, and the animals, although they are handled naturalistically, often also evoke a mythical ambience, particularly when they are portrayed in the legendary southern continent of Jambhudvipa, a region of bliss and abode of many mythical creatures, identified with the Himalayas.

(ii) Sculpture in the round.

(a) Stone. As in preceding periods, images continued to be erected on pedestals in the sanctuaries where they were worshipped. They were therefore generally portrayed standing in a frontal pose, although the Buddha and some Mahayana deities were sometimes seated cross-legged. There are hardly any stone sculptures of this period showing figures in movement. A fragment (Hô Chi Minh City, N. Mus.) discovered in south Vietnam shows the bodies of Candaka and Kanthaka, the Buddha's coachman and horse, one weeping and the other dying of sorrow after their master's departure. The large stone group erected in the pool surrounding the temple of Neak Pean at Angkor representing the horse Balaha, an incarnation of the *bodhisattva* Avalokiteshvara, bringing his disciples to salvation, is exceptional. The four colossal faces on the Bayon towers, the four separate heads on the gates of Angkor Thom and the giants holding the *nāgas* on the causeways leading into the city are primarily architectural in conception (*see* §II, 1(iv)(c) above).

The image of the Buddha seated in *samādhi* (meditation), protected by the seven-headed serpent king (*nāgarāja*), Muchilinda, is most characteristic of the period. Statues of the Buddha with hands raised in the gesture of dispelling fear (*abhaya mudrā*) are also important, particularly towards the end of the period. The same is true of the image of the Buddha conquering Mara (*Māravijaya*), which occurs more often in bas-relief than in the round during this period. Bayon style iconography gives a major place to the *bodhisattvas*.

Iconographically, the most original sculptures in the Bayon style are undoubtedly the portrait-statues. The depiction of deceased royal or princely personages as deities is certainly earlier than the end of the 12th century; references to it occur in 9th-century inscriptions. The originality of the Bayon style lies in the representation of the deities with the dead person's features without idealizing them: for example the head with heavy face and small slit eyes (Paris, Mus. Guimet, no. 17582) or the image of Prajnaparamita represented as a little girl (Phnom Penh, N. Mus.). There is also the series of remarkable statues thought to represent Jayavarman VII in meditation, found at various sites (see fig. 24). Stripped of all royal attire and ornaments, the sovereign is shown merely as an adherent of the Buddhist religion.

Since the Hindu gods are an integral part of Buddhist cosmology, their cult was not supplanted by Buddhism, and such images as Vishnu seated, Shiva dancing and Shiva the ascetic continued to be favoured. On the internal walls of the gallery at Bayon, Shaivite scenes were carved, probably during the 13th century, most likely following the return to influence of certain important Hindu families. On these reliefs Ravana shaking Mt Kailasa, Shiva overcoming Kama and the myth of the origin of the *liṅga* (Skt: the symbolic representation of Shiva as a stylized phallus, which became the palladium of the Khmer rulers) are all portrayed.

The depiction of clothing on stone sculptures in the round was usually very simple, and figures were often entirely unadorned. Indeed, the inscriptions state that the images were given real clothes and adornments that could be changed. The only male garment sculpted in stone was a short, vertically striped *sampot* worn round the hips and fastened with a simple anchor device in front and with the edges passed between the legs and tucked behind into a wide belt decorated with four-petalled flowers carved in squares. The dress of female deities consisted of a skirt decorated with a regular pattern of fleurets and draped so as to form a large, triangular front panel. The real clothes must certainly have been far richer, similar to those worn by the princely figures in the bas-reliefs and the images of *dvārapāla*s and *devatā*s. The dignitaries in the bas-reliefs, as well as some *dvārapāla*s, wore draped costumes with long panels at the side. Their belts were decorated with pendants. The skirts of the *devatā*s and of the princesses were edged with a wide braid embroidered with pearls, denticles and stripes. Hair was dressed in stylized plaits with small crescents and piled on the top of the head. Avalokiteshvara and deities wore their hair in the ascetic's style, in a cylindrical braided chignon (*jaṭāmukuṭa*). If the figure, whether male or female, wore a decorated headdress, this would consist of a diadem shaped like a crown and carved with a row of flowers, pearls and a border of denticles, and a covering for the chignon decorated with rows of lotus-petals. Deities in their terrifying aspect wore a sort of helmet decorated on the brow with a diadem of leaves.

On some early images in the Bayon style the Buddha seated in meditation is portrayed apparently wearing only the monk's undergarment (*antaravāsaka*), draped round the lower half of the body. As the style developed, he is shown wearing the *uttarāsanga* (monastic robe) with the right shoulder bare and the end folded over the left shoulder. In standing images of the Buddha the *uttarāsanga* covers both shoulders. The Buddha's hair is dressed either in tight curls or small stylized plaits and has a conical covering decorated with lotus-petals on the *uṣṇīṣa*.

In Angkor sculpture there has always been a tendency to simplify the anatomy, and only rarely is there any hint of musculature. At the end of the 12th century and the beginning of the 13th, the development of personal cults produced a large number of orders from individual patrons. As a result, sculptors had to produce pieces very quickly, following a prescribed pattern, and so could pay little attention to the modelling of the body. Furthermore, they often used soft sandstone of indifferent quality, which did not hold together well, so that to ensure the statue's stability they had to exaggerate the size of the legs. In some statues there is a striking contrast between the rather coarse and heavy treatment of the body and the finely modelled face with its closed eyes and natural, meditative expression (for example, the Avalokiteshvara of Preah Khan of Angkor; Phnom Penh, N. Mus.). Only the most outstanding pieces reveal the sculptor's powers of observation, and these do so even though the anatomy is only suggested.

24. *Jayavarman VII*, sandstone, h. 440 mm, Bayon style, from Preah Khan of Kompong Svay, late 12th century to the early 13th (Phnom Penh, National Museum)

(b) Bronze. While the stone statues in the Bayon style tend towards uniformity in the arrangement of their dress and their adornments, the bronze images are richly adorned, and their clothes are draped in a variety of ways. Some still have costumes similar to those of the preceding era, of the Angkor Vat and even the Baphuon style; others show the changes characteristic of the Bayon style. Most of these bronzes are small statuettes made, no doubt, for

veneration in private oratories or to be carried in processions. Hindu deities are fairly numerous: Shiva, Vishnu on Garuda, and Vishnu's consort, Lakshmi. The Mahayana Buddhist images include the Buddha protected by the *nāga*, sitting in meditation between Avalokiteshvara and Prajnaparamita, and such Mahayana deities as Hevajra, a ferocious manifestation of the transcendental Buddha Akshobya, dancing on a demon (beautiful examples of these are in Phnom Penh, N. Mus. and Bangkok, N. Mus.).

Although the production of the Bayon period consisted chiefly of small statuettes, the bronzesmiths maintained their mastery of their art, as is shown by several large pieces that were taken to Thailand after the conquest of Angkor in 1431 and then to Burma after the sack of Ayutthaya in 1767, where they are kept in a Mandalay monastery (Arakan Pagoda). These include lions, an adorned three-headed elephant and two *dvārapālas*, of which one, almost complete, must originally have been about 2 m high. Various other small bronze objects of this period demonstrate the same fine workmanship and elegant proportions. The National Museum, Phnom Penh, possesses parts of a lotus motif, including buds and a leaf, that were fixed by lugs to a slightly curved stem. Small bells, *vajras* (thunder-bolt images), conches and other objects made of bronze were used in Mahayana cults. The conches are especially elegant and are usually decorated with an image of Hevajra surrounded by dancing figures (Phnom Penh, N. Mus.; Bangkok, N. Mus.). Gilded bronze ornaments decorated chariot poles and palanquin fastenings (hooks and rings). The poles end in a five- or seven-headed *nāga*; sometimes a *garuḍa* is mounted on the *nāga*, sometimes the *nāga* has the head of a *garuḍa* (Bangkok, N. Mus.). The finials of some poles are in the form of a shelter for a Buddha image or a Vajrasattva, the Supreme or Primordial Buddha, holding a small bell and a *vajra* (Phnom Penh, N. Mus.).

BIBLIOGRAPHY

H. Dufour and C. Carpeaux: *Le Bayon d'Angkor Thom* (Paris, 1910–14)

P. Stern: 'Le Bayon d'Angkor Thom et l'évolution de l'art khmer', *An. Mus. Guimet*, xlvii (1927) [whole issue]

G. Coedès: 'Le Portrait dans l'art khmer', *A. Asiatiques.*, vii/3 (1960), pp. 179–98

J. Boisselier: 'Notes sur les bas-reliefs tardifs d'Angkor Vat', *J. Asiat.*, ccl (1962), pp. 35–48

G. Coedès: 'La Date d'exécution des deux bas-reliefs tardifs d'Angkor Vat', *J. Asiat.*, xxii (1962), pp. 244–8

P. Stern: *Les Monuments khmers du style de Bayon et Jayavarman VII* (Paris, 1965)

J. Boisselier: 'Notes sur l'art du bronze dans l'ancien Cambodge', *Artibus Asiae*, xxix/4 (1967), pp. 275–334

5. AFTER *c.* 1220. By the mid-13th century the Khmers were beginning to adopt Theravada Buddhism. In the same period, the rulers of Angkor lost their control over the Chao Phraya basin and had to endure repeated Thai attacks, as a result of which they were finally compelled to abandon Angkor soon after the Thai conquest of 1431–2. One king, probably Ang Chan I (*reg c.* 1510–*c.* 1560), transferred his court to Angkor for a brief period in the mid-16th century, and it was at this time that the bas-reliefs were carved on the north-east quadrant of Angkor Vat (*see* §3(i) above), probably from a canvas sketched in the 12th century, as well as those at the end of the Elephant Terrace in Angkor Thom, in Temple 486 and in Temple X at Preah Pithu.

25. Four-armed deity, sandstone, Vat Srei Sar Chhor, 16th century

In 1594 the Thais conquered Lovek. This disaster greatly weakened the Khmer kingdom for a long time, and once again the forest reclaimed Angkor. However, the Khmers did not forget the old capital's existence. They continued to go on pilgrimage to Angkor Vat, by then transformed into a Buddhist temple, as is shown by inscriptions recording the offering of gifts, especially statues, to the temple. Some of the fine images at Preah Pean of Angkor Vat may also have been such offerings. Important statuary dating from this period has been conserved in two monasteries of Srei Santhor, Vat Srei Sar Chhor (see fig. 25) and Vat Vihear Suor. Throughout the 17th–20th century Buddhist sculpture continued to be produced in traditional style and with traditional iconography, and even during the period of French rule there was scarcely any discernible influence of Western, colonial styles.

(i) Late 13th century–the 16th. (ii) 17th–19th centuries. (iii) 19th–20th centuries.

(i) Late 13th century–the 16th. Towards the end of the 13th century Temple 486 at Angkor was at least partly reconstructed as a Theravada sanctuary, and images of the Buddha were carved on its pediments and false doors. The serene faces of these effigies are in the tradition of the Bayon style. Probably also dating from this period are some large stone statues at Preah Pean of Angkor Vat, but these are not of such high quality. A group of wooden

statues (Angkor, Depôt Conserv. Mnmts) representing the standing Buddha displaying the *abhaya mudrā* proclaim the far-reaching influence of Dvaravati art (*see* THAILAND, §IV, 1(i)). The *uttarāsanga* covers both shoulders, allowing the *antaravāsaka*, revealed by the luminosity of the Buddha's body, to be seen at the waist. These images have the discreet naturalism and meditative expression characteristic of Bayon art. However, some wooden statues of the standing Buddha adorned are inspired by models of the Angkor Vat style, which sought above all to express majesty, as indicated by the spreading diadem, the conical hair-cover and necklace pendants. Sculpture in this style, although it diminished in importance, continued to be produced during the following centuries. The most recent of the works found at Srei Santhor is a large wooden statue of the standing Buddha (Vat Srei Sar Chhor Monastery) adorned in the *abhaya mudrā*, which differs greatly from the Angkor tradition and with its rich dress is similar in style to Ayutthaya images of the late 16th century and early 17th.

The late bas-reliefs of Angkor Vat retain many features of the Angkor Vat and Bayon styles. The figures in these reliefs resemble the statues of deities in the monasteries of Srei Santhor. Several of the seated statues in the sanctuaries have four arms, but unfortunately they do not have any attributes that would make it possible to establish whether they are Hindu or Mahayana Buddhist. The modelling of their bodies is rather heavy and lacking in vigour. Their heads, however, are more individualized. The square-jawed face of Deity A at Vat Srei Sar Chhor, probably the oldest in this series, is reminiscent of some figures in the late reliefs of Angkor Vat.

The headdresses of the Srei Santhor statues are also similar to those of the deities on the late reliefs at Angkor Vat and include a sort of tiara joining the diadem, a hair-cover and neck-shield. The diadem, which is still spread out on Deity A at Vat Srei Sar Chhor, already has a vertical fold on each side reminiscent of the more pronounced folds on the diadems of later Buddha images of the Ayutthaya period in Thailand; these folds also appear on several tiaras in the Angkor Vat reliefs. On the oldest pieces at Vat Srei Sar Chhor, the necklace is decorated with parallel bands and pendants following an Angkor model; on the later images it is replaced by a pectoral ornament descending in a triangle on to the chest and chased with volutes. Both of these types of adornment can be found on the late reliefs at Angkor Vat; however, all the ornamentation, both at Srei Santhor and at Angkor Vat, displays a flower-shaped motif with two lateral flamelike petals characteristic of post-Angkor art. As the Srei Santhor images are seated, there is no indication of their garb. The figures on the reliefs wear a *sampot* often with a basque covering the hips and a sort of scarf with two long, floating panels knotted at the belt and sometimes worn over trousers.

Several statues of this period are of seated figures with their hands joined in veneration; similar images occur in Thailand. Eight such praying figures made of stone were placed around the Vat Tep Pranam sanctuary at Udong. A particularly fine, wooden statue of a praying figure (Phnom Penh, N. Mus.) from Angkor Vat is seated on the left side, with legs crossed and a contemplative expression on his face. On his head, which is slightly inclined towards his joined hands, he wears a decorated tiara, and his neck-shield is adorned with a remarkable pattern of volutes round a large flower with flame-shaped lateral petals.

(ii) 17th–19th centuries. After the end of the 16th century, Khmer sculptures, whether in the round or in relief, were generally made from wood. As they were easy to transport in consequence, few have been found *in situ*. A number of statues were placed in Angkor Vat; but images of high quality were also made for the monasteries of large towns and at royal courts such as Udong, which was the main royal residence at this time, Battambang, Siem Reap, Pursat and Kompong Cham.

The sculptors of Angkor had always represented the Buddha in an idealized but naturalistic manner, and in the early post-Angkor period this tradition was maintained. However, during the period following the capture of Lovek by the Thais in 1594 sculptors increasingly abandoned attempts at naturalism and turned their attention to representing the Buddha as a superhuman being, whose transcendence was revealed by the 32 major *lakṣaṇa*s (auspicious signs) described in the Buddhist texts. This new concept of the Buddha's image also indicates that there were influences from the Theravada Buddhist art of Ayutthaya.

Representations of the standing Buddha are the most numerous, no doubt partly because the natural form of the tree trunks from which they were carved lends itself to this type of image particularly well. However, the hands and lateral dress panels of the garment were carved separately and fixed later to the statues. The gesture most often represented is the *abhaya mudrā*, performed either by both hands or by one, with the other hanging down beside the body. The seated Buddha is often represented calling the earth to witness with his right hand (*bhūmisparśa mudrā*) at the moment of his triumph over Mara (*Māravijaya*). The image of the Buddha in meditation with his hands resting in his lap (*samādhi*), protected by the *nāga*, became rarer. In standing images of the Buddha in *abhaya mudrā*, the *uttarāsanga* covers both shoulders and the *antaravāsaka*, held at the waist by a wide belt and draped to form a vertical panel in front, falls below the *uttarāsanga* to the ankles. In seated images of the Buddha the *uttarāsanga* leaves the right shoulder bare and the shawl (*sanghāṭī*) is folded and placed over the left shoulder. The curls on the Buddha's head are rendered simply as squares. The statues were generally given two coats of lacquer, one black and one red, and then gilded to evoke two of the *lakṣaṇa*s: the luminosity of the body and the skin's golden sparkle.

From the beginning of the 17th century to the end of the 19th, there were numerous studios producing many Buddha images, but none of these had any real artistic merit, and only a few produced truly original works, such as the statues from one studio at Siem Reap, which are of an extreme simplicity and have a gentle, meditative and slightly melancholy facial expression.

Many representations of the Buddha from this period are in royal attire, in reference to his royal birth and his role as a *cakravartin* (Skt: universal monarch) and teacher of the Law that governs the world. Whether in royal attire or in a simple monastic robe, he is represented in the same postures. His adornments include a tiara (though not invariably), a breastplate (sometimes decorated with pendant chains), bracelets and armlets. The belt and the folded edge and front panel of the *antaravāsaka* are covered with decoration, sometimes embroidered instead of worked in gold. Many images have a sort of basque or two winglike motifs covering the hips below the belt. What appear to be the earliest pieces are decorated with carvings and are lacquered and gilded. The top of the tiara is usually conical; the diadem is welded to the neck-shield and has a vertical leafy branch or a fold (as mentioned above) above the ear; on the forehead volutes are arranged around a flower with burnished side petals. On one of the most beautiful statues of this type (Angkor, Depôt Conserv. Mnmts, no. 5533) the facial features are so distinctive that it appears to be a portrait.

During the 17th century ornaments made of pearls and lacquer filigree were added, like braid, in patterns of scrolled leaves, volutes and flowers. This technique may owe something to Burmese art. During the 18th century, the lacquer was no longer only worked into filigree or pearls but also inlaid with glass beads and thickly coated mouldings. Lacquered images decorated in this way usually have a tiara with a tapering crown. In the 17th- and 19th-century pieces the lateral folds (as above) of the diadem behind the ears were replaced by finely cut wings made of lacquer set in a metal frame. The breastplate is adorned with crossed or hanging chains. The influence of late Ayutthaya art on these pieces is unmistakable. Two beautiful assemblages of Buddha images attired in this way were set out on the altars of two of the sanctuaries of Leach (Pursat). These statues are elegantly and richly attired. The monastery of Vat Preah Eynkosei at Siem Reap has two later images, probably dating from the end of the 18th century, each wearing a winged tiara that frames the face, which is leaning slightly forward with an expression of great gentleness. There are only a few statues of figures in an attitude of worship, two of which (Phnom Penh, N. Mus.) come from a monastery at Babor (Kompong Chhnang), a town that was one of the royal residences. Their adornment is similar to that of the carved adorned Buddhas of the end of the 17th century, and they are dressed in a *sampot* with a basque draped over trousers.

Nothing remains of any sanctuaries built during the 17th and 18th centuries, and if they were decorated with reliefs these have disappeared with them. The only elements to have been preserved are some fragments of reliefs on wood from Babor that must have formed the wall of one or two small temples there. On these fragments (Phnom Penh, N. Mus.) scenes from the life of the Buddha and the *jātakas* (stories of the Buddha's former lives) are identifiable, as well as episodes from the *Reamker*, the Khmer version of the *Rāmāyaṇa*. The costumes and adornments of the figures are of the same type as those of the praying figures from Babor mentioned above. More interesting are the female figures, as no female images in the round have survived. They appear in several scenes, but most notably as large guardian figures analogous to the celestial *devatās* (*apsarasas*; deities) of the temples of Angkor. Their dress includes a fine scarf covering the bosom and a draped skirt with soft panels at the front, held on the hips by a belt and basques. Their tiaras are similar to those worn by the male figures; however, one of these *devatās* wears three flowering branches above a narrow diadem, probably inspired by the headdresses of some *devatās* in the Angkor Vat style.

(iii) 19th–20th centuries. During the 19th century images of the Buddha continued to be made in the 18th-century tradition, but these became increasingly lifeless. During the 20th century there was a proliferation of statues cast in cement that contributed to this decadence. The revival of Cambodian arts under the direction of Georges Groslier was mainly concerned with work in precious metals and with weaving. The Pursat School of Art has produced many statuettes made from the local marmoreal stone; but most of this work lacks originality, and original pieces are more likely to be made in local studios. Thus the monastery of Vat Samrong Khnong at Battambang housed a touching statue of a worshipping nun made from limestone mortar (late 19th century–early 20th). In a more populist style, a relief in cast cement on an enclosing wall of Vat Kdol at Battambang, dating from the beginning of the 20th century, illustrates scenes from the *Reamker* in a humorous way, sometimes with an element of burlesque, but often with a touch of poetry (see fig. 26).

Colonial styles had little influence on Cambodian sculpture. A statue of King Norodom (*reg* 1860–1904) on

26. Scene from the *Reamker*, cement relief, Vat Kdol, Battambang, early 20th century

horseback was made in Europe in the 1860s and placed to the east of the Silver Pagoda, Phnom Penh; only the head is a likeness of the King. The monument raised in the 1920s in honour of King Sisowath (*reg* 1904–27) on the slopes of Phnom Penh hill (a hundred metres to the south of the Vat Phnom sanctuary) is also a Western work. The bronze image of the King was destroyed after the fall of the monarchy in 1970; only the ceramic screen remains. This is decorated with *devatā*s, dressed like dancers of the Royal Ballet coming to pay homage to the King. Another Western work, the monument to the fallen of World War I, was dismantled and the bronze elephant antefixes that decorated it were placed in the National Museum of Phnom Penh.

BIBLIOGRAPHY

J. Boisselier: *La Statuaire khmère et son évolution*, 2 vols, Pubns Ecole Fr. Extrême-Orient, xxxvii (Saigon, 1955)

——: 'Note sur les bas-reliefs tardifs d'Angkor Vat', *J. Asiat.*, ccxl/2 (1962), pp. 244–8

J. Coedès: 'La Date d'exécution des deux bas-reliefs tardifs d'Angkor Vat', *J. Asiat.*, ccxl/2 (1962), pp. 235–44

M. Giteau: *L'Iconographie du Cambodge post-angkorien*, Pubns Ecole Fr. Extrême-Orient (Paris, 1975)

MADELEINE GITEAU

27. Wall painting of a scene from the *Reamker*, cloister of Vat Preah Keo (Silver Pagoda), Phnom Penh, late 19th century

IV. Painting.

There is virtually no surviving Cambodian painting dating from before the end of the 19th century, and what there is seems to owe everything to Thai painting. It is recognized, however, that an earlier, authentic Khmer school once existed and that its disappearance was due less to the hazards of tropical climate than to the vicissitudes of history and to human neglect. Nothing is left of pre-Angkor painting, and all that survives of the Angkor period are the wall paintings in the two sanctuaries of Prasat Neang Khmau at Chok Gargyar (Koh Ker), dating from the reign of Jayavarman IV (*reg* AD 921[928]–441). These paintings are characterized by an unerring sureness of outline and employ only four colours (white, brown, red and black), applied with uniform brushstrokes. They may originally have been embellished with details in other colours. The architectural style of the composition is suggestive of bas-relief rather than painting. From the early 14th century, the Thais of Sukhothai and Ayutthaya reduced their former Khmer suzerain to the status of a Thai province, which, while still rebellious and desirous of preserving its own culture, became progressively more subject to Thai influence. Because nothing remains, it is impossible to discern how this fusion of Thai and Khmer painting styles came about during the post-Angkor period.

Paintings chiefly adorned the interior walls of monasteries as well as ceilings and wooden panels on doors and window shutters. Textiles such as cotton and silk, as well as paper, were also used as painting surfaces, but illuminated manuscripts are relatively rare in Cambodia, and their illustrations are usually schematic. Prior to painting, all these surfaces were systematically prepared. The surfaces of walls were usually thoroughly washed with a special preparation to rid them of mineral salts. They were then covered with a coat of plaster made with lime; a tamarind extract served as the binding agent. After polishing, the plastered wall was painted. The fragility of the paintings produced in this manner is understandable in a country with heavy seasonal rainfalls that can irreparably damage them through spreading damp. Moreover, the rain often attacked the paintings directly because dislodged roof tiles were not always replaced. In Cambodia, unlike Thailand, wooden and canvas surfaces were apparently untreated before being painted and are consequently better conserved.

The Khmer painters, like their Thai masters, employed only natural colours made by the maceration of certain plants and extraction from clay (particularly ochres). Gold leaf was used only in the richest monasteries to embellish certain details; most painters tried to achieve the same effect by using a luminous yellow outlined in red. Paint brushes were made from vegetable fibres or animal hair.

Khmer painting, although decorative, is primarily didactic and religious; its chief aim is to edify the faithful, and it is found almost exclusively within the confines of monasteries. The subject-matter and themes include the life of the Buddha, episodes from the *jātaka*s (stories of the Buddha's former lives), especially the *Story of Vessantara*, and evocations of the world of the gods and of hell. Non-Buddhist themes, such as those of the *Reamker*, the Khmer version of the *Rāmāyaṇa* epic (see fig. 27), and narrative literature (e.g. the *Story of Preah Chinavong*) are treated less often, although more in Cambodia than in Thailand. The fact that these themes are of Brahmanic origin has never been an obstacle to their representation in places of Buddhist worship, since the heroes have always been seen as *bodhisattva*s.

Because Cambodian painting is essentially didactic, it also conforms to strict iconographic conventions. In the late 19th century these rules were less strictly observed, but the best paintings basically conform to them. They were intended to ensure that the characters depicted could be recognized by everyone and the story easily followed. The painter had to serve a long apprenticeship to master the artistic techniques and the canons that governed them.

The gestures, poses and clothing he gave to the figures had to establish clearly their individual identities. Of uniform size, whatever their place in the painting, boldly outlined and coloured with unshaded brushstrokes, they are two-dimensional representations in a purely decorative pictorial universe. Similarly, buildings are traditionally depicted using an isometric projection and scale unrelated to the figures. The landscape, also accessory, is often treated with feeling and even a certain humour, as when, for example, the artist introduces small animals. It is here also that we see the first signs of Western influence with the introduction of realism and the use of perspective. The traditional treatment of landscape, unlike that of human figures and architectural elements, could accommodate this influence because the depiction of successive planes (foreground, middleground and background) already existed in Khmer painting. Additionally, the rendering of indirect lighting in the landscape created half-tones that softened and transformed line, whereas line, rather than depth, still dominated in the treatment of the other elements of the painting.

Since the late 19th century the various elements of paintings have been rendered according to slightly more elastic rules than had existed previously, but representations of the same subject differ very little one from another. Nevertheless, there are clear differences of style between artists, of whom the more gifted are distinguishable by their greater sensibility and skill in composing and harmonizing the scenes, by the purity and sureness of their line and brushstrokes and by their choice of colours.

BIBLIOGRAPHY

J. Boisselier: *Le Cambodge* (Paris, 1966)
M. Giteau: *Iconographie du Cambodge post-angkorien* (Paris, 1975)
J. Boisselier: *La Peinture en Thaïlande* (Paris, 1976); Eng. trans. as *Thai Painting* (Tokyo, 1976)
M. Jacq-Hergoualc'h: *Le Roman: Source d'inspiration de la peinture khmère* (Paris, 1982)

MICHEL JACQ-HERGOUALC'H

V. Textiles.

The Khmer empire grew out of the Indianized states of Funan and Zhenla, and the influence of Indian textiles on techniques, style, design and symbolism in Cambodia has been profound. Khmer textiles in turn influenced those of Thailand: after the Thais conquered Angkor in 1431/2, the courts of Ayutthaya and Bangkok received tribute in the form of cloth and other precious goods until French colonization in the late 19th century. When the frontiers of Cambodia were drawn up by the French, the Khmer people were split in two. The textiles, like the language, of the Khmers in Thailand (Khmer Sung) and in Cambodia (Khmer Tam) developed along somewhat divergent paths. As a consequence of the catastrophic political events of 1975–8 there was little opportunity for the Khmers of Cambodia to weave at all. The continuity of tradition was, however, maintained in Thailand, and a survey of the textiles and dress of the Khmers of Thailand is therefore included here.

28. Silk weft ikat *pidan* cloth depicting heaven with dancing girls and elephants, 1.55×0.79 m, Khmer, 1989 (Chiang Mai, private collection)

1. KHMER. The available information about Khmer Tam textiles from Cambodia is restricted to a few articles by French writers and to records of court textiles collected by the National Museum of Phnom Penh. These articles describe all types of textiles as *sampot*, including ikats and embroidered and supplementary weft cloths, although, strictly speaking, the Khmer word is *sompruat*, which means 'cloth for wearing'. The *sampot* listed by Stoeckel are of six main types. The first, called *pamuong*, is a shot silk or cotton woven with two shafts (thus producing the simplest weave) and is categorized by colour, such as violet (*svai*), green (*baitang*), yellow (*luong*), red (*kraham*) or black (*khman*). The second type is called *kaniuh*, the Khmer name for a textile woven with a twisted, two-coloured yarn in the weft. These cloths are called *kaniuh saut* if they are of pure silk, *kaniuh ambas* if pure cotton and *kaniuh saut leai ambas* if cotton and silk mixed; all are also woven with two shafts. The *sampot anlunh* is a chequered silk fabric woven with three shafts and using multicoloured warp and weft. The *sampot lobak* has supplementary weft designs. The use of up to 18 shafts has been recorded, but Stoeckel did not say what materials were used. The cloths may be categorized according to the design of the supplementary pattern, for example *sampot lobak krachap* (a fruit). Twelve designs are recorded, together with the number of shafts required for the design and an illustration. The *sampot sarabap* was made using gold yarns in a brocade decoration. These cloths were for the rich, and by the 1920s their production had stopped. The word *sarabap* may derive from *yerabub*, a Persian gold brocade cloth copied by Thai and Lao weavers. The sixth type described by Stoeckel was the *sampot holl*, a silk ikat that is further categorized by the various designs, of which Stoeckel records 14, for example *sampot holl kum pich*, a diamond-and-lantern pattern ikat.

The textiles woven by the Khmers include different types for clothing, for religious wall hangings and for household use. The textiles in the National Museum of Phnom Penh, recorded by its former curator, Madeleine Giteau, include ikats, usually used as pantaloons (*chong kraben*), in which the long cloth is wrapped round the waist, and the loose ends are twisted together, passed between the legs, tucked in at the waist at the back and secured with one or more silver belts. *Chong kraben* cloths were worn by both men and women, either as pantaloons or as long skirts with pleats at the front (Thai *pha na nang*). Traditionally, no top was worn by men or women until the introduction of Western-style shirts and coats by the French in the late 19th century. A smaller ikat silk cloth (*pidan*) documented by Giteau depicted temple scenes with elephants, dancing girls and Khmer monuments, in a style that shows least Indian influence (see fig. 28). The designs of temples, people and elephants are said to depict heaven, and it is used as a wall hanging for the room of a dying person or in temples. These cloths, still woven in Cambodia, are similar to those recorded by Madeleine Giteau in the early 20th century.

The traditional pantaloon or *chong kraben* cloth is approximately 4×1 m and is woven in a variety of techniques, including ikat (*see* TEXTILE, §III, 1(ii)(a)) and plain and two-coloured twisted yarns. Formerly, the ikat was made in a three-shaft twill weave with over-dye techniques in the ikat. The dominant colours were red, yellow and green with a dark maroon ground colour. Designs were geometric, small and mostly based on Indian sari designs. The most popular was the *sompruat holl* cloth, based on the classic double-ikat *patola* sari design involving a framed central panel of small motifs surrounded on the long edges by a patterned band and, on the ends, by *kruai choeng* points. This cloth is often referred to by Thai names, such as *pha thai that* (meaning that one cloth could buy freedom for a slave), or *pha pum* or *sompuk pum*, names taken from the *sompak lai* embroidered Thai designs that the Khmer weavers were commissioned to incorporate. The size, decoration and number of rows of *kruai choeng*, together with the type of design, indicated status. It is likely that these textiles were used by the Thai court and royalty from the Ayutthaya period (1351–1767) until the time of Rama V (*reg* 1868–1910). After that the ikat *chong kraben* was woven only for use in ordination ceremonies or by the Khmer aristocracy in Thailand and Cambodia. The mass of the people used cloths of plain yarns or two-coloured yarns twisted together. Green and purple were favourite colours.

Modern Khmer Sung textiles are predominantly silk; even poor Khmer farmers living in Thailand may wear silk for work. The *chong hol* (*mi hol*), is worn by women as a tubular skirt. It measures 2×1 m and is patterned in the weft with narrow rows of arrow-shapes in ikat, alternating with thin stripes of plain colours. These are always woven in a three-shaft twill. The dominant colours are yellow, green, black and white designs on a red ground. This textile was sometimes decorated with a separate ikat hem piece, called the *chong hol pha bol*, that was sewn on separately, in imitation of the borders on the *sompruat holl*. It is no longer woven, except for use in the theatre.

A silk cloth called *rabue* is worn by men as a shoulder-cloth or loincloth. It is made using four shafts and in a complex design of six colours, creating a tiny chequer pattern. Dominant colours are orange, black and green. Another version, the *pha kama*, made by Thais as well as by Khmers, is woven in large chequers with dominant colour combinations originating from different areas, such as red and white, black and white, yellow, green and black, or purple and turquoise. The Khmers make these in silk or, increasingly, in synthetic yarns. Another cloth woven for men's use is the silk sarong made in a chequer pattern of twisted yarns in which orange and green predominate. This 2×1 m textile is sewn into a tube. The women's shoulder-cloth is a narrow, plain white (black for funerals) silk cloth woven in a diamond twill using 4–8 shafts. Today it is worn over a modern shirt.

An interesting Khmer Sung textile is the silk *am prom*, which is woven with a tiny white double ikat on a dark red ground. The warp and weft ikat designs create small crosses scattered at random throughout the cloth.

BIBLIOGRAPHY

J. Stoeckel: 'Etude sur le tissage au Cambodge', *A. Archéol. Khmers*, i/4 (1921–3), pp. 387–402

J. Galotti: 'Les Sampots du Cambodge', *A. & Déc.*, l (1926), pp. 161–8

Art of Ikat (exh. cat. by F. Skyring, Watson, ACT Craft Cent., 1981)

PATRICIA NAENNA

2. MINORITY PEOPLES. Among the 10% of the Cambodian population who are not Khmer, a substantial proportion are Vietnamese or Chinese. The other minorities include Thais, Laos, Chams and several small but distinct groups of hill people. Cham traditional dress resembles that of the Malays, the main item of clothing being the skirt sarong. Cham cloth (of silk or cotton) is traditionally decorated by means of a wax or starch batik resist. Imported Javanese cloths have become popular. Cham women wear close-fitting dark green tunics with tight sleeves and open at the neck. Men's shirts are often worn with an open robe extending to the ankles, white cloth with red and green stripes being specially favoured. Cham brides dress in royal attire, wearing elaborate headdresses with gilded pins, large fabric collars with pendants and armbands. The Chams also use banners and parasols during rituals and demarcate sacred areas with textiles. On ceremonial occasions they display palm fronds and numerous fabric hangings decorated with appliqué, embroidery and tassels. The Jarai and Rhadé peoples, who live on the Darlac Plateau in contiguous areas of Vietnam and eastern Cambodia, have more in common with the Chams than with the Khmers. The men of both groups wear jackets and small turbans, and the women short skirts and sleeveless bodices.

BIBLIOGRAPHY

D. J. Steinberg: *Cambodia: Its People, its Society, its Culture* (New Haven, 1959)

J. Baccot: *Syncrétisme religieux dans un village cham du Cambodge (On G'Nur et Cay a O Russei)* (diss., U. Paris, 1968)

Area Handbook for the Khmer Republic (Cambodia) (Washington, DC, 1973)

MICHAEL HITCHCOCK

VI. Theatre.

Cambodian theatre reflects the prolonged influence of Indian models, modified by indigenous forms and influences from other parts of South-east Asia. The bas-reliefs of Angkor Vat (first half of the 12th century) depict dancing *apsaras*, an Indian motif common throughout South-east Asia. Chinese influence is also present, although less obviously, in Cambodian theatre. The *lakhon bassac*, a dance drama originating among the Khmers of southern Vietnam, reveals both Indian and Chinese influences. The shadow theatre of Cambodia, in its repertory, the structure of its performances and the technique of manipulating the puppets, is related to that of Thailand, Malaysia and the south-east Indian state of Andhra. There are few historical data on the origin and development of the genre in

Cambodia, and more comparative research on the different traditions is needed.

1. Costumes and masks. According to the chronicles, after the collapse of Angkor in the mid-15th century the entire Khmer court with its skilled craftsmen was taken to the Thai court of Sukhothai, where Khmer theatrical forms were introduced, and were, it seems, thereafter largely lost to Cambodia. Whether this is true or not, it is certain that in the 19th century Thai dancers reintroduced Khmer dance in a slightly modified form to the Khmer court of Phnom Penh under the patronage of King Ang Duong (*reg* 1841–59). Cambodian theatre falls into several categories: classical dance, popular dance drama, pure dance and folk-dance. Classical dance was originally performed within the court by female courtiers and female members of the royal family. It takes its themes from the *Reamker*, the Khmer *Rāmāyaṇa*, and is characterized by graceful and refined movements. Dance drama is a more popular form originally performed only by men, but now by both sexes. In the pure dance form no story is enacted; the Candle Dance, popular throughout South-east Asia and performed by a group of young girls, is an example of this style. Folk-dance includes harvest and rain-invoking dances and courtship dances such as the *lamthong* or *rom vung*, in which couples or mixed groups of dancers move together in a flirtatious manner without actually touching.

Costumes worn in Khmer dance and dance drama are of a single basic type. Both male and female performers wear a piece of cloth called a *sampot* (*see* §V above) wrapped around the waist, usually with front pleats drawn between the legs and tucked into a belt at the back to form loose pantaloons. Costumes worn by kings, princes and gods are particularly ornate and consist of a tight-fitting, long-sleeved, silk brocade jacket with wing-shaped epaulettes and embroidered collar, a *sampot* of gold or silver secured by two belts, and a narrow panel of cloth flanked by side panels hanging from the waist. Their jewellery consists of several bracelets on each arm, anklets, chains over the chest, earrings and a pendant in the shape of a banyan leaf. They also wear a tall, tapering crown or *mkot*, which is treated with great veneration. The feet are bare; in the bas-reliefs of Angkor female dancers are also portrayed bare-breasted, though nowadays, perhaps as a result of Thai influence in the 15th and 16th centuries, they wear a piece of cloth tied around the chest, tucked into the waist on the dancer's right and draped over the left shoulder. Over this hangs a stiff brocade shawl that reaches to mid-calf at the back. Goddesses, queens and princesses wear a gold or silver lamé *sampot*, a tall *mkot* similar to the man's but lighter, and heavy earrings, armlets and anklets (see fig. 29). They also dance barefoot. Costumes worn by lesser characters are less ornate and sumptuous, according to their status. *Sampot* may vary in quality from plain silk to cotton, and jewellery is present in varying quantities or even absent. Smaller crowns, coronets or flowers may be worn instead of the *mkot*. Costumes worn in folk-dances are also simpler and made of cotton.

Masks are not worn by human characters or by gods in Cambodian theatre, but only by demons, monkeys and

29. Costume of the Royal Cambodian ballet

some other animals and birds. The mask, which is made of a substance like papier mâché, covers the entire head and has eye-holes but no holes for mouth or nose. The features are usually grotesque, monkey masks having exaggerated wide, grinning mouths. *Yaksha*s (Skt: demons) also have wide, fanged mouths and wear a tall *mkot*, which adds to the weight of the already heavy mask. The most feared and revered mask is that of Ravana (Khmer: Rab), the wicked ruler of Lanka, whose battle against Rama is one of the principal themes of the *Rāmāyaṇa*. Rab's mask has long tusks and a tall *mkot* with nine heads carved on it, which, together with the face beneath the crown, make up the ten heads of the demon king.

BIBLIOGRAPHY

Chaufea Veang Samdach Thiounn: *Danses cambodgiennes* (n.p., n.d.); rev. and augmented by J. Cuisinier as *Danses cambodgiennes d'après la version originale du Samdach Chaufea Thiounn* (Phnom Penh, 1968)

A. Leclère: *Le Théâtre cambodgien* (Paris, 1911)

G. Groslier: *Danseuses cambodgiennes anciennes et modernes* (Paris, 1913)

A. Danielou: *La Musique du Cambodge et du Laos* (Pondicherry, 1957)

Area Handbook for the Khmer Republic (Cambodia) (Washington, DC, 1973)

P. R. Cravath: *Earth in Flower: An Historical and Descriptive Study of the Classical Dance Drama of Cambodia* (diss., U. HI, 1985; microfilm, Ann Arbor, 1987)

Chan Moly Sam: *Khmer Court Dance* (Newington, 1987)

MIRANDA BRUCE-MITFORD

2. Puppets. The most elaborate type of shadow theatre performed in Cambodia is the 'large hides' (Khmer *nang*

sbek thom, *nang sbek* or *sbek thom*), which was associated with court rituals and entertainments. The puppets may represent either individual figures or group scenes (see fig. 30). The name is derived from their great height, which is on average about 1.25 m, though puppets of 2 m exist. The figures are first drawn in great detail on ox- or cowhides, according to strict conventions, and then cut out with the utmost care.

The different types are divided into five categories: royalty, demons, nature spirits, mythical monkeys and secondary characters, such as farmers. It is in the last category that the puppetmaker is allowed some freedom of interpretation. The shadow puppets are supported by two bamboo sticks that serve as handles for the puppeteer. The whole process of making the puppets and performing with them is surrounded by a number of rituals to protect both makers and puppeteers from the powers attributed to the puppets, which are all characters from the *Reamker*. There are obvious similarities of iconography between the puppets, the carved stone figures at Angkor and the costumes of the Royal Ballet, although these have been little studied.

Performances are usually in the open as part of religious festivals, but may also be staged to avert drought or other catastrophes. The centre of the performance area is a large screen of some 7–10 m in width and 3 m in height, elevated about 1 m from the ground. The shadows are manipulated behind or in front of the screen, which is illuminated from behind by an open fire or, nowadays, more usually by electric light. An orchestra that may consist of eight to ten musicians is seated in front of the screen. Their instruments consist of two or three buffalo-hide drums, xylophones (*roneath*), gongs (*khong*), wind instruments (*sralai*) and small brass cymbals (*ching*). There may be 100 or more shadow puppets in a single set. During a performance these are placed on a horizontal beam behind the screen.

The performance starts at nightfall and is preceded by a number of rituals that have to be performed to protect the puppeteer and let the spirits take possession of the puppets. The puppeteers are trained from a very early age to perform elegant dance movements while manipulating the puppets. There are no written texts and the performances are improvised by two narrators (*kru*), who are seated at each side of the screen and represent the powers and characters of good (Rama) and evil (Ravana) respectively. While the narrators are reciting the dialogue, the puppets are held motionless against the screen. When the narrator has finished a part of the story the orchestra starts to play and that part is illustrated by the dancing puppeteers.

The movements of the shadow puppets and the dancing puppeteers are directed by the orchestra and follow strict conventions, while the structure of the performance is determined by the narrators, who decide on the order and length of the spoken episodes and the dance interludes. The performance of the whole *Reamker* generally lasts about seven consecutive nights, but performances outside a religious context are now much shorter. As the genre is so closely related to royal rituals, there is little room for interpretation or innovation in the *nang sbek thom*, and many elements of the classical dance theatre have been retained.

The other type of Khmer shadow theatre is the 'little hides' (*nang sbek touch* or *nang trolung*), a popular version of the *nang sbek thom* and free of its strict conventions. The puppets represent individual characters and are on average 300 mm in height. They are made according to the same process as the 'large hides', but their limbs are often movable by means of small sticks. The features of the puppets are less refined than those of the *nang sbek thom*, and the comic figures especially are very crude. Performances mainly take place in a religious context, but may also be presented as pure entertainment. There is only one narrator; he is seated with the puppeteers, of whom there may be as many as five in a company, behind a screen about 3 m wide and 1.5 m high. The screen is illuminated from behind by oil lamps or electric lights. The puppeteers do not dance but only manipulate the puppets behind the screen. The orchestra may consist of six musicians, and the instruments used are similar to those in the *nang sbek thom*. The repertory is not restricted to the *Reamker*. Khmer stories are frequently adapted and, indeed, any theme or shadow, including the silhouettes of aeroplanes, may be incorporated. Because it can make use of popular themes and characters in this way, the *nang sbek touch* has long had a wide following in rural Cambodia.

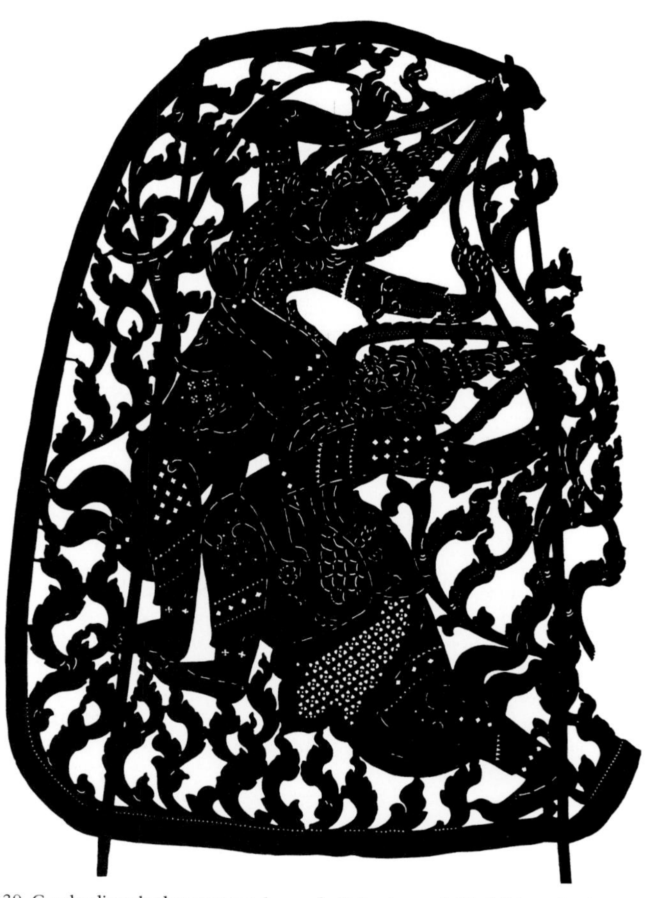

30. Cambodian shadow puppet (*nang sbek*), leather, *c.* 1.25×0.84 m; the figures represent the *Battle of Lakshmana and Indrajit*

BIBLIOGRAPHY

Dato Haji Mubin Sheppard: 'The Khmer Shadow Play and its Links with Ancient India', *J. Malay. Branch Royal Asiat. Soc.*, xli/1 (1968), pp. 199–204

J. Brunet: *Nang Sbek: Théâtre d'ombres dansé cambodge* (Berlin, 1969)

ROBIN RUIZENDAAL

VII. Ceramics.

The earliest ceramics found in Cambodia are utilitarian earthenware vessels decorated with simple geometric designs. They were shaped by striking a paddle on wet clay held against a fired clay anvil, a technique known from other early sites in South-east Asia. This basic type of pottery was made from the 4th millennium BC until the 9th century AD, and similar wares are again being produced in Cambodia for domestic use. A technological transition from this low-fired, unglazed earthenware to high-fired, glazed stoneware took place at the end of the 9th century or perhaps earlier. It marked the beginning of a distinctive ceramic tradition that lasted for about 500 years and roughly parallels the dates of the Khmer empire of Angkor (early 9th century to mid-15th). 'Khmer ceramics' is a collective term assigned to these wares, since they were undoubtedly made under the cultural direction and influence of Angkor. They reached a peak of artistic excellence in the 12th century, but subsequently production decreased and quality deteriorated and because of the decline of the empire and the growth in popularity of Chinese trade wares, it is unlikely that any Khmer ceramics were made after the 14th century.

Several probable Khmer ceramics production sites and kilns have been identified in Cambodia and Thailand; the Kulen Plateau, 40 km north-east of Angkor, is the most likely area known in Cambodia. Though no kilns have been found here, surface finds include kiln debris and green-glazed sherds. Sherds found elsewhere in Cambodia are similar in shape but different in body and glaze, a characteristic attesting to regional variations caused by the use of local materials.

31. Bird-shaped ceramic pot with brown glaze, diam. 100 mm, Khmer, late 11th century (Toronto, Royal Ontario Museum)

The kilns were capable of reaching and sustaining a temperature high enough to produce a hard and non-porous body. The clay has a high iron and sand content and after firing looks coarse and grainy, with the colour ranging from buff to grey or reddish. Although some Khmer ceramics were thrown on a potter's wheel, and some evidence exists for the use of moulds, most were made with coils and then finished on a turning table. The ridges of the coils can be felt on the interior of larger pieces. Such shapes as knobs on covers and conches were modelled by hand. Two glazes, green and brown, were used, both colours sometimes appearing on a single piece. However, although brown-glazed sherds have been excavated at temples in Angkor, it is not thought that Angkor was itself a production site, and brown-glazed wares have not been found at any of the probable kiln sites in Cambodia. It is therefore possible that these wares were made only in the Khmer-ruled areas of Thailand and were then transported to such places as Angkor. (For a description of Khmer brown glaze *see* THAILAND, §V, 5.) The green glaze is thin, translucent and mottled, the colour ranging from clear to yellowish or light green. Crazing is always visible. An uneven flaking of the glaze, which exposes the colour and texture of the body, is also characteristic.

Decoration on all Khmer ceramics is restrained, but horizontal rings around the neck or shoulder (see fig. 31) and such geometric patterns as arrows or short vertical lines are common. A diagnostic feature is the rimless base, which on green wares is frequently glazed. It is roughly finished on larger pieces, but on small pieces it is often in the shape of a flat button, with an impression that looks like a thumbprint. It is thought these prints were formed when the pieces were separated from the wheel or turning device. A potter's mark incised on the base of green-glazed wares is also common. Each mark is different, but all consist of one to four lines roughly cut in a geometric configuration, for example a triangle or a cross. The purpose of these marks is unknown.

The shapes of these green-glazed wares are simple, well-balanced and functional. They include architectural tiles and finials, covered jars, boxes, bowls, small jars, pots (some elephant-shaped), bottles and conches. All served either a utilitarian or a ceremonial purpose. One of the longest enduring shapes in the Khmer ceramic tradition is the conical bowl. Its only decoration consists of a deeply carved ring on the exterior round the lower section, and it has firing scars, caused by the small clay balls used to separate individual bowls in a stack, in the form of a ring of unglazed marks on both the interior and exterior of each bowl. Also common are round, covered boxes with broad bases. These are shaped like fruit, with segmented sides and a stem on the cover. The base is usually glazed and has a potter's mark. Typical of the green-glazed form are cylindrical covered jars. The covers are deep and dome-shaped, with a tiered knob and a lotus-bud tip. Modelled or carved petals and horizontal rings decorate the jars' shoulders. Pots with attachments modelled into animal forms, for example a caparisoned elephant, have also been excavated. Traces of finely ground lime on their interiors suggest that they were utilized as containers in betel sets.

Foreign influences on Khmer ceramics came from India and China. Indian influences probably reached the early Khmer empire via Java, for which one source of evidence is provided by the remarkably similar depictions of vessels on stone-carvings at both Borobudur in Java and Angkor in Cambodia, and is seen in such shapes as conches and baluster-shaped urns. Positive evidence that China was a source of technological influence was found in the 1970s, when quantities of Chinese trade wares similar in shape, glaze and decoration to Khmer ceramics were found in Butuan, on the north coast of Mindanao Island in the southern Philippines. Guangdong Province, in southern China, has been identified as the provenance of these wares, apparent in such shapes as bottles with tiered mouth rims and round boxes with lobes, all dating from between the 10th and 12th centuries. Despite these obvious foreign influences, the shapes and glazes of Khmer ceramics in Cambodia and Thailand are unknown in any other ceramic tradition, and their style is unique.

BIBLIOGRAPHY

D. Stock, ed.: *Khmer Ceramics, 9th–14th Century* (Singapore, 1981)

D. Rooney: *Khmer Ceramics* (Kuala Lumpur, 1984)

R. Brown: *The Ceramics of South-East Asia: Their Dating and Identification* (Singapore, 1988)

H. Fujiwara: *Khmer Ceramics from the Kamrātaṅ Collection*, intro. by D. F. Rooney (Singapore and Bangkok, 1990)

DAWN F. ROONEY

VIII. Other arts.

1. Coins. 2. Crematory pavilions. 3. Metalwork. 4. Musical instruments. 5. Wood-carving.

1. COINS. Spanish missionaries first recorded a gold and silver coinage in the vicinity of Battambang in north-western Cambodia during the late 16th century. Of these, only silver specimens survive, usually of the 1 *pe* denomination. The designs only appear on one side of these finely executed coins and are very diverse, ranging from crabs and flowers to the *garuḍa* (mythical bird with human arms and torso, and head, wings and claws of an eagle) and *haṁsa* (sacred goose). Because the coins do not possess an identifying inscription, the significance of their designs remains uncertain, although some (such as the *garuḍa*) probably represent personal marks of the Cambodian or Thai rulers who controlled the Battambang region between the 16th and 19th centuries. One of the last indigenous issues, a copper coin with a silver wash displaying a *haṁsa* with scrolls emanating from its beak, was struck during the third quarter of the 19th century. Western-style minting machinery was first imported into Cambodia under King Ang Duong (*reg* 1841–59). A mint was established at Udong in 1853 and struck silver and bronze coins with a *haṁsa* and date on the obverse and a stylized representation of Angkor Vat on the reverse. The coins range in size from a 44–5 mm 4-*bat* piece to the 30 mm *bat* and 20 mm *sling* and *pe*. The first dies used to strike the coins were prepared by Ralph Heaton & Son of Birmingham, England. Locally made dies were also used to strike smaller denomination issues, such as the bronze *pe*.

BIBLIOGRAPHY

H. A. Ramsden: 'The Coins of Battambang', *Numi. & Philat. J. Japan*, iii/6 (1914), pp. 201–7

C. K. Panish: 'The Coins of North Cambodia', *Amer. Numi. Soc. Mus. Notes*, xx (1975), pp. 161–74

J. Cribb: 'The Introduction of European Style Coins in Cambodia', *Seaby Coin & Medal Bull.* (Feb 1982), pp. 45–50

R. S. Wicks: *A Survey of Native Southeast Asian Coinage Circa 450–1850: Documentation and Typology* (PhD diss., Ithaca, NY, Cornell U., 1983)

ROBERT S. WICKS

2. CREMATORY PAVILIONS. As in other Buddhist countries, cremation of the dead is generally practised in Cambodia. The deceased is usually incinerated in a crematory pavilion called a *men*, which forms the focus of the funeral ceremony and represents Mt Meru, the sacred mountain and abode of the gods. The size of the *men* reflects the social status of the deceased and the wealth of the relatives. At a humble cremation, bamboo and the soft trunks of banana trees are the main building materials used for the *men*, which in its simplest form consists merely of a roof supported at each corner by four banana trunks. The structure is then wrapped with a white cloth spangled with stars cut out of gold and silver paper. A pyre is constructed inside the area marked by the four posts and the corpse is placed directly on top of this. In more elaborate cremations, the *men* has to last for a month, so wood is used instead of banana trunks. Wooden *men* are tall, square structures, open on all four sides. The roof is pyramidal and multi-tiered, and the number of tiers indicates the rank of the deceased, a nine-tiered roof being reserved for kings and queens. The structure is richly decorated with motifs either painted on to the wood or cut out of paper, and the interior is covered with white cloth spangled with stars and other motifs.

Surrounding this pavilion is a square enclosure; the four sides of the square are aligned with the cardinal points of the compass, a tradition dating back to the time of Angkor, and pierced by four axial entrances. At the corners of this enclosure small structures are erected, where Buddhist monks take turns to recite prayers throughout the night. At a princely funeral this complex is in turn surrounded by a further enclosure that forms a covered gallery, which is open on its inner side. Towers are erected at each corner of the outer enclosure, from which gifts are distributed to the mass of people attending the cremation. A particularly ornate *men* was constructed in January 1970 for the cremation of Chuon Nath, Supreme Buddhist Patriarch of Cambodia.

BIBLIOGRAPHY

P. Collard: *Cambodge et Cambodgiens* (Paris, 1925)

C. Fillieux: *Merveilleux Cambodge* (Paris, 1962)

HAK SREA KUOCH

3. METALWORK. Metal was first worked in the region now known as Cambodia between 2000 and 1500 BC, shortly after agriculture was introduced into the area. Metalwork, particularly work in gold and silver, is highly prized, and levels of craftsmanship are high. In technique, function and design Khmer metalwork shows clear affinities with that of other South-east Asian work, particularly that of the mainland; both Indian and Chinese influences are also present.

MIRANDA BRUCE-MITFORD

32. Betel box in the shape of a frog, silver with incised decoration, h. 45 mm, diam. 200 mm, mid-20th century (London, private collection)

(i) Betel sets. Betel sets have long been widely used in Cambodia, where the use of betel is a universal and ancient custom. Betel containers depicted on stone carvings at Angkor and references to royal betel-nut bearers in Chinese records attest to its use by the Khmers in the 12th century. Silver or an alloy of silver and copper was the primary metal used. Betel sets for royalty, however, were made of gold or silver and inlaid with hardstones. Few old examples exist because they were often melted down and the metal recycled. The earliest surviving silver betel set dates from the early 20th century and was most likely made at Phnom Penh, the modern centre of silversmithing. In the 1920s French assistance for the craft resulted in improved quality of workmanship. After the 1950s boxes were mass-produced and quality declined. An effort in the early 1980s to revive the craft enabled the production of silver betel sets to resume.

Khmer betel sets characteristically consist of a wooden or lacquer tray with three or more silver animal-shaped boxes containing individual ingredients for betel chewing. Both real and mythical animals are depicted. Typical forms include a crouching dog with a long neck, a reclining deer and a kneeling elephant with an upturned trunk. Other popular animal shapes are puffer fish, frog (see fig. 32), pig, lion, goat, rabbit, cock, hen and duck. The finest boxes are skilfully decorated with detailed patterns in which fur, feathers and fishscales are realistically imitated with swirling lines, spirals and dots. Elaborate floral and flame patterns, sometimes superimposed on a decorated body, are common. Each box was handmade by annealing, cutting, hammering, incising and punching. Some boxes have inscriptions written in Khmer or Chinese on the base.

BIBLIOGRAPHY

K. I. Matics: 'Khmer Silver in Animal Shapes', *A. Asia*, xviii (July–Aug 1988), pp. 81–90

DAWN F. ROONEY

(ii) Other objects. Apart from fine jewellery and animal-shaped betel boxes, precious metals have traditionally been used in the manufacture of royal regalia, such as the king's sacred sword and sceptre and the great throne. Palanquins and chariots were of carved wood covered with gold and silver, and royal elephants were caparisoned in gold brocade with gold tusk-sheaths. The parasols of royal personages and dignitaries had gold handles. Zhou Daguan, a Chinese envoy who was in Angkor in 1296–7, stated that the palace windows were framed in gold, the doors gilded and that there was a tower of gold, presumably of brick covered with gold leaf or perhaps with bronze. The so-called Silver Pagoda of the Royal Palace, Phnom Penh, built in the late 19th century, is so named because the floor is made up of over 5000 large silver tiles, each weighing 1 kg.

The Khmers' love of fine jewellery is very evident in the bas-reliefs of Angkor Vat and other temples built between the 9th and 13th centuries. Buckles, hairpins and hair-combs used by royalty and other wealthy families and worn by dancers are frequently of gold or silver, usually finely chiselled and worked in gold.

Zhou Daguan mentioned the demand in Cambodia for Chinese gold, silver and tin, iron pots and copper plates, as well as the use of lances and small shields or bucklers, but stated that neither armour nor bows and arrows were used. The reliefs of Angkor Vat show battles in which some shields are embossed with *kalā* or lion masks, and others are decorated with concentric rings or patterns made up of small circles. Lances and spears were made of iron. Offering-plates and serving utensils may be of embossed silver, and silver water cups, spittoons and bowls are also found. These are usually ornate and embossed with strong swirling shapes and foliage in shallow relief.

MIRANDA BRUCE-MITFORD

4. MUSICAL INSTRUMENTS. Khmer musical instruments have much in common with those of Thailand, Laos and Burma; like them they display some Indian and Chinese influence. The 12th-century bas-reliefs at Angkor Vat and the Bayon include some of the earliest representations of court musical instruments, among them barrel-shaped drums of a type still used throughout the region, gong-chimes and harps. The harp is no longer used in Cambodia: in South-east Asia, it now occurs only in Burma. Instruments played in village orchestras in the late 20th century are similar to court instruments, but more simply decorated.

Gong-chimes (*khong vong*) are placed on upright horse-shoe-shaped frames sometimes carved and gilded with foliage motifs, or on horizontal circular frames of turned wood or bamboo. Larger gongs are hung from heavily decorated stands. Xylophones (*roneath aek* and *roneath dham*) sometimes also have carved, lacquered and gilded frames. The decoration often comprises flower and foliage motifs, sometimes with *nāgas*. Stringed instruments include two- or three-stringed fiddles (*dra u* and *dra khmer*), with sound-boxes made from jackfruit, wood, bamboo, ivory or buffalo horn, covered with snakeskin or elephant-trunk skin. The *takhe* is a three-stringed zither, with a sound-box traditionally carved in the form of a crocodile and ivory or wooden pegs. Drums (*skor*) are generally plain, with wooden bodies, but often sit on ornate carved and gilded stands. The Cambodians also use a goblet drum, with a waisted earthenware body. A more unusual instrument, possibly introduced by early Indian missionaries for use in both Hindu and Buddhist temple rituals, is the conch-shell trumpet. This is still occasionally used at important ceremonies.

BIBLIOGRAPHY

Grove Instr.; Grove 6: 'Kampuchea'
E. Taylor: *Musical Instruments of South-East Asia* (Singapore, 1989)

SIAN E. JAY

5. WOOD-CARVING. Cambodian wood-carving has much in common with that of other South-east Asian countries, particularly Thailand and Burma, where similar techniques and decorative motifs are used. The wood is carved into foliate and scroll designs, the whole piece being roughly hewn before the more intricate details are carved with chisels and knives. Many houses in Cambodia are of wood, especially in rural areas. These are largely unadorned, although the wealthiest have carved gables, balustrades and access staircases (*see* §II, 2 above). Monasteries usually have carved pillars and doorframes. The Royal Palace in Phnom Penh houses carved wooden sedan-chairs, litters and beds, many of which are heavily gilded or inlaid with glass mosaic and hardstones. Wooden images, mostly heads of the Buddha, are carved in the traditional manner in ebony or hardwood. The features are distinctively Khmer, with a broad face, wide cheekbones, long eyes set far apart and a wide, faintly smiling mouth. Hair curls are usually tight, and there is an *uṣṇīṣa* (cranial protuberance) on the top of the head. (For a fuller account of wooden sculpture in the post-Angkor period, *see* §III, 5 above.) Most everyday wooden objects are simple and unadorned, but some are decorated. Boats, oxcarts and the handles of rice-harvesting sickles are often carved with traditional designs, found also in stone as well as wood-carving, such as floral patterns and the heads of dragons and *nāgas*. *Nāgas* are a common decorative motif and traditionally represent both the fertility of the waters and the power of the rulers of Angkor, who claimed descent from the union of a *nāga* princess with a Brahman prince (*see* §I, 3 above).

The art of the wood-carver declined during the 19th century and into the 20th. The French attempted to halt this decline by establishing a School of Cambodian Arts, where young apprentices could be trained in this and other crafts. During the Communist regime (1975–9) creative work ceased altogether but the school has been re-established and wood-carving is once more being produced, partly to satisfy the demand of tourists but also in an effort to revive Buddhism and Buddhist art in Cambodia.

BIBLIOGRAPHY

Area Handbook for the Khmer Republic (Cambodia) (Washington, DC, 1973)
T. R. Newman: *Contemporary South-east Asian Arts and Crafts* (New York, 1977)

MIRANDA BRUCE-MITFORD

Cambó y Batlle, Francisco de Asís (*b* Vergés, Gerona, 2 Sept 1876; *d* Buenos Aires, 30 April 1947). Spanish lawyer, politician, patron and collector. He was of Catalan origin and inherited a large fortune, which he subsequently increased. He studied philosophy and letters and also law at the University of Barcelona, graduating, respectively, in 1895 and 1898, and practised as a lawyer as well as writing for the periodical *La veu de Catalunya*. In 1901 Cambó began a political career in the administration of Barcelona, including acting as commissioner for the International Fair there in 1929. He was elected to the Spanish Cortes several times and held various ministries; as Minister of Finance he introduced the first limits on the export of works of art in 1922, and further similar laws followed in 1926 and 1933. He explained his policy in a speech to the Cortes on 6 December 1935, when he intended to modify the 'Ley del Tesoro Artístico' of 1933 and improve the conditions for private collecting by making it possible to re-export works in the course of a number of years; he believed that legislation, which was centred exclusively on protecting the national heritage, should also help to increase it. He left politics before the beginning of the Civil War to pursue his financial activities.

Cambó was an outstanding collector. He privately initiated a practice of benefiting public collections by acquiring works himself, which he kept in his house in the Via Layetana, Barcelona, and which he would then donate to fill gaps in public museums. At the beginning of the 1920s his collection of some 65 works of art, mainly bought on the advice of Joaquín Folch i Torres (*b* 1886), the art historian and critic, already included the portrait of *Lady Georgina Poyntz, Countess Spencer* by Thomas Gainsborough and *St John the Baptist and St Francis of Assisi* attributed to El Greco (both Barcelona, Mus. A. Catalunya). From the Joseph Spiridon collection he bought 27 of the 79 paintings auctioned (Berlin, 31 May 1929), including 3 panels by Sandro Botticelli on the *Story of Nastagio degli Onesti* (1468 or 1487) and 2 attributed to Taddeo Gaddi on the *Life of St Eligius* (mid-14th century; now attributed to the Master of the Madonna of Mercy), all of which he bequeathed in 1941 to the Prado, Madrid. He bought works by contemporary artists—mainly Catalans such as Isidro Nonell y Monturiol, Santiago Rusiñol, Joaquim Mir, Olegario Junyent (*b* 1876) and Ramon Casas (including his portrait, *Francisco de Asís Cambó*; Barcelona, Mus. A. Catalunya)—and paid for the completion of the mural decoration (1920–36; destr. 1936) of Vic Cathedral by José María Sert (1874–1945). Part of his collection was destroyed in July 1936 and part was dispersed to Switzerland and Argentina, where Cambó lived in exile. Cambó's collection centred principally on earlier painting. He preferred Italian primitives, and he gave the Prado Museum several of these, including Giovanni dal Ponte's *Seven Liberal Arts* (1435) as well as a *bodegón* by Francisco de Zurbarán. He donated other works to the Capuchin friars at Sarriá and to José Bertrán (*b* 1873). Except for Botticelli's portrait of *Michele Marullo Tarkaniota*, inherited by his daughter, Helena Cambó, and a panel from the *Birth of the Virgin*, attributed to the Master of the Cini Madonna of the Rimini School, which he gave to the Musée Cantonal des Beaux-Arts in Lausanne, Cambó bequeathed his collection to the Museu Municipal de les Belles Artes in

Barcelona (now Barcelona, Mus. A. Catalunya). This donation comprised some 50 works representing Italian, Spanish, Flemish, Dutch, French and other schools. Among the most outstanding of the works are Titian's portrait of *Laura Dianti*, the portrait of *Alathea Howard, Countess of Arundel* by Peter Paul Rubens and the portrait of the notary *Pierre-Louis Laideguive* by Maurice-Quentin de La Tour (all Barcelona, Mus. A. Catalunya).

Cambó also founded various cultural and artistic institutions: in Barcelona the foundations of Bernat Metge (1921), the Bíblica Catalana (*c.* 1925) and the Monumenta Catalana (*c.* 1925) and in Paris the Fundación Cambó at the Sorbonne. A journalist and writer of distinction, he produced several books (mostly in Catalan), including *Visions d'Orient* (Barcelona, 1921), *Entorn del Feixisme Italià* (Barcelona, 1925), *Les Dictadures* (Bilbao, 1929), *Per la concòrdia* (Barcelona, 1930), *Memòries: 1876–1936* (Barcelona, 1981) and *Meditacions: Dietari, 1936–1946* (Barcelona, 1982).

BIBLIOGRAPHY

J. Pla: *Materials per una història d'aquests últims anys*, 3 vols (Barcelona, 1928–30), pp. 256–337
F. J. Sánchez-Cantón: 'El donativo de Cambó al Museo del Prado', *A. Esp.*, xiv/1 (1942), pp. 7–14
J. Pijoan: 'En Cambó', *Quad. Exili*, xvi (1945), pp. 10–15
F. J. Sánchez-Cantón: 'Cambó y el Museo del Prado', *Arbor*, xxiii (1947), pp. 260–65
Tristán: 'El testamento de D. Francisco Cambó', *Destino* (20 Dec 1947), pp. 4–5
N. Luján: 'El legado de D. Francisco Cambó: Pequeña historia de una colección', *Destino* (20 Jan 1951), pp. 16–18
J. Pabón: *Cambó*, 3 vols (Barcelona, 1952–1969), ii, pp. 539–73; iii, pp. 496–527
E. Molist Pol: 'El legado Cambó', *Revista* (15 July 1954), pp. 1–6
J. Benet Aurell: 'Un coleccionista con sentido social', *Revista* (13 Oct 1955), pp. 13–19
F. J. Sánchez-Cantón: 'El legado Cambó a Barcelona', *Goya*, ix (1955), pp. 154–61
——: *La colección Cambó* (Barcelona, 1955)
J. Álvarez Lopera: 'Coleccionismo, intervención y mercenazgo en España, 1900–36: Una aproximación', *Fragmentos*, xi (1987), pp. 33–47
Colección Cambó (exh. cat., Madrid, Prado, 1990)

MIGUEL CABAÑAS BRAVO

Cambrai, Jean de. *See* JEAN DE CAMBRAI.

Cambrai, Nicolas de. *See* GUILLAIN, (1).

Cambray-Digny, Luigi de. *See* DE CAMBRAY-DIGNY, LUIGI.

Cambridge (i). City in England, seat of the country's second oldest university, and county town, with a population of *c.* 100,000. Named after a bridge over the River Cam, Cambridge was a centre of feudal power and commerce before the foundation of the university at the beginning of the 13th century. Since then, however, the university has dominated the town and influenced its development. As Cambridge lies in level country, its expansion has been easy, with more trouble from waterlogged ground than from hills. The surrounding area is poor in durable stone. Clunch, a local soft limestone, has been used for building, as has oolite brought in from Peterborough. Brick is more characteristic of the area, with red brick coming from the north of Cambridgeshire and paler yellow, grey, brown or pink bricks and tiles being manufactured from gault clay deposits near the Cam.

1. History and urban development. 2. King's College Chapel.

1. History and urban development.

(i) Before 1800. (ii) 1800 and after.

(i) Before 1800. A Romano-British civilian town (Durovigutum) covered about 25 acres on comparatively high ground on the west bank of the river; it was probably a staging post with a ford through the Cam on the route between Colchester (Camulodunum) and the Midlands. The Anglo-Saxon town was a dual settlement, the Mercian part in the upland area west of the river and the other, more populous East Anglian town partly on a low gravel ridge east of the Cam. The best relic of this settlement, which probably had several churches, is the tower of St Benet's, which may date from a rebuilding after King Sweyn of Denmark (*reg* 985–1014) burnt the town in 1010. There seems to have been a Scandinavian trading community closer to the bridge, with its own church of St Clement.

William I built a castle at Cambridge in 1068; some Saxon houses were pulled down to make land available. The motte is the castle's chief surviving feature, but an impressive gate-house, great hall and other buildings were built in stone under Edward I in the late 13th century and early 14th. The river carried barge traffic, and Milne Street (now largely covered by King's College; *see* §2 below), lined with wharves, lay parallel to it. The town was elongated, small and unfortified, with cornfields close to its eastern and western sides. Across the river the town was restricted by what is now known as King's Ditch, but beyond it two religious houses (the Augustinian priory of Barnwell and St Radegond's Benedictine nunnery, now Jesus College) were founded in the first half of the 12th century. Late Romanesque and Early Gothic work appears in St Radegond's north transept (*c.* 1150–75; rest. 1846–9 by A. W. N. Pugin) and in some parish churches: significant are the circular nave of Holy Sepulchre Church (*c.* 1130; rest. 1841 by Anthony Salvin) and Early Gothic fragments surviving from St John's Hospital Chapel (*c.* 1267–*c.* 1280; destr.; fragments in Cambridge, St John's Coll., and U. Cambridge, Mus. Archaeol. & Anthropol.). There are fine Decorated windows in Little St Mary's (12th century; rebuilt *c.* 1340–52) and in St Michael's (early 14th century).

The arrival *c.* 1209 of the scholars, lecturers and students of the university had little immediate effect on the city's architecture, although the Franciscan, Dominican, Carmelite and Augustinian friaries founded in the 13th century on the periphery of the town were important additions. Private houses served as university lecture rooms and lodgings; some became student hostels. The university itself still had no corporate buildings. Colleges were eventually endowed and provided permanent lodgings for graduates and teachers. Hugh de Balsham, Bishop of Ely (*reg* 1256–86), founded the first Cambridge college, eventually known as Peterhouse, in the buildings of St John's Hospital (now St John's College) in 1280. Four years later the college moved to accommodation near St Peter's (now Little St Mary's), which served as its college chapel until the 17th century. The hall (1286; altered 15th century; rest. 1870 by George Gilbert Scott II) was the first building specifically constructed to meet the needs of scholars in Cambridge.

Seven more colleges were founded in the 14th century. In 1324 Hervey de Stanton (*d* 1327) founded Michaelhouse (now part of Trinity College), little of which survives. Two years later the Chancellor of the University, Richard Badew (*fl* 1320–30), founded University Hall, refounded in 1338 by Elizabeth de Burgh (?1295–1360), Lady of Clare, as Clare Hall (now Clare College; completely rebuilt 1638–1715). In 1337 Edward III formalized the royal maintenance of a few scholars at Cambridge, a practice started in 1317 by Edward II (*reg* 1307–27), creating King's Hall. Most of its 14th-century buildings were demolished after Henry VIII amalgamated it with Michaelhouse to found Trinity College in 1546. Pembroke College was founded in 1347 by Marie de St Pol, Countess of PEMBROKE, and the Divinity School, begun *c.* 1350, was the first university building. William Bateman, Bishop of Norwich (*reg* 1344–54), established Trinity Hall in 1350, and on the death of Edmund Gonville in 1351 took control of the foundation of Gonville Hall, established three years earlier. Trinity Hall's chapel was licensed in 1352, but Gonville Hall's chapel (*c.* 1370; altered 1637 and 1870) was the first to be completed in Cambridge at a time when members of other colleges worshipped in nearby parish churches. In 1352 the tradition of royal and aristocratic endowment at Cambridge was broken by the unparalleled foundation of Corpus Christi College by two town guilds.

The component parts of a college—hall, chapel, master's lodge and living rooms—gradually became established. Pembroke Old Court brought all these elements together. The Front Court (1448–9) of Queens' College (see fig. 1), founded by Andrew Docket (*d* 1484) in 1446, was the first college structure in Cambridge combining all these elements to be designed and built as a unit, probably by Reginald of Ely (*fl* 1438; *d* 1471). Reginald also worked on Henry VI's grandiose scheme for King's College (founded 1441; *see* §2 below), the spacious site of which was acquired at the expense of some houses, much of Milne Street and the church of St John the Baptist.

Some college courts built of the friable local clunch, such as Gonville Court, were later faced with ashlar, which Georgian dons found more sophisticated, but the earlier building technique is visible in the Old Court of Corpus Christi. By contrast, Queens' Front Court is brick-faced clunch. By 1475 the Old Schools Court—comprising the Schools of Divinity, Law and Arts and the Library—was finished. Across the river the only college was the Benedictine Buckingham College (founded 1428; refounded in 1542 as Magdalene College); most of the late medieval First Court (*c.* 1430–*c.* 1580), with an early Tudor hall, remains. The Late Perpendicular nave (completed 1508) of Great St Mary's is a fine example of the East Anglian style built by the university mason John Bell (*fl* 1476–1503) and possibly designed by John Wastell. Brick and stone gate-towers are prominent features of some colleges. The gate-houses at Christ's College and St John's College (both founded by Margaret Beaufort, Countess of Richmond and Derby, in 1505 and 1511 respectively) have elaborate heraldic carving above the entrances, as does that of Trinity College.

1. Cambridge, Queens' College, Front Court, 1448–9

Some late medieval and 16th-century colleges were created by the conversion of existing institutions. St Radegond's Priory, for instance, became Jesus College when Bishop Alcock of Ely (*reg* 1486–1500) took over its buildings in 1497. St John's College succeeded the Hospital of St John the Evangelist, and Emmanuel College, founded in 1584 by Sir Walter Mildmay (?1520–89), eventually used some of the buildings of the Dominican friary. Sidney Sussex College was founded by Lady Frances Sidney, Dowager Countess of Sussex (1531–89), on the site of the Franciscan convent in 1594.

Late Tudor and Jacobean Gothic, with increasing classical detail, appears in the addition of Caius Court (1565 and 1567) and the Gate of Honour (1575; see fig. 2) to Gonville Hall, which John Caius (1510–73) refounded as Gonville and Caius College in 1557; in the chapel (1555–67; rest.), hall (1604–5, by Ralph Simons (*fl* 1584–1604)) and other buildings round the Great Court at Trinity College, designed by Thomas Nevile, Master of Trinity (*d* 1615); in the brick step-gabled library (16th century) at Trinity Hall; and in St John's spacious Second Court (1598-1602, by Ralph Simons and Gilbert Wigge). John Westley (*d* ?1644) continued this trend with Clare College East Range (1638–40) and Emmanuel Old Court (1663–4). Except for the library at St John's (1623–4) and the chapel of Peterhouse (consecrated 1632), Cambridge has few equivalents to the sophisticated survivalist Gothic at Oxford.

In 1640–43 more typically Renaissance taste influenced the Fellows' Building at Christ's. After the Restoration, Wren's fully Renaissance architecture arrived at Cambridge in the new chapels at Pembroke (1663–5) and Emmanuel (1666–74), together with the rectangular library at Trinity (1676–84), which needed specially strong foundations because it was built on soft alluvial soil near the Cam (*see* WREN, CHRISTOPHER and LIBRARY, fig. 2). In 1674 important Renaissance rebuilding started at St Catharine's, founded in 1473 by Robert Wodlark (*d* 1479).

The area of the town hardly increased during the 18th century, but Cambridge was much beautified by the

2. *Gate of Honour, Gonville and Caius College, Cambridge*, engraving by J. Le Keux, 1841

creation of the landscaped pleasance of The Backs, extending to and beyond the river, which by now was spanned by various college bridges. Among the best buildings of the period are James Gibbs's classical Senate House, built in 1722–30, and the dignified Gibbs' Building, begun in 1724 south of King's Chapel to expand the living accommodation of the college. Many medieval college ranges were refaced in ashlar, and classical panelling adorned halls and chapels. Some new buildings were completed: James Essex continued the fine Neo-classical chapel at Clare (1764–9), designed by his mentor, the amateur architect James Burrough (1691–1764). Essex was solely responsible for an important riverside building (*c.* 1756) for Queens', of which only the Essex Building was constructed; for a three-arched bridge for Trinity (1765); and for an Ionic street front at Emmanuel (1769). He also designed a simple Guildhall to replace its ramshackle predecessor (1782–4; destr.).

(ii) 1800 and after. Soon after 1800 the number of students and dons in the colleges greatly increased. The campus-style buildings of Downing College, founded by Sir George Downing (?1684–1749), were started in 1807 and constitute one of William Wilkins's most important Grecian designs. The rest of his work in Cambridge—Trinity New Court (1821–7), Corpus Christi's Second Court (1822–6) and King's screen and hall range (1823–8)—is Perpendicular Gothic Revival; the same idiom was achieved by different architects in Jeffry Wyatville's work (1821–32) at Sidney Sussex, in Gisborne Court (1825–6) at Peterhouse by W. McIntosh Brooks (*d* 1849), in St John's New Court (1825–31) by Thomas Rickman and Henry Hutchinson, and elsewhere. Edward Blore's Pitt Building (1831–3) for the University Press, with its prominent tower, is Gothic Revival. Other Neo-classical buildings include Charles Robert Cockerell's University Library (1837–42; now the Squire Law Library), which was designed as part of a dramatic Grecian composition of four blocks with an Ionic portico facing Great St Mary's (only one wing was built); and the Fitzwilliam Museum, started in 1837 to designs by George Basevi, with a Corinthian portico.

Important changes were introduced to the city in the 1840s, including the railway; in subsequent decades more employment in the university and colleges, the general prosperity of arable farmers in the eastern counties and new housing for dons, who were now allowed to marry, led to the expansion of the town itself, particularly in the eastern area of Barnwell, in Chesterton to the north, and southwards down Hills Road. Growth to the west was largely collegiate, with the Gothic Revival Selwyn College for men (1882–9), by A. W. Blomfield (1829–99), founded in memory of G. A. Selwyn (1809–78), and with Girton and Newnham for women; some dons' houses were also built. New university buildings, mostly for science teaching, were built much closer to the centre.

Gothic Revival churches include the Perpendicular-style Christ Church (1837–9), St Paul's (1841) and St Andrew the Great (1842–3), all by Ambrose Poynter (1796–1886), and G. F. Bodley's All Saints' (1861–71) in the Decorated Revival style. George Gilbert Scott I designed a large new chapel (built 1863–9) with a massive tower for St John's, while Dunn & Hansom of Newcastle built the completely vaulted Catholic church of Our Lady and the English Martyrs (1885–90). Alfred Waterhouse designed the Cambridge Union in 1866 and the first buildings of Girton College in 1873. For the Corporation R. R. Rowe (1824–99) built the Byzantine Revival Corn Exchange (1874), with multicoloured brickwork. Basil Champneys designed the Queen Anne Revival buildings in ornamented brickwork for Newnham College from 1874.

Revivalist references continued into the 20th century with a slight acceptance of the Modern Movement in a few private houses after World War I. An important group, by Giles Gilbert Scott, consists of Clare Memorial Court (1923–34), with pale grey brick and classical details in stone, and the new University Library (opened in 1934), the tower of which dominates the city skyline.

The academic character of Cambridge has been maintained, with extensions to the University Library (completed in 1972 and 1992), the founding or relocation of colleges and the building of separate courts for such colleges as Caius (St Michael's Court, 1903, by Sir Aston Webb) and Clare (Castle Hill Hostel, 1957–8, by David Roberts (1911–82)). The creation of the Arts and Science Precincts and of imposing new quarters for the Cavendish Laboratory (1909, by W. K. Marshall) have increased the density of academic buildings. The Sidgwick Avenue Arts Precinct, mostly by Casson, Conder & Partners from 1958 onwards, is opposite the step pyramid of the History Faculty Library (1964–7), with its tall enclosing blocks, by James Stirling. More Brutalism appears near by in Caius's Harvey Court (from 1958, by Sir Leslie Martin and Colin St John Wilson), one of many college extensions outside original sites. The George Thomson Building (1963–4), by Philip Dowson of Ove Arup & Partners, in Corpus Christi's Leckhampton complex, has a concrete hanging frame. Fitzwilliam College (founded 1889; present buildings begun 1958), built in brick by Denys Lasdun, and New Hall (founded 1954; built 1962–5), mostly in white concrete by Chamberlin, Powell & Bon, were relocated on new sites.

The new undergraduate colleges are Churchill (founded 1958 by Senate vote) and Robinson (founded by Sir David Robinson). At Churchill College (begun 1959, by Richard Sheppard, Robson & Partners) central buildings and interlocked residential courts are set in a large campus site (see fig. 3). At Robinson, by Gillespie, Kidd & Coia, the brick main buildings, in the south-east corner of a garden site sluggishly permeated by Bin Brook, are in two main blocks enclosing a sequence of untypically narrow courts. The most notable blocks, facing Grange Road, are the somewhat daunting gate-tower and the chapel with two windows by John Piper, one rising so high that its top is difficult to view.

In 1987 a new settlement of *c.* 6000 houses was projected beyond Milton, north of the city. On the Milton Road the Science Park has been developed by Trinity College on a 130-acre site opposite the Business Park. The site includes three shallow artificial lakes, and the present buildings are mostly on the park's eastern side. The most striking, sometimes likened to a stranded whale, is the Napp Laboratories (1979–83) by Arthur Erickson.

3. Cambridge, Churchill College, by Richard Sheppard, Robson & Partners, begun 1959

BIBLIOGRAPHY

R. Willis and J. W. Clark: *The Architectural History of the University of Cambridge, and at the Colleges of Cambridge and Eton*, 4 vols (Cambridge, 1886/*R* 1992)

T. D. Atkinson and J. W. Clark: *Cambridge Described and Illustrated* (London, 1897)

A. Gray: *The Town of Cambridge: A History* (Cambridge, 1925)

——: *Cambridge University: An Episodical History* (Cambridge, 1926)

J. Steegman: *Cambridge, As It Was and Is Today* (London, 1940, rev. 5/1954)

N. Pevsner: *Cambridgeshire*, Bldgs England (London, 1954, 2/1970/*R* 1989)

An Inventory of the Historical Monuments in the City of Cambridge, Royal Comm. Anc. & Hist. Mnmts & Constr. England, 2 vols (London, 1959)

J. P. C. Roach, ed.: *The City and University of Cambridge* (1959/*R* 1967), iii of *A History of the County of Cambridge and the Isle of Ely*, Victoria Hist. Co. England (London, 1938–)

B. Little: *Cambridge Discovered* (Cambridge, 1960)

N. Taylor and others: *Cambridge New Architecture* (Cambridge, 1964, rev. London, 3/1970)

C. R. Benstead: *Portrait of Cambridge* (London, 1968)

T. Rawle: *Cambridge Architecture* (London, 1985)

BRYAN LITTLE

2. King's College Chapel. King's College was the second royal foundation in Cambridge, inaugurated by Henry VI in 1441. Work began in 1443 slightly north of the present site, with three ranges and a gateway (partly surviving in the Old Schools). Henry's Will and Intent of 1448 launched a new scheme of buildings round a square court roughly the size of the existing one, with library, hall, Provost's Lodge and chambers, a gate in the east wall and a chapel on the north side. The chapel, dedicated to SS Mary and Nicholas, built from 1448 to 1515, is the only surviving part of this second plan.

(i) Architecture. The chapel is an aisleless limestone building *c.* 90 m long and 30 m to the crown of the vault. It is divided internally into choir and antechapel. Only the

antechapel was intended to have low side chapels, but more were added when building began. The principal (south) elevation has tall windows above the chapels between staged buttresses, and the north elevation is similar though obscured. Four identical angle turrets complete the symmetrical exterior profile. The end bays, where college buildings were intended to adjoin, have no chapels.

The first campaign, under REGINALD OF ELY, was hampered by lack of funds and by the civil war from 1455. Work stopped temporarily under Edward IV after 1461. By then, ground courses for the whole building existed, with the socle walls of the choir bays. Before 1476–7 some of the north chapels were in use, and the four easternmost side windows were under construction. The second master mason, John Wolryche, was succeeded in 1477 by SIMON CLERK, who amended the design. Edward IV funded another phase in 1479, which continued under Richard III (*reg* 1483–5) but was stopped by Henry VII. The construction to 1485 involved the roofing but not the vaulting of six eastern bays, more of the side chapels and fragmentary sections of the antechapel. Henry VII paid for the completion of the structure from 1508; his executors finished the antechapel and built the high vaults and the exterior battlements and towers.

The style of the antechapel differs from the choir by its greater degree of enrichment, a feature of the original design. The choir has bare socle walls where woodwork, or painting as at Eton College Chapel, was intended (see fig. 4). Sculpted half figures of angels define the base of an upper zone with tall, transomed, five-light Perpendicular windows. The variation in the tracery after the third bay denotes the arrival of Clerk in 1477. The choir vault supports indicate that a simplified, cheaper design was adopted after 1461. The antechapel by contrast has panelled walls pierced by traceried closet screens, more complex vault supports on high pedestal bases at floor level, and additional jamb niches. The pier south of the pulpitum mostly predates 1461 and confirms that the extra elements in the antechapel formed part of the 1448 design and are not Tudor enrichments.

4. Cambridge, King's College Chapel, choir, 1448–1515

In the rapid Tudor campaign the antechapel and fan vault were constructed by JOHN WASTELL; the style is related to contemporary royal work but is more restrained. Those bays completed before 1485 were altered to accommodate the existing fan vault. Extensive Tudor documentation has enabled a complete analysis of this campaign to be made.

The oak pulpitum, possibly by JOHN LEE, dates from *c.* 1532–6. It has a jettied loft and carries a great organ that is also partly 16th-century; the screen has early Renaissance detailing and fine sculpture. The contemporary stalls have canopies of 1675–8. There is a fine lectern of 1509–28 and the altarpiece is Rubens's *Adoration of the Magi* of 1634.

BIBLIOGRAPHY

Harvey
T. Carter: *King's College Chapel: Notes on its History and Present Condition* (London, 1867)
G. G. Scott: *Essay on the History of English Gothic Architecture* (London, 1881)
J. Saltmarsh: *King's College Chapel Cambridge* (Cambridge, 1959)
H. M. Colvin, ed.: *The Middle Ages* (1963), i–iii of *The History of the King's Works*, 6 vols (London, 1963–82)
R. Tibbs: *King's College Chapel Cambridge* (Lavenham, 1970)
F. Woodman: *John Wastell of Bury, Master Mason* (diss., U. London, 1978)
——: *The Architectural History of King's College Chapel* (London, 1986)
For further bibliography *see* §1 above.

FRANCIS WOODMAN

(ii) Stained glass. There are 26 windows, of which the west window, made in 1878 by Clayton & Bell, depicts a *Last Judgement.* The remaining windows constitute the most complete glazing programme to survive from the reign of Henry VIII, and it is the best-integrated ensemble of stained glass in Britain.

The glazing programme links the Apocryphal *Life of the Virgin* in windows 1–2 (reading from the west) with the *Life of Christ* in windows 3–12 on the north side and windows 14–20 on the south. Apart from the great east window (13), which contains scenes of the *Passion* centring on the *Crucifixion*, windows 2–20 are arranged typologically in the manner of the *Speculum humanae salvationis* and *Biblia pauperum* (*see* TYPOLOGICAL CYCLES). New Testament scenes appear in the lower outer lights, with appropriate Old Testament types above; in the central of the five lights are messengers carrying inscribed scrolls. The last windows on the south side illustrate the *Acts of the Apostles.*

Glazing began in 1515, when building finished. In that year the north German Barnard Flower (*d* 1517) is named as glazier. A second campaign is documented in 1526, when two contracts name Galyon Hone (*fl c.* 1517–51), James Nicholson, Richard Bond and Thomas Reve, who were to continue the original scheme. Two other contracts name Francis Williamson and Simon Symondes. The final windows date from 1537–45, and one of the last to be completed was the great east window of the choir. Bishop Fox of Winchester (*d* 1528) was responsible for the initial programme, to be based on that of the windows (destr.) of Henry VII's Chapel in Westminster Abbey. Wayment (1972) has clarified the relationship of the early glass with that of Fairford, Glos, and designers have been identified, one of the earliest being known as the Fairford designer. Another has been recognized as DIRK VELLERT of Antwerp, who was responsible not only for the vidimus or small design but also for the final full-scale cartoon. The side windows are 13.4 m high and 4.7 m wide, the east window slightly larger.

There are significant changes in style from window to window: for instance, the Late Gothic of the Fairford-style *Agony in the Garden* (9) is succeeded by a fully Renaissance, almost Mannerist *Noli me tangere* (17; see fig. 5). Window 1 was designed in 1517 but executed only in 1527, which indicates that the glazing campaign was not straightforward.

Although influences are detectable from Normandy and Brabant and from the work of individual artists including Rogier van der Weyden, Hugo van der Goes, Leonardo da Vinci and Michelangelo, in terms of glazing, glass-painting, staining and enamelling the windows are prodigious. The pot-metals can be brilliant, as in the *Fall of Manna* (9), exploiting the potentialities of the medium. There were often problems in integrating figures and landscape, as with *Reuben Finds the Pit Empty* (17), although Reuben's flock is finely detailed. In the later windows designers and glaziers achieved great success using architectural settings, as in the *Trial before Pilate* (13), with Renaissance detailing in stain and very expressive painting for faces. The glaziers were always at a disadvantage, however, in having to fit scenes across two or more lights.

5. Cambridge, King's College Chapel, *Noli me tangere* (detail, *Christ and St Mary Magdalene*), south nave, window 17, *c.* 1530; head of Mary restored *c.* 1845

BIBLIOGRAPHY

H. G. Wayment: *The Windows of King's College Chapel, Cambridge*, Corp. Vitrearum Med. Aevi: Great Britain, suppl. i (London, 1972)

——: *King's College Chapel, Cambridge: The Great Windows, Introduction and Guide* (Cambridge, 1982)

——: *King's College Chapel, Cambridge: The Side Chapel Glass* (Cambridge, 1988)

M. Q. SMITH

Cambridge (ii). *See under* BOSTON.

Camden, William (*b* London, 2 May 1551; *d* Chislehurst, London, 9 Nov 1623). English antiquary, historian and collector. The son of a painter, Camden was educated at Christ's Hospital, St Paul's School and Oxford. Unable to obtain a fellowship, he moved to London in 1571 and began collecting material that would later form the basis of his greatest work, the *Britannia*, the foundation of antiquarian studies in Britain. Camden was persuaded to systematize his researches by the cartographer ABRAHAM ORTELIUS, who was visiting London in 1577. Camden wrote both of his debt to Ortelius and of his own ambitions: '[Ortelius] did very earnestly sollicit me to acquaint the World with *Britain* that ancient Island; that is, to restore Britain to its antiquities, and its Antiquities to Britain, to renew the memory of what was old, illustrate what was obscure, and settle what was doubtful.' The *Britannia* appeared on 2 May 1586, dedicated to William Cecil, 1st Baron Burghley, who was the foremost patron of scholarship at the time. It was largely topographical and historical, though with significant elements of heraldry and genealogy. It was an immediate success, running to three English editions in four years. It was both the beneficiary and the fullest expression of the scholarship and historical methods of JOHN LELAND and other Tudor antiquaries whose work had been the first attempt at a comprehensive topographical survey of England.

From 1593 to 1597 Camden was headmaster of Westminster School, where proximity to Parliament, the Inns of Court and the College of Heralds helped him to become the central figure in a great age of English antiquarian studies. In 1597 he left to become Clarenceux King of Arms. His effect on Jacobean scholarship was incalculable; ROBERT BRUCE COTTON was only the most famous of his protégés. Together they made a tour of the Picts Wall in 1599–1600, subsequently presenting their findings in papers delivered to the Society of Antiquaries, of which Camden had been a leading force since its inception in 1586. He was also the first Englishman since Thomas More to correspond regularly with the scholarly community of Europe, a practice that was to have such fruitful consequences for 17th-century English culture. Camden gave an impetus to the development of the monument in English sculpture with the publication of the epitaphs in Westminster Abbey (1600). He was buried in Westminster

Abbey in 1623, where a sophisticated classicizing tomb was erected showing him at half-length holding a copy of the *Britannia*, a motif based upon a panel portrait of Camden by Marcus Gheeraerts (ii) (1609; Oxford, Bodleian Lib.). The Westminster monument is taken to be the work of Nicholas Stone I on the grounds of quality, though Stone makes no mention of it in either his notebook or account book. There is also a medal of Camden by A. Caque (1823; London, BM).

WRITINGS

Britannia (London, 1586, rev. 6/1607); Eng. trans. by R. Gough as *Camden's Britannia*, 3 vols (London, 1789, rev. 2/1806)

Reges, reginae, nobiles, et alii in ecclesia collegiata B. Petri Westmonasterii sepulti (London, 1600)

BIBLIOGRAPHY

T. Smith: *G. Camdeni et illustrium virorum ad G. Camdenum epistolae* [The letters of W. Camden and of famous men to W. Camden] (London, 1691)

E. Gibson: *Camden's Britannia* (London, 1695)

T. D. Kendrick: *British Antiquity* (London, 1950)

S. Piggott: *William Camden and the Britannia*, Reckitt Archaelogical Lecture (Edinburgh, 1953)

J. Evans: *A History of the Society of Antiquaries* (Oxford, 1956)

S. Piggott: *Ancient Britons and the Antiquarian Imagination* (New York, 1989)

DAVID HOWARTH

Camden Town Group. Exhibiting society of 16 British painters that flourished between 1911 and 1914. It was created from the inner core of artists who regularly attended the informal Saturday afternoon gatherings first established by Walter Sickert in 1907 in a rented studio at 19 Fitzroy Street, London. Sickert, Lucien Pissarro, Spencer Gore, Harold Gilman and Robert Bevan, together with disciples, pupils and sympathetic colleagues, met weekly to display their work to each other and to a small band of patrons while discussing the politics of art in London. Although Fitzroy Street was never intended to represent a movement or school, between 1907 and 1911 it did nurture a distinct episode in the history of British art, which is most suggestively described as Camden Town painting. The pictures tended to be small: 'little pictures for little patrons', to quote one of the latter, Louis Fergusson. A Sickert-inspired vocabulary of favourite themes was established: nudes on a bed or at their toilet, informal portraits of friends and coster models in shabby bed-sitter interiors, mantelpiece still-lifes of cluttered bric-à-brac, and views of commonplace London streets, squares and gardens. Every theme was treated with objective perceptual honesty. The handling developed by many of these painters, influenced above all by Lucien Pissarro, represents a late and temperate flowering in England of French Impressionism. With qualifications, interest in colour analysis and the development of a broken touch were characteristics common to the inner core of 'Camden Town' painters.

By the end of 1910 the Fitzroy Street gatherings were patronized by a large circle of painters representing a complex jigsaw of friendships and professional relationships. Recruits were discovered at exhibitions, notably those of the Allied Artists' Association (AAA). In 1909 and 1910 the establishment of the New English Art Club (NEAC) admitted work by several Fitzroy Street artists for exhibition. During the winter of 1910–11 Roger Fry staged the exhibition *Manet and the Post-Impressionists* at the Grafton Gallery. The public, most of the critics and the figureheads of the art world united to condemn the exhibition as an outrage. The old guard of the NEAC were among the most hostile, and it became obvious that the grudging tolerance recently displayed towards Fitzroy Street and its allies would be abruptly withdrawn. This revived antagonism was the main impetus behind the creation of the Camden Town Group.

Disaffection with the NEAC was the chief topic of discussion among members and satellites of Fitzroy Street early in 1911. The relative merits of capturing control of its jury or setting up a rival exhibiting society were hotly debated. Dining at Gatti's (probably in April), Sickert, Charles Ginner, Bevan, Gore and Gilman decided to create a new society. Discussion continued at Fitzroy Street, over dinner at the Criterion (when it was decided whom to invite as members) and in a restaurant in Golden Square when, according to Walter Bayes (1869–1956), Sickert is said to have invented the name Camden Town Group because 'that district had been so watered with his tears that something important must sooner or later spring from its soil'. Bayes, who had been recruited to Fitzroy Street in 1908 when Sickert admired his work in the AAA exhibition, had evidently joined the original Gatti's set to become a founder-member of the new society, as had James Bolivar Manson, more recently introduced to Fitzroy Street by Pissarro. Manson was elected Secretary and Gore President of the new society. Ginner recorded that the founder-members of the Group wished to create a limited circle of those painters whom they considered to be the best and most promising of the day. This ideal explains the recruitment of Percy Wyndham Lewis (proposed by Gilman) and Maxwell Gordon Lightfoot, both outside the Fitzroy Street circle, and perhaps Augustus John and J. D. Innes, who sometimes attended the Saturday gatherings but were not within its inner core. Lesser credentials were demanded when the founders wished to invite friends, pupils and disciples. Sickert and Ginner proposed Malcolm Drummond (1880–1945), who had been a pupil at Rowlandson House, the private school where Sickert taught etching, drawing and painting from 1910 to 1914. Drummond's painting of *Brompton Oratory* (*c.* 1910; AC Eng) had been exhibited at the AAA in 1910. His *19 Fitzroy Street* (*c.* 1913–14; Newcastle upon Tyne, Laing A.G.; see fig.) documents one of the Group's meetings and probably depicts Manson, Gore and Ginner examining pictures taken from the stack in the studio. Gilman proposed William Ratcliffe; Gore proposed his deaf pupil Doman Turner (*c.* 1873–1938). Henry Lamb, a neighbour with a studio in Fitzroy Street, was invited. Lastly, Gilman, strongly supported by Sickert, insisted that the Group should exclude women. Thus a finite membership of 16 was achieved: founder-members were Bayes, Bevan, Gilman, Ginner, Gore, Pissarro, Sickert and probably Manson; invited members were Drummond, Innes, John, Lamb, Lewis, Lightfoot, Ratcliffe and Doman Turner. Sickert persuaded Arthur Clifton of the Carfax Gallery in Bury Street, St James's, to lend his basement premises in June 1911 for their first exhibition.

Each of the members was entitled to show four works, which were to be hung together rather than mixed on the walls. In fact at the first exhibition only 55 instead of 64

Malcolm Drummond: *19 Fitzroy Street*, oil on canvas, 710×508 mm, *c*. 1913–14 (Newcastle upon Tyne, Laing Art Gallery)

pictures were shown; Innes did not exhibit, while Lamb with three and Lewis and John with two pictures each did not take up their full quota. Sickert's four contributions included two related figure subjects, now titled *What Shall We Do for the Rent?* (*c*. 1909; Kirkcaldy, Fife, Mus. & A.G.) and *Summer Afternoon* (*c*. 1909; priv. col., see L. Browse: *Sickert*, London, 1943, pl. 61), but then both called *Camden Town Murder*, probably for publicity reasons. Lewis contributed two angular pen-and-ink drawings of a man's head, one now titled *The Architect* (1909; priv. col., see Baron, 1979, p. 259). These excited much derision, but otherwise there was little to offend the critics: fresh urban and rural landscapes, Camden Town figures in interiors, two cab-yard scenes by Bevan, and two music-halls by Gore. John's presence was reassuring, and every critic could recognize the qualities of design, draughtsmanship and the technical fluency of Lightfoot and Lamb.

The second exhibition of the Group was held at the Carfax Gallery in December 1911, when 53 pictures were included. Duncan Grant, elected to replace Lightfoot, who had resigned, contributed one picture; John did not exhibit; Bayes and Lewis with three pictures each and Lamb with two explain the shortfall. At a meeting attended by all members except Grant, Innes and John, the idea of expanding the Group was first debated but finally voted down. However, a motion that new and larger premises be sought for their exhibitions was carried unanimously and effectively delayed active consideration of their next exhibition, which did not take place until December 1912.

At the third and last Camden Town Group exhibition, again held at the Carfax Gallery because larger premises had not been found, 13 of the 16 members showed 45 pictures. Grant, John and Innes abstained; each, having closer artistic and commercial allegiances to rival societies and galleries, had exhibited only once with the Group. Their absence meant that the overall character of the paintings on view was more cohesive than in 1911. Only Bayes, Lamb and Lewis remained to represent styles developed outside the influence of the original nucleus of Fitzroy Street painters. The year between shows had allowed time for the talents of less experienced exhibitors to mature and this third exhibition included Drummond's *St James's Park* (1912; Southampton, C.A.G.) and Ratcliffe's *Clarence Gardens* (*c*. 1912; London, Tate). Ginner also showed *Piccadilly Circus* (1912; London, Tate), one of his earliest brilliantly coloured and tautly constructed cityscapes. Bevan showed his first London horse-sale paintings (for an example of 1913 *see* ENGLAND, fig. 22). Three artists exhibiting with the Camden Town Group, Lewis, Lamb and Gore, were also invited by Fry to contribute to his *Second Post-Impressionist Exhibition* at the Grafton Gallery, which opened in October 1912, and which was extended in December, thus overlapping the Carfax Gallery offering. The coincidence of these two exhibitions tended to polarize their respective characters in the eyes of critics and public. The viability of the Camden Town Group was threatened when it was relegated to a neutral position between the radicalism of Fry's selection and the conservatism of the NEAC.

During 1913 Clifton continued to sponsor the work of individual members of the Camden Town Group, as he had done in 1912, by offering them separate exhibitions. As in previous years, 19 Fitzroy Street (still chaired by Sickert) remained a central meeting-point where members of the finite Camden Town Group were joined by an ever-expanding number of visitors, many of whom became members of the parent society. Thus Jacob Epstein was admitted to membership in April 1913. Radical art politics were in a state of constant flux during this year as rival factions formed, overlapped and re-formed. Things came to a head in the autumn when the Fitzroy Street group reassembled after a summer recess to face decisions about the expansion of the Camden Town Group. It was decided to form a new society, the London Group, through the amalgamation of the two. Thus the Camden Town Group, after less than three years independence, was reabsorbed into the parental fold.

The Camden Town Group gradually petered out. Its last gesture was to respond to the invitation to select an exhibition of English Post-Impressionists, Cubists and others to be held at the Brighton Art Gallery from December 1913 until January 1914. However, this exhibition was also the first gesture as a corporate body of the London Group. Not only did all 11 active members of the Camden Town Group exhibit (those absent being Doman Turner, Grant, Innes, John and Lamb), so too did all the Fitzroy Street founder-members of the London Group and eight of the nine artists elected before the first exhibition in March 1914.

WRITINGS

Work by English Post-Impressionists, Cubists and Others (exh. cat., ed. W. Lewis and J. B. Manson; Brighton, A.G. & Mus., 1913), pp. 5–12
C. Ginner: 'Neo-Realism', *New Age* (1 Jan 1914)
W. Bayes: 'The Camden Town Group', *Sat. Rev.* (25 Jan 1930)
C. Ginner: 'The Camden Town Group', *Studio*, cxxx/632 (1945), pp. 129–36
W. R. Sickert: *A Free House: Or the Artist as Craftsman*, ed. O. Sitwell (London, 1947) [anthol. of Sickert's writings]

BIBLIOGRAPHY

F. Rutter: *Some Contemporary Artists* (London, 1922)
——: *Since I was Twenty-five* (London, 1927)
——: *Art in my Time* (London, 1933)
A. Rutherston: 'From Orpen and Gore to the Camden Town Group', *Burl. Mag.*, lxxxii (1943), pp. 201–5
M. de Saumarez: 'Camden Town Group Pictures in the Leeds Collection', *Leeds A. Cal.*, iii/12 (1950), pp. 10–22, 28
J. Rothenstein: *Modern English Painters*, 2 vols (London, 1952–6, rev. 1976)
D. Sutton: 'The Camden Town Group', *Country Life Annu.* (1955), pp. 97–100
Q. Bell: 'The Camden Town Group I: Sickert and the Post-Impressionists', *Motif*, 10 (1962–3), pp. 36–51
——: 'The Camden Town Group II: Opposition and Composition', *Motif*, 11 (1963–4), pp. 68–85
——: 'Sickert and the Post-Impressionists', *Victorian Artists* (London, 1967), pp. 85–94
M. Easton: '"Camden Town" into "London": Some Intimate Glimpses of the Transition and its Artists, 1911–1914', *Art in Britain, 1890–1940* (exh. cat., U. Hull, A. Col., 1967), pp. 60–75
Camden Town Recalled (exh. cat. by W. Baron, London, F.A. Soc., 1976)
W. Baron: *Miss Ethel Sands and her Circle* (London, 1977)
R. Shone: *The Century of Change: British Painting since 1900* (London, 1977)
W. Baron: *The Camden Town Group* (London, 1979) [bibliog. and list of exhs]
S. Watney: *English Post-Impressionism* (London, 1980)
The Camden Town Group (exh. cat. by W. Baron and M. Cormack, New Haven, CT, Yale Cent. Brit. A., 1980)
C. Harrison: *English Art and Modernism, 1900–1939* (London, 1981)
For further bibliography *see* individual biographies of Camden Town Group artists.

WENDY BARON

Camelford, 1st Baron. *See* PITT, THOMAS.

Camelio [Camelius; Camelus]. *See* GAMBELLO, (2).

Camelot. *See* AVED, JACQUES.

Cameo. Design engraved, carved or moulded in relief on gemstones, glass, ceramics etc; it uses layers of different colours, which can be transparent or opaque, so that the background and raised ground contrast. There are often just two colours: one dark colour, the other lighter, often white. The most common form is a medallion with a profile portrait (*see* GEM-ENGRAVING; for illustration *see* HARDSTONE, colour pl. II, fig. 2).

Camera (i). Term used in ancient architecture for an arched roof, ceiling or covering, as well as a vault. The term came to refer to a vaulted hall or a room with an arched ceiling and later to any small room, hall or chamber. □

Camera (ii). *See under* PHOTOGRAPHY, §I.

Camera lucida [Lat.: 'light chamber']. Optical device used as an aid for drawing or copying. Its somewhat misleading name is derived from the fact that it performs the same function as the CAMERA OBSCURA but in full daylight. Far more easily portable than a camera obscura, a camera lucida basically consists of a prism mounted on an adjustable stand and a drawing-board. The prism has to have one right angle, two of 67.5° and one of 135°. When the stand is adjusted so that the prism half covers the pupil of the eye, the draughtsman using it has the illusion of seeing both the object he wishes to draw, which is reflected through the prism by rays of light, and its outlines on the drawing-board. If paper is placed on the drawing-board the outlines can easily be traced off.

A much more sophisticated apparatus than the camera obscura, the camera lucida was perhaps invented, and certainly given its final form, by Dr William Hyde Wollaston, who patented it in 1807. Examples have been found as parts of portable drawing outfits used by amateur sketchers as well as by professional draughtsmen and artists (see fig.). The apparatus has also been adapted for use with a microscope. Various examples of sketches made with a camera lucida are known, such as that of the *Temple of Juno at Grigenti, Sicily* (pencil, 110×160 mm; London, Sci. Mus.) made by Sir JOHN HERSCHEL. While unmistakably mechanical in appearance, this illustrates the kind of virtuoso effects that could be achieved and is free of the sort of distortion at the edges of the image that could result from the use of a camera obscura with its much more primitive lens.

The camera lucida could also be used to make enlargements or reductions from an original, depending on how the user altered the distances between the copy being made, the prism and the object being copied. It did have

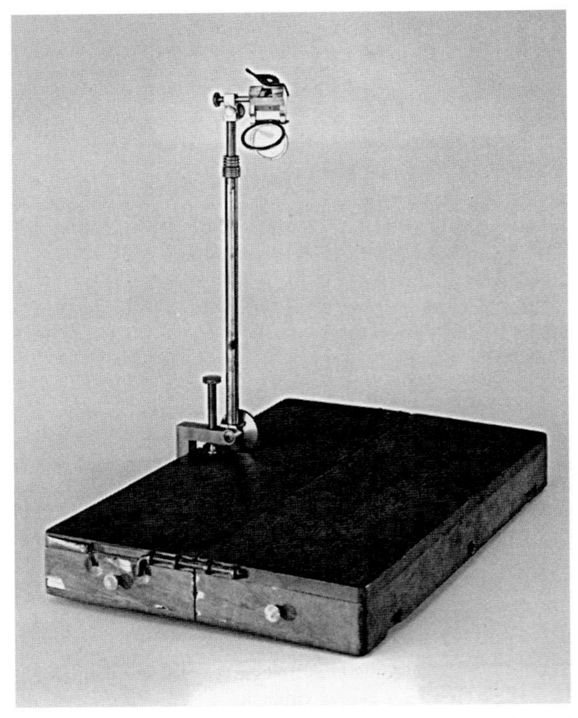

Camera lucida as part of a portable drawing outfit, brass, glass and mahogany, box 30×300×200 mm, early 19th century (London, Science Museum)

its disadvantages, however: the draughtsman had to be able to manoeuvre himself, or move the image on the board, so that it was possible to see both it and the pencil-point; any movement of the head made accuracy difficult; and in bright sunlight prolonged use of the camera lucida must have been very tiring.

See also VARLEY, (2).

BIBLIOGRAPHY

D. Brewster: *A Treatise on Optics* (London, 1831), p. 195
H. Hutter: *Die Handzeichnung* (Vienna, 1966); Eng. trans. as *Drawing, History and Technique* (London, 1968), pp. 145–6
H. Osborne, ed.: *The Oxford Companion to Art* (Oxford, 1970)
C. Ashwin: *Encyclopedia of Drawing* (London, 1982)

Camera obscura [Lat.: 'dark chamber']. Light-tight box with a small hole in one side, sometimes fitted with a lens, through which light from a well-lit scene or object enters to form an inverted image on a screen placed opposite the hole (see fig.). A mirror then reflects the image, right way up, on to a drawing surface where its outlines can be traced. The camera obscura was the direct precursor of the modern camera, and its use by earlier artists can be compared to that made of the camera by artists of the 19th and 20th centuries. Moreover, a camera obscura was the device used by Thomas Wedgwood and Humphry Davy in the late 18th century in their attempts to project an image on to paper and leather coated with a silver nitrate solution; the image was finally fixed by Nicéphore Niépce in 1826–7.

The origins of the camera obscura go back at least to Aristotle, who noted the principle on which it works in his *Problems*. This was also noted by the Arabian philosopher Ibn al-Haytham (Alhazen; *c.* 965–1039) who recommended it to astronomers as a means of observing eclipses safely; it was frequently used for this purpose, often in conjunction with an astronomer's reticle. This appears to have been its main use at least until the 16th century, though the English scholar Roger Bacon (1214–94) appears to have known of the mirror device by which the camera obscura was of interest and value to artists. Giorgio Vasari mentions an invention of Leon Battista Alberti that sounds as if it may have been a camera obscura, but it was not until the publication of the Neapolitan physician Giovan Battista della Porta's *Magia Naturalis* (Naples, 1558) that the camera obscura became popularized as a mechanical aid to drawing, and not until the early 1600s that Johann Kepler gave it the name by which it is now known.

Following this the camera obscura became increasingly popular and important. Both Johannes Torrentius and Johannes Vermeer are known to have used it (the former thus laying himself open to a charge of witchcraft); so, notably, did Canaletto, who had a camera obscura made by the Venetian optical-instrument maker Domenico Selva. Among other painters who enthusiastically adopted it were Francesco Guardi, Michele Giovanni Marieschi, Luca Carlevaris and Sir Joshua Reynolds. John Harris mentions the camera obscura in his *Lexicon Technicum* (London, 1704) as being on sale in London; indeed, throughout the 18th century their use became a craze. They were enjoyed equally for the views they made possible, particularly the chiaroscuro effects produced by

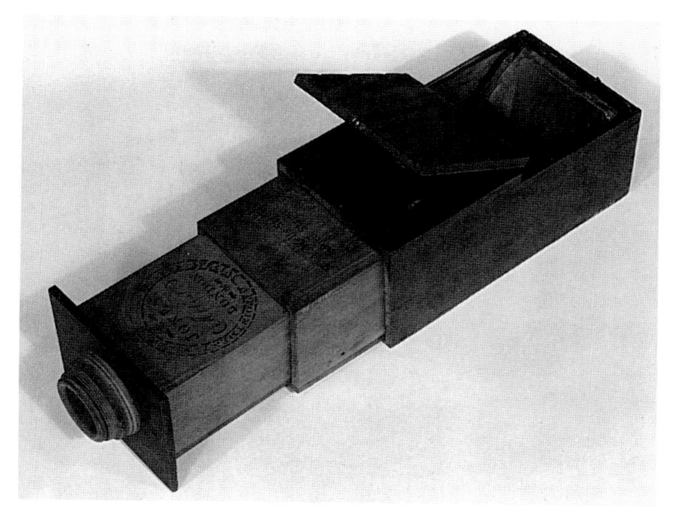

Camera obscura by Jones of London, mahogany and glass, 89×203×102 mm, late 18th century (London, Science Museum)

looking from or through a darkened area at a well-lit subject (perhaps similar to those created by the Claude glass and satisfying a similar 18th-century taste). Horace Walpole and Goethe are among those known to have owned and used a camera obscura, presumably for this reason. In 1747 the London instrument maker John Cuff published an anonymous contemporary poem praising the camera obscura, which gives some indication of the healthy market there was for these instruments. It contains much fulsome praise:

> Say, rare Machine, who taught thee to design?
> And mimick Nature with such Skill divine . . .
> Exterior objects painting on the scroll
> True as the Eye presents 'em to the Soul. . . .

The camera obscura came in many sizes, some large enough, though portable, to warrant being covered with a tent; these could easily accommodate a man standing (and drawing) inside. Others, like sedan-chairs, were fitted with bellows, which the artist or viewer worked with his feet to improve ventilation. Sir Joshua Reynolds owned one (London, Sci. Mus.) that, with great ingenuity, collapsed down to the size and appearance of a book and could be stored as such.

BIBLIOGRAPHY

G. Vasari: *Vite*, ii (1550, rev. 2/1568); ed. G. Milanesi (1878–85), pp. 535–48
H. Hutter: *Die Handzeichnung* (Vienna, 1966); Eng. trans. as *Drawing, History and Technique* (London, 1968), p. 145
H. Osborne, ed.: *The Oxford Companion to Art* (Oxford, 1970)
H. Schwarz: 'An Eighteenth Century English Poem on the *camera obscura*', *Festschrift für Beaumont Newall* (Albuquerque, 1975), pp. 127–38
Thomas Gainsborough's Exhibition Box and Transparencies (exh. cat., Gainsborough's House, Sudbury, Suffolk, 1979)
J. H. Hammond: *The Camera Obscura: A Chronicle* (Bristol, 1981) [with bibliog.]
C. Ashwin: *Encyclopedia of Drawing* (London, 1982), pp. 16–20

JACQUELINE COLLISS HARVEY

Camerino. *See under* VARANO.

Camerino, Arcangelo di Cola da. *See* ARCANGELO DI COLA DA CAMERINO.

Camerino, Giovanni Angelo di Antonio. *See under* MASTERS, ANONYMOUS, AND MONOGRAMMISTS, §I: MASTER OF THE BARBERINI PANELS.

Camerino, Girolamo di Giovanni da. *See* GIROLAMO DI GIOVANNI DA CAMERINO.

Cameron, Charles (*b* London, 1745; *d* St Petersburg, 1812). English architect of Scottish descent, active also in Russia. One of the most interesting exponents of Neo-classicism in architecture, he was a fervent admirer of antiquity and at the same time a follower of Palladio. In England he was known as an authority on Roman baths, but in Russia he worked on buildings and landscape design. Although he belonged to the school of James Adam and Robert Adam (i), his work also shows the influence of earlier styles, especially the work of Richard Boyle, 3rd Earl of Burlington, and William Kent.

In 1760 Cameron was apprenticed to his father, Walter Cameron, who was a member of the Carpenters' Company in London and who also undertook the erection of new buildings. Charles Cameron's skill as a draughtsman attracted the attention of Isaac Ware, who invited him to collaborate on a new edition of a book by Burlington, *Fabbriche antiche disegnate da Andrea Palladio* (1730), which contained Palladio's measurements of Roman baths. Cameron decided to publish his own work on Roman baths after Ware's death in 1766, using Burlington's and Ware's material. In 1768 he travelled to Rome to gather more precise measurements and to carry out the partial excavation of the Baths of Titus. In 1772 he published *The Baths of the Romans*, in a lavish folio edition with many engravings and a long scholarly treatise on Roman baths. Based during this period in his father's house in White Horse Street, Piccadilly, London, he had lost his collection of books and engravings when his father went bankrupt in 1768. He took his father to court in an attempt to save some of his property, but the consequent damage

Charles Cameron: Cameron Gallery, Tsarskoye Selo (now Pushkin), 1783–6

to his reputation ensured that for several years he received no architectural commissions in England.

At the end of 1779 Cameron arrived in St Petersburg, invited as an expert on Roman baths, in order to build the 'Roman House' in the garden of Catherine II's favourite summer residence, Tsarskoye Selo (now PUSHKIN), *c.* 22 km south of St Petersburg. He was also commissioned to build classical pavilions at nearby PAVLOVSK for the heir to the throne, the future Emperor Paul I (*reg* 1796–1801). Cameron told Catherine that he was related to the Camerons of Lochiel and gave himself out to be a Jacobite. This obfuscation of the truth went unchallenged for 200 years and formed the basis of biographies of Cameron.

During his time as Catherine's court architect Cameron worked exclusively on buildings at Tsarskoye Selo and Pavlovsk and refused private commissions. His principal work was the Roman Baths (Rus. *termy*) at the south-east corner of the Great or Yekaterininsky Palace on a falling site; the building was reached from the Empress's favourite suite, the interior of which Cameron began to decorate from 1780. The Baths consisted of the Cold Baths (*kholodnyye bani*), with the Agate Pavilion (*agatovyye komnaty*) above them (completed 1785); next came a hanging garden, the colonnaded Cameron Gallery, named in honour of the architect (*kameronovaya galereya*; 1783–6; see fig.); and finally a gentle ramp to the gardens, the Pente Douce (*pandus*; 1792). This set of buildings, complex in construction and function, is notable for its elegance and unity of style. Cameron used architectural forms close to those of antiquity but at the same time often displayed great creative audacity, as when he made the spaces between the columns in the covered Cameron Gallery very much wider than Classical prototypes.

In the Great or Yekaterininsky Palace (*bol'shoy dvorets*), built by Bartolomeo Francesco Rastrelli, Cameron's interiors make a complete stylistic break with earlier work. He started with a suite of eight rooms at the north end of the building (damaged in World War II and restored). These included the Green Dining-room (*see* STUCCO AND PLASTERWORK, fig. 17), the Blue Chinese Drawing-room and the Bedroom of the Grand Dukes. Then followed work on the official suite at the opposite end of the palace, with the Rotunda and Chinese Hall beside the Lyons Drawing-room and the Arabesque Room, and finally the Empress's private apartments with small rooms, delicately and intricately decorated, especially the Empress's Bedroom. All the decorations were extraordinarily varied and, in contrast to the work of the Adam brothers, did not consist mainly of architectural motifs: Cameron created a theatrical, refined environment with soft, delicate colours, using many materials, such as cast silver, porcelain, glass, marble, amber, jasper and lapis lazuli, silk and fine woods. He also contributed to the design of the park (*novyy sad*), where the Englishman John Busch, who became Cameron's father-in-law, was head gardener from the early 1770s until 1789. Cameron worked also on the Chinese Village, made up of 17 buildings (1786–96), four Chinese bridges (1780–82), a pyramid, a Neo-classical temple (1792) and a church (1796). Next to the park and between Tsarskoye Selo and Pavlovsk he devised a grandiose scheme in the form of an idealized town called Sofia (dest. 1808, except the church). Here his plans for the church of St Sofia (*sofiyskiy sobor*;

1782–7), the post office (1782–5) and 20 or so houses were carried out. Three-storey blocks of houses with richly decorated façades form a magnificent frame turned towards the park. At Sofia, Cameron established a colony of Scottish craftsmen whom he had persuaded to move with their families from Edinburgh in 1784. Among them were Adam Menelas, or Menelaws, and William Hastie, who later became well-known architects in Russia.

At Pavlovsk, 6 km to the south-east, Cameron built a palace and a park ensemble (*see* GARDEN, fig. 55). First he designed the pavilions for the park: the round-domed Doric Temple of Friendship (1779–82), the circular Colonnade of Apollo (1780–83; ruined), an aviary and an obelisk (both 1782) in antique taste; he also designed a dairy (1782) and a kitchen (1781; ruined) in the style of rustic huts, modelled on the park buildings on the Württemberg estates in Germany. (Paul's wife, the Grand Duchess Mariya Fyodorovna, was of that family.) The park—the area next to the palace and the valley of the River Slavyanka—was replanned according to his suggestions between 1781 and 1787. Cameron designed and built the Great Palace (1782–7) in the form of a Palladian country mansion, with a central block and two wings joined to it by curved colonnades. He started work on and designed the interiors of the Grecian and Italian halls, but owing to a disagreement, principally with the Grand Duchess, he was replaced in 1786 by the Italian architect Vincenzo Brenna. Brenna completed the palace and was involved in the layout of the gardens in the 1790s. Cameron was reinstated by Paul I in 1800, and from 1801 to 1803 he was back at Pavlovsk, where he built the famous Pavilion of the Three Graces, with its Ionic columns and perfect proportions, and other monuments.

In 1801 Cameron unsuccessfully entered the competition to design the cathedral of Our Lady of Kazan in St Petersburg. During his brief period out of office he designed a palace for Count Kirill Razumovsky and his family at Baturino in Little Russia (now in Ukraine). In 1802 Emperor Alexander I (*reg* 1801–25) appointed Cameron architect-in-chief to the Admiralty. As the official architect to the navy he erected a large naval hospital in Oranienbaum (1803–6; now Lomonosov), consisting of 16 buildings, and a large number of utilitarian naval structures in St Petersburg, but he was not responsible for the rebuilding of the Admiralty building, which was given in 1806 to Andreyan Zakharov. At the end of his life Cameron's work became unfashionable, and although he remained court architect until his death, none of his final projects was built.

BIBLIOGRAPHY

Charl'z Kameron: Sbornik statey [Charles Cameron: a collection of essays] (Petrograd, 1924)
V. N. Taleporovsky: *Charl'z Kameron* (Moscow, 1939)
G. K. Loukomsky: *Charles Cameron* (London, 1943)
Charles Cameron (exh. cat., ed. T. Talbot Rice; London, ACGB, 1968)
I. Rae: *Charles Cameron: Architect to the Court of Russia* (London, 1971)
V. Kennett and A. Kennett: *The Palaces of Leningrad* (London, 1973)
D. Shvidkovsky: 'Cameron Discoveries', *Archit. Rev.* [London], clxxii (Dec 1982), pp. 42–51
E. Harris: *British Architectural Books and Writers, 1556–1785* (Cambridge, 1990), pp. 136–9
J. M. Robinson: 'A Dazzling Adventurer. Charles Cameron: The Lost Early Years', *Apollo*, cxxxv (Jan 1992), pp. 31–8

D. O. SHVIDKOVSKY

Cameron, Sir **D(avid) Y(oung)** (*b* Glasgow, 28 June 1865; *d* Perth, 16 Sept 1945). Scottish painter and etcher. He trained at the Glasgow and Edinburgh Schools of Art in the early 1880s and was at first associated with the Glasgow Boys. He became a leader in the Scottish etching revival, having been encouraged to take up the medium by George Stevenson in 1887. From 1887 to 1892 he was a member of the Royal Society of Painter-Etchers. His first published prints were the Clyde Set (1889; Rinder, 1912, nos 30–49), followed by his London Set (1899; Rinder, 1912, nos 289–301) and a number of continental sets: North Holland, 1892; North Italian, 1894–6; Paris, 1904; Belgian, 1907 (Rinder, 1912, nos 115–36, 202–29, 361–6, 387–96). These show the influence of Seymour Haden, Whistler and Charles Meryon. Cameron's prints include many architectural subjects such as old city streets, and workshop and church interior views such as the *Five Sisters, York Minster* (1907; Rinder, 1912, no. 397). They moved from a picturesque, illustrative approach in the early works to a highly symbolic use of central shadow or emanating light. Architecture was increasingly treated as expressive in its own right and in several cases this was achieved through a radical reworking which eliminated human forms, as in *Rosslyn* (1899; Rinder, 1912, no. 303). From Rembrandt, Cameron evolved a style of large tonal masses and, in late prints, virtually abandoned middle tones.

In the 20th century, Scottish mountain landscape, rendered with strong chiaroscuro, replaced architecture as his chief interest. After *Dark Angers* (Manchester, C.A.G.) of 1903 Cameron's oils adopted brighter light values, encouraged by a trip to Egypt in 1908–9. Paintings introducing increasingly high colour include his Ben Ledi pictures (following from his famous etching of 1911; Rinder, 1912, no. 424) and the *Hills of Skye* (Glasgow, A.G. & Mus.). During World War I he was commissioned by the Canadian Government to contribute to its War Record paintings: this resulted in such works as the *Garment of War* (Edinburgh, City A. Cent.). Cameron held many titles and honours, including election as a member of the Royal Scottish Academy in 1918 and of the Royal Academy in 1920. In later life he supervised the murals for St Stephen's Hall, Palace of Westminster, London, and was closely involved in the development of the British School at Rome. He was knighted in 1924 and appointed King's Painter and Limner in Scotland in 1933.

BIBLIOGRAPHY

DNB
D. Martin: *The Glasgow School of Painting* (London, 1897/*R* 1976), pp. 1–2
J. L. Caw: *Scottish Painting Past and Present, 1620–1908* (Edinburgh, 1908/*R* 1975), pp. 457–60
F. Rinder: *D. Y. Cameron: An Illustrated Catalogue of his Etched Work* (Glasgow, 1912)
A. J. Finberg: *The Paintings of D. Y. Cameron, ARA, RSA* (London, 1919)
A. M. Hind: *The Etchings of D. Y. Cameron* (London, 1924)
D. S. Meldrum: 'Sir David Cameron's Watercolours of the Highlands', *Apollo*, x (1929), pp. 220–22
F. Rinder: *David Young Cameron: Etchings and Drypoints from 1912–1932* (Glasgow, 1932)
A Selection from the Works of D. Y. Cameron: Paintings, Drawings and Etchings (exh. cat. by T. J. Honeyman, ACGB, Scottish Committee, 1947)
Sir D. Y. Cameron Centenary Exhibition (exh. cat. by A. Auld, ACGB, Scottish Committee, 1965)

Charles Meryon. David Young Cameron (exh. cat., ed. A. Cortez, P. J. Jouve, P. Junod and R. M. Mason; Geneva, Mus. A. & Hist., 1981)
J. Halsby: *Scottish Watercolours, 1740–1940* (Braintree, 1986), pp. 151–2
D. Macmillan: *Scottish Art, 1460–1990* (Edinburgh, 1990), pp. 302–3
B. Smith: *D. Y. Cameron: The Vision of the Hills* (Edinburgh, 1992)
C. Willsdon: *Mural Painting in Britain, 1840–1940* (Oxford, in preparation)

CLARE A. P. WILLSDON

Cameron [née Pattle]**, Julia Margaret** (*b* Calcutta, 11 June 1815; *d* Dikoya Valley, Ceylon [now Sri Lanka], 26 Jan 1879). English photographer and writer. Her father was an official in the East India Company. She therefore spent a number of years in Calcutta, but she was educated by her maternal grandmother in France and in England. In 1838 she married Charles Hay Cameron, a distinguished jurist. She brought up six children, who were born between 1839 and 1852. In 1848 the Cameron family settled permanently in England, living first in London and from 1860 at Freshwater, Isle of Wight. Cameron was a frequent visitor to the literary and artistic salon conducted by her sister, Sara Prinsep, at Little Holland House, Kensington, London. In 1847 she published a translation of Gottfried August Bürger's *Leonora*; she also wrote poetry, and apparently began a novel.

Julia Margaret Cameron was given her first camera in 1864 to occupy her time while her husband and sons were on the family coffee estates in Ceylon. Photography was not a common amateur recreation in the 1860s; she described her eventual commitment to the difficult wet collodion negative and albumen print positive process in a letter to Sir John Herschel (31 December 1864) as fired by her ambition to 'ennoble Photography' (see Ford, pp. 140–41). She was also inspired by the fancy dress portrait photographs taken in 1863 by the English painter David Wilkie Wynfield (1837–87). George Frederick Watts, whom Cameron had met at Little Holland House, supported her work and used her images as painting studies. She was elected a member of photographic societies in London and Scotland in 1864.

Julia Margaret Cameron: *Mary Mother*, albumen print, 1867 (Rochester, NY, International Museum of Photography at George Eastman House)

Like other members of her social group, Cameron regarded recent technical developments in photography, including such forms as *carte-de-visite* portraiture, as threats to established values of photographic representation. She inscribed her photographs as 'From Life' and refused to retouch defects on the negative, believing such an action mitigated the authenticity of the material connection between the photographic negative and her subject. Her controversial soft-focus technique gave animation and breadth to her forms and rejected the perfection of detail prized in commercial photography; her expressive and symbolic uses of lighting were distinguished from the generalized illumination characteristic of commercial work. In her bust portraits of notable Victorian men, Cameron referred to ideal types and to compositions from Old Master paintings to communicate her idea of heroic individuals. An example of this approach is *Henry Taylor: A 'Rembrandt'* (*c.* 1866; see 1984 exh. cat., p. 111). Her narrative photographs, derived from *tableaux vivants* and amateur theatricals, dealt largely with women, in particular with idealizations of the Victorian roles of wife and mother, for example *Mary Mother* (1867; see fig.). Cameron's major work of narrative photographs was her *Illustrations to Tennyson's 'Idylls of the King' and Other Poems* (London, 1874–5), published in two volumes, in which she represented the female characters of Camelot, such as Guinevere in *The Parting of Sir Lancelot and Queen Guinevere* (see 1984 exh. cat., p. 78).

Cameron actively sought both to place her inspirational subjects before the public and to achieve sales and recognition for her work. She was not obliged to earn a living from her photographs but hoped purchases would aid her family's ailing finances. She registered over 500 photographs for copyright protection and sold her work through the London print-sellers Colnaghi & Company. Cameron regularly contributed to exhibitions of photographic societies in London, Edinburgh, Paris and Berlin, and to international exhibitions in London, Dublin, Paris, Vienna and Philadelphia; she also organized three one-woman shows in London. In her search for sitters and for reviewers of her work, she drew upon her extensive contacts among the Victorian intelligentsia, many of whom wrote favourable notices about her work for prominent journals. She made numerous portrait studies of close friends, including *Alfred Tennyson* (see Weaver, pp. 99–101) and *Sir John Herschel* (see 1984 exh. cat., pp. 108–9).

Commercial photographers resented Cameron's contempt for photographic proprieties and her easy access to famous sitters and to publicity. Their hostility to her technique abated, however, when they realized her work was not a serious threat to their market. The pictorial qualities of her photography were appreciated by her select audience but were inapplicable to the values of the mass audiences. Cameron produced few photographs after she moved to Ceylon with her family in 1875. The Arts and Crafts movement revived interest in Cameron's work in the 1890s, and Virginia Woolf, Cameron's great-niece, published a selection of her photographs.

BIBLIOGRAPHY

V. Woolf, ed.: *Victorian Photographs of Famous Men and Fair Women*, essay by R. Fry (London, 1926/*R* 1973)

H. Gernsheim: *Julia Margaret Cameron: Her Life and Photographic Work* (London, 1948, rev. Millerton, 1975)

C. Ford: *The Cameron Collection: An Album of Photographs by Julia Margaret Cameron Presented to Sir John Herschel* (London, 1975)

Julia Margaret Cameron, 1815–1879 (exh. cat. by M. Weaver, ACGB, 1984)

M. Weaver: *Whisper of the Muse: The Overstone Album and Other Photographs by Julia Margaret Cameron* (Malibu, 1986)

Cameron: Her Work and Career (exh. cat. by J. Lukitsh, Rochester, NY, Int. Mus. Phot., 1986)

JOANNE LUKITSH

Cameroon, Republic of [Cameroun, République du]. Country in west-central Africa, stretching from the Gulf of Guinea in the south-west to Lake Chad in the north. To the west, Cameroon borders on Nigeria, to the east on Chad and the Central African Republic and to the south on the Congo, Gabon and Equatorial Guinea. The capital is Yaoundé. French and English are both official languages.

1. GEOGRAPHY AND CULTURAL HISTORY. Cameroon's geography comprises the full range of climatic and scenic variations found in Africa: virgin forest in the south, grasslands in the west, scrubby savannah with the Massif de l'Adamaoua in the north, and savannah with the Mandara Mountains in the far north. The population of Cameroon (11,540,000; UN estimate, 1989) is made up of a number of peoples who traditionally followed their own religions, each speaking their own language. Through the Arabs, the north came under Islamic influence at a very early stage, while the south was later converted to Christianity by European missionaries. From 1884 to 1916 Cameroon was a German protectorate; subsequently the western part became a British colony, and the larger, eastern part a French colony. The country became independent in 1960, and in 1961 the eastern and western sectors were united to form the present state. This entry covers the art produced in the area since colonial times. For art of the region in earlier periods, *see* AFRICA, §VII, 5(i).

See also BAMILEKE AND RELATED PEOPLES, BAMUM, BANGWA, CHAMBA (ii) and FANG.

2. CONTINUING TRADITIONS. Cameroon's traditional arts are rich and varied. Special mention may be made here of the spindle-shaped pieces of nut shell (30–50 mm long) used by the Beti and Ewondo of southern Cameroon in the game of *abbia*, on which are drawn an infinite variety of schematic representations of men and women, animals, objects and symbols. In the south-west the Douala produce ornamental carvings on canoe prows, as well as filigree model canoes, geometrically painted animal masks and squat, rectangular chiefs' stools with animal motifs. In the grasslands of the north-west, rich traditions of masking, figure sculpture and wood-carving have continued, as well as beadwork, ivory and bronze-working. While many of these arts were traditionally dependent on royal patronage, since colonization they have become increasingly secularized. In 1922 the establishment by Mosé Jegab in Bamun of the 'Street of Artists', in which craftsmen worked in studios, became a model for several similar organizations in Cameroon. After a while, however, the quality of the objects produced began to decline, resulting in the production of much souvenir or 'airport' art. Isolated projects, like that of Father Engelbert Mveng in Yaoundé, to revitalize such traditional arts as *abbia* motifs in new contexts, had little lasting effect. For further information on continuing traditions, *see* BAMILEKE AND RELATED PEOPLES, BAMUM, BANGWA, CHAMBA (ii) and FANG.

3. ARCHITECTURE. At the beginning of the colonial period (*c.* 1885) buildings were varied, having developed to accord with the landscape and the materials to hand. The most lavish buildings were those belonging to the indigenous rulers. During colonization German architects analysed traditional architecture and developed a synthesis of this and Western styles, resulting in 'German tropical architecture', as exemplified by David Mandessi-Bell's residence (1904), a two-storey, pergola-type design on a rectangular ground-plan, providing optimum ventilation. The people of Cameroon have been aware of the importance of these buildings to their own history, and some were still in use in the 1990s. Following World War I and the takeover of the colony by the French there was a break in architectural developments. Bauhaus Functionalism reached Cameroon only in the 1920s and 1930s, as an offshoot of the European Modern Movement. The bank and post office in Yaoundé and the post office, Douala, are examples of this style.

After World War II a new awareness of the value of the forms and expressions of African culture developed. As Westerners began to appreciate African Art, the European architects who continued to dominate Cameroonian building projects went on using peusdo-African attributes as stylistic elements until ten years or so after independence. Examples of this tendency include the cinema at Abbia and various ministries in Yaoundé. In the 1970s and 1980s a new functionalism became more widespread as multi-storey buildings, formally reminiscent of the work of Le Corbusier, began to make their mark on the townscapes of Douala and Yaoundé. In the 1990s there were 40 to 50 native Cameroon architects, but because building contracts were still placed mainly with foreign firms, no truly individual style, adapted to the region, had yet evolved. In addition, traditional dwellings, which originally differed markedly from one region to another, were becoming increasingly uniform. Roofs made of natural materials were giving way to corrugated iron, and the wide variety of building materials was being replaced by concrete blocks.

4. PAINTING AND SCULPTURE. Cameroon artists became aware of European painting as a result of colonial influences, and some were inspired to adopt its content and styles. There was, however, no systematic training in fine art until the early 1970s, when a few artists received scholarships to study art, first of all in France and then in

Joseph-Francis Sumegne: *Motherhood*, woodcut, 300×400 mm, 1988 (private collection)

other overseas countries. Pascal Kenfack (*b* 1950), who studied painting and sculpture at the Ecole Régionale des Beaux-Arts, Besançon, and the Ecole des Beaux-Arts, Paris, and René Tchébétchou, who also studied in Paris, were among these. Kenfack's paintings and his sculptures, carved from tree trunks, are concerned mainly with the history and mythology of his people, although his creative methods bear a European stamp. In Tchébétchou's work, subjects relating to the African philosophy of life predominate. His work is in an objective, figurative style with a suggestion of Cubist influence. In 1986 he was commissioned by Misereor, a German Catholic charity, to design the *Hungertuch*. A few Cameroon artists who studied abroad took up residence there. Francis Mbella (*b* 1961) studied in 1983 at the Ecole des Beaux-Arts, Paris, and lives mainly in France. His African and European landscapes and still-lifes in intense, often dark shades convey a superficially abstract pictorial structure.

The majority of self-taught artists stayed in Cameroon and developed their talents in a variety of ways. Joseph-Francis Sumegne treated themes from the mythology of the Bamileke without completely moving away from the contemporary situation (see fig.). He appropriated a number of old techniques and—like the wood-carvers of earlier times—made use of the materials that he found in his surroundings. Jean-Baptiste Ngnetchopa (*b* 1953), another wood-carver, came from a family of traditional sculptors and received his training in the form of a seven-year apprenticeship. His early works are large mahogany or iroko panels depicting, in high relief, village life, traditional ceremonies and portraits of, for example, President Mitterrand of France and Queen Elizabeth II. In 1985 he began a series of banknotes, carved in high relief in wood (see exh. cat. 1991–2).

In the field of sculpture there was a wide gulf between those who still followed traditional models in their work and those who created their own interpretations, appropriate to the present. Among the latter group Maître Gédéon Pando may be singled out. His sculptures are impressive for the understanding of material and the expression that they display.

5. Art life and organization. By the early 1990s there was only a small demand in Cameroon for fine art, with neither the public nor the government buying works of art in significant quantities. The lack of patronage was filled partly by foreign embassies and their cultural institutes in the capital, some of which organized exhibitions and short seminars for Cameroon artists both in Cameroon and abroad. Occasional exhibitions were also held by larger hotels. Scholarships for foreign art schools or study tours were occasionally made available by a number of

countries, but within Cameroon there was no systematic art tuition at either secondary or tertiary levels. Attempts to introduce specialist teaching at grammar schools and art education as a teaching subject at the teachers' training college fell into abeyance with the departure of the German teaching force. In the early 1990s the one-time Minister for Education, Adamou Ndam Njoya, started a promising initiative to build up an integrated training that included handicrafts and fine art. Collections of Cameroonian art are held by the Musée National, Yaoundé, and the private Petit Musée d'Art Camerounais, Yaoundé, as well as by various national, provincial, municipal and local museums in Bamenda, Buea, Douala, Dschang, Foumban, Kousseri, Maroua and Mokolo. A number of artists have been employed as conservators or administrators in some of these museums.

BIBLIOGRAPHY

E. Mveng: 'Die afrikanische Kunst von gestern und heute', *Neues Afrika*, iii (1961), pp. 475–9
W. Hirschberg: *Die Künstlerstrasse: Auf Studienreise durch Kamerun* (Vienna, 1962)
E. Mveng: 'L'Art camerounais', *Abbia*, 3 (1963), pp. 3–24
R. Gardi: *Unter afrikanischen Handwerkern: Begegnungen und Erlebnisse in West-Afrika* (Wabern, 1969)
L. Marfurt: *Abbia: Un Jeu des Beti du Sud-Cameroun* (Yaoundé, 1970)
P. Gebauer: 'Architecture of Cameroon', *Afr. A.*, v/1 (1971), pp. 40–49
——: 'Art of Cameroon', *Afr. A.*, iv/2 (1971), pp. 24–35
A. Debel: *Kamerun in Farbe* (Paris, 1977) [guidebook]
H.-J. Koloss: *Kamerun: Könige-Masken-Feste* (Stuttgart, 1977)
D. J. Crowley: 'The Art Market in Cameroon and the Central African Empire', *Afr. A.*, xii/3 (1979)
R. P. E. Mveng: *L'Art et l'artisanat africains* (Yaoundé, 1980)
J. Etienne-Ngue: *Artisanats et arts de vivre au Cameroun* ([1982])
The Cultural Identity of Cameroon (Yaoundé, 1985)
Deutsche Architektur in Kamerun, 1884–1914, ed. W. Lauber (Stuttgart, 1988) [Ger., Eng. and Fr. text]
Cameroun art et architecture (exh. cat., Paris, Mus. N. A. Afr. & Océan., 1988–9)
N. W. Edelman, ed.: *L'Art camerounais* (Yaoundé, 1989)
F. Mbella: *Les Reflets de la couleur* (Yaoundé, 1991)
'Jean-Baptiste Ngnetchopa', *Africa Now* (exh. cat., Las Palmas de Gran Canaria, Cent. Atlantic. A. Mod.; Gronigen, Groniger Mus.; Mexico City, Cent. Cult. A. Contemp.; 1991–2), pp. 151–7

GLORIA J. UMLAUFT-THIELICKE

Cametti, Bernardino (*b* Rome, 1669; *d* Rome, July 1736). Italian sculptor. His family came from Gattinara in Piedmont—a town famous for its engravers—and he served a long apprenticeship in the workshop of Lorenzo Ottoni in Rome. His first known works are the marble relief of the *Canonization of St Ignatius* (1695–8; Rome, the Gesù, chapel of S Ignazio), based on a design provided by Andrea Pozzo, and the monument to *Count Vladislav Constantine Wasa* (1698–1700; Rome, Stimmate di S Francesco), commissioned by Cardinal Giovanni Francesco Albani (later Clement XI). In the Lazio region Cametti was also active at Frascati, where he produced a relief (1704) for the façade of the cathedral; and at Palestrina, with the funerary monuments to *Prince Taddeo Barberini* and *Cardinal Antonio Barberini* (both 1704; S Rosalia), where he experimented with a new concept in tomb design which he used again in the monument to *Gabriele Filippucci* (*c.* 1706; Rome, S Giovanni in Laterano).

Cametti's masterpiece is his *Diana the Huntress* (*c.* 1720; Berlin, Gëmaldegal.), which was originally located in the centre of a fountain at the Palazzo Orsini in Rome. It combines the elegance of French sculpture with Baroque monumentality. The sculptor was the only Italian artist to enjoy the privilege of having a studio at the Académie Française, Rome, and to maintain close links with the French artists living in the city. For the chapel of the Monte di Pietà in Rome, Cametti sculpted his *Almsgiving* (1721–4), while the *St Cesario* (*c.* 1723–4) was placed adjacent to the high altar of the Pantheon. The monuments to *Giovanni Andrea Muti* and his wife *Maria Colomba Muti* (both 1725; Rome, S Marcello) demonstrate the artist's remarkable aptitude for portraiture, inherited from Ottoni, as well as the meticulous care that he lavished on sculptural details.

Besides his work in Rome, Cametti provided numerous works for other locations in Italy. He sent his *SS Simon and James the Lesser* (1722; Mus. Opera Duomo) to Orvieto and his statues of *St Luke* and *St Mark* (1716; Madonna di S Luca) to Bologna. Victor-Amadeus II of Savoy commissioned him to carry out two marble bas-reliefs in Turin, the *Annunciation* (1729) and the *Intercession of the Blessed Amadeus in the Victory by the House of Savoy over the Armies of Louis XIV* (1735; both Superga, Basilica).

BIBLIOGRAPHY

DBI; Thieme–Becker
N. Pio: *Vite* (1724); ed. C. Enggass and R. Enggass (1977), pp. 152–3
U. Schlegel: 'Bernardino Cametti', *Jb. Berlin. Mus.*, v (1963), pp. 151–200
R. Enggass: *Early Eighteenth-century Sculpture in Rome: An Illustrated Catalogue Raisonné* (University Park, PA, 1976), pp. 149–58
A. Nava Cellini: *La scultura del settecento* (Turin, 1982), pp. 20–23
V. Martinelli, ed.: *Le statue Berniniane del colonnato di S Pietro* (Rome, 1987), pp. 142, 205
P. Ferraris: 'La fabbrica della chiesa delle Stimmate in Roma e la statua di S Francesco di Bernardino Cametti', *Stor. A.*, lxv (1989), pp. 69–86

DONATELLA GERMANÒ SIRACUSA

Camilliani, Camillo (*fl c.* 1574–?1603). Italian sculptor and military engineer. He moved to Palermo from Florence in 1574, to assemble and enlarge (with the collaboration of Michelangelo Naccherino) the fountain executed in the 1550s by his father, Francesco Camilliani (*d* 1586), a pupil of Baccio Bandinelli, for the Florentine villa of Pietro di Toledo. This had been sold to the city of Palermo by Pietro's son Luigi di Toledo, to be erected in the newly built Piazza Pretoria in front of the Palazzo Senatorio. It was much praised by Vasari and represented the introduction of Mannerist sculpture to Palermo. Many documents relate to Camilliani, although only a few works survive. In 1586 he was appointed viceregal architect and custodian of coastal fortifications, in which role he played an important part in the defence of Sicily. In 1585 he was responsible for the construction of the military quarter at Milazzo. His busy studio supplied fountains, statues, funerary monuments and silver objects to churches and noble patrons. His statue of *Glaucus* (mid-1580s; Palermo, Gal. Reg. Sicilia) was executed for the Palazzo Reale. In 1590 he designed the tribune of S Giovanni di Malta in Messina, which was completed by Giacomo del Duca, and in 1592 he agreed to make an elaborate fountain (destr. 19th century) for the city of Caltagirone. The remains of a rich silver tabernacle, which was originally decorated with twelve apostles and the four evangelists, are preserved in the church of S Maria in Caltagirone. In

1593 he planned the triumphal arch for the Florentines in honour of S Ninfa. In 1599 he was commissioned by Baroness Laura Valdina to produce a monument to her son Mauro Valdina, for the Chiesa Madre in Rocca. Enriched with marble inlay, it forms an important precedent for the style of decoration that prevailed in Sicilian churches during the 17th and 18th centuries. The plans for the Chiesa Madre in Milazzo and the courtyard of the Rocca Valdina Castle in Rocca have also been attributed to Camilliani (Samona).

BIBLIOGRAPHY

G. Vasari: *Vite* (1550, rev. 2/1568); ed. G. Milanesi (1878–85)
G. di Marzo: *I Gagini e la scultura in Sicilia de' secoli XV e XVI* (Palermo, 1880)
G. Samona: 'L'opera dell'architetto fiorentino Camillo Camilliani in Sicilia', *Riv. Reale Ist. Archeol. & Stor. A.*, iv (1932–3), pp. 227–8
D. Garstang: *Giacomo Serpotta and the Stuccatori of Palermo, 1560–1790* (London, 1984)

DONALD GARSTANG

Camillo, Giulio (*b* Friuli, *c.* 1480; *d* Milan, 15 May 1544). Italian writer. He held a professorship in Bologna for some time, but dedicated the greater part of his life to elaborating his Teatro del Mondo (destr.). This was a wooden amphitheatre in Venice, constructed after the Vitruvian model, divided by seven gangways into seven sections that corresponded to the seven pillars of wisdom of the Temple of Solomon. The theatre was built on seven levels: the first, governed by the seven planets, was followed by others embodying a series of allegories dominated by mythological themes (Apollo, the Cave, the three Gorgons, Pasiphaë and the Bull, Mercury's sandals, and Prometheus). Derived from both the Classical mnemonic and the hermetic tradition (Yates), the Teatro was intended to guarantee instant access to universal knowledge. Giovanni Paolo Lomazzo's *Tempio della pittura* (Milan, 1590) took its inspiration from this. Towards 1530, Camillo wrote a treatise on imitation, in which he argued against Erasmus's *Ciceronianus* (1528). The treatise concludes with a comparison between the visual arts and eloquence. Camillo examines the two disciplines through seven degrees, from matter to concept, thereby transferring the figures of rhetoric to the visual arts. In addition, several documents testify to his impact on the imagery of the Renaissance and confirm his links with Sebastiano Serlio, Titian, Lorenzo Lotto and Pordenone (Bolzoni).

WRITINGS

L'idea dell'eloquenza (MS.; *c.* 1530); ed. L. Bolzoni (Padua, 1984)
Della imitatione (Venice, 1544); ed. B. Weinberg in *Trattati di poetica e retorica del cinquecento*, i (Bari, 1970), pp. 159–85
L'idea del teatro (Florence, 1550)

BIBLIOGRAPHY

DBI
L. Bernheimer: 'Theatrum mundi', *A. Bull.*, xxviii (1956), pp. 225–31
F. A. Yates: *The Art of Memory* (London, 1966), pp. 129–59
L. Bolzoni: *Il teatro delle memoria: Studi su Giulio Camillo* (Padua, 1984)

FRANÇOIS QUIVIGER

Camilo, Francisco (*b* Madrid, *c.* 1615; *d* Madrid, 1673). Spanish painter of Italian origin. His father was Italian and his mother Spanish. Her second husband, Pedro de las Cuevas, ran an excellent school of painting and drawing in Madrid, where Camilo trained along with many contemporary artists. Here Camilo would have been aware of the changes in painting that occurred *c.* 1630–40 as a result of the diffusion of prints by Peter Paul Rubens and the arrival at the court of paintings commissioned from Rubens by Philip IV. These made a deep impression on the Madrid school. With Francisco Rizi, Camilo was the earliest exponent of the High Baroque style in Madrid.

There is no work identified as being by Camilo before 1649, but there is evidence that he began painting when very young. According to Palomino, he painted a *St Francis Xavier* (untraced) for the Casa Profesa of the Jesuits, Madrid, in 1633, and in 1649 he was working in the Alcázar, Madrid, on the decoration of the Salón de Comedias. Between 1649 and *c.* 1655 he was employed by the Carthusian monastery of El Paular, Madrid, where he painted *St James* (Madrid, Prado, on dep. Salamanca, Cathedral of Ciudad Rodrigo) and *SS Anthony Abbott and Paul the Hermit* (Madrid, Prado).

Camilo preferred elongated proportions and undulating outlines for his figures and tended to depict rather gentle, sentimental and devout expressions. The colouring, often deep blues, greens and yellows, is always elegantly harmonized. Palomino stressed Camilo's expression of devotional tenderness and relates how when Philip IV saw the paintings of *Jupiter* and *Juno* (1643) by Camilo on the vaults of the Galería del Príncipe, Alcázar, Madrid, he observed that 'Jupiter looked like Jesus Christ and Juno the Virgin Mary'; this story illustrates the lack of heroic spirit in his painting.

Franciso Camilo: *Ascension*, oil on canvas, 2.07×1.37 m, 1651 (Barcelona, Museu d'Art de Catalunya)

Camilo's liking for movement is evident both in the arrangement of his compositions, where the figures never appear static, and in his treatment of fabrics, which are always floating and undulating. These elements and his individual sense of composition are apparent in the *Ascension* (1651; Barcelona, Mus. A. Catalunya; see fig.) and in the *Martyrdom of St Batholomew* (1651; Madrid, Prado). These qualities are also seen in his two paintings, *St Joseph* and *St Joachim* (1662), for an altarpiece in the church of La Fuencisla, Segovia, in his paintings of *St Joseph* and *St Benedict* (1663) for the altarpiece in the convent of Las Benitas, Toledo, and in the paintings showing two episodes from the *Images of Christ* series for the Oratory of Cristo de las Injurias, or de la Paciencia, Madrid (1649 and 1651; Madrid, Prado). His late works include the large-scale *St Peter Consecrating St Torquatus as Bishop* (*c.* 1665–70; Madrid, Prado, on dep. Toledo, Hosp. Tavera) and *St Carlo Borromeo with those Afflicted by the Plague* (*c.* 1665–70; Salamanca Cathedral).

BIBLIOGRAPHY

A. A. Palomino de Castro y Velasco: *Museo pictórico* (1715–24/*R* 1947), p. 970

D. Angulo Iñiguez: 'Francisco Camilo', *Archv Esp. A.*, xxxii/126 (1959), pp. 89–107

——: 'Nuevas obras de Francisco Camilo', *Archv Esp. A.*, xxxviii/149 (1965), pp. 59–61

F. Collar Cáceres: 'Más pinturas de Francisco Camilo en Segovia', *Archv Esp. A.*, lix/235 (1986), pp. 277–90

ALFONSO E. PÉREZ SÁNCHEZ

Camino Brent, Enrique (*b* Lima, 22 July 1909; *d* Lima, 15 July 1960). Peruvian painter and teacher. He attended the Escuela Nacional de Bellas Artes in Lima from the age of 12 or 13, studying under José Sabogal, Daniel Hernández and Manuel Piqueras Cotoli. In 1930 in Lima he exhibited Indigenist-style paintings inspired by his travels in Cuzco, Puno and Ayacucho, and he finally completed his studies in 1932 and began teaching at the Escuela Nacional. He began to exhibit outside Peru in the late 1930s and in 1941 he set up the Galería de Lima. Over the next two decades he travelled extensively, including to the USA, Europe and North Africa. Notable among the commissions Camino Brent received was that for the Corporación Nacional de Turismo for its chain of hotels throughout Peru. In these and other paintings he displayed his distinctive form of Indigenism, characterized by distorted figures and architecture—often dilapidated buildings in remote villages—full of movement and contrast (e.g. *Herod's Balcony* and *Church of S Sebastián at Huancavelica*, both 1937; both Lima, Mus. Banco Central de Reserva).

BIBLIOGRAPHY

J. Villacorta Paredes: *Pintores peruanos de la República* (Lima, 1971), pp. 51–3

J. A. de Lavalle and W. Lang: *Pintura contemporánea*, Colección arte y tesoros del Perú, ii (Lima, 1976), pp. 88–97

W. IAIN MACKAY

Cammarano, Michele (*b* Naples, 23 Feb 1835; *d* Naples, 21 Sept 1920). Italian painter. He came from a family of artists of Catalan origin and was taught by his grandfather Giuseppe (1766–1850) and his great-uncle Antonio before enrolling at the Naples Accademia di Belle Arti in 1853. He studied under Gabriele Smargiassi (1798–1882), an exponent of traditional, composed, Romantic landscape, but was soon impressed by the *plein-air* landscape painting of Giacinto Gigante and by the work of the landscape painters of the Scuola di Posilippo, Alessandro La Volpe (?1820–87) and Vincenzo Franceschini (1812–85). Between 1854 and 1855 Cammarano entered the studio of Nicola Palizzi and devoted more time to studies from the live model and of landscape *en plein air*, with stays on Capri and at Cava Campobasso. This led to a break with Smargiassi, but Cammarano continued to attend evening life classes at the Accademia and to take part in competitions. Early works, such as *Winter Landscape* (1857; Naples, Accad. B.A.), are close in style to the work of Nicola Palizzi. Cammarano also studied figure painting with Giuseppe Mancinelli (1813–75) and took a greater interest in history and literature, with the aim of finding subjects for compositions such as the *Massacre of Altamura* (sketch 1863; Naples, Mus. N. S Martino). He also joined Filippo Palizzi's life drawing class and retained a close attachment to Palizzi for the rest of his life. He realized, however, that he should not allow himself to be trapped into excessive analytic precision in his painting and that he should aim for a more concise and expressive effect. His Realism, above all manifest in studies of rocks, trees, water and dilapidated walls, was free from Palizzi's descriptive nuances and was based on a system of vigorous and constructive brushstrokes. In 1861 he took part in the artistic debate on the *macchia* technique, which linked the Tuscan Macchiaioli and the artists of the Scuola di Resina. The importance of subject-matter for Cammarano at this time, however, is evident in *Earthquake at Torre del Greco* (1862; Naples, Mus. N. S Martino) and in *Idleness and Work* (1863; Naples, Capodimonte), which marked the beginning of his concern with social problems.

In 1865 Cammarano went to Rome where he met many Italian artists, for example the numerous pupils of Tommaso Minardi still faithful to Classical themes and styles, and also many foreign artists, such as the Spaniard Mariano Fortuny y Madrazo and the German August Riedel. Cammarano's views had a demonstrable influence on the Roman circle of Italian artists, in particular Cesare Fracassini (1838–68), who asked him to collaborate on two works. During this period Cammarano extended his studies on light, and chiaroscuro came to be a unifying feature of his work. In 1867 Cammarano exhibited the *Resources of the Poor* (priv. col.; see Biancale, pl. xxvii), a painting that attracted the young Venetian artists Luigi Nono (1850–1918) and Giacomo Favretto. In Venice in 1868 he painted another work on a pressing social theme, *Encouragement to Vice* (priv. col., see Biancale, pl. xxi). In 1868 he returned to Rome where he met and admired Federico Faruffini. In Cammarano's night scene, *Piazza San Marco* (1869; Rome, G.N.A. Mod.), he combined Realist detail and a modern *à plat* application of paint. In Paris in 1870 he was able to see the work of Eugène Delacroix, Théodore Géricault and others. Above all he was able to meet Gustave Courbet, to whom he was linked by similar attitudes to subject-matter and a similar painting technique, using wide constructive brushstrokes. On his return from Paris, Cammarano dedicated himself to large paintings on military subjects, such as the *Charge of the Bersaglieri* (1871; Naples, Capodimonte). These works are indeed impressive for their size, their wealth of detail and their complexity of internal movement, created in such a way as to capture and maintain the spectator's attention. During this period Cammarano also carried out small works such as studies of mountains, rustic interiors and women in costume. In 1885, with works such as *Workers on the Land* (priv. col., see Biancale, pl. lxvi), Cammarano abandoned Naturalism and produced a series of intensely dramatic works, as in a *Game of 'Briscola'* (1887; Naples, Accad. B.A.). Here he used a diagonal viewpoint to portray the tragic outcome of a game of cards: in one corner lies the dead body of one of the players, while a crowd breaks through a side door, along with a stream of light that illuminates the scene theatrically. In 1888 the Italian Government commissioned Cammarano to paint a large picture, entitled *Dogali* (1896; Rome, Pal. Braschi), to commemorate the 500 Italians killed by the natives of Massaua. Cammarano spent five years on the spot making sketches and plans for this work. In 1900 he succeeded Filippo Palizzi as Professor of Landscape Painting at the Naples Accademia. The last years of his life were principally dedicated to teaching.

BIBLIOGRAPHY

DBI; Thieme–Becker
M. Biancale: *Michele Cammarano* (Milan, 1936)
C. Lorenzetti: *L'Accademia di Belle Arti di Napoli* (Florence, 1952), pp. 268–71, 285–7
Michele Cammarano (exh. cat., ed. L. Autiello and P. Ricci; Naples, Villa Com., 1959)
R. Causa: *Napoletani dell'ottocento* (Naples, 1966), pp. 51–9
R. Mormone: 'Michele Cammarano e il tramonto dell'ottocento', *La Galleria dell'Accademia di Belle Arti in Napoli* (Naples, 1971), pp. 67–87
P. Ricci: *Arte e artisti a Napoli, 1800–1943* (Naples, 1981)

MARIANTONIETTA PICONE PETRUSA

Cammas, Lambert-François-Thérèse (*b* Toulouse, 12 Nov 1743; *d* Toulouse, 31 Jan 1804). French painter and architect. He was the son of Guillaume Cammas (1698–1777), a painter and architect in Toulouse, who is known principally for having designed the first municipal theatre (1737) in Toulouse and the façade of the Capitole (1749–52), as well as for having carried out the decoration of the Salle des Illustres at the Hôtel de Ville. Lambert-François-Thérèse Cammas studied at the Académie Royale de Peinture in Toulouse, where in 1765 he won the Grand Prix with an *Allegory on the Death of the Dauphin* (Paris, Ecole B.-A.). The prize money was used to finance a trip to Italy. Cammas remained in Rome from 1767 to 1771, in 1770 being admitted to the Accademia di S Luca with the *Accession of Pope Clement XIV* (Rome, Accad. N. S Luca). In Rome, Cammas made many architectural studies and drew antique remains, but he was also interested in the problem of restoring ancient monuments. He may have carried out some architectural work; a chapel at the church of Pátrica, near Frosinone, is attributed to him.

On his return to Toulouse, Cammas enjoyed a successful career as both painter and architect. He succeeded Jean-Pierre Rivalz as painter and architect of the Capitole in 1779 and exhibited regularly in the Salons of the Académie. In 1775 he won first prize for the *Allegory on the Restoration of Parliament* (Toulouse, Mus. Augustins), a subject typical of his oeuvre, which consists mainly of historical and allegorical topics. These are provincial competition productions that lack distinction. As an architect Cammas worked principally for the Carthusian Order in Toulouse. Between 1780 and 1788 he designed and supervised the erection of the dome and high altar of the church in the Carthusian monastery. His collaborators included the sculptors Jean-Baptiste Julia (*d* 1803), for the stuccowork, and François Lucas, for the angels in marble for the high altar (1785); Cammas himself painted the monochrome figures in the pendentives of the dome. He went on to provide designs for such Carthusian churches as those at Castres, Cahors, Villefranche and Rodez. For the charterhouse of Saïx, near Castres, he painted the *Consecration of the Charterhouse to the Sacred Heart*, but the Revolution prevented him from delivering it. He was an ambivalent supporter of the Revolution. Appointed a Justice of the Peace, he was imprisoned from 7 January to 9 October 1801 for not having 'shown enough enthusiasm in the service of the executive power'. During his imprisonment at Castres he painted *Totila, King of the Goths, Calling on St Benedict* (Castres Cathedral).

UNPUBLISHED SOURCES

Toulouse, Mus. Dupuy and Mus. Vieux-Toulouse [one album of drgs in each: Roman sketches, decorative designs and architectural drgs]

BIBLIOGRAPHY

B. Guibal: 'Notice biographique sur Lambert-François-Thérèse Cammas, peintre-architecte-ingénieur', *Acad. Sci. Inscr. B.-Lett. Toulouse*, 5th ser., ii (1858), p. 394
Le Dessin toulousain de 1730 à 1800 (exh. cat. by R. Mesuret, Toulouse, Mus. Dupuy, 1954)
R. Mesuret: *Inventaire général des dessins des musées de province: Toulouse, Musée Paul-Dupuy* (Toulouse, 1958)
——: *Toulouse, Musée Paul-Dupuy: Dessins antérieurs à 1830*, Toulouse, Mus. Dupuy cat. (Toulouse, 1958)
O. Michel: 'Lambert-François Cammas et l'Académie romaine de Saint-Luc', *Mél. Archéol. & Hist.: Ecole Fr. Rome*, lxxxii (1970), pp. 501–24
R. Mesuret: *Les Expositions de l'Académie royale de Toulouse de 1751 à 1791* (Toulouse, 1972) [incl. 50 works by Cammas that were exhibited at places other than the Académie]

BRUNO TOLLON

Camoin, Charles (*b* Marseille, 23 Sept 1879; *d* Paris, 20 May 1965). French painter. After the death of his father, he was brought up by his mother alone, whose endless travels seem to have affected his studies. At 16 he simultaneously enrolled at the Ecole des Beaux-Arts, Marseille, which he attended in the morning, and at the Ecole de Commerce. After winning a prize for drawing, he was encouraged by his mother to enter Gustave Moreau's studio at the Ecole des Beaux-Arts in Paris, which he did in May 1898, shortly before Moreau's death. Although he barely had time to derive any benefit from Moreau's teaching, he formed several lasting friendships among fellow students later associated with FAUVISM: Manguin, Puy, Rouault, Matisse and especially Marquet, with whose work his own shows marked affinities.

After Moreau's death, when Camoin's fellow students enrolled in other studios or private art schools, he worked alone or else with Marquet in the streets of Paris during the few hours that Marquet was not at the Académie Carrière. Camoin's portrait of *Albert Marquet* (1904–5; Paris, Pompidou; see fig.), now generally considered his masterpiece, was formerly believed to be a self-portrait by Marquet. Although it avoids the violent colour contrasts characteristic of the Fauves, it shows an awareness of contemporary trends in its rejection of chiaroscuro and

Charles Camoin: *Albert Marquet*, oil on canvas, 920×725 mm, 1904–5 (Paris, Pompidou, Musée National d'Art Moderne)

modelling, in its treatment of the picture as a flat surface by means of a rough black outline and a frontal presentation, and in its rejection of illusionism by stressing the material identity of the image as broadly brushed paint on bare canvas.

Camoin was called up for military service in 1900 in Arles, where he chose subjects that had already been singled out earlier by van Gogh and Gauguin. In 1901, after being transferred to Aix-en-Provence, he met Cézanne and thereafter began regular correspondence with him, referring to him as an evangelist of painting. These diverse influences are clearly evident in works such as *Self-portrait as a Soldier* (1901; Aix-en-Provence, Mus. Granet) and *Portrait of the Artist's Mother* (Marseille, Mus. Cantini). The painting *La Cabaretière* (1900; Sydney, A.G. NSW) was for a long time attributed to Gauguin, while *Mme Matisse Tapestry-making* (1904; Strasbourg Mus. B.-A.) bears comparison with the work of Vuillard. In 1904 Camoin met Monet at Giverny and had his first one-man exhibition at Berthe Weill's gallery in Paris, where Marquet and Dufy also showed. He was one of the artists represented in the room at the Salon d'Automne of 1905 that gave rise to the term Fauvism. During this period he travelled extensively, visiting Naples in 1904; in 1906 staying with Marquet in the south of France, where they met Manguin, Signac and Cross; and travelling to Corsica, Tangiers, London, Frankfurt and Morocco in 1912–13 with Marquet and Matisse. In 1913 he was one of the exhibitors at the Armory Show, New York, which introduced modern art to the USA.

Camoin experienced a severe crisis of confidence in his work in 1913 and destroyed more than 80 canvases that were in his studio. The remnants were gathered up by collectors, and this gave rise to a lawsuit, Camoin objecting not to their possessing his works, but to their claiming they could completely restore them to their original state; in 1927 the court found in his favour. During World War I he was mobilized; while at the front he continued to work mainly in watercolour and pastel. Just after the war Camoin accompanied Matisse to Cagnes and there met Renoir. The influence of Renoir may be seen in the change in Camoin's work towards paintings where he concentrated on colour reflections. Thereafter he made studies both in the studio and directly from nature. An example of his work from this period is *Girl with Bouquet* or *Girl with Fan* (1919; Paris, Mus. A. Mod. Ville Paris). During World War II Camoin lived mainly in St Tropez and produced few works because of the scarcity of materials, but he otherwise maintained a high level of production in his later years, on his own estimate completing 50 or 60 canvases a year.

BIBLIOGRAPHY

Gustave Moreau et ses élèves (exh. cat., Marseille, Mus. Cantini, 1962)
Charles Camoin (exh. cat. by M. Latour, Marseille, Mus. B.-A., 1966)
Le Fauvisme Français et les débuts de l'Expressionisme Allemand (exh. cat., Paris, Mus. N. A. Mod., 1966)
D. Giraudy: *Camoin: Sa vie, son oeuvre* (Marseille, 1972)

VANINA COSTA

Camón Aznar, José (*b* Saragossa, 5 Oct 1898; *d* Madrid, 14 May 1979). Spanish art historian and critic. From 1927 he taught literary and artistic theory at the Universidad de Salamanca, and from 1939 he taught history of art, first at the Universidad de Zaragoza and from 1942 at the Universidad de Madrid, where he was Dean of the arts faculty. He became a member of the Consejo Superior de Investigaciones Científicas, Madrid, where he founded and directed the *Revista de ideas estéticas* (1943). In 1950 he became Director of the Museo Lázaro Galdiano, Madrid, and in 1954 created the review *Goya*, published by the museum. An increasing interest in Cubism in the 1950s led him to write *Picasso y el cubismo* (1956). He was elected in 1956 as an academician of the Real Academia de Bellas Artes de S Fernando, Madrid. He was also a Patron of the Museo del Prado and of the Museo Español de Arte Contemporáneo, both in Madrid, and President of the Asociación Española de Críticos de Arte from its inception in 1960. He wrote on contemporary art, architecture, El Greco, Goya and Velázquez, as well as producing essays on aesthetic theory. Shortly after his death the Instituto y Museo Camón Aznar was inaugurated in Saragossa, housing his collection of art and publishing a *Boletín* that aimed to continue the writer's work.

WRITINGS

Dominico Greco (Madrid, 1950)
Los disparates de Goya y sus dibujos preparatorios (Barcelona, 1951)
Picasso y el cubismo (Madrid, 1956)
Las artes y los días (Madrid, 1965)
José Camón Aznar: Perfil autobiográfico (Saragossa, 1984)

BIBLIOGRAPHY

J. A. Gaya Nuño: *Historia de la crítica de arte en España* (Madrid, 1975)

PALOMA ALARCO CANOSA

Camondo. French family of collectors. (1) Isaac de Camondo and (2) Moïse de Camondo were cousins and lived next door to each other in Paris; both left their considerable acquisitions to the French nation, to form part of public collections.

(1) Comte **Isaac de Camondo** (*b* 1851; *d* Paris, 7 April 1911). Banker and collector. He began collecting in 1880; his paintings, tapestries, furniture, 18th-century *objets d'art*, medieval and Renaissance sculptures and Japanese prints were housed in his home in Rue de Monceau, Paris. Among his most prized objects were a clock with the *Three Graces* by Etienne-Maurice Falconet and a relief attributed to Donatello (both Paris, Louvre). Camondo was a major collector of late 19th-century painting: at the time of his death he owned 19 works by Degas, including *Absinthe* and *Ironing Women*; 14 by Monet, including a set of four paintings from the series of *Rouen Cathedral*; 9 paintings by Manet, among them the *Fifer*, and 8 paintings by Sisley. The collection also included important works by Corot, Delacroix, Ingres, Jean-François Millet, Daumier, Puvis de Chavannes, van Gogh and Cézanne. In 1908 Camondo presented his entire collection to the French state, stipulating that it was to be kept together at the Louvre for 50 years after his death, in a suite of adjoining rooms bearing his name; he donated 100,000 francs for this purpose.

BIBLIOGRAPHY

E. Molinier: 'Un Don au Musée du Louvre: La Collection du comte I. de Camondo', *Gaz. B.-A.*, n. s. 2, xvii (1897), pp. 89–103
A. Alexandre: 'Collection de M. le comte Isaac de Camondo', *Les Arts* [Paris], vii (1908), pp. 2–32
Catalogue de la collection Isaac de Camondo, Musée National du Louvre (Paris, *c.* 1911–17)
C. Dreyfus: 'La Collection Camondo: Le Mobilier et les objets d'art du XVIIe siècle', *Gaz. B.-A.*, n. s. 3, xi (1914), pp. 469–82
P. Jamot: 'La Collection Camondo au Musée du Louvre', *Gaz. B.-A.*, n. s. 3, xi (1914), pp. 388–404
——: 'La Collection Camondo au Musée du Louvre: Les Peintures et les dessins', *Gaz. B.-A.*, n. s. 3, xi (1914), pp. 441–60
G. Migeon: 'La Collection Camondo: Les Oeuvres d'art d'Extrême Orient', *Gaz. B.-A.*, n. s. 3, xi (1914), pp. 483–90
G. Migeon, P. Jamot, P. Vitry and C. Dreyfus: *La Collection Isaac de Camondo au Musée du Louvre* (Paris, 1914) [republication of *Gaz. B.-A.* articles]
P. Vitry: *Catalogue de la collection Camondo* (Paris, 1914)
——: 'La Collection Camondo: Les Sculptures et les objets d'art du Moyen Age et de la Renaissance', *Gaz. B.-A.*, n. s. 3, xi (1914), pp. 461–8
S. Monneret: *L'Impressionisme et son époque: Dictionnaire international illustré*, i (Paris, 1978)

(2) Comte **Moïse de Camondo** (*b* 1860; *d* Paris, 1935). Banker and collector. He was head of the family bank in Paris; around 1900 he began to collect seriously. In addition to paintings by Jean-Baptiste Oudry, Francesco Guardi, Jean-Baptiste Huet, Elisabeth Vigée-Lebrun and Hubert Robert, the collection included the Buffon service from Sèvres, Savonnerie carpets, part of the silver service commissioned by Catherine the Great for Prince Orlov, and a lady's writing desk by the *ébéniste* Martin Carlin. It occupied the house in the Rue de Monceau that Camondo had commissioned from René Sergent in the Louis XVI style of Anges-Jacques Gabriel's Petit Trianon.

Camondo was an active supporter of the arts: in 1920 he was appointed Vice-President of the Société des Amis du Louvre, and in 1930 he became Vice-President of the Union Centrale des Arts Décoratifs, to which in 1935 he bequeathed his house and collections. These became the Musée Nissim de Camondo, named after Camondo's father and also after his son, killed in battle in 1917. Camondo hoped that the museum would contribute to the education of artists and craftsmen.

BIBLIOGRAPHY

Musée Nissim de Camondo, Union Centrale des Arts Décoratifs (Paris, 1936, rev. 1954)
Musée Nissim de Camondo, Union Centrale des Arts Décoratifs (Paris, 1973)
G. Mabille: *Orfèvrerie française des XVIe, XVIIe, XVIIIe siècles* (Paris, 1984)
O. Aaron: 'The Rebirth of the Musée Nissim de Camondo', *Apollo*, cxxvi (1987), pp. 33–7

AMY WALSH

Camouflage [Fr. *camoufler*: 'to hide or disguise'; It. *camuffare*: 'to disguise or deceive']. Term used to describe the means of disguising or hiding an object, vehicle or vessel used on combat. Throughout both World Wars the great majority of French, British, German and American artists (whether soldiers or civilians) were employed as camouflage experts. After developments in photography and in aviation, camouflage was evolved in an attempt to conceal weapons from aerial surveillance. The French were among the first to seek the help of artists in such attempts, and the first *service de camouflage* in military history was established on 12 February 1915, in response to a proposal by Lucien-Victor Guirand de Scevola (1871–1950), an artist in the infantry who painted disruptive patterns on the surface of the artillery to reduce its visibility. The word 'camouflage' was quickly accepted, as was the deployment of artists as 'camoufleurs', resulting in Britain in the establishment of the British Camouflage Service as part of the Royal Engineers in 1916 and in the USA as the American Camouflage Corps in 1917. The latter was partly the consequence of the enthusiasm of Abbott Handerson Thayer, co-author of *Concealing Coloration in the Animal Kingdom* (1909), who was an heroic example for dozens of young American artists, led by Homer Saint-Gaudens (son of Augustus Saint-Gaudens), who enlisted in the war on the understanding that they would be used as camouflage experts. During World War I, in addition to camouflaging equipment, Allied artists such as Jacques Villon, André Dunoyer de Segonzac, Jean-Louis Boussingault, Henri Bouchard, Pierre Laprade, Jean Puy, Charles Dufresne, Luc-Albert Moreau, Barry Faulkner, Louis Bouché (*b* 1896) and Grant Wood were typically asked to design armour-plated observation posts consisting of realistic replicas of dead tree trunks, periscopes disguised as tree branches, papier mâché listening posts in the form of hollow horse carcasses, disruptively patterned sniper suits, overhanging nets garnished with strips of osnaburg, false heads, life-size dummies, concealed foxhole covers, miles of painted canvas roads suspended above ground to conceal troop movements, and the alteration of landmarks in the hope of diverting attacks from the air.

There was a significant increase in the wartime role of artists when in 1917 the British marine painter Norman Wilkinson (1878–1971) invented a method of ship camouflage called 'dazzle painting', in which a confusing assortment of shapes was painted on the sides of ships to prevent German submarines from obtaining an accurate reading of the ship's course. Under Wilkinson's direction the Dazzle Department was set up in the classrooms of the Royal Academy of Art in London, where women art students were hired to apply dazzle patterns to ship models. The patterns were drawn up as blueprints and used in the painting of actual ships under the supervision of dock officers, one of whom was Edward Wadsworth, who depicted the ships in such paintings as *Dazzle Ships in Drydock at Liverpool* (see fig.). In 1918 Wilkinson was loaned to the American Navy in order to set up an orderly way to apply dazzle patterns to more than 1000 American ships.

During World War II the roster of those who were actively used as camouflage experts, whether military or civilian, is extraordinary: the painters Roland Penrose (author of *The Home Guard Manual of Camouflage*, 1941), Julian Trevelyan (1910–88), Arshile Gorky and Gyorgy Kepes (*b* 1906) taught camouflage to soldiers or civilians. László Moholy-Nagy was a consultant to the Mayor of Chicago in connection with a plan to disguise the Lake Michigan shoreline. The many artists, designers and architects engaged in camouflage during World War II included Ellsworth Kelly, theatre designer Jo Mielziner (*b* 1901), fashion designer Bill Blass (*b* 1922), stage designer Donald Oenslager (*b* 1902), Noel Martin, Victor Christ-Janer, S. W. Hayter, Leon Underwood, Oskar Schlemmer, Oliver Messel, Percyval Tudor-Hart (1873–1954), Basil Spence and Charles Payne. In 1942 the American artist Eric Sloane both wrote and illustrated a book entitled *Camouflage Simplified*, and civilian animators at the Walt Disney Studio volunteered to camouflage the Lockheed Aircraft plant in Burbank, CA.

Edward Wadsworth: *Dazzle-ships in Drydock at Liverpool*, oil on canvas, 3.04×2.43 m, 1919 (Ottawa, National Gallery of Canada)

BIBLIOGRAPHY

G. H. Thayer: *Concealing Coloration in the Animal Kingdom: An Exposition of the Laws of Disguise through Color and Pattern, Being a Summary of Abbott H. Thayer's Discoveries*, intro. A. H. Thayer (New York, 1909, 2/1918)
H. B. Cott: *Adaptive Coloration in Nature* (London, 1940)
R. Penrose: *The Home Guard Manual of Camouflage* (London, 1941)
E. Sloane: *Camouflage Simplified* (New York, 1942)
S. Reit: *Masquerade: The Hidden War: The Amazing Camouflage Deceptions of World War II* (New York, 1978, 2/London, 1980)
G. Hartcup: *Camouflage: A History of Concealment and Deception in War* (New York, 1980)
N. Wilkinson: *A Brush with Life* (London, 1969) [autobiog. account of his development of dazzle painting]
R. Behrens: *Art and Camouflage: Concealment and Deception in Nature, Art and War* (Cedar Falls, 1981)
——: 'The Art of Dazzle Camouflage', *Defense Analysis*, iii (1987), pp. 233–43
R. R. Behrens: 'Blend and Dazzle: The Art of Camouflage', *Print* (1991), pp. 92–8 [full-colour illus.]

ROY R. BEHRENS

Campagna, Girolamo [Gerolamo] (*b* Verona, 1549; *d* Venice, *c.* 1625). Italian sculptor. He was one of the most important sculptors working in Venice and the surrounding region in the late 16th century and the early 17th. Although his older rival Alessandro Vittoria was a more versatile artist, Campagna's talents centred on a remarkable gift for religious statuary. In this he was unrivalled in Venice and scarcely equalled elsewhere in Italy. Among his most impressive achievements are the high altars for the Venetian churches of Il Redentore and S Giorgio Maggiore. His brother Giuseppe Campagna (*d* 1626) was also a sculptor and assisted him.

1. Training and early work, to *c.* 1580. 2. Major commissions, *c.* 1580–*c.* 1600. 3. Works after *c.* 1600.

1. TRAINING AND EARLY WORK, TO *c.* 1580. Campagna was the son of a furrier and trained under Danese Cattaneo, probably when he was engaged on the Fregoso monument in S Anastasia, Verona (1562–5). Campagna was described as the 'garzone et lavorante' of Cattaneo in 1571 when the latter was nominated to appraise the value of Jacopo Sansovino's bronze sacristy door for S Marco in Venice. In 1572 Cattaneo won the commission to carve the last marble relief, of *St Anthony Raising the Youth in Lisbon*, in the cycle for the saint's chapel in Il Santo, Padua, and Campagna moved there with him. Later that year Cattaneo died, leaving his disciple all his drawings and plaster casts; among them, presumably, were some inherited from Jacopo Sansovino (*d* 1570). In December 1573 Campagna received the contract for the completion of Cattaneo's relief, against competition from Francesco Segala and Antonio Gallini (*fl* 1566–73). Work on it was interrupted by a period restoring antiquities for Hans Fugger in Augsburg, but he completed the relief by the beginning of 1577. The style follows the example of Sansovino's second relief in the same cycle, the *Miracle of the Maiden Carilla.*

Campagna's first work in Venice was a marble *Pietà* relief, with the Dead Christ supported by angels, and a bronze panel of the *Resurrection* for the altar of the Holy Sacrament in S Giuliano (begun *c.* 1578). The altar was designed by Giovanni Antonio Rusconi and executed by

Cesare Franco (*fl* 1578–99), who apparently subcontracted part of the work to Campagna. Campagna's *Pietà* (finished by 1580) contrasts strongly with the more mannered figures of the *Virgin* and *St John* supplied for the flanking niches by Alessandro Vittoria. Campagna combined stylistic characteristics drawn from Cattaneo's work with inspiration from Classical sculpture such as the *Laokoon*.

Campagna's most important early independent commission was for a marble statue of *St Giustina* for the land entrance of the Arsenale in Venice in 1578. The figure is posed in dynamic contrapposto, inspired by Michelangelo's *Rachel* (Rome, S Pietro in Vincoli). Possibly around the same time he carved a statue of the *Virgin and Child* (destr. 1808) for the chapel of the Arsenale. In 1579 he won the competition against Vittoria for the new high altar (destr. 1895) and tabernacle for Il Santo in Padua (he again shared the execution with Cesare Franco). It was under construction from 1580 to 1584 and replaced the old high altar by Donatello, although it incorporated his statues and reliefs. Campagna contributed marble reliefs of prophets and angels, together with bronze statuettes for the tabernacle, the Evangelists and Church Fathers anticipating his mature style. These are now in the Museo Antoniano at Il Santo.

2. Major commissions, *c.* 1580–*c.* 1600. In the 1580s Campagna emerged as Vittoria's chief rival in Venice. In 1582 he executed stucco statues of two *Sibyls*, the *Virgin* and the *Archangel Gabriel* for the choir of S Sebastiano. Probably in the same year he carved the marble statuettes of *Hercules* and *Mercury* for the chimneypiece of the Sala del Collegio of the Doge's Palace. This was followed by allegorical figures of *War*, *Peace* and *Minerva* (*c.* 1585) for a door in the Sala delle Quattro Porte of the palace. All these works demonstrate Campagna's worth as an interpreter of the style of Sansovino. His figures are weightier and display a surer grasp of anatomy than those of Vittoria. Also in 1582 Campagna was commissioned to execute six marble statues of Virtues for the tomb of Doge Nicolò da Ponte designed by Vincenzo Scamozzi for S Maria della Carità (now the Accademia). Vittoria's contribution was limited to carving the bust of the Doge, and Campagna's major role in this collaboration indicates that he had impressed Marc'Antonio Barbaro, the Doge's executor, a patron of Palladio and a discerning connoisseur.

1. Girolamo Campagna: *Christ*, bronze, 1589–90 (Venice, Il Redentore)

Barbaro may have obtained for Campagna further state commissions. Campagna collaborated again with Scamozzi in the Doge's Palace, executing two marble atlantes (*c.* 1587) for a chimneypiece by Scamozzi in the Sala dell' Anticollegio. These demonstrate his skill in carving the nude figure. They also worked together on the completion of Sansovino's Library in the Piazzetta, for which Campagna and his brother supplied six marble statues of gods and goddesses between 1588 and 1591. In addition Campagna received notable private commissions, including those for a marble statue of the *Redeemer* (*c.* 1581–8) in S Moisè and for a marble *Virgin and Child with Angels* (*c.* 1585–8) in S Salvatore, executed for the Dolfin family. The latter, his first surviving attempt at this theme, betrays an obvious debt to Sansovino, but Campagna invested his figures with the more monumental forms of late Cinquecento art also to be seen in the paintings of Tintoretto and the sculpture of Giambologna.

On 3 November 1590 Campagna and Tiziano Aspetti each agreed to carve a colossal marble figure for the land entrance of the Public Mint (now the Libreria Marciana). Campagna's pre-eminent position was threatened by Aspetti, a younger sculptor, alongside whom he had previously worked in the Doge's Palace, and relations were strained. Aspetti's *gigante*, however, suffers by comparison with the overpowering menace of Campagna's figure. The threat from the younger sculptor was momentary, and Campagna went on to receive the two most important Venetian sculptural commissions of the late 16th century, for the high altars of Il Redentore and S Giorgio Maggiore. These altars represent Campagna's first known attempt at bronze statuary and include the first monumental bronze figures cast in Venice since those for the Zen Chapel in S Marco (1504–22). The figures of the crucified *Christ* (see fig. 1), *St Mark* and *St Francis* for the altar of Il Redentore were executed in 1589–90. Campagna later described the *Crucifixion* as 'famosissimo', and its combination of pathos and beauty must have excited admiration at the time. The sensuous treatment of the nude male figure is inspired by Donatello's bronze *Christ* in Il Santo in Padua. The poses of the two saints (originally placed nearer to the cross) complement its sinuous contrapposto. The *St Mark*'s dynamic gesture and expressive features have the proto-Baroque style of many of Campagna's later figures. A pair of small bronze angels holding candlesticks were probably made around the same date for the church of S Maria del Carmelo (the Carmini) in Venice.

Campagna was commissioned to execute the bronze high altar of S Giorgio Maggiore on 20 January 1592. He is said to have worked after a design and several sketches by the painter Antonio Vassilacchi (called Aliense). One drawing that may be by Campagna survives (Toronto, A.G. Ont.), and it shows that various refinements were made to the original design as the project evolved. The subject is the Trinity, with the four Evangelists supporting on their shoulders a large copper globe, on which stands God the Father (see fig. 2). The theme extends back to early Christian iconography but is uncommon for a high altar; the source for Campagna's unusual interpretation may have been a woodcut in Achille Bocchi's *Symbolicarum quaestionum* (Bologna, 1555), which illustrates Socrates supporting the globe on his shoulders with the Trinity hovering above. Campagna here transformed the theme into a three-dimensional composition of compelling authority.

The altar was finished in 1593 and clearly met with approval since the abbot of S Giorgio ordered a marble altarpiece of the *Virgin and Child with Angels* from Campagna in August 1595. This work, completed the following year, can be seen as a revised version of the earlier group in S Salvatore; it initiated a new type of Virgin and Child composition, which served as a model for bronze versions by Nicolò Roccatagliata and others. During this period Campagna also made a colossal stone *Angel* (destr.) for the campanile of S Giorgio. Other lost works of a similar date include the over life-size marble statues of *St Rose* and *St Thomas Aquinas* (badly damaged by fire, 1867) for the chapel of the Rosary at SS Giovanni e Paolo and a colossal statue of *Neptune* in plaster for the coronation of the Dogaressa Morosina Grimani in 1597. A marble group of *Hercules and Antaeus*, commissioned in 1597 by Girolamo Verità for the Villa Il Boschetto at San Pietro in Lavagno, near Verona, is another, less successful, example of his rare attempts at mythological subjects.

2. Girolamo Campagna: bronze high altar, 1592–3, S Giorgio Maggiore, Venice

3. Works after *c.* 1600. Between 1600 and 1604 Campagna produced two tombs in Venice for the Doges Pasquale Cicogna and Marino Grimani. The first, now in Il Gesuiti (S Maria Assunta), consists of a triumphal arch with an applied Composite order framing the semi-recumbent marble figure of Cicogna on his sarcophagus in the central bay. The architecture recalls that of Scamozzi, but the chief novelty lay in the presentation of the Doge. Although Palladio had incorporated the semi-recumbent effigy into his designs for tombs in the middle of the 16th century, this composition was used rarely in Venice and the Veneto. Campagna's revival did not prove influential, possibly because this pose lacked the dignity appropriate for a ruler. The Grimani monument is a double tomb for the Doge and Dogaressa, filling virtually the whole of one wall of their parish church of S Giuseppe. Campagna was inspired by Palladio's imposing double monument to *Doge Alvise Mocenigo and his Wife* (Venice, SS Giovanni e Paolo), although in Campagna's case the architecture serves merely as an imposing framework on to which marble statues, caryatids and reliefs are applied. More influential was the seated marble statue of *Doge Leonardo Loredan* (completed *c.* 1605) in SS Giovanni e Paolo. The design for the figure was probably conceived by Cattaneo before his death, but Campagna executed it, introducing a new iconographic type into Venetian funerary monuments. The commemorative marble statue of *Federigo da Montefeltro* (1604–6), commissioned by the Duke of Urbino, Francesco-Maria II della Rovere, was apparently the only work by Campagna to have been badly received. Criticism of his model stung Campagna into producing an apologia that is valuable for the list of his works and reveals his self-regard. The statue was eventually installed on the palace staircase at Urbino in 1606.

At around this date Campagna returned to the use of bronze, producing the statue of *St Anthony Abbot* for S Giacomo di Rialto in 1605, bronze statuettes of *St Agnes* and *St Anthony of Padua* for S Maria Gloriosa dei' Frari in 1608–9, and the high-relief figures of the *Angel* and *Virgin Annunciate* for the Loggia del Consiglio (now Castelvecchio), Verona, in 1609–10. The *St Anthony Abbot* evokes the proto-Baroque style of Palma Giovane's figures in his later paintings, while the Annunciation figures exploit the dramatic contrasts of the theme in a manner reminiscent of Veronese. Campagna's last major commissions, for the high altar of S Lorenzo, with marble statues of *St Lawrence* and *St Sebastian* (1615–17), and for the series of saints and prophets for the Scuola Grande di S Rocco (*c.* 1610–20), while undiminished in technical skill, are more subdued in style.

BIBLIOGRAPHY

DBI [with full bibliog.]

G. Gronau: 'Die Statue des Federigo da Montefeltro im herzoglichen Palast von Urbino', *Mitt. Ksthist. Inst. Florenz*, iii (1919–32), pp. 254–67

J. Pope-Hennessy: *Italian High Renaissance and Baroque Sculpture* (1958, rev. 3/1986), iii of *Introduction to Italian Sculpture* (Oxford, 1955–63), pp. 101–2, 413–15

P. Rossi: *Girolamo Campagna* (Verona, 1968)

W. Timofiewitsch: *Girolamo Campagna: Studien zur venezianischen Plastik um das Jahr 1600* (Munich, 1972) [fundamental]

S. Mason Rinaldi: 'La cappella del SS Sacramento in San Zulian', *Atti Ist. Veneto Sci., Lett. & A.*, cxxxiv (1975–6), pp. 439–56

W. Timofiewitsch: 'Marginalien zur Grabmalskulpture des Danese Cattaneo', *A. Ven.*, xxxii (1978), pp. 230–37

B. Boucher: 'A Statuette by Girolamo Campagna and a Portrait by Leandro Bassano', *A. Ven.*, xxxiv (1980), pp. 159–64

D. McTavish: 'A Drawing by Girolamo Campagna for the High Altar of San Giorgio Maggiore', *A. Ven.*, xxxiv (1980), pp. 165–8

BRUCE BOUCHER

Compagno di Pesellino. *See* APOLLONIO DI GIOVANNI.

Campagnola. Italian family of draughtsmen, printmakers and painters. (1) Giulio Campagnola was the son of Girolamo Campagnola (1433/5–1522), a humanist scholar and writer on art. Vasari mentioned a once-famous Latin letter by Girolamo describing the achievements of contemporary Paduan artists. (2) Domenico Campagnola was Giulio's adopted son, and the prints of both artists were important in spreading an awareness of Venetian landscape through Europe.

(1) Giulio Campagnola (*b* Padua, *c.* 1482; *d* Venice, after 1515). Contemporary humanists such as Matteo Bosso praised his precocious artistic gifts, his knowledge of Greek, Latin and Hebrew, and his skills as a musician, singer and lute-player. In 1497 his father sought to secure him a place at the court of Francesco II Gonzaga, 4th Marchese of Mantua, where it is possible that Giulio came into contact with Andrea Mantegna. By 1499 Giulio was at the Ferrarese court of Ercole I d'Este. His earliest engravings, datable between 1497 and 1506, were influenced by Mantegna and by Albrecht Dürer: for instance, in the *Ganymede and Zeus* (*c.* 1500–03; see Hind, no. 4) the figure style is indebted to Mantegna, while the rustic landscape is directly inspired by Dürer's *Virgin with the Monkey* (B. 42).

In 1507 Giulio was recorded in Venice, and his art from the period 1507–13 must be seen in the context of Venetian painting in the first decades of the 16th century. The dominant influence was the circle of Giorgione, and Giulio's engravings, such as the *Old Shepherd* (*c.* 1507–9; H 8), the *Astrologer* (1509; H 9), his only dated print, and the *Young Shepherd* (*c.* 1510–12; H 10) spread to a wider public an awareness of Giorgione's pastoral themes and arcane subjects as explored in such paintings as the *Three Philosophers* (*c.* 1508–10; Vienna, Ksthist. Mus.). Giulio was evidently close to the humanist circles of the Veneto, and Marcantonio Michiel recorded ten miniatures on vellum by him in the house of the poet Pietro Bembo, one of which represented a 'nude woman, after Giorgione, reclining and viewed from behind'. This description recalls Giulio's engraving of *Venus Reclining in a Landscape* (*c.* 1510; H 13; see fig.), perhaps based on a lost painting

Giulio Campagnola: *Venus Reclining in a Landscape*, stipple engraving, 112×159 mm, *c.* 1510 (London, British Museum)

by Giorgione, which is the most perfect example of his innovative stippling technique (*see also* PRINTS, §III, 7(iv) and fig. 12). The development from a purely linear treatment of form to an overall dotted surface of light and shade may be seen as an attempt to find a graphic equivalent to the tonal painting of Giorgione. It is not clear whether Giulio, in this or in other prints, collaborated directly with Giorgione (and later with Titian) or whether he made free interpretations of other artist's ideas.

In 1515 the celebrated Venetian printer Aldo Manuzio left instructions in his will that Giulio should cut the italic type he had invented. Giulio was himself probably dead by *c.* 1517, when his unfinished print *Shepherds in a Landscape* (H 6), which he had prepared in a delicate and poetic pen-and-brown-ink drawing (Paris, Louvre), was completed by Domenico Campagnola in a bolder style.

(2) Domenico Campagnola (*b* ?Venice, 1500; *d* Padua, 10 Dec 1564). Adopted son of (1) Giulio Campagnola. He was of German extraction and was apprenticed to Giulio in Venice *c.* 1507. A group of drawings of pastoral subjects, indebted to Giorgione and to Dürer, includes the slightly tentative *Landscape with Two Youths* (London, BM) and *Landscape with Boy Fishing* (Washington, DC, N.G.A.) and may be dated to his earliest years, perhaps before 1517. His independent career began in 1517–18 with a group of engravings and woodcuts that are largely independent of Giulio Campagnola but clearly indebted to the work of Titian. Indeed, the close correspondence between Domenico's work and Titian's has led to suggestions that Domenico was responsible for the forged Titian drawings (e.g. New York, Met.) taken from counterproofs of the master's woodcuts (see Dreyer; Byam Shaw). Domenico's own prints are executed in an unusually flowing and sketchy technique and include enigmatic, pastoral themes, such as the *Shepherd and Old Warrior* (1517; H 9), which recalls the moody poetry of Giorgione, and religious subjects, such as the *Assumption of the Virgin* (1517; H 3). This latter depends on Titian's painting of that subject (Venice, Frari), completed the following year, which suggests that Domenico had access to Titian's workshop. Domenico's main innovation was in the technique of the woodcut, and it is evident that he cut the blocks himself rather than relying on a professional cutter. The energy of the unusually bold *Vision of St Augustine* (1517; see 1976–7 exh. cat., no. 19) is indebted to such works as Titian's woodcut of *St Jerome*, cut by Ugo da Carpi (1976–7 exh. cat., no. 18).

Perhaps by 1520 Domenico had moved to Padua, where he became a leading painter, executing frescoes and easel paintings for churches and palaces. His fresco of *Joachim and Anna* (*c.* 1520; Padua, Scu. Carmine) is indebted to Titian, whose influence remains strong in such mature works as the *Virgin and Child Enthroned with Saints and a Donor* (Prague, N.G., Šternberk Pal.). Here the asymmetrical composition and the high pedestal on which the Virgin sits are derived from Titian's *Pesaro Madonna* (Venice, Frari), while the rich treatment of fabrics is close to the painting of Paolo Veronese.

However, in this period Domenico was most celebrated for his landscape drawings and woodcuts, which are deeply influenced by Titian's woodcuts, as in the *Landscape with Milkmaid* (*c.* 1520–25; see 1976–7 exh. cat.). In such woodcuts as *Landscape with a Wandering Family* (1535–40; see 1976–7 exh. cat., no. 28) and *Landscape with a Hurdy-gurdy Player and a Girl* (*c.* 1540; see 1976–7 exh. cat., no. 29) and in drawings such as *Landscape with a Dragon* (Vienna, Albertina) he created, with flowing, rhythmic strokes, decorative panoramic landscapes. The foregrounds are raised, and beyond extend vistas of twisting paths, castles, bridges and ruins, leading to the jagged peaks of distant mountains. Such works introduced a new speciality into Venetian art, and they were sought after by such cultivated collectors as Gabriele Vendramin and Marco di Mantova Benavides (Michiel). Hieronymous Cock, Pieter Bruegel the elder, Hendrick Goltzius and Peter Paul Rubens are among the artists whose landscapes were influenced by Domenico's drawings and prints. This influence continued into the 18th century, when Antoine Watteau copied Domenico's drawings.

BIBLIOGRAPHY

DBI [with bibliog.]

M. Bosso: *Familiares et secundae epistulae* (Mantua, 1498), pp. 75, 86, 211

G. Vasari: *Vite* (1550, rev. 2/1568); ed. G. Milanesi (1878–85), iii, pp. 225, 385, 634, 639

M. A. Michiel: *Notizie d'opere di disegno nella prima meta del secolo XVI, pubblicata e illustrata da D. Jacopo Morelli* (Bassano, 1800), pp. 19, 130 [Giulio]; (Bologna, 1884), pp. 23, 69 [Domenico]

P. Kristeller: *Giulio Campagnola Kupferstiche und Zeichnungen* (Berlin, 1907) [good illus.]

G. Fiocco: 'La giovanezza di Giulio Campagnola', *L'Arte*, xviii (1915), pp. 137–56

A. M. Hind: *Early Italian Engraving* (London, 1938–48), v, pp. 189–205, 207–15 [H]

H. Tietze and E. Tietze-Conrat: *The Drawings of Venetian Painters in the XVth and XVIth Centuries* (New York, 1944)

R. Colpi: 'Domenico Campagnola, nuove notizie biografiche e artistiche', *Boll. Mus. Civ. Padova*, xxxi–xliii (1952–4), pp. 81–111

Early Italian Engravings from the National Gallery of Art (exh. cat., ed. J. Levenson; Washington, DC, N.G.A., 1973), pp. 390–436

Titian and the Venetian Woodcut (exh. cat. by D. Rosand and M. Murano, Washington, DC, N.G.A.; Dallas, TX, Mus. F.A.; Detroit, MI, Inst. A.; 1976–7), pp. 120–39, 154–71

P. Dreyer: 'Tizianfälschungen des sechzehnten Jahrhunderts: Korrekturen zur Definition der Delineatio bei Tizian und Anmerkungen zur Datierung seiner Holzschnitte', *Pantheon*, xxxvii (1979), pp. 365–75

J. Byam Shaw: 'Titian's Drawings: A Summing up', *Apollo*, cxii (1980), pp. 386–91

M. J. Zucker: *Early Italian Masters* (1980), 25 [XIII/ii] of *The Illustrated Bartsch*, ed. W. Strauss (New York, 1978–), pp. 463–95 [Giulio]; pp. 497–516 [Domenico]

The Genius of Venice, 1500–1600 (exh. cat., ed. J. Martineau and C. Hope; London, RA, 1983–4), pp. 248–53 [drgs], pp. 310–15, 320–21, 324–8 [prts]

R. Cafritz, L. Gowing and D. Rosand: *Places of Delight* (London, 1989)

□

Campaña, Antoni (*b* Arbucies, nr Gerona, 1906). Spanish photographer. After finishing his studies as a commercial technician in Barcelona, he started work at the age of 16 as a photographer's assistant. This early contact with photography made Campaña aware of the need to broaden his knowledge of the medium. In 1934 he moved to Munich to study with Willy Zielke. On his return to Barcelona, Campaña established himself as a specialist in the bromoil technique. He combined his own personal work with that of sports photojournalism.

PHOTOGRAPHIC PUBLICATIONS

Orientaciones fotográficas (Barcelona, 1946)

BIBLIOGRAPHY

Photographies catalanes des années trente (exh. cat., Paris, Cent. Etud. Cat., 1982)

Idas y caos: Aspectos de las vanguardias fotograficas en España (exh. cat., ed. J. Fontcuberta; Madrid, Salas Picasso; New York, Int. Cent. Phot.; 1984–6)

MARTA GILI

Campana (di Cavelli), Giampietro, Marchese (*b* Rome, 1808; *d* Rome, 10 Oct 1880). Italian collector and archaeologist. He came from a wealthy family of Roman bankers and inherited his passion for archaeology from his grandfather Giampetro Campana (*d* 1793). As a young man he began to excavate necropolises in Etruria and Antique villas in Latium and Magna Graecia and built up a large collection of antique artefacts through purchases from dealers. Later he acquired a number of works by 14th- and 15th-century painters from Siena, Florence and Venice, as well as by artists from smaller centres of production in Umbria, Romagna, Emilia, Sicily and the Marches. In 1843 and 1845 he bought several pictures from the collection of Joseph Fesch, among them a *Sacra conversazione* (*c.* 1500) by Vittore Carpaccio (Avignon, Mus. Petit Pal.). The size and diversity of his collection grew to such an extent that he eventually needed three buildings in which to house it. His own house on Monte Celio in Rome was a veritable museum of Antique art that attracted royalty, artists and connoisseurs. However, in order to indulge his passion for collecting he began to borrow large sums of money from the Monte di Pietà deposit bank, of which he was Director. As a result he was arrested in 1857 for misappropriation of funds, his collection was seized by the papal government and put up for sale, and he was banished by Pope Pius IX. He travelled to Geneva and Paris and in 1870 returned to Rome, where he unsuccessfully attempted to recoup some of his finances and where he died ten years later.

In December 1860 a number of works of art from his collection, mostly maiolica and Renaissance sculptures, were purchased for the South Kensington Museum in London (now the Victoria and Albert Museum), which was about to open. The Imperial Hermitage Museum (now the State Hermitage Museum) in St Petersburg also acquired works from his collection, among them Antique statues and portrait busts, the Cumae vase (4th century BC), Euphronios' psykter of *Hétaïres Banqueting* (*c.* 515–10 BC) and nine frescoes of the school of Raphael that were formerly in the casino at the Porta Pinciana in Rome. The remaining works, of which there were almost 12,000, the bulk of the collection, were bought in April 1861 by Napoleon III and the following year were displayed, under the title of 'Musée Napoléon III', at the Palais de l'Industrie, Paris, from May to October. As quarters there were

Musée Napoléon III: Terracotta Room in the Louvre, also called the Galerie Campana by Charles Giraud (1819–92), oil on canvas, 1866 (Paris, Musée du Louvre)

found to be too cramped, Napoleon decided to transfer the most important pieces from the collection to the Louvre, while duplicates and works of art not considered to be of superior quality were sent to museums in the provinces (*see* BONAPARTE, (8)). Works from Campana's collection that remained in the Louvre included a krater by Euphronios depicting *Herakles Struggling to Raise Antaeus off the Ground* (5th century BC), a marble portrait head of *Emperor Augustus* (after AD 14) from Cerveteri in Etruria, a fragment of the frieze from the Ara Pacis (consecrated 9 BC) and the Etruscan Epouz sarcophagus (520–510 BC). These pieces, along with other vases, reliefs and small terracotta statues, marble and bronze objects, paintings, glassware and jewellery, were displayed in nine rooms, named 'Galerie Campana', which were opened to the public on 15 August 1863 (see fig.). Campana's collection of paintings in the Louvre is especially rich in Gothic and Renaissance works from Italy, the most important of which is one of the three panels of Paolo Uccello's *Rout of San Romano* (1455–60). Other paintings of the period include a triptych (2nd quarter of 14th century) from the studio of Bernardo Daddi, a lunette of the *Lamentation* (*c.* 1474; Paris, Louvre) by Cosimo Tura, an *Annunciation* (1477–8) by Lorenzo di Credi and paintings of the *Virgin and Child* by Lorenzo Monaco, Sassoferrato and Bernardino Pinturicchio. Approximately 300 paintings that had been allocated to smaller museums were brought together in the 1950s and carefully restored to hang in the Petit Palais (14th/15th century) in Avignon, which was specially renovated. Most of Campana's paintings in this museum (opened 1976) are Italian works from the 14th and 15th centuries, including a *Virgin and Child* (*c.* 1467–70) by Botticelli, an early 16th-century *Adoration of the Magi* from the school of Lombardy and an altarpiece of *St Jerome* by the Master of the Buckingham Palace Madonna.

BIBLIOGRAPHY

E. Galichon: *Des Destinées du musée Napoléon III: Fondation d'un musée d'art industriel* (Paris, 1862)

S. Reinach: *Esquisse d'une histoire de la collection Campana: Extrait de la 'Revue archéologique'* (Paris, 1905)

P. Perdrizet and R. Jean: *La Galerie Campana et les musées français* (Bordeaux, 1907)

E. Schlumberger: 'L'inépuisable Collection Campana', *Conn. A.*, 144 (1964), pp. 38–49

M. Laclotte and E. Mognetti: *Peinture italienne: Musée du Petit Palais, Avignon*, xxi, Inventaire des collections publiques françaises (Paris, 1976)

FRANÇOISE MAISON

Campaña, Pedro. *See* KEMPENEER, PETER DE.

Campanato, Pietro di Giovanni Battista [Pietro delle Campane] (*b* ?Venice, *c.* 1460; *d* Venice, 18 Oct 1542). Italian bronze-caster. During a period of revival in bronze-casting, he was trained in the workshop of Alvise Campanato in the parish of S Luca, Venice, establishing his own bronze foundry probably during the 1480s and becoming prominent as a caster of cannons. From 1504 to 1515, with Giovanni Alberghetti and Paolo di Matteo Savin, Campanato was involved in bronze-casting from models by Alessandro Leopardi, Tullio Lombardo §II and Antonio Lombardo for the chapel of Cardinal Zen in S Marco, Venice. The bronze statue of the *Virgin and Child* for this chapel by Antonio Lombardo (*see* LOMBARDO, §II(3)) bears the inscription PETRI IOANNIS CAMPANATI M.DXV. In 1521 Pietro also cast one of the bronze doors. Of his eighteen children, three were employed in his large workshop.

BIBLIOGRAPHY

Thieme–Becker

J. Pope-Hennessy: *Italian Renaissance Sculpture* (London, 1958, rev. New York, 1985), pp. 344–5

STEVEN BULE

Campanile [It.: 'bell tower']. Italian church belfry, often freestanding.

□

Campbell, Colen (*b* 1676; *d* London, ?13 Sept 1729). Scottish architect and writer. He was the key propagandist for the Palladian revival in early 18th-century England (*see* PALLADIANISM). First as an architectural publisher and then as an architect, he did as much as any contemporary to determine the lines of development of secular architecture for a generation.

Campbell was a nephew of Sir Hugh Campbell of Cawdor, Nairnshire, and his first career was as an advocate in Edinburgh, where he began to establish a reputation at the outset of the 18th century. Between *c.* 1708 and 1712 Campbell abandoned his legal practice to begin a career as an architect in London. By December 1708 he was in London hoping to become Master of the [Royal] Works in Scotland. This post, then unpaid, was currently held by James Smith, an architect by whom Campbell was to be significantly influenced. It is known that Campbell had been abroad before 1716. His architectural apprenticeship was completed in the preparation of engravings of prominent British buildings, the *Vitruvius Britannicus* (1715–25). This served to introduce both Campbell himself and his public to the variety of British architecture and to launch his name as a notable new architect in London. It also inaugurated an entirely new phase of English architectural publishing.

1. *Vitruvius Britannicus*. 2. Architectural practice.

1. 'VITRUVIUS BRITANNICUS'. *Vitruvius Britannicus* was a cooperative venture that appears to have developed out of the desire of a group of booksellers to capitalize on an already established taste for topographical illustration. Published in 1715 and 1717, the two original volumes each consisted of 100 large folio plates of plans, elevations and sections chiefly illustrating contemporary secular buildings. Many of these provided lavish illustration of the best-known houses of the day, such as Chatsworth, Derbys, or Blenheim Palace, Oxon (for illustration *see* BLENHEIM PALACE), intended to appeal to the widespread desire for prints of such buildings and to provide their architects with a chance to publicize their current work. More humble owners were also given the chance to display their recently built country seats alongside such palaces. The result was a miscellaneous collection of houses built during the previous two centuries showing every kind of style, including the restraint of Christopher Wren's Marlborough House, London, and the Baroque extravagance of Thomas Archer's Roehampton House, Surrey.

The final form of the book was decisively affected, however, by the threat of competition provided by Giacomo Leoni's forthcoming translation of Palladio. More by luck than foresight, the booksellers were prevailed upon to employ Campbell as draughtsman and architectural adviser and to allow the reorganization of the contents of the volumes in ways that made it serve his own purposes. The most prominent of these was the introduction to the first volume, in which Campbell inveighed against the excesses of Italian Baroque architecture and called for a return to the decorum and correctness of the ancients, of whom Andrea Palladio was the most recent exemplar. This anti-Baroque manifesto took up ideas recently stated in France, but Campbell significantly adapted it to English conditions. He refuted the 'general Esteem that [English] Travellers have for Things that are Foreign', and the book demonstrated impressively the wealth of home-grown architectural talent. Moreover, Campbell claimed that the true heir of Palladio's classic correctness was Inigo Jones. To support this, *Vitruvius Britannicus* illustrated a series of buildings that Campbell attributed to Jones, including the Banqueting House, Whitehall, London, and Wilton House, Wilts. Research into Jones's work was an influential part of Campbell's architectural education. In some cases he had to rely on uncertain attributions and on drawings provided by others. These he altered to conform with what he thought were correct standards of purity.

Having established Jones as the touchstone of reformed taste, Campbell claimed that his own works continued that tradition and would mark the rejection of the 'odd and chimerical Beauties' of the Baroque. The principal evidence for this in the first volume were the designs of 1713 for Wanstead House, Essex (destr. 1824; see fig. 1). His other published designs were mostly unexecuted projects, each dedicated to a public figure from whom he hoped for professional employment. He dedicated the plates of Jones's works in the same way.

Campbell's designs in *Vitruvius Britannicus* illustrate the state of his stylistic development in 1715–17. He leaned heavily and obviously on Palladio, some of his designs consisting of a fusion of Palladian buildings to create the large country house required by the English landowning aristocracy. There is little sign that he had yet acquired sufficient discrimination to separate Palladio's more Mannerist designs, such as the Palazzo Valmarana, Vicenza, from those that expressed the classical decorum he claimed to admire. Other designs were based on the eclectic projects made by James Smith, many of whose drawings, including more obviously Palladian derivatives, were in Campbell's collection.

In retrospect the publication of *Vitruvius Britannicus* marks the launch of the Palladian phase of English architecture more distinctly than any other event. At the time, the novel doctrines that Campbell outlined and the rather heterogeneous stylistic ideas of his own designs were less important than the great popularity of the book—shown by its large and increasing list of subscribers—and its influence on the development of Campbell's career and on architectural publishing in general. Henceforth, as shown in the career of Isaac Ware or Robert Adam, book publishing became a customary means of bringing a young architect's name before the public. None of his successors followed exactly the same formula as Campbell, with his unique mixture of his own and others' designs, popular prints and polemic, but this was because the forms of architectural publication developed rapidly after 1715. Of these forms, one of the most enduring was the illustrated review of contemporary architecture. This preserved Campbell's title without any of his reforming zeal, in the *Vitruvius Britannicus* of 1737, 1767 and 1771, *Vitruvius Scotticus* of *c.* 1812 and the abortive *Vitruvius Hibernicus.*

The publication of the second volume of *Vitruvius Britannicus* in 1717 allowed Campbell to leave architectural publishing to concentrate on the practice; but he realized too well the advantages of publication to neglect it entirely. A third volume of *Vitruvius Britannicus* appeared in 1725, which, besides handsome perspectives and estate plans of some houses, concentrated on the display of Campbell's own works. At the end of his life Campbell began working on a translation of Palladio's *I quattro libri dell'architettura.* Although he published only the first of the four books, he

1. Colen Campbell: Wanstead House, Essex, second design for west front, 1713; from *Vitruvius Britannicus*, i (1715), pls 24–5

intended them to supersede the expensive, inaccurate or incomplete existing translations.

2. Architectural practice. The development of Campbell's architectural career was indebted throughout to private patronage. Despite two attempts to gain employment from the Fifty New Churches Commission, he had no success as a church designer, and his contact with royal patronage in the Office of Works was particularly unfortunate. In September 1718 he was appointed Deputy Surveyor under the leadership of William Benson following the deposition of Christopher Wren, but he was dismissed with Benson ten months later due to the latter's arrogant mismanagement of the Office. During this public humiliation, however, Campbell replaced James Gibbs in charge of the modernization for Richard Boyle, 3rd Earl of Burlington, of Burlington House, London, where he designed a façade heavily dependent on Palladio's Palazzo Iseppo Porto, Vicenza. Although Campbell did not retain Burlington's patronage once the Earl emerged as an architect himself, this was his first aristocratic commission and his first in fashionable Westminster. Equally significant, it led to Campbell's participation in the design of houses on the estate that Burlington laid out to the north of his house. Here Campbell developed a simple terrace design, in which the details of the façade were controlled by Palladian proportions but could be easily and cheaply copied. Campbell also designed a more utilitarian sequence of terrace houses in Chancery Lane, London (1719), and a pair in Brook Street, London (1726), where he spent his last years. A very grand version, for seven houses to take up the east side of Grosvenor Square, London, was designed in 1725 but not executed.

The most significant area of architectural design for the generation after 1720 in England was the country house, whether on the palatial scale of Wanstead or the more usual size of the villa. For the grand house, Campbell's Wanstead design, with its rectilinear façade and projecting portico that derived as much from Vincenzo Scamozzi as from earlier English models, provided a fashionable pattern for several houses in the 1730s. An alternative model, Houghton, Norfolk, designed for the Prime Minister, Sir Robert Walpole, in 1722, was derived from the south front of Wilton and made good Campbell's claim to base his Neo-classical revival on the example of Jones. Adapted by Lord Burlington and William Kent at Holkham Hall, Norfolk, this proved an even more influential model than the Wanstead design.

Campbell received at least five commissions for smaller country houses, and here the development of his style can be observed most clearly. His first villa, at Newby, now Baldersby, N. Yorks (*c*. 1720), still used the language of the English Baroque in the heavy half columns and balustrade of the elevation, even while the plan adapted Palladio's Villa Emo, Fanzolo. At Stourhead, Wilts (1721–4; see fig. 2), and Waverley, Surrey (*c*. 1725), however, Campbell refined his understanding of a limited, orthodox vocabulary, while increased flexibility was introduced through the relationship of basement and principal floor and expressed by variations in the handling of string courses and other details. All was contained within the triadic discipline of such Palladian elevations as the Villa

2. Colen Campbell: Stourhead, Wiltshire, first design, 1720–22; from *Vitruvius Britannicus*, iii (1725), pls 41–3

Emo or the project for Giulio Capra. As in the case of the urban terrace, the final result of this design was to establish a routine, anonymous pattern for the smaller Georgian house that proved as long-lasting as it was versatile. Apart from this sequence, Campbell's most remarkable villa design was Mereworth, Kent (*see* PALLADIANISM, fig. 2), where he built an intelligent adaptation of Palladio's Villa Capra or Villa Rotonda, Vicenza. The clarity and simplicity of the Villa Rotonda had fascinated James Smith among other previous British architects, and Campbell's drawings show that he experimented on this famous Palladian idea in association with Lord Burlington, who was shortly to provide his own synthesis at Chiswick, near London.

Little survives upon which to base an assessment of Campbell's treatment of interiors. As with his villas, he seems to have come to terms only slowly with the programme enunciated in *Vitruvius Britannicus*. At Wanstead the hall had a simple bolection-moulded chimney-piece set between giant pilasters in the panelling. By the end of his career, at Stamp Brooksbank's house, Hackney, near London (1728; destr. *c*. 1790), Campbell was drawing on Jones's ideas for increasingly elaborate chimney-pieces and complex plasterwork. A few of his plans show that he did grasp the system of interrelated room proportions that underlay Palladio's aesthetic ideas.

Campbell's architectural style spread among groups of patrons, including the courtiers of George, Prince of Wales. His association with Roger Morris, with whom he worked on at least three buildings, ensured the continuation of a Palladian tradition separate from that of Lord Burlington.

Since the 1730s Campbell's reputation has been eclipsed by that of Lord Burlington, whose aristocratic status gained him undue respect as progenitor of Palladianism. Campbell's role was reassessed following the rediscovery of many of his drawings and the reappraisal of the role of publications in the process of stylistic change. Campbell was fortunate that the decade of his greatest influence, after 1715, saw the final stabilization of an oligarchic society whose architectural needs were to change little for many years. For these needs, Campbell provided a series of lastingly satisfactory solutions. His buildings lack the vitality of John Vanbrugh, the idiosyncrasy of Nicholas Hawksmoor or the subtlety of Burlington, but Campbell was a pioneer in the use of easily recognizable symbols, notably the free-standing portico or the cubic hall, which gave his buildings the air of antique dignity suitable to the classicist culture of the élite.

WRITINGS

trans.: *Andrea Palladio's First Book of Architecture* (London, 1728) [original in It., pubd Venice, 1570; contains 5 pls of Campbell's work]

PRINTS

Vitruvius Britannicus, 3 vols (London, 1715–25)

BIBLIOGRAPHY

Colvin
F. W. Sheppard, ed.: *The Parish of St James's Piccadilly: North of Piccadilly* (1963), xxxii of *Survey of London* (London, 1900–)
H. E. Stutchbury: *The Architecture of Colen Campbell* (Manchester, 1967)
G. Goodfellow: 'Colen Campbell's Last Years', *Burl. Mag.*, cxi (1969), pp. 185–91
L. Boynton: 'Newby Park, the First Palladian Villa in England', *The Country Seat*, ed. H. Colvin and J. Harris (London, 1970), pp. 97–105
J. Harris, ed.: *Catalogue of the Drawings Collection of the Royal Institute of British Architects* (Farnborough, 1973)
H. M. Colvin and others: *1660–1782* (1976), v of *History of the King's Works*, ed. H. M. Colvin (London, 1963–76)
T. P. Connor: 'The Making of *Vitruvius Britannicus*', *Archit. Hist.*, xx (1977), pp. 14–30
——: 'Colen Campbell as Architect to the Prince of Wales', *Archit. Hist.*, xxii (1979), pp. 64–71
——: 'Architecture and Planting at Goodwood, 1723–1750', *Sussex Archaeol. Cols*, cxvii (1980), pp. 185–93
——: 'A Late Villa by Colen Campbell', *Burl. Mag.*, cxxiv (1982), pp. 36–7
E. Harris: '"Vitruvius Britannicus" before Colen Campbell', *Burl. Mag.*, cxxviii (1986), pp. 340–46
——: *Architectural Books in England before 1780* (in preparation)

T. P. CONNOR

Campbell, George (*b* Arklow, Co. Wicklow, 29 July 1917; *d* Dublin, 1979). Irish painter and writer. After leaving school in Dublin, he lived with his widowed mother and brothers in Belfast and worked in various jobs. He published *Now in Ulster* (Belfast, 1944), a volume of verse and short stories, with his brother Arthur. He began painting during the blitz of Belfast, when he was working in an aircraft factory, taking the bomb damage as his subject-matter. Working with the painter Daniel O'Neill (1920–74) reinforced his romanticism. His association with Gerard Dillon (1916–71), with whom he travelled to Connemara (to paint landscapes) and later to London, likewise intensified an interest in bohemian characters that led him to visit Spain in the early 1950s. His frequent prolonged stays in Catalunya and Malaga, and his contact with Spanish art, had a lasting effect, epitomized in the isolated dignity of the figure in *Spanish Match-seller* (*c*. 1959; Cork, Crawford Mun. A.G.).

Campbell's paintings until the 1960s were generally dark in tone and mysterious in mood, dramatized by accents of lighter tone that were likened by Eric Newton to 'little climaxes that emerge like fireworks in the night' (White, p. 28). During the 1970s, however, he began to lighten his palette, at the same time loosening the construction of his landscapes, as in *Road to Clifden* (*c*. 1975; Dublin, Allied Irish Bank).

BIBLIOGRAPHY

J. White, ed.: *George Campbell RHA*, text by E. Newton (Dublin, *c*. 1970)
M. Catto: *Art in Ulster 2* (Belfast, 1977), pp. 18–20

□

Campbell, John (*b* Glasgow, 4 July 1857; *d* Wellington, New Zealand, 4 August 1942). New Zealand architect of Scottish birth. He served his articles in Glasgow under John Gordon (1835–1912) and arrived in New Zealand in 1882. Although he worked briefly as a draughtsman for the firm of Mason and Wales, almost his entire career was spent working for the Public Works Department, to which he was first appointed in 1883. He was promoted to draughtsman in charge of the design of government buildings in New Zealand in 1888 and held the newly created title of Government Architect in 1909, retiring in 1922. His early buildings were generally designed in the Queen Anne style, often incorporating Baroque elements; examples include his additions to the Government Printing Office (1894–6; destr.), Wellington, and his Police Station (1895–9) in Dunedin, modelled on New Scotland Yard, London. He later designed the Dunedin Law Courts

(1899–1902) in Gothic Revival style with a Scottish Baronial inflection. In the early part of the 20th century Campbell established Edwardian Baroque as the official architectural style for government buildings in New Zealand by means of his consistent use of the style. In works such as the Government Buildings (1902–7; destr. 1931), Napier, the Public Trust Office (1905–9) and Chief Post Office (1908–12; destr. 1974, see *A Brief History of Public Buildings*, p. 5) in Wellington, as well as numerous provincial and suburban government offices, Campbell used a range of Baroque elements that became almost synonymous with New Zealand government architecture of the time. In 1911 Campbell and one of his staff, Claude Paton, won the national competition for the design of Parliament House, Wellington. Their Edwardian Baroque design was only partially built (1912–22) but is nevertheless the crowning achievement of Campbell's career. Parliament House and many of Campbell's government offices were subsequently recognized as especially significant examples of Edwardian Baroque architecture in New Zealand and an important part of the legacy of such buildings throughout the former British Empire.

BIBLIOGRAPHY

A Brief History of Public Buildings in New Zealand (Wellington, 1970) [Ministry of Works pubn]

P. G. Richardson: *An Architecture of Empire: The Government Buildings of John Campbell in New Zealand* (diss., Christchurch, NZ, U. Canterbury, 1988)

PETER RICHARDSON

Campbell, John, 1st Baron Cawdor (*b* ?Stackpole, 24 April 1755; *d* Bath, 1 June 1821). English politician and collector. He was the elder son of Pryse Campbell (*d* 1768), MP, of Cawdor, Nairnshire (now Highland), and he succeeded his grandfather, John Campbell, MP, of Stackpole, Pembrokeshire (now Dyfed), in 1777. He was MP for Nairnshire in 1777–80 and for Cardigan Boroughs from 1780 until his elevation as Baron Cawdor in 1796. Campbell's first major commission was the full-length portrait (Cawdor Castle, Highland) by Reynolds exhibited at the Royal Academy in 1778. He visited Italy in 1784 and 1786–8 and his interest in collecting seems to have been encouraged by his friendship with the Hon. Charles Francis Greville. He sat to Christopher Hewetson for a bust (Cawdor Castle) in 1784 and purchased pictures from the dealer James Durno in 1788 and antiquities from Thomas Jenkins. One of Canova's first British patrons, he commissioned the sculptor's *Cupid and Psyche* (Paris, Louvre) and also patronized John Charles Felix Rossi.

In 1789 Campbell married Lady Caroline Howard, daughter of the 5th Earl of Carlisle. In 1790 he purchased a house in Oxford Street, London, where, on Greville's advice, he constructed a 'passage gallery' to house the collection, which included such marbles as the Villa Lante Vase (Woburn Abbey, Beds) and over 120 'Etruscan' vases. However, his expenses exceeded his resources and his 'Museum' was sold by the auctioneers Skinner and Duke, 5–6 June 1800. He was a pioneer in the appreciation of early Italian pictures, and in addition to the antiquities there were a number of pictures, including two 'Masaccios' (predella panels by Perugino and associate; Liverpool, Walker A.G.; Polesden Lacey, Surrey, NT), two 'Dürers' and Italian views by Tito Lusieri (*fl* from 1785), A.-L.-R. Ducros and Henry Tresham. The most remarkable of Cawdor's pictures, Bellini's *Doge Leonardo Loredan* (London, N.G.), was sold privately. Cawdor returned to Italy in 1814–15 and renewed his association with Canova, but his collecting days were over.

UNPUBLISHED SOURCES

Carmarthen, Dyfed Archvs Serv. [Cawdor MSS]

BIBLIOGRAPHY

[G. E. Cokayne]: *The Complete Peerage*, 14 vols (London, rev. 1910–59)

L. Namier and J. Brooke: *The House of Commons, 1754–1790*, 3 vols (London, 1964), ii, p. 190

F. Russell: 'The Cawdor Collection', *Country Life*, clxxv/4530 (14 June 1984), pp. 1746–8

FRANCIS RUSSELL

Campbell, Ralph (*b* Kingston, Jamaica, 13 March 1921; *d* Kingston, 26 Nov 1985). Jamaican painter and teacher. He received his early artistic training under Edna Manley at the Junior Centre of the Institute of Jamaica and at the Jamaica School of Art and Crafts, both in Kingston. He later attended Goldsmiths' College, London, and the Chicago School of Interior Decoration. He taught intermittently at the Jamaica School of Art and several high schools in Kingston. Although he is best known for his expressionist religious works and his atmospheric landscapes, his work is characterized by variety in terms of subject-matter, styles and techniques. His many experiments were not always equally successful and the quality of his work is somewhat uneven, although his best works, such as *Sea of Galilee* (1975; Kingston, Inst. Jamaica N.G.), are among the finest of the early Jamaican Art Movement.

BIBLIOGRAPHY

Jamaican Art 1922–1982 (exh. cat. by D. Boxer, Washington, Smithsonian Inst.; Kingston, Inst. Jamaica, N.G.; 1983), pp. 17–19, 61

VEERLE POUPEYE

Campelo, António (*b* c. 1530; *d* before 1580). Portuguese painter. He served his apprenticeship in Rome, and his work closely adheres to the tenets of Mannerism. It is possible that in August 1552 he participated in the fresco decoration of the Montepulciano Apartment at the Vatican, which was the residence of Cardinal Giovanni Ricci, formerly nuncio in Portugal. Ricci may have arranged the apprenticeship for Campelo, although he is usually thought to have been among the artists, including Gaspar Dias, sent to Rome by King John III. From Campelo's Roman period are several vigorous and theatrical drawings (Lisbon, Mus. N.A. Ant.). Three of these (inv. nos 58, 381 and 382) are copies of sections of the painted façade of the Palazzo Milesi (destr.), Rome, with scenes from the *History of Ancient Rome* by Polidoro da Caravaggio and Maturino of Florence. The *Allegory of Prudence* (Lisbon, Mus. N.A. Ant., 137) faithfully duplicates a section of the painted façade at the Villa of Vicolo Savelli, Rome, by Pellegrino Tibaldi (1552), and the drawing *Strength* (Lisbon, Mus. N.A. Ant., 383) is based on a fresco by Giulio Romano in the Psyche Loggia, Palazzo della Farnesina, Rome. These show the freedom of his draughtsmanship and his sureness of composition. Da Costa noted that Campelo followed the school of Michelangelo as much in the strength of the drawing as in his use of colours and cited the panel of *Christ Carrying the Cross* (*c*. 1570;

Lisbon, Mus. N.A. Ant., reserve), then in the Monastery of Jerónimos, Lisbon. Though in poor condition, it conveys Campelo's sense of plasticity in the pose of the soldiers, the dramatic depiction of Christ and the fresh colouring used for the draperies and armour.

BIBLIOGRAPHY

F. da Costa: *Antiguidade da arte da pintura* (MS.; 1696); ed. G. Kubler (New Haven and London, 1967), p. 265

A. de Gusmão: *A pintura antiga no Mosteiro dos Jerónimos* (Lisbon, 1950)

V. Serrão: 'António Campelo, um pintor do tempo do Camões', *Camões*, 2–3 (1980), pp. 19–34

——: *A pintura maneirista em Portugal* (Lisbon, 1982), pp. 51–7

VITOR SERRÃO

Campen, Jacob van (*b* Haarlem, 2 Feb 1595; *d* Randenbroek, nr Amersfoort, 13 Sept 1657). Dutch architect and painter. He received his training as a painter from Pieter de Grebber in Haarlem, becoming a member of the Guild of St Luke there in 1614. On the death of his parents within the next two years, he received a considerable inheritance and the title of Lord of Randenbroek. He did not have the benefit of a formal architectural training; Weyerman's account of a stay made by van Campen in the Veneto, Italy (1615–21), and his acquaintance with Vincenzo Scamozzi has been discounted by later scholars. His first known work (1624) is the façade of a double house for the brothers Balthasar and Johan Coymans in Amsterdam (Keizersgracht 177). His façade differs from the traditional narrow canal house with a stepped gable by having eight bays, of which the middle four project slightly. Constructed of brick, the façade consists of a low ground-floor, above which are two storeys articulated by tiers of pilasters—Ionic below, Corinthian above—capped with a shallow attic. By Dutch standards the roof is rather low. This rigorous articulation of the façade by pilasters was entirely new in the Netherlands. In addition, the pilasters do not stand on a plinth, as was usual. With this design, which was immediately admired and incorporated in Salomon de Bray's *Architectura moderna* (1631), van Campen introduced a new development in Dutch architecture that became known as Dutch Classicism. This movement reached maturity in 1633 with van Campen's Mauritshuis (see fig.) in The Hague, designed for Johan Maurits, Count of Nassau-Siegen. The building is free-standing, its façade articulated on all sides by a colossal order of Ionic pilasters resting on a plinth storey. The façade is surmounted by a pediment, above which rises a steeply inclined roof with two chimneys. The front façade is seven bays wide; the outer ones and the middle three project slightly. The central projection with the entrance is entirely constructed of sandstone and is crowned with a pediment containing the Nassau coat of arms. The central projection of the rear, five-bay façade is also in stone, as are the other decorative parts such as the festoons under the windows on the first floor.

Van Campen was also responsible for major alterations (1633–5) at the Municipal Orphanage in Amsterdam and in 1639 produced a design for rebuilding the Oude Hof (1553; now Pal. Noordeinde; *see* THE HAGUE, fig. 1), an existing town palace owned by the Stadtholder's family in The Hague. His façade has two tiers of pilasters and a pediment crowning the three central bays. Two projecting wings flanking a courtyard separate the main block from

Jacob van Campen: view of the Mauritshuis (Royal Cabinet of Paintings), The Hague, 1633; from a drawing by Jan de Bisschop, *c.* 1660 (Dresden, Kupferstichkabinett)

the street, but unlike the Parisian hôtel they are the same height as the *corps de logis* and are opened up as arcaded galleries at ground-level. A few years after his work in The Hague, van Campen returned to Haarlem, where he was commissioned by the burgomasters to design the church of St Anna or Nieuwe Kerk (from 1645). An existing tower, which Lieven de Key had added in 1613 to a former medieval church, had to be worked into the design: van Campen built a sober brick church against this feature. The plan takes the form of a Greek cross inscribed in a square, with four piers at the angles. The four subsidiary squares thus created have lower, flat coffered ceilings. The arms of the cross are barrel-vaulted and run into a central cross vault constructed in timber. Van Campen refrained from using a dome at this point, to avoid expense and visual distraction from the picturesque tower. The longitudinal arms span uninterruptedly from wall pilaster to central pier, whereas an intermediate column is inserted to help support each cross arm span. The longitudinal columns were probably omitted to improve the view of the free-standing square pulpit, also designed by van Campen and located beneath the southern cross arch. At St Anna, which is closely related to Venetian churches built during the second half of the 16th century, van Campen created a church type that proved very suitable for Protestant services, since the congregation could gather around the pulpit. It may have inspired Christopher Wren's St Martin's Ludgate (1677–84), London. During the construction of St Anna, van Campen also designed the town hall of Amsterdam (now the Royal Palace; *see* AMSTERDAM, §V, 2, and TOWN HALL, fig. 3), a scheme for which the old town hall and 69 houses had to be demolished. Van Campen introduced a strict classicism into the architecture of the northern Netherlands; his distinguished birth, financial independence and influential connections all helped him to attract important commissions. He followed the work of Scamozzi through books of engravings, and by adapting and developing his own style he became involved with the direction of international classicism in architecture. He greatly influenced other Dutch architects—for example Pieter Post—whom he advised or allowed to amend and execute some of his designs. His version of classicism was brought to England by returning refugees from the Commonwealth, and it found ready acceptance there, notably by Hugh May and Roger Pratt.

See also THEATRE, fig. 10.

BIBLIOGRAPHY

Macmillan Enc. Architects; Thieme–Becker

J. C. Weyerman: *De levensbeschryvingen der Nederlandsche kunstschilders* [Biographies of Dutch artists] (The Hague, 1729–69)

M. D. Ozinga: *Protestantse kerkenbouw in Nederland* (Amsterdam, 1929)

F. A. J. Vermeulen: *Handboek tot de geschiedenis der Nederlandsche bouwkunst* [History of Dutch architecture], ii (The Hague, 1941)

S. J. Fockema Andreae and others: *Duizend jaar bouwen in Nederland* [Thousand years of Dutch architecture], ii (Amsterdam, 1957)

K. Fremantle: *The Baroque Town Hall of Amsterdam* (Utrecht, 1959)

J. Rosenberg, S. Slive and E. H. Ter Kuile: *Dutch Art and Architecture*, Pelican Hist. A. (Harmondsworth, 1966/*R* 1977)

J. H. Kluiver: 'De orgelarchitectuur van Jacob van Campen', *Bull. Kon. Ned. Oudhdkd. Bond.*, lxxiii/1 (1974), pp. 1–18

W. Kuyper: *Dutch Classicist Architecture* (Delft, 1980)

PAUL H. REM

Campendonk, Heinrich (*b* Krefeld, 3 Nov 1889; *d* Amsterdam, 9 May 1957). German painter, printmaker and stained-glass artist. He attended the Fachschule für Textilindustrie and the Kunstgewerbeschule in Krefeld (1905–9), where his teacher Johan Thorn Prikker showed him the power of line and colour and introduced him to the work of Vincent van Gogh and Paul Cézanne. In 1911 he was invited by Franz Marc and Vasily Kandinsky to Sindelsdorf in Upper Bavaria. They knew of his work through August Macke whose cousin, Helmut, shared a studio with Campendonk. While Campendonk's harmonious and often transparent application of luxurious Fauvist colours reflects the influence of Robert and Sonia Delaunay and of Macke, Marc's geometric compositional approach is clearly visible in the experimental style of such paintings as *Leaping Horse* (1911; Saarbrücken, Saarland Mus.), shown in the first exhibition of Der Blaue Reiter in 1911–12 in Munich and illustrated in the almanac *Der Blaue Reiter*. Unlike Marc, however, he included figures in his mystical portrayals of animals in nature. This subject-matter was also explored in his first tentative graphic works, published in 1912 in Herwarth Walden's periodical *Der Sturm*. He continued to experiment with styles such as Cubism (e.g. *Composition with Horse*, 1912; Bonn, Städt. Kunstmus.), Futurism (e.g. *Yellow Animal*, 1914; The Hague, Gemeentemus.) and Orphism (e.g. the *Sixth Day*, 1914; Duisburg, Lehmbruck-Mus.), and exhibited with the Expressionist group the 'Rheinische Expressionisten' before World War I.

The war years and the deaths of Marc and Macke were a turning-point for Campendonk. In 1916, after two years of military service, he moved to Seeshaupt. Campendonk destroyed much of his earlier work and, in response to the work of Marc Chagall, moved toward depicting representational fantasies in works such as *The Poor* (1918; Krefeld, Kaiser Wilhelm Mus.). Concurrently his woodcuts evolved with heraldic presentations of fish, cats, goats, cows, figures and profuse vegetative ornament, in a style derived from such sources as African tribal art, Egyptian shadow play figures and Russian folk prints. Most of Campendonk's 77 woodcuts were produced at this time from highly finished preparatory drawings, making variant states rare. Many of the woodcuts have black backgrounds that contrast with radiant accents of watercolour, evoking the luminosity of stained glass and accruing symbolic power.

In 1920 Campendonk travelled to Italy to study the frescoes of Giotto and Fra Angelico as well as the Early Christian mosaics in Ravenna. Subsequently an architectonic construction of space appeared in his paintings, for example *Interior* (1920; The Hague, Gemeentemus.). In 1922 he returned to Krefeld and developed a more abstract and decorative style, while producing stage designs for the theatre as well as boldly simplified woodcuts. Having occasionally painted on glass throughout the previous decade, he turned in earnest to stained-glass design in 1923. During this year he also began exhibiting at the Société Anonyme, New York, which sponsored his first American one-man show in 1925. In 1926 he took the position vacated by Thorn Prikker at the Kunstakademie, Düsseldorf.

After receiving numerous commissions for monumental frescoes and stained-glass windows over the next several years, Campendonk abandoned woodcuts to concentrate on public art. When his position in Düsseldorf was discontinued in 1933, he emigrated to Belgium, where he worked on an unfinished series of stained-glass icons entitled *Stations of the Cross.* In 1935 he took a position at the Rijksakademie van beeldende Kunsten in Amsterdam and devoted the next decade primarily to stained-glass commissions. His *Passion Window* won the Grand Prix when shown at the Dutch Pavilion at the Exposition Universelle, Paris (1937). Although more withdrawn after World War II, Campendonk resumed painting and continued to receive numerous stained-glass commissions. Often praised for his dreamlike imagery, his style is a contemplative blending of fantasy with a reserved and exacting precision, at once imaginary and concrete.

BIBLIOGRAPHY

W. Schürmeyer: *Heinrich Campendonk* (Frankfurt, 1920)
G. Biermann: 'Heinrich Campendonk', *Junge Kst* (1921)
M. T. Engels: *Heinrich Campendonk*, Monographien zur rheinisch-westfälischen Kunst der Gegenwart (Recklinghausen, 1958)
——: *Campendonk: Holzschnitte* (Stuttgart, 1959) [cat. rais.]
P. Wember: *Heinrich Campendonk* (Krefeld, 1960) [cat. rais. of ptgs with extensive bibliog.]
M. T. Engels: *Campendonk als Glasmaler* (Krefeld, 1966)
Heinrich Campendonk: Gemälde, Aquarelle, Hinterglasbilder, Grafik (exh. cat., Bonn, Städt. Kstmus., 1973)
Die rheinische Expressionisten: August Macke und seine Malerfreunde (exh. cat., Bonn, Städt. Kstmus., 1979)
A. Firmenich: *Heinrich Campendonk (1889–1957): Lebensgeschichte und stilkritische Analyse seines expressionistischen Werkes mit Werkkatalog des malerischen Oeuvres* (Recklinghausen, 1989)

TIMOTHY O. BENSON

Campeny y Estrany, Damián (*b* Mataró, 12 April 1771; *d* Barcelona, 7 July 1855). Spanish sculptor and teacher. He began studying at the Escuela de Bellas Artes de la Lonja in Barcelona at the age of 14, and he worked in the studio of Salvador Gurri (*fl* 1756–1819), a late Baroque sculptor with Neo-classical tendencies. Campeny left the studio after he was attacked by Gurri, who, as a teacher at the Escuela (1785), continued to persecute him and threw him out. Campeny then worked in Lérida, Cervera and Montserrat. He produced his first major work, *St Bruno* (1795; destr. 1831), in carved polychromed wood. He also trained with Nicolás Traver and José Cabañeras, both late Baroque artists. Stylistically, Campeny began with a moderate and personal naturalism, later assimilating some of the Baroque influences from his Catalan teachers. Readmitted to the Escuela, in 1795 he won a scholarship to complete his studies in Rome, where he went in 1796 and had his own studio for 17 years. He was at the Accademia di S Luca, worked in the restoration department of the Museo Capitolino and also studied with Antonio Canova, who had a decisive influence on his work and became a close friend. In Italy he became such a pure Neo-classicist that he was called the 'Spanish Canova'. Various works from this period are held at the Lonja in Barcelona, for example *Paris* (1808) and Campeny's masterpiece the *Dying Lucretia* (plaster, 1803; marble, 1834). The collection also contains a statue of the Virgin as *Ianua Coeli* (1815), made using various hard coloured stones.

Because of Campeny's success in Rome he was appointed teacher of sculpture at the Escuela de Bellas Artes in Barcelona, where he returned in 1816 and taught for 39 years, becoming Director of Sculpture in 1819 and then Director-general from 1827. Following his return to Spain, his work included the *Catalan Mercenary Killing a French Horseman* (1819; Barcelona, Real Acad. Cat. B.A. S Jorge). His main religious work is the *Holy Sepulchre* float (1816), consisting of five life-size figures, with heads, hands and feet of moulded papier-mâché and the rest in cloth and wood, made for the Maundy Thursday procession. In 1825 the Junta de Comercio de Cataluña signed a contract with Campeny for several works, although only a few were executed. Campeny's fame was widespread and he was appointed court sculptor by King Ferdinand VII. He joined the Academia de Bellas Artes de San Carlos of Valencia (1820), the Academia de Ciencias y Artes de Barcelona (1838; President from 1841) and the Academia de Nobles y Bellas Artes de San Luis of Saragossa (1845). He was a respected teacher and theoretician, although he left no writings. His later works possessed a certain idealized naturalism, Romantic in feeling. However, Neo-classicism was his predominant style and he was perhaps the best Neo-classical artist in Spain, being a master of technique, composition and chiaroscuro. Although his works are mostly of mythological and other pagan subjects, he made many religious sculptures, especially after 1830, in which he tried to combine traditional Spanish imagery with a Neo-classical style.

BIBLIOGRAPHY

C. Cid: 'La decoración de la Casa Lonja de Barcelona', *Bol. Mus. A. Barcelona*, vi/3–4 (1948), pp. 423–62
F. Marés: 'El escultor Damián Campeny Estrany', *Ensay*, 5 (1951)
C. Cid: 'Una obra maestra del neoclasicismo español: La *Lucrecia muerta* de Damián Campeny', *Archv Esp. A.* (1952), pp. 15–25
——: 'Damián Campeny artista mitológico', *Goya*, 16 (1957), pp. 221–4
J. Bassegoda Nonell: *La Casa Llotja de Mar de Barcelona* (Barcelona, 1986)

CARLOS CID PRIEGO

Camphuyzen [Camphuysen], **Govert** [Govaert] **(Dircksz.)** (*b* ?Gorinchem, 1623–4; *d* ?Amsterdam, *bur* 4 July 1672). Dutch painter. He was working as a portrait painter in Amsterdam by 1643, and in 1652 an inventory of his house and possessions was drawn up before their sale to pay off his debts. He is next recorded in 1655 working in Stockholm for the dowager Queen Hedvig Eleonora and as a court portrait painter for such patrons as the Chancellor, Count Magnus Gabriel De La Gardie (1622–86). Camphuyzen's work comprises mostly animal paintings reminiscent of the work of Paulus Potter as well as landscapes with low horizons and figures in the style of Aert van der Neer that reveal an interest in the depiction of unusual light effects; the finest of such works is the *Dutch Farm at Sunset* (London, Wallace). He also executed a number of more specifically topographical works, including his best-known painting *Stockholm Castle* (1661; Stockholm, Stat. Hist. Mus.), which successfully combines accuracy with atmospheric effects. It is painted with almost poetic understanding: the building rises like a fairy-tale castle above the gloom of the moat and the dark foliage, the sunlight reflected on its rough walls, its spires silhouetted against the sky. At the same time, however, in the Dutch tradition, it also presents quite accurately the appearance of the castle after it was remodelled in the late

1500s. Camphuyzen returned to Amsterdam *c.* 1665, and in 1667 he drew up his will.

BIBLIOGRAPHY

Thieme–Becker

S. Strömbom: 'Camphuysens målning av Stockholms slott' [Camphuyzen's painting of Stockholm Castle], *St Eriks Åb.* (1948)

B. Rapp: *Djur och stilleben i karolinsky måleri* [Animals and still-lifes in Caroline painting] (Stockholm, 1951)

B. Haak: *The Golden Age: Dutch Painters of the Seventeenth Century* (London and New York, 1984), pp. 305–6

TORBJÖRN FULTON

Campi. Italian family of artists. From Cremona, they were active there and elsewhere in Italy from the late 15th century to the late 16th. Galeazzo Campi (*b* Cremona, *c.* 1477; *d* Cremona, 1536) and Sebastiano Campi (*fl* 1522–31), sons of Antonio Campi, were both painters who probably shared a workshop. Galeazzo's sons, (1) Giulio Campi and (2) Antonio Campi were painters and architects who collaborated on many decorative cycles in the mid-16th century. After Giulio's death, Antonio began to paint in a more naturalistic manner, and in this he was followed to some extent by his youngest brother, (3) Vincenzo Campi, who had also almost certainly studied earlier with Giulio. The third generation of the Campi included Antonio's son, Claudio Campi, who signed his own name to his father's drawings.

BIBLIOGRAPHY

DBI

G. Vasari: *Vite* (1550, rev. 2/1568); ed. G. Milanesi (1878–85)

A. Perotti: *I pittori Campi da Cremona* (Milan, 1932)

I Campi e la cultura artistica cremonese del cinquecento (exh. cat., ed. M. Gregori; Cremona, Mus. Civ. Ala Ponzone, 1985)

(1) Giulio Campi (*b* Cremona, *c.* 1508; *d* 5 March 1573). Painter and architect. He probably trained with his father, Galeazzo Campi. His first signed and dated painting, the altarpiece of the *Virgin and Child with SS Nazarius and Celsus* (1527; Cremona, S Abbondio), shows the influence of the Brescian painting of Moretto and Romanino. His development was rapid, and within a few years he showed an interest in the art of Pordenone, Giulio Romano and Raphael. This is evident in two altarpieces, *Nativity with Saints* and *Virgin and Saints with a Marchese Stampa as Donor* (1530; both Milan, Brera), and in the frescoes (1530) in S Maria delle Grazie, Soncino. Apart from a few works of interest such as the *Game of Chess* (Turin, Mus. Civ. A. Ant.), in the 1530s Giulio concentrated on an important fresco cycle for S Agata, Cremona, with scenes from the *Life of St Agatha* (1537); and from 1539 to 1542 he decorated the two transepts of S Sigismondo, Cremona. The rich and varied style of these works, which combined elements from Mannerism and the work of Pordenone, influenced Cremonese painting in the following decades. In a major commission to decorate the whole of S Margherita, Cremona, which he also probably rebuilt (1547), he attained a high degree of sophistication and complexity. With his brother, (2) Antonio Campi, he then painted some canvases for the Palazzo della Loggia, Brescia, illustrating *Stories of Justice* (*in situ* and dispersed in Brescia, Pin. Civ. Tosio-Martinengo; Budapest, Mus. F.A.). He probably visited Rome in the mid-1550s; his subsequent decoration (1557) of the first bay of S Sigismondo, Cremona, with the *Pentecost* and two *Prophets* shows a new monumentality and daring illusionism. In the 1560s he painted a large *Crucifixion* for S Maria della Passione, Milan, an altarpiece with *SS Philip and James* (1565) for S Sigismondo, Cremona, and *St Lawrence* for Alba Cathedral (all *in situ*). In his last years Giulio executed numerous works for Cremona Cathedral, including the vast organ shutters. These paintings show a gradual transition from complex compositions to simpler ones, reflecting the requirements of the Counter-Reformation. At his death he left incomplete the decoration of the presbytery of S Maria di Campagna, Piacenza, and of S Abbondio, Cremona.

BIBLIOGRAPHY

S. Zamboni: 'Per Giulio Campi', *A. Ant. & Mod.*, x (1960), pp. 170–73

G. Bora: 'Note Cremonese, II: L'eredità di Camillo e i Campi', *Paragone*, 311 (1976), pp. 49–74

G. Godi and G. Cirillo: *Studi su Giulio Campi* (Milan, 1978)

G. Bora: 'Giulio e Antonio Campi architetti', *Per A. E. Popham* (Parma, 1981), pp. 21–41

(2) Antonio Campi (*b* Cremona, 1523; *d* Cremona, Jan 1587). Painter, engraver, architect and writer, brother of (1) Giulio Campi. He probably trained with Giulio in a style tending towards Mannerism. His first signed and dated work, the *Virgin and Child with SS Jerome and Joseph, with Donor* (1546; Cremona, S Ilario), reflects the style of Camillo Boccaccino, himself inspired by Parmigianino, and the influence of Boccaccino on Antonio increased in the following years and is particularly marked in a series of chiaroscuro engravings (1547 to the early 1550s; e.g. *Adoration of the Magi*, 1547). Around 1547 Antonio collaborated with Giulio on frescoes in S Margherita, Cremona. Still working with Giulio, from 1549 he painted at least half of the eight canvases for the Palazzo della Loggia, Brescia, illustrating *Stories of Justice* (*in situ* and dispersed in Brescia, Pin. Civ. Tosio-Martinengo; Budapest, Mus. F.A.), and in 1557 he frescoed part of the first bay of S Sigismondo in Cremona.

Also in the 1550s Antonio worked on the decoration of two rooms in the Palazzo Pallavicini in Torre Pallavicina and possibly on its architectural plan. The decoration of the presbytery of S Paolo Converso, Milan, dates from before 1564. The rich and forceful Mannerist style of these works is also evident in the *Resurrection* (1560; Milan, S Maria presso S Celso) and is even more striking in the *Beheading of St John the Baptist* (1567), in the chapel of S Giovanni in S Sigismondo, Cremona, which was entirely decorated by Antonio over a period of almost 20 years.

During the 1560s Antonio veered between different styles: the *Pietà* (1566) in Cremona Cathedral is starkly devotional; the *Holy Family* (1567; Cremona, S Pietro al Po) conveys a sense of grandeur; and the *Sacra conversazione* (Milan, Brera) displays sumptuous elegance. Possibly because of his contact with the Archbishop of Milan, Carlo Borromeo (1538–84; canonized 1610), from the late 1560s Antonio's devotional subjects became more expressive. Examples include *Scenes from the Passion* (?1569; Paris, Louvre); frescoes of the *Three Marys at the Tomb* and a *Pietà* (Meda, near Milan, S Vittore); *St Jerome* (Madrid, Prado), painted for El Escorial; and the *Beheading of St John the Baptist* (1571; Milan, S Paolo Converso). In the *Adoration of the Shepherds* (1575; Crema, S Maria della Croce) the intimate devotional atmosphere is emphasized by the use of a nocturnal setting.

Antonio Campi: *St Catherine in Prison*, oil on canvas, 4.0×5.0 m, 1584 (Milan, S Angelo)

Apart from these experiments, Antonio's activity in the 1570s included works of such diverse character as his stately signed *Virgin with Saints* (1575), now part of the main altar of S Pietro al Po in Cremona; the mannered *St Sebastian* (1575; Milan, Castello Sforzesco); and the triptych of the *Assumption* (1577; Milan, S Marco), which recalls Brescian painting in its light and colour, as does the *Adoration of the Magi* (1579) in S Maurizio al Monastero Maggiore in Milan. He also completed the decoration of the transepts of S Pietro al Po in Cremona, with scenes from the *Life of St Peter* (1575–9). He then worked on important paintings in S Paolo Converso in Milan, including the *Adoration of the Shepherds* (1580) and the *Martyrdom of St Lawrence*; both are interesting for their strong naturalism, which anticipates Caravaggio.

From 1580 Campi served as architect for the Fabbrica del Duomo, Cremona, for which he also painted the fresco of the *Centurion Kneeling before Christ* for the apse (*in situ*). This fresco, commissioned in 1582, was probably completed after a journey to Rome, where Antonio is said to have worked in the Vatican and been made a *cavaliere aurato* in 1583 by Gregory XIII for his work as an architect. Campi's high standing in Cremona was confirmed with the publication of his important *Cremona fedelissima* in 1585, though a first incomplete edition had probably appeared in 1582. This is a history of the city illustrated with elaborate engravings.

Antonio Campi's last important paintings were done in Milan in the chapel of S Caterina in S Angelo (*in situ*). These are the *Martyrdom of St Catherine* (1583) and *St Catherine in Prison* (1584; see fig.); the former is characterized by formal devices and elaborate drapery, the latter by a masterly nocturnal play of light and shadow. A similar theatricality, although obtained here by the use of *sotto in sù* perspective, is found in the *Presentation in the Temple* (1586; ex-Milan, S Marco; Naples, S Francesco di Paola). Also in 1586, with his brother (3) Vincenzo Campi, Antonio began to paint the ceiling of S Paolo Converso, Milan. For this (*in situ*) he designed a false portico and an architectural backdrop by means of the *quadratura* devices for squaring up already used by Giulio Romano in Mantua and by his own brother, Giulio, in S Sigismondo, Cremona, and recently codified in the treatise by Jacopo Vignola, *Le due regole della prospettiva practica* (Rome, 1583). These advanced conceptions were probably sketched out by Antonio before his death and completed by his brother Vincenzo.

WRITINGS

Cremona fedelissima città e nobilissima colonia de' Romani . . . (Cremona, 1585)

BIBLIOGRAPHY

R. Longhi: 'Quesiti caravaggeschi, II: I precedenti', *Pinacotheca*, v–vi (1929), pp. 258–329

F. Bologna: 'Antonio Campi: La *Circoncisione* del 1586', *Paragone*, 41 (1953), pp. 46–51

R. Longhi: 'Un *San Sebastiano* di Antonio Campi', *Paragone*, lxxx/8 (1957), pp. 66–7

M. L. Ferrari: 'La "maniera de' Campi cremonesi" a Torre Pallavicina', *An. Scu. Norm. Sup. Pisa*, 3rd ser., iv/3 (1974), pp. 805–16

G. Bora: 'Note Cremonesi, II: L'eredità di Camillo e i Campi', *Paragone*, 327 (1977), pp. 54–88

——: 'Giulio e Antonio Campi architetti', *Per A. E. Popham* (Parma, 1981), pp. 21–41

(3) Vincenzo Campi (*b* Cremona, 1530–35; *d* Cremona, 1591). Painter, brother of (2) Antonio Campi. He trained in the family workshop in Cremona, absorbing from (1) Giulio Campi a formal and complex style of composition and from Antonio an expressive pathos. His earliest surviving works, which show little originality, were executed in the 1560s—altarpieces such as the *Deposition* (Cremona, SS Siro e Sepolcro) and the *Pietà* for S Facio in Cremona (Cremona, Osp. Nuovo). In the *Pietà* in the chapterhouse at Cremona Cathedral he attempted, through naturalism and illusionism, to express the new iconographical precepts of the Counter-Reformation. Similar and interesting paintings, which also show Vincenzo's characteristic sentimentality, are the *Pietà* (Bordolano, S Giacomo) and the *Pietà* now in the Museo Civico Ala Ponzone at Cremona. He worked in fresco on the *Prophets* (1573) on the nave arches in Cremona Cathedral.

In *Christ Being Nailed to the Cross* (1575; Pavia, Mus. Certosa) Vincenzo began to develop a richer and mellower palette to portray more naturalistic figures from contemporary life. The later *Christ Being Nailed to the Cross* (1577; Madrid, Prado), with its naturalistic motifs, which Caravaggio may have seen in his years in Lombardy, is similar in conception. At the same time Vincenzo was experimenting with his treatment of altarpieces, using simpler but more intense colour, as in the *Virgin in Glory with Saints* (1577; Cremona, S Maria Maddalena) and the *Trinity with SS Apollonia and Lucy* (1579; Busseto, Oratory of the Trinity). In the *Annunciation* (1581) in the oratory of S Maria Annunciata at Busseto, Vincenzo emphasized colour and chiaroscuro, almost certainly following recent developments in Venetian painting. In the same period he was influenced by such Flemish artists as Joachim Beuckelaer and Pieter Aertsen to paint humorous, naturalistic scenes with titles such as *Fishwives*, *Fruit-sellers* and *Cooks* (e.g. series 1580–81; Kirchheim im Schwaben, Schloss Fugger), and *Fish Market* (*c.* 1580; Milan, Brera; *see* GENRE, fig. 1).

Between 1586 and 1589, at first with his brother Antonio, and then on his own, Vincenzo worked on the ceiling frescoes of S Paolo Converso in Milan (*in situ*). These depict the *Ascension*, the *Assumption of the Virgin* and, theatrically framed in *trompe l'oeil* colonnades, the *Apostles*. One of his last works, *St Matthew with the Angel* (1588; Pavia, S Francesco Maggiore), shows an intensity of feeling and direct naturalism that anticipates Caravaggio.

BIBLIOGRAPHY

A. Venturi: *Storia* (1901–40), ix/6, pp. 887–900
A. Puerari: 'Due dipinti di Vincenzo Campi', *Paragone*, iv/37 (1953), pp. 41–5
S. Zamboni: 'Vincenzo Campi', *A. Ant. & Mod.*, xxx (1965), pp. 924–47
——: '*La cucina* di S Sigismondo', *Atti & Mem. Accad. Clementina Bologna*, ix (1970), pp. 31–3
M. Gregori: 'Note su Vincenzo Campi, pittore di naturalia, e su alcuni precedente', *Paragone*, xlii/501 (1991), pp. 70–86

Campi, Bernardino (*b* Cremona, 1522; *d* Reggio Emilia, 18 Aug 1591). Italian painter. He was almost certainly not related to the CAMPI family of artists from Cremona, although Claudio Campi, son of (2) Antonio Campi, married Bernardino's niece. The main source of information about Bernardino's life is Lamo's *Discorso* (1584). He trained in Cremona with his father, Pietro Campi, a goldsmith, with the painter Giulio Campi and then (after moving to Mantua) with Ippolito Costa. After his return to Cremona in 1541, Bernardino painted the *Assumption of the Virgin* (1542) for S Agata, and in S Sigismondo he executed frescoes (1546), including the *Prophets* in the nave. His work, always characterized by attention to detail, was influenced by Giulio Romano, Pordenone, Giulio Campi and especially by Camillo Boccaccino, with whom he seems to have collaborated from 1544. Bernardino's fame grew during the 1550s, after he had moved to Milan, where he executed numerous works for the nobility (all untraced). Surviving altarpieces painted for Milanese churches in the 1560s include the *Transfiguration* (S Fedele) and the *Virgin with Saints* (1565; S Antonio), both executed with Carlo Urbino, and the *Crucifixion* (Florence, Fiesolana Abbey) for the Scuola dei Genovesi, Milan. After returning to Cremona, he painted the elegant altarpiece with *SS Cecilia and Catherine* (dated 1566) and the dome decorations (1570) for S Sigismondo. For Cremona Cathedral he produced a series of canvases and, for the apse, a fresco with the *Entry into Jerusalem* (1573). Bernardino's work of the 1570s includes the *Pietà* (1574; Milan, Brera) and two altarpieces (1575) in S Maria della Croce at Crema. In 1582 he was in the service of Duke Vespasiano Gonzaga in Sabbioneta, where he carried out decorations for the Palazzo del Giardino (*in situ*); from 1587 to 1590 he was employed at Guastalla on decorations (destr.) in the palace of Ferrante Gonzaga. Bernardino's last documented paintings are the frescoes (1589) in the choir of S Prospero in Reggia Emilia.

BIBLIOGRAPHY

DBI
A. Lamo: *Discorso intorno alla scoltura, e pittura dove ragiona della vita, ed opere in molti luoghi . . . fatte dall'eccellentissimo cremonese M. Bernardino Campo* (Cremona, 1584)
G. B. Zaist: *Notizie istoriche de' pittori, scultori ed architetti cremonesi* (Cremona, 1774/*R* Cremona, 1975), pp. 186–214 [incl. Lamo]
F. Zeri: 'Bernardino Campi: Una *Crocifissione*', *Paragone*, iv/27 (1953), pp. 36–41
M. Di Giampaolo: 'Bernardino Campi a Sabbioneta e un'ipotesi per Carlo Urbino', *Antichità Viva*, xiv/3 (1975), pp. 30–38
G. Bora: 'Note cremonesi, II: L'eredità di Camillo e i Campi', *Paragone*, 327 (1977), pp. 54–88
I Campi e la cultura artistica cremonese del cinquecento (exh. cat., ed. M. Gregori; Cremona, Mus. Civ. Ala Ponzone, 1985)

G. BORA

Campi, Pietro Paolo (*b* Massa Carrara, 1668; *d* Rome, 17 Aug 1764). Italian sculptor. Nothing is known of his apprenticeship, but at the age of 34 he was awarded third prize for sculpture in the Concorso Clementino. In Rome, where he lived with his brother Andrea Campi, also a sculptor, he was employed in the workshop of Pierre Legros (ii), whose assistant he became until the master's death in 1719. Having been introduced to the Abbot of Montecassino by Legros, Campi sent numerous sculptures to the abbey, taking full advantage of his brother's assistance. He was commissioned to execute eight monumental statues for the cloisters: *Pope Gregory II* and *Duke Gisulf I* (both 1712), the *Popes Zacharias and Alexander II* and *Conrad I* (both 1717), *Victor III* (1720), *Benedict XIII* (1726), and *St Benedict* and *St Scholastica* (both 1735). He also completed (1720) the statue of *Charlemagne* begun by Legros in 1714. All the works for Montecassino were dispatched by sea, which allowed the sculptor to continue working for his Roman patrons. For the series of sculptures representing the founders of the religious orders for St Peter's in Rome, Campi took particular care in the execution of the *St Giuliana Falconieri* (1732; north transept), in which, in the modelling of the mantle and dress, as well as in the languidly pious facial expression, the influence of Legros can clearly be observed. *St Pietro Nolasco* (1742; Rome, St Peter's, north transept) is Campi's last dated work.

BIBLIOGRAPHY

Thieme–Becker
E. Schwarzenberg: 'From the *Alessandro morente* to the Alexandre Richelieu: The Portraiture of Alexander the Great in Seventeenth-century Italy and France', *J. Warb. & Court. Inst.*, xxxii (1969), pp. 398-405 (p. 400)
R. Enggass: *Early Eighteenth-century Sculpture in Rome* (University Park, PA, 1976), pp. 179–82 [with bibliog.]
A. Nava Cellini: *La scultura del settecento* (Turin, 1982), p. 39

DONATELLA GERMANÒ SIRACUSA

Campidoglio, Michele Pace del [Michelangelo di]. *See* PACE DEL CAMPIDOGLIO, MICHELE.

Campigli, Massimo (*b* Florence, 4 July 1895; *d* St Tropez, 31 May 1971). Italian painter. He was brought up in Milan after his family moved there in 1904. At the age of 19 he published a poem in the Florentine Futurist periodical *Lacerba* and met Umberto Boccioni and Carlo Carrà. During World War I he was sent to the front (1916) and after capture and imprisonment in Hungary, he escaped to Russia. When the war ended he resumed his literary activities, becoming a journalist with the newspaper *Corriere della Sera*, which in 1919 posted him to Paris. There he started teaching himself to paint, at first producing works that showed the influence of Picasso and Fernand Léger. In 1923 he had his first one-man show at the Galleria Bragaglia in Rome. By the mid-1920s he had evolved a style characterized by well-rounded forms like those of wooden dolls. While Campigli's often bizarre subject-matter recalls Pittura Metafisica, the influence of the Purist journal *Esprit Nouveau* is also apparent in the structure of his compositions. In *Female Acrobats* (1926; priv. col., see Serafini, p. 41) the near-symmetry of the two figures, one of which is upside down, lends poise and stability to the composition. Campigli later considered such works to be too rigorous.

Campigli was a habitual visitor to the Egyptian collections in the Louvre but while on a visit to Rome in 1928 he discovered the Etruscan Museum at the Villa Giulia. In Etruscan art Campigli found compositional methods that were not reliant on symmetry, until then his most important tool. At the same time the texture of Ancient wall-painting also began to interest him. There followed a period of intense activity, resulting in a successful show at Jeanne Bucher's gallery in Paris in 1929. The works exhibited featured wasp-waisted women inhabiting an archaic world and engaged in timeless activities such as drawing water at a fountain. Combined with the heavily worked paint are areas of reduced detail and others that are simply sketched in. This transitional period was short, and by 1931 his personal style was established. In the park and beach scenes such as *Fishermen's Wives* (1934; Rome, G.N.A. Mod.), the figures are isolated and schematically rendered in controlled, flat forms. From this date the female figure continued to be a dominant theme in Campigli's work.

In the 1930s Campigli was relatively successful; he had a series of four exhibitions in New York and, together with Gino Severini and Mario Tozzi, participated in the *Italians in Paris* show. He also exhibited with the Novecento Italiano group in Italy. On his return to Italy from Paris in 1933, he signed the *Manifesto della pittura murale* (*see* SIRONI, MARIO) and executed a mural for the Milan Triennale of decorative arts. He received public commissions, the most notable of which were his works in the Palazzo di Giustizia, Milan (1938), and his huge decorative mural in the University of Padua. As a result of these experiences, he painted larger canvases in the post-war years when he divided his time between Milan, Rome, Paris and St Tropez. During the 1940s he painted a series of works inspired by the theatre, in which busts peer from the bursting theatre boxes. This theme reaches its most powerful expression in the large *Red Theatre* (1960; priv. col., see Russoli), which unites colour, texture and form. Campigli's continual reconsideration of the same themes over a 40-year period reflected his search for the ultimate image; infinitely variable in its details, infinitely repeatable in its archaic strength.

WRITINGS

'Giornale-strada: Parole in libertà', *Lacerba*, ii/14 (July 1914), p. 213
Campigli: Prefazione dello stesso, xx of *Arte moderna italiana* (Milan, 1931)

BIBLIOGRAPHY

A. Chastel: *Les Idoles de Campigli* (Paris, 1961)
F. Russoli: *Campigli pittore* (Milan, 1965)
Campigli (exh. cat., Milan, Pal. Reale, 1967)
G. Serafini, ed.: *Omaggio a Campigli* (Rome, 1968, 2/1972)
Omaggio a Campigli (exh. cat., intro. M. Carrà; Cortina d'Ampezzo, Gal. A. Mod. Falsetti, 1973)
Massimo Campigli (exh. cat., intro. U. Apollonio; Ferrara, Gal. Civ. A. Mod., 1979)

MATTHEW GALE

Campin, Robert (*b c.* 1375–9; *d* Tournai, 1444). South Netherlandish painter. He is first mentioned in 1405–6 as a painter in Tournai. As he purchased citizenship there in 1410, he may have been born elsewhere. There is evidence of some connection with Valenciennes, where the name Campin is said to have been common, but nothing certain is known of his artistic training and background.

Campin's career can be traced through various Tournai records. He was frequently employed by the municipality from 1408 to 1441 for banners and other decorative ephemera. He also worked on more considerable paintings, in particular in 1428 on a mural in the Halle des Jurez depicting SS Piat and Eleuthère and the King, Queen and Dauphin of France. Alterations to the Halle led to the mural's destruction in 1436, but it was sufficiently esteemed to be copied by another artist before demolition. Campin's polychromy of statues brought him into direct contact with the flourishing Tournai sculptural tradition: he worked not only for the town, as in 1425 when he coloured the figures decorating the Halle des Doyens, but also for various churches, notably that of St Brice in 1408–9. He knew the sculptors as well as their works, for in 1406–7 he appears in the accounts of the executors of the famous sculptor Jacques de Braibant, to whom he had supplied a picture and a cross. Other citizens also employed him: for the executors of Regnault de Vesrain in 1438 he designed a series of paintings on the *Life of St Peter*, to include portraits of Regnault and his wife. The series was executed on cloth by Henri de Beaumetiel to hang like fictive tapestries in the chapel of St Pierre.

Campin was clearly successful, for he owned various properties and had sufficient surplus capital to invest in Tournai stock. He was active in the Corporation of Goldsmiths and Painters and is said to have been sub-dean in 1423 or 1424 and Eswardeur in 1425 and 1427. Through the guild, he was involved in the more democratically organized town government that had ousted the established patrician authorities. When the revolt was crushed, various leaders were punished, and in 1429 Campin was penalized for refusing to testify against one of them. He was sentenced to go on pilgrimage to St Gilles en Provence and to pay a fine. Lingering resentment among the authorities may have contributed to a further prosecution. In 1432 his immorality in living with Laurence Polette in spite of being married to Ysabiel de Stocquain was punished by the sentence of a year's banishment. It was only on the intercession of Margaret of Burgundy, Countess of Hainault and Holland, that this was commuted to a fine. This intervention is Campin's only proven connection with the high nobility of the Netherlands, although he was certainly known to artists outside Tournai. In addition to such associations with independent artists, Campin ran a workshop, employed assistants and took apprentices. His *valets* were given presents by the church of St Brice in 1409–10. In 1419 the son of the painter Gheeraert de Stoevere of Ghent was working in Campin's shop, presumably to acquire skills and expertise unavailable at home. Four of Campin's apprentices are named in the guild list of 1426–8, one of whom, Jacques Daret, had been a member of his household from at least 1418 without the formality of an apprenticeship. A second, Rogelet de Pasture, is reasonably identified with Rogier van der Weyden and would then have been some 27 years old when apprenticed. Like Daret therefore, he is likely to have worked with Campin for some years before registration.

Despite his 'criminal' record, Campin continued to be employed by the municipality, churches and citizens of Tournai until at least three years before his death in 1444. Of all the works documented as his, nothing survives in a satisfactory state to serve as a basis for further attribution. He was paid in 1428 for colouring statues of the *Virgin Annunciate* and the *Archangel Gabriel* (Tournai, Ste Marie-Madeleine) carved by the sculptor JEAN DELEMER for the church of St Pierre in Tournai. The very damaged fragment of a mural *Annunciation*, with two angels, found in the church of St Brice, can be associated with payment to 'Mestre Robert le pointre' in 1406–7. These works provide the best, if tantalizingly inadequate, yardstick by which to judge other attributions, since it is only supposition that tapestries of the *Life of St Peter*, given to Beauvais Cathedral by Bishop Guillaume de Hellande in 1460, reflect Campin's designs for the cloth paintings executed by Beaumetiel. Common features in the works of the MASTER OF FLÉMALLE (*see* MASTERS, ANONYMOUS, AND MONOGRAMMISTS, §I) and those of JACQUES DARET and Rogier van der Weyden (*see* WEYDEN, (1)), both apprenticed to Robert Campin but not otherwise known to have been in contact with each other, have led to a general acceptance of Campin as the artist of the Flémalle oeuvre.

BIBLIOGRAPHY

A. Pinchart: 'Roger de la Pasture dit van der Weyden', *Bull. Comm. Royale A. & Archéol.*, vi (1867), pp. 408–94

——: 'Quelques artistes et quelques artisans de Tournai des XIVe, XVe et XVIe siècles', *Cl. Lett. & Sci. Mor. & Polit.: Bull. Cl. Lett. & Sci. Mor. & Polit. & Cl. B.-A.*, 3rd ser., iv (1882), pp. 559–615

A. de la Grange and L. Cloquet: *Etudes sur l'art à Tournai et sur les anciens artistes de cette ville*, Mémoires de la société historique et littéraire de Tournai, xx, xxi (Tournai, 1887–8)

M. Houtart: *Jacques Daret, peintre tournaisien du XVe siècle* (Tournai, 1907)

E. J. Soil de Moriame: 'L'Eglise-Saint-Brice à Tournai', *An. Soc. Hist. & Archéol. Tournai*, n. s., xii (1908), pp. 73–638

G. Hulin de Loo: 'An Authentic Work by Jacques Daret Painted in 1434', *Burl. Mag.*, xv (1909), pp. 202–8

——: 'Jacques Daret's *Nativity of Our Lord*', *Burl. Mag.*, xix (1911), pp. 218–25

M. Houtart: 'Quel est l'état de nos connaissances relativement à Robert Campin, Jacques Daret et Roger van der Weyden?', *An. Féd. Archéol. & Hist. Belgique XXIIIe congrès: Ghent, 1913*, iii, pp. 88–108

V. van der Haeghen: 'Autour des frères Van Eyck, Cartulaire', *Bull. Soc. Hist. & Archéol. Gand*, xv (1914), pp. 3–67

E. Renders with J. de Smet and L. Bayaert-Carlier: *La Solution du problème van der Weyden-Flémalle-Campin*, 2 vols (Bruges, 1931)

P. Rolland: 'Quelques textes relatives à Robert Campin', *Rev. Belge Archéol. & Hist. A.*, ii (1932), pp. 335–45

——: *Les Primitifs tournaisiens, peintres et sculpteurs* (Brussels and Paris, 1932)

——: *La Peinture murale à Tournai* (Brussels, 1946)

——: 'Les Impératifs historiques de la biographie de Roger', *Rev. Belge Archéol. & Hist. A.*, xviii (1949), pp. 145–61

P. H. Schabacker: 'Notes on the Biography of Robert Campin', *Acad. Anlct.: Kl. S. Kst.*, xli/2 (1980), pp. 1–14

——: 'Observations on the Tournai Painters' Guild with Special Reference to Rogier van der Weyden and Jacques Daret', *Acad. Anlct.: Kl. S. Kst.*, xliii/1 (1982), pp. 9–28

CATHERINE REYNOLDS

Campionesi. Term coined by critics in the 19th century to designate a group of sculptors and architects who were active in northern Italy and elsewhere from the mid-12th century to the late 14th; the name derives from their place of origin, Campione (Campigliono) di Lugano, which in documents often appears after their baptismal names. Some of the masters were related. A distinctive style, marked by solid forms and a robust realism, becomes apparent only in the second half of the 12th century and the first half of the 13th; later it merges with the more general manner of north Italian sculptors and builders from Arogno, Bissone and other places between Lake Como and Lake Lugano.

1. 12TH–13TH CENTURIES. The earliest document mentioning the masters from Campione is a contract dated 30 November 1244 between Ubaldino, Director (*Massaro*) of the Cathedral Works of Modena from 1230 to 1263, and Enrico di Ottavio da Campione, who undertook, on behalf of himself and his heirs, to work for the cathedral *in perpetuum*. This contract was a renewal of an earlier one drawn up between Alberto, Director from 1190 to 1208, and Anselmo, the grandfather of Enrico. The names of Anselmo's three sons, Alberto, Jacopo and Ottavio (father of Enrico), are also cited in the document. From the chronology it can be deduced that in the second half of the 12th century a master from Campione named Anselmo was installed as Master of the Works at the Cathedral, which was consecrated in 1184.

A document dated 1261 mentions that the workshop of the Campionesi was situated on cathedral property between the church and the Ghirlandina bell-tower, but there are no documents allocating responsibility for particular works within the cathedral to a specific master. The rood screen (*see* MODENA, fig. 3) is unanimously attributed to Anselmo and his collaborators; however, its sculptures, datable between *c.* 1175 and 1184, show affinities with Provençal Romanesque (as at Saint-Gilles-du-Gard Abbey, St Trophîme, Arles, and the frieze at Beaucaire), as well as with the work of Benedetto Antelami. Anselmo himself is credited with the *Passion* scenes, from *Christ Washing the Feet of the Disciples* to *Christ Carrying the Cross*. The work of four collaborators can also be identified on the screen. Other works at the cathedral attributed to Anselmo's followers are the pulpit (erected under Bozzalino, Director from 1208 to 1225), the altar, the crypt capitals, work on the façade, including the rose window, and the Porta Regia (1209–31) on the south flank of the nave, which has a porch supported by two columns of ophite, one twisted and the other hexagonal, a characteristic feature of later works by the Campionesi. The last of these masters active at Modena was Enrico II, who completed the Ghirlandina bell-tower (1319) and the free-standing pulpit in the nave (1322).

A number of works have been attributed to the circle of the Modena Campionesi, with varying degrees of certainty. They include the reliefs (1171) of the Porta Romana, Milan (now Milan, Castello Sforzesco), signed by ANSELMUS, whom some critics identify as Anselmo da Campione; four pairs of *Apostles* in red Verona marble (*c.* 1185–7; see fig.) from the old cathedral in Milan, perhaps from its rood screen, built into the inside wall of the north aisle of the present cathedral; the figure of *St Stephen* (Bologna, Mus. S Stefano); and the sculptures praised by Vasari on the Porta dei Leoni (1220; destr.) of

Campionesi (attrib.): *Apostles*, Verona marble, *c.* 1185–7 (Milan Cathedral)

the old cathedral at Bologna (fragments in Bologna Cathedral and Bologna, Pal. Arcivescovile). The masters also worked north of the Alps; they are credited with the sculptures from the dismembered rood screen of Chur Cathedral (*c.* 1178), Switzerland, and the paired *Apostles* at Basle Cathedral, which show the influence of Late Antique models. The capitals (mid-12th century; dispersed, but some, including one bearing the *Last Supper*, still in the church) from S Vitale, Carpineti, probably from a screen, should be considered as antecedents of Antelami's work rather than that of the Campionesi. The red marble shrine under the altar of Parma Cathedral is the work of the Master of Abdon and Sennon (Quintavalle, 1990), a sculptor active in the late 12th century whose style lies midway between that of Antelami and the Campionesi.

Classical influence is also apparent in the style of another sculptor related to the Campionesi: Guido Bigarelli da Arogno (*see* GUIDO DA COMO), who worked in Tuscany *c.* 1250 with his half-brother Lanfranco and other assistants. He made the octagonal font in the baptistery of Pisa (1249) and the pulpit (1250) of S Bartolomeo in Pantano, Pistoia; the architrave of the main portal and some sculptures on the portico of Lucca Cathedral (S Martino) are also attributed to him, while the scenes from the *Life of St Regulus* in the cathedral may be by Lanfranco or a Lombard sculptor of Guido's circle. The work of Adamo d'Arogno and his descendants shows the same artistic background. They built the choir of Trento Cathedral, which, according to an inscription dated 1295, was begun in 1212. The north portal tympanum, representing *Christ in Majesty*, shows the fusion of the Campionesi masters' style with that of Antelami. The workshop responsible for it also produced the porch of Bolzano Cathedral and some sculptures from the old portal of the Franciscan church in Salzburg, of the first half of the 13th century (Salzburg, Burgmus.).

In the second half of the 13th century the style of the Campionesi became less distinctive, as can be seen from such workshop pieces as the *Wheel of Fortune* on the transept façade of Trento Cathedral (by Egidio da Campione), the lions on the porch of Parma Cathedral (by Giambono da Bissone, 1291) and the font of Varese Cathedral. Their interest in early French Gothic sculpture is apparent in the tomb of *Ottone Visconti* (1295) in Milan Cathedral and in that of *Berardo Maggi* (1308) in the old cathedral of Brescia.

2. 14TH CENTURY. In the works of the Campionesi masters active in the 14th century in Lombardy, Romanesque structural elements are blended with Gothic details. Among the most important examples are the tomb of *Cardinal Guglielmo Longhi* (*d* 1319; Bergamo, S Maria Maggiore), attributed to Ugo da Campione, and some of the statues of the Loggia degli Osii (1316–30), Milan. The only personality who emerges clearly is Giovanni da Campione, who signed the baptistery in Bergamo in 1340, one of the porches of S Maria Maggiore, Bergamo, in 1351, and the equestrian statue of *St Alexander*, now in S Maria Maggiore, in 1353. Giovanni is recorded as foreman in the ledger of S Maria Maggiore (1361–3) and as master builder and wood-carver in Bellano. His work shows an

awareness of the sculptures of Nicholaus Balducci and GIOVANNI BALDUCCI (e.g. the *Virtues* on the shrine of St Peter Martyr, 1339; Milan, S Eustorgio), and he favoured such typical motifs of the Campionesi as twisted columns. He was perhaps most adept as an architect, at least to judge by his work on the Bergamo baptistery, an octagonal structure with a colonnade encircling its upper storey. Originally inside S Maria Maggiore, the baptistery was inaccurately rebuilt outside the church; a drawing made in 1660 (see D. Calvi: *Effemeride* (Milan, 1676–7)) shows the main lines of the original structure and reveals that the sculptural cycles have been rearranged. The last Campionesi master active in Bergamo was Nicolino di Giovanni (*d* 1364).

Among the Campionesi active in the second half of the 14th century, the most eminent was Bonino da Campione (*fl* 1357; *d* ?1397), who was probably trained in Bergamo under Giovanni. Gothic elements appear in three dated works by him: the signed tomb of *Folchino degli Schizzi* (*d* 1357) in Cremona Cathedral; the monument to *Bernabò Visconti* (equestrian statue, 1363, sarcophagus, 1380–85; both Milan, Castello Sforzesco), formerly in S Giovanni in Conca, Milan; and the signed tomb of *Cansignorio della Scala* (*d* 1375) at S Maria Antica, Verona (*see* VERONA, §3(iii); for illustration *see* SCALA, DELLA). The last, dated 1370–76, includes a recumbent effigy, guardian angels and three reliefs on the sarcophagus; signed BONINUS DE CAMPIGLIONO MEDIOLANENSIS DIOCESIS, it also shows the work of collaborators, both Campionesi and local assistants. Works attributed to Bonino include the tomb of *Bishop Balduino Lambertini* (*d* 1349) in the old cathedral at Brescia; parts of the restored mausoleum of *Stefano and Lambertina Visconti* (1352; Milan, S Eustorgio); the frontal of the sarcophagus of *Protaso Camaini* (Milan, S Eustorgio); and probably the tomb of *Regina della Scala* (1384; Milan, Castello Sforzesco).

The last of the Lombard Campionesi was Matteo da Campione (*d* 1396), architect and sculptor at Monza Cathedral; he built its façade (characterized by an abundance of decorative elements), the pulpit and the baptistery (destr.). In 1388–9 he was in Milan, working at the cathedral, and in 1390 he refused to become director of the cathedral works. The cathedral annals cite the names of numerous other Campionesi architects and sculptors, including Zeno (whom some critics consider to be its first architect), Giacomo, who carved the relief above the sacristy door (1390) and Alberto II (*fl* 1404).

BIBLIOGRAPHY

DBI; *EWA*; Thieme–Becker

[C. Borghi]: *Il Duomo ossia Cenni storici e descrittivi della Cattedrale di Modena* (Modena, 1845), pp. 33–4, 77–81

G. Campori: *Gli artisti italiani e stranieri negli stati estensi* (Modena, 1855), pp. 116–17

G. Merzario: *I maestri comacini: Storia artistica di mille duecento anni (600–1800)*, i (Milan, 1893), pp. 242–52

A. Dondi: *Notizie storiche ed artistiche del Duomo di Modena* (Modena, 1896), pp. 16–18, 53–5, 185–6

A. Venturi: *Storia* (1901–40)

C. Baroni: *Scultura gotica lombarda* (Milan, 1944)

P. Toesca: *Il trecento* (Turin, 1951)

G. de Francovich: *Benedetto Antelami architetto e scultore e l'arte del suo tempo*, i–ii (Milan and Florence, 1952), pp. 45–109

E. Arslan: 'La scultura romanica', *Storia di Milano*, iii (Milan, 1954), pp. 591–600

F. De Maffei: *Le arche scaligere di Verona* (Verona, 1954), pp. 73–87

C. Baroni: 'La scultura gotica', *Storia di Milano*, v (1955), pp. 729–812

A. C. Quintavalle: *La Cattedrale di Modena: Problemi di romanico emiliano* (Modena, 1964), pp. 247–55

R. Salvini: *Il Duomo di Modena* (Modena and Milan, 1972), pp. 55–61

W. Montorsi: *La Torre della Ghirlandina: Comacini e Campionesi a Modena* (Modena, 1976), pp. 135–54

——: *Iscrizioni modenesi romaniche e gotiche: Duomo e Palazzo del Comune con un'appendice sulla Torre* (Modena, 1977), pp. 277–83

A. C. Quintavalle: *Benedetto Antelami* (Milan, 1990)

G. L. Mellini: 'L'arca di Cansignorio di Bonino da Campione a Verona', *I maestri campionesi*, ed. R. Bossaglia and G. A. Dell'Acqua (Bergamo, 1992) pp. 173–97

ROBERTO CORONEO

Campo, Pedro Fernández del. *See* MEJORADA, Marqués de.

Camponovo, Antonio (*b* Medrissio, Ticino, 1850; *d* Buenos Aires, 1938). Swiss architect, active in Bolivia. He studied at the Politecnico, Turin. At the end of the 1860s he emigrated to Argentina and was later in Sucre, Bolivia, where with his brother Miguel Camponovo he planned and built the Banco Nacional (begun 1872). Its style is derived from early Renaissance forms, with characteristic mullioned windows, and it is among the first examples in Bolivia of eclecticism, which was then in fashion in the European academies. He also worked on the Palacio de Gobierno (begun 1892), Sucre (*see* BOLIVIA, §II, 2(i)), and designed private houses, such as the country house (*quinta*) El Guereo, outside Sucre, and the Palacio de la Glorieta (*c*. 1900), Sucre, for the Argandoña family, which combines elements of the Romanesque, Renaissance, Arabic and neo-classical styles in one of the most richly eclectic buildings in Bolivia. In 1900 he went to La Paz, which had been made the capital of Bolivia in the previous year, to oversee the completion of the cathedral (for illustration *see* LA PAZ), begun *c*. 1830 by Manuel de Sanahuja. After disputes with the Jesuit architect Eulalio Morales, Camponovo's neo-classical design, which conformed with that of Sanahuja, was accepted. By 1905 he had completed the interior decoration (using a Corinthian order), the second storey of the main façade and the dome above the transept. He also built the Palacio Legislativo (1900–08), La Paz, a neo-classical structure focused on two main debating halls. His other works in La Paz include his own house in El Prado, a building of elegant eclecticism, and a new façade and the interior decoration (1909) for the Teatro Municipal.

WRITINGS

La catedral de La Paz (La Paz, 1900)

BIBLIOGRAPHY

T. Gisbert and J. de Mesa: *Monumentos de Bolivia* (La Paz, 1978), pp. 128, 132–3, 150–52

TERESA GISBERT

Camporese. Italian family of architects. Their building activities in Rome and its vicinity span the century between the Enlightenment and the Risorgimento, throughout which they maintained ties with the Accademia di S Luca in Rome as students, professors and administrators. They were also linked by Pasquale Belli, who was taught by (1) Pietro Camporese (i), became his assistant and later taught Pietro's sons (2) Giulio Camporese and (3) Giuseppe Camporese and Giulio's son (4) Pietro Camporese (ii).

(1) Pietro Camporese (i) (*b* Rome, 20 Oct 1726; *d* Rome, 1781). He studied at the Accademia di S Luca with

Francesco Nicoletti (*c.* 1700–76). A student competition project for a cathedral complex (1754; Rome, Accad. N. S Luca; see Marconi, nos 500–03) suggests that he began his career with a conservative temperament, favouring neither the waning Rococo nor the emerging Neo-classicism of Giovanni Battista Piranesi's generation. This conservatism is also apparent in his completion (1774) of the upper register of the façade of S Maria in Aquiro, Rome; Francesco da Volterra's design remained unfinished from 1590, and Pietro remained faithful to the original style.

Pietro was admitted to membership of the Accademia in 1775, upon the accession of his principal patron, Pius VI. At about that time Pius commissioned him to build the cathedral of S Andrea at Subiaco. In the intervening decades since his competition design, however, he had settled upon a personal compromise between his academic training and recent architectural trends. The cathedral is comprised of traditional, 16th-century forms expressed in a Neo-classical language. Together with the adjoining Palazzo del Seminario (1715), the extension of which he took over from Carlo Colombi di Merate (*fl* mid-18th century), the cathedral forms a complex of severe masses standing like a fortress on the high escarpment overlooking the valley of the River Aniene. The buildings were completed to Pietro's designs by his sons in 1789. The family's work at Subiaco, which also included an arch dedicated to Pius VI, began to establish its reputation for stone- and brickwork of the highest technical quality, reviving ancient practices on the advice of such contemporary theorists as Johann Joachim Winckelmann.

After 1775 Pietro collaborated with Michelangelo Simonetti on the construction of the Museo Pio-Clementino in the Vatican, where (3) Giuseppe Camporese also worked (see below; *see also* MUSEUM, fig. 4, and DISPLAY OF ART, fig. 2). About 1779 he restored the church of S Orsula for the Ursuline convent (now the Conservatorio di S Cecilia) at Rome. The interior (now a theatre) is entirely white and detailed with austere elegance. Also by Pietro, but of unknown date, is the Palazzo del Collegio Germanico, on the Via della Scrofa in Rome. Its brick veneer is meant to echo the nearby façade of the Palazzo di S Apollinare (1745) by Ferdinando Fuga, but its severity and brooding melancholy are Pietro's.

(2) Giulio Camporese (*b* Rome, 1754; *d* Rome, 1 Nov 1840). Son of (1) Pietro Camporese (i). He studied with his father and Pasquale Belli. All his building activity was carried out as assistant to his father or in partnership with his brother (3) Giuseppe Camporese. The last decades of his career were spent solely as lecturer in architecture at the Accademia di S Luca, of which he became a member in 1812. The politics of the period may have cost him commissions, since he seems to have had liberal leanings that supported Napoleon's new order in Italy. His admission piece for the Accademia (Rome, Accad. N. S Luca; see Marconi, nos 2242–4) was a *mnemacheo* or 'archive-cum-memorial' to Napoleon's victories, military and cultural. It is a blatant example of Roman revival architecture as imperial propaganda.

(3) Giuseppe Camporese (*b* Rome, 1763; *d* Rome, 15 March 1822). Son of (1) Pietro Camporese (i). He studied with his father and with Pasquale Belli. Together with his contemporary Raffaele Stern he must be considered among the first architects to define 19th-century Roman architecture by merging academic traditions with Neo-classical purism. Between 1786 and 1791, while finishing his father's projects in Subiaco, Giuseppe joined the work on the Vatican museums (see above). He finished the rooms left incomplete at Simonetti's death and made his own contribution in the design of the Atrio dei Quattro Cancelli, the monumental entrance to the museums. The exterior of this two-storey, domed structure is a hybrid of Roman tomb architecture and Jacopo Vignola's classicism, executed in the family tradition of the finest quality of materials and workmanship. The upper level contains the Sala della Biga, a rotunda articulated by engaged columns with an alternating scheme of niches and arched window bays. The rather mechanical coolness and precision of this classicism extends even to the colours and grains of the marbles.

In 1798 Giuseppe was admitted to the Accademia di S Luca. During the period of French rule (1809–14) he directed the commission on highways and bridges for the region around Rome, and within the city he oversaw excavations in the Forum Romanum (1810–13) and the Forum of Trajan (1812–13). His designs for the parish churches of Genzano di Roma and Carbognano (nr Caprarola), Lazio, perpetuated the ideals set forth by his father at Subiaco. In 1821 Giuseppe saw to the remodelling, along similar lines, of the church and convent of S Maria di Monserrato in Rome. The church, begun in 1518 by Antonio da Sangallo (ii), was remade into a 19th-century purist's version of the church architecture of Andrea Palladio.

(4) Pietro Camporese (ii) (*b* Rome, 22 May 1792; *d* Rome, 1873). Son of (2) Giulio Camporese. He studied at the Accademia di S Luca with his father and Pasquale Belli, and nearly all his work was carried out in Rome. In 1823 fire destroyed the basilica of S Paolo fuori le Mura, and Pietro was appointed to the committee of architects that oversaw its rebuilding under Belli's direction. His experiences here no doubt reinforced his familial inclinations toward a dry, rational and academic classical revivalism. Between 1831 and 1846 he restored the hospital of S Giacomo in Augusta (degli Incurabili) and remodelled the façades adjacent to its church and along the Via Antonio Canova. Here antique and Renaissance motifs were distilled to the simplest possible contours and details and yet powerfully modelled, as proof of the architect's pedigree. He also restored the church of SS Vito e Modesto (1834) and the Teatro Argentina (1837).

Pietro's façade for the Palazzo Wedekind on the Piazza Colonna dates from 1838. To what was then a pontifical post office, he added a Renaissance Revival front and attached a portico of 16 Ionic columns supporting a terrace. 12 of the columns came from the Porticus Augusta (late 1st century BC) excavated at Veii in 1812–17, but accents at the centre and ends of the colonnade give it a 16th-century character as much as an antiquarian one. The real success of the design lies in the way that the 'stoa' gives new sense to the urban space of the piazza, dramatizing its relationship to the column of Marcus Aurelius and Via del Corso beyond while providing more shelter for public activity. In the design of the Istituto di Belle Arti (1845) for Gregory XVI, Pietro again tried to draw advantage from a difficult urban situation. With its back to the River Tiber and its front on the narrow Via di Ripetta, the building embraces the street through the horseshoe plan at the centre of the façade and in turn enlivens an otherwise monotonous and confining street contour. The design fails in its detailing, however, which lacks the grandeur appropriate to the plan and is executed in the poorest materials. In that regard, the impoverishment of the papacy in recent years could no longer support the standards that the Camporese family had once championed. The same could be said of his reconstruction of the Ospedale degli Orfanelli on the Piazza Capranica, with its plain stuccoed façades and courtyard arches of brick in thin beds of mortar.

In the early 1870s Pietro was put in charge of the commission planning the expansion of the city as the new capital of a united Italy. As president of the Accademia di S Luca, he also served on the jury for the design of the façade of Florence Cathedral.

BIBLIOGRAPHY

E. Lavagnino: *L'arte moderna dai neoclassici ai contemporanei*, 2 vols (Turin, 1956), pp. 20–21, 52–4, 274–6
C. L. V. Meeks: *Italian Architecture, 1750–1914* (New Haven, 1966)
P. Marconi, A. Cipriani and E. Valeriani: *I disegni di architettura dell'archivio storico dell'Accademia di San Luca*, 2 vols (Rome, 1974)

GIL R. SMITH

Campori, Giuseppe, Marchese (*b* Modena, 17 Jan 1821; *d* Modena, 19 July 1887). Italian historian and collector. He began his publications in 1844 with a guide to the paintings from Modena in the Belvedere, Vienna. In 1846 he began his long association with the journal *Archivio storico italiano*, where many of his studies of Modena and the Este (i) family were published, the only interruption coming after the unification of Italy, when he was briefly involved in politics, holding public office in 1860 and again in 1864. In the early 1860s the archives of the Este family were opened, and this led Campori to supervise the printing of several collections of documentary material, notably those published in 1866 and 1870. He collaborated on many of the new periodicals in Italy, in particular the *Nuova antologia* in Florence and the *Giornale storico della letteratura italiana* in Turin. All this time he was writing, and at his death his publications numbered more than 225 items. He left his numerous works of art to the Galleria e Museo Estense in Modena; they now form the Galleria Campori. His books, prints and letters were given to the Biblioteca Estense, Modena, where they constitute the Fondo Campori, as well as to the Biblioteca Comunale and the Biblioteca dell' Accademia Nazionale di Scienze, Lettere ed Arti.

WRITINGS

Delle opere di pittori modenesi che si conservano nell'imperiale Galleria del Belvedere in Vienna (Modena, 1844)
Lettere artistiche inedite (Modena, 1866)
Raccolta di cataloghi ed inventarii inediti di quadri, statue, disegni, bronzi, dorerie, smalti, medaglie, avorii, ecc dal secolo XV al secolo XIX (Modena, 1870)

BIBLIOGRAPHY

DBI

DAVID CAST

Camprobín (Passano), Pedro de (*b* Almagro, 1605; *d* Seville, 22 July 1674). Spanish painter. The son of a silversmith, he was apprenticed between 1619 and 1624 to Luis Tristán de Escamilla in Toledo, where he became acquainted with developments in the new genre of still-life. He was examined and certified as *maestro pintor* in Seville in June 1630, after which his activity there as a painter is documented with regularity. His earliest dated painting and only known religious work is a signed *Magdalene* (1634; Seville, El Salvador). In 1660, together with Bartolomé Esteban Murillo, Francisco de Herrera (ii) and Juan de Valdés Leal, he was among the founders of the Academia de Bellas Artes.

Camprobín's earliest signed still-lifes (Santander, Botín priv. col., and Madrid, priv. col.) clearly reveal the influence of Francisco and Juan de Zurbarán and must date from the late 1630s or 1640s. His earliest dated still-lifes, for instance *Still-life with Game Fowl* (1653; Dallas, TX, S. Methodist U., Meadows Mus. & Gal.), reveal an independent spirit. His best-known works are his elegant, airy flower pieces, still-lifes of fruit and banquet pieces, some with landscape or architectural vistas, painted in the 1660s (e.g. *Bodegón*; Madrid, priv. col., see exh. cat., 1983, p. 77).

Camprobín's delicate technique involved the application of fluid paint and thin glazes of colour over a rather friable ground and has rendered his canvases especially vulnerable to careless restoration. His well-preserved still-lifes reveal an artist of unexpected finesse.

BIBLIOGRAPHY

Céan Bermúdez
H. Sancho Corbacho: *Documentos para la historia del arte en Andalucía* (Madrid, 1930), ii, p. 270
J. Cavestany: *Floreros y bodegones en la pintura española* (Madrid, 1936–40), pp. 78–9
I. Bergström: *Maestros españoles de bodegones y floreros del siglo XVII* (Madrid, 1970), pp. 43–5
E. Valdivieso: 'Nuevos datos y obras de Pedro Camprobín', *Rev. A. Sevill.*, iii (1983), pp. 72–5
Pintura española de bodegones y floreros de 1600 a Goya (exh. cat. by A. E. Pérez Sánchez, Madrid, Prado, 1983), pp. 77–8
Spanish Still-life in the Golden Age: 1600–50 (exh. cat. by W. B. Jordan, Fort Worth, TX, Kimbell A. Mus., 1985), pp. 23–5

WILLIAM B. JORDAN

Camuccini. Italian family of dealers, collectors and painters.

(1) Pietro Camuccini (*b* Rome, 1 July 1761; *d* Rome, 1833). During the early 19th century he was one of the most prominent dealers in Rome and, with his brother (2) Vincenzo Camuccini, the owner of a fine collection of Old Masters. After giving up his apprenticeship with Domenico Corvi in 1783 or 1784 in favour of his brother, whose talent as a painter was greater than his, he began dealing in antiquities, prints and paintings. He was able to support Vincenzo (both parents having died) and introduced him to artists, dealers and collectors espousing Neo-classicism, including Angelica Kauffman, Antonio Zucchi, Thomas Jenkins, Giovanni Volpato and Alexander Day. Among the foreign collectors of his acquaintance was the eccentric Frederick Augustus Hervey, Bishop of Derry (later 4th Earl of Bristol), for whom Pietro acquired several antiquities and 16th- and 17th-century paintings. It was with Pietro acting as intermediary that Hervey commissioned Vincenzo in 1793 to paint the *Death of Caesar* and in 1800 the companion piece, the *Death of Virginia* (both Naples, Capodimonte). From the 1780s Pietro's taste and artistic interests influenced Vincenzo, who first came across the works of earlier masters, notably Poussin, through engravings collected by Pietro, who also suggested that Vincenzo make an intense study of works by Raphael and Michelangelo in the Vatican, Rome.

The collection formed by the two brothers consisted of 74 paintings, mostly acquired from Roman palaces, including a *Sunset Landscape* by Claude, a *Crucifixion* by Guercino (both Alnwick Castle, Northumb.) and *Feast of the Gods* (Washington, DC, N.G.A.) by Giovanni Bellini (finished by Titian). The collection was sold by Vincenzo's son in 1853 to Algernon Percy, 4th Duke of Northumberland (whose agent had valued it at £2500 in 1850). With the proceeds the former bought a castle at Cantalupo in Sabina, near Rome.

UNPUBLISHED SOURCES

Cantalupo in Sabina, Pal. Camuccini [MS. of T. Barberi: *Catalogo ragionato della Galleria Camuccini* (*c.* 1851); another copy Alnwick Castle, Northumb. Archv]

BIBLIOGRAPHY

DBI

A. Constantin: *Idées italiennes sur quelques tableaux célèbres* (Florence, 1840)

C. Falconieri: *Vita di V. Camuccini* (Rome, 1875)

Vincenzo Camuccini, 1771–1844: Bozzettie disegni dallo studio dell'artista (exh. cat., ed. G. P. De Angelis; Rome, G.N.A. Mod., 1978)

I. Ceccopieri: *Miscellanea della società romana di storia patria XXXII, l'archivo Camuccini: Inventario* (Rome, 1990)

Exploring Rome: Piranesi and his Contemporaries (exh. cat., ed. C. D. Denison; Montreal, Cent. Can. Archit.; New York, Pierpoint Morgan Lib.; 1993–4)

(2) Vincenzo Camuccini (*b* Rome, 22 Feb 1771; *d* Rome, 2 Sept 1844). Brother of (1) Pietro Camuccini. From an early age he was assisted and encouraged by Pietro, who had given up his place in the studio of Domenico Corvi to Vincenzo. The younger brother's earliest known painting, the *Sacrifice of Noah* (1785; Cantalupo in Sabina, Pal. Camuccini), is a competent work demonstrating his use of Corvi's technique of chiaroscuro. Between 1787 and 1789, on the advice of Pietro, Vincenzo undertook an intensive study of Michelangelo's and Raphael's frescoes at the Vatican. He also studied archaeology with Ennio Quirino Visconti, who introduced him to leading ecclesiastics within the papal court of Pope Pius VI. It was probably through his brother that Vincenzo met Frederick Augustus Hervey, Bishop of Derry (later 4th Earl of Bristol), who commissioned from him a copy (1789) of Raphael's *Entombment* (both Rome, Gal. Borghese). His familiarity with the art of the High Renaissance and with 17th-century Roman art is eloquently displayed in his drawings from *c.* 1787. In *Joseph Interpreting the Dreams* (*c.* 1795; Florence, Uffizi), for example, he is clearly influenced by the monumental quality of Michelangelo's figures. He produced drawings of antique sculpture after plaster casts and such originals as Trajan's Column, the heroic reliefs of which helped shape his interpretation of Roman history. His many drawings reveal a fluid technique and lively artistic imagination.

The Classical tradition in Rome was sustained in the 17th century, particularly through the work of Poussin, and was reinforced in the early 18th century by archaeological excavations at Pompeii and Herculaneum. For Camuccini's circle, Winckelmann's writings on the Antique were an important source of inspiration, as were Neo-classical works by such foreign artists resident in Rome as Anton Raphael Mengs (e.g. *Parnassus with Apollo and the Muses*, 1760–61; Rome, Villa Torlonia) and Gavin Hamilton (e.g. *Helen and Paris*, 1782–4; ex-Gal. Borghese, Rome; Rome, Pal. Braschi). Indeed, Camuccini's *Finding of Paris* (*c.* 1796; Rome, Gal. Borghese) is close to Hamilton's style. Artists who painted in a similar style, for example Pietro Benvenuti, Giuseppe Bossi and Luigi Sabatelli, had all worked in Rome and had known Camuccini well but had moved to either Milan or Florence in the early years of the 19th century, leaving him as the pre-eminent painter in Rome. The profound influence of Jacques-Louis David on Neo-classical artists in Rome cannot be underestimated, particularly after the *Oath of the Horatii* (1784; Paris, Louvre) was exhibited there in 1785. This painting marks a final break with the rhythmic fluency of earlier paintings with strong classicizing tendencies, and its subject-matter—the superseding of personal loyalty by civic duty—also set a new standard. Although Camuccini aspired to paint such themes, those paintings of his most like David's (e.g. *Pompey Urged to Defend the State*, *c.* 1810; Rome, Pal. Taverna Monte Giordano) were not painted until over 20 years later during the French occupation of Rome (1809–14).

In 1793 Camuccini was commissioned by Hervey to do a large painting of the *Death of Caesar* (Naples, Capodimonte). The cartoon was completed and exhibited in 1796 and achieved immediate fame. He then began work on the painting, completing it in 1799. When exhibited, it was criticized as having 'no depth' and being 'dull and dark' in colour (Falconieri, p. 46). He destroyed it and by 1818 had produced a new version, now in Naples (*see* ITALY, fig. 42). The subject was highly topical, giving full expression to Republican ideals. He was exact in his interpretation of the source (Plutarch's writings) and, assisted by Visconti, endeavoured to depict the setting and costumes as accurately as possible; for example, the statue of Pompey on the left side of the painting was modelled on the statue of the same subject in the Galleria Spada in Rome. He chose the moment before Julius Caesar was stabbed to death, using as his source the scene described in Vittorio Alfieri's play *Brutus II* (1789). The painting's companion piece, the *Death of Virginia* (Naples, Capodimonte), was commissioned in 1800 and finally completed in 1804. In this case, the subject was taken from Livy's *History of Rome* and from Charles Rollin's *Histoire romaine* (1738–48). Camuccini depicted the moment when Virginia's father curses the tyrant Appius, who has attempted to enslave his daughter and who is prevented from doing so by the father, who kills his daughter with his sword. The theme of the painting is again a noble one: the shedding of innocent blood to preserve virtue and freedom. The success of these works established Camuccini's reputation in Rome and abroad.

In 1802 Camuccini became a member of the Accademia di S Luca, his presentation piece being a *bozzetto* of the

Death of Virginia (Rome, Gal. Accad. N. S Luca). He taught at the Accademia and was its Principal from 1806 to 1810. A contemporary source recording his election as Principal commented on his youth and said that, more than any other painter, he had 'studied Raphael in great depth' (Missirini, p. 345). In 1803 Pope Pius VII nominated him Director of the mosaic workshop at St Peter's, and he executed for the church a mosaic of the *Incredulity of Thomas* (1806–22). The Pope appreciated his abilities and in 1814 made him Superintendent of the Apostolic Palaces. In his religious paintings (*c.* 1800–10) he still used chiaroscuro in the manner of his early teacher, Corvi (e.g. *Presentation of the Virgin*, 1806; Piacenza, S Giovanni in Canale). In addition to the large number of commissions for biblical or historical scenes, he executed several portraits, somewhat reluctantly as he considered this to be an inferior genre. Among the most striking are those of family or friends (e.g. *Bertel Thorvaldsen*, 1808; Rome, Gal. Accad. N. S Luca). In more formal commissions he combined acute observation with an awareness of regal dignity (e.g. *Maria Luisa Bourbon, Duquesa di Lucca*, *c.* 1811; Florence, Pitti). In the most sensitive of his official portraits—*Pius VII* (1815; Vienna, Ksthist. Mus.; see fig. 1)—the pose is taken from Raphael's portrait of *Julius II* (Florence, Uffizi). The portrait of the King of Naples, *Ferdinand I* (1819–20; Naples, Pal. Reale), was painted in the grandiose manner of Pompeo Batoni. He also painted a later, unfinished *Self-portrait* (*c.* 1830; Cantalupo in Sabina, Pal. Camuccini).

In 1810 Camuccini visited Paris and Munich and was received with suitable honours. In Paris he was presented to Napoleon and was invited to dine with David. It was probably on this visit that Vincenzo bought the most outstanding acquisition in the brothers' collection, the

1. Vincenzo Camuccini: *Pius VII*, oil on canvas, 1.36×1.13 m, 1815 (Vienna, Kunsthistorisches Museum)

Madonna dei Garofani by Raphael (London, N.G., on loan). However, the painting, which was from a French collection, was not in Rome until the late 1820s. In Munich he made a study (Cantalupo in Sabina, Pal. Camuccini) after Poussin's *Lamentation* (Munich, Alte Pin.), paying particular attention to the painter's subtle gradations of light and dark to enhance compositional structure. He returned to Rome in 1811 and was chosen, along with such artists as Gaspare Landi and Felice Giani, to assist in the redecoration of the Palazzo del Quirinale for the proposed arrival of Napoleon. Camuccini was allowed to select for the central salon two subjects based on the theme of the illustrious patronage of arts and letters. Using Raphael's Stanze in the Vatican as his inspiration, he painted *Charlemagne Summoning Italian and German Scholars to Found a University of Paris* and *Ptolemy III among Scholars Brought to the Library of Alexandria* (both 1811–13; ex-Pal. Quirinale, Rome; Rome, Pal. Montecitorio).

After the French occupation of Rome, he remained pre-eminent in the art life of the city. In 1826 Ferdinand I put him in charge of the reorganization of the royal picture collection at Naples, and in 1830 Pius VIII made him a baron and entrusted him with the reorganization of the art collection at the Vatican museums. In 1833, when Raphael's body was exhumed from the Pantheon, he was asked by the Accademia dei Virtuosi to provide the official drawing of his remains. In the 1830s and 1840s he employed several studio assistants, including Francesco Podesti and Natale Carta (1790–1884), to help him with his numerous commissions. From this time his subjects were derived almost entirely from Roman sources. *Virgil Reading the Aeneid to the Family of Augustus* (*c.* 1819; Cantalupo in Sabina, Pal. Camuccini) was published in an edition by Annibale Caro of Virgil's *Aeneid* (Rome, 1819), and the *Continence of Scipio* (*c.* 1833; see fig. 2) was composed in the manner of a Roman frieze. His last Roman subject—*Camillus Liberating the Capitol from the Gauls* (1840; Genoa, Pal. Reale)—was commissioned by Charles-Albert, King of Sardinia, and fulfils all the formal and aesthetic ideals of Neo-classicism that were beginning to be challenged by the Puristi (*see* PURISMO) and by the emerging Romantic movement. The Nazarene painter Friedrich Overbeck openly expressed his criticism of Camuccini's *Deposition* (*c.* 1836; Cantalupo in Sabina, Pal. Camuccini), and it remained unfinished for lack of payment (Falconieri, p. 266). The Puristi also criticized his use of references to the 17th century found in *St Paul Raised to the Third Heaven* (1840; Ostia, Basilica). Such references also appear in an earlier series of 84 scenes of the *Life of Christ* (Cantalupo in Sabina, Pal. Camuccini). These were published as lithographs (Rome, 1829) and formed a significant contribution to the religious art of the pontificate of Leo XII.

Camuccini suffered a stroke early in 1842; although he continued to paint, most of his late works remain unfinished. He was aware of the changes in artistic taste and the move away from academicism, and after his death the considerable reputation he had enjoyed was undermined by the disdain of the Puristi for moralizing history painting. Willard (p. 249) has attributed the decline of his reputation to the poor quality of engravings after his works. Another factor is that his portraits, which are among his best works,

2. Vincenzo Camuccini: *Continence of Scipio*, oil on canvas, *c.* 1833 (Vienna, Kunsthistorisches Museum)

have been scattered in various collections, and there is scant knowledge of the approximately 300 drawings and oil sketches preserved by his heirs.

UNPUBLISHED SOURCES

Cantalupo in Sabina, Pal. Camuccini Archv [lett. and ntbks]

BIBLIOGRAPHY

M. Missirini: *Memorie per scrive alle storia Romana Accademia di S Luca* (Rome, 1823)
C. Falconieri: *Vita di V. Camuccini* (Rome, 1875)
A. R. Willard: *History of Modern Italian Art* (London, 1889)
F. Pfister: 'Disegni di Vincenzo Camuccini', *Boll. A.: Min. Pub. Istruzione*, n.s., viii (1928), pp. 21–30
U. Heisinger: 'The Paintings of Vincenzo Camuccini', *A. Bull.*, ix (1978), pp. 297–313
Vincenzo Camuccini: Bozzetti e disegni (exh. cat., ed. G. P. De Angelis; Rome, G.N.A. Mod., 1978)
N. Penny: 'Raphael's *Madonna dei garofani* Rediscovered', *Burl. Mag.*, cxxxiv (1992), p. 67
Exploring Rome: Piranesi and his Contemporaries (exh. cat., ed. C. D. Denison; Montreal, Cent. Can. Archit.; New York, Pierpont Morgan Lib.; 1993–4)

LUCINDA LUBBOCK

Camus, Louis-Denis Le. *See* LE CAMUS, LOUIS-DENIS.

Camus, Pierre Duval Le. *See* DUVAL LE CAMUS, PIERRE.

Camus de Mézières, Nicolas Le. *See* LE CAMUS DE MÉZIÈRES, NICOLAS.

Canaanite. People who inhabited coastal Syria, Lebanon and Palestine between *c.* 3000 BC and *c.* 1200 BC. Although there were dialects and regional variations, the Canaanites shared a common language and material culture. 'Canaanite' is an ethnic name possibly derived from the Akkadian word *kinahna* (purple), referring to the purple dye produced from a gland of the murex snail. Similarly, the descendants of the Canaanites, the PHOENICIANS, bore a name derived from the Greek word for purple, *phoinikes*. The dye, which varied in colour from scarlet to purple, was the most conspicuous and expensive product of the coastal region of the eastern Mediterranean and became closely linked with royalty. The date of origin of the Canaanites is disputed, although there is a growing recognition of continuity from *c.* 3000 BC. The distinction between Canaanites and Phoenicians in *c.* 1200 BC is artificial: there is no evidence to suggest that the Phoenicians came from elsewhere, and every reason to treat them as autochthonous.

The Canaanites spoke a West Semitic language closely related to Hebrew and Arabic. Their most outstanding achievements were linguistic. The Ugaritic texts (*see* UGARIT) reveal their religion and literature and show that the poetry of the Hebrew Bible owes much to Canaanite literature. Even more important was their invention of the alphabet (*c.* 1400 BC). All present-day alphabets are derived from the Canaanite original. Canaanite religion was essentially a nature/fertility cult in keeping with an agriculture-based economy and society. The most important deity, Baal, was both a weather god and a chthonic deity; his spouse, Anat, was a fertility goddess (*see also* SYRIA-PALESTINE, §I, 3(ii)). Canaanite social organization was feudal, with a multitude of local baronies. It is possible that in the Middle Bronze Age (*c.* 2000–*c.* 1600 BC) there was a larger kingdom in southern Canaan with its capital at HAZOR.

The most important aspects of Canaanite art are its eclecticism and aniconic tendency. Canaanite artists drew inspiration from their more powerful neighbours in all periods. This reflects both their strategic position between the Aegean, Anatolia, Mesopotamia, inland Syria and Egypt, and their role as traders between these regions.

Nevertheless it would be a mistake to see Canaanite art as derivative and unoriginal since it is also distinctively Canaanite, the borrowed motifs being altered to suit their tastes and express their themes. The potency of this art may be judged from its effect on the Greeks: the Greek sphinx, for example, which is winged and female, is derived from the Canaanite sphinx, which combines both Egyptian and Mesopotamian elements. From the beginning the Canaanites were artistically impoverished compared with their neighbours. Rather than religious images, their temples contained aniconic standing stones; non-geometric decoration on pottery was rare. It is no accident that the aniconic Jewish and Islamic religions later emerged from this region, as well as the Iconoclastic movement in the Byzantine Christian community.

The Canaanites excelled in metalwork—such as the repoussé bowls known from Ugarit—and ivory-carving. A fragment of ivory inlay from Megiddo shows a Canaanite king receiving a victorious army with prisoners. The side of the throne is in the form of a Canaanite sphinx (see fig.). Their pottery, however, was dull and uninspired compared with Minoan and Mycenaean products. Red slip and burnish was used throughout their ceramic tradition. Middle Bronze Age pottery was decorated with horizontal lines of red-and-black paint, often separated by pendent or upright triangles, or by a zigzag line. Late Bronze Age pottery (*c.* 1600–*c.* 1200 BC) was decorated with bands of red-and-black paint arranged in a pattern of triglyphs and metopes, which were frequently filled with the Tree of Life motif, sometimes with goats or ibexes rampant on either side of the tree.

In the Early Bronze Age (*c.* 3500–*c.* 2000 BC) cylinder seals with geometric motifs were produced. In the Late Bronze Age they produced vast numbers of scarabs, which used hieroglyphics purely as decorative motifs without regard to their meaning in the Egyptian script. They produced no large-scale sculpture; the small-scale works—metal and ceramic figurines—are crude compared with works from Mesopotamia and Egypt. The Middle Bronze Age tombs of JERICO (19th–17th centuries BC) yielded attractively simple furniture imitating the Egyptian style. Wooden items, such as boxes, were inlaid with ivory, bone or mother-of-pearl. Canaanites depicted in Egyptian tomb paintings are shown producing cloth dyed or woven in brightly coloured stripes, a practice recalled in the biblical story of Joseph's 'coat of many colours' (Genesis 37:3).

The architecture of the Canaanites is limited by their poor economic status. Only at Ugarit is there known to have been a wealthy polity whose rulers could afford large-scale building projects. The Canaanite house followed no standard plan but was built to suit the available space and had a courtyard with a number of small rooms opening off it. There are no indications of stairs to an upper storey, but the roof, reached by wooden ladders, was used as a living area. The royal palace at Ugarit represents the summit of Canaanite architecture (for illustration *see* UGARIT). At first it was a small building comprising two wings. The public wing was entered via a small portico, and the entrance hall was flanked by a guardroom, from which a door opened into the throne-room; this arrangement is known as a *bit hilani.* The private wing, reached by a doorway from the throne-room, consisted of a series of rooms surrounding a small courtyard. The thickness of the walls indicates that there was an upper storey. Through the course of the Late Bronze Age successive Ugaritic kings added larger and more elaborate versions of the original *bit hilani*, as well as a multitude of small rooms and courtyards for the domestic and administrative functions of the palace. Canaanite religious architecture was quite varied (e.g. *see* LACHISH). At MEGIDDO, in the Early Bronze Age, three megaron temples were constructed. In the Middle and Late Bronze Ages at several sites 'migdol' or 'tower' temples with an entrance porch supported by two columns and flanked by towers leading to a rectilinear sanctuary, often with a niche behind an altar at the far end, were built. Elsewhere, smaller temples with indirect access are found. As yet there is no clear linkage between temple-plan and deity worshipped. Canaanite military architecture reflected a high incidence of warfare, between local rulers and with foreign invaders. City gates had indirect entrance ramps and multiple internal piers. The curtain walls were massive and solid, built of mud-brick on stone foundations and rendered with a thick clay coating. From the Early Bronze Age particularly vulnerable points were protected with a low external covering wall. Towers were also a feature at vulnerable points along the circuit.

See also SYRIA–PALESTINE.

Canaanite ivory inlay fragment, from Megiddo, *c.* 1250–*c.* 1150 BC (Jerusalem, Rockefeller Museum)

BIBLIOGRAPHY
H. Frankfort: *The Art and Architecture of the Ancient Orient*, Pelican Hist. A. (Harmondsworth, 1954, rev. 4/1970)
J. Gray: *The Canaanites*, Ancient Peoples and Places (London, 1964)
K. M. Kenyon: *Archaeology in the Holy Land* (London, 1964, 4/1979)
G. Saadé: *Ougarit: Métropole cananéenne* (Beirut, 1979)
Y. Aharoni: *The Archaeology of the Land of Israel: From the Prehistoric Beginnings to the End of the First Temple Period* (London, 1982)

RUPERT L. CHAPMAN

Canada, Dominion of. Country in North America, bounded to the north by the Arctic Ocean, to the west by the Pacific and to the east by the Atlantic; the only land borders it shares are with the USA, on the south and between the Yukon and Alaska in the north-west (see fig. 1). Canada is comprised of ten provinces and two territories, and although it occupies almost 10,000,000 sq. km, the vast majority of the population (*c.* 25,000,000) live within 160 km of the Canada–US border. Canada is a parliamentary democracy and a member of the Commonwealth. The Prime Minister is political head of state, while the reigning member of the British royal family serves as titular head of state, represented by the Governor-General.

This article is a survey of Canadian art since the beginning of European colonization in the early 17th century. For its earlier history and information on the continuing traditions of its native peoples *see under* NATIVE NORTH AMERICAN ART.

See also HALIFAX (ii), MONTREAL, OTTAWA, QUEBEC, TORONTO, VANCOUVER and VICTORIA.

I. Introduction. II. Architecture. III. Painting and graphic arts. IV. Sculpture. V. Interior design. VI. Furniture. VII. Ceramics. VIII. Glass. IX. Gold and silver. X. Textiles. XI. Patronage. XII. Collecting and dealing. XIII. Museums. XIV. Art education. XV. Art libraries and photographic collections.

I. Introduction.

Although there had been some previous explorations of Canada, the first permanent settlements were established by the French in the early 17th century in the east and along the St Lawrence River, in 'New France'. Both the French and the British sought to exploit the great natural resources of the country and especially to gain monopolies in the lucrative fur trade. Franco-British rivalry led eventually to the capture of Quebec by the British in 1759 and the granting of New France to the British in the Peace of Paris in 1763. Following the American Revolution there was an influx from the south of United Empire Loyalists, settlers who wished to remain loyal to the crown. To ease conflicts caused by combining the British and French systems, the colony was divided in 1791 into Upper Canada (Ontario) and Lower Canada (Quebec), each with its own legislature. In 1867 the British North America Act united the provinces into the Dominion of Canada. The west, largely unsettled until this date, was made more accessible by the completion of the nationwide Canadian Pacific Railway in 1885. From the early 20th century there has been rapid urban growth, with further waves of immigrants arriving from around the world. The multicultural atmosphere this has created is dynamic but has contributed to the lack of a specific national and cultural identity. From the earliest settlement to the present, Canadian art has been marked by its assimilation of the traditions and styles brought by immigrants and the innovation required by circumstances of climate and available materials.

BIBLIOGRAPHY
Encyclopedia Canadiana, 10 vols (Ottawa, 1958)
K. McNaught: *The Pelican History of Canada* (London, 1969, rev. 1982)
J. H. Marsh, ed.: *The Canadian Encyclopedia*, 4 vols (Edmonton, 1985, 2/1988)
R. Cole Harris, ed.: *The Historical Atlas of Canada* (Toronto, 1987)

□

II. Architecture.

1. Before 1867. 2. 1867 and after.

1. BEFORE 1867. The predominating influences on Canadian architecture during the colonial period were the tastes and traditions of the two principal groups of European settlers, the French and the British. The architectural forms that they imported were modified by a number of factors, including the materials available for construction, the extreme climate, the vast distances that impeded settlement and movement and the scarcity of skilled labour. Neither group drew on the impermanent construction techniques of the native peoples.

Apart from the settlement at L'Anse aux Meadows on the Newfoundland coast, thought to date from the 11th century, the earliest European buildings in Canada date from the early 17th century, when the French settled along the St Lawrence River and in certain bays and inlets of the Atlantic coast. The earliest structures were built of upright timber posts set on the ground or on a sill; frame construction was also used, in which vertical members were infilled with rubble, then strengthened with short, horizontal timbers slotted in between. Timber construction remained common, but once settlement became more established the French began to build in stone, erecting structures of rubble masonry covered with stucco as a protection against rain and frost. Ashlar construction was expensive; it was at first used as a trim for doors and windows and only later as a finished dressing for the main façade. Throughout the 18th century timber construction still predominated, though stone construction became more widespread, especially in towns where the threat of fire was great.

These early buildings were quite plain in appearance, with little or no surface ornament and with openings spaced for convenience rather than for appearance. Their traditional designs became the foundation of regional architecture in Quebec (exhaustively studied and catalogued (1937–53) by GÉRARD MORISSET), a characteristic of which is heavy, prominent roofs. The earliest roofs were usually hipped, replaced later by gable roofs; dormers were a common feature, as was the flare outwards along the eaves. More ambitious buildings, such as churches and certain government structures, were given slightly more architectural detailing. A few major buildings in Quebec City, such as the Episcopal Palace (1692–7; destr.) by CLAUDE BAILLIF and the château of Vaudreuil (1723–7; destr.), were in a provincial form of French classicism, especially in the treatment of windows, symmetry, applied orders and pediments. Church architecture was slightly more ambitious, and the interior decoration was often highly elaborate, following norms established in France;

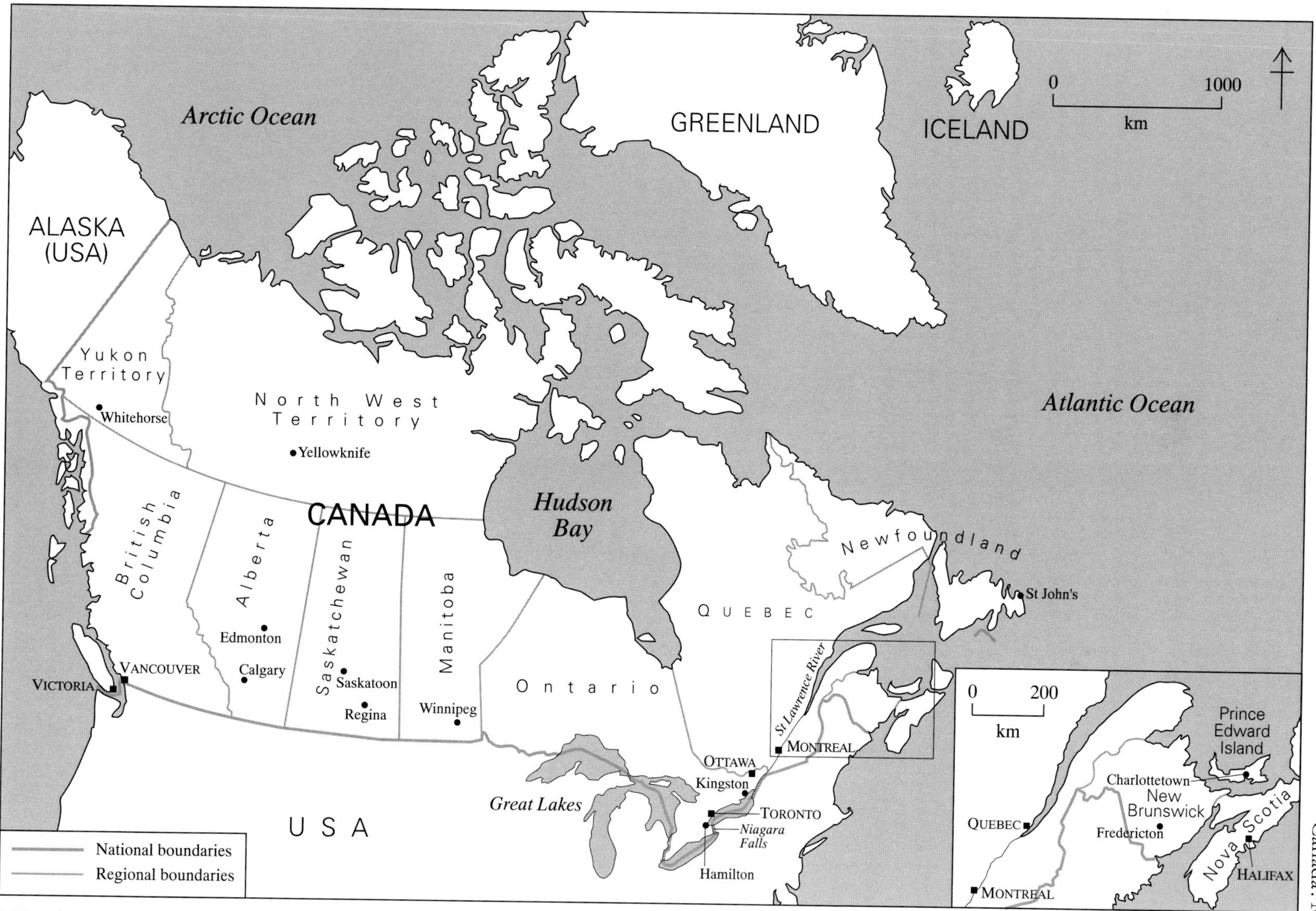

1. Map of Canada; those areas with separate entries in this dictionary are distinguished by CROSS-REFERENCE TYPE

examples include the cathedral (begun 1646) and the parish church of Notre-Dame-des-Victoires (rebuilt 1723; by JEAN-BAPTISTE MAILLOU), both in Quebec City.

Like those of the French, the buildings in early British and Loyalist settlements were constructed by craftsmen who used inherited vernacular traditions or had been trained through apprenticeship. Stone tended to dominate in urban centres in Quebec and where larger and more ambitious public buildings were required. Wood was favoured in Atlantic Canada and in south-western Ontario. Brick, increasingly used in the 19th century, was favoured in and around York (now Toronto), which initially lacked nearby supplies of stone. In the British community, classical design inspired by Palladianism was the dominant style for churches, State buildings and larger houses, even into the 19th century. Buildings were generally horizontally proportioned and symmetrical, with evenly spaced openings, shallow hipped or gable roofs and handsome but restrained decoration of a classical nature, including fanlights, columns, pilasters, Venetian windows and classical mouldings. A superb example is the Holy Trinity Anglican Cathedral (1800–04; see fig. 2), Quebec City, by the British artillery officers William Robe (1765–1820) and William Hall (*d* 1814), modelled, like many other churches of the period, on the parish church of St Martin-in-the-Fields (1720–26), London, by James Gibbs. At first Quebec architecture remained unaffected by these new British influences, but British tastes gradually affected local design. Among its leading architects was François Baillairgé, who actively transmitted French architectural ideas to church interiors in Quebec. His son Thomas Baillairgé elaborated a forceful classical church architecture that was applied in Quebec, notably in the twin-towered façade (1843) he added to the Roman Catholic Cathedral, Quebec City (*see* BAILLAIRGÉ). By the early 19th century Quebec architects had absorbed much of current English taste into their work.

2. William Robe and William Hall: main façade of the Holy Trinity Anglican Cathedral, Quebec City, 1800–04

During the second decade of the 19th century there was increased demand for building following a massive influx of settlers, mainly from Great Britain, and the opening up of new areas to the west of existing settlements. Among the new arrivals were architects bringing ideas current in British practice, which were also spread by the increasingly available architectural pattern books. With the beginnings of industrialization such construction materials as milled timber and prefabricated metalwork were produced. Improvements in transportation (e.g. the construction of national railways) helped to spread building materials and components, settlers and ideas farther across British North America, factors that contributed to the creation of a more sophisticated architecture. Historical revivalism, in the shape of Neo-classicism and Gothic Revival, swept Canada in the 1820s and determined the appearance of the majority of buildings for the rest of the century. The ideology of the PICTURESQUE informed a great deal of this work, awakening architects and patrons to the dramatic potential of the Canadian landscape. Picturesque villas and cottages appeared in areas of concentrated British settlement, particularly for the use of middle-class administrators and army officers. An example is Colborne Lodge (1836), Toronto, a *cottage orné* built by the architect JOHN G. HOWARD for himself. The style also influenced the design of other types of buildings, especially churches.

Neo-classical architecture was inspired principally by the works of British Neo-classicists, such as John Soane and John Nash (i), and features flattened surfaces, blind arcades and antique orders typical of the style. Two particularly fine examples are the City Hall (1843–4) in Kingston, Ontario, by the Irish-born GEORGE BROWNE and Province House (1843–8), Charlottetown, Prince Edward Island, designed by Isaac Smith (1795–1871). The Frontenac County Court House (1855–8), Kingston, by EDWARD HORSEY indicates Neo-classicism shading into eclecticism, with its mixture of Greek Revival and Renaissance Revival details. The refined and restrained qualities of British Neo-classicism were also applied to Quebec vernacular construction, with classically inspired buildings preserving the prominent roof-lines, casement windows and masonry techniques typical of local practice (e.g. the Anglican Deanery, 1841, Desjardins Street, Quebec City, by Frederick Hacker (*c.* 1802–46) and Edward Taylor Fletcher (1817–97)). The American Federal style also had a certain influence, often manifested in Greek Revival, temple-form designs for churches and houses, for example Plymouth Trinity Church (1848), Sherbrooke, and the County Building (1859), Brome Lake, both in Quebec.

The earliest Gothic Revival buildings were largely inspired by the decorative approach to the style established by the models of the Commissioners' Churches in Britain, that is, buildings largely classical in design and elevation but given a superficial dressing of Gothic Revival detail, as exemplified by the Roman Catholic church of Notre-Dame (1823–9), Montreal, by James O'Donnell (1774–1830). The influence of the Ecclesiologists (*see* ENGLAND, §II, 5(c)) in Gothic Revival church design strongly influenced religious architecture in Canada. Their journal, *The Ecclesiologist*, gave advice on church design throughout the British Empire, and for Canada it advised less ornamentation and simpler, bolder outlines as a way of dealing with the demands of a rigorous climate. Numerous Gothic Revival churches were erected, including the particularly striking Christ Church Cathedral (1845–53) in Fredericton, New Brunswick, built to separate designs by FRANK WILLS and WILLIAM BUTTERFIELD. A number of churches were erected in timber, cleverly adapting Ecclesiological ideology to this common Canadian material (e.g. Frank Wills's Christ Church Anglican, 1856, Maugerville, NB). Ecclesiology influenced the church design of all of the Christian sects; to one architect alone, VICTOR BOURGEAU, who worked for the Roman Catholic diocese of Montreal, some 200 churches in the Gothic Revival style are attributed. However, churches built in distant missions tended to follow conservative, pre-Ecclesiological designs, as these forms were more suitable for evangelical purposes.

By the mid-19th century it was common to find individual architects who built both Gothic Revival and Neo-classical buildings as required, as is exemplified by the careers of WILLIAM HAY and FREDERIC W. CUMBERLAND in Toronto and JOHN OSTELL in Montreal.

A third form of revivalism based on the Italian Renaissance style became popular in the 1840s and remained current to the end of the century. It was manifested initially in public buildings, urban dwellings and commercial blocks based loosely on Charles Barry's clubhouses in London. The palazzo-type design of cubic volume, articulated with a prominent base storey, emphasized main entrance, bold cornice and richly sculptural decoration, was adopted in numerous accomplished examples, including Keith Hall (1863), Halifax, Nova Scotia, by David Stirling (1822–87). A related type of Picturesque villa also appeared, distantly inspired by the villas of Tuscany and more directly by Italianate villas in Britain. The Canadian versions were asymmetrical designs with off-centre towers, French windows and verandahs.

Despite waves of temporary fashions in Canadian architecture, certain strong traditions survived, sometimes incorporating and often outlasting passing tastes. These included traditional Quebec house and church architecture, the symmetrical buildings inspired by British classicism and the architecture of smaller, less influential, groups of immigrants, such as the Hebron Moravian Mission (1771–1904), Newfoundland. The most characteristic works of the end of this period are the Parliament Buildings (1859–66; for illustration *see* FULLER, THOMAS), Ottawa, by Thomas Fuller and others. Originally intended for the united provinces of Canada East (Quebec) and Canada West (Ontario), they became the Parliament Buildings of the new nation following Confederation in 1867 (*see* OTTAWA, §2). Robust, polychromatic, Ruskinian works, in a High Victorian Gothic Revival style, they were dramatically unlike anything built in Canada before and symbolized the country's new status.

BIBLIOGRAPHY

J. Rempel: *Building with Wood and Other Aspects of Nineteenth Century Building in Central Canada* (Toronto, 1967, rev. 1980)
M. Lessard and H. Marquis: *Encyclopédie de la maison québecoise: Trois siècles d'habitations* (Montreal, 1972)
L. Noppen and others: *Québec: Trois siècles d'architecture* (Quebec, 1979)
M. Brosseau: *Gothic Revival in Canadian Architecture* (Ottawa, 1980)
A. Duffus and others: *Thy Dwellings Fair: Churches of Nova Scotia, 1750–1830* (Hantsport, 1982)
M. Carter, ed.: *Early Canadian Court Houses* (Ottawa, 1983)
E. Pacey and others: *More Stately Mansions: Churches of Nova Scotia, 1830–1910* (Hantsport, 1983)
N. Clerk: *Palladian Style in Canadian Architecture* (Ottawa, 1984)
L. Maitland: *Neoclassical Architecture in Canada* (Ottawa, 1984)
J. Wright: *Architecture of the Picturesque in Canada* (Ottawa, 1984)
H. M. S. Smith: *The Historic Churches of Prince Edward Island* (Erin, 1986)
——: *The Historic Houses of Prince Edward Island* (Erin, 1986)
M. de Caraffe and others: *Town Halls of Canada* (Ottawa, 1987)
J. Blumenson: *Ontario Architecture: A Guide to Styles and Building Terms, 1784 to Present* (Markham, 1990)
G. Simmins, ed.: *Documents in Canadian Architecture* (Peterborough, Ont., 1992)

For further bibliography *see* §2 below.

LESLIE MAITLAND

2. 1867 AND AFTER. From Confederation to the end of World War I Canadian architecture was largely fashioned by contemporary British and American developments. The impact of these external influences varied, depending on the density and patterns of settlement, the severity of the climate and the resilience of existing architectural traditions. As a result, architecture from this period has a distinctly regional flavour. Generally, the well-established centres of Toronto and Montreal provided styles, new technology and ideas on the nature of Canadian architecture to such rapidly expanding cities as Winnipeg, Vancouver, Edmonton and Calgary.

Architectural styles initially remained firmly rooted in historicism, becoming bolder and more eclectic as the century drew to its close. Following Confederation the Second Empire style was dominant. Buildings such as the grandiose Hôtel de Ville (1874–8; rebuilt 1922), Montreal, by HENRI-MAURICE PERRAULT and the Assemblée Nationale (1877–86), Quebec City, by EUGÈNE-ETIENNE TACHÉ were modelled on French prototypes. Others, such as the Market Hall (1876) in Saint John, New Brunswick, by McKean & Fairweather are muted by the strong classical tradition of Atlantic Canada, while the idiosyncratic City Hall (1878, 1881 and 1890) in Victoria, British Columbia, by John Teague (1833–1920) reflects that city's distance from the eastern centres of fashion. The arrival in the mid-1880s of the CHÂTEAU STYLE, the Queen Anne Revival and H. H. Richardson's version of the Romanesque Revival signalled the high-water mark of Victorian architecture. Of the many excellent buildings of this period, outstanding are the picturesque Château Frontenac Hotel (1892–5) in Quebec City, designed by the American Bruce Price, and the Richardsonian Romanesque Old City Hall (1889–99), Toronto, by E. J. LENNOX. In addition the federal Department of Public Works, based in Ottawa, became an important source of accomplished architecture under its talented Chief Architect THOMAS FULLER. Its distinctive Romanesque Revival post offices and public buildings helped to establish the federal government's presence across the country.

Late 19th-century Canada was marked by a rapid increase in urbanization and by a demand for new types of buildings, particularly commercial and industrial structures. A notable development was the early adoption of the structural and technical innovations used for the warehouses and tall buildings of Chicago and New York, for example in the five-storey Equity Chambers office building (1878), Toronto, and the eight-storey New York Life Assurance Company building (1887), Montreal, by Babb, Cook & Willard. Structural steel came into general use in the mid-1890s, enabling buildings to rise above eight storeys. The first fireproof, self-supporting steel-frame building in Canada was the second Robert Simpson Department Store (1895), Toronto, by Edmund Burke (1850–1919) and John Horwood (1864–1938). By 1910, medium-height, steel-frame buildings had become a conspicuous feature of all major Canadian cities. Winnipeg still boasts one of the best-preserved Chicago-style commercial districts in North America, while in Vancouver the 13-storey Dominion Building (1905–10) by J. S. Helyer (1857–1919) and the 17-storey Sun Tower (1909–12) by W. T. Whiteway (1856–1919) in turn claimed title as the tallest building in the Commonwealth. Contemporaneous with the first skyscrapers was a growing acceptance of the timber 'balloon' frame construction technique; this combines a light frame with an external cladding of wood or brick, making it economical and fast to erect. In western Canada its popularity contributed to the particular character of the architecture.

Many of the best buildings from these years were designed by foreign, particularly American, architects, who were the products of teaching methods increasingly modelled on those of the Ecole des Beaux-Arts, Paris. Canadian interest in the classicist Beaux-Arts style intensified following the success of the World's Columbian Exposition (1893) in Chicago, and the style appeared in Canada in the first decade of the 20th century. It was most popular with the chartered banks, who furnished an early and important example in the extension (1904) to the Bank of Montreal, Montreal, by the American firm McKim, Mead & White assisted by ANDREW T. TAYLOR. A number of Canadian architects also won important commissions, notably JOHN M. LYLE, who conducted a Beaux-Arts atelier in Toronto from 1906. The 18-storey Toronto–Dominion Bank (1913–14), Toronto, by the local firm of DARLING & PEARSON, with its combination of classical formality and opulence, marked the beginning of a general transformation of banking districts in Canadian cities. The firm of Edward and William S. MAXWELL in Montreal designed several excellent Beaux-Arts buildings, including the winning design for the Saskatchewan Parliament Buildings (1908–12), Regina, one of three similarly domed Beaux-Arts legislature buildings erected in the western provinces. One of the most important examples of the style is the monumental, colonnaded Union Station (1911–27), Toronto, by Ross and Macdonald (*see* ROSS, GEORGE), Hugh Jones and John Lyle.

The Arts and Crafts Movement was another of the many currents that informed architecture at the turn of the century. Its ideals were adopted by the architecture department at McGill University, Montreal, under its second director, PERCY NOBBS. Teaching focused on the regional nature of Canadian architecture and stressed the need for designs appropriate to the country's history and climate. The curriculum also promoted contemporary British classicism, which, it was argued, was more suited to Canada than the 'American' Beaux-Arts version. This nationalistic emphasis led to many federal buildings being given an English Edwardian flavour. It was in Vancouver, however, that Arts and Crafts ideals blossomed into an important regional style. Taking established idioms (e.g. Early Tudor and Queen Anne Revival), such architects as the gifted SAMUEL MACLURE and his occasional collaborator FRANCIS MAWSON RATTENBURY fashioned a West Coast domestic style, distinctive in its respect for native woods, its craftsmanship and its sensitivity to the spectacular surroundings.

In the 1920s and 1930s examples of the Art Deco style, such as the high-rise Marine Building (1928–30), Vancouver, by MCCARTER NAIRNE, added a flamboyant note to the scene. In general, though, buildings of this period tend to be conservative, as architects proved reluctant to abandon historical styles or take advantage of developments in modern building materials. A more radical modernism appeared in Montreal in the 1930s. The sleek, planar design of ERNEST CORMIER's own house (1930–31; see fig. 9 below), for example, displays a subtle understanding of contemporary French design, as does the equally sophisticated, Le Corbusier-inspired house (1936) that belonged to Marcel Parizeau (1898–1945).

Full acceptance of Modernist architecture did not emerge until the 1950s and 1960s, during a period of exceptional growth. The early initiative was taken by the Vancouver firm SHARP, THOMPSON, BERWICK, PRATT and Partners, whose Vocational Institute (1948–9), Vancouver, was one of the earliest large-scale, Modernist projects in Canada. This firm's employees included two leading members of Canada's avant-garde architectural movement: ARTHUR ERICKSON, whose first major project was the bold and superbly sited Simon Fraser University (1963–5), Burnaby, British Columbia, and RON THOM, a subtle designer whose particular talents are evident at Trent University (1963–71), Peterborough, Ontario, a reinterpretation of the traditional Oxbridge quadrangle. JOHN B. PARKIN from Toronto was another early and talented practitioner of the International Style; his design for the Railway Station (1966), Ottawa, pays homage to Mies van der Rohe. In the 1960s the scale of Canada's development encouraged leading architects from overseas to contribute to the proliferation of Modernist architecture in major cities. The Australian John Andrews designed innovative university residences (1965) for Scarborough College, near Toronto. Montreal was transformed by developments at Place Ville Marie (1958–63), based on linking underground walkways and elegant towers designed by the American I. M. Pei and a consortium of local architects led by RAY AFFLECK, and at Place Victoria (1965), designed by the Italians Luigi Moretti and Pier Luigi Nervi. This process culminated in Expo 67, when Montreal's exhibition site became a showcase for experimental architecture. Among the most internationally influential projects were MOSHE SAFDIE's Habitat '67 (see fig. 3), consisting of modular precast concrete flats, and the American pavilion, a version of the geodesic dome by R. Buckminster Fuller. Other

3. Moshe Safdie: Habitat '67, Montreal, 1964–7

major cities were similarly transformed by dazzling arrays of steel-and-glass towers, as multi-national corporations vied with each other for domination of the skyline.

Parallel to the implementation of international Modernism, local and vernacular traditions were reinvigorated in small-scale projects. Using a subjective style, Roger D'Astous (*b* 1926) and Paul Marie Coté (1921–63) completed a transformation (begun in the 1940s) of Quebec's religious architecture with an expressive group of reinforced concrete churches, the romantic and energetic forms of which contain echoes of several Latin cultures. The vast spaces and brilliant skies of the prairies inspired DOUGLAS CARDINAL to create the small St Mary's Church (1967–8) in Red Deer, Alberta, a poetic masterpiece of curving, textured brick forms. The double helical structure of the Eglise du Précieux Sang (1968) in St Boniface, Manitoba, designed by ETIENNE-JOSEPH GABOURY is an interesting reinterpretation of an established tradition.

During the 1970s the development of Modernism continued apace, with several notable examples of international trends represented in Canada. Craig, Zeidler & Strong (*see* ZEIDLER, EBERHARD) designed Ontario Place (1970), Toronto, an early and highly successful theme park sited over water. The Citadel Theatre (1976) in Edmonton, Alberta, by Diamond, Myers & Wilkin is a lucid composition sheathed in steel and glass, which incorporates theatres, restaurants and a pedestrian mall. Other western Canadian contributions include the Winnipeg Art Gallery, a monolithic wedge of smooth Manitoba limestone designed by Gustavo da Roza (*b* 1933) and the Number Ten Architectural Group, and Erickson's splendid Museum of Anthropology (1971–6; for illustration *see* ERICKSON, ARTHUR), University of British Columbia, Vancouver. At the same time hindsight suggested that Expo 67, with its emphasis on the unlimited possibilities of modern technology and growth, marked a watershed for the more extreme manifestations of the International Style. Public distaste for increasingly massive commercial developments, coupled with a concern for the survival of inner cities, brought about a change in direction in architecture. With their master-plan for the False Creek housing project (1974–7) in Vancouver, Thompson, Berwick, Pratt and Partners successfully launched the redevelopment of a depressed industrial area. RAYMOND MORIYAMA reintroduced the sense of responsive government with his welcoming design of simplified masses for the Civic Centre (1972–3), Scarborough. Irony and wit appeared in the best Post-modern buildings, such as the Bradley House (1977), North Hatley, Quebec, by Peter Rose (*b* 1943) and the City Hall (1982–7), Mississauga, Ontario, by Jones & Kirkland; both make reference to building types familiar in Canada since the 19th century.

See also §V, 1 below.

BIBLIOGRAPHY

H. A. Brooks: *The Prairie School Architecture* (Toronto, 1975)
C. Cameron and J. Wright: *Second Empire Style in Canadian Architecture* (Ottawa, 1980)
R. Cawker and W. Bernstein: *Contemporary Canadian Architecture: The Mainstream and Beyond* (Toronto, 1982)
John M. Lyle: Toward a Canadian Architecture (exh. cat. by G. Hunt, Kingston, Ont., Agnes Etherington A. Cent., 1982)

L. Whiteson: *Modern Canadian Architecture* (Edmonton, 1983)
J. Bingham: *Samuel Maclure: Architect* (Ganges, BC, 1985)
Historical Architecture of Saskatchewan (Regina, 1986)
T. Boddy: *Modern Architecture in Alberta* (Edmonton, 1987)
K. Crossman: *Architecture in Transition: From Art to Practice, 1885–1906* (Montreal, 1987)
A. Erickson: *The Architecture of Arthur Erickson* (Vancouver and Toronto, 1988)
C. Bergeron: *L'Architecture des églises au Québec, 1940–1985* (Montreal, 1989)
——: *Architectures du XXe siècle au Québec* (Montreal, 1989)
R. Cawker: *Viewpoints: One Hundred Years of Architecture in Ontario, 1889–1989* (Toronto, 1989)
A. Freedman: *Sight Lines: Looking at Architecture and Design in Canada* (Toronto, 1990)
L. Maitland: *The Queen Anne Revival in Canadian Architecture* (Ottawa, 1990)
J. Bland and others: *The Architecture of Edward and W. S. Maxwell* (Montreal, 1991)
H. Kalman: *History of Canadian Architecture* (Toronto, 1993)
N. Clerke: *Le Style Beaux-arts au Canada* (in preparation)

JACQUELINE HUCKER

III. Painting and graphic arts.

1. Before 1867. 2. 1867–1938. 3. 1939–60. 4. After 1960.

1. BEFORE 1867. The earliest depictions by Europeans of Canadian subject-matter appeared in the decorated margins of maps from the mid-16th century. These often inaccurate illustrations were made by artists who had never been to Canada and were based on the accounts by travellers. Subsequently, painting was dominated by the amateur and professional artists who came in the wake of the French colonization of Quebec. Most of the early French painters in Canada were either priests, nuns or soldiers; few were professionally trained. Among them were such figures as L'Abbé Hugues Pommier (1637–86), a parish priest at the Séminaire de Québec, Michel Dessailliant de Richeterre (*fl* 1701–23), an itinerant artist, and Paul Beaucourt (1700–56), a sergeant in the French army. Though rather crude, their work was typical of the period and consisted largely of portraits and ex-voto paintings. Numerous untrained itinerant artists also specialized in ex-voto works. Among professional artists was the painter and wood-carver Jacques Leblond dit La Tour (1671–1715), who arrived in Canada in 1690. The most important painter from this early period was CLAUDE FRANÇOIS, Frère Luc. A Récollet friar and a pupil of Simon Vouet, he spent 18 months in Quebec (1670–71), where he painted such Baroque religious works as the *Holy Family* (1671; destr. 1759) for Notre-Dame-de-Québec Cathedral and the *Assumption of the Virgin* (1671; *in situ*) for the Hôtel-Dieu Chapel in Quebec City, as well as others for the chapel of the Hôpital-Général in Quebec and elsewhere. He continued to produce works for churches in Canada after his return to France in 1671.

Following the British conquest of Canada, a new artistic tradition and aesthetic were grafted on to the French stock. This led to the first landscape works in Canada, reflecting the growing interest in this genre in England with the concomitant taste for the picturesque and the Sublime. The French had largely ignored landscape, as their work was for the embellishment of churches. Père Louis Hennepin (1626–*c.* 1705), a Récollet priest, had drawn Niagara Falls in 1678, and Père Jean Pierron (*fl* 1660–73) had made various sketches around Quebec between 1660 and 1673, but little else was produced until the arrival of the British. Many of the English artists were soldiers who were either keen amateur painters or were engaged as topographers; most of them remained in Canada only for the term of their military duty. Their work ranged from the topographic to more romantic contemplations of nature. Many had been trained at the Royal Military Academy, Woolwich, and they painted in watercolour, as this was the most convenient and portable medium given the difficult working conditions. One of the earliest English landscape painters was Capt. THOMAS DAVIES, who made various watercolours between 1757 and 1790 while stationed at Halifax, Montreal and Quebec; six of his views of waterfalls were engraved and printed (London, *c.* 1768). Lt James Peachey (*d* 1797) spent the last ten years of his life painting views of Lower Canada. Richard Short (*fl* 1759–61) had a series of views of Halifax published in 1759 and of Quebec City in 1761. Later, watercolours were also produced by Lt-Col. JAMES PATTISON COCKBURN, who arrived in Quebec in 1826 and remained in Canada until 1836. His views of Upper Canada, Montreal and Quebec, for example the *Gate of the Citadel at Quebec* (1831; Quebec, Mus. Qué.), are some of the best of the period. William Henry Bartlett arrived in the USA in 1838; his months in Upper and Lower Canada resulted in *Canadian Scenery* (2 vols; London, 1842), which he both wrote and illustrated. Other English landscape painters included William Eagar (*c.* 1796–1839), Capt. Hervey Smyth (1738–?1811), GEORGE HERIOT and Colonel Alexander Cavalie Mercer (1783–1868). This 'topographical' approach flourished between 1770 and 1840, though there were notable exponents after this, for example Capt. Henry James Warre (1819–98), who was one of the first to paint the Rocky Mountains during a trip to the Oregon Territory (1845–6).

By the late 18th century various native and European artists began to take up portraiture. Among them was Paul Beaucourt's son François Malepart Beaucourt (1740–94), the first native-born Canadian painter of note. After spending his earliest years in Quebec, he lived in France and elsewhere in Europe for 15 years before settling in Montreal. He specialized in portrait painting and produced rather stiff, formal works, for example *Eustache Ignace Trottier* (1793; Quebec, Mus. Qué.). Another early Canadian portrait painter was François Baillairgé (*see* BAILLAIRGÉ, (2)). Louis Dulongpré (1754–1843), a French soldier, was supposed to have painted over 3000 portraits between 1785 and 1815, among them *James McGill* (1806; Quebec, Mus. Qué.). Other Europeans included WILLIAM BERCZY, who painted the *Woolsey Family* (1809; Ottawa, N.G.), and GEORGE THEODORE BERTHON, who settled in Toronto in 1844. The Canadian ANTOINE PLAMONDON achieved great success in the genre with such formally posed works as the *Pigeon Hunt* (1853; Toronto, A.G. Ont.). He taught THÉOPHILE HAMEL, who adopted much the same style and achieved similar renown.

Daniel Fowler (1810–94) came to Canada in 1843, and after a brief return trip to England in 1857, he spent the remainder of his life producing landscapes, flower pictures and still-lifes with dead game in pen and ink and watercolour. His more distinctive contemporary was the Irish-born PAUL KANE, who came to Canada *c.* 1818 and

4. Paul Kane: *The Chief and his Companions*, oil on canvas, 640×764 mm, *c.* 1856 (Ottawa, National Gallery of Canada)

travelled with the Hudson's Bay Company in western Canada from 1846 to 1848. The sketches he made were later incorporated into paintings, often of Native Americans, such as *The Chief and his Companions* (*c.* 1856; Ottawa, N.G.; see fig. 4); his paintings constitute the main record of such tribes as the Assiniboine and Blackfoot at this time. The most able of the settlers of this period, however, was the Dutch-born CORNELIUS KRIEGHOFF, who concentrated on genre subjects (e.g. *Habitant Farm*, 1854; Ottawa, N.G.). His popular romantic works appealed primarily to English patrons and to the habitants themselves; wealthier French settlers thought them a vulgar caricature of their own lifestyle (see also fig. 10 below).

BIBLIOGRAPHY

E. Morris: *Art in Canada: The Early Painters* (Toronto, 1911)
N. MacTavish: *The Fine Arts in Canada* (Toronto, 1925)
A. H. Robson: *Canadian Landscape Painting* (London and Toronto, 1932)
G. McInnes: *A Short History of Canadian Art* (Toronto, 1939)
W. Colgate: *Canadian Art: Its Origin and Development* (Toronto, 1943/*R* 1967)
D. W. Buchanan: *The Growth of Canadian Painting* (London and Toronto, 1950)
L'Art au Canada (exh. cat. by G. Martin-Méry, Bordeaux, Mus. B.-A., 1962)

For further bibliography *see* §3 below.

□

2. 1867–1938. Confederation in 1867 did not immediately affect painters and graphic artists. For the next few years they continued to pursue the themes and styles that they had practised before the political union of the provinces. Coincidentally, they found it helpful to establish artistic societies (*see* §XIV below) through which they could promote their ideas and exhibit their work. Frederic Marlett Bell-Smith (1846–1923), a central member of the Society of Canadian Artists (founded in Montreal in 1867), worked initially as a photographer, illustrator and teacher and later turned to oil and watercolour to paint landscapes and genre scenes. Much artistic activity in Montreal centred around the photographic firm of WILLIAM NOTMAN, which regularly hired painters to colour photographs and to create backgrounds. One such painter was JOHN ARTHUR FRASER, a British-born artist who was involved in the establishment of the Society of Canadian Artists. In 1867 he was sent to Toronto to set up a photographic

office; he soon became an important catalyst in encouraging artistic activity in Ontario, including the creation in Toronto of the Ontario Society of Artists in 1872. A prominent member of this society, LUCIUS R. O'BRIEN, disagreed with Fraser and in 1880, with the help of two governors-general, established the first truly national arts organization, the Royal Canadian Academy of Arts in Ottawa. Both the organization and the artist achieved prominence. O'Brien's sublime *Sunrise on the Saguenay* (1880; Ottawa, N.G.) reflected the dominant style of Canadian painting, one shared by FREDERICK A. VERNER, who travelled west to depict the native peoples and the countryside, emphasizing atmospheric qualities of quiet, light and colour in a sublime landscape.

By about 1875 the French academic style assumed new importance in Canadian art. Genre subjects, portraits and figure scenes, and large, epic themes executed with incredible detail and high finish became important. WILLIAM BRYMNER, one of the first Canadians to study in Paris, returned to Montreal to paint domestic figure scenes, and PAUL PEEL did slick and sentimental subjects that embody academic painting. Another French-trained artist, Robert Harris (*see* HARRIS, (1)), from Prince Edward Island, was considered the master of monumental history painting, and for this reason he was given the most important contemporary commission, a large group composition of the *Fathers of Confederation* (*c*. 1885, destr.; oil sketch, *c*. 1883, Charlottetown, Confed. A.G. & Mus.). Other painters of the then popular genre scene were Sophie Pemberton (1869–1959) from Victoria, BC, and Charlotte Schreiber (1834–1922) from Toronto. Schreiber was one of the first Canadian women to do illustrations. A second wave of Canadian students in Paris included GEORGE A. REID and MARC-AURÈLE DE FOY SUZOR-COTÉ. Reid persisted with the academic style of monumental figure painting, producing not only immense canvases but also ambitious murals (1897–9) for the City Hall, Toronto, before developing an interest in landscape painting after the turn of the century. Suzor-Coté, working in Quebec, also depicted both academic subjects and landscape themes.

The landscape was entirely dominant for two painters whose influence came partly via the American Hudson River school. In the *Flood Gate* (1900; Ottawa, N.G.) HOMER WATSON worked one grand theme, man against the elements. HORATIO WALKER, influenced by the Barbizon school, sought a quieter theme and a looser technique in such work as *Oxen at the Trough* (1899; Ottawa, N.G.). In Quebec the religious painter OZIAS LEDUC approached his work in a manner similar to Watson. Leduc also favoured intense examination, initially preferring still-life to landscape. Only towards the end of his life did he pursue dreamlike, spiritual landscapes of great poignancy.

In the graphic arts, after Confederation, J. W. Bengough (1851–1923) gained a special reputation for his cartoons. Opportunities increased when O'Brien edited *Picturesque Canada: As it Was and Is* (Toronto, 1882) and commissioned illustrations from artists. Another fine illustrator was C. W. Jefferys (1869–1951), who specialized in historical depiction. The surge of painting activity found its counterpart in graphics, with many artists working in both areas. Contemporary societies soon reflected the new emphasis on the graphic arts. With the formation in 1886 of the Toronto Art Students' League, a sketching club, came the production of yearly illustrated calendars. The Graphic Arts Club appeared *c*. 1904 and a decade or so later the Society of Canadian Painter–Etchers and Engravers.

By 1907 a number of artists, reacting against the old-fashioned look of much Canadian painting, formed the CANADIAN ART CLUB, a private exhibiting society based in Toronto. Both Walker and Watson were important members, as were Brymner and MAURICE CULLEN, both from Montreal and both painting atmospheric, quasi-Impressionistic landscapes. Another member was CLARENCE GAGNON, who also favoured landscapes but was as well a renowned illustrator. The most important contributor to this group was James Wilson Morrice. Though he lived for the most part in Paris, he still found inspiration in Canada and returned every year until World War I. In *Return from School* (*c*. 1900; Toronto, A.G. Ont.) Morrice captured the snow-laden sky and the spring dampness with an economy of means and a painterly elegance, a style he continued to refine (e.g. *Landscape, Trinidad*, *c*. 1921; Ottawa, N.G.; for illustration *see* MORRICE, JAMES WILSON).

Contemporaneously, a group of commercial artists in Toronto became friends and started to go on sketching and fishing holidays together. A seminal canvas was A. Y. JACKSON's stark *Terre sauvage* of 1913 (Ottawa, N.G.; for illustration *see* GROUP OF SEVEN), depicting autumnal leaves and spindly pines on Pre-Cambrian rock. In the same year two others, J. E. H. MACDONALD and Lawren S. Harris, visited an exhibition of Scandinavian art at the Albright–Knox Art Gallery in Buffalo, NY, and were greatly impressed. Gradually these designers determined to concentrate on landscape painting, favouring the rugged Canadian north as their theme. Slowly they adopted the prevailing geographic nationalism, presenting their work as technically home-grown instead of imported from Europe. In 1914 they painted mainly in Algonquin Park, Ontario, where Tom Thomson relished the brash autumn colours. The war separated these intrepid experimenters. Thomson continued to paint in Algonquin Park until his death in 1917, producing such arresting canvases as the *Jack Pine* (1916–17; Ottawa, N.G.; for illustration *see* THOMSON, TOM), a lone pine set in front of a serene evening lake, a canvas that became a Canadian icon. MacDonald, in Toronto, created a few intense and misunderstood canvases, including the *Tangled Garden* (1916; Ottawa, N.G.). Jackson, Franz Johnston (1888–1949), ARTHUR LISMER and FRED VARLEY all participated in the Canadian War Records. Varley was deeply moved by the atrocities of war and painted some of his most successful works, including *For What?* (Ottawa, Can. War Mus.).

In 1920 these painters decided to exhibit together under the name the Group of Seven. Harris provoked exploration further afield, into Algoma, northern Ontario. Here MacDonald was inspired to paint his commanding *Falls, Montreal River* (1920; Toronto, A.G. Ont.). In 1921 Harris went to the north shore of Lake Superior, where, in a landscape recently ravaged by forest fire, he isolated bare tree trunks and rounded islands, situating them in mystical light, as in the monumental *North Shore, Lake Superior*

5. David B. Milne: *Ollie Matson's House is Just a Square Red Cloud*, oil on canvas, 460×560 mm, 1931 (Ottawa, National Gallery of Canada)

(1926; Ottawa, N.G.; for illustration *see* HARRIS, LAWREN S.). Both Jackson and Harris eventually went as far north as possible, painting in the Arctic. Meanwhile, in the Algonquin area, Lismer and Varley created some of their most famous canvases depicting single pine trees. Jackson sketched in all parts of Canada, promoting the land-based nationalism that characterized the philosophy of these friends. This informal association lasted for 13 years, with a certain shift in membership. In 1924 Johnston left the Group while, two years later, A. J. Casson (1898–1992) joined it; in 1931 EDWIN H. HOLGATE became a member, as did LIONEL LEMOINE FITZGERALD the next year. In 1933 the Group expanded into the Canadian Group of Painters.

In Montreal another group of painters, the Beaver Hall Hill Group, included Randolph Hewton (1888–1960), Holgate and a strong phalanx of women such as Lilias Torrance Newton (1896–1980) and PRUDENCE HEWARD. They not only painted landscapes, as was the pervading mood, but also did strong figure painting, something much less common at the time; a notable combination of landscape and figure painting is Holgate's *Nude* (1930; Toronto A.G. Ont.). These painters became dominant members of the Canadian Group of Painters. Carl Schaefer (*b* 1903) and Charles Comfort, two other members, pursued individualistic landscape themes, while BERTRAM BROOKER and JOCK MACDONALD pioneered Canadian abstract art. Another member was Emily Carr. Initially drawn to recording the declining Native American culture, especially totem poles, Carr worked on the West Coast, often in remote Indian villages. Having studied in France, she preferred bold colours and broad forms. In 1927 she went to eastern Canada, where she encountered Harris and other members of the Group of Seven. Greatly encouraged, she renewed her efforts, simplified her forms and clarified her aims. *Big Raven* (*c.* 1928; Vancouver, A.G.; for illustration *see* CARR, EMILY), which depicts a native carving set in a swirling sea of forest, pulses with energy and vision.

DAVID B. MILNE also pursued a rural vision. As intellectual as Carr was emotional, Milne went to New York in 1903 to become an illustrator. After studying at the Art Students League and exhibiting in the Armory Show in 1913, he returned to Canada in 1929. Producing both watercolours and oils, he favoured landscapes (see fig. 5), although figures often appear in his early work. He invented a method of making colour drypoints, a medium in which he produced pared-down, scintillating jewels.

BIBLIOGRAPHY

D. Reid: *Le Group des Septs/The Group of Seven* (Ottawa, 1970)

J.-R. Ostiguy: *Un Siècle de peinture canadienne, 1870–1970* (Quebec City, 1971)

B. Lord: *The History of Painting in Canada: Towards a People's Art* (Toronto, 1974)

Canadian Painting in the Thirties (exh. cat. by C. C. Hill, Ottawa, N.G., 1975)

'Our Country Canada': Being an Account of the National Aspirations of the Principal Landscape Artists in Montreal and Toronto, 1860–1890 (exh. cat. by D. Reid, Ottawa, N.G., 1979)

A Distant Harmony: Comparisons in the Painting of Canada and the United States of America (exh. cat. by A. Davis, Winnipeg, A.G., 1982)

The Mystic North (exh. cat. by R. Nasgaard, Toronto, A.G. Ont.; Cincinnati, OH, A. Mus.; 1984)

Douglas Fetherling, ed.: *Documents in Canadian Art* (Peterborough, Ont., 1987)

A. Davis: *The Logic of Ecstasy: Canadian Mystical Painting, 1920–1940* (Toronto, 1992)

For further bibliography *see* §3 below.

ANN DAVIS

3. 1939–60. A new era in the development of modern painting in Canada began on 15 February 1939, when JOHN LYMAN launched the Contemporary Arts Society in Montreal. Lyman resented the Group of Seven's claim to be the only authentic representatives of Canadian painting. He felt that their exclusive devotion to landscape painting was both too narrow and dépassé, that modern art was more interested in form than subject-matter and that the Society should reflect this clearly in a well-organized programme of annual exhibitions. The Contemporary Arts Society existed until 1948 and during this period showed the more lively Canadian painters, including GOODRIDGE ROBERTS, Philip H. Surrey (*b* 1910), MILLER BRITTAIN, PAUL-EMILE BORDUAS, who was its first vice-president, and some of his protégés, for example JEAN-PAUL RIOPELLE and Marcel Barbeau (*b* 1925). Although he was not very active in the Contemporary Arts Society, the painter ALFRED PELLAN made a considerable impact when he returned to Quebec in 1940 after living in Paris for 14 years. Shortly after his return he had exhibitions both in his native Quebec City and in Montreal, showing a group of 161 works, including what the catalogue described as *décorations non figuratives.* Such critics as Maurice Gagnon (1904–56), Marcel Parizeau (1898–1945) and Robert Elie (1915–73) responded warmly to this first opportunity to see work by a member of the Parisian avant-garde who also happened to be a French-Canadian.

6. Guido Molinari: *Black Angle noir*, enamel paint on canvas, 1.52×1.83 m, 1956 (Ottawa, National Gallery of Canada)

After the *Exposition des Indépendants*—a new group exhibition organized in 1941 by Father Marie-Alain Couturier (1897–1954) and shown in Quebec City and Montreal, in which both Pellan and Borduas participated—the next sensation on the Montreal art scene was an exhibition in 1942 by Borduas of 45 Surrealist gouaches, which demonstrated the principle of automatic writing as defined by André Breton in *L'Amour fou* (Paris, 1937). The group known as LES AUTOMATISTES emerged soon after. Its members included Riopelle, Barbeau, FERNAND LEDUC, Pierre Gauvreau (*b* 1922), Jean-Paul Mousseau (*b* 1927) and others who signed the REFUS GLOBAL manifesto in 1948. Aside from the PRISME D'YEUX group, the collective show held at the Place des Artistes, Montreal, in May 1953 was the first challenge—in the works of GUIDO MOLINARI in particular—to the aesthetic of Les Automatistes. It was, however, the manifesto of LES PLASTICIENS, written by the painter and critic Rodolphe de Repentigny (1926–59) and launched on 10 February 1955, that marked a real turning-point in the development of painting in Quebec. The signatories of the new manifesto rejected the need to go back to such pioneers of European abstract art as Mondrian; their desire for 'order' was expressed in geometric abstraction, as shown in the paintings of Fernand Toupin (*b* 1930), with their irregularly shaped canvases covered by hard-edge, two-colour painted stripes. The first Plasticiens, among them Jean-Paul Jérôme (*b* 1928) and Louis Belzile (*b* 1929), were soon overtaken by the more radical minimal abstractionists Molinari (see fig. 6) and CLAUDE TOUSIGNANT. Plasticism dominated the Montreal scene well into the 1960s, only partly challenged by such brilliant painters as JEAN MCEWEN, Jacques Hurtubise (*b* 1939) and CHARLES GAGNON, the latter two of whom were more open to the influence of American art than their elders.

A similar development took place in Toronto in the 1950s. The initiator of the modern movement, Jock Macdonald, had taught art at the Ontario College of Art, Toronto, since September 1947 and was as important an art teacher there and in Vancouver as Borduas had been in Quebec. The show that marked a new departure in Toronto painting was called *Abstracts at Home.* It was organized by WILLIAM RONALD, a student of Macdonald, and took place at Simpson's department store in October 1953. The idea was to promote modern furniture and new interior decoration ideas for the middle-class home. Seven painters took part, among them Kazuo Nakamura (*b* 1926), JACK BUSH and Oscar Cahén (1916–56). This was the first time most of the artists had met, but these initial meetings gave rise to the group of abstract painters known as PAINTERS ELEVEN, one of whose better-known members was HAROLD TOWN.

The most significant centre in the western part of Canada was Emma Lake, northern Saskatchewan, the venue for an annual art summer camp developed by the

University of Saskatchewan on land originally belonging to Augustus Kenderline (1870–1947), an artist born and trained in England and the founder of the art department at Regina College (now the University of Regina). The organizers of the summer school, in particular Kenneth Lochhead (*b* 1926), Arthur McKay (*b* 1926), Roy Kiyooka (*b* 1926) and RONALD BLOORE, invited important international artists and critics to the school, among them the painter Barnett Newman (1959). Such visitors were attracted not only by the personalities of the organizers but also by the fact that at the time Saskatchewan was the first region of North America to have elected a socialist government (1944–64) and was therefore of particular interest to the American intelligentsia. Whatever the reasons behind their visits, their mere presence and their continued interest helped to maintain the position of western Canadian painters in the mainstream of American art (*see also* §4 below).

The development of the graphic arts during this period owes much to ALBERT DUMOUCHEL and his influential teaching career in Montreal.

BIBLIOGRAPHY

J. R. Harper: *Painting in Canada: A History* (Toronto and Buffalo, 1966, rev. 2/1977)

D. Reid: *A Concise History of Canadian Painting* (Toronto, 1973, rev. 2/1988)

FRANÇOIS-MARC GAGNON

4. AFTER 1960. By the 1960s abstract painting was firmly entrenched in Montreal and Toronto (*see* §3 above). In Toronto, Jack Bush continued to have a strong influence after the formal dissolution of Painters Eleven in 1960, although painterly abstraction was tempered by figurative and landscape references in the paintings of GRAHAM COUGHTRY, John Meredith (*b* 1933), Gordon Rayner (*b* 1935) and Gershon Iskowitz (1921–88). JOYCE WIELAND and MICHAEL SNOW integrated collage elements into their painting and experimented with film and, in Snow's case, photography. Snow's multimedia work marked the beginnings of conceptual art in Canada.

Smaller, regional centres played an important role in the 1960s and 1970s. In London, Ontario, JACK CHAMBERS and GREG CURNOE espoused a strongly regionalist point of view, emphasizing closely observed local themes, while Ron Martin (*b* 1943) pursued a phenomenologically based abstraction. Landscape has been the subject of the weather paintings (see fig. 7) of Paterson Ewen (*b* 1925) since he abandoned abstraction after leaving Montreal in 1968.

The response to modernism in western Canada was quite varied. In Vancouver JACK LEONARD SHADBOLT continued to be engaged by the landscape. The hard-edge optical style that predominated in the 1960s, seen in the work of Gordon Smith (*b* 1919), Takao Tanabe (*b* 1926) and Brian Fisher (*b* 1939), yielded in the 1970s to an eclecticism informed by intermedia and communications theories. Foremost among the exponents of a more conceptual approach was Iain Baxter (*b* 1936), working under the name of the N. E. Thing Co.

Perhaps the purest response to the influential theories of the American formalist critic Clement Greenberg occurred in the Prairies. Greenberg (1962) and the colour field painters Kenneth Noland (1963) and Jules Olitski (1964) gave workshops at Emma Lake (*see* §3 above) that

7. Paterson Ewen: *Moon over Tobermory*, acrylic and metal on gouged plywood, 2.44×3.36 m, 1981 (Ottawa, National Gallery of Canada)

inspired the painters Kenneth Lochhead (*b* 1926), Ronald Bloore, Arthur McKay (*b* 1926), Ted Godwin (*b* 1933) and Douglas Morton (*b* 1926), who formed the Regina Five. Greenberg's influence also extended to Saskatoon, where Dorothy Knowles (*b* 1927) and her husband, William Perehudoff (*b* 1919), were working. Here, however, landscape painting remained a major force that strongly affected the work of younger artists. In Edmonton, Alberta, a number of formalist painters, including Doug Haynes (*b* 1936) and Bob Scott, maintained close contact with Greenberg, working away from the aesthetic developments occurring elsewhere in Canada.

Figurative painting held its own in many parts of the country. Some painters, such as Ivan Eyre (*b* 1935) in Winnipeg or John Hall (*b* 1943) in Calgary, developed original figurative styles in relative isolation. In the Atlantic provinces a highly realistic figurative style was dominant, as seen in the work of ALEX COLVILLE and Tom Forrestall (*b* 1936) of Nova Scotia or Christopher Pratt (*b* 1935) and Mary Pratt (*b* 1935) of Newfoundland, although since the 1970s the Nova Scotia College of Art and Design, Halifax, under Garry Neill Kennedy (*b* 1935) has provided an alternative orientation towards conceptual art, stimulated by the presence of an international faculty.

In the 1970s the predominant position of painting was challenged, as conceptual art, multimedia work and experimentation with such new media as video opened up a variety of new avenues of artistic expression. Canadian video artists in particular, among them Vera Frenkel, Paul Wong, Colin Campbell, GENERAL IDEA, Julien Poulin and Pierre Falardeau and Norman Cohn, have received widespread recognition for their reshaping of the image of reality presented by the media. Painting and graphic arts in the 1980s were not guided by any one theoretical perspective. Its very openness again made it an attractive vehicle for a wide variety of ideas and styles, from the feminism of Mary Scott to the existential expressionism of BETTY GOODWIN. Perhaps the most important development was the emergence of a newly critical approach to representation, as seen in the work of Joanne Tod (*b* 1953), Shirley Wiitasalo (*b* 1949) and many other painters.

BIBLIOGRAPHY

R. Bringhurst and others, eds: *Visions: Contemporary Art in Canada* (Vancouver and Toronto, 1983)

D. Burnett and M. Schiff: *Contemporary Canadian Art* (Edmonton, 1983)

DIANA NEMIROFF

IV. Sculpture.

1. BEFORE 1960. Academic sculpture was relatively slow in its development in Canada, with little activity before 1880. There was a well-established tradition of wood-carving in Quebec dating back to the 17th century; the majority of products of such sculptors as LOUIS QUÉVILLON served decorative or religious purposes. Early sculptural activity occurred in the major centres of Upper Canada and Lower Canada. The first academically trained sculptors to work in Canada were of foreign birth, and the first sculptures to be exhibited were copies after famous antique and European models. One of the few sculptors doing original work was English-born Samuel Gardner (1817–93), a stone-carver from near Hamilton, Ontario, who modelled a bust of *Governor-General Lord Metcalfe* (*c.* 1847; Toronto, A.G. Ont.). In 1856 the eminent educationist Dr Egerton Ryerson imported many reproductions for his Educational Museum of Upper Canada, Toronto, later commissioning original work; this collection was decentralized when the picture galleries were closed in 1912. In the absence of a large pool of local talent, commissions were often awarded to foreign sculptors; one early exception was the Limeridge monument (1870), Toronto, by the Montreal sculptor Robert Reid, erected in memory of those volunteers who were killed in the raids (1866) made by the Fenians (the Irish Republic Brotherhood) over the Canadian–American border.

By the 1880s there were enough professional sculptors to fill the growing demand for portrait busts and commemorative and historical monuments, which arose from an increased national pride and the concomitant wish to record Canada's history and immortalize her most distinguished citizens. Among those commissioned to model portrait busts for Ryerson's museum were Mildred Peel (*c.* 1855–*c.* 1916), F. A. T. Dunbar (1849–1921) and the two most prolific sculptors of their day, Hamilton MacCarthy (1847–1939) in Ontario and Louis-Philippe Hébert (*see* HÉBERT (ii), (1)) in Quebec. MacCarthy, who arrived from England in 1885, was responsible for the monument to *Sir John A. MacDonald* (1893) at the Provincial Legislative Building in Toronto and monuments to *Samuel de Champlain* (Ottawa, 1915; Saint John, NB) and for numerous monuments commemorating the Boer War. Hébert executed two allegorical groups and six niche figures (1886–96) on the façade of the Assemblée Nationale at Quebec City, whose monumental programme, first envisaged by its architect, Eugène-Etienne Taché, was carried out in altered form by Elzéar Soucy (1876–1970), ALFRED LALIBERTÉ, Henri Hébert (1884–1950), Joseph Brunet (1884–1950), Sylvia Daoust (*b* 1902) and others. Louis-Philippe Hébert also undertook the monuments to *Sir George-Etienne Cartier* (1885), *Sir John A. MacDonald* (1895), *Queen Victoria* and *Alexander Mackenzie* (both 1901), all on Parliament Hill, Ottawa. MARC-AURÈLE DE FOY SUZOR-COTÉ and Laliberté recorded Quebec's history on a more modest scale: the former modelled a number of habitant types, which were cast in bronze between 1911 and 1927 (plaster models, Quebec, Mus. Qué.), and the latter executed 214 small bronze figures depicting the lives of the early Québecois (1928–32; versions, Quebec, Mus. Qué.).

Some sculptors spent prolonged periods abroad, seeking the training, materials or better markets that were lacking in Canada. George Hill (1861–1934) of Montreal studied in Paris and later undertook the memorials to *Queen Victoria* in Ottawa (1901) and Hamilton (1907), the Boer War memorial (1907) in Dominion Square, Montreal, and the nurses' national memorial (1926) in the Parliament Buildings, Ottawa. Alexander Phimster Proctor (1862–1950), an animal sculptor, emigrated to the USA but sent work to Canada for exhibition through the Canadian Art Club. Robert Tait Mackenzie (1867–1938), whose work as a medical doctor took him to Philadelphia in 1904, also exhibited his idealized athletic figures in Canada and undertook such monumental works as *The Call* (the Scottish–American memorial; 1923–7) in Edinburgh and the Rosamund war memorial (1923) at Almonte, Ontario.

The demand for war memorials, especially after World War I, provided such Canadian sculptors as Alfred Howell (1889–1978) and Coeur de Lion MacCarthy (1881–1979) with unprecedented opportunities to practise their art. Walter Allward (1876–1955), one of the foremost sculptors of the early 20th century, had to his credit the Northwest Rebellion monument (1885), the South African memorial (1910; both in Toronto), among others, when he received the commission for the Canadian war memorial (1922–36) at Vimy Ridge, France. His work, like that of Emanuel Hahn (1881–1957), Florence Wyle (1881–1968) and FRANCES N. LORING, demonstrates the contemporary taste for Auguste Rodin and Symbolist sculpture. Hahn designed the Lindsay war memorial (1922) at Lindsay, Ontario, the *Edward Hanlan* memorial (1926), Toronto, and various coins, including the 1935 and 1939 silver dollars. He was influential as a teacher (*c.* 1912–51) at the Ontario College of Art, Toronto, where Stephen Trenka (*b* 1909), Donald Stewart (*b* 1912) and ELIZABETH WYN WOOD, whom he subsequently married, were among his students.

Wyle and Loring, two expatriate Americans, initially worked in a romantic-realist style typified by Loring's series of 15 bronze figures of munition workers commissioned for the Canadian War Records (1918; examples in Ottawa, Can. War Mus.). Both undertook garden, architectural and monumental sculpture: Loring was particularly active in the last and was responsible for the Galt war memorial (1930) at Cambridge, Ontario, for example. In the late 1920s their work began to demonstrate the influence of the more conservative strain of modernism, as practised by the American sculptor Paul Manship, among others. Henri Hébert and Elizabeth Wyn Wood were two major proponents of this style, as exemplified by Wyn Wood's *Reef and Rainbow* (1927, realized in tin on a black marble base, 1935; Toronto, A.G. Ont.; see fig. 8).

In 1928 Wyn Wood, Hébert, Hahn, Loring and Wyle founded the Sculptors' Society of Canada, which signalled the rising status of sculpture in Canada. Its ranks grew to

8. Elizabeth Wyn Wood: *Reef and Rainbow*, cast tin on a black marble base, l. 955 mm, 1935 (Toronto, Art Gallery of Ontario)

include sculptors from across the country: Charles Marega (1875–1939), Beatrice Lennie (1905–87) and Lilias Farley (*b* 1907) from Vancouver; H. McRae Miller (*b* 1895), Pierre Normandeau (1906–65) and Orson Wheeler (*b* 1902) from Montreal; as well as Arthur Tracy (*b* 1910), Alvin Hilts (*b* 1908), Cleeve Horne (*b* 1912) and Jean Horne (*b* 1914), John Sloan (1890–1970), Frances Gage (*b* 1924), William McElcheren (*b* 1927) and Jacobine Jones (1898–1976). During the 1930s and 1940s such sculptors as Jones collaborated with architects on the decoration of new buildings. Of increasing popularity were smaller works scaled for domestic settings, as exemplified by the work of Eugenia Berlin (*b* 1905), Pauline Redsell (*b* 1908), Gloria Jeffries (*b* 1923) and Dora Wechsler (1897–1952).

After World War II Canadian sculptors gradually became aware of recent developments abroad, experimenting with new techniques and participating in international shows and competitions. Such emigré artists as Leo Mol (*b* 1915), Dora de Pedery-Hunt (*b* 1913) and SOREL ETROG contributed to the development of Canadian sculpture in the post-war years. Quebec sculptors led the way towards more contemporary modes of expression, beginning with Louis Archambault (*b* 1915), Charles Daudelin (*b* 1920) and Anne Kahane (*b* 1924). Archambault's *Iron Bird* (1950; Ottawa, N.G.) was the only Canadian work exhibited at the International Exhibition of Sculpture in London in 1951, and Kahane, who became best known for her figurative wood-carvings, won a prize for the *Unknown Political Prisoner* (maquette; Quebec, Mus. Qué.), her entry in an international competition sponsored in 1953 by the Institute of Contemporary Arts, London. Sibyl Kennedy (*b* 1899), who had studied with Alexander Archipenko in New York, specialized in expressively elongated figures inspired by contemporary German sculpture, and E. B. Cox (*b* 1914) similarly showed an awareness in the early 1950s of European sculpture, as well as of native West Coast masks.

BIBLIOGRAPHY

N. MacTavish: *The Fine Arts in Canada* (Toronto, 1925)
Canadian Sculpture (exh. cat., Toronto, A.G., 1928)
M. Ormond Hammond: *Painting and Sculpture in Canada* (Toronto, 1930)
G. McInnes: *A Short History of Canadian Art* (Toronto, 1939)
W. Colgate: *Canadian Art: Its Origin and Development* (Toronto, 1943/*R* 1967)
M. Ross, ed.: *The Arts in Canada: A Stocktaking at Mid-century* (Toronto, 1958)
Panorama de la sculpture au Québec, 1945–1970 (exh. cat., Montreal, Mus. A. Contemp., 1970)
L. Noppen and G. Deschenes: *L'Hôtel du parlement: Témoin de notre histoire* (Quebec City, 1986)
Loring and Wyle: Sculptors' Legacy (exh. cat., Toronto, A.G. Ont., 1987)
R. Shipley: *To Mark our Place: A History of Canadian War Memorials* (Toronto, 1987)
Statues of Parliament Hill: An Illustrated History, National Capital Commission (Ottawa, 1988)
La Sculpture au Québec, 1946–1961: Naissance et persistance (exh. cat. by M. Martin and G. Saint-Pierre, Quebec, Mus. Qué., 1992)

CHRISTINE BOYANOSKI

2. 1960 AND AFTER. In the early 1960s certain European tendencies held sway, as shown in the Expressionist, cast-aluminium sculptures of Walter Yarwood (*b* 1917), who had been a member of Painters Eleven, the 'nail-collage' sculptures of David Partridge (*b* 1919) and the Cubist-inspired bronzes of Sorel Etrog. At Expo 67, Montreal, the Canadian sculpture exhibits ranged from 1950s-style 'scorched and tortured metal' pieces to cool, formal, geometric constructions, exemplified in the work of HENRY SAXE and of Robert Murray (*b* 1936), who made large, angled forms in painted Cor-ten steel (e.g. *Haida*, 1973; Ottawa, Dept. Ext. Affairs). Artists who worked with steel in a similarly expansive vein were Kosso Eloul (*b* 1920) and Ted Bieler (*b* 1938), with his outdoor piece *Tetra* (1976; Kingston, Ont.). Hugh Leroy (*b* 1939) and Ed Zelenak (*b* 1940) also made pieces intended for public spaces, but they used cast or laminated fibreglass (e.g. Zelenak's *Stratford Piece*, 1972; Stratford, Ont.). Government, corporate and gallery sources provided support for work to complement the building boom in the 1970s.

Pop, Minimalism, conceptual and land art all had their adherents in the late 1960s and the 1970s. Such painters as MICHAEL SNOW turned to sculpture; he made a series of stiff, upright, cut-out female figures (e.g. *Expo Walking Woman*, 1966–7; Toronto, A.G. Ont.) to express his view of uniformity and alienation in modern life. Françoise Sullivan (*b* 1925) moved from welded metal constructions in the 1950s to wall-hung, shaped and stretched raw canvases linked with floor sculptures, often of piles of stones (e.g. *Tondo 7*, 1980; Ottawa, Canada Council A. Bank). The minimalist work of the RABINOWITCH brothers is concerned with the relationship between the viewer and the sculpture. Liz Magor (*b* 1948) constructed mixed-media assemblages evocative of time, memory and place (e.g. *Time and Mrs Tiber*, 1976; Ottawa, N.G.), while MURRAY FAVRO created such installations as *Van Gogh's Room* (Toronto, A.G. Ont.). Wood, water and living moss were used for indoor sculptures; animal forms reappeared, sometimes as a comment on human activity, as in *Dogface Boys' Picnic* (1974–5; Ottawa, N.G.) by Sherry Grauer (*b* 1939). In the 1980s there was a preoccupation with sculpture as architecture and as non-functioning machines, and with sculpture built from electronic gadgetry, often incorporating video. Eva Brandl (*b* 1951) filled gallery spaces with structures akin to Aztec temples or built tall, isolated towers; witty, electromechanical pieces by Roland Brener (*b* 1942) utilized sound, signs and movement (e.g. *Small Talk*, 1987; Victoria, BC, A.G. Gtr Victoria). Michel Goulet (*b* 1944) assembled sundry objects to create narrative set pieces, as in his *Factitious Faction* (1988; Montreal, artist's col.), which includes a row of rifles and books.

Sculptors continue to explore viewer participation, cinematic display and storytelling. Aside from his controversial use of raw meat as a medium, Jana Sterbak (*b* 1955) has constructed sleek wooden sculptures; *Sisyphus* (1990) is an upturned 'bell', into which he climbed to rock around the floor, maintaining direct engagement with the object. Kim Adams (*b* 1951) piled car trailers with models of fantasy islands, replete with tiny houses, farms, trees, people and animals (e.g. *Earth Wagons*, 1989–91; Montreal, Gal. Christiane Chassay).

BIBLIOGRAPHY

D. Burnett and M. Schiff: *Contemporary Canadian Art* (Edmonton, 1983)
D. Fetherling, ed.: *Documents in Canadian Art* (Peterborough, Ont., 1987)

□

V. Interior design.

1. Architectural. 2. Decorative.

1. ARCHITECTURAL. With the gradual establishment of permanent settlements in Quebec and on the eastern seaboard, building forms of European character were introduced, and ideas on the internal treatment of rooms began to spread. The early evolution of interior architecture in Canada can be characterized by movement through various stylistic phases: the Baroque and French Neo-classical, followed by Georgian, Classical Revival, Gothic Revival, Italianate, Second Empire, Romanesque Revival and Queen Anne, to a return of classicism at the end of the 19th century. The first artisans and builders who came to Canada were specialized and skilled craftsmen who probably played a dominant role in the way buildings looked, over that of the individual designer (architect or engineer). Craftsmanship of exceptionally high quality was practised, notably in religious institutions in Quebec; examples include the 17th-century square-framed wooden staircase in the Aile St-Augustin at the Ursuline convent and the carving by Pierre Emond (1738–1808) in Monsig. Briand Chapel in the Séminaire de Québec, both in Quebec City.

The introduction of plaster at the beginning of the 19th century led to fine work, notably in the decoration of ceilings. The work of the late 1820s and 1830s in the old part of Quebec City is outstanding, with designs of great delicacy and linear quality featuring swags, garlands and torches in the style of Robert Adam, edged with modillion cornices. In Toronto, of particular interest is Osgoode Hall (begun 1829) by Frederic William Cumberland and William G. Storm, the Great Library (1857; part of the centre block rebuilt 1856–60) of which is perhaps the finest room in Canada. The proportions are almost equal to the triple cube, and the detail is classical. The richly ornamented plasterwork of the domed and vaulted ceiling, the double columns, pilasters and pedimented doorways contribute to the overall impression of sumptuous elegance.

With Confederation in 1867, the symbol of self-government became the Parliament Buildings in Ottawa, designed in the Gothic Revival style and possessing the impressive interior of the Parliamentary Library (1878) by John William Hurrell Watts (1850–1917). The use of coloured floor-tiles and window glass throughout the complex illustrates the taste for polychromy that had developed in the 1850s.

The McGill University Union Building (1904–6) in Montreal, designed by PERCY NOBBS, is a good example of a building by an architect interested in total design. His plans included furniture, plaster decoration and wrought-iron fittings in the tradition of the Arts and Crafts Movement, with such Canadian motifs as the McGill shield and heraldic devices of the provinces playing an important part in the decorative scheme. Nobbs's use of plaster to impart beauty and character to an interior is illustrated in the Faculty Room (*c.* 1916) of the Arts Building at the University of Alberta, Edmonton. Oval in shape, the richly garlanded high ceiling crowns a room whose plain walls are enriched with shallow niches containing flower baskets filled with stylized vegetation.

SAMUEL MACLURE, a British Columbia-based architect, is noted for his domestic interiors, which invariably display two distinct features: a cross-axial ground-floor plan with rooms arranged around a central hall, often containing a fireplace flanked by built-in chimney-corner seats in the best Arts and Crafts manner, and finely detailed hand-crafted furniture and fittings. Maclure was responsible for the interiors of Government House (1903) in Victoria, BC, in collaboration with the architect FRANCIS MAWSON RATTENBURY. The firm of Henry Bloomfield & Sons executed the large oriel window on the staircase, incorporating British Columbian coastal themes, while James J. Bloomfield (1872–1951), son of British-born Henry Bloomfield (*fl* 1887–1900), designed and painted the murals for the ballroom ceiling, featuring stencilled figures from ten local native tribes, one over each of the arched openings and spandrels.

The search for an identifiably Canadian style of architecture was a major concern of JOHN M. LYLE, a Toronto-based architect. His interior schemes, especially those of the numerous office buildings for the Bank of Nova Scotia in the 1920s and 1930s, are characterized by their bold planar forms, light, clear colours and stylized ornament based on Canadian flora and fauna, historical figures and local industry. St Anne's Church in Toronto is one of the few public buildings in Canada with a complete interior decoration scheme planned from inception and fully realized. Designed in the Byzantine Revival style by the architect William Ford Howland (1874–1948) in 1907, the decoration took place from 1923 to 1925 under the direction of the architect William Rae (1867–1957), with J. E. H. MacDonald, a member of the Group of Seven, as overall designer. The plan of the church is in the form of a Greek cross, dominated by a dome supported on four arches. The colour palette is in a limited range of earth-tones with the addition of ultramarine blue and gold. Figural works by Herbert H. Stansfield (1881–1937), Herbert Sydney Palmer (1881–1970), Fred Varley and MacDonald fill the pendentives, while four huge heads of Old Testament prophets painted by Varley and sculpted plaques of the symbols of the four Evangelists by Frances N. Loring and Florence Wyle (1881–1968) were placed around the base of the dome.

In spite of the Depression of the 1930s Canadian interiors were created that made inventive use of luxurious materials. The interior of the Cormier House (1930–31) in Montreal is an outstanding example (see fig. 9). The architect ERNEST CORMIER designed the house for himself and was responsible for all interior design, furnishings and fixtures. Most notable is the use of decorative floor materials in different patterns throughout the five-level house, related to the status of various rooms. A simple rectangular design in cork for a bathroom on the fifth level carries through to the immense studio space, its magnificent terrazzo floor interlaced with large interlocking circles and squares inlaid in marble. Wall treatments feature exotic materials in two patterns—horizontal bands and a chequer-board. In the studio, alternating bands of Japanese pear-wood veneer were hand-tinted in dark mahogany and silver blue. The consistency expressed throughout in material, pattern and colour distinguish the house as one of the most mature examples of the Art Deco style in Canada. Elsewhere, the architect Marcel B. Parizeau (1898–1945), head of the Interior Decoration Department (1936–45) of the Ecole de Meuble in Montreal, created Le Corbusier-influenced interiors that offered a strongly individual approach to the Art Deco style, characterized by simplification of form, clean lines, fine workmanship and the use of natural materials.

9. Ernest Cormier: living-room of Cormier House, Montreal, 1930–31

The International Style was introduced in Canada during the 1960s through the rationalized building methods of Ludwig Mies van der Rohe as developed by the American building industry and its corporate clientele. His approach was to design a system of building that required the maximum utilization of highly refined technology; internal spaces expressed the programme of Purism through the precise use of materials, repeated elements and total absence of ornament. The best example in Canada is the Toronto–Dominion Centre (1963–9) in Toronto, designed by Mies van der Rohe with local architectural consultants John B. Parkin Associates and Bregman & Hamann. The rough texture and cool colour of the grey granite floor and natural surface of the beige travertine walls in the ground-floor lobbies are part of a vocabulary of materials that includes black-painted steel members and clear and bronze-tinted glass.

The decoration of the National Arts Centre in Ottawa was the federal government's major centennial project (1967) for the nation's capital. The talents of many artists were incorporated into the interior of the building, particularly in the treatment of ceilings, walls, screens and doors. Two Canadian textile artists contributed important works: Micheline Beauchemin (*b* 1930) designed one of the most dramatic components in the form of an Opera Hall curtain in panels of looped nylon fibre in graded shades of red; the Theatre curtain by Mariette Rousseau-Vermette (*b* 1926) is a large, three-dimensional, abstract composition in colours ranging from deep purple and blue through olive green to golden yellow. Notable among interior spaces at Expo 67 in Montreal were the 12 exhibition suites in Habitat '67, the modular multiple housing complex (see fig. 3 above) designed by architect Moshe Safdie. Each suite was designed by a Canadian architectural firm or interior designer, including Dudas Kuypers Rowan Ltd, Jacques S. Guillon and Associates, Forrest, Bodrug & Associates, Webb Zerafa Menkes, Architects (Alison Hymas (*b* 1932), interior designer), Sigrun Bulow-Hube, Robert Kaiser, John Gallop, Howard Taylor and Christen Sorensen, and furnished by Canadian manufacturers. It afforded an important showcase for Canadian products and such innovative furnishing materials as fibreglass, reinforced plastic and acrylic plastic sheeting, as well as novel lighting techniques, including interior-lit upholstered chairs.

In the 1970s the demand for consumer goods led to the construction of such shopping facilities as enclosed malls, the interior surfaces of which afforded space for large-scale art works. At the Eaton Centre (1977) in Toronto, a multi-level glass-enclosed galleria, the South Court is enlivened with the sculpture *Flight Stop* (1979) by Michael Snow, representing a flock of 60 Canada geese, individually suspended and descending from a height of 36.6 m. More recently, interior architecture has reflected the impact of innovative technology, specifically in the areas of communications, climate control, lighting, security and sound. Nowhere has this been more dramatically demonstrated than in the Canadian Centre for Architecture (1989), Montreal. Designed by the architect Peter Rose (*b* 1943) in collaboration with the founder of the centre, the architect Phyllis Lambert (*b* 1927), the building epitomizes the most advanced techniques in museum design. The clarity of organization of the interior volumes, together with the meticulous detailing of the materials—Trenton limestone, the material of 19th-century Montreal, maple panelling and anodized aluminium—and the restrained use of colour, combine to make the interior spaces among the most memorable of the late 20th century.

See also §II above.

BIBLIOGRAPHY

E. Arthur: *Toronto: No Mean City* (Toronto, 1964)
A. Gowans: *Building Canada: An Architectural History of Canadian Life* (Toronto, 1966)
J. Parkin: *Art in Architecture* (Toronto, 1982)
S. Wagg: *Percy Erskine Nobbs: Architect, Artist, Craftsman* (Montreal, 1982)
John M. Lyle: Towards a Canadian Architecture (exh. cat. by G. Hunt, Kingston, Ont., Queen's U., Agnes Etherington A. Cent., 1982)
J. Bingham: *Samuel Maclure, Architect* (Ganges, BC, 1985)
Seduced and Abandoned (exh. cat. by V. Wright, Toronto, A.G. Harbourfront, 1985–6)
C. Cameron and M. Trepanier: *Vieux Québec: Son Architecture intérieure* (Ottawa, 1986)
W. Dendy and W. Kilbourn: *Toronto Observed* (Toronto, 1986)
G. Lesser: *Ecole du meuble, 1930–1950* (Montreal, 1989)

OLGA M. WILLIAMS

2. DECORATIVE. The founding of Quebec in 1608 introduced into the St Lawrence River valley the French furniture styles and decorative tastes that were to dominate interiors for the following 150 years. Although ecclesiastical communities, government officials and the military brought personal belongings and furniture with them in the early years of settlement, the difficulties of survival were such that one can hardly speak of interior decoration during the first half-century. The first domestic buildings of New France usually consisted of one large, all-purpose room with a fireplace on each end wall or, alternatively, an interior wall with fireplace separating working and living space from sleeping space. Most floors were of butted cedar or pine boards; walls were rough plastered and whitewashed over masonry or timber construction. Houses of the merchant and seigneurial classes normally had more internal divisions and showed some interest in decoration and material comfort as social life and a local economy developed. Because it was practical as insulation, readily available and could be decoratively treated, wooden panelling soon became a common form of internal finish in the homes of the wealthier classes from the late 17th century well into the 19th. As early as 1662 the inventory of Lambert Closs (E.-Z. Massicotte: 'L'inventaire de Lambert Closs', *Bull. Rech. Hist.*, xxv/1 (Jan 1919), pp. 16–31) mentions that 'The said house [has] three rooms, two with fireplace, of which the first is panelled all round.' In addition to plain panels, motifs of the successive Louis styles created an *en suite* effect in keeping with the Louis XIV aesthetic of the late 17th century. An advertisement in the *Quebec Gazette* (18 Oct 1764) describes the interior organization and decoration of the former governor's house then for sale, including the 'pier glasses, and the pieces of painting placed over the doors', as was the custom in France.

Until the end of the 17th century most furniture was considered a part of the architectural décor and was ranged stiffly around the walls of the room. Tables and benches were frequently placed against an end wall, and diners would sit with their backs to the wall when eating. In domestic interiors many tables were drop-leaf or of trestle construction, drawn forward into the room for use, dismounted and stored against a wall at other times. Such case furniture as armoires, dish dressers and buffets were sometimes built into the thick walls. The description by Swedish botanist Pehr Kalm, who travelled through Canada in 1749, of a seigneurial interior gives a precise picture of the high end of interior decoration in French Canada: 'The interior of the houses is well furnished; different sorts of tapestries, as we have, a commode with many drawers placed between two windows, a large mirror with a gilded frame hanging above the commode; various likenesses on the walls, among which a good number of priests and monks.' Habitant interiors of the same period were furnished more sparsely, the furniture itself, in local adaptations of the Louis XIII, XIV or XV styles, providing the only decorative elements in an otherwise plank-floored and whitewashed room. Inventories made after the deaths of peasants, merchants and tradesmen confirm the presence in the 18th century of common furniture forms in modest numbers, as well as some textiles, particularly bed-hangings, candlesticks, open animal-oil lamps and lanterns, but very little to suggest other than utilitarian objects.

When the British took Quebec in 1759 a new decorative vocabulary of forms and motifs introduced Chippendale, then Adam and finally Sheraton and Empire styles for furniture and interiors. Neo-classical elements began to appear in woodwork—doorjambs, window-frames, cornices and panelling. The tariff tables of 1748 indicate that imported textiles, carpets and wall hangings were becoming widely available as the population grew to about 55,000, and commercial activity increased. The interior of a house for sale in Montreal was described in the *Quebec Gazette* (9 Nov 1769) as 'neatly finished, wainscotted, painted and papered in the English manner'. A largely American taste for painted surfaces applied to pine and birch for interior finish, creating *trompe l'oeil* effects that imitated oak, mahogany, rose-wood and even local bird's-eye or tiger maple, began to displace to some extent plain painted surfaces. This practice satisfied a growing desire for exotic but unavailable or expensive woods while updating older pieces and panels in the taste of the day.

10. Cornelius Krieghoff: *Officer's Trophy Room*, oil on canvas, 445×635 mm, 1846 (Toronto, Sigmund Samuel Building)

In the Maritime provinces, the settlement along the south shore of Nova Scotia of so-called 'foreign protestants' from Germany and Switzerland in 1753 added to the Georgian tastes of the British at Halifax a whole new range of folk motifs, such as hearts and flowers, rosettes and sun discs, compass stars and birds, as well as a predilection for polychrome painted surfaces and painted canvas floor coverings that combined the practical advantages of easy cleaning with the pleasures of decorative effect and the ordered stability of geometrically marked motifs. The influx of Loyalists after the American Revolution contributed a New England version of modified British forms to this mix. At first, interiors were simply furnished with late Chippendale pieces and adaptations of American Windsor chairs and of the Federal style. Portraits of family members and of ships reflected the clannish nature and the commercial bases of the maritime economy as well as the practical and conservative attitudes of the community. In the 19th century a fashion for scenic and stylized ceilings and murals produced a remarkable number of painted interiors, of which the Croscup Room (*c.* 1848; Ottawa, N.G.) is the most developed example. Based on images drawn from the *Illustrated London News*, the decoration demonstrates the imagination and ingenuity of the folk artist in adapting the materials at hand to situations in which the products and technical means of high-style design were unavailable or too costly. About 100 surviving examples of rooms with decorative schemes in this tradition trace the path of itinerant artists along the settled shores of Nova Scotia and display stylized images of the Tree of Life, framing effects of swags and garlands, and abstract designs that reveal a delight in colour and line.

In central Canada, as in the Maritime provinces, 19th-century decoration was for the most part Victorian in essence and derivative in style, although it reflected local circumstances and conditions in terms of objects, materials and finish. The influence of Anglo-American taste was pervasive, as was the growing presence of mass-produced industrial products and eclectic forms, imported at first and then imitated by local manufacturers, including Thomas Nisbet in Saint John, New Brunswick, William Drum (1808–76) in Quebec City and Jacques & Hay in Toronto. With such merchandizing phenomena as the mail-order catalogue, stylistically watered-down, inexpensive and commercial versions of revival styles and designs were brought to country and city dwellers alike towards the end of the century. Climate and a scattered population reinforced the inward-looking tendencies of the Victorian aesthetic at both the centre and the periphery of the country. Social life was inevitably more conservative and introverted, parlour-based and familial than in warmer countries, and the Victorian interior provided a kind of psychological antidote to the overwhelming presence of the natural forces that had so intimidated the first settlers. Cornelius Krieghoff's painting *Officer's Trophy Room* (1846; Toronto, Sigmund Samuel Bldg; see fig. 10), reproduced in the round in the Musée Canadien des Civilisations (Hull, Quebec), provides an exceptional image of a

Canadian interior of the mid-19th century. The young officer's collections of such ethnographic and site-specific objects as snowshoes, bearskin rugs and military paraphernalia reflect both the Canadian scene and the European tradition of the cabinet of curiosities within the overall clutter and disorganization of a Victorian aesthetic. In this bric-à-brac view of domestic interiors no space is left unfilled, no object can be out of place. Paintings, including Krieghoff's own in miniature, harness, books, stuffed birds, moccasins and a bust of Shakespeare all share the dark interior, unlit from without, a kind of psychological repository of personal tastes, interests, occupations and curiosities. The natural world intrudes only as a cultural artefact, created and mediated by the artist himself, into the European space of military and cultural conquest.

In Montreal, the commercial and financial heart of the country, the evolving forms of Victorian style appeared at their most elaborate in the mansions of the ruling élite from about 1850 to 1930. At first colourful and overstated, heavy with mouldings, marble mantels surmounted by gilt-framed mirrors, brightly coloured wallpapers, thick velour curtains and an excess of furniture, this taste became more subdued towards the end of the century. Dark wood panelling, beamed or coffered ceilings, mantels with shelves above for small objects and massive furniture mirrored medieval and Renaissance furnishings. The Arts and Crafts Movement soon purged the excesses of these variants of Victorian décor without changing entirely some of its psychological effects. The simplified rectilinear lines of oak furniture, the sombre tones of varnished panelling, the suppression of unintegrated objects and overstocked rooms created a more masculine atmosphere without eliminating the darkness and the inward-looking ambience associated with medievalism in its Victorian guise. The shift in emphasis from surface decoration to structure suggested stability, security and the exclusion of the external world. In a similar vein Toronto developed what might be called the 'inglenook' syndrome: small-paned, leaded windows with built-in window-seats below, stained-glass transoms and secondary windows, varnished panelling, Arts and Crafts-style furniture, Gothic framed fireplaces flanked by inset seating as a decorative focus in principal rooms and Oriental carpets on oak strip or parquet flooring. The domestic interiors of western Canada, settled from about the mid- to late 19th century, reflected either the simplicity and austerity of immigrant life in its meagre beginnings or the post-industrial tastes of already established eastern traders and businessmen. The railway to the Pacific, completed in 1885, and the mail-order catalogue of the T. Eaton Co., first published in 1884, brought to these newcomers, according to their means, the industrial styles of machine-made furniture and household items in a proliferation unthinkable before steam and the Industrial Revolution. The log-cabin technology of early Canadian settlement and the turf-hut expedient of the treeless prairie landscape soon gave way to frame houses, wood-stove heating, embossed tin panelling of ceilings and walls, press-back chairs, fancy oil lamps and chandeliers, inexpensive pottery and decorative china from the rapidly industrializing urban centres of North America. Despite this product-driven decoration, which proposed more or less the same possibilities to everyone, certain Canadian motifs emerged—the beaver, the buffalo, the maple leaf—that could not be assimilated with international concepts of design or function.

Mid- to late 20th-century interior decoration, in one manifestation at least, still contained the same impulses towards the appropriation of personal space as those seen in an *Officer's Trophy Room.* The turn towards country furnishings and the icons of domestic life is in a direct line of descent from the values expressed in Krieghoff's painting: a nostalgia for reassuring and familiar objects, the spice of the exotic safely tamed and flight from the high-tech, synthetic materials and aggressively geometric, mechanical forms that characterize the other dominant trend in contemporary decoration, formal Modernism and its Post-modern successors. The former style is most clearly seen in such magazines as *Century Home* (1983–) and *City and Country Home* (1982–), in which antique and reproduction furniture of an earlier age is combined with traditional handmade textiles (quilts, coverlets, hooked rugs), folk-art objects, collections of country pottery, early advertising items and the like arranged for the most part in 'cosy' and anachronistic settings that idealize the gritty living conditions and hard times of pre-20th-century North America. The opposite trend is minimalist, modernist and international, anchored in clean, open interior spaces with furniture in metal, glass, plastics, leather and wood, with large abstract paintings and little surface ornament other than material textures. It is a style that is functional, often austere, impersonal and non-specific, very unlike the 'country' look that emphasizes the decorative, sentimental, eccentric and circumstantial.

BIBLIOGRAPHY

L. Russell: *Heritage of Light: Lamps and Lighting in Early Canadian Homes* (Toronto, 1968)

E. Colchester and G. Colchester: 'Domestic Interiors', *Can. Colr*, xi/3 (1976), pp. 70–75

J. Bernier: *Les Intérieurs domestiques des menuisiers et charpentiers de la région de Québec, 1810–1819* (Ottawa, 1977), p. 83

P. Kalm: *Voyage de Pehr Kalm au Canada en 1749*, ed. and trans. J. Rousseau and G. Béthune (Montreal, 1977)

C. Cameron: *Index of Houses Featured in 'Canadian Homes and Gardens' from 1925 to 1944* (Ottawa, 1980)

C. Greenaway: *Interior Decorative Painting in Nova Scotia* (Halifax, 1986)

F. Rémillard and B. Merrett: *Mansions of the Golden Square Mile: Montreal, 1850–1930* (Montreal, 1987)

VI. Furniture.

The history of furniture-making in Canada has its beginnings in style migration and is closely tied to ethnic origins and political realignments. Unlike the machine-made products of the mid- to late 19th century and the international styles of the 20th, all of the distinct furniture forms of Canada reflect their ethnic origins in style survivals easily identified with European traditions.

1. Before the mid-19th century. 2. Mid-19th century and after.

1. Before the mid-19th century.

(i) Quebec. (ii) The Maritime provinces. (iii) Ontario.

(i) Quebec. By the time of the first nominal census of New France in 1666, the population of about 3200 included 65 artisans directly connected to either carpentry or joinery. Along with the other woodworking trades, these craftsmen

constituted about 35% of the skilled workmen in the colony and continued until the end of the 18th century to be the largest single group of tradesmen. Although hundreds of names of joiners and turners occur in documents of the period, none of their furniture appears to have been signed. Unlike the closely controlled guild system in France, there was no requirement in French Canada to present a masterpiece to a jury in order to practise. This freedom encouraged a highly personal character in the unsigned pieces of French Canada, very different from the identifiable but rigidly controlled and more predictable furniture of France.

The traditional forms of French–Canadian furniture, based on the Louis XIII, XIV and XV styles, evolved slowly from the foundation of Quebec City in 1608 until its capture by the British in 1759. The first of these Louis styles to be used in Canada favoured the square in structural terms and the equilateral triangle as the basic decorative motif: the lozenge, the cross of St Andrew and the diamond point. Tables and chairs had supports and stretchers turned in spirals, columns and baluster shapes; case furniture (chests, armoires etc) was often framed with symmetrical mouldings. The overall effect was of simplicity, mass and stability. The Louis XIV style continued but modified these geometric preferences with an insistence on rectilinear simplicity, an emphasis on parallel lines, curves of short radius and a general architectural effect of formality and imposing scale. The gilding, veneering and marquetry found in France were replaced in Canada with vigorously carved geometric shapes and plain painted surfaces. As the Louis XIV style evolved into the Louis XV, which was to be the last metropolitan influence to affect directly the furniture of French Canada, the curvilinear replaced the rectilinear as the dominant line, and asymmetrical decoration in the form of vines, shells, S- and C-curves, volutes and scrolls proclaimed a growing interest in natural forms, greater comfort and a taste for movement and life.

The arrival in Quebec of the British and then the Americans in lesser numbers led to a reorientation of tastes. French styles, cut off from Continental models, began to assimilate Anglo-American forms and motifs in unusual and sometimes very successful new hybrids. Even a return to the straight lines of Neo-classicism at the end of the 18th century came through Anglo-American sources rather than directly from the Louis XVI idiom. The Anglo-American influence was mainly of a practical rather than a bookish nature. British officers, merchants and administrators brought with them quantities of furniture, usually of mahogany, in the latest British styles, which must have set new fashions in motion among the French élite. The sale of the household furniture of a Colonel Irving, advertised in the *Quebec Gazette* (23 April 1767), mentions 'very handsome mahogany four post bedsteads . . . field bedsteads, mahogany chairs, black birch ditto, mahogany desks, walnut ditto, mahogany tables, birch ditto' etc. The birch furniture may well have been made locally in the new styles, since birch, along with white pine, was the principal wood used in the making of furniture during the French regime. Some of the mahogany pieces may have been the work of one of the several British craftsmen recently established in Quebec (*see* MONTREAL, §3 and QUEBEC, §2). As early as 26 June 1766 Henry O'Neill, a joiner, and Henry Dunn, a cabinetmaker, were advertising in the *Quebec Gazette* for 'an apprentice boy, of a good character'.

Much of the early French–Canadian furniture that survives was made between 1760 and 1820 and combines traditional French models of provincial inspiration with certain of the more formal decorative features of the work of Thomas Chippendale and particularly of Robert Adam. The COMMODE, which was perhaps the most sophisticated of the forms made during this period, is often purely French in the shape and line of the case (*arbalete*, *bombe* etc) but with Chippendale claw-and-ball feet. One playful example, a finely executed, sophisticated commode (Montreal, Mus. F.A.), has boot feet, illustrating the tendency to anomalous folk interpretation of high-style forms in 18th-century Canada. While maintaining essential French characteristics of proportion, line and construction, armoires also frequently show the decorative vocabulary of the Adam style in the execution of cornice, frieze and panel.

At least one form unique to French Canada, the *capucine* chair (see fig. 11), developed during the latter half of the 18th century. The French prototype was the straw chair, a simply made, undecorated ladder-back with a straw seat.

11. *Capucine* chair, birch-wood and rush, h. 991 mm, made in Quebec, second half of the 18th century (Toronto, Royal Ontario Museum)

12. Mahogany sofa table by Thomas Nisbet, h. 705 mm, made in Saint John, New Brunswick, *c.* 1825 (Toronto, Royal Ontario Museum)

In contrast, the Canadian *capucine* has baluster turnings in the Louis XIII fashion, strong shaping of the horizontal back splats and a rather more imposing size and gives an overall impression of lightness and good proportion.

An unusual aspect of the Anglo-American influence on the basic French styles of the *ancien régime* was the frequent stylistic updating, particularly of case pieces that had been painted originally in a characteristic blue, green or red, by repainting in imitation of such woods as the native bird's-eye and tiger maple or imported mahogany and rose-wood. This practice (used, for example, by the TWISS family of clockmakers) provided a popular solution to an economic problem—the cost of imported and unusual woods—and the dilemma of keeping up with changing fashions. At times the technique resulted in exceptional effects of *trompe l'oeil* or fanciful abstract decoration quite unlike European decorative painting of either architecture or furniture.

(ii) The Maritime provinces. With the arrival of Governor Edward Cornwallis, accompanied by about 2500 English colonists, and the founding of Halifax, Nova Scotia, in 1749, a parallel to the French settlement was born in the Maritime regions of eastern Canada. Apparently 14 joiners and 3 turners came with Cornwallis, and a further 35 arrived in 1753. Very little documented furniture of the 18th century has been identified, however, other than a few Windsor chairs stamped by Joseph Degant, who worked in Halifax *c.* 1780. This was an industry of individual craftsmen tied to the British and American style tradition, which eventually flourished in the first half of the 19th century with such makers as THOMAS NISBET in St John, NB; the firm of Tulles, Pallister & McDonald in Halifax; James Cole, the Windsor chairmaker, also in Halifax; and JOSEPH SIBLEY and his son and nephews in Wittenburg, NS.

The other major group of early settlers was American (from *c.* 1750), first the pre-Loyalists, then Loyalists after the American Revolution and finally those who simply imagined a better life in new surroundings. Some brought furniture with them, and it may be assumed that the craftsmen in the group were subject to continuing strong influences from the nearest centres of commerce and supply—Boston, New York and the New England states generally, where an American interpretation of Georgian styles had already occurred. The predominant use of mahogany in the prevailing Anglo-American styles (e.g. a sofa table by Nisbet, *c.* 1825; Toronto, Royal Ont. Mus.; see fig. 12) coincided with ready access to mahogany returned as ballast in ships trading with the West Indies out of Halifax and Saint John.

The principal local woods used in the St John River valley were birch, pine, maple, cherry and butternut. The styles at first were interpretations of the late Georgian versions (American Federal style) of Adam, Hepplewhite and Sheraton, or French Neo-classical then Empire forms as seen through American eyes. Windsor chairs became an altogether independent form in North America, without the central pierced splat common in Britain, constructed rather with multiple spindles and vigorous turnings of legs and stretchers. Many of these chairs were branded or stencilled with makers' names, unlike the more important cabinet pieces, which seldom had paper labels or other identification. In such rural areas as outpost Newfound-land, traditional furniture continued to be made well into the 20th century.

One other ethnic group contributed to the decorative vocabulary of Maritime furniture forms from about 1753 to the 19th century, the so-called 'foreign protestants' recruited in Germany and Switzerland to balance the French presence in the St Lawrence River valley and the French-speaking Acadians in New Brunswick and Nova Scotia. The German speakers, who settled mainly in Lunenburg and along the south shore of Nova Scotia, left a strong visual record of their origins. It is the decorative aspects of Lunenburg furniture that reveal a Germanic presence, however, rather than the furniture forms them-selves, which are essentially British in line and proportion. Such motifs as hearts, stylized floral elements, swirls, stars of various sorts and whirling swastikas are frequent, as are chip-carving of edges in framing and textured effects of depth. These are motifs that are part of the folk traditions in many European countries, here used obsessively and in simple ways. For the most part, the individual elements are spaced over the surface rather than being continuous and stand in strong contrasting colours against a unified field of different hue. English-style cupboards in Neo-classical and Empire shapes often received another kind of decorative treatment in the form of overall painted designs in imitation of exotic woods or simply in free-hand, abstract patterns of black over red.

(iii) Ontario. Like the Maritime provinces, Upper Canada was settled mainly by Loyalists. A second large group was made up of Pennsylvania Germans, many of whom were Mennonites, and Quakers, whose pacifism and generally disinterested political attitude were at odds with the prevailing climate in the USA. Both the American and German Loyalists carried to Upper Canada the styles of Britain and the Continent as modified by the American experience; thus Regency and later Empire characteristics

appear in Upper Canadian furniture through American Federal and Empire forms rather than directly from either British, German or French models. By the early 19th century emigration from Britain brought the direct influence of Chippendale, Adam, Hepplewhite and Sheraton to exist side by side with the American adaptations of these styles. Similarly, Pennsylvania German furniture forms found themselves in company with German styles introduced by immigrants arriving directly from the German-speaking areas of Western Europe from *c.* 1820 to 1860. The settle bed, a distinctive vernacular type, was made in areas of Irish settlement.

Maple (bird's-eye and curly), cherry and walnut were the cabinet hardwoods used in Upper Canada, with pine as a secondary wood. Finished with a clear sealer, hardwood furniture had relatively little elaborate inlay in spite of a frequent mixing of such woods as maple and walnut in simple geometric patterns. Pine and basswood were the chief softwoods used for less formal furniture; they were either plain painted or more skilfully executed in imitation of native fancy woods or such exotic imports as mahogany and rose-wood. The Pennsylvania Germans particularly favoured these *trompe l'oeil* graining effects and strongly abstract decoration. While they preserved the Pennsylvania tradition of painted or inlaid dates, initials and names to identify or commemorate important events, they did not in the main continue the practice of elaborate floral and folk motif embellishment found in Pennsylvania.

The first furniture-maker to advertise in the *Upper Canada Gazette* (23 Jan 1802) was Daniel Tiers (*b c.* 1777) of York (now Toronto), a chairmaker. Like many other artisans of the early 19th century, he was obliged to combine this profession with other activities in order to survive. As the colony grew, however, some small factory operations developed. American-born Chester Hatch (*b* 1796), who began operations in Kingston in 1816, had opened a branch in the rival town of York by the summer of 1823 and offered 'fancy, bamboo and Windsor chairs . . . for cash or produce' (*Upper Canada Gazette*, 21 Aug 1823). These and similar advertisements indicate the beginnings of a specialized local industry in the Anglo-American Neo-classical and Empire styles, as well as an ever present American influence, which increased through the various furniture revivals of the Victorian era. Such Canadian manufacturers as JACQUES & HAY fought back with their own versions of popular American revival styles, while Canadian chairmakers imitated the painted American Hitchcock chair of Sheraton inspiration and the Windsor in simplified form. These were for the most part factory-made chairs that sold at modest prices. Although immigrant craftsmen from Britain and imported furniture undoubtedly maintained a British presence in some fashionable parlours, the common man was increasingly furnished by American industry and enterprise or local versions of the product.

There are no developed Upper Canadian styles with a central body of characteristic structures, profiles and decorative features, but there are distinctive pieces that adapt or combine in original ways both materials and elements of high-style inspiration. A corner cupboard from eastern Ontario (*c.* 1820–30; Toronto, Royal Ont. Mus.), made of painted pine rather than mahogany, combines Adamesque elements of architectural detail and such motifs as urns, fans and paterae with half columns that extend into turned feet suggestive of Sheraton and even Empire influences. The overall execution of the decorative elements, with the exception of the finely glazed doors, is heavily exaggerated, the work of a skilled but unsophisticated artisan. Eventually the influence of Victorian revivals, of the Arts and Crafts Movement and of Charles Locke Eastlake and others as interpreted by the American furniture industry obscured whatever Canadian characteristics of motif and material had existed earlier in the less commercialized, more individualistic craft tradition, and the styles of New York and other American centres came to dominate the trade after about 1850.

2. MID-19TH CENTURY AND AFTER.

(i) Immigrant and religious sect styles. During the latter half of the 19th century a further influx of European immigrants brought German speakers and Poles to Renfrew and Wilno in eastern Ontario and, into the empty spaces of western Canada, such ethnic religious sects as the Dukhobors and Hutterites from Russia, the Mennonites and the Ukrainians, who were fleeing persecution or looking for land and the freedom to pursue their own ways unhindered. Each of these groups had distinctive craft traditions of furniture-making with origins in the late medieval, Renaissance or Baroque forms of Eastern Europe. Because they organized in communal groups according to religious belief and closely held social custom, they stood apart from the mainstream and thus preserved, until the coming of the mail-order catalogue and increasing external pressure, elements of line, proportion, colour and style belonging to a distant tradition.

The Germans of Renfrew County came from the Baltic areas of north-eastern Germany. The *Milchschrank* (food locker), with single or double doors, an open, vertical grille at the top and panelled bottom, and the glazed or open dish dresser are the most important of their furniture forms and relate directly to European prototypes. Most of these pine pieces have a minimal cornice or curved pediment and are plain painted in blue, red or green. Occasional carving or cut-out hearts and tulips discreetly maintain a traditional folk presence of Germanic origin.

The Poles, who also came to Renfrew County, brought with them the peasant traditions of the Kaszub people of northern Poland. The dish dressers, storage chests and wardrobes they made reflect in both form and decoration a taste for simple curves. The painted decoration of chests is, in contrast, well developed: stylized floral motifs, stars and sunbursts in bright contrasting colours, or plain painted surfaces with mouldings or borders in opposing colours (blue, red, yellow, green). The pediments of dressers and wardrobes are consistently formed by two elongated, rather flattened C-scrolls end-to-end, with a simple shell or sheaf carving at the juncture. The storage boxes have high bracket bases with a bulbous inner contour; tables are similar to the cleated-top tables of their Germanic neighbours, without stretchers but sometimes with rustic bracket cut-outs spanning leg and apron.

The Mennonites of southern Manitoba, like their brethren in Waterloo County, Ontario, used paint to protect and decorate the surfaces of their simple rectilinear sleeping benches, wardrobes, chests and tables. The high-style British forms filtered through Pennsylvania, so common in the early Germanic furniture of Ontario, are largely missing in western Canada. Standing cupboards often have small turned or tiny cabriole legs, and hanging corner cupboards rest normally on triangular shelves or wainscot. The doors of case pieces are usually plain panelled, and pediments appear as flattened vestigial forms of the broken arch shape.

In contrast, the Dukhobor furniture of western Canada is exuberant in line and vivid in colour. Rectangular tabletops with large lateral overhangs rest on solidly constructed, well-turned legs, joined by box stretchers that taper gracefully to the floor. The turnings and proportions suggest Renaissance prototypes, while the scrolls and volutes of some table aprons and the flattened curves of cornices and skirts, with biomorphic forms worked into the decorative profile, recall elementary Baroque shapes in which the twisting line and the effects of shifting perspective have become planimetric. Most of these pieces are painted in bright colour combinations that accentuate turnings, mouldings, drawer fronts and the hollow cut corners of panels. Such pieces as boxes and chests may have stylized painted flowers, pinwheels, roundels or other folk-inspired motifs. Similarly, Ukrainian furniture is vigorously curvilinear and bright in the colours used to protect the surface and to conceal the poverty of the woods (spruce, fir, ash, pine).

(ii) Other developments. In the 20th century the stylistic and decorative shapes of Canadian furniture took two very different directions. The first looked back nostalgically to the styles of the 18th century and the early 19th and imitated either the country forms of softwood furniture, mainly in pine but without painted decoration, or the formal hardwood furniture of birch, cherry, walnut and maple, as exemplified by contemporary adaptations of French and English period styles. The second looked forward and participated in the movements of international modernist style. Unlike the Scandinavians, Canadian designers and makers did not develop a specific national style, in spite of certain natural advantages of material supply. In the late 20th century individual designers experimented with modernist forms and new materials, but the influence of Jacques Guillon (*b* 1922), Douglas Ball (*b* 1935), Julien Hébert (*b* 1917) and Thomas Lamb (*b* 1938), to mention a few, cannot be compared to that of the designers of the Bauhaus or of Charles and Ray Eames in the USA. Theirs are, in any case, individual designs attached to specific names, which participate in the international movements of modern aesthetics.

BIBLIOGRAPHY

G. MacLaren: *Antique Furniture by Nova Scotia Craftsmen* (Toronto, 1961)
H. Ryder: *Antique Furniture by New Brunswick Craftsmen* (Toronto, 1965)
J. Palardy: *The Early Furniture of French Canada* (Toronto, 1965)
P. L. Martin: *La Berçante québécoise* (Montreal, 1973)
E. Collard: 'Montreal Cabinetmakers and Chairmakers: A Checklist', *Antiques*, cv (1974), pp. 1132–46
H. Dobson and B. Dobson: *The Early Furniture of Ontario and the Atlantic Provinces* (Toronto, 1974)
D. B. Webster, ed.: *The Book of Canadian Antiques* (Toronto, 1974)
C. Foss: *Cabinetmakers of the Eastern Seaboard* (Toronto, 1977)
J.-P. Hardy and D.-T. Ruddel: *Les Apprentis artisans à Québec, 1660–1815* (Montreal, 1977)
L. Musson Nykor and P. Musson: *Mennonite Furniture* (Toronto, 1977)
H. Pain: *The Heritage of Upper Canadian Furniture* (Toronto, 1978)
D. B. Webster: *English Canadian Furniture of the Georgian Period* (Toronto, 1979)
Mat. Hist. Bull., 11 (1980) [issue devoted to furn. stud.; incl. annotated bibliog. of Can. furn., pp. 36–56]
M. Bird and T. Kobayashi: *A Splendid Harvest: Germanic Folk and Decorative Arts in Canada* (Toronto, 1981)
H. Dobson and B. Dobson: *A Provincial Elegance: Arts of the Early French and English Settlements in Canada* (n.p., 1982)
W. Peddle: *The Traditional Furniture of Outport Newfoundland* (St John's, Nfld, 1983)
W. J. McIntyre: 'From Workshop to Factory: The Furnituremaker', *Mat. Hist. Bull.*, 19 (1984), pp. 25–35
B. Lee-Whiting: *Harvest of Stones: The German Settlement in Renfrew County* (Toronto, 1985)
D. K. Burnham: *Unlike the Lilies: Doukhobor Textile Traditions in Canada* (Toronto, 1986)
J. A. Fleming: 'The Ethnic Furniture of Western Canada', *Bull. Can. Soc. Dec. A.*, I, vi/4 (spring, 1988); II, vii/1 (summer, 1988)
——: *The Painted Furniture of French Canada, 1700–1840* (Hull, Qué., 1994)
M. S. Bird: *Canadian Country Furniture, 1675–1950* (Toronto, 1995)
J. A. Fleming: *The Painted Furniture of French Canada, 1700–1840* (Toronto, 1995)

JOHN A. FLEMING

VII. Ceramics.

The earliest records of potting by European settlers go back to the days of New France and include evidence, such as notarized agreements of 1688 and 1694, that coarse earthenware was made in the 17th century. In the rest of what now constitutes Canada, documented references to ceramic production come after the British conquest of 1760. A potter was mentioned in Nova Scotia's assessment rolls in 1786. The first recorded potter in Upper Canada was settled on a land grant by 1796. Another potter in New Brunswick was noted in a register of voters in 1797. The first official mention of potting in western Canada, where permanent settlement began later, was an act to incorporate a Manitoba brickyard and pottery in 1871. As late as the 1880s Canadian pottery was referred to as 'an infant industry'. Imported British ceramics dominated the Canadian pottery trade, and it was the British ceramic tradition that was the strongest influence on the industry as it developed.

1. UTILITARIAN WARES. Clay that burned red or buff in the kiln was readily available in Canada. In the early 19th century newspapers carried advertisements for locally made 'brown earthenware', the work of potters who flourished briefly; John Thomas (*b* 1810–11; *d* 1889) in Saint John, New Brunswick, John Martindale in Niagara, Ontario, and Michael Whitmore in York (now Toronto) were among those advertising brown earthenware before 1830. An English visitor reported in 1825 that this Canadian earthenware was of good quality, but from the time of the British conquest those working near ports or such inland waterways as the St Lawrence River were in competition with overseas suppliers. British earthenware—bowls, milk pans, baking dishes—was imported into Canada in large quantities, often underselling indigenous goods. In 1855, for example, 40,000 pieces of Newcastle brown earthenware arrived in Montreal in a single shipment. It was in the face of such massive competition that

Canadian makers of common earthenware persevered, the more isolated of whom fared the best.

In efforts to compete a significant role was played by British-born potters. Robert Malcolm jr, for example, came from England and in 1856 opened the Elmsdale Pottery, near Halifax, Nova Scotia, where all the principal workmen were from 'pottery districts at home'. Another Englishman, John Brown (1814–66), patented in Toronto in 1859 an earthenware body that was suitable for improved drainpipes or 'yellow earthenware'. JOSEPH WHITE of Bristol arrived in Saint John in 1864 and within weeks was offering moulded earthenware in English designs. English wares—teapots, jugs and figures of dogs—also served as models for French-Canadian and German-born potters. Canadian makers of dark-bodied earthenware produced simple, utilitarian wares. Aesthetic effect was not the goal, yet German-Canadian potters, a number of whom arrived in Upper Canada in the 19th century by way of the USA, achieved distinctive results with mottled green, brown and orange glazes over a red body. Such French-Canadian potters as the DION family also used streaked and mottled glazes, as in a tobacco jar and stand with mottled brown glaze (*c.* 1885; Hull, Qué., Can. Mus. Civiliz.; see fig. 13). In all regions a growing awareness of Canadian identity was evident in the use of such decorative motifs as beavers and maple leaves. Thomas A. Joyce (*b* 1831), working in Nova Scotia from the 1850s, produced red earthenware bowls with moulded maple leaves around the rim. The Cap Rouge Pottery, Quebec, advertised moulded, brown-glazed beaver jugs in 1862. The Glasgow Pottery, Iberville, Quebec, produced ringed, buff-bodied spittoons with beavers in the 1880s.

The slow decline of common earthenware in Canada began during the mid-19th century, when stoneware production was introduced to Canada by Americans. Common stoneware had been imported from Great Britain since the 1760s. From 1840 it was made in Canada, initially at St Johns, Quebec (now St Jean), by members of the FARRAR family. The first stoneware potteries in Upper Canada were founded by Americans in 1849 at Picton and Brantford. More potteries were established in all parts of the country, but because stoneware clays were sparingly distributed in Canada, most potters imported American clay. One of the first to use Canadian clay was Malcolm, who by 1862 was using clay found at Stewiacke, Nova Scotia, for his stoneware. Salt-glazing was used by most Canadian potters, although some, for example Joseph White, used a liquid glaze after the manner of Bristol potters in England. Stoneware products were utilitarian, chiefly storage vessels. Such items as sap crocks for maple sugaring met specific Canadian needs. Decoration was sprigged, incised or blue-painted, and birds or flowers were popular motifs.

In the 20th century changing conditions eliminated much of the need for stoneware in kitchens and dairies. A few 19th-century potteries survived for a time (11 were in operation in 1904), one of them owned by Simon Thomas HUMBERSTONE. The discovery of stoneware clay in Alberta led to a late development there, but generally stoneware production declined.

13. Tobacco jar and stand, red earthenware body and mottled brown glaze, h. 248 mm, made at the Dion pottery, Ancienne Lorette, Quebec, *c.* 1885 (Hull, Québec, Canadian Museum of Civilization)

2. TABLEWARES. Although coarse earthenware and stoneware were the staple products of Canadian potters in the 19th century, at the St Johns Stone Chinaware Co., founded in 1873 in St Johns, Quebec, a higher grade of ware was successfully produced for a sustained period. There, a dense earthenware of a kind first made in the early 19th century in Staffordshire, known as ironstone, stone china or white granite, was made as tableware using imported English clay. Initially English moulds and patterns were used, but later original patterns were introduced, including a fern and fleur-de-lis pattern and a moulded maple-leaf pattern. By 1880 it was Canada's largest pottery and at one time employed 400 workers, half of whom were Staffordshire-trained. Its success was based on two factors: it produced a type of earthenware for which British imports had already created a strong demand, and it had the financial backing of two influential businessmen, Edward C. Macdonald and Duncan Macdonald. In 1877, when the company was in difficulties, Edward Macdonald bought the business. In 1896 it was sold to potters from France, but within two years it was bankrupt. Other 19th-century potteries tried to follow the lead of the St Johns Stone Chinaware Co. in tablewares, for example the Stafford Pottery in St Cunegonde, Quebec, and the British Porcelain Works, in St Johns itself, which lasted for only a few years. The lack of suitable indigenous clays and the flood of imported wares rendered their efforts futile. A survey of the Canadian ceramic industry made in 1931 by the National Development Bureau, Ottawa, discovered that no pottery in the country was making whitewares for the table. Even in the 1980s Canada imported all but a small fraction of the tablewares used.

In 1983 an effort to encourage Canadian manufactured tablewares was made when the Ontario Potters Association, under the patronage of Lily Schreyer, wife of the Governor-General Edward Schreyer, organized a competition for a table service to be used in Rideau Hall, Ottawa. Entries in earthenware, stoneware and porcelain, from traditional to free-form contemporary styles, were submitted and included work from small-scale industrial potters, studio potters and teachers of ceramics. Submissions from 17 potters were selected for a nationwide exhibition. The winner was Jan Phelan, from Hillsdale, Ontario, known for her sculptural forms in stoneware and decorative, often carved, functional porcelain. She entered a wheel-thrown, porcelain place setting with irregular edges and a flowing, floral border design (Ottawa, Rideau Hall).

3. Ornamental wares and studio pottery. Ornamental wares formed an important part of the output of modern Canadian potters. This was not the case in earlier days when potters existed on the practical. An increasing emphasis on ornaments marked the Victorian years, however, and brought incentive to produce them. Makers of common earthenware and stoneware began to produce figures of dogs, picture frames, flower containers and wall plaques. As early as 1851 an English-born potter, James Bailey, of Bowmanville, Upper Canada, was advertising 'toys' (ornaments). His Staffordshire-type dogs sometimes had green-tinted lead glazes over red bodies. Brown- or green-glazed picture frames came from other Upper Canadian potters in the 1860s. In the 1880s relief-decorated terracotta plaques depicting coalminers at work were made at the Prescott Pottery, Enfield, Nova Scotia.

Forerunners of modern studio potters were in evidence in Canada in the 1890s, and their work was promoted by such organizations as the Montreal branch of the Women's Art Association, which in 1896 opened a craft shop where pottery was displayed. An outcome of this venture was the founding in 1906 of the Montreal-based Canadian Handicrafts Guild. Other guilds followed elsewhere. Organizations relating purely to ceramics were founded later: the Canadian Guild of Potters in 1936 and the Ontario Potters Association in 1948. In 1955 the first all-Canadian ceramic exhibition took place at the Montreal Museum of Fine Arts. In addition to showing their work at home, Canadian potters began winning recognition outside the country, notably at the annual Ceramic National Exhibition in Syracuse, NY. In particular, the New Brunswick potters Kjeld Deichmann (1900–63) and Erica Deichmann (*b* 1914) became well known for their stoneware, which was characterized by simplicity and unusual glazes. From the 1960s Raku-wares (simply moulded, low-fired earthenwares with thick lead glazes, traditionally associated with the Japanese tea ceremony) caught the imagination of such Canadian potters as Monique Bourbonnais Ferron (*b* 1927), Walter Dexter (*b* 1931), Agnes Olive and Christopher Thompson (*b* 1952), who adapted the technique in their own work. East Asian influence of another kind can be seen in the work of Harlan House, who in the mid-1970s was one of the few Canadian potters working exclusively in porcelain. Such works as House's 'Tree Peony' vase (1988; Harlan House priv. col., see fig. 14) typify an underlying characteristic of Canadian ceramics in the late 20th century: the assimilation of European, American or East Asian influences, which results in an individual or personal expression rather than a distinctive Canadian style.

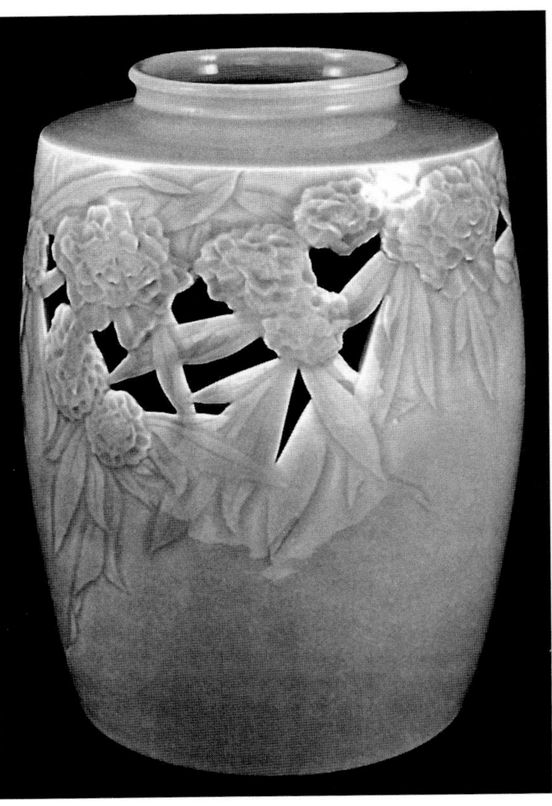

14. 'Tree Peony' vase by Harlan House, porcelain with celadon glaze, h. 320 mm, 1988 (Harlan House private collection)

BIBLIOGRAPHY

The Ceramic Industry of Canada, National Development Bureau, Department of the Interior (Ottawa, 1931)
E. Collard: *Nineteenth-century Pottery and Porcelain in Canada* (Montreal, 1967, rev. 2/1984) [incl. a dictionary of Can. potters]
D. B. Webster: *Early Canadian Pottery* (Toronto, 1971)
G. MacLaren: *Antique Potteries of Nova Scotia* (Halifax, 1972)
D. L. Newlands: *Early Ontario Potters* (Toronto, 1979)
R. Fortin: *Poterie et vaisselle: Saint-Jean et Iberville* (St Jean, 1982)
M. Gaumond: *La Poterie de Cap-Rouge* (Quebec, 1984)
S. Inglis: *The Turning Point: The Deichmann Pottery 1933–63* (Hull, Qué., 1991)

ELIZABETH COLLARD

VIII. Glass.

Because of Canada's initial colonial role as a marketplace for British manufacturers, it was only after the Rebellion of 1837–8 that Canada began to produce glass; the first glasshouse, the Mallorytown Glass Works, was founded in Mallorytown, Ontario, in 1839. As with several of its successors, it concentrated on the manufacture of such functional glass products as lamp chimneys, fruit jars and bottles, using iron moulds, and it was characteristically short-lived, closing in 1840. Most decorative glass at this time was freeblown. Such whimseys as hats or caps, drapes of chains, twisted walking canes and paperweights were fashioned by glassblowers as personal gifts.

Between 1860 and 1898 four major companies operated near shipping and railway facilities. The Canada Glass Works (1864–72), Hudson, Quebec, and the Hamilton Glass Co. (1865–96), Hamilton, Ontario, produced *Waldglas* that ranged in colour from light aquamarine to amber. In contrast, the St Lawrence Glass Co. (1867–73), Montreal, and the Burlington Glass Co. (1874–98), Hamilton, produced lead glass, which was colourless and was used for finer glass lamps and tablewares. Daily washing of fragile lampshades created a large demand and has resulted in many surviving, but mismatched, shades and bases.

With the adoption of the mechanical press, an American innovation of the 1820s (*see* UNITED STATES OF AMERICA, §VIII, 2), glassware became more affordable, allowing Canadians of ordinary means to set a lavish table for the first time. Pressed-glass tableware sets of the 1860s are characterized by bold geometric designs, while the compôtes and fruit nappies of the 1880s feature delicately rounded birds, flowers and berries. Pressed glass imitated commemorative medallions, moulded ceramics and most notably cut glass, as seen, for example, in a plate (*c.* 1887; Toronto, Royal Ont. Mus.; see fig. 15) made by the Nova Scotia Glass Co. (1881–92), Trenton, to commemorate the 50th anniversary of the reign of Queen Victoria. By the 1890s patterns were once again more emphatic, sometimes organized in panels and later executed in clear, emerald-green glass and opal, white or blue glass. By the mid-1920s cut glass was no longer a strong influence on pressed-glass design, and pastel shades in simple shapes came into favour.

All of the major glass factories employed glasscutters or engravers from 1867 to 1900. Using wheel-engraving, they added monograms to presentation pieces and decorated table sets with incised lines and simple, stylized patterns. With the invention in the 1890s of acid polishing (immersion in a bath of hydrofluoric and sulphuric acid), dull engraved or cut glass was quickly given a sparkling appearance. Cut glass enjoyed an upswing in popularity, and small, independent engraving shops sprang up to handle the demand for American-inspired hobnails and pinwheels and such distinctively Canadian floral patterns as 'Primrose', 'Cornflower' and 'Maple Leaf'. Crystal blanks were increasingly imported from Belgium (Cristalleries du Val-Saint-Lambert), France (Baccarat) and the USA (Libbey Glass Co., C. Dorflinger & Sons and the Mount Washington Glass Works).

From the 1930s the Canadian glass market was dominated by mass production and competition from foreign—in particular American—imports. In 1968, however, decorative glass in Canada took a radical departure under the leadership of Robert Held (*b* 1943), who transplanted the excitement and technology of the studio glass movement from the USA (*see* UNITED STATES OF AMERICA, §VIII, 2) to Canada, in particular to the Sheridan School of Crafts and Design in Oakville (formerly in Mississauga), Ontario. The opportunity to work in glass, independent of a factory, attracted those eager to integrate the roles of designer and maker. The Sheridan School began to train artist-craftsmen formally, and from 1971 several of its faculty and graduates began to develop glass programmes in other colleges across Canada. By 1988 the country's only all-glass educational facility, Le Centre des Métiers du Verre du Québec, in Montreal, was opened, combining a gallery with teaching studios under the direction of the sculptor François Houdé (1950–93).

In 1978 Held left Sheridan to found Skookum Glass (now Robert Held Art Glass), based in Calgary, Alberta (previously also in Vancouver, British Columbia); it is noted for Art Nouveau-style glass, and in the late 1980s it was the largest producer of freeblown, decorative glass in Canada. The balance of decorative glass was made by small, one- or two-man shops, where the influence of

15. Pressed-glass plate with profile of Queen Victoria, diam. (with handles) 293 mm, made by the Nova Scotia Glass Co., Trenton, *c.* 1887 (Toronto, Royal Ontario Museum)

process on design is evident. Perhaps due to the merging of the designing and making processes, the smaller studios capitalized on the inherent properties of hot glass; paperweights, perfume bottles, vases and goblets made in the 1970s and 1980s characteristically accentuate the transparency and fluidity of the medium. Decorative work of the late 1980s reflected dominant trends in North American glass sculpture, particularly the combination of such materials as stone or concrete with glass. In June 1993 the Canadian Clay and Glass Gallery opened in Waterloo, Ontario.

BIBLIOGRAPHY

H. Spence and K. Spence: *A Guide to Early Canadian Glass* (Toronto, 1966)
G. Stevens: *Canadian Glass, c. 1825–1925* (Toronto, 1967)
J. Alyuia: *Glassware from Eastern Canada* (Ottawa, 1981)
T. King: *Glass in Canada* (Erin, Ont., 1987)
Patterns in Light: The John & Mary Yaremko Collection (exh. cat. by J. Holmes, Toronto, Royal Ont. Mus., 1987)
G. Hickey: 'Gathering Momentum: The Studio Glass Movement in Canada', *Glass in Sculpture*, Toronto, Koffler Gal. cat. (Toronto, 1988), pp. 6–16
New Work Glass, 36 (1989) [special issue covering contemp. Can. glass; full colour pls]

GLORIA HICKEY

IX. *Gold and silver.*

Although silversmiths are recorded in the 1660s, an indigenous tradition did not begin until 1700, when Michel Levasseur (*fl* 1700–12) moved from France, followed over the next six decades by some thirty French silversmiths. They in turn trained colonial apprentices, and by this means silversmithing was implanted in Quebec and Montreal. A guild system was never established, and few silversmiths were able to gain a livelihood from silversmithing alone. Among the exceptions were François Chambellan (*c.* 1688–1747), Paul Lambert dit Saint-Paul (1691–1749) and Ignace-François Delezenne (1718–90).

Silver production was constrained by Canada's lengthy colonial status, which favoured importation from Europe. Nevertheless, silversmithing reached a thriving level early in the 18th century through patronage by the clergy and a well-to-do class of military officers, civil officials, merchants and landowners. Early colonial silverware was in a provincial Louis XIV style, and besides flatware, the most common articles were écuelles, tumblers, wine-tasters, plates and candlesticks; articles that were larger, more elaborate or of contemporary Rococo design were imported. Roman Catholic parish churches and religious communities were often well endowed with silver imported from Parisian suppliers. Early colonial makers for the Church were headed by Lambert and Delezenne. The former worked in a provincial Louis XIV style, the latter in a more classical version of the same style. The more common wares were chalices and ciboria, but the range was wide and included censers, sanctuary lamps and monstrances. By the mid-1750s Indian trade silver—given to Indians by traders in return for fur—emerged as a highly lucrative commodity. Most of this market was controlled by Delezenne and Alexandre Picard (*c.* 1727–99) of Quebec.

Among the first Anglophone immigrants after the ceding of Canada to Britain were a few silversmiths, but their large-scale influx came during the American Revolution, when some four dozen Loyalist silversmiths moved from the USA to eastern and central Canada; they were in such surplus numbers that many were compelled to abandon silversmithing altogether. Over the next few decades the majority of silversmiths were occupied with making flatware or Indian trade silver. A great deal of church silver was made, but, because of the engulfing effect of importation, domestic hollowware production was spasmodic. Canadian silversmiths found it difficult to compete with the mechanized processes of British silver manufacturers.

By 1774 Montreal had replaced Quebec as the capital of the fur trade, and there was a corresponding relocation of silversmiths. Large silver workshops to supply the fur trade with Indian trade silver were established in Montreal by Robert Cruickshank (1767–1809), Pierre Huguet, Joseph Schindler (*fl* 1760–86) and others. The new political ascendancy of the British also encouraged an assertion of English tastes in styles and articles, although such traditional French articles as the ecuelle, tumbler and ragout spoon, made by French-Canadian silversmiths, were perpetuated for a time. The most common silverwares in this period were the sugar bowl, cream jug, sauceboat, salt, snuff-box, pap boat and ladle. Of newly introduced articles, the most consequential were the silver teapot and associated tea equipment, for until this time Canadians were coffee drinkers, in accordance with French custom. No surviving Canadian-made teapot would appear to date before the 1780s. Early teapots were in the Adam style, either oval or drum shaped and plain or ornamented with bright-cut engraving. Complete tea services are not common before 1800, but one by Robert Cruickshank dates from 1797 (Toronto, Royal Ont. Mus.). While such other articles as ewers, candlesticks, soup tureens and trays were made, their relative infrequency suggests a supplementary place in the trade: that is, a local silversmith was resorted to in cases when a dealer did not have an imported piece in stock.

In the immediate post-conquest period, Protestants were allowed to worship publicly in Quebec for the first time; while they were preoccupied with organizing themselves, the Francophone Catholic Church not only continued to be a formidable client but also redirected almost all of its substantial patronage to colonial silversmiths. Even the ordinary rural parish church possessed, on average, one or more chalices and ciboria, a sanctuary lamp, altar crucifix, censer and processional cross, as well as such smaller pieces as an incense-boat, chrismatory, pax and cruets. Local clergy recognized the usefulness, in the colonial context, of tradition as a symbolic affirmation of the uninterrupted presence of the French Church in Canada in the face of its precarious position under early British rule. As a result, the late Louis XIV style flourished in church silver until the end of the 18th century.

Delezenne bridged the French and English regimes as maker to churches in Quebec. His successor was his former apprentice, FRANÇOIS RANVOYZÉ, who from about 1771 dedicated himself to producing church silver. Ranvoyzé proved to be one of the most original Canadian silversmiths, when, by 1782, he invented a highly personal style of free-form, generalized floral and vegetal motifs, rendered by chasing, which had a distant debt to the Rococo. This decorative style culminated in a rare solid gold altar garniture, consisting of a ciborium, monstrance and chalice, for the parish church of L'Islet (1810–12; Quebec, Mus. Qué; see fig. 16). Nevertheless, by 1798 Ranvoyzé was already beginning to relinquish this personal style for another of Louis XVI derivation, which was borrowed from LAURENT AMIOT. Following his return in 1787 to Quebec from France, where he had trained for five years, Amiot had induced a stylistic rupture. The clergy wholeheartedly endorsed the current Louis XVI designs that he promoted, and he soon became an overpowering rival to Ranvoyzé. Amiot's success was based on a concise series of design formulae, incorporating the harmonious articulation of a classical vocabulary, which could be repeated while allowing for minor variations between individual pieces.

The contemporary course of Montreal silversmiths was more conservative, possibly because many of them, including Schindler, Cruickshank and Michael Arnoldi (1763–1807), were Anglophones working for a Francophone clergy. Louis XIV designs were adhered to until the end of the 18th century. For many years most Protestant liturgical silver was imported, some being donated by sponsors overseas, some through royal patronage. One of the earliest pieces actually made in Canada was a paten of 1786 by Cruickshank for the Protestant Church of Montreal (now Christ Church Cathedral). Protestant silver, whether imported or made locally, usually conformed to plain Reformation types, whether for Anglicans, Presbyterians or other denominations. One of the earliest Gothic Revival services made in Canada was by Robert Hendery (1814–97) for Christ Church Cathedral, Montreal, in 1861. There was, however, a reluctance to adopt the Gothic designs of the Anglo-Catholic Tractarian party, and they were not generally accepted for Anglican communion plate until the end of the century.

In contrast, Catholic silver of the early 19th century was fundamentally Louis XVI-inspired, with a local flavour often invested in the translations; such cross-cultural adaptations were more likely in Montreal than in Quebec. Huguet, for example, reproduced Louis XVI decorative motifs by means of the English technique of bright-cut engraving. Salomon Marion also reworked traditional motifs with hints of Regency influence. This same tendency applies to a change in the Catholic baptismal ewer, which assumed the form of miniature English teapots or cream jugs. The Bourbon Restoration of 1814 and its concomitant Catholic Renaissance led to a renewed susceptibility to current artistic impulses from France. The Restoration style was revivalist with an injection of Baroque lavishness, which was tempered in the hands of Canadian silversmiths. Huguet, Marion and Paul Morand (*d* 1854) in turn dominated the market of the Montreal region. Their counterparts in Quebec were Amiot, Joseph Sasseville (*fl* 1776–1831) and his son François Sasseville (*fl* 1797–1864). A monument of this period is a silver statue of the *Virgin* by Marion (Ottawa, N.G.).

In domestic silver of the same period the Adam style lingered on, while a subdued version of the English Regency style was introduced in several tea services by Marion. From the 1790s Amiot made occasional Louis

16. Gold liturgical vessels made for the parish church of L'Islet, Quebec, by François Ranvoyzé (left to right): ciborium, h. 245 mm, 1810; monstrance, h. 388 mm, 1812; chalice, h. 241 mm, 1810 (Quebec, Musée du Québec)

XVI pieces of masterful design, particularly ewers and coffeepots. In the case of two soup tureens, he effected an exquisite synthesis of the English Rococo and Louis XVI styles, and in the 1830s he even experimented with the Rococo Revival. The spectre of importation was never far away, and a hiatus in silverware production occurred in the 1830s and 1840s. Much still came from Britain, but the USA also entered the trade. Flatware continued to be made locally in great quantities, with Nelson Walker, who also made presentation cups, and Peter Bohle (1786–1865) to the fore in Montreal.

The general state of silversmithing did not differ substantially in the rest of Canada. Whether in Upper Canada or the Atlantic provinces, flatware was the mainstay of most silversmiths. The only significant quantity of hollowware was made by Peter Nordbeck (1789–1861) of Halifax, Nova Scotia, who had emigrated from Germany. Much of this consisted of chalices and ciboria for the Catholic Church, in the English Recusant (Catholic) style of the 18th century.

After the mid-19th century a more resolute challenge to the importation of foreign silverware was offered by such silversmiths as Hendery, J. G. Joseph & Co. (*fl* 1857–77) of Toronto and William Herman Newman (1826–94) and M. S. Brown & Co. (*fl* 1886–1919) of Halifax, while in Quebec the longstanding tradition in church silver was maintained by François Sasseville, his nephew Pierre Lespérance (*fl* 1819–82) and Ambroise-Adhémar Lafrance (*fl* 1822–1908) in turn. Of these, Hendery built the largest enterprise, and from 1887, in the successor firm of Hendery & Leslie, it was the leading maker to the trade, supplying retail silversmiths virtually across the country. Some of the most accomplished work of the later 19th century consisted of presentation pieces that in stylistic terms accorded with British fashion. Hendery dominated this sphere, producing many elaborate centrepieces and trophies, some of which are more properly called sculpture in silver, for example a centrepiece commissioned in 1863 for the Hon. Sir George-Etienne Cartier, MP, by the constituents of his riding. Hendery also expanded into the church market, making for Catholic, Jewish and Protestant purposes alike. By the end of the century Hendery & Leslie was making an unprecedented array of silver hollowware. New silver manufacturers arose in Toronto at the end of the 19th century, and in Montreal in 1899 Hendery & Leslie was taken over by Henry Birks & Sons, which expanded across the country to become the largest silversmithing firm; it continued in the late 20th century to supply most of Canada's silver.

BIBLIOGRAPHY

R. Traquair: *The Old Silver of Quebec* (Toronto, 1940)

G. Morisset: *François Ranvoyzé* (Quebec, 1942)

——: *Paul Lambert dit Saint-Paul* (Quebec, 1945)

J. E. Langdon: *Canadian Silversmiths, 1700–1900* (Toronto, 1966)

François Ranvoyzé: Orfèvre, 1739–1819 (exh. cat. by J. Trudel and A. Juneau, Quebec, Mus. Qué., 1968)

J. E. Langdon: *American Silversmiths in British North America, 1776–1800* (Toronto, 1970)

D. C. MacKay: *Silversmiths and Related Craftsmen of the Atlantic Provinces* (Halifax, 1973)

R. Derome: *Les Orfèvres de Nouvelle-France* (Ottawa, 1974)

Silver in New France (exh. cat. by J. Trudel, Ottawa, N.G., 1974)

R. Fox: *Quebec and Related Silver at the Detroit Institute of Arts* (Detroit, 1978)

——: *Presentation Pieces and Trophies from the Henry Birks Collection of Canadian Silver* (Ottawa, 1985)

ROSS FOX

X. Textiles.

Canada does not have a long textile tradition. It was only in the 19th century that production became important, after the colonial settlements became secure but before the effects of the Industrial Revolution made an impact. Early colonists showed little interest in making textiles, attaching more importance to such profitable activities as fur trading. European imports still prevailed in the early 18th century, even though settlers then began to weave druggets and fabric for clothing and household linen, but no examples of these are known to survive. The import of textiles, including printed cottons and serge for blankets, continued, and local production remained relatively rare until 1806, when Napoleon's trade blockade against Britain restricted imports. By this time increasing importance was attached to personal goods, including household linens and clothes, and so local production expanded until factory-made textiles became widely available in the early 20th century.

Canadian textiles were influenced by the national origins of the settlers, though to some extent their traditions became mingled. The French, although settled from the 17th century, started to weave only in the 18th century. Although colonial interiors in Quebec appear to have been sparsely decorated, some textiles were used to supply a touch of colour, especially in urban areas. In the convents the nuns produced finely embroidered ecclesiastical goods and imparted their skills to girls of French and Native American origin. In rural homes, spinning and weaving on two-shaft looms took place. The weaves were simple tabby or twill, plain, striped or checked.

The work of the United Empire Loyalists shows many similarities with that of the USA. They brought with them more complex weaves, in particular double weave and reversible summer-and-winter weave, for which they used multiple-shaft looms. Some of the immigrants who arrived directly from Britain in the early 19th century might have lost their weaving skills, since the Industrial Revolution was well underway in their homeland. Among them, though, were the Highland Scots, who were accustomed to weaving tweeds and blankets at home, and professional weavers of Lowland Scotland and Northern Ireland, who used four-shaft looms and specialized in overshot weaving. These immigrants were also known for their linen shirts and petticoats, woollen blankets, hooked rugs and patchwork quilts.

The Germans who settled in Waterloo County, Ontario, from the mid-19th century came from the USA and directly from Europe. They too included professional weavers, who used multiple-shaft looms for the production of twill diaper, complex point twills, star-and-diamond patterns and double cloth. They were known for their decorative coverlets and horse-blankets.

In the French-Canadian tradition much of the work was done by women, who integrated it with their other domestic tasks, but the professional weavers of the Scottish and German communities were men, many of them farmers. These weavers often used materials supplied by the customer. Flax, hemp and wool were produced on farms, but cotton was imported, becoming more widespread from the early years of the 19th century. The textiles were dyed, as yarn or in the piece, with imported indigo, cochineal and madder for blues and reds, and with local dyeplants for yellows and browns. All materials were precious, and wool in particular was in short supply, so worn-out textiles were recycled (which might account for the lack of early examples).

Among the most important Canadian textiles were coverlets, vital in the harsh climatic conditions. The French cut discarded furnishings—old serge blankets for example—into long, narrow strips, which they used as a thick weft (on a cotton warp) to produce *catalogne.* Related to the *lirette* of western France, *catalogne* first appeared in the 18th century, when it was imported for making into bedcovers, but in the following century it was made in Acadia (an area of Francophone settlement in the Maritime provinces) and Quebec. Usually the coverlets were simply patterned with weft stripes in contrasting colours, but more elaborate versions were made with warp and weft stripes, with variable warp spacing to alter the texture, and in combination with other decorative techniques. Sometimes the warp or weft was made of two colours twisted together. Most *catalogne* was woven in widths of about 1.10 m, and two widths were joined together to make a coverlet. In the late 19th century and the 20th, wider pieces were woven for carpeting.

One of the decorative techniques sometimes combined with *catalogne* was *à la planche*, a form of weaving done, as the name implies, with the aid of one or two narrow boards or rods inserted behind the shafts to enable an additional pattern weft to be used when required to create small squares of floating threads; with the use of a second board a chequered effect could be achieved.

The most spectacular of the coverlets are the *boutonnue* or weft-loop ones done on a ground of *catalogne* or plain-weave wool. They feature a weft loop in relief, produced by lifting up, with the fingers or with the aid of a hook, the loops or *boutons* drawn from the main weft or from a supplementary weft that was often inserted where required by the pattern as a brocading weft. The motifs thus formed by the loops are sometimes the same colour as the ground, sometimes not. The designs include the fir tree, the birch, the eight-pointed star (said to be from Charlevoix, Qué.), various flowers and leaves and geometric motifs (see fig. 17). Frequently, the techniques of *boutonnue* and *à la planche* weaving are combined to further enhance the decorative effect.

17. *Boutonnue* coverlet in a star pattern, from Charlevoix, Québec, 0.92×1.40 m, *c.* 1905 (Quebec, Université Laval, Archives de Folklore)

Paralleling production in the USA, but also developing independently, was the weaving of overshot coverlets. Introduced by Scottish and Irish weavers in the late 18th century, they had a second, pattern weft that overshot the plain tabby ground. The earliest had white linen grounds, subsequently replaced by hand-plied cotton, and pattern wefts of hand-spun wool dyed blue, red, brown or yellow. Eventually both cotton and wool were machine-spun. Such coverlets were economical in their use of wool but also warm, because the air was trapped in the loose weave.

Geometrically patterned coverlets formed part of the same German tradition that was responsible for the double-cloth and multiple-shaft coverlets of the USA. The introduction of the Jacquard loom enabled weavers to produce floral and realistic patterns. The coverlets were often commissioned to celebrate a marriage, and many of the designs, even the cards, were taken from the USA, the most popular being the four-rose pattern with a rose-and-crow border. Jacquard weaving was done by professionals, generally Loyalists of German and Swiss extraction working in southern Ontario, but the business died out at the beginning of the 20th century.

The production of quilted covers was part of the French tradition; made with plain tops and of two or three layers of fabric, they were stitched together in patterns based on stars, flowers, concentric circles and various geometric shapes. English settlers introduced PATCHWORK covers of small, geometric pieces joined edge-to-edge. American patchwork techniques were also used, with larger pattern pieces joined to form bold designs or applied to plain tops in floral and pictorial patterns (*see* UNITED STATES OF AMERICA, §XI, 2).

The range of Canadian textiles was enriched in the 19th and 20th centuries by numerous carpets. Besides those made of *catalogne*, there were three non-woven types: braided, hooked and sewn. The most widespread technique, universal by its simplicity, is braiding by hand, which consists of plaiting three or more strands of material to form a braid. This is afterwards rolled spirally and sewn to produce a hard-wearing carpet usually the size of the threshold of a door. Flat braided rugs made by joining wide braids together edge to edge were introduced by Swedish settlers. It is the play of colours that determines the pattern of braided carpets, forming concentric circles, V-shapes or parallels. The dark colours of the wool, which do not readily show the dirt, mix with some reds to give a harmonious appearance. Hooked rugs came to Canada directly from Britain and through the USA. They were first made in the Maritime provinces but later spread, each region developing its own styles. Nova Scotia is particularly rich in these rugs. The technique of hooking thin strips of fabric through a canvas (*see* RUG, §1), following a drawn design, allows for great creativity, and hooked rugs show an interesting variety of patterns, the simplest of which are geometrical. Flower-and-leaf designs, disseminated by catalogues and periodicals, were widely used, but the carpets most characteristic of popular taste are those with animal motifs or rustic scenes, the originality of each one arising from the different environment in which it was created. Hooked rugs are pieces of whimsy, products of patient and refined workmanship: they were reserved for the best decorated and least frequented places in the house, the bedrooms and the living-room. Sewn rugs were decorative but fragile. In Quebec, for example, mats called *tapis à languette* were decorated around the edges with tabs or tongues of cloth and in the centre with applied roundels, often double-layered, arranged in geometric, star or simple floral patterns. These were most often used to adorn furniture. In the 20th century simple rag rugs were woven on a wooden frame, strips of material being secured to the frame as a warp and other strips being worked over and under them by hand to produce a hard-wearing carpet.

Canadian settlers also wove shawls and yardage fabric for dresses and shirts. Made of wool or wool and cotton, these fabrics were often patterned with stripes or checks. Domestic linen with diaper and occasionally more elaborate patterns, although never produced in large quantities, was still being woven, mostly in German communities, in the late 19th century. A distinctively Canadian item of clothing is the *ceinture fléchée* or arrow-head sash, which was worn by *voyageurs* around the waist. The sashes were braided in a technique using very tightly spun wools. The arrowhead or heart motif, usually red, was flanked by blue, yellow, green or white in a forked-lightning motif. Both Native American and French traditions seem to have contributed. The best-known is the 'Assomption' sash, so called from the name of the village in the Montreal area where an important craft industry in these sashes flourished in the 19th century. It is characterized by its arrowhead pattern, also called the heart, on each side of which are blue, yellow, green and white zigzags. In the 20th century, handweaving largely died out in eastern Canada, though there was a brief revival during the Depression of the 1930s. In the west, however, an entirely separate tradition was maintained by the Ukrainian and Dukhobor settlers, who had arrived from Russia from 1890 and continued to weave bedcovers, wall hangings, rugs and clothing fabric in the styles of their native lands. Their work includes geometrically patterned tabbies and pile and tapestry weaving with Caucasian designs.

BIBLIOGRAPHY

J.-N. Fauteux: *Essai sur l'industrie au Canada sous le régime français*, ii (Quebec City, 1927), pp. 444–82
C. M. Barbeau: 'Assomption Sash', *N. Mus. Canada Bull.*, xciii (1938) [whole issue]; repr. as *Ceintures fléchées* (Ottawa, 1945/*R* Montreal, 1973)
——: *Maîtres artisans de chez nous* (Montreal, 1942)
——: *Saintes artisanes*, 2 vols (Montreal, 1944–6)
R. L. Séguin: *La Civilisation traditionnelle de 'l'habitant' aux 17e et 18e siècles* (Montreal, 1967), pp. 386–99, 492–8, 619–25
——: *Le Costume civil en Nouvelle-France* (Ottawa, 1968), pp. 1–21, 262–91
H. B. Burnham and D. K. Burnham: *Keep Me Warm One Night: Early Handweaving in Eastern Canada* (Toronto, 1972)
L. Dechêne: *Habitants et marchands de Montréal au XVIIe siècle* (Montreal, 1974), pp. 151–5
C. Simard: *Les Bois et les textiles*, i of *Artisanat québécois* (Montreal, 1975), pp. 167–468
M. Conroy: *300 Years of Canada's Quilts* (Toronto, 1976)
D. K. Burnham: 'Constructions used by Jacquard Coverlet-weavers in Ontario', *Studies in Textile History in Memory of Harold B. Burnham*, ed. V. Gervers (Toronto, 1977), pp. 31–42
J. Beaudoin-Ross: 'An Early-eighteenth-century Pieced Quilt in Montreal', *RACAR*, i–ii (1979–80), pp. 105–9
J. Mathieu: *Faire ces tapis à la mode de l'Ile d'Orléans* (Montreal, 1980)
D. K. Burnham: *The Comfortable Arts: Traditional Spinning and Weaving in Canada* (Ottawa, 1981)
M. Laurent: 'Bouclé par la trame (dit boutonné)', *Boutonné d'hier et d'aujourd'hui* (Quebec City, 1983) pp. 7–16, 49
J. Mathieu: 'Les Textiles dans l'intérieur domestique: Etude comparative Perche-Québec, XVIIe–XVIIIe siècles', *Can. Flklore Can.*, v (1983), pp. 38–59
D. K. Burnham: *Unlike the Lilies: Doukhobor Textile Traditions in Canada* (Toronto, 1986)
J. Mathieu: 'La Récupération des tissus dans la production domestique québécoise', *Bull. Liaison Cent. Int. Etud. Textiles Anc.*, 63–64 (1986), pp. 151–7
B. Audet: *L'Etablissement agricole de l'Ile d'Orléans, XVIIe siècle–début du XVIIIe: Etude de culture matérielle* (diss., Quebec City, U. Laval, 1987), pp. 126–40, 233–8
'Mode et costumes et les textiles traditionnels', *Objets de civilisation* (exh. cat., intro. R. Arpin; Hull, Qué., Can. Mus. Civiliz., 1990), pp. 61–77

JOCELYNE MATHIEU

XI. Patronage.

Canada has a scant record of private art philanthropy; even government patronage was not a factor until the mid-20th century. The Roman Catholic Church in Quebec, particularly the Jesuit Order and the Ursuline Sisters, was a major patron of architecture and the fine and decorative arts (especially of gold and silver; *see* §IX above) well into the late 19th century. There was, however, no entrepreneurial parallel among Canada's *haute bourgeoisie* or its corporate community, with the exception of Sir WILLIAM VAN HORNE's commissions on behalf of the Canadian Pacific Railway. The founding of the National Gallery of Canada, Ottawa, in 1880 was a singular act by a parliament that would demonstrate little interest in Canadian art and artists until almost a century after Confederation. In the first half of the 20th century the few government art programmes, such as the War Memorial projects instigated by WILLIAM MAXWELL AITKEN, 1st Baron Beaverbrook, and the short-lived Overseas Fellowship Programme (1952–7), were rare examples of public patronage of individual artists.

Art patronage on a significant scale occurred with the founding of the Canada Council in 1957. This developed out of the Royal Commission on National Development in the Arts, Letters and Sciences (1949). It was initiated by grass-roots demands for an assessment of Canada's cultural needs and the financial resources required for a national response to an impoverished situation. The ensuing Massey Report of 1951, named after its chairman, the Canadian diplomat VINCENT MASSEY, led to the establishment of the Canada Council six years later. It is the most important cultural vehicle in the country and the prime patron of the national art community. Modelled on the Arts Council of Great Britain, its mandate has been to fulfil the recommendation of the Massey Report that the Canadian community has a deep responsibility to those in the visual and performing arts and in the area of literature. The existence of the Canada Council influenced the establishment of provincial arts councils, which also provided grants for institutions and organizations and, in a few cases, for individual artists. In 1968 the formation of the federal Museums Assistance Programme led to further government patronage. Another source of patronage was the programme set up by the Department of Public Works, whereby 1% of the construction cost of each federal building was dedicated to the commissioning of works of art to enhance the structure. It was terminated in 1978, although a similar programme on a 1.5% expenditure exists in Quebec. Since 1980 art galleries and museums have received 80% of their funding from the government.

Corporate patronage, active in Canada since the early 20th century, usually takes the form of architectural competitions and the occasional commissioning of a work of art for a building's public spaces. Since the 1970s Canadian businesses have helped to sponsor museum exhibitions, but only about 10% of all Canadian corporations support the fine arts. The strongest corporate activity has been the building of collections, as in the case of the Toronto-Dominion Bank. Many collectors and segments of the art community itself regard collecting as the essential act of patronage. The private sector has contributed to the construction costs of art museums and has donated funds and art works to collections, and thus the emphasis of patronage has been on the institution, not on the artist. Whether or not this has occurred because of the history of government support of institutions, it has given Canada a particular pattern of art patronage.

BIBLIOGRAPHY

V. Massey and others: *Royal Commission on National Development in the Arts, Letters and Sciences, 1949–1951* (Ottawa, 1951)
Annual Reports, Canada Council (Ottawa, 1958–91)
A. Jarvis and others: 'The Patrons', *Can. A.*, xix (1962), pp. 187–221
D. McConathy: 'The Canadian Cultural Revolution', *A. Canada*, xxxii (1975), pp. 38–92
S. Crean: *Who's Afraid of Canadian Culture?* (Don Mills, 1976)
B. Ostry: *The Cultural Connection* (Ottawa, 1978)
L. Applebaum and J. Hébert: *Report of the Federal Cultural Policy Review Committee* (Ottawa, 1983)
G. Woodcock: *Strange Bedfellows* (Victoria, 1985)
E. Bovey and others: *Funding of the Arts in Canada to the Year 2000: The Report of the Task Force on Funding of the Arts* (Ottawa, 1986)

XII. Collecting and dealing.

Since the second half of the 19th century, those who have collected art have also been responsible for the establishment and growth of Canadian museums (*see* §XIII below). Prior to the 1880s the acquisition of European or Canadian art by individuals or institutions was sporadic. The most notable exception was the Desjardins collection of about 200 paintings brought to Quebec from France in 1817 (for further discussion *see* LÉGARÉ, JOSEPH). From 1880 to 1920 Montreal experienced the most ambitious and energetic amassing of art ever to occur in Canada, and the city gained an international reputation for its private collections. Henry Birks collected Canadian domestic and ecclesiastical silver and gold, while approximately 100 collectors were associated with the Canadian Pacific Railway, either directly or indirectly. Sir WILLIAM VAN HORNE, Sir GEORGE A. DRUMMOND and Charles Hosmer (1851–1925), among others, were also founder-patrons of the Art Association of Montreal (later the Montreal Museum of Fine Arts). They aggressively collected British and academic European art, and this was made all the more unusual by their early interest in Impressionism. Their collections were purchased through auctions and dealers in New York, London and Paris, as well as through William Scott & Sons in Montreal, and reflected diverse tastes and personal ambitions. While some works were gifted to the Museum, by the 1920s most of these collections had been sold internationally. Collecting in Toronto, beginning at the turn of the century, was a less voracious activity. The few collections were more conservative and reflected little interest in contemporary art. English and Scottish painting, especially portraiture, was more popular than in Montreal. Sir EDMUND WALKER was the most renowned collector of the period, and Frank P. Wood (1883–1955), through the English dealer Joseph Duveen, assembled the first collection of Old Master paintings in Canada, part of which is now housed in the Art Gallery of Ontario, Toronto. Unlike Montreal, the impetus for private collecting in Toronto was largely fuelled by international dealers, such as Knoedler and Durand-Ruel. The acquisition of Canadian art was seen as the responsibility of the National Gallery of Canada in Ottawa.

After World War I the imposition of income tax, as well as the scarcity and cost of works, curtailed the collecting of international art. In the 1920s Canadian art was first acquired in large quantities by such private collectors as Charles Band (1885–1969) and the meat packer and philanthropist James Stanley McLean (1876–1954), both of Toronto, as well as by such corporations as Canada Steamship Lines Inc. in Montreal. One of the most important collectors of Canadian art was G. Blair Laing (1911–91), who was an art dealer in Toronto from the 1930s to the 1950s. The Laing Galleries specialized in works by Cornelius Krieghoff, Tom Thomson and the Group of Seven. Laing himself showed special interest in the work of James Wilson Morrice, donating 83 of the artist's paintings to the National Gallery of Canada in 1990. Douglas M. Duncan (1902–68), another art dealer, whose bequest went to the National Gallery, was a foremost collector of Canadian art and particularly supported the career of David B. Milne. Sigmund Samuel's large collection of 18th- and 19th-century Canadian art and furniture was set up in 1951 in Toronto as the Sigmund Samuel Canadiana Gallery. In 1965 approximately 5000 works of art by the Group of Seven and its contemporaries were given to the Province of Ontario by Robert and Signe McMichael and are housed in an extensive building at Kleinburg, north of Toronto. The Zacks amassed a substantial collection of modern art and contemporary Canadian work, and the Sobey family of Stellarton, NS, collected late 19th-century and 20th-century Canadian art up to and including the Group of Seven. There were some collectors who still had an interest in British art: VINCENT MASSEY's collection, for example, was formed in the mid-1940s and was later given to the National Gallery of Canada.

The founding of the Canada Council in 1957 fostered the acquisition of contemporary Canadian art. Within a decade Canadian art became the primary focus of private, corporate and public collections, as well as of dealers such as Av Isaacs in Toronto and Agnes Lefort in Montreal. The Canadian art market gained added international importance when Sotheby's opened an auction house in Toronto in 1967. In 1972 the Art Bank, the 'purchasing arm' of the Canada Council, was set up for the purpose of acquiring works of art, mainly for office buildings and other public spaces. This was followed by the establishment of similar institutions in various provinces, although with a regional emphasis. Such galleries as the Mendel Art Gallery in Saskatoon, the Norman MacKenzie Art Gallery at the University of Regina and the Lord Beaverbrook Art Gallery in Fredericton, New Brunswick (*see* AITKEN, WILLIAM MAXWELL), were founded in the 1950s on the private collections of their namesakes. This reflected a general trend that continued throughout the second half of the 20th century when, for example, the Thomson Gallery opened in Toronto in 1990 to display more than 300 pieces of 19th- and 20th-century Canadian art from the collection of businessman Kenneth Thomson (*b* 1923).

BIBLIOGRAPHY

R. H. Hubbard: *European Paintings in Canadian Collections*, 2 vols (Toronto, 1956)
Canada Collects (exh. cat. by E. Turner, Montreal, Mus. F.A., 1960)
G. B. Laing: *Memoirs of an Art Dealer*, 2 vols (Toronto, 1983)
G. Loranger: *An Essay on Private and Public Art Collecting in Canada* (Toronto, 1985) [privately published]
Discerning Tastes: Montreal Collectors, 1880–1920 (exh. cat. by J. Brooke, Montreal, Mus. F.A., 1989)
Gainsborough in Canada (exh. cat. by I. Lumsden, Fredericton, NB, Beaverbrook A.G., 1991)
C. C. Hill: *Morrice: A Gift to the Nation: The G. Blair Laing Collection* (Ottawa, 1992)

SANDRA PAIKOWSKY

XIII. Museums.

Despite its relatively small population, Canada has approximately 2000 museums, representing a wide range of types. Besides over 100 museums and galleries administered by provincial and federal governments, there are many smaller, community-based museums of local history. The museum system is a mixture of private and public non-profit institutions, run by either government, societies or individuals. Some of these receive a certain amount of government support, but all benefit from having active museum and gallery associations and a high degree of public involvement in their activities. Although 80% of museums existing in the 1990s were established after 1945, the earliest ones can be traced back to the first European settlement in the 17th century, and their subsequent development parallels that of museums in Great Britain, France and the USA.

The earliest collections were formed by the explorers and administrators of the colony of New France and the territory of British North America, but these ultimately became part of British and French museums and galleries when their owners returned to Europe. Museum history in Canada itself began with the creation of collections mainly for religious, educational, scientific or private purposes. In the 17th and 18th centuries members of the seminaries in Quebec City assembled collections to support their educational work, many of the pieces having since found their way into the Musée du Québec and the Université Laval. After the British conquest many private museums and museums founded by societies were established, such as the Literary and Historical Society of Quebec in 1823 and the Montreal Natural History Society in 1830. In Quebec City in 1833 the artist Joseph Légaré opened the first art gallery in Canada. There were several profit-making museums in other parts of British North America as well, for example the Niagara Falls Museum (now the Niagara Falls Art Gallery and Museum), established in 1827. In 1828 and 1830 several Mechanics Institutes were set up as museums in Montreal, Quebec, Toronto, and St John's, Newfoundland, that of Halifax eventually becoming the Nova Scotia Museum in 1868. Universities and colleges also created museums as testimonies to their educational purposes: the museums of King's College in Windsor, Nova Scotia (1803), Pictou Academy, Nova Scotia (1819), the University of New Brunswick in Fredericton (1841) and the University of Toronto (1841) are examples. In Montreal in 1881 Sir William Dawson turned the small collection owned by McGill University into the Redpath Museum, the first purpose-built museum in Canada. By the late 19th century the college and university museum was the dominant type of museum in Canada.

The early years of Canada's museum history were characterized by lack of interest or occasional grudging support on the part of the government. The role of the federal government in the making of museum policy was initially established in Montreal in 1841 with the creation of the Museum of the Geological Survey of Canada, whose purpose it was to demonstrate the results of the Survey's work to the public and to legislators. The Museum was represented at the Great Exhibition of 1851 in London, where, as a vehicle for government policy, displays from New Brunswick, Nova Scotia, Newfoundland and the Province of Canada (now Ontario and Quebec) convinced visitors that these areas were a source for raw materials and were capable of supporting investment and settlement. Such interest led the provinces to establish museums of a similar sort, Quebec City's Musée de l'Instruction Public (1883–1920) and the British Columbia Provincial Museum in Victoria (1889) being two examples. The National Gallery of Canada owes its origins to the interest of the Governor-General, John Campbell, the Marquis of Lorne, and his wife, Princess Louise, daughter of Queen Victoria, who helped establish the Royal Canadian Academy of Arts, the structure of which was based on its parent institution, the Royal Academy in London. The inaugural exhibition was held in Ottawa in 1880, the diploma works deposited by the academicians forming the nucleus of the

Gallery's collection. As with many of Canada's government-supported museums in the 19th century, the National Gallery's subsequent life was somewhat precarious. In 1907 a new Advisory Arts Council guided the Gallery to a broader collection policy involving the purchase and donation of both Canadian and foreign works. It was not until 1913 that the Gallery was established in legislation, and it continued to have problems of organization, funding and housing.

From the 1880s a large number of both art and historical museums were created by societies and associations. The celebration in the 1880s of the centennials of English settlement in Canada generated a historical consciousness that resulted in the founding of several museums by provincial and local historical societies, such as the Vancouver Art, Historical and Scientific Association (later to become the Vancouver Museums and Planetarium), the Niagara-on-the-Lake Historical Society in 1895 and the Brôme County Historical Society in Quebec. The Art Association of Montreal established the Montreal Museum of Fine Arts in 1879, and the Ontario Society of Artists set up the Art Museum of Toronto (later the Art Gallery of Ontario) in 1911. Other major art galleries were established within the next 15 years: the Winnipeg Art Gallery in 1912, the Art Gallery of Hamilton in 1914, the Edmonton Art Gallery in 1924 and the Vancouver Art Gallery in 1926.

There was also a growing professional awareness of museum problems. As part of a series on the museums of Britain and her colonies, Sir Henry Miers and Frank Markham published a report in 1932 that was a critique of the Canadian museum system. Only 19 of the 125 museums studied were found to have full-time curators, while the annual expenditures of the British Museum in London or the Field Museum of Natural History in Chicago were more than twice that of the total expenditures of all museums in Canada. Nevertheless, the National Gallery of Canada, for example, was actively involved with such extension programmes as the series of travelling exhibitions sent to smaller galleries in all parts of the country. Public awareness was further increased by various radio broadcasts on cultural matters. There was also a concerted effort to reach children by means of series of art reproductions sent out to public schools. By the 1940s there were several regional art circuits throughout Canada that hosted or originated travelling shows as part of a policy of gallery decentralization.

After World War II museums were affected by the rise in nationalism. There was now more government support for the wide range of museums existing in the country. In 1947 the Canadian Museums Association was formed to help improve museum services in Canada, and in the 1960s this led to the establishment of professional programmes and to widespread growth of provincial and regional museum and gallery associations. Following the Miers and Markham Report, the report of the Massey–Levesque Commission in 1952 outlined and commented on the problems of Canada's cultural development. In 1957 the Americans Carl and Grace Guthe, commissioned by the Canadian Museums Association, reported on the state of two-thirds of museums, finding that only 50 had an annual budget of over £Can. 15,000 and were able to employ full-time staff. These critical assessments led such provinces as Ontario and Nova Scotia to begin direct funding of local museums. At the federal level, the Canada Council, founded in 1957, established support in the form of a variety of grants to artists and art galleries (*see* §XI above). In 1963 the federal government created the Department of the Secretary of State, one of whose responsibilities it was to coordinate cultural policies and programmes. In 1967 the celebration of Canada's centenary led to the creation of projects for 150 museums, the total cost of which was more than £Can. 15 million. Money from these funds was used for the building of new quarters for larger museums in British Columbia (the British Columbia Provincial Museum), Alberta (the Provincial Museum of Alberta), Manitoba (the Manitoba Museum of Man and Nature), Nova Scotia (the Nova Scotia Museum) and Ontario (the Ontario Science Center), as well as a range of smaller museums throughout the country. By the 1980s provincial and municipal support for museums was beginning to match that of the federal government, resulting in the establishment of such museums as the Musée de la Civilisation in Quebec City in 1987. During this decade there was a marked decrease in federal support to museums outside the capital region of Ottawa and a concentration on the building of new museum and gallery structures within the city itself. A more centralized structure seemed to result, with the new National Gallery, designed by Moshe Safdie, opening in 1988 and the Canadian Museum of Civilization, by Douglas Cardinal, in 1989. The National Museums of Canada, the federal body founded in 1927 and responsible for the administration of these and other museums, ceased to exist in 1990, when the various museums and galleries under its jurisdiction became self-determining. In the 1980s and 1990s there was widespread growth of alternatives to the traditional museum, such as the eco-museum, the native-run museum and the artist-run centre.

BIBLIOGRAPHY

H. A. Miers and S. F. Markham: *A Report on the Museums of Canada to the Carnegie Corporation of New York: To Which is Appended a Directory of Canada and other Parts of the British Empire on the American Continent* (Edinburgh, 1932)

M. Ross, ed.: *The Arts in Canada: Stock-taking at Mid-century* (Toronto, 1958)

J. S. Boggs: *The National Gallery of Canada* (Ottawa, 1971)

A. F. Key: *Beyond Four Walls: The Origins and Development of Canadian Museums* (Toronto, 1973)

B. Dixon: *The Museum and the Canadian Public* (1974)

Museums, Art Galleries and Related Institutions in Canada, 1972, Statistics Canada (Ottawa, 1975)

2001, the Museum and the Canadian Public: Lake Couchiching, Ont., 1976

The Works of Joseph Légaré, 1795–1855 (exh. cat. by J. R. Porter, Ottawa, N.G., 1978)

To Found a National Gallery: The Royal Canadian Academy of Arts, 1880–1913 (exh. cat., Ottawa, N.G., 1980)

The National Gallery of Canada: Past and Prologue (Ottawa, 1986)

D. V. Verney: *Three Civilizations, Two Cultures, One State: Canada's Political Traditions* (Durham, NC, 1986)

G. F. MacDonald and S. Alsford: *A Museum for the Global Village: The Canadian Museum of Civilization* (Hull, Qué., 1989)

J. LYNNE TEATHER

XIV. Art education.

In the 17th and 18th centuries art education in Canada was largely based on a system of apprenticeship or was dependent on the courses irregularly offered by itinerant European or American artists. During the French regime European-trained artists passed on their knowledge, particularly of the decorative arts, in small workshop settings. The Saint-Joachim Ecole des Arts et des Métiers was founded *c.* 1668 by Bishop François de Montmorency-Laval (1623–1708) at Cap Tourmente, near Quebec City, to train painters, wood-carvers and silversmiths. A major wave of immigration occurred after 1783, mainly from the USA, which vastly expanded the population, but the teaching of art continued to take place in informal settings and on an intermittent basis until 1815. After this time, many artists, mostly from Great Britain, emigrated and set up more formal art schools. In 1818 George Ramsay, 9th Earl of Dalhousie (1770–1838), Lieutenant-Governor of Nova Scotia from 1816 to 1820, initiated the foundation of Dalhousie College (now Dalhousie University), Halifax, which began offering art classes regularly in 1829. In the 1820s and 1830s Mechanics Institutes were also set up throughout the colonies to provide a more popular outlet for the teaching of art in a wide range of areas.

Formal art exhibitions and artistic criticism began as early as 1828 in Quebec, 1830 in Halifax and 1834 in Toronto. By the 1850s art exhibitions had become a regular feature of Canadian life, prizes being awarded in a variety of categories at local and provincial exhibitions. Most of the exhibitors received their art education by attending lectures at the mechanics institutes or studying with private tutors or in private academies, but after 1850 art education based on the copying of classical models became a regular feature of the public education system. By Confederation in 1867, art education was also being undertaken through artists' societies, including the Art Association of Montreal (founded 1860), the Ontario Society of Artists (1872), Toronto, and the Royal Canadian Academy of Arts (1880), Ottawa. These organizations provided academic instruction, either through their own classes or by building the curriculum for such schools as Toronto's Ontario College of Art, founded in 1876. Alternately, such institutions as the Ecole Nationale des Beaux-Arts (now the Ecole des Beaux-Arts), founded in Montreal in 1870, and the Victoria School of Art and Design (now the Nova Scotia College of Art and Design), founded in Halifax in 1887, provided a link between art and the needs of the commercial world. Artists also formed more informal associations such as the Toronto Art Students' League (1886) and the CANADIAN ART CLUB (1907–15), which provided a freer atmosphere for the study of newer developments in the fine arts. The Guild of Sculpture of Ontario (1895) provided encouragement and training for sculptors. In 1896 a department of architecture was opened at McGill University, Montreal. Art education continued essentially unchanged until the 1930s, when new approaches to art education began to occur. In 1939 Mount Allison University in Sackville, New Brunswick, was the first institution to offer a Bachelor of Fine Arts degree, and within the next 30 years other universities followed its lead. Arthur Lismer, Group of Seven member and an art educator, promoted a less restrictive approach to the teaching of art, first in Halifax (1916–19) and then in Toronto (1919–38) and Montreal (1942–67), considering it a social science and emphasizing the student's natural creativity.

After World War II a return to apprentice-style teaching and artists' workshops began to occur at such schools as the Banff School of Fine Arts in Alberta, founded in 1933, the Emma Lake workshops in Saskatchewan, established in 1936, and Le Centre des Métiers du Verre du Québec, opened in 1988. These trends have continued to predominate in the teaching of art in Canada, although the commercial approach is still reflected in the curricula of the Nova Scotia College of Art and Design and the Ecole du Meuble in Montreal (founded 1930), where furniture and interior design and textile production are taught.

BIBLIOGRAPHY

J. D. Wilson, R. M. Stamp and L. P. Andet, eds: *Canadian Education: A History* (Scarborough, Ont., 1970)

100 Years: Evolution of the Ontario College of Art (exh. cat., Toronto, A.G. Ont., 1976–7)

D. Leighton and P. Leighton: *Artists, Builders and Dreamers: 50 Years at the Banff School* (Toronto, 1982)

J. G. Reid: *Mount Allison University: A History, to 1963* (Toronto and London, 1984)

L. Lacroix: 'Art Education', *The Canadian Encyclopedia*, ed. J. H. Marsh, i (Edmonton, 1985, rev. 2/1988), pp. 126–7

G. Lesser: *Ecole de meuble, 1930–1950* (Montreal, 1989)

JIM BURANT

XV. Art libraries and photographic collections.

The oldest art library in Canada, founded by the Art Association of Montreal, first opened to the general public in 1882 in the Association's quarters. The libraries of the National Gallery of Canada (1918) in Ottawa, the Art Gallery of Ontario (1906) in Toronto and the Museum of Fine Arts in Montreal (the latter an outgrowth of the Art Association of Montreal), as well as several other museum and gallery libraries across Canada, concentrate on building collections of artists' files and exhibition catalogues that document Canada's cultural heritage and its contemporary scene. The library (1914) of the Royal Ontario Museum in Toronto reflects an institutional mandate to collect material relating to native and decorative arts and archaeological artefacts, and similarly the National Museum of Canada (by 1986 the Canadian Museum of Civilization) in Hull, Quebec, emphasizes folk arts and native arts. The libraries of some of the older universities, such as at the University of Toronto (1892), at McGill University, Blackader-Lauterman Library of Architecture and Art (1922), Montreal, at the University of British Columbia, Fine Arts Division Library (1915), Vancouver, and at the Université Laval (1852) in Quebec, have developed strong all-round holdings of material on art and architecture. The Ontario College of Art (1876) in Toronto and the Nova Scotia College of Art and Design (1887) in Halifax serve a broad art community with library collections developed for practising artists. Both the Metropolitan Toronto Reference Library, Fine Art Dept (1960), and the Vancouver Public Library, Art Division (1929), for many decades have maintained extensive artists' files and card indexes that focus on regional artistic activity. The Canadian Centre for Architecture in Montreal (founded in 1979; opened in 1989) has become a particularly rich repository of monographs, periodicals, photographs, drawings and models for advanced research in the history and understanding of architecture and the built environment. Canadian architecture prior to 1914 is being documented by the Canadian Inventory of Historic Building (1970) in Ottawa, which has gathered information and photographs relating to over 200,000 structures.

BIBLIOGRAPHY

Fine Arts Library Resources in Canada, 2 vols, National Library of Canada (Ottawa, 1978)
M. F. Williamson: 'The Tyranny of Distance: Art Libraries in Canada', *A. Libs J.*, viii/1 (1983), pp. 59–72
Guide, Canadian Inventory of Historic Building (Ottawa, 1987)
Centre canadien d'architecture; Les Débuts, 1979–1984/Canadian Centre for Architecture: The First Five Years, 1979–1984 (Montreal, 1988) [bilingual text]

MARY F. WILLIAMSON

Canadian Art Club. Society of artists active in Toronto from 1907 to 1915. Among its 20 members were William Brymner, Maurice Cullen, Clarence Gagnon, James Wilson Morrice, Edmund Morris (1871–1913), A. Phimister Proctor (1860–1950), Horatio Walker, Homer Watson and Curtis Williamson (1867–1944). The Club was formed in reaction to the low standards and 'truth to nature' aesthetics of the Ontario Society of Artists and was modelled on Whistler's International Society of Sculptors, Painters and Gravers. Its eight exhibitions concentrated on small, carefully hung groups of works by leading Canadian artists and attempted to establish a high standard for other artists. The Club applauded individual achievement and was nationalistic in persuading expatriates to exhibit at home but, unlike the Group of Seven, defined nationality in only the broadest terms. The artists who exhibited at the Club were influenced by the Barbizon school, the Hague school and British *plein-air* painting, by Whistler and the Impressionists. Their works were well received by critics, and the Club's activities were an important catalyst for artistic and institutional change. Its major influence was that of its Quebec Impressionist members on the emerging Group of Seven. After the death of Morris in 1913, however, and with the distractions of World War I, the Club disbanded; personalities clashed, finances were shaky and the membership was too dispersed to sustain the enthusiasm to keep it alive.

BIBLIOGRAPHY

The Canadian Art Club, 1907–1915 (exh. cat. by R. J. Lamb, Edmonton, Alta, A.G., 1988)

ROBERT J. LAMB

Canal, Ramón Alva de la. *See* ALVA DE LA CANAL, RAMÓN.

Canales, Alejandro (*b* Managua, 1945). Nicaraguan painter. He studied drawing, painting and sculpture at the Escuela Nacional de Bellas Artes, Managua, under a scholarship from 1961 to 1970. Throughout the 1970s he struggled to make a living by selling his art and in 1977 joined the revolutionary movement that overthrew the dictatorship of General Somoza in 1979. He was commissioned in 1980 by the newly established Ministerio de Cultura to paint a mural, *Literacy Campaign* (4×22 m; Managua, Parque Velásquez), about the highly successful national literary crusade that took place in that year, deftly synthesizing elements from European modernism, Mexican muralism and Pre-Columbian art.

Canales executed two more murals near Parque Velásquez: *Coffee Harvest* (2×7 m, 1982) and the huge, boldly-coloured *Communication Past and Present* (30×14 m, 1984), a synthesis of Nicaraguan history that extends several stories in height on the side of the Telcor Building, which dominates downtown Managua near the lake front. There are also murals by Canales in the Teatro Rubén Darío and the Instituto Nacional de Securidad Social, Managua. His growing international reputation led to further invitations to paint murals in other countries, including Mozambique and the USA, and was an important factor in establishing Nicaragua's influential role in the revitalization of mural painting.

BIBLIOGRAPHY

E. Cockcroft and D. Kunzle: 'Report from Nicaragua', *A. Amer.*, lxx/5 (1982), pp. 51–9
D. Craven and J. Ryder: 'Nicaragua's Revolution in Culture', *A. Mag.*, lviii/5 (1984), pp. 83–6
J. Weber: 'Sandinista Arts', *New A. Examiner* (Oct 1985), pp. 42–4
L. Morales Alonso: 'Reflexiones sobre el muralismo', *Ventana* (23 Nov 1985), p. 2
D. Craven: *The New Concept of Art and Popular Culture in Nicaragua Since the Revolution in 1979* (Lewiston, 1989), pp. 189–207

DAVID CRAVEN

Canaletto [Canal, Giovanni Antonio] (*b* Venice, 17 Oct 1697; *d* Venice, 10 April 1768). Italian painter, etcher and draughtsman. He was the most distinguished Italian view painter of the 18th century. Apart from ten years spent in England he lived in Venice, and his fame rests above all on his views (*vedute*) of that city; some of these are purely topographical, others include festivals or ceremonial events. He also painted imaginary views (capriccios), although the demarcation between the real and the invented is never quite clearcut: his imaginary views often include realistically depicted elements, though in unexpected surroundings, and in a sense even his Venetian *vedute* are imaginary. He never merely re-created reality. He was highly successful with the English, helped in this by the British connoisseur JOSEPH SMITH, whose own large collection of Canaletto's works was sold to King George III in 1762. The British Royal Collection has the largest group of his paintings and drawings.

1. Life and work. 2. Working methods and technique.

1. Life and work.

(i) Early works, *c.* 1716–30. (ii) Views of Venice and the patronage of Joseph Smith, 1730–39. (iii) Etchings and capriccios, 1740–45. (iv) England, 1746–55. (v) Last years, 1756–68.

(i) Early works, c. *1716–30.*

(a) Rome and Venice: Theatre and early capriccios. His father, Bernardo Canal (1674–1744), was a well-established painter of theatrical scenery. The earliest source on Canaletto as a painter records that from 1716 to 1718 he was working with Bernardo and an uncle, Cristoforo Canal (*d* before 10 June 1730), on stage sets for operas by Antonio Vivaldi at the theatres of S Angelo and S Cassiano in Venice (Orlandi, p. 75). Around 1719 he travelled to Rome, again as his father's assistant, to paint scenery for Alessandro Scarlatti's operas *Tito Sempronico Gracco* and *Turno Aricino*, which were performed at the Teatro

Capranica during Carnival 1720. This experience of scenery painting gave him a thorough grounding in draughtsmanship, perspective and *quadratura*. None of his stage sets has survived, but the designs for them were highly praised by Anton Maria Zanetti the younger (1771, p. 462), who also recorded that Canaletto could not adjust to working with theatre people and soon directed his talents to painting views, both real and imaginary (p. 463). Canaletto's Roman sojourn was crucial to his artistic formation and may have been much longer than the few months usually suggested. He was inscribed in the Venetian painters' guild, the Fraglia, in 1720, but this inscription could have been made during a brief visit home or even while he was still in Rome.

An important set of architectural drawings numbered 1 to 23 (all London, BM, except no. 19, Darmstadt, Hess. Landesmus.) have come to be viewed as the artist's earliest known works. They represent Roman sites or monuments, both ancient and modern, and bear inscriptions that are considered autograph (1981 exh. cat., no. 93, p. 81). But for several reasons—they differ markedly in quality and style, they are based in part on engravings by Giovanni Battista Falda and Etienne Dupérac and were used by Canaletto for paintings of his middle years—the questions of when and why they were made require further elucidation (Corboz, 1985, i, p. 30).

Having, in his own words, 'solemnly excommunicated the theatre' (Zanetti, 1771, p. 462), Canaletto appears to have tried his hand next at fantasy views and landscapes while gradually working his way into the more exacting art of realistic view painting. His early capriccios were probably made during or just after his stay in Rome. This early phase of his career remains insufficiently known, as many of the pictures are privately owned and not easily accessible, yet several have been identified (Morassi, 1956 and 1966). Most of these depict decaying edifices and architectural fragments, usually overgrown with foliage, or else Roman ruins, some real and some fantastic, often placed in a lagoon-like setting. They are painted in broad, loose brushstrokes on a dark ground and no doubt reflect Canaletto's stage-design manner. The few lively, sketchy figures serve mainly as colour accents. Two such typical early views are the pendants in the Cini collection in Venice (see 1982 exh. cat., nos 76–7). A large capriccio in a private Swiss collection (see Puppi, 1968, pl. 1) is inscribed 'Io Antonio Canal 1723'. The *Landscape with Ruins and a Renaissance Building* (Hartford, CT, Wadsworth Atheneum) is a particularly attractive painting and, significantly, it was formerly attributed to Marco Ricci.

Canaletto certainly saw Luca Carlevaris's capriccios and imaginary harbour scenes during his formative years in Venice. In Rome he must have encountered Baroque architectural compositions, such as those by Viviano Codazzi and Giovanni Ghisolfi, as well as Gaspar van Wittel's Roman *vedute* and possibly even Giovanni Paolo Panini's very early ruinscapes. Yet Ricci's works, often confused with Canaletto's, provided the greatest inspiration. The personal connection between the two artists was probably closer than has been suspected: in 1718 Ricci worked as stage designer in the same Venetian theatres as did the Canal family, and he, like Canaletto, may have been in Rome *c.* 1719–20.

Around 1725 Canaletto collaborated with Giovanni Battista Piazzetta and Giovanni Battista Cimaroli (*fl c.* 1700–after 1753) on the allegorical tomb painting *Capriccio: Tomb of Lord Somers* (*c.* 1725; Birmingham, Mus. & A.G.), and with Giambattista Pittoni and Cimaroli on *Capriccio: Tomb of Archbishop Tillotson* (priv. col., see 1989 exh. cat., nos 12–13), both part of a series commissioned by Owen McSwiny for Charles Lennox, 2nd Duke of Richmond. Canaletto's contribution was to paint the extensive architectural settings and the sarcophagi. These, probably the last in date of Canaletto's youthful imaginary views, show the influence of Marco Ricci, who was also a contributor to the series. In 1727 McSwiny wrote to the Duke that 'Canal has more work than he can doe in any reasonable time and well' (quoted in Constable, 1962, i, app. II).

(b) Early Venetian townscapes. In the 1720s Canaletto also painted realistic views, from 1725 to 1740 devoting himself almost exclusively, and with unrivalled success, to this genre. Some of his early townscapes appear to have been adapted from engravings and even from paintings by Carlevaris, supporting the hypothesis that after his return from Rome to Venice he spent some time in Carlevaris's studio. Among the earliest are four companion pieces: the *Piazza S Marco* and *Grand Canal from the Campo S Vio* (Lugano, Col. Thyssen-Bornemisza) and a less celebrated view, the shabby *Rio dei Mendicanti*, with *Grand Canal from the Palazzo Balbi* (Venice, Correr), which may be dated, on topographical evidence, to *c.* 1724. His first documented paintings, executed between August 1725 and July 1726, for Stefano Conti, a merchant of Lucca, were two pairs, the *Grand Canal: Looking North from near the Rialto Bridge* with the *Grand Canal: The Rialto Bridge from the North*, and the *Grand Canal: From S Maria della Carità* with *SS Giovanni e Paolo and the Scuola di S Marco* (all Montreal, priv. col., see Constable, 1962, i, pls 42, 48–9 and 58).

The letters (some in Canaletto's own hand) and memoranda pertaining to the Conti deal provide the richest single source of information on Canaletto in the 1720s (Haskell, 1956). They show that by 1725–6 he was very much in demand as a specialist of Venetian townscapes, having apparently surpassed Carlevaris's reputation in this genre; that he was particularly skilled at 'making the sun shine' in his pictures; that it was his custom to prepare his paintings outdoors 'on the spot' and 'not at home after an idea' as was Carlevaris's practice; that one of his views had entered the prestigious Sagredo collection and was hanging in the Sagredo family palazzo; and that on St Roch's feast day in 1725 he had astounded everyone in Venice with a picture of *SS Giovanni and Paolo* (untraced), which Conte Colloredo Waldsee, the Imperial Ambassador, had bought even though he already owned a picture by Canaletto.

The paintings themselves form the basis for dating a number of views painted *c.* 1722–8. These early works, including the Conti pictures, are mostly large and painted on dark reddish ground, hence dark in appearance. The paint is applied in thick, loose brushstrokes, with a ragged touch. The exaggerated foreshortenings and intense contrasts of light and shadow endow the views with a vivid

1. Canaletto: *Stonemason's Yard*, oil on canvas, 1.24×1.63 m, 1726–7 (London, National Gallery)

immediacy, further enhanced by threatening storm clouds. Their theatricality may owe something to Canaletto's apprenticeship in scene painting, but the humid atmosphere of Venice is realistically rendered and the sketchy, incidental figures, always active and moving, attest to the artist's keen observation of daily life. The five large pictures in the Gemäldegalerie Alte Meister, Dresden, depicting similar subjects but compositionally more sophisticated, can be dated a little later.

The poetry and lofty mood of the townscapes of the 1720s, when Canaletto was not yet concentrating on celebrated sites for the tourist market, were never to be surpassed. The essence of his romantic style shows most vividly in a series of companion pieces, two horizontal and four upright, painted as part of a decorative ensemble depicting six sites in Venice as seen from the Piazza and Piazzetta (*c.* 1725; Windsor Castle, Berks, Royal Col.). These were either acquired early on or, probably, commissioned by Joseph Smith. The powerfully realistic *Stonemason's Yard* (1726–7; London, N.G.; see fig. 1), a vivid and intimate view of everyday life in Venice and of weathered and decaying buildings, is perhaps his masterpiece. The *View of Murano from the Fondamente Nuove* (Windsor Castle, Berks, Royal Col.) and the *Molo Looking West: Fonteghetto della Farina* (Venice, A. Giustiniani priv. col., see Puppi, 1968, pls 47–8) date from the same period.

The two sun-drenched views commissioned by the Conte Giuseppe di Bolagno, the *Bucintoro Returning to the Molo on Ascension Day* (1730; Windsor Castle, Berks, Royal Col.; *see* VEDUTA, fig. 1) and the *Reception of the Ambassador* (priv. col., see 1982 exh. cat., no. 84), and the famous *Venice: The Feast Day of St Roch* (London, N.G.; see fig. 2), all painted *c.* 1730, mark the grand culmination of Canaletto's youthful period while heralding his mature style at its best.

(ii) Views of Venice and the patronage of Joseph Smith, 1730–39. Canaletto was at his most productive and commercially successful during the 1730s, the decade in which he painted the views of Venice with which his name is associated. The majority of these works were made for affluent English patrons, who desired mementos of a visit to Venice, often made on the GRAND TOUR. These clients approached Canaletto directly on occasion but usually through Joseph Smith, who had lived in Venice since *c.* 1700. Banker, shipping agent and, from 1744, consul, Smith was also a keen connoisseur of art, a great patron and a formidable collector. His palazzo, packed with pictures, was the chief meeting-place for English tourists. That Canaletto was working exclusively for Smith, as maintained by the Swedish diplomat Count Carl Gustav Tessin in 1736 (Links, 1977, p. 37) and again by Horace

2. Canaletto: *Venice: The Feast Day of St Roch*, oil on canvas, 1.47×1.99 mm, *c.* 1730 (London, National Gallery)

William Walpole in 1741 (Links, 1977, p. 37), overstates the case. Though the relationship with Smith must have started in the 1720s and lasted until Canaletto's death, no contract between the two men is known to have existed; rather theirs was an informal partnership that benefited both. Establishing contacts for Canaletto with prospective patrons and shipping his paintings to them in England put Smith in an advantageous position to acquire works by Canaletto for his own collection.

In 1735 the publishing firm of Giambattista Pasquali issued the *Prospectus Magni Canalis Venetiarum*, an album of 14 prints of Venetian views (12 of the Grand Canal, 2 of Venetian festivals; Windsor Castle, Berks, Royal Col.); these were engraved by Antonio Visentini after paintings by Canaletto described on the title page as being in Smith's residence. In 1742 Smith had a new edition of the *Prospectus* published: to the first set it added 24 new prints, again engraved by Visentini, based on yet another cluster of Canaletto townscapes that Smith had acquired in the 1730s. By 1742 these view paintings, apart from 15 that Smith kept for himself, had been sold to various members of the English nobility. They were painted with tourists in mind and show noted Venetian sites, always in bright sunlight. On average they are of smaller size than his view paintings of the 1720s; the 34 *vedute* included in the two editions of the *Prospectus* are of uniform size, *c.* 480×800 mm, which was evidently a size that Smith liked to handle for Canaletto's run-of-the-mill output in those years (both size and format were particularly suitable for pictures that came in large sets). Among the English aristocrats who bought these view paintings were John Russell, 4th Duke of Bedford (1710–71), and Francis Osborne, 4th Duke of Leeds (1685–1741), while no fewer than nine were acquired for an unidentified member of the Duke of Buckingham's entourage. By the 19th century Richard Grenville, 3rd Duke of Buckingham and Chandos (1823–89), owned 19 pictures (dispersed, but known as the Harvey group; see Constable, 1962, ii, p. 277, no. 188); 22 of 24 *vedute* commissioned by the 4th Duke of Bedford remain at Woburn Abbey, Beds. These two sets, roughly of *Prospectus* size and showing the Grand Canal, the area around the Piazza and various churches and campi, epitomize the style of the 1730s.

Although Canaletto occasionally still used the reddish-brown ground he had favoured in the 1720s, he painted most of his views for export on white, light grey or light cream grounds. His skies turned serenely blue, with spare white clouds; the atmosphere evaporated; the subdued colours of the juvenilia disappeared; bright local colours were applied to the costumes. The advent of the high Rococo in Venice brought a similar lightening of the palette to certain works by Pittoni, Piazzetta and Giambattista Tiepolo. It is a more pronounced feature of some of Canaletto's works than others, leading critics to speculate that he was consciously using two different modes according to his patrons' taste. But whether his style was influenced to this extent by his market is impossible to determine. Although some paintings of that era are visibly straight commercial products done to a formula, at full speed, the craftsmanship is always impeccable even when the overall effect is prosaic. Canaletto did not simply repeat compositions; in fact autograph replicas are extremely rare. It was during the 1730s that he developed the calligraphic shorthand of blobs, short curves and rigid short lines that he used most noticeably in painting the staffage, thereby rendering it more static. But however

3. Canaletto: *Bacino di S Marco*, oil on canvas, 1.25×2.05 m, *c.* 1735 (Boston, MA, Museum of Fine Arts)

hasty the creation, the arrangement of stereotyped figures was always masterly. Corboz (1985, ii) catalogued some 200 Canaletto paintings as executed between 1731 and 1746. Not all of these were handled by Joseph Smith; unaccountably the loftiest of them seem to have eluded him (Links, 1977, p. 41). The famous *Bacino di S Marco* (*c*. 1735; Boston, MA, Mus. F.A.; see fig. 3) and the pendants depicting the *Entrance to the Grand Canal* and *Piazza S Marco* (Washington, DC, N.G.A.) did not pass through his hands. They may have been acquired directly from the artist by Henry Howard, 4th Earl of Carlisle. The only adequately documented work of Canaletto's maturity is a superb painting of unusual iconography, *Riva degli Schiavoni: Looking West* (London, Soane Mus.). In February 1736 it was completed and delivered to Johann Matthias, Marshal von der Schulenburg, military commandant of Venice, who had commissioned it directly from Canaletto for the handsome sum of 120 sequins (Binion, 1990, p. 118). By late 1739 Canaletto was acclaimed by Charles de Brosses (*Lettres familières écrites d'Italie en 1739 et 1744*; ed. Paris, 1885, p. 399) as the greatest townscape painter of all time.

(iii) Etchings and capriccios, 1740–45. In the early 1740s Canaletto gave up painting Venetian *vedute* almost entirely and devoted himself mostly to drawing and, probably for the first time, to etching. The change was largely due to the decline in English patronage after the outbreak of the War of the Austrian Succession (1741), which made travelling hazardous and sending paintings to England risky. His change in medium was accompanied to a certain extent by a change in subject-matter: he gave preference to capriccios and landscapes over realistic townscapes. In 1740–41 he made a tour of the Brenta canal, as far as Padua, with his nephew Bernardo Bellotto, during which he made around 30 drawings from nature, such as the luminous *Farm on the Outskirts of Padua* (Windsor Castle, Berks, Royal Col.), which show a fresh and spontaneous response to a new source of inspiration.

Throughout this period Canaletto was also working on etchings, which rank with the best ever produced. They fall within the great revival of etching in Venice that is represented in the work of Tiepolo, Piazzetta and Michele Giovanni Marieschi. Canaletto's style, though varying considerably from print to print, is distinguished by a wide range and great subtlety of tonal variation and a delicate, poetic rendering of light. Of the 34 items of his etched oeuvre, 31 were published in bound sets, with one third representing actual Venetian sites and the rest imaginary and untitled landscapes, suggestive of the countryside around Padua and along the Brenta canal. The etchings may have been commissioned and financed by Joseph Smith, for the title-page of the bound edition bears the dedication *Giuseppe Smith Console di S.M. Britanica.* The date of Smith's appointment to the post of consul, 6 June 1744, provides the *terminus post quem* for the collection's publication, and the year of Canaletto's departure for London, 1746, provides an *ante quem.* As the paper used for the etchings is said to have been produced between 1740 and 1743 (see 1986 exh. cat., p. 109), these years may well be considered as Canaletto's etching period, although the variety of technique and style within the set suggests that he experimented with the medium over an extended period, possibly between 1735 and 1744 (Bromberg, 1974). The sequence in the surviving original sets, such as that which belonged to Anton Maria Zanetti the elder (Berlin, Kupferstichkab.), was not based on chronology; what determined it remains to be discovered.

Etching may have been Canaletto's main preoccupation at this time, yet in 1743 he also received a large commission from Joseph Smith for 13 'pieces over doors', all of which were capriccios. Most of Canaletto's capriccios were executed after 1740, his interest in this form of painting perhaps reawakened because of the declining demand for topographical views. These later capriccios differ from his earlier ones in containing fewer invented architectural elements. *Capriccio: The Horses of S Marco in the Piazzetta* (1743; Windsor Castle, Berks, Royal Col.) places the famous horses in a different, but real, setting. Sometimes the fancifully juxtaposed elements are taken from more widely separated locations and assembled in an imaginary setting, as in the capriccio that shows the Colleoni statue near a Renaissance church and Roman ruins, including the Colosseum (priv. col., see Constable, 1962, i, pl. 88, no. 477).

(iv) England, 1746–55. In 1746 Canaletto, prompted by the decline of commissions in Venice, moved to England; George Vertue recorded his arrival in London in May of that year. Smith had provided letters of introduction, and McSwiny presented him to the Duke of Richmond. Canaletto was based in England until at least 1755, interrupting his stay in 1750–51 and again in 1753 to revisit Venice. In his first two years in England, he chose the Thames and the area around Westminster Bridge as his subject-matter. The bridge was then under construction and its supporting framework, scaffolding, crossed planks and poles gave him a series of attractive motifs, as in *London: Seen through an Arch of Westminster Bridge* (*c*. 1746–7; Alnwick Castle, Northumb.), which was painted for Hugh Smithson (later 1st Duke of Northumberland). The two imposing pictures *London: The Thames on Lord Mayor's Day* and *London: The Thames with Westminster Bridge in the Distance*, purchased by Ferdinand Filip, Prince of Lobkowitz (Prague, N.G., Kinský Pal.), were probably painted *c*. 1747. In the late summer of that year the Duke of Richmond permitted him to make drawings from the windows of Richmond House, overlooking the Thames, which resulted in two of his greatest English paintings, *London: Whitehall and the Privy Garden* and *London: The Thames and the City of London from Richmond House* (both Goodwood House, W. Sussex). London remained the centre of his activity, but after 1748 he spent prolonged periods away from the city, painting his patrons' country seats and domains. For Charles Noel Somerset, 4th Duke of Beaufort (*d* 1756), for instance, he painted *Views of Badminton* (1749; Badminton House, Glos; *in situ*). Towards the end of his stay in England he received a major commission from a friend of Joseph Smith, Thomas Hollis, and the paintings produced for this eccentric individual illustrate the varied quality of Canaletto's English output. Thus *Ranelagh: Interior of the Rotunda* (1754; London, N.G.) is unusually pedestrian, while *Old*

4. Canaletto: *Old Walton Bridge over the Thames*, oil on canvas, 488×767 mm, 1754 (London, Dulwich Picture Gallery)

Walton Bridge over the Thames (1754; London, Dulwich Pict. Gal.; see fig. 4) is a spirited masterpiece. His English oeuvre is not massive; no more than 40 paintings of English subjects are known. It may be that he went on producing Roman and Venetian *vedute*, even in the form of drawings, and that many of his imaginary views and capriccios that cannot be dated were made in England. Judgements of this period range from high praise to denigration. That he 'saw London through Venetian eyes' (Constable) is true, but that he never succeeded in capturing and rendering the poetry of the northern light is debatable. The claim that he developed his mechanical touch in England is inaccurate, for his calligraphic mannerisms are evident in works made in Venice many years earlier.

(v) Last years, 1756–68. Though the year of Canaletto's return from England to Venice is not known, he seems to have spent at least the last decade of his life in Venice. Some 40 paintings—both townscapes and architectural landscapes—and just over 100 drawings from these years have been identified (Corboz, 1985, ii). The drawings show a marked preference for fanciful compositions and capriccios over topographical views.

Canaletto was not among the 36 founder-members of the Accademia Veneziana di Pittura e Scultura (founded 1750, officially recognized 1756); only in 1763 did he become a member. He submitted his reception piece in 1765, choosing as its subject an architectural capriccio, a *Colonnade Opening on to the Courtyard of a Palace* (Venice, Accad.). That increasing age and illness accounted for the relatively slim output of his last ten years is questionable. His style had become highly mannered and is often viewed as dry and hard; yet most of the works are vigorous and remarkably well conceived, among them the untitled series of capriccios engraved by Fabio Berardi (1728–88) and published by Joseph (Giuseppe) Wagner (1706–80) and the ten very large drawings of the ducal ceremonies and festivals (one in London, BM) engraved by Giambattista Brustolon and published soon after 1763. The latter series proves that his skill in rendering large crowd scenes effectively was altogether unimpaired. The last dated work from Canaletto's hand is a drawing of the *Cantoria of S Marco with its Musicians* (Hamburg, Ksthalle). It bears an autograph inscription stating that he made it in 1766 at the age of 68 'without spectacles'. Canaletto died two years later after a short illness and was buried where he had been baptized, in the parish of S Lio. His three sisters inherited his estate, which the inventory made on his death reveals to have been modest. There were 28 pictures found in his studio, presumably unsold works by him; to posterity he left over 500 paintings and an even greater number of drawings of inestimable value.

2. Working methods and technique.

(i) Drawings and etchings. Canaletto was a superb and prolific draughtsman, and his 500 known drawings represent only a fraction of his total graphic output. The vast majority consist of elaborate, nearly finished compositions; a mere handful of his figure studies have been identified, for example *Three Groups of Figures: Market Scenes* (pen and brown ink; Rotterdam, Mus. Boymans–van Beuningen), and first thoughts and compositional studies are extremely rare. During the later part of his career many were made for the engraver or as ends in themselves. He

used white paper to draw, no doubt because of his constant interest in rendering light, primarily sunlight, and its effects. He drew with the pen, using various types of quill, occasionally a reed and even metallic pens (Parker, 1948, p. 22). A graphite or chalk foundation or rough tracings in chalk can almost always be detected under the actual penwork, as in *Two Studies of Men Standing* (New York, Met.). In the early part of his career Canaletto used tight pen hatchings for his shadows; then, from the mid-1730s, he switched to ink washes instead, probably to save time. He used rulers and dividers extensively. He used sketchbooks and albums for drawing, as is suggested by the numbers on some isolated sheets, but these were dismantled and have been reassembled only in part.

The Cagnola sketchbook (early 1730s; Venice, Accad.) is particularly informative on Canaletto's working methods. Its 75 numbered sheets contain 138 diagrammatic sketches of Venetian architectural sites, especially of buildings on the Grand Canal always viewed from the water. Profusely annotated in Canaletto's hand, it contains factual material set down by the artist on the spot in black or red chalk, then apparently gone over with the pen later in the studio and expanded. The question of whether Canaletto used the camera obscura for the diagrams has been debated hotly but inconclusively (Pignatti, 1958; Gioseffi, 1959). That he used mechanical aids such as dividers, rulers, compasses and, presumably, optical instruments, has never been seriously denied. Zanetti (1771, p. 462) speaks of his using the camera obscura and knowing how to correct for its distortions. In all likelihood he used it as an aide-mémoire for jotting down an overall view of some site, which he called a *scaraboto*, or some rough outline of a scene. He certainly did not use it for a careful and detailed recording of scenes to be transposed unchanged on to canvas. The works themselves belie such a procedure. His *vedute* are never topographically accurate even though they remain convincing as such, as they did to his patrons. A careful scrutiny of his views shows that he always manipulated the topography, at times extensively, combining two or more viewpoints, then unifying the whole through the fall of light. The departures from reality in the interest of overall design led him to change the proportions of the buildings and to widen and narrow the distances between them. Frequently he would suppress specific architectural elements (e.g. one of St Mark's cupolas) to achieve a better composition.

The purpose of many of Canaletto's drawings is unclear. A group of 142 drawings made in the 1730s is particularly puzzling. All were in Joseph Smith's collection. There is no evidence that anyone besides Smith showed interest in Canaletto's drawings at that time. It is not unlikely that Smith in his role of impresario assembled these drawings in a catalogue of Venetian subjects from which prospective customers might pick. Alternatively he may have kept them as mementos or records of the pictures that had passed through his hands. Or perhaps he was simply the first to recognize Canaletto's genius as draughtsman.

Canaletto's etching style is highly individual. He probably learnt to etch on his own, drawing directly on the copper plate, although some reminders of Marco Ricci's etching style can be detected, as in the handling of the sky. No trace of elaborate preparations or of counterproofs has emerged.

(ii) Studio practice and influence. Many of Canaletto's works of the busy 1730s were copied. There is no reason to believe that these copies were produced in his workshop or even that he had a large team of assistants. In all likelihood his studio was a family workshop. His father, Bernardo, only 56 years old in 1730, did more than just lend a hand. And his nephew, the precocious and highly gifted Bernardo Bellotto, who became a member of the Fraglia as early as 1738, no doubt supplied substantial help during an apprenticeship that must have lasted from 1734 to 1740. No serious evidence has emerged to date of Michele Marieschi or Francesco Guardi having spent any time in Canaletto's studio or having collaborated with him. His influence on the English school of painting, especially Samuel Scott, has not been sufficiently investigated. In the opinion of Waterhouse (1969), when Canaletto left England in 1755 he had established the vogue for views of London, especially the reaches of the Thames, and had laid the groundwork for an English school of topographical art.

See also ARCHITECTURAL PICTURES, fig. 4.

BIBLIOGRAPHY

EARLY SOURCES

P. A. Orlandi: *Abecedario pittorico* (Venice, 1753) [with additions by Guarienti]

A. M. Zanetti [the younger]: *Della pittura veneziana e delle opere pubbliche de' veneziani maestri* (Venice, 1771), pp. 462–4

'The Note-books of George Vertue', *Walpole Soc.*, xxii (1934), pp. 130, 132

GENERAL

F. Haskell: *Patrons and Painters* (London, 1963, rev. New Haven and London, 2/1980)

E. Waterhouse: *Painting in Britain, 1530 to 1790*, Pelican Hist. A. (Harmondsworth, 1969)

F. Vivian: *Il Console Smith mercante e collezionista* (Vicenza, 1971)

A. Binion: *La Galleria scomparsa del maresciallo von der Schulenburg* (Milan, 1990)

MONOGRAPHS AND CATALOGUES

D. von Hadeln: *Die Zeichnungen von Antonio Canal genannt Canaletto* (Vienna, 1930)

R. Pallucchini and G. F. Guarnati: *Le acqueforti del Canaletto* (Venice, 1945)

K. T. Parker: *The Drawings of Antonio Canaletto in the Collection of His Majesty the King at Windsor Castle* (Oxford and London, 1948)

F. J. B. Watson: *Canaletto* (London and New York, 1949)

V. Moschini: *Canaletto* (Milan, 1954)

M. Levey: *The Eighteenth-century Italian Schools*, London, N.G. cat. (London, 1956), pp. 10–37

A. Pallucchini: *Canaletto* (Milan, 1958)

T. Pignatti: *Il quaderno di disegni del Canaletto alle Gallerie di Venezia* (Milan, 1958)

Disegni veneti di Oxford (exh. cat., ed. K. T. Parker; Venice, Fond. Cini, 1958)

D. Gioseffi: *Canaletto: Il quaderno delle Gallerie veneziane e l'impiego della camera ottica* (Trieste, 1959)

W. G. Constable: *Canaletto*, 2 vols (Oxford, 1962, rev. by J. G. Links, 3/1989)

Canaletto e Guardi (exh. cat., ed. K. T. Parker and J. Byam Shaw; Venice, Fond. Cini, 1962)

M. Levey: *Canaletto: Paintings in the Collection of Her Majesty the Queen* (London, 1964)

——: *The Later Italian Pictures in the Collection of Her Majesty the Queen* (London, 1964)

Canaletto (exh. cat., ed. W. G. Constable; Toronto, A.G., 1964)

J. Kainen: *The Etchings of Canaletto* (Washington, DC, 1967)

L. Puppi: *L'opera completa del Canaletto* (Milan, 1968, rev. 1981)

T. Pignatti: *Canaletto* (Florence, 1970)

M. Levey: *The Seventeenth and Eighteenth-century Schools*, London, N.G. cat. (London, 1971)
J. G. Links: *Views of Venice by Canaletto Engraved by Antonio Visentini* (New York, 1971)
R. Bromberg: *Canaletto's Etchings* (London, 1974)
W. L. Barcham: *The Imaginary View Scenes of Antonio Canaletto* (New York, 1977)
J. G. Links: *Canaletto and his Patrons* (London and New York, 1977)
T. Pignatti: *Canaletto: Disegni scelti ed annotati* (Florence, 1979)
Disegni veneti della collezione Lugt (exh. cat., ed. J. Byam Shaw; Venice, Fond. Cini, 1981), no. 93, p. 81
J. G. Links: *Canaletto* (Ithaca, 1982)
Canaletto: Disegni—dipinti—incisioni (exh. cat., ed. A. Bettagno; Venice, Fond. Cini, 1982)
C. Miller: *Fifty Drawings by Canaletto from the Royal Library, Windsor Castle* (London and New York, 1983)
A. Corboz: *Canaletto: Una Venezia immaginaria*, 2 vols (Milan, 1985)
Canaletto e Visentini: Venezia e Londra (exh. cat., ed. D. Succi; Venice, Ca' Pesaro, 1986)
Canaletto (exh. cat., ed. K. Baetjer and J. G. Links; New York, Met., 1989)

SPECIALIST STUDIES

H. F. Finberg: 'Canaletto in England', *Walpole Soc.*, ix (1920–21), pp. 21–76
——: 'The Lovelace Capricci', *Burl. Mag.*, lxxii (1938), pp. 69–70
F. J. B. Watson: 'Some Unpublished Canaletto Drawings of London', *Burl. Mag.*, lxxviii (1950), pp. 315–19
M. Levey: 'Canaletto's Regatta Paintings', *Burl. Mag.*, xcv (1953), pp. 365–6
H. Zimmerman: 'Über einige Bilder der Sammlung Streit im Grauen Kloster zu Berlin', *Z. Kstgesch.*, vii (1953), pp. 197–224
F. Haskell: 'Stefano Conti, Patron of Canaletto and Others', *Burl. Mag.*, lxxxiv (1956), pp. 296–300
A. Morassi: 'Considerazioni sugli inizi del Canaletto', *Venezia e l'Europa: Venezia, 1956*, pp. 356–60
——: 'Settecento inedito', *A. Ven.*, xvii (1963), pp. 143–50
T. Miotti: 'Tre disegni inediti del Canaletto', *A. Ven.*, xx (1966), pp. 275–8
A. Morassi: 'La giovinezza del Canaletto', *A. Ven.*, xx (1966), pp. 207–17
R. Pallucchini: 'Appunti per il vedutismo veneziano del settecento', *Muzeum i Tworca* (Warsaw, 1969), pp. 141–55
T. Pignatti: 'Sei villaggi campestri dal Canaletto', *Boll. Mus. Civ. Ven.*, xiv (1969), pp. 23–8
R. Palluchini: 'Per gli esordi del Canaletto', *A. Ven.*, xxvii (1973), 155–88
A. Corboz: 'Sur la prétendue objectivité de Canaletto', *A. Ven.*, xxviii (1974), pp. 205–18
A. Binion: 'Some New Drawings by Canaletto', *Master Drgs*, xiv (1976), pp. 390–96
——: 'Three Drawings by Canaletto', *Master Drgs*, xviii (1980), pp. 373–5
L. Puppi: 'The Drawings of Antonio Canaletto', *Masterpieces of Eighteenth-century Venetian Drawing* (London, 1983), pp. 133–56
F. Russell: 'Canaletto and Joli at Chesterfield', *Burl. Mag.*, cxxx (1988), pp. 627–30

ALICE BINION

Canaletto, Bernardo. *See* BELLOTTO, BERNARDO.

Canard. *See* BROADSIDE.

Canavesio, Giovanni (*b* Pinerolo, Piedmont; *fl* 1450–1500). Italian painter. He was registered in Pinerolo as a 'master painter' in 1450, but no early works by him are known. In 1472 he was commissioned in Albenga (Liguria) to paint a *Maestà* (untraced) for the church of Oristano in Sardinia, and from that date his career in western Liguria and the region of Nice is documented by signed and dated works. These include two important fresco cycles, that of the *Passion* and *Last Judgement* (1482) in S Bernardo, Pigna (Liguria), and that of the *Life of Christ* and the *Last Judgement* (1492) in Notre-Dame-des-Fontaines near La Brigue (Alpes Maritimes), as well as three large polyptychs, two of which depict the *Virgin and Child with Saints* (1491, Turin, Gal. Sabauda; and 1499, Verderio Superiore, nr Como, parish church, formerly in Pornassio, S Dalmazzo), while the third represents *St Michael* (1500; Pigna, S Michele). With Giovanni Baleison, Canavesio signed the frescoes in the chapel of St Sébastien, Saint-Etienne-de-Tinée (Alpes Maritimes).

Several other works are attributed to Canavesio, some of which are dated; among these are the heraldic decoration on the façade of the Bishop's Palace at Albenga (1477), the *Passion* frescoes in the chapel of Notre-Dame-des-Douleurs, Peillon (Alpes Maritimes), and the polyptychs of the *Virgin and Child* (Genoa, Pal. Bianco), of a *Dominican Saint* (either St Dominic or St Thomas Aquinas) in S Domenico, Taggia (Liguria), of *St Anthony of Padua* and of *St Bernardino*, both in Ste Rosalie, Lucéram (Alpes Maritimes), and of *St Christopher* (Florence, Banca Toscana). To these should be added the central figure of the polyptych of *St Biagio* (Pornassio, S Dalmazzo).

Canavesio's style is idiosyncratic, containing south Netherlandish elements and features from the schools of the Nice region and Provence, recognizable in the bright colours enhanced by strong lighting and also in the expressionistic traits derived from the figure style of north Piedmont. His activity in western Piedmont contributed to the formation of a style that combined characteristics from both Ligurian and Piedmontese painting, which survived until the mid-16th century in the work of local artists.

BIBLIOGRAPHY

DBI
M. Roques: *Les Peintures murales de sud-est de la France: XIIIe au XVIe siècle* (Paris, 1961), pp. 112–14, 341–52
G. V. Castelnovi: 'Il quattro e il primo cinquecento', *La pittura a Genova e in Liguria*, ed. E. Poleggi, i (Genoa, 1987), pp. 118–21, 151–2

GIOVANNA ROTONDI TERMINIELLO

Canberra. Capital of Australia. Founded as a result of the federation of the Australian colonies (1901), the city (population *c.* 270,000) is noted for its urban plan, a remarkable combination of garden city and Beaux-Arts ideals. The inland site for Canberra was established in the Australian Capital Territory *c.* 250 km south-west of Sydney and *c.* 480 km north-east of Melbourne. An international competition for the design of the urban plan was won in 1912 by the American architect Walter Burley Griffin. His scheme (for illustration *see* GRIFFIN) combines formality, befitting the ceremony of state, and informality, reflecting the democratic structure of Australian society. The plan is closely related to the undulating topography of the site, with prominent hills employed as radial hubs for a system of formal axes that are in turn aligned to distant topographical features. The focus of the entire plan is Capital Hill, site of the parliament, which forms the apex of the Parliamentary (or Federal) Triangle where the principal government buildings are located. A central, tree-lined land axis links Capital Hill with Mt Ainslie to the north (site of the Australian War Memorial, 1941, by Emil Sodersten); the Molonglo River valley between them was flooded to form a lake as the principal cross axis. Two street axes, Commonwealth Avenue and Kings Avenue, define the sides of the Parliamentary Triangle and cross the lake to link Capital Hill respectively with Civic, the main commercial district, and Mt Pleasant, site of the Royal Military College.

Canberra, aerial view of Parliament House (1980–88) by Mitchell/Giurgola & Thorp, looking north across Lake Burley Griffin to Mt Ainslie

Construction of services and roads was begun after Griffin arrived in Australia in 1913. There was, however, considerable opposition to his scheme, partly because of cost, and although it was finally given official approval in 1918, control of the project passed to a committee in 1920, and Griffin resigned. The first private leases were sold in 1924, residential areas were subdivided and houses built, and the commercial centre was established; extensive tree-planting was also begun, initiating Canberra's 'garden city' appearance. Progress on the work accelerated after the appointment of the Federal Capital Commission (1925), when Griffin's plan was published with the stipulation that any deviations must be approved by parliament. Nevertheless 'utilitarian development' was initially recommended for reasons of economy, and a 'provisional' parliament building (1923–7; by George Sydney Jones) was constructed below Capital Hill, together with ancillary government offices and housing, and the first residential suburbs (by Kingston and Griffith). Canberra was inaugurated as the seat of government in 1927, but its development languished during the Depression of the 1930s and then during World War II and after.

In 1958, when Canberra's population totalled only about 39,000, the National Capital Development Commission (NCDC) was established to continue the city's construction. Rapid growth thereafter was accompanied by extensive suburban expansion in large sub-centres (e.g. by Woden, Belconnen and Tuggeranong), which contain notable buildings by many of Australia's leading architects, including Harry Seidler, John Andrews, Philip Cox, Daryl Jackson and Peter Corrigan. In the city itself Griffin's plan began to take shape when Lake Burley Griffin was finally created (1964). Work also began on the monumental public buildings in the Parliamentary Triangle along the southern shore of the lake, notably the National Library (1968; by Bunning & Madden with T. E. O'Mahoney); and the High Court (1972–80; *see* AUSTRALIA, fig. 6) and adjacent Australian National Gallery (1973–82; both by Edwards, Madigan Torzillo & Briggs). In 1979 a competition was held for a new Parliament House, which was completed in time for Australia's Bicentenary in 1988. It is built behind the old one, on top of Capital Hill; Griffin had intended this site for a 'people's Capitol' above the parliament, which he planned for a smaller rise below. His aim is reflected in the new building by Mitchell/Giurgola & Thorp (see fig.): the structures appear to be carved out of the hill within two monumental outward-curving walls that mark the lines of Griffin's diagonal axes and are ramped and roofed in turf. Above the 'hill' thus re-created flies an enormous national flag supported on a stainless-steel mast. The building is finished with Australian marble and timber and filled with Australian paintings, sculpture and decorative arts. Other new public buildings planned for the Parliamentary Triangle include the National Science & Technology Centre and National Archive & Exposition Building. The site for the new Museum of Australia is on the northern shore of the lake.

Plans for a national art collection, now housed in the Australian National Gallery, originated in 1911 with the foundation of the Historic Memorials Committee 'to secure portraits of representative men' and the Commonwealth Art Advisory Board to advise on purchases. For many years visual arts activity in Canberra was centred around the Canberra Arts Society (1927), which held regular local exhibitions. Other established galleries include the Nolan Gallery (1980), the Canberra School of Art Gallery (1981) and Canberra Contemporary Art Space Inc. (1987).

See also AUSTRALIA, especially §§II, 2; XI; and XII.

BIBLIOGRAPHY

H. L. White, ed.: *Canberra: A Nation's Capital* (Canberra, 1954)
D. L. Johnson: *The Architecture of Walter Burley Griffin* (Melbourne, 1977), pp. 14–25
Canberra: An Architectural Guide to Australia's Capital, Royal Australian Institute of Architects (Manuka, 1982)
R. Pegrum: *The Bush Capital: How Australia Chose Canberra as its Federal City* (Canberra, 1983)
J. Taylor: *Australian Architecture since 1960* (Sydney, 1986), pp. 93–115
T. Aslanides and J. Stewart: *Canberra and the Australian Capital Territory: A Heritage Field Guide* (Sydney, 1988)
H. Beck, ed.: *Parliament House, Canberra: A Building for the Nation* (Sydney, 1988)

MICHAEL SPENS

Candela (Outeriño), Félix (*b* Madrid, 27 Jan 1910). American architect of Spanish birth, active mainly in Mexico. He trained at the Escuela Superior de Arquitectura, Madrid. After graduating in 1935, Candela opened a small studio and applied to the Real Academia de Bellas Artes de S Fernando for a travel scholarship to Germany, where he intended to study the theory of shell structures. The Civil War in Spain (1936–9), however, shattered these plans. Candela joined the Republican forces, fleeing across the frontier into France after the Nationalist victory in 1939. Briefly interned in a camp in Perpignan, he then emigrated to Mexico, where, with his younger brother Antonio Candela, he opened a construction company.

At the beginning of his professional career Candela yielded to the conservative tastes of his clients, setting aside his passion for thin-shell structures until 1951, when he was commissioned to build the cosmic ray laboratory at the University of Mexico. The laboratory's two hyperbolic paraboloid concrete vaults, 15 mm thick and spanning over 10 m, brought instant recognition and led to many building commissions and lecture invitations. More importantly, however, Candela was finally able to pursue his own particular interests. Over the period that followed he broke the monopoly of academic science in thin shells that had been held hitherto by German and British theoreticians. In this he was strongly influenced by such architects as Antoni Gaudí and Eduardo Torroja y Miret, whose experiments with vault designs differed from conventional solutions used by Italian and German architects, emphasizing formal variety and exploring the possibilities for slender, ribless structures. The *c.* 1000 structures erected by Candela ranged from simple 'umbrella' roofs to the most sophisticated shells. Examples from the early 1950s include the Florería Ras Martín (1951; with Cayetano de la Jara), Chapultepec, and the Escuela Hidalgo (1953; with Luis Rivadaneyra) in Mexico City, and the umbrella structure (1953–4; with Alejandro Prieto) at the entrance to the Laboratorios CIBA, Churubusco.

Perhaps Candela's best-known work from the 1950s, however, is the church of the Miraculous Virgin (1955; see fig.) in Mexico City. The beauty of the church's interior is reinforced by warped columns integrated with the hyperbolic paraboloid roof vaulting. This was followed a year later by the church of S Antonio de las Huertas (with Enrique de la Mora and Fernando Lopez Carmona), which exemplifies Candela's characteristic use of shells with free edges (without reinforcing arches to support their outer edges). Here light penetrates to the interior through clerestories between the vaults to give splendid architectural effects. There were also a number of commercial and industrial buildings built by Candela during this period, including such multiple umbrella structures as the Mercado de Coyoacán (1956; with Pedro Ramírez Vázquez and Rafael Mijares) and single or multiple shells, as in the vast twin vaults of Las Aduanas (1954), Vallejo, Mexico City. His own favourite structure, however, was the restaurant at Xochimilco (1957–8; with Joaquin Alvárez Ordóñez and Fernando Alvárez Ordóñez; *see* CONCRETE, fig. 4). This consists of eight groin vaults formed by four intersecting hypars; the undulating outside edges of the shells, apparently unsupported, allow for the full appreciation of the slenderness of the roof, which is only 40 mm thick, despite spanning a distance of 42.5 m. Another important building of the late 1950s was the open chapel (1959; with Guillermo Rossell and Manuel de la Rosa) on the top of a hill near the Lomas de Cuernavaca Valley. This is planned in the tradition of a Classical Greek theatre and has an asymmetrical saddle roof, which spans 31 m, rises to 22 m at its crown and is a mere 40 mm in thickness.

During the 1950s and early 1960s Candela benefited from the oil boom that stimulated the Mexican economy. Apart from the impetus it naturally gave to local building activity, the oil boom led to considerable migration by the rural poor into large cities, and this provided Candela with the cheap labour necessary for shell construction. He continued to produce important work, however, even as the effects of the boom faded throughout the 1960s. In 1963 he built the Bacardi Bottling Plant in Cuatitlán, and in 1966 he built the church of S Monica, Mexico City. Then in 1968 he won first prize in the competition for the Palacio de Deportes for the Olympic Games, which were held in Mexico City that year. The palace has an impressive roof, built with intersecting steel arches 135 m long and

Félix Candela: church of the Miraculous Virgin, Mexico City, 1955

covered with copper. In the 1970s he settled in the USA, establishing a practice in Chicago in 1971 and becoming an American citizen in 1978. He was also professor of architecture at the University of Illinois at Chicago Circle until 1978. In 1980 he left for Madrid but after several years returned to the USA and settled in Raleigh, NC, where he was active as a consultant and visiting lecturer. His international reputation brought him several honorary doctorates.

Candela considered creativity in art and in science to be close, if not identical. He strongly objected to the indiscriminate application of the theory of elasticity for shell design, and the pedantic requirements of local building codes based on this theory. He also never lost sight of aesthetic criteria or allowed his intuitive feel for structure to be outweighed by other factors. Thus, while his projects were masterpieces of logic, blending skills of construction, economy and function, this logic was inseparable from an appreciation of the architectural merits of a structure, and all Candela's collaborations bear the stamp of his personality and style.

WRITINGS

D. Billington and others: *New Architecture; Maillart Papers* (Princeton, 1973)

En defensa del formalismo y otros excitos (1985)

Félix Candela, arquitecto (Madrid, 1994)

BIBLIOGRAPHY

C. Faber: *Candela: The Shell Builder* (New York, 1963)

C. Bamford Smith: *Builders in the Sun: Four Mexican Architects* (New York, 1967), pp. 93–130

J. A. Starczewski: 'Spotkanie z Felixem Candelą: Twórcą konstrukcji łupinowych', *Inżyn. & Budownictwo*, xl/5 (1984), pp. 161–6

——: *Félix Candela: The Structure and Form of Reinforced Concrete Shells* (Atlanta, 1992)

H. Ursula, ed.: *Zum Werk von Félix Candela: Die Kunst der leichten Schalen* (Cologne, 1992)

JERZY ANDRZEJ STARCZEWSKI

Candela, José María Galván. *See* GALVÁN CANDELA, JOSÉ MARÍA.

Candelabrum. A support for one or more lights, consisting of a base, usually three-footed, a shaft and a receptacle or tray, which became a highly developed decorative art form in the ancient world.

The Latin word *candelabrum* derives from the more ancient form of the implement, used by the Etruscans, which held wax or tallow candles or torches by means of vertical or horizontal spikes. In Hellenistic, late Republican and Imperial times the earlier form tended to be replaced by a more luxurious, singly or multiply branched type designed to hold one or more oil lamps. Ancient authors spoke of candelabra made of gems, gold, silver, bronze and wood.

Candelabrum, marble, h. 1.85 m, *c.* 100 BC (Tunis, Musée National du Bardo)

Especially prized were those bronzes with trays from Aigina and shafts from Taras. The most renowned candelabra of the ancient world were undoubtedly the seven-branched candelabrum from the Temple in Jerusalem, taken by the Romans in AD 70, and the one described by Pliny (*Natural History* XXXIV.xiv) as a tree laden with fruit that was removed from Thebes by Alexander the Great and later brought to the Temple of Apollo on the Palatine, Rome. On his visit to the Erechtheion on the Acropolis at Athens, Pausanias (*Guide to Greece* I.xxvi.6) saw a candelabrum made by KALLIMACHOS which held enough oil to burn for an entire year.

The excavations of Herculaneum and Pompeii have produced hundreds of bronze candelabra in a rich variety of types. Most are clearly objects of luxury intended for use at banquets. A standard type consists of a zoomorphic tripod base supporting a fluted shaft which ends in a calyx-capital with a tray for a lamp. Lamp-trays are also supported by branched arboriform shafts, with or without accompanying statues. Another class of Pompeian candelabra employs scrolling branches for the suspension of oil lamps. The ultimate in luxury candelabra were undoubtedly the *epheboi lychnophoroi*, statues of youths holding lamps. One such life-size bronze (Naples, Mus. Archeol. N., 143 753) stood in the House of the Ephebe in Pompeii, where it illumined nocturnal banquets by means of lamps suspended from scrolls attached to the hands.

Marble candelabra consist of a calyx-topped baluster supported on a triangular altar on zoomorphic feet. The sides of the altar-bases are often sculpted in relief, usually showing single figures from a repertory common to other forms of decorative marble sculpture such as the WELL-HEAD, *oscillum* (mask hung from a tree) and *pinax* (rectangular relief). In form and function marble candelabra are connected only remotely with their metal counterparts. A formal connection with Greek *thymiateria* (incense burners) has often been suggested. They are found principally in Italy, where they served mostly as outdoor decorative sculpture at luxurious villas. In a study of 165 examples Cain has suggested that the class began not earlier than the mid-2nd century BC with Athenian sculptors producing for a Roman market. The earliest type would thus be represented by five examples from the MAHDIA shipwreck (*c.* 100 BC; Tunis, Mus. N. Bardo; see fig.). By the time of Julius Caesar (*d* 44 BC) production had shifted from Athens to Rome, with the greatest number of candelabra produced under Augustus (*reg* 27 BC–AD 14). A later revival of the form occurred during the reign of Hadrian (*reg* AD 117–38) and is represented by a number of splendid examples found in Hadrian's Villa at Tivoli (Paris, Louvre; Rome, Vatican, Gal. Candelabri).

See also GREECE, ANCIENT, §X, 8, and ROME, ANCIENT, §X, 6.

BIBLIOGRAPHY

Enc. A. Ant.: 'Candelabro'

C. Daremberg and E. Saglio, eds: *Dictionnaire des antiquités grecques et romaines d'après les textes et les monuments*, I/ii (Paris, 1887), pp. 869–75

E. Pernice: *Gefässe und Geräte aus Bronze* (1925), iv of *Die hellenistische Kunst in Pompeji*, ed. E. Pernice and F. Winter (Berlin and Leipzig, 1925–41)

A. Merlin and L. Poinssot: *Cratères et candélabres de marbre, trouvés en mer près de Mahdia* (Tunis and Paris, 1930)

H.-U. Cain: *Römische Marmorkandelaber*, Beiträge zur Erschliessung hellenistischer und kaiserzeitlicher Skulptur und Architektur (Mainz, 1985)

A. Testa: *Candelabra e thymiateria* (Rome, 1989)

L. Pirzio Biroli Stefanelli and others: *Il bronzo dei Romani: Arredo e suppellettile* (Rome, 1990)

EUGENE DWYER

Candella. *See* CHANDELLA.

Candelottaro. *See* CERRUTI, MICHELANGELO.

Candia. *See under* CRETE, §5.

Candid, Peter [Candido, Pietro di Pietro; Witte, Pieter de] (*b* Bruges, *c.* 1548; *d* Munich, March 1628). Netherlandish painter, tapestry designer and draughtsman, active in Italy and Germany. He was one of several Italian-trained Mannerist artists employed by the courts of Europe and was the leading figure in Munich from 1600 to 1628. His versatility led Sandrart to describe him as a 'universal painter'. When he was about ten years old he emigrated to Florence with his parents—his father, Pieter de Witte (*fl* *c.* 1547–62), being a tapestry weaver who found employment in the Medici tapestry factory founded in 1546. The family name later changed to Candido, but the son was usually called Candid north of the Alps, where he returned in 1586. Very little is known about him as a person, and there is no portrait of him. He married and had five children, including a son Wilhelm (*fl* 1613–25), who was a painter though he later (1625) became a court *Silberdiener*, and a daughter who married the engraver Filips Sadeler in 1624.

1. FLORENCE, TO 1586. Candid probably started his apprenticeship in the early 1560s, but his teacher is unknown. He is first mentioned in documents in 1569 regarding a payment for materials for a fresco he had executed in the Cappella di S Luca (Florence, Santissima Annunziata), where members of Florence's Accademia del Disegno assembled and were buried; he is not himself mentioned as a member until 1576. In 1583, on his return from a year spent in Rome, he became an officer of the Accademia and held various posts in the following years. Further biographical information comes from Karel van Mander I, who knew Candid personally in 1574, among the circle of Netherlanders living in Florence. His biography of Candid describes him as a good exponent of both fresco and oil painting, who could also model in clay, a skill that was very useful to him in his painting. According to van Mander, Candid collaborated with Vasari on the interior decoration of the Sala Regia in the Vatican, Rome, and the cupola of Florence Cathedral, as well as executing tapestry designs and other assignments for Cosimo I de' Medici, Grand Duke of Tuscany. This work would have been done before 1574, although there are no documents confirming it.

Candid's first dated painting depicts a *Sacra conversazione with Donor (Francesco Buini)* (1578; Volterra Cathedral); it is Mannerist in the style of Bronzino, with monumental figures distributed over the entire surface of the picture that nonetheless remain isolated; their lively gestures impart a certain restlessness to the composition. The most important of his other early works (almost all of which are altarpieces, except for a portrait of *Giuliano de' Medici, Duke of Nemours*; Florence, Pal. Medici–Riccardi) is a *Lamentation* (*c.* 1580–86; Volterra, Pin. Com.). The composition is harmonious and strictly planned, with large figures arranged in a confined area along the picture plane, filling the space and thus obstructing any perspective view. The colouring is reminiscent of Jacopo Pontormo and Rosso Fiorentino, characterized by lively iridescent hues; adjacent contrasting colours project jaggedly into one another. Candid signed a fresco of the *Virgin and SS Nicholas and Jerome* (1585; Florence, S Niccolò del Ceppo), the lower part of which was damaged in the floods of 1966; its composition is harmonious, close in style to Andrea del Sarto's *Madonna del Sacco* fresco (1525; Florence, Santissima Annunziata). A return to vivid colours, in contrast to the pale, washed-out tones used by the Mannerists, an increased sobriety in composition and more naturally proportioned figures are typical of Florentine painting *c.* 1580, and Candid's *Lamentation* and the fresco in S Niccolò are in line with these tendencies. By and large his style in Florence developed under the influence of Italian paintings of the school of Michelangelo, although closer in manner to Bronzino and Alessandro Allori than to Vasari. The Netherlandish tradition is also discernible.

2. MUNICH, 1586–1628. Candid was recommended to the court at Munich by the sculptor Giambologna—who taught his brother, the sculptor Elia Candido (*d* 1574)—and was summoned by Duke William V of Bavaria in 1586. He served there for more than 40 years as a court painter. On his arrival he became part of a team of Italian artists working under the direction of his fellow countryman Friedrich Sustris, who had also been in Florence. He painted frescoes to Sustris's designs in the Grottenhof of the Residenz, parts of the vaulting of two chapels and various other work for the court, including ephemeral decorations for the theatre and for processions. However, altarpieces were his main activity, and by 1600 he had painted about 20 pictures with religious content for the Duke and other patrons (e.g. *Annunciation*, 1587; and *Martyrdom of St Ursula*, 1588; both Munich, St Michael). Carrying on where he had left off in Italy, he created strictly planned compositions, which he developed two-dimensionally. The elements of the pictures are arranged symmetrically, with a clear distinction between heaven and earth. The colours are beautiful and luminous; his characteristic iridescent tones gradually become less arbitrary, the colours blend and the surface of the painting shimmers like silk. Decorative elements akin to still-life paintings show his delight in detail: flowers, plumes, brooches, trimmings, fringes, transparent veils and sashes. His inventiveness was widely imitated, reproductive engravings playing a large part in this. He also drew plates of his own, many of which were engraved by the Sadeler

family (e.g. *Christ at Emmaus*, Chicago, IL, A. Inst.; engraving by Aegidius Sadeler; see Hollstein, xxii, no. 62).

Candid's activities expanded once Duke (later Elector) Maximilian I of Bavaria came to power (1598) and Sustris had died (1599). In 1604 the Duke set up a tapestry workshop with craftsmen from the Netherlands, who executed four extensive series of tapestries comprising about 50 hangings worked through with gold on the *Deeds of Otto von Wittelsbach*, the founder of the Duke's dynasty, *The Months* (see fig. 1), *The Seasons* and *The Times of Day*. Candid designed them and produced the cartoons for this, his largest commission (1604–18). Because of the experience he had acquired in Florence, he was made responsible for planning and supervising the execution of the tapestries by the weavers, down to the last detail. He managed to ensure that the differentiated colours, with the light, at times iridescent, tones seen in his paintings, were transferred exactly into the medium of textiles. The tapestries are among the most beautiful and qualitatively best examples of their kind made in the 17th century. Attention to detail and precision show Candid to have been an outstanding cartoon-maker in the Netherlandish tradition.

Cartoons for tapestries made by the low-warp method present the design in reverse to enable it to be executed, and Candid's drawings include versions both ways round. The initial preparatory drawings are done as for paintings, up to the point immediately preceding the cartoon, when it is technically necessary to concentrate on emphasizing the outlines and forego the spontaneous touch of the artist. Candid always drew very purposefully and with a view to a planned composition; his skill can be best seen in the pages from his sketchbook, mainly figure studies and details of figures drawn from a model. They are on a reddish paper, which further enhances the pictorial effect, in red-and-black chalk or in ink, with a light wash, often highlighted with white, a favourite touch. About 130 drawings, including detailed studies and complete designs for paintings, tapestries and prints, survive, mostly done between 1600 and 1620, the majority for tapestries; there is no evidence that Candid designed sculpture or architecture.

Candid was in charge of all interior paintings at the new buildings added by Duke Maximilian to the Residenz in Munich and the Altes Schloss at Schleissheim, near Munich. The size of the Residenz was more than doubled from 1612 by adding three new wings to the north, with a Great Hall (the Kaisersaal) and two guest suites known as the Steinzimmer and Trierzimmer. Only the ceilings and friezes were painted; the walls were decorated with tapestries. The paintings by Candid and his collaborators were inserted into the wooden ceiling (only preserved and *in situ* in the Trierzimmer). Each presents a monumental allegorical figure in front of a landscape or a building—the

1. Peter Candid: *March*, from *The Months*, tapestry series manufactured to the artist's design in the Munich workshop of Hans van der Biest, 4.10×5.19 m, 1612 (Munich, Residenz)

friezes also show allegorical scenes. Candid's Netherlandish origins are more apparent in some of these pictures than in his altarpieces—in the realism of the detail, the features typical of genre painting and the atmospheric landscape backgrounds. The latter probably give some idea of the pure landscapes he is known to have painted, none of which survives.

Candid had a large staff of assistants at the Residenz and at the Altes Schloss, decorated in 1617. For the main pictures on the ceiling of the Kaisersaal, preparatory drawings show that he himself made studies from models for the single figures and planned the composition down to the last detail. Elsewhere, he produced only small, quickly drawn sketches of his ideas, leaving his collaborators to work them up. In 1619 he was asked to produce designs for painting the interior of the Goldener Saal of the Rathaus at Augsburg: a prestigious commission for which the paintings were executed by the Augsburg painter Johann Matthias Kager.

In spite of his other commissions and although he was restricted as early as 1611 by illness, Candid continued to paint altarpieces. He liked returning to successful figure types and compositions, so little variation is evident. Compared with the early Munich altarpieces, a freer, simpler arrangement of the component parts of the picture is evident, as is his renewed preoccupation with High Renaissance style. In his *Visitation of the Virgin* (*c.* 1612; Freising Cathedral; see fig. 2), the model, Pontormo's fresco on the same theme (Florence, Santissima Annunziata), can certainly be recognized, but at the same time the dominant position of the powerful main figures, the heavy robes and the colouring show that Candid had made the transition to early Baroque. The high altarpiece for the Frauenkirche in Munich (1620; broken 19th century but still *in situ*) marks a highpoint of his final years; the main panel, *c.* 8 m high, with an *Assumption of the Virgin* (Munich, Frauenkirche), brings together Italian and northern elements.

2. Peter Candid: *Visitation of the Virgin*, oil on panel, 2.50×1.75 m, *c.* 1612 (Freising Cathedral)

Candid painted small copper panels on religious, mythological and allegorical themes in the precise style so favoured in the Mannerist period (e.g. *Sacra conversazione*, Oldenburg, Landesmus.; and *Apotheosis of Aeneas*, Berlin, Bodemus., drawing, Philadelphia, PA Acad. F.A.). He was also active as an art dealer and did business with Philipp Hainhofer.

BIBLIOGRAPHY

Hollstein: *Dut. & Flem.*; Thieme–Becker
K. van Mander: *Het schilder-boeck* ([1603]–1604), fols 184f, 291
J. von Sandrart: *Teutsche Academie* (1675–9); ed. A. R. Pelzer (1925), pp. 81, 150
P. J. Rée: *Peter Candid: Sein Leben und seine Werke* (Leipzig, 1885)
E. Bassermann-Jordan: *Die dekorative Malerei der Renaissance am bayerischen Hofe* (Munich, 1900), pp. 84–178
K. Steinbart: 'Die niederländischen Hofmaler der baierischen Herzöge', *Marburg. Jb. Kstwiss.*, iv (1928), pp. 89–165
——: 'Peter Candid in Italien', *Jb. Preuss. Kstsamml.*, lviii (1937), pp. 63–80
Aufgang der Neuzeit: Deutsche Kunst und Kultur von Dürers Tod bis zum Dreissigjährigen Kriege, 1530–1650 (exh. cat., Nuremberg, Ger. Nmus., 1952)
B. Knüttel: *Peter Candid (um 1548–1628): Hofmaler Maximilians I. von Bayern* (diss., U. Frankfurt am Main, 1964)
——: 'Zur Geschichte der Münchner Residenz, 1600–1616 (I)', *Münchn. Jb. Bild. Kst*, xviii (1967), pp. 187–210
B. Volk-Knüttel: *Wandteppiche für den Münchener Hof nach Entwürfen von Peter Candid* (Munich, 1976) [most detailed biography]
Peter Candid: Zeichnungen (exh. cat. by B. Volk-Knüttel, Munich, Staatl. Graph. Samml., 1978–9)
Zeichnung in Deutschland: Deutsche Zeichner, 1540–1640, 2 vols (exh. cat. by H. Geissler, Stuttgart, Staatsgal., 1979–80), i, pp. 146–8
Welt im Umbruch: Augsburg zwischen Renaissance und Barock, 2 vols (exh. cat., ed. B. Bushart; Augsburg, Städt. Kstsammlungen, 1980), ii, nos 463, 618–19
H. Glaser, ed.: *Um Glauben und Reich: Kurfürst Maximilian I* (1980), II/i of *Wittelsbach und Bayern*, Beiträge zur Bayerischen Geschichte und Kunst, 1573–1657 (Munich, 1980)
Um Glauben und Reich: Kurfürst Maximilian I (exh. cat., ed. H. Glaser; Munich, Residenz, 1980), II/ii of *Wittelsbach und Bayern* (Munich, 1980)
Elias Holl und das Augsburger Rathaus (exh. cat., ed. W. Baer, H.-W. Kruft and B. Roeck; Augsburg, Stadtarchv, 1985)
A. Bauer-Wild and B. Volk-Knüttel: *München, Profanbauten*, III/ii of *Corpus der barocken Deckenmalerei*, ed. H. Bauer and B. Rupprecht (Munich, 1989–) [documents, lost as well as surviving paintings]
B. Volk-Knüttel: 'Der Hochaltar der Münchener Frauenkirche von 1620 und seine Gemälde von Peter Candid', *Monachium sacrum: Festschrift zur 500-Jahr-Feier der Metropolitankirche zu unserer lieben Frau: München, 1994*, ii, pp. 203–32

BRIGITTE VOLK-KNÜTTEL

Candida, Giovanni (di Salvatore Filangieri) [Jean de; Jehan de] (*b* Naples, before 1450; *d* after 1499). Italian medallist and diplomat. He was descended from the Candida branch of a noble Neapolitan family. His father carried the title of Baron of San Niccolò. Although Candida spent most of his life in the diplomatic service of various patrons, and followed his medallic activity only as an amateur, his contribution to this branch of art is significant.

Some of his medals may have been intended to further his career by flattering their sitters. After working for the Anjou family in Naples, in 1472 Candida became secretary to Charles the Bold, Duke of Burgundy and, after Charles's death, to Maximilian of Austria and Mary of Burgundy from 1477–80. In 1473 he travelled to Venice in a vain attempt to win the services of Bartolommeo Colleoni for his master. Subsequently various other diplomatic missions took him to Rome, Naples and Milan.

Candida's medallic style shows considerable diversity. It evolves through various phases from Burgundian to Italian (betraying the influence of LYSIPPUS THE YOUNGER and also touches of the Florentine school), to Italianizing French. Secure assignment of unsigned medals to Candida has been fraught with difficulty. Only three signed medals have been recorded: the earliest (1476–7; Berlin, Bodemus.) portrays *Charles the Bold and his Future Son-in-law*, later Maximilian I; another (1478; Paris, Bib. N.) depicts *Antonio Graziadei* who was in Maximilian's employ; and a third piece (1479; Berlin, Bodemus.) shows the portraits of *Jean de la Gruthuse and Jean Miette*, commander and gaoler of the Lille citadel where Candida was briefly imprisoned in 1479; the reasons for his imprisonment presumably were because of remarks he had made about Maximilian or his father Frederick III in a letter that was intercepted, or perhaps due to his having slandered Pope Sixtus IV while in Rome. It is likely that this medal was made in gratitude to Gruthuse for having obtained his release; its reverse is inscribed CVSTOS CARCER[is] CANDIDE INSVLIS 1479. A closed group of four unsigned medals (1472–80) originating at the Burgundian court has been tentatively assigned to Candida. It needs to be mentioned, however, that stylistically this group stands apart from the rest of Candida's oeuvre. Portrayed are *Charles the Bold*, his brother *Antoine, le Grand-Bâtard* (both London, BM), *Jean le Tourneur*, chamberlain to Charles (Brussels, Bib. Royale Albert 1er, Cab. Médailles), and *Jacopo Galeota* (Paris, Bib. N.). A widely appreciated unsigned medal whose attribution to Candida is secured by its close stylistic affinity to his signed medal of Charles and Maximilian, celebrates the *Wedding of Maximilian of Austria to Mary of Burgundy* (1477; Washington, DC, N.G.A.). It depicts on the obverse the youthful myrtle-wreathed Maximilian, and on the reverse his bride. In 1480 Candida left the Low Countries for the French court of Louis XI, and under Charles VIII wrote a short history of France in support of Charles's claim to the Kingdom of Naples. Candida was granted French citizenship and appointed Royal Councillor and Ambassador to the Holy See (1491). In 1493 he again undertook a diplomatic mission to Rome, where upon the King's request the Pope named him Protonotary Apostolic. Medals attributed to his French period (1480–1500) include portraits of *Pierre de Courthardy*, advocate-general (after cast, Paris, Bib. N.), *Guillaume des Perriers*, French representative at the court of the Rota (London, V&A), and a medal of *Giuliano della Rovere* (later Julius II), paired with the portrait of *Clemente della Rovere*, Bishop of Mende (London, BM). An undated letter by Guillaume de la Mare, secretary to Robert Briçonnet, Archbishop of Reims, mentions a silver medal of *Robert Briçonnet* made by Candida. Two unsigned varieties of *Briçonnet* medal survive: both are bronze, and none seems to be extant in silver. One legend refers to him before (e.g. Washington, DC, N.G.A.), the other after (e.g. Berlin, Bodemus.) his appointment as Archbishop (27 Oct 1493). There is another small group of medals of French sitters from the early 16th century; while Candida's influence can be discerned, they may not stem from his own hand, but may be products of one of his French followers. Documentary evidence of Candida ends in 1499 and it is not clear whether he died in that year or lived for several more years in obscurity. Two medallic portraits of *Candida* himself exist. One shows him as a boy (perhaps a self-portrait) (Modena, Gal. & Mus. Estense), the other, a unique oblong lead (Washington, DC, N.G.A.) as a young man. The latter piece has at times been attributed to Lysippus. Candida is also thought by some to be represented in Memling's *Portrait of a Man Holding a Nero Sestertius* (Antwerp, Kon. Mus. S. Kst.), though it differs somewhat from his own medallic portraits. Candida's medals are characterized by a bold ductus of lettering and by candid portraiture; the relief is generally low. Reverse types are straightforward, often of heraldic devices. The subsequent development of medallic art in Flanders and northern France was strongly influenced by Candida's work.

BIBLIOGRAPHY

DBI; Forrer; Thieme–Becker

A. Armand: *Les Médailleurs italiens* (Paris, 2/1883–7), i, pp. 58, 106

A. Heiss: 'Jean de Candida', *Rev. Numi.*, n.s. 3, viii (1890), pp. 453–79

F. Mazerolle: *Les Médailleurs français du XVème au milieu du XVIIème* (Paris, 1902–4), i, pp. xi, xvi, xxiii; ii, pp. 19–22

C. von Fabriczy: *Medaillen* (Leipzig [1904]; Eng. trans., London, 1904), pp. 161–7

V. Tourneur: 'Jehan de Candida, diplomate et médailleur au service de la maison de Bourgogne, 1472–1480', *Rev. Belge Numi.*, lx (1914), pp. 381–411; lxv (1919), pp. 7–48, 251–300

C. Hulin de Loo: 'Le Portrait du médailleur par Hans Memlinc: Jean de Candida et non Niccolò Spinelli', *Festschrift für Max J. Friedländer* (Leipzig, 1927), pp. 103–8

G. F. Hill: *Corpus* (1930), i, pp. 211–19

G. F. Hill and G. Pollard: *Renaissance Medals of the Samuel H. Kress Collection in the National Gallery of Art* (London, 1967)

U. Middeldorf: 'On the Dilettante Sculptor', *Apollo*, cvii (1978), pp. 310–22

——: *Collected Writings* (Florence, 1981), pp. 186–91

U. Middeldorf and D. Stiebral: *Renaissance Medals and Plaquettes* (Florence, 1983), pp. vi–viii

G. Pollard: *Medaglie italiane del rinascimento*, Museo Nazionale del Bargello, 3 vols (Florence, 1985), p. 344

L. Waldmann: 'Giovanni Filangieri Candida', *The Currency of Fame: Portrait Medals of the Renaissance* (exh. cat., ed. S. K. Scher; New York, Frick, 1994), pp. 121–6

MARK M. SALTON

Candilis–Josic–Woods. French architectural and urban planning partnership formed in 1955 by Georges Candilis (*b* Baku, Azerbaijan, 11 April 1913), Alexis Josic (*b* Stari Becej, Serbia, 24 May 1921) and Shadrach Woods (*b* New York, 30 June 1923; *d* New York, 31 July 1973). Candilis, who was of Greek origin, graduated in architecture (1936) from the Institute of Technology in Athens and worked as an architect for the Ministry of Aviation, Athens (1937–40). He emigrated to France in 1945 and worked briefly for André Lurçat and then for Le Corbusier (1948–50), where he was involved in the construction of the Unité d'Habitation (1945–52), Marseille, and where he met Woods, who studied engineering at New York University (1940–42) and literature at the University of Dublin (1945–

8). In 1951 Candilis and Woods, with the engineer Henri Piot, were asked to head ATBAT-Afrique, the Moroccan office of ATBAT, the Atelier des Bâtisseurs, a multidisciplinary organization founded on Le Corbusier's initiative in 1947 and headed by the engineer Vladimir Bodiansky. Their major concern was to find collective housing solutions for the rapidly urbanizing Islamic countries and their mushrooming shanty towns by combining low-cost prefabrication construction techniques with traditional residential patterns. This led to the development of experimental units such as the Beehive Block (1952) and the Semiramis Block (1953) that were cross-ventilated and included private patios suited to the traditional practice of open-air cooking. In Oran, Algeria, and Casablanca, these units were assembled in linear, low rise blocks, enlivened by an abstract play of balconies and external corridors. Candilis and Woods, who were members of CIAM, presented the units at CIAM IX (1953), Aix-en-Provence, where they proved highly influential in consolidating the ideas of TEAM TEN, the group that emerged from CIAM in 1956 to promote the importance of individual architectural and social identity, scale and meaning in place of the rigid Functionalism of CIAM's Athens Charter (1933).

Candilis returned to the headquarters of ATBAT in Paris in 1954. There he met Josic, who had studied painting in Belgrade with his father Mladen Josic and had also studied architecture at the University of Belgrade, graduating in 1948. Josic had worked as an architect for the Ministry of Construction, Belgrade (1945–7), taught in his father's art school and was a scenographer (1948–50) before moving to Paris and joining ATBAT (1953). The partnership of Candilis–Josic–Woods was formed in 1955 when Woods returned to France; other associates at the time were Piot, the architect Guy Brunache and the engineer Paul Dony. The three principals took full advantage of their diverse backgrounds and complementary skills: Candilis attracted commissions, Josic was the artist and Woods the theoretician. Their practice maintained a multi-disciplinary nature; to them, as to many members of their generation, the individualistic attitude and working methods of most pioneers of the Modern Movement could not address the realities of urban growth after World War II. Such views led Candilis and Woods to become founding members of Team Ten in 1956 and their office attracted a number of young American architects, including Charles Gwathmey.

In 1955 Candilis–Josic–Woods won the national competition 'Opération Million', which was organized to improve the planning of government housing; it involved the construction of 3600 housing units in France, particularly in the Paris suburbs. This placed the practice at the forefront of research into low-cost housing; its theoretical research, based on the articulation of mass and the separation of specific and general functions in plan, focused on the organization and assembly of modular units. The goal was to provide an alternative both to the German *Siedlungen* housing model of the 1920s and 1930s, and also to Le Corbusier's Unité d'Habitation of the 1940s and 1950s. Although still relying on mass production, their alternative was intended to be more flexible and humanly scaled than its predecessors. In France, where the housing crisis reached dramatic proportions, Candilis–Josic–Woods built thousands of low-cost units using industrialized components. Their concepts for façades, with high-level strip windows and projecting balconies, were widely copied. Their most successful designs were perhaps the smaller scale developments with a Mediterranean feel, such as the terrace housing (1961), Aix-en-Provence. However, workmanship and detailing were often disappointing, and some of their large-scale developments, such as Marseille-La Viste (1959), seem as drab and inhuman as any other French *grand ensemble* in the suburbs of large cities. They also designed a number of housing projects in Islamic countries and in Martinique and Guadeloupe, in which their concern for the respect of vernacular features was contradicted by their unwillingness to use local materials.

Research by Candilis–Josic–Woods in the field of low-cost housing naturally led to work in urban planning, in which Woods played a prominent role. In 1956 the office won a competition for, and subsequently built, the extension of Bagnols-sur-Cèze, a small town north of Avignon that had been selected as the site for the first atomic plant in France. They also produced master-plans (unexecuted) for new towns on the periphery of Caen (1961), Hamburg (1961) and Fort-Lamy (now N'Djamena) (1963), Chad. Rejecting both the formal planning principles of the French academic tradition and Le Corbusier's Athens Charter, whose zoning they considered too monolithic and inhuman, they aimed to restore the interrelationships of urban functions and of built space and open space, using modular and cluster plans. These theories were applied to the award-winning master-plan for Toulouse-Le-Mirail (1961; see fig.), a satellite town first planned for 100,000 inhabitants; it included a centrally located, regional commercial and administrative centre, together with industrial zones to provide local employment, and a university, built in part by Candilis and Josic (1965–75). Dwellings were conceived as linear, mid-rise or low-rise structures. The original scheme called for a strong separation between traffic circulation and protected pedestrian 'spines' leading to schools grouped in educational parks, but it was subjected to major alterations. Perhaps their most interesting urban design project was a proposal for the centre of Frankfurt-Römerberg (1963; with Manfred Schiedhelm). Covering the area between the town hall and the cathedral, destroyed during World War II, the organizing principle was an orthogonal grid of pedestrian ways from which stemmed a group of non-intrusive, low-rise structures and open spaces, incorporating shops, dwellings and offices, with underground parking. Similar principles were used in the French primary school (1962), Geneva, and the Cité Artisanale (1965), Sèvres, as well as in the Freie Universität Berlin, Dahlem (1963–73; with Jean Prouvé), which suffered from the absence of an urban context.

The formal partnership of Candilis–Josic–Woods broke up in 1963. Candilis subsequently focused on leisure developments, for example the Languedoc-Roussillon coastline (1964–75); he also designed an acclaimed hotel (1966) in Caesarea, Israel, as well as hotels in Tahiti and Saudi Arabia and other projects in the Middle East. Josic was responsible for the award-winning design of the new town of Lille-Est (1972–8; with François Calsat) and he participated in the redevelopment of Vanves and Sèvres

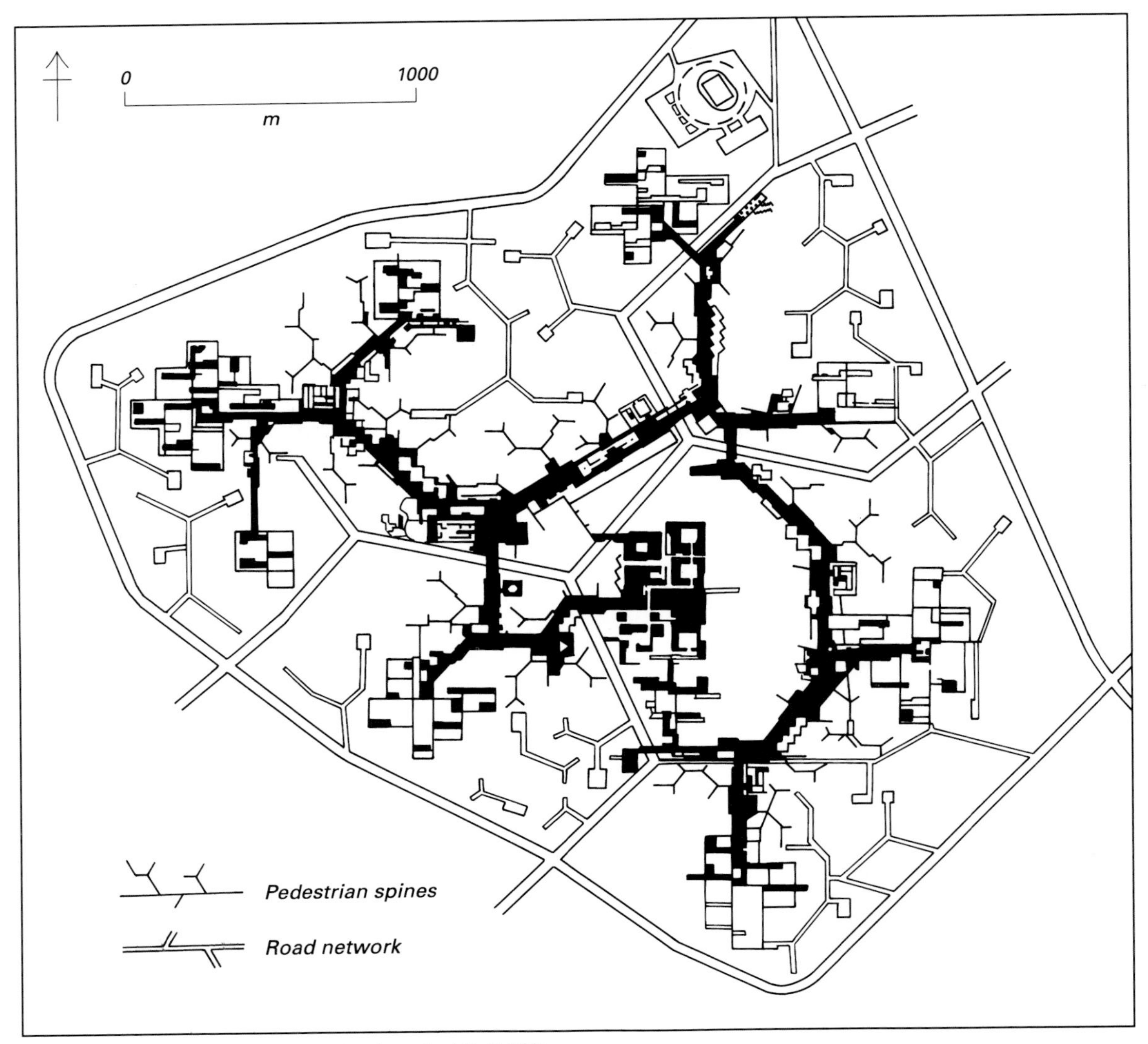

Candilis–Josic–Woods: master-plan for Toulouse-Le-Mirail, 1961

in the suburbs of Paris. Candilis and Josic worked together on some projects, including the Hilton Hotel (1970), Lahore, and several competition entries. Woods also worked with Candilis from 1963 to 1967 on such projects as the ski resort (1964–5), Vallée de Belleville, and the Steilshoop regional centre (1966), Hamburg. In 1967 he returned to the USA; his planning proposal for the small-scale transformation of the SoHo district of New York (1969) offered an alternative to drastic redevelopment projects still current at the time. He was a popular lecturer in American schools and had just been appointed Henry Bishop Visiting Professor of Architecture at Yale University, New Haven, CT, at the time of his death.

WRITINGS

G. Candilis: 'Bagnols-sur-Cèze', *Archit. Des.*, xxx/5 (1960), pp. 181–5
——: 'Problèmes d'urbanisme', *Archit. Aujourd'hui*, 118 (1964), pp. 33–5
A. Smithson, ed.: *Team 10 Primer* (London, 1968) [several contributions]
G. Candilis, A. Josic and S. Woods: *Toulouse-Le-Mirail: Birth of a New Town* (Stuttgart, 1975)
S. Woods: *The Man in the Street: A Polemic on Urbanism* (Baltimore, 1975)

BIBLIOGRAPHY

M. Besset: *New French Architecture* (Stuttgart and London, 1967)
Candilis-Josic-Woods (Stuttgart, 1968)
P. Smithson: 'Toulouse-Le-Mirail', *Archit. Des.*, xli (1971), pp. 599–604
'Team 10+20', *Archit. Aujourd'hui*, 177 (1975), pp. 44–53
Guide de l'architecture dans les villes nouvelles de la région parisienne, intro. J. E. Roullier and G. Salmon-Legagneur (Paris, 1979)

ISABELLE GOURNAY

Candlestick. Portable stand for a candle. From the ancient Roman period until the introduction of gas and oil lighting in the 19th century, artificial light was primarily provided by candles, though oil lamps and partly-stripped rushes soaked in fat or wax were also used (*see* LIGHTING, §2). Candles were shaped from a dough of fat, cast in moulds, rolled out from sheets of wax or dipped. Wicks were made of cotton, flax or rushes; candles were made from beeswax, tallow (animal fat), bayberry wax and, later, mineral wax.

One of the earliest extant candlesticks is of silver and was made in the reign of the Emperor Justinian I (AD 527–65; London, BM). Medieval candlesticks, however, were made from iron, brass or wood and had a pricket—a thin spike of metal—on which the candle was impaled. Few pricket candlesticks dating before 1400 survive. Some 12th-century candlesticks include representations of beasts and human figures, for example the Gloucester Candlestick (1104–13; London, V&A; *see* ROMANESQUE, fig. 76) and the surviving fragments of a candlestick made near Reims (late 12th century; Reims, Mus. St Rémi; *see* ROMANESQUE, fig. 73), with a foot in the form of a winged dragon. In the 12th and 13th centuries copper candlesticks with champlevé enamel decoration were made at Limoges (e.g. London, V&A).

Candle holders or sockets, in which the candle was set, appeared in Europe in the late 13th century, in particular on domestic candlesticks. Until about 1500 the pricket form of candlestick and the type with a socket were used concurrently. A cup was also incorporated at the top of the stem below the pricket or socket to hold the accumulation of wax. In the 16th century a drip tray, often halfway up the stem, was added, while many candlesticks were made with a concave depression in the base.

During the late Middle Ages most pricket candlesticks had three feet, but *c.* 1450–1500 a new style with a round base appeared. This form is probably derived from earlier Near Eastern brass candlesticks that have drum-shaped bases (e.g. base of a candlestick probably from Iran, first half of the 14th century; Edinburgh, Royal Mus. Scotland; *see* ISLAMIC ART, fig. 147). In the late 15th century socketed candlesticks were made with notches to facilitate the removal of the stub; the notches were often crudely cut, rectangular and usually carrying file marks that show they were cut after casting. Notches were replaced in the late 16th century by a round, drilled hole, in which a lever could be inserted to eject the spent candle. Mouldings or knops also appear on 16th-century brass candlesticks (e.g. Flemish brass candlestick, *c.* 1500–50; priv. col.; see fig.).

Brass candlestick, knobbed with stepped foot, drilled hole and aperture, h. 1356 mm, Flemish, *c.* 1500–50 (private collection)

Pewter candlesticks were particularly popular in the 17th century. Few silver candlesticks made before 1600 survive: extant examples from the 17th century follow the form of those in base metals (e.g. pair of silver trumpet-shaped candlesticks, 1649; Boston, MA, Mus. F.A.). Candlesticks in wood, bone or ceramic (e.g. English Delft trumpet-based candlestick, *c.* 1660; priv. col., see *The Somerset House Art Treasures Exhibition, 1979*, exh. cat., London) from this period are also similar to base metal examples. During the 17th century baluster stems were introduced, the drip tray having become unfashionable. At this time candle holders or sockets were made without apertures, and in the 18th century mechanical grips and other devices (often patented) that ejected the stubs were developed.

In the late 17th century and early 18th candlesticks were produced in a wide variety of fashionable styles. While certain features that were common to all areas of production appeared, each region developed its own variations of the main forms. Silver and brass were the most commonly used materials. Small silver candlesticks on square bases, often with elaborate embossed decoration, formed part of the large toilet services of the Baroque period (e.g. pair in French toilet service from Paris, 1658–76; Copenhagen, Rosenborg Slot; *see* FRANCE, fig. 76).

Octagonal faceted brass candlesticks were also popular, as improvements in casting ensured that a greater variety of forms could be produced: most candlesticks were cast in two halves (including stem, base and socket) and then soldered together. During the 1730s and 1740s elaborate Rococo candlesticks in silver, porcelain and earthenware were made (e.g. pair in silver by Robert Calderwood, 1746; priv. col.; *see* IRELAND, fig. 22). George Michael Moser produced designs for candlesticks that incorporate twisted human figures supporting the socket (e.g. of 1740; London, V&A). Paktong, an artificial silver alloy of 20% nickel with brass, began to be used for candlesticks during the first half of the 18th century, but the cost of production and a shortage of the zinc-based alloy meant that it was not widely popular. By the 1760s developments in core-casting (i.e. casting in one piece using a removable core) enabled candlesticks to be produced more inexpensively by using less metal. Simpler Neo-classical forms appeared with reeded or fluted stems on a square base and sockets in the form of Corinthian capitals. This type of hollow candlestick often has a loaded base to provide stability. Candlesticks in the Neo-classical style were designed by such architects as Robert Adam (i) in order to harmonize with other interior furnishings (e.g. pair of 1767; Leeds, Temple Newsam House).

During the 19th century ornamental candlesticks continued to be made in the prevailing styles (e.g. pair of Gothic Revival candlesticks designed by A. W. N. Pugin, 1844–5; London, V&A), although a number of more practical forms were introduced. Telescopic candlesticks were patented in 1795: they are in the form of a cylindrical stem with a number of telescopic slides and are adjustable from about 5 cm to 50 cm. Sheffield plate was also a popular material for candlesticks during the early 19th century. By the mid-19th century, however, candle lighting had been superseded by oil lamps.

It is often difficult to date candlesticks by style, as many forms, for example chamber candlesticks, continued to be manufactured over a long period. Ecclesiastical candlesticks with triangular stems and bases were made in southern Europe from the 16th to the 19th century. The use of special silver candlesticks for the *havdalah* ceremony remains traditional in Jewish communities (*see* JEWISH ART, §VI, 2). Candlesticks continued to be made in modern styles after 1900 (e.g. pair of modernist pewter candlesticks by Reed & Barton, 1928; New Haven, CT, Yale U. A.G.; *see* PEWTER, fig. 3), although antique styles remained popular.

See also CANDELABRUM, CHANDELIER and SCONCE.

BIBLIOGRAPHY

Early Lighting (Hartford, 1972) [The Rushlight Club]
G. Wills: *Candlesticks* (London, 1974)
R. Michaelis: *Old Domestic Base Metal Candlesticks* (Woodbridge, 1978)
S. Wechssler: *Lampen, Leuchten und Laternen* (Munich, 1983)
J. Burke: *Birmingham Brass Candlesticks* (Charlottesville, VA, 1986)
J. Bourne and V. Brett: *The Art of Lighting in the Domestic Interior* (London, 1991)

PETER HORNSBY

Candounis, Nikolaos. *See* KANTOUNIS, NIKOLAOS.

Candrātreya [Candrella]. *See* CHANDELLA.

Cane. The stem of the rattan palm. The technique of interweaving split cane to form an open mesh originated in East Asia; it was first used in England during the Restoration period in the second half of the 17th century for the bottoms and backs of seat furniture, supplies of the palm being shipped to Europe from the Malay Peninsula by the East India Co. Caning was also widely used by Dutch Colonial furniture-makers (*see* INDONESIA, §VIII, 8). After declining in favour, caning again became popular in the late 18th century for chairs, cradles, bedheads and, as Thomas Sheraton observed, 'anything where lightness, elasticity, cleanness, and durability, ought to be combined'. In the late 19th century and the early 20th there was a worldwide demand for furniture constructed entirely of the tough, fibrous core of the rattan palm; a wide range of articles, often described as 'art cane furniture', was available for gardens, conservatories, steamers, cafés, drawing-rooms and hotels. The cane is sometimes combined with fixed upholstery, and some makers used brightly coloured stains. A large collection of Edwardian trade catalogues issued by leading cane manufacturers, including W. T. Ellmore & Son (Leicester), E. A. Day and Morris Wilkinson & Co. (both Nottingham), is owned by the City Art Gallery, Leeds.

See also BAMBOO, BASKETWORK and WICKER.

BIBLIOGRAPHY

P. Macquoid and R. Edwards: *The Dictionary of English Furniture*, 3 vols (London, 1924–7, rev. 1954/*R* 1983)
P. Kirkham: 'Willow and Cane Furniture in Austria, Germany and England *c*. 1900–14', *Furn. Hist.*, xxi (1985), pp. 128–33

CHRISTOPHER GILBERT

Cane, Louis (*b* Beaulieu, Alpes-Maritimes, 13 Dec 1943). French painter and writer. He studied at the Ecole des Arts Décoratifs in Nice and then at the Ecole des Arts Décoratifs in Paris. He had his first one-man show at the Galerie Givaudan in Paris in 1969. His early works were 'painted papers', for example *Collage* (1967; see Bielefeld exh. cat., p. 51). These were followed by the 'stamped works' of 1968 to 1969, created using a repeated design stamped onto canvas, such as *Untitled* (1968; see Bielefeld exh. cat., p. 48). From 1970 to 1971 he participated in the Supports-Surfaces group, though he was not included in the first exhibition (1970). In 1971 he co-founded and thereafter directed the review *Peinture/Cahiers théoriques*, originally intended as a mouthpiece for this group. At this time he began to produce his large 'floor-wall' canvases, painted in a few colours, which hung from the wall and extended on to the floor at the base. Those of 1974 and 1976 are mainly in black.

In his subsequent works Cane made increasing use of tradition and was particularly influenced by the architecture of Brunelleschi and 14th- and 15th-century Tuscan painting. He produced a series of works based on Giotto's *The Crucifix of St Damien Speaks to St Francis* (1290–95), for example *St Damien Speaks to St Francis, No. 52* (1976; see 1977 exh. cat.). Cane's work of the 1980s shows a return to figuration, again inspired by a study of famous paintings such as Velázquez's *Las Meninas*. He painted a number of works showing the influence of Picasso, de Kooning and primitive rock painting, such as *The Deluge* (1982; see 1983 exh. cat., fig. 21).

BIBLIOGRAPHY

Louis Cane (exh. cat. by M. Pleynet, Paris, Pompidou, 1977)
Louis Cane: Werke 1968–1978 (exh. cat. by M. Pauseback and others, Bielefeld, Städt. Ksthalle, 1978)
Louis Cane, 1968–1978: The First Ten Years of a Painter (exh. cat., Jerusalem, Israel Mus., 1978)
Louis Cane (exh. cat., Saint-Paul-de-Vence, Fond. Maeght, 1983)

□

Caneja, Juan Manuel [Díaz] (*b* Palencia, 1905). Spanish painter. He moved to Madrid to study architecture but soon abandoned this career to devote himself to painting. For several years he attended the studio of Daniel Vázquez Díaz, and he actively participated in the cultural life of avant-garde circles in Madrid, becoming a member in 1927 of the Primera Escuela de Vallecas, a group of artists and intellectuals centred around the painter Benjamín Palencia and the sculptor Alberto. Together they travelled around the outskirts of Madrid, in particular to Vallecas, in search of artistic inspiration.

Caneja familiarized himself with Cubism and the work of Matisse during a stay in Paris in 1929, and he exhibited several works influenced by Cubism at his first one-man exhibition (Madrid, Mus. A. Mod., 1934). After the declaration of the Spanish Republic in 1931 he joined the Confederación Nacional del Trabajo; this involvement in leftist politics later led to his imprisonment for three years under the regime of General Franco. At the close of the Spanish Civil War in 1939 he became interested in landscape painting, a genre with no problems of censorship. Appraising the Castilian landscape without anecdote through a schematized language derived from Cubism, he created virtually abstract paintings representing sections of land structured by colour and light.

BIBLIOGRAPHY

Juan Manuel Caneja (exh. cat., Madrid, Min. Cult., 1984)
C. Alonso de los Ríos: *Díaz Caneja* (Palencia, 1985)

PALOMA ALARCÓ CANOSA

Canet, Antoni (*fl* 1394; *d* by April 1431). Catalan architect and sculptor, probably of Mallorcan origin. In 1394 he was working as a highly paid apprentice of Pere Ça Anglada on the choir carving of Barcelona Cathedral. He was briefly involved in the decoration of the Portal del Mirador of Palma de Mallorca Cathedral (1397). In 1405 he executed some of the ornamental detail of the portal of the former chapter house (now Capella del Santíssim) in the cloister of Barcelona Cathedral. His most important sculptural work is the alabaster tomb of *Bishop Ramon d'Escales* in the Capella de les Ànimes in the Cathedral, commissioned in 1409. The sarcophagus bears the recumbent effigy of the Bishop and a frieze of weeping figures on the front, which reveal that Canet, who was familiar with the Franco-Flemish models derived from Claus Sluter, was one of the most outstanding craftsmen of the international style in Catalan sculpture.

As an architect Canet was Master of the Works of Seu d'Urgell Cathedral until 1416, when he attended the famous meeting of architects and sculptors at Girona Cathedral (*see* MASON (i), §IV, 3(ii)). He was against the initial scheme for a three-aisled plan for the nave; immediately afterwards the Chapter commissioned him to design a single-cell nave and to co-direct the works with Guillem Bofill. Canet was in Girona until 1426, when he built the first two bays of the nave (23 m wide) and carved the *Virgin and Child* on the first vault boss (1424). He was also commissioned to make a wooden tabernacle for S Domingo, Girona (1423; untraced).

BIBLIOGRAPHY

A. Duran Sanpere: 'Un gran escultor medieval desconocido', *La Vanguardia* (Barcelona, 26 May 1938)
——: 'Visita a la Catedral, Octava Jornada: La Capilla del Obispo Escales y el Coro', *Divulgación Hist.*, ii (1946), p. 340
E. Serra i Ràfols: 'La nau de la Seu de Girona', *Miscellània Puig i Cadafalch* (Barcelona, 1947–51), pp. 185–204
M. Durliat: 'Le Portail du Mirador de la Cathédrale de Palma de Majorque', *Pallas*, ix (1960), pp. 245–55
A. Cirici i Pellicer: *Arquitectura Gòtica Catalana* (Barcelona, 1968)
P. Freixas: 'Antoni Canet, maestro mayor de la Seu de Gerona', *Rev. Gerona*, lx (1972), pp. 50–60
A. Duran Sanpere: 'Antoni Canet: Un gran escultor medieval', *Barcelona i la seva Història: L'Art i la cultura* (Barcelona, 1975), pp. 52–6
N. de Dalmases and A. José Pitarch: *L'Art gòtic: S. XIV–XV*, Història de l'Art Català, iii (Barcelona, 1983)
P. Freixas: *L'Art gòtic a Girona: Segles XIV–XV* (Barcelona, 1983)
M. Rosa Terés: 'Una nova aportació a l'obra d'Antoni Canet', *D'Art* [Barcelona], viii–ix (1983), pp. 201–4

PERE FREIXAS

Canevale [Canevalle]. Italian family of architects, active in Bohemia. Marcantonio Canevale (*b* Lanzo d'Intelvi, northern Italy, 28 Sept 1652; *d* Prague, *bur* 15 Dec 1711) and his brother Giovanni Canevale (*d* Orlík, Bohemia, 11 Nov 1706) were both enrolled in the Old Town Guild in Prague on 20 May 1674. Marcantonio acquired citizenship in the New Town there on 16 October 1680 and subsequently worked for aristocratic families in Bohemia (e.g. the Ditrichštejn, Wallenstein and Pachta). In 1694–6 he built the church of the Holy Cross at Reichenberg (now Liberec) at the expense of the count of the Holy Roman Empire Franz Ferdinand von Gallas, but it was later remodelled (1753–6) by Johann Josef Kuntze (1724–1800). His finest work was created for the Ursuline Order in Prague: the church of St Ursula (1699–1704) in Prague New Town, with its three-bay nave, shows a striving towards a rhythmical and centralized treatment of the internal volumes and has an advanced form of vaulting—two wide domical vaults with a central, barrel-vaulted bay. This church is one of the best works in Bohemia from the period around 1700. Among Marcantonio's most interesting secular buildings is the palace (1697–1702) in Mnichovo Hradiště, which has three wings and a tower built over the central projecting bay. His brother Giovanni worked from 1686 as architect to Prince Eggenberg on his estates in southern Bohemia. Among Giovanni's various works and many restorations, the simple church in Brloh (1694–1704) and the church towers in Ktiš (1688–99) and Kájov (Gojau; 1691–93) are notable. Marcantonio's son Carlo Antonio Canevale (*b* Prague, *bapt* 19 Feb 1688; *d* Prague, *bur* 2 May 1740) acquired citizenship in the New Town, Prague, on 11 April 1712. Two attractive churches in Maková Hora (1719–22) and Vraclav (1724–6) are attributed to him.

BIBLIOGRAPHY

DBI; Thieme–Becker
K. B. Mádl: 'Marcantonio Canevalle', *Památky Archeol.*, xxxiii (1923), pp. 105–10
P. Toman: *Nový slovník československých umělců* [New dictionary of Czechoslovak artists], i (Prague, 1947), pp. 123–4
H. Machálková: *Marco Antonio Canevale* (diss., Prague, Charles U., 1951)
P. Preiss: *Italští umělci v Praze* [Italian artists in Prague] (Prague, 1986), pp. 340–42

VĚRA NAŇKOVÁ

Canevale, Isidore [Marcell Armand] (*b* Vincennes, 1730; *d* Vienna, 2 Nov 1786). French architect and landscape designer, active in Austria. He trained in Paris under Giovanni Niccolò Servandoni, whom he followed to

Vienna in 1760. There he worked for the Crown Prince (later Emperor Joseph II (*reg* 1765–90)), and in 1776 he became Court Architect with responsibility for work in the suburbs of Vienna. Besides numerous architectural monuments, including a triumphal arch (1765) in Innsbruck, Canevale was also commissioned by the Emperor to design several private buildings, as well as summer houses for him in the Prater district of Vienna (1781–4) and on the Laaerberg (1786). Canevale also redesigned the Allgemeines Krankenhaus (the 'Narrenturm'; 1783), the Josephinum (1783–5; *see* AUSTRIA, fig. 7), a military medical school founded by the Emperor, and the anatomical theatre in the old university, all in Vienna (*see* AUSTRIA, §II, 4). Other works included the garden 'castle' known as 'Josephstöckl' (1780–83) for Joseph II, in the Augarten, Vienna, and a scheme commissioned by the Emperor for a building ('Neugebäude', 1776; destr. 1897–1900) in Budapest.

Canevale also worked for numerous secular and religious patrons in Austria, Moravia, Silesia and Hungary. His work for the Liechtenstein princes on their estates in Valtice and Lednice, Moravia (now the Czech Republic), is documented from 1768. For Bishop Christoph Anton Migazzi, Canevale designed the cathedral (1763–72) in VÁC, Hungary; its central dome, coffered ceiling and giant portico of detached columns carrying a heavy attic announced the arrival of Neo-classicism in Hungary. Canevale's plans for the archiepiscopal cathedral of St Adalbert, Esztergom, and the Esterházy palace in Tata were not carried out, but he probably designed the Wiener Neudorf parish church (1778–80). His landscape designs included the pleasure gardens (1763) for Graf Franz Esterházy in Bernolákovo (now Slovakia), and from 1782 he played a major part in redesigning the gardens for the castle at Laxenburg, Austria, in the English landscape style. Canevale's simple Neo-classical style, with its exploitation of basic geometric forms on a monumental scale, recalls the aesthetics of his contemporaries, Etienne-Louis Boullée and Claude-Nicolas Ledoux.

BIBLIOGRAPHY

M. Mojzer: 'Canevale in Ungarn', *Mitt. Ges. Vergl. Kstforsch. Wien*, xxii (1970), p. 34

R. Wagner-Rieger: 'Vom Klassizismus bis zur Sezession: Geschichte der Architektur in Wien', *Gesch. Stadt Wien*, vii/3 (1973), pp. 93–6

W. G. Rizzi and M. Schwarz: 'Die Architektur zur Zeit Josephs II', *Österreich zur Zeit Kaiser Josephs II* (exh. cat., ed. K. Gutkas; Melk, Stiftsmus., 1980), pp. 202–6, 210, 566–9

G. Hájos: *Romantische Gärten der Aufklärung* (Vienna, 1989), pp. 132–5

PETER FIDLER

Canevari, Antonio (*b* Rome, 1681; *d* Naples, April 1764). Italian architect. He was a pupil of Antonio Valeri (1648–1736) and Pierfrancesco Garolli (1638–1716) and first achieved prominence with his design for a papal residence (1703; Rome, Acad. N. S Luca, Archivio Storico, Dis. architett. 452–4) in a competition held by the Accademia di S Luca, Rome. In 1715 he took part in a competition for the new sacristy of St Peter's, Rome, and from 1715 to 1718 he restored the church of SS Giovanni e Paolo, also in Rome. In 1717 he took over the direction of the rebuilding of the church of Stimmate di S Francesco from Giovanni Battista Contini. He modified the design and conceived the façade, which, with its large statue of *St Francis* before the middle upper window, was a novelty in Rome, although there were precedents in Cosimo Fanzago's church façades, such as S Giuseppe degli Scalzi a Pontecorvo (1643–60), Naples. From 1724 Canevari continued the modernization of the church of S Eustachio, Rome, completing the transept and apse, and in 1725 claimed responsibility for rebuilding the portico of S Paolo fuori le Mura (destr. 1823).

John V of Portugal paid for the Bosco Parrasio on the Janiculum, where the literary Arcadian Academy held its meetings. Canevari, a member of the Academy since 1716, devised its garden in 1725 as a series of visually stimulating terraces and staircases, centring on a small amphitheatre. From 1727 he lived in Lisbon, where he contributed to the restoration and enlargement of the royal residence (destr. 1755) and was responsible for the design of court festivities. He was involved in the completion of Mafra, but in 1732 errors in the construction of the Águas Livres aqueduct at Lisbon led to his dismissal.

In the same year Canevari entered the competition for the façade of S Giovanni in Laterano, Rome, for which he had already produced designs in 1722. In 1737 he entered the service of Charles III of Naples, where he was responsible for constructing the Capodimonte hunting lodge in collaboration with Giovanni Antonio Medrano (*b* 1703) and the Villa Reale in Portici (1738–59). His other works include a design for the 'ziborium' of the high altar (destr.) of the church of Montecassino (1727), a festival design *al Sedile di Porto* in Naples (1740) and the baldacchino in S Nicola, Bari (1743).

BIBLIOGRAPHY

DBI

N. Pio: *Vite* (1724); ed. C. Enggass and R. Enggass (1977), pp. 153–4

F. Milizia: *Le vite de' più celebri architetti d'ogni nazione e d'ogni tempo* (Rome, 1768); rev. as *Memorie degli architetti antichi e moderni*, ii (Bassano, 4/1785), p. 251

R. C. Smith: 'João Frederico Ludovice, an Eighteenth Century Architect in Portugal', *A. Bull.*, xviii (1936), pp. 286–9

R. Pane: *Ville vesuviane del settecento* (Naples, 1959), pp. 193–8

R. Mormone: 'Documenti per la storia dell'architettura napoletana del settecento', *Napoli Nob.*, n. s. 2, iii (1963–4), p. 120

H. Hager: *Filippo Juvarra e il concorso di modelli del 1715 bandito da Clemente XI per la nuova sacristia di S Pietro* (Rome, 1970), pp. 39–42, 55

A. Vendetti: 'Note su Antonio Canevari architetto', *Stud. Romani*, xxi (1973), pp. 358–65

P. Ferraris: 'Antonio Canevari', *In urbe architectus—modelli, disegni, misure: La professione dell'architetto a Roma, 1680–1750* (exh. cat., ed. B. Contardi and G. Curcio; Rome, Mus. N. Castel S Angelo, 1991), pp. 331–2

ANJA BUSCHOW OECHSLIN

Cangianti [It.: 'colour changes', from present participle of *cangiare*: to change; Fr. *changeant*; Eng. changeables]. The practice of using two or more hues of different lightness to imitate the effects of light and shadow on a surface. *Cangianti* often imitate the appearance of shot silk where the woof and the warp are two different colours, a weaving practice that causes the fabric to appear to change in colour with its orientation to the light. *Cangianti* modelling emerged in 14th-century Italian painting as an alternative to CHIAROSCURO modelling. Its greatest exponents in later centuries were Michelangelo and Federico Barocci.

JANIS CALLEN BELL

Cangzhen. *See* HUAISU.

Can Hasan [now Alaçatı]. Site dating from the 7th millennium BC, about 13 km east-north-east of Karaman, Turkey. Can Hasan lies on the border of the Konya basin at the northern foot of the Taurus Mountains. One of the two main mountain crossings providing access between the Mediterranean coast and the Anatolian plateau descends to the Konya plain at Karaman. There are three mounds at Can Hasan: the first and largest, Can Hasan I, has been dated by radiocarbon analysis to the 6th–4th millennium BC; Can Hasan II, from the evidence of coins and potsherds, belongs to the Hellenistic, Roman and early Byzantine periods; Can Hasan III has been dated by radiocarbon analysis to the 7th millennium BC. Can Hasan I was excavated by David French in 1961–7 and Can Hasan III in 1969–70. Finds are in the Museum of Anatolian Civilizations in Ankara and in the Archaeological Museum, Karanan.

Can Hasan I (see fig.) and III belong to a phase that followed the earliest experiments in agriculture and animal husbandry. They both have an agglomeration of densely packed structures. Each building was independent from but juxtaposed to its neighbour. Evidence of planning is clearly visible in the layout of the settlement. This arrangement, which is known from other sites in the Konya plain, such as Çatal Hüyük, is not characteristic of 7th- and 6th-millennium BC sites (e.g. Hacılar) in south-west Anatolia. The structures were made from mud-brick without stone foundations. The flat roofs, supported by timber posts, provided access to buildings at the centre of the site. There is evidence for two storeys. Wall and floor surfaces were painted red; at Can Hasan I they were patterned with red paint on a white clay ground. The basic pattern is a meander and diamond motif, intricately arranged, with a large dot painted in the centre of each diamond.

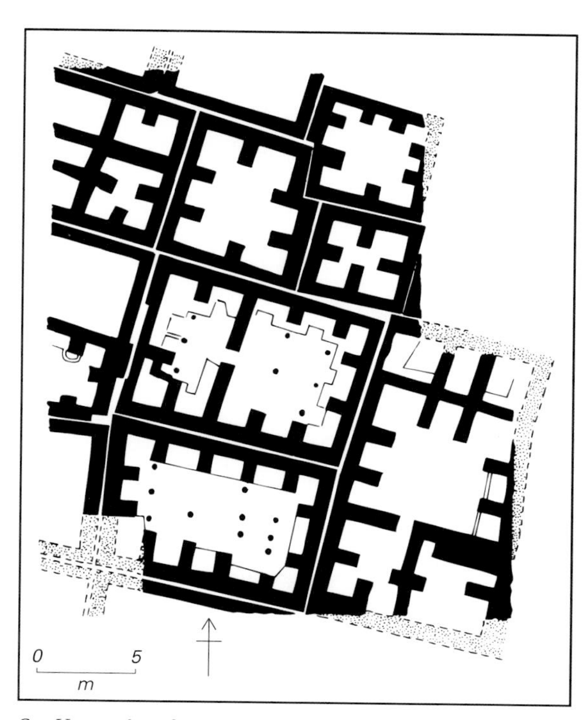

Can Hasan, plan of Can Hasan I, level 2b, 6th millennium BC

Although Can Hasan III was aceramic, pottery was common at Can Hasan I. The earliest type is a plain, dark-coloured, burnished ware. This gave way to a pale-coloured pottery with simple, red-painted patterns. In the next phase there was an expanded range of shapes, and though some pottery was left plain, most was painted, particularly with meander and diamond patterns. This motif is also found on fine incised ware unique to Can Hasan, of which one piece is decorated with sun and animal symbols. In a later phase the meander and diamond motif was replaced by hatched squares and curvilinear designs. Finally, two-colour patterns (red and black) were introduced.

In the last phase of occupation at Can Hasan I (4th millennium BC) the close agglomeration of structures was replaced by an arrangement of small, simple buildings, courtyards and open areas. The pottery characteristic of this level is a black burnished ware, sometimes white patterned, which is quite different from earlier fashions both in technique and in appearance.

The worked bone and stone tools used at Can Hasan III are typical of the period (only at Can Hasan I is metal found: a copper macehead). The use of obsidian and flint declined at Can Hasan I, and the types are simple. Some of the tools were marked with simple linear motifs. Worked clay figurines include sheep, goats, donkeys and cows. Small and large human figurines were produced, clearly male, but generally only the head (?female) is represented, shaped in a stylized and exaggerated manner; at Can Hasan I hair, eyes, ears, nose and even dress were emphasized by red paint. An ivory bracelet, stone trinkets and worked seashells are evidence for personal adornment. Simple linear patterns were cut or drilled on the stone and shell. Objects or raw materials came to Can Hasan from some distance: Mediterranean seashells, central Anatolian obsidian, south-east Anatolian pottery and ivory (possibly from Africa).

BIBLIOGRAPHY

D. French: 'Excavations at Can Hasan', *Anatol. Stud.*, xii (1962), pp. 27–40; xiii (1963), pp. 29–42; xiv (1964), pp. 125–34; xv (1965), pp. 87–94; xvi (1966), pp. 113–24; xvii (1967), pp. 165–78; xviii (1968), pp. 45–53

——: 'Excavations at Can Hasan III, 1969–70', *Papers in Economic Prehistory*, ed. E. S. Higgs (Cambridge, 1972), pp. 181–90

DAVID FRENCH

Canina, Luigi (*b* Casale Monferrato, 24 Oct 1795; *d* Florence, 17 Oct 1856). Italian architect, archaeologist and architectural historian. He studied architecture at the University of Turin (1810–12) under Ferdinando Bonsignore (1767–1843) and his assistant Giuseppe Talucchi (1782–1863). After serving (1812–14) in the fortress of Alessandria, he resumed his studies and obtained a degree in architecture in 1814. He served a period of apprenticeship under Talucchi, who helped him obtain a three-year grant from the Court of Turin for further study in Rome, where Canina settled in January 1818. He worked on engravings of Roman monuments under the antiquarian, scholar and publisher Mariano Vasi (1744–1820), and at the end of his three-year period as *pensionato*, he presented a survey of the Colosseum (*Anfiteatro Flavio descritto, misurato e restaurato*; dispersed) to the architects of the

Luigi Canina: Egyptian propylaeum (1826–7), Villa Borghese, Rome

Accademia di S Luca, including Giuseppe Valadier, who were much impressed.

In 1824 Canina was appointed to execute his scheme for the expansion of the park of the Villa Borghese, Rome. Canina's plan (10 watercolours, 1820–22; Rome, Bib. Casanatense) was modelled on Hadrian's Villa at Tivoli (*see* TIVOLI, fig. 2), providing an architectural solution for the new main entrance near the Porta del Popolo and the two bridges crossing the Via delle Tre Madonne. On the first bridge, the road is flanked on each side by Egyptian propylaia: two obelisks and two truncated, pyramidal pylons linked by porticos with lotus-shaped capitals (1826–7; see fig.). The road on the second bridge passes under the Roman triumphal arch of Septimius Severus. This was designed with a single barrel vault and simplified decoration. The attic is replaced by a three-stepped platform, which supports a restored ancient statue (*Septimius Severus*), part of a former garden monument. The main entrance (on the present Piazzale Flaminio) is emphasized by large Ionic propylaia (1827–33). The elegant iron gate, decorated with Greek motifs, is flanked by two porticos with tympani, which are surmounted by acroteria with eagles and griffins in low relief. The square in front of the gate was also designed by Canina.

After succeeding Virgilio Fontana as architect of the Borghese properties, Canina continued (1825–7) with lesser projects in the Villa Borghese. He worked on the Greek-style façade and the Egyptian room in the Casino Vagnuzzi (partially destr. 1849) near the Porta del Popolo and did maintenance and renovation in the Palazzo Borghese and Cappella Paolina (or Borghese Chapel) in S Maria Maggiore. A mechanical chair lift was designed by him for the Palazzo Borghese. Over a period of 20 years he also supervised the renovation of buildings surrounding the Piazza Borghese and in the adjacent quarter.

Canina pursued his archaeological and historical interests throughout his life. In 1827 he published the first volume of his monumental work, *L'architettura dei principali popoli antichi considerata nei monumenti*, which covers archaeology, architectural history and civic architecture in three sections on Greece, Rome and Egypt. The second section, *L'architettura romana*, began to appear in instalments from 1830, published by Canina's own printing and engraving establishment. This work began a period of intense typographical and editorial activity throughout the Roman publishing trade. *L'architettura egiziana*, which came out in 1839, actually included all non-Classical styles of ancient architecture. In 1839, after directing excavations in the Borghese properties (e.g. the Torrenova mosaic in 1834; excavations on the Esquilino, 1848–50), Canina was named Commissario alle Antichità di Roma and appointed director of the excavations at Tuscolo and Veio. In the latter post he succeeded Luigi Biondi (1776–1839), with whom he had collaborated since 1825. His archaeological writings were criticized, however, by proponents of new philological methods, and a number of his reconstructions of ancient monuments were accused of excessive fantasy.

Canina's relations with the Piedmontese court continued with a journey to Turin (1843) in the entourage of Mary Christina, who commissioned Canina's study of Christian architecture and the proposals for the cathedral of S Giovanni in Turin. The work (1843) was an important contribution to 19th-century architectural theory, including the debate on the forms of churches, for which Canina proposed the basilical type. Around this time Canina completed a supplement to Antoine Desgodets's work on the ancient buildings of Rome and wrote on the architecture of the ancient Hebrews and the Temple of Jerusalem (1845), attempting a reconstruction of the latter. Canina also visited London in 1845, where he built on existing contacts with members of the Royal Institute of British Architects, in particular C. R. Cockerell and T. L. Donaldson. In the same year he was entrusted with a project for the church of the Sanctuary at Oroppa, Biella, for which he produced large-scale drawings and a wooden model (Biella, Archv & Mus. Santuario). He visited London again in 1851 to visit the Great Exhibition, and the following year, in a publication with numerous plates, he proposed a Pompeian decoration for Joseph Paxton's Crystal Palace, as well as the application of decorations derived from the most diverse ancient civilizations, in iron and wood, to various types of modern buildings.

In the early 1850s Canina focused his archaeological studies on excavations in the Roman Forum, at the location of the Basilica Giulia (1850), and in the Via Appia (1850–53). He also contributed to the preparatory work for the drainage of the Pontine swamps and planned the reactivation of the Aqua Marcia in Rome. In 1855 he was elected president of the Museo Capitolino and enrolled in the Roman nobility. Canina's pupil and collaborator Giovanni Montiroli (1817–91) was sent by Canina to Algernon Percy, 4th Duke of Northumberland, in 1854; Montiroli was followed by the painter Alessandro Mantovani (1814–92), who headed a group of Italian craftsmen working on the modernization of the interior of Alnwick Castle (Northumb.). In 1856 Canina himself went to Alnwick; he died in Florence on his return journey and was buried there in the church of Santa Croce.

UNPUBLISHED SOURCES

Casale Monferrato, Bib. Civ. [Canina's archives]

Turin, Archv Stato, sezione Corte, Fondo Canina, bb. 1–21 [Canina's archives]

WRITINGS

L'architettura dei principali popoli antichi considerata nei monumenti, 9 vols (Rome, 1827–39)

Le nuove fabbriche della Villa Borghese denominata Pinciana (Rome, 1828)

Esposizione storica e topografica del Foro Romano e sue adiacenze, 2 vols (Rome, 1834, rev. 2/1845)

L'architettura antica descritta e dimostrata con i monumenti: Opera divisa in tre sezioni riguardanti la storia, la teoria e le pratiche dell'architettura egiziana, greca, romana, 9 vols (Rome, 1834–44)

Aggiunte e correzioni (o supplemento) all'opera di A. Desgodetz sugli edifizi antichi di Roma (Rome, 1843)

Ricerche sull'architettura più propria dei tempi cristiani, ed applicazione della medesima ad una idea di sostituzione della Chiesa cattedrale di S. Giovanni in Torino (Rome, 1843, rev. 2/1846)

Ricerche sul genere di architettura proprio degli antichi Giudei ed in particolare sul tempio di Gerusalemme (Rome, 1845)

Gli edifizi di Roma antica e dei contorni di Roma, 6 vols (Rome, 1848–56)

Particolare genere di architettura domestica decorato con ornamenti di svelte forme ed impiegato con poca varietà dai più rinomati popoli antichi ora solo ordinato con metodo e proposto alla applicazione delle fabbriche moderne in parte costrutte col legno e ferro fuso (Rome, 1852)

with C. R. Cockerell and J. S. Harford: *Illustrations, Architectural and Pictorial of the Genius of M. A. Buonarroti, with Descriptions of the Plates* (London, 1857)

Regular contributions to *Mem. Romane Ant. & B.A.* (from 1825), *AION* and *Bull. Inst. Corr. Archeol.* (1833–55) and *Diss. Pont. Accad. Romana Archeol.* (1835–60)

BIBLIOGRAPHY

DBI; *Enc. A. Ant.*; *Enc. It.*; *Macmillan Enc. Architects*; Thieme–Becker

T. L. Donaldson: *A Brief Memoir of the Late Commendatore Canina, Architect* (London, 1856)

O. Raggi: *Della vita e delle opere di Luigi Canina architetto ed archeologo di Casal Monferrato* (Casale Monferrato, 1857)

G. Bendinelli: *Luigi Canina (1795–1856): Le opere, i tempi* (Alessandria, 1953)

P. Hoffman: *La casina Vagnuzzi sulla Flaminia* (Rome, 1965)

C. Meeks: *Italian Architecture, 1750–1914* (New Haven and London, 1966), pp. 115, 118, 314, 340

W. Oechslin: 'Dekor und Architektur: Caninas Kritik an Paxtons Crystal Palace', *Kunstchronik*, xxx (1977), pp. 120–22

A. Jacobini: 'Concetto e progetto di villa in Luigi Canina', *Urbe*, 3–4 (1983), pp. 112–19; 1–2 (1984), pp. 3–27

M. Rovigatti: 'I progetti di Luigi Canina per l'ampliamento di Villa Borghese a Roma', *Ric. Stor. A.*, 22 (1984), pp. 55–63

B. Di Gaddo: *Villa Borghese: Il giardino e le architetture* (Rome, 1985), pp. 155–88

A. Sistri: 'Il Fondo Canina all'Archivio di Stato di Torino', *Dis. Archit.*, iii (1991), p. 25

S. Pasquali: 'Luigi Canina architetto ed archeologo', *Rassegna*, iv (1993), pp. 44–52

VALERIA FARINATI

Canneri [Canera; Caneri; Canerio; Carlerio]**, Anselmo** (*b* Verona, 1522–34; *d* Verona, 1584–6). Italian painter. He was a pupil of Giovanni Caroto (Vasari) and worked mainly in Verona and the Veneto. He was one of a group of Veronese painters who often worked together, frequently on decorations for buildings by Michele Sanmicheli and Andrea Palladio, and was also an early collaborator of PAOLO VERONESE (see Gisolfi Pechukas, 1987 and 1988).

In 1551 Canneri worked with Veronese and Battista Zelotti on frescoes in Sanmicheli's Villa Soranzo (mostly destr. 1816) at Castelfranco. (Fragments by Canneri are at: Castelfranco Cathedral sacristy, two putti; Venice, Semin. Patriarcale, Gloria; Paris, Sambon Col., putto; Padua, Favaretti Col., putto; priv. cols, *Rhetoric and Dialectic*, sold London, Christie's, 1962, and *Minerva between Geometry and Arithmetic*, sold Verona, Arte Antica, 1993; see Gisolfi Pechukas, 1987). Drawings by Canneri related to the Villa Soranzo fresco decorations are looser than those by Zelotti (see Gisolfi Pechukas, 1988, and Gisolfi, 1989–90). This was soon followed by collaboration with Bernardino India and Domenico Brusasorci on the decoration of Palladio's Palazzo Thiene, Vicenza (see Magagnato). Canneri's frescoes in both these schemes show flaccid physical types and clumsy foreshortening. The forms are, however, superficially close to those of Veronese while the colours are more muted and more diffusely lit than in contemporary examples by the latter. During the 1560s Canneri collaborated with Brusasorci, Paolo Farinati and Battista dell'Angolo del Moro in frescoing the exterior of the Palazzo Murari (later Bocca-Trezza) in Verona (see Schweikhart). Canneri's (damaged) frieze, representing emperors' busts and fallen warriors, is characterized by heavy forms.

Of three known altarpieces by Canneri for churches in Verona, two—*Trinity with St Fermo and Another Saint* (ex-S Fermo) and the *Pentecost* (ex-SS Nazaro e Celso)—are untraced and the third, the *Circumcision* (1566; ex-S Zeno; Verona, Castelvecchio) is damaged, though not so much as to obscure the artist's now fuller forms and sensitive use of colour (for colour illustration see 1988 exh. cat.; see Gisolfi, 1989–90, for Zancon's engraving of the picture prior to its bisection). Later Canneri collaborated with Brusasorci and Farinati on a series of three oil paintings illustrating the *Life of Moses* for the Palazzo Ridolfi, Verona (see dal Pozzo and Corso). Figures in his severely damaged canvas of *Moses Affronting the Pharaoh* (1584; Verona, Castelvecchio) seem heavy and their finish is rather harsh. Yet the very same figure types in his smaller, better preserved *Finding of Moses* (Hagerstown, MD, Washington Co. Hist. Soc. Mus.) are more graceful and softer (see Gisolfi Pechukas, 1988).

BIBLIOGRAPHY

G. Vasari: *Vite* (1550, rev. 2/1568); ed. G. Milanesi (1878–85), v, pp. 290–91

B. dal Pozzo: *Le vite de' pittori, degli scrittori et architetti veronesi* (Verona, 1718), pp. 27, 255, 294

G. B. Lanceni: *Recreazione pittorica* (Verona, 1720), i, pp. 245, 303

D. Zannandreis: *Le vite dei pittori, scultori, ed architetti veronesi* (Verona, 1891), pp. 144–5

G. Corso: 'I. Nella quadreria di Luigi Ravignani una trilogia pittorica di Mosè di Felice Brusasorzi, Anselmo Canerio e Paolo Farinati', *Madonna Verona*, xiv (1920), pp. 33–40

——: 'II. Note per la biografia del pittore Anselmo Canerio', *Madonna Verona*, xiv (1920), pp. 41–3

L. Magagnato: *Palazzo Thiene sede della Banco Populare di Verona* (Verona, 1966), pp. 81–7, 117–30

G. Schweikhart: *Fassadenmalerei in Verona* (Munich, 1973), p. 253, figs 226–9

Palladio e la maniera (exh. cat., ed. V. Sgarbi; Vicenza, S Corona, 1980), pp. 74–5

D. Gisolfi Pechukas: 'Veronese and his Collaborators at La Soranza', *Artibus & Hist.*, xv (1987), pp. 67–108

——: 'Paolo Veronese ed i suoi primi collaboratori', *Atti del convegno internazionale di studi e nel quatro centenario della morte di Paolo Veronese: Venezia, 1988*

Veronese e Verona (exh. cat., ed. S. Marinelli and others; Verona, Castelvecchio, 1988)

D. Gisolfi: '"L'anno veronesiano" and Some Early Questions about Early Veronese and his Circle', *A. Ven.*, xliii (1989–90), pp. 30–42

DIANA GISOLFI

Cano, Alonso (*bapt* Granada, 19 March 1601; *d* Granada, 3 Sept 1667). Spanish painter, sculptor and architect. He was an artist of rare versatility in 17th-century Spain, although his architectural work was not extensive. While he is also known for his drawings, only about 60 of these are definitely attributable to him, despite the many extant sketches with the name 'Cano' carelessly added by later hands. Unlike most of his Spanish contemporaries, such as Zurbarán or Velázquez, whose artistic styles did not outlive them, Cano's artistic legacy is measured in part by the number of artists who trained in his workshop and went on to become important masters in their own right: the painters Pedro Atanasio Bocanegra, Juan de Sevilla (1643–95) and, more distantly, José Risueño, and the sculptors Pedro de Mena and José de Mora, who began by following Cano's models and then continued to produce polychrome sculpture in a distinctive style typical of Granada.

1. Seville, to 1638. 2. Madrid, 1638–52. 3. Granada, from 1652.

1. SEVILLE, TO 1638. Cano's father, Miguel Cano (*d* after 1630), worked as an *ensamblador* (designer of altarpieces) and in 1614 moved his family from Granada to Seville. This was probably because artistic activity there was far greater than in Granada as a result of the wealth brought to Seville by its trade with the Indies. In August 1616 Alonso Cano began his apprenticeship in the workshop of Francisco Pacheco, where Velázquez was just completing his own training. Cano and Velázquez, two years his elder, became lifelong friends.

Lazaro Díaz del Valle, who was in the service of Philip IV and knew Cano during his period at Court, wrote in 1659 that the young apprentice had remained only eight months in Pacheco's workshop. Nevertheless, Cano's earliest known paintings, such as *St Francisco de Borja* (1624; Seville, Mus. B.A.) and the portrait of *An Ecclesiastic* (*c.* 1625–30; New York, Hisp. Soc. America), are so close in style to the meticulous technique practised by Pacheco that they suggest that Cano spent the entire five years stipulated in the apprenticeship contract under the master's tutelage. Indeed Pacheco, a learned if not a gifted painter, probably contributed significantly to Cano's distinctive aesthetic. In his treatise *Arte de la pintura* (Seville, 1649), Pacheco advocated the supremacy of drawing over colour, and the purity of line, elegance of contour and classical feeling that distinguish Cano's style from that of his Spanish contemporaries reveal his own attitude to have been the same. The sources of his style and his talents as a designer of the architectural framework of altarpieces and of sculpture were further enriched by work in his father's shop. He also absorbed stylistic traits from the sculptor Juan Martínez Montañés and from painters such as Francisco Varela, Juan de Uceda Castroverde and especially Juan del Castillo, who supplied paintings for altarpieces designed by Miguel Cano. In January 1626 Alonso married María de Figueroa, who came from a family of artists but who died only two years later. In April 1626 he became a *maestro pintor*, and in 1630 he was appointed head of the Painters' Guild of Seville.

Cano's earliest large independent commission was for the architecture and sculpture of the high altar of S María, or Nuestra Señora de la Oliva, at Lebrija, south of Seville. It was assigned to him by his father in August 1629. Pablo Legot collaborated on the project, providing the paintings and gilding. The finished work indicates that Cano's talent and originality were already in evidence by this date. The architecture of the altarpiece is basically Palladian in design and reveals the classicizing tendencies in Cano's work. He broke dramatically with the traditional form of Sevillian altarpieces by employing a single giant order to unite the two lower storeys and by using a deep cornice above these, effectively reducing the third tier to the height of an 'attic'. He also increased the traditional width of the 'attic' to three sections instead of one, an arrangement reflecting the disposition of the lower storey. The artist's wooden polychrome sculpture of the *Virgin and Child*, which rests just above the altar, is even more innovative. Sevillian sculptors such as Martínez Montañés had previously sculpted the draped figure in order to maximize the play of light and shade. Cano simplified the surfaces, thus emphasizing instead the graceful contours of the figure.

1. Alonso Cano: *St John the Evangelist's Vision of the Heavenly Jerusalem*, oil on canvas, 826×438 mm, 1636–7 (London, Wallace Collection)

The only altarpiece by Cano in Seville to survive intact is that dedicated to St John the Evangelist in the convent church of S Paula. The semi-circular top of the altarpiece provides a clean, simple contour and is a fine example of Cano's work as an *ensamblador*. As at Lebrija, the middle storey of the altarpiece is marked by columns in a giant order, which frame the central figure of St John the Evangelist, carved by Martínez Montañés. The classically inspired architectural details, including several Italianate putti, are richer and more profuse than in the earlier work. The paintings, executed between late 1635, when the contract for the altarpiece was signed, and 1638, were dispersed in 1810. They included *St James the Great* and *St John the Evangelist with the Chalice* (both Paris, Louvre), *St John's Vision of God* and *St John's Vision of the Lamb* (both Sarasota, FL, Ringling Mus. A.), the *Communion of the Virgin* (attributed to Juan del Castillo by Wethey; Genoa, Pal. Bianco) and *St John the Evangelist's Vision of the Heavenly Jerusalem* (London, Wallace; see fig. 1). All six paintings portray large-scale figures set close to the picture plane, which would have been clearly legible within the complex ornamental framework. Cano's elegance of line and clear, pale colours bear more resemblance to the paintings of contemporary Bolognese classicizing artists than to the dark, sculptural images still being produced by his contemporaries in Seville. *St John the Evangelist's Vision of the Heavenly Jerusalem* is a particularly fine example of Cano's painting style during his Sevillian period. The craggy, expressive head of the saint is the only detail that reflects the forceful naturalism typical of much early Baroque painting in Spain. Although the angel is convincingly modelled and foreshortened, its graceful posture, the smooth anatomical rendering and elegance of line typify Cano's idealizing style. His use of colour is equally distinct from the rather sober range of local colours used by his contemporaries. The grey-green and yellow-green of the angel's drapery contrast delicately with the white and rose tones of St John's clothing. The figures are silhouetted against a pale green sky illuminated with soft, golden clouds, from which emerges the shimmering white visionary Jerusalem.

2. MADRID, 1638–52. In January 1638 Cano left Seville for Madrid as painter and Ayudante de Cámara to the Conde Duque de Olivares, first minister of Philip IV. The completion of the altarpiece in the church of S Paula was left to Cano's friend Juan del Castillo. Cano may have come to Olivares's attention at the suggestion of Velázquez, who had been in Madrid as painter to the King for some years. The continued friendship of the artists is attested by the fact that Velázquez and his assistant-servant Juan de Pareja acted as witnesses in the sale of Cano's house in Seville. The two painters worked together on several projects during Cano's years in Madrid.

Little is known of Cano's work for Olivares. He may have carried out few commissions for him other than the *Crucifixion* (Madrid, priv. col., see Wethey, 1955, pl. 105) painted for the Dominican nuns of the convent of Loeches. The convent itself was given to them by Olivares, who retired to Loeches when he fell from power in 1643. Cano's first commission from the King (1639–40) was to paint some of the 16 imaginary portraits of early kings of Spain, to be placed high on the walls of the Salón Dorado of the Alcázar in Madrid. The double portrait of *King Ferdinand II and Queen Isabella* known to have been commissioned from Cano is lost, but the dramatically foreshortened figures in two pictures, *A Spanish King* and *Two Spanish Kings* (both Madrid, Prado), firmly attributed to Cano on the basis of style, probably echo the composition of the missing picture.

2. Alonso Cano: *St Isidore and the Miracle of the Well*, oil on canvas, 2.16×1.49 m, *c*. 1646–8 (Madrid, Museo del Prado)

On 20 February 1640 the royal palace of El Buen Retiro was damaged by fire, and Cano was sent with Velázquez through Old Castile to gather paintings to replace those lost. He was also contracted to restore 160 of the canvases that were not irreparably damaged, giving him an unparalleled opportunity to study the royal collection. His close scrutiny of a collection rich in late 16th-century Venetian painting was reflected by a change in Cano's style, which became more fluid and painterly, as in *St Isidore and the Miracle of the Well* (*c*. 1646–8; Madrid, Prado; see fig. 2). The high degree of finish found in Cano's works during his period in Seville is tempered here by looser brushwork. Freely applied white highlights suggest the influence of the Venetian paintings he had studied and demonstrate his familiarity with the work of Velázquez.

Cano's life had already been marked by personal difficulties. In 1636 he had been in debtors' prison in Seville; he was bailed out by his friend Juan del Castillo. When Olivares resigned as minister to Philip IV in 1643, Cano must have felt insecure about his status in Madrid, for he wrote to Toledo Cathedral to apply for the position of Maestro Mayor (architect). Although he was unsuccessful, his application can be seen as an interesting reflection of his confidence as an architect. This was followed by more serious personal trouble. After the death of his first wife, in 1631 Cano had married Maria Magdalena de Uceda, the 12-year-old daughter of the painter Juan de Uceda Castroverde. Her extreme youth at the time of her marriage may be explained by the death of her father only a few months later; Castroverde must have been anxious to secure his daughter's future before he died. On 10 June 1644 Maria Magdalena was found in her bed, murdered by stab wounds. Cano was absolved of the murder, but he was tortured under suspicion of having hired her assassin. He was eventually declared innocent but nevertheless left Madrid to spend a year in Valencia. His return to the capital is documented by the contract of 20 September 1645 for the altarpiece dedicated to Our Lady of Peace in the church of La Magdalena at Getafe, near Madrid. The four studies he executed in preparation for the painting of the two lateral altars in La Magdalena document his working procedures. The bistre and wash *Annunciation* (Madrid, Prado), which shows the whole composition and was probably submitted to the donor for approval, was preceded by more rapid sketches in pen and bistre and by a pencil sketch of a single figure. The painting itself (*in situ*; see Wethey, 1952, fig. 4) was then executed by Cano's assistants.

Some of Cano's finest paintings date from between 1645 and 1652. Apart from the *Miracle of the Well*, these include the *Noli me tangere* (Budapest, Mus. F.A.), quite evidently based on the painting of the same subject by Correggio, which was in the royal collection (Madrid, Prado); the *Descent into Limbo* (Los Angeles, CA, Co. Mus. A.); one of the finest of Cano's depictions of the *Virgin of the Immaculate Conception* (Vitoria, Mus. Prov. B.A.); and a handsome example of the *Crucifixion*, of which he made a number of versions (one in Madrid, Real Acad. S Fernando, Mus.). His most notable architectural design during his period in Madrid was the triumphal arch at the Puerta de Guadalajara, part of the decorations for the royal entry in 1649 of Mariana of Austria, second wife of Philip IV. It was said to have been strikingly original, and Cano's reputation as an architect was sufficient for his advice to be sought on the building of the Ochavo Chapel in Toledo Cathedral in 1650.

3. GRANADA, FROM 1652. Having applied in a letter of 28 July 1651 for a position as prebendary in Granada Cathedral, and with the support of Philip IV for his appointment, Cano was given a conditional prebendary, which stipulated that he be ordained as a priest within the year and that he work on the unfinished decorations for the Cathedral, begun during the reign of Charles V. He complied by executing designs for a choir lectern and silver lamps for the altar and by beginning work on a series of seven large paintings (4.6 m high) based on scenes from the *Life of the Virgin* for the Cathedral sanctuary. He also designed a church and convent (*c.* 1652–3) for the nuns of the Angel Custodio, as well as painting fourteen pictures and carving five statues for them. The convent and church were both destroyed by the French in 1810; however, the church of La Magdalena, also in Granada, begun ten years after Cano's death, is undoubtedly an adaptation of his design. Three arches enclose a deep portico, reflecting the plan of the interior. The rather dry severity of the architectural details accords with Cano's classicizing taste.

The five statues for the Angel Custodio represent a return to the art of sculpture, which Cano had not practised during his years in Madrid. The little polychrome cedarwood *Virgin of the Immaculate Conception* (1655–6; Granada Cathedral, Sacristy) is one of his best-known sculptures. The pensive Virgin, her blue mantle forming a dramatically tapered, scalloped profile, is a more youthful interpretation of the *Immaculate Conception* he had painted while in Madrid and is the model for the painted version in the Cathedral sanctuary. It was widely copied and determined the style for renderings of the subject by artists in Granada such as Pedro de Mena and José de Mora during the following decades. The most impressive sculptures produced by Cano in Granada are the monumental polychrome wooden figures of *St Anthony of Padua with the Christ Child*, *St Joseph with the Christ Child* and *St James of Alcalá* (all Granada, Pal. Carlos V). These were designed for the Angel Custodio and executed with the assistance of Pedro de Mena between 1653 and 1657. The figures are shown walking, and the folds of the drapery provide richly varied surfaces. The suggestion of activity is simultaneously stilled by the figures' contemplative expression.

Cano delayed ordination, however, and in February 1655 the King granted him a further year to prepare himself. In October 1656 the Cathedral canons took Cano's prebendary from him, as he had failed his Latin examination. In 1657 he went back to Madrid to seek help from the King, who again intervened on his behalf, ensuring that the painter passed his examinations before the papal nuncio in Madrid. When Cano finally received holy orders, he was officially reinstated by royal edict in April 1658.

Between 1660, when he returned to Granada, and 1664 Cano completed the series of the *Life of the Virgin*, still *in situ* in the rotunda of Granada Cathedral. The *Presentation of the Virgin*, the *Annunciation*, the *Visitation* and the *Purification of the Virgin* were already finished, although the *Presentation* was reworked after 1660; the canons had initially rejected the work, apparently because the figures were too small to be clearly legible from below. In the three succeeding canvases—the *Birth of the Virgin*, the *Immaculate Conception* and the *Assumption of the Virgin*—Cano depicted fewer figures, which were much larger in scale. Clearly inspired by the large scale of the Venetian paintings in the royal collection, these paintings are fine examples of Cano's ability to create monumental architectural settings, strongly illusionistic heavenly vistas and large-scale figures of solemn grandeur.

When Cano completed his work for Granada Cathedral, the canons ordered him to vacate the space in one of the Cathedral towers that he had been using as a studio. He went to Málaga, where his most important legacy is the *Virgin of the Rosary* in the Cathedral, painted between 1665 and 1666. He returned to Granada in 1666 or 1667. On 4 May 1667 the Cathedral canons approved his design for the façade of the Cathedral, and he was appointed its architect. This was by far his most important work as an architect. The Cathedral was designed in the early 16th century by Diego de Siloe, and the *basamento* of the façade was already in place and one of the towers built when Cano contracted to complete it. The sculptural decoration was added in the 18th century. Cano probably based his design on Siloe's original plans for the façade, at least in the adaptation of a triumphal arch format and in the use of circular windows. Cano's design seems to have been inspired by the Isabelline style of portals protected by deep niches used, for example, on Salamanca Cathedral, but without the ornamental profusion characteristic of that style. The completed façade has the appearance of being composed of elements too thin and delicate for the scale, producing the beautiful but disquieting effect of an enormous altarpiece without paintings. Cano did not live to see the façade completed, however. He died only four months after his design was accepted, and his request to be buried in the Cathedral crypt was granted.

BIBLIOGRAPHY

M. Gómez-Moreno: 'Alonso Cano, escultor', *Archv Esp. A. & Arqueól.*, xi (1926), pp. 177–213
H. E. Wethey: 'Alonso Cano's Drawings', *A. Bull.*, xxxiv (1952), pp. 217–34
M. E. Gómez Moreno: *Alonso Cano: Estudio y catálogo de la exposición celebrada en Granada en junio de 1954* (exh. cat. by M. E. Gómez Moreno; Madrid, 1954)
H. E. Wethey: *Alonso Cano: Painter, Sculptor and Architect* (Princeton, 1955)
E. Rosenthal: *The Cathedral of Granada* (Princeton, 1961)
F. Chueca Goitia: 'Alonso Cano y su influjo en la arquitectura barroca', *Centenario de la muerte de Alonso Cano en Granada 1667–1967: Estudios* (Granada, 1969), pp. 111–27
J. Bernales Ballesteros: *Alonso Cano en Sevilla* (Seville, 1976)
N. A. Mallory: 'Notas sobre Alonso Cano', *Goya*, clxxx (1984), pp. 437–9
J. M. Serrera: 'Alonso Cano y los Guzmanes', *Goya*, clxcii (1986), pp. 336–47

SUZANNE STRATTON

Caño, El. Pre-Columbian site, sometimes referred to as the Temple Site, near Penonomé on the Río Caño, Coclé Province, central Panama. Major excavation was undertaken in 1925 by Hyatt Verrill, who referred to El Caño as a large ceremonial precinct with rows of stone columns, of which at least 100 had carved human or animal figures up to 2.1 m tall. The ceramics from El Caño are so similar to the elaborate polychrome ware from SITIO CONTE, *c.* 5 km to the south, that the two sites must have been contemporaneous. Olga Linares interpreted El Caño as a funerary or ceremonial centre or both, used from *c.* AD 500 until *c.* 900 and then abandoned. Nevertheless, the site was occupied at the time of the Spanish Conquest in the mid-16th century. The sculptures and associated ceramics have been acquired by numerous collections, including the Museo Nacional de Panamá, Panama City; the Museum of the American Indian, Heye Foundation, New York; and the Museum Rietberg, Zurich.

Verrill described the site as an area covering *c.* 40 ha, but only the central portion of *c.* 4 ha was cleared and excavated. His site plan shows a rectangular, north–south layout, with several groups of huge, roughly shaped, basalt phallic columns up to 6 m high, arranged in rows around a large central column. Verrill claimed that the rows were spaced to form lines radiating from the central column like the rays of the sun. To the sides of the rows of columns were rows of sculpted columnar human, anthropomorphic and animal figures facing east. Wolfgang Haberland divided the sculptures into two groups, labelled Penonomé I and II styles, but he made no suggestion that one group preceded the other. The first group comprises figures with only the heads carved in the round, while the limbs and details are carved in low relief on the surfaces of the columns. They represent tall, slim figures with no distinction between column and image. The Penonomé II group comprises figures carved in deeper, more rounded and naturalistic relief: much smaller figures are perched upon square columns, confined to the top or upper portion and not incorporated into them.

In addition to the large columnar and shaft sculptures, Verrill collected a number of smaller stone figures. Most are compact standing or squatting male images with arms attached and flexed across the abdomen. Some have one hand raised or freed from the body. All have elaborately arranged hair or wear a head covering. Most are crudely carved from porous stone, with few details and facial features discernible. All are boulder-like but vary in shape from rounded to elongated, from having legs to having a peg base. In general, they relate to some of the large columnar figures with neckless heads set directly on the shoulders, limbs in relief, legs drawn up as if squatting and arms across the torso.

For discussion of Pre-Columbian Panama *see also* SOUTH AMERICA, PRE-COLUMBIAN, §II.

BIBLIOGRAPHY

A. H. Verrill: 'Excavations in Coclé Province, Panama', *Ind. Notes*, iv (1927), pp. 47–61
S. K. Lothrop: 'Coclé: An Archaeological Study of Central Panama, Part 1', *Mem. Peabody Mus. Archaeol. & Ethnol.*, vii (1937) [whole issue]
——: 'Coclé: An Archaeological Study of Central Panama, Part 2', *Mem. Peabody Mus. Archaeol. & Ethnol.*, viii (1942) [whole issue]
R. G. Cooke: *The Archaeology of the Western Coclé Province of Panama* (diss., U. London, 1972)
R. Torres de Arauz: *Arte precolombino de Panamá* (Panama City, 1972)
W. Haberland: 'Stone Sculpture from Southern Central America', *The Iconography of Middle American Sculpture*, New York, Met. cat. (New York, 1973), pp. 134–53
O. F. Linares: *Ecology and the Arts in Ancient Panamá: On the Development of Social Rank and Symbolism in the Central Provinces*, Studies in Pre-Columbian Art and Archaeology, xvii (Washington, DC, 1977)

JOAN K. LINGEN

Cano de la Peña, Eduardo (*b* Madrid, 1823; *d* 1897). Spanish painter, watercolourist and illustrator. He trained at the Escuela de Nobles Artes in Seville (1833–40) and subsequently at the Real Academia de S Fernando in Madrid. He became a member of the Academia de S Isabel de Hungria of Seville in 1848, where he taught from 1859 and reformed the teaching of art. His early work shows traces of Neo-classicism, although his art is essentially based on Romanticism. Between 1851 and 1861 he concentrated on portrait painting, depicting mainly female subjects or children; examples include *Youth with a Dog* (Seville, Neana Col.), *Self-portrait* (Seville, Mus. B.A.) and *Josefa Garvey* (Seville, priv. col.). He was an important link between Romanticism and Realism and stimulated a renewed interest in history painting in Spain, a genre he established at the Exposición Nacional in 1856 with his painting *Christopher Columbus in the Convent of La Rábida* (Madrid, Pal. de las Cortes), which was awarded first prize. He won the same prize in 1858 with the *Burial of Don Alvaro de Luna* (Jaén, Mus. Prov.), and both of these paintings reflect the artist's interest in faithfully recording historical scenes. He also produced small-scale, costume paintings, which have a distinctive regional quality and sensual colouring, as in *Genre Scene in Seville* (1871; Brunswick, ME, Bowdoin Coll. Mus. A.), and was active as a muralist and as a watercolourist. In addition, he was an accomplished engraver, and among his illustrations are those for *La Sevilla pintoresca* (1844) by Amador de los Rios.

BIBLIOGRAPHY

J. Cascales y Muñoz: 'Eduardo Cano de la Peña', *Ilus. Esp. & Amer.* (1897), p. 263
——: *Las bellas artes plásticas en Sevilla* (Toledo, 1929)
A. Muro Orejon: *Apuntes para la historia de la Academia de Bellas Artes de Sevilla* (Seville, 1961)
G. Pérez Calero: *El pintor Eduardo Cano de la Peña, 1823–97* (Seville, 1979)
E. Valdivieso González: *Pintura sevillana del siglo XIX* (Seville, 1981)
G. Pérez Calero: 'Eduardo Cano y Mariano Fortuny', *Archv Esp. A.*, lix (1986), p. 418
C. Reyero Hermosilla: *Imagen histórica de España, 1850–1900* (Madrid, 1987)
G. Pérez Calero: 'Cano de la Peña, Eduardo', *Cien años de pintura en España y Portugal*, i (Madrid, 1988)
C. Reyers Hermosilla: *La pintura de historia en España* (Madrid, 1989)
La pintura de historia del siglo XIX en España (exh. cat., Madrid, Prado, 1992)

GERARDO PÉREZ CALERO

Canogar, Rafael (*b* Toledo, 17 May 1935). Spanish painter. In the late 1940s he studied privately under various painters, including Daniel Vázquez Díaz, also drawing in the afternoons at the Círculo de Bellas Artes in Madrid. He painted briefly in the style of Vázquez Díaz but in the early 1950s became interested in the work of major modernists such as Picasso, Braque and Miró. After the failure of his first commercial show, held in 1954 at the Galería Altamira in Madrid, he established contact with other painters, many of them trained by Vázquez Díaz, who joined together in 1957 as El Paso, through which *Art informel* became established as an influential current in Spanish art. Most of his paintings at this time, like those of his colleagues, were abstract, such as *Painting No. 41* (2×1.5 m, 1959; Madrid, Mus. A. Contemp.), typical in its sombre palette and violent, impulsive brushwork.

In the 1960s Canogar began to reintroduce imagery, sometimes using retouched press photographs as a starting-point for socially concerned images such as *Composition with Soldier* (Madrid, Mus. A. Contemp.). He soon applied this system of reworking found images to other types of material including well-known paintings from the history of art (e.g. *Portrait of a Woman, After Rubens*, 1966; Madrid, Mus. A. Contemp.), and in the early 1970s he began to experiment technically to obtain a variety of chromatic and textural effects, especially in figure sculptures and in painted reliefs such as *Urban Scene* (wood and polyester construction, 1.7×5 m, 1970; Madrid, Mus. A. Contemp.), in which he represented a crowd of silhouetted people. In the mid-1970s he began again to paint abstract pictures, some of them very large (e.g. the triptych *Painting P-22-78*, oil on canvas, 1.95×3.9 m, 1978; artist's priv. col., see exh. cat., pp. 130–31), combining a geometric structure with a simple (often monochromatic) colour scheme and a surface activated by gestural brushstrokes.

BIBLIOGRAPHY

Rafael Canogar: 25 años de pintura (exh. cat., essays E. Crispolti, M. Logroño and M. Padorno, Madrid, Bib. N., 1982)

MARÍA TERESA DABRIO GONZALEZ

Canon. *See under* MASTERPIECE.

Canonica, Luigi (*b* Roveredo di Tesserete, nr Lugano, 9 March 1762; *d* Milan, 7 Feb 1844). Italian architect and designer. He was a pupil of Giuseppe Piermarini at the Accademia di Brera, Milan, and later his assistant and collaborator. After the establishment of French rule in 1796, Canonica was appointed State Architect of Milan, replacing Piermarini who was too closely identified with the previous Habsburg regime. He was influenced by contemporary work in France and produced designs conforming closely to the directives of the French administration in Milan under Eugène de Beauharnais. He was not interested in the political and moral aspects of his work but designed formal and functional Neo-classical buildings.

In 1800 Canonica made a plan for a 'Città Bonaparte' to be built on an area to be made available by the demolition of parts of Milan's Castello Sforzesco. This was the first idea for the 'Foro Bonaparte', a new administrative centre for the city, for which GIOVANNI ANTONIO ANTOLINI also submitted a proposal that was initially accepted but subsequently rejected (1802) on grounds of cost (*see* MILAN, §I, 4). In 1805 Canonica submitted another design for the area, which responded more effectively to the prevailing economic and political circumstances. His plan differed from Antolini's in its 'liberal' character: it was concerned only with the general layout of the urban area and the façades of the buildings, behind which people could build their living quarters and shops according to their needs. The scheme was never completely realized and parts of the site were simply laid out as wooded landscape; the main work carried out involved the enlargement of the Piazza d'Armi at the castle and construction of the Arena, public gardens and tree-lined avenues. The triumphal arch planned for the end of the road to Paris, the Strada del Sempione, at the convergence of the avenues following the city walls, was built as the Arco della Pace (*see* MILAN, fig. 6) by Luigi Cagnola. In designing the Arena (1805; completed 1813) Canonica studied the surveys and the ideal reconstruction of the Circus of Caracalla made by Angelo Uggeri for G. L. Bianconi's *Descrizione dei circhi particolarmente di quello di Caracalla* (Rome, 1789), and as a result it was strongly imitative of ancient arenas.

As State Architect, Canonica supervised all the decorations erected in Milan for Napoleon's coronation as King of Italy in 1805. In preparation, he first visited Fontainebleau and Saint-Cloud. His designs included decorations, furnishings, furniture, illuminations, a covered walkway from the Palazzo Reale to the cathedral, and the uniforms of the dignitaries present at the ceremony; he thus acted as court architect, decorative designer and costume designer. The decorative structures included a number of temporary triumphal arches: of these, the one built at the Porta Vercellina was later re-erected in stone, the first permanent triumphal arch to be built during the Neo-classical period in Milan.

Following the success of the Arena, Canonica was commissioned to build a series of theatres. He used as his model the tradition of the tiered auditorium, of which the unsurpassed example was La Scala, Milan, built by Piermarini. Canonica's theatres included the Teatro Carcano (1803), Milan; Teatro della Concordia (1808), Cremona; Teatro Grande (interior, 1811), Brescia; Teatro Re (1813), Milan; and Teatro Sociale (1820–24), Sondrio. At La Scala he enlarged the stage and the adjacent areas (1814). His theatres were designed on a horseshoe plan, with tiers of private boxes placed directly one above the other and a relatively small entrance lobby.

When the Austrians returned to Milan, Canonica's public commissions were cancelled and in 1817 he was dismissed from his post as State Architect. From then on he worked mainly for private or religious patrons and built mostly villas and town houses, such as his own house in Via S Agnese (*c*. 1815); the Casa Porro Lambertenghi in Via Monte di Pietà (before 1816); Casa Brentani-Greppi in Via Manzoni (1829–31; now the Banca Commerciale Italiana); and Palazzo Anguissola-Traversi (1829–31), all in Milan. For these buildings he worked to a format consisting of a ground floor with smooth rustication, an optional mezzanine floor and two more floors divided by a string course and a balcony with an iron parapet. This approach produced façades that could be inserted into the most diverse environments. It also created continuous and uniform surfaces that threw into relief their few decorative details. It was immediately imitated and so widely diffused that it gave a characteristic look to the Neo-classical cityscape, which can be considered Canonica's most significant legacy.

BIBLIOGRAPHY

[G. Ricci: 'Voce Canonica Luigi', xviii (Rome, 1975)]
DBI
L'età neoclassica in Lombardia (exh. cat., ed. A. Ottino Della Chiesa; Como, Villa Olmo, 1959), pp. 76–9
C. L. V. Meeks: *Italian Architecture, 1750–1914* (New Haven and London, 1966), pp. 101, 106, 396
G. Mezzanotte: *Architettura neoclassica in Lombardia* (Naples, 1966), pp. 281–315
A. M. Brizio: 'Interventi urbanistici e architettonici a Milano durante il periodo napoleonico', *Atti del convegno sul tema: Napoleone e l'Italia: Rome, 1969*, pp. 413–27
Mostra dei maestri di Brera (1776–1859) (exh. cat., Milan, Pal. Permanente, 1975), pp. 70–72
R. Middleton and D. Watkin: *Architettura moderna* (Milan, 1977), pp. 68, 300, 422

GIANNI MEZZANOTTE

Canonica, Pietro (*b* Turin, 1 March 1869; *d* Rome, 8 June 1959). Italian sculptor, teacher, composer and musician. He studied sculpture from 1880 at the Accademia Albertina di Belle Arti in Turin, under Odoardo Tabacchi, and initially adhered to the traditions of Naturalism, with Romantic and Renaissance influences. He later turned to Realism, making no concessions to the more avant-garde artistic tendencies of the 20th century. He established his reputation with a series of portraits of society personalities, including *Emily Doria-Pamphili* (marble, h. 570 mm, 1904; Rome, Gal. Doria-Pamphili; copies, Rome, G.N.A. Mod. and Mus. Canonica) and *Donna Franca Florio* (marble, h. 1050 mm, *c*. 1903–4; Rome, Mus. Canonica), and also members of the British royal family, such as *Edward VII* (marble, h. 570 mm, 1903; London, Buckingham Pal., Royal Col.). His vast output includes many works with symbolic or sacred subject-matter, as well as numerous funereal and commemorative monuments. These include the model (plaster, h. 330 mm) and statue (marble, h. 3.28 m) of *Tirreno* (1907–11) for the monument to *Victor-Emanuel II* in Rome, the model for the monument to *Tsar Alexander II* (plaster, h. 2.48 m, 1912–14) at Petrodvorets, and the equestrian statue of *Kemal Ataturk* (bronze and marble, h. 10 m, 1927; Ankara). Other notable works include the *Alpino* (bronze and stone, h. 4 m, 1922) in Courmayeur and the funerary monuments to *Benedict XV* (marble and bronze, h. 12 m, 1928) in St Peter's, Rome, and to *Pius XI* (marble, 1941–9) in the Palazzo Laterano, Rome. After World War II Canonica executed mainly religious works, including the doors for the abbeys of Montecassino (1951) and Casamari (1959). He was professor of sculpture at the Accademia di Belle Arti in Venice (1910) and later at the Accademia di Belle Arti, Rome. He was elected Accademico d'Italia (1929) and a member of the Accademia Nazionale di San Luca (1930), eventually becoming a senator for life (1950) for his outstanding artistic achievements.

BIBLIOGRAPHY

F. Sapori: *Pietro Canonica scultore* (Rome, 1960)
M. A. Canonica: *Museo Canonica: Guida* (Rome, 1969)
N. Cardano and M. Caraci: *Canonica scultore e musicista* (Rome, 1985)

ANA MARIA RYBKO

Canonici, Matteo Luigi (*b* Venice, 1727; *d* Venice, *c*. 1805). Italian collector. He entered the Society of Jesus in Bologna in 1743 and was ordained in 1757, making his solemn profession to the Society in Parma in 1761. He collected his first historical manuscripts and medals in Parma but had to relinquish them when the Jesuits were expelled in 1767. He also collected paintings: for example he owned Correggio's *Zingarella* (Naples, Capodimonte), which he ceded to Prince Chigi. After the suppression of the Jesuits in 1773, Canonici returned to Venice and started seriously collecting books, especially Bibles, and manuscripts of all kinds. In forming his collection he corresponded and competed with all the best-known Italian scholars and bibliophiles, frequently making exchanges. His greatest coup was probably the acquisition *c*. 1780 of a large part of the famous collection of Jacopo Soranzo (1686–1761), which included many manuscripts from Bernardo Trevisan (1652–1720). Canonici's library was famous among his contemporaries, and after his death Giacomo Morelli tried unsuccessfully to negotiate its purchase for the Biblioteca Marciana in Venice. In 1817 Canonici's heirs sold the 'non-Venetian' part of his collection, nearly 3000 manuscripts, to the Bodleian Library, Oxford, for £5500. As well as 301 Italian and 1394 Latin manuscripts, many of them with fine illumination, the collection also included 124 Greek codices and 143 in Oriental languages (mainly Hebrew). A few Canonici manuscripts were sold in the Celotti sale in London, 26 February 1821, but most of the remaining manuscripts (*c*. 1000) were sold to the Rev. Walter Sneyd in 1835. The Canonici manuscripts bought by Sneyd were partly sold at Sotheby's in London on 25 June 1836; there were further sales on 16 December 1903 (the most important), 28 November 1927, 26 March 1929 (at Hodgson's), 27 June 1932 and 23 April 1934.

BIBLIOGRAPHY

I. Merolle: *L'Abate Matteo Luigi Canonici e la sua biblioteca* (Rome and Florence, 1958)

J. B. Mitchell: 'Trevisan and Soranzo: Some Canonici Manuscripts', *Bodleian Lib. Rec.*, viii/3 (1969), pp. 125–35 [with pls]

A. C. DE LA MARE

Canons Regular. *See* AUGUSTINIAN CANONS.

Canon table. Numerical list of concordant passages in the Gospels, devised in the early 4th century by the historian Eusebios of Caesarea. Such tables indicate passages to be found in all four Gospels, those found in two or three of the Gospels and those unique to a particular Gospel. In medieval manuscripts they appear as a series of pages, varying from seven to as many as nineteen, placed at the front of Gospel books and often included, preceding the Gospels, in full Bibles. It was customary to surround them with ornament and, despite the wide geographical and chronological range of this practice, the basic decorative format remained fairly constant. The tables are divided and framed by representations of architectural columns surmounted by arcades or, occasionally, pediments; pictorial matter is concentrated in the upper part of the design, which might contain decorative and symbolic bird and plant motifs as well as more explicit illustrative features, such as the Evangelist symbols or the Twelve Apostles. In Eastern manuscripts the tables are sometimes preceded by two or three pages of introductory text, similarly framed by architectural designs, and a further page of related ornament (e.g. a tempietto) might be included at the beginning or end.

It is probable that the architectural decoration of canon tables existed in the early 4th century, but the earliest extant examples are from the 6th century: fragments of an Italian Gospel book (Rome, Vatican, Bib. Apostolica, MS. Vat. lat. 3806) and the RABBULA GOSPELS (Florence, Bib. Medicea-Laurenziana, MS. Plut. I. 56), which is of Mesopotamian provenance and has canon tables bordered by a lengthy series of scenes from the *Life of Christ*. In the Gospel books produced by early medieval Insular artists, the canon tables are usually decorated with abstract devices characteristic of the Hiberno-Saxon style, although a more illustrative content appears in the BOOK OF KELLS (Dublin, Trinity Coll. Lib., MS. 58). Among the many sets of canon tables in Carolingian Gospel books and Bibles, those in the Gospel books of the late 8th-century First Court School of Charlemagne (Ada Group) are especially handsome, as exemplified by the tables in the Soissons Gospel book (St Médard Gospels; Paris, Bib. N., MS. lat. 8850, fol. 10*v*; see fig.). The distinctive canon table pages in the Ebbo Gospels (Epernay, Bib. Mun., MS. 1), a masterwork of the Carolingian Reims school, are illustrated with small genre figures at the top of the architectural patterns. Carolingian canon table decoration provided models followed in northern manuscript art during the 10th and 11th centuries, with particularly impressive results in many of the Ottonian Gospel books. By the end of the 12th century in western Europe, the making of luxury Gospel books had declined sharply with a consequent decline in the artistic importance of canon tables (*see* CAROLINGIAN ART, §IV, 3).

The early history of canon tables in the Byzantine East is difficult to follow due to the paucity of surviving manuscripts, although there was no doubt a strong tradition, continued in the sumptuous canon table pages in Byzantine Gospel books of the 11th and 12th centuries and later. Here, and generally in Eastern manuscripts, complex, predominantly geometric designs are used to ornament the architectural frames of the tables. In Armenian manuscripts of the Gospels (e.g. the ÉDJMIADZIN GOSPELS and the VEHAP'AR'S GOSPELS), still produced long after the medieval period, the ornamentation of the canon tables often recalls the rich intricate rhythms of Islamic art (*see* EARLY CHRISTIAN AND BYZANTINE ART, §V, 2 (ii) and (iii)). Related traditions of canon table design existed all round the peripheries of Eastern Christendom, as in the brightly painted Gospel books from Ethiopia, of which there are examples from as late as the 17th century (London, BL, MS. Orient. 481).

See also GOSPEL BOOK.

Canon table, 362×267 mm; from the Soissons Gospel book (St Médard Gospels), late 8th century (Paris, Bibliothèque Nationale, MS. lat. 8850, fol. 10*v*)

BIBLIOGRAPHY

C. Nordenfalk: *Die spätantiken Kanontafeln*, 2 vols (Göteborg, 1938)

J. Leroy: 'Recherches sur la tradition iconographique des canons d'Eusèbe en Ethiopie', *Cah. Archéol.*, xii (1962), pp. 173–204

Architectural canopy by Jan Gossart: *Virgin and Child with SS Catherine and Barbara* (the Malvagna Triptych), oil on panel, after 1511 (Palermo, Galleria Nazionale della Sicilia)

C. Nordenfalk: 'The Apostolic Canon Tables', *Gaz. B.-A.*, n. s. 5, lxii (1963), pp. 17–34

E. Klemm: 'Die Kanontafeln der armenischen Handschrift Cod. 697 im Wiener Mechitaristenkloster', *Z. Kstgesch.*, xxxv (1972), pp. 69–99

DON DENNY

Canopic jars. Set of four vases into which a mummy's internal organs were deposited. *See* EGYPT, ANCIENT, §§XII, 2(vi)–(vii).

Canopy (i). In architecture, a projecting, often ornamented roof above a stall, altar (see fig.), pulpit, screen, niche or effigy (*see also* GIOTTO, fig. 6).

See also CIBORIUM (ii).

Canopy (ii). Covering, usually of upholstery, positioned over or behind a bed or throne etc (*see* CLEVE, VAN (i), (1), fig. 1, and MEMLING, HANS, fig. 3).

□

Canossa, Matilda of. *See* MATILDA OF CANOSSA.

Canova, Antonio (*b* Possagno, nr Treviso, 1 Nov 1757; *d* Venice, 13 Oct 1822). Italian sculptor, painter, draughtsman and architect. He was the most innovative and widely acclaimed sculptor of NEO-CLASSICISM. His development during the 1780s of a new style of revolutionary severity and idealistic purity led many of his contemporaries to prefer his ideal sculptures to such previously universally admired Antique statues as the Medici *Venus* and the Farnese *Hercules*, thus greatly increasing the prestige of 'modern' sculpture. He was also much in demand as a portrait sculptor, often combining a classicizing format with a naturalistic presentation of features.

I. Life and work. II. Working methods and technique. III. Critical reception and posthumous reputation.

I. Life and work.

1. Sculpture. 2. Painting. 3. Other activities.

1. Sculpture.

(i) Training and early years in Venice, to 1779. (ii) Rome: papal tombs and other works of the early 1780s. (iii) The Cupid and Psyche theme and other works of the later 1780s. (iv) Works of the 1790s. (v) Funerary monuments and portraits, *c.* 1800–15. (vi) Ideal works, from *c.* 1800. (vii) Last works and the Temple at Possagno.

(i) Training and early years in Venice, to 1779. Antonio Canova was the son of Pietro Canova (1735–61), a stonecutter of Possagno. He was brought up by his grandfather, Pasino Canova (1714–94), a mediocre sculptor who specialized in altars with statues and low reliefs in late Baroque style (e.g. *Angels*; Crespano, S Marco, and Galliera Veneta, S Maria Maddalena). In 1770 or 1771 Antonio was apprenticed to the sculptor Giuseppe Bernardi (*d* 1774) in Pagnano, near Asolo, later following him to Venice. After Bernardi's death he worked for a few months in the studio of the sculptor Giovanni Ferrari (1744–1826). In Venice he studied the nude at the Accademia and the plaster casts of famous antique sculptures in Filippo Farsetti's collection. It was on the great stairway of Farsetti's palazzo on the Grand Canal that Canova's own first independent works—two *Baskets of Fruit* (marble, 1774; Venice, Correr)—were placed.

In 1775 Canova won second place in a competition at the Accademia with a small terracotta group of *Wrestlers* (Venice, Accad.), copied from a plaster cast owned by Farsetti of the famous antique group in the Uffizi, Florence. In the mid-1770s he was commissioned by Senator Giovanni Falier to carve stone statues of *Eurydice* and *Orpheus* (1775–7; Venice, Correr) for the garden of the Villa Falier at Pradazzi di Asolo. These works won him the favour of the Venetian patriciate: Marino Grimani commissioned a small marble replica of the *Orpheus* (St Petersburg, Hermitage); and the Procurator Lodovico Rezzonico commissioned six statues for his villa in Bassano (not carried out). Canova carved *Alvise Valaresso as Aesculapius* (marble, 1777–8) and *Giovanni Poleni* (limestone, 1779–80; both Padua, Mus. Civ.) for Andrea Memmo's scheme to adorn the Prato della Valle, Padua, with statues of illustrious men, the commissions being provided by the Marchesa Ernestina Stahrenberg Spinola and Leonardo Venier. The masterpiece of his early period, the marble group of *Daedalus and Icarus* (1778–9; Venice, Correr), was produced for the Procurator Pietro Pisani. Like *Eurydice* and *Orpheus*, these works represent the protagonists as nude figures, a decision that was particularly audacious in the case of *Alvise Valaresso.*

Canova moved from a strongly late Baroque orientation in the statues for the Falier garden towards a tempered classicism in the two works created for the Prato della Valle. A more complex aesthetic appears in *Daedalus and Icarus,* which earned him wide acclaim. The nude figures, posed with 'natural' attitudes and gestures, show Canova developing a new language, balanced between the naturalist tradition and the growing late 18th-century movement towards classicist idealization. The naturalistic figure of the old man, which is clearly influenced by the paintings of Giovanni Battista Piazzetta (especially his famous 'character heads'), is contrasted with the idealized figure of the young Icarus.

In 1779 Canova was nominated as a member of the Venetian Accademia, to which he offered a terracotta statue of *Apollo* (Venice, Accad.). This is a small model for one of the statues he had planned to produce for the Villa Rezzonico at Bassano and was inspired by Bernini's *Apollo and Daphne* (Rome, Gal. Borghese), of which there was a small plaster reproduction in the Farsetti gallery.

(ii) Rome: papal tombs and other works of the early 1780s. In October 1779 Canova went to Rome to study both ancient and modern art, a necessary step for an ambitious young artist. He gave a critical account of his experiences on the journey and in Rome in his *Quaderni di viaggio.* In Rome he was the guest of the Ambassador of the Venetian Republic, Girolamo Zulian, who was the main engineer of Canova's success in Rome. Canova was also patronized by the Venetian patrician Abbondio Rezzonico, a member of the Roman senate and nephew of Clement XIII. Canova made contact with artists, archaeologists, scholars and connoisseurs of classicist inclinations such as the painter Gavin Hamilton. He studied and sketched from antique sculptures and from the works of painters (especially Michelangelo) and frequented the studios of the most important artists working in Rome. He particularly admired the art of Pompeo Girolamo Batoni.

To introduce his own work to Roman society Canova sent to Venice for a plaster cast of *Daedalus and Icarus.* This had a moderate reception, but some reservations were expressed by critics who found it too far from antique prototypes. Canova, like nearly all the Roman sculptors of the time, refused to make copies of antique statues for Girolamo Zulian: he wished to emulate, not copy, the Ancients. In 1780 he visited Naples and the ancient sites at Pompeii, Herculaneum and Paestum, returning to Rome after a short stay in Venice to complete his statue of *Giovanni Poleni.*

For Abbondio Rezzonico Canova carved a marble statuette of *Apollo Crowning Himself* (Bahamas, priv. col., see Pavanello, 1990), inspired by the *Apollo of the Parnassus* fresco by Anton Raphael Mengs at the Villa Albani, Rome. The first important work in which he followed Neo-classical principles is *Theseus and the Minotaur* (marble, 1781–3; London, V&A), carved for Ambassador Zulian, who left Canova free to choose his own subject. In 1781 the ambassador also managed to obtain a three-year grant for Canova from the Venetian government, enabling him to continue working in Rome. Hamilton admired *Theseus and the Minotaur* and the French critic Antoine-Chrysostôme Quatremère de Quincy described it in 1834 as the first example in Rome of the true resurrection of antiquity. Canova represented Theseus in a tranquil moment after his victory, rather than representing the figures in action, as in the Baroque tradition, and while the Minotaur's body is naturalistically rendered, the figure of Theseus, inspired by the Ludovisi *Mars* (Rome, Mus. N. Romano), is classically idealized.

Canova's greatness and stylistic innovation were revealed to the wider public in the funerary monument he executed for *Clement XIV* (marble, 1783–7; Rome, SS Apostoli; *see* NEO-CLASSICISM, fig. 2), which was carved at the same time as Jacques-Louis David was painting his great statement of Neo-classical style, the *Oath of the Horatii* (Paris, Louvre). The ideas concerning sculpture of such Neo-classical theorists as Johann Joachim Winckelmann found expression in Canova's monument. The critic Francesco Milizia eulogized the monument, praising its repose, elegance and simplicity: to Winckelmann simplicity was the supreme aim of art (Cicognara, 1824). The monument follows the same general plan as that of the papal tombs of Bernini, but Canova reduced it to essentials: the seated statue of the pope occupies the place of honour at the summit of the triangular composition, and allegorical figures of the Virtues frame the sides of the sarcophagus. However, the triumphalistic accents of its Baroque prototypes have disappeared and the chosen Virtues are Humility and Temperance. The pope's gesture is no longer one of benediction: it is sacramental, indeed baptismal, recalling Jean-Antoine Houdon's statue of *St John the Baptist* (plaster, 1767–8; Rome, Gal. Borghese), which Canova had obviously studied closely, together with its pendant *St Bruno* (Rome, S Maria degli Angeli). Canova's extensive use of white Carrara marble and the formal geometry of his work testify to his renunciation of the Baroque.

Canova was also working on the funerary monument for *Clement XIII* (marble, 1783–92; Rome, St Peter). He again used the traditional pyramidal scheme, but spaces have an essential function, and figures are independent of one another. Piety and doctrine serve the theme of meditation on death. As in the monument for *Clement XIV*, the observer is invited to look upwards, into a symbolic space: from the lions at its base, custodians of the entrance to the sepulchre, to the idealized nude Genius of Death derived from Classical models, and the theological Virtues carved on the sarcophagus beside it, then to the colossal statue of Religion. The monument culminates in the figure of the pope kneeling in prayer with lowered eyes, his tiara beside him on the ground. His face is an excellent portrait in the Venetian realist tradition. The Genius of Death in particular was much admired by Canova's contemporaries. It has been suggested that this beautiful adolescent male figure is one of the most perfect realizations of Winckelmann's artistic ideal (Honour, *Neo-classicism*, 1968).

(iii) The Cupid and Psyche theme and other works of the later 1780s. Canova continued to explore the Neo-classical ideal of grace represented by the youthful nude body in the later 1780s in a series of statues and groups slightly less than life-size. Among them are the portrait of *Prince Henryk Lubomirski as Eros* (marble, 1786–8; Łańcut Castle, Poland), *Cupid* (marble, 1787–9; Anglesey Abbey, Cambs, NT) and the famous groups of *Cupid Awakening Psyche* (marble, 1783–93; Paris, Louvre; see fig. 1; replica with variations, 1794–6; St Petersburg, Hermitage) and *Cupid and Psyche Standing* (marble, 1796–1800; Paris, Louvre; replica, 1800–03; St Petersburg, Hermitage).

The myth of Psyche, with its theme of spiritual love transcending the senses, was of particular interest for Canova and clearly struck a responsive chord in the sensibilities of his contemporaries. In *Cupid Awakening Psyche* he drew inspiration from an ancient painting of a *Faun and Bacchante* discovered at Herculaneum, as is obvious from his terracotta sketch models (Venice, Correr; Possagno, Gip. Canoviana). Two figures clinging violently to each other are refined to more relaxed and balanced forms, but without any suppression of emotion. This passion contrasts with the more platonic *Cupid and Psyche Standing*, which Cicognara (1824) described as a 'delicate and gentle work, with figures that seem more like soft flesh than like hard stone'. The life-size marble *Venus and Adonis* (1789–94; Geneva, Villa La Grange), with its extremely refined modelling of the nude bodies and the skilful complexity of their entwining, continues this vein of delicate sensuality and is a prelude to Canova's masterpiece, the *Three Graces* (*see* §(vi) below). When it was first shown to the public, in Naples in 1795, *Venus and Adonis* was greeted with extraordinary enthusiasm, and Canova was described as the greatest contemporary sculptor in the erotic–mythological genre.

From 1787 to 1792 Canova produced a series of low reliefs in plaster with episodes from the life of Socrates, and from the *Iliad*, the *Odyssey* and the *Aeneid* (e.g. Possagno, Gip. Canoviana; Venice, Correr; Padua, Pal. S Bonifìcio). Taking 15th-century Tuscan sculpture, Gavin Hamilton's paintings and Attic vases as his stylistic sources, he experimented with new themes: sublime, tragic and violent (e.g. the *Imprisonment and Death of Socrates*, the *Death of Priam*, 1787–90), as well as graceful (the *Dance of the Children of Alcinous*, 1790–92). In these works Canova evoked Greek civilization through a style of Apollonian clarity, utilizing the possibilities of frieze composition and linear profiles in the subtlest ways.

1. Antonio Canova: *Cupid Awakening Psyche*, marble, 1.55×1.68 m, 1783–93 (Paris, Musée du Louvre)

(iv) Works of the 1790s. During the 1790s Canova continued to work with originality and variety of invention. He introduced a radical new development in the typology of the funerary monument with a scheme for a tomb for *Titian* to be erected in S Maria Gloriosa dei Frari, Venice (not executed; terracotta models, 1790–95; Possagno, Gip. Canoviana, and Venice, Correr). (The design was later adapted for the monument to *Maria Christina of Austria*; *see* §(v) below.) In the stele for *Admiral Angelo Emo* (marble, 1792–5; Venice, Mus. Stor. Navale), commissioned by the Republic of Venice, Canova authoritatively revived the model of the Classical stele. For this work he received a life pension, which was confirmed by the subsequent rulers of Venice, the French and the Austrians. In his stelae he tended progressively to reduce the depth of the relief. The *Emo* stele has almost fully rounded figures, whereas in the stele for *Nicola Antonio Giustiniani* (see fig. 2) he isolated the noble and magnificently draped personification of Padua against a smooth background plane.

The statue of the *Penitent Magdalene* (marble, 1794–6; Genoa, Mus. S Agostino) is a moving expression of religious sentiment, displaying an almost 19th-century sensibility in the accentuated naturalism of the semi-nude figure, weeping, crouched on the ground. The marble statues of the pugilists *Creugas* (1795–1801) and *Damoxenos* (1795–1806; both Rome, Vatican, Mus. Pio-Clementino) and the colossal marble *Hercules and Lichas* (1795–1815; Rome, G.N.A. Mod.), demonstrate Canova's ability to produce heroic and sublime statuary centred on the themes of strength, physical pain and madness. Foremost is *Hercules and Lichas*, in which Canova depicted the

2. Antonio Canova: stele for *Nicola Antonio Giustiniani*, marble, 1.86×1.27 m, 1796–7 (Padua, Museo Civico)

3. Antonio Canova: tomb of *Maria Christina of Austria*, in the Augustinian church, Vienna, marble, h. 5.74 m, 1798–1805; from an engraving by Pietro Bonoto, 1805 (Vienna, Österreichische Nationalbibliothek)

madness of Hercules flinging young Lichas into the sea. Clearly Canova wished to create a modern equivalent of the antique Farnese *Hercules*. Drawing inspiration from the Greek tragedies, he portrayed Hercules, the traditional symbol of virtuous strength, subjugated by irrational forces. The engraving after *Hercules and Lichas*, commissioned by Canova, was dedicated to Melchior Cesarotti (1730–1808), the translator of Homer and Ossian, who played an essential role in Canova's artistic development. In translating from the Greek, Cesarotti sought to interpret the spirit of the text, maintaining its original life and grace. Similarly Canova reinterpreted antique statuary, eschewing copies or casts, seeking to express a free and modern version of Classical style and sensibility.

(v) Funerary monuments and portraits, c. *1800–15.* From the early years of the 19th century Canova was the most celebrated artist in Europe. It was largely thanks to his reputation that Rome continued to be a prestigious centre of contemporary art. He was in demand for the most important occasions and received countless commissions, many of which remained unfinished. His most remarkable and prestigious monumental work of the 19th century is the tomb of *Maria Christina of Austria* (see fig. 3) in the Augustinian church, Vienna. This was commissioned by Herzog Albrecht von Sachsen Teschen, the husband of Maria Christina, during a visit made to Vienna by Canova in 1798 and is among the most notable creations of Neo-classical art. While the earlier monuments to *Clement XIV* and *Clement XIII* are Neo-classical reinterpretations of Baroque funerary monuments, that to *Maria Christina* is a completely original work, in which statues are totally independent of the architectural structure. Here, Canova developed the scheme originally intended for the monument to *Titian*, with the idea of a cortège of people moving—like a secular version of the procession of the Marys to the sepulchre—towards the open door of the tomb. The pyramidal tomb recalls the tombs of ancient Egypt, and the tomb of *Caius Cestius* in Rome. All traces of the traditional sarcophagus have disappeared. The deceased is no longer exalted: she is remembered only in a portrait medallion high up on the pyramid. The whole is a meditation on the theme of death and the inexorable progress of humanity towards it.

Smaller in scale, but also striking, is Canova's monument to the great Italian tragic poet *Vittorio Alfieri* (marble, 1804–10; Florence, Santa Croce). This consists of a rectangular sarcophagus raised on a simple two-tier podium and decorated with a portrait medallion of the poet. The geometrical perfection of the structure and the single colossal figure of Italy weeping at the sarcophagus (the first personification of the Italian nation) were greatly admired by contemporaries. Canova made a series of studies for a monument to *Horatio, Viscount Nelson* (*c.* 1806; e.g. plaster, wax and terracotta sketch; Possagno, Gip. Canoviana) and numerous marble stelae, in which he strove for neo-Attic purity through increasingly formal abstraction. These show enormous care in the modulation of the relationships between the figures and the background plane. Examples include that for *Giovanni Volpato* (1804–7; Rome, SS Apostoli), the *Orange-Nassau* stele (1806–8; Delft, Nieuwekerk), two *Mellerio* stelae (1812–

13; Palermo, Sopr. Beni Cult. & Amb.) and the *Trento* stele (1813–15; Vicenza, Chiostro di S Pietro).

Canova was a prolific portrait sculptor, and after 1800 was in great demand among European sovereigns and other notables. He could employ traditional naturalism in the rendering of features and drapery, as in two busts of *Pius VII* (both marble, 1803–4; Versailles, Mus. Hist.; 1806–7, Rome, Protomoteca Capitolina), or combine a classicizing format with a moderated naturalism in the treatment of character, derived from Roman portrait sculpture of the Republican period, e.g. bust of *Domenico Cimarosa* (marble, 1808; Rome, Protomoteca Capitolina). Canova also produced a colossal heroic nude statue portraying *Napoleon as Mars the Pacifier* (marble, 1803–6; London, Apsley House; bronze replica, 1809; Milan, Brera), and planned a bronze equestrian statue of the Emperor, which was later completed as a statue of *Charles III of Naples and Spain* (1807–19; Naples, Piazza Plebiscito). Among his other portrait statues are those of *Ferdinand IV of Naples as Minerva* (marble, 1800–20; Naples, Capodimonte), a colossal work whose rhetorical emphasis on majesty contrasts with the uncompromisingly truthful depiction of the king's rather unattractive features, and of *George Washington* portrayed as an ancient legislator (marble, 1817–21; destr.; plaster model, Possagno, Gip. Canoviana) for the Capitol at Raleigh, NC.

Canova's portraits were particularly in demand from members of Napoleon's family and entourage, of whom he made numerous busts, such as those of *Cardinal Joseph Fesch*, Napoleon's uncle (marble, 1807–8; Ajaccio, Mus. Fesch), and *Alexandrine Bleschamps*, the wife of Lucien Bonaparte (plaster, 1808; Possagno, Gip. Canoviana). Among his portrait statues of the Bonaparte family were those of Napoleon's mother, *Letizia Ramolino ('Madame Mère')*, seated (marble, 1804–7; Chatsworth, Derbys) and of the *Empress Marie Louise as Concordia*, also seated (marble, 1810–14; Parma, G.N.). The most famous and fascinating portrait is that of *Paolina Borghese Bonaparte as Venus Victorious* (marble, 1804–8; Rome, Gal. Borghese), in which Canova revived the Venuses of the Venetian school of the 16th century. The sensuality of the nude figure, modelled with exquisite softness, contrasts with the artificiality of the pose; the face is in profile and the subject seems to be trying to evade the gaze of the onlooker. The refinement with which the marble is finished was brought out to the full by the artificial light in which the work was originally shown, in a room set aside for it alone.

(vi) Ideal works, from c. *1800.* In 1811 Canova began a series of ideal heads in marble (e.g. *Clio*, Montpellier, Mus. Fabre; *Calliope*, Florence, Pitti; *Helen*, Venice, Pal. Albrizzi), a genre in which he achieved some singular results in his search for ideal beauty—notably the *Vestal Tuccia* (Milan, Gal. A. Mod.). He had already begun work on the colossal marble group of *Theseus and the Centaur* (1804–19; Vienna, Ksthist. Mus.), which, like *Hercules and Lichas*, presents a rigorously frontal view. Canova again reinterpreted the Baroque tradition in Neo-classical terms: he froze movement and gesture in calculated correspondences, within a syntax of abstract articulations. There is an obvious reference to the antique *Laokoon* group (Rome, Vatican, Mus. Pio-Clementino) in the face of the defeated centaur.

In the first decades of the 19th century Canova produced a remarkable series of ideal masterpieces in an erotic vein: *Venus Emerging from the Bath* (*Venus Italica*, marble, 1804–12; Florence, Pitti; replica made for Ludwig I of Bavaria, 1807–10; Munich, Residenz), *Paris* (marble, 1807–12; St Petersburg, Hermitage; replica made for Ludwig I of Bavaria, 1810–16; Munich, Neue Pin.), the *Three Graces* (marble, 1812–16; St Petersburg, Hermitage; replica made for John Russell, 6th Duke of Bedford; see fig. 4), *Mars and Venus* (marble, 1815–22; London, Buckingham Pal., Royal Col.) and *Endymion Sleeping* (marble, 1819–22; Chatsworth, Derbys).

The statue of *Venus Italica* was intended for the *Tribuna* of the Uffizi in Florence, to replace the Medici *Venus*, which the French had carried off to the Louvre. Only Canova was considered worthy of competing with ancient Greek and Roman sculpture. The statue of *Paris*, carved for the Empress Josephine, was particularly admired by Cicognara, who wrote: 'if one could make statues by caressing marble, I would say that this statue was formed by wearing out the marble that surrounded it with caresses

4. Antonio Canova: *Three Graces*, marble, h. 1.67 m, 1815–17 (on view at Edinburgh, National Gallery of Scotland, or London, Victoria and Albert Museum)

and kisses' (Cicognara, 1973, p. 54). In *Paris* Canova again achieved the extraordinary softness of touch inspired by Correggio and the great painters of the Venetian Renaissance. The grace of Correggio also seems to underlie the *Three Graces* carved for Josephine. This was Canova's masterpiece, and perhaps the most representative work of Neo-classical taste—classicizing, yet in form and sentiment quite distinct from any work of antiquity. Three young female figures in whispered conversation are linked in soft intertwinings of arms and bodies. The mythological archetype is brought to life in the present, in the sphere of ideal beauty. It was praised, almost without exception, by Canova's contemporaries, including Quatremère de Quincy, and inspired poems by Ugo Foscolo and Ludwig I of Bavaria.

Canova also experimented with the movement of the female body in three marble statues: *Dancer with her Hands on her Hips* (1805–12; St Petersburg, Hermitage; replica, 1818–22; Ottawa, N.G.), *Dancer with a Finger Touching her Chin* (1809–14; untraced; plaster model, Possagno, Gip. Canoviana) and *Dancer with Crotal* (an antique clapper or castanet) (1811–15; Berlin, Skulpgal.). The extraordinary technical virtuosity of these works creates a new rhythm of grace, elegance and poised movement, in which the boundary between the nude and the draped figure almost disappears; the anatomical forms and the light veils reveal the body more than they hide it and together define a new canon of beauty.

Canova continued to explore the artistic possibilities of groups of figures after the *Three Graces*, returning to the sensuality of his early *Venus and Adonis* with *Mars and Venus*, carved for the Prince Regent, later George IV. He interpreted the longing for peace that filled Europe after the Napoleonic Wars by portraying Mars conquered by his love for Venus. Other reclining nude figures carved for the Prince Regent include the *Naiad* (marble, 1815–17) and the unfinished *Dirce* (marble, 1819–22; both London, Buckingham Pal., Royal Col.).

In the reclining marble statue of *Endymion Sleeping*, taking his inspiration from the funerary genius of the monument to *Clement XIII* of 30 years before, Canova expressed a new ideal of male beauty, captured in the young sleeping shepherd about to be visited by Diana. The marble is worked with astounding virtuosity to render the different surfaces: skin, hair, cloth, the dog's coat, the rocky outcrop. This can be compared with the unfinished *Sleeping Nymph* (marble, 1820–22; London, V&A; plaster model, 1820; Possagno, Gip. Canoviana), which was inspired by the antique Borghese *Hermaphrodite* (Paris, Louvre). The sensual softness of the *Sleeping Nymph*, modulated with exquisite elegance, bears further comparison with the nudes of Jean-Auguste-Dominique Ingres.

(vii) Last works and the Temple at Possagno. In his last years Canova showed himself to be a sensitive interpreter of changing tastes in the art world, moving towards great formal purity while retaining a Romantic sensibility. In the funerary genre he showed particular inventiveness in the cenotaph to the *House of Stuart* (marble, 1817–19), commissioned by the British Government and erected in St Peter's, Rome, to commemorate the Old and Young Pretenders and Cardinal York. At the top, on a corbel, are the busts of the three subjects and the family crest. Emphasis is on the closed door of the cenotaph and the nude mourning geniuses that stand beside it with reversed torches. These two youthful figures, which Stendhal admired to the point of hyperbole, are modelled with extreme refinement, so that again the marble becomes 'soft flesh' and the carving of the drapery seems designed to reveal the nude. As in the monuments to *Clement XIII* and *Maria Christina of Austria*, the fugitive beauty of the adolescent is intimately linked with the thought of death and is designed to inspire meditation on the transcendent idea of beauty fixed by art.

Canova also sought new forms of expression in his sacred sculpture. Returning to the theme of Mary Magdalene, which was particularly suitable for rendering in the nude, he carved a statue of the *Fainting Magdalene* (marble; untraced; plaster model, 1819–22; Possagno, Gip. Canoviana), for Robert Banks Jenkinson, 2nd Earl of Liverpool (1770–1828), in which the figure lies in a pose of languid abandon, suffused with pathos. In November 1821 Canova also finished modelling his last completed work, a *Lamentation* (plaster model; Possagno, Gip. Canoviana), returning to the subject of his painted altarpiece (Possagno, Temple) retouched for the last time that same year (*see* §2 below). Formal simplicity expresses a resigned view of the mystery of death.

In his late portraits Canova, following the example of his passionate *Self-portrait* (marble, 1812; Possagno, Temple), accentuated the inner nobility of the subjects. In 1822, on his own initiative, he made colossal portrait busts of his three dearest friends: *Antonio d'Este* (plaster; untraced), the director of his Roman studio, *Leopoldo Cicognara* (unfinished, marble; Ferrara, Certosa) and the *Abate Giambattista Sartori* (1775–1858; bust unfinished, marble; Bassano, priv. col.; see 1992 exh. cat., no. 141), his half-brother, who was his personal secretary from 1800. A marble statue of *Pius VI* (Rome, Grotte Vaticane), commissioned in 1817 for the Confession in St Peter's, was also left partly unfinished. For the portrait of the pope, who died in exile in 1799, Canova repeated the pose of the statue of *Clement XIII*, with greater emphasis on the attitude of fervent oration expressed by the open mouth and the eyes raised to heaven, as in the saints of Guido Reni's altarpieces.

To celebrate the return of Pius VII to Rome in 1814 Canova offered to the Basilica of St Peter a colossal statue (h. 8 m) of *Religion* (half-size plaster model; Possagno, Gip. Canoviana). When this was refused he decided to build a new church in his native Possagno. The construction of the Temple of Possagno began in 1819, and Canova devoted the last years of his life to it.

Canova conceived a combination of the Doric portico of the Parthenon with the circular, domed, space of the Pantheon to create a symbolic synthesis of the Greek, Roman and Christian civilizations, and to represent the rebirth of religious sensibility. For the entablature of the porch of the Temple he modelled seven metopes (plaster, 1820–22; Possagno, Temple) with episodes from the Old and New Testaments, in which he was clearly inspired by the work of 15th-century Italian sculptors. The Temple also became Canova's mausoleum, for while his heart is preserved in the monument to *Canova* in the Church of the Frari, Venice, and his right hand in a vase at the Accademia di Belle Arti, Venice, the rest of his body was placed in a tomb at Possagno constructed from the funeral monument to the *Marchese Beriò*, which Canova left unfinished in 1822, and which again shows the influence of the 15th century. Sartori, who was named by Canova as his sole heir, finished the construction of the Temple in 1830. He also had the Gipsoteca Canoviana (Francesco Lazzari, 1834) built next to the house where the artist was born, to hold the original plasters, terracotta and marble works and paintings that remained in the artist's studio in Rome. These works, which were installed in the Gipsoteca in 1836, form a fascinating museum of Canova's figurative ideas.

2. PAINTING. In 1780 Canova began painting under the guidance of his friend Martino de Bonis, working in a style reminiscent of Giorgione (e.g. *Venus with a Mirror*, *c.* 1785; Possagno, Gip. Canoviana). At first these exercises had the character of a hobby, although some contemporary critics admired them. However Cicognara suggested their real value lay in their function as studies of ideas to be worked out in sculpture.

Canova used painting to explore figurative themes and to develop new ideas, often well before they entered his sculptural works. He created a canon of feminine beauty that contained elements taken from Leonardo and Correggio. Canova's painting—together with his drawings and sketches—is fundamental to the creative process. His masterpiece is the large altarpiece for the parish church of Possagno (later placed in the Temple), painted in 1798–9 and retouched in 1810 and 1821. This depicts the *Lamentation*, and was inspired by Anton Raphael Mengs's altarpiece (Barcelona, Pal. Pedralbes) of the *Apparition of God the Father over the Dead Christ*. The Possagno altarpiece is a sublime meditation on the theme of death and on the end of a historical epoch, marked by the fall of the Republic of Venice in 1797 and the imprisonment of Pius VI. In this altarpiece Canova showed a marked interest in the art of the Italian painters of the 14th century and in John Flaxman's austere line engravings on Classical themes. The upper part of the composition is dominated by the radiant halo of the Eternal Father, inspired by the *Zeus* of Otricoli (Rome, Vatican, Mus. Pio-Clementino). As Argan (1970) pointed out, this iconographic borrowing reveals a profound certainty that the ideal form of art could be produced only by 'a syncretism of the Classical and the Christian'.

3. OTHER ACTIVITIES. Canova worked tirelessly in the service of the arts, often spending large sums of his own money to aid artists and cultural institutions and to promote the conservation of the artistic heritage. In 1802 he was nominated by Pius VII as Ispettore Generale delle Antichità e Belle Arti of the Papal States. He took a great interest in archaeological excavations, in acquiring works of art for the Vatican Museums and in stemming the export of works of art. He antagonized Ludwig I of Bavaria by denying him permission to export the Barberini *Faun* (Munich, Glyp.) to Munich. (The permission was later extorted from Pius VII by Francis I of Austria.) Although his early election to the Accademia di S Luca in Rome was blocked by the jealousy of rival sculptors until 1800, he was elected president in 1810 and perpetual president in 1814. He devoted much of his large income to helping students. In Paris in 1815 (after the final fall of Napoleon) Canova worked to recover the works of art removed by the French from the Papal States and from Italy during the Napoleonic Wars. This was a difficult task, in which he was helped by several illustrious Englishmen, including Arthur Wellesley, 1st Duke of Wellington; William Richard Hamilton (1777–1859); Charles Long, 1st Baron Farnborough; and Robert Stewart, Viscount Castlereagh (1769–1822), to whom in 1818 he presented some of his ideal heads as a sign of gratitude. Pius VII, for his part, named Canova Marchese d'Ischia. In 1815 the artist went to London to certify the authenticity of the Phidian marbles of the Parthenon (taken to England by Thomas Bruce, 7th Earl of Elgin), which made a tremendous impression on him. With great critical acumen, he advised that they should not be subjected to restoration.

II. Working methods and technique.

Canova's working methods were intended to allow him the greatest possible freedom while completing the maximum number of commissions. He even contrived to continue with literary and historical study by having selected texts read to him while he worked. Following a practice begun in Venice and perfected in the execution of the monument to *Clement XIV*, certain stages of production were delegated to his studio assistants (who were in fact workmen rather than pupils).

'Sketch with fire and execute with phlegm': this maxim of Winckelmann's could be taken as a summary of Canova's method. From the clay sketch to the finished marble the work was rigorously controlled so that Canova could check the results and make corrections at every stage of the process. From the drawings (almost all in Bassano del Grappa, Mus. Civ.) and from the clay sketch that fixed his first intuition (sometimes anticipated by paintings), Canova went on to execute a small model, to which he then devoted a deeper study, in which the invention was subjected to further exploration and testing. When he was satisfied he would produce a full-size clay model, from which a plaster cast was made. On this he would mark the key points for measurement, and his studio workers would then proceed to rough out the figure in marble. Canova himself did the finishing, giving the work what he and his contemporaries called the last touch: this very important part of the process was made by candlelight using special tools. After the 'polisher' had given the marble a diaphanous luminosity, Canova applied a patina (now lost) on the skin surfaces. This brought out the tonal difference between skin and clothing, giving to flesh an immaculate whiteness.

The artist's last touch was a seal of authenticity, and it was in that process that Canova made the most decisive modifications with respect to the plaster model. For this reason it is not legitimate to assign to Canova—except as regards the basic idea—the marble statues that remained uncompleted in the studio at his death. On the other hand, the replicas of his statues and groups may be considered authentic, even when these were made several years apart and for different patrons, since he kept in his studio not only the original models but also plaster casts made from the finished marble works before they were sent to their owners; patrons often visited the studio and made their selection from among these.

Canova's system of work concentrated on the initial idea, and on the final carving of the marble. It encompassed a rigorous process of sublimation of the image: from the violence of the first intuition, captured so roughly as to be almost formless, to the meditative serenity of pure form, placing great emphasis on concentration and reflection.

Canova never had pupils nor wanted them: the workers in his studio cannot be considered as such. His reluctance to take pupils derived from an awareness that while he might be able to teach a method of work he could not transmit the secret of his art. Canova's consciousness of the originality of the artist, and the singularity of his every expression, was one of the major marks of his modernity.

III. Critical reception and posthumous reputation.

Few artists have been so highly praised in their lifetime as Canova or have seen their art so widely acclaimed by critics, connoisseurs, poets and writers. Winckelmann's aspiration towards an art that would transcend time to radiate the serenity of ideal Beauty seemed finally to have been realized. In an age that insisted on the will and moral energy of single individuals as a prerequisite for progress and for any possible redemption, Canova's life was exemplary. His achievements far transcended his modest beginnings, and he lived his commitment to art with total dedication as if it were a new form of lay priesthood.

Much was written about Canova during his lifetime, from newspaper and magazine articles to more scholarly monographic studies, and engravings of his works occupied a special sector of the art market and were in demand everywhere. His death provoked universal mourning: there was an awareness that Canova was the last heir of the great Italian artistic tradition. On the wave of emotion surrounding his death, between 1822 and 1825, many volumes of essays, biographies and collections of verses were published—all eulogistic in character. This body of writing was crowned by the work of Quatremère de Quincy (1834) and by the *Memorie* of d'Este (1864).

The critics of the Romantic period included Canova's works in their condemnation of Neo-classicism, and the artist was soon forgotten. Only the works of his early period in Venice, and a few isolated sculptures, such as the papal monuments to *Clement XIV* and *Clement XIII* and the statue of *Paolina Borghese Bonaparte* were exempt from this blanket judgement, because they were considered free of Neo-classical traits. Only in the second half of the 20th century did Canova re-emerge, not only as a sculptor, but also as the creator of a taste and the protagonist of a crucial moment at the dawn of the modern epoch. The importance and value of Canova's art is now recognized as holding in balance the last echo of the Ancients and the first symptom of the restless experimentation of the modern age.

WRITINGS

E. Bassi, ed.: *I quaderni di viaggio* (Venice and Rome, 1959)
H. Honour, ed.: *A. Canova: Scritti* (Rome, 1994)

BIBLIOGRAPHY

EARLY SOURCES

F. Tadini: *Le sculture e le pitture di A. Canova pubblicate fino a quest'anno 1795* (Venice, 1796)
C. L. Fernow: 'Über den Bildhauer Antonio Canova und dessen Werke', *Romische Studien*, i (Zurich, 1806)
Catalogo cronologico delle sculture di A. Canova (Rome, 1817)
I. Teotochi-Albrizzi: *Opere di scultura e di plastica di A. Canova*, 14 vols (Pisa, 1821–4)
P. A. Paravia: *Notizie intorno alla vita di A. Canova* (Venice, 1822)
Alcune lettere di A. Canova ora per la prima volta pubblicate [per nozze Emo Capodilista-Maldura] (Venice, 1823)
L. Cicognara: *Biografia di A. Canova* (Venice, 1823)
G. Falier: *Memorie per servire alla vita del marchese A. Canova* (Venice, 1823)
G. Tambroni: *Intorno alla vita di A. Canova* (Venice, 1823)
Biblioteca canoviana, 4 vols (Venice, 1823–4)
L. Cicognara: *Storia della scultura dal suo risorgimento in Italia fino al secolo di Canova*, vii (Prato, 1824)
M. Missirini: *Della vita di A. Canova* (Prato, 1824)
H. Moses: *The Works of A. Canova* (London, 1824)
J. S. Memes: *Memoirs of Canova* (Edinburgh, 1825)
G. Rosini: *Saggio sulla vita e sulle opere di A. Canova* (Prato, 1825)
Lettere inedite di Antonio Canova (Padua, 1833)
A.-C. Quatremère de Quincy: *Canova et ses ouvrages* (Paris, 1834)
Lettere familiari inedite di A. Canova e di Giannantonio Selva (Venice, 1835)
Lettere inedite di Leopoldo Cicognara ad A. Canova (Padua, 1839)
D. Anzelmi: *Opere scelte di A. Canova* (Naples, 1842)
Lettere scelte dall'inedito epistolario di A. Canova [per nozze Lampertico-Colleoni] (Vicenza, 1854)
P. Giordani: *Epistolario*, ed. A. Gussalli (Milan, 1854–5)
G. J. Ferrazzi: *Nelle solenni esequie di Monsignore Giambattista Sartori-Canova* (Bassano, 1858)
A. d'Este: *Memorie di A. Canova* (Florence, 1864)
V. Malamani: *Un'amicizia di A. Canova: Lettere di lui al conte L. Cicognara* (Città di Castello, 1890)
L. Cicognara: *Lettere ad A. Canova*, ed. G. Venturi (Urbino, 1973)

GENERAL

DBI
R. Zeitler: *Klassizismus und Utopia* (Stockholm, 1954)
C. Maltese: *Storia dell'arte in Italia, 1785–1943* (Turin, 1960)
M. Praz: *Gusto neoclassico* (Naples, 1961)
G. Hubert: *La Sculpture dans l'Italie napoléonienne* (Paris, 1964)
——: *Les Sculpteurs italiens en France sous la Révolution, l'Empire et la Restauration, 1790–1830* (Paris, 1964)
Arte neoclassica: Atti del convegno 12–14 ottobre, 1957 (Venice and Rome, 1964)
H. Honour: *Neo-classicism*, Style & Civiliz. (Harmondsworth, 1968)
F. Boyer: *Le Monde des arts en Italie et la France de la Révolution et de l'Empire* (Turin, 1969)
G. C. Argan: 'Studi sul neoclassico', *Stor. A.*, 7–8 (1970), pp. 249–66
The Age of Neoclassicism (exh. cat., London, RA and V&A, 1972), pp. 195–214

MONOGRAPHS

A. G. Meyer: *Canova* (Bielefeld and Leipzig, 1898)
V. Malamani: *Canova* (Milan, 1911)
E. Bassi: *Canova* (Bergamo, 1943)
A. Muñoz: *A. Canova: Le opere* (Rome, 1957)
A. González-Palacios: *A. Canova* (Milan, 1966)
G. C. Argan: *Antonio Canova* (Rome, 1969)
G. Pavanello: *L'opera completa del Canova* (Milan, 1976)
F. Licht: *Canova* (New York, 1983)
G. Barbieri and M. Pavan: *Canova scultore pittore architetto a Possagno* (Citadella, 1990)
Antonio Canova (exh. cat. by G. Pavanello and G. Romanelli, Venice, Correr, 1992)

DRAWINGS

G. M. Pantaleoni: *Disegni anatomici di A. Canova* (Rome, 1949)
E. Bassi: *A. Canova* (Milan, 1957)
C. L. Ragghianti: 'Studi sul Canova', *Crit. A.*, xxii (1957), pp. 3–102
E. Bassi: *Il Museo Civico di Bassano: I disegni di Antonio Canova* (Venice, 1959)
Antonio Canova Tegninger fra Museet i Bassano (exh. cat. by B. Passamani, Copenhagen, Thorvaldsens Mus., 1969)
H. Ost: *Ein Skizzenbuch A. Canovas* (Tübingen, 1970)

A. González-Palacios: 'Sei fogli di A. Canova', *A. Illus.*, v (1972), pp. 160–62
U. Ruggeri: 'Un taccuino del Canova', *Crit. A.*, xxix (1974), no. 136, pp. 65–80; no. 137, pp. 77–88; no. 138, pp. 47–58
Disegni di Canova del Museo di Bassano (Milan, 1982)
G. L. Mellini: *Canova: Disegni* (Florence, 1984)
A. Mariuz and G. Pavanello: 'Disegni inediti di Antonio Canova da un taccuino "Canal"', *Saggi & Mem. Stor. A.*, xix (1994)

POSSAGNO GIPSOTECA AND TEMPLE

M. Missirini: *Del tempio eretto in Possagno* (Venice, 1833)
A. Nani: *Il Tempio Canoviano illustrato* (Treviso, 1863)
——: *Canova ed il suo Tempio di Possagno* (Treviso, 1882)
E. Bassi: *La Gipsoteca di Possagno* (Venice, 1957)
H. Wischermann: 'Canovas Panteon: Überlegungen zum Tempio Canoviano von Possagno', *Architectura* [Munich] (1980), pp. 134–63
E. Paolin: *Canova e Possagno* (Asolo, 1987)
G. Pavanello: 'La Gipsoteca di Possagno', *Antonio Canova* (exh. cat., Venice, Correr, 1992)

SPECIALIST STUDIES

R. Bratti: 'A. Canova nella sua vita artistica privata', *Archv Ven.*, xvii (1917), pp. 281–450
L. Coletti: 'La fortuna del Canova', *Boll. Reale Ist. Archeol. & Stor. A.* (1927), pp. 21–96 [contains full bibliog. to 1924]
A. Sorbelli: *Inventare dei manoscritti delle biblioteche d'Italia. Volume lviii. Bassano del Grappa* (Florence, 1934)
Mostra canoviana (exh. cat., ed. L. Coletti, Treviso, Pal. Trecento, 1957)
F. J. B. Watson: 'Canova and the English', *Archit. Rev.* [London], cxxxii (1957), pp. 403–6
H. Honour: 'A. Canova and the Anglo-Romans', *Connoisseur*, cxliii (1959), pp. 241–5; cxliv (1959), pp. 225–31
S. Krasa: 'A. Canovas Denkmal der Erzherzögin Marie Christine', *Albertina-Stud.*, v–vi (1967–8), pp. 67–134
P. Fehl: 'Thomas Appleton of Livorno and Canova's Statue of G. Washington', *Festschrift Ulrich Middeldorf* (Berlin, 1968), pp. 523–52
H. Honour: 'Canova's Statue of a Dancer', *N.G. Canada Bull.*, vi (1968), pp. 2–13
G. C. Argan: 'Il filo del Canova', *Momenti del marmo* (Rome, 1969), pp. 103–9
H. Hawley: 'A. Canova Terpsichore', *Bull. Cleveland Mus. A.*, lvi/8 (1969), pp. 287–304
H. Honour: 'Canova's *Theseus and Minotaur*, *V&A Mus. Yb.*, i (1969), pp. 1–15
O. Raggio: 'Canova's *Triumphant Perseus*', *Connoisseur*, clxxii (1969), pp. 204–12
H. Honour: 'Canova and David', *Apollo*, xcvi (1972), pp. 312–17
——: 'Canova's Statues of Venus', *Burl. Mag.*, cxiv (1972), pp. 658–70
——: 'Canova's Studio Practice', *Burl. Mag.*, cxiv (1972), pp. 146–59, 214–29
E. Debenedetti and others: *Studi canoviani* (Rome, 1973)
H. Honour: 'Gli Amorini del Canova', *A. Illus.*, vi (1973), pp. 312–20
——: 'Canova's Napoleon', *Apollo*, xcviii (1973), pp. 180–84
M. Pavan: 'A. Canova e la discussione sugli *Elgin Marbles*', *Riv. Ist. N. Archeol. & Stor. A.*, xxi–xxii (1974–5), pp. 219–344
G. Pavanello: 'Due Muse di A. Canova', *Per Maria Cionini Visani: Scritti di amici* (Turin, 1977), pp. 136–7
Venezia nell'età di Canova, 1780–1830 (exh. cat. by G. Pavanello, Venice, Correr, 1978)
A. Corboz: 'Pygmalion, serviteur des deux maîtres', *Genava*, xxvi (1979), pp. 165–75
F. Boggero: 'Una rilettura critica del Canova: La *Maddalena penitente*', *A. Lombarda*, xxv (1980), pp. 386–92
S. Rudolph: 'Il monumento Stuart del Canova: Un committente dimenticato e il primo pensiero ritrovato', *Antol. B.A.*, iv (1980), pp. 44–54
O. Stefani: *La poetica e l'arte del Canova* (Treviso, 1980)
A. Pinelli: 'La sfida rispettosa di A. Canova: Genesi e peripezie del *Perseo trionfante*', *Ric. Stor. A.*, iv/13–14 (1981), pp. 21–39
U. Schlegel: 'Canova Tänzerin', *Jb. Preuss. Kultbes.*, xviii (1981), pp. 187–200
P. Fehl: 'Canova's Tomb and the Cult of Genius', *Labyrinthos*, i (1982), pp. 46–66
E. Debenedetti: 'Canova e il suo tempo', *Scritti in onore di Giulio Carlo Argan*, i (Rome, 1984), pp. 431–51
G. Pavanello: 'A. Canova: I bassorilievi *Rezzonico*', *Boll. Mus. Civ. Padova*, lxxxiii (1984), pp. 145–62
M. E. Michele: 'Le raccolte di antichità di Antonio Canova', *Riv. Ist. N. Archael. & Stor. A.*, viii–ix (1985–6), pp. 205–322
C. Del Bravo: '*Idee* del Canova', *Intersezioni*, vii (1987), pp. 73–83
G. Pavanello: 'Domenio Zoppetti', *Una città e il suo museo. Un secolo e mezzo di collezioni civiche veneziane* (exh. cat., Venice, Correr, 1988), pp. 117–121
E. Bassi and L. Paduan Urban: *Canova e gli Albrizzi, tra ridotti e dimore di campagna nel tempo* (Milan, 1989)
A. Cuozzo: 'Due bassorilievi inediti del Canova', *Venezia A.*, iii (1989), pp. 173–4
J. Wardropper and Th. F. Rowlands: 'Antonio Canova and Quatremère de Quincy: The Gift of Friendship', *A. Inst. Chicago Mus. Stud.*, xv/1 (1989), pp. 38–44
S. Zamboni: 'Un carteggio inedito di Antonio Canova', *An. Fac. Magistero U. Cagliari*, xii (1989), pp. 193–212
G. L. Mellini: 'Canoviana', *Ant. Viva.*, xxix/1 (1990), pp. 21–30
——: 'Presenza dell'antico nella pittura di Antonio Canova', *Venezia e l'archeologia* (Rome, 1990)
M. G. Miggiani: 'Documenti sul bozetto per il monumento a Francesco Pesaro di Antonio Canova', *Venezia A.*, iv (1990), pp. 176–85
G. Pavanello: 'Antonio d'Este, amico di Canova, scultore', *Antol. B.A.*, ix/35–8 (1990), pp. 13–22
——: 'Una scheda per l' "Apollo che si incorona" di Antonio Canova', *Antol. B.A.*, ix (1990), pp. 4–12
O. Stefani: *I rilievi del Canova* (Milan, 1990)
H. Honour: 'A Bust of *Sappho* by Antonio Canova', *Artibus & Hist.*, xxiv (1991), pp. 193–200
Alle origini di Canova: Le terrecotte della collezione Farsetti (exh. cat., ed. S. O. Androsov, Rome, Fondazione Memmo Palazzo Ruspoli, 1991–2)
Canova all'Ermitage. Le sculture del Museo di San Pietroburgo (exh. cat., Rome, Pal. Ruspoli, 1991–2)
G. Pavanello: 'Collezioni di gessi canoviani in età neoclassica: Padova', *A. Friuli, A. Trieste*, xii–xiii (1993), pp. 167–90
——: 'Sulla collezione di Antonio Canova: I cassoni degli Argonauti di "Ercole da Ferrara"', *Boll. Mus. Civ. Padova*, xcii (1993)
——: 'Antonio Canova per il Re di Spagna', *A. Ven.*, xlvi (1994), pp. 72–8

GIUSEPPE PAVANELLO

Cánovas del Castillo, Antonio. *See* KAULAK.

Cansever, Turgut (*b* Antalya, 1922). Turkish architect and writer. He studied architecture at the Fine Arts Academy in Istanbul. As a student of SEDAD HAKKI ELDEM, and later as his teaching assistant, he was influenced by Eldem's ideas on the nature of national architecture. Cansever began his career working in urban planning in Istanbul. During the 1950s, however, he began to attract attention with buildings and designs that incorporated new technology and materials but also referred to the past. His KARATEPE Museum (1954–61) near Adana, for example, had slab roofs of poured concrete, but the open porches and corner windows refer to historical and regional architectural traditions. He adopted this approach for other buildings, including the Anadolu Club (1959; with Abdurrahman Hancı) at Büyükada, Istanbul, which combines a traditional T-plan with a meticulous treatment of details, particularly the windows; a block of flats in Çiftehavuzlar, Istanbul; and the partly realized Terakki Foundation School in Istanbul. This approach also inspired the Turkish Historical Society Building (1966; with Ertur Yener; *see* TURKEY, fig. 2) in Ankara. This influential building, which won an Aga Khan Award for Architecture in 1980, had a protected interior space consisting of a three-storey covered court with traditional features. The exterior of the building, which had an overhang on pilotis, employed red Ankara stone for its cantilevered upper walls and painted raw cement for the lower structural elements. Like his earlier designs, it was significant for its historical and regional connotations. Cansever advanced his ideas further by writing about architecture.

WRITINGS

Thoughts and Architecture (Ankara, 1981)

BIBLIOGRAPHY

R. Holod and D. Rastorfer, eds: *Architecture and Community: Building in the Islamic World Today* (Millerton, NY, 1983), pp. 139–50

'Turgut Cansever', *Mimar*, 11 (1983), pp. 4–67 [Turk. text]

R. Holod and A. Evin, eds: *Modern Turkish Architecture* (Philadelphia, 1984), pp. 113–5, 124–7, 139, 141–8

S. Tansuğ: *Çağdaş Türk sanatı* [Contemporary Turkish arts] (Istanbul, 1986), pp. 316–7, 393 [Turk. text]

□

Cantacuzino, G(eorge) M(atei) (*b* Vienna, 23 May 1899; *d* Iaşı 1 Nov 1960). Romanian architect, urban planner, painter, theorist and restorer. Descended from a Wallachian family of statesmen and scholars, he studied (1920–29) at the Ecole des Beaux-Arts, Paris, with Gustave Umbdenstock and G. Gromort. His work consistently showed Neo-classical and Renaissance influences, from the Palladian-style Chrissoveloni Bank (1928; with A. Schmiedigen), Bucharest, to the substantial number of buildings he completed in Romania during the 1930s. In many of these the classicist forms overlaid a sophisticated functionality in the planning, for example the IAR aeroplane factory (1933), Braşov. He also designed houses (e.g. in Amza Square, Bucharest, 1935), hotels (e.g. the Hotel Bellona on the Black Sea coast, 1934) and churches, such as those at Tetcani and Flămânda (1939), and he participated in the production of the master plan of 1935 for Bucharest. He was commissioned to design the Romanian Pavilion for the World's Fair, New York (1939), the first occasion on which Romanian architecture was represented internationally. The enduring influence of classical examples is visible in such late works as the pavilions at Iaşı, a continuation of the Palladian idiom. He was also active as a restorer, for example at the Mogoşoaia Palace (1920–28), Bucharest, the country house (1938–40) at Drugăneşti-Stoeneşti, and various churches in northern Moldavia. In addition to his work as an architect and restorer, Cantacuzino was a frequent exhibitor of paintings and drawings; he also broadcast radio lectures on architectural subjects, contributed numerous articles to architectural magazines and produced a translation of Vitruvius. His theoretical investigations into the relationship between modern functionalist architecture and national style led him to emphasize the priority of spiritual over formal considerations. From 1942 to 1948 he was professor of architectural history and theory at the Ion Mincu Academy of Architecture, Bucharest.

WRITINGS

Palladio, essai critique avec douze dessins de l'auteur (Bucharest, 1928)

ed. *Caiete de estetică: Simetria* [Notebooks on aesthetics: symmetry] (Bucharest, 1939–47)

trans. Vitruvius: *De architectura*

Introducerea la cercetarea textelor lui Vitruviu (Bucharest, 1947); *R* as *Introducere la opera lui Vitruviu scrisori catre Simon* (Bucharest, 1993)

Izvoare şi popasuri [Springs and halts], intro. A. Anghelescu (Bucharest, 1977)

BIBLIOGRAPHY

R. Patrulius: 'George Matei Cantacuzino', *Architectura*, 4–5 (1975)

ALEXANDRU BELDIMAN

Cantagallina, Remigio (*b* Borgo San Sepolcro, *c.* 1582; *bur* Florence, 1656). Italian etcher and draughtsman. He did not study at the 'academy' of Giulio Parigi in Florence, as has been claimed, although he did collaborate with the architect in 1608 when he engraved prints of two of Parigi's theatre sets. His first documented work is from 1603, the date of a series of landscape etchings. Northern influences in his early prints can be traced to Paul Bril, but his way of creating perspective by the intensification of shadow is reminiscent of Antonio Tempesta. It is significant that Cantagallina was one of the first artists to abandon the late-Mannerist vision of nature as fantastic and frightening for a genuine interest in themes from daily life. Among his most notable drawings are the splendid *Village Piazza* (1633; Princeton U., NJ, A. Mus.) and the large *View of Siena* (Florence, Uffizi). In 1612–13 he was in the Netherlands, where he produced such detailed drawings as the *Palace of Brussels* and *Sulphur-making at Franc Mont* (both Brussels, Musées Royaux B.-A.). Some of his etchings also are known: the *Death of St Francis* (1605); *Bona, City of Barbary* (1607); four etchings on biblical subjects (1609); a series of 14 landscapes (1627; London, BM); and 12 undated landscapes (Vienna, Albertina). His last known engraving dates from 1635, a *Landscape with Travellers* that is notable for the delicacy of its execution and for the masterly handling of space. The latest drawing (Florence, Uffizi) is dated 1655.

BIBLIOGRAPHY

C. Thieme: *Florentiner Zeichner des Frühbarocks* (Munich, 1977), p. 350

A. Negro Spina: *Giulio Parigi e gli incisori della sua cerchia* (Naples, 1983), pp. 161–78

——: 'Le incisioni di paesaggio di Remigio Cantagallina', *Studi di storia dell'arte in memoria di Mario Rotili* (Naples, 1984), pp. 403–11

ANNAMARIA NEGRO SPINA

Cantanhede, 3rd Conde de. *See* MARIALVA, 1st Marquês de.

Cantarini, Simone [il Pesarese] (*b* Pesaro, *bapt* 21 Aug 1612; *d* Verona, 15 Oct 1648). Italian painter and engraver. He was one of the most eminent pupils of Guido Reni and one of the most gifted engravers in the tradition of the Carracci. He had a strong personality and developed a highly original style, which united aspects of Bolognese classicism with a bold naturalism.

Cantarini was the son of a merchant. He first trained with the Late Mannerist painter Giovanni Giacomo Pandolfi (*c.* 1570–*c.* 1640), a follower of Federico Zuccari. He made a brief visit to Venice, where he absorbed the Venetian interest in light and colour. On his return to Pesaro he studied with Claudio Ridolfi (*c.* 1570–*c.* 1644), from whom he acquired an appreciation of the art of Federico Barocci. Barocci inspired the soft *sfumato* of the faces of his Virgins and saints, their idyllic mood and tender feeling, and the echoes of Raphael and early Correggio. Early on in his career, and still in the Marches, Cantarini saw the paintings of Orazio Gentileschi and Giovan Francesco Guerrieri, works that provoked his interest in a powerful naturalism, which is often apparent even in his more classical paintings. To this early period belong his paintings of *St Rita* (Pesaro, S Agostino), the *Crucifixion* (Pesaro, S Veneranda) and the altarpiece depicting the *Virgin with SS Barbara and Terenzio* (Aicurzio, nr Milan, S Andrea).

Around 1632 Cantarini saw, in Pesaro Cathedral, Guido Reni's *Virgin and Child with SS Thomas and Jerome* (Rome,

Pin. Vaticana), his *Annunciation* (Fano Cathedral) and the *Delivery of the Keys to St Peter* (ex-Fano Cathedral; Paris, Louvre). This had a profound impact on his later development. He made copies and drawings of these paintings, the success of which won him important commissions: for *St Peter Healing the Lame Man* (Fano, S Pietro in Valle), *St Thomas of Villanueva* and the *Virgin of the Girdle* (both Fano, Pin. Civ.). In 1635 he moved to Bologna with the specific intention of meeting Reni, and he went to work in Reni's studio. His bold and ambitious nature and his growing awareness of his own potential, however, soon led him to reject the subordinate position of disciple and to assume a provocative stance. Their relationship developed into full-blooded rivalry, so that in 1637 they abandoned any contact. After this, Cantarini's economic difficulties and continual quarrels with clients made it necessary for him to leave Bologna (*c.* 1638). His profound response to the poetry of Reni's art is apparent in works that may be dated to this early period in Emilia, such as the *Virgin of Monserrato* (*c.* 1637; Stuffione, Modena, S Maria delle Grazie), *St Stephen* (Bazzano, Bologna, Parish Church) and the *Transfiguration* (*c.* 1637; Rome, Pal. Cancelleria). Probably contemporary with these are his paintings of the *Virgin with Saints* and *St Anthony and the Child Jesus* (Bolognina, Bologna, S Antonio da Padova), the *'Great Saints'* (Rimini, Tempio Malatestiano) and *Lot and his Daughters* (Bologna, Neri priv. col., see Ferretti Colombo, p. 23, fig. 6), which, in its refined colour, is close to the late style of Reni.

Cantarini returned to Pesaro in 1639. In the following years, although Reni's influence remained strong, the rupture in their relationship encouraged him to search for a more personal style. He moved away from academic classicism, renewed his early interest in naturalism and developed a freer, more lyrical vein. This was the period of the *Rest on the Flight into Egypt* (Paris, Louvre), *Mary Magdalene* and *St Joseph* (Pesaro, Mus. Civ.), *St James* (*c.* 1640; Rimini, Pin. Com. & Mus. Civ.) and *Susanna and the Elders* (*c.* 1640; Bologna, Pin. N.). About 1640–42 he visited Rome; the paintings conceived during and following his stay reveal a desire to move closer to the tradition of Raphael, yet without rejecting naturalism: the *Rest on the Flight into Egypt* (Milan, Brera) is based on Raphael's *Madonna del Velo* (Chantilly, Mus. Condé). Other contemporaneous works, such as the *Holy Family* (Rome, Gal. Borghese), the *Rest on the Flight into Egypt* (Rome, Gal. Doria-Pamphili) and *Atalanta and Hippomenes* (Ferrara, Dell'Acqua priv. col., see Mancigotti, p. 131, fig. 70), suggest an interest in the trend towards Venetian art, displayed in the work of Francesco Mola, Pietro Testa and Andrea Sacchi. Attributable to his later years, but nevertheless still related to this tendency, are his *Virgin with SS Vincent and Benedict* (Gandino, Bergamo, Parish Church) and *St Matthew and the Angel* (Washington, DC, N.G.A.), the latter distinguished by unusually free brushwork.

On his return to Bologna, probably in 1642, the year of Reni's death, Cantarini opened his own studio in the Palazzo Zambeccari, which was attended by artists such as Lorenzo Pasinelli, Flaminio Torri and the engraver Girolamo Rossi (*fl* 1632–64). During this last period of the artist's life he renewed his interest in the Carracci and painted the *Adoration of the Magi* (Florence, Torrigiani-Salina priv. col., see Mancigotti, p. 157, figs. 93–4, pl. 22) and the *Holy Family with the Infant St John* (Rome, Gal. Borghese; see fig.), paintings that are characterized by balanced composition and rigorous draughtsmanship. In 1647 Cantarini was invited to Mantua by Carlo II Gonzaga of Nevers (1629–65); however, he took so long over the portrait the Duke had commissioned that he was relieved of his duties. He became seriously ill and moved to Verona, where he died.

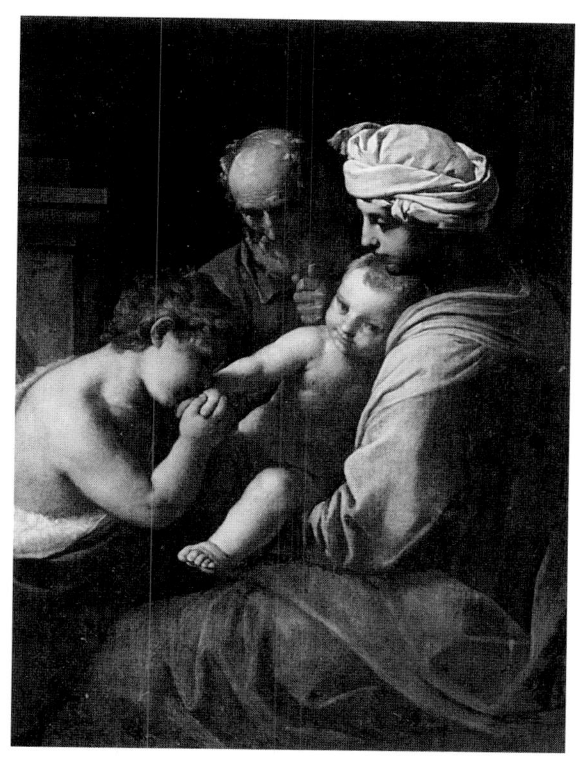

Simone Cantarini: *Holy Family with the Infant St John*, oil on canvas, 960×730 mm, early 1640s (Rome, Galleria Borghese)

Cantarini's work as an engraver has been recorded and praised by various sources for its extraordinary delicacy and its vibrant and luminous quality. Many works are attributed to him but at present the actual number of engravings with a rightful claim to his authorship is restricted to 37 plates of mythological and religious subjects, all of exceptional quality (see Spike).

BIBLIOGRAPHY

DBI; Thieme–Becker

C. C. Malvasia: *Felsina pittrice* (1678); ed. M. Brascaglia (Bologna, 1971), pp. 587–601

F. Baldinucci: *Notizie* (1681–1728); ed. P. Barocchi and A. Boschetto (Florence, 1974–5), iv, pp. 40–49

A. Emiliani: 'Simone Cantarini: Opera grafica, I', *A. Ant. & Mod.*, viii (1959), pp. 438–56

I maestri della pittura del Seicento emiliano (exh. cat., ed. F. Arcangeli, M. Calvesi and G. C. Cavalli; Bologna, Pal. Archiginnasio, 1959), pp. 114–28

Mostra di disegni del Seicento emiliano nella Pinacoteca di Brera (exh. cat., ed. A. Emiliani; Milan, Brera, 1959), pp. 27–57, 69–84

E. Borea: *Pittori bolognesi del Seicento nelle gallerie di Firenze* (Florence, 1975)

M. Mancigotti: *Simone Cantarini il Pesarese* (Pesaro, 1975)
L'opera incisa di Simone Cantarini (exh. cat., ed. P. Bellini; Milan, Castello Sforzesco, 1980)
J. T. Spike: *Italian Masters of the 17th Century* (1981), 42 [XIX/ii] of *The Illustrated Bartsch*, ed. W. Strauss (New York, 1978–)
A. Ferretti Colombo: 'Simone Cantarini: Dalla Marca Baroccesca alla Bassa Padana', *Boll. A.*, lxvii/13 (1982), pp. 19–34
The Age of Correggio and the Carracci (exh. cat., Washington, DC, N.G.A.; New York, Met.; Bologna, Pin. N.; 1986), pp. 398–405
L'arte degli Estensi: La pittura del Seicento e del Settecento a Modena e Reggio (exh. cat., ed. A. Emiliani; Modena, Pal. Musei, 1986)
M. Cellini: 'Un nuovo Cantarini', *Paragone*, xxxviii/445 (1987), pp. 40–44
A. Emiliani: 'Simone Cantarini', *La pittura in Emilia e in Romagna: Il Seicento*, ed. A. Emiliani, i (Milan, 1992), pp. 207–18

MARINA GAROFOLI

Canterbury. English city in Kent on the River Stour, seat of the southern metropolitan see, with a population of *c.* 48,000.

I. History and urban development. II. Centre of manuscript production. III. Cathedral.

I. History and urban development.

1. Before *c.* 1530. 2. *c.* 1530 and later.

1. BEFORE *c.* 1530. The site at a major ford crossing the River Stour was first settled at the end of the 1st century BC, perhaps as an *oppidum* for the local tribes of the Cantiaci or Kentish people. The Cantiaci were prosperous and traded across the English Channel with Gaul. After the Roman invasion of AD 43 their prosperity continued; but it was not until the beginning of the 2nd century AD that their settlement was laid out as a Roman *civitas* with baths, a theatre and a temple precinct. The forum and basilica of Durovernum Cantiacorum have not yet been definitely identified. There were large town houses with tessellated pavements, workshops and pagan shrines. West of the Stour crossing was an industrial suburb where metalwork and pottery were produced. The city was encircled with walls and gates between *c.* AD 270 and 290 (see fig. 1). Along the main roads leaving the town were extensive cemeteries. After the withdrawal of the Roman army by *c.* 410, evidence suggests that the city, which had continued as a market for the Cantiaci, declined. For a time it may have been deserted: the fine hoard of Roman Christian silver buried outside the western walls before AD 411 bears witness to fear of unsettled times. The Anglo-Saxons, who had probably arrived by the 490s, built sunken-floored huts (*Grubenhäuser*) among the ruined Roman buildings, sometimes straddling old streets, which eventually created a different street system, although the gates remained in use. The western area near the river was left as pasture.

Possibly the earliest recorded event in Canterbury was the arrival in 597 of Augustine (*d* 604), sent as a missionary by Pope Gregory I to the territory of King Ethelbert I of Kent (*reg* 550–616), whose Frankish wife, Queen Bertha (*d* before 616), was a Christian. Augustine and his party were given lodgings in the town and worshipped in the small chapel of St Martin (now part of St Martin's Church; 1a) on a villa site east of the walls with the Queen and her chaplain, Bishop Liudhard (*d c.* 603). When the mission flourished, Ethelbert gave Augustine a church 'built in ancient times by the hands of Roman believers' (Bede:

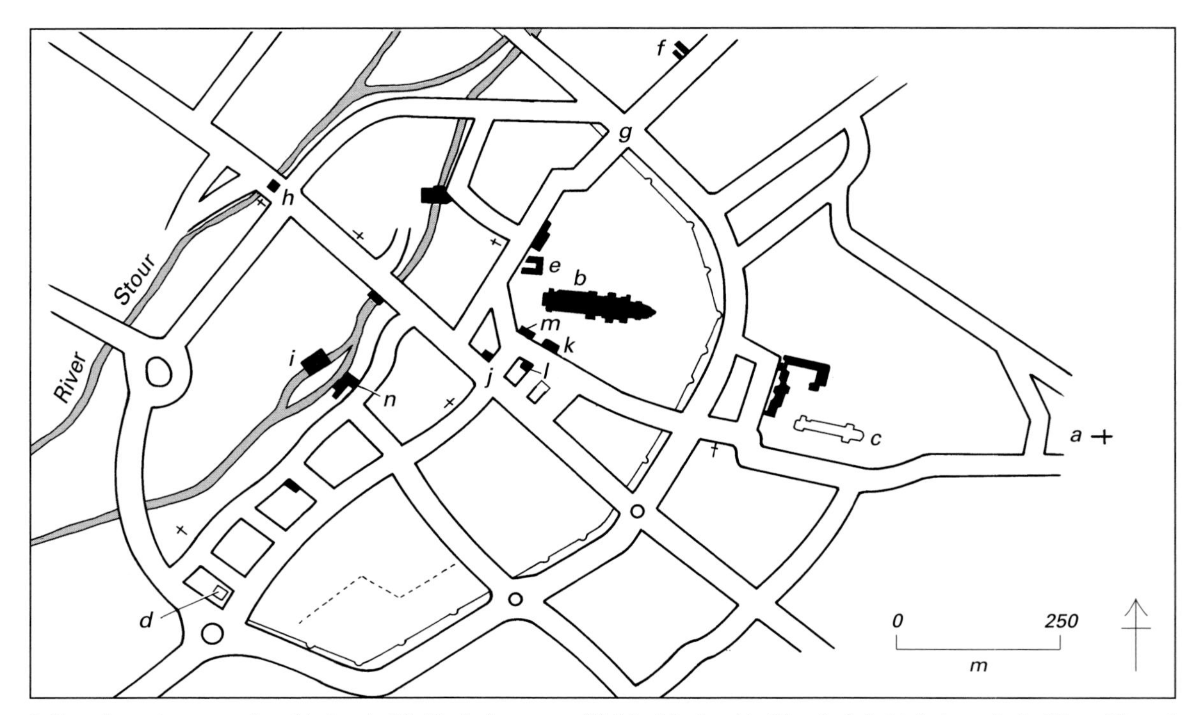

1. Canterbury city centre, plan: (a) chapel of St Martin (now part of St Martin's church); (b) cathedral; (c) St Augustine's Abbey; (d) royal castle; (e) archiepiscopal palace; (f) St John's Hospital; (g) Northgate; (h) Westgate; (i) Franciscan friary; (j) Cheker of the Hope Inn; (k) Sun Inn; (l) White Bull Inn; (m) Christ Church Gate; (n) Poor Priests' Hospital

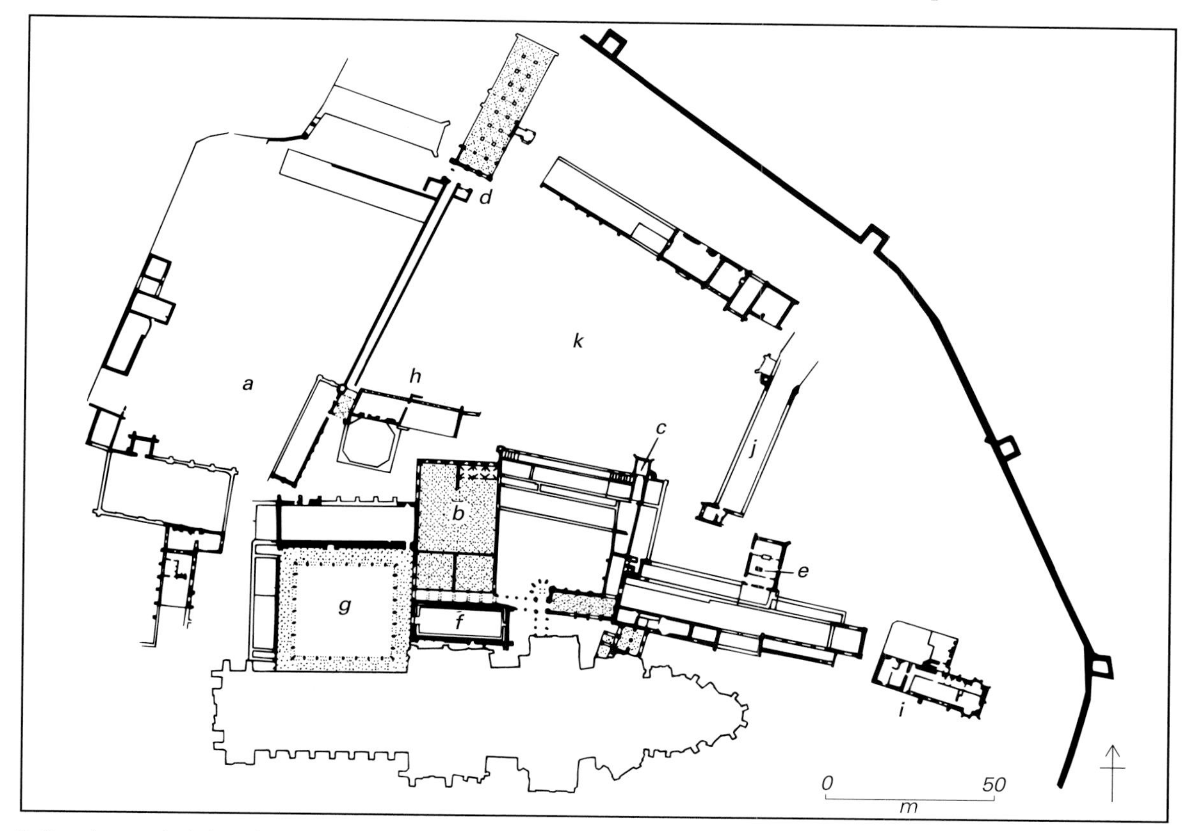

2. Canterbury, cathedral precinct, plan: (a) archiepiscopal palace; (b) dormitory; (c) Dark Entry; (d) Court Gate; (e) Table Hall (now Choir House); (f) chapter house; (g) Great Cloister; (h) guest house; (i) Meister Omers; (j) Deanery; (k) Green Court

Ecclesiastical History of the English People (MS.; 731), i, chap. xxxiii. 3–4; ed. B. Colgrave and R. A. B. Mynors (Oxford, 1969), p. 115)—Christ Church—as his cathedral (1b), and a site for a monastery outside the city walls to the east (SS Peter and Paul, ded. 613, reded. as St Augustine's in 978; 1c). Pope Gregory intended that the two metropolitan bishoprics in Britain should be at London and York. Although Augustine consecrated a bishop for London, he consecrated Lawrence (*reg* 604–19) as his successor at Canterbury, presumably because the mission had not prospered sufficiently for a change of headquarters. Since then the metropolitan of southern England has remained at Canterbury, with the title of archbishop, which has profoundly influenced the development of the city.

Cantawaraburh, as it was known, flourished as a centre of continental and Kentish trade from the 7th to the 10th century, troubled by occasional incursions from the Vikings, especially in 851 and 1011. In spite of this the cathedral community of Christ Church as well as St Augustine's Abbey grew and obtained houses and land in the city. Manuscripts were produced in Canterbury from the 8th century (*see* §II below). From the 9th century Christ Church charters give an impression of a well-settled city with some form of corporate organization. The city invaded by William, Duke of Normandy, in 1066 was therefore a commercial settlement with small industries, two large religious houses, perhaps four small churches and probably the ruins of the large Roman theatre. The Normans immediately built a motte-and-bailey castle in the south-west corner of the enclosure, reusing a Roman burial mound. Between 1085 and 1125 a three-storey rectangular royal castle was built of stone on a site a little to the west (1d) to defend the Stour Valley. It stood largely intact until the 18th century; in 1826 it became a gas- and water-works, and only two storeys now remain. The period from 1070 to 1170 was a time of architectural activity in Canterbury. Archbishop Lanfranc (*reg* 1070–89) laid out new monastic buildings at Christ Church, erected a new cathedral (*see* §III below) and built a T-shaped archiepiscopal palace (excavated 1986; see fig. 1e and fig. 2a) on the continental model. Further he built two almshouses or hospitals, St Nicholas's (founded *c.* 1084) at Harbledown, west of Canterbury, and St John's (1f) in the suburb of Northgate (1g). Opposite St John's he established a community of priests to serve the hospital, which later became St Gregory's Priory of Augustinian Canons, with extensive domestic buildings and a very large early 12th-century church (excavated 1989). To the east of the city a small suburb developed near St Martin's Church. From 1070 a new church and monastic buildings were laid out by Abbot Scotland (*reg* 1073–87) at St Augustine's Abbey (all destr.; see fig. 3). A few examples of good Romanesque sculpture were found in excavations (1900–31). The number of small churches in and near the city increased to 22.

In 1170 Archbishop Thomas Becket was martyred in his cathedral, and from then until the destruction of his shrine in 1538 Canterbury was the goal of international pilgrimage. About 1180 St Thomas' Hospital (now an almshouse) on Eastbridge was endowed as a pilgrim hostel: its original undercroft still stands. Much is known of the city *c.* 1200 from a study of Christ Church Priory rentals. Most of the eastern area within the walls was occupied, including the large Christ Church Precinct in the north-east corner, which still dominates the plan of the inner city. West of the intramural arm of the river there were few houses except along the street towards the Westgate (1h). There were suburbs at Northgate, Longport and Oaten Hill (east), along Wincheap (south) and up towards St Dunstan's Church in the archbishop's estate of Westgate; they were not greatly extended until the 19th century. Within the city, some merchants had stone houses with stone cellars; some of the latter remain. Moneyers, goldsmiths, tanners, weavers and Jewish financiers worked in the city.

The cathedral precincts have contained a variety of buildings over the centuries, several of which have been exceptionally large. The dormitory (before 1093; mostly destr.; 2b), for instance, built by Lanfranc to accommodate around 150 monks measured 24×45 m; the surviving shafts in the Dark Entry (2c) running beneath it are incised with striking patterns. Prior Wibert (*reg* 1151–67) built the Court Gate (*c.* 1155; 2d; *see* GATEHOUSE, §2) with finely carved capitals and arch rolls, as well as the North Hall (*c.* 1153; mostly destr.; rest., of which the exterior staircase survives). The treasury (*c.* 1155–60; additional storey late 13th century; now the canons' vestry) has the only surviving octopartite rib vault in England. Many of the monastic buildings have been largely destroyed, for example the reredorter, kitchen, refectory, infirmary cloister, prior's chapel (*c.* 1260), cellarer's hall (east wall, parts of south wall and bases of sub-vault columns preserved) and Pentise Gate (staircase and part of east wall preserved). The Table Hall (now Choir House; 2e) dates from *c.* 1265, when it was used as a refectory. Prior Eastry (*reg* 1285–1331) rebuilt the chapter house (completed 1305; 2f); it measured 9×27 m and was later altered by Prior Chillenden, who did much building in the precincts. He rebuilt the Great Cloister (*c.* 1395–1414; 2g), which contains nearly 850 heraldic bosses, constructed the timber pentise, and built the adjoining guest house (1394; 2h). Meister Omers (completed 1447; rest.; 2i) was built by Cardinal Beaufort (*c.* 1377–1447) to accommodate guests. The King's School now occupies Meister Omers, the Brewhouse and the Bakehouse (both *c.* 1100; Brewhouse destr. 1942), as well as other more recent buildings in the precincts. The medieval Prior's House (later Deanery; 2j) was rebuilt after a fire in 1570; it was later damaged by bombs in World War II and restored, as was the north side of Green Court (2k).

Outside the precincts, in 1224 the Franciscans (Greyfriars) were given marshy land not used for housing in the south-western quarter within the walls, where they gradually set up their friary; one small building (1i) astride the river remains. The Dominicans (Blackfriars) settled under royal patronage in 1236. In the north-eastern quarter they built a large church and domestic buildings, of which the refectory (*c.* 1250) and guest hall (*c.* 1320) remain. Then, as now, there was much open ground to the west within the walls. The Augustinian Friars (Whitefriars) erected buildings (destr.) south of St George's Street in 1326. All the friars had generally good relations with the citizens, whose guilds met in their churches and who were buried

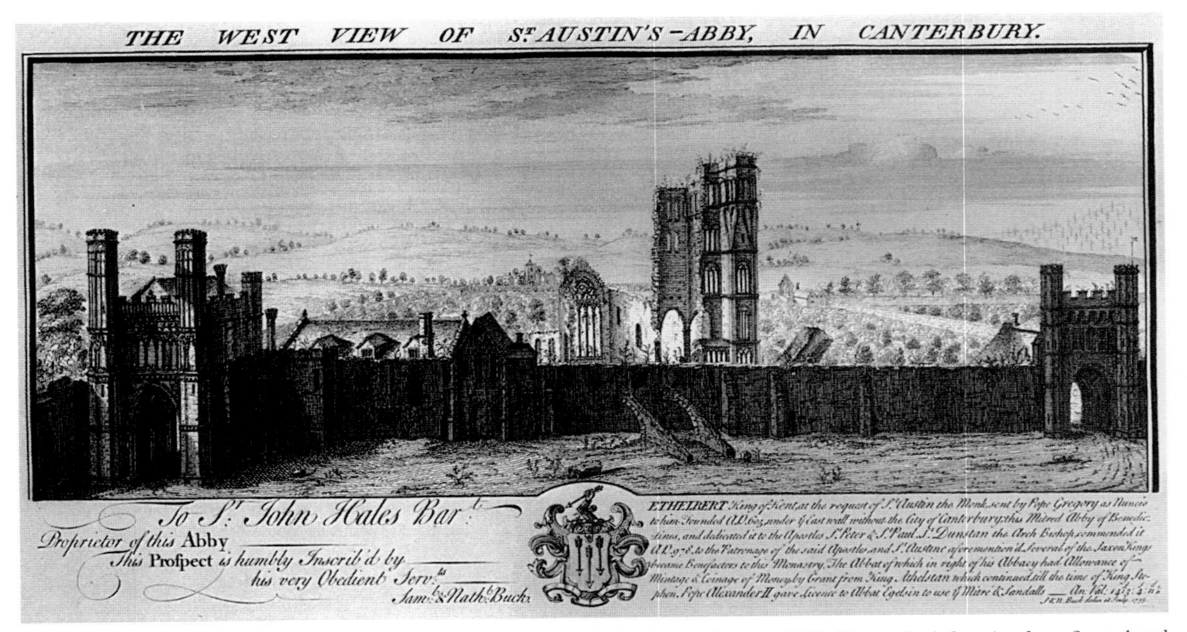

3. Canterbury, west view of St Augustine's Abbey, begun 1070, with the Great Gateway, 1300–09, on the left; print from Samuel and Nathaniel Buck: *Venerable Remains of above 400 Castles, Monasteries, Palaces, etc.*, begun 1720

4. Canterbury, courtyard of the Cheker of the Hope Inn, 1392–5, with the gateway opening on to High Street; from a 19th-century engraving by F. W. Fairholt, 191×231 mm (Canterbury, Royal Museum and Art Gallery)

in their churchyards. The Great Gateway, or Fyndon Gate (1300–09; see fig. 3) of St Augustine's Abbey is magnificent in scale; it has octagonal corner turrets and is covered with elaborate carving, including foliage, ballflower and figures.

The city remained mostly within its patched Roman walls. In 1363 a commission ordered the repair of the walls, which was undertaken *c.* 1378–1409. The Westgate was in progress in 1380, probably designed by Henry Yevele. Long stretches of the rebuilt wall with half round or square towers survive. Burgate (destr.) was reconstructed *c.* 1475, Newingate (destr.) by 1495 and the eastern walls by 1494. Much rebuilding of small houses, shops, and large inns or pilgrim hostels took place in the 15th century. They were timber-framed with tiled roofs, later disguised by stucco or mathematical tiles. Inns were built by Christ Church Priory and can be accurately dated: the Cheker of the Hope (1392–5; partly destr.; see figs 1j and 4), the Sun (1437–8; partly rebuilt; 1k) and the White Bull (1468; 1l). The timber-framed Guildhall (destr.) was rebuilt in 1438, and the indenture survives. Reconstruction drawings suggest that 15th-century Canterbury resembled some of the surviving small German towns with stout framing. It was reasonably prosperous: many prominent citizens owned land or houses in nearby villages as well as working within the walls. Despite their wealth, the city's churches remained largely unmodernized, apart from the occasional enlargement of windows to allow light. Christ Church Gate (1517–*c.* 1520/1; rest.; 1m), which leads into the precincts, was built; the pilasters on either side of its two arches have inlaid stone panels, carved with Renaissance motifs.

2. *c.* 1530 AND LATER. The Reformation of the 1530s and 1540s had a serious effect on the city, although welcomed by some leading citizens. The pilgrimage trade ceased: the friaries and monastic houses, which had provided employment, were dissolved. Several friaries became private houses. Apart from one courtyard in use as a royal posting house, St Augustine's Abbey was destroyed and used as a source of stone. Christ Church Priory buildings were adapted to make houses for the clergy and their staff. Few new houses were built then or later, so that Canterbury lacks the architecturally distinguished houses to be seen in, for example, Winchester Cathedral Close.

Poverty and plague ravaged Canterbury in the 1560s. By 1572 the city authorities rented the Poor Priests'

Hospital (founded *c.* 1220; 1n) in Stour Street for the use of the poor. Its mostly 14th-century buildings were later used as a workhouse and are now the Canterbury Heritage Museum; they stand on the site of an earlier stone house (excavated 1979–81). The city was revived by the arrival after 1548 and 1567 of French-speaking Protestant refugees from what is now Belgium and northern France. They used the cathedral crypt as their church and settled particularly in the west of Canterbury. Weaving and market-gardening were their specialities. They remained a separate community within the city for several generations, joined after 1660 by Huguenot refugees. The population increased from *c.* 3000 in the 1520s to 6000 in the 1660s.

Canterbury suffered during the Civil War and Commonwealth (1642–60). The cathedral and precinct houses were damaged, parts of the city walls destroyed, and the wooden gates burnt. After the Restoration repairs and rebuilding took place. By 1697 a traveller noticed the houses were 'neat but not very lofty, most are of brickwork'. Silk-weaving and paper-making were practised by the refugee community. The 18th century was not a time of change, although stucco and sash windows were added to some medieval houses. Few 18th-century houses remain other than Westgate House and Barton Court. In the 1770s a flurry of modernizing by the city authorities began. They demolished more of the city walls and, between 1781 and 1801, three of the gates. The streets were paved and lit between 1787 and 1789, involving the ruthless trimming back of bay windows, porches, and even a church tower that extended too far into the street.

The beginning of the Napoleonic Wars in 1803 placed Canterbury near the enemy. Barracks were laid out to the north, and ever since then soldiers have been stationed at Canterbury. In 1792 a local entrepreneur, James Simmons (*d* 1807), rebuilt one of the water mills (destr. 1932) to a design by James Smeaton (*d* 1792). Simmons also created the city's first public garden, turning the former castle motte (known as Dane John) into a small hill with paths, providing a 'prospect' of the city. In the 1790s the population increased from *c.* 9000 to 11,000, creating the need for a hospital, begun 1791–2, and a prison (1806–10) by George Byfield (*c.* 1756–1813). The sale of drawings and engravings, mostly of the cathedral and the ruins of St Augustine's, continued into the 1850s. A. J. B. Hope and WILLIAM BUTTERFIELD built St Augustine's College (completed 1848) in the grounds of the former abbey.

The railway linked Canterbury to Whitstable in 1830, and to London and Ramsgate in 1845. The West Railway Station was built in 1846, but a station on the line to Dover was not completed until 1861. The trains brought visitors, and also children to Canterbury's boarding-schools—the Gothic Clergy Orphan School (1852), and the King's School (founded 1541 by Henry VIII) in the precincts. Suburban houses spread beyond the stations, but Canterbury remained a small, unindustrialized city. The population was *c.* 15,000 in 1841 and *c.* 21,000 in 1881.

In 1942 the eastern half of the city was severely damaged by bombing. Rebuilding after World War II and the construction in the 1960s of a partial ring road outside the city walls totally altered the eastern approach to the city. A boom in education provided the university (founded 1962) on a hillside to the north-west and Christ Church College by Robert Matthew, Johnson-Marshall & Partners (1962–4) on part of the St Augustine's Abbey site. Housing estates and much private housing were built on other hills. Traffic and parking remain unsolved problems, since Canterbury is still the shopping centre for the people of east Kent, as for the Romanized Cantiaci. The modern city is one of contrasts—modern shops and educational buildings together with medieval streets, remnants of the city walls and one gate (Westgate).

BIBLIOGRAPHY

W. Somner: *The Antiquities of Canterbury* (London, 1640, rev. 1703)
W. Gostling: *A Walk in and about the City of Canterbury* (Canterbury, 1774, rev. 6/1825) [useful references]
F. W. Cross: *History of the Walloon and Huguenot Church at Canterbury* (London, 1898)
J. C. Cox: *Ancient Cities: Canterbury, a Historical and Topographical Account of the City* (London, 1905)
C. Cotton: *The Grey Friars of Canterbury* (Manchester, 1924)
A. R. Martin: 'The Dominican Priory at Canterbury', *Archaeol. J.*, lxxxvi (1930), pp. 152–77
W. Urry: *Canterbury under the Angevin Kings* (London, 1967)
M. Sparks, ed.: *The Parish of St Martin and St Paul Canterbury: Historical Essays in Memory of James Hobbs* (Canterbury, 1980)
T. Tatton-Brown, P. Bennett and M. Sparks: 'The Poor Priests' Hospital in Canterbury', *Collectanea Historica: Essays in Memory of Stuart Rigold*, ed. A. Detsicas (Maidstone, 1981), pp. 173–86
The Archaeology of Canterbury, Canterbury Archaeological Trust (1982–)
P. Clark and J. Clark: 'The Social Economy of the Canterbury Suburbs: The Evidence of the Census of 1563', *Studies in Modern Kentish History* (Maidstone, 1983), pp. 65–86
N. Brooks: *The Early History of the Church of Canterbury: Christ Church, from 597 to 1066* (Leicester, 1984)
J. Peters: *A Family from Flanders* (London, 1985)
F. H. Panton: 'James Simmons: A Canterbury Tycoon', *Archaeol. Cantiana*, cv (1988), pp. 215–44
D. Sherlock and H. Woods: *St Augustine's Abbey: Report on Excavations, 1960–78* (Maidstone, 1988)
T. Tatton-Brown: 'The History of St Gregory's Priory', *Archaeol. Cantiana*, cvii (1989), pp. 314–27
——: 'The History of the Archbishop's Palace in Canterbury', *J. Brit. Archaeol. Assoc.*, cxliv (1991), pp. 1–60

MARGARET SPARKS

II. Centre of manuscript production.

The chief importance of Canterbury for manuscript illumination was in the early medieval and Romanesque periods. In the 6th century, however, to meet the needs of the new ecclesiastical foundations after Augustine's mission, manuscripts were imported to Canterbury from the Continent. An important surviving example of such a Late Antique Mediterranean import is the late 6th-century Gospels of St Augustine (Cambridge, Corpus Christi Coll., MS. 286). By the middle of the 8th century the Canterbury scriptoria were producing notable manuscripts under Late Antique influence, such as the VESPASIAN PSALTER (London, BL, Cotton MS. Vesp. A. I) and the Stockholm Codex Aureus (Stockholm, Kun. Bib., MS. A. 135).

With the revival of artistic production during the monastic reform movement of the 10th century (*see* ANGLO-SAXON ART, §I), the Christ Church scriptorium in the time of Archbishop Dunstan created such high-quality works as the Bosworth Psalter (*c.* 975–1000; London, BL, Add. MS. 37517; see fig. 5), which contains elaborate enlarged painted initials of foliage, interlace and animal heads. The significant development of the late 10th century, however, was the evolution of the outline drawing style, which appears in several manuscripts attributed to St Augustine's Abbey (e.g. Oxford, St John's Coll., MS. 28; Cambridge, Trinity Coll., MS. 0.3.7) and to Christ Church (London, BL, Cotton MS. Cleop. C. VIII). This style was given added impetus by the arrival of the Carolingian UTRECHT PSALTER (Utrecht, Bib. Rijksuniv., MS. 32) in Canterbury in the late 10th century. This important example of the animated linear manner of the school of Reims exerted a continuing influence. The first of several copies made at Canterbury was the Harley Psalter (London, BL, Harley MS. 603; *see* ANGLO-SAXON ART, fig. 10), illustrated by several artists with over 100 coloured and shaded drawings in a highly expressive style.

A more fully painted style is associated with the early 11th-century manuscripts produced by the Christ Church scribe EADUI, for example the Eadui Gospels (Hannover, Kestner-Mus., MS. WM. XXIa 36) and the Eadui Psalter (London, BL, Arundel MS. 155; *see* BENEDICTINE ORDER, fig. 1). In the productions of both the Winchester and Canterbury scriptoria of this period influence from the more painterly style of the 10th-century Winchester school is combined with the linear manner derived from Reims (*see* CAROLINGIAN ART, §IV, 3). With the continuing exchange of influences and ideas between England and the Continent during the years around 1066, the early post-Conquest Canterbury manuscripts show the influence of various Norman painting styles and an emphasis on the painted initial, as well as the continued use of the linear manner associated with pre-Conquest work, as seen in a Passional (London, BL, Arundel MS. 91; for illustration *see* SAINTS' LIVES) and Martyrology (London, BL, Cotton MS. Vitell. C. XII(i)) produced at St Augustine's Abbey in the early 12th century.

The scriptoria of both foundations flourished during the 12th century. The Christ Church scriptorium is credited with the production of numerous manuscripts with impressive cycles of fully painted, historiated initials (e.g. *c.* 1130; Flavius Josephus: *Jewish Antiquities*, Cambridge, U. Lib., MS. Dd.1.4; Cambridge, St John's Coll., MS. A.8; *see* ROMANESQUE, fig. 61); the illustrated Psalter leaves (*c.* 1140; New York, Pierpont Morgan Lib., MSS M. 724 and 521; London, BL, Add. MS. 37472(i); London, V&A, MS. 661) with 12 detailed biblical vignettes on each page; and the second copy of the Utrecht Psalter, the Eadwine Psalter (*c.* 1150–60; Cambridge, Trinity Coll., MS. R.17.1; see fig. 6), containing 156 tinted outline drawings in a firmly controlled linear manner. The Dover Bible (Cambridge, Corpus Christi Coll., MSS 3–4) may also be a product of the Christ Church scriptorium, commissioned in connection with the foundation of St Martin's Priory (1139), Dover. Ecclesiastical relations between Canterbury, Dover and Rochester resulted in much textual and artistic influence between the manuscripts produced in and for these houses. The painted initials in the Rochester Bible (*c.* 1130; London, BL, Royal MS. 1. C. VII; Baltimore, MD, Walters A.G., MS. 18) seem clearly dependent on Canterbury influence, which also occurs in a number of other Rochester books.

The attribution of the fine mid-12th-century Lambeth Bible (London, Lambeth Pal. Lib., MS. 3; *see* BIBLE, fig. 4; Maidstone, Mus. & A.G.) to the scriptorium of St Augustine's has been questioned, and stylistic relations with Bury

5. Canterbury, Christ Church: 'Q', historiated initial from the Bosworth Psalter, *c.* 975–1000 (London, British Library, Add. MS. 37517, fol. 33*r*)

6. Canterbury, Christ Church: *Eadwine the Scribe*, miniature from the Eadwine Psalter, *c.* 1150–60 (Cambridge, Trinity College, MS. R.17.1, fol. 283*v*)

St Edmunds Abbey and St Albans Abbey (now Cathedral) have been noted. The latest surviving version of the Utrecht Psalter (Paris, Bib. N., MS. lat. 8846) was produced at Christ Church *c.* 1180–90, although this was not a direct copy after the original. The heavily modelled style and extensive use of gold reveal the strong Byzantine influences generally pervasive during these years. Such influences may also be seen in other late 12th-century Christ Church books (e.g. London, BL, Royal MS.10.A.XIII and Cotton MS. Claud. B. II).

Changing patterns of patronage and manuscript production from the end of the 12th century mark a general shift from monastic scriptoria to itinerant and lay workshop production. There are thus far fewer manuscripts with a secure Canterbury provenance from this period. Possible examples include a small Bible (London, BL, Burney MS. 3) made before the middle of the 13th century for Robert de Bello, Abbot of St Augustine's, the Bible of William of Devon (London, BL, Royal MS.1.D.1; *see* BORDER, MANUSCRIPT, fig. 1) and several related manuscripts, all in a style that reveals strong influence from contemporary French manuscripts. Some 13th-century illustrated Apocalypses may derive from Canterbury (e.g. London, Lambeth Pal. Lib., MS. 209) but this is not certain.

BIBLIOGRAPHY

M. R. James: *The Ancient Libraries of Canterbury and Dover* (Cambridge, 1903)
——: *The Canterbury Psalter* (London, 1934)
F. Wormald: *English Drawings of the Tenth and Eleventh Centuries* (London, 1952)
C. R. Dodwell: *The Canterbury School of Illumination, 1066–1200* (Cambridge, 1954)
——: *The Great Lambeth Bible* (London, 1954)
D. Wright and A. Campbell: *The Vespasian Psalter* (Copenhagen, 1967)
C. M. Kauffmann: *Romanesque Manuscripts, 1066–1190*, A Survey of Manuscripts Illuminated in the British Isles, iii (London, 1975)
E. Temple: *Anglo-Saxon Manuscripts, 900–1066*, A Survey of Manuscripts Illuminated in the British Isles, ii (London, 1976)
W. Cahn: *Romanesque Bible Illumination* (Ithaca, NY, 1982)
N. Morgan: *Early Gothic Manuscripts (1), 1066–1190*, A Survey of Manuscripts Illuminated in the British Isles, iv (London, 1982)
J. Backhouse: 'The Making of the Harley Psalter', *BL J.*, x/2 (1984), pp. 97–113
English Romanesque Art, 1066–1200 (exh. cat., ed. G. Zarnecki, J. Holt and T. Holland; London, Hayward Gal., 1984)
The Golden Age of Anglo-Saxon Art (exh. cat., ed. J. Backhouse, D. Turner and L. Webster; London, BM, 1984)
The Making of England: Anglo-Saxon Art and Culture, AD 600–900 (exh. cat., ed. L. Webster and J. Backhouse; London, BM, 1991)
M. Gibson, T. A. Heslop and R. W. Pfaff, eds: *The Eadwine Psalter: Text, Image, and Monastic Culture in Twelfth-century Canterbury* (London and University Park, PA, 1992)

LESLIE ROSS

III. Cathedral.

Seat of the metropolitan archbishopric, the monastic cathedral was founded by Augustine in 597. Originally dedicated to St Saviour (Christ Church), by 990 it was dedicated also to the Trinity. The Anglo-Saxon buildings were burnt in 1067, and Archbishop Lanfranc reformed and rebuilt the monastery and cathedral. Lanfranc's choir was rebuilt from 1096 by Archbishop Anselm, but this building was substantially damaged by fire in 1174. The present choir, built 1175–84, is the successor to that of Anselm, while the nave, crossing tower and main transept were enlarged and rebuilt from 1377 to replace those of Lanfranc. The main patrons were the monastic priors and the archbishops.

The eastern arm is both choir and martyrium, the shrine of the murdered archbishop St Thomas Becket. The shrine itself was obliterated in 1538, although the monastery was not dissolved until 1540, when Christ Church was refounded as a secular cathedral. The monastic buildings, north of the church, were largely demolished except for the cloister ranges, but the cathedral fabric survived; since the 17th century it has undergone almost continual repair and restoration.

The historically significant parts of Canterbury Cathedral are Lanfranc's lost building and the present choir (see fig. 7), both of which developed the foremost contemporary ideas from Europe and transmitted them to English architecture. The buildings before 1174 are known from documents and from fragments surviving in the plan and proportions of the existing building, where they dictate the length of the nave and the plan and height of the choir.

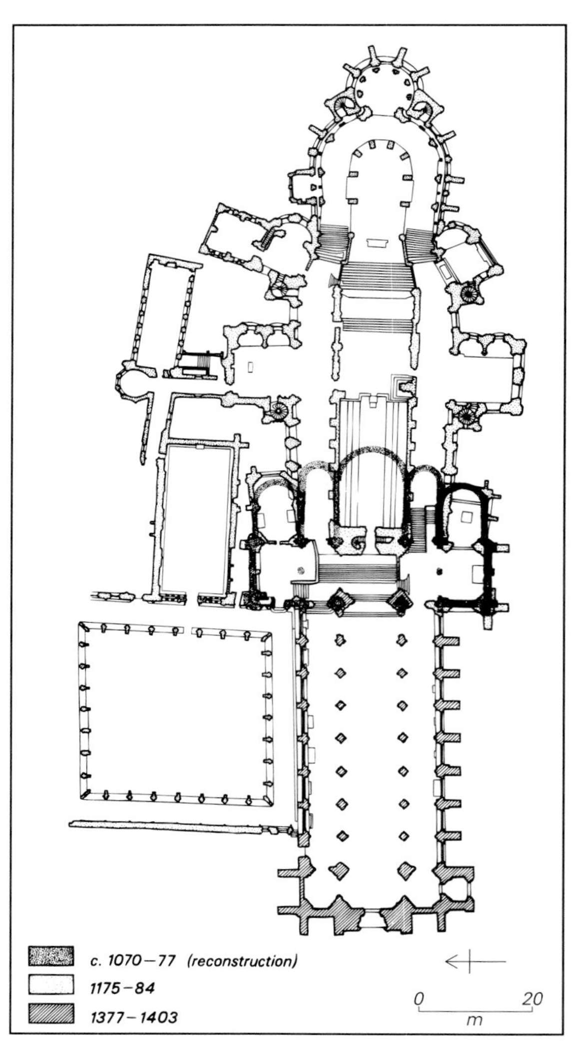

7. Canterbury Cathedral, plan of the present building, begun 1174

Valuable documentary sources include the writings of two 12th-century Christ Church monks, Eadmer and Gervase. Gervase's tract, 'The burning and repair of the church at Canterbury', is of special interest, not only describing both the present choir and its predecessor but also giving a detailed account of the building campaign after 1174: a unique medieval record, which, within the limits of Gervase's interests (which are not those of architectural historians), is accurate.

1. Architecture. 2. Sculpture. 3. Stained glass.

1. Architecture.

(i) Anglo-Saxon cathedral. (ii) Archbishop Lanfranc's cathedral. (iii) Archbishop Anselm's choir. (iv) 1174–84. (v) After 1184.

(i) Anglo-Saxon cathedral. After 597 Augustine 'recovered' a Romano-British church, which Eadmer believed to survive until the fire of 1067 (see below). Archbishop Cuthbert (*reg* 740–60) built a church of St John the Baptist immediately to the east both as a baptistery and a burial church for the archbishops. The main church may have been restored by Archbishop Wulfred, who reformed and rebuilt the monastery in the early 9th century; Archbishop Oda (*reg* 942–58) repaired the roof and raised the walls by *c.* 6 m, perhaps because the lower windows were obscured by porticus. The crypt and choir may have been altered when St Dunstan was entombed there in 988; and the Danes ransacked and burnt the church in 1011.

The form of the baptistery is unknown, but by the mid-11th century Christ Church was an oblong *c.* 41 m long, divided into unequal halves by projecting north and south towers, with altars possibly in their upper levels. The south tower was the main entrance to the church. At the west was an apse marking the altar of St Mary and the archbishop's throne. The apsed eastern sanctuary was raised over a confessio crypt, which was related to Roman liturgical practices. Double-ended churches are found in the Rhineland; but it is equally possible that the final arrangement at Canterbury was the result of piecemeal development. Traces of the pre-Conquest building were discovered under the floor of the present nave in 1993.

(ii) Archbishop Lanfranc's cathedral. This was built around the site of its predecessor and was ready for use *c.* 1075–7. Its appearance is known from references by Eadmer and Gervase and from fragments in the present building. Like its successors, it was built of limestone. The plan was cruciform, with a crossing tower and five apses in echelon, the outer two being transept chapels. The sanctuary was raised over a crypt reached by stairs from the presbytery aisles and the crossing. The presbytery and aisles were divided by solid walls, but the nave had an arcade of eight bays with gallery and clerestory, the gallery continuing round the transept to give access to the upper chapels. There is no firm evidence of a clerestory passage. The west façade had twin towers delineated from the ground up and masking the aisles; the north-west tower survived until 1832. The main entrance to the cathedral was probably on the south side, as it is today.

Decoration included cushion capitals and external blind arcading between the buttresses, over the clerestory windows. Stylistically, Lanfranc's church was indebted to Norman architecture, especially the contemporary St Etienne, Caen; but there are elements from elsewhere, such as the cushion capitals derived from Germany. The building was a formative influence on the development of Anglo-Norman architecture.

(iii) Archbishop Anselm's choir. By the late 11th century, owing to the large number of monks, a substantial new east end was required. This was almost a complete church in itself, an aisled basilica with transept, ambulatory and three attached chapels; and the monks' choir was wholly contained within it. Prior Ernulf (1096–1114) supervised the construction, and his successor Conrad (1114–26) was responsible for the decoration. The choir was consecrated in 1130.

The floor-level was raised *c.* 3 m above the crossing, underpinned by a crypt extending beneath the entire superstructure, its central vessel subdivided by a double row of columns, some with incised patterns, surmounted by carved and painted block capitals (see fig. 10 below). The central entrance to the old crypt was blocked. The choir was *c.* 70 m long internally and *c.* 22 m high, with nine bays. The ambulatory chapels, now dedicated to SS Andrew and Anselm, were originally towers, and their apses are angled towards the east end. The rectangular eastern chapel housed the Trinity altar. Square eastern transepts, with angle stair-turrets and two apsed chapels on each arm, opened off the sixth bay, but the main arcade was continuous and there was no marked crossing. The elevation, destroyed in 1174, can be surmised from Gervase's description and extant remains, but the evidence is not conclusive; Willis's reconstruction (1845) has been modified by later scholars. The three-storey elevation had a columnar arcade with tau-cross capitals, a gallery with windows in the outer wall and a clerestory with passage. The arched divisions of the upper storeys cannot certainly be determined. The aisle walls were articulated with a decorative blind arcade and huge round-headed windows, the stained glass of which, with the painted wooden ceiling, would have flooded the interior with the colour for which it was praised by William of Malmesbury. Sources for the eastern towers, angled chapels and hall crypt have been sought in the Empire, and the raised choir hints at Anselm's native Italy, although columnar piers were commonplace in Anglo-Norman architecture. No close parallels for Anselm's choir survive in Britain.

Between 1130 and 1174 the only active builder was Prior Wibert (1151–67; *see* §2 below). In the cathedral he heightened and decorated the transept turrets and altered the ambulatory tower-chapels, apparently to avert collapse, adding extra masonry at crypt and ground-floor level and rebuilding the vaults. Both towers were dismantled before 1336.

(iv) 1174–84. The choir and martyr's shrine chapel built after the 1174 fire survive architecturally intact (see fig. 8). The exact responsibility of each of the two architects in the final design is uncertain. William of Sens (1174–8) devised the scheme and built most of the choir and presbytery. William the Englishman (1179–84) finished the work in progress and built the Trinity Chapel and corona (eastern tower). The monks entered their choir at Easter 1180, and with one season's interruption in 1183,

8. Canterbury Cathedral, choir, begun 1174, interior looking east

building was finished by 1184. Decoration continued at least until 1220, when the shrine of St Thomas was translated to the Trinity Chapel (*see* §3 below).

The fire destroyed the roof and central vessel of Anselm's choir but left the outer walls standing almost to their full height. The new choir, *c.* 4 m higher than its predecessor, was built within the shell of the old walls, which thus dictated both the plan and the proportions. Two of the old piers were reused as extra supports in the crypt. The monks' choir and presbytery were positioned as before, but a significant new feature was the proper crossing to the eastern transept (the entrances of which were widened by cutting back masonry and realigning the main piers). The tower-chapels were retained from Anselm's choir, so the presbytery, now with four bays, narrows towards the east before opening out into the huge new Trinity Chapel, which, with the corona, extends *c.* 38 m beyond the line of the old ambulatory wall, which was cut away. The Trinity Chapel has two straight bays and a five-part hemicycle, with an ambulatory leading to the corona. For the first time Canterbury had a principal saint whose remains were placed behind the high altar, as in other English great churches; but here the shrine was sited directly over the saint's original tomb in the crypt (as at Saint-Denis Abbey, France), and it was housed in its own martyrium. The Trinity Chapel is approached through rising floor levels, with the intensity of decoration greatly increased in the vicinity of the shrine. Despite controversy over the question, it seems clear that such an emphasis was intended from the start, and the alterations apparent at the junction of presbytery and Trinity Chapel do not represent a substantive change in ideas.

The three-storey elevation has sexpartite rib vaults (except over the eastern crossing and adjacent bays, and the Trinity Chapel, where they are quadripartite). The choir arcade has alternate round and octagonal columns; the crossing piers have applied Purbeck shafts, and extra shafting gives greater variety to the presbytery piers. The Purbeck vault shafts descend to the abaci of the large acanthus capitals. The gallery has Purbeck-shafted twin-arched openings, and the clerestory has single lancets to the exterior and triple, Purbeck-shafted openings on the inner plane of the wall. Although there is a clerestory passage, this is not a thick-wall structure: the passage is supported on transverse arches in the gallery that rest on the aisle vaults. There is evidence that it was intended to vault the gallery with transverse barrel vaults, but although the south side is lit by the outer windows that these would allow, masonry breaks imply that this was a later arrangement, and the lean-to roof of the north side probably represents an early solution. The adaptations of Anselm's structure to the new building are most apparent in the aisles: their height includes the old gallery level, with new upper windows but the main windows retained, in a unique two-storey elevation. New wall arcading was inserted alongside the old, and vault ribs were positioned to connect existing outer responds with newly aligned piers.

The Trinity Chapel and corona have a different elevation from the choir: the higher floor level changes the proportions of the arcade and upper storeys, and the middle storey resembles a triforium. The clerestory and exterior parapet are slightly higher, and the shallow flying buttresses are among the earliest known, if of no obvious use. Inside the colour is far more intense, with the *opus Alexandrium* floor, the twinned marble columns of the main arcade and huge aisle windows, set just above the floor and framed by Purbeck shafts set forward of the wall.

Stylistically, the squat, wide proportions of the choir, with its dark gallery, insofar as they are not the outcome of existing constraints, are descended from such churches as Abbot Suger's Saint-Denis; and while the chevron and dogtooth in all the arch and vault mouldings are English, the use of coloured shafting to this extent derives from such north-east French churches as the cathedrals of Arras and Valenciennes (both destr.), although the capitals have close parallels at Notre-Dame, Paris. The elevation of the Trinity Chapel, with passages on two levels, is more up to date, grouping Canterbury with a series of buildings identified by Bony (1957–8), scattered in a wide arc north and east of Paris, south to Geneva; the main source of the twinned columns and acanthus capitals seems to have been Arras Cathedral.

The Trinity Chapel and its crypt were entirely built by William the Englishman, who Caviness (1979) has suggested brought a new team of craftsmen. The stylistic and structural evidence is inconclusive. Despite their names, both William of Sens and William the Englishman were evidently trained in north-east France, and it could be argued either that the choir and Trinity Chapel represent the designs of two different people, or that the differences are explicable in terms of the physical limits imposed on the one and their relative absence on the other. Structurally, there are similar ambiguities. At the junction of the presbytery and Trinity Chapel, aisle wall arcading inserted by William of Sens is partly concealed by the steps up to the Trinity Chapel; the half-submerged main piers change from octagonal to circular; colonnette fragments and a marble string course embedded in the later masonry imply an abandoned plan for a screen and another arrangement for the Trinity Chapel piers; and the Trinity Chapel capitals appear to have been designed for extra shafts. For over a century scholars followed Willis's interpretation that the floor level was heightened after William of Sens left, and that the Trinity Chapel is exclusively William the Englishman's work, Caviness (1979) and Woodman (1981) arguing that the plan for the latter was altered and enlarged. Draper (1983), however, has demonstrated that the higher floor level, with concomitant alterations, must be associated with William of Sens, which implies that the elevation of the Trinity Chapel was also decided by him. This has reopened the question of the plan, and of individual responsibility for the whole; but whoever designed the present building, an enlarged saint's chapel must have been envisaged from the start.

(v) After 1184. No more major structural work was done until the nave was rebuilt from 1377 to 1403, although the monastic buildings and arrangements for the cult received attention. The chapter house fittings and choir-screen of Prior Eastry (1285–1331) were made by masons who had recently worked at Westminster; they introduced ogee arches and such decorative motifs as pinnacles and gables. In 1336 the east window of St Anselm's Chapel was remade with an elaborate curvilinear design using Kentish tracery, a type used also in the remodelled Infirmary chapel.

The nave, probably by Henry Yevele and Stephen Lote (*fl* 1381; *d* 1417/8), was based on the building it replaced, the aisles encompassing Lanfranc's arcade and tribune; but the main vessel was heightened to match vault levels further east. The nave (see fig. 9) shows the first use at Canterbury of the Perpendicular style for monumental purposes: such earlier works as the Black Prince's chantry (1363) used the delicate, angular mouldings of Perpendicular purely decoratively. The three-storey nave elevation, based on work in London and the choir of York Minster, has strong vertical emphasis, the arcade very high in proportion to the blank middle storey and squat clerestory, set slightly back in the wall plane and high under the vault. The rectilinear lierne vault, based on wide, shallow arches, descends to shafts that rise continuously from the floor, interrupted only by moulded capitals, and shaft rings (a revived Early Gothic motif, seen also in Yevele's nave of Westminster Abbey). The immense aisle windows and the great west window have a reticent pattern of simple rectilinear panels.

Stephen Lote was also engaged by Prior Chillenden (*reg* 1391–1411), who finished the nave, to rebuild the cloister and the pulpitum under the main crossing. The west transept was remade during the 15th century; the south-west tower 1424–34. The last main addition was the central tower (Bell Harry), completed by John Wastell from 1494. It is vaulted with fan vaults sprung from the

9. Canterbury Cathedral, nave, 1377–1403, interior looking east

corners and sides, the crisp clarity of the mouldings anticipating Wastell's later vaults in King's College Chapel, Cambridge. Four angle turrets, with tiers of stepped niches, crown the exterior.

For further illustration *see* GOTHIC, fig. 7.

BIBLIOGRAPHY

William of Malmesbury: *Gesta pontificum Anglorum* (1125); ed. N. E. S. A. Hamilton, Rolls Ser. (London, 1870), p. 138

Gervase: *Tractatus de combustione et reparatione Cantuariensis ecclesiae* (*c.* 1200), in *Gervasii Cantuariensis opera historica*, i, ed. W. Stubbs, Rolls Ser. (London, 1897), pp. 3–29

R. Willis: *The Architectural History of Canterbury Cathedral* (London, 1845); repr. in *The Architectural History of Some English Cathedrals* (Chicheley, 1972) [incl. a trans. of Gervase, pp. 36–52, and extracts from Eadmer]

J. Bony: 'The Resistance to Chartres in Early 13th-century Architecture', *J. Brit. Archaeol. Assoc.*, n.s. 2, xx–xxi (1957–8), pp. 35–52

P. Kidson: 'Canterbury Cathedral: The Gothic Choir', *Archaeol. J.*, cxxvi (1969), pp. 244–6

British Archaeological Association Conference Transactions: Medieval Art and Architecture in Canterbury before 1200: Canterbury, 1979 [incl. article by M. Caviness]

F. Woodman: *The Architectural History of Canterbury Cathedral* (London, 1981)

P. Draper: 'William of Sens and the Original Design of the Choir Termination of Canterbury Cathedral', *J. Soc. Archit. Hist.*, xlii (1983), pp. 238–48

N. Brooks: *The Early History of the Church of Canterbury* (Leicester, 1984) [incl. discussion of the Anglo-Saxon cathedral, pp. 37–59]

NICOLA COLDSTREAM

2. SCULPTURE. The architectural sculpture of Canterbury Cathedral is among the most important Romanesque sculpture in England. The crypt, surviving from Archbishop Anselm's choir (from 1096; *see* §1(iii) above), has

10. Canterbury Cathedral, stone capital in the crypt, late 11th century

11. Canterbury Cathedral, fragment of a stone screen, 1180

a series of capitals carved with fantastic grotesques (see fig. 10) and foliage motifs borrowed heavily from contemporary Canterbury manuscripts. Two cushion capitals, carved with Winchester acanthus foliage, masks and dragons, were extremely influential at other Benedictine houses as far afield as Durham Cathedral priory and Worcester Cathedral priory, as well as the royal foundation of Reading Abbey. Most of the other capitals are block form, and, although less popular elsewhere, they are also imaginative works of high quality. The subject-matter has no religious content. Each face is carved with an independent motif, although there are occasional thematic similarities on the adjoining faces of individual capitals (e.g. a grotesque holding a fish and an empty bowl on one side, and the same, with a full bowl, on the other). Other motifs include goats and grotesques playing musical instruments, acrobats, griffins and riders. The surviving remains of the outer walls of Anselm's choir give an idea of its sculptural decoration. The window and arch heads have simple geometric motifs carved in low relief. The tau-cross capitals in the ambulatory, reused in the crypt, are of a similar type to those used at JUMIÈGES ABBEY and in London (St John's Chapel in the Tower of London (*see* LONDON, §V, 4) and the dormitory of Westminster Abbey) a few decades earlier.

The vast building programme initiated by Prior Wibert in the third quarter of the 12th century included the installation of a new water system, which is recorded in two drawings (after *c.* 1160) in the Eadwine Psalter (Cambridge, Trinity Coll., MS. R.17.1); the water tower is carved with geometric motifs that also appear on the treasury abutting St Andrew's Chapel. The same ornamental repertory was used on a number of other monastic buildings and on certain additions made to the cathedral. The distinctive types of ornament can be traced to Normandy, and there are especially close links with the abbey of La Trinité at Caen. Although not notable sculptors, this workshop was outstanding technically, and indeed it may have been specially called to Canterbury for its engineering skills to install the new water system.

Wibert's building programme appears still to have been in progress in 1174, for there is evidence that after the fire the team worked alongside the foreign masters in the reconstruction of the choir. This is apparent both in the choir aisle mouldings and in the sculptural decoration. The very high quality sculpture discovered during the restoration of the cloister in 1972 (see fig. 11) falls into two groups: three-quarter figures of kings in quatrefoils, and roundels filled with grotesque and human heads. All the pieces are strongly modelled and stylistically unified, closely related to Transitional sculpture in the Ile de France (for further discussion *see* TRANSITIONAL STYLE). The shapes, even the subjects, suggest that the most likely provenance for the fragments was the choir screen, which Gervase recorded was erected in time for Easter 1180. Stylistically similar to the screen fragments are the capitals inserted into the choir aisle wall arcade, presumably after the great fire. Both the screen and these capitals were carved at the same time as the Gothic choir capitals, revealing the co-existence of the two workshops and showing how misleading stylistic divisions can be as dating evidence.

Besides Prior Eastry's choir screen (*see* §1(v) above), the non-architectural sculpture in the cathedral includes wall monuments and tombs dating from 1205 to the present day. The medieval tombs represent the development of English tomb sculpture throughout the Middle Ages. The tomb of *Archbishop Hubert Walter* (*d* 1205) is a Purbeck marble sarcophagus with a gable roof decorated with roundels containing human heads in relief. The wall tomb of *Archbishop Pecham* (*d* 1294) is one of the so-called Court series, with canopy, weepers and effigy (in this instance, a wooden one) comparable to contemporary tombs at Westminster Abbey and elsewhere. The free-standing tomb of *Archbishop Meopham* (*d* 1333) is decorated with small sculptures of angels, Evangelists and monks. It has a horizontal tester, as do the tombs of *Edward the Black Prince* (*d* 1376) and *Henry IV* (*d* 1413) and his queen: both are decorated with heraldry and paintings, and the Black Prince's tomb displays his achievements.

BIBLIOGRAPHY

G. Zarnecki: *Regional Schools of English Romanesque Sculpture* (diss., U. London, 1950)

L. Stone: *Sculpture in Britain: The Middle Ages*, Pelican Hist A. (Harmondsworth, 1955, rev. 2/1972), pp. 116, 147–9, 192

D. Kahn: *Romanesque Architectural Sculpture in Kent* (diss., U. London, 1982)

English Romanesque Art, 1066–1200 (exh. cat., ed. G. Zarnecki, J. Holt and T. Holland; London, Hayward Gal., 1984), pp. 195–8

D. Kahn: 'Recently Discovered Eleventh-century Reliefs from Canterbury', *Gesta*, xxvii/1 (1989), pp. 53–60

For further bibliography *see* §1 above.

DEBORAH KAHN

3. STAINED GLASS. Canterbury Cathedral has more surviving medieval stained glass than any other English cathedral except York. It is of three main periods: first that of *c.* 1180–1220 in the choir, choir aisles, eastern transepts, presbytery, Trinity Chapel, Corona and the south window of the south-west transept; second that of the late 14th century in the west window of the nave; and third that of the late 15th century in the north window of the north-west transept. There are also some windows containing glass from various periods, mostly removed from other locations, in the crypt, the chapel of St Edward the Confessor and the water tower.

The glass of the early period is of major importance as the earliest comprehensive scheme of stained-glass decoration surviving in England. The clerestory windows of the presbytery and choir have a series of figures of the *Ancestors of Christ.* Many panels of this series are now in the south window of the south-west transept, and several, including the figure of *Adam*, are in the west window of the nave. As a consequence of these removals many of the series now in the clerestory windows date from the 19th and 20th centuries. In the choir aisle windows was an extensive series, surviving in part, of typological windows (*see* TYPOLOGICAL CYCLES), paralleling Old Testament scenes with episodes from the *Life of Christ.* In the rose window of the north-east transept are figures of prophets and personifications of the virtues, and in the upper windows of the choir aisles are scenes from the *Lives of SS Dunstan and Anselm.* The latest windows are the *Miracles of St Thomas Becket* (*see* GOTHIC, fig. 68) in the ambulatory of the Trinity Chapel, and a typological window and part of a *Tree of Jesse* window in the Corona. The *Miracles of St Thomas* correspond to the position of his shrine in the centre of the Trinity Chapel.

The chronology of these windows is complicated. It is reasonable to assume that by the translation of the relics of St Thomas in 1220 the windows depicting his miracles were mostly completed. The *Ancestors of Christ* series in the clerestory windows was begun perhaps as early as 1180

12. Canterbury Cathedral, *Queen of Sheba before Solomon* (detail), stained glass, from the second typological window, north choir aisle, *c.* 1200 (rest.)

and completed at the latest by *c.* 1200. They are by several artists working in slightly differing styles. Many of these figures have a stylistic similarity to such late 12th-century English painting as that of the Master of the Gothic Majesty in the WINCHESTER BIBLE (Winchester, Cathedral Lib.) and of the English painter of the wall paintings of Sigena chapter house (*see* SIGENA MONASTERY, §1). Others are clearly related to French stained glass at St Remi, Reims (*see* REIMS, §IV, 3(iii)), and the surviving panels of another sacred genealogy from St Yved, Braine, now in Soissons Cathedral.

Contemporary with these clerestory windows are the typological windows in the choir aisles. They may be as early as *c.* 1180–90, but the dating is controversial and some scholars have dated them as late as the early 13th century. There were originally 18 such windows in the choir aisles and east transepts; the iconographic programme of a series of scenes from the *Life of Christ*, each flanked by two Old Testament parallels (see fig. 12), is known from a medieval transcript of the verse inscriptions accompanying them. There were precedents for such a programme in lost wall paintings in the chapter house of Worcester Cathedral, also known through a medieval description. The style of these windows, by several artists, is characterized by elongated figures in dynamic postures with a great variety of pose and facial type. These medallion windows feature square and circular panels alternating in various patterns, with wide ornamental foliage borders.

The *Miracles of St Thomas Becket* date from *c.* 1200–20. They depict the miracles of healing and other acts of salvation through the saint's intercession, and several show scenes at his tomb (for further discussion *see* STAINED GLASS, §III, 1; *see also* GOTHIC, fig. 68). They are a rare survival of glass representing near-contemporary events with genre details of costume, location and action. Several artists were involved, some perhaps influenced by French glass at Sens Cathedral (*see* SENS, §1(iii)) and Chartres Cathedral. The scenes are set in complex designs of quatrefoil-, diamond-, vesica- and square-shaped panels set against ornamental patterned grounds, with wide ornamental foliage borders.

The great west window of the nave was glazed at the end of Richard II's reign *c.* 1395–9 and is a major Late Gothic work of English stained glass. In the tracery lights are prophets and saints, and below is part of a series of large standing figures of the *Kings of England* (see fig. 13). Some of the figures of the kings were lost, and in the late 18th century the gaps were filled with panels of the late 12th-century *Ancestors of Christ* series from the choir clerestory. The reason for the choice of a royal genealogy and the circumstances of patronage of the window are unclear. The style has some similarity to the work of Thomas of Oxford (*fl c.* 1380–95) at New College, Oxford, and Winchester College.

13. Canterbury Cathedral, *English King* (detail), stained glass, from the west window in the nave, *c.* 1395–9 (rest.)

The latest medieval glass is in the great north window (*c.* 1475–85) of the north-west transept. The donor was Edward IV, who is depicted kneeling with his wife, Elizabeth Woodville (1437–92), and their children, in the centre of the window, with angels above holding shields with their heraldry. The tracery lights, in a different style, are of prophets, apostles and saints. Above the royal donors were a series of panels of the *Joys of the Virgin* and saints (destr. 1643). The figures of the royal family are in part restored, but those of the King and Queen are relatively complete and represent the Flemish style favoured by the court of Edward IV. They contrast with the rather hard, dry manner of the indigenous English style in the tracery lights.

There are also a small number of 19th- and 20th-century windows, mostly of little artistic distinction. The *Peace* and *Salvation* windows of 1950–60 by the Hungarian artist Ervin Bossanyi (1891–1975) in the south-east transept are exceptions.

BIBLIOGRAPHY

B. Rackham: *The Ancient Glass of Canterbury Cathedral* (London, 1949)

M. H. Caviness: *The Early Stained Glass of Canterbury Cathedral, c. 1175–1220* (Princeton, 1977)

——: *The Windows of Christ Church Cathedral, Canterbury*, Corp. Vitrearum Med. Aevi (London, 1981)

NIGEL J. MORGAN

Canterbury, Michael of. *See* MICHAEL OF CANTERBURY.

Canterbury, Thomas of. *See* THOMAS OF CANTERBURY.

Cantilever. Structural system in which a member is rigidly fixed at one end in a supporting structure and free at the other, for example a balcony overhang or a tall building. Although in common usage the term is most frequently applied to horizontal members, the structural behaviour of all cantilevers is similar irrespective of direction. The cantilever is the most commonly used structural system both in nature and in architecture. Rock overhangs or vertical rock outcrops, trees and insect termitaries are all natural examples of cantilevers. The Eiffel Tower in Paris, the leaning towers of Pisa and Bologna, and the CN Tower in Toronto are examples of architectural cantilevers; in civil engineering they are used, for example, for cantilever bridges (*see* BRIDGE, §1), electricity transmission towers or pylons.

The asymmetrical behaviour of the cantilever is the key to its successful use and of vital importance to its safety: the stresses are zero at its free end and at a maximum at the fixed end. The cross-section of the cantilever is therefore a minimum at the free end and a maximum at the fixed end. If wind load is the primary load on the cantilever, as in a tower, the increase in cross-section of the cantilever follows the increase in wind stresses nearer the fixed supports, as in the Eiffel Tower, the most famous historical cantilever of all time (*see* EIFFEL, GUSTAVE). The deflections of a cantilever are at a maximum at the free end, and very often limiting these deflections may be the governing criterion of design.

Cantilevered reinforced-concrete structure of Fallingwater, Bear Run, near Pittsburgh, Pennsylvania, by Frank Lloyd Wright, 1935–7

The development of the cantilever took place in many different regions of the world. In China the *dougong* or bracket system was a device used to project the eaves from the line of the timber columns. The pieces of the *dougong* fitted within each other providing further cantilever extension of the roof-line. In medieval Italy it found expression in the building of towers; unfortunately the urge to build tall towers was far ahead of the knowledge of soil mechanics or the foundations that would be necessary to anchor such tall structures safely. This led to towers leaning out of plumb, such as the towers of Bologna (Asinelli and Garisenda) or the Leaning Tower of Pisa.

Gradually the structural behaviour of the cantilever was studied by many notable physicists and engineers, of whom one of the earliest was Galileo Galilei. His analysis of the behaviour of the cantilever was, however, incorrect; he assumed that the cantilever bends about its lower axis, when in fact it bends about its centroidal axis. The latter idea was proposed *c.* 200 years later in 1826 by the French civil engineer Claude-Louis-Marie-Henri Navier (1785–1836). In tall, vertically cantilevered structures, such as towers, chimney stacks or multi-storey high-rise buildings, it should be realized that the overall structure is a cantilever, although there can be other non-cantilever structural systems within the overall system: for example the structural system in a transmission tower is a space frame, although in overall behaviour it is a cantilever.

The development of increased understanding of cantilever behaviour became an important influence on architecture in the late 19th century and the 20th. In the work of Frank Lloyd Wright and subsequent architects the horizontal cantilever in the form of balconies, canopies or decorative elements became a recognizable motif that identified a building as 'modern' (see fig.). Vertical cantilever theory underlay the construction of increasingly tall structures; by the end of the 1970s structures had reached heights of *c.* 500 m. The Sears Tower (1974), Chicago, by Fazlur Khan (*b* 1929) is an office building 110 storeys and 442 m high (*see* SKYSCRAPER, fig. 3). Its structure consists of nine framed 'tubes' of various heights, each *c.* 23 m square in plan; they are bundled together at the base and function in an overall manner as cantilevers from the ground. The CN Tower in Toronto has a total height of 553 m, with a main concrete structure 446 m high, and was completed in 1975. It is a cantilever, consisting of three legs or buttresses; each leg is *c.* 28 m×7 m at its base and tapers upward. Transmission towers taller than the CN Tower exist, but they are 'guyed towers' with stay-wires, which help to reduce deflections at the top, and are thus not true cantilever structures but propped cantilevers.

See also CHINA, §II, 1(i)(c) and BRACKET SYSTEM.

BIBLIOGRAPHY

B. S. Benjamin: *Structures for Architects* (Lawrence, 1974, rev. New York, 2/1984, rev. Lawrence, 3/1992)

T. Copplestone and others: *World Architecture: An Illustrated History* (London, 1976)

H. J. Cowan: *The Master Builders* (New York, 1977)

M. Salvadori: *Why Buildings Stand Up* (New York, 1980)

D. P. Billington: *The Tower and the Bridge* (New York, 1983)

B. S. Benjamin: *Structural Evolution: An Illustrated History* (Lawrence, 1990)

B. S. BENJAMIN

Canton. *See* GUANGZHOU.

Cantón, Francisco Javier Sánchez. *See* SÁNCHEZ CANTÓN, FRANCISCO JAVIER.

Cantone, Bernardino (*b* Pieve di Balerna, nr Como, 1505; *d* Genoa, 1576–80). Italian architect, urban planner, surveyor and engineer. The son of a family of craftsmen, he arrived in Genoa in 1519 and enrolled in the guild of the Maestri Antelami Lombardi, completing his apprenticeship as a mason, architect and surveyor during the early 1520s. From around 1527 he took part in several projects to renovate and expand the medieval city, including the clearing of the Piazza Ferraria (now Piazza Matteotti). He played a key role in this phase of Genoese urban development (*see* GENOA, §1), firstly as architect to the Magistrates of the Padri del Comune (1531) and then as Architetto di Camera from 1546 until retirement in 1576. His early projects included the expansion of the eastern suburbs (1535–8) in conjunction with the modernization of Genoa's 14th-century fortifications; the enlargement of the Piazza Fossatello (1539–40) as a family enclave and marketplace; and the reconstruction of the Lanterna (1543), the beacon to ships at the harbour entrance.

In the same period Cantone built a palazzo (1542) for Nicola Cicala on the Piazza dell'Agnello in the Early Renaissance style prevalent in Genoa during the first half of the 16th century. However, the arrival of Galeazzo Alessi to build the church of S Maria Assunta di Carignano (1549–1603) radically changed the predominant building style in Genoa to Roman High Renaissance. Alessi's designs were all closely supervised in construction by Cantone and other artists associated with the '*scuola di Carignano*'.

As Architetto di Camera, Cantone took charge of work on the Strada Nuova (1550–51, 1557–60) starting from Alessi's plan to create a monumental axial street on the northern fringe of the medieval city. He adapted Alessi's design, which was influenced by the Via Giulia (1508–11) in Rome, to the insular interests of the Genoese patriciate, creating, in a street closed at one end, an aristocratic residential neighbourhood for the élite families of bankers and merchants who built palaces there.

Cantone's mastery of Alessi's Roman style is evident in the Palazzo Pallavicino (1558–63; now Banco di Napoli), on the Strada Nuova, which he supervised according to Alessi's plans. This features a façade with a sophisticated Mannerist interplay of rusticated and dressed marble frames with grey *pietra di Promontorio* mouldings. Cantone also built the Palazzo Spinola (1558–66; now Banca d'America e d'Italia), with its more austere, tripartite façade decorated with painted Classical architecture, reliefs and figures. Both buildings continue the traditional Genoese atrium-staircase-loggia entrance and interior courtyard with the rich combinations of classical architecture, grotesque decoration and ceiling *quadro riportato* frescoes, characteristic of palaces by Alessi.

Cantone also collaborated with Giovanni Battista Castello on the Palazzo Spinola (now Doria, 1563–6, altered in the 17th century), the Palazzo Lomellino (now Podestà, 1563–5), both on the Strada Nuova, and the Palazzo Imperiale on the medieval Piazza di Campetto (1560). Cantone's Villa Lercari, 'la Semplicità', in S Pier d'Arena (1558–63, destr.), was particularly striking in its placement of a monumental building cube over a formal terraced garden, descending down to the sea with nymphaea and other garden structures. It contributed significantly to the development of the suburban residence for which Genoa became famous during the Late Renaissance and Baroque eras.

BIBLIOGRAPHY

DBI
E. De Negri and others: *Il catalogo delle ville genovesi* (Genoa, 1967)
E. Poleggi: *Strada Nuova, una lottizzazione del cinquecento a Genova* (Genoa, 1968/*R* 1982)
Galeazzo Alessi e l'architettura del cinquecento. Atti del convegno internazionale di studi: Genova, 1974
I palazzi delle Strade Nuove (Genoa, 1986)
Le Strade Nuove (Genoa, 1986)
Le ville di Genova (Genoa, 1986)

GEORGE L. GORSE

Cantoni, Simone (*b* Mendrisio, Ticino, 2 Sept 1739; *d* Gorgonzola, 18 March 1818). Italian architect. He came from a family of artists and architects who worked in Genoa. He first studied with his father, an engineer, but in 1763 he moved to Rome, where he worked under Luigi Vanvitelli and surveyed ancient Roman remains with Francesco Lavega. He completed his studies in 1768 at the new academy at Parma under Ennemond-Alexandre Petitot. He built extensively in Lombardy and contributed to the introduction of French-inspired classicism into Milan. Cantoni chose to establish himself in Milan in 1768, rather than in Genoa like his family, but he was faced with strong competition from Giuseppe Piermarini, who eventually took over all the official commissions of the period. Cantoni found patronage among the Milanese nobility, for whom he built numerous palazzi and villas in and around Milan in the fashionable Neo-classical style. His first commission in Milan was for the renovation of the Palazzo Mellerio (1772–4). The commission for the Palazzo Serbelloni (1775–1814), built in a resolutely Neo-classical style, occupied Cantoni for the rest of his life. The façade comprises fifteen bays and three storeys; the three central bays project slightly and feature a pedimented loggia of free-standing Ionic columns, which occupies the two upper floors. There is a bas-relief frieze above the *piano nobile* and a lunette forming another loggia in the tympanum. The building was chosen for the reception of Napoleon in Milan in 1796. Cantoni also designed the cemetery and other small buildings in Gorgonzola in a restrained Neo-classical style for the Serbelloni family. Cantoni's only official commission was for the renovation (1778–83) of the façade and salon of the Palazzo Ducale, Genoa, for which he presented a speculative competition entry in 1778. The façade is in seven bays over a rusticated basement, with three central projecting bays; there are paired engaged columns on the two lower floors, Doric below and Ionic above.

By the end of the 18th century Cantoni had established himself and thereafter never lacked commissions: in a letter of 1794 he listed 21 works in progress (Rodi). In his later years he travelled extensively between Milan, Como, Bergamo and Ticino; among his most important works of the period are the enormous Neo-classical church (1781–1832) at Porto Maurizio; the Palazzo Vailetti (1783–91),

Bergamo; the Palazzo Pertusati (1789–91; destr.), Milan, arranged around a garden courtyard like a Parisian hôtel; the staircase and courtyard of the Palazzo Affaitati (1794), Cremona; and the Villa Olmo (1780–94; *see* ITALY, fig. 23), Como. The Villa Olmo incorporated Palladian elements within a severe Neo-classical framework, notably the colonnade of six engaged Ionic columns above a rusticated ground-floor. His last work was the church of SS Protasio e Gervasio (1818), Gorgonzola, based on an earlier design of 1802. The church is centrally planned and was possibly based on Francesco Borromini's S Agnese (1653) in the Piazza Navona, Rome; a wide porch ends in pedimented pavilions that dwarf the central portico.

UNPUBLISHED SOURCES

Bellinzona, Archv Cant. [drgs, some of which are pubd in Rodi below]

BIBLIOGRAPHY

C. L. V. Meeks: *Italian Architecture, 1750–1914* (New Haven, 1966)
G. Mezzanote: *Architettura neoclassica in Lombardia* (Naples, 1966)
C. Rodi: *Simone Cantoni architetto* (Como, 1973)
R. Middleton and D. Watkin: *Neoclassical and Nineteenth Century Architecture*, Hist. World Archit. (New York, 1980), pp. 295, 299, 392
V. Zanella: 'Progetti minori di Simone Cantone per Bergamo', *A. Lombarda*, 50–52 (1980), pp. 275–83
M. Morandi: 'Un progetto cremonese di Simone Cantone: La ristrutturazione del palazzo Affaitati-Magio', *A. Lombarda*, 92–3 (1990), pp. 117–22

□

Cantré, Jozef (*b* Ghent, 26 Dec 1890; *d* Ghent, 29 Aug 1957). Belgian sculptor and printmaker. From 1901 he went to classes at the Koninklijke Academie in Ghent, and from 1907 he attended day classes in drawing and modelling. He was taught by Jean Joseph Delvin (1853–1922). In 1908 he made his first book illustrations and woodcuts, for the *Boek der Maagden*; in 1909 he made his first sculpture in plaster, the *Weeping Woman* (priv. col., see De Ridder, pl. 1). His early sculptures, influenced by George Minne and Constantin Meunier, are realist in style. Apart from a period in Berlin (1923), he lived in the Netherlands from 1918 to 1930, in Blaricum and Oisterwijk, where he met Gustave De Smet and Frits Van den Berghe.

Cantré's contacts with Expressionists in Belgium and elsewhere, together with his introduction to non-Western sculpture, led him to change his work. During his years in the Netherlands he gave up modelling for direct carving in wood or stone. His sculptures are angular in shape, heavily stylized and loaded with emotional content. Over the years he abandoned closed, geometrical structures in favour of more dynamic forms, depicting drapery with a linear elegance. He also produced statues and monumental work for churches and gravestones. One of his most impressive monuments is that for the Socialist leader *Eduard Anseele* (Balmoral granite, h. 5 m, 1938–48) in Ghent. As a printmaker, with Frans Masereel and others he was one of the so-called Vijf who revived the Flemish woodcut. He illustrated many books including Karel van De Woestijne's *De boer die sterft* (The dying peasant; Antwerp, 1932).

BIBLIOGRAPHY

A. De Ridder: *Jozef Cantré* (Antwerp, 1952)
L'Oeuvre gravé de Jozef Cantré (exh. cat., Brussels, Bib. Royale Albert 1er, 1959)

ELS MARÉCHAL

Cantú, Federico (*b* Cadereyta, nr Monterrey, 3 March 1908; *d* Mexico City, 29 Jan 1989). Mexican painter, sculptor and printmaker. He studied at the Escuela de Pintura al Aire Libre at Coyoacán, in the early 1920s and independently with Spanish sculptor Mateo Hernández and the Catalan José de Creeft. Although younger than the major figures of post-revolutionary Mexican art, his work reflected their influence in the use of Pre-Columbian themes in his mural and sculptural work and in occasional references to indigenous types. In general, however, it was distinguished by the ephemeral, melancholic, linear quality of his figures, clearly influenced by Botticelli and by Picasso's Blue Period; harlequins, romantic poets and women with flowing hair were common subjects in his paintings, which were primarily portraits, religious scenes and allegorical compositions. In 1945 he began an association with the printmaker Carlos Alvarado Lang, and the resulting engravings showed fine linear elegance (e.g. the *Communion Rail*, 1945–6; Monterrey, La Purísima). Throughout the 1960s he produced sculpted reliefs and free-standing sculptures for the buildings of the Instituto Mexicano de Seguridad Social; in these works Cantú came close to the massive qualities associated with the Mexican school, but his figures' volume was still tempered by linear detailing.

BIBLIOGRAPHY

Eduardo P. Blackaller: *Federico Cantú: Seis décadas de trabaio* (Mexico City, 1980)
Federico Cantú: Ciclos y reencuentros (exh. cat., Mexico City, Mus. Pal. B.A., 1986)
A. Arteaga: *Federico Cantú: Una nueva visión* (Mexico City, 1989)

KAREN CORDERO REIMAN

Canuti, Domenico Maria (*b* Bologna, 5 April 1625; *d* Bologna, 6 April 1684). Italian painter. After training in Bologna under Guido Reni, Guercino, Giovanni Andrea Sirani and Francesco Gessi, he was in Rome from 1651 to 1655 under the patronage of Abbot Taddeo Pepoli, a distinguished Bolognese scholar. His Bolognese origins, specifically a debt to Reni and the Carracci, are apparent in the *Ecstasy of St Cecilia* (Imola, S Maria di Valverde), considered to be his first work. The *Universal Judgement* (Bologna, S Girolamo della Certosa), signed and dated 1658, shows the development of a more Baroque style. That he was also aware of Venetian painting is apparent in his first ceiling fresco, the *Triumph of Bacchus and Ariadne* (*c.* 1664; Bologna, Palazzo Fibbia, now Masetti-Calzolari), executed in collaboration with the *quadraturista* Domenico Santi, called Mengazzino (1621–94). Here Canuti tried to conceal any distinction between the real space of the hall and his illusionistic spatial cone traversed by bands of radiating light.

Canuti executed various decorative works for the Palazzo Pepoli Campogrande in Bologna. By March 1665 he had finished his first commission there: two frescoes (*in situ*) on the grand staircase ceiling, set within medallion-shaped stucco frames and showing the outstanding events of the life of the distinguished 14th-century Bolognese figure Taddeo Pepoli—his *Election as Prince of Bologna in 1338* and *Appointment to the Apostolic Vicarage by Benedict XII.* Here the architectural settings reveal a specific debt to Veronese. Three preparatory studies for the work survive; a drawing (London, BM) for the first, and *bozzetti*

Domenico Maria Canuti: *Apotheosis of Hercules on Olympus* (1660–70), fresco, Gran Salone, Palazzo Pepoli Campogrande, Bologna

for both (Milan, Treccani priv. col.). These demonstrate Canuti's usual habit of diverging, in the completed work, from all preparatory sketches.

Between 1660 and 1670, in collaboration with an ex-pupil, the *quadraturista* Giovan Gioseffo Santi (1644–1719), Canuti painted his outstandingly successful *Apotheosis of Hercules on Olympus* (see fig.) on the ceiling of the Gran Salone in the Palazzo Pepoli Campogrande (*in situ*). This work, which alludes by association to the glorious distinction of the Pepoli, achieves a compelling illusion of vast aerial space through a careful balancing of light and mass. It also achieves a perfect balance between figure painting and *quadratura*. For Canuti its precedents would have been the celebrated ceiling decorations in Rome: Annibale Carracci's for the Farnese Gallery (*see* ITALY, fig. 36) and Pietro da Cortona's for the Palazzo Barberini (*see* ROME, fig. 61). He was probably also familiar with Cortona's ceilings for the State rooms of the Palazzo Pitti in Florence (for illustration of ceiling in Sala di Giove, *see* CORTONA, PIETRO DA, fig. 2). Santi's preparatory sketch for the *quadratura* setting (Windsor Castle, Berks, Royal Col.) shows the influence of the designs made by Angelo Mitelli Colonna and Agostino Mitelli for the Palazzo Pitti. The final plan, however, abandoned the rectangular format of the sketch in favour of an oval and an even more daring perspective. It is clear from the Palazzo Pepoli *quadratura*, among the most intricate of its time, that Canuti was attracted less by the dominantly architectural scheme of Colonna and Mitelli than by the ornamental and decorative possibilities of the form. His gift for using such effects to enhance the figure painting enabled him to impart a new vigour and sense of opulence to an established Roman Baroque genre. Several preparatory sketches for the ceiling survive: three oval drawings for the central scene (Munich, Staatl. Graph. Samml.; Venice, Fond. Cini; London, Flavia Ormond F.A.) and two *bozzetti* (both priv. col.). The project was completed in August 1671 and its success brought Canuti immediate invitations to work in Rome. Before he went to Rome, however, he painted a somewhat different work, the *Death of St Benedict* (*c*. 1671; Bologna, Pin. N.), which, in its spirit and strong, dark tonality, anticipates the early work of Giuseppe Maria Crespi (ii).

In Rome by 4 April 1672, Canuti was enrolled as a member of the Accademia di S Luca in September. His most important Roman commission was for the *Apotheosis of St Dominic*, painted (1673–5; *in situ*) on the vault and apse of SS Domenico e Sisto, with Enrico Giovanni Haffner as *quadraturista*. It was also Canuti's only commission for a nave vault. Haffner conceived his framework as the continuation of the actual architecture of the walls of the church. Frescoed corbels appear below frescoed windows (matching the real ones) and appear to support frescoed balconies and bridges, features that both define and contain the limitless space of the ceiling. Canuti's careful grouping of the figures and his adept handling of perspective and light effects give a strong sense of upwardly swirling movement to the dramatic central scene of the *Apotheosis*. The *quadratura* is lavish to a degree not previously encountered in Rome. However, this new type of scenographic fresco painting attracted few followers in that city, apart from Andrea Pozzo in his painting (1688–94) of the vault of S Ignazio. The style had more success in Genoa, where Canuti's love of a sensual profusion of flowers, fruit and half-naked figures appealed to native taste, and flourished in the decorative ensembles of Gregorio de Ferrari and the *quadraturista* Antonio Maria Haffner. In Rome Canuti and Enrico Giovanni Haffner also frescoed the *Apotheosis of Romulus* (1675–6; *in situ*) on the large antechamber ceiling in the Palazzo Altieri. The vitality of this work, another triumph of illusionistic space, is also found in a surviving preparatory drawing (Madrid, Prado).

Canuti returned to Bologna, where between 21 June 1677 and 24 January 1678 he provided decorations (*in situ*) for the library of the convent of S Michele in Bosco for Abbot Taddeo Pepoli. In the central salon the theme of knowledge covers the three domes and is continued on the wall lunettes with allegories of the sciences (preparatory drawing, Florence, Uffizi). The style anticipates the Rococo decoration of 18th-century libraries. Neither this commission nor the *Jupiter Delivering Bacchus to Mercury* that Canuti frescoed on a ceiling in Palazzo Marescotti, Bologna (*in situ*), display his previously characteristic preoccupation with ceiling depth and irradiating light. The Marescotti fresco, for which preparatory drawings exist (Paris, Louvre; Budapest, N. Mus.), is Canuti's only known ceiling without *quadratura*. Apart from his obviously significant contribution to Italian ceiling painting, Canuti is notable as a sensitive draughtsman, whose drawings owe much to those by Ludovico Carracci and Guercino. He had a flourishing studio in Bologna, where Giuseppe Maria Crespi (ii) worked.

BIBLIOGRAPHY

E. Feinblatt: 'The Roman Work of Domenico Maria Canuti', *A. Q.* [Detroit], xv (1952), pp. 45–65

——: 'Some Drawings by Canuti Identified', *A. Q.* [Detroit], xxiv (1961), pp. 262–82

T. Poensgen: 'Some Unknown Drawings by Domenico Maria Canuti', *Master Drgs*, v/2 (1967), pp. 165–8

E. Feinblatt: 'D. M. Canuti and Giuseppe Rolli: Further Studies for Frescoes', *Master Drgs*, vii (1969), pp. 164–5

S. Stagni: *Domenico Maria Canuti* (Rimini, 1988)

E. Feinblatt: *Seventeenth-century Bolognese Ceiling Decorators* (Santa Barbara, 1992)

FLAVIA ORMOND

Canvas. Type of strong, substantial cloth originally made of hemp (*Cannabis sativa*, from which it takes its name) but more likely to be of a coarse flax or tightly woven linen; similar textiles of cotton or jute are also called canvas. A cloth type rather than a specific cloth, with varied practical applications, canvas is important as a material used for making painting supports. 'Canvas' has therefore come to mean not only the raw cloth but also a piece of fabric mounted on a stretching frame and prepared for use in painting or a finished painting, usually in oils, painted on a textile support.

1. Properties and types. 2. History and use. 3. Conservation.

1. Properties and types.

(i) Properties. Canvas is most often a plainly woven cloth with a weft that passes alternately under and over each warp thread. The warp and weft are usually of equal strength, but the tightness of the weave may vary: substantial canvases might have coarse, robust threads, loosely

woven, or fine ones tightly packed together. The weave affects the stability of the cloth, the ease with which it can be prepared for painting and the texture (tooth) that the prepared surface presents. The choice of canvas, although often based on practicalities, therefore has an influence on the final appearance of the painting. The more complex twill weaves sometimes used for canvas produce a pronounced surface pattern either of parallel diagonal lines or of a herringbone design. Such cloth is a particular feature of the work of Veronese (see fig. 1). Sir Joshua Reynolds used it in imitation of Veronese , and in some works by Camille Pissarro and Paul Gauguin (see fig. 2) its employment also seems intentional. However, its early use by Andrea Mantegna and the unusual occurrence of an even more complex damask cloth beneath *Erminia and the Shepherds* (*c.* 1623–5; Paris, Louvre) by Domenichino rather suggest the ad hoc use of any suitable fabric. The development of CRAQUELURE, accretions of dirt and varnish and certain types of paint loss are subsequently attributable to the type of canvas weave.

The transition from hand weaving to machine weaving effected a slight change in the character and behaviour of canvas cloths. Later machine-woven canvases tend to be smoother and more tightly woven. Wider cloth can be made by machine, but since canvas can always be joined easily to make larger pieces this has not affected its use.

1. Paolo Veronese: *Allegory of Peace*, oil on canvas, 1.05×0.64 m, 1551 (Rome, Protomoteca Capitolina)

Being a loose and flexible material, canvas is not fit to be painted on in its natural state. It must first be stretched taut across a frame to create a flat and relatively firm surface. Canvases are generally prepared from unfinished cloth, the deep, variable colour and fibrous nature of which are also unhelpful to the artist, so it is usual to prepare the cloth before painting on it. A coating of SIZE stabilizes the stretched canvas and prevents the paint from soaking into it, a potentially destructive occurrence in the case of oil paint; for most purposes a GROUND preparation is applied on top of that. Nevertheless, the inherent properties of the raw cloth are not entirely suppressed. A stretched and prepared canvas remains semi-flexible and will continue to respond to temperature and humidity changes, mostly at its unprimed reverse side. This causes continual movement due to the fluctuating tension in the threads and renders the support technically unstable, though within certain tolerable limitations.

Although the life-expectancy of a painting on canvas is often less than the supposed durability of the fabric employed would suggest (*see* §3 below), the conveniences of canvas outweigh its disadvantages. Its low cost and light weight are in its favour, while its tooth and the slight give of its surface when painted on are felt by many artists to add to the pleasures of painting.

(ii) Types. True hemp comes from the Indian plant *Cannabis sativa*, but the name is loosely applied to other vegetable fibres used for similar purposes. Hemp was originally used for ropemaking and for coarse cloth for sails. Tintoretto and Nicolas Poussin are known to have used cloth of hemp, and its employment probably continued into the 19th century. It is easily confused with flax, the plant *Linum usitatissimum*, from which linen is made (and which also yields linseed oil). The names flax and linen both apply to this cloth and may be used indiscriminately, though flax usually refers to a heavy, coarse version of the cloth with robust threads, and linen to the finer-quality fabrics made from the same fibre. The raw cloth is grey-brown, sometimes with specks of woody matter enmeshed in the weave. Flax has a rougher, more fibrous surface than linen. Linen and flax are strong, hard-wearing fabrics, with a theoretical life-expectancy of up to 1000 years, and their use has largely dominated painting on canvas. Handmade linen canvas continued to be used into the 19th century. Probably since the 19th century specific qualities of 'artists' linen' have been manufactured in Belgium and Ireland. Different weave qualities and weights may be used selectively for different styles or subject-matter. The most finely woven ones are sometimes referred to as 'portrait linen'. Ticking, onion bag, holland and cambric are some of the now defunct or little-used terms for canvas varieties.

Cotton is softer and less durable than linen. It is produced in a great variety of weights and weave qualities; the heavier qualities of cotton 'duck' are sometimes described as canvas, and it is usually these that are employed in painting. Cotton is naturally a creamy off-white in colour and has a smoother surface than linen.

2. Paul Gauguin: *Te Reroia*, oil on canvas, 0.95×1.30 m, 1897 (London, University of London, Courtauld Institute Galleries)

Although the cotton industry was mechanized before the linen industry, it was only in the 20th century that cotton canvas supplanted linen, largely because cotton was more economical to use. Cotton canvases are widely used by amateur painters and students but since the 1960s have enjoyed a popularity at all levels of activity. David Hockney's *A Bigger Splash* (1967; London, Tate), for example, is on a cotton duck.

Hessian is a coarse cloth made from jute, the fibre from the inner bark of *Corchorus capsularis* and *Corchorus olitorius.* It has large fibrous threads and presents a rough, hairy surface, giving a canvas with a bold and pronounced tooth when prepared. It is a slightly orange yellow-brown in colour. Hessian has a short life-expectancy and becomes brittle and friable after 50–100 years. It is nevertheless occasionally used by painters, especially where a rugged surface texture is desired. Gauguin's *Te rerioa* (1897; U. London, Courtauld Inst. Gals) is on a hessian canvas, perhaps improvised from discarded sacking or a bale covering.

Synthetic fibres have as yet found little use in artists' canvases, as their preparation presents difficulties and most painters have a conservative attitude towards them. They are now being employed, though not very extensively. Synthetic fibres would potentially make durable and stable canvases, but they are not sympathetic towards some of the established practices of painting and at present are of greater interest to conservators.

BIBLIOGRAPHY

M. Doerner: *Malmaterial und seine Verwendung im Bilde* (Munich, 1921, rev. 4/1933); Eng. trans. as *The Materials of the Artist* (London, 1935/*R* 1979)

R. Mayer: *Dictionary of Art Terms and Techniques* (London, 1969)

J. Stephenson: *The Materials and Techniques of Painting* (London, 1989)

2. HISTORY AND USE. Canvas was originally used for ships' sails, tents, sacking and similar practical applications. Its adoption for painting has been conditioned by local availability, fashion, cost and, perhaps, personal preference. The early evidence of painting on cloth is circumstantial or consists of isolated examples. As the materials involved are perishable, the incidence of their use and the relative importance of such works cannot be established. Painted linen has been found in an Egyptian tomb of El-Ghebeleń dating from *c.* 3500 BC (Turin, Mus. Egizio), the painted decoration of textiles features in Pre-Columbian South American art, and paintings on silk were an established art form of the Chinese Han dynasty (206 BC–AD 220). Pliny the elder mentioned the use of canvas for a portrait, 36 m high, of the Roman emperor Nero. It is generally accepted that in Western art the transition from using panels to using canvases for important paintings began during the 15th century, but there is documentary evidence from the 14th century that painting on cloth was then already widely practised. At least one of the methods in use was German or English in origin, while another was probably Flemish. An Italian public record dated 1335

refers to 'pictures on cloth in the German method' (Eastlake, i, pp. 90–91) by a Maestro Marco and his brother Paolo, living in Venice, who had either learnt or copied the method from a German friar who had painted similar works on cloth. The early date is significant, but so too is the location: Venetian artists developed an enthusiasm for canvas before the rest of Italy, and its exploitation there during the Renaissance more than 100 years later represents a turning-point in art history.

A manuscript (Paris, Bib. N., MS. 6741) of 1410 confirms that the English painted on cloth at about this time and describes a method of painting on cloth using transparent watercolours. Finely woven linen was soaked in gum solution and, when dry, stretched out and laid flat on an absorbent layer of coarse woollen cloth. The artists walked over it with clean feet and painted as they went with colours that might well have been organic dyes rather than pigmented paints. The woollen cloth covering the floor absorbed the excess moisture, while the gum prevented the colours from running. (This unusual method of working on cloth probably accounts for the confused distinction between 'painters' and 'stainers' that surfaced later in the English guild system: 'painters' worked on panels, 'stainers' on cloth.) Whether the English and German methods were the same is not known, but evidently a similar technique was known in Germany as, according to Vasari, Albrecht Dürer sent Raphael a painting in transparent watercolours on fine linen that could be viewed from both sides, the highlights being derived from the cloth without the use of white. Leonardo da Vinci may also have known this method of painting.

Other methods of working on cloth were given by Cennino Cennini in *Il libro dell'arte* (*c.* 1390): linen or silk was used to make religious processional banners; black or blue cloths were used for painted decorative hangings, probably in imitation of tapestries; silk painted on both sides is mentioned for palls, ensigns and again banners; and the painting and gilding of velvet to make sumptuous, exotic cloths and of woollen cloth for heraldic devices on noblemen's apparel are discussed. In the case of religious banners, the preparation for painting involved stretching the cloth on a frame, although Cennini referred to its being rolled or folded, implying that it was later removed. His suggestions that a size solution weaker than usual might be used and that starch or sugar should be added (to act as a plasticizer) and his concern for the thinness of the gesso ground all indicate the need for maximum flexibility and tend to confirm that the finished paintings hung loosely. The *Virgin of Humility* (late 14th century; London, N.G.; see fig. 3) by Lippo di Dalmasio, contemporary with Cennini's account, is probably the remnant of a processional banner such as he described. Canvas was also used for other short-lived decorations at festivals and, as today, for theatrical scenery.

In this early period a connection existed between painters, embroiderers and tapestry-makers. The English method of painting detailed above was actually related by an embroiderer, and Cennini wrote of painting on to cloth to provide designs for embroiderers to work over. Other instances of cooperation between these activities are also indicated. Tapestry cartoons were provided by painters, as the later examples (London, V&A) by Raphael confirm.

3. Lippo di Dalmasio: *Virgin of Humility*, tempera on canvas, 1.10×0.87 m, late 14th century (London, National Gallery)

It is quite likely that some of these were executed on to cloth as a convenient way of achieving the large scale needed. Painted imitations of tapestries were also produced as a less costly alternative to them. Large painted hangings were a particular product of the Netherlands in the early 15th century. Karel van Mander I commented on their frequent use as room decorations there and expressed the opinion that some that he had seen were by Roger of Bruge (?Rogier van der Weyden). These 'Flemish cloths' reached Italy in quantity, and it is generally supposed that they provided the inspiration for the north Italian artists who then began painting on canvas supports, though, as discussed above, painting on cloth had been introduced to Venice much earlier.

Canvas was also applied to the wooden panels employed for tempera painting, as a cover either for the joints where stress might occur or for the whole of the surface to be worked on. Its use in this context was mentioned by Theophilos in *De diversis artibus* (1110–40) and afterwards by Cennini and others. Painting directly on to canvas need not have involved a radical change in concept. The earliest works on canvas were probably painted that way for ease of transportation and were then installed *in situ* on top of a panel. Andrea Mantegna's *Virgin and Child with St Mary Magdalene and St John the Baptist* (*c.* 1495; London, N.G.) was formerly mounted in that fashion, and his *Presentation in the Temple* (*c.* 1454–5; Berlin, Gemäldegal.) still is. Other canvases of this period show signs of having originally been fixed over panels.

Cennini's method of preparing canvas for banners was sensitive to the shortcomings of textile supports generally, and the progression from there to the fixed canvas supports of the 15th and 16th centuries involved little more than leaving the canvas on its stretcher and painting on only one side of it. Apparently the typical practice was to prepare and paint the canvas on a temporary stretcher and to transfer it to another one, probably of lighter construction, or to a panel for display. This could permit an adjustment to the pictorial space if necessary and certainly favours easy transportation. Mantegna noted that canvas could be 'wrapped around a rod when being moved', showing his awareness of its portable nature. Until the 17th century depictions of artists at work often showed canvases lashed to temporary frames while being painted on, as for example in the *Artist as Zeuxis Painting an Ugly Old Woman* (?*c.* 1670–80; Frankfurt am Main, Städel. Kstinst. & Städt. Gal.) by Arent de Gelder. Thomas Gainsborough was still doing this in the 18th century, but by then it would have been unusual.

Netherlandish and northern Italian painters started to use canvas for quality work in the 15th century. Some early examples are in size colour, suggesting a possible link with the English and German methods noted, but it was the combination of oil paint with canvas that ensured its future success. The focal point of this development was Venice. Although Mantegna was not a Venetian painter, his father-in-law, Jacopo Bellini, was, and these two artists represent the obvious beginnings of painting on canvas in Italy. Bellini's sons Gentile and Giovanni also favoured canvas, and together they dominated Venetian painting for the rest of the century. Giorgione, Titian and Sebastiano del Piombo trained in Giovanni Bellini's studio, and in the hands of Titian in particular the dominance of canvas was finally confirmed. Tintoretto and Veronese took still more advantage of the potential scale on which canvas could be used. The inability of frescoes and tempera paintings on wooden panels to survive in Venice's humid, salty atmosphere explains the Venetian willingness to adopt both oil paint and canvas, but the suitability of that combination was probably known already. Canvas was cheap, lightweight and readily available, especially in a maritime nation such as Venice, and pieces could be sewn together to make supports of any size. These factors were enough to guarantee its popularity from the late Renaissance onwards, since when its essential use has not changed. The type of ground applied to it and the techniques used over it have evolved, but these are separate issues (*see* GROUND).

In the 17th century a full-length portrait painted on canvas commonly corresponded in width to the typical width of handmade cloth, a factor determined by how far the shuttle could be thrown. In the sale of Peter Lely's studio contents in 1682, some items were described as canvas, others as sacking, some indeterminately as 'cloth'. Canvas sizes relating to portraiture were quoted as whole length and half length, but it cannot be supposed that these were an exact specification. In the 18th century, when the commercial production of artists' canvases replaced their preparation within the studio, there was increasing standardization of canvas sizes and the frames that went with them, and by the 19th century a full range of sizes for landscape and portraiture had been developed. Commercial production favoured the preparation of large pieces that were then cut down to make smaller sizes. This eventually led to the introduction of the now-familiar wedged stretcher that permits an already primed canvas to be tightened by a slight expansion of its carrying frame.

BIBLIOGRAPHY

C. Cennini: *Il libro dell'arte* (*c.* 1390); Eng. trans. and notes by D. V. Thompson jr (1933)
G. Vasari: *Vite* (1550; rev. 2/1568); ed. G. Milanesi (1878–85)
C. Eastlake: *Materials for a History of Oil Painting* (London, 1847); repr. as *Methods and Materials of Painting of the Great Schools and Masters*, 2 vols (New York, 1960) [esp. vol. i]
M. K. Talley: *Portrait Painting in England* (diss., U. London, 1978; privately pubd, London, 1981)
Paint and Painting (exh. cat., London, Tate, 1982)
J. Ayres: *The Artist's Craft* (London, 1985)
A. Callen, ed.: *Techniques of the Great Masters of Art* (London, 1985)
Z. Veliz: *Artists' Techniques in Golden Age Spain* (Cambridge, 1986)
D. Wolfthal: *The Beginnings of Netherlandish Canvas Painting, 1400–1530* (Cambridge, 1989)
J. Dunkerton and others: *Giotto to Dürer: Early Renaissance Painting in the National Gallery* (London, 1991)

3. CONSERVATION. Canvas is susceptible to rot, pest attack, accidental damage and the general degradations of time. It is, in fact, quite fragile when stretched and is easily cut or punctured. The conservation of canvas is often a matter of restoration and repair (*see* CONSERVATION AND RESTORATION, §II, 1 and 2(i)). The primary object is to preserve and conserve the painting on the canvas, and to achieve that end the integrity of the cloth support is often compromised. In extreme circumstances the canvas has been removed entirely and the paint layers and ground transferred to another support. Only in comparatively recent times has attention been given to the notion of keeping a work of art intact by slowing down, arresting or reversing the degradation of its fabric support with the minimum of alteration to that support. In less than ideal conditions canvases do not age well, so the vast majority of works on canvas have already been committed to the traditional processes of restoration that are mostly variants of lining or relining the canvas (*see* RELINING). Once (re)lining has been decided on, the process must be repeated at periodic intervals, as, although relining is in some degree reversible, it is not possible to go back to an even earlier stage in the canvas's history and choose an alternative form of conservation action.

Where a canvas has not been relined, it may be possible to consider other methods of conservation, although much depends on the condition of the canvas. A gentle reintroduction of moisture can partially rejuvenate a canvas, by regenerating the layer of size and relaxing the threads of the canvas, allowing the distortion in the paint layers to be corrected. This reintroduction of moisture takes place during the old-fashioned glue relining process. Vapour treatment on a vacuum hot-table or a low-pressure table is a modern, controlled method of achieving the same result. Vapour treatment was used successfully to conserve *Mr and Mrs Coltman* by Joseph Wright of Derby (London, N.G.), a painting dated to *c.* 1771 that had never been lined. Remounting the treated canvas on a blind stretcher, with solid panels fitted between the members of the frame, was then sufficient to conserve the canvas in its existing condition.

Control of temperature and humidity is of major importance in the conservation of canvas, as changes in these cause movement in the canvas, subject it to stress and promote differential behaviour between the canvas, paint and ground layers. Unfavourable conditions also promote biological attack. A constant temperature of 18°C and a relative humidity of between 50% and 55% is considered the most suitable environment for canvas. Such conditions, of course, are only likely to exist in galleries or museums. In less favourable circumstances, some means of preventing the surrounding atmosphere from gaining access to the back of the canvas, where it is most vulnerable, is usually beneficial. Mounting canvas on panel, not permanently as in the 'Marouflage' technique where it is glued down, but with the panel acting merely as a stretcher, or alternatively using a blind stretcher greatly reduces the effects of temperature and humidity changes on the canvas. It will also protect against accidental damage to the canvas from the rear. Thin sheets of metal and plastic have been used to back canvases successfully in a similar manner, but in using these materials there is a potential danger from condensation or trapped moisture. Generally, anything that encloses the back of the canvas and creates a more stable micro-climate is advantageous. Even a piece of lightweight card or strong paper used to enclose the back of the stretching frame will be beneficial. The use of a double canvas will also protect the canvas from changes in temperature and humidity: a second canvas stretched on the same frame can act to reinforce the one that is painted, also creating a barrier or buffer between the painted canvas and the atmosphere. In the 19th century a number of artists' colourmen used this method. Many of Turner's later paintings are or were originally 'loose lined' in this way. *Our English Coasts* by William Holman Hunt (1852; London, Tate) is an example of a painting backed by a second, primed canvas, a more effective protection than the unprimed backing cloths that were sometimes used.

Even when a canvas is carefully prepared and well looked after, it is still inclined to wear at the edges where it is in contact with the stretcher. Stretchers with rounded edges are much less damaging than ones with angled edges. Strip-lining an affected canvas to repair damage at the edges involves minimal interference with the canvas. Unless the stretcher is original to the painting and therefore part of its history, it may be preferable to replace the stretcher with a better one. Rough handling is bad for canvases and shock or vibration should be guarded against during transportation. Other risks to canvases include oxidation of the canvas caused by air pollution and the detrimental effects of ultraviolet light. A controlled environment is again the solution to these problems.

If the canvas is penetrated by oil, it will become brittle and decay. Proper preparation of the canvas and the employment of sensible techniques by the painter should substantially prevent this. However, even with the greatest of preparatory care, canvas inevitably becomes acidic and brittle with age. Treatments of oil to the back of canvases as a protection against damp must be avoided. The preservation of present and future works would be greatly enhanced if painters and the art materials trade took greater notice of some of these conservation factors. Poor preparation and the unsuitability of the materials and techniques used are likely to pose major threats to the life-expectancy of some modern works, which may require serious intervention rather than minor conservation procedures to preserve them for the future.

BIBLIOGRAPHY

C. Wolters and others: 'The Care of Paintings & Fabric Paint Supports', *Mus. Rev. Trimest.*, xiii (1960), pp. 134–71

J. Lodewijks: 'The Latest Developments in the Conservation of Old Textiles by Means of Heat Sealing', *ICOM, Mixed Conference: Laboratories and Treatment of Paintings: Brussels, 1967*

W. P. Prescott: 'The Lining Cycle', *Conference on Comparative Lining Techniques: London, 1974*

G. Berger: 'Unconventional Treatments for Unconventional Paintings', *Stud. Conserv.*, xxi/3 (1976), pp. 115–28

G. Emile-Mâle: *The Restorer's Handbook of Easel Painting* (New York, 1976)

M. Watherston: 'Treatment of Cupped and Cracked Paint Films Using Organic Solvents and Water', *Conservation and Restoration of Pictorial Art*, ed. N. Bromelle and P. Smith (London, 1976), pp. 110–25

D. Bomford: 'Moroni's *Canon Lodovico di Terzi*: An Unlined Sixteenth Century Painting', *N.G. Tech. Bull.*, iii (1979), pp. 34–42

A. Reeve: 'A New Multi-purpose Low-pressure Conservation Table for the Treatment of Paintings', *Stud. Conserv.*, xxix/3 (1984), pp. 124–8

M. Wyld and D. Thomas: 'Wright of Derby's *Mr and Mrs Coltman*: An Unlined English Painting', *N.G. Tech. Bull.*, x (1987), pp. 28–32

JONATHAN STEPHENSON

Canyon de Chelly. Archaeological zone in north-west Arizona. Pre-Columbian sites here are attributed to the Anasazi culture (*c.* 200 BC–*c.* AD 1350) and were built between the 12th and 14th centuries AD when the Anasazi began to abandon their scattered small hamlets on cliff tops for fewer but larger settlements of cliff dwellings. These were constructed in the steep-sided, stream-cut main and subsidiary canyons with numerous overhanging cliffs; on the shelves of such overhangs the Anasazi built blocks of apartment-like structures constructed of adobe bricks or stone blocks (e.g. White House ruins). The removal of the Anasazi from plateau dwellings to cliff dwellings may have been for defence as aggression increased between groups (*see also* MESA VERDE). The earliest rooms often became storage rooms as later dwellings were built above and in front of them. The blocks were multi-storey and terraced, with access between terraces by wooden ladders. Inter-storey floors–ceilings were made with log rafters. Walls had key-hole and trapezoidal doorways and in some cases square windows. Open spaces in front of the blocks were excavated and filled to create level ceremonial areas, and circular, semi-subterranean *kivas* were dug for use as men's ritual meeting places (*see* KIVA). Society was matrilineal, and the houses were owned by women. Crop failure and possibly invasion by Navajo and Apache groups may have caused the abandonment of Canyon de Chelly *c.* 1350.

For further discussion of the indigenous arts and architecture of the Southwest region of the USA *see* NATIVE NORTH AMERICAN ART.

BIBLIOGRAPHY

P. S. Martin and F. Plog: *The Archaeology of Arizona: A Study of the Southwest Region* (New York, 1973)

A. Ortiz, ed.: *Southwest*, Hb. N. Amer. Ind., ix (1979) [whole vol.]

——: *Southwest*, Hb. N. Amer. Ind., x (1983) [whole vol.]

L. S. Cordell: *Prehistory of the Southwest* (New York, 1984)

——: 'Southwest Archaeology', *Annu. Rev. Anthropol.*, xiii (1984), pp. 301–32

M. Coe, D. Snow and E. Benson: *Atlas of Ancient America* (Oxford, 1986), pp. 68–79

DAVID M. JONES

Cao Zhibai [Ts'ao Chih-pai; *zi* Zhensu; *hao* Yunxi] (*b* Huating (modern Songjiang, Shanghai Municipality), 1272; *d* 1355). Chinese painter, poet and engineer. Born into a family of prominent officials, he lost his father during infancy and was brought up by his mother and grandfather. He received a traditional education in the Chinese Confucian classics. He distinguished himself first as a hydraulic engineer, serving in 1294 and again in 1298 as an imperial adviser. His engineering achievements earned him great repute and doubtless contributed to his becoming one of the richest men in the Huating district. By reclaiming large areas of local wetland, he developed a large estate and farm. In the early 1300s he became a teacher in the nearby district of Kunshan but soon resigned. Later he visited the capital, Dadu (Khanbalik; now Beijing), where many aristocrats and high officials were interested in befriending him. Cao declined all offers of patronage, however, saying that he was not one of the vulgar people who went to the capital to seek high position.

He returned to the south and lived a hermit's life on his estate, reading the Daoist *Yijing* ('Book of Changes'). He launched a lavish building programme there, eventually consisting of over 80 structures, including various types of hall, studios, libraries, pavilions, towers and terraces, with picturesque garden embellishments such as rocks, caves and bridges; he also took a hand in planting flowers and trees. He collected several thousand volumes of books and several hundred scrolls of calligraphy and painting. Some of his early extant paintings, such as *Wintry Trees* (album leaf, ink on silk, 1325; Beijing, Pal. Mus.), *Two Pines* (hanging scroll, ink on silk, 1329; Taipei, N. Pal. Mus.) and *Rocks and Trees* (album leaf, ink on silk, n.d.; Princeton U., NJ, A. Mus.), reflect his interest in the trees and plants around his estate. They were works in the Li–Guo landscape tradition of the Northern Song (960–1127) masters Li Cheng and Guo Xi, who took a special interest in wintry trees and pines and based their work on direct experience of nature.

In his later years Cao was well known for his generosity: he often invited men of letters and the arts to be his house guests, sometimes for long periods of time. Among frequent visitors were such prominent literati artists as Huang Gongwang, Ni Zan, Yang Weizhen (1296–1370), Wang Mian and many poets of the period. At their literary gatherings, they moved around the grounds, drinking wine, composing poetry, writing essays, talking about Daoist ideas and mysticism, playing the *qin* (lute) and singing songs, in the manner of the ancient literati. During this period China was ruled by the alien Yuan dynasty (1279–1368). Scholars who would have held official bureaucratic posts in earlier periods of native rule rejected offers of Mongol patronage, instead devoting themselves to self-cultivation through painting, calligraphy and poetry and meetings with like-minded friends.

In his later paintings Cao seems to have been influenced by the works of friends such as Huang Gongwang. Guo Xi ceased to attract his interest; instead he turned his attention to the work of DONG YUAN, which by this time had made a great impact on literati painters. This new direction can be seen in extant works from the last period of his life, such as *Mountains Covered with Snow* (hanging scroll, ink on paper, 1350; Taipei, N. Pal. Mus.) and *Landscape with Trees* (hanging scroll, ink on paper, 1351; Beijing, Pal. Mus.). In these paintings he adopted some elements characteristic of the monumental landscapes of the Northern Song period, such as high mountains in the background dominating the whole composition and a tripartite composition. However, he combined these features with the type of long, wavy, 'hemp-fibre' texture strokes (*pima cun*) associated with Dong Yuan.

BIBLIOGRAPHY

O. Sirén: *Chinese Painting: Leading Masters and Principles* (London and New York, 1956–8), iv, pp. 69–70

Chu-tsing Li: '*Rocks and Trees* and the Art of Ts'ao Chih-po', *Artibus Asiae*, xxiii/3–4 (1960), pp. 153–92

J. Cahill: *Hills Beyond a River: Chinese Painting of the Yuan Dynasty, 1279–1368* (New York and Tokyo, 1976), pp. 80–84

Chen Gaohua: *Yuan dai huajia shiliao* [Historical sources on Yuan-period painters] (Shanghai, 1980), pp. 391–402

CHU-TSING LI

Capa, Robert [Friedman, André] (*b* Budapest, 22 Oct 1913; *d* Thai-Binh, Vietnam, 25 May 1954). American photographer of Hungarian birth. He studied political science at Berlin University from 1931 to 1933. A self-taught photographer, as early as 1931 he worked as a photographic technician for the Ullstein publishing house and as a photographic assistant for Dephot (Deutscher Photodienst) cooperative photographic agency. In 1933 he emigrated to Paris, where he and his friend Gerda Pohorylles (1901–37) invented the American-sounding name Robert Capa, initially to publish photo-stories for which she wrote the text. This unsettled period in Paris offered numerous opportunities to work as a freelancer and to publish successfully. Although Lucien Vogel, the publisher of the magazine *Vu*, had revealed Capa's use of a pseudonym, he kept the name and flew to Spain as a reporter on the Spanish Civil War. With Pohorylles (using the pseudonym Gerda Taro) he published *Death in the Making*, which contained his most famous photograph *Death of a Spanish Loyalist*, a soldier falling at the moment of being hit by a bullet. This picture made his reputation as a talented war reporter.

In 1938 Capa travelled to China and reported on the Japanese invasion; from 1941 to 1945 he was war correspondent for *Life* magazine, photographing in Italy, France, Germany and many other European countries. However, he intended to give up this occupation after World War II and lived in Paris for a time as part of a circle that included Pablo Picasso, Ernest Hemingway and John Steinbeck. During this period he also became friendly with Chim (David Seymour), Henri Cartier-Bresson, George Rodger (*b* 1908) and the *Life* photographer Bill Vandivert and joined them in founding the cooperative photographic agency Magnum in 1947. Membership of the agency was later to become a mark of high quality. Between 1948 and 1950 he photographed the unrest surrounding the establishment of the state of Israel; in 1954 he travelled to Indo-China as a temporary war correspondent for *Life* and was fatally wounded in Vietnam. His death was the tragic consequence of his basic principle: 'If your pictures aren't good enough, you aren't close enough.'

Capa's ability to capture in one picture the feelings of a people in rebellion or at war brought him the great admiration of his contemporaries and later generations. Many world-famous photographs show this ability: the weeping child in an Israeli camp in *Israel, 1948*, swimming soldiers in *D-Day, Omaha Beach, June 6, 1944*, hysterical Neapolitan mothers weeping over their sons in *Italy, 1944* (all in Capa, 1969). A common feature is that the narrative moment does not predominate; they are imbued with humanity but also bear witness to Capa's fascination with the human tight-rope walk between the will to live and the tendency to self-destruction.

Capa not only set new standards in photography, acting as a model for others; his work, full of commitment and human partisanship, is also a manifesto against war, injustice and oppression. Numerous awards were established in his name.

PHOTOGRAPHIC PUBLICATIONS

Death in the Making, text by G. Taro (New York, 1937)
The Battle of Waterloo Road (New York, 1943)
Slightly out of Focus (New York, 1947)
The Russian Journal, text by J. Steinbeck (New York, 1948)
Report on Israel, text by Irving Shaw (New York, 1950)
Images of War (New York, 1964)

BIBLIOGRAPHY

R. E. Hood: *Twelve at War* (New York, 1967)
A. Farova: *Robert Capa* (New York, 1968)
C. Capa, ed.: *The Concerned Photographer* (New York, 1969)
——: *Robert Capa, 1913–1954* (New York, 1974)
R. Martinez: *Robert Capa* (Milan, 1979)
G. Soria: *Les Grandes Photos de la guerre d'Espagne* (Paris, 1980)
C. Capa and R. Whelan, eds: *Robert Capa Photographs* (New York, 1985; Ger. edn., Cologne, 1985)

REINHOLD MISSELBECK

Capacha–Opeño. Pre-Columbian culture and ceramic assemblage found in Mexico. It is named after the Capacha ceramics from Colima and part of Jalisco and the site of El Opeño in Michoacán, which flourished during the Early Pre-Classic period (*c.* 2000–*c.* 1000 BC). Similar ceramic assemblages from these sources, along with other shared cultural features, indicate early contact between Mesoamerica and north-west South America (see below).

The Capacha ceramic assemblage, radiocarbon dated to *c.* 1350 BC, was named by Isabel Kelly. It consists largely of pottery once placed in graves or tombs but subsequently looted. Although no living sites or mounds are known, the ceramics are the oldest so far found in Colima. The pottery is predominantly monochrome and made of a thick, heavy, grainy paste. The most common form is a large, open-mouthed jar with a cinctured body, measuring up to 380 mm high and locally called a *bule*. Other forms include *tecomates* (or *tecomatl*), spherical vessels in imitation of gourds, with restricted openings and no collar, animal effigies, one stirrup-spouted vessel and a trifid form comprising a compound vessel of upper and lower bodies connected by three tubes to create a kind of modified stirrup-spouted form (see fig.). Capacha vessels are typically decorated with broad-line incision and punctation combined with sunburst patterns. A few vessels and fragments were painted with a rose-red slip or with a combination of red and purple-black. Designs are delineated by incisions and zoning. Some figurines are reminiscent of the Tlatilco style of the Central Highlands. Most Capacha ceramics are believed to come from looted shaft and chamber tombs.

Capacha–Opeño, black compound vessel, h. 280 mm, Colima style, *c.* 1350 BC (Washington, DC, Smithsonian Institution)

Two unlooted tombs were discovered at El Opeño near Jacona, Michoacán. Excavated by the Mexican archaeologist Arturo Oliveros, they were found to contain skeletons accompanied by rich offerings. One tomb had been reused and contained the remains of ten individuals. The other contained two male skeletons and pottery and has been dated by radiocarbon analysis to *c.* 1500 BC. Some of the forms and decorations in the El Opeño ceramic assemblage have parallels in the Capacha material, including painted sherds with zoning and incision. The Capacha–Opeño sample is small, but differences include types of clay figurines and an absence of stirrup-spouted vessels at El Opeño. At the same time, both areas lack many elements of contemporary ceramics found elsewhere in West Mexico, including tall necked bottles, spouted trays, excised decoration, rocker stamping, kaolin ware and polished black ware.

The Capacha–Opeño shaft tombs are also important for their probable relationship to cultures in north-west South America. Although the tomb chronology for Colombia and Ecuador is still uncertain, it is generally agreed that they are roughly contemporary (*see* SOUTH AMERICA, PRE-COLUMBIAN, §II, 2). West Mexican shaft tombs, such as those at El Opeño, form part of the wider Capacha complex and resemble those of the Cauca Valley and central Andes of Colombia. In general the Capacha culture shows stronger similarities to north-west South America than to Mesoamerica at this time. Other parallels are seen with the VALDIVIA culture and with the Machalilla culture of the Ecuadorian coast: the latter shared with Capacha the practice of a particular type of cranial deformation known as *tabula erecta*. The most convincing ceramic links are some distinctive similarities in ornamentation and in the form of stirrup-spouted vessels. These specialized vessels, including the Capacha trifid variant, are thought to have a single origin, although their distribution throughout West Panama, Colombia and Ecuador is discontinuous. If contact between these areas had been made by following the Pacific coast, the Capacha culture would have occupied a key position and provided a foothold for penetration inland, eventually into central Mesoamerica.

For discussion of the arts of Pre-Columbian Mexico *see also* MESOAMERICA, PRE-COLUMBIAN.

BIBLIOGRAPHY

J. A. Oliveros: 'Nuevas exploraciones en El Opeño, Michoacán', *The Archaeology of West Mexico*, ed. B. Bell (Ajijíc, 1974), pp. 182–201

I. Kelly: *Ceramic Sequence in Colima: Capacha, an Early Phase*, Anthropological Papers of the University of Arizona, xxxvii (Tucson, 1980)

MURIEL PORTER-WEAVER

Capalatitis, Giovanni Battista. *See* CAVALLETTO, GIOVANNI BATTISTA.

Capanna, Puccio (*fl* Assisi, 1341–7). Italian painter. Vasari described him as one of Giotto's most important pupils, but he identified him with the painter Puccio di Simone who is documented in Florence, although he included among the works attributed to this artist numerous paintings in Assisi and noted that the inhabitants of Assisi considered him to be a fellow citizen. A document of 1341, however, confirms the existence of an Assisi painter named Puccio di Capanna: the authorities commissioned 'Puccius Cappanej et Cecce Saraceni, pictores de Assisio' to paint images of the Virgin and Child with Saints on the 'Porta externa platee nove' and the 'Porta Sancti Ruphini' (see Abate). Puccio Capanna is also documented in Assisi in 1347 (Cenci).

On the basis of this document, a fresco fragment from the Porta di S Rufino representing the *Christ Child Turning towards St Francis* (Assisi, Mus. & Pin. Com.) has been identified as Puccio Capanna's work; it is clearly part of a larger composition of the *Virgin and Child with Saints* (Marcucci). The fragment is a member of a stylistically homogeneous group of works formerly attributed to various artists, including Stefano Fiorentino (Longhi). It comprises the frescoes of the *Coronation of the Virgin* and two scenes from the *Life of St Stanislas* in the choir of the Lower Church of S Francesco, Assisi, and the *Crucifixion* in the chapter house; a detached fresco of the *Crucifixion* from the oratory of S Ruffinuccio (Assisi, Mus. Opera Duomo); fragmentary frescoes of the *Annunciation* and the *Crucifixion* in the convent of S Giuseppe, Assisi; a fresco of the *Virgin and Child Enthroned with Saints* in the chapel of S Giorgio, S Chiara, Assisi; and a small diptych composed of the Kress *Crucifixion* (Raleigh, NC, Mus. A.) and the *Virgin and Child Enthroned with Two Angels and Ten Other Small Figures* (Rome, Vatican, Pin.). Despite the fact that the document of 1341 also mentions another artist, Cecce di Saracino (otherwise unknown), and that it refers to the commissioning not the execution of the frescoes, the attribution of this group of paintings to Puccio Capanna has been generally accepted.

These paintings are so close to the work of Giotto that they have more in common with the work of Maso di Banco and Giottino than with local Umbrian painters (e.g. Mello di Gubbio, *fl* early 14th century). The roots of Puccio Capanna's style lie in the frescoes executed by Giotto's workshop in the chapel of the Maddalena and in the south transept of the Lower Church of S Francesco, Assisi, particularly the *Crucifixion*, which is characterized by an airy monumentality, delicacy of colour and a mood of sublime pathos. Unlike Maso di Banco and Taddeo Gaddi, who developed the skill of representing depth, Puccio Capanna concentrated on the human figure, investing it with a more ample monumentality and increasing and deepening the range of expressions and attitudes, creating a soft and mellow style. He was one of the most original of Giotto's followers, and his work anticipated many of the naturalistic tendencies of later 14th-century painting (e.g. the work of Altichiero).

BIBLIOGRAPHY

DBI

G. Vasari: *Vite* (1550, rev. 2/1568); ed. G. Milanesi (1878–85), i, pp. 130–31

Fra Ludovico da Pietralunga: *Descrizione della basilica di S Francesco e di altri santuari di Assisi* (Assisi, 1570–80); ed. P. Scarpellini (Treviso, 1982), pp. 63–4, 292–304

R. Longhi: 'Stefano Fiorentino', *Paragone*, xiii (1951), pp. 18–40

G. Abate: 'Per la storia e l'arte della basilica di S Francesco in Assisi', *Misc. Francesc.* (1956), pp. 3–36

L. Marcucci: 'Dal maestro di Figline a Giottino', *Jb. Berliner Mus.*, v (1963), pp. 14–43

P. Scarpellini: 'Di alcuni pittori giotteschi nella città e nel territorio di Assisi', *Giotto e i giotteschi in Assisi* (Rome, 1969), pp. 211–70 (242–62)

C. E. Caldora: 'Capanna, Puccio', *Dizionario enciclopedico Bolaffi dei pittori e degli incisori italiani*, iii (Turin, 1972), p. 6

C. Cenci: *Documentazione di vita assisiana*, i (Grottaferrata, 1974), pp. 85, 100

B. Zanardi: 'Da Stefano Fiorentino a Puccio Capanna', *Stor. A.*, xxxiii (1978), pp. 115–27

F. Todini and B. Zanardi: *La Pinacoteca comunale di Assisi: Catalogo dei dipinti* (Florence, 1980), pp. 56–8

C. Volpe: 'Il lungo percorso del "dipingere dolcissimo e tanto unito"', *Storia dell'arte italiana*, ed. G. Bollati and P. Fossati, v (Turin, 1983), pp. 231–304

LUCIANO BELLOSI

Capdevila, Francisco Moreno. *See* MORENO CAPDEVILA, FRANCISCO.

Cape Cormorin. *See* KANYAKUMARI.

Cape Dutch style. Architectural style developed at the Cape of Good Hope, South Africa, during the period of Dutch East India Company rule (1652–1795). Despite subsequent British stylistic innovations, its use continued in country districts until the 1880s. The term was first acknowledged, with reservations, by G. E. Pearse in 1933 but was given authority only in 1953 by C. de Bosdari. It covers three main building types: farmhouses, town houses and public buildings.

Cape Dutch farmhouse, Groot Constantia, Cape Province, *c.* 1792; restored by F. K. Kendall, 1926

The early development of both domestic types followed similar lines, with the availability of materials being the major determining factor. Local bricks were under-fired and insufficiently water-resistant, which led to the use of lime plaster on exteriors, creating a white-walled aesthetic. Experiments with tiled roofs were unsuccessful, resulting in the adoption of thatch. Roofs were hipped at first, but were gradually replaced with half-hipped or gabled ends; the latter were given decorative outlines from an early date. Most early houses were rectangular in plan and only one room deep. However, the larger residences of the officials had more complex plans and triple-gabled façades with a central full-height gable flanked by dwarf gables.

The Cape Dutch farmhouse was descended from these early prototypes and achieved its definitive form by 1750. A variety of plan types was used, the U-plan, the T-plan and the H-plan being the most common. These were characterized by wings meeting at right angles, necessitated by the limitations of roof span to about 6 m. All were entered from the centre of the façade and had an entrance hall (*voorhuis*) linked to an inner hall of the same width behind (*galderij* or *achterhuis*). A central gable was placed above the entrance, with end gables terminating the wings; by mid-century the flanking gables had been omitted. The entrance door was usually elaborated with mouldings and in later years was enclosed by a classical surround. It was reached from the *stoep*, a raised terrace extending the full width of the façade. Earlier houses had casement windows, but these were gradually replaced by sliding sashes. Notable examples of Cape Dutch farmhouses include Groot Constantia (see fig.), Stellenberg, on the Cape Peninsula.

In contrast with the farmhouse, the town house, and LA PROVENCE, at Fransch Hoek took a form influenced by the narrowness of building plots and the fire risks inherent in the use of thatch. The adoption of flat roofs was first considered as early as 1717, but it was not until the 1770s that the majority of houses were rebuilt in this form. The flat roof permitted the introduction of the double-pile plan, with a two room depth, as the problem of valley gutters in parallel pitched roofs was eliminated. Other differences involved the use of a narrower *voorhuis* and a wider *achterhuis*. Town houses were also often extended to an upper storey, a rare occurrence in farmhouses.

The town house faced the street directly, separated from it only by the *stoep*. Like the farmhouse it usually had a symmetrical façade, but the decorative emphasis of a central gable was difficult to achieve with a flat roof. This was at first overcome by the use of a curvilinear parapet; in the 1780s the *dakkamer* was introduced: a gable-like extension of the wall surface above the cornice, with a room behind it for stability. In the 1790s a pediment, often containing relief sculpture, was used over the central bay of the façade, which was often articulated with pilasters.

The third category of Cape Dutch architecture is that of public buildings, of which few have survived. Most public buildings followed the academic classicism favoured by military engineers, notably Louis Michel Thibault (e.g. drostdy at Graff-Reinet; 1804), who had studied under Ange Jacques Gabriel in Paris. He worked closely with the sculptor Anton Anreith (1754–1822) from Freiburg im Breisgau and the builder Hermann Schutte from Bremen, both of whom also worked as architects in their own right.

See also SOUTH AFRICA, §VI, for a discussion of the interior decoration of Cape Dutch houses.

BIBLIOGRAPHY

G. E. Pearse: *Eighteenth Century Architecture in South Africa* (London, 1933)
C. de Bosdari: *Cape Dutch Houses and Farms* (Cape Town, 1953)
J. van der Meulen: *Die europäische Grundlage der Kolonialarchitektur am Kap der Guten Hoffnung* (Marburg, 1962)
H. Fransen and M. A. Cook: *The Old Buildings of the Cape* (Cape Town, 1980)
A. Obholzer, M. Baraitser and W. A. Malherbe: *The Cape House and its Interior* (Stellenbosch, 1985)
J. Walton: *Old Cape Farmsteads* (Cape Town, 1989)

R. H. FITCHETT

Čapek, Josef (*b* Hronov, 23 March 1887; *d* Bergen-Belsen, April 1945). Czech painter, printmaker and writer. He studied weaving (1901–3) in Vrchlabí and then from 1904 to 1910 decorative painting at the School of Applied Arts in Prague, where he was influenced by the highly decorative art of the Secession. During this period he wrote stories with his brother, the novelist Karel Čapek (1890–1938). In 1910 they went to Paris for nearly a year, where Josef Čapek studied painting at the Académie Colarossi and became a friend of Apollinaire. In 1911 he and his brother co-founded the Cubist-orientated Group of Plastic Artists. Čapek attempted to modify Cubism by introducing elements of Expressionism and Symbolism. His efforts dumbfounded some members of the group, and in 1912 he and various of his friends parted company with it. From 1915 he began to achieve a synthesis of Cubism, Neo-classicism and a personal symbolism (e.g. the *Man in the Hat*, 1915; Hradec Králové, Reg. Gal.), and in 1917 he participated in the first and subsequent exhibitions of the group Tvrdošíjní (The Stubborn Ones) and began to produce a number of prints for the magazine *Červen*, including the poster design for Arnošt Dvořák's *Mrtvá* at the Červná Sedma theatre in Prague (colour lithograph, 1920; Prague, Mus. App. A.). In the 1920s his paintings and prints became more densely woven, more expressive and more concerned with issues of civilian and suburban life. He also undertook theatre design, journalism and book illustration as well as publishing his own theoretical essays. In the late 1920s he became greatly influenced by folk art, painting simplified images of houses and countryside in bold strokes of bright colour. In 1933 he became a member of the editorial board of the magazine *Život*; by then his expressionistic painting had become somewhat oppressive, as in *Cloud* (1933; Ostrava, A.G.). In 1938 he painted the first pictures of his cycle *Fire*, whose large, gesturing figures played out a warning against war (e.g. *Fire (1)*, 1938; Prague, N.G.). His last cycle of paintings, *Longing*, dating from 1939, is symbolic of a despair with contemporary events. On 1 September 1939 he was arrested by the Germans and taken to Dachau, and later to Bergen-Belsen concentration camp, where he died.

WRITINGS

Nejskromnější umění [The most modest art] (Prague, 1920)
Kulhavý poutník [The limping pilgrim] (Prague, 1936)
Umění přírodních národů [The art of natural peoples] (Prague, 1938)
J. Slavík, ed.: *Dvojí osud: Dopisy Josefa Čapka* [The double face of destiny: letters of Josef Čapek] (Prague, 1980)

BIBLIOGRAPHY

J. Pečírka: *Josef Čapek* (Prague, 1961)
K. Srp: 'Josef Čapek', *1909–25 Kubismus in Prag* (exh. cat., ed. J. Švestka and T. Vlček; Düsseldorf, Kstver., 1991), pp. 158–65

VOJTĚCH LAHODA

Capernaum [Capharnaum, Kafarnaum; now Kefar Nahum]. Town located on the north-west shore of the Sea of Galilee (Lake Kinneret), Israel. Mentioned in the New Testament as a place visited by Jesus, it is traditionally held to have been the home of St Peter. Two synagogues have been identified in Capernaum, the second built on the remains of the first, as well as an octagonal area thought to be the site of a church of St Peter, built where his house was believed to have stood. The town was destroyed in the 7th century AD.

The earlier synagogue, dated to the 1st century AD, has been tentatively identified with the synagogue at Capernaum, the building of which is mentioned in Luke 7:5. Excavators have found a basalt cobbled pavement and several basalt walls, which run under the south wall and the east and west stylobates of the main hall of the later limestone synagogue. Benches along the walls are assumed, but no entrance has been found. The dating of the limestone synagogue is in dispute. In 1916 H. Kohl and C. Watzinger dated it as built in the late 2nd century and destroyed in the early 4th century. More recent excavators (see Corbo, Loffreda and Spijkerman) assert that construction began *c.* 350–400 and was completed in 450 and destroyed *c.* 680–750. The synagogue consisted of a two-storey main hall (20.40×18.65 m) with an adjoining court (11.25×11.25 m) on the east side. It was built on an artificial platform, the foundations of which were the walls of the earlier synagogue. In front of the building's decorated south façade ran a raised platform. The façade, orientated towards Jerusalem, had three entrances on the ground floor, with a semicircular lunette above the central entrance. The hall was divided by two rows of columns, terminated by a lateral row of columns, into a central nave surrounded by three aisles. Benches were built along the east and west walls. The small columns, capitals and frieze fragments found in the hall suggest that the upper storey may have been a gallery.

Inside the south façade, two platforms were bases for aediculae, which probably served both as the Torah shrine and as the place for the menorah. A flagstone pavement formed the floor of the hall and the court; the latter, entered from the hall, was trapezoid in outline. It had three rows of columns forming a portico; all three exterior walls had entrances. The synagogue ornamentation consisted of architectural decoration of the façade. The lintels, cornice and arch were all moulded and carved with floral, figurative and geometric designs. Corinthian capitals and frieze fragments inside the hall suggest that there had been elaborate interior ornamentation.

To the south of the synagogue an octagonal area, paved with mosaic, represents the sanctuary of a mid-5th-century church built on the site of the supposed house of St Peter, the octagon occupying the space of the actual house. The mosaic has a peacock in the centre and a border of lotus flowers. To the east of this there is an apse, which may have been the baptistery.

BIBLIOGRAPHY

H. Kohl and C. Watzinger: *Antike Synagogen in Galilaea* (Leipzig, 1916), pp. 4–40
G. Orfali: *Capharnaum et ses ruines, 1905–1921* (Paris, 1922)
V. Corbo: *The House of St Peter at Capharnaum* (Jerusalem, 1969)
V. Corbo, S. Loffreda and A. Spijkerman: *La sinagoga di Cafarnao dopo gli scavi del 1969* (Jerusalem, 1970)
L. I. Levine, ed.: *Ancient Synagogues Revealed* (Jerusalem, 1981), pp. 52–62
V. Corbo: 'Resti della sinagoga del primo secolo a Cafarnao', *Stud. Hierosolym.*, iii (1982), pp. 273–357
J. E. Strange and H. Shanks: 'Synagogue Where Jesus Preached Found at Capernaum', *Bibl. Archaeol. Rev.*, ix/6 (1983), pp. 24–31
L. I. Levine, ed.: *The Synagogue in Late Antiquity* (Philadelphia, 1987)

RACHEL HACHLILI

Capet. French dynasty of rulers, collectors and patrons. Hugh Capet, Duke of the Franks, succeeded the last Carolingian ruler, Louis V (*reg* AD 986–7), as King of France (*reg* AD 987–96). There were no outstanding patrons until the 13th century, when (1) Blanche of Castile became Queen of France as a consequence of her marriage (1200) to Louis VIII (*reg* 1223–6). Her patronage is sometimes difficult to distinguish from that of her son (2) Louis IX, particularly during his minority, when they were jointly involved in the foundation and endowment of several monastic institutions and the rebuilding of Saint-Denis Abbey. Nevertheless, their individual tastes are evident: for instance in Blanche's patronage of manuscript illumination and her preference for Cistercian foundations. Among Louis IX's architectural projects, his foundation and embellishment of the Sainte-Chapelle, Paris, is outstanding. His grandson (3) Philip IV was particularly active as a patron in Paris, his interests ranging from manuscript illumination, goldsmithswork and ivory-carving to more monumental projects; he also employed Italian artists. (4) Mahaut, Countess of Artois, was a great-granddaughter of Blanche and great-niece of Louis IX. Although little survives of her patronage, her household accounts reveal a sophisticated taste for artistic luxury and monumental decoration characteristic of contemporary aristocratic patronage. Philip IV's son Charles IV (*reg* 1322–8) married (5) Joanna of Evreux. One branch of the Capet family, the counts of VALOIS, inherited the throne in 1328.

(1) Blanche of Castile, Queen of France (*b* Palencia, before 4 March 1188; *d* Paris, 26–7 June 1252). She was the wife of Louis VIII (*reg* 1223–6) and the mother of (2) Louis IX, becoming Regent during the latter's minority (1226–34) and during the Sixth Crusade (1248–52). A strong and capable ruler, Blanche defended royal authority against rebellious barons after the death of Louis VIII. In 1230 she defeated an attempt by Henry III, King of England, to recapture Plantagenet possessions in France. Blanche has been described as the first important royal patron of the 13th century, yet the extent of her patronage and her personal taste are difficult to establish. Until the majority of Louis IX in 1234, Blanche was associated with her son's patronage. In 1228 he founded the Cistercian abbey of Royaumont (Oise) in fulfilment of Louis VIII's will. Although the will had specified a Victorine foundation, the substitution of a Cistercian monastery may reflect Blanche's own predilection: her father, Alfonso VIII, King of Castile (*reg* 1158–1214), had founded four Cistercian abbeys, including Las Huelgas, Burgos. According to Guillaume de Nangis, Blanche and Louis IX were involved before 1231 in the decision to rebuild the church of Saint-Denis Abbey, which is decorated with the arms of Castile and the fleur-de-lis. There is less evidence, however, for the tradition that Blanche was actively involved in the reconstruction of Tours Cathedral (after 1233).

After 1234 Blanche's patronage became more personal and independent, although she and Louis continued to patronize many of the same monasteries, and she remained his most trusted adviser. She founded two richly endowed Cistercian convents: Notre-Dame-la-Royale, Maubuisson (nr Pontoise), little of which survives, and Notre-Dame-du-Lys, Dammarie-les-Lys (nr Melun, Seine-et-Marne). Maubuisson was begun in 1236, and by 1242 the church was complete; it was consecrated in the presence of Louis and Blanche in 1244. Total costs for the church and conventual buildings were 24,431 livres, and Blanche endowed the convent with 100 livres per annum in addition to tithes from her properties at Etampes, Dourdan and elsewhere. She was buried there in the Cistercian habit in 1252. Notre-Dame-du-Lys was founded in 1244; by 1248 the buildings were sufficiently advanced to accommodate the nuns. Although less lavishly endowed than Maubuisson, more survives of the original church: the austerity and simplicity of the design (a flat-ended chevet and large expanses of unadorned wall) suggest that Blanche maintained the architectural simplicity traditional to the Cistercian Order. This is far more apparent at Maubuisson and Lys than at her son's foundation of Royaumont and may reflect Blanche's own endorsement of the Cistercian aesthetic. Her heart was buried at Notre-Dame-du-Lys in 1253, presumably after the completion of the church. Both convents were decorated with the arms of Castile and of France.

As with Louis IX, there seems to have been considerable variety and flexibility in Blanche's taste. Her patronage of the Cistercians might suggest that her own tastes were severe, but this is contradicted by the lavish scale and decoration of the few surviving manuscripts that can be associated with her. The royal accounts suggest that she commissioned elaborate illuminated books for her Cistercian foundations, for the royal chapel and for herself and members of her family. In 1241 she paid for a Psalter, commissioning three more in 1242. According to tradition, Blanche gave a fine Bible (Paris, Bib. N., MS. fr. lat. 14397) to St Victor Abbey in Paris. An extant Psalter (Paris, Bib. Arsenal, MS. fr. 1186) is traditionally held to be Blanche's. Her name has been associated with two large and lavish *Bibles moralisées* in several volumes, one of which includes an image of a king and a queen (New York, Pierpont Morgan Lib., MS. M.240, fol. 8*r*; *see* GOTHIC, fig. 72), the latter possibly Blanche herself. She also owned a late 12th-century English Psalter (Leiden, Bib. Rijksuniv., MS. lat. 76A) from which Louis IX is said to have learnt to read.

BIBLIOGRAPHY

H. de l'Epinois: 'Comptes relatifs à la fondation de l'abbaye de Maubuisson', *Bib. Ecole Chartes*, xix (1858), pp. 550–67

A. Dutilleux and J. Depoin: *L'Abbaye de Maubuisson (Notre-Dame-la-Royale): Histoire et cartulaire*, 2 vols (Pontoise, 1882–5)

E. Berger: 'Histoire de Blanche de Castille, reine de France', *Bib. Ecoles Fr. Athènes & Rome*, lxx (1895)

'Après sept siècles: L'Abbaye du Lys', *Archéologia*, xxxi (1970), pp. 31–3

For further bibliography *see* (2) below.

(2) Louis IX, King of France [St Louis] (*b* Poissy, 25 April 1214; *reg* 1226–70; *d* Carthage, 25 Aug 1270; *can* 1297; *fd* 25 Aug). Son of (1) Blanche of Castile. Under Louis IX, France enjoyed unprecedented prosperity and peace; during his lifetime he was already seen as the ideal Christian monarch. Pious, a good administrator and an effective diplomat, Louis simplified the royal administration and did much to assure justice and fair taxation. He initiated two crusades, the first from 1248 to 1254 and the second in 1270. He was described by his biographer Jean de Joinville as having 'illuminated his kingdom with beautiful abbeys...and a great number of hospitals and convents of the Dominicans, Franciscans and other religious orders'. Other 13th-century authors, such as Guillaume de Saint-Pathus and Guillaume de Nangis, also enumerated his foundations and emphasized the King's personal involvement in construction projects. His artistic patronage seems to have been primarily architectural, although he also donated windows, manuscripts and reliquaries. Several of the buildings associated with him were richly decorated with sculpture; he may also have participated in the decision to create the series of tombs of royal ancestors at Saint-Denis Abbey.

Louis founded the Cistercian abbey of Royaumont (Oise) in 1228. His name is also associated with the reconstruction, beginning in 1231, of Saint-Denis Abbey, where he was subsequently buried. During the 1230s he commissioned the reconstruction of the chapel at Saint-Germain-en-Laye, which closely resembles Saint-Denis and has been attributed to the same architect. Louis's most prominent foundation, however, was the Sainte-Chapelle in Paris, begun *c.* 1240 and consecrated on 26 April 1246, a building designed to house the recently acquired relic of the Crown of Thorns. The chapel unites architectural structure with stained glass, sculpture and painting (*see* PARIS, §V, 2 and fig. 34). Louis also rebuilt the choir of the Benedictine priory at Nogent-les-Vièrges (Oise) *c.* 1242–3. The crusade of 1248–54 prompted the development of the port of Aigues-Mortes (Gard), from which Louis and his army departed for both crusades. While in the Holy Land, he substantially rebuilt the walls of Jaffa, strengthened those of Acre, Haifa and Caesarea and founded a Franciscan house in Jaffa.

The evidence, although scanty, suggests that Louis's taste may have changed on his return from the failed crusade in 1254. He seems to have seen its failure as a reflection of his own imperfections; he became increasingly penitential and more austere in his dress and demeanour, and he contemplated joining the Francisan Order. In any event, his patronage after 1254 was almost exclusively directed towards mendicant foundations, hospitals and private chapels. He established Franciscan houses in Paris, Vernon, Rouen, Senlis and Compiègne; Dominican houses in Paris, Compiègne, Caen, Macon, Carcassonne and Rouen; a Carmelite abbey in Paris; houses for the Brothers of Penitence, the Blancs-Manteaux and the Brothers of the Cross, and Carthusian and Guillemite abbeys in Paris. Louis also founded a house for the Trinitarians at Fontainebleau and participated in the foundation of a Franciscan convent by his sister Isabella at Longchamp. He continued to be a patron of Royaumont and the two Cistercian convents founded by his mother, Blanche of Castile, at Maubuisson and Lys (*see* (1) above). He founded a number of hospitals (Pontoise, Compiègne and the Quinze-Vingts in Paris). He also erected chapels in the royal residences at Rouen, Vincennes, Pontoise, Corbeil and Senlis and rebuilt the royal palace at Tours. He supported other building projects as well, for example giving wood and stone from royal properties for the construction of Tours Cathedral. His religious foundations from after 1254 are largely destroyed. Those of the mendicants in particular seem to have been austere and utilitarian, consisting often of large, single-volume churches covered with wooden ceilings rather than vaults; whether this reflects the King's own taste or simply that of the orders in question is difficult to assess.

Branner (1965) suggested that the King and his circle initiated a 'court style' in architecture that became fashionable throughout the kingdom and in all Europe. There is good evidence, however, that an elegant style was already flourishing in Paris (the nave chapels at Notre-Dame and the refectory and Lady chapel at St-Germain-des-Prés, for example) independently of royal patronage. The early buildings erected by Louis vary in style, reflecting the character and function of each building rather than a single and consistent royal taste in architecture. The austere, flat wall surfaces of Royaumont result from its Cistercian affiliation, while the Sainte-Chapelle is as lavishly decorated as a metalwork reliquary. The ornate tracery patterns at Nogent-les-Vièrges contrast with flat panels of wall to either side of the windows, a detail reminiscent of Royaumont. Yet at Saint-Denis and Saint-Germain-en-Laye there are delicate shifts in wall planes set off against rich bundles of shafts, reflecting the influence of Burgundian architecture.

Louis's patronage of other arts is more difficult to assess. It is generally agreed that he and his mother donated the north transept rose at Chartres Cathedral, *c.* 1230. Although he established a library for scholars in the annexe of the Sainte-Chapelle, the books were theological texts devoid of illumination. Little is known about his personal library; from the small number of manuscripts that can be associated with the King, it has been assumed (Branner, 1977) that Louis was not a great collector of books. Illuminated books that can be connected with him are rare: the exceptionally beautiful and lavish ST LOUIS PSALTER (Paris, Bib. N., MS. lat. 10525) was his own prayerbook. Probably produced after Louis's return from his first crusade, the Psalter emphasizes the Old Testament story of Joseph, suggesting a parallel between Louis's captivity in Egypt and Joseph's sale into slavery to Egyptian merchants (Jordan, 1980). The closely related Isabella Psalter (Cambridge, Fitzwilliam, MS. 300) was produced either for the King's sister or his daughter. Branner has associated two leaves (both New York, Pierpont Morgan Lib., MS. G. 37), perhaps from Gratian's *Decretal*, with Louis's own library, as well as a small Bible (Paris, Bib. N., MS. 10426). A *Bible moralisée* (Toledo Cathedral) was perhaps commissioned by Blanche or Louis in the 1220s. The grace and elegance of painting produced in court circles can also be judged from the stained glass (*see* PARIS, fig. 36) and painted medallions (*see* GOTHIC, fig. 6) of the Sainte-Chapelle, although the latter are heavily repainted. The scant remains indicate that there was considerable variety in the styles of illuminated books and painted decoration commissioned by Louis IX and his immediate family.

BIBLIOGRAPHY

L. de Tillemont: *Vie de Saint Louis*, 6 vols (Paris, 1849)

A. Haseloff: 'Les Psautiers de Saint Louis', *Mém. Soc. N. Antiqua. France*, lviii (1899), pp. 17–42

M. Aubert and others: *Les Vitraux de Notre-Dame et de la Sainte-Chapelle de Paris*, Corp. Vitrearum Med. Aevi (Paris, 1959)

R. Branner: *Saint Louis and the Court Style in Gothic Architecture* (London, 1965)

——: 'The Painted Medallions in the Sainte-Chapelle in Paris', *Trans. Amer. Philos. Soc.*, lviii/2 (1968), pp. 1–42

M. Harrison-Caviness and L. Grodecki: 'Les Vitraux de la Sainte-Chapelle', *Rev. A.*, i–ii (1969), pp. 9–16

Actes des colloques de Royaumont et de Paris—Septième centenaire de la mort de Saint Louis: Paris and Royaumont, 1970

R. Pernoud, ed.: *Le Siècle de Saint Louis* (Paris, 1970)

G. S. Wright: 'A Royal Tomb Program in the Reign of St Louis', *A. Bull.*, lvi (1974), pp. 224–43

A. Erland-Brandenburg: *Le Roi est mort* (Paris, 1975)

R. Branner: *Manuscript Painting in Paris during the Reign of Saint Louis* (Berkeley, 1977)

W. Jordan: *Louis IX and the Challenge of the Crusade* (Princeton, 1979)

H. Stahl: 'Old Testament Illustration during the Reign of St Louis: The Morgan Picture Book and the New Biblical Cycles', *Acts of the XXIVth International Congress on the History of Art: Bologna, 1979*, ii, pp. 79–93

W. Jordan: 'The Psalter of Saint-Louis (B.N. MS. lat. 10525): The Program of the Seventy-eight Full-page Illustrations', *Acta*, vii (1980), pp. 65–91

C. BRUZELIUS

(3) Philip IV [Philip the Fair; Philippe le Bel], King of France (*b* Fontainebleau, 1267–8; *reg* 1285–1314; *d* Fontainebleau, 29 Nov 1314). Grandson of (2) Louis IX. He was the son of Philip III (*reg* 1270–85) and Isabella of Aragon. Philip expanded the power and size of the royal administration and was the first French monarch to impose general taxation. His struggle with the papacy, evolving from fiscal policies, led to the so-called 'Babylonian captivity' (1309–1408), which had enduring artistic consequences with Italian artists regularly travelling north of the Alps. Although Philip used controversial means to pursue his politics, his determination to enhance the crown's prestige resulted in the most significant artistic undertakings since the time of Louis IX. Indicative of this is the first use during his reign of the title Peintre du Roi. In 1298 Philip sent the painter Etienne d'Auxerre (*fl* 1292–1301) to Rome to familiarize himself with the artistic circle of Pietro Cavallini. By 1304–5 the King had engaged the services of Roman painters Filippo Rusuti (Rizuti; *fl* 1297–1317) and Giovanni Rizuti (*fl c.* 1300), who worked in the royal castle (mostly destr.) at Poitiers until 1317, and Nicolaus Desmarz (Nicolò de Marzi; *fl* 1309), who was active at Saint-Denis Abbey.

Philip improved his capital, rebuilding fortifications and paving streets. From 1299 he ordered the enlargement of the Palais de la Cité, including the construction (1301–13), under Jean d'Esserent and Nicolas de Chaume (*fl* first half 14th century), of a vast reception hall (Grand' Salle), the long Galerie des Merciers (both destr. 1618) and the Petite Salle. The master carpenter Jean de Gisors made the tripartite keel-shaped ceiling of the Grand' Salle, while Nicolas le Loquetier furnished the floor (1312) with black marble with white streaks, imported from the Rhineland. EVRARD D'ORLÉANS probably made the series of statues of French kings (destr.) for the Palais de la Cité. On the portal of the chapel (1309) of the Collège de Navarre, an important Parisian scholastic complex founded in 1304 by Philip's wife, Queen Joanna of Navarre (*c.* 1270–1305), were placed statues of *Philip* and *Joanna* and of their son, the future *Louis X*.

Philip took every opportunity to bolster the Capet dynasty. He ordered a tomb from Jean d'Arras for his father *Philip III* (Saint-Denis Abbey) and honoured his grandfather Louis IX by achieving his canonization (1297) and by establishing two foundations: the Dominican priory of St Louis (mostly destr.), Poissy, and Royallieu (founded 1303) at Neuville-aux-Bois. The church at Poissy was built on the plan of Royaumont in the Parisian court style and had a large, glazed rose window with spandrels; Evrard d'Orléans may have worked on the sculptural programme there.

Philip's patronage of goldsmiths, particularly GUILLAUME JULIEN, and his control, through the guild, of high standards, made Paris the centre of the jewellery and enamel trades in early 14th-century Europe (*see* PARIS, §IV, 1). Among Guillaume Julien's works for the King was a life-size reliquary bust of *St Louis* (1298–9; mostly destr. 1791) for the Sainte-Chapelle. Ivory-carvers also benefited from royal patronage: a mirror-back (*c.* 1300; Paris, Mus. Cluny, CL 404) depicting a king, a queen and their children in a bold, calligraphic style probably represents Philip and his family. Philip also had literary interests: he and his wife sponsored translations of ancient and contemporary writings into French, supported writers and exempted university booksellers from taxation. The foundation charter (1306) of the University of Orléans was confirmed by Philip. The *Life and Miracles of St Denis* (Paris, Bib. N., MSS fr. 2090–92, lat. 13836), with 77 full-page miniatures providing lively tableaux of 14th-century life in Paris, was commissioned by Philip. The royal accounts mention the acquisition of liturgical books, and the King owned illuminated manuscripts, including a Bible in two volumes (Paris, Bib. N., MSS lat. 248[1,2]); Boethius's *Consolation of Philosophy* (Paris, Bib. N., MS. fr. 1097); a volume of fables, the *Livre de Dina et Calila* (late 13th century; Paris, Bib. N., MS. lat. 8504); and a Breviary (?before 1297; Paris, Bib. N., MS. lat. 1023) ascribed to Master Honoré (*see* HONORÉ, MASTER and fig.).

BIBLIOGRAPHY

B. Prost: 'Recherches sur les peintres du roi antérieurs au règne de Charles IV', *Etudes d'histoire du moyen-âge dédiées à Gabriel Monod* (Paris, 1896), pp. 388–403

C. Enlart: 'L'Emaillerie cloisonnée à Paris sous Philippe le Bel et le maître Guillaume Julien', *Mnmts Piot*, xxix (1927–8), pp. 1–97

J. Viard: *Les Journaux du trésor de Philippe IV le Bel* (Paris, 1940)

J. Guérout: 'Le Palais de la Cité des origines à 1417', *Mém. Féd. Soc. Hist. & Archéol. Paris & Ile-de-France*, i (1949), pp. 57–212; ii (1950), pp. 21–204

A. Erlande-Brandenburg: 'La Priorale Saint-Louis de Poissy', *Bull. Mnmtl*, cxxix (1971), pp. 85–112

PATRICK M. DE WINTER

(4) Mahaut, Countess of Artois (*b* before 1275; *reg* 1302–29; *d* Paris, 27 Nov 1329). Great-niece of (2) Louis IX. She was the daughter of Robert II, Count of Artois (*d* 1302), and Amicie de Courtenay (*d* 1275). Mahaut was a child when her mother died, and in 1285 she married Otto IV, Count of Burgundy (*d* 1303), by whom she had four children. Her two daughters married sons of Philip IV; the elder, Joanna, later became Queen of France as wife of Philip V (*reg* 1316–22). In 1302 she inherited the title and lands of Artois, to which were added the Burgundian holdings of her husband on his death. She was thus one of the great magnates of France and a politically significant figure. Her resources and status enabled her to exercise extensive patronage, as is reflected in her household accounts (Arras, Archvs Dépt. Pas-de-Calais), which indicate a steady flow of commissions and payments for objects from the date of her accession. Indeed, these accounts are the crucial evidence for Mahaut's activities as a patron, since very few of the objects concerned survive. The accounts reveal an energetic patron of considerable discernment who formed long-term links with particular artists and craftsmen and was prepared to spend freely.

Of the range of objects mentioned in the accounts, those that survive are sculptural. Mahaut's most fruitful association was with Jean Pépin de Huy, although other sculptors are recorded, notably Pierre Boye and Jean de Brequessant, both of whom collaborated with Jean Pépin de Huy. Together with Evrard d'Orléans, all three worked on the tomb of *Otto IV* (*c.* 1312–14; mostly destr. 1793) for the abbey church of Cherlieu (Haute-Saône), of which a weeper (Paris, Louvre) and part of a figure (Vesoul, Caisin priv. col.) survive. JEAN PÉPIN DE HUY also worked on the tombs of Mahaut's father and two sons at Maubuisson Abbey (nr Pontoise). The accounts indicate a payment to the sculptor and metalworker Guillaume le Perrier for a silver effigy for the tomb of Robert II. It seems that Mahaut also made provision for a monument for herself (destr.), to be placed in the La Thieulloye Abbey (nr Arras). This is now known only from a drawing (1602; Brussels, Bib. Royale Albert 1er) and was possibly by the Tournais sculptor Jean Aloul (*fl c.* 1305–42). It showed Mahaut in a Dominican habit holding the abbey church in her hand.

The accounts also mention manuscripts, both secular and ecclesiastical, intended for Mahaut's personal use and as gifts for family, members of the household and institutions (e.g. *see* ROMANCE, MANUSCRIPT, §2(ii)). For example, in 1312 Marie, described as 'l'ecrivain', was paid for a copy of the Hours of the Cross. The accounts also contain numerous references to jewellery and metalwork, such as payment in 1302 for a gilded goblet and in 1319 for a silver and enamel tabernacle made in Arras (all untraced).

Another aspect of Mahaut's patronage was connected with the building and refurbishment programmes undertaken at her residences, mainly the châteaux of Hesdin and Conflans (both destr.). The accounts record many payments to craftsmen and merchants for decorations and furnishings; for example from 1316 to 1317 she bought 20 tapestries from Jean de Meaux in Paris. Between 1314 and 1330 there was major work at Conflans, including an extensive programme of wall painting, specific elements of which are detailed in the accounts, for example the type and cost of pigments used. In 1320 Pierre de Bruxelles (*fl* 1318–29) was asked for a series of paintings to commemorate Otto, including depictions of his Sicilian campaign. It is known that Mahaut was involved with several religious houses, including Maubuisson Abbey, where she chose to be buried alongside her father, and particularly with La Thieulloye Abbey, which she founded in 1323 and for which she provided gold and silver vessels, silver-gilt images and liturgical vestments. Mahaut ordered an alabaster figure of the *Virgin and Child* (Gosnay Parish Church, Pas-de-Calais) from Pépin de Huy as a gift to the nuns at Gosnay in 1329.

BIBLIOGRAPHY

DBF

M. le Chanoine Dehaisnes: *Documents et extraits divers concernant l'histoire de l'art dans la Flandre, l'Artois et le Hainault*, i (Lille, 1886)

——: *Histoire de l'art dans la Flandre, l'Artois et le Hainault avant le XVe siècle* (Lille, 1886)

J. M. Richard: *Une Petite-nièce de Saint-Louis: Mahaut, Comtesse d'Artois et de Bourgogne, 1302–29* (Paris, 1887)

A. Kemp-Welch: *Of Six Medieval Women* (London, 1913), pp. 83–115

J. Lestocquoy: *L'Art de l'Artois: Etudes sur la tapisserie, la sculpture, l'orfèvrerie, la peinture* (Arras, 1973), pp. 97–8

F. Baron: 'Le Gisant de Jean de Bourgogne, fils de Mahaut d'Artois: Oeuvre de Jean Pépin de Huy', *Bull. Soc. N. Antiqua. France* (1985), pp. 161–3

R. W. Lightbown: *European Mediaeval Jewellery* (London, 1992)

Dictionnaire des sculpteurs français du moyen âge (Paris, 1992)

PIPPA SHIRLEY

(5) Joanna of Evreux, Queen of France (*b* 1310; *d* 1371). Daughter-in-law of (3) Philip IV. She was married to Charles IV of France (*reg* 1322–8) between 1325 and 1328, and is associated with several important works, including the silver-gilt *Virgin and Child* (Paris, Louvre; *see* GOTHIC, fig. 86), with an enamelled base, which she donated to Saint-Denis Abbey in 1339. In her will Joanna bequeathed a small Book of Hours, commissioned by her husband from Jean Pucelle, to Charles V: this work has been identified with a grisaille manuscript (New York, Cloisters, MS. 54. 1. 2.) known as the Hours of Jeanne d'Evreux (*see* PUCELLE, JEAN, §1; GRISAILLE, §1; and GOTHIC, fig. 80).

□

Cape Town. South African city, legislative capital of the Republic and capital of Cape Province. It is situated at the tip of the continent on Table Bay below the broad plateau of Table Mountain (see fig.). Cape Town (metropolitan population *c.* two million) is the second largest city in South Africa and is an important port and rail terminal. It was the first settlement founded by Europeans in Southern Africa and retains a rich heritage of its colonial architecture.

A replenishment station for the Dutch East India Company was established at Table Bay in 1652 by Jan van Riebeeck; it consisted of a large market garden protected by a fort, later the Castle of Good Hope (1666–77), built in a star-shaped plan. The outpost grew slowly; early buildings made use of readily available local materials and were influenced by Dutch domestic architecture, leading to the development of the CAPE DUTCH STYLE (*see also* SOUTH AFRICA, §§I and III). In 1770, during the war between the Netherlands and England, French mercenaries were drafted in to protect the Cape. Among them was L. M. THIBAULT, a military engineer who had trained at the Académie Royale d'Architecture, Paris. He worked under both Dutch and British rule at the Cape and was responsible for most of the government buildings of the period, many of which show a pronounced French Neo-classical influence. Thibault worked with Anton Andreith (1754–1822), a sculptor and architect who executed numerous decorative schemes, including the pedimental relief at the wine store of Groot Constantia (1791). British rule was established in 1806, and thereafter Georgian and Regency town houses became fashionable (e.g. 33 Bree Street, 1830). The city expanded with a regular grid plan, and during the 19th century building types became more varied, reflecting the commercial expansion and social diversification of the city. The Groote Kerk, Adderley Street, was rebuilt to a design by the German architect Herman Schutte (1761–1844) with a mixture of Gothic and classical elements. Several public buildings were erected around the original Company market gardens (later the Botanic Gardens), for example the Renaissance Revival Public Library (1858–60) and the House of Assembly (1875) by H. E. Graves, and the Neo-Egyptian South African College by James Adamson and Colonel John Lewis.

In 1860 the maritime role of Cape Town was strengthened by the extension of the Alfred Docks with the Victoria Basin. The discovery of diamonds and gold quickened the pace of development, as did the Anglo-Boer War (1899–1902), which brought a flood of people and equipment through the port. In 1892 HERBERT BAKER arrived, and his eclectic Arts and Crafts style was blended with Cape Dutch in such buildings as Groote Schuur, which he rebuilt (1893, 1897) for Cecil Rhodes and is now the official residence of South Africa's prime ministers. The cathedral of St George (begun 1897) was rebuilt by Baker and his partners FRANCIS MASEY and F. K. KENDALL in sandstone from Table Mountain in Norman Revival style. Masey and Kendall were responsible for several other notable buildings in Cape Town, including the Renaissance-inspired Rhodes Building (1900–08), with Dutch gables and Etruscan columns and shutters, which proved such a compelling mix that its influence retarded the introduction of modern developments.

Cape Town, view of the city and Table Mountain

Classicism, which persisted in Cape Town until World War II, gave the city centre its present homogeneity, while the continuing influence of the Cape Dutch style is apparent in the South African National Gallery (1928–9), designed by Public Works Department architects. Art Deco was introduced through the moulded geometric façades of the Market House (1928–9), Greenmarket Square, by W. H. Grant, while Max Policansky (*b* 1909), a graduate from Liverpool University, introduced the Modern Movement with the Judge Clothing Factory (1937), Victoria Road. In the same year the Old Mutual Building, by Fred Glennie and Louw & Louw, blended glittering Art Deco architecture with a frieze by Ivan Mitford-Barbarion (1896–1976) depicting black Africans and native animals.

After the war Cape Town underwent dramatic change following an influx of new settlers, new land reclamation and direct experience of overseas developments. The foreshore had a rigidly planned and monotonous framework imposed on it, and when the National Government came to power many of the houses in District Six were demolished and their inhabitants rehoused on the bleak Cape Flats. Notable commercial buildings of the period include the International Style glass Trust Bank Centre (1966) by Colyn & Meiring and the BP Centre (1973) by REVEL FOX, which is clad in dark Paarl granite and was designed to respond to the intersecting city grids. The political isolation of the 1970s was relieved by the work of ROELOF UYTENBOGAARDT, who had studied in Rome and worked in the USA and was responsible for the Truworth Factory (1970) and Werdmuller Commercial Centre (1973). As political dialogue reopened in the 1980s the universities began to expand; the buildings of the Middle Campus (1984–6) for the University of Cape Town, by JULIAN ELLIOTT, were modelled on the African *kraal*. The almost contemporary Woolman House (1985) by Douglas Robertson is an energy-efficient commercial building that complements the adjacent Victorian City Hall (completed 1905).

The South African Fine Arts Association was established in Cape Town in 1851, and in 1864 William Foster opened the Roeland Street Art School (later the Cape Town School of Arts). The South African Drawing Club was formed in 1899, with the English artist J. S. Morland as teacher and examiner; this led to semi-professional artists forming the South African Society of Artists in 1902. The most important art collections in Cape Town include those of the South African National Gallery (founded 1871) and the Michaelis Collection (founded 1916), housed in the Old Town House (1755; formerly the Burghers' Watch House), Greenmarket Square, which was remodelled by J. M. Solomon after the bequest by Sir Max Michaelis.

See also SOUTH AFRICA, §§IV–VI and XI–XIII.

BIBLIOGRAPHY

J. van der Meulen: 'Cape Dutch Architecture of the Eighteenth Century', *Bouwknd. Wkbld.*, 24 (1956), pp. 294–300
H. Fransen: 'Cape Baroque', *Apollo*, cii/164 (1975), pp. 252–61
The Buildings of Central Cape Town, 3 vols (Cape Town, 1978)
H. Fransen and M. A. Cook: *The Old Buildings of the Cape* (Cape Town, 1980)

RODNEY HARBER

Capgrave, John (*b* ?Kings Lynn, 21 April 1393; *d* Kings Lynn, 12 Aug 1464). English writer, translator and scribe. He entered the Augustinian monastery at Kings Lynn,

Norfolk, *c.* 1410, was ordained priest in 1416–17 and then studied in London (1417–22). By 1422 he had completed a verse translation of the *Life of St Norbert.* He studied at Cambridge from 1422, preaching his sermon, the *Tretis of the Orders that be Undyr the Reule of Oure Fader Seynt Augustin*, in that year. He became a bachelor in theology in 1423 and gained his doctorate in 1425. He is not recorded between 1427 and 1437, during which time he may have composed works now lost, for example, the *Commentary on Kings*, dedicated to Humfrey, Duke of Gloucester, and John Lowe, Bishop of St Asaph (*d* 1467), which is referred to in the preface to Capgrave's *Commentary on Genesis* (1437–8; Oxford, Oriel Coll.), a copy of which was presented to Duke Humfrey at Woodstock on 1 January 1439. Capgrave was present at the laying of the foundation stone of King's College, Cambridge, on 2 April 1441. On 1 August 1446, as prior, he acted as host to Henry VI on his visit to the Augustinian friary at Lynn, as described in *De illustribus Henricis* ('On the Famous Henrys'). In February 1447 he visited Rome, which he described in *The Solace of Pilgrimes.* On 22 July 1453 he was elected Prior Provincial of the Augustinian Order in England and was re-elected on 6 August 1445. He wrote the *Commentary on the Acts of the Apostles* (1457) and *c.* 1462 *De fidei symbolis* ('On the symbols of the Faith') concerning creeds, both dedicated to William Gray, Bishop of Ely, to whom the lost *Commentary on Revelation* (*c.* 1460) may also have been dedicated. The *Abbreviacion of Cronicles* was probably an earlier work, revised for presentation to Edward IV *c.* 1462–3. Many of the surviving manuscripts of Capgrave's works are in his own hand or were copied under his supervision at Kings Lynn.

BIBLIOGRAPHY

A. de Meijer: 'John Capgrave, O.E.S.A.', *Augustiniana*, v (1955), pp. 400–40; vii (1957), pp. 118–48, 531–75

P. J. Lucas: 'John Capgrave, O.S.A. (1393–1464), Scribe and "Publisher"', *Trans. Cambridge Bibliog. Soc.*, v (1969), pp. 1–35

J. C. Fredeman: 'The Life of John Capgrave, O.E.S.A. (1393–1464)', *Augustiniana*, xxix (1979), pp. 197–237

P. J. Lucas: 'A Fifteenth-century Copyist at Work under Authorial Scrutiny: An Incident from John Capgrave's Scriptorium', *Stud. Bibliog.*, xxxiv (1981), pp. 66–95

P. J. Lucas, ed.: *John Capgrave's Abbreviacion of Cronicles*, Early English Text Society, original ser., cclxxxv (Oxford, 1983)

JEREMY GRIFFITHS

Capiello, Leonetto (*b* Livorno, Tuscany, 9 April 1875; *d* Cannes, 5 Feb 1942). French poster designer, painter, draughtsman and caricaturist of Italian birth. He had his first exhibition at the age of 17 in Florence and in 1896 published his first album of caricatures, entitled *Lanterna magica* (Livorno). He moved to Paris in 1898, later becoming naturalized, and there began work for the periodical *Le Rire.* Until 1904 his main occupation was as a caricaturist, and he worked also for the journals *Revue blanche*, *Assiette au beurre* and others. In 1899 the *Revue blanche* published an album of 18 of his caricatures, entitled *Nos Actrices*, with a preface by Marcel Prévost. In the same year Capiello created his first advertising poster for the comic journal *Frou-Frou* (see Viénot, pl. 12). As a poster designer he was a great innovator, producing dynamic works in strong colour. Other works included *Chocolat Kraus* (1903; see Viénot, pl. 18), *Cinzano* (1910; see Viénot, pl. 21) and *Kub* (1931; see Viénot, pl. 34). He then gave up creating caricatures to devote himself to posters; his last volume of caricatures from an earlier period appeared in 1905. He was a regular exhibitor at the Salon des Humoristes, first organized by Arsène Alexandre at the Palais de Glace, Paris, in 1908.

Capiello also painted many portraits and decorative panels. In 1912 he was commissioned to decorate the tearooms of the Galeries Lafayette and in 1935 painted the immense fresco *Festival in Paris* (see Viénot, pl. 43) for the Dupont restaurant on Boulevard Barbès in Paris. At the Exposition Internationale des Arts et Techniques dans la Vie Moderne, in Paris (1937), Capiello painted the decorative panel *Motive Force* for the pavilion of publicity (see Viénot, pl. 40). He also illustrated various books, such as Voltaire's *La Princesse du Babylon*, and he provided a cover for Guillaume Apollinaire's *Poète assassiné.*

BIBLIOGRAPHY

DBF; Edouard-Joseph

J. Viénot: *L. Capiello: Sa Vie et son oeuvre* (Paris, 1946)

□

Capists. *See* KAPISTS.

Capital. The upper part or crowning feature of a column or pilaster, set on top of the shaft. Capitals act as a transition between the shaft and the element they support,

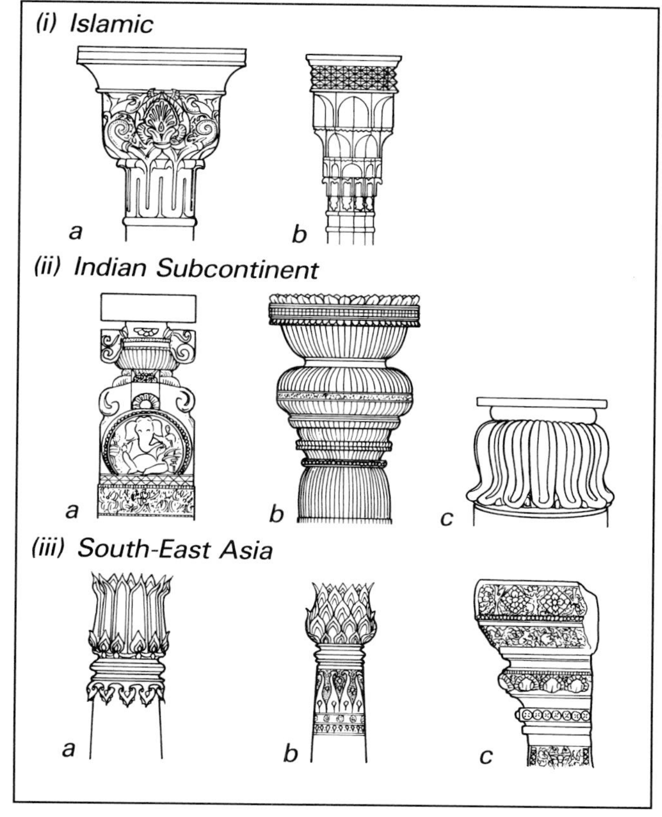

1. Capital types: (i) Islamic: (a) Western Islamic Composite, (b) *Muqarnas*; (ii) Indian subcontinent: (a) 'Vase of plenty' (*ghatapallava*), (b) cushion, (c) lotus; (iii) South-east Asia: (a) Thai water lily, (b) Thai lotus bud, (c) Khmer

usually an architrave, lintel or arcade; a square, circular or polygonal impost block or abacus above the capital often helps to reconcile the form of the shaft with that of the element above.

Capitals generally have highly distinctive sculptural decoration (see figs 1 and 2). In Classical architecture the form of the decoration is an essential attribute of each of the orders (*see* ORDERS, ARCHITECTURAL). In medieval architecture several decorative types of capital evolved, but they were executed in a huge range of individual examples and thus came to serve an important role in dating buildings.

Similarly, in Islamic architecture distinctive types of capitals that evolved from Classical prototypes can be seen, particularly in the Mediterranean Islamic lands. In India and South-east Asia capitals are often characterized by very elaborate decoration; some forms found in traditional temple architecture were used in secular buildings

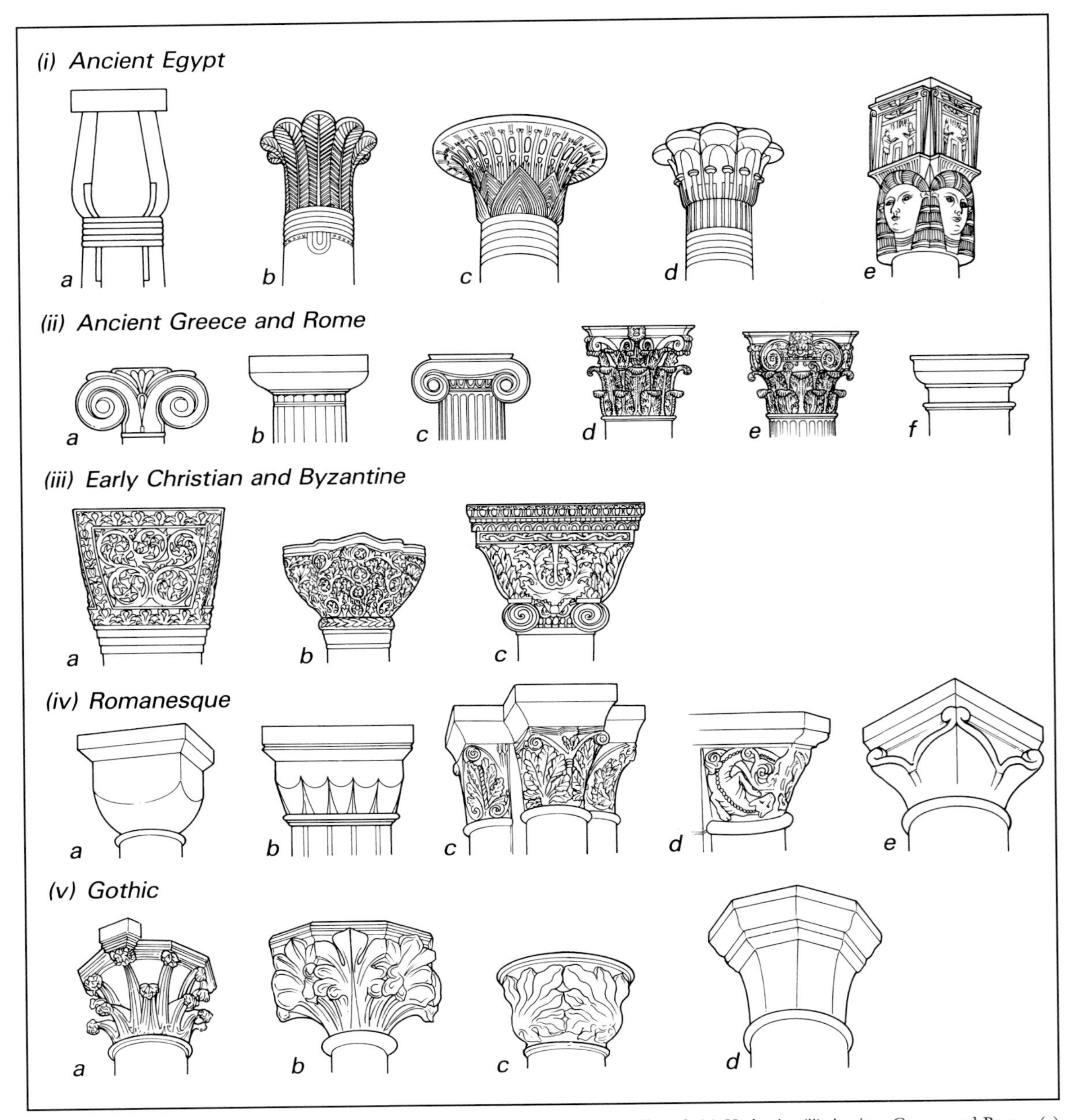

2. Capital types: (i) Ancient Egypt: (a) lotus, (b) palm-leaf, (c) papyriform, (d) scalloped, (e) Hathoric; (ii) Ancient Greece and Rome: (a) Aiolic, (b) Greek Doric, (c) Ionic, (d) Corinthian, (e) Composite, (f) Tuscan; (iii) Early Christian and Byzantine: (a) truncated cone, (b) fold, (c) Composite; (iv) Romanesque: (a) cushion, (b) scalloped, (c) foliate, (d) figural, (e) waterleaf; (v) Gothic: (a) crocket, (b) foliate, (c) foliate, (d) moulded

in the 20th century in an attempt to impart a vernacular or indigenous character.

□

Capitino, Giunta di. *See* GIUNTA PISANO.

Capodimonte Porcelain Factory. Italian porcelain factory. It was founded in 1743 in the grounds of the Palazzo Reale di Capodimonte by Charles VII, King of Naples (later Charles III, King of Spain). The clear, white, soft-paste porcelain was developed by Livio Schepers (*d* 1757) and Gaetano Schepers (*d* after 1764). The chief modeller was GIUSEPPE GRICCI and the principal painters were Giovanni Caselli (1698–1752), Giuseppe della Torre (*fl* 1744–*c*. 1764) and Johann Sigismund Fischer (*fl* 1750–58). The factory produced useful wares, sculpture and snuff-boxes. Some early decorative schemes were based on prototypes from the Saxon factory of Meissen. Painted subjects included battle scenes, allegorical figures and still-lifes stippled or painted in a subdued palette of browns, blues and greens and chinoiseries in brilliant colours. Religious figures were also produced, but most were of peasants or characters from the *commedia dell'arte*, composed as narrative couples or groups. Modelling was simple and effective more through mood and gesture than detail. Figures were sparsely decorated and costumes were simply trimmed with coloured or gilded borders. One of the factory's most extraordinary achievements was the *Salottino di Porcellana* of painted and relief chinoiserie tiles created for the Palazzo Reale in Pórtici between 1757 and 1759 (now Naples, Capodimonte; *see* ITALY, fig. 71). When Charles succeeded to the Spanish throne in 1759, the factory closed and was transferred to the new building in the Buen Retiro, Madrid (*see* MADRID, §III, 2).

BIBLIOGRAPHY

F. Stazzi: *Capodimonte* (Milan, 1972)
A. Caròla-Perrotti: *Le porcellane dei Borbone di Napoli* (Naples, 1986)
Porcellana di Capodimonte: La Real Fabbrica di Carlo di Borbone, 1743–1759 (exh. cat., Naples, 1993)

CLARE LE CORBEILLER

Capogrossi, Giuseppe (*b* Rome, 7 March 1900; *d* Rome, 9 Oct 1972). Italian painter. After taking a degree in law in 1922 he decided to become a painter and attended the atelier of Felice Carena, at the same time forming a very close friendship with the Italian painter Emanuele Cavalli (1904–81), an almost symbiotic association that lasted until about 1945. He first exhibited his work in 1927 alongside Cavalli; their combination of primitivism with an intellectual approach influenced the formative work of Gino Bonichi Scipione, Mario Mafai and Antonietta Raphaël (?1895–1975).

After a trip to Paris in 1929 Capogrossi returned to Rome where, with Cavalli and Corrado Cagli, he elaborated a type of painting based on a magical and esoteric conception of colour. All three were among the loose association of painters that came to be known as the SCUOLA ROMANA. The compositions of paintings made by Capogrossi during these years, such as the *Tiber in Full Spate* (1934; priv. col., see 1986 exh. cat., pl. 20), the *Tiber Poet* (*c*. 1933; priv. col., see 1986 exh. cat., pl. 16) and *The Rowers* (*c*. 1933; priv. col., see 1986 exh. cat., pl. 19), executed in pale colours similar to those employed in fresco, have the measured cadence of Piero della Francesca's geometrical schemes. Their subject-matter, alluding to obscure myths hidden beneath the everyday, bears a considerable resemblance to a form of Magic Realism promoted by the theorist and writer Massimo Bontempelli (1878–1960).

In the late 1930s Capogrossi began to employ darker tones, gradually evolving a post-Cubist vocabulary between 1945 and 1948. In 1949 he painted his first abstract works, and towards the end of that year he arrived at a formalized language of signs that he continued to explore until his death in works such as *Surface 38* (1952; Rome, G.N.A. Mod.). He constructed these pictures by arranging and linking together, in countless variations, a regular or irregular comb-shaped matrix that determined the internal space of the work. His search for essences cannot be defined as formalist; the free composition of colours and signs according to an empirical logic, instantaneous yet meditated and profoundly rational, is nearer to the sensibility of *Art informel*. In 1951, along with Mario Ballocco (*b* 1913), Alberto Burri and Ettore Colla, Capogrossi helped found the Gruppo Origine, a group of Roman artists who promoted abstract art in response to realism; one of their central concerns was to seek maximum simplicity of expression by reduction, which they saw as a return to first principles. In 1952 Capogrossi participated in Milanese SPAZIALISMO, taking part in several group shows. His work attracted critical attention internationally, his originality and singular independence earning him a place in the history of post-war abstract painting in Italy.

BIBLIOGRAPHY

M. Seuphor: *Capogrossi* (Venice, 1954)
M. Tapié: *Capogrossi* (Venice, 1962)
G. C. Argan and M. Fagiolo: *Capogrossi* (Rome, 1967)
M. Calvesi: *Le due avanguardie* (Bari, 1975)
Capogrossi: Fino al 1948 (exh. cat. by B. Mantura, Spoleto, Pal. Rosario Spada, 1986)
Capogrossi: Opere dal 1947 al 1972 (exh. cat. by M. Apa, Urbino, Pal. Ducale, 1987)
F. Benzi: 'Capogrossi e Cavalli: Storia di un sodalizio "platonico"', *Le Scuole Romane* (exh. cat., ed. F. Benzi; Verona, Gal. Civ. A. Mod. & Contemp., 1988)

FABIO BENZI

Capon, Kenneth. *See under* ARCHITECTS' CO-PARTNERSHIP.

Caponigro, Paul (*b* Boston, MA, 7 Dec 1932). American photographer. He studied music at Boston University College of Music (1950–51). In 1953 and again in 1956, when he also studied with Alfred W. Richter, Caponigro studied photography with Benjamin Chin, former student of Ansel Adams and Minor White at the California School of Fine Art. From 1957 to 1959 he was associated with Minor White, first as a student in Rochester, New York, at workshops in White's home and then as an assistant during the summers of 1958 and 1959. His association with White provided the basis for his mature style. A delicate tonal balance and mystical view of nature typify black and white images such as *Running White Deer, County Wicklow, Ireland* (1967; see *Landscape: Photographs by Paul Caponigro*, New York, 1975, no. 27). Throughout his career he repeatedly returned to the examination of particular forms in nature. Close-up views of sunflowers constitute one series (*Sunflower*, New York, 1974); another is devoted to the ancient stone monuments of England and Ireland, for example *Ardara Dolmen, County Donegal, Ireland* (1967; New York, MOMA, see Szarkowski, p. 193) and the later portfolio *Stonehenge* (Santa Fe, 1978).

PHOTOGRAPHIC PUBLICATIONS

M. White, ed.: *Aperture*, xiii/1 (1967) [issue devoted to Caponigro]; rev. as *Paul Caponigro: Photographs* (New York, 1972)

BIBLIOGRAPHY

J. Szarkowski: *Looking at Photographs* (New York, 1973), pp. 192–3
Paul Caponigro Photography: 25 years (exh. cat., intro. P. C. Bunnell, ed. D. W. Mellor; Philadelphia, PA, Phot. Gal., 1981)

CONSTANCE W. GLENN

Caporali. Italian family of artists.

(1) Bartolomeo (di Segnolo) Caporali (*b* Perugia, *c.* 1420; *d* Perugia, *c.* 1505). Painter. He seems to have been working as a painter in Perugia by 1442 but is first documented on 24 December 1454, when he received payment for a *Pietà* and a *Maestà* (both untraced) executed for the shoemakers' guild in Perugia. In 1457–8 he was treasurer of the painters' guild, and in 1462 he was elected a civic prior for March and April. On 6 May 1467 he received payment, in Rome, for gilding the ceiling of S Marco. On 18 July of the same year he and Benedetto Bonfigli were paid by the merchant Lancillotto di Ludovico to execute a panel for the chapel of S Vincenzo in S Domenico, Perugia (untraced; unconvincingly associated with a reconstructed polyptych, Perugia, G.N. Umbria), and on 14 July the following year they received the balance due for their finished work.

Caporali's first extant work is the triptych depicting the *Virgin and Child Enthroned with Two Angels, a Sylvestrine Monk and a Lay Brother* executed for the Confraternita della Giustizia, Perugia (ex-S Mustiola, Perugia; Perugia, G.N. Umbria), sometimes attributed to Fiorenzo di Lorenzo. Several payments are recorded between October 1475 and April 1476 from the Confraternita di S Andrea, which commissioned the work, to Caporali and Sante d'Apollonio (*d* 1484), with whom he may have collaborated on a series of stylistically similar works, such as the *Virgin and Child with Angels* and *St Sebastian* (both Perugia, G.N. Umbria), a triptych (London, N.G.) and *St Eligius* and *St John the Baptist* (both Copenhagen, Thorvaldsens Mus.). Between 1477 and 1479 Caporali painted the *Adoration of the Shepherds* (Perugia, G.N. Umbria) for the convent in Monteluce, Perugia. In 1487 he signed and dated an altarpiece for the Cacciatori di Castiglione del Lago (fragments Perugia, G.N. Umbria; Udine, Mus. Civ., and Mentana, Zeri priv. col., see Gardner, pp. 47–9). On 26 November 1487 Evangelista di Francesco de' Rossi paid for a fresco, executed by Caporali, depicting the *Virgin and Child with SS Jerome and Anthony Abbot* (*in situ*) for the parish church of Rocchicciola, near Assisi. Another fresco, in S Francesco, Montone, depicting *St Anthony of Padua between St John the Baptist and the Archangel Raphael with Tobias*, commissioned by Bernardino Fortebraccio, is signed and dated 1491.

Caporali's style was derived primarily from Verrocchio and his followers and then modified through contacts with Umbrian artists younger than himself, such as Fiorenzo di Lorenzo, Perugino and Pinturicchio. Other works attributable to Caporali on stylistic grounds include a miniature depicting the *Porta Sant'Angelo* (1486; Vienna, Akad. Bild. Kst.) and two painted *gonfaloni* (1482; Montone, S Francesco; 1492; Civitella d'Arno, parish church). Among less secure attributions to Caporali are a series of works in the style of Benozzo Gozzoli and Bonfigli, sometimes dated to his early career (Bombe, Gnoli, Santi), and his participation in the *Tavolette di St Bernardino* (1473; Perugia, G.N. Umbria). Caporali's work as a miniaturist is unclear, but it is linked to the career of his brother Giapeco Caporali (*d* 1478), whose one certain work is a large, signed initial in the *Registro dei Consigli e Riformanze del Comune di Perugia* (1474; Perugia, Archv Stato).

BIBLIOGRAPHY

DBI
W. Bombe: *Geschichte der Peruginer Malerei* (Berlin, 1912)
U. Gnoli: *Pittori e miniatori nell'Umbria* (Spoleto, 1923), pp. 47–51, 348
C. Gamba: *Pittura umbra del rinascimento* (Novara, 1949), pp. xvi–xvii, xxiv–xxviii
F. Zeri: 'Appunti nell'Ermitage e nel Museo Pusckin', *Boll. A.*, iii (1961), pp. 219–36
F. Santi: *La nicchia di San Bernardino a Perugia* (Milan, 1963), p. 5
E. E. Gardner: 'I disegni di G. B. Cavalcaselle e la pala di Bartolomeo Caporali a Castaglione del Lago', *Quaderni d'Emblema*, ii (Bergamo, 1973)
——: *Galleria Nazionale dell'Umbria: Dipinti, sculture e oggetti de secoli XV–XVI* (Rome, 1985), pp. 51–9
B. Toscano: 'La pittura in Umbria nel 400', *La pittura in Italia: Il quattrocento*, ed. F. Zeri, 2 vols (Milan, 1987), p. 369
F. Todini: *La pittura umbra dal duecento al primo cinquecento* (Milan, 1989), i, pp. 49–52; ii, pp. 356–64
M. Bury: 'Bartolomeo Caporali: A New Document and its Implications', *Burl. Mag.*, cii (1990), pp. 469–75
P. Scarpellini: 'Bartolomeo Caporali', *Galleria Nazionale dell'Umbria. Dipinti, sculture e ceramiche: Studi e restauri* (Florence, 1994), pp. 235–8

P. SCARPELLINI

(2) Giovan Battista Caporali [il Bitte; il Bitti] (*b* Perugia, *c.* 1475; *d* Perugia, *c.* 1555). Painter, architect, illuminator and writer, son of (1) Bartolomeo Caporali. A follower of Perugino, he collaborated in 1503 with Bernardino Pinturicchio on the *Coronation of the Virgin* (Rome, Pin. Vaticana) for S Maria della Fratta, Umbertide. In 1508–9 he was in Rome, probably assisting Pinturicchio on the frescoes in S Maria del Popolo, and the influence of Raphael's works there can be seen in his fresco of *Christ Enthroned with Saints* (*c.* 1510; Cereseto, Parish church). His mature style is demonstrated in the *Adoration of the Shepherds* (*c.* 1519; Panicale, S Michele Arcangelo), the panel of the *Virgin and Child with Saints* (Perugia, G.N. Umbria) and frescoes including those in S Pietro, Perugia (1521), S Agostino, Montefalco (1522), and S Maria della Luce, Perugia (1532). In the 1520s he undertook a major architectural commission, a villa near Cortona, 'il Palazzone', for Cardinal Silvio Passerini. Caporali also executed some of the decoration of the interior, with Tommaso Bernabei Papacello (1500–59), including grisaille frescoes of mythological subjects. His writings included poetry (London, BM, C106.a.3) and an annotated Italian edition of Vitruvius's *De architectura*, essentially repeating Cesare Cesariano's translation of 1521. Among his illuminations is a signed portrait of *Pope Julius III* in the *Annale decemvirale* of 1553 (Perugia, Bib. Augusta). He trained the architect Galeazzo Alessi, and his son Giulio Caporali (*fl* 1559–94) was a painter.

WRITINGS

Marcus Vitruvius Pollio, de architectura, con il suo comento et figure Vetruvio in volgar lingua raportato per M. Gianbatista Caporali di Perugia (Perugia, 1536)

BIBLIOGRAPHY

DBI

G. Vasari: *Vite* (1550, rev. 2/1568); ed. G. Milanesi (1878–85), iii, pp. 597, 696 [as 'Benedetto' Caporali]

B. Frescucci: *Il Palazzone* (Sondrio, 1965)

P. Scarpellini: 'Giovan Battista Caporali e la cultura artistica perugina', *Atti del XII Convegno di studi Umbri: Perugia, 1981*, pp. 22–79 [with bibliog.]

La pittura in Italia: Il cinquecento (Milan, 1988), ii, p. 666

□

Cappadocia. Region of central Anatolia, now in Turkey.

1. Introduction. 2. Early Christian and Byzantine.

1. INTRODUCTION. The region known in ancient times as Greater Cappadocia extends from Lake Tatta eastwards to the River Euphrates. It was bordered to the south by Cilicia, and to the north lay Pontus, which before the late 4th century BC had also formed part of Cappadocia. The region consists largely of a plateau divided by the Taurus and Antitaurus mountains, with volcanic areas in the west and around Erciyas Dağı (anc. Mt Argaeus) in the centre. Cappadocia has been continuously inhabited since prehistoric times, and during the 2nd millennium BC it was part of the Hittite empire. Conquered by the Persians in 585 BC, it was ruled during the 4th–1st centuries BC by the descendants of the satrap Ariarathes (*b c.* 404 BC). In AD 17 Cappadocia became a Roman province, with its capital at Caesarea (now Kayseri).

Material from the Greco-Roman period is mostly limited to funerary stelae of poor quality found at various sites, but an inventory of Greco-Roman necropoleis has revealed that there was continuity between the pagan and Christian population. The medieval development of Göreme simply followed the foundations of Çavüşin and Maçan, which themselves had originated in the ancient settlement of Venasa (now Avanos), a sacred town dedicated to Zeus (Strabo: *Geography* V.vi.9).

Cappadocia was converted to Christianity very early, and by the 2nd century AD it already had numerous Christian communities. In AD 370 the bishopric of Caesarea alone had 50 suffragan bishops, and St Gregory of Nyssa wrote of its churches in his second letter: 'so many could not be counted in all the rest of the world together'. It is with the religious art and architecture of Cappadocia between the 4th and 13th centuries that this article is mainly concerned, in particular the many rock-cut churches and monasteries and their wall paintings.

From the 8th century to the mid-9th, seasonal invasions by the Arabs resulted in considerable depopulation. With the reconquest of the eastern provinces of the Byzantine empire came a period of peace and prosperity, and from the late 9th century churches and small monasteries multiplied. The 10th century and the first three-quarters of the 11th mark the medieval apogee of Cappadocia. The arrival of the Turks (Caesarea was captured in 1081) occurred in the midst of a period of prosperity and was final, though the Greek Christian population persisted for centuries. After the state of war in the 12th century, the economic revival that the Seljuk, and later Mongol, peace brought to Anatolia in the 13th century also affected the Greek colonies. Many churches were restored and painted in this period. It will be noted that the main centres of religious and urban activity changed between the Roman period and the early Middle Ages. In the Ottoman period the religious communities stagnated, and it was not until the 19th century that a certain tolerance and a moderate increase in wealth led to the appearance of new foundations. The exchange of populations in 1924 put an end to the Greek presence.

2. EARLY CHRISTIAN AND BYZANTINE. The arts of Cappadocia during the period discussed here should also be considered in the wider context of EARLY CHRISTIAN AND BYZANTINE ART.

(i) Architecture. (ii) Wall painting.

(i) Architecture.

(a) Rock-cut structures. (b) Built churches.

(a) Rock-cut structures. Rock-cut 'architecture' is found in other parts of the Byzantine world: in Phrygia, west of Cappadocia; in Midye in Thrace; in Sille, near Konya to the south; and near Chersonesos on the north coast of the Black Sea (*see also* ROCK CHURCH). These monuments are, however, linked only by their rock-cut nature, suggesting that such architecture is likely to appear in any region having rock soft enough for easy excavation.

Cappadocia is now best known for the region immediately around Erciyas Dağı, where soft rock formed from volcanic ash has been eroded by the weather to form many interlacing valleys. These are often steep-sided and lined with cone-shaped formations into which cavities have been cut. Occasional rock-cut tombs with pillared 'temple' fronts date from at least as early as Classical antiquity, but most rock-cut monuments are Byzantine or post-Byzantine. Many cavities serve domestic or agricultural purposes: there are rock-cut villages (e.g. Çavüşin); pigeon houses, which supply fertilizer for local agriculture and consist of irregular cavities excavated at several levels, linked by vertical 'chimneys' (e.g. Ortahisar); and subterranean labyrinths forming 'underground cities' (e.g. Kaymaklı). The latter are said to have housed sizeable communities, but they must have functioned primarily as storage areas; the use of subterranean warehousing is still a local practice.

Rock-cut architecture must have been quicker and cheaper than building, requiring no quarrying or hauling of materials, and the soft rock is easily cut. A tunnel must first have been cut into the cliff or cone, followed by the enlargement of its far end to create the roughed-out shape of a church or other structure. Finishing would have been sculptural, starting at the top and working downwards, probably with wooden scaffolding set into the roughed-out walls, which would then have been cut back as work progressed. A small church might have been completed in a few weeks by only two or three workers. Since the process could clearly not have started with the laying out of a ground-plan, much must have depended on the 'eye' of individual masons.

Since the granular rock does not lend itself to intricate carving, carved decoration is largely confined to simple cornices and mouldings with occasional scroll or foliage

1. Cappadocia, Göreme, rock-cut interior of Tokalı Kilise (New Church), ?*c.* 950–60, showing the north-east corner with barrel vault, carved and painted screen and horseshoe-shaped arches

ornament. Capitals are usually slabs or tapering blocks, sometimes decorated with incised geometric ornament (e.g. the church at Şahinefendi Monastery). The capitals of the church at Hallaç Monastery are unusual in having rudimentary volutes and horned animal heads. The monastery also has a unique high-relief human figure of uncertain subject in the vaulting of one of its rooms. By far the most common carved motif is the horseshoe-shaped blind niche that decorates the interiors of many churches. It is also the basic motif of the decorated façades that are a conspicuous feature of many rock-cut monuments. Several registers of blind arcades formed of rows of horseshoe-shaped niches front large monuments, such as the monasteries and the complexes of Açık Saray, and can be very elaborate.

Donor images and invocations in the painted decorations (*see* §(ii) below) suggest that the patrons of cave monuments were usually gentry rather than aristocracy. Many are identified by first names only, and where family names are given they are seldom traceable in documentary records. The titles found, such as *protospatharios*, *domestikos* and *kleisouriarchos*, are those of middle rank. There is only one imperial portrait, that of Nikephoros II Phokas (*reg* 963–9) and his immediate family, in the Pigeon House Church at Çavüşin, but it was probably not commissioned by the emperor himself.

Churches. Possibly as many as 500 cavities are Byzantine churches or chapels, densely grouped in some valleys, scattered in others; some are part of monastic complexes, others are solitary. There is virtually no documentary evidence for these monuments, most of which are known only by descriptive Turkish names, such as Karanlık Kilise ('the dark church'). Occasionally the original dedication of the church is given by an inscription (e.g. Soğanlı, St Barbara). The first detailed accounts of these churches were published by Hans Rott (1908), and Guillaume de Jerphanion later provided much fuller descriptions of their painted decoration, after several visits to the area in 1907 and 1911–13. The often well-preserved polychrome painting cycles (*see* §(ii) below) are particularly important for the history of Byzantine monumental art in Anatolia, of which very little has survived elsewhere.

The 'cave' churches are finished to resemble built architecture. Vaulting, columns, blind arcading, cornices and other details are reproduced with care and are often emphasized with borders of geometric patterns in red paint, which was also occasionally used to imitate masonry lines. A few churches have inscriptions giving dates ranging from the 10th century to the 13th, but for many others the attribution of date depends on the style of their painting or architecture and its relationship to dated examples. Some churches have been placed as early as the 7th century AD (e.g. Açıkel Ağa Kilise, Belisırma), but most probably fall between the 9th and 11th centuries. The production of rock-cut churches then declined, but occasional church decorations with 13th-century inscriptions attest the religious tolerance of the Sultanate of Konya (e.g. Kırk Dam Altı Kilise, Belisırma).

There is no local 'Cappadocian' church type, since the several schemes found are all familiar from contemporary built Middle Byzantine architecture. These layouts are widely distributed and include the single-naved, barrel-vaulted church or chapel, which tends to be small (e.g. Göreme, Chapel 9, *c.* 3×4 m; Çavüşin, Pigeon House Church, *c.* 6×8 m). Such churches usually have a single apse (e.g. Göreme, Chapel 8), but occasionally a large main apse is flanked by small side apses (e.g. Göreme, Chapel 9); apses are partly closed by rock-cut parapets flanking a central opening. A common variant on this plan is the twin-aisled church with a connected pair of barrel-vaulted aisles, one of which often served as a funerary chapel with graves in tomb niches cut into its walls (e.g. Ayvalı Kilise). The domed free cross (e.g. Göreme, Chapel 27) and the cross-in-square (e.g. Göreme, 'Column Churches') are also common; their domes are carried on rudimentary pendentives with no evidence of squinches. Cross-in-square churches usually have columns, but occasionally piers were used (e.g. Direkli Kilise); cross-arms are barrel-vaulted; corner bays may have domes, barrel vaults or cross vaults, although often more than one form appears in the same church. Three apses open off the eastern bays of the nine-bay square, each partly closed either by rock-cut parapets or by taller screens with central horseshoe-shaped openings and flanking 'windows' (e.g. Göreme, Chapel 21). The larger, three-aisled basilica is represented by a few examples: they have rather squat proportions and are usually divided by arcades on columns (e.g. Çavüşin, St John the Baptist, 17×10 m). Only in the Selime Monastery church do columns and piers alternate. Less common plans include the transverse barrel-vaulted nave (e.g. Tokalı Kilise, New Church; see fig. 1), which has parallels in the church architecture of the ṬUR ʿABDIN, and in the triconch (e.g. Tağar), best known on MT ATHOS. Whether occurrence of these plans indicates Mesopotamian and Athonite influence in Middle Byzantine Cappadocia—which was indeed a centre of pilgrimage—or simply shows that such layouts were much more widely distributed than the surviving built examples suggest, is uncertain. Whatever the architectural form of the church, there is usually a rock-cut altar attached to the back wall of each apse and flanked by one or more seats behind the parapets or screens. Uniquely, Durmuş Kilisesi in Avcılar also has a rock-cut ambo towards the east end of its nave.

Hermitages and monasteries. There are several hermitages, each generally consisting of a small chapel, a cell and a tomb. Inscriptions sometimes name the hermit or his patron, as at the Hermitage of Niketas the Stylite at Güllü Dere. Hermitages appear early in the sequence of cave monuments, in the late 9th century and the early 10th, some possibly earlier still. Hermits were probably drawn by the desert-like appearance of the volcanic valleys and in turn attracted pious visitors, who were then responsible for the excavation and decoration of the rock-cut churches.

The larger monasteries belong to the first half of the 11th century and may be seen as the final episode in the development of Byzantine ecclesiastical rock-cut architecture in Cappadocia. They are of two types: courtyard monasteries and refectory monasteries. Courtyard monasteries are scattered throughout the region and resemble built monasteries of the kind still seen in Greece. Each consists of a series of rooms and a church set around an open courtyard. Subterranean labyrinths provided storage space, which could be sealed by large rock discs rolled across the entrances. Monasteries of this type generally have a single, cross-in-square church, with a prominent tomb chamber attached to it for the burial of the founder (e.g. Hallaç Monastery; see fig. 2). The rooms, seldom more than six, include a large hall (probably the refectory) and a kitchen with a conical or domed vault. Other rooms were probably dormitories, since there are no cells: their small size suggests that there were few monks. At Açık Saray (the Open Palace) on the Nevşehir–Gülşehir road, there is a group of similar complexes that appear to have been secular, since most lack churches; these may have been stopping places for merchant caravans or troops.

The refectory monasteries are without formal arrangement. Each consists of a church, a refectory and a cluster of roughly-cut rooms (e.g. Çarıklı Kilise Monastery). The refectories have rock-cut tables and benches and are often large enough to seat about 30 people, probably including visitors, since again there are no cells, and the resident community must have been small. The church is usually of cross-in-square or free-cross plan, with a large narthex, often with many graves cut into its floor and walls. Refectory monasteries are concentrated in the Göreme valley region, which may have been a centre of pilgrimage with Tokalı Kilise as its focus. This site, which probably began as a hermitage, was clearly a place of pilgrimage, since its earliest monument, a small, single-nave chapel (the Old Church) hewn in the early 10th century, was extended about 50 years later by excavation through its apse to create a larger and more elaborate New Church (see fig. 1) with a side chapel and funerary crypt.

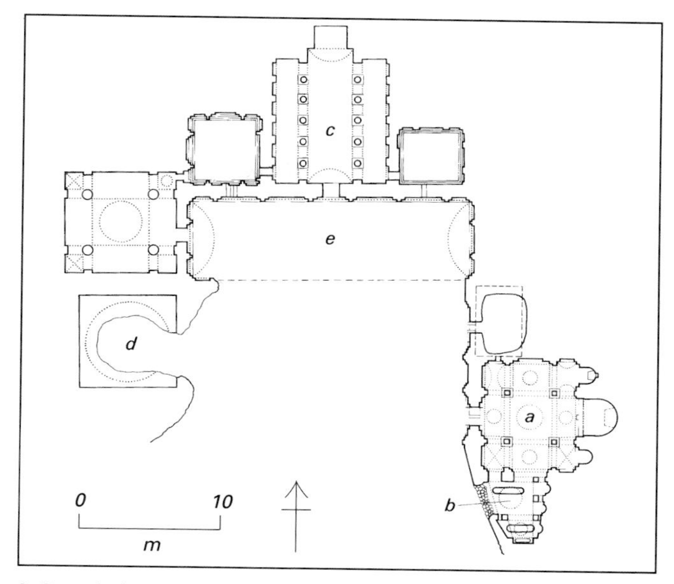

2. Cappadocia, near Ortahisar, rock-cut Hallaç Monastery, early 11th century, plan: (a) church; (b) tomb chamber; (c) hall; (d) kitchen; (e) courtyard and vestibule

(b) Built churches. Early Christian architecture in Cappadocia is represented by about 30 built churches (4th–6th centuries), concentrated in the Hasan Dağı region south of Aksaray but also scattered at other sites between Aksaray, Niğde and Kayseri. Several architectural types are found: the barrel-vaulted single nave (e.g. Sarıgöl), free-cross (Sivrihisar), basilica (Eski Andaval) and domed octagon (Sivasa). The churches are built of ashlar masonry, and their windows and entrances are usually horseshoe-shaped and often framed by linked hood mouldings. Capitals and occasional lintels and cornices are decorated with the stylized acanthus ornament used widely in Early Christian architecture. In style and technique these churches resemble those of BINBIRKILISE (the Thousand and One Churches) in the Karaman region further to the south-west.

Building in Cappadocia declined between the mid-7th century and the 9th, following the Arab incursions and concomitant changes to the Byzantine social and administrative structure. Territorial recovery beginning in the late 9th century is signalled by the repair and remodelling of some of the Early Christian churches and by the appearance of the cross-in-square, the most common and widespread of Middle Byzantine church plans. Examples at Çeltek and Belisırma are, like their Early Christian predecessors, built of ashlar masonry and use the horseshoe arch.

BIBLIOGRAPHY

H. Rott: *Kleinasiatische Denkmäler aus Pisidien, Pamphylien, Kappadokien und Lykien* (Leipzig, 1908)

G. de Jerphanion: *Une nouvelle province de l'art Byzantin: Les Eglises rupestres de Cappadoce*, 2 vols (Paris, 1925–42)

N. Thierry and M. Thierry: *Nouvelles églises rupestres de Cappadoce: Région du Hasan Dağı* (Paris, 1963)

S. Kostof: *Caves of God: The Monastic Environment of Byzantine Cappadocia* (Cambridge, MA, 1972)

M. Restle: *Studien zur frühbyzantinischen Arkitektur Kappadokiens* (Vienna, 1979)

L. Rodley: *Cave Monasteries of Byzantine Cappadocia* (Cambridge, 1985)

LYN RODLEY

(ii) Wall painting.

(a) Introduction. (b) Historical survey.

(a) Introduction. While the many examples of wall painting known from Cappadocia range in date from the painted Roman tombs in the village of Kavak near Göreme

3. Cappadocia, wall painting of the *Virgin Enthroned*, triumphal arch of the church of Joachim and Anna, Kızıl Çukur, early 7th century (*in situ*)

to the works of the Greek Christian community in the early 20th century, most survive in the Byzantine rock-cut churches of the 10th–13th centuries (*see* §(i)(a) above). Some 200 examples of pictorial art are known from rock-cut churches, mostly in the region of Avanos and Ürgüp, near Kızıl Irmak, and near Aksaray in the Hasan Dağı. Of these, only a few can be precisely dated by inscriptions. Two decorative schemes date from the beginning of the reign of Constantine VII Porphyrogenitus (*reg* 913–59): Tavşanlı Kilise near Ortahisar, and St John at Güllü Dere, near Çavüşin. Another scheme dates from the joint reign of Constantine VII and Romanos Lekapenos (*reg* 921–44): Eğri Taş Kilisesi near Ihlara in the Hasan Dağı. The Pigeon House Church of Çavüşin commemorates the victories of Nikephoros Phokas (*reg* 963–9) and may therefore date from 965–9. The slightly earlier New Church of Tokalı Kilise (?*c.* 950–60; see fig. 1 above) has been attributed to the patronage of the Phokas family. The other painted churches that can be firmly dated are Direkli Kilise (*c.* 976–1025) and St Michael at Ihlara (*c.* 1055–6), St Barbara (1006 or 1021) and Karabaş Kilise (1060) in the Soğanli valley, together with Karşi Kilise (1212), the Forty Martyrs at Suveş (1216–17) and St George at Belisirama (*c.* 1283–95).

Most Cappadocian wall paintings are executed in *a secco* technique on surfaces varying from pure plaster in the early Middle Ages to a mixture of cob plaster and lime later on. The pigments used were from materials found locally, such as iron oxide, haematite, chalk and goethite; the most common binding agent was casein. Other pigments include one made out of a mixture of mercury dust and sulphur found in Asia Minor, and an ultramarine blue obtained from lapis lazuli, a product of Afghanistan.

(b) Historical survey. The attribution of certain church paintings to the period between the mid-6th century and the end of iconoclasm in 843 (see below) is largely based on analogies with comparable works from other parts of the Byzantine empire, although, with the discovery since 1960 of many more painted churches, several schemes assignable to dates before the mid-9th century are now available for study. For paintings from the 10th–13th centuries, stylistic comparisons between the few dated examples (*see* §(a) above) and the paintings in undated Cappadocian churches make it possible to establish a general chronology, which can be related to the painting workshops active in different localities.

Roughly 15% of known Cappadocian paintings date from the mid-6th century to the mid-9th; 30–35% from the late 9th century to the mid-10th; 10–15% from the middle and second half of the 10th century; 25–30% from the first three quarters of the 11th century; and some 15% from the 13th century. The 12th century seems to have been a period of almost total inactivity.

Early works, 6th century to the mid-9th. The paintings that predate the period of iconoclasm (726–843), when figural representations in religious art were officially banned, are characterized by the artists' desire to exalt the omnipotence of God and his divine nature in human form. The images are dogmatic and symbolic, with the cross, as the sign of Christ, having a prominent place in the programmes of votive panels. Typical programmes depict key images from the Life of Christ: for example from Çavüşin, church of St John the Baptist, the *Infant Christ Praying in his Bath* and the *Incredulity of Thomas* (in which the apostle recognizes the sovereignty of Christ without touching his wounds). Some theophanic images are very elaborate, for example an *Ascension* that shows Christ preaching (Balkanderesi, Church 1) and the triumphal scene of the *Crucifixion* presented by St John the Baptist and flanked by a double row of apostles in arcades in the chapel of the hermitage of Niketas the Stylite at Güllü Dere. In the church of Joachim and Anna at Kızıl Çukur the *Conception and Infancy of the Virgin* is presented as a series of divine interventions, serving as pendants to the image of the *Virgin Enthroned* in a mandorla adored by angels (early 7th century; see fig. 3). This is one of two surviving representations of this scheme; the other, the fragmentary 6th-century apse mosaic in the Panagia Kanakaria at Lythrankomi on Cyprus, has been stolen.

In the early 8th century crosses were used to decorate large votive panels. Ceilings and vaults are often covered with large Latin crosses set against a background of vine *rinceaux*. Sometimes a cross against a starry ground replaces the image of Christ in the apse, above the Virgin flanked by archangels. The votive panels emphasize the effect of divine grace through such scenes as Daniel in the Lions' Den, the Burning Fiery Furnace and the Vision of St Eustace. Saints are rarely depicted, except for St John the Baptist and a few military and physician saints. Finally, some wall paintings of this period are distinguished by their extensive decoration, as in the churches of St Stephan and SS Peter and Paul at Meskendir, the chapel in the hermitage of Niketas the Stylite and the tombs at Maçan-Avcılar. These decorative schemes are derived from the repertory of Greco-Roman art and are related to contemporary decoration in Visigothic Spain, Lombard Italy, the pre-Arab Transcaucasus and Byzantine and Ummayad Syria.

As first noted by Millet and Jerphanion, the paintings of the church of St Basil near Cernil belong to the iconoclastic period (726–843). Their stylization is still linked to Greco-Oriental art, and crosses take the place of busts of patriarchs in the conch of the apse. Similarly, in the 'iconoclast' church of Yaprakhisar (Davullu Kilisesi) a lion replaces St Eustace hunting the cross-bearing deer, while the funerary decoration at Karacaören, near Ürgüp, which shows flowering *rinceaux* framing crosses, is reminiscent of Ummayad art.

'Archaic', late 9th century–the early 10th. After the prohibition of images during the iconoclastic period, walls were covered with figurative decoration. Gradually scenes from the Life of Christ came to predominate, filling several registers and accompanied by detailed saints' lives. Ornament was reduced to a few friezes, and the great votive crosses were replaced by representations of the True Cross flanked by Constantine I (*reg* 306–37) and his mother, Helena (255–330). Paintings of this period were called 'archaic' by their discoverer, Guillaume de Jerphanion, who believed them to be the earliest in Cappadocia; and despite the subsequent discovery of earlier painting (see above), the term remains in use. The Life of Christ is portrayed in narrative sequences, illustrating the Infancy, the Ministry, Passion and Post-Resurrection Appearances. Such key symbolic images as the Transfiguration and Ascension are often moved out of chronological sequence, with the former placed on tympana or triumphal arches and the latter in the centre of the vault or in the dome. The loss of almost all Middle Byzantine painting in Constantinople means that the numerous Cappadocian churches of this period constitute a unique repertory of iconography, particularly for scenes of the Passion, Dormition, Visions of the Prophets, Deësis and Last Judgement.

Painters were clearly allowed a degree of individual initiative, which explains the existence of unusual images drawn from apocryphal writings; examples are the *Transfiguration* accompanied by a *Vision of Paradise*, as described in the Apocalypse of Peter, in the church of St Theodore near Ortahisar; the *Visions of the Magi* at Eğri Taş Kilesesi, illustrating the polymorphism of God; and the *Judgement of Pilate* at Kokar Kilise, where Christ is shown in a luminous mandorla that gives objective form to his divinity. Some other subjects are totally unscriptural, for example the *Devil Defying Christ at the Last Supper* in the churches at Ihlara, in particular a well-preserved painting in Yılanlı Kilise.

These numerous 'archaic' programmes are differentiated by their extremely varied styles. The handling of form and drapery in the church of St John at Güllü Dere (*c.* 913–20; see fig. 4) is similar to that found in the 9th-century dome mosaic of Hagia Sophia at Thessaloniki (*see* THESSALONIKI, §III, 5(ii)). Kılıclar Kilise has paintings that equal the best products of the early 10th century, while Tavşanlı Kilise (913–20) is evidence of the survival of artistic traditions of the Late Antique period. The paintings of Eğri Taş Kilisesi (921–44) are related to the art of Rome in the 8th and 9th centuries, and those at St Eustace at Göreme to contemporary popular art. It seems, then, that painters in this period, from the most sophisticated to the most provincial, borrowed from many traditions, both older and contemporary; among the latter must be counted certain details taken from the neighbouring Muslim world, such as the 'kiss-curl' coiffure of St Catherine in the Old Church of Tokalı Kilise.

4. Cappadocia, wall painting of the *Apostle Andrew*, church of St John, Güllü Dere, *c.* 913–20 (*in situ*)

Mid- and late 10th century. The paintings of this period seem to mark a refinement both in style and in the exegesis of the texts illustrated, leading some to argue that Cappadocia participated in the creative activity of the 'Macedonian Renaissance' at its apogee (*see also* MACEDONIAN DYNASTY). In Balı Kilise near Belisirama, a painter called Leo used the *Annunciation* for an apse programme and accompanied it with a poem in honour of the Archangel Gabriel. At the New Church of Tokalı Kilise, where the paintings have been restored, important innovations occur in the New Testament sequence, and the *Pentecost* scene is expanded to include tribes and peoples depicted behind four nimbed kings. The *Crucifixion* in the apse is flanked and commented upon by figures of *Jeremiah* and *Ezekiel*, and a beautiful image of the *Virgin of Tenderness* (Theotokos Eleousa) in the niche between the prothesis and sanctuary apses emphasizes the human nature of the Child. In St Barbara at Soğanlı (1006 or 1021), which is faithful to 10th-century tradition, Adam and Eve are depicted throwing themselves at the feet of *Christ Pantokrator* enthroned in the apse, and the traditional *Harrowing of Hell* is turned into an image of universal resurrection by the addition of tombs from which the dead are rising.

The Pigeon House Church at Çavüşin contains remarkable decorations commemorating the victorious campaigns of Nikephoros Phokas against the Arabs in 964 and 965. In the north absidiole, as if in a tribune, are depicted the Emperor with his wife Theophano, their son Basil, the Emperor's father Caesar Bardas, and his brother the *kuropalates* Leo; advancing on horseback along the north wall are the two leaders of the Byzantine army, John Tzimiskes (*reg* 969–76) and Melias, filing past as if on parade. This scene of imperial triumph is completed by a reference to a heavenly intervention, the arrival of the Archangel Michael to reinforce the armies of Joshua at the capture of Jericho.

11th century. The stylistic developments of the preceding period continued with decorative programmes falling into two types. One is almost entirely hagiographical, as in Sümbüllü Kilisesi and Direkli Kilise at Belisirama (late 10th century or early 11th) and in Yusuf Koç Kilisesi (first quarter of the 11th century). The other consists of the illustration of the *Twelve Feasts of the Church*, as in the three 'column churches' of Çarıklı Kilise, Elmalı Kilise and Karanlık Kilise at Göreme. It is a programme related to those at Constantinople, but unlike the metropolitan schemes, which have the Virgin or Virgin and Child in the main apse, it still has Christ in that position, though now as part of a Deësis instead of being enthroned or in a mandorla and surrounded by the symbols of the Evangelists and his angelic bodyguard.

Four different styles may be identified. The 'classical style' follows on from the art of the 10th century (e.g. Sümbüllü Kilisesi, Direkli Kilise and Ala Kilise at Belisirama, St Barbara at Soğanlı, Tağar and the north wall of Eski Gümüş). The 'precious style' is represented by the paintings of the three 'column churches'; it derives from the aristocratic art of the late 10th century and led to a certain academicism in the treatment of portraits, though it achieved felicitous mannerist effects in such bravura pieces as the *Ascension.* Despite some awkward features, these paintings are reminiscent of Constantinopolitan art, a fact perhaps explained by the presence among the donors at Karanlık Kilise of a dignitary sent to the region by the Patriarch of Constantinople. In a similar style are some rather provincial paintings of Yusuf Koç Kilisesi. The 'realist and expressionist' style is represented by the decorations of Karabaş Kilise in the Soğanli valley, commissioned by a member of the landed nobility of the region, the *protospatharios* Michael Skepidis. Lastly, the 'schematic style', derived from a structural analysis of Classical models, is exemplified by the paintings of the church of Ayvalı Köy, the apse of Eski Gümüş, Meryemana at Göreme and the Cistern Church at Maçan-Avcılar.

12th and 13th centuries. The 12th century in Cappadocia was a period of warfare from which hardly any paintings survive. Once Turkish hegemony over the region was established, the Greek communities of Cappadocia had little contact with the Byzantine empire, and this explains the conservative, even fossilized, character of 13th-century works. The painters copied the subject-matter and ornament of the best local works, but their execution was usually mediocre. Even the decoration of Karşi Kilise near Gülşehir (1212), which was done for an important female donor, is of a poor quality, its only point of interest being the picturesque details in the *Last Judgement.* In the built church at Ortaköy, however, the layer of 13th-century paintings is stylistically superior to the two previous schemes, and the hagiography is a combination of survivals (e.g. the *Angel Appearing to Joshua* and the *Vision of St Eustace*) and revivals (e.g. the *Human-headed Dragon Defeated by St Theodore* and the *Bishops Officiating* in the apse). An example of good provincial work is in a church at Ortahisar, now a villager's house in Ali Reis Street; two depictions of the *Pantokrator* are preserved, one in the apse and the other in the dome.

The more sophisticated decorative schemes displaying influences from Latin art in Bezirhanı Kilisesi, near Belisirama, and in the church in the village of Yükseklı north of Kızıl Irmak and opposite Gülşehir, can be attributed to two itinerant painters from the Byzantine empire. The paintings can be dated to the late 13th century by many of their details, in particular the nimbi of Christ painted in imitation of goldsmith's work and, in the second church, a *Baptism* in which the River Jordan is accompanied by a personification of the Sea holding a boat and wearing a sailing ship, complete with crew, on his head.

BIBLIOGRAPHY

G. Millet: *Recherches sur l'iconographie de l'Evangile aux XIVe, XVe et XVIe siècles* (Paris, 1916)
G. de Jerphanion: *Une nouvelle province de l'art byzantin: Les Eglises rupestres de Cappadoce*, 2 vols (Paris, 1925–42)
——: *La Voix des monuments*, 2 vols (Paris, 1930–38)
N. Thierry and M. Thierry: *Nouvelles eglises rupestres de Cappadoce: Région du Hasan Dağı* (Paris, 1963)
M. Restle: *Die byzantinische Wandmalerei in Kleinasien* (Recklinghausen, 1967; Eng. trans. Shannon, 1969)
L. Giovannini, ed.: *Arts of Cappadocia* (London, 1971)
N. Thierry: *Peintures d'Asie Mineur et de Transcaucasie aux Xe et XIe siècles* (London, 1977)
——: 'Un problème de continuité ou de rupture: La Cappadoce entre Rome, Byzance et les Arabes', *Acad. Inscr. & B.-Lett.: C. R. Séances* (1977), pp. 88–144
——: 'La Vierge de tendresse a l'époque macédonienne', *Zograf*, x (1979), pp. 59–70
Atti del 5o Convegno internazionale di studi sulla civiltà rupestre medioevale nel mezzogiorno d'Italia: Lecce-Nardo, 1979
N. Thierry: 'L'Iconoclasme en Cappadoce d'après les sources archéologiques: Origines et modalités', *Rayonnement grec: Hommages à Charles Delvoye*, ed. L. Hadermann-Misguich and G. Raepsaet (Brussels, 1982), pp. 389–403
——: *Haut moyen âge en Cappadoce: Les Eglises de la région de Çavuşin*, i (Paris, 1983)
——: 'Découvertes à la nécropole de Göreme', *Acad. Inscr. & B.-Lett.: C. R. Séances* (1984), pp. 656–91
A. W. Epstein: *Tokalı Kilise: Tenth-century Metropolitan Art in Byzantine Cappadocia* (Washington, DC, 1986)
Constantine VII Porphyrogenitus and his Age: 2nd International Byzantine Conference: Delphi, 1987, pp. 217–84
C. Jolivet-Lévy: *Les Eglises byzantines de Cappadoce: Le Programme iconographique de l'abside et de ses abords* (Paris, 1991)

NICOLE THIERRY

Cappa magna. *See under* VESTMENTS, ECCLESIASTICAL, §1(iii).

Capparoni [Caparroni; Capparone; Capperoni], **Gaspare** (*b* Rome, 20 June 1761; *d* Rome, 13 Dec 1808). Italian gem-engraver. He won prizes in sculpture at the Accademia di S Luca, Rome, in 1780, 1782 and 1783. He is documented as an engraver from 1790 with a cameo bearing the *Head of Maecenas*, executed for the Pallavicini family. His works, signed ΚΑΠ, ΚΑΠΠΑ, ΚΑΠΠΑΡΟΝΙ and CAPPARONI, include engravings in both intaglio and cameo, although he seems to have preferred the latter technique. Among his documented signed works are: *Maecenas* (Rome, priv. col., see Pirzio Biroli Stefanelli, no. 1); *Hebe Giving Water to the Eagle* (Vienna, Ksthist. Mus.); *Ganymede and the Eagle* (see Guattani, 1807, p. 135); a *Veiled Head of a Woman* (St Petersburg, Hermitage); *Paris* (PBS 5); *Brutus*, in intaglio (PBS 6); and a bust of *Napoleon* (PBS 8), copied from a statue by Antonio Canova (London, Apsley House). Contemporary sources attribute about 20 other unsigned works to Capparoni; the most notable of these is the *Birth of Telephus* (PBS 20), mentioned by Guattani, from an antique bas-relief in the Villa Borghese, Rome. He was considered one of the most accomplished engravers of his time.

Capparoni took an active part in the cultural life of the time; among his friends were Gavin Hamilton, Canova, Vincenzo Camuccini and Giuseppe Cades. He bought and sold works of art. He edited the seventh volume of *Il Museo Pio Clementino descritto da Ennio Quirino Visconti* (Rome, 1807) and, together with Antonio d'Este, the first volume of *Il Museo Chiaramonti* (Rome, 1808).

BIBLIOGRAPHY

G. A. Guattani: *Memorie enciclopediche romane sulle belle arti e antichità*, i (Rome, 1806), p. 79; ii (Rome, 1807), pp. 135–6; iv (Rome, 1808), p. 125

R. Righetti: *Incisori di cammei a Roma* (Rome, [1954/5]), pp. 44–5

L. Pirzio Biroli Stefanelli: 'Gaspare Capparoni, scultore in gemme', *Xenia*, ii (1981), pp. 85–98 [PBS]

LUCIA PIRZIO BIROLI STEFANELLI

Cappelen, (Herman) August (*b* Skien, Telemark, 1 May 1827; *d* Düsseldorf, 8 July 1852). Norwegian painter, active in Germany. From a well-to-do family, he studied at Christiania (now Oslo) Universitet and then became a private pupil of Hans Fredrik Gude before going to Düsseldorf in 1846; he spent the rest of his life there, except for summer visits to Norway and a longer stay in Christiania (1848–9). Johann Wilhelm Schirmer's traditional technique and Dutch landscape art were important influences. In contrast to other Norwegian Düsseldorf painters, Cappelen was not especially attracted by mountain scenery. His most successful work, *Waterfall in Lower Telemark* (1852; Oslo, N.G.), probably developed from sketches made in 1851. The waterfall runs diagonally through the picture, and the mist hangs low over the wooded hillside that frames the scene. The diminutive figures of men working logs over the falls create a romantic contrast with the monumentality of the natural surroundings.

Melancholy pervades Cappelen's paintings despite the happy and lively nature apparent in his correspondence. His great unfinished work, *Decaying Forest* (1852; Oslo, N.G.), reveals a macabre quality underlying his lyrical and dramatic perception of nature. In this fantastic and semi-symbolic scene, clefts open in the mountainside, and rotting and broken tree trunks run from foreground to background, with pine trees silhouetted against the evening sky. Cappelen avoided panoramic views, preferring close observation of isolated sections of terrain, which he treated with a sure sense of colour and form. He was the most natural Romantic painter among the Norwegian Düsseldorf painters and in his brief working life he succeeded in revealing the mystical side of nature.

WRITINGS

E. Østvedt, ed.: *Auguste Cappelens brev* [Letters] (Oslo, 1952)

BIBLIOGRAPHY

NKL

S. Willoch: *August Cappelen og den romantiske landskapskunst* (Oslo, 1928)

August Cappelen (exh. cat. by O. Thue, Oslo, Kstforen., 1957)

E. Østvedt: 'August Cappelen: Mennesket og maleren' [A. Cappelen: the man and the painter], *Pa gamle tufter: Ti Telemarksprofiler* [On old foundations: ten profiles from Telemark] (Skien, 1975), pp. 8–27

ERNST HAVERKAMP

Cappellari, Bartolommeo Alberto. *See* GREGORY XVI.

Cappelle, Jan van de (*bapt* Amsterdam, 25 Jan 1626; *bur* Amsterdam, 22 Dec 1679). Dutch businessman, collector, painter, draughtsman and etcher. Though now considered the outstanding marine painter of 17th-century Holland, he was not a professional artist nor a member of the Amsterdam Guild of St Luke. His father owned a successful dye-works in Amsterdam, in which both Jan and his brother Louis were active. Their father enjoyed a long life and probably managed the firm until close to his death in 1674, when Jan inherited it. This left Jan with plenty of spare time to pursue his hobby, painting. He married Annetje Jansdr. (Anna Grotingh) before 1653. He died a widower, survived by his seven children, who inherited his considerable fortune. His last will shows that in addition to the dye-works and immense cash assets, van de Cappelle owned extensive properties and an art collection that must be rated among the most important of his time.

Apart from his involvement with the arts, Jan shared his countrymen's love of ships and sailing. He owned a pleasure yacht, moored in the 'oude yacht haven', which must have taken him on many trips along the Dutch coast and rivers, giving him an opportunity to sketch and draw from nature.

1. Art collection. 2. Paintings. 3. Drawings and prints.

1. ART COLLECTION. The inventory of the collection, dated 1680, lists 200 paintings and more than 7000 drawings by a wide range of artists. The drawings included 798 by the artist's own hand (mostly untraced), 900 by Hendrick Avercamp, 300 by Esaias van de Velde, 400 by van Goyen and a few by Willem van de Velde the elder. By far the largest number of drawings, 1300, was by Simon de Vlieger, probably acquired after the artist's death in 1653. There were no less than 500 drawings by Rembrandt, most of them acquired at the artist's insolvency sale in 1658; they included nearly 300 (almost all) of Rembrandt's landscape sketches. Among the paintings were portraits of van de Cappelle and his wife by Rembrandt, Frans Hals, Gerbrandt van den Eeckhout and Jan van Noort (all untraced). There were in total seven paintings by Rembrandt, five by Hercules Segers and three by Rubens, as well as a copy by van de Cappelle after a painting by de Vlieger and another after Jan Porcellis, whose autograph work was represented by sixteen examples. Van de Cappelle may have used works in the collection for his own study purposes, but most of the items were acquired long

after he had developed his own style. The quality of the works shows the taste and discrimination of a true collector and patron.

2. PAINTINGS. Van de Cappelle was a prodigy, whose own dated pictures range from as early as 1644 (*Winter Scene*; untraced) to 1663. In 1654 Gerbrand van den Eeckhout, Rembrandt's pupil and friend, wrote a quatrain in the *album amicorum* of the humanist Jacob Heyblocq, praising the 'art of Johannes van de Cappelle who taught himself to paint out of his own desire'. This confirms that van de Cappelle was self-taught, but the quality of his paintings suggests that he must have practised rigorously from an early age, seeking advice and guidance from established marine painters in Amsterdam. A close relationship with Simon de Vlieger in his formative years seems certain, but Willem van de Velde the elder, who shared van de Cappelle's enthusiasm for shipping, also seems to have played a part in his development. Van de Cappelle's oeuvre is small: fewer than 150 paintings are known, most of which are marine scenes, with a small proportion treating the subject of winter landscape. He greatly influenced the marine painters of his generation, particularly Hendrick Dubbels and Willem van de Velde II. His winter landscapes were copied and emulated by Jan van Kessel and others.

(i) Marine subjects. Van de Cappelle's early picture of *Shipping in a Calm* (1645; England, D. Robarts priv. col.) is a fully fledged masterpiece by an artist not yet 20, pioneering a new approach to MARINE PAINTING. While sharing the new luminosity of sky and water of de Vlieger's beach scenes of the 1640s, it introduces a novel compositional system, with a group of large ships set close to the picture plane and the diminishing forms of other ships leading in strict linear perspective towards the far horizon. This perspective device lends great depth to the picture space and is not seen in de Vlieger's paintings before 1649. However, a signed and dated sheet of perspective studies by de Vlieger (1645; London, BM) indicates that he was also experimenting with ship perspective in the very year that van de Cappelle painted his picture. It seems that the young student translated into paint the older master's theoretical studies. Experiments based on new optical discoveries were probably, in fact, carried out jointly by de Vlieger and van de Cappelle. One of Jan's rare beach scenes (1651) seems to echo de Vlieger's earlier *Beach* (1643; both The Hague, Mauritshuis). However, van de Cappelle's painting transcends those of the older master by introducing new subtleties in the treatment of light and reflections. This new fascination with light effects culminated in van de Cappelle's masterpiece, *A Calm* (Cologne, Wallraf-Richartz-Mus.), in which the cool radiance of a rising sun over the water, accentuated by the single figure of a fisherman and two groups of small boats, is the dominating motif in a deceptively simple composition.

In the late 1640s and the early 1650s van de Cappelle perfected the type of marine painting first represented in the picture of 1645, which is known as a 'parade' (i.e. a formal gathering of ships for a ceremonial occasion). He was clearly interested in the pictorial effects of ships

1. Jan van de Cappelle: *State Barge Saluted by the Home Fleet*, oil on panel, 640×925 mm, 1650 (Amsterdam, Rijksmuseum)

2. Jan van de Cappelle: *Winter Scene*, oil on canvas, 432×514 mm, 1653 (Paris, Fondation Custodia, Institut Néerlandais)

anchored in smooth water, their hulls and sails bathed in sparkling light and echoed in the luminous, faintly broken reflections underneath the surface. The geometric precision of the ships' alignment and the architectural clarity of their forms lend firm structure to a composition largely depending on vaporous skies filled with billowing clouds over a very low horizon. The contrast of rigid masts and hulls with the fluidity of light, reflections and atmosphere is epitomized in such 'parades' as the *River Scene with a State Barge* (1650; London, N.G.) and the *State Barge Saluted by the Home Fleet* (1650; Amsterdam, Rijksmus.; see fig. 1). The 'parade' boats are filled with elegantly dressed people. Their costumes provide touches of local colour, but the figures are always carefully integrated into the overall composition.

Other paintings feature small craft and more humbly dressed fishermen at work or passenger barges peacefully drifting along the banks of a river (e.g. *River View with Boats*, 1651; Zurich, Ksthaus). These paintings are distinguished by an all-pervading luminous atmosphere that softens all outlines and unifies forms and local colours. Linear perspective in the formation of ships and boats is complemented by the masterly treatment of aerial perspective. The saturation of colours is reduced, while the brightness of light is increased towards the horizon. The intensity of light just above the horizon line suggests the infinite continuity of space. More than any other artist of his time, with the exception only of Rembrandt, van de Cappelle was a painter of light.

Van de Cappelle's earlier works recall the cool silvery hues of de Vlieger, but carefully controlled local colours in costumes, sails and coastal motifs, together with the rainbow tints of clouds and the fiery red of smoke billowing from gun salutes, combine to enliven the uniform greyness prevalent in marines of the so-called 'tonal school' of painting in Haarlem. In his later works van de Cappelle used a warmer golden tonality, exceptionally allowing himself a greater colouristic exuberance when setting the rosy glow of a sunset sky against water of a deep turquoise blue, as in the *River Scene with Sailing Vessels* (Rotterdam, Mus. Boymans–van Beuningen). This must be a late work, influenced by the sunsets of Salomon van Ruysdael's late paintings.

The majority of van de Cappelle's marine paintings feature ships or boats seen from an expanse of calm water.

The view is flanked unobtrusively on one or both sides by a jetty, a narrow promontory or strip of beach with boats at anchor and fishermen at work. Only a handful of van de Cappelle's known works are scenes with rough water (e.g. *The Beach*; The Hague, Mauritshuis), and none shows a storm at sea. The painting of a 'Storm by the deceased' mentioned in the artist's inventory after his death has never been found.

(ii) Winter scenes. Fewer than 20 fully authenticated winter scenes by van de Cappelle are known; these range in date from 1652 to 1654 (the *Winter Scene* of 1644 being untraced). He derived his motifs and compositional ideas for winter landscapes from earlier Dutch masters, notably Hendrick Avercamp, Isaac van Ostade and Esaias van de Velde. His winter scenes have many affinities with those of Aert van der Neer, but they are more austere. Only a few figures of skaters or players of *kolf* (a simple type of ice hockey) appear on the frozen canals or rivers, and they are incidental to the study of nature. The silvery sparkle of a winter sky, often mingled with the rosy hues of a sunset, is integrated with the reflecting surface of an expanse of frozen water. Light bounces off the snow-covered branches of bare trees, their diminishing forms leading the eye towards the far horizon in a perspective formation that resembles the rows of ships in the 'parade' pictures. Figures are arranged in depth strictly according to the rules demonstrated in de Vlieger's sheet of perspective studies (see fig. 2; other masterpieces of this type of winter landscape are in Amsterdam, Rijksmus., and Madrid, Mus. Thyssen–Bornemisza.) Two winter landscapes in upright format—*Frozen Canal* (Enschede, Rijksmus. Twenthe) and *Winter Landscape* (England, priv. col., see Russell, fig. 30)—are pure studies of nature, eliminating the genre element of skating figures; they seem to belong to a later period, probably the late 1650s and early 1660s.

3. DRAWINGS AND PRINTS. Most of the artist's drawings listed in the 1680 inventory have been lost, and signed and dated examples are extremely rare; only one of them, the *Barge with Soldiers* (16[4]6; Berlin, Kupferstichkab.), is a marine scene. This close-up study of a boat and figures demonstrates van de Cappelle's skill in rendering figures in convincing poses, with only a few delicate strokes of the pen. Subtle washes add the effects of atmosphere and diffused light. Even more atmospheric is the unsigned *Ferry Boat with Travellers and Three Horses* (Hamburg, Ksthalle), which is a preparatory drawing for the painted *Marine* (Antwerp, Kon. Mus. S. Kst.). Its careful execution implies that the artist worked painstakingly and slowly on even the simplest motifs to arrive at the mastery of his finished paintings.

Drawings of winter scenes are relatively more frequent. Of particular interest is the sketch of a frozen river with *kolf* players in Heyblocq's *album amicorum*, which is accompanied by van den Eeckhout's rhyme. The same album contains one of the more crowded and animated winter scenes by Aert van der Neer, contrasting with the serene calm of van de Cappelle's composition. (More finished drawings are in Paris, Fond. Custodia, Inst. Néer., and Haarlem, Teylers Mus.) A late drawing (1662; Berlin, Kupferstichkab.), though still impressive in the treatment of light and reflections, is less delicate. Two other drawings of winter scenes (both Hamburg, Ksthalle) must also be late; they lack the compositional harmony of the 'golden' period, which culminated in the 1650s.

Only two etchings signed by van de Cappelle are known. One is of a *Wide River with Fishing Boats* (Hollstein, no. 1), signed in reverse *J. V. Capel.* The form of signature and manner of execution confirm a date before 1650. The *Winter Landscape with a Stone Bridge* (Hollstein, no. 2) must date from the 1650s. The composition is derived from Rembrandt's painting of a *Landscape near Ouderkerk* (Amsterdam, Rijksmus.). A third etching, also a winter scene (Hollstein, no. 3), seems to be by a follower. The eight etchings of pure landscapes attributed to van de Cappelle (Hollstein, nos 4–11) and variously carrying the signatures of Jan van Goyen and Jacob Esselens are uncharacteristic of the artist's style and are not accepted by Stechow and other experts.

BIBLIOGRAPHY

Hollstein: *Dut. & Flem.*
A. Bredius: 'De schilder Johannes van de Cappelle', *Oud-Holland*, x (1892), pp. 26–40, 133–6
C. Hofstede de Groot: *Holländischen Maler*, vii (1918)
W. Stechow: *Dutch Landscape Painting in the Seventeenth Century* (London, 1968), pp. 95–8, 106–8
M. Russell: *Jan van de Cappelle, 1624/6–1679* (Leigh-on-Sea, 1975) [with full bibliog., docs & complete cat. rais. by Hofstede de Groot, with revisions and addenda]
Mirror of Empire: Dutch Marine Art of the Seventeenth Century (exh. cat. by G. S. Keyes, Minneapolis, MN, Inst. A.; Toledo, OH, Mus. A.; Los Angeles, CA, Co. Mus. A.; 1990–91), nos 10–12

MARGARITA RUSSELL

Cappelle, Jean-Baptiste van de. *See* VAN DE CAPPELLE, JEAN-BAPTISTE.

Capponi. Italian family of patrons, merchants and statesmen. From the 14th century the family was a powerful force in the political and economic life of Florence. A focus for their patronage was the family chapel in the church of S Spirito, Florence, which contains the sarcophagus (1458) of *Neri di Gino Capponi* (1388–1457) by Bernardo Rossellino. In 1521 Ludovico Capponi (*d* 1534), having pursued a banking career in Rome, returned to Florence and in 1525 bought the Annunziata Chapel (attributed to Brunelleschi) in the church of S Felicità. For it he commissioned from Pontormo, assisted by his pupil Bronzino, decorations (1525–8) that included an altarpiece of the *Lamentation* (*in situ*; *see* PONTORMO, JACOPO DA, fig. 2), which has subsequently been regarded as both Pontormo's masterpiece and a key work of Mannerism. Bronzino later executed a portrait (*c.* 1550; New York, Frick) of Ludovico's son, also named Ludovico Capponi (1534–1614). The Marchese Alessandro Gregorio Capponi (1683–1746), the last member of the Roman branch of the family, helped supervise the restoration (1731), by Filippo Barigioni (1672–1753), of the Arch of Constantine, and in 1734 Pope Clement XII gave him charge for life of the new Capitoline museums. He assembled a notable collection of paintings and prints (which passed to his sister), medals and antiquities (which now form part of Rome's Museo Nazionale Romano (Museo delle Terme)) and rare books and manuscripts, which constitute the *Codici Capponiani* (Rome, Vatican, Bib. Apostolica, 9265).

Other members of the family became leading merchant bankers in Tuscany, Rome and the financial centres of northern Europe.

DBI BIBLIOGRAPHY

G. Vasari: *Vite* (1550, rev. 2/1568); ed. G. Milanesi, iii (1878), p. 292; vi (1881), pp. 270–72

A. Pieraccini: *La famiglia Capponi di Firenze* (Pisa, 1882)

G. S. Cozzo: *I Codici Capponiani* (Rome, 1897)

JANET SOUTHORN

Capponi, Raffaelle de'. *See* RAFFAELLINO DEL GARBO.

Cappuccino, il. *See* STROZZI, BERNARDO.

Capralos, Christos (*b* Panaitolion, 16 Nov 1909; *d* 20 Jan 1993). Greek sculptor. He studied painting at the Higher School of Fine Arts in Athens and sculpture in Paris with Marcel Gimond (*b* 1894) and at the Académie de la Grande Chaumière and the Académie Colarossi. From 1940 to 1946 he worked in isolation in his village, inspired by the people around him, especially his mother. The solid structure, dense shapes, simplified planes and regular distribution of light on surfaces reveal the influence of Emile-Antoine Bourdelle, Aristide Maillol, Charles Despiau and Gimond, and of archaic Greek sculpture. These works were exhibited at the Parnassos Gallery, Athens, in November 1946 and established his reputation. After 1946 he lived and worked in Athens. His Pindos Monument (1.1×40.0 m, 1952–6; Aigina, the artist's studio), a stone frieze planned during World War II, tells the epic story of war and peace. The composition, inspired by Egyptian carvings, ancient Greek stelae and folk art, is simple, ordered and rhythmic. The harsh lines of the carving, in varying relief, are combined with a slightly undulated surface. After 1957 Capralos returned to such traditional methods as hammering and bronze-casting with the lost-wax technique. Hammering imposed taut outlines, dense masses and economy of line. At the same time he worked the casts for the bronzes straight on to sheets of wax, using heat. In the workshop he built in Aigina in 1962 he made a series of anthropomorphic stone objects and carvings that revive the Cycladic tradition. From 1965 he began to work also in wood. The organic shapes of the eucalyptus inspired his highly expressive monumental sculptures (e.g. *Crucifixion: Parody of the East Pediment of the Temple of Zeus at Olympia*; Aigina, the artist's studio). Capralos also made innumerable figurines in clay and many ceramics. A year before his death he founded the Christos and Souli Capralos Foundation, to which he donated all his works.

BIBLIOGRAPHY

Capralos (exh. cat. by A. Xydis, Athens, Parnassos Gal., 1946)

Christos Capralos (exh. cat., intro. C. Christou; Athens, N.G., 1981)

MARINA LAMBRAKI-PLAKA

Caprarola, Cola da. *See* COLA DA CAPRAROLA.

Caprarola, Villa [Palazzo] **Farnese.** Italian estate near Viterbo, *c.* 55 km north-west of Rome. It stands on a hilltop site overlooking the medieval village of Caprarola and was built for Cardinal Alessandro Farnese, grandson of Pope Paul III, by Jacopo Vignola and his successors from 1557 to 1583. The interior contains a series of frescoes that constitute one of the most important decorative cycles of the later 16th century. The lower gardens were built in 1557–83 to Vignola's designs, while the upper garden and casino (*palazzina*) were built *c.* 1584–6 to designs by Giacomo del Duca.

Caprarola, Villa Farnese, by Jacopo Vignola, 1557–83

1. ARCHITECTURE AND DECORATION. The Villa Farnese was constructed on the foundations of a fortress begun *c.* 1521 for Pope Paul III by Antonio da Sangallo (ii) and Baldassare Peruzzi. This accounts for its unusual pentagonal plan with arrowhead bastions, although the circular courtyard at the centre of the structure was Vignola's own design. Vignola also designed the axial, terraced approach to the villa, with a straight road ascending from the village to an oval forecourt with a rusticated loggia facing a fish pond (filled in before 1600). The forecourt is embraced by two symmetrical semicircular horse-ramps rising to a second, larger, trapezoidal court, with staircases leading up to the villa itself (see fig.). These elements provide a magnificent spatial setting for the drafted masonry façade of the villa, articulated by two orders of pilasters in local volcanic stone. The design drew extensively on architecture at the Vatican in Rome, the seat of the patron's power: the tripartite, fortified façade with central loggia (originally open) recalls Innocent VIII's Villa Belvedere (1480s), while the double-ramped staircase in front of the villa and the triumphal-arch motif on the upper portico were derived from Bramante's Cortile del Belvedere (begun 1505). The contrast between the solid, massive lower storey and the flat, abstract, geometrical upper storeys, however, was characteristic of Vignola's own classicizing Mannerist style (for further discussion *see* VIGNOLA, JACOPO).

The ground floor and *piano nobile* of the villa were planned with two sets of summer apartments on the north side and two of winter apartments on the south, each with salon, antechamber, bedroom, dressing room and study.

The basement housed service areas, while the small rooms in the top storeys housed staff and retainers. In one of the angles at the front of the building is a monumental two-storey spiral staircase; opposite is a guard room and circular armoury on the ground floor and a loggia and circular chapel on the *piano nobile* above.

The summer apartments were frescoed by Taddeo Zuccaro and Federico Zuccaro (*see* ZUCCARO), although the illusionistic architecture on the walls of the Sala di Giove and the vault of the armoury were designed by Vignola. After Taddeo's death (1566), Federico painted the Gabinetto dell'Ermatena, the circular chapel and part of the Sala d'Ercole, all on the *piano nobile*. He also painted the guard room and four rooms of the winter apartment on the ground floor (excluding the salon). JACOPO BERTOIA completed the Sala d'Ercole (1569), executed the vaults of the stanze della Penitenza, dei Guidizi and dei Sogni in the winter apartment on the *piano nobile*, and began work on the Sala degli Angeli (also in the winter apartment) shortly before his death in 1572. About 1574–5 Giovanni de' Vecchi and his assistants painted the walls of the Sala degli Angeli and all of the Sala del Mappamondo (restored 1960s), which is decorated with maps of four continents, Italy and the Holy Land (for further discussion and illustration *see* MAP). The remaining frescoes, including the salon of the ground-floor winter apartment, the spiral staircase and the internal courtyard porticos, were supervised by Antonio Tempesta from 1579 to 1583.

The complex iconographical programme, glorifying the Farnese family and addressing major political, economic, spiritual and intellectual concerns of Cardinal Farnese, was worked out in consultation with the patron by such scholarly advisors as Onofrio Panvinio, who devised the scheme for the Sala dei Fasti Farnese; Paolo Manuzio (1512–74), the Venetian and Roman publisher; Annibal Caro, the humanist secretary to Cardinal Farnese; and perhaps also Fulvio Orsini, the Farnese librarian.

2. GARDENS. The two walled lower gardens of the Villa Farnese were laid out to Vignola's designs, in square parterres, with sculpture and fountains symbolizing the seasons and the regenerative cycles of nature. In the west garden—once linked by a pergola—are statues of *Autumn* and *Winter* and the Grotto of the Rain, a cave seemingly supported by six stucco satyrs with moisture dripping from the vault into a pond below. On the terrace above the grotto is the Fountain of Unicorns. The north garden contains statues of *Spring* and *Summer* and the Fountain of Venus, with Venus flanked by two satyrs. At the junction of the two gardens is the Fountain of the Shepherd; water was designed to cascade down a rustic hill from two satyrs or fauns at the top, over a shell held by two nude water deities, to two herms and two reclining river gods flanking a statue of *Mercury* as the good shepherd.

The upper gardens and casino were laid out by Giacomo del Duca in the 1580s. He incorporated into the design terraces, fountains and sculpture. They are remarkable for the synthesis of natural and manmade elements. The discovery of a new vein of water in 1616 led Cardinal Odoardo Farnese to expand the upper gardens by adding two lower pavilions, 24 herms surrounding the parterres in front of the casino, gardens and fountains at the rear of the casino, and ramps connecting the front and rear gardens. The architect was probably Girolamo Rainaldi. The programme of the upper gardens has never been worked out in detail, but the major elements include statues of *Oblivion* and *Silence* flanking the Lily Fountain, a dolphin water-chain flowing from the Fountain of the Chalice, which is in turn flanked by two river gods with cornucopias, and two unicorn and dolphin fountains.

BIBLIOGRAPHY

L. Sebastiani: *Descrizione e relazione istorica del nobilissimo e real palazzo di Caprarola* (Rome, 1741)

C. Trasmondo-Frangipani: *Descrizione storico-artistica del R. Palazzo di Caprarola* (Rome, 1869)

G. Balducci: *Il palazzo Farnese in Caprarola illustrato nella storia e nell'arte* (Rome, 1910)

F. Baumgart: 'La Caprarola di Ameto Orti', *Studi Romanzi*, xxv (1935), pp. 77–179

I. Faldi: *Gli affreschi del Palazzo Farnese di Caprarola* (Imola, 1962)

S. Benedetti: 'Sul Giardino Grande di Caprarola ed altre note', *Quad. Ist. Stor. Archit.*, xvi/91 (1969), pp. 1–44

G. Labrot: *Le Palais Farnèse de Caprarola: Essai de lecture* (Paris, 1970)

L. Partridge: 'Vignola and the Villa Farnese at Caprarola', *A. Bull.*, lii (1970), pp. 81–7

——: 'The Sala d'Ercole in the Villa Farnese at Caprarola', *A. Bull.*, liii (1971), pp. 267–86; liv (1972), pp. 50–62

——: 'Divinity and Dynasty at Caprarola: Perfect History in the Room of Farnese Deeds', *A. Bull.*, lx (1978), pp. 494–530

I. Faldi: *Il Palazzo Farnese de Caprarola* (Turin, 1981)

E. Polla: 'Anomalie costruttive e dimensionali nel Palazzo Farnese a Caprarola', *Saggi in onore di Guglielmo de Angelis d'Ossat*, ed. S. Benedetti and G. Miarelli Mariani (Rome, 1987), pp. 351–64

L. Partridge: *Caprarola, Palazzo Farnese, FMR* Grand Tour (Milan, 1988)

——: 'Discourse of Asceticism in Bertoja's Room of Penitence in the Villa Farnese at Caprarola', *Mem. Amer. Acad. Rome* (in preparation)

——: 'The Room of the Maps at Caprarola, 1573–75', *A. Bull.* (in preparation)

LOREN PARTRIDGE

Capreae [now Capri]. Island in the Bay of Naples, Italy. Its name is derived from the ancient Greek for 'boar'. The island remained insignificant until the emperor Augustus (*reg* 30 BC–AD 14) visited it in 29 BC and fell in love with it; he and his successor, Tiberius (*reg* AD 14–37), who withdrew from public life to live there permanently between AD 27 and 31, constructed a number of villas there—12 if Tacitus is to be believed—of which there are substantial surviving remains of three. Least well preserved, but the favoured residence of Augustus, is the 'Palazzo a Mare' in the middle of the north coast, spread out on a series of terraces over a strip *c.* 800 m long and 200 m wide. The main residential block lies to the east with a bath suite immediately behind it; there is also an adjacent artificial harbour for ease of access.

Tiberius' favoured palace was the Villa Jovis ('Villa of Jupiter'; see fig.) recorded by Pliny and Suetonius, on a magnificent, precipitous site at the north-east corner of the island, with stupendous views and sheer drops to the sea 300 m below. First explored in 1827 and completely excavated in 1932–5, this mountain-top villa, covering an area of *c.* 7000 sq. m, has rooms arranged in four wings around a central square courtyard, below which are four enormous rock-cut cisterns for storing rain-water. There is skilful use of ramps and staircases to link the constituent parts of a complicated split-level building in a cohesive, tight-knit unit. The baths occupy much of the south wing, and the landward west wing contains the service quarters and a spacious kitchen. The emperor's private quarters were in the north wing, and the main reception room or dining-room (with projecting semicircular bay) is in the middle of the east wing. To the north of the main villa a staircase leads down to a long corridor (perhaps for exercise and contemplation), off which open small rooms.

The third villa (Damecuta), excavated in 1937–48, lies on another impressive site at the north-west corner of the island: a block of rooms at the west end, including one with a projecting semicircular bay similar to that in the Villa Jovis, is linked by a long corridor to further rooms (perhaps the emperor's private quarters) at the east end, partly destroyed by a 12th-century tower that stands on top. All three villas were badly plundered at various times before the 20th century, so that little now remains of the marble and mosaic floors with which the principal rooms must have been adorned, and few pieces of sculpture have been recovered. Despite this the villas do provide a precious insight into the private lifestyle of Rome's first two emperors and illustrate the skill of Roman architects at adapting difficult mountain-top sites to the needs of their imperial patrons.

BIBLIOGRAPHY

A. Maiuri: *Capri: Storia e monumenti* (Rome, 1956)

J. B. Ward-Perkins: *Roman Imperial Architecture*, Pelican Hist. A. (Harmondsworth, 1981), pp. 198–201

R. J. A. WILSON

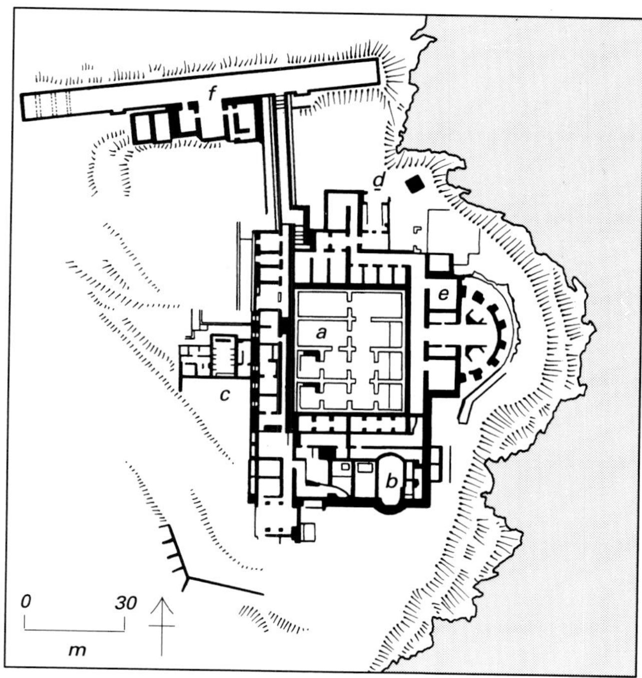

Capreae, Villa Jovis, 1st half of 1st century AD, plan: (a) courtyard above cisterns; (b) baths; (c) service quarters and kitchen; (d) emperor's quarters; (e) reception room or dining-room; (f) corridor

Capriani, Francesco. *See* VOLTERRA, FRANCESCO DA.

Capriccio [It.: 'caprice']. A drawing or painted or engraved composition combining features of imaginary and/or real architecture, ruined or intact, in a picturesque setting. In its fantasy element it is the opposite of the VEDUTA. It reached its apogee as a popular genre during the era of the Grand Tour of Europe, which produced a heavy demand for pictorial souvenirs. Italy, in particular, offered real landscapes with Classical ruins; all that was required to elaborate and combine existing remains within a picturesque setting was a degree of poetic licence. Architectural fantasy in paintings, drawings and engravings had also a creative function, as an outlet for artists' and architects' imaginative expression or experiments, uninhibited by the prescriptive terms of commissions or by practical needs. The capriccio fulfilled in addition a decorative role, ranging from large-scale painted images within room decoration to miniature painted scenes on furnishings and ceramics.

Emerging as a mature art form during the early 18th-century Rococo period, the capriccio eventually declined during the early part of the next century in the face of the greater depth and imaginative range of Romantic painting as well as the demands by the academies for more 'serious' subject-matter. However, as a vehicle for creative licence, the architectural fantasy has never completely died out and continues to thrive on a minor level, either as a lighthearted decoration or serving the need for extreme visual experiment in architectural design.

The term 'capriccio', which derives from the Italian for the unpredictable jumping of a young goat, covers also a rarer form of subject-matter, defined by the 17th-century theorist Filippo Baldinucci as expressing an 'idea of invention' or the product of an unfettered imagination. Such an application of the term is pre-eminently represented by the etched, dreamlike figure compositions in the print series of Giambattista Tiepolo (*I Capricci*; Venice, *c*. 1750) and Goya (*Los Caprichos*; Madrid, 1796/8–1803).

1. EARLY MANIFESTATIONS. Some of the earliest imaginative compositions of architecture appear in surviving wall paintings from Herculaneum and Pompeii, where they served both to amplify restricted spaces and to enliven large areas of wall surface in top-lit urban buildings. Painted fantasy architecture was also incorporated into the decorative schemes of Roman Imperial dwellings, as in the remains of Nero's Domus Aurea, the rediscovery of which, near the Roman Colosseum during the late 15th century, had far-reaching artistic consequences. Significantly, in the late quattrocento a conscious revival of fantastic architectural compositions occurred, particularly in the work of Andrea Mantegna and his contemporaries in northern and central Italy. While imaginary architectural compositions had occurred throughout medieval and early Renaissance paintings, Mantegna's works display a new preoccupation with reconstructing ancient Rome; in them, ancient buildings and ruins are fantastically juxtaposed in the background (e.g. *St Sebastian*, *c*. 1460; Vienna, Ksthist. Mus.). At the end of the century this concern is found among the esoteric woodcuts illustrating Francesco Colonna's dream-bound novella, the *Hypnerotomachia Poliphili* (Venice, 1499).

Predictably, Mannerist artists and decorators developed the scope for architectural fantasy; but the emergence of this subject-matter as a genre in its own right is closely bound up with Baroque stage design. This reached unprecedented heights of expression in the late 17th century in the complex perspectival compositions of the Galli-Bibiena family (chiefly disseminated through their engraved works) and continued well into the early 18th century with designers such as Filippo Juvarra and Luigi Vanvitelli. An early pioneer of the capriccio within this theatrical context was François de Nomé. His highly distinctive style, characterized by febrile figures set against architecture undergoing cataclysmic decomposition, was to make a strong impression on 20th-century Surrealists such as Dalí.

2. THE 18TH CENTURY. It was in early 18th-century Venice, where topographical art developed alongside the experimental world of the theatre, that the architectural capriccio emerged as an independent art form under Marco Ricci. The small etchings of Classical ruins published posthumously in Carlo Orsolini's *Varia Marci Ricci experimenta* (1730) combined the poetic essence of Giorgione's idylls with keenly observed Roman monuments. The apotheosis of this formula was achieved in a series of ambitious canvases of allegorical tombs, commissioned in the early 1720s by the impresario Owen McSwiny; it was to involve, among others, Marco Ricci and his uncle Sebastiano Ricci, together with Canaletto, Giambattista Pittoni and Giovanni Battista Piazzetta. Eventually 10 of the projected 24 paintings were acquired by Charles Lennox, 2nd Duke of Richmond, to decorate the dining-room at Goodwood House, W. Sussex. The Venetians were particularly swift to adopt the genre. Among the foremost was Canaletto, who etched and painted several ambitious fantasies, such as the *Capriccio Palladiano* (Bergamo, priv. col.), a painting of Palladio's unexecuted Rialto Bridge across the Grand Canal, juxtaposed to his Vicentine Basilica. Other outstanding capriccio painters were Antonio Visentini and, pre-eminently, Francesco Guardi, whose vibrant painterly techniques produced a range of works in the genre with atmospheric nuances of mood that have never been rivalled.

Meanwhile in Rome, Giovanni Paolo Panini developed the range of the capriccio in the form of decorative compositions recording groups of the principal monuments seen on the Grand Tour in order to satisfy the demands of visitors, especially the 'milordi Inglesi'. Panini, established in Rome by 1717, through his skills as a *vedutista* and decorator, became a member of the Académie de France in Rome and professor of perspective at its headquarters in the Palazzo Mancini-Salviati. His extensive output was to culminate in two pendant compositions of great virtuosity for Etienne-François, Duc de Choiseul, *Roma antica* and *Roma moderna* (1757; versions Boston, MA, Mus. F.A., and Stuttgart, Staatsgal.). In these works, painted views of antique and recent Roman architecture

1. Capriccio by Hubert Robert: *Discovery of the Laokoon*, oil on canvas, 1.19×1.62 m, 1773 (Richmond, Virginia Museum of Fine Arts)

are displayed on the walls of vast thermal halls filled with sculpture and populated by admiring connoisseurs with their ciceroni.

During this period Piranesi had been deliberately exploiting the capriccio as an experimental means of arriving at new concepts in architectural design. In his first publication, the *Prima parte di architetture e prospettive* (1743), he used a sequence of capriccio etchings to stimulate the imagination of contemporary architects towards free experiment with antique forms. The first state of his celebrated suite of etched prison scenes (published anonymously, 1749–50) was significantly entitled *Invenzioni capric di carceri.* These plates were reissued in 1761 in a heavily reworked state as the *Carceri d'invenzione.* It was clear from the start that the penal imagery was of less significance to the artist than the opportunities that these stark utilitarian structures provided for spatial experiment. Moreover, Piranesi's extravagantly fanciful view of the Appian Way, which he used as the frontispiece to volume II of his major archaeological work, *Le antichità romane* (1756), also presented a visual challenge. This bizarre composition, involving a plethora of monuments, was intended to symbolize the Roman genius for funerary architecture, as borne out by the variety of tombs illustrated with technical thoroughness in that volume.

It was above all Piranesi's transforming vision that ensured the survival of the capriccio into the early phase of Romanticism represented by the work of the Frenchman Hubert Robert, arguably the greatest exponent of the painted capriccio. He endowed Panini's formulas with a heightened sense of drama, exploiting Piranesi's lighting, exaggerated scale and perspective and juxtaposing the monumental with scenes of everyday life in order to amplify the heroic stature of the past. After spending 11 years in Italy, Robert returned to Paris in 1765 and the following year was accepted by the Académie Royale as a 'painter of ruins', the highest accolade yet conferred on capriccio painting. Some of his greatest Roman compositions were produced in the following years: notably his masterpiece, the *Discovery of the Laokoon* (1773; Richmond, VA, Mus. F.A.; see fig. 1). In this work he combined the theatrical recession of Bernini's Scala Regia in the Vatican palace with the plan of the Grande Galerie of the Louvre as a cavernous setting for the writhing Hellenistic group that dwarfs the pullulating humanity surrounding it.

While the painted capriccio featured in wall schemes of interior decoration throughout the 17th and 18th centuries, by the 1760s the revelations at Herculaneum and Pompeii gave a new authority to the use of large inset ruin scenes with a carefully contrived perspective. In England, Robert Adam was swift to exploit most effectively the skills of Antonio Zucchi (1726–95) in ambitious compositions that act as focal-points in his interiors, notably the Eating Room (*c.* 1767) of Osterley Park House, London, and the Music Room (1771) of Harewood House, W. Yorks. The architectural fantasy as a means of conveying visionary and impracticable designs was frequently adopted by the radical designers of Neo-classicism. Some architects of the French Revolutionary era presented their most radical

2. The Painted Room by Rex Whistler (1936–7), Plas Newydd, Gwynedd, NT

conceptions through engravings, as did Claude-Nicolas Ledoux in his *L'Architecture considérée sous le rapport de l'art, des moeurs et de la legislation* (1804). In the case of Etienne-Louis Boullée this was done through finished drawings with highly emotive lighting effects and exaggerated scale (e.g. *Design for a Cenotaph to Newton*, 1784; Paris, Bib. N.; for illustration *see* BOULLÉE, ETIENNE-LOUIS). Similarly, Sir John Soane's frustrated aspirations to produce monumental public buildings were immortalized through the outstanding skill of his assistant Joseph Michael Gandy in a series of sublime panoramas, such as *Architectural Visions of Early Fancy and Dreams* (1820; London, Soane Mus.).

3. LATER MANIFESTATIONS. While this experimental role of the capriccio has survived into the 20th century, the decorative use of the architectural fantasy, after a long period of neglect, achieved an unexpected and tragically brief revival in the career of Rex Whistler. As part of an awakening interest in the 18th century during the inter-war years, Whistler, before his death in action, left behind a small group of exceptional painted interiors. In these the capriccio, using a range of *trompe l'oeil* techniques and based on scholarly research, was extended to an entire interior scheme. His earliest and best-known work, the *Pursuit of Rare Meats* (1926–7) in the Tate Gallery restaurant, London, was followed by commissions for several country houses, such as Sir Philip Sassoon's Port Lympne, Kent (1930–33). Whistler's undoubted masterpiece remains the dining-room commissioned by the 6th Marquess of Anglesey for Plas Newydd, Gwynedd, completed by June 1937 (see fig. 2). The main painting in oils on a single canvas 17.68 m long, which continues on the return walls, features a panoramic harbour scene that echoes the view through the windows opposite over the Menai Strait, with Renaissance townscapes containing buildings of every style and period, bathed in a Claudian light. While there have been several extremely competent imitators since the last war, Whistler's unique blend of elusive meaning, visual wit and nostalgia for a lost Classical world—the essence of the capriccio—is unlikely ever to be repeated.

BIBLIOGRAPHY

P. de Nolhac: *Hubert Robert* (Paris, 1910)
R. Wittkower: *Art and Architecture in Italy, 1600–1750*, Pelican Hist. A. (Harmondsworth, 1958, rev. 3/1973, *R* 1982)
M. Levey: *Painting in 18th-century Venice* (London, 1959, 2/1980)
F. Arisi: *G. P. Panini* (Piacenza, 1961)
E. Croft-Murray: *Decorative Painting in England, 1537–1837*, ii (London, 1970)
R. Bromberg: *Canaletto's Etchings* (London, 1974, San Francisco, 2/1993)
J. Wilton-Ely: *The Mind and Art of Piranesi* (London, 1978)
F. Haskell: *Patrons and Painters: Art and Society in Baroque Italy* (New Haven and London, 1980), pp. 287–91
L. Whistler: *Rex Whistler* (London, 1985)
J. Wilton-Ely: *Giovanni Battista Piranesi: The Complete Etchings* (San Francisco, 1994)
The Glory of Venice: Art in the 18th Century (exh. cat., ed. J. Martineau and A. Robinson; London, RA, 1994)

JOHN WILTON-ELY

Caprino, Meo da. *See* MEO DA CAPRINO.

Capriolo, Domenico (di Bernardino) (*b* Venice, *c.* 1494; *d* Treviso, 8 Oct 1528). Italian painter. He moved from Venice to Treviso *c.* 1517, where he is well documented (though there is little about his painting). In 1518–19 he married Camilla, daughter of the painter Pier Maria Pennacchi. A coherent body of work executed between 1518 and 1528 has been reconstructed. Capriolo's first secure work, the *Adoration of the Shepherds* (Treviso, Mus. Civ.), signed and dated 1518, has a formal structure reminiscent of the late style of Giovanni Bellini, with the broader chromatic range of Palma Vecchio and a crepuscular light that recalls the Venetian works of Giovanni Girolamo Savoldo or Giovanni da Asola (*fl* 1512–31). The *Assumption* in Treviso Cathedral, commissioned in 1520, shows, in its spiralling movement, the influence of the contemporary frescoes of Pordenone in the nearby Malchiostro Chapel. In the *Legend of the Doubting Midwife* (Treviso, Mus. Civ.), signed and dated 1524, the influence of Savoldo is greater than that of Palma. This is also apparent in the altarpiece of the parish church of Ponzano Veneto (Treviso), dated 1525. The portrait of *Lelio Torelli* (Barnard Castle, Bowes Mus.), signed and dated 1528, Capriolo's last known work, seems by contrast to reflect local models of portraiture and lies somewhere between the styles of Sebastiano Florigerio and Bernardino Licinio. Other works assigned to Capriolo include: the altarpieces of the parish churches of Cavasagra and Spercenigo, near Treviso; the *Adoration of the Shepherds* in the sacristy of Serravalle Cathedral at Vittorio Veneto; a fragment of a *Nativity* (Venice, Mus. Correr); two paintings of the *Virgin and Child with Saints* (Bucharest, Mus. A.; Conegliano, Mus. Civ. Castello); and the *Portrait of a Musician* (Vienna, Ksthist. Mus.), previously attributed to Pordenone. Capriolo was murdered by his wife's stepfather, after years of litigation about her dowry.

BIBLIOGRAPHY

DBI; Thieme–Becker
M. Lucco: 'Domenico Capriolo', *Proposte di restauro: Dipinti del primo cinquecento nel Veneto* (Florence, 1978), pp. 97–100
G. Fossaluzza: 'Profilo di Domenico Capriolo', *A. Ven.*, xxxvii (1983), pp. 49–66
E. Manzato: 'Opere trevigiane di Domenico Capriolo', *Stud. Trevi.*, i (1984), pp. 85–93
M. Lucco: 'I pittori trevigiani e "l'effetto Malchiostro"', *Il Pordenone: Atti del Convegno internazionale di studio: Pordenone, 1985*, pp. 141–8

MAURO LUCCO

Caprotti, Gian Giacomo [Salaì] (*b* Oreno, nr Monza, *c.* 1480; *d* Milan, 19 Jan 1524). Italian painter. In 1490, aged 10, he joined the workshop of Leonardo da Vinci in Milan. In his notebooks Leonardo described him as a 'lying, obstinate, greedy thief' but also considered him an able pupil. He was nicknamed Salaì (or Salaino, the name of a demon) because of his lively and irascible character. He remained with Leonardo for about 30 years. In 1499 he accompanied him to Mantua, Venice and Florence. By 1505 he had achieved some fame as a painter; Alvise Ciocha, an agent of Isabella d'Este, Marchioness of Mantua, described him as 'very able for his years' and invited him to advise Pietro Perugino who was working for her. He accompanied Leonardo to Rome in 1513 and three years later to France, with Francesco Melzi. In 1519, following his master's death, Salaì settled in Milan on property that Leonardo had bequeathed him. He died a violent death. An inventory of his possessions shows that he inherited many works by Leonardo, including the *Mona Lisa* and the *Infant St John the Baptist* (both Paris, Louvre). No signed works by Caprotti are known; documents mention two paintings of the *Penitent St Jerome* (untraced) in the monastery of S Gerolamo in Milan. It is assumed that his work adheres closely to that of Leonardo. According to this hypothesis, the *Virgin and Child with St Anne* (Los Angeles, UCLA, Wight A. G.) and *St John the Baptist* (Milan, Ambrosiana), copies of paintings by Leonardo (both Paris, Louvre), have been attributed to him.

BIBLIOGRAPHY

J. P. Richter, ed.: *The Literary Works of Leonardo da Vinci*, ii (London, 1888, rev. 1970), pp. 363–5
W. Suida: *Leonardo und sein Kreis* (Munich, 1929), p. 306
J. Shell and G. Sironi: 'Salaì and Leonardo's Legacy', *Burl. Mag.*, cxxxiii (1991), pp. 95–108 [good bibliog.]

ANNA MARIA FERRARI

Capua. Italian town in Campania. In Roman times Casilinum was the harbour town of the important ancient city of Capua (*see* SANTA MARIA CAPUA VETERE, §1); the town fell into decline from the 1st century AD but was refounded by the Lombards and repopulated by the people of ancient Capua, whose city had been destroyed by the Saracens in AD 841. Capua flourished under the Lombards and then under the Normans, who conquered it in the 11th century. The town still retains its medieval aspect, although many of its early churches have been remodelled or rebuilt. The cathedral was founded in the 9th century, reconstructed in the 12th and rebuilt after it was destroyed in World War II, but the 9th-century bell-tower still stands, and mosaics are preserved in the crypt. Three churches also built by the Lombards are substantially remodelled: S Michele a Corte (9th century), and S Giovanni a Corte and S Salvatore Maggiore a Corte (both 10th century). The 13th-century Norman castle, the Castello delle Pietre, still stands. Only fragments remain of the fine Capua Gate built by Emperor Frederick II (see below). After the Middle Ages Capua suffered numerous sackings and gradually lost its importance. With the Aragonese occupation of the 15th century some Catalan influences were introduced into the architecture, evident in the transitional Late Gothic–early Renaissance portal of the Museo Campano. The church of San Prisco south-east of Capua contains Early Christian mosaics in the tomb chapel of S Matrona (*see* SANTA MARIA CAPUA VETERE, §2), while the basilica of SANT'ANGELO IN FORMIS, 4 km north-east of Capua, contains 11th-century frescoes of Old and New Testament scenes.

The Capua Gate was built between 1234 and 1240 by Frederick II to fortify the bridgehead where the Via Appia from Rome crossed the Volturno River. Partially demolished in 1557, tower bases survive *in situ*, and the Museo Campano in Capua houses the extant sculptures. Imperial chronicles mention the construction of bridge towers and imply that they follow Frederick's own design. Medieval and Renaissance descriptions and 16th-century drawings suggest the original appearance of the monument: polygonal towers flanked a three-storey façade with Roman sculptures and classicizing medieval works (for illustration *see* HOHENSTAUFEN, (2)). The upper storey arcade contained statues, supposedly Roman spolia from Capua Vetere (Capua, Mus. Prov. Campano). Below, three arcuated niches displayed a life-size enthroned togate statue of *Frederick II*, flanked by ancient statues of *Diana* and possibly *Apollo*. Three inscribed roundels with busts ringed the archway. A Classical-style female bust captioned *Custodia* (also termed *Justitia* and *Capua*) was installed below the Emperor's effigy, and in the spandrels on either side were classicizing busts of identical bearded men, imperial counsellors and the judges Petrus di Vinea and Thaddeus Suessa. Lion *protomes*, male and female heads, and capitals also survive.

The gate's design imitated ancient Roman city gates and triumphal arches, and in intent it paralleled the revived Roman ceremonies that followed Frederick's victory over the Lombards at Cortenuova in 1237. Its unprecedented classicism articulated Frederick's attempts to renew the Augustan Age of Peace, much like the Roman rhetoric of Imperial documents and ceremonies. The secular iconography enunciated the imperial justice of his law code, the *Liber Augustalis*, and doctrines of statecraft. The gate, facing Rome itself, wooed the chauvinistic Roman aristocracy as it challenged the Papacy with its Solomonic overtones. This classicizing monument inspired later sculptures by Nicola Pisano and Arnolfo di Cambio and the 15th-century triumphal arch built by Alfonso V at the Castel Nuovo, Naples.

BIBLIOGRAPHY

C. Shearer: *The Renaissance of Architecture in Southern Italy* (Cambridge, 1935)
C. A. Willemsen: *Kaiser Friedrichs II: Triumphtor zu Capua* (Wiesbaden, 1953)
M. Cordaro: 'La porta di Capua', *Annu. Ist. Stor. A.* (1974–6), pp. 41–63
G. Scaglia: 'La "Porta delle Torri" di Federico II a Capua in un disegno di Francesco di Giorgio', *Napoli Nob.*, 20 (1981), pp. 203–22; 21 (1982), pp. 123–34
J. Meredith: 'The Revival of the Augustan Age in the Court Art of Emperor Frederick II', *Artistic Strategy and the Rhetoric of Power: Political Uses of Art from Antiquity to the Present*, ed. D. Castriota (Carbondale, 1986), pp. 39–56
P. C. Claussen: 'Die Statue Friedrichs II. vom Brückentor in Capua (1234–1239)', *Festschrift für Hartmut Biermann*, ed. C. Andreas, M. Bückling and R. Dorn (Weinheim, 1990), pp. 19–39
J. Meredith: 'The Arch at Capua: The Strategic Use of *Spolia* and References to the Antique', *The Intellectual Life of the Court of Frederick II*, ed. W. Tronzo (in preparation)

JILL MEREDITH

Capuchins. Religious order of mendicants. It was founded in 1529 by Matteo da Bascio, and it was the last of a number of movements in the Franciscan order that sought a return to the supposed pristine form of the rule and a greater austerity than that of such orders as the Observants, to whom da Bascio had belonged. This asceticism involved da Bascio's followers being discalced, wearing beards and incorporating a conspicuously pointed hood (*cappuccio*) in their habit. Opposition to the Capuchins' independence from other branches of the Franciscan movement was only finally overcome by papal approval in the early 17th century. The Capuchins nevertheless spread not only within Italy but also to Spain (particularly after the death in 1598 of Philip II), Portugal, France and beyond. From their foundation, the Capuchins concentrated on apostolic preaching and spiritual ministry to the poor and oppressed. This and their evident poverty and detachment from family relations caused them to be widely admired among the lower orders of society. This admiration was enhanced by their heroic care of the sick in epidemics, and their services were also sought to reconcile feuds or to appeal to rulers for fiscal relief for their subjects, as St Lawrence of Brindisi did on behalf of South Italian subjects of Spain. Entry to political circles also led to a few Capuchins being employed in secret diplomacy, and the close association of the Capuchins with papal authority caused them to be excluded for a short time from the Venetian Republic during the Interdict of 1606–7.

While the conspicuous poverty of the Capuchins potentially limited the display of their churches, they still received paintings by major artists, and even in an architectural context they were occasionally supported by powerful patrons. For example, after the epidemic of 1575, the Venetian Senate determined to erect a commemorative church; although the simple splendour of Palladio's design for Il Redentore (*see* PALLADIO, ANDREA, fig. 7) caused the Capuchins at first to decline the custody of the church as too magnificent for them, they were subsequently persuaded to accept it. While the influences on the groundplan of the church include that of the evolving design of the Observant Franciscans' churches, with a large nave suitable for preaching as a traditional mendicant feature, the final form of the costly basilica owes much to its function in the annual public ceremonies commemorating the epidemic and its relief. This is nevertheless combined with a restrained emphasis on the cruciform that also does justice to Capuchin tradition. Many notable artists were also commissioned by powerful patrons to paint altarpieces and other works for Capuchin churches, despite the Order's desire for simplicity. In 17th-century Italy, for example, Cardinal ANTONIO BARBERINI, the brother of Pope Urban VIII, was himself a Capuchin. His patronage led to Giovanni Lanfranco painting a *Nativity* (1631; *in situ*) and an altarpiece of the *Immaculate Conception* (*c*. 1630; untraced) for the Capuchin church in Rome. In Venice in the 18th century, at a time when a member of the Order had exceptionally become patriarch of the city, Giambattista Tiepolo depicted the *Invention of the True Cross* (1740–43; Venice, Accad.) for the Capuchin church.

The image of St Francis was naturally important in the iconography of the Capuchins, as it was with other branches of the Franciscans, although the Capuchins were anxious to portray the saint with the features that they believed they alone had preserved authentically (e.g. Murillo's *St Francis at the Porziuncola*, painted *c*. 1655-6 for the Capuchin church in Seville; now Cologne, Wallraf-Richartz Mus.). The emphasis on the cross and the crucified Christ was if possible even more marked than in the rest of the Franciscan movement (e.g. Murillo's the *Crucified Christ and St Francis Embracing*, *c*. 1668, also for the Capuchin church in Seville; now Seville, Mus. B.A.).

Crypt of Capuchin church of S Maria della Concezione, Rome, by Michele da Bergamo and Antonio Casone, 1626

The Christocentric devotion associated with the Order's preaching is also reflected in the dedication of their church in Venice. In Rome the Capuchins became noted not least for the decoration, composed of skeletons and bones arranged in patterns (see fig.), of the crypt at the church of S Maria della Concezione (1626). Here the patronage of the Barberini family also allowed for the acquisition of Guido Reni's *St Michael as the Champion of the Holy Souls* (oil on silk, 1635; *in situ*) and Pietro da Cortona's the *Healing of Saul by Ananias* (oil on canvas, 1631; *in situ*). The Capuchins also shared the wider Franciscan enthusiasm for the cult of St Michael and for the Immaculate Conception as well as the Franciscan devotion to the Nativity. Paintings of Franciscan saints were featured in their churches (e.g. Murillo's *St Anthony of Padua*, *c*. 1664–6, for the Capuchin church in Seville; now Seville, Mus. B.A.), while the striking scene of the nocturnal papal recognition of *Pope Nicholas V at the Tomb of St Francis of Assisi* (Paris, Louvre) was painted in 1630 by Laurent de La Hyre for the Capuchin church in Paris.

BIBLIOGRAPHY

Father Cuthbert: *The Capuchins*, 2 vols (London, 1928)
M. a Mercato Saraceno: *Relationes de origine ordinis capuccinorum* (Assisi, 1937)
A. Huxley: *Grey Eminence: A Study in Religion and Politics* (London, 1942)
A. d'Ascoli: *La predicazione dei cappuccini nel '500 in Italia* (Loreto, 1956)
T. Graf: *Die Kapuziner* (Freiburg, 1957)
Le origini della riforma cappuccina: Atti del convegno di studi storici: Camerino, 1978
A. Foscari and M. Tafuri: *L'armonia e i conflitti: La chiesa di S. Francesco della Vigna nella Venezia del '500* (Turin, 1983)
M. Tafuri: *Venezia e il rinascimento: Religione, scienza, architettura* (Turin, 1985)

A. D. WRIGHT

Capus, Jean. *See* CHAPUS, JEAN.

Carabin, (François-)Rupert (*b* Saverne, Lower Rhine, 17 March 1862; *d* Strasbourg, 1932). French sculptor, decorative artist and draughtsman. He moved to Paris with his family after the Franco-Prussian War in 1870 and worked as an ornamental sculptor in a cabinetmaker's studio in 1878. In the early 1880s he befriended painters such as Georges Seurat, Claude Monet and Toulouse-Lautrec. He is best known for the small number of pieces of furniture made before he became Director of the Ecole des Arts Décoratifs in Strasbourg in 1920. These objects had more in common with sculpture than with the work of traditional cabinetmakers. He often made use of female nudes in his furniture, not as decoration but literally as construction, for example in one of his earliest works, a wooden table (h. 760 mm; Paris, Maurice Rheims priv. col., see exh. cat., p. 98), in place of conventional legs he used carved human figures depicted as if supporting the table-top with their uplifted arms.

Carabin's interest in the female form is further attested to by life drawings. Apart from the furniture, he also produced small decorative objects and medals (e.g. a commemorative medal for the magazine *Le Journal*, silver, diam. 50 mm, 1898; Hamburg, Ksthalle), several funerary monuments and more conventionally sculptural carved figures, for example *Voluptuousness* (h. 1.2 m, 1902; Strasbourg, Mus. B.-A.).

BIBLIOGRAPHY

L'oeuvre de Rupert Carabin, 1862–1932 (exh. cat., texts by Y. Brunhammer and C. Merklen; Paris, Pal. Luxembourg, 1974)

VANINA COSTA

Caracas [Santiago do Leon de los Caracas]. Capital of Venezuela. It was founded in 1567 by Diego de Losada on a strategic location on fertile land in the foothills of the Cordillera about 11 km from the coast. It was laid out by Diego de Henares on a grid-plan, as was characteristic of most of the cities founded by the colonizing Spaniards in the Americas and in general accordance with the 'Leyes de Indias' (1573) of Philip II, King of Spain. In the first plan (1578) houses were located around a main, central square, and each city block was divided into four. Throughout the period of colonial rule (until 1821) Caracas developed slowly, the result of limited economic activity, recurrent earthquakes and devastating epidemics. No buildings survive from the 16th century. In the mid-17th century, however, Caracas took on the role of civic and religious authority that had previously rested with the city of Coro. The most significant building from this period is the cathedral, begun in the mid-1660s to replace an earlier cathedral destroyed by earthquake. It has five naves and owes much to Coro Cathedral (1583–1617). The façade (*see* VENEZUELA, fig. 3) was executed by Francisco Andrés Meneses in 1711. The architecture of southern Spain, particularly of Andalusia, influenced colonial dwellings, few examples of which survive. Houses were usually single storey with plain exteriors and windows with grilles. Decorative features were generally confined to sculptural details above windows and doors. All rooms connected with a central patio; some dwellings had secondary patios and gardens. Red-tile roofs projected deeply over exterior walls.

In the 18th century cultivation of cacao made Venezuela a prosperous agricultural dominion of Spain and stimulated the creation of the Real Compañía Guipuzcoana. In 1728 the company made an agreement with the Crown by which the colony would be sent two warships a year in return for the company's sole right to import European goods to Venezuela. Since the port of La Guaira was of more importance to the Real Compañía Guipuzcoana, they erected no notable building in Caracas. At the instigation of Governor Felipe Ricardos stores were constructed around the Plaza Mayor in 1755, but these were demolished by President Guzmán Blanco in the mid-19th century when the Plaza Mayor was converted into the Plaza Bolívar. A number of goldsmiths operated in Caracas at this time, and a silversmiths' guild was also established in the 18th century. Works were generally Hispanic in character, and there were some notable ecclesiastical commissions (*see* VENEZUELA, §V).

A powerful earthquake devastated Caracas in 1812, killing some 12,000 people. Furthermore, the wars of independence and subsequent civil unrest also detracted from any impetus for urban development and architectural planning. The portrait painter JUAN LOVERA was based in Caracas in this unstable period. The city was recorded in oil sketches by Ferdinand Bellermann (1814–89) and in drawings by Camille Pissarro, who visited in 1852–4, establishing a studio in the city. Bellermann emphasized the melancholy majesty of the ruined churches of Santísima Trinidad (*c.* 1720; now the site of the Pantéon Nacional) and Las Mercedes (1698), set among tropical vegetation and against the impressive Cordillera.

The first art institution in Caracas was established in 1835, and painters were greatly influenced by developments and teaching in Paris (*see* VENEZUELA, §IX). A cholera epidemic struck the city in 1855, resulting in the building of the Neo-classical Hijos de Dios cemetery by Olegario Meneses (*c.* 1810–60). From the late 19th century Caracas began to spread along the east–west axis of its valley. Guzmán Blanco (President, 1870–90) was responsible for the first sustained programme of public building and did much to develop the arts. He commissioned the European-trained architect Juan Hurtado Manrique (1837–96) for such projects as the Palacio del Gobierno (1856–60), the Universidad façade (1876), the Museo Nacional (1883; now the Museo de Bellas Artes), the Masonic temple, the church of the Calvario and the Plaza Bolívar (1886–90). Manrique's most important religious work was the Neo-classical church of S Teresa (1876; see fig.). By the late 19th century Caracas's once uniform skyline of red roofs was punctuated by a number of stately, Neo-classical buildings.

A marked eclecticism appeared in public building works in the early 20th century, notably by Alejandro Chataing (1874–1928), while a simplified version of colonial architecture also prevailed. Another building boom began in 1936, when the International Style was established in Venezuela under the leadership of the French urban planner Maurice Rotival. Although not accepted in its entirety, elements survived of Rotival's design for a modern Caracas. CARLOS RAÚL VILLANUEVA, who had trained in Paris and was a member of the Rotival team, was responsible for El Silencio (completed 1943), Caracas's first multi-functional urban complex. This ambitious project replaced slum dwellings with six-storey blocks of flats joined by an unbroken street-level arcade. Villanueva was also involved in the nearby Avenida Bolívar project (1946–7) and in the construction of the Centro Simón Bolívar (1952–4), which, with its two thirty-storey towers providing office and commercial space and separate levels for pedestrians and vehicles, became symbolic of a dynamic, future-orientated Caracas. Works for the Ciudad Universitaria (1944–59) were probably Villanueva's greatest achievement. These buildings exhibit a fusion of architectural styles based on colonial, local and modern European aesthetics, and the design of the complex was likened by Villanueva to musical movements (for illustration *see* VILLANUEVA, CARLOS RAÚL). In addition, the university was conceived as an open-air museum and adorned with sculptures in open spaces and murals on exterior walls by such 20th-century artists as Fernand Léger, Hans Arp and Alexander Calder. Projects of superblocks for urban workers by Villanueva and others in the mid-20th century were intended to be independent, self-contained units making the most of sculptural forms and vibrant colours.

Caracas, S Teresa by Juan Hurtado Manrique, 1876

In the second half of the 20th century a new generation of architects produced a range of complexes, parks and buildings such as the Museo de Arte Contemporaneo (1974–82; *see* VENEZUELA, §VIII) and the Teatro Teresa Carreño (*see* VENEZUELA, fig. 5), while the Metro train system, with its two routes across the city, was opened in 1983, with ongoing plans for expansion. By the 1990s Caracas's population numbered some 4 million, and in conjunction with an oil boom and land speculation, a rather chaotic urban sprawl developed.

BIBLIOGRAPHY

C. R. Villanueva: *La Caracas de ayer y de hoy, su arquitectura colonial y la reurbanización de El Silencio* (Paris, 1950)

G. Gasparini and J. P. Posani: *Caracas a través de su arquitectura* (Caracas, 1969)

G. Gasparini: *Caracas: La ciudad colonial y guzmancista* (Caracas, 1978)

J.-P. Cousin and others: 'Caracas, Venezuela', *Archit. Aujourd'hui*, 247 (1986), pp. 70–95 [Fr. and Eng. text]

F. Irace: 'Caracas, un dramma urbano', *Abitare*, 253 (1987), pp. 206–31 [It. and Eng. text]

ANTHONY PAEZ MULLAN

Caraccetto, il. *See* LAPIS, GAETANO.

Caracciolo, Giovanni Battista [Battistello] (*b* Naples, *bapt* 7 Dec 1578; *d* Naples, 1635). Italian painter. He was one of the greatest Caravaggesque painters and the founder of Neapolitan Caravaggism. His *Liberation of St Peter* (*c.* 1615; Naples, Pio Monte della Misericordia; see fig. 1) and *Christ Washing the Feet of the Disciples* (1622; Naples, Certosa di S Martino; see fig. 2 below) are masterpieces of 17th-century Neapolitan art, and attain a powerful and tragic grandeur. Unlike Caravaggio, he also worked in fresco.

1. Training and early works, to 1617. 2. Mature and late works, 1618–35.

1. TRAINING AND EARLY WORKS, TO 1617. Although the biographer of Neapolitan artists, BERNARDO DE DOMINICI, reports that he studied with Francesco Imparato, Caracciolo probably trained in the workshop of Belisario Corenzio (documented in Naples 1590–1646), an accomplished fresco artist and elegant draughtsman. His first documented work is a fresco of six putti on the façade of the Monte di Pietà in Naples (ruined), for which he was paid in 1601 and which formed part of a fresco cycle executed by the Corenzio workshop. Inside, the chapel is decorated with frescoes of scenes from the *Passion* (1602–18), mature works by Corenzio, which reveal his knowledge of the works painted by the Cavaliere d'Arpino in the Certosa di S Martino. It is not easy to distinguish the different hands within this cycle, but it is likely that Caracciolo painted the allegory of the *Soccorso* ('succour') in the rooms adjacent to the chapel. It seems probable, too, that he assisted Corenzio in the ceiling frescoes, which move beyond straightforward narrative and create dramatic contrasts of light and dark, as in the *Agony in the Garden and the Sons of Zebedee.* This training with Corenzio was of fundamental importance to Caracciolo, whose achievement as a fresco painter and draughtsman distinguishes him from other Caravaggesque painters. Furthermore, Corenzio's workshop kept abreast of the most advanced tendencies in contemporary art. A signed drawing by Belisario records an intermediate stage in the development of Caravaggio's *Calling of St Matthew* (Rome, S Luigi dei Francesi), and suggests how responsive Corenzio's circle was to innovation.

The *Immaculate Conception with SS Dominic and Francis of Paola* (Naples, S Maria della Stella), painted in 1607, is the only fully signed altarpiece by Caracciolo and suggests that he went with Belisario to study Caravaggio's Roman works. While it seems likely that its overall arrangement was based on the *Seven Acts of Mercy* (1606–07), which Caravaggio painted in Naples for one of the seven altars of the Pio Monte della Misericordia, Caracciolo's altarpiece was also indebted to the scene from the *Life of Matthew* (1599–1600; Rome, S Luigi dei Francesi) and the *Death of the Virgin* (1601–06; Paris, Louvre). The complex building up of the composition is similar in plan to that of the *Madonna of the Pilgrims* (1603–06; Rome, S Agostino) and especially to that of the *Madonna of the Rosary* (1604–06; Vienna, Ksthist. Mus.). Caracciolo's *Immaculate Conception* was of outstanding importance in the development in Neapolitan painting away from Late Mannerism towards Caravaggesque naturalism.

After 1607 and before 1610 (the date of Caravaggio's second Neapolitan period) Caracciolo painted the *Holy Family with St John* (Naples, Mus. S Martino) and the half-length *Ecce homo*, of which several versions are known (e.g. Los Angeles, CA, Warschaw Col.). All these are related to the *Immaculate Conception.* In 1607 he painted two works for Francesco Antonio Ametrano: a *St Peter* (untraced) and a *David*, perhaps identifiable with a painting in the Borghese Gallery in Rome, which Longhi attributed to Orazio Borgianni. A fresco of *Putti and Drapery* around the organ of the church of Monteoliveto, Naples, may be dated to *c.* 1607.

De Dominici says that Caracciolo made copies of works by Caravaggio but this is not verifiable, partly because all documented works from 1608–10 have been lost. Yet a number of works show his assimilation of Caravaggio's art. It has been suggested that the composition of the *Virgin and Child in Glory* (Catanzaro, Mus. Prov.) was based on Caravaggio's first idea for the *Seven Acts of Mercy.* The *Decapitation of St Januarius* (Palestrina, S Antonio Abate), which some scholars attribute to Caravaggio, is in style and subject typical of Caracciolo and perhaps directly inspired by a lost original by Caravaggio. The *Crucifixion* (Naples, Mus. Civico di Castelnuovo) is a free interpretation of Caravaggio's *Crucifixion of St Andrew* (Cleveland, OH, Mus. A.).

In other paintings datable *c.* 1610 or shortly after, Caracciolo created more personal variations on Caravaggesque themes that were destined to exert a powerful influence on Neapolitan naturalism. Among them are many versions (in private collections or on the art market) of *Salome with the Head of John the Baptist.* Finally, a direct debt to Caravaggio is evident in two contemporaneous versions of *St John the Baptist*: an engraving signed with Caracciolo's three initials interlaced, and a painting of *St John the Baptist* (Berkeley, U. CA, A. Mus.). These were probably done before 1615, and may perhaps be associated with Caravaggio's painting of the same subject for the Fenaroli Chapel.

Around 1610, Caracciolo painted the *Baptism* (Naples, Pin. Girolamini), in which, rejecting the Late Mannerist emphasis on drawing, he began to paint more rapidly, as he had seen Caravaggio do during his second visit to Naples in such works as the *Martyrdom of St Ursula* (1610; Naples, Banca Commerciale). In the *Baptism* Caracciolo interprets the tragic self-expressiveness of Caravaggio's late work in terms of a characteristic grave pathos.

In 1610 Lanfranco Massa, an art collector and procurator of the Doria family, wrote from Naples to Marcantonio Doria, the patron of Caravaggio's *St Ursula*, describing the progress on this painting, and requesting paintings by Caracciolo, whom Massa considered a disciple of Caravaggio. Caracciolo's fame had evidently spread beyond Naples. In 1614 he visited Rome, where he met Orazio Gentileschi (Pacelli and Bologna). On his return he painted the *Liberation of St Peter* (Naples, Pio Monte della Misericordia; see fig. 1), paid for in September 1615 by the governors of the Pio Monte della Misericordia, a charitable institution that had commissioned Caravaggio's *Seven Acts of Mercy.* A comparison between the male nude in chains in the foreground of Caracciolo's painting with the male nude at the bottom left of Caravaggio's picture reveals that Caracciolo was also influenced by Gentileschi's more delicate art; the light caresses the surfaces, the colours are refined and the rendering of St Peter's and the Angel's drapery recalls Gentileschi's meticulous surface detail. Nonetheless, in its treatment of space, and narrative tension, it surpasses Gentileschi's works up to this date, and is one of the masterpieces of Italian Caravaggesque painting. The *Beheading of St John the Baptist* (Seville, Mus. B.A.) again re-interprets a Caravaggesque subject in the light of contemporary developments in Roman art; here, especially in the female figures, Caracciolo was responsive to Gentileschi's *Choir of Muses*, painted in the casino of

1. Giovanni Battista Caracciolo: *Liberation of St Peter*, oil on canvas, 3.10×2.07 m, *c.* 1615 (Naples, Pio Monte della Misericordia)

Palazzo Rospigliosi in Rome, and to the facial types of Antiveduto Gramatica.

Between May and August 1617 Caracciolo frescoed the 13 sections, later heavily repainted, of the chapel of the Blessed Simon Stock (Naples, S Teresa agli Studi), enriching his fresco technique through his study of developments in Rome. His *Trinitas terrestris* ('Earthly Trinity', Naples, Pietà dei Turchini) also dates from 1617. Caracciolo's name appears in the margin of the 'statutes of reform' of the Accademia di S Luca in Rome at this period.

2. Mature and late works, 1618–35. In the first few months of 1618 Caracciolo was in Florence, at the court of Grand Duke Cosimo III de' Medici, where he painted the *Rest on the Flight into Egypt* (1618; Florence, Pitti) for his patron's private chapel. Yet the motive for his move to Tuscany was Cosimo's desire to have his portrait painted, as well as that of his wife, the Grand Duchess Maria Maddalena of Austria. Only two portraits by Caracciolo are now in evidence, that of *Pietro Bernini* (Turin, priv. col., see 1991 exh. cat., p. 226) and that of the poet *Basile* (untraced; documented by an engraving by Nicholas Perrey from Basile's *Teagene*, Rome, 1637), but he was known as a portrait painter, and numerous portraits for Neapolitan, Genoese and Florentine patricians are recorded.

At the cosmopolitan court of Cosimo, he came into contact with the art of Artemisia Gentileschi and Filippo Napoletano, of Jacques Callot, and of northern landscape painters, such as Cornelis van Poelenburch, Bartholomeus Breenbergh and Jacob Pynas. He also studied the Tuscan approach to the portrayal of expression and gesture, and in his religious pictures he experimented with new, more informal relationships between the figures, and compositions built up on diagonals and on an oblique placement of the figures, as in *SS Cosmos and Damian* (Berlin, Gemäldegal.), *Noli me tangere* (Prato, Mus. Com.), *Joseph and Potiphar's Wife* (Zurich, Rau Found. priv. col.), and *Tobias and the Angel* (London, priv. col., see 1982 exh. cat., p. 71). All these were painted during Caracciolo's visit to Florence.

From 1610 he increasingly worked for patrons in Genoa, which he visited several times between 1618 and 1624. A bill of payment dated December 1618 mentions pictures 'both in oil and in fresco'. The frescoes were evidently those in the loggia of Marcantonio Doria's casino, or country villa, at Sampierdarena near Genoa, which are further documented in a letter from Lanfranco Massa of 1624. In 1605 Caravaggio had refused a commission to fresco the loggia; then Caracciolo came and painted at least one scene from the *Life of Abraham*; and before the end of 1624 Orazio Gentileschi also contributed. Unfortunately the whole fresco cycle was destroyed in the 19th century.

In April 1619 Caracciolo received the final payment for the large altarpiece of the *Virgin in Paradise* (Stilo Cathedral), which he painted for his physician Tiberio Carnevale. In the early 1620s he developed a more monumental Caravaggesque style, creating ambitious compositions and an exceptionally broad treatment. This phase is introduced by the *Miracle of St Anthony of Padua* (Naples, S Giorgio dei Genovesi), the complex conception of which is made clear in a small preparatory study (Naples, Pisani priv. col., see 1991 exh. cat., p. 231). Yet it reaches its fullest expression in the large *Christ Washing the Feet of the Disciples* (1622; see fig. 2), for the choir of the church of the Certosa di S Martino, one of the masterpieces of 17th-century Neapolitan painting. In 1624–5 Caracciolo painted the fresco decoration of *Tobias and the Archangel* in the Severino Chapel, S Marina la Nova, Naples. One of the four putti in the vault reappears with little change in the *Judgement of Solomon* (Florence, Serlupi Col.).

Meanwhile Caracciolo's reputation among Neapolitan patrons was growing. Some documents from those years mention portraits painted by him, but none of these have survived. Inventories also suggest that he may have painted still-lifes: in 1672, in the collection of Davide Imperiale in Naples, there was a 'small painting four palms in size, with fruits and other things, by Battistello'. The inventory of Gaspare San Giovanni Toffetti, prepared in 1651, lists a 'Putto sleeping surrounded by many flowers, in an octagon, with frame gilded by Battistello of Naples'. These two paintings have not yet been found; but a close study of certain works painted after *c.* 1620 reveals still-life details that show their origins in a Caravaggesque tradition: the loaves of bread, bunch of grapes and flask in *Lot and his Daughters* (Milan, Volponi priv. col., see 1991 exh. cat.,

2. Giovanni Battista Caracciolo: *Christ Washing the Feet of the Disciples*, oil on canvas, 2.2×3.0 m, 1622 (Naples, Certosa di S Martino)

pp. 246–7); the large fish in *Tobias and the Angel* (mentioned above); the roses in the oval portrait of a *Young Girl* (Rome, Gal. Pal. Corsini), which some scholars attribute to Angelo Caroselli or Artemisia Gentileschi; the basket with bread and the other symbols of the passion in the *Infant Jesus* (Naples, priv. col., see 1991 exh. cat., p. 239).

In the 1620s Caracciolo painted both frescoes and altarpieces, particularly for the Certosa di S Martino, Naples. His decoration of five sections of the vaulted ceiling of the Palazzo Reale in Naples with *Exploits of the Great Captain Consalvo de Cordova* (*in situ*) probably took place between 1625 and 1630. This history painting was an unusual commission for a Caravaggesque painter, and Caracciolo elaborated motifs from the many historical cycles painted by Belisario, and also from the decorations of Roman, Florentine and Genoese palazzi.

In the first half of the 1620s Caracciolo painted the side panels (now in very poor condition) with the *Martyrdom of St Januarius* for the chapel of that name (Naples, S Martino), *St Martin and Four Angels*, the *Adoration of the Magi* (1626) and the pendants of *St Martin and St John the Baptist* (all Naples, S Martino). In these last works, and particularly in the superb *St Onuphrius* (Rome, Pal. Barberini), he was influenced by Jusepe de Ribera, who was in Naples from 1616. In 1626 Caracciolo acted with him as witness to the marriage of Giovanni Do. Three years later, in 1629, Caracciolo figured in a document as a Knight of the Garment of Christ of Portugal.

In March 1631 he completed the *Assumption of the Virgin* in the chapel of the Assumption (Naples, S Martino). The side panels have been lost (they were replaced in the 18th century with two canvases by Francesco de Mura). In these late works he moved away from the sculptural forms and cold colours of the 1620s, and painted in lighter, brighter colours, reminiscent of Domenichino and Guido Reni.

In the ceiling and centre panels of the chapel dedicated to St Gennaro in S Martino, painted from the end of 1632, the decline in quality suggests the intervention of assistants, perhaps including the artist's son Pompeo. Four *bozzetti*, of scenes from the *Life of St Januarius* survive (Naples, Mus. S Martino). Caracciolo's last known large work is the fresco cycle in the large chapel at the end of the church of S Diego at the Ospedaletto, which even de Dominici considered weak; nonetheless, the powerful figures of prophets and the ancestors of Christ in the ceiling are evidently from Caracciolo's hand, as are the eight lunettes depicting scenes from the *Lives of Abraham and Jacob*, which show an awareness of contemporary landscape painting and themselves influenced Roman landscape after *c.* 1640.

Of the many children of Caracciolo's marriage at the age of 20 to Beatrice di Mario, one son, Pompeo Caracciolo (*b* 1606), produced works that have survived—paintings whose style links them with the followers of Massimo Stanzione.

BIBLIOGRAPHY

B. de Dominici: *Vite* (1742–1745)
G. A. Galante: *Guida sacra della città di Napoli* (Naples, 1872/*R* 1985)
R. Longhi: 'Battistello', *L'Arte*, xviii (1915), pp. 58–75, 120–37; also in *Opere complete: Scritti giovanile, 1912–1922* (Florence, 1961)
——: 'Un *San Tommaso* del Velazquez e le congiunture italo-spagnole tra il cinque e il seicento', *Vita Artistica* (1927), pp. 4–12; also in *Saggi e ricerche 1925–1928* (Florence, 1967)
H. Voss: *Neuen zum Schaffen des Giovanni Battista Caracciolo*, *Jb. Preuss. Kstsamml.* (1927), pp. 19–27
R. Longhi: 'Ultimi studi sul Caravaggio e la sua cerchia', *Proporzioni*, i (1943), pp. 5–63
R. Causa: 'Aggiunte a Battistello', *Paragone*, i/9 (1950), pp. 42–5
Caravaggio e dei caravaggeschi (exh. cat. by R. Longhi, Milan, Pal. Reale, 1951)
R. Causa: *Pittura napoletana dal XV secolo al XIX secolo* (Bergamo, 1957)
M. Gregori: 'Un nuovo Battistello', *Paragone*, viii/85 (1957), pp. 105–08
R. Longhi: 'Due dipinti del Battistello', *Paragone*, viii/85 (1957), pp. 102–04
——: 'Un *San Giovanni Battista* del Caracciolo', *Paragone*, viii/109 (1957), pp. 58–60
F. Bologna: 'Altre aggiunte a Battistello Caracciolo', *Paragone*, xi/129 (1960), pp. 45–51
Caravaggio e caravaggeschi nelle Gallerie di Firenze (exh. cat. by E. Borea, Florence, Pitti, 1970)
R. Causa: 'La pittura del seicento a Napoli dal naturalismo al barocco', *Storia di Napoli* (Cava dei Tirreni, 1972), v, pp. 915–94
——: *L'arte nella Certosa di San Martino a Napoli* (Naples, 1973)
M. Stoughton: *The Paintings of Giovan Battista Caracciolo* (diss., U. MI, Ann Arbor, 1973)
W. Prohaska: 'Beiträge zu Battistello Caracciolo', *Jb. Ksthist. Samml. Wien*, lxxiv (1978), pp. 153–269
M. Stoughton: 'Giovanni Battista Caracciolo: New Biographical Documents', *Burl. Mag.*, cxx/905 (1978), pp. 204–15
V. Pacelli and F. Bologna: 'Caravaggio 1610: La *Sant'Orsola confitta dal tiranno* per Marcantonio Doria', *Prospettiva*, xxiii (1980), pp. 23–44
Painting in Naples, 1606–1705: From Caravaggio to Giordano (exh. cat., ed. C. Whitfield and J. Martineau; London, R.A.; Washington, DC, N.G.A.; 1982)
V. Pacelli: *Caravaggio: Le 'Sette Opere di Misericordia'* (Salerno, 1984)
Civiltà del '600 a Napoli, 2 vols (exh. cat., ed. S. Cassani; Naples, Capodimonte, 1984–5)
M. Causa Picone: 'Battistello frescante nel Palazzo Reale di Napoli', *Paragone*, xxxviii/443 (1987), pp. 3–25
——: 'Corenzio e Battistello nel Monte di Pietà a Napoli', *Paragone*, xl/469 (1989), pp. 68–79
Battistello Caracciolo e il primo naturalismo a Napoli (exh. cat., ed. F. Bologna; Naples, Castel Sant'Angelo and Certosa di S Martino, 1991)
Battistello pittore di storia (exh. cat., Naples, 1991)
M. Causa Picone: 'Giunta a Battistello: Appunti per una storia critica di Battistello disegnatore', *Paragone*, xliv/519–21 (1993), pp. 24–87

STEFANO CAUSA

Caracol. Site of one of the largest Pre-Columbian MAYA cities, on the eastern edge of the Maya mountains in the Vaca Plateau, Belize. It was occupied from *c.* 300 BC to AD 1250 and remained active during the Maya hiatus of *c.* AD 550–650. Although some distance from water, it had easy access to resources in the Maya mountains. Caracol was discovered in 1938 and first explored by Linton Satterthwaite (University of Pennsylvania) and A. Hamilton Anderson (first archaeological commissioner of Belize) in the 1950s. The central part of the site was mapped, several buildings and tombs were excavated, and a series of carved stone monuments was discovered. The iconography of the monuments indicates that Caracol developed a distinct regional style during the Early Classic period (*c.* AD 250–*c.* 600); this style was subsequently adopted in much of the Maya region. A. F. Chase and D. Z. Chase have documented the dominance of Caracol during the so-called Maya hiatus of *c.* AD 550–650. Monuments and artefacts from the site are in Belize City (Bliss Inst.), Philadelphia (U. PA, Mus.) and Denver (A. Mus.).

The earliest evidence of Maya occupation at Caracol dates to the Late Pre-Classic period (*c.* 300 BC–*c.* AD 250). In the Early Classic period monumental architecture was constructed at the site centre and at the end of at least one of seven intra-site causeways. During the transition from the Early Classic to Late Classic period (*c.* AD 550–650) the inhabitants of Caracol dominated the southern Maya lowlands through successful wars against Maya TIKAL (562) and Naranjo (631) and built the tall Caana structure (42 m). From *c.* 700 to *c.* 780 no monuments were erected, but by the end of the Classic period (*c.* 900) Caracol was once more prospering and the raising of stelae had resumed. There is only slight evidence for Post-Classic (*c.* 900–1521) occupation.

Most ceramics from Caracol fall into a tradition separate from those found in the central Petén region of north-eastern Guatemala or in the Belize Valley. Caracol's Early Classic carved stone monuments presage iconographic developments later utilized elsewhere in the Maya lowlands, specifically with regard to the use of multiple human figures and ancestral figures in earth-monster imagery. Classic period monuments include red-painted tomb capstones with black-line hieroglyphic texts and wall texts in tombs. The textual capstones are unique in the southern Maya lowlands and suggest that Caracol retained some stylistic anachronisms well into the Late Classic period (*c.* 600–*c.* 900). Caracol's final monuments display foreign costumes and manner of portraiture, possibly suggesting political contacts with northern Maya cities.

BIBLIOGRAPHY

L. Satterthwaite: 'Reconnaissance in British Honduras', *Bull. U. Mus.*, xvi (1951), pp. 21–37
——: 'Sculptured Monuments from Caracol, British Honduras', *Bull. U. Mus.*, xviii (1954), pp. 1–45
A. H. Anderson: 'Recent Discoveries at Caracol Site, British Honduras', *Proceedings of the 32nd International Congress of Americanists: Copenhagen, 1956*, pp. 494–9
——: 'More Discoveries at Caracol, British Honduras', *Proceedings of the 33rd International Congress of Americanists: San José, Costa Rica, 1958*, pp. 211–18
C. P. Beetz and L. Satterthwaite: *The Monuments and Inscriptions of Caracol, Belize* (Philadelphia, 1981)
A. F. Chase: 'Troubled Times: The Archaeology and Iconography of the Terminal Classic Southern Lowland Maya', *Fifth Palenque Round Table, 1981*, vii, ed. M. G. Robertson and V. M. Fields (San Francisco, 1985), pp. 104–14
A. F. Chase and D. Z. Chase: *Glimmers of a Forgotten Realm: Maya Archaeology at Caracol, Belize* (Orlando, 1987)
——: *Investigations at the Classic Maya City of Caracol, Belize: 1985–1987* (San Francisco, 1987)

ARLEN F. CHASE, DIANE Z. CHASE

Caradosso [Foppa, Cristoforo] (*b* Mondonico, nr Pavia, *c.* 1452; *d* between 6 Dec 1526 and 1 April 1527). Italian goldsmith, coin- and gem-engraver, jeweller, medallist and dealer. Son of the goldsmith Gian Maffeo Foppa, from 1480 he served at the Milanese court with his father, eventually becoming personal goldsmith and jeweller to Ludovico Sforza (il Moro), Duke of Milan. In 1487 Caradosso was in Florence, where his appraisal of an antique cornelian was highly esteemed. He worked in

Hungary in the service of King Matthias Corvinus, probably in August 1489; a later visit to the court was cut short by the King's death (1490). Between 1492 and 1497 Caradosso travelled to various Italian towns to buy jewels and other precious objects for Ludovico il Moro. He visited Rome, Viterbo and Florence early in 1496, when the Medici family's possessions were sold off after the expulsion of Piero de' Medici (1471–1503) from Florence. After the fall of Ludovico il Moro in 1500, Caradosso remained for some years in Lombardy. In 1501 he was involved in negotiations to sell a number of marble busts and statues, presumably antique, to Ludovico Gonzaga, Bishop of Mantua; in 1503 he formed part of a committee to judge the plans for a door in Milan Cathedral; in 1505 he tried to persuade Isabella d'Este, Marchesa di Mantua, to buy a vase (untraced) he had made of 49 engraved crystals set in enamelled and gilt silver, but she rejected it because it was too big. He was in contact with the Mantuan court again in 1512 and in 1522–4.

Caradosso moved to Rome in 1505 and received a constant stream of commissions, from the popes from Julius II to Clement VII and from members of the papal court; he was also given a pension from the Camera Apostolica. In 1509 he was a founder-member of the Università degli Orefici (the goldsmiths' guild) in Rome. In 1526 he made a will in which several of his works are mentioned. Vasari stated that he portrayed Caradosso among the papal entourage in the fresco of the *Entry of Leo X into Florence* (Florence, Pal. Vecchio).

To his contemporaries, Caradosso was most famous as a jeweller. Although none of his jewellery works can be identified, his career can be traced from 1495 when he designed a gorget ('gorzarino') for Ludovico il Moro, until 1524, when he contracted to make a tabernacle for the Volto Santo in the Sancta Sanctorum in St Peter's, Rome; this was left unfinished at his death. His most famous work was a papal tiara made for Julius II in 1509–10 and recorded in a drawing (*c.* 1725; London, BM) by Francesco Bartoli (*c.* 1675–*c.* 1730). Caradosso also made a matching clasp for the Pope's cope; this was of sheet-gold and silver, with the Four Doctors of the Church grouped around a magnificent diamond. Cellini wrote that Caradosso was the finest craftsman of his day and described how he hammered gold and silver sheets finer than anyone else. Using this technique, he made hat badges, paxes, crucifixes and other decorative and functional objects. He made an inkwell for which John of Aragon was reputed to have offered 1500 gold pieces; Ambrogio Leone's description (*Dialogus de nobilitate rerum*, 1525) of this piece has led to the identification of numerous replicas of two of the reliefs that originally decorated it: the *Rape of Ganymede* and *Battle of the Lapiths and Centaurs* (specimens of both in Washington, DC, N.G.A.); other plaques have, consequently, also been attributed to Caradosso. He carved gemstones with such skill that they were mistaken for antique works. Lomazzo and Vasari reported that he made portrait medals of Gian Giacomo Trivulzio, Julius II and Bramante, and this has provided the basis for all the additional attributions made by modern writers, although none of his coins or medals is documented.

The attribution of the base of the *Calvary* of Matthias Corvinus (Esztergom, Mus. Christ.) to Caradosso would seem to be correct on both historical and technical grounds, but other attributions, such as Pius IV's pax (Milan, Tesoro Duomo), are much more problematical. Lomazzo stated that a terracotta frieze of putti and heads (Milan, S Satiro) was by Caradosso, but it is documented as the work of Agostino Fonduli. Teseo Ambrogio (*Chaldaicam linguam*, Pavia, 1539, introduction, p. 182) described a bronze *Cupid* or *Apollo* (untraced) by Caradosso, his only recorded sculptural work.

BIBLIOGRAPHY

Thieme–Becker
P. Gauricus: *De sculptura* (1504); ed. and Fr. trans. by A. Chastel and R. Klein (Geneva, 1969), pp. 246, 263
G. Vasari: *Vite* (1550, rev. 2/1568); ed. G. Milanesi (1878–85), iii, p. 535; iv, p. 161
B. Cellini: *La vita* (MS., *c.* 1558–62), in *B. Cellini: Opere*, ed. O. Bacci (Florence, 1901), I, xxvi, xliii, liv
G. Lomazzo: *Trattato della pittura* (Milan, 1584), in *Lomazzo: Scritti sulle arti*, ed. R. P. Ciardi (Florence, 1973–4), i, p. 325; ii, pp. 287, 534, 549, 550
B. Cellini: *I trattati dell'oreficeria e della scultura*, ed. G. Milanesi (Florence, 1857), pp. 30–31, 72–5, 89–90, 95–6
A. Bertolotti: *Artisti lombardi a Roma nei secoli XV, XVI e XVII* (Milan, 1881), i, pp. 240–41, 258, 272–81; ii, pp. 274, 313
A. Luzio and R. Renier: 'Il lusso di Isabella d'Este. II. Gioielli e gemme', *Nuova Antol.*, xxxi/xiv (1896), pp. 294–324 [306–8]
A. Armand: *Les Médailleurs italiens des quinzième et seizième siècles* (Paris, 1883–87), i, pp. 107–12; ii, pp. 291–2; iii, pp. 34–44
E. Molinier: *Les Plaquettes*, i (Paris, 1886), pp. 99–108
E. Müntz: 'La Tiare pontificale du VIIIe au XVIe siècle', *Mém. Inst. Nat. Fr., Acad. Inscr. & B. Lett.*, xxxvi (1898), pp. 235–324 [303]
H. Thurston: 'Two Lost Masterpieces of the Goldsmith's Art', *Burl. Mag.*, viii (1905–6), pp. 37–43 [43]
F. Malaguzzi Valeri: *La corte di Lodovico il Moro* (Milan, 1913–23), iii, pp. 325–39
W. von Bode: 'Caradossos Plaketten und Bramantes Anteil daran', *Z. Numi.*, xxxiii (1922), pp. 145–55
J. Balogh: *Contributi alla storia delle relazioni d'arte e di cultura tra Milano e l'Ungheria* (Buda, 1928), pp. 63–4
G. F. Hill: *Corpus*, i (London, 1930), pp. 166–74
E. Schaffran: 'Mattia Corvino Re d'Ungheria ed i suoi rapporti col rinascimento italiano', *Riv. A.*, xv (1933), pp. 191–201 [193–4]
P. Bondioli: 'Per la biografia di Caradosso Foppa', *Archv Stor. Lombardo*, lxxv–lxxvi (1948–9), pp. 241–2
D. W. H. Schwarz: 'Eine Bildnisplakette des Gian Giacomo Trivulzio', *Jber.: Schweiz. Landesmus. Zürich*, lxvi (1957), pp. 39–47
C. G. Bulgari: *Argentieri, gemmari e orafi d'Italia: Roma*, i (Rome, 1958), p. 246
R. Weiss: 'The Medals of Pope Julius II (1503–1513)', *J. Warb. & Court. Inst.*, xxviii (1965), pp. 163–82 [169–79]
E. Steingräber: 'Lombardisches Maleremail um 1500', *Festschrift Wolfgang Braunfels* (Tübingen, 1977), pp. 371–87 [375–9]
Y. Hackenbroch: *Renaissance Jewellery* (Munich, 1979), pp. 17–22
J. Pope-Hennessy: 'The Italian Plaquette', *The Study and Criticism of Italian Sculpture* (Princeton, 1980), pp. 192–222 [204–6]
Natur und Antike in der Renaissance (exh. cat., Frankfurt am Main, Liebighaus, 1985), pp. 446–8

MARCO COLLARETA

Carafa. Italian family of patrons. Its origins are obscure, but by the 14th century it was one of the leading Neapolitan noble families with an archbishop of Bari (Bartolomeo Carafa, *fl* 1325; *d* 16 March 1367) and prior of the Knights Hospitaller in Cyprus (Bartolomeo Carafa, *fl* 1378; *d* 1405) among its members. During the period of Aragonese rule in southern Italy (1442–1501), the Carafa extended their influence through military, administrative and diplomatic undertakings on behalf of the new rulers, thereby acquiring extensive feudal holdings in and around Naples that were consolidated and extended in later centuries. Apart from service as soldiers and statesmen, they also acquired pre-eminence in the Church, providing from the late 15th century onwards a veritable dynasty of archbishops of Naples, cardinals, including (1) Oliviero Carafa, and a pope, (2) Paul IV. There are Carafa monuments in Rome, but most are in Naples. Within the Seggio di Nido (one of the city's ancient city wards) are several Carafa palaces dating from the 15th and 16th centuries with later additions and restorations. The façade of the 15th-century Palazzo Carafa di Maddaloni, built by Diomede Carafa (1406–87), has the decorative stonework and classical ornament typical of the best of south Italian Renaissance architecture and once contained a remarkable collection of antique sculpture. As regards ecclesiastical patronage, the Carafa initially concentrated on the 14th-century Dominican church of S Domenico Maggiore at the heart of their family enclave. They contributed to the fabric of the priory and endowed the church with several chapels and tombs. While S Domenico continued in use as burial place for later generations of the Carafa, in 1497 (1) Cardinal Oliviero Carafa commissioned a funerary chapel in Naples Cathedral, where members of his immediate family were later buried.

BIBLIOGRAPHY

DBI

B. Aldimari: *Historia genealogica della famiglia Carafa*, 3 vols (Naples, 1691)

F. Scandone: 'I Carafa di Napoli', *Famiglie celebri italiane*, 2nd ser. (Turin, 1902–23), i, table 19

(1) Cardinal **Oliviero Carafa** (*b* Naples, 10 March 1430; *d* Rome, 20 Jan 1511). He studied civil and canon law at the universities of Perugia, Ferrara and Naples and was appointed Archbishop of Naples in 1458 by Pius II and vice-president of the Sacro Regio Consiglio (the supreme tribunal for the kingdom of Naples) by King Ferdinand I. With the latter's support, Carafa was made a cardinal by Paul II in 1467. His long experience and his abilities as a diplomat and jurist finally won him (1503) the supreme position within the College of Cardinals of Dean and Cardinal Bishop of Ostia. However, although thrice a powerful contender, he was never elected pope.

Carafa's will (1509) reveals his immense income from his many ecclesiastical benefices, and the few surviving documents concerning the financing of his artistic schemes suggest that he was willing to pay well above the standard fees. As Cardinal Protector of the Dominicans, he was a generous patron in several respects and contributed to the fabric of the principal Dominican church and priory in Rome, S Maria sopra Minerva. While his commission for a second cloister now remains in only a fragmentary state, his chapel at the end of the south transept of the church survives in much better condition, although its mural paintings, executed by Filippino Lippi between 1488 and 1493 (*see* LIPPI, (2)), have suffered a number of depredations, most notably those on the east wall, which was rebuilt in 1566 to install the tomb of *Pope Paul IV* (*see* (2) below). The paintings relate to the chapel's twin dedication to the Virgin Annunciate and to S Thomas Aquinas. On the altar wall is the *Assumption of the Virgin* and a fresco altarpiece of the *Annunciation with St Thomas Aquinas Presenting Cardinal Carafa to Mary*. On the west wall are two hagiographic scenes relating to Aquinas: the *Miracle of St Thomas* and the *Triumph of St Thomas*. In the vault are four of the sibyls (one repainted in the 17th century). A tomb chamber (now concealed by the tomb of *Pope Paul IV*) contains a stuccoed and painted vault, embellished with Carafa emblems and attributed to Raffaellino del Garbo.

Although Carafa lived mainly in Rome, only occasionally visiting Naples, he acted as a patron to his family, especially deeming the archiepiscopal see to be his family's property and retaining control of the title by bestowing it on a succession of close relatives. Such considerations motivated his second and much larger chapel commission in the crypt of Naples Cathedral. Known popularly as the Succorpo, the chapel was built between 1497 and 1506 both as a funerary chapel for Carafa and his immediate family and as a reliquary chapel for St Januarius, patron saint of Naples. The saint's remains were rediscovered in 1480 at the abbey of Montevergine and, due to Carafa's efforts, translated to Naples in 1497 and placed in the Succorpo. The architectural design of the chapel is sometimes attributed to Bramante; the intricately carved marble relief work of the 12 altar niches lining the walls is more securely assigned to Tommaso Malvito (*fl* 1476–1508) and his workshop. There is no tomb, but a focal feature of the decorative scheme is a life-size carved statue of Carafa at prayer. Religious imagery is largely confined to the carved marble ceiling, where seven bishop saints of Naples are prominent. Elsewhere the ornament is overwhelmingly classical in detail and furnishes a vivid instance of Carafa's taste for the Antique.

Carafa also commissioned (*c.* 1508) from Perugino a high altarpiece for Naples Cathedral, the *Assumption of the Virgin with St Januarius and Cardinal Carafa* (*in situ*). As Cardinal Protector of the Canons Regular of the Lateran Congregation, he commissioned Bramante to design and supervise the building of the cloister at S Maria della Pace, Rome, as attested by the frieze inscription, which gives the date 1504 and names Carafa as the founder. Other evidence suggests that Carafa was also responsible for the construction of the adjacent convent. Other projects financed by Carafa (for which little or no physical evidence now survives), included the restoration and embellishment of the Roman churches of S Maria in Aracoeli and S Lorenzo fuori le Mura and the Neapolitan cemetery church of S Gennaro *extra moenia*. He also founded a hospital adjacent to S Gennaro.

Within the private sphere, Carafa built a villa in Rome on the site of the present Palazzo del Quirinale. A modest building, it contained a display of ancient funerary monuments inscribed with epigrams. This lost collection confirms his role as a patron of humanism, attested by dedications to him in numerous scholarly works and by his promotion of an annual literary festival that took place beside an antique sculpture nicknamed 'Pasquino', which Carafa set up on the street corner of his city residence, near Piazza Navona. While most of his commissions were religious, many of Carafa's artistic schemes were distinctive for their allusion to Classical prototypes: a striking instance of the influence of antiquity, even over ostensibly conservative Renaissance patrons.

BIBLIOGRAPHY

DBI

B. Chioccarello: *Antistitum praeclarissimae Neapolitanae ecclesiae catalogus* (Naples, 1643), pp. 286–309

F. Strazzullo: 'Il Card. Oliviero Carafa mecenate del rinascimento', *Atti Accad. Pontaniana*, n. s., xiv (1966), pp. 139–60
G. L. Geiger: *Filippino Lippi's Carafa Chapel: Renaissance Art in Rome* (Kirksville, MO, 1986)
D. Norman: 'The Succorpo in the Cathedral of Naples: "Empress of all Chapels"', *Z. Kstgesch.*, xlix (1986), pp. 323–56
——: 'The Library of Cardinal Oliviero Carafa', *Bk Colr*, xxxvi (1987), pp. 354–71, 471–90
——: 'In Imitation of Saint Thomas Aquinas: Art, Patronage and Liturgy within a Renaissance Chapel', *Ren. Stud.*, vii (1993), pp. 1–42

DIANA NORMAN

(2) Pope **Paul IV** [Gian Pietro Carafa] (*b* Sant'Angelo a Scala, nr Avellino, 28 June 1476; elected 1555; *d* Rome, 18 Aug 1559). After an exemplary life, first as a reform-minded bishop (1506), then as one of the founders of the Theatine order (1524), he was elected pope at the age of 79. He was learned and interested in the arts but achieved comparatively little as a patron; his finances were limited, and he judged artists and the arts with the same severity that he showed in other affairs. Churches in Rome, such as S Maria Maggiore, were cleared of indecorous works of art, and in one case a painter was brought before the Inquisition for having made a crucifix that was deemed unfitting. An *Index* of forbidden books was issued, and the Pope ordered Michelangelo to make his *Last Judgement* in the Sistine Chapel more modest. However, Michelangelo refused, and the Pope did not pursue the matter, being afraid of losing Michelangelo's services as architect of St Peter's. (Only after Michelangelo's death in 1564 was much of the nudity in the *Last Judgement* covered, by order of Pius IV.) It is symptomatic of his rule that such patrons as the cardinals Giovanni Ricci and Girolamo Capodiferro, whose recently finished palaces in Rome were being decorated, decided to leave the city. In the Vatican Palace Paul IV had the apartment of Julius III expanded and redecorated by Pietro Mongardini [Venale] (*fl* 1541–83), though no trace of the decoration survives. The loggia with scenes of the *Exploits of Hercules* by Taddeo Zuccaro was turned into a chapel by Giovanni Sallustio Peruzzi, who was then papal architect. Also in the Vatican Palace Paul IV made alterations to the Sala dei Palafrenieri, which involved sacrificing frescoes by Raphael. In 1557 Pirro Ligorio, a fellow Neapolitan, was created architect to the Vatican palace, where his most important commission was for a new casino in the Vatican gardens, which was finished in 1563 by Pius IV (*see* LIGORIO, PIRRO, fig. 1). In addition Paul IV was concerned with the construction of St Peter's, bringing it explicitly to the attention of the cardinals on his deathbed, but he was never personally able to make a contribution of any importance to it. His tomb, designed by Ligorio, is in S Maria sopra Minerva.

BIBLIOGRAPHY

Ludwig, Freiherr von Pastor: *Geschichte der Päpste* (1886–9)
T. Torriani: *Una tragedia nel cinquecento romano: Paolo IV e i suoi nipoti* (Rome, 1951)
D. Redig de Campos: *I palazzi vaticani* (Bologna, 1967), pp. 140–46

J. L. DE JONG

Caraglio, Giovanni Jacopo (*b* Verona or Parma, *c.* 1500–05; *d* ?Kraków, 26 Aug 1565). Italian engraver, goldsmith and medallist, active also in Poland. He is first recorded in 1526 in the entourage of Marcantonio Raimondi in Rome. There the printer and publisher Baviera introduced him to Rosso Fiorentino, whose allegory *Fury* he engraved (B. 58). Caraglio continued to collaborate with Rosso and engraved several suites, such as the *Labours of Hercules* (B. 44–9), *Pagan Divinities in Niches* (B. 24–43) and *Loves of the Gods* (B.9–23; two after Rosso and eighteen after Perino del Vaga). After the Sack of Rome (1527), Caraglio took refuge in Venice, where he made engravings after Titian (B. 3, 64). His presence is recorded there until 1537. By 1539 he was in Poland, probably at the recommendation of his friend Pietro Aretino, who had contacts in the court of Bona Sforza (1494–1557), wife of Sigismund I, King of Poland. By 1545 Caraglio entered the service of the King as goldsmith, medallist and engraver of hardstones. Surviving works include two signed intaglios (Paris, Bib. N.; New York, Met.), two medals (Padua, Mus. Civ.; Venice, Correr) and a cameo (Munich, Staatl. Münzsamml.). According to Vasari, he retired to Parma after the death of Sigismund I in 1548; other writers suggested he remained in Poland in the service of Sigismund II Augustus, who knighted him in 1552, an event probably commemorated in his portrait by Paris Bordone (Kraków, N. A. Cols).

Numbered with Agostino dei Musi and Marco Dente in the Roman school of engravers in the circle of Raimondi, Caraglio showed a greater freedom of line. With Rosso Fiorentino and Parmigianino he discovered new modelling effects with subtler lighting and more animated forms, for example in his engraving of *Diogenes* (B. 61) and in the first state of the *Rape of the Sabine Women* (B. 63). His oeuvre comprises about 70 engravings (65 listed by Bartsch) on religious, mythological and allegorical themes after Rosso Fiorentino (almost half), Raphael, Perino del Vaga, Parmigianino, Titian, Giulio Romano and Baccio Bandinelli. He used various signatures: *Jacobus caralius Veronensis*, *Jacobus Veronensis* and *Jacobus Parmensis*.

BIBLIOGRAPHY

DBI
A. von Bartsch: *Le Peintre-graveur* (1803–21), XV/i, pp. 61–100 [B.]
J. D. Passavant: *Le Peintre-graveur* (Leipzig, 1860–64), vi, pp. 95–8
H. Zerner: 'Sur Giovanni Jacopo Caraglio', *Actes du XXIIe Congrès international d'histoire de l'art: Budapest, 1969*, pp. 691–5
S. Boorsch, J. T. Spike and M. C. Archer: *Italian Masters of the 16th Century* (1985), 28 [XV/i] of *The Illustrated Bartsch*, ed. W. Strauss (New York, 1978–)

FRANÇOISE JESTAZ

Caraman, Duc de [Riquet, Victor-Louis-Charles de] (*b* 24 Dec 1762; *d* Paris, 1839). French diplomat, soldier and collector. He was born into a family with a long military history. At the age of 18 he left France to travel around Europe and while abroad met, among others, Frederick II, King of Prussia, Catherine II, Empress of Russia, Gustav III of Sweden, William Pitt the younger and Charles James Fox. Back in France from 1785, he initially supported the Revolution but soon became disillusioned by its excesses and joined the Prussian army. On returning to France in 1801 he was arrested, and his freedom was curtailed until the Restoration of 1814, when he briefly became ambassador in Berlin. He then spent 14 years in Vienna before returning to France in 1828 when he was made Duc de Caraman. After a period in Spain he volunteered for the unsuccessful campaign (1830) to take Constantine in Algeria. Thereafter he devoted himself to problems of industry and political economy and was on the jury of the Exposition des Produits de l'Industrie Nationale of 1834 in Paris. He was a great art lover and accumulated a number of paintings by Old Masters and contemporary artists. A sale of some of these, mainly of Old Masters, was held in 1830 and included works by Giovanni Bellini, Canaletto, Claude Lorrain, Correggio, Carlo Dolci, Francia, Jean-Baptiste Greuze, Guercino, Rembrandt, Guido Reni, Vermeer and Joseph Vernet. Most notable were Claude's *Landscape with the Judgement of Paris* (*c.* 1645) and Vermeer's *Woman Weighing Pearls* (*c.* 1665; both Washington, DC, N.G.A.).

BIBLIOGRAPHY

*Catalogue de tableaux anciens choisis dans les diverses écoles et formant le riche cabinet de M. le Duc de C**** (Paris, 1830)

Biographie Universelle Ancienne et Moderne (Paris, 1843–57)

□

Caramuel de Lobkowitz, Juan (*b* Madrid, 23 May 1606; *d* Vigevano, 7 Sept 1682). Spanish cleric, theorist, writer and architect. He was an eminent exponent of Counter-Reformation thought, who sought to bring all contemporary knowledge within a unified system. His career was marked by controversy, however, as his advocacy of Cartesian rationality—to which he was not fully committed—brought him into conflict with the Catholic Church. He was a prolific author, writing 260 works (69 of which were published) on theology, history, politics, law, language and music; his best-known contribution to architectural theory is his treatise *Architectura civil, recta y obliqua* (1678–9).

Caramuel's father, Lorenzo Caramuel de Lobkowitz, was descended from a noble Flemish family and had been an astronomer to Charles V; his mother, Catarina Frisse, was related to the Danish royal family. Caramuel received his early education from his father. From the age of ten he studied under the Jesuits at the university of Alcalá de Henares, graduating in 1629; he then studied at Salamanca and Valladolid, where he became a Reader in theology. Because of his ecclesiastical connections he was able to travel extensively throughout the Holy Roman Empire, to Flanders, the Palatinate, Austria and Bohemia. In 1655 he was called to Rome to intervene between the Bohemian princes and Pope Alexander VII. He was effectively exiled in 1657, however, when he was appointed Bishop of Campagna and Satriano; he took up his appointment in Naples (1659), where he acted as intermediary between the Accademia degli Investiganti and the Church. In 1673 he was appointed Bishop of Vigevano, and there he was able to indulge his interests in architecture, publishing his treatise five years later.

Caramuel's *Architectura civil, recta y obliqua* was produced in three volumes. The first provided a theological justification for the development of architecture from the Temple of Solomon, Jerusalem, to the Escorial (completed 1584), Madrid. Continuing a theme from Vitruvius (*On Architecture* I.i), he also expounded at length on the natural sciences that an architect should know: arithmetic, geometry, astronomy and music—the *ars antiqua* and *ars nova*. The principal innovation of the treatise was contained in the second volume in a discussion of *architectura recta* ('orthogonal architecture'; Tratado V) and *architectura obliqua* ('oblique architecture'; Tratado VI), which dealt respectively with the orders and the distortions (anamorphosis) that he believed were necessary to accommodate them to the more dynamic contemporary architecture. The third volume contained the illustrations, drawn by Caramuel himself; he described numerous variations on setting out the orders, including an Ionic order designed by Michelangelo for his buildings on the Capitoline Hill (begun 1560s), Rome; he also showed indigenous architecture from the New World, including a plan of the settlement of Hochelaga on the site of modern Montreal.

Caramuel claimed that his ideas on anamorphosis dated from 1624. Architects were already designing buildings with complex plan shapes, but Caramuel sought to extend the distortions from the wall surface to the orders themselves, so that all sloping elements in a building would involve the use of equivalent oblique members such as balusters, column capitals and architraves (see fig.). This theory met with little application among practising architects because it necessitated the abandonment of the modular basis of Classical architecture in favour of a geometrical basis. Jacopo Vignola had, however, moved in this direction in his Villa Farnese (begun 1557), Caprarola, and Caramuel owned a copy of Vignola's *Regola delli cinque ordini di architettura* (Rome, 1562). Much of Caramuel's theory was sophistry; for example, he criticized Gianlorenzo Bernini's design for the piazza of St Peter's (1656–67), Rome, and described his alternative, with anamorphic columns (Tratado VIII.x).

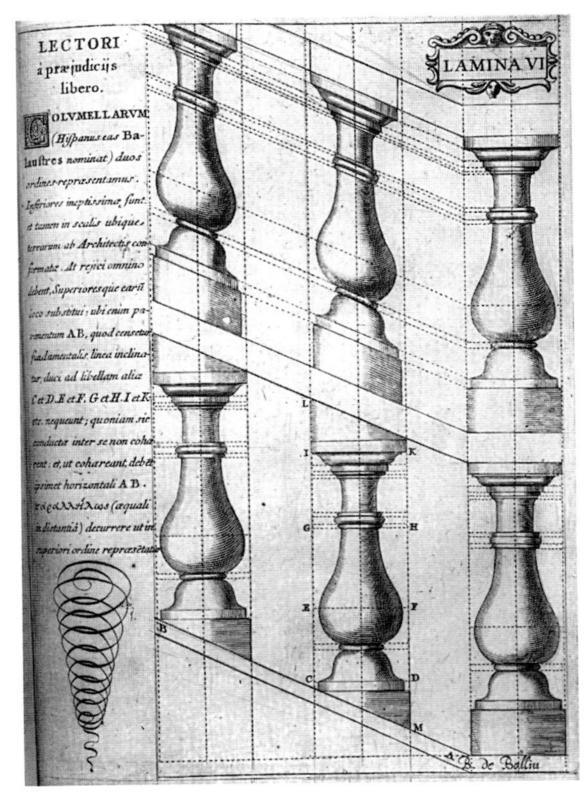

Juan Caramuel de Lobkowitz: *architectura obliqua* and *architectura recta*; from his *Architectura civil, recta y obliqua* (Vigevano, 1678–9)

Guarino Guarini, who was also both a cleric and a scientist, commented on Caramuel's theories of 'orthogonal' and 'oblique' architecture in his almost contemporaneous *Architettura civile.* Writing as a practising architect, Guarini condemned Caramuel for his lack of experience in the use of the 'oblique'; he denied the relevance of the 'oblique' and 'semi-oblique', believing that an architect should confine himself to simple obliquities, which meant, in practice, confining them to the plinths and entablatures of the orders. Luigi Vanvitelli may have been familiar with Caramuel's theories of planning on a geometrical basis, in which the dimensions and layout of a building are linked through numerical formulae, and he may have utilized them in his design for the Palazzo Reale at Caserta (see Hersey). The abstract, yet mystical, basis of this theory, based on the analysis, via Vitruvius, of such ancient buildings as the Temple of Diana, Ephesos (Tratado VIII), could perhaps be more readily applied to those structures that are closer to Neo-classicism rather than fully within the Baroque.

The only work of architecture by Caramuel is the façade of Vigevano Cathedral (1673–?1682). The main piazza in Vigevano had been laid out by Ludovico Sforza, Duke of Milan, in the 1490s with a regular arcade, possibly to a design by Donato Bramante, to accommodate the ducal palace, but this resulted in a misalignment with the cathedral. Caramuel attempted to resolve this situation by designing a symmetrical, concave oval façade that was offset from the centre-line of the cathedral itself; this disguised the difference in alignment and provided a termination to the piazza, although it resulted in the central motif of the façade being formed by a pair of pilasters rather than a window. The façade is reminiscent of Francesco Borromini's S Ivo alla Sapienza (1640s), Rome, and there are also similarities to Lombard Baroque architecture, such as the Collegio Elvetico (1627), Milan, by Francesco Maria Ricchini, which has a concave façade. Caramuel's façade, like his treatise, had little influence on future developments, however; he remains better known for his theological works.

See also ORDERS, ARCHITECTURAL, §I, 2(iii)(c).

WRITINGS

Architectura civil, recta y obliqua, considerada y dibuxada en el templo de Jerusalem, 3 vols (Vigevano, 1678–9/*R* Farnborough, 1964)

BIBLIOGRAPHY

G. Guarini: *Architettura civile*, ed. B. Vittone (Turin, 1737); ed. B. Tavassi La Greca (Milan, 1968) [II.viii.1 contains criticism of *architectura obliqua*]
J. Tadisi: *Memorie della vita di Giovanni Caramuel di Lobkowitz* (Venice, 1760)
D. de Bernardi Ferrero: 'Il conte Ivan Caramuel di Lobkowitz, vescovo di Vigevano architetto e teorico dell'architettura', *Palladio*, 15 (1965), pp. 91–110 [on the façade of Vigevano Cathedral]
A. Guidoni-Marino: 'Il colonnato di Piazza S Pietro dall'architettura obliqua di Caramuel al "Classicismo" Berniniano', *Palladio*, 23 (1973), pp. 81–120
D. Pastine: *Juan Caramuel: Probabilismo ed enciclopedia* (Florence, 1975)
P. Bellazzi: *Juan Caramuel* (Vigevano, 1982)
Atti del convegno internazionale di studi: Le meraviglie del probabile Juan Caramuel (1606–1682): Vigevano, 1982
G. L. Hersey: *Architecture, Poetry and Number in the Royal Palace at Caserta* (Cambridge, MA, 1983)
W. Oechslin: 'Anotaciones a Guarino Guarini y a Juan Caramuel de Lobkowitz', *An. Arquit.*, 2 (1990)

ZILAH QUEZADO DECKKER

Caran d'Ache [Poiré, Emmanuel] (*b* Moscow, 1859; *d* Paris, 26 Feb 1909). French draughtsman and illustrator. Born into a French family in Moscow, he was the grandson of a squadron leader in Napoleon's Guides who had remained in Russia after being wounded in the Battle of Moscow. He left Russia in 1878 and enlisted in the French army in Paris. After designing uniforms for the army, he worked on the *Chronique parisienne* in 1880 and then on a number of other French as well as American, Italian and Russian magazines. He adopted as his pseudonym the Russian word for pencil ('karandash') and specialized in amusing military scenes, some of which were published in *Nos soldats du siècle* (1890). His 'Lundis' in *Le Figaro*, a series of satirical drawings that appeared each Monday from 1899, were particularly celebrated and many of his satirical plates on the Dreyfus affair appeared there. He also co-founded with Jean-Louis Forain the anti-Dreyfus weekly satirical journal *Psst!*, which ran from 1898 to 1899. In addition Caran d'Ache was a co-founder of the paper the *Tout Paris* and provided illustrations for a number of books, such as Albert Millaud's *La Comédie du jour sous la république athénienne* (Paris, 1886) and Nikolai Dmitrievich Benardaki's *Prince Kozakokoff* (Paris, 1893). He had made a fortune by 1900, becoming one of the celebrities of the 'Belle Epoque'. In his work he created a completely linear style, schematized like shorthand, and developed his stories through a succession of pictures, usually grouped together under one title but without captions. In this sense he can be seen as a precursor of the modern cartoon, breaking up the story into a sequence of extremely simplified images.

WRITINGS

Nos soldats du siècle (Paris, 1890)

BIBLIOGRAPHY

DBF
H. M. Bateman: *Caran d'Ache the Supreme* (London, 1933)
Inventaire du fonds français après 1800, Paris, Bib. N., Cab. Est. cat., iv (Paris, 1949), pp. 64–83

MICHEL MELOT

Caratti [Carata], **Francesco** (*b* Bissone, Ticino, 1615–20; *d* Prague, Jan 1677). Swiss architect, active in Bohemia. In the mid-17th century he and his father-in-law Pietro Materna (*fl* 1632–48) constructed two fountains in Valtice (S. Moravia) for Prince Liechtenstein. From 15 June 1652 to 16 March 1656 he was in the employ of Prince Libochovice in Roudnice nad Labem (N.E. Bohemia), where he began the extensive reconstruction of the castle (completed by Antonio Porta in 1684). He built the two ashlar-faced lower storeys of the shorter east wing of a 16×19 bay oblong block with an inner courtyard, a design that foreshadowed the enormity of the Černín Palace (from 1668). In 1656 Caratti left Roudnice to work for Count Michna in Prague, where he adapted Michna's palace (*c.* 1640; architect unknown) in the Malá Strana quarter. Between 1656 and 1678 he built the Dominican church of St Mary Magdalene (closed 1786 and later reconstructed), which had a longitudinal nave and a *trompe l'oeil* dome over the crossing. Around 1660 he probably designed Count Nostic's palace in Malá Strana. In 1668 Caratti was commissioned to design a palace for Count Humprecht Czernin on a wide but shallow site on the

Hradčany in Prague. The resulting work, which the architect continued to supervise for the rest of his life, is an enormous structure, the largest private palace in Central Europe. Its 29 bays are articulated by giant three-quarter columns running through two storeys and surmounted by capitals, where grimacing heads look out between Ionic volutes. These columns, which support small, fragmented lengths of entablature framing a range of mezzanine windows, stand on a massive plinth of eight courses of diamond-rusticated blocks. The fragmentation of the entablature makes it visually too light to counter the colonnade's upward thrust, which is dissipated in Mannerist fashion at the thin roof-line. Apart from a series of minor buildings, which have not survived, Caratti built a church (1669) and a belfry (1673) for Czernin at Kosmonosy in Mladá Boleslav (central Bohemia). A number of aristocrats sought his services but all that remains is his design of a palace (*c.* 1673; unexecuted) for Count Dietrichstein on the Hradčany. Caratti's monumental architectural style was never really developed in Bohemia. His work, which incorporates elements of Viennese art and Lombard architecture, was also influenced by Andrea Palladio, whose theories served as a basis for Caratti's secular buildings.

BIBLIOGRAPHY

DBI; Thieme–Becker

J. J. Morper: *Das Czernin-Palais in Prag* (Prague, 1940)

E. Hempel: *Baroque Art and Architecture in Central Europe*, Pelican Hist. A. (Harmondsworth, 1965)

J. Tříska and V. Lorenc: *Černínský palác v Praze* [The Černín Palace in Prague] (Prague, 1980)

P. Vlček: 'Francesco Caratti', *Umění*, xxxii (1984), pp. 1–22

PAVEL VLČEK

Caravaggino, il. *See* DONINI, TOMMASO.

Caravaggio, Cecco del [Buoneri, Francesco] (*fl* Rome, *c.* 1610–20). Painter active in Italy. His nationality is not known. He was a follower of Caravaggio, and his rare works reveal a highly original and idiosyncratic response to that artist's naturalism. Agostino Tassi mentioned him as involved, with several French artists, in the decoration of the Villa Lante at Bagnaia between 1613 and 1615, and Giulio Mancini noted a 'Francesco detto Cecco del Caravaggio' who was close to Caravaggio.

Richard Symonds, who visited Rome in 1650, mentioned that the model for Caravaggio's *Amore vincitore* (Berlin, Alte N.G.) was one 'Checco da Caravaggio', 'his owne boy or servant that laid with him' (quoted Papi, 1992). The central work in Cecco's oeuvre is *Christ Driving the Money-changers from the Temple* (Berlin, Alte N.G.), which Longhi (1943) identified as the work, formerly in the collection of Vicenzo Giustiniani, that had been referred to in G. M. Sylos's *Pinacotheca sive Romana pictura et scultura* (Rome, 1673, p. 116) as by 'Checcus a Caravaggio'. This picture is clearly indebted, in its surface realism, the raking sidelight and the staging of the protagonists, to Caravaggio's *Calling of St Matthew* (1600; Rome, S Luigi dei Francesi) and may date from *c.* 1610. A large and dramatic *Resurrection* (Chicago, IL, A. Inst.), formerly attributed to Louis Finson, is stylistically very close to this picture and is generally accepted as a secure attribution to Cecco del Caravaggio. Other works attributed to him include a strange *Cupid at the Spring* (Rome, Vitti priv. col., see 1989 exh. cat., fig. 2), with a striking *trompe l'oeil* effect, a *Musical Instrument Maker* (London, Apsley House) and a *Flute-player with Still-life* (Oxford, Ashmolean). These works are distinguished by sharp lighting and by a veracity of surface texture derived from Caravaggio. Several art historians have believed Cecco to be a northern European artist, either French or Flemish, while Marini has suggested that he might be of Spanish origin. Papi (1991) has identified the artist with an unknown painter called Francesco Buoneri, who executed an altarpiece for the Cappella Guicciardini in S Felicità in Florence; the altarpiece was rejected by the patrons, and Papi believed it to have been the Chicago *Resurrection*, which may thus be dated 1619–20. He also suggested (1992) that the artist may be Italian and published a checklist of works attributed to him.

BIBLIOGRAPHY

G. Mancini: *Considerazione sulla pittura* (MS., *c.* 1617–21); ed. A. Marucchi and L. Salerno, i (Rome, 1956), p. 108

A. Bertolotti: 'Agostino Tassi, suoi scolari e compagni pittori in Roma', *G. Erud. A.*, v (1876), p. 208

R. Longhi: 'Ultimi studi sul Caravaggio e la sua cerchia', *Proporzioni*, i (1943), pp. 5–63

Caravaggio and his Followers (exh. cat., ed. R. Spear; Cleveland, OH, Mus. A., 1971), pp. 82–7

M. Marini: 'Cecco del Caravaggio', *La Casana*, ii (1979), pp. 11–15

——: '*San Pietro Nolasco trasportato dagli angeli*: Bartolommeo Cavarozzi e Cecco del Caravaggio', *Antol. B.A.*, iii/9–12 (1979), pp. 68–77

B. Nicholson: *The International Caravaggesque Movement* (Oxford, 1979), pp. 43–4

Fall Exhibition: Old Master Paintings (exh. cat., New York, Piero Corsini, 1989), pp. 21–3

G. Papi: 'Pedro Nuñez del Valle e Cecco del Caravaggio (e una postilla per Francesco Buoneri)', *A. Cristo*, 742 (1991), pp. 39–50

——: *Cecco del Caravaggio* (Florence, 1992)

□

Caravaggio, Michelangelo Merisi da [Merisi, Michelangelo] (*b* Milan or Caravaggio, autumn 1571; *d* Porto Ercole, 18 July 1610). Italian painter. After an early career as a painter of portraits, still-life and genre scenes he became the most persuasive religious painter of his time. His bold, naturalistic style, which emphasized the common humanity of the apostles and martyrs, flattered the aspirations of the Counter-Reformation Church, while his vivid chiaroscuro enhanced both three-dimensionality and drama, as well as evoking the mystery of the faith. He followed a militantly realist agenda, rejecting both Mannerism and the classicizing naturalism of his main rival, Annibale Carracci. In the first 30 years of the 17th century his naturalistic ambitions and revolutionary artistic procedures attracted a large following from all over Europe.

I. Life and work. II. Working methods and technique. III. Character and personality. IV. Influence. V. Critical reception and posthumous reputation.

I. Life and work.

1. Background and training in Lombardy, to 1592. 2. Early years in Rome, 1592–*c.* 1596. 3. Rome, *c.* 1596–*c.* 1599: The emergence of the mature manner. 4. Rome, 1599–1606: Years of success and fame. 5. Flight to Latium, 1606. 6. Last years in Naples, Malta and Sicily, 1606–10.

1. BACKGROUND AND TRAINING IN LOMBARDY, TO 1592. Michelangelo (or Michele) was the first child of Fermo Merisi (*d* 1577) and his second wife, Lucia Aratori

(*d* 29 Nov 1590). A plausible speculation (of Maurizio Calvesi) has his birthday falling on or near 29 September, the feast day of his name saint, the Archangel Michael. Fermo Merisi hailed from Caravaggio, after which Michelangelo was to be called, and was majordomo and architect to Francesco Sforza, Marchese di Caravaggio (*d* 1583), who had residences both in the Lombard capital, Milan, and his nearby ancestral seat of Caravaggio, near the border with Venetian territory. A preponderance of documents places the Merisi family in Milan until Fermo's death, from plague, in Caravaggio on 20 October 1577, but they must have moved freely between the two places and may have retreated to Caravaggio in the late 1570s. Michelangelo was again living in Milan before 6 April 1584, when he was apprenticed there to the Bergamasque painter Simone Peterzano, a pupil of Titian, for a period of four years. A succession of legal documents, in which Michele and his brother Giovan Battista Merisi (*b* 21 Nov 1572) disposed of their shares of various inherited properties, next records him as a resident of Caravaggio (25 Sept 1589; 20 June 1590; 21 March and 1 April 1591). On 11 May 1592 a final division of the family estate was made between the three surviving children (Michelangelo, Giovan Battista and Caterina (*b* 12 Nov 1574)). Caravaggio sold his remaining share, a small piece of agricultural land, the same day, and the lack of subsequent references to him in Lombardy suggests that he left his native land at once, never to return. He may simply have been seeking professional advancement; yet, according to Bellori (1672), he left because of 'certain quarrels'; and an almost indecipherable passage in the manuscript of Caravaggio's first and arguably most objective Italian biographer, Giulio Mancini, suggests that he may have spent time in prison in Milan for his part in the wounding of a constable. Although there are neither references to, nor examples of, specific works painted by Caravaggio during his youth in Spanish Lombardy, his north Italian background and training had far-reaching consequences for his art. Whether Caravaggio travelled immediately to Rome (Mancini said that he arrived there at about the age of 20) or went first to Venice, as Bellori claimed, remains an open question. Since no trace of activity in Venice has been unearthed, it is more likely that he moved straight to Rome in the summer of 1592. It would, however, be surprising if Caravaggio had not previously visited Venice, given Peterzano's admiration for Titian and Caravaggio's display, in his own paintings, of a knowledge of works in the city. Peterzano's influence on the young Michelangelo should not be underestimated. He combined an interest in evocative light and colour, inspired by Titian, with more characteristically Lombard qualities and concerns: a precise handling of paint, which was more finished than that of the Venetians, even while retaining traces of their textured brushwork; a fondness for the sometimes ugly detail of nature; and, despite the fact that he was predominantly a painter of religious subjects, an interest in still-life detail and portraiture. Bellori asserted that while in Milan Caravaggio concentrated on portraits, and, given his later insistence on painting his subject pictures from posed models, a background in portrait painting would make sense.

The striking originality of Caravaggio's art renders assessment of his other artistic influences difficult. However, it is clear that he was well versed in the various naturalistic traditions of 16th-century northern Italy: he knew the works of the Venetian painters Lorenzo Lotto, the Bassani and, especially, Titian, all of whom had left important paintings in the churches either of Milan or of the cities of the western Veneto (e.g. Titian's *Resurrection*, Brescia, SS Nazaro e Celso). Brescia and Bergamo also contained a large, and for Caravaggio perhaps even more influential, group of pictures by the 16th-century Brescian masters Giovanni Girolamo Savoldo, Gerolamo Romanino, Moretto and Giovanni Battista Moroni. Their direct yet poetic naturalism drew jointly on Lombard and Venetian priorities, redirecting the Venetian fondness for expressive light and atmosphere into a concern with shadowy interiors and, on occasion, night scenes. In Milan, Caravaggio was to encounter a third tradition, that of Leonardo and his Milanese followers, whose naturalistic style placed particular emphasis on chiaroscuro as a device for enhancing the three-dimensionality of figures (e.g. Leonardo's *Virgin of the Rocks* (London, N.G.; *see* LEONARDO DA VINCI, fig. 2), then in the Milanese church of S Francesco Grande). It seems, too, that Caravaggio may have been responsive to the art of the Campi brothers, especially to their ruggedly realistic night pieces, painted in Cremona and Milan in the mid- to late 16th century.

Caravaggio's artistic personality was also forged by the Counter-Reformationary climate nurtured by Archbishop Carlo Borromeo in Milan and by the character of the Lombard people themselves. The renewed seriousness and fervour that Borromeo had instilled in the religious life of the city, as well as his advocacy of naturalism and simplicity in religious art, are echoed in Caravaggio's subsequent religious paintings. Equally, the Lombard peoples enjoyed a reputation for vigorous, even wily independence and retained affinities with their origins in the Germanic world, not least in a tribalism that harboured egalitarian notions. Caravaggio's forceful idiosyncracy of character and populist inclinations, together with his northern passion for realism, were all, to some degree, rooted in this inheritance, which later fuelled his wholesale assault on the very different cultural traditions of late Mannerist Rome.

Caravaggio was to be aided in that enterprise by the long arm of his family's feudal masters and by the many Lombards he encountered on his travels. The Sforza–Colonna connection, in particular, was to serve him in good stead throughout his career. On Francesco Sforza's death, his widow, Costanza Colonna, became Caravaggio's protector, and her good offices and dynastic links were to provide Caravaggio with useful contacts, protection, and even commissions, in later life. The Colonna were tied by marriage to both the Milanese Borromeo and the Genoese Doria families, both of whom were to commission paintings from Caravaggio.

2. EARLY YEARS IN ROME, 1592–*c*. 1596. Caravaggio's early Roman years are undocumented in contemporaneous records, but 17th-century accounts and a group of extant paintings permit a tentative reconstruction of his movements from one studio or dealer to another in search

of employment. It is, however, not always possible to link particular paintings precisely with the phases, episodes and patrons mentioned in these accounts, and it is virtually impossible to arrange all of the phases in an exact order.

Of all Caravaggio's purported early Roman residences, the first may have been with Monsignor Pandolfo Pucci of Recanati, a beneficed priest of St Peter's, for Pucci was head of the household of Camilla Peretti, the sister of Pope Sixtus V, and the Peretti had close links with the Marchesi di Caravaggio. But Caravaggio, forced to do unpleasant household chores and fed on a diet of salad, left within a few months, dubbing his benefactor 'Monsignor Insalata' (Monsignor Salad). He is said by Mancini to have produced copies of devotional paintings for Pucci, who allegedly took them back to Recanati (untraced).

It was perhaps after leaving Pucci's household that Caravaggio worked for Lorenzo Siciliano (*fl* Rome, 1590s), who specialized in manufacturing crudely painted 'heads' (i.e. head-and-shoulder or half-length figures) for the art market and for whom, 'being very poor indeed, and virtually naked, he painted heads for a groat apiece and produced three a day' (Bellori's marginal notes to Baglione). It may have been here that Caravaggio met the Syracusan painter Mario Minniti. There probably followed an interlude, mentioned only by Bellori, with the Sienese painter Antiveduto Gramatica. Gramatica was apparently a masterly manufacturer of portrait heads and small pictures of saints (untraced), and Bellori claimed that Caravaggio churned out half-lengths for him.

The period spent in the house of the celebrated late Mannerist painter, the Cavaliere d'Arpino, and his brother Bernardino, which lasted eight months (Mancini), is, by contrast, mentioned by all the early biographers, although their accounts lack clarity and consistency. It is unlikely to have occurred before June 1593, when Bernardino arrived in Rome. Such an invitation implied a significant recognition of Caravaggio's talent, and it presumably occurred after his activity for Lorenzo and Gramatica. However, Bellori is the only writer to state in what capacity Caravaggio was employed: to paint flowers and fruit. Since Arpino's own surviving pictures contain neither, these must either be lost paintings in which Caravaggio supplied the still-life details or, more probably, independent still-lifes by Caravaggio that Arpino sold under his imprimature. The problem is compounded by the fact that still-life was a new genre whose emergence and development around this time are poorly understood and the fact that Caravaggio's only securely attributed still-life, the *Basket of Fruit* (*c.* 1598–1601; Milan, Ambrosiana; *see* STILL-LIFE, fig. 4), done for Cardinal Federico Borromeo, is later in date.

1. Caravaggio: *Rest on the Flight into Egypt*, oil on canvas, 1.35×1.66 m, *c.* 1595–6 (Rome, Galleria Doria-Pamphili)

Attempts by Federico Zeri (1976) to identify such pictures have met with a mixed response. However, since two of Zeri's attributions (both Rome, Gal. Borghese) probably formed part of the substantial collection of pictures confiscated from Arpino by the Borghese in 1607, the proposal deserves further attention.

Two half-length figure paintings that contain masterly still-lifes of fruit (both Rome, Gal. Borghese), the so-called *Sick Little Bacchus* and the *Boy with a Basket of Fruit* or '*Fruit Vendor*', along with another of a *Boy Peeling Fruit*, now known only through copies, were also part of the confiscation from Arpino and have not unreasonably been assumed to date from Caravaggio's time with him. Their appearance could provide a clue to the kind of work Caravaggio had previously executed for Lorenzo Siciliano and Gramatica. The *Sick Little Bacchus* is almost certainly the *Self-portrait as Bacchus* referred to by Baglione, who asserted that Caravaggio used himself as a model in a number of pictures painted after he had left Arpino's house and was trying to set up on his own.

All the biographers also mentioned a stay in the hospital at Santa Maria della Consolazione. For Baglione this preceded the period in the Arpino household, while Mancini said that it was occasioned by a horse kick while Caravaggio was living with Arpino and his brother and concluded his period of residence with them. Mancini also stated that Caravaggio, both during and for a long time after his convalescence, painted 'many pictures' for the hospital's prior (who has not been securely identified), who took them to his homeland in either Sicily or Seville (depending on which version of Mancini's MS. is consulted). If the latter, their possible impact on the young Velázquez is intriguing.

The biographers are united in claiming that, after leaving Arpino and the hospital, Caravaggio worked on his own behalf. It was during this phase, according to Mancini, that he was given a room in the house of another churchman, the Umbrian Monsignor Fantino Petrignani, a stay unlikely to predate 1595, as Petrignani was absent from Rome in 1594. But Mancini's reference to the 'many' pictures done 'at that time', among which he singled out *A Gypsy Telling a Young Man's Fortune* (probably *The Fortune-teller* in Rome, Mus. Capitolino), the *Rest on the Flight into Egypt* and the *Penitent Magdalene* (both Rome, Gal. Doria-Pamphili) does not make it clear whether 'that time' refers to the period spent with Arpino and Petrignani as a whole or that with Petrignani alone. Neither did Mancini indicate whether any of them were painted for Petrignani himself. Petrignani's inventory of 18 March 1600 does not refer to paintings by Caravaggio; however, it is possible that Petrignani, who was well connected, presented Caravaggio's pictures to high-ranking ecclesiastics or arranged for them to buy Caravaggio's works. The *Rest on the Flight into Egypt* (see fig. 1) and the *Penitent Magdalene* seem to have been in the Aldobrandini collection from the early 17th century and may have been bought, commissioned or received as gifts during the mid-1590s by Cardinal Pietro Aldobrandini. Caravaggio's unassertive, even delicate style in these works owes much to the art of northern Italy. Aspects of the composition, lyrical colouring and humble rural piety of the *Rest on the Flight* are close to Venetian tradition (Lotto; Jacopo Bassano; Savoldo). At the same time the modelling is relatively flat and there are marked infelicities of drawing and foreshortening. Neither had Caravaggio yet evolved a dramatic language of posture and gesture. The simple, passive poses are closely dependent on studio models; Caravaggio seems to have used the same slight, adolescent girl for both the Virgin in the *Rest on the Flight* and for the figure in the *Magdalene*—a practice that he would continue to follow, though with more sophistication, in subsequent years (*see* §II below). These two pictures contain other signs of Caravaggio's preference for constructing an imagined world out of the building blocks of mundane reality, as in the wicker-covered flask, pigeon-winged angel, fungus-dotted oak tree, luxuriating weeds and scattered stones of the *Rest on the Flight*. In the same picture Caravaggio introduced a characteristically deft piece of illusionism, foreshortening one of the angel's wings so that its edge abuts the picture plane, at right angles to it, a device that he would subsequently revert to and strengthen in the similarly foreshortened window-shutter in the *Calling of St Matthew* (see fig. 4). Furthermore, while the *Rest*'s poetic landscape is essentially retrospective, Caravaggio effected in the *Magdalene* a radically prophetic decontextualization, at once modernizing (as seen in the tiled floor and the girl's dress) and universalizing. The setting of a dim, bare chamber punctuated by light from an external source became the preferred existential space of his mature art—although the contrast between light and shadow was by then greatly enhanced.

3. ROME, *c.* 1596–*c.* 1599: THE EMERGENCE OF THE MATURE MANNER. In the mid-1590s, as Caravaggio was beginning to attract the attention of the Roman *cognoscenti*, a French art dealer, Maestro Valentino, sold some of his pictures—perhaps including *The Fortune-teller* and *The Cardsharps* (Fort Worth, TX, Kimbell A. Mus.; see fig. 2)—to Cardinal Francesco Maria del Monte, who was to become one of the artist's most important patrons. In these anecdotal genre scenes of contemporary subjects, with half-length figures, Caravaggio first developed his skill at dramatic narrative. These picturesque parables of deceit were of ultimately Netherlandish inspiration (e.g. Bosch, Bruegel and Lucas van Leyden); but whereas the early Netherlandish masters had often treated such scenes in a grotesque or comic manner as part of more extensive images that included other examples of depravity and folly, Caravaggio isolated the single episode in order to subject it to re-enactment with posed models dressed for the part. Aspects of the pictures anticipate his evolved Roman style: the archlike groupings of figures and diagonal axes of *The Cardsharps* feature prominently in later works; while the triangular wedge of the backgammon board, foreshortened illusionistically over the edge of the table, prefigures, in embryo, the same shape vastly magnified of the tombstone supporting the several actors of the Chiesa Nuova *Entombment* (1602–4; *see* §4 below).

Cardinal del Monte was Grand Duke Ferdinando I de' Medici's ambassador at the papal court and lived in one of the Medici residences, the Palazzo Madama. He was a late Renaissance polymath with a keen interest in music,

2. Caravaggio: *The Cardsharps*, oil on canvas, 915×1280 mm, *c.* 1595–6 (Fort Worth, TX, Kimbell Art Museum)

the theatre, alchemy and painting. His brother, Guidubaldo, was the foremost mathematician of the age, and Galileo was one of their friends. About 1596–7 Caravaggio joined the del Monte household as a paid retainer and was still there on 19 November 1600, although he left soon after. The Cardinal is known to have owned ten paintings by him. This arrangement influenced Caravaggio's art directly and indirectly. Del Monte's passion for music and alchemy found issue in at least three commissions, the *Concert of Youths* (*c.* 1595–7; New York, Met.); *The Lute-player* (New York, Wildenstein's, on loan to New York, Met.) and *Jupiter, Neptune and Pluto*, painted in oils on the ceiling of del Monte's alchemical laboratory (now the Casino Ludovisi); while the atmosphere of empirical science must have been congenial to the young naturalistic painter. Caravaggio may have continued to work for del Monte after 1600, for the beautiful and freely painted *Lute-player* has some claim to be considered a later product, although the current orthodoxy puts it firmly in the 1590s. The picture is a later autograph variant (see 1990 exh. cat.; Christiansen, 1990; Mahon, 1990) of *The Lute-player* (*c.* 1595–7; St Petersburg, Hermitage; see fig. 3) that was almost certainly commissioned by the Marchese Vincenzo Giustiniani, a close friend of del Monte and a distinguished intellectual.

Giustiniani's inventory of 1637 lists 13 paintings by Caravaggio, making him quantitatively his most important patron. The Hermitage *Lute-player* epitomizes the complex cross-currents of Caravaggio's early Roman style. Like the majority of his secular pictures from the 1590s, it is a half-length, almost certainly painted direct from life (it may even represent a specific musician) and also features a prominent still-life. It is essentially a demonstration piece, designed to show off Caravaggio's skill at representing both the human figure and naturalistic still-life. It may have been in connection with this painting that Caravaggio remarked, as reported by Guistiniani, that it was as difficult to paint a good picture of flowers as one of figures. It brings to a high-point of resolution the formula pioneered in such early works as the *Sick Little Bacchus*, the *Boy Peeling Fruit* and a *Boy Bitten by a Lizard* (Florence, Fond. Longhi; also known, uniquely for Caravaggio, in an autograph later replica in London, N. G.). In all of them a half-length figure of a scantily clad youth is seated behind a table on which Caravaggio has arranged a naturalistic still-life made up of one or more of the following elements: fruit, vegetables and flowers placed in a glass vase that also contains a reflection.

Caravaggio even included flowers in two of the only three portraits from the 1590s to have survived. The figure in Giustiniani's *Courtesan Phyllis* (*c.* 1597–8; ex-Kaiser-Friedrich Mus., Berlin, destr. 1945; see Cinotti, 1991, pl. 19) held a posy of jasmine; and the portrait of *Maffeo Barberini*, the future Pope Urban VIII (Florence, Gal.

Corsini), of disputed but not unconvincing attribution, includes a cut crystal vase of flowers on a table.

In the genre paintings themselves Caravaggio was not bound by any single iconographic convention or intent, and all modern attempts to seek a unifying key to their meaning have signally failed. Rather, having alighted on a formula that was ideal for asserting his naturalism in a Rome still half-attached to the non-naturalistic aesthetic values of Mannerism, Caravaggio proceeded to tailor it to the requirements or opportunities of an expanding art market or of individual patrons. In these imaginative genre concoctions, he drew on a north Italian tradition of depicting figures with fruit or flowers—either as personifications of the seasons (Dosso Dossi's *Boy with a Basket of Flowers*, Florence, Fond. Longhi), as mythological figures (e.g. Titian's *Flora*, Florence, Uffizi) or as allegorical portraits. He also responded to 16th-century Lombard and Venetian paintings of musicians, shown either singly or in groups, such as (?)Giorgione's *Concert* (Florence, Pitti).

The intensity of presence and idiosyncracy of mood of the genre paintings is the result of painting directly from posed models and objects placed in the studio. Caravaggio reconstructed the reality of a corner of a room, with all its accidents of light and shadow. Nothing that will enhance the illusion of reality is ignored, from keenly observed details to the strategic foregrounding of objects. His insistence on recording and even exaggerating distinctive details runs contrary to the generalizing conventions of Renaissance art, though it had precedents in that of northern Italy and northern Europe: maggot holes in an apple; drops of water on a leaf or decanter; the curl of a sheet of music; an excessive length of gut string crinkling out of the pegbox of a lute or violin. This passion for verisimilitude extends also to the human models, who seem to be rendered with remarkably little idealization and even with such features as dirty fingernails emphasized polemically (e.g. in *Bacchus*, *c.* 1597–8; Florence, Uffizi).

Caravaggio's evocative and spatially suggestive observation of the play of light includes both cast shadows and the reflections of windows, buildings and even people in water- or wine-filled glass vases or decanters. This preoccupation with the effects of light (which is prefigured by such artists as Savoldo) has the additional naturalistic function of positing a world of (reflected) objects and light sources beyond the picture space. Caravaggio also introduced in such works as the *Boy Bitten by a Lizard* and the St Petersburg *Lute-player* another device that was to become central to his mature religious art: a diagonal shaft of light slanting across the back wall. It is first and foremost a function of his studio-based naturalism, the source of light by implication a high window in the room in which he placed his models. But the shaft of light also assumes other functions, both pictorial and expressive.

3. Caravaggio: *The Lute-player*, oil on canvas, 0.94×1.19 m, *c.* 1595–7 (St Petersburg, Hermitage)

For it not only animates the monotony of the back wall but also serves to emphasize a dramatic moment or indicate the presence of the Divine. This 'cellar lighting', as it came to be known, was developed by Caravaggio into one of the hallmarks of his mature style, its naturalistic, spiritual and dramatic dimensions increasingly integrated.

In his incipiently Baroque effort to abolish the distinction between the world of the picture and that of the spectator, Caravaggio dramatically located objects right up against the picture plane, displaying or even proffering them to the viewer (sheet music; a violin or flute; a basket of fruit; Bacchus's glass of wine). Neither did he stop there. He sought to cap this sense of presence in several instances through the added dimension of sound—adumbrating in the cry of the *Boy Bitten* or the parted lips of his singing lute-players the recurrent motif of an open mouth in his mature art.

Caravaggio linked figures and still-life together with ingenuity and flair. That the formula is geared to an evocation of sensual beauty is clear from the poetic interaction that he articulated between the figures and their inanimate equivalents, for example the chord created between the soaringly elegant flower arrangement in the Giustiniani *Lute-player* and the ornately coiffured lutenist whose curly hairdo it pointedly echoes. The fact that all of the youths are clad either in loose shirts with plunging necklines or pseudo-antique off-the-shoulder garments may well imply a deliberate eroticism. It would be surprising if some of Caravaggio's patrons were not attracted by this aspect of his pictures. Del Monte was cited by one contemporary source as having acquired a taste for the company of boys in his old age after a youth misspent with women; while Giustiniani, though a married man and the owner of the *Courtesan Phyllis*, commissioned from Caravaggio not only the androgynous *Lute-player* singing Jacob Arcadelt's madrigal, 'You know that I love you', but also (*c.* 1603) the scurrilously suggestive *Victorious Cupid* (for illustration *see* GIUSTINIANI (i), (2); *see also* §4 below).

Perhaps, too, the effeminate appearance of some (not all) of these boys reflects the particular contexture of certain subcultures. Did the *bardassi* (catamites) who flourished in Counter-Reformation Rome, as they had in antiquity, dress up like the *Boy Bitten* or *The Lute-player*? Did musicians dress like this in order to accentuate the elegance and refinement of their performances? And how did the culturally sanctioned deviation of castrato singers fit into the equation— especially if, as seems possible from the heavy, rounded features, the del Monte *Lute-player* is a portrait of one?

If the stage for the emergence of Caravaggio's mature manner was fully set by the last quarter of the 1590s, the precise mechanics of the transition to it remain obscure. The two or three years leading up to the decisive breakthrough of the Contarelli Chapel paintings (1599–1600) are conventionally associated with a preparatory strengthening of the contrasts of light and shade, a concomitant increase in the three-dimensionality of figures and a heightened fluency of dramatic articulation. The works widely associated with this phase are, however, not especially homogeneous in technique or style. They include del Monte's *Ecstasy of St Francis* (*c.* 1597–8; Hartford, CT, Wadsworth Atheneum) and *St Catherine of Alexandria* (*c.* 1597–8; Madrid, Mus. Thyssen-Bornemisza); a *Medusa* (*c.* 1597–9; Florence, Uffizi), which may, as was probably the case with the Uffizi *Bacchus*, have been commissioned by the Cardinal as a gift for Ferdinando I de' Medici; a *Conversion of the Magdalene* (Detroit, MI, Inst. A.), which seems to have been owned in the 17th century by the Aldobrandini; and a *Judith Beheading Holofernes* (Rome, Pal. Barberini), which belonged to Ottavio Costa, a rich banker.

The three paintings done for del Monte are the strongest candidates for this moment, possibly beginning with the *St Francis*. It is a small, unusually freely brushed cabinet picture, whose silvery light and lyrical sentiment recall Savoldo, while the boy angel who, innovatively, supports the swooning saint is in the sensual vein of the half-lengths. The picture's marked chiaroscuro derives from the fact that St Francis's stigmatization occurred at night, and it seems probable that this accident of subject-matter played its part in alerting Caravaggio to the potential of chiaroscuro as a metaphor for spiritual experience—reawakening in the process memories of many dark Lombard paintings. Such an approach had the undoubted advantage for a self-consciously naturalistic painter that the presence of the divine could be rendered by light alone, without resort to apparitions in the sky.

Caravaggio's other route to a fully fledged chiaroscuro lay in his observation of the form-enhancing properties of light entering dim rooms from high windows. In this respect the *St Catherine* really does seem to represent something of a turning-point, for in it, as Bellori noted, Caravaggio began to strengthen his shadows significantly. The *Medusa* also uses chiaroscuro and an even more restricted palette as a means of enhancing three-dimensionality and horror. The Gorgon's wide-mouthed scream lifts Caravaggio's early fascination with sound on to the more melodramatic plane that would characterize his efforts in the early years of the 17th century.

The *Conversion of the Magdalene* and *Judith Beheading Holofernes* also slot conceptually into this pattern of evolution. In the *Conversion*, Caravaggio not only employed the same model as in the *St Catherine* but developed further the formula of figures seated dramatically around a table—halfway, it could be argued, between *The Cardsharps* and the more complex arrangements of the later *Calling of St Matthew* and the two paintings of the *Supper at Emmaus*. Equally it could be said of the *Judith*, which like the *St Francis* is iconographically a night scene, that the Jacobean intensity of its treatment of a violent subject, replete with spurting blood, precisely echoes the *Medusa*, as well as having close affinities with the *Martyrdom of St Matthew*. Furthermore, its very bold contrasts of light and shade, which may have been achieved by Caravaggio painting by lamplight in order to emulate the effect of torches in Holofernes' tent, would help to explain the otherwise unprecedented force of the chiaroscuro in the *Martyrdom*. However, there is no overriding reason for placing either the *Conversion* or the *Judith* before 1600.

4. ROME, 1599–1606: YEARS OF SUCCESS AND FAME. Between 23 July 1599 and 4 July 1600 Caravaggio painted two large canvases, the *Calling of St Matthew* and

the *Martyrdom of St Matthew* (see figs 4 and 5) for the side walls of the Contarelli Chapel in S Luigi dei Francesi, Rome—his first public commission. The commission was awarded by the Fabbrica of St Peter's, probably on the advice of Cardinal del Monte, in final fulfilment of the will of the French cardinal Matthieu Cointrel (Italianized as Matteo Contarelli), to celebrate his memory through the deeds of his name saint, and only after Arpino had failed to honour a prior contract to fresco them. Together with two smaller lateral canvases of the *Crucifixion of St Peter* and the *Conversion of St Paul*, executed in 1601 for the chapel of Tiberio Cerasi in the Augustinian church of S Maria del Popolo, Rome, these two large wall paintings won Caravaggio immense fame as a painter of religious subjects and led to an uninterrupted flow of commissions, both for churches and private collections. He was elected to the Accademia di S Luca *c.* 1600–01.

In the two *St Matthew* histories Caravaggio created a new and emotive combination that remained fundamental to his art: realistic figure types allied to bold chiaroscuro (*see also* TENEBRISM). The pictures appear to relate to two alternative kinds of studio lighting used by Caravaggio during the ensuing years: sunlight from a high side window, as seen in the *Calling*, and illumination in a dark room from a lamp placed high above the models, which may have been employed in the *Martyrdom*. Bellori claimed that the latter was Caravaggio's habitual practice, and it would have had the advantage over natural lighting of providing a constant source of illumination. It is likely, however, that he resorted to both procedures, sometimes within a single painting.

The fact that Caravaggio always lit his models from above indicates that he was well aware that such lighting enhances three-dimensionality. Indeed, unlike several of

4. Caravaggio: *Calling of St Matthew*, oil on canvas, 3.22×3.40 m, 1599–1600 (Rome, S Luigi dei Francesi, Contarelli Chapel)

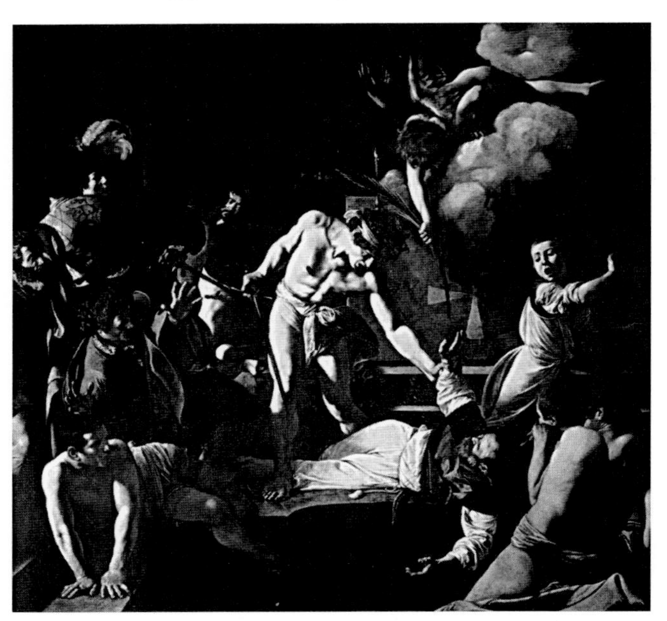

5. Caravaggio: *Martyrdom of St Matthew*, oil on canvas, 3.23×3.43 m, 1599–1600 (Rome, S Luigi dei Francesi, Contarelli Chapel)

his imitators, particularly such northern painters as Honthorst, he rarely used an internal light source, as this type of radiance flattens the appearance of forms. Caravaggio's lighting was part of the same militantly realist agenda that informed his close adherence to the appearance of his models, an uncompromising aesthetic neatly encapsulated in his statement at the Baglione libel trial that 'a good painter is one who knows how to paint well and imitate natural things well'.

This agenda alone, however, would not have been sufficient to create such remarkable images, were it not for Caravaggio's intuitive grasp of dramatic form. In the *Calling* the main source of illumination is high up on the right, in the *Martyrdom* on the left. This corresponds to the direction of the action in both pictures, with the light in them intended to mimic the daylight entering the chapel from a window above the altar—as is made specific in the *Calling* by a widening beam of light that slants across the back wall. The light in both cases can be read either as a symbol, or even the agent, of the divine will. A slanting beam of light, at once natural and divine, develops into one of Caravaggio's favourite metaphors. In the *Calling*, the light on the wall sweeps past the figures of Christ and his companion, who have just entered the counting-house, as if it were a superior force directing their endeavours, paralleling Christ's gathering gesture as he summons the tax-gatherer Levi (Matthew) to the discipleship. In the *Martyrdom* the pools of light that pick out the saint and his assassin alike, as well as parts of the sinuous angel who leans down from a cloud to hand Matthew his palm of martyrdom, forcefully convey the idea of heavenly sanction for this second and final harvesting of the saint back to God.

At the same time Caravaggio is skilful in his location of scatterings of light to signpost individual indicators of dramatic response and shape the overall pattern of the action. Indeed, he used light as much to convey human alarm at the workings of providence as the nature of the Godhead itself. It is only one of many examples of dramatic irony in his art. Another is the way in which Caravaggio cast Matthew's slayer in the *Martyrdom* as one of the nude figures he had been baptizing—suddenly risen from the font to transform a tranquil scene into one of sound and fury. This dramatic flair, which would often override the finer points of iconography without subverting the central significance of the subject, extended to the inclusion of his self-portrait in religious pictures. In the *Martyrdom* this takes the form of a conceit: Caravaggio, as one of the fleeing crowd, looks back over his shoulder to witness the holy mystery and his own mastery in recreating it.

The Contarelli narratives are great pieces of theatre, paralleling the pyrotechnics of the Elizabethan–Jacobean stage and heralding the theatricality of High Baroque art. Their consummate illusion is to make it appear as if sacred events are taking place in the space of the chapel. It is an impression that is heightened, here as elsewhere, by Caravaggio's eloquent deployment of both modern and biblical costume.

The X-ray of the *Martyrdom* confirms Bellori's claim that Caravaggio reworked the design three times. Some of the underlying figures (indebted to Raphael's fresco of the *Battle of Ostia* in the Vatican Stanze) and those of the saint, executioner and acolyte on the final surface (dependent on Titian's subsequently destroyed *Martyrdom of St Peter*) also confirm that Caravaggio was not as neglectful

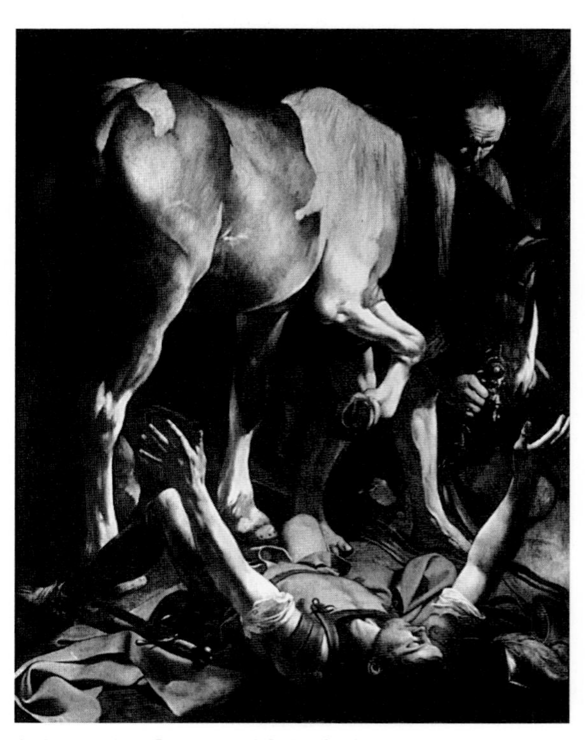

6. Caravaggio: *Conversion of St Paul*, oil on canvas, 2.30×1.75 m, 1601 (Rome, S Maria del Popolo, Cerasi Chapel)

of artistic precedent as his stance as doctrinaire realist might lead one to suppose.

The *Crucifixion of St Peter* (1601) and the *Conversion of St Paul* (1601; see fig. 6) in the Cerasi Chapel of S Maria del Popolo show an even greater economy of dramatic means and a more insistent foregrounding of the figures. The particular pattern of the chiaroscuro and quality of light in both works suggest that Caravaggio used a hanging lamp for illumination, as the main figures are bathed in a centralized pool of light, which has the effect of projecting them forward on to the viewer's attention. It goes hand in hand with a mastery of dramatic moment, as Caravaggio compactly directed all his resources towards involving the viewer in the drama: St Peter turns on his cross to address the crowd/onlooker, and Saul's arms are thrown back in rapture towards the picture plane, embracing the light of conversion virtually from the spectator's point of view. Caravaggio may have intensified his illusionism in the Cerasi Chapel out of rivalry with Annibale Carracci, who had been commissioned to do the altarpiece, the *Assumption of the Virgin*. Each artist asserted the distinctiveness of his approach, with Annibale pushing his fondness for Raphaelesque idealization, even lighting and colouristic delicacy to a new pitch, and Caravaggio countering with his vigorous anti-classicism. The backside and muddy feet of one of Peter's executioners are thrust ostentatiously against the picture plane, while the rump of Saul's horse (a tired Roman dray horse on a hot day) is unceremoniously directed at Annibale's altarpiece.

Such boldness on Caravaggio's part is remarkable given the fact that these two pictures were, in all probability, replacements for two others by him, in a different style, which, according to Baglione, were found unsatisfactory by the patron and one of which, a *Conversion of St Paul*, has been identified as the picture now in the Odescalchi collection, Rome (see Cinotti, 1991, pl. 33). What precisely it was about this attractively coloured, if somewhat Mannerist composition that failed to please remains conjectural.

In the early 1600s, flushed with success, Caravaggio pursued his at times provocative agenda in a succession of altarpieces for side chapels in churches and easel paintings for private collectors. However, his ostentatious rhetoric of the real was not always to the liking of church authorities, who considered that many of the sacred figures lacked decorum. Three out of five of the altarpieces that he delivered between 1602 and 1606 were either rejected outright or soon taken down: *St Matthew and the Angel*, commissioned on 7 February 1602 to complete his work on the Contarelli Chapel (ex-Kaiser-Friedrich Mus., Berlin, destr. 1945; see Cinotti, 1991, pl. 40) and for which Caravaggio made a replacement (1602–3; *in situ*); the *Death of the Virgin* (1601–2/3, or later; Paris, Louvre) for Laerzio Cherubini's chapel in S Maria della Scala; and the *Madonna of the Serpent* (*c*. 1605–8 April 1606; Rome, Gal. Borghese), painted for the altar of the Papal Grooms (Palafrenieri) in St Peter's. This last was immediately snapped up by Cardinal Scipione Borghese, who was to become the last great collector of Caravaggio's works. Only the *Entombment* (1602–4; Rome, Pin. Vaticana) for the Vittrice Chapel in the Chiesa Nuova and the *Madonna of Loreto* (or *Madonna of the Pilgrims*, 1604–5; Rome, S Agostino) prospered, both destined to become highly popular devotional works, not least with the poor.

Caravaggio was given a freer rein to pursue his experiments by a number of sympathetic and wealthy private collectors, notably Vincenzo Giustiniani, who bought the rejected first version of *St Matthew and the Angel*, and the Roman nobleman, Ciriaco Mattei. In the first half of 1601 Caravaggio moved into the palace owned jointly by Ciriaco and his brothers Asdrubale and Cardinal Bernardino, probably staying there until his imprisonment for several months in the summer of 1603, when he was involved in a libel trial for writing scurrilous verses about Giovanni Baglione. He seems to have spent the rest of his Roman sojourn in rented accommodation, punctuated by very brief trips to the Marches around the turn of 1603–4, allegedly to paint an unidentified altarpiece for the Capuchin church of S Maria di Costantinapoli in Tolentino, and to Genoa for two weeks in early August 1605, to escape arrest for wounding a notary. While in Genoa he was probably given shelter by Giovanna Colonna, wife of Giovanni Andrea Doria II, and turned down a commission from Marcantonio Doria to fresco the loggia of his villa at Sampierdarena, near Genoa.

For Ciriaco Mattei, his main patron within that family, Caravaggio painted the *Supper at Emmaus* (1601; London, N.G.), *St John the Baptist* (?1602; Rome, Pin. Capitolina) and the *Taking of Christ* (1602; Dublin, N.G.). Among the works that he executed for Giustiniani were the *Incredulity of St Thomas* (1602–3; Potsdam, Schloss Sanssouci) and the *Victorious Cupid* (*c*. 1603; Berlin, Gemäldegal.; for illustration *see* GIUSTINIANI (i), (2)).

Both the *Supper* and the *Incredulity of St Thomas* are replete with virtuoso naturalistic flourishes and, in their desire for immediacy of dramatic impact, pay scant regard to the niceties of decorum. In the *Supper*, an obsession with displaying his skill at foreshortening and still-life painting tempted Caravaggio into a number of transgressions, whether of convention or logic—from the inclusion of a basket of fruit seasonal to the autumn of 1601 when the picture was painted, but not to Easter when the episode is meant to have occurred, to the fact that it is perched implausibly over the front edge of the table. In the *Incredulity of St Thomas* his wish to convey the sensation of touch induced a very literal and equally melodramatic interpretation: the farouche Christ guides Thomas's finger right inside his wound and both he and the onlookers wince at the impact. Their wrinkled brows are a favourite, at times overblown, device of Caravaggio's for conveying psychological tension. Furthermore, as if to lay all doubts about Christ's physical presence to rest, Caravaggio dwelt intently on his body, gratuitously hitching up his robe to reveal his thigh.

The indulgence, perhaps even encouragement, of Ciriaco and Giustiniani enabled Caravaggio to carry this polemical programme one stage further, for the *St John the Baptist* (with a ram, rather than the customary Lamb of God) and the *Victorious Cupid* are ebullient pederastic fantasies, burlesques on the high-flown Platonic poetry of Michelangelo's idealized *ignudi*. The *St John*, however, is also the first in a succession of increasingly serious single-figure paintings of this saint, which became the vehicle for the study of the young male nude (examples after *c*. 1603,

Kansas City, MO, Nelson–Atkins Mus. A. and Rome, Pal. Corsini). These paintings are paralleled by a series of studies of *St Jerome* that enabled Caravaggio to explore the appearance of age (examples 1605–6, Rome, Gal. Borghese; ?1605–8, Monserrat, Mus. Adadia).

The insistent realism of Caravaggio's private religious commissions of *c.* 1601–3 was not, however, exclusively stylistic, for he was always conscious of the need to focus the significance of the image through some striking piece of theatre. In the *Supper at Emmaus*, for example, the right-hand apostle's double armspan of surprise, which could be viewed simply as a gratuitous piece of illusionism, equally serves as the man's bewildered assertion that he had last seen the Christ with whom he is now confronted dead on the cross. Similarly, in the public commission of the *Entombment*, the outstretched arms of the Virgin double as a protective gesture and an allusion to the crucifixion, while the raised arms of Mary Cleophas incorporate a climax to the mourners' grief and hint at Christ's future resurrection. The quality of ritualistic mime that Caravaggio thereby brings to his gripping *tableaux vivants* has much in common with the modern theatre. However, Caravaggio's overriding sense of dramatic moment was bound, on occasion, to put him at odds with Counter-Reformation orthodoxy, especially when he presented those moments in terms of very ordinary human types and situations, as his rejected works and their 'corrected' replacements make clear.

In the case of the *St Matthew and the Angel*, there seems no reason to doubt Bellori's explanation that 'the priests took it down, saying that the figure [of St Matthew] with its legs crossed and its feet rudely exposed to the public had neither decorum nor the appearance of a saint', for in the second version Matthew's bare legs are covered and the soles of his feet (one of which had been thrust forward over the centre of the altar) turned into profile on the picture plane. In addition, the androgynous angel who nestles up against the gormless saint and guides his hand in its writing has been made more masculine and banished to a respectable distance up in the sky.

Similar factors seem to have pertained in the case of the *Death of the Virgin*, not least as regards the 'indecorous' portrayal of the Virgin. According to different accounts, Caravaggio had used either a live or drowned prostitute as his model—and there is certainly a corpse-like cast to his plain and bloated Virgin, with her lower legs exposed to reveal swollen ankles and twisted toes. In his replacement (1610–12; Rome, S Maria della Scala) Carlo Saraceni prettified her countenance and covered her legs. He also took account of what must have been another fundamental objection to Caravaggio's work: that it too much resembles an ordinary deathbed situation, for he not only depicts the Virgin seated and dying rather than prostrate and stone-dead, but indicates her imminent heavenly ascent by populating the upper part of the canvas with a choir of angels.

The *Madonna of the Serpent*, a politically correct work that symbolizes the extirpation of heresy, was also thought to be flawed in its characterization of sacred figures. Bellori, again, was surely right when he pinpointed the vulgar depiction of the Virgin and the nude Christ Child. The full frontal nudity of this urchin-like and somewhat over-aged Jesus and the (slight) décolletage of his mother were the culprits. However, it is not clear who it was within the individual church establishments, or perhaps even from higher ecclesiastical authority, who insisted on the unacceptability of these works. Reformed religious orders, which upheld the fundamentalist ideals of poverty and humility, may well have been attracted to Caravaggio's art, and the Augustinians, the Oratorians (in the Chiesa Nuova) and, increasingly, the Franciscans and the Capuchins seem to have had few problems with his down-to-earth vision.

The pressures of success (and criticism) may have played their part in further destabilizing Caravaggio's volatile character, and in the period from 1600 to 1606 he was frequently arraigned before the courts for a variety of offences. The picaresque saga culminated in his fateful killing of Ranuccio Tommasoni in Rome, on 29 May 1606, during a brawl occasioned by a disputed bet on a game of tennis—an event that forced him to flee the city under threat of capital punishment.

5. Flight to Latium, 1606. Caravaggio fled for protection to the estates owned by his Milanese feudal lords, the Colonna, south-east of Rome (at Paliano, Zagarolo and Palestrina), apparently painting while there a second version of the *Supper at Emmaus* (1606; Milan, Brera; see fig. 7) and a *Magdalene* (usually identified with a lost *Magdalene in Ecstasy* known through copies; see Cinotti, 1991, pl. 56). Comparison of the Brera *Supper* with the earlier version (London, N. G.) pinpoints Caravaggio's shift away from his mesmeric but ostentatious earlier rhetoric towards a much more assured integration of naturalism with content and expression. In the later picture gesture is more restrained, and sensuous surface detail gives way to a much darker pictorial field, on which only essential objects or actions are highlighted. The brushwork is more fluid and expresses mood and atmosphere while enhancing pictorial unity. Although this characteristic had begun to manifest itself in the later Roman years (e.g. in the *Madonna of Loreto*) and was in part simply the result of growing technical assurance, it became far more marked in his pictures from 1606 onwards, prompted by the increasing urgency of his life as a fugitive.

6. Last years in Naples, Malta and Sicily, 1606–10. Caravaggio's last four years were restless ones after the lengthy Roman sojourn. He travelled from the Colonna estates to Naples, where he stayed from before 6 October 1606 to early July 1607. A commission from the Conde de Benavente, Viceroy of Naples, for a *Crucifixion of St Andrew* (1607; Cleveland, OH, Mus. A.) demonstrates that he continued to receive patronage at the highest level. His last years were ones of considerable artistic experiment, and if pictures such as the *Madonna of the Rosary* (Vienna, Ksthist. Mus.) and the *Flagellation* (Rouen, Mus. B.-A.) were done in Naples in 1606–7, as seems probable, rather than in Rome, then his first Neapolitan period was productive and varied. The *Madonna of the Rosary* is both more lightly coloured and somewhat more idealized than the generally gloomy pictures done in Naples in the wake of the Brera *Supper*. Apart from the *Crucifixion of St Andrew* for the Viceroy, these include a small horizontal

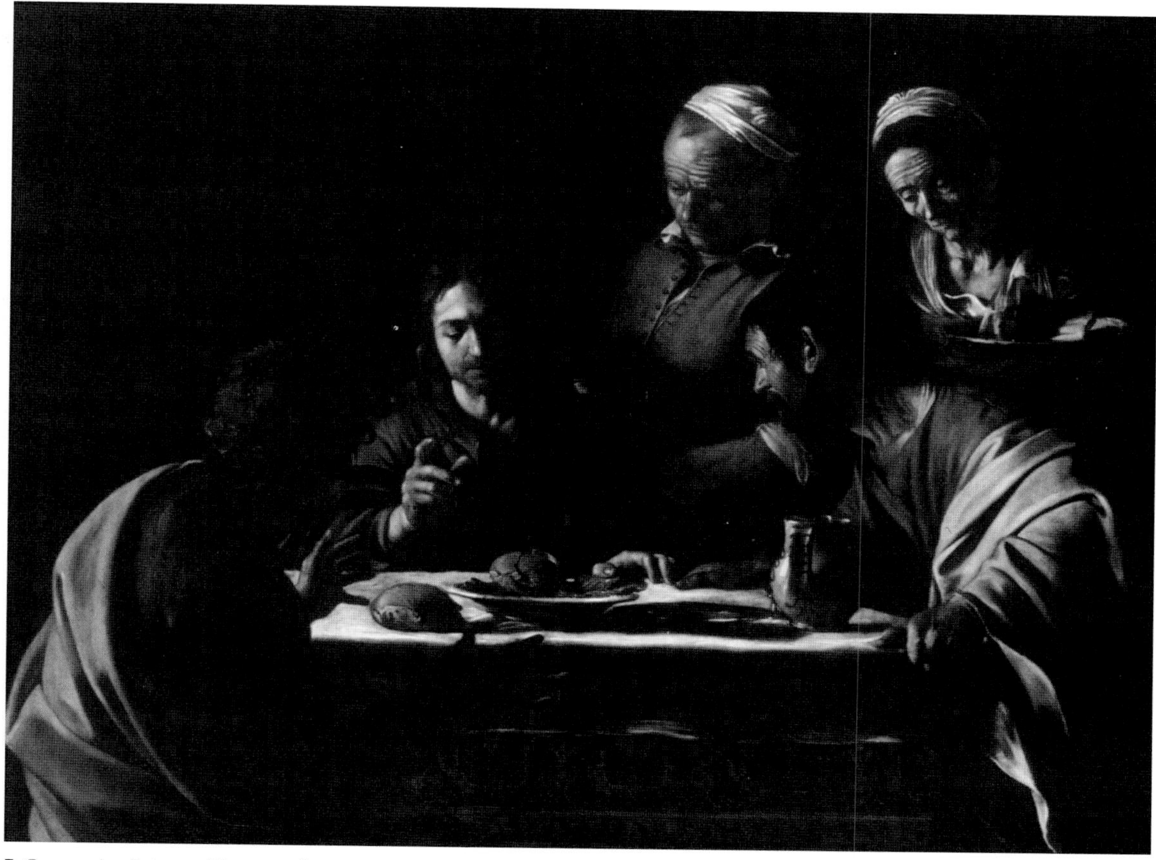

7. Caravaggio: *Supper at Emmaus*, oil on canvas, 1.41×1.75 m, 1606 (Milan, Pinacoteca di Brera)

painting, *David with the Head of Goliath* (Vienna, KSthist. Mus.), and two large altarpieces, the *Seven Works of Mercy*, completed by 7 January 1607, for the charitable confraternity, the Pio Monte della Misericordia (*in situ*), and the *Flagellation* (*c.* May–June 1607; Naples, Capodimonte) for the de Franchis Chapel in S Domenico Maggiore.

In these pictures Caravaggio maintained and even extended his passion for foregrounding his figures with bold foreshortenings against dark backgrounds, so preventing the eye from wandering too far into depth. Dramatic impact remains a top priority—so much so that the crowded *Seven Works of Mercy* is, in its complex, dynamic illusionism, perhaps the first fully Baroque altarpiece. These paintings are also distinguished by a new, unblinking sobriety of mood. In them Caravaggio's insights into human nature come closer than ever to the ardent ideals of the Counter-Reformation. It is a mood that is further enhanced by the emotive brushwork (the flesh of Christ's leg in the *Flagellation* has a transfigured quality that anticipates Rembrandt). The *Flagellation* also introduces, in the substantial gap over the heads of the figures, a compositional device that is developed in Caravaggio's subsequent Maltese and Sicilian canvases.

Caravaggio travelled next to Malta, in order to become a Knight of St John, and stayed there from 12 July 1607 to early October 1608. He was elected a Knight of Obedience of the Order of St John on 14 July 1608, and the huge, horizontal *Beheading of St John the Baptist* (see fig. 8), which he executed for the oratory of the conventual church, now co-cathedral, in Valletta in 1608 was probably his obligatory gift of passage into the Order. Among his other Maltese works are a *St Jerome* (1607–8; Valletta, St John), a portrait of the *Grand Master of the Knights Hospitallers, Alof de Wignacourt, with a pageboy* (1607–8; Paris, Louvre) and an unknown *Knight of Malta* (1607–8; Florence, Pitti). However, after 'an ill-considered quarrel' (Bellori) with a senior member of the Knights Hospitallers in the summer of 1608, Caravaggio was imprisoned. He escaped and fled to Sicily. Although he was under a capital sentence of banishment from Rome, he was never actively pursued by the papal authorities, and it is only at this point that a genuine threat arose to exacerbate his inner demons. For it is likely that the Knights pursued him in search of revenge. Bellori wrote of fear hunting him from place to place, and he made a fairly rapid progress around the Sicilian coast: to Syracuse (Oct–?Dec 1608), where Mario Minitti was responsible for gaining him the commission to paint the *Burial of St Lucy* (Syracuse, S Lucia al Sepolcro); Messina (?Jan–Aug 1609), where he left the *Adoration of the Shepherds* (see fig. 9) and the *Raising of Lazarus* (both Messina, Mus. Reg.); and finally to Palermo (?Aug–Sept 1609), where he painted the *Nativity with SS*

8. Caravaggio: *Beheading of St John the Baptist*, oil on canvas, 3.61×5.20 m, 1608 (Valletta, co-Cathedral of St John)

Francis and Lawrence (ex-Oratory of S Lorenzo, Palermo; stolen 1969).

In these Maltese and Sicilian canvases Caravaggio reiterated and expanded the empty space introduced in the Naples *Flagellation*, transforming the upper part of the picture into an assertive void. In three of them (the *Beheading*, the *Burial of St Lucy* and the *Adoration of the Shepherds*) it is accompanied by a greater perspectival depth. These new spatial modes are finely tuned to another development: the location of figures back from the picture plane, usually in tightly knit geometric groupings in which they are bound to each other with a minimum of gesture (e.g. in the arch formed by all the main actors in the *Beheading*, emphatically located in front of a stone gateway; and the friezes of figures slotted, coulisse-like, into the near or middle distance of the Sicilian paintings). Figures are now smaller in relation to the setting and, because of this and their loss of assertive individuality, more insignificant.

The combined effect of these strategies is to encourage a more detached and contemplative reading of the drama, at arm's length, and a related sense of the fixed and tragic fate of man. Caravaggio's conversion to this new mode was, however, not total, and in the Palermo *Nativity* he mixed it with the foregrounded illusionism of his previous work. These pictures attain a new emotional intensity, conveyed primarily by an almost total abandonment of any but the most essential gestures and a corresponding channelling of feeling into restrained postures and intense facial expressions. The downcast gaze, always a favourite of Caravaggio but now imbued with a deeper sense of melancholy and pathos, becomes a leitmotif. In the Maltese and Sicilian altarpieces it acquires added resonance from the fact that the focus of attention for the onlookers is invariably on or near the ground: the corpses of St John, St Lucy and Lazarus or the figure of the Christ Child in the Messina *Adoration* and Palermo *Nativity*. In the Sicilian paintings Caravaggio may have been encouraged in this path of humility by the fact that most were done for Mendicant churches (Capuchins; Franciscans). But he equally took advantage of the archetypal subject-matter to transform them into more generalized discourses on life and death.

Caravaggio returned to Naples in September or October 1609. Here, having unsuccessfully tried to placate the Grand Master of the Order of St John, Alof de Wignacourt, with a *'Herodias' with the Head of St John the Baptist in a Basin* (either the *Salome* in the Pal. Real, Madrid, or that in the N. G., London), Caravaggio was surrounded outside the notorious Locanda del Cerriglio by a group of armed men (probably Knights of St John or their agents) and badly wounded in the face (as reported in a letter of 24 Oct 1609). Despite this near fatal incident, Caravaggio produced a remaining handful of masterpieces, mainly towards the end of this second Neapolitan period; his one altarpiece, for the church of S Anna dei Lombardi, a *Resurrection*, was apparently destroyed in 1805, although it may be reflected in the *Resurrection* by Louis Finson (1610; Aix-en-Provence, St Jean-de-Malte). In the *Denial of St Peter* (Switzerland, priv. col., see Cinotti, 1991, pl. 81), the

9. Caravaggio: *Adoration of the Shepherds*, oil on canvas, 3.14×2.11 m, 1609 (Messina, Museo Regionale Messina)

St John the Baptist and *David with the Head of Goliath* (both Rome, Gal. Borghese) he kept the figures well up towards the picture plane and filling much of the canvas. In one very late work, however, the *Martyrdom of St Ursula* (before 11 May 1610; Naples, Banca Commerciale Italiana) for Marcantonio Doria, he combined a fully foregrounded relief of figures with an echoing void above their heads. The two Borghese pictures, both executed in the fluid and painterly manner of Caravaggio's final years, are distinguished by his propensity for harnessing his own increasingly melancholic insights into the human condition to the iconography of Christian art. The young nude in the *St John the Baptist* is a far cry from his ebullient predecessor (Rome, Pin. Capitolina) or the somewhat contrived brooding of Ottavio Costa's late Roman version (*c.* 1603–5; Kansas City, MO, Nelson–Atkins Mus.); he merely asserts his presence by his existence. It is Caravaggio's last, affectionately lingering essay on a favourite theme. The *David with the Head of Goliath* (see fig. 10 below), by contrast, transforms the more transcendental mood of the slightly earlier Vienna version into a brooding, poetic meditation on the artist's own mortality. For the head of Goliath, proffered to the viewer by David, who glances down at it with a sad (perhaps valedictory) look, bears the features of Caravaggio himself—ravaged, as might be expected by the summer of 1610.

The *St John* formed part of the cargo Caravaggio had with him as he sailed north in July 1610; the *David* may have been sent to Rome in advance or left behind in Naples for the time being. They were apparently gifts for Pope Paul V and Cardinal Scipione Borghese, part of a deal brokered above all, it would seem, by Cardinal Ferdinando Gonzaga and Caravaggio's feudal mistress, Costanza Colonna, whereby Caravaggio was to be pardoned for the murder of Tommasoni and allowed to return to Rome. In such a context, the *David with the Head of Goliath* acquires an altogether new significance—as a characteristically pungent conceit, with Caravaggio offering up to the art-loving Borghese his fictive head instead of the real one that he might have been obliged to forfeit. But he was not to enjoy the pleasure of delivering it in person. When his boat put in to Porto Ercole, Caravaggio was mistaken for someone else and arrested. Although released after two days, he died of fever within a week.

II. Working methods and technique.

Caravaggio was credited by his early biographers with introducing two radical working procedures aimed at enhancing the effect of reality: painting his pictures directly from posed models and illuminating the models (and by extension the pictures) with directed light from a high source, variously identified as a window or lamp (for discussion of Caravaggio's lighting, *see* §I above). Visual and technical analysis alike confirm the essential accuracy of this account.

There are precedents for such approaches both as regards lighting and the use of models. However, their combination and sustained application by Caravaggio in his mature religious art did constitute a significantly novel agenda, especially when viewed, as he surely intended, in opposition to the more idealized formulation of the human figure and more calculated articulation of movement that his great classicizing contemporary Annibale Carracci arrived at through extensive use of preparatory drawings and then subjected to a generally much more even lighting in his finished paintings.

Not one drawing by Caravaggio has been identified; he undoubtedly limited his drawing to the most ephemeral of compositional studies, which he discarded as soon as they had served their purpose as guides to the posing of models from whom he would then paint. There is some evidence that such procedures were not altogether unknown in northern Italy during the 16th century, especially in a Venice that reputedly advocated the primacy of painting over drawing. But the precise nature of Venetian practice and the extent, therefore, to which Caravaggio may have pushed it to extremes, remains conjectural. His devotion to the medium of oil paint was also rooted in Venetian priorities, although Caravaggio went further than most of his north Italian precursors in totally avoiding fresco. Nearly all of Caravaggio's paintings were on canvas. The weaves vary greatly over the course of his career to include almost all of those available at the time.

Only two of Caravaggio's surviving paintings are on panel—the Odescalchi *Conversion of St Paul* (cypress) and the Vienna *David* (poplar). The fact that cypress is one of the most expensive and durable of woods, that Cerasi was one of the richest men in Rome and that Caravaggio's replacement version, probably done after Cerasi's death, was on canvas confirm that the choice of support was the patron's and that the artist himself preferred the more receptive and pliable nature of canvas—as might be expected from a painter trained in northern Italy, devoted to naturalistic effects and intent on working '*alla prima*'. The Vienna *David* was painted on top of a pre-existing Mannerist-style picture of vertical alignment, but Caravaggio turned it on its side, in keeping with his regular preference for the horizontal in private commissions of more than one figure. This may have been related to the greater ease with which posed models could be accommodated to such a format.

Caravaggio seems often in his early years in Rome to have employed a grey or grey–green ground characteristic of 16th-century Lombard painters such as Moretto, Moroni and Peterzano. It is apparently evident in the *Sick Little Bacchus*, the *Boy with a Basket of Fruit*, the *Penitent Magdalene*, *The Fortune-teller* and *The Cardsharps* (Christiansen, 1986). Schneider (restorer, and contributor to the 1991–2 monographic exh. cat.), however, first cast doubt on the findings and then, according to Christiansen (1992), conceded them—while maintaining that the grey was superimposed on an underlying brown ground. Whatever the case, the presence of grey immediately beneath the final picture layer in these works now seems agreed and plays a part in determining the comparatively light tonality of the finished paint surface. Whether it is also an indication of the pictures' priority among the early works is less certain.

At some point Caravaggio switched wholesale to darker grounds—especially the reddish-brown that was favoured by those in contemporary Roman circles (including Arpino) and was to become almost universal in the 17th century. But it is likely that Caravaggio experimented occasionally with brown grounds at a very early stage (e.g. in the Longhi *Boy Bitten by a Lizard*). Caravaggio's subsequent devotion to dark grounds was closely bound up with the evolution of his chiaroscuro. They helped to absorb the middle tones and intensify shadows—the former enhancing tonal unity, the latter augmenting the effect of relief by establishing sharper contrasts with the strongly lit areas. In later years, when he worked more rapidly and was less concerned with finish, he allowed the ground to show through in several places and to act as a middle tone in its own right.

The precise colours of Caravaggio's dark grounds are only gradually offering up their secrets to technical analysis. They can be made up of several different colours (as in the Detroit *Magdalene*), thereby engendering some very vibrant effects. While the overall appearance in his middle years was, more often than not, of a deep reddish-brown (as in the London *Supper at Emmaus*), it could also veer more towards umber or even pure red (as in the Capitoline *St John*). Towards the end of his career, he sometimes opted for even darker grounds, which included a good deal of black (e.g. the National Gallery *Salome*).

That Caravaggio used two principal techniques for establishing the outlines of his figures on the ground, brush drawing in a light value and incisions with a sharp instrument such as a stylus, is confirmed by X-rays, infrared reflectography, raking light and the evidence of the naked eye. The fact that both procedures are evident only along certain contours does not necessarily imply that they were not more extensive. Some of the lines may be concealed by paint, which is, in several instances, impervious to X-ray. Indeed, the brush-drawn outlines are likely to have extended throughout the composition.

The incised lines are more problematical. While the use of incisions for transferring whole cartoons to plaster or panel was traditional, as was the technique of incising straight lines to mark out the edges of architectural or semi-architectural elements such as tables, Caravaggio's employment of them in a sporadic fashion along the curved contours of parts of limbs or faces has no known precedent in Renaissance art. Yet this might simply be due to the fact that so few 16th- and 17th-century pictures have been examined with a view to finding them. It may also be that there are more of them underneath the rather thick paint of pictures such as the London *Supper at Emmaus*, but it is more likely that Caravaggio used them only to mark summarily the position of certain key contours, either in order to 'fix' the position of a model's pose on the canvas or as guidelines to composition, perhaps both. While the latter procedure could have been an established one (and had certainly been followed by ancient Roman wall painters), the former may have been a relative novelty generated by his practice of working directly from the model.

Apart from these enigmatic incisions, Caravaggio also sometimes used the end of a brush handle to scrape away surface paint and to create an embossed effect, as in the drapery of the *St Catherine*; while on at least one occasion, in *The Cardsharps*, he resorted to the Titianesque expedient of using the tips of his fingers (to dab on the decorative markings on the older cheat's doublet).

The evidence for Caravaggio having painted directly from models is more substantial than the speculation about the role of incisions. In the first instance, he clearly used the same model for different pictures—most unequivocally in the *St Catherine* and the *Conversion of the Magdalene*. Correspondingly, there is a succession of strikingly different models for the same character in different pictures. Such a policy did not prevent him from making minor adjustments to their features to improve characterization. Indeed X-ray and infra-red photographs of one picture, the *Sacrifice of Isaac* (*c.* 1603; Florence, Uffizi), seem to indicate that he used the same model in two different poses for the figures of both Isaac and the angel, modifying his features considerably on the final paint surface, especially for the angel. It is doubtful, however, that this was his normal practice as regards facial appearance. It seems to have been determined in this instance by the apparently unusual circumstance of him using the same model for different figures within a single painting.

This case raises equally fundamental (and as yet unanswered) questions as to whether Caravaggio always painted from one model at a time, and then collaged the individual life studies together, or whether, as might be assumed, he sometimes posed more than one figure. Indeed, it is difficult to imagine him not resorting at some stage in the pictorial process to group posing in order to calculate the full effects of composition and lighting.

The comparatively few surviving works by Caravaggio need not suggest that he was a slow worker. Indeed the implication of van Mander's account that he did not work steadfastly is that he worked relatively quickly when he did (*see* §III below). The grainy texture of a number of pictures suggests that he used a drying agent (perhaps litharge) in order to expedite production. For all that, his early and middle period works are immaculately finished, in the best Lombard traditions. The degree of smooth-finished detail that he achieved would have been possible only with a fluid oil medium (probably linseed), perhaps diluted with turpentine, and applied with soft brushes. The paint surface in the early works, however, tends to be thinner than in the usually dense application of his maturity.

Despite Caravaggio's predominantly smooth application of paint, there is a marked undercurrent in his work of more expressive, Venetian-type brushwork. It is especially evident in his handling of draperies, not least in the multidirectional and fluid brushstrokes of such early works as the *Concert of Youths* and the *Ecstasy of St Francis*; or in the green drape of the Magdalene in the Detroit *Conversion*, where he built the colour effect out of juxtaposed patches of variously brushed colour, rather than through his usual superimposition. Such effects go hand in hand with an equally Venetian concern with beautiful colour chords. Several of the works of the 1590s are distinguished by an almost equal fascination with both colour and texture, and while both are, at least superficially, subordinated in the middle years to tone and finish, closer inspection often reveals even there beautifully subtle passages of colour and a controlled mastery of the interaction of smooth, glazed areas with brief flourishes of impasto or dexterously free brushwork.

Caravaggio's tendencies towards the Venetian tradition acquired a renewed and highly individualistic lease of life in his last years. By then he had abandoned his previous obsession with the minute imitation of nature, opting instead for a much freer technique. It is as if his masterly brush-drawing method, originally used primarily for preparatory purposes, had come to the surface and dictated the aesthetic tenor of the image. A mixture of free-flowing and sporadic brushwork allows the priming to show through in several places, acting as a middle tone. Impastoed highlights and glazed shadows are applied in a bold, schematic fashion that is highly evocative of form when seen from a distance, but almost abstract at close quarters. The pools of shadow overlaying eye sockets, for example, become either like Giant Panda markings, barely translucent, or like ragged stains, while the highlights that indicate their raised surrounds are regular, broad sweeps of impastoed white.

Caravaggio's limited palette from the time he espoused chiaroscuro onwards (*c.* 1598–9) was dominated by red and yellow ochres, earth colours (such as umber), charcoal black, lead white, lead tin yellow, green resinate of copper and cinnabar red. Earths and ochres predominated, and brighter colours were always veiled. Bellori's assertion that Caravaggio considered cinnabar red and azure blue poisons among the colours and that, when he did use them, he toned them down is borne out both by observation and technical analysis. He used blue very rarely outside the Virgin's mantle, and his cinnabar reds (vermilions) are muted with earth and other dark colours in the drape of the Capitoline *St John.* While he obviously mixed colours (both on the palette and the canvas), he tended to keep his pigments pure and extended this habit to his treatment of shadows, where he usually darkened with deeper tints of the underlying object rather than with some other dark colour.

III. Character and personality.

Caravaggio's widely mythologized character and personality remain an enigma. His fiery temper, arbitrary behaviour, propensity for violence and bohemian way of life are amply documented in strictly contemporary records. His subsequent 17th-century aesthetic detractors (especially Bellori) had no need of exaggeration when they invoked his remarkably unstable mentality in explanation of his, to them, deviant art. Yet it is important to guard against reductive interpretations: his demonization by 17th-century critics was by turns crude and subtle, and modern assessments can be equally one-track, either in the inclination to brand him a psychopath or in the tendency to give centre-stage to his homosexuality.

The few contemporary characterizations were, for the most part, neither precise nor judgemental. What they agreed on was Caravaggio's extreme strangeness. An adjective that occurs twice is 'stravagantissimo', which can be rendered, roughly, as 'very strange/bizarre/eccentric'. 'Stravagante' is difficult to translate from the Italian, since its meaning depends on the context in which it is used and, even then, does not always have a precise focus. It always implies a transgression of normal behaviour, but this can assume many forms, from foibles and mild eccentricities to actions bordering on, and crossing, the threshold of sanity. It is often used indulgently in connection with the artistic temperament. In Caravaggio's case, however, the use of the superlative form, 'stravagantissimo', implies an unusual degree of 'extravagance', even for an artist.

The word first surfaces in a letter of 24 August 1605, from Fabio Masetti to Count Giovanni Battista Laderchi, in which Masetti quotes Cardinal del Monte as saying that Caravaggio is 'uno cervello stravagantissimo' ('an extremely odd person'), in a context that implies that this made him very unreliable. The designation probably soon became common currency and was used by Giulio Mancini, who believed that Caravaggio's 'stravaganze' served to shorten his life by at least ten years and partly to diminish the glory he had gained through his profession. Mancini's deployment of the noun in this extended sense to hint at a life of excess as well as an unusual character indicates the flexibility of the term. Neither can such views be dismissed as the spiteful gossip of the Roman intelligentsia. A provincial Sicilian patron in Messina, Niccolò di Giacomo, arrived at a remarkably similar conclusion in the summer of 1609, when he referred to Caravaggio in a memorandum as 'this painter with a highly disturbed brain ["cervello stravolto"]'.

Caravaggio's quick temper and provocative speech were intimately implicated in the series of violent incidents that punctuated his life. Karel van Mander (1604) wrote that he 'does not pursue his studies steadfastly; so that after a fortnight's work he will swagger about for a month or two with a sword at his side and with a servant following him, from one tennis-court to the next, ever ready to engage in a fight or an argument, with the result that it is most difficult to get along with him'. Some of the details of this account are verifiable from trial records and newspaper reports. The former show that Caravaggio was brought to trial no less than 11 times between October 1600 and September 1605. The charges ranged widely. They included beating an acquaintance with a stick; wounding with a sword or hunting-knife (twice); throwing stones (twice, including once at the window of his ex-landlady); throwing a plate of artichokes at a waiter whom he deemed to have insulted him; carrying a sword and dagger without a licence; swearing crudely at a constable; and, together with the painter Orazio Gentileschi and the architect Onorio Longhi, writing satirical verses about the painter Baglione. If Caravaggio's hot temper and sharp tongue were often the immediate catalysts of hostilities, more deep-seated causes were obviously at work. The strongest impression to emerge is of Caravaggio's enduring anger. Its roots in early experience may have included feelings of resentment at the loss of his father when he was only six and of his mother when he was eighteen (for psychoanalytic interpretations, see Röttgen, 1974, and Hibbard, 1983).

There was also a social dimension to Caravaggio's delinquency, as his adversary, Baglione, conceded when he stated that Caravaggio was often in the company of men who were as belligerent as he was. He moved in a bohemian circle, which included soldiers of the papal guard, a bookseller, a perfumier and the Brescian painter Prospero Orsi, as well as Longhi and Gentileschi. Its members often accompanied him on his perambulations and were always among the first to give evidence in his favour or bail him out when he was apprehended. There is no reason to believe that Caravaggio was the undisputed leader of the clique, and some to show that others, such as Onorio Longhi, played an equally prominent part. Sandrart claimed that the group took as its motto the Stoic tag 'nec spe, nec metu' (Lat.: 'without hope or fear'), which gives a self-consciously philosophical twist to Baglione's avowal of Caravaggio's excessively fearless nature.

However, there is also evidence to suggest that Caravaggio's acts of violence were, to some degree, rooted in traditional conceptions of 'honour'—as when, on his own testimony, he wounded Mariano Pasqualone in the back of the head for having insulted him and then refusing to settle the matter with swords; or, if Sandrart is to be believed, when he issued a similar duelling challenge to the Cavaliere d'Arpino. Whatever its causes, Caravaggio's extremism had important implications for his art. The bold contrasts of his chiaroscuro, the sharp intensity of his characterizations and his insistence on the superiority of the seen over the ideal do not seem unconnected with his uncompromising way of seeing the world in terms of polarities, and other people as either for him or against him.

Caravaggio's self-absorption also manifests itself artistically in the self-portraits that he introduced in several pictures. They have no simple explanation. An element of attitudinizing seems to co-exist, in some instances, with genuine exploration of his own emotions. There is also, perhaps, a hint of narcissism. Two other documented aspects of Caravaggio's personality could also be loosely termed narcissistic: a preoccupation with his own sartorial elegance and his homosexual leanings (which psychoanalysis explains in terms of narcissistic object-choice). Knowledge of the former is based on Bellori's backhanded observation that Caravaggio 'availed himself of only the finest materials and velvets worn by noblemen; but once he had put on a suit of clothes, he changed it only when it had fallen into rags'—a plausibly bohemian detail.

The precise nature of Caravaggio's sexuality remains controversial, perhaps because the evidence points so unequivocally towards his having been bisexual. The only references to the matter in his lifetime (in the Roman trial transcripts) indicate that he consorted with prostitutes and had a kept boy. A certain Lena 'who stood in the Piazza Navona' was, according to Mariano Pasqualone's testimony on 29 July 1605, 'Caravaggio's girl'. While in his testimony of 28 August 1603, at the Baglione libel trial, Mao Salini claimed that one of the people who distributed copies of the satirical verses was a youth called Giovan Battista, a *bardassa* of Caravaggio and Onorio Longhi. Some modern commentators have claimed that *bardassa* in this context may simply mean servant, but this is unlikely. A *bardassa* was a bardash or catamite—a boy kept for sexual favours.

10. Caravaggio: *David with the Head of Goliath*, oil on canvas, 1.25×1.01 m, 1610 (Rome, Galleria Borghese)

The subsequent 17th- and early 18th-century sources refer only to boys, thereby reinforcing the impression of a predominantly homosexual reputation. Manili, in his guide to the Villa Borghese (1650), stated that the figure of David in the Borghese *David with the Head of Goliath* (see fig. 10) was modelled on the artist's *Caravaggino* (his 'little Caravaggio'); while the English writer Richard Symonds was informed about the same time by those in the Palazzo Giustiniani that the model used by Caravaggio for Vincenzo Giustiniani's provocative Cupid was the future Caravaggist painter Cecco del Caravaggio, 'who was his servant or boy that laid with him'. Such perceptions were doubtless also fortified through scrutiny of Caravaggio's art. The aura of homoeroticism that Caravaggio's half-lengths and 'Michelangelesque' nudes exude both enhances and receives corroboration from the rumoured tradition of his pederasty. Nevertheless, Cavavaggio's female figures can also be strongly sensual.

IV. Influence.

Caravaggio's bold style, naturalistic ambitions and revolutionary working procedures attracted a large artistic following in the first 30 years of the 17th century. For much of this period Caravaggism was the main stylistic alternative in Italy to the classicism of the Carracci. It also held a great appeal for many of the northern European artists visiting Rome and Naples (perhaps in part because of its compatibility with traditional Netherlandish conceptions of naturalism) and was soon transported back to their native lands. It did not survive as a movement much beyond 1630 (except in provincial locations), yet, in a broader sense, Caravaggio's influence was pervasive throughout the century, with his realism and chiaroscuro making more than a passing impression on such major figures as Rubens, Rembrandt, Velázquez and Murillo.

However, Caravaggism was never a homogeneous studio style like those propagated by the Carracci, Rubens and Rembrandt. It was, rather, disseminated through direct contact with his works and those of his close followers. A familiarity with at least some of Caravaggio's paintings, usually in Rome (or, to a lesser extent, Naples) and an inclination to adopt both his motifs and the idiosyncracies of his iconography are essential conditions of a genuine Caravaggism. However, for the very reason that such influence usually derived from study of Caravaggio's paintings rather than personal tuition, the boundaries of the movement were always loosely defined, with the majority of Caravaggists selecting only certain elements of the master's art and grafting them on to their own, sometimes quite different, regional or national traditions.

The process of emulation began in Caravaggio's own lifetime. Baglione, Orazio Gentileschi, Orazio Borgianni, Guido Reni and, probably, Carlo Saraceni all adopted aspects of his style while he was still in Rome. He seems to have had at least one pupil/assistant in Rome, Cecco del Caravaggio, and conceivably another, Bartolomeo Manfredi. After Caravaggio's flight from Rome in 1606, a Caravaggist movement began to develop there, with Orazio Gentileschi, Carlo Saraceni and Bartolomeo Manfredi in the vanguard. It was Manfredi, above all, who popularized the Caravaggesque style in the second decade of the 17th century. One of his most influential contributions was to reinvigorate the subject-matter of Caravaggio's early narrative genre pictures with the chiaroscuro of his mature art. Manfredi had a strong impact on the many artists who passed through his flourishing studio in the period *c.* 1615–22, not least on a large contingent of northern Europeans.

Among the Dutch Caravaggists (who hailed mainly from Utrecht), Hendrick ter Brugghen alone does not seem to have responded to Manfredi. In fact he left Rome in 1614. By contrast, Dirck van Baburen, Gerrit van Honthorst and Jan van Bijlert, as well as the Walloon painter Nicolas Régnier, were all greatly influenced by the 'Manfredi Manner', as were the Frenchmen Simon Vouet, Valentin de Boulogne and Nicolas Tournier, and the probably French Master of the Judgement of Solomon. Their respective styles drew freely on the works of Caravaggio, Manfredi and even other Caravaggists of the first generation (*see* UTRECHT CARAVAGGISTI).

Caravaggio's last four *Wanderjahre* also spawned Caravaggist enclaves in the south, most notably and enduringly in Naples, where Carlo Sellitto and Giovanni Battista Caracciolo were among his closest disciples. Other Caravaggists operating in Italy in the period *c.* 1610–40 included the Italians Artemisia Gentileschi, Giovanni Serodine, Orazio Riminaldi, Giovanni Antonio Galli (lo Spadarino), Rutilio Manetti, Pietro Paolini, Bartolomeo Cavarozzi and Angelo Caroselli; the Frenchmen Claude Vignon, Guy François, Trophime Bigot and the Pensionante del Saraceni; the Lorraine artists Jean Leclerc and Georges de la Tour (one of the greatest and most original of Caravaggio's disciples); the Flemings Louis Finson, Theodoor Rombouts and Gerard Seghers; the Dutchman Matthias Stom; the Spaniards Alonzo Rodriguez, Jusepe de Ribera and Juan Bautisto Maino; and the Maltese Andrea Risto.

V. Critical reception and posthumous reputation.

The preoccupations and boundaries of nearly all subsequent Caravaggio criticism were set by an exceptionally rich crop of written responses to his art during the 17th century. Contrary to received opinion, none of these was unreservedly hostile, and some were strongly affirmative. All praised his tremendous powers of imitation and his colouring. The early commentators and those from northern Europe were the most enthusiastic—not afraid of voicing specific objections, but without seeking to minimize his stature. They included the Dutch artist Karel van Mander (1604), the papal physician and connoisseur Giulio Mancini (*c.* 1617–30), Caravaggio's patron Vincenzo Giustiniani (*c.* 1620–30) and the German painter Joachim von Sandrart (1675–9). Nonetheless, the classic–idealist objection to the unadorned quality of his naturalism, already implicit in Federico Zuccaro's reputed disdain for the 'Giorgionismo' of the Contarelli laterals, received a remarkably early written airing in the manuscript treatise on painting (*c.* 1607–15) of Monsignor Giambattista Agucchi, a close friend of Annibale Carracci and Domenichino. For him, Caravaggio, like the ancient sculptor Demetrios of Alopeke, had 'abandoned the idea of beauty, intent only on the attainment of likeness'. Such views became increasingly the common currency of art criticism, reinforced no doubt by the enduring popularity of Bolognese classicism as an aesthetic yardstick.

Gradually, certain criticisms raised in an even-handed way by Mancini—about Caravaggio's excessive dependence on the model and consequent shortcomings in the articulation of dramatic narrative and the convincing portrayal of movement, as well as about his 'unnatural' lighting—became, in the hands of academically minded painters and literati of the mid-century (Carducho, 1633; Baglione, 1642; Scannelli, 1657; Bellori, 1672; and Scaramuccia, 1674), the linchpin of a sustained drive to marginalize his achievement. These academic critics vied with one another in their search for the most damning epithet, but they also frequently used each other's terminology. The language of criticism was self-perpetuating. Carducho's witty diatribe, in which he demonized Caravaggio as the artistic equivalent of the Anti-Christ—an alluring 'Anti-Michelangelo', whose 'impetuous, unheard-of and outrageous technique of painting without preparation' had seduced all too many artists from the 'true doctrine' of study and draughtsmanship—was only the most colourful formulation of what was fast becoming a critical cliché.

More subtle, and much more influential, was Bellori's long and detailed *Vite*, a rhetorical masterpiece that all the more effectively damns Caravaggio with faint praise by setting his art for the first time within a coherent framework of historical development. Caravaggio's distinction was to have supplanted the artifice of the late Maniera with a vigorous naturalism rooted in his Lombard heritage. 'But', added Bellori with schoolmasterly aplomb, 'how easy it is to fall into one extreme while fleeing another.' Caravaggio and his followers departed from Mannerism only to imitate nature *too* closely. Running through Bellori's seemingly judicious and detached analysis, which deftly uses the paraphernalia of scholarship to legitimize his prejudices, is an unrelenting vein of opposition. He orchestrated all the previously voiced criticisms into a finely textured onslaught, in which every individual observation is ingeniously slotted into the overall pattern of disapproval. Caravaggio's temperamental behaviour, for instance, is a manifestation of his 'dark nature', which, in turn, is reflected in his dark style. Moral overtones permeate the essay. For Bellori, Caravaggio's dependence on the model was doubly pernicious. On the one hand, it was too easy, encouraging young artists to think that they could neglect study and take a short-cut to fame. On the other, it engendered contempt for beautiful things and destroyed the 'authority' of Raphael and the Antique. In their place it put the 'vile' things of unidealized nature. Indeed, there is a clear element both of class distinction and aesthetic disgust in Bellori's critique. He claimed that Caravaggio's followers gratuitously sought out vulgar and ugly forms, including working-class costume, rusty armour, chipped pottery, wrinkled and blemished skin, and limbs disfigured by disease. Caravaggio's rejection of the Platonism, which was central to Bellori's conception of an improving art, was a threat at one and the same time to religion, high culture and social hierarchy. Bellori also coined one influential critical refinement: that 'his first style, sweet and pure in colour, was his best'.

Bellori's classicizing critique held absolute sway for well over a century and remained a major force for much longer. Some of his more purely art-historical judgements (about Caravaggio's chronology and stylistic development, for example) even continue to guide the view of the artist today, perhaps more than they should. On the other hand, while several 19th-century critics accepted Bellori's idealizing perspective, the impact of the Romantic movement, with its stress on individual genius and artistic temperament, made others more indulgent to Caravaggio's personal and artistic idiosyncracies. The re-espousal of the legitimacy of individualism in art went hand-in-hand with a new relativism that had developed, from the 18th century onwards, along with the discipline of art history itself. Caravaggio's style became merely one among the available alternatives.

The 20th century has spawned a veritable Caravaggio industry, which has become fixated, at different stages, on a wide variety of issues—from his anticipation of the techniques of the cinema (Longhi) to his status as an icon for the gay community. Style, iconography and, latterly, technique have been extensively (though not exhaustively) explored. Moving through the sometimes confusing plethora of analysis has been a stabilizing core of solid connoisseurship, which has often served to focus wider discussions. Its most brilliant practitioners have been Roberto Longhi, Denis Mahon and Mina Gregori. The attributional debate has witnessed both increases and contractions of Caravaggio's oeuvre. However, it now stands on the threshold of a new phase. For as our knowledge of the individual styles of Caravaggio's followers grows, so the rapid expansion of the master's own oeuvre in recent years will need to be put to the test.

BIBLIOGRAPHY

EARLY SOURCES

The most important of the biographies and critical accounts listed below are van Mander, Mancini, Baglione and Bellori. Most of the relevant passages from these four sources are given in English in H. Hibbard: *Caravaggio* (London, 1983).

K. van Mander: *Schilder-boeck* ([1603]–1604)

G. B. Agucchi: *Trattato dellpittura* (MS.; Rome, *c.* 1607–15); in D. Mahon: *Studies in Seicento Art and Theory* (London, 1947) [brief but pregnant critique from a classicizing stand-point]

G. Mancini: *Considerazioni sulla pittura* (MS.; Rome, *c.* 1617–30); ed. A. Marucchi and L. Salerno, 2 vols (Rome, 1956–7)

V. Giustiniani: 'Letter on Painting to Theodor Ameyden' (MS., Rome, *c.* 1620–30); in *Lettere memorabili dell'Ab. Michele Giustiniani* (Rome, 1675); also in G. Bottari and S. Ticozzi, eds: *Raccolta di lettere sulla pittura* (Milan, 1822–5), vi; Eng. trans. in R. Enggass and J. Brown: *Italy and Spain, 1600–1750*, Sources & Doc. Hist. A. (Englewood Cliffs, 1970)

V. Carducho: *Diálogos de la pintura* (Madrid, 1633); Eng. trans. in R. Enggass and J. Brown: *Italy and Spain, 1600–1750*, Sources & Doc. Hist. A. (Englewood Cliffs, 1970)

G. Baglione: *Vite* (1642); ed. V. Mariani (1935)

F. Scannelli: *Il microcosmo della pittura, overo trattato diviso in due libri* (Cesena, 1657); ed. R. Lepori, 2 vols (Bologna, 1980); Eng. trans. in Hibbard (London, 1983)

G. P. Bellori: *Vite* (1672); ed. E. Borea (1976)

L. Scaramuccia: *Le finezze de' pennelli italiani* (Pavia, 1674); Eng. trans. in Hibbard (London, 1983) [only contains a brief but critically interesting ref. to Caravaggio's lost painting of the *Resurrection* in S Anna dei Lombardi, Naples]

J. von Sandrart: *Teutsche Academie* (1675–9); ed. A. R. Peltzer (1925); Eng. trans. in Hibbard (London, 1983)

F. Susinno: *Le vite de' pittori messinesi e di altri che fiorirono in Messina* (MS.; Messina, 1724); ed. V. Martinelli (Florence, 1960); Eng. trans. of parts of his life of Caravaggio in Hibbard (London, 1983)

GENERAL

D. Mahon: *Studies in Seicento Art and Theory* (London, 1947)
R. Wittkower: *Art and Architecture in Italy, 1600–1750*, Pelican Hist. A. (Harmondsworth, 1958, rev. 1973 and 1980)
S. Freedberg: *Circa 1600: A Revolution of Style in Italian Painting* (Cambridge, MA, and London, 1983)

MONOGRAPHS, EXHIBITION CATALOGUES, SYMPOSIA

M. Marangoni: *Il Caravaggio* (Florence, 1922)
Mostra del Caravaggio e dei Caravaggeschi (exh. cat. by R. Longhi and others, Milan, Pal. Reale, 1951)
R. Longhi: *Il Caravaggio* (Milan, 1952, Rome, 2/1968, 3/1982, with intro. by G. Previtali)
R. Hinks: *Michelangelo da Caravaggio* (London, 1953)
F. Baumgart: *Caravaggio: Kunst und Wirklichkeit* (Berlin, 1955)
W. Friedlaender: *Caravaggio Studies* (Princeton, 1955, rev. New York, 1969)
Artists in 17th-century Rome (exh. cat., ed. D. Mahon and D. Sutton; London, Wildenstein's, 1955) [entry by D. Mahon on *St John the Baptist* (?1602; Rome, Pin. Capitolina)]
R. Jullian: *Caravage* (Lyon and Paris, 1961)
M. Kitson: *The Complete Paintings of Caravaggio* (London, 1969, rev. Harmondsworth, 1985)
Caravaggio e Caravaggeschi nelle gallerie di Firenze (exh. cat., ed. E. Borea; Florence, Pitti, 1970)
Caravaggio and his Followers (exh. cat. by R. Spear, Cleveland, OH, Mus. A., 1971) [cat. rev. New York, 1975]
Immagine del Caravaggio (exh. cat., ed. M. Cinotti; Bergamo, Pal. Ragione; Caravaggio; Brescia; 1973)
Caravaggio y el naturalismo español (exh. cat. by A. Pérez-Sánchez, Seville, Alcázar, 1973)
Burl. Mag., cxvi (1974) [special issue on Caravaggio and followers; includes several articles on the *Conversion of the Magdalene* (Detroit, MI, Inst. A.)]
M. Marini: *Io Michelangelo da Caravaggio* (Rome, 1974)
H. Röttgen: *Il Caravaggio: Ricerche e interpretazioni* (Rome, 1974)
Colloquio sul tema Caravaggio e i Caravaggeschi: Roma, 1974
M. Cinotti, ed.: *Novità sul Caravaggio* (Regione Lombardia, 1975)
F. Bardon: *Caravage, ou l'expérience de la matière* (Paris, 1978)
The Church of St John's in Valletta, 1578–1978 (exh. cat., ed. J. Azzopardi; Malta, St John's, 1978)
J. Gash: *Caravaggio* (London, 1980, 2/1988)
A. Moir: *Caravaggio* (New York, 1982, concise edn 1988)
Painting in Naples, 1606–1705: From Caravaggio to Giordano (exh. cat., ed. C. Whitfield and J. Martineau; London, RA; Washington, DC, N.G.A.; Paris, Grand Pal., Turin, Fond. Agnelli; 1982–4)
M. Cinotti: *Michelangelo Merisi da il Caravaggio: Tutte le opere*, introd. G. A. dell'Acqua (Bergamo, 1983) [the most complete cat.]
H. Hibbard: *Caravaggio* (London, 1983) [the most well-rounded modern study in Eng., with trans. of the main 17th-century biogs and crit.]
Caravaggio in Sicilia: Il suo tempo, il suo influsso (exh. cat. by V. Abbate and others, Syracuse, Pal. Bellomo, 1984)
The Age of Caravaggio (exh. cat., New York, Met.; Naples, Capodimonte; 1985)
M. Calvesi and L. Trigilia, eds: *L'ultimo Caravaggio e la cultura artistica a Napoli, in Sicilia e a Malta* (Syracuse, 1987)
M. Gregori: 'Michelangelo Merisi da il Caravaggio', *Dopo Caravaggio: Bartolomeo Manfredi e la Manfrediana Methodus* (exh. cat., ed. M. C. Poma; Cremona, 1987), pp. 50–57
M. Marini: *Michelangelo Merisi da Caravaggio 'pictor praestantissimus'* (Rome, 1987; rev. 1989)
D. Bernini, ed.: *Caravaggio: Nuove riflessioni* (Rome, 1989)
M. Calvesi: *La realtà del Caravaggio* (Turin, 1990)
M. Cinotti: *Caravaggio: La vita e l'opera* (Bergamo, 1991) [good critical biog.; excellent pls]
Michelangelo Merisi da Caravaggio: Come nascono i capolavori (exh. cat., ed. M. Gregori; Florence, Pitti; Rome, Pal. Ruspoli; 1991–2) [extensive disc. of technique, as well as questions of attrib.; excellent pls; indispensable distillation of recent scholarship]
F. Bologna: *L'incredulità del Caravaggio* (Turin, 1992)
S. Corradini: *Caravaggio: Materiali per un processo* (Rome, 1993) [contains new docs]
R. Bassani and F. Bellini: *Caravaggio assassino* (Rome, 1994)
J. Gash: *Caravaggio* (New York, 1994)
S. Macioce: 'Caravaggio a Malta e i suoi referenti: Notizie d'archivio', *Stor. A.*, lxxxi (1994), pp. 207–28
Caravaggio e la collezione Mattei (exh. cat., Rome, Pal. Barberini, 1995)

SPECIALIST STUDIES

Individual works

R. Hinks: *Caravaggio's 'Death of the Virgin'* (Oxford, 1953)
R. Longhi: 'Un originale del Caravaggio a Rouen e il problema delle copie caravaggesche', *Paragone*, xi/121 (1960), pp. 23–36
H. Röttgen: 'Die Stellung der Contarelli-Kapelle in Caravaggios Werk', *Z. Kstgesch.*, xxviii (1965), pp. 47–68 [redates the Contarelli Chapel pictures on doc. evidence]
D. Heikamp: 'La *Medusa* del Caravaggio e l'armatura dello Scià Abbâs di Persia', *Paragone*, xvii/199 (1966), pp. 62–76
R. Enggass: 'La virtù di un vero nobile: L'Amore Giustiniani del Caravaggio', *Palatino*, xi (1967), pp. 13–20
I. Lavin: 'Divine Inspiration in Caravaggio's Two St Matthews', *A. Bull.*, lvi (1974), pp. 59–81
——: 'Addenda to "Divine Inspiration"', *A. Bull.*, lvi/4 (1974), pp. 590–91
H. Potterton: *'The Supper at Emmaus' by Caravaggio*, N.G. series: Painting in Focus, 3 (London, 1975)
M. Gregori: 'Addendum to Caravaggio: The Cecconi *Crowning with Thorns* Reconsidered', *Burl. Mag.*, cxviii (1976), pp. 671–80
A. Lurie and D. Mahon: 'Caravaggio's *Crucifixion of St Andrew* from Valladolid', *Bull. Cleveland Mus. A.* (Jan 1977), pp. 3–24
C. Scribner III: '*In alia effigie*: Caravaggio's London *Supper at Emmaus*', *A. Bull.*, lix/3 (1977), pp. 375–82
G. Wright: 'Caravaggio's *Entombment* Considered *in situ*', *A. Bull.*, lviii/1 (1978), pp. 35–42
F. Bologna and V. Pacelli: 'Caravaggio, 1610: La *Sant' Orsola confitta dal tiranno* per Marcantonio Doria', *Prospettiva*, xxiii (1980), pp. 24–45
M. Cordaro: 'Indagine radiografica sulla *Buona Ventura* dei Musei Capitolini', *Ric. Stor. A.*, 10 ('Roma nell' anno 1600') (1980), pp. 100–06
W. Prohaska: 'Untersuchungen zur *Rosenkranz Madonna* Caravaggios', *Jb. Ksthist. Samml. Wien*, lxxvi (1980), pp. 111–32
V. Pacelli: *Caravaggio: La sette opere di misericordia* (Salerno, 1984)
V. Pacelli and A. Brejon de Lavergnée: 'L'Eclisse del committente? Congetture su un ritratto nella *Flagellazione* di Caravaggio rivelato dalla radiografia', *Paragone*, xxxvi/419–23 (1985), pp. 209–18
R. Parks: 'On Caravaggio's *Dormition of the Virgin* and its Setting', *Burl. Mag.*, cxxvii (1985), pp. 438–48
K. Wolfe: 'Caravaggio: Another *Lute Player*', *Burl. Mag.*, cxxvii (1985), pp. 450–52
M. Wiemers: 'Caravaggios *Amore vincitore* im Urteil eines Romfahres um 1650', *Pantheon*, xliv (1986), pp. 59–61
K. Christiansen: 'Technical Report on *The Cardsharps*', *Burl. Mag.*, cxxx (1988), pp. 26–7
D. Mahon: 'Fresh Light on Caravaggio's Earliest Period: His *Cardsharps* Recovered', *Burl. Mag.*, cxxx (1988), pp. 10–25
P. Askew: *Caravaggio's 'Death of the Virgin'* (Princeton, 1990); review by J. Gash, *Burl. Mag.*, cxxxiv (1992), pp. 186–8
G. Correale, ed.: *Identificazione di un Caravaggio: Nuove tecnologie per una rilettura del 'San Giovanni Battista'* (Venice, 1990); review by J. Gash, *Burl. Mag.*, cxxxiv (1992), pp. 186–8
K. Christiansen: 'Some Observations on the Relationship between Caravaggio's Two Treatments of the *Lute-player*', *Burl. Mag.*, cxxxii (1990), pp. 21–6
D. Mahon: 'The Singing "Lute-player" by Caravaggio from the Barberini Collection, Painted for Cardinal del Monte', *Burl. Mag.*, cxxxii (1990), pp. 4–20
A Caravaggio Rediscovered: The 'Lute Player' (exh. cat. by K. Christiansen, New York, Met., 1990)
S. Benedetti: *Caravaggio: The Master Revealed* (Dublin, 1993) [on the *Taking of Christ*]
——: 'Caravaggio's *Taking of Christ*: A Masterpiece Rediscovered', *Burl. Mag.*, cxxxv (1993), pp. 731–41
F. Cappelletti: 'The Documentary Evidence of the Early History of Caravaggio's *Taking of Christ*', *Burl. Mag.*, cxxxv (1993), pp. 742–5

Other

D. Mahon: '*Egregius in urbe pictor*: Caravaggio Revised', *Burl. Mag.*, xciii (1951), pp. 223–34
——: 'Addenda to Caravaggio', *Burl. Mag.*, xciv (1952), pp. 3–23
L. Venturi and G. Urbani: 'Studi radiografici sul Caravaggio', *Atti Accad. N. Lincei, Mem. Cl. Sci. Morali, Stor. & Filol.*, viii/5 (1952), pp. 37–46
D. Mahon: 'On Some Aspects of Caravaggio and his Times', *Bull. Met.*, xii (1953), pp. 33–45
J. Hess: 'Modelle e modelli del Caravaggio', *Commentari*, v (1954), pp. 271–89

L. Salerno: 'Caravaggio e il priore della Consolazione', *Commentari*, vi (1955), pp. 258–60
R. Longhi: *Opere complete*, 10 vols (Florence, 1961–)
D. Macrae: 'Observations on the Sword in Caravaggio', *Burl. Mag.*, cvi (1964), pp. 412–16
L. Salerno, D. Kinkead and W. Wilson: 'Poesia e simboli nel Caravaggio', *Palatino*, x (1966), pp. 106–17
A. Moir: *The Italian Followers of Caravaggio*, 2 vols (Cambridge, MA, 1967)
P. Askew: 'The Angelic Consolation of St Francis of Assisi in Post-Tridentine Italian Painting', *J. Warb. & Court. Inst.*, xxxii (1969), pp. 280–306
A. Moir: 'Did Caravaggio Draw?', *A. Q.* [Detroit], xxxii/4 (1969), pp. 354–72
H. Röttgen: 'Caravaggio-Probleme', *Münchn. Jb. Bild. Kst*, xx (1969), pp. 143–70
C. Frommel: 'Caravaggios Frühwerk und der Kardinal Francesco Maria del Monte', *Stor. A.*, 9–10 (1971), pp. 5–52
D. Posner: 'Caravaggio's Homo-erotic Early Works', *A. Q.* [Detroit], xxxiv (1971), pp. 301–24
L. Spezzaferro: 'La cultura del Cardinale del Monte e il primo tempo del Caravaggio', *Stor. A.*, 9–10 (1971), pp. 57–92
S. Vsevolozhskaya and I. Linnik: *Caravaggio and his Followers: Paintings in Soviet Museums* (Leningrad, 1975)
B. Wind: 'Genre as Season: Dosso, Campi, Caravaggio', *A. Lombarda*, xlii/3 (1975), pp. 70–73
A. Moir: *Caravaggio and his Copyists* (New York, 1976)
F. Zeri: 'Sull'esecuzione di "nature morte" nella bottega del cavalier d'Arpino, e sulla presenza ivi del giovane Caravaggio', *Diari di lavoro*, ii (Turin, 1976), pp. 92–103
J.-P. Cuzin: *La Diseuse de bonne aventure de Caravage*, Louvre: Les dossiers du département des peintures, 13 (Paris, 1977)
V. Pacelli: 'New Documents Concerning Caravaggio in Naples', *Burl. Mag.*, cxix (1977), pp. 819–29
B. Nicolson: *The International Caravaggesque Movement* (Oxford, 1979); rev. and enlarged by L. Vertova as *Caravaggism in Europe*, 3 vols (Turin, 1989) [very useful lists of ptgs attrib. to Caravaggio and his followers; numerous pls in rev. edn]
L. Sebregondi Fiorentini: 'Francesco d'Antella, Caravaggio, Paladini e altri', *Paragone*, xxxiii/383–5 (1982), pp. 107–22
F. Trinchieri Camiz and A. Ziino: 'Caravaggio: Aspetti musicali e committenza', *Stud. Mus.*, i (1983), pp. 67–90
R. Spear: 'Stocktaking in Caravaggio Studies', *Burl. Mag.*, cxxvi (1984), pp. 162–5
G. Previtali: 'Caravaggio e il suo tempo', *Prospettiva*, xli (1985), pp. 68–80
D. Cutajar, ed.: 'Malta and Caravaggio', *Mid-Med Bank Ltd: Report and Accounts* (Malta, 1986; rev. 2/1989)
K. Christiansen: 'Caravaggio and "L'esempio davanti del naturale"', *A. Bull.*, lxviii/3 (1986), pp. 421–45 [a good disc. of Caravaggio's working procedures and technique]
D. Jarman and G. Incandela: *Derek Jarman's 'Caravaggio'* (London, 1986)
F. Trinchieri Camiz: 'The Castrato Singer: From Informal to Formal Portraiture', *Artibus & Hist.*, ix/18 (1988), pp. 171–86
F. Cappelletti and L. Testa: 'I quadri di Caravaggio nella collezione Mattei: I nuovi documenti e i riscontri con le fonti', *Stor. A.*, lxix (1990), pp. 234–44
F. Trinchieri Camiz: 'Music and Painting in Cardinal del Monte's Household', *Bull. Met.*, xxvi (1991), pp. 213–26
K. Christiansen: 'Caravaggio's Second Versions', *Burl. Mag.*, cxxiv (1992), pp. 502–3
J. Gash: 'Painting and Sculpture in Early Modern Malta', *Hospitaller Malta, 1530–1798*, ed. V. Mallia-Milanes (Malta, 1993), pp. 509–603
S. Macioce: 'Un cavaliere magistrale', *A. & Dossier*, 85 (1993), pp. 19–21
V. Pacelli: *L'ultimo Caravaggio: Dalla Maddalena a mezza figura ai due San Giovanni (1606–1610)* (Todi, 1994)

JOHN GASH

Caravaggio, Polidoro da. *See* POLIDORO DA CARAVAGGIO.

Caravanserai [Pers. *kārvānsarāy*]. Inn for caravans, merchants and their wares. Found in cities and along routes in most Islamic lands, caravanserais and related institutions are known by a wide variety of terms, including *dār*, *funduq*, *khān*, *manzil*, *qaysariyya*, *ribāt* and *wakāla* in Arabic, *bazār*, *bazistān*, *chahār-sū[q]* and *tīm* in Persian and *çarsi*, *bedesten* and *han* in Turkish. Whatever the name, a caravanserai is usually a secure rectangular building with an open (or vaulted) courtyard surrounded by stables, lodgings and storerooms. Traditionally, massive gates protected the entrance, which contained porters' rooms. A well or fountain stood in the courtyard, and space or a separate room was reserved as a mosque. There might also be a bath. Rural caravanserais were often established as pious foundations to provide travellers with a needed service (*see* ISLAM, §III). The revenues from urban caravanserais often supported a madrasa or a mosque.

Rural caravanserais were staging-posts and way-stations usually spaced a day's journey (30 km) apart. The form evolved from the staging-posts maintained by the Achaemenid and Byzantine empires on major communication routes, but their development in the Islamic world is particularly tied to the domestication of the camel and the replacement of wheeled traffic with caravans. Where necessary, caravanserais provided separate quarters for horses, donkeys and camels, since they could not be stabled together. The earliest known example is the Lesser Enclosure at QASR AL-HAYR EAST, founded in the early 8th century AD in the Syrian desert between Palmyra and the River Euphrates. It was a two-storey square structure with a single gate leading to a courtyard surrounded by a peristyle with a gallery above. A small bathhouse stood near by. The Abbasid caliphs (*reg* 749–1258) and their families built caravanserais along the pilgrimage route from Iraq to the Holy Cities of Arabia, but only ruins remain. Under the Saljuq sultans of Iran (*reg* 1038–1194), magnificent caravanserais were erected to encourage international trade. Two of the most important are RIBAT-I SHARAF in north-east Iran and RIBAT-I MALIK in Uzbekistan. Both are free-standing courtyard buildings with regular exteriors and an elaborate façade; they are known for their intricate brickwork. Ribat-i Sharaf was of such high quality that Turkan Khatun, the wife of Sultan Sanjar (*reg* 1118–57), had it refurbished as a palace in 1154. The Saljuq rulers of Anatolia (*reg* 1077–1307) built three types of stone caravanserai, comprising a closed vaulted hall, rooms surrounding an open courtyard or a combination of both (*see* ISLAMIC ART, §II, 5(iii)). Most have spectacular carved portals; two of the most impressive are the Sultan Hans erected by Sultan 'Ala' al-Din Kayqubadh on the roads between Konya and Aksaray (1229; rest. 1278) and at Tuzhisar between Sivas and Kayseri (1236–7).

The Ayyubid (*reg* 1169–1260) and Mamluk (*reg* 1250–1517) rulers of Syria and Egypt erected caravanserais along the trade routes between Cairo and Aleppo, but few are of architectural significance. Under the Safavid dynasty of Iran (*reg* 1501–1732), such rulers as 'Abbas I encouraged international trade by building caravanserais along major routes, particularly those to India. Most are rectangular structures set in the open countryside with rounded towers at the corners, three plain walls and a fourth marked by a boldly projecting portal. A vaulted vestibule leads to the interior, a court surrounded by one or two storeys of vaulted rooms linking iwans in the middle of each of the four sides. The number and similarity of the buildings suggest that plans were issued from a central office. In the

Caravanserai courtyard, Rüstem Paşa Han, by Sinan, Edirne, Turkey, 1560–61

17th century, complex octagonal plans with monumental gates and round towers were introduced (e.g. ʿAminabad).

The urban caravanserai functioned as a terminus for the journey, a depot for goods and a place for commercial transactions. The terminology shows that its origins lie in the commercial architecture of the Hellenistic and Byzantine world. The term *qaysariyya*, from the Greek 'imperial [market]', was used in Mediterranean regions that had been under Byzantine rule. It usually denoted a system of buildings laid out in cloisters of shops, workrooms, warehouses and frequently living quarters. In North Africa the term came to mean 'central market', while in Egypt it was replaced by *wakāla*. *Funduq*, derived from the Greek *pandoxeion* (housing attached to a church or synagogue for needy strangers), was commonly used in North Africa to refer to an urban hostelry, particularly those for foreign (i.e. Jewish, Christian and European) merchants. *Khān*, a word of Persian origin that became common in Arabic and Turkish, began to be used only under the Mamluk and Ottoman (*reg* 1281–1924) dynasties. Urban caravanserais were often named after the special products traded in them (e.g. Khan al-Sabun ['Soap'], Ipek ['Silk'] or Bal ['Honey'] Han).

Urban caravanserais (usually known as *dār*) were built from early times in such cities as Baghdad and Cairo, but the oldest surviving example is the Khan al-Mirjan in Baghdad, built in 1359 by the Jalayirid governor to support his adjacent funerary complex. The innovative transverse vaulting covering the central hall shows that the patron considered the caravanserai as important artistically as he did economically. The burgeoning Levantine trade in the later Middle Ages and the commercial prosperity of Syrian cities resulted in the building of caravanserais with elaborate decoration, such as striped ashlar façades and richly carved window embrasures, although they show little architectural evolution. At first the caravanserais of Aleppo and Damascus were built in the suburbs, but they soon came to be built in the heart of the city, and their street façades contained rows of shops. The Khan al-Gumruk (Customs) in Aleppo (1574), for example, had a total of 344 shops, two fountains, a mosque, two stone markets and a monumental entrance. In Cairo, *wakāla*s were built in the heart of the city, and there were more than 200 by the 17th century. Typically, two or more storeys of maisonettes were added above the caravanserai on the lower floors to provide rental housing and increase revenues for the establishment. The *wakāla* built by the Mamluk sultan Qansuh al-Ghawri in 1504–5 near the Azhar Mosque is the best-preserved example. The Ottoman caravanserais of Bursa and Edirne (see fig.) had space for large and impressive courtyards, but those of Istanbul often had to be built on constricted sites.

The Safavids also built caravanserais in Iranian cities. Under ʿAbbas I, the bazaar in Isfahan was extended several kilometres from the old maidan to the new. Rows of shops lined the main street, and gateways and alleys led to many caravanserais. The largest and most spectacular is the caravanserai (early 18th century) attached to the Madar-i Shah Madrasa, which was supported by the revenues of the commercial structure. The caravanserai is approached from the Chahar Bagh, the main avenue in this part of the city, through a bazaar of 43 bays and a portal into a courtyard about 76 m square. It was surrounded by 100 single rooms and suites arranged on two storeys. A smaller courtyard was used for stabling animals. It was transformed into a luxury hotel in the mid-20th century.

The standard type of urban caravanserai is found as far west as Morocco and Spain. The Funduq al-Tattawiniyyin ('of the Tetouan [merchants]') in Fez stands adjacent to the 'Attarin and Misbahiyya madrasas, which its revenues once supported. The elaborate wooden ceiling of the vestibule is similar to woodwork in the 'Attarin Madrasa (1323–5), suggesting that both are of the same date. The Corral del Carbón, erected by the Nasrid sultans of Granada (*reg* 1230–1492) in the 15th century, is the only surviving caravanserai in Granada. It has an exuberant monumental portal with a large awning and *muqarnas* vault. The interior, similar to the *funduq* in Fez, is a sober courtyard (16 m square) surrounded by porticos and galleries giving access to the individual rooms. Stairways on each side lead from the portico to the two upper floors.

BIBLIOGRAPHY

Enc. Islam/2: 'Bezzāzistān', 'Khān'

J. Sauvaget: 'Caravansérails syriens du Hadjdj de Constantinople', *A. Islam.*, iv (1937), pp. 98–121

——: 'Caravansérails syriens du moyen âge', *A. Islam.*, vi (1939), pp. 46–55 and vii (1940), pp. 1–19

M. Siroux: *Caravansérails d'Iran et petites constructions routières* (Cairo, 1949)

G. Marçais: *L'Architecture musulmane d'occident* (Paris, 1954)

K. Erdmann: *Das anatolische Karavansaray des 13. Jahrhunderts*, 3 vols (Berlin, 1961–76)

G. Goodwin: *A History of Ottoman Architecture* (London and Baltimore, 1971)

M. Siroux: *Anciennes voies et monuments routiers de la région d'Ispahān* (Cairo, 1971)

A. Raymond: *Artisans et commerçants au Caire au XVIIIe siècle* (Damascus, 1974)

O. Grabar and others: *City in the Desert: Qasr al-Hayr East* (Cambridge, MA, 1978)

M. Scharabi: 'Drei traditionnelle Handelsanlagen in Kairo: Wakālat al-Bāzara, Wakālat Du l'Fiqar und Wakālat al-Quṭn', *Mitt. Dt. Archäol. Inst.: Abt. Kairo*, xxxiv (1978), pp. 127–64

E. Sims: 'Trade and Travel: Markets and Caravanserais', *Architecture of the Islamic World*, ed. G. Michell (London, 1978), pp. 80–111

R. Hillenbrand: *Islamic Architecture: Form, Function and Meaning* (Edinburgh, 1994), pp. 331–76

□

Carbone, Giovanni Bernardo (*bapt* Albaro, 12 May 1616; *d* Genoa, 11 March 1683). Italian painter. One of the finest though one of the least known Genoese painters, he studied with Giovanni Andrea de' Ferrari (i) in the late 1620s, a period when he could have known Giovanni Benedetto Castiglione and Giovanni Andrea Podesta, who were also in the studio. His trips to Venice of *c.* 1643–4 and 1650, his friendships with Valerio Castello in the 1650s and with Casone and Giovanni Battista Carlone in the 1670s indicate some further influences on his work. He is chiefly known as a portrait painter who followed the manner of Anthony van Dyck closely enough to confuse clients in the 17th and 18th centuries. His earliest dated painting, a portrait of the *Imperial Family* (1642; Terralba, Villa Imp.; see Martinoni, fig. 3), is highly ambitious, showing the family crowded into a room with a perspective view of their villa and gardens in the background. Many of his portraits are refined depictions of full-length figures, ranging from distinguished ecclesiastics to elaborately dressed children in the manner of van Dyck, standing on balconies with highly detailed baskets of fruit (e.g. *Portrait of a Child*, Madrid, Prado). His splendid portrait of *Paolo Gerolamo Franzone* (Nîmes, Mus. B.-A.) shows the sitter full-length on the terrace of a Genoese palace, turning to receive a letter from a black servant. In its modelling and inclusion of still-life, his work relates to the portraits by Luciano Borzone; he may have derived his interest in Flemish realism from the works of Anton Maria Vassallo.

Carbone's skill in depicting still-life, facial features and fabrics is also apparent in his religious paintings. His altarpiece of *St Michael with SS Jerome and Bernardo* (*c.* 1640; Marassi, S Margherita) shows figures highly charged with light and colour and with sharply articulated contours, similar to those in works by de Ferrari and Domenico Fiasella. Three dated paintings, the *Visitation* (1647; Lerici, Parish Church), *Virgin and Child with Six Saints* (1663; Genoa, S Teodoro) and the *Virgin and Child with St Anthony of Padua and St Stephen* (1665; Celle Ligure, Parish Church), indicate that his sweet-faced figure types and softly flowing draperies continued throughout his career but gained a silkier *sfumato*, in keeping with the Venetianizing style and the open brushwork of his friend Castello, whose fresco, the *Presentation of the Virgin* (*c.* 1659; Genoa, S Maria del Zerbino), Carbone finished in a style that was very close to that of its initiator.

Carbone's most panoramic religious painting is the large altarpiece *St Louis Adoring the Cross* (*c.* 1663; Genoa, SS Annunziata), which contains carefully described still-life and fabrics, strongly lit angels and numerous charming foreground and background figures depicted in velvety shadows. The multi-figured composition is in the same tradition as paintings by Casone and Carlone, but its strong *sfumato* offers an alternative to their colourful narratives of the 1660s and 1670s. To these paintings can be added the vividly realistic *Adoration of the Magi* (Genoa, Mus. Accad. Ligustica B.A.). The artist's delicate modelling, refined figure style and skill for precisely describing still-life are seen also in chalk drawings (e.g. *Virgin and Child Entrusting the Keys to a Saint*, Florence, Uffizi) that approach the softness of Strozzi, who was also in Venice in the 1640s, and the lyrical Baroque figures of Castello.

BIBLIOGRAPHY

DBI

R. Soprani: *Vite* (1674); enlarged, ed. C. G. Ratti, ii (Genoa, 1797), pp. 18–21

O. Grosso: 'Giovanni Bernardo Carbone', *Dedalo*, viii/1 (1927–8), pp. 109–34

Genoese Masters (exh. cat. by B. Manning and R. L. Manning, Dayton, OH, A. Inst.; Hartford, CT, Wadsworth Atheneum; 1962–3)

C. Marcenaro: *Pittori Genovesi a Genova* (Genoa, 1969), pp. 107–10

L. Alfonso: 'Carbone, Gio. Bernardo', *La Berio*, ii (1970), pp. 41–4; iii (1970), pp. 37–42

V. Belloni: *Pittura genovese del seicento*, ii (Genoa, 1974), pp. 98–107

E. Baccheschi: *Il Museo dell'Accademia Ligustica di Belle Arti* (Genoa, 1983)

R. Martinoni: *G. V. Imperiale* (Padua, 1983), pp. 113–15, 279

Disegni genovesi dal XVI al XVIII secolo (exh. cat. by M. Newcome, Florence, Uffizi, 1987), cat. 57, 58

M. NEWCOME

Carbonel, Alonso de (*b* Albacete, *c.* 1590; *d* Madrid, 31 Aug 1660). Spanish architect and sculptor. The son of a carpenter, he trained as a sculptor with Antón de Morales (*fl* 1586–1625). He designed the altarpiece (1612–18) for S María Magdalena in Getafe, near Madrid, in the classical style. With the Conde-Duque de Olivares as his patron, he turned to architecture and at the court of Philip IV was appointed second Aparejador to the royal works (1627), then Aparejador Mayor (1630) and finally Maestro Mayor (1643). Carbonel's style was similar to the classicism of Juan Gómez de Mora (i), for whom he had worked, although his façades, doors and windows tended to be more decorative. His most important work was the construction of the Buen Retiro (1630–33; *see* MADRID, §IV, 1), which was built with low-quality materials, such as brick; stone was used only for door- and window-frames. The building consisted of a square block with corner towers terminating in slate capitals, as was usual for a Spanish fortress, and had an interior courtyard. The existing Gothic church of the monastery of St Jerónimo, joined to the palace by a small cloister, served as the chapel. The interior of the palace was decorated with paintings by Diego Velázquez and others, sculptures and furniture. The most spectacular room was the Salón de Reinos (completed 1635). In the large gardens, Carbonel built five rustic chapels or hermitages dedicated to different saints. He was also involved in the completion of the royal Pantheon at the Escorial, which had been started by Gómez de Mora and Giovanni Battista Crescenzi; Carbonel built the vault, the marble and bronze altarpiece and the staircase. The Pantheon was finally inaugurated in 1654. He also built a country palace (1635; ruined) for the Conde-Duque de Olivares at Loeches, near Madrid. The church and Dominican convent near by, where Olivares was buried, is attributed to Carbonel on stylistic grounds.

BIBLIOGRAPHY

R. Martorell: 'Alonso Carbonel, arquitecto y escultor del siglo XVII', *A. Esp.*, xxxi (1958), pp. 50–58
J. M. de Azcárate: 'Datos para las biografías de los arquitectos de la corte de Felipe IV', *Rev. U. Madrid*, xlii–xliii (1962), pp. 517–46
——: 'Anales de la construcción del Buen Retiro', *An. Inst. Estud. Madril.*, i (1966), pp. 99–135
J. Brown and J. Elliot: *A Palace for a King: The Buen Retiro and the Court of Philip IV* (London and New Haven, 1980)

ALFONSO RODRÍGUEZ CEBALLOS

Carbon print. *See under* PHOTOGRAPHY, §I.

Carborundum print [Fr. *Gravure au carborundum*]. Print made by combining carborundum—a carbon and silicon compound customarily used for polishing by abrasion—with synthetic resin or varnish (*see also* PRINTS, §III, 8). The mixture is then hardened on a plastic or metal support. The process was invented during the 1960s by the French artist Henri Goetz (1909–89), who realized that the carborundum provided an ink-holding 'tooth'. The technique can be combined with intaglio processes or used as an alternative to them.

Goetz approximated conventional intaglio effects either by using heated tools to cut into a coating of varnish hardened on its support, or by suspending grains of carborundum in liquid varnish before it dried. The materials specified in his 1968 treatise included carborundum in eight gradations from 80–1200, synthetic varnishes and resins in crystal and liquid form, appropriate solvents, pyrogravure tools, emery and glass papers, and intaglio printing equipment, including a hot-plate. The technique's outstanding advantage, in addition to its speed, is that corrections can be made by dissolving the varnish with trichlorethylene, which also allows economic recycling of the support. The quality of line is determined by the thickness of the varnish and the temperature and nature of the point. Pastel or lithographic crayon marks, or textural impressions executed on the varnish in thinned typographic ink, can be sprinkled with carborundum dust, which is fixed to the varnish by passing a flame over it. The carborundum's fineness or coarseness determines the character of the mark. Effects similar to aquatint can be created by mixing ground resin crystals with colorant, solvents and various grades of carborundum. Such mixtures can be brushed on to the support or applied thickly by palette knife. For finer applications Goetz suspended carborundum in ether and devised a pseudo-mezzotint by spreading salt on a thick layer of varnish, heating it, then, after cooling, washing the salt away to leave ink-retaining indentations. Although much work with carborundum resembles intaglio printing, pyrogravure in thick varnish produces an idiosyncratic weal in the printed sheet, while built-up textures, requiring simultaneous printing from the relief and the intaglio, palpably emboss and/or deboss the paper.

Combined colour carborundum and intaglio print by Joan Miró: *La Sorcière*, etching, aquatint and carborundum, 1055×705 mm, 1969 (Paris, Galerie Lelong); printed in an edition of 75

Goetz made many abstract prints employing his discoveries, as did another French artist, Max Papart (*b* 1911). The Spaniards Antoni Clavé and Antoni Tapiés also employed carborundum, but its most celebrated exponent was their countryman, Joan Miró (see fig.), who, in experiments from 1967, often built out a thickened paste well above the support, to suggest impasto strokes and textures in the print. Working with Dutrou, Morsang or Arte Adrien for Maeght Editeur, Miró enjoyed the grand scale and liberation the process afforded and wrote to Goetz enthusing about the freshness and spontaneity of the technique compared to conventional processes. Kelpra Studio, London, introduced the technique to Britain in the early 1980s and worked with John Piper and Jim Dine. Joe Tilson has also used carborundum to brilliant large-scale effect.

BIBLIOGRAPHY

H. Goetz: *Gravure au carborundum: Nouvelle technique de l'estampe en taille douce* (Paris, 1968, rev. 2/1974)
G. Bergström: *L'Oeuvre gravé de Henri Goetz, 1940–72* (Stockholm, 1973)
Miró: L'Oeuvre graphique (exh. cat., Paris, Mus. A. Mod. Ville Paris, 1974)
K. Masrour, ed.: *L'Oeuvre gravé de Goetz* (Paris, 1977)
R. Passeron: *Antoni Clavé: Graphic Work, 1939–1976* (Fribourg, 1977)
S. Lohensson, M. Bohbot and M. Papart: *Catalogue de l'oeuvre gravé de Max Papart* (Stockholm, 1979)
H. Goetz: 'Goetz, un dernier mot', *Cah. Est. Contemp.*, i ([1990])

PAT GILMOUR

Çarça, Diogo de. *See* SARÇA, DIOGO DE.

Carcano, Filippo (*b* Milan, 25 Sept 1840; *d* Milan, 19 Jan 1914). Italian painter. He enrolled in 1857 at the Accademia di Brera in Milan, where he was taught by Francesco Hayez and Giuseppe Bertini, and where he became friendly with Tranquillo Cremona. Carcano's talent was immediately evident and he won many prizes. In 1860 he presented a large-scale history painting, *Federico Barbarossa and the Duke Enrico Leone at Chiavenna* (Milan, Brera), which clearly reveals the influence of his teachers. On leaving the Accademia, however, Carcano became interested both in the new Realism and in the techniques of GLI SCAPIGLIATI. In 1860 he visited both London and Paris, examining the recent work of both English and French landscape painters. Carcano first experimented with interior scenes, genre scenes and sentimental subjects. One of his most impressive early works, remarkable for its freshness of approach, is the *Dancing Class* (1865; Turin, Gal. Civ. A. Mod.). On exhibition in 1865 the painting provoked strong reactions: in its almost photographic approach to detail and its unusual treatment of light and shade it marks a bold departure from Carcano's previous academic style. In 1867 he exhibited *Game of Billiards* (Milan, Brera). This also provoked considerable debate because of its style, which included a rudimentary form of the painting technique of the Divisionists in parts of the composition. Among the distinctly sentimental subjects in Carcano's early work is the *Goodhearted Boys* (1878; Milan, Brera).

With the encouragement of Carlo Pittara (1836–91), one of the leading exponents of the Piedmont landscape school, Carcano started to paint landscape. In 1880 his painting *First Snow in the Mountains* won the prize for landscape painting at the Quarta Esposizione di Belle Arti held in Turin, and in 1882 *Piazza San Marco* (Rome, G.N.A. Mod.) won the Principe Umberto Prize at the annual Brera exhibition in Milan. Following these successes, Carcano dedicated himself for a time almost exclusively to landscape painting, and he gradually became recognized as one of the most innovative exponents of the genre. With pictures that conveyed the majestic qualities of the north Italian landscape in wide views painted on large canvases, Carcano introduced the concept of naturalistic landscape painting to Milan. His work was much in demand during these years and he travelled frequently, exhibiting paintings at national and international exhibitions. From the 1880s onwards he also treated landscape as setting rather than subject, as in *Grazing* (1884; Udine, Mus. Civ.), which was probably influenced by the work of the Dutch painter Paulus Potter. Carcano also treated still-life in a novel manner: *Just Arrived* (1886; Milan, Gal. A. Mod.) shows a sharply angled view of a box of oranges against a black background.

Carcano experimented with a variety of different types of brushwork. He used long brushes, which enabled him to view his large canvases from a distance as he worked, and he painted with short, very wide strokes. He also used a palette-knife with a serrated edge to produce a sensation of light and movement in the sky. Carcano influenced the landscape painting of many Italian artists, in particular that of Eugenio Gignous.

BIBLIOGRAPHY

DBI
G. Cesura: *Filippo Carcano* (Milan, 1986)
M. Valentini and A. Scotti: *Filippo Carcano (1840–1914): Vedute milanesi e panorami lombardi* (Milan, 1987)

CLARE HILLS-NOVA

Carcassonne. Medieval fortified town in Languedoc, southern France. Situated on a plateau dominating the plain of the Aude, the walled town of Carcassonne is roughly rectangular in shape, up to 525 m long and 250 m wide (see fig. 1 and CASTLE, fig. 1). It is still surrounded by its medieval double enclosure wall: the inner curtain is *c.* 1245 m in length, with 29 towers, while the outer has 18 towers and is *c.* 1320 m long. The Château Comtal and the former cathedral of St Nazaire also survive.

1. HISTORY AND URBAN DEVELOPMENT. The site was occupied as early as the 6th century BC, when its strategic defensive position must already have been recognized. The oldest parts of the inner curtain wall date either from the late Roman period (before AD 333, the date at which Carcassonne is mentioned as a *castrum* on the route from Bordeaux to Jerusalem) or from Visigothic times. There are traces of several campaigns of work on the north front (from the Tour du Moulin du Connétable to the Tour de la Chapelle) and the west front (from the Tour de la Justice to the Tour Visigothe). During the minority of Louis IX (1226–39) the seneschals of Carcassonne raised the inner wall by several metres and added an outer wall preceded by a moat. After the revolt of 1240, Louis razed the Faubourg St Michel, which abutted the east front of the outer wall, and rebuilt the section of the rampart running from the Tour de la Vade to the Barbicane St Louis. A section of the inner wall (780 m), evidently still considered weak, was rebuilt by Philip III (*reg* 1270–

85) and Philip IV (*reg* 1285–1314) between 1280 and 1287. Finally, between 1852 and 1879, Viollet-le-Duc carried out substantial restorations, adding crenellations to the walls and giving the towers slate roofs (for part of his reconstruction *see* CURTAIN WALL (i)). The use of slates has been strongly criticized, however, and restorers are replacing them with clay ridge tiles.

The curtain walls of the earliest enclosure wall are 6–7 m high and 2 m wide. The surviving towers, which straddle the wall about every 20 m, are horseshoe-shaped and filled in at the base, but each has a chamber lit by three round-arched windows at the level of the parapet walls. The early 13th-century exterior wall demonstrated a more active concept of defence: its towers are hollow at the base and contain superimposed, vaulted chambers with numerous arrow loops. The improvement in weaponry and the pronounced projection of the circular towers from the wall enabled them to be spaced further apart, at rough intervals of 60–70 m. The walls rebuilt from 1280 to 1287 are thinner, with rusticated masonry, many more arrow loops on several levels and six towers *à bec* for defence against direct attack. The Porte Narbonnaise, built during this campaign, is exceptional, defended by two formidable spurred towers, a drawbridge and the St Louis barbican.

The Château Comtal, running along the west side of the inner rampart, was built by the Vicomtes de Trencavel between 1120 and 1150. The buildings, altered in part in the 13th, 15th and 18th centuries, were residential and administrative: they comprised two buildings placed end-to-end parallel to the rampart and a third, built at right angles, oriented east–west; a chapel was added in the north-west corner *c.* 1180. In the 12th century the building was described as a palace but it was transformed into a genuine fortress when the earliest enclosure wall was consolidated and the second rampart built. Three curtain walls were built to the south, east and north of the palace, preceded by a moat and flanked by six round towers with the same characteristics as those of the outer wall: battered bases, superimposed, rib-vaulted chambers and stirrup-shaped loop holes. There was provision for hoardings at the tops of the towers and curtain walls, and a bridge preceded by a barbican defended the access to the castle. The defences were directed against the city to resist uprisings against the new royal administration.

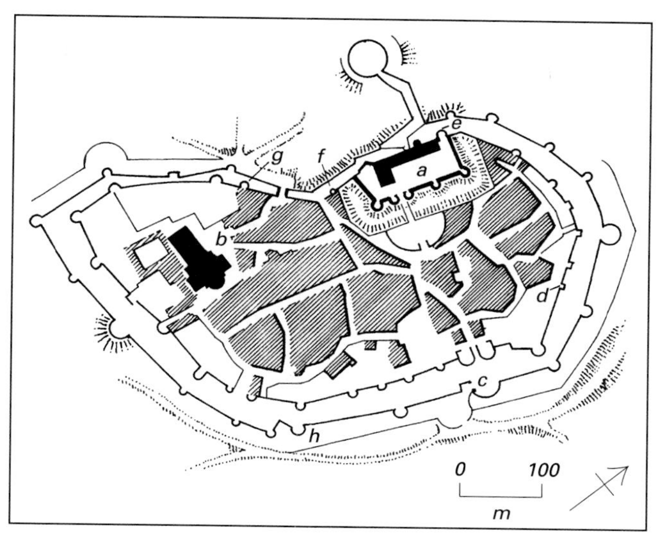

1. Carcassonne, plan: (a) Château Comtal; (b) St Nazaire; (c) Porte Narbonnaise and Barbicane St Louis; (d) Tour du Moulin du Connetable; (e) Tour de la Chapelle; (f) Tour de la Justice; (g) Tour Visigothe; (h) Tour de la Vade

2. ST NAZAIRE. It was a cathedral until 1801, when the episcopal seat was moved to the lower town; restorations were carried out by Viollet-le-Duc from 1844. The church has a Romanesque nave and a Gothic transept, choir and apse. In 1096 Pope Urban II (*reg* 1088–99) blessed the stones intended for the construction of the nave; the style of the portal and several of the capitals suggests that this was built by 1125. The aisled nave, 59 m long and 16 m wide, has square piers with engaged shafts alternating with circular piers. The half-barrel vaults of the aisles are almost as high as the pointed barrel vault of the main vessel, providing safer buttressing but precluding direct lighting.

Between 1269 and 1330 the east end was replaced by a Gothic transept and choir. The decision to retain the Romanesque nave, as well as the restricted space to the east, dictated the dimensions of the new work, which was much wider than the old but shallow and relatively low. The plan, a seven-sided apse preceded by a choir bay and flanked on either side by three rectangular chapels grafted on to a strongly projecting transept, was inspired by Cistercian buildings and was also adopted in some Franciscan churches during the same period. The choir bay has a sexpartite vault and the transept arms are rib-vaulted; they each have three bays skirted on the east by an aisle opening into the chapels (see fig. 2). There was a change of plan during the course of construction, when the chapel vaults were heightened to the same level as the aisle vaults. The tall, slender supports are braced by iron tie-bars. This device imparts a light and airy character to the architecture; both the apse and transept are flooded with light through the many tall stained-glass windows of the eastern walls and the roses at the transept ends.

The impact of Parisian Gothic, especially of the Sainte-Chapelle, Paris, can be recognized both here and in the arrangement of the sculptural decoration, which vividly demonstrates the influence of French Gothic sculpture in the region in the second half of the 13th century. At the east end a group of 22 statues, dated *c.* 1280–1300, is attached to the pier shafts under the vault springings, an arrangement identical to that of the Sainte-Chapelle. The tomb of *Bishop Guillaume Radulphe* (1266) also exemplifies Parisian styles: its funeral procession was to be widely diffused locally, as well as the naturalistic foliage of which it is one of the earliest examples in the Languedoc. The pier statues, representing the Apostles, the *Annunciation*, the *Virgin and Child*, Christ with an angel and five saints, constitute an iconographic programme like that of a portal. Three sculptors worked on this group; one was directly influenced by the statues of the Sainte-Chapelle and the last workshop of Reims Cathedral, while the others developed a novel style characterized by the monumental proportions of the figures, the abundance of broken folds

2. Carcassonne, St Nazaire, interior view of south transept, 1269–1330

in the draperies and the decorative refinement of the faces and wavy locks of hair. This style appeared elsewhere in the region in the first half of the 14th century and is also seen on the tomb of *Bishop Pierre de Rochefort* (*d* 1322), in his funerary chapel on the north side of the cathedral.

There are nine stained-glass windows at the east end; the two flanking the axial window were renewed at the beginning of the 16th century. The axial window has scenes of the *Infancy and Passion of Christ*, while the western two apse windows show the *Lives of SS Peter and Paul* (north side) and *SS Nazaire and Celsius* (south). The north transept is devoted to the Virgin, the central subject of the rose and the main figure in the *Tree of Jesse* in the chapel closest to the choir, while the south transept is dedicated to the glorification of Christ, who is enthroned in the middle of the rose and appears again in the *Tree of Life* window (chapel next to the choir); the other transept windows are decorated with grisaille. The brightly coloured windows were executed between 1280 and 1322. The axial window is stylistically isolated and relates to the style of the mid-13th century. The north transept windows date from the 1300s and were influenced by the stained glass of the cathedrals of Clermont-Ferrand and Tours. Although the windows dating from the period of Pierre de Rochefort in the western part of the apse and south transept were executed by local artists, they are heavily dependent on Ile-de-France models.

BIBLIOGRAPHY

J. P. Cros-Mayrevieille: 'Mémoire sur la chapelle et le mausolée de l'évêque Guillaume Radulphe', *Mém. Soc. Archéol. Midi France*, iv (1840–41), pp. 185–94
E. Viollet-le-Duc: 'Rapport sur l'église Saint-Nazaire de Carcassonne', *Rev. Aude*, i (1845–6), pp. 394–8
——: *Rapports sur les restes de l'ancienne cité de Carcassonne* (Paris, 1858)
J. P. Cros-Mayrevieille: *Les Monuments de Carcassonne* (Paris, 1859)
A. Blanchet: 'A propos de l'enceinte de Carcassonne', *Rev. Etud. Anc.*, n. s. 4, xxiv (1922), pp. 313–16
J. Poux: *La Cité de Carcassonne: Histoire et description* (Toulouse, 1925)
G. J. Mot: 'Les Tombeaux gothiques de Saint-Nazaire de Carcassonne', *Bull. Mnmt.*, cxi (1953), pp. 125–40
P. Héliot: 'L'Age du château de Carcassonne', *An. Midi*, lxxviii (1966), pp. 7–21
C. Bourély: 'Essai de datation du Château Comtal de Carcassonne', *Actes des congrès de la fédération historique du Languedoc méditerranéen et du Roussillon et de la fédération des sociétés académiques et savantes du Languedoc-Pyrénées-Gascogne: Carcassonne et sa région, 1970*, pp. 89–96
Y. Bruand: 'La Cité de Carcassonne', *Congr. Archéol. France*, cxxxi (1973), pp. 496–551
——: 'Chronologie et tracé de l'enceinte Wisigothique de Carcassonne', *Mélanges d'archéologie et d'histoire médiéval en l'honneur du doyen Michel de Boüard* (Geneva and Paris, 1973), pp. 29–37
M. Durliat: 'L'Ancienne Cathédrale Saint-Nazaire de Carcassonne', *Congr. Archéol. France*, cxxxi (1973), pp. 548–72
M. Pradalier-Schlumberger: 'Le Décor sculpté de la cathédrale Saint-Nazaire de Carcassonne', *Congr. Archéol. France*, cxxxi (1973), pp. 573–94
——: 'La Naissance de la sculpture gothique à Carcassonne', *Cah. Fanjeaux*, ix (1974), pp. 317–29
J. P. Suau: 'Les Verrières de la cathédrale Saint-Nazaire de Carcassonne', *Les Vitraux de Narbonne* (Narbonne, 1992), pp. 53–6

HENRI PRADALIER

Carchemish [Lat. Europus; now Jerabis, Jerablus]. Site in Turkey on the west bank of the River Euphrates, now on the Turkish-Syrian border. This ancient city is extensively attested in cuneiform records from the mid-3rd to mid-1st millennia BC and mentioned in New Kingdom Egyptian records, *c.* 1500–1200 BC, and in the Old Testament. It is the source of indigenous sculpture and associated hieroglyphic Luwian inscriptions dating *c.* 1000–700 BC. Excavations commissioned by the British Museum (1878–81) recovered some inscribed sculptures. Regular excavations under C. L. Woolley (1911–14 and 1920) were broken off by war, and latterly the establishment of the Turkish–Syrian frontier immediately to the south of the site has precluded further excavation. Finds are in the British Museum in London and in the Museum of Anatolian Civilizations in Ankara.

Carchemish has produced evidence of occupation stretching back to the Chalcolithic period (*c.* 5300 BC) and has a long recorded history. First attested in the Ebla archives *c.* 2500–2300 BC, it is better known from *c.* 1800 to *c.* 1600 BC from the Mari and Alalakh texts as the seat of an independent dynasty. Thereafter it became incorporated in the kingdom of Mitanni and was captured by the Hittite king Suppiluliuma I *c.* 1350 BC, becoming the capital of the Hittite empire in Syria under its own Hittite dynasty. This line of kings endured for at least five generations in direct descent, and at the collapse of the Hittite empire *c.* 1200 BC it is likely that the city itself escaped destruction and preserved a continuity of occupation through the subsequent Dark Age. After 1000 BC Carchemish reappears as the main Neo-Hittite centre, with a tradition of architecture, sculpture and inscriptions descending from its imperial past.

The excavated remains of the city belong almost exclusively to the Early Iron Age (*c.* 1000–600 BC), apart from the extensively traced fortifications, which incorporate earlier work, and a group of miniature gold, lapis lazuli and steatite figures of deities (*c.* 1400–1200 BC; London,

BM) that was found in a later cremation burial. The site divides into three sectors: the high Citadel mound on the riverbank; the Inner Town embracing it from west to south sides; and the Outer Town similarly embracing the Inner Town. The fortifications stretching from the Citadel west and south along the river were stone-built, but their ends were joined by an arc of earth rampart protecting the Inner Town. Typical Hittite stone gateways were excavated, the Water Gate on the river and West and South gates piercing the earth rampart. The ancient appearance of the Citadel mound seen from the river, with towers, gates and crenellated battlements, is suggested by its representation on the bronze gates of Shalmaneser III from Balawat (*c.* 850 BC; London, BM).

The external history of Carchemish for this period can be gathered from Assyrian records, and its internal dynastic history from its own inscriptions. An archaic stele names King Ura-Tarhunzas (early 10th century BC), whose dynasty was superseded by a four-generation line, the house of Suhis (early 10th century BC–early 9th). The excavated area of the Inner Town was largely the work of this dynasty, particularly its last two kings, Suhis II and Katuwas, with some later rebuilding and additions. The Water Gate building was faced with poorly preserved, sculpted orthostat blocks, archaic in appearance and uninscribed, probably attributable to Suhis I or his son and paralleled in age only by sculpture at Ain Dara. A road ran west from the Water Gate to the Storm-god Temple and the adjoining Great Staircase, ascending through an elaborate gate-house towards the Citadel. Opposite this was the King's Gate, which comprised the Herald's Wall, the Royal Buttress and the Processional Entry. The only complete building plans were those of the Storm-god Temple and a *hilani* building (*see* SYRIA–PALESTINE, §II, 1) to the south of the road. Of the other buildings only the sculpted orthostat façades were recovered. The building techniques were typically Hittite, with timber-frame and mud-brick walls on rubble foundations and basalt and limestone orthostats as wall facings.

Suhis II built an exterior façade of the Storm-god Temple (the Long Wall of Sculpture), showing a procession of gods followed by victorious chariotry and infantry ascending to the Citadel. Katuwas built the temple itself, the Processional Entry with its processions of the goddess Kubaba and the god Karhuha (missing), and the gate chamber of the King's Gate with the statue of the god Atarsuhas on a double lion base outside on the right. His inscriptions also describe a wooden upper storey, the women's quarters. Fragments of a colossal ruler statue on another double lion base, similar to the colossus from Zincirli, represent a funerary statue of Suhis II. Either ruler could have built the Herald's Wall, with its antithetical groups of fabulous beasts and mythological scenes. The Suhis–Katuwas style is typical early Neo-Hittite and recognizable at other contemporary sites.

During the period *c.* 870–830 BC there was strong Assyrian pressure on Carchemish, which had to pay much tribute, and no major works definitely attributed to this period have been found. Thereafter the house of Astiruwas can be seen from its sculpture and inscriptions to have ruled Carchemish for three to five generations. Work associated with the Regent Yariris and his protégé the young Kamanis, later king, preserves good examples of the middle Neo-Hittite style (early 8th century BC); in particular, the Royal Buttress was added, and Katuwas's Processional Entry was remodelled, showing the Regent with the Prince and his brothers (see fig.). The last king of Carchemish, Pisiri, ruled *c.* 740–717 BC. Some reliefs from the gate-house of the Great Staircase and a colossal seated statue from the South Gate can be attributed to this period and seem to have been deliberately destroyed. They show the late Neo-Hittite style known from better-preserved examples at Zincirli, Sakca Gözü and Arslantepe-Malatya.

Carchemish, Royal Buttress, detail from a row of reliefs showing the brothers of Prince Kamanis at play, h. 1.12 m, early 8th century BC (Ankara, Museum of Anatolian Civilizations)

In 717 BC the Assyrians seized the city, removed the king and constituted Carchemish as a province under an Assyrian governor. This they held until 605 BC, when Nebuchadnezzar (*reg* 605–562 BC) annihilated the Assyrian remnant, which was supported by the Egyptian army based in the city; Carchemish itself was destroyed. Substantial Roman building indicates that later it was again an important centre. Its name then seems to have been Europus, which probably survives in the modern village name.

BIBLIOGRAPHY

RLA: 'Karkamiš'

D. G. Hogarth: *Introductory* (1914), i of *Carchemish* (London, 1914–52)

C. L. Woolley: *The Town Defences* (1921), ii of ibid.

C. L. Woolley and R. D. Barnett: *The Excavations in the Inner Town* (1952), iii of ibid.

W. Orthmann: *Untersuchungen zur späthethitischen Kunst* (Bonn, 1971)

J. D. Hawkins: 'Who was Yariris?; Kamanis and Sasturas', *Anatol. Stud.*, xxix (1979), pp. 157–62

——: 'Kubaba at Karkamiš and Elsewhere', *Anatol. Stud.*, xxxi (1981), pp. 147–76

——: 'Rulers of Karkamiš: The House of Astiruwas', *IX Türk Tarih Kongresi: Ankara, 1981*

I. J. Winter: 'Carchemish *ša kišad Puratti*', *Anatol. Stud.*, xxxiii (1983), pp. 177–97

J. D. HAWKINS

Carchera, Nicolas. *See* KARCHER, NICOLAS.

Cárcova, Ernesto de la (*b* Buenos Aires, 3 March 1867; *d* Buenos Aires, 28 Dec 1927). Argentine painter. He studied painting in the mid-1880s at the Academia de la Sociedad Estímulo de Bellas Artes in Buenos Aires, and then in Turin and Rome. On his return to Buenos Aires in 1893 he showed one of his most representative works, *Without Bread and without Work* (1893; Buenos Aires, Mus. N. B.A.), which in its application of a naturalistic style to subjects drawn from the lives of ordinary people revealed the influence of contemporary Italian art and of his socialist convictions; although painted in Italy it related to the desperate situation in which many found themselves in Argentina. He also produced portraits and still-lifes in oils and pastels, and he became preoccupied with problems of light and atmosphere that led him to adopt an increasingly light palette and linked him to the Impressionist aesthetic, as in *Silent Nature* (1927; Buenos Aires, Mus. N. B.A.).

Cárcova was outstanding among Argentine painters working at the turn of the century. He was also influential on many artists who later became prominent in Argentina: in Buenos Aires in 1921 he co-founded and directed the Escuela Superior de Bellas Artes (later renamed the Escuela Superior de Bellas Artes Ernesto de la Cárcova); he was also Director of the Patronato de Becarios en Europa (which awarded scholarships for study in Europe), president of the Sociedad Estímulo de Bellas Artes and Director of the Museo de Calcos y Escultura Comparada. He was awarded the gold medal at the International Exhibition held in St Louis, MO, in 1904.

BIBLIOGRAPHY

C. Córdova Iturburu: *La pintura argentina del siglo veinte* (Buenos Aires, 1958), p. 20
Arte Argentina dalla Independenza ad oggi, 1810–1987 (exh. cat., Rome, Ist. It.-Lat. Amer., 1987), p. 54
J. E. Payró: 'La pintura', *Historia general del arte en la Argentina*, vi (1988), pp. 162–4

NELLY PERAZZO

Cárdenas, Agustín (*b* Matanzas, 10 April 1927). Cuban sculptor, active in France. He studied under Juan José Sicre, and at the Escuela Nacional de Bellas Artes 'San Alejandro' in Havana (1943–9). He settled in Paris in 1955 and became involved with the Surrealists. He also started to consider his African heritage and to incorporate Dogon totems in his work (e.g. *Sanedrac*, 1957; bronze cast, 1974; see exh. cat., p. 5). Brancusi and Arp were significant influences, and affinities can also be traced between Cárdenas's use of line to evoke magical transformations and the works of two other Cubans based in Paris, Wifredo Lam and Jorge Camacho. Working in marble, bronze and stone, he often used familiar images such as birds, flowers or the female nude as the bases for his lyrical abstractions (e.g. *Engraved Torso*, marble, 1976; see exh. cat., p. 22). The combination of these images of life with patterns suggesting infinite repetition became a central element in his work, and constitute a synthesis of abstraction and reference. He undertook monumental commissions in France, Israel, Austria, Japan and Canada, and his works are housed in collections worldwide, including the Museo de Arte Contemporáneo, Caracas, the Musée d'Ixelles, Bruxelles, and the Musée d'Art et d'Industrie, St Etienne, France.

BIBLIOGRAPHY

A. Breton: *Le Surréalisme et la peinture* (Paris, 1928, rev. 1965; Eng. trans., London and New York, 1972), pp. 322–3
J. Pierre: *La Sculpture de Cárdenas* (Brussels, 1971)
Cárdenas: Trente ans de sculpture (exh. cat. by J. Pierre, Paris, JGM Gal., 1988)

RICARDO PAU-LLOSA

Cardenas, Bartolomé de. *See* BERMEJO, BARTOLOMÉ.

Carder, Frederick (*b* Brockmoor, Staffs, 18 Sept 1863; *d* 10 Dec 1963). American glass designer and technician of English birth. He trained as an assistant in his father's salt-glazed stoneware factory in Stourbridge, Staffs, and attended evening classes at the Stourbridge School of Art and the Dudley Mechanics Institute, Dudley, W. Midlands, where he came under the tutelage of John Northwood (1836–1902). In 1880, after a recommendation by Northwood, Carder was employed as a designer and draughtsman at the Stourbridge firm of Stevens & Williams. During this period Carder developed his Mat-su-no-ke glass (which uses the application of clear or frosted glass in high relief outside the vessel). He also collaborated with Northwood to make coloured art glass and cut and cased glass.

In 1902, after a research trip to the USA for Stevens & Williams, Carder established a factory at Corning, NY, to produce blanks for T. G. Hawkes & Co. In 1903 Carder, who was inspired by the Art Nouveau style, joined with Thomas G. Hawkes (1846–1913) to found the STEUBEN GLASS WORKS, Corning, for the production of ornamental art glass. During his 30 years as Art Director, Carder developed new techniques of enamelling and etching. Some of the types of art glass produced include 'Aurene', 'Calcite' and 'Tyrian' glass. In 1918 Steuben became a subsidiary of the Corning Glassworks, and Carder continued as Art Director. The huge range of ornamental glasswares developed by Carder has resulted in him being generally regarded as the founder of the modern tradition in American art glass. He retired from Corning in 1933.

BIBLIOGRAPHY

P. V. Gardner: *The Glass of Frederick Carder* (New York, 1971)
M. J. Madigan: *Steuben Glass: An American Tradition in Crystal* (New York, 1982)
Steuben Glass: The Carder Years (exh. cat., St Petersburg, FL, Mus. F.A., 1984)

K. SOMERVELL

Cardew, Michael (*b* Wimbledon, London, 26 May 1901; *d* Truro, Cornwall, 11 Feb 1983). English potter. As a young boy he watched Edwin Beer Fishley (1832–1911) potting at Fremington, Devon. He won a scholarship to Oxford University but almost failed to graduate because he made pots rather than study in the holidays. In 1923 he joined BERNARD LEACH as a student in the Leach Pottery at St Ives, Cornwall. They shared an interest in English slipware, and in 1926 Cardew left St Ives to set up his own workshop where he planned to revive the tradition. He leased the pottery at Greet, near Winchcombe, Glos, where, from 1926 until 1939, he worked with earthenware clay (e.g. earthenware pie dish, *c.* 1938;

Bristol, Mus. & A.G.), assisted by Elijah Comfort (*d* 1945), Sidney Tustin (*b* 1914), Charles Tustin (*b* 1921) and Raymond Finch (*b* 1914), his partner and ultimate owner of Winchcombe Pottery. In 1939 Cardew moved to St Tudy on the edge of Bodmin Moor, Cornwall, where he founded Wenford Bridge pottery, which was to be his base for the remainder of his life.

In 1942 Cardew began his long association with Africa when he went as Pottery Instructor to Achimota College on the Gold Coast (now Ghana). Here he built and ran Alajo Pottery, making domestic ware and tiles and training West African potters. When the project closed in 1945 Cardew moved to Vumé Dugamé, on the Volta River, where he built a pottery and made stoneware pots glazed a dark bronze-green (e.g. stoneware jar, 1947–8; Brit. Council Col.). His health broke down in Africa, and he returned to Wenford Bridge; here he made stoneware pots from 1949 to 1951, when he returned to West Africa as Pottery Officer for the Nigerian Government. His job was to protect native women potters from exploitation and to teach pottery skills. He built the pottery and training centre at Abuja, where he again made stoneware pots with dark-toned glazes, working with such colleagues as Clement Kofi Athey (*b* 1925) and Ladi Kwali.

Cardew 'retired' to Wenford Bridge in 1965. During the next 18 years he made stoneware pots in between teaching or demonstrating in Britain, the USA, Canada, New Zealand and Australia, where, in 1968, he worked for six months with Aborigines in the Northern Territory. He also wrote *Pioneer Pottery*, a masterpiece of technical information. His pots have been widely exhibited in Britain and Europe and are in public and private collections throughout Britain.

WRITINGS

Pioneer Pottery (London, 1969/*R* 1975)
A Pioneer Potter: An Autobiography (London, 1988)

BIBLIOGRAPHY

Michael Cardew, Crafts Advisory Committee (London, 1976)
G. Clark: *Michael Cardew* (London, 1978)
Michael Cardew and Pupils (exh. cat. by T. Sidey, York, C.A.G., 1983)

KATHY NIBLETT

Cardi, Lodovico. *See* CIGOLI, LODOVICO.

Cardiff [Welsh Caerdydd]. Commercial centre and port on the Severn Estuary, the largest city and, since 1955, capital of the Principality of Wales, a separately administered part of the UK. The Norman castle, established *c.* 1100, occupies the remains of a Roman fortress, founded 2 km from the mouth of the River Taff *c.* AD 60. Next to it developed a medieval borough with a bishopric at Llandaff (3 km north-west), a mid-6th-century Celtic foundation. The modern city, which encloses these sites, is the creation of 19th-century commerce, mainly in the export of iron and coal. This activity reached its peak around 1910, since when the city has evolved into the national administrative centre, with a population nearing 300,000.

The castle retains its Norman keep and the core of its late 3rd-century Roman walls, refaced 1900–30. The residential west range, rebuilt 1777–8 by Henry Holland, was extended for John Patrick Crichton-Stuart, 3rd Marquess of Bute (*see* STUART, (2)), from 1868 to 1893 to designs

Cardiff, Civic Centre: Law Courts (left) and City Hall, both 1897–1904, by Edwin Rickards

by William Burges. It is one of the most elaborate of his medieval fantasy buildings (*see* BURGES, WILLIAM, fig. 1, for illustration of the interior). South and east of the castle and around the Pierhead (2 km south-east of the centre) extend streets with some good Victorian commercial and public buildings, but this period of growing prosperity is best represented architecturally by several fine churches. The decayed cathedral at Llandaff was rebuilt (1843–69) by John Prichard and John Pollard Seddon; serious war damage forced a second restoration in 1949–63 by George Pace (1915–75). Some of the earlier fittings survive, notably a triptych, the *Seed of David* (1858–64) by Dante Gabriel Rossetti, and windows by Morris, Marshall, Faulkner & Co.; Pace added the concrete parabolic organ arch, carrying Jacob Epstein's sculpture *Christ in Majesty* (aluminium; 1956). In 1864–6 William Butterfield built the spacious St Augustine, Penarth, 'one of his most majestic achievements' (Thompson, 1971, p. 243), enriched by his characteristic polychromy. Equally grand is St German (1884), Adamsdown, by G. F. Bodley and Thomas Garner (1839–1906), which is as dignified as Llandaff Cathedral and more elegant. Commercial prosperity up to 1910 also produced attractive shopping arcades and handsome residential streets, for example Ninian Road, Roath, and Cathedral Road, Riverside, with richly gabled and bay-windowed house fronts.

The summit of public ambition in Cardiff is marked by the Civic Centre in Cathays Park, the finest group of early 20th-century Neo-classical buildings in Britain (see fig.). The grid layout presents major designs by young architects, such as Edwin Alfred Rickards' City Hall (1897–1904), in astylar Baroque Revival with lavish exterior reliefs and a tall clock tower, and his Law Courts (1897–1904), in the Tuscan order; E. Vincent Harris's Glamorgan County Hall (1908–10), a Roman Corinthian design based on George Basevi's Fitzwilliam Museum, Cambridge; and the University Bute Building (1911–16) by Percy Thomas (1883–1969), in free-style Roman Doric. Among works by established architects are Ninian Comper's World War I *Memorial* (1924–8), using the Corinthian order from

Epidauros, Smith & Brewer's National Museum of Wales (built 1910–27), in a stately simplified Greek Doric, and University College (1903–9) by William Douglas Caröe (1857–1938), a rich but over-extended scheme in Ionic Baroque Revival. Public sculpture includes the South African *War Memorial* by Albert Toft (1862–1949) and several figures by Sir William Goscombe John. In 1937–9 Sir Percy Thomas added the Temple of Peace and Health, in a stripped Neo-classical style. Apart from the austere New Welsh Office (1977–80) by Sir Alex Gordon (*b* 1917), which dominates the earlier buildings of Cathays Park in size and scale, and the acoustically successful St David's Hall (1979–83) by the Seymour Harris Partnership, few buildings from the period 1945–90 are of special note. Interest now centres on the Bay Scheme for the Pierhead and docks area, where Alsop & Lyall's tubular Visitor Centre initiated in 1989 a new surge of activity in public art and architecture. In 1994 the competition for the new Cardiff Bay Opera House was won by Zaha Hadid.

The National Museum of Wales houses, in galleries opened 1987–93, the national collection of fine and applied art. It contains European and British works from the 16th century onwards and is particularly strong in portraiture, landscape and porcelain. There are also three special collections: works by Welsh artists, with stone-carving of the Celtic/Early Christian period, paintings by Richard Wilson and David Jones and sculpture by William Goscombe John and Ivor Roberts-Jones (*b* 1913); 19th-century French art (the Davies Bequests), with paintings by Monet, Renoir, Manet, Jean-François Millet and Honoré Daumier and sculpture by Rodin; and fine Welsh porcelain from the Nantgarw factory (1813–22) and the Swansea potteries (*c.* 1767–1870). Cardiff also has the National Industrial and Welsh Folk museums, while several galleries, including Oriel, Ffotogallery, The Old Library and Chapter Arts Centre, show temporary exhibitions.

BIBLIOGRAPHY

J. H. James: *History and Survey of the Cathedral Church of Llandaff* (Cardiff, 1929)
W. Rees: *Cardiff: A History of the City* (Cardiff, 1969)
P. Thompson: *William Butterfield* (London, 1971)
J. Hilling: *Cardiff and the Valleys: Architecture and Townscape* (London, 1973)
M. J. Daunton: *Coal Metropolis, Cardiff, 1870–1914* (Leicester, 1977)
J. Davies: *Cardiff and the Marquesses of Bute* (Cardiff, 1980)
J. Mordaunt Crook: *William Burges and the High Victorian Dream* (London, 1981)
I. N. Soulsby: *The Towns of Medieval Wales* (Chichester, 1983)
——: *Cardiff: A Pictorial History* (Chichester, 1989)
M. Evans and O. Fairclough: *The National Museum of Wales: A Companion Guide to the National Art Gallery* (Cardiff and London, 1993)

JEREMY LOWE

Cardigan, Earls of. *See* BRUDENELL.

Cardinal, Douglas (Joseph) (*b* Calgary, Alta, 7 March 1934). Canadian architect. He studied at the University of British Columbia, Vancouver (1953–4), and at the University of Texas in Austin (1956–63; BArch.). He worked for Bissell & Holman in Red Deer, Alberta (1963–7), and opened his practice there in 1964. In 1967 he opened a second office in Edmonton, where he practised from 1976. He was of North American Indian descent, and from the outset of his career in northern Alberta he endeavoured to weld indigenous philosophy, especially that of the Plains Indians, with contemporary material culture and technology. His earliest completed building, Guloien House, Sylvan Lake, Alberta (1967), was one of a series of commissions for social and educational facilities to serve the native peoples in north-western Canada. Besides expressing his aim of combining native tradition with modern practice, it also indicated his consistent social concern by the involvement of the client in the design process; through that same process he developed a Master Plan for the Alberta Indian Education Centre at Edmonton (from 1970).

Cardinal's predilection for fluid, organic forms with curvilinear profiles and plans, with a preference for natural or hand-finished materials, particularly brick, is exemplified in his best-known early work, St Mary's Roman Catholic Church, Red Deer, Alberta (1967–8). The curving brick walls of the church seem to coalesce with the more massive undulations of the surrounding landscape while also symbolizing its significance and religious purpose; they also support a technically sophisticated suspended concrete roof.

During the 1970s Cardinal completed a series of institutional commissions throughout western Canada. The Hay River High School, Northwest Territories (1972–3), achieved a blend of serviceable plan and naturalized form, intended to accommodate the provincial educational system to the native environment. It led to further commissions for schools in rural Alberta: at Bow Island (1973), Kehewen (1975), Ile à La Crosse (1976) and at Spruce Grove (1980). The design of the Regional College and Theatre at Grande Prairie, Alberta (1975–6), displayed particular refinement in the plastic articulation of mass and volume. He also adapted his regulated but informal concept of spatial organization to a conventional urban setting in Holy Trinity Catholic High School, Edmonton (1983–4). At the same time that he demonstrated analysis of purpose and user preference in other types of community building, he undertook a development study for drop-in centres in the predominantly native communities bordering Slave Lake.

Undulating profiles and plans and variegated brick facing continued to be motifs in Cardinal's work, for example the Alberta Government Services Centre at Ponoka (1977). For him curved forms were both an expression of basic tenets of native culture and philosophy and a reaction at the practical level to the rather severe rectilinear architecture that was still dominant at the beginning of his career. The grandest expression of his 'cultural shell' is the Canadian Museum of Civilization, Hull, Quebec (1985–9); its rhythmic and richly textured, poured- and hammered-concrete exterior fabric contains diversely articulated exhibition spaces and provides a symbolic ensemble with the federal parliament buildings, which face it across the river. In his book *Of the Spirit* (1977) he stressed the desire to realize individual and societal needs in order to 'reinstate our humanness as the most important element in all our efforts'. In 1993 Cardinal won the prestigious commission for the new Smithson Museum of Native American History in Washington, DC, confirming his reputation as a highly inventive manipulator of organic form.

WRITINGS

Of the Spirit: Writings by Douglas Cardinal, (Edmonton, Alta, 1977)
'In Harmony with the Land, Compatible with Man', *Habitat*, 3–4 (1977), pp. 25–7

BIBLIOGRAPHY

Contemp. Architects
C. M. Ede: *Canadian Architecture, 1960/1970* (Toronto, 1971), pp. 198–206
A. Rogatnick and A. Balkind: 'The Work of Douglas Cardinal: An Evolving Indian Architecture', *Artscanada*, xxxiii/3 (1976), pp. 35–42
L. Whiteson: *Modern Canadian Architects* (Edmonton, 1983), pp. 70–73
C. Bergeron: *Canadian Architectural Periodicals Index* (Quebec, 1986), p. 293
R. Cawker: *Contemporary Canadian Architecture: The Mainstream and Beyond* (Markham, Ont., 1988), pp. 130–33
T. Boddy: *The Architecture of Douglas Cardinal* (Edmonton, 1989)

R. WINDSOR LISCOMBE

Cardo. Term for a longitudinal street in a Hellenic or ancient Roman city. The *cardo maximus* was the main street running north–south (*see* ROME, ANCIENT, §III, 2).

Cardon. Flemish family of sculptors. The brothers (1) Servaes Cardon and (2) Joannes Cardon were the sons and pupils of the decorative sculptor Forci [Fursy] Cardon (*c.* 1577–1651), who was responsible for some of the sculptural decorations of the chapel of the Mercers' Guild in Onze-Lieve-Vrouw Cathedral in Antwerp, as well as for some sculpture for their guildhall. What little remains of the brothers' work is in a typically robust Flemish Baroque style, although some of the sculptures associated with Joannes display the greater degree of elegance and sophistication of the High Baroque style.

(1) Servaes [Servais] **Cardon** (*b* Antwerp, *bapt* 19 April 1608; *d* ?Antwerp, between 11 Jan and 4 Nov 1649). He became a master sculptor in the Antwerp Guild of St Luke in 1628–9. During the 1630s he made a number of stone statues of the *Virgin* for street-corner shrines in Antwerp. His most important creation was the pulpit (1642; destr.) for the Benedictine abbey church at Afflighem, near Brussels. He also carved a touchstone and white marble altar for the church of St Jacobus in Antwerp (dedicated in 1642; destr.). About 1648 he made the stone high altar for the church of Ste Amelberga in Zandhoven, in the province of Antwerp, and in 1648 a marble altar for the charterhouse at Lier (since 1784, St Lambertus, Gestel near Lier). A number of terracotta statuettes by him survive, signed and in some instances dated; they include an ?*Apostle* (Paris, Louvre) and *Bacchus* (ex-Capouillet col., Brussels). A signed terracotta portrait bust of a man, dated 1646, was formerly in an Amsterdam private collection (see *Grande Encyclopédie de la Belgique et du Congo*, ii, Brussels, 1952, p. 199, fig. 167). There is an oak *Virgin and Child*, attributed to Servaes Cardon, in the Musée de la Ville de Bruxelles, Brussels.

(2) Joannes [Jan; Jean] **Cardon** (*b* Antwerp, *bapt* 25 Jan 1614; *d* ?Antwerp, before 7 April 1656). Brother of (1) Servaes Cardon. He became a master in the Guild of St Luke in Antwerp in 1643. During the 1640s he visited France to perfect his skills. Like Servaes, he worked for the abbey church of Afflighem, where he carved the wooden stalls (1651; untraced). In 1654–5 Peter Verbrugghen (i) is recorded as making the rood screens for several altars in the church of St Paulus in Antwerp (one survives) from the designs of 'Monsieur Cardon'. This was presumably Joannes, since Servaes had died in 1649. At least two graceful signed and dated terracotta statuettes by Joannes survive. They include a *Virgin and Child* (1643; Antwerp, priv. col., see *Le siècle de Rubens*, exh. cat., Brussels, Musées Royaux B.-A., 1965, p. 354). However, their attribution is not entirely secure, since another sculptor called Jan Cardon, born in Douai in 1605 or 1612, is recorded in Antwerp. A similar uncertainty hangs over several small, secular, terracotta sculptures by 'Cardon' that appear in 17th- and 18th-century inventories.

UNPUBLISHED SOURCES

Brussels, Bib. Royale Albert 1er, MS. 17.649.51 [P. Baert: *Recueil de documents pour servir à l'histoire de la sculpture et de l'architecture en Belgique* (late 18th-century)]

BIBLIOGRAPHY

NBW: 'Cardon (Forci)'
A. Pinchart: 'Documents inédits', *Archvs A., Sci. & Lett.*, i (1860), pp. 254–5
P. Rombouts and T. van Lerius: *De Liggeren en andere historische Archieven der Antwerpsche Sint-Lucasgilde* [The Liggeren and other historic archives of the Guild of St Luke, Antwerp], ii (The Hague, 1872), pp. 117, 122–4, 127, 133, 140, 150–51, 154, 160, 203–4
Exposition des anciens métiers d'art malinois, d'art religieux de la Province d'Anvers et de folklore local: Edition définitive (exh. cat., ed. H. Dierickx-Beke fils; Mechelen, Kon. Acad. Beeld. Kst., 1911), p. 48
J. Casier and P. Bergmans: *L'Art ancien dans les Flandres (Région de l'Escaut): Mémorial de l'exposition rétrospective organisée à Gand en 1913* (Brussels and Paris, 1914), i, pp. 90–91, fig. 121
M. Casteels: 'De beeldhouwers de Nole te Kamerijk, te Utrecht en te Antwerpen' [The sculptors of Nole at Kamerijk, Utrecht and Antwerp], *Acad. Anlct: Kl. S. Kst.*, xvi (1961), pp. 40, 49, 52, 107, 247, 251–5, 304, 344–5, 354
La Sculpture au siècle de Rubens dans les Pays-Bas méridionaux et la principauté de Liège (exh. cat., Brussels, Mus. A. Anc., 1977), pp. 33–5
G. Persoons: *Sebastiaen de Neve's Communiebank uit 1655–1657 in Sint-Pauluskerk Antwerpen* [Sebastiaen de Neve's communion bench of 1655–7 in St Paul's Church, Antwerp] (Antwerp, 1981), pp. 9, 14–15
M. Vandenven: 'Van Diepenbeeck-Boeyermans-van der Sluysen: Enkele archivalische gegevens' [Van Diepenbeeck-Boeyermans-van der Sluysen: some archival material], *Feestbundel: Bij de opening van het Kolveniershof en het Rubenianum* (Antwerp, 1981), pp. 117–18

HELENA BUSSERS

Cardon, Anthony [Antoine] (*b* Brussels, 15 May 1772; *d* London, 16 April 1813). Flemish engraver and print publisher, active in London. The son of Antoine Alexandre Joseph Cardon (1739–1822), a painter and engraver in Brussels, he was persuaded by the troubled times to go to London in 1792. He entered the Royal Academy Schools on 3 November 1792 and was engaged by Paul Colnaghi to engrave, under the direction of Luigi Schiavonetti, three of the *Cries of London* after Francis Wheatley in 1794–6. Cardon was an enterprising man, soon establishing himself as an independent publisher. He took advantage of the peace of 1801, in that year engraving and publishing in Paris and London Joseph Boze's painting of *The First Consul and General Berthier at the Battle of Marengo* (untraced) jointly with the painter. He was known to Joseph Farington, who noted some of his activities, such as his purchase of two paintings by Philippe Jacques de Loutherbourg for engraving (4 March 1805) and his defeat by Thomas Landseer in a ballot at the Royal Academy for Associate Engravers (10 Feb 1806). He was the joint proprietor of four large plates of the *Storming of Seringapatam* after Robert Ker Porter with Luigi Schiavonetti and his brother Niccolo Schiavonetti, with whom he frequently worked. In 20 years Cardon produced a great number of plates of historical subjects as well as portraits and was thought to have died as a result of over-application.

BIBLIOGRAPHY

O'Donoghue; Thieme–Becker

J. Farington: *Diaries* (1793–1821), ed. K. Garlick, A. Macintyre and K. Cave as *The Diaries of Joseph Farington* (New Haven and London, 1978–84), vii, pp. 2528, 2681

DAVID ALEXANDER

Cardona, S Vicente. Former collegiate church in Catalonia, Spain. The first reference to a church dedicated to St Vincent in Cardona Castle dates to AD 980. By the end of the century the canons were already following the rule established at Aachen, but the crucial stage in the church's development took place under Bremon, Vizconde de Cardona (*d* 1029). In 1019, following the advice of Oliba, Abbot of Ripoll, he restored religious life in the church and endowed it generously. Shortly before his death Bremon began work on a new church, which was consecrated in 1040; according to the surviving record of the endowment, the lords of Cardona promised to protect the religious community in their castle. In 1090 the Augustinian rule was introduced.

S Vicente is perhaps the boldest yet most harmonious example of First Romanesque architecture in Catalonia (*see* ROMANESQUE, §II, 1 and fig. 1). The church is 57 m long and is built of *petit appareil* with thick mortar layers, characteristic of Lombard masons. The stones are regular in size, especially in the piers and arches. The nave is wide, with very narrow aisles. The last and shortest of the four nave bays is the narthex, which gives access to the church. Two other doors, on the northern and southern sides, were reserved for the use of the canons. The transept (14.5 m high) is lower than the nave (19 m), but in width it equals the dimensions of the main nave bays. In plan the transept barely projects beyond the aisle walls. There is an eastern apsidal chapel on each arm, corresponding to the nave aisles. The raised presbytery has a straight bay preceding the main apse.

The spiral staircases in the side walls of the narthex now lead to the aisle roofs. Although it has been suggested that the staircases belonged to towers, which would have given the church a two-tower façade, supporting evidence has not been found. The stairs also give access to a tribune gallery above the narthex, which was possibly for the use of the count and his family during the services.

Inside the church the main supports are cruciform piers, with pilasters on the main faces leading to transverse arches under the barrel vault. Each side-aisle bay contains three small groin vaults, and the narthex is also groin-vaulted. The transept and presbytery are barrel-vaulted, the apses have semi-domes, and over the crossing is a dome on squinches enclosed within an octagonal tower. The church is well lit, with clerestory and aisle windows; there are also windows in the dome, the transept ends, the presbytery and the apses. All the windows except those in the west façade and the transept walls are double chamfered. The nave has a stretch of wall above the crossing arch to compensate for the lower height of the transept. This aesthetically displeasing solution has been interpreted as evidence of a decision to build the nave higher than the side aisles. There can be no doubt, however, that the church was built in one campaign.

Access to the crypt was originally by means of lateral staircases; the flights of stairs flanking the central doorway were the result of subsequent alterations. The crypt, like

Cardona, S Vicente, exterior from the south-east, consecrated 1040; from a photograph, 1910, before restoration

its contemporaries, such as the first crypt of Vic Cathedral, has four bays with three aisles and groin vaults springing from monolithic columns topped by simple, undecorated capitals.

The raised presbytery, which has parallels with North Italian architecture, is extremely effective. The inside walls of the presbytery and main apse are articulated by niches rising from the floor and delineated by pilaster strips. This system of wall articulation was to develop into the columnar arcading of mature Romanesque architecture.

The exterior of the building clearly emphasizes and demonstrates the organization of the interior spaces (see fig.). The walls are decorated with hanging arches and Lombard bands, and the arcading round the main apse, the presbytery and the east sides of the transept is punctured with openings, which simulate an exterior gallery and accentuate the chiaroscuro effects of the design. The pilaster strips rise from a high socle, which emphasizes the slender proportions of the building. S Vicente became a model for many other more modest structures built in Catalonia during the 11th century.

In the 12th century the narthex vaults were decorated with a painted cycle of complex iconography focused on the majestic image of *Christ Pantokrator* in the central vault and New Testament scenes in the side vaults (the *Presentation in the Temple* and the *Flagellation*). In 1592 the building became a collegiate church, but from the late 18th century it was used as barracks, causing considerable damage. In the 20th century successive restorations were carried out, modifying the interior proportions of the building by lifting the old irregular paving stones. The west staircases and the dome were reconstructed, and the remains of the plaster on the walls were removed, leaving a pock-marked surface.

See also ROMANESQUE, §II.

BIBLIOGRAPHY

J. Sureda: *La pintura románica en Cataluña* (Madrid, 1981)
Catalunya romànica, ix: *El Bages* (Barcelona, 1984), pp. 151–71

M. GUARDIA

Cardona, Segorbe y. *See* SEGORBE Y CARDONA.

Carducho [Carduccio]. Italian family of artists, active in Spain. The brothers (1) Bartolomé Carducho and (2) Vicente Carducho settled in Spain after moving there in 1585 to work at the Escorial.

BIBLIOGRAPHY

J. J. Martín González: 'El arte y las artistas en la corte en el siglo XVII', *Archv Esp. A.*, xxxi/121 (1958), pp. 125–42
S. Jacob: 'Elemente florentinische in der spanischen Malerei des frühen 17. Jahrhunderts', *Mitt. Ksthist. Inst. Florenz*, xiii (1967), pp. 115–64
D. Angulo and A. E. Pérez Sánchez: *Historia de la pintura española: Pintura madrileña del primer tercio del siglo XVII* (Madrid, 1969)
J. Brown and R. Engass: *Italy and Spain, 1600–1750*, Sources & Doc. Hist. A. (Englewood Cliffs, NJ, 1970)
S. Schroth: *The Private Picture Collection of the Duke of Lerma* (diss., New York U., 1990)

ALFONSO E. PÉREZ SÁNCHEZ,
MARY CRAWFORD VOLK

(1) Bartolomé [Bartolomeo] **Carducho** (*b* Florence, *c.* 1560; *d* Madrid, 1608). Painter, sculptor and architect. He trained in Florence with Bartolomeo Ammanati in painting, sculpture and architecture, and at the age of 18 he was working under Federico Zuccaro on the painting of the dome of the cathedral of S Maria del Fiore in Florence. He then accompanied Zuccaro to Rome, where he executed various commissions for Pope Gregory XIII and became implicated in the legal case of 1581 against Zuccaro and Domenico Passignano over the engravings of the *Porta Virtutis*, considered insulting by their detractors. Pardoned by the Pope, he continued to work under Zuccaro in all the latter's papal commissions.

In 1585 Bartolomé travelled to Spain to paint the cloister at the Escorial with his master and a team of assistants. He appears to have been the only assistant to please Philip II for he remained in the Spanish royal service after his companions left in 1586 and when Zuccaro returned to Italy in 1589. Bartolomé continued to work on court commissions and also acted as a dealer, selling paintings for such fellow Tuscans as Lodovico Cigoli and Domenico Passignano, with whom he remained in contact and whose work was much admired in Spain. In 1592 he married Jerónima Capello, the widow of a joiner who had worked at the Escorial. In 1598 he was appointed Pintor del Rey and executed the series of scenes from the *Life of St Lawrence* (Madrid, Escorial). In 1599 he collaborated with Luis de Carvajal and Pompeo Leoni on the triumphal arches erected in Madrid for the entry of Margaret of Austria, the queen of Philip III. Bartolomé was a close friend of Leoni and on several occasions acted for the sculptor in financial matters. In 1600 he painted the *Adoration of the Magi* (Segovia, Alcázar chapel) and was proposed by El Greco as an appraiser of the latter's paintings for the Colegio de Doña María de Aragón, Madrid (dispersed), jointly with Juan Pantoja de la Cruz, who was appointed by the college. At the same time he became the favourite painter of the powerful Francisco Gómez de Sandoval y Rojas, Duque de LERMA, the King's favourite and first minister, who entrusted him with many commissions in Madrid and more especially in Valladolid between 1601 and 1606, when the court was established there. During the first decade of the 17th century his younger brother (2) Vicente Carducho worked as his assistant and collaborator, for example on the altar paintings (1604–10) for the Franciscan church of S Diego, Valladolid. Much of the biographical information available on Bartolomé comes through Vicente; for example the fact that when he came to Spain he abandoned sculpture and architecture and devoted himself entirely to painting and decorative work in fresco.

Bartolomé's work was a point of departure for naturalistic painting in Castile; it provided a bridge between the austere Counter-Reformation painting of the reign of Philip II and the pre-Baroque character of Spanish art in the first third of the 17th century. He was trained in academic Vasarian Mannerism, with its emphasis on draughtsmanship and composition, but he was also familiar with Correggio's use of *sfumato*, as well as the looser technique and rich colouring of the Venetian school. At the same time Bartolomé's taste for realistic detail and the attempt to achieve a unified atmosphere in his treatment of light brought him nearer to the naturalism of the succeeding generation of Spanish artists. For example, in the *Death of St Francis* (1593; see fig.) he anticipated the naturalistic style of Zurbarán's generation in the still-life objects painted with exceptional intensity, in the realism

Bartolomé Carducho: *Death of St Francis*, oil on canvas, 1.15×1.53 m, 1593 (Lisbon, Museu Nacional de Arte Antiga)

of the faces and in the intense, direct lighting. His *Deposition* (1595; Madrid, Prado) demonstrates a light, fluid technique in the Venetian manner and a refined palette of pinks, mauves and deep greens that was to become popular with other, younger artists in Madrid such as Eugenio Cajés and Jusepe Leonardo. The *Adoration of the Magi* of 1600 and the *Last Supper* (1605; Madrid, Prado) are similarly fluid in execution, with rich Venetian colouring and intense expressions on some of the faces.

ALFONSO E. PÉREZ SÁNCHEZ

(2) Vicente Carducho (*b* Florence, 1570–76; *d* Madrid, 1638). Painter and theorist, brother of (1) Bartolomé Carducho. He became a prolific painter for both the church and the court in Castile, adapting a late 16th-century Italianate style, introduced into Spain in the 1580s, to Spanish themes and settings. After his death this style was superseded in monastic programmes by Zurbarán's pietistic simplicity and in altarpieces and devotional painting by the elegant compositions of van Dyck and Rubens, while Velázquez was unrivalled as a portrait painter. Of more enduring influence than Vicente's paintings, however, was his *Diálogos de la pintura* (Madrid, 1633), an erudite defence of painting as a noble pursuit and of the artist as a learned humanist. While painters in Spain struggled until the 18th century to attain freedom from artisanship, the *Diálogos* featured significantly in 17th-century efforts to achieve that goal, and with Francisco Pacheco's *Arte de la pintura* (Seville, 1649), is one of the most important 17th-century theoretical writings in Spanish.

1. Religious painting. 2. Career at court. 3. The *Diálogos de la pintura*.

1. RELIGIOUS PAINTING. Vicente's service to the Spanish crown began with his apprenticeship with Bartolomé at the Escorial. By 1601 he was working at Valladolid, the seat of the court until 1606, and at Lerma, the personal fiefdom of Philip III's first minister, Francisco Gómez de Sandoval y Rojas, Duque de Lerma. His first important commission (1604–10) involved collaboration with Bartolomé in the church of S Diego, Valladolid. The large central painting, dedicated to S Diego de Alcalá de Henares (Valladolid, Sección Pint.), portrays the saint in ecstasy, a theme Vicente repeated in later years. It is flanked by scenes of the *Annunciation* and the *Stigmatization of St Francis* (Valladolid, Sección Pint.). Vicente executed at least five other altar paintings of the Annunciation, all variations on the composition at Valladolid, for churches in Castile during the subsequent 15 years. The principal stylistic features of his work were developed at this date: careful drawing, smooth surfaces and classicizing compositions that caught figures in tableau-like arrangements. Iconographically the paintings for S Diego reveal Vicente's preference for lucid, orthodox formulation, which contributed to his success in such commissions. For the next

decade and a half, he supplied numerous altarpieces for Franciscan, Hieronymite and Augustinian churches and monasteries in the region.

In 1626 Vicente contracted for his single most important religious commission, a cycle of 56 paintings for the Carthusian monastery of El Paular, near Segovia. The first 27 episodes illustrate scenes from the *Life of St Bruno*, the 11th-century founder of the Order (see fig. 1). The major events in the ordinal history itself are depicted in a further 27 images, with two additional panels showing the escutcheons of Philip IV and of the Order. Vicente made numerous drawings and oil sketches for this commission, which reveal his working methods more completely than for any other work (some Madrid, Bib. N.; Madrid, Real Acad. S Fernando; and Florence, Uffizi). Dispersed when El Paular was suppressed in 1836, the paintings are in Spanish museums and institutions on deposit from the Museo del Prado, Madrid.

Vicente's paintings at El Paular comprised the most extended monastic cycle in 17th-century Europe at a time when such commissions were proliferating in Italy and France as well as Spain. He drew inspiration from Giovanni Lanfranco's cycle for the church of S Martino in the Carthusian monastery at Naples in 1620, probably known through engravings, and set an example for Francisco Zurbarán's work (1638–9) in the charterhouse at Jérez de la Frontera and for Eustache Le Sueur's paintings (1645–8; Paris, Louvre) for the charterhouse in Paris. Vicente's cycle has been compared in Spain with the work of Zurbarán, whose career was more completely concerned with monastic programme painting than Vicente's. The latter's paintings, however, display little of Zurbarán's austerity. His gestures are more rhetorical, the costumes more elegant and the choice of moment more dramatic while his composition is marked by violent action and theatrical arrangement. The choice of episodes from the lives of St Bruno and his most illustrious successors in the Order reflects a specifically 17th-century reading of Carthusian history. The dramatic programme of paintings was devised by the reformist prior of the Order, Juan de Baeza (*d* 1641), who stressed the mystical yet violent nature of Carthusian history, from St Bruno's miraculous conversion around 1082 to the Counter-Reformation martyrdoms of friars in England and Germany. Vicente displayed similar affinities with a Baroque viewpoint in his late works for other religious establishments, such as the *Martyrdom of St Peter Armengol* (Madrid, S Jeronimo), one of twelve works painted (1632–5) for the Trinitarians at Madrid, and the *Return of St John of Matha from Tunis* (Villanueva y Geltrú, Mus. Balaguer, see M. Crawford Volk, 1977, pl. 132), one of three paintings executed in 1631–2 for the Mercedarians at Madrid.

2. CAREER AT COURT. From 1609 Vicente's official position was Pintor del Rey, although he continued to produce religious works. His knowledge of the royal collections, extremely rich in Venetian works and especially those of Titian, is evident in the three paintings he executed between 1614 and 1616 for the main altar of the newly built royal establishment of the Encarnación in Madrid. The flanking paintings, of *St Margaret* and *St Philip* (*in situ*), honouring the patron saints of the founders, Philip

1. Vicente Carducho: *Finding a Miraculous Spring*, oil on canvas, 3.45×3.15 m (Madrid, Museo del Prado); from the series the *Life of St Bruno*, 1626–32

III and his queen, Margaret of Austria, reveal Vicente's knowledge, for example of Titian's *St Margaret* of *c.* 1564–8 (Madrid, Prado). They also introduce the bi-level compositional organization that he later frequently employed.

In 1627 Vicente participated in the competition for a painting showing the expulsion of the Moors in 1609 under Philip III. The winning work was to hang in the Alcázar's Salón Nuevo, an important room on the south façade of the building in which receptions and official ceremonies took place. It would join a group of newly installed paintings from the royal collections, including Titian's *Allegory of the Battle of Lepanto* (*c.* 1572–5; Madrid, Prado), with subjects relating to the Spanish Habsburg monarchy's historic defence of the faith. Diego Velázquez, court painter since 1623, won the competition, which marked the ascendancy of the talented Sevillian over Vicente and the other court painters, Angelo Nardi and Eugenio Cajés. Velázquez's work was destroyed, however, in the fire at the Alcázar in 1734, and ironically only the drawing for Vicente's composition survives from this episode (Madrid, Prado).

Vicente's official duties included collaboration with other court painters to act as a restorer, consultant and connoisseur. During the 1620s and 1630s in particular Philip IV was acquiring new works of art and engaged in extensive projects of decoration at the Alcázar and El Buen Retiro. In this connection Vicente was called upon in 1625 to enlarge three paintings in the royal collection, including Titian's *Allegory of the Battle of Lepanto* and his *Allegory of Religion* (*c.* 1575; Madrid, Prado), that were to be rehung in the Salón Nuevo. In 1629 he carried out repair work, including some painting, in several rooms on the western façade of the Alcázar. In October 1633 he was working with Velázquez, who as portrait painter to the king was responsible for the creation of the royal image, inspecting the likenesses and decorum of some 37 portraits of the royal family collected from shops and other public places where they were being offered for sale. Vicente was probably included because of his long years of service at court and well-known belief in high artistic standards.

Vicente also participated in the next great painting commission given to painters at court, the decoration of the Salón de Reinos at El Buen Retiro (begun *c.* 1634). Twelve paintings of historic battles won by Spanish arms since Philip IV's ascent to the throne in 1621 were required to complete a pictorial ensemble presided over by five equestrian portraits of the royal family. As the senior court painter, Vicente contributed three canvases (all 1634; Madrid, Prado), showing the battles at Rheinfelden (see fig. 2) and Fleurus in 1622, and the relief of Constance in 1633. In these works he displayed both an ability to render the bravura effects suitable for images of victory and considerable skill as a portrait painter. His contribution was again overshadowed, however, by that of Velázquez, the celebrated *Surrender at Breda* (1634–5; Madrid, Prado).

No clear evidence of active rivalry between the two painters is currently known, but from 1623 their professional lives constantly touched. In their art, as in their training and experience, they represented distinct viewpoints, and the greater talent of the younger painter is indisputable. In a passage in the *Diálogos* Vicente seemed to express an anti-naturalist position (unsustained by his own painting) that has been interpreted as a veiled attack on Velázquez. Moreover, Velázquez's entrance into court had enjoyed strong support from Philip IV's first minister, Gaspar de Guzmán y Pimentel, the Conde Duque de Olivares, and his rise in favour was steady and rapid, whereas Vicente's appointment had sprung from an apprenticeship of over ten years with the community of Italian artists called by Philip II to the Escorial. In his ambition to achieve noble rank, however, Velázquez had to overcome objections from the nobility, who still considered painting to be a craft, and Vicente demonstrated his sympathetic involvement in the common struggle by painters in Castile to achieve status as professionals when he published his *Diálogos* in 1633.

2. Vicente Carducho: *Battle of Rheinfelden, 1622*, oil on canvas, 2.97×3.57 m, 1634 (Madrid, Museo del Prado)

3. THE 'DIÁLOGOS DE LA PINTURA'. Adopting the form of eight short dialogues between a master painter and his pupil, Vicente presented a literary argument for painting as a liberal art and, more importantly, described a contemporary cultural context at Madrid within which painters were the intimates of connoisseurs, the literati and courtiers. From the second to the seventh dialogues he surveyed the history, methods, most celebrated practitioners and chief components of painting as an art and included a section on the proper treatment of religious subject-matter. Adhering largely to an established body of theoretical writing produced in Italy during the 15th and 16th centuries, he cited above all the late 16th-century ideas expounded by Giovanni Paolo Lomazzo in *Trattato dell'arte della pittura, scultura et architettura* (Milan, 1584) and by Federico Zuccaro in *L'idea de' pittori, scultori ed architetti* (Turin, 1607). He used Zuccaro especially in emphasizing an intellectual dimension in painterly accomplishment and the limits of pure naturalism. He differed from his Italian sources in eschewing philosophical speculation in favour of practical prescription.

Vicente's remarks in the dialogues about the character of painting were guided in part by a pedagogical purpose. The first dialogue details a study tour abroad from which the pupil has just returned, and includes a survey of the major artistic monuments seen in Flanders, France and especially Italy. This travel is undertaken to complement the young student's education after extensive reading about the arts in ancient and Renaissance texts. Vicente relied heavily in his choice and estimation of the Italian monuments on Vasari's *Vite* (Florence, 1568). The discussion may be a record of an actual trip, perhaps made by the author, or an imaginary journey intended to demonstrate the need for direct visual experience in a young artist's training.

The eighth dialogue is the most original. After offering a glossary of terms and definitions of artistic materials and techniques, Vicente introduces (fol. 147v) a sequence of visits to outstanding collections in Madrid, mentioning a group of courtiers that includes Diego Messia Felípez de Guzmán, Marqués de Leganés; Juan Alfonso Pimentel de Herrera, Conde de Benavente; Francisco de Borja y Aragón, Prince of Esquilache; and Manuel de Acevedo y Zúñiga, Conde de Monterrey. The device drew attention to the cultivated circles around the court in order to enlist aid in the painters' struggle to achieve recognition. At the same time these passages comprised the principal published reference in Spanish to collecting activity at the Spanish court during the 17th century.

The *Diálogos*, illustrated with eight full-page engravings allegorically related to the text, show Vicente as a theorist using Mannerist sources to demonstrate the importance of the idea of the learned artist in the Baroque age. Bound with certain editions of the *Diálogos* was the *Memorial informativo*, a collection of essays by six prominent men of letters, including Lope de Vega (1562–1635), defending the idea of painting as a liberal art. Published in 1629, it had originally been written in response to a legal case in which a group of painters in Madrid had refused to pay taxes levied on them on the basis that they were engaged in commerce. Litigation had not resolved the issue, and Vicente's writing contributed a shrewd and erudite further testimony in favour of the noble status of painting.

WRITINGS

Diálogos de la pintura: Su defensa, origen, essencia, definición, modos y diferencias (Madrid, 1633); ed. F. Calvo Serraller (Madrid, 1979)

Artists' Techniques in Golden Age Spain: Six Treatises in Translation, trans. Z. Veliz (Cambridge, 1986)

BIBLIOGRAPHY

G. Cruzada Villaamil: 'Conatos de formar una academia o escuela de dibujo en Madrid en el siglo XVII', *A. España*, v (1866), pp. 167–72, 258–70

A. Fumagalli: 'I trattatisti e gli artisti italiani en un trattato d'arte spagnolo', *The Athenaeum*, ii (1914), pp. 292–309

B. Cuartero y Huerta: 'La cartuja de S María de El Paular y su colección de cinquenta y seis lienzos pintados por Vicente Carducho', *A. Esp.*, v (1921), pp. 266–82

J. J. Martín González: 'Relaciones entre Nardi, Carducho y Velázquez', *Archv Esp. A.*, xxxi/121 (1958), pp. 59–66

J. Baticle: 'Les Peintres de la vie de Saint Bruno au XVIIe siècle: Carducho, Lanfranc, Le Sueur', *Rev. A.* [Paris], viii (1959), pp. 17–28

G. Kubler: 'Vicente Carducho's Allegories of Painting', *A. Bull.*, xvii/4 (1965), pp. 439–45

M. L. Caturla: 'Documentos en torno a Vicencio Carducho', *A. Esp.*, iii (1968–9), pp. 146–231

J. Gállego: *El pintor, de artesano a artista* (Granada, 1976)

M. Crawford Volk: *Vicencio Carducho and 17th-century Castilian Painting* (New York and London, 1977)

——: 'Velázquez and the Liberal Arts', *A. Bull.*, lviii/1 (1978), pp. 69–86

——: 'Addenda: The Madrid Academy', *A. Bull.*, lxi/4 (1979), p. 627

J. M. Moran Turina: 'Felipe III y las artes', *An. Hist. A.*, 1 (1989), pp. 159–79

S. Schroth: *The Private Picture Collection of the Duke of Lerma* (Diss., NYU., 1990)

S. Orso: *Velasquez, Los Borrachos, and Painting at the Court of Philip IV* (Cambridge, 1993)

E. Umberger: 'Velasquez and Naturalism: Interpreting *Los Borrachos*', *Res*, 24 (Autumn 1993), pp. 21–43

MARY CRAWFORD VOLK

Careaga, Enrique (*b* Asunción, 30 Aug 1944). Paraguayan painter. He studied in Asunción in the studio of the painter and teacher Cira Moscarda, who helped to reform the artistic values of the younger generation in the 1960s. In 1964 Careaga helped found Los Novísimos, a group concerned with revitalizing Paraguayan art and introducing into it a more cosmopolitan style. He began in his paintings to develop geometrical arrangements that showed a debt to Constructivism (e.g. *Structures III*, 1979; Maldonado, Museum of American Art) and to Op art (e.g. *Diagonal Progression*, 1968–70; Asunción, Mus. Parag. A. Contemp.; and *Chromatic Transparencies*, 1971–2; Paris, Bib. N.). In 1964 he won a scholarship to go to Paris, where he was strongly influenced by Victor Vasarely and the Groupe de Recherche d'Art Visuel, which confirmed his interest in using optical effects to generate the image, as in *Spatial–Temporal Spheres BS 7523* (1975; Washington, DC, Mus. Mod. A. Latin America). The first stage of this work was based on the representation of two-dimensional fields in which effects of vibration and instability were created by the interreaction of strongly contrasting colours. Towards 1972 Careaga introduced three-dimensionality in spatial projects: the structure of a work no longer depended on oscillatory effects that play on perception through light and colour, but it was defined by the presence of weightless volumetric bodies shifting in space, which in their final stage explode and disintegrate. He also used metal in constructions based on geometric shapes (e.g.

Revolving Structure Zama 7916, 1978–9, using stainless steel).

BIBLIOGRAPHY

O. González Real: 'La abstracción geométrica en la plástica paraguaya', *Anticipación y reflexión* (Asunción, 1980), pp. 83–6

O. Blinder and others: *Arte actual en el Paraguay* (Asunción, 1983)

TICIO ESCOBAR

Carena, Felice (*b* Cumiana, nr Turin, 13 Aug 1879; *d* Venice, 10 June 1966). Italian painter. He began his studies at the Accademia Albertina in Turin where he was a pupil of Giacomo Grosso. His early painted works demonstrate his interest in Symbolism, Eugène Carrière, the bourgeois Intimism of the Nabis (Maurice Denis in particular), the painting of Arnold Böcklin and the references to classical mythology in the work of Franz von Stuck, Hermenegild Anglada Camarasa, Ignacio Zuloaga and Leonardo Bistolfi. After 1906 he lived in Rome for almost 20 years. His initial associations there with Ferruccio Ferrazzi (1891–1978) and Felice Casorati, and subsequent involvement with the Secessione romana, imposed an edge of realism on his Symbolist training. During these years he produced the *Portrait of his Mother* (1912; Rome, G.N.A. Mod.) and *Portrait of a Priest* (1913; Venice, Ca' Pesaro). Encouraged by Armando Spadini he developed a 'precious' style of painting, rich with luminous blends of colour and acknowledging a debt to the paintings of the seicento and to classical forms. The *Pilgrims in Emmaus* (1922) and *The Apostles* (1924; both Florence, Pitti) reveal a sympathy with the ideals of the artists who gathered around the Valori plastici. After World War I came official recognition with his appointment in 1924 as a professor at the Accademia di Belle Arti in Florence. At the end of World War II he retired to the lagoon town of Cannaregio, where he lived as a recluse for the last 20 years of his life.

BIBLIOGRAPHY

L. Ozzola: 'Artisti contemporanei: Felice Carena', *Emporium* (June 1914), pp. 403–16

C. L. Ragghianti: 'Carena', *Crit. A.* (1935–6), pp. 148–51

SAVERIO SIMI DE BURGIS

Caresme [Carême], **Jacques-Philippe** (*b* Paris, 25 Feb 1734; *d* Paris, 1 March 1796). French painter, engraver and illustrator. He was the son of the painter Claude-François Caresme (*b* 1709) and studied with his cousin Charles-Antoine Coypel. In 1753 he was a pupil at the Académie Royale, where in 1761 he won second place in the Prix de Rome competition with *Judith and Holofernes* (untraced). Following his acceptance by the Académie in 1766, he was able to exhibit regularly at the Salon until his expulsion in 1778. In 1768 he received a commission for a *Presentation of the Virgin*, one of a group of three paintings destined for Bayonne Cathedral, where it still remains. The following year Caresme showed an oil sketch for the picture at the Salon. Shortly after this he was one of a number of painters selected to work at the Petit Trianon, Versailles, where he was commissioned to produce two overdoors for the antechamber: *Myrrha Changed into Myrrh* and *The Nymph Minthe Changed into Mint* (both *in situ*). The latter work, dated 1772, was exhibited at the Salons of 1775 and 1777, the year in which the Académie commissioned from Caresme, as his *morceau de réception*, a painting for the ceiling of the Galerie d'Apollon in the Louvre, Paris; his failure to produce this work resulted in his expulsion from the Académie at the end of 1778.

The production of Caresme is very various and includes portraits, still-lifes, *fêtes galantes* reminiscent of paintings by Antoine Watteau, Nicolas Lancret or even Jean-Honoré Fragonard (e.g. *Harlequin*; Paris, Mus. Cognacq-Jay) and tavern scenes in the Flemish 17th-century style, as well as landscapes, historical, mythological, and religious subjects, bacchanals and other light-hearted themes. Although he had been accepted into the Académie as a history painter, he is best known as a painter of gallant themes and as an illustrator of risqué subjects. His engravings (see Portalis–Béraldi) enabled him to reach a wide public: he provided illustrations for La Fontaine's *Fables* (Paris, 1765–75) and for *Le Décaméron français* (Paris, 1762). During the French Revolution, which inspired him to produce several works, he adopted a severe classicizing style, as in the *Market-women going to Versailles on 5 October 1789* and the *Execution of the Marquis de Favras on 19 February 1790*.

BIBLIOGRAPHY

Portalis–Béraldi

P. Mantz: 'Jacques-Philippe Caresme', *Chron. A. & Curiosité*, i/5 (21 Dec 1862), pp. 37–9

M. Roux: *Inventaire du fonds français: Graveurs du dix-huitième siècle*, Paris, Bib. N. Dépt. Est. cat., iii (Paris, 1934), pp. 432–3

HÉLÈNE GUICHARNAUD

Carew, John Edward (*b* Tramore, Co. Waterford, *c.* 1782; *d* London, 30 Nov 1868). British sculptor. Possibly the son of an Irish sculptor, he may have received some instruction in Dublin before going to London, where he assisted Sir Richard Westmacott from 1809 to 1823 and set up his own studio in 1821. His marble *Arethusa* (Petworth House, W. Sussex, NT) was bought by George Wyndham, 3rd Earl of Egremont, in 1823. This led to a close association with Egremont; Petworth House has a superb collection of Carew's work in marble, including *Adonis and the Bear* (1826), *The Falconer* (1831) and *Prometheus and Pandora* (1838), all examples of his Neo-classical mythologies, and a series of busts, one of which is a portrait of Egremont (1831).

Carew also made commemorative marble statues of public figures, including *William Huskisson* (1833; Chichester Cathedral), *Edmund Kean* (1835; London, Drury Lane Theat.) and his best-known, *Sir Richard Whittington Listening to the London Bells* (1844; London, Royal Exch.). In these works he eschewed antique dress in favour of modern or historical dress. He contributed *Henry Gratten* (1844) to the important series of statues in St Stephen's Hall, Westminster Palace, London, and made the bronze relief of *The Death of Nelson* (1850) on the base of Nelson's Column in Trafalgar Square. He made a number of religious works, among which were two altarpieces of a Baroque character: the *Baptism of Christ* (1837) for the church of St John the Baptist in Brighton, and the *Assumption* (1853), for the church of the Assumption and St Gregory, Warwick Street, London. More Neo-classical in style were the memorial to *Mrs Fitzherbert* (1837), also in St John the Baptist, Brighton, and the Percy family monument (1837) in Petworth parish church. Carew's sculpture has Neo-classical *gravitas*, tempered by a sense of realism and emotion, particularly in religious and portrait subjects. He ceased to exhibit after 1848 due to failing eyesight.

BIBLIOGRAPHY

Gunnis

R. H. C. Finch: 'The Life and Work of J. E. Carew', *Bull. Irish Georg. Soc.*, ix/3–4 (1966), pp. 84–96

B. Read: *Victorian Sculpture* (New Haven, 1982)

JOHN TURPIN

Carey, William Paulet (*b* Dublin, 1759; *d* Birmingham, 21 May 1839). British writer and dealer. He first trained as a painter and subsequently became an engraver, but an eye injury forced him to turn to art criticism, journalism and dealing. He settled in London before 1792 but travelled extensively throughout Britain, promoting and publicizing the arts. Carey was well-known in artistic circles and was friendly with John Raphael Smith, Francesco Bartolozzi and Benjamin West PRA; he was among the first (1805) to recognize the gifts of Francis Chantrey and was acquainted with Henry Raeburn, whom he visited in Edinburgh in 1818. However, his notices earned him the hostility of Benjamin Robert Haydon, while John Constable dismissed his articles on modern British art for the *Worcester Guardian* (1835) as 'a parcel of sad stuff'.

In his writings Carey lamented the absence of a tradition of history painting in Britain and advocated the claims of a modern and national art. These views recommended him to Sir John Fleming Leicester, later Baron de Tabley, who had formed an important collection of modern British pictures. He opened it to the public in 1818; the following year Carey supplied it with a catalogue raisonné and in 1826 published an extended account of the Tabley collection. In 1837, on a visit to the United States, Carey delivered a lecture to the Artists' Fund Society in Philadelphia and published a pamphlet on the national and commercial benefits of the arts. Before his return in 1838 he consigned a substantial number of paintings and drawings to sales in Philadelphia and Baltimore. Carey was a vigorous participant in the often vitriolic debates that arose out of the exhibitions at the British Institution and elsewhere. His writings, often under a pseudonym such as 'Lorenzo', were strident in tone and essentially conservative and did little to foster the progressive elements in British art.

WRITINGS

Thoughts on the Best Mode of Checking the Prejudices against British Works of Art (York, 1801)

A Critical Description of the Procession of Chaucer's Pilgrims to Canterbury (London, 1808) [critique of Thomas Stothard's *Pilgrimage to Canterbury*, 1806; London, Tate]

Letter to J. A. Esq., a Connoisseur in London (Manchester, 1809)

Cursory Thoughts on the Present State of the Fine Arts (Liverpool, 1810)

Critical Description and Analytical Reviews of Death upon the Pale Horse Painted by Benjamin West (London, 1817) [painting 1817; Philadelphia, PA, Acad. F. A.]

A Descriptive Catalogue of a Collection of Paintings by British Artists in the Possession of Sir John Fleming Leicester, with occasional remarks, etc, by Sir Richard Colt Hoare (London, 1819)

The National Obstacle to the National Public Style Considered (London, 1825)

Some Memoirs of the Patronage and Progress of the Fine Arts, in England and Ireland, During the Reign of George the Second, George the Third, and his Present Majesty; with Anecdotes of Lord de Tabley, of Other Patrons, and of Eminent Artists, and Occasional Critical References to British Works of Art (London, 1826)

Appeal to the Directors of the Royal Irish Institution (Dublin, 1828)

Observations on the Primary Object of the British Institution for the Promotion of the Fine Arts (Newcastle, 1829)

Brief Remarks on the Anti-British Effect of Inconsiderate Criticism on Modern Art and the Exhibition of the Living British Artists (London, 1831)

BIBLIOGRAPHY

C. R. Leslie: *Memoirs of the Life of John Constable RA* (London, 1843, rev. 1845), p. 246

W. T. Whitley: *Art in England 1800–37*, 2 vols (London, 1930–32)

D. Hall: 'Tabley House Papers', *Walpole Soc.*, xxxviii (London, 1960–62), pp. 59–122

□

Caria. Ancient country in south-west Asia Minor (now Turkey), south of the Maeander (Menderes) River and west of modern Fethiye (excepting the coastal cities of IONIA). The Carians claimed to be an indigenous people of mainland Asia Minor, though in Greek tradition they were originally islanders. Until the 4th century BC they lived mainly in mountain villages organized into local federations and grouped around sanctuaries such as that of Carian Zeus at Mylasa (Milas). The Carian language is imperfectly understood, owing to a paucity of surviving inscriptions. The script is alphabetic, and some forms are the same as Greek letters, but surviving fragments are virtually unintelligible, and it is not even certain that the language is Indo-European.

Minoan, Mycenaean and Greek colonization of the region touched only the coasts, leaving the interior Carian until the arrival of the Romans. At Muskebi, near Halikarnassos (Bodrum), there is evidence of Mycenaean settlement, possibly refugees from the upheavals of the Greek mainland at the end of the Bronze Age; Minoan imports found at Iasos and at Miletos in Ionia testify to Cretan settlement there as early as the Middle Bronze Age (*c.* 2050–*c.* 1600 BC), followed by Late Bronze Age Mycenaeans (*c.* 1600–*c.* 1050 BC). Tombs at several sites near Halikarnassos, notably at Asarlik and Dirmil, have produced Proto-Geometric pottery similar to Attic products, possible evidence for Greek settlement; the finds date no earlier than the 8th century BC. At Sinurin, a Carian temple site near Mylasa, a local style of figure-decorated pottery has been identified, and at other Carian sites such as Kaunos, Late Geometric bowls similar to Greek prototypes have been found; these areas later produced local varieties of the East Greek Wild Goat style of orientalizing pottery. The extent of fusion of foreigners and natives at the two main Greek settlements—Halikarnassos and Knidos—remains unclear, as Carian names occur frequently in inscriptions from Halikarnassos, while at Knidos they are virtually unknown.

Caria was subjugated by the Lydians during the 7th and 6th centuries BC and by the Persians in the late 6th century BC, after Lydia and Ionia had already been subsumed into the Persian empire. Attic and East Greek wares began to appear in increasing numbers at this time. The Carians joined the Ionians in the failed revolt against Persia in 499 BC; later in the 5th century BC they were enrolled with the rest of the Greek cities and towns of coastal Asia Minor in the so-called Delian League, set up by Athens to prevent a revival of Persian power in Greek lands.

In 387 BC, under the King's Peace treaty agreed to by Greece and Persia, the Asian cities were recognized as belonging to Persia, and Caria became a Persian satrapy under the Hekatomnid dynasty. The third satrap of Caria was MAUSOLOS (*reg* 377–352 BC), whose first capital was

Caria, Temple of Zeus at Euromos, probably *c.* AD 117–38

at Mylasa. Mausolos moved the capital to Halikarnassos in the 370s BC and devoted his reign to the Hellenization of Caria. His sister and wife, Artemisia, succeeded him and had his tomb, the Mausoleum, built (*see* HALIKARNASSOS, §2). Caria was included in Attalus III's kingdom of Pergamon, which was bequeathed to Rome in 133 BC, when the country became part of the Roman province of Asia. Although it suffered under the Republic and during the civil wars of the 1st century BC, Caria prospered under the Roman Empire, including even the small inland cities, which were still occupied by native Carians. Decline set in during the 3rd century AD, and eventually the emperor Diocletian (*reg* AD 284–305) made Caria a separate province. Bishoprics were established in a number of Carian cities under the Byzantine empire. After the battle of Manzikert in 1071, Seljuk Turks swept across Anatolia and captured most of Caria by the end of the 12th century. In the 14th century Mylasa became the capital of the short-lived Menteşe rulers, predecessors of the Ottoman Turks in Caria; during the 15th century the area was absorbed by the Ottoman empire.

The main coastal cities of ancient Caria were HALIKARNASSOS and KNIDOS, HERAKLEIA UNDER LATMOS, LABRAUNDA (a sacred precinct, not a city proper), Mylasa and Stratonikeia. Iasos and Euromos are among cities known today because of the extent of their surviving ruins, though they appear not to have been among the most important ancient towns. Away from the coast, settlement tended to concentrate along the Maeander River and its tributaries; towns included Tralles (Aydın), Nysa, Alinda, Alabanda (considered by Strabo one of the three most important cities of Caria, with Mylasa and Stratonikeia), APHRODISIAS and HIERAPOLIS. (For further discussion of the main ancient cities of Caria *see* their individual site articles.)

The site of Euromos was originally known as Kyromos or Hyromos, words of non-Greek origin. Its indigenous character can be seen in the Carian-type graves in the area: rectangular tombs cut from the rock, covered with huge stone lids. Euromos is today the site of one of the best preserved temples in Turkey, dedicated to Zeus (see fig.). A Hellenistic inscription (*c.* 320–*c.* 30 BC) from the site mentions Zeus Lepsynos as the titular deity at that time, possibly an assimilation of a Carian god and the Greek Zeus. The surviving structure (probably Hadrianic, AD 117–38) is a Corinthian peripteral temple of 6 by 11 columns on a stylobate measuring 14.4×26.8 m. There were four additional columns in front of the pronaos, the opisthodamos had two columns *in antis*, and inside the cella was a naiskos with a niche that held the cult statue. Sixteen columns remain standing, supporting sections of the architrave; some of the columns are unfluted, implying that the temple was never completed. Excavations carried out during the 1970s produced several terracotta slabs with chariots, birds and floral motifs that suggest that a shrine of some sort existed on the site from as early as the 6th century BC.

Further down the coast at the village of Kuren is the site of Iasos, excavated by Italian archaeologists since 1960. Middle Minoan pottery and remains of Minoan houses date the settlement to as early as *c.* 2000–*c.* 1550 BC, and there are also Mycenaean remains of the Late Bronze Age. In the 9th century BC the site was recolonized by Greeks, who must have appreciated its favourable location on a bulbous peninsula with excellent harbours and nearby marble quarries. The surviving remains are mainly from the Roman period and include a mausoleum in the form of a Syrian-style temple tomb, with a burial chamber surmounted by a small Corinthian temple *in antis* on a 10-step krepidoma. Stoas surrounding the mausoleum now contain some finds from the site; other artefacts are held by the Archaeological Museum at Izmir. The colonnade around the Roman agora has been partially restored, and remains of other buildings may be seen in the area; at the southern end of the city wall stand the ruins of a villa, with floor mosaics and fragments of wall painting. Tombs outside the city wall date from the 3rd millennium BC to the Roman period and include some of Carian type, while Proto-Geometric and Geometric graves have been discovered in the later agora. Post-Classical remains include an early Christian basilica on the site of the earlier Temple of Zeus Megistos overlooking the east harbour, and several Byzantine churches.

Mylasa, capital of the Persian satrapy of Caria under Mausolos before the capital was moved to Halikarnassos, was also the main cult centre of Caria: a single Corinthian column in the centre of the modern town is all that remains standing of the Temple of Carian Zeus (1st century BC), common sanctuary of all the Carians. The most important surviving remains are those of a tomb (2nd–1st century BC) called the Gëmüşkesen (Turk.: 'silver purse'); its design, supported by the proximity of Mylasa to Halikarnassos and the political connections between them, suggests that it was influenced by, or even intended as a smaller copy of, the Mausoleum at Halikarnassos. The structure consists of a square burial chamber of fine masonry on a stepped base. Above the tomb chamber a colonnade made up of four Corinthian pillars at the corners and two Corinthian columns between each pillar supports a shallow pyramid, now mostly destroyed; the roof above the colonnade is decorated with elaborate geometric patterns and foliage motifs. A hole in the floor of the colonnaded platform presumably was used for pouring libations to the dead.

The ancient city of Tralles (now Aydın), was excavated in 1902–3; there is little to see on the ground. Most of the finds, dating from the prehistoric period to the Byzantine era, are in the Archaeological Museum at Istanbul, and there is also a small museum in Aydın. The finest artefact recovered from the site is the so-called Ephebe of Tralles (h. 1.48 m, 1st century BC–1st century AD; Istanbul, Archaeol. Mus.). This marble statue of a youth draped in a thick cloak depicts the subject (possibly a pugilist) leaning in exhaustion against a pillar after an athletic contest.

Sherds from the site of Kaunos suggest that settlement there began as early as the 9th century BC; this original settlement appears to have been exclusively Carian. Hellenistic and Roman remains are well-preserved in many cases, but perhaps more interesting are the rock-cut tombs (mid-4th century BC) across the Dalyan River. The lower levels of the cliff face in which the tombs are cut contain simple chambers carved out of the rock; above are elaborate temple tombs. The use of Greek architectural forms on indigenous Carian rock burials may have much to do with the attempts by the Hekatomnid dynasty to Hellenize the satrapy of Caria. Most of the temple tombs have two or more Ionic columns *in antis*, with a pediment and frieze; some have a surrounding passageway, some an open space above the flat or barrel-vaulted roof; inside there were usually three stone benches on which the dead were laid. The tombs were reused continuously down to the Roman period.

BIBLIOGRAPHY

L. Robert: *La Carie* (Paris, 1954)

J. Boardman: *The Greek Overseas* (London, 1964/*R* 1973, rev. 1980)

E. Akurgal: *Ancient Civilizations and Ruins of Turkey* (Istanbul, 1969, 5/1985)

G. E. Bean: *Turkey Beyond the Maeander* (London, 1971, 2/1980)

G. M. A. Hanfmann: *From Croesus to Constantine: The Cities of Western Asia Minor and their Arts in Greek and Roman Times* (Ann Arbor, 1975)

G. Pugliese Carratelli and others: *Arslantepe, Hieropolis, Iasos, Kyme: Scavi archeologici italiani in Turchia* (Venice, 1993)

□

Cariani [de' Busi]**, Giovanni** (*b* San Giovanni Bianco, nr Fuipiano al Brembo, *c.* 1485; *d* Venice, after 1547). Italian painter. He moved with his family *c.* 1505 to Venice, where he is first described as a painter in a Venetian document of 29 April 1509. His early style was deeply influenced by that of Sebastiano del Piombo rather than by that of Giorgione or Titian. This is evident in such paintings as *St Agatha* (Edinburgh, N.G.) and the *Sacra conversazione* (Venice, Accad.). Even the double *Portrait of Two Young Men* (Paris, Louvre) seems to be based on Sebastiano's portrait *Verdelot and Ubrecht* (untraced). After Sebastiano's departure for Rome (1511), Cariani became interested in the work of Titian, creating a style close to that of his fellow Bergamesque, Palma Vecchio. This is demonstrated in a group of paintings that includes Cariani's first reliably dated work, the *Virgin and Child with Saints and Donors* (Bergamo, priv. col., see Pallucchini and Rossi, pl. I), which once bore the date 1514. Probably datable to the same period is *The Concert* (Warsaw, N. Mus.).

In 1517 Cariani was in Bergamo, where he was commissioned by the Scuola di S Giuseppe to paint an altarpiece, the *Virgin and Saints* (1517–18; Milan, Brera), for S Gottardo. This painting marked a definitive break with his Venetian style, in which his finest works were executed, and a turning towards a drier style featuring angular planes. It is a manner derived from Palma and Titian but more deeply rooted in a local tradition and not equal to that of Lorenzo Lotto, the most distinguished painter then active in Bergamo. Though less original than that of his earlier period, this is Cariani's most characteristic style. In 1519, still in Bergamo, Cariani signed and dated a portrait of *Seven Members of the Albani Family* (Bergamo, Roncalli priv. col., see 1983 exh. cat., p. 61) and in 1520 completed the *Virgin and Child with a Worshipper* and the *Resurrection* (both Milan, Brera), commissioned by Ottaviano Vimercati for S Pietro at Crema. Dating from the same period are the portraits of *Giovanni Benedetto Caravaggi* (Bergamo, Gal. Accad. Carrara) and *Giovan Antonio Caravaggi* (Ottawa, N.G.; see fig.).

Giovanni Cariani: *Giovan Antonio Caravaggi*, oil on canvas, 935×937 mm, *c.* 1520 (Ottawa, National Gallery of Canada)

Towards the end of 1523 Cariani returned to Venice, where much had changed; Titian now dominated the Venetian school. Cariani seems to have drawn closer to the style of Bonifazio Veronese and, possibly through the example of Giovanni Girolamo Savoldo, to have discovered the fascination of northern engravings. He also seems to have reconsidered the art of Lorenzo Lotto and Gerolamo Romanino. Such influences are apparent in the paintings of the *Road to Calvary* (Milan, Ambrosiana; Brescia, Pin. Civ. Tosio–Martinengo), in the *Visitation* (Vienna, Ksthist. Mus.) and in the so-called *Invention of the Cross* (Bergamo, Gal. Accad. Carrara), dating from some years later.

Between 1528 and 1530 Cariano was again working in Bergamo, painting a triptych (Bergamo, Gal. Accad. Carrara, and Venice, priv. col.) for the church of Locatello.

During the 1530s, in Venice, although he produced some distinguished works, such as *Lot and his Daughters* (Milan, Castello Sforzesco), which reflects the art of Bonifazio Veronese, his stylistic uncertainty became ever more evident, and his art increasingly provincial. In certain portraits of this period, such as the *Old Man of Nuremberg* (1536; Vienna, Ksthist. Mus.) and also in works such as the *Sacra conversazione* (London, N.G.), he came strikingly close to Bernardino Licinio. It seems likely, too, that he painted less, since few works painted between 1530 and 1547, when he is last documented, have been identified. However, in 1541, he was paid for an altarpiece of *St Roch* (destr.), executed for the Busi Chapel in SS Filippo e Giacomo, Fuipiano.

BIBLIOGRAPHY

DBI [with bibliog.]
M. A. Michiel: *Notizie d'opere di disegno* (*c*. 1534–40); ed. G. Frizzioni (Bologna, 1884), pp. 125, 138, 139, 144, 185
G. Mariacher: 'Giovanni Busi, detto Cariani', *Pittori bergamaschi dal XIII al XIX secolo: Il cinquecento*, i (Bergamo, 1975), pp. 247–313
R. Pallucchini and F. Rossi: *Giovanni Cariani* (Milan, 1983)
V. Sgarbi: '1518: Cariani a Ferrara e Dosso', *Paragone*, xxxiv/389 (1983), pp. 3–18
The Genius of Venice, 1500–1600 (exh. cat., ed. C. Hope and J. Martineau; London, RA, 1983), pp. 160–66
E. Safarik: 'Una monografia su Giovanni Cariani e un contributo alla conoscenza del suo primo periodo', *A. Ven.*, xxxviii (1984), pp. 230–32
F. Frangi: 'Giovanni Cariani', *La pittura in Italia: Il cinquecento*, ed. G. Briganti, 2 vols (Milan, 1987, rev. 1988), ii, pp. 667–8 [with bibliog.]
A. Ballarin: 'Giovanni Busi, Called Cariani', *Gothic to Renaissance: European Painting, 1300 to 1600*, ed. D. Garstang (London, 1988), pp. 27–32
F. Rossi: 'Cariani', *Pinacoteca di Brera: Scuola veneta* (Milan, 1990), pp. 406–19

MAURO LUCCO

Carib. One of several groups of Amerindian peoples inhabiting pockets of the Caribbean and northern countries of South America. They were particularly dominant in the Lesser Antilles until the European colonies began to be established in the late 15th century.

For main discussion *see* ANTILLES, LESSER, §II, 1.

□

Caribbean Islands. Archipelago in the Caribbean Sea, comprising numerous islands scattered in a wide arc stretching from Cuba to Aruba. The islands may be divided into three groups: the Greater Antilles, consisting of CUBA, Hispaniola (divided into HAITI and the DOMINICAN REPUBLIC), PUERTO RICO and JAMAICA; the chain of small islands from the Virgin Islands to Aruba known as the LESSER ANTILLES; and the islands to the north of the Greater Antilles that form THE BAHAMAS (see fig. 1). This article provides a general discussion of the major cultures found throughout the Caribbean Islands and their influence and importance within the region. For more detailed surveys of specific arts and artists, *see* the individual islands surveys.

I. Introduction. II. Cultures.

I. Introduction.

1. GEOGRAPHY AND HISTORY. The islands cover a total land area of 234,000 sq. km and their geology falls into three areas: the faultblock mountains of the Greater Antilles, Trinidad and Tobago and the islands close to the north coast of South America; the volcanic peaks of the inner arc of the Lesser Antilles; and the limestone plateaux of parts of Cuba, the Bahamas and the outer arc of the Lesser Antilles. The climate is marine tropical, with local variations based on wind direction and altitude. There is a risk of hurricanes in summer months. Rainfall largely determines vegetation, but most of the original forest has been cleared for cultivation.

The population of the islands (32.3 million in 1989) is predominantly Afro-Caribbean, but it also includes people of Amerindian, European, Indian, and Chinese origin. The diversity of religions in the Caribbean Islands reflects the variety of the region's settlers. The influences that have come to bear on Caribbean art and architecture include the shamanism of the Amerindians; Christianity and Judaism of the European colonists; the West African religions of imported slaves; and Hinduism and Islam of indentured labourers from south Asia.

The Spaniards concentrated on mainland spoils and neglected the islands themselves, which came to be used in the 16th century as trading and raiding posts from which the Dutch, French and English harassed the passage of Spanish treasure fleets. Permanent agricultural settlements followed, but it was the Dutch-led transition to sugar production in the middle of the 17th century that provided the real foundations of the Caribbean experience. The plantation system under which sugar was produced determined not only the physical landscape but also Caribbean social structure and patterns of life, including attitudes towards race and colour. The white plantation owners satisfied the need for manual labour through the large-scale importation of African slaves, and, after emancipation in the 19th century, by various forms of contract labour from Asia and Portugal. This accounts for the diverse character of Caribbean populations. When great fortunes were possible, as in the period up to 1800, men of substance and taste chose to live in the metropolis, where they spent their money and educated their children. This absentee tradition influenced the development of Caribbean ideas. Those among the élite who stayed had to contend with the ever-present threat of slave uprisings, and they regarded the Caribbean as a place of transitory exile. This may explain why European visitors to the plantation 'Great Houses' often found them bereft of style and adornment.

A major process of localization nevertheless took place, which affected every group in the Caribbean. This was known as creolization: 'creole' was originally applied to black slaves born in the Caribbean but was later used to refer to anyone born locally, and then extended to local things, habits and ideas. A major role in this process was played by the so-called free people of colour, the mixed offspring of white masters and their slaves. Although they suffered from a series of legal and other disabilities and they were distrusted by the black slaves, they formed the group that provided the leadership for the constitutional struggles of the post-slavery period. Generally, in the Caribbean the ending of slavery was associated with the rise of the peasantry, and in villages off the plantations some scope was found for a revitalization of African

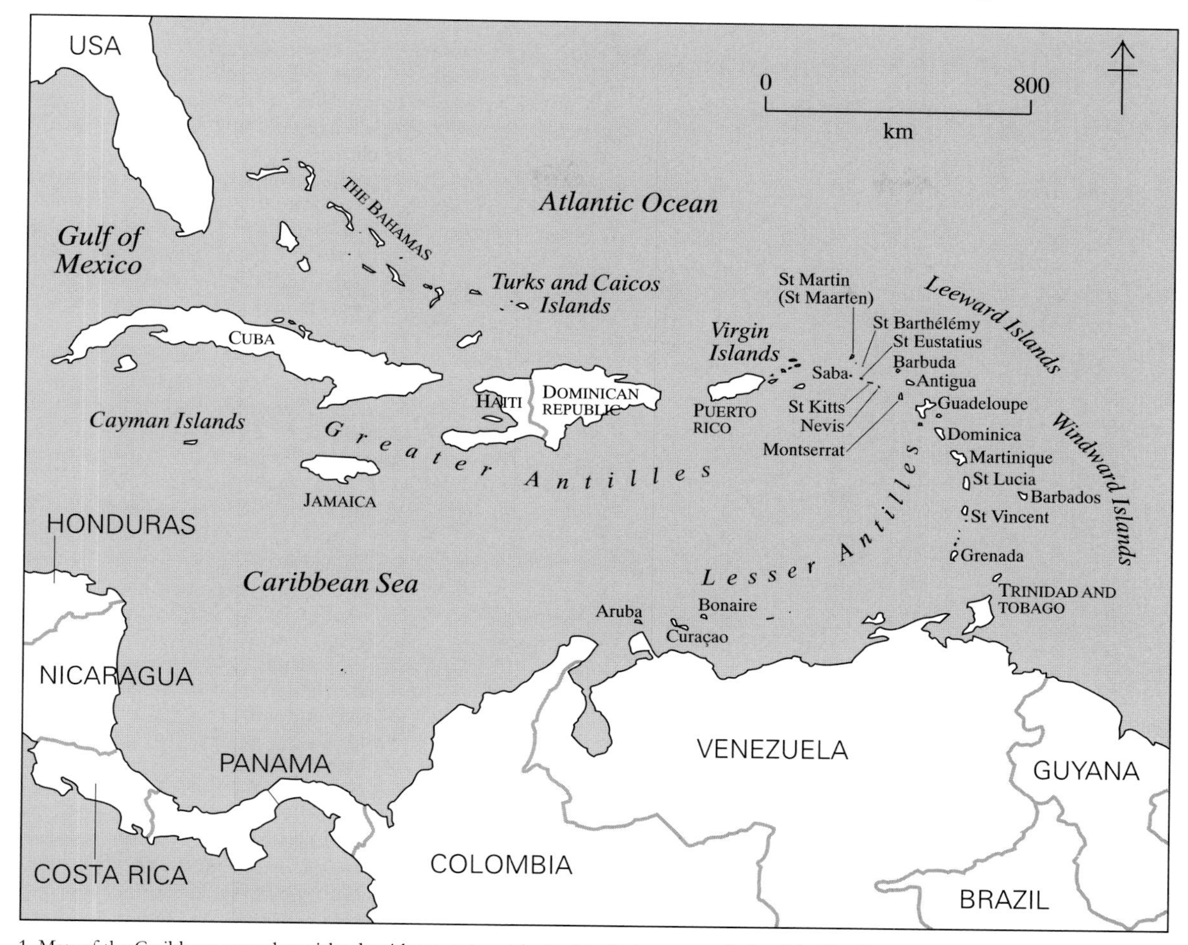

1. Map of the Caribbean area; those islands with separate entries in this dictionary are distinguished by CROSS-REFERENCE TYPE

cultural traits. Creolization had, however, made great progress, and the emerging middle class was more likely to be the product of Western, often missionary, education. This group gradually demanded a greater say in the process of administration. After World War I and particularly following the depression of the 1930s a rising labour movement added fuel and mass support to these claims. The scene was set for a process of constitutional devolution, which, after a brief flirtation with the notion of a Caribbean federation, peaked in the 1960s with the independence of the small states of the Caribbean. In the period following, the heightening of American economic, political and cultural influence took place, but strong ethnic concerns also grew, as expressed, for example, in the Black Power movement of the 1970s, and a continuing, though at the time not so urgent, search for a Caribbean cultural identity.

BIBLIOGRAPHY

E. V. Govela: *Slave Society in the British Leeward Islands at the End of the 18th Century* (New Haven, 1965)
E. Williams: *From Columbus to Castro: A History of the Caribbean, 1492–1969* (London, 1970)
E. Brathwaite: *The Development of Creole Society in Jamaica* (Oxford, 1971)
D. Lowenthal: *West Indian Societies* (London, 1972)
H. Blume: *The Caribbean Islands* (London, 1974)
M. Cross: *Urbanization and Urban Growth in the Caribbean* (Cambridge, 1979)
D. Watts: *The West Indies: Patterns of Development, Culture and Environmental Change Since 1942* (Cambridge, 1987)

JANET HENSHALL MOMSEN, C. J. M. R. GULLICK, KUSHA HARAKSINGH

2. EXHIBITIONS. Major exhibitions of Caribbean art took place from the second half of the 19th century, triggered by the enthusiastic response of the Caribbean Islands when they participated in the Great Exhibition of the Industry of All Nations at the Crystal Palace in London in 1851. They included the Trinidad Exhibition (1868) and the Jamaica International Exhibition (1891), which incorporated exhibits of local artwork. From the 1890s museums played a central role in establishing the importance of national exhibitions as a tool for development in the arts. In 1890 in the Dominican Republic the establishment of the Salon Artistique provided the first opportunity for artists to exhibit their work locally.

During the 20th century Caribbean exhibitions began to gain a popular audience. The development of schools of fine arts in the Spanish islands influenced the creation of national exhibitions as a forum for exchange. During the 1920s the Salon of the Association of Painters and Sculptors of Havana created a regular schedule of shows. In 1927 the Exhibition of New Art in Havana established the impact of modernism on the visual arts in the Spanish islands. In Jamaica the *All Island Exhibition* (1938) was organized in Kingston to exhibit the best in local art and craft, and many unknown Jamaican artists emerged for the first time.

During the 1940s and 1950s the surge of nationalist sentiment found a response among the visual artists of the Caribbean; in the Dominican Republic the first National Biennial of the Plastic Arts was held in 1942. In Barbados the local Arts and Craft Society initiated an annual exhibition, which included artists invited from other islands. In 1944–5 the British Council assisted in the organization of an exhibition of work from the larger countries of the English-speaking Caribbean. In 1955 an exhibition of *Fine Art from the Caribbean*, sponsored by the Alcoa Steam Ship Company of New York, was the first show to represent the region's artistic expression. The paintings were drawn from the Dutch, Spanish, English and French Caribbean territories, and they focused primarily on naive artists. The Riverside Museum in New York organized the first recorded exhibition of Puerto Rican art in 1956 to almost universal criticism, the works exhibited being rejected as mediocre copies of European art. By this date the São Paulo Biennale in Brazil had become the mecca for all artists from the Spanish islands. By the 1960s exhibitions of Caribbean art contributed to expressions of radicalism in local culture. The *Backyard Exhibition* in Trinidad and the *Sidewalk Exhibition* in Barbados were examples of this activity in the English-speaking Caribbean. In 1970 the Instituto de Cultura Puertorriqueña established the first Biennial Exhibition of Graphic Art of Latin America. Its impact can be clearly defined in the following flowering of graphic arts in the Spanish-speaking islands. Since 1976 the Carifesta Exhibition has been the single most important agent for exchange among the visual artists of the Caribbean.

In the late 20th century the art of the Caribbean Islands became the subject for a number of international exhibitions. In 1983 an exhibition on 19th-century Cuban art was held at the Museo del Prado in Madrid; in the same year *Jamaican Art, 1922–1982* was the subject of a Smithsonian Institution travelling exhibition; and *Caribbean Art Now*, organized by the Commonwealth Institute of London in 1986, attempted to bring the work of English-speaking Caribbean artists into focus. As a counter-balance the Caribbean turned its attention on itself, attempting to reconstruct its national art histories for the first time through well-documented, penetrating retrospectives and national exhibitions. Jamaica led the way with the exhibition *Five Centuries of Jamaica Art*, organized in 1976 by the National Gallery. A number of retrospectives of individual artists were held by the Museo de Arte, Ponce (*Francisco Oller*, 1984; *José Campeche*, 1988), and by the Barbados Museum, St Michael (*Golde White*, 1987; *Hector Whistler*, 1988; *Ivan Payne*, 1990). In 1991 the *Gala di arte* brought together important artists of the Dutch Antilles for the first time. In the Dominican Republic in 1992 the first Biennial of Painting of the Caribbean and Central America was held in Santo Domingo, at the Galeria de Arte Moderno.

BIBLIOGRAPHY

N. Connell: 'Artists of the Caribbean', *The Studio*, cliii/770 (1957)

D. Boxer: *Jamaican Art, 1922–1982* (Washington, DC, 1983)

A. Cummins: *The History and Development of Museums in the English-speaking Caribbean* (diss., U. Leicester, 1989)

Art in Latin America: The Modern Era, 1820–1980 (exh. cat. by D. Ades, London, Hayward Gal., 1989)

Gala di Arte: An Exhibition of Works by Antillean and Aruban Artists (exh. cat. by H. Block-Storm, Curaçao, 1991)

ALISSANDRA CUMMINS

II. Cultures.

1. Native American. 2. Western. 3. Afro-Caribbean. 4. Indo-Caribbean.

1. NATIVE AMERICAN. The Greater Antilles and the Bahamas were inhabited by Taino Native Americans when they were the first lands visited by Columbus during his early voyages of discovery. The Lesser Antilles were inhabited at the time by the fierce Carib Native Americans, who had migrated a few centuries before from the coast of South America, displacing the earlier inhabitants, Saladoids of Arawak stock. These comprise the three main groups of Pre-Columbian Native Americans in the Caribbean Islands.

(i) Saladoid. (ii) Carib. (iii) Taino.

(i) Saladoid. The finest Pre-Columbian artefacts of the Lesser Antilles are the pottery, amulets and personal ornaments of the Saladoids (also known as Igneris) who inhabited the islands *c.* AD 1200. They migrated from the north-eastern coast of South America *c.* 400 BC. The Saladoids were the best potters of the ancient Caribbean. Their ceramic tradition, imported from South America, enabled them to produce a fine, high-fired, thin-walled ware usually decorated with white-on-red designs of exceptional beauty. Typical forms included bell-shaped bowls, sometimes ornamented with modelled zoomorphic and anthropomorphic lugs and D-shaped strap-handles. Exotic pieces shaped as fishes, crabs, birds, turtles and humanoid heads were also produced; these were ceremonial wares dedicated to spirits or mythological beings believed to be essential to their subsistence. Some of the most elaborate vessels were covered with red paint and decorated with thin, incised lines filled with white paint; others were adorned with small, delicately modelled lugs. Paints, made from mineral oxides, kaolin and charcoal, were used to create mostly geometric ornamental designs; these were generally restricted to borders, although the inner surfaces of plates and bowls were totally decorated. When the background colour of the vessel was incorporated into the red-and-white painted decoration, beautiful polychromeware resulted. Fine crosshatched incision, sometimes filled with red or white paint, and modelled lugs on the flaring rims of unpainted bowls are common and are considered a characteristic trait of early Saladoid pottery.

Personal ornaments and amulets made from polished hardstones such as amethyst, cornelian and quartz, as well as marble and granite, are among the finer examples of Saladoid art. Miniature silhouettes of frogs, birds, fishes and humanoid figures were also carved from mother-of-pearl, conch-shell or bone and perforated for attachment to cotton clothing; *naguas* (short, apron-like garments), belts and bindings are also common. The finest examples of early Saladoid pottery and personal ornaments in the Lesser Antilles (examples San Juan, U. Puerto Rico Mus.; New Haven, CT, Yale U., Peabody Mus. Nat. Hist.; and Fort de France, Musée d'Archéologie) have been found in Martinique, Guadaloupe and Monserrat, but with the conquest of the Lesser Antilles by the Caribs, the production of pottery and other expressions of Saladoid culture ceased.

(ii) Carib. The Caribs, a warlike people who used large, powerful bows and poisoned arrows, were the best navigators of the Caribbean, which they travelled in large canoes (*piraguas* or *pirogues*) made from tree trunks and impelled by oars. They practised ritual cannibalism, believing, in common with other American aborigines, that by eating human flesh they would be endowed with the victims' strength and courage. Because of this practice and their hostility towards the colonists, the Spaniards punished them with slavery. From their islands in the Lesser Antilles—especially their strongholds of Guadeloupe, Martinique, Dominica and St Vincent—the Caribs organized war parties of 15–20 canoes to raid the Greater Antilles, robbing the Taino inhabitants of food and women. The Spaniards were not interested in colonizing the Lesser Antilles, mainly because the islands lacked gold, but they were also deterred by the Caribs' poisoned arrows. The Caribs continued their attacks on the Greater Antilles during the early phase of Spanish colonization, sacking coastal settlements, burning plantations and capturing Spaniards, Tainos and African slaves. During the second decade of the 17th century, French and English corsairs and pirates established settlements in the islands, sometimes warring and sometimes making peace with the Caribs. Gradually the Carib populations of most of the islands were exterminated by the Europeans. In St Vincent and Dominica, however, many Caribs survived and intermixed with African slaves captured during attacks on Spanish settlements or rescued from sunk slave ships. These people were called Black Caribs, and in 1797 the English made a treaty by which they were resettled in the island of Routan, off the coast of Honduras; they later expanded into inland Honduras and Guatemala, where they are known as Garifunas.

From the discovery of the islands in 1493, Spanish chroniclers described aspects of Carib art and culture, noting the Caribs' excellence as weavers. Woven cotton, produced by women—(both Caribs and captured Tainos)—was used for *naguas* and cotton bindings used as arm and leg decoration. Basketry was also produced by women. Personal ornaments—mostly amulets—and ceremonial objects were made by men from stone, conchshell, bone and clay. Special value was assigned to the *caracoli*, a greenstone ornament resembling a batlike creature that was worn as a pendant over the chest. This ornament was also sometimes made from *guanin*, a gold and copper alloy obtained by trade from Colombia. The pottery, made by women, was crude and more functional and domestic in character. Both cooking pots and the large *ouicu* vessels, used in the fermentation of a manioc beverage, were simple, unadorned, low-fired ware with a grainy texture; some archaeologists have identified it with the Swazey culture. The best description of Carib culture is found in the writings of such French missionaries as Dutertre, J. B. Labat (*Nouveau Voyage aux isles de l'Amérique*, 6 vols (Paris, 1722), Charles de Rochefort (*Natuurlijke en zedelyke historie van d'eylanden de voor-eylanden van Amerika* (Rotterdam, 1662; Eng. trans., London, 1666)) and others, who describe the Caribs' excellent basketry, woven cloth and personal ornaments.

(iii) Taino. The Tainos were Arawak-speaking Native Americans, whose ancestors were the Saladoids (*see* §(i) above). The Tainos were agriculturalists, cultivating yucca (manioc; from which they made cassava bread), maize and various edible roots. Their complex political system was based on powerful hereditary chiefs called *caciques*, who exercised political and religious power over a number of villages. The Tainos believed in the existence of a creator god, Yocahu, and a goddess of fecundity, Atabey. They also had other gods associated with rain, storms and other inexplicable natural phenomena. Ancestor cults were common, and some deceased *caciques* or other extraordinary individuals were considered demi-gods, to be embodied in myths. Their remains, especially the skulls, were encased in woven cotton or put inside sacred wooden idols (*zemis*). When the Spaniards arrived Taino culture was flourishing, as can be seen from the centralization of chieftainship, the hierarchically structured society, organized worship and the construction of impressive ceremonial centres with multiple plazas, in which ball-games, ceremonies and ritual practices were held. However, within a century of the Spanish Conquest the Tainos had disappeared from the Greater Antilles and the Bahamas. Wars and forced labour, for which they were ill prepared, together with new illnesses brought to the islands by Africans and Europeans, were among the causes of their demise.

Taino art was mostly linked to religious belief and ceremonial practice, personal ornament and the decoration of tools and implements. The most striking artefacts are associated with the esoteric *cohoba* ritual, in which the practising *cacique* or shaman attained a hypnotic state through the inhalation of the sacred *cohoba* (*Anadenanthera peregrina*; *see* SOUTH AMERICA, PRE-COLUMBIAN, §I, 3(ii)) powder. The *cohoba* idols, mostly made from wood, represent Yocahu, squatting nude in what seems to be a ceremonial posture; a round, slightly concave dish on the idol's head held the hallucinogenic powder. Among the many beautiful examples of these idols is a dark, highly polished piece, 1.03 m high, from Jamaica, in the British Museum, London (see fig. 2). Another large example from the Dominican Republic and held by the Smithsonian Institution, Washington, DC, represents two squatting figures on a low ceremonial stool (*dujo*) with a vertical, rodlike projection supporting the round *cohoba* dish. The two figures seem to allude to twins, a common theme in Taino mythology; and gold-leaf or conch-shell inlays were probably set in the concave eyes and mouths, as was common in Taino sculpture. The Metropolitan Museum of Art in New York has a fine specimen from Hispaniola, carved, like other *cohoba* idols, from *guayacan* wood, which still retains its inlaid teeth of conch-shell. There are only a

2. Taino wooden *cohoba* idol representing the god Yocahu, h. 1.03 m, from Jamaica (London, British Museum)

few carved stone *cohoba* idols. Other elaborate and decorated artefacts, such as inhaling tubes, vessels and sticks used to induce vomiting were also associated with the *cohoba* ceremony.

The Tainos wore hardly any clothing, although they decorated their bodies with ornaments and paint, and married women wore a *nagua*, sometimes painted with red and black geometric designs or decorated with applied bone, conch-shell or stone beads. Red, white and black vegetable pigments were also used as body paint. The typical Taino designs used in personal art were also applied to ceramics, wooden implements, rock drawings and sculpture. Tubes of bone, pierced stones and conch-shells and ceramic beads of various sizes were strung on fibre cords to create elaborate and striking necklaces and pendants, while woven cotton and feathers were used to make beautiful head ornaments. Small anthropomorphic or zoomorphic amulets of coloured stones, conch-shell, bone or modelled clay were also worn, and lips and ears were perforated to take ornaments.

The Tainos had not learnt the art of casting metals, but they pounded gold nuggets found in riverbeds into thin sheets to create amulets and other ornaments or inlays for sculptures. The technique of stone-carving and polishing reached a climax with the manufacture of monolithic stone belts and 'elbowstones' used during the ceremonial ball-game. Stone belts have a convex decorative field, generally decorated with carved human, animal or geometric designs. The elbowstones are similar, but are smaller, representing only the main section or boss, which was protective and also served for hitting the rubber ball (*c.* 9 lbs) used in the ceremonial game. They have carved grooves at either end, where curved wood branches were attached with twigs to complete the belt. *Bateyes* or ballcourts were lined with monoliths, sometimes carved with elaborate petroglyphs, delimiting the long sides of the rectangular fields (*see* BALLCOURT, §1). In Puerto Rico and the Dominican Republic, the Tainos carved their petroglyphs not only in the *bateyes* but also on rocks in rivers, creeks, caves and other isolated places, where they seem to mark important or sacred events. They usually represent human or animal figures, large anthropomorphic heads or mythical figures with combined human and animal features. Ovoid anthropomorphic stone masks with open mouths and large eyes seem to represent a ritual expression and are another important manifestation of Taino sculpture. They are carved from stone nodules and are slightly hollowed and unpolished on the reverse, suggesting that they were made to attach to other objects. The occurrence of small figurines with similar masks attached to their forearms has led scholars to believe that they formed part of the ball-player's ceremonial paraphernalia. The original masks probably had inlaid eyes and mouths.

Dujos, ceremonial stools carved from wood or stone, represent another important category of Taino sculpture. Zoomorphic *dujos*, probably of mythic or totemic significance, have the animal's head projecting from between the front legs of the stool, while the narrow and slightly concave seat extends upwards and backwards, simulating its tail and forming the backrest. The faces have deep-set eyes and expressive open mouths, occasionally inlaid with gold, as in the case of one example from the Dominican Republic conserved in the British Museum, London. The backrests of *dujos* were sometimes carved with central decorative panels composed of concentric circles, triangles and chevrons. Anthropomorphic *dujos* usually have the head protruding from the back; some also have arms incised along the borders of the seat. The most sculptural, interesting and abundant objects of magico-religious paraphernalia are *zemis*, three-pointed idols of diverse types: archaeologists have associated their various forms with mountains, germinating yucca and women's breasts as well as with gods or tutelary spirits. Sculptural *zemis* represent anthropomorphic, zoomorphic or anthropozoomorphic figures. The head is usually carved on the front projection, while the back cone represents the posterior extremities, generally in the form of a frog's hindquarters.

Areytos were ceremonial celebrations held to mark noteworthy events such as the inauguration or death of a *cacique* or other important figure, a military victory or a significant birth, initiation or marriage. Songs, dances and recitals of myths were employed as means of narrating communal history. Participants in these events decorated themselves with personal ornaments (headdresses, ear-rings, necklaces, lip-ornaments, rings and bracelets) and with body paint and elaborate hairstyles. The *areytos* represent the union of all the arts practiced by the Tainos: narrative, song, dance, costume, paint, personal ornament and ritual sculpture.

BIBLIOGRAPHY

Père R. Breton: *Relations de l'isle de la Guadaloupe* (1647)
C. de Rochefort: *Histoire naturelle et morale des Iles Antilles de l'Amérique* (Rotterdam, 1658, 2/1665)
J. B. Du Tertre: *Histoire générale des Antilles* (Paris, 1667–71)
T. A. Joyce: *Central American and West Indian Archaeology* (London, 1916)
J. W. Fewkes: *A Prehistoric Island Culture Area of America* (Washington, DC, 1922)
S. Loven: *Origins of the Tainan Culture, West Indies* (Göteborg, 1935)
M. MacKusick: *Distribution of Ceramic Styles in the Lesser Antilles* (microfilm, Ann Arbor, 1960)
Proceedings of the International Congresses for the Study of Pre-Columbian Cultures of the Lesser Antilles: Montreal (1961–)
E. Tabio and E. R. Tabio: *Prehistoria de Cuba* (Havana, 1966)
G. Willey: *An Introduction to American Archaeology*, i: *North and Middle America* (Englewood Cliffs, 1966)
E. Fernández Méndez: *Art and Mythology of the Taino Indians of the Greater West Indies* (San Juan, 1972)
M. Veloz Maggiolo: *Arqueología prehistórica de Santo Domingo* (Singapore, 1972)
L. Allaire: *Vers une préhistoire des Petites Antilles* (Montreal, 1973)
M. García Arévalo: *El arte Taíno de la República Dominicana* (Santo Domingo, 1977)
M. Pons-Alegría: 'Taino Indian Art', *Archaeology*, xxxiii/4 (1980), pp. 8–15
Crónicas francesas de los indios caribes, Sp. trans., abridged, by M. Cardenas Ruiz, intro. R. E. Alegría, Centro de Estudios Avanzados de Puerto Rico y el Caribe (San Juan, 1981)
R. E. Alegría: *Ball Courts and Ceremonial Plazas in the West Indies*, Yale U., Pubns Anthropol., lxxix (New Haven, 1983)
I. Rouse: *The Tainos: Rise and Fall of the People who Greeted Columbus* (New Haven, 1992)

RICARDO E. ALEGRÍA, MELA PONS-ALEGRÍA

2. Western.

(i) Architecture. (ii) Painting, graphic arts and sculpture. (iii) Decorative arts.

(i) Architecture. The first European colony in the Caribbean region was Santo Domingo (now Dominican Republic), founded in 1496. Within 50 years the city had acquired the appearance of a Spanish city. The architecture owed nothing to antecedent Amerindian tradition; rather its principal buildings were the work of Castilian and Sevillian designers. The Alcazar del Almirante (1510–14; partly ruined, partly restored), Santo Domingo, was a primary example of early Caribbean architecture. Although Amerindians and later Africans, formed a major part of the workforce, they did not significantly influence the stylistic approach to the design. The use of local cut stone for the façades of these buildings was perhaps the most important contribution of the West Indian environment.

Elsewhere in the Caribbean, by the mid-17th century the Leeward Islands were extensively settled by the French and English. Simple one-room wooden or wattled cottages gave way to more palatial stone buildings as the wealth of the plantation class increased. Richard Ligon, in *A True and Exact History of the Island of Barbados* (London, 1657), was critical of the hot, stuffy low-ceilinged rooms that he encountered; however, his ideas for using shuttered windows to enhance ventilation found little response at this time among the conservative planters. By the 1660s Nicholas Abbey and Drax Hall in Barbados were constructed along the lines of Jacobean country houses. These were among the first to be built in local limestone, since brick was not widely available and the local hardwoods were disappearing rapidly. In Jamaica Stokes Hall, (*c.* 1710), St Thomas, and Colbeck Castle (*c.* 1748), St Catherine, much later in origin, were clearly influenced by military design. On Curaçao the Brievengat Land House with its tiled roof, dormer windows and massive shutters, showed little evidence of tropical adaptation. Château Murat on Marie-Galante, Guadeloupe, resembled a typical 18th-century French country house, while Whim Great House (now Estate Whim Plantation Museum) on St Croix, with its extended oval shape, was an elegant late 18th-century architectural fantasy. In Jamaica great houses, such as Rose Hall, St James, bore little evidence of adaptation but reflected the style of the English 18th-century country mansion; built between 1770 and 1780, Marlborough, Manchester, was clearly designed in the Palladian style, while Bellevue, St Andrew, with its colonnaded entrance and row of sash windows, was unmistakably Georgian in style. In general by the late 18th century English style had become the model for much of the region, except on the Spanish islands. From the 18th century the single most important influence on Caribbean architecture was probably the *Book of Architecture* (1728) by James Gibbs, and Caribbean Georgian (incorporating corner quoins, pediments and engaged pilasters) became the accepted style. After 1760 a new prosperity in the Spanish islands brought an influx of architects from Cádiz. Havana became the centre for this later flowering of Spanish colonial architecture. Such late 18th-century buildings as the Casa de Correos (*c.* 1770–92) and the Casa de Gobierno (*c.* 1776–92), both in Havana, are characteristic of the severity of Spanish Neo-classicism.

By the end of the 18th century smaller Caribbean houses showed more evidence of creolization and modification. In most cases the whole structure was raised off the ground to allow for circulation; a double entrance staircase, often with a vaulted area under the central section (used as a hurricane shelter), was a characteristic feature. Multiple hipped roofs (occasionally with dormer windows in the French and Dutch islands) protected the buildings during hurricanes. The ground-floor often had many apertures, some filled with jalousies (louvres), and often incorporated a verandah with intricately carved rail and bargeboard; this gingerbread fretwork often formed the most attractive feature of the house. At the turn of the 19th century the vogue for the styles of European Gothic Revival and Italianate villas found expression in Caribbean architecture. In Haiti local architects, trained in Paris, embellished these styles, using multicoloured wood and brick to create the airy confection of the gingerbread style embodied in the Grand Hotel Oloffson (1887), Port-au-Prince. In Trinidad the migration of European merchants at the end of the 19th century led to the creation in the early 1900s of the 'Magnificent Nine' in St Clair, Port of Spain. In the Dominican Republic the expansion of such provincial cities as Santiago and Puerto Plata easily lent itself to a similar process of transculturation. The influx of workers from the English and Dutch islands were reflected in the construction of Victorian gingerbread style wooden houses, their exteriors painted in bright colours with the balconies, columns, doors and windows painted in contrasting tones. These features came to be regarded as elements of a quintessentially Caribbean style.

ALISSANDRA CUMMINS

(ii) Painting, graphic arts and sculpture. The earliest form of Western culture to appear in the Caribbean was religious art. The Spaniards who arrived in the Greater Antilles brought with them Spanish and Flemish religious paintings. Sculpture as an art form appeared in churches and official buildings; the New Seville Carvings (*c.* 1530; Kingston, Inst. Jamaica, N.G.) are among the earliest-known examples of European craftsmen incorporating specifically Caribbean themes into their work. Most of the early Christian art came via Seville, but there was some input from Mexico in the 17th century. In the Roman Catholic areas of the Caribbean religious forms of folk art, santos, were produced. These were small wooden carvings of saints and other holy figures (see fig. 3). The earliest ones were in a style reminiscent of Spanish Baroque and were probably imitations of imported icons and may have been carved by priests. These were replaced by indigenous styles, which in Puerto Rico were similar to European Gothic, and finally by so-called 'primitive' santos with little emotion. The tradition of producing these figures survived longest in Puerto Rico, and their production flourished between 1750 and 1950. After the 1950s santos declined in quality and were mainly replaced by plaster casts or plastic figures. There were fewer flowerings of religious art in the Protestant areas of the Caribbean. As there were no saints to merge with African and Native American spirits, little religious syncretism occurred. Hardly any religious art from before the late 18th century has survived hurricanes, wars and religious conflicts in the region.

3. Wooden santos carved by Pedro Rinaldi, Ponce, Puerto Rico

Between the late 15th century and the 17th artists in the Caribbean were for the most part anonymous recorders of the exotic landscape. Prints of the Caribbean area were produced as part of the first European books and albums on the region, following Columbus's arrival in the New World. In the 16th century the growing popular interest and investment in commercial ventures in the region fuelled a profitable industry in the production of illustrative maps and prints. By the 1590s the engraver and publisher Jean Theodor de Bry, based in Frankfurt am Main, was firmly established as one of the most important suppliers of 'Caribbeana'; his copperplate engravings for Girolamo Benzoni's *Americae pars quinta ... secundae sectionis hispanorum* (Frankfurt, 1595) seem to have attracted popular attention. During the 17th century European engravers, particularly the Dutch, exploited the popularity of exotic Caribbean scenes, borrowing freely from every source. The *Prospect of Bridge Town in Barbados* (1695; St Michael, Barbados Mus.; see fig. 4) by Samuel Copen (*c.* 1663–1717) is a fine example of this type of typographical engraving. It was not, however, until the 18th century that printing presses were introduced into most of the islands. Even then these remained limited for the most part to letterpress printing. The interest in rational and scientific discipline gave rise to a more formal development in the graphic arts to aid the systematic recording of the flora and fauna of the West Indies. The book of *The Natural History of Barbados* (1750; St Michael, Barbados Mus.) by the Rev. Griffith Hughes was illustrated by the celebrated Georg Dionysius Ehret.

Also during this period some wealthy plantation owners in the larger islands began to commission large numbers of works of art both at home and abroad. The Spanish court painter Luis Paret stimulated the development of art in Puerto Rico, where he had been banished in 1775; he was one of the few professional artists known to have been active in that country. The emergence of José Campeche (1751–1809) as a major portrait painter owes a debt to Paret's presence. His *Lady on Horseback* (1785; Ponce, Mus. A.) is considered to be his first masterpiece. Campeche was the first major Caribbean artist to turn from religious to secular topics. His father had produced altar frontals in Puerto Rico, with which he assisted. In the Lesser Antilles, Italian artist Agostino Brunias (?1785–96), active in the region from 1770, concentrated his attention on the lower echelons of society, including slaves and mulattos. From the 1770s there developed an interest in panoramic landscapes favoured by travelling artists from Europe. Minor English painters Philip Wickstead (*d* 1790s) and George Robertson (1748–88), who travelled to Jamaica in 1773 under the patronage of Jamaican historian William Beckford, concentrated their attention on painted topographical scenes, while Robertson, James Hakewill (1778–1843) and Bartholomew Kidd (1808–89)

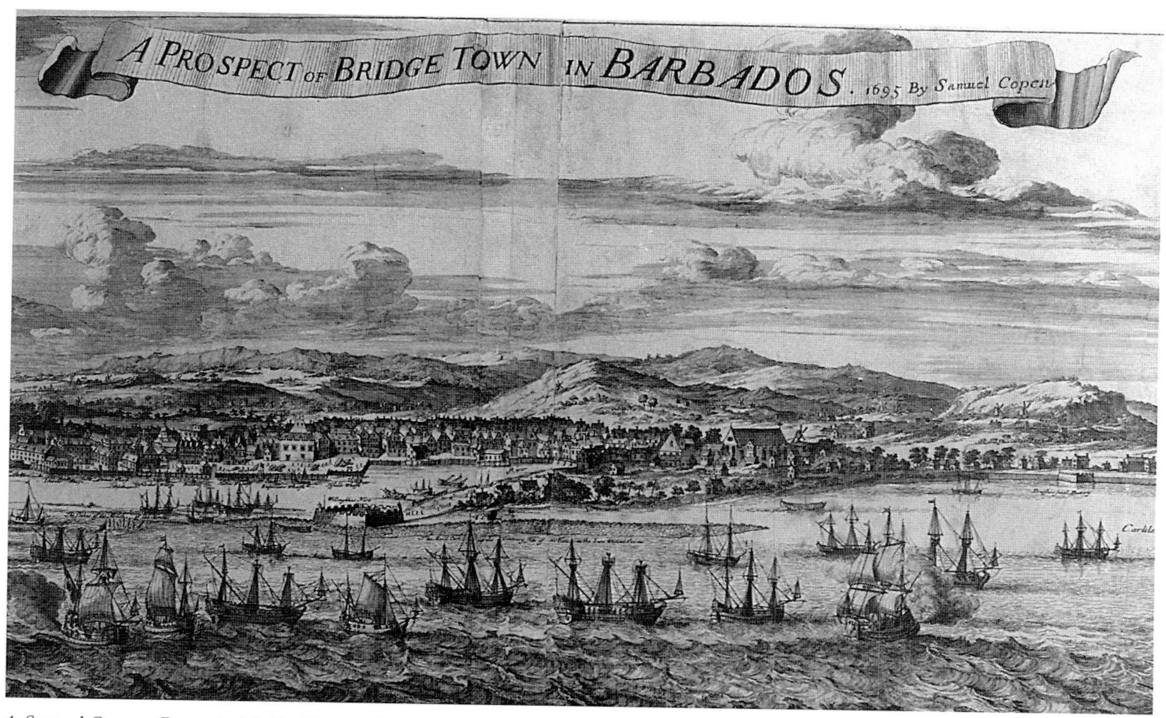

4. Samuel Copen: *Prospect of Bridge Town in Barbados*; topographical engraving by Johannes Kip, 189×511 mm, 1695 (St Michael, Barbados Museum)

all produced albums of prints of Jamaican views. The first prints known to have been published in Jamaica were the lithographs, by Adolph Duperly sr, of Jamaican artist Isaac Mendes Belisario's sketches, for example *Koo Koo, or the Actor Boy* (St Michael, Barbados Mus.; *see* JAMAICA, fig. 3).

Between the 17th and 19th centuries sculpture came primarily from European sources, commissioned by the wealthy classes and by government. Several churches in Jamaica and Barbados boast superb examples of English commemorative sculpture. The many memorials that were executed include John Cheere's monument to *James Lawes* (*c.* 1740; Jamaica, St Andrew), John Bacon's memorial to *Sir Walter Rodney* (1789; Jamaica, Spanish Town) and John Flaxman's Brathwaite Memorial (1800; Barbados, St Michael's Cathedral). Other sculptors whose work is represented in the Caribbean include Joseph Wilton, John Steell, Edward Hodges Bailey, Joseph Nollekens and John Gibson, firmly establishing the Neo-classical image of the English colonies of the period. Sir Richard Westmacott's bronze of *Horatio Nelson* (*c.* 1812–13; Bridgetown, Trafalgar Square) and the bust of *Augustus Frederick Ellis* (1824; Kingston, N.G.) by Francis Chantrey are among the examples of portrait sculpture that are still extant.

The impact of growing independence movements in the Spanish colonies and in Haiti encouraged the search for national identities, which greatly influenced the development of art in those islands. In addition the printing press became a powerful instrument for social and political reform, and in the 1930s a number of Spanish engravers escaping the Spanish Civil War (1936–9) arrived in the Caribbean, including Joaquin de Alba and Blas, who made their protests from the Dominican Republic. The founding of art academies in Cuba and Haiti during this period was a part of the process of seeking Caribbean identities. In the Lesser Antilles minor European artists such as Percy William Justyne, William Carpenter and Lionel Grimstone Fawkes gained popular patronage for their literal renderings of Caribbean scenes. It was, however, only in the latter part of the 19th century that local artists began to establish themselves, though typically under the influence of European academic training.

During the first decades of the 20th century art continued to be influenced by European culture, and, for the most part, landscapes, portraits and genre painting continued to form the main themes, rendered in a Realist or Neo-Impressionist style. Nevertheless the radical artistic tendencies developing in Europe did enter Caribbean expression, adapted by avant-garde artists, who, returning home in the 1920s, became involved with the anti-colonialist movements developing in the islands. Also during the 1920s Caribbean sculpture began to emerge from the shadow of European domination. In 1937 Caribbean nationalist fervour reached its peak, expressed by extensive rioting among the islands' working classes. From the 1940s Caribbean artists focused deliberately on the establishment of an authentic national identity. Foreign artists continued to influence Caribbean artistic development as they settled in the islands, often playing a teacher–mentor role to local artists. In Haiti, American De Witt Peters established the Centre d'Art in Port-au-Prince, thus becoming a catalyst for the development of Haitian art from 1943.

From the early 1950s Caribbean art developed rapidly, as artists were brought into contact with various trends in European and American art through either visits and training abroad or the Western-orientated training systems adopted in local art schools, debating the balance of power between dependency and identity. By the late 20th century art schools and museums had been largely responsible for the creation of an environment more receptive to art, particularly as an expression of national identity and multiculturalism, in islands that more often than not were newly independent. Throughout the Caribbean artists continued to explore and adapt a multiplicity of styles that bear witness to the diversity of Caribbean culture and its synthesism in the consciousness of its people.

ALISSANDRA CUMMINS, C. J. M. R. GULLICK

(iii) Decorative arts. From the establishment of the first Spanish colonies *c.* 1493 until the late 16th century the majority of manufactured goods in the New World came from Europe rather than local sources. From the late 16th century ceramic production of unglazed and lead-glazed utilitarian earthenware had begun on the island of Hispaniola, while in the other islands such production was started only in the latter half of the 17th century in response to the rapid development of the sugar industry and continued until well into the 20th century. There is no evidence of glass production in the Caribbean Islands; glassware remained an imported item throughout the history of the region, the primary sources being England and the Netherlands until the 19th century, when North American products were favoured.

From the 16th century in the Spanish-speaking colonies jewellery and tableware made in Mexico and Peru were probably distributed to the islands. Blacksmiths in the Spanish settlements worked with imported raw iron, producing domestic and military hardware and developing an exuberant creole style by the 19th century, reflected in the fashionable house balconies of wrought-iron. Accounts of the 16th and 17th centuries, from both Barbados and Jamaica, reveal a large number of jewellers and goldsmiths working with imported material, despite the scarcity of mineral resources in the islands. In the French islands by the 18th century a thriving goldsmithing industry had developed, which serviced the other smaller English and Dutch islands; this trade existed into the 20th century. In the Dominican Republic the existence of significant sources of hardstones, such as amber and larimar, led to the development of a prosperous jewellery-making industry by the 19th century, which continued to be popular in the late 20th century. In the English islands a small but significant metalworking industry emerged in the early 20th century.

Little remains of the furniture used in the early island settlements before the 18th century. From the simple, crudely constructed joint-stools, plank-tables and forms that were constructed during the 16th century, the local craftsmen progressed to deft reproductions of European-made furniture, while the wealthy landowners continued to import large quantities of furniture in the popular styles of the day. It was only during the 19th century that a true Caribbean style may be said to have emerged, utilizing the excellent local hardwoods available. Essentially the creolization of European 19th-century styles took the form of a broader, more exuberantly carved design, less graceful and heavier proportions, the incorporation of Caribbean floral elements to replace the European, a preponderance of native woods (including the popularization of mahogany), caned backs and seats and a heavy, dark finish, which contrasted well with the pale plastered walls of Caribbean interiors. In the 20th century Caribbean furniture design continued to be influenced primarily by European and American sources, although traditional domestic styles remained popular.

BIBLIOGRAPHY

R. S. Dunn: *Sugar and Slaves: The Rise of the Planter Class in the English West Indies, 1624–1713* (North Carolina, 1972)

Five Centuries of Art in Jamaica (exh. cat. by D. Boxer, Kingston, N.G., 1976)

D. Buisseret: *Historic Architecture of the Caribbean* (London, 1980)

P. Gosner: *Caribbean Georgian: The Great and Small Houses of the Caribbean* (Washington, DC, 1982)

R. Taylor: *Francisco Oller: A Realist-Impressionist* (Puerto Rico, 1983)

E. Perez Montas: *Colonial Houses of Santo Domingo* (Santo Domingo, 1984)

R. Taylor: *José Campeche and his Time* (New York, 1988)

P. Archer-Shaw and K. Morrison: *Jamaican Art* (Kingston, 1990)

V. Poupeye-Ramelaar: *1940–1990: Jamaica School of Art* (Kingston, 1990)

A. Cummins: 'European Prints and Paintings as Markers in Ethnohistorical Research on the Caribbean', *Proceedings of the 14th Congress of the International Association for Caribbean Archaeology: Barbados, 1991*

L. Mezin: 'Portrayals of West Indian Carib and the Amerindian of the Guyanas', *Proceedings of the 14th Congress of the International Association for Caribbean Archaeology: Barbados, 1991*

ALISSANDRA CUMMINS

3. AFRO-CARIBBEAN. The term Afro-Caribbean is applied in a number of ways, so that the boundaries of its meaning have become blurred. Usage tends to differ between discussions of the period of slavery and post-emancipation. With reference to the period of slavery it includes free persons of colour; in Cuba, the Dominican Republic and Puerto Rico slaves were more readily freed than in other islands. Those freed in Spanish colonies tended to be more hispanicized, and some of their arts and crafts relate to European vernacular arts. The slaves of subsequent importations to Cuba and Puerto Rico in the 19th century were less often freed and less acculturated. Even within the more racially segregated British Caribbean not all the free people of colour were brought up within a cultural tradition rooted in African heritage. For example, the wealthy illegitimate sons of plantation owners in the British Caribbean could be brought up within an élite European tradition. As élite free persons of colour have been marginalized in discussions of Afro-Caribbean culture of the pre-emancipation period, the complications of the role of ancestry and culture in the definition of Afro-Caribbean is generally ignored; rather they concentrate on the arts and crafts produced by the slaves and maroon (runaway slave) population.

Abolition of the slave trade and emancipation occurred at different times throughout the Caribbean Islands. Following emancipation acculturation continued throughout the region. This merging of traditions has contributed to the problems of the use of the term Afro-Caribbean to describe peoples and artefacts of the late 19th century and the 20th. A narrow definition considers cultural items within an African tradition that are produced in the

Caribbean by people of African descent. A wide-ranging use of the term includes people and their products, with at least one African ancestor, whose descendants live or once lived in the Caribbean; such people form the majority on all the Caribbean islands except Puerto Rico.

The African slaves imported to the Caribbean came mainly from West Africa initially, passing through ports on the coast of the area that now comprises Guinea, Sierra Leone, Ghana and Nigeria. The African origins frequently mentioned in West Indian slave lists include Asante, Efik, Dahomey, Moco, Fante and Yoruba. The major arts of these peoples included wood-carving, bronze- and brass-casting, goldwork, textiles and architecture. Metalworkers often belonged to a separate group or caste, and skilled carvers, potters and weavers could become full-time specialists. Other slaves came from further south along the West African coast, where fewer specialists were found; raffiawork, cloth and carvings in wood and ivory were the major arts of this area.

Despite the fact that the British, French and Dutch planters in the Caribbean systematically split groups of peoples in an attempt to reduce chances of rebellions, their specific cultural traditions survived, although not as well as in Brazil, where the Portuguese retained groupings of peoples. A major exception is Haiti, which retained many African traits as a partial consequence of its slave revolution; similarly maroon settlements in Jamaica and Surinam also preserved some African traits. Generally slaves brought their skills with them from Africa and practised those that their masters permitted; more African traditions survived in areas where there was a larger proportion of Africans to Europeans. Commonly reported were basketwork chairs and containers; straw plaiting for ropes and bed mats; leatherwork and pottery. Little African-style metalwork survived, except in Haiti, nor sculpture, except in some religious cults. Slave housing appears to have had some African input, but the amount is debated; Haitian examples have arguably more. Dance and the accompanying costumes survived and developed as part of performances in the period leading up to Christmas and New Year as precursors of CARNIVAL; after emancipation many celebrations in the Catholic areas of the Caribbean moved from the Christmas period to being pre-Lenten. The continuing of African traditions was not always consistent in an area. Some pre-Lenten carnival celebrations in the southern Caribbean have come indirectly via Trinidad. The emphasis on artistic designers for a set of related costumes is particularly Trinidadian. The carnival of St Kitts and Nevis similarly influenced the Christmas celebrations of the Dominican Republic; Jamaican Jonkonnu is thought to have influenced the celebrations of the same name in the Bahamas and elsewhere, held at Christmas.

Many aspects of Afro-Caribbean culture are associated with religion and ritual. African religious practices frequently combined with Catholicism in parts of the Caribbean Islands. Visual puns due to similarities in iconography resulted in the equation of Roman Catholic saints with African gods; for example St Patrick became equated with Damballah-wedo, the serpent spirit in Haitian Vodoun, and some crosses are for Baron Samedi. Other Haitian religious art is less multi-vocal; the *vévé* or ritual ground drawings from Vodoun ceremonies for Damballah clearly illustrate a serpent. *Vévé* have in turn influenced Haitian secular art. Many of the works of Hector Hyppolite, who was a Vodoun functionary, make reference to them. Indeed, it could be argued that Vodoun and its images and symbols were the most common topic of the naive school of Haitian painting. There are some similarities between the *vévé* and the artefacts of Pentecostal sects, for example the drawings used by Vincentian shakers in mourning rituals and the similar diagrams of Trinidadian shouters. Once in the Caribbean, African religious carvers appear to have been put to work carving furniture for their masters. Only a few slaves seem to have found time to carve ancestor figures, but drums were produced and some other musical instruments. The more artistic examples tend to be the most African-influenced. Traditional Cuban carving and masks and traditional Haitian sculpture have African parallels and probably ancestry, as do some of the drums and occasionally other musical instruments used in rituals in Cuba and Haiti.

In the Protestant islands those Afro-Caribbeans who were the most successful at retaining their African beliefs and related art forms were the descendants of maroons.

5. Ronald Moody: *The Mother*, concrete, h. 1.6 m, 1958–9 (Leicester, Leicestershire Museum and Art Gallery)

6. Afro-Caribbean decorated vehicle, late 20th century

The major maroon communities of the Caribbean Islands were in Jamaica and St Vincent. The descendants of the Jamaican maroons have a syncretic Protestant belief system. The majority of Vincentian maroons inter-married with Carib Indians, and they were deported to the Bay Islands of Central America in 1797; their descendants, the Garifuna, have merged with shamanism, ancestor worship and Roman Catholicism. The major Jamaican maroon art forms are performing arts and involve few aesthetic artefacts other than costumes and drums.

In the 20th century Afro-Caribbean art becomes much harder to define precisely. Throughout the history of the region professional Caribbean artists have (with the partial exception of the naive arts of Haiti) been influenced by Western fine arts. Materials other than wood tend to be non-traditional, as are the tools used, and the ideas behind much art are 'Westernized', even when the artist attempts to reach back to African roots. Some major 20th-century Afro-Caribbean artists, such as Ronald Moody (see fig. 5), received some of their training in Europe, while others, such as Dennis Williams (*b* 1923), were academics with Westernized education. The Jamaican sculptor Edna Manley, the wife of one prime minister and the mother of another, produced many sculptures affirming the Afro-Caribbean way of life and encouraging the development of the arts in Jamaica.

Since the majority of Afro-Caribbeans are Christian, Christian themes are also frequently represented in 20th-century painting and sculpture. Black Power orientated cooperatives have used African religious themes in items of tourist art, but these rarely have religious significance, since their purpose is to emphasize the enslavement of their ancestors. Other tourist art, which need not be considered as strictly Afro-Caribbean, includes work in shell, straw and fibre. Carved wood, bamboo products, cloth, ceramic and seed works are also produced in most islands, while embroidery and leatherwork are sold on some islands. Vehicle decoration is another form of 20th-century art in the Caribbean (see fig. 6); vehicles decorated with the most African stylization are produced by or for Rastafarians and reggae musicians.

BIBLIOGRAPHY

Carib. Q., iv/3 (1956); iv/4 (1956) [special issues on carnival]

The Art Heritage of Puerto Rico (exh. cat., New York, Met., 1974)

Haitian Art (exh. cat. by U. Stebich, New York, Brooklyn Mus., 1978)

C. J. M. R. Gullick: 'West Indian Artefacts: A Bibliographical Essay', *Mus. Ethnographers' Grp Newslett.*, 19 (1985), pp. 26–53

J. W. Nunley and J. Bettelheim: *Caribbean Festival Arts* (St Louis, 1988)

C. J. M. R. GULLICK

4. INDO-CARIBBEAN. The Asian population of the Caribbean Islands are descendants of the indentured labour force of the 19th century. They are more heavily represented in the south than in the northern population, and in Trinidad they constitute the largest ethnic group. The workers came mainly from the rural areas of the eastern Gangetic plain but with smaller numbers from the south of the Indian Subcontinent; the legacy of the latter is especially noticeable in the French territory of Guadeloupe. Until the 1940s a sizeable proportion of the Caribbean Indian population was born in India, but indenture was terminated in 1917, and in the late 20th century it was rare to find an Indian who was not born locally. Until the 1940s, also, the majority of Asians lived in rural districts, and they were engaged in agriculture, which was natural considering their introduction to the Caribbean Islands to work on sugar plantations; thereafter, however, there was a significant move into new occupations, and some residential drift to the towns.

The rural origins of the Asian population and their adherence to Hinduism and Islam help to account for the features of Indian art and culture in the Caribbean. Though a variety of traditions defined by locality and caste categories were evident in the original population of migrants, on the plantations of the Caribbean these were telescoped into a small space. Initially, there was some jostling for status and pre-eminence, but before long a process of homogenization was underway, in which the Bhojpuri tradition of eastern India was to emerge as dominant. This was characterized in language by Bhojpur (a variant of Hindi) and in religion by devotional Hinduism, based particularly on the *Rāmāyaṇa* epic and the myths of the Puranas. These provided the basis not only for the view of the ideal life but also for folk songs, stories and dramatic presentations, and a range of icons and imagery available for replication in folk art. Homogenization was further fuelled by the exodus from plantation or estate residence to village life in the later 19th century, as Asians exchanged their guaranteed return passage to India, but in particular their savings, for land, and by ethnic competition in the 20th century, both of which further minimized regional or other peculiarities and precipitated the formation of an Indo-Caribbean identity.

Although those recruiting in India had sought to concentrate on agricultural labour, they in fact took in a fair cross-section of the catchment area; accordingly, a variety of caste-specific skills, such as those of the potter and the jeweller, crossed the seas and have been handed down in the Caribbean Islands. Domestic and ritual occasions provided the early field of practice and remain significant. Especially important, for example, is the decoration of the altar for ritual observances, and the platform on which the priest sits. Folk artists decorate the marriage tent and other spaces that are consecrated for ritual performances, such as annual celebrations of the *Ramlīlā* and *Kṛṣṇālīlā* village theatre based on the exploits of Rama and Krishna as recorded in the epics. The materials used are coloured rice and paper. Cheap prints imported from India, with framed images of the deities of the Hindu pantheon, have been supplemented by local paintings in oils, which are highly stylized and sometimes include motifs from films produced in Bombay. Much folk art is functional and destroyed after the event. Indeed, Hindu religious paraphernalia is destroyed in flowing water courses after the occasion, and so too are the elaborate replicas of Muslim tombs constructed in bamboo and paper for the annual celebration of the Shi'ite Muharram festival known locally as 'Hosay'. Hosay takes place in Trinidad and Jamaica. The festival commemorates the martyrdom on 10 Muharram 680 of Muhammad's grandson Husayn. Also, gold and silver jewellery were routinely and repeatedly melted down to make new or more pieces as gifts to keep up with additions to the family.

The more permanent arts include the temples and mosques that are a common feature of the landscape of the southern Caribbean (see fig. 7). These betray a variety of styles and materials, from early crude and makeshift structures in mud and wood to elaborate and spacious concrete buildings, particularly those erected since the 1970s. In some of the earlier temples representations of gods and goddesses were roughly carved in stone. In modern structures, it is more common to find icons brought from India and installed after due ceremony. The characteristic type of mosque structure is hypostyle, with symbolic domes and minarets attached after completion of the central building. Ancillary features include arches, cupolas, façades, towers and representations of a star and moon.

BIBLIOGRAPHY

A. Niehoff and J. Niehoff: *East Indians in the West Indies* (Milwaukee, 1960)
M. Klass: *East Indians in Trinidad* (New York, 1961)
V. S. Naipaul: *A House for Mr Biswas* (London, 1961)
D. Lowenthal: *West Indian Societies* (London, 1972)
Singaravelou: *Les Indiens de la Guadeloupe* (Bordeaux, 1975)
I. J. Bahadur Singh, ed.: *Indians in the Caribbean* (London, 1987)
S. Vertovec: *Hindu Trinidad: Religion, Ethnicity and Socio-economic Change* (London, 1992)

KUSHA HARAKSINGH

Caricature. Type of art in which the characteristic features of the human figure are exaggerated for amusement or criticism. The term *caricatura* (from It. *caricare*: 'to load or change') was probably invented by Annibale Carracci. It appeared in print, possibly for the first time, in a preface by Giovanni Atanasio Mosini (a pseudonym for Monsignor Giovanni Massani, house master to Pope Urban VII) to Agucchi's *Trattato* (1646) and two years later by Bernini.

Caricature appears as an art form throughout the world. Of all its international forms, however, the Western tradition has probably been studied the most, and this article therefore concentrates on this aspect; besides the overview in §2 below, further references to caricature elsewhere may appear within country and regional survey articles of the ancient world and of Asian and African art.

7. Hindu temple, Reform Village, Trinidad, 1940s

1. Western. 2. Elsewhere.

1. WESTERN. In Western art there are essentially two traditions of caricature. The first derives from Italy, where caricature was seen as primarily a humorous, exaggerated portrait. In northern Europe, especially in 18th-century London and 19th-century Paris, its scope widened to include both individuals and human types, who were caricatured in political, social and moral prints for satirical effect. This latter use became the most prevalent, and thus much caricature falls under the more specific category of SATIRE.

In contrast, however, not all satire need be caricatural, as it can be effective through the use of symbolism or content without relying solely on exaggeration. Whatever the intention, caricature invariably rests on the premise that outward appearances can be suitably exaggerated so as to emphasize personality traits. The devices of caricature have therefore been used to study human character, especially under the auspices of the pseudo-science of physiognomy.

(i) Before 1720. (ii) 1720–1870. (iii) After 1870. (iv) Historiography.

(i) Before 1720. Sketches of grotesque heads may be considered precedents to caricatures, although the best known, by Leonardo da Vinci, were apparently intended as physiognomic studies. Giuseppe Arcimboldo composed facial features from combinations of such unlikely elements as vegetables and pots and pans for comic effect (*see* ARCIMBOLDO, GIUSEPPE, fig. 2). During the Renaissance, caricature developed as a counterpart of the Ideal. The term was first applied to the variety of caricatural heads (*c.* 1590) by Annibale Carracci and Agostino Carracci. One of the first surviving caricatures of an individual

1. Caricature by Pier Leone Ghezzi: *Joseph Henry of Straffon, Co. Kildare*, pen and brown ink, over traces of black chalk, 311×213 mm, *c*. 1750 (New York, Metropolitan Museum of Art)

is the *Theologian of the Aldobrandini Household* (*c*. 1634; Chatsworth, Derbys) by Domenichino. Guercino drew scatological caricatures. It is thought that these artists drew caricatures for private amusement, but in 17th-century Rome caricature became a fad: Pier Francesco Mola was prolific in his production of pornographic caricatures. Stefano della Bella drew sieges and entertainments that were influenced by the work of Jacques Callot.

Gianlorenzo Bernini drew pen-and-ink caricatures of individual figures; eight of these survive, including that of *A Marshal-in-chief of Pope Urban VIII* (Rome, Gab. N. Stampe) and *? Cardinal Scipione Borghese* (Rome, Vatican, Bib. Apostolica), with its remarkable economy of line. Bernini probably introduced caricature to the portrait painter Pier Leone Ghezzi, considered to be the first artist to make the production of caricatures his primary activity. His 2000 surviving caricatures, carried out between 1693 and his death in 1755, depict Roman society, musicians and tourists, for example *Joseph Henry of Straffon, Co. Kildare* (*c*. 1750; New York, Met.; see fig. 1). Etchings of Ghezzi's drawings were popular in Germany and England, where they contributed to the taste for caricature, especially among the upper classes. Anton Maria Zanetti (i) is said to have brought the art of caricature from Rome to Venice, where the genre was further developed by Giambattista Tiepolo, who drew types rather than individuals and whose work was popular among English Grand Tourists. He was succeeded as a caricaturist by his son Giandomenico Tiepolo. Jacques Callot caricatured dwarfs of the Medici court and *commedia dell'arte* characters, emphasizing the mask rather than the face. After being summoned by Richelieu, he returned in 1628 to Paris, where his reputation as one of the most important comic artists persisted until the 19th century. Caricature was also occasionally practised in France after Bernini visited in 1665 (several drawings by Watteau exist).

There was little original caricature in England during this period, apart from polemical prints, pamphlets and broadsheets produced during the Civil War (1642–9). The best satirical printmaker working in England was the Bohemian Wenceslaus Hollar; the development of English caricature was also influenced by Dutch social and political satires. In the Netherlands itself Cornelis Dusart drew political caricatures in reaction to the vices associated with the French and later turned his attention to individuals. Romeyn de Hooghe was employed in the 1670s and 1680s by the Dutch stadholder William, Prince of Orange, to make polemical prints about James II's attempt to re-establish Catholicism in Britain. Dutch caricaturists also attacked Louis XIV's policies towards the Protestant Netherlands, the Thirty Years' War and the Revolution of 1688 in England.

(ii) 1720–1870. The satirical broadsheets popular in northern Europe together with the portrait caricature typical in Italy formed the basis of English caricature. A popular album of 25 caricatures by Carracci, Ghezzi, Guercino, Watteau and others was published in facsimile by Arthur Pond in London in 1737–9, so increasing access to Italian models. William Hogarth, called 'the father of English caricature', developed a new genre of satirical narrative etchings, which were often based on paintings. He exposed social ills and hoped to encourage reform through such series of 'modern moral subjects' as the *Harlot's Progress* (1731), the *Rake's Progress* (1733–4), *Marriage à la Mode* (1743; *see* SATIRE, fig. 1) and *Industry and Idleness* (1747). Reacting against Italian dilettantish caricature, he made satirical printmaking a profession, in part through his central role in agitating for the Copyright Act of 1735. The publication of copyrighted broadsheets and caricatural series made more copies of prints by identified artists available to a larger public. James Gillray specialized in political cartoons, which he began making in 1778. The impact of the French Revolution and Napoleon prompted him to produce such caustic caricatures as the *Plumb-pudding in Danger* (1805; London, BM; see fig. 2). Gillray also coined the image of 'Little Boney' for Napoleon, the first figure to be universally caricatured (*see* ENGLAND, fig. 19). Isaac Cruikshank and George Cruikshank picked up the theme and also satirized Charles James Fox, William Pitt the younger and George III. In England caricature enjoyed a greater degree of freedom than elsewhere in Europe. In addition to his political caricatures of the 1780s, Thomas Rowlandson produced thousands of caricatural drawings of English social life and invented the pedantic character of Dr Syntax. Gillray, Rowlandson and the Cruikshank, as well as William Dent (*fl* 1783–93) and the young Richard Newton (1777–98),

2. Caricature by James Gillray: *Plumb-pudding in Danger*, hand-coloured etching, 256×356 mm, 1805 (London, British Museum)

flourished in the period that has come to be known as the Golden Age of English caricature.

In Spain, Goya responded to the Napoleonic campaigns with some of the most powerful images in the history of caricature. His series of prints, the *Caprichos* (1799), the *Disasters of War* (*c.* 1820) and the *Disparates* (1816–23, pubd as the *Proverbios*, 1864), show the horror, superstition, violence and suffering caused by war and the Inquisition (*see* AQUATINT, fig. 2). In France caricature became common practice only in the late 18th century. The watercolours of fashionable society by Philibert-Louis Debucourt exemplify the polite social satire of the *ancien régime.* Caricature came to the fore as a political force during the French Revolution (1789–95). From 1789 to 1799 there are prints and broadsheets attacking the monarchy, clergy, émigrés and the Third Estate, showing the influence of German, Dutch, English and French popular prints. These range from several sophisticated prints by the painter Jacques-Louis David (e.g. the *English Government*, 1793–4) to caricatures employing obscene imagery and crude broadsheets. After the Revolution, the taste for genre images, the flourishing print market and the invention of lithography by Alois Senefelder in 1798–9 contributed to the further growth of caricature. Its increasing popularity coincided with the interest in physiognomy, to the extent that the representation of grimaces became fashionable in the 1820s. Louis-Léopold Boilly's *Recueil de grimaces* (Paris, 1823–8) contains 94 lithographs that combine caricature and physiognomy.

The union of caricature and journalism was initiated by Charles Philipon, publisher of *La Caricature* (founded 1830), one of the first comic newspapers, and of its successor *Le Charivari* (founded 1832). He was the major force behind the publication of political caricatures and, later, social caricature and satirical books. Philipon drew an analogy between Louis-Philippe's head and a pear (*poire* or fathead), which led to fines and imprisonment, though the symbol took hold. The most important political and social caricaturist of this time was Honoré Daumier, who made some 4000 lithographs between 1832 and 1875, mostly for *Le Charivari* as well as some for *Le Journal amusant.* His early caricatures were predominantly political (*see* SATIRE, fig. 2) and contributed to the downfall of Charles X. Under the censorship laws of September 1835 journals were forbidden from satirizing the king and court. Consequently, there was a major shift from political to social satire, with an emphasis on daily life, which continued throughout the Second Empire. With the growth of Paris, caricature took part in the fashion for classifying and codifying the population, and caricature journals became increasingly numerous and popular. Daumier created a human comedy in his satire of Parisian types, habits and manners, with a particular focus on the bourgeoisie. He also developed and employed such emblematic figures as Robert Macaire, the quintessential con man, and

Joseph Prudhomme, the ultimate bourgeois (introduced by Henry Monnier). When censorship was lifted during the Second Republic (1848–52), Daumier created Ratapoil, an *agent provocateur.* Ratapoil provides a rare example of caricatural sculpture (plaster, *c.* 1851; Buffalo, NY, Albright–Knox A.G.; numerous casts in bronze). With the more liberal laws of 1866, Daumier returned to political caricature, taking on issues of European politics, universal suffrage, budgetary excesses, German militarism, disarmament and, above all, the price of war. Other major 19th-century French caricaturists include J. J. Grandville, who produced political caricatures in the early 1830s and then prints and illustrated books with imaginative morphological transformations of humans, animals and objects, which prefigure Surrealism. Joseph Traviès represented the under class. He devised Mayeux, a hunchback embodying prejudice, vanity and lasciviousness. Paul Gavarni drew the elegant world, the demi-monde, particularly women of easy pleasure, and some workers. Cham produced a range of social and political themes, while Gustave Doré, as well as illustrating books, drew caricatures of Parisian life, its theatres and other diversions.

The death of Gillray in 1815 marked an end of the first major phase of caricature in England, although caricatures continued to be published, culminating in agitation for the Reform Bill of 1832. Caricature then shifted from the political to the social, as seen in *Punch: The London Charivari*, the first English journal dedicated to caricature, founded in 1841. There were also albums of caricature appealing to a growing middle- and lower middle-class public. Among the most important of the cartoonists was John Leech, who joined *Punch* in its first year. His drawing *Substance and Shadow: Cartoon No. 1* (*Punch*, v (1843), p. 23) led to the term 'cartoon' being adopted for caricatures of topical events. Leech's early work focused on street scenes and politics; during his 23 years with *Punch*, he contributed 700 cartoons and 3000 illustrations. His successor as *Punch*'s principal cartoonist was John Tenniel, best known for his illustrations for Lewis Carroll's *Alice's Adventures in Wonderland* (London, 1865) and *Through the Looking Glass* (London, 1872).

There are only 78 known caricatures for the period 1764 to 1822 in the USA, although caricature became more common in broadsheets after 1828. The *American Comic Almanach* (founded 1841) was followed by *Punchinello* (referring to the English *Punch*). *Harper's Weekly* began publication in 1857 and was followed two years later by *Vanity Fair.*

The one German caricaturist of note in the 18th century was Daniel Nikolaus Chodowiecki, who drew *c.* 2000 caricatures of the aristocracy, clergy and military. He illustrated Johann Kaspar Lavater's *Physiognomische Fragmente* (Leipzig and Winterthur, 1775–8), which also appeared in French and English editions. Late 18th-century and 19th-century German caricature tended to be derivative, with such few exceptions as Gottfried Schadow's satirical sketches of Napoleon and his generals. The original and influential Swiss Rodolphe Töpffer interwove text and illustration in continuous narratives called 'comic picture novels', for which he invented such characters as Messieurs Jabot, Crepin and Vieuxbois, as in *Histoire de M. Jabot* (?1835). Equally important is the German Wilhelm Busch, whose picture stories in successive frames prefigure comic-strips in their structure and Surrealism in their comic absurdity. His best-known work, *Max und Moritz* (Munich, 1865), was translated into 30 languages. He also contributed to the journals *Fliegende Blätter* (founded 1845) and *Fischietto* (founded 1848), which were among the new publications founded around the time of the Revolution of 1848. Other major journals established in this period include *Punsch* (1847), *Leuchtkugeln* (1848), *Düsseldorfer Monatschefte* (1849), *Leipziger Charivari* (1858), *Berliner Charivari* (1847) and the particularly popular *Kladderadatsch* (1848).

(iii) After 1870. From 1870 to 1900 no fewer than 139 journals specializing in caricature were published in Paris, including *Le Chat noir* (1882–97), founded by the owners of the cabaret of the same name. Between 1900 and 1914 another 94 journals appeared, including *L'Eclipse* (later called *La Lune*), for which André Gill, their principal contributor, drew portrait caricatures. *L'Assiette au beurre* published *c.* 10,000 drawings between 1901 and 1912. There was a general shift from works of physiognomic interest to caricatures of situations. Jean-Louis Forain, one of the few right-wing caricaturists, left *Le Figaro* in the 1890s because of his anti-Dreyfus position and co-founded the anti-Semitic journal *Psst!* (1898–9) with Caran d'Ache. By the end of the 19th century in Germany an important group of caricaturists were producing work related to the emerging Expressionist movement. The most significant of their publishing outlets was the periodical *Simplicissimus*, founded in 1896, which satirized the Church, the military, bureaucracy, the middle class and the Kaiser's foreign policy. Its contributors included Alfred Kubin, Théophile-Alexandre Steinlen, Adolphe Willette and Käthe Kollwitz, although its leading cartoonist after 1902 was the Norwegian Olaf Gulbransson, whose portrait caricatures were influential both in Germany and on the *New Yorker* in the USA. After World War I *Simplicissimus* supported the government and declined. In reaction to World War I, George Grosz fiercely caricatured the corruption and violence associated with militarism (*see* SATIRE, fig. 3), capitalism and the rise of fascism, for example in the drawing *The Robbers* (1923; Washington, DC, N.G.A.), and he often published his work in Communist journals. In the 1930s John Heartfield and Hannah Höch used photomontages to attack the Nazis.

English caricatures before World War I tended to be mild, such as those by Max Beerbohm of elegant celebrities, including the pen-and-ink *Mr H. G. Wells and his Patent Mechanical Republic* (*c.* 1903; New Haven, CT, Yale U., Beinecke Lib.); many of these appeared in the English edition of *Vanity Fair* (founded 1868). The illustrated press flourished between the wars, and political cartoons reflected editorial policy. The most important caricaturist was David Low, who worked in London from 1920 to 1963, particularly for the *Evening Standard* (1926–50) and *The Guardian* (1953–63). Low created Colonel Blimp, who personified Reaction, and caricatured Adolf Hitler, Neville Chamberlain and Franklin Delano Roosevelt. Ronald Searle (*b* 1920), one of *Punch*'s leading cartoonists from 1949, later joined the more scurrilous and barbed *Private Eye*, founded in 1961. He influenced Gerald Scarfe

3. Caricature by Saul Steinberg: *Conversation (Three Women)*, pen and ink and crayon, 1968 (collection of Mr and Mrs Jacob M. Kaplan)

(*b* 1936), who became known for his savage attacks on political figures and for his caricatural sculpture, film and opera design. In addition to political cartoons, Ralph Steadman (*b* 1936) illustrated a number of books, including *I Leonardo* (London, 1982).

In the USA Thomas Nast, 'the father of American political cartooning', created the symbols of the elephant and the donkey for the Republican and Democratic parties respectively. He began as a pictorial journalist during the Civil War, and in his commitment to the Union cause and social change he attacked the politician William Marcy Tweed and big city corruption. There was a proliferation of newspaper cartoons from the 1890s. *The Masses*, the leading journal to include cartoons, employed a number of artists from the Ashcan school, and William Gropper (1897–1977) drew for its successor, *Americana*, in the 1930s. By this date comic-strip art was a growing art form: most important were Winsor McCay, creator of Little Nemo, George Herriman for Krazy Kat (for illustration *see* COMIC-STRIP ART) and Oliver Harrington for Bootsie. The *New Yorker* (founded 1925) published visually sophisticated caricatures and cartoons, often about art, urban and suburban life. James Thurber (1894–1961), Managing Editor in 1927, focused on imaginative ventures and the war of the sexes. The Mexican Miguel Covarrubias, the most fashionable caricaturist of the 1920s and 1930s, drew performers and public figures. Charles Addams (1912–88) was known for his macabre scenes and ghoulish characters, including the *Addams Family* cartoon, Peter Arno (1904–68) for his situation jokes. Saul Steinberg, one of the most brilliant caricaturists of the 20th century, created plays on words, signs and images (see fig. 3) and parodied drawing and style, as in the caricature from the collection *The Catalogue* (Cleveland and New York, 1945). Other leading *New Yorker* cartoonists of the late 20th century include Booth, Edward Koren, Arthur Spiegelman (the creator of *Maus*) and William Steig (*b* 1907). Significant social cartoonists include Jean-Jacques Sempé (*b* 1932) and Claire Bretcher (*b* 1940).

In Russia three artists working together from 1924 have collectively produced cartoons under the anagram 'Kukryniksy'. First publishing works in *Pravda* (1933) on politics and daily life, they also contributed to the satirical journal *Krokodil*, as did Boris Yefimov. The leading French political and social caricaturist, 'Tim' Louis Mitelberg (*b* 1919), born in Poland, focused on individual political figures; he began publishing in *Action* (1945), then in

L'Humanité (1952–8) and thereafter primarily for *L'Express*. He became known for his illustrated books, parodies of art styles and for his sculpture of *Dreyfus* (1988) on the corner of the Boulevard Raspail and the Rue Stanislas, Paris.

(iv) Historiography. Theoretical writings on Western caricature appeared first in Italy. After Mosini used the term *caricatura*, Bernini introduced it to France *c.* 1665. There it first appeared in André Félibien's *Principes* (Paris, 1676), in his discussion of the *portrait chargé*. In his life of Annibale Caracci in *Le vite de' pittori, scultori et architetti* (Rome, 1672), Giovanni Pietro Bellori referred to the artist's 'burlesque or caricatured portraits'. Filippo Baldinucci, in his *Vocabulario toscano dell'arte del disegno* (Florence, 1681), discussed portrait caricature for the sake of humour. The first definition in English was made by Sir Thomas Brown, who published *A Letter to a Friend* (London, 1690) and *Christian Morals* (Cambridge, 1716). Werner Hofmann noted that 'it was only in the 18th century that it found its way into the dictionaries and gradually passed into common speech'. Hogarth illustrated and commented on the distinction between 'caricature', which reflects an artist's response to his subject, and 'character', or the portrayal of a likeness. Denis Diderot and Jean Le Rond d'Alembert appreciated caricature for its 'unbridled imagination' (*Encyclopédie*, ii, Paris, 1757). Francis Grose's *Rules for Drawing Caricatures* (1788) furthered the analysis of caricature. Compendium volumes of European caricature were published by E. Jaime in *Musée de la caricature* (1834–8).

In the mid-19th century histories of caricature began to appear. Among the first was Thomas Wright's *A History of Caricature and Grotesque in Literature and Art* (London, 1865), in which caricature is viewed as a primitive form of art. In *Histoire générale de la caricature* (1865–88), Champfleury discussed caricature from a Realist perspective. In 'De l'essence du rire et généralement du comique dans les arts plastiques' (1855) and 'Quelques caricaturistes français' (1857), Charles Baudelaire was the first to write about the philosophical and spiritual element in caricature, its eternal and temporal aspects, its mysterious and diabolical qualities and its defiance and Romantic appreciation of ugliness. Hugo von Hofmannsthal saw caricature as anticipating modern art in its concern for everyday life and abstract form (*Kunstkritiken: Prosa*, i, 1893). Heinrich Brauer and Rudolf Wittkower explained the rise of caricature by pointing to the emergence of the concept of the individual and the concomitant development of a spirit of mockery (*Die Zeichnungen des Gianlorenzo Bernini*, 1931). In his essay 'The Psychology of Caricature' (1935), Ernst Kris drew on Freudian theory to explore the psychological mechanisms of caricature, particularly the relationships between wit, caricature and dreams. In a further study with Ernst Gombrich, *Caricature* (1940), they examined the sources of caricature in aggression, according to the theories of Freud. Gombrich's essays 'The Experiment in Caricature' (*Art and Illusion*, 1960) and 'The Cartoonist's Armoury' (*Meditations on a Hobby Horse*, 1963) are of major importance for understanding the psychological and perceptual mechanisms of the making and reading of caricature. Werner Hofmann placed caricature in the context of the history of art in *Caricature from Leonardo to Picasso* (1957) and argued that the formal means of caricature have much in common with abstract art. In his essay 'Bernini and the Art of Social Satire' (1981), Irving Lavin suggested that the early history of caricature can be seen as part of the history of art theory, with its focus on style. The interaction of caricature and physiognomy in codifying and classifying the urban population and the relationship to such other popular arts as pantomime was discussed by Judith Wechsler in *A Human Comedy: Physiognomy and Caricature in 19th Century Paris* (1983).

BIBLIOGRAPHY

GENERAL

F. Grose: *Rules for Drawing Caricatures* (London, 1788)
E. Jaime: *Musée de la caricature* (Paris, 1834–8)
C. Baudelaire: 'De l'essence du rire et généralement du comique dans les arts plastiques', *Le Portefeuille* (8 July 1855); repr. in *Charles Baudelaire, oeuvres complètes*, ii, ed. C. Pichois (Paris, 1976), pp. 525–43
T. Wright: *A History of Caricature and Grotesque in Literature and Art* (London, 1865/*R* New York, 1968)
Champfleury: *Histoire générale de la caricature*, 6 vols (Paris, 1865–88)
E. Kris: 'The Psychology of Caricature' (1935); repr. in *Psychoanalytic Explorations in Art* (New York and London, 1952), pp. 173–88
E. H. Gombrich and E. Kris: 'The Principles of Caricature', *Brit. J. Medic. Psychol.* xvii (1938), pp. 319–42; repr. in E. Kris: *Psychoanalytic Explorations in Art* (New York and London, 1952), pp. 189–203
——: *Caricature* (Harmondsworth, 1940)
W. Hofmann: *Caricature from Leonardo to Picasso* (New York and London, 1957)
E. H. Gombrich: 'The Experiment in Caricature', *Art and Illusion* (New York and London, 1960), pp. 330–58
——: 'The Cartoonist's Armoury', *Meditations on a Hobby Horse* (London, 1963), pp. 127–42
M. D. George: From Hogarth to Cruikshank: Social Change in Graphic Satire (London, 1967)
R. Shikes: *The Indignant Eye: The Artist as Social Critic in Prints and Drawings from the Fifteenth Century to Picasso* (Boston, 1969)
B. Hillier: *Cartoons and Caricatures* (London, 1970)
Caricature and its Role in Graphic Satire (Providence, 1971)
D. Kunzle: *The History of the Comic Strip: The Early Comic Strip* (Berkeley and Los Angeles, 1973)
B. Bornemann, C. Roy and R. Searle: *La Caricature: Art et manifeste, du XVIe siècle à nos jours* (Geneva, 1974)
K. Herding and G. Otto, eds: *Karikaturen* (Giessen, 1980)
W. Feaver: *Masters of Caricature from Hogarth and Gillray to Scarfe and Levine* (New York, 1981)
E. Lucie-Smith: *The Art of Caricature* (Ithaca, 1981)
J. Wechsler: *A Human Comedy: Physiognomy and Caricature in 19th Century Paris* (London and Chicago, 1983)
J. Wechsler, ed.: 'The Issue of Caricature', *A.J.* [New York], xliii (Winter 1983) [issue devoted to caricature]
R. Shikes and S. Heller: *The Art of Satire: Painters as Caricaturists and Cartoonists from Delacroix to Picasso* (New York, 1984)

SPECIALIST STUDIES

C. Baudelaire: 'Quelques caricaturistes français', *Le Présent* (1 Sept 1857); repr. in *Charles Baudelaire, oeuvres complètes*, ii, ed. C. Pichois (Paris, 1976), pp. 544–63
J. Grand-Carteret: *Les Moeurs et la caricature en Allemagne, en Autriche, en Suisse* (Paris, 1885)
——: *Les Moeurs et la caricature en France* (Paris, 1888)
A. Alexandre: *L'Art du rire et de la caricature* (Paris, 1892)
H. von Hofmannstahl: *Kunstkritiken: Prosa*, i (1893); repr. in *Gesammelte Werke, Prosa I* (Frankfurt-am-Main, 1950), pp. 162–9
M. H. Spielmann: *The History of 'Punch'* (London, 1895)
H. Brauer and R. Wittkower: *Die Zeichnungen des Gianlorenzo Bernini*, 2 vols (Berlin, 1931)
F. D. Klingender: *Hogarth and English Caricature* (New York and London, 1944)
M. D. George: *English Political Caricature: A Study of Opinion and Propaganda*, 2 vols (Oxford, 1959)
I. Lavin: 'Bernini and the Art of Social Satire', *Drawings by Gianlorenzo Bernini from the Museum der Bildenden Künste, Leipzig* (exh. cat., ed. I. Lavin and others; Princeton U., NJ, A. Mus., 1981), pp. 25–52; repr.

in *Modern Art and Popular Culture: Readings in High and Low*, ed. K. Varnedoe and A. Gopniz (New York, 1990), pp. 19-50
English Caricature, 1620 to the Present (exh. cat., ed. R. Godfrey; London, V&A; 1984)
J. Cuno, ed.: *French Caricature and the French Revolution, 1789–1799* (Los Angeles, 1988)

JUDITH WECHSLER

2. ELSEWHERE. Outside the West, caricature occurs not only in paintings and drawings but also in, for example, African masquerade (*see* AFRICA, §VI, 3), Pre-Columbian ceramics and in South-east Asian relief sculptures illustrating *jātaka* stories and the burlesque characters of shadow plays (*wayang*). In East Asia the use of caricature includes Zen Buddhist paintings of patriarchs and other figures. The work of the Chinese painter Liang Kai includes humorous depictions of such figures as a Chan priest.

(i) African. In African art, caricature is used generally to condemn inappropriate actions, to affront rivals and to mock outsiders and foreigners. The Yoruba of Nigeria sometimes address improper sexual behaviour and other socially unacceptable activities in the imagery of their Gelede masqueraders, as in the figure of Asewo the Prostitute, whose name literally means 'we do it for money'. Similarly, improper sexual acts are sometimes graphically represented in Igbo *m'bari* house sculpture. Caricaturing such unacceptable societal behaviour reinforces the moral code while entertaining the viewer. Ridicule of rivals for the purpose of competitive positioning, sometimes by demeaning their symbols, is found throughout Africa. Among the Fante of coastal Ghana, for example, fishermen aligned to the Asafo companies use relief imagery on their canoe gunwales to impugn their rivals. A sea snake, a symbol of good fortune, may be represented in a rival's colour as a helpless victim being eaten by a more powerful sea snake. The satirizing of outsiders is very common. Among such masked caricatures are the Colonialist in a pith helmet, the Anthropologist, taking notes and asking silly questions, the European Woman with vivid red lips, clutching her handbag, and the bedraggled Hausa Trader. The Yoruba Oyinbo (White Man) mask has a long, narrow, straight nose, elliptical slits for eyes and straight hair (all non-Yoruba features) and a costume of European cloth (Pemberton, 1989, p. 180). This form of caricature is also characteristic of the *m'piko* masks of the Makonde of Mozambique. In a modern context caricature is an essential ingredient of the cartoons that appear in many African newspapers and periodicals, as well as appearing in the work of such modern painters as Stephen Kappata (*see* ZAMBIA, §3).

BIBLIOGRAPHY

S. Ottenberg: 'Humorous Masks and Serious Politics among Afikpo-Igpo', *African Art and Leadership*, ed. D. Fraser and H. M. Cole (Madison, 1972)
H. M. Cole: *Mbari: Art and Life among the Owerri Igbo*, Trad. A. Africa (Bloomington, IN, 1982), pp. 202–3
H. J. Drewal and M. T. Drewal: *Gelede: Art and Female Power among the Yoruba*, Trad. A. Africa (Bloomington, IN, 1983/*R* 1990), pp. 197–201
J. Pemberton III: 'The Oyo Empire', *Yoruba: Nine Centuries of African Art and Thought*, by H. J. Drewal and J. Pemberton III with Rowland Abiodun (New York, 1989), pp. 147–87

PATRICIA CORONEL, MICHAEL CORONEL

(ii) Islamic. In the Islamic world the intentional exaggeration and distortion of likenesses for humorous or satiric effect is relatively rare, since representation plays only a minor role (*see* ISLAMIC ART, §I, 7). Caricature is found only in the few periods when figural representations were relatively common. One example is in a well-known manuscript (Paris, Bib. N., MS. arab. 5847) of al-Hariri's *Maqāmāt* ('Assemblies'), copied and illustrated by Yahya al-Wasiti in 1237, probably at Baghdad. In an image such as *Abu Zayd before the Governor of Rahba* (fol. 26*r*) the painter has emphasized the hooked nose of the roguish hero Abu Zayd and the foppish beard worn by the governor. Caricature was more developed in Persian painting of the 17th century, in the works of RIZA and his followers. His painting of *Nashmi the Archer* (Cambridge, MA, Sackler Mus.), dated 4 Rabi 'II AH 1031/25 (February 1622), depicts a pot-bellied and slip-shod character smoking an opium pipe. Riza's caricature alludes to the momentous change in contemporary society brought about by the acceptance of firearms that made a traditional soldier, such as Nashmi, superfluous.

BIBLIOGRAPHY

R. Ettinghausen: *Arab Painting* (Geneva, 1962/*R* 1977)
S. R. Canby: 'Age and Time in the Work of Riza', *Persian Masters: Five Centuries of Painting* (Bombay, 1990), pp. 71–84

SHEILA BLAIR, JONATHAN BLOOM

(iii) Pre-Columbian American. In the Pre-Columbian Americas caricature confirmed an élite or supernatural status to the individual being portrayed. Its religious nature and its presence in only those Pre-Columbian cultures with a tradition of realism distinguish it from the Western tradition of caricature. One of the earliest cultures to make use of the art form was the Olmec (Pre-Classic period, *c.* 2000 BC–AD 250) of the Gulf Coast region of modern Mexico. A fragment of a greenstone-carving from southern Veracruz of the *Head and Shoulders of a Woman* (*c.* 400 BC; Washington, DC, Dumbarton Oaks) exhibits naturalistic features, although the mouth is strangely distorted by large, fleshy lips. This same treatment of the mouth, seen on many Olmec figures, is interpreted as central to a religious cult centred around the jaguar. Among the Classic period Maya (*c.* AD 250–*c.* 900) a superb calligraphic tradition flourished, and caricature was most often employed on two-dimensional figures painted on pottery or carved in shallow relief on stone. The god known as GIII has a number of pictorial forms, ranging from purely human with slightly distorted features to combinations of humans and animals and completely abstracted human forms. Each of these represents a different 'guise' of the god. In South America the Moche culture (north coast of Peru, *c.* AD 100–700) made extensive use of caricature in ceramic art. Startlingly realistic, fully three-dimensional representations of human heads were fashioned into vessels. Features were frequently distorted by battle scars (suggesting leadership and high status) and bloated by parasitic disease, perhaps indicating supernatural or otherworldly associations. Also common are pottery figures with enormous phalli, the tips of which become the vessels' spouts.

BIBLIOGRAPHY

E. Benson: *The Mochica, a Culture of Peru* (New York, 1972)
M. Miller: *The Art of Mesoamerica from Olmec to Aztec* (London, 1986)
L. Schele and M. Miller: *The Blood of Kings: Dynasty and Ritual in Maya Art* (Fort Worth, 1986)

E. MICHAEL WHITTINGTON

Caričin Grad [Tsaritsin Grad, Tzaritchingrad; Lat. Justiniana Prima]. Site of an early Byzantine city located 30 km south-west of Leskovac in Serbia. The name means 'the emperor's fortress', and it can almost certainly be identified with Justiniana Prima, which, according to Prokopios (*b c.* AD 500), Justinian I founded *c.* AD 525–50 in honour of his birthplace, Tauresium. The site occupies a high plateau between the rivers Svinjarica to the west and Caričina to the east; an aqueduct also brought water from the Petrova Gora, 17 km to the south, and entered the city at the south-west corner. Fortifications strengthened with towers and wide ditches surround the city (*c.* 500 m north–south by *c.* 215 m east–west), which is divided into two parts: an upper city area that contains a polygonal acropolis and a lower city to the south-east. Excavations, first undertaken in 1912 and continued from the 1940s, have shown that the city was destroyed within a century of its foundation, probably by the Avaro-Slavs, but it was briefly revived in the 9th and 10th centuries. Many of the finds are in the National Museum at Leskovac.

The acropolis contained the episcopal palace, ecclesiastical and administrative buildings, including a three-aisled basilica with a western narthex and atrium and three eastern apses. Beneath the centre of the atrium is a rock-cut cistern (9.5×6.5 m) that was supplied by a spring; there is also a three-aisled vaulted crypt. To the south of the basilica is a quatrefoil baptistery with a cruciform *piscina* and mosaics; to the north a street runs between the basilica and the remains of the episcopal palace and other administrative buildings. The remains of an elaborate circular forum (diam. *c.* 22 m) stand to the east of the acropolis. Four paved, colonnaded streets radiate from the forum's centre: east to a large gate through the city wall and west to the acropolis; the streets to the north and south have not been fully excavated. Other buildings in this part of the city include a basilica with a large crypt, at least two further churches (one a basilica and the other, to the south, a vaulted, cross-shaped church) and several unidentified structures.

Although an east–west cross-wall divides the upper from the lower city, the two parts are linked by a single main street running north–south. Among the other structures uncovered in the lower city are a bathing complex, a double basilica composed of two parallel, apsed halls, a barrel-vaulted triconch chapel and a three-aisled basilica with a tripartite transept (30.0×18.5 m) and a colonnaded atrium to the west. Remains of the synthronon (bishop's bench) and canopy survive in the eastern apse. Remnants of the church's sculptural decoration include Ionic capitals carved with fine-toothed acanthus and bearing Justinian's monogram, thus suggesting that it was built *c.* 525–50. The floors of the narthex and central nave are decorated with mosaic representations of the *Good Shepherd*, hunters, savage beasts, centaurs and Amazons in a style similar to the mosaics from the Great Palace in Constantinople (*see* ISTANBUL, §III, 12) and NIKOPOLIS.

BIBLIOGRAPHY

Stillwell: 'Justiniana Prima'

D. Mano-Zissi: 'Caričin Grad', *Velika Arheološka Nalazišta u Srbiji* [Important archaeological sites of Serbia] (Belgrade, 1974), pp. 78–88

V. Kondić and V. Popović: *Caričin Grad* (Belgrade, 1977)

SUSAN PINTO MADIGAN

Carignano, Princes of. *See under* SAVOY.

Carings, Alexander. *See* KEIRINCKX, ALEXANDER.

Carini Motta, Fabrizio (*b* Viadana; *d* Mantua, 1700). Italian architect, stage designer and writer. He was the brother-in-law of Giacomo Francesco Motta, superintendent of the Teatro Grande in Mantua, whose surname he adopted and who probably assisted him in his youth. He began working at the court of Mantua as a painter *c.* 1650, later becoming general superintendent of buildings and prefect of theatres. In 1668 he built a theatre (destr.) for Luigi Fedeli at Mantua, with a proscenium arch similar to that introduced by Giovanni Battista Aleotti at the Farnese Theatre (1618–19), Parma. It had a central space bounded by two stepped levels, three tiers of boxes and an upper balcony. This theatre was the site of Carini Motta's only documented stage designs, those for the *Torneo a'piedi* (1674), recorded in engravings accompanying the libretto published in Mantua. In 1688 he designed the Teatro dei Comici, Mantua, with five tiers of boxes as well as the parterre. Carini Motta also produced a considerable number of stage devices and machines; firework displays and ceremonial structures for the coronations of Popes Clement IX (1667) and Clement X (1670); stage devices for the productions of *Gran Costanzo* (1670) and *Ottaviano Cesare Augusto* (1682); and funeral accoutrements for Eleonora Gonzaga (1687), Margherita d'Este (1693) and Eleonora Maria Gioseffa (1698). Carini Motta's most important work, however, was the first book exclusively devoted to theatre design. This treatise, with 11 plates, published at Guastalla in 1676, is valuable not least for the account it gives of the design of early Italian theatres. It defines two general types: those for princely or noble audiences, and those for the general public. The rules given for planning and construction derive from Carini Motta's own experience. A later treatise (1688) on the construction of theatres and theatrical machinery shows auditoria with bell-shaped and horseshoe plans.

UNPUBLISHED SOURCES

Milan, Castello Sforzesco [*Disegni e figure di facili compartimenti delli cinque ordini d'adornati d'architettura*]

WRITINGS

Trattato sopra la struttura de theatri e scene (Guastalla, 1676); ed. E. A. Craig (Milan, 1972)

O. K. Larson, ed.: *The Theatrical Writings of Fabrizio Carini Motta* (Carbondale, IL, 1987)

BIBLIOGRAPHY

P. Carpeggiani: 'Teatri e apparati scenici alla corte dei Gonzaga tra cinque e seicento', *Boll. Cent. Int. Stud. Archit. Andrea Palladio*, xv (1975), pp. 101–18

A. Cavicchi: 'Scenotecnica e macchinistica teatrale in un trattato inedito di Fabrizio Carini Motta (Mantova, 1688)', *Venezia e il melodramma nel seicento* (Florence, 1976), pp. 359–77

O. K. Larson: 'New Evidence on the Origins of the Box Set', *Theat. Surv.: Amer. J. Theat. Hist.*, xxi (1980), pp. 79–91

G. Ricci: 'Note sull'attività di Fabrizio Carini, architetto teatrale e scenotecnico', *Il seicento nell'arte e nella cultura con riferimenti a Mantova* (Cinisello Balsamo, 1985), pp. 148–63

GIULIANA RICCI

Carjat, Etienne (*b* Fareins, Ain, 1 April 1828; *d* Paris, ?1906). French photographer, caricaturist and writer. He was trained as an industrial designer, then, like Nadar, he embarked on a career as a caricaturist. He was passionately fond of the theatre and published a series of lithographs, *Le Théâtre à la ville*, in Paris in 1854. He founded literary reviews, among which was *Le Boulevard* (1861), which established his reputation. After an apprenticeship in 1858 with Pierre Petit, he began to photograph artistic, literary and political personalities with whom he was associated politically, including the composer *Gioacchino Rossini* (pubd 1877; e.g. in Rochester, NY, Int. Mus. Phot.) and *Emile Zola* (pubd 1877; e.g. in Rochester, NY, Int. Mus. Phot.). He also photographed actors, including *Sarah Bernhardt* and the mime artist *Charles Deburau* on stage. Some friends, including *Gustave Courbet* (e.g. pubd 1878; Rochester, NY, Int. Mus. Phot., *see* PHOTOGRAPHY, fig. 9), were the object of a series of photographs. He was also the accredited photographer of *Victor Hugo* (*c.* 1870; pubd 1876; Paris, Bib. N., Cab. Est.), with whom he corresponded.

Like his friend and rival Nadar, Carjat aimed for the direct approach, rejecting any form of artifice. The figure is placed against a bare background, often three-quarter length, which allows concentration on the face. The gaze itself often takes on a disturbing intensity, as in the portrait of *Charles Baudelaire* (several versions, 1861–5; e.g. pubd 1878; Rochester, NY, Int. Mus. Phot.). Many of these images were published in woodburytype in the *Galerie contemporaine, littéraire, artistique*, published intermittently in Paris between 1876 and 1884. Carjat used the collodion glass negative process, the most appropriate for portraits at that time, but his prints are inferior in quality to Nadar's, and many have survived yellowed with age. The partial dispersal of his studio stock makes it impossible to judge his work as a whole. Working on his own, he never had a studio with the scope of Nadar's, nor did he achieve such fame as his.

BIBLIOGRAPHY

J. Adhémar: 'Carjat', *Gaz. B.-A.*, n.s. 6, lxxx (Aug, 1972), pp. 71–82

Etienne Carjat photographe (exh. cat., text S. Heftler; Paris, Carnavalet, 1982–3)

E. Fallaire: *Etienne Carjat and 'Le Boulevard' (1861–1863)* (Paris, 1987)

HÉLÈNE BOCARD

Carl. German family of builders and architects. Peter Carl (*b* Helling, 1541; *d* Sandhofen, 12 Feb 1617) became a master builder at Nuremberg and entered the service of the Nuremberg council as a municipal carpenter and waterway engineer (1580). His most important work here, done in collaboration with the architects Jakob Wolff I and II, was the Fleischbrücke (1596–8) over the river Pegnitz, modelled on the Rialto Bridge in Venice. In 1616 he was summoned to Heidelberg by Elector Frederick V (*reg* 1610–23) of the Palatinate to solve structural problems at the construction of the Dicker Turm (begun 1614), in the north-west of the palace complex. For the Heidelberg 'Theatrum' housed in it, he contrived a grandiose suspended construction. He was then commissioned by the Elector to work on the fortifications at Mannheim and to collaborate in restoration work at Frankenthal and Sandhofen.

Peter's son Hans Johann Carl (*b* Nuremberg, 13 Jan 1587; *d* Nuremberg, 14 June 1665) trained originally in pewterwork, although he was also taught perspective by Jakob Wolff I. About 1609 Hans studied mathematics, perspective and surveying in Ulm with the engineer Johann Faulhaber. In military service to the Elector of Brandenburg he trained in fortifications construction, gaining further experience with the Dutch artillery. In 1614 the council of Nuremberg secured his services for the city, where he collaborated in the building of the new Rathaus, reinforced the city's fortifications and improved its artillery. He also designed and built the Dreieinigkeitskirche (1627–31) in Regensburg in an intermediate style between Gothic and Renaissance, with vaults articulated by a cross between coffering and ribwork. In 1631 the Nuremberg council appointed him municipal armourer, a post he held until his death. From *c.* 1625 he assembled the 'Kleine Zeughaus', a collection of scale models representing a complete army camp (preserved almost complete in Nuremberg, Ger. Nmus.).

BIBLIOGRAPHY

L. Fehrle-Burger: 'Das Heidelberger Hoftheater', appendix to *Ruperto-Carola*, ed. G. Hinz, xvi/35 (Heidelberg, 1964)

E. Königer: 'Das kleine Nürnberger Zeughaus', *Bildhft. Ger. Nmus.*, iii (Nuremberg, 1967)

K. Pechstein: 'Allerlei Visierungen und Abriss wegen der Fleischbrücken 1595', *Anz. Ger. Nmus.* (1975), pp. 72–89

K. Möseneder: 'Die Dreieinigkeitskirche in Regensburg: Ein protestantischer Kirchenbau', *Martin Luther: Eine Spiritualität und ihre Folgen*, Schriftenreihe der Universität Regensburg, ed. H. Bungert, ix (Regensburg, 1983), pp. 171–255

SONJA WEIH-KRÜGER

Carl August, (Grand) Duke of Saxe-Weimar. *See* WETTIN, (11).

Carlerio, Anselmo. *See* CANNERI, ANSELMO.

Carles, Arthur B(eecher) (*b* Philadephia, PA, 9 March 1882; *d* Philadelphia, PA, 18 June 1952). American painter and teacher. As a student at the Pennsylvania Academy of the Fine Arts, Philadelphia, between 1900 and 1907, he won numerous prizes, including fellowships to travel abroad. Modern French art was Carles's primary source of inspiration; he lived in France between 1907 and 1910 and returned there in 1912, 1921 and 1929. Cézanne and Matisse inspired his use of colour for both structure and expression, as in *The Church* (1908–10; New York, Met.). Close to Edward Steichen and John Marin, Carles associated with Alfred Stieglitz's circle, and in 1912 he had the first of four solo exhibitions in New York at the 291 gallery. He showed at the Armory Show in 1913 and at annuals in Philadelphia and across the country. As an influential teacher he inspired students at the Pennsylvania Academy from 1917 to 1925 and then in private classes, opening their eyes to colour and to modern art.

Carles was one of the finest colourists among the early American modernists. His favourite subjects were the female nude, flower-pieces and French landscapes, treated in a variety of styles but with painterly colour always dominant. In the late 1920s he began to break up forms with Cubist planes of colour, as in *Arrangement* (1925–7; Chicago, IL, A. Inst.). *Abstraction (Last Painting)* (1936–41; Washington, DC, Hirshhorn), on which he was working when he was incapacitated by a fall and stroke in 1941, was prophetic of Abstract Expressionism.

BIBLIOGRAPHY

H. G. Gardiner: 'Arthur B. Carles: A Critical and Biographical Study', *Bull. Philadelphia Mus. A.*, lxiv (1970), pp. 139–89

Arthur B. Carles: Painting with Color (exh. cat. by B. A. Wolanin, Philadelphia, PA, Acad. F.A., 1983)

BARBARA ANN BOESE WOLANIN

Carleton, Sir **Dudley**, 1st Viscount Dorchester (*b* Brightwell, Oxon, 10 March 1573; *d* London, 15 Feb 1632). English diplomat, politician, collector and patron. At Westminster School, London, Carleton was taught by William Camden, author of *Britannia* (1586), a topographical survey of England that had given its author an international reputation. Carleton went on to Christ Church, Oxford, and later married the daughter of Sir Henry Savile, a great benefactor of Oxford University. He then became secretary to Francis Norris, Earl of Berkshire, ambassador to Madrid, where Carleton saw the Habsburg Titians—an experience that prepared him for his years in Venice. Carleton arrived in Venice in 1610 as ambassador and immediately began to assist those English visitors interested in art. His chief concern was to please Robert Carr, 1st Earl of Somerset, the current favourite of James I, by buying antiquities for his collection. But Carleton was obliged to retain them, since Somerset fell from favour in 1615, just as Carleton was shipping them to England.

In March 1616 Carleton became ambassador at The Hague, where he stayed for 12 years, apart from one short interlude in Paris. During this time he was in contact intermittently with Rubens. In the spring of 1618 he asked Rubens to swap some of his own paintings for those antiquities Carleton had bought earlier for Somerset. The prelude to what turned out to be hard bargaining was a letter from Carleton to Rubens: 'Sir, you may calculate on having in this collection of marbles, the most costly and most precious *in hoc genere*, which no prince or private person, whoever he may be, on this side the mountains can have.' Although Carleton was wrong (Thomas Howard, 2nd Earl of Arundel, had a better collection), Rubens was sufficiently impressed to buy them. Thus Rubens acquired 123 pieces (mostly busts and statues) and Carleton received nine paintings by Rubens, three by Tintoretto and a set of tapestries of unknown authorship illustrating the life of Scipio Africanus. The Rubens paintings included *Daniel in the Lion's Den* (Washington, DC, N.G.A.), *Prometheus* (Philadelphia, PA, Mus. A.) and *St Sebastian* (probably the picture in Berlin, Gemäldegal.), as well as a *Susanna and the Elders* (untraced), which, Carleton declared, made even an old man amorous. Among those by Tintoretto was *Apollo and Marsyas* (Hartford, CT, Wadsworth Atheneum), one of the painter's earliest works, and a *Rape of Proserpina* (Rotterdam, Mus. Boymans–van Beuningen; attrib.).

The correspondence between Carleton and Rubens during this exchange reveals that Carleton was worried because not all the paintings were entirely autograph. In this he betrayed a typically English suspicion of Rubens's method of delegating work to others. The eagle in the *Prometheus*, for instance, was by Frans Snyders. But in fact Carleton had acquired a cache of pictures by Europe's leading painter; no Englishman was to equal it until George Villiers, 1st Duke of Buckingham, bought Rubens's own private collection in 1627.

Carleton continued to take a close interest in contemporary artists because he was buying both for himself and others, including Charles, Prince of Wales (later Charles I), who was developing a marked interest in art. Consequently, in the summer of 1621 Carleton again became involved with Rubens when Henry Danvers, later Earl of Danby, approached him with a view to commissioning a picture of a lion hunt for the Prince. While Carleton tried to satisfy the future King, he endeavoured also to flatter the court. On 22 June 1621 he presented Arundel with Gerrit van Honthorst's *Aeneas Fleeing from the Sack of Troy* (untraced), which may have been the first work by the most distinguished northern follower of Caravaggio to arrive in London. In November 1624 Carleton sent his wife to Middelburg and Flushing to buy pictures for Buckingham. Lady Carleton informed her husband: 'be assured here are very rich and raire thinges, sufficient to make my Lord of Buckingham a wonderfull sumtious present', and she then went on to spend £627. This proved a good investment: Carleton was raised to the peerage in 1626 and two years later finally returned home to be created Viscount Dorchester. In December 1628 he was made one of the two Secretaries of State. He had thus arrived at the summit of the English political system, and although he did so by having been the outstanding diplomat of his age, his involvement with art had given him an edge over his rivals.

Carleton was acquainted with the disreputable Daniel Nys, middleman involved in selling the Gonzaga collection to Charles I in 1628, and he was called on therefore to mediate in the dispute over the massive sums that Nys claimed from the King. Carleton was also still in touch with artists in the Low Countries; in 1631 he ordered, through Rubens, a picture by Frans Snyders, and other paintings by now unknown artists recommended by Rubens. He had meanwhile been elected Chancellor of Oxford University, for which he promoted a scheme of embellishment that prompted the Vice-Chancellor to write: 'though others have provided for her necessities yet yr L[ord]ship is ye first that ever thought of ornament and delight for her'. His interest in architecture extended to advising his stepson Paul, 1st Viscount Bayning, with expensive and expansive plans to transform his house and gardens at Bentley, Oxon, into something more elegant and Italianate.

On Carleton's death in 1632, he was buried in Westminster Abbey. Nicholas Stone (i) carved a full-length effigy for his tomb (1640), which combines the recumbent figure *all'antica* with the Elizabethan vernacular tradition of representing great men in their robes of office. There is also a half-length of *Carleton* (London, N.P.G.) by M. J. van Mierevelt.

BIBLIOGRAPHY

P. Yorke, ed.: *Letters from and to Sir Dudley Carleton* (London, 1757)
W. N. Sainsbury: *Original Unpublished Papers Illustrative of the Life of Sir Peter Paul Rubens, as an Artist and Diplomatist* (London, 1859)
T. Longueville: *Policy and Paint* (London, 1913)
D. Howarth: *Lord Arundel and his Circle* (New Haven, 1985)

DAVID HOWARTH

Carlevaris [Carlevarijs], **Luca** (*b* Udine, 20 Jan 1663; *d* Venice, 12 Feb 1730). Italian painter, engraver and architect. 'The first of any note who painted views of Venice' was how he was described in 1789 by John Strange (sale

Luca Carlevaris: *Arrival of the 4th Earl of Manchester in Venice in 1707*, oil on canvas, 1.32×2.64 m, 1707 (Birmingham, City of Birmingham Museum and Art Gallery)

catalogue, London, 10 Dec), the British Resident in Venice from 1773. Although Carlevaris was more than simply a view painter, much of his work was certainly in the genre later made popular by Canaletto and Francesco Guardi (*see also* VEDUTA). Carlevaris's artistic inclinations were probably inherited from his father, a painter and designer who died when his son was very young. In 1679 Carlevaris moved to Venice and was discovered by the Zenobio family, whose palace was near where he lived. He is said to have made a trip to Rome, from which he returned to Venice in 1698, and while there must have become aware of view paintings and *capricci* by artists such as Gaspar van Wittel (Vanvitelli). On his return he established himself by painting similar works (e.g. *Seaport* and *Piazzetta*; both Udine, Mus. Civ.). In 1703 he published *Le fabriche e vedute di Venezia disegnate poste in prospettiva et intagliate da Luca Carlevaris*: 104 views of Venice. It was the most complete survey of the fabric of the city ever produced and served as a model for Venetian view painters throughout the 18th century.

Carlevaris's first recorded commission for a painting is dated 1704. Partly because of the patriotism associated with his *Fabriche e vedute* and partly because of his friendship with the Zenobio family, he was actively patronized by Venetians, unlike Canaletto. When Charles Montagu, the 4th Earl of Manchester (*d* 1722), arrived on an official visit in 1707, Carlevaris was the obvious choice to document the scene, as he did in the *Arrival of the 4th Earl of Manchester in Venice in 1707* (1707; Birmingham, Mus. & A.G.; see fig.), a scene rich in colour and detail, which not only documents an event but also accurately renders the many beauties of a lavishly decorative city. Carlevaris's other views, depicting regattas and similar events, also convey something of the air and drama of Venice's grander spaces, such as canals, campi or the Piazza; this quality was absent in the work of his predecessors in the genre, whose works suffer somewhat from *horror vacui*. Carlevaris's small, personal drawings and oil sketches (53 examples of the latter, London, V&A) are like shorthand notes, with a freedom and life that convey the vivacity of a busy city.

Carlevaris's name appeared on the list of the confraternity of Venetian painters from 1708 to 1713, in 1726 and in 1727. In 1712 he was in Conegliano, and in 1714 he worked in Udine as an architectural supervisor. That he had had some sort of mathematical training is clear from his portrait in old age (Oxford, Ashmolean), painted by Bartolommeo Nazari (1699–1758), which portrays him with a pair of dividers in addition to a pencil; the engraving after the portrait describes him not only as a Venetian painter but also as a 'Mathematicae cultor egregius'. His reputation for depicting views and events did not diminish and when the Imperial Ambassador made a visit to Venice in 1727, Carlevaris was commissioned to record the scene; the result was *Cesareo Conte di Colloredo Entering the Doge's Palace* (Dresden, Gemäldegal. Alte Meister). There is no evidence that Canaletto ever studied with him, but the younger artist must have been influenced by Carlevaris's pictures and engravings. Carlevaris was plagued with a progressive paralysis from 1728 until his death.

BIBLIOGRAPHY

M. Levey: *Painting in Eighteenth-century Venice* (London, 1959, rev. 2/1980)
W. G. Constable: *Canaletto*, 2 vols (Oxford, 1962, rev. 3/1989)
A. Rizzi: *Luca Carlevarijs* (Venice, 1967)
Da Carlevarijs ai Tiepolo: Incisori veneti e friulani del settecento (exh. cat. by D. Succi, Venice, Correr; Gorizia, Mus. Prov. Pal. Attems; 1983)
The Genius of Venice, 1500–1600 (exh. cat., ed. J. Martineau and C. Hope; London, RA, 1983)

JOHN WILSON

Carli, Raffaelle de'. *See* RAFFAELLINO DEL GARBO.

Carlier. French family of architects and decorators. They were in the service of the Spanish kings of the Bourbon dynasty, Philip V and Ferdinand VI, in the 18th century. René Carlier (*b* Paris, *fl* 1712; *d* Madrid, 15 Aug 1722) and his son François Antoine Carlier (*b* Paris, 1707; *d* Bayonne, 29 Dec 1750) introduced the late Baroque style of Louis XIV and the taste for French Regency and Louis XV decoration to Spain. René Carlier was a pupil of Robert de Cotte. In 1712 he was sent by Louis XIV to Spain to execute de Cotte's designs for the new palace and gardens of Buen Retiro, Madrid. Work on the palace was abandoned because of the War of Succession, although Carlier was able to carry out the modernization of the staterooms and bedrooms of Philip V and Queen María Gabriela of Savoy in the old castle of Madrid, a project also conceived by de Cotte, which included wood panelling, fireplaces and furniture in the French style. Carlier was also involved with designs for the garden statues at La Granja de San Ildefonso, Segovia.

François Antoine Carlier accompanied his father to Spain but returned to Paris with a grant from Philip V to study architecture at the Paris Académie, where he received first prize for architecture in 1726. In 1734 he returned to Spain and was appointed Architect to the King. In 1738 he designed the plan and elevations for the new chapel of the palace of El Pardo, near Madrid (executed by Manuel López Corona). The cross-shaped church is dominated by a low dome, linked to a short nave, at the foot of which is the royal gallery. Carlier's main work was the convent and church of the Visitation in Madrid, founded by Queen Barbara of Braganza, the wife of Ferdinand VI. Carlier drew up the plans and elevations that were executed by his follower Francisco Moradillo between 1750 and 1757. Only the church survives (the convent was remodelled in 1880 to house the Palace of Justice). In style the church is more Italian than French, with Rococo decoration only in the Queen's gallery and in the pulpit. His retables were not made of wood, in the Spanish tradition, but of marble and bronze; the paintings and sculptures were made in late Italian Baroque style.

BIBLIOGRAPHY

Y. Bottineau: *L'Art de cour dans l'Espagne de Philipe V, 1700–1746* (Bordeaux, 1962), pp. 275–80, 401–2, 427–8

T. Martin: 'La capilla del Palacio Real de "El Pardo"', *Reales Sitios: Rev. Patrm. N.*, lix (1979), pp. 29–36

Y. Bottineau: 'L'Art de cour dans l'Espagne de Philipe V: Mise au point 1962–1980', *Mél. Casa Velázquez*, xviii (1982), pp. 477–93

——: *L'Art dans l'Espagne des Lumières, 1746–1808* (Paris, 1986)

ALFONSO RODRÍGUES CEBALLOS

Carlier, Jean-Guillaume (*bapt* Liège, 3 June 1638; *d* Liège, 1675). Flemish painter. He was a pupil of Bertholet Flémal, with whom he probably collaborated on several pictures. In his youth he probably also copied works by Gérard Douffet, founder of the Liège school. The anachronistic vigour of his known paintings (about 12) suggests that he may have visited Italy. His stylistic development is difficult to establish, since none of his works is dated. Two of his paintings, possibly the earliest known, pendants of the *Baptism of Christ* (Liège, St Paul) and the *Healing of the Possessed Man* (Mainz, Landesmus.), seem to be of quite different temperaments: the first unmistakably in the harshly realistic style of Caravaggio, the second more modern. He subsequently combined strength of expression with a more considered and balanced style influenced, through Flémal, by the French, as for example in the *Martyrdom of St Denis* (lost during the French Revolution but known from a sketch in Brussels, Mus. A. Anc.), *St Joseph Adoring the Infant Jesus* (Mainz, Landesmus.), *Christ and the Children* (priv. col.) and two pendants: the *Mystic Marriage of the Holy Hermann-Joseph* (Liège, Mus. A. Wallon) and the *Virgin Giving the Habit of his Order to St Norbert* (Munich, Alte Pin.). The last two were restored to his oeuvre in 1987 (see 1987 exh. cat.). Late in life he returned to the realist vein, as in the moving *Crucifixion* (*c.* 1670; Verviers, Mus. B.-A. Cér.). Many writers have judged Carlier to be the best painter Liège produced in the 17th century.

BIBLIOGRAPHY

F. Van Hulst: *Notice sur Jean G. Carlier* (Liège, 1837)

J. Helbig: *La Peinture au pays de Liège et sur les bords de la Meuse* (Liège, 1903)

J. Hendrick: *La Peinture au pays de Liège: XVIe, XVIIe, XVIIIe siècles* (Liège, 1987)

Walthère Damery (1614–1678) (exh. cat., Bilzen, Château Oude Biezen, 1987)

PIERRE-YVES KAIRIS

Carlile [née Palmer], **Joan** (*b* ?London, *c.* 1606; *bur* Petersham, nr London, 27 Feb 1679). English painter. She was the daughter of William Palmer (*d* 1634), an official in the Royal Parks. She married the minor poet and court dramatist Ludowick Carlile in 1626 and later lived at Petersham Lodge in Richmond Park, where her husband was appointed a keeper in 1637. She is one of the first recorded female English painters, and she achieved a surprising degree of contemporary recognition, though little of her work can be traced. According to Buckeridge, who mistakenly called her Anne, she 'copy'd the Italian masters so admirably well, that she was much in favour with King Charles I, who became her Patron'. Her work was undisturbed by the Civil War and Interregnum, and in 1654 she moved to Covent Garden, where she 'resolved to use her skill for something more than empty fame'. She attracted influential patrons, producing single and group portraits on a pleasing and intimate scale, often set in a landscape. *Stag Hunt* (*c.*1649–50; Lamport Hall, Northants), a rare firmly attributed picture, is an important early sporting painting that foreshadows the 18th-century English conversation piece. The hunting party, which includes the artist and her family, was probably painted to commemorate the visit of the Royalist Sir Justinian Isham (1610–74) to Petersham. The characteristically stout, frozen figures are awkwardly posed in front of an unconvincing landscape backdrop. A similar staged arrangement occurs in the *Tollemache Family* (*c.*1650; Ham House, Surrey, NT), a clumsy attempt at re-creating the fashionable open-air group portrait type, in which the voluptuous, heavy-lidded beauties made popular by Lely have given way to poorly drawn, defective forms and exaggerated gestures.

BIBLIOGRAPHY

B. Buckeridge: 'Essay towards an English School of Painters', *The Art of Painting*, ed. R. De Piles (London, 1754)

M. Toynbee and G. Isham: 'Joan Carlile (1606?–1679): An Identification', *Burl. Mag.*, xcvi (1954), pp. 273–7

M. K. Talley: *Portrait Painting in England: Studies in the Technical Literature before 1700* (London, 1981), pp. 144, 236

JOHN SHEERAN

Carlin, Martin (*b* nr Freiburg im Breisgau; *d* Paris, 6 March 1785). French cabinetmaker of German birth. Although nothing is known about his training, he was working in the workshop of Jean-François Oeben when he became the latter's brother-in-law in 1759. He became a *maître-ébéniste* on 30 July 1766. He set up a workshop in the Rue du Faubourg Saint-Antoine, Paris, and produced luxurious furniture, which was sold by the dealers Simon-Philippe Poirier, Dominique Daguerre and Darnault to a distinguished clientele including the Comtesse de Provence, the Herzogin von Saxe-Teschen, Louise-Jeanne de Durfort, the Duchesse de Mazarin, the Marquise de Brunoy and the daughters of Louis XV, who decorated the Château Bellevue in Paris with some of Carlin's most beautiful, lacquered furniture. Carlin was very assured in his use of materials and choice of bronzes. These characteristics are best illustrated in his construction of numerous pieces of furniture inset with porcelain plaques from the factory of Sèvres. His masterpieces include two commodes (*see* CERAMICS, colour pl. I, fig. 2) and a *guéridon* table (Paris, Louvre) and a writing-table with porcelain plaques (Lisbon, Mus. Gulbenkian) for the Comtesse Du Barry, a commode (London, Buckingham Pal., Royal Col.) with panels of pietra dura for Mademoiselle Laguerre, a lacquered commode (Paris, Louvre) for Madame Victoire and a writing-desk with porcelain plaques (Malibu, CA, Getty Mus.) for Empress Marya Fyodorovna. Among Carlin's most sophisticated pieces are his *bonheurs du jour* (e.g. Paris, Mus. Nissim de Camondo), which combined a writing-table and toilet accessories decorated with porcelain plaques and similarly decorated secrétaires (e.g. of 1776–7; Malibu, CA, Getty Mus.).

BIBLIOGRAPHY

F. de Salverte: *Les Ebénistes du XVIIIème siècle: Leurs oeuvres et leurs marques* (Paris, 1923, rev. 5/1962)

J. Viaux: *Bibliographie du meuble (Mobilier civil français)*, 2 vols (Paris, 1966–88)

P. Lemonnier: 'Les Commodes de Martin Carlin', *L'Estampille*, 171–2 (1984), pp. 6–19

JEAN-DOMINIQUE AUGARDE,
JEAN NÉRÉE RONFORT

Carlini, Agostino [Augustino] (*b* Genoa, *c.* 1718; *d* London, 15 Aug 1790). Italian sculptor, active in England. He had arrived in London by 1760 and in 1768 became, with Joseph Wilton and William Tyler (*d* 1801), one of the three sculptors to be appointed Foundation Members of the Royal Academy. He subsequently became the second Keeper of the Royal Academy in 1783, a position he retained until his death, when he was succeeded by Wilton. Carlini exhibited at the Society of Artists between 1760 and 1768 and at the Royal Academy between 1769 and 1787.

Carlini competed for, but failed to win, several major commissions, including that for a statue of Admiral Lord Rodney for Jamaica, but was fortunate in receiving patronage from friends intent on keeping him in England. His earliest datable work, a marble statue of the 'quack' doctor *Joshua Ward* (*c.* 1760–64; London, V&A) was commissioned by the sitter in exchange for an annuity. Carlini's bold carving, technically superior to many of his British contemporaries, is evident in his marble bust of *George III* (1773; London, RA), which originally stood on the library chimney-piece at Somerset House, London. More visible are three colossal keystone masks representing the rivers Dee, Severn and Tyne and statues of *Prudence* and *Justice* (Portland stone, 1776–8) on the Strand façade of Somerset House. His funerary monuments include marble memorials to *Lady Bingley* (*d* 1771; Bramham Park Chapel, W. Yorks) and the *Countess of Shelburne* (*d* 1771; All Saints, High Wycombe, Bucks). The marble sarcophagus of *John, 1st Earl of Shelburne*, carved after a design by Robert Adam (1765; Mausoleum, Bowood House, Wilts), is traditionally attributed to him. His masterpiece is the monument to *Lord and Lady Milton* (1775; Milton Abbas Church, Dorset). This follows the 17th-century formula for monuments: the deceased appears as a recumbent effigy admired by the figure of the widower lying alongside, on a Gothick base designed by Adam. Carlini's work is marked by the scale and vigour of the European Baroque. Charles Maucourt painted a portrait miniature of Carlini (London, N.P.G.), and John Francis Rigaud's portrait *Giovanni Battista, Francesco Bartolozzi and Agostino Carlini* (London, N.P.G.) was exhibited at the Royal Academy in 1777.

BIBLIOGRAPHY

Gunnis

H. Walpole: *Anecdotes of Painting in England* (Strawberry Hill, 1762–71, rev. New Haven, 1937), v, pp. 140–41

M. Trusted: '"A Man of Talent": Agostino Carlini (*c.* 1718–90)', *Burl. Mag.*, cxxxiv (1992), pp. 776–84; cxxxv (1993), pp. 190–201

JULIUS BRYANT

Carlisle, Earls of. *See* HOWARD (ii).

Carlo, Ferrante [Gianfattori, Carlo Ferrante] (*b* Parma, 18 April 1578; *d* Rome, 9 June 1641). Italian writer, patron, collector and amateur dealer. He was educated in philosophy, law and letters, and in 1604 he journeyed to Rome, where he became the private secretary of Cardinal Paolo Camillo Sfondrato. In 1605 he was admitted to the Accademia degli Umoristi and by this time appears to have assumed the name Ferrante Carlo, by which he remains generally known. He became one of Rome's foremost men of letters, a notable poet and a prolific correspondent (Bottari). He befriended numerous artists, including Giulio Cesare Procaccini, Lavinia Fontana, Guercino, Simon Vouet and Alessandro Tiarini, while his abundant correspondence with Ludovico Carracci (Nicodemi) from between 1606 and 1619 is among the most significant of the surviving letters.

He became private secretary to Cardinal Scipione Borghese, occupying private apartments in the Palazzo Borghese, including a picture gallery. He was appointed by Pope Paul V to write a history, the *Templum Vaticanum* (MS., Rome, Vatican, Bib. Apostolica), of the Old Basilica of St Peter's, to be illustrated by the architect Martino Ferrabosco, and he worked on this from *c.* 1620 to 1629. He left both this and a biography of Paul V incomplete. During the 1620s he led attacks against Bernini's alterations to the dome of St Peter's, coming to be called Bernini's *nemico* (It.: adversary) (Fraschetti).

He is perhaps best known for his friendship with Giovanni Lanfranco, and he was identified by Passeri as one of the artist's strongest supporters during the renowned controversy between Lanfranco and Domenichino over the commission for paintings in S Andrea della Valle, Rome. Turner has suggested he may have assisted Lanfranco in devising the iconographic programme (*Assumption of the Virgin*) executed in the cupola.

During 1631–2 he was involved in the scandal surrounding the Sicilian entrepreneur Don Fabrizio Valguarnera, who was arrested in Rome for diamond theft and died in prison there in 1632. Paintings were acquired from him by Valguarnera and his testimony (Costello) at Valguarnera's trial provides a rare insight into his enigmatic activities as an amateur picture dealer (Haskell). He is thought to have owned a considerable picture collection and is known to have favoured pictures by Bolognese artists and to have both commissioned works and acted informally as an agent between his preferred artists and potential clients. When he died his private papers passed to Cassiano dal Pozzo (Lumbroso), in whose library they were almost certainly consulted by Giovanni Pietro Bellori (Turner).

BIBLIOGRAPHY

G. P. Bellori: *Vite* (1672); ed. E. Borea (1976), pp. 375–96
G. B. Passeri: *Vite* (1679); ed. J. Hess (1934), pp. 65, 150, 151, 154, 155, 157, 251, 346
G. Bottari: *Raccolta di lettere sulla pittura, scultura ed architettura scritta da' più celebri personaggi dei secoli XV, XVI e XVII* (Rome, 1757–68); enlarged S. Ticozzi (Milan, 1822–5/*R* Olms, 1976), i, pp. 271–94, 297–328, 334
I. Affò: *Memorie degli scrittori e letterati parmigiani* (Parma, 1797), v, pp. 21–54
J. Dumesnil: *Histoire des plus célèbres amateurs italiens* (Paris, 1853), pp. 334–401
G. Lumbroso: *Notizie sulla vita de Cassiano dal Pozzo* (Turin, 1875), p. 23 [the association with Ferrante Carlo]
S. Fraschetti: *Il Bernini* (Milan, 1900), p. 71 [contains letter from the Mantuan Ambassador describing Ferrante Carlo's attitudes towards Bernini]
A. Borzelli: *'L'Assunta' del Lanfranco in S Andrea della Valle giudicata da Ferrante Carlo* (Naples, 1910) [incl. Carlo's *Descrittione*, Naples, Bib. N., MS. XII. G. 27, fols 11–31]
G. Nicodemi: 'Otto lettere di Ludovico Carracci a Don Ferrante Carlo', *Aevum* (1935), pp. 305–13
J. Costello: 'The Twelve Pictures "Ordered by Velásquez" and the Trial of Valguarnera', *J. Warb. & Court. Inst.*, xiii (1950), pp. 237–84
N. Turner: 'Ferrante Carlo's *Descrittione della Cupola di S Andrea della Valle depinta dal Cavalier Gio: Lanfranchi*: A Source for Bellori's Descriptive Method', *Stor. A.*, xii (1971), pp. 297–325
F. Haskell: *Patrons and Painters, Art and Society in Baroque Italy* (New Haven and London, 1980), pp. 123–4, 402
G. P. Bernini: *Giovanni Lanfranco (1582–1647)* (Parma, 1982, 2/1985) [corr. with Lanfranco, originally pubd by Bottari, pp. 341–9]

□

Carlo Alberto, King of Sardinia. *See under* SAVOY, §I, 2.

Carlo Borromeo. *See* BORROMEO, (1).

Carlo da Milano. *See* BRACCESCO, CARLO.

Carlo di Cesari [Cesare] **del Palagio** [Cesari, Carlo de; Pallago, Carlo; Palazzo, Carlo; Zeherin, Karl] (*b* Florence, 1540; *d* Mantua, *c.* 1598). Italian sculptor, stuccoist and bronze-caster. His work was considered to be by two artists until Keutner (1991–2) proposed that Carlo di Cesari and Carlo Pallago were the same person. Most of his creative career was spent working at the courts of German princes; so far his name has been connected with surviving works only north of the Alps. He is documented as working, in his early years, as an assistant to Vasari and Giambologna at the Medici court in Florence. In 1565 he was accepted as a member at the Accademia del Disegno in Florence, continuing to pay his subscription until 1568. From 1569 to 1573 he worked for Hans Fugger in Augsburg (*see* FUGGER, (3)), making sculptural decorations in stucco and terracotta for his house (partly destr. 1944) as part of Friedrich Sustris's decorative scheme. Twelve pairs of almost life-size terracotta satyrs have survived in the library, which remains intact. In 1573 he was employed by the Crown Prince of Bavaria (from 1579 Duke William V), who wanted to have his castle, Burg Trausnitz in Landshut, furnished along the same lines as Hans Fugger's house. From 1574 Carlo di Cesari divided his time between Munich, where he produced marble busts for the Antiquarium in the Residenz, and Landshut, where he worked on the stucco decoration (destr. 1961) in Burg Trausnitz and on bronze figures for a fountain (two satyrs, some putti and a Venus are believed to survive; Munich, Residenz and Washington, DC, N.G.A.). He cast the figures himself, thus initiating the casting of figures in bronze at the court of the Dukes of Bavaria.

Between 1579 and 1581 Carlo di Cesari was in Florence, and from 1581 he again worked for the Fuggers; thereafter, almost all his work in Augsburg and Munich was done in collaboration with the sculptor HUBERT GERHARD. Between 1582 and 1585 they created 12 over life-size figures of famous men and women (*in situ*) for the hall of the palace (1578–83) built for Hans Fugger in Kirchheim an der Mindel. Between 1585 and 1588 Carlo di Cesari received large sums of money from the Munich court, probably relating to interior decoration (lost) in the new wings of the Residenz. In 1588 he returned briefly to Florence, but was engaged that year to work for Christian I, Elector of Saxony (*reg* 1586–91). From 1590 to 1593 he was engaged on the sculptural furnishing of the choir of Freiberg Cathedral, Saxony, which was being altered by Giovanni Maria Nosseni into a burial chapel for the Wettin family. Nosseni's decorated walls are entirely covered with life-size figures: at the bottom are the electors and their consorts, five portrait figures in bronze kneeling in adoration; on the altar, the *Crucifixion with SS John the Baptist and Paul* (in bronze), and above the *Resurrection* (in stucco); and on the ceiling, the *Last Judgement*, a painted panorama with stucco figures. As well as these there are eight stucco figures of prophets and music-making putti. All these were cast by Carlo di Cesari himself, which was not the case later with the figures in Munich. While he was still working in Saxony, the Holy Roman emperor Rudolf II tried to engage him for a project in Prague. In 1592 Duke William V of Bavaria requested his presence, no doubt in connection with the large project for his tomb, on which he collaborated with Gerhard in 1593. Intended for the church of St Michael, Munich, the installation was never completed. Of the surviving bronze figures, those documented as being by Carlo di Cesari comprise two knights (Munich, Frauenkirche, tomb of Ludwig; *see*

KRUMPPER, HANS, fig. 2), two lions (Munich, Residenz, west façade) and four richly decorated bronze candelabra (Munich, St Michael). The decorative bronze cartouche with a coat of arms on the façade of St Michael is also authenticated as his. In 1597 Carlo di Cesari returned to Italy and made his will in Mantua the following year, shortly before his death.

BIBLIOGRAPHY

W. Holzhausen: 'Die Bronzen der kurfürstlich sächsischen Kunstkammer zu Dresden', *Jb. Preuss. Kstsamml.*, liv (1933), pp. 45–88
H. W. Frey, ed.: *Neue Briefe von Giorgio Vasari. Der literarische Nachlass Giorgio Vasaris*, iii (Burg bei Magdeburg, 1940)
B. P. Baader: *Der bayerische Renaissancehof Herzog Wilhelms V. (1568–1579). Ein Beitrag zur bayerischen und allgemeinen Kulturgeschichte des 16. Jahrhunderts* (Leipzig and Strasbourg, 1943), pp. 285, 293
T. Müller: 'Berichte der Staatlichen Kunstsammlungen. Bayer. Nationalmuseum', *Münchn. Jb. Bild. Kst*, iii–iv (1952–3), p. 341
M. Baxandall: 'Hubert Gerhard and the Altar of Christoph Fugger', *Münchn. Jb. Bild. Kst*, xvii (1966), pp. 127–44
H. Magirius: *Der Dom zu Freiberg* (Berlin, 1977)
D. Diemer: 'Quellen und Untersuchungen zum Stiftergrab Herzog Wilhelms V. von Bayern und der Renata von Lothringen in der Münchner Michaelskirche', *Quellen und Studien zur Kunstpolitik der Wittelsbacher vom 16. bis zum 18. Jahrhundert*, ed. H. Glaser (Munich and Zurich, 1980), pp. 7–82
Welt im Umbruch: Augsburg zwischen Renaissance und Barock (exh. cat., Augsburg, Städt. Kstsammlungen, 1980), ii, pp. 174–81
D. Diemer: 'Bronzeplastik um 1600 in München. Neue Quellen und Forschungen', *Jb. Zentinst. Kstgesch.*, ii (1986), pp. 107–77 (esp. 135–55)
E. Weski and H. Frosien-Leinz: *Der Antiquarium der Münchner Residenz* (Munich, 1987), p. 61, n. 170 [ref. to Carlo di Cesari's will in Mantua]
D. Diemer: 'Hubert Gerhard und Carlo Pallago als Terrakottaplastiker', *Jb. Zentinst. Kstgesch.*, iv (1988), pp. 19–141
H. Lietzmann: 'Unbekannte Nachrichten zur Biographie von Antonio Abondio und Carlo Pallago', *Jb. Zentinst. Kstgesch.*, v–vi (1989–90), pp. 327–50 (esp. from p. 337)
M. Meine-Schawe: 'Giovanni Maria Nosseni, ein Hofkünstler in Sachsen', *Jb. Zentinst. Kstgesch.*, v–vi (1989–90), pp. 283–325
H. Keutner: 'The Venus Anadyomene Attributed to Carlo di Cesare del Palagio (1540–1598)', *Christie's Int. Mag.* (Winter 1991–2), pp. 8–11 [identifying Carlo Pallago with Carlo di Cesari]
M. Meine: *Die Grablege der Wettiner im Dom zu Freiberg. Die Umgestaltung des Domchores durch Giovanni Maria Nosseni, 1585–1594* (Munich, 1992)
D. Diemer: 'Hans Fuggers Sammlungskabinette', *Die Fugger und die Musik* (exh. cat., Augsburg, Fuggerei-Mus., 1993), pp. 13–14

DOROTHEA DIEMER

Carlo Emanuele I, 11th Duke of Savoy. *See* SAVOY, §II(3).

Carlo Emanuele II, 14th Duke of Savoy. *See* SAVOY, §II(8).

Carlo Emanuele III, King of Sardinia. *See* SAVOY, §II(12).

Carlo Felice, King of Sardinia. *See under* SAVOY, §I, 2.

Carlone (i). Italian family of artists. Taddeo Carlone (1543–1615) and his brother Giuseppe Carlone were, like their father Giovanni Carlone, sculptors. Born in Rovio (Lombardy), they moved to Genoa *c*. 1560. Another member of the family was Pietro Carlone, who with his son Francesco Carlone was a bronze-caster. Taddeo's sons (1) Giovanni Carlone and (2) Giovanni Battista Carlone became painters, probably working together in Genoa and Milan and perhaps in Rome and Florence before 1630. The Carlone brothers' sculptural heritage and their education in Rome and Florence differed from that of their Genoese contemporaries who had studied under Giovanni Battista Paggi, and together with Domenico Fiasella they stimulated a revival of fresco decoration in Genoa. Frescoes painted in the 1620s by the Carlone brothers and Fiasella and by Lazzaro Tavarone, Andrea Ansaldo and Bernardo Castello are close in composition, colour, figures and subject-matter. (2) Giovanni Battista Carlone's studio produced a vast quantity of brilliantly coloured frescoes, which were highly proficient and popular; these are best seen on the nave vaults of the large Genoese churches, S Ambrogio and S Siro. He relied on family members, and among his 24 children were Simon Carlone, Niccolò Carlone (1644–1714) and (3) Giovanni Andrea Carlone, who assisted him and kept the studio alive until the end of the 17th century.

(1) Giovanni (Andrea) Carlone (*b* Genoa, *bapt* 24 April 1584; *d* Milan, 1630). Painter. His first teacher was his father, Taddeo, who then sent him to study with Pietro Sorri (1556–1621), who was in Genoa from 1595 to 1597 and from 1612 to 1613. Giovanni's early works, such as a drawing of *Venus with Cupid* (1607; Providence, RI Sch. Des., Mus. A.), a fresco of *Samson Slaying the Lion* (1607; Genoa, Villa Imp. Scassi) and an altarpiece of the *Crucifixion with SS Bartholomew and Longinus* (1610; Albisola Marina, Parish Church), reveal the strong influence of Bernardo Castello, whose daughter Carlone married in 1609. Other chalk drawings, such as the *Child with Puppy* (Florence, Uffizi), have a charming naturalism that is close not only to the art of Castello and of Lazzaro Tavarone, but also to the genre painting of Bernardo Strozzi, who studied with Sorri in the late 1590s. The influence of Castello remained strong in the *Crucifixion with the Virgin and SS John, Mary Magdalene and Carlo Borromeo* (1614; Rovio, Parish Church).

In 1616 Giovanni is recorded in Rome, where he probably worked as Castello's assistant on frescoes in the Palazzo del Quirinale and in the Palazzo Rospigliosi–Pallavicini, for which Castello was paid in 1616. It is impossible to separate his work from that of either Castello or (2) Giovanni Battista Carlone, who may have accompanied him to Rome and may have studied with Domenico Passignano in Florence on the return journey.

Giovanni Carlone's activity from 1610 to 1620 is incompletely documented. Among the works of this period are his frescoes of scenes from the *Lives of Christ and the Virgin* (*c*. 1619; Genoa, S Ambrogio, nave, transept and dome), the frescoed scenes celebrating the patron's family at the Villa Spinola di S Pietro at Sampierdarena (see Pesenti, pls 127–30) and frescoes in Santissima Annunziata, Genoa (1627–8). All these display his expertise in depicting many sweet-faced figures in complex compositions, which often include highly naturalistic still-life details and architectural backgrounds. His figure style, a blend of the lean, muscular figures of Tavarone with the softer, heavier figures of Castello, is strikingly close to that of Fiasella. Giovanni died while working on frescoes in S Antonio Abate, Milan, which were then finished by his brother, Giovanni Battista, 'with such uniformity and similarity that the work seems of the same hand' (Soprani-Ratti).

(2) Giovanni Battista Carlone (*b* Genoa, 16 Feb 1603; *d* Genoa, 1684). Painter, brother of (1) Giovanni Carlone. He probably went to Rome with his brother and studied in Florence with Domenico Passignano on the way back to Genoa. The many frescoes datable to the 1620s suggest that the brothers probably worked as a team. Giovanni Battista's independent activity is not documented before 1630–32, when he finished the frescoes begun by his brother in S Antonio Abate in Milan. His earliest dated work is a canvas of *St James Opening the Door for King Ferdinand* (1632; Genoa, oratory of S Giacomo della Marina), which shows figures with sharp facial features and twisting, tight drapery folds—a figure style indebted to Salvator Rosa and distinctly different from the slightly swollen faces and hands in the figures by Giovanni Carlone I.

The Carlone workshop was influenced by the Roman decorative fresco painting of Pietro da Cortona; indeed, commissions received by the Carlone family for frescoes at the Villa Vascella, Rome (with Cortona, Francesco Allegrini and Giovanni Francesco Grimaldi, 1643; destr.), and at the Certosa di Pavia (1660) imply that they had numerous artistic contacts outside Genoa. Giovanni Battista was an extremely prolific artist. From the 1640s and 1650s his dated paintings include *St James on the Way to Martyrdom Healing a Man* (1646; Genoa, S Giacomo della Marina); the *Birth, Baptism and Beheading of St John the Baptist* (1644; Chiavari, S Giovanni Battista); and a fresco, perhaps with Giulio Benso, in the chapel of the Palazzo Ducale at Genoa (1655). His most accomplished works are the decoration of the nave, apse and dome of S Siro, Genoa (1652–70), and the frescoes of the *Story of Aeneas* in brilliant reds, greens and purples, reminiscent of the sumptuous decorations of Cortona in the Palazzo Airoli-Negrone, Genoa (see Pesenti, pls 190–93). In 1661 Giovanni Battista competed with Domenico Piola for the commission for the dome of S Siro and here he created an illusionist vision of *Paradise* that follows Correggio and Giovanni Lanfranco.

Giovanni Battista's late work is contemporary with the High Baroque style of Domenico Piola's workshop, the Casa Piola. Perhaps as early as 1661, stimulated by his contact with Piola and later by his friendship with the Baroque sculptor Pierre Puget (to whom he acted as an agent in 1671), he began to create figures that are more undulating. Late works include the *Martyrdom of St Benigno* (1672; Genoa, Albergo Poveri) and frescoes in Bosio Marlugo (1676) and in S Sebastiano, Genoa (*c.* 1680; destr.).

(3) Giovanni Andrea Carlone (*b* Genoa, 16 May 1639; *d* Genoa, 4 April 1697). Painter, son of (2) Giovanni Battista Carlone. He was educated first by his father and then went to Rome to study under Carlo Maratti; in Rome he came into contact with Giovanni Battista Gaulli, with whom he shared patrons and who influenced his early decorative style. In this decade (1660s) he also worked in Perugia, painting frescoes in the church of S Filippo Neri (1662–9), with scenes from the Old Testament; he also worked in the church of Il Gesù (1666–7).

In the 1670s, between visits to Genoa, Giovanni Andrea travelled extensively from Naples, Messina and Palermo to Venice, Padua, Ferrara, Bologna, Modena, Parma and Piacenza. He was active in Roman artistic circles, becoming a member of the Accademia di S Luca in 1675, and he worked closely with Gaulli on frescoes in Il Gesù in Rome, showing the *Life of St Francis* (1673–8), and with Maratti in the Palazzo Altieri (1674–7), where he executed a frieze of the *Four Seasons* in the Sala Verde in brilliant oranges and pinks, greens and golds (see Gavazza, 1987, fig. 175). In these years he also worked in Foligno (*c.* 1670), Assisi (1663–77) and again at Perugia (1672, 1675). In the 1680s and 1690s he was based mainly in Genoa, where, with his brother Niccolò, he frescoed two rooms in the Palazzo Rosso with an *Allegory of the Arts* and an *Age of Mankind* (1691–2); he also made short trips to Rome (1680, 1686) and to Monaco.

This constant travelling provided him with a wide range of styles. His paintings in Perugia and Foligno resemble those of Umbrian artists. His Roman works reflect the style of Maratti, while his Genoese frescoes unite the decorative style of his father, influenced by Cortona, with the High Baroque art of Gaulli and Maratti. At the end of the century the artists of the Casa Piola, partly in response to Carlone's works, had absorbed this High Baroque style.

BIBLIOGRAPHY

DBI

R. Soprani: *Le vite de' pittori, scoltori, et architetti genovesi* (Genoa, 1674), pp. 113–14 [Giovanni]; 114, 238, 304 [Giovanni Battista]

R. Soprani and C. G. Ratti: *Delle vite de' pittori, scultori, ed architetti genovesi*, i (Genoa, 1768), pp. 261–5 [Giovanni]; p. 265 [Giovanni Battista]; ii (Genoa, 1769, rev. 1797), pp. 1–9 [Giovanni Battista]; pp. 91–102 [Giovanni Andrea]

M. Marangoni: *I Carloni* (Florence, 1925)

V. Belloni: *Pittura genovese del seicento* (Genoa, 1969), pp. 135–53

C. V. Castelnovi: 'La pittura nella prima metà del seicento dall'Ansaldo a Orazio de' Ferrari', *La pittura a Genova e in Liguria*, ii (Genoa, 1971, rev. 1987)

Genoese Baroque Drawings (exh. cat. by M. Newcome, Binghamton, SUNY; Worcester, MA, A. Mus.; 1972), nos 27–8 [Giovanni]; nos 51–3 [Giovanni Battista]; nos 107–10 [Giovanni Andrea]

V. Belloni: *Penne, pennelli e quadrerie* (Genoa, 1973), pp. 33–9

G. Biavati: 'Precisazioni su Giovanni Andrea Carlone', *Paragone*, xxv/297 (1974), pp. 62–73

E. Gavazza: *La grande decorazione a Genova*, i (Genoa, 1974)

L. Alfonso: 'I Carlone a Genova', *La Berio*, xvii/1–2 (1977), pp. 43–94

G. R. Terminiello and M. Semino: 'Le volte della chiesa di S Siro a Genova', *Il restauro nell'attività della soprintendenza*, i (Genoa, 1978), pp. 15–35

F. Boggero: 'Gli affreschi di Giovanni Battista Carlone nella chiesa genovese di S Siro', *Stud. Stor. A.* (1978–9), pp. 149–61

L. Barroero and V. Casale: *Pittura del '600 e '700: Ricerche in Umbria*, ii (Rome, 1980), nos 4–14, 18–21, 568–76

M. Newcome: 'Genoese Baroque Decoration in SS Giacomo e Filippo', *A. Crist.*, dclxix (1983), pp. 317–26

——: 'Giovanni Andrea Carlone', *Paragone*, xxxv/409 (1984), pp. 40–61

F. R. Pesenti: *La pittura in Liguria: Artisti del primo seicento* (Genoa, 1986)

E. Gavazza: 'Il momento della grande decorazione', *La pittura a Genova e in Liguria*, ii (Genoa, 1987)

Disegni genovesi dal XVI al XVIII secolo (exh. cat. by M. Newcome, Florence, Uffizi, 1987), no. 45 [Giovanni]; nos 46–8 [Giovanni Battista]

E. Gavazza, F. Lamera and L. Magnani: *La pittura in Liguria: Il secondo seicento* (Genoa, 1990)

E. Lunghi: 'Documenti per l'attività di Giovanni Andrea Carlone ad Assisi', *A. Crist*, dccxlii (1991), pp. 55–62

Kunst in der Republik Genua (exh. cat. by M. Newcome, Frankfurt am Main, Schirn Ksthalle, 1992)

M. NEWCOME

Carlone (ii). Italian family of artists. They came from Valle d'Intelvi, near Lake Como. Active since the 16th century, one branch of the family settled in Styria, Austria, in the mid-17th century. The numerous members worked variously as architects, master builders, sculptors, stuccoists and painters, often using their powerful family ties to promote one another's work and earn new commissions. They were mainly active in Austria and Germany as well as in their native Italy, their influence extending into the first half of the 18th century. Among the most prominent were the stuccoist (4) Giovanni Battista Carlone II and his son (7) Diego Francesco Carlone, the architect (3) Carlo Antonio Carlone and his nephew the decorative painter (8) Carlo Innocenzo Carlone. Giovanni Battista II founded the famous stucco workshop that operated mainly in southern Germany and Upper Austria and was taken over after his death by Diego Francesco. Carlo Antonio worked at Kremsmünster Abbey and, most notably, began work on the abbey church of St Florian. One of the most sought after decorative painters of his time, Carlo Innocenzo executed frescoes for royal and aristocratic patrons as well as for many churches.

BIBLIOGRAPHY

Macmillan Enc. Architects; Thieme–Becker

A. Hajdecki: 'Die Dynastenfamilien der italienischen Bau- und Maurermeister des Barocks in Wien', *Ber. & Mitt. Altert.-Ver. Wien*, xxxix (1906), pp. 1–83

M. Maragoni: *I Carloni* (Florence, 1925)

J. Tuschnig: *Die steierischen Zweige der Künstlerfamilie Carlone* (diss., U. Graz, 1935)

E. Guldan: *Die jochverschleifende Gewölbedekoration von Michelangelo bis Pozzo und in der bayerisch-österreichischen Sakralarchitektur* (diss., U. Göttingen, 1954)

J. Sturm: *Beiträge zur Architektur der Carlone in Österreich* (diss., U. Vienna, 1969)

Ostbair. Grenzmarken, xi (1969) [contains several articles on Carlone (ii) family members]

P. Fidler: 'Zur Architektur des 17. Jahrhunderts im Raum Wien', *Akten des XXV: Internationalen Kongresses für Kunstgeschichte: Wien, 1985*, ix, pp. 133–8

(1) Giovanni Battista Carlone I (*b* Verna, 1580–90; *d* Vienna, 28 Dec 1645). Architect. From *c.* 1614 to 1627 he worked for Charles Eusebius, Prince of Liechtenstein, in Moravia, where he became involved in the building of the manor house at Lednice and in the alterations to the Liechtenstein palace at Valtice. He also drew up a town plan (1614) for Valtice. From 1620 to 1637 he was architect to the imperial court of Ferdinand II, Holy Roman Emperor: his works include a banqueting hall in the Hofburg, Vienna, and the rebuilding of the royal castle in Bratislava, both in 1630. About 1630 he also worked for Graf von Harrach, Archbishop of Prague, and in 1630 he designed a *castrum doloris* for Conte Collalto. From 1637 to 1645 he was attached to the court of the Dowager Empress Eleonora Gonzaga, while the residence of Count Palffy in Bratislava was erected to his plans in 1637. Carlone also supervised the alterations (1634–45) to the monastery at Klosterneuburg and carried out work (1638–44) for Graf von Verdenberg. In 1642 he repaired and designed the architecture for a pleasure lake at the imperial summer residence on the River Wieden. He may also have collaborated in building the chapels of the Michaelerkirche, Vienna.

BIBLIOGRAPHY

R. Kohlbach: *Steierische Baumeister* (Graz, n.d.)

V. and D. Mencel: *Bratislava, Stavební obraz města a hradu* [Bratislava, townscape of the city and the castle] (Prague, 1936)

P. Fidler: *Architektur des 16. Jahrhunderts: Architekten, Baumeister und Bauten des Wiener Hofkreises* (Innsbruck, 1990), pp. 63–123

(2) Peter Franz [Pietro Francesco] **Carlone** (*b* 1606; *d* Seckau, 1680). Architect and master builder. He built the chapel of St Sebastian in Frohnleiten (1625), the novices' quarters for the Jesuits at Leoben (1630), and erected part (1652–4) of the convent at Göss (destr. 1828). The new wing of the chapter house and the priory in Gurk, Carinthia, were built (1637–64) to his plans but have been characterized as purely functional buildings of no artistic significance. In 1654 he submitted plans for the new monastery building at St Georgen on the Längsee. Between 1658 and 1679 he was working on alterations to the enormous monastery at Seckau. The west front, which runs three storeys high with octagonal corner towers crowned with onion domes, is arcaded on the side towards the courtyard. Ceremonial rooms (Kaisersaal, Huldigungssaal) of great pomp, richly stuccoed, are located on the first floor. The Jesuit church (1660–65) in Leoben, an early example of the wall-pillar church later developed by his son (3) Carlo Antonio Carlone, is attributed to him. From 1668 to 1671 he was involved in rebuilding the cathedral church at Passau. A period at the monastery at Garsten is documented in 1677, where the collegiate church was built to his plans. In Upper Austria the Jesuit church of St Ignatius (1669–78) in Linz, the Cölestinerkirche in Steyr (1676–81) and the monastery church at Schlierbach (1680–83) are attributed to him.

Carlone's works were often constrained by his patrons' fixed ideas and modest budgets and in later life frequently demonstrate a substantial contribution by his son Carlo Antonio. Nevertheless, Peter Franz is regarded as the most important architect of the 17th century in Styria: he added a new element to the so-called Carlone type of church interior—the wall-pillar church, with its characteristically rich stucco decoration.

BIBLIOGRAPHY

R. Kohlbach: *Steierische Baumeister* (Graz, n.d.)

B. Roth: *P. F. Carlone als Seckauer Baumeister, 1658–82*, Seckauer geschichtliche Studien, xvii (Seckau, 1962)

(3) Carlo Antonio Carlone (*b* Scaria, nr Como, 1635; *d* St Nicola, nr Passau, *bur* 1 May 1708). Architect, son of (2) Peter Franz Carlone. He worked *c.* 1654 for his father at the convent at Göss. By 1658 he is documented as collaborating on the alterations to the cathedral chapter at Gurk, and in 1661 he was working at the monastery at Seckau. For the Jesuit church of the Nine Angelic Choirs in Vienna (1662), Carlone, pressed for space, set back the upper two storeys of the elevation but ran the ground-floor through, flush with the wings of the Casa Professa that flank it, in a design that compromises with the secular. In 1671 he submitted plans for the tower of the parish church at Vilshofen in Bavaria. He had evidently worked previously in Passau on the Jesuit church of St Ignatius (1669–78; later made Linz Cathedral). From 1679 the chapel of the Virgin at Kremsmünster Abbey was constructed to his plans as an aisleless hall in three bays perpendicular to the axis of the church. He subsequently designed the church towers and most of the Fischbehälter, the latter combining arcades, sculpture, wrought-iron grilles and ponds to constitute an idiosyncratic work of art (*see* KREMSMÜNSTER, §1).

Other works of this period include the monastery church at Garsten (1677, with the Losenstein Chapel of 1685) and the reconstruction (1683–7) of the pilgrimage church of Maria Kulm at Frauenberg bei Admont, both of them displaying Carlone's development of the wall-pillar church type. In 1686 he is documented as working at the monastery at Spittal am Pyhrn, but his most notable move that year was to commence work on the abbey church of St Florian (1686–95; *see* ST FLORIAN ABBEY, §1), the interior of which is undoubtedly his masterpiece (see fig.). Giant half columns on high pedestals articulate the four bays of its nave, supporting a powerfully projecting entablature that runs round the whole interior, the triple extrusion of which, over a multiplicity of supporting members, announces the crossing, surmounted by a great drumless dome on pendentives. The nave is roofed by a succession of *Platzlgewölbe* (cap vaults), the shallow dome system that Carlo Antonio was the first to introduce into Austria and Germany at the beginning of the High Baroque period. It facilitated the painting of unified ceiling frescoes and led to the predominance of ceiling painting over stucco decoration in German Baroque. At St Florian, the frescoes cover the whole area of the vaulting. They display painted reproductions of the minor order used in the nave at the side chapel arcades and at the high altar, where they are superimposed in two storeys.

Carlo Antonio Carlone: interior of St Florian abbey church, 1686–95

In 1688 Carlone worked on the great court of the monastery at Reichersberg on the River Inn. The following year, the Ägidiuskirche in Vöcklabruck was built to his plans, and from 1697 to 1700 he supervised the construction of the parish church at Rohrbach. The monastery of Niederaltaich (from 1698) was built to his designs and is important for the development of Bavarian monastic architecture. The monastery church at Baumgartenberg, completed in 1697, is also attributed to him, and documents show him to have worked at the Gleink foundation in 1700. The plan for the small centralized pilgrims' church at Christkindl, diversified internally by four niches and finished after Carlone's death by Jakob Prandtauer, dates from 1702.

Carlo Antonio Carlone is primarily known as the creator of religious buildings during the Baroque period in Upper Austria, although his influence extends as far as Passau and Styria. As an architect he coordinated the work of the Carlone group of stuccoists, who can be shown to have collaborated on almost all his projects, contributing much to the uniform stylistic character of his buildings. Carlone has also been credited with disseminating some of the stylistic motifs of the Baroque architecture of Francesco Borromini and Guarino Guarini.

BIBLIOGRAPHY

T. Korth: *Stift St Florian* (Nuremberg, 1975)

(4) Giovanni Battista Carlone II (*b* Scaria, nr Como, *c.* 1650; *d* 1707). Stuccoist and sculptor, brother of (3) Carlo Antonio Carlone. He began his artistic career in Passau, where he worked on the decoration of the Jesuit church in 1675. From 1677 he produced the interior stucco for Passau Cathedral, where for the first time he introduced human figures into the architectural framework (*see* GERMANY, fig. 32). From 1677 to 1679 he also worked for Count Sinzendorf in the Passau area (tomb chapel in the Capuchin church). In 1682 he went to Garsten, where he created the stucco decoration for the monastery church and the summer refectory. From 1684 to 1685 the Carlone workshop was at work in the monastery church at Schlierbach. Carlone returned to Garsten in 1687 to work on the stucco for the Losenstein tomb chapel. Before 1690 he decorated the altars of the Ägidiuskirche in Vöcklabruck and those in the castle chapel at Marbach. From 1689 to 1693 he produced the stuccowork for the pilgrimage church at Gartlberg, and from 1690 to 1695 he was engaged on the stucco decoration for the abbey church at St Florian. He worked in the monastery at Schlägl in 1693 but left the Passau–Upper Austria area in 1695 to move to the Upper Palatinate. From then until 1698 he worked at the monastery church at Waldassen, which he filled with an amazing wealth of stuccowork: swelling foliage, richly turned cartouches and innumerable figures ranging from Old Testament prophets to the Persian and Phrygian sibyls. From 1696 to 1699 he was employed in the Salesian church in Amberg and from 1702 to 1707 in the pilgrimage church of Mariahilf, where he was responsible for the high altar. Carlone also decorated (1697) the dome (destr.) over the crossing in Regensburg Cathedral.

Giovanni Battista Carlone's stucco decoration is distinguished by massive voluminous forms with naturalistic ornamentation. His works fill all the available space on walls and vaulting or frame fresco areas with heavy stucco garlands. By their size and creative force his decorations constitute an important part of the architectural ensemble, contributing to the spatial effects in a building.

BIBLIOGRAPHY

E. Guldan: 'Quellen zu Leben und Werk italienischer Stukkatoren des Spätbarock in Bayern', *Arte e artisti dei laghi Lombardi*, ii (Como, 1964), pp. 165–290

F. Engl: 'Die Stuckarbeiten G. B. Carlones, in der St Ägidiuskirche zu Vöcklabruck, in der Schlosskapelle zu Marbach, im Pfarrhof zu Ried und im Stifte Reichersberg', *A. Lombarda*, ii (1966), pp. 149–54

W. Luges: 'Die Stukkateure', *Linzer Stukkateure* (exh. cat., Linz, Stadtmus., 1973), pp. 61–8

(5) Johann Joachim Carlone (*bapt* Graz, 22 July 1653; *d* Graz, 12 Nov 1713). Architect and master builder. From 1667 to 1671 Carlone was apprenticed to his father, the master builder Franz Isidor Carlone. He worked for him at Schloss Eggenberg and at the Graz church of Mariahilf, where he built the summer refectory in a conservative style. His main independent works are palaces, including those in Graz-Wagensberg (1689) and Stubenberg (1689). In 1700 he was appointed regional Master Mason. From 1701 he worked on the monastery church at Pöllau.

(6) Bartolomeo Carlone (*fl c.* 1686). Stuccoist, cousin of (3) Carlo Antonio Carlone. From 1686 to 1708 he worked at the abbey church of St Florian in Austria and on the Leopoldine wing there (1701). In 1693 he was also employed at Schlägl Abbey in Upper Austria. He later worked on the stucco decoration (1698) at Schloss Weinberg and in *c.* 1700 was documented as being employed at the Ursuline church in Linz and at the parish church in Mauthausen, Upper Austria.

BIBLIOGRAPHY

E. Guldan: 'Quellen zu Leben und Werk italienischer Stukkatoren des Spätbarock in Bayern', *Arte e artisti dei laghi Lombardi*, ii (Como, 1964), pp. 165–290

W. Luges: 'Die Stukkateure', *Linzer Stukkateure* (exh. cat., Linz, Stadtmus., 1973), pp. 61–8

(7) Diego Francesco Carlone (*b* Scaria, 1674; *d* Scaria, 25 June 1750). Stuccoworker, son of (4) Giovanni Battista Carlone II. He learnt his trade in his father's workshop in Passau Cathedral. About 1695 he was in Rome, and in 1701 he worked at the Salesian church at Amberg and the Carmelite church at Straubing. By then he was already in charge of his father's firm, with Paolo Allio I (*see* ALLIO (ii), (1)) as his leading collaborator; they worked together until 1720. In 1702 the workshop provided stucco decorations for the pilgrimage church of Mariahilf, near Amberg, and in 1704–5 for the abbey church at St Florian, Upper Austria, and for the collegiate church in Salzburg. Carlone and Allio worked in the priory church at Rattenberg from 1706 to 1712 and at the religious foundation in Lambach from 1707 to 1709. In 1708 Carlone alone worked on the stucco decoration of the interior of Schloss Klesheim near Salzburg. The stucco in the sacristy of the parish church at Müll also suggests his hand. Later he worked in the Carmelite church in Linz and the Jesuit church at Passau. In 1718 he stuccoed rooms in the hunting lodge at Thyrnau and in 1719–20 he worked in the summer refectory of the monastery of Kremsmünster. In 1719 and again in 1725 he was active in the ducal residence at Ludwigsburg. The works of the first quarter of the 18th century are undoubtedly Carlone's best.

In 1723 Carlone worked on the high altar of the priory church of Weingarten, where he later built the side altars. From 1730 he worked on altars in the monastery church at Einsiedeln, Switzerland, and in 1734 in Schloss Ansbach, another of his most striking achievements. In 1739 he worked on the altar figures in S Maria di Carignano, Genoa, to designs by the sculptor Francesco Maria Schiaffino. Shortly before his death he produced the stucco figures in the parish church at Scaria. Carlone owed his many commissions to his close contacts of blood or friendship with leading architects: in Germany he was associated with the court architects Donato Giuseppe Frisoni (1683–1735) and Paolo Retti (1661–1748), while in Salzburg he was engaged to work on the buildings of Johann Bernhard Fischer von Erlach. In some room decorations he collaborated with his younger brother, (8) Carlo Innocenzo Carlone.

Throughout his work Carlone was able to merge the artistic legacy of his father with impulses coming from Roman sculpture after Bernini. His pleasing stucco figures and his highly developed sense for decorative pose and drapery earned him great popularity among the patrons of his time. For a period his workshop had a dominant position in Austria and southern Germany, and was even able to resist the growing influence of the stuccoworkers of Wessobrunn. Carlone's artistic strength lies in the figure components of his decoration rather than in the ornamentation. His figures have light, loose forms. As a stuccoworker and sculptor, he had a strong feeling for soft, naturalistic forms with plastic modelling and shallow, delicate relief. He often worked from models and showed a good understanding of the peculiarities of different modes of decoration. The large number of his commissions was not generally detrimental to the quality of his works, but it often forced him into typological repetition. His figures have a limited range of postures and facial expressions. This suggests the mass-production of altars, with the individual components, putto groups and heads being cast. A similar method is evident in Carlone's ornamental decorations. He was generally able, however, to keep the overall design in view: his decorations combine with the interior architecture to form an imposing whole. Carlone did not follow the mid-18th-century trend of merging individual genres in the service of a notion of the unified room but instead allowed the optical peculiarities of architecture, stucco and painting to develop freely and individually.

BIBLIOGRAPHY

A. Brini: *La vita e l'opera di Carlo e Diego Carloni di Scaria* (diss., U. Pavia, 1948)

E. Guldan: 'Quellen zu Leben und Werk italienischer Stukkatoren des Spätbarock in Bayern', *Arte e artisti dei laghi Lombardi*, ii (Como, 1964), pp. 165–290

H. Vagt: *Untersuchungen zum Werk Diego Francesco Carlones* (diss., U. Munich, 1970)

W. Luges: 'Die Stukkateure', *Linzer Stukkateure* (exh. cat., Linz, Stadtmus., 1973), pp. 61–8

E. Ascarelli d'Amore: 'I Carloni Diego Francesco e Carlo Innocenzo', *A. Crist.*, xliii (1975), pp. 51–8

(8) Carlo Innocenzo Carlone (*b* Scaria, 1686; *d* Como, 17 May 1775). Painter, brother of (7) Diego Francesco Carlone. He was apprenticed at the age of 12 to Giulio Quaglio III in Venice. After 1700 he worked with Quaglio in Udine and Laibach (now Ljubljana, Slovenia), and from 1706 to 1711 he continued his studies in Rome, at the workshop of Francesco Trevisani and at the Accademia di S Luca. He was also influenced by the work of leading Italian 17th-century painters: he made a careful study of works by Pietro da Cortona, Luca Giordano, Francesco Solimena and others. He left Rome in about 1711, and his first securely attributed work is dated 1712 (altarpiece in Kirchberg am Wagram, Lower Austria). By 1716 at the latest, he was in Vienna, where with Marcantonio Chiarini (1652–1730) he painted the fresco of the *Triumph of Apollo* in the Belvedere summer palace of Prince Eugene. In 1721–3 he worked at the Belvedere again with the illusionist room-painter Gaetano Fanti (1687–1759), and with Chiarini he provided frescoes for the banqueting halls, the *sala terrena* and the chapel. Also with Chiarini, he decorated the ceiling of the staircase and the banqueting hall in the Palais Daun-Kinsky, Vienna. In Schloss Hetzendorf (nr Vienna) he frescoed the ceremonial rooms for the Princess of Liechtenstein. The frescoes from Carlone's early period in Vienna show both a bravura mastery of technique and the effects of his time in Italy, but there is little trace in these grandiose decorations of the spectacular colour and light compositions of his later work. The calm, balanced groups of figures are matched by balanced relationships of light and shade. The Hetzendorf frescoes, however, do hint at the new decorative qualities of his work.

In 1717 Carlone was at work on a fresco (destr.; oil sketch Salzburg, Barockmus.) in the Council Chamber in the Landhaus at Linz, where he worked with the architectural painter Francesco Messenta (*c*. 1675–1745). The two men also collaborated on the painted decoration of the Wallfahrtskirche at Stadl Paura, Upper Austria (altars and dome frescoes). Carlone's first works in Germany were the frescoes (1720–21) in the chapel and rooms in the castle at Ludwigsburg, where he worked with his brother Diego Francesco. Carlone obtained the Ludwigsburg commission through the mediation of his relatives, the master builders Donato Giuseppe Frisoni (1683–1735) and Paolo Retti (1661–1748). His Viennese patrons, meanwhile, recommended him to paint a fresco in the Kurfürstenkapelle in the cathedral of Breslau (now Wrocław, Poland) in 1721. During the 1720s Carlone's style changed: his compositions became clearer and more expansive, his

Carlo Innocenzo Carlone: *Allegory of Peace and Justice*, *bozzetto* for a ceiling fresco, oil on canvas, 360×440 mm, *c*. 1717 (Vienna, Belvedere, Österreichische Galerie)

figures lighter and more graceful, with a slightly Mannerist quality. The colours of his frescoes lost their earthiness and became more radiant. In 1727 Carlone completed the frescoes in the parish church at Gross-Siegharts, Lower Austria, and painted those for the ceiling of the castle chapel in Schlosshof. From 1727 to 1729 he painted frescoes for the staircase, the main hall and the library of the Palais Clam-Gallas in Prague. His altarpiece in the castle chapel at Smiřice, Czech Republic, is dated 1724 (or possibly 1727). Many of his works from this period are now thought to have been lost, while some were ordered but not executed. A staircase fresco for Schloss Mirabell in Salzburg was never executed but is recorded in a *bozzetto.*

From 1725 Carlone habitually returned for the winter months to Italy, where he continued his work in a more congenial climate. In 1725 he worked in Como on the frescoes and paintings in SS Annunziata del Crocifisso and at the same time on the fresco decorations for the palace of Conte Gallio. It is possible that the four altarpieces in S Fedele in Como were painted by him as early as 1720. In the 1730s Carlone worked predominantly in Germany and Italy. In 1733 he painted decorative frescoes for the outside staircase of the Villa Colleoni in Calusco d'Adda. For Graf Wilhelm von Grävenitz he decorated (1730) the ceiling of the castle hall at Heimsheim. In 1734 he worked with his brother Diego Francesco (who provided stucco decoration) on the ceiling of the castle hall in Ansbach. He also worked for religious foundations in Weingarten, Germany (altarpieces, 1731), and in Einsiedeln, Switzerland (altarpieces, 1739–41). In 1736–7 he was commissioned by Duke Charles Alexander to work at the Schlossresidenz in Stuttgart. At Schloss Ludwigsburg he provided frescoes for the dining room and the ancestors' hall in 1730–33 as well as portraits (untraced) of his patron Eberhard-Ludwig, Duke of Württemberg, and his wife. In 1750–52 Carlone worked for the last time in Germany at SCHLOSS BRÜHL, where he was commissioned by the Elector-Archbishop of Cologne, Clemens August, to provide frescoes for the guardroom, main staircase, music room and chapel.

Throughout his maturity, Carlone carried out important work in his native Italy. Between 1738 and 1745 he painted frescoes in the nave, aisles and transept of Monza Cathedral. In 1745 he worked at the Villa Lechi in Montirone, Brescia, and in 1745–7 he painted frescoes in the parish church at Tagliuno, Bergamo. Commissioned by Conte Lechi, he also frescoed the parish church at Calvisina, Brescia. With his brother Diego Francesco, he decorated the parish church at Scaria. His frescoes for S Michele all'Arco in Bergamo were produced in 1750. After 1745 Carlone also executed frescoes in Brescia, in the Palazzo Gaifami and the churches of S Eufemia and S Maria degli Angeli. His frescoes in S Filippo and S Maria Maddalena in Lodi date from 1756. In 1759 Carlone is documented as at work in Castel San Pietro near Mendrisio, executing paintings in the choir. In 1760 he began painting frescoes in the parish church in Scovole on Lake Garda; after his death these were finished by Giosué Scotti (1729–85). Carlone's last work, the frescoes in Asti Cathedral, were undertaken when he was 80.

A large number of *bozzetti* by Carlone survive (Salzburg, Barockmus., Germany, priv. cols and elsewhere; see fig.) and reveal his ideas and principles of composition. He probably influenced a number of contemporary painters in southern Germany, but his pupils, apart from Giuseppe Delai (*b* 1732) from Bolzano, have remained anonymous. Carlone's early work was influenced by his Venetian and Roman impressions, but he was later attracted to the work of Giambattista Tiepolo; and when his activity became more centred in Lombardy, he devoted increasing attention to the tradition of that region. His work, however, always retained the elegant manner of his youth, his strength lying in the sophisticated use of colour shown in his frescoes and altarpieces.

BIBLIOGRAPHY

J. C. Füssli: *Geschichte und Abbildung der besten Künstler in der Schweiz*, iv (Zürich, 1779), p. 224

A. Brini: *La vita e l'opera di Carlo e Diego Carloni di Scaria* (diss., U. Pavia, 1948)

H. Voss: 'L'attività di C. Carlone in Austria e in Germania', *Barocco europeo e barocco veneziano* (Florence, 1963), pp. 147–57

A. Barrigozzi Brini and K. Garas: *Carlo Innocenzo Carlone* (Milan, 1967)

D. McRae: 'Another *Catalogo* of the Sketches of C. Carlone', *A. Lombarda*, xii/1 (1967), pp. 143–9

K. Rossacher: 'Der junge Maulpertsch und C. I. Carlone', *Alte & Mod. Kst*, xvi (1971), pp. 22–4

I. Manke: 'Die Fresken von C. Carlone in der Ahnengalerie des Ludwigburger Schlosses', *Pantheon*, xxxii (1974), pp. 261–72

E. Ascarelli d'Amore: 'I Carloni Diego Francesco e Carlo Innocenzo', *A. Cris.*, xliii (1975), pp. 1–32, 51–8

W. Hansmann: 'Eine rheinische Carlone-Sammlung', *Wallraf-Richartz-Jb.*, xxxvii (1975), pp. 185–204

PETER FIDLER

Carlos, Frei (*fl* 1517–35). South Netherlandish painter, active in Portugal. He is the most obviously Flemish of the artists working in Portugal during the first half of the 16th century. His earliest-known work may have been painted before he went to Portugal: the *Mystic Marriage of St Catherine* (London, N.G.), clearly influenced by the triptych of the same subject by Hans Memling (1479; Bruges, Memlingmus.). This affinity with the Bruges school and with Memling is apparent in all of Frei Carlos's work, which is close to that of other painters then working in Évora, such as Francisco Henriques. Their marked Netherlandish characteristics derive in part from the panels of the great altarpiece dedicated to the *Life of the Virgin* (*c.* 1500; Évora, Mus. Évora), painted for Évora Cathedral by Netherlandish artists, which recalls the art of Hugo van der Goes, Gerard David and Quinten Metsys. Between 1510 and 1512 Carlos collaborated with the Master of Lourinhã on the *Triptych of the Infantes* (Lisbon, Mus. N. A. Ant.).

In 1517 Carlos made his profession as a monk at the Hieronymite monastery of Espinheiro, Évora, describing himself as 'Frey Carlos de Lisboa framengo'. From then on his work was mainly devoted to the houses of the Hieronymite Order. The paintings attributed to him indicate that he had an organized workshop, with several painters imitating his work. Between 1517 and 1521 he was commissioned by Manuel I to paint the altarpieces (untraced) for the high and side altars in the church of the convent of Espinheiro, Évora. A *Virgin and Child* (Lisbon, Mus. N. A. Ant.) for the Jerónimos Monastery at Belém dates from about 1522. The *Annunciation* (1523; Lisbon,

Mus. N. A. Ant.) includes a picture within a picture: a little panel depicting the Old Testament scene of the *Burning Bush*, hanging in the Virgin's oratory. In *Christ Appearing to the Virgin* (1529; Lisbon, Mus. N. A. Ant.) the figure of the Virgin is reminiscent of that in *Christ Appearing to the Virgin, with St Paul and Donor* attributed to the Master of the Legend of St Ursula (i) (*c.* 1480–88; New York, priv. col.). Frei Carlos's interest in depicting precious objects is seen in the beautiful processional cross of gold and crystal held by Christ. The setting is also typical of Netherlandish tradition in the attention given to detail, such as the linenfold carving and the early Renaissance columns in the background. The scene is enacted in two separate spaces, an interior and an outdoors. This type of composition also suggests the influence of the multiple scenes of contemporary Portuguese theatre, as in the pieces by the goldsmith and dramatist Gil Vicente. Carlos's last recorded work is a *Deposition* (1535; untraced) for the monastery of S Marinha da Costa, Guimarães.

BIBLIOGRAPHY

J. Couto: *A oficina de Frei Carlos* (Lisbon, n.d.)
W. H. James Weale: '*The Risen Saviour Appearing to his Mother*: A Masterpiece by Roger de la Pasture', *Burl. Mag.*, xvi (1909), pp. 159–60
A. Gusmão: 'Os primitivos e a renascença', *Arte portuguesa: Pintura* (Lisbon, 1950), pp. 245–51
H. J. Friedländer: *Early Netherlandish Painting* (1967–76), vi

DAGOBERTO L. MARKL

Carlos I de Bragança. *See* BRAGANZA, (14).

Carlos III, King of Spain. *See* BOURBON, §II(4).

Carlos IV, King of Spain. *See* BOURBON, §II(6).

Carlotto. *See* LOTH, (2).

Carlsbad [Karlsbad]. *See* KARLOVY VARY.

Carlsen, Frederik Wilhelm (Christian). *See* FREDDIE, WILHELM.

Carlsund, Otto G(ustaf) (*b* St Petersburg, 11 Dec 1897; *d* Stockholm, 25 July 1948). Swedish painter and critic. From 1922 to 1923 he studied at the Konstakademien in Oslo. The Swedish painter Adrian-Nilsson was influential in his development, notably with regard to his 'musical' paintings, in which he attempted through visual elements to achieve an auditory effect; the music of J. S. Bach inspired him in this. He maintained contact with, among others, Fernand Léger, Amédée Ozenfant and Mondrian while in Paris from 1924 to 1930, and during this period he was primarily interested in Cubism and geometric abstraction, influences reflected in *The Chair* (1926; Stockholm, Mod. Mus.). In 1929 he co-founded the Art Concret group in Paris with Theo van Doesburg, Jean Hélion, and the Armenian painter Leon Tutundjian (1905–68), and in 1930 he published their manifesto *The Basis of Concrete Art* in the first and only edition of *Art Concret* (*see* CONCRETE ART). Carlsund underwent a severe crisis in connection with an exhibition in Stockholm in 1930; he had difficulty in communicating through his modernist works, and from 1932 to 1945 he devoted himself less to painting, choosing instead to write prolifically. His radicalism was also reflected in his writing, which included art criticism, and his ideas often met with opposition, although in later years they attracted greater interest. He published his own magazine, *Konstvärlden*, from 1941 to 1945.

WRITINGS

T. Brunius and U. T. Moberg, eds: *Otto G. Carlsund skriver om konst* [Otto G. Carlsund writes on art] (Stockholm, 1988)

BIBLIOGRAPHY

O. Reutersward: *Otto G. Carlsund i fjärrperspektiv* [Otto G. Carlsund in long perspective] (Åhus, 1988)

JACQUELINE STARE

Carlu, Jacques (*b* Bonnières-sur-Seine, 7 April 1890; *d* Paris, 3 Dec 1976). French architect. He studied at the Ecole des Beaux-Arts in Paris and then spent some time in Bucharest. In 1913 he began his unusual transatlantic career when he went to Canada to work for the planner Thomas Hayton Mawson on various projects in Calgary and Ottawa; he also worked in the office of Henry Hornbostel (1867–1961) in Pittsburgh (1914). After returning to France, he won the Premier Grand Prix de Rome (1919) as a student of Victor Laloux; while still completing his unorthodox fourth-year submission—reconstructions of the Capitoline Hill, Rome, during the Etruscan period, which were brightly coloured in a manner reminiscent of Art Deco—Carlu was appointed as the first director of the Ecole d'Art Américaine en France, Fontainebleau, which he headed until 1937.

Carlu's popularity among American students at Fontainebleau led to his appointment (1924) as Professor of Advanced Design at the Massachusetts Institute of Technology, Cambridge, where he played a significant role in promoting French decorative fashion in North America; he also produced some interior designs (completed 1930) for the T. Eaton department stores in Toronto and Montreal that introduced the 'ocean liner' style to Canada and were forerunners of the streamlined aesthetic that became prevalent in the 1930s. His top-floor restaurant in the Montreal store remained almost unaltered into the 1990s. This period in the USA also resulted in Carlu becoming an unexpected advocate of the development of high-rise buildings in France, and his designs (1931 and *c.* 1943) for La Défense, Paris, appear quite prophetic. The *c.* 1943 drawing is in the collection of the Canadian Center for Architecture in Montreal.

After his return to France in 1933, Carlu was involved with proposals to rebuild Gabriel Davioud's Palais du Trocadéro for the Exposition Internationale (1937) in Paris. Working with Robert Mallet-Stevens, he first proposed to transform the obsolete structure into a Musée de la République; instead he designed the Palais de Chaillot (with Louis Hippolyte Boileau and Leon Azéma (1888–1978)), enclosing within its two curved wings parts of the original structure. A monumental but well-proportioned building, it reflected the austere neo-classicism of the 1930s; its terraces form a strong perspective across the River Seine to the Eiffel Tower and the Champ de Mars.

After a period in the USA during World War II, Carlu returned to France once more and, during the 1950s and 1960s, carried out a number of large public commissions, including the NATO headquarters (1955–9), Paris, now the Université de Paris IX-Dauphine; this building reflected only to a certain extent the powerful massing and monumental simplicity of the Palais de Chaillot. Other examples of his later work include the Maison de la Radio (1956), Rennes, and the Faculté des Lettres et des Sciences Humaines Censier (1964), Paris. Carlu became a member of the Institut de France in 1957.

BIBLIOGRAPHY

E. S. Campbell: 'French Comrades in America: Jacques Carlu', *Pencil Points*, vii/4 (1926), pp. 267–89

I. Gournay: 'Jacques Carlu et le style paquebot outre-atlantique', *Mnmts Hist.*, 130 (1983–4), pp. 71–4

——: *Le Nouveau Trocadéro* (Liège, 1985)

——: 'Architecture at the Fontainebleau School of Fine Arts', *J. Soc. Archit. Hist.*, xlv/3 (1986), pp. 270–85

ISABELLE GOURNAY

Carlyle, Thomas (*b* Ecclefechan, nr Dumfries, 4 Dec 1795; *d* London, 4 Feb 1881). Scottish writer and historian. He studied at the University of Edinburgh from 1809 to 1818. In the 1820s he wrote numerous articles and reviews that helped to introduce English readers to contemporary German philosophy and German romantic literature, and established his reputation. Among the most important were 'Schiller's Life and Writings' (*London Magazine*, 1823–4), 'The State of German Literature' (*Edinburgh Review*, 1827) and 'Goethe' (*Foreign Review*, July 1828). Towards the end of the 1820s he began to address social concerns. In his essay 'Signs of the Times' (1829) he attacked what he saw as the 'mechanical' nature of English society and the equally mechanical thought that characterized it. In 'Characteristics' (1831) he criticized the 'self-consciousness' of the whole cultural environment. In subsequent writings he argued that modern society's loss of religious belief and consequent lack of spiritual or emotional guidance led to materialism, spiritual emptiness and an inability to act spontaneously. In such works as *Past and Present* (London, 1842) he evoked, by contrast, the image of a medieval English society permeated by religious faith. He criticized both the *laissez-faire* economic doctrines prevalent at the time and the movement for democracy, arguing in *On Heroes, Hero Worship and the Heroic in History* (London, 1841) that society could only be restored to spiritual health by strong leadership.

Although Carlyle apparently took little interest in the visual arts, at times even explicitly disparaging them as worthless, his low estimation of their role arose from a conviction that the artist in modern society was hampered by the spiritual emptiness of the age. Whereas, he suggested in *On Heroes*, during the Renaissance the poet acted as an interpreter of human life, a 'heroic' function akin to that of the prophet in earlier times, the modern artist, no matter which discipline he worked in, was at best a source of harmless amusement and at worst a worthless dilettante. Carlyle nevertheless exerted a considerable influence on the fine arts, mainly through Ruskin, whom he met *c.* 1850. Ruskin adopted many elements of Carlyle's thought and developed the latter's idea of the intimate connection between a society's art and its social structure and values, a theme that was later to be explored by such writers as William Morris. Ruskin also shared Carlyle's belief that as social roles became more specialized in a modern society, both the artist and the critic would become increasingly marginal figures, less able and less concerned to represent and address the whole of society or the totality of human experience. Partly through Ruskin's efforts, Carlyle's belief that any art of value must embody a set of strongly felt and enunciated beliefs was to some extent taken up by members of the Pre-Raphaelite Brotherhood in their attempt to embody a sort of spiritual reawakening and in their rejection of what they saw as the outdated and empty academicism of the work of their contemporaries. Carlyle himself, however, does not seem to have entertained any particularly paternal feelings towards the Pre-Raphaelites, and, although he continued to maintain a close friendship with Ruskin, he remained more impressed by the latter's writings on social and economic matters. Carlyle was the subject of paintings by Whistler (*Arrangement in Grey and Black, No. 2*, 1872–3; Glasgow, A.G. & Mus.) and John Everett Millais (1877; London, N.P.G.) and was represented in Ford Madox Brown's *Work* (1852, 1856–63; Manchester, C.A.G.).

WRITINGS

H. D. Traill, ed.: *Collected Works*, 30 vols (New York, 1896–9)

G. A. Cate, ed.: *The Correspondence of Thomas Carlyle and John Ruskin* (Stanford, 1982)

G. B. Tennyson, ed.: *A Carlyle Reader: Selections from the Writings of Thomas Carlyle* (Cambridge, 1984)

BIBLIOGRAPHY

J. A. Froude: *Thomas Carlyle: A History of his Life in London* (London, 1884)

C. F. Harrold: *Carlyle and German Thought, 1819–1834* (London, 1934)

R. Williams: *Culture and Society, 1780–1950* (London, 1958, rev. Harmondsworth, 1963), pp. 85–98

MATTHEW TAYLOR

Carmelite Order [Order of the Blessed Virgin Mary of Mt Carmel]. Monastic order apparently founded *c.* 1150 near the fountain of Elijah on Mt Carmel in the Holy Land. The earliest Carmelites were hermits living in conditions of great austerity. Around 1240 they fled from Saracen invaders and re-established themselves as a mendicant order in Western Europe, where they substituted white, hooded habits for their striped robes and subsequently became known as the White Friars. They were no longer eremetical except in a few rural houses such as Hulne in Northumberland, England. From their monasteries in such university towns as Oxford, Cambridge, Paris and Bologna they took a full part in university life as both students and teachers and acquired a reputation for scholarship.

The Carmelite Order was subject to one of the most important reforms of the Counter-Reformation. Its leader was the devout Spanish mystic St Teresa of Ávila (1515–82; *can* 1622), whose reformed branch, known as the Discalced (or barefoot) Carmelites, was founded in 1562. Her aim was to return to the original asceticism and devotion of the earliest hermits on Mt Carmel. From 1568 another Spaniard, St John of the Cross (1542–91; *can* 1726), extended these reforms to male Carmelite houses. Both St Teresa and St John experienced remarkable visions and states of religious ecstasy, while enduring unimaginable physical deprivations. The Discalced Carmelites remained a cloistered order, devoted above all to prayer and personal spiritual salvation. After the religious disruptions of the French Revolution (1789–99) the Order never recovered its former strength.

1. ICONOGRAPHY. Lifelike portrayals of Carmelites appear in the fine miniatures of the late 14th-century English Carmelite Missal (London, BL, Add. MSS 29704–5, 44892), reconstructed from fragments. The relaxation of the Carmelite rule by Pope Eugenius IV (*reg* 1431–47) in 1433 was depicted in fresco (1421; partly destr.) by the Carmelite artist Fra Filippo Lippi, in the cloister of his monastery, S Maria del Carmine, Florence (for an alternative dating and interpretation of subject-matter *see* LIPPI, (1)). Stocky, white-robed Carmelite friars also appear in Masaccio's Pisa Polyptych (1426; dispersed; for locations *see* MASACCIO) for S Maria del Carmine, Pisa, as well as in his depiction of *St Peter Enthroned as Bishop of Antioch* (1427–8; see fig.), part of the fresco cycle in the Brancacci Chapel, S Maria del Carmine, Florence.

Scenes from the life of Elijah, who was regarded by the Carmelites as their founder, became popular themes in the art of the Order. (For a discussion of Pietro Lorenzetti's representation of the Carmelites' foundation legend *see* PREDELLA.) A fine example is Gaspard Dughet's series of landscape frescoes (1647–51) with scenes from the *Lives of the Prophets Elijah and Elisha* in the Carmelite church of S Martino ai Monti, Rome. Both St Teresa and St John of the Cross were represented in Carmelite art. The most striking portrayal of St Teresa is Gianlorenzo Bernini's sculpture of the *Ecstasy of St Teresa* in the Cornaro Chapel in the Carmelite church of S Maria della Vittoria, Rome. Bernini shows the saint swooning in ecstasy on a bed of clouds, at the climax of a visionary experience, while a smiling angel points an arrow towards her heart. St Joseph also became a popular figure in Carmelite imagery, as did St Simon Stock (*d c.* 1265), the English Carmelite who was chosen as the first Western prior-general of the Order in 1247. In 1251 he had a vision of the Virgin offering him the scapular, the monastic cape said to protect the wearer from the fires of Purgatory. This was the event depicted by Giambattista Tiepolo in 1740–49 on the ceiling of the Sala Capitolare of the Scuola Grande dei Carmini in Venice. St Joseph was greatly revered by St Teresa, who dedicated her nunnery in Ávila to him; in 1628 he was made the patron saint of the whole Discalced Carmelite Order.

Carmelite friars in a painting by Masaccio: *St Peter Enthroned as Bishop of Antioch* (1427–8), fresco, Brancacci Chapel, S Maria del Carmine, Florence

Marian themes also played an essential part in Carmelite iconography from the Middle Ages onwards. Representations of the Trinity were often illustrated in conjunction with Marian subjects. The Carmelites included the Immaculate Conception in their Marian imagery in the Counter-Reformation fight against heresy; for instance, Diego Velázquez's *Immaculate Conception* (*c.* 1620; London, N.G.) was originally in the Carmelite monastery in Seville. The Immaculate Virgin figured prominently in Tiepolo's huge fresco (1745; destr. 1915) for the ceiling of the Discalced Carmelite church of S Maria degli Scalzi in Venice. This fresco depicted the *Translation of the Santa Casa di Loreto* miraculously carried by angels from Nazareth to Italy at the time of the Saracen invasions. The Carmelites, who had themselves left the Holy Land to escape the Saracens, were made guardians of the Santa Casa at its final resting place, LORETO, in 1489.

2. PATRONAGE. The early Carmelites in Western Europe enjoyed both royal and noble patronage; their benefactors included the English Plantagenet kings. In the Middle Ages, however, they were not as richly endowed as the larger mendicant orders. The monks usually lived in individual cells, sharing a common refectory. This arrangement can be seen in their largely 15th-century monastic buildings at Aylesford, England, founded in 1242. The ruins of the priory at Hulne, which was established at the same time, preserve the aisleless church plan with a long chancel and two cross walls, as preferred by the English Carmelites. Since the Order was dependent on donations from the faithful, the most conspicuous works of art in Carmelite churches were often to be seen in family chapels, in which private families could display their own importance as well as their pious donations. A well-known example is the fresco cycle begun by Masaccio in S Maria del Carmine, Florence, commissioned by Felice Brancacci, a prosperous silk merchant. Similarly, Bernini's *Ecstasy of St Teresa* was endowed by the wealthy family of the Venetian Cardinal Federigo Cornaro (*d* 1653; *see* BERNINI, (2), §I, 1 (iii)).

Despite their simple ideals the Discalced Carmelites themselves attracted donations on such a large scale that they became extremely wealthy and erected magnificent churches. A prominent example is S Maria degli Scalzi (S Maria di Nazareth), Venice, begun by Baldassare Longhena in 1656. In reply to criticism of the extravagance of their church, in 1734 they claimed that the Venetian monastery was no more splendid than the sister church of S Maria della Vittoria (1608–12), Rome, by Carlo Maderno. They further defended their position by arguing that St Teresa herself had preferred magnificence in churches, although living-quarters should, of course, be as simple as possible.

BIBLIOGRAPHY

[Teresa of Ávila]: 'Libras de livra de St Teresa', *Obras completas*, ed. Louis de Lyon (Salamanca, 1588); trans. by J. M. Cohen as *The Life of St Teresa by herself*, Penguin Classics (Harmondsworth, 1987)
E. Mâle: *L'Art religieux après le Concile de Trente* (Paris, 1932)
L. C. Sheppard: *The English Carmelites* (London, 1943)
D. Knowles: *The Religious Orders in England*, i (Cambridge, 1948); ii (Cambridge, 1955)
M. Rickert: *The Reconstructed Carmelite Missal: An English Manuscript of the Late XIV Century in the British Museum* (London, 1952)
W. J. McDonald, ed.: *New Catholic Encyclopaedia*, iii (New York, 1967), pp. 113–26
J. J. Bardel: 'Gaspard Dughet and San Martino ai Monti', *Stor. A.*, xxvi (1976), pp. 45–60
W. Barcham: 'Giambattista Tiepolo's Ceiling for S Maria di Nazareth in Venice: Legend, Traditions, and Devotions', *A. Bull.*, lxi (1979), pp. 430–47
J. Cannon: 'Pietro Lorenzetti and the History of the Carmelite Order', *J. Warb. & Court. Inst.*, i (1987), pp. 18–20
C. Gilbert: 'Some Special Images for Carmelites, circa 1330–1430', *Christianity and the Renaissance: Image and Religious Imagination in the Quattrocento*, ed. T. Verdon and J. Henderson (Syracuse, NY, 1990), pp. 161–207

DEBORAH HOWARD

Carmichael, Peter. *See under* COCKS AND CARMICHAEL.

Carmina figurata. Term used to describe poems in which certain letters or words are contained within patterns or compositions to form independent phrases or verses within regular lines of continuous text (see fig. in which, for example, Christ's halo contains the words 'Rex regum et dominus dominorum'). Anticipated in Hellenistic poetry, *carmina figurata* were introduced to the Latin world *c.* AD 320 by Publilius Optatianus Porfyrius, court poet of Constantine the Great. Porfyrius' poems were widely copied and imitated in the early Middle Ages because the juxtaposition of poetic and visual configurations lent itself to the exposition of layers of theological thought. They were composed by Venantius Fortunatus (*fl c.* 530–610) and St Boniface (*c.* 680–754), among others, and appealed particularly to scholars of the Carolingian Renaissance. Alcuin of York (*fl c.* 735–804), his pupil Josephus Scotus (*d* 791) and Theodulph, Bishop of Orléans, all wrote *carmina figurata*, but the most influential work was created *c.* 810 by Alcuin's pupil Hrabanus Maurus (*fl c.* 776 or 784–856), later Abbot of Fulda (822–42) and Archbishop of Mainz (847–56). His *De laudibus sanctae crucis* is a collection of 28 poems accompanied by prose versions and explanations, the whole presenting the cross in different permutations as the mystical structure of the cosmos, which embraces and clarifies every aspect of creation and salvation. There are 48 surviving copies of the work, and the lost luxury editions that Hrabanus is also known to have had made for Louis the Pious (*reg* 781–840), Pope Gregory IV (*reg* 827–44) and Otgar, Archbishop of Mainz (*reg* 826–47), are reflected by the exceptional quality of the finest of the extant copies (Rome, Vatican, Bib. Apostolica, MS. Reg. lat. 124; and Vienna, Österreich. Nbib., Cod. 652).

BIBLIOGRAPHY

E. Kluge: 'Studien zu Publilius Optatianus Porfyrius', *Münchn. Mus. Philol. Mittelalt. & Ren.*, iv (1924), pp. 323–48
K. Holter, ed.: *Hrabanus Maurus, Liber de laudibus sanctae crucis: Vollständige Faksimile Ausgabe des Codex Vindobonensis der Österr. Nationalbibliothek* (Graz, 1973)
H.-G. Müller: 'Hrabanus: De laudibus sanctae crucis', *Beihft Mittelaltein. Jb.*, xi (1973), pp. 1–409

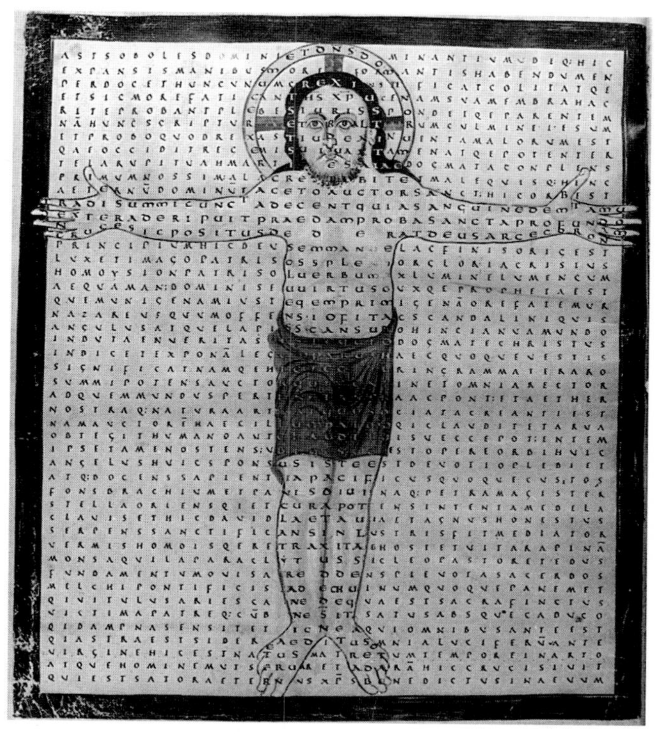

Carmina figurata in Hrabanus Maurus: *De laudibus sanctae crucis* with illumination of *Christ*, Corbie, 9th century (Amiens, Bibliothèque Municipale, MS. 233, fol. 6*v*)

F. Mütherich: 'Die Fuldaer Buchmalerei in der Zeit des Hrabanus Maurus', *Hrabanus Maurus und seine Schule: Festschrift der Hrabanus-Maurus-Schule, 1980* (Fulda, 1980), pp. 94–125

JOACHIM E. GAEHDE

Carmona, Salvador. *See* SALVADOR CARMONA.

Carmontelle, Louis de [Carrogis, Louis] (*b* Paris, 15 Aug 1717; *d* Paris, 26 Dec 1806). French draughtsman, designer and writer. He began his career as tutor to children of nobility, among them those of the Duc de Luynes at the château of Dampierre, where in 1754 he redesigned the park in the English manner. During the Seven Years' War he worked as a topographical artist for Pons de Saint-Maurice and made portraits and caricatures of the soldiers in his regiment. Pons de Saint-Maurice recommended him to Louis-Philippe, Duc d'Orléans (1725–85), who in 1763 appointed him *lecteur* to his son Philippe, Duc de Chartres. Carmontelle quickly became involved in all aspects of the ducal household, notably in the theatre; he wrote 'proverbes' (playlets illustrating a moral point) for it and supervised their production to his own designs. His texts were published as *Proverbes dramatiques* between 1768 and 1787, but his illustrations to them remained unpublished until 1933 (original drawings at Chantilly, Mus. Condé). He also recorded the members of the ducal household at the Palais Royal and at Villers-Cotterets in a series of portrait drawings, in pencil and watercolour or gouache. These were made rapidly, often in less than two hours, and almost all show the sitter full-length in profile. They are an invaluable record of both courtiers and distinguished visitors, such as the young *Mozart with his Father and Sister* (1763) and *David Hume* (*c.* 1763–5; Edinburgh, N.P.G.). Carmontelle retained most of these drawings himself but occasionally gave replicas to the sitters. At his posthumous sale on 17 April 1807, some 750 of his drawings, uniformly mounted, were sold; the largest surviving group is now at the Musée Condé, Chantilly. Such was their renown that 27 were engraved at the request of Catherine the Great of Russia. Among his other activities, from 1783 Carmontelle painted panoramas 'en transparence' for projection in a magic lantern and made six etchings, five after his own portraits. More important, he designed the parks at Le Raincy, near Paris and Monceau (now in Paris); his account of the Parc Monceau, illustrated with engravings after his drawings, amounts to a theoretical treatise against the monotony of the *jardin anglais.* Instead, he wished 'to reunite in one garden all times and places', which resulted in the extraordinary theatrical variety of the Parc Monceau. Carmontelle is traditionally assumed to be the author of a substantial body of art criticism, written in response to the Salons held between 1779 and 1789 and published anonymously. Although the attribution of these pamphlets has recently been disputed (see Crowe, p. 261), their importance remains indisputable, for they provide very clear indications of the political context of pre-Revolutionary painting.

WRITINGS

Jardin de Monceau, près de Paris, appartenant à S.A.S. Mgr le Duc de Chartres (Paris, 1773)
Coup de patte sur le sallon de 1779: Dialogue précédé et suivi de réflexions sur la peinture (Paris, 1779)
La patte de velours pour servir de suite à la seconde édition du Coup de patte, ouvrage concernant le sallon de peinture. Année 1781 (London, 1781)
Le Triumvirat des Arts, ou Dialogue entre un peintre, un musicien et un poète sur les tableaux exposés au Louvre. Année 1783 ([Paris], 1783)
Le Frondeur ou Dialogues sur le Sallon par l'auteur du Coup-de-patte et du Triumvirat ([Paris], 1785)
Vérités agréables ou le Salon vu en beau par l'auteur de Coup de patte (Paris, 1789)

Carnac, megalithic alignments, Late Neolithic period, *c.* 3000 BC

BIBLIOGRAPHY

DBF
F.-A. Gruyer: *Chantilly: Les Portraits de Carmontelle* (Paris, 1902) [catalogue of 484 drawings in the Musée Condé]
Louis de Carmontelle: Lecteur du duc d'Orléans (1717–1806) (exh. cat. by L. Vauxcelles, Paris, Gal. André Weil, 1933)
M. Roux: *Inventaire du fonds français: Graveurs du dix-huitième siècle*, Paris, Bib. N., Cab. Est. cat. (Paris, 1934), pp. 434–6
J. Mierral-Guérault: 'L'Oeuvre pictural de Carmontelle', *Positions des thèses des élèves de l'Ecole du Louvre, 1948–1952* (Paris, 1956), pp. 301–8
T. Crowe: *Painters and Public Life in Eighteenth-century Paris* (New Haven and London, 1985)

RICHARD JOHN

Carnac. Region of north-west France, centre of the principal concentration of prehistoric megalithic monuments (*see* MEGALITHIC ARCHITECTURE, §2) in Brittany. Situated south-west of Vannes, the area includes the parishes of Carnac and Locmariaquer, extending to Quiberon. The monuments include more than a hundred passage graves (dolmens) and many standing stones (menhirs) arranged singly or in groups including large alignments (*see also* DOLMEN and MENHIR). Curiously, these numerous and often huge stones did not attract the attention of scholars before the 18th century.

The typical large alignments, three of which are at Carnac and another at Erdeven, have one or two oval structures of contiguous stones at each end. Between these, ten to twelve apparently parallel lines of more or less equally spaced stones extend over a distance that can exceed a kilometre (see fig.). In reality, these lines are irregular and undulating, and the structures are very ruined; some stones are missing, while others have been restored. The stones decrease in size from the ends of the alignments towards their centres. Neolithic-period material, including flints, stone axes and pottery, has been found in the packing around their bases. The blocks are of local granite; a few are quite large and heavy. Wild speculations concerning their alignments' ritual or symbolic significance have flourished, particularly in the 19th century, when the first theories about astral worship and astronomical use originated. The alignments differ in orientation, however, and there is no scientifically conclusive evidence to support even the most recent hypotheses, although some large isolated menhirs could have served as foresights for solar or lunar observation.

Early in the Neolithic period the largest surviving stone of all, at Locmariaquer (*h* 20 m), and other decorated menhirs from Locmariaquer were broken and their fragments reused as capstones in neighbouring passage graves and also for GAVRINIS. As in the case of many large elements at Locmariaquer, these granite blocks came from some distance away, implying that the builders were skilled in moving large stones. Stones and slabs from older dismantled monuments, sometimes decorated, were also reused in other tombs. A few huge cairns and mounds of both the round and the elongated types contain closed chambers, sometimes with smaller satellite rooms; the longer structures have an independent passage grave at the end. The grave goods found in these closed chambers are exceptional and include prestige stone implements of rare materials, such as beautiful jadeite axes, and pendants and beads of hard stone. These are found in individual graves, presumably of upper-class people belonging to a ranked society of some kind. In contrast, the passage graves were used as collective tombs. The covers of these mounds may have different layers, and their structures sometimes show accretion.

The passage graves can be typologically classified into several varieties; the sequence of grave goods confirms their chronology. The orthostats of the earlier monuments can have a slightly anthropomorphic outline; more often anthropomorphic 'escutcheons' are pecked or incised on them. Other more or less recognizable motifs include 'croziers', hafted axes and stylized 'animals'. They can be deliberately grouped or randomly associated: in the later angled passage graves there is a more integrated and distinctive use of the 'escutcheon' idols. Evidence from those districts (such as Normandy and Poitou) where bones have been preserved shows that these collective tombs were only used for the burials of certain people and indicates that their function was not purely funerary. Always situated on slightly elevated ground, these monuments were often reused in the Late Neolithic period and Early Bronze Age (*c.* 3000–*c.* 2000 BC). Late Neolithic gallery graves are known but are not common in this region, although they are numerous elsewhere in Brittany.

Traces of contemporary settlement sites are rare; in the later Neolithic period there was a tendency to regroup habitations in slight elevations that may have been fortified, as at Le Lizo, Carnac. The rising sea-level would have inundated the best low-lying ground, but around the monuments at Locmariaquer and elsewhere there are traces of diverse activities. Also, earth from occupation levels, full of debris, has often been utilized in the building of the mounds, and numerous postholes of an earlier building were discovered under the cairn of the impressive passage grave known as the Table des Marchands at Locmariaquer. Bronze Age and Iron Age occupation is less evident in the district, but Locmariaquer was an important Gallo-Roman site.

For further discussion of the art and architecture of Neolithic Europe *see* PREHISTORIC EUROPE, §IV.

BIBLIOGRAPHY

P. R. Giot, J. L'Helgouach and J. L. Monnier: *Préhistoire de la Bretagne* (Rennes, 1979)
P. R. Giot, J. Briard and L. Pape: *Protohistoire de la Bretagne* (Rennes, 1979)

P. R. GIOT

Carnegie, Andrew (*b* Dunfermline, Scotland, 25 Nov 1835; *d* Lenox, MA, 11 Aug 1919). American industrialist and patron of Scottish birth. He emigrated with his family to the USA in 1848 and settled in poverty with them in Allegheny, near Pittsburgh, PA. Entirely self-educated from the age of 11, by his own efforts and skilful investment he acquired an enormous fortune in railways, oil, and the iron and steel industry. He donated more than £350 million to a variety of social, educational and cultural causes, the best-known of which was his support of the free public library movement with grants for buildings, which he believed would provide opportunities for self-improvement without any taint of charity. Carnegie's first library gift went to his native city of Dunfermline in 1881, followed by a library and clubhouse complex for Braddock, PA (opened 1889), where his principal steel plant was located, and a library and opera house for Allegheny (opened 1890). His most ambitious cultural creation was the Carnegie Institute at Pittsburgh, where a city library, concert hall, natural history museum, architecture hall and art gallery complex was built in stages by the architects Alden and Harlow between 1891 and 1907. Altogether *c.* 3000 libraries and city branches were constructed throughout the English-speaking world in the main period of his philanthropy, which extended from the late 1890s to 1917, when America's entry into World War I curtailed non-essential building. The USA received half of these libraries, typically costing between £10,000 and £20,000 and located in the small towns of the Midwest and the West Coast, as well as in the industrial cities. Communities were expected to engage their own architects, and they were required to provide a site and promise annual support for the library of not less than 10 per cent of Carnegie's grant. Almost every architectural style is represented, the so-called 'Carnegie Classical' predominating simply as the conventional style for public architecture of the period.

See also LIBRARY, §II, 3.

BIBLIOGRAPHY

T. W. Koch: *A Book of Carnegie Libraries* (New York, 1917)
B. J. Hendrick: *Andrew Carnegie*, 2 vols (New York, 1932)
G. S. Bobinski: *Carnegie Libraries: Their History and Impact on American Public Library Development* (Chicago, 1969)
J. D. Van Trump: *An American Palace of Culture: The Carnegie Institute and Carnegie Library of Pittsburgh* (Pittsburgh, 1970)
J. F. Wall: *Andrew Carnegie* (London and New York, 1970)
The Taste of Andrew Carnegie (brochure by A. Blaugrund and S. M. Sivard, New York, NY Hist. Soc., 1991)

SIMON PEPPER

Carneiro, António Teixeira (*b* Amarante, 16 Sept 1872; *d* Oporto, 31 March 1930). Portuguese painter, draughtsman and illustrator. He was brought up in an orphanage in Oporto, where he attended the drawing class of the Escola de Belas-Artes; there he was a pupil of António Soares dos Reis and then studied painting from 1890 to 1896. In 1897 he went to Paris with a grant from the Marquês de Praia e Monforte. From 1897 to 1899 he attended the Académie Julian, where he was a pupil of Jean-Paul Laurens and Benjamin Constant. The Parisian *fin-de-siècle* ambience helped form his style. The influence of Pierre Puvis de Chavannes, Eugène Carrière and the Symbolism of Edvard Munch were important in his work. In his first major painting, the triptych *Life* (1899–1901; Vila Nova de Famalicão, Fund. Cupertino de Miranda), Carneiro developed his personal vision of Symbolism on the theme of hope, love and *saudade* (longing or nostalgia), inspired by Puvis de Chavannes and with the crisp, sweet drawing and pale colours of that artist.

In 1899 Carneiro travelled in Italy and afterwards returned to settle in Oporto, where he taught drawing at the Escola de Belas-Artes from 1918. He also devoted himself to portrait painting in oils and red crayon. He counted intellectuals and poets among his friends and illustrated their works and did their portraits. His interest in self-analysis is seen in the fine *Self-portrait* (*c.* 1903; Oporto, Casa–Oficina Carneiro). In 1907 he decorated the Oporto Stock Exchange with allegorical murals.

The work of Carneiro possesses a tendency towards Naturalism combined with idealism and mysticism, and he shows a need to imbue concrete forms with symbolic meaning. His land- and seascapes, such as *Landscape at Melgaço* (1921; Lisbon, Mus. Gulbenkian), are especially lyrical and evocative. He created his own vision of the world in dreamy and mysterious images seen in a series depicting the beaches at Leça da Palmeira (1911–17; Matosinhos, Col. Mun.). These luminous compositions are painted in shades of pink and green, and scenes of dusk are in tones of blue.

Carneiro belonged to the group of intellectuals known as the *Renascença Portuguesa* whose neo-Romantic, nationalistic and reactionary ideas were expressed in the magazine *A Águia*, of which he was artistic director from 1917 to 1927. He produced many sanguine drawings and book illustrations, often for authors from the group. His 42 drawings for Dante's *Inferno* (1928) were part of an incomplete project to illustrate the *Divine Comedy*. He also wrote a collection of sonnets, *Solilóquios*, which were published posthumously (Lisbon, 1936). One of his last paintings, *Camões Reading the Lusiads to Dominican Friars* (1927; Oporto, Casa–Oficina Carneiro), is more decorative and marks the end of a series of church interiors.

BIBLIOGRAPHY

J. Alves: *António Carneiro e a pintura portuguesa* (Oporto, 1972)
António Carneiro (exh. cat. by J.-A. França, Lisbon, Gulbenkian Mus., 1973)
Soleil et ombres: L'Art portugais du XIXème siècle (exh. cat. by J.-A. França, Paris, Petit Pal., 1987–8), pp. 278–83

RUTH ROSENGARTEN,
LUCÍLIA VERDELHO DA COSTA

Carneo [Carniello]**, Antonio** (*b* Concordia Sagittaria, nr Venice, 26 Nov 1637; *d* Portogruaro, 16 Dec 1692). Italian painter. He was a highly original artist, whose eclectic style is dazzlingly varied, and who brought new vigour to painting in the Veneto. His life and career are sparsely documented. His father, Giacomo Carneo, was an artisan and bell-ringer, and it is not clear how Antonio acquired his knowledge of painting, which was rooted in the art of the Venetian Mannerists such as Pordenone, Tintoretto, Veronese and Palma Giovane, yet extended to the painterly Baroque style of Rubens, Johann Liss, Bernardo Strozzi, Francesco Maffei, Bernhardt Keil, Sebastiano Mazzoni, Giovanni Battista Langetti and Luca Giordano. A period of about ten years in Cordovado, beginning in or before 1658, is documented. It has been suggested (Pallucchini) that sometime in the 1660s he worked in Pietro della Vecchia's studio.

In 1664, shortly before moving to Udine, he painted an *Immaculate Conception* (untraced) for S Paolo al Tagliamento, Cordovado. Udine became his adopted home, and there he enjoyed the generous support of Conte Leonardo Caiselli and Conte Giovan Battista Caiselli. He probably had connections with Giuseppe Cosattini (1625–99), a pupil of Alessandro Varotari, whose influence can be seen in the rather mechanical *Holy Family Revered by the Lieutenant and Deputies* (1667; Udine, Mus. Civ.). In the same years Carneo developed a highly realistic style of portraiture, as in the portrait of *Ferdinando Prampero* (1668; Udine, Mus. Civ.) and his portraits of *Giovan Battista Caiselli* and *Leonardo Caiselli* (Udine, priv. col.), which alternated with the vivid Caravaggesque naturalism of his early genre scenes, such as *The Fortune-teller* (Udine, Banca del Friuli) and *The Vagabond* (Udine, Mus. Civ.). There followed, between 1680 and 1690, the *Martyrdom of St Bartholomew* (Udine, Basilica delle Grazie), distinguished by an increasingly Baroque, vibrant touch, and a series of violent scenes of death and torture, such as the *Death of Lucretia* (Warsaw, N. Mus.), which are influenced by the Venetian tenebrists, and in which the dark, thick paint echoes the handling of Langetti.

In 1689 Carneo retired to Portogruaro, where he finished the altarpiece of the *Virgin, St Zeno and Mary Magdalene* for the church of Fossalta. In his later works, beginning with the *Education of the Virgin* (1690; Udine, S Cristofero) he returned to his roots. His palette became lighter, and closer to Veronese, and his compositions attained a new classical simplicity and clarity. Among his last works were the small genre scenes formerly in the Caiselli collection in Udine, of *Shepherds*, *Travellers*, *Soldiers Resting*, *Card-players*, which are rather lifeless copies after prints by Abraham Bloemaert.

BIBLIOGRAPHY

DBI
A. Rizzi: *Antonio Carneo* (Udine, 1960)
B. Steinborn: 'Un Tableau d'Antonio Carneo à Wroclaw', *A. Ven.*, xxvi (1972), pp. 204–7
R. Pallucchini: *La pittura veneziana del seicento* (Milan, 1981), p. 272
G. Bergamini and S. Tavano: *Storia dell'arte nel Friuli–Venezia Giulia* (Reana del Rojale and Udine, 1984), pp. 439–43
C. Donazzolo Cristante: 'Antonio Carneo', *La pittura in Italia: Il seicento*, ed. M. Gregori and E. Schleier, ii (Milan, 1988, rev. 1989), pp. 671–2

GIUSEPPE PINNA

Carnevale [Carnovale]**, Fra** [Bartolomeo di Giovanni Corradini] (*fl* Florence, 1445; *d* Urbino, 1484). Italian painter. On 28 November 1445 he was described as a pupil of Fra Filippo Lippi. He was active in his home town of Urbino by 1451, when he received payments on behalf of the syndics of S Domenico for the doorway and glazed terracotta lunette commissioned from Maso di Bartolommeo and Luca della Robbia in Florence. He was absolved from painting an altarpiece in 1456. From 1461 he was parish priest at San Cassiano di Cavallino, near Urbino, but he appears to have been active in Urbino, where in 1467 he received payments for an altarpiece of the *Birth of the Virgin* for S Maria della Bella. This was his most famous work, which Vasari said influenced Bramante. The picture was confiscated by Cardinal Antonio Barberini in 1631 and has been identified with two panels from his collection (New York, Met., and Boston, MA, Mus. F.A.). Carnevale is listed in a later *memoria* among the engineers and architects of Federigo II da Montefeltro, Duke of Urbino.

See also MASTERS, ANONYMOUS, AND MONOGRAMMISTS, §I: MASTER OF THE BARBERINI PANELS.

BIBLIOGRAPHY

A. Schmarsow: *Melozzo da Forlì: Ein Beitrag zur Kunst und Kulturgeschichte Italiens im XV. Jahrhundert* (Berlin, 1886), pp. 361–2
K. Christiansen: 'For Fra Carnevale', *Apollo*, cix (1979), pp. 198–201
M. Strauss: *The Master of the Barberini Panels: Fra Carnevale* (diss., New York U., Inst. F. A., 1979)

KEITH CHRISTIANSEN

Carnevali [Carnovali]**, Giovanni** [il Piccio] (*b* Montegrino, Luino, Varese, 29 Sept 1804; *d* Caltaro sul Po, Cremona, 5 July 1873). Italian painter. He was sponsored by Conte Giovanni Spini to study at the Accademia Carrara, Bergamo. Here Carnevali was subject not only to the influence of his teacher, the Neo-classical painter Giuseppe Diotti, a former pupil of Andrea Appiani, but also to the great variety of Venetian Old Master paintings available to him in the academy's collection. Carnevali rapidly became one of Bergamo's most sought-after portrait painters, his work being much in demand among the intellectual élite of the town, such as *Giovanni Maironi da Ponte* (1826) and *Conte Guglielmo Lochis* (1835; both Bergamo, Gal. Accad. Carrara). His first public commission was the *Education of the Virgin* (1826) for the parish church of Almenno S Bartolomeo, near Bergamo. The altarpiece clearly shows the influence of Appiani, while for his portraits Moretto da Brescia and G. B. Moroni were also an important source of inspiration.

In 1831 Carnevali travelled to Rome. He also visited Parma, where he was attracted more by the soft outlines and colours in the work of Correggio and Parmigianino than by the Neo-classical artists. He returned to Lombardy in 1832 and opened a studio in Cremona. Two outstanding examples of his portraiture during this period are *Giovanni Beltrami* (1832–5; Cremona, Mus. Civ. Ala Ponzone) and *Conte Giuseppe Manara with a Negro Servant* (1842; Bergamo, priv. col.), both of which clearly refer to 16th-century Italian portraiture. In 1835 Carnevali transferred his studio to Milan, where it remained until his death.

A solitary and retiring character, he did not frequent Milanese artistic circles, acquiring a reputation for unconventionality in his life-style and in his art. Carnevali did not acquire great artistic renown in Milan, his style being the antithesis of that practised by the highly successful Francesco Hayez. Both artists have been identified as early exponents of the Italian form of Romanticism, but whereas Hayez tended towards the academic, Carnevali was more emotive and atmospheric. He placed many small touches of different colours on the canvas to produce a shimmering, luminous effect. Despite his artistic isolation in Milan, Carnevali was in contact with people connected with La Scala, and a number of important, full-length portraits such as that of *Rosa Mariani* (Cremona, Mus. Civ. Ala Ponzone) derive from this association.

In 1845 Carnevali visited Paris with Giacomo Trécourt (1812–82), head of the art school in Pavia and former fellow student at the Accademia Carrara. Both were primarily interested in seeing Delacroix's works, but Carnevali was also attracted by the light effects and the use of colour in the work of Jean-Baptiste-Camille Corot and the Barbizon school artists, which were reflected in his own *Landscape with Large Trees* (1850; Milan, Gal. A. Mod.), and in the work of Watteau, Jean-Honoré Fragonard and Correggio, whose influence can be seen in *Ariadne Abandoned* (*c.* 1850; Pavia, Pin. Malaspina).

The fruit of these multiple influences can be seen in three important late works. The church of S Martino in Alzano Maggiore, near Bergamo, probably commissioned the first of these, *Hagar in the Desert* (Bergamo, Gal. Accad. Carrara), around 1840, but Carnevali did not begin work on it until about 1855. Many related preparatory drawings and sketches for this painting survive. When completed in 1863, its grandiose, sweeping forms, combined with Carnevali's atmospheric interpretation of light

Giovanni Carnevali: *The Bather*, 1869 (Milan, Galleria d'Arte Moderna)

and colour, were so different from contemporary religious works that the paintings proved unacceptable to the church commissioners. Following a heated debate among Bergamo intellectuals, and despite Trécourt's defence of the work, it was eventually rejected. *Moses Rescued from the Waters* (1866; Bergamo, priv. col., see 1986 exh. cat., pl. 36) is perhaps one of Carnevali's most representative works. Its dream-like combination of landscape and figures, in which the action seems suspended in a pearly luminosity of fragmented brushstrokes, was of great importance to SCAPIGLIATI artists and remains one of Carnevali's most imposing and successful works. *The Bather* (1869; Milan, Gal. A. Mod.; see fig.) reveals yet another element in Carnevali's constantly evolving style, since it has been interpreted both as the culmination of his work in the Romantic vein and, in its treatment of the figure, as a parallel to Realism.

BIBLIOGRAPHY

DBI

Il piccio e artisti bergamaschi del suo tempo (exh. cat., Bergamo, Pal. Ragione, 1974) [incl. comprehensive bibliog.]

1886–1986. La Permanente: Un secolo d'arte a Milano (exh. cat., Milan Pal. Permanente, 1986)

CLARE HILLS-NOVA

Carnicero. Spanish family of artists. (1) Alejandro Carnicero taught three of his sons: Gregorio Carnicero (*fl c.* 1800), a sculptor and engraver, (2) Antonio Carnicero and Isidro Carnicero (1736–1804), a sculptor and painter, who became a director of the Real Academia di S Fernando, Madrid.

(1) Alejandro Carnicero (*b* Iscar, Valladolid, 17 June 1693; *d* Madrid, 6 Oct 1756). Sculptor and engraver. He trained in Salamanca under José de Larra, the nephew of Alberto Churriguera. Between 1726 and 1731 Carnicero collaborated with de Larra and others on the choir-stalls of Salamanca Cathedral, and he probably completed the choir-stalls in the monastery at Guadalupe between 1742 and 1744. In 1728 he was commissioned by the Carmelites of the Third Order (of which he had become a member in 1726) to do a polychromed wooden figure group of the *Virgin of Carmen with St Simon Stock and an Angel* for the chapel of the Carmelitas, Salamanca. From 1730 to 1732 he carved stone medallions with busts of kings for the façades in the Plaza Mayor at Salamanca. He carved a figure in wood of *St Michael* for the hospital of Navas del Rey, Castile (*in situ*). Between 1745 and 1750 he carved four wooden figures for the organ-case in León Cathedral (now dismantled, in store, León Cathedral). In 1749 Carnicero went to Madrid, where he had been commissioned to do three stone statues of Spanish kings for the Palacio Real (now in the park in front of the Palacio Real). A polychromed wooden figure of *Christ Falling under the Cross* (London, V&A) is based on a composition by Alessandro Algardi. The Baroque movement of Carnicero's figures is combined with the influence of a French courtly style typical of Spanish sculpture of the first half of the 18th century. He also made engravings after his own sculpture and was one of the first teachers of MANUEL FRANCISCO ALVAREZ DE LA PEÑA.

BIBLIOGRAPHY

Ceán Bermúdez
B. Velasco: 'Esculturas de Alejandro Carnicero en Salamanca', *Bol. Semin. Estud. A. & Arqueol.*, xl–xli (1975), pp. 679–82
J. J. Rivera: 'Alejandro Carnicero y el organo de la catedral de León', *Bol. Semin. Estud. A. & Arqueol.*, xliv (1978), pp. 485–90
J. J. Martín González: *Escultura barroca en España, 1600–1770* (Madrid, 1983), pp. 436–44

MARJORIE TRUSTED

(2) Antonio Carnicero [Carnicero Mancio] (*b* Salamanca, 10 Jan 1748; *d* Madrid, 21 Aug 1814). Painter and draughtsman, son of (1) Alejandro Carnicero. He arrived at the Court in Madrid with his father in 1749 and took part in the competitions held by the Real Academia de S Fernando, winning second prize in 1769 with the *Coronation of Alfonso XI and Queen Mary in the Monastery of Huelgas de Burgos* (Madrid, Real Acad. S Fernando, Mus.). In 1760 he won a scholarship to Rome, subsequently winning prizes from the Accademia di S Luca. On his return to Madrid in 1766 he worked as a portrait painter, producing works such as the portrait of *Doña Tomasa de Aliaga, Widow of Salcedo* (Madrid, Prado). In 1788 he was elected an honorary member of S Fernando. Under the protection of the Spanish prime minister, Manuel Godoy, Príncipe de la Paz, whom he painted on several occasions (e.g. *Portrait of Godoy*, Madrid, Real Acad. S Fernando, Mus.), and after painting the portraits of *Charles IV* and *Maria Luisa* (both Madrid, Monasterio de la Encarnación), he was appointed Pintor de Cámara in 1796. In 1798 he applied unsuccessfully for the post of drawing-master to the Prince of Asturias, the future Ferdinand VII, although by 1806 he was teacher of the Infante Princes. He was a refined draughtsman and prepared illustrations for the editions of Cervantes's *El ingenioso hidalgo Don Quixote de la Mancha* published by the Real Academia Española (Madrid, 1780; 1782). He also made the drawings for the handsome engravings (Madrid, Calcografía N.) of the Real Picadero (Royal Riding School). In addition to his portraiture, which displays a talent for realism and wit, although at times combined with slightly garish colours, Carnicero executed attractive and descriptive *costumbrista* paintings, depicting everyday life, popular gatherings and hunting scenes, for instance *Duck Shooting on the Albufera, Valencia* (*c.* 1802; Madrid, Pal. Real). His landscapes are less intuitive and appear rather schematic. One of his best-known narrative paintings is the *Ascent of a Montgolfier Balloon in Aranjuez* (*c.* 1783–90; Madrid, Prado), in which his descriptive method is evident.

BIBLIOGRAPHY

M. A. Martínez Ibáñez: 'La Tauromaquia de Carnicero', *Cuad. Cult.*, 14 (1979)
——: 'Dibujos inéditos de Antonio Carnicero Mancio de su etapa romana', *Archv. Esp. A.*, 211 (1980), pp. 384–6
——: 'Aportaciones de la figura del pintor Antonio Carnicero Mancio', *Archv. Esp. A.*, 214 (1981), p. 221
J. Camón, J. L. Morales and E. Valdivieso: *Arte español del siglo XVIII*, Summa A., xxvii (Madrid, 1984)
M. A. Martínez Ibáñez: *Antonio Carnicero Mancio: Pintor* (diss., U. Complutense de Madrid, 1987)

JUAN J. LUNA

Carnival. Term used to describe public revelling that includes music, dance or performance. It is characterized mainly by the elaborate costumes that are created specifically for it. In countries where the Roman Catholic tradition is dominant, carnival denotes a period of variable duration that ends at midnight before Ash Wednesday, although in some localities the latter day can also be included. In these contexts, therefore, it is a specific calendrical event generally associated with forthcoming Lent. It is often referred to with the French Mardi Gras, which properly applies to only Shrove Tuesday. The term has, however, become used more generally; it may entail demonstrating, occasionally with explicit, if satirical, political overtones. It also denotes indoor partying and feasting of the kind arranged by community organizations or private individuals. The English equivalent of carnival as an annual event, Shrovetide, seems to be disappearing with the decline of the activities customarily connected with the period in the popular culture of the British Isles.

This article is a general discussion of the history of pre-Lenten carnival. For a discussion of the ephemeral art and architecture associated with such public festivities as pageants or royal entries, *see* PAGEANT AND FESTIVAL ARTS. For a discussion of mask and masquerade in Africa, on which a number of Afro-Caribbean cultures draw for carnival, *see* AFRICA, §VI, 3.

1. Origins. 2. Symbolism. 3. Modern development.

1. ORIGINS. The etymology of the term has long been debated, but consensus concentrates on a root *carnem levare* (Lat. 'to put away the flesh [as food]'), from which derive *carnis levamen*, *carnelevarium*, *carnilevaria* and other terms. This makes 'carnival' an inverted metonymy of

Lent and its fasting connotations. In German, however, the term for carnival is *Fastnacht* ('the night of fasting'). In considering carnival not as an isolated event but as part of the wider cycle of Christmas and Easter celebrations, there appears to be continuity between it and the winter masquerades that in Europe mark the Christmas season; the relation of opposition between carnival and Lent is crucial to the definition of both. The structural relation between the two periods is still explicit in Provence in France, where carnival is known as Carêmentrant ('coming Lent'), in Belgium, where Mardi Gras is called Quaresmel (from *Quaresima*, the Roman Catholic term for Lent) and in several other variants on the basic form. The opinion widely held by folklorists is that carnival is a historical and structural transformation of pre-Christian winter festivals, such as the Roman Saturnalia (kalends of January), Lupercalia (15 and 16 February), Brumalia (late February) and Matronalia (kalends of March). The overall symbolism of Saturnalia, for example, is considered by many to be the most probable historical model of carnival-like behaviour. One hypothesis is that carnival is also linked etymologically with *carrus navalis*, a boat-shaped wagon drawn by horses, which carried the revellers. Livy (*History of Rome* II.xxi) tells of how the Saturnalia were officially established in 495 BC, although some authorities maintain that the festival must have been older. Tacitus (*Annals* XIII.xv) mentions the custom of electing a King of the Saturnalia, a feature of carnival celebrations throughout Europe. The Saturnalia fell in the last days of December through to the beginning of January, and it was characterized by the inversion or disregard of normal social rules. According to Virgil (*Georgics* II.387), the earliest masks were made of bark; other materials were introduced later, while mask types multiplied into a wide range of characters. Lupercalia was explicitly linked to women's fertility, a theme recurrent in Matronalia, while at Brumalia men and women revelled in the streets, wearing animal skins and ivy garlands and hailing the end of winter. Some historians, on the other hand, claim that carnival is a specific development of the Christian era, dating only to the Middle Ages.

In synthesis, although carnival as such is probably a medieval development that became increasingly influenced by Lent in both its timing and symbolism, it grew out of a pan-European complex system of winter masquerading related to the seasonal passages still recognizable in European folklore. Church policies succeeded, at least partially, in absorbing by assimilation the masquerades of the Christmas–Epiphany cycle. This was achieved occasionally through the provision of official functional equivalents for masquerading and revelling, such as the Festum Stultorum or Asinaria Festa (Feast of Fools), celebrated by the lower clergy on the day of the Holy Innocents (28 December) and the New Year well into the 17th century. What remained of winter masquerading was then pushed further along the Christian liturgical calendar to become 'squeezed' between the Epiphany and Lent, a period of low ebb between two strongly characterized cycles.

2. SYMBOLISM. The symbolism of carnival includes a large variety of forms according to time and place. The earliest documents concerning winter masquerading and carnival proper refer to masks and performances still largely present in contemporary celebrations. The 13th-century document *De ludo carnelevar* is considered the earliest known description of carnival. The event described took place in the presence of the Pope in Testaccio, a quarter in Rome where public festivals had been held since antiquity. At the core of the event were a bear hunt, a bullock hunt and a cock hunt. The three animals are interpreted as embodiments of the Devil, Pride and Lust respectively. The killing of the animals was said to be a metaphor for the renunciation of vices in the forthcoming Lent.

Contest is one of the characteristics of carnival involving games and competitions between opposed groups. In Rome, the Feste di Testaccio (see fig. 1) involved a sequence of hotly contested horse races and tournaments. These provided the core of carnival celebrations until the 1870s and 1880s, when they were repeatedly banned by the authorities due to their alleged 'uncivilized' nature. In those years the Roman carnival was performed only intermittently, until its final death at the beginning of the 1890s. In England 'wild football' contests were (and occasionally still are) played in several towns at Shrovetide. Mock battles were fought on the river in Lille in France in the 18th century, in Trento, northern Italy, and in the Schembart Carnival of Nuremberg, Germany, in the 15th and 16th centuries. The latter is a well-known and exemplary case of carnival celebrations as they were staged by guild corporations throughout urban Europe in the late Middle Ages and the Renaissance. Revelling factions would antagonize one another either in formalized contests or simply by trying to outsmart one another in the pageants. The line between ritualized rivalry and open hostility would often be crossed, leading to violent outbursts of civil unrest. In Romans-sur-Isère near Valence, southern France, the carnival of 1580 ended in a bloodbath after the nobility and the craftsmen parties had worked each other up to a frenzy through staging provocative masquerades. Another instance of the contest paradigm turning into an occasion of open political revolt is that of the Keyenoba masquerade of Georgia: in 1894 the enactment of a mock battle between the Georgian king and the Keyen, a Georgian equivalent of the Carnival King in western Europe, was abolished after the festival turned into an overt attack against the tsar.

Throughout its history carnival took on increasingly overt political overtones, often stemming directly from the deliberate manipulation of its traditional symbolism. Between 1520 and 1543 in Germany a number of Fastnacht celebrations poked fun at the papacy through grotesque masquerading. Similarly, the execution of a puppet in Vibaudan, southern France, during the carnival of 1850 was perceived by the town authorities as a provocative reference to the revolution of 1848. Overall, the contest paradigm embraces the entire history of carnival as represented in the widespread iconography of the Battle between Carnival and Lent (*see* BRUEGEL, (1), fig. 1).

Another symbolic element of carnival is the execution of the scapegoat, often staged at the climax of celebrations throughout Europe. The propitiatory sacrificial victim is

1. Feste di Testaccio, Rome, mid-16th century (Rome, Gabinetto Nazionale delle Stampe)

widely identified with carnival itself, personified by overfed, lascivious and generally intemperate Kings of Misrule such as Hans Wurst (Hans the Sausage) in German contexts. The final pantomime would then entail the trial, sentencing and execution of the Carnival King, responsible for all that the masqueraders would judge as sin and misfortune. In Rome, well into the 19th century, Martedì Grasso was the day when criminals were publicly executed. The victims would often include a convicted Jew. Until abolition of this act by Pius IX in 1848, the Jewish community was forced to organize a running contest and to hand over a substantial sum of money, used by the Roman Senate to finance the carnival celebrations, amid the jibes and abuses of the populace.

Until abolition in the 1960s, the role of the scapegoat in southern Spain was sustained by La Mahoma, a gigantic representation of the head of the prophet Muhammad exploded at the end of a mock battle between Christians and Moors. If criminals, Jews and Moors often became the living targets for the 'Expulsion of Evil' during carnival, the personifications of carnival maintained more symbolic, as well as ritual overtones in rural areas. The hunt of mythical characters, such as the Salvanel of the Val di Fiemme in the Dolomites and of the Bear in the Pyrenees and Romania, went side by side with the slaughtering of 'carnivalesque', 'intemperate' animals such as the cock, the goose or the pig thrown into the crowd or awarded in contest-like performances. However, from Spain to the Pyrenees, across France and into Switzerland, the Italian peninsula, Central Europe and the Caucasus, carnival still 'dies' in comic fashion, its belly bursting open with sausages and wine, its testament full of promise for next year's revels. Variations on this theme often feature the resurrection of carnival, realized by mock surgical operations to free it of its overload of food and drinks.

In rural areas masquerades carry explicit connotations that betray their pre-Christian origins. The Schöneperchten and Schiacheperchten of southern Austria are a case in point. Perchta (or Berchta/Bertha) was a female civilizing hero in Germanic lore. The masquerades are arranged in contrasting sets of beautiful, gentle and 'positive' characters (Schöneperchten) in opposition to the monstrous and aggressive Schiacheperchten. Such contrast between 'positive' and 'negative' characters is widespread, as in the case of the ugly Tschäggäta and the gentle Otschi of Lötschental in Switzerland, the Schöne- and Wüeschte Schuppeln of Urnäsch in Switzerland, the Mascarade Rouge and the Mascarade Noire of the Basque region, the Mescres a Bel and the Mescres a Burt of the Dolomite Ladins and so on. Rural masquerades often feature characters related to Harlequin (from hell, *Hölle*) not only in their name but also sometimes in their attire and demeanour. The character appears in medieval manuscripts as the leader of the Mesnie Hellequin ('the family [or company] of Harlequin'), the Wild Hunt of ghosts and spirits of the underworld that all over Europe was said to haunt the nights in search of human game, especially on equinoxes and solstices.

European masks also have infernal origins. Maska appears in the Edict of Rotarius (AD 643) as a witch, a ghost or a spirit. Moreover, the array of masquerades between Christmas and Epiphany that feature monstrous and horrifying characters relates masks to the cluster of pan-European beliefs concerning the need to propitiate the infernal powers unleashed during the Twelve Nights that encompass the New Year festivities. Research in the 1980s tried to unravel the complex web of relationships between the historical, the mythical and the ritual aspects of masquerade. The association between masks and the underworld also makes sense of carnival as a rite of passage when the relationship between 'This' and the 'Other World' is renegotiated. In many instances from rural areas, masks of the Harlequin type plough the still-frozen land in what has been interpreted as a ritual of increase for the forthcoming agricultural season. Similarly, the leaps of the masks can be explicitly associated to the growth of the crops.

The symbolism of carnival as both a cosmic and a human rite of passage, entailing sacrifice to and propitiation of the chthonic forces, has helped to interpret some of its core sociological features. To date, across the more conservative cultural areas of the Alps, carnival marks the coming of age of a new generation. The youths celebrating their rite of passage to adulthood take the lead in the masquerades, often to the exclusion of all other social groups. From at least the Middle Ages carnival linked the mythical motif of the return of the dead to the initiation of young males in an explicit, if complex, network of symbolic relations. This led, in the Modern Age, to the development of more secular (or rather desymbolized) youth associations, such as the French *Bachelleries*, the historical antecedents of contemporary carnival societies.

The historical demise of the prescriptive, mandatory aspects of carnival as a rite of passage has favoured an explosion of creativity both in the masks' appearance and in the patterns of performance to be found in late 20th-century urban festivals. In this sense, it has been argued that the dilution of the masks' implicit ritual symbolism has transferred some of their dramatic strength from the masks' behaviour to their very appearance: for example, the Mescres a Burt (Ugly Masks) of the Dolomite Ladins performed in the past according to deviant, licentious and aggressive patterns; in modern times their behaviour has been greatly tamed, while their attire and facial disguises have become all the more grotesque and transgressive.

Some structural elements have, however, been retained, such as inversion. Its primary form involves the crossing of the divide between humans and animals. The latter include those who are the epitome of anti-human, anti-cultural behaviour and who are most likely to feature in the masquerades. Lustful cocks, stubborn donkeys, ferocious bears and irate, oversexed bulls predominate over animals perceived as 'closer' to human beings: dogs, cats and sheep do not enter the metaphorical bestiary. From cross-referencing the animal and the human world, a whole kaleidoscope of miscegenation develops, with monsters and hybrids articulating both moral and aesthetic metaphors and paradoxes.

Back in the realm of humans, ordinary clothes are often worn inside-out and back-to-front. Cross-dressing also occurs. Since masking is still often an exclusively male affair, male cross-dressing predominates, although in Germany and Sicily there are instances of carnivals involving exclusively women dressing as men. Cross-dressing may entail the exaggeration of primary and secondary sexual characteristics, while the whole of the body often becomes the privileged ground for the same aesthetic exercise. Limbs, appendages and other anatomical parts (hair, mouth, teeth, nose, eyes and ears) are stretched and enlarged by means of a variety of dramatic props, occasionally leading to the transgressive and grotesque satirization of well-known public figures, politicians, actors and fictional characters of the media industry being the favourite subjects.

Exaggeration may also take quite a different turn. In Caribbean carnival and increasingly in those American and European celebrations that are in one way or another related to them, exaggeration takes the form of glamorizing the (especially female) body. Multicoloured ribbons and veils, feathers, sequins, mirrors, lycra textiles and other such materials are arranged in oversized extensions of the bodily coverings, often inspired by local and global mythologies. The intention appears to be to expand the bodily space, both towards the transgressive, repulsive and grotesque as well as towards the alluring and seductive end of the dramatic spectrum.

3. MODERN DEVELOPMENT. The birth of a distinctly urban, modern tradition of carnival was due largely to transformations in the symbolism of masks introduced by the Renaissance development of the Italian *commedia dell'arte* (*see also* THEATRE, §III, 2(i)(b)). The masks shed both their wider symbolic connotations and their mythological references and came to embody individual psychological types. The chthonic underpinnings of such masks as Pulcinella (Punch), Arlecchino (Harlequin) and Zanni turned into definite comic characters (hence 'zany'). In the 16th century Harlequin wore a black mask and a patched costume and carried a bat, but by the 18th century he wore the more familiar diamond-patterned costume. Carnival became all the more an expression of individual creativity. The traditions of the Venice, Rome, Nice, Basle, Binche, Viareggio and other major historical and contemporary carnivals acquired their present structures mainly in the second half of the 19th century.

Parallel to that process, the confrontation of the colonizing powers of Portugal and Spain with the cultural traditions of the indigenous and slave populations in the American colonies paved the way to the development of what has become a carnivalesque tradition unparalleled in participation and magnificence. In Mexican popular culture, elements of the yearly, pre-Conquest ritual cycle merged with the popular traditions introduced by Spanish missionaries and lay colonizers. In the late 20th century the variety of Mexican masquerades reflects the highly diversified patterns of both native and Spanish inputs. In Brazil and the Caribbean the early disappearance of Amerindian culture fostered a pattern of development of urban masquerades in which the African element has become predominant. In Rio de Janeiro the Samba schools,

2. Carnival parade in Trinidad, showing Roman centurion costumes designed and made by Ken Morris, 1983

although rooted in the culture of the underclasses, draw to their carnival parades large numbers of middle- and upper-class revellers in what has been analysed by sociologists as a phenomenon underpinned by strong ideological and nationalistic overtones. In Haiti, carnival, mainly attended by the middle and the upper classes, is not particularly structured, focusing on individual masquerading. It is followed during Lent by the Rara festival celebrated by the Maroon population. The symbolism of Rara is rooted in the Haitian revolution of 1791 and in elements of Vodoun, in turn derived from the articulation of Yoruba and Kongo religious traditions with popular Roman Catholicism (*see* HAITI, §II, 2).

Elements of British and continental European folklore, such as the Mummers' Plays and the Hobby Horse, merged in the Christmas Jonkonnu (John Canoe) masquerades with African motifs introduced by the plantation workforce in Jamaica, Belize and the Bahamas (*see* JAMAICA, fig. 3). As well as John Canoe, characters include Pitchy Patchy, Horsehead and Amerindian. Masks are generally of decorated wire mesh. Variations of the Jonkonnu-type of celebration take place at Christmas and in the New Year in St Kitts and Nevis, the Dominican Republic and Bermuda. Costumes for these include capes decorated with mirrors, ribbons, or beads. Wire-screen masks are often attached to the sides of headdresses. Elements derived from the secret societies of Kongo as well as from the Ekoi and Efik societies of the Cross River area of Eastern Nigeria were at the roots of the Cabilda associations, which form the core of the *comparsas* of Cuban carnival. The *comparsas* are formed from groups of musicians, families or neighbourhoods. In Cuba and elsewhere throughout the Caribbean carnival traditions are strictly linked with the fight for emancipation from slavery and the subsequent struggle to impose the legitimacy of Black West Indian cultural expressions. The myriad symbolic costumes, motifs and music documented in Trinidad and Tobago over two centuries constitutes such an example (*see* TRINIDAD AND TOBAGO, §II, 2). The heart of this carnival is the period of two days and nights before Ash Wednesday. In 1983 the characters included Roman Centurions wearing copper armour and masks that drew upon African forms (see fig. 2).

The specific dynamics and complexities of the history of Caribbean carnival have developed its contemporary political significance as a fundamental (if disputed and contested) symbol of cultural and national identity. The late 20th-century carnivals of Toronto, Paris and Notting Hill in London are modelled on the carnival Mas ('mask') celebrations of Trinidad and Antigua (and to a lesser extent Rio); in their complex interplay of revivalist pan-African and militant symbolism, they articulate issues of ethnicity and cultural identity also detectable in the New Orleans Mardi Gras and in the Brooklyn Carnival in New York. Having borrowed symbolic and cultural elements from imported African traditions, by the end of the 20th century carnival had come almost full-circle back to the African continent: the Ode-lay masquerades of Freetown in Sierra Leone, although originating in the secret societies of the freed Yoruba slaves, came to be advertised as 'carnivals'.

For further illustration *see* ANTILLES, LESSER, fig. 2.

BIBLIOGRAPHY

J. Savaron: *Traité contre les masques* (Paris, 1608)
E. K. Chambers: *The Mediaeval Stage*, 2 vols (Oxford, 1903)
G. Antonucci: 'Carnis Levamen: Charivarium', *Flclor. It.*, second year, no. 1 (Oct 1926), pp. 9–13
F. Clementi: *Il carnevale romano nelle cronache contemporanee*, 2 vols (Città di Castello, 1938–9)
S. Sumberg: *The Nürnberg Schembart Carnival* (New York, 1941)
D. J. Crowley: 'The Traditional Masques of Carnival', *Carib. Q.*, iv/3 & 4 (March & June 1956), pp. 194–223 [double issue]
J. Caro Baroja: *El carnaval: Análisis historico-cultural* (Madrid, 1965)
E. Hill: *The Trinidad Carnival: Mandate for a National Theatre* (Austin, 1972)
L. Schmidt: *Perchtenmasken in Österreich* (Vienna, 1972)
C. Gaignebet and M.-C. Florentin: *Le Carnaval: Essais de mythologie populaire* (Paris, 1974)
S. Glotz, ed.: *Le Masque dans la tradition européenne* (Mons, 1975)
M. Mesnil: 'The Masked Festival: Disguise or Affirmation?', *Cultures*, ii (1976), pp.11–29
P. Burke: *Popular Culture in Early Modern Europe* (London, 1978)
B. Scribner: 'Reformation, Carnival and the World Turned Upside-down', *Soc. Hist.*, iii/3 (Oct 1978), pp. 303–29
A. Cohen: 'Drama and Politics in the Development of a London Carnival', *Man*, i (1980), pp. 65–87
J.Le Goff and J.-C. Schmitt, eds: *Le Charivari* (Paris, 1981)
R. da Matta: *Carnavais, malandros e heróis* (Rio de Janeiro, 1981)
E. Le Roy Ladurie: *Carnival in Romans: A People's Uprising at Romans, 1579–1580* (Harmondsworth, 1981)
M. Grinberg and S. Kinser: 'Les Combats de Carnaval et de Carême: Trajets d'une métaphore', *Annales*, i (1983), pp. 65–98
F. Manning, ed: *The Celebration of Society: Perspectives on Contemporary Cultural Performance* (Bowling Green, 1983)
T. Seboek, ed.: *Carnival!* (Berlin, 1984)
S. Kinser: 'Presentation and Representation: Carnival in Nuremberg, 1450–1550', *Representations*, ii (1986), pp. 1–41
J. Nunley: *Moving with the Face of the Devil: Art and Politics in Urban West Africa* (Urbana, 1986)
J.-C. Schmitt: 'Les Masques, le diable, les morts dans l'occident médiéval', *Razo*, vii (1986), pp. 87–119
J. Nunley and J. Bettelheim, eds: *Caribbean Festival Arts* (Seattle, 1988)
C. Poppi: 'Il bello, il brutto e il cattivo: Elementi d'analisi simbolica ed estetica delle maschere della Val di Fassa', *Faceres: Maschere lignee del carnevale di Fassa*, ed. F. Chiocchetti (Vigo di Fassa/Vich, 1988)
——: 'Il sesso degli angeli: Strutture simboliche e riti di passaggio nei carnevali dell'arco alpino', *Il carnevale: Dalla tradizione arcaica alla*

traduzione colta del rinascimento, ed. M. Chiabò and F. Doglio (Rome, 1989)
S. Kinser: *Carnival, American Style: Mardi Gras at New Orleans and Mobile* (London, 1990)

CESARE POPPI

Caro, Annibal [Annibale] (*b* Civitanova, Marches, 18 June 1507; *d* Rome, 20 Nov 1566). Italian writer and artistic adviser. The son of a merchant, he received a Classical education in Civitanova from the poet Rodolfo Iracinto before moving in 1525 to Florence, where he became secretary to Giovanni de' Gaddi. He accompanied his patron to Rome, where Gaddi was appointed Clerk of the Apostolic Chamber in 1529. He met many artists in Gaddi's circle, some of whom he subsequently assisted in obtaining commissions. These included Benvenuto Cellini, Alessandro Cesati, Niccolò Tribolo, Bartolomeo Ammanati and Giulio Clovio. Michelangelo was a friend and Caro owned a bronze head of the artist (Florence, Casa Buonarroti), possibly by Daniele da Volterra. In 1543 after Gaddi's death Caro entered the service of Pier Luigi Farnese, Duke of Parma, for whom he worked until the Duke's assassination in 1547. He then became secretary and chief artistic adviser to Pier Luigi's son, Cardinal Alessandro Farnese. His duties included supervising the execution of the Cardinal's commissions and devising iconographic programmes. He assisted Francesco Salviati in obtaining the commission (1548) from Cardinal Farnese for the Cappella del Pallio in the Cancelleria, Rome, and apparently recommended Daniele da Volterra to paint the frieze of scenes from the *Life of Bacchus* for the Cardinal's bedroom in the Palazzo Farnese. In 1551 Caro was responsible for overseeing the execution of Guglielmo della Porta's marble and bronze tomb of *Paul III* (Rome, St Peter's) and determining the allegorical figures for it.

Caro had a lasting and productive friendship with Giorgio Vasari. He was among those who first urged the artist to write the *Vite* (1550, rev. 2/1568), and he helped edit an early draft. In 1548 he commissioned Vasari to paint a *Venus and Adonis* (untraced), based on an *Idyll* of Theocritus. Caro also used Theocritus and other Hellenistic texts as the basis for the iconographic programmes that he wrote for Vasari during the 1550s. These include the frescoes that decorated two loggias of the palazzo and villa of BINDO ALTOVITI; (e.g. *Worship of Ceres*, Rome, Pal. Venezia) and those (destr.) for the loggia above the nymphaeum of the Villa Giulia, Rome. Caro's most important iconographic programmes are the sophisticated and erudite *invenzioni*, characteristic of Mannerist taste, for the Villa Farnese at Caprarola. The surviving decorations there, by Taddeo Zuccaro, are indicative of Caro's intentions and methods. For composing programmes he consulted handbooks of mythology such as Vincenzo Cartari's *Imagini delli dei degl'antichi* (1556), which supplied information about the appearance and attributes of individual figures, allowing the iconographer to concentrate on their meanings and disposition. Caro's programmes were extremely complex, even including instructions to the artist about colours and poses.

Caro owned a modest collection, which included several antique sculptures and some Classical manuscripts (inventory pubd in Greco, 1950). His portrait was painted by Agnolo Bronzino and by Salviati (both untraced). A posthumous bronze and marble bust by Antonio di Bernardino Calcagni survives (1566–72; London, V&A; for illustration *see* CALCAGNI, ANTONIO). Caro's collection contained portraits of relatives and friends, a miniature by Clovio and paintings of both religious and secular subjects, none of which can be identified. He also collected antique coins and wrote a treatise on the iconography of coins and medals (untraced). In 1563 he retired from Farnese service to Frascati, where he had built a villa (now part of the Villa Torlonia), although he continued to advise Onofrio Panvinio and Fulvio Orsini about iconography for the Cardinal. At Frascati, he completed a verse translation of Virgil's *Aeneid*. He was buried in S Lorenzo in Damaso, Rome; his funeral monument (1567–70) is by Giovanni Antonio Dosio.

WRITINGS

Opere, 8 vols (Milan, 1807–12)

BIBLIOGRAPHY

DBI
F. Sarri: *Annibal Caro* (Milan, 1934)
A. Greco: *Annibal Caro: Cultura e poesia* (Rome, 1950)
F.-E. Keller: *Zum Villenleben und Villenbau am römischen Hof der Farnese: Kunstgeschichtliche Untersuchung der Zeugnisse bei Annibal Caro* (Berlin, 1980)
C. Robertson: *Annibal Caro and the Visual Arts* (diss., U. London, 1981)
——: 'Annibal Caro as Iconographer: Sources and Method', *J. Warb. & Court. Inst.*, xlv (1982), pp. 160–81

CLARE ROBERTSON

Caro, Sir **Anthony** (*b* New Malden, Surrey, 28 March 1924). English sculptor. He had a conservative training from 1947 to 1952 at the Royal Academy Schools, London, which was greatly enriched by the two years (1951–3) he spent as assistant to Henry Moore, learning not only from his ideas but from the books in Moore's library. *Woman Waking* (1959; London, Tate) exemplifies Caro's work of the 1950s when he modelled figural works in a loosely expressionist vein that sought to express how the body felt from the inside out. The lumpy, awkward and ponderous masses of these works owe much to Picasso and Dubuffet, especially the latter's *Corps de dames* series of 1950. By the end of the decade Caro's growing dissatisfaction with this mode of working led him to experiment with other materials and more spontaneous effects, often explored during teaching projects at St Martin's School of Art, London, where he worked part-time from 1953. These experiments bore fruit after a visit to the USA from 1959 to 1960 during which he was influenced by the critic Clement Greenberg and by the work of such artists as Kenneth Noland and David Smith. On his return Caro began welding standardized metal units into abstract configurations, which were then further unified by being painted in a single primary colour. Although their syntax was derived from Cubism and was uncompromisingly abstract, these open form sculptures placed directly on the ground still related to the figure through their gestural or bodily calligraphy and scale. They rapidly took on a predominantly horizontal axis, a lyrical mood and a light open infrastructure of cantilevered planes and lines as in *Early One Morning* (1962; London, Tate; see fig.). Caro denied the weight, appearance and attendant connotations of the material and made sculpture which seemed almost to hover above the ground, touching it lightly at several discrete points. Throughout the later 1960s Caro also

Anthony Caro: *Early One Morning*, acrylic, plastic and synthetic resin, h. 2.90 m, 1962 (London, Tate Gallery)

made a number of small sculptures known as *Table Pieces*, incorporating tools, handles and other manual references in which he maintained an equivalence between size and scale without sacrificing that anonymous handling of material central to his practice. Caro's first solo show at the Whitechapel Art Gallery in London brought him considerable critical attention. He was quickly regarded as a major figure for his role, both through his work and his teaching, in re-orientating the mainstream of modernist British sculpture into an abstract constructed mode. The previous decade had been dominated by the monumental monolithic sculpture of Moore, and by the so-called 'Geometry of Fear', eviscerated figurative sculpture by artists such as Reg Butler and Lynn Chadwick. Caro's example can be said to have created a new school in its wake.

In 1972 Caro was invited to Verduggio in Italy where he found a factory that could provide him with a plentiful supply of irregularly shaped soft steel offcuts. Leaving the material raw, protected only by a coat of varnish, he manipulated these components into relatively simple planar configurations, often with a vertical orientation. His new-found affirmation of the literalness of the metal was offset by the associative character of its surfaces and textures as well as by the irregular shapes of the forms. These were akin to those found in the earlier paintings of Helen Frankenthaler, who had worked in his studio several months previously, and to the work of Jules Olitski. Following his major exhibition at MOMA, New York (1975), which subsequently toured the USA, his reputation in that country was high, notably in circles influenced by Greenberg's formalist aesthetic. A rare example of a public sculpture by Caro is *National Gallery Ledge Piece* commissioned by the National Gallery in Washington, DC, for the east building in 1978.

By the end of the decade Caro's growing fascination with freely formed metal had led him to experiment in welding sheet bronze, in addition to casting from found objects like pots, both whole and broken. The resulting sculptures were more insistently Cubist in character than his work of previous years, and became looser and grander during the early 1980s. By mid-decade the organic, even figurative, associations generated in his abstract metal sculpture had acquired a fully representational counterpart in the series of small-scale modelled sculpture of female figures derived from life drawings. References to the art of the past, which in later work informed Caro's sculpture more overtly, erupted in 1986 into a series of paraphrases made after an 11th-century sandstone Indian carving which he greatly admired. As a result of these investigations he alternated between the two idioms of abstract constructed sculpture and modelled figural bronzes.

BIBLIOGRAPHY

Anthony Caro (exh. cat. by M. Fried, ACGB, 1969)

Anthony Caro (exh. cat. by W. Rubin, New York, MOMA, 1975)

D. Blume and others: *Anthony Caro: Catalogue raisonné*, 5 vols (Cologne, 1982)

D. Waldman: *Anthony Caro* (Oxford, 1982)

Anthony Caro, Sculptor, 1969–84 (exh. cat. by T. Hilton, ACGB, 1984)

LYNNE COOKE

Caro, Lorenzo de (*fl* Naples, 1740–61). Italian painter. He is among the most individual and whimsical figures in 18th-century Neapolitan painting, although few of his works are known. He was probably a pupil of Francesco Solimena and adopted the brilliant painterly effects and bold brushwork of Solimena's late style. In 1740 he painted some canvases (dispersed) for the parish church of Cassino and worked in the church of the Cesarea in Naples at least until 1761, the date of the overarch painting. Most of his numerous works for Neapolitan churches and palazzi have been lost. He is most famous for his canvases depicting saints (1757–8) in SS Filippo e Giacomo, Naples. These are stylistically close to his *Charles of Bourbon Visiting the Abbey of Montecassino* (Naples, Pisani priv. col., see 1979 exh. cat., p. 247), which may be dated to the same period. The strongly characterized portraits in the latter work suggest contact with the work of Giuseppe Bonito.

Notable for their extraordinary spontaneous quality are two small canvases of the *Conversion of St Paul* and the *Triumph of Judith* (*c*. 1758; Marano di Castenaso, Molinari Pradelli priv. col., see 1979 exh. cat., p. 249). In these the composition is reminiscent of Solimena, but the interpretation is spirited, the touch rapid and the surface rich. In similar style is the *Immaculate Conception* (Naples, Palmieri priv. col., see 1979 exh. cat., p. 251), where the sumptuous colour and flickering effects of light and shade are analogous to those produced by contemporary Bohemian and Austrian artists. Indeed, de Caro has been confused with these painters, who were influenced by Piazzetta's response to the art of Solimena.

BIBLIOGRAPHY

DBI

Civiltà del settecento a Napoli, 1734–1799 (exh. cat., ed. N. Spinosa; Naples, Capodimonte, Pal. Reale and elsewhere; 1979–80), i, pp. 135–47, 246–51

La raccolta Molinari Pradelli: Dipinti del sei e settecento (exh. cat., ed. C. Volpe; Bologna, Pal. Podestà, 1984), p. 150

UGO RUGGERI

Caro, Rodrigo (*b* Utrera, nr Seville, 4 Oct 1573; *d* Seville, 10 Aug 1647). Spanish antiquarian, collector and writer. He came from a family of minor gentry. He studied canon law at the University of Osuna and obtained his degree at the University of Seville in 1596. Shortly afterwards he took holy orders and embarked on a career with the archbishopric of Seville. His life was uneventful, except for petty squabbles with other clerics and a brief banishment to Portugal in 1632 on account of a dispute with the king's tax collectors.

Caro was passionately interested in antiquity. Around 1595, when still a student at the University of Seville, he visited the ruins of the nearby Roman town of Italica. This inspired a poem, *Canción a las ruinas de Itálica*, in which he expressed his sorrow at the transience of greatness. Through these interests he became acquainted with men of letters in Seville in the circle of the painter and art theorist Francisco Pacheco (a group often misleadingly referred to as an 'academy'). Its members included the poets Francisco de Rioja (*c*. 1600–59) and Fernando de Herrera (1534–97), humanists and historians such as Juan de Robles (1574–1649) and Tomas Tamayo de Vargas (1588–1641) and such aristocrats as the erudite Fernando Enríquez de Ribera, 3rd Duque de Alcalá. Caro dedicated to Alcalá his *Relación de las inscripciones y antigüedad de la villa de Utrera* (1622) and to Alcalá's son, the Marqués de Tarifa, *Días geniales o lúdicros* (first pubd 1884). These works are antiquarian studies showing profound scholarship. Caro's position as visiting judge of the archbishopric enabled him to travel extensively within his jurisdiction and to gather first-hand information about coins, inscriptions and other antiquities. As his letters reveal, there was established a network of like-minded friends who shared their discoveries. Caro appears to have been partly motivated by an intense local patriotism and his aim to prove the antiquity and greatness of Utrera. His enthusiasm led to his deception by the forgeries of the Jesuit Jerónimo Román de la Higuera, author of the apocryphal 'Chronicals' of Dextrus and Maximus, which Caro himself edited in 1627. Caro's own works, such as *Antigüedades y principado de la ilustrissima ciudad de Sevilla* (1634), with the *Adiciones* (first pubd 1932), are scholarly and provide valuable information for modern archaeologists. He often mentioned his own collection in his writings; it was divided between his house at Utrera, where he kept the sculptures and larger pieces, and Seville, where he kept the coins, medals and smaller bronzes; it was apparently dispersed after his death. He made numerous gifts to other collectors in Seville, including the Duque de Arcos (1602–72) and Sancho Hurtado de la Puente.

Caro's late years were marked by poor health and disappointment that he did not receive anticipated favours through Francisco de Rioga, librarian to the all-powerful Prime Minister, the Conde Duque de Olivares.

WRITINGS

Antigüedades y principado de la ilustrissima ciudad de Sevilla y chorographia de su Convento Iuridico o antigua Chancilleria (1634, ed. facs. Seville, 1982)

Días geniales o lúdicros (1884, 2/Madrid 1978)

Varones insignes en letras naturales de la ilustrísima ciudad de Sevilla [y] Epistolario (Seville, 1915)

Adiciones al principado y antigüedades de la ciudad de Sevilla y su Convento Jurídico (Sevilla, 1932)

VICENTE LLEÓ CAÑAL

Carocci, Baverio de'. *See* BAVIERA.

Carocci, Guido (*b* Florence, 16 Sept 1851; *d* Florence, 20 Sept 1916). Italian art historian and writer. After leaving school at the age of 16, he briefly studied drawing and painting, and from 1866 he engaged in journalism. He wrote for *Fieramosca*, *Nazione* and other newspapers while pursuing an independent interest in history and art. He maintained a close connection between art and history in his thought and work as a writer and as a public official. His plainly composed writings focused on the history, arts, genealogy and topography of Florence and Tuscany and, as in *I dintorni di Firenze* (1881), showed him to be a meticulous researcher, a keen observer and an erudite historian. In 1882 he founded *Arte e storia*, a weekly (later monthly) journal, which he directed until his death and which achieved a wide circulation, becoming one of the most important periodicals of the time. It was designed to promote interest in the arts and encourage the study of history, and together with leading scholars and artists, he contributed numerous articles to it during his lifetime. From 1887 he held various offices in the administration of the regional office for the Belle Arti, culminating in the posts of Ispettore Regionale dei Monumenti (1891) and director of the Museo di S Marco (*de facto* 1892, officially 1909). In these various capacities he worked indefatigably to protect the integrity of Tuscany's artistic patrimony. Over the years Carocci compiled the *Schedario*, a comprehensive index—nearly 100,000 handwritten cards—of buildings, monuments, works of art, religious orders, families and coats of arms in Tuscany. This served as the basis for his major work, the catalogue of works of art and architecture in Tuscany, which was commissioned by the government. He began the *Catalogo* in 1887 and it comprises 25,000 cards divided into three parts, each part covering a different field. Each of the cards is located in the same province as the work of art to which it refers.

WRITINGS

I dintorni di Firenze (Florence, 1881, rev., 2 vols, 1906–7)

A. & Stor., founder and editor (1882–1916)

BIBLIOGRAPHY

DBI

G. Di Cagno: *Arte e storia: Guido Carocci e la tutela del patrimonio artistico in Toscana (1870–1915)* (Florence, 1991)

EFREM GISELLA CALINGAERT

Carol I, King of Romania [Carol of Hohenzollern-Sigmaringen, Prince of Romania] (*b* Sigmaringen, 20 April 1839; *reg* 1866–1914; *d* Peleş Castle, 27 Sept 1914). Romanian ruler, collector and patron. He was the son of Karl Anton, Prince of Hohenzollern-Sigmaringen (1811–85), who formed a large collection of German art (Sigmaringen, Fürst. Hohenzoll. Samml. & Hofbib.). Carol, who was elected Prince of Romania in 1866 and crowned king in 1881, benefited from a refined intellectual education enriched by visits to France, Italy, Spain and Portugal. During his brief period as a student at Bonn University in 1862, he was introduced to the history of art by Anton Springer, with whom he maintained contact, inviting him to Romania in 1871. From Carol Pop de Szathmari, his court painter and photographer, Carol commissioned photographic (1867) and chromolithographic (1868, 1883) albums with Romanian views and subjects (Bucharest, N. Mus. A. and Roman. Acad. Lib.).

Under the King's patronage, the architect André Lecomte du Noüy (1844–1914) restored several religious buildings in Romania, among them the episcopal church of CURTEA DE ARGEŞ (1517; rest. 1875–86), where members of the royal family are buried. Peleş Castle, initially designed by Wilhelm von Doderer (1825–1900), was built from 1875 to 1883 in the German Renaissance Revival style under the direct guidance of Carol I. The interior decoration in carved wood was executed by Martin Stöhr (1819–96), who had been brought by Carol I from Sigmaringen. In 1883 Gustav Klimt, his brother Ernst Klimt (1863–92) and their collaborator Franz von Matsch (1861–1942) executed historical portraits and decorative paintings for some of the halls of this castle.

Carol started to acquire Old Masters systematically in 1879. He bought them mainly from an important collection owned by Felix Bamberg (*b* 1820), a scholar and German consul. Carol's taste for Spanish painting was particularly evident in his purchases, which included nine canvases by El Greco, only three of which are still in Romania, for example the *Adoration of the Shepherds* (1600) and the *Betrothal of the Virgin* (*c.* 1613–14), as well as works by Francisco Zurbarán, Alonso Cano, José Antolínez and Juan de Valdés Leal. Italian schools occupied the largest part of Carol I's collection. He chose Quattrocento paintings by Domenico Veneziano and Marco Zoppo, works by Renaissance and Mannerist masters (Jacopo Bassano, Bernardino Licinio, Agnolo Bronzino and Pellegrino Tibaldi) and works of the Baroque period (by Pier Francesco Mola, Orazio Gentileschi, Mattia Preti, Luca Giordano and Jacopo Amigoni).

Carol also owned a small number of German works, including a *Venus and Cupid* (1520) by Lucas Cranach the elder. Flemish and Dutch schools were well represented in this rich ensemble. It comprised a portrait by Rubens, *Haman Praying Esther to be Forgiven* (*c.* 1660) by Rembrandt, biblical scenes by Jan Sanders van Hemessen, Bartholomäus Spranger and Pieter van Mol and flower pictures by Jan Breughel the elder and Rachel Ruysch. The entire collection was bequeathed to the Romanian crown, to be kept permanently in Romania, and formed the nucleus of the Universal Art Gallery of the National Museum of Art, Bucharest.

BIBLIOGRAPHY

Aus dem Leben König Karls von Rumänien: Aufzeichnungen eines Augenzeugens, 4 vols (Stuttgart, 1894–1900)

L. Bachelin: *Tableaux anciens de la Galerie Charles 1er, roi de Roumanie* (Paris, 1898)

P. Lindenberg: *König Karl von Rumänien* (Berlin, 1906, rev. 3/1923)

A. Tzigara-Samurcaş: 'Carol I şi monumentele străbune' [Carol I and the ancestral monuments], *Convorbiri Lit.*, xliii/4 (1909), pp. 358–71

A. Busuioceanu: *Ecoles italiennes du XIVe au XVIe siècle*, I/i of *La Galerie de peintures de sa majesté le roi Charles II de Roumanie* (Paris, 1939)

T. Enescu: 'La collezione di pittura europea del museo nazionale d'arte di Bucarest', *Capolavori europei dalla Romania* (exh. cat., Venice, Doge's Pal., 1991), pp. 21–4

REMUS NICULESCU

Caroline, Duchesse de Berry. *See* BOURBON, §I(15).

Caroline Islands. *See* MICRONESIA; PALAU.

Caroline Louise, Margravine of Baden-Durlach. *See* ZÄHRINGEN, (3).

Carolingian art. The art associated with CHARLEMAGNE, King of the Franks, from the last quarter of the 8th century AD, and with his successors, to the beginning of the 10th century. The territories they ruled comprise parts of present-day France, Switzerland, Germany, Austria and Italy, an area that in the 9th century enjoyed great cultural and artistic unity derived from the fusion of Insular and other recent art forms with those of late antiquity. In its strictest sense, the term does not cover Charlemagne's ancestors, the so-called Pepinists, nor the last Carolingian kings of France, Louis IV (*reg* 936–54), Lothair (*reg* 954–86) and Louis V (*reg* 986–7), although it is sometimes applied more widely. The term Carolingian was used as an art-historical concept by Kugler in 1837, followed in 1839 by Waagen. Kugler was also the first scholar to characterize the style of Carolingian art.

I. Introduction. II. Architecture. III. Sculpture. IV. Painting. V. Metalwork. VI. Ivories. VII. Rock crystal.

I. Introduction.

As the stewards of the Merovingian Frankish kings (*see* MEROVINGIAN ART), Charlemagne's forebears became increasingly powerful, exercising power over the kings themselves. Charlemagne became sole ruler in 771 and King of the Lombards in 774. He was crowned in Rome by Pope Leo III in 800 and, to reflect his avowed revival of the idea of the Roman Empire (*renovatio Romanorum imperii*), was called Emperor from 801. He extended the Frankish empire south, east and north, conquering the Saxons beyond the River Elbe, forcing their conversion to Christianity and establishing missionary bishoprics at Osnabrück, Paderborn, Minden and Münster.

The art that was created in Charlemagne's newly conquered territories during his reign can be described as Carolingian only if it is connected with his court or with the bishops and abbots associated with it, and the aims and initiatives of their artistic policies. After the court was permanently established at Aachen from 794 it became the point of departure for Charlemagne's religious and cultural reforms based on the *renovatio*, which aimed to revive specifically the Christian empire of Constantine. Charlemagne's team of international scholars re-established high standards in the study and dissemination of Classical and biblical texts, for which the Caroline minuscule was developed, and enriched the liturgy with pomp and ceremony. The artistic *renovatio*, expressed in architecture, sculpture, manuscript illumination and liturgical objects, was the consequence of this policy. Charlemagne's annexation of the Italian territories was extremely important, as they contained most of the buildings and works of art that Carolingian craftsmen used as models. Although Charlemagne's son, Louis the Pious (*reg* 814–40), extended Carolingian rule into the Iberian peninsula as far as the River Ebro, and contact with the Islamic world is documented, Islam made scarcely any impression on Carolingian art.

In 843 the three surviving sons of Louis the Pious, Lothair I (*reg* 840–55), Louis the German (*reg* 843–76) and CHARLES THE BALD divided the empire between them at the Treaty of Verdun. Charles the Bald took over the western third from the Pyrenees to the Scheldt, Louis acquired the lands east of the Rhine and the Aar, while Lothair had Italy, together with a strip of land between his brothers' kingdoms extending from the Mediterranean to the North Sea, and the title of Emperor. Shortly before his death Lothair again subdivided his kingdom between his three sons, with Louis II (*reg* 855–75) receiving Italy and the title of Emperor, Lothair II (*reg* 855–69) LOTHARINGIA (now Lorraine), and Charles (*reg* 855–63) Provence. In 870 after the death of Lothair II, Charles the Bald and Louis the German divided Lotharingia between themselves at the Treaty of Meersen. At the death of Louis II, Charles the Bald acquired Italy and the title of Emperor. Charles the Fat (Emperor Charles III from 884), a son of Louis the German, reunited Charlemagne's empire in 885 after the death of his father, his brothers and King Carloman of France (*d* 884), but by 886 he was forced to abdicate from kingship of France by the Vikings and the Capetian Odo (*reg* 887–98), and in the eastern Frankish kingdom by his nephew Arnulf of Carinthia (Emperor 896; *d* 899). Arnulf was succeeded by his young son Louis the Child (*b* 893, *reg* 899–911). After the death of Odo the Carolingian Charles the Simple (*d* 929) was recognized as the west Frankish (French) king, but he was imprisoned in 923.

In the last decades of the 9th century and the first half of the 10th, the fighting between Charlemagne's successors and the Viking raids, as well as the threat from the Huns from 862, led to heavy cultural losses and reductions in artistic output, though production continued uninterrupted in such centres as Metz, Reims and Reichenau.

BIBLIOGRAPHY

B. de Montfaucon: *Les Monumens de la monarchie française, qui comprennent l'histoire de France, avec les figures de chaque règne, que l'injure des tems a épargnées*, i (Paris, 1729)

F. Kugler: *Handbuch der Geschichte der Malerei seit Constantin dem Grossen*, i (Berlin, 1837)

G. F. Waagen: *Kunstwerke und Künstler in England und Paris*, iii (Berlin, 1839)

D. Bullough: *The Age of Charlemagne* (London, 1965, 2/1973)

Karl der Grosse: Werk und Wirkung (exh. cat., Aachen, Rathaus, 1965)

W. Braunfels, ed.: *Karl der Grosse: Lebenswerk und Nachleben*, 5 vols (Düsseldorf, 1965–8)

W. Braunfels: *Die Welt der Karolinger und ihre Kunst* (Munich, 1968)

J. Hubert, J. Porcher and W. Volbach: *L'Empire carolingien* (Paris, 1968); Eng. trans. as *Carolingian Art* (London, 1970) and *The Carolingian Renaissance, 750–950* (New York, 1970) [esp. good illus.]

ULRICH KUDER

II. Architecture.

Although the term Carolingian is strictly applied to the art associated with Charlemagne and his descendants, in architecture it may be applied more widely to buildings from the middle of the 8th century AD. Few Carolingian buildings survive, but detailed archaeological investigations together with careful studies of written sources make it possible to establish the general design of many of the most important monuments.

In this period many important developments in architecture were initated that altered church building forever in western Europe. On the one hand the *renovatio* of Charlemagne and his court promoted the assimilation of the monumental tradition of Early Christian architecture in northern Europe. At the same time, the relatively simple design of the standard basilica was gradually transformed through the introduction of towered façades, the multiplication of altars and apses, the compartmentalization of space and an elaboration of crypts and vaulted passageways, so that from the 10th century early Romanesque architecture developed on a new footing.

1. Buildings of the *renovatio*. 2. AD 814–40. 3. After AD 840.

1. BUILDINGS OF THE 'RENOVATIO'. The first building that can be called Carolingian is the abbey church of Saint-Denis, as rebuilt between 754 and 775 (destr.; *see* SAINT-DENIS ABBEY, §I, 1). Renowned for the tomb of the first bishop and martyr of Paris, the site had long been a favoured burial place for Frankish kings, including Charlemagne's father, Pepin the Short (*reg* 751–68). Following the example of Old St Peter's in Rome, the 8th-century church was an aisled basilica terminated by a projecting transept and an apse housing an annular or semicircular crypt (see fig. 1a and b). A contemporary literary description also indicates that, like its Early Christian model, the church of Saint-Denis was preceded by an atrium (Soclet; Bischoff; Jacobsen, 1983). The Roman features of the Carolingian church were meant to equate St Denis, the Apostle of the Gauls, with St Peter, the Apostle of the Romans, and to symbolize the new alliance

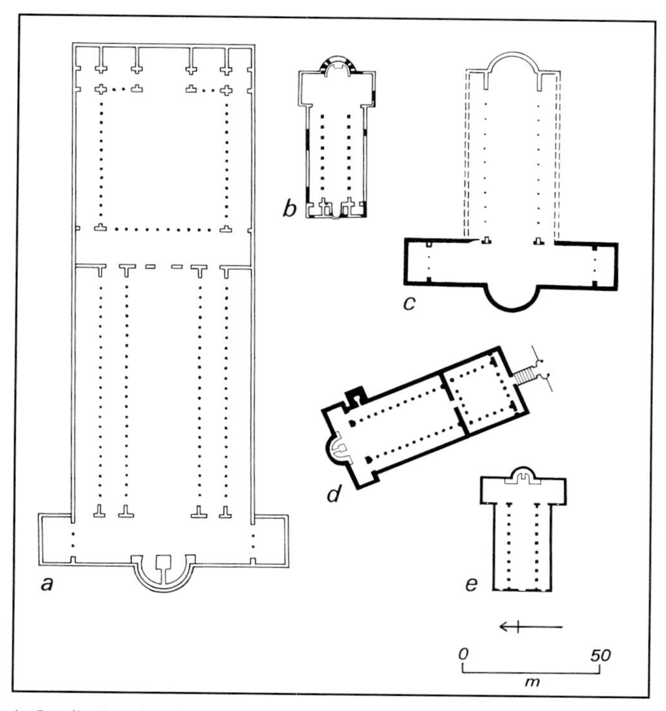

1. Carolingian churches, plans based on Old St Peter's, Rome: (a) Rome, Old St Peter's, *c.* 320–29/30; (b) Saint-Denis Abbey, AD 754–75; (c) Fulda Abbey, begun *c.* 790; (d) Rome, S Prassede, *c.* 820; (e) Seligenstadt, SS Peter und Marcellinus, 830s

between the papacy and the Franks made manifest in 754 by a visit to the abbey by Pope Stephen II (*reg* 752–7). At the same time, two towers surmounting the façade, mentioned by Abbot Suger in the early 12th century, followed local tradition. It is this synthesis of northern and Roman features that makes Saint-Denis such a potent symbol of the new Carolingian era.

The contemporary abbey church (767–74; destr.) at Lorsch also possessed a massive western entrance but seems to have had no transept. The best preserved Carolingian feature at Lorsch is the free-standing Torhalle (gateway; for illustration *see* LORSCH ABBEY, with further discussion of the building), with its triple-arched opening and classicizing capitals derived from such Roman monuments as the 4th-century Arch of Constantine and the gateway (destr.) to the atrium of Old St Peter's. Opinions differ as to the exact date of the Lorsch gateway. There are stylistic affiliations with the funerary chapel, the Ecclesia varia (*c.* 880; destr.), but the monument could also fit into the last quarter of the 8th century, and it was perhaps set up to commemorate Charlemagne's visit to Lorsch in 774 after his conquest of Lombard Italy.

Ideas of the *renovatio* appeared most strongly in Carolingian architecture in the ten years around 800, with building on a scale not seen since the reign of Emperor Justinian in the early 6th century. The prime example of this stage is the palace complex (partly destr.) at Aachen, which Charlemagne designated as his permanent capital in the last years of his reign. Here the polygonal chapel, basilican audience hall and monumental gateway recall Early Christian models at Trier, Ravenna, Rome and Constantinople. Even luxurious building materials, such as columns and marble revetment, were transported north of the Alps from ancient ruins in Rome and Ravenna. The royal palace (destr. 1689) at Ingelheim, begun a few years earlier and on a smaller scale, demonstrates a similar revival of Late Antique villa designs with a semicircular colonnaded entrance and an aisleless audience hall.

Renovatio ideals were carried over into monastic architecture as well. Under the leadership of Angilbert, a friend and adviser to Charlemagne, the abbey (destr.) at Centula, for example, was built on a monumental scale, with three churches interconnected by a portico *c.* 275 m long (*see* SAINT-RIQUIER ABBEY, fig. 1). One of the churches, dedicated to St Mary, was a copy one-third the size of the palatine chapel at Aachen; a similar influence may be behind the design of the oratory at GERMIGNY-DES-PRÉS, built for Theodulf, the Abbot of Fleury and another member of the élite circle of scholars at Charlemagne's court.

The abbey church (destr.) at Fulda, begun *c.* 790 by Abbot Baugulf, followed Old St Peter's in Rome in both plan and size (see fig. 1c). Although Fulda was not a complete copy of the Vatican church, aspects of the design followed Rome so literally that the apse and transept at Fulda were built at the west end of the basilica instead of the east, as had long been the custom in church building both north and south of the Alps. Indeed, contemporaries referred to the western placement of the apse as 'following Roman custom' (*Romano more*; *see* FULDA, §1). The resultant double-apse plan, with an apse at either end of the church, also appeared at approximately the same time at Saint-Maurice d'Agaune (destr.) in present-day Switzerland and at the cathedral (destr.) of Cologne. At Fulda, as at Saint-Denis, the design of the church reflected a desire to associate with Rome the remains of a saint, in this case those of the missionary, martyr and founder of the abbey, St Boniface (680–754), whose body was housed in the western apse. This movement towards closer links with Rome coincided with the introduction and promotion of the Roman liturgy by the Frankish Church. As described by Angilbert and others, the daily life of the monk was centred about a continuous round of prayers and processions. Similarly, subsidiary chapels and secondary apses served the multiplication of altars and their relics.

2. AD 814–40. Immediately after the death of Charlemagne in 814, there was a dramatically changed attitude towards such ambitious building. Louis the Pious, Charlemagne's son and successor, intervened at Fulda to bring a halt to what he termed the 'enormous buildings and unnecessary work', and he convened two synods at Aachen in 816 and 817 to legislate monastic reform. He was guided in this process by Benedict of Aniane (*c.* 750–821), whose monastery (destr.) near Aachen at Inden (now Kornelimünster) had a church notable for its small size and lack of Roman features. The nave was short and flanked by single aisles with rectangular piers instead of columns; to the west stood a compact block made up of a central projecting porch; and to the east was a staggered arrangement of three horseshoe-shaped apses. This rejection of the grandiose schemes of the previous generation set a new standard. Even Einhard's abbey church (begun 815), at Steinbach, near Michelstadt, followed the design of Kornelimünster save for the presence of a corridor crypt. Ironically, it was during this same period that the revival of Early Christian architecture reached its zenith in Rome under the patronage of PASCHAL I. The church of S Prassede, for example, is a copy of Old St Peter's with atrium, transept and annular crypt (see fig. 1d), albeit on a reduced scale, and is decorated with luxurious figural mosaics.

After the death of Benedict of Aniane, the initial fervour of monastic reform began to subside north of the Alps and a more tempered eclectic approach prevailed. Einhard abandoned his church at Steinbach after he obtained relics from Rome in 827, and between 831 and 840 he built a new church at Seligenstadt (Hessen; rest.; see fig. 1e) following the Roman formula of T-shaped basilica and annular crypt popular in the days of Charlemagne. Similarly, Paderborn Cathedral was enlarged at the west end in 836 by a continuous transept and an apse housing an annular crypt. At the abbey church of Hersfeld, on the other hand, a new church was built (831–50; ruined) that followed the triple-apse and segmented transept design of Kornelimünster but at twice the size. Thus, in the later 820s and 830s there was not so much a wholesale return to the architectural precepts of an earlier age as a process of assimilation and compromise whereby elements of both Roman influence and more recent monastic reform could be combined to suit the needs of a given situation.

Such an attitude helps to explain the seemingly contradictory elements of the remarkable parchment sheet known as the St Gall Plan (St Gall, Stift.-Bib., MS. 1092;

see ST GALL ABBEY, §2), which bears the detailed plan of a monastery, including an abbey church, a cloister walk surrounded by a dormitory, refectory and cellar, and numerous subsidiary buildings, all carefully identified by Latin inscriptions. The size and complexity of the plan reflect the importance of monasteries in the Carolingian realm as centres of learning and economic self-sufficiency. Most striking are the orderliness and regularity of the monastic layout created by a taut network of parallel and perpendicular axes of individual buildings and building groups (*see* MONASTERY, §I). The resemblance to a small Roman town or military camp cannot be coincidental and must be the result of the study of the architectural treatise of Vitruvius and ancient surveying manuals known to have been copied in Carolingian scriptoria.

All is not uniform, however. Although the design of the abbey church with its two apses, dedicated to St Peter and St Paul respectively, seems to echo the *renovatio* of Charlemagne's reign, the length of the church as labelled is considerably shorter (200 ft instead of 300 ft) than the 40 ft width of the nave indicates, which suggests a desire to reduce the size of the building. More important, the internal space of the nave and aisles is shown broken up by a multitude of subsidiary altars and their surrounding barriers, presumably low screens. Immediately adjoining the abbey church to the south is the cloister, approximately 100 ft square. The first archaeological evidence for cloisters is found at Lorsch and at Mittelzell, Reichenau, and dates from the mid-8th century. These early internal courtyards seem to have been relatively primitive arrangements, but the St Gall Plan shows the cloister fully formulated with masonry arches and a central garden. The plan was drawn up specifically for Abbot Gozbert (816–37) as he prepared to rebuild St Gall Abbey from 830. Its ideal nature is evident by the fact that its rectangular format was ill-suited to the irregular site at St Gall, and Abbot Gozbert did not follow the plan closely in rebuilding the abbey church. Thus it represents an ideal more than a reality. Nonetheless, the notion of the tight integration of the abbey church and cloister as the core of a monastic complex would prevail throughout the Middle Ages.

3. AFTER AD 840. The period of later Carolingian architecture, from the death of Louis the Pious until the end of the 9th century, was perhaps the most innovative. Among various features, two in particular stand out—the westwork and the outer crypt—both of which were used at the abbey church of Corvey as completed in 885. The core of the church was similar in size to that represented on the St Gall Plan, but at the west end was added a massive westwork (see fig. 2), which is still visible today with flanking stair-towers and several internal storeys, while at the east end a series of narrow passageways enveloped the main apse and culminated in a cruciform chapel, which protruded *c.* 18 m beyond the main body of the church. Westworks and the outer crypts had originated decades earlier. The specific reasons for their development are not fully known but they were no doubt liturgical (for further discussion *see* WESTWORK). The first preserved example of a westwork is at Charlemagne's palatine chapel at Aachen; earlier examples are documented at Saint-Denis, Lorsch and Saint-Riquier. At Aachen the westwork

2. Corvey Abbey church, westwork, AD 873–85

marked the position of Charlemagne's throne and may have carried connotations of kingship; this aspect may have pertained at other sites as well. At Corvey, the primary motivation seems to have been to provide an upper gallery for monastic choirs as well as room for secondary altars (*see* WESTWORK, fig. 1).

The development of the outer crypt (*see* CRYPT) was related to the expansion of the cult of relics and the concomitant multiplication of altars, together with the need to accommodate a growing desire by privileged members of the Church and laity to be buried *ad sanctos*, to use the medieval term (i.e. near relics associated with the high altar). In 832, a semi-subterranean chapel was attached to the apex of the apse and annular crypt at Saint-Denis; thereafter, crypts in increasingly complex forms came to surround the eastern apses of churches in many parts of northern Europe, for example at Saint-Philibert-de-Grandlieu (begun 836), St Pierre (864–78) at Flavigny-sur-Ozerain, St Germain at Auxerre (841–59; *see* AUXERRE, §2), Lorsch and Corvey (for discussion of a further type of elaborate crypt *see also* GRENOBLE, §2). Later

Carolingian architecture, therefore, is characterized by an aggrandizement of the eastern and western ends of the church in order to suit new liturgical and political demands.

BIBLIOGRAPHY

EWA

R. Krautheimer: 'The Carolingian Revival of Early Christian Architecture', *A. Bull.*, xxiv (1942), pp. 1–38; rev. in *Studies in Early Christian, Medieval and Renaissance Art* (New York and London, 1969), pp. 203–56

F. Oswald, L. Schaefer and H. R. Sennhauser: *Vorromanische Kirchenbauten: Katalog der Denkmäler bis zum Ausgang der Ottonen*, 3 vols (Munich, 1966–71/*R* 1990); suppl. by W. Jacobsen, L. Schaefer and H. R. Sennhauser (Munich, 1991)

F. Möbius: *Westwerkstudien* (Jena, 1968)

H. E. Kubach and A. Verbeek: *Romanische Baukunst an Rhein und Maas: Katalog der vorromanischen and romanischen Denkmäler*, 4 vols (Berlin, 1976–89)

W. Horn and E. Born: *The Plan of St Gall: A Study of the Architecture and Economy of, and Life in, a Paradigmatic Carolingian Monastery*, 3 vols (Berkeley, Los Angeles and London, 1979)

C. Heitz: *L'Architecture religieuse carolingienne: Les Formes et leurs fonctions* (Paris, 1980)

R. Krautheimer: *Rome: Profile of a City, 312–1308* (Princeton, 1980), pp. 109–42

A. J. Soclet: 'La *Descriptio Basilicae Sancti Dyonisii*: Premiers Commentaires', *J. Sav.* (1980), pp. 104–17

B. Bischoff: 'Eine Beschreibung der Basilika von Saint-Denis aus dem Jahre 799', *Kunstchronik*, xxxiv (1981), pp. 97–103

W. Jacobsen: 'Saint-Denis im neuen Licht: Der neuentdeckten Baubeschreibung aus dem Jahre 799', *Kunstchronik*, xxxvi (1983), pp. 301–8

——: 'Gab es die karolingische 'Renaissance' in der Baukunst?', *Z. Kstgesch.*, li (1988), pp. 313–47

A. Zettler: *Die frühen Klosterbauten Reichenau* (Sigmaringen, 1988)

W. Jacobsen: *Der Klosterplan von St Gallen und die karolingische Architektur* (Berlin, 1992)

CHARLES B. McCLENDON

III. Sculpture.

Except for a stone head of a youthful figure (*c.* 800; h. 220 mm; Darmstadt, Hess. Landesmus.) excavated at Lorsch, large-scale figure sculpture has not survived from the Carolingian period, and although stucco decoration was often combined with frescoes in Carolingian churches, such as at S Salvatore, Brescia, and S Benedetto, Málles Venosta, very little sculpture in this medium remains from the period. Decorative sculpture, however, does seem to have played a significant part in the Carolingian *renovatio.* In the palace chapel at Aachen not only do the bronze railings show Classical capitals and *rinceaux* (*see* §V, 1 below), but on the exterior Classical capitals crown engaged pilasters. The composite capitals on the Torhalle of Lorsch Abbey (*c.* 800) could easily be confused with late Roman capitals, with their fleshy acanthus leaves, bold scrolls, and bead and reel motifs. The Ionic pilasters on the upper level of the gateway, although less Classical in form, are obviously based on Roman prototypes. Decorative motifs derived from designs originating in Syria and Constantinople were widespread in the Carolingian period. Patterns include interlace, rosette designs, star patterns, *rinceaux* and guilloche, and they were to become part of the standard repertory of later Ottonian and Romanesque sculptors.

The largest corpus of surviving Carolingian stone sculpture comprises chancel parapets or closure slabs used to partition off the altar area from the main body of the church. Several hundred are known in Italy, Switzerland, Germany and France. A workshop that produced many of the relief sculptured panels was probably located near the major quarries on the modern borders of Italy, Switzerland and Austria. A handsomely carved closure slab (Bolzano, Mus. Civ.; see fig. 3) from S Benedetto at Málles Venosta has an intricate design comprising a rosette enclosed within a circular frame, which in turn is framed on the diagonal by a square and subsequently enclosed within a circular knot frame. Residual spaces are filled by abstract floral designs. An even more complex design appears in S Ambrogio, Milan, on a closure slab (re-used as an altar frontal) in the chapel of S Vittore. Here a Greek cross decorated with a guilloche pattern is surrounded by an interweaving knot pattern from which emerge rosettes and grape-cluster motifs. Simpler examples can be found in the Musée d'Art et d'Histoire at Metz, Schänis Church (Switzerland) and the Musée Granet at Aix-en-Provence. At least two Carolingian semicircular ambos (both late 8th century) are to be found in Switzerland, in the abbey churches at Romainmôtier and Saint-Maurice d'Agaune. Here the Latin cross motif dominates, enframed by knot patterns.

A handsome and well-preserved ciborium (806–16) still stands in S Apollinare in Classe, Ravenna. It is inscribed with the name of the commissioner, the priest Peter. This stone canopy, originally placed over the main altar, also employs intricate knot patterns, grape-vine motifs, abstract animals and birds. The four arches rest on freely interpreted Corinthian capitals, which in turn are supported by spirally fluted columns. An impressive marble cross (1.50×2.00 m; *c.* 827) at Budrio, near Bologna, has rich decoration on both sides employing *rinceaux* and guilloche motifs. An inscription on the front, INDI NO RENOVA

3. Closure slab with carved ornament, marble, from S Benedetto, Málles Venosta (Bolzano, Museo Civico)

CRUX TEMPORIBU DOM VITALE EPSC., names the donor as Vitalis, Bishop of Bologna from 789 to 844.

BIBLIOGRAPHY

M. Prou: 'Chancel carolingien orné d'entrelacs à Schaenis (canton de Saint-Gall)', *Mém. Acad. Inscr. & B.-Lett.*, xxxix (1912), pp. 122–38

A. DEAN MCKENZIE

IV. Painting.

Monumental painting is poorly represented by the few and fragmentary examples of wall painting and mosaic decoration, the dating of which is often controversial. Our understanding of Carolingian painting is, therefore, largely based on manuscripts, which survive in relatively great number and are in many cases datable through inscriptions and other indications of patronage.

1. Wall. 2. Mosaic. 3. Manuscript.

1. WALL. Examples of wall painting from the last quarter of the 8th century to the end of the 9th represent only a small fraction of what once existed and are often fragmentary or damaged, many of them suffering from heavy restoration; literary sources provide evidence for some of the lost cycles.

(i) Literary evidence. In a poem eulogizing Louis the Pious, Ermoldus Nigellus (*d c.* 835) described the sequence of paintings in the palace chapel and audience hall (*aula regia*) at Ingelheim Palace. According to this account scenes from the Old and New Testaments decorated the nave walls of the chapel, presumably laid out in registers as at Brescia and Müstair (*see* §(ii) below). The programme of the *aula regia*, on the other hand, was devoted to legitimizing the Carolingian dynasty and comprised two sequences of rulers, Classical and Christian, apparently accompanied by scenes depicting their most glorious deeds. The date of the paintings is controversial. Although it is generally assumed that Louis the Pious, to whom the poem was addressed, commissioned them, neither Louis nor events subsequent to Charlemagne's Saxon wars were depicted. Against a date in Charlemagne's reign, however, is the fact that there is no evidence of comparable cycles dating from *c.* 800; references to the decoration of the palatine chapel at Aachen with scenes from the Old and New Testaments, and to representations of the Liberal Arts and Charlemagne's Spanish campaigns in the palace itself, can be traced back only to doubtful 12th-century sources (Pseudo-Turpin's *Historia Karoli Magni*), and were not confirmed by the traces of the original decoration that were uncovered in the 19th century. Preserved *tituli* from the paintings that once adorned the monastery church of St Gorgonius, Gorze (consecrated 765), refer only to a depiction of Christ in Majesty in the apse. Evidence for the existence of extensive cycles is later in date; Sedulius Scottus's *tituli* describing lost wall paintings in Liège were composed in the mid-9th century; the sequence of 40 scenes from the New Testament, also known by surviving verses, that once decorated the walls of Abbot Gozbert's church at St Gall, can be dated to the time of Hartmut (deputy abbot from 841; abbot 872–83).

(ii) Chronological survey. The few surviving remnants of wall painting dating from the early Carolingian period are primarily ornamental remains of the decoration, preserved in the excavated apse of Saint-Denis Abbey and the ring crypt at St Emmeram, Regensburg, as well as fragments excavated in Paderborn Cathedral and on Reichenau (Mittelzell Minster and Niederzell), including marbling, bands of inscription and decorative friezes.

Several datable wall paintings belong to the period of Louis the Pious. In Einhard's church (consecrated 827) at Steinbach, near Michelstadt, a corbel frieze along the upper walls of the nave provides evidence of the original decoration of the church. Its illusionistic effect may well have been similar to work at Brescia or S Martino ai Monti, Rome. Later fragments excavated at Mittelzell Minster, Reichenau, are assigned to the building dedicated in 816 under Abbot Heito (*reg* 806–23). The remains of wall paintings uncovered in the crypt of the church at Petersberg, near Fulda, are associated with Rabanus Maurus, Abbot of Fulda (*reg* 822–42). The *Virgin* surrounded by bust medallions of virgins and standing saints in the middle barrel vault, the (overpainted) angels in the south vault and the *Lamb of God* and *Baptism* on the north vault correspond to *tituli* and altar inscriptions composed by Rabanus; the paintings may therefore belong to the building consecrated in 836. In the abbey church at Corvey, endowed by Louis the Pious in 822 and consecrated in 844, numerous excavated fragments have made it possible to reconstruct part of its original interior decoration, which consisted of a medallion frieze running round the clerestory of the nave.

The extensive cycle of frescoes at S Salvatore, Brescia, is accompanied by an inscription naming a young hero (*tiro*) called *HLVdovicus* or *HLVtharius*, which has been related to Louis the Pious as well as to his sons Lothair I and Louis II (Jacobsen). The illusionism, seen in the better-preserved areas of the painting, with its rich tonal values, would seem to indicate a date in the second quarter of the 9th century. The paintings in three registers on the nave walls, although damaged, combined with the partly preserved stucco decoration on the transverse arches, give a unique impression of the spatial effect of Carolingian church decoration. The programme includes not only the *Infancy of Christ* in the window area, but also the lives of local saints (at least in the lowest register) and bust medallions in the spandrels of the arches. Not yet fully clarified is the relationship with the more hieratic representations of saints standing in front of perspectively rendered architecture in the church of S Maria in valle at Cividale (Friuli); here, too, a close connection with complementary stuccowork can be demonstrated.

There are general correspondences, in the horizontally consecutive zone-by-zone arrangement of the sequence of scenes and in some decorative details, between Brescia and frescoes at the monastery church of Müstair in Grisons (*see* MÜSTAIR, ST JOHANN). The church contains the most extensive painting cycle to survive from the Carolingian period, comprising five registers containing scenes from the *Life of David* and *Life of Christ* on the nave walls (the *David* scenes and remains of the *Ascension of Christ* from the triumphal arch are now in Zurich, Schweizer. Landesmus.). Below the (heavily restored) vault of the three apses (on which the *Traditio legis* and a *Cross* or *crux gemmata* alongside the *Christ in Majesty* are represented) are scenes from the lives of the saints to whom the altars were dedicated, partly covered by Romanesque paintings of the same subjects. The west wall has a monumental *Last Judgement.* The scenes, nearly 100 in all, were separated by bands entwined by garlands similar to those found at CASTELSEPRIO (*see also* EARLY CHRISTIAN AND BYZANTINE ART, §III, 3(ii)) and in Carolingian manuscripts. The decorative richness—for example in the background buildings, which are decorated with precious stones and strands of pearls—works together with the effect of highly contrasted light and shadow. While a date around 800 is suggested for the church building it seems more likely that the paintings were created in the second quarter of the 9th century (Davis-Weyer).

The subtle differences between the paintings in Müstair and those in the small Benedictine church at nearby Málles Venosta (Mals) remain unexplained (*see* MÁLLES VENOSTA, S BENEDETTO). Despite coincidences in the programmes and similarities in details of the figure style of the central niche, there is no parallel at Müstair for the very differentiated and subtle painting found in the two famous portraits on the east wall, showing an ecclesiastical (see fig. 4) and a secular donor. It is possible to see reflections of the Müstair paintings at St Peter's at Mistail in Grisons. Sketchy remains of the original painting indicate that there were considerable iconographical similarities, at least in the *Last Judgement* scene on the west wall. The paintings in the small church of S Procolo, Naturno (Naturns), not far from Málles, show other artistic trends. A marked, almost ornamental stylization in the figures and a repertory of motifs that has as yet barely been interpreted (e.g. a herd of cattle on the entrance wall), secure a special place for these pictures within early medieval wall painting. Because of the archaizing forms in which pre-Carolingian traditions were obviously being continued, these frescoes have often been dated to the 8th century, although a date in the 9th century appears more likely.

4. *Ecclesiastical Donor* (?2nd quarter of the 9th century), detail of wall painting on the east wall, S Benedetto, Málles Venosta

The remains of a painted interior in the Torhalle at Lorsch Abbey show that Carolingian painters were capable of superb illusionism and technical brilliance. The widely accepted assignment of the paintings to the period of Charlemagne has been challenged and a later dating during the reign of Louis the German (*d* 876) or Louis the Younger (*reg* 876–82) proposed. After the elimination of modern restorations, the architectural painting of the upper stage revealed a quality and a technical mastery hitherto unknown. Resting on a base of multicoloured fictive marble, painted columns supporting a high entablature show deftly applied mottled effects suggesting costly types of stone. It is probable that this impressive classicism coincided with the heyday of the monastery, before 850.

The only west Frankish example of Carolingian wall painting that can be adduced is the painting in the crypt of St Germain at Auxerre (dedicated 859; *see* AUXERRE, §2). The scenes depicted between the vaults refer to the patron saints to whom the two side chapels were dedicated (scenes from the *Life of St Stephen* in the north aisle, *St Laurence before Christ in Majesty* in the south). The decorative richness of the floral friezes reveals parallels with contemporary book illumination (e.g. the Court school of Charles the Bald; *see* §3(iii) below).

Important in the late phase of Carolingian wall painting are the cycles at Corvey (second phase) and Trier. The interior decoration of the westwork of Corvey can largely be reconstructed on the basis of the painting on the inner arch mouldings. Here, fictive architecture, complementing and continuing the three-dimensional imposts, forms the framework for geometric and floral motifs in a comparatively wide range of colours. In the western part, above a painted cornice, the underpainting of an extensive frieze of sea monsters has been discovered to which belongs the scene of *Odysseus Fighting against Scylla.* This decoration, with its astonishingly Classical character, can be reliably dated between 873 and 885.

Finally, in the crypt of St Maximin in Trier, the west wall, a parapet built in front of it and the vaults were completely repainted in the course of restoration work after the destruction by the Normans in 882. The paintings on the west wall and parapet show the *Nailing of Christ to the Cross,* unusual in Western art at this period, and a *Procession of Martyrs* (Trier, Bischöf. Dom- & Diözmus.; see fig. 5). In a section of the barrel vault preserved as a result of being walled up in the Ottonian period, the paintings (largely lost since they were uncovered) showed standing Prophets, writing Evangelists and other seated figures. The paintings, which can presumably be associated with Archbishop Radpod of Trier (*reg* 883–915), still betray the tradition of, for example, Auxerre in some more general traits, not least the range of colours, but they clearly reveal diagrammatic tendencies and a hardening in style, also characteristic of book illumination at the end of the 9th century.

5. *Procession of Martyrs*, wall painting from St Maximin, Trier, after AD 882, (Trier, Bischöfliches Dom- und Diözesanmuseum)

2. MOSAIC. Owing to the scarcity of evidence for mosaic decoration, the preliminary drawings (Brauweiler, Rhein. Amt Dkmlpf.) for the original dome mosaic in the palatine chapel at Aachen are important documents for Carolingian monumental painting; together with 17th-century sketches, they enable us to form a fairly complete picture of the ceiling programme. These indicate a *Christ in Majesty* surrounded by the 24 elders standing in front of their thrones and holding crowns. The use of dramatic lighting and zigzag folds in the preliminary drawings suggests links with the manuscript painting of the Court school of Charlemagne (*see* §3(ii) below). The apse mosaic of the oratory at Germigny-des-Prés, consecrated in 806, may perhaps be seen as a continuation of the activity of the mosaicists who were at work at Aachen, even though the angels flanking the *Ark of the Covenant* in the former appear more animated (*see* GERMIGNY-DES-PRÉS, §3).

BIBLIOGRAPHY

RDK: 'Farbigkeit der Architektur'

F. F. Leitschuh: *Geschichte der karolingischen Malerei: Ihr Bilderkreis und seine Quellen* (Berlin, 1894)

P. Clemen: *Die romanische Monumentalmalerei in den Rheinlanden*, Ges. Rhein. Geschknd., xxxii (Düsseldorf, 1916)

E. S. King: 'The Carolingian Frescoes of the Abbey of Saint Germain d'Auxerre', *A. Bull.*, xi (1929), pp. 359–75

L. Birchler: 'Zur karolingischen Architektur und Malerei in Münster-Müstair', *Frühmittelalterliche Kunst in den Alpenländern. Akten zum III. internationalen Kongress für Frühmittelalterforschung: Olten–Lausanne, 1951*, pp. 167–252

A. Grabar and C. Nordenfalk: *Das frühe Mittelalter* (Geneva, 1957; Eng. trans., New York, 1957), pp. 1–89 [see A. Grabar]

H. Schnitzler: 'Das Kuppelmosaik der Aachener Pfalzkapelle', *Aachen. Kstbl.*, xxix (1964), pp. 17–44

N. Rasmo: 'Gli affreschi carolingi di Malles', *Arte in Europa: Scritti di storia dell'arte in onore di Edoardo Arslan* (Milan, 1966), pp. 189–202

Kunst und Kultur im Weserraum, 800–1600, ii (exh. cat., Corvey, Abbey, 1966), nos 380–82, pp. 645–8 [see H. Claussen]

Aufnahmen von Wandmalereien und Mosaiken aus dem Zeitalter Karls des Grossen (exh. cat., ed. W. Beeh and others; Michelstadt, Schloss Fürstenau, 1968; rev. Darmstadt, 1979)

W. Lammers: 'Ein karolingisches Bildprogramm in der Aula Regia von Ingelheim', *Festschrift für Hermann Heimpel*, iii, Veröffentlichungen des Max-Planck-Instituts für Geschichte, xxxvi (Göttingen, 1972), pp. 226–89

C. Eggenberger: 'Die frühmittelalterlichen Wandmalereien in St. Prokulus zu Naturns', *Frühmittelalt. Stud.*, viii (1974), pp. 303–50

B. Anderson: *The Frescoes of San Salvatore at Brescia* (diss., Berkeley, U. CA, 1976)

W. Bornheim: 'Bemalte und gemalte karolingische Architektur', *Dt. Kst- & Dkmlpf.*, xxxvi (1978), pp. 7–20; also in *Dkmlpf. Rheinland-Pfalz Jber.*, xxxi–xxxiii (1976–9), pp. 31–51

St. Peter Mistail GR., Schweizerische Kunstführer (Basle, 1979)

L. Wüthrich: *Wandgemälde. Von Müstair bis Hodler: Katalog der Sammlung des Schweizerischen Landesmuseums Zürich* (Zurich, 1980), nos 1–21, pp. 17–41

N. Rasmo: *Karolingische Kunst in Südtirol* (Bolzano, 1981)

S. Spada Pintarelli: *Pittura carolingia nell'Alto Adige: Note bibliografiche* (Bolzano, 1981)

Seminario internazionale sulla decorazione pittorica del San Salvatore di Brescia: Brescia, 1981

A. Peroni: 'San Salvatore di Brescia: Un ciclo pittorico altomedievale rivisitato', *A. Med.*, i (1983), pp. 53–80

H. R. Sennhauser: 'Das Münster des Abtes Gozbert (816–37) und seine Ausmalung unter Hartmut (Proabbas 841, Abt 872–83)', *Unsere Kstdkml.*, xxxiv (1983), pp. 152–67

H. Claussen: *Kloster Corvey* (Munich, 1985; rev. St Gall, 1988)

K. Hauck: 'Karolingische Taufpfalzen im Spiegel hofnaher Dichtung: Überlegungen zur Ausmalung von Pfalzkirchen, Pfalzen und Reichsklöstern', *Nachr. Akad. Wiss. Göttingen Philol.-Hist. Kl.*, i (Göttingen, 1985)

W. Jacobsen: 'San Salvatore in Brescia', *Studien zur mittelalterlichen Kunst, 800–1250: Festschrift für Florentine Mütherich zum 70. Geburtstag* (Munich, 1985), pp. 75–80

H. Claussen: 'Die Wandmalereifragmente', *Die Ausgrabungen im Dom zu Paderborn 1978–80 und 1983*, xi of *Dkmlpf. & Forsch. Westfalen* (Bonn, 1986), i, pp. 247–79

A. Peroni: 'Stucco e pittura nel S Benedetto di Malles', *Festschrift Nicolò Rasmo* (Bolzano, 1986), pp. 77–89

C. Davis-Weyer: 'Müstair, Milano e l'Italia carolingia', *Il Millenio Ambrosiano*, ed. C. Bertelli, i (Milan, 1987), pp. 202–37

M. Exner: *Die Fresken der Krypta von St Maximin in Trier und ihre Stellung in der spätkarolingischen Wandmalerei*, Trierer Zeitschrift, x (Trier, 1989) [suppl.]
T. Ludwig: *Michelstadt-Steinbach: Einhardbasilika* (Bad Homburg vor der Höhe, 1989)
H. Claussen and M. Exner: 'Abschlussbericht der Arbeitsgemeinschaft für frühmittelalterliche Wandmalerei', *Z. Ksttech. & Konserv.*, iv (1990), pp. 261–90
W. Kofler Engl, H. Nothdurfter and H. Stampfer, eds: *St Prokulus, Naturns: Archäologie, Wandmalerei* (Bolzano, 1990)
O. Emmenegger and H. Stampfer: 'Die Wandmalereien von St Benedikt in Mals im Lichte einer maltechnischen Untersuchung', *Die Kunst und ihre Erhaltung: Festschrift für Rolf E. Straub zum 70. Geburtstag* (Worms, 1990), pp. 247–68
M. Exner: 'St Prokulus, Naturns: II. Zu den Ergebnissen von Grabung und Restaurierung', *Kunstchronik*, xliii (1990), pp. 557–74
Saint-Germain d'Auxerre: Intellectuels et artistes dans l'Europe carolingienne, IXe–XIe siècles (exh. cat. by C. Sapin, Auxerre, 1990), pp. 121–43
E. Rüber: *St Benedikt in Mals*, Eur. Hochschschr., ser. xxviii, cxxx (Frankfurt am Main, 1991)
M. Exner: 'Die Reste frühmittelalterlicher Wandmalerei in der Lorscher Torhalle: Bestand, Ergebnisse, Aufgaben', *Kst Hessen & Mittelrhein*, xxxii–xxxiii (1992–3), pp. 43–63
H. Claussen: 'Les Frises d'acanthe et géométriques du Westwerk de Corvey', *Edifices et peintres aux IVe–XIe siècles. Actes du colloque C.N.R.S.: Auxerre, 1994*, pp. 99–113
R. McKitterick, ed.: *Carolingian Culture* (Cambridge, 1994)
For further bibliography *see* articles on individual sites.

MATTHIAS EXNER

3. MANUSCRIPT. As an historical phenomenon, Carolingian manuscript painting hinged on the reforms instigated by Charlemagne and was the outcome of the demands he made on manuscript production, as demonstrated by his great decrees: the *Admonitio generalis* (789), the *Epistola de litteris colendis* (before 800) and the missive with which he introduced the book of homilies by Paul the Deacon.

(i) Introduction. (ii) Before *c.* AD 850. (iii) After *c.* AD 850.

(i) Introduction. The demand for new, carefully laid out editions of the sacred books with the correct text was an integral part of the renovation of the liturgy that was taking place. Three types of manuscript, important for book illumination, were expressly mentioned: Gospel books, Psalters and Sacramentaries. A further category to be added was the Bible; the new, single-volume edition (pandect) was the largest undertaking that Charlemagne set the scriptoria. Evangeliaries (containing those parts of the Gospels read during Mass) were already appearing alongside Gospel books; Charlemagne and his wife commissioned a costly example, the Godescalc Evangeliary (*see* §(ii) below).

The centre of Charlemagne's endeavours was his court, especially once established at Aachen in 794 (*see* AACHEN, §2). There had been earlier attempts to reform manuscript production in the Frankish kingdom, particularly at the monasteries at Corbie and Chelles, but these attempts had not resulted in any far-reaching and lasting success. Only with the 'Court school' of Charlemagne, supported by the sovereign's authority and systematically concerned for the content, writing and decoration of manuscripts, was the ground laid for a lasting *renovatio* with a decisive impact on the future. Sample editions, exempla, of the most important types of manuscript were produced and these were then disseminated throughout the empire to serve as models. Examples made at the Court school for the Gospel book and Psalter have been preserved (*see* §(ii) below); the Sacramentary, based on a model ordered from Rome, has been lost but there survives a copy of it produced in 812 (Cambrai, Bib. Mun., MS. 164). Only the new edition of the Bible was not undertaken at court: it was entrusted to Charlemagne's closest confidant, the Anglo-Saxon Alcuin (*c.* 740–804), Abbot of St Martin, Tours, where the production of large, richly decorated pandects remained the foremost concern for half a century (*see* §(ii) below). Charlemagne was concerned not only with liturgical manuscripts but also with illustrated secular texts. This interest is demonstrated by a manual of astronomy and computus, written after an assembly of scholars had been summoned to Aachen in 809, which was systematically distributed through copies to various parts of the empire. The original is lost and is best conveyed by a copy produced *c.* 840 (Madrid, Bib. N., MS. 3307).

With the tasks divided between Charlemagne's Court school and the monastery at Tours, two different types of schools of illumination emerged right at the beginning of the Carolingian period, and were to have important implications for the 9th century. The Court school, connected to the person of the ruler, was relatively small and short-lived, mainly concerned with the production of luxury manuscripts intended for the sovereign himself and his entourage. The Court school of Charlemagne was followed by those of his grandsons Lothair I and, especially, Charles the Bald. The monastery school, by contrast, with a large available workforce, was more enduring and able to take on time-consuming, large-scale tasks; producing work for export, it developed fixed types for certain categories of manuscripts, which were widely distributed. Examples of the classic Carolingian monastic school are Tours and the Franco-Saxon school of the northern French monasteries. The schools of the great bishops were similar to the court schools, dependent on and influenced by individual patronage. Among these were the scriptoria working for Ebbo, Archbishop of Reims (*reg* 816–35, 840–41), and Drogo, Bishop of Metz (*reg* 823–55).

The Carolingian schools, however, were not only of different type but also of different artistic character. The determining factor was their relationship to the renaissance movement at Charlemagne's court, with its aim of reviving the antique art of book illumination. This meant using images to convey three-dimensional figures in a spatial setting instead of using organic figures in ornamental and abstract patterns in the way typical of Insular and pre-Carolingian art. While these aims were accepted and developed by many of the Carolingian schools, others adhered to the old traditional forms or—to some extent influenced by Insular art—evolved an abstract, ornamental, two-dimensional repertory in which figural images, with a very few exceptions, had no place. The contrast between these two trends continued right through the 9th century.

The great source on which the schools of the Carolingian renaissance could draw was the painting of the Late Antique period. To what extent and where the last remains of this tradition may have been still active is almost unanswerable in view of the few fragments of monuments that have survived from Italy or Byzantium. The links, however, with older examples of illuminated books—Late

Antique, Byzantine and Italian codices—can be reconstructed more clearly. The many copies of Classical codices played a special role in the Carolingian perception of antiquity, especially the accurate copies of Late Antique models, in which not only the iconography but also the style of the model was imitated. Some of these are of such excellent quality that they make an important contribution to our knowledge of Late Antique book illumination, now largely lost, as well as occupying a place in Carolingian book illumination. This is particularly true of secular texts, scientific, poetic or didactic works, but above all of astronomical tracts, which were produced in large number because of the interest in astronomy and computus at that time. These included illustrations of catalogues of constellations from tracts and scholia, as well as illustrations of the most famous antique work on astronomy, Aratus' *Phaenomena*, of which there are illustrated copies of both the translations of Germanicus and Cicero (*see* ASTROLOGICAL AND ASTRONOMICAL MANUSCRIPTS and §(ii) below).

Other notable copies of Classical manuscripts include the earliest surviving illustrated *Physiologus*, in Berne, and the most significant of a number of copies of an illustrated edition of Terence's *Comedies* in the Vatican Library, which can probably be traced back to a 5th-century original (*see* TERENCE and fig.), while a collection of tracts by Roman land surveyors, the *agrimensores*, goes back to a 6th-century original (*see* §(ii) below). A manual on midwifery (Brussels, Bib. Royale Albert 1er, MS. 3724) demonstrates the wide range of interests of the period. Both the Carolingian copy and the original of the famous Calendar of 354, created by the Roman calligrapher Filocalus, have been lost; a compendium of antique state imagery, it has come down to us only in later copies (*see* §(iii) below). The illustrations for the *Psychomachia* by Prudentius, depicting the struggle between virtues and vices, are examples of transpositions of antique models (*see* §(iii) below), as is the well-known Trier Apocalypse (Trier, Stadtbib., MS. 23), which is based on a 6th-century Roman model. Late Antique cycles were not only copied directly from the originals, but were also adapted from intermediate manuscripts produced in the British Isles, as demonstrated by the Valenciennes Apocalypse (Valenciennes, Bib. Mun., MS. 99) and Sedulius' *Carmen Paschale* (Antwerp, Mus. Plantin–Moretus, MS. M. 174).

The determining factor in the development of Carolingian book illumination, however, was the new formulation of the pictorial themes by artists as they freely assimilated and transformed their models. These new formulations, conditioned by the circumstances then prevailing, left their stamp on the character of the individual schools, along with characteristic ornamental forms in which antique motifs were linked with elements derived from Insular art, for example the large decorated initial letter as well as individual motifs (*see* INSULAR ART, §3).

(ii) Before c. AD *850.* The earliest extant work in the new Carolingian style is the Godescalc Evangeliary (781–3; Paris, Bib. N., MS. nouv. acq. lat. 1203; *see* GODESCALC and MANUSCRIPT, fig. 9), which was written in gold on purple ground by the scribe after whom it is named as a commission by Charlemagne and his wife. Despite its imperfections it demonstrates the new aims, in script, decoration and miniatures (see fig. 6), which were perfected and extended in the following period. In the years immediately following, the surviving manuscripts of the Court school have only ornamental decoration; even the Dagulf Psalter (Vienna, Österreich. Nbib., Cod. 1861) intended for Pope Adrian I (*reg* 772–95) is decorated with ornamental pages only. From the late 790s, however, the Gospel books produced by the Court school take up the pictorial world of the Godescalc Evangeliary, expanding it by using new models to produce magnificent portraits of the Evangelists, superb canon tables and monumental decorative pages, all of which convey the impression of imperial grandeur so characteristic of the Court school. With the insertion of figures and scenes into the letters on the decorative pages, a form of historiated initial, already known in Insular art, was developed and would become the distinctive hallmark of medieval decoration (*see* INITIAL, MANUSCRIPT). The Court school's supreme achievement was the Soissons or St Médard Gospels (Paris, Bib. N., MS. lat. 8850; for illustrations *see* CANON TABLE and SYMBOL); with its monumental miniatures, canon tables and decorative pages it epitomizes 'le style Charlemagne'. The final work of the Court school of Charlemagne is the Lorsch Codex Aureus (Alba Iulia, Batthyaneum Lib.; Rome, Vatican, Bib. Apostolica, MS. Pal. lat. 50), the miniatures of which had a strong impact even in the Ottonian period.

6. *St Matthew*, miniature from the Godescalc Evangeliary, AD 781–3 (Paris, Bibliothèque Nationale, MS. nouv. acq. lat. 1203, fol. 1*r*)

7. *St Matthew*, miniature from the Coronation Gospels, from Aachen, late 8th century (Vienna, Schatzkammer, fol. 15*r*)

Parallel with the work produced by Charlemagne's Court school, the quite different style of the Coronation Gospels (Vienna, Schatzkam.; see fig. 7), also originating at the court, marked the emergence of what might be termed the classical style. The *Evangelists*, depicted as antique philosopher types, refer back to the illusionistic style of the Late Antique, and the classicizing arcades of the canon tables use the same vocabulary. This style was continued in a small number of books, for example in the Aachen Gospels (Aachen, Domschatzkam.). One of its distinguishing features is the lack of emphasis on the decoration of initial letters.

Various schools, generally under the influence of former members of the court, followed these two groups; Charlemagne's Court school was emulated primarily in the east and the group represented by the Vienna Gospels had its following primarily in the west.

After Charlemagne's death the court itself soon lost its pre-eminence. During the reign of Louis the Pious, humanist and antiquarian interests were popular at court, as reflected in a number of superb copies of Classical manuscripts, among which are a Terence (Rome, Vatican, Bib. Apostolica, MS. Vat. lat. 3868; for illustration *see* TERENCE), the *agrimensores* codex (Rome, Vatican, Bib. Apostolica, MS. Pal. lat. 1569), the *Aratea* copies (Leiden, Bib. Rijksuniv., MS. Voss. lat. Q. 79; *see* ASTROLOGICAL AND ASTRONOMICAL MANUSCRIPTS, fig. 1; London, BL, Harley MS. 647) and the later copies of the Calendar of 354 (e.g. 15th century; Vienna, Osterreich. Nbib., Cod. 3416). For Louis's successor, Emperor Lothair I, a cycle of representations of the months was created for an edition of Wandalbert of Prüm's martyrology (*see* §(iii) below). The most important work of the Court school in Aachen is a Psalter made for the Emperor (London, BL, Add. MS. 37768).

Meanwhile, however, the legacy of art from Charlemagne's court had emerged elsewhere, in Reims. Under Archbishop EBBO, a confidant of Louis the Pious, a number of manuscripts were produced at the abbey of Hautvillers. These continued the tradition of painterly illusionism of the group associated with the Vienna Coronation Gospels, but in a new form, marked by a dynamic sense of movement and heightened expressivity. A new image of the Evangelists emerged in the Ebbo Gospels (Epernay, Bib. Mun., MS. 1; for illustration *see* AUTHOR PORTRAIT), in which they are portrayed as inspired seers, differing both from the imposing figures depicted by the Court school and the Classical philosopher types of the Vienna Gospels. Together with the canon tables illustrated with genre scenes and figures inspired by antique models, and initial pages with abstract gold decorative work, they represent a new type of Gospel book, which was to become extremely influential. Traces of Reims models in both the west and east of the empire are evidence of the impact of the art of Ebbo's period.

Besides the Ebbo Gospels, another masterpiece of the Reims group associated with Ebbo is the UTRECHT PSALTER (816–34; Utrecht, Bib. Rijksuniv., MS. 32), one of the outstanding achievements of medieval graphic art. The psalms and canticles are accompanied by drawn, mostly literal illustrations, sometimes historical scenes and occasional references to the events of the New Testament. The Late Antique elements in the images and the similarities between the content of the illustrations here and in other Psalter cycles suggest the existence of an earlier model, although there is controversy about its extent and character; nonetheless, it is generally agreed that there is a significant Carolingian contribution. Two other manuscripts belonging to the Ebbo group demonstrate the influences underlying them: the Berne *Physiologus* (Berne, Burgerbib., MS. 318), which copies an antique manuscript, and a codex in Paris (Paris, Bib. N., MS. lat. 265) the miniatures in which repeat those that appear in the Vienna Gospels.

When Ebbo as a supporter of the lost cause of Lothair I was forced to leave Reims in 835 and go into exile, the scriptorium of St Martin in Tours (*see* TOURS, §2(i)) was reaching its peak. It was under Alcuin's successor, Fridugisus (*reg* 807–834), that the school started to expand, and during the tenure of Abbot Adalhard (*reg* 834–43) and Abbot Vivian (*reg* 844–51) a series of Gospels, Sacramentaries and Bibles was produced that demonstrated the ability of the artists at Tours to master the Classical heritage in both figural and decorative art and make it their own. Decoration was developed to become an instrument serving to structure and punctuate the layout of the huge pandects (*see* TOURS, fig. 2). Miniatures were introduced *c.* 830, as in the Stuttgart Gospels (Stuttgart,

Württemberg Landesbib., MS.II.40). The *Christ in Majesty* and the *Evangelist* portraits form a programme that became a classic component of the Tours Gospels and continued to be used as a model further afield for centuries. With the Moutier-Grandval Bible (London, BL, Add. MS. 10546; *see* BIBLE, fig. 3) figural illustrations also started to appear in the Bibles, serving as frontispieces for the biblical books. In the Vivian Bible (Paris, Bib. N., MS. lat. 1), where the number of miniatures was doubled to eight, one of the great artists of medieval book illumination, known as Master C (Koehler, 1930–82) emerged; his most beautiful work is in the Lothair Gospels (Paris, Bib. N., MS. lat. 266). Among the school's patrons were emperors and kings, temporal and spiritual princes, including Lothair I, the Empress Irmingard and Charles the Bald, and consequently portraits of the rulers were featured in the manuscripts. Tours' finest period was rapidly followed by its demise. In 853 the city was attacked by the Vikings; although a few manuscripts were produced after that, even a Bible (Cologne, Erzbischöf. Dioz.- & Dombib., MS. 1), the school did not recover its former importance.

An important school in the Carolingian revival of Classical painting after Reims and Tours was Metz. Once again the initiative came from a member of the court, Drogo, the illegitimate son of Charlemagne. Drogo became Bishop of Metz in 823 and served as archchaplain to his brother, Louis the Pious, and his nephew Lothiar I for many years. A small number of manuscripts were created in Metz, which are among the finest achievements of medieval decorative art. The main work is the Sacramentary made for Drogo (Paris, Bib. N., MS. lat. 9428; *see* MISSAL, fig. 1); the decoration consists of ornamentation of the initial letters with gold acanthus tendrils encompassing small figures and scenes. Thus a motif already used in the initial pages of the Gospels produced at Charlemagne's Court school was taken up in a new form. The small scenes are of great iconographic interest as they form a New Testament cycle, rare in Carolingian book illumination.

Another place of manuscript production was the scriptorium of THEODULF, Bishop of Orléans; as the author of the *Libri Carolini*, Theodulf had played an important role at Charlemagne's court in the iconoclastic dispute. Like Alcuin, he too had undertaken a new edition of the Bible, as attested by several copies. The two most significant (Paris, Bib. N., MS. lat. 9380 and Le Puy, Trésor Cathédrale Notre-Dame) are written in tiny minuscule script and decorated with gold on purple parchment, but are without miniatures, in line with the author's standpoint. A Gospel book (Berne, Burgerbib., MS. 348), created in Theodulf's sphere of influence, probably at Fleury where he was abbot, also has no miniatures other than a representation of the *Evangelist Symbols*, with the Hand of God.

In the east, the scriptorium at Fulda is of particular interest. As part of the area evangelized by Anglo-Saxon missionaries, Fulda adhered to the Insular tradition in its manuscripts well into the 9th century, as demonstrated by a Psalter (Frankfurt am Main, Stadt- & Ubib., MS. Barth. 32). Rabanus Maurus, Abbot of Fulda (822–42), is associated with the famous CARMINA FIGURATA of his *De laudibus sanctae crucis* (e.g. Rome, Vatican, Bib. Apostolica, MS. Reg. lat. 124), which includes an image of *Louis the Pious*. Elaborately produced Gospels attest to the school's importance in the second quarter of the century (Erlangen, Ubib., MS. 9; Würzburg, Ubib., MS. M.p.th.f.66). The Evangelist portraits and canon tables indicate that among their models was a manuscript from Charlemagne's Court school. In Salzburg, too, the Evangelist portraits from the second quarter of the 9th century (e.g. in Paris, Bib. N., MS. lat. 8849) reveal the influence of a manuscript from the Court school. The same is true of the Middle Rhine where Charlemagne's Court school served as a model in Mainz (e.g. Munich, Bayer. Staatsbib., Clm. 4451) and in Lorsch (e.g. Manchester, John Rylands U. Lib., MS. 9). Completely different from all of these schools is the style of manuscripts from the northern French monastery of St Bertin, Saint-Omer, which had purely ornamental decoration. The frames and initials have a light, delicate decoration, particularly noticeable in the Psalter (Berlin, Staatsbib. Preuss. Kultbes., MS. theol. lat. fol. 58) destined for King Louis the German. This is the early stage of what is described as Franco-Saxon illumination, centred in the monasteries of northern France (*see* §(iii) below).

(iii) After c. AD *850.* In the second half of the 9th century the situation had changed. The school of Tours had ceased to function, the Court school of Emperor Lothair came to an end with his death in 855 and Metz soon ceased to figure among the important renaissance schools. Only in Reims, under the aegis of Archbishop Hincmar (*reg* 845–82), did manuscript production continue to develop out of the preceding great period, building on it, but nonetheless distinct. The use of gold and purple is characteristic, as in the Purple Psalter (Oxford, Bodleian Lib., MS. Douce 59). The main works are the Gospels, which originally belonged to St Remi (New York, Pierpont Morgan Lib., MS. M. 728) and those that were at St Thierry (Reims, Bib. Mun. MS. 7). The richly decorated Achadaeus Psalter (Cambridge, Corpus Christi Coll., MS. 271), made under Hincmar's successor, is especially interesting as it is precisely dated to 886–7 by the inclusion of the names of the king, pope and archbishop, thus documenting the late stage of the Reims school.

The group of manuscripts associated with Archbishop Hincmar were not the only important representatives of book illumination in Reims in the third quarter of the 9th century. A second group of manuscripts was created in these years, linked in script and ornamentation, but produced in another Reims scriptorium. The most impressive of all Carolingian Bibles, the BIBLE OF SAN PAOLO fuori le Mura (*c.* 870; Rome, S Paolo fuori le Mura; see fig. 8), belongs to this group; it was one of the presents Charles the Bald gave to win the Pope's support for his coronation as Emperor in 875. Decorated with 23 (originally 24) full-page miniatures to introduce the books in the Old and New Testaments, a dedicatory miniature of *Charles the Bald and Richildis* (his second wife), as well as a plethora of decorated pages, title-pages and initial letters, it far exceeds all the Tours Bibles in richness and splendour. In the dedicatory poem the writer Ingobertus compares himself with antique calligraphers. The Bible, which is the work of a team of scribes and illuminators, brings together not only a variety of models, but also the influences of the

8. *Story of San Girolamo*, miniature from the Bible of San Paolo, Reims, *c.* AD 870 (Rome, S Paolo fuori le Mura, fol. 3*v*)

great renaissance schools of Tours, Reims and the Court school of Charles the Bald.

Charles the Bald's Court school, the last of the great schools of the Carolingian renaissance, is associated with the ruler and his court through numerous allusions in poems, litanies and prayers. While the actual location of the school is still a matter of conjecture, it is nonetheless clear that it must have been in close proximity to the ruler, at a place in the heartland of his territory. The name of the principal scribe, Liuthard, which recurs in several manuscripts—for example in the Codex Aureus of St Emmeram along with that of his brother, Beringar—is another unifying factor in the school. One of the earliest manuscripts written for Charles is especially memorable, a prayer book intended for the sovereign's personal use (Munich, Residenz), which is the earliest surviving prayer book made for a medieval king. The masterpiece of this school, the CODEX AUREUS OF ST EMMERAM (Munich, Bayer. Staatsbib., Clm. 14000; for illustration *see* PURPLE CODEX), is very splendidly decorated with pictorial and ornamental pages and canon tables in imitation of Charlemagne's Court school. The images of Charles developed a new and very important iconography for the ruler portrait.

The second group of manuscripts that dominated the third quarter of the 9th century alongside the Court school of Charles the Bald was in complete contrast to it. They were produced in the monasteries of the region of north France adjacent to the English Channel, following on from the school of St Bertin (*see* §(ii) above), which operated there in the second quarter of the century, but using a new vocabulary more heavily influenced by Insular art. The decoration is concentrated on frames, canon tables and initials. The main location of the school has been given as the monastery of Saint-Amand, where an abstract, linear style of ornament was consistently used. The school was geared towards export, producing series of Gospel books and Sacramentaries. Miniatures occurred only in exceptional cases, the best-known being in the Francis II Gospels (Paris, Bib. N., Mus. lat. 257), with not only the *Four Evangelists* but also—iconographically unusual—a miniature of the *Crucifixion*. The school's supreme achievement is the Second Bible of Charles the Bald (Paris, Bib. N., MS. lat. 2). Adorned with decorative pages and initials, it is a masterpiece of graphic art, and an example of the consistent use of abstract ornament (see fig. 9). Another school was at the monastery of Saint-Vaast where the linear abstract style was less consistently adhered to, being mixed with vegetal motifs. More miniatures were also used, the best-known being the double portraits of the *Evangelists* in the richly decorated Prague Gospels (Prague Cathedral, Cim. 2): beside the figures of the *Evangelists* are representations of their vocations, legitimizing the authors of the sacred texts.

Because of their geographical position, the Franco-Saxon monasteries were particularly vulnerable to attacks

9. *In principio*, decorated initial page to Genesis from the Second Bible of Charles the Bald, from Saint-Amand, AD 871–3 (Paris, Bibliothèque Nationale, MS. lat. 2, fol. 11*r*)

from the Normans; as the monks fled, manuscripts, illuminators and scribes moved eastwards, establishing themselves in new monasteries, which they encouraged to start production on their own account. This applies to Corvey or Echternach, for instance, where manuscripts produced *c.* 900 show the influence of Franco-Saxon models.

From among other east Frankish schools of the second half of the 9th century Freising can be singled out; a group of Gospel books was created there during the tenure of Bishop Anno (*reg* 854–75), influenced by manuscripts from Reims. In the late 9th century two important cycles of miniatures were produced on the island of Reichenau; the first, a copy (Rome, Vatican, Bib. Apostolica, MS. Reg. lat. 438) intended for Louis the German of the martyrology of Wandalbert of Prüm, a work originally dedicated to Lothair I; the second, the most important copy of the *Psychomachia* by Prudentius (Berne, Burgerbib., MS. 264).

It was, above all, the school of St Gall, however, where a fine Carolingian scriptorium that had been evolving steadily over decades, reached its peak, as at Freising, in the late 9th century. Initially concentrating on ornamental decoration, miniatures were now included in its most important manuscripts, such as the Folchart Psalter (St Gall, Stift.-Bib., Cod. 23) and especially the Psalterium Aureum (St Gall, Stift.-Bib., Cod. 22). Besides miniatures of *David* and *Jerome* it has a unique cycle of 15 illustrations for the titles of the Psalms, as well as richly decorated initials. The final manuscript to be produced was a manuscript of *Maccabees* (Leiden, Bib. Rijksuniv., MS. Perizoni 18). An attack by the Hungarians in 925 led to the dissolution of the last of the important Carolingian schools.

BIBLIOGRAPHY

H. Janitschek: 'Zwei Studien zur Geschichte der karolingischen Malerei', *Strassburger Festgruss an Anton Springer zum 4. Mai 1885* (Berlin and Stuttgart, 1885), pp. 1–30

——: *Geschichte der deutschen Kunst*, iii (Berlin, 1890), pp. 1–51

E. H. Zimmermann: *Die Fuldaer Buchmalerei in karolingischer und ottonischer Zeit* (Vienna, 1910)

H. Omont: *Bibliothèque Nationale: Bibles de Charles le Chauve II (lat. 2)* (Paris, 1911)

F. Landsberger: *Der St. Galler Folchart-Psalter: Eine Initialenstudie* (St Gall, 1912)

A. Merton: *Die Buchmalerei in St. Gallen vom neunten bis zum elften Jahrhundert* (Leipzig, 1912/*R* 1923)

A. Boinet: *La Miniature carolingienne* (Paris, 1913)

G. Leidinger, ed.: *Der Codex Aureus der Bayerischen Staatsbibliothek in München*, 6 vols (Munich, 1921–5) [facs.]

A. Goldschmidt: *Die karolingische Buchmalerei* (1928), i of *Die deutsche Buchmalerei* (Munich and Florence, 1928; Eng. trans., Florence and Paris, 1928)

W. Koehler: *Die karolingischen Miniaturen*, 6 vols (Berlin, 1930–94) [vols iv, v and vi with F. Mütherich; i, *Die Schule von Tours*; ii, *Die Hofschule Karls des Grossen*; iii, *Die Gruppe des Wiener Krönungsevangeliars: Metzer Handschriften*; iv, *Die Hofschule Kaiser Lothars: Lotharingische Einzelhandschriften*; v, *Die Hofschule Karls des Kahlen*; vi, *Die Schule von Reims*]

C. Nordenfalk: 'Ein karolingisches Sakramentar aus Echternach und seine Vorläufer', *Acta Archaeol. [Copenhagen]*, ii (1931), pp. 207–44

E. T. De Wald: *The Illustrations of the Utrecht Psalter* (Princeton, London and Leipzig, [1932])

A. Grabar and C. Nordenfalk: *Das frühe Mittelalter* (Geneva, 1957; Eng. trans., 1957), pp. 89–217 [esp. C. Nordenfalk on manuscript painting]

O. Homburger: 'Eine spätkarolingische Schule von Corbie', *Forschungen zur Kunstgeschichte und christlichen Archäologie*, iii (Wiesbaden, 1957), pp. 412–26

C. von Steiger and O. Homburger: *Physiologus Bernensis: Faksimile-Ausgabe des Codex Bongarsianus 318 der Burgerbibliothek Bern* (Basle, 1964)

F. Mütherich: 'Die Buchmalerei am Hofe Karls des Grossen', *Karl der Grosse; Lebenswerk und Nachleben*, iii, ed. W. Braunfels and H. Schnitzler (Düsseldorf, 1965), pp. 9–53

B. Bischoff and others: *Der Stuttgarter Bilderpsalter: Bibl. fol. 23 Württembergische Landesbibliothek, Stuttgart*, 2 vols (Stuttgart, 1965–8) [facs. and commentary]

W. Braunfels, ed.: *Das Lorscher Evangeliar* (Munich, 1967) [facs. and intro.]

W. Koehler: *Buchmalerei des frühen Mittelalters: Fragmente und Entwürfe aus dem Nachlass*, ed. E. Kitzinger and F. Mütherich (Munich, 1972)

Hrabanus Maurus: Liber de laudibus sanctae crucis. Faksimile-Ausgabe des Codex Vindobonensis 652 der Österreichischen Nationalbibliothek (Graz, 1972–3) [facs. and commentary by K. Holter]

Codex Millenarius (Graz, 1974) [facs. and commentary by W. Neumüller and K. Holter]

F. Mütherich, ed.: *Drogo-Sakramentar: Manuscrit latin 9428, Bibliothèque nationale, Paris*, Codices Selecti, xlix (Graz, 1974) [commentary vol. by W. Koehler]

Trierer Apokalypse: Faksimile-Ausgabe des Codex 31 der Stadt-bibliotek Trier (Graz, 1975) [facs. and commentary by R. Laufner and P. Klein]

F. Mütherich and J. E. Gaehde: *Karolingische Buchmalerei* (Munich, 1976; Eng. trans., London, 1977)

H. L. Kessler: *The Illustrated Bibles from Tours* (Princeton, 1977)

S. Dufrenne: *Les Illustrations du Psautier d'Utrecht: Sources et apport carolingien* (Paris, 1978)

K. Holter, ed.: *Der Goldene Psalter: Dagulf-Psalter: Vollständige Faksimile-Ausgabe im Originalformat von Codex 1861 der Österreichischen Nationalbibliothek*, Codices Selecti, lxix (Graz, 1980)

K. van der Horst and J. H. A. Engelbregt, eds.: *Utrecht-Psalter: Vollständige Faksimile-Ausgabe im Originalformat der Handschrift 32 aus dem Besitz der Bibliothek der Rijksuniversiteit te Utrecht*, 2 vols, Codices Selecti, lxxv (Graz, 1982–4) [facs. and commentary]

C. Eggenberger: *Psalterium aureum Sancti Galli: Mittelalterliche Psalterillustration im Kloster St. Gallen* (Sigmaringen, 1987)

B. Bischoff and others: *Aratea Kommentar zum Aratus des Germanicus MS. Voss. Lat. Q. 79. Bibliotheek der Rijksuniversiteit Leiden* (Lucerne, 1987–9) [facs. and commentary]

F. Mütherich and K. Dachs, eds: *Das Quedlinburger Evangeliars* (Munich, 1991)

La bibbia di San Paolo fuori le Mura, Codex membranaceus saeculi, ix (Rome, 1993) [facs. and commentary]

FLORENTINE MÜTHERICH

V. Metalwork.

The revival of metalworking in the Carolingian period was brought about by the reform and enrichment of the liturgy under Charlemagne. The revised liturgy required more sacred vessels, the most important manuscripts needed lavish book covers, and many churches were now wealthy enough to commission works of the highest quality. An increasing interest in relics, encouraged by Charlemagne, necessitated elaborate reliquaries to house them. Around his own court in Aachen, Charlemagne revived the craft of monumental bronze-casting on a scale not seen since the Roman Empire. The bronze works were a conscious reference to the grandeur and authority of ancient Rome.

The artistic unity that was apparent around Charlemagne's court was replaced after the Treaty of Verdun in 843 by a greater diversity of styles, developing especially in the newly revitalized regions of Lombardy, north-east France, south Germany and north Spain. The spectacular ecclesiastical metalwork surviving from the Carolingian empire represents only one aspect of the smiths' achievements; such secular objects as swords, buckles, brooches and belts, preserved in earlier Frankish graves, were no longer buried and have thus largely disappeared.

1. Before AD 843. 2. AD 843 and later.

1. Before AD 843. At the start of Charlemagne's reign the main cultural and intellectual impetus in continental Europe came from the Insular monasteries of Ireland and Northumbria, with missionary monks bringing their manuscripts and art as far as Fulda and Echternach. The chalice (Kremsmünster, Stiftskirche, Schatzkam.) given by Tassilo III, Duke of Bavaria, to Kremsmünster between 777 and 788 and the back cover of the Lindau Gospels (*c.* 800; New York, Pierpont Morgan Lib.) are examples of the restless interlacing animal ornament from Britain being used on south German work. Although Insular in appearance, the Lindau Book Cover is made with cloisonné enamel panels. Cloisonné, a technique practised by craftsmen in the Byzantine empire, did not find favour with Insular craftsmen who tended to use the champlevé technique for applying enamels (*see* Enamel, §2(i) and (ii)). A mixture of style and technique is also found on the house-shaped reliquary (Sion Cathedral, Treasury) inscribed with the name of Altheus, Bishop of Sion between 780 and 799. The animal ornament is Germanic but the bright cloisonné enamel plaques of the *Evangelists* are executed in the north Italian manner. Two reliquaries, made away from the dominant influence of Charlemagne's court, show the continuation of earlier Merovingian designs: the Enger Burse (purse-shaped) Reliquary (*c.* 800; Berlin, Bodemus.) and the Pepin Burse Reliquary (Conques, Trésor Ste Foy). The Enger Reliquary combines Merovingian garnet and paste inlay in gold cells with more classically inspired figures under arcades. The earliest part of the Pepin Reliquary, a primitive embossed *Crucifixion* plaque with an 8th-century inscription, was used to repair the reliquary in the 9th century (*see* Reliquary, §I, 3).

A further injection of outside influence came with the defeat of the Avars in 796. Fifteen wagon-loads of precious eastern booty were brought to Aachen. It is quite likely that the sword known as Charlemagne's (Vienna, Schatzkam.) arrived in the West at this time: the copper inlay and gilt dragons are reminiscent of Hungarian or south Russian work. The ewer reliquary (St Maurice, Abbey Treasury) was reputedly given to Charlemagne by Harun ar-Rashid of Baghdad (*reg* 786–809). Certainly the large hemispherical enamels are of Middle-Eastern design, and the entire container, made of somewhat ill-fitting pieces, may be of similar manufacture.

Charlemagne's endeavour to confirm his status with all the visible trappings of imperial Rome extended to the field of metalwork, in which his most monumental achievement was the revival of Classical bronze-casting. For his imperial chapel at Aachen he commissioned five pairs of solid cast bronze doors, the largest almost 4 m high (four pairs survive). Their ornament is severely restrained but impressive. The doors are divided into plain panels surrounded by frames in low-relief Classical ornament. Each leaf has a lion-head ring mount based on Classical designs. Remains of a foundry and even moulds for the door frame have been excavated, revealing that the doors were made locally. Another possible product of this foundry is the pine-cone fountain in the chapel vestibule. It appears to be a copy of the pine-cone fountain (Rome, Vatican, Cortile Pigna) symbolizing the fountain of life in the centre of the atrium at St Peter's, Rome. Charlemagne's founders had great difficulty in making their copy of the pine-cone: it could not be cleanly removed from its mould and was left partially complete and unpolished (*see also* Aachen, §2(ii)(a) and (b)). Technically simpler and more successful were the bronze railings around the upper gallery of the chapel. They are made with tall, slender pilasters topped by accurate Corinthian capitals and framed by delicate acanthus scrollwork.

The bronze life-size equestrian statue (untraced) of a Roman emperor that Charlemagne brought from Ravenna may have been the inspiration for an unusual bronze equestrian statuette (Paris, Louvre; see fig. 10), traditionally identified as a portrait of Charlemagne. With the characteristic Frankish moustache, large eyes, gartered leggings, tunic and cloak, the statuette is not unlike the vivid description of Charlemagne given by Einhard (p. 77). Another bronze-casting known as the Throne of Dagobert (Paris, Bib. N., Cab. Médailles; *see* Throne, §II, 1(ii)) is also of debatable date. Although the back and sides were probably added by Abbot Suger of Saint-Denis in the 12th century, the accurate Classical design of the base could well date from Charlemagne's time. Only a drawing survives of the embossed silver triumphal arch (*c.* 815), designed as a cross base and commissioned by Einhard. Its decoration is arranged in the same manner as a Roman imperial archway but the subject-matter is the triumph of Christianity (*see* Reliquary, §I, 3). The arch and the equestrian statuette are examples of Classical forms reproduced in miniature.

10. *Equestrian figure of ?Charlemagne*, bronze, h. 235 mm, from Metz, early 9th century (Paris, Musée du Louvre)

Three other objects are closely associated with the Emperor: the Talisman (or Amulet) of Charlemagne, the 'Escrin (shrine) de Charlemagne' and an almost life-size silver crucifix probably given to Pope Leo III by Charlemagne after his coronation in Rome in 800. The dainty amulet (late 8th century; Reims, Pal. Tau), shaped like an ampulla, originally contained a relic of the Virgin's hair, visible behind a sapphire and an emerald. The stones, attached by acanthus claw settings, are surrounded by a rich border of gold filigree, embossed foliage, gemstones and pearls. The 'Escrin', once in the abbey treasury at Saint-Denis and drawn by Labarre in 1794 before it was destroyed in the French Revolution, was of an extraordinary design, with tiers of open bejewelled arches surmounted by an open roof-type structure. The scaffold of arches stood on a box base and dozens of jewels hung in all the apertures. It was clearly enriched several times during the thousand years it survived. The only part that remains is the crest (Paris, Bib. N., Cab. Médailles), a Roman intaglio with gemstones and pearls radiating around it. The great silver crucifix was melted down in the 16th century, but before then an unusual copy (1540; Rome, Vatican, Mus. Sacro Crist.) was made with cuir-bouilli (leather moulded through water). The massive style of the figure of *Christ* and the restrained treatment of drapery are paralleled in later manuscripts from the Court school of Charles the Bald. The iconographical arrangement of the cross, with the risen *Christ* at the top and the *Virgin* and *St John* on the lateral arms, is the earliest example of its kind.

Charlemagne's son Louis the Pious (*reg* 814–40), while a great lover of learning, was less impressed by material splendour than his father. He distributed the greater part of the imperial treasure at Aachen to Pope Leo III and to the poor. Only two significant pieces of precious metalwork come from his reign; they give no indication of an imperial provenance. The Ardenne Processional Cross (*c.* 830; Nuremberg, Ger. Nmus.) is completely studded with gems, fairly crudely surrounded with pearled wire and interspersed with small raised cross motifs (also found on the Milan Altar, *c.* 835; *see* §2 below). It is one of the earliest jewelled crosses to survive. The other object is the St Stephen Burse Reliquary (*c.* 830; Vienna, Schatzkam.), which is related to the earlier Enger Reliquary. One side is completely studded with gold and gems while the back and sides are decorated with figurative roundels struck from a die.

2. AD 843 AND LATER. The development of local centres after the division of the empire in 843 was reflected in metalwork as in other media. Under Lothair I (*reg* 840–55) the strong cultural traditions of north Italy reasserted themselves. The Golden Altar (0.85×1.22 m, *c.* 835) of S Ambrogio, Milan, is the finest product of this period. An inscription indicates that it was commissioned by Archbishop Angilbert II of Milan (*reg* 824–59) and two scenes show St Ambrose giving crowns both to the archbishop, who presents the altar to him, and to Vuolvinius the Smith (see fig. 11; *see also* RELIQUARY, §I, 3). All four sides of the altar are decorated with embossed sheets (gold on the front, silver gilt elsewhere) surrounded by enamel and jewel-studded frames. The centre of the altar front is

11. *Vuolvinius the Smith Receiving a Crown from St Ambrose*, silver gilt, detail of roundel on the back of the Golden Altar, 1.22×2.20×0.85 m, S Ambrogio, Milan, *c.* AD 835

divided into a cross shape with a panel of *Christ Enthroned* in the middle. Accompanying scenes are a rare early cycle of the *Life of Christ* and the *Life and Miracles of St Ambrose*. Both the style and the iconography of the altar derive from Late Antique models. Vuolvinius the Smith produced a work of rare technical excellence. The cloisonné enamels are particularly delicate and colourful.

Other pieces of north Italian metalwork may be related to the altar. The Iron Crown of Lombardy in the chapel of Theodolinda, Monza Cathedral, is made of an iron band surrounded by a jewelled diadem. The blue, green and white enamel plaques that surround the gemstones suggest that the crown could have come from the same workshop as the Milan Altar. The internal iron ring is traditionally a relic of Christ's Passion and the whole object may have been designed for a votive purpose. The burse reliquary (see fig. 12) also at Monza Cathedral, heavily encrusted with gold and gemstones on one side, shows some technical similarities with the Milan Altar too. The other side, with a *Crucifixion* punched into sheet gold, shares the same iconographic traditions as the *Crucifixion* panel on the altar. They both show Longinus and Stephaton and Classical busts of the sun and moon.

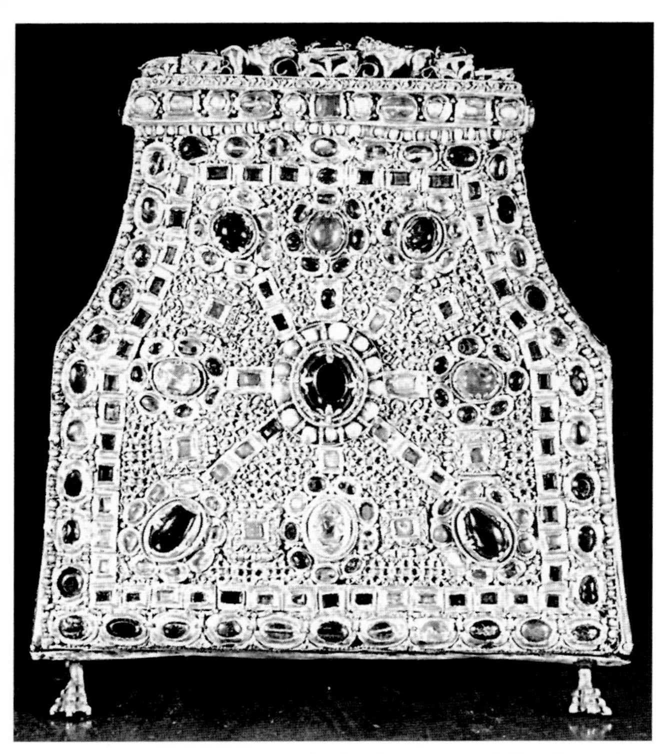

12. Burse reliquary (front), gold studded with gemstones, 333×260 mm, from north Italy, mid-9th century (Monza, Museo F. Serpero del Tesoro)

The Pepin Reliquary at Conques, a composite piece (*see* §1 above), has several oddly shaped enamel plaques attached, for instance as capitals on the rear. Their pattern of gold and enamel is just like that on the borders of the *Christ in Majesty* on the Milan Altar. As they were clearly not made for their present position they must have reached Conques from Milan, perhaps as part of another reliquary, some time after the mid-9th century. The Lantern of St Vincent (Conques, Trésor Ste Foy) was probably given (*c.* 880) to the abbey at Conques by Abbot Bégon I (*see* CONQUES, §2). The reliquary is a miniature representation of a Roman funerary monument such as that (1st century AD) at Glanum (Saint-Rémy-de-Provence). On a square base, a drum is surrounded by six columns topped by a conical roof. The bust of *Christ Blessing*, repeated six times around the drum, probably relates the reliquary to Conques, which at that time was dedicated to Christ. The style of the busts, with long faces, closely set eyes, long noses and sharply creased drapery, is reminiscent of the Milan Altar. The influence of the Milan Altar persisted as far as Oviedo: in 908 King Alfonso III gave Oviedo Cathedral the Cross of Victory (Oviedo Cathedral, Camara Santa), which has 28 enamel plaques on the front. These show animal and foliate motifs executed with the same exquisite technique and colour range as the Milan work. Its shape also reflects the design of the Ardenne Cross made in the reign of Louis the Pious. The Tuotilo Book Cover (*c.* 900; St Gall, Stift.-Bib.) also has technical connections with the Milan Altar. The book cover has ivory plaques surrounded by metal frames. On both the altar and the book cover the embossed foliage is not simply hammered out of a single sheet, but each leaf is embossed separately and soldered on to the backing.

Charles the Bald, youngest son of Louis the Pious, inherited the western part of the empire in 843 and eventually secured the central domain of Lotharingia. Under Charles, Saint-Denis Abbey superseded Aachen as the centre of royal patronage. Although the abbey suffered some incursions from the Vikings, between 867 and 885 Charles the Bald, as lay abbot, secured a period of relative peace there. Most of the treasures of Saint-Denis were lost in the French Revolution (*see* SAINT-DENIS ABBEY, §IV). Early in his reign, before Charles was able to assemble craftsmen of high quality, the covers for the Psalter of Charles the Bald were made (*c.* 850–60; Paris, Bib. N., lat. 1152). Its central ivories were reused, from *c.* 820–30, and the metal borders are coarse and unimaginative; the gemstones are large, the filigree heavy. This contrasts with the outstanding covers of the CODEX AUREUS OF ST EMMERAM (Munich, Bayer. Staatsbib. Clm. 14000; *see* BOOKBINDING, colour pl. IV, fig. 2). Precisely dated by an inscription to 870, it was at St Emmeram, Regensburg, by the 10th century. The front cover has a stunning arrangement with rich borders of blue and green gems regularly interspersed with pearls held by chalice-shaped fittings. In the centre is a plaque of *Christ in Majesty* and around him are the *Evangelists* and scenes from the Gospels, all in embossed gold. Small acanthus leaves clasp the gemstones and the filigree scrolls end in silver pearls, features also found on Charlemagne's talisman. The figure style is of clearly northern origin, deriving from the taut figures of the Reims and Tours manuscript tradition.

During the French Revolution, Saint-Denis lost the golden altar probably given to it by Charles the Bald after he became lay abbot. It is known from early descriptions and from a late medieval painting, the *Mass of St Giles* (London, NG), in which it is illustrated. The richness of decoration and diversity of motifs find their match only in the Milan Altar. The frontal is divided by three arches with *Christ in Majesty* in the centre. Hanging from the side arches are jewelled votive crowns, like the iron crown at Monza, another indication of north Italian influence.

The ciborium of King Arnulf (Munich, Residenz) is another Carolingian treasure designed like a miniature architectural structure. Four columns supporting arches stand on the corners of a square portable altar base. Above the arcade four short columns support a gabled roof. An inscription cites King Arnulf of Bavaria as the donor. He must have given the ciborium to St Emmeram, Regensburg, during his reign (887–96). Like the Codex Aureus, it has heavily beaded frames around the repoussé gold figurative plaques. The fluttering style of the figures is reminiscent of Reims manuscripts.

The front cover of the Lindau Gospels (New York, Pierpont Morgan Lib.) can be classed as another product of Charles the Bald's Court school. The slim, fluttering angels on gold plaques surrounding the central *Crucifixion* are similar in style to those of the Codex Aureus. The solid monumental *Christ* harks back to the Court school of Charlemagne; however, the decorative borders appear more cluttered than those on the Codex Aureus because of the pearls and the gemstones of various shapes and colours (reds, greens and blues). The busy surface is achieved by a layer of acanthus foliage forming a total background.

The eclectic style of Charles the Bald's Court school, the location of which is uncertain (*see* §VI, 2 below), may be due to the use of a wide variety of sources, many of which are now lost, and also to genuine artistic inventiveness. The dogged adherence in Charlemagne's reign to authoritative Classical models indicates a culture trying to find its roots in a somewhat selfconscious way. By the end of the 9th century the cultural *renovatio* was reaching fulfilment. Skilled and educated artists now existed all across the empire. Their visual vocabulary drew on a wide range of foreign and native sources. The result was an artistic climate in which artists felt free to develop in their own way. The first few decades of the 10th century were spent trying, often in vain, to preserve these spectacular treasures from the pillaging of the Vikings, Slavs and Hungarians.

BIBLIOGRAPHY

Einhard and Notger the Stammerer: *Two Lives of Charlemagne* (early 9th century); trans. L. Thorpe (Harmondsworth, 1974)
D. M. Félibien: *Histoire de l'abbaye de Saint-Denis* (Paris, 1706)
P. E. Schramm and F. Mütherich: *Denkmale der deutschen Könige und Kaiser: Ein Beitrag zur Herrschergeschichte von Karl dem Grossen bis Friedrich II, 768–1250* (Munich, 1962)
F. Steenbock: *Der kirchliche Prachteinband im frühen Mittelalter von den Anfängen bis zum Beginn der Gotik* (Berlin, 1965)
Les Trésors des églises de France (exh. cat., Paris, Mus. A. Déc., 1965)
P. Lasko: *Ars sacra, 800–1200*, Pelican Hist. A. (Harmondsworth, 1972)

JANE GEDDES

VI. Ivories.

Before the establishment of the Carolingian dynasty, the craft of ivory-carving was almost extinguished, partly owing to the spread of Islam, which interrupted the supply of ivory from India and North Africa. Carolingian ivories, most of which are relief plaques made to adorn luxury book covers, are closely related in composition, framing, ornament and drapery styles to contemporary illuminated manuscripts. The same models were used for both, and in some instances the same person may have been both the ivory-carver and the illuminator. The two main groups of ivories are those associated with the Court school of Charlemagne, and those from the workshops of Charles the Bald; ivories can also possibly be associated with the reign of Charlemagne's son, Louis the Pious (*reg* 814–40).

1. Before AD 843. 2. AD 843 and later.

1. BEFORE AD 843. Ivory-carving played an important role in the Carolingian *renovatio.* Compared to the few attempts at monumental sculpture in stone and stucco (*see* §III above), the reliefs are a remarkable achievement. The main stylistic feature of many in this group is the return to antique naturalism, learned through copying Late Antique models. The dependence on the Early Christian tradition can occasionally be demonstrated by the survival of both the model and the Carolingian copy: one survivor, clearly instrumental in the genesis of Carolingian ivories around 800, is the fragmentary five-part diptych (Berlin, Staatl. Museen; Nevers, Mus. Blandin; Paris, Louvre) produced in Rome *c.* 400, the scenes from which were faithfully copied on a book cover (Oxford, Bodleian Lib., MS. Douce 176) depicting *Christ Triumphant* surrounded by scenes of his life. The latter originally adorned a manuscript written at the royal abbey of Chelles, whose abbess was Gisela, Charlemagne's sister, and it was certainly produced at the Court school at Aachen.

13. Book cover of the Dagulf Psalter showing scenes of *David* and *St Jerome*, ivory, h. 168 mm, from Aachen, AD 783–95 (Paris, Musée du Louvre)

The Oxford book cover is stylistically linked to the only securely dated ivory: the cover (Paris, Louvre; see fig. 13) of the Dagulf Psalter (Vienna, Österreich. Nbib., Cod. 1861), dated between 783 and 795, which contains scenes of *David* and *St Jerome.* These ivories became the nucleus of the works produced during the reign of Charlemagne, displaying strong Early Christian influences in the physical type of the figure with youthful heads, wide-open eyes, elegant folds and classic orientation. Another pivotal work presumably produced about 810, but dated by Harbison to the 820s, is the celebrated cover (front, London, V&A; back, Rome, Vatican Mus. Sacro Bib. Apostolica), of the Lorsch Gospels (Alba Iulia, Batthyaneum Lib.; Rome, Vatican, Bib. Apostolica, MS. Pal. lat. 50), which promotes a more calligraphic rather than plastic treatment of the drapery. Each cover is divided into five parts, with the incorporation of some elements of a 6th-century consular diptych: the top panel of the London cover may be the vestige of an original Early Christian ivory. With the increased demand for ivory during the Carolingian period, the limited supply of late Classical decorated panels, usually consular diptychs, were planed down to provide a new working surface. The Lorsch Gospel covers not only reveal a profound indebtedness to earlier models but they are the most lavish ivories to survive from the early 9th century.

Other ivories either display characteristics of both the Dagulf and Lorsch ivories or seem to be independent of them. These include the beautiful *Ascension* (Darmstadt, Hess. Landesmus.; see fig. 14) with its rich dramatic qualities, the *St John the Evangelist* (New York, Cloisters), whose opulent drapery goes beyond the *all'antica* effects of the earlier models, and the *St Michael* ivory (Leipzig, Mus. Ksthandwks), which is noted for its ornamental abundance. Because of the strong stylistic and compositional similarities to manuscripts produced for the court, for example the Trier Gospels (Trier, Stadtbib., MS. 22) and the Soissons Gospels (Paris, Bib. N., MS. lat. 8850), and the fact that many of the ivories were destined for book covers, they were probably produced in the same workshop. Thematically, ivories associated with the court mostly emphasize the triumphal, celestial, miraculous and redemptive qualities of Christ. Narrative, where present, is in the service of these qualities. Some ivories, such as the unique iconographic image of the *Virgo militans* (New York, Met.) or the *Majestas Domini* (Berlin, Staatl. Museen), appear to be later manifestations of the Court school, and their disputed dating depends on whether they are survivals or revivals.

The continuation of ivory-carving after the death of Charlemagne in 814 is indicated by the multiplicity of styles evident both in manuscripts and in ivories. The role of Louis the Pious as patron of the arts is becoming increasingly recognized, but the number of ivories secured to this period is disputed. If the Lorsch Covers are as late as the 820s, the continuation of the styles, motifs and themes of the court of Charlemagne must be reassessed. It has also been postulated that the so-called Liuthard Group of ivories (*see* §2 below) should be associated with Louis the Pious (Harbison).

14. Ivory of the *Ascension*, 140×93 mm, *c*. AD 800 (Darmstadt, Hessisches, Landesmuseum)

2. AD 843 AND LATER. The first ivories to display a high-relief style that contrasts with those of the Court school of Charlemagne were made for Charles the Bald. Their style derives from the Utrecht Psalter (Utrecht, Bib. Rijksuniv. MS. 32) and other works produced in Reims during the tenure of Archbishop Ebbo (816–35). Several ivories (e.g. Zurich, Schweiz. Landesmus.) are directly based on the themes of the Utrecht Psalter, with tiny, deeply undercut figures in rhythmic compositions driven into action with nervous energy. The cover of the Psalter of Charles the Bald (Paris, Bib. N., MS. lat. 1152) illustrates Psalms 50 and 56 but displays a less expressionistic style than is found in the Utrecht Psalter. Central to this group is the large and elaborate *Crucifixion* panel placed before 1014 on the cover of the book of Pericopes of Henry II (Munich, Bayer. Staatsbib., Clm. 4452). It must originally have adorned a major Carolingian manuscript and it has been linked to the Codex Aureus of St Emmeram (Munich, Bayer. Staatsbib., Clm. 14000; *see* §V, 2 above). This ivory and others related to it are named after Liuthard, the scribe–illuminator of the manuscript; if the entire Liuthard Group can be associated with Louis the Pious, this would provide a closer chronological link to the Utrecht Psalter and indicate that ivories were often reused.

Metz became a principal artistic centre under Archbishop Drogo (*reg* 845–55), whose Sacramentary (Paris, Bib. N., MS. lat. 9428) is covered with openwork ivory panels of the *Life of Christ* and liturgical scenes composed of flat, thickset figures. This and other Metz works form the first workshop of Charles the Bald, although Reims and Saint-Denis Abbey have also been suggested as possible centres of production. A second workshop, the Late Metz Group, also produced ivories for Charles the Bald (see fig. 15). Most of these can be dated *c*. 870 by the so-called Cathedra Petri (the coronation throne of Charles the Bald; now Rome, St Peter's), which was richly decorated with openwork ivories and inlaid with gold, a distinctive feature of many of the late Metz ivories. The throne displays a rich programme of imagery: imperial (a portrait of *Charles the Bald*), cosmological (figures of the *Constellations*) and mythological (the *Labours of Hercules*).

The more massive and solid figure style of these ivories is also related to a group of panels mostly depicting New Testament scenes, especially a series of *Crucifixion* plaques (London, V&A; Munich, Bayer. Staatsbib.; New York, Met.; Paris, Bib. N.). This group, which is composed of several sub-groups, shares many qualities with the manuscripts produced for the Emperor at both Metz and Reims. Significantly, iconography, style and even technique in the later Metz ivories had an impact on both late 9th-century continental art and on the Anglo-Saxons, and they also established the essential tendencies of Ottonian art (*see* OTTONIAN ART, §VI). The only Carolingian ivory-carver known by name was the monk Tuotilo, recorded at St Gall Abbey between 895 and 912, who was also renowned as a goldsmith, sculptor and musician. Several Gospel book covers by his hand, one with a unique *Ascension of*

15. Book cover showing the *Crucifixion* and the *Three Marys at the Tomb*, ivory, 237×124 mm, from ?Metz, *c.* AD 870 (New York, The Cloisters)

the Virgin (St Gall, Stift.-Bib., Cod. 53), echo a Carolingian tradition with harder, more simplified forms and a continued interest in floral ornamentation.

BIBLIOGRAPHY

A. Goldschmidt, P. G. Hübner and O. Homburger: *Die Elfenbeinskulpturen aus der Zeit der karolingischen und sächsischen Kaiser, VIII–XI Jahrhundert*, i (Berlin, 1914)

T. P. F. Hoving: *The Sources of the Ivories of the Ada School* (diss., Princeton U., 1959)

A. L. Vandersall: *The Ivories of the Court School of Charles the Bald* (diss., New Haven, Yale U., 1965)

S. H. Ferber: 'Crucifixion Iconography in a Group of Carolingian Ivory Plaques', *A. Bull.*, xlviii (1966), pp. 323–34

H. Fillitz: 'Die Elfenbeinreliefs zur Zeit Kaiser Karls des Grossen', *Aachen. Kstbl.*, xxxii (1966), pp. 14–45

A. von Euw: 'Studien zu den Elfenbeinarbeiten der Hofschule Karls des Grossen', *Aachen. Kstbl.*, xxxiv (1968), pp. 36–60

'La Cattedra lignea di S Pietro in Vaticano', *Mem. Pont. Accad. Romana Archeol.*, 3rd ser., x (1971) [whole issue]

A. Vandersall: 'Two Carolingian Ivories from the Morgan Collection in the Metropolitan Museum of Art', *Met. Mus. J.*, vi (1972), pp. 17–57

H. Fillitz: 'Die Cathedra Petri zur gegenwärtigen Forschungslage', *Archv Hist. Pont.*, xi (1973), pp. 353–73

W. Sanderson: 'A Group of Ivories and Some Related Works from Late Carolingian Trier', *A. Bull.*, lvi/2 (1974), pp. 159–75

H. Fillitz: 'Elfenbeinreliefs vom Hofe Kaiser Karls des Kahlen', *Beiträge zur Kunst des Mittelalters: Festschrift für Hans Wentzel zum 60. Geburtstag* (Berlin, 1975), pp. 41–51

D. Gaborit-Chopin: *Ivoires du moyen âge* (Fribourg, 1978)

H. Fillitz: 'Die religiöse Reform und die bildende Kunst der Karolingerzeit: Die Elfenbein', *Atti del XXIV Congresso internazionale di storia dell'arte. Riforma religiosa e arti nell'epoca carolingia: Bologna, 1979*, i, pp. 59–69

S. Lewis: 'A Byzantine *Virgo Militans* at Charlemagne's Court', *Viator*, xi (1980), pp. 71–93

W. Sanderson: 'Trierer Elfenbeinarbeiten vom 4. Jahrhundert bis zum Ende der karolingischen Renaissance', *Festschrift 100 Jahr: Rheinisches Landesmuseum, Trier* (Mainz, 1980), pp. 319–46

——: 'Archbishop Radbod, Regino of Prüm and Late Carolingian Art and Music in Trier', *Jb. Berlin. Mus.*, xxiv (1982), pp. 41–61

R. Melzak: *The Carolingian Ivory Carvings of the Later Metz Group* (diss., New York, Columbia U., 1983)

J. Duft and J. R. Schnyder: *Die Elfenbein-Einbände der Stiftsbibliothek St. Gallen* (Beuron, 1984)

P. Harbison: 'Earlier Carolingian Narrative Iconography: Ivories, Manuscripts, Frescoes, and Irish High Crosses', *Jb. Röm.-Ger. Zentmus.*, xxxi (1984), pp. 455–71

V. H. Elbern: 'Ornamentum oder Bildwirklichkeit', *Celica Iherusalem: Festschrift für Erich Stephany* (Cologne, 1986), pp. 186–95

C. T. Little: 'A New Ivory of the Court School of Charlemagne', *Studien zur mittelalterlichen Kunst, 800–1250: Festschrift für Florentine Mütherich zum 70. Geburtstag* (Cologne, 1986), pp. 11–28

M. Collareta: 'Per la ricostruzione di un capolavoro della scultura carolingia in avorio', *Paragone*, xxxviii/445 (March, 1987), pp. 3–12

U. Surmann: *Studien zur ottonischen Elfenbeinplastik in Metz und Trier*, Beitr. Kstgesch. (Bonn, 1990)

CHARLES T. LITTLE

VII. Rock crystal.

The 9th century was marked by a revival of gem engraving, practised only sporadically in the early medieval west. Intaglio-cut transparent quartz appeared *c.* 825–50 and continued to be produced until the mid-10th century. During this period rock crystal was as valuable as rubies and sapphires; known patrons are all of high rank. The gems were commissioned as seal-dies and for use on altars, reliquary crosses and other liturgical implements. The surviving crystals, 34–158 mm in length, form two major groups of different style and format: eleven flat or shallowly curved gems, the most famous of which was made for King Lothair II of Lotharingia (*reg* 855–69), illustrating *Susanna and the Elders* (115 mm; London, BM; for illustration *see* GEM-ENGRAVING, fig. 9), and six more strongly convex stones (including five showing the *Crucifixion*; London, BM; London, V&A; Conques, Trésor Ste-Foy; Esztergom, Cathedral Treasury). Two agates (Florence, Mus. Archeol.; Remiremont, Mus. Mun. Charles de Bruyères) and a jet seal (Zurich, Schweiz. Landesmus.) are closely related to the crystals.

The gems can be linked to workshops at Metz, Trier, Aachen and the court of Charles the Bald. They do not copy works in other media, but share common styles with manuscripts and ivories. They are technically related to early Carolingian coins. Earlier proposals of connections to Byzantine glyptic have been disputed. The crystals are iconographically innovative. Scenes of the Crucifixion (Paris, Bib. N.; Venice, Col. Cini; Freiburg im Breisgau,

Augustinmus.) and *Baptism* (Freiburg im Breisgau, Dom-Mus.; Rouen, Mus. Ant.) reflect current liturgy and theology. The *Susanna* cycle is generally linked to events surrounding the attempted divorce of Lothair II, and may be a sophisticated evocation of Justice. In all cases the symbolism of the stone itself, evoking purity and innocence, conversion, baptism, the Incarnation, the Passion and the nature of angels, reinforces the message of the imagery.

BIBLIOGRAPHY

J. Baum: 'Karolingische geschnittene Bergkristalle', *Actes du IIIe Congrès international pour l'étude du haut moyen âge: Olten, 1951*, pp. 111–17, 125–6

G. Kornbluth: *Like to a Precious Stone: Engraved Gems from the Carolingian Empire* (in preparation)

GENEVRA KORNBLUTH

Carolis, Marchese **Livio de** (*b* Pofi, Lazio, 1680; *d* Rome, 1 Sept 1733). Italian patron and collector. He and his father, Giovanni Battista de Carolis (1645–1718), made their fortune from grain trading, a business that expanded when they moved to Rome from Pofi. In the 1720s Livio de Carolis enjoyed the patronage of Pope Benedict XIII, who made him General of the Pontifical Post and in 1726 granted him the fief of Prossedi in Lazio and with it the title of marchese. He was a pious man, a member of the Roman Confraternità delle Stimmate, and a generous supporter of a Florentine Jesuit named Antonio Baldinucci, later beatified (1839) for his sanctity. But it was worldly ambition that motivated his purchase in 1714 of the large island site adjoining the Via del Corso for the family palace (now the Palazzo del Banco di Roma, Piazza S Marcello). Existing buildings were demolished and the Roman architect and engraver Alessandro Specchi was commissioned to design a new three-storey palace (with a balcony from which to watch the traditional horse-races in the Corso) large enough to accommodate Livio, his brothers Michele and Pietro de Carolis and their uncle, the prelate Giuseppe de Carolis (*d* 1742). It was built between 1716 and 1722. The ceilings of the principal rooms on the *piano nobile* were decorated with mythological and allegorical paintings on canvas (*in situ*), commissioned from the most fashionable artists in Rome, among them the Venetian Francesco Trevisani, the Neapolitan Sebastiano Conca, the Florentine Bernardino Luti and Carlo Maratti's pupil Giuseppe Bartolomeo Chiari. Collected pictures also decorated the palace, including overdoors and overwindows painted by Gaspard Dughet in the 1650s for the Palazzo Costaguti and purchased by de Carolis *c*. 1722. The palace was one of the grandest new buildings of early 18th-century Rome but its cost all but ruined de Carolis, who died deeply in debt. He was buried in the chapel of the Confraternità delle Stimmate, S Pietro in Montorio. The fief of Prossedi had to be disposed of in 1746 and the palace itself was sold at auction in 1750.

BIBLIOGRAPHY

U. Barberini and others: *Via del Corso* (Rome, 1961), pp. 229–39

A. Bocca: *Il Palazzo del Banco di Roma già de Carolis* (Rome, 1967)

A. Giuggoli: *Il Palazzo de Carolis in Roma* (Rome, 1980), pp. 149–66

JANET SOUTHORN

Carolsfeld, Schnorr von. *See* SCHNORR VON CAROLSFELD.

Carolus-Duran [Durand, Charles-Emile-Auguste] (*b* Lille, 4 July 1837; *d* Paris, 1917). French painter. He came from a humble background and by the age of 11 was taking lessons at the Académie in Lille from the sculptor Augustin-Phidias Cadet de Beaupré (*b* 1800) who taught him to sketch. At 15 he began a two-year apprenticeship in the studio of one of David's former pupils, François Souchon (1787–1857), whose name he still referred to several years later when he exhibited at the Salon. In 1853 he moved to Paris. He copied in the Louvre where he must have met Henri Fantin-Latour, then taking life classes at the Académie Suisse (1859–60). He exhibited at the Salon for the first time in 1859. His first period in Paris, from 1853 to 1862 (interspersed with visits to Lille, where he received portrait commissions and an annuity in 1861), shows the influence of Gustave Courbet, whose *After Dinner at Ornans* (1849) he had been able to see in the Musée des Beaux-Arts at Lille. Thanks to Fantin-Latour or Zacharie Astruc, whom he had known in Lille, he soon befriended Courbet, Manet and the Realist artists, painting their portraits with a serious Realism full of concentrated energy: *Fantin-Latour and Oulevay* (1861), *Zacharie Astruc* (*c*. 1860–61; both Paris, Mus. d'Orsay) and *Claude Monet* (1867; Paris, Mus. Marmottan).

The award of the Wicar prize in 1860 made it possible for Carolus-Duran to visit Rome from 1862 to 1866. He stayed at Subiaco, in the Franciscan convent, where he did the *plein-air* painting *Evening Prayer* (1863). On his return to Paris he received a medal at the Salon of 1866 for the *Assassination* (Lille, Mus. B.-A.), a dramatic genre scene inspired by Italian life and the examples of Léopold Robert and Victor Schnetz. Carolus-Duran's journey to Spain from 1866 to 1868 confirmed his admiration of Spanish painting (his change of name during the first Paris trip had been its outward sign). *The Kiss* (1868; Lille, Mus. B.-A.; *see* LILLE, fig. 2), painted on his return, bears traces of his study of Spanish painting, with a sombre palette and rich impasto. It is probably a self-portrait with his wife, Pauline-Marie-Charlotte Croizette, who exhibited pastel portraits between 1864 and 1875. He portrayed her again in the *Woman with the Glove* (1869; Paris, Mus. d'Orsay), in muted colours and with energetic handling. The fallen glove accentuates the spontaneous appearance of the genre scene.

After staying in Brussels during the Commune (1870), Carolus-Duran opened a studio in Paris in 1872, which was visited regularly by Americans, including John Singer Sargent. A fashionable portrait painter, he stayed close to artistic and literary circles and did several portraits of Manet (e.g. 1872, U. Birmingham, Barber Inst.; *c*. 1880, Paris, Mus. d'Orsay) and a portrait of *Emile de Girardin* (1875; Lille, Mus. B.-A.) who had founded *La Presse* in 1836. His portraits of men sometimes recall Degas, as in those of the picture dealer *Etienne Haro* (1873; Paris, Petit Pal.) or of *Gustave Doré* (1875; Strasbourg, Mus. B.-A.). However, it was his portraits of women that made him famous. Besides the spontaneous images of his family, such as the *Laughing Women* (1870; Detroit, MI, Inst. A.), Carolus-Duran specialized in portraits of the aristocratic women who reigned over the Paris salons, such as *Woman with a Dog* (1870; Lille, Mus. B.-A.); his sister-in-law, the actress Sophie Croizette, in *Mlle Croizette on Horseback*,

Carolus-Duran: *Mlle Croizette on Horseback*, oil on canvas, 2.99×3.17 m, 1873 (Tourcoing, Musée Municipal des Beaux-Arts)

painted in Trouville in 1873 (Tourcoing, Mus. Mun. B.-A.; see fig.); or *Mme Sainctelette* (1871; Brussels, Mus. A. Mod.). He also painted portraits of children, as, for example, in *Blue Child* (1873; Paris, Brame & Lorenceau Col.).

A one-man show in 1874–5 at the Cercle des Mirlitons confirmed Carolus-Duran's success. Although he was still using clear contrasts of light and shade in the portrait of *Nadezhda Polovtsova* (St Petersburg, Hermitage), painted during a trip to Russia in 1876, settings became sumptuous and the colour vivid. A *plein-air* setting accentuated the naturalism of the portrait of his sister-in-law, revealing an interest in the experiments in landscape painting then being undertaken by the Impressionists. Although the poses became mannered his technique was always dazzling, as in *Anna Alexandrovna Obolenskaya* (1887; St Petersburg, Hermitage). The portrait of *Mme Georges Feydeau* (1897; Tokyo, N. Mus. W. A.) shows the influence of Anthony van Dyck on his sophisticated compositions.

Carolus-Duran won a commission to paint a ceiling in the Palais du Luxembourg, Paris, the *Glorification of Marie de' Medici* (1878; now Paris, Louvre). He painted several religious pictures such as the *Last Hour of Christ* and the *Embalming of Christ* (both St Aygulf, Notre-Dame de l'Assomption). In 1890 he was a founder-member of the Société Nationale des Beaux-Arts, whose president he became in 1900. In 1904 he was elected a member of the Institut and in the same year he was made Director of the Académie de France in Rome.

BIBLIOGRAPHY

A. Alexandre: 'Carolus-Duran', *Rev. A. Anc. & Mod.*, xiii (1903), pp. 185–200; xiv (1903), pp. 289–304

Carolus-Duran (exh. cat., Paris, Gal. Flavian, 1973)

Ingres and Delacroix through Degas and Puvis de Chavannes: The Figure in French Art, 1800–1870 (exh. cat., New York, Shepherd Gal., 1975)

VALÉRIE M. C. BAJOU

Caron, Antoine (*b* Beauvais, 1521; *d* Paris, 1599). French painter and draughtsman. He started his career modestly in his native city, then a relatively important artistic centre, where he painted some religious pictures (e.g. the *Resurrection*; Beauvais, Mus. Dépt. Oise) and designed cartoons for stained-glass windows; both demonstrate his innate taste for decorative work. Caron was later active in the workshops at Fontainebleau, and his name appears in the royal accounts of Henry II between 1540 and 1550. He later became court painter to Catherine de' Medici, the Queen Regent (1560–63). Besides Jean Cousin the younger, he was the only French artist from this period with a recognizable artistic personality and was an important witness to the activities of the Valois court during the reigns of Charles IX (*reg* 1560–74) and Henry III (*reg* 1574–89) and the violent Wars of Religion (1562–98) between Catholics and Huguenots. Like his royal patrons, Caron was an ardent Roman Catholic; he was connected with the Catholic League and a friend of its poet and pamphleteer, Louis d'Orléans.

At Fontainebleau, Caron worked under the direction of Francesco Primaticcio and alongside Nicolò dell'Abate, and so his style is essentially Italianate and Mannerist (*see* FONTAINEBLEAU SCHOOL). His figures are always elongated, with tapering limbs and small heads. These features remained constant, even after Caron had withdrawn in 1561 from the team of artists working at Fontainebleau. The following year he began an association with the apothecary and humanist art patron Nicolas Houel (*c.* 1524–87), for whom he made drawings illustrating his four-volume manuscript poem the *Legend of Artemisia* (Paris, Bib. N.). This project was initiated by Houel to console Catherine de' Medici after the death of Henry II in 1559 and also to glorify her reign. Queen Artemisia of Halicarnassus, the grief-stricken and faithful widow of King Mausolus, was an obvious allusion to Catherine. Caron's drawings, 59 of which survive (Paris, Bib. N. and Louvre), later served as cartoons for the tapestry series of the same subject (*c.* 1607; set of 10 surviving tapestries, Minneapolis, MN, Inst. A.; other individual panels elsewhere). Caron also illustrated Houel's manuscript *Histoire françoyse de nostre temps* (*c.* 1562–72; Paris, Louvre), in which the subjects, with a sonnet by Houel on the *verso* of each folio, illustrate scenes from the reigns of Francis I to Charles IX.

Caron's violent *Massacres of the Triumvirate* (1566; Paris, Louvre), likely to be a direct reference to the bloody Wars of Religion, and the calmer *Tiburtine Sibyl* (*Augustus and the Sibyl*, *c.* 1575–80; Paris, Louvre) are both characteristic paintings. They are populated by numerous graceful figures set in expansive scenes of extraordinary architectural fragments with exaggerated perspective. Painted in bright colours, the compositions have a curious dreamlike atmosphere and balletic quality.

The same spirit is reflected in the extravagant festivals and pageants Caron was called on to arrange for the court. Early on in his career for the Queen Regent he was entrusted with the decoration for the ceremonial entry of Charles IX into Paris. In 1572 Caron organized the festivities for the marriage of Margaret of Valois and the King of Navarre (later Henry IV), and the following year, together with Germain Pilon and the poet Jean Dorat (*c.* 1508–88), he arranged the fêtes in the Tuileries Gardens for the reception of the Polish ambassadors and the grand entry of the Duke of Anjou (the future Henry III), whom they had elected King of Poland. Caron was also involved in 1581 in the celebrations for the marriage of the Duc de Joyeuse. A fascinating series of six drawings by Caron (Cambridge, MA, Fogg; Edinburgh, N.G.; U. London, Courtauld Inst. Gals (2); New York, Pierpont Morgan Lib.; and Paris, Louvre) depicts some of the festivals that occurred between 1564 and 1575; they provide an insight into these remarkable occasions and ample proof that Catherine de' Medici spared no expense in the creation of her 'magnificences'. The aquatic spectacles (see fig.) were particularly popular and must have been viewed with awe by the huge numbers of spectators that could be accommodated at such royal fêtes. These events also served as subjects for the subsequently woven Valois Tapestries (*c.* 1582; Florence, Uffizi).

Caron's last years were spent living in the Rue Montorgueil, Paris, the quarter where most engravers and woodcutters resided. His drawings were reproduced by numerous late 16th-century printmakers, including Denis de Mathonière, Etienne Delaune, Léonard Gaultier and his own son-in-law Thomas de Leu. Mathonière's six woodcuts of the *Story of Esther* after Caron were published in 1580. Caron also provided the original designs for the engraved illustrations in *Les Images ou tableaux de plate peinture des deux Philostrate* (Paris, 1614/15), which was published posthumously in a sumptuous folio edition by the archaeologist and art critic Blaise de Vigenère (1523–96). A popular and influential book with observations on Renaissance art and artists in Italy and France, it attempted to re-create the Roman paintings described by Philostratos. It was reprinted numerous times and was especially praised by Nicolas Poussin.

BIBLIOGRAPHY

Thieme–Becker
J. Guiffrey: *Les Dessins de l'histoire des rois de France par Nicolas Houel* (Paris, 1920)
L. Dimier: *La Peinture française au XVIe siècle* (Marseille, 1942)
A. Blunt: *Art and Architecture in France, 1500–1700*, Pelican Hist. A. (Harmondsworth, 1953), pp. 152–4
J. Adhémar: *Le Dessin français au XVIe siècle* (Lausanne, 1954)
J. Ehrmann: 'Caron et les tapisseries des Valois', *Rev. A.*, vi (1956), pp. 9–14
——: 'Drawings by Antoine Caron for the Valois Tapestries in the Uffizi, Florence', *A. Q.* [Detroit], xxi/1 (1958), pp. 47–65
F. Yates: *The Valois Tapestries* (London, 1959)
S. Béguin: 'Une *Résurrection* d'Antoine Caron', *Rev. Louvre*, 4–5 (1964), pp. 203–13
W. McAllister Johnson and G. Monnier: 'Caron antiquaire: A propos de quelques dessins du Louvre', *Rev. A.*, xiv (1971), pp. 23–30
L'Ecole de Fontainebleau (exh. cat. by S. Béguin and others, Paris, Grand Pal., 1972); rev. as *Fontainebleau: Art in France, 1528–1610*, 2 vols (exh. cat. by S. Béguin and others, Ottawa, N.G., 1973)
U. von Haumeder: *Antoine Caron: Studien zu seiner 'Histoire d'Artemise'* (diss., U. Heidelberg, 1976)
R. Strong: *Art and Power: Renaissance Festivals, 1450–1650* (Woodbridge, 1984)
J. Ehrmann: *Antoine Caron: Peintre des fêtes et des massacres* (Paris, 1986)

Antoine Caron: *Water Festival at Bayonne, 24 June 1565*, black chalk, pen and brown ink, a few touches of black ink, grey-brown wash, heightened with white, 348×492 mm, 1565 (New York, Pierpont Morgan Library)

Französische Zeichnungen im Städelschen Kunstinstitut, 1550 bis 1800 (exh. cat. by M. Stuffmann, Frankfurt am Main, Städel. Kstinst. & Städt. Gal., 1986–7), pp. 4–7

S. J. TURNER

Caroselli, Angelo (*b* Rome, 10 Feb 1585; *d* Rome, 8 April 1652). Italian painter. He was the son of a dealer in second-hand goods and taught himself to paint. According to Baldinucci, he knew Caravaggio, who fled Rome in 1606, and this association may have encouraged his decision to become a painter. After visits to Florence (1605) and Naples (1613), Caroselli settled in Rome, where, in 1615, he married a Sicilian, Maria Zurca. His weakness for beautiful women was notorious (Baldinucci; Passeri). His second marriage, to Brigitta Lauri, daughter of the Flemish painter Balthasar Lauwers or Lauri (1578–1645), took place in 1642.

Caroselli was mentioned on the lists of artists at the Accademia di S Luca, Rome, in 1608. Around 1619 he shared a workshop with the Lucchese painter Pietro Paolini, in which Filippo Lauri and Francesco Lauri (1612–37) later became his pupils and assistants. He was well known as a talented imitator of the Old Masters, and examples of his imitations, such as a *Virgin* after Raphael, which Nicolas Poussin could not distinguish from the original, and a *St Helen* after Titian, were cited by Baldinucci. A small *St Matthew*, based on a painting by Caravaggio, was mentioned in a 1638 inventory of the Giustiniani collection. Caroselli was also famous for his portraits and painted one of Caravaggio. All these works remain untraced.

Caroselli's work was greatly influenced by Caravaggio well into the 1620s. His oeuvre is small, and most of his surviving works were painted for private patrons. The *Allegory of Vanity* (Florence, Fond. Longhi, see A. Boschetti, ed.: *La Collezione Roberto Longhi*, Florence, 1991, pl. 64), an early work, clearly shows the influence of the paintings that Caroselli copied. Both the soft effects of light and the composition are derived from Caravaggio's *Mary Magdalene* (Rome, Gal. Doria-Pamphili); the warm colour, however, is indebted to 16th-century Venetian art. Caravaggio's influence is again revealed in the *Portrait of a Man* (Berlin, Gemäldegal.), in the effects of light, the brutal realism and the sharp precision of detail. In the 1620s, like other followers of Caravaggio, Caroselli moved away from Caravaggism. This is clear in the *St Wenceslas* (1630; untraced) painted for St Peter's, Rome. The altarpiece was replaced in 1743 by a mosaic copy made by Pietro Paulo Cristofari (1685–1743), which lacks the power suggested by the surviving oil sketch (1630; Rome, Pal. Braschi). The saint stands before a theatrical architectural setting, and his billowing drapery and fervent expression attain a High Baroque intensity. The *St Gregory the Great* (1631; Rome, S Francesca Romana) shows a similar development, away from Caravaggio towards the contemporary Baroque style. In 1635-6 Caroselli's name is listed among the academicians of the Accademia di S Luca.

The later pictures, made for private patrons, are more interesting than the religious works and illustrate Caroselli's ability to adopt different styles. In his paintings of the *Virgin and Child* (e.g. Manchester, C.A.G., and Rome, Pal. Barberini) he returned to patterns established in the Renaissance. Yet he also painted small scenes of witchcraft and sorcery, such as *The Conjurors* (Ancona, Pin. Com.) and *The Magician* (Arezzo, Pal. Bruni–Ciocchi), where the figures, arrayed in fantastic 16th-century dress, are placed among strange and mysterious objects. Such works have parallels in the art of Salvator Rosa and of François de Nomé, who was Caroselli's brother-in-law. Carlo Caroselli, Angelo's son from his first marriage, also became a painter.

BIBLIOGRAPHY

DBI [with earlier bibliog.]
G. B. Passeri: *Vite* (Rome, 1679); ed. J. Hess (1934), pp. 189–94
F. Baldinucci: *Notizie* (1681–1728); ed. F. Ranalli (1845–7), iii, pp. 739–47
A. Ottani: 'Su Angelo Caroselli, pittore romano', *A. Ant. & Mod.*, xxix (1965), pp. 289–97 [with illus.]
A. Moir: *The Italian Followers of Caravaggio* (Cambridge, MA, 1969)
Elisabetta Giffi: 'Per il tempo romano di Pietro Paolini e gli inizi di Angelo Caroselli', *Prospettiva*, xlvi (1986), pp. 22–30 [with illus.]

RENATE MÖLLER

Caroto. Italian family of painters, prominent in Verona during the first half of the 16th century. (1) Gian Francesco Caroto, who is the better known of the brothers on account of his greater productivity, travelled widely, and his work is noted for its eclecticism. His younger brother (2) Giovanni Caroto's development is, in contrast, gradual, conservative and based on local sources. There are some disputed attributions between the two brothers, but these appear to derive from the mistaken assumption that works of lesser quality can be assigned to Giovanni. Fewer works can be assigned with confidence to him, but these are more consistent in quality than Gian Francesco's more numerous paintings. There appear to be only two clear instances of collaboration.

(1) Gian [Giovan] **Francesco Caroto** (*b* Verona, *c.* 1480; *d c.* 1555). According to Vasari he was trained by Liberale da Verona, but there is no clear evidence of this in his earlier works. A chronological review of his securely attributed works reveals a series of identifiable influences including Lorenzo Costa the elder, Leonardo and his followers, Raphael, Giulio Romano, Parmigianino and Correggio. His earliest known work is a *Virgin and Child* (Modena, Gal. & Mus. Estense), signed and dated 1501. It recalls more readily the sculptural qualities of Francesco Bonsignori than the linear emphasis of Liberale. A fresco depicting the *Annunciation* (1508; Verona, S Gerolamo) retains some of this sculpted sense, but the figure types are clearly influenced by Leonardo, probably the effect of a sojourn in Milan in 1507. The *Pietà* (Turin, Fontana priv. col., see Franco Fiorio, fig. 17), signed and dated 1515, resembles the style of Leonardo's Milanese followers. Lombard influence is also evident in the frescoes depicting *Tobias* and the canvas of *Three Angels* executed for the Spolverini Chapel, S Eufemia, Verona, variously dated between 1508 and 1520. A portrait of a *Red-headed Youth Holding a Drawing* (Verona, Castelvecchio) also belongs to this period.

A new phase revealing central Italian influence is evident in the altarpiece depicting the *Virgin and Child with Four Saints* (1528; Verona, S Fermo Maggiore). Raphael's works and the presence of Giulio Romano in Mantua from 1524 seem to be the sources. In the *Raising of Lazarus* (1531; Verona, Pal. Vescovile) Caroto achieves a nice balance:

the figures are classically proportioned, but their muscularity is not exaggerated; a view of the River Adige provides a pleasingly lyrical setting. Six panels of landscapes viewed through illusionistic arched windows, decorating the choir-stalls in S Maria in Organo, Verona, are also datable to around 1530. *Christ Washing the Feet of the Disciples* (Verona, Castelvecchio) would seem to belong to the same period but is dated 1545–50 (dal Bravo; Franco Fiorio). Frescoes depicting scenes from the Old Testament (Verona Cathedral, nave) probably belong to the late 1530s. In the altarpiece depicting *St Ursula* (1545; Verona, S Giorgio in Braida) and *Christ Taking Leave of his Mother* (1546; Verona, S Bernardino, Avanzi Chapel), Gian Francesco's figures have acquired longer proportions and mannered poses. Some of Gian Francesco's works on canvas are executed in tempera (1987 exh. cat.). In the Villa del Bene, Volargne, decorated by the Caroto brothers and Domenico Brusasorci around 1551, the frescoes attributed to Gian Francesco include some extremely fine passages, such as the horn-blowing angel in scenes from the *Apocalypse* in the main hall. Gian Francesco's pupils included Domenico Brusasorci and Antonio Badile.

(2) Giovanni (Battista) Caroto (*b* Verona, 1488; *d* Verona, 1563–6). Brother of (1) Gian Francesco Caroto. His training is undocumented, and some writers have assumed that Giovanni studied with his brother. His work shows the influence of Girolamo dai Libri (1474–1555) and Francesco Morone. Giovanni's work moves from an early classical style that includes detailed representation of texture, fabric and landscape background to a fully High Renaissance style around 1530. His earliest extant work is probably the *Annunciation* on two canvases (Verona, S Giorgio in Braida), traditionally dated 1508 but possibly slightly later. It appears to refer both to Gian Francesco's contemporary fresco of the same subject (Verona, S Gerolamo) and to Leonardo's early *Annunciation* (Florence, Uffizi). Although the figures are somewhat stiff, the work shows Giovanni to be gifted and skilful. The depiction of the Virgin's luminous dress is masterful, and the attention to detail in the sunset and wintry landscape

Giovanni Caroto: *Baptism* with illusionistic frame, shadow and hooks, detail from fresco (*c.* 1551), Villa del Bene, Volargne

behind Gabriel recalls Netherlandish painting. Similar qualities recur in the *Virgin and Child Enthroned with SS Stephen and Martin* (signed and dated 1514; ex-S Giovanni in Fonte, Verona; Verona Cathedral). In the *Virgin and Child Enthroned with SS Peter and Paul* (1516; Verona, S Paolo, main altar) the detail in the landscape and the sharply illuminated, rich materials is reduced to achieve an immediate sense of unity and grandeur, fostered by the huge, barrel-vaulted setting and a more pervasive, even light.

The pair of canvases representing *St Paul* and *St George* (Verona, Castelvecchio) probably belong to the early 1520s. The figure types are more generalized, and detail is further reduced in the landscape background. Their cool afternoon light resembles that in earlier examples by Morone and Paolo Cavazzola. Giovanni's *Self-portrait with Wife Placida* (1530; Verona, Castelvecchio), a fragment of high quality from an altarpiece formerly in the chapel of S Niccolò (S Maria in Organo)—which, Vasari claims, was frescoed by Gian Francesco and is an example of the brothers' collaboration—has great dignity and calm in its image of the praying couple: all stiffness and sharp detail seen in earlier works have gone, and the cool light casts delicate, coloured shadows. Frescoes of the archangels *Michael* and *Gabriel* on the exterior of the Fontanelli Chapel, S Maria in Organo, also from 1530, likewise show mastery of a High Renaissance style. The angle at which the light falls is coordinated with the actual window to enhance the illusion that the sun is shining on the archangels in their *trompe l'oeil* niches.

Giovanni's activity as a student of antiquity may explain his smaller output in painting than his brother. In 1540 a series of his drawings of Verona's Roman remains—the only documented works by Giovanni from this decade—were printed as woodcut illustrations to the first, Latin, edition of Torello Saraina's *De origine et amplitudine civitatis Veronae*. They were published under his own name in 1560. These drawings show, in comparison with drawings of the same monuments by contemporaries, that Giovanni imaginatively 'restored' the antiquities, adding, for example, sculpted decorations on the Arco Leoni. The drawings for the 1546 vernacular edition (1546 edn and original drgs; Verona, Bib. Civ.) include a *Self-portrait* and a draped female niche figure, matronly and severe, labelled .GAVIA M.F. In the Villa del Bene, Volargne, where the Caroto brothers collaborated *c.* 1551, the room whose decoration is attributed to Giovanni has a striking monochrome frieze depicting animals, cornucopias, men and coats of arms. Below, six *trompe l'oeil* frescoes of biblical scenes appear as framed paintings with hooks and cast shadows (see fig.). Within this playful illusion, Giovanni's forms, illuminated by cool light, display their customary gravity and classical features.

The portrait of a *Young Benedictine Monk* (Verona, Castelvecchio) has variously been assigned both to Gian Francesco (Franco Fiorio) and to Giovanni (Baron). Its calm classicism, cool light and difference in handling in comparison with Gian Francesco's portrait of the *Red-headed Youth Holding a Drawing* (Verona, Castelvecchio) argue for the latter view. According to Vasari, Giovanni taught both Veronese and Anselmo Canneri.

PRINTS

De le antiquità de Verona con novi agointi da M. Zoane Caroto pittore (Verona, 1560)

BIBLIOGRAPHY

T. Saraina: *De origine et amplitudine civitatis Veronae* (Verona, 1540; vern. edn, 1546)
G. Vasari: *Vite* (1550, rev. 2/1568); ed. G. Milanesi (1878–85)
B. dal Pozzo: *Le vite de' pittori, scultori e architetti veronesi* (Verona, 1718), pp. 25–7
G. Biermann: 'Die beiden Carotos in der Veroneser Malerei', *Kunstchronik*, iv (1903–4), pp. 7–20
L. Simeoni: 'Nuovi documenti sui Caroto', *L'Arte*, vii (1904), pp. 64–7
B. Baron: 'Giovanni Caroto I', *Burl. Mag.*, xviii (1910), pp. 41–4
——: 'Giovanni Caroto II', *Burl. Mag.*, xviii (1910), pp. 176–83
G. Trecca: 'Giovanni Caroto', *Madonna Verona*, iv/16 (1910), pp. 190–96
C. Garibotto: 'Affreschi di Giovanni Caroto in S Maria in Organo di Verona', *Madonna Verona*, xv/58–60 (1921), pp. 32–4
C. del Bravo: 'Per Giovan Francesco Caroto', *Paragone*, xv/173 (1964), pp. 3–16
M. T. Franco Fiorio: 'Appunti su Giovan Francesco Caroto', *A. Lombarda*, 11 (1966), pp. 33–42
P. Marchiori: 'Giovanni Caroto (cenni biografici)', *Vita Veron.*, xx (1967), pp. 94–6
——: 'Giovanni Caroto disegnatore', *Vita Veron.*, xx (1967), pp. 173–4
——: 'Giovanni Caroto pittore', *Vita Veron.*, xx (1967), pp. 340–44
M. T. Franco Fiorio: *Giovan Francesco Caroto* (Verona, 1971)
D. Gisolfi Pechukas: *The Youth of Veronese* (diss., U. Chicago, 1976), chaps ii and iii
Proposte e restauri (exh. cat., ed. S. Marinelli; Verona, Castelvecchio, 1987), pp. 128–40
G. Ericani: 'La stagione pre veronesiana e la pittura di paesaggio a Verona', *Veronese e Verona* (exh. cat., ed. S. Marinelli; Verona, Castelvecchio, 1988), pp. 7–15

DIANA GISOLFI

Carove, Carlo (*fl* 1667; *d* 1697). Italian stuccoist, active in Sweden. His earliest known work is the stuccowork (1667) in the mortuary chapel of General Lars Kagg at the parish church of Floda in Södermanland. The walls of the chapel's lofty hall are crowded by fluted Corinthian pilasters carrying a heavy and richly ornamented entablature. Between the pilasters are rounded niches with large statues of Virtues, trophies and putti. The large vault contains double rows of heraldic shields and vegetative ornament, centred on a larger shield in the middle of the vault. The whole of this ambitious and ostentatious interior is a curious mixture of humanist learning, genealogical and martial pride and pompous naivety. From 1669 onwards Carove was occupied with major decorative schemes at the royal Drottningholm Castle, Stockholm, including work on the main staircase, the two large anterooms of the upper storey and the state bedchamber in the lower storey. Here, in one of his most notable works, the limited use of stuccowork is supplemented by wood-carving, metalwork and painting (*see* SWEDEN, fig. 19).

During his time in Sweden, Carove also became head of a large workshop of stuccoists. Thus work attributed to him may in fact have been executed by other stuccoists associated with his workshop. Among these were his relation or possibly his brother Giovanni Carove (*fl* Drottningholm, 1664–74), Giovanni Brentano (*fl* 1670–80), the Swedes (apparently apprentices of the workshop) Erik Niure (*fl* 1670) and Simon Nauclerus (*fl* 1675), and perhaps Christoffer Tessel, who decorated the Mariedal Mansion (1670s) in Västergötland. This able group of artists moved around the country at the request of the land-owning nobility, and great country houses decorated by Carove and his colleagues include Karlberg Castle (early to mid-17th century; now within the boundary of Stockholm), Ericsberg, Nynäs and Mälsåker Palace (all early to mid-17th century; all in Södermanland), Sjöö in Uppland and Finspång in Östergötland. At Mälsåker the walls of the great hall are decorated with fluted Corinthian pilasters, and there is a heavy, very richly ornamented entablature. The cavetto vault features sweeping acanthus tendrils and putti. Thus many of the elements of the Kagg Chapel are repeated, but the overall impression is quite different: while the chapel is exuberant, the hall of Mälsåker is restrained and dignified. Whether this is a result of the artist maturing, the views of the client or the palace's architect, Nicodemus Tessin (*see* TESSIN, (1)), or of all of these factors combined, is hard to say. The octagonal bathroom at Ericsberg is notable for its fluted pilasters, garlands and putti, and the upper hall of Sjöö is also among Carove's most successful works. Carove's workshop also stuccoed the mortuary chapel (1680s) of Erik Dahlbergh in Turinge, Södermanland, and worked in Stockholm, where important works included those (1680s to before 1697) in the royal castle (destr. 1697) and those (*c.* 1669) in the city palace of Seved Bååth, then owned by Admiral Gustaf Otto Stenbock. The magnificent two-storey great hall of the Bååth Palace is decorated with groups of Michelangelesque slaves, trophies and dolphins.

Stylistically, Carove and his group employed a typical mixture of Italian and French ornament, the former consisting of cartouches and scrollwork, and the latter of vegetative elements derived from Roman antiquity with added floral motifs derived from ornamental engravings by Jean Le Pautre. The workshop leant rather heavily on the designs of this master, a few of their ceilings being simply transferred directly from the engravings to stucco. Also characteristic of the group is the brilliant handling of the ornamental parts of their works, while their figure sculptures vary in quality from sensitive (as at Mälsåker) to stiff and awkward. At Carove's death, the Swedish heyday of stucco decoration was already coming to an end, and the tradition of Italian artistry was not continued.

BIBLIOGRAPHY

E. Andrén: *Mälsåker* (Stockholm, 1945)
T. O. Nordberg: *Karlberg* (Stockholm, 1945)
S. Karling: 'Les Stucateurs italiens en Suède', *Arte e artisti dei laghi lombardi, 2 della Rivista archeologica dell'antica Provincia e Diocesi di Como: Como, 1964*, pp. 291–301
G. Beard: *Stucco and Decorative Plasterwork in Europe* (London and New York, 1983)

TORBJÖRN FULTON

Carpaccio. Italian family of painters. (1) Vittore Carpaccio was one of the most gifted painters in early Renaissance Venice. His artistic reputation far outweighs that of his two sons, Pietro Carpaccio (*fl c.* 1510–30) and (2) Benedetto Carpaccio, neither of whom remained in Venice. Presumably his principal pupils and assistants, they inherited a provincial, conservative and socially modest clientele from their father. Pietro was presumably the elder (since according to Venetian custom he was named after Vittore's father); he is first documented in Venice in 1513, but by 1526 he had set up shop in Udine. No certain works by him are known.

(1) Vittore Carpaccio [Carpathius; Carpatio; Scarpaza; Scharpaza; Scarpazza; Scarpatia] (*b* Venice, ?1460–6;

d Venice, 1525–6). His name is associated above all with the cycles of lively and festive narrative paintings that he executed for several of the Venetian *scuole*, or devotional confraternities. He also seems to have enjoyed a considerable reputation as a portrait painter. While evidently owing much in both these fields to his older contemporaries, Gentile and Giovanni Bellini, Carpaccio quickly evolved a readily recognizable style of his own which is marked by a taste for decorative splendour and picturesque anecdote. His altarpieces and smaller devotional works are generally less successful, particularly after about 1510, when he seems to have suffered a crisis of confidence in the face of the radical innovations of younger artists such as Giorgione and Titian.

1. Life and commissions. 2. Work. 3. Working methods and technique. 4. Critical reception and posthumous reputation.

1. Life and commissions. Vittore was the son of Pietro Scarpazza, a Venetian furrier. A will made by his uncle in 1472 naming Vittore as a beneficiary has been used as evidence that the painter had reached the age of 15 by that date and therefore that he must have been born before 1457. But under Venetian law, a child could be named as a future, if not immediate, beneficiary of a testamentary bequest and the stylistic evidence of his work indicates that Vittore may have been born as late as 1465. This later birthdate is supported rather than contradicted by a document of 1486, which records him still living in his father's house.

1. Vittore Carpaccio: *Presentation of Christ in the Temple*, oil on panel, 4.21×2.36 m, 1510 (Venice, Galleria dell'Accademia)

Carpaccio's earliest dated work is the *Arrival of St Ursula at Cologne* (1490; Venice, Accad.), the first of nine canvases executed for the Scuola di S Orsola and depicting the life of the confraternity's patron saint. Other paintings in the cycle are dated 1491, 1493 and 1495. Almost certainly earlier than 1490 is the *Salvator Mundi with Four Apostles* (Florence, ex-Contini–Bonacossi priv. col.), in which the artist's signature uniquely appears in its Venetian form of 'Vetor Scarpazo'. The stylistic evidence of these and of other putative early works, some of them controversial attributions, provides the only source of knowledge of Carpaccio's artistic training and has been interpreted in a number of different ways. The traditional view that he was a pupil of the Bellini brothers was first challenged by Molmenti and Peter Ludwig, who proposed Lazzaro Bastiani as his master. Emphasis has also been placed on the formative influences of Antonello da Messina, Ferrarese painting, Giovanni Bellini and Jacometto Veneziano. Gentile Bellini also seems a likely candidate while the inclusion of Roman motifs in the St Ursula cycle, combined with apparent echoes of the art of Perugino, has led to speculation that Carpaccio paid an early visit to Rome (Zampetti, 1966 monograph).

From the 1490s onwards, Carpaccio regularly inscribed his most important works with dates and signatures, and a number of documents also survive that refer to lost works and to other aspects of his professional career. In 1508 he served as a member of a committee convened to evaluate the recently completed frescoes by Giorgione on the Fondaco de' Tedeschi and in 1511 he corresponded with Francesco Gonzaga, Marquis of Mantua, in the hope of persuading him to buy a large canvas referred to as '*uno Jerusalem*' (presumably a religious subject with a background townscape identifiable as that of Jerusalem). Among Carpaccio's most important dated altarpieces, most of which were painted in his later career, are *St Thomas Aquinas Enthroned* (1507; Stuttgart, Staatsgal.), the *Presentation of Christ in the Temple* (1510; Venice, Accad.; see fig. 1) and the *Martyrdom of the Ten Thousand* (1515; Venice, Accad.). These three works were all painted for churches in Venice; but from about 1510 Carpaccio worked increasingly for provincial customers, sending altarpieces to destinations such as Treviso, Capodistria (now Koper, Slovenia), Pirano (near Trieste), Brescia and Pozzale di Cadore in the Dolomites.

It has sometimes been suggested that Carpaccio was the preferred artist of a particular social or cultural group, such as the *lunghi* faction within the ruling Venetian patriciate (so-called because their families had held power for many generations), or of leading Venetian humanists and intellectuals. But a survey of all the artist's known employers shows that, on the contrary, he never enjoyed the consistent support of any one type of patron and that his association with the ruling classes was sporadic. For all his talents as a narrative painter, he worked only briefly on the great history cycle in the Sala del Maggior Consiglio in the Doge's Palace, assisting Giovanni Bellini in 1507. Perhaps even more surprisingly, he only ever painted one work for a *scuola grande*, contributing, in 1494, a canvas to the *Miracles of the True Cross* cycle for the Scuola Grande

2. Vittore Carpaccio: *Miracle at Rialto*, oil on canvas, 3.65×3.89 m, 1494 (Venice, Galleria dell'Accademia)

di S Giovanni Evangelista (Venice, Accad.; see fig. 2). On at least two occasions he lost competitions for commissions held by the Scuola Grande della Carità to lesser artists. His four independent narrative cycles were all painted for *scuole piccole*; and although in the case of the Scuola di S Orsola at least some of the canvases were paid for and presumably also supervised by the patrician Loredan family, his employers at the *scuole* of the Schiavoni, the Albanesi and S Stefano consisted chiefly of tradesmen, artisans, sailors and the like. The donors of Carpaccio's metropolitan altarpieces were of a similarly varied social standing, ranging from the patrician Sanuto family, to the citizen families of Ottoboni and Licinio, to a confraternity of artisans such as the Scuola dei Tessitori di Lana (woolweavers). Beyond Venice, Carpaccio is known to have had contacts with members of princely families of the Italian mainland: the *Portrait of a Young Knight* (1510; Madrid, Mus. Thyssen-Bornemisza; see fig. 3) has been associated with the della Rovere of Urbino (or with the Aragonese dynasty at Naples). However, most of Carpaccio's mainland commissions came from clients of a much lower social status, such as the devotional confraternity in Udine who commissioned the *Blood of the Redeemer* (1496; Udine, Mus. Civ.), or the parish church of Grumello de' Zanchi near Bergamo (dismembered polyptych *in situ*).

2. WORK.

(i) Narrative cycles. The canvases painted in the mid-1490s for the Scuola di S Orsola already show Carpaccio at his best. In the largest of the series, the *Departure of St Ursula* (1495; Venice, Accad.; see fig. 4), the scene on the right is typically one of pageantry and ceremony, with gaily dressed figures set against a townscape teeming with incident. Although supposedly set in 4th-century Brittany, the scene is clearly meant to evoke the splendour of late 15th-century Venice, with marble-encrusted palaces rising

3. Vittore Carpaccio: *Portrait of a Young Knight*, oil on canvas, 218×152 mm, 1510 (Madrid, Mus. Thyssen-Bornemisza)

from the waves, floating domes and bell-towers, ships at anchor, festive processions, displays of rich fabrics and shimmering reflections. In the scene on the left, set in pagan England, the backdrop is even more exotic. Here Carpaccio is known to have based his architectural designs on woodcuts showing views of buildings in the eastern Mediterranean, apparently with the intention of creating an appropriately outlandish setting. He is evidently in full command of the laws of geometric perspective and plots the recession into depth with logic and consistency; yet the effect of deep space is counteracted by the frieze-like treatment of the figure composition, and especially by the highly decorative use of colour, which creates a pattern of reds and greens that decisively reasserts the picture plane.

By the 1490s such features were conventional in Venetian cyclical narrative painting, as was the group portrait in the lower left corner, which presumably represents the current office-holders in the confraternity. Important precedents for Carpaccio's approach to narrative painting were the cycle of Old Testament scenes painted in the 1460s and 1470s by various artists for the Scuola Grande di S Marco (destr. by fire in 1485), and the prestigious history cycle in the Doge's Palace (destr. by fire in 1577), with its many scenes of pageantry and of ambassadorial reception and departure. With the unfortunate loss of both these cycles, it is not easy to assess either the originality of Carpaccio's contribution to the type or his artistic relationship to its leading practitioner, Gentile Bellini. What does seem clear, however, is that the St Ursula cycle is characterized by a spirit of poetic fantasy that eluded the more soberly literal Gentile, and that with his feeling for the expressive qualities of light, Carpaccio had as much in common with Giovanni Bellini as with Gentile.

In the six or seven years during which Carpaccio was engaged on the St Ursula cycle, his art matured rapidly. In the *Arrival of St Ursula at Cologne* (1490; Venice, Accad.) the treatment of light and atmosphere is still comparatively primitive, and the ostentatious but naive use of perspective foreshortening recalls the work of Jacopo Bellini. In the *Reception of the Ambassadors* (*c.* 1496; Venice, Accad.) the balance between effects of spatial recession and flat decoration has become much more subtle and harmonious: virtuoso feats of *trompe l'oeil* illusionism in the foreground and effects of distance achieved through

4. Vittore Carpaccio: *Departure of St Ursula*, oil on canvas, 2.80×6.11 m, 1495 (Venice, Galleria dell'Accademia)

atmospheric softening do not disrupt the orderly pattern of shapes and colours whose arrangement reasserts the two-dimensional nature of the canvas.

The pictorial sophistication of the later St Ursula scenes is preserved in at least some of the canvases that Carpaccio painted for the Scuola di S Giorgio degli Schiavoni between 1502 and about 1508. This series, which today enjoys the distinction of being the only Venetian narrative cycle of the early Renaissance to survive in its original building, comprises four separate groups of scenes rather than a continuous narrative, as at the Scuola di S Orsola. The individual compositions are accordingly conceived less in a frieze-like than in a centripetal manner, while the narratives are treated with greater simplicity and clarity, particularly in the three scenes of the *Life of St Jerome.* In keeping with the smaller scale of the canvases, the mood is more intimate and the scene of *St Jerome Leading the Lion into the Monastery* conveys a sense of humour all too rare in Italian Renaissance painting. The colour has become deeper and more glowing than in the St Ursula cycle, perhaps partly in response to the contemporary work of Giorgione, and this gives an appropriate warmth and richness to the exotic environment in the three scenes from the *Life of St George.* For information about Islamic buildings and costumes Carpaccio drew extensively on woodcuts published in Bernhard von Breydenbach's account of his pilgrimage to the Holy Land (Mainz, 1486) as a means of lending his stories verisimilitude, while at the same time freely rearranging his borrowings according to his own poetic invention.

The last of the Scuola degli Schiavoni series, *St Tryphonius Exorcizing the Demon* (*c.* 1507–8), shows a loss of inspiration compared with the St Jerome and St George scenes, appearing almost like a pastiche of the opening scenes of the St Ursula cycle. Comparable tendencies towards slack and mechanical draughtsmanship, hard and dull colour and self-repetition are already to be found in the six canvases of the Scuola degli Albanesi cycle (*c.* 1500–10; dispersed among Venice, Ca' d'Oro and Correr; Bergamo, Gal. Acad. Carrara; Milan, Brera). The explanation in both cases may be that Carpaccio was already making extensive use of workshop assistance. However, the decline in his art was not consistent from this time onwards, and all four of the canvases for the Scuola di S Stefano (1511–20; dispersed among Paris, Louvre; Berlin, Gemäldegal.; Milan, Brera; Stuttgart, Staatsgal.) are superior in invention and execution to those of the Albanesi. The *Stoning of St Stephen* (1520; Stuttgart, Staatsgal.) may even be interpreted as a brave attempt by the artist to revolutionize his style in accordance with 16th-century ideals: the figures are large in relation to the picture field and organized into more compact groups than in his earlier cycles, while the landscape is conceived in terms of loose and cursive rhythms rather than step-by-step spatial recession. But Carpaccio was only moderately successful in his attempt to modernize himself: his actors lack the mobile fluency and heroic dimension of the High Renaissance figure style, and their draperies are very stiff and angular. Furthermore, his art had largely lost the very qualities that made the earlier cycles so appealing: the picturesque details, the vividness of anecdote, the mood of festive gaiety. The *Stoning* is not only stylistically archaic for its date—by 1520 Titian had already completed his *Assumption of the Virgin* (Venice, S Maria Gloriosa dei Frari) and at least one of his mythologies for the Duke of Ferrara—but it also compares unfavourably with Carpaccio's own work of two or three decades earlier.

(ii) Devotional works and portraits. In the field of large-scale public works, Carpaccio's talents were undeniably best suited to narrative painting, and even at the height of his powers, he was much less successful as a painter of altarpieces. Models for his most ambitious works of this type would have been provided by the altarpieces of Giovanni Bellini, but Carpaccio lacked Bellini's ability to combine gentle dignity with calm grandeur. The wit and inventiveness with which the narrative scenes of St Ursula's life on earth are portrayed make the representation of her apotheosis in the accompanying altarpiece (1491; Venice, Accad.) appear dull and contrived by comparison; the figures seem artificially inflated rather than truly grandiose, and the symmetry of their grouping monotonous rather than impressively solemn. Carpaccio's metropolitan altarpieces of the first decade of the 16th century are somewhat more effective, but it is unfortunate that he received most of his altarpiece commissions in the last 15 years of his life, during the very period when his creative powers were in decline.

As a painter of devotional subjects, Carpaccio was much more comfortable when working on a relatively small scale or on pictures intended for an informal, domestic setting. The *Virgin and Child with St John the Baptist* (Frankfurt am Main, Städel. Kstinst.) has an anecdotal charm that has much in common with the narrative cycles and constitutes a highly personal contribution to the well-established genre of the half-length Virgin and Child. In another vein, the *Meditation on the Passion of Christ* (New York, Met.) reveals an ability to communicate feelings of religious seriousness rarely found in his larger, more public works. This has been associated with the spiritual climate emanating from the circle of reforming clerics in Venice that centred around the personality of Paolo Giustinian (Perocco, 1960).

Carpaccio's devotional works vary in dimension, style and quality according to their subject-matter and typology, and probably also according to the type of client who commissioned them. They are consequently often very difficult to date, despite the fact that the comparatively large number of dated works by the artist ought to provide a clear chronological framework. The *Meditation on the Passion*, for example, is sometimes regarded as an early work of *c.* 1490 (Hartt, 1940; Lauts, 1962) and sometimes (and probably more plausibly) as a late work of *c.* 1510. Similarly, the polyptych in Zara (Zadar, S Anastasia) has been seen as early (Longhi, 1932, 1946; Pallucchini, 1961; Zampetti, 1966 monograph), middle (Pignatti, 1955; Perocco, 1960; Lauts, 1962), late (Tietze, 1944) and even as a work executed piecemeal in all three phases (Muraro, 1966).

Carpaccio's fame as a portrait painter is attested in general terms by Vasari, and more specifically by three separate contemporary sources, which refer to portraits by him of certain eminent men and women of letters. None of these can be identified with extant works of art, and most modern attributions remain controversial. Nevertheless, the number of individually characterized heads, including obvious group portraits, that appear in the narrative cycles (see fig. 4), together with a number of fine portrait drawings, make the testimony of the sources entirely credible. One of the characteristics most admired by the Tuscan poet Girolama Corsi Ramos in Carpaccio's portrait of her was that it made her 'seem about to speak'. In other words, the artist must have consciously departed from the characteristically reticent and timeless type of portraiture practised by Giovanni Bellini, and in this respect his portraits may have constituted an important link between those of Antonello da Messina and Giorgione. For most of his portraits Carpaccio would have adopted the standard bust-length, three-quarter view formula, but in the highly original *Portrait of a Young Knight* (see fig. 3 above) the figure is seen in full-length against a richly detailed landscape background. To account for this exceptional arrangement, it has been suggested that this was a posthumous portrait, in which the sitter is commemorated in the full-length pose often adopted for funerary effigies, especially for warriors (Goffen, 1983). In any case, Carpaccio deserves credit here for producing what is probably the first independent full-length portrait in Italian painting, a type that was later developed by Titian.

3. Working methods and technique. Information about the composition and running of Carpaccio's workshop has to be inferred from visual and biographical evidence since there are no documents or early sources. The weaknesses of the Albanesi cycle suggest that by about 1500 Carpaccio employed at least one trained assistant in addition to the customary shop apprentice. The date is probably too early to allow an identification of this assistant with either of his sons, but it is normally assumed that they provided extensive assistance in the artist's later years.

Many of Carpaccio's works are executed on the traditional panel support, but to a greater extent than most of his contemporaries he also made frequent use of canvas, a support that only became normal in Venetian painting during the course of the 16th century. This was a direct consequence of his activity as a painter of narrative cycles, a context in which Jacopo and Gentile Bellini had already employed canvas for some decades. Carpaccio, however, was a pioneer in the use of canvas for altarpieces (as in the *Apotheosis of St Ursula*), and in exploiting its physical properties for new expressive ends. His priming is normally very thin, scarcely covering the rough weave, and his handling of the new medium of oil paint is often sketchy and suggestive. Bold touches of pure colour anticipate the pictorialism of Giorgione and Titian. While Carpaccio's technique lacked the careful, methodical craftsmanship of his contemporaries Giovanni Bellini and Cima, at its best it expressed a greater vivacity and spontaneity; at its worst it can look undisciplined and even incompetent. Analysis of the pigments has shown that Carpaccio moved from a relatively restricted palette in early works such as the St Ursula cycle to a much richer one in a latish work such as the *Presentation in the Temple* (1510; Venice, Accad.), perhaps with the aim of rivalling the chromatic effects of his younger contemporaries.

The comparative freedom of Carpaccio's pictorial technique was nevertheless combined with a traditional dependence on preliminary drawing as a means of working out his compositions and defining form. Scientific analysis has revealed sharp incisions into the gesso ground of architectural orthogonals and the outlines of figures. More drawings by Carpaccio survive than by any other Venetian painter before the later 16th century. Most of them can be related to paintings, and they appear to reflect all the main stages in the preparatory process, ranging from rapid, very free sketches corresponding to early compositional ideas, to more careful compositional studies in which effects of space and light are worked out, to detailed studies from life of individual figures and heads. In compositional studies, such as the preparatory drawing (London, BM) for *St Augustine in his Study* (*see* Collecting, fig. 2) in the Scuola degli Schiavoni, Carpaccio reveals his essentially 15th-century habits of mind by concentrating on generating, by means of geometric perspective, a lucid three-dimensional space, into which his figure is later inserted. At the same time, by making frequent use of ink washes and of coloured (normally blue) papers, he used drawing in a characteristically Venetian fashion to suggest pictorial effects that would be fully realized only in the medium of paint.

In addition to their preparatory function, Carpaccio's drawings, especially the detailed figure studies, also served as records to be preserved in the workshop for use in subsequent commissions. This habit of reusing old designs was shared by most of his contemporaries, including Giovanni Bellini, but after about 1510 Carpaccio tended to indulge in it excessively, and this certainly contributed towards the mechanical dullness that prevails in so many of his later works.

4. Critical reception and posthumous reputation. Despite the artistic decline of his later years, which must have been perfectly apparent to any discerning contemporary, Carpaccio was consistently regarded by subsequent generations as the most important of Giovanni Bellini's Venetian contemporaries. Daniele Barbaro speaks of him respectfully in his treatise on perspective (Daly Davis, 1980), and Vasari chose the biography of Carpaccio as the broad umbrella under which miscellaneous lesser north Italian painters of the 14th and 15th centuries could shelter. But for Vasari, followed by the main Venetian sources, Carpaccio himself stood very much in the shadow of the Bellini brothers, and it was not until John Ruskin's passionate reappraisal of his work in the 1860s that Carpaccio emerged as a fully autonomous artistic personality. Ruskin was attracted by the wealth of detail in Carpaccio's paintings, which he regarded as the outward manifestation of a touchingly sincere Christian reverence and sense of morality. In a characteristic overstatement he declared Carpaccio's message to be 'the sweetest, because the truest, of all that Venice was born to utter' (*Fors Clavigera*, Letter 71, 4 Oct 1876). Ruskin's often misplaced eloquence nonetheless aroused a greater general interest in the artist, and this in turn led to the detailed documentary study by Molmenti and Ludwig (1906), which provided the essential factual basis for all subsequent research. Molmenti and Ludwig shared the later 19th-century view

of Carpaccio as essentially a genre painter, concerned with chronicling the people and events of his time; but, in the 1930s, critics of the Cubist generation such as Roberto Longhi and Giuseppe Fiocco emphasized the very different qualities that they saw as part of the heritage of Piero della Francesca and Antonello da Messina: crystalline perspectival space, reduction of forms to simple volumes rounded with light, clarity of formal structure, emotional impassiveness. A great variety of different approaches to Carpaccio were adopted by the many critics and historians who contributed to the discussion of his art at the time of, and immediately after, the comprehensive exhibition of his works held in the Doge's Palace in 1963.

(2) Benedetto Carpaccio (*fl c.* 1520–60). Son of (1) Vittore Carpaccio. The first documented references to Benedetto occur in 1530 and 1533 when he was still living in Venice, but by 1540 he had become a citizen of Capodistria (now Koper, Slovenia), where he apparently spent the rest of his life. A number of signed and dated altarpieces made for churches in Istria provide a fairly clear idea of his artistic personality: these include a *Coronation of the Virgin* (1537; Koper, Prov. Mus.), a *Virgin and Child with SS Justus and Sergius* (1540; Trieste, S Giusto) and a *Virgin and Child with SS George and Lucy* (1541; Pirano, nr Trieste, Municipio). These show Benedetto to have been an artist of greatly inferior talents who perpetuated an enfeebled 15th-century style up to the middle of the 16th century. After his father's death he continued to produce paintings that were little more than assemblages based on existing motifs from the family stock of drawings. However, it is almost certainly thanks to their preservation by Benedetto that so many of Vittore Carpaccio's drawings, many of them of very high quality, have survived. Giovanni Bellini and Cima probably drew just as much as Carpaccio, but they lacked artistic heirs within their families, and it is likely that most of their drawings were lost soon after their deaths. Benedetto is last heard of in 1560, apparently having attained a position of considerable respectability in his adopted city.

BIBLIOGRAPHY

DBI; Thieme–Becker

EARLY SOURCES

G. Vasari: *Vite* (1550, rev. 2/1568); ed. G. Milanesi (1878–85), iii, pp. 627–42

F. Sansovino: *Venetia città nobilissima et singolare* (Venice, 1581, 2/1663)

C. Ridolfi: *Meraviglie* (1648); ed. D. von Hadeln (1914–24/*R* 1965)

M. Boschini: *Le miniere della pittura* (Venice, 1663)

A. M. Zanetti: *Della pittura veneziana e delle opere pubbliche de' veneziani maestri* (Venice, 1771)

G. A. Moschini: *Guida per la città di Venezia*, 2 vols (Venice, 1815)

GENERAL WORKS

J. Crowe and G. B. Cavalcaselle: *A History of Painting in North Italy* (London, 1871, rev. 2/1912)

J. Ruskin: *Fors Clavigera* (Orpington, 1871–87)

——: *St Mark's Rest* (Orpington, 1877–84)

L. Venturi: *Le origini della pittura veneziana* (Venice, 1907)

——: *Giorgione e il Giorgionismo* (Milan, 1913)

H. Tietze and E. Tietze-Conrat: *The Drawings of the Venetian Painters in the 15th and 16th Centuries*, 2 vols (New York, 1944)

R. Longhi: *Viatico per cinque secoli di pittura veneziana* (Florence, 1946)

B. Berenson: *Venetian School* (1957), i, pp. 56–9

M. Bonicatti: *Aspetti dell'umanesimo nella pittura veneta dal 1455 al 1515* (Rome, 1964)

A. Parronchi: 'La prospettiva a Venezia tra quattro e cinquecento', *Prospettiva*, 9 (1977), pp. 7–16

G. Bellavitis: 'La *Pala di Castelfranco*: Analisi prospettica', *Giorgione: Atti del convegno internazionale di studio per il 5to centenario della nascita: Venezia, 1979* [for technical analysis]

F. Ames-Lewis: *Drawing in Early Renaissance Italy* (London, 1981)

T. Pignatti, ed.: *Le scuole di Venezia* (Milan, 1981)

L. Lazzarini: 'Il colore nei pittori veneziani tra il 1480 e il 1580', *Boll. A.*, n. s. 6, 5 (1983), suppl., pp. 135–44

M. Lucco: 'Venezia fra quattro e cinquecento', *Storia dell'arte italiana*, ed. G. Bollati and P. Fossati, v (Turin, 1983), pp. 457–9

N. Huse and W. Wolters: *Venedig: Die Kunst der Renaissance* (Munich, 1986)

P. Fortini Brown: *Venetian Narrative Painting in the Age of Carpaccio* (London and New Haven, 1988)

MONOGRAPHS, EXHIBITION CATALOGUES, SYMPOSIA

P. Molmenti and G. Ludwig: *Vittore Carpaccio: La vita e le opere* (Milan, 1906; Eng. trans., 1907)

G. Fiocco: *Carpaccio* (Rome, 1931)

T. Pignatti: *Carpaccio* (Milan, 1955)

G. Perocco: *Carpaccio*, Tutta Pitt. (Milan, 1960)

R. Pallucchini: *I teleri del Carpaccio in San Giorgio degli Schiavoni* (Milan, 1961)

J. Lauts: *Carpaccio: Paintings and Drawings* (London, 1962) [cat. rais. and illus.]

Vittore Carpaccio (exh. cat., ed. P. Zampetti; Venice, Doge's Pal., 1963); review by G. Robertson in *Burl. Mag.*, cv (1963), pp. 385–90

M. Muraro: *Carpaccio* (Florence, 1966)

P. Zampetti: *Vittore Carpaccio* (Venice, 1966)

L'opera completa del Carpaccio, notes by G. Perocco, intro. M. Cancogni, Class. A. (Milan, 1967) [cat. and colour illus.]

G. Perocco: *Carpaccio: Le pitture alla Scuola di San Giorgio degli Schiavoni* (Treviso, 1975) [with Eng. trans.]

M. Serres: *Esthétiques sur Carpaccio* (Paris, 1975)

M. Muraro: *I disegni di Vittore Carpaccio* (Florence, 1977) [cat. and illus.]

V. Sgarbi: *Carpaccio* (Bologna, 1979)

F. Bardon: 'La Peinture narrative de Carpaccio dans le cycle de Ste Ursule', *Mem. Ist. Veneto Sci. Lett. & A.*, xxxix/4 (1985)

SPECIALIST STUDIES

R. Fry: 'A Genre Painter and his Critics', *Q. Rev.* ccviii (1908), pp. 491–504

O. Böhm: 'The Calling of St Matthew, by Carpaccio', *Burl. Mag.*, xvi (1909–10), pp. 228–33

T. Hetzer: 'Tizian und Carpaccio', *Mhft. Kstwiss.*, vii (1914), pp. 317–22

R. Longhi: 'Per un catalogo del Carpaccio', *Vita A.*, iii (1932), pp. 4–13; also in *'Me pinxit' e quesiti caravaggeschi* (Florence, 1968), pp. 75–9

F. Hartt: 'Carpaccio's *Meditation on the Passion*', *A. Bull.*, xxii (1940), pp. 25–35

N. di Carpegna: 'Il restauro dei Carpaccio di S Giorgio degli Schiavoni', *A. Veneta*, i (1947), pp. 67–8

B. Maier: 'Benedetto Carpaccio', *Pagine Istria.*, iii (1950), p. 93

H. Roberts: 'St Augustine in *St Jerome's Study*: Carpaccio's Painting and its Legendary Source', *A. Bull.*, xli (1959), pp. 284–97

T. Pignatti: 'Rapporti fra il Cima ed il Carpaccio attorno al primo decennio del cinquecento', *Prov. Treviso*, v (1962), pp. 9–11

R. Gallo: 'La Scuola di S Orsola: I teleri del Carpaccio e le tombe di Gentile e Giovanni Bellini', *Boll. Mus. Civ. Venez.*, viii (1963), pp. 1–24

R. Weiss and V. Branca: 'Carpaccio e l'iconografia del più grande umanista veneziano (Ermolao Barbaro)', *A. Veneta*, xvii (1963), pp. 35–40

K. Ambrozic: 'Due dipinti di Vittore Carpaccio', *A. Veneta*, xviii (1964), pp. 162–4

W. Pokorny: 'Carpaccio's Alcyone Cycle', *Burl. Mag.*, cviii (1966), pp. 418–21

P. Zampetti: 'L'oriente del Carpaccio', *Venezia e l'oriente fra tardo medioevo e rinascimento*, ed. A. Pertusi (Florence, 1966), pp. 511–26

Z. Wazbinski: 'Portrait d'un amateur d'art de la Renaissance', *A. Veneta*, xxii (1968), pp. 21–9

M. Muraro: 'Vittore Carpaccio o il teatro in pittura', *Studi sul teatro veneto fra rinascimento ed età barocca*, ed. M. Muraro (Florence, 1971), pp. 7–19

G. Pochat: 'Bemerkungen zu Carpaccio und Mantegna', *Kstbist. Tidskr.*, xl (1971), pp. 99–106

J. Fletcher: 'Sources of Carpaccio in German Woodcuts', *Burl. Mag.*, cxv (1973), p. 599

V. Sgarbi: 'Vittore Carpaccio: Poetica e committenza', *Prospettiva*, xiv (1978), pp. 31–46

S. Vărzaru: 'Tre fonti letterarie riguardanti l'opera di Vittore Carpaccio', *Rev. Roum. Hist. A.* (Série Beaux-Arts), xv (1978), pp. 117–20

M. Daly Davis: 'Carpaccio and the Perspective of Regular Bodies', *La prospettiva rinascimentale*, ed. M. Dalai Emiliani, i (Florence, 1980), pp. 183–200
J. Bernasconi: 'The Dating of the Cycle of the Miracles of the Cross from the Scuola di San Giovanni Evangelista', *A. Veneta*, xxxv (1981), pp. 198–202
P. Reutersward: 'The Dog in the Humanist's Study', *Ksthist. Tidskr.*, 1 (1981), pp. 53–69
R. Goffen: 'Carpaccio's Portrait of a Young Knight: Identity and Meaning', *A. Veneta*, xxxvii (1983), pp. 37–48
M. Pedrocchi: 'La tavola con i Santi Giovanni Evangelista, Antonio Abate, Giacomo, Domenico, Lorenzo e Nicola di Bari dell'Accademia Carrara di Bergamo attribuita a Carpaccio', *Boll. A.*, n. s. 6, 5 (1983), suppl., pp. 145–50
A. Rona: 'Zur Identität von Carpaccios Ritter', *Pantheon*, xli (1983), pp. 295–302
D. Marshall: 'Carpaccio, St Stephen and the Topography of Jerusalem', *A. Bull.*, lxvi (1984), pp. 610–20
P. Scarpa: 'Disegni sconosciuti di Vettor Carpaccio', *Interpretazioni veneziani: Studi di storia dell'arte in onore di Michelangelo Muraro*, ed. D. Rosand (Venice, 1984), pp. 133–5
A. Gentile: 'Nuovi documenti e contesti per l'ultimo Carpaccio. I: *L'incontro di Gioacchino e Anna* per San Francesco di Treviso', *Artibus & Hist.*, vii/13 (1986), pp. 55–65
L. Zorzi: *Carpaccio e la rappresentazione di Sant'Orsola* (Turin, 1987)
A. Gentile: 'Nuovi documenti e contesti per l'ultimo Carpaccio. II: I teleri per la scuola di Santo Stefano in Venezia', *Artibus & Hist.*, ix/18 (1988), pp. 79–109

PETER HUMFREY

Carpeaux, Jean-Baptiste (*b* Valenciennes, 11 May 1827; *d* Courbevoie, 11 Oct 1875). French sculptor, painter, draughtsman and etcher. He was one of the leading sculptors of the Second Empire (1852–70) in France.

1. Training and early sculpture. 2. Architectural sculpture and public monuments. 3. Portraits. 4. Painting.

1. TRAINING AND EARLY SCULPTURE. He was born into poor circumstances as the son of a lacemaker and bricklayer who wanted him to be a mason. He made friends easily throughout his life, including the painters Bruno Cherier, Eugène Giraud and Jospeh Soumy and the architect Charles Garnier, together with writers, actors and highly placed patrons. In 1838 his family moved to Paris although Carpeaux always retained strong links with his native town. When his family went to the USA, Carpeaux was left in Paris and from 1844 worked ceaselessly for ten years at the Ecole des Beaux-Arts to obtain the Prix de Rome. For the first six years he was a pupil of the sculptor François Rude and then of Francisque-Joseph Duret. To make a living he modelled popular subjects for reproduction in bronze and gave classes at the Petite Ecole, the predecessor of the Ecole des Arts Décoratifs.

A sculptor could not survive without official commissions, and, before those that the Prix de Rome would later bring him, Carpeaux attempted to attract the attention of Emperor Napoleon III and his wife Empress Eugénie with the historic relief the *Reception of Abd-el-Kader at Saint-Cloud* (plaster, 1853; Versailles, Château; marble, 1896, executed by Charles Romain Capellaro; Valenciennes, Mus. B.-A.) and the *Empress Eugénie Protecting Orphans and the Arts* (plaster, 1854; Valenciennes, Mus. B.-A.), a work of pious propaganda. In 1854 he won the Grand Prix de Rome with his *Hector Imploring the Gods to Save his Son Astanyax* (plaster; Paris, Ecole B.-A.; Valenciennes, Mus. B.-A.). While at the Académie de France in Rome, where he stayed until 1862, he produced such works as the *Fisherboy Listening to a Seashell* (plaster, 1857; Paris, Louvre; Valenciennes, Mus. B.-A.), in homage to Rude's *Neapolitan Fisherboy* (marble, 1833; Paris, Louvre), and the group *Count Ugolino and his Sons* (plaster, 1857–61; bronze, 1860, Paris, Mus. d'Orsay). This powerful work proceeds from the ideal aspiration of 19th-century sculpture to combine both skill and competition with the works of the past from which might spring vigorous new growth. Carpeaux himself explained this progression in a letter to Chérier, 'a statue imagined by the poet of the *Divine Comedy* and created by the father of *Moses* [i.e. Michelangelo]—that would indeed be a masterpiece of the human spirit'.

2. ARCHITECTURAL SCULPTURE AND PUBLIC MONUMENTS. Before his departure for Rome, Carpeaux produced the *Genius of the Navy* (1854) for the attic storey of the Pavillon de Rohan, at the Louvre, Paris. On his return from Rome in 1862, he was entrusted by the architect Hector-Martin Lefuel with producing two stone groups (*in situ*) for the south side of the Pavillon de Flore, which Lufuel had just rebuilt, at the Louvre: *Imperial France Bringing Enlightenment to the World and Protecting Science and Agriculture*, which was close to Michelangelo, and *Flora*, evoking the ballet danced by Louis XIV at the Louvre in 1669 and after which the pavilion was named. The putti in this relief were called 'Rubenesque' by art historians, who recalled, in this connection, Carpeaux's journey to Bruges, Antwerp and Ghent in 1863. This was the first time that Carpeaux introduced the complex, diagonally placed figures and the circular, dance-like compositions that he explored in his later groups. Both groups dominate the façade, projecting beyond the lines of the building in a way that Lefuel never intended, and the work was only accepted after the intervention of the Emperor.

His group *Temperance* (1863–6; destr.; replaced by a modern copy) for Théodore Ballu's church of La Trinité (1861–7), Paris, depicting qualities Carpeaux most lacked, would be equally suited to secular surroundings. If the completion of the Louvre proclaimed the continuity and hence the legitimacy of Napoleon III's regime, the great work of the second decade of the Second Empire, the Paris Opéra, affirmed the triumphant prosperity that flowed from it. The architect of the Opéra, Charles Garnier, Carpeaux's friend from the Petite Ecole, suggested that Carpeaux should sculpt a group depicting the Dance of Bacchus for the main façade of the Opéra 'in the spirit of the Arc de Triomphe' (Carpeaux to his friend Dutouquet, 25 December 1863), and three untitled figures were commissioned from him on 17 August 1865. After attempting another subject, *Drama and Comedy* (two plaster sketches; Paris, Mus. d'Orsay), Carpeaux decided upon the subject of *The Dance* (1866; Paris, Mus. d'Orsay; see fig. 1; copy *in situ* in 1964) adding, as Garnier wrote jokingly in *Le Nouvel Opéra de Paris* (Paris, 1878), up to one figure a day; the final work comprises seven figures, surrounding a winged genius.

The sculpture was carved in echaillon stone and unveiled 27 July 1869, and immediately provoked a public scandal: 'It is the very personification of art under the Second Empire... it is the unleashing of appetites...Carpeaux's girls say "To pleasure!" Rude's woman cries "To arms"' (Claretie, pp. 26–8). A bottle of ink was thrown at the

1. Jean-Baptiste Carpeaux: *The Dance*, high relief, echaillon stone, h. 4.5 m, 1866–9 (Paris, Musée d'Orsay)

work a month after the unveiling. Public opinion demanded its removal, and Garnier was forced to commission a new group from Charles Gumery (1827–71). Although a plaster version (1870; untraced) and the stone version (1873; Angers, Mus. B.-A.), which was finished by Gumery's pupils, were made, the group was never erected because of the Franco-Prussian War of 1870 and because, after Carpeaux's death in 1875, the criticism of Carpeaux's work turned to praise.

In 1861 a competition was launched for a monument to be erected in Paris commemorating the defence of Paris against the Russians in 1814 at the Porte de Clichy. Although Carpeaux's submission did not win, in 1910 his widow presented the Petit Palais with a striking maquette of *Maréchal Moncey* on horseback scaling a bristling array of soldiers and guns. Carpeaux's entry for the international competition of 1864, for the erection of a monument to Peter IV, King of Portugal (*reg* 1826) (also Emperor Peter I of Brazil; *reg* 1822–31), in Lisbon was again unsuccessful (maquette; Valenciennes, Mus. B.-A.).

In 1867 the architect Gabriel-Jean-Antoine Davioud commissioned a monumental fountain for the gardens of the Observatoire, Paris, from Carpeaux, Emmanuel Fremiet, Eugène Legrain (1837–1915) and Louis Villeminot (1826–after 1914). In a letter to E. Chesneau in November 1872 Carpeaux described his intentions: 'I have represented the four cardinal points turning to follow the rotation of the globe. Their attitudes follow their polar arrangement, so that there is one full face, one three-quarters, one profile and one rear.' The model was accepted and shown at the Salon of 1872, the first since the Franco-Prussian War. The casting was carried out by Matifat and the figures were erected in 1873–4. The figures were not, however, polychromed as had been Carpeaux's wish.

In addition to these monumental works in Paris, Carpeaux contributed to the reconstruction of the Hôtel de Ville in his home town of Valenciennes. The architect Batigny (*b* 1838) commissioned the city artists of Valenciennes (the 22 winners of the Prix de Rome) to provide the decoration of the façade. In disagreement with his uncle, the academician and sculptor Henri Lemaire, Carpeaux saw his project—an allegorical statue of Valenciennes repulsing an attacking army—reduced to just one figure, *Valenciennes* (stone, 1868–70; destr. 1940; replaced with a copy), which was severely criticized because of its nudity and 'disturbed' appearance. His other work for Valenciennes was the monument to the 18th-century painter Antoine Watteau. Carpeaux first suggested to the mayor on 16 July 1860 that he should execute a statue of Watteau for the Grand Place in Valenciennes. His project was accepted but not the proposed site, and Carpeaux dropped the idea until 1867 by which time he had decided to execute the figure in marble instead of the bronze originally planned. The plaster model (h. 2.5 m; Valenciennes, Mus. B.-A.) was shown in Paris during the 1870 Salon in front of the Palais de l'Industrie and was moved to Valenciennes in 1875. After Carpeaux's death a fund was opened in 1880 for the completion of the monument, which consisted of the figure of *Watteau*, finally in bronze, supported on a fountain decorated with children dressed in costumes of the *commedia dell'arte*, swans—the symbol of Valenciennes—and bas-reliefs inspired by Watteau's paintings. Ernest-Eugène Hiolle completed the monument, which was installed in front of the church of St Géry on 12 October 1884. Carpeaux had therefore lost on two counts: the site and the material.

3. Portraits. In 1862 Carpeaux was presented to Princess Mathilde Bonaparte, Napoleon III's cousin, by his patrons from Rome (the Marquis de Piennes, the Marquise de La Valette, Comte de Nieuwerkerke). He executed two busts of her at Saint-Gratien, her summer residence outside Paris. In the official bust (Paris, Mus. d'Orsay; see fig. 2), which she bequeathed to the Louvre in 1904, tiara, ermine and jewels show the imperial pose to advantage. The other (1863), which was more intimate, was intended for friends; a plaster copy (Paris, Mus. d'Orsay) was dedicated to the writer Charles-Augustin Sainte-Beuve. In appreciation the Princess presented Carpeaux at the court of Napoleon III and in 1864 he was appointed drawing-master to Eugène-Louis-Jean-Joseph Bonaparte, Prince Imperial (1856–79). Carpeaux produced a full-length portrait sculpture (marble, 1867; Paris, Mus. d'Orsay) of his 11-year-old pupil in a simple everyday pose. After the fall of the Second Empire (1870), this made it possible for the Sèvres Porcelain Factory to continue to reproduce the figure in biscuit porcelain under

2. Jean-Baptiste Carpeaux: *Princess Mathilde*, marble, h. 970 mm, 1862 (Paris, Musée d'Orsay)

the title *Boy with a Dog*. The Empress Eugénie commissioned a posthumous portrait of Napoleon III (1873; New York, Met.; unfinished marble copy, Compiègne, Château), and Carpeaux completed his court sketches (Compiègne, Château) with those of the Imperial Mortuary Chapel in the church of St Mary, Chislehurst, Kent.

Carpeaux also executed portraits of celebrities who were often seen around the Tuileries, including *Ernest André* (marble, 1862), deputy for the Gard, his son *Edouard André* (marble, 1863; both Mus. d'Orsay), banker, deputy and art collector. While in exile in London (1871–3) Carpeaux executed busts of *Madame Lefèvre* (marble, 1871; Paris, Mus. d'Orsay), *Madame de Fontreal* (1873) and *Madame Turner* (1871–2; London, V&A). On his return to France he made those of *Alexandre Dumas the Younger* (marble, 1873; Paris, Comédie Française) and *Madame Dumas* (orig. plasters for both; Paris, Mus. d'Orsay).

Among Carpeaux's well-known works, the portraits of the women he loved are calm and sad: '*La Palombella*', who died during his stay in Rome and whose 'antique' features are seen in the face of *Imperial France* (1863, model, Paris, Mus. d'Orsay; limestone, S. façade, Pavillon de Flore, Louvre), and *Amélie de Montfort* (1869; Paris, Mus. d'Orsay; Valenciennes, Mus. B.-A.), his wife from 1869. Nine years earlier Carpeaux's vitality had absorbed the laughter of the fifteen-year-old Anna Foucart, whose portrait he carried out in 1860; it is her smile that can be seen in the *Laughing Girl* (1860), *Flora* (1863), the *Mischievous Child* (1865; all Valenciennes, Mus. B.-A.) and the *Kneeling Flora* (marble, 1873; Lisbon, Mus. Gulbenkian). The series of sketches produced from Carpeaux's studio recall 18th-century taste, which was brought back into fashion by the French family of writers and critics the Goncourts. This taste gained a wide appreciation because Carpeaux reproduced in his lifetime terracotta sketches of the *Dance* (Valenciennes, Mus. B.-A.) and put forward as examples the bust of *Asia* or the *Mater Dolorosa* in two versions—one finished, the other 'sketched'.

4. Painting. His painted work, mostly in the form of oil sketches, includes a series of introspective self-portraits (e.g. *Self-portrait in a Red Shirt*, 1862; Valenciennes, Mus. B.-A.), in which his pain and illness caused by cancer are increasingly evident. There are also evocative scenes of balls (e.g. *Masked Ball at the Tuileries*, 1867; Paris, Mus. d'Orsay) and such visionary works as the *Berezowski's Attempt on the Life of Tsar Alexander II* (1867; Paris, Mus. d'Orsay).

A man of intense emotions, Carpeaux found expression through drawing in notebooks, which he took everywhere. His inner turbulence led him to follow the path that links romanticism to expression: 'You tell me that I'm too enthusiastic, *e caro mio*, if I did not have these flights of admiration, which the public take for exaggeration, I would not be capable of expressing myself' (letter to his friend Foucart, 29 June 1861).

UNPUBLISHED SOURCES

Paris, Louvre, and Mus. d'Orsay [main archives, incl. notebooks]
Valenciennes, Mus. B.-A. [archives of Valenciennes and drawings]

BIBLIOGRAPHY

J. Claretie: *J.-B. Carpeaux, 1827–1875* (Paris, 1875)
L. Delteil: *Le Peintre-graveur illustré*, vi (Paris, 1906–26; Eng. trans., New York, 1969)
L. Clément-Carpeaux: *La Vérité sur l'œuvre et la vie de J. B. Carpeaux 1827–1875*, i (Paris, 1934), ii (Nemours, 1935)
Sur les traces de J. B. Carpeaux (exh. cat., ed. V. Beyer; Paris, Grand Pal., 1976)
A. Hardy and A. Braunwald: *Catalogue des peintures et sculptures de J. B. Carpeaux à Valenciennes* (Valenciennes, 1978)
D. Kocks: *Jean Baptiste Carpeaux: Rezeption und Originalität* (Cologne, 1981)
A. M. Wagner: *Jean-Baptiste Carpeaux: Sculptor of the Second Empire* (New Haven and London, 1986)
L. de Margerie: *Carpeaux: La Fièvre créatrice*, Découvertes Gallimard, no. 68 (1989)

ANNE PINGEOT

Carpegna, Ambrogio, Conte (*d* Rome, 14 March 1643). Italian patron. He came from the Duchy of Urbino, which was absorbed into the Papal State by Pope Urban VIII (Maffeo Barberini) in 1631. Although most of his family supported the claims of the Medici to the papal succession, Ambrogio moved to Rome to espouse the Barberini cause. He served the Pope on diplomatic missions and collaborated on the creation of the Piazza Trevi (1641–3), a project that involved enlarging the medieval piazza, moving the aqueduct, replacing Leon Battista Alberti's fountain with a new one designed by Gianlorenzo Bernini and rebuilding the Palazzo Carpegna. Francesco Borromini projected a new palace designed around an ingenious oval courtyard extending across a public street; the surrounding oval loggia would have continued over the street on two bridges, while the view from the courtyard was to focus on the statue of the *Acqua Vergine*, placed at the centre of Bernini's fountain. After the deaths of Ambrogio and Urban VIII (1644) these ambitious schemes were abandoned, although the Palazzo Carpegna was completed on a greatly reduced scale (attrib. a follower of Giacomo della Porta; enlarged by Borromini) for Ambrogio's brother, Cardinal Ulderico Carpegna (1595–1679), during 1643–9. Today it is the seat of the Accademia di S Luca (*see* ROME, §VI).

BIBLIOGRAPHY

DBI

P. A. Guerrieri: *Genealogia di Casa Carpegna* (Rimini, 1667), iv of *La Carpegna abbellita et il Monte Feltro illustrato* (Urbino, 1667)

M. Tafuri: 'Borromini in Palazzo Carpegna: Documenti inediti e ipotesi critiche', *Quad. Ist. Stor. Archit.*, lxxix–lxxxiv (1967), pp. 85–107

J. Connors: 'Alliance and Enmity in Roman Baroque Urbanism', *Röm. Jb. Bib. Hertz.*, xxv (1989), pp. 207–94 (233–45)

JOSEPH CONNORS

Carpenter, Andrew [Carpentière, Andries] (*b c.* 1677; *d* London, July 1737). English sculptor, of French or Flemish descent. According to Vertue, he learnt 'the rudiments of drawing' from Peter Eude, a portrait and history painter trained at the Académie Royale, Paris, who settled in England and later in Scotland. Carpenter became principal assistant to John van Nost (i), and he is recorded as present in London in 1702 by Ralph Thoresby, the Leeds historian. Thoresby regarded Carpenter's marble statue of *Queen Anne*, commissioned *c.* 1710–12 by Alderman William Milner for Moot Hall, Leeds (*c.* 1710–12; Leeds, C.A.G.), as 'generally esteemed. . .the best that was ever made' and included an engraving of it in his *Ducatus Leodiensis* (1715). The statue of the Queen, in her Parliament robes with crown, globe, sceptre and Order of the Garter, demonstrates Carpenter's ability to handle marble competently on a monumental scale. From 1716 to 1717 he was associated with Francis Bird in the production of statues for the pediment of St Paul's Cathedral.

Carpenter's work moved from the semi-Baroque style of Nost to a new manner derived from James Gibbs. In 1725 he executed the monument to *Montague Garrard Drake and Jane Drake* at the church of St Mary, Amersham, Bucks, to Gibbs's design, later published in the latter's *Book of Architecture* of 1728 (pl. 121). His most important monuments are at St Mary's Church, Bowdon, Ches, to *Langham and Henry Booth* (1727) and to *Henry Booth, 3rd Earl, and the Countess of Warrington.* The latter, erected in 1734, consists of a large sarcophagus flanked by female figures representing Learning and Truth and is based on the monument to *Mrs Katherine Bovey* in Westminster Abbey, which was designed by Gibbs and executed by Michael Rysbrack. This in turn was modelled on Giovanni Battista Foggini's *Feroni* monuments (1691–3) in SS Annunziata, Florence.

Vertue noted that besides monumental work, Carpenter specialized in the leaden figures used to animate the skylines of great houses and to adorn formal gardens. He worked in 1722 for James Brydges, Duke of Chandos at Cannons, Edgware, Middx. In 1722–3 he supplied Viscount Dillon with a *Fame* and a *Roman Soldier*, both 2.18 m high, for the parapet at Ditchley, Oxon. In 1723 Lord Carlisle ordered from him a *Farnese Hercules*, *Spartan Boys*, a *Sitting Venus* and a *Faunus* for the gardens at Castle Howard, Yorks. The price list for Castle Howard itemizes the 24 different statues in Carpenter's repertory (Gunnis), including *Cain and Abel*, *Venus de Medici*, the *Duke of Marlborough*, a *Bagpiper*, an *Indian*, a *French Peasant and Paisanne* and *Love and Disdain.* Further lead statues were supplied to Moulsham Hall, Essex, in 1730–32. Carpenter's most remarkable extant lead statues are those executed for the Duke and Duchess of Kent at Wrest Park, Beds (1730). These groups include the *Rape of the Sabines* and *Aeneas and Anchises* and are remarkably ambitious in composition. According to Vertue, the exhausting work on these commissions hastened Carpenter's death, 'aged about 60'.

BIBLIOGRAPHY

Gunnis

R. Thoresby: *Ducatus Leodiensis: Or the Topography of the Ancient and Populous Town and Parish of Leeds* (1715)

L. Weaver: *English Leadwork, its Art and History* (London, 1909)

'The Note-books of George Vertue', *Walpole Soc.*, xxii (1933–4), pp. 83, 111; xxiv (1935–6), p. 35

C. H. Collins-Baker and M. I. Collins-Baker: *The Life and Circumstances of James Brydges, First Duke of Chandos* (London, 1949)

M. Whinney: *Sculpture in Britain, 1530–1830*, Pelican Hist. A. (Harmondsworth, 1964)

T. Friedman: 'A Noble Magnificent Statue', *Leeds A. Cal.*, lxxii (1973), pp. 5–13

F. Haskell and N. Penny: *Taste and the Antique* (London, 1981)

T. Friedman: *James Gibbs* (London, 1984)

TESSA MURDOCH

Carpenter [née Geddes], **Margaret Sarah** (*b* Salisbury, 1793; *d* London, 13 Nov 1872). English painter. Encouraged by Jacob Pleydell-Bouverie, 2nd Earl of Radnor, she established herself in London at the age of 20 after winning a Salisbury Society of Arts gold medal for a study of a boy's head. Regarded as 'the best woman portrait painter of her time' (Whitley, p. 162), she did portraits of many notable men, including *Patrick Fraser Tytler* (1845) and *Archbishop Sumner* (1852; both London, N.P.G.). Carpenter's work was admired for its artistic qualities, independent of the subject's identity. When she exhibited *Head of a Polish Jew* (untraced) at the British Institution in 1823, a reviewer wrote: 'It very rarely happens that a specimen of art like this is produced from the hand of a lady: here are colour, strength and effect, and anatomical drawing.' Carpenter exhibited at the Royal Academy between 1818 and 1866, as well as at the British Institution and the Society of Artists. Her output is estimated at 1000 paintings.

It is likely that James Carpenter, the prosperous bookseller and publisher, acted as agent for Carpenter when she first arrived in London. He was known as a zealous dealer with an eye for young talent. Margaret married Carpenter's son, William Hookham Carpenter (1792–1866), who, after working in his father's line of business, became Keeper of Prints and Drawings at the British Museum in 1845. Their children, William (*c.* 1819–99) and Jane Henrietta (*fl* 1847–57), were also artists. Through her father-in-law, Carpenter met Richard Parkes Bonington who advised her on the practicability of sending her work to the Paris Salon. She executed a chalk study of Bonington (London, N.P.G.), which was engraved as the frontispiece to J. D. Harding's portfolio after Bonington's work, published in 1829.

UNPUBLISHED SOURCES

Collection of press cuttings, London, V&A, vol. v, 1283
Sitters Book, London, N.P.G. Archv [transcription of Carpenter's 'Client List' (*c.* 1812–64)]

BIBLIOGRAPHY

DNB
W. T. Whitley: *Art in England, 1821–1837* (Cambridge, 1930), p. 162
R. Smith: 'One Face to Remember', *Women's A. Mag.*, no. 54 (Sept/Oct 1993), pp. 26–7

MARCIA POINTON

Carpenter, R(ichard) C(romwell) (*b* Middlesex, 21 Oct 1812; *d* London, 27 March 1855). English architect. He was articled to John Blyth (1806–78), a little-known London architect, who encouraged him to pursue his interest in ecclesiastical architecture. He studied the books of John Britton, A. W. N. Pugin and others and visited medieval buildings. In 1830 he exhibited a design for a cathedral transept at the Royal Academy. His earliest executed ecclesiastical commissions were the churches of St Stephen (1843–4; destr.) and St Andrew (1844–6) in Birmingham. St Andrew's is in correct 14th-century style, with a deep chancel, and is very much in the manner of Pugin, of whom Carpenter was a friend and close follower. Carpenter was the favourite architect of the Cambridge Camden (later Ecclesiological) Society. His best-known churches are St Paul's (1846–8), Brighton, Sussex, and St Mary Magdalene's (1849–52), Munster Square, London, which *The Ecclesiologist* called 'the most artistically correct new church yet consecrated in London'. Neither received the tall spire designed for it. Carpenter also made some sensitive and learned restorations, including Chichester Cathedral, W. Sussex (1847–9), and Sherborne Abbey, Dorset (nave and transept, 1849–51, choir, 1856–8 by William Slater). He played an important part in the 'revival' of stained glass and was the first to employ John Richard Clayton (1827–1913; later of the firm of Clayton & Bell) to make cartoons.

Carpenter's domestic work consisted mostly of schools and parsonages: the latter included one in Scottish medieval style at Burntisland, Fife (1850–54). He worked on two country houses: at Campden House (1846), Glos, for Charles Middleton, the 1st Earl of Gainsborough, he made extensive additions, including a chapel; and at Bedgebury Park (1854–5), Kent, he used a French château style to suit the 17th- and 18th-century house of his client, the ecclesiologist Alexander John Beresford Hope, for whom he also designed a screen, stalls and tomb in his church at Kilndown, Kent, as well as a parsonage. His most important school commissions came from the Rev. Nathaniel Woodard, for whom he designed Lancing College (designed 1848; begun 1854), W. Sussex, and St John's College (1851–3), Hurstpierpoint, W. Sussex. At his death Hope, Woodard and others arranged that his practice should be taken over by his former pupil William Slater (1819–72), who in 1863 took into partnership Carpenter's son, Richard Herbert Carpenter (1841–93), the designer of the chapel (begun 1868) at Lancing College.

BIBLIOGRAPHY

Obituary, *Builder*, xiii (1855), p. 165; *The Ecclesiologist*, xvi (1855), pp. 137–41

PETER HOWELL

Carpentier, Eugène (*b* Courtrai [Flem. Kortrijk], 20 May 1819; *d* Beloeil, 10 March 1886). Belgian architect. One of the most distinguished Belgian architects of the second half of the 19th century who designed in several styles, he won a first prize at the Académie Royale des Beaux-Arts in Brussels in 1845 and specialized in the study of medieval architecture under Joseph Jonas Dumont. Around 1852 he established himself in Bruges, where he collaborated with Jean-Baptiste Charles François Bethune on the chapel of the Sisters of Charity (1858); before 1861, however, he moved to Beloeil, where he was employed on alterations to the Prince de Ligne's château (which was then largely rebuilt following a fire in 1900). Carpentier was most influential in the field of ecclesiastical architecture. His churches at Beloeil (1862), Châtelet (1867; destr. by fire 1937), Thollembeek (1869), Antoing (1869) and Awenne (1881) show a personal interpretation of High Victorian Gothic, whereas St Remacle (1880) in Spa is an advanced exercise in the archaeological Romanesque Revival manner. His most conspicuous civilian building is the Hôtel Continental (1874; interior and roof destr. by fire), which marks the crossing of Boulevard Anspach with boulevards A. Max and E. Jacqmain in Brussels and is conceived in a typical Second Empire style. He had made an interesting contribution to the Renaissance Revival in 1859 when building the Château de Calmont at Ruyen, and his designs for hospitals at Maldegem (1867–76) and Ath (1876) and school buildings at Tournai (1874–6) and Menin (1881) were selected for several exhibitions. A member of the Royal Commission on Monuments, Carpentier also did much restoration, where his skill in understanding the structure of medieval buildings was particularly useful. Examples of his restorations are at St Ursmer (1863) in Lobbes, at Huy (1876), at St Martin (1876) in Courtrai, St Nicolas (1878) in Tournai, Het Rubenssteen (1875) at Elewijt and the belfry and former Cloth Hall (1881) of Tournai.

BIBLIOGRAPHY

BNB; Thieme–Becker
Exposition nationale d'architecture (exh. cat., Brussels, Pal. B.-A., 1883), p. 74
'Eugène Carpentier', *L'Emulation*, xi (1886), pp. 3–4
H. Rousseau: 'Eugène Carpentier: Notes biographiques', *Bull. Comm. Royale A. & Archéol.*, xxxi (1892), pp. 147–61
——: 'Biographie: Eugène Carpentier', *L'Emulation*, xviii (1893), pp. 73–8
J. van Cleven: 'Neogotiek en neogotismen: De neogotiek als component van de 19de eeuwse stijl in België', *De Sint-Lucasscholen en de neogotiek*, ed. J. De Maeyer (Leuven, 1988), pp. 44–6

JEAN VAN CLEVEN

Carpet. Originally a thick cover for a bed, table etc. From the 16th century the term included knotted carpets from the Middle East; it gradually became exclusively associated with knotted carpets placed on the floor. By the early 18th century other forms of fabric floor covering had assumed the same name. (*See also* RUG.)

I. Types and techniques. II. History.

I. Types and techniques.

1. Hand-knotted. 2. Tapestry-woven. 3. Flat-woven. 4. Embroidered and needle-worked. 5. Pile-woven. 6. Power-loom woven. 7. Warp-printed. 8. Machine-tufted.

1. HAND-KNOTTED. This is considered the quintessential carpet. Woven originally in Asia, such carpets were

highly prized and later copied in many parts of Europe. The knots, tied in cut lengths of yarn, the ends of which formed the pile, were inserted during the process of construction, or weaving; they were tied in rows across the warps, each row of knots being separated by one, two or three picks of weft, laid in as alternate rows of plain weave (*see* TEXTILE, §II, 1). Hand-knotted carpets can be divided into several categories, according to the knot used; this is, consequently, a means of establishing a carpet's provenance. There are four types of knot, each type known by several names. The first is the Turkish, Ghiordes or symmetrical knot (see fig. 1a and colour pl. II) and the second the Persian, Senna or asymmetrical knot (1b and colour pl. III). A third type, based on the first two but worked over four warps instead of two, is known as the jufti knot; depending on the style, this may be the Turkish jufti or the Persian jufti (1c). The fourth type of knot is the Spanish or single-warp symmetrical knot (1d).

The warp of Middle Eastern carpets was almost exclusively tightly spun wool, often a dark natural colour (see colour pl. IV); in some very fine Persian carpets, tightly spun silk was used for the warps, as it was stronger and less bulky than wool, and a loosely spun silk for the wefts. In Persian and Indian carpets the silk warps were later replaced by factory-spun cotton. In Turkish carpets wefts were usually of a softer wool, often dyed red; cotton was sometimes used, especially in Caucasian rugs. In 19th- and 20th-century rugs a combination of materials has sometimes been used for the weft, and some late Indian carpets have employed jute. The knots of Middle Eastern carpets were almost invariably of wool, although of widely differing qualities. Silk was used in particularly rich carpets, and occasionally small amounts of cotton were used. The density of the knots varied enormously according to the quality of the carpet, and could range from 5 knots to 2000 knots per 25 sq. mm, a broad average lying between 10 and 40 knots per 25 sq. mm.

A different form of hand-knotted carpet are the *ryijy* and *ryer* rugs woven in Finland and Norway. They were made entirely of wool, the knots being worked in rows between larger areas of plain weave. A group of yarns, sometimes of contrasting colours, was used for each knot, which was worked in the Turkish or symmetrical fashion across the warps. The weaving was much coarser than that of the classic Eastern carpets; in each pick there might be only three knots per 25 mm, and the rows of knots were spaced on average about 25 mm apart, giving only three knots per 25 sq. mm. The pile was generally much longer than that of Eastern carpets, up to 25 mm long. Early *ryijy* and *ryer* are found with pile on both front and reverse, but fewer knots were worked on the reverse, and the pile was left longer. The front and reverse knots were usually worked at the same time along the same row or pick.

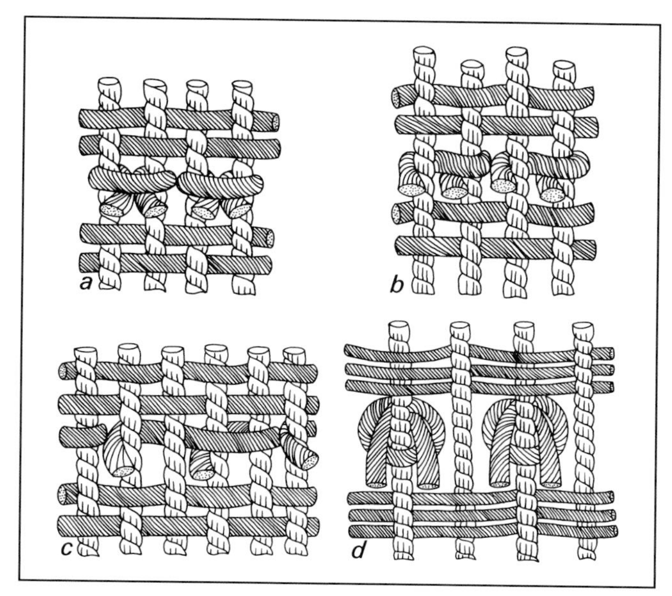

1. Types of knot used in hand-knotted carpets: (a) Turkish, Ghiordes or symmetrical knot; (b) Persian, Senna or asymmetrical knot; (c) jufti knot; (d) Spanish knot

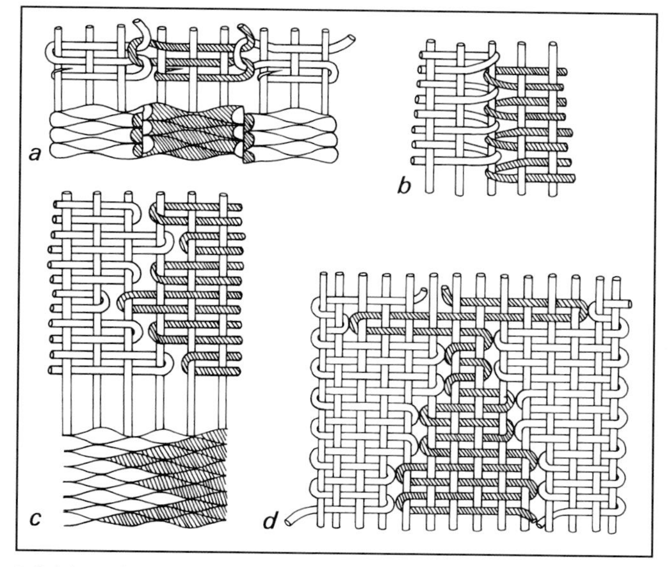

2. Joining techniques in tapestry-woven carpets: (a) double interlock joins; (b) dovetailing; (c) hatching; (d) stepped joins

2. TAPESTRY-WOVEN. Such carpets and rugs, which have been woven in many parts of the world, have a plain woven weft-faced structure in which the weft is beaten down very hard to cover the warp entirely (*see* TAPESTRY, §I). Their distinctive feature is the use of discontinuous coloured weft threads, which travel only a short distance along the pick in creating the pattern. Differently coloured areas of the pattern are not necessarily joined in the weaving process, and slits running in the direction of the warps may form between two colours. In the type produced in West Asia, known as kelims, kilims, khelims or ghilleems (*see* KILIM), such slits are common, but they are not invariable, and various joining methods are employed. Interlocking techniques are found in early Peruvian tapestry, in Navajo rugs (*see* TEXTILE, colour pl. IV, fig.2) and blankets and in Swedish and Norwegian *rølakan* rugs.

With single interlocked joins, like those found in Norwegian *rølakan*s and in some kilims from central to south-west Persia, the finish is the same on both sides of the weaving. With double interlock joins, as used on Swedish *rølakans* and some Persian kilims, particularly those woven by the Baktari tribes, although the front looks the same as single interlock, on the back the join is more obvious, and a ridge is visible (see fig. 2a). Another method of making vertical joins is dovetailing, which gives a jagged saw-tooth line (2b); it is used in kilims from Thrace and north-west Persia. Hatching is a steep zigzag joining technique that gives a softer edge (2c). In intricate or curved areas of the design, wefts sometimes travel around a contrasting pattern area, instead of remaining strictly perpendicular to the warp; known as eccentric or curved-weft tapestry, this is also found mainly in Thracian kilims. In large areas of a single colour, 'lazy lines' can sometimes be seen; these were created when the weaver, having taken the weft over a limited number of warps, moved it along to work on the next area, forming a diagonal line in the weave. Such lines have sometimes been used as a pattern feature, progressing across one or two warps at a time to produce a smooth line, while a stepped diagonal line was a distinctive feature of patterns in kilims (2d). Soumak and small areas of brocading (*see* §3 below) were occasionally used in kilims.

3. Flat-woven. Rugs and carpets woven without a pile or raised surface texture have been made in all parts of the world and vary from the highly prized and richly adorned to the simplest and most basic of matting. Carpets can be woven using basic plain weave, with simple or complex patterns ranging from warp- or weft-faced stripes to intricate designs. Looms with three, four, six and eight shafts give vast scope for pattern and surface texture on the warp or weft face; these range from simple twills, with all their variations of diaper and broken twills, to shadow weave, spot weave, honeycomb, block patterns and brocades.

Warp-faced carpets and rugs, in which only the warp yarns are visible, are considered to be more hard-wearing, because warp yarns have generally tended to be stronger and more tightly spun. Examples include Bedouin saha or tent curtains made of goat hair, and Venetian carpets, first recorded in 1803, which had a striped worsted warp and a wool weft (by the end of the 19th century this was often replaced by jute). References to Venetian carpeting show that it was used for halls and stairs; it is known to have been made in Kidderminster, Yorkshire and Scotland and had no known connection with Venice. List carpets, first recorded in 1747 and noted to be like an inferior version of the Venetian, were wiry, plain-weave coarse carpets in which the weft was made of selvages, then called lists, cut from other fabrics. Such carpets were made of cotton, with narrow, coloured stripes; seldom found in Britain, they were quite popular in America.

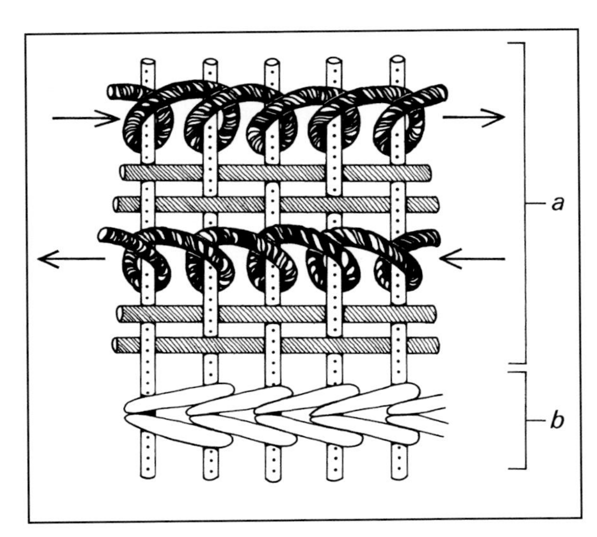

3. Soumak technique of rug-making

Soumak is a weft-faced technique, used in Caucasian rug-making, that involved repeatedly wrapping the weft yarn around the warps to create a distinctive surface texture (see fig. 3). The yarn may travel from selvage to selvage, using a continuous weft, but its path is not direct; it can be wrapped around each individual warp or around two or more, while the progress of the weft moves one warp along with each wrap (rather like backstitch in needlework), giving a diagonal appearance to the surface. This diagonal can be alternated with the ground weave, in which case it is called soumak brocading, or it can be worked without any ground weaving in between, called soumak wrapping. The diagonal can also be reversed, giving a zigzag effect. There are many different variations: the soumak wefts are sometimes used for patterning across part of the warp, employing discontinuous wefts, to produce blocks of different colours or textures.

Hard-wearing double and triple cloths used as floor coverings are known as Kidderminster, Scotch, Ingrain, Union or two- or three-ply carpets. A double cloth has two independent sets of warps and wefts of plain weave, one on top of the other. They can be crossed, so that the top set intersects the lower one and changes places with it. If different colours are used for each set of warps and wefts, a pattern can be formed by moving the sets back and forth at chosen intervals. This method gives a reversible product with a choice of two sets of colours. Triple cloth works in a similar fashion, but with three sets of warps and wefts, giving a choice of three sets of colours. The first mention of carpets of Kidderminster cloth is found in 1634 in an inventory of the Countess of Leicester, but it is not known whether that cloth corresponded to Kidderminster double cloth, first made there in 1735. Double-cloth carpets were introduced in 1778 to Kilmarnock, Scotland, where in 1824 the triple-cloth technique was perfected. These types of carpet were mainly all-wool products and tended to have worsted yarn in the warp and wool in the weft. Early carpets using double and triple cloths were made by sewing together strips 910 mm wide, with approximately 15 ends and picks per 25 mm. By the early 20th century improved technology had made possible the weaving of wide seamless carpets (*see also* §6 below).

4. Embroidered and needle-worked. Embroidered carpets could be worked in a variety of stitches on a canvas ground. Early embroidered carpets, dating from the 16th century, were on single-thread canvas; those of the 19th century and after seem to have favoured double-thread canvas. As early as the 17th century patterns already drawn on the canvas were sold with a set of wools or silks,

ready to be executed. The stitches, although sometimes coarser, were the same as those used for other canvaswork, using primarily wool and occasionally small amounts of silk. The most common stitches found in early examples are tent stitch and cross stitch; from the 19th century embroiderers made use of variations of cross stitch, half-cross stitch and herringbone stitch, as well as knotted stitch, chain stitch and rice stitch.

Two types of hand-knotted pile rug that were popular in the late 19th century and the 20th were the long-pile rug and the short-pile rug. Both used a canvas ground and almost exclusively used wool for the pile. The long-pile method used pre-cut lengths of wool (an instrument known as a 'turkey gauge' was sometimes used to ensure evenness of length) that were drawn through the canvas and knotted one at a time using a latched hook. In the short-pile method, a needle threaded with a long piece of yarn was used to make a knot or double stitch on the canvas; the thread was taken around a gauge, and a second knot or double stitch was made one space further along. Repeating this process created a row of the pattern; the loops were cut before the gauge was moved on to a new area.

5. PILE-WOVEN. The techniques employed for these carpets contributed towards the eventual mass production of carpets; the looms used to produce them were subsequently fitted with jacquard montures (a mechanism for controlling the selection of heddles to be lifted in weaving) and were later adapted to become power looms (*see* §6 below).

In Chenille carpets, originally called Patent Axminsters, the pile was created by means of a specially prepared form of chenille yarn, made by weaving a flat cloth with a wool weft, and a warp, usually of linen, arranged in groups with spaces between. The cloth was then cut along the length of the warp between the groups. The resulting long strips were used as pile warps in the carpets; the cut wool wefts formed the tufts. In the weaving of the chenille cloth, the colour of the weft could be changed, so that the cut strips used as pile warps formed the pattern. Colour changes along the strip could range from 12 to 20 per 25 mm. The density of chenille in construction is 3.5–5 per 25 mm, corresponding roughly to 42–100 knots per 25 sq. mm. In weaving chenille carpets, it was difficult to maintain accurate registering of the pattern; also, the chenille was apt to break away from the surface of the carpet, as it did not have a very strong anchor, while a binding warp that was too strong sometimes crushed the pile.

The looped-pile or Brussels carpet was first patented in England at Wilton in 1741 and the first loom for weaving it was built at Kidderminster in 1749. The construction was like that of terry-towelling but woven with multi-coloured supplementary warps, from which groups of threads were looped proud of the ground warp when required to form the pattern (see fig. 4a). Up to six colours could be used, but often only two were required, and self-coloured Brussels carpets were also made. Brussels carpet was considered durable and clean and could render a wide variety of patterns, although the complicated shedding motion made it unsuitable for long pattern repeats. It was uneconomic in patterning, as much expensive worsted yarn lay below the surface. The weaving of wide carpets was impractical, and even with a jacquard monture, the heavy machinery could not be worked at great speed. The carpets were usually 700 mm wide and up to 46 m long; several widths could be joined, the borders being woven separately. There were 40 to 100 loops per 25 sq. mm. The surface quality was considered to be lacking in richness, and on poorer versions the foundation weave showed through.

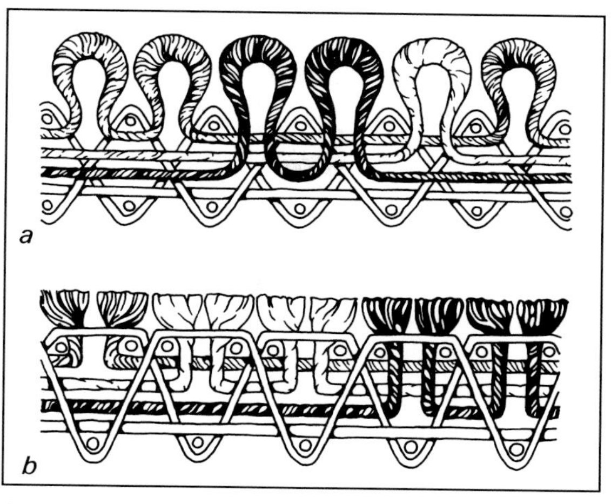

4. Looped-pile carpet: (a) Brussels carpet; (b) Wilton carpet

Wilton carpets were originally made around Wilton, near Salisbury, in large quantities. The technique was almost the same as that of Brussels, but the pile was cut (see fig. 4b). The number of colours, or pattern warps, varied from two to six, although again, self-coloured carpets of this type were also made. The carpets were woven in widths ranging from 690 mm to 910 mm, with 50–150 loops per 25 mm. Carpets up to 2.7 m wide were known, but they were rare, being technically difficult and therefore expensive. Wilton had the same disadvantages as Brussels, but the cut pile gave it a richer surface texture and more covering power. It was considered the best kind of machine-made carpet; the close-piled quality was sometimes called velvet carpeting (*see also* WILTON, §2).

6. POWER-LOOM WOVEN. Up to the 1830s and 1840s the looms used in factories to produce Kidderminster, Ingrain, Brussels and Wilton carpets did not differ greatly from those used domestically. In 1825 a jacquard monture was first used in Kidderminster for Ingrain carpets and soon after for Brussels and Wilton. This simplified the weaving process and made possible looms operated by only one person. In 1842 Wood of Pontefract patented the first steam loom to be used for Brussels carpets. In 1847 John Crossley of Halifax purchased Wood's patent and tried it for tapestry, or warp-tinted carpets (*see* §7 below). In 1839 Erastus Brigham Bigelow (1814–79), an American engineer, had begun to work on perfecting a power loom for Ingrain carpets (*see* §3 above). The early results were technically excellent, producing a superior article, but the loom did not at first increase speed or productivity. In 1846, when his Ingrain loom was being launched, Bigelow took out a British patent for a new

power loom for Brussels carpet (*see* §8 below). The final version was said to combine the driving motions of Bigelow's Ingrain loom, the power of the Jacquard loom and, for the pile, a terry wire mechanism that Bigelow had previously devised for a coach-lace loom. It was only after he had displayed his looms in London at the Great Exhibition of 1851 that carpet manufacturers began to show enthusiasm for power-loom weaving. Crossleys of Halifax bought Bigelow's patent for £10,000 and proceeded to sell licences to build the looms to various British manufacturers.

7. WARP-PRINTED. These are sometimes misleadingly known as tapestry carpets, although they are not tapestry-woven but have a ground warp and a pattern warp and are woven in a similar way to velvet (*see* TEXTILE, §III, 1(i)). The pattern warp is six times longer than the ground warp and is woven in over rods to create a looped pile, which can, as in velvet, be cut or can be left in loops. Before weaving, the pattern warp is dyed or printed in different colours so as to form a pattern in weaving. Because the quality of dyefastness is poorer in partially dyed or printed textiles, these carpets were not considered to have the durability of other carpets, where the whole yarn was immersed in the dye vats. Another disadvantage was that the pattern did not always register perfectly in the weaving. This kind of carpet could be woven up to 2.7 m or 3.65 m wide, with 7–9 tufts per 25 mm, 64 per 25 sq. mm.

8. MACHINE-TUFTED. Although AXMINSTER was known as a weaving centre for carpets, the carpet known as machine-tufted, and also as Axminster, has apparently no connection with the town. It was Tomkinson & Adam who introduced machine-tufted carpets, which were woven on a loom (see fig. 5) developed from a patent bought from Halcyon Skinner, an American. They were known as Royal Axminster carpets and were closer in general appearance to hand-knotted carpets than anything so far achieved. Unlike Brussels and Wilton carpets, they entailed no waste of valuable worsted. A separate row of warp rollers, sometimes known as spools, was made up for each line or pick of pattern in the carpet; these rotated in sequence above the loom, and at the appropriate time the correct roller was presented to the loom. The necessary amount of yarn was then taken for each tuft and cut. The row of rollers then moved on, and the next one in the sequence was presented. The texture was not very fine; the first Royal Axminsters had about 30 tufts per 25 sq. mm, and the Imperial Axminsters marketed by Tomkinson & Adam in 1893 had 48 tufts per 25 sq. mm. By the 1930s this had improved to 63 tufts per 25 sq. mm. The number of colours that could be used was virtually unlimited, and carpets up to 2.7 m wide could be woven. In 1910 Tomkinson & Adam acquired machines from the French company of Renard, which made knotted carpets resembling hand-made ones. In 1927 Jacquard or Gripper Axminsters were introduced, dispensing with the need to pre-arrange colours on a series of rollers or spools. The colours required for the whole pattern were set up; the jacquard device selected those that were needed for each row and, by means of a gripper, pulled off the required lengths of yarn, cut them and took them to the correct place on the loom. Up to 16 colours were practicable, which was ample for most designs. These carpets wasted less wool than Imperial Axminsters, and the method could be used for making both small and large quantities. The spool and gripper methods were later combined in the Spool Gripper Axminster to maximize the advantages of both types.

5. Axminster weaving loom (Wakefield, W. Yorks, Calderdale Archives)

Since World War II many changes in carpet-making have taken place. In the 1950s looms that weave face-to-face carpets were introduced. Two separate backings were woven, with a single set of loops between them, which, when cut, produced two identical carpets. New synthetic fibres, such as nylon, acrylic, rayon, polyester and polypropylene, were introduced. Perhaps the most radical change was mechanical tufting, introduced by an American carpet manufacturer. Instead of weaving the pile in, cut tufts were attached to a ready-made backing; this was at first a woven backing and later a sheet backing. This method was found to be 10 to 20 times faster than any other method of carpet weaving. In the 1960s and 1970s methods of introducing patterns to tufted carpets were explored. First, the tufts could be made high or low, giving a self-coloured, raised pattern. Then printing of colours on to an uncoloured tufted base was developed, using machinery that resembled sets of hypodermic needles. A third way was to move the backing back and forth during tufting to produce simple geometric patterns. Since the 1970s hand-held tufting guns have been used by designer-craftsmen to make one-off gallery pieces or individual commissions.

For types and techniques of carpet-making from specific regions, *see under* the particular country or culture survey.

BIBLIOGRAPHY
C. E. C. Tattersall: *Notes on Carpet Knotting and Weaving* (London, 1920/*R* 1927)
A. B. Roth: 'A Brief Survey of Carpet Manufacture', *J. Textile Inst.*, xxv (1934), pp. 134–43
C. E. C. Tattersall: *A History of British Carpets* (London, 1934)
A. H. Cole and H. F. Williamson: *The American Carpet Manufacture* (Cambridge, MA, 1941)
J. S. Ewing and N. P. Norton: *Broadlooms and Businessmen: A History of the Bigelow Sanford Company* (Cambridge, MA, 1955)
A. Crossland: *A Modern Carpet Manufacture* (Manchester and London, 1958)
A. F. Stoddard: *The Carpet Makers* (Elderslie, 1962)
G. Robinson: *Pitmans Common Commodities and Industries: Carpets* (London, 1966)
P. Collingwood: *The Techniques of Rug Weaving* (London, 1968/*R* 6/1979)
A. F. Stoddard: 'The Story of British Carpets', *Carpet Rev.* (1972)
I. Bennett, ed.: *The 'Country Life' Book of Rugs and Carpets of the World* (London, 1978)
J. N. Bartlett: *Carpeting the Millions* (Edinburgh, 1978)
Y. Petsopoulis: *Kilims: The Art of Tapestry Weaving in Anatolia, the Caucasus and Persia* (London, 1979/*R* 1982)
The Eastern Carpet in the Western World (exh. cat., ed. D. Sylvester and D. King; London, Hayward Gal., 1983)
W. Shea: *Carpet Making in Durham City* (Durham, 1984)
For further bibliography *see* §II below.

MARGARET ROBERTS

II. History.

1. Introduction. 2. Western world.

1. INTRODUCTION. It is not possible to establish when and where carpets were first produced, but the survival of the PAZYRYK Carpet in a burial mound in the Gorno-Altay Mountains, on the border between Russia, Kazakhstan and Mongolia, shows that the knotted-pile technique (*see* §I, 1 above) was well understood by the 4th century BC. Excavated fragments from various sites, including Turfan, Loulan, Xinjiang (all Xinjiang Uygur Autonomous Region, China), the At-Tar Caves in Iraq and Fustat, Old Cairo, show that the use of the technique was widespread from the 3rd century BC to the 6th century AD, but it is not known if it spread from one centre or developed independently in several places. It seems probable that the technique was introduced into much of Europe from the Islamic world, but independent discovery remains a possibility.

Documents show that fine carpets were being woven in Spain in the 12th century (*see* SPAIN, §V, 1); surviving fragments (Quedlinburg, St Servatius) from a convent in Quedlinburg, Germany, show that the technique was being practised in central Europe at the end of the 12th century (*see* §2(i) below). Documents and, more importantly, paintings in the 14th and 15th centuries attest to the spread of Turkish carpets along trade routes in Europe. What are considered to be the finest and the most important carpets were woven in Persia in the 16th century and in Mughal India in the 17th (*see* ISLAMIC ART, §VI, 4(iii)(c) and INDIAN SUBCONTINENT, §VI, 2). By then the number of Persian carpets being traded in Europe had increased considerably; documents and surviving pieces show that European merchants were commissioning carpets from the Middle East. They continued to take an interest even when production in the weaving centres of Turkey and Persia declined in the 18th century as a result of economic and political turmoil. The continuing demand for imported carpets prompted the establishment of carpet-weaving workshops in several European centres, leading eventually to the mechanization of the industry in the 19th century.

By the middle of the 19th century the carpet industry in the Middle East had revived, but it came under direct European influence; traditional designs and palettes were adapted to suit European and American tastes, and new designs were introduced for the Western market. At the same time, private and public collections of antique carpets were formed, and exhibitions and publications were used to introduce oriental carpets to a wider audience. Because few antique carpets were available in the 20th century, interest was focused on tribal pieces: domestically woven carpets and storage bags made and used by nomadic tribes in the Middle East. Because of their functional nature, no examples have survived from before the middle of the 19th century, but the variety of techniques used and the exuberance of the designs have proved just as challenging as the classic carpets of four centuries before.

The following survey is concerned primarily with the history of carpet production in the Western world. Further information on carpets is given within the relevant country and civilization surveys under the headings 'Textiles' or 'Other arts'.

2. WESTERN WORLD.

(i) Before 1500. (ii) 1500–1680. (iii) 1681–1800. (iv) 1801–1914. (v) After 1914.

(i) Before 1500. It is not known how or when the art of carpet-knotting was introduced into Europe. It is apparent that carpet-weaving was well established in the southern provinces of Spain by the 12th century and that the products of these looms were of high quality: carpets from Andalusia were used at the court of the Fatimid caliphs in Cairo, and in 1154 the Arab geographer El Idrisi mentioned that it would be difficult to surpass the quality of the woollen carpets from Chinchilla de Monte Aragón and Cuenca. Two other 12th-century Arab authors, Ibn Sa'id and El Saqundi, confirmed that Spanish carpets were being exported to the Middle East. From the 13th century there is increasing evidence that Spanish carpets were also being traded northwards into Europe: when Eleanor of Castile arrived in London in 1254 to marry Prince Edward (later Edward I), she brought carpets and textiles from Spain that aroused the admiration and envy of many. So well organized was the industry that Pope John XXII (*reg* 1316–34) was able to order carpets to be woven in Spain for the episcopal palace in Avignon, and Spanish carpets are listed in several other European inventories of the period.

It is possible that attempts were made to copy Spanish carpets in other areas of Europe. Parts of a large hanging woven in the Spanish manner have survived in Germany (Quedlinburg, St Servatius); it was made by nuns in Quedlinburg in the Harz Mountains under the supervision of Abbess Agnes between 1186 and 1203. The sisters may have developed the technique independently, but it is more probable that they were copying a Spanish or Middle Eastern prototype. Throughout the medieval period textiles were being brought from the Middle East to Europe by merchants and soldiers returning from the Crusades, and cargoes carried up the rivers Danube and Rhine could have introduced the idea of knotted pile to weavers in central and western Europe. There is, however, nothing to indicate that carpet-weaving ever became established in medieval Europe, except in Spain.

The oldest, almost complete Spanish carpet to have survived is probably that in the Islamisches Museum, Berlin: it appears to date from the 14th century. Sometimes called the Synagogue carpet because the main motif is thought by some to resemble or represent the Ark of the Covenant, it is a unique piece and one that illustrates the characteristic feature of Spanish carpet-weaving: the knot is always tied around a single warp thread, unlike the symmetrical or asymmetrical knots of the Middle East, which encircle two warp threads (*see* §I, 1 and fig. 1 above). The single-warp knot has been found in early carpet fragments from Central Asia (3rd–6th century AD; some on loan to London, V&A), and it was used by Coptic weavers in Egypt to produce a looped pile; it is, however, not possible to establish what connection, if any, existed between these three areas, although it is known that Coptic weavers were employed in Spain in the 10th century. From the 11th century the carpet-weaving towns referred to in medieval texts gradually came under Christian rule, but it is thought that the weavers continued to be Muslims, or *mudéjar*s, who had chosen to remain.

In the 15th century the main centres of production that can be identified from texts include Liétor, Letur and Alcaraz, in Murcia, but it should be noted that surviving carpets cannot be attributed to specific towns with any degree of certainty. It is known that quantities of Turkish carpets were imported to Spain, some of which were faithfully copied by local weavers while others were adapted to include elements of native art. Large-pattern Holbein carpets (see ISLAMIC ART, §VI, 4(iii)(a)), which were very popular in Europe, were copied in Spain and appear in inventories as 'wheel' carpets. They combine the large octagons of the Turkish originals with the detailed interlacing of Hispano-Moresque art (see fig. 6). Frequently an additional border at the top and bottom was decorated with human figures, birds and animals, probably derived from Iberian folk art.

The successful adaptation of a foreign weaving technique to a local artistic tradition is evident in an important group of armorial carpets (*see* SPAIN, fig. 59) thought to have been woven in Letur in the first half of the 15th century. About 18 examples have survived, many bearing the coats of arms of Alfonso Enríquez, Almirante de Castilla (1354–1429), and members of his immediate family. Like many Spanish carpets, these are very long in relation to their width, and they were probably made for the long, narrow corridors of local houses. The fields of the armorial carpets are composed of a honeycomb of small octagons and diamonds, which are filled with geometric forms, stylized animals and other creatures. Although comparisons have been drawn with the carpets depicted in contemporary Timurid miniatures, it is more probable that the geometric field was inspired by the tiled floors of Christian houses in Spain.

From the late 15th century carpet-weavers began to copy contemporary Spanish and Italian textile designs, especially those based on pomegranate or lobed-leaf motifs. Such patterns, with their fine, curving lines, made great demands on the skill of the weaver. The end of the

6. Carpet, 1.85×0.93 m, Spanish, first half of the 15th century (Washington, DC, Textile Museum)

15th century was a turning-point in carpet design: until then the Spanish had coloured their wool with rich vegetable dyes—predominantly red, dark blue, green and yellow—used for centuries throughout the Mediterranean, but after the discovery of the Americas in 1493 cochineal became available, enabling the weavers to experiment with new shades. Also, in 1492 King Ferdinand and Queen Isabella finally expelled the Moors from Spain, and thereafter the country looked increasingly towards Renaissance Europe for its artistic inspiration.

(ii) 1500–1680. Although by the early 16th century artistic patronage in Spain lay entirely in the hands of Christian

Savonnerie carpet, wool knotted pile, 6.12×3.58 m, from Paris, 1660–65 (New York, Metropolitan Museum of Art)

Star Ushak carpet, wool knotted pile, 4.27×2.13 m, from Ushak, Turkey, first half of the 17th century (New York, Metropolitan Museum of Art)

Prayer rug, wool knotted pile, 1.65×0.80 m, from Beshir, Turkmenistan, 19th century (Munich, Staatliches Museum für Völkerkunde)

Wagner Garden Carpet, woollen pile, cotton warps, cotton and wool wefts, 5.31×4.32 m, from Iran, 17th century (Glasgow, Burrell Collection)

nobles, Turkish carpets were still being imported and copied. In the Turkish models the strong geometric patterns of the previous century were gradually being replaced by a curvilinear court style based on floral motifs, but when copied by Spanish weavers the proportions of these new designs were frequently distorted, probably unintentionally, and the predominant reds of the originals were often replaced with blues and yellows to make them more acceptable to European taste. Other European elements were introduced, including the double-headed eagle of the Habsburg dynasty and religious symbols. The latter indicate that particular carpets were commissioned for church use; the practice seems to have become more common as the Counter-Reformation progressed. Contemporary silk patterns and fashionable Renaissance motifs continued to influence carpet design, and by the end of the 16th century Spanish carpets had become entirely European in style (see fig. 7). The single-warp knot, which was difficult to tie but had enabled the weavers to produce fine, curving lines and detailed patterns, was replaced in the mid-17th century by the Ghiordes (symmetrical) knot, and the main areas of production moved north to be centred on Cuenca and Madrid.

Outside Spain, knotted pile carpets were almost unknown in Europe until the beginning of the 16th century: even in grand houses rushes were still scattered on the floors, and as late as 1598 it was reported by a German traveller, Paul Hentzer, that Elizabeth I's chambers at Greenwich Palace, London, were strewn with hay. Records show that Turkish carpets were imported into England at the beginning of the 16th century, but they must have been rare and expensive. It took Cardinal Thomas Wolsey, one of the most powerful men in England, over two years to obtain 60 carpets in 1520 as part of a diplomatic agreement. When he fell from power in 1528 his possessions were forfeited to the Crown, and his carpets were presumably added to those belonging to Henry VIII. The King and his family were often painted standing on carpets (though in that period carpets were usually placed on tables, not on the floor), and so accurate are the portraits by Hans Holbein the younger (e.g. *Henry VIII and the Barber-Surgeons*, 1543; London, Barbers' Co.) that we can confidently identify the carpets depicted by him as Turkish. There are, however, other 16th- and early 17th-century portraits (e.g. by William Larkin: *Diana Cecil, Countess of Oxford*, before 1619; London, Ranger's House) in which the carpets appear to be English or Flemish copies of Turkish imports. It is recorded that Pierce Butler, 8th Earl of Ormonde (*d* 1539), ordered a 'Turkey' carpet to be made on his estate at Kilkenny, Ireland, and to that end brought weavers from Flanders, where a carpet-weaving industry must have been already well established, but nothing more is known of his venture. The oldest surviving carpet made in England, in East Anglia, is dated 1570 (Earl of Verulam priv. col.; for illustration see Tattersall, pl. I). It is 8 m long, and the design contains the royal arms, the arms of the Harbottle family and those of Ipswich. Three surviving Star Ushak carpets (Duke of Buccleuch priv. col.; for illustration see Tattersall, pls II, III) are thought to have been made in Norwich. They are woven on a hemp warp, and each contains the arms of Montagu and Harrington; two are dated, one 1584 and the other 1585. Like the Spanish nobility, English patrons often commissioned weavers to include heraldic devices in the design.

7. Carpet, 2.97×1.85 m, Spanish, 16th century (London, Victoria and Albert Museum)

By the end of the 16th century the English had adapted Turkish weaving techniques to local artistic traditions and were weaving carpets with designs based on the common flowers and shrubs found in many English gardens—roses, honeysuckle, pansies, strawberries and oak leaves. From the late 16th century inventories in England began to differentiate between 'turkie carpetts', which were imported from the Middle East, and carpets of 'turkie work', meaning the knotted carpets made in England. As large carpets were expensive, small panels suitable for cushion-covers (see fig. 8) and upholstery became popular; they were often made domestically as well as commercially. These remained in demand throughout most of the 17th century, and production did not decline until the 1680s, when the importation of Turkish and Persian carpets increased. Then, with the greater use of Eastern carpets and the popularity of inlaid floors, almost all production of knotted carpets in England seems to have ceased. It was not revived until the middle of the 18th century, and then only with help from France.

Although it is known that copies of imported carpets had been woven in France in the 15th century by weavers

8. Turkey-work panel, 49×61 mm, English, early 17th century (London, Victoria and Albert Museum)

called *tapissiers sarrazinois*, the craft seems to have fallen into disuse at an earlier date than it did in England. In 1601 Henry IV appointed a commission to establish new trade and manufacture within his kingdom. In 1604 a certain Jean Fortier proposed to this commission that factories be set up in Paris to weave carpets in the Turkish manner. Nothing seems to have been done until Pierre Dupont (*d* 1640) obtained a licence in 1608 to use a workshop under the Palais du Louvre in Paris in which to manufacture carpets in the *façon du Levant* and the *façon de Turquie*. In 1627 he took one of his former pupils, Simon Lourdet (*d* 1666), into partnership and installed him in a former soap factory near Colline de Chaillot, Paris. Lourdet began to weave carpets, screens, seat-covers and wall hangings, and the name SAVONNERIE was applied to all the products of his workshop. Dupont continued to work at the Louvre.

The Savonnerie continued to enjoy royal patronage: the importation of Eastern carpets into France was prohibited, and Dupont and Lourdet were granted an 18-year concession for the making of carpets. In 1663 Jean-Baptiste Colbert, Louis XIV's chief minister, conferred a new constitution on the Savonnerie and placed it with the newly established Manufacture des Gobelins under the direction of the court painter Charles Le Brun. Few pieces have survived from the early years of the Savonnerie, but a study of the existing records indicates that several very expensive carpets were woven in silk with gold and silver threads. However, the carpets that have survived, from the 1660s onwards, are made of wool and are usually small with designs of multicoloured flowers standing out against a black ground (see colour pl. I). These were designed to complement contemporary ebony furniture inlaid with floral motifs. This attempt to create stylistic uniformity within an interior may owe much to the direction and teaching of Le Brun and other artists from the Académie Royale. Le Brun was the inspiring force behind the production, beginning in 1666, of more than 100 superb carpets for the Palais du Louvre and the Palais des Tuileries (many of those that survive from the Louvre are under the charge of the Mobilier National). The complex designs were based on the combination of brightly coloured flowers and a dark ground; at each end there were monochrome tableaux representing allegories or landscapes, and the Classical allusions were often continued in the central medallion, which usually contained an oblique reference to the Sun King—the head of Apollo, a sunflower or the sun itself (see fig. 9). Although this basic format is to be found in most of the carpets, the wealth of detail and the ingenuity of the designers were such that no two

9. Carpet, 9.14×4.57 m, made at the Savonnerie, Paris, 1673–81 (New York, Metropolitan Museum of Art)

seem alike. These carpets are rightly held to be the finest products of the Savonnerie looms.

(iii) 1681–1800. The fortune of the Savonnerie workshops, so intimately linked with royal patronage, fluctuated with the size of the king's purse, and from the second half of the 17th century the weavers experienced both frenzied activity and idleness. The harassment of Protestants, which culminated in the Revocation of the Edict of Nantes in 1685, had caused many skilled artisans to leave France during the 17th century. In addition, the financial crisis caused by a series of unsuccessful military campaigns towards the end of the century had an adverse effect on the demand for luxury items and left many looms at the Savonnerie standing idle. In 1712, in an effort to improve the situation, orders were placed for the furnishing of rooms in the châteaux at Versailles and Fontainebleau, and the Savonnerie was given the title Manufacture des Meubles de la Couronne de Tapis Façon de Perse et du Levant. The architect Robert de Cotte, also director of the Gobelins, was put in charge. There was a noticeable collaboration between the tapestry workshops at the Gobelins and the carpet workshops at the Savonnerie: not only did they have the same director, but they frequently shared the same designers, including Jean-Baptiste Belin, Pierre Josse Perrot (*fl* 1724–35) and François Boucher. Under their influence the designs were changed to mirror contemporary taste; although the carpets continued to be enormous, graceful curvilinear lines and Rococo motifs began to replace the landscapes and allegorical tableaux of the previous century. It was not uncommon for two or three carpets to be woven from the same cartoon. In one case three identical carpets were required to cover the dais of the king's throne at Versailles, and in another, three identical ones were sent to three châteaux, at La Muette, Choisy-le-Roi and Fontainebleau (all these carpets now Paris, Mobilier N.).

Since the Savonnerie worked exclusively for the monarch and as imported carpets were not always easy to obtain, nor in keeping with French taste, there was considerable incentive for enterprising manufacturers to produce reasonably priced alternatives. Louis XV's Intendant des Finances, Jean-Henri-Louis Orry de Fulvy (*d* 1751), suggested that the tapestry workshops at Aubusson should weave carpets to meet this demand (*see* AUBUSSON, §2). In 1743, with financial assistance from the King, vertical looms, tools and samples of Turkish carpets were sent to Aubusson, and work began. The Crown continued to finance the venture until the workshops were taken over as a private enterprise in 1746. Initially, the carpets were based on Turkish models, but although a government inspector considered that these copies were comparable to any woven in Turkey, it was apparent by 1750 that customers did not want imitations but something new, something French. So in 1753 the painter Louis-Joseph Le Lorrain created a new style known as *à grande mosaïque.* He avoided elaborate patterns and bright colours, which he feared would deaden other furnishings in the room, and instead based his designs on scattered blossoms and delicate garlands of flowers picked out in white, yellows and blues. In many ways these were similar to contemporary Savonneries, which had developed to reflect the new tastes of the 18th century. In keeping with the more informal atmosphere of the age, many of the great rooms at Versailles had been subdivided into small, intimate ones, and in response carpet designs had become less crowded, more floral and lighter in colour. By the second half of the 18th century two types of carpet were being made at Aubusson: knotted pile ones woven on vertical looms and tapestry-woven ones made on traditional horizontal looms. The late 18th century was a turbulent period in France, and both the Savonnerie and Aubusson suffered badly from lack of orders within the country and from the complete cessation of trade abroad. It was not until the proclamation of the First Empire in 1804 that the situation improved.

The art of carpet-knotting was reintroduced into England in 1750 by two disgruntled craftsmen from the Savonnerie. One of the men, Pierre Poiré (*b c.* 1710), was said to have been a mediocre workman who was found copying a portrait in his own house, contrary to the regulations, and fled to London to avoid punishment. He and his fellow émigré, Louis Théau, were befriended by a defrocked Capuchin friar, Pierre Parisot, and after taking rooms in Westminster they began to make carpets. They soon obtained the patronage of William Augustus, Duke of Cumberland, moved to Paddington and presented him with their first carpet for his sister-in-law, Augusta, the Dowager Princess of Wales. Although receiving fulsome praise for their work, they seem to have become disobliging and were dismissed. In 1753 they moved to Fulham to share a tapestry-weaving studio, but the venture failed, and the premises were sold at public auction in July 1755. The carpet looms and designs were bought by a Swiss Huguenot, Claude Passavant of Exeter, who took them and some of the workmen back to Exeter. The workshop seems to have lasted only six years. Three signed carpets have survived: one dated 1757 (see fig. 10), the other two 1758 (Petworth House, W. Sussex, NT; priv. col.). All three exhibit marked French qualities in both composition and palette, with Rococo designs in strong reds and blues on a black ground. It is probable that the weavers brought French designs with them, and it is known that at least one of the Fulham men employed by Passavant had worked at the Gobelins. In his letters this weaver, J.-B. Grignon, stated that the English were interested only in Savonnerie-type pile carpets and not in tapestry ones (*see also* EXETER, §2).

After the sale of the Fulham workshop, some of the weavers stayed in London and were employed by Thomas Moore (*c.* 1700–88) of Chiswell Street, Moorfields. This workshop quickly gained a reputation for fine carpets that were said by many to be superior to imported ones. Moore acted as a wholesaler for upholsterers and seems, from an early date, to have supplied clients with Brussels, Wilton and Ingrain carpets (see below). In 1763 he received a royal warrant, and after his death the workshop continued to be run by his family until 1793, when it seems to have ceased production. Its output included carpets for the Prince of Wales (later George IV) and even, it is said, one designed by the Prince himself.

A third important English workshop also owed its existence to the Fulham enterprise. Thomas Whitty (*d* 1792), a weaver from Devon, had been inspired by the sight of a Turkish carpet but had found the English horizontal loom unsuited to its manufacture. It was not until he persuaded an apprentice to show him the Fulham workshop that he realized that vertical looms were needed.

10. Carpet, 3.65×4.49 m, Exeter, 1757 (London, Victoria and Albert Museum)

He began work on his first carpet in AXMINSTER in 1755. The following year the Royal Society of Arts, in an attempt to improve the design and quality of British goods, decided to offer an annual prize for, among other things, carpets woven in the Turkish manner. At that time it was estimated that £16,000 p.a. were being spent on imported carpets, and it was desirable that at least part of that money should go instead to British manufacturers. In the first year, 1757, the prize was shared by Thomas Moore and Thomas Whitty; in 1758 Whitty shared the prize with Passavant; and in 1759, the final year of the prize, Whitty was the sole recipient.

One of the most characteristic features of both English and French carpets of this period is the way in which the designs and colours echo the decoration of the rooms in which they were to be displayed, especially the ceiling designs. Determined to create integrated interiors, architects began to design carpets for specific settings. Robert Adam (i), for example, often worked closely with Thomas Moore (e.g. London, Syon House, 1769, and Osterley Park House, NT, 1775–8). Under Adam's influence, Moore's designs became more classical, incorporating Etruscan and Pompeian motifs. Thomas Chippendale (i) worked in a similar way with the workshops at Axminster.

All hand-knotted carpets, imported or locally made, were expensive and beyond the means of all but the most prosperous. There were, however, cheaper alternatives. From at least the 16th century strong woollen cloth had been used as a relatively inexpensive floor covering. From the mid-17th century a patterned worsted double cloth known as an Ingrain, Kidderminster, Scotch or Union carpet was very popular in Britain and North America. It remained in use until *c.* 1914 and in the 19th century was also woven as a triple cloth (*see* §I, 3 above). It was made on horizontal looms in long strips 915 mm wide, which could be stitched together to form wide carpets, often with contrasting borders. Records from the 17th century frequently mention 'Kidderminster stuff', and it is known that it was used for carpeting parts of Worcester Cathedral. It was woven by outworkers in Scotland and northern England, and the first factory devoted to its production was established by a Mr Pearsall in KIDDERMINSTER in 1735. Despite its popularity, it was not as durable as pile carpet, and the number of colours that could be used was limited.

A looped-pile carpet called Brussels, woven in the manner of an uncut velvet, was very hard-wearing. It too was produced in long lengths, but usually only in widths of 69 mm. Although woven before then in Tournai, the first patent to weave such carpeting was taken out in 1741 by a London merchant and two Wilton men, John Barford, an upholsterer, and William Moody, a clothier. It was possible to weave a great variety of designs, but the foundation was apt to show through in poor-quality pieces, and the looped pile did not produce a rich, luxurious texture. This, however, could be achieved by cutting the pile to give a type of carpet called Wilton (*see* WILTON, §2).

Both types proved popular, and by the 1750s they were being supplied to the royal family. They represent a technological breakthrough necessitated by the growing demand for good-quality floor coverings—weavers were now able to produce a sturdy pile carpet without having to tie each knot by hand. Not only were the carpets quicker to make and therefore cheaper than hand-knotted ones, but the purchaser could have the strips cut and sewn to cover the entire floor, fitting into alcoves and around hearths, and he could order the design and colours of his choice, advantages seldom available with imported Eastern carpets. Brussels carpets were also widely used in France, where they were known as *moquette*. There, as in England, they helped fill the increasing market for carpets.

(iv) 1801–1914. In France the establishment of the First Empire in 1804 marked the beginning of a period of prosperity. This gave a new lease of life to both the Savonnerie and Aubusson workshops, with orders from the imperial household for magnificent carpets to replace those damaged or lost in the Revolution. The designs of most of these were inspired by the work of Percier and Fontaine, the creators of the Empire style, but although many of the carpets woven for the imperial palaces were decorated with such classical war motifs as shields, helmets, spears and trophies, the floral tradition continued, often with the addition of classical muses, graceful swans and peacocks. Work slowed down a little after the fall of Napoleon, but large carpets continued to be woven at the Savonnerie. In 1825 the Savonnerie was finally amalgamated with the Gobelins workshops, and after this its carpet designs were influenced increasingly by those of the tapestry-weavers. By the end of the 19th century it was common for the same cartoons to be used in both techniques. The privately owned Aubusson workshops

11. Warp-printed carpet, 2.26×1.7 m, English, mid-19th century (London, Victoria and Albert Museum)

found themselves competing with industrial manufacturers in the 19th century, and demand for their hand-knotted products declined rapidly in the 1830s, when even the royal household was ordering machine-woven carpets for the Grande Galerie of the Palais des Tuileries. In order to survive, Aubusson employed English workmen to set up looms for weaving Brussels and Wilton carpets, and by the 1850s their products were rivalling English ones in their quality and beauty. Although a few hand-knotted carpets were commissioned, from the 1840s the workshops produced mainly machine- and tapestry-woven ones.

In the 19th century there were similar changes in England. After the demise of the Moorfields workshop, Thomas Witty of Axminster was the sole producer of hand-knotted carpets. He followed the French fashion for enriched classical designs so closely that some of his carpets are almost replicas of contemporary Savonnerie products. In 1828 his factory, by then run by his sons, was nearly destroyed by fire. It never recovered: the stocks and surviving looms were bought by a Mr Blackmore in 1836 and transferred to Wilton, where production continued side by side with the increased use of mechanical and power looms. Technological advances followed in quick succession as manufacturers sought to provide cheap floor coverings to satisfy a growing market. In 1832 Richard Whytock of Edinburgh adapted a method of pre-printing the required colours on to the warp before weaving. With this he produced 'Tapestry Brussels' and 'Tapestry Velvet' carpets with up to 150 colours in the pattern (see fig. 11). In 1839 James Templeton, a shawl manufacturer in Glasgow, developed a way of weaving carpets with chenille thread. These were known as Chenille Axminsters. The pile was woven separately, with tufts of the correct number and colour to form the pattern, then inserted as weft on the surface of a linen or jute base. This had the advantage of keeping all the expensive wool on the surface, and there was practically no limit to the number of colours that could be used, but the resulting fabric was intrinsically fragile and not really suited to its purpose. In 1841 his firm was asked to weave a chenille carpet for St George's Chapel, Windsor Castle, for the baptism of Prince Edward (later Edward VII), and among other royal commissions was a chenille carpet for the opening of the Great Exhibition of 1851 in London. In the USA, Erastus Brigham Bigelow (1814–79) of Massachusetts invented a power loom *c.* 1839 that could weave both double and triple cloth, and in 1848 he invented one that could weave Brussels and Wilton carpets; these machines were eventually capable of weaving up to 50 m per day, compared with a hand-loom weaver's daily 6.5 m. In 1878 Tomkinson & Adam of Kidderminster purchased from New York a loom for making machine-tufted carpets, and in 1910 they introduced one that could make knotted pile. These, and many other inventions, made it possible to weave carpets in a fraction of the time that it would have taken to knot the pile by hand. Production costs dropped dramatically, and by the end of the 19th century reasonably good-quality, durable floor coverings were available to most people. The use of jute from the 1830s, however, limited the life of these carpets, becoming brittle as it aged. Also, the new dyestuffs were not always satisfactory: they faded badly, and wool from different dye batches gave a striped effect.

As the mechanized production of carpets increased in Europe, the number of Eastern carpets being imported also increased. Both had their critics, of whom the most prominent was William Morris. He decried in British carpets the prevalent taste for extravagant and full-blown floral patterns, with such disparate elements as scrolls, landscapes and urns, and in imported carpets the indiscriminate use of aniline colours and Westernized designs.

12. Carpet designed by Vanessa Bell, 92×184 mm, from the Omega Workshops, London, 1914 (London, Victoria and Albert Museum)

Morris had designed carpets for several machine techniques since 1875, but in 1878 he began to weave small carpets in his studio in Hammersmith, developing the designs from classical Persian models. Larger hand-knotted carpets were subsequently commissioned, but the venture was never commercially viable, and in 1912 the carpet looms were transferred to the Wilton Royal Carpet Co. Another attempt to re-establish the production of hand-knotted carpets took place in western Ireland. In 1896 the government asked Alexander Morton (1844–1921) to provide work in the Donegal area to alleviate economic distress. Initially, Morton started a workshop to make lace, but he then established a factory to make hand-knotted carpets in Killybegs. It proved to be very successful and quickly gained a reputation for quality in both material and design, but the social and economic face of Europe was changing, and the market for exclusive, expensive carpets was growing smaller.

It was only in some of the non-industrialized countries of Europe that the hand-knotting tradition flourished, and then on a domestic scale. The knotted *ryijy* carpets of Finland (*see* FINLAND, §XI), mentioned in inventories as early as 1451–2, continued to be made in the 19th century. Flat-woven carpets, heavily influenced by Anatolian kilim designs, were traditionally produced in the Balkans, and most of the surviving examples date from the 19th century.

(v) After 1914. Just as William Morris had condemned British design in the late 19th century, so Roger Fry and his fellow artists rejected both the Arts and Crafts Movement and the Art Nouveau style. In 1913 they had formed the Omega Workshops in London to produce commissioned works heavily influenced by Continental design—by the Post-Impressionists, Paul Poiret and the Wiener Werkstätte. The Omega Workshops were a short-lived but important enterprise that used strong geometric and abstract designs (see fig. 12) in complete contrast to the uninspired decoration of the time in Britain. Carpet design was being freed from the rather heavy and traditional influence of the Savonnerie and Aubusson, and such French interior designers as Paul Follot, Louis Süe and André Mare (1887–1932) were reinterpreting garlands, trellises and medallions, using vibrant new colour combinations.

In France several exhibitions of Algerian and Moroccan art (1917, 1919 and 1923) included thick-pile Berber carpets, which caught the imagination of such designers as Da Silva Bruhns and Stéphany. The effect of these ethnic influences, combined with contemporary artistic trends, especially with Cubism, was to change attitudes towards carpet design to such an extent that even well-established, traditional workshops began to commission modern designs from artists. Designs by Robert Bonfils (1886–1971) and Gaudissart were used at the Savonnerie, and the small-scale patterns of Edouard Bénédictus (1878–1930) were used by the Beauvais carpet factory to produce machine-made *moquettes*. By the 1920s, however, good-quality machine-made carpets were within the budget of most middle-class people, and since the importation of carpets from Turkey, Persia and further afield had increased, it might have seemed that there was no future for hand-knotted carpets in Europe. This was not so: the Exposition des Arts Décoratifs in Paris in 1925 confirmed that there really was a revival in the craft. Amid the modern, stark interiors of the exhibition brilliantly coloured carpets, especially those designed by Jean Lurçat and by Mlle Max Vibert, were used to add texture and warmth.

British designers in the 1930s responded well to France's challenge. It is to the credit of such firms as the Wilton Royal Carpet Co. and the Edinburgh Weavers that they could risk moving away from tried and tested patterns to experiment with designs based on the work of Picasso and Georges Braque and interpreted by such artists as E. McKnight Kauffer, Marion Dorn (1899–1964), Betty Joel and Ronald Grierson (*b* 1901; see fig. 13). These carpets were usually machine-woven, either for individual clients or for hotels, cinemas or luxury liners. Such large workshops and factories as Donegal Carpets Ltd in Ireland and the Wilton Royal Carpet Co. continued to weave hand-knotted carpets, but less for private houses and increasingly for government property, embassies and international companies. The designs tended to be copies or pastiches of late 18th-century and early 19th-century carpets, which gave a sense of classical grace to well-proportioned state rooms and boardrooms. By the late 20th century commissions for large hand-made carpets had diminished dramatically, and at one time even these large workshops were facing the serious threat of extinction. Ironically, many commissions came from the royal houses of the Middle East.

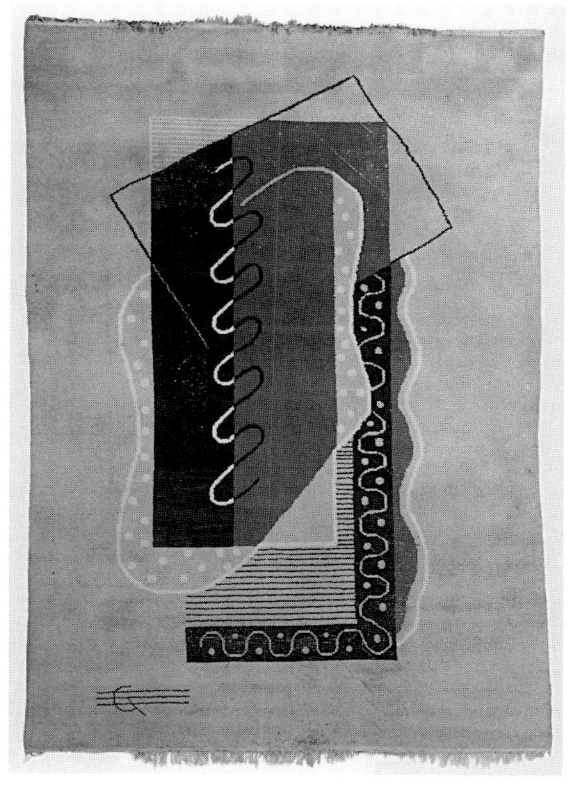

13. Carpet designed by Ronald Grierson, 2.72×1.89 m, from an Indian workshop, 1935 (London, Victoria and Albert Museum)

The interior designers of the 1950s and 1960s exploited the texture and colour of carpets to contrast with the white walls and light woods that were typical of the popular Scandinavian style. Such flatweaves as kilims and durries were imported into Europe from as far afield as Mexico and India and were used with machine-woven shag-pile carpeting. In the 1970s, perhaps in reaction, there was a revival of interest in the even-textured, machine-woven Axminsters and Wiltons, which were produced in an eclectic repertory of designs incorporating both traditional and modern elements. Imported Eastern rugs continued to be popular, and some European artists and craftsmen, for example Helen Yardley (*b* 1954) and Grace Erickson (*b* 1950), made rugs and small carpets, sometimes hand-knotted and sometimes machine-tufted, with designs similar to those of the 1930s.

BIBLIOGRAPHY

A. F. Kendrick and C. E. C. Tattersall: *Handwoven Carpets, Oriental and European* (London, 1926)
U. T. Sirelius: *The Ryijy Rugs of Finland* (London, 1926)
V. Sylwan: *Svenska ryor* [Swedish long-pile carpets] (Stockholm, 1934)
C. E. C. Tattersall: *A History of British Carpets* (Benfleet, 1934)
F. L. May: 'Hispano-Moresque Rugs', *Notes Hisp.*, iv–v (1944–5), pp. 31–69
H. Engelstad: *Norske ryer* [Norwegian shag rugs] (Oslo [1946])
E. Kühnel and L. Bellinger: *Spanish Rugs, 12th Century to 19th Century*, ii of *The Textile Museum Catalogue* (Washington, DC, 1953)
M. Jarry: *The Carpets of the Manufacture de la Savonnerie* (Leigh-on-Sea, 1966)
C. E. C. Tattersall and S. Reed: *British Carpets* (London, 1966)
M. Jarry: 'Designs and Models for Savonnerie Carpets in the 18th Century', *Burl. Mag.*, cx (1968), pp. 258–62
B. Jacobs: *Axminster Carpets* (Leigh-on-Sea, 1969)
M. Jarry: *Carpets of Aubusson* (Leigh-on-Sea, 1969)
——: 'Design in Aubusson Carpets', *Antiques*, xcv (1969), pp. 702–7
——: 'Savonnerie Panels and Furnishing Materials of the 17th and 18th Centuries', *Connoisseur*, clxx (1969), pp. 211–19
S. B. Sherrill: 'The Islamic Tradition in Spanish Rug Weaving', *Antiques*, c (1974), pp. 532–49
C. Gilbert, J. Lomax and A. Wells-Cole: *Country House Floors*, Temple Newsam Country House Studies, no. 3 (Leeds, 1987)

JENNIFER WEARDEN

Carpi, Aldo (*b* Milan, 6 Oct 1886; *d* Milan, 27 March 1973). Italian painter. He devoted himself to painting from an early age, and from 1906 he studied with Cesare Tallone at the Accademia di Belle Arti di Brera in Milan, where he met the painters Achille Funi (1890–1972), Carlo Carrà and Siro Penagini (1885–1952). He moved in the same Milanese avant-garde circles as Umberto Boccioni, Gaetano Previati, Filippo Tommaso Marinetti and others. His paintings often took lyrical themes, but they were treated in a highly individual expressionistic style. In 1914 he took part in the Venice Biennale, where he received a prize for *After Supper* (1913; Florence, Pitti). In the following year he began the theme of masks, which was to remain a constant feature of his output. He was active during World War I on the Albanian front (1915), where he created a series of drawings published in Milan in 1917 under the title *Serbia eroica*. After demobilization (1919) he resumed his painting career, depicting not only masks but also marine subjects, portraits and domestic scenes (e.g. *Family Portrait*, 1927; Milan, Gal. A. Mod.). He also designed a number of stained-glass windows in Milan, for example in S Simpliciano (1928) and for the cathedral (begun 1932–4, completed 1947). In 1930 he became Professor of Painting at the Accademia in Milan; however, in 1944 he was deported to the concentration camp of Mauthausen and later to Gusen, where he remained until 1945. He relived this dramatic experience in the surviving pages of the *Diario di Gusen* (published 1971) and, more especially, in a series of drawings made either from life in the concentration camp itself or later from memory. On his return to Milan he was appointed Director of the Accademia and in 1950 he began another cycle of masks, entitled *Carabinieri*; from 1962 he concentrated on the series *Circus* and *Clowns*. In 1968 he provided the cartoons for the decoration of the Church of the Annunciation, Nazareth.

WRITINGS

Diario di Gusen (Milan, 1971)

BIBLIOGRAPHY

M. De Micheli: *Aldo Carpi* (Milan, 1963)
Aldo Carpi (exh. cat. by M. De Micheli, Milan, Rotonda Besana, 1972)

DANIELA DE DOMINICIS

Carpi, Girolamo da [Sellari, Girolamo; Ferrara, Girolamo da] (*b* Ferrara, *c.* 1501; *d* Ferrara, ?1 Aug 1556). Italian painter, architect and stage designer. His father Tommaso (*fl* 1503–23) was a painter and decorator at the court of the Este in Ferrara, and Girolamo was trained in the workshop of Garofalo. He visited Rome in the early 1520s (Fioravanti Baraldi) and was in Bologna in 1525, where he worked with Biagio Pupini and Giovanni Borghese on the decoration of the sacristy of S Michele in Bosco. Around this time (1525) he painted the altarpiece of the *Virgin Enthroned with Saints* (Dresden, Gemäldegal. Alte Meister; destr.) for S Biagio in Bologna.

From these early works onwards da Carpi developed a pictorial language that combined the Ferrarese models of Garofalo and Dosso Dossi with the influence of such works by Raphael as the *St Cecilia* (Bologna, Pin. N.), which he saw in Bologna, the *Madonna of Foligno* (Rome, Pin. Vaticana) and the frescoes in the loggia of the Villa Farnesina in Rome. Da Carpi's *Adoration of the Magi* (*c.* 1528; Modena, Gal. & Mus. Estense) shows the influence of the cartoon (London, N.G.) on the same subject executed in Bologna *c.* 1523 by Baldassare Peruzzi for Conte Giovan Battista Bentivoglio. In 1530 da Carpi was again in Ferrara, where he worked with his father on the decoration of the cupola (destr.) and friezes in the nave of S Francesco. Some of the ideas in his *SS Catherine and Ursula* in S Francesco were clearly suggested by his meeting with Parmigianino in Bologna, *c.* 1527–30. Parmigianino's influence is strong also in the *Adoration of the Magi* (*c.* 1532; Bologna, S Martino), the *Mystic Marriage of St Catherine* (*c.* 1534; Bologna, S Salvatore) and the later *St Jerome* (Ferrara, S Paolo). In these works he combined the inspiration of Parmigianino with a monumental style derived from Giulio Romano.

Parmigianino's influence proved fundamental also for da Carpi's portrait painting, a field in which he was very active, according to Vasari. Important examples include the portraits of *Onofrio Bartolini Salimbeni* (1528–9; Florence, Pitti), *Cardinal Ippolito de' Medici and Monsignor Mario Bracci* (1532–3; London, N.G.; see fig.) and *Girolamo de' Vincenti* (1535; Naples, Capodimonte). Between 1531 and 1537 da Carpi settled in Ferrara, although he

Girolamo da Carpi: *Cardinal Ippolito de' Medici and Monsignor Mario Bracci*, panel, 1.38×1.12 m, 1532–3 (London, National Gallery)

maintained close relations with patrons in Bologna. Around 1532–3, for S Francesco, Ferrara, he painted the altarpiece of the *Apparition of the Virgin* (Washington, DC, N.G.A.), which includes a portrait of the donor, Giulia Muzzarelli. This was his most mature work, in which he profited from his youthful study of Titian and Giulio Romano and his keen interest in the art of Correggio, which he saw in Modena and Parma (Vasari).

From 1536 da Carpi's relations with the Este court intensified. In 1537 his name first appeared in the accounts for frescoes painted (1537–41) in the Este villa at Belriguardo (nr Ferrara; destr.), where he worked with Garofalo, Dossi, Camillo Filippi (*see* FILIPPI, (1)) and others. In this period he also worked on the construction of the Palazzo Naselli Crispi in Ferrara and on the decoration of other Este buildings including the Palazzo della 'Montagna di Sotto' or Montagnola (1541; destr.) and the villa at Copparo (1545), near Ferrara. In addition he created the sets for the tragedy *Orbecche* (1541) and the pastoral fable *Egle* (1545), both written by the humanist Giovan Battista Giraldi Cinzio. During the same years he painted several works on allegorical and mythological themes for Ercole II d'Este, including *Opportunity and Repentance* (1541), *Ganimede* (1541) and the *Venus on the Eridano* (1546; all Dresden, Gemäldegal. Alte Meister) for the 'camera del poggiolo' in the Castello Estense.

In 1549 da Carpi was called to Rome by Cardinal Ippolito II d'Este to work on the excavation of Hadrian's Villa at Tivoli and the arrangement of the gardens of the palace at Monte Cavallo, on the Quirinal hill in Rome. His interest in antiquity is attested by his drawings (London, BM; Philadelphia, PA, Rosenbach Mus.; Turin, Bib. Reale). In 1550 he entered the service of Pope Julius III as architect in charge of modifications to the Villa Belvedere in the Vatican. After his return to Ferrara in 1553, he worked on the reconstruction of the Castello Estense, which was damaged by fire in 1554.

BIBLIOGRAPHY

G. Vasari: *Vite* (1550, rev. 2/1568); ed. G. Milanesi (1875–85)

F. Antal: 'Observations on Girolamo da Carpi', *A. Bull.*, xxx (1948), pp. 81–103

N. W. Canedy: 'Some Preparatory Drawings by Girolamo da Carpi', *Burl. Mag.*, cxii (1970), pp. 86–94

R. Roli: 'Quattro secoli di pittura', *San Michele in Bosco*, ed. R. Renzi (Bologna, 1971), pp. 204–9

N. W. Canedy: *The Roman Sketchbook of Girolamo da Carpi*, Stud. Warb. Inst., xxiv (London, 1976)

A. Mezzetti: *Girolamo da Ferrara detto da Carpi: L'opera pittorica* (Milan, 1977)

A. M. Fioravanti Baraldi: 'Girolamo Sellari detto da Carpi', *La pittura bolognese del '500*, ed. V. Fortunati Pierantonio (Bologna, 1986), pp. 209–35 [good bibliog.]

——: ' "Apollo, anchor che tu cantassi in rime . . .". Eros e Voluptas in alcuni disegni di Girolamo da Carpi, in Musei Ferraresi, 1985–1987', *Boll. Annu.*, xv (1988)

E. Sambo: 'Girolamo da Carpi/Girolamo Sellari', *La pittura in Italia: Il cinquecento*, ii (Milan, 1988), pp. 733–4

ANNA MARIA FIORAVANTI BARALDI

Carpi, Pio da. *See* PIO.

Carpi [Panico]**, Ugo da** (*b* Carpi, *fl c.* 1502–32). Italian woodcutter. He trained as a type-founder and painter and *c.* 1509 moved to Venice, where he was employed for five or more years making woodcut book illustrations. Despite the menial nature of his work, which involved copying 15th-century designs, he broke with custom by signing his blocks. By 1515 he had secured an important commission from the Venetian publisher Bernardino Benalius to cut blocks for the *Sacrifice of Abraham*, a large black-and-white print on four joined sheets (Berlin, Altes Mus., 15.15). The composition is a pastiche of elements taken from Dürer and Titian and was designed perhaps by Ugo himself. Benalius sought a copyright for the print, and, probably as a result, the following year Ugo sought the protection of the Venetian Senate for a colour-printing process he was now using, the chiaroscuro woodcut (*see* WOODCUT, CHIAROSCURO, §§1 and 2). He claimed to have invented the technique, although it was not patented, as is often thought; he did, however, copyright all his chiaroscuro designs, past and future, doubtless due to the plagiarism of earlier works such as the *Sibyl Reading* (B. 6). German chiaroscuro woodcuts, in fact, predate his by at least six years, and he probably encountered examples in Venice. Several of these employ three blocks, but Ugo began in the more usual two-block style. A series of *Hercules* subjects (B. 14, 15), printed with detailed black key-blocks over muted background blocks (usually blue), show his rapid progress towards more flexible line and more ingenious schemes of shading. He progressed to four blocks for his next print, the *Massacre of the Innocents* (B. 8), a skilful interpretation of an engraving by Marcantonio Raimondi after Raphael (B. 18).

Probably in late 1517 Ugo moved to Rome and sought work in the thriving print industry surrounding Raphael's studio. Nearly all his subsequent chiaroscuro prints, in three to five blocks, reflect the broad massing of colour areas found in the works of Raphael's circle, as well as the planes of tone increasingly used by engravers to interpret them. Ugo's main contribution to the chiaroscuro woodcut, therefore, was stylistic: the abandonment of closed contours and linear crosshatching in the key-block for strokes of emphasis and massed shadows, and in his tone-blocks the transformation of shapes into flat planes and silhouettes. By 1518, the date of the copyright granted him by the Vatican, he was fully in control of his medium, as can be seen in such prints as *David Slaying Goliath* (B. 8) and *Ananias Struck Dead* (B. 27–I), and was acting as his own printer. Perhaps his most remarkable work, with its simple, stylized background, is *Aeneas Fleeing Troy with Anchises and Ascanius* (B. 12), also dated 1518. Ugo must have begun work not long after this on woodcut typefaces for Lodovico Arrighi's *La operina di Lodovico Vicentino da imparare di scrivere littera cancellarescha* (Venice, 1522–3); in 1525, after a dispute with Arrighi, Ugo published another edition, with newly cut blocks. The same year he compiled, cut and published his *Thesauro de' scrittori*, a similar treatise on writing.

After the Sack of Rome in 1527, Ugo moved to Bologna, where, according to Vasari, he cut his masterpiece, the magnificent *Diogenes* (B. 10; *see* PRINTS, colour pl. VI) after Parmigianino, or perhaps after Gian Jacopo Caraglio's engraving (B. 61) of the subject. Ugo's editions of his woodcuts are of high quality, usually printed in subdued graduated greens or blues, apart from the striking green and gold contrasts of the *Diogenes*. Numerous chiaroscuro woodcuts after Parmigianino and others have been attributed to him, despite their relatively superficial resemblance to his 14 documented works, and it is often assumed that he supervised a workshop.

WRITINGS

Thesauro de' scrittori (Venice, 1525); facs. edn with Eng. intro. by E. Potter (London, 1968)

BIBLIOGRAPHY

G. Vasari: *Vite* (1550, rev. 2/1568); ed. G. Milanesi (1878–85), pp. 420–21
A. von Bartsch: *Le Peintre-graveur* (1803–21), xii, pp. 11–13 [B.]
L. Servolini: 'Ugo da Carpi', *Riv. A.*, xi (1929), pp. 174–94, 297–319
A. Petrucci: 'Di Ugo da Carpi e del chiaroscuro italiano', *Boll. A.*, xxvi (1932–3), pp. 277–81
W. Suida: 'Tizian, die beiden Campagnola u. Ugo da Carpi', *Crit. A.*, i/6 (1936), p. 285
P. Hofer: 'Variant Issues of the First Edition of Ludovico Arrighi Vicentino's "*Operina*"', *Calligraphy and Palaeography: Essays Presented to Alfred Fairbank on his 70th Birthday* (London, 1965)
L. Servolini: *Ugo da Carpi: I chiaroscuri e le altre opere* (Florence, 1977)
K. Oberhuber: *Marcantonio Raimondi, Part One* (1978), 26 [XIV/i] of *The Illustrated Bartsch*, ed. W. Strauss (New York, 1978–)
M. Zucker: *Early Italian Masters* (1980), 24 and 25 [XIII/i and XIII/ii] of *The Illustrated Bartsch*, ed. W. Strauss (New York, 1978–)
J. Johnson: 'Ugo da Carpi's Chiaroscuro Woodcuts', *Prt Colr/Conoscitore Stampe*, 57–8 (1982), pp. 2–87

JAN JOHNSON

Carpio, Marquéses del [Avellaneda y Haro; Haro y Guzmán]. Spanish family of statesmen, patrons and collectors. Few private collections in 17th-century Europe rivalled the immense holdings of (2) the 6th Marqués del Carpio and (3) the 7th Marqués del Carpio. They were powerful and wealthy relatives of the families of Olivares and Monterrey, and from 1620 to 1687 they amassed over 3000 pictures, as well as hundreds of drawings, sculptures and objects of vertu.

(1) Conde de **Castrillo** [García Avellaneda y Haro] (*fl* Madrid, 1620–40). He was the brother of Diego López de Haro, 5th Marqués del Carpio. Castrillo rose in prominence at the Spanish court in the 1620s, becoming President of the Council of the Indies. Part of the immense wealth that he controlled on behalf of Philip IV was diverted to building and furnishing the Buen Retiro palace (begun 1630; *see* MADRID, §IV, 1). Although documents from the 1660s recording the collection of the Conde mention few pictures of interest, contemporary sources cite important gifts from the Conde to Philip IV, including 14 paintings of the *Plagues of Egypt* (untraced), possibly by Pedro Orrente, in addition to furnishings, silverware, paintings and tapestries bought with funds for the royal palaces.

BIBLIOGRAPHY

J. de Barrionuevo: *Avisos*, ii (1640), p. 334
J. Brown and J. Elliott: *A Palace for a King* (New Haven, 1980), pp. 106–7, 120–23
M. Burke: *Private Collections of Italian Art in 17th-century Spain* (diss., New York U., 1984; microfilm, Ann Arbor, 1986), i, pp. 84–5; ii, docs 2.9–2.11

(2) 6th Marqués del **Carpio** [Luis Méndez de Haro y Guzmán] (*b* Valladolid, 1598; *d* Madrid, 1661). Nephew of the (1) Conde de Castrillo. He was the son of Diego López de Haro, 5th Marqués del Carpio, whom he succeeded in 1648. Don Luis followed his uncle, Gaspar de Guzmán y Pimental, Conde-Duque de Olivares, as the favourite (*valido*) of Philip IV in the 1640s; he is best known for negotiating peace with France in 1660. When Philip IV redecorated parts of the Escorial in the 1650s, Don Luis sought pictures for the project. Correspondence from 1654 to 1655 between the Spanish Ambassador to London, Don Alonso de Cárdenas, and Don Luis records the latter's purchases from the estate of Charles I, including a *Self-portrait* by Albrecht Dürer (1498; Madrid, Prado), the *Death of the Virgin* by Andrea Mantegna (*c.* 1462; Madrid, Prado) and the *Holy Family*, also known as *La Perla* (*c.* 1518; Madrid, Prado), by Raphael, as well as works by Andrea del Sarto, Titian and Veronese. Several of the paintings from Charles I's collection, for example Correggio's *Mercury Instructing Cupid before Venus* (*c.* 1525; London, N.G.), passed into Don Luis's own collection, which included works attributed to Titian (possibly the *Adoration of the Magi*, *c.* 1560; Madrid, Prado) and by Tintoretto, Veronese (e.g. *Kneeling Magdalene*, 1583; Madrid, Prado), Federico Barocci, Guido Reni, Peter Paul Rubens and Anthony van Dyck. Like the 1st Marqués de Leganés and other noble collectors, Don Luis entailed part of his collection into the estates attached to his titles.

(3) 7th Marqués del **Carpio** [Marqués de Eliche; Gaspar de Haro y Guzmán] (*b* 1 June 1629; *d* Naples, 16 Nov 1687). He was one of the more flamboyant figures of the 17th century. At different times in his career he was a debauched womanizer, a conspirator in an attempt in 1662 to blow up the theatre at the Buen Retiro palace, a soldier, the instigator of a peace treaty with Portugal in 1668, a distinguished ambassador to the Holy See (1674–82), a reforming Viceroy of Naples (1682–7) and the supporter and reorganizer of the theatre companies of Madrid. During the 1650s Don Gaspar produced dramas, masques, operas and other royal entertainments at the Buen Retiro palace. He was also among the foremost private collectors and patrons of his age and by 1651 had formed a fine collection of contemporary Spanish, Flemish and Italian masters, including Velázquez's *Toilet of Venus* (or *Rokeby Venus*, *c*. 1648–50; London, N.G.), which first appears in the inventory of the collection made in June 1651. Bellori cites Don Gaspar's collection and his patronage of Carlo Maratti during his embassy to Rome, a period in which he also supported what Sebastiano Resta called a *scuola platonica* of artists and aesthetes (Bottari and Ticozzi). Despite demanding political duties as Viceroy of Naples, Don Gaspar continued to collect paintings and began shipping works back to Spain. At his death his collection comprised over 1400 works in Spain and approximately 1800 in Italy, including Raphael's Alba *Madonna* (*c*. 1509; Washington, DC, N.G.A.; see fig.), which he had acquired from the church of Monte Oliveto, near Naples, Antonello da Messina's *Ecce homo* (New York, Met.), Correggio's *Madonna del latte* (possibly that in Budapest, Mus. F.A.), 18 works by Maratti, over 150 attributed to Tintoretto, numerous pieces by Titian and other Venetian painters and a wide range of works of the Bolognese school.

Don Gaspar's collections were partially dispersed in sales of his estate. A group of paintings was transferred to the Spanish royal collection in payment of claims made by the royal treasury, but many of the finest works were inherited by his daughter, Doña Catalina Méndez de Haro y Guzmán (*b* 1672), whose husband later became the 10th Duque de Alba. The Carpio collection, including paintings and sculpture, the library of the Conde-Duque de Olivares and a large armoury, passed into the collection of the Duques de Alba in 1733.

BIBLIOGRAPHY

G. P. Bellori: *Vite* (1672); ed. E. Borea (1976), iii, pp. 136–210
G. Bottari and S. Ticozzi: *Raccolta di lettere sulla pittura, scultura et architettura, scrite dai più celebri personaggi di secolo XV, XVI e XVII*, 8 vols (1822–5)
J. M. Pita Andrade: 'Los cuadros que poseyó el séptimo marqués del Carpio', *Archv Esp. A.*, xxv (1952), pp. 223–36
G. de Andrés: *El marqués de Liche: Bibliófilo y colleccionista de arte* (Madrid, 1975)
M. Burke: *Private Collections of Italian Art in 17th-century Spain* (diss., New York U., 1984; microfilm, Ann Arbor, 1986), i, pp. 101–29, 130–201; ii, docs 3.1–3.12, 4.1–4.14d [further bibliog.]

MARCUS BURKE

Carpioni, Giulio (*b* Venice, 1613; *d* Venice, 29 Jan 1678). Italian painter and etcher. He was a pupil of Alessandro Varotari, through whom he was drawn to the early works of Titian, though he also responded to the Venetian Caravaggesque works of Carlo Saraceni and Jean Leclerc. Around 1631 he and Varotari made a brief visit to Bergamo, where he came into contact with Lombard art. On his return to Venice he became acquainted with Pietro della Vecchia; the etchings of Simone Cantarini and Odoardo Fialetti as well as Nicolas Poussin's bacchic scenes (through the etchings of Pietro Testa) were further influences. In 1638 he settled in Vicenza and executed most of his work there. His first dated works are two vast lunettes, the *Apotheosis of Vincenzo Dolfin* (1647) and the *Apotheosis of Girolamo Bragadin* (1648; both Vicenza, Mus. Civ. A. & Stor.), which are close in style to similar works by Francesco Maffei. There followed the *Martyrdom of St Catherine* (1648; Vicenza, S Caterina), a *Self-portrait* (Milan,

Raphael: *Madonna and Child with the Young St John the Baptist* (the Alba *Madonna*), oil on panel, transferred to canvas, diam. 945 mm, *c*. 1509 (Washington, DC, National Gallery of Art)

Brera) in which he depicted himself crowned with laurel drawing an antique procession, and the mythological frescoes (*c*. 1650) in a small room in the Villa Caldogno-Nordera at Caldogno, Vicenza. At this time the Baroque style of Maffei dominated art in Vicenza, and Carpioni only gradually moved away from his influence. His *Adoration of the Magi* (mid-1650s; Vicenza, Mus. Civ. A. & Stor.), painted for the oratory of the Zitelle in Vicenza, reflects Maffei's mannered elegance and brilliant painterly freedom, while *St Nicholas Exorcising the Demons* (*c*. 1656; Vicenza, oratory of S Nicola) suggests a reaction against this decorative exuberance and a return to the naturalism of Caravaggio (Pilo). After Maffei's departure to Padua in 1657 Carpioni entered the most productive phase of his career. Of his canvases in the oratory of S Chiara, Vicenza, only one is dated, the *Five Saints* of 1663; they are in an unusual vertical format and include the Baroque *St Clare Repulsing the Saracens* and the warmly realistic *Miracle of the Mule*. There followed a series of decorative friezes, which renew a Vicentine tradition, among them the unusually long frieze of putti, allegories and grisaille sibyls (*c*. 1665; Vicenza, Mus. Civ. A. & Stor.) for the Palazzo Negri, Vicenza, and an allegorical frieze (*c*. 1665) in the Palazzo Giustiniani Baggio, Vicenza; for the latter he collaborated with the sculptor Giambattista Barberini (*d* 1666), the *quadratura* specialists Giuseppe Arighini and Giambattista Gattucci and the fresco painters Pietro Ricchi and Giovanni Ghisolfi. His most important late decorative work dates from 1671 and consists of 11 canvases showing the *Triumph of St Nicholas* and the *Virtues*, for the ceiling of the oratory of S Nicola, Vicenza. His most original works, however, are his small bacchanals, indebted to Titian and to Testa, which he interpreted with wit and a melancholy charm. Orlandi (p. 311) described them as 'perfect conceptions, such as dreams, sacrifices, bacchanals, triumphs, dances of putti, the most attractive caprices and fantasies that a painter, inclined to work on a small scale, has ever conceived'. His favourite subjects were the *Triumph of Silenus* (e.g. Venice, Accad.) and the *Realm of Hypnos* (e.g. *c*. 1656, Vienna, Ksthist. Mus.; *c*. 1665, New Haven, CT, Yale U. A.G.). Carpioni was also a gifted etcher, of religious and mythological subjects (e.g. *The Elements*, B. 82–5), and there are collections of his drawings at the Uffizi, Florence, and the Ashmolean Museum, Oxford.

BIBLIOGRAPHY

DBI
P. A. Orlandi: *Abecedario pittorico* (Bologna, 1704, rev. 1753)
G. M. Pilo: *Carpioni* (Venice, 1961) [with full bibliog.]
G. G. Zorzi: 'Il testamento del pittore Giulio Carpioni: Alcune notizie della sua vita e delle sue opere', *A. Ven.*, xv (1961), pp. 219–22
C. Donzelli and G. M. Pilo: *I pittori del seicento veneto* (Florence, 1967), pp. 111–20
F. dal Forno: 'Aggiunte al Carpioni', *Vita Veron.*, xiii/6 (1970), pp. 7–19
M. Carter Leach and R. W. Wallace: *Italian Masters of the Seventeenth Century (1982)*, 45 [XX/ii] of *The Illustrated Bartsch*, ed. W. Strauss (New York, 1978–) [B.]

□

Carr, Alwyn (Charles Ellison). *See under* RAMSDEN, OMAR.

Carr, (M.) Emily (*b* Victoria, BC, 13 Dec 1871; *d* Victoria, 2 March 1945). Canadian painter and writer. She studied art from 1891 to 1894 at the California School of Design in San Francisco. She lived in England from 1899 to 1904, studying at the Westminster School of Art in 1899, and settled in Vancouver on her return. Her stay in Paris in 1910–11, during which she had a painting shown at the Salon d'Automne in 1911, proved far more influential on her art, familiarizing her with Impressionism, with Post-Impressionism and with Fauvism.

Carr returned to Canada in 1911, living in Vancouver from 1912. Until 1913 she continued work on the study of Indian sites that she had initiated in 1908. The art and artefacts of the Northwest Coast Indians had, even by this time, been seriously depleted by American and European museums and collectors. Anxious to record what she described as the 'real art treasures of a passing race', she travelled widely to some of the most remote settlements. Her interest, however, went beyond recording material culture and she sought, through her paintings, to grasp the character and the spirit of the Indian villages and the central place occupied in their culture by carvings, totem poles and other objects. *Skidegate* (oil on board, 1912; Vancouver, A.G.), a close-up study of a totem pole, is typical of these works. The exhibition of these pictures held by Carr in Vancouver in 1913 was a commercial failure. She returned to Victoria and built a block of four flats in the hope of supporting herself as a painter from the rent, but the managerial responsibility occupied her fully (and unhappily) and she did no painting for the next 15 years.

Emily Carr: *Big Raven*, oil on canvas, 0.87×1.14 m, *c*. 1928 (Vancouver, Vancouver Art Gallery)

In 1927 Carr travelled to Ottawa to visit an exhibition at the National Gallery of Canada of art from the west coast of Canada, in which 26 of her paintings were included alongside work by other white and Indian artists. There she met Lawren S. Harris and other members of the GROUP OF SEVEN. Both they and their work were a revelation to her, and immediately on her return to Victoria she began painting again. Her new paintings, such as *British Columbian Indian Village* (1930; Vancouver, A.G.) and *Big Raven* (*c*. 1928; Vancouver, A.G.; see fig.), were quite different in character from her previous pictures, bolder in drawing and colour, more monumental in form and more imaginative in the presentation of the imagery, whether of the rich coastal forests or of Indian totems. In paintings such as *Scorned as Timber, Beloved of the Sky* (1935; Vancouver, A.G.) she was deeply influenced by the mystical interpretations of the landscape in Harris's recent work. She exhibited with the Group of Seven in 1930 and in the course of the decade began to gain recognition and appreciation, first in the east and then in the west with a major exhibition in 1938 at Vancouver Art Gallery.

In 1937, following a heart attack that curtailed but did not stop her painting activity, Carr began to write, winning the Governor-General's Award for Literature in 1942. Her seven books, including *Klee Wyck* (1941), a collection of stories about her life with the Indians, shed interesting light on her paintings and their subject-matter.

WRITINGS

Klee Wyck (Toronto, 1941)
Growing Pains: The Autobiography of Emily Carr (Toronto, 1946)
Hundreds and Thousands: The Journals of Emily Carr (Toronto, 1966)

BIBLIOGRAPHY

E. Hembroff-Schleicher: *M. E.: A Portrayal of Emily Carr* (Toronto, 1969)
——: *Emily Carr: The Untold Story* (Saanichton and Seattle, 1978)
D. Shadbolt: *The Art of Emily Carr* (Vancouver, 1979)
M. Tippett: *Emily Carr: A Biography* (Vancouver, 1979)
Emily Carr: The Mature Years (exh. cat. by D. Shadbolt, Vancouver, A.G., 1979)
R. Gowers: *Emily Carr* (Leamington Spa, Hamburg and New York, 1987)
D. Shadbolt: *Emily Carr* (Vancouver, 1990)

DAVID BURNETT

Carr, John (*b* Horbury, W. Yorks, 15 May 1723; *d* Askham Richard, N. Yorks, 22 Feb 1807). English architect. He was the son of Robert Carr, a mason and county surveyor, with whom he trained and later collaborated; together they surveyed the county bridges of West Riding, Yorks, from around 1752. Carr built mostly in the north of England, where his contacts with the county magistrates in Yorkshire and his support for the Whig Party brought him to the notice of influential patrons, who furthered his professional career. This proved to be prolific and wide-ranging. Though it was based on Burlingtonian principles his style was eclectic enough to accommodate Baroque, Rococo or Neo-classical motifs, and he was influenced by his rivals William Kent, James Paine, William Chambers and Robert Adam, although his work is readily distinguishable from theirs. Early houses such as Huthwaite Hall (1748), N. Yorks, or Arncliffe Hall (*c.* 1750–54), N. Yorks, owed much to contemporary pattern books, but at Harewood House (1758–71), W. Yorks, his motifs were unequivocally fresh and Neo-classical. Most of his subsequent houses are two- or three-storey cubes in a style typical of English Palladianism, enlivened externally by bay windows and internally by varied room shapes. The interior decoration of such houses as Lytham Hall (1757–64), Lancs, is Rococo, while that of Thoresby (1767–71; destr.), Notts, is characteristic of the transition from Rococo to Neo-classicism, and Constable Burton (*c.* 1762–8), N. Yorks, is in a Néo-Grec style. At Denton (1770–81) and Norton Place (1776), Bishops Norton, both Lincs, on the other hand, the manner of Robert Adam prevails. He also successfully remodelled houses (e.g. Raby Castle (1768–88), Durham), and his numerous stable blocks are models of variety and ingenuity, the most notable feature being the circular courtyard used, for example, at Buston (*c.* 1780–90), Derbys.

Carr also designed numerous public buildings, including Newark Town Hall (1773–6), Notts, York Assize Courts (1773–7) and the Assembly Rooms at Nottingham (1778), as well as the new hospital of S Antonio, Oporto, Portugal, begun in 1770. He also designed over 60 bridges, many of which (e.g. at Skipton, N. Yorks) flouted orthodox practice and were notable for their use of vernacular masonry types. His church commissions included examples both in a classical style, for example at Bierley (1766), W. Yorks, and in Gothick, for example at Ravenfield (1756), W. Yorks, while his new village (1759–71) at Harewood, W. Yorks, included building types of a widely varied character.

Carr was noted for the professionalism of his approach. The excellence of his planning was allied to constructional systems that were sound but economical, and these were judged to take precedence over surface decoration, where a patron might reasonably demand some personal choice. His detailed knowledge of the orders and of theories of proportion meant that both were integrated within a consistent personal style. His response to developments in landscape design was reflected in both the siting of out-offices and the care he took with secondary elevations. Despite the modest size of his drawing office, he rarely delegated work to either of his successive chief assistants, William Lindley (*c.* 1739–1818) and Peter Atkinson (1735–1805). His trusted craftsmen did, however, have some freedom in their choice of minor decorative detail.

BIBLIOGRAPHY

York Georgian Society: *The Works in Architecture of John Carr of York* (York, 1973)
W. A. Eden and R. B. Wragg: 'John Carr Stonecutter Extraordinary and the Architectural Virtuosi', *Trans. Anc. Mnmt Soc.*, xxiv (1980), pp. 23–48
I. Hall: *Georgian Buxton* (Derby, 1984)

IVAN HALL

Carr, Robert, 1st Earl of Somerset (*fl* 1601; *d* July 1646). Scottish collector and courtier. He enjoyed only a brief period of pre-eminence (1612–15) at the court of James I (James VI of Scotland) but, following the example of Henry, Prince of Wales (*see* STUART, House of, (3)), he quickly amassed his own collection. The core of it, like Henry's, was bought in Venice. Somerset was no connoisseur but seems to have been well advised by the courtier and miniaturist James Palmer and others; his agent in Venice was the English ambassador Sir DUDLEY CARLETON, 1st Viscount Dorchester, who bought from the dealer Daniel Nys. The principal consignment arrived in London in June 1615. It contained pictures attributed to Tintoretto (probably including *A Maze*; London, Hampton Court, Royal Col.), Paolo Veronese, Jacopo Bassano (*Beheading of St John the Baptist*; Copenhagen, Stat. Mus. Kst.), Titian and Andrea Schiavone. Carleton also dispatched 98 antique heads and figures of marble. An inventory of Somerset's Whitehall residence, made in November 1615 (after his arrest on suspicion of complicity in the murder of Sir Thomas Overbury), noted other pictures besides the principal Venetian acquisitions, indicating that there had been other sources of supply. Carleton repossessed the pictures that he had acquired (for which he had not been paid) and sold them to Thomas Howard, 2nd Earl of Arundel (*see* HOWARD (i), (1)), to whom the king also awarded other confiscated parts of Somerset's collection.

BIBLIOGRAPHY

N. Sainsbury, ed.: *Original Unpublished Papers Illustrative of the Life of Sir P. P. Rubens as an Artist and Diplomat* (London, 1859), pp. 273–9
M. Hervey: *The Life, Correspondence and Collections of Thomas Howard, Earl of Arundel* (Cambridge, 1921)
P. Seddon: 'Robert Carr, Earl of Somerset', *Ren. & Mod. Stud.*, xiv (1970), pp. 48–68
T. Wilks: 'The Picture Collection of Robert Carr, Earl of Somerset (*c.* 1587–1646), Reconsidered', *J. Hist. Col.*, i/2 (1989), pp. 167–77
A. R. Braunmuller: 'Robert Carr, Earl of Somerset, as Collector and Patron', *The Mental World of the Jacobean Court*, ed. L. Levy Peck (Cambridge, 1991), pp. 230–50

TIMOTHY WILKS

Carr, William Holwell (*b* Exeter, 1758; *d* London, 24 Dec 1830). English collector, dealer and painter. He began collecting while abroad in 1781. On returning to England he took the living of the parish of Menheniot, Cornwall, but as a non-resident priest spent his life in London. An amateur painter, he was an honorary exhibitor at the Royal Academy, London, between 1797 and 1820. Through Arthur Champernowne he joined a syndicate formed by the dealer William Buchanan in 1805; his curb on acquisitions proved unwelcome and provoked his dismissal in 1806, but he thus became outright owner of some distinguished pictures bought by Buchanan's associate James Irvine. A founder-member and director of the British

Institution, London, Carr lent significantly to its controversial exhibitions of Dutch and Flemish pictures (1815) and Old Masters (1816). He was among the first in England to acquire Italian pictures dating from before 1500, although his collection comprised mainly 16th- and 17th-century works. Besides pictures by Domenichino, Pier Francesco Mola, Guercino and Annibale Carracci, he owned important examples of the work of Bernardino Luini, Titian, Tintoretto, del Sarto, Sebastiano del Piombo, Garofalo, Rembrandt, Rubens, Claude and Gaspard Dughet. These, together with his own portrait (1820–30) by John Jackson, were among the 35 pictures he bequeathed to the National Gallery, London.

BIBLIOGRAPHY

DNB
C. Holmes and C. H. C. Baker: *The Making of the National Gallery* (London, 1924)

DAVID BLAYNEY BROWN

Carrà, Carlo (Dalmazzo) (*b* Quarguento, Piedmont, 11 Feb 1881; *d* Milan, 13 April 1966). Italian painter, critic and writer. He was apprenticed to a team of decorators at the age of 12, after the death of his mother. His work took him to Milan, London and Switzerland, as well as to the Exposition Universelle in Paris in 1900. He visited museums, and in Milan in 1906 he enrolled at the Accademia di Belle Arti di Brera, studying under Cesare Tallone. By 1908 he was arranging shows for the Famiglia Artistica, an exhibiting group. He met Umberto Boccioni and Luigi Russolo, and together they came to know Filippo Tommaso Marinetti and to write the *Manifesto dei pittori futuristi* (1910; *see* FUTURISM). Carrà continued, however, to use the technique of DIVISIONISM despite the radical rhetoric of Futurism. In an attempt to find new inspiration Marinetti sent them to visit Paris in autumn 1911, in preparation for the Futurist exhibition of 1912. Cubism was a revelation, and in 1911 Carrà reworked a large canvas that he had begun in 1910, the *Funeral of the Anarchist Galli* (New York, MOMA; see fig.). He had witnessed the riot at the event in 1904. The crowd and the mounted police converge in violently hatched red and black, as Carrà attempted the Futurist aim to place the spectator at the centre of the canvas. In the reworking he attempted to make the space more complex and the lighting appear to emerge from within.

The Paris trip also established personal contacts, with Guillaume Apollinaire, Amedeo Modigliani and Picasso. Carrà returned in 1912 and 1914, punctuated by a year of collaboration with Giovanni Papini's and Ardegno Soffici's Florentine periodical *Lacerba*. Soffici's close association with Paris may have reinforced Carrà's intense investigation of Cubism and encouraged him to reconsider the

Carlo Carrà: *Funeral of the Anarchist Galli*, oil on canvas, 1.98×2.66 m, 1910–11 (New York, Museum of Modern Art)

structure of his paintings, leading him to explore collage. In the *Interventionist Demonstration* (1914; Milan, G. Mattioli priv. col., see M. Carrà, 1967–8, i, p. 259) he combined collage with Marinetti's words-in-freedom and Apollinaire's ideograms, creating one of the most memorable Futurist images.

Carrà's disillusionment with Futurist aims and his intensifying rivalry with Boccioni became apparent from 1915 in paintings that concentrated on the human figure. They owed something to African sculpture and culminated in the *Antigrazioso* of 1916 (priv. col., see M. Carrà, 1967–8, i, p. 303), in which an awkward figure with a huge head stands on a chequered floor next to a trumpet; in the background a house floats on an ochre ground. These four elements struggle between independence and interdependence, and their lumpy solidity is reminiscent of Giotto's work, rather than employing Futurist dynamics. Carrà had been reconsidering Giotto in 1915 and 1916, probing the compositional force and the humanity of the people. He published an article on him in 1916 and later a book, and this understanding became the basis of his aesthetic.

Carrà was called-up at the beginning of 1917 and was posted to a unit near Ferrara, where he met Giorgio De Chirico and Alberto Savinio through Soffici. This signalled the beginning of the collaboration between Carrà and De Chirico that gave rise to PITTURA METAFISICA. Working at the hospital for nervous diseases, Carrà painted the *Metaphysical Muse* and the *Mother and Son* (both 1917; Milan, Brera), depicting mannequins derived from those of De Chirico. Despite the similarities, there is an independence from De Chirico: the tonality and colour are restricted; the mannequins are direct in their presentation, factors that indicate his continuing investigation of Giotto's work.

By winter 1917 Carrà was in Milan, where he held an exhibition. Over the following three years a profound crisis meant that he painted only four canvases, but he continued to draw and to write theoretical articles for *Valori plastici*, as well as his book *Pittura metafisica*, propagating the new art. A reconsideration of nature on the Ligurian coast resolved the crisis in 1921. *Pine by the Sea* (priv. col., see M. Carrà, 1967–8, i, p. 343) is a distillation of four elements isolated against the beach, through which Carrà expressed the substantiality that he found in Giotto's work, giving weight and solidity to the intervening spaces as well as the objects. He also achieved a unity based on surface composition rather than classical perspective or imitation of nature.

Between 1922 and 1939 Carrà made numerous contributions as art critic to the Milan newspaper *L'ambrosiano*. During the early 1920s he returned periodically to a metaphysical style, but most of his work was concentrated on the resolution of structure through landscapes and seascapes, and a reassessment of Cézanne, who had been a strong influence since his trips to Paris. He painted several bather compositions, including *Summer* (1930; Milan, Gal. A. Mod.), blending the earthy and the bold anatomical approaches of Giotto and Cézanne to monumental effect. In 1933 Carrà signed the *Manifesto della pittura murale* with Mario Sironi, Massimo Campigli and Achille Funi, and in 1936 he applied the monumental style that they advocated in the execution of frescoes (destr.) for the Milan Triennale of decorative arts. His frescoes of 1938 for the Palazzo di Giustizia in Milan (*in situ*) show a simplicity of colour and line. The number of figures is limited and the style severe. He emphasized the interplay between the solidity of the elements, avoiding the heroic muscularity favoured by the Fascist regime.

Carrà returned to the Accademia di Belle Arti di Brera as professor of painting (in 1941). Over the next 20 years his style gradually took on a more scumbled effect with rich combinations of colour, although his subject-matter changed very little, still dominated by particular motifs: the breakwater, the beach cabins, rural landscapes and views of Venice from which figures were excluded.

WRITINGS

Pittura metafisica (Florence, 1918, 2/1945)
Giotto (Florence, 1924; Eng. trans., 1925)
La mia vita (Milan, 1943/*R* 1981)
M. Carrà, ed.: *Tutti gli scritti* (Milan, 1978)

BIBLIOGRAPHY

Carrà (exh. cat., Milan, Pal. Reale, 1962)
M. Carrà: *Carlo Carrà: Tutta l'opera pittorica*, 3 vols (Milan, 1967–8)
M. Carrà, ed.: *Metafisica* (Milan, 1968; Eng. trans., abridged, 1971) [selected articles, 1916–20]
M. Carrà and M. Valsecchi: *Carrà: Opera grafica, 1922–64* (Vicenza, 1976)
Carlo Carrà (exh. cat., Ferrara, Gal. Civ. A. Mod., 1977)
M. Carrà: *Carlo Carrà: Disegni, acquaforti, litografi* (Florence, 1980)
Carlo Carrà: Mostra antologica (exh. cat., ed. M. Carrà; Milan, Pal. Reale, 1987)

MATTHEW GALE

Carracci. Italian family of artists. The family, originally from Cremona, had settled around the middle of the 15th century in Bologna, where its male members earned their living as tradesmen. A genealogical tree (excluding the female family members) was drawn up around 1600 by (2) Agostino Carracci (London, BM; Malvasia, i, p. 326). Three members of the family, (1) Ludovico Carracci and his cousins (2) Agostino Carracci and (3) Annibale Carracci, rose to artistic prominence in the last quarter of the 16th century. Jointly they effected an artistic reform that overthrew Mannerist aesthetics and initiated the Baroque. Among their many pupils were three younger members of the Carracci family. Of these, only Agostino's natural son (4) Antonio Carracci achieved significant originality vis-à-vis his more famous father and uncles. The other two, Ludovico's younger brother Paolo Carracci (1568–1625) and Francesco or Franceschino Carracci (1595–1622), the son of Agostino's and Annibale's brother Giovanni Antonio Carracci, were mediocre talents who produced no works of importance to the history of art.

I. Introduction. II. Family members.

I. Introduction.

1. The Carracci reform and the Accademia degli Incamminati. 2. Collaboration.

1. THE CARRACCI REFORM AND THE ACCADEMIA DEGLI INCAMMINATI. The Carracci's artistic reform was rooted in a profound disaffection with current Mannerist practice and an equally deep commitment to north Italian naturalism and *colore*. In order to escape the sterility of *maniera*, they turned to the study of nature on the one hand and of the paintings of non-Mannerist artists such

as Correggio, Titian and Veronese on the other. Incorporating elements of these masters' styles into their own works, they sought to combine truth to nature with a direct appeal to the beholder's sentiments. Within a decade, they overcame the initial opposition to their new style and were acknowledged as the leading artists in Bologna. In the early 1590s Annibale and Agostino began to expand the foundations of their style, admitting elements of central Italian *disegno* and fusing them with northern Italian colourism and chiaroscuro. The Carracci's conscious imitation of aspects of their predecessors' works later earned them the epithet of 'eclectics' and led in due time to a rejection of their accomplishment as cerebral, unfeeling and academic. Such an attitude rests on a misreading of their historical position and disregards the emotional content of their work. The Carracci's synthesis of stylistic elements from different sources was not an end in itself, but a means to create a new and vital style that was as much an expression of personal conviction as it was of contemporary artistic and religious concerns. It was the persuasive power of verisimilitude that the Carracci sought. Their religious paintings especially possess a marked didactic component and seek to persuade the viewer of the historical or moral truth of the representation. In this respect, their works are in harmony with the precepts of the Counter-Reformation, which stressed that religious painting should display truth to common experience and above all inspire a simple, human faith. Bologna was an important centre of post-Tridentine theology, and the fact that the city's archbishop, Cardinal Gabriele Paleotti, was the author of a treatise on religious painting (1582), underscores the currency of such ideas at the time the Carracci initiated their reform movement.

The first steps leading to the reform are difficult to reconstruct. Dated engravings from Agostino's hand exist from 1574 onwards, but no securely dated paintings are known by any of the Carracci before 1583, by which time the crucial steps towards the reform had been taken. Hence it is impossible to decide which of the three took the leading role in breaking with existing Mannerist practice. Nonetheless, it is quite clear that the Carracci formulated the premises of their attack on Mannerism jointly and jointly elaborated the approach that enabled them to overcome that style. Probably in 1582 Agostino and Annibale Carracci opened an academy called the Accademia degli Desiderosi in the studio of Ludovico, the only one of them to have joined the Bolognese painters' guild. Surviving evidence concerning the academy and its activities dates mainly from after 1600 and cannot be assumed to reflect accurately its aims at the time of its inception. Most likely the Carracci Academy, sometimes called the Accademia del Disegno or the Accademia del Naturale, started as a largely informal gathering of like-minded young artists fired by a common enthusiasm and dedicated to common goals. The academy acquired plaster casts, a skeleton and similar teaching tools, yet functioned as an extended painters' workshop. About 1590 it changed its name to the Accademia degli Incamminati (Academy of 'those who are making progress') and turned into a teaching institution with an overtly didactic curriculum. From the start, great stress was placed on the study of nature. Hence the importance accorded to drawing from life, not only from the posed model, either nude or clothed, but also from animals, plants, landscapes and inanimate objects. In later years, competitions were organized between the members, with prizes awarded for the best drawing in various categories. Due attention was paid to the sciences of perspective, colour and optics. Agostino's well-attested interest in artistic theory, music, rhetoric and poetry would have stimulated other members of the academy to study and discuss these subjects. Later reports of regular contacts with leading members of Bologna's intellectual community are probably greatly exaggerated. There is no doubt, however, that the continuous exchange of views and criticisms within the academy compelled the Carracci to define their theoretical standpoint; in addition, the daily discipline of teaching forced them to articulate the intellectual as well as the technical underpinnings of their style.

2. COLLABORATION. The close partnership between the Carracci can be deduced from a number of decorative projects that they undertook in Bologna and elsewhere between 1583 and 1594. In the Palazzo Fava, Bologna, they painted two small friezes in 1583–4 (*Stories of Europa* and *Stories of Jason*), followed *c.* 1586 by a larger frieze with *Stories of Aeneas* in the same palazzo. The Carracci's joint masterpiece is the frieze with *Stories of the Founding of Rome* in the Palazzo Magnani–Salem (now Credito Romagnolo), Bologna, executed *c.* 1589–90. In 1592 they supplied a number of ceiling paintings on canvas representing the *Gods of Olympus* (Modena, Gal. & Mus. Estense) for the Palazzo dei Diamanti, Ferrara. In 1593–4 the Carracci again joined forces in the Palazzo Sampieri–Talon in Bologna, decorating three rooms with frescoes on the ceilings and chimneys; concurrently they painted overdoors with New Testament subjects for the same palazzo (Milan, Brera). In most of these projects, especially the decorative friezes, their collaboration extended to the very conception and design of individual scenes. Surviving drawings show that a particular scene initially designed by one of the Carracci might well be executed by a second, using the other's drawings; collaboration of two members of the studio within a single scene seems also to have occurred. Despite much debate, there is no consensus among scholars as to the attribution of several scenes. This indicates that the Carracci collaborated in these cycles with an unusually free interchange of ideas, criticisms and drawings. Their much-quoted response to the question as to which one of them had painted the frieze in the Palazzo Magnani–Salem plainly was the literal truth: 'It is by the Carracci; all of us made it'. Similar reciprocation may have occurred where easel paintings were concerned, though the evidence here is less conclusive.

The Magnani frieze affirmed the success of the Carracci, and with this their need to present a united stylistic front decreased and the individuality of the three artists became more apparent. Still it was as 'the Carracci' that they were approached in 1593 by the leading members of the Farnese family, Ranuccio VI, 4th Duke of Parma and Piacenza, and his younger brother Cardinal Odoardo. Ludovico and Agostino were invited to enter the Duke's service in Parma, while Annibale was to travel to Rome and work for Cardinal Odoardo in the Palazzo Farnese. In the event, it was Agostino and Annibale who went to Rome late in the summer of 1594 to enter into negotiations with the Cardinal; Ludovico chose to remain in Bologna. This summons signalled the end of the joint Carracci studio. After a brief return to Bologna, Annibale moved to Rome in 1595 and remained there until his death in 1609. In 1598 Agostino joined him, but the brothers soon fell out and in 1599 Agostino attached himself to the court of Duke Ranuccio in Parma. Ludovico, meanwhile, carried on the academy in Bologna until his death.

BIBLIOGRAPHY

A. Bolognini Amorini: *Le vite di Ludovico, Agostino, Annibale ed altri dei Carracci* (Bologna, 1840)

A. Foratti: *I Carracci nella teoria e nella pratica* (Città di Castello, 1913)

H. Bodmer: 'Drawings by the Carracci: An Aesthetic Analysis', *Old Master Drgs*, viii (1933–4), pp. 51–66

——: 'L'accademia dei Carracci', *Bologna: Riv. Mens. Com.*, xiii/8 (1935), pp. 61–74

C. G. Marchesini: 'Le incisioni dei Carracci e della loro scuola', *Guthenberg Jb.* (1944–9), pp. 161–78

A. Petrucci: 'L'incisione carraccesca', *Boll. A.*, xxxv (1950), pp. 131–44

R. Wittkower: *The Drawings of the Carracci in the Collection of Her Majesty the Queen at Windsor Castle* (London, 1952)

D. Mahon: 'Eclecticism and the Carracci: Further Reflections on the Validity of a Label', *J. Warb. & Court. Inst.*, xvi (1953), pp. 303–41

Mostra dei Carracci: Catalogo critico, 2 vols (exh. cat., Bologna, Pal. Archiginnasio, 1956) [i: *I dipinti* by C. Gnudi and others; ii: *I disegni* by D. Mahon]

D. Mahon: 'Afterthoughts on the Carracci Exhibition', *Gaz. B.-A.*, xlix (1957), pp. 193–207; 267–98

The Carracci: Drawings and Paintings (exh. cat., ed. R. Holland; U. Newcastle upon Tyne, Hatton Gal., 1961)

Dessins des Carraches (exh. cat. by R. Bacou and D. Mahon, Paris, Louvre, 1961)

J. R. Martin: 'The *Butcher's Shop* of the Carracci', *A. Bull.*, xlv (1963), pp. 263–6

M. Calvesi and V. Casale: *Le incisioni dei Carracci* (Rome, 1965)

A. Ottani: *Gli affreschi dei Carracci in Palazzo Fava* (Bologna, 1966)

C. Volpe: *Il fregio dei Carracci e i dipinti di Palazzo Magnani in Bologna* (Bologna, 1972)

D. De Grazia: *Prints and Related Drawings by the Carracci Family* (Washington, DC, 1979)

L. Spezzaferro: 'I Carracci tra naturalismo e classicismo', *Le arti a Bologna e in Emilia dal 16 al 17 secolo: Atti del 24 congresso internazionale di storia dell'arte: Bologna, 1979*, pp. 203–28

Bologna 1584: Gli esordi dei Carracci e gli affreschi di Palazzo Fava (exh. cat., ed. A. Emiliani; Bologna, Pin. N., 1984)

R. Zapperi: 'The Summons of the Carracci to Rome: Some New Documentary Evidence', *Burl. Mag.*, cxxviii (1986), pp. 203–5

Les Carraches et les décors profanes: Atti del convegno: Roma, 1986

The Age of Correggio and the Carracci (exh. cat. by C. Dempsey, D. Posner and A. Ottani Cavina, Bologna, Pin. N.; New York, Met.; Washington, DC, N.G.A.; 1986–7)

C. Goldstein: *Visible Fact over Verbal Fiction: A Study of the Carracci and the Criticism, Theory and Practice of Art in Renaissance and Baroque Italy* (Cambridge, 1988)

C. Dempsey: 'The Carracci Academy', *Academies of Art between Renaissance and Romanticism*, ed. A. W. A. Boschloo (The Hague, 1989), pp. 33–43

A. Emiliani: *Le 'Storie di Romolo e Remo' di Ludovico, Agostino e Annibale Carracci* (Bologna, 1989)

G. Feigenbaum: 'Drawing and Collaboration in the Carracci Academy', *IL 60: Essays Honoring Irving Lavin on his Sixtieth Birthday*, ed. M. A. Lavin (New York, 1990), pp. 145–55

G. Perini: *Gli scritti dei Carracci*, Villa Spelman Colloquia, ii (Bologna, 1990)

C. Robertson: 'The Carracci and Others in the Camera del Poggiolo at Ferrara', *Burl. Mag.*, cxxxiv (1992), pp. 417–27

G. Feigenbaum: 'Practice in the Carracci Academy', *The Artist's Workshop*, ed. P. M. Lukehart (Washington, DC, 1993), pp. 59–76

C. VAN TUYLL VAN SEROOSKERKEN

II. Family members.

(1) Ludovico [Lodovico] **Carracci** (*b* Bologna, *bapt* 19 April 1555; *d* Bologna, 13 or 14 Nov 1619). Painter, draughtsman and etcher. His father, Vincenzo Carracci, was a butcher, whose profession may be alluded to in Ludovico's nickname 'il Bue' (It.: 'the Ox'), though this might also be a reference to the artist's own slowness. Ludovico's style was less classical than that of his younger cousins Agostino and Annibale, perhaps because of a mystical turn of mind that gave his figures a sense of other-worldliness. Like his cousins, he espoused the direct study of nature, especially through figure drawing, and was inspired by the paintings of Correggio and the Venetians. However, there survives in his work, more than in that of his cousins, a residue of the Mannerist style that had dominated Bolognese painting for most of the mid-16th century. Ludovico maintained a balance between this Mannerist matrix, his innate religious piety and the naturalism of the work of his cousins. With the exception of some travels during his training and a brief visit to Rome in 1602, Ludovico's career was spent almost entirely in Bologna. In the first two decades of the 17th century he lost touch with the activities of his more up-to-date Bolognese compatriots—contemporaries and pupils alike—who were then active in Rome, including his cousin Annibale. Ludovico's later work became overblown and eccentric. This curious 'gigantism' was first evidenced in paintings of the late 1590s, but the tendency seems to have been reinforced by the monumental classicism of Annibale's ceiling of the Galleria Farnese in the Palazzo Farnese, Rome, which Ludovico saw on his visit in 1602. In spite of his isolation in Bologna, Ludovico strongly influenced the subsequent development of painting in his native city and elsewhere, especially through his pupils, who included Guido Reni, Giacomo Cavedone, Francesco Albani, Domenichino and Alessandro Algardi.

1. Life and work. 2. Working methods and technique. 3. Critical reception and posthumous reputation.

1. Life and work.

(i) Training and early work, before *c.* 1590. (ii) Middle years, *c.* 1590–1601. (iii) Late work, 1602 and after.

(i) Training and early work, before c. *1590.* Probably sometime after 1567 Ludovico trained in Bologna with the Mannerist painter Prospero Fontana, though the precise date of his apprenticeship is unknown: to judge from his few surviving early pictures, he carried over little or nothing of Fontana's style into his subsequent work. On 23 March 1578 Ludovico requested admission as master to the Corporazione dei Pittori in Bologna. According to Malvasia, at about this period he travelled to Florence, Parma, Venice and Mantua. On 28 June 1582 Ludovico was elected a member of the council of the Compagnia dei Bombasari e Pittori, Bologna.

The earliest known paintings by Ludovico were made shortly after *c.* 1580; they reveal the influence of Federico Barocci, though they also hark back to an earlier tradition of Emilian painting, most notably to the work of Niccolò dell'Abate. Examples include the *Mystic Marriage of St Catherine* (*c.* 1581–2; Bologna, priv. col., see 1993–4 exh. cat., no. 1) and the *St Vincent Martyr* (*c.* 1580–83; Bologna,

1. Ludovico Carracci: *Madonna and Child Adored by Saints and Donor* (the Bargellini *Madonna*), oil on canvas, 2.82×1.88 m, 1588 (Bologna, Pinacoteca Nazionale)

Credito Romagnolo). In composition and handling, the *St Vincent* is indebted to both Correggio and Barocci, the latter's print of the *Virgin and Child* (B. 2) providing the model, in reverse, for Ludovico's figure group in the upper right of the picture. Also datable from the first half of the 1580s are the *Sacrifice of Isaac* (Rome, Pin. Vaticana), though it is often dated rather later, and the *Mystic Marriage of St Catherine, with SS Francis and Joseph and Two Angels* (Göteborg, Kstmus.). The best-known work from the first half of the 1580s—and the one that shows Ludovico's early style at its most elegant and attractive—is the *Annunciation* (1583–4; Bologna, Pin. N.), which was commissioned by Giulio Cesare Guerini for the room of the Compagnia del Santissimo Sacramento, adjacent to the former church of S Giorgio in Poggiale, Bologna. The colours, form and sentiment are still Baroccesque, though there is now a stronger element of Correggio's presence. Yet in spite of these influences, the idiom is also now clearly Carraccesque in form and style. In 1584, together with Agostino and Annibale, Ludovico completed for Filippo Fava the fresco cycle of the *Stories of Jason* on the frieze of the Gran Salone in the Palazzo Fava, Bologna. Ludovico's share may be only surmised from stylistic evidence: it is now widely agreed that he was responsible for much of the *Enchantment of Medea* and the *Rejuvenation of Aeson.*

Some two years earlier, also together with his two cousins, Ludovico had founded the Accademia dei Desiderosi (the so-called Carracci Academy), of which he was nominated head. The three artists treated the academy as yet another of their collaborative enterprises, and it enabled them to explore their artistic reforms with greater independence. The academy was also a channel through which commissions flowed from the city's churches and the local nobility, commissions that were then diverted by Ludovico to whichever of the three artists were available or most suited to execute the project.

In the second half of the 1580s Ludovico began to receive commissions from leading Bolognese families for altarpieces in important local churches, among them S Francesco, where the *Conversion of St Paul* (1587–8; Bologna, Pin. N.) was painted for the family chapel of Emilio Zambeccari. Another example is the *Madonna and Child Adored by Saints and Donor* (1588; Bologna, Pin. N.; see fig. 1), painted for the Bargellini family, who installed it in the Buoncompagni Chapel of the church of the Monache Convertite in Via Lame (now S Maria del Buon Pastore). Signed and dated LVD. *Caratius* F. MDLXXXVIII, the Bargellini *Madonna* is Ludovico's first signed painting; it marks his full maturity as a painter and it is also one of his most successful works. The majestic composition, clearly inspired by the airy altarpieces of the great Venetians, such as Titian and Veronese, represents a new departure in his style. The graceful movement and gentle humanity of expression attained in his figures became a hallmark of his style during this and the following decade. Also probably painted in the mid- to late 1580s

2. Ludovico Carracci: *Tacconi Family*, oil on canvas, 970×760 mm, *c.* 1588–90 (Bologna, Pinacoteca Nazionale)

(though sometimes dated early in the next decade) is another celebrated altarpiece, the *Immaculate Virgin Adored by Saints* (the '*Madonna degli Scalzi*'; Bologna, Pin. N.), which was painted for the Bentivoglio Chapel in the church of the Madonna degli Scalzi in Strada Maggiore.

In the early part of his career, Ludovico also specialized in two other categories of painting: portraits and small-scale works on copper, painted either as devotional pieces or cabinet pictures. Highly finished, the latter are exquisite in handling and iridescent in colour. The jewel-like appearance of the *Marriage of the Virgin* (1588; London, priv. col., on loan to N.G.) is also a consequence of the elegant poses of the figures and the complexity of the whole composition. Such pictures later exerted a strong influence on the young Centese painter Guercino.

Ludovico was also successful as a portraitist, capturing a likeness as well as conveying something of the personality and mood of the sitter. The well-known portrait of the *Tacconi Family* (*c.* 1588–90; Bologna, Pin. N.; see fig. 2) is among his best works of the type. Malvasia mentioned it when it belonged to the Bonfiglioli family, pointing out that Prudenza Tacconi was Ludovico Carracci's sister; she is shown alongside her husband Francesco and their two children Gasparo Gilippo and Innocenzo, who was later to become a painter. In the second part of his career, Ludovico seems to have more or less given up portraiture; at least few or no independent painted portraits have survived.

(ii) Middle years, c. *1590–1601.* The 1590s mark yet another step in Ludovico's development. As if he had already determined to stay in his native city for good, the painter declined an invitation to enter into the service of the Farnese family in Rome, an offer subsequently taken up in 1595 by both Agostino and Annibale. Ludovico's work of the 1590s is characterized by a more sombre palette, suggesting that the early influence of Barocci had finally been supplanted by that of the Venetians: rich earth colours, with the occasional dark blue, green and purple, are bathed in a more broken, uneven light. Typical of this new painterly direction is the *Holy Family with St Francis and Donors* (1591; Cento, Pin. Civ.), which was commissioned by Giuseppe Piombini of Cento for the altar of his family chapel in the church of the Cappuccini at Cento. The patron is depicted as St Joseph, while members of his family, Pietro Antonio Piombini and his wife, Elisabetta Dondini, appear in contemporary dress at the lower right of the picture. The exciting potential of this great altarpiece was recognized some 25 years later by the young Guercino, who acknowledged its strong impact on him by the nickname he gave it, '*La cara cinna*' (or 'Dear mother's breast'), referring to the nourishment it had provided in his tender years. These same qualities are more strikingly present in another altarpiece, the *Martyrdom of St Ursula* (1592; Bologna, Pin. N.), formerly placed in the church of S Girolamo, Bologna; it is similarly Venetian in feel and, perhaps more than any other of Ludovico's pictures, owes the greatest debt to the work of Veronese.

The daylight ambience that Ludovico favoured in his altarpieces of the 1580s was increasingly replaced in his work of the succeeding decade by more dramatically lit nocturnes. Accompanying this darkening of the palette and pictorial setting was an intensification of the emotional states of the participating figures, features seen in a number of other altarpieces made for Bolognese churches at this time: the *St Hyacinth* (1594; Paris, Louvre), painted for the Turrini Chapel in S Domenico; the *Transfiguration* (*c.* 1595–6; Bologna, Pin. N.), commissioned by Dionigio Ratta for S Pietro Martire; and the *Probatica piscina* (1595–6; Bologna, Pin. N.), commissioned by Giovanni Torfanini for the then new church of S Giorgio in Poggiale.

Ludovico's collaboration with his two cousins on decorative fresco cycles in the palazzi of wealthy Bolognese patrons also continued into the mid-1590s. They worked together on the decoration of the Palazzo Magnani–Salem; the date 1592 is inscribed on the fireplace of the Gran Salone, which contains frescoes with *Stories of the Founding of Rome.* The extent of Ludovico's share of the decoration, probably begun *c.* 1589, remains controversial: it seems to include the *She-wolf*, though the preparatory drawing for this (Paris, Louvre) is unquestionably by Annibale, the *Rape of the Sabines* and the *Sabine Women Intervening in the Battle between the Romans and the Sabines*, though, again, the related preparatory drawing (Chatsworth, Derbys) is by Annibale. In 1592 Ludovico and Annibale were commissioned to decorate two chimney-breasts in the Palazzo Lucchini, for which Ludovico painted *Alexander and Thais Setting Fire to Persepolis* (detached fresco now Bologna,

3. Ludovico Carracci: *Ascension*, oil on canvas, 2.14×1.66 m, 1597 (Bologna, S Cristina)

Pal. Francia). In 1593–4 he helped decorate a number of rooms in the Palazzo Sampieri–Talon.

Towards the end of the decade, Ludovico began to make his figures colossal in size, one of the first examples of this 'gigantism' being the *Ascension*, painted for the high altar of the church of S Cristina, Bologna (1597; *in situ*; see fig. 3). By the end of the 1590s Ludovico's position as Bologna's pre-eminent painter had been earned by the consistently high quality and originality of his pictures. He painted another version of the *Martyrdom of St Ursula* (?1600; Imola, S Domenico) and the *Birth of the Baptist* (Bologna, Pin. N.), which was commissioned in 1600 by Dionigio Ratta for the high altar of the church of S Giovanni Battista, Bologna, but apparently erected only in 1604. This was also the time when younger rivals appeared on the scene and began to establish themselves at Ludovico's expense. In 1598 Guido Reni was chosen in preference to both Ludovico and Bartolomeo Cesi to decorate the *apparati* (temporary structures) erected in Bologna in honour of Pope Clement VIII, and he nearly supplanted Ludovico in the commission from Ratta for S Giovanni Battista. According to Malvasia, Reni offered to paint this altarpiece for half the price that Ludovico was asking and even presented the patron with a beautiful drawing showing a preliminary idea for the composition (possibly Windsor Castle, Berks, Royal Lib., 2328).

(iii) Late work, 1602 and after. Ludovico's visit to Rome, documented as having taken place between 31 May and 13 June 1602, gave him the opportunity to see at first hand the new, classicizing style that his cousin Annibale had evolved in his decorations of the Palazzo Farnese. Malvasia, who all too frequently championed Ludovico's interests at the expense of those of his cousins in his lives of the three painters, claimed, rather improbably, that a motive for Ludovico's visit was to 'raggiustare la galleria Farnese' (to retouch or correct the frescoes in the gallery), a statement made all the more implausible by the fact that the ceiling had been unveiled the previous year. Nevertheless, Ludovico's Roman journey did seem to mark a milestone in his career: from then on the 'visionary' or 'neo-Gothic' element in his style became more pronounced, becoming the hallmark of his last phase.

On 18 January 1603 the funeral celebrations in honour of Agostino Carracci that Ludovico had organized, together with other members of the Carracci Academy, took place in Bologna. A pamphlet entitled *Il funerale d'Agostino Carraccio fatto in Bologna sua patria*, with engravings by Francesco Brizio and Guido Reni, said to have been based on drawings by Ludovico, was published soon after by Benedetto Morelli. In the spring of the same year Monsignor Giovanni Battista Agucchi put forward Ludovico's name to the Fabbriceria of St Peter's, Rome, as an artist ideally qualified to paint one of the altarpieces for the basilica. The recommendation proved abortive and the commissions were instead shared among the members of the Tusco-Roman faction of painters then active in Rome, such as Cristofano Roncalli, Giovanni Baglione, Bernardo Castello, Domenico Passignano and others.

The following spring Ludovico began one of the largest decorative undertakings of his late period, the fresco cycle of the *Story of St Benedict* in the octagonal cloister of the convent of S Michele in Bosco, Bologna. The commission, which Ludovico seems to have begun planning as early as 1602–3, was completed in April 1605, together with members of the by then renamed Accademia degli Incamminati, mostly members of his workshop. The cycle is now a ruin, with only the odd passage of original paintwork surviving. The 37 frescoes of which it is composed are subdivided by caryatids and are contained within an elaborate architecture. Ludovico painted seven of the scenes; the remainder was divided between his pupils and associates. Although the subject-matter is religious, the conception of the whole has been seen as a response on the part of Ludovico to Annibale Carracci's secular compositions on the ceiling of the Galleria Farnese.

Ludovico was next engaged by Bishop Claudio Rangoni on the decoration of the choir of Piacenza Cathedral, with *Stories from the Life of the Virgin*, a commission on which he worked together with Camillo Procaccini. The only surviving payment to the artist is dated 11 June 1605, but work continued until 1608, when the decoration was unveiled. Ludovico's share comprised some of the large-scale canvases that formerly decorated the walls of the choir, including the massive *Funeral of the Virgin* and the *Apostles at the Tomb of the Virgin* (both Parma, G.N.), which were removed *c.* 1800 when the interior of the cathedral was 'restored'. Still *in situ* are his frescoes of the *Glory of the Heavens* occupying three of the four spaces of the vault (the fourth, the *Assumption of the Virgin*, was painted by Procaccini). Ludovico's contribution is memorable for the colossal scale of the figures, whose exaggerated proportions mark the culmination of the process begun a decade earlier.

During the last ten years of his life, Ludovico was increasingly eclipsed by younger rivals, most notably by Guido Reni who returned from Rome in 1613 to take up work on two prestigious commissions, the decoration of the apse of the chapel of S Domenico in the church of S Domenico, Bologna, and the high altar of the church of the Mendicanti. In contrast to the suave modernity and brightness of colour of Guido's mature work, the paintings of Ludovico's declining years seem drab and remote. Nevertheless, the best of them have an eccentricity and mystical power, the like of which was only to reappear in English history painting of the late 18th century, in the work of such painters as James Barry and Fuseli.

Ludovico's late pictures include the *Calling of St Matthew* (probably *c.* 1606–7; Bologna, Pin. N.), painted for the chapel of the Compagnia dei Salaroli, S Maria della Pietà, Bologna; the *Crucifixion* (*c.* 1610–13; Ferrara, S Francesca Romana); the *Preaching of St Antony* (*c.* 1614–15; Milan, Brera), done originally for the high altar of S Antonio Abate, the Collegio Montalto; the *Martyrdom of St Margaret* (1616) for the Gonzaga Chapel of the Theatine church of SS Maurizio and Margherita, Mantua (*in situ*); and the justifiably famous *Paradiso* (1617; S Paolo Maggiore, Bologna).

2. Working methods and technique. Ludovico's working method combined long-standing, traditional procedures of painting and drawing with a new attitude towards pictorial conception that he and his cousins introduced into their work in the 1580s. The basic practices of preparing pigments and other materials, making detailed

4. Ludovico Carracci: *St Carlo Borromeo Adoring the Virgin and Child*, compositional study, red chalk, heightened with white, 180×146 mm (Paris, Musée du Louvre)

preliminary studies on paper for a given work, enlarging and transferring compositions from one surface to another, making cartoons, painting from scaffolding (in the case of large-scale wall and ceiling decorations) and so on were, in essence, those that had been employed and perfected in painters' workshops in Italy during the preceding hundred years or more, though, doubtless, with a few 'house' variations, as there would have been in any other painter's studio or workshop of the period.

The well-known Carracci reform of painting, in which Ludovico played his part, was therefore not so much a revolution in the use of materials or particular practical methods but in the presentation of pictorial subject-matter. Annibale was the first to realize fully a more lucid, naturalistic conception of a given composition and to give form to this idealized view of the world in his mature work; he was followed at the outset of his quest by both Agostino and Ludovico. The Carracci's pursuit of a more naturalistic conception of the subject gave drawing an important role, enabling them to confront nature and to obtain a more truthful rendering of reality. Ludovico's drawings of the 1580s and 1590s, together with those of his cousins from the same period, show this striving towards a more naturalistic rendering of the human figure.

More personal to Ludovico was his method of preparing a composition by means of a series of preparatory drawings that differ widely in design, even though they were all conceived for the same work. He seems to have considered many possible solutions for a given composition before finally opting for one. Sometimes no strong formal development seems to link together a sequence of drawings for a given composition. Yet for such a seemingly erratic creative process, Ludovico had a distinguished Emilian forerunner in Parmigianino, whose preparatory drawings for pictures reveal a similar richness of invention; and it can be no accident that Ludovico's compositions are sometimes strongly redolent of those of Parmigianino. Another trick of Ludovico's drawing technique finds an echo in his finished painting. This was his adoption of a paper cut-out correction, which was laid down on to the compositional study, usually to alter the position of a figure. Such a correction was used for the kneeling figure of the saint in a preparatory drawing (Paris, Louvre; see fig. 4) for the altarpiece of *St Carlo Borromeo Adoring the Virgin and Child* (Forlì, Pin. Civ.). The consequent silhouetting effect is often carried over into the pictures; it is, for example, especially marked in the *Ascension* (Bologna, S Cristina), where the background figures do indeed look like cut-outs silhouetted against the sky.

3. Critical reception and posthumous reputation. Ludovico's considerable influence on the evolution of 17th-century Bolognese painting was due to a number of factors, including his long-held position as head of the Carracci Academy. He seemed to regard his tenure of this office as a personal calling and, in spite of pressing invitations on the part of influential patrons to work outside the city, he was not prepared to relinquish it. He was also undoubtedly effective as a teacher and organizer, a quality well exemplified in the decoration of the cloister of S Michele in Bosco, which brought together many of his pupils and associates from the academy. Moreover, his ability as a teacher and communicator enabled him to pass on to a succeeding generation of painters the essential lessons of the Carracci reforms. This ensured that his compositional vocabulary, his penchant for sombre colours and dramatic lighting and, indeed, his personal brand of religious devotion were echoed throughout the century and beyond. The impact of his art was therefore felt by Bolognese painters as diverse as Guercino and Giovanni Andrea Donducci, called Mastelletta, at the beginning of the 17th century, and Domenico Maria Canuti and Giuseppe Maria Crespi at the end.

Although highly regarded in England in the 18th century by such critics as Joshua Reynolds, Ludovico's work fell out of fashion in the 19th century, along with that of his cousins and, indeed, the whole of the rest of the Bolognese school of painting of the 17th century and the early 18th. Interest in Ludovico's work was rekindled just before the middle of the 20th century, along with the general revival of interest in the Carracci. A milestone in this process was the monograph on the painter published in 1939 by the German art historian Heinrich Bodmer. Thereafter Ludovico's work began to receive the re-evaluation that it deserved, though interest in his work has tended to lag behind that of his more famous cousin Annibale. The process of reassessment has continued, as exemplified by the monographic exhibition held in Bologna and Fort Worth, TX, in 1993–4. Nevertheless, this process is far from complete: problems of chronology and the attribution of several paintings remain, while the considerable task of gauging his work as a draughtsman requires further attention.

BIBLIOGRAPHY

EWA; Thieme–Becker

EARLY SOURCES

G. Baglione: *Vite* (1642); ed. V. Mariani (1935), pp. 105–6, 381
G. P. Bellori: *Vite* (1672); ed. E. Borea (1976)
C. C. Malvasia: *Felsina pittrice* (1678); ed. G. Zanotti (1841), i, pp. 263–97
F. Belvisi: *Elogio storico del pittore Lodovico Carracci* (Bologna, 1825)
S. Muzzi: *Notizie intorno al pittor maestro Lodovico Carracci* (Bologna, 1843)

MONOGRAPHIC WORKS

H. Bodmer: *Lodovico Carracci* (Burg bei Magdeburg, 1939); rev. by W. Arslan, *Riv. A.*, xxiii (1941), pp. 268–72; and by W. Friedländer, *A. Bull.*, xxiv (1942), pp. 190–95
G. Feigenbaum: *Lodovico Carracci: A Study of his Later Career and a Catalogue of his Paintings* (diss., Princeton U., 1984; microfilm, Ann Arbor, 1985)
Ludovico Carracci (exh. cat., ed. A. Emiliani; Bologna, Pin. N.; Fort Worth, TX, Kimbell A. Mus.; 1993–4)
G. Feigenbaum: *Lodovico Carracci* (New York, 1994)

DRAWINGS

D. Miller: 'A Drawing by Ludovico Carracci for his Lost *Penitence of St Peter*', *Burl. Mag.*, cvi (1964), p. 374
J. R. Judson: 'A Study of Ludovico Carracci for his Scalzi *Madonna*', *Master Drgs*, v/4 (1967), pp. 387–9
R. E. Spear: 'A Late Drawing by Ludovico Carracci', *Master Drgs*, xvii/1 (1979), pp. 51–2
B. Bohn: *The Drawings of Lodovico Carracci* (diss., New York, Columbia U., 1982; microfilm, Ann Arbor, 1986)
——: 'The Chalk Drawings of Lodovico Carracci', *Master Drgs*, xxii/4 (1984), pp. 402–25
M. Newcome: 'Ludovico Carracci, Jacopo da Empoli, Giovanni Andrea de Ferrari: Notes on Three Drawings in the Palazzo Rosso in Genoa', *Master Drgs*, xxiii–xxiv/2 (1985–6), pp. 204–8
B. Bohn: 'Lodovico's Last Decade', *Master Drgs*, xxv/3 (1987), pp. 219–36
A. Brogi: 'Disegni di Ludovico Carracci: Alcune precisazioni', *A. Bologna: Boll. Mus. Civ. A. Ant.*, i (1990), pp. 34–45
B. Bohn: 'Malvasia and the Study of Carracci Drawings', *Master Drgs*, xxx/4 (1992), pp. 396–414

SPECIALIST STUDIES

W. Friedländer: 'Contributo alla cronologia e all'iconografia di Ludovico Carracci', *Cron. A.*, iii (1926), pp. 133–44
M. L. Blumer: 'Un quadro di Lodovico Carracci a Notre Dame di Parigi', *Riv. A.*, xxi (1939), pp. 51–7
R. E. Righi: '*L'Erede* di Lodovico Carracci già nel palazzo Grassi', *Strenna Stor. Bologn.*, v (1955), pp. 103–9
M. Pinnell: 'Lodovico Carracci's *Assumption of the Virgin*', *NC Mus. A. Bull.*, i/4–5 (1957–8), pp. 1–7
M. Rosci: 'Un Ludovico inedito e l'iconografia di San Carlo', *A. Ant. & Mod.*, 31–2 (1965), pp. 335–8
S. Zamboni: 'Ludovico Carracci e Francesco Gessi: Due dipinti inediti', *Ant. Viva*, vii/1 (1968), pp. 1–10
L. Street: 'Lodovico Carracci's *Assumption of the Virgin* in Modena', *A. Q.* [Detroit], xxxiii (1970), pp. 379–92
——: 'La vendita Ellesemere di disegni dei Carracci', *A. Illus.*, iii (1970), pp. 255–8
——: '*Una Navita* di Lodovico Carracci', *A. Illus.*, iv/43–4 (1971), pp. 52–7
C. Volpe: 'Sugli inizi di Ludovico Carracci', *Paragone*, xxvii/317–19 (1976), pp. 115–29
G. Bertini: '*Rinaldo e Armida* di Ludovico Carracci', *Paragone*, xxxvi/406 (1983), pp. 60–61
L. Galante: 'Un Ludovico Carracci e una copia dal Barocci a Gravina di Puglia', *Prospettiva* [Florence], 43 (1985), pp. 61–4
N. Turner: 'Two Paintings Attributed to Lodovico Carracci', *Burl. Mag.*, cxxvii (1985), pp. 795–6
M. Fioravanti Baraldi: 'Un'*Assunta* di Ludovico Carracci per i Bentivoglio', *Il Carrobbio*, xiii (1987), pp. 159–67
G. Feigenbaum: 'The *Kiss of Judas* by Lodovico Carracci', *Rec. A. Mus., Princeton U.*, xlvi/1 (1989), pp. 3–18
E. Marchetti: 'Appunti per una nuova ipotesi di attribuzione di un dipinto già ritenuto di L. Carracci un tempo nella chiesa parrocchiale di Semelano, ora al museo Beaux Arts di Rennes', *Atti & Mem. Reale Deput. Stor. Patria Prov. Moden.*, xi (1989)
G. Feigenbaum: 'The Early History of Lodovico Carracci's *Annunciation* Altarpiece', *Burl. Mag.*, cxxxii/1050 (1990), pp. 616–22
C. H. Wood: 'Agucchi, Lodovico Carracci and the Monument to Cardinal Sega at Piacenza', *Burl. Mag.*, cxxxii/1060 (1991), pp. 429–33
G. Perini: 'L'effigie di Ludovico: Contributo all'iconografia del Carracci maggiore', *Atti & Mem. Accad. Clementina Bologna*, xxxii (1993), pp. 355–85

NICHOLAS TURNER

(2) Agostino Carracci (*b* Bologna, 15 Aug 1557; *d* Parma, 22 March 1602). Painter, engraver and draughtsman, cousin of (1) Ludovico Carracci. He abandoned his profession as a tailor, which was also that of his father, Antonio, and began training as a painter. According to Faberi, he studied first in the workshop of the painter Prospero Fontana (like Ludovico), then trained under the engraver and architect Domenico Tibaldi and under the sculptor Alessandro Menganti (1531–*c.* 1594). However, it is likely that Faberi's account was influenced by his desire to present Agostino's career as an example of the versatile '*cursus studiorum*' advocated by the Accademia degli Incamminati. Other sources (Mancini, Malvasia, Bellori) agree that it was his cousin Ludovico who was responsible for directing him towards painting. Only recently has it been assumed that he was a pupil of Bartolomeo Passarotti.

The earliest surviving works by Agostino are engravings. Engraving was an extremely profitable practice, to which he dedicated himself wholeheartedly in the first part of his career and in which he attained new heights of perfection. Although the attribution to him (Malvasia) of the frontispiece (B. 257) for the new edition of the *Symbolicae quaestiones* by A. Bocchi is uncertain, his first dated engravings go back to 1576 (*Holy Family*, from a prototype by Marcantonio Raimondi; *Holy Family with SS Catherine and John the Baptist*, B. 94). Between the end of the 1570s and the beginning of the 1580s Agostino made engravings after original works by Girolamo da Treviso, Orazio Samacchini, Lorenzo Sabatini, Raffaellino da Reggio and Denys Calvaert; engravings after prints by Cornelis Cort and Federico Barocci; and, finally, prints of his own composition, among them a *Frieze above the Map of Bologna* (1581; B. 263) and the so-called *Santini* ('Little saints'), some of which are dated *Rome 1581*. In 1582 he was in Cremona, where he executed the illustrations for *Cremona fedelissima*, published by Antonio Campi in 1585 (B. 192–230). Some engravings after Tintoretto and Paolo Veronese also date to 1582.

It is difficult, on the basis of his engraved work alone, to put forward a convincing reconstruction of Agostino's early activity as a painter. However, by the end of the 1570s he was beginning to work within the local tradition. Faberi's mention of his work on a fresco in the locality of 'I Ronchi' (Bologna, Ronchi di Crevalcore) allows parts of the surviving decoration in the Palazzo Caprara to be attributed to him (Benati and Peruzzi). It is likely that Agostino not only engraved the works of the Bolognese masters of the previous generation but also improved his painting technique by copying their works. An example of this is the *Judith* (Bologna, Banca Carimonte), a copy of a painting by Sabatini (fragment, Berea Coll., KY; attributed to Parmigianino). He also made an engraving after this painting (B. 4).

Agostino's engravings indicate that he made trips to Rome (1581: though not absolutely certain), Cremona

(1582) and Venice (1582) and make clear that these were opportunities to free himself from the local late Mannerist tradition. In this period he studied, among others, the great Venetian painters, which enabled him to establish the basis of his expressive style. Like Ludovico and Annibale, he became convinced of the need for an intense study of nature, which is evident in a series of rapidly executed portrait drawings and oil sketches on paper (e.g. *Portrait of a Boy*; Parma, G.N.). He began to produce caricatures, perhaps a little ahead of his brother and cousin, a genre already practised by the Mannerists, such as Passarotti, who had developed its literary implications.

Between 1583 and 1584 Agostino worked with Ludovico and Annibale on the frieze decorations of the *Stories of Europa* and the *Stories of Jason* in the Palazzo Fava, Bologna. Here the critics agree that Agostino should be credited with the scenes in which the Venetian influence is strongest: the *Meeting of Jason and Pelias*, *Jason Stealing the Golden Fleece* and *Jason Giving the Golden Fleece to Pelias*. The *Fête champêtre* (Marseille, Mus. B.-A.) can be dated to the same period (Malvasia). The *Death of Adonis* (Raleigh, NC Mus. A.) may have been painted a little before the Fava frescoes and can perhaps be identified with a painting that Malvasia saw in the Donnoli house.

In 1586 Agostino was in Parma with Annibale, where he made engravings after works by Correggio, painted a *Holy Family* in fresco in the Capuchin church and a *Virgin and Child with SS Nicholas, Cecilia, Margaret and the Infant St John* (dated 1586; both Parma, G.N.) for the monastery of S Paolo. In comparison to the assured style of his earlier works, here he seems to have been intimidated by the proximity of his brother, even though the turgid forms and their Correggesque softness are highly personal. Between 1587 and 1589 Agostino was again in Venice, where he worked on more engravings after Veronese and Tintoretto. He returned to Bologna and executed a *Communion of St Jerome* (Bologna, Pin. N.; see fig.) for the Carthusian monastery in Bologna, having elaborated the composition in a series of detailed preparatory drawings, some of which have survived (Bologna, Pin. N.; Florence, Uffizi; Vienna, Albertina). In 1590 an edition of *Gerusalemme liberata* by Torquato Tasso was published in Genoa, containing ten engravings (B. 182–91) by Agostino, copied from drawings by Bernardo Castello. About the same time he worked with Annibale and Ludovico on the frescoed frieze depicting the *Stories of the Founding of Rome* in the Palazzo Magnani-Salem, Bologna. He was responsible for the scenes of the *Refugees Seeking Shelter on the Campidoglio*, *Romulus with the Spoils of Acronus*, the *Battle between the Romans and the Sabines*, the *Captain of the Veienti Derided* and *Romulus Appearing at Proclo*. From the same period are the *Ecce homo* (Genoa, Pal. Durazzo Pallavicini), noted by Malvasia in 1678 in the Melari house in Bologna, the *Portrait of a Woman Dressed as Judith* (ex-Matthiesen F.A., London), the *Virgin and Child with the Infant St John* (Louisville, KY, Speed A. Mus.) and *St Jerome in Meditation* (Rome, Gal. Doria-Pamphili; attributed to Annibale).

Agostino collaborated with his relations for a few more years. Of the ovals (1592) commissioned by Cesare d'Este for a ceiling of the Palazzo dei Diamanti in Ferrara, surviving letters state that, in addition to a *Pluto* (Modena, Gal. & Mus. Estense), Agostino also executed an *Aeolus*

Agostino Carracci: *Communion of St Jerome*, oil on canvas, 3.76×2.24 m, 1591–2 (Bologna, Pinacoteca Nazionale)

(untraced), which is recorded in a preparatory drawing (Modena, Gal. & Mus. Estense). In the Palazzo Sampieri–Talon, Bologna, where the three Carracci frescoed three rooms of the ground floor (1593–4), Agostino was responsible for the two chimney-pieces depicting *Hercules and Cacus* and *Enceladus Struck by Lightning*. The canvas of *Christ and the Woman of Samaria* (Milan, Brera) comes from the same palazzo and belongs to a series of overdoors (1593–4) by the three Carracci, depicting the three female sinners of the Gospels.

After his second trip to Venice, Agostino also worked on the series known as *Le lascivie* ('The lusts'), which are his most famous engravings (B. 114 and 123–36). The *Nativity* in S Maria della Pioggia, Bologna, and the great *Last Supper* (Madrid, Prado) date to the same period. According to a letter of 8 July 1595 from Annibale to Giulio Fossi, in 1594 the two brothers went to Rome in order to negotiate with Cardinal Odoardo Farnese the contract for the decoration of the Palazzo Farnese, Rome (*see* (3), §I, 1(ii) below). While he was in Rome, Agostino made a renewed study of the work of Michelangelo, which inspired the large *Assumption* (Bologna, Pin. N.), a painting he left unfinished. In Bologna he painted the dated portrait of *Anna Parolini Guicciardini* (1598; Berlin, Gemäldegal.). At the end of the same year he moved to Rome, where he worked with his brother on the vault of the Galleria Farnese. Agostino worked on the two scenes facing each other on the long walls: the subjects, which are difficult to identify, are *Glaucus and Scylla*, beneath which the date 1598 is inscribed, and *Aurora and Cephalus*. He also painted the flanking imitation bronze medallions and *ignudi*. In the vault of the gallery his hand can be distinguished from that of Annibale because of its Raphaelesque sentiment and the less illusionistic rendering of form. Agostino also painted some individual canvases for the Farnese, such as the triple portrait of the *Dwarf Amon, Mad Peter and Hairy Arrigo* (three clowns belonging to the court of Odoardo), *Democritus Laughing*, the *Holy Family with St Margaret and the Infant St John* and *St Jerome Praying* (all Naples, Capodimonte).

Disagreements with his brother and an invitation to Parma by Ranuccio II persuaded Agostino to leave Rome in autumn 1599, at which time he may already have been suffering from poor health (Mancini). In Parma he began to decorate the vault of a room of the Palazzo del Giardino, but it remained unfinished at his death. At the centre are *Three Cupids*; on the three sides, separated by stucco decorations, are scenes depicting *Galatea and the Argonauts*, *Venus and Mars* and a *Warrior Resisting the Enchantment of a Siren*, which Bellori interpreted as being allegories of venal love, lascivious love and virtuous love. Agostino achieved an almost 'purist' elegance in this work. A few small-scale paintings such as the *Holy Family* and *Mary Magdalene Meditating* (both Genoa, Pal. Durazzo Pallavicini) can be dated to the same period. Other works executed for the Farnese and recorded in the inventories, such as the *Galatea*, known through preparatory drawings (Vienna, Albertina) and a number of copies (Parma, Pal. Giardino) or else mentioned by Faberi (two portraits of Ranuccio Farnese, one depicting him dressed in armour and the other in adoration before the Virgin), have not been traced.

Agostino was buried in Parma Cathedral. On 18 January 1603 the Accademia degli Incamminati held a solemn funeral service for him in the church of the Ospedale della Morte in Bologna, in which his commemoration became the pretext for a celebration of the academy itself, as had been the case at Michelangelo's funeral celebrated in Florence by the Accademia del Disegno.

BIBLIOGRAPHY

DBI; *EWA*

L. Faberi: *Orazione in morte di Agostino Carracci* (1603); repr. in C. C. Malvasia: *Felsina pittrice* (1678), ed. G. Zanotti (1841), i, pp. 306–11

G. Mancini: *Considerazioni sulla pittura* (*c.* 1617–21); ed. A. Marucchi and L. Salerno (Rome, 1958), i, pp. 217–18

G. P. Bellori: *Vite* (1672); ed. E. Borea (1976), pp. 115–29

C. C. Malvasia: *Felsina pittrice* (1678); ed. G. Zanotti (1841), i, pp. 263–368

E. Bodmer: 'Le note marginali di Agostino Carracci nell'edizione del Vasari del 1568', *Il Vasari*, x (1939), pp. 89–128

H. Bodmer: 'Die Entwicklung der Stechkunst des Agostino Carracci', *Graph. Kst*, n. s. 1, v (1940), pp. 121–42

T. Mullaly: 'A Self-portrait of Agostino Carracci Painting his Brother Annibale', *Burl. Mag.*, xciii (1951), p. 88

L. Durand: *Les Estampes composant 'Le lascivie' du graveur Agostino Carracci* (Lyon, 1957)

A. De Vita: 'L'animosità di Agostino Carracci contro il Vasari', *Il Vasari*, xvi (1958), pp. 64–78

C. Dempsey: 'Two "Galateas" by Agostino Carracci Re-identified', *Z. Kstgesch.*, xxix (1966), i, pp. 67–70

S. E. Ostrow: *Agostino Carracci* (diss., New York U., 1966)

J. Anderson: 'The Sala di Agostino Carracci in the Palazzo del Giardino', *A. Bull.*, lii (1970), pp. 41–8

L. S. Crandall: 'A Version of Agostino Carracci's *Omnia vincit amor*', *Register* [Lawrence, U. KS] (1970), pp. 25–39

D. S. Pepper: 'Agostino Carracci: Maître et dessinateur', *Rev. A.*, xiv (1971), pp. 39–44

D. DeGrazia Bohlin and B. Bohn: *Italian Masters of the Sixteenth Century (1980)*, 39 [XVIII/i] of *The Illustrated Bartsch*, ed. W. L. Strauss (New York, 1978–) [B.]

A. Nova: 'Postille al giovane Cerano: La data di nascita, un committente e alcune incisioni inedite di Agostino Carracci', *Paragone*, 397 (1983), pp. 46–64

J. Anderson: 'Agostino Carracci', *Around 1610: The Onset of the Baroque* (exh. cat., London, Matthiesen F.A., 1985), pp. 18–25

R. Zapperi: 'Arrigo le Velu, Pietro le Fou, Amon le Nain, et autre bêtes: Autour d'un tableau d'Agostino Carracche', *An., Econ., Soc., Civilis.*, xl (1985), pp. 307–27

G. Bertini: *La Galleria del Duca di Parma: Storia di una collezione* (Bologna, 1987)

D. Benati: 'Agostino Carracci', *La pittura in Italia: Il cinquecento*, ed. G. Briganti (Milan, 1988), ii, pp. 668–9

M. Di Giampaolo: 'Da Venezia a Bologna: Un importante disegno di Agostino Carracci', *Prospettiva*, 57–60 (1989–90), pp. 153–5

D. Benati and L. Peruzzi: 'La decorazione pittorica', *Castello dei Ronchi* (Crevalcore, 1990), pp. 21–9

D. Benati: 'Agostino Carracci', *Disegni emiliani del sei–settecento: Quadri da altare e da stanza*, ed. D. Benati (Milan, 1991), pp. 28–44

M. Di Giampaolo: 'Agostino Carracci', *Disegni emiliani del sei–settecento*, ed. J. Bentini and A. Mazza (Milan, 1991), pp. 26–9

A. Brogi: 'Su un dipinto di Agostino Carracci, e il suo disegno', *Paragone*, 503 (1992), pp. 38–44

R. Williamson: '*Omnia vincit amor*: Un dipinto di Agostino Carracci', *Atti & Mem. Accad. Clementina Bologna*, n.s., 30–31 (1992), pp. 111–50

V. Birke: 'A New Study by Agostino Carracci for the *Last Communion of St Jerome*', *Master Drgs*, xxxi (1993), pp. 404–7

DANIELE BENATI

(3) Annibale Carracci (*b* Bologna, *bapt* 3 Nov 1560; *d* Rome, 15 July 1609). Painter, draughtsman and printmaker, brother of (2) Agostino Carracci. Since his lifetime, he has been considered one of the greatest Italian painters of his age. His masterpiece, the ceiling (1597–1601) of the Galleria Farnese, Rome, merges a vibrant naturalism with the formal language of classicism in a grand and monumental style. Annibale was also instrumental in evolving the 'ideal', classical landscape and is generally credited with the invention of CARICATURE.

I. Life and work. II. Working methods and technique. III. Character and personality. IV. Critical reception and posthumous reputation.

I. Life and work.

1. Paintings. 2. Drawings. 3. Prints.

1. PAINTINGS.

(i) Bologna, 1560–95. (ii) Rome, 1595–1601. (iii) Rome, 1601–9.

(i) Bologna, 1560–95. According to his biographer Malvasia, Annibale was taught painting by his cousin Ludovico, who early recognized the younger man's talents and sent him on a study trip through northern Italy—the so-called *studioso corso*—to acquaint him with the great tradition of Lombard and Venetian Renaissance painting. Malvasia published two letters purportedly written by Annibale to Ludovico in April 1580 from Parma, in which he expressed his enthusiasm at discovering Correggio's art. Whether or not these letters are fabrications, as has been alleged, it is beyond question that Annibale visited

Parma, Venice and other north Italian cities in the early 1580s and that he made careful study of the paintings he saw there.

Since nothing certain is known of Ludovico's work before *c.* 1584, the actual extent of his influence on his cousin's formation cannot be determined. That Annibale was also influenced—if not necessarily taught—by Bartolommeo Passarotti, one of Bologna's chief Mannerist artists, can be deduced, however, from his earliest surviving paintings. These depict genre subjects of a kind popularized by Passarotti and are executed in a broad technique that resembles that used by the older master for such works. Annibale's early genre paintings (*c.* 1581–4) vary from unassuming head studies and exercises in foreshortening, such as a *Drinking Boy*, known in several versions, and the *Dead Christ* (Stuttgart, Gemäldegal.), to more complex pieces, such as the large and ambitious *Butcher's Shop* (Oxford, Christ Church Pict. Gal.) or the stupendous *Bean Eater* (Rome, Gal. Colonna; see fig. 1). Despite their superficial resemblance to works produced by Passarotti and his studio, these pictures are remarkable for the unprecedented directness and sympathy with which they present their simple subjects; light and colour are handled to a maximum effect of naturalism, and the summary brushwork helps to render a first impression as directly as possible.

This freshness of vision also distinguishes Annibale's first major religious work, the *Crucifixion with Saints* (1583; Bologna, S Maria della Carità), a surprisingly powerful work for a 23-year-old artist. The composition—six figures crowded together in the foreground, arranged symmetrically around the cross—derives from Passarotti, but the bold naturalism with which the massive and slightly awkward figures are presented is novel. There is little sense of elegance or artifice. Annibale presented the sacred figures as belonging to the same world as that inhabited by the butchers and tradesmen of his genre pictures, using the same vigorous, at times coarse, technique, though there are also passages of great painterly beauty, which indicate direct knowledge of Venetian painting. The transposition of an 'informal' technique appropriate to low-life paintings to a religious work destined for a public location was deemed revolutionary. Not surprisingly the *Crucifixion* was vehemently attacked by older Bolognese artists, who were offended by the absence of finish and artifice. The fact that the Carracci had by 1583 set up their own academy and were attracting students away from the

1. Annibale Carracci: *Bean Eater*, oil on canvas, 570×680 mm, *c.* 1583–4 (Rome, Galleria Colonna)

established studios no doubt played its part in the *Crucifixion*'s critical reception. Despite all censure, the work evidently impressed local patrons enough to ensure that further commissions soon followed.

The *Baptism* in S Gregorio, Bologna (commissioned in 1583, installed in 1585), shows the artist widening his horizons. The figure style and the clumsy composition attempt to emulate Correggio; the high-keyed palette of the upper portion of the painting, showing God the Father in a glory of angels, reveals the impact of the work of Federico Barocci. Over the next few years, Annibale continued to explore what Barocci and especially Correggio could teach him. The lithe and supple figures and the warm local colours that characterize his contributions to the friezes in the Palazzo Fava, Bologna (1583–4; *see* §I, 2 above), derive from lessons learnt from them. The altarpiece that Annibale executed in 1585 for the Capuchin church in Parma, the *Pietà with SS Francis and Clare* (Parma, G.N.; see fig. 2), reveals a deeper reflection on the art of Correggio. Its composition is more tightly structured than before, and the figures, particularly those in the lower half of the painting, move within a believable space; through pose and gesture, they actively engage the viewer's response. Annibale adopted a Correggesque *sfumato* within a restricted range of warm, earthy browns and reds. The fall of light serves to heighten the painting's expressive impact. In all respects the *Pietà* heralds later developments, and it has rightly been called the 'first Baroque picture' in Italy (Mahon, 1947, p. 274). Baroque tendencies are even more explicit in the *Assumption of the Virgin* (1587; Dresden, Gemäldegal.), painted for the Confraternity of St Roch in Reggio Emilia.

2. Annibale Carracci: *Pietà with SS Francis and Clare*, oil on canvas, 3.74×2.38 m, 1585 (Parma, Galleria Nazionale)

The frieze with the *Stories of the Founding of Rome* (Bologna, Pal. Magnani-Salem) most likely dates from 1589–90. Annibale painted three of the narrative frescoes (*Remus Fighting the Cattle Thieves*; *Remus Brought before King Amulius* and *Romulus Marking the Boundaries of Rome*) and contributed designs for some of the other scenes. The ornamental framework, richer and more complex than that of the Fava friezes, was probably also designed by Annibale, who executed at least one of the groups separating the panels. The increased complexity and energy of the Magnani frieze owe much to Annibale's study of the great Renaissance masters of the Venetian school. Between 1588 and 1595 Venetian influences dominated his work. Agostino's prints after Venetian paintings provided a rich source of inspiration, but presumably Annibale also visited the city again in late 1587 or 1588. He explored the various possibilities offered by the different painters of Venice, testing their solutions against what he could observe in nature. Thus the *Virgin of St Matthew* (1588; Dresden, Gemäldegal. Alte Meister) is an obvious paraphrase of Veronese, but transposes the latter's courtly idealism into a more robust, almost homely realism. The *Venus, Satyr and Two Cupids* (*c.* 1588; Florence, Uffizi), a free variation on a composition by Titian, heightens the sensuousness of its model to a marked degree.

Venetian and Veneto-Flemish examples also influenced Annibale's early landscape paintings, such as his *Hunting* and *Fishing* scenes (*c.* 1587; Paris, Louvre). These pendant canvases are essentially genre scenes set out of doors, with numerous figures in contemporary dress engaged in everyday activities in a landscape setting. Presumably the genre pictures and landscapes were mainly produced for decorative settings, but after *c.* 1588 Annibale no longer felt the need to accept minor commissions for decorative settings or portraits, although he seems to have painted the occasional landscape for his own pleasure. The *River Landscape* (*c.* 1589–90; Washington, DC, N.G.A.; see fig. 3) is an early example of a 'pure' landscape, in which the human presence has become incidental. Portrait painting, a genre that Annibale had occasionally practised in his early years (e.g. the portrait of ?*Claudio Merulo*, 1587; Naples, Capodimonte), likewise virtually disappeared from his oeuvre at this time.

Annibale next attempted to unite powerful Lombard naturalism with central Italian principles of design. A first indication of this process is found in the *Virgin of St Louis* (probably *c.* 1589–90; Bologna, Pin. N.). The rich painterly effects and colour remain Venetian, but the figures are given a new compactness, and their gestures and expressions are more idealized. The composition itself, a design of subtly balanced diagonals, is symmetrical and essentially static. Such features indicate that Annibale consciously sought to moderate the Baroque tendencies of his earlier work with a measure of classical restraint. The increasingly

3. Annibale Carracci: *River Landscape*, oil on canvas, 885×1482 mm, *c.* 1589–90 (Washington, DC, National Gallery of Art)

monumental, dated altarpieces of 1592–3 document his striving towards a new equilibrium: the *Assumption of the Virgin* (1592; Bologna, Pin. N.), the *Virgin of St Luke* (1592; Paris, Louvre) and the *Virgin with SS John and Catherine* (1593; Bologna, Pin. N.). The outcome is magnificently illustrated by the *Resurrection* (1593; Paris, Louvre; see fig. 4). Powerful and clearly delineated figures are set before a splendidly poetic landscape. A suggestion of explosive movement is created by the pattern of diagonals emanating from the sealed tomb in the picture's centre, but these forces remain firmly contained within a closed and harmonious composition. While the figures have the solidity and formal regularity of Classical sculpture, the power of naturalistic description is such that they remain convincing as living beings. By such means, the viewer is persuaded to accept the reality of the supernatural event, even as the degree of idealization removes it from everyday experience. The closely contemporary *Venus Adorned by the Graces* (*c.* 1594; Washington, DC, N.G.A.) illustrates this stylistic phase in a more sensuous mode.

In the late summer of 1594 Annibale left Bologna, with Agostino, in response to an invitation received from Cardinal Odoardo Farnese. Before moving definitively to Rome in 1595, Annibale briefly returned to Bologna in order to finish outstanding commissions. Chief among these was *St Roch Distributing Alms* (Dresden, Gemäldegal. Alte Meister), which had been commissioned as early as *c.* 1587 for the church of S Prospero in Reggio Emilia. The huge canvas, containing many more figures than any previous work by Annibale, thus became the final statement of his Bolognese period and his most felicitous synthesis of classical rhetoric and Lombard naturalism to date. The composition's firm structure owes as much to Raphael as it does to Veronese; as in the late works of Raphael, the many figures all contribute to convey the moral sense of the event. With the *St Roch*, Annibale created the first great history painting of the Baroque.

(ii) Rome, 1595–1601.

(a) Camerino Farnese, c. *1596–7.* On arriving in Rome, Annibale was given lodgings in the Palazzo Farnese. Here he was asked to paint the ceiling of the Cardinal's private study (*c.* 1596–7). This room, known as the Camerino Farnese, is small (*c.* 4.8×9.4 m) with a coved ceiling penetrated by six triangular spandrels over semicircular lunettes. The iconographical programme of the frescoes, probably devised by the Farnese librarian Fulvio Orsini, alludes allegorically to the virtues of the patron. The principal scenes show *Hercules Bearing the Globe*, *Hercules Resting from his Labours* and *Hercules at the Crossroads.* These are treated as *quadri riportati* (simulated easel paintings), the last-named central scene being actually painted on canvas (Naples, Capodimonte; replaced with copy in Rome). A network of gilt stucco bands connects the three scenes and further divides the ceiling into irregular fields, filled with painted ornament simulating stuccowork. Small mythological and allegorical figures are contained within fictitious reliefs painted in chiaroscuro. In the four lunettes on the walls, Annibale represented *Ulysses and Circe*, *Ulysses and the Sirens*, *Perseus and Medusa* and the *Catanian Brothers Carrying their Parents.*

The decorative scheme of the ceiling, indebted to Mantegna's Camera degli Sposi (Mantua, Pal. Ducale; *see* ILLUSIONISM, fig. 1), is north Italian in origin, and the same holds true for the style of the ceiling paintings.

4. Annibale Carracci: *Resurrection*, oil on canvas, 2.17×1.60 m, 1593 (Paris, Musée du Louvre)

Though the first traces of Annibale's direct observation of Roman antiquities and of Michelangelo are visible in some compositions and individual figures, such quotations are contained within a whole that does not, as yet, differ significantly from his most recent Bolognese work. Only in the central canvas, *Hercules at the Crossroads*, is there a more insistent reference to antique sculpture, a tautening of outline and an aggrandizement of forms that serve to give the figures an appropriately 'antique' air.

Annibale's development during the years 1597–1601 is one of progressive assimilation of the principles of Roman classicism: the confrontation with the city's artistic monuments, both ancient and modern, prompted him to adjust his synthesis of northern colourism and central Italian design. There is no sudden shift of allegiance: on the contrary, the influence of Correggio, in abeyance since the late 1580s, enjoyed a sudden and remarkable revival in Annibale's early Roman works (e.g. the *Coronation of the Virgin*, New York, Met.; the *Archangel Gabriel*, Chantilly, Mus. Condé), though now seen through a Raphaelesque prism.

(b) Ceiling of the Galleria Farnese, 1597–1601. A wholehearted conversion to classical ideals was powerfully supported, however, by the requirements of Annibale's next major task, the decoration of the ceiling of the Palazzo Farnese's gallery (for central fresco see fig. 5 below; for whole scheme *see* ITALY, fig. 35). The Galleria Farnese is a long and relatively narrow room (20.14×6.59 m) covered by a barrel vault. Annibale illustrated the set theme—the power of love—with scenes from Classical mythology, which unequivocally and joyfully celebrate profane love as an all-conquering force to which even the Olympian gods are subject. It is unlikely that the programme was intended to convey a moral or religious message, as was formerly thought; the frescoes offer little support for Bellori's reading of them as an allegory of the struggle between Heavenly and Earthly love. The choice of mythological subject-matter appears to have been prompted largely by the fact that the gallery contained some of the finest antique statues of the Farnese collection. Nor does it seem that Annibale was given a highly detailed programme to follow: his preparatory drawings show that devising the ornamental framework took precedence over, and in some cases even determined, the choice of incidents to be included.

The vault confronted the artist with a task unlike any he had undertaken before, both in terms of size and of complexity. For an indeterminate period between October 1598 and the autumn of 1599, he was helped by Agostino, who painted the two large narrative scenes above the gallery's long walls. Others assisted in painting minor parts of the frescoes, but the ceiling is to all intents and purposes Annibale's single-handed creation. Actual execution was probably begun in 1598; the preceding months were used to work out a satisfactory framework for the frescoes. Surviving studies and copies of lost drawings document the evolution of the design (*see* §II, 2 and fig. 6 below), which combines elements from various sources in a novel and inventive way. The vault is conceived as being open to the sky. A painted frieze of alternating mythological paintings and feigned bronze roundels, separated by pairs of atlantids and terms painted to resemble stucco sculptures, illusionistically continues the architectural division of the gallery's lower walls on the ceiling. In front of the frieze and partly obscuring it are four *quadri riportati* in gilt frames, one on each wall, showing episodes from Ovid's *Metamorphoses*. These pictures are imagined as being propped on top of the gallery's walls; the two vertical ones on the short walls illusionistically project forward into space. Other *quadri riportati*, some in the guise of tapestries, others framed as if they were easel pictures, are strung across the crown of the vault. Interspersed among these make-believe paintings and sculptures are various flesh-and-blood figures: putti who play on top of the roundels in the frieze, satyrs seated on the frames of the vertical paintings and nude youths who sit at the terms's feet holding garlands punctuated with masks. Where the painted friezes meet at the four corners of the room, pairs of cupids (Eros and Anteros) are seen playing against a backdrop of blue sky.

The germs of Annibale's invention are to be found in Raphael's Vatican Loggie and, above all, in Pellegrino Tibaldi's frescoes in the Sala di Ulisse (Bologna, Pal. Poggi; *see* TIBALDI, (1), fig. 1), where a similar mixture of *quadratura* framework, simulated easel paintings and 'living' beings is found. Several ornamental motifs recall the Carracci frieze in the Palazzo Magnani, in particular the combination of 'stone', 'bronze' and 'living' figures peopling the vault, while others refer to Raphael's Farnesina Loggia. The decoration's firm integration into the room's

5. Annibale Carracci: *Triumph of Bacchus and Ariadne* (1597–1601), central fresco of the ceiling of the Galleria Farnese, Palazzo Farnese, Rome

architecture—real and imagined—also owes much to the ceiling of the Sistine Chapel; the *ignudi* are only the most obvious references to Michelangelo. Significantly, Annibale rejected Parmese solutions entailing a pronounced *sotto-in-sù* illusionism in favour of Roman prototypes. But, while the decorative structure of the gallery is in a sense a compendium of 16th-century Roman ideas, the sheer inventiveness of its organization and its brilliant naturalism opened up the way for the great Baroque ceilings of the 17th century. The levels of fictitious reality in the Galleria Farnese are both more complex and are handled with much greater logic and persuasiveness than in any of its predecessors. The effect of the whole is that of a colourful imaginary 'picture gallery', richly decorated with bronze and stone sculpture, placed on top of the real sculpture gallery below.

This effect relates to a secondary theme of the frescoes, which is the power of art, and of the art of painting in particular. Annibale's frescoes can be interpreted as a mock-serious statement of his views on the PARAGONE, the 16th-century debate concerning the relative merits of sculpture and painting. Such an interpretation is supported by the many allusions to sculpture to be found in the paintings, most obviously in the 'bronze' reliefs and 'stucco' sculptures but also in the narrative scenes, which contain numerous quotations of renowned statues. In the ceiling Annibale used his command of optical verisimilitude to conjure up various levels of reality, each equally persuasive, in a dazzling and witty display of painterly virtuosity. The *ignudi* and the putti, imagined as being part of the spectator's world, are distinguished from the mythological beings peopling the *quadri riportati*, who are treated in a more idealizing manner, which again invites comparison with ancient sculpture. Yet at the same time supposedly sculpted figures such as the stucco terms and atlantids or the masks seem equally alive; they exchange glances, grimace and otherwise react to events in the narrative scenes or to the spectator on the gallery's floor. The frescoes thus proclaim the painter's skill in creating a duplicate world and encourage the viewer to marvel at the power of his art.

The rich profusion of decorative elements endows the Farnese ceiling with an air of festivity and joyous energy that is maintained within the single scenes. The largest *quadro riportato*, the *Triumph of Bacchus and Ariadne* placed in the centre of the vault (see fig. 5), shows a romping train of satyrs and maenads accompanying the god of wine and his bride. The impression may be of riotous abandon, but the figure groups are contained within a symmetrical and carefully balanced composition of strict classical design. For inspiration, Annibale turned to ancient Bacchic sarcophagi; other famous prototypes, both antique and modern, served for individual figures. In general, the Farnese ceiling exhibits a degree of idealization and classicism greater than anything Annibale had painted before. The figures are aggrandized far beyond the norms set by his previous works, with enlarged features and heroic, sculptural bodies. Outline assumes a greater importance in communicating shape and content; the use of colour tends to isolate each figure from its surroundings. In part such features would have been prompted by the formal requirements of the decoration: the legibility of the frescoes from the gallery's floor some 10 m below was clearly an important consideration. The Classical imagery of the ceiling must also have stimulated Annibale to develop an appropriately classicizing language, as must the inevitable comparison with Raphael's Loggia of Cupid and Psyche in the Villa Farnesina (*see* MYTHOLOGICAL PAINTING AND SCULPTURE, fig. 3).

(c) Other works. The gallery's vault was finished and unveiled in May 1601. Despite the fact that the ceiling occupied most of Annibale's time and energy between 1597 and 1601, a considerable number of easel works can also be dated to the same years. These include the *Adoration of the Shepherds* (Orléans, Mus. B.-A.), a 'romanized' version of a composition created by Correggio; the small *Temptation of St Anthony* on copper (London, N.G.); the large *Nativity of the Virgin* for the basilica in Loreto (Paris, Louvre) and a medium-sized altarpiece commissioned by Cardinal Odoardo Farnese, *Christ in Glory with Four Saints and the Donor* (Florence, Pitti). The most impressive religious picture of these years is the *Pietà* (*c.* 1599–1600; Naples, Capodimonte), likewise painted for Cardinal Odoardo. It blends memories of Correggio and Michelangelo in an image of great emotional power. The *Pietà* is to 16th-century religious painting what the gallery's ceiling is to secular decoration: a recapitulation of past achievements and a signpost to new developments. The *Landscape and River Scene* (*c.* 1596; Berlin, Gemäldegal.) occupies a similar position for landscape painting, integrating Venetian naturalistic elements into a firmly structured design and pointing forward to the invention of the ideal landscape.

(iii) Rome, 1601–9. Before the unveiling of the Farnese ceiling, Annibale was relatively little known in Rome. The first painting by his hand to appear in a public location within the city was a small altarpiece of *St Margaret* in S Caterina dei Funari (installed 1599), a variant replica of a figure in the *Virgin of St Luke* of 1592 and stylistically still part of his late Bolognese years. The radical transformation of his style since he came to Rome could not be appreciated fully until his altarpiece of the *Assumption of the Virgin* for the Cerasi Chapel in S Maria del Popolo was unveiled early in 1601 (*in situ*). Despite the panel's relatively modest size, it has an overpowering impact. Supported by angels, the Virgin erupts from the empty tomb around which the apostles crowd, compressed together in the immediate foreground. Forms are simplified, and the almost geometrical solidity of the figures is intensified by the bright colours and sharp focus typical of panel painting. A staccato tempo of abrupt gestures, sudden twists and turns and unexpected juxtapositions forcefully communicates the picture's dramatic content, replacing the gentler, lyrical rhythms of the *Pietà* or the Farnese ceiling. The fact that the *Assumption* was to be flanked by two paintings by Caravaggio no doubt contributed to its extremist position. Faced with the challenge posed by Caravaggio's anti-idealist style, Annibale took the opposite course. His altarpiece polemicizes Caravaggio's non-selective naturalism, countering it with a conception of religious painting in which sacred figures of idealized perfection are depicted with the greatest possible verisimilitude; a conception that, moreover, had the full authority of tradition behind it.

In his pursuit of an ideal truth that would be emotionally compelling, Annibale turned to the late works of Raphael. It is the latter's designs for the Sistine Chapel tapestries and the *Transfiguration* (*see* RAPHAEL, figs 5 and 6) that determine the last distillation of Annibale's classical style. The Cerasi altarpiece initiates that final development, which has been termed 'hyper-idealism' and which took place in the years 1601–4. These were some of the busiest years of Annibale's life. Cardinal Odoardo put him in charge of the decoration of the Palazzetto Farnese, a *casino* in the garden of the Palazzo Farnese. Within the palazzo itself, the walls of the gallery awaited decoration. The unveiling of the gallery's ceiling, moreover, multiplied demand for Annibale's work, and he accepted several prestigious commissions from other patrons. It must have been obvious that the amount of work awaiting him called for the help of more, and abler, assistants than he had had so far. It seems he used a visit to Bologna, occasioned by Agostino's death in February 1602, to persuade a number of students working in the Carracci Academy to join him in Rome. Francesco Albani, Domenichino and Agostino's young son Antonio soon arrived from Bologna, while Lanfranco and Badalocchio, previously Agostino's pupils in Parma, likewise joined the studio. The first task awaiting the students was the decoration of the Palazzetto Farnese. The walls and ceilings of the *casino*'s rooms were to be adorned with paintings and frescoes, many of them supplied by Annibale's shop, in some cases following his designs. Surviving pictures by the master himself from this project are the *Sleeping Venus* (*c.* 1602; Chantilly, Mus. Condé), an intensely classicizing work illustrating a text by Philostratus Lemnius, and the *Rinaldo and Armida* (Naples, Capodimonte), executed with the help of an assistant.

Payments for scaffolding for the decoration of the walls of the Galleria Farnese start in May 1603; the frescoes were finished before the end of 1604. Annibale himself painted relatively little, leaving most of the project to his assistants. With some studio intervention, he executed the two large scenes on the short walls: the *Rescue of Andromeda* and *Perseus and Phineus*. Above the central doorway facing the windows is a fresco of the *Virgin with a Unicorn*, painted by Domenichino from Annibale's cartoon. Interspersed among the stucco decorations along the long walls are small mythological scenes painted by assistants from sketches provided by the master. Members of the shop were responsible also for the four *Virtues* painted in the end bays of the long walls and for the *imprese* of various members of the Farnese family.

The frescoes on the gallery's walls differ markedly in temper from the *Loves of the Gods* on the ceiling. Whereas the ceiling exudes an air of libidinous festivity, the wall paintings display a sombre, moralistic mood. According to Bellori, they are to be interpreted as allegories of the virtues possessed by the Farnese family. Thus *Perseus Rescuing Andromeda* would symbolize Reason freeing the Soul from Vice, and its pendant, *Perseus and Phineus*, the Triumph of Virtue over Lust. The presence of *Virtues*, the *Virgin and the Unicorn* and the Farnese *imprese* lend some support to such an allegorical reading. It has also been suggested, though, that the wall frescoes continue and expand a theme adumbrated in a more playful fashion on the ceiling, namely the allusion to *paragone* and the nature of art. The two Perseus episodes, concerned with living beings turned into stone, most obviously lend themselves to such a reading, but many of the smaller scenes along the long walls—the *Fall of Icarus* and the Prometheus scenes, among them—can also be seen as allegories of the power of art. If the thematical divergence of the frescoes on the walls from those on the ceiling may therefore have been overestimated, there is no questioning their great disparity in style. Instead of the joyous interweaving in bright sunshine of plastically rounded forms seen on the vault, the wall frescoes display a harsh and stony world of muted colours, where block-like figures are frozen in angular attitudes and from which all sensuousness of depiction has been banned. This is particularly so in the two Perseus scenes painted by Annibale himself, where the geometrical, hard-edged style first encountered in the Cerasi *Assumption* is further developed.

One of Annibale's most admired paintings, the *Pietà* (or the '*Three Maries*'; London, N.G.), displays many of the same characteristics and is most likely to date from the same years. It is the final result of a lifelong fascination with Correggio's painting of the subject in Parma. Though the influence of this prototype is still perceptible, its emphasis on the *affetti*, the 'movements of the soul', gives it a wholly new meaning and places it squarely within the 17th century. A similar emotionality invests the *Pietà with St Francis* (Paris, Louvre), painted for the Mattei Chapel in S Francesco a Ripa, a work largely executed in 1603 but left unfinished until *c.* 1607, and the small *Stoning of St Stephen* on copper (*c.* 1603; Paris, Louvre). The latter work is particularly innovative in that it applies the rules of monumental design to small-scale history painting.

Early in 1605 Annibale succumbed to an apoplectic attack brought on, it seems, by physical exhaustion. Though he recovered enough to accept new commissions later that year, the attack left him prey to a profound melancholy, which was exacerbated by the lack of appreciation shown him by his main patron, Cardinal Odoardo Farnese, who paid a mere 500 scudi for his labours in the Galleria Farnese. Annibale, deeply wounded by this slight to his honour, left the Cardinal's service in August 1605 and found lodgings on the Quirinal Hill. Illness and depression compelled him to relinquish most of his outstanding commissions to his pupils. In 1603–4 he had agreed to paint six lunettes with New Testament scenes in a landscape setting for the chapel in the palazzo of Cardinal Pietro Aldobrandini (Rome, Gal. Doria-Pamphili). Before 1605 he had painted one of the lunettes, the *Flight into Egypt*, and designed the *Entombment*. The *Flight into Egypt* (*see* LANDSCAPE PAINTING, fig. 6) is the archetypal statement of what has come to be known as the 'ideal landscape', a rationally constructed landscape in which human figures, buildings and nature are held in perfect balance. In 1605 the commission was turned over to Albani, who finished the *Entombment* and, with the help of other assistants, executed the remaining four lunettes. Annibale had in 1604 also contracted to paint the chapel of Juan Enriques de Herrera (destr.) in S Giacomo degli Spagnuoli (frescoes and altarpiece divided between Madrid, Prado; Barcelona, Mus. Catalunya; and Rome, S Maria di Montserrato). The master designed all the frescoes and executed some of them before March 1605, when illness forced him to put Albani in charge of the remainder. Despite the resulting unevenness of execution, the spare and sober Herrera frescoes are important testimonies to the final phase of Annibale's development.

Annibale's last years were marked by deep melancholia and artistic sterility. He appears to have worked only sporadically, though continuing to supervise the few paintings put forth in his name by his students (altarpieces in S Onofrio, Rome, and in the Farnese Chapel in the abbey church at Grottaferrata). In July 1608, in an attempt to get him to work again, his remaining students drew up a contract in which each member of the studio undertook to finish at least one small painting every five weeks. The attempt seems to have had little, if any, effect. Following a visit to Naples in the company of the young Bolognese painter Baldassare Aloisi (1577–1638), Annibale died in Rome. An inventory of his meagre belongings drawn up shortly afterwards lists several unfinished paintings, none of them identifiable. According to his wish, Annibale was buried in the Pantheon.

2. DRAWINGS. All three Carracci were consummate draughtsmen, but Annibale especially has always been esteemed as one of the greatest draughtsmen in Western art. His drawings show an apparently effortless grasp of shape and structure, together with an extraordinary sensitivity to light and atmosphere. Thematically they cover a wide range. Figure studies and other kinds of preparatory drawings predominate, but there are also numerous sheets without such a specific purpose, particularly from his early years. These document his lively interest in the world around him and his keen powers of observation; among them are domestic scenes, portrait studies, sketches of beggars and vagrants, and scenes witnessed in the streets of Bologna. In the 1580s Annibale produced a series of drawings of ambulant tradesmen in characteristic costumes (one survives; Edinburgh, N.G.). These drawings, apparently made for the artist's own pleasure, were later engraved and published by Mosini as the *Arti di Bologna* (Rome, 1630).

Another area of interest was landscape: drawn landscape studies survive from all phases of his career. Mostly in pen and ink, they generally appear to have been done in the studio; none can be related to extant paintings or prints. Early landscape drawings show clear Venetian influence in arrangement and poetical mood, while the landscapes of the last Roman years are much starker, becoming almost 'stenographic' in their economical notation of form and light. Relatively few life studies of a model in an 'academic' pose can reliably be attributed to Annibale; generally accepted examples all date from his early years.

Most of Annibale's surviving drawings were made in preparation for painted compositions. Early figure drawings and composition studies are concerned with the distribution of light and shadow rather than outline; they exploit a variety of colouristic techniques in strong chiaroscuro. Influenced by Correggio's draughtsmanship, the young Annibale preferred red chalk for figure studies, often smudging the chalk or combining it with red wash or white heightening to obtain a richer, more atmospheric effect. Occasionally he used a lightly oiled black chalk or charcoal in a similarly soft manner. Pen drawings of the early years are frequently enriched with differently coloured washes or make use of tinted paper; unlike the chalk drawings, they show a clear debt to the older generation of Bolognese draughtsmen. As his style matured, Annibale's drawings became more disciplined. The predominance of black chalk from *c.* 1588 onwards, often in combination with white chalk on blue or grey paper, appears to be due to Venetian influence.

Once Annibale had moved to Rome, the graphic definition of form and anatomical structure assumed greater importance. The celebrated figure studies for the Farnese ceiling (see fig. 6) show a simplified chalk technique: shading is used mainly within well-defined contours to modulate form, and the painterly softness of earlier studies gives way to a more sculptural treatment. Human form is now conceptualized and idealized beyond the particular. Annibale's later pen drawings likewise became more sparing in their use of wash, until in his last years they acquired a harsh, inelegant aspect that is as expressive as it is unprecedented.

6. Annibale Carracci: *Polyphemus*, black chalk, heightened with white, 521×385 mm, *c.* 1598 (Paris, Musée du Louvre); study for the ceiling of the Galleria Farnese, Palazzo Farnese, Rome

Always admired, Annibale's drawings were collected from an early date. In the 17th century, the Roman Francesco Angeloni, a friend of Agucchi and Bellori, owned no less than 600 drawings connected with the Galleria Farnese; these were acquired by the French painter Pierre Mignard and were subsequently owned by Pierre Crozat and Pierre-Jean Mariette before being dispersed. (The two largest actual holdings are in the Louvre, Paris, and in the Royal Library at Windsor Castle. Important and representative groups are also to be found at Chatsworth House, Derbys; the Uffizi, Florence; the Metropolitan Museum of Art, New York; the Ashmolean, Oxford; and the Albertina, Vienna. Most print rooms contain at least some examples.)

Sources from the 17th century almost unanimously credit Annibale with the invention of caricature. However, no true caricatures survive that can be securely attributed to him. It therefore remains speculative whether it was Annibale or Agostino (by whom true caricatures are known) who was primarily responsible for the invention of the genre.

3. PRINTS. Annibale's proficiency as a draughtsman relates directly to his accomplishment as a printmaker. Though his output in the medium is limited—only seven finished engravings and twelve etchings can be attributed to him—his prints are of exceptional quality. Apart from two reproductive engravings produced at the beginning of his career, he worked only from his own inventions. It was Agostino who instructed Annibale in the technique of engraving, and the earliest prints reliably attributed to the latter (e.g. the *Crucified Christ*, 1581; B. 5) follow the older brother's manner. A more personal style of engraving is first encountered in the small *St Jerome* (*c.* 1583–5; B. 13). Annibale's engravings reveal a greater feeling for texture and atmosphere than do Agostino's, and he showed more interest in establishing mood. He had a marked preference for etching, exploiting its spontaneity and resemblance to pen drawing to great effect. The etching of the *Holy Family with St John the Baptist* (1590; B. 11), a tender domestic scene rendered with short, vibrant strokes creating a soft luminosity, is a typical example. This etching manner is developed in the *St Jerome in the Wilderness* (B. 14) and the *Susanna and the Elders* (B. 14), both datable to the early 1590s.

The *Pietà* (or '*Christ of Caprarola*', 1597; B. 4) is Annibale's most famous work in the medium. It combines the techniques of engraving, etching and drypoint in a technically intricate image of great originality and emotional power. The only other print dating from Annibale's years in the service of the Farnese is the engraving of the *Drunken Silenus* (*c.* 1598–1600; B. 18). It was pulled from a silver platter that he engraved, the so-called Tazza Farnese (Naples, Capodimonte). A companion piece, a silver bread basket known as the Paniere Farnese (Naples,

Capodimonte), was likewise designed by Annibale but was engraved by Francesco Villamena. In imagery and style, both works are intimately related to the Farnese ceiling.

Annibale returned to printmaking in 1606, the date of the *Madonna della scodella* (B. 9) and *Christ Crowned with Thorns* (B. 3). Both are powerful examples of his expressive late style, with simplified, bulky forms looming large in the picture field. An undated *Adoration of the Shepherds* (B. 2) was designed in 1606 or possibly even later.

II. Working methods and technique.

The Carracci reinstated the Renaissance practice of making life studies in preparation for painted compositions. Annibale carefully considered beforehand a picture's composition, the poses of individual figures it contained and the distribution of light and shadow within it, before actually beginning to paint. Surviving drawings, especially of his Bolognese period, provide ample evidence of his continuous referral to nature and the model. In Rome, faced with the vastly more complex decorative projects for Cardinal Farnese, Annibale's preparatory processes became even more laborious, as the numerous studies for the Camerino and especially those for the ceiling of the Galleria Farnese attest. All the classic preparatory stages are represented in the surviving material related to these projects: rapid compositional sketches, more elaborate general studies that clarify the distribution of light, life studies of individual figures and anatomical details and full-scale cartoons. His working methods thus conformed to established central Italian traditions. Annibale is said by Bellori to have made preparatory colour sketches or oil *bozzetti* in the Venetian tradition, but no undisputed examples are known.

Whether in oils or fresco, Annibale's painted works display an admirable crispness of detail and a masterly technique. The roughness of touch that characterizes the early genre paintings and the *Crucifixion* of 1583 was supplanted soon thereafter by a smoother handling influenced by Correggio's carefully glazed paintings. Yet the Bolognese canvases in general continue to display a fondness for painterly effects of Venetian origin; the variegated texture of brushstrokes helps create an impression of movement and shifting light, and a more refined variant of the broken touch of the genre paintings occasionally resurfaces in paintings with a decorative purpose (e.g. the *River Landscape* of 1590). Even in his Roman period, when naturalism was no longer a function of technique but of drawing and the paint surface of his pictures had generally become tighter and more uniform, Annibale remained sensitive to painterly effects, as demonstrated in the marvellous suggestion of nature in movement in the Aldobrandini *Flight into Egypt*.

Annibale has generally not been rated very highly as a colourist. It is true that he was not particularly innovative in his use or choice of colours, and colouring in his paintings—even the earliest ones—is usually subservient to design. That he nonetheless had a thorough understanding of the laws of colour and optics is clear from his Bolognese paintings, which contain splendidly poetic passages of pure colour. In its different way, the Farnese ceiling is an unparalleled masterpiece of bright, naturalistic colour applied in true fresco. It is only in the works of his last years that Annibale renounced altogether the sensuous appeal of colour to concentrate on the rendering of the *affetti* through gesture and facial expression.

Annibale transmitted his working methods to his pupils. According to 17th-century writers, Annibale's training of studio assistants to imitate his manner was a second aspect of his reform: not since Raphael had Rome witnessed a comparable school of talented artists harmoniously working together under the direction of one master. In Bologna, Annibale did not have pupils in the strict sense: students attending the Carracci Academy were instructed by all three leading members of the family. And while he did have assistants, such as Innocenzo Tacconi between 1595 and 1602, who helped him paint the Farnese ceiling and other works, it was not until 1602 that a true school formed around the artist. Its members, most of them far more talented than Tacconi, included Albani, Domenichino, Lanfranco, Badalocchio, Antonio Carracci and the Milanese G. A. Solari (*c.* 1581–1666). More loosely associated with the studio were Antonio Maria Panico (*c.* ?1570–*c.* 1620), in the service of another member of the Farnese family, and the landscape specialist Giovanni Battista Viola.

It was thus only from 1602 that Annibale had an opportunity to mould the talents of young artists. He taught them not only through his own example but also by encouraging them to study the monuments of Roman art on which he had based his late manner: works such as the *Laokoon* (Rome, Vatican, Mus. Pio-Clementino), the Vatican Stanze and the Sistine Chapel, Raphael's Loggie and the like were copied, dissected and analysed by the master and his students. Annibale used his pupils' assistance in various ways. In a large commission, such as the walls of the Galleria Farnese, he let them execute subsidiary scenes according to his designs and under his close supervision. In the Palazzetto Farnese, on the other hand, the pupils contributed frescoes and canvases with minimal help from the master. The easy partnership between peers that had characterized the Carracci shop in Bologna appears to have influenced Annibale's collaboration with his pupils in his Roman studio. He sometimes let them execute minor passages in his own works, and at other times he intervened in works substantially designed by one of the pupils, either by providing drawings or by correcting or adding some passages himself. The students were given considerable stylistic latitude, even in projects for which Annibale bore nominal responsibility; the walls of the Galleria Farnese and the Herrera Chapel frescoes are cases in point. However, the circumstances under which these works had to be executed, under great pressure of time and speed, and the illness that struck Annibale early in 1605 no doubt made this a practical rather than a desirable solution. Through his teaching and example, Annibale successfully inculcated the principles of his style in his pupils, thus initiating a school, the influence of which was to last well over two centuries.

III. Character and personality.

Very little written material survives by Annibale Carracci's own hand. Most revealing are his marginal notes in a copy of Vasari's *Vite* (Bologna, Bib. Com. Archiginnasio), in which he vented his fierce indignation at the historian's Tuscan bias and expressed his admiration for those Venetian painters whose achievements Vasari, in his eyes, had belittled. The impromptu annotations provide fascinating insights into Annibale's temperament as well as his stylistic allegiance—virtually all the notes deal with Venetian artists, and the only Bolognese painter to receive favourable mention is Pellegrino Tibaldi—but unfortunately it cannot be established exactly when they were written. Though it has been argued on circumstantial evidence that they were written only after the artist settled in Rome in 1595, the very impulsiveness and indignation of the notes seem more characteristic of Annibale's youth. The strong pro-Venetian sentiment suggests that they were written shortly after a trip to the Republic, perhaps in the years 1588–90, when Venetian influence on Annibale's painting was at its peak.

Aside from these notes, only one letter (Reggio Emilia, Archv Stato), addressed to Giulio Fossi, a patron, in 1595, is indisputably Annibale's. Malvasia published some otherwise unknown letters (and fragments), which he attributed to the artist, but their authenticity has not been universally accepted. Despite the paucity of the evidence, a consistent picture of Annibale's personality emerges from it, when amplified by the accounts of his biographers. They portray him as a warm-blooded man, as choleric as he was compassionate, a man of few words, to whom his personal independence was paramount. Annibale saw himself first and foremost as a painter and preferred the company of craftsmen to that of persons of more elevated rank; the status of courtier, forced on him during his years in the service of Cardinal Farnese, did not suit him and ultimately contributed to his breakdown. Annibale took little heed of his outward appearance, dressing casually like an artisan, and—in contrast to his brother Agostino—set little store by social accomplishments or laymen's acclaim. There are several anecdotes about him sharply deflating Agostino's pretensions by reminding his brother that they were the sons of a tailor, and themselves craftsmen. On the other hand, Annibale took his profession extremely seriously, reacting violently to any real or imagined slight to his stature as a painter. He could be intensely jealous of other artists, notoriously so in the case of the much younger Guido Reni; yet he was an extremely generous teacher.

At several points in his life Annibale painted his own portrait (e.g. *c.* 1585, Milan, Brera; 1593, Parma, G.N.). The most revealing is the unparalleled *Self-portrait on an Easel* (*c.* 1603; St Petersburg, Hermitage), which shows Annibale's portrait on an easel from which his palette hangs, in a gloomy, ill-defined interior. A dog and cat lurk in the foreground; further back, before a window, either a sculpture or a plaster model is seen. Roughly painted with evident haste, this sombre work reduces the artist's portrait to one of several objects in a nondescript space. The artist thus dissociated himself from his own image and work and subjected both to the judgement of the viewer.

IV. Critical reception and posthumous reputation.

Annibale's standing as one of the foremost painters of his generation was recognized by his contemporaries, as the earliest biographical notices attest (Mancini; Mosini; Baglione). The two standard biographies of the artist were published a generation later, by Giovanni Pietro Bellori (1672) and Carlo Cesare Malvasia (1678): although generally reliable, both are biased, Bellori in favour of the Roman Annibale, Malvasia of the Bolognese. These biases reflect a debate that sprang up shortly after, if not during, Annibale's lifetime, namely whether he had been the greater painter in Bologna or in Rome. It was Bellori's view that Annibale was able to achieve that synthesis of *colore* and *disegno* that so successfully restored the art of painting only after he had seen the marvels of Rome; the artist's Emilian period is consequently presented as a prelude to that crowning achievement. The Bolognese Malvasia, on the other hand, sought to emphasize the north Italian roots of the Carracci reform. He believed Ludovico to have been its prime instigator and repeatedly challenged the received opinion that Annibale was pre-eminent. In his eyes, Annibale had abandoned the cause of Emilian painting by defecting to Rome, and he held that the qualitative level of Annibale's art had suffered as a consequence. On the whole, it is Bellori's view, that it was precisely by going south that Annibale was able to consolidate the achievements of the Bolognese reform movement, that has prevailed.

Well into the 19th century, the position of Annibale Carracci as one of Italy's greatest painters remained unassailable. It was not until the advent of Romanticism that the Carracci 'restoration' of painting came to be seen as a reactionary rather than a progressive act. For the first time, the concept underlying the reform—the conciliation of disparate elements of style coupled with renewed study of their basis in nature—was regarded with suspicion and labelled 'eclecticism'. In a remarkably short time this derogatory view of the Carracci's achievement led to a wholesale rejection of it as merely technical and sterile.

Annibale's reputation was slowly revived only in the second quarter of the 20th century, at the hands of a few scholars such as Roberto Longhi, Heinrich Bodmer, Rudolph Wittkower and Denis Mahon. Their publications rescued the Carracci from critical oblivion; Mahon, in particular, sought to remove the stigma of eclecticism that still clung to their works. A large loan exhibition of paintings and drawings of the Carracci, held in Bologna in 1956, offered both a consecration of these efforts and a first possibility for stocktaking.

Other scholars continued to research Annibale's oeuvre, its chronology and its iconographical aspects, culminating in Donald Posner's monograph (1971). Since the later 1970s the scholarly debate has shifted away from problems of attribution and interpretation and come to focus on the role played by theoretical concerns in the daily practice of the Carracci, especially Annibale. At issue is the question of whether or not the Carracci conceived of their pictorial style as a 'method', based in objective theory and therefore capable of being taught to others, or whether the intuitive aspects of painting prevailed in their artistic practice. Those who defend the latter view (including Mahon and Posner) see the Carracci Academy as little different from an extended painters' workshop, despite its somewhat grandiose title, and characterize Annibale as an intuitive artist to whom theory and learning were of little practical value. Others—Dempsey foremost among them—emphasize the role played by theory in the Carracci's practice and contend that the academy was modelled on contemporary literary academies and functioned much as an institution of higher education might. In their eyes, Annibale's approach to painting was shaped by intellectual concerns. The debate hinges to a large extent on the interpretation of two specific sources: the funeral oration for Agostino Carracci, pronounced by Lucio Faberio in 1603, and Malvasia's biographies of the three Carracci, published in 1678. Virtually all current knowledge of the Accademia degli Incamminati and its curriculum depends on these two sources. Whereas Faberio's oration has been shown to be a rhetorical exercise that reveals little about daily practice in the academy in its pre-1595 heyday, Malvasia's account is less easily dismissed. His credibility has been questioned on numerous occasions, but the evidence is far from unequivocal, and in recent years strong arguments have been put forward in support of his essential reliability. Archival research may ultimately resolve the issue. Detailed investigations of Annibale's social background and professional milieu may help to confirm or refute his biographers' otherwise unsubstantiated statements.

There has never been any question, however, that Annibale's achievement was of the highest order or that it brought about a revitalization of the great tradition of Italian Renaissance painting. The principles of the Carracci reform set the course for painting in Italy and France in the 17th century. With greater clarity of purpose and intellectual force than either Ludovico or Agostino, Annibale demonstrated how the past could be revitalized and adapted to contemporary ends. His later Roman work prepared the way for the classical strain of Baroque art, exemplified by his pupil Domenichino and perpetuated by Poussin, Le Brun and the French academic tradition. At the same time Annibale's example helped shape the 'anti-classical' Baroque: Lanfranco, its first great practitioner, was no less receptive a student of his work than was Domenichino. Historically, Annibale's role in Italian painting can be compared only to Raphael's before him. It is evident that the artist himself and his admirers were well aware of the parallel, and it is only fitting that Annibale should be buried in the Pantheon, next to the tomb of Raphael.

BIBLIOGRAPHY

Exhaustive bibliographies may be found in *Mostra dei Carracci: I dipinti* (exh. cat. by G. C. Cavalli, Bologna, Pal. Archiginnasio, 1956), pp. 251–64; and in D. Posner's article on Annibale Carracci in the *DBI*. Of the items published before 1977, the present bibliography includes only the most essential.

EARLY SOURCES AND DOCUMENTS

G. Mancini: *Considerazioni sulla pittura* (1614–30); ed. A. Marucchi and L. Salerno, 2 vols (Rome, 1956)

G. Baglione: *Vite* (1642); ed. V. Mariani (1935)

G. P. Bellori: *Vite* (1672); ed. E. Borea (1976)

——: *Le Vite de' Annibale e Agostino Carracci* (Rome, 1672); Eng. trans. by C. Enggass, foreword by R. Enggass (University Park, PA, and London, 1968)

C. C. Malvasia: *Felsina pittrice* (1678); ed. G. Zanotti (1841)

K. Andrews: 'Annibale Carracci's Last Residence in Rome', *Burl. Mag.*, cxvi (1974), pp. 32–4

M. Fanti: 'Le postille carraccesche alle *Vite* del Vasari', *Il Carrobbio*, v (1979), pp. 147–64

R. Zapperi: 'L'inventario di Annibale Carracci', *Antol. B.A.*, iii/9–12 (1979), pp. 62–7

M. Fanti: 'Ancora sulle postille carraccesche alle *Vite* del Vasari: In buona parte sono di Annibale', *Il Carrobbio*, vi (1980), pp. 136–41

C. Dempsey: 'The Carracci *postille* to Vasari's *Lives*', *A. Bull.*, lxviii (1986), pp. 72–6

GENERAL

D. Mahon: *Studies in Seicento Art and Theory* (London, 1947)

S. J. Freedberg: *Circa 1600: A Revolution in Style in Italian Painting* (Cambridge, MA, and London, 1983)

MONOGRAPHS

D. Posner: *Annibale Carracci: A Study in the Reform of Italian Painting around 1590*, 2 vols (London, 1971); review by A. W. A. Boschloo in *Paragone*, xxiii/269 (1972), pp. 66–79

A. W. A. Boschloo: *Annibale Carracci in Bologna: Visible Reality in Art after the Council of Trent*, 2 vols (The Hague, 1974)

C. Dempsey: *Annibale Carracci and the Beginnings of Baroque Style* (Glückstadt, 1977); review by D. Posner in *Burl. Mag.*, cxxi (1979), pp. 44–5

P. J. Cooney and G. Malafarina: *L'opera completa di Annibale Carracci*, Class. A., 87 (Milan, 1979)

R. Zapperi: *Annibale Carracci: Ritratto di artista da giovane* (Turin, 1989)

CAMERINO FARNESE AND GALLERIA FARNESE

J. R. Martin: 'Immagini della Virtù: The Paintings of the Camerino Farnese', *A. Bull.*, xxxviii (1956), pp. 91–112

R. Bacou: 'Two Unpublished Drawings by Annibale Carracci for the Palazzo Farnese', *Master Drgs*, ii/1 (1964), pp. 40–44

W. Vitzthum: 'Two Drawings by Annibale Carracci in Madrid and a Comment on the Farnese Gallery', *Master Drgs*, ii/1 (1964), pp. 45–9

J. R. Martin: *The Farnese Gallery* (Princeton, 1965)

E. Battisti and others: '*Amore carnale e divino*: Discussione sulla galleria dei Carracci', *Marcatrè* (1966), pp. 298–304

C. Dempsey: '*Et nos cedamus amori*: Observations on the Farnese Gallery', *A. Bull.*, l (1968), pp. 363–74

R. Distelberger: 'Beobachtungen zur Wanddekoration der Galleria Farnese', *Wien. Jb. Kstgesch.*, xxv (1972), pp. 210–17

F.-C. Uginet: *Le Palais Farnèse à travers les documents financiers, 1535–1612* (Rome, 1980)

C. Dempsey: 'Annibale Carrache au Palais Farnèse', *Le Palais Farnèse* (Rome, 1981), i/1, pp. 269–311

R. Zapperi: 'Per la datazione degli affreschi della Galleria Farnese', *Mél. Ecole Fr. Rome: Moyen Age, Temps Mod.*, xciii/2 (1981), pp. 821–2

C. Thiem: 'A Newly Discovered Sketch by Annibale Carracci for the Farnese Ceiling', *Burl. Mag.*, cxxvii (1985), pp. 525–6

I. Marzik: *Das Bildprogramm der Galleria Farnese in Rom* (Berlin, 1986)

Les Carrache et les décors profanes: Actes du colloque organisé par l'Ecole française de Rome: Rome, 1986

A. Chastel, G. Briganti and R. Zapperi: *Gli 'Amori degli dei': Nuove indagini sulla Galleria Farnese* (Rome, 1987)

C. Robertson: '*Ars vincit omnia*: The Farnese Gallery and Cinquecento Ideas about Art', *Mél. Ecole Fr. Rome: Moyen Age, Temps Mod.*, cii/1 (1990), pp. 7–41

A. Reckermann: *'Amor Mutuus': Annibale Carraccis Galleria Farnese-Fresken und das Bild-Denken der Renaissance* (Cologne and Vienna, 1991)

DRAWINGS

D. DeGrazia Bohlin: 'The Influence of Parmigianino on the Drawings of Agostino and Annibale Carracci', *Le arti a Bologna e in Emilia dal 16 al 17 secolo: Atti del 24 Congresso internazionale di storia dell'arte: Bologna, 1979*, pp. 141–50

P. Rosenberg: 'Un Carton de Baroche et un dessin d'Annibal Carrache inédits', *Per A. E. Popham*, ed. I. Consigli and A. Consigli (Parma, 1981), pp. 131–3

D. DeGrazia Bohlin: 'Un'*Adorazione dei pastori* di Annibale Carracci', *Ant. Viva*, xxii/ii (1983), pp. 38–9

C. R. Puglisi: 'Two Newly Identified Drawings by Annibale Carracci for the Herrera Chapel', *Master Drgs*, xxii (1984), pp. 310–15

M. Jaffé: 'A Drawing by Annibale in the Fitzwilliam', *Burl. Mag.*, cxxvii (1985), p. 776

A. Weston-Lewis: 'Annibale Carracci and the Antique', *Master Drgs*, xxx/3 (1992), pp. 287–313

PRINTS

H. Bodmer: 'Bemerkungen zu Annibale Carraccis graphischem Werk', *Graph. Kst.*, iii/3–4 (1938), pp. 107–17

O. Kurz: 'Engravings on Silver by Annibale Carracci', *Burl. Mag.*, xcvii (1955), pp. 282–7

D. DeGrazia Bohlin and B. Bohn: *Italian Masters of the Sixteenth Century (1980)*, 39 [XVIII/i] of *The Illustrated Bartsch*, ed. W. Strauss (New York, 1978–) [B.]
Italian Etchers of the Renaissance and Baroque (exh. cat., Boston, MA, Mus. F.A., 1989), pp. 105–12

SPECIALIST STUDIES

H. Tietze: 'Annibale Carraccis Galerie im Palazzo Farnese und seine römische Werkstätte', *Jb. Ksthist. Samml. Allerhöch. Ksrhaus.*, xxvi (1906–7), pp. 49–182
H. Bodmer: 'Die Jugendwerke des Annibale Carracci', *Z. Bild. Kst*, lviii (1924), pp. 104–13
R. Longhi: 'Annibale, 1584?', *Paragone*, viii/89 (1957), pp. 33–42
D. S. Pepper: 'Annibale Carracci ritrattista', *A. Illust.*, vi (1973), pp. 127–37
C. Dempsey: 'Annibale Carracci's *Christ and the Canaanite Woman*', *Burl. Mag.*, cxxiii (1981), pp. 91–5
M. Jaffé: 'The *Penitent Magdalene in a Landscape* by Annibale Carracci', *Burl. Mag.*, cxxiii (1981), pp. 88–91
M. Royalton-Kisch: 'Annibale's Altarpiece for the Palazzo Farnese', *Burl. Mag.*, cxxiii (1981), p. 488
A. Brogi: 'Considerazioni sul giovane Annibale Carracci e qualche aggiunte', *Paragone*, xxxv/413 (1984), pp. 36–49
S. Ginzburg: 'The Portrait of *Agucchi* at York Reconsidered', *Burl. Mag.*, cxxxvi (1994), pp. 4–14

(4) Antonio Carracci (*b* Venice, ?1583; *d* Rome, 8 April 1618). Painter, son of (2) Agostino Carracci. He was born either *c.* 1583 (Baglione) or in 1589 (Bellori). His mother was a Venetian courtesan named Isabella. After his father's death, he joined the Roman household of his uncle Annibale Carracci. While Antonio may have collaborated with other studio assistants on the wall frescoes (1603–4) of the Galleria Farnese and the decoration (1606; commissioned from Francesco Albani) of some rooms in the Palazzo Mattei di Giove, Rome, his earliest undisputed works date from after Annibale's death in 1609. At that time, according to Monsignor G. B. Agucchi (Malvasia), Antonio returned briefly to Bologna, with the intention of joining Ludovico Carracci's studio, but the proposed collaboration came to nothing. A frescoed *Vision of St Francis* in the lower oratory of S Colombano was most probably painted during this Bolognese sojourn, and his *Burial of Christ* (Rome, Gal. Borghese) dates from *c.* 1609. He returned to Rome in 1610 and assisted Guido Reni in the Pauline Chapel of the Palazzo del Quirinale, where he painted *Virtues* and other subsidiary figures on the walls. Shortly afterwards he collaborated with other former pupils of Annibale Carracci in S Sebastiano fuori le mura, where he executed a fresco (now damaged) on the sacristy ceiling.

Antonio's style displays an attractive blend of Emilian naturalism and Roman classicism. Strongly influenced by Reni, he developed a delicate manner that combines graceful purity of line with a strong narrative impulse. The decoration of three chapels in S Bartolomeo all'Isola, Rome, commissioned by Cardinal Michelangelo Tonti (probably in 1611), constitutes his major public work. One chapel contains scenes from the *Passion*, another episodes from the *Life of the Virgin*. More accomplished and better preserved than these are the frescoes (?1614) in the third chapel, dedicated to Carlo Borromeo. Antonio also provided an altarpiece for the same chapel, showing the saint kneeling before an altar, which is now in the church's sacristy.

In 1615 Antonio married the Cypriot Rosa Leoni. The following year he decorated the Stanza del Diluvio in the Palazzo del Quirinale with a ceiling fresco of angels supporting the papal coat of arms and a frieze of sibyls and putti alongside octagonal panels showing biblical scenes set in extensive landscapes. These works reveal that he was briefly influenced by Agostino Tassi and Orazio Gentileschi. One scene from the frieze, the *Deluge*, reappears in Antonio's best-known easel painting (1616–17; Paris, Louvre). Other reliably attributed works of this period include an altarpiece of the *Virgin and Child with Saints* from S Giovanni a Capo di Borgo, Lucca (*c.* 1615; Berlin, Gemäldegal.), and an oval panel with *Alexander and King Porus* (*c.* 1616; priv. col., see Schleier, fig. 7), painted for Cardinal Alessandro Montalto. He also supplied an *Annunciation* (*c.* 1616) for the chapel of the Madonna della Colonna in Savona Cathedral. His last paintings, such as the *Death of St Cecilia* (Montpellier, Mus. Fabre), are striking anticipations of the classicism of Nicolas Poussin or Eustache Le Sueur.

BIBLIOGRAPHY

DBI [with full bibliog.]
G. Mancini: *Considerazioni sulla pittura* (1614–30); ed. A. Marucchi and L. Salerno, 2 vols (Rome, 1956)
G. Baglione: *Vite* (1642); ed. V. Mariani (1935), pp. 150–51
C. C. Malvasia: *Felsina pittrice* (1678); ed. G. Zanotti (1841), i, pp. 369–73
F. Frisoni: 'Antonio Carracci: Riflessioni e aggiunte', *Paragone*, xxxi/367 (1980), pp. 22–38
E. Schleier: 'Ancora su Antonio Carracci e il ciclo di Alessandro Magno per il cardinal Montalto', *Paragone*, xxxii/381 (1981), pp. 10–25
R. Zapperi: 'I ritratti di Antonio Carracci', *Paragone*, xxxviii/449 (1987), pp. 3–22
C. van Tuyll van Serooskerken: 'Two Preparatory Drawings by Antonio Carracci', *Master Drgs*, xxxi (1993), pp. 428–32

C. VAN TUYLL VAN SEROOSKERKEN

Carrand, Louis (*b* Lyon, 22 April 1827; *d* Florence, 21 Sept 1888). French collector. His father Jean-Baptiste Carrand (1792–1871) was a collector of medieval and Renaissance decorative objects (Byzantine and Gothic ivories, Renaissance maiolica, enamelwork, arms, bronzes and coins) and a connoisseur of manuscripts and documents, first in Lyon and then in Paris, where Louis worked in partnership with him. Their most prestigious purchases were some early medieval and Gothic ivory pieces and the famous flabellum (9th century, court of Charles the Bald) from the Benedictine abbey of Tournus in Burgundy. In 1867 they exhibited ivories, bronzes, arms, wood-carvings and secular gold items in the Exposition Universelle, Paris. After his father's death Louis continued to enlarge the collection. In particular he added early medieval and Renaissance textiles. In 1880 he moved to Nice and in 1881 to Pisa, where he remained until 1886, continuing to buy artefacts not only from French and Italian sales but also from England, Germany, Greece and Turkey. In 1886 he moved to Florence, where he took an active part in the city's cultural life as a member of the committee that organized the Donatello exhibition and that also included the antiquarian Stefano Bardini and the restorer and painter Gaetano Bianchi. In the Donatello exhibition of 1887 Carrand showed precious enamel pieces, maiolica ware, ivories, leather items and textiles. On his death he bequeathed his collection of 3305 objects, including Byzantine, late medieval, French Gothic and Islamic ivories, Limoges enamels dating from the 13th to the 16th century, gems, cameos, gold, cutlery, Islamic and Indian metalwork, tooled leather, Byzantine and Renaissance fabrics, medals, wood-carvings, domestic objects, maiolica, glass objects and bronzes to the city of Florence, with the stipulation that it be displayed solely and permanently at the Museo Nazionale del Bargello. The Carrand collection, together with works from the Uffizi, became the nucleus of the collection of decorative arts at the Bargello.

BIBLIOGRAPHY

J. F. Garmier: 'Le Goût du moyen âge chez les collectionneurs lyonnais du XIXème siècle', *Rev. A.*, xlvii (1980), pp. 53–64

P. Barocchi and G. Gaeta Bertelà: 'La fortuna di Donatello nel Museo Nazionale del Bargello', *Omaggio a Donatello, 1386–1986* (Florence, 1985), pp. 77–121

P. Barocchi and G. Gaeta Bertelà: 'La genesi della collezione Carrand', *Arti del medio evo e del rinascimento: Omaggio ai Carrand, 1889–1989* (Florence, 1989), pp. 39–131

G. Gaeta Bertelà: 'La donazione Carrand al Museo Nazionale del Bargello', *Arti del medio evo e del rinascimento: Omaggio ai Carrand, 1889–1989* (Florence, 1989), pp. 1–38

G. GAETA BERTELÀ

Carraquiri, Nazario (*b* Pamplona, 28 July 1809; *d* ?1899). Spanish collector. The son of a French coppersmith who had settled in Pamplona, he was engaged in commerce and in politics and was elected deputy for Tafalla (Pamplona) several times. An active and enterprising man, he moved to Madrid in 1837 where he was a director of many companies, acquired a considerable fortune and became influential in the court of Isabella II. He was intellectually accomplished and interested in both art and literature (he was a patron of the TALIA society, which encouraged writers of drama). According to Madoz, in his house in Calle Jacometrezo, Madrid, he brought together an important collection of over two hundred pictures, the titles of which are not given but which include six works by Murillo, four by Titian, three by Alonso Cano, three by Zurbarán, two by Pedro Orrente and others by Rembrandt, Parmigianino, Reni, Tristán de Escamilla, Veronese, José del Castillo and the Romantic painter Antonio María Esquivel, who painted a portrait of *Carraquiri* (Madrid, Mus. Romántico), in the background of which are some of the paintings of his collection. There is evidence to suggest that in the 1860s he returned to his native region, where he bred bulls for the arena.

BIBLIOGRAPHY

P. Madoz: *Diccionario geográfico-estadístico-histórico de España y sus posesiones de ultramar*, x (Madrid, 1847), p. 863

Baron de Parla-Verdades: *Madrid al daguerrotipo: Colección de cuadros políticos, morales, literarios y filosoficos* (Madrid, 1849), pp. 97–8

M. Rodriguez de Rivas: *Guía del Museo Romántico* (Madrid, 1955), p. 23

PILAR BENITO

Carrara, da [Carraresi]. Italian family of rulers and patrons. Though Giacomo I da Carrara (*d* 22 Nov 1324) was elected Capitaneus et Dominus Generalis of Padua in 1318, he relinquished power in 1320, and the family did not secure an independent and unassailable hold on the city until Marsiglio I da Carrara (*d* 21 March 1338) expelled the della Scala family of Verona (who had controlled Padua from 1328) and became Signore in August 1337.

Carrarese patronage on any substantial scale evidently started during the rule of Marsiglio's successor Ubertino (*reg* 1338–45), who began to build the Reggia on a site possibly earmarked by Cangrande della Scala for his own palace in Padua. The western section, the Palazzo di Ponente, was completed by 1345, and the eastern section, the Palazzo di Levante, was at least under construction by then. Much of the Reggia was demolished in the 19th century, but its general layout—a series of interconnected courtyards, loggias and apartments of various sizes—can be understood from maps and other reliable records. The initial decorative campaign continued through the rule of Giacomo II da Carrara (*reg* 1345–50). Several frescoed apartments from different dates survive, but documents provide a more or less complete list of a much richer series of fresco cycles. The subject-matter of these, either heraldic and chivalric or based on themes from the Antique, perfectly reflects the tastes and interests of 14th-century court patrons. Parts of two rooms decorated with purely heraldic motifs survive, but the most important apartment, according to later accounts, was the Sala Thebana, with frescoes (destr.) based on Statius's epic poem *Thebaid*. The choice of such a subject may reflect the long-standing humanist tradition in Padua, but Statius's epic appealed equally to a broad chivalric and courtly audience. Only with Petrarch's visits to Padua during the rules of Giacomo and Francesco I (*reg* 1355–88) did Carrarese patronage turn towards the more serious moralizing classicism of the 14th-century humanists. Though the majority of the palace frescoes, including those in the later Camera Herculis (decorated by 1363) and the Camera Camilli (by 1366), are lost, the high quality of early Carrarese commissions can be judged from the tombs of *Ubertino da Carrara* and *Giacomo II da Carrara* by Andriolo de' Santi of Venice (ex-S Agostino, Padua; Padua, Eremitani), the latter decorated with a *Coronation of the Virgin* fresco by Guariento (di Arpo), and from Guariento's frescoes and ceiling panels from the palace chapel (after 1345).

With the patronage of the family and court of Francesco I, painting in Padua became for a time the most innovative in Italy. Major court commissions went to the Florentine Giusto de' Menabuoi and ALTICHIERO. Giusto's frescoes (e.g. *Crucifixion*; *see* MENABUOI, GIUSTO DE', fig. 2) of *c.* 1376 in the cathedral baptistery were commissioned by Francesco's wife, Fina Buzzacarina, who turned the baptistery into a mausoleum for herself and her husband. Giusto's frescoes share a grounding in Giotto's work with Altichiero's surviving fresco cycles for Francesco's courtiers. These, for example the cycle in the Oratorio di S Giorgio, Padua, may reflect the culture of a court connected by many political, commercial and intellectual ties to Florence. Furthermore, Petrarch, who spent his last years in Padua, left a painting of the *Virgin* (untraced) by Giotto, 'whose beauty the ignorant do not understand', to Francesco I, his final patron. The advanced pictorial and humanist interests of the Carrarese court were combined in Francesco's most important commission, the Sala Virorum Illustrium (destr.), a great hall painted, almost certainly by Altichiero, with an elaborately didactic scheme based on Petrarch's *De viris illustribus*. Petrarch, and then Lombardo della Seta, undertook the completion of *De viris illustribus* at Francesco's request. Several of Petrarch's works were copied for Francesco, and the illumination in some of these manuscripts has also been attributed to Altichiero.

The Carrarese library, removed wholesale by Gian Galeazzo Visconti after he took Padua in 1388, was one of the greatest of its time. The subsequent collection of Francesco II da Carrara (*reg* 1390–1405) contained many medical texts, including the sumptuously and scientifically illustrated *Liber aggregatus* of Serapion, the so-called Carrarese Herbal (London, BL, Egerton MS. 2020). During the final years of Carrarese rule the proto-humanist culture encouraged by earlier Carrarese patrons bore fruit in the remarkable Carrarese portrait medals (Padua, Mus. Civ.), made in close imitation of Roman coin-portraits. These are of fundamental importance in the history of the early Renaissance medal.

BIBLIOGRAPHY

H. H. Brown: 'The Carraresi', *Studies in the History of Venice*, i (London, 1907, New York, 2/1973), pp. 107–51
E. Levi: *Francesco di Vannozzo e la lirica nelle corti lombarde durante la seconda metà del sec. XIV* (Florence, 1908)
T. E. Mommsen: 'Petrarch and the Decoration of the Sala Virorum Illustrium in Padua', *A. Bull.*, xxxiv (1952), pp. 95–116
S. Bettini: *Le pitture di Giusto de' Menabuoi nel Battistero del Duomo di Padova* (Padua, 1960)
F. d'Arcais: *Guariento* (Venice, 1965)
J. K. Hyde: *Padua in the Age of Dante* (Manchester, NY, 1966)
C. Gasparotto: 'La Reggia dei da Carrara', *Atti & Mem. Accad. Patavina Sci., Lett. & A.*, lxxix (1966–7), pp. 71–116
——: 'Gli ultimi affreschi venuti in luce nella Reggia dei da Carrara e una documentazione inedita sulla Camera di Camillo', *Atti & Mem. Accad. Patavina Sci., Lett. & A.*, lxxxi (1968–9), pp. 237–61
Da Giotto al Mantegna (exh. cat., ed. L. Grossato; Padua, Pal. Ragione, 1974) [with articles and bibliog. on Paduan art in the Carrarese period]
L. Lazzarini: 'La cultura delle signorie venete e i poeti di corte', *Storia della cultura veneta: Il trecento*, ed. G. Folena (Vicenza, 1976), pp. 477–516
W. Wolters: *La scultura veneziana gotica, 1300–1460*, i (Venice, 1976), pp. 168–9

JOHN RICHARDS

Carrara, Giacomo, Conte (*b* Bergamo, 9 June 1714; *d* Bergamo, 20 April 1796). Italian patron and collector. He was educated in letters and philosophy in his native city and studied drawing, in which he gained some proficiency, in Verona, Venice and Bologna. The death of his father, Conte Carlo Carrara, in 1755, left him free to pursue his artistic interests, and from 1756 to 1758 he travelled in Italy, visiting Parma, Bologna, Rome, Florence and Pisa to study paintings and build up his own collection of art.

Though his means were fairly modest, which encouraged the development of a selective approach to collecting, by the time of his death Carrara's palazzo in the Via Pignolo, Bergamo (no. 56, now Palazzo Berizzi), contained some 1500 pictures and many more prints and drawings. His collection (inventoried by Bartolomeo Borsetti in 1796) was particularly rich in 16th-century Veneto art, including works by Old Masters associated either by birth or by patronage with Bergamo: Lorenzo Lotto's *Mystic Marriage of St Catherine with Niccolò Bonghi* (Bergamo, Gal. Accad. Carrara) was one such painting. Contemporary art was also represented in the collection; for example Carrara's portrait (Bergamo, Gal. Accad. Carrara) was painted by Giuseppe Ghislandi from Bergamo.

Carrara's interest in art also embraced art history. He collected documents and studied pictures with a view to correcting published errors and establishing the details of an artist's life and work. He exchanged information and opinions about art with scholars elsewhere in Italy, including Girolamo Tiraboschi (1731–94), the librarian of the Este family in Modena, and the Vatican librarian Giovanni Gaetano Bottari, to whose published collection of letters on art and artists he made several contributions in the 1760s. Carrara was a friend of Francesco Maria Tassi (*d* 1782) and prepared additions and annotations to Tassi's book (published posthumously in 1793) on the lives of artists from Bergamo.

In 1766, Carrara contributed towards the costs of founding a museum of antiquities in Bergamo, and in 1780 he acquired a site in Via della Noce for a public art gallery combined with a school for painters. He employed an architect from Bergamo, Costantino Gallizioli (1720–99), and two Milanese painters, Federico Ferraris and Domenico Riccardi (*fl* 1765–78), to build and decorate the new institution, to which, in his will of 1795, he bequeathed all his possessions. The gallery opened in 1785 and the school in 1793, under the direction of the Milanese artist Dionigi Sadis. As a result, perhaps, of the school's conservative curriculum (which was modelled on the late 16th-century academy of the Carracci in Bologna) and restricted intake (entry was open only to around 12 pupils from disadvantaged backgrounds), it did not remain independent for long and soon after Carrara's death it became affiliated to the Accademia di Brera in Milan. The gallery of paintings underwent change in the 19th century, but nevertheless still survives today (augmented by the collections of Conte Guglielmo Lochis in 1859 and of the art historian Giovanni Morelli in 1891) as the Accademia Carrara, where Carrara's personal papers are also preserved.

Carrara's interest in local artists was shared by his brother Francesco (1716–93), who became a cardinal in 1785 and was the protector in Rome of two artists from Bergamo, the sculptor Alessandro Benedetto Possenti (1738–68) and his brother, the painter and sculptor Pier Giuseppe Possenti (1750–1810/16).

BIBLIOGRAPHY

G. Bottari: *Raccolta di lettere sulla pittura, scultura ed architettura scritte da' più celebri personaggi dei secoli XV, XVI e XVII* (Milan, 1754–73); enlarged by S. Ticozzi (Milan, 1822–5/*R* Olms, 1976), iv, pp. 132–42, 463–5, 477–81; vi, p. 236
F. M. Tassi: *Vite de' pittori, scultori e architetti bergamaschi* (Bergamo, 1793); ed. F. Mazzini (Milan, 1969), ii, p. 282
G. Frizzoni: *Le Gallerie dell'Accademia Carrara* (Bergamo, 1907)
A. Pinetti: *Il conte Giacomo Carrara e la sua galleria secondo il catalogo del 1796* (Bergamo, 1922)
F. Russoli: *Accademia Carrara catalogo* (Bergamo, 1967), pp. 5–8

JANET SOUTHORN

Carrarino, il. *See* BOLGI, ANDREA.

Carrasco, Ted (*b* La Paz, 1933). Bolivian sculptor. He taught himself to sculpt by studying Pre-Columbian sculpture and ceramics. Between 1959 and 1961 he travelled in several Latin-American countries; he then lived in Europe for 12 years, working in Holland, Belgium, France and Switzerland. While in Europe he married the Swiss sculptor Francine Secretan, with whom he returned to Bolivia in 1974, settling in La Paz. In 1964 he was awarded the first 'Queen Elizabeth' prize in the 10th International Sculpture Biennale in Brussels. Carrasco's preferred materials were stone and bronze. His subject-matter was based on the knowledge of the age-old traditions of native peoples and on their relation to nature, although his work is modernist in appearance. His earliest works represent seated women and later the *munachis*, or love and fertility amulets. In the early 1970s his art became more synthetic, more cryptic and abstract. During this period his interpretation of the genesis of life was notable, conveyed in enormous spheres that were split open to reveal magical interior worlds. After returning to Bolivia his art became more figurative, as in *Pachamama*, the Andean goddess of the earth, *Andes* (1988; Seoul, Olymp. Village, Sculp. Gdn), and the monument to *Marshal Andrés de Santa Cruz* (1990; La Paz).

WRITINGS

with P. Querejazu: *Ted Carrasco* (La Paz, 1988)

BIBLIOGRAPHY

P. Querejazu: *La pintura boliviana del siglo XX* (Milan, 1989)

PEDRO QUEREJAZU

Carreño, Mario (*b* Havana, 24 June 1913). Cuban painter. He studied at the Academia de S Alejandro in Havana (1925–*c.* 1930), at the Academia de S Fernando in Madrid (1932–5) and at the Ecole des Arts Appliqués in Paris (1937–9). He subsequently lived in New York from 1944 to 1950. During the 1940s he was part of the Caribbean avant-garde that applied Cubist and Surrealist approaches to regional themes, producing paintings such as *Caribbean Enchantment* (1949; Washington, DC, Mus. Mod. A. Latin America). Widely travelled and stylistically diverse, in the 1950s he worked primarily in geometric abstraction, but after settling permanently in Santiago, Chile, in 1957, he integrated these Constructivist forms into dreamlike settings influenced by the Andean landscape and by the poetry of his friend, Pablo Neruda (1904–73), as in *Land of Volcanoes* (1974; Santiago, Manuel Agosín priv. col., see 1976 exh. cat., p. 26). In the 1960s and early 1970s he treated the threat of nuclear war in paintings such as *20th-century Totem* (1973; priv. col., see 1976 exh. cat., p. 41), which depicts a column of mannequin fragments over a desolate terrain. In 1948–9, and again in the early 1980s, Carreño worked on the *Antillanas* series, which celebrates the lore and colours of the Caribbean. In 1982 he received the National Prize for Art in Santiago, Chile.

BIBLIOGRAPHY

J. Gómez-Sicre: *Pintura cubana de hoy* (Havana, 1944)
E. Ellena: *Mario Carreño: 24 dibujos* (Santiago, 1973)
Carreño (exh. cat., Santiago, Gal. Imagen, 1976)
R. Pau-Llosa: 'Contemporary Central American and Caribbean Painting', *A. Int.*, xxvii (1984), pp. 28–33
Outside Cuba/Fuera de Cuba (exh. cat., New Brunswick, NJ, Rutgers U., Zimmerli A. Mus., 1987)

RICARDO PAU-LLOSA

Carreño, Omar (*b* Porlamar, 7 Feb 1927). Venezuelan painter and sculptor. He studied at the Escuela de Artes Plásticas y Aplicadas in Caracas (1942–50). He lived for over 12 years in Europe from 1951, studying at the Académie de la Grande Chaumière and at the Ecole du Louvre in Paris, where he was a member of the group Los Disidentes (1951). He also studied conservation and restoration in Rome. In Caracas he was a member of the influential Taller Libre de Arte (from 1948), and in 1966 he began promoting the expansionist movement in Venezuela. After briefly working in an *Art informel* style, Carreño adopted geometric abstraction from the late 1960s until the mid-1980s, at which point he turned to figuration. In 1972 he received the Premio Nacional de Artes Plásticas in Caracas.

BIBLIOGRAPHY

F. Paz Castillo and P. Rojas Guardia: *Diccionario de las artes plásticas en Venezuela* (Caracas, 1973), pp. 61–3

ELIDA SALAZAR

Carreño de Miranda, Juan (*b* Avilés, nr Oviedo, 25 March 1614; *d* Madrid, 3 Oct 1685). Spanish painter. One of the most important painters in Spain in the 17th century, he executed many religious works in oils, tempera and fresco and was considered to be, after Velázquez, the most accomplished portrait painter of his day.

1. Early and middle years, to 1666. 2. Royal success, 1667 and after.

1. Early and middle years, to 1666. He was the son of Juan Carreño de Miranda, a painter of modest talent who also traded in paintings; his uncle, Andrés Carreño (*c.* 1591–1660), was also a painter, active in Valladolid. At an early age Carreño went with his father to Madrid, where he entered the studio of Pedro de las Cuevas, an artist highly esteemed as a teacher; the basis of Cuevas's teaching was a thorough instruction in draughtsmanship. In the studio Carreño came into contact with fellow pupils of his own age, among them Antonio de Pereda, Francisco Camilo and Antonio Arias Fernández. According to Palomino, Carreño then left to study colour with Bartolomé Román, a pupil of Vicente Carducho. Through Román, he probably established contact with Carducho himself, for his earliest works show the influence of the older master. It is likely that Carreño had become a recognized artist by 1634, when he was working on commissions for several churches in Madrid, although no paintings have survived from these early years. From 1640 to 1650 he was probably employed by ecclesiastical patrons, though few works from this period are known. His first known signed and dated painting is *St Anthony Preaching to the Fishes* (1646; Barcelona, Mus. Balaguer de Villanueva & Geltrú). The *Holy Family* (Madrid, S Martín) is dated 1649, and the *Annunciation* and *Betrothal of St Catherine* (both 1653; Madrid, Hosp. Order Tercera) show his fully developed and unique manner of combining compositional schemes inspired by Rubens and other Flemish artists with a rich technique acquired from a careful study of Venetian masters, especially Titian. Also from this period are the *Magdalene* (1654; Madrid, Real Acad. S Fernando, Mus.) and *St Sebastian* (1656; Madrid, Prado), both of which show a strong Venetian influence. At this time he began to establish relations with the court of Philip IV and frequently acted as valuer of paintings belonging to the estates of recently deceased nobility. He resided in the house of Don Gaspar de Fuensalida, a court official and close friend of Velázquez.

In 1658, when he was elected a representative of the city of Madrid for the estate of nobles, Carreño testified in favour of Velázquez in the investigation undertaken for the latter's eligibility for the Order of Santiago, stating that he had known him for over 34 years. It was apparently at this time—almost as a reward for his warm recommendation—that Velázquez offered him a position as a painter in the Alcázar. In 1658, under the direction of the Italian artists Agostino Mitelli and Angelo Michele Colonna, who had both recently arrived in Madrid, he began to participate in the decoration of the Alcázar with mythological scenes

1. Juan Carreño de Miranda: *Founding of the Trinitarian Order*, oil on canvas, 1666 (Paris, Musée du Louvre)

(destr.) in fresco and tempera. In this project he collaborated with Francisco Rizi (*see* RIZI, (2)), who became his close friend and with whom he established a working relationship that resulted in many joint commissions in succeeding years. Although the paintings were destroyed when the Alcázar burnt in 1734, their style was probably greatly influenced by Titian. During the 1650s Carreño's reputation became more widespread, and commissions increased. He took on many apprentices and assistants in his workshop, including Juan Martín Cabezalero, who was still in his employ in 1666, and possibly Mateo Cerezo.

Carreño was extremely prolific in the 1660s, and much of his work and activity during this time is documented. In 1660 he signed the large canvas of *St James Mounted* (Budapest, Mus. F.A.) and the portrait of *Don Bernabé de Ochoa Chinchetru* (New York, Hisp. Soc. America Mus.), the latter being the first of a fine series of portraits of members of court society. The *Immaculate Conception* (1662; Granada, Fund. Moreno) initiated an iconographical type of majestic solemnity that he was to use often during his career (versions, 1666, Vitoria, Old Cathedral; *c.* 1665–70, Bilbao, Mus. B.A.). In 1663 he undertook, with Rizi, a commission for paintings of the *Life of St Isidore the Farmer* (completed 1668; destr. 1936) in S Isidro Chapel, S Andrés, Madrid (church destr. 1936; chapel remains). In 1664 he and Rizi contracted to execute tempera paintings on the vault of the Atocha Church, which they later repainted in fresco (church and paintings destr. 1936). In the following year he again began a collaboration with Rizi in the painting of scenes from the *Life of St Anthony* in S Antonio de los Portugueses o Alemanes, Madrid. Carreño executed figures of great solemnity, and Rizi created the ornamentation of simulated architecture, urns and festoons; after 1695 the whole was reworked by Luca Giordano. In 1665 Carreño and Rizi also began the execution of paintings (completed 1669; destr.) in the Capilla de las Reliquias in Toledo Cathedral; they also worked on the Holy Week monument (destr.) in the cathedral. The large altarpiece of the *Founding of the Trinitarian Order* (Paris, Louvre; see fig. 1) was executed in 1666 for the Trinitarians of Pamplona: Rizi made the sketches, and Carreño painted the final composition. During the 1660s Carreño was assisted by his pupils, and a large part of the work of repeating such successful compositions as the various Immaculate Conceptions was certainly theirs. His workshop at this time included artists who would eventually become established in their own right, for example Francisco Ignacio Ruiz de la Iglesia and José Jiménez Donoso.

2. ROYAL SUCCESS, 1667 AND AFTER. Carreño's growing prestige encouraged him to try to secure a position at court, where since 1656 Rizi had been Pintor del Rey. In 1667 Carreño petitioned to replace Sebastián de Herrera Barnuevo, Pintor de Cámara, on account of his 'absences and illnesses', but this was refused, as it was considered an unusual request. In September 1669 he obtained the title of Pintor del Rey through the Queen Mother, Mary Anne of Austria, mother and regent of Charles II. This was the beginning of a swift rise to a successful career as court painter, such as Velázquez had enjoyed during the reign of Philip IV. In December 1669 Carreño was appointed Ayuda de la Furriera (Aide to the Keeper of the Keys of the King's Palace) and in 1671 was given the position of Pintor de Cámara. The latter appointment was made over the head of Rizi, the senior Pintor del Rey, and henceforth resulted in cool relations between the two artists.

In his new position Carreño was chiefly engaged in painting portraits, and he rendered expressive studies of the sickly child-king *Charles II* (version, 1671; Oviedo, Mus. B.A.) and several of his mother, *Queen Mary Anne of Austria* (version, *c.* 1669; Madrid, Prado), in severe widow's weeds, the latter portraits influenced by those of the Queen (version, 1666; London, N.G.) by Juan Bautista Martínez del Mazo. Later paintings of the King depict him wearing the robes of the Golden Fleece (1677; Rohrau, Schloss; see fig. 2) and dressed in military uniform (1679; untraced; versions, 1681, Toledo, Casa & Mus. El Greco; 1683, Guadalupe, Monastery de Nuestra Señora de Guadelupe). As Velázquez had done earlier, Carreño also painted a series of portraits of members of the court, including the highest nobility, court dwarfs and clowns, foreign ambassadors and distinguished visitors. Examples include *Doña Francisca de Velasco, Marquesa de Santa Cruz* (*c.* 1665–70; Madrid, Marqueses de Santa Cruz priv. col.), *Inés de Zúñiga, Condesa de Monterrey* (*c.* 1670; Madrid, Mus. Lázaro Galdiano), a *Woman of the Medinaceli Family* (version, *c.* 1675; Toledo, Hosp. Tavera), *Piotr Ivanowitz Potemkin, the Russian Ambassador* (1681; Madrid, Prado)

2. Juan Carreño de Miranda: *Charles II*, oil on canvas, 2.17×1.41 m, 1677 (Rohrau, Graf Harrach'sche Familiensammlung, Schloss Rohrau)

and the opulent *Don Sabas Millini, Papal Nuncio* (version, 1683; Guadalupe, Monastery de Nuestra Señora de Guadalupe). The *Duque de Pastrana* (*c.* 1670; Madrid, Prado) is an effective example of the fusion of Spanish severity and Flemish complexity. Among his more unusual portraits are one of *Michol the Dwarf* (*c.* 1680; Dallas, TX, S. Methodist U., Meadows Mus. & Gal.) and two of *Eugenia Martínez Vallejo, the Freak*, an excessively obese child presented to the court of Madrid. In one painting she is wearing clothes presented to her by Charles II, and in the other she is nude as Bacchus (both 1680; Madrid, Prado). Carreño's court activity grew, and he undertook other commissions in addition to portraits, ranging from the supervision of the restoration of the monastery of the Escorial after a fire in 1671, to painting a copy (1674; Madrid, Real Acad. S Fernando, Mus.) of Raphael's large canvas *Road to Calvary* (*'Lo Spasimo di Sicilia'*, 1517; Madrid, Prado) for the Convento de las Descalzas Reales, Madrid. In 1680, when Marie Louise of Orleans arrived in Madrid to marry Charles II, Carreño supervised the important celebrations connected with the event and oversaw the contributions of temporary decorations made by his fellow artists.

Carreño's relations with other artists were apparently always cordial, and Palomino praises his good nature, modesty and prudence. Documents referring to the last years of his life are particularly concerned with his petitions to the court for money, as payments from commissions were frequently late in arriving. In his last years he often painted religious subjects. In 1682 he executed two large paintings for S Juan (destr.), Madrid, the church adjoining the Alcázar: the *Baptism* (version, Madrid, parish church of Santiago) and the *Feast of Herod* (destr.; sketch Madrid, Prado). One of his many versions of the *Immaculate Conception* (Madrid, Convento Encarnación) is dated 1683, and when he died in 1685 he left unfinished a painting of *St Damasus* that had been commissioned by the Ayuntamiento of Madrid. Completed by Palomino, it is now in the Museo Municipal de Madrid. Carreño also left unfinished a copy (1685; Madrid, Prado) of Reni's *Judith and Holofernes* (Rome, Gal. Spada). His wife, who outlived him, made out a will that provided for his various friends and pupils, including Ruiz de la Iglesia, Pedro Ruíz González and Jerónimo Ezquerra (*fl c.* 1700).

Although Carreño's religious paintings show him to have been strongly influenced by the Baroque style of Rubens, there is an element of severe classicism in his work that is especially evident in his simplest compositions, in which Venetian models, based on Titian, are given a restrained sensuality. His portraits, similar to those of Velázquez, have an air of stern elegance and reveal an intimate approach to his sitters, no matter what their social position. At the same time, he brought to Spanish portrait painting a courtly gallantry reminiscent of van Dyck, whose works he surely admired.

BIBLIOGRAPHY

A. A. Palomino de Castro y Velasco: *Museo pictórico* (1715–24)

D. Berjano Escobar: *El pintor don Juan Carreño de Miranda (1614–1685): Su vida y sus obras* (Madrid, 1925)

R. A. Marzolf: *The Life and Work of Juan Carreño de Miranda (1614–1685)* (Ph.D. diss.; microfilm, Ann Arbor, 1961)

L. Castañón: *Pintores asturianos: I. Carreño* (Oviedo, 1970)

J. Barretini Fernández: *Juan Carreño: Pintor de Cámara de Carlos II* (Madrid, 1972)

A. E. Pérez Sánchez: *Juan Carreño de Miranda (1614–1685)* (Avilés, 1985) [with comprehensive illustrations and extensive bibliog.]

——: *Carreño, Rizi, Herrera y la pintura madrileña de su tiempo* (Madrid, 1986) [with extensive bibliog.]

ALFONSO E. PÉREZ SÁNCHEZ

Carrera, José Antonio Jimeno y. *See* JIMENO Y CARRERA, JOSÉ ANTONIO.

Carrère & Hastings. American architectural partnership formed in 1885 by John Merven Carrère (*b* Rio de Janiero, 9 Nov 1858; *d* New York, 1 March 1911) and Thomas Hastings (*b* New York, 11 March 1860; *d* New York, 22 Oct 1929). Carrère studied in Lausanne and at the Ecole des Beaux-Arts, Paris (1877–82), in the atelier of Victor-Marie-Charles Ruprich-Robert. On his return to New York, Carrère worked in the office of McKim, Mead & White (1883–5) before setting up practice with his fellow employee Hastings. Hastings had studied more briefly at the Ecole des Beaux-Arts in 1884 in the atelier of Louis-Jules André.

The practice was launched with commissions from the developer Henry Morrison Flagler (1830–1913), for whom Carrère & Hastings designed the Ponce de Leon Hotel (1885–8; later Flagler College), the Alcazar Hotel (1888–9), the Memorial Presbyterian Church (1889–90) and other Spanish–American Renaissance-style buildings in Palm Beach and Saint Augustine, Florida. For more northerly latitudes Carrère and Hastings developed the Renaissance classicism of McKim, Mead & White with great success, winning the competition for the New York Public Library in 1897 (built 1902–11; *see* NEW YORK, fig. 3). The clear, functional planning and refined use of stylistic ornament distinguished these buildings. Other works include the Russell Senate and Cannon House office buildings (1905–10), and the Carnegie Institution (1909), all in Washington, DC, and the New Theatre (1911–12), New York. Both partners were involved in the movement towards urban planning that accompanied the American Beaux-Arts style. Carrère was architectural director for the Buffalo Exhibition (1901) and drew up plans for Ohio, Baltimore, MD, and Grand Rapids, MI (1909). He originated the Art Commission of the City of New York and was a notable campaigner for architectural education and the improvement of architectural ethics.

After Carrère's death in a motor car accident, Hastings, who had been the principal designer of the two, continued the practice, specializing in tall office buildings adapted to the New York zoning restrictions, for example the Cunard Building (1919–21), the Macmillan Building (1924) and the Standard Oil Building (completed 1926). He was an articulate advocate of American classicism and remained closely in touch with the design work of his office. Other works include the Memorial Amphitheatre at Arlington Cemetery, VA, and the temporary Victory Arch (1918; destr.) in New York. In London, Hastings designed Devonshire House (1924–6), Piccadilly, a block of luxury apartments (now offices) for which the consultant architect was Charles H. Reilly. Hastings had had an association with Reilly and the Liverpool University School of Architecture since 1909.

WRITINGS

Carrère with A. W. Brunner: *Preliminary Report for a City Plan for Grand Rapids* (1909)

Hastings: 'On the Evolution of Style', *Amer. Architect*, xcvii (1910), p. 71

BIBLIOGRAPHY

'The Work of Messrs Carrère & Hastings', *Archit. Rec.*, xxvii (1910), pp. 1–120

Obituary [Carrère], *RIBA J.*, xviii (1910–11), p. 352; *Amer. Architect*, xci (1911), pp. 131–2

F. S. Swales: 'John Merven Carrère, 1858–1911', *Archit. Rev.* [London], xxix (1911), pp. 283–93

E. Clute: 'Master Draftsmen' [Hastings], *Pencil Points*, vi (1925), pp. 49–60, 88

Obituary [Hastings], *Amer. Architect*, cxxxvi (1929), p. 55; *Archit. Forum* (Dec 1929), p. 35; *Archit. Rec.*, lxvi (1929), p. 596; *RIBA J.*, xxxvi (1929–30), pp. 24–5

D. Gray: *Thomas Hastings, Architect: Collected Writings* (Boston, 1933)

C. Condit: 'The Pioneer Concrete Buildings of St Augustine', *Prog. Archit.* (Sept 1971), pp. 128–33

□

Carrey, Jacques (*b* Troyes, 12 Jan 1649; *d* Troyes, 18 Feb 1726). French painter and draughtsman. His reputation is founded on the series of drawings he made of the Parthenon, Athens, in 1674. Carrey was one of several young artists who accompanied Charles-Henri-François Olier, Marquis de Nointel, in his embassy to Constantinople in August 1670. Louis XIV had commanded Nointel to purchase manuscripts, medallions and sculptures while abroad, and the Premier Peintre du Roi, Charles Le Brun, recommended that Carrey, a pupil of his, should be included in the entourage in order to make drawings of the most significant buildings and settings. As a result of this, between 1670 and 1679 Carrey executed over 500 drawings of towns, antiquities, ceremonial displays and examples of local festivities and customs in Asia Minor, Greece and Palestine.

Nointel's party visited Athens in November 1674; in a two-week period Carrey produced about fifty-five drawings of the sculptures on the Parthenon (*see* ATHENS, §II, 1(ii)). Thirty-five of these, showing details of the pediments, metopes and friezes, survive (Paris, Bib. N.). Much of the Parthenon's sculpture was destroyed in 1687, and as the sole record of this lost work, Carrey's drawings are vital documentation of the building's former embellishments. In his red and black chalk drawings, probably made on the spot, Carrey meticulously recorded the cracks and other damage, making no attempt to complete missing details. Nine further drawings he made of scenes and antiquities in Athens also survive (Paris, Bib. N.).

On his return to Paris in 1679 Carrey presented Le Brun with the large number of drawings he had made at Constantinople; several (recently rediscovered) are in the Cabinet des Dessins at the Louvre, Paris. Three paintings known to have been made by Carrey in 1675 are untraced, but the enormous canvas depicting *The Marquis de Nointel before the City of Athens* (Chartres, Mus. B.-A.) is almost certainly his work.

BIBLIOGRAPHY

P.-J. Grosley: 'Jacques Carrey', *Le Grand Dictionnaire historique*, ed. L. Moréri (Paris, 1674, rev. 20/1753), iii, p. 270

H. Omont: *Athènes au XVIIe siècle: Dessins du Parthénon attribués à J. Carrey et conservés à la Bibliothèque Nationale* (Paris, 1898)

R. Heberdey: 'Untersuchungen zu den Zeichnungen Jacques Carreys', *Jhft. Österreich. Archäol. Inst. Wien*, xxxi (1939), pp. 96–141

T. Bowie and D. Thimme: *The Carrey Drawings of the Parthenon Sculptures* (London, 1971)

THOMAS NICHOLS

Carrhae. *See* HARRAN.

Carrick, William [Karrik, Vil'yam; Karrik, Vasily (Andreyevich)] (*b* Edinburgh, 31 Dec 1827; *d* St Petersburg, Nov 1878). Scottish photographer, active in Russia. He was the son of a Scottish timber merchant living in St Petersburg. He studied architecture and painting at the Academy of Arts in St Petersburg from 1844 to 1853, when he went to Rome to further his studies in painting. On his return to St Petersburg in spring 1856 he had already decided to take up photography for financial reasons, and he became the assistant to a portrait photographer named Hoch. In 1857 he travelled to Edinburgh, where he studied photography briefly with James Good Tunny and met the photographer John McGregor (*d* 1872). McGregor agreed to travel to St Petersburg, and the two opened a portrait studio there in September 1859, making albumen prints using wet collodion plates. Their photographs received approval from the imperial household, and Carrick developed a relationship with the court painter Mihály Zichy, with whom he embarked on a project of photographing the works of artists (e.g. Zichy's watercolour of the *Russian Emperor Shooting a Bear*, 1864;

see Ashbee, 1978, fig. 11), one of the first to do so professionally.

When portrait trade was slack Carrick began to take pictures of ordinary people in St Petersburg, first in the studio and later in the streets; he later published *cartes-de-visite* as the series *Russian Types* (1860s). Intended for the tourist trade as genre photographs, they show Carrick indulging his interest in and warmth for the city street sellers, who generally appear relaxed before the lens, for example *Milkmaid* (F. Ashbee priv. col., see Ashbee and Lawson, pl. 16). Carrick's interest in the lives of ordinary people prompted him to make a journey with McGregor into the Simbirsk region in 1871, where he again attempted to document people in their daily occupations. His vision of the nobility of labour was borne out in the many shots of peasants at work, possibly inspired by French Realism, for example *Fieldworker, Simbirsk* (1871–5; E. Sommer priv. col., see Ashbee and Lawson, pl. 6), yet Carrick's photographs remain natural and unposed and divorced from straightforward ethnographic photography. After McGregor's death Carrick made another trip to Simbirsk in 1875 and completed another innovative series documenting life in the region.

BIBLIOGRAPHY

F. Ashbee: 'William Carrick: A Scots Photographer in St Petersburg (1827–1878)', *Hist. Phot.*, ii/3 (1978), pp. 207–22

S. Morozov: *Tvorcheskaya fotografiya* [Creative photography] (Moscow, 1986), pp. 72–4, 78–9, 93

F. Ashbee and J. Lawson: *William Carrick, 1827–1878* (Edinburgh, 1987)

KEVIN HALLIWELL

Carrick Fox, Ethel. *See* FOX, ETHEL CARRICK.

Carriera, Rosalba (*b* Venice, Oct 1675; *d* Venice, 15 April 1757). Italian pastellist and painter. She was a daughter of Andrea Carriera, who worked in the mainland *podesteria* of the Republic of Venice, and of Alba Foresti, an embroiderer. She had two sisters: Angela, who married the painter Giovanni Antonio Pellegrini, and Giovanna, who, like Rosalba herself, never married. Pier Caterino Zeno (see Campori, 1886) and other, anonymous sources recorded that she was a pupil of Giuseppe Diamantini; according to Mariette, she originally painted snuff-boxes and later became a pupil of Federico Bencovich. There are more precise records of her life and of some of her works from 1700 onwards, when she started keeping the letters she received and rough copies of those she sent (Florence, Bib. Medicea-Laurenziana, MS. Ashburnham 1781).

During the early years of the century Carriera painted mainly miniature portraits on small pieces of oval-shaped ivory (e.g. *Mrs Summers*; London, V&A), which were often intended to adorn the inside of snuff-box lids. However, the portrait of *Antonio Maria Zanetti* (Stockholm, Nmus.), painted when Zanetti was no more than 20 years old, proves that she was already producing the pastel portraits for which she would become most renowned. Her international clientele, composed principally of British, French and German travellers, provided her with a lifelong source of commissions for miniature portraits for snuff-box lids or medallions, cabinet paintings and portraits in pastel. As a result of the interest of Christian Cole, secretary to Charles Montagu, 1st Duke of Manchester (then ambassador extraordinary in Venice), Carriera was admitted to the Accademia di S Luca in Rome on 27 September 1705, submitting the *Girl with Dove* (Rome, Accad. N. S Luca) as her reception piece. Carlo Maratti, principal of the Accademia, much admired this miniature, the undulating brushstrokes of which are reminiscent of Pellegrini's Rococo style. A number of Carriera's early miniatures, such as the *Flute-player, Woman Playing the Harpsichord* and *Lady Cutting her Hair* (all St Petersburg, Hermitage), take women's everyday activities as their subject; others, for example *Flora* (Munich, Bayer. Nmus.) and *Venus and Cupid* (Copenhagen, Kon. Dan. Kstakad.), explore mythological themes connected with women's lives. There are rather fewer portraits of men.

Around 1708 Carriera painted a pastel *Self-portrait* (Florence, Uffizi) for the collection of artists' self-portraits belonging to the Grand Duke Cosimo III de' Medici. This work, which is mentioned in a letter of 1709, was painted in a style similar to that of the French pastellist Joseph Vivien. From 1711 to 1720 she brought a more personal style to her pastel portraits, with more delicate and subtly blended colours, the drawing less marked and facial expressions more indicative of the subject's psychological state. Although they could be categorized as official State portraits, her depictions of aristocrats are distinguished by their lack of severity, as can be seen in her *Portrait of a Man in Armour* (Dresden, Gemäldegal. Alte Meister), which may be identified as Augustus III of Poland (Sani, 1988), and in her portrait of *Philip, Duke of Wharton* (London, Buckingham Pal., Royal Col.). In this ten-year period Carriera came into contact with the French painter Nicolas Vleughels, the important connoisseur of prints and drawings Pierre-Jean Mariette and the collector Pierre Crozat, who invited her to Paris. On 14 January 1720 she was admitted to the Accademia Clementina in Bologna and in March that year went to Paris with Pellegrini, who had been commissioned to paint the ceiling of the Banque Royale (1720–21; destr.).

While in Paris, Carriera was Crozat's guest at his house in the Rue de Richelieu. Her visit, which lasted until 11 March 1721, was a triumphant success. She painted portraits of *Louis XV as a Child* (versions, Dresden, Gemäldegal. Alte Meister; Boston, MA, Mus. F.A.) in pastel and also in miniature, as mentioned in her diary. Her sitters also included some of the most fashionable ladies at the French court; her portrait of *Mlle de Clermont* (Chantilly, Mus. Condé) is among the few of these paintings that survive. She made friends with many of the artists living in Paris, including Hyacinthe Rigaud, Nicolas de Largillierre, Jean-François de Troy and Antoine Watteau, who was impressed by her miniatures and exerted great influence on her work. On 26 October 1721 she was received (*reçue*) into the Académie Royale de Peinture et de Sculpture with the *Nymph of the Train of Apollo* (Paris, Louvre) as her *morceau de réception.* At this time her work became increasingly mature and refined; her ability to give deeper expression to faces is exemplified in the portrait of *?Antoine Watteau* (1720; Treviso, Mus. Civ. Bailo; see fig.).

After her return to Italy, Carriera was invited in 1723 to the Este court at Modena, where she painted portraits

Rosalba Carriera: *?Antoine Watteau*, pastel on card, 550×430 mm, 1720 (Treviso, Museo Civico Luigi Bailo)

of each of the three daughters of Duke Rinaldo d'Este (versions of each, Dresden, Gemäldegal. Alte Meister; Florence, Uffizi; Munich, Residenz). She also gained an important patron in Joseph Smith, the British consul in Venice, who bought a considerable amount of her work, part of which was later acquired by George III for the royal collections in England.

In 1730 Carriera left Italy again, this time for Vienna, where Pellegrini had been summoned to paint the cupola of the Salesian church. While there she made portraits of the *Empress Amalia* (Munich, Residenz; Dresden, Gemäldegal. Alte Meister) and of the poet and librettist *Pietro Metastasio* (Dresden, Gemäldegal. Alte Meister). These works represent a new stage in her development, in which she brought out the more austere characteristics of her sitters, with less emphasis on Rococo playfulness.

In later years Carriera underwent an eye operation, but this did not, apparently, interfere seriously with her painting. She continued to receive important sitters and was also commissioned to paint a series of the *Four Elements* for Frederick-Augustus II, Elector of Saxony (Augustus III of Poland from 1733), with whom she had contact through Francesco Algarotti. Augustus was the leading collector of her pastels; his gallery in Dresden, described by 18th-century sources as one of the wonders of the age, contained more than 100 of them in the Rosalba Room. His son Frederick-Christian (1722–63) added Carriera's miniatures to the collection. Most of these works were either sold by the Dresden Gemäldegalerie or destroyed in World War II.

See also PASTEL, §2, and colour pl. IV.

WRITINGS

A. Sensier, ed.: *Journal de Rosalba Carriera pendant son séjour à Paris en 1720 et 1721* (Paris, 1865)

B. Sani, ed.: *Rosalba Carriera: Lettere, diari, frammenti*, 2 vols (Florence, 1985)

BIBLIOGRAPHY

Mariette

'Elogio di Rosalba Carriera', *Mercure France*, ii (1722), pp. 114–16

G. L. Bianconi: *Elogio storico del Cavaliere Anton Rafaele Mengs con un catalogo delle opere che esso fatte* (Pavia, 1795), pp. 18–20

L. Lanzi: *Storia pittorica dell'Italia* (Bassano del Grappa, 1795–6)

G. Campori, ed.: *Lettere artistiche inedite* (Modena, 1886) [see letter of 1729 from Pier Caterino Zeno to Marmi]

V. Malamani: 'Rosalba Carriera: Per l'inaugurazione delle sale degli autoritratti nella R. Galleria degli Uffizi', *Gal. N. It.*, iv (1899), pp. 27–149

——: *Rosalba Carriera* (Bergamo, 1910)

P. Ratouis de Limay: *Le Pastel en France au XVIII siècle* (Paris, 1946)

R. Pallucchini: *La pittura veneziana del settecento* (Venice, 1960)

J. Cailleux: 'Un Portrait de Watteau par Rosalba Carriera', *Miscellanea I. Q. van Regteren Altena* (Amsterdam, 1969), pp. 174–7, fig. p. 345, no. 2

G. Gatto: 'Per la cronologia di Rosalba Carriera', *A. Ven.*, xxi (1971), pp. 182–93

B. Sani: 'Lo studio del Correggio in alcuni pastelli di Rosalba Carriera', *An. Scu. Norm. Sup. U. Pisa*, i (1978), pp. 203–12

——: 'La terminologia della pittura a pastello e in miniatura nel carteggio di Rosalba Carriera', *Convegno nazionale sui lessici tecnici del sei e settecento: Pisa, 1980*, pp. 387–417

——: 'Pastelli e miniature di Rosalba Carriera nelle collezioni di Giovanni Guglielmo Pfalz', *Itinerari*, ii (1981), pp. 133–43

——: *Rosalba Carriera* (Turin, 1988)

BERNARDINA SANI

Carrier-Belleuse [Carrier], **Albert-Ernest** (*b* Anizy-le-Château, Aisne, 12 June 1824; *d* Sèvres, 3 June 1887). French sculptor and designer. He was one of the most prolific and versatile sculptors of the 19th century, producing portrait busts, monuments and ideal works, as well as exploiting to the full the commercial opportunities offered by developing technology for the mass production of small-scale sculpture and decorative wares. His style ranged from the unembellished Realism of his male portraits to the neo-Baroque exuberance of his architectural decoration, and his art is particularly associated with the amiable opulence of the Second Empire. He signed his works A. Carrier until *c*. 1868, thereafter adopting the name Carrier-Belleuse.

Carrier-Belleuse began a three-year apprenticeship with a goldsmith at the age of 13, a training that gave him a lifelong sensitivity to intricate surfaces. In 1840 David d'Angers sponsored his entry to the Ecole des Beaux-Arts, Paris, but his straitened financial circumstances led him to study decorative arts at the Petite Ecole. This left him free to produce small models for such commercial manufacturers of porcelain and bronze as Michel Aaron, Auguste Lemaire, Vittoz and Paillard, who were beginning to flourish in the 1840s. Few examples of his work of this period are identifiable. By 1850 he was in England, employed as a designer at the Minton ceramic factory, though it is not clear if the revolutionary political events of 1848 were the cause of his departure from France. In addition to the many decorative objects and statuettes that he modelled for Minton, such as *Seahorse with Shell* (1855; London, V&A), he supplied models for ceramics and metalwork to other English companies, including such Staffordshire-based firms as Wedgwood and William Brownfield & Sons. In 1855 he returned to France but continued to collaborate with English firms until his death.

From 1857 Carrier-Belleuse regularly exhibited large-scale sculpture at the Salon. His first important success was in 1863 when Napoleon III bought the life-size marble *Bacchante with a Herm of Dionysus* (Paris, Jard. Tuileries). He often repeated the theme of the beguiling female nude, notably in *Sleeping Hebe* (marble, 1869; Paris, Mus. d'Orsay; see fig.). As in the work of his contemporary Jean-Baptiste Carpeaux, the neo-Baroque opulence of these statues is tempered by a strain of closely observed Realism.

Carrier-Belleuse also produced religious statuary, notably the *Messiah* (marble, 1867; Paris, St Vincent-de-Paul), which earned him the Médaille d'Honneur, and a number of ambitious public monuments, including *General Massena* (bronze, 1867; Nice, Place Massena) and *Alexandre Dumas père* (bronze, 1884; Villers-Cotterêt, Rue Alexandre Dumas). He supplied monuments abroad, and the large number of works by him in Argentina, including the marble monument to *General St Martin* (1879) in Buenos Aires Cathedral, raises the possibility that he might have maintained a workshop there to execute his designs.

Carrier-Belleuse was one of many sculptors to benefit from Baron Haussmann's rebuilding of Paris, begun during the Second Empire (1851–70), although in 1870 he was in Brussels working on the decoration of the Bourse and was therefore spared the privations of the siege of Paris in the following year. He contributed to the embellishment of the Louvre, the Tribune du Commerce, the Théâtre de la Renaissance, the Banque de France and Charles Garnier's Opéra. His magnificent electrotyped *torchères* (1873; *in situ*) for the grand staircase of the Opéra, each with its three over-life-size figures derived from the work of such 16th-century sculptors as Jean Goujon and Germain Pilon, perfectly illustrate Carrier-Belleuse's talent for combining historicist styling with the most recent technical innovations.

Albert-Ernest Carrier-Belleuse: *Sleeping Hebe*, marble, h. 2.07 m, 1869 (Paris, Musée d'Orsay)

In his many portrait busts, Carrier-Belleuse contributed to the reaction against the static poses and idealizing tendencies of Neo-classicism. He preferred to draw his inspiration from the 18th-century tradition of lively Realism, and in such lifelike male portraits as the bust of *Honoré Daumier* (patinated plaster, *c.* 1865–70; Versailles, Château) he used contemporary dress. Among his few court commissions are two portraits of *Napoleon III* (e.g. patinated plaster, 1864; Paris, Carnavalet); most of his sitters, however, were well-known artists, writers and politicians, often drawn from his circle of friends. A number of his elegant female portraits were reworked as fantasy busts, the features of Marguerite Bellanger, for instance, reappearing in the guises of *Diana* (tinted plaster; Paris, Martin de Nord priv. col.) and *Winter* (plaster; Paris, Mus. A. Déc.). The basic cast would often be varied by changing accessories, costumes or patinas. His portraits of historical figures include a statuette of *Michelangelo* (bronze, 1855; Berlin, Bodemus.) and a miniature portrait bust of the same artist (silvered version, *c.* 1860; New York, Met.) and are distinguished by the high quality of their chasing in examples from the artist's studio. Carrier-Belleuse sold reproduction rights to commercial manufacturers who executed many of these works in metal, terracotta, ceramic and marble without such careful attention to finish.

Carrier-Belleuse produced his own terracotta editions of gallant themes in the Rococo spirit, sometimes reductions of his Salon exhibits. Statuettes and groups were cast in moulds and then reworked while still wet to ensure a fresh, crisp surface. These pieces were sold by the artist, sometimes at auction. A similar diversity of themes and media characterized his applied designs. Supported by his reputation as a serious sculptor, he executed lavish one-off pieces, for instance a silvered bronze chimney-piece (1866) for the mansion of the courtesan and patron Païva, on the Champs-Elysées, Paris. He also continued to collaborate with commercial manufacturers to exploit the opportunities inherent in mass production, devoting as much care to the design of such a mass-produced object as his zinc clockcase (e.g. 1867; London, V&A) as to a unique de luxe one. In order to sustain his many activities, Carrier-Belleuse maintained a busy studio, in which some of the leading sculptors of the next generation, including Auguste Rodin, Jules Dalou and Alexandre Falguière, learnt to appreciate the value of the applied arts and the benefits of working in series, editions and variations.

In 1876 Carrier-Belleuse was made artistic director of the Sèvres porcelain manufactory to reform what were seen at the time as the aesthetic excesses of the previous decades. He devoted himself to revitalizing Sèvres with dozens of new designs, such as the 'Vase Carrier-Belleuse' (e.g. 1883; Paris, Hôtel du Sénat). In 1884 he published *L'Application de la figure humaine à la decoration et à l'ornementation industrielles*, a collection of 200 designs of anthropomorphic objects, which underlined his belief that since the human figure was traditionally the focus of art, its application to everyday objects would elevate their status. In the same year he was made an officer of the Légion d'honneur for his services to the decorative arts.

BIBLIOGRAPHY

A. Segard: *Albert Carrier-Belleuse* (Paris, 1928)

J. Hargrove: *The Life and Work of Albert Carrier-Belleuse* (New York, 1977)

P. Ward-Jackson: 'A.-E. Carrier-Belleuse, J.-J. Feuchère and the Sutherlands', *Burl. Mag.*, cxxvii (1985), pp. 147–53

JUNE HARGROVE

Carrière, Eugène (*b* Gournay, Seine-et-Oise, 27 Jan 1849; *d* Paris, 27 March 1906). French painter and printmaker. The eighth of nine children of a poor insurance salesman, he was brought up in Strasbourg, where he received his initial training in art at the Ecole Municipale de Dessin as part of his apprenticeship in commercial lithography. In 1868, while briefly employed as a lithographer, he visited Paris and was so inspired by the paintings of Rubens in the Louvre that he resolved to become an artist. His studies under Alexandre Cabanel at the Ecole des Beaux-Arts were interrupted by the Franco-Prussian War (1870–71), during which he was taken prisoner. In 1872–3 he worked in the studio of Jules Chéret. In 1878 he participated in the Salon for the first time, but his work went unnoticed. The following year he ended his studies under Cabanel, married and moved briefly to London where he saw and admired the works of Turner. Success eluded him for a number of years after he returned to Paris and he was forced to find occasional employment, usually with printers, until as late as 1889, to support his growing family. Between 1880 and 1885 his brother Ernest (1858–1908), a ceramicist, arranged part-time work for him at the Sèvres porcelain factory. There he met Auguste Rodin who became and remained an extremely close friend.

Carrière had great admiration for many of the Old Masters, but in his early work he was mainly influenced by his contemporary Jean-Jacques Henner. In the early 1880s Carrière requested Henner's comments on his work.

Eugène Carrière: *Maternity*, oil on canvas, 504×613 mm, *c.* 1889 (Philadelphia, PA, Museum of Art)

Carrière increasingly used a near monochromatic brown palette with occasional touches of other colours and a painterly technique somewhat like that of Henner, and by the mid-1880s Carrière's work was characterized by a dense brown atmosphere out of which the images emerged. *Sick Child* (1885; Paris, Mus. d'Orsay) is an example of the theme of a mother and her child that Carrière often used and that has come to be regarded as typifying his work.

Carrière described at length the manner in which he worked (*Ecrits et lettres choisies*, ed. J. Delvolvé (Paris, 1907), pp. 321–3). This was similar to the Old-Master method of laying in the preliminary underpainting. His innovative idea was to develop this underpainting by modifications of value and sparse additions of subtle colour, and to present the result as a finished work of art. He said that painting is the logical development of light, and his earth tone palette and the effect of light picking out images from a vaporous environment produced works that illustrated his belief, as a spiritualist, in creation as a continuing process of coalescence out of primal, universal forces.

At the Salon of 1884 one of Carrière's paintings received an honourable mention, and the influential art critic Roger Marx became a champion of his work. Thereafter, Carrière found friends in most of the important artists, critics, writers and collectors of his time.

Carrière occupies an important place in the Symbolist movement, which developed in the visual arts from the mid-1880s. The quality of poetic, dreamlike reverie that pervades his work particularly appealed to Symbolist critics such as Charles Morice and Jean Dolent; the latter described Carrière's art as reality having the magic of dreams. Carrière also frequented the Café Voltaire and was involved in Symbolist theatre, bringing him into the main stream of Symbolism. By employing a monochromatic brown palette, softening the focus and enveloping his figures in a thick, dark atmosphere, as in *Maternity* (*c.* 1889; Philadelphia, PA, Mus. A.; see fig.), Carrière achieved a natural sense of space, light and colour. His ethereal images have a quality of pervasive stillness.

Carrière's strong belief in the essential brotherhood of man led him to consider his family as a microcosm of mankind. Though most of his paintings are of family members or family relationships, his interest in the universal rather than the specific usually resulted in figures without much individuality presented in a formless environment. He also produced a number of portraits, however; most notable is that of *Verlaine* (Paris, Mus. d'Orsay).

From the late 1880s Carrière's work in oil and graphic media developed an emphasis on technique. There is evidence of stroking, wiping and scratching in the textural surfaces of his pictures. The limited range of colours and the apparentness of the technique and medium, as in *Self-portrait* (*c.* 1903; Paris, Grunbaum Col.), further underline his concern to present the spiritual aspect, rather than the physical appearance, of objects.

Carrière received many honours during his career. He was a founder member of the Société Nationale des Beaux-Arts and of the Salon d'Automne (of which he was named honorary president). Carrière also exhibited with the Libre Esthétique in Brussels (in 1894, 1896 and 1899), the Munich Secession (in 1896, 1899, 1905 and 1906) and the Berlin Secession in 1904. After his death from cancer of the throat, the Société Nationale des Beaux-Arts and the Salon d'Automne in 1906, as well as the Ecole Nationale des Beaux-Arts and the Libre Esthétique in 1907, held major retrospective exhibitions. The Musée d'Orsay in Paris owns a large collection of his work.

BIBLIOGRAPHY

C. Morice: *Eugène Carrière—l'homme et sa pensée, l'artiste et son oeuvre: Essai de nomenclature des oeuvres principales* (Paris, 1906)
E. Faure: *Eugène Carrière: Peintre et lithographe* (Paris, 1908)
L. Delteil: *Eugène Carrière* (1913), viii of *Le Peintre-graveur illustré*, 31 vols (Paris, 1906–30/*R* New York, 1969)
J.-R. Carrière: *De la vie d'Eugène Carrière* (Toulouse, 1966)
R. J. Bantens: *Eugène Carrière: His Work and his Influence* (diss., Penn. State U., 1975; microfilm, Ann Arbor, 1976)
The Other Nineteenth Century (exh. cat., ed. L. d'Argencourt and D. Druick; Ottawa, N.G., 1978), pp. 63–71
R. J. Bantens: *Eugène Carrière: The Symbol of Creation* (New York, 1990)

ROBERT J. BANTENS

Carriès [Cariès], **Jean(-Joseph-Marie)** (*b* Lyon, 15 Feb 1855; *d* Paris, 1 July 1894). French sculptor and ceramicist. He was brought up in an orphanage and in 1868 entered the studio of a sculptor of religious images named Vermare. In 1874 he became a probationary pupil of Augustin-Alexandre Dumont at the Ecole des Beaux-Arts in Paris but, having failed the tests for full admission, left to set up on his own. He made his début at the Salon of 1875; his first success, however, came after that of 1881, and above all from a private exhibition organized by the Cercle des Arts Libéraux in 1882. Most of his sculptural work, principally bronze portrait busts cast by the lost-wax method, was carried out between 1881 and 1888. It includes portraits of contemporaries, for example *Jules Breton* and *Léon Gambetta* (plaster casts of both, Paris, Petit Pal.); historical representations, for example of *Frans Hals* and *Diego Velázquez* (plaster casts of both, Paris, Petit Pal.); and a number of ideal busts—Symbolist reinterpretations of the academic *tête d'expression*—for example *The Desperate* (plaster cast, Paris, Petit Pal.) and *The Nun* (bronze, Lyon, Mus. B.-A.). He also produced studies of various heads of babies (examples in Paris, Petit Pal.). From 1888 Carriès was able to fulfil a long-standing desire to experiment with ceramics. His most ambitious work in this medium, a monumental Symbolist doorway (destr.) commissioned in 1889 by Winaretta Singer (1865–1943), Princesse de Scey-Montbéliard, was intended to adorn the room in which she kept the manuscript of Wagner's opera *Parsifal*. He died before it was completed, but the plaster maquette, together with a collection of works by Carriès donated by his friend Georges Hoentschel (1855–1915), is at the Musée du Petit Palais, Paris. He signed his works *Joseph Carriès* until 1890–91 and *Jean Carriès* thereafter.

BIBLIOGRAPHY

A. Alexandre: *Jean Carriès, imagier et potier: Etude d'une oeuvre et d'une vie* (Paris, 1895)
P. Thiébaut: 'A propos d'un groupe céramique de Jean Carriès: *Le Grenouillard*', *Rev. Louvre*, 2 (1982), pp. 121–8

PHILIPPE THIEBAUT

Carrillo, Lilia (*b* Mexico City, 2 Nov 1930; *d* Mexico City, 6 June 1974). Mexican painter and stage designer. She studied at the Escuela de Pintura y Escultura la Esmeralda in Mexico City and later in Paris at the Académie de la Grande Chaumière. One of the pioneers of *Art informel* in Mexico, like her husband, Manuel Felguérez (whom she married in 1960), she formed part of a group of young painters who rebelled against the Mexican art establishment in the 1950s. Exhibiting her work widely during the 1960s, she aroused controversy by winning second prize with an abstract work at the Salón Esso (1965; Mexico City, Pal. B.A.). In 1968 she also helped set up the Salón Independiente as a protest against the government-subsidized Salón Solar on the occasion of the Olympic Games in Mexico City. She made several murals, but her most important works were her abstract easel paintings, displaying a fine use of colour. In the 1960s she also worked as a stage designer.

BIBLIOGRAPHY

Homenaje a Lilia Carrillo (exh. cat., Monterrey, Nue. León, Promoc. A., 1979)

LEONOR MORALES

Carrington, Dora (de Houghton) (*b* Hereford, 29 March 1893; *d* nr Newbury, Berks, 11 March 1932). English painter and decorative artist. Daughter of a Liverpool merchant, she was brought up in Bedford. She trained at the Slade School of Fine Art in London where she met John Nash, who aroused her interest in wood-engraving, and Mark Gertler, whose powerful figure paintings influenced her own approach to portraiture. She rejected Gertler as a lover and set up home with the homosexual essayist and biographer Lytton Strachey (1880–1932), first at Tidmarsh Mill, near Pangbourne, Berks, then at Ham Spray, between Newbury and Hungerford, Berks. In 1921 she married Ralph Partridge, living with him and Strachey in a *ménage à trois*, surrounded mainly by literary friends and receiving little encouragement to exhibit. She turned instead to decorative work, emulating Vanessa Bell and Duncan Grant but in a style more native in inspiration and more naive. She designed tiles and inn signs, experimented with painting on glass and tinfoil, decorated furniture and designed the library at Ham Spray. Emotional relationships further diversified her interests and much of her creative energy went into her letters which, with their mongrel prose, inimitable spelling and spontaneous illustrations, provide an exceptional insight into her life and character. As a painter she is uneven, at times awkward, at others, as in *The Mill at Tidmarsh* (1918; priv. col., see Carrington, pl. 5), bringing poetic vehemence to her well-constructed image. She is aligned more with her Slade contemporaries than with Bloomsbury. The example of French art did not loosen her touch, and her obsession with her subject denied a more abstract perception of form. Often she is more Pre-Raphaelite than Post-Impressionist. The 'preternatural acuteness' that Julia Strachey observed in her view of others sharpens the fun in her letters and can give a startling intensity to her portraits and landscapes.

WRITINGS

D. Garnett, ed.: *Carrington: Letters and Extracts from her Diaries* (London, 1970)

BIBLIOGRAPHY

M. Holroyd: *Lytton Strachey: A Critical Biography*, 2 vols (London, 1967–8)

Dora Carrington: Paintings and Drawings (exh. cat., Oxford, Christ Church Pict. Gal., 1978)
N. Carrington: *Carrington: Paintings, Drawings and Decorations* (Oxford, 1978)
G. H. Gerzina: *Carrington: Another Look at Bloomsbury* (Ann Arbor, 1985)
J. Hill: *The Art of Dora Carrington* (London, 1994)

FRANCES SPALDING

Carrington, Leonora (*b* Clayten Green, nr Chorley, Lancs, 6 April 1917). Mexican painter and writer of English birth. In 1936 she travelled to London, where she studied under Amédée Ozenfant and in 1937 met Max Ernst, with whom she became involved artistically and romantically, leading to her association with Surrealism. They moved to Paris together in 1937. At the outbreak of World War II, Ernst was interned as an enemy alien, and Carrington escaped to Spain, where she was admitted to a private clinic after having a nervous breakdown; she later recounted the experience in her book *En bas* (1943). After marrying the Mexican poet Renato Leduc in 1941 (a marriage of convenience), she spent time in New York before settling in Mexico in 1942, devoting herself to painting. There she and Remedios Varo developed an illusionistic Surrealism combining autobiographical and occult symbolism. Having divorced Leduc in 1942, in 1946 she married the Hungarian photographer Imre Weisz.

Carrington remained committed to Surrealism throughout her career, filling her pictures with strange or fantastic creatures in surprising situations, notably horses, which appear in *Self-portrait* (1938; priv. col., see Chadwick, p. 77), as well as unicorns, owls, dogs and lizards; she sometimes also combined features of animals and human beings. Her references were wide-ranging, whether to ancient Babylonian, Assyrian and Egyptian mythology (e.g. *Palatine Predella*, 1946; priv. col., see Chadwick, pl. XIX) or to visions reminiscent of the Middle Ages. The strange, enigmatic and subtly humorous anecdotes that appear in her work were the expression of a profound inner world, a mythology of her own making, which although terrifying protected her from the aggressive banality of the external world. A prolific painter, she combined technical refinement with a careful but at the same time extremely free design, as in *The Chrysopeia of María de Jesús* (1964; priv. col., see Rodríguez Prampolini, pl. XIII).

WRITINGS

En bas (Paris, 1943), xviii of *L'Age d'or*, ed. H. Parisot; Eng. trans. as *Down Under* (New York, 1944, Paris, 2/1973)

BIBLIOGRAPHY

I. Rodríguez Prampolini: *El surrealismo y el arte fantástico de México* (Mexico City, 1969), pp. 73–5
J. García Ponce: *Leonora Carrington* (Mexico City, 1974)
T. del Conde: 'Pintura fantástica y nueva figuración' (1982), xv of *El arte mexicano*, ed. J. A. Manrique, pp. 2276–98
W. Chadwick: *Women Artists and the Surrealist Movement* (London, 1985), pp. 67–8, 74–86, 191–201

JORGE ALBERTO MANRIQUE

Carrión, de. Spanish family of illuminators and painters. Juan de Carrión, who is first mentioned in Ávila in the early 1470s, and his brother Pedro are known primarily for the illumination of the choir-books (early 1470s; all Ávila, Mus. Catedral) of Ávila Cathedral. Juan used to be credited with the authorship of all the miniatures decorating these books, but the publication of the payment records of Ávila Cathedral has now revealed that the miniature of *Pentecost* (MS. III, fol. 30*r*) is the work of Pedro. Juan's personal style is also securely documented, and to him can be attributed the miniatures of the *Adoration* (MS. I, fol. 102*r*), the *Resurrection* (detached leaf), the *Nativity* (MS. I, fol. 92*r*) and a detached leaf depicting *Eight Saints* (Paris, Ecole N. Sup. B.-A., no. 152). The Carrión group, composed of fifteen liturgical and secular manuscripts and three detached leaves, dating from *c*. 1470–85, is one of the most important of Spanish 15th-century manuscript illumination. Also attributed to Juan de Carrión is the panel painting of *Anna Selbdritt with SS Christopher and Barbara* (Ávila, Mus. Catedral), which reveals his familiarity with contemporary Netherlandish painting. On the basis of internal evidence it can be established that Juan de Carrión guided a workshop with both royal and aristocratic patronage, including King Henry IV of Castile, his father John II of Castile and Alfonso Carrillo, Archbishop of Toledo. The workshop possessed a timely awareness of the work of such leading European artists as Jan van Eyck, Rogier van der Weyden and Martin Schongauer, thus expressing a taste for northern European art that must have been favoured by its patrons.

See also MASTERS, ANONYMOUS, AND MONOGRAMMISTS, §I: MASTER OF THE CYPRESSES.

BIBLIOGRAPHY

J. Domínguez Bordona: 'Las miniaturas de Juan de Carrión', *Archv Esp. A.*, vi (1930), pp. 17–20
——: 'Dos dibujos de Juan de Carrión', *Archv Esp. A.*, viii (1932), p. 95
A. Saulnier: 'Oeuvres inédites de l'enlumineur Juan de Carrión', *Rev. A.* [Paris], lvii (1982), pp. 56–60
M. P. Silva Maroto: 'La miniatura hispano-flamenca en Ávila: Datos documentales', *Miscelánea de arte* (Madrid, 1982), pp. 55–8
M. Gómez-Moreno: *Catálogo monumental de la provincia de Ávila* (Madrid, 1983), i, pp. 119–20
L. M. F. Bosch: *Manuscript Illumination in Toledo (1446–1482): The Liturgical Books* (diss., Princeton U., 1985), pp. 424–513
——: 'Iluminación en Ávila y Segovia durante el siglo XV: Los libros litúrgicos del grupo de Juan de Carrión', *Archv Esp. A.* (1991), pp. 471–87
——: 'Les manuscritos abulenses de Juan de Carrión', *Archv Esp. A.*, lxiv (1991), pp. 55–64

LYNETTE BOSCH

Carrión de los Condes. Town in Palencia province, Old Castile, Spain. Today a modest agricultural town, Carrión de los Condes flourished from the late 11th century to the mid-13th, when its place at the border of Castile and León on the pilgrimage road to Santiago de Compostela brought economic prosperity and strategic importance. A county seat from the late 10th century, Carrión was the stronghold of the Beni Gómez clan, who established their burial place in the monastery of S Zoilo, affiliated with Cluny Abbey in 1076 and the site of Church councils in 1103 and 1130. A shafted window and some masonry are all that remain of the church of *c*. 1100, but several tombs of the late 11th century and early 12th bear fine inscriptions; others, from the first half of the 13th century, have extensive figure-carving attributable to a local workshop also responsible for tombs at the nearby Augustinian house of Benevivere. The richly sculpted Romanesque façades of the churches of S María del Camino and Santiago (*see* §§1 and 2 below) attest to the town's importance in the 12th century, when it was the setting for the marriage of Sancho III of Castile (*reg* 1157–8) and Blanche of Navarre (*d* 1156) in 1151, the arming of Alfonso VIII of Castile (*reg* 1158–1214) in 1169 and of his cousin Alfonso IX of León (*reg* 1188–1230) in 1188.

After the 13th century the importance of Carrión de los Condes declined, and its churches and their furnishings—mainly of the late 16th century and 17th—are comparable to those of surrounding towns. Most notable are the cloister of S Zoilo, begun by Juan de Badajoz el Mozo in 1537, continued by local artists and completed in 1604; the Crucifix and *Pietà* of Gregorio Fernández in the early 17th-century domed church of the convent of S Clara; the tomb (*c.* 1630) of *Melchor Álvarez de Vozmediano, Bishop of Guadix* in the 16th-century hall church of S Andrés; and the Plateresque retable of the sanctuary of Belén, a church begun in the mid-15th century. Civic monuments include a medieval bridge of nine arches, modest remains of the town walls, and three town houses with heraldic shields.

BIBLIOGRAPHY

J. Urrea Fernández and J. C. Brasas Egide: *Inventario artístico de Palencia y su provincia*, ii (Madrid, 1980)

1. S MARÍA DEL CAMINO. The remaining sculpture of the Romanesque church of S María del Camino is concentrated on the projecting south portal. The five arches, supported by alternating stepped jambs and columns, are flanked by reliefs of *Samson* astride a lion and a large equestrian figure; above the portal are corbels, metopes carved with a fragmentary *Zodiac* cycle and a frieze with scenes of the *Magi*. On one of the arches, radiating voussoirs bear 37 human figures, some with musical instruments. There are parallels for the capitals and imposts at Segovia and Fuentidueña (Old Castile), suggesting a date of *c.* 1150, and there are also similarities to radiating voussoirs at Oloron Sainte-Marie (France) and Uncastillo (Saragossa), both sources for Fuentidueña. Independent links with western France, where radiating voussoirs were common, could, however, explain the presence of the prominent equestrian figure.

2. SANTIAGO. Only the west façade of the church of Santiago survives, dominated by a high-relief frieze with *Christ in Majesty* and the Evangelist symbols flanked by the *Twelve Apostles* under arched canopies (for illustration, *see* ROMANESQUE, fig. 31). Below is an arched doorway with craftsmen and secular activities carved on the radiating voussoirs, which are supported by two columns, each adorned with an angel in low relief over spiral mouldings studded with flowers. The representation of the Apostles was traditional in Spain, while craftsmen accompanying the *Last Judgement* or *Weighing of Souls* appear at Uncastillo (Saragossa), Sanguesa and Tudela (Navarre), suggesting a moralizing content for those at Carrión. The overall design echoes the south portal of S María, the sculptors of which also carved the outermost *Apostles* and some of the ornament at Santiago. The remaining figures are the earliest surviving work of one of the most important ateliers in late 12th-century Spain. On the voussoirs drilled decoration, acanthus borders and backgrounds and delicately carved facial features recall sculpture at La Charité-sur-Loire and Souvigny in Burgundy. The figures of the voussoirs have the same facial types and channelled draperies as the frieze, where rippling, windswept robes fall and flutter, carved in thin sheets of stone with a baroque exuberance akin to late Burgundian sculpture at Donzy-le-Pré and Charlieu Abbey. Earlier Spanish sculpture must have also impressed these artists as they turned to the large figures: arching ridges of drapery, the occasional cross-legged pose and the fully rounded heads show the influence of the style of the transept sculpture of Santiago de Compostela Cathedral.

Santiago, Carrión, was highly influential. At S María, Piasca (Cantabria), many motifs were copied by a sculptor responsible for minor decoration at Carrión. In the northern parts of the modern province of Palencia craftsmen were depicted on archivolts at Perazancas and Arenillas de San Pelayo, the *Apostles* inspired those at Moarves and Zorita del Páramo, and capitals from S María, Aguilar de Campóo (Madrid, Mus. Arquel. N.), show the style of Carrión. In Galicia the *Christ in Majesty* of the north transept portal of Lugo Cathedral reflects that of Carrión, and sculptural fragments at Santiago de Compostela Cathedral associated with the western crypt resemble the *Apostles*. Finally, the workshop completed the decoration of S Vicente, Ávila, carved a shrine for its patron saints and prepared capitals for Ávila Cathedral. A dedicatory inscription of 1172 on the west façade of S María, Piasca, makes a date of *c.* 1165 plausible for Santiago, consistent with its relationship to S María del Camino and influence elsewhere.

BIBLIOGRAPHY

M. A. García Guinea: *El arte románico en Palencia* (Palencia, 1961, rev. 2/1975)
S. Moralejo Alvárez: 'Esculturas compostelanas del último tercio del siglo XII', *Cuad. Estud. Gallegos*, xxviii (1973), pp. 294–310
B. Mariño: 'Die Fassade der Kirche von Santiago de Carrión de los Condes: Ein Beitrag zur Ikonographie der Arbeit in der mittelalterlichen Kunst', *Med. Aevum Quotidianum*, iii (1984), pp. 50–59
M. F. Cuadrado Lorenzo: 'Un posible zódiaco alegórico en las metopas de la portada meridional de Santa María de Carrión de los Condes', *Bol. Semin. Estud. A. & Arqueol. Valladolid*, li (1985), pp. 440–46
J. D'Emilio: 'Tradición local y aportaciones foráneas en la escultura románica tardía: Compostela, Lugo y Carrión', *Actas. Simposio Internacional sobre: 'O Pórtico da Gloria e a arte do seu tempo'* (Santiago de Compostela, 1992), pp. 83–101

JAMES D'EMILIO

Carritt, (Hugh) David (Graham) (*b* London, 15 April 1927; *d* London, 3 Aug 1982). English connoisseur, dealer and critic. He was educated at Rugby School and won a scholarship to Christ Church, Oxford. Possessing what Bernard Berenson described as 'the finest eye of his generation' and a phenomenal visual memory, he repeatedly made the vital correlation that led to a previously unsolved attribution or brought to light an important picture. In 1956 Albrecht Dürer's study of a lion in the Kunsthalle, Hamburg, provided the clue for Carritt's fully accepted attribution to Dürer of *St Jerome in the Wilderness* (Norfolk, Bacon priv. col., see Carritt, 1957, p. 360), formerly considered to be Italian. He also found in private ownership Caravaggio's untraced *Concert of Youths* (New York, Met.), five large mythological canvases by Giovanni Antonio Guardi (two in Washington, DC, N.G.A.) and

Giambattista Tiepolo's lost *Venus Entrusting Eros to Chronos* (London, N.G.).

In 1964 Carritt's growing reputation led to his joining Christie's, London, where his expertise and flair made a notable contribution to the revival of the firm's fortunes. While there he discovered the portrait of *St Ivo of Chartres* by Rogier van der Weyden (London, N.G.). He left Christie's in 1970 to found Artemis, the international art dealing consortium, with the Belgian banker Baron Léon Lambert (1928–87). Although he was not wholly suited to the role of art dealer, Carritt's connoisseurship and international contacts ensured the firm's success. Of his discoveries made while with Artemis the most important were the *Baptism* by Giovanni di Paolo (Pasadena, CA, Norton Simon Mus.) and Jean-Honoré Fragonard's early masterpiece, *Psyche Showing her Sisters Cupid's Presents* (London, N.G.), which he alone recognized, wrongly catalogued, in the widely publicized Mentmore sale in 1977.

WRITINGS

'Dürer's *St Jerome in the Wilderness*', *Burl. Mag.*, xcix (1957), pp. 360–66

'Mr Fauquier's Chardins', *Burl. Mag.*, cxvi (1974), pp. 502–9

BIBLIOGRAPHY

DNB

D. Wintersgill and I. McNicholl: 'Profile: David Carritt', *A. & Auction*, v (Oct 1982), pp. 44–8

J. Herbert: *Inside Christie's* (London, 1990)

COLIN ANSON

Carroll, Lewis [Dodgson, Charles L(utwidge)] (*b* Daresbury, Ches, 27 Jan 1832; *d* Oxford, 14 Jan 1898). English mathematician, writer and photographer. Well-known as the author of children's books with a logical philosophical undercurrent, he was active as an amateur photographer, using wet collodion plates, from May 1856 to July 1880, according to his diary. His portraits of Victorian luminaries include *Dante Gabriel Rossetti* (1863; see Gernsheim, pl. 21), *Arthur Hughes* (1863; see Gernsheim, pl. 32), *John Everett Millais* (1865; see Gernsheim, pl. 48), *Alfred Tennyson* (1857; see Gernsheim, pl. 8) and many churchmen. His portraits of children are often elegantly composed: *The Ellis Children* (1865; see Ovenden and Melville, pl. 2), for example, lie, sit and stand to form a white triangle of dresses on the dark landscape. *Effie Millais* (1863; see Gernsheim, pl. 50) in her white flannel night-gown swirls within an oval frame. His letters suggest that he made numerous nude studies of children. Four hand-tinted examples of these may be found in the Rosenbach Museum and Library, Philadelphia.

Carroll occasionally strove for an effect very similar to Julia Margaret Cameron's Pre-Raphaelitism. *Florence Bickersteth* (1865; see Gernsheim, pl. 54) shows white hands gripping a black hat, dark hair rippling over a white blouse. Carroll wrote 'Photographers are a blind race at best; . . . we learn to look at even the prettiest faces as so much light and shade' (Gernsheim, p. 121). Yet the direct, controlling gaze of many of his young female models suggests the curious humility of his camera; they can appear imperious (especially Alice Liddell) or sensuous when presented as draped nudes. On the whole they are inviting, innocent and, at the same time, wise representations of the sexuality of Victorian girlhood.

BIBLIOGRAPHY

H. Gernsheim: *Lewis Carroll, Photographer* (London and New York, 1949)

G. Ovenden and R. Melville: *Victorian Children* (London, 1972)

M. Cohen: *Lewis Carroll, Photographer of Children: Four Nude Studies* (New York, 1978)

A. Clark: *Lewis Carroll: A Biography* (New York, 1979)

C. Mavor: 'Dream Rushes: Lewis Carroll's Photographs of the Little Girl', *The Girl's Own*, ed. C. Nelson and L. Vallone (London, 1994)

LESLIE WILLIAMS

Cars, Laurent (*b* Lyon, 28 May 1699; *d* Paris, 14 April 1771). French printmaker, print publisher and print-seller. Early in his life his family removed to Paris. His father, Jean-François Cars (1661–1730), an engraver and publisher, was his first teacher. He next studied painting under Joseph Christophe (1662–1748) and François Lemoyne and then completed his studies in engraving under Nicolas-Henry Tardieu. In 1729 he was approved (*agréé*) by the Académie Royale and on 31 December 1733 was received (*reçu*), on presentation of the engraved portraits of *Michel Anguier* after Gabriel Revel and of *Sébastien Bourdon* after Hyacinthe Rigaud. From 1750 he gradually abandoned engraving in favour of print-selling, particularly those of his father's collection. In 1757 he was appointed a Conseiller. His work included nearly 190 prints; he engraved portraits, historical and mythological subjects after Lemoyne, such as *Hercules and Omphale* and the *Bath of Iris*, and genre subjects after Watteau, such as *Figures de différents caractères* and *Fêtes vénitiennes* (generally considered Cars's masterpiece). He also engraved after Chardin (e.g. the *Bird-song Organ*) and Greuze, among others. Cars illustrated Molière's *Oeuvres* with engravings after Boucher (1734) and Jean de la Fontaine's *Fables choisies* after Oudry (1755–9). He also contributed prints to the *Galerie de Versailles* (1753). He was among the best reproductive engravers of his time; his design was masterly and his handling fluid and expressive, and such contemporaries as Charles-Nicolas Cochin *le fils* and Louis-Simon Lempereur stressed that he was an interpreter and not merely a copyist. His numerous pupils included Jacques-Firmin Beauvarlet, Jean-Jacques Flipart, François Flipart and Augustin de Saint-Aubin. His portrait by Cochin was engraved in 1750 by Saint-Aubin Cochin; his portrait by Jean-Baptiste Perronneau was engraved in 1759 by Simon-Charles Miger (1736–1820).

BIBLIOGRAPHY

M. Roux: *Inventaire du fonds français: Graveurs du dix-huitième siècle*, Paris, Bib. N., Dept Est. cat., iii (Paris, 1934), pp. 454–517

P. Jean-Richard: *L'Oeuvre gravé de François Boucher dans la collection Edmond de Rothschild* (Paris, 1978), pp. 128–41

M. Préaud and others: *Dictionnaire des éditeurs d'estampes à Paris sous l'Ancien Régime* (Paris, 1987), p. 74

V. Meyer: 'Le Commerce des thèses au XVIIIe siècle', *Nouv. Est.* (in preparation)

VÉRONIQUE MEYER

Carse, Alexander (*b c.* 1770; *d* Edinburgh, Feb 1843). Scottish painter. He originally worked as a wigmaker. In the 1790s he produced topographical illustrations in Edinburgh and reputedly trained under David Allan and at the Trustees' Academy. Turning to figure subjects *c.* 1800, he contributed to the development of Realism in Scottish genre. He evolved a frank but subtle style with a sensitive response to character and the nuances of light, seen in

Arrival of the Country Cousins (*c.* 1812; Duke of Buccleuch priv. col.). His art was admired by the young David Wilkie, who based his *Pitlessie Fair* on Carse's *Oldhamstock Fair* (1796; both in Edinburgh, N.G.). Wilkie also took up many of the subjects that Carse had already derived from Allan, such as *Penny Wedding*, which Carse had painted in 1819 (G. N. Statham priv. col., on dep. Edinburgh, N.G.).

Carse contributed to the exhibitions of the Society of Incorporated Artists in Edinburgh from their inception in 1808. He also became a regular and popular exhibitor in London, where he lived from 1812 to 1820. His works depicted contemporary domestic life and humorous and literary subjects such as *Tam o'Shanter* (1815; Edinburgh, N.G.) and the *Troops of Tweeddale* from Penicuik's poems, depicted on the ceiling panel (destr.) for Newhall House, near Edinburgh. He also wrote a Romantic poem which he illustrated, *The Witches' Late Wake* (1815; Edinburgh, N.G.). In 1831 he was elected an Artist Associate of the Royal Institute in Edinburgh, but he produced little in his later years.

BIBLIOGRAPHY

J. L. Caw: *Scottish Painting Past and Present, 1620–1908* (Edinburgh and London, 1908/*R* Bath, 1978), p. 106

L. Errington: Untitled article on Carse's *Penny Wedding*, *Nat. Gals Scotland Bull.*, 1 (1975)

D. Irwin and F. Irwin: *Scottish Painters at Home and Abroad, 1700–1900* (London, 1975), pp. 190–91

W. R. Hardie: *Scottish Painting, 1837–1939* (London, 1976, rev. 2/1990), pp. 34, 42

J. Halsby: *Scottish Watercolours, 1740–1940* (Braintree, 1986), pp. 59–60

Town and Country: The Social Scene in Scotland, 1850–1920 (exh. cat., ed. C. A. P. Willsdon; U. Glasgow, Hunterian A.G., 1986)

L. Errington: *Alexander Carse (c. 1770–1843)*, Scottish Masters, 2 (Edinburgh, 1987) [incl. checklist of major extant works]

D. Macmillan: *Scottish Art, 1460–1990* (Edinburgh, 1990), pp. 165, 179–80

CLARE A. P. WILLSDON

Carstens, Asmus Jakob (*b* Sanct Gürgen, nr Schleswig, Denmark [now Germany], 10 May 1754; *d* Rome, 2 May 1798). Danish–German painter and draughtsman. Both Denmark and Germany claim him as their own in their national histories of art, but his greatest impact was on the international group of artists gathered in the last decade of the 18th century in Rome, where Carstens spent his last and most productive years. His severe Neo-classical drawing style and, to an even greater extent, his romantically charged commitment to art influenced such younger artists as Bertel Thorvaldsen and Joseph Anton Koch. Carstens's life is excellently documented by Karl Ludwig Fernow, who knew the artist as a young man in Germany and was his closest friend during his mature years in Rome.

1. Early years, to 1791. 2. Rome, 1792–8.

1. Early years, to 1791. According to Fernow, Carstens spurned as too stifling an offered apprenticeship with Johann Heinrich Tischbein (i); instead he trained for five years as a cooper. In 1776 he began his fine arts studies at the Copenhagen Academy, where his masters included Nicolai Abraham Abildgaard. Distrustful of the academic discipline of direct copying after plaster casts, he studied the works in the galleries, later drawing the forms from a combination of memory and inspiration.

Like Abildgaard and many north European artists of the late 18th century, Carstens was determined to go to Rome to immerse himself in the study of ancient art. Denied a first prize at the Academy and with it a scholarship to study in Rome, he nonetheless travelled to Italy in 1783. There he was deeply impressed by the powerful forms of Giulio Romano's frescoes at the Palazzo del Tè in Mantua.

After running out of funds Carstens returned to north Germany and eked out a living through a variety of minor commissions, including portraits (which he despised). He also received financial assistance from, among others, Christian Overbeck, a town official in Lübeck and father of the painter Friedrich Overbeck. In 1788 Carstens went to Berlin, where he obtained an appointment as a teacher at the Akademie and found favour as a muralist, decorating rooms both for the royal family and for the minister of education, Karl Friedrich von Heinitz.

Little of Carstens's early work, including the murals and a proposed monument to Frederick II, King of Prussia, survives. His early drawings collected at Copenhagen (Copenhagen, Stat. Mus. Kst) are, despite his self-advertised anti-academicism, unexciting student exercises, but an augury of his later success can be found in the coloured chalk *Self-portrait* (Hamburg, Ksthalle) traditionally dated to 1784, when the artist was living in Lübeck. Heavily idealized, the portrait is a powerful testament to his emerging style and nascent sensibility. From his Berlin years a large (940×1160 mm) black chalk drawing of the *Rape of Ganymede* (Weimar, Schlossmus.) survives, one of four illustrations contributed by Carstens to Karl Philipp Moritz's *Götterlehre* (Berlin, 1791). Nearly life-size in scale, the *Ganymede* is stylistically ambitious, contrasting the steely, obsessive, feather-by-feather realism of Jupiter as an eagle with the pliant, softly modelled, almost waxen figure of the youth. Emblematic of the new seriousness that Carstens and his generation brought to art is the austere frontality of both subjects. Also notable is the composition, in which the figures of Jupiter and Ganymede are held close to the picture plane and fill virtually its entire extent.

2. Rome, 1792–8. In 1792, through the good offices of von Heinitz, Carstens obtained a leave of absence from his teaching duties and a stipend from the Prussian government to travel to Rome. There he took up quarters in the studio previously occupied by Pompeo Girolamo Batoni in Via Bocca di Leone. Immersed in the artistic life of the city, Carstens almost completely ignored his obligations to the Berlin Akademie (he was, for example, supposed to submit regular reports on his progress). Finally, in December 1795, von Heinitz wrote from Berlin demanding that Carstens fulfil the terms of the agreement and return immediately to his teaching position. Carstens's lengthy, indignant reply has often been cited as an early manifestation of the burgeoning romantic self-definition of the artist: 'I must also tell your Excellency that I belong not to the Berlin Akademie but to mankind. . . I renounce all benefits, preferring poverty, an uncertain future and perhaps a hopelessly infirm old age. . ., so that I may do my duty to art and fulfil my calling as an artist' (Fernow). Carstens stayed in Rome for the few remaining years of his life.

Asmus Jakob Carstens: *Night with her Children Sleep and Death*, black chalk, 745×985 mm, *c.* 1795 (Weimar, Schlossmuseum)

In 1795 Carstens held at his studio a one-person exhibition of drawings and paintings in tempera, having by this time totally abandoned oil painting. He included such works as *Night with her Children Sleep and Death* (Weimar, Schlossmus.; see fig.), *Time and Space* (inspired by the writings of Immanuel Kant; untraced) and *Heroes in the Tent of Achilles* (Weimar, Schlossmus.). One of several attempts by late 18th-century artists to establish alternatives to traditional resources for exhibition or patronage, this show was widely hailed. While there is considerable variety in the styles, media and iconographic sources of Carstens's mature works, certain characteristics recur. During this period he was influenced by the works of Michelangelo, even proposing a monumental *Battle between the Titans and the Gods* loosely modelled on, and on the scale of, Michelangelo's *Last Judgement* in the Sistine Chapel, Rome, and a corresponding grandeur hangs over most of his Roman production. Also, even though Carstens moved towards a pure outline style only at the very end of his life, all his Roman work is marked by a reductive purification of means, one result of which was his near total interest in drawing rather than oil painting. Finally, he supported his ambition to be all-encompassing or universal, rather than specific or parochial, by depicting allegorical rather than historical subject-matter. A similar outlook (and sometimes a similar style) is found in the work of several other late 18th-century artists, including Les Primitifs in France and Johann Heinrich Füseli and William Blake in England.

Carstens took no students into his studio, but his art and, more particularly, his ideas profoundly influenced a number of younger artists, including Bertel Thorvaldsen, Joseph Anton Koch (who in 1799 engraved a series of the *Voyage of the Argonauts* after Carstens's 24 preliminary drawings), Eberhard Wächter and Bonaventura Genelli (nephew of the architect Hans Christian Genelli, with whom Carstens collaborated in Berlin). Without many direct connections to Carstens, the NAZARENES—particularly Peter Cornelius—owe much to his art. In the long term, however, his example (defiant, proud and grand) more than his art (fragmentary, incomplete, often clumsy and soon outdated) inspired the Romantics.

BIBLIOGRAPHY

K. L. Fernow: *Leben des Künstlers Asmus Jakob Carstens* (Leipzig, 1806); rev. H. Riegel as *Carstens: Leben und Werke* (Hannover, 1867)

F. Noack: *Das Deutschtum in Rom*, i (Stuttgart, 1927), pp. 349–51

A. F. Heine: *Asmus Jakob Carstens und die Entwicklung des Figurenbildes* (Strasbourg, 1928)

A. Kamphausen: *Asmus Jakob Carstens*, Stud. Schleswig-Holstein. Kstgesch., v (Neumünster in Holstein, 1941)

H. von Einem: *Asmus Jakob Carstens: Die Nacht mit ihren Kindern* (Cologne, 1958)

R. Rosenblum: 'German Romantic Painting in International Perspective', *Yale U. A.G. Bull.*, xxxiii/3 (1972), pp. 23–6

W. Busch: 'Der sentimentalische Klassizismus bei Carstens, Koch und Genelli', *Kunst als Bedeutungsträger*, ed. W. Busch, R. Hausherr and E. Trier (Berlin, 1978)

P. Springer: 'Das Grabdenkmal Asmus Jacob Carstens' an der Cestius-Pyramide', *Röm. Jb. Kstgesch.*, xvii (1978), pp. 185–208

PETER WALCH

Cartagena (de Indias). City on the Caribbean coast in northern Colombia, in the department of Bolívar, with a population in the late 20th century of *c.* 500,000. Founded in 1533 on a strategically important bay, throughout the colonial period it was the principal port for trade with Spain and the importation of slaves from Africa. This commercial activity and the immediate need to fortify the city from attack were reflected in a rapid consolidation that made it the first well-established site on Colombian territory. It achieved city status in 1575. Ground-floor trading arcades and religious buildings were almost complete by the early 17th century. The cathedral (begun 1575, damaged 1586, restored and completed 1600–21 by Simón Gonzáles; *d* 1627) was one of the most influential religious buildings in the Spanish viceroyalty of Nueva Granada. The church of S Pedro Claver (1695–1736), designed by Jesuit architects and the most monumental church in the city, was inspired by Il Gesù in Rome. Opposite it, Palacio de la Inquisición (1770) has a massively arched portal that is perhaps the most elaborate example of Baroque in Colombia.

Surviving examples of domestic colonial architecture are usually of two or three storeys, some with *Mudéjar* ceilings and towers facing the sea (e.g. the 17th-century house of the Marqués de Valdehoyos in Calle de la Factoria); others are single-storey (e.g. in the San Diego district and the Getsemani suburb). Cartagena's houses were notable throughout Nueva Granada for their elegance and often had large bay windows; the appearance from the end of the 16th century of overhanging balconies (see fig.) shows the influence of craftsmen from the Canary Islands. The Spanish wars with France and England paralysed much Caribbean trade, with repeated attacks continuing until the mid-18th century. It was only in the late 18th century that renewed prosperity made possible the completion of the modern defensive system. The military engineer appointed to the task, Antonio de Arévalo (*b* 1715), like his predecessors Juan Bautista Antonelli the younger, Juan Bautista McEvan (*d* 1715) and Juan de Herrera y Sotomayor (*d* 1732), made use of the abundant supply of slave labour and the nearby quarries to restore the old forts of S José (dating from 1698) and S Fernando de Bocachica (1759), the impressive castle of S Felipe de

Barajas (1657) and the city wall, with its vaults for supplies and munitions and its elegant Neo-classical gateway.

In the early 19th century epidemics and social and economic unrest during the struggle for independence dramatically reduced the population and growth of Cartagena, and the city only began to recover towards the end of the century. Traditional architectural crafts using wood and bamboo provided an economical alternative for builders, as exemplified in the houses of El Cabrero and Torices, districts near the city walls; ranches (*quintas*) on Manga island were eclectically designed by their socially aspiring owners and foreign builders in predominantly French Neo-classical, Moorish or Caribbean styles, incorporating tiles and shutters as well as grilles, attics, pediments and gardens. One of the most significant 20th-century buildings is the Casa de Huéspedes Ilustres de Colombia, built in 1980–81 by Rogelio Salmona (*b* 1929). It combines Salmona's contemporary design with the restoration by German Tellez (*b* 1931) of the arsenal of the fort (built 1741) of S Juan de Manzanillo. The modern city has numerous museums, many of them housed in historic buildings. The Museo de Arte Religioso, for example, is housed in the Casa S Pedro Claver, while the Palacio de la Inquisición now houses the Museo Colonial, the Museo Antropológico and the Museo Histórico. The Museo de Arte Moderno and the Museo Naval del Caribe are contained in the Claustro de S Juan de Dios, and the Bartolomé Calvo Library is located in a former Republican bank. In addition, the Museo del Oro y Arqueológico specializes in Precolumbian Sinú culture.

BIBLIOGRAPHY

E. Marco Dorta: *Cartagena de Indias, puerto y plaza fuerte* (Madrid, 1960)
J. M. Zapatero: *Historia de las fortificaciones de Cartagena de Indias* (Madrid, 1979)

FERNANDO CARRASCO ZALDÚA

Cartagena, Alonso de. *See* ALONSO DE CARTAGENA.

Cartari, Vincenzo (*b* Reggio Emilia, ?1531; *d* after 10 Sept 1569). Italian writer. He apparently spent his life in the service of the Este family, to whom most of his published works are dedicated. In all his writings he was preoccupied with the diffusion of Classical knowledge in the vernacular. In 1551 he published a translation of Ovid's *Fasti*; in his dialogue *Il Flavio intorno ai Fasti Volgari* (Venice, 1553) he commented on this, also adding much material on Roman myths, religion and ceremonies. His most important work, however, is the *Imagini delli dei de gl'antichi* (Venice, 1556, 2/1571; facs. ed. M. Bussagli, Genoa, 1987), a handbook for artists, which the preface states would give them 'material for a thousand beautiful inventions with which to adorn their statues and paintings' (1556 edn, p. 3). In practice, however, the book was used more by iconographic advisers than by artists themselves. It contains information about the gods of antiquity, each chapter devoted to one of the gods and the myths associated with them and their descendants. Cartari concentrated on their appearances and attributes, as well as their various symbolic significances, an innovative emphasis on the visual aspects of myth. Although he insisted in his preface that all his sources were 'worthy ancient authors', in fact he relied considerably on Late Antique writers on myth, such as Martianus Capella (*fl* 410–39)

Cartagena, colonial houses with overhanging balconies, 17th–18th century

and Fulgentius (*c*. 467–552). Two contemporary works on mythology were also among his sources: Giovanni Boccaccio's *Genealogia deorum* (Venice, 1373), which provided his exegetical method and some material; and Lilio Gregorio Giraldi's *De deis gentium* (Basle, 1548), from which he took large sections with little alteration, also following its structure instead of Boccaccio's genealogical arrangement. He described many antique statues and images on coins, but his knowledge of these was evidently derived exclusively from literary texts, such as Pausanias and Philostratus the elder; he may also have consulted contemporary numismatic manuals.

The arrangement and comprehensive index of the *Imagini* made it particularly easy to use, and it rapidly became popular as an iconographic sourcebook all over Italy. For example, many figures in Veronese's frescoes of *c*. 1560 in the Villa Barbaro at Maser were derived from this book. Cosimo Bartoli, one of Vasari's advisers on the Palazzo Vecchio decorations, and Giuseppe Betussi (1512–?1573), author of the scheme for the Villa Obizzi near Padua, also used it. The *Imagini* was also the major source for Annibal Caro's elaborate scheme for the Camera dell'Aurora in the Villa Farnese at Caprarola, painted by Taddeo Zuccaro in 1562. This cycle, which shows Dawn chasing away Night, accompanied by numerous figures related to these personifications, illustrates well how the arrangement, the stress on appearances and the detailed listing of attributes in the *Imagini* could be used. They enabled the composer of iconographic schemes to evolve a new kind of programme, in which a number of *all'antica* figures were combined to express an abstract idea or allegory, rather than to illustrate a mythological narrative. *Il Flavio*, though not intended specifically as an iconographic handbook, was also used by Caro to supplement the *Imagini*. The second, greatly expanded, edition of Cartari's manual, published in 1571, is accompanied by woodcuts by Bolognino Zaltieri (*fl* 1560–80). These were influential, despite being of mediocre quality and not always closely related to the text. Cartari's continuing popularity is attested by the numerous editions and translations of the *Imagini* printed throughout the rest of the 16th century and the early 17th.

BIBLIOGRAPHY

DBI
J. Seznec: *La Survivance des dieux antiques*, Stud. Warb. Inst., 11 (London, 1940, Paris, 2/1980), pp. 206–78
T. Puttfarken: 'Bacchus und Hymenaeus in der Villa Maser', *Mitt. Ksthist. Inst. Florenz*, xxxiv (1980), pp. 1–19
Giorgio Vasari (exh. cat., ed. L. Corti and M. D. Davis; Arezzo, Mus. Casa Vasari, 1981), pp. 183–5
C. Robertson: 'Annibal Caro as Iconographer: Sources and Method', *J. Warb. & Court. Inst.*, xlv (1982), pp. 160–81
C. Hope: 'Veronese and the Venetian Tradition of Allegory', *Proc. Brit. Acad.*, lxii (1986), pp. 388–428

CLARE ROBERTSON

Cartaro, Mario (*b* Viterbo; *fl* 1560; *d* Naples, 16 April 1620). Italian printmaker and cartographer. He was in Rome by 1560, the date of his first known engraving, the *Adoration of the Shepherds* (B. 2), after Heinrich Aldegrever. Bartsch recorded 28 prints by him, to which Passavant added a further 27. Mainly engravings, his works include *St Jerome* (B. 14), after Albrecht Dürer, *Christ Descending into Limbo* (B. 7), after Andrea Mantegna, the *Last Judgement* (B. 18), after Michelangelo, and a *Landscape* (B. 26), after Titian. Until 1577 he collaborated with the publisher Antoine Lafréry, providing illustrations for the *Speculum Romanae magnificentiae*, a collection of plans and views issued between 1545 and 1577, and for *Le tavole moderne di geografia* (*c*. 1580). After this he turned increasingly to the more profitable activity of print selling. He spent his last years in Naples making drawings for printed maps of the kingdom of Naples (e.g. B. 27) with the help of the mathematician Niccolò Antonio Stelliola (1547–1623).

BIBLIOGRAPHY

DBI
A. von Bartsch: *Le Peintre-graveur* (1803–21), xv, pp. 520–32 [B.]
J. D. Passavant: *Le Peintre-graveur* (Leipzig, 1860–64), vi, pp. 157–61
S. Boorsch and J. T. Spike: *Italian Masters of the Sixteenth Century* (1986), 31 [XV/iv] of *The Illustrated Bartsch*, ed. W. Strauss (New York, 1978–)

FRANÇOISE JESTAZ

Cartaud, Jean-Silvain (*b* Paris, 1675; *d* Paris, 15 Feb 1758). French architect. He studied in Italy from 1695, but his subsequent work shows little influence from the Italian Baroque. In 1703 he designed the façade of the Barnabite church, Paris, although his earliest project of note was the hôtel (1704; destr.) designed in Paris for Pierre Crozat; it was greatly admired by contemporaries and established Cartaud's reputation in Paris. The plan of the building, which attracted most attention, grouped living rooms symmetrically around a small central courtyard, and a large gallery housing part of Crozat's art collection closed the scheme at the rear, overlooking the elaborate garden. A smaller gallery at first-floor level faced the courtyard. Cartaud's design for the château of Montmorency (1708), a country retreat built for Crozat, was also symmetrical in plan and featured a large oval salon in the manner of Louis Le Vau's Vaux-le-Vicomte (1657–61), which projected into the garden, each bay of the façade divided by stately Corinthian pilasters. Cartaud worked for several other powerful patrons, including, from 1711 to 1714, the Duc de Berry. Most of his designs reflect the reserved elegance of the work of Jules Hardouin Mansart. This is true of his best-known work, the Hôtel de Janvry (1732–3; destr.), Paris, where he used rusticated pilasters to mark the ends of the only slightly projecting *avant-corps*. Both the courtyard and garden façades incorporated windows spanned by depressed arches topped by decorative masks or trophies, while the parapet of the *avant-corps* displayed ornamental urns. Cartaud built several other houses in Paris, and among his later works is the façade (1738) of Notre Dame des Victoires, Paris. He became a member of the Académie in 1742 and worked for Louis-Philippe, Duc d'Orléans, for the last six years of his life, during which time he designed the service buildings of the Palais Royal, Paris.

BIBLIOGRAPHY

G. Brice: *Nouvelle description de la ville de Paris*, i (Geneva, 1698)
J. Mariette: *L'Architecture française*, 5 vols (Paris, 1727–38/*R* 1927–9)
A. J. Dézallier d'Argenville: *Voyage pittoresque de Paris* (Paris, 1749)
J. F. Blondel: *L'Architecture françoise*, 8 vols (Paris, 1752–6/*R* 1904–5)
V. Champier and R. Sandoz: *Le Palais Royal*, 2 vols (Paris, 1900)
R. Bloomfield: *History of French Architecture*, ii (New York, 1911/*R* 1974)
L. Hautecoeur: *Architecture classique*, iii (1950)
M. Gallet: *Paris Domestic Architecture of the Eighteenth Century* (London, 1972)
W. G. Kalnein and M. Levey: *Art and Architecture of the Eighteenth Century in France*, Pelican Hist. A. (Harmondsworth, 1972)

KATHLEEN RUSSO

Carte-de-visite. *See under* PHOTOGRAPHY, §I.

Cartellier, Pierre (*b* Paris, 22 Dec 1757; *d* Paris, 12 June 1831). French sculptor. He was the son of a locksmith and studied at the Ecole Gratuite de Dessin, Paris, and then in the studio of Charles-Antoine Bridan and at the Académie Royale. He failed to win the Prix de Rome and began to earn his living modelling decorative motifs for bronze founders. He also worked as an assistant to Joseph Deschamps (1743–88) on decorative sculpture for Queen Marie-Antoinette at the châteaux of Trianon and Saint-Cloud, near Versailles, taking over from Deschamps on his death. During the French Revolution he was one of a number of sculptors who collaborated on Antoine Quatremère de Quincy's scheme to turn the church of Ste Geneviève, Paris, into a mausoleum, the Panthéon, to which he contributed a stone relief representing *Force and Prudence* (1792–3; destr.). He exhibited a terracotta statuette of *Friendship* (priv. col., see Hubert, 1980, p. 7, fig. 4) in the 1796 Salon and in 1801 achieved his first major success when he exhibited the plaster version (untraced) of his statue of *Modesty*, based on the antique Capitoline *Venus* (Rome, Mus. Capitolino); the marble version (exh. 1808 Salon; Amsterdam, Hist. Mus.), executed for Empress Josephine, demonstrates not only his commitment to the prevalent Neo-classical style but his distinctive personal grace of composition and delicacy of execution.

Cartellier contributed to many of Napoleon's schemes for embellishing Paris. For Jean-François-Thérèse Chalgrin's project to adapt the Luxembourg Palace for the use of the Senate he executed high-reliefs of *Peace* and *War* (stone, after 1800; *in situ*) as well as statues of *Aristides* (plaster, exh. 1804 Salon; untraced) and *Pierre-Victurnien Vergniaud* (plaster, 1804–05; Bordeaux, Mus. Aquitaine, on deposit from Versailles, Château), the latter a powerful, draped effigy of the Girondin orator. For the Salle de Diane at the Louvre he produced a plaster bas-relief of the *Dance of the Spartan Maidens* (1802; *in situ*). His contribution to the series of portraits depicting great Frenchmen, intended for the Tuileries, was an austere marble bust of *Maurice, Maréchal de Saxe* (Versailles, Château). Other official commissions included statues of *Napoleon as Legislator* (marble, 1803; Versailles, Château) for the Ecole de Droit, of *Louis Bonaparte, King of Holland* (marble, exh. 1810 Salon; Versailles, Château) and of *General Roger Valhubert* (marble, 1810–15; Avranches, Jar. Plantes), intended for the Pont de la Concorde, Paris. Cartellier also carved the Antique-inspired stone relief *Glory Distributing Crowns* (1807; *in situ*) over the portal of the Louvre colonnade and the marble relief of the *Capitulation before Ulm* (1806–09; *in situ*) on the east face of the Arc de Triomphe du Carrousel, Paris. He continued to work as a decorative sculptor under the Empire, making the models for the feet of the imperial throne at Saint-Cloud and for putti decorating Empress Marie-Louise's famous jewel cabinet (1812; Paris, Louvre), designed to complement one made for Josephine in 1809. In 1808 he was rewarded with the Cross of the Légion d'honneur and in 1810 he was elected to the chair at the Institut de France vacated by the death of Antoine-Denis Chaudet, some of whose works he helped to complete.

Cartellier was equally in demand as an official sculptor under the Restoration after 1815, now taking royalist heroes as his subject-matter. He produced the monumental equestrian relief of *Louis XIV* (stone, 1814–16) for the tympanum of the entrance façade of the Hôtel des Invalides, Paris, to replace a badly damaged work by Guillaume Coustou (i). He also made a bronze statue of *Louis XV* to replace a destroyed work by Jean-Baptiste Pigalle in the Place Royale in Reims (*see* REIMS, fig. 1) and a statue of *General Charles Pichegru* (marble, 1815–19; Versailles, Château). His marble statue of *Minerva* (1818–22; Versailles, Château) is a somewhat doctrinaire Neo-classical exercise. In 1816 Cartellier became a professor at the Ecole des Beaux-Arts, where his many pupils included some of the foremost sculptors of the next generation, notably François Rude and Louis Petitot. He was awarded the Order of Saint-Michel by Charles X at the Salon of 1825.

The Revolution of 1830 prevented the completion of two royal commissions of the 1820s, a bronze equestrian statue of *Louis XV* to replace Edme Bouchardon's destroyed work in the Place Louis XV (Place de la Concorde), Paris, and a memorial to *Charles, Duc de Berry*, which he began after the Duc's assassination in 1820 in collaboration with Louis-Marie-Charles Dupaty (1771–1825) and Jean-Pierre Cortot (fragments, marble; Saint-Denis Abbey). He did, however, model a horse which was cast in bronze in 1834 and, provided with an accompanying statue of *Louis XIV* by Petitot, this now stands in the Cour d'Honneur of the château of Versailles. Among Cartellier's late works on a more modest scale are the touching marble statue for the funerary monument of *Empress Josephine* (1814–25; Rueil-Malmaison, Hauts de Seine, SS Pierre et Paul), which portrays the Empress at prayer; the marble portrait relief on the tomb of *Mgr de Juigné, Archbishop of Paris* (1825; Paris, Notre-Dame); and the lifelike, bronze, seated statue for the tomb of *Dominique-Vivant Denon* (1826; Paris, Père Lachaise Cemetery).

Cartellier was unusual among contemporary French sculptors in that his training was as much that of a craftsman as that of an academic sculptor. Despite his attachment to the Neo-classical aesthetic, he never visited Rome. The demands of his monumental commemorative commissions often obliged him to seek inspiration in the realist aspects of the tradition of French sculpture of the 17th and 18th centuries.

BIBLIOGRAPHY

Lami

G. Hubert: 'Pierre Cartellier, statuaire: Oeuvres et documents inédits: Ancien Régime, Révolution, Consulat', *Bull. Soc. Hist. A. Fr.* (1976), pp. 313–29

——: 'L'Oeuvre de Pierre Cartellier: Essai de catalogue raisonné', *Gaz. B.-A.*, 6th ser., xcvi (1980), pp. 1–44

La Sculpture française au XIXe siècle (exh. cat., ed. A. Pingeot; Paris, Grand Pal., 1986)

GÉRARD HUBERT

Cartellino. Small, illusionistically rendered scroll or piece of paper that carries a signature, inscription, motto or religious invocation on a work of art. The cartellino may be attached to the background or placed in the foreground of a picture, often on a plinth or parapet (*see* CIMA DA CONEGLIANO, fig. 2).

RUPERT FEATHERSTONE

Carter, Howard (*b* London, 9 May 1874; *d* London, 2 March 1939). English archaeologist, epigrapher and copyist. Howard and his sister Amy (later Walker), a miniaturist, and brother William (1863–1939), a society portrait painter, were taught to paint by their father, Samuel John Carter (1835–92), who was a successful animal painter and watercolourist in Norfolk and London. Between 1889 and 1891 Howard Carter drew and catalogued the Egyptological collection of William Tyssen-Amherst, 1st Baron Amherst of Hackney (1835–1909), whose influence enabled him in 1891 to join the Archaeological Survey of Egypt, for which he drew reliefs and inscriptions from the Middle Kingdom tombs at Beni Hasan and Deir el-Bersheh. His work on the temple reliefs and inscriptions of Deir el-Bahri (*see* THEBES (i), §IV) established his reputation as the finest Egyptological copyist and epigrapher since Achille Prisse d'Avennes (1807–79). The six volumes of Carter's drawings at Deir el-Bahri were reproduced between 1893 and 1899 in the then innovative medium of collotype, which gave a very accurate copy of his originals.

As a result of his epigraphic work at Deir el-Bahri, Carter was appointed Inspector of the Antiquities of Lower Egypt in 1903, but resigned in 1905 after a petty squabble at Saqqara and worked in Egypt as a commercial watercolourist. While in London in 1908 he met George

Herbert, 5th Earl of Carnarvon (1866–1923), whose financial help enabled Carter to pursue his archaeological work. By 1919 he had discovered five royal tombs in the Theban necropolis. However, his discovery of the tomb of TUTANKHAMUN in November 1922 was to dwarf all his other work, for it became the most important single excavation in Egyptological history. His painstaking excavation methods helped preserve many of the fragile organic items, and his method of drawing and recording objects in strict relation to each other ensured the accuracy of the record. To document the tomb in such fine detail took Carter ten years. Despite all his labours, however, a definitive catalogue of the tomb has never been published.

WRITINGS

with P. E. Newberry: *The Tomb of Thontmosis IV* (London, 1904)
with Lord Carnarvon: *Five Years Exploration at Thebes* (Oxford, 1912)
with A. Mace: *The Tomb of Tut.Ankh.Amen Discovered by the Late Earl of Carnarvon and Howard Carter*, 3 vols (London, 1923–33)

BIBLIOGRAPHY

W. R. Dawson: *Who Was Who in Egyptology* (London, 1951; ed. E. P. Uphill, 1972)
N. C. Reeves: *Ancient Egypt at Highclere Castle* (Highclere, 1989)
H. V. F. Winstone: *Howard Carter and the Discovery of the Tomb of Tutankhamun* (London, 1991)
T. G. H. James: *Howard Carter: The Path to Tutankhamun* (London, 1992)
Howard Carter before Tutankhamun (exh. cat. by N. C. Reeves and J. H. Taylor, London, BM, 1992)

□

Carter, John (*b* London, 22 June 1748; *d* London, 8 Sept 1817). English antiquary, draughtsman and writer. Eccentric, obstinate, zealous and courageous, Carter called himself, as it suited him, artist, painter, architect and antiquary. He started as a draughtsman in the building trades. Between 1774 and 1778 he made drawings for the *Builder's Magazine*, a builder's dictionary of terms that appeared monthly from 1774. His design of a sessions house was cribbed by someone else and submitted as the winning entry in an architectural competition. An introduction to the Society of Antiquaries in 1780 brought him work sketching medieval buildings, sculpture, paintings, stained glass and metalwork. Antiquarian patrons wrote scholarly commentaries for his picturebook of medieval art, *Specimens of Ancient Sculpture and Painting* (London, 1780–94, rev. 1838/*R* 1887). Sketching in and around the Palace of Westminster in 1790 for the Society of Antiquaries, he produced measured architectural drawings of St Stephen's Chapel published in 1795. This was the first serious archaeological reconstruction of an English Gothic building, which now provides important documentation for the royal chapel (partly destr. 1834). The Society proposed to publish all the ecclesiastical buildings in England with Carter doing the work. He turned out large, beautifully finished, delicately tinted drawings at an impressive rate, producing detailed plans, elevations and views for the Society of Antiquaries of Exeter Cathedral (1797), Bath Abbey (1798), Durham Cathedral (1801), Gloucester Cathedral (1809) and St Albans Cathedral (1813). His drawings for Wells Cathedral were never published. The Society elected him a fellow but trouble followed: outraged at destruction during restorations at Durham Cathedral, he attacked James Wyatt, the architect in charge. The Society of Antiquaries elected Wyatt a fellow and censured Carter. Until his death he contributed to the *Gentleman's Magazine*, passionately condemning the destructive restoration of medieval buildings. Rejecting the term 'Gothic' because of its pejorative connotations, Carter wrote *The Ancient Architecture of England* (1795–1814), asserting that pointed architecture was an English invention; this argument, however, was soon disproved. A more lasting contribution lies in his 109 plates of architectural details arranged in chronological order, which provide the rudiments for more recent stylistic analysis.

WRITINGS

The Ancient Architecture of England (London, 1795–1814; rev. by J. Britton 1837/*R* 1887)
The Progress of Architecture (London, 1830)

BIBLIOGRAPHY

Colvin; *DNB*
Obituary: *Gent. Mag.*, lxxxvii (1817), pp. 363–8; lxxxviii (1818), pp. 273–6, 382
J. Britton: 'On the Life, Professional Works, Writings and Character of John Carter, F.S.A. and Draughtsman', *Builder*, viii (1850), pp. 302–4
C. Eastlake: *A History of the Gothic Revival* (London, 1872), pp. 103–8
J. Evans: *A History of the Society of Antiquaries* (Oxford, 1956), pp. 182–207
H. Colvin: 'Views of the Old Palace of Westminster', *Archit. Hist.*, ix (1966), pp. 23–184
T. Mowl: 'Designs by John Carter for Lea Castle, Worcestershire', *Archit. Hist.*, xxv (1982), pp. 47–55
M. E. Roberts: 'John Carter at St Stephen's Chapel: A Romantic Turns Archaeologist', *England in the Fourteenth Century*, ed. W. M. Ormrod (Woodbridge, 1986), pp. 202–12

MARION ROBERTS

Cartesianism. *See under* DESCARTES, RENÉ.

Carthage. Ruined city on the North African coast at the end of a narrow peninsula pointing into the Bay of Tunis. Now an archaeological site at the edge of Tunis itself, Carthage was founded, according to legend, by the Phoenician queen Elyssa in 814 BC. It became a major Mediterranean power until its destruction by the Romans in 146 BC. Carthage flourished as a Roman city, Christianity reaching it by the 2nd century AD. The city was revived by Emperor Justinian, but it was finally destroyed by the Arabs in AD 698.

For later history *see* TUNIS.

1. PUNIC. In the 6th and 5th centuries BC the city's interventions in disputes between the Greek and Phoenician city states of Sicily made Carthage the leading western Phoenician colony, and it formed a close alliance with the Etruscans. From the 5th century BC the Carthaginians spread into the African hinterland, eventually controlling the area that is today the northern half of Tunisia. They also concluded three alliances with the newly emergent power of Rome. Further conflict in Sicily, however, precipitated (264 BC) the Punic Wars, which eventually led to the total destruction of Carthage.

Carthaginian art reflected the dominant Mediterranean styles of the time. During the Archaic period Carthaginian artists copied such oriental objects as the scarab seals of the Egyptian pharaohs, but afterwards they followed the styles of Classical and Hellenistic Greece. Tin may have been imported from Cornwall, while copper and other metals were brought in from Spain, where the colony of Nova Carthago was founded in 228 BC. The only surviving Carthaginian literary work, *The Periplous of Hanno* (before

480 BC), records a voyage down the west coast of Africa, perhaps to the modern Ivory Coast. Carthage appears to have been more a trading centre than a centre of production, but some Carthaginian imitations of foreign products have now been identified. For example, some black slipped 'Campanian' pottery of the 4th–2nd century BC is now regarded as Carthaginian rather than Italian.

The centre of the city was the acropolis on the Byrsa hill (see fig. 1a), and the original settlers lived between here and the coast. At first the sides of the Byrsa accommodated only stone vaulted tombs, but by the 5th century BC the south slope was occupied by the small houses of metalworkers and other artisans. Later houses opened on to a street that probably ran south-east directly from the acropolis to the harbours and along which the Romans had to fight, house by house, when they took the city in 146 BC. It seems from an inscription to have been financed by the guilds of cloth merchants, goldsmiths and other trades. By the 3rd century BC Carthage had a regular street grid and large peristyle houses, like contemporary Greek cities.

In the 5th century BC a massive defensive wall was built along the sea front, but the line of the city wall inland is not yet clearly established. Little is known of the city's public buildings. In the 3rd or 2nd century BC the well-protected Circular and Rectangular enclosed harbours (1b and 1c) were built, while the quayside and the central island of the Circular Harbour were covered with ship sheds or dry docks for the navy that fought Rome.

The *tophet* ('sanctuary') of Tanit, chief deity of the city, lay close to the harbours (1d). It is an open precinct, still containing hundreds of stelae marking the cremation urns of one- to three-year-old children sacrificed to the goddess. Early stelae (7th–4th century BC) were decorated with architectural elements and a *betile*, or bottle shape, carved in high relief. The later stelae (4th–2nd century BC) were finely engraved with a variety of magic symbols and inscriptions recording the genealogy of the victims (see fig. 2; *see also* PUNIC ART, fig. 1). Grave goods found in other cemeteries include an interesting series of half life-size pottery masks with leering smiles. Two large marble sarcophagi (late 4th century BC; Carthage, Mus. Lavigerie) from the St Monique cemetery have full-length high relief sculptures of a priest and priestess on their lids. The priestess wears a headdress in the form of a bird, and her garments still bear traces of black and gold paint. The priest has a full beard and an earring in his left ear. Each figure holds a small urn in the left hand, and the priestess clasps a small bird in her right. An almost exact duplicate of the priest's sarcophagus has been found at Tarquinii (Tarquinia, Pal. Vitelleschi), demonstrating the close links between the Etruscans and Carthage. The principal Punic finds from Carthage are divided between the Musée National de Carthage on the Byrsa hill and the Musée National du Bardo, Tunis.

Carthaginian influence on African towns is best seen in the Punic town of Kerkouane in north-east Tunisia, which was not built over in later times. The buildings line a single main street that spirals round through the settlement; they include several large houses, all with separate bathrooms, as well as temples and other public buildings.

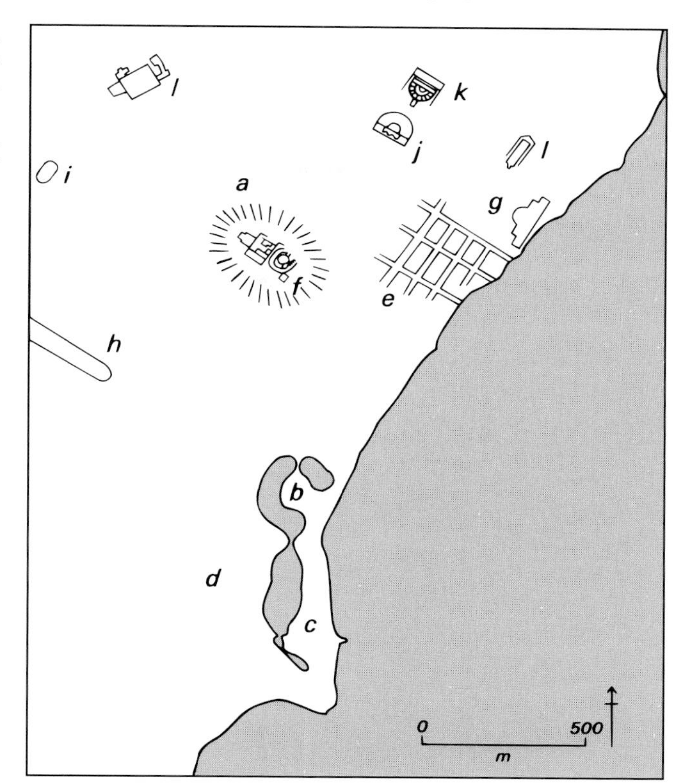

1. Carthage, plan showing main sites and buildings, *c.* 8th century BC–2nd century AD: (a) Byrsa hill; (b) Circular Harbour; (c) Rectangular Harbour; (d) *tophet* of Tanit; (e) forum; (f) governor's palace; (g) Antonine Baths; (h) circus; (i) amphitheatre; (j) theatre; (k) odeion; (l) cisterns

2. ROMAN. Less than 25 years after the destruction of the Punic city the Romans considered refounding the site as a colony. Gaius Gracchus in 122 BC and Julius Caesar in 44 BC proposed new settlements, but there is little archaeological evidence that occupation took place before Augustus refounded the city in 29 BC as capital of the province of Africa.

It was once thought that the whole Roman street system, consisting of some 430 blocks covering 3 ha, was laid out under Augustus; but the original colony probably covered little more than the south-east quarter of the city between the Byrsa and the Punic ports (see fig. 1 above); the rest of the Roman city was developed in several phases between the 2nd and 5th centuries AD. The Punic acropolis on the Byrsa remained the city's administrative centre in Roman times and was extended by the construction of huge terraces. In the centre was the forum (1e), flanked to the west by the capitolium (under the French colonial cathedral) and to the east by the civic basilica (both 2nd century AD). To its south was another public square flanked by a temple, while on the southern edge of the whole hill was the palace (2nd century AD) of the Roman governor of Africa (1f). In the later 1st and 2nd centuries AD a ring of public buildings was built around the earlier colony. These included the Antonine Baths (AD 143–62; 1g) and the circus (1h), which were the largest buildings of their kind outside Rome itself. The citizens of Roman

2. Carthage, *tophet* of Tanit, Punic stele (detail) depicting a priest carrying a child to a sacrifice, 5th or 4th century BC (Tunis, Musée National du Bardo)

Carthage took an enthusiastic interest in the circus, and several mosaics depict popular charioteers and horses with identifying inscriptions. (The circus continued in use through the 5th century (*see* §3 below), after which it became a rubbish dump.) Other public buildings in his group include an amphitheatre, theatre, odeion and several groups of public cisterns (1i–l). Unfortunately only the heavily robbed foundations of these important buildings survive, the best preserved being the Antonine Baths, where re-erected columns give some idea of its impressive size.

The wealth that financed these buildings was generated by the rich farmland of the Medjerda Valley to the south-west of the city. Each year the Roman fleet left Carthage with grain for the free bread dole at Rome; wine and olive oil were also exported. The Punic ports were redeveloped in the 2nd and 3rd centuries AD, when porticos were built around the quay and island of the Circular Harbour. At the beginning of the 5th century what may have been a huge warehouse complex *c.* 70 sq. m was built on top of 18 masonry vaults to the west of the Rectangular Harbour.

The most important works of art from Roman Carthage are probably the fine floor mosaics. Major Roman sculptures were also discovered during early excavations at the theatre and the odeion, while a life-size statue of a late Roman circus official has been uncovered more recently. Other finds include a cache of late Roman silver bowls, one inscribed with the name of the Cresconius family (*c.* AD 400; London, BM).

BIBLIOGRAPHY

A. Audollent: *Carthage romaine* (Paris, 1901)
A. Lézine: *Carthage-Utique: Etudes d'architecture et d'urbanisme* (Paris, 1968)
J. de Moreuil, ed.: *Carthage: Its Birth and Grandeur* (Paris, 1969)
P. Cintas: *Manuel d'archéologie punique*, i–ii (Paris, 1970–76)
J. Feron: *Mort-Dieu de Carthage*, 2 vols (Paris, 1975)
J. G. Pedley, ed.: *New Light on Ancient Carthage* (Ann Arbor, 1980)
H. Benichou-Safar: *Les Tombes puniques de Carthage* (Paris, 1982)
Carthage: U. du Québec à Trois-rivières, 1984
J. H. Humphrey, ed.: *The Circus and a Byzantine Cemetery at Carthage*, i (Ann Arbor, 1988)
D. L. Bomgardner: 'The Carthage Amphitheater: A Reappraisal', *Amer. J. Archaeol.*, xciii (1989), pp. 85–103
F. Rakob: *Karthago 1: Die deutschen Ausgrabungen in Karthago* (Mainz, 1991)
A. Ennabli, ed.: *Pour sauver Carthage* (Tunis, 1992)
S. Lancel: *Carthage* (Poitiers, 1992)

3. CHRISTIAN. Christianity reached Carthage early and was a significant force by the 2nd century AD. Following the Edict of Milan (313) numerous churches were built, among them the Circular Monument (mid-4th century), a rotunda with an attached basilica modelled on Constantine's basilica of the Holy Sepulchre at Jerusalem (*see* JERUSALEM, §II, 2(i)); its dedication is uncertain. Another 4th-century church in the centre of the city near the ports was excavated by Tunisian archaeologists in the early 1980s, and 19th-century explorations uncovered several early cemeterial churches outside the city walls. In layout these churches seem to have followed the norms established over the rest of North Africa in the 4th century. These include the division of the nave into several aisles separated by paired columns. Many churches had an apse at each end of the nave with a processional path between them, and their altar and ambo might be set some way into the nave. The floor was usually of fine mosaic, that of cemeterial basilicas often consisting of tomb mosaics.

In 439 Carthage fell to the Germanic Vandals, but despite the latter's Arianism there is little evidence of alteration or disturbance in the ecclesiastical remains. The capture of the city in 534 by the Byzantine general Belisarios (505–65) was seen by Emperor Justinian I (*reg* 527–65) as the first step in the reconquest of the Roman Empire, and the city had to be rebuilt to suit his vision of imperial renewal. Many churches, such as the Columned Monument and the 4th-century church excavated by the Tunisian team, were rebuilt to twice their previous size, while outside the walls the Damous El Karita basilica (l. *c.* 65 m) reached its fullest extent with 13 aisles. Many of the streets were repaved, and new drains were installed. The mosaicists who worked on some of the new buildings may have come from Constantinople and then been active at Ravenna. Justinian put great pressure on the African clergy to conform to his beliefs, but the new churches seem to have maintained their African characteristics rather than adopting Byzantine features.

The Justinianic programme was the last great building period in ancient Carthage. Perhaps the drain on public funds was too much, or the buildings proved sufficient to meet all subsequent demands. For much of the later 6th century the Byzantines were occupied with rebellions among the Berber tribes and in the army: peace, with a certain economic and cultural prosperity, returned in the first half of the 7th century. During this time African pottery still controlled much of the western Mediterranean market, as it had since the 4th century. In 698, however, the city finally fell to the Arabs, who already held the rest of North Africa. Nearby Tunis became the dominant centre, and in the 8th century Carthage served as a quarry for the columns used in the mosques of KAIROUAN and Córdoba.

BIBLIOGRAPHY

J. Vaultrin: 'Les Basiliques chrétiennes de Carthage', *Rev. Afr.*, lxxiii (1932), pp. 182–318

N. Duval: 'Etudes d'architecture nord-africaine, I: Les Monuments de Carthage, étude critique', *Mél. Ecole Fr. Rome: Moyen Age, Temps Mod.*, lxxxiv (1972), pp. 1072–88

L. Ennabli: 'Results of the International Save Carthage Campaign: The Christian Monuments', *World Archaeol.*, xviii (1987), pp. 291–311

S. T. Stevens: 'Bin El Knissia at Carthage: A Rediscovered Cemetery Church', *J. Roman Archaeol.* (1993) [suppl. 7]

SIMON P. ELLIS

Carthusian Order [Fr. Chartreux, It. Certosini, Ger. Kartäuser]. Monastic order founded in 1084 by St Bruno (*c.* 1030–1101; *can* 1514), a canon of St Cunibert in Cologne. The Order took its name from that of the mountainous site of the mother house at La Grande Chartreuse in the diocese of Grenoble (Isère). The Order has never been reformed; such continuity over more than 900 years is unique. The way of life of the first Carthusians, characterized by total dedication to contemplation through silence, assiduous prayer, poverty, penance and almost continuous occupancy of a solitary cell, impressed contemporaries with its novelty. Bruno set out to deepen the essential ideals of monasticism through the strictest separation from the world, combined with an intense desire to set aside time for God ('vacare Deo'). His followers led an eremitical life, inspired by biblical models and the Fathers of Egypt and Palestine, but partially tempered by cenobitism, which allowed for the practicalities of survival in the particularly harsh environment chosen by the Order. The early Carthusians did not represent a criticism of established Benedictine monasticism (*see* BENEDICTINE ORDER), and relations remained close with both the CLUNIAC ORDER and the CISTERCIAN ORDER. The severity of the Carthusian way of life limited the Order's appeal, and consequently it did not challenge other orders.

1. History. 2. Architecture. 3. Iconography and patronage.

1. HISTORY. The foundation of the Order was the fruit of a collaboration between three men: St Bruno, Abbot Seguin (*fl c.* 1082) of La Chaise Dieu (founded 1043; Haute-Loire) and Bishop Hugh of Grenoble (1052–1132). Bruno, master of the cathedral school at Reims, declined the archbishopric and withdrew from Reims to live as a hermit. His fame attracted visitors, however, and so he enlisted Abbot Seguin's support and approached the Bishop of Grenoble seeking a site where, undisturbed, Bruno and six companions might follow the eremitical life. Of his companions, four were clerics and two were laymen, the first *conversi* (lay brothers) of the Order. Like the clerics, they lived apart from the world, but their responsibility for the manual work of the community allowed the clerics to live the desert ideal. Bishop Hugh granted the group the 'desert' called Cartusia in the remote mountains above Grenoble, and in 1084 he led Bruno and his companions there. When Urban II (*reg* 1088–99), Bruno's former pupil and colleague, summoned him to Rome in 1090 to advise on a resolution of the papal schism, Bruno appointed Landuin of Lucca prior. To prevent the disintegration of the community in Bruno's absence, Bishop Hugh entrusted the oversight of Cartusia to Abbot Seguin. When Landuin regrouped the hermits, at Bruno's instigation Urban ordered Seguin to return the 'desert' to the Carthusians, thus indirectly approving Bruno's foundation. In Rome, Bruno briefly established a hermitage in the Baths of Diocletian, but having refused the bishopric of Reggio, he was allowed to return to his solitary vocation, founding another hermitage at Santa Maria della Torre in Calabria at the end of 1091. When he died, his profession of faith was attached to the mortuary roll sent out from S Maria della Torre.

Bruno provided the initiative and the inspiration behind the Order, yet he spent only six years at Cartusia and left no written rule or any instructions concerning the structure of the mother house and its relationship with other houses. Custom and example were transmitted orally to houses of the emerging Order until *c.* 1127, when Prior Guigo I (*reg* 1109–36) wrote down the *Customs* (*Consuetudines*). Although the *Customs* did not constitute an actual rule, they became the Order's first legislative document. Laying down many practical details in 80 chapters, and sensitive to the spirit as well as to the letter of the observances, the clarity of the *Customs* helps to explain the success of the Order. Guigo regulated the relationship between the distinct groups of monks and lay brothers. The first 41 chapters concern the monks: the disciplinary provisions combine elements from both the Rule of St Benedict and the writings of St Jerome. The next 38 chapters deal with the *conversi*, and the final chapter provides a eulogy on the solitary life. This eulogy describes the unique contemplative rest enjoyed by the Carthusian, whose cell represents Bethlehem. In the solitude of the cell, away from tumultuous crowds, Guigo says that study of the Old and New Testaments will teach the greatest and most subtle secrets (*Customs* 80).

The Carthusians tried to restore what they saw as the fundamental elements in the original Benedictine ideal: total obedience and surrender, a combination of eremitism and poverty, and a much reduced monastic life. Poverty was an instrument of the spiritual life that enabled the hermit to engage in undisturbed contemplation. It was the achievement of Bruno and his early successors to combine in a semi-eremitical way of life a strict interpretation of the Rule of St Benedict with a severe, but not excessive, asceticism. The Carthusian vision could not have been realized without the *conversi* to perform such specialist tasks as agriculture and tending flocks, which allowed for the survival of the group under the harshest conditions and protected the monks from all temporal concerns. The *conversi*, who inhabited a separate building (the Lower House at La Grande Chartreuse) also had individual cells and took the same vows as the monks. The Lower House lay within the heart of the 'desert'. Relations between the two Houses were strictly regulated. Every other Sunday the *conversi* went to the Upper House to hear the communal service, while the prior spent one week in five in the Lower House. The lay brothers gave the Order its particular characteristic and enjoyed a strong spiritual union with the monks, with whom they were interdependent.

While Guigo I was prior, new Carthusian foundations were made at Portes (Ain) in 1115 and at Les Ecourges (Isère), Durbon (Gap), La Sylve-Bénite (Isère) and Meyriat (Ain) in 1116. Guigo's *Customs* of *c.* 1127 were approved by Innocent II in 1133. These early houses, although living according to identical constitutions, were independent; but in 1140 Anthelme, the sixth prior, summoned the first General Chapter at La Grande Chartreuse, where it was agreed that the prior of the mother house should be confirmed as dealing with the government of what was henceforth to be an established Order. Expansion was not rapid. Remote sites were sought in the Alps in 1146, Dalmatia in 1160, Sweden in 1162, Spain in 1163, England in 1178 and Ireland by 1279. Later charterhouses included S Martino, Naples (1325; *see* NAPLES, §IV, 3), Galluzzo, Florence (1341), founded by Niccolo Accaioli, and Pavia (1390; *see* PAVIA, §2(i)), founded by Giangaleazzo Visconti. At its greatest extent the Order numbered 196 houses, of which 100 were in France and 41 in Italy.

2. ARCHITECTURE. The vivid description of Cartusia by Guibert de Nogent, who visited the monastery *c.* 1115–17, reveals that the first house there was constructed in wood on a desolate and rocky promontory, which, at an altitude of 1175 m, was more or less permanently inaccessible and buried deep in snow for the greater part of the year. On 31 January 1132 the original building was overwhelmed by an avalanche in which more than half of the brothers died, and Guigo I decided to rebuild at a slightly lower level and on a less exposed site. This second site is La Grande Chartreuse.

The vision of the interior vocation of the Carthusians had a profound effect on the Order's architecture and artistic production. The equilibrium of the solitary, semi-eremitic life could be maintained only by the establishment of the separate houses, the Upper House for the monks and the Lower House for the lay brothers. Each community of monks was limited to the apostolic number of 12, headed by the prior, and there were a maximum of 16 *conversi*. Twelve simple, detached wooden cells opened to a common cloister that contained a refectory and chapter house. From the *Life* of Bruno it is clear that between 1084 and 1100 the monks lived two to a cell, the individual cell, in which each monk read, prayed, copied manuscripts, ate, slept and drew water from a conduit that ran round the cloister, all in the strictest silence, being a later development. The monks gathered together for Matins, Mass and Vespers in the conventual church. The other Hours were recited privately in the cell. Only on feast days did the whole community say the Hours together in the choir and eat together in silence in the refectory.

There is little surviving evidence for the earliest buildings, as almost all the oldest Carthusian houses were destroyed and rebuilt several times over. The ideal plan seems to have been based on the quadrangular cloister, the central element of monastic life (see fig.). The cells were small cottages, each with three rooms, opening out of three sides of the cloister (*see* MONASTERY, fig. 7). On the fourth side lay the church, refectory, chapterhouse, kitchen and storerooms. The complex was surrounded by a wall. The earliest surviving monastery (1165–90), at Žiče in Slovenia, retains its enclosing wall and parts of the great cloister. The Carthusian ground-plan was highly inventive, including systems of passages, courtyards and openings through which food was handed. The prior had to be able to overlook the whole complex.

While the early Carthusians were not opposed to the principle of donations made to found a cell, the *Customs* laid down that churches were to be utterly simple, without gold or silver ornaments, rugs or tapestries, and with only one chalice in precious metal (*Customs* 41). The churches were small, with a single nave and ample choir divided transversely by a high screen, which separated the monks from the *conversi*. The scarcity of windows and candles did not encourage elaborate ornament within the church. Such early foundations as Le Liget (Indre-et-Loire), founded in 1176 by Henry II of England, were simple and austere, but an interesting evolution occurred from the 13th century onwards. The generosity of wealthy patrons inaugurated a new era of accessible, larger buildings. The first such large grant to the Order was the gift of Château

La Grande Chartreuse, interior of cloister, late 12th century

de Vauvert (Gard) by Louis IX of France. In 1356 Pope Innocent VI (*reg* 1352–62) founded Villeneuve-lès-Avignon; it originally had two cloisters, the larger surrounded by cells and the smaller by the chapterhouse, the refectory and the entrance to the church (*see* VILLENEUVE-LÈS-AVIGNON, §1). The charterhouse (mostly destr.) at Champmol, near Dijon (*see* DIJON, §IV, 1), was founded in 1385 by Philip the Bold, Duke of Burgundy, for 25 monks (twice the usual number). It had two cloisters, as did Villefranche-de-Rouergue (Aveyron), founded in 1456 by Vésian Valette, a rich merchant. Other examples of the classic double cloister were at Buxheim (Bavaria) and Tückelhausen in Germany, and at Parkminster (W. Sussex). Seven charterhouses were erected in England between 1343 and 1414, but the London Charterhouse (1370–1436) was the first intended to accommodate a double community. Thomas Holland, Duke of Surrey (1374–1400), founded Mount Grace (N. Yorks) in 1398 for a prior and 16 monks, and Henry V's foundation of 1414 at Sheen (destr.; Surrey) was the grandest, although only 30 of the proposed 40 cells were executed. Urban charterhouses had to be defensible, and several developed fortified gateways with cylindrical corner turrets. La Grande Chartreuse was rebuilt in the 16th and 17th centuries, and Pavia, Galluzzo and Buxheim were entrusted to estimable architects.

3. ICONOGRAPHY AND PATRONAGE. Apart from the severity of their lifestyle, the most recognizable attribute of the Carthusians is their white, full-length, cowled habit. St Bruno was not represented until after his canonization by Pope Leo X on 19 July 1514; he is usually shown at prayer, hands crossed over his breast, reading from a book that rests on a skull. St Hugh of Lincoln (*d* 1200) appears on the late 15th-century altarpiece at Thuison (Amiens diocese) wearing the Carthusian habit beneath his episcopal robes and with his swan at his side. The Order's patron was St John the Baptist, but by the 15th century scenes from the *Life of the Virgin* and representations of the *Crucifixion* and of the Carthusian saints were all deemed worthy subjects of meditation. The Order's symbol was the cross, and its motto was 'stat crux dum volvitur orbis' ('the cross stands while the world revolves').

The earliest Carthusian frescoes at Le Liget date from the end of the 12th century and include a remarkably complete cycle of the *Life of the Virgin*. At Champmol, Philip the Bold (*see* BURGUNDY, (1)) ordered JEAN DE BEAUMETZ to decorate the church and paint a picture for each cell and commissioned a circular devotional painting of the *Trinity* (*c*. 1420; Paris, Louvre), to which the house was dedicated. The latter work, probably by JEAN MALOUEL, depicts God the Father supporting the dead Christ while the Holy Spirit, in the guise of a tiny bird, pecks at the Crown of Thorns, and the Virgin and St John look on. John the Fearless continued the Burgundian patronage of Champmol, commissioning the *Martyrdom of St Denis* (*c*. 1416; Paris, Louvre; for illustration *see* BELLECHOSE, HENRI). Another *Crucifixion* (*c*. 1420), which has been attributed to Bellechose, portrays the dead Christ surrounded by the three Marys, St John the Evangelist and St George, perhaps the patron saint of the Carthusian donor, who kneels beneath the cross with a scroll emerging from his mouth, on which is written 'Miserere Mei Deus'. The same emotional intensity is evoked by the *Pietà* (*c*. 1440; Paris, Louvre) from Villeneuve-lès-Avignon. A stained-glass window of the *Virgin and Child* in the sacristy at Villefranche-de-Rouergue also contains representations of the heads of Carthusian saints, including *Guigo I* and *St Basil*.

Every Carthusian was a potential scribe and every cell a scriptorium in miniature. Nearly all the monks were literate. As they spent so much of their time copying manuscripts, the Carthusians claimed to preach the word of God with their hands rather than with their mouths. Guigo I insisted on the care needed to handle books and on the value of the skill of copying manuscripts, which, whenever possible, was to be taught to all monks (*Customs* 27). A 13th-century Carthusian Bible (Grenoble, Bib. Mun., MS. 14, fol. 158*v*) has a decorated letter showing a monk writing. The *Customs* detail the contents of the cell, complete with all the requisite tools for a copyist. To write, a monk needed a desk, chalk, two pumice stones, two inkwells, a knife, two razors to level the surface of the parchment, a stiletto, a lead line, a ruler, a little board for marking out the page, wax tablets and a stylus. If a trained craftsman became a monk, he was allowed to have the appropriate tools and to practise his art. Each monk was permitted to take two books from the library to read in his cell. The so-called Revelation of 100 Paternosters is a 15th-century devotional book (London, BL, Lansdowne MS. 379, fols 41–54) associated with Sheen Charterhouse and attributed to the circle of Margaret Beaufort and Henry V. It is a Passion devotion in the form of an extended meditation on the Seven Wounds of Christ, a popular theme among English Carthusians.

Although the *Customs* specifically states that no founder or benefactor should be buried within the enclosure or commemorated, the Order attracted considerable patrons from its earliest days. Comtesse Jeanne d'Alençon gave 14 cells to the Paris Chartreuse. Her gift was commemorated in a low relief that showed her presenting the 14 Carthusians to the Virgin and St John the Baptist. A similar tablet depicted Peter of Navarre with the four Carthusians whose cells he donated in 1396. Philip the Bold's Charterhouse of Champmol was conceived as a quasi-royal necropolis to supersede the burial site of his ducal ancestors at Cîteaux Abbey. The building project took nearly 20 years to complete. It was almost completely destroyed in 1792, leaving only the portal of the conventual church and remains of the so-called Well of Moses (*see* FRANCE, fig. 33) by CLAUS SLUTER; it was originally a fountain, the centrepiece of the Great Cloister. The surviving works from Champmol include the Duke's magnificent tomb (1404; Dijon, Mus. B.-A.), which shows him clothed as a Carthusian with 40 weepers (for illustration *see* WEEPER), and the two great altarpieces (1390–99; Dijon, Mus. B.-A.; *see* GOTHIC, §III, 2(ix)(a) and fig. 51) by JACQUES DE BAERZE and MELCHIOR BROEDERLAM. The strong lay influence there indicates that while Carthusian ideals remained much the same, by the later Middle Ages the lay contribution had been greatly enhanced from that of the original *conversi*, although their role remained important.

BIBLIOGRAPHY

Vita S Brunonis; ed. in *PL*, clii (1853), cols 481–92

Guibert of Nogent: *De vita sua* (*c*. 1115–17); ed. in *PL*, clvi (1853), cols 853–6

A. Wilmart: 'La Chronique des premiers Chartreux', *Rev. Mabillon*, xvi (1926), pp. 77–142

F. Wormald: 'The Revelation of a Hundred Paternosters: A Fifteenth-century Meditation', *Laudate*, xv (1936), pp. 165–82

J. Evans: *Art in Mediaeval France, 987–1498* (Oxford, 1952)

B. Bligny: *Recueil des plus anciens actes de la Grande Chartreuse, 1086–1198* (Grenoble, 1958)

A. Oswald: 'The London Charterhouse Restored', *Country Life*, cxxvi (1 Oct 1959), pp. 418–21; (8 Oct 1959), pp. 478–81

B. Bligny: 'L'Eglise et les ordres religieux dans le royaume de Bourgogne aux XIe et XIIe siècles', *Cah. Hist. A. Contemp.: Doc.*, iv (1960) [whole issue]

——: 'L'Erémitisme et les Chartreux', *L'eremitismo in Occidente nei secoli XI e XII*, Miscellanea del Centro di Studi Medioevali, iv (Milan, 1965), pp. 248–63

——: 'Les Chartreaux dans la société occidentale du XIIe siècle', *Cah. Hist. A. Contemp.: Doc.* (1975) [whole issue]

——: *Saint Bruno: Le Premier Chartreux* (Rennes, 1984)

'Un Chartreux', ed.: 'Guigues Ier: Coutumes de Chartreuse', *Sources Chrétiennes*, cccxiii (1984)

BRENDA M. BOLTON

Cartier-Bresson, Henri (*b* Chanteloup, Seine-et-Marne, 22 Aug 1908). French photographer, painter and draughtsman. He not only shaped and extended the concept of photography but through it achieved a psychological penetration and formal perfection equal to other kinds of serious image-making. He began to study painting and drawing at the age of 15 and in Paris was a student in the atelier of André Lhote in 1927–8, a painter whom he remembered with affection and respect. Lhote's Synthetic Cubist methods and high valuation of the 'lightning sketch' as a source of ideas seem to have proved fruitful for him.

Cartier-Bresson spent a year in the French army in 1930, and then he visited the Côte d'Ivoire in 1931, followed by a period of convalescence in France from Blackwater fever contracted during his travels. His serious interest in photography began at the time of his return (although photographs from 1929 are known). From 1932 he used the Leica camera, his chief mentor being André Kertész, whom Cartier-Bresson later described as 'my poetic well-spring'. The Leica, with its excellent lenses, transformed the aesthetic possibilities of the miniature camera. It allowed photographers to fulfil the dream of entering the crowd as a passionate observer, described by Charles Baudelaire in *Le Peintre de la vie moderne* (1863). Cartier-Bresson is known to have read Baudelaire in his youth.

From 1932 to 1933 Cartier-Bresson brought elements from Post-Impressionism and Surrealism to bear on the new technology in photographs taken first in the streets of Paris, then during his travels in Italy and Spain. A famous photograph simply titled *Andalusia* (1933; see *Images à la sauvette*, pl. 11) includes two young boys in a maze of shadowed alleyways. The arrangement and the mood of troubled mystery are unprecedented in photography and suggest an adaptation of a key painting by De Chirico (one that Cartier-Bresson may have seen in André Breton's *Le Surréalisme et la peinture*, 1928), *Melancholy and Mystery of a Street* (1914). The deep, angular shadows, the steeply tilted perspective, the claustrophobic oppressiveness of the architectural forms, the children themselves (with the suggestion of the fears and fantasies of puberty) and the way shadows stand in for realities not shown: all of these elements of Cartier-Bresson's photograph can be traced to his study of De Chirico's painting, and it is possible to think of Cartier-Bresson as pioneering a 'metaphysical' photography in emulation of De Chirico's Pittura Metafisica period. Other images from this time of intense discovery by Cartier-Bresson include swarming children in ruins—the forms creating echoes, harmonies and metaphors, as in *Seville* (1933; see Bonnefoy, p. 28)—or street scenes in which dark heads 'rhyme' with shadowed windows, for example *Madrid* (1933; see fig.), and in which the flickering grace of the children is perfectly foiled by the deliberate progress of a portly, middle-aged pedestrian. The formal logic cannot be dissociated from the psychological perception of the narrative.

During the 1930s Cartier-Bresson's work was credited to 'Henri Cartier'. He made his first photo-reportage in a contribution to the Parisian illustrated magazine *Vu* in 1932; a year later his work was exhibited for the first time at the Julien Lévy Gallery in New York. Lévy recalled how Cartier-Bresson would slap down on the desk a batch of prints, eschewing that devotion to the fine print perfectly positioned on its rag mount favoured by 'fine art' photographers.

Despite his lively curiosity and adeptness in cultural matters, Cartier-Bresson personified the field photographer, traveller and eyewitness of history. He joined an ethnographic expedition to Mexico in 1934 and put the finishing touches to his strict and incisive style in such images as *Alicante* (1932 and 1933; see Bonnefoy, pp. 21–2) and *Mexico* (1934; see Bonnefoy, pp. 23, 25). He photographed the prostitutes of the Calle Cuauhtemocztin, a set of vivid social portraits in which the women look out from rectangular apertures cut into doors; in another photograph transvestites prance before the camera; another image shows copulation in a brothel. Cartier-Bresson's volatile temperament transgressed the boundaries of decorum in composition and in subject-matter. His appreciation of innocence, abundantly revealed in his photographs, was accompanied by a hatred of pretension.

In 1935 he lived in the USA, studying cinematic technique with Paul Strand (whom he always chose to refer to as 'Maître'). On his return to France, Cartier-Bresson worked with film maker Jean Renoir on a Front Populaire film, *La Vie est à nous* (1936). He was Renoir's assistant on *La Règle du jeu* (1939) and directed *Victoire de la vie* (1937), on hospitals in Republican Spain; he co-directed *Le Retour* (1944–5) and directed two documentaries for CBS (1969–70). In 1940 he was imprisoned by the Germans, but he escaped and participated in MNPGD, a French underground photographic unit that helped prisoners to escape. He made portraits of painters and writers, such as Matisse, Bonnard and Braque (pubd as *Photo Portraits*, 1985). From 1944 to 1945 he was one of a group of professional photographers who recorded the liberation of Paris. In Dessau he photographed the moment when a Gestapo informer was identified and denounced by one of his victims, *Dessau: Exposing a Gestapo Informer* (1945; see Bonnefoy, p. 68).

Few photographs of the 20th century encompass so much of its history. The image perfectly fulfils the aesthetic

Henri Cartier-Bresson: *Madrid*, 1933

of the 'decisive moment' formulated in the text of Cartier-Bresson's major collection of his work, *Images à la sauvette* (1952). He prefaced his original and compelling remarks with one sentence quoted from Cardinal de Retz: 'There is nothing in this world that does not have a decisive moment.' In his concluding paragraphs he wrote: 'A photograph is for me simultaneous recognition, in a fraction of a second, of an element of meaning of a detail, on the one hand, and on the other, of a rigorous organization of visually perceived forms expressing this detail.' The era of the 'decisive moment', allied to Cartier-Bresson's distaste for flash or other intrusive forms of artificial lighting, and his embargo on the cropping of his photographs, dominated the medium of photography during the next three decades and set a standard that remained an inspiration to later photographers.

After the war Cartier-Bresson's work was published in illustrated magazines through the Magnum cooperative, which he and fellow photographers Robert Capa, David Seymour ('Chim') and George Rodger (*b* 1908) established in 1947. In the previous year he was honoured by a retrospective exhibition at the Museum of Modern Art, New York, planned as a memorial exhibition before it emerged that the photographer had survived the war; it included 300 photographs.

Cartier-Bresson visited the USA from 1946 to 1947, and then from 1948 to 1950 India, Burma, Pakistan, China and Indonesia. He stationed himself in China during the last six months of the Kuomintang and the first six months of the People's Republic, producing a body of work published as *D'Une Chine à l'autre* (1954). He was in Indonesia at the moment of its independence. In 1954 he was the first Western photographer to be admitted to the USSR as part of the thaw that followed the death of Stalin. His Russian photographs appeared in 1955 as *Moscou, vu par Henri Cartier-Bresson* (1955). In 1958–9 he revisited China for three months for the tenth anniversary of the People's Republic, and he published his photographs as *China* (1964). He followed this by periods of work in Cuba, Mexico, Canada, India, Japan and, of course, France. He became a pervasive inspiration and model for photographers, his influence and stature comparable to that of Le Corbusier in architecture. In 1966 he left Magnum, and from 1974 he devoted himself to drawing and to his first (and never completely abandoned) love, painting. These works, such as the drawing *Muséum d'histoire naturelle* (1976; see exh. cat., 1984, pp. 26–8), often revealing his great admiration for his friend Alberto Giacometti, have also been exhibited and published.

PHOTOGRAPHIC PUBLICATIONS

Images à la sauvette (Paris, 1952); Eng. trans. as *The Decisive Moment* (New York, 1952)
D'Une Chine à l'autre (Paris, 1954)
Moscou, vu par Henri Cartier-Bresson, ed. R. Delpire (Paris, 1955)
China (New York, 1964)
The Face of Asia (London, 1972)
Photo Portraits (London, 1985)
Henri Cartier-Bresson in India (London, 1987)
America in Passing (London, 1991)
A propos de Paris (Paris, 1994)

BIBLIOGRAPHY

L. Kirstein and B. Newhall: *The Photographs of Henri Cartier-Bresson* (New York, 1947, rev. 1963)

A. Farova: *Henri Cartier-Bresson* (Prague, 1958)
C. Roy: *Henri Cartier-Bresson* (Paris, 1976)
Y. Bonnefoy: *Henri Cartier-Bresson, Photographer* (London, 1981)
Henri Cartier-Bresson, Drawings and Paintings (exh. cat. by D. Elliot, J. Levy and A. B. Joffroy, Oxford, MOMA, 1984)
Henri Cartier-Bresson: The Early Work (exh. cat. by P. Galassi, New York, MOMA, 1987)
J. Claire: *Line by Line: The Drawings of Henri Cartier-Bresson*, foreword by J. Russell (London, 1989)

MARK HAWORTH-BOOTH

Cartography. *See under* MAP.

Carton, Enguerrand. *See* QUARTON, ENGUERRAND.

Cartoon. Drawing, sometimes coloured, made specifically as a pattern for a painting, textile or stained-glass panel. It is produced on the same scale as the final work and is usually fairly detailed. The transfer of the image works best if the drawing in the cartoon is of a linear nature and if the composition has crisp, clear outlines.

1. TECHNIQUE. In painting there are two methods of transferring a cartoon to the support, which may be a canvas, panel or wall. The first is similar to TRACING. The back of the cartoon is rubbed over with chalk; the paper is attached to the support; and the main lines are drawn over with a stylus, thus transferring the chalk from the back of the cartoon to the new support. In the second method, which is called POUNCING, the main lines of the cartoon are pricked through with a needle or stylus, the size and closeness of the holes varying according to the detail in the drawing. Sometimes in order to preserve the drawn cartoon, a supplementary cartoon or *spolvero* is made by pricking through the original cartoon and a blank sheet of paper at the same time. The cartoon or supplementary cartoon is then laid flat against the support, and the pricked lines firmly dabbed with a muslin bag containing powdered charcoal. The charcoal dust penetrates the pounce bag and is forced through the holes in the cartoon on to the support beneath. Another method of transfer is to rub over the holes with a large stick of soft charcoal or red chalk and then to smear the medium through the holes and on to the support by using a finger.

When the cartoon is removed from the support the original drawing is duplicated in a series of dots, which can be joined up to make a complete drawing using whatever instrument or medium the artist prefers. The original can be referred to if necessary to supply any details missing from the transfer. If a reversed image is required the *spolvero* is turned over before it is used. In surviving cartoons it is possible to tell which method was used for transfer from the prick marks or from the indentation of the lines.

2. HISTORY. Cartoons were used by illuminators, textile workers and stained-glass artists from the early medieval period, but their first appearance in painting occurs only in the second half of the 14th century. Cennini, writing *c.* 1390, gave detailed instructions for the execution of textile patterns using a parchment cartoon, a procedure that has been verified in Tuscan panel paintings of the period. In the following century such artists as Piero della Francesca began to use cartoons for figure compositions, whereas previously they had been employed only for the repetition of decorative motifs.

From the late 15th century cartoons became an essential part of studio practice, particularly with the systematic working methods of such artists as Raphael (for illustration *see* POUNCING). For important areas of a painting, faces for example, auxiliary cartoons were made: outlines were pounced from the main cartoon on to a further sheet of paper, which was worked up in greater detail before transfer (see fig.). Since cartoons were used again and again, for copying whole compositions or for reproducing individual figures, they were considered valuable studio property. Cartoons by the greater artists were especially prized: those, for example, by Leonardo and Michelangelo for the Sala della Signoria in the Palazzo Vecchio, Florence (1504–5), were copied until they disintegrated. However, one cartoon by Leonardo does survive, the *Virgin and Child with SS John the Baptist and Anne* (black and white chalk on tinted paper, *c.* 1507–8; London, N.G.); although it seems to have been intended for a painting, it has not been pricked or incised.

In fresco painting cartoons were rarely used alone. Until the 16th century they were combined, to a greater or lesser extent, with *sinopia* underdrawing, and later they were employed in conjunction with freehand drawing, squaring up and other quick methods of transfer. They were much used by Annibale Carracci in the 17th century, with his deliberate emulation of Raphael's technique, and again by the Nazarenes in the 19th century for the same reason (*see*

Auxiliary cartoon for the *Transfiguration* (1520) by Raphael: *Head of a Youthful Bearded Man Looking Downwards over his Right Shoulder* (detail), black chalk over pounced underdrawing, 375×278 mm (Chatsworth, Derbys)

CORNELIUS, PETER, fig. 2), but in the 20th century they were finally superseded by photoprojection.

In textile design cartoons have always been necessary. Silk-weavers used to work from full-colour cartoons that reproduced one section of the repeat, and embroiderers still pounce designs through to the ground fabric. In tapestry-weaving the cartoons were coloured (e.g. the series by Raphael depicting the *Missions of SS Peter and Paul*, *c.* 1514–17; British Royal Col., on loan to London, V&A) until the 20th century, when outline drawings became more usual (*see* TAPESTRY, §I).

See also FRESCO, §1(ii) and STAINED GLASS, §I, 6. For cartoon in the sense of a humorous image *see* CARICATURE, COMIC-STRIP ART and SATIRE.

BIBLIOGRAPHY

C. Cennini: *Il libro dell'arte* (*c.* 1390); Eng. trans. and notes by D. V. Thompson jr as *The Craftsman's Handbook: 'Il libro dell'arte'* (New Haven, 1933/*R* New York, 1954), pp. 87, 111
G. Vasari: *Vite* (1550, rev. 2/1568); Eng. trans. by L. S. Maclehose, ed. G. B. Brown, as *Vasari on Technique* [intro. prefixed to the *Vite*] (London, 1907/*R* New York, 1960), pp. 213–15
J. Watrous: *The Craft of Old-Master Drawings* (Madison, 1957)
P. Goldman: *Looking at Drawings: A Guide to Technical Terms* (London, 1979)
P. Joannides: *The Drawings of Raphael, with a Complete Catalogue* (Oxford, 1983)
P. Mora, L. Mora and P. Philippot: *Conservation of Wall Paintings* (London, 1984)
Art in the Making: Italian Painting before 1400 (exh. cat. by D. Bomford and others, London, N.G., 1989–90), pp. 130–35

SHIRLEY MILLIDGE

Cartouche. Ornamental tablet or shield bearing an inscription, monogram or heraldic arms framed in elaborate scrolls, shell-shaped volutes or similar devices. The term has been extended to include the lozenge-shaped frames inscribed with the names of pharaohs in Egyptian hieroglyphs. The cartouche was a minor ornament in the vocabulary of European Renaissance and Mannerist design. Used in both ecclesiastical and secular contexts, it adorned exterior and interior walls and furniture (e.g. cassone with shield cartouche flanked by putti, carved wood and gilt, Roman, mid-16th century; London, V&A). It also embellished manuscripts and prints, used as a motif to enclose titles and brief texts, notably in architectural elevations and maps (*see* MAP).

The use of the cartouche developed more fully in the Baroque era, however, and in its more opulent 17th-century form it spread rapidly as a decorative device throughout Europe and eventually to the New World. It became the dramatic focus of pedimental designs above façades, doorframes and windows, as well as in chimney-pieces, keystones and balconies (see fig.). Deeply carved in stone, marble and wood or in cast plaster or stucco, its commonly shared characteristics were lavish back or forward scrolls resembling parchment or a profusion of scrolling plant forms. Shields were frequently surmounted by crowns or mantled helmets and flanked by figures, animals or birds and heavy floral swags (e.g. shield cartouche flanked by ostriches, carved and painted wood, façade, Uppark, W. Sussex, *c.* 1686); variations included trophies, flags and sunburst surrounds. In the first half of the 18th century cabinetmakers used cartouches in the open pediments of armoires, cabinets and tallboys. During

Cartouche of the arms of the Pamphili family on the façade of S Andrea al Quirinale, Rome, by Gianlorenzo Bernini, 1658–70

the Neo-classical period following the 1750s, the cartouche was largely replaced by evenly dispersed roundels, urns and vases executed in shallow relief. It was reintroduced with the revival of interest in Baroque forms at the end of the 19th century.

PRINTS

H. Vredeman de Vries: *Recueil de cartouches* (Antwerp, 1555 and 1557/*R* Brussels, 1870) [two suites of cartouche designs]

BIBLIOGRAPHY

B. Fletcher: *A History of Architecture* (London, 1896; rev. 19/1987)
E. Hempel: *Baroque Art and Architecture in Central Europe*, Pelican Hist. A. (Harmondsworth, 1965)

□

Cartwright, Julia (*b* Edgcote, Northants, 7 Nov 1851; *d* Oxford, 24 April 1924). English critic and historian. In her writing she combined the results of methodical scholarship with a passionate enthusiasm to give a vivid picture of her subjects. She respected the new 'scientific' approach to art led by Giovanni Morelli, and her favourable reviews of Bernard Berenson's early publications were partly responsible for the warm reception some of the new ideas received in England. Among 19th-century artists, she wrote a monograph on *Jules Bastien-Lepage* (1894), a biography of *Jean-François Millet* (1896)—possibly under the influence of her one-time editor and friend W. E. Henley—and articles on other French painters. She was a fervent admirer of the Arts and Crafts Movement and her monographs on *Sir Edward Burne-Jones* (1894), *G. F. Watts* (1896) and *Lawrence Alma-Tadema* were greatly admired, not least by the artists themselves, who became her firm friends. She also championed the Italian landscape artist Giovanni Costa.

Cartwright's chief work, however, was on the Italian Renaissance. The times in which she wrote witnessed a change in taste resulting in growing interest in and awareness of this period. Her monographs *The Painters of Florence* (1901), *Sandro Botticelli* (1903) and *Raphael* (1905) were, together with her biographies of *Beatrice d'Este* (1899) and *Isabella d'Este* (1903), a major contribution to the understanding of Italian art and history, although she incurred the wrath of the archivist Alessandro Luzio, who had published many of the documents about Isabella d'Este that Cartwright drew on. Her writings exemplified the didactic approach so loved by Victorians. Her opinion was sought by museum directors, connoisseurs and the general public. She belonged to a group of English writers, including Sir George Hill and Claude Phillips, whose major works were completed before the arrival in England of the more rigorous and analytical art historians of the German school.

WRITINGS

Mantegna and Francia (London, 1881)
The Early Work of Raphael (London, 1895, rev. 1907)
Raphael in Rome (London, 1895, rev. 1907)
Christ and his Mother in Italian Art (London, 1897)
Baldassare Castiglione, the Perfect Courtier: His Life and Letters, 1478–1529, 2 vols (London, 1908)
Hampton Court (London, 1910)
Christina of Denmark (London, 1913)
San Bernardino in Art (London, 1913)
Italian Gardens of the Renaissance (London, 1914)
Regular contributions to *Argosy*, 1872–5; *Portfolio* [London], 1880–92; *Mag. A.*, 1882–7; *New Q.*, 1887; *19th C.* [London], 1888–1910; *A. J.* [London], 1891–1900; *Nat. Rev.*, 1891–1904; *Q. Rev.*, 1896–1900; *Burl. Mag.*, 1904; the *Manchester Guardian*

BIBLIOGRAPHY

A. Emanuel, ed.: *The Diaries of Julia Cartwright, 1867–1910: A Bright Remembrance* (London, 1988)

ANGELA EMANUEL

Cartwright, Richard. *See* ROYLEY, RICHARD.

Cartwright, William (*bapt* London, 1 Jan 1606; *d* London, 17 Dec 1686). English actor and collector. He was the son of an actor who was a friend of Edward Alleyn, founder of Dulwich College. He was himself first recorded on the stage in Norwich in 1635, but when the theatres closed down during the Commonwealth period he seems to have made his living as a bookseller in London. In 1658 he apparently published *Actor's Vindication*, a version of Thomas Heywood's *Apology for Actors.* With the Restoration of Charles II in 1660 he returned to the stage as a member of the refounded King's Company, in which he played a prominent part as both actor and shareholder.

Cartwright was a keen collector, especially of pictures, and he bequeathed to Dulwich College his collection of 239 paintings, together with an inventory in his own hand. Only about 75 of these paintings survive in Dulwich Picture Gallery, the remainder having been stolen by his servants or subsequently lost. They constitute a remarkably important survival, from a late 17th-century collection made by a person of adequate but not great means. The surviving pictures include works by John Greenhill and L. A. Castro, little represented elsewhere, and exhibit Cartwright's interest in acquiring pictures by such British contemporaries as Robert Streeter, Parry Walton (*d* 1702) and Isaac Fuller. Copies after Jacopo Bassano indicate a wish to give the collection a taste of the Old Masters; and the inclusion of landscapes, seascapes, mythological scenes and genre paintings as well as family portraits reveal Cartwright's ambitions in terms of subject if not always of quality. The collection includes a group of rare theatrical portraits of the period, including the only authenticated portrait of the actor Richard Burbage.

BIBLIOGRAPHY

DNB
G. Warner: *Catalogue of the Manuscripts and Muniments at Dulwich* (London, 1881)
E. Boswell: 'Young Mr Cartwright', *Mod. Lang. Rev.*, xxiv (1929), p. 225
N. Kalinsky and G. Waterfield, eds: *Mr Cartwright's Pictures* (London, 1987)

GILES WATERFIELD

Caruana, Pietro Paolo (*b* Valletta, 4 Jan 1793; *d* Valletta, 23 April 1852). Maltese painter and lithographer. He was the most significant Maltese disciple of Tommaso Minardi, whom he met and befriended while studying in Rome at the Accademia Nazionale di San Luca. In Malta he established himself as one of the leading artists of his generation and received prestigious commissions from both the Church and the British administration. He also produced prints intended for the tourist market and was the first Maltese to own a lithographic press. In 1831 he was appointed Professor of Drawing in the School of Design at the University of Malta, in Msida. His works are uneven in quality but they share a common indebtedness to the ideals of Minardi's Purismo, to which he remained faithful all his life. His major painting, the *Visitation of the Virgin* (Valletta, Portosalvo Church), demonstrates his admiration for the Renaissance, but he was also influenced by such Neo-classical artists as David, to whom he paid tribute in his large canvases with episodes from the life of St George, *St George in the Temple of Apollo* and *St George before Diocletian* (1843; parish church of St George, Qormi). Caruana's *Plague of 1813* (Valletta, Mus. F.A.) is Malta's first Romantic painting. His son Raffaele Caruana (1820–86) was also a painter, but he rarely rose above mediocrity, and his works are generally dry and academic because of his sterile imagination and technical rigidity. Raffaele Caruana's most remarkable work is probably the portrait of *Salvatore Borg* (Valletta, Mus. F.A.); he produced mostly church paintings, including the altarpiece of the *Ascension* (St Julian's, Old Parish Church).

BIBLIOGRAPHY

A. Ganado: 'Pietro Paulo Caruana: The First Lithographs Produced in Malta', *Proceedings of History Week, 1981*, ed. M. Buhagiar (Valletta, 1982), pp. 49–60
M. Buhagiar: *The Iconography of the Maltese Islands, 1400–1900: Painting* (Valletta, 1988), pp. 162–6

MARIO BUHAGIAR

Carucci, Jacopo. *See* PONTORMO, JACOPO DA.

Caruelle d'Aligny, Théodore. *See* ALIGNY, THÉODORE CARUELLE D'.

Carus, Carl Gustav (*b* Leipzig, 3 Jan 1789; *d* Dresden, 28 July 1869). German painter and draughtsman. As well as being an artist, he achieved considerable success as a doctor, a naturalist, a scientist and a psychologist. As an artist, he was concerned almost exclusively with landscape painting, although he never practised it professionally. While still at school in Leipzig, he had drawing lessons from Julius Diez; he subsequently studied under Johann Veit Schnorr von Carolsfeld (1764–1841) at the Oeser drawing academy. From 1813 he taught himself oil painting, copying after the Dresden landscape painter Johann Christian Klengel, whom he visited in his studio. In 1811 after six years at university he graduated as a doctor of medicine and a doctor of philosophy. In 1814 he was appointed professor of obstetrics and director of the maternity clinic at the teaching institution for medicine and surgery in Dresden.

Carus showed his work as an artist publicly for the first time when he exhibited several landscapes at the Dresden Kunstakademie exhibition in 1816. Shortly afterwards he came to know Caspar David Friedrich, and the two artists became lifelong friends. Between 1817 and 1823, under Friedrich's influence, Carus painted a large number of works on subjects Friedrich had often chosen: lonely coasts, megalithic graves, ruins or cemeteries. Carus's paintings, however, did not achieve the formal tension and intellectual depth of Friedrich's pictures. Carus's principal works for this period are *Moonlit Night on Rügen* (1819), *Woman on a Balcony* (1824; both Dresden, Gemäldegal. Neue Meister), *Spruce Wood under Snow with a Stone Cross* (1823; Frankfurt am Main, Goethemus.), *Graveyard on the Oybin in Winter* (1828; Leipzig, Mus. Bild. Kst.; see fig.) and *Window Overlooking the Oybin in Moonlight* (*c.* 1828; Schweinfurt, Samml. Schäfer). At Friedrich's instigation, Carus went on study tours across the island of Rügen (1819) and to the Riesengebirge (1820). In 1821 he made a journey to Switzerland and Italy.

When Carus visited Johann Wolfgang von Goethe in Weimar in 1821, Goethe took a lively interest not only in Carus's scientific investigations but also in his work as a painter. The interaction of the artistic and scientific was as important for Carus as for Goethe: pragmatic, even scientific observation of nature had played a major role in Carus's development as an artist. From the mid-1820s pictorial realism, with a preference for close-range subjects and strong mood, became more marked, especially in the series of small studies inspired by J. C. Dahl: for example the small picture *Painter's Room in Moonlight* (1826; Karlsruhe, Staatl. Ksthalle). In other works there is a marked sense of comfort and emotional calm, as in *Boat Trip on the Elbe* (1827; Düsseldorf, Kstmus.). Carus travelled to Italy for a second time in 1828, as medical adviser to Prince Frederick Augustus of Saxony, and he made a third Italian journey in 1841. In 1844 he visited England and Scotland. The oil studies made on the spot during these journeys, as well as the paintings executed from them later, show a spontaneous realism (e.g. *Balcony in Naples*, 1829–30; destr.; see Prause, pl. 35). Some works reveal Carus's interest in geology and the formation of the earth's surface. Even in his late work, however, there are constant reminders of the Romantic subject-matter of the early paintings. Pictures such as *Oaks by the Sea* (1835; Dresden, Gemäldegal. Neue Meister) and the numerous charcoal drawings executed after 1851 are proof of this.

Carl Gustav Carus: *Graveyard on the Oybin in Winter*, oil on canvas, 670×520 mm, 1828 (Leipzig, Museum der Bildenden Künste)

It is not possible to separate Carus's work as a painter from his theoretical ideas on nature and landscape painting. These were set down in the *Neun Briefe über Landschaftsmalerei*, first published in 1831, and had been formulated, from 1815 onwards, under the influence of Friedrich's concept of art. Carus's arguments relating to the perception of nature, however, go beyond Friedrich. With his concept of the *Erdlebenbild* Carus sought to convey the notion that the landscape painter, like the scholar, must not conceive of nature as a fixed form but as a living organism. Carus's autobiographical account, *Lebenserinnerungen und Denkwürdigkeiten* (Leipzig, 1865–6), also provides valuable information about his artistic activity.

WRITINGS

Neun Briefe über Landschaftsmalerei (Leipzig, 1831; *R*, ed. D. Kuhn, Heidelberg, 1972)

Lebenserinnerungen und Denkwürdigkeiten (Leipzig, 1865–6)

E. von Sydow, ed.: *Reisen und Briefe* (Leipzig, 1926)

BIBLIOGRAPHY

M. Prause: *Carl Gustav Carus: Leben und Werk* (Berlin, 1968)

C. G. Carus in mortis centenarium (exh. cat., Dresden, Gemäldegal. Neue Meister, 1969)

Carl Gustav Carus und die zeitgenössische Dresdner Landschaftsmalerei: Gemälde aus der Sammlung Georg Schäfer, Schweinfurt (exh. cat., Schweinfurt, Samml. Schäfer, 1970)

W. Genschorek: *Carl Gustav Carus: Arzt, Künstler, Naturforscher* (Leipzig, 1978)

E. Meffert: *Carl Gustav Carus: Sein Leben, seine Anschauung von der Erde* (Stuttgart, 1986)

HANS JOACHIM NEIDHARDT

Carvajal, Luis de (*b* Toledo, *c.* 1556; *d* Madrid, 1607). Spanish painter. He was a half-brother of the sculptor and architect Juan Bautista Monegro. Having trained with Juan de Villoldo (*fl* 1508–51) in Toledo, he went to Italy and in 1577 is documented in Rome at the Accademia di S Luca. The *Penitent Magdalene* (1579; Toledo, Mus. Santa Cruz) shows the influence of late Roman Mannerism. Between 1579 and 1590 he is documented at the Escorial, carrying out numerous commissions for Philip II. From about 1583 he settled in Madrid. Most of his surviving paintings are to be seen at the Escorial, including ten canvases for the minor altars of the royal basilica, depicting life-size pairs of saints. Outstanding among these is *St John Chrysostom and St Gregory Nazianzus* (1582). The two Greek Doctors of the Church are strongly modelled in light and shade; their lean, ascetic faces partly cast in shadow have the authenticity of portrait likenesses, and their rich brocade copes are decorated with exquisite miniature scenes on the orphreys. His paintings for the Escorial show that Carvajal had a highly developed technique in the use of light and shade, a strong interest in naturalism and the ability to imbue his figures with a sense of piety and devotion. He was influenced by Jacopo Bassano and Titian, of whose work he made copies. A late work, *St Blaise*, in the parish church at Yepes, shows the combined influence of Titian and El Greco, and in *St Nicholas of Tolentino* (1604; Toledo, Casa & Mus. El Greco) his tendency towards naturalism is very advanced.

BIBLIOGRAPHY

J. Zarco Cuevas: *Pintores españoles en San Lorenzo el Real de el Escorial* (Madrid, 1931) [illustrations and documents]

C. R. Post: *A History of Spanish Painting*, xvi: *The Later Renaissance in Castile* (Cambridge, MA, 1966)

T. de Antonio Sáenz: *Pintura española del último tercio del siglo XVI en Madrid: Juan Fernández de Navarrete, Luis de Carvajal y Diego de Urbina*, 3 vols (diss., Madrid, U. Complutense, 1987)

ROSEMARIE MULCAHY

Carvajal y Lancaster, José de (*b* 1698; *d* Madrid, 8 April 1754). Spanish politician and patron. His brilliant political career began when he was young. After becoming Judge of the Royal Chancellery of Valladolid, in 1742 he was appointed Governor of the Council of the Indies and in 1746 President of the Real Junta de Comercio y Moneda. Ferdinand VI made him Minister of State and Gentilhombre de Cámara, and he eventually became President of the Council of State. During the years of his ministerial activity he showed himself to be politically in favour of England and Portugal against the general preference of the Spanish Bourbon monarchy for France and Italy.

José de Carvajal y Lancaster was among those who promoted the creation (by royal decree of 12 April 1752) of the Real Academia de Bellas Artes de S Fernando, Madrid, the first such academy to be founded in Spain in the 18th century. He was appointed its Director in 1752, a post he held until his death, and he always saw the Real Academia as an establishment of the arts in the service of the monarchy. He patronized many foreign artists in Spain, among them the architects Giambattista Novelli and Giovanni Battista Sacchetti; the sculptor Giovanni Domenico Olivieri; and the portraitist Louis-Michel van Loo who came to Spain in 1737. He personally gave bursaries to Spanish painters to study abroad, such as José del Castillo, who between 1751 and 1753 trained in the workshop of Corrado Giaquinto in Rome. The painter Francisco Preciado de la Vega and the sculptor Felipe de Castro worked for Carvajal y Lancaster; owing to the high esteem in which his patron held him, the latter played an important role in the new Real Academia. The appearance of José de Carvajal y Lancaster is known from a bust by Felipe de Castro and a posthumous portrait by Andrés de la Calleja (both Madrid, Real Acad. S Fernando, Mus.).

BIBLIOGRAPHY

Conde de Fernan Nuñez: *Vida de Carlos III* (Madrid, 1898), pp. 3, 110, 164, 168, 171–2, 174, 178, 215

D. Ozanam: *La diplomacia de Fernando VI: Correspondencia reservada entre D. José de Carvajal y el Duque de Huescar, 1746–9* (Madrid, 1975)

Y. Bottineau: *El arte cortesano en la España de Felipe V, 1700–46* (Madrid, 1986)

MERCEDES AGUEDA

Carvalheira, Rosendo (Garcia de Aráujo) (*b* Lisbon, 1863; *d* Lisbon, 21 Jan 1919). Portuguese architect. He was born of a poor family but came to the notice of Alexandre Herculano (1810–77), the famous historian, who supervised his studies. Carvalheira trained at the Instituto Industrial, Lisbon, in a tradition based on Neoclassicism but was also sensitive to historicist trends, which in Portugal derived from the Manueline style of the 16th century, and to the decorative aesthetic of Art Nouveau propagated by French periodicals. In a short period up to 1910, when the Portuguese monarchy ended, Carvalheira divided his activity between commissions for private houses, outstanding among which is the chalet (1893), Monte Estoril, for the queen, Maria Pia (1847–1911), and the planning of several shops in the commercial centre of Lisbon, including Tabacaria Mónaco (1894) in the Rossio, with Art Nouveau decoration. He also designed the Sanatoriòm de Sant'Ana (1901–4), Parede, one of the most important Art Nouveau complexes in Portugal, with a functional plan, skilfully designed elevations and furnishings and outstanding *azulejo* (glazed tile) decoration; and an anti-tuberculosis welfare centre (1906), Avenida 24 Julho, Lisbon, commissioned by Queen Amalia (1863–1951). The concept of architecture as one of the fine arts, which was characteristic of the profession throughout the 19th century, led Carvalheira, like others of his generation, to an interest in the restoration of historic buildings; his main achievements in this context were his involvement with the final stages of the work on the Hieronymite Monastery at Belém and the restoration of Guarda Cathedral. He was a founder-member (1906) of the Sociedade dos Arquitetos Portugueses and vice-president of the Associação dos Arquitetos e Arqueólogos Portugueses; he was also active as an architectural critic and defender of the national heritage and the interests of the architectural profession.

BIBLIOGRAPHY

J.-A. França: *A arte em Portugal no século XIX*, ii (Lisbon, 1966), pp. 130–31, 175, 179

E. Martins Bairrada: *Arquiteto Rosendo Carvalheira: Um filho adoptivo de Alexandre Herculano na arte de construir* (Lisbon, 1981)

RAQUEL HENRIQUES DA SILVA

Carvalho, Flávio de (Resende) (*b* Barra Mansa, 10 Aug 1899; *d* Valinhos, 4 June 1973). Brazilian painter, draughtsman, architect and sculptor. He was in Europe from 1910 to 1922 and lived first in Paris and then in London; he studied civil engineering at Armstrong College, University of Durham, and painting in the evening at the King Edward VII School of Fine Arts. On his return to Brazil he settled in São Paulo. His design of 1927 for the headquarters of the government of São Paulo state, although never realized, made him one of the pioneers of modern Brazilian architecture (Dahler, pp. 130–31). During the 1930s in particular he was one of the liveliest figures in the cultural life of the country, responsible for radicalizing the initial successes of modernism. In 1931 his interest in the psychology of the masses led him to put on the performance *Experience No. 2* in São Paulo. In the same city in 1932 he founded the Clube dos Artistas Modernos and the Teatro de Experiência where he mounted, to great public scandal, his *Bailado do Deus morto*, later publishing a text related to it, *A origem animal de Deus e O bailado do Deus morto* (São Paulo, 1973). From 1937 to 1939 he also led the May Salon group. In 1947 he executed the *Tragic Series*, drawings of his mother on her deathbed (U. São Paulo, Mus. A. Contemp.). His varied production was recognized at the São Paulo Biennale with a gold medal for ballet design in 1953, the international prize for drawing in 1967 and the posthumous tribute of a retrospective in 1983.

Carvalho was consistently in step with the international movements of his time, especially between the 1920s and 1940s, but his work is essentially rooted in Viennese Expressionism with a Surrealist inflection. Among his best-known works are *Final Ascension of Christ* (1932; São Paulo, Pin. Estado) and the portrait of the poet Ungaretti (1941; Rome, G. N. A. Mod.). His sculpture included a monument to the Spanish poet *Federico García Lorca* in São Paulo. In painting and drawing he focused on the human figure, especially the female body, treating it with a violence and brutality rare in Brazilian art at any time, for example *Despised Woman Curls into a Foetal Position* (1932; São Paulo, Mus. A. Assis Châteaubriand).

BIBLIOGRAPHY

P. M. Almeida: *De Anita ao museu* (São Paulo, 1961)
P. M. Bardi: *Profile of the New Brazilian Art* (Rio de Janeiro, 1970)
Flávio de Carvalho (exh. cat. by W. Zanini and others, São Paulo, XVII Biennale, 1983)
L. C. Dahler: *Flávio de Carvalho e a volúpia da forma* (São Paulo, 1984)
Expressionismo no Brasil: Heranças e afinidades (exh. cat. by S. T. Barros and I. Mesquita, São Paulo, XVIII Biennale, 1985)

ROBERTO PONTUAL

Carvalho, José Rodrigues de. *See* RODRIGUES DE CARVALHO, JOSÉ.

Carvalho, Pedro Alexandrino (*b* Lisbon, 27 Nov 1729; *d* Lisbon, 27 Jan 1810). Portuguese painter, draughtsman, teacher and writer. He was apprenticed to João de Mesquita, an obscure painter–decorator who specialized in ornamentation, and he also studied painting and drawing under Bernardo Pereira Pegado. His early training coincided with the end of the reign of John V, during which time a lavish and ostentatious courtly Baroque style predominated in Portugal. He learnt easel painting from a friend, the somewhat older André Gonçalves, in whose studio he became acquainted with examples of the Italian Baroque style that dominated Portuguese painting. Gonçalves's own work, however, did not greatly influence that of Carvalho, who adhered to a Late Baroque Italian style, painting works with clear and luminous colours deriving from Rubens.

In 1755 Lisbon was devastated by a powerful earthquake, and shortly after Carvalho was commissioned to paint a series of altarpieces and ceilings for the new churches that were built. He became the most sought-after church decorator of his day, painting an extensive series of panels of religious subjects for such churches as the Mártires, S António da Sé and S Pedro de Alcántara. He won significant recognition, however, for the *Salvator mundi* (destr.), painted in 1778 for the Sé (Lisbon Cathedral). A study for it in the Museu Nacional de Arte Antiga, Lisbon, is a dynamic composition rendered with free and supple brushstrokes in a palette of gentle tonalities and shows little evidence of the academicism found in much of his work. His several *quadratura* ceilings for churches and other buildings in Lisbon and the surrounding area include the *trompe l'oeil* low relief of the *Annunciation*, in Nossa Senhora de Encarnação, and an *Allegory of Time* (*c.* 1792) in the chamber of the Conselho de Estado (Council of State) in Queluz Palace. His more purely decorative works include panels (1790) for a sedan chair designed for the occasion of the inauguration of the Basílica da Estrêla. He also executed several portraits, including a *Self-portrait* (1755; Lisbon, Acad. B.A.). Due to the wide diversity of genres in which he practised and to the great number of commissions that he could not resist accepting, Carvalho's paintings often have a certain academic rigidity and sometimes lack character. He was perhaps more talented as a draughtsman, especially in studies for figures, draperies and architectural details and in preliminary sketches of landscape, all of which are drawn with a free and supple line (e.g. the *Adoration of the Shepherds*, Lisbon, Mus. N. A. Ant.).

At the request of the Real Academia de la Historia de Madrid, he wrote *Relação dos pintores e escultores que florescerão no século de 1700, de que ha obras públicas* ('Account of the painters and sculptors who flourished in the 18th century, by whom there are public works'), a catalogue (lost) that was one of the basic sources for *Colecção de memórias relativas às vidas dos pintores, escultores, architectos e gravadores portuguezes* ('Collection of reminiscences concerning the lives of Portuguese painters, sculptors, architects and engravers'; Lisbon, 1823) by Cirilo Wolkmar Machado (1748–1823). In 1785 Carvalho was appointed Professor at the Academia de Desenho do Nu (Academy of Figure Drawing) in Lisbon and from 1788 was a member of the Irmandade de S Lucas (Confraternity of St Luke), an association of painters, sculptors and architects.

BIBLIOGRAPHY

Machado
J. da C. Taborda: *Regras da arte da pintura* [Principles of the art of painting] (Lisbon, 1815/*R* Coimbra, 1992) [includes bibliog.]
R. Santos: *Oito séculos de arte portuguesa*, i (Lisbon, 1964)
J.-A. França: *Lisboa pombalina e o Iluminismo* [Pombaline Lisbon and the Enlightenment] (Paris, 1965, Lisbon, 3/1987)
——: *A Arte em Portugal no século XIX* (Lisbon, 1967)
N. Correia Borges: *Do barroco ao rococó: História da arte em Portugal*, ix (Lisbon, 1986)

LUISA ARRUDA

Carvalho e Melo, Sebastião José de. *See* POMBAL, 1st Marquês de.

Carvalho Mange, Ernest Robert de. *See* MANGE, ERNEST.

Carvallo, Feliciano (*b* Naiguatá, Vargas, 11 Nov 1920). Venezuelan painter. He was self-taught as an artist. His naive painting first came to the public's attention in 1949, in a one-man show at the Taller Libre de Arte in Caracas. Carvallo's appearance on the art scene marked the beginning of the boom in naive painting in Venezuela. His main subject was the various Venezuelan folk festivals, which he depicted in fabulous jungles populated by numerous native animals. His detailed technique was based on the elaborate intertwining of different elements in the painting, achieving attractive decorative effects. He exhibited at an international level, and in 1966 he was awarded the Premio Nacional de Pintura and the Premio Armando Reverón at the Salón Oficial Anual de Arte Venezolano.

BIBLIOGRAPHY

Feliciano Carvallo (exh. cat. by G. Diehl, Paris, Gal. Villand & Galanis, 1966)

ELIDA SALAZAR

Caryatid. Sculpted female figure (equivalent to the male ATLANTID) used in place of a column. Caryatids first appeared in ancient Greek architecture around the mid-6th century BC; they were also used in Roman architecture, and these models were revived in the 18th and 19th centuries (*see* §2 below). Classical caryatids are always clothed; they may be dressed in the Ionic style and may have either a *polos* or a high-sided crown on their heads, or a wider drum representing a basket containing sacred objects. When dressed in Doric costume, however, caryatids bear the capital directly on their heads. Where hands survive, they may hold ceremonial religious vessels.

1. Caryatids, marble, in the Porch of the Maidens, Erechtheion, Athens, *c.* 421–405 BC (partly restored)

1. Greece and Rome. 2. Later history.

1. GREECE AND ROME. Although Vitruvius (*On Architecture* I.i.5) is incorrect in suggesting that caryatids were not used in Greece until after the Persian Wars (490–479 BC), their traditional association with Karyai in the Peloponnese and their alleged connection with the cult of Artemis Karyatis (Pausanias: *Description of Greece* III.x.6–7) seem convincing. Caryatid-like figures appear in the decoration of ceramic vessels in the 7th century BC, but the earliest surviving examples of true caryatids in an architectural context occur in the Ionic Knidian Treasury at Delphi (mid-6th century BC), where two caryatids *in antis*, wearing Ionic dress and standing on pedestals, replaced the usual columns. The closely related Siphnian Treasury (*c.* 525 BC), also at Delphi, again had two caryatids *in antis* as part of its elaborate sculptured decoration (*see* DELPHI, §2). The most influential caryatids in architectural history were, however, those in the south porch of the Erechtheion on the Athenian Acropolis (*see also* ATHENS, §II, 1(i) and (ii)). Instead of two maidens, *in antis* and on separate pedestals, the Erechtheion was given six standing prostyle on a high parapet (see fig. 1). These were copied at a Late Classical shrine on the acropolis at Limyra in Lycia, and coin evidence suggests that there were further copies in several sanctuaries in the Hellenized eastern Mediterranean. One of the largest pairs of Greek caryatids, now badly damaged, adorned the Lesser Propylaia at the Sanctuary of Demeter at Eleusis, given in fulfilment of vows by the Roman consul Appius Claudius Pulcher in the mid-1st century BC. Unlike earlier caryatid groups with matched mirror-image pairs, they appear to have differed in dress. The fragmentary upper half of one (Cambridge, Fitzwilliam) is 2.09 m high and carries a drum-shaped casket on its head.

Matched pairs of caryatids modelled on those at the Erechtheion were later used in a semi-religious context in the portico on three sides of the Forum of Augustus in Rome, which had the Temple of Mars Ultor (ded. 2 BC) dominating its north-east side. Since these caryatids adorned the upper storey, they stood far higher above ground than did their prototypes. By contrast, copies of the same caryatids were placed at ground level on the edge of the Canopus in the gardens of Hadrian's villa at Tivoli (*c.* AD 120–30). Further copies and adaptations of the Erechtheion caryatids have been discovered associated with villas and elaborate tombs in the vicinity of Rome. Other, non-architectural, caryatid figures occur as decorative elements in the minor arts of Greece, Etruria and Imperial Rome. The most notable are the stands supporting mirror-discs, usually dating from the 6th and 5th centuries BC.

BIBLIOGRAPHY

E. E. Schmidt: 'Die Kopien der Erechtheionkoren', *Ant. Plast.*, xiii (1973) [whole issue]

L. O. Keene Congdon: *Caryatid Mirrors of Ancient Greece* (Mainz, 1981)

G. LLOYD-MORGAN

2. LATER HISTORY. References to architectural caryatids did not reappear in the West until the Renaissance (the column statues of such medieval buildings as Chartres Cathedral being sculptural reliefs and not separate architectonic elements), although small, free-standing allegorical figures were used to support sarcophagi in Italy (e.g. Nicola Pisano's *Arca di S Domenico*, 1264–7, in the church of S Domenico, Bologna). In the 15th and 16th centuries, however, speculative illustrations derived from Vitruvius's single mention of caryatids (*On Architecture* I.i.v) appeared in many of the translations and treatises of Renaissance theorists, who showed considerable liberty in interpretation, mixing contemporary and antique forms in a variety of poses. Fra Giovanni Giocondo's edition of Vitruvius (*M. Vitruvius per jocundem*, Venice, 1511) was the first attempt to illustrate them; Francesco di Giorgio Martini, in his translation of Vitruvius, the *Magliabechiano* (Florence, Bib. N. Cent.), postulated that columns contained hidden human figures; Cesaro Cesariano, in his *Di Lucio Vitruvio Pollione de Architectura* (Como, 1521), interpreted the orders as simplified versions of human figures, with terms being a transitional stage; and Serlio ascribed human qualities to the orders in *Regole generali di architettura* (Venice, 1537), book iv of his treatise. These interpretations, however, did not carry much conviction in 16th- and 17th-century practice. Although caryatids occurred in small-scale ornamental designs and also in painting (e.g. Daniele da Volterra's decoration for the Orsini Chapel at Santa Trinità dei Monti, Rome; *c.* 1541–5), they are virtually unknown in an architectural context until the 18th century, with the exception of the four (1550–51) by JEAN GOUJON that support a gallery in the Salle de Bal in Pierre Lescot's new wing of the Louvre, Paris.

The caryatids at the Erechtheion were first accurately illustrated in *The Antiquities of Athens* (London, 1762–1816) by James Stuart and Nicholas Revett, and they began to feature in the work of the 18th- and 19th-century Neo-classicists. John Soane used a version with arms in an oval lantern that lit the staircase at Buckingham House (1793; destr.), London, and the caryatid became a favourite motif of his: in the Bank of England (1792–1833), London, caryatids appeared in the domes of the Consols Office (1797–9) and, more prominently, the Old Dividend Office (1818–23; destr. 1927; *see* SOANE, JOHN, fig. 1). HENRY INWOOD, who published an important study on *The Erechtheion in Athens* (London, 1827), used two literal reproductions of the Erechtheion's caryatid porch at St Pancras New Church (1819–22), London, but these were considered abhorrent by contemporary architects. Léon Vaudoyer used twin caryatids in the entrance gateway (1838) to the Conservatoire des Arts et Métiers, Paris, and Karl Friedrich Schinkel used four caryatids in the Roman bathhouse (1835; with Ludwig Persius) at Sanssouci, Potsdam, and a caryatid porch overlooking the Black Sea in his unexecuted design (1838) for the imperial pleasure palace of Orianda, near Yalta, in the Crimea. Caryatids also appeared in the 20th century, notably at Highpoint Two (1935–8), Highgate, London, a block of flats designed by the Modernist Berthold Lubetkin and Tecton: two caryatids copied from the Erechtheion figures in the British Museum were used to support the entrance canopy (see fig. 2), the architects claiming that they would be in place only temporarily pending the creation of their modern

2. Caryatids at Highpoint Two, Highgate, London, by Berthold Lubetkin and Tecton, 1935–8

equivalents. At the end of the 20th century they were still in position.

BIBLIOGRAPHY

'Highpoint 2: Footnote on Sculpture', *Archit. Rev.* [London], lxxxiv (1938), p. 176

A. Blunt: *Art and Architecture in France, 1500–1700*, Pelican Hist. A. (Harmondsworth, 1953/*R* 1988)

B. Davidson: 'Daniele da Volterra and the Orsini Chapel', *Burl. Mag.*, cix (1967), pp. 553ff

E. Schmidt: *Geschichte der Karyatide* (Würzburg, 1982)

G. Hersey: *The Lost Meaning of Classical Architecture: Speculation on Ornament from Vitruvius to Venturi* (London, 1988)

J. Onians: *Bearers of Meaning: The Classical Orders in Antiquity, the Middle Ages and the Renaissance* (Princeton, 1988)

□

Carysfort, 5th Earl of. *See* PROBY, WILLIAM.

Casa, Nicolò della [La Case, Nicolas de] (*fl* 1543–8). French engraver. All that is known besides the fact that he produced five engravings is that, as he himself indicated, he was from Lorraine and worked in Rome between 1543 and 1548, if not over a longer period. While there he Italianized his name, perhaps to recall the Florentine origins of his family. Della Casa may have gone to Rome at the same time as Nicolas Beatrizet, who was also from Lorraine. Like Beatrizet, he had some works published by Antonio Salamanca; again like Beatrizet, but some years before him, he engraved Michelangelo's *Last Judgement* in 11 plates (1543–5; see Robert-Dumesnil, 1) and engraved a portrait of *Henry II* (1547; RD 5). There is also considerable vigour in his portraits of the sculptor *Baccio Bandinelli* (RD 2), of Emperor *Charles V* (after Enea Vico; RD 3) and of *Cosimo de' Medici* (after Bandinelli; RD 4).

BIBLIOGRAPHY

A. P. F. Robert-Dumesnil: *Le Peintre-graveur français*, ix (Paris, 1865), pp. 180–83 [RD]

A. Linzeler and J. Adhémar: *Inventaire du fonds français: Graveurs du XVIe siècle*, Paris, Bib. N., Dépt Est. cat. (Paris, 1932–8), i, pp. 209–12; ii, p. 265

Abbé J. Choux: 'Nicolas de la Case, graveur lorrain du XVIe siècle', *Pays Lorrain*, lvi/4 (1975), pp. 175–80

MARIANNE GRIVEL

Casado del Alisal, José María (*b* Villada, Palencia, 24 March 1831; *d* Madrid, 9 Oct 1886). Spanish painter and illustrator. He began his studies at the Escuela Municipal de Dibujo in Palencia and continued in 1850 at the Escuela Especial de Pintura in Madrid. In 1855 he was awarded a fellowship by the Real Academia de Bellas Artes de San Fernando in Madrid for his *Resurrection of Lazarus* (Madrid, Real Acad. S Fernando, Mus.). He then spent several years in Rome, where he painted such works as *A Prisoner* (1856; Madrid, U. Complutense) and *Semiramis in Dante's Inferno* (1858; Madrid, U. Complutense and Pal. Real), which are notable for their skilful drawing and anatomical correctness. His history paintings of this period include the *Death of the Conde de Saldaña* (Palma de Mallorca, Mus. Mallorca), and his treatments of this genre led to numerous other successes, such as the *Last Moments of Ferdinand IV, 'El Emplazado'* (Madrid, Senate) exhibited at the Exposición Nacional de Bellas Artes in 1857. When his fellowship was renewed in 1860 he moved to Paris, where he executed *Taking the Oath in the Cortes of Cádiz of 1810* (Madrid, Pal. de las Cortes), for the Congreso de los Diputados in Madrid, a painting clearly reminiscent of David's work. The composition of his *Surrender of Bailén* (Madrid, Prado), another painting from his Parisian period, shows the marked influence of Velázquez. This and the splendid *Portrait of a French Lady* (Madrid, Prado) were both exhibited at the Exposición Nacional of 1864.

In Madrid, as *pintor honorario de cámara* to Isabella II, Casado del Alisal painted the elegant portrait of *Isabella II* (1865; Madrid, Pal. Real) in court dress, a work notable for its rich colours and is more successful in its composition than the slightly earlier *Queen Isabella II with her son Alfonso* (1864; U. Valladolid), which was a highly theatrical and allegorical work. Casado del Alisal now combined painting with teaching at the Escuela Superior de Pintura in Madrid, and other works of this period with contemporary historical subjects include the *Two Caudillos* (Madrid, Senate) and a portrait of *Amadeus I of Savoy* (Valencia, priv. col.). Around this time Casado del Alisal collaborated on the illustrations for the review *La ilustración de Madrid* and painted canvases on popular subjects as well as portraits of such contemporary political figures as *Baldomero Espartero, Duque de la Victoria y Príncipe de Vergara* and *Alejandro Mon* (both Madrid, Pal. de las Cortes).

After his appointment in 1873 as Director of the Academia Española de Bellas Artes in Rome, Casado del Alisal concentrated more on colour in his painting, using subject-matter similar to that of such painters as Mariano Fortuny y Marsal, Vicente Palmaroli González (1834–96) or Francisco Pradilla. This is seen in *La Tirana*, *Lady with a Fan* and *Woman with a White Mantilla* (all *c.* 1875–80; Madrid, Prado). In 1881 he completed the history painting, the *Legend of the Monk King*, better known as the *Bell of Huesca* (Huesca, Ayuntamiento), which is distinguished by its fine composition and sense of atmosphere. After resigning his position in Rome, Casado del Alisal returned to Madrid and taught at the Escuela de Artes y Oficios. In 1883 he was elected a member of the Real Academia de Bellas Artes de San Fernando. His late works include small paintings of Romantic subjects, many of which are untraced, and several highly realistic portraits with simple compositions such as those of *Práxedes Mateo Sagasta* (Madrid, Pal. de las Cortes) and *Alfonso XII* (Madrid, Pal. Real). Casado del Alisal also collaborated on the decoration of the basilica of S Francisco el Grande in Madrid, painting the *Apparition of St James at the Battle of Clavijo* (1885).

WRITINGS

Discurso leído ante la Real Academia de Bellas Artes de San Fernando (Madrid, 1885)

BIBLIOGRAPHY

F. J. Portela Sandoval: *Casado del Alisal, 1831–86* (Palencia, 1986)

FRANCISCO PORTELA SANDOVAL

Casala. *See under* K'ASAGH.

Casali, Andrea, Cavaliere (*b* Rome, 17 Nov 1705; *d* Rome, 7 Sept 1784). Italian painter and dealer, active in England. A pupil in turn of Sebastiano Conca and Francesco Trevisani, Casali received, in 1728, his first important commission, painting the cloister of S Sisto Vecchio, Rome, which was being restored for Benedict XIII. He was rewarded for this cycle of 32 lunettes depicting the *Life of St Dominic* by being made a Knight of the Golden Spur the following year. In 1729, he painted *S Filippo Neri* *in Ecstasy* for S Gregorio della Divina Provvidenza in Rome and two oval works of Franciscan saints—*Margherita da Cortona* and *Giacinta Marescotti*—facing one another in the church of S Antonio al Monte, Rieti. Casali's commissions in the early 1730s include the *Virgin in Glory* (1730) at Collevecchio, the *Martrydom of St Cristina* (1732) for the main altar of the collegiate church at Bolsena and his work for Cardinal Pietro Ottoboni's chapel of the Holy Sacrament at S Lorenzo in Damaso, Rome. This consists of an *Adoration of the Mystic Lamb* in fresco on the vault, since his altarpiece in oils of the *Holy Trinity* is now untraced.

In 1735 Trevisani recommended Casali, his favourite pupil, to the architect Filippo Juvarra, who was seeking a group of artists to decorate the palace of La Granja de San Ildefonso near Madrid. Casali's resultant *Tuccia* and *Death of Sophonisba* (both Madrid, Pal. Real) are his first public treatments of themes from ancient history, which hitherto he had restricted to easel paintings made for private collectors. Casali's *Annunciation* and *Adoration of the Magi* (both 1738; Turin, Accad. Albertina) are the last known works of his Roman period.

Following Ottoboni's death in 1740 Casali left Rome. Travelling via Paris, where in 1741 he was approved (*agréé*) by the Académie Royale de Peinture et de Sculpture, he reached England. He was drawn there by the promises of Grand Tourists for whom he had acted as cicerone in Rome, among them Sir Charles Frederick and Henry Howard, 4th Earl of Carlisle. At first he made small easel paintings and portraits. In 1743 he was commissioned by Lord Castlemaine to provide six large history paintings for Wanstead House, Essex (e.g. *Coriolanus*; now Burton Constable, Humberside). In 1747 Casali returned to an earlier type of subject, with his *Dead Christ* (sold London, Christie's, 1972), painted for the chapel of the Bavarian Embassy in London. The peace treaty of Aix la Chapelle in 1748, which marked the end of a four-year war between Britain and France, allowed Casali to travel to Prussia via Holland, where he worked for the court, but he returned to London almost immediately to collaborate on the celebratory Royal Fireworks, a display in Green Park supervised by Servandoni, the music for which was composed by George Frideric Handel.

During the 1750s Casali was much sought after; indeed, his status was such that even William Hogarth was happy to accept Casali's *Adoration of the Magi* (1748–50) as a gift to be hung in the chapel of the Foundling Hospital, London (*in situ*). The continuing vogue for Italianate decoration favoured such artists as Casali. He carried out commissions throughout England, including Asgill House, Richmond, London, and Hovingham Hall, N. Yorks, for the staircase dome of which he made a copy (*c*. 1760) of Guido Reni's widely admired *Aurora*, in the Casino dell'Aurora of the Palazzo Rospigliosi, Rome. At Holkham Hall, Norfolk, he painted a gallery of portraits illustrating the line of descent of its owner Thomas Coke, 1st Earl of Leicester. Casali's greatest patron, however, was William Beckford the elder (1709–70) who, after a fire in 1755 at Fonthill, his country house in Wiltshire, replaced it with a Palladian house (*c*. 1757–*c*. 1770; destr.), and filled it with pictures. Casali's works were dispersed in 1801 by the younger William Beckford; examples are at Bath (U. Bath, Holburne of Menstrie Mus.), Dyrham Park, Avon, NT (e.g. *Allegories of the Arts*), and Burton Constable, Humberside (e.g. *Edward and Elfrida*). Casali's religious works for the chapel in London of the Sardinian embassy (1762) and for St Margaret, Westminster, London (1763; *SS Peter and Paul*) are untraced. These were produced during the same period that Casali painted a series of feigned low reliefs for interiors at Syon House, London, under the direction of Robert Adam; they reveal a radical change in Casali's style as a consequence of his contact with Adam. The close of these fruitful years in England was marked by two sales in London in 1766 of Casali's own works and of some of the paintings that he bought and sold as a dealer.

Casali continued to paint after his return to Rome in 1766, and he regularly sent pictures to exhibitions in London. He also completed 16 religious compositions in the 1770s for Santa Trinità dei Spagnoli, Rome. Despite his successes, however, Casali was never admitted to the Accademia di S Luca.

BIBLIOGRAPHY

DBI

E. Croft-Murray: *Decorative Painting in England*, ii (London, 1970), p. 181

J. Urrea Fernandez: *La pintura italiana del siglo XVIII en España* (Valladolid, 1977), p. 253

J. Christian, ed.: 'A. Casali: Portrait of *Sir Charles Frederick*, 1738', *National Art Collection Fund: Annual Report* (Oxford, 1980), pp. 88–9, no. 2871

OLIVIER MICHEL

Casanova. Italian family of artists. The travelling Venetian actors Gaetano Giuseppe Casanova (*d* 1733) and Giovanna Zanetta Farussi produced six sons, the second of whom was the adventurer Giovanni Giacomo Casanova (*b* Venice, 2 April 1725; *d* Château Dux, Bohemia, 4 June 1798), notorious for his amorous pursuits. He is best-known for his *Mémoires*, which include generally reliable information about the lives and careers of two of his brothers: (1) Francesco Casanova, known for his battle and equestrian pictures, and (2) Giovanni Battista Casanova, a Neo-classical draughtsman, painter, forger and writer.

WRITINGS

There have been numerous editions of the *Mémoires* of Giovanni Giacomo Casanova. The two given here represent the earliest, as well as an acclaimed modern edition.

W. von Schütz, ed.: *Aus den Memoiren*, 13 vols (Leipzig, 1822–8)

F. A. Brockhaus, ed.: *Histoire de ma vie*, 6 vols (Wiesbaden and Paris, 1960–62)

BIBLIOGRAPHY

DBI; Thieme–Becker

C. van Heyden de Lancey: 'Les Portraits de Jacques et de François Casanova', *Gaz. B.-A.*, xi (1934), pp. 99–107

C. Donzelli: *I pittori veneti del settecento* (Florence, 1957), pp. 57–9

(1) Francesco Casanova (*b* London, *bapt* 7 June 1727; *d* Brühl, nr Vienna, 8 July 1803). Painter. Born in London, where his parents were touring, he spent his youth in Venice. The influence of Venetian art was an important feature of his work. In the *Mémoires* of his brother Giovanni Giacomo Casanova, it is said that in Venice he studied drawing with Giovanni Antonio Guardi during a 10-year period ending around 1749. The *Fortune-teller* (*c*. 1749; Rome, priv. col., see Kuhn, fig. 1) may be among Francesco's earliest surviving works. In Venice he made copies after the work of the history and battle painter Francesco Simonini whose pupil in Florence he probably was from *c.* 1749 to 1751. In that year he moved to Paris but in 1752 left for Dresden, where he came in contact with the work of Charles Parrocel and Philips Wouwerman.

In 1757 Casanova returned to Paris where, according to the *Mémoires*, he exhibited a picture at the Louvre, and rapidly became a much sought-after court painter of battle, hunting and equestrian scenes. Around 1760 he executed *Surprise Attack on a Wagon* (Moscow, Pushkin Mus. F.A.) and the *Camp* (Schleissheim, Neues Schloss). Between 1761 and 1771 he exhibited at the Salon to much critical acclaim. On his marriage certificate of 1762 he was designated 'Peintre du Roi', a position he retained until 1783. He became a member of the Académie Royale de Peinture et de Sculpture in 1763, and paintings from this period include *Landscape with Shepherds* (*c.* 1770; Béziers, Mus. B.-A.) and two pictures executed for Louis-Joseph, Prince de Condé (1736–1818), shown at the Salon of 1771—*Battle of Lens* and *Battle of Fribourg* (both *c.* 1771; Paris, Louvre). By about 1772 he had begun designing tapestry cartoons for the royal factories in Beauvais and Aubusson, including the fragment representing a *Kneeling Man* (*c.* 1772; Paris, Louvre) and the study of a *Fishing Scene* (early 1770s; St Petersburg, Hermitage). Between 1779 and 1783 he continued to exhibit at the Salon and executed, for example, *Landscape with Rider* (1780; Moscow, Pushkin Mus. F.A.).

In 1783 Casanova settled in Vienna. His paintings from this period include the *Equestrian Portrait* (*c.* 1783; Klosterneuburg, Mus. Chorherrenstiftes) and *Cavalry Battle* (1792; Vienna, Ksthist. Mus.). During the early 1790s he was probably commissioned by Catherine II of Russia to paint a cycle of pictures representing the *Russian Victory over the Turks*, with which some preparatory studies (Vienna, Albertina) may be associated. In 1795 he travelled with Prince Nicolas Esterházy to Hungary, where he is said to have executed numerous equestrian sketches, and in 1797 he completed paintings for Ferdinand IV, the Bourbon King of Naples (1759–1825), including *Fox Hunting* (Naples, Capodimonte). His most significant pupil was Philippe Jacques de Loutherbourg, who studied with him in Paris.

BIBLIOGRAPHY

DBI; Thieme–Becker

H. Leporini: 'Francesco Casanova', *Pantheon*, xxii (1964), pp. 173–83

E. Martini: *La pittura del settecento veneto* (Udine, 1982), pp. 75, 530–31

B. Kuhn: 'Der Landschafts- und Schlachtenmaler Francesco Casanova (1727–1803)', *Wien. Jb. Kstgesch.*, xxxvii (1984), pp. 89–118, 223–36

(2) Giovanni Battista Casanova (*b* Venice, 2 Nov 1728 or 4 Nov 1730; *d* Dresden, 7 Dec 1795). Draughtsman, painter, forger and writer, brother of (1) Francesco Casanova. He was brought up in Dresden, where he studied with Louis de Silvestre and Christian Wilhelm Ernst Dietrich. According to the *Mémoires*, he returned to Venice in 1746, and between about 1749 and 1752 is said to have studied with Giovanni Battista Piazzetta. He moved in 1752 to Rome, where he studied, worked and resided with Anton Raphael Mengs. In Rome he also studied from nature and from the works of Old Masters, especially Raphael, but was to become best known for his masterful drawings after the Antique. In 1754 he was elected to the Society of Arcadia. After 1755 he became closely associated with Johann Joachim Winckelmann, whom he is said to have taught drawing in Rome. Among his few surviving paintings the best known is a gesso copy (*c.* 1762; London, V&A) of Raphael's *Transfiguration* (1518–20; Rome, Pin. Vaticana), although he also executed portraits and pictures with allegorical themes. Many of his drawings after the Antique were engraved as illustrations for Winckelmann's publications, but in the early 1760s, when his relationship with the archaeologist was becoming strained, he conspired with Mengs to deceive Winckelmann with three forged antique wall paintings. The most famous and probably the only one fully realized as a painting is the *Jupiter and Ganymede* (1760; Rome, Pal. Corsini) by Mengs. There were also two drawings (untraced) of fictitious wall paintings representing the *Dancing Maenads* and the *Education of Erechtheus*, both of which Winckelmann unwittingly used to illustrate the first edition of *Geschichte der Kunst des Alterthums* (1764, pp. 262–3; see also Pelzel, figs 3–4).

In 1764 Casanova made a portrait drawing of *Winckelmann* (Leipzig, Mus. Bild. Kst.). In the same year he took up a professorship at the Akademie in Dresden. In 1765 many of his finest drawings were published as illustrations to the *Antichità di Ercolano* (*see* HERCULANEUM, §VI), commissioned by Charles III, the Bourbon King of Naples, and continued by his son Ferdinand IV. At this time Winckelmann, discovering the forgeries, initiated a scurrilous attack on Casanova in a series of letters, to which Casanova replied in kind (see *Briefe*). In 1766 a portrait of *Winckelmann* in profile (untraced; see Schulz, fig. 11) drawn by Casanova and engraved by Bartolomeo Follin was published as the frontispiece to a periodical, which included a critical essay by Casanova on topics such as Mengs's *Ascension of Christ* (1752; Dresden, Katholische Hofkirche). The following year numerous drawings prepared earlier were published in Winckelmann's *Monumenti antichi inediti*. In 1770 he published a critical essay on the nature of the Antique (*Discorso*), and in 1776 he became a director of the Dresden Akademie. He bequeathed his substantial library and collection of small works of art to his brother Francesco, although they were later sold at auction in 1797. Many of his drawings are in the Albertina, Vienna.

WRITINGS

'Mengs Altarblatt, die Himmelfahrt Christi vorstellend', *Neue Bibliothek der schönen Wissenschaften und der freien Künste*, iii (1766), pp. 132–44

Discorso sopra gl'antichi, e vari monumenti loro, per uso degl'alunni dell'elettoral' Accademia delle bell'Arti di Dresda (Leipzig, 1770)

PRINTS

Le antichità di Ercolano esposti, Accademia Ercolanese, 8 vols (Naples, 1757–92), iv (1765); viii (1792) [illustrations throughout]

J. J. Winckelmann: *Geschichte der Kunst des Alterthums* (Dresden, 1764), pp. 262–78; illus. pp. 262–3

——: *Monumenti antichi inediti*, 2 vols (Rome, 1767) [illustrations throughout]

Indice descritto de' monumenti incisi restati inediti nella Stamperia Reale appartenenti alle antichità di Ercolano e di Pompei (Naples, 1844) [includes 12 plates engraved from Casanova's drawings]

BIBLIOGRAPHY

DBI; *NDB*; Thieme–Becker

H. Keller: *Nachrichten von allen in Dresden lebenden Künstlers* (Leipzig, 1788), pp. 25–31

Catalogue d'une collection d'estampes délaissé par feu Jean Casanova, Professeur et Directeur de l'Académie Electorale de Dresde (Dresden, 1797)
E. Lavagnino: *Gli artisti italiani in Germania*, iii of *I pittori e gl'incisori* (Rome, 1943), pp. 140–44, 163
J. J. Winckelmann: *Briefe*, ed. H. Diepolder and W. Rehm (Berlin, 1952–7), iii, pp. 22–3, 151–2; iv, pp. 388–90
A. Schulz: *Die Bildnisse J. J. Winckelmanns* (Berlin, 1953), p. 55
T. Pelzel: 'Winckelmann, Mengs and Casanova: A Reappraisal of a Famous Eighteenth-century Forgery', *A. Bull.*, liv (1972), pp. 300–15
S. Roettgen: 'Storia di un falso: Il Ganimede di Mengs', *A. Illus.*, vi (1973), pp. 256–70

JUDITH L. CARMEL

Casanova, Antonio Maria. *See under* ANTONIO MARIA DA VILLAFORA.

Casas (i Carbó), Ramon (*b* Barcelona, 5 Jan 1866; *d* Barcelona, 29 Feb 1932). Catalan painter. Born into a wealthy family, he was a pupil of Joan Vicens (1830–86) and published his first drawing in the magazine *L'Avenç* of Barcelona in 1881, the same year in which he went to Paris. There he studied under Carolus-Duran and exhibited his chiaroscuro *Self-portrait as Andalusian* (Barcelona, Mus. A. Mod.) at the Salon des Champs-Elysées (1883). At the Académie Gervex he knew another Catalan painter Laureà Barrau (1863–1957), and they went together to Granada in 1884. In this year his painting *Bullfight* (Montserrat, Mus. Montserrat), already sketchy and luminous, was considered too avant-garde by the critics when it was exhibited at the Sala Parés of Barcelona. Casas's main period of work began in 1890, when he returned to Paris with his close friend the painter and writer Santiago Rusiñol. They lived with Miquel Utrillo (1862–1934) at the Moulin de la Galette in Montmartre. His painting now focused on views of suburban Paris and interiors with figures; it used grey tones, seeking poetry in vulgar or everyday themes. Works such as *Plein air* (*c.* 1890; Barcelona, Mus. A. Mod.) and *Interior of the Moulin de la Galette* (*c.* 1890; Sitges, Mus. Cau Ferrat; see fig.) show Degas's influence in their compositions, and Whistler's in their sense of colour. At that time he began to exhibit his works at the Salon du Champ de Mars, also showing twice at the Salon des Indépendants. When he exhibited the Parisian paintings in Barcelona (Sala Parés, 1890 and 1891; Exposició General de Belles Arts, 1891), the critics began to talk about his 'modernism'; the term soon became associated with the new generation of Catalan artists that used to meet at Els Quatre Gats café in Barcelona (1897–1903), established by Casas.

In Barcelona again, after the years spent in Paris, Casas's paintings were almost journalistic in their subject-matter, for example *Garrote vil* ('Evil garrotte', 1894; Madrid, Casón Buen Retiro) and *Procession of Corpus at Santa Maria del Mar* (1898; Barcelona, Mus. A. Mod.), and his female figures became the prototype of the Catalan women of his time. A large group of charcoal drawings published in his magazines *Quatre gats* (1899) and *Pel & ploma* (1899–1903), many of them portraits of intellectuals and artists, made him very famous (229 in Barcelona, Mus. A. Mod.). He was also celebrated for his commercial posters (e.g. *Anis del Mono* and *Champagne Codorniu*, both 1898; see 1982 *Ramon Casas* exh. cat., pp. 122, 133). In 1899 he became a member of the International Society of Painters. The synthesis of his art is characterized by the series of 12

Ramon Casas: *Interior of the Moulin de la Galette*, oil on canvas, 1.00×0.82 m, *c.* 1890 (Sitges, Museu del Cau Ferrat)

large paintings (1902) for the private club Cercle del Liceu in Barcelona (see Bassegoda Nonell), but in the early 1900s his art became more academic (e.g. *The Charge*, 1899–1903; Olot, Mus. A. Mod.), and in 1908 and 1924 he visited the USA due to his friendship with the collector Charles Deering. For his earlier work he continued to be regarded as the best painter of Catalan modernism, admired and envied by the young Pablo Picasso, despite Casas having been one of his first protectors.

BIBLIOGRAPHY

J. F. Ràfols: *Ramon Casas, dibujante* (Barcelona, n.d.)
——: *Ramon Casas, pintor* (Barcelona, n.d.)
J. M. Jordà: *Ramon Casas, pintor* (Barcelona, 1932)
Ramon Casas y su época (exh. cat. by A. del Castillo, Barcelona, Junta Museus, 1958)
J. Bassegoda Nonell: *El círculo del Liceo: 125 aniversario, 1847–1972* (Barcelona, 1973)
F. Fontbona: *Casas* (Barcelona, 1979)
Ramon Casas (exh. cat., ed. C. Mendoza; Barcelona, Pal. Virreira, 1982)
Ramon Casas: Retrats al carbó (exh. cat., ed. C. Mendoza; Barcelona, Pal. Virreira, 1982)
F. Fontbona and others: *El cercle del Liceu* (Barcelona, 1991)

FRANCESC FONTBONA DE VALLESCAR

Casas Grandes. Pre-Columbian site, also the name given to an archaeological culture and region of northern Chihuahua, Mexico. Between *c.* 1060 and *c.* 1340 the site of Casas Grandes was an administrative centre and emporium, known as Paquimé, for a vast region of some 87,000 sq. km of northern Mexico. Paquimé may have been established by merchant groups from Mesoamerica to the south. The evidence of trade throughout the region, and of the influence of Mesoamerican religious cults, demonstrates extensive contact with the cities of Pre-Columbian Mesoamerica (*see* MESOAMERICA, PRE-COLUMBIAN, §I, 4) and with the communities of the Southwest USA (*see* NATIVE NORTH AMERICAN ART, §§I, 2(i) and V, 1(i)). Trade items included marine shells, turquoise and other minerals, exotic birds, and finished decorative pieces made of shell, pottery and stone.

Throughout the region the inhabitants built integrated systems of check dams, terraces, ditches and reservoirs to collect run-off water in order to increase agricultural productivity. Between *c.* 1060 and *c.* 1205 (termed the Medio phase) Paquimé consisted of 20 individual house clusters around plazas. These were single-storey adobe structures, all served by a single water distribution system. Internal arrangements included cast mud load-bearing walls, T-shaped doorways, square-columned frontages, stairways and raised hearths. In one housing complex there were rows of rectangular macaw breeding boxes, in which archaeologists found nesting materials, eggshell fragments and macaw skeletons.

In the Paquimé phase (*c.* 1205–60) the city was rebuilt and extended to cover an area of *c.* 36.5 ha. It comprised a core area of multi-storey apartment-like blocks of dwellings—with walls of 'marly concrete, mixed with pebbles and small stones' (Di Peso, Rinaldo and Fenner, v, p. 440), wooden roof beams, stairways, and internal water supplies and drainage channels—and surrounding public and ceremonial areas. About 1600 rooms housed a population of over 2200. More than half the rooms had raised sleeping platforms *c.* 1 m off the floor. The ceremonial and public areas included a stone-faced platform, earthen platform mounds and truncated pyramids around public plazas, and several earthen-sided I-shaped ball courts. Beneath the playing field of one ball court there were burials of apparently ritually dismembered individuals. There was a market area, a subterranean walk-in well, a reservoir and stone slab-covered drains. Throughout the region there was also a system of trails, wayhouses, signal stations and forts.

In the Diablo phase (*c.* 1261–*c.* 1340) the population increased still further. Civil construction and the maintenance of public buildings ceased, and the population began to encroach on the public plazas by building crude dwellings within them and by subdividing the existing apartment complexes.

Throughout all three phases there was abundant evidence of craft specialization. Pottery production included bowls, jars and other shapes painted with black and red on white or buff, and having incised decoration. Several of the pottery storage jars found had capacities of nearly 70 litres. Shell objects included engraved *Strombus* shells and other marine molluscs, *Strombus* trumpets and turquoise-inlaid shells. The lost-wax casting technique was used to make ceremonial copper axes and elaborate copper bells. Sheet copper was hammered and rolled into armlets, disc beads, rings and pendants. Collections are held at the Museo Regional, Chihuahua, and in the Museo Nacional de Antropología, Mexico City.

BIBLIOGRAPHY

M. P. Weaver: *The Aztecs, Maya and their Predecessors: Archaeology of Mesoamerica* (New York, 1972, rev. 3/1993)
C. C. Di Peso: *Casas Grandes: A Fallen Trading Center of the Gran Chichimeca*, i–iii (Dragoon, AZ, 1974)
C. C. Di Peso, J. B. Rinaldo and G. Fenner: *Casas Grandes: A Fallen Trading Center of the Gran Chichimeca*, iv–xiii (Dragoon and Flagstaff, 1974)
W. D. Lipe: 'The Southwest', *Ancient Native Americans*, ed. J. D. Jennings (San Francisco, 1978), pp. 327–401
L. S. Cordell: *Prehistory of the Southwest* (New York, 1984)

DAVID M. JONES

Casasola, Agustín Víctor (*b* Mexico City, 1874; *d* Mexico City, 1938). Mexican photographer and collector. He worked as a reporter for the Catholic newspaper *El tiempo* during the 1890s, becoming a staff photographer by 1900. He not only recorded the official functions and daily life in Mexico City under President Porfirio Díaz but also began to take an interest in social conditions, despite strict government censorship preventing publication of anything other than the most anodyne of images. He also began to collect the work of other photographers, which with his own work provide an invaluable record of Mexican life before, during and after the Revolution (1910–17). Few of the photographs in the Casasola archive are credited, making it almost impossible to attribute images to him. The subjects included political demonstrations, insurrections, the poor, factories, executions (see 1985 exh. cat., pp. 24–5) and music-hall performers (see 1985 exh. cat., pp. 78–9). Casasola did not, however, comment on events or display the passion for social improvement found in the work of Jacob A. Riis and Lewis W. Hine.

After working on a freelance basis as a photographer for *El imparcial* and *El mundo ilustrado* during the first decade of the 20th century, Casasola established the Society of Press Photographers (1911). While Díaz's dictatorship was beginning to crumble, the Society documented Francisco Madero's 'No Re-election' presidential campaigns throughout the country, resulting in many striking photographs of the bloody uprising in the north led by Pascual Orozco and Francisco (Pancho) Villa (see 1985 exh. cat., pp. 32–3). At the end of 1911 Casasola organized an exhibition of this material in Mexico City, to which the newly elected President Madero was invited. In 1914 Casasola founded the Photographers' Information Agency, which both commissioned and bought news photographs from other photographers.

Following the Revolution, Casasola received many official commissions from the Obregón and Calles governments. In 1921 his son, Gustavo Casasola, became the archivist of the family firm and published the *Album histórico gráfico*, which set out to provide a visual record of the Mexican Revolution; the album was expanded and published as the *Historia gráfica de la Revolución Mexicana* and in more comprehensive form as *Seis siglos de historia gráfica de México*. Few of the photographs in the archive document the battles of the Revolution but rather are records of leading personalities and of the context of the struggles. During the 1920s and 1930s they were valuable reference material for the Mexican muralist painters. In the early 1970s the archive was purchased by the Mexican government and went into the custodianship of the National Institute of Anthropology and History (INAH), being housed at the Fototeca of the Ex-Convento de San Francisco, Pachuca, Hidalgo in Mexico.

PHOTOGRAPHIC PUBLICATIONS

G. Casasola, ed.: *Historia gráfica de la Revolución Mexicana, 1900–1960*, 10 vols (Mexico City, 1964)

——: *Seis siglos de historia gráfica de México, 1925–1970*, 7 vols (Mexico City, 1976)

BIBLIOGRAPHY

The World of Agustín Víctor Casasola, 1900–1938 (exh. cat., ed. M. Zuver; Washington, DC, Fondo del Sol Visual A. Media, 1984)

Tierra y libertad: Photographs of Mexico, 1900–1935, from the Casasola Archive (exh. cat., ed. D. Elliott; Oxford, MOMA, 1985)

DAVID ELLIOTT

Casas y Nóvoa, Fernando (*b* Santiago de Compostela, *bapt* 16 Aug 1691; *d* Santiago de Compostela, 1749). Spanish architect. A pupil and follower of Domingo de Andrade (*c*. 1639–1712), he became a leading architect of the mid-18th century in Galicia. His first significant work is the cloister (1711–14) of Lugo Cathedral, in which he incorporated classical round-headed arches, separated by paired pilasters in the manner of Andrade, within an existing medieval form. Later works were more Baroque in style: the church of Las Capuchinas (1715), La Coruña; the altar of the chapel of Pilar (1718), Santiago de Compostela Cathedral, which resembles the retables that Casas y Nóvoa had seen in his travels in Portugal; the convent of S Domingo (1725), Santiago de Compostela; the circular chapel of Nuestra Señora de los Ojos Grandes (1726), Lugo Cathedral; the church of the Benedictine monastery (1735), Lugo; and the important *Churrigueresque* principal altar and cloister at S Martín Pinario, Santiago de Compostela. The principal altar (1730–33), carved by Miguel de Romay, is in the form of a baldacchino and is open to both the nave and the choir. The main cloister (1741) is attributed to him and has a free-standing coupled giant order reminiscent of Michelangelo. Casas y Nóvoa's greatest works were part of the renovations (1738–50) of Santiago de Compostela Cathedral. The key project was the construction of the Fachada del Obradoiro, the Baroque west façade of the cathedral, which was added to the Romanesque building (*see* SANTIAGO DE COMPOSTELA, fig. 1). It protects the Pórtico de la Gloria (by Maestro Mateo, 1188) and contains the Espejo, a two-storey glass panel which admits light to the nave. The north tower duplicated Andrade's Campanas Tower (1667–70) on the south side. The Obradoiro, with its uniform ornament and use of Classical orders within a Romanesque composition, has been regarded as a forerunner of 19th-century eclecticism (Kubler, 1959).

BIBLIOGRAPHY

M. Chamoso Lamas: *La arquitectura barroca en Galicia*, Artes y Artistas (Madrid, 1955)

G. Kubler: *Arquitectura de los siglos XVII y XVIII*, A. Hisp., xiv (Madrid, 1957)

G. Kubler and M. Soria: *Art and Architecture in Spain and Portugal and their American Dominions, 1500–1800*, Pelican Hist. A. (Harmondsworth, 1959)

M. T. Rios Miramontes: 'Estudio arquitectonico de la capilla del Pilar de la catedral de Santiago de Compostela', *Archv Esp. A.*, lxi (1988), pp. 337–54

□

Casaubon. *See* KERSEBOOM.

Cascalls, Jaume [Castayls, Jaime] (*b* ?Berga; *fl* 1345–79). Catalan sculptor, painter and architect. A citizen of Barcelona, he must have been trained among Italians, but in a school that was acquainted with developments in France and receptive to Sienese influences—possibly Pisa or Naples. Mallorcan painting—especially manuscript illumination, which was influenced by Pisan art—and the work of the Master of the San Michele in Borgo Pulpit (a Pisan sculptor who worked on the shrine of S Eulalia, 1327–39, in Barcelona Cathedral) also constituted important formative influences on his style. He married the daughter of Ferrer Bassa and was associated with the Bassa workshop in a commission for works for Saragossa in 1346. Like Ferrer Bassa, he was responsible for introducing Italianizing elements into Catalonia.

No authenticated paintings by Jaume Cascalls survive, however, and he is now known primarily for his sculpture, notably for the signed alabaster retable of the *Virgin* (*c*. 1345; 2.07×3.35 m) in S María, Cornellà del Conflent, which shows Italian characteristics in the treatment of continuous narrative and in the technique, in which some areas are deliberately left unfinished for expressive effect. At about this time, Jaume worked in Perpignan for the Aragonese crown. By 1349 and possibly as early as 1347, when he is mentioned as an associate of Master Aloi, he was working on the royal tombs at the Cistercian abbey of Poblet (Tarragona). He was appointed Master of the Works at the Seu Vella, Lleida (Sp. Lérida), in 1361 and carried out work on the cloister, the Puerta de los Apóstoles and the bell-tower. His final works, sometimes workshop productions, were at Tarragona Cathedral (1375; sculptural remodelling and completion of the façade) and Poblet (1377; oratories). Among the works that may be attributed to him are the polychrome alabaster figure of *'Charlemagne'* (Girona, Mus. Catedralici), the *Holy Sepulchre* of S Feliú, Girona, of which the principal figure of *Christ* remains in the church (other fragments in Girona, Mus. Arqueol.), and the figure of a king (Barcelona, Mus. A. Catalunya).

BIBLIOGRAPHY

A. Duran i Sanpere: *Els retaules de pedra*, i (Barcelona, 1932)

C. Pérez Gimeno: 'En torno a Jaume Cascalls: Su obra en Gerona', *D'Art* [Barcelona], v (1979), pp. 65–77

R. Alcoy: *La introducción y derivaciones del italianismo trescentista en la pintura gótica catalana: 1325–1350* (diss., U. Barcelona, 1988)

——: 'Jaume Cascalls: Un nombre para el Maestro del triptico de Baltimore', *J. Walters A. Gal.* (in preparation)

R. Alcoy and P. Beseran: 'Cascalls i les escoles de la Italia Meridional a Catalunya: L'escultura del Tresents' (in preparation)

ROSA ALCOY

Cascella, Pietro (*b* Pescara, 2 Feb 1921). Italian sculptor, painter, ceramicist, mosaicist and designer. He learnt the first rudiments of his art in the workshop of his father Tommaso, experimenting with painting, sculpture and applied arts. At the end of the 1930s, he moved to Rome, where he studied at the Accademia di Belle Arti. He was initially a painter and after World War II collaborated with architects on various decorative projects, including the base of the Palazzo delle Esposizioni in Genoa and the ceiling of the Salone delle Riunioni in the Ministry of Foreign Affairs in Rome (1955–6). At the same time he was active as a ceramicist and mosaicist, and between 1949 and 1956 he produced large polychrome compositions that were influenced by Picasso (e.g. a mosaic made in collaboration with his first wife, Maria Cesarini Sforza, *c.* 1949; Rome, Stazione Termini). In 1950 he exhibited for the first time at L'Obelisco in Rome, with his brother the sculptor Andrea Cascella (*b* 1920), his frequent collaborator. This was followed by one-man shows at the Galleria del Naviglio in Milan in 1954 and at the Venice Biennale of 1966.

Cascella started to concentrate on sculpture at the end of the 1950s, combining the influence of Constantin Brancusi with that of primitive art. His sculpture became progressively more monumental, as in the famous monument to the *Martyrs of the Polish People and of other Peoples* (1958–67) in Auschwitz in Poland. In this work Cascella collaborated with his brother Andrea, the Spanish architect Julio Lafrente, the Italian architect Giorgio Simoncini, and the Polish sculptor Jerzy Jamuszkiewicz. The monument, which consists of cyclopean masonry, established 'the wall' as a major iconographic theme in Cascella's work. He was also active as a designer of objects, for example lamps, and open-air works such as fountains and memorial tablets, for example the monument in memory of *Judge Alessandrini* (1979) in the Palazzo di Giustizia in Pescara.

BIBLIOGRAPHY

Gruppo Valle d'Inferno (exh. cat., Rome, Obelisco, 1949–50)
G. Vergami: *Pietro Cascella* (Milan, 1974)
La scultura di Pietro Cascella: I segni della memoria dell'uomo (exh. cat., intro. E. Crispolti, ed. M. Crescentin; Siena, Pal. Pub., 1984)

SILVIA LUCCHESI

Čaše, Ivan. *See* ZASCHE, IVAN.

Casé, Paulo Hamilton (*b* Rio de Janeiro, 1931). Brazilian architect. He graduated in 1957 from the Faculty of Architecture at the National University of Brazil and in 1958 he went into partnership in Rio de Janeiro with Luiz Acioli (*b* 1933). In 1964 he began to teach architecture at the Federal University of Rio de Janeiro. He belonged to a new generation of Brazilian architects whose intention was to go beyond the formalism and functionalism of international styles and to promote, through their teaching, an authentically Brazilian character in architecture. In his design for the Hotel Porto do Sino (1966), his planning and use of local materials and building techniques countered both the aesthetic ideas of Le Corbusier, which dominated the Rio de Janeiro school, and the Brutalism seen in the obsessive use of reinforced concrete that dominated architecture in São Paulo. Other hotel designs were also characterized by a wealth of space and use of local materials and building techniques, as in the Porto do Sol hotel (1973–6) at Guarapari, a horizontal building formed by groups of white-walled blocks with balconies and mud-tiled roofs, stretching out rhythmically along a rocky point overlooking the sea. His most characteristically Brazilian works were private houses, such as the Manga Larga house (1968) at Itaipava and the João Dalmacio house (1978) at Vitória. In his commercial work, a great inventiveness of form and use of reinforced concrete was allied to complex planning: examples include the Banco Mercantil do Brasil (1969) and the Bank of Tokyo (1972) in São Paulo, and the Fininvest headquarters (1983) in Rio de Janeiro in which a 12-storey lightwell organizes the internal space, protecting it from noise and sun. Several of his buildings won prizes from the Institute of Architects of Rio de Janeiro.

BIBLIOGRAPHY

'Brazilian Hotels with International Standards', *Constr. São Paulo*, 1391 (1974), pp. 13–15
'Projects for Hotels in Brazil', *Arquit. Brasil*, 10 (1977–8), pp. 39–48
'Fininvest, Rio de Janeiro', *Projeto*, 63 (1984), pp. 39–42

PAULO J. V. BRUNA

Casein. Complex protein found in milk that may be used as a glue (*see* ADHESIVES, §§1(i) and 2) or as a binding medium for paint (*see* PAINT, §1). It exists in different forms, isolated from the milk and activated for use by various methods. There are significant differences in the properties of the casein obtained by each method of preparation. Casein was originally produced by reacting curd or skim milk directly with an alkali, originally lime and later ammonia. Monoamvonium caseinate is easier to employ and is generally of good quality, but a purer type of casein in powder form is now more widely used, and the convenient tube colours are most generally employed.

Lime casein, being practically insoluble in water and possessing great adhesive strength, has been important as a glue. Casein is likely to have been employed for bonding wood in ancient Egypt, Greece and Rome and perhaps also on the Indian subcontinent and in China. Firm evidence of its use in Europe is found from the Middle Ages; descriptions of its preparation from cheese, probably a reference to some form of purified curd, appear in several manuscripts, including Theophilus's *De diversis artibus* (12th century). Cennino Cennini described casein in *Il libro dell'arte* (*c.* 1390) specifically as a woodworker's glue and mentioned its use for joining pieces of wood to make up large panels for painting (*see* PANEL PAINTING, §2).

Although the use of casein in fine art painting has been limited, it may have been quite extensively employed for durable decorative coatings. References to the use of curd in decorative painting appear in ancient Hebrew texts. Casein has been identified in 18th-century vernacular ceiling paintings in Bavaria and the Tyrol and is sometimes associated with wall painting (*see* WALL PAINTING, §I and CONSOLIDANT). Its application as a medium for fine art painting from at least the 19th century stems from its industrial and commercial use at that time. The confused rediscovery of materials for tempera painting during the 19th century also enhanced its status as a painting medium. In North America the availability of a commercially manufactured brand of casein colour in tubes has ensured its use for painting during the 20th century. Despite its unique matt or semi-matt appearance, no specific style or method of painting has been associated with the medium, and it tends to be employed as an alternative form of tempera; it has also been used in mixed-media work.

When applied as a paint, casein presents difficulties: its adhesive strength and brittleness may provoke defects, and the paint film is susceptible to mould (*see* PLASTIC, §3). Tube casein must be well thinned with water, and brushes must be wetted before being placed in the paint. Although not an emulsion, casein may be emulsified with oil, but the resulting medium yellows badly.

BIBLIOGRAPHY

Theophilus: *De diversis artibus* (?1110–40); Eng. trans. by J. G. Hawthorne and C. S. Smith as *On Divers Arts* (Chicago and London, 1963)

C. Cennini: *Il libro dell'arte* (MS.; *c*. 1390); trans. and notes by D. V. Thompson jr (1933)
C. Eastlake: *Methods and Materials of Painting of the Great Schools and Masters*, 2 vols (London, 1847/*R* New York, 1960)
R. J. Gettens and G. L. Stout: *Painting Materials: A Short Encyclopaedia* (New York, 1942, rev. 1966)
A. Dehn: *Watercolour, Gouache and Casein Painting* (New York, 1955)
S. Quiller and B. Whipple: *Water Media: Processes and Possibilities* (New York, 1986)

JONATHAN STEPHENSON

Caselli [Castelli] **(da Parma), Cristoforo** [Temperelli; Temperello, il] (*b* Parma, *c*. 1460; *d* Parma, before 27 June 1521). Italian painter. He was the son of Giovanni di Cristoforo, who may also have been a painter. His style seems to have been based on a provincial Parmese version of Antonello da Messina's—which he could have learnt from Bartolomeo Montagna in Vicenza—and on that of Piero della Francesca. In 1488 Caselli was recorded in Venice, where he painted the organ shutters of the *Annunciation with SS Elijah and Albert* (destr.) for the church of the Carmine in 1489; also in 1489 he began to work with Giovanni Bellini, Alvise Vivarini, Lattanzio da Rimini and others on the painted decoration (destr. 1577) of the Sala del Maggior Consiglio in the Doge's Palace. There he presumably developed his individual narrative style, superficially close to Vittorio Carpaccio but fundamentally indebted to Giovanni Bellini. A triptych (1495; Venice, Semin. Patriarcale) of the *Virgin and Child with Two Saints*, a *Donor Bishop* and *God the Father* was made for S Cipriano, Murano. The *SS Francis and Louis of Toulouse with the Blessed Giovanni da Capestrano* (*c*. 1495; Baltimore, MD, Walters A.G.) and the *Virgin and Child* (sold London, Sotheby's, 7 April 1982) were also painted at this time.

In 1495 Caselli returned to Parma, where he undertook a series of important commissions, including the *Nativity with SS Peter and John the Baptist* (Castell'Arquato, S Maria, Mus.); this seems slightly earlier than the *Adoration of the Magi* (1499; Parma, S Giovanni Evangelista; see fig.), although it has been dated 1502 (Quintavalle; *DBI*). On 10 March 1496 he signed the contract to paint a large altarpiece of the *Virgin and Child with SS Hilary and John the Baptist and Angels* for the Consorzio dei Vivi e dei Morti in Parma Cathedral (1499; Parma, G.N.). The large scale of the figures, the articulation of planes by means of architectural elements and the spaciousness of the scene would seem to be derived from a Lombard rather than a Venetian tradition, perhaps stemming from Donato Bramante. A synthesis of Venetian and Lombard traditions is evident in the *Adoration of the Magi* (ex-Nemes priv. col., Munich; see Berenson, 1957, i, pl. 527). Another signed work of *c*. 1499 is *St Peter Enthroned* in the parish church of Almenno San Bartolomeo (nr Bergamo), the central panel of a polyptych whose side panels show *SS Paul and James* and *SS Matthew and Sebastian* (both Detroit, MI, Inst. A.). The upper register of the polyptych consisted of three panels of *SS John the Baptist and Catherine*, the *Virgin and Child* and *Mary Magdalene and an Apostle* (all Bergamo, Gal. Accad. Carrara).

Between 1500 and 1507 Caselli was not recorded in Parma; he may have visited Venice again and seen Giovanni Bellini's S Zaccaria altarpiece (*in situ*). In 1507 he was back in Parma and painted *God the Father* in

Cristoforo Caselli: *Adoration of the Magi*, oil on panel, 1.90×1.35 m, 1499 (Parma, S Giovanni Evangelista)

imitation mosaic in a semi-dome of the cathedral; it is obviously influenced by Giovanni Battista Cima, and Coletti suggested that it was derived from a drawing by that artist. The signed grisaille of the *Dead Christ between Two Angels* on the Montini monument in Parma Cathedral probably dates from 1507, the year of Canon Montini's death. In the frieze decoration with scenes of sacrifice (Parma, S Giovanni Evangelista), formerly attributed to Giovanni Antonio da Parma, Caselli united elements from Bramante with the late style of Giovanni Bellini. In 1515 he made armorial designs (destr.) for Giuliano de' Medici, Duc de Nemours, and designed those for Francis I, King of France, which were painted by Alessandro Araldi (1521; destr.).

BIBLIOGRAPHY

DBI; *Enc. It.*; Thieme–Becker
G. Vasari: *Vite* (1550, rev. 2/1568); ed. G. Milanesi (1878–85), vi, p. 485 [referred to as Castelli]
A. Venturi: *Storia* (1901–40), VII/iv, pp. 256, 604, 606–8, 616
J. A. Crowe and G. B. Cavalcaselle: *A History of Painting in North Italy* (London, 1912), i, p. 164; ii, pp. 300–02
B. Berenson: *Dipinti veneziani in America* (Milan, 1919), pp. 58–9
A. Venturi: *La pittura del quattrocento in Emilia* (Bologna, 1931), p. 74
E. Sandberg-Vavalà: 'Attribution to Cristoforo Caselli', *A. Amer.*, xx (1932), pp. 195–201
Catalogo della mostra parmense di dipinti noti ed ignoti dal XIV al XVII secolo (exh. cat. by A. Quintavalle, Parma, G.N., 1948), pp. 9–11
B. Berenson: *Venetian School* (1957), i, pp. 60–61
C. Coletti: *Cima da Conegliano* (Venice, 1959), pp. 57, 91
F. Heinemann: *Bellini e i Belliniani* (Venice, 1962), pp. 98–100
A. Quintavalle: 'Christoforo Caselli', *A. Emilia*, ii (1962), pp. 52–3
K. Rusk Shapley: *Paintings from the Samuel H. Kress Collection, Italian Schools, XV–XVI Century* (London, 1968), p. 61

F. Zeri: *Italian Paintings in the Walters Art Gallery*, i (Baltimore, 1976), pp. 274–80
C. Volpe: 'Una Madonna di Cristoforo Caselli e un prototipo di Piero per il Veneto', *Notizie da Palazzo Albani*, xii/1–2 (1983), pp. 34–7

MARIA CRISTINA CHIUSA

Casentino, Jacopo del. *See* JACOPO DEL CASENTINO.

Caserta, Palazzo Reale [Reggia]. Large 18th-century palazzo situated in Italian town of Caserta, the successor of ancient and medieval Capua. The town is the capital of a province of the Campania region and is situated 28 km from Naples. Its growth dates from the 19th century. The Bourbon king Charles VII of Naples (from 1759 King Charles III of Spain) decided to make Caserta the site of a royal residence in imitation of Versailles. His choice was based on the excellent local hunting and the vulnerability of his palazzo at Naples in the event of a popular uprising or an attack from the sea. The building was designed by Luigi Vanvitelli and executed between 1752 and 1772. It was inhabitable from 1775 onwards and in the late 1770s and during the 1780s such artists as Fidele Fischetti and Domenico Mondo produced frescoes for various rooms (e.g. Mondo's *Classical Heroes*, 1781, for the overdoors of the Sala delle Dame, and *Apotheosis of the Bourbon Arms*, 1789, for the Salone degli Alabardieri; *see also* ITALY, §V, 6 and fig. 72). It was not fully furnished until the mid-19th century. Charles of Bourbon never lived in it; his son Ferdinand IV did so only occasionally, and it only fulfilled its intended purpose as a royal residence for the Bourbons between 1830 and 1860.

The palazzo, standing as a self-contained block (253×190 m) in a flat site, is of striking appearance (see fig.). The five-storey façade (253 m×49 m) has, however, a certain monotonous quality exacerbated by the absence of the architectural and ornamental additions intended by Vanvitelli. The interior is more animated: it is divided into four equal-sized oblong courts radiating from a dramatic central octagonal vestibule, where Vanvitelli employed scenographic principles to lead the viewer through a series of imposing vistas. The main axis is primarily for communication, while the transverse axis leading from the vestibule contains the ceremonial staircase (*see* VANVITELLI, LUIGI, fig. 2), chapel and theatre. The chapel and to a certain extent the theatre were modelled on those at Versailles. The chapel presents a lavish display of marble work and incorporates several paintings, including a *Presentation in the Temple* by Anton Raphael Mengs and an *Immaculate Conception* (1780s) by Giuseppe Bonito. Although the grand marble staircase is the area of greatest magnificence, the masonry throughout the building is beautiful in its precision.

Caserta, aerial view of the Palazzo Reale, by Luigi Vanvitelli, 1752–72

The formal gardens were laid out according to French textbook rules by Martin Biancour under Vanvitelli's supervision. The dominating axis is about 3 km long from the palace entrance to the waterfall at the end of the park and was intended to be prolonged in the opposite direction as a road reaching all the way to Naples. A broad stretch of water, the *canalone*, with large fountains, occupies the length of the vista which ends at the great cascade at the foot of the mountain. To one side is a garden in the English style with rare plants (from 1782). The system by which water is conveyed to the park (1753–69) is one of the greatest technical achievements of the 18th century; 42 km long, it includes a spectacular aqueduct, the Archi della Valle, of antique proportions (528 m l.×60 m h.).

On the city side of the palazzo, Vanvitelli developed only the schematic design seen in the bird's-eye view in his *Dichiarazione*, with an oval forecourt housing barracks and stables and roads radiating outwards. The town later developed to one side of the palazzo and not in front of it as originally envisaged.

BIBLIOGRAPHY

L. Vanvitelli: *Dichiarazione dei disegni del real Palazzo di Caserta* (Naples, 1756)
G. Chierici: *La Reggia di Caserta* (Rome, 1937)
F. De Filippis: *Caserta e la sua reggia* (Naples, 1954)
M. Fagiolo dell'Arco: *Funzioni, simboli, valori della Reggia di Caserta* (Rome, 1963)
M. R. Caroselli: *La Reggia di Caserta: Lavori, costo, effetti della costruzione* (Milan, 1968)
C. de Seta: 'I disegni di Luigi Vanvitelli per la Reggia di Caserta ed i progetti di Carlo Fontana per il palazzo del principe di Liechtenstein', *Stor. A.* (1974), pp. 267–76

JÖRG GARMS

Cashel [Cashel of the Kings]. Fortified ecclesiastical site in Co. Tipperary, Ireland. The rock of Cashel, surmounted by its cluster of medieval buildings, rises high above the surrounding plain (see fig.). The limestone outcrop was a natural fortress, occupied from the 4th century AD by the kings of Munster. Its known architectural history did not begin until 1101, when King Murtough O'Brien (*d* 1119) handed it over to the Church. In 1111 Cashel became one of the major ecclesiastical centres of Ireland through the establishment of an archbishopric there. As well as the ruins of the Gothic cathedral, there survive a round tower,

Cashel, view from the north-east showing the 12th-century Round Tower and the 13th-century Gothic cathedral

an exquisite Romanesque chapel, the Hall of the Vicars-choral and the remains of a fortified house belonging to the archbishops.

1. Architecture. 2. Sculpture.

1. ARCHITECTURE. The earliest building is the Round Tower (27.94 m high), evidently erected shortly after 1101, a date that accords with its well-dressed sandstone masonry (there is no evidence to support traditional claims for a date in the 9th or 10th century). Originally free-standing, the tower heralded the new religious status of the rock. Doorways in round towers usually point towards the main church, and at Cashel this indicates that the first cathedral was located at the east end of the later Gothic chancel. The first cathedral was replaced by a second in 1169, but nothing is known of the design of either.

The most important building, Cormac's Chapel (*see* ROMANESQUE, fig. 20), was built between 1127 and 1134 by Cormac mac Carrthach (*d* 1138), King of Desmond. The consecration ceremony in 1134 was a major event. It has been convincingly argued that the chapel was the first serious piece of Romanesque architecture in Ireland. Although simple in plan, with an aisleless nave (9.04×5.38 m) and a small chancel (4.17×3.30 m), the architecture is surprisingly rich, with many of the attributes of mature Romanesque design. The nave is barrel-vaulted, with a series of closely spaced transverse arches, and the chancel is covered by a miniature ribbed vault, the first of its kind in Ireland; above both vaults are spacious crofts reached by a spiral stair in the south tower. The interior walls are lined with arcades. There is an elaborate chancel arch in four orders and an abundance of grotesque human and animal heads. Fragments of wall and ceiling painting survive (recently rest.). All this was apparently new to Ireland; the towers flanking the east end of the nave also depart from Irish tradition in being square rather than round. The roof of stone corbels is, however, the finest example of a distinctively Irish mode of construction. The exterior masses of the building are crisply articulated, with a series of steep gables at the east end and string courses, corbel tables and wall arcades underlining the geometry of the design. There are two portals, each decorated with chevron arches and carved tympana, the latter a feature seldom found in Irish Romanesque. The north door, originally the main entrance but later blocked by the Gothic cathedral, was sumptuously treated. There are two anomalies in the plan of the chapel: the building is not orientated, deviating by about 15° to the north, and the chancel is not aligned on the same axis as the nave. Both anomalies are best explained by the cramped site and the presence of earlier buildings, now destroyed.

The building's purpose is not clear. Although its ornate appearance suggests that it was the private chapel of a king or bishop, there is no documentation to support this, and the building may have been intended for the use of Benedictine monks who settled at Cashel about this time. Its ostentation suggests it served as an architectural manifesto of the reform party in the Irish Church, of which King Cormac was a promoter. The reformers looked abroad for encouragement, which no doubt explains the foreign elements in the designs. Apart from the corbelled roof and the simple plan, no other features of the building have native origins; England, Germany and France have each been suggested as major sources of inspiration. Precedents for the towers exist in Germany, and religious connections between Cashel and Regensburg have been emphasized, but it is generally agreed that both architecture and sculpture have their principal roots in the west of England and south Wales, and that a number of English masons were present when the chapel was under construction.

Cormac's Chapel introduced a new ornamental architecture to Ireland in place of the austere masonry of the past and served as a catalyst for the development of Irish Romanesque. Although its architectural influence was limited, individual features had a significant impact on subsequent church building.

The chapel and early Round Tower were retained and integrated into the fabric of the Gothic cathedral (*c.* 1240–*c.* 1300), the chancel of which was extended to an unusual length (28.35 m) at the expense of the nave. This enabled the south transept to fit around the chapel. The internal length of the chancel stands in the ratio of 1:√2 to the length of the transepts (40.23 m), underlining the careful planning of what seems to be a straightforward design (*see* ARCHITECTURAL PROPORTION, §I). Although grand in scale, the cathedral lacks the sophistication of European Gothic architecture. The plan is simple, with no aisles and no stone vaults (except over the crossing and south porch). The long chancel, lit by a sequence of Early Gothic lancets, has many parallels in Ireland and Scotland; the lancet windows in the transept, with cusped oculi above, can be related to the Cistercian Abbey of Dunbrody (Co. Wexford), and so too can the wall passages below them. The design is thus second-generation Gothic in Ireland, rather than the product of ideas freshly imported from England. Nevertheless, there are many features of interest: the attractive niches that embellish the exterior of the transepts, the curious windows in the spandrels of the choir lancets and the presence of over 100 carved heads, chiefly label stops and corbels. The stark crossing tower, which now dominates the rock, was heightened in the 15th century, and the whole nave was remodelled for the benefit of the archbishops. A dour fortified house, usually attributed to Archbishop O'Hedian (1406–40), was inserted at the west end, and a second floor, linked to the house, was constructed across what was left of the nave. It is not clear if this functioned as a great hall or a gallery open to the church. The archbishops thus integrated their 'palace' with the cathedral, a combination of church and dwelling for which there were many precedents in Ireland. Archbishop O'Hedian was also responsible for the Hall of the Vicars-choral (rest.). The cathedral was badly damaged in the Cromwellian siege of 1647, and it was abandoned altogether a century later. Although its silhouette of gables, turrets and towers makes a splendidly romantic ruin, as a piece of architecture it lacks the pioneering qualities of Cormac's Chapel.

BIBLIOGRAPHY

A. Hill: *A Monograph of Cormac's Chapel, Cashel, County Tipperary* (Cork, 1874)

A. C. Champneys: *Irish Ecclesiastical Architecture* (London, 1910)

J. Gleeson: *Cashel of the Kings* (Dublin, 1927)

H. G. Leask: *St Patrick's Rock, Cashel, Co. Tipperary* (Dublin, [1940])

——: *Irish Churches and Ecclesiastical Buildings*, 3 vols (Dundalk, 1955–60)

L. de Paor: 'Cormac's Chapel: The Beginnings of Irish Romanesque', *North Munster Studies, Essays in Commemoration of Monsignor Michael Moloney*, ed. E. Rynne (Limerick, 1967), pp. 133–45

F. Henry: *Irish Art in the Romanesque Period, 1070–1170 AD* (London, 1970)

R. A. Stalley: 'Three Irish Buildings with West Country Origins', *Medieval Art and Architecture at Wells and Glastonbury: British Archaeological Association Conference Transactions: Wells, 1978*, pp. 62–5

2. SCULPTURE. The monuments of Cashel provide some outstanding examples of Irish Romanesque carving, illustrating Ireland's increasing awareness of European art in the 12th century. St Patrick's Cross originally stood to the south of the cathedral, where it has been replaced by a facsimile. The original (now in the Hall of the Vicars-choral) is 3.43 m high and decorated with large reliefs of the *Crucifixion* (west face) and a *Bishop* (east face), a common formula in Romanesque Ireland. The iconography of the *Crucifixion*, with Christ wearing a long tunic (*colobium*) and short belt, follows a type popularized by the wooden crucifix called the Volto Santo (Lucca Cathedral). It is essentially a sandstone version of a standard wooden rood, close in design to the Langford rood (Langford, Oxon, St Matthew). The structure of the cross is exceptional. Vertical stays were left in place to support the outstretched arms, which in turn may have supported angels either side of Christ's head. The bishop depicted on the east face, popularly interpreted as St Patrick, was evidently designed to assert episcopal authority at a time when a new diocesan system was being implemented.

The rich, eclectic sandstone sculpture of Cormac's Chapel is noticeably lacking in indigenous motifs. The two tympana, one depicting a lion and centaur, the other a grotesque beast, can be related to carvings in the west of England, such as those at Milborne Port, Dorset, and a similar source is likely for the variety of carved corbels, capitals and chevron ornament. The human heads set in the archivolts round the chancel arch are among the first examples of a motif that became popular in Irish Romanesque. Although the arrangement is foreign, possibly French, in origin, related to that in the church at Bellegarde du Loiret, the style of the sculpture is close to that of carvings discovered in Cork, where Cormac mac Carrthach founded an Augustinian abbey.

A magnificent sandstone sarcophagus, 2.34 m long, is now stored within the chapel. Cut in solid stone and intended to be visible above ground, such a sarcophagus was unprecedented in Ireland. Presumably it was derived from a country with a much stronger Classical tradition. Decidedly unclassical, however, is the ornament carved in false relief on one of the sides. Depicting two interlocked beasts, entangled by snakes, this is the largest stone example of the Irish version of the Scandinavian Urnes style. The sarcophagus is usually attributed to the second quarter of the 12th century, and its monumental opulence implies royal patronage.

Cashel also retains a wealth of limestone Gothic sculpture, including numerous head stops and corbels on the cathedral and a series of late medieval tomb chests.

BIBLIOGRAPHY

H. G. Leask: 'St Patrick's Cross, Cashel, Co. Tipperary: An Enquiry into its Original Form', *J. Royal Soc. Antiqua. Ireland*, lxxxi (1951), pp. 14–18

J. Bradley: 'The Sarcophagus at Cormac's Chapel, Cashel, Co. Tipperary', *N. Munster Antiqua. J.*, xxvi (1984), pp. 14–35

P. Harbison: *The High Crosses of Ireland* (Bonn, 1992), i, pp. 34–5

ROGER STALLEY

Casilear, John William (*b* New York, 25 June 1811; *d* Saratoga Springs, NY, 17 Aug 1893). American engraver, draughtsman and painter. At 15 he was apprenticed to the engraver Peter Maverick (1780–1871) and then to Asher B. Durand. Casilear and his brother George formed a business partnership that eventually developed into the American Bank Note Co., the principal private bank-note engravers in America. He was perhaps the most fluent and accomplished draughtsman of his generation, and important collections of his landscape drawings are in the Detroit Institute of Arts and the Boston Museum of Fine Arts.

Casilear was an exponent of the HUDSON RIVER SCHOOL of landscape painting. Such works as *Lake George* (1860; Hartford, CT, Wadsworth Atheneum) and his views of Genesee Valley, NY, and Niagara Falls manifest the refined colour, restrained brushwork and ordered composition typical of that group. Casilear's compositions are firmly drawn and articulated through a subtle palette that explores the value and saturation of hues.

In 1833 Casilear was elected an Associate at the National Academy of Design, New York, based on his engravings and in 1851 an Academician based on his painting. In 1840 Casilear, Durand, John Frederick Kensett and Thomas Rossiter (1818–71) travelled to Europe to study, visiting London, Paris and Rome. Casilear was a regular exhibitor at the National Academy of Design (1833–90), the Apollo Association (1838–43), the American Art-Union (1847–51), the Pennsylvania Academy of the Fine Arts, Philadelphia (1855–65), and elsewhere.

BIBLIOGRAPHY

D. Stauffer: *American Engravers upon Copper and Steel* (New York, 1907)
American Paradise: The World of the Hudson River School (exh. cat. by J. K. Howat, New York, Met., 1987)

JOHN DRISCOLL

Casilinum. *See under* CAPUA.

Casimir. *See* KARPFF, JEAN-JACQUES.

Casimir III, King of Poland. *See* PIAST, (1).

Casino [It.: 'little house'] **(i).** Term used in Italian Renaissance and Baroque architecture for the house of a *villa suburbana*. A good example is the casino of the Villa Giulia, Rome, by Jacopo Vignola. By extension, the term came to refer to an ornamental pavilion or small house, usually in the grounds of a large house or palazzo.

Casino (ii). Term used in the 18th century for a public room for music or dancing; it later came to refer to a building for gambling.

□

Casket. A small case or lidded box for storing various objects. (For reliquary caskets *see* RELIQUARY, §I, 1 and ROMANESQUE, §VII and fig. 77.) Among the early types are nuptial caskets, which functioned as courtship gifts or marriage chests, miniature precursors of the Italian CASSONE. They were popular from the 4th century AD and were usually made of ivory or wood. An outstanding Early Christian example in silver is Projecta's Casket (4th century; London, BM; see fig.), which combines a Christian inscription and secular scenes. In the Byzantine period ivory caskets were produced with rosettes, scrollwork and delicately carved figural reliefs (*see* EARLY CHRISTIAN AND BYZANTINE ART, §VII, 9). About 50 complete examples survive, including the 10th- or 11th-century Veroli Casket (London, V&A; *see* EARLY CHRISTIAN AND BYZANTINE ART, fig. 9). Some of the Byzantine caskets (e.g. Troyes, Trésor Cathédrale) appear to have had an ecclesiastical use, as storage boxes for pyxes, incense boats and other small liturgical utensils. Secular ivory caskets were produced in France in the 14th century. They were usually decorated with low reliefs illustrating romances (e.g.

Projecta's Casket, silver, Rome, 4th century AD (London, British Museum)

London, V&A) or allegorical scenes, but their function is unclear.

Caskets were also used for storing important books and papers. For example, bible boxes were used by both ecclesiastic and lay owners for storing Bibles. They were particularly common in the Renaissance and made of wood, usually walnut or oak, with either a flat or a slanting hinged lid. They were decorated with foliate strapwork or similar designs and were sometimes inscribed and dated. Epistolary cases are another type of wood casket, used especially from the 11th century to the 16th for storing important letters or documents. They were frequently covered with cuir-bouilli (boiled leather), which was applied when soft to take its required form. They were made with hinged lids, sometimes with iron locks, and various ornamentation, usually incised or punched. Small bronze epistolary caskets were also produced, for example *c.* 1500 in Padua, with reliefs of classical figures and foliate ornamentation.

In France during the Baroque period porcelain and faience caskets were produced, the latter, for example, at Marseille. Some of these were in the form of miniature armoires, with *fête champêtre* representations or heraldic coats of arms on the doors. The shelved interiors were painted with floral sprays, with gilt fleurs-de-lys. A distinctive type of English casket developed in the early 17th century. These boxes were used for storing jewellery or toilet articles and were usually made of wicker or embroidered, with glass beadwork, stumpwork and petit point decoration and such ornaments as glass-bead flowers attached to the lid. Other types of English casket were metal, or of wood veneered with oyster marquetry and with elaborate gilt-bronze hinges and a fall front, or with two doors opening at the front to reveal small drawers. They were commonly owned by the aristocracy and royalty (e.g. jewel casket of Mary II, *c.* 1690; London, V&A; *see* ENGLAND, §IX, 2(iii) and fig. 86) and were frequently depicted in European painting of the period. In the 19th century English caskets were also produced in agate ware and contained animal figures on the lid in a manner typical of Romantic art.

BIBLIOGRAPHY

A Catalogue of the Very Choice Collection of Old French Snuff Boxes, Bonbonnières, Etuis, Caskets, etc. (sale cat., London, 1897)

P. Williamson, ed.: *The Medieval Treasury*, London, V&A cat. (London, 1986)

JOHN N. LUPIA

Casnedi, Raffaele (*b* Runo, Varese, 24 Sept 1822; *d* Milan, 29 Dec 1892). Italian painter. From 1840 he studied under Luigi Sabatelli at the Accademia di Belle Arti di Brera, Milan. There he was awarded many prizes, including the Premio Roma in 1852, which enabled him to spend five years in Rome. His work from this period included the *Widow's Mite* (1854; Milan, Brera). In 1856 Casnedi returned to Milan and in 1860 became Professor of Drawing at the academy. His teaching and that of his fellow professors, Francesco Hayez and Giuseppe Bertini, was of considerable importance to future generations of artists based in Milan. Among his pupils were the Scapigliati artists Pietro Bouvier and Francesco Didioni, and the Divisionists Angelo Morbelli and Giovanni Sottocornola.

In his easel paintings, Casnedi's subject-matter tended to consist of genre scenes and historical or literary themes, such as the *Prisoner of Chillon* (1855; Milan, Brera; sketch, Milan, Gal. A. Mod.), which was awarded a prize at the Brera annual exhibition in 1855.

Casnedi was equally well known for his frescoes. He and Bertini decorated the backdrop of the Teatro alla Scala (*The Birth of the Theatre: Fabulae Atellanae*; destr.). In 1864–5 Casnedi frescoed the ceiling of the main hall in Milan's old central railway station with allegories of the Italian provinces (destr.). Between 1865 and 1867 he frescoed one of the lunettes in the central crossing of the Galleria Vittorio Emanuele, Milan, with the figure of America and later the allegory of Art at one of its main entrances. Because of their exposed position these frescoes deteriorated rapidly and were replaced by mosaics of the same subjects in 1911–12.

Casnedi executed a large number of frescoes around Milan, mainly for churches in the Brianza region. He worked in SS Pietro e Marcellino, Bresana Brianza, between 1873 (the *Doctors of the Church*) and 1877 (*Christ's Entry into Jerusalem*).

BIBLIOGRAPHY

Comanducci; *DBI*; Luciani

L. Caramel and C. Pirovano: *Opere dell'ottocento*, Milan, Gal. A. Mod. cat., i (Milan, 1975), p. 40

I maestri di Brera (exh. cat., Milan, Pal. Permanente, 1975), pp. 204–5

CLARE HILLS-NOVA

Casorati, Felice (*b* Novara, 4 Dec 1883; *d* Turin, 1 March 1963). Italian painter, sculptor and printmaker. Casorati spent his formative years in Padua where he developed a passion for music and literature. He began to paint in 1902 but to please his mother he read law at the University of Padua, graduating in 1906. He continued to paint meanwhile and to frequent the studio of Giovanni Viannello (1873–1926). In 1907 he exhibited at the Venice Biennale and his *Portrait of a Woman* (Turin, priv. col., see 1985 exh. cat., p. 242), an elegant portrait of his sister Elvira, was praised by the jury. It is representative of his early works, which were marked by the influence of the Viennese Secession, Art Nouveau and Symbolism. From 1908 Casorati lived in Naples where he first saw works by Pieter Bruegel I at the Museo di Capodimonte. He was also in touch with contemporary northern European artistic circles. He continued to exhibit at the Venice Biennale where, in 1910, he met Gustav Klimt, whose work he had admired since 1905.

Between 1911 and 1914 Casorati was in Verona where he collaborated on the *Via Lattea*, a review for which he produced a series of graphic works. These were stylized and recherché images, recalling the illustrations of Jan Toorop or Aubrey Beardsley. Casorati's paintings of this period, such as the *Dream of the Pomegranate Tree* (1913; Turin, Lattes Col., see 1985 exh. cat., p. 246) and *Scherzo: Eggs* (1914; Turin, Carluccio Col., see 1985 exh. cat., p. 78), are highly refined and decorative and have a symbolic richness reminiscent of Klimt's works, though they lack the latter's decadent and haunting atmosphere. During World War I and until 1920, Casorati was associated with the artists of Ca' Pesaro in Venice, who, under the direction of Nino Barbantini, called for a renewed form of classicism and the negation of naturalism. Casorati was often loosely associated with artistic groups or organizations in the course of his career (he exhibited with the Novecento Italiano in 1926 and 1929) but he regarded these as practical arrangements that had little bearing on his own work. Before being mobilized in 1915 he had a one-man show at the Rome Secession, which included his first sculptures of varnished terracotta.

Casorati was discharged from the army on the death of his father in 1917. During a visit to Turin he met Piero Gobetti and a year later he moved there with his mother and two sisters. Casorati was intrigued by the decadent atmosphere of Turin with its sinister views. Through his friendship with Gobetti, who in 1921 took on the role of critic to champion him in Antonio Gramsci's newspaper *Ordine nuovo*, and his adhesion until 1922 to Gobetti's own political group Amici di Rivoluzione Liberale, Casorati became aware of the harsher social and political realities of post-war Italy.

The periodical *Valori plastici* was published for the first time in 1918 and Casorati shared with its contributors a desire to re-establish a link with the art of the past and to disregard the innovations of Futurism. After the war, Casorati's attitude towards painting changed dramatically and he considered his pre-war work experimental and immature. In works such as *Man with Barrels* (1919; Turin, Gal. Civ. A. Mod.; see fig.) and *Eggs on a Chest of Drawers* (1920; Turin, priv. col., see 1985 exh. cat., p. 79) the decorative symbolism has been replaced by a sober tectonic solidity. A direct light negates tonal gradations, creating a psychological tension, and the emphasis is on forms rather than detail. Though related to Pittura Metafisica, Casorati's works do not share the jarred syntax and irony of Giorgio De Chirico or Carlo Carrà's work of the same period.

Felice Casorati: *Man with Barrels*, tempera on canvas, 1.72×1.47 m, 1919 (Turin, Galleria Civica d'Arte Moderna)

Casorati exhibited with the dissidents of the Ca' Pesaro group in 1920. According to Lionello Venturi, the Paul Cézanne exhibition at the Venice Biennale of that year was instrumental in encouraging Casorati's search for a balance between space, form and colour. In 1921 he exhibited at the Galleria Centrale in Turin, where he showed a series of graphic works with the artists who were later to form the Sei a Torino group. Works of the early 1920s, such as *Silvana Cenni* (1922; Turin, priv. col., see 1985 exh. cat., p. 87) and *Meriggio* ('Midday'; 1922; Trieste, Mus. Civ. Revoltella; *see* TURIN, fig. 5), attest to Casorati's interest in 15th-century painting, especially the mathematical constructions of Piero della Francesca and the highly foreshortened figures of Mantegna. From 1923 his studio in Via Mazzini and later in Via Gallinari became a school for young artists in Turin. In 1924 he received critical acclaim for his one-man show at the Venice Biennale.

While continuing to exhibit widely in the late 1920s and 1930s he also experimented with decorative arts as a means of bringing art into everyday life. He worked with Alberto Sartoris on the project for the Piccolo Teatro in the Casa Gualino, Turin, and designed costumes and sets for La Scala, Milan, and the Maggio Musicale in Florence in the 1930s and after World War II. Also with Sartoris he designed the slaughterhouse (*macelleria*) for the commercial street that formed part of the Piedmontese Pavilion at the International Biennale of decorative arts held in Monza in 1927. In 1928 he accepted the chair of interior design at the Accademia Albertina in Turin and in 1941 he became head of painting at the same Academy. In 1933 he collaborated on the Architectural Pavilion at the Milan Triennale of decorative arts. By the 1930s he had become part of the art establishment. The Stampa Gallery of Turin organized a major retrospective of his work in 1937 and he won the Venice Biennale Award for painting in 1938. In 1942 Casorati retired to Pavorolo, outside Turin.

Throughout his career, Casorati's oeuvre retained an intense psychological import. He continued to paint familiar themes, including female figures and nudes, still-lifes, desolate houses and landscapes, but by the 1930s the rigid spatial compositions of the previous decade had been superseded by freer constructions, the tones had softened and the use of shadows was gentler, as in *The Ladle* (1933; Milan, Gal. A. Mod.). After 1945 his palette brightened considerably as he used colour as a means of expression, blocking out his figures with heavy contours. In 1952 he received the Premio Speciale della Presidenza at the Venice Biennale.

BIBLIOGRAPHY

P. Gobetti: *Felice Casorati, pittore* (Turin, 1923)
L. Venturi: 'Il pittore Felice Casorati', *Dedalo*, iv (1923), pp. 238–61
Felice Casorati (exh. cat., intro. L. Venturi; Venice, XIV Esposizione Internazionale d'arte, 1924)
Casorati (exh. cat., ed. L. Carluccio; Turin, Gal. Civ. A. Mod., 1964)
F. Tempesti: *Arte dell'Italia fascista* (Milan, 1976)
M. Valsecchi: *Casorati* (Rome, 1977)
Omaggio a Felice Casorati (exh. cat., ed. M. Valsecchi; Sasso Marconi, Casa A., 1980)
Casorati (exh. cat., ed. M. Valsecchi; Ferrara, Gal. Civ. A. Mod., 1981)
G. Perocco: *I maestri di Ca' Pesaro, 1908–1923* (Venice, 1982)
Gli anni Trenta (exh. cat., ed. G. Perocco; Milan, Pal. Reale, 1982)

Il novecento italiano, 1923–1933 (exh. cat., ed. G. Perocco; Milan, Pal. Permanente, 1983)
Felice Casorati, 1883–1963 (exh. cat., ed. M. M. Lamberti and P. Fossati; Turin, Accad. Albertina B.A., 1985)

SIMONETTA FRAQUELLI

Caspicara [Chili, Manuel] (*fl* Quito, 18th century). Ecuadorian sculptor. An Indian nicknamed *Caspicara* (wooden face), he lived in Quito, and his name and work were discovered in 1791 by the doctor and journalist Eugenio Espejo. He was a pupil of Bernardo de Legarda. He is considered the outstanding sculptor of religious images in polychromed wood of the colonial period in Quito because of the delicacy, grace and feeling that he gave to human expressions and his attention to the details of anatomy and the movement of his figures. The elegant but natural carving of the drapery adds a Baroque quality to his sculptures. The most outstanding of his works in Quito, all of unknown date, include the *Four Virtues* and the *Holy Shroud* in Quito Cathedral; *St Francis*, the *Twelve Apostles* and the *Assumption of the Virgin* in S Francisco; and *La Virgen del Carmen*, *St Joseph* and the *Coronation of the Virgin* in the Museo Franciscano in Quito. In certain of his works he grouped the figures as if in a painting, as in the *Holy Shroud*, and the *Assumption of the Virgin* mentioned above.

RICARDO DESCALZI

Cassai, Tommaso di Ser Giovanni di Mone. *See* MASACCIO.

Cassana, Niccolò (*b* Venice, 1659; *d* London, 1714). Italian painter. He was apprenticed to his father, the Genoese painter Giovanni Francesco Cassana (1611–90), and from him learnt to paint in the tenebrist style. In 1684 he was enrolled in the guild of Venetian painters. After the death of Giusto Suttermans (1681), the official portraitist of the Medici court, Cassana tried to win favour by sending a *Self-portrait* (1683) to Florence to form part of the collection of self-portraits in the Uffizi. Yet this work, the earliest example of his prolific output as a portrait painter, was rejected and relegated to the gallery's storeroom (see Chiarini). Few of his numerous early portraits for the Venetian nobility and clergy survive; some are known through engravings. Among those that have been identified are those of a *Notary* (Venice, Doge's Pal.), *Giambattista Doria* (Venice, Correr) and various others (Lovere, Gal. Accad. B.A. Tadini; Genoa, Pal. Rosso).

In 1688 Grand Prince Ferdinando de' Medici met Cassana in the course of a visit to Venice (*see* MEDICI, DE', (28)). They formed a sincere and long-lasting friendship. Cassana visited Florence many times and painted many portraits for the Medici court, including *Cosimo III*, his daughter *Anna Maria Luisa* (*c.* 1690), *Ferdinando* and his wife *Violante Beatrice of Bavaria* and *Cardinal Francesco Maria de' Medici* (all Florence, Uffizi). In addition to official portraiture Cassana also painted more naturalistic and modest portraits, for example the portraits of *Alberto Tortelli* and *Giuliano Baldassarini* (both Florence, Uffizi), in which Ferdinando's much admired and talented gamekeepers are depicted in relaxed, conversational poses. The *Portrait of a Cook* (1707), in which the theme and freedom of handling are reminiscent of Bernardo Strozzi, belongs to the same series as the *Dwarf* (Florence, Pitti); both of these are enlivened by a vivid realism, enhanced by the presence of animals and objects. Cassana conducted a long and frequent correspondence with Ferdinando (Venice, Bib. N. Marciana), which reveals that he acted as an agent of the Medici court for the purchase of works of art and also as a copyist; his copy of Salvator Rosa's *Oath of Catiline* (untraced) is in the Palazzo Pitti, Florence. Cassana must have been less enthusiastic about his work as restorer, for he completed and touched up the ruined or missing parts of paintings in a way that seems excessively offhand.

According to Ratti (1769), Cassana also produced history paintings. His religious pictures include a copy of Titian's *St Peter Martyr*, painted to replace that work (destr.) in SS Giovanni e Paolo, Venice (*in situ*). His only surviving mythological work is a *Bacchanal* (St Petersburg, Hermitage), a large work in which he moved away from the tenebrist style towards the classicism of Nicolas Poussin and Sebastiano Ricci. In 1709, during the royal visit to Venice, Cassana painted portraits of *Frederick IV, King of Denmark* (untraced) and the court dignitary *Ivor Rosenkranz* (Hillerød, Frederiksborg Slot). Guarienti's revision of Orlandi states that after sending two portraits to England (untraced) Cassana was summoned by Queen Anne and died in London during that visit.

BIBLIOGRAPHY

DBI [with bibliog. to 1978]
P. A. Orlandi: *Abecedario pittorico* (Bologna, 1704); rev. P. M. Guarienti (Venice, 1753)
C. G. Ratti: *Delle vite de' pittori scultori ed architetti genovesi*, ii (Genoa, 1769), pp. 14–16
G. Fogolari: 'Lettere pittoriche del Gran Principe Ferdinando di Toscana a Niccolò Cassana (1698–1709)', *Riv. Reale Ist. Archeol. & Stor. A.*, vi (1937), pp. 145–86
N. Ivanoff: 'Ritratti dell'Avogaria', *A. Ven.*, viii (1954), p. 278
M. Chiarini: 'Niccolò Cassana, Portrait Painter of the Florentine Court', *Apollo*, c (1974), pp. 234–9
F. Zava Bocazzi: 'Niccolò Cassana a Venezia', *Atti Ist. Ven. Sci., Lett. & A.*, cxxxviii (1978–9), pp. 611–34
R. Pallucchini: *La pittura veneziana del seicento* (Milan, 1981), pp. 309–11

MARCO CARMINATI

Cassandre [Mouron, Adolphe Jean-Marie] (*b* Kharkiv, Ukraine, 24 Jan 1901; *d* Paris, 17 June 1968). French designer, painter and writer. His family settled in Paris in 1915. After very briefly attending the Ecole des Beaux-Arts in Paris in 1918, he studied in Lucien Simon's studio, at the Académie de la Grande Chaumière and at the Académie Julian. In 1922 he began designing posters (for an illustration, *see* POSTER, fig. 5), using the name 'Cassandre'. His first notable success was *The Woodcutter* (1923; Paris, Mus. Affiche & Pub.), executed in clear, simplified forms, somewhat influenced by Cubism. In 1926 he published his first text on poster design in *Revue de l'Union de l'Affiche Française*, in which he emphasized the poster artist's connection with the ancient and medieval traditions of communicating messages through pictures. He designed his first typeface, the advertising Bifur face, in 1927 and in 1930 designed the sanserif Acier display face; these reflected his growing interest in the typographic elements of his posters. In the 1930s his output of posters for French and foreign firms was prolific. It included the popular triptych *Dubo Dubon Dubonnet* (1932; New York,

MOMA), which illustrated the pleasure of drinking Dubonnet by increasing the coloured areas of the design. Others, such as *Paris* (1935; see Mouron, pl. 53), were influenced by Surrealism, in particular the empty, haunting spaces of De Chirico's works. In 1935 a collection of Cassandre's posters was published as *Le Spectacle est dans la rue*, with a preface by Blaise Cendrars. He spent the winters of 1936–7 and 1937–8 in New York, where he worked for *Harper's Bazaar*, and in 1937 he designed his first all-purpose typeface, Peignot. After returning to Paris in 1938 he concentrated on painting until 1944, producing austere, realistic portraits such as that of *Pierre Reverdy* (1943; see Mouron, p. 121), as well as landscapes. After earlier commissions in the 1930s, in the 1940s and 1950s Cassandre was much occupied with stage designs, such as those for the ballet *Les Mirages*. This was performed in 1947 and had a narrative written by Serge Lifar and Cassandre himself. He designed a few posters in the 1940s and 1950s and in 1958 designed a typeface for Olivetti. His productivity waned in the 1960s, but he did design the famous logo for Yves Saint Laurent and produced tempera paintings such as the bleak *The Frontier* (1962; see Mouron, p. 151), as well as occasional posters, before his suicide.

BIBLIOGRAPHY

Le Spectacle est dans la rue, preface B. Cendrars (Paris, 1935)
Posters by Cassandre (exh. cat. by E. M. Fantl, New York, MOMA, 1936)
A. M. Cassandre: Un Précurseur de l'art présent (exh. cat. by R. Mason, Geneva, Gal. Motte, 1966)
H. Mouron: *Cassandre* (Munich, 1985; Eng. trans., London, 1985) [includes article by Cassandre, pubd in *Rev. Un. Affiche Fr.*]

□

Cassano, Marchese di. *See* SERRA, GIOVAN FRANCESCO.

Cassas, Louis-François (*b* Azay-le-Ferron, Indre, 3 June 1756; *d* Versailles, 1 Nov 1827). French draughtsman, engraver, sculptor and archaeologist. He received instruction in drawing from Joseph-Marie Vien, Jean-Jacques Lagrenée and Jean-Baptiste Le Prince. In 1778 he departed for Italy, where he developed his landscape draughtsmanship and his passion for antiquity. He travelled incessantly, recording everything he saw and venturing out from Rome to Venice, Naples and Sicily. An example of the numerous drawings he produced is the *Ruins of the Baths of Titus Seen from the Colosseum* (Paris, Ecole N. Sup. B.-A.). In 1782 a group of amateurs, under the patronage of Emperor Joseph II, commissioned from him a series of views of the Istrian and Dalmatian coast; these were eventually published in J. Lavallée's *Voyage pittoresque et historique de l'Istrie et de la Dalmatie*. After a brief spell in France, Cassas followed Marie-Gabriel, Comte de Choiseul-Gouffier, to his new ambassadorial post in Constantinople in 1784. He subsequently visited Syria, Egypt, Palestine, Cyprus and Asia Minor, recording his impressions of Alexandria, Cairo, Smyrna, the Temple of Diana (Artemis) at Ephesos and the Palmyra and Baalbek ruins. Many of the 250 drawings dating from this trip were of hitherto unrecorded sights. With Choiseul's assistance Cassas published these works in the *Voyage pittoresque de la Syrie, de la Phoenicie, de la Palaestine et de la Basse Aegypte*, though only 30 copies were printed. In 1787 Cassas left Constantinople, returning to France via Rome and reaching Paris in 1792. After the Revolution he was appointed drawing-master at the Gobelins, where he remained until his death. He also produced 74 models in cork and terracotta of the principal ancient monuments for the Ecole des Beaux-Arts, Paris, influencing the development of Neo-classicism at the beginning of the 19th century.

PRINTS

Voyage pittoresque de la Syrie, de la Phoenicie, de la Palaestine et de la Basse Aegypte (Paris, 1799)
J. Lavallée: *Voyage pittoresque et historique de l'Istrie et de la Dalmatie* (Paris, 1802)

BIBLIOGRAPHY

R. de Portalis: *Les Dessinateurs d'illustrations au dix-huitième siècle* (Paris, 1877), pp. 49–58
French Landscape Drawings and Sketches of the Eighteenth Century (exh. cat., London, BM, 1977), pp. 105–6

JOSHUA DRAPKIN

Cassatt, Mary (Stevenson) (*b* Allegheny City [now in Pittsburgh], 25 May 1844; *d* Le Mesnil-Théribus, France, 14 June 1926). American painter and printmaker. Having settled in Paris, she became a member of the Impressionist circle. The quality of her draughtsmanship is evident in all the media in which she worked, notably pastel. She is particularly associated with the theme of mother and child.

1. LIFE AND WORK. Daughter of a Pittsburgh banker, Mary Cassatt received a cultured upbringing and spent five years abroad as a child (1851–5). In 1860, at the age of 16, she began classes at the Pennsylvania Academy of the Fine Arts, Philadelphia, and in 1866 sailed again for Europe. During the next four years she studied in Paris with Jean-Léon Gérôme and Charles Chaplin, in Ecouen with Paul Soyer (1823–1903), in Villiers-le-Bel with Thomas Couture and in Rome with Charles Bellay (1826–1900). She concentrated mainly on figure painting, often posing her models in picturesque local costume. When she returned to Europe after 16 months in the USA (1870–71), she painted and copied in the museums of Parma, Madrid, Seville, Antwerp and Rome, finally settling in Paris in 1874. Until 1878 she worked mainly as a portrait and genre painter, specializing in scenes of women in Parisian interiors. She exhibited regularly in the USA, particularly in Philadelphia, and had paintings accepted in the Paris Salons of 1868, 1870 and 1872–6.

Cassatt's study of Velázquez and Rubens, coupled with her interest in the modern masters Thomas Couture, Courbet and Degas, caused her to question the popular Salon masters of the 1870s and to develop her own increasingly innovative style. This led to rejection of some of her Salon entries in 1875 and 1877 but also prompted Degas to invite her to exhibit with the Impressionists. She made her début with them at their fourth annual exhibition (1879), by which time she had mastered the Impressionist style and was accepted as a fully fledged member by artists and critics alike. She went on to participate in the Impressionist exhibitions of 1880, 1881 and 1886.

In 1877, when her parents and older sister Lydia arrived to settle with her in Paris, she exchanged her youthful lifestyle, living alone in her studio, for a more family-orientated existence. Their more spacious and comfortable accommodation also encouraged Cassatt's two brothers and their families to make frequent visits from Philadelphia. Family members often figure in Cassatt's Impressionist portraits and scenes of daily life during this period (e.g. *Lydia Crocheting in the Garden at Marly*, 1880; New York, Met.; *see also* IMPRESSIONISM, colour pl. VIII).

Cassatt began to revise her Impressionist style in the 1880s, and after the last Impressionist exhibition (1886) she developed a refined draughtsmanship in her pastels, prints and oil paintings. After exhibiting with the new Société des Peintres-Graveurs in 1889 and 1890, she had her first individual exhibition of colour prints and paintings in 1891 at the Galerie Durand-Ruel, Paris. In 1892 she was invited to paint a large tympanum mural, *Modern Woman*, for the Woman's Building at the World's Columbian Exposition (Chicago, 1893). Although the mural itself does not survive, many paintings (e.g. *Nude Baby Reaching for an Apple*, 1893; Richmond, VA, Mus. F.A.), prints (e.g. *Gathering Fruit*, drypoint with aquatint, *c.* 1895) and pastels (e.g. *Banjo Lesson*, 1894; Richmond, VA Mus. F.A.; see fig.) based on Cassatt's mural designs reflect her concept of modern woman 'plucking the fruits of knowledge or science'. She exhibited these in her first major retrospective exhibition in 1895 at Durand-Ruel's gallery in Paris and again in 1895 at his gallery in New York.

Cassatt's success in Europe and the USA was such that in 1894 she was able to purchase the Château de Beaufresne in Le Mesnil-Théribus (*c.* 90 km north-west of Paris) from the sale of her work. Thereafter she alternated between Paris and the country, with a few months every winter in the south of France. She increasingly concentrated on the mother-and-child theme and on studies of women and young girls, often turning to the Old Masters for inspiration. For this work she was recognized on both

Mary Cassatt: *Banjo Lesson*, pastel on paper, 710×572 mm, 1894 (Richmond, VA, Virginia Museum of Fine Arts)

continents, and, in addition to receiving a number of awards, including the Légion d'honneur in 1904, she was called 'the most eminent of all living American women painters' (*Current Lit.*, 1909, p. 167). She spent much of her time during these years helping her American friends build collections of avant-garde French art and works by Old Masters. Those she advised included Henry and Louisine Havemeyer, Mrs Montgomery J. Sears, Bertha Honoré Palmer and James Stillman.

Cassatt painted until 1915 and exhibited her latest work that year in the *Suffrage Loan Exhibition of Old Masters and Works by Edgar Degas and Mary Cassatt* at the Knoedler Gallery, New York; but soon afterwards cataracts in both eyes forced her into retirement. She continued to be actively interested in art, however, and until her death she vigorously expressed her own views and opinions to the many young artists who visited her seeking advice.

2. WORKING METHODS, TECHNIQUE AND SUBJECT-MATTER. Cassatt's own experimentation and her openness to new ideas caused her style to change many times during her long career. In her early years (1860–78) she practised a painterly genre style in dark, rich colours as in *A Musical Party* (1874; Paris, Petit Pal.); during her Impressionist period (1879–86) she used a pastel palette and quick brushstrokes in such works as *Cup of Tea* (*c.* 1880; New York, Met.); in her mature period (1887–1900) she developed a style that was more finished and dependent on abstract linear design, for instance in *The Bath* (1893; Chicago, IL, A. Inst.); and in her late period (1900–26) she often used colour combinations with a sombre cast, as in *The Caress* (1903; Washington, DC, N. Mus. Amer. A.).

As a student and young artist, Cassatt avoided the academic emphasis on drawing and concentrated instead on painting techniques. But as her career progressed, particularly after 1879 when she took up pastels and printmaking, she developed a refined and original drawing style that blended European and oriental effects. Her first efforts in printmaking were in a collaboration with Degas, Pissarro and others to produce a journal combining art criticism and original prints. Although the journal, *Le Jour et la nuit*, never appeared, Cassatt went on to finish several complex prints in etching, aquatint and drypoint, such as *The Visitor* (softground, aquatint and drypoint, *c.* 1880; see Breeskin, 1948, no. 34). In the late 1880s she turned to drypoint for a spare and elegant effect, as in *Baby's Back* (*c.* 1889; see Breeskin, 1948, no. 128). Her greatest achievement in printmaking, however, was the group of 18 colour prints she produced during the 1890s. The first ten were completed and exhibited as a set in 1891 and are highly prized for their skilful use of aquatint, etching and drypoint and for Cassatt's hand-inking and wiping of the plates for each print. Prints from this set, such as *The Letter* (drypoint and aquatint, 1890–91; see Breeskin, 1948, no. 146), show her successful synthesis of the abstract design of Japanese colour prints and the atmospheric qualities of Western art.

Cassatt's pastels are equally important to her development as an artist. Although she used pastel as a sketching tool from the first, it was not until she joined the

Impressionist circle that she began to produce major finished works in this medium. Pastel became increasingly popular in both Europe and the USA in the 1870s and 1880s, and Cassatt was one of the first to exploit the properties of pastel in conveying the vibrancy of 'modern' life. As in oil, she tailored her application of the pastel pigment to fit her changing style: exuberant strokes and rich colours during her Impressionist phase gave way to a calmer, more monumental style (exemplified by *Banjo Lesson*) as she matured. In the 1890s she returned often to the study of pastel techniques of 18th-century masters, particularly Maurice-Quentin de La Tour.

In the late 1880s Cassatt began to specialize in the mother-and-child theme (e.g. *The Family*, 1893; Norfolk, VA, Chrysler Mus.). This developed from her interest in the monumental figure and the depiction of modern life and was also in tune with late 19th-century Symbolism. She soon became identified with the theme and continues to be considered one of its greatest interpreters.

BIBLIOGRAPHY

J. K. Huysmans: *L'Art moderne* (Paris, 1883), pp. 6, 110, 231–4 [reviews of Salon of 1879, Impressionist exhibitions of 1880 and 1881]

Exposition Mary Cassatt (exh. cat., preface A. Mellério; Paris, Gal. Durand-Ruel, 1893)

W. Walton: 'Miss Mary Cassatt', *Scribner's Mag.*, xix (1896), pp. 353–61 [review of Cassatt's exhibition in New York, 1895]

'Most Eminent of All Living American Women Painters', *Current Lit.*, xlvi (1909), pp. 167–70

A. Segard: *Mary Cassatt: Une Peintre des enfants et des mères* (Paris, 1913) [first complete study of Cassatt's life and work, based on interviews with her]

A. D. Breeskin: *The Graphic Work of Mary Cassatt: A Catalogue Raisonné* (New York, 1948, rev. Washington, DC, 2/1979)

L. W. Havemeyer: *Sixteen to Sixty: Memoirs of a Collector* (New York, 1961)

F. A. Sweet: *Miss Mary Cassatt: Impressionist from Pennsylvania* (Norman, OK, 1966)

A. D. Breeskin: *Mary Cassatt: A Catalogue Raisonné of the Oils, Pastels, Watercolours, and Drawings* (Washington, DC, 1970, rev. 2/ in preparation)

Mary Cassatt, 1844–1926 (exh. cat., Washington, DC, N.G.A., 1970)

N. Hale: *Mary Cassatt* (New York, 1975)

Mary Cassatt at Home (exh. cat. by B. S. Shapiro, Boston, MA, Mus. F.A., 1978)

Mary Cassatt and Edgar Degas (exh. cat. by N. M. Mathews, San Jose, CA, Mus. A., 1981)

N. M. Mathews, ed.: *Cassatt and her Circle: Selected Letters* (New York, 1984)

Mary Cassatt and Philadelphia (exh. cat. by S. G. Lindsay, Philadelphia, PA, Mus. A., 1985)

F. Weitzenhoffer: *The Havemeyers: Impressionism Comes to America* (New York, 1986) [explains Cassatt's role as adviser to the Havemeyer collection]

N. M. Mathews: *Mary Cassatt* (New York, 1987)

Mary Cassatt: The Color Prints (exh. cat. by N. Mowll Mathews and B. Stern Shapiro, Washington, DC, N.G.A.; Williamstown, Williams Coll. Mus. A.; Boston, MA, Mus. F.A.; 1989)

N. M. Mathews: *Mary Cassatt: A Life* (New York, 1994)

NANCY MOWLL MATHEWS

Cassel. *See* KASSEL.

Cassinari, Bruno (*b* Piacenza, 29 Oct 1912; *d* Milan, 27 March 1992). Italian painter. He trained initially at the Gazzola school of art in Piacenza and from the age of 17 took evening classes at the Accademia di Belle Arti di Brera in Milan. He made his début as a painter in 1940 with a one-man show in the Galleria di Corrente. At that time the Corrente was the artistic circle most concerned with introducing Italian culture to the rest of Europe. During World War II Cassinari moved first to Brianza, then to Venice and finally to Milan where he settled in 1945. In 1946 he was one of the signatories of the manifesto of the Nuova Secessione Artistica Italiana, which became known as the Fronte Nuovo delle Arti in 1947; in this year Cassinari resigned from the group. The work of van Gogh and then Modigliani exercised a profound and liberating influence on Cassinari. However, after meeting Picasso in 1949 in Antibes, he abandoned the tonal qualities in the spirit of the traditional Lombard painters in favour of a prismatic and strident coloration (e.g. *Still-life in Pink*, 1952; Rome, G.N.A. Mod.). His friendship with Picasso led to a one-man show in 1950 at the Musée Picasso in Antibes. Cassinari remained in Antibes until 1953. In 1950 he was awarded the Gran Premio for painting at the Venice Biennale, and in the following year he was invited to exhibit in a one-man show at the São Paulo Biennale. Cassinari also worked in other media and techniques, including sculpture, illustration, printmaking and design, and as a designer of cartoons for tapestries.

BIBLIOGRAPHY

C. Pirovano: *Cassinari* (Milan, 1969)

Cassinari: Olii, gouaches, sculture (exh. cat. by A. Sala, Milan, Gal. Levi, 1973)

Cassinari (exh. cat. by G. A. Dell'Acqua and G. Anzari, Piacenza, Mus. Civ., 1983)

Corrente: Il movimento d'arte e cultura di opposizione, 1930–1945 (exh. cat., ed. C. Ragghianti; Milan, Pal. Reale, 1985)

Cassinari (exh. cat. by E. Crispolti, R. Bossaglia and G. Anzari, Milan, Pal. Reale, 1986)

SILVIA LUCCHESI

Cassiodorus, Flavius Magnus Aurelius (*c*. AD 485–580). Roman statesman, monk and writer. He was a relation of the philosopher Boethius (*c*. 480–525) and was born into a leading south Italian family of landowners and civil servants. His rhetorical talents commended him to Theoderic the Great, the Ostrogothic ruler of Italy (*reg* 493–526); he served as consul in 514 and was intermittently a prominent minister and propagandist of successive Ostrogothic rulers. He was a friend of the scholar–monk Dionysius Exiguus (*fl* 520) and, with Pope Agapetus I (535–6), planned a Christian university at Rome. Following the Byzantine reconquest of Italy in 542, he moved to Constantinople. He returned to Italy *c*. 552 to live a religious life in the monastery of Vivarium, which he founded on his Calabrian estates. His numerous writings include a collection of state documents, the *Variae*, which reveal much about the culture and values of the Ostrogothic regime and about Rome's public monuments, buildings and conservation under it. His *Institutiones*, an educational handbook written for his monks, which was widely influential in the 6th and 7th centuries, and later between the 9th and 11th centuries, and helped to establish the trivium and quadrivium, did not reject Classical and secular learning, but stressed the importance in monastic life of scholarship and the copying and binding of manuscripts. Many manuscripts, including the Codex Amiatinus (*c*. 690–700; Florence, Bib. Medicea-Laurenziana, MS. Amiatinus 1), may have a Vivarian ancestry. It is an exaggeration, however, to see Vivarium as a vital link in the transmission of the Classical heritage to the Middle Ages.

WRITINGS

Institutiones (*c.* AD 552–80); Eng. trans. by L. W. Jones as *Cassiodorus Senator: An Introduction to Divine and Human Readings* (New York, 1946)

Variae (*c.* AD 540); Eng. trans., abridged, by T. Hodgkin as *The Letters of Cassiodorus* (London, 1886); exact and unabridged Eng. trans. as *Variae of Magnus Aurelius Cassiodorus Senator* by S. J. Barnish (Liverpool, 1992)

BIBLIOGRAPHY

P. Courcelle: *Les Lettres grecques en Occident de Macrobe à Cassiodore* (Paris, 1948; Eng. trans., Cambridge, MA, 1969), pp. 313–88

J. J. O'Donnell: *Cassiodorus* (Berkeley, 1979)

B. Ward-Perkins: *From Classical Antiquity to the Middle Ages: Urban Public Building in Northern and Central Italy, AD 300–850* (Oxford, 1984)

S. J. B. BARNISH

Cassirer [Cahrs], **Paul** (*b* Görlitz, 21 Feb 1871; *d* Berlin, 7 Jan 1926). German dealer, publisher and journalist. After studying art history at the University of Munich, where he was co-editor of *Simplicissimus* from 1896 to 1898, he established himself in 1898 as a publisher and dealer in Berlin, helping contemporary artists towards international recognition. In 1908 he founded Verlag Paul Cassirer, a firm that published belles-lettres, especially Expressionist literature, and that promoted such artists as Ernst Barlach. In 1910 he married Ottilie Godefroy, who wrote her memoirs many years later under her stage name of Tilla Durieux.

Cassirer founded the Pan-Presse in 1909, edited the bimonthly *Pan* in 1910 and in 1913 founded the journal *Die Weissen Blätter*, containing comment on literature and art, which he published until 1921. Already President of the Berlin Secession, in 1913 he founded the Freie Sezession, whose exhibitions he planned. In the years preceding World War I Cassirer became a friend of Paul Durand-Ruel and promoted the work of the French Impressionists, and that of Wilhelm Trübner, Max Liebermann, Lovis Corinth, Max Slevogt, Fritz Klimsch, Heinrich Hübner (*b* 1869), Ulrich Hübner (1872–1932), Konrad von Kardorff (1877–1945), Leo von König (1871–1944) and August Gaul. After enlisting in 1914 he returned from service as a conscientious objector, living for the rest of World War I in Berne and Zurich. He died in 1926, but his gallery and publishing firm continued to operate until 1933, and his art-dealing businesses in Amsterdam, Zurich and London were run by Walter Feilchenfeldt (1894–1953) and Grete Ring. The Cassirer collection is now the Green Library at Stanford University in California.

BIBLIOGRAPHY

T. Durieux: *Meine ersten neunzig Jahre* (Berlin, 1971)

G. Brühl: *Die Cassirers: Streiter für den Impressionismus* (Leipzig, 1991), pp. 65–104

INGRID SEVERIN

Cassock. *See under* VESTMENTS, ECCLESIASTICAL, §1(i).

Casson, Sir **Hugh (Maxwell)** (*b* London, 23 May 1910). English architect and designer. He was educated at Eastbourne College, St John's College, Cambridge, and the Bartlett School of Architecture, University College, London. In 1933 he was Craven Scholar at the British School at Athens. As assistant and later partner to Christopher Nicholson (1904–48) he was involved in the Modern

Hugh Casson and Neville Conder: Elephant House, Zoological Gardens, Regent's Park, London, 1962–5

Movement but also worked on the Surrealist transformation of Monkton House (1936–8), West Dean Park, Chichester, W. Sussex (originally designed by Lutyens), for the collector and patron Edward James. Casson served as a Camouflage Officer (1940–44) in the Air Ministry and as Technical Officer in the Ministry of Town and Country Planning (1944–6). In 1946 he established a partnership with Neville Conder (*b* 1922), who had been educated at Charterhouse School, Surrey, and the Architectural Association School, London. In 1948 Casson was appointed Director of Architecture for the Festival of Britain, coordinating the brilliant display of modern architecture for the arts complex on the South Bank, London (opened May 1951), with attention to vistas, landscape and colour. He was knighted in 1952 in recognition of this achievement.

Casson and Conder sought to adapt their designs to historic environments, producing, in Casson's phrase, 'herbivore modernism'. They made the Cambridge University Faculty of Arts masterplan (1952) and executed a quadrangle of faculty and lecture buildings (1958–66), adding the Department of Classics building in 1980. The main buildings are raised on sculptural concrete piloti. Some are faced in stone, others in brick. This was followed by a plan for Birmingham University (1958), involving landscaping and halls of residence; the flexibility of the plan allowed for such later additions as the School of Education (1972) and Computer Centre (1975). The King George VI Memorial Hostel (1956–8), Holland Park, London, the restored east wing of Holland House (destr. World War II), is partly inspired by Swedish modernism and introduces a characteristic use of the mansard roof, while the Elephant House (1962–5; see fig.) at London Zoo, Regent's Park, plays with themes from New Brutalism. The District Bank (1966–9), King Street, Manchester, is a six-storey building faced in ribbed granite.

Casson was personally involved with the interior design work of the practice and served as Professor of Environmental Design at the Royal College of Art (1953–75). He designed some of the interiors for the Time & Life Building (1953), New Bond Street, London, the royal yacht *Britannia* (1955), the *SS Canberra* (1960) and the London Hilton Hotel (1963), Park Lane, as well as private interiors for Windsor Castle and Buckingham Palace. He was coordinating designer of the street decorations in Westminster for the coronation of Queen Elizabeth II (1953). He also designed sets for operas, notably that for the première of William Walton's *Troilus and Cressida* (1954) at the Royal Opera House, London.

Later works of the partnership include Wyvern Theatre (1968–71), Swindon, the Civic Centre (1971–6), Derby, the General Dental Council Building (1973), Wimpole Street, London, and the Ismaili Centre (1979–81), Cromwell Gardens, London, a rich and decorative granite-clad building. Hobhouse Court (1980), Leicester Square, London, is a sensitive example of urban infill. The partnership also acted as consultants for Lansdowne House (1985), Berkeley Square, London. Casson's high public profile was largely maintained through his publishing, broadcasting and lecturing on architecture and design. He also made a reputation for his watercolours, many of which illustrate his *Diary* (1981). He was Provost of the Royal College of Art in 1980–86 and President of the Royal Academy in 1976–84, a period during which the Academy adopted a more public and forceful role.

WRITINGS

New Sights of London (London, 1937)

Homes by the Million: An Account of the Housing Achievement in the USA, 1940–1945 (London, 1947)

An Introduction to Victorian Architecture (London, 1948)

ed.: *Inscape: The Design of Interiors* (London, 1968)

Diary (London, 1981)

BIBLIOGRAPHY

Contemp. Architects

'Civic Pride', *Architects' J.*, clxvi/49 (1977), pp. 104–6

A. Williams and others: 'Mini profile: Casson Conder and Partners', *Building* (25 Aug 1978), p. 54

——: 'Ismaili Centre', *Building* (24 Feb 1984), pp. 35–42

ALAN POWERS

Illustration Acknowledgements

We are grateful to those listed below for permission to reproduce copyright illustrative material and to those contributors who supplied photographs or helped us to obtain them. The word 'Photo:' precedes the names of large commercial or archival sources who have provided us with photographs, as well as the names of individual photographers (where known). It has generally not been used before the names of owners of works of art, such as museums and civic bodies. Every effort has been made to contact copyright holders and to credit them appropriately; we apologize to anyone who may have been omitted from the acknowledgements or cited incorrectly. Any error brought to our attention will be corrected in subsequent editions. Where illustrations have been taken from books, publication details are provided in the acknowledgements below.
Line drawings, maps, plans, chronological tables and family trees commissioned by the *Dictionary of Art* are not included in the list below. All of the maps in the dictionary were produced by Oxford Illustrators Ltd, who were also responsible for some of the line drawings. Most of the line drawings and plans, however, were drawn by the following artists: Diane Fortenberry, Lorraine Hodghton, Chris Miners, Amanda Patton, Mike Pringle, Jo Richards, Miranda Schofield, John Tiernan, John Wilson and Philip Winton. The chronological tables and family trees were prepared initially by Kate Boatfield and finalized by John Johnson.

Brugghen, Hendrick ter *1* Rijksmuseum, Amsterdam; *2* North Carolina Museum of Art, Raleigh, NC (Gift of David M. Koetser in honour of W.R. Valentiner); *3* Metropolitan Museum of Art, New York (Purchase, funds from various donors, 1956; no. 56.228); *4* Trustees of the National Gallery, London
Brunei *2–3* Brunei Museums
Brunel, Isambard Kingdom Photo: Anthony Kersting, London
Brunelleschi, Filippo *2, 5–8* Photo: Archivi Alinari, Florence
Bruni, Fyodor David King Collection, London
Brunsberg, Hinrich Institute of Art PAN, Warsaw (neg. no. 70686)/ Photo: Z. Swiechowski
Brunswick Städtisches Museum, Brunswick
Brus, Günter Samuel Fogg Rare Books and Manuscripts, London
Brush *1–3* Winsor & Newton, London
Brushline *2* Tokyo National Museum, Tokyo
Brussels *1* Bibliothèque Royale Albert 1er, Brussels; *2* Ministerie van de Vlaamse Gemeenschap, Monumenten en Landschappen, Brussels; *3, 9* Photo: © ACL Brussels; *4* Photo: Economic Union Publications Division, Brussels; *5* Photo: S.T.I.B./© DACS, 1996; *6* Metropolitan Museum of Art, New York (Gift of Mrs Frederic R. Coudert, Jr, in memory of Mr and Mrs Hugh A. Murray, 1957; no. 57.62); *7–8* Photo: Patrimonio Nacional Archivo Fotográfico, Madrid
Brustolon, Andrea Civici Musei Veneziani d'Arte e di Storia, Venice
Brutalism British Architectural Library, RIBA, London
Bruyn: (1) Bartholomäus Bruyn (i) *1* Bayerische Staatsgemäldesammlungen, Munich; *2* Photo: Rheinische Bildarchiv, Cologne
Bryullov: (2) Karl Bryullov Russian Museum, St Petersburg
Bubastis Trustees of the British Museum, London
Bucharest *1* Photo: Alina-Ioana Şerbu; *2* Photo: ROMPRES, Bucharest
Bückeburg Board of Trustees of the Victoria and Albert Museum, London
Bučovice Czech Academy of Sciences, Prague/Photo: Paul Prokop
Budapest *1* Historical Museum, Budapest; *2* National Commission for the Protection of Monuments, Budapest; *3* Photo: Tihanyi Bence, Budapest
Buddhism *1–2, 4, 9, 12, 15* Trustees of the British Museum, London; *3* British Library, London (MS. Or. 6902); *5* Syndics of Cambridge University Library; *6* British Library, London (no. V23154); *7–8* Photo: Werner Forman Archive, London; *10* Photo: David Snellgrove; *11* Photo: © RMN, Paris; *13* Royal Academy of Fine Arts Library, London (Art Documentation); *14* National Museum of Korea, Seoul; *16* Cleveland Museum of Art, Cleveland, OH
Budhanilkantha Photo: Mary Shepherd Slusser
Buenos Aires South American Pictures, Woodbridge, Suffolk/Photo: Tony Morrison
Bugatto, Zanetto Photo: Scala, Florence
Buggiano Photo: Archivi Alinari, Florence
Building regulations *3* Museum of Modern Art, New York
Bukhara *1* Freer Gallery of Art, Smithsonian Institution, Washington, DC; *2* Hutchison Library, London/Photo: Trevor Page; *3* Photo: SCR Photo Library, London
Bulfinch, Charles Library of Congress, Washington, DC
Bulgaria *2* Yale University Press Photo Library, London/Photo: Peter Hlebarov; *3* Photo: Juliana Nedeva-Wegener; *4* Photo: Robert Harding Picture Library, London; *5* Photo: Tania Velmans; *6* National Art Gallery, Sofia/Photo: Yale University Press Photo Library, London; *7* British Library, London (neg. no. 59799); *8* National Art Gallery, Sofia; *9* Ethnographic Museum, Plovdiv; *10* National Gallery of Decorative and Applied Arts, Sofia/© Yevgeniya Racheva-Manolova; *11* Rila Monastery Museum, Bulgaria; *12* National Gallery of Decorative and Applied Arts, Sofia
Bulgarini, Bartolommeo Harvard University Art Museums, Cambridge, MA (Gift of Friends of the Fogg Museum of Art Fund and Henry Goldman Fund)
Bundzhikat Photo: Donish Institute of History, Dushanbe
Bungalow British Architectural Library, RIBA, London
Buon (i): (1) Bartolomeo Buon Photo: Archivi Alinari, Florence
Buonconsiglio, Giovanni Photo: Archivi Alinari, Florence
Buonconsiglio Castle Photo: Maria Angela Mattevi
Buontalenti, Bernardo *1* Photo: Archivi Alinari, Florence; *2* Photo: © RMN, Paris
Buqras Biologisch Archeologisch Instituut des Rijksuniversiteits, Groningen
Burchfield, Charles Munson–Williams–Proctor Institute, Museum of Art, Utica, NY
Bureau *1* Landesdenkmalamt Baden-Württemberg, Karlsruhe; *2* Photo: © RMN, Paris
Burges, William *1* Photo: Conway Library, Courtauld Institute of Art, London; *2* Photo: Anthony Kersting, London
Burgkmair: (2) Hans Burgkmair I *1* Trustees of the British Museum, London; *2* Bayerische Staatsgemäldesammlungen, Munich
Burgos *1* Photo: Anthony Kersting, London; *2–3* Photo: Ampliaciones y Reproducciones MAS, Barcelona
Burgundy: (1) Philip the Bold Bibliothèque Royale Albert 1er, Brussels
Burgundy: (3) Philip the Good Bibliothèque Royale Albert 1er, Brussels
Burgundy: (5) Charles the Bold Photo: © ACL Brussels
Burkina Faso Photo: Christopher D. Roy
Burle Marx, Roberto Photo: Marcel Gautherot
Burma *2–3, 5–10, 14* Photo: Pierre Pichard; *4* Photo: Wim Swaan, London; *11–13* Photo: Marie Gatellier; *15* British Library, London (MS. Or. 14178, fol. 10); *16* British Library, London (MS. Or. 5757, fols 17–18); *17, 27* Photo: Noel F. Singer; *18* Royal Pavilion, Art Gallery and Museums, Brighton; *19* Board of Trustees of the Victoria and Albert Museum, London; *22, 25* Board of Trustees of the Theatre Museum, London; *23* Museum of Fine Arts, Boston, MA; *24, 26* Photo: Sylvia Fraser-Lu

Burnacini, Lodovico *1* Bildarchiv, Österreichische Nationalbibliothek, Vienna
Burne-Jones, Edward *1* Metropolitan Museum of Art, New York (Alfred N. Punnett Endowment Fund, 1947; no. 47.26); *2* Tate Gallery, London
Burney, Edward Francesco Photo: Bridgeman Art Library, London
Burnham, Daniel H. *1* Chicago Historical Society, Chicago, IL/Photo: C.D. Arnold; *2* Architectural Association, London/Photo: Karin Hay
Burra, Edward Photo: Lefevre Gallery, London
Burri, Alberto Tate Gallery, London
Burrini, Gian Antonio Photo: Archivi Alinari, Florence
Bursa Photo: Anthony Kersting, London
Bury St Edmunds *1* Photo: Francis Woodman; *2* Pierpont Morgan Library, New York
Busch, Wilhelm Photo: Hans Georg Gmelin
Büsinck, Ludolph Courtauld Institute of Art, London
Bust *1* J. Paul Getty Museum, Malibu, CA; *2*, *4* Photo: Archivi Alinari, Florence; *3* Kunsthistorisches Museum, Vienna; *5* Statens Konstmuseer, Stockholm; *6* Musée Carnavalet, Paris; *7* Musée Rodin, Paris (inv. no. S. 1063)/Photo: Bruno Jarret/© DACS, 1996
Butinone, Bernardino Photo: Archivi Alinari, Florence
Butkara *1–2* Photo: Anna Maria Quagliotti
Butterfield, William *1* Photo: Anthony Kersting, London; *2* Photo: RCHME/© Crown Copyright; *3* Oxfordshire Photographic Archive, D.L.A., O.C.C.
Buytewech, Willem *1* Hamburger Kunsthalle, Hamburg; *2* Trustees of the British Museum, London
Bwa and Gurunsi *1–2* Photo: Christopher D. Roy
Byblos Trustees of the British Museum, London
Byōdōin Photo: © RETORIA/Y. Futagawa & Associated Photographers
Cabanel, Alexandre Photo: Giraudon, Paris
Cabinet (i) *1* British Library, London (no. 459.e.22); *2* Photo: Meredith Chilton
Cabinet (ii) Board of Trustees of the Victoria and Albert Museum, London
Cabinet picture *1* Photo: Archivi Alinari, Florence; *2* Soprintendenza per i Beni Artistici e Storici, Rome
Caccini, Giovanni Battista *1* Metropolitan Museum of Art, New York (Haris Brisbane Dick Fund, 1967; no. 67.208); *2* Photo: Conway Library, Courtauld Institute of Art, London
Cáceres Photo: Ampliaciones y Reproducciones MAS, Barcelona
Cades, Giuseppe Photo: M. Teresa Caracciolo Arizzoli
Cádiz Photo: Ampliaciones y Reproducciones MAS, Barcelona/TAF Helicopters, S.A.
Cadouin Abbey Photo: Branger-Viollet, Paris
Caen *1–2* Photo: Conway Library, Courtauld Institute of Art, London; *3* Photo: Bildarchiv Foto Marburg
Caernarfon Castle *2* Photo: Anthony Kersting, London
Caffa, Melchiorre Photo: Gabinetto Fotografico Nazionale, Istituto Centrale per il Catalogo e la Documentazione, Rome
Caffiéri: (4) Jean-Jacques Caffiéri Trustees of the Wallace Collection, London
Cagnacci, Guido Kunsthistorisches Museum, Vienna
Cagnola, Luigi Photo: Prof. Gianni Mezzanotte
Caillebotte, Gustave Musée d'Art Moderne, Petit Palais, Geneva
Cairo *3* Ashmolean Museum, Oxford; *4* Photo: Bernard O'Kane; *5* Photo: Jonathan M. Bloom; *6* Photo: Robert Harding Picture Library, London
Cairo, Francesco *1* Photo: G. Chiolini and Co., Pavia; *2* Museo del Prado, Madrid
Caja-espiga Photo: Henri Stierlin, Geneva
Calcagni, Antonio Board of Trustees of the Victoria and Albert Museum, London
Calcutta *1–2* Photo: Philip Davies; *3* Board of Trustees of the Victoria and Albert Museum, London
Calder: (3) Alexander Calder Whitney Museum of American Art, New York (Gift of the Friends of the Whitney Museum of American Art; no. 62.18)/Photo: Otto E. Nelson/© ADAGP, Paris, and DACS, London, 1996
Calendar *1* British Library, London (MS. A VI, fol. 5*v*); *2* J. Paul Getty Museum, Malibu, CA
Calendario, Filippo Photo: Osvaldo Böhm, Venice
Callot, Jacques *1* National Gallery of Art, Washington, DC (R. L. Baumfeld Collection); *2* National Gallery of Art, Washington, DC
Cals, Adolphe-Félix Bowes Museum, Barnard Castle, Co. Durham
Calvaert, Denys Staatliche Kunstsammlungen Dresden
Calvary Pierpont Morgan Library, New York
Calvinism Photo: Bildarchiv Foto Marburg
Camaldolese Order Photo: Archivi Alinari, Florence
Camassei, Andrea Gabinetto Fotografico Nazionale, Galleria Nazionale d'Arte Antica, Rome
Cambiaso, Luca *1* Photo: Archivio Fotografico SAGEP, Genoa; *2* Photo: Patrimonio Nacional Archivo Fotográfico, Madrid
Cambodia *2*, *22* Photo: Werner Forman Archive, London; *3–5*, *7*, *9* Photo: Henri Stierlin, Geneva; *6* Photo: Wim Swaan, London; *8*, *10–14*, *17* Photo: Guy Nafilyan; *15* Photo: P. Ian Page; *16*, *18* Photo: Hans Hinz, Allschwil; *19* Asian Art Museum of San Francisco, CA (Avery Brundage Collection); *20*, *24* Photo: © RMN, Paris; *21* Loke Wan-Tho, Singapore/Photo: Overseas Agenzia Fotografica, Milan; *23*, *25–7* Photo: Madeleine Giteau; *28* Photo: Patricia Naenna; *29* Photo: Robert Harding Picture Library, London; *30* With permission of the International Institute for Traditional Music, Berlin/Photo: Jacques Brunet; *31* Royal Ontario Museum, Toronto (Gift of Herman Levy); *32* Photo: John Villiers
Cambridge *1* By permission of Queens' College, Cambridge; *2* British Library, London (no. 010358.r.8); *3* Cambridge University Collection of Air Photographs; *4* Photo: Anthony Kersting, London; *5* Provost and Scholars of King's College, Cambridge/Photo: P.A.L. Brunney
Camden Town Group Laing Art Gallery, Newcastle upon Tyne (Tyne and Wear Museums)
Camera lucida Trustees of the Science Museum, London/Photo: Science and Society Picture Library
Camera obscura Trustees of the Science Museum, London/Photo: Science and Society Picture Library
Cameron, Charles Photo: Aurora Art Publishers, St Petersburg
Cameron, Julia Margaret International Museum of Photography at George Eastman House, Rochester, NY
Cameroon Photo: Gloria J. Umlauft-Thielicke
Camilo, Francisco Photo: Ampliaciones y Reproducciones MAS, Barcelona
Camoin, Charles Musée National d'Art Moderne, Paris
Camouflage *1* National Gallery of Canada, Ottawa (Transfer from the Canadian War Memorials, 1921)/© Estate of Edward Wadsworth, 1996. All rights reserved DACS
Campagna, Girolamo *1* Photo: Osvaldo Böhm, Venice; *2* Photo: Conway Library, Courtauld Institute of Art, London
Campagnola: (1) Giulio Campagnola Trustees of the British Museum, London
Campana, Giampietro Photo: © RMN, Paris
Campbell, Colen *1* British Architectural Library, RIBA, London; *2* *Vitruvius Britannicus* (1725), iii, pl. 270
Campen, Jacob van Staatliche Kunstsammlungen Dresden
Campi: (2) Antonio Campi Museo d'Arte Antica, Castello Sforzesco, Milan
Campionesi Fototeca, Fabbrica del Duomo, Milan
Camuccini: (2) Vincenzo Camuccini *1–2* Kunsthistorisches Museum, Vienna
Canaanite Israel Antiquities Authority, Jerusalem
Canada *2* Parks Canada, Heritage Recording and Technical Data Services; *3* Architectural Association, London/Photo: R. De Pierro; *4* National Gallery of Canada, Ottawa (Transferred from Parliament of Canada, Ottawa, 1888); *5* National Gallery of Canada, Ottawa (Vincent Massey Bequest, 1968); *6* National Gallery of Canada, Ottawa; *7* National Gallery of Canada, Ottawa/Photo: Paterson Ewen; *8* Art Gallery of Ontario, Toronto (Gift from the Albert H. Robson Memorial Subscription Fund, 1950; Estate of Elizabeth Wyn Wood and Emanuel Hahn); *9* Centre Canadien d'Architecture, Montreal; *10* Royal Ontario Museum, Toronto (Sigmund Samuel Collection); *11–12* Royal Ontario Museum, Toronto; *13* National Museums of Canada, Ottawa/Photo:H. Foster; *14* Harlan House, Marysville, Ontario; *15* Royal Ontario Museum, Toronto (John and Mary Yarenko Collection of Canadian Glass); *16* Musée du Québec/Photo: Patrick Altman, 1977; *17* Archives Nationales du Québec/Photo: O. Bériau
Canaletto *1–2* Trustees of the National Gallery, London; *3* Museum of Fine Arts, Boston, MA (Abbott Lawrence Fund, Seth K. Sweetser Fund and Charles Edward French Fund); *4* Trustees of Dulwich Picture Gallery, London
Canberra Image Library, State Library of New South Wales, Sydney/ Photo: Heide Smith for Mitchell, Giurgola and Thorp
Candela, Félix Photo: Ramiro Romo
Candelabrum Deutsches Archäologisches Institut, Rome (neg. no. 61.482)
Candid, Peter *1* Photo: Bildarchiv Foto Marburg; *2* Freising Cathedral
Candlestick Photo: Peter Hornsby

Canina, Luigi Photo: Andrea Tonolo, Rome
Cano, Alonso *1* Trustees of the Wallace Collection, London; *2* Museo del Prado, Madrid
Canon table Bibliothèque Nationale de France, Paris
Canopy (i) Photo: Scala, Florence
Canova, Antonio *1* Photo: © RMN, Paris; *2* Museo Civico, Padua; *3* Bildarchiv, Österreichische Nationalbibliothek, Vienna; *4* Photo: Conway Library, Courtauld Institute of Art, London
Cantarini, Simone Photo: Scala, Florence
Canterbury *3* British Library, London (no. G.2256, vol. 2); *4* Canterbury Museums Collection; *5* British Library, London (Add. MS. 37517); *6* Master and Fellows of Trinity College, Cambridge/Photo: Conway Library, Courtauld Institute of Art, London; *8, 10–11* Photo: Conway Library, Courtauld Institute of Art, London; *9* Photo: Anthony Kersting, London; *12* Board of Trustees of the Victoria and Albert Museum, London; *13* Photo: RCHME/© Crown Copyright
Cantilever Architectural Association, London/Photo: Andrew Higgott
Canuti, Domenico Maria Gabinetto Fotografico Soprintendenza ai Beni Artistici e Storici, Bologna
Canvas *1* Photo: Scala, Florence; *2* Courtauld Institute Galleries, London; *3* Trustees of the National Gallery, London
Capacha–Opeño National Museum of the American Indian, Smithsonian Institution, Washington, DC
Cape Dutch style South African Library, Cape Town
Cape Town Images of Africa Photobank, Lichfield/Photo: Johann van Tonder
Cappadocia *1* Photo: Lyn Rodley; *3–4* Photo: Nicole Thierry
Cappelle, Jan van de *1* Rijksmuseum, Amsterdam; *2* Photo: Bridgeman Art Library, London
Caprarola, Villa Farnese Photo: Gabinetto Fotografico Nazionale, Istituto Centrale per il Catalogo e la Documentazione, Rome
Capriccio *1* Virginia Museum of Fine Arts, Richmond, VA (Arthur and Margaret Glasgow Fund); *2* National Trust Photo Library, London/Photo: John Bethell
Capuchins Photo: Archivi Alinari, Florence
Caracas South American Pictures, Woodbridge, Suffolk/Photo: Tony Morrison
Caracciolo, Giovanni Battista *1–2* Photo: Archivi Alinari, Florence
Caramuel de Lobkowitz, Juan *1* British Library, London (no. 559.f.9)
Caravaggio, Michelangelo Merisi da *1, 3, 7* Photo: Bridgeman Art Library, London; *2* Kimbell Art Museum, Fort Worth, TX; *4* Photo: Archivi Alinari, Florence; *5* San Luigi dei Francesi, Rome/Photo: Bridgeman Art Library, London; *6, 8–10* Photo: Scala, Florence
Caravanserai Photo: Godfrey Goodwin
Carborundum print Photo: Archives Succession Miró
Carcassonne *2* Photo: Anthony Kersting, London
Carchemish Trustees of the British Museum, London
Cardiff Photo: Jeremy Lowe
Cardona, S Vicente Photo: Ampliaciones y Reproducciones MAS, Barcelona
Carducho: (1) Bartolomé Carducho Museu Nacional de Arte Antiga, Lisbon
Carducho: (2) Vicente Carducho *1–2* Museo del Prado, Madrid
Caria Photo: Michael House
Cariani, Giovanni National Gallery of Canada, Ottawa
Caribbean Islands *2* Trustees of the British Museum, London; *3* Photo: Oliver Benn; *4* Photo: Alissandra Cummins; *5* Leicestershire Museums, Arts and Records Service; *6* Photo: Spectrum Colour Library, London; *7* Photo: Dr Kusha Haraksingh
Caricature *1* Metropolitan Museum of Art, New York (no. 1973.67); *2* Trustees of the British Museum, London; *3* Photo: British Library, London
Carlevaris, Luca Birmingham Museums and Art Gallery
Carlone (ii): (3) Carlo Antonio Carlone Photo: Bundesdenkmalamt, Vienna
Carlone (ii): (8) Carlo Innocenzo Carlone Österreichische Galerie im Belvedere, Vienna/Photo: Bildarchiv, Österreichische Nationalbibliothek, Vienna
Carmelite Order Photo: Archivi Alinari, Florence
Carmina figurata Bibliothèque Municipale, Amiens
Carnac Robert Harding Picture Library, London/Photo: Adam Woolfitt
Carnevali, Giovanni Photo: Scala, Florence
Carnival *1* Gabinetto Nazionale delle Stampe, Rome/Photo: Alessandro Vasari, Rome (neg. no. 39897); *2* Photo: John Nunley
Caro, Anthony Tate Gallery, London
Carolingian art *1* Yale University Press from K. J. Conant, *Carolingian and Romanesque Architecture 800–1200*; *2, 11* Photo: Bildarchiv Foto Marburg; *3–4* Museo Civico, Bolzano; *5* Rheinisches Landesmuseum, Trier (photo no. B.1794); *6, 9* Bibliothèque Nationale de France, Paris; *7* Kunsthistorisches Museum, Vienna; *8* Photo: Scala, Florence; *10, 13* Photo: © RMN, Paris; *12* © Parrocchia di San Giovanni Battista/Museo del Duomo, Monza; *14* Hessisches Landesmuseum, Darmstadt; *15* Metropolitan Museum of Art, New York
Carolus-Duran Photo: Giraudon, Paris
Caron, Antoine Pierpont Morgan Library, New York (acc. no. 1955.7)
Caroto: (1) Gian Francesco Caroto Photo: Diana Gisolfi
Carpaccio: (1) Vittore Carpaccio *1–2* Photo: Osvaldo Böhm, Venice; *3* Museo Thyssen-Bornemisza, Madrid; *4* Soprintendenza ai Beni Artistici e Storici, Venice
Carpeaux, Jean-Baptiste *1–2* Photo: © RMN, Paris
Carpet *5* Calderdale Leisure Services, Museums and Arts, Halifax; *6* Textile Museum, Washington, DC; *7–8, 10–13* Board of Trustees of the Victoria and Albert Museum, London; *9* Metropolitan Museum of Art, New York (Gift of the Samuel H. Kress Foundation, 1958; no. 58.75.129)
Carpi, Girolamo da Trustees of the National Gallery, London
Carpio: (3) 7th Marqués del Carpio National Gallery of Art, Washington, DC (Andrew W. Mellon Collection, 1937)
Carr, Emily Vancouver Art Gallery/Photo: © Robert Keziere
Carrà, Carlo Museum of Modern Art, New York (Acquired through the Lillie P. Bliss Bequest)
Carracci: (1) Ludovico Carracci *1* Photo: Scala, Florence; *2–3* Photo: Archivi Alinari, Florence; *4* Photo: © RMN, Paris
Carracci: (2) Agostino Carracci Photo: Scala, Florence
Carracci: (3) Annibale Carracci *1–2*, Photo: Scala, Florence; *3* National Gallery of Art, Washington, DC (Samuel H. Kress Collection); *4, 6* Photo: © RMN, Paris
Carreño de Miranda, Juan *1* Photo: © RMN, Paris; *2* Photo: Ampliaciones y Reproducciones MAS, Barcelona
Carriera, Rosalba Museo Civico 'Luigi Bailo', Treviso
Carrier-Belleuse, Albert-Ernest Photo: © RMN, Paris
Carrière, Eugène Philadelphia Museum of Art, Philadelphia, PA
Carstens, Asmus Jakob Kunstsammlungen zu Weimar
Cartagena Photo: Fernando Carrasco Zaldua
Carthage *2* Musée National du Bardo, Tunis
Carthusian Order Photo: Arch. Phot. Paris/© DACS, 1996
Cartier-Bresson, Henri Photo: John Hillelson Agency Ltd
Cartoon Devonshire Collection, Chatsworth, Derbys. By permission of the Duke of Devonshire and the Trustees of the Chatsworth Settlement/Photo: Courtauld Institute of Art, London
Cartouche Photo: Archivi Alinari, Florence
Carus, Carl Gustav Museum der Bildenden Künste, Leipzig
Caryatid *1* Photo: Archivi Alinari, Florence; *2* British Architectural Library, RIBA, London
Casas, Ramon Photo: Ampliaciones y Reproducciones MAS, Barcelona
Caselli, Cristoforo Soprintendenza per i Beni Artistici e Storici di Parma e Piacenza
Cashel Office of Public Works, Ireland
Casket Trustees of the British Museum, London
Casorati, Felice Museo Civico d'Arte Antica, Turin
Cassatt, Mary Virginia Museum of Fine Arts, Richmond, VA
Casson, Hugh Photo: Conway Library, Courtauld Institute of Art, London